Contents

The MILEPOST
All-The-North Travel Guide

GEICO.

COMBINE
HOME & AUTO

insurance and you could save.

geico.com | 1-800-947-AUTO | Local Office

A typical view along the Denali Highway of snow-capped peaks in the Alaska Range, scattered spruce and pothole lakes. (©Bill Rome)

Welcome to the North Country

The North Country is the land north of 51° 16' latitude. Geographically, it encompasses Alaska, Yukon, Northwest Territories, northern British Columbia and Alberta. Following are some facts and figures about each of these areas.

Alaska

Population: 737,625
Capital: Juneau
Largest City: Anchorage
Area: 571,951 square miles
Coastline: 6,640 miles
Shoreline: 33,904 miles
Highest Point: Denali, 20,310 feet

Lowest Point: Pacific Ocean, sea level
State Flower: Forget-me-not
State Tree: Sitka spruce
State Bird: Willow ptarmigan
State Motto: North to the Future
Major Industries: Tourism, petroleum, fishing
Drinking age: 21. *(NOTE: The sale and/or importation of alcoholic beverages is prohibited in more than 100 bush communities.)*
Visitor Information: Alaska Travel Industry Association; www.travelalaska.com

Alaska is the largest state in the union in area (twice the size of Texas), but ranks 48th in population, based on recent census estimates. Approximately 16 percent of the population is Alaska Native: Inupiaq, Yupik, Cupik, Aleut, Alutiiq, Athabascan, Tlingit, Haida and Tsimshian.

Alaska has 17 of the 20 highest mountains in the United States, including the highest peak in North America—Denali, the crown jewel of Denali National Park, elev. 20,310. Named by a prospector in 1896, for presidential nominee William McKinley of Ohio, the mountain returned to its original Alaska Native name—Denali—with passage of the Alaska National Interest Lands Conservation Act of 1980. However, it was still named McKinley according to the U.S. Board of Geographic Names until it was changed at the federal level in 2015.

The state falls into 6 natural geographical regions: Southeastern, Southcentral, the Interior, Southwestern, Western and the Brooks Range/Arctic.

Southeastern Alaska is a moist, luxuriantly forested panhandle extending some 500 miles from Dixon Entrance south of Ketchikan to Icy Bay on the Gulf of Alaska coast. This narrow strip of coast, separated from the mainland and Canada by the Coast Mountains and the hundreds of islands of the Alexander Archipelago, form the Inside Passage water route used by ships and ferries. Cruise ships bring over 1 million passengers through the Inside Passage each summer. Alaska's capital city, Juneau, is the largest city in Southeast and the second largest city in the state at pop. 32,269. Prince of Wales Island is the third largest island in the nation (behind Hawaii and Kodiak).

The Southcentral region of Alaska curves 650 miles north and west from the Gulf of Alaska coast to the Alaska Range. This

region's varied geography includes the Matanuska–Susitna river valleys, the Chugach and Wrangell–St. Elias mountain ranges, the Kenai Peninsula and the Prince William Sound glaciers. Anchorage, the state's largest city, is the hub of Southcentral.

Interior Alaska lies cradled between the Brooks Range to the north and the Alaska Range to the south, a vast area that drains to the Yukon River, the Kuskokwim River and its tributaries. It is a climate of extremes, holding both the record high (100°F at Fort Yukon) and the record low (-80°F at Prospect Creek). Fairbanks, pop. 31,905, is the hub of the Interior and a jump-off point for bush communities in both the Interior and Arctic.

Southwestern Alaska takes in Kodiak Island, the Alaska Peninsula and Aleutian Islands. Kodiak, less than an hour's flight from Anchorage and 9.5 hours by ferry from Homer, is the largest island in Alaska and second largest in the United States (the largest being Hawaii). Kodiak was Russian Alaska's first capital city and is home to the largest bears in the world. Brown bear viewing is an attraction on Kodiak and at Katmai National Park and Preserve near King Salmon. The Alaska Marine Highway Southwest/Aleutian route, provides ferry service from Kodiak to Unalaska/Dutch Harbor.

Western Alaska stretches from the head of Bristol Bay north along the Bering Sea coast to the Seward Peninsula near the Arctic Circle. This region extends inland from the coast to encompass the Yukon–Kuskokwim Delta. Nome is one of the best known destinations in Western Alaska.

Arctic Alaska lies above the Arctic Circle (latitude 66°33′), between the Brooks Range to the south and the Arctic sea coast to the north, and from the Canadian border to the east westward to Kotzebue. Day and overnight trips to Nome, Utqiagvik (formerly known as Barrow) and Prudhoe Bay are popular packages offered out of Anchorage and Fairbanks.

If you include the Alaska Marine Highway (ferry) System, all regions of Alaska are connected by highway with the exception of Western Alaska. And that region's hub cities—Bethel and Nome—are less than 2 hours from Anchorage by air.

Canada

Yukon

Population: 39,000
Capital: Whitehorse
Largest City: Whitehorse
Area: 186,661 square miles/482,443 square km
Highest Point: Mount Logan, 19,550 feet/5,959m
Lowest Point: Beaufort Sea/Arctic Ocean, sea level
Territorial Flower: Fireweed
Territorial Bird: Raven
Territorial Tree: Subalpine Fir
Major Industries: Tourism, mining
Drinking age: 19. Packaged liquor, beer and wine are sold in government liquor stores and licensed off-sales outlets.
Visitor Information: Tourism Yukon, Box 2703, Whitehorse, YT Y1A 2C6; phone 1-800-661-0494; email vacation@gov.yk.ca; www.travelyukon.com

Shaped somewhat like a right triangle, Yukon is bordered on the west

by Alaska at 141° longitude; on the north by the Beaufort Sea/Arctic Ocean; on the south by British Columbia at latitude 60°; and on the east by the Northwest Territories.

The Indigenous Peoples of Yukon are referred to as First Nations. There are 14 Yukon First Nations each with their own rich culture and history: Carcross/Tagish First Nation, Champagne and Aishihik First Nation, Kluane First Nation, Kwanlin Dün First Nation, Liard First Nation, Little Salmon/Carmacks First Nation, First Nation of Na-Cho Nyäk Dun, Ross River Dena Council, Selkirk First Nation, Ta'an Kwäch'än Council, Teslin Tlingit Council, Tr'ondëk Hwëch'in, Vuntut Gwitchin First Nation and White River First Nation. Yukon also has eight Indigenous language groups: Gwich'in, Han, Northern Tutchone, Southern Tutchone, Kaska, Tagish, Inland Tlingit and Upper Tanana.

Yukon was made a district of the Northwest Territories in 1895, and became a separate territory in June of 1898, propelled by the influx of people and commerce that arrived with the great Klondike Gold Rush.

Dawson City, in the heart of the Klondike, became the new territory's first capital. At the height of the gold rush, an estimated 30,000 people lived in Dawson City. By 1903, as other gold stampedes drew off much of Dawson's population, the city's boom days were over, although mining continued to support the community for many years. Whitehorse, however, was thriving, both as terminus of the White Pass & Yukon Route railway from Skagway and as a major service stop on the Alaska Highway, which had opened to public travel in 1948. Whitehorse also had a large airport—today's Erik Nielsen Whitehorse International Airport—and on March 31, 1953, Whitehorse replaced Dawson City as capital of Yukon.

Yukon has 3 national parks, 2 of which are fly-in. Kluane National Park and Reserve, a UNESCO World Heritage Site, located along the Haines and Alaska highways, contains Canada's highest peak, Mount Logan (elev. 19,550 feet/5,959m). Vuntut National Park, located in the northwestern corner of Yukon, is 50 km/31 air miles from Old Crow. Ivvavik National Park, the first national park in Canada resulting from a Yukon First Nation's land claim, is 200 km/124 air miles west of Inuvik, NT. Yukon also has 4 territorial parks, 4 new territorial parks in the planning stages and 4 Canadian Heritage Rivers.

British Columbia

Population: 4,817,200
Capital: Victoria
Largest City: Vancouver
Area: 364,764 square miles/944,735 square km
Highest Point: Fairweather Mountain 15,299 feet/4,663m
Lowest Point: Pacific Ocean, sea level
Provincial Flower: Pacific dogwood
Provincial Tree: Western redcedar
Provincial Bird: Steller's jay
Provincial Mammal: Spirit Bear (also known as the Kermode Bear)
Provincial Motto: Splendor Without Diminishment

Major Industries: Construction, manufacturing, forestry, mining and energy, tourism, film and television productions, food processing, agriculture, seafood products
Drinking age: 19. Packaged liquor, beer and wine are sold in government liquor stores and various private retail outlets.
Visitor Information: Destination British Columbia; www.hellobc.com

Canada's most westerly and third largest province, British Columbia stretches 808 miles/1,300 km from its southern border with the United States to the northern boundaries with Yukon and Northwest Territory. It is bounded on the east by Alberta and on the west by the Pacific Ocean. The province includes Vancouver Island, site of the capital city of Victoria. Slightly more than half the province's population resides in the Victoria–Vancouver area.

The region was important in early fur trade, and expansion of the province came with the 1860s Cariboo gold rush, followed by the completion of Canada's first transcontinental railway—the Canadian Pacific. British Columbia entered the Dominion of Canada on July 20, 1871, as the 6th province.

Popular tourist destinations include Vancouver and Whistler; Victoria and Vancouver Island; the Gulf Islands; the Sunshine Coast; the Okanagan Valley; the Cariboo; the Kootenay Rockies; Northern BC and Haida Gwaii. BC has 7 national parks, one marine conservation area, 13 National Historic Sites and 1,030 parks, reserves, protected areas, conservancies and recreation sites. The province's national parks—Glacier, Gulf Islands, Gwaii Haanas, Mount Revelstoke, Kootenay, Pacific Rim and Yoho—are among the most spectacular in North America.

Mile Zero of the Alaska Highway is located in Dawson Creek, BC (not to be confused with Dawson City, YT).

Alberta

Population: 4,291,980
Capital: Edmonton
Largest City: Calgary
Area: 255,540 square miles/661,848 square km
Highest Point: Mount Columbia, 12,294 feet/3,747m
Lowest Point: Slave River Valley at 573 feet/175m
Provincial Flower: Wild rose
Provincial Tree: Lodgepole pine
Provincial Bird: Great horned owl
Provincial Motto: Strong and Free
Major Industries: Petrochemicals, forest products, agriculture, food processing, tourism, machinery, electronics and telecommunications, business services
Drinking age: 18. Liquor, beer and wine are sold in private liquor stores.
Visitor Information: Travel Alberta, Calgary; Phone 1-800-ALBERTA; travelinfo@travelalberta.com; www.travelalberta.com

The Province of Alberta is bordered to the west by British Columbia, to the south by Montana, to the east by Saskatchewan and to the north by the Northwest Territories. Among the dramatic features of this geographically fascinating area are the vast Canadian Rockies, the Columbia Icefields, unique geological formations of the Canadian Badlands around Drumheller and central Alberta, home to some of the world's

largest deposits of dinosaur fossils. View these displayed at the Royal Tyrrell Museum in Drumheller and the Philip J. Currie Dinosaur Museum near Grande Prairie.

Indigenous people include the Assiniboine, Blackfoot, Cree and Sarcee. The first European settlers—fur traders—arrived in the 18th century. In 1905, Alberta became a province of Canada. Discoveries of oil and natural gas deposits in the early 1900s caused economic growth, and in the 1970s, 1980s and 1990s, these deposits brought prosperity. Edmonton in central Alberta and Calgary and Lethbridge to the south are the most populated cities and are major destinations. Grande Prairie in Alberta's northwest, offers travelers all services en route to the Alaska Highway.

Banff and Jasper are 2 of Alberta's 5 national parks and are located in the Canadian Rockies. These parks host several million visitors a year. Alberta has 59 National Historic Sites.

Northwest Territories

Population: 44,469
Capital: Yellowknife
Largest City: Yellowknife
Area: 452,480 square miles/1,171,918 square km
Highest Point: Unnamed peak, 9,062 feet/2,762m
Lowest Point: Beaufort Sea, sea level
Territorial Flower: Mountain aven
Territorial Tree: Tamarack
Territorial Bird: Gyrfalcon
Major Industries: Mining, fishing, tourism, government
Drinking age: 19. Packaged liquor, beer and wine are sold in government liquor stores. Sale and possession of alcohol is prohibited in several communities.
Visitor Information: Northwest Territories Tourism, Yellowknife; Phone (867) 873-5007 or toll-free within the U.S. and Canada at 1-800-661-0788; email info@spectacularnwt.com; spectacularnwt.com

On April 1, 1999, Northwest Territories was divided into 2 territories. This division created Nunavut and its capital, Iqaluit on Baffin Island, in what was the eastern half of the old Northwest Territories. The new Northwest Territories—the western half of the former Northwest Territories—comprises a sixth of Canada and is about the size of Alaska. Roughly half of the population of Northwest Territories is Aboriginal, including Dene, Inuvialuit and Métis.

Northwest Territories' has 5 national parks, including Wood Buffalo National Park. Established in 1922, Wood Buffalo is one of the largest national parks in the world and the largest in Canada. There are also over 40 Canadian historic places.

Access to Northwest Territories is from Alberta via the Mackenzie Highway or from British Columbia via the Liard Highway both with year-round access to Yellowknife. (Both routes are found in the Deh Cho Route section.) Road access from Yukon is via the Dempster Highway to Inuvik or the North Canol Road which deadends at the NWT border. A major road-building project in the 1960s constructed most of the highway system in western Northwest Territories.

How to Use The MILEPOST®

The *MILEPOST*® provides mile-by-mile descriptions of all major highways and roads in Alaska and northwestern Canada; detailed information on all major destinations (cities, communities, national parks, attractions) and "how-to" help for various modes of transportation (air, ferry, railroads, etc.). *Refer to the Contents on page 1 and the Index on pages 702–704.*

The *MILEPOST*® will work for you regardless of how you plan to travel—whether by car, by plane, on a tour bus, ferry, cruiseship or by bicycle. It will help you plan your trip, as well as act as a valuable guide during your trip.

The highway logs in *The MILEPOST*® are the backbone of the text. These mile-by-mile descriptions of highways and byways of the North contain campgrounds, dining, lodging, gas, grocery and other services, attractions, fishing spots, road conditions, geography, history and much more.

The Key to Highways maps on pages 8–10 show you driving distances and which highways are covered within *The MILEPOST*®. The Basic Itineraries on pages 11–14 offer ideas of how to put together your trip.

To the right is an abbreviated version of part of the Parks Highway log, keyed to help you understand how to read all highway logs in *The MILEPOST*®.

1. A boldface paragraph appears at the beginning of each highway log showing beginning/ending destinations and the boldface letters representing them. In this log A represents **Anchorage**, C is **Cantwell** and F is **Fairbanks**. We've also added direction and arrows in some logs to indicate whether you read fron to back or back to front.

2. The boldface numbers following the letters represent the distance in miles from the beginning and ending destinations. (In Canada, the metric equivalent in kilometers follows the boldface mileage.) In this example, the Denali National Park entrance is located at **A 237.4 C 27.4 F 124.6** or 237.4 miles from Anchorage, 27.4 miles from Cantwell and 124.6 miles from Fairbanks.

3. **Junctions** with other logged roads are accented by a color bar. The cross-referenced section is uppercased: e.g. DENALI NATIONAL PARK section is referenced here. (*If a page number is not given, refer to Contents, page 1.*)

4. "Log" advertisements are classified-type advertisements that appear in the text. These are identified by the boldface name of the business at the beginning of the entry and "[ADVERTISEMENT]" at the end. These log advertisements are written by the advertiser.

5. Display advertisements are keyed in the log by a boldface entry at their highway locations, followed by the words "See display ad." Their advertisement will appear near this entry or a page and/or section will be referenced.

It may also help you to know how our field editors log the highways. *The MILEPOST*® field editors drive each highway, taking notes on facilities, features and attractions along the way and note the mile at which they appear. Mileages are measured from the beginning of the highway, which is generally at a junction or the city limits, to the end of the highway, also usually a junction or city limits. Most highways in *The MILEPOST*® are logged either south to north or east to west. If you are traveling the opposite direction of the log, you will read the log back to front. To determine driving distance between 2 points, simply subtract from the first mileage figure.

The introduction to each highway logged in *The MILEPOST*® includes a chart of mileages between major points (see below).

Maps also accompany highways logged in *The MILEPOST*®, each with a key explaining the abbreviations (see example at bottom). Key to mileage boxes reflect rounded off mileages.

The following symbols appear in *The MILEPOST*® logs:

Symbol	Meaning	Symbol	Meaning
⛺	Campground	⛽	Gas station
🎣	Fishing	⛽	Gas station with diesel
➕	Medical aid	🔭	Wildlife/Birding views
↓↑	Direction	♿	Handicap Accessible

Parks Highway Log

Northbound: Distance from Anchorage (A) is followed by distance from Cantwell (C) and distance from Fairbanks (F). Read log: ❶ ↓

❷ **A 237.4 C 27.4 F 124.6 Denali National Park and Preserve** entrance. Turnoff to west on Park Road for access to Denali National Park and Preserve.

❸ **Junction** 92-mile-long Park Road, which provides access to visitor services and attractions in Denali National Park. See DENALI NATIONAL PARK section on page 427 for Park Road log and details on park entrance fee, campgrounds, transportation and activities in the park.

Begin paved pedestrian path on west side of Parks Highway, which leads north along the highway to Denali Park commercial area.

Begin posted speed zone northbound.

A 238 C 28 F 124 Third bridge northbound over the Nenana River. Access to west Glacier Way. Access to west for double-ended **Mile 238 Rest Area**; parking, toilets, tables and access to the pedestrian path. *CAUTION: Supervise children; pets must be on a leash. It is a long drop to the river from the rest area.*

❹ **A 238.1 C 28.1 F 123.9 Grande Denali Lodge.** Panoramic views from our perch on Sugarloaf Mountain. Enjoy our fireside lobby, dine at award-winning Alpenglow Restaurant, or grab a bite at Peak Spirits. 160 guest rooms, 6 cozy cabins, private meeting room. Rooms have WiFi, Keurig coffee maker, A/C, fridge. Tour desk, free shuttle, on-site laundry.1-855-683-8600. [ADVERTISEMENT]

A 238.7 C 28.7 F 122.9 Sourdough Road. Access east to **Denali Rainbow Village RV Park and Motel**, located behind the Boardwalk Mall. Urgent Care to west.

➕ ⛺

❺ **Denali Rainbow Village RV Park and Motel.** See display ad on page 433 in the DENALI NATIONAL PARK section.

Distance in miles	Anchorage	Denali Park	Fairbanks	Talkeetna	Wasilla
Anchorage		237	362	113	42
Denali Park	237		125	153	195
Fairbanks	362	125		278	320
Talkeetna	113	153	278		71
Wasilla	42	195	320	71	

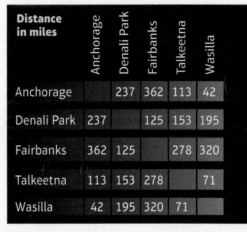

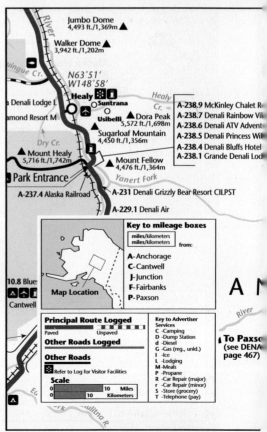

Jumbo Dome 4,493 ft./1,369m ▲
Walker Dome 3,942 ft./1,202m ▲
N63°51' W148°58'
Healy ▢
Suntrana
Denali Lodge L
amond Resort M
Usibelli
Dora Peak 5,572 ft./1,698m ▲
Sugarloaf Mountain 4,450 ft./1,356m ▲
Dry Cr.
▲ Mount Healy 5,716 ft./1,742m
Mount Fellow 4,476 ft./1,364m ▲
Park Entrance
A-237.4 Alaska Railroad
A-231 Denali Grizzly Bear Resort CILPST
A-229.1 Denali Air
Yanert Fork
Healy Cr.
A-238.9 McKinley Chalet
A-238.7 Denali Rainbow Vil
A-238.6 Denali ATV Advent
A-238.5 Denali Princess Wi
A-238.4 Denali Bluffs Hotel
A-238.1 Grande Denali Lod

10.8 Blues
Cantwell

Key to mileage boxes
miles/kilometers
miles/kilometers from:
A-Anchorage
C-Cantwell
J-Junction
F-Fairbanks
P-Paxson

Map Location

Principal Route Logged
Paved ‖ Unpaved
Other Roads Logged
Other Roads
Refer to Log for Visitor Facilities

Key to Advertiser Services
C -Camping
D -Dump Station
d -Diesel
G -Gas (reg., unld.)
I -Ice
L -Lodging
M -Meals
P -Propane
R -Car Repair (major)
r -Car Repair (minor)
S -Store (grocery)
T -Telephone (pay)

Scale
0 | 10 Miles
0 | 10 Kilometers

A N
River
To Paxso
(see DENA
page 467)

Map 1

INTRODUCTION

Key to Highways Map 1 Miles(Kilometers) between junctions and communities

© 2019 The MILEPOST®

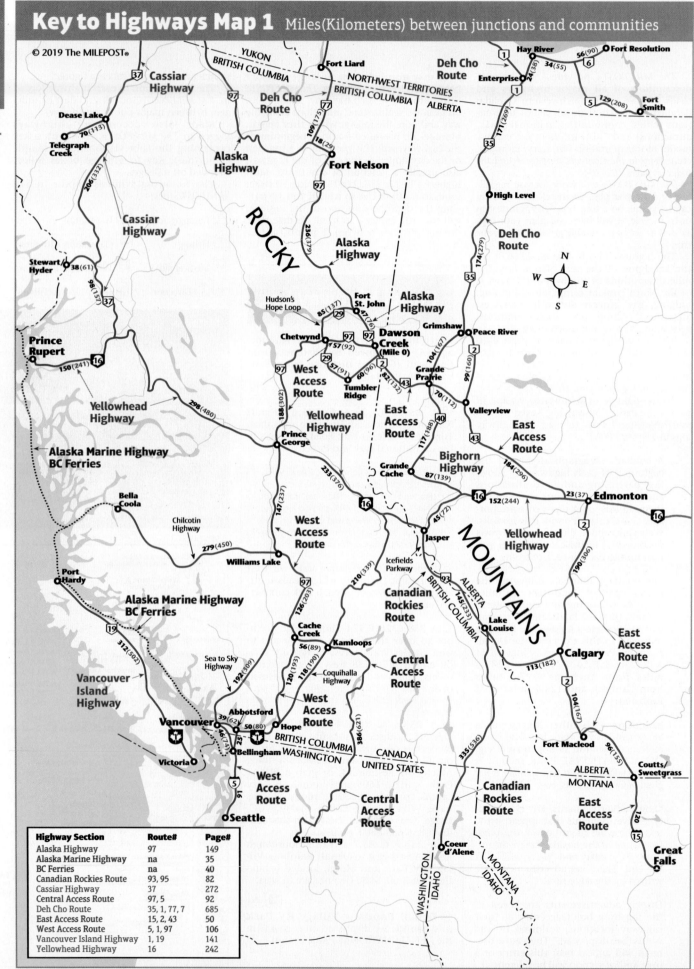

YUKON
BRITISH COLUMBIA

Cassiar Highway

Deh Cho Route

NORTHWEST TERRITORIES
BRITISH COLUMBIA
ALBERTA

Fort Liard

Deh Cho Route

Hay River

Enterprise

34(55)

56(90)

Fort Resolution

Fort Smith

Dease Lake

70(113)

Telegraph Creek

206(332)

Alaska Highway

109(175)

77

18(29)

Fort Nelson

236(379)

97

High Level

174(279)

35

Deh Cho Route

171(269)

35

129(208)

5

6

Stewart Hyder

38(61)

98(157)

37

Cassiar Highway

ROCKY

Alaska Highway

Hudson's Hope Loop

85(137)

29

Fort St. John

47(76)

Alaska Highway

Grimshaw

Peace River

Prince Rupert

150(241)

16

Chetwynd

57(92)

97

97

Dawson Creek (Mile 0)

104(167)

99(160)

2

Yellowhead Highway

298(480)

188(302)

97

West Access Route

29

57(91)

60(96)

Tumbler Ridge

2

82(132)

43

Grande Prairie

70(112)

Valleyview

43

East Access Route

Alaska Marine Highway
BC Ferries

Yellowhead Highway

Prince George

233(376)

East Access Route

117(188)

40

Bighorn Highway

184(296)

Bella Coola

147(237)

Grande Cache

87(139)

16

152(244)

23(37)

Edmonton

16

Chilcotin Highway

279(450)

Williams Lake

West Access Route

16

45(72)

MOUNTAINS

2

Port Hardy

97

126(203)

210(339)

Jasper

Icefields Parkway

93

ALBERTA

Yellowhead Highway

190(306)

19

312(502)

Cache Creek

56(89)

Kamloops

Canadian Rockies Route

145(233)

BRITISH COLUMBIA

Lake Louise

East Access Route

Sea to Sky Highway

192(309)

120(193)

118(190)

Coquihalla Highway

Central Access Route

113(182)

Calgary

Vancouver Island Highway

39(62)

Abbotsford

West Access Route

386(621)

2

104(167)

Vancouver

50(80)

Hope

335(536)

Fort Macleod

96(155)

Coutts/Sweetgrass

Victoria

46(73)

Bellingham

BRITISH COLUMBIA

WASHINGTON

CANADA

UNITED STATES

ALBERTA

MONTANA

5

West Access Route

19

Canadian Rockies Route

East Access Route

120

Seattle

Central Access Route

15

Ellensburg

Coeur d'Alene

WASHINGTON
IDAHO

MONTANA
IDAHO

Great Falls

Highway Section	Route#	Page#
Alaska Highway	97	149
Alaska Marine Highway	na	35
BC Ferries	na	40
Canadian Rockies Route	93, 95	82
Cassiar Highway	37	272
Central Access Route	97, 5	92
Deh Cho Route	35, 1, 77, 7	685
East Access Route	15, 2, 43	50
West Access Route	5, 1, 97	106
Vancouver Island Highway	1, 19	141
Yellowhead Highway	16	242

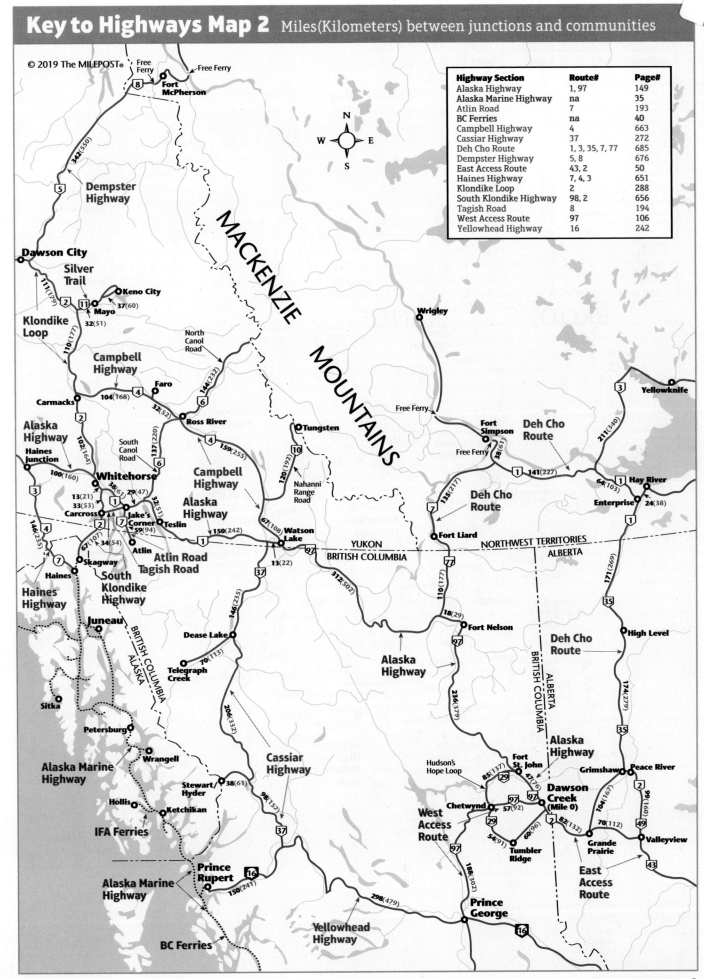

© 2019 The MILEPOST®

Highway Section	Route#	Page#
Alaska Highway	1, 97	149
Alaska Marine Highway	na	35
Atlin Road	7	193
BC Ferries	na	40
Campbell Highway	4	663
Cassiar Highway	37	272
Deh Cho Route	1, 3, 35, 7, 77	685
Dempster Highway	5, 8	676
East Access Route	43, 2	50
Haines Highway	7, 4, 3	651
Klondike Loop	2	288
South Klondike Highway	98, 2	656
Tagish Road	8	194
West Access Route	97	106
Yellowhead Highway	16	242

Free Ferry

Free Ferry

8 Fort McPherson

342(550)

5 Dempster Highway

Dawson City

Silver Trail

111(179)

2 11 Mayo 37(60) Keno City

32(51)

Klondike Loop

110(177)

Campbell Highway

Carmacks

104(168) 4 Faro

North Canol Road

144(232)

32(52) 6 Ross River

Alaska Highway

102(164)

Haines Junction

100(160)

South Canol Road

137(220)

4 159(255)

MACKENZIE MOUNTAINS

Wrigley

Tungsten

120(192)

Nahanni Range Road

10

3 Yellowknife

Free Ferry

Fort Simpson

Deh Cho Route

38(61) Free Ferry

1 141(227)

211(340)

64(103) Hay River

Enterprise 24(38)

Whitehorse

13(21) 38(61)

33(53) 1 29(47)

3

Carcross 32(51)

146(235) 2 7 Jake's Corner

4 67(107) 34(54) 59(94) Teslin

Atlin

7 Skagway

Haines

Haines Highway

South Klondike Highway

Juneau

Atlin Road Tagish Road

Campbell Highway

Alaska Highway

150(242)

1 67(108) Watson Lake

97

13(22)

37

312(502)

YUKON
BRITISH COLUMBIA

Deh Cho Route

7 135(217)

Fort Liard

NORTHWEST TERRITORIES
ALBERTA

110(177)

77

1

BRITISH COLUMBIA
ALASKA

Dease Lake

70(113)

Telegraph Creek

Sitka

Petersburg

Wrangell

Alaska Marine Highway

Hollis

Ketchikan

IFA Ferries

206(332)

Cassiar Highway

Stewart/ Hyder 38(61)

98(157)

37

18(29) Fort Nelson

97

Alaska Highway

236(379)

Deh Cho Route

High Level

171(269)

35

174(279)

35

Alaska Highway

Hudson's Hope Loop

85(137)

Fort St. John

29 47(76)

Grimshaw Peace River

Dawson Creek (Mile 0)

97

104(167)

2 66(106)

West Access Route

Chetwynd 57(92)

29

54(91) 60(96) Tumbler Ridge

2 82(132)

70(112) 49

Grande Prairie

Valleyview

97

188(302)

East Access Route

43

Prince Rupert 16

150(241)

Alaska Marine Highway

BC Ferries

Yellowhead Highway

298(479)

Prince George

16

Map 3 · INTRODUCTION

Key to Highways Map 3 · Miles(Kilometers) between junctions and communities

© 2019 The MILEPOST®

Highway Section	Route#	Page#
Alaska Highway	1, 2	149
Alaska Marine Highway	na	35
Atlin Road	7	193
Campbell Highway	4	683
Dalton Highway	11	492
Dempster Highway	5, 8	676
Denali Highway	8	467
Edgerton Highway/		
McCarthy Road	10	457
Elliott Highway	2	485
Glenn Highway	1, 4	318
Haines Highway	7, 4, 3	651
Klondike Loop	2, 9, 5	288
Parks Highway	3	374
Richardson Highway	4, 2	437
Seward Highway	1, 9	511
South Klondike Highway	98, 2	656
Steese Highway	6	476
Sterling Highway	1	538
Tagish Road	8	194
Taylor Highway	5	310
Tok Cutoff	3	318
Top of the World Highway	9	308

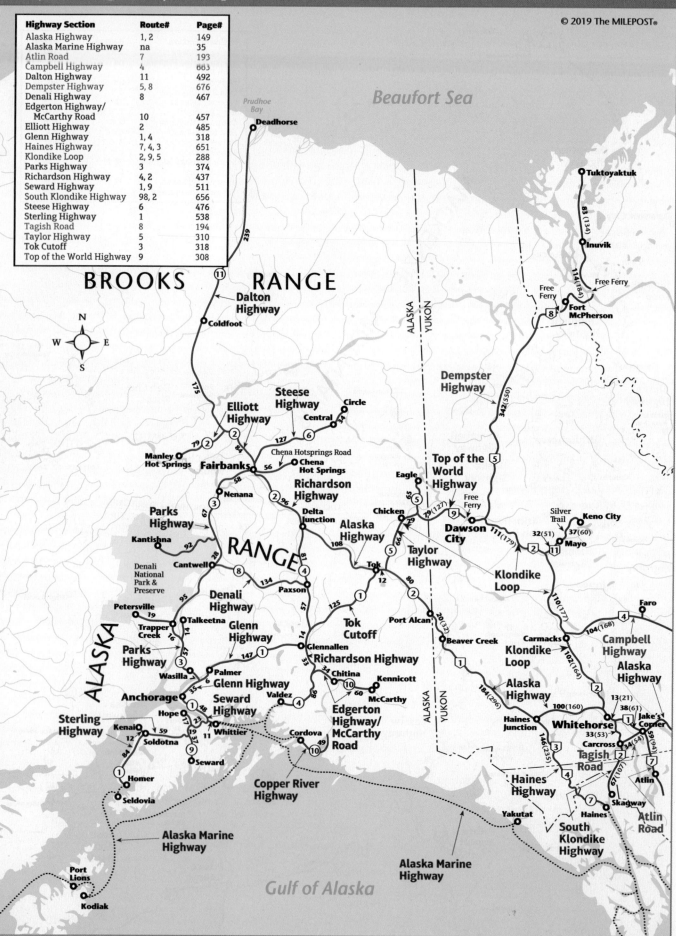

Basic Itinerary #1:

Inbound: Alaska Highway via West Access Route

Outbound: Inside Passage

Major Attractions

1. Sea to Sky Highway
2. Barkerville
3. Muncho Lake
4. Liard Hotsprings
5. Sign Post Forest
6. SS Klondike
7. Kluane Lake
8. Fairbanks
9. Denali National Park
10. Glenn Highway Scenic Byway
11. Southeast Alaska/ Inside Passage

The classic itinerary for Alaska-bound travelers on the West Access route is to drive the Alaska Highway one-way, and take the Alaska Marine Highway the other way via the Inside Passage from Haines, AK, to Bellingham, WA. The ferry portion of the itinerary requires advance reservations. Travelers should work backwards from their ferry departure date when estimating travel time for the driving portion of the trip.

Depart Seattle on the West Access Route, but cross the international border at Blaine (instead of Sumas), and follow Highway 99 through Vancouver to Horseshoe Bay and the start of the Sea to Sky Highway. This stunning highway, a former logging road, is a slight twist in the traditional West Access approach to the Alaska Highway. And it is, indeed, a twisting road, but Highway 99 also offers an exciting route into British Columbia's Cariboo country. North of Cache Creek on Highway 97 turn off to Wells and Barkerville for part of the Gold Rush Circle Route side trip.

Leave Prince George via the Hart Highway to Dawson Creek. Stop in Chetwynd for a root-beer float and a look at some amazing chainsaw sculptures. Take a Tumbler Ridge side trip to see Kinuseo Falls or drive the Hudson's Hope Loop and tour the huge W.A.C. Bennett Dam.

Heading north up the Alaska Highway, allow enough time to stop and enjoy wildlife viewing, scenic lakes and historic lodges along the way. Stop for a soak at Liard River Hotsprings. At Watson Lake, first stop in Yukon, photograph the famous Sign Post Forest. From Watson Lake it is just 164 miles to Teslin, home of the George Johnston Museum and the Tlingit Heritage Center.

Next stop is Whitehorse, capital of Yukon and home to many of Yukon's best known attractions, including the SS *Klond-*

ike, Yukon Beringia Interpretive Center and the Yukon Transportation Museum. Side trips include scenic Atlin on Atlin Road and/or Emerald Lake and Carcross on the South Klondike Highway. Ride the historic White Pass & Yukon Route Railway roundtrip between Carcross and Skagway.

Continuing north from Whitehorse, you will visit Haines Junction, the Kluane Lake area and Beaver Creek just before the border of Alaska at Port Alcan. Your first stop in Alaska will probably be Tok, which has all services and 2 visitor information centers. Delta Junction also has all services and is the official end of the historic Alaska Highway. Stop at the Big Delta State Historical Park just beyond Delta Junction and before driving on to Fairbanks.

Fairbanks has many attractions: Allow time for side trips to gold mines, Chena Hot Springs, the trans-Alaska pipeline, as well as visits to the Large Animal Research Station, Museum of the North and Pioneer Park.

Plan on at least 2 days (or more) to drive the Parks Highway from Fairbanks south to Anchorage. There's quite a bit to see and do on this highway, from horseback riding to touring sled dog kennels. Denali National Park is a must stop as is the short side trip to Talkeetna. Anchorage side trips include Prince William Sound and the Kenai Peninsula.

From Anchorage, take the Glenn Highway Scenic Byway, with views of Matanuska

Glacier, to the Tok Cutoff to Tok. From Tok, go southeast on the Alaska Highway to Haines Junction, YT, then south on the Haines Highway to Haines, AK, where you catch the Alaska state ferry south to Bellingham, WA. If time allows, include stopovers at Southeast ports along the Inside Passage/ Alaska Marine Highway portion of your trip.

Inbound mileage: 2,701 miles
Detail: Seattle to Dawson Creek 853 miles
Dawson Creek to Fairbanks 1,486 miles
Fairbanks to Anchorage 362 miles

Outbound mileage: 771 miles. Ferry travel is 68 hours (about 3 days).
Detail: Anchorage to Tok 328 miles
Tok to Haines 443 miles

FOLLOWING THIS ITINERARY IN The MILEPOST

NOTE: For reverse itinerary, read sections from bottom to top and reverse page numbers.
Page numbers for major attractions and side trip options are found on the Contents page and/or in the Index.

Map labels: ALASKA, Fairbanks, Delta Junction, Tok, Anchorage, YUKON, Whitehorse, Haines, Juneau, Watson Lake, Fort Nelson, Petersburg, BRITISH COLUMBIA, Ketchikan, Prince Rupert, Dawson Creek, ALBERTA, Prince George, Bellingham, WASHINGTON, Seattle

Basic Itinerary #2:

Inbound: Central Access/Hart Hwy. to Alaska Hwy. and Klondike Loop

Outbound: Inside Passage to Yellowhead Hwy. to Canadian Rockies Route

This itinerary uses the Central Access route and part of the West Access route inbound to reach the Alaska Highway. Drive north to Whitehorse and enter Alaska via the Klondike Loop. On the return, take the Alaska Marine Highway from Haines to Prince Rupert, BC, and drive east on the Yellowhead Highway to Jasper and follow the Icefields Parkway south. The ferry portion of this itinerary requires advance planning. Check current summer schedules and time your itinerary accordingly.

Head up the Central Access Route from Ellensburg, WA, through British Columbia's Okanagan region. Follow Yellowhead Highway 5 north to Clearwater, making time to stop and see the spectacular waterfalls at Wells Gray Provincial Park. At Tete Jaune Cache, where Yellowhead 5 junctions with Yellowhead 16, drive west to Prince George and follow the Hart Highway northeast to Dawson Creek, BC, Mile Zero of the Alaska Highway.

Head north on the Alaska Highway, allowing enough time to stop and enjoy wildlife viewing, rivers, historic lodges, beautiful Muncho Lake and Liard River Hotsprings. At Watson Lake, first stop in Yukon, don't miss the famous Sign Post Forest. Continue on to Whitehorse, capital of Yukon and home to many of Yukon's best known attractions, including the SS *Klondike*, Yukon Beringia Interpretive Center and the Yukon Transportation Museum.

Just northwest of Whitehorse, turn off the Alaska Highway onto the Klondike Highway, which leads to the historic gold rush town of Dawson City. After exploring Dawson, line up early for the ferry ride across the Yukon River to the Top of the World Highway. The ride only takes a few minutes, but on busy summer days, Alaska-bound traffic can stack up. You will also want to allow plenty of time to drive the Top of the World Highway; winding, narrow road and gravel breaks make this scenic drive a slow one.

After crossing into Alaska, you will junction with the Taylor Highway, which leads north to Eagle on the Yukon River and south through Chicken to the Alaska Highway. At Chicken, don't miss the Pedro gold dredge, Tisha's schoolhouse or Beautiful Downtown Chicken. The Taylor Highway from Chicken south to the Alaska Highway junction is paved. It is only 12 miles from this junction to Tok.

Tok is an important service stop on the Alaska Highway and it is also decision-making time: Do you first head southwest on the Tok Cutoff/Glenn Highway to Anchorage, or continue on the Alaska Highway to Delta Junction and on to Fairbanks? Since any driving tour of Alaska should include Anchorage, Fairbanks and Denali National Park, it may be a question of timing, with events like Fairbanks' Midnight Sun Baseball Game (June 21st) or salmon runs on the Kenai Peninsula helping decide your route.

Outbound from Tok, take the Alaska Highway southeast to Haines Junction and the Haines Highway to Haines (or the South Klondike Highway to Skagway). Arrange for ferry passage through Southeast Alaska to Prince Rupert, BC. From Prince Rupert, it is a 682-mile drive via Yellowhead Highway 16 to Jasper. From Jasper, head south on the Icefields Parkway to junction with Trans-Canada Highway 1. Head east to Castle Junction, then south on BC Highway 93 to Radium Hot Springs. BC Highways 93/95 take you south to the U.S. border and U.S. Highway 95 to Coeur d'Alene, ID.

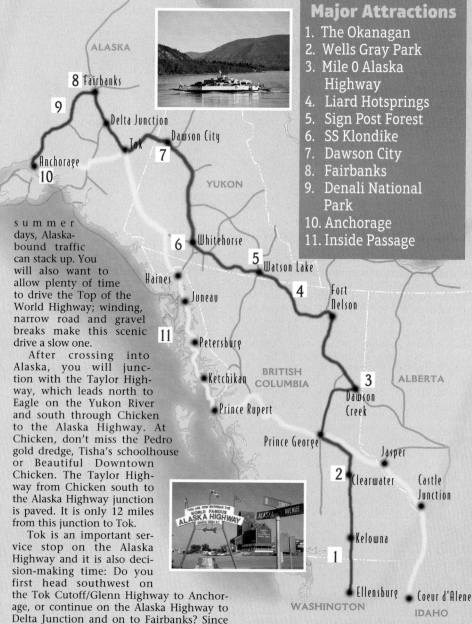

NOTE: For reverse itinerary, read sections from bottom to top and reverse page numbers.
Page numbers for major attractions and side trip options are found on the Contents page and/or in the Index.

Major Attractions

1. The Okanagan
2. Wells Gray Park
3. Mile 0 Alaska Highway
4. Liard Hotsprings
5. Sign Post Forest
6. SS Klondike
7. Dawson City
8. Fairbanks
9. Denali National Park
10. Anchorage
11. Inside Passage

Inbound mileage: 2,985 miles
*Detail: Ellensburg to Dawson Creek 1,012 miles
Dawson Creek to Whitehorse 895 miles
Whitehorse to Tok 510 miles
Tok to Fairbanks 206 miles
Fairbanks to Anchorage 362 miles*

Outbound mileage: 1,932 or 2,109 miles.
Ferry travel is 42 hours.
*Detail: Anchorage to Haines 771 miles
(OR Anchorage to Skagway 948 miles)
Prince Rupert to Jasper 682 miles
Jasper to Coeur d'Alene 479 miles*

Basic Itinerary #3:

Inbound: Inside Passage/Klondike Loop
Outbound: Alaska & Cassiar highways to West Access

This inbound itinerary combines ferry travel on the Alaska Marine Highway through the Inside Passage (Bellingham, WA, to Skagway, AK), with the Klondike Loop route into Alaska, while the outbound is an all-land route via the Alaska Highway, Cassiar and Yellowhead highways to the West Access Route with return to Seattle, WA. Reserve in advance for ferry travel.

This sample itinerary allows 8 to 10 days for exploring Southeast Alaska by ferry and road. Or you can choose to stay on the ferry for the 3-day trip from Bellingham to Skagway.

Ketchikan is first port of call in Alaska. The morning arrival allows you much of the day to explore the town and approximately 30 miles of road. Saxman Totem Park is just 2 miles from downtown; Totem Bight State Historical Park is just 10 miles north.

The following day, take the Inter-Island Ferry Authority (IFA) from Ketchikan to Hollis on Prince of Wales Island, the third largest island under the American flag. Spend a full day exploring the island and return to Ketchikan the next day and ride the mainline state ferry route to Wrangell.

Wrangell attractions include Chief Shakes Island and Tribal House in the harbor. If you have the time, book a boat trip with one of the local outfitters to Anan Wildlife Observatory to see the bears or up the Stikine River to see glorious scenery. Experience one of the best campground views in Alaska at Nemo Point.

Depart Wrangell for Petersburg with the Alaska Marine Highway. (State ferries dock a short walk from downtown.) Petersburg attractions include whale watching and tours out to LeConte Glacier.

From Petersburg, continue by ferry to Juneau, Alaska's capital. Allow time to see Mendenhall Glacier and other Juneau sights.

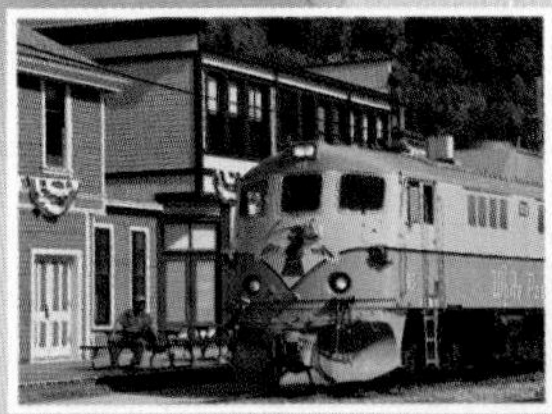

Continue by ferry to Skagway, home of Klondike Gold Rush National Historial Park. Don't miss the White Pass & Yukon Route Railway excursion out of Skagway!

It is only a 2½-hour drive from Skagway, AK, to Whitehorse, YT, via the South Klondike Highway and it is a beautiful drive in clear weather. After sightseeing Whitehorse, drive up the Alaska Highway a few miles and turn on to the North Klondike Highway to Dawson City, which forms the first part of the Klondike Loop. It is a day's drive from Whitehorse, capital of Yukon, to Dawson City, the first capital of Yukon, longer if you allow time to visit Takhini Hot Springs and the Yukon Wildlife Preserve.

Cross the Yukon River by ferry at Dawson City and follow the gravel Top of the World Highway into Alaska, where the Taylor Highway winds south through Chicken and the historic Fortymile gold mining district before it junctions with the Alaska Highway just 12 miles east of Tok. Continue west on the Alaska and Richardson highways to Fairbanks. After taking in Fairbanks area attractions like Pioneer Park, Chena Hot Springs and the University of Alaska's Museum of the North, drive down the Parks Highway to Denali National Park, Talkeetna and Anchorage.

Explore the Kenai Peninsula before heading out the Glenn Highway/Tok Cutoff from Anchorage to Tok. At Tok, take the Alaska Highway east to Watson Lake to see the Sign Post Forest, then backtrack 13 miles west and head south on the Cassiar/Highway 37 into British Columbia.

Cassiar Highway 37 is popular with motorists who have driven the Alaska Highway and are looking for an alternate route for the drive back. The Cassiar accesses Stewart, BC, and Hyder, AK, an interesting side trip with glaciers (Bear and Salmon) and bear viewing (at Fish Creek).

Major Attractions

1. Inside Passage
2. Klondike Gold Rush National Historical Park
3. Whitehorse
4. Dawson City
5. Big Delta Historical Park
6. Denali National Park
7. Anchorage
8. Kenai Peninsula
9. Glenn Highway
10. Stewart/Hyder
11. Fraser Canyon
12. Barkerville

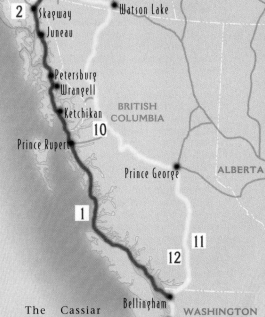

The Cassiar junctions with Yellowhead Highway 16, which takes you east to Prince George, where you pick up the West Access Route south. Take a side trip to Wells and Barkerville for part of the Gold Rush Circle Route then continue to the international border at Sumas and back down I-5 to Seattle, WA.

Inbound mileage: 1,195 miles plus 3 to 10 days ferry travel time.
Detail: Skagway to Dawson City 442 miles
Dawson City to Fairbanks 391 miles
Fairbanks to Anchorage 362 miles

Outbound mileage: 2,320 miles
Detail: Anchorage to Tok 328 miles
Tok to Watson Lake 669
Watson Lake to Prince George 761
Prince George to Seattle 562

Map labels: ALASKA, Fairbanks, Delta Junction, Tok, Dawson City, YUKON, Anchorage, Whitehorse, Skagway, Watson Lake, Juneau, Petersburg, Wrangell, Ketchikan, BRITISH COLUMBIA, Prince Rupert, Prince George, ALBERTA, Bellingham, WASHINGTON, Seattle

Basic Itinerary #4:

Inbound: Deh Cho Route, Alaska Highway, Klondike Loop
Outbound: Cassiar & Yellowhead highways to East Access

Major Attractions

1. Icefields Parkway
2. Alexandra Falls
3. Yellowknife
4. Dawson City
5. Fairbanks
6. Anchorage
7. Salmon Glacier

This all-land itinerary features a lot of wilderness driving and offers an off-the-beaten-path choice on the inbound portion via the Deh Cho Route through Northwest Territories to junction with the Alaska Highway. Also in the mix: The less traveled Bighorn Route coupled with the wildly popular Icefields Parkway (both in Alberta).

Head north on the East Access Route from Great Falls, MT, crossing into Alberta at Sweetgrass, MT/Coutts, AB, and continue north to Calgary, one of the province's 2 largest population centers. Turn west on Trans-Canada Highway 1 to the spectacular Icefields Parkway. From Jasper, at the north end of the Icefields Parkway, drive east 45 miles to reach the Bighorn Highway and take it north to Grande Prairie.

From Grande Prairie, one of the portals to Alberta's Peace River region, continue driving north. Stop at the remarkable Dunvegan Provincial Park and Historic Site en route. Continue on to Grimshaw, which is Mile Zero of the Mackenzie Highway. The Mackenzie Highway is part of the Deh Cho Route itinerary through Northwest Territories.

A well-maintained, two-lane highway, the Mackenzie Highway travels straight through northern Alberta, and into Northwest Territories about 400 miles north of Grande Prairie. From the Alberta/NWT border, the Deh Cho Route continues as NWT Highway 1, the aptly named Waterfalls Route, featuring the spectacular Alexandra and Louise waterfalls.

A number of NWT highways connect with the Deh Cho Route, each with its own attractions. We suggest you take the Frontier Trail (Highway 3) to Yellowknife. Along the way see herds of bison. This highway crosses a pre-Cambrian shield to a modern city on the territory's largest lake.

The Deh Cho Route follows Highway 1 to junction with the Liard Trail south to the Alaska Highway. Make the 76-mile round-trip side trip to Fort Simpson before continuing on to Fort Liard and then junctions with the Alaska Highway 17 miles west of Fort Nelson.

From the Liard Trail junction, drive northwest 312 miles to Watson Lake, first stop in the Yukon. At Watson Lake, you continue northwest on the Alaska Highway to just beyond Whitehorse, where it junctions with the Klondike Highway to Dawson City (for more details see Itinerary #2).

After exploring Dawson City, the first capital of Yukon and a Klondike Gold Rush heritage site, take the 5-minute ferry ride across the Yukon River. (See the KLONDIKE LOOP section for details on when the customs station is open here.) On the other side you will follow the Top of the World Highway into Alaska, then the Taylor Highway south through Chicken and the historic Fortymile gold mining district to the Alaska Highway 12 miles east of Tok. From Tok, continue west on the Alaska/Richardson Highway to Fairbanks, then south on the Parks Highway to Anchorage.

The outbound portion of this trip takes the Glenn Highway/Tok Cutoff from Anchorage to Tok, then the Alaska Highway from Tok east and south to the Cassiar Highway/Highway 37. The Cassiar offers an easy access 2-lane highway to Stewart, BC, and Hyder, AK, via Highway 37A. This is a photo worthy side trip with Bear and Salmon glaciers and bear viewing (Fish Creek).

The southern terminus of the Cassiar Highway junctions with Yellowhead Highway 16. Travel east to Edmonton on the East Access Route then south to Calgary (or veer south at Jasper for Icefields Parkway to Cal-

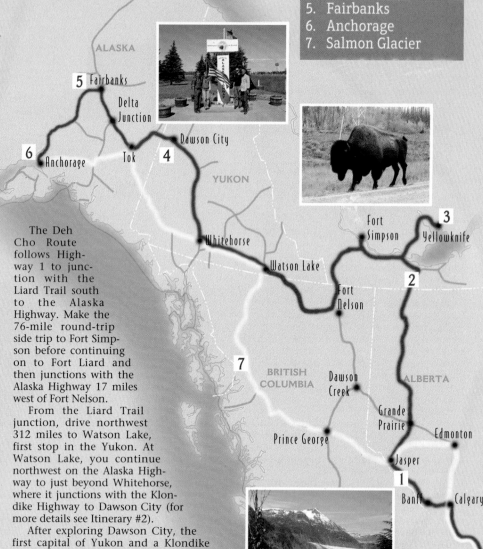

gary) and continue south to Great Falls, MT.

Inbound mileage: 3,875 miles.
Detail: Great Falls to Calgary 320 miles
Calgary to Grande Cache 374 miles
Grande Cache to Yellowknife 843 miles
Yellowknife to Fort Simpson 390 miles
Fort Simpson to Watson Lake 595 miles
Watson Lake to Whitehorse 275 miles
Whitehorse to Dawson City 323 miles
Dawson City to Fairbanks 390 miles
Fairbanks to Anchorage 364 miles

Outbound mileage: 2,669 miles.
Detail: Anchorage to Tok 328 miles
Tok to Whitehorse 396 miles
Whitehorse to Dease Lake 395 miles
Dease Lake to Prince George 602 miles
Prince George to Edmonton 454 miles
Edmonton to Great Falls 494 miles

NOTE: For reverse itinerary, read sections from bottom to top and reverse page numbers.
Page numbers for major attractions and side trip options are found on the Contents page.

Travel Planning

Denali is shrouded in clouds while Dall sheep soak in the sun. (©Donna Dewhurst)

Accommodations

Accommodations in the North can range from luxurious to utilitarian to downright funky. Along these roads there are fine lodges and major-chain hotels/motels (Best Western, Canada's Best Value Inn, Princess Lodges, Westmark Hotels and others); bed and breakfasts; hostels; log cabins; and yurts.

Considering the remoteness of many communities and the seasonal nature of Northern travel, you may be surprised at the wide variety of lodging available.

The larger cities along these routes, such as Anchorage, Fairbanks and Whitehorse, for example, have room quantities and options that you would expect in similarly sized communities down south, but in midsummer, even those locations can fill up quickly. The smaller communities provide a lesser number of rooms and options. Whether your destination is a major city or a small highway community, you should consider reserving ahead, if possible, to ensure a room is available.

Some facilities along highways of the North may be more rustic than you are used to. This is, after all, the Last Frontier! You will also find some first-class establishments in surprisingly remote locations along the highways, accommodations deemed interesting enough and charming enough to be included in the "best of" lists of various travel publications. Some of the amenities that you would find in large cities may be missing, but the hospitality of the North will typically make up for it.

NOTE: We do not rate accommodations. In our experience, you can have a 5-star experience in a 1-star hotel (or vice versa), and sometimes the remote location and lack of lodging options make ratings a moot point. Paid advertisements for accommodations appearing in *The MILEPOST®*—whether display ads or "log ads" placed in the highway log—are written by the advertisers themselves (these are followed by [ADVERTISEMENT]).

We do not endorse or guarantee any of these advertising facilities or services, but we trust that they will live up to their promises. If you feel that they do not, please write, phone or email us. We do not mediate disputes, but if we get enough complaints about a business not living up to its advertisement, we will ask the advertiser to do a reality check. Keep in mind that businesses may be summer seasonal, smaller locations may close unexpectedly due to unforeseeable events and rates can change.

Again, please call ahead if you want to ensure that you have a place to stay.

Air Travel

More than half of all visitors to Alaska arrive by air, more than 6 million people are served in Anchorage and Fairbanks International airports annually (this number includes Alaskans traveling within state). Air travel is one of the most common forms of transportation within the North. You can fly just about anywhere with wheels, skis or floats (some floatplanes will have wheels embedded in their floats and those are called "amphibs," short for amphibian). If there is no scheduled service to where you want to go and for what you want to do, you can almost always charter a plane to get there.

You will find charter planes at local airstrips. Most communities have a state-maintained airstrip or private airstrip. But keep in mind that not all airstrips have airports. You will find links to Alaska airport information at website: dot.alaska.gov/airport-portal.shtml.

Major communities such as Anchorage, Fairbanks and Juneau have a selection of companies offering air tours to glaciers and mountaintops in fixed-wing aircraft or helicopters. Other tour options include wildlife viewing (see more under "Wildlife Viewing" near the end of this section). For example, Rust's Flying Service out of Anchorage and Natron Air out of Soldotna offer bear viewing tours that will fly across Cook Inlet to Katmai National Park.

An air carrier must be licensed by the Federal Aviation Administration to fly passengers commercially. Many offer flights in small planes under Visual Flight Rules (VFR), which means the flight can take place only when weather and visual conditions permit the pilot to see 2 miles ahead, and the cloud ceiling is at least 1,000 feet. Passengers should be prepared to have a flight postponed or canceled if conditions are unsafe. For information on the FAA's Circle of Safety aviation education program, visit www.dot.alaska.gov/stwdav/forms/CircleofSafetyHANDBOOK.pdf or phone 1-866-357-4704. For information on flight delays from major airports, please check www.fly.faa.gov/flyfaa/usmap.jsp.

Airlines flying passengers within Alaska include Alaska Airlines, Grant Aviation, Ravn Alaska and PenAir.

Airlines flying passengers in Alaska include Air Canada, Alaska Airlines, Ameri-

Charter and scheduled air service are available to just about any destination in the North.
(©Judy Nadon, staff)

can Airlines, Condor, BP/ConocoPhillips, Delta Airlines, IcelandAir, Japan Airlines, Jet-Blue, Korean Air, Sun Country, TransNorthern, United Airlines and Yakutia Airlines.

Air Canada, Air North, Condor, Air North and West Jet serve Whitehorse, YT, while several major carriers serve larger cities such as Edmonton and Calgary, AB. International carriers from Asia and Russia also offer scheduled or charter flights.

There are more than 250 certified charter/air taxi operators in Alaska. Air taxi rates may vary from carrier to carrier. Most operators charge an hourly rate either per plane load or per passenger; others may charge on a per-mile basis.

Aside from offering transportation from one place to another, many flying services also offer—or specialize in—flightseeing. For a fixed fee, you can fly around mountains, look for wildlife, or land on a glacier and go dogsledding or hiking. Flightseeing by fixed wing or helicopter trips to area attractions are often available at a fixed price per passenger. Charter fares vary greatly between companies, planes and destinations (see the communities of Anchorage, Talkeetna, Seward, Soldotna and Denali National Park for flightseeing providers).

Luggage space is often limited and dependent on number of passengers. Don't be offended when the pilot or ticketing agent asks your weight; they need that data to ensure an accurate balance within the plane. See ads in *The MILEPOST®* and contact local companies for more information.

The MILEPOST® highway logs include the location of most airstrips along the highways and in communities. *NOTE: The brief description of airstrips given in The MILE-POST® is in no way intended as a guide for pilots. Pilots should have a current copy of the Alaska Supplement (www.faa.gov/ air_traffic/flight_info/aeronav/productcata log/supplementalcharts/supplementalaska), charts and appropriate radio frequencies.*

Bicycling in Alaska

Road conditions vary throughout Alaska from newly-paved highways to unimproved dirt roads. The summer bicycle routes discussed here are on Alaska's paved highways. These major routes generally have good shoulders. Bicyclists will have to share the highways with vehicles but you can avoid traffic by riding in the early morning and on weekdays. One advantage of Alaska touring

in summer are the long daylight hours.

What to take

Bike shops are few and likely only in larger communities so planning is essential. Bring the tools (and skills) necessary to repair your bike as well as extra gear and brake cables, inner tubes, patch kit and pump. Pack wind/waterproof gear, layers

©Sharon Nault

for fluctuating temperatures, water (and a method to purify water), freeze-dried/ lightweight food, cook stove, camera, tent or bivy sack, sleeping pad and sleeping bag in waterproof panniers or packs. We recommend saddlebag-style bicycle packs over a back wheel with fender. Remember to keep bear spray and bug spray readily available to you while you ride, just in case you need it. Perhaps most important of all, wear reflective/high visibility gear and outfit your bicycle with lighting to make certain that traffic will see you as you ride.

Suggested Routes

Anchorage to Denali National Park (237 miles) **or Fairbanks** (363 miles) via the Parks Highway. Ride northeast out of Anchorage on the Glenn Highway 35 miles which veers north and becomes the Parks Highway. Services are available prior to as well as in Wasilla at Milepost 42, and then approximately every 30–50 miles to Fairbanks. Broad Pass is the highest point at 2,400 ft. and the route is largely flat with good shoulders. Milepost 237 is the entrance to Denali National Park and Preserve. Don't miss your chance to explore the park. Campgrounds and all services may be found in the park vicinity. If you continue on to Fairbanks, it is another 125 miles with small communities along the way at Healy at Milepost 249 and Nenana at Milepost 304 (58 miles outside of Fairbanks).

Return to Anchorage via the Alaska Railroad from either Denali National Park or from Fairbanks.

Anchorage to Valdez Loop (304 miles). Head northeast out of Anchorage on the Glenn Highway and stay on it, turning east toward Palmer at the Parks Highway junction. Palmer, at Milepost 42, has all services. This route becomes challenging at Milepost 66, as the next 25 miles eastbound include narrow, winding road, few turnouts, and 7 percent grades. If possible, do this early in the day when there is less traffic sharing the road. There are several lodging and camping locations along the way to get water, a meal, or spend the night, but the next community is Glennallen at Milepost 189. From Glennallen, go south 115 miles on the Richardson Highway to Valdez. Tonsina River Lodge is en route, 36 miles south of Glennallen, with food, lodging and tenting. The remaining 79 miles to Valdez include a 20-mile climb up Thompson Pass followed by 35 miles of mostly downhill into Valdez (all services). (NOTE: The last 200 miles of this route

is used for the Fireweed 400 bicycling race on July 12–13, 2019.)

From Valdez, take the Alaska Marine Highway ferry system across Prince William Sound to Whittier, then, either pedal back to Anchorage (60 miles) via the Seward Highway or take the Alaska Railroad.

Golden Circle Loop: Skagway–Haines–Juneau (355 miles). Named for the gold rush history in this area, this route spans 2 countries (must have passport for border crossings—crossing hours open daily 7 A.M. to 11 P.M. Alaska standard time) and takes in a UNESCO World Heritage Site. The tour can begin in any of the 3 communities and includes a ferry ride from Juneau to your starting/ending points (Haines or Skagway); biking the highways between Skagway to Haines; and ending with a ferry ride back to Juneau. Regardless of direction, this route climbs from sea level to 3,500 ft., but you also have a nice downhill on the other end. (Skagway offers bicycle tours that drop riders off at Milepost 14.3 north of town so they can coast the 11 percent downgrade to town.)

On the Haines Highway, all services are available in Haines, AK; dining, water and lodging at the 33 Mile Roadhouse; water and tenting at Milepost 93.5 Million Dollar Falls Yukon government campground; and all services in Haines Junction, YT, at the junction with the Alaska Highway. From Haines Junction go east 20 miles to Otter Falls Cutoff (dining, water, cabins and camping): the next 80 miles on the Alaska Highway has campgrounds (with water) until you reach Whitehorse, YT, with all services. Continue southeast from Whitehorse 12 miles to the South Klondike Highway, then pedal south 36 miles to Carcross (most services). From Carcross you can hop on the White Pass & Yukon Route Railway to Skagway, AK, or pedal the last 65 miles south. Finish off the Golden Circle Route with a ferry transport back to Alaska's capital and the state's second largest city, Juneau.

Bus Lines

Transportation in this category ranges from no frills shuttle van service to narrated motorcoach tours. Most scheduled bus service between or to cities in the North is seasonal (summer-only). Also check under "Transportation: Bus" within text for the communities you visit for information regarding metro transit systems.

Alaska Cruise Transportation, phone (907) 350-6010, toll-free 1-888-257-8527; info@alaskacruisetransfer.com; www.alaskacruisetransfer.com Provides narrated day tours and direct transfers between Seward and Anchorage and Whittier and Anchorage.

Alaska Park Connection/Alaska Tour & Travel, 3900 Arctic Blvd., Ste. 304, Anchorage, AK 99503. 1-800-266-8625; info@Alaskacoach.com; www.alaskacoach.com. Twice daily deluxe scheduled motorcoach service between Anchorage, Whittier, Seward, Talkeetna and Denali National Park. Call our reservations office or book online. Custom tour packages also available.

Alaska/Yukon Trails, P.O. Box 84608, Fairbanks, AK 99708. (907) 888-5659; info@AlaskaShuttle.com; www.alaskashuttle.com. Daily shuttle Anchorage to Talkeetna, Denali Park and Fairbanks (and in reverse) April 20–Sept. 30; and from Fairbanks to Dawson City, YT May 26–Sept. 15, 3-times a week.

Dalton Highway Express, P.O. Box

82991, Fairbanks, AK 99708. (907) 474-3555; adventure@northernalaska.com; www.daltonhighwayexpress.com. One-day van service in summer between Fairbanks and Deadhorse/Prudhoe Bay. Drop-offs and pickups for bicyclists arranged. Departs Fairbanks at 6 A.M., arrives Deadhorse at 10 P.M. Advance reservations strongly recommended to ensure service.

Denali Overland Transportation Co., P.O. Box 330, Talkeetna, AK 99676. Phone (907) 733-2384; info@denalioverland.com; www.denalioverland.com. Charter van service based in Talkeetna offers 24-hour daily service April 1 to Oct. 1 between Anchorage, Talkeetna and Denali National Park. Catering largely to mountain climbers, it offers plenty of cargo space for passengers.

Gray Line Alaska, 720 W. 5th Ave., Anchorage, AK 99501; 1-888-425-1737. Offering vacation packages May-September with a seasonal Anchorage office; www.graylinealaska.com. Motor coach package tours with accommodations and some sightseeing included throughout Alaska.

Interior Alaska Bus Line. P.O. Box 635, Tok, AK 99780. Phone 1-800-770-6652; email: akbus2@aptalaska.net. Transportation from Anchorage, Fairbanks, Tok and Northway. Call for reservations.

Kennicott Shuttle, HC 60 Box 284M, Copper Center, AK 99573. Phone (907) 822-5292; kennicottshuttle@gmail.com; www.kennicottshuttle.com. Shuttle service connecting Glennallen, Copper Center, Kenny Lake, Chitina Airport, and Chitina Wayside to Kennicott River Footbridge. (Transportation from footbridge to Kennicott and McCarthy provided by local van services like Wrangell Mountain Transport (907/554-4492).

The Klondike Experience, Box 336, Dawson City, YT Y0B 1G0. Phone (867) 993-3821, www.klondikeexperience.com. Scheduled service 3 times weekly from Dawson City (departure at noon, arrival Whitehorse at 7 P.M.) and Whitehorse (departure at 10 A.M., arrival Dawson City 5 P.M.). Daily tours and backcountry packages to Tombstone Territorial Park. Many other destinations and locations available. Inquire for options, tours & charters. Able to transport canoes, kayaks and more.

Seward Bus Lines, depot locations at 539 3rd Ave., Seward and 1130 W. International Airport Rd., Anchorage AK 99518; toll-free phone 1-888-420-7788; phone in Seward, (907) 224-3608; phone in Anchorage, (907) 563-0800; sewardbuslines@acsalaska.net; www.sewardbuslines.net. Daily summer (May 1–Sept. 15) schedule has twice daily departures from Anchorage and Seward. This provider also provides transportation between Seward and Whittier.

Soaring Eagle Transit, P.O. Box 254, Gakona, AK 99586. Phone (907) 822-4545; soaringeagletransit@gulkanacouncil.org; www.soaringeagletransit.com. Operates year round in the Glennallen/Copper Center vicinity. Transport to Anchorage and Valdez Tuesday, Thursday and Saturday in summer. They connect with Interior Alaska Bus Line at some points.

The Stage Line, 1242 Ocean Dr., Homer, AK 99603; phone in Homer (907) 235-2252; phone in Anchorage (907) 868-3914; stage.line@hotmail.com; www.stagelineinhomer.com. Passenger transportation, freight, parcel, and courier service, between Anchorage and the Kenai Peninsula and between Kenai Peninsula communities.

Camping

Campers will find snug campsites at private and public campgrounds along Northern highways.
(Judy Nadon, staff)

Alaska and Canada have both government and private campgrounds. With few exceptions, these campgrounds are located along the road system, and most roadside campgrounds accommodate both tents and RVs. Wilderness camping is also available in most state, federal, provincial and territorial parklands.

The MILEPOST® logs all public roadside campgrounds, and includes facilities (water, toilets, firewood, tables, firepits, etc.), camping fees, length of stay limits and other information. *The MILEPOST®* highway logs also include private campgrounds. Keep in mind that government campgrounds generally do not offer hookups or other ameni-

ties, and may not be able to accommodate large RVs and 5th-wheelers. Additionally, each location may have hours when their electricity and/or water services are curtailed. Be sure to read posted notices or inquire with campground host, if you are concerned. Out of respect for other campers, please use your generators judiciously. Many choose to stay in state, federal, provincial and territorial campgrounds because they prefer peace and quiet.

Season dates for most campgrounds in the North depend on weather, i.e. freezing temperatures can freeze waterlines. Campgrounds are generally open from mid- to late-May until early- to late-September. As a rule, the farther north the campground, the shorter the season.

Keep in mind that although campground information may indicate the presence of water pumps, they are sometimes not working or users may have to boil the water (the text will note that when the information is available to us). Always carry your own water as backup and/or be prepared to purify or boil water if necessary.

NOTE: Campers are urged to use established campgrounds. Overnighting in rest areas and turnouts may be unsafe and is illegal unless otherwise posted. Something else to consider before adventuring out is the midnight sun in these areas. If you have difficulty sleeping in daylight, you may want to bring blackout shades for your RV or a sleeping mask for nighttime use.

The MILEPOST® indicates both private and public campgrounds with tent symbols in the highway logs.

Alaska

Government agencies offering recreational campsites in Alaska are the Alaska Dept. of Natural Resources (DNR) Alaska State Parks, the Bureau of Land Management (BLM), the National Park Service (NPS), the U.S. Forest Service (USFS) and the U.S. Fish & Wildlife Service (USF&WS). These agencies each honor the inter-agency pass that offers discounts to pass holders. These include: America the Beautiful (annual), Senior (lifetime), Access (for permanently disabled persons) and Military (annual) passes and offer half-price discount on camping and park admissions.

Alaska State Parks. The largest state park system in the United States, DNR maintains more than 2,400 campsites within the 121-unit state park system. Camping areas include state recreation sites (SRS), 7 state parks (Chugach, Denali, Chilkat, Kachemak Bay, Wood-Tikchik, Afognak Island and Shuyak Island), State Recreation Areas (SRA), State Historical Sites (SHS), State Historical Parks (SHP), State Marine Parks (SMP) and a Bald Eagle Preserve. State campgrounds generally do not accept reservations, although state campgrounds operated by private contractors may have a reservation system in place. A few campgrounds are reservable. Updates will be posted at the Alaska State Parks website and campsites are reserved at www.reserveamerica.com.

Camping fees (subject to change) range from $10–$45/night. Day-use parking fees are $5–$10/vehicle. Boat launch fees are $10–$20/day; sani-dump stations $10 and firewood up to $8 per bundle where available. Alaska State Parks also offers 66 public use cabins for rent. These cabins are in 29 state park units. Fees range from $35–$165/night and may be reserved at www.reserveamerica.com.

Many areas utilize a fee station located on site. Electronic pay stations that accept credit card payments have been added to several park units and more will be added in the future. To obtain an annual pass for day use or boat launches, go to www.dnr. alaska.gov/parks/asp/fees. You may fill out the online parks pass order form or mail in the paper park pass order form. Annual park passes may also be purchased in person (see list of locations online). Paper forms need to be mailed with check or money order payable to the State of Alaska, or with credit card information, and sent to DNR Public Information Center, Alaska Park Pass, 550 W. 7th Ave., Ste. 1260, Anchorage, AK 99501. Online passes are only payable with credit card. Decals are mailed within 2 business days of receipt of online request. For more information phone (907) 269-8400, or the Anchorage Public Information Center at (907) 644-3661 or 1-866-869-6887; or visit www.alaskacenters.gov. State recreation areas operated by concessionaires and may not honor the annual passes.

The Bureau of Land Management (BLM) maintains 11 campgrounds along the Steese, Richardson, Denali and Dalton highways; fees range from $6–$12/night. Unless otherwise posted, all undeveloped BLM public lands are open to free camping, usually for a maximum of 10 days per stay. The Bureau of Land Management, Alaska State Office is located at 222 W. 7th Ave., Suite 13, Anchorage, AK 99513-7599; phone (907) 271-5960 and has a public information center, open 8 A.M. to 4 P.M. weekdays (closed holidays) at 605 W. 4th St.; phone (907) 644-3661. In Fairbanks, stop by the BLM office at 222 University Ave., phone (907) 474-2200. In Glennallen, stop by the BLM office at Mile 186.5 Glenn Highway. Open 8 A.M. to 4:30 P.M. weekdays, phone (907) 822-3217; www.blm.gov/ak.

The National Park Service maintains 6 campgrounds in Denali National Park and Preserve (see DENALI NATIONAL PARK section); fees are $15–$30. Other national parks included in *The MILEPOST®* are: Glacier Bay in Southeast Alaska *(see page 640)* and Kenai Fjords, accessible by tour boat out of Seward *(page 537)*; Klondike Gold Rush National Park in Skagway *(page 650)*; and Wrangell-St. Elias National Park & Preserve *(page 466)*.

U.S. Forest Service campgrounds are available in Alaska's 2 national forests: Tongass and Chugach. USFS campgrounds charge a fee of $8–$28 per night depending on facilities; primitive campgrounds have no fees. There is a 14-day limit at most campgrounds. Some campsites may be reserved. For more information and reservations, visit the National Recreation Reservation Service (NRRS) at www.recreation.gov, phone toll-free 1-877-444-6777. For information on all recreation in Alaska's national forests, visit www.fs.usda.gov/chugach and www.fs.usda.gov/tongass.

U.S. Fish & Wildlife Service manages more than 120 campsites in camping areas along Skilak Lake Road and Swanson River/Swan Lake Roads within Kenai National Wildlife Refuge. Fees are $5–$10 per night and some campgrounds are free of charge. Contact the Refuge Manager, Kenai National Wildlife Refuge, P.O. Box 2139, (Ski Hill Road), Soldotna, AK 99669, phone (907) 262-7021; or visit www.fws.gov/refuge/Kenai/visit/visitor_activities/camping.html.

Canada

Provincial and territorial government campgrounds and recreation sites as well as private campgrounds are readily available along the Alaska Highway and connecting routes in British Columbia, Alberta, Yukon and the Northwest Territories.

A park sticker—purchased at entrance stations—is required for motorists staying overnight in Canada's national parks. National Park campsites may have electrical hookups. Firewood is supplied for free (bring your own ax for kindling). Kathleen Lake Campground on the Haines Highway now has oTENTik sites; details at www.pc.gc.ca (go to Plan your visit>Camping & accommoations).

Yukon has 42 territorial government campgrounds and many recreation sites located along its road system. The well-maintained campgrounds have picnic tables, firepits, firewood, water supply, outhouses, playgrounds, wheelchair-accessible facilities, a picnic shelter and often, boat launches.

NOTE: Use firewood responsibly and heed fire bans. It is against the law to remove firewood from a Yukon government campground. Do not carry firewood from one campground to another (thereby transferring devastating bugs or invasive species).

Sites are fully serviced from mid-May to mid-September. 10 campgrounds are serviced one week earlier and stay open until Sept. 30. Gated campgrounds close Oct. 1. There is a 14-day limit in any 30-day period. Campsites with a registered occupant are not allowed to be left unoccupied for more than 24 hours.

Campsites are first-come, first-serve. A camping permit ($12 CAD/night) is required, and you may purchase your daily campground permits in advance (www.env. gov.yk.ca/camping-parks/CampingPermits. php) or self-register when you arrive. There are no sani-dump stations in Yukon government campgrounds. For predicted site availability for all Yukon government campgrounds and recreation sites go to www. env.gov.yk.ca/camping-parks/campground_availability.php and click on the campground you are interested in .

Campground quiet hours are from 11 P.M. to 7 A.M. and require that all generators be turned off during this time. Visit website for complete campground rules: http://www.env.gov.yk.ca/camping-parks/campgrounds.php. For more information, contact the Parks Branch at (867) 667-5648; in Yukon/NWT 1-800-661-0408 ext. 5684; email yukon.parks@gov.yk.ca.

British Columbia has an extensive provincial park system, with 10,700 campsites, available at more than 340 vehicle accessible campgrounds. Park gates are generally open from 7 A.M. to 11 P.M. Camping fees range from $11–$35 CAD per camping party per night, depending on facilities (which tend to include: picnic tables, firepits, firewood, water supply, outhouses, wheelchair-accessible facilities and often, boat launches). There is a 14-day limit for most parks and a 7-day limit in 5 of the busiest parks. Some campsites may be reserved; visit www.discovercamping.ca for a list of provincial parks accepting campsite reservations and to make online reservations.

In all provincial parks, conservancies, protected areas and recreational areas, generators are restricted to use between 9 A.M. to 11 A.M. and from 6 P.M. to 8 P.M. Generators must be placed on designated campsite pads and not in surrounding vegetation. Generators will not be allowed in walk-in campsites.

For more information on BC Parks, visit

Highway signs alert travelers to Yukon government campgrounds 2 kilometers/1.2 miles ahead of turnoff. (©Sharon Nault)

www.bcparks.ca. Reservations can be made via the reservation link found at that website. Phone in Canada 1-800-689-9025, or outside Canada (519) 826-6850, daily 7 A.M. to 7 P.M. (Pacific standard time); (closed Christmas and New Years Day).

Alberta's provincial park system includes 108 provincial parks and recreation area campgrounds and 79 forest provincial recreation areas. Online booking for provincial parks is available beginning each February at Reserve.AlbertaParks.ca or phone 1-877-537-2757. Fees are $5–$26 CAD per night, additional fees for hook-ups, sani-dump, showers. There is a 16-day-consecutive limit for stays in campgrounds (5-days for group campsites). Quiet hours are 11 P.M. to 7 A.M. Campgrounds tend to include: picnic tables, firepits, firewood, water supply, outhouses, playgrounds, wheelchair-accessible facilities, a picnic shelter and often, boat launches. For more information, go to www.alberta parks.ca. To receive a campground guide, phone Travel Alberta 1-866-427-3582.

Northwest Territories operates more than 20 public campgrounds, many with walking trails and natural features, such as waterfalls. Fees range from $15–$32 CAD per night and payment and must be in Canadian currency/Canadian check. Fred Henne, Fort Providence, Queen Elizabeth, Twin Falls Gorge and Hay River Territorial parks have a 14–day limit during peak season. Firewood is available for a fee. Campgrounds tend to include: picnic tables, firepits, firewood, water supply, outhouses, playgrounds, wheelchair-accessible facilities, a picnic shelter and often, boat launches. Visit NWT parks.ca for reservations. Online reservations are available in mid-April 2019.

Multiple day-use areas are available for highway travelers to enjoy an open-air picnic or stretch their legs.

NWT has 5 national parks: Tutkut Nogait, Aulavik, Nahanni, Nááts'jhch'oh and Wood Buffalo. The only national park with highway access is Wood Buffalo. Stop by a Parks Canada office or check their website (www.pc.gc.ca/en/index) or call **Simpson Air** (867) 695-2505 for details on fly-in trips to remote Nahanni National Park.

Crossing the Border

Crossing the U.S.–Canada international border is usually not a problem for most travelers.
(©Sharon Nault)

Firewood

Firewood can transport harmful pests!

Help keep invasive species out of the Last Frontier.

Firewood can harbor pests that threaten the health of Alaska's forests. Please buy and burn firewood locally.

To protect our trees:

- Don't bring firewood into or out of the state.

- Purchase or collect firewood near your destination.

- Leave unused firewood behind; do not transport it to a new location.

- Report unusual or suspect insects immediately to the UAF Cooperative Extension Service:

www.uaf.edu/ces • 877-520-5211

UAF is an AA/EO employer & educational institution.

Firewood can harbor many different kinds of invasive pests and diseases that are harmful to Alaska's trees—both in forest and urban settings. Inadvertent transportation of insect larvae and tree diseases in infested materials like firewood, has greatly increased the distribution of pests and diseases such as gypsy moth, oak wilt, the emerald ash borer into previously unaffected, healthy areas. This poses a serious threat to trees such that several states have firewood and quarantine regulations in place to try to slow the spread of wood pests. In 2008, APHIS issued a Federal Order requiring heat treatment for shipments of all firewood made of hardwood species entering the U.S. from Canada.

The emerald ash borer (*Agrilus planipennis*), is an invasive, wood-boring beetle that attacks ash trees (*Fraxinus spp.*), including white, green, black, and blue ash. Mountain ash (*Sorbus spp.*), not a true ash, is unaffected. While ash trees are not part of Alaska's natural hardwood forest component, hundreds of ash trees are planted throughout the urban landscape. Early detection and isolation of infestations are the best defenses against the ecological and economic damage caused by wood pests and diseases. Stay alert to large or colorful insects such as the Asian longhorn beetle and emerald ash borer.

Visitors are encouraged to take a role in helping ensure the healthy future of the state's parks, forests, and trees. Please report unusual or suspect materials or insects immediately by submitting a report if possible online at www.uaf.edu/ces/ipm/cmp/sample-submission/; or phone UAF Cooperative Extension Service at 1-877-520-5211.

To protect our forests and cities from these firewood hitchhikers, do not transport firewood beyond where you bought it or collected it and definitely not across state/international lines.

Scrap lumber is a good alternative for campfires as it is fully dried and debarked and cannot harbor pests and diseases of living trees like raw wood or logs can. Disassembled pallets are typically safe.

NOTE: Painted, treated, or composites of wood and glue such as chipboard and plywood should not be burned as the fumes put off are a serious health hazard.

Travel between the United States and Canada is usually fairly straightforward. There are various documentation requirements and regulations that we highlight below. All travelers and their vehicles may be searched at the discretion of the customs officials whether or not the traveler feels that he or she has complied with customs requirements. When in doubt, declare it.

Following is a brief description of border crossing requirements for the U.S. and Canada. Regulations and procedures change frequently. Travelers are urged to check with customs offices or online sources for the most current restrictions and regulations on topics pertaining to them, prior to traveling. For Canada customs information, go to the Canada Border Services Agency website at www.cbsa.gc.ca/travel-voyage/ivc-rnc-eng.html. You may also contact Canada Border Services Agency, through the 24-hour Border Information Services line (BIS) at 1-800-461-9999 within Canada; (204) 983-3500 outside Canada.

For detailed U.S. customs information go to the Travel section of the U.S. Customs & Border Protection website at www.cbp.gov. You may also contact your nearest U.S. customs office; 1-877-CBP-5511. For border crossing wait times, check U.S. website: bwt.cbp.gov/index.html or Canada's website: www.cbsa-asfc.gc.ca/bwt-taf/menu-eng.html.

Entry into Canada from the U.S.

Identification: If you are a U.S. citizen crossing into Canada, a passport WILL BE REQUIRED to return back into the United States so please have a passport before you try to enter Canada. All travelers should visit www.cbp.gov/travel/us-citizens/know-before-you-go and www.cbp.gov/travel/us-citizens/whti-program-background for information on the U.S. Western Hemisphere Travel Initiative (WHTI) and requirements to enter or return to the United States.

Traveling with children: Children under the age of 18 are classified as minors and are subject to the entry requirements set out under the Immigration and Refugee Protection Act.

If you are traveling with minors, you must carry proper identification for each child such as a birth certificate, passport, proof of citizenship, permanent resident card or Certificate of Indian Status. If you are not the parent or guardian of the children, you should also have written permission from the parent/guardian authorizing the trip. We strongly recommend that they have a letter from both parents (where applicable or whomever has guardianship of the child) detailing the length of stay, and identifying and authorizing who will take care of them while they are in Canada. The letter should include addresses and telephone numbers of where the parents or guardian can be reached.

Divorced or separated parents traveling with children should carry copies of the legal custody agreements for the children. If you are traveling with a group of vehicles, make sure you arrive at the border in the same vehicle as your children to avoid any confusion.

Admissibility: Admissibility of all travelers seeking to enter Canada is considered on a case-by-case basis and based on the specific facts presented by the applicant at the time of entry. If you have ever been arrested for a crime, we recommend that you review this section carefully.

Under the Immigration and Refugee

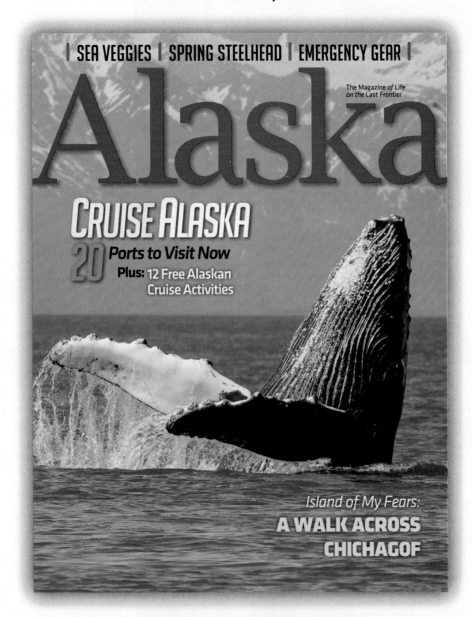

Joint border facility on Top of the World Highway—U.S. Poker Creek and Canada Little Gold Creek Customs—is the farthest north U.S.–Canada border for motorists. (©Sharon Nault)

Protection Act (IRPA), a person may be deemed inadmissible for a number of reasons. A criminal conviction—including a conviction of Driving Under the Influence (DUI)—could make a person inadmissible to Canada. For that reason, be prepared to discuss any criminal history with a border services officer when arriving in Canada.

When planning a trip to Canada, visitors are encouraged to visit the CBSA or Immigration, Refugees and Citizenship Canada (IRCC) websites in order to ensure that they are admissible to Canada. People with criminal convictions can apply to be deemed rehabilitated or they may be eligible for a temporary resident permit. For more information on overcoming criminal inadmissibility please visit the IRCC website at www.cic.gc.ca/english/information/inadmissibility/conviction.asp.

What you can bring: Visitors may bring "personal baggage" into Canada free of duty. This includes clothing, camping and sports equipment, cameras, CD players and iPods, computers, vehicles, boats, etc. Gifts up to $60 CAD per gift, excluding alcohol and tobacco, permitted, duty free. Alcohol and tobacco are admitted if the visitor meets the age requirements of the province or territory where they are entering Canada. Visitors are permitted the following amounts without paying duty, on all of the following: 200 cigarettes, 50 cigars or cigarillos, 200 tobacco sticks and 200 grams (7 oz.) of manufactured tobacco. Visitors are permitted 1 of the following amounts without paying duty: 1.5 liters of wine or 1.14 liters (40 oz.) of liquor, or 24 355-ml (12 oz.) cans or bottles (8.5 liters) of beer or ale provided that it is for personal use. You may bring additional quantities but you will have to pay full duty and taxes on the excess.

Canada has restrictions and limitations that apply to importing meat, eggs, dairy products, fresh fruit, vegetables, dog food (see *Traveling with Pets page 32*) and other food and non-food items. See details at www.inspection.gc.ca/food/information-for-consumers/travellers/what-can-i-bring-into-canada-/eng/1389648337546/1389648516990 and follow links specifically pertaining to

the item with which you are traveling.

Canada also follows CITES guidelines regarding the import/export of endangered species of wild fauna and flora including parts or products. For details on restrictions and permits, visit https://travel.gc.ca/travelling/documents/cites-permits.

©Kris Valencia, staff

Pets: Dogs and cats from the U.S. that are at least 3 months old need a signed and dated certificate from a veterinarian verifying that they have a current vaccination against rabies. This certificate must clearly identify the animal in your possession. If your pet appears unwell, a veterinary health certificate prepared within the last 30 days may be requested at the border. Read additional details at: www.inspection.gc.ca/animals/terrestrial-animals/imports/policies/live-animals/pets/dogs/eng/1331876172009/1331876307796.

Firearms: Canada vigorously enforces its firearms importation laws. Border officials may, at their discretion, search any vehicle

for undeclared firearms and seize any vehicle and firearm where such firearms are found. Possession of an undeclared firearm may result in arrest or imprisonment. Go to this webpage for additional information to help you ascertain if your firearm would be permissible for transport and for the form that you can download, fill out, and be ready to present at the border, when you declare it. www.rcmp-grc.gc.ca/cfp-pcaf/fs-fd/visit-visite-eng.htm. Phone 1-800-731-4000 with questions.

Firearms in Canada are classified as restricted, non–restricted or prohibited. ALL handguns are either restricted or prohibited. Visitors CANNOT import a prohibited firearm into Canada. They must be at least 18 to import other firearms. Restricted firearms are only allowed to cross Canada and re-enter the United States or for approved purposes such as participation in target–shooting competitions where the importation is allowed for special purposes, with a temporary registration (nonresident fee of $25 CAD).

Pepper spray is allowed if it is clearly labeled as an animal repellent, e.g. bear spray. "Mace," tasers and similar products intended to incapacitate a person are considered illegal weapons and are prohibited. Read additional information here: www.cbsa-asfc.gc.ca/import/iefw-iefa-eng.html.

For additional details and documents required to lawfully import and possess firearms in Canada, as well as the rules for storing and transporting firearms, visit the Canada Firearms Center online at www.rcmp-grc.gc.ca/cfp-pcaf/ or phone 1-800-731-4000. See Canada Border Services Agency online at www.cbsa.gc.ca for information on border controls.

Cannabis: Cannabis is legal or decriminalized in all of Canada and in some U.S. states, including Alaska and Washington, but it is illegal under U.S. federal law. Therefore, the transport of cannabis or any product containing cannabis across the U.S.–Canada border is illegal, even if you are traveling from states that have legalized or decriminalized cannabis. This applies to recreational and medical cannabis. For more information visit www.canada.ca/en/services/health/campaigns/cannabis/border.html and dhss.alaska.gov/dph/director/pages/marijuana/law.aspx.

Fireworks: An import permit issued by Natural Resources Canada is required. Additional information and forms are at: www.nrcan.gc.ca/explosives/importation/9911.

Returning Canadian Residents: Personal exemptions from duty on imported goods is based on how long you have been absent: $200 worth of goods for 24+ hours; $800 of goods for 48+ hours; and $800 for 7 days or more (does not apply to tobacco products and alcoholic beverages).

Entry into the U.S. from Canada

Identification: All U.S. residents aged 16 and older, must present a valid, acceptable (WHTI-compliant) travel document that denotes both identity and citizenship when entering the United States by land or sea. WHTI-compliant documents include U.S. passports, Trusted Traveler Card (NEXUS, SENTRI, or FAST), U.S. Passport Card, Military ID (when traveling on orders), U.S. Merchant Mariner card (when on official business) state or province-issued Enhanced Driver's License, American Indian Card or Enhanced Tribal Card when and where available. U.S. and Canadian citizens under 16 must have a birth certificate issued by federal, state, provincial, county or municipal authority or alternative proof of citizenship when entering by land or sea. For more information please visit www.cbp.gov/travel/us-citizens/western-hemisphere-travel-initiative for requirements and information.

Canadian citizens over the age of 16 may present a valid Canadian Passport, a Trusted Traveler Card (NEXUS, SENTRI, or FAST), or Enhanced Drivers License for entry.

A valid, unexpired passport and visa are required for all other foreign nationals. Nationals of countries participating in the Visa Waiver Program may present unexpired machine-readable passports. The Electronic System for Travel Authorization (ESTA) is accessible via internet for citizens and eligible nationals of Visa Waiver Program (VWP) countries to apply for advance authorization to travel to U.S. under VWP. Certain persons may require specific supporting documentation such as an employment petition, student authorization, or approval notice. For more details, visit: travel.state.gov/content/travel/en/us-visas/tourism-visit/visa-waiver-program.html.

Foreign visitors entering the U.S. for the first time are required to pay a paper processing fee of $6 U.S. per person. (This fee does not apply to Canadian citizens.) This fee is payable in U.S. currency, U.S. travelers checks, credit cards and debit cards with the VISA logo at most ports of entry, although some of the very small, remote border crossings will not accept credit cards, only accept U.S. currency and U.S. travelers checks. Have U.S. funds prior to arriving at the U.S. border or call ahead at the port of entry and inquire about credit cards.

What you can bring: Visitors to the U.S. may bring in duty-free all personal effects (apparel, jewelry, hunting, camping and fishing equipment, cameras, portable radios, etc.), household effects (furnishings, dishes, linens, books, etc.), and vehicles for personal use and not for resale.

Non-residents who are at least 21 years old may bring in, free of duty, up to 1 liter of alcoholic beverage (beer, wine, liquor) for personal use. Quantities above 1 liter are subject to duty and internal revenue tax. Tobacco products included in your personal exemption are 200 cigarettes (one carton) or 50 cigars or 2 kg. (4.4 lbs.) of smoking tobacco, or proportional amounts of each.

If you require medicine containing habit-forming drugs, make sure it is properly identified, carry only the quantity normally needed and have a prescription or written statement from your physician that the medicine is necessary for your physical well-being.

The U.S. Dept. of Agriculture's Animal and Plant Health Inspection Service (APHIS) requires that travelers entering the United States from a foreign country declare all fruit, vegetables, plants and plant products, meat and meat products, animals, birds and eggs. This includes agricultural products of U.S. origin. Fruits, vegetables, meats, and birds taken out of the United States cannot always be reentered into the country. APHIS offers traveler tips for facilitating inspection at the international border at www.cbp.gov/travel/international-visitors/agricultural-items.

When purchasing Canadian or Alaska Native arts made with wildlife parts (e.g. bone, hide, fur, claws, feathers, etc.) ask about possible problems crossing the border, or check regulations beforehand. For exam-

U.S–Canada border crossings often have hours posted along the approach route as well as reader-boards with border wait times posted. (©Kris Valencia, staff)

ple, mammoth and mastodon ivory do not require paperwork, but walrus ivory does. The U.S. Fish & Wildlife Service and Alaska State Council on the Arts have issued *A Customs Guide to Alaska Native Arts* specifically for items bought in Alaska that are being exported out of the U.S. Go to www.eed.state.ak.us/aksca/pdf/customs_guide_to_ak_native_arts.pdf. You may download a copy there or call the U.S. Fish and Wildlife Service Import Export Office (Anchorage, AK); phone (907) 271-6198.

Other restricted or prohibited items may include: cigars, liquor-filled candy; firearms and ammunition; hazardous articles (fireworks, dangerous toys, toxic or poisonous substances); lottery tickets; exotic pets; pet birds; obscene articles and publications; switchblade knives; trademarked items; wildlife and endangered species, including any part or product. Please check this list for additional information: www.cbp.gov/travel/us-citizens/know-before-you-go/prohibited-and-restricted-items.

Personal exemptions for U.S. residents are dependent on how long you have been out of the country; if you have been out of the country more than once in a 30-day period; and the total value of the merchandise you are bringing back with you, as well as its country of origin. Personal exemptions are $200, $800, or $1,600. There are limits on the amount of alcoholic beverages, cigarettes, cigars, and other tobacco products that may be included in a resident's personal exemption. Differences are explained in "Know Before You Go" at www.cbp.gov/travel/us-citizens/know-before-you-go.

Pets: A valid rabies vaccination certificate that clearly identifies the dog or cat you are traveling with *must* accompany the animal and be available for customs review. If your pet appears ill, a health certificate issued by your vet within 30 days of travel, may be requested for review by agent.

Invasive Species: When crossing the border by ferry or automobile, you may unintentionally transport invasive weeds and other pests that can damage Alaska's ecosystems.

Spotted knapweed has been identified as a high priority species for prevention and eradication, due to its potential

to severely harm moose, deer, caribou, elk and salmon. Introduced to North America a couple hundred years ago, spotted knapweed has severely infested the northwestern U.S. and southern British Columbia. Knapweeds replace native grass species, which can decrease forage for livestock and wildlife. It also increases soil erosion, which degrades fish habitat. Once established, controlling spotted knapweed is difficult and costly.

Small populations of spotted knapweed have been found in Alaska. To prevent the spread of spotted knapweed and other unwanted invasives: Wash vehicles thoroughly and often, especially before entering Alaska; pay special attention to areas where soil is likely to be trapped, such as on the insides of wheels and anywhere beneath the vehicle; clean ATVs, trailers, bicycles, boats, and footwear thoroughly after use and before you resume your travel.

Go to website: plants.alaska.gov/invasives/index.htm and look for the link where you can email a request for the free pocket weed guide.

Cannabis: Cannabis is legal or decriminalized in all of Canada and in some U.S. states, including Alaska and Washington, but it is illegal under U.S. federal law. Therefore, the transport of cannabis or any product containing cannabis across the U.S.–Canada border is illegal, even if you are traveling from states that have legalized or decriminalized cannabis. This applies to recreational and medical cannabis. For more information visit www.canada.ca/en/services/health/campaigns/cannabis/border.html and dhss.alaska.gov/dph/director/pages/marijuana/law.aspx.

Cruising to Alaska

Cruise ships docked along Juneau waterfront. (©Kris Valencia, staff)

Alaska's massive coastline features extraordinary beauty and fascinating, small-town ports to explore. A destination sought by many, Alaska welcomed more than a million cruising visitors in 2018. This route of travel is much-loved because it combines the comfort of a largely prepaid and often luxurious accommodation with the wild beauty of Alaska. And the choices of port-side experiences vary to please any cruiser. Whether you wish to shop for Alaska jewelry or Alaska Native artwork, flightsee over natural wonders (fixed-wing or helicopter), take a thrilling zipline tour, kayak in glacial waters, ride behind a dog team or hike glaciers, the opportunities are endless.

The most frequently chosen cruise is the week-long roundtrip Inside Passage itinerary which departs from Seattle or Vancouver and stops at several Southeast Alaska ports. The second most common would be a one-way, north or southbound through the Inside Passage and crossing the Gulf, with one direction traveled by sea and the other by air. This option allows for add-on days to explore within Alaska's interior. There are many shorter and longer trips that range from sailing to cruising, often in a more boutique-styled vessel (see small-sized cruises). These voyages may stay solely in the Inside Passage, Cross Sound or the Prince William Sound area. And lastly, a few longer voyages include those that cross trans-Pacific to Russia or Japan, or turn north for the Northwest Passage (stops on these may include the Alaska Gulf, Aleutian Islands and Southwest Alaska ports).

Among the choices to make in this vacation decision are: What size of vessel and quantity of fellow travelers appeals to you? Ships to Alaska vary from several thousand guests on mega cruiseships down to just a handful of fellow travelers on the smallest boats.

Next, when do you want to cruise? Cruising season is largely mid-May to mid-September for the most options but both pre-season and post-season choices can offer unusual port stops and extraordinary experiences. The warmest weather is likely in July or August but salmon runs and whale watching may be better in June or September. And finally, which type of experience are you after and which ports do you hope to explore? With those decisions made, you can begin to examine the options of cruise-line and sailing date that works best for you.

Read through the following overview of cruise lines serving Alaska in 2019, and contact the cruiseship company with the amenities and itineraries that meet your needs.

When thinking about what excursions and opportunities are available at your ports of call, remember that *The MILEPOST®* covers many if not most of these within the SOUTHEAST, ANCHORAGE, SEWARD HIGHWAY, STERLING HIGHWAY and KODIAK sections of this book and you can use it to arrange your own shore excursions.

Large to "Mega" Cruiseships

Carnival Cruiselines: The Carnival *Legend* (2,124 guests/963 ft. in length) offers summer-long Tuesday departures from Seattle, WA roundtrip with visits to Ketchikan, Juneau and Skagway, Glacier Bay and Victoria. The final 2 trips are 8-nights Seattle roundtrip with the same port itinerary. The Carnival *Splendor* (approx. 3,000 guests) offers one, 14-day Long Beach, CA roundtrip to Skagway/Glacier Bay, AK and back on Aug. 25. For more information call/go to: 1-800-CARNIVAL; www.Carnival.com.

Celebrity Cruiselines: The *Infinity*, *Millennium* and *Solstice* all tour Alaska waters (approx. 1,814 guests/843 ft. in length). Cruises begin May 10 and range from 7–8days in length with multiple focuses to choose between. Roundtrip voyages are from Seattle, WA, and Vancouver, BC, to Skagway and Hubbard Glacier in Alaska. Ports include Ketchikan and Icy Straits among others. Some itineraries end or begin in Seward, AK. For more information call/go to: 1-800-647-2251; www.celebritycruises.com.

Disney Cruiselines: Disney's *Wonder* departs Vancouver, BC, in summer season on Mondays May 21–Sept. 3 (2,400 passenger/964 ft. in length). The 7-night roundtrip cruise goes through Alaska ports and attractions like Tracy Arm to Juneau, Skagway and Ketchikan. There is one 5-day and one 9-day trip offered. For more information call/go to: 1-800-951-3532, www.disneycruise.com.

Holland America: is like a small-sized Large/Mega cruiseline with approx. 1,400 guests/800 ft. in length. The *Eurodam*, *Westerdam*, *Nieuw Amsterdam*, *Amsterdam*, *Noordam*, *Volendam* and *Zaandam* do 7-night cruises that include one-way and roundtrip cruises from Seattle and Vancouver, and visit Ketchikan, Juneau and Skagway among other ports. The southbound cruises depart from Seward, AK. The *Amsterdam* and *Westerdam and Zaamdam* also offer a 14-day roundtrip from Vancouver, BC that includes Haines, AK. For more information call/go to: 1-877-932-4259; www.hollandamerica.com.

Cruise ship docked along Marine Way in downtown Juneau, near the Red Dog Saloon, a local landmark. (©Kris Valencia, staff)

Norwegian Cruiselines: The Norwegian *Pearl, Jewel* (approx. 2,394 guests/695 ft. in length) and *Bliss* (in her debut season with 4,004 guest capacity). Offering cruises throughout the summer of 7 days in length, departure ports include Seattle, WA, and Vancouver, BC. One trip of 9 days is May 26 with departure from Seattle and return to Vancouver. For more information call/go to: 1-866-234-7350; www.ncl.com.

Princess Cruiselines: This cruiseline schedules 8 ships for its Alaska itineraries: *Star Princess, Coral Princess, Emerald Princess, Golden Princess, Island Princess, Ruby Princess* and *Grand Princess.* The season kickoff is on Apr. 27 as the Emerald Princess begins a 12-night roundtrip voyage from Los Ange-

les. There are 7-night roundtrips from Seattle, WA and Vancouver, BC, and 10-day roundtrips from San Francisco, CA. Also available are 1-way 7-night cruises (north or southbound) from Vancouver and Whittier (Anchorage), AK. Ports-of-call, which vary depending on itinerary, include Alaska features: Ketchikan, Sitka, Juneau, Skagway, Glacier Bay, Tracy Arm Fjord, College Fjord, Hubbard Glacier; and Victoria, BC. For more information call/go to: 1-800-774-6237; www.princess.com.

Royal Caribbean Cruiseline: *Radiance of the Seas* and *Explorer of the Seas* (approx. 2,139 guests/962 ft. in length). These two ships depart from Vancouver, BC, Seattle WA, and Seward, AK for 7–night voyages with attractions that may include Juneau, Skagway, Tracy Arm Fjord, Icy Strait, Hubbard Glacier (in Alaska) and/or Victoria, BC. For more information call/go to: 1-866-562-7625; www.royalcaribbean.com.

Cruise ships include plenty of options for exploring attractions on land at port cities. This is Mendenhall Glacier in Juneau. (©Kris Valencia, staff)

Mid-Size Cruise Vessels

Oceania Cruiseline: This 11-night season opener begins in San Francisco to Southeast ports then to Vancouver, BC, May 19. The *Regatta* offers several 7-night and 10-night and 1, 12-night and two 15-night cruises departing from either Seattle, WA or Vancouver, BC. Itineraries include the Inside and/or Outside Passages, stops in some of the lesser visited ports and offers a luxurious onboard experience. For more information call/go to: 1-800-386-9283; www.cruiseocea nia.com.

Regent Seven Seas Cruises: The *Seven Seas Mariner* travels Alaska waters with 7-night one-ways departing either from Seward, AK, or Vancouver, BC. These cross the Gulf of Alaska and traverse the Inside Passage. There are 3, 10-night and 1, 11-night cruises offered. The season ends with a 12-night Vancouver to Los Angeles cruise beginning on Sept. 18, 2019, directly followed by a 15-night Los Angeles to Miami cruise. This cruise company offers all-inclusive package. For more information call/go to: 1-844-473-4368; www.RSSC.com.

Silversea Cruises: From Vancouver, BC to Seward, AK (or in reverse), the *Silver Muse* offers 7-day voyages throughout the summer. The route includes Ketchikan, Juneau, Skagway, Sitka, Tracy Arm and Hubbard Glacier AK. For more information call/go to: 1-888-978-4070; www.silversea.com.

Small Cruise Vessels

Alaska Dream Cruises: The *Alaskan Dream, Admiralty Dream, Baranof Dream, Chichigof Dream* and *Misty Fjord* offer 5 cruise ship options (approx. 10–76 guests/60–207 ft. in length). There are 7 cruise itinerary options to choose between 5–11 night trips and land extensions possible. For more information call/go to: 1-855-747-8100; www.AlaskanDreamCruises.com.

All Aboard Yacht Charters: The historic 87-foot, 6 cabin, 1931-vintage yacht *Discovery* features 7-night/8-day Inside Passage cruises north or south between Ketchikan and Juneau, and Juneau and Sitka, and round-trip voyages from Juneau. They also offer an 11-night cruise at the start and end of the season from Seattle, WA to Ketchikan, AK. Each cruise provides 6–12 guests with fishing opportunities, wildlife viewing, rowing skiffs and kayaks for guest adventures. Book early to travel with this provider (they book up early). For more information call/go to: 1-800-767-1024; aclassicyacht. com.

American Cruise Lines: The season begins with an Inside Passage, 14-night cruise from Seattle, WA to Juneau, AK and ends with its return to Seattle, WA. In between, the *American Constellation* shifts to the core season 7-night southeastern Alaska itinerary. Ports and attractions include Glacier Bay, Kake, Haines, Skagway, Petersburg, and Tracy Arm/South Sawyer Glacier with return to Juneau. For more information call/go to: 1-800-460-4518; www.americancruise lines.com.

The Boat Company: This cruiseline emphasizes environmental awareness. Two vessels—the 20-guest *Liseron*, a now-upscale converted 1940s minesweeper, and the 24-guest *Mist Cove*, a decidedly upscale replica—sail 7-night voyages between Sitka and Juneau, AK. The itinerary is flexible and spontaneous. Guests can spend as much time off the boat as they like, hiking, fishing, canoeing, kayaking or beachcombing. For more information call/go to: 1-877-647-8268; www.theboatcompany.org.

Custom Alaska Cruises: With a maximum of 12 guests for 7-day cruises aboard the MV *Sikumi* or via the 8–12 guest MY *Golden Eagle*, these trips include wildlife viewing including bear and whale watching, glacier viewing, photography, kayaking, daily beach excursions, visits to hot springs, fishing, pulling crab or shrimp pots and fulfilling requests. For more information call/go to: (970) 217-6359; www.sikumi.com.

Discovery Voyages: This pioneering small ship cruise company operates the comfortably refurbished former missionary vessel *Discovery* (12 guests/65 ft.) in Prince William Sound. Cruise and cruise-tour itineraries range from 2–5 nights. Its varied-length sightseeing vessel trips include a hike and kayak voyage, Classic Discovery, Grand Alaska Journey (includes Denali National Park), Photo Voyages and more. For more information call/go to: 1-800-324-7602; www.discoveryvoyages.com.

Fantasy Cruises: A full summer season of mostly 8-night voyages aboard the 32 passenger *Island Spirit* includes the Inside Passage voyages, wilderness cruises, discovery cruises and Captain's Choice cruises. All trips include glacier viewing, beach hikes, exploring small coves, forest trail walks, and other outdoor activities. Initial and final voyages for the year will be a 14-day Juneau, AK to Seattle, WA voyage. For more information call/go to: 1-800-234-3861; www.smallalaska ship.com.

Lindblad Expeditions/National Geographic: The *Sea Bird* and *Sea Lion* both provide 62 guests accommodations in 31 outside suites and the *Quest and Venture*, for 100 guests. The 6-, 8-, 14-, and 15-day journeys. Itineraries may feature Alaska's Tracy Arm Fjord and Sawyer glaciers, Ford's Terror wilderness, Petersburg, whale watching in Frederick Sound, Chatham Strait, Point Adolphus, and Inian Pass plus cruising a full day in Glacier Bay; the 15-day includes time in Haida Gwaii, BC. For more information call/go to: 1-800-397-3348; www.expedi tions.com.

Maple Leaf Adventures: The MV *Swell*, a renovated tugboat (accommodates 12 guests/88 ft.), offers 9–night trips from Petersburg to Sitka or the Supervoyage, 10-night Sitka to Ketchikan, AK. Trips include kayaking, hikes, glacier and wildlife viewing. It also offers trips in BC. For more information call/go to: (250) 386-7245; www.MapleLeafAdventures.com.

Sea Wolf Adventures: The 97-foot-long expedition vessel *Sea Wolf* accommodates up to 12 guests and offers active small ship cruising adventures suitable for people of all abilities. 6-day Glacier Bay and 10-day Glacier Bay–Sitka, Sitka–Juneau and Juneau–Ketchikan trips. Hiking, wildlife viewing and kayaking. Handicap accessible. For more information call/go to: (907) 957-1438; www.seawolfadventures.net.

Sound Sailing: The vessel is a modern, fast, Catalina/Morgan 50-foot sailboat, with 3 guest cabins (large double berth with private head and shower). They offer customized itineraries for 7- or 10-day trips. It operates between Sitka, Juneau, Petersburg and Glacier Bay. For more information call/go to: (907) 887-9446 or www.soundsailing.com.

Un-Cruise Adventures: April to September, these boats (22–84 guests) offer 11 itineraries ranging from 7–14 nights. Cruises may focus on whales and glaciers, Inside Passage cultures, or expedition-style explorations, such as kayaking and paddle-boarding. The luxury cruise options include extra amenities, soft-adventure, and exclusive excursions. For more information call/go to: 1-888-862-8881/www.uncruise.com.

Driving North

Always be prepared for wildlife crossing the road on your journey North. Moose are also quite common on Anchorage streets. (©Donna Dewhurst)

Driving to the North is no longer the ordeal it was in Alaska Highway's early days. Images of vehicles stuck in mud up to their hubcaps are far removed from the asphalt-surfaced Alaska Highway of today.

Motorists can still expect delays for road construction and some rough, dusty road, but have patience, these projects help to improve road conditions

Roads in the North range from multi-lane freeways to 1-lane dirt and gravel roads. The more remote roads are gravel. Motorists are much farther from assistance, and more preparation is required for these roads.

Major highways in Alaska are paved with the exception of the following highways that are at least partially gravel: Steese Highway (Alaska Route 6), Taylor Highway (Alaska Route 5), Elliott Highway (Alaska Route 2), Dalton Highway (Alaska Route 11), Denali Highway (Alaska Route 8) and Edgerton Highway/McCarthy Road (Alaska Route 10).

In Yukon, the Alaska Highway, the Haines Highway and the Klondike Highway from Skagway to Dawson City are asphalt-surfaced.

Major routes through Alberta and British Columbia are paved. The Cassiar Highway (BC Highway 37) is paved with rare gravel breaks. On the Deh Cho Route, the Liard Trail, BC Highway 77 from the Alaska Highway and connecting British Columbia and Northwest Territories, is paved for its 86 miles. Its extension north via NWT Highway 1 includes 23 miles of pavement and 133 of gravel. Paving extends north from the

Alberta border/Highway 35 to Yellowknife via NWT Highways 1 and 3 and past Hay River via routes 2/5.

Know your vehicle, its limitations and the road conditions. Some Northern roads may not be suitable for a large motorhome or trailer, but most roads will present no problem to a motorist who allots adequate time and uses common sense. It is always a good idea to empty your gray water tanks before you embark, to decrease weight on tougher roads.

Keep in mind the variable nature of road conditions. Some sections of road may be in poor condition because of current construction or recent bad weather. Other highways—particularly gravel roads closed in winter—may be very rough or very smooth, depending on when maintenance crews last worked on the road.

Asphalt surfacing for most Northern roads is Bituminous Surface Treatment (BST), an alternative to hot-mix pavement which involves application of aggregates and emulsified asphalt. Also known as "chip seal," recently applied or repaired BST is as smooth as any Lower 48 superhighway. However, weather and other factors can lead to failures in the surfacing including potholes and loss of aggregate.

Also watch for "frost heaves" caused by subsidence of the ground under the road.

Many gravel roads in the North are treated with magnesium chloride as a dust-control measure. This substance corrodes paint and metal; wash your vehicle as soon as possible after exposure. In heavy rains, magnesium

chloride and mud combine to make a very slippery road surface; drive carefully!

Safeguard against theft while at campgrounds, rest stops or in the cities. Always lock your vehicle, be sure valuables are out of sight in an unattended vehicle and report any thefts to the authorities.

NOTE: Drive with headlights and seat belts on at all times.

Windshield damage is possible but largely avoidable. BE COURTEOUS, don't follow vehicles too closely and always watch for flying rocks in gravel portions. SLOW DOWN to avoid throwing rocks at the windshields of fellow travelers. Truckers and other travelers will respond to your driving and if you barrel down the road and are discourteous, they will be less likely to slow to avoid throwing rocks as they pass you (just as you are throwing rocks into their vehicle if you drive at high speeds).

Car Rentals

To do a fly/drive trip using a car rental rather than a motorcoach tour package can be the best choice for the independently-minded traveler. Most national car rental companies are found in Alaska and Canada and are located at or near major airports.

There are several complications with car rentals in the far north however, the first being that few allow for travel on gravel roads. In Alaska, those roads include the Denali, Dalton, Steese, Taylor and Elliott highways and the McCarthy Road.

There are also difficulties taking rental cars across the border between the U.S. and

Canada. Inquire about policies regarding international travel prior to renting.

For most travelers who want to fly in and do a week-long trip in the Anchorage/ Kenai Peninsula/Denali National Park and Fairbanks area, car rentals will be simple. For those who are looking to get off the beaten track to more remote roads, there are rental companies (e.g. alaskaautorental.com and www.arctic-outfitters.com) who rent specific vehicles with extra amenities that make them suited for remote gravel roads.

Electric vehicles (EV)

Electric vehicles are becoming more common in the western provinces and as such, we have begun to note **EV plug-ins** (charging stations) along these highways. Visitor information centers within the larger communities of western provinces, frequently have charging stations. Noted charging stations include: the Dawson Creek Visitor Center at Mile Zero, Alaska Highway; the Houston Visitor Center on Yellowhead Highway 16; all across Vancouver Island; and at multiple locations in between. EV plug-ins are harder to find as you go north although hotels in the North often offer parking lot electric plugins (to help cars start in extreme cold). Be sure to talk to the hotel before plugging in your electric vehicle. If you are an EV driver, let us know your experiences on the road so that we can expand this information in the next edition.

Emergency Services Along the Way

Major cities and many mid-size towns in the North have hospitals, ambulance service and police on the 911 system. Out on the highway it is often a different story, with some stretches of road outside the 911 service area or without cell phone reception.

Emergency Services are noted in all highway communities in *The MILEPOST®*, with phone numbers for Alaska State Troopers and RCMP, city police, ambulances, hospitals and health clinics. In the event of an injury accident, first try 911, then the number of the nearest law enforcement.

Because of the long distances between services on most Northern highways and byways, travelers and locals in the North stop to help motorists in trouble. Read "Highway Safety Tips" several topics further down, for tips on how to safely and effectively provide and/or receive aid.

Gasoline/Diesel

Gasoline and diesel are readily available in Alaska and Canada. The more remote you are, the further between service stations. Look ahead in the highway log for fuel pro-

viders and when in doubt, call to confirm that small businesses are open.

In the North, as elsewhere, gas prices vary. Generally, gas prices are higher in Canada and Alaska than the Lower 48, but this is not a hard and fast rule. A general rule of thumb: The more remote the gas station, the higher the price. Gas prices may vary considerably at service stations within the same community. For current gas prices go to www.themilepost.com and click on Alaska, British Columbia and Alberta gas

price links at the bottom of the home page. And don't forget to factor in prevailing exchange rates (see chart, this page).

It is a good idea to carry some cash, since a few gas stations in Alaska and along some Canadian highways are independents and may not accept credit cards. Most do. Alberta stations have switched over entirely to "chip" technology credit cards so if you don't have a credit card with a "chip," you will have to enter the station to pay using credit card. British Columbia stations are

2019 Gas Chart for Gas/Diesel Cost in U.S. Funds per Gallon

Choose the posted liter price, then the current Exchange Rate below to see U.S. cost per gallon.

Liter Price	1.05	1.10	1.15	1.20	1.25
$0.79	$2.85	$2.72	$2.60	$2.49	$2.39
$0.81	$2.92	$2.79	$2.67	$2.55	$2.45
$0.83	$2.99	$2.86	$2.73	$2.62	$2.51
$0.85	$3.06	$2.92	$2.80	$2.68	$2.57
$0.87	$3.14	$2.99	$2.86	$2.74	$2.63
$0.89	$3.21	$3.06	$2.93	$2.81	$2.69
$0.91	$3.28	$3.13	$3.00	$2.87	$2.76
$0.93	$3.35	$3.20	$3.06	$2.93	$2.82
$0.95	$3.42	$3.27	$3.13	$3.00	$2.88
$0.97	$3.50	$3.34	$3.19	$3.06	$2.94
$0.99	$3.57	$3.41	$3.26	$3.12	$3.00
$1.01	$3.64	$3.48	$3.32	$3.19	$3.06
$1.03	$3.71	$3.54	$3.39	$3.25	$3.12
$1.05	$3.79	$3.61	$3.46	$3.31	$3.18
$1.07	$3.86	$3.68	$3.52	$3.37	$3.24
$1.09	$3.93	$3.75	$3.59	$3.44	$3.30
$1.11	$4.00	$3.82	$3.65	$3.50	$3.36
$1.13	$4.07	$3.89	$3.72	$3.56	$3.42
$1.15	$4.15	$3.96	$3.79	$3.63	$3.48
$1.17	$4.22	$4.03	$3.85	$3.69	$3.54
$1.19	$4.29	$4.09	$3.92	$3.75	$3.60
$1.21	$4.36	$4.16	$3.98	$3.82	$3.66
$1.23	$4.43	$4.23	$4.05	$3.88	$3.72
$1.25	$4.51	$4.30	$4.11	$3.94	$3.79
$1.27	$4.58	$4.37	$4.18	$4.01	$3.85
$1.29	$4.65	$4.44	$4.25	$4.07	$3.91
$1.31	$4.72	$4.51	$4.31	$4.13	$3.97
$1.33	$4.79	$4.58	$4.38	$4.20	$4.03
$1.35	$4.87	$4.65	$4.44	$4.26	$4.09
$1.37	$4.94	$4.71	$4.51	$4.32	$4.15
$1.39	$5.01	$4.78	$4.57	$4.38	$4.21
$1.41	$5.08	$4.85	$4.64	$4.45	$4.27
$1.43	$5.15	$4.92	$4.71	$4.51	$4.33
$1.45	$5.23	$4.99	$4.77	$4.57	$4.39
$1.47	$5.30	$5.06	$4.84	$4.64	$4.45
$1.49	$5.37	$5.13	$4.90	$4.70	$4.51
$1.51	$5.44	$5.20	$4.97	$4.76	$4.57
$1.53	$5.52	$5.26	$5.04	$4.83	$4.63
$1.55	$5.59	$5.33	$5.10	$4.89	$4.69
$1.57	$5.66	$5.40	$5.17	$4.95	$4.75
$1.59	$5.73	$5.47	$5.23	$5.02	$4.81
$1.61	$5.80	$5.54	$5.30	$5.08	$4.88
$1.63	$5.88	$5.61	$5.36	$5.14	$4.94
$1.65	$5.95	$5.68	$5.43	$5.20	$5.00
$1.67	$6.02	$5.75	$5.50	$5.27	$5.06
$1.69	$6.09	$5.82	$5.56	$5.33	$5.12
$1.71	$6.16	$5.88	$5.63	$5.39	$5.18
$1.73	$6.24	$5.95	$5.69	$5.46	$5.24
$1.75	$6.31	$6.02	$5.76	$5.52	$5.30

also switching to this technology. If the pump doesn't accept your card, just go inside. The attendant can run it manually. To avoid the hassle, ask your credit card company for a chipped card for travel in Canada. Most credit card companies do offer this now and your card may already have the electronic chip on it.

Like everywhere else, pay attention. Watch for posted gas prices that are for cash, but not noted as such. Some northern Canadian gas stations have begun "pay inside only" due to drivers leaving without paying. Gas stations may have dollar limits on the number of gallons pumped using a credit card or they may put a "hold" for a fixed amount on your credit card but then charge only the pump total.

Some stations are automated and there is no attendant on duty. These accept credit cards. CardLock gas stations are noted as such within our text. They vary in that they are unmanned and typically used by company vehicles (often truckers) with fleet management cards. If noted "public" anyone can use them. If you're not used to this type of gas pump, take your time and read the directions posted on or near the pump. They may ask for additional identification like your billing zip code or vary in process of unlocking pump and fueling. If you choose, you could get a Cardlock Fuel Card that works at the non-public pumps as well. The CFN card works at 2,300 cardlock locations while the Pacific Pride Fuel Card works at 1,300 fuel stations. It is NOT necessary to get these cards; The MILEPOST® staff has long traveled these roads without cardlock fuel cards.

IMPORTANT: Make sure you are at the right pump for the fuel you need and check with attendant if you are confused by which is gas or diesel. Do not assume type of gas by pump handle color. Diesel is usually identified by a green pump handle in the U.S., while in Canada a green handle may be gas and a yellow or red handle may be diesel (we have seen this in NWT).

Canadian gas stations use the metric system; quantity is by liters. There are 3.785 liters per U.S. gallon or .2642 gallons per liter. The chart on page 26 shows actual cost per gallon, figured from cost per liter and factoring in the exchange rate. Canadian gas stations, like U.S. stations, grade gasoline according to the octane rating, but they use the designations Bronze (87), Silver (89) and Gold (91) instead of regular, plus, and super/supreme/premium. Some northern gas stations may only have regular gas available. Consider bringing a booster additive with you if your vehicle requires a super/supreme level gas. ULSD (Ultra Low Sulfur Diesel) is available across Canada and Alaska.

Highway Safety Tips

If you need to stop because your vehicle is in trouble, or you have stopped to help someone else in trouble—pull your vehicle off the main highway onto the shoulder or use a turnout (turnouts are logged in The MILEPOST®). Injuries and fatal accidents have occurred after someone has stopped along the road either because they are experiencing car problems or to help someone who is having trouble.

Carry an emergency road kit with flares and/or reflectors. In the event of an accident or vehicle breakdown, create a safety zone around the vehicle using at least 3 flares. Place flares/reflectors starting at least 300 feet behind your vehicle on the edge of the roadway to adequately warn oncoming traffic. Tie a white cloth to the radio antenna or a door handle. Make sure it is clearly visible.

If you do not have flares/reflectors, turn on your vehicle's emergency flashers or leave your headlights on low beam and turn on your turn signal. Put up the hood of the car. The highway flares, white cloth and flashers are all distress signals that will let law enforcement officers know you need help.

Stay with your vehicle until help comes (this is essential in winter). If you must leave your vehicle, carry a flashlight or lightstick. Walk on road shoulder, facing traffic.

Insurance

Auto insurance is mandatory in Alaska and all Canadian provinces and territories. Proof of insurance is required and U.S. issued policies are accepted, as are U.S. Driver's Licenses. Visiting motorists are required to produce evidence of insurance should they be involved in an accident. There is an automatic fine if visitors involved in an accident are found to be uninsured. Your car could be impounded.

Motorcycles

Almost every make of motorcycle, in every shape and size, has made the trip to Alaska. The most common concern expressed by motorcyclists we've talked to along the way was the distance between gas stops that can be 100 miles or more on some highways. Many were using The MILEPOST® to figure their gas stops in advance of each day's travel and most carry extra gas.

Many motorcyclists were pulling trailers and there were no significant challenges to report despite driving many miles of road that included stretches of gravel, potholes and frost heaves. We did meet up with a motorcyclist on the Alaska Highway one year who was on the return portion of his trip back to the Lower 48. He had found out the hard way that he was pulling too heavy a trailer for Northern roads. He had had a miserable time negotiating the frost heaves and potholes that plague some roads.

Lighter bikes are more suitable for gravel roads while larger bikes are definitely more comfortable for long highway trips. If you prefer, you can fly or cruise to Alaska then rent a motorcycle out of Anchorage and skip the extra miles and wear on your own bike. Power cruisers and touring bikes are popular choices, especially with those pulling trailers.

Regardless of what you ride, perform major maintenance on your bike before heading North. If you break down on the road, towing distances to the next repair shop can be several hundred miles.

There are motorcycle repair shops in Alaska and Canada, but you will usually find well-stocked motorcycle shops only in the cities. Many riders prefer the comfort designed models made for touring and these are serviced in major cities, just as they are in the lower 48.

Windshields are essential to protect riders from gravel and dust. Some bikers also use Plexiglas headlight shields and hand guards. A fairing, while not completely protecting you from rocks, will offer good protection against insects, rain, wind and cold. Case guards are good insurance against damage to the bike should you go down. Consider taking a good competition air filter to improve engine performance and gas mileage. Heated handgrips are also recommended for colder temperatures. A skid plate will help protect the engine from rocks kicked up by the front wheel, and a center stand can be a great help when parking on gravel, fixing a flat or lubing a chain. For additional security, carry a light nylon cover for your bike. Keep your radiator safe from flying rocks with a perforated guard in front of it, as suggested by riders we met on the road.

Gravel roads are rough on tires, and flats are common, so start out with new tires. A complete tire repair kit is essential. Also, bring a valve stem tool, a mini bicycle pump and dish soap to aid in tire changes.

Some northern bridges present challenges to motorcyclists. There are numerous narrow 2-lane bridges, many with metal-grated decks that can be *very slippery* when wet and have longitudinal grooves that tend to cause motorcycles to sway. Go with the sway rather than fighting it. There are also wood-deck bridges that are very slippery when wet. Slow down when crossing these bridges.

Be wary when driving on roads with rumble strips. Some roads will have rumble strips down the center lines so that people who wander into the center of the highway will be alerted to their location. These rumble strips can startle a biker while pulling out to pass a vehicle ahead and cause them to overcorrect. These grooves have been studied and determined to not be a danger, but can impact a rider if surprised by them.

A final word to both motorcyclists and vehicle drivers: Be safe out there! Don't exceed the speed limit and be willing to go much slower need be. Be alert for potholes, loose gravel on pavement, soft shoulders and other road damage such as frost heaves and deeply rutted pavement that can fatally hinder your ability to maneuver at normal driving speeds. Road construction areas can be challenging for both motorcycles and vehicles depending on the weather and current conditions of the road surface. The MILEPOST® was behind a group of motorcyclists on a stretch of deep gravel road where the Alaska Highway was under reconstruction. A motorcyclist pulling a trailer fishtailed in the gravel and went over. (He and the bike were fine, except for a bruised leg.) Another time we spotted an RV tipped onto its side because it had driven too far onto a narrow shoulder (on the Cassiar Highway).

There are quite a few moose-vehicle collisions each year and some stretches of highway are designated Moose Danger Zones. Be especially vigilant of wildlife.

Planning your trip

Depending on where you want to stop and how much time you have to spend, you can count on driving anywhere from 150 to 500 miles a day. On most roads in the North, you can figure on comfortably driving 250 to 300 miles a day.

In the individual highway sections, log mileages are keyed on the highway strip maps which accompany each highway section in The MILEPOST®. You may also use the mileage boxes on these maps to calculate mileages between points, or refer to the mileage box at the beginning of the highway. There is a Mileage Chart on the back of the pull-out Plan-A-Trip Map, and mileages between junctions and communities are also given on the Key to Highways maps (see pages 8–10).

Four suggested itineraries are located in the front of the book, *pages 11–14,* to serve as trip ideas for those looking for a bit more instruction. These basic routes include varied inbound and outbound routes to maximize your Alaska/Canada experience by not having to retrace your steps. The major attractions are listed with each itinerary to assist you with your decision.

Normally, May through October is the best time to drive to Alaska. A severe winter or wet spring may affect road conditions, and there may be some rough road until road maintenance crews get out to upgrade and repair. Motels, hotels, gas stations and restaurants are open year-round in the cities and on many highways. On more remote routes, such as the Cassiar Highway, not all businesses are open year-round. Check road conditions and weather outlook before traveling. Also call ahead for accommodations and gas if traveling these roads in winter.

Most people are familiar with the Walmart brand and what it offers and Walmarts are common in Canada. A similar brand store in Canada is Canadian Tire—despite its name, it isn't just a tire store. It offers many Walmart-like necessities for travelers including oil changes, camping equipment, some groceries and much more.

VISA and MasterCard are readily accepted all along the highways of Alaska and Canada. Still, it is wise to carry enough cash for souvenirs, gas or lodging at that random place that may not accept credit cards.

Campgrounds in Provinces and Territories do not accept credit cards or U.S. checks. Be sure to carry Canadian cash including loonies and toonies ($1 and $2 coins) so that you can put the correct amount in self-registering envelopes and to pay for coin-op showers found in many campgrounds.

Police

Travelers will see the Alaska State Troopers in Alaska and the Royal Canadian Mounted Police (RCMP) in Canada. In addition, many Northern communities have city or municipal police forces.

The RCMP was established in Yukon during the Klondike Gold Rush, when it was called the Northwest Mounted Police. Later the RCMP began patrolling the newly constructed Alaska Highway in the 1940s, with detachments at Whitehorse, Haines Junction, Teslin and Watson Lake. Today, the RCMP is responsible for policing services at the federal, provincial and municipal level in Canada.

The Alaska State Troopers is a statewide law enforcement agency with Trooper Posts throughout the state and detachments in Ketchikan, Palmer, Anchorage, Fairbanks and Soldotna.

Like their Canadian counterparts, Alaska's law enforcement evolved largely in response to the influx of gold seekers, followed by the need to patrol the state's growing number of roads in the 1940s. The Territory of Alaska Highway Patrol was established in 1941, and given policing powers in 1948. The Alaska State Trooper Museum in Anchorage traces this history.

Phone numbers for city police, RCMP detachments and Alaska State Troopers posts are noted in community descriptions.

Road Condition Reports

General road conditions are noted in the introduction to each highway in *The MILE-POST®.* Specific areas of concern are also called out in the logs. Current seasonal road conditions provided by government agencies may be obtained at the following:

Alaska road conditions. The Alaska Department of Transportation (DOT) has traveler information via phone and website. This 511 system provides current driving conditions, current and future road construction, closures, incidents and urgent reports, weather cameras (check the weather camera box to see real-time web cam views of highways), winter driving tips, route summary reports and mountain pass locations. From within Alaska phone 511, or online at 511.alaska.gov. (The National Weather Service also provides weather information at www.weather.gov/arh.)

Statewide updates for Very Difficult and/or Hazardous driving condition will be tweeted to the Twitter handle @alaska511. Travelers can follow either the statewide handle @alaska511 or the following area Twitter accounts preceded by ak511_ (for example ak511_Anchorage): Anchorage, Fairbanks, Southeast, Peninsula, Mat-Su, Tok, Tazlina, Valdez, Dalton and Denali.

Yukon road conditions: For year-round daily recorded updates, phone (867) 456-7623. Yukon Highways & Public Works Dept.'s Road Report online at www.511yukon.ca. Reports are up-to-the-minute and include road construction. Also visit the Visitor Centers for reports and conditions.

British Columbia road conditions: General automated road information is available 24 hours-a-day phone 1-800-550-4997 (cell *4997); for road reports. Or go to www.drivebc.ca. BC web cams show real-time conditions at: images.drivebc.ca/bchighway-cam/pub/html/www/index-Northern.html.

Northwest Territories road conditions: Phone 1-800-661-0750 or go to www.dot.gov.nt.ca/Highways/Highway-Conditions for highway conditions and ferry schedules. The DOT twitter feed is at: mobile.twitter.com/GNWT_DOT.

Alberta road conditions: Alberta Transportation provides the official road report. In Alberta dial 511 or outside of Alberta 1-855-391-9743. Or visit: 511.alberta.ca and click on the map for road and weather conditions where you intend to travel.

Roundabouts

Since 2000, the Alaska Dept. of Transportation has built numerous roundabouts—in Anchorage, Fairbanks, North Pole, Fort Wainwright, Denali National Park, Wasilla (there are more than 10 in the Mat-Su area), Juneau and Sitka—and more are planned, so both residents and visiting motorists need to know how to negotiate these unique traffic patterns. Essentially, roundabouts are 1- to 2-lane continuous traffic intersections. Traffic moves in a counter-clockwise direction and there are no traffic signals. The most important rule to remember is: Motorists already in the roundabout have the right-of-way. Vehicles must yield to vehicles already in the roundabout, when entering the roundabout.

Finally, follow posted speed limits and drive defensively. For more information, go to: dot.alaska.gov/stwddes/dcstraffic/roundabouts.shtml.

Speed Limits/Driving Laws

Travelers may plan to average 55-mph on most of the paved highways. For more remote gravel roads, such as the Taylor Highway and Denali Highway, a safe average might be 20- to 45-mph. Actual driving time may vary due to weather, road construction, road conditions, traffic, time of day, season, driver ability and rest stops.

The MILEPOST® references speed limits on some sections of highways to give an idea of travel time. But we do not include all posted speed limits, which on paved highways in Alaska range from 55- to 65-mph on major highways to 30-mph through communities.

In British Columbia, if you are caught speeding more than 40-kmph/25-mph above the speed limit, your vehicle will be impounded for 7 days. The cost of towing and the impound storage fee is at least $210, in addition to your fine of $368 (and 3 demerits).

The Alaska DMV states that the average cost of a first DUI is $22,740 based on days in jail, court fines, vehicle impound, attorney, loss of car and other consequences. Of particular note in Canada is British Columbia's drinking limit for drivers, because of its severity compared to other provinces, territories and U.S. states. A 0.05 blood alcohol concentration has a first offense of 3-days driving ban, $200 fine, possible vehicle impound for 3 days (with all associated fees for towing and impound) and a $250 reinstatement fee for your driver's license (this totals at least $600 for the first offense).

Distracted Driving laws are in place in Yukon, British Columbia, Alberta and Northwest Territories banning the use of handheld cell phones and other electronic devices including iPods, laptops and GPS units. Fines in British Columbia begins at $167/3 demerits; Alberta $172; Northwest Territories $100/3 demerits and Yukon $250/3 demerits against your record.

One-touch or voice activated phones are allowed except by British Columbia who bans hand-held and hands-free devices for novice drivers. Alaska bans texting while driving; first offense is a Class A Misdemeanor and a $500 fine; if the texting causes an accident or harm, these penalties go up exponentially.

Tires

On gravel, the faster you drive, the faster your tires will wear out so take it easy. You should have no tire problems provided you have the right size for your vehicle, with the right pressure, not overloaded, and not already overly worn. Belted bias or radial ply tires are recommended for gravel roads. Studded tires are legal in Alaska from Sept. 15–May 1 and from Oct. 1–April 30 in BC. Yukon's rules on studded tires are in conjunction with Alaska and BC dates. BC *also requires* passenger vehicles to use winter tires on BC Highways from Oct. 1–March 31 and you may be delayed, have your car impounded or get fined if you are not in compliance.

Carry 1 good spare. Consider 2 spares if you are traveling remote gravel roads such as the Dempster, Taylor and Dalton highways. The space-saver (doughnut) spare tires found in some passenger cars are not adequate for use as a spare on these roads.

Avid RVer Gerald Kreimeyer and his wife have driven to Alaska from Florida almost every year since he retired in 2009, driving an average of 14,000 miles round trip. He asked us to remind travelers about the importance of tire maintenance. "Check

Traveling with Pets

Pets on leash is the rule on trails, and the best way to keep your dog safe. (©Kris Valencia, staff)

For those traveling with pets, many of *The MILEPOST®* staff travel with pets too. These tips are from our personal experience as well as tips from other travelers.

Keep your pets on leashes whenever they are outside your vehicle. We mention wildlife cautions often but take it to heart. A dog can quickly dash up to a bear or moose just inside the woods or underbrush at a turnout and you may suddenly face an unwelcome and possibly lethal situation.

Make sure your pet is microchipped and has current ID tags so that if you lose a pet and it is found, you may be reached. One tip provided by Ronald Jones in *RVing to Alaska*, is to "put emergency contact information and a picture of your animal somewhere in the coach—a sort of mini-passport... If the animal has an identification chip, include that information..."

If you do lose your dog, check with the vet's office or animal shelter in the next town. Animal shelters are generally found only in the larger communities and not all communities have vets, so if the town has neither one, ask around. Also ask about broadcasting a lost dog message on the local radio station.

If you use a special pet food, bring enough to feed the animal for the entire trip because you might not be able to get it in Canada or Alaska." *(NOTE: Be sure to leave the food in its original bag with ingredients listed. If you don't, it may be confiscated at the border for unknown content.* Additionally, Canada's border crossing limits import to 20 kg/44 lbs of pet food).

You must have proper proof of rabies vaccination documentation for your pet when crossing the U.S.–Canada border, and, if your pet appears unwell, see a vet and get a health certificate for transport (dated within 30 days of travel) or you may be turned away at the border.

Treat for fleas and ticks before traveling north. Alaska does not have fleas or ticks; *please do not bring them with you.*

Respect the highway businesses who are tired of picking up after canine visitors and have posted notices requesting that pets stay in their vehicles. There are plenty of turnouts to stop at and walk your dog. Remember to pick up after them; litter bins are located at many turnouts.

Animal injuries occur in the North as they do anywhere else, but there are a few special considerations to keep in mind. Smaller communities may not have a resident vet. If your dog is injured, help may be several hours away. Bring a pet first aid kit that includes self-sticking bandage tape, gauze, antiseptic, antibiotic cream, Benadryl (for allergic reactions) and a non-steroidal anti-inflammatory like Rimadyl (doggie Advil). You may want to download the American Red Cross app in advance to help with pet first aid at www.redcross.org/mobile-apps/pet-first-aid-app.

Small dogs are vulnerable to predation by eagles and foxes. Bears and moose may go after any size dog if provoked. Also keep an eye out for porcupines. Dog fights with loose or unfriendly local dogs are also a possible cause of dog injuries.

If you take your pet fishing, boat and water safety should apply to both pet and owner. Fast-moving, powerful rivers, such as the Kenai, are difficult for even strong swimmers (canine or human) to negotiate. Consider a life preserver for your dog or board them for the day. Local businesses will help you understand your options.

10 Highest Highway Passes in Alaska

Mentasta Summit *Glenn Highway (2,434 ft. /742m)*

Thompson Pass *Richardson Highway (2,678 ft. /816m)*

Tahneta Pass *Glenn Highway (3,000 ft. /914m)*

Twelvemile Summit *Steese Highway (3,190 ft. /972m)*

Isabel Pass *Richardson Highway (3,280 ft. /1,000m)*

White Pass *Klondike Highway 2 (3,292 ft. /1,003m)*

Eureka Summit *Glenn Highway 2 (3,322 ft. /1,012m)*

Eagle Summit *Steese Highway (3,685 ft. /1,123m)*

Maclaren Summit *Denali Highway (4,086 ft. /1,245m)*

Atigun Pass *Dalton Highway (4,800 ft. /1,463m)*

your tires' manufacture date. If the tires are 4 or 5 years old or show signs of cracking, you need new ones, especially driving Northern roads. It is not just the inconvenience of a flat tire: Tire blowouts can inflict tremendous damage to the undercarriage of your rig and, if a rear dually is affected, can wipe out electric, plumbing or even worse. I've had one front blowout, and 2 rear blowouts that caused $5,000 to $8,000 in damage."

Vehicle Preparation

Make sure your vehicle and tires are in good condition. Paved highways have cut down on the problems with dust and mud in the North, though you may run into both on gravel roads or in construction areas. When driving gravel in dry weather, keep the windows on your vehicle closed and check your air filter periodically.

A high clearance vehicle is best for some of the rougher gravel roads. Good windshield wipers and a full windshield washer (or a bottle of wash and a squeegee) will make travel safer.

On gravel roads, drive at slow, safe speeds to keep down the dust for drivers behind you, and to avoid spraying other vehicles with gravel (and damaging windshields). Gravel breaks are noted by "Loose Gravel" signs. *Slow down for gravel breaks!*

Although auto shops in Northern communities are generally well-stocked with parts, carry tools and a first-aid kit. If you are driving a vehicle which may require parts not readily available up North, carry whatever you think necessary. You may wish to carry a few extra gallons of gas, water, and fluid for brakes, power steering and automatic transmissions.

RV preparation tips: Know the height of your vehicles in metric measurements, as bridge heights in Canada are noted in meters.

Diesel pushers can suffer from a "street sweeping" type of injury when traveling through gravel. The mud/rock guards that are installed on most of these RVs can actually end up bouncing rocks and gravel back into the fan, which then propels those items into the radiator at penetrable speeds. To prevent this, Tim Anderson, owner of Anchorage's **Alaska Performance RV** says, to "consider installing rock guards behind the rear wheels, install tow car shields, and if possible, install protection around the radiator and fan blades." Simple aluminum screening on both sides of the RV, held in place by plastic zip ties is one reader's fix for this problem. Towing costs and repair costs can be exorbitant in out-of-the-way places, so plan ahead.

As often as we give advice about driving in the North Country, we also hear from our readers who have additional comments that may be helpful to others. Gerry Kreimeyer had this to say about protecting RVs:

"Dirty windows, damaged paint or finishes, and constant cleaning can all take away from the enjoyment of seeing Canada and Alaska on your trip north. There are some preparations and precautions you can take before you leave home that will lessen the workload. Whether you own or rent an RV, keeping the RV clean and damage-free is easier when you plan ahead.

"First: Make sure the RV is water tight. Check and reseal any caulk that is cracked, damaged or missing. A good self-leveling lap sealant is best.

"Second: Wash, degrease, clean and wax. There are products made for fiberglass boats in salt-water (go to www.collinitemarine.com for wax and cleaner/degreaser) that work great for RVs.

"Third: Apply a barrier to help prevent or minimize damage from rocks, dirt and bugs. Inexpensive surface protectors like www.surfacearmor.com work well on RVs."

Gerry has also observed that driving on badly frost-heaved road, or even dropping off a large curb, can really torque a motorhome or camper. "It is possible that slides—if not secured with braces—could shift on rough roads like the Top of the World Highway or sections of the Alaska Highway between Destruction Bay and Beaver Creek.

Winter Driving

Tips to help with winter driving include: keep the windshield clear of ice, check antifreeze and reduce driving speeds on icy roads and equip your vehicle with survival gear. Consider carrying: traction material (ashes, kitty litter, wood chips); chains (even with snow tires); shovel, ice scraper, flashlight, flares; fire extinguisher; extra warm clothing (including gloves, boots, hat and extra socks), blankets or sleeping bags; food; tools; first-aid kit; and an extension cord to plug the car into a block heater. Other items to include: a tow rope or cable, ax, jumper cables and extra gas. For additional information, go to: www.themilepost.com/articles/faq-driving-the-alaska-highway and look at topic 10.

Renting an RV

Rental RV at Chicken, AK, a favorite stop on the Klondike Loop. (©Milton & Kelley Barker, staff)

Renting an RV can be a relatively economical way to explore Alaska and Canada at your own pace, enjoying the solitude that camping offers but with the luxury of a soft bed, your own bathroom and an indoor space in case of rain. First-timers should be assured that it really isn't that hard to drive a RV, even a "big rig" (30 feet plus). The pros at RV rental agencies say you get the hang of it within 15 minutes or by the first 100 miles out of town.

The rental agency should demonstrate the basic operation of the motorhome for you before you take off. Learning about "off tracking," "swing out" (or "tail swing") and the other effects of driving a 10-foot-wide vehicle with 12 or more feet of overhang behind the rear wheels is important if you're unaccustomed to big rigs.

Some of the key points to remember in driving an RV: Do not start turning until your back wheels are past the obstacle; drive slowly and at an angle over dips in the road, such as gutters, so that the overhang doesn't "bottom out"; accelerate slowly; and allow 4 to 5 times the stopping and following distance you do in a car. It is also recommended you use an outside spotter when backing up, in addition to the rearview mirrors, and that you make sure to check for obstructions at campsites. Trees and tree branches are the number one cause of damage to rental RVs.

Upon making your reservation, a deposit is usually required and you may be given a check-in time frame to pick up your rental vehicle, as well as a return time. Do not plan to put in a lot of miles the first day of your trip. You will spend some time doing paperwork, familiarizing yourself with the RV, packing up the RV, buying food and other supplies, then driving through town traffic before you reach the open road.

The RV should come supplied with linens, towels, pots and pans, cutlery and dishes. Toasters and coffee makers may be made available free on request or for an extra charge. Other items often available for rent include ice chests, extra lawn chairs, bike racks and fishing rods.

There are a number of reputable rental agencies to choose from in Anchorage, where most visitors land, including Alaska Motorhome Rentals (www.BestofAlaska Travel.com), ABC Motorhome & Car Rentals (www.abcmotorhome.com) and Go North Car & RV Rental (www.gonorth-alaska.com).

You will find most RV rental rates are quite comparable. Generally, rates vary depending on the size of the RV, with the daily rate higher in mid-summer and lower at the beginning of the season (April–May) and at the end of the season (September–October). Daily rates are usually based on a 7 days or more rental period; expect to pay an extra charge for 4- to 6-day rentals.

Mileage options may be offered as well, with a daily rate plus per mile charge or a higher daily rate with unlimited mileage. Return rental with full gas and propane tanks or incur additional charges.

Ask what kind of extra services and items they supply. Do they have courtesy van service to and from the airport? What is included in the basic rental fee? What are the extra costs, such as cleaning fees?

Also ask about insurance coverage. Most dealers include comprehensive coverage, but with a high deductible. Talk to your own insurance agent about whether you should purchase the dealer's Collision Damage Waiver or if your policy will cover the deductible.

When choosing a vendor, you will need to look at what they have available in terms of makes and models of RVs. Check web sites and brochures for particulars on their rental RVs. How many does the unit sleep? Do they have slideouts? Also key to making a decision is what units are available for your vacation dates.

A good dealer will provide you with plenty of information upon receiving your inquiry and even more information after taking your reservation. I received a confirmation packet that detailed my motorhome pickup time and all fees to be charged. This 10-page booklet included general arrival information, what to do if arriving after hours, pickup particulars, credit card requirements, return times, driver's license requirements, and answers to some commonly asked questions.

If you have only 1 or 2 weeks, have some kind of itinerary in mind before you arrive. Alaska's road system is relatively limited, and distances are not great, but there's a lot to see. And you may want to make advance reservations for the Alaska State ferry across Prince William Sound between Whittier and Valdez, or for campsites in popular areas like Denali Park and the Kenai Peninsula.

If you arrive in Anchorage, you can take off in 3 directions: South down the Seward Highway; east on the Glenn Highway; and north up the Parks Highway (see Key to Highways Map 3 on page 10). Read through the highway logs in *The MILEPOST®*, noting campground locations, attractions, fishing opportunities, and mileages between points, to come up with a trip that will fit your interests and your timetable.

One-way RV rentals to Alaska are hard to find but inquire with ABC Motorhomes (phone 1-800-421-7456/www.abcmotor home.com) or with Go North Car & RV Rental (phone 1-866-236-7272/www.gonorth-alaska.com).

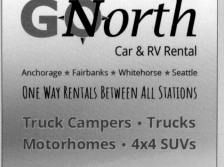

Ferry Travel

The Alaska Marine Highway ferry system connects 33 coastal Alaska communities.
(©Kris Valencia, staff)

Ferry travel to and within Alaska is provided by the state ferry system—the Alaska Marine Highway System (AMHS)—which serves Bellingham, WA, Prince Rupert, BC, and 33 coastal Alaska communities from Ketchikan to Unalaska.

The Marine Highway in Southeast Alaska runs through the Inside Passage and spans from Bellingham, WA, to Skagway, AK. The Southcentral/Southwest route serves Prince William Sound, Homer, Kodiak and the Aleutian Islands. *(See maps on pages 36–38).*

The Inside Passage route for the Alaska Marine Highway, follows the coast of British Columbia and uses the protected waterways between the islands and the mainland of Southeast Alaska. (The Inside Passage is also commonly used to refer to Southeast Alaska and its communities.)

British Columbia Ferry Services, Inc. (BC Ferries) also serves the Inside Passage, providing passenger/vehicle ferry service between Port Hardy and Prince Rupert, BC. Port Hardy is located at the north end of Vancouver Island, 312 miles/502 km north of Victoria via Trans-Canada Highway 1 and BC Highway 19; the ferry terminal is at Bear Cove *(see VANCOUVER ISLAND HIGHWAY section on pages 141–148).* Prince Rupert is also the farthest north of the ports served by BC Ferries, and the southern port for many Alaska state ferries serving Southeast Alaska.

BC Ferries schedules, information and reservations for the Inside Passage, along with details on tariffs and vessels, appear under "BC Ferries" *beginning on page 40 this section.* Visit BC Ferries online at www.bcferries.com or phone 1-888-223-3779.

Motorists often use the Alaska Marine

Ferry Routes
Washington and British Columbia from Puget Sound to Hecate Strait

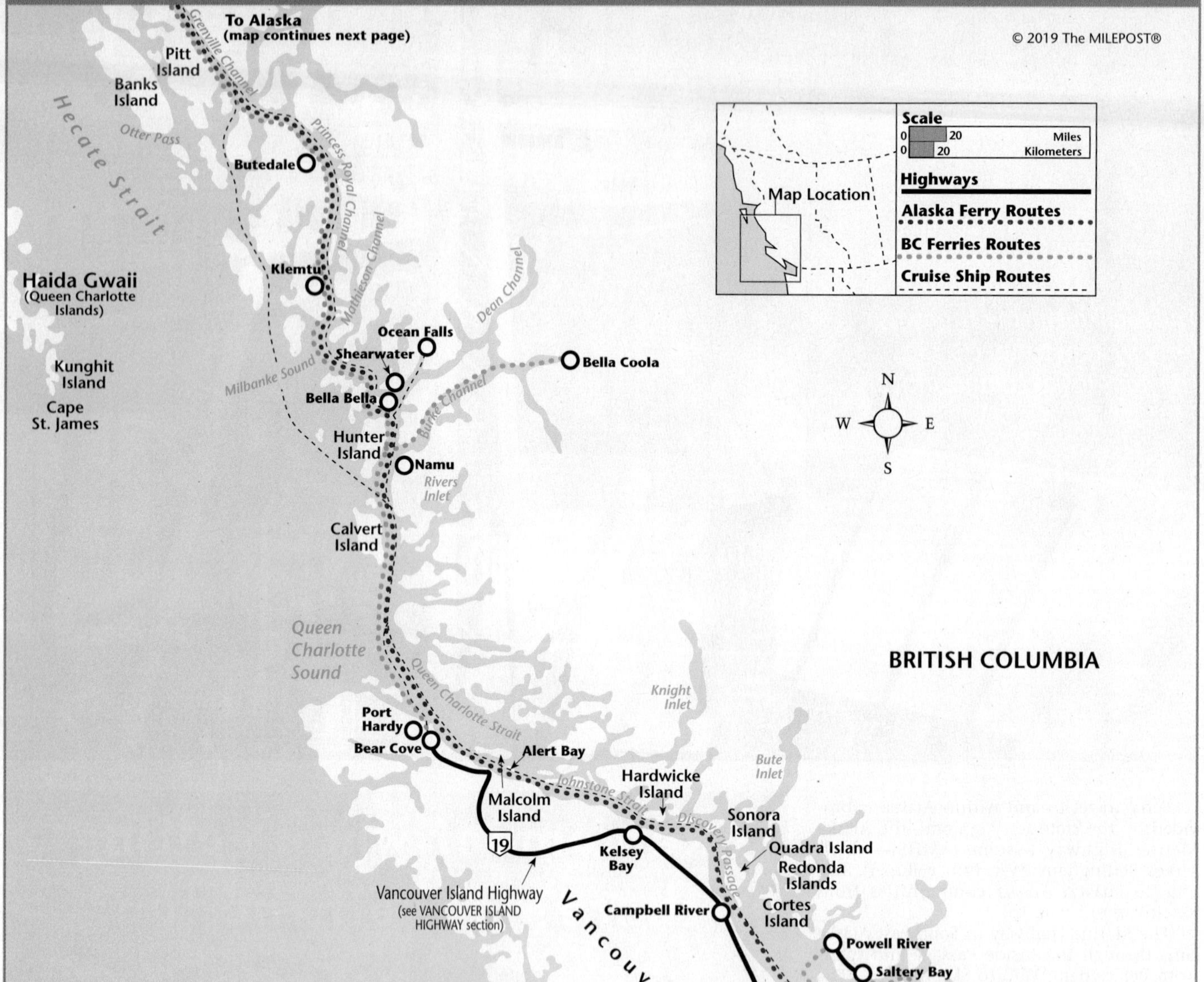

© 2019 The MILEPOST®

Scale

| 0 | 20 | Miles |
| 0 | 20 | Kilometers |

Map Location

Highways
Alaska Ferry Routes
BC Ferries Routes
Cruise Ship Routes

To Alaska
(map continues next page)

Pitt
Island

Banks
Island

Hecate Strait

Otter Pass

Grenville Channel

Princess Royal Channel

Butedale

Mathieson Channel

Klemtu

Haida Gwaii
(Queen Charlotte
Islands)

Ocean Falls

Shearwater

Dean Channel

Bella Coola

Kunghit
Island

Cape
St. James

Milbanke Sound

Bella Bella

Hunter
Island

Burke Channel

Namu

*Rivers
Inlet*

Calvert
Island

*Queen
Charlotte
Sound*

BRITISH COLUMBIA

N
W — E
S

*Knight
Inlet*

Queen Charlotte Strait

Port
Hardy

Bear Cove

Alert Bay

Hardwicke
Island

*Bute
Inlet*

Malcolm
Island

Johnstone Strait

Sonora
Island

Quadra Island

Redonda
Islands

19

Kelsey
Bay

Discovery Passage

Cortes
Island

Vancouver Island Highway
(see VANCOUVER ISLAND
HIGHWAY section)

Campbell River

Powell River

Saltery Bay

Vancouver Island

Courtenay

Texada
Island

Earls Cove

19

Langdale

Horseshoe Bay

Port Alberni

Highway to
Horseshoe Bay

Strait of Georgia

Vancouver

Vancouver Island Highway
(see VANCOUVER ISLAND
HIGHWAY section)

Nanaimo

Tsawwassen

CANADA
U.S.A.

Bellingham

Saltspring
Island

Swartz Bay
Sidney

Anacortes

Victoria

CANADA
U.S.A.

San
Juan
Islands

5

Pacific Ocean

Strait of Juan de Fuca

101

Port Angeles

Everett

WASHINGTON

101

Seattle

*Puget
Sound*

5

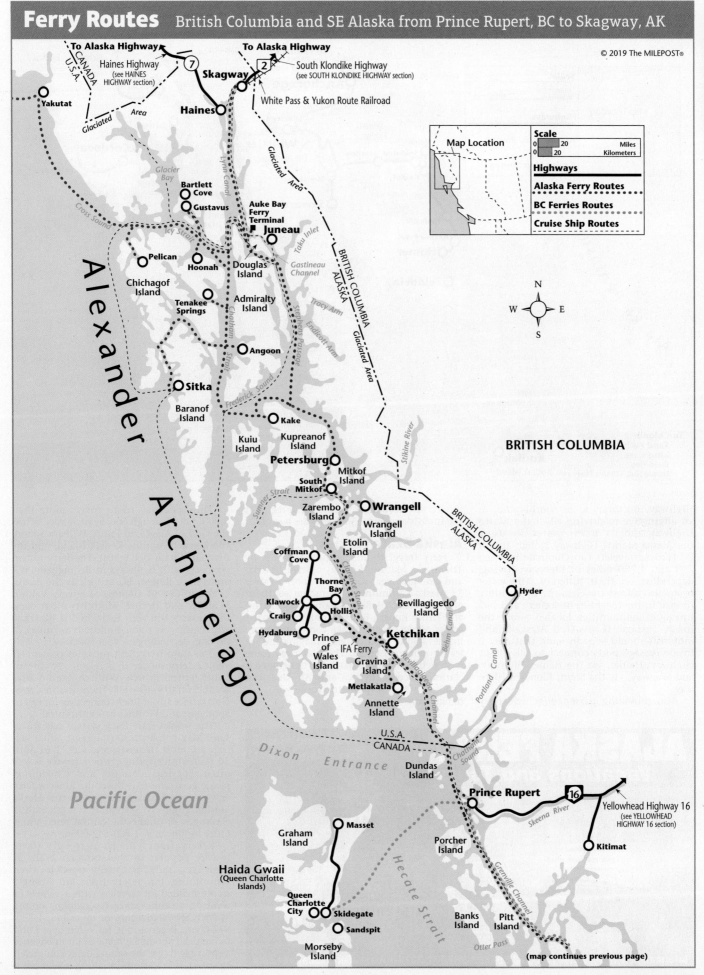

Ferry Routes
British Columbia and SE Alaska from Prince Rupert, BC to Skagway, AK

To Alaska Highway

Haines Highway
(see HAINES
HIGHWAY section)

Skagway

South Klondike Highway
(see SOUTH KLONDIKE HIGHWAY section)

To Alaska Highway

White Pass & Yukon Route Railroad

Haines

CANADA
U.S.A.

Glaciated
Area

Lynn Canal

Glaciated Area

Glacier
Bay

Cross Sound

**Bartlett
Cove**

Gustavus

Icy Strait

Auke Bay
Ferry
Terminal

Juneau

Taku Inlet

BRITISH COLUMBIA
ALASKA

Glaciated Area

Pelican

Hoonah

Douglas
Island

Gastineau
Channel

**Chichagof
Island**

**Tenakee
Springs**

Admiralty
Island

Chatham Strait

Stephens Passage

Tracy Arm

Endicott Arm

Alexander

Angoon

Sitka

Baranof
Island

Frederick Sound

Kake

Archipelago

Kuiu
Island

Kupreanof
Island

Petersburg

Mitkof
Island

**South
Mitkof**

Summer Strait

Stikine River

BRITISH COLUMBIA

Wrangell

Zarembo
Island

Wrangell
Island

Etolin
Island

**Coffman
Cove**

**Thorne
Bay**

Klawock

Hollis

Craig

Hydaburg

Prince
of
Wales
Island

IFA Ferry

Clarence Strait

Revillagigedo
Island

BRITISH COLUMBIA
ALASKA

Hyder

Ketchikan

Gravina
Island

Metlakatla

Behm Canal

Revillagigedo Channel

Portland Canal

Annette
Island

U.S.A.
CANADA

Pacific Ocean

Dixon   Entrance

**Dundas
Island**

Chatham Sound

Prince Rupert

Yellowhead Highway 16
(see YELLOWHEAD
HIGHWAY 16 section)

Skeena River

Kitimat

Masset

Graham
Island

**Porcher
Island**

Grenville Channel

Haida Gwaii
(Queen Charlotte
Islands)

Hecate Strait

**Queen
Charlotte
City**

Skidegate

Sandspit

**Banks
Island**

**Pitt
Island**

Otter Pass

Morseby
Island

(map continues previous page)

Scale
Map Location

| 0 | 20 | Miles |
| 0 | 20 | Kilometers |

Highways
Alaska Ferry Routes
BC Ferries Routes
Cruise Ship Routes

N
W — E
S

Yakutat

Southcentral/Southwest Ferry Routes

© 2019 The MILEPOST®

Map Location

Scale
0 — 20 Miles
0 — 20 Kilometers

Highways ━━━━━
Alaska Ferry Routes ●●●●●
Cruise Ship Routes ----

Knik Arm

To Fairbanks (see PARKS HIGHWAY section)

Anchorage

Glaciated Area

Columbia Glacier

Richardson Highway (see RICHARDSON HIGHWAY section)

Valdez

Turnagain Arm

Portage

Tatitlek

Seward Highway

Whittier

Cordova

No thru-traffic past this point

Kenai
Soldotna   Sterling

The Alaska Railroad

Prince William Sound

Copper River Highway (see COPPER RIVER HIGHWAY log)

Kasilof

Skilak Lake

Moose Pass

Hinchinbrook Island

Cook Inlet

Tustumena Lake

Seward

Chenega Bay

Sterling Highway

Ninilchik

Montague Island

Anchor Point

Homer

Seldovia

Gulf of Alaska

N W E S

Alaska Peninsula

Afognak Island

To Chignik
Sand Point
King Cove
Cold Bay
Unalaska/Dutch Harbor

Port Lions

Kodiak

Kodiak Island

Highway, northbound or southbound, as an alternative to driving all of the Alaska Highway and its access routes. By using the Alaska Marine Highway System and/or BC Ferries, travelers can eliminate between 700 and 1,700 miles of highway driving, depending on their itinerary. The water route also allows travelers the opportunity to take in the magnificent scenery and picturesque communities located along the Inside Passage. (Cross-Gulf Alaska-bound motorists should keep in mind that only 2 Inside Passage ports connect to the Alaska Highway: Haines, via the Haines Highway; and Skagway, via the South Klondike Highway.

Also providing passenger/vehicle ferry

service within Alaska's southeastern region is the Inter-Island Ferry Authority *see page 41.*

Alaska State Ferries

Ferry travel to and within Alaska is by The Alaska Marine Highway System (AMHS) and provides year-round transport to over 33 Alaska communities from the southern gateway cities of Bellingham, Washington and Prince Rupert, British Columbia to ports across Alaska. Many Alaska communities are inaccessible to road systems, making the sea travel option, essential. This waterway route is so extraordinary it has been designated a National Scenic Byway and All-American Road; it is the only marine route with this designation.

This waterway route covers more than 3,500 miles through Southeast Alaska, across the Gulf of Alaska, to Prince William Sound, the Kenai Peninsula, Kodiak Island, and the Aleutian Chain (see maps). The ferry system connects with highways in Bellingham, WA and Prince Rupert, BC as well as the Alaska communities of Haines, Skagway, Valdez, Whittier and Homer. Motorists often combine a ferry trip with their driving itinerary, which can save you hundreds of miles of driving, depending on your itinerary.

The state ferry fleet provides passenger/vehicle ferry service in 3 regions: Southeast, Southcentral/Prince William Sound and Southcentral/Southwest. There is also Cross-Gulf service in summer connecting Juneau in Southeast and Whittier in Southcentral.

The Alaska state ferry system has 2 seasons: May 1 to Sept. 30 (summer), when sailings are most frequent; and Oct. 1 to April 30 (fall/winter/spring), when service is less often. For trip planning and scheduling, please go to the AMHS website at www.ferry alaska.com. Email questions to the Alaska Marine Highway System at dot.ask.amhs@ alaska.gov or phone the central reservations office in Juneau at 1-800-642-0066.

Reservations: Alaska state ferry travel is very popular in the summer. Walk-on passenger traffic is usually possible, even last-minute, but reservations are strongly recommended for travelers with a vehicle or wanting a cabin. Make reservations online at www.ferryalaska.com or by calling 1-800-642-0066. Reservations for cabin space and for vehicles should be made as far in advance as possible to get the sailing dates you prefer. However, don't assume a sailing is sold out if

Approximate Running Times
(* indicates fast ferry times)

Southeast/Inside Passage

Prince Rupert to Ketchikan	6 hrs.
Bellingham to Ketchikan	38 hrs.
Ketchikan to Wrangell	6 hrs.
Wrangell to Petersburg	3 hrs.
Petersburg to Juneau	8 hrs.
Petersburg to Sitka	10 hrs. 45 min.
Sitka to Juneau	8 hrs. 45 min.
Juneau to Haines	4 hrs. 30 min.
Haines to Skagway	1 hr.

Southeast Feeder Routes

Ketch. to Metlakatla/Annette Bay	45 min.
Juneau to Sitka	4 hrs. 30 min. *
Juneau to Petersburg	4 hrs. *
Juneau to Gustavus	4 hrs. 15 min.

Cross Gulf

Juneau to Yakutat	17 hrs.
Yakutat to Whittier	22 hrs.

Prince William Sound

Whittier to Valdez	5 hrs. 45 min.
Whittier to Cordova	6 hrs. 45 min.
Valdez to Cordova	13 hrs. 45 min.

Southcentral

Homer to Kodiak	9 hrs. 30 min.
Homer to Seldovia	1 hr. 30 min.
Whittier to Kodiak	19 hrs. 30 min.

Southwest

Kodiak to Chignik	18 hrs. 45 min.
Chignik to Sand Point	9 hrs. 15 min.
Sand Point to King Cove	6 hrs. 45 min.
King Cove to Cold Bay	2 hrs.
Cold Bay to False Pass	4 hrs. 15 min.
False Pass to Akutan	10 hrs. 30 min.
Akutan to Dutch Harbor	3 hrs. 30 min.

Please visit www.FerryAlaska.com
or call 1-800-642-0066
for reservations
or visit: FerryAlaska.com

Email: dot.ask.amhs@alaska.gov
AMHS Reservations Office
6858 Glacier Highway
P.O. Box 112505
Juneau, AK 99811-2505

For road conditions and
vessel tracking information dial 511

Deck passengers can put up tents on specified decks or find a lounge chair to sleep on.
(©Kris Valencia, staff)

you suddenly decide to include the ferry in your itinerary; phone or check online to see if there is space available.

Vehicles: Vehicle fares depend on the size of your vehicle and the distance you travel. You are charged by how much space you take up, so a truck with trailer is measured from the front of the bumper to the end of the trailer, including hitch space. Charges are also applied to motorcycles, bikes and kayaks. Do not attempt to estimate your vehicle length; you must accurately measure your vehicle to avoid additional charges and the potential for being moved to a later sailing due to size restrictions. Maximum length allowed is 48 feet, for a single unit.

Some exceptions and/or restrictions apply to certain ports and vessels. Please visit www.ferryalaska.com or call 1-800-642-0066 for more information. U.S. Coast Guard safety regulations prohibit travel on the car deck; passengers are not allowed to sleep or dine in their vehicles.

Cabins: If you are traveling on one of the longer ferry runs, such as the 38-hour trip between Bellingham, WA and Ketchikan, AK, you should reserve a cabin well in advance. Cabin fares are charged per unit, not by the number of people using the cabin. Cabins are outfitted with single or double bunk bed-style berths and vary in size and availability. Some cabins have a toilet, shower and linens (towel, sheets, blankets). Pick up keys from the purser's office when you board. You can also rent blankets, pillows, and towels for a fee from the Purser on mainline vessels.

Other Sleep Options: If cabin space is sold out or you wish to save a few dollars and travel without a cabin, the inside recliner lounges and the covered solarium located on the upper deck serve as sleeping areas. Just bring your own sleeping bag and find yourself the perfect spot to relax for the evening. Small, free-standing tents are also permitted on the solarium deck (but not under the heated covered area) and on the stern of the cabin deck. Be sure to bring duct tape to secure your tent to the deck as strong winds can pick up while the ferry is underway.

Food & Beverage Service: Food service varies from vessel to vessel. Hot meals, snacks, and beverages are available in cafeterias, or snack bars on all vessels, except the Lituya. Food service hours vary based on sailing departure times. You can bring your own food and beverages, but keep in mind that refrigeration is not available on board. For guest convenience, there are microwaves, coin-op ice and soft drink/snack vending machines.

Luggage: You are responsible for your own luggage. Foot passengers may bring up to 100 lbs. of hand luggage. There is no limit on weight carried in a vehicle. Baggage carts for carry-on luggage are driven between the terminals and the car deck. Baggage handling is NOT provided and the Alaska Marine Highway System is not responsible for lost, stolen, or damaged luggage.

Pets: For a pet to be transported via ferry between Bellingham, WA or Prince Rupert, BC and Alaska ports, they must have a valid rabies certificate and it must clearly identify your animal and be presented at check-in. (See "Crossing the Border" in the TRAVEL PLANNING section for requirements for pets.) Dogs and other pets are not allowed in cabins and must be transported on the vehicle deck only. When prior approval has been obtained, there may an exception made for a certified service animal. Pets are to be transported inside a vehicle or in kennels furnished by the passenger (on the car deck). Pets must be cared for by the owner. On long sailings, you may feed, water and/or walk your pet on the car deck during one of the 15-minute announced car deck calls. You may also walk your pet at port stops. Keep in mind that some port stops are very brief and that sailing time between some ports will be as long as 38 hours (Bellingham to Ketchikan). Car deck calls are dependent on weather conditions and other variables.

Accessibility: Each vessel has a few cabins that are equipped to accommodate passengers with disabilities and every vessel has elevator access to cabin decks.

Hazardous Materials: Hazardous materials may not be transported on the ferries. The valves on propane or similar type tanks must be turned off and sealed by an AMHS employee. Portable containers of fuel are permitted but must be stored with vessel personnel while en route.

ID Requirements: All AMHS customers are required to show proper valid government ID, meaning photo identification issued by a government authority such as a state or provincial driver's license, passport, official government issued ID, or military ID. Passengers traveling in or out of Prince Rupert, BC, or who plan on driving through Canada, are required to show their passport. (Also check "Crossing the Border" in the TRAVEL PLANNING section for ID requirements.) Passengers onboard AMHS vessels between Bellingham, WA, and Ketchikan, AK, are not required to show a passport as the ship does not stop in a Canadian port along the way.

BC Ferries MV Northern Expedition plies the Inside Passage between Port Hardy and Prince Rupert, BC. *(©David L. Ranta, staff)*

Vessels

Aurora (AUR) began service 1977; carries 250 passengers, 33 vehicles; cafeteria, heated solarium.

Columbia (COL) began service 1974; carries 499 passengers, 133 vehicles, 104 cabins; dining room, cafeteria, heated solarium.

Fairweather (FWX) Fast Ferry, began service 2004; scheduled to retire in 2019.

Kennicott (KEN) began service 1998; carries 450 passengers, 78 vehicles, 109 cabins; cafeteria, heated solarium.

LeConte (LEC) began service 1974; carries 225 passengers, 33 vehicles; cafeteria, solarium.

Lituya (LIT) began service 2004; carries 125 passengers, 15 vehicles.

Malaspina (MAL) began service 1963; carries 450 passengers, 83 vehicles, 72 cabins; cafeteria, heated solarium.

Matanuska (MAT), began service 1963; carries 450 passengers, 83 vehicles, 106 cabins; cafeteria, heated solarium.

Tazlina, scheduled to begin service May 2019, in Lynn Canal as a day boat. 300 passengers, 53 vehicles.

Tustumena (TUS) began service 1964; carries 160 passengers, 34 vehicles, 24 cabins; dining room, heated solarium.

BC Ferries

BC Ferries provides year-round service on 24 routes throughout coastal British Columbia, with a fleet of 35 passenger- and vehicle-carrying ferries. The ferry route of special interest to Alaska-bound travelers is the "Inside Passage" service between Port Hardy (on Vancouver Island) and Prince Rupert, and service to Vancouver Island from mainland ports out of Vancouver, BC at Tsawwassen and Horseshoe Bay.

Inside Passage service between Port Hardy and Prince Rupert offers a convenient connection with the Alaska Marine Highway at Prince Rupert. Prince Rupert is located 450 miles/724 km west of Prince George via the Yellowhead Highway *(see YELLOWHEAD HIGHWAY 16 section; see description of Prince Rupert beginning on page 270)*. Port Hardy is 312 miles/502 km north of Victoria via Trans-Canada Highway 1 and BC Highway 19 *(see VANCOUVER ISLAND HIGHWAY log on pages 141–148)*. NOTE: *The Port Hardy ferry leaves from Bear Cove terminal, which is 6 miles from Port Hardy.*

©David L. Ranta, staff

Inside Passage summer service between Port Hardy and Prince Rupert is aboard the MV *Northern Expedition*, carrying 600 passengers and 130 vehicles. This ferry has an expanded range of cruise-ship-like food service options to include a fine dining buffet, a relaxed atmosphere grill/cafeteria, as well as solarium seating, a gift shop, lounge, children's playroom, 55 modern staterooms, travel information and many other amenities.

Summer service on this route is during daylight hours, so cabins are not necessary for the 16-hour trip, although cabins are available for day-use or round-trip passengers. (Passengers cannot stay onboard while ferry is in dock due to Transport Canada Regulations.) The ferry goes up one day and comes back the next. (Winter sailings include an overnight aboard the *Northern Adventure* with fewer scheduled sailings than in summer.) Check-in time is 2 hours prior to departure.

Keep in mind that both the northbound and southbound Inside Passage sailings arrive at Prince Rupert and Port Hardy respectively at 11:30 P.M. By the time you drive off the ferry, it will be midnight. Local campgrounds in both Prince Rupert and Port Hardy will accommodate RV guests arriving at this late hour, but it is a good idea to call ahead for reservations and let them know you will be on the ferry.

Inside Passage travelers can extend their visit from Prince Rupert out to Haida Gwaii (formerly the Queen Charlotte Islands) via the MV *Northern Adventure*. BC Ferries provides 5-day-a-week service to Skidegate on Graham Island in Haida Gwaii. Crossing time is about 7 hours, with one overnight sailing a week (cabins are available).

To reach Vancouver Island, travelers may use the passenger and vehicle ferry service to Victoria out of Port Angeles, WA, available from Black Ball, or take BC Ferries passenger and vehicle service from Tsawwassen, south of Vancouver, to Swartz Bay.

Travelers may also take BC Ferries service from Tsawwassen to Duke Point/Nanaimo (2 hours) or from Horseshoe Bay, west of Vancouver, to Departure Bay/Nanaimo (1 hour and 40 minutes). Be aware that during commuting hours around weekends and holidays, lines can be long. From Nanaimo it is 251 miles/405 km—or about a 5 hour drive—to Port Hardy, the departure point for BC Ferries Inside Passage service. If you are

---

BC FERRIES SUMMER 2019 INSIDE PASSAGE
June 19–September 14, 2019, M.V. *Northern Expedition*

NORTHBOUND

Dep. **Port Hardy** 7:30 A.M.-Arr. **Prince Rupert** 11:30 P.M.
Dates: June: 19, 21, 23, 25, 27, 29; July odd-numbered days
August even-numbered days; Sept. 1, 3, 5, 7, 9, 11, 13

En Route Stop: **Bella Bella** 12:50 P.M.-Dep. 1:50 P.M.
Dates: June: 19, 23, 25, 27; July odd-numbered days except 5, 13, 19, 27
August even-numbered days except 2, 10, 16, 24, 30; Sept. 1, 3, 5, 9, 11

En Route Stop **Klemtu** 3 P.M., Dep. 4 P.M.
Dates: June: 21, 29; July 5, 13, 19, 27; August 2, 10, 16, 24, 30; Sept. 7, 13

SOUTHBOUND

Dep. **Prince Rupert** 7:30 A.M.-Arr. **Port Hardy** 11:30 P.M.
Dates: June 20, 22, 24, 26, 28, 30; July even-numbered days;
August odd-numbered days; Sept. 2, 4, 6, 8, 10, 12, 14

En Route Stop: **Bella Bella** 5:10 P.M., Dep. 6:10 P.M.
Dates: June 20, 22, 24, 28, 30; July even-numbered days except 2, 10, 16, 24, 30;
August odd-numbered days except 7, 13, 21, 27; Sept. 2, 6, 8, 12, 14

En Route Stop: **Klemtu** 3 P.M., Dep. 4 P.M.
Dates: June 26; July 2, 10, 16, 24, 30; Aug. 7, 13, 21, 27; Sept. 4, 10

NOTE: Mid-Coast passengers transfer from
M.V. *Northern Expedition* to M.V. *Northern Sea Wolf* in Bella Bella

driving from Victoria to Port Hardy, allow at least 7 hours. Ferry routes connecting Vancouver and Vancouver Island are serviced by a modern fleet of ferries including 3 Super C class vessels providing the ultimate in comfort for your passage.

Vancouver Island is a popular destination for vacationing mainland resident. Alaska-bound motorists taking the BC Ferries Inside Passage route should allow plenty of time in their itinerary to visit the island's many attractions. (See VANCOUVER ISLAND HIGHWAY log on pages 141–148.)

Schedules: BC Ferries Summer 2019Inside Passage (Port Hardy–Bella Bella/Klemtu–Prince Rupert) schedule appears on facing page. Sailing schedules for other months/ports are available online at www.bcferries.com. Travelers are advised to check the online schedule prior to traveling.

Tsawwassen–Swartz Bay, Horseshoe Bay–Departure Bay, and Tsawwassen–Duke Point ferries sail daily year-round, with frequent (only TSA–SWB is hourly in the summer) sailings from early morning to late evening during summer with naturalists onboard in summer. Schedules are no longer printed, visit www.bcferries.com for current schedules on all routes.

Fares: Inside Passage peak (regular) season passenger fares are from May 1 to Oct. 1. Shoulder and off-peak season rates are reduced. These lower fares are available during the fall, winter and spring when service is less frequent.

All fares shown are in Canadian funds. Terminals accept Visa, Mastercard, American Express or cash, but most terminals cannot accept debit cards (the exceptions are Port Hardy/Bear Cove and McLoughlin Bay, which can accept debit cards for payment).

At press time, Inside Passage regular passenger fares (in CAD) one-way to/from Port Hardy and Prince Rupert were: (peak/off peak) $175 regular/$102.75 adult passenger; $87.50 regular/$51.40 child, 5 to 11 years; under 5 years of age, free. (Special fares apply for BC residents on school events and for disabled and senior BC residents.) Vehicle fares one-way for vehicles up to 7 feet high, up to 20 feet in length: $398.65 regular/$223.95, plus an additional $34 regular/$19.10 for each extra foot over 20 feet. Other one-way fares: Motorcycle, $199.25 regular/$111.95 (with sidecar or trailer, $303.25 regular/$163.40); bicycle, $5; stowage (canoe, kayak, etc.) $10.

Summer cabin rates for the *Northern Expedition* day-cruise between Port Hardy and Prince Rupert are: Inside and wheelchair cabins, $100; outside cabins, $130.

Reservations: Passenger and vehicle (private passenger or recreational vehicle with or without a trailer) reservations are strongly advised for the Inside Passage. Reservations are less essential, but still recommended for the frequent Island to Vancouver routes. For reservations, phone 1-888-223-3779 in North America; phone 250-386-3431 from outside North America.

Reservations can be made online at www.bcferries.com. Cancellations made fewer than 30 days prior to departure for Inside Passage trip are subject to a cancellation fee.

Information: BC Ferries phone in North America 1-888-223-3779, Ext. 3; from outside North America, phone 250-386-3431; email customerservice@bcferries.com; online at www.bcferries.com.

For a complete array of vacation package options go to: www.bcferriesvacations.com.

Inter-Island Ferry Authority (IFA)

The IFA dock in Ketchikan for the MV Stikine and MV Prince of Wales is adjacent the Alaska State Ferry dock. *(©Kris Valencia, staff)*

KETCHIKAN TO HOLLIS
MV *Stikine* or MV *Prince of Wales*

Daily year-round service
(except for Thanksgiving Day & Christmas Day)

Depart Hollis 8:00 A.M.-Arrive Ketchikan 11:00 A.M.
Depart Ketchikan 3:30 P.M.-Arrive Hollis 6:30 P.M.

Formed in 1997 to improve transportation to island communities in southern Southeast Alaska, the IFA is a Port Authority organized under Alaska's Municipal Port Authority Act.

The IFA's MV *Stikine* or MV *Prince of Wales* are both 198 feet in length and 95-gross tons. Their capacity is 190 and 160 passengers respectively, and 30 vehicles and is operated by a staff of 7. These vessels offer daily passenger and vehicle service between Ketchikan and Hollis/Clark Bay on Prince of Wales Island. Crossing time is about 3 hours. The IFA ferry departs Ketchikan from a dock adjacent the Alaska Marine Highway terminal. An IFA reservation desk is located inside the Alaska Marine Highway Ketchikan terminal building. IFA maintains its own terminal at Hollis/Clark Bay. The IFA vessels fill in for the Alaska Marine Highway during repairs or maintenance.

Check-in for your reservation with a vehicle is one hour prior to departure or your space may be released to stand-by vehicles. Walk-on passengers must check in one-half hour prior to departure or the seats may be released to stand-by passengers.

An important addition to the economy and Southeast population, the IFA carries an average of 52,000 passengers and 12,335 vehicles annually. It provides transportation to commuters for those in logging, seafood processing and even some of the Alaska Marine Highway staff living on Prince of Wales Island.

The IFA provides the essential reliable and speedy transport necessary for the shipment of 3 million pounds of seafood annually. This fast-expiring freight is worth $15 million. The seafood must reach the market quickly to avoid spoiling and complete loss. These fisheries include geoduck, halibut, winter kings, roe, black cod, shrimp, sea cucumbers and other salmon species that are harvested by fishermen on Prince of Wales.

A paved highway begins at the Clark Bay ferry terminal near Hollis on Prince of Wales Island and leads 23 miles to the coast at Klawock with connections to Craig, Hydaburg, Thorne Bay, Coffman Cove, Naukati and Whale Pass; this route takes motorists through the temperate rainforest environment typical of Southeast Alaska. *See Prince of Wales Island description and road logs on pages 609–617.*

For information and reservations on IFA vessels, phone 1-866-308-4848 or visit www.interislandferry.com.

IFA Terminal Phone #s
Clark Bay/Hollis Terminal:
Phone (907) 530-4848
Ketchikan Terminal:
Phone (907) 225-4848

The famous Kenai River has many public fishing access points. This is at the Funny River Recreation Site. (©Kris Valencia, staff)

Fishing & Hunting

Hunting and fishing are popular sports in the North and a way of life for many residents. Both resident and nonresident sport fishermen and hunters must be aware of rules and regulations before going out in the field. Failure to comply with state hunting and fishing regulations can result in monetary fines and loss of trophies or property.

Regulation booklets are available from the government sources listed below and may also be found at a variety of outlets, including outdoor stores. Visitors will also find all the outdoor gear they need for fishing, hunting, boating or camping.

Alaska Department of Fish and Game (ADF&G): Located at 1255 W. 8th St., in Juneau; license information, phone (907) 465-2376; email adfg.license@alaska.gov; www.adfg.alaska.gov/. Hunting and fishing licenses are available by mail or online at www.adfg.alaska.gov/Store or through one of 1,000 license vendors throughout Alaska.

Alberta Fish & Game Association: phone 1-877-944-0313 or (780) 944-0313; visit their website at: mywildalberta.com/; or for licenses, www.albertarelm.com/licensing.page. Click on Alberta Regulations and read online or order a print copy of the fishing and hunting regulations.

British Columbia Fish & Game: Fish & Wildlife Branch, Ministry of Environment, phone 1-877-855-3222; email FishandWildlife@gov.bc.ca; visit www.env.gov.bc.ca/fw/fish/regulations/ for fishing regulations. Hunting information categories at www.env.gov.bc.ca/fw/wildlife/.

NWT Fish & Game: Wildlife & Fisheries, Dept. of Environment & Natural Resources, phone (867) 767-9055; www.enr.gov.nt.ca for links to hunting and fishing licenses.

Yukon Fish & Game: Hunting, Fishing and Wildlife Viewing: Dept. of Environment, Fish & Wildlife Branch, phone (867) 667-5652; email: environment.yukon@gov.yk.ca.; or visit www.env.gov.yk.ca. Click on the Hunting, Fishing & Trapping tab at top to see Fishing Regulations, Hunting

Regulations and other publications available to download. Hunting licenses and fishing licenses may be purchased online.

Fishing (Alaska)

The biggest challenge for visiting anglers is the sheer number and variety of fishing opportunities available. Many fishing guides and charter operators advertise in *The MILEPOST®.* The ADF&G has dozens of pamphlets on fishing regional waters, as well as online regional sport fishing updates. An annual resident sport fishing license is $29. Resident Senior Citizen and Disabled Veteran license applications are only available in person through local Fish and Game offices or by contacting the Fish and Game Licensing office.

A nonresident annual sport fishing license is $145. Nonresident fees are as follows: 1-day sport fishing licenses $25; 3-day licenses $45; 7-day licenses $70; and 14-day licenses $105.

To fish for chinook salmon, residents and nonresidents must also purchase a King Salmon Stamp. An annual resident king salmon stamp is $10. Nonresidents fees are: $15 for a 1-day stamp; $30 for 3 days; $45 for 7 days; $75 for 14 days; and $100 for an annual nonresident King Salmon Stamp.

Salmon are the most popular sport fish in Alaska, with all 5 species of Pacific salmon found here: chinook, coho, pink, chum and sockeye. Other sport fish include halibut, rainbow trout and steelhead, Dolly Varden and Arctic char, cutthroat and brook trout, northern pike, Arctic grayling and lake trout.

Knowing the kind of fish and fishing you want may help plan your trip. For example, chinook fishing in Southeast is restricted to saltwater, but cutthroat are common on the mainland and every major island in Southeast. Alaska's Interior has the largest Arctic grayling fishery in North America. Northern pike is the most sought-after indigenous sport fish in Interior Alaska after the Arctic grayling. These fish are the main sport fish species in the Tanana River drainage.

Excellent fishing is available north or south within a day's drive of Anchorage. The Kenai Peninsula offers streams

where chinook, sockeye, coho, pink and chum salmon may be caught during the summer. Dolly Varden, steelhead and rainbow trout also run in Peninsula streams. Several lakes contain trout and landlocked salmon. In-season saltwater fishing for halibut, rockfish and several salmon species is excellent at many spots along the Peninsula and out of Whittier, Homer, Seward and Valdez. For specific fishing spots both north and south of Anchorage, see the PRINCE WILLIAM SOUND, SEWARD, STERLING, GLENN and PARKS HIGHWAY sections. *Because of the importance of fishing to Alaska, both commercially and for sport, regulations are updated yearly by the state and are strictly enforced, so it is crucial to obtain a current regulations book. There are often last-minute closures too, so you must check just prior to fishing, to ensure compliance.* Go to the ADF&G home page, www.adfg.alaska.gov, and click on Licenses & Permits under the Fishing and Hunting category tabs.

Most fishing enthusiasts focus their trips between April and October, when the weather is milder, but anglers have great success during the colder months as well. The Alaska Dept. of Fish and Game Sport Fish Division gives a run timing for all fisheries by region. Also check local newspapers for ADF&G regional fishing updates.

Where to fish is probably the most difficult choice, with the huge number of fishing destinations available. Throughout *The MILEPOST®* you will see the friendly little fish symbol at the end of some paragraphs. Wherever you see one, you will find a description of the fishing. Fishing spots are also listed under the "Area Fishing" heading in the Attractions section of each community.

You can fish any body of water that is legal, but local knowledge of whether or not it contains fish, helps. *NOTE: We are very grateful to the Alaska Department of Fish and Game who has provided us with information on which lakes are stocked and what fisheries are along the highways.*

There is a long tradition of harvesting shellfish in Alaska. *However, shellfish harvested in Alaska waters can contain the toxin causing PSP (paralytic shellfish poisoning).* This includes clams, mussels, oysters, cockles, geoducks and scallops. Crabmeat is not known to contain the toxin causing PSP, but crab viscera can contain unsafe levels of toxin and should be discarded. According to the Alaska Dept. of Health and Social Services, the toxin that causes PSP cannot be cooked, cleaned or frozen out of shellfish. Early signs of PSP include tingling of the lips and tongues, which may progress to tingling of fingers and toes, loss of control of arms and legs, followed by difficulty breathing. PSP can be fatal in as little as 2 hours.

Hunting (Alaska)

Nonresident hunters in Alaska must be accompanied by an Alaska-licensed guide or an Alaska resident 19 years of age or older within second degree of kindred and holding a current Alaska hunting license when hunting brown bear, Dall sheep or mountain goats. A resident annual hunting license costs $45. An annual nonresident hunting license costs $160.

A combined annual hunting and sport fishing license is $69 for residents or a cost of $305 for nonresidents. Nonresidents may also purchase a combined annual hunting and one-day fishing license for $185, annual hunting and three-day license for $205; 7 days for $230; and 14 days for $265.

There are 26 game management units in Alaska and wide variation in hunting seasons and bag limits for various species. Check for special regulations in each unit. Information on hunting in Alaska, game animals, regulations and more is available at www.adfg.alaska.gov/index. cfm?adfg=hunting.main.

Big game includes black and brown/grizzly bears, deer, elk, mountain goats, moose, wolves and wolverines, caribou, Dall sheep, musk-oxen and bison. Big game tags are required for residents hunting musk-ox and brown/grizzly bear and for nonresidents hunting any big game animal. These non-refundable, nontransferable metal locking tags (valid for the calendar year) must be purchased prior to the taking of the animal. A tag may be used for any species for which the tag fee is of equal or lesser value. Examples of nonresident tag prices: brown/grizzly bear/$1,000, Dall sheep/$850, and mountain goat/$600.

Small game animals include grouse, ptarmigan and hares. Fur animals that may be hunted are coyote, fox and lynx. Waterfowl are also abundant. There is no recreational hunting of polar bear, walrus or other marine animals.

The Alaska Department of Fish and Game's Division of Wildlife Conservation has an entire web section devoted to providing information for hunters/trappers. Go to www.adfg.alaska.gov and find "Trapping" in the Hunting subhead menu.

Holidays

The following dates are for 2019. Be sure to check for special events under the "Attractions" heading in each of the community descriptions within *The MILEPOST®* for additional holidays/events.

January

Holidays: Jan 1 New Year's Day (USA/Canada); Jan. 21 Martin Luther King, Jr. Day (USA)

February

Holiday: Feb. 18 Presidents Day (USA)

March

Holidays: March 27 Seward's Day (Alaska),

April

Holidays: April 19 Good Friday (USA/Canada); April 21 Easter Sunday (USA/Canada), April 22 Easter Monday (Canada)

May

Holidays: May 20 Victoria Day (Canada); May 27 Memorial Day (USA)

July

Holidays: July 1 Canada Day (Canada); July 4 Independence Day (USA).

August

Holidays: Aug. 5 Civic Holiday (Canada); Aug. 19 Discovery Day (Yukon)

September

Holidays: Sept. 2 Labor Day (USA)/Labor Day (Canada)

October

Holidays: October 14 Alaska Indigenous Peoples Day (Alaska)/Thanksgiving (Canada); Oct. 18 Alaska Day (Alaska)

November

Holidays: Nov. 11 Veterans Day (USA)/Remembrance Day (Canada); Nov. 28 Thanksgiving (USA)

December

Holidays: Dec. 25 Christmas Day (USA/Canada); Dec. 26 Boxing Day (Canada)

Internet/Cell Phones

Cell phone coverage and reception is unpredictable and sporadic outside the cities. Staff has received and placed calls on our cell phones in some out-of-the-way places but have been unable to raise a signal just a few miles outside Fairbanks or south of Anchorage along Turnagain Arm. Adding to the unpredictability is your cell phone provider's roaming agreements, which may black out certain areas.

Most hotels, motels, lodges, bed-and-breakfasts, hostels and RV parks offer some form of internet access for their guests. Internet cafes are found in larger northern communities (Starbucks is a good bet). WiFi is also increasingly available at hotels, local libraries, visitor centers and even campgrounds. Schools and community centers may also offer internet access for travelers.

In the North, especially along the highways where businesses are "off grid," broadband usage is very expensive, limited and slow. You may be asked to refrain from sending videos or photos, streaming videos and other high download activities/websites.

For availability of internet access along the highways, see highway businesses advertising in *The MILEPOST®*.

Use 10-digit phone numbers for all calls in Alberta and British Columbia.

British Columbia, Yukon, Alberta and Northwest Territories have "distracted driving" laws regarding handheld cell phones or other electronic devices while driving *(see penalties under Speed Limits/Driving Laws on page 31 in "Driving North").*

Metric System

Metric conversions of special interest to cross-Canada travelers are as follows: 1 mile=1.609 kilometers; 1 kilometer=0.621 miles; 1 meter=3.3 feet; 1 yard=0.9 meters; 1 gallon=3.785 liters; 1 liter=.2642 gallons. See chart on this page for additional conversions.

Money/Credit Cards

©Kris Valencia, staff

The monetary system in Canada is based on dollars and cents like the U.S., but there are differences. Canada has nickels, dimes, quarters, 1-dollar coins ("loonies") and 2-dollar coins ("toonies"), but no longer uses pennies, so cashiers round-off up or down as needed. Paper currency comes in $5, $10, $20, $50, $100, etc. bills.

U.S. currency is accepted as payment in most places in Canada, but not NWT campgrounds. Merchants give change in Canadian currency and they may or may not give you the prevailing exchange rate.

The Canadian dollar and American dollar (Continues on page 47)

METRIC CONVERSIONS
Temperatures, distance and speed limits

Fahrenheit	Celsius
122°	50°
120°	49°
110°	43°
104°	40°
100°	38°
90°	32°
86°	30°
80°	27°
70°	21°
68°	20°
60°	16°
50°	10°
40°	4°
32°	0°
30°	-1°
20°	-7°
14°	-10°
10°	-12°
0°	-18°
-4°	-20°
-10°	-23°
-20°	-29°
-22°	-30°
-30°	-34°
-40°	-40°

Miles	Kilometers
1	1.6
2	3.2
3	4.8
4	6.4
5	8.0
6	9.7
7	11.3
8	12.9
9	14.5
10	16.1
20	32.2
30	48.3
40	64.4
50	80.5
60	96.5
70	112.6
80	128.7
90	144.8
100	160.9

Kilometers	Miles
1	0.6
2	1.2
3	1.9
4	2.5
5	3.1
6	3.7
7	4.3
8	5.0
9	5.6
10	6.2
20	12.4
30	18.6
40	24.8
50	31.0
60	37.2
70	43.4
80	49.6
90	55.8
100	62.0

KPH	MPH
30	20
50	30
70	40
90	55
100	60

Railroads

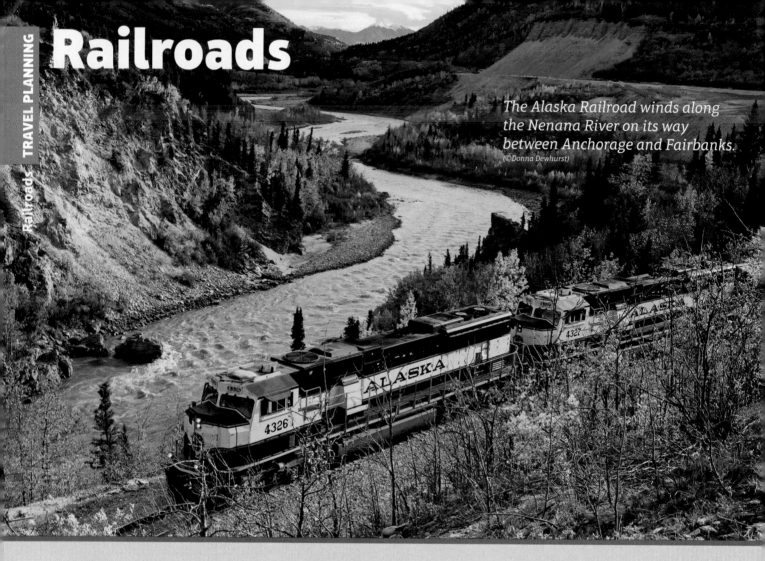

The Alaska Railroad winds along the Nenana River on its way between Anchorage and Fairbanks.
(©Donna Dewhurst)

Although no railroads connect Alaska or the Yukon with the Lower 48, there are 3 railroads in the North—the Alaska Railroad, the White Pass & Yukon Route and the trans-Canada service provided by VIA Rail.

Construction of the Alaska Railroad began in 1915 under Pres. Woodrow Wilson. On July 15, 1923, Pres. Warren G. Harding drove the golden spike at Nenana, signifying completion of the Railroad. The main line extends 470 miles from Seward to Fairbanks, with spurs to Whittier and Palmer. The Alaska Railroad is an iconic part of Alaska history, connecting some of Alaska's best-loved destinations for over 90 years! The Alaska Railroad operates daily summer service between Anchorage, Denali Park, Fairbanks, Seward, Girdwood, Whittier, Portage, Grandview and Spencer Glacier, and year-round service between Anchorage and Fairbanks.

The White Pass & Yukon Route (WP&YR) is a narrow-gauge (36-inch) privately owned railroad built during the Klondike Gold Rush. Construction of the WP&YR began in May 1898 and reached White Pass in February 1899 and Whitehorse in July 1900. It was the first railroad in Alaska and at the time, the most northern of any railroad in North America.

The WP&YR has one of the steepest railroad grades in North America. Starting at sea level in Skagway the railroad climbs to 2,865 feet/873m at the Summit of White Pass in only 20 miles/32 km of track. In 1994, it was declared an International Historic Civil Engineering Landmark, one of

only 42 in the world today. From 1900 until 1982, the WP&YR provided passenger and freight service between Skagway, AK, and Whitehorse, YT. Today, it operates passenger service from Skagway, AK, to Carcross, YT; the tracks to Whitehorse are inactive. Bus service fills in to/from Whitehorse.

For summer visitors, the WP&YR offers daily train service and sightseeing excursions from May through September (see details on page 44 under White Pass and Yukon Route heading).

VIA Rail operates Canada's only national passenger rail service. VIA Rail serves all regions of southern Canada, from the Atlantic to the Pacific. VIA Rail's Jasper/Prince Rupert service may be included in itineraries for Alaska-bound travelers departing from Prince Rupert, BC, on the Alaska Marine Highway System. VIA Rail's *Canadian* transcontinental service, "the ultimate Canada train trip," connects Toronto, ON, with Vancouver, BC, departure point for some Alaska-bound cruise ships.

The Alaska Railroad

Following are schedules and adult fares (peak season) on Alaska Railroad routes in summer 2019: Peak Season is June 1 to August 31; Value Season pricing available May 11–31 and Sept. 1–17. Children ages 2 through 11 ride for 50 percent of adult fare; under 2 ride free if infant in lap. U.S. Military receive a 20 percent discount off retail rail fares with military ID required at boarding.

The following schedules and fares are

subject to change without notice. Check train schedules at www.AlaskaRailroad.com for updates.

Reservations and information: Reservations are recommended on all routes. Tickets may be purchased in advance by mail. Checks, VISA, MasterCard, AMEX and Discover are accepted. Phone (907) 265-2494; 1-800-544-0552; www.AlaskaRailroad.com.

Anchorage–Wasilla–Talkeetna–Denali–Fairbanks (Denali Star Train): Daily passenger service on the *Denali Star* from May 11–Sept. 17, 2019 (peak season June 1 to August 31). Dining, baggage service, no-smoking cars, wheelchair access. Northbound train departs Anchorage at 8:15 A.M., arrives Wasilla 9:30 A.M., departs Wasilla at 9:35 A.M., arrives Talkeetna 11:05 A.M., departs Talkeetna at 11:20 A.M., arrives Denali Park 3:40 P.M., departs Denali Park at 4 P.M. and arrives Fairbanks 8 P.M.

Southbound train departs Fairbanks at 8:15 A.M., arrives Denali Park at 12:10 P.M., departs Denali Park at 12:30 P.M., arrives Talkeetna at 4:40 P.M., departs Talkeetna at 5 P.M., arrives Wasilla 6:15 P.M., departs Wasilla at 6:20 P.M., and arrives Anchorage 8 P.M.

One-way peak season (June 1–August 31) Adventure Class fares are: Anchorage–Fairbanks, $249; Anchorage–Talkeetna, $106; Anchorage–Denali Park, $174, Fairbanks–Denali Park, $77; Fairbanks–Talkeetna, $147. The Alaska Railroad's premium glass-domed GoldStar railcars are also available for booking on this route. GoldStar Service is inclusive of onboard meals and beverages.

Luxury railcars are also available on this route through cruise ship companies. Go to www.alaskatrain.com for details.

Talkeetna–Hurricane (Hurricane Turn Train): Round-trip summer service between Talkeetna and Hurricane Gulch, departing Talkeetna on Thursdays–Mondays between May 16 and Sept. 16, 2019. One of America's last flag stop trains, the *Hurricane Turn* takes you into rural Alaska where local residents have used the train for transportation to their remote homes or recreational property since 1923. This is a great day trip for visitors and/or access for those who wish to camp in the backcountry (train stops for drop-off/pick-up).

Departs Talkeetna 1:00 P.M., arrives Hurricane 3:30 P.M., leaves Hurricane at 4:30 P.M. arrives back in Talkeetna at 7:15 P.M. (all times are approximate). Roundtrip fare (Adventure Class only available) between Talkeetna and Hurricane is $108 in summer. The *Hurricane Turn* will stop wherever people want to get on or off. NOTE: There is no dining car on the Hurricane Turn Train. Passengers are encouraged to bring snacks/beverages.

Anchorage–Girdwood–Seward (Coastal Classic Train): Operates daily in summer from May 11 to Sept. 16, 2019 (peak season June 1 to Aug. 31). Dining, baggage service, no-smoking cars, wheelchair access.

Southbound train departs Anchorage at 6:45 A.M., arrives Girdwood 8 A.M., arrives Seward 11:05 A.M. Northbound train departs Seward at 6 P.M., arrives Girdwood 8:50 P.M., arrives Anchorage 10:15 P.M.

Round-trip adult fare from Anchorage or Girdwood to Seward is $175 for Adventure Class, $360 for GoldStar Service. One-way fare from Anchorage to Girdwood is $84 Adventure Class, $176 GoldStar Service. One-way adult fare Anchorage or Girdwood to Seward is $110 Adventure Class, $218 Goldstar Service.

Anchorage–Girdwood–Portage–Whittier–Spencer Glacier–Grandview (Glacier Discovery Train): Daily round-trip service from May 25 to Sept. 16, 2019, between Anchorage, Girdwood, Portage, Whittier, Spencer Glacier and Grandview, with motorcoach return from Portage to Anchorage or Girdwood on Spencer Glacier service and Grandview service. Dining, baggage service, no-smoking cars, wheelchair access.

The *Glacier Discovery* follows Turnagain Arm to Portage, then goes through the Anton Anderson Memorial Tunnel to Whittier. The train backtracks to Portage to board passengers before continuing on to Spencer Glacier Whistle Stop, a remote area in the Chugach National Forest where there is a boarding platform, shelter, restrooms, interpretive signs and trail to glacier views and campsites. Free guided hike led by a USFS ranger. At Spencer Glacier the railroad also offers optional tours: rafting, kayaking, hiking and ice climbing. (Reservations required for these optional tours.) After departing Spencer Glacier, the train climbs some of the railroad's steepest grade to Grandview (stunning alpine views). Departs Anchorage at 9:45 A.M., arrives Girdwood 10:55 A.M., departs Girdwood 11:00 A.M., arrives Portage 11:30 A.M., departs Portage 11:35 A.M., arrives Whittier 12:05 P.M., departs Whittier 12:45 P.M., arrives Portage at 1:15 P.M., departs Portage at 1:25 P.M., arrives Spencer Glacier 1:45 P.M., departs Spencer Glacier 1:55 P.M., arrives Grandview

The Alaska Railroad stops at the Denali Park depot from both Anchorage and Fairbanks.
(©Serine Reeves)

3:20 P.M.

Return train departs Grandview at 3:30 P.M., arrives at Spencer Glacier at 4:30 P.M., departs Spencer Glacier 4:40 P.M., arrives Portage at 5:15 P.M., departs Portage at 5:30 P.M., arrives Whittier at 6:05 P.M., departs Whittier at 6:45 P.M., arrives Portage at 7:05 P.M., departs Portage at 7:20 P.M., arrives Girdwood at 7:35 P.M., departs Girdwood at 7:40 P.M. and arrives Anchorage 9:15 P.M. (Rafting participants as well as Grandview sightseeing guests disembark in Portage for motorcoach transfer to Girdwood and Anchorage, arriving 6:15 P.M. and 6:45 P.M.)

Round-trip adult fares from Anchorage to Girdwood, $109; 1-way fare $69. Round-trip adult fare Anchorage to Spencer Glacier Whistle Stop, $129, or to Grandview $139 (both include motorcoach transfer from Portage to either Anchorage or Girdwood). Adventure Class only available on this route.

Reservations and information: Reservations are recommended on all routes. Tickets may be purchased in advance by mail. Checks, VISA, MasterCard, AMEX and Discover are accepted. Trains are cashless so all purchases onboard must be made with credit card. Phone (907) 265-2494; 1-800-544-0552; www.AlaskaRailroad.com.

A photo ID is required at depot check-in. Passengers may have 2 pieces of checked baggage and 1 carry-on for no charge, 2 extra pieces of baggage (for a total of 4) for an additional fee. No single piece may weigh more than 50 lbs. A special handling fee of $20 per item applies to oversized bags, bicycles and other recreational equipment.

Special firearms restrictions apply. Fed-

The White Pass & Yukon Route excursions out of Skagway are not to be missed.
(©Kris Valencia, staff)

eral Railroad Administration regulations prohibit the transport of fuel, with the exception of five liters or less of white gas per container in the bag car. No propane is allowed in bag cars, but kerosene and propane may be transported aboard the Glacier Discovery Train only, which is outfitted with a special transport compartment; these fuels must be checked with the conductor at the time of boarding. Other hazardous items are not permitted. Animals must be transported in kennels in the baggage car. The Alaska Railroad accommodates visitors with disabilities.

White Pass & Yukon Route

Following are schedules and fares for White Pass & Yukon Route in 2019. All times indicated in schedules are Alaska standard time. Skagway is on Alaska standard time, which is 1 hour earlier than White-horse, which is on Pacific standard time. Reservations a must!

Fares in U.S. dollars and include taxes; half price for children 12 and under. Cancellation fees apply. Schedules and fares are subject to change without notice.

Contact the White Pass & Yukon Route at Box 435, Skagway, AK 99840. Phone (907) 983-2217 or 1-800-343-7373; email info@wpyr.com; www.wpyr.com.

White Pass Summit Excursion: Available April 29 to Oct. 3, 2019. This 3- to 3½-hour, 40-mile fully narrated round-trip features 2 tunnels, trestles, waterfalls and more. Passport not required. Train is wheelchair accessible. Visit www.wpyr.com/excursions for additional information on availability and exceptions to schedule.

Bennett Scenic Journey: Passport required. Follow the trail of the Klondike stampeders between Skagway, AK, and Car-cross, YT. Guests enjoy a stop at our restored 1903 Bennett Station for a visit to the Bennett Museum and a self-guided walking tour around the old town site. Lunch is served on board the train upon departing Bennett. Motorcoach transfer to/from Skagway via the Klondike Highway with a stop at Emerald Lake. Available May 21 to Sept. 8, 2019. Departs 7:30 A.M. on Tuesday–Friday and Sunday (train to Carcross with bus return to Skagway); departs 9:30 A.M. Tuesday–Thursday, Saturday–Sunday (bus to Carcross with train return to Skagway). Passport required. Visit www.wpyr.com/excursions for additional details and pricing.

Train and Motorcoach Connections via Carcross: Passport required. A boxed lunch on board the train is included in all tours. Reservation agents are available to customize rail and highway trips between Whitehorse, YT and Skagway, AK. Please visit www.wpyr.com/excursions for more details.

Laughton Glacier Hiker Service: Passport required. This 14-mile train ride leads to a 5- to 8-mile self-guided hike through old growth forest to Laughton Glacier. Departs Skagway daily at 7:40 A.M. and 12:10 P.M. April 29 to Oct. 3, 2019. Visit www.wpyr.com/excursions for exceptions to schedule, pricing and more information.

Denver Glacier Service: Passport required. Board in Skagway for a round-trip train to the Denver trailhead. Self-guided walking tour to view Denver Glacier, recommended for those in fair physical conditions. Departs Skagway daily at 7:40 A.M. and 12:10 P.M. between April 29 to Oct. 3, 2019. Visit www.wpyr.com/excursions for exceptions to schedule, pricing and more information.

Chilkoot Trail Hiker Service: Passport required. Operates May 21 to Sept. 8, 2019. Northbound train departs Bennett on Tuesday–Friday and Sunday at 11 A.M. for Carcross. Southbound train departs Bennett for Fraser and Skagway on Tuesday–Thursday and Saturday–Sunday at 3:15 P.M. For details visit www.wpyr.com/excursions. Hiker lunches are available for advance purchase.

VIA Rail

VIA Rail's famous *Canadian* departs Toronto for Vancouver on Tuesdays, Thursdays and Saturdays during peak season (May to mid-October, 2019) with stops in Winnipeg, Saskatoon, Edmonton and Jasper and Kamloops North over the train's 3-day, 4-night journey. The *Canadian's* schedule provides for same-day connections in Toronto and other eastern destinations and daylight viewing of the Canadian Rockies. Travelers can choose between Economy class or Sleeper Plus or Prestige class, VIA's premier service with sleeping car accommodations, delicious meals prepared by onboard chefs, showers, and dome cars.

The other Rockies and Pacific VIA service in Western Canada is between Jasper, AB, and Prince Rupert, BC, with an overnight layover in Prince George (passengers must book their own hotel room). The 2-day trips depart 3 times per week on Wednesdays, Fridays, and Sundays. Choose between Economy or Touring class. Touring class is available mid-June to late September on select dates (check schedule) and includes complimentary food service as well as access to a dome car and a panorama car with 360 degree views.

Reservations and information: Phone 1-888-842-7245, or visit: www.viarail.ca.

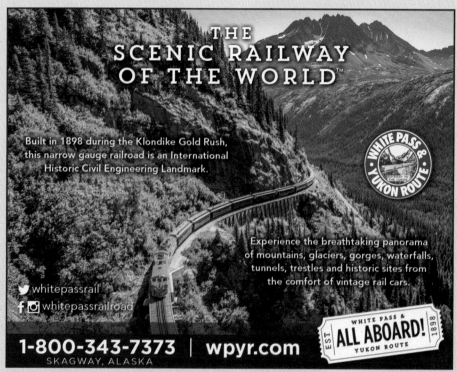

(Continued from page 43)

are 2 separate currencies and the rate of exchange varies. Not all banks in the U.S. have foreign currency on hand, so exchange your U.S. currency for Canadian currency at a bank in Canada. You will probably get a better rate of exchange at a bank, although there is still a fee.

Major American bank and credit cards are accepted in Canada. Credit card purchases are billed at the U.S. dollar equivalent at the current exchange rate and often a pesky "Foreign Transaction Fee" is included.

Many cities in Alaska and Canada have automated teller machines (ATMs)—MasterCard/Cirrus ATM Network, Nexxus and others—and they usually accept bank debit cards regardless of country of origin. It is important to carry some cash since some merchants may not accept plastic.

NOTE: Always remember to call your credit card company and file a trip plan with them before you embark on a trip so that they know where to expect charges and don't turn off your credit card when you are mid-trip.

Shipping

Whether you are moving to Alaska, or planning to ship your vehicle one way and drive the other, there is a shipper to accommodate your needs.

Vehicles: Carriers that will ship cars, campers, trailers and motorhomes between Anchorage and Seattle/Tacoma include the following:

Alaska Marine Highway System; phone 1-800-642-0066; www.dot.state.ak.us/amhs. Vehicle must be loaded and unloaded by owner or designated 3rd person. AMHS will not load or unload vehicle. Reservations for unaccompanied vehicles must be made over the phone or in person.

Alaska Marine Lines (Lynden family of companies); phone (206) 764-8346 or 1-800-326-8346; email amlcsc@lynden.com; www.lynden.com/aml. Ships vehicles, boats, campers, trailers, motorhomes, recreational vehicles, and household goods. Twice-weekly barge service between Seattle, WA and multiple points in Southeast Alaska and Central Alaska. Seasonal service to Western Alaska.

Alaska Vehicle Transport (United Road Services Inc.), in Anchorage phone (907) 561-2899 or toll-free 1-800-422-7925; www.alaskavehicletransport.com. Transports vehicles to, from and around Alaska.

Matson, in Anchorage, AK and Tacoma, WA; (907) 263-5073/(253) 882-1620; www.matson.com/matnav/services/alaska.html. Ships vehicles, household goods, general cargo and other materials twice-weekly to Alaska from Tacoma, WA.

Tote Maritime (TOTE), Anchorage, AK and Federal Way, WA; 1-800-426-0074; www.totemaritime.com. Ships freight, vehicles, boats and RVs between Federal Way, WA, and Anchorage, AK.

Persons shipping vehicles between Seattle/Tacoma and Anchorage are advised to shop around for the carrier that offers the services and rates most suited to the shipper's needs. Freight charges are dependent upon the carrier and the size of the vehicle.

Household Goods and Personal Effects: Most moving van lines have service to and from Alaska through their agency connections in most Alaska and Lower 48 cities. To

initiate service, contact the van line agents nearest your origin point.

Northbound goods are shipped to Seattle and transferred through a port agent to a water vessel for carriage to Alaska. Few shipments go over the road to Alaska. Southbound shipments are processed in a like manner through Alaska ports to Seattle, then on to the destination.

U-Haul (www.uhaul.com) provides service into the North Country for those who prefer to move their goods themselves. There are many U-Haul dealerships in Alaska and several in northwestern Canada for over–the–road service. Note weight restrictions on some routes, such as the Icefields Parkway *(log starts on pages 89)*, when choosing your itinerary. Other restrictions may apply to U-Haul vehicles and trailers.

Time Zones

Most of Alaska is on Alaska standard time, which is 1 hour earlier than Pacific standard time, 2 hours earlier than Mountain standard time, 3 hours earlier than Central standard time and 4 hours earlier than Eastern standard time. St. Lawrence Island (Alaska) and part of the Aleutian Islands are on Hawaii–Aleutian standard time.

Yukon and most of British Columbia are on Pacific standard time. (Exceptions in British Columbia include Rocky Mountain communities and the Dawson Creek area, which observe Mountain standard time.)

Northwest Territories and Alberta are on Mountain standard time.

Daylight Saving Time in the U.S. and Canada is March 10–Nov. 3, 2019 and is observed in Alaska except in the Aleutian Islands and St. Lawrence Island.

Time zone crossings are posted along the highways and noted within *The MILEPOST®* highway logs.

Tours

Tours can range from a day cruise to see wildlife and glaciers to a multi-day package or custom tour that may use several different vendors to provide transportation, accommodations and sightseeing/activities.

Booking agents can include wildlife touring in your customized package. Also check with tour desks at motels/hotels or ask your bed-and-breakfast or campground host about wildlife viewing tour operators available locally.

Air services offer aerial bear viewing, guided land-based bear viewing tours and round-trip transportation to bear viewing camps and lodges. Tour operators often offer sport fishing, bird watching and other activities along with bear viewing. Natron Air in Soldotna and Rust's Flying Service out of Anchorage both offer bear viewing air excursions (see display ads in Anchorage and Soldotna's city descriptions). There are a few tour operators that offer coastal brown bear viewing by boat.

Package tours with a reservation service like Viking Travel/www.AlaskaFerry Vacations.com, often include cruise; fly/cruise; cruise plus land tour by motor-

coach, rail, etc.; and customized itineraries with optional add-ons, such as destinations and activities that are not part of the basic package.

Tour packages may be put together by a tour company, a travel agent, a travel wholesaler or you, the independent traveler. There is an incredible list of travel options to choose from in Alaska, as well as a huge geographical area. Your time, budget and interests will help narrow down the choices.

Tour costs vary and may or may not include all transportation, lodging and activities, meals, tips, taxes, etc. These types of tours are usually not cheap, although for many travelers the expense of a packaged tour is offset by the convenience of reserved lodging and pre-arranged transportation and activities The larger tour companies in Alaska, such as Gray Line Alaska and Alaska Tour & Travel, offer package tours using their own motorcoaches, cruiseships, railcars and motels. Other major Alaska tour companies use their own facilities (boats, motorcoaches, etc.) and contract with other vendors to provide other forms of transportation, lodging, sightseeing and activities on their packaged tours.

A travel agent can acquaint you with what package tours are available and their cost. If you are considering a package tour to Alaska by cruise ship there are many cruise companies and experiences to choose between (see "Cruising to Alaska" pages 24–26). Travelers who do not wish to join a large tour may customize their own package tour, either with the help of a travel agency or by using information within The MILEPOST®.

Read through the descriptions of major destinations in Alaska, such as Southeast Alaska/Inside Passage, Prince William Sound, Denali National Park, Kenai Peninsula, Anchorage, Fairbanks, etc. Everything from half-day motorcoach trips, sightseeing cruises, heli-tours over glaciers, or fly-in bear viewing to overnights on islands or on the North Slope, are covered in both the editorial and in the advertising. Or take a rail tour with Alaska Railroad and skip the rental car with overnights in Seward, Anchorage, Talkeetna, Denali National Park and Fairbanks.

Independent travelers can book any tour that might interest them, but they may also have to make arrangements for additional lodging and transportation. For example, a visitor might make independent arrangements for a flight to Anchorage and lodging for a night, then book a tour to Denali National Park or Utqiagvik (formerly Barrow) or some other destination that would include transportation and lodging. The options are almost limitless. You can even purchase portions of the packaged tours (if space is available), such as the land tour portion from a cruiseline.

When to go/Weather

One of the frequent questions is, "When is the best time to travel?" Many Alaskans recommend May and June as the most favorable months for travel to the North, as well as probably the most promising period for views of Denali. The high season for travel in the North is June through August, usually the warmest months. But summer can also be the wettest months. The weather is as variable and unpredictable in the North as anywhere else.

An often asked question about travel to the North is "when can I avoid the bugs?" The answer is mid-winter. Summer is bug season and you will run into mosquitoes, black flies (also called white-sox, simulids and buffalo gnats) and no-see-ums (also known as punkies).

Mosquitoes emerge from hibernation before the snow has entirely disappeared. They peak in June but continue to harass humans and wildlife through the fall. Mosquitoes are especially active in the early morning and at dusk. They hatch their eggs in water, so the North—with its marshy tundra and many lakes—is a fertile breeding ground.

The National Weather Service website for Alaska is www.weather.gov/arh. Or phone the Alaska Weather Information Line: in Anchorage or from Outside, phone (907) 266-5105 and press option 1 for recorded forecast. To view weather conditions at various airports in Alaska, go to the FAA web site at: avcams.faa.gov. For seasonal weather data, visit the Alaska Climate Research Center at: climate.gi.alaska.edu. For Road Weather Information System (RWIS) reports, choose an area or corridor map at: roadweather.alaska.gov/iways/roadweather/forms/AreaSelectForm.html then click on blue icons to display road temperatures and weather conditions..

Current weather and 5-day forecasts for Alberta, British Columbia and Yukon communities are available from Environment Canada at www.weatheroffice.ec.gc.ca/canada_e.html. 24-hour recorded weather reports and forecasts are available by phone for: Whitehorse, YT, (867) 456-7623 (includes road report); Fort Nelson, BC, 250-774-6461; and for Dawson Creek, Chetwynd, Fort St. John and Fort Nelson, BC, Peace River and Grande Prairie, AB, phone 250-785-7669.

One advantage of summer travel to the North is the long hours of daylight: 19 hours and 21 minutes in Anchorage at summer solstice (June 21) and 21 hours and 49 minutes of daylight in Fairbanks. If you are traveling in winter, the reverse is true: 3 hours and 41 minutes of daylight in Fairbanks at winter solstice (December 21) and 5 hours and 27 minutes in Anchorage. The farther north you go, the longer (or shorter) the days get (see chart).

You can obtain a table of the times of sunrise/sunset, moonrise/moonset, or the beginning and end of twilight, for any year at: aa.usno.navy.mil/data/docs/RS_OneYear.php.

Because most people travel in the summer and fill up hotels, motels, campgrounds and ferries, you might consider an early spring (April or May) or fall (late August into October) trip, when there's usually more room at lodges, campgrounds and on the ferries. Keep in mind, however, that some tours, attractions, lodges, campgrounds and other businesses may not be open outside of the summer season. Check the advertisements in The MILEPOST® for details on seasonal opening and closing dates. Also, snowstorms are not uncommon in spring and fall (and sometimes summer) in the North.

Alaska winter is amazing and Alaskans have found ways to embrace the short days and long nights. Hearty visitors who don't mind a little cold now make up more than 10 percent of the more than 2 million who travel here each year.

DAYLIGHT HOURS

Summer Maximum

	Sunrise	Sunset	Daylight
Utqiagvik	May 11	Aug. 2	continuous
Fairbanks	2:57 A.M.	12:47 A.M.	21:49 hours
Anchorage	4:20 A.M.	11:42 P.M.	19:21 hours
Juneau	3:51 A.M.	10:07 P.M.	18:16 hours
Ketchikan	4:04 A.M.	9:32 P.M.	17:27 hours
Adak	6:27 A.M.	11:09 P.M.	16:42 hours

Winter Minimum

	Sunrise	Sunset	Daylight
Utqiagvik	Jan. 24	Nov. 19	none
Fairbanks	10:58 A.M.	2:40 P.M.	3:41 hours
Anchorage	10:13 A.M.	3:41 P.M.	5:27 hours
Juneau	8:44 A.M.	3:07 P.M.	6:22 hours
Ketchikan	8:12 A.M.	3:18 P.M.	7:06 hours
Adak	9:52 A.M.	5:37 P.M.	7:46 hours

One popular winter destination is the Hotel Alyeska/Alyeska Resort (www.alyeskaresort.com), a 304-room hotel 40 miles south of Anchorage in the town of Girdwood. The resort features world-class skiing.

Fairbanks offers many great reasons to visit in winter. From February 14–March 31, 2019, check out the BP World Ice Art Championships. And just 60 miles northeast of Fairbanks is the Chena Hot Springs Resort (chenahotsprings.com). A winter visit to see the Northern Lights from the resort is truly a memorable experience. Tour the resort's unique Aurora Ice Museum, kept at a cool 25°F year-round.

In Anchorage, the annual Fur Rendezvous Festival (known locally as "Rondy") takes place February 22–March 3, 2019. The 10-day festival includes carnivals, sled dog races and the "Running of the Reindeer." It is capped by a fireworks show. The ceremonial start of the Iditarod Sled Dog Race™ on downtown's Fourth Avenue is March 2, 2019.

For more winter events and ideas, look under the "Attractions" editorial in community descriptions.

Wildlife Viewing

The opportunity to see wildlife is a major attraction for many visitors to the North Country. The MILEPOST® highway logs point out spots along the highways where travelers may see Dall sheep, moose, caribou, bear and other mammals. Wildlife and bird viewing areas of particular interest are highlighted by this symbol:

Booking agents packaging custom Alaska vacations can include wildlife touring on your trip. Also check with tour desks at motels/hotels or ask your bed-and-breakfast or campground host about wildlife viewing tour operators available locally.

A good resource for wildlife viewing information is the Alaska Dept. of Fish and Game (ADF&G). Check out their list of Alaska wildlife viewing sites at www.adfg.alaska.gov at "Where to Go" under the Viewing subhead.

Birding

Alaska has nearly 500 species of birds, so visitors have a good chance of seeing many varieties without even trying. Birding newsletters and statewide bird checklists are available at the Alaska Dept. of Fish and Game's Wings Over Alaska web site at www.adfg. alaska.gov/index.cfm?adfg=birdviewing. wings.

Enjoy spring and summer birding in Fairbanks at Creamer's Field Migratory Waterfowl Refuge or in Anchorage at the Anchorage Coastal Wildlife Refuge/Potter Marsh. If your travel plans are flexible, plan ahead to take in one of the many festivals that celebrate birds in Alaska.

With all of Alaska's shoreline, migrating shorebird festivals are held in multiple locations, feature birding experts and celebrate the return of millions of shorebirds: Wrangell's Stikine River Birding Festival is held April 25–27, 2019; Cordova's Copper River Delta Shorebird Festival is held May 2–5, 2019; Homer's Kachemak Bay Shorebird Festival is May 9–12, 2019.

The Alaska Bald Eagle Festival takes place Nov. 13–16, 2019, in Haines, AK with 1,000–3,000 bald eagles congregating on the Alaska Chilkat Bald Eagle Preserve. The Tanana Valley Sandhill Crane Festival at Creamer's Field takes place in Fairbanks Aug. 23–25, 2019.

There are more festivals than what we can cover in this space. Look for additional details within our text or at the Wings Over Alaska website noted above.

Bear Viewing

There are 3 types of bears in Alaska: polar bears, black bears and brown bears. Viewing Ursus arctos, the brown bear or grizzly, ranks high on visitors' wish lists of activities during a trip to Alaska. Most private bear viewing businesses offer day trips to see brown bears, although overnight and multi-day trips with lodging or camping are available. The hot spots for bear viewing tours in Southcentral and southwestern Alaska are West Cook Inlet, Kodiak Island and the Alaska Peninsula, where coastal brown bears congregate in large numbers to fish at stream mouths or graze sedge fields.

Access is mainly by small plane, on floats or wheels, out of Homer, Kodiak, Kenai–Soldotna, Anchorage and Seward. Air services offer aerial bear viewing, guided land-based bear viewing tours and round-trip transportation to bear viewing camps and lodges.

Air service to bear viewing destinations is offered by Natron Air in Soldotna and Rust's Flying Service and Ravn Air out of Anchorage (Ravn goes to Kaktovik for polar bears).

Kodiak National Wildlife Refuge, accessible by air charter or boat, is home to about 3,000 bears. The refuge offers a bear viewing platform at the O'Malley River where visitors can observe bears in the wild. Contact the refuge for details at: www.fws.gov/refuge/kodiak.

On the Alaska Peninsula, bears congregate at Brooks Falls, near Brooks Camp in Katmai National Park (www.nps.gov/katm/index.htm), for the sockeye salmon run. Camping is available at the park's Brooks Camp and lodging is available at Brooks Lodge through the park concessionaire.

The McNeil River State Game Sanctuary, about 100 miles southwest of Anchorage, is a favorite site of photographers and videographers intent on documenting brown bears. Visits to McNeil are by permit only, selected in an annual lottery. Information on permits is available online from Alaska Dept. of Fish and Game at www.adfg.alaska.gov/index.cfm?adfg=mcneilriver.main.

Dall sheep inhabit Alaska mountain ranges. The rams are distinguished by their massive curling horns, while females have shorter, slightly curved, thinner horns. (©Amy Bragg)

In Southeast Alaska, the U.S. Forest Service manages 5 bear viewing sites: **Margaret Creek** at Ketchikan (accessible only by boat or floatplane, check with Visit Ketchikan for local guide suggestions: www.visitketchikan.com); **Dog Salmon Creek** at Prince of Wales Island; **Anan Wildlife Observatory**, accessible by boat, located southeast of Wrangell (check for local guide suggestions at www.wrangell.com); **Stan Price State Wildlife Sanctuary** at Pack Creek, located on Admiralty Island; and **Fish Creek Wildlife Observatory** near Hyder, where both brown and black bears may be photographed here as they fish for salmon from mid-July to early September.

Wildlife Cruises

Both charter cruises and scheduled day cruises are available to view wildlife along Alaska's magnificent coastline. Passengers on day cruises have the opportunity to see some of Alaska's most famous glaciers and also its wildlife like sea otters, Steller sea lions, dolphins, harbor seals, Dall porpoises, whales (minke, gray, fin, humpback), puffins, eagles, black-legged kittiwakes, common murres, cormorants, and parakeet and rhinoceros auklets.

In Southeast Alaska, whale watching, glacier tours and custom sightseeing cruises are arranged by Viking Travel in Petersburg. Day cruises concentrate on whale watching and sightseeing in such gems as Misty Fjords National Monument (out of Ketchikan), Tracy Arm (out of Juneau) and Glacier Bay (also out of Juneau). Juneau's *Adventure Bound* Alaska Cruises offers daily trips to Tracy Arm, a long, narrow fjord that extends into the heavily glaciated Coast Mountain Range, 50 miles southeast of Juneau, to see wildlife, waterfalls and glaciers.

Glacier Bay National Park offers wildlife and spectacular glacier scenery. Glacier Bay is on the itinerary of many Inside Passage cruiseships and is on the Alaska Marine Highway ferry system. It is also a popular destination for day cruises out of Juneau. Charter boat tours of Glacier Bay, Icy Strait and Point Adolphus are available in Gustavus, the small

community just outside the park boundary. Wildlife cruises may be arranged through local accommodations, such as Annie Mae Lodge and Glacier Bay Lodge.

Full-day, half-day and dinner cruises of Kenai Fjords National Park depart daily from Seward, located 127 miles south from Anchorage. These scheduled cruises explore the park's glaciated coastline and the substantial populations of marine mammals and birds that make it their home. Full-day cruises also visit Chiswell Islands National Wildlife Refuge. Operators include: Major Marine Tours; and Sunny Cove Sea Kayaking Co. Charter boats are also available out of Seward for wildlife viewing. (While in Seward, visit the Alaska SeaLife Center to see coastal birds and marine mammals).

Daily scheduled cruise tours and custom sightseeing cruises of Prince William Sound's glaciers and wildlife depart from Whittier and Valdez. Tour operators include: Major Marine Tours, Phillips' Cruises & Tours, Stan Stephens Glacier & Wildlife Cruises and Lu-Lu Belle Glacier Wildlife Cruises. Pangaea Adventures in Valdez offers guided sea kayaking trips to glaciers.

Wildlife Parks & Tours

The Alaska Wildlife Conservation Center at **Milepost S 79** Seward Highway, 48 miles south of Anchorage is a drive-through animal park, the center is dedicated to the rehabilitation of wild orphaned and injured animals. Rescued black and grizzly bears, lynx, caribou, moose, musk-oxen, bison, elk, Sitka black-tailed deer, eagles and other raptors are among the residents at the park.

For extensive musk-ox viewing see the Musk-Ox Farm in Palmer (muskoxfarm.org) and the UAF Large Animal Research Station in Fairbanks (www.lars.uaf.edu). LARS also has reindeer for visitor viewing.

The Yukon Wildlife Preserve, located about a half-hour's drive from Whitehorse, is a 700-acre animal park. A 1½-hour passenger van tour reveals mountain goats, caribou, moose, elk, wood bison, musk-oxen, mule deer and mountain sheep in their natural habitat.

Alaska Highway via
East Access Route

CONNECTS: Great Falls, MT, to Dawson Creek, BC

Length: 869 miles   **Road Surface:** Paved   **Season:** Open all year

(See maps, pages 51-52)

 **15** **2** **3** **4** **43**

Most of the East Access Route lies within Alberta, Canada's 4th largest province.
(©Earl L. Brown)

Distance in miles	Calgary	Dawson Creek	Edmonton	Grande Prairie	Great Falls	Lethbridge	Valleyview
Calgary		550	190	468	320	134	398
Dawson Creek	550		360	82	869	702	152
Edmonton	190	360		277	510	324	208
Grande Prairie	468	82	277		787	602	70
Great Falls	320	869	510	787		186	717
Lethbridge	134	702	324	602	186		532
Valleyview	398	152	208	70	717	532	

The East Access Route from Great Falls, MT, is one of 2 major access routes logged in *The MILEPOST®*—along with the West Access Route from Seattle, WA—that take you to Dawson Creek, BC, and the start of the Alaska Highway. (Three other approaches logged as driving routes are the Canadian Rockies Route from Coeur d'Alene, ID, to Jasper, AB; the Central Access Route from Ellensburg, WA, to Tete Jaune Cache, BC; and Vancouver Island Highway.)

The East Access Route was the first and only access route to Dawson Creek, BC—and the start of the Alaska Highway—when the Alaska Highway opened to civilian traffic in 1948. The original route differed from today's route because Highway 43 was not completed until 1955. Instead, motorists had to drive north from Edmonton via Highway 2 to Athabasca, then west to High Prairie, then south to Grande Prairie, AB. Today's route goes directly from Edmonton to Grande Prairie and Dawson Creek through Whitecourt and Valleyview via Highway 43. Total driving distance via the East Access Route is 869 miles/1,399 km.

Alternate routes in Alberta that are logged in the East Access Route section are Trans-Canada 1 Highway to its junction with the Icefields Parkway, and the Devonian Way Bypass at Edmonton.

The following driving log of the East Access Route is divided into 3 sections: Great Falls, MT, to the U.S.-Canada shared border crossing station at Sweetgrass, MT/Coutts, AB; from the border to Edmonton; and from

Major Attractions:

©Sharon Nault

Fort Whoop-Up, West Edmonton Mall, Philip J. Currie Museum

Edmonton to Dawson Creek, BC, via Valleyview and Grande Prairie.

All highways logged in this section are paved primary routes, with visitor services readily available along the way. Most of the

East Access Route
Great Falls, MT, to Edmonton, AB

© 2019 The MILEPOST®

To Grande Cache
40
16
To Mayerthorpe
43
Chip Lake
Wabamun Lake
16
(map continues next page)
To Slave Lake
Devonian Bypass
Edmonton
N53°33' W113°30'
16 To Saskatoon

4.5/7.2km Glowing Embers →
RV Park & Travel Centre CDIST
60
Devon
22
19
625
Nisku
E-21/34km
CB-368/593km

39
Leduc
2A

To Prince George
16
Jasper
C-258/414km

DC-360/579km
E-0
CB-390/627km
PG-450/724km

2
Wetaskiwin

CB-293.7/472.6km
RV There Yet
Campground C

Ponoka

93
Icefields Centre
Icefields Parkway

11
Rocky Mountain House
11
Lacombe
E-103/165km
CB-287/462km

North
Saskatchewan River

Red Deer

ROCKY

Saskatchewan River Crossing

BRITISH COLUMBIA   ALBERTA

Red Deer River

93
Icefields Parkway

22
Innisfail
Bowden

C-113/182km

Olds

Red Deer River

Carstairs

J-60/97km

Golden
Lake Louise
1
Crossfield
72
9
Drumheller

95
Castle Junction
Banff

Airdrie
Balzac
N51°05' W114°05'

To Revelstoke

93
Bow River
1

Calgary

Okotoks
E-190/306km
CB-200/321km
C-0

95

Sheep River
High River
S40
Cowboy Trail
2

Bow River

To Regina

22
Nanton
E-294/474km
CB-96/154km

Columbia River
Kootenay River
Columbia Lake

Stavely

Willow Creek

CB-121.3/195.2km
Lazy J Motel L

Claresholm

CB-67.8/109.1km
Bridgeview RV Resort CDS
N49°42' W112°50'
To Regina

Head-Smashed-In Buffalo Jump World Heritage Site

Crowsnest Pass
4,534 ft./1,382m

Frank

95
93

785
Fort Macleod
Oldman R.

CB-65.5/105.4km Fort Whoop-Up
Lethbridge
E-324/522km
CB-66/105km

3
Stirling
52
New Dayton
4
Warner

Cranbrook

3
6
505
Raymond
Milk River

To Hope
3
Kingsgate
Eastport

Waterton Lakes National Park

Waterton Park
5
Cardston
501
Coutts
N49°00' W111°57'

BRITISH COLUMBIA   CANADA
IDAHO   UNITED STATES
ALBERTA   MONTANA
Sweetgrass

E-390/627km
CB-0
GF-120

89

To Medicine Hat

95
2

Glacier National Park

2
To Medicine Hat

93

Browning

Shelby
GF-86 Lewis & Clark RV Park CDP
87

37
Lake Koocanusa

Conrad

To Spokane
Sandpoint

2

Kalispell

2

Brady

89

15

N47°5' W111°3'
Great Falls

GF-0
S-120

15
To Helena

87
To Billings

Principal Route Logged
Paved   Unpaved
Other Roads Logged
Other Roads   **Ferry Routes**
Refer to Log for Visitor Facilities
Scale
0   20   Miles
0   20   Kilometres

Key to Advertiser Services
C -Camping
D -Dump Station
d -Diesel
G -Gas (reg., unld.)
I -Ice
L -Lodging
M -Meals
P -Propane
R -Car Repair (major)
r -Car Repair (minor)
S -Store (grocery)
T -Telephone (pay)

Map Location

Key to mileage boxes
miles/kilometres
miles/kilometres
from:
C - Calgary
CB - Canadian Border
DC - Dawson Creek
E - Edmonton
GF - Great Falls
J - Junction
PG - Prince George
S - Sweetgrass

East Access Route Edmonton, AB, to Dawson Creek, BC

© 2019 The MILEPOST®

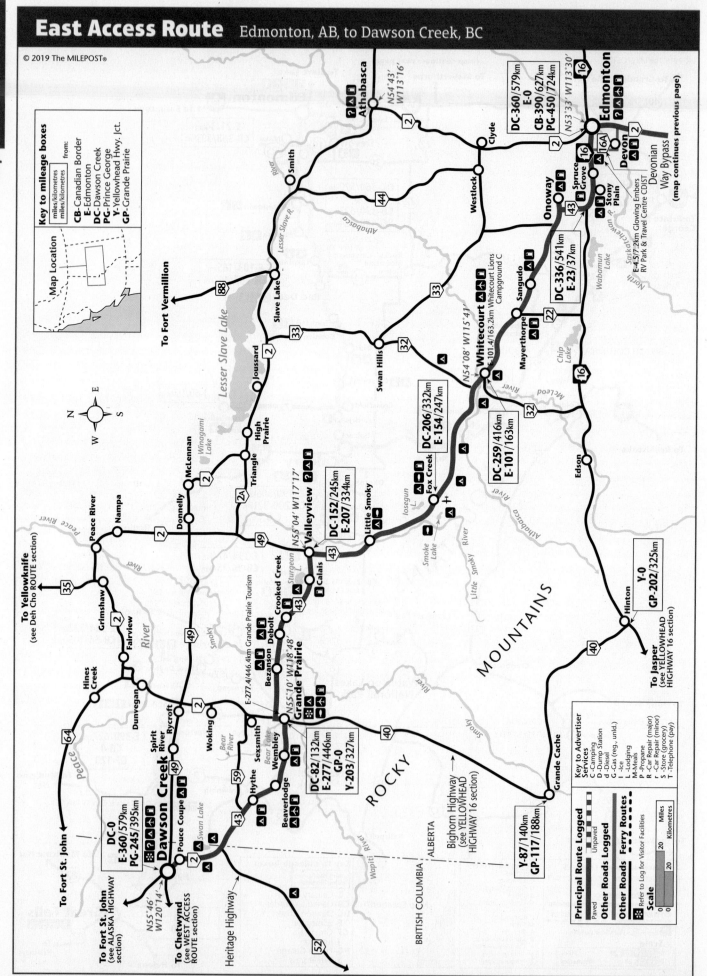

Key to mileage boxes

miles/kilometres   from:
miles/kilometres

CB-Canadian Border
E-Edmonton
DC-Dawson Creek
PG-Prince George
Y-Yellowhead Hwy. Jct.
GP-Grande Prairie

Map Location

To Fort Vermillion

DC-360/579km
E-0
CB-390/627km
PG-450/724km
N53°33' W113°30'

DC-336/541km
E-23/37km

DC-259/416km
E-101/163km

DC-206/332km
E-154/247km

DC-152/245km
E-207/334km

Y-0
GP-202/325km

DC-82/132km
E-277/446km
GP-0
Y-203/327km

DC-0
E-360/579km
PG-245/395km

Y-87/140km
GP-117/188km

Athabasca N54°43' W113°16'

Edmonton N53°33' W113°30'

Devon Devonian Way Bypass (map continues previous page)

Clyde

Smith

Westlock

Onoway

Spruce Grove

Stony Plain

Sangudo

Mayerthorpe

Whitecourt N54°08' W115°41' E-101.4/163.2km Whitecourt Lions Campground C

E-4.5/7.2km Glowing Embers RV Park & Travel Centre CDIST

Slave Lake

Joussard

High Prairie

McLennan

Triangle

Donnelly

Nampa

Peace River

Grimshaw

Fairview

Hines Creek

Dunvegan

Rycroft

Woking

Sexsmith

Wembley

Hythe

Beaverlodge

Pouce Coupe

Dawson Creek N55°46' W120°14'

Valleyview N55°04' W117°17'

Little Smoky

Fox Creek

Iosegun L.

Smoke Lake

Crooked Creek

Calais

Debolt

Bezanson

Grande Prairie N55°10' W118°48' E-277.4/446.4km Grande Prairie Tourism

Hinton

Edson

Grande Cache

To Jasper (see YELLOWHEAD HIGHWAY 16 section)

Bighorn Highway (see YELLOWHEAD HIGHWAY 16 section)

MOUNTAINS

ROCKY

BRITISH COLUMBIA ALBERTA

To Yellowknife (see Deh Cho ROUTE section)

To Fort St. John

To Fort St. John (see ALASKA HIGHWAY section)

To Chetwynd (see WEST ACCESS ROUTE section)

Heritage Highway

Lesser Slave Lake

Winagami Lake

Chip Lake

Wabamun Lake

North Saskatchewan River

Athabasca River

Lesser Slave R.

Smoky River

Peace River

Spirit River

Bear River

Swan Lake

Sturgeon L.

Little Smoky River

Wapiti River

McLeod River

Swan Hills

Key to Advertiser Services
C -Camping
D -Dump Station
d -Diesel
G -Gas (reg., unld.)
I -Ice
L -Lodging
M -Meals
P -Propane
R -Car Repair (major)
r -Car Repair (minor)
S -Store (grocery)
T -Telephone (pay)

Principal Route Logged
Paved
Unpaved
Other Roads Logged
Other Roads   Ferry Routes
Refer to Log for Visitor Facilities

Scale
Miles
Kilometres

N W E S

88 44 2 33 32 16 43 22 2 24 49 35 64 2 59 43 40 52

EAST ACCESS ROUTE is multi-lane, divided highway.

East Access Route Log

Distance from Great Falls (GF) is followed by distance from the international border crossing at Sweetgrass (S).

Exit numbers and mileposts on Interstate 15 reflect distance from the Idaho–Montana border.

INTERSTATE HIGHWAY 15

GF 0 S 120 Exit 278 to **GREAT FALLS** (pop. 58,950, elev. 3,300 feet) via 10th Avenue South. Exit here for food, gas/diesel, lodging, private RV park, Market Place shopping mall and hospital.

Great Falls, located at the confluence of the Sun and Missouri rivers, is Montana's third largest city (after Billings and Missoula). University of Providence, Great Falls College MSU, Montana Air National Guard and Malmstrom AFB are located here. Local attractions include the 60-mile River's Edge Trail, Electric City Water Park, Montana ExpoPark, Centene Stadium and Riverside Railyard Skateboard Park. See next exit for additional attractions.

GF 2 S 118 Exit 280 to Great Falls City Center via Central Avenue West/U.S. 87 North. **Visitor Information:** Tourism's Basecamp in Downtown Great Falls, 100 1st Ave N. Open year-round Monday to Friday from 8 A.M. to 5 P.M. A direct 1.7 miles from Exit 280.

Also access this exit to Gibson Park Historic Walking Tours, unique shopping and dining, and River's Edge Trail and Elk's Riverside Park; take River Street past Black Eagle Dam views to Lewis and Clark National Historic Trail Interpretive Center, Giant Springs Heritage State Park Picnic Area with playground (day use only), trout hatchery, Veterans Memorial and miles of multi-use trails; the Charles M. Russell Museum; Children's Museum of Montana; downtown shopping, dining and lodging; and the Paris Gibson Square Museum of Art (between 14th and 15th streets).

Continue north on Interstate 15 for the Canadian border. The posted speed limit is 80 mph (65 mph for trucks).

GF 5.3 S 114.7 Distance marker northbound shows Vaughn Jct. 7 miles, Shelby 80 miles, Lethbridge 179 miles.

GF 6 S 114 Paved turnout to east.

GF 8 S 112 Exit 286 to Manchester.

GF 12 S 108 Vaughn. Exit 290 to U.S. Highway 89 North/MT Highway 200 West; to Choteau and Missoula. Gas/diesel, lodging, camping, restaurants, Lewis and Clark Trail.

GF 13 S 107 Distance marker northbound shows Dutton 22 miles, Shelby 72 miles, Lethbridge 171 miles.

GF 19.5 S 100.5 Exit 297 to Gordon; no services.

GF 20.8 S 99.2 Distance marker northbound shows Power 5 miles, Conrad 40 miles, Lethbridge 164 miles.

GF 23.4 S 96.6 Teton County.

GF 24.5 S 95.5 Exit 302 to Power and Highway 431. Teton County.

GF 25.4 S 94.6 Distance marker northbound shows Dutton 10 miles, Shelby 60

River's Edge Trail offers miles of multi-use pathway along the Missouri River.

(©Claire Torgerson, staff)

miles, Lethbridge 159 miles.

GF 32 S 88 Physical mileposts 309 and 310 are only 0.7 mile apart.

GF 35 S 85 Exit 313 to Highway 379 East and Highway 221 West to Dutton (gas/diesel, restaurant and picnic tables).

GF 36.2 S 83.3 Distance marker northbound shows Brady 14 miles, Conrad 25 miles, Lethbridge 148 miles.

GF 40.7 S 79.3 Rest areas both sides of freeway at Teton River bridge. Next rest area 23 miles.

GF 43 S 77 Exit 321 to Collins Road; Collins 5 miles west, no services.

GF 44 S 76 Distance marker northbound shows Brady 6 miles, Shelby 41 miles, Lethbridge 140 miles.

GF 45.7 S 74.3 Entering Pondera County northbound.

GF 46 S 74 Physical mileposts 323 and 324 are only 0.5 mile apart.

GF 49.5 S 70.5 Exit 328 west to Brady (gas/diesel) and east to Highway 365.

GF 51 S 69 Distance marker northbound shows Conrad 10 miles, Shelby 34 miles, Lethbridge 133 miles.

GF 57.5 S 62.5 Exit 335 to Midway Road, Conrad (4 miles) via Business Loop 15.

GF 61 S 59 Exit 339 for **CONRAD** (pop. 2,488) grocery store, casino, restaurant, gas/diesel, lodging (Super 8), RV park and hospital. Weigh station and rest area, just off exit to east.

GF 62.5 S 57.5 Distance marker northbound shows Ledger Road 5 miles, Shelby 23 miles, Lethbridge 122 miles.

GF 64 S 56 Railroad crossing.

GF 67.3 S 52.7 Exit 345 to Highway 366 east, Ledger Road and Tiber Dam; no services.

GF 70 S 50 Exit 348 to **junction** with MT Highway 44 West to Valier Road. Valier and Lake Frances Recreation Area (with campground) are 15 miles to the west; Lewis and Clark trail, restaurant, gas, lodging.

GF 71 S 49 Distance marker northbound shows Shelby 14 miles, Kevin-Oilmont 30 miles, Lethbridge 113 miles.

GF 74 S 46 Exit 352 to Bullhead Road; no services.

GF 76.3 S 43.7 Toole County.

GF 77.5 S 42.5 Highway descends 7 percent grade northbound.

CAUTION: Watch for deer next 3 miles.

GF 79 S 41 Marias River.

GF 80.5 S 39.5 Exit 358 to Marias Valley Road to east, camping; Golf Course Road to west.

GF 81 S 38.5 Distance marker northbound shows Shelby 4 miles, Kevin-Oilmont 20 miles, Lethbridge 103 miles.

GF 83 S 37 Double-ended paved roadside parking area northbound with litter barrel.

GF 85 S 35 Exit 363 to Business Loop 15 to **SHELBY** (pop. 3,376); food, gas, diesel, lodging and access to Marias Medical Center. Visitor information at the Chamber of Commerce next to the City Park. Marias Museum of History and Art is located at 1129 1st St. N. and the Carousel Rest Area is located at 441 11th Ave. N.

Junction with U.S. Highway 2 west to Cut Bank and Glacier National Park at this exit.

Camping at **Lewis & Clark RV Park** at Exit 364; campgrounds also next to Comfort Inn, Best Western hotels and Glacier Motel; and at the Lake Shel-oole Campground.

GF 86 S 34 Exit 364 to Shelby via Busi-

Dinosaur at the Milk River Travel Information Center is a popular photo op.
(©Earl L. Brown)

ness Route 15; access to airport and to campground at **Lewis & Clark RV Park**; pull-throughs, laundry, full hookup 30/50 amp, propane, satellite TV. ⛺

Lewis & Clark RV Park. See display ad on page 53.

Sign northbound shows: Port of Sweetgrass 34 miles, open 24 hours.

GF 87.4 S 32.6 Distance marker northbound shows Sunburst 24 miles, Sweetgrass 32 miles, Lethbridge 98 miles.

GF 90.6 S 29.4 Exit 369 to Bronken Road; no services.

GF 92 S 28 Distance marker northbound shows Kevin-Oilmont 9 miles, Sweetgrass 27 miles, Lethbridge 93 miles.

GF 95 S 25 Exit 373 to Potter Road; no services.

GF 96 S 24 Distance marker northbound shows Kevin-Oilmont 5 miles, Sweetgrass 23 miles, Lethbridge 89 miles.

GF 101 S 19 Exit 379 to Kevin/Highway 215 to west and Oilmont/Highway 343 to east; restaurants and other services.

GF 102 S 18 Distance marker northbound shows Sunburst 9 miles, Sweetgrass 17 miles, Lethbridge 83 miles.

GF 108 S 12 Exit 385 to Swayze Road; no services.

GF 112 S 8 Exit 389 to city of Sunburst to west/Highway 552, all services. 🅱

GF 112.7 S 7.3 Distance marker northbound shows Sweetgrass 7 miles, Lethbridge 73 miles.

GF 116 S 4 Exit 394 Ranch access; no services. *CAUTION: Deer and high winds.*

GF 119.7 S 0.3 Exit 397 to Sweetgrass; restaurant, gas/diesel, lodging and rest area. Last turn back northbound before border. Southbound, the rest area is to the right, immediately after going through U.S. customs. 🅱

GF 120 S 0 Shared 24-hour **U.S.–Canada Port-of-Entry** at international border (Sweetgrass, MT/Coutts, AB). Make sure you have your passport.

See Crossing the Border in the TRAVEL PLANNING section for more details on crossing the border and customs requirements.

ALBERTA HIGHWAY 4

Distance from U.S.–Canada border (CB) is followed by distance from the junction with Highway 16A at Edmonton (E).

CB 0 E 389.7 (627 km) Shared 24-hour **U.S.–Canada Port-of-Entry** at international border. Duty-free shop southbound. Community of **COUTTS** (pop. 277); Coutts Traveler Operations, phone 403-344-3766, www.couttsalberta.com. Nearest hospital is in Milk River, phone 403-647-3500.

There is a campground to the west, just north of the border.

NOTE: Seat belts are required in Alberta. Speed limits in Alberta are in metric. Alberta has a Distracted Driving Law. Posted highway speed limit is 110 kmph/68 mph on 4-lane highway northbound.

CB 0.7 (1.1 km) **E 389** (626 km) Exit for Highway 500 East to Aden and Highway 880 (30 miles/49 km).

CB 1 (1 km) **E 388.7** (625.6 km) Commercial vehicle inspection to west (RVs and autos exempt); County of Warner roadside turnout and Welcome to Alberta sign to east. Memorial to the First Special Service Force. Litter bins and interpretive signs about Alberta's fossil trail. Elk farm visible to the southeast at this turnout.

CB 1.5 (2.4 km) **E 388.2** (624.7 km) Distance marker northbound shows Milk River 18 km/11 miles, Lethbridge 103 km/64 miles.

CB 4.1 (6.6 km) **E 385.6** (620.6 km) Red Creek.

CB 7.5 (12.1 km) **E 382.2** (615 km) Turnoff for Gold Springs campground 4 km/2.5 miles east. ⛺

CB 10 (16.1 km) **E 379.7** (611 km) Junction with Highway 501 to Del Bonita which leads 108 km/67 miles west to junction with Highways 2 and 5 at Cardston, home of the **Remington–Alberta Carriage Center**, one of the world's foremost collections of horse-drawn vehicles. From Cardston, Highway 5 leads 40 km/25 miles west to Waterton Park, tourist centre for Waterton Lakes National Park.

Distance marker northbound Milk River 4 km/3 miles, Warner 21 km/13 miles, Leth-

bridge 90 km/56 miles.

CB 12 (19.3 km) **E 377.7** (607.7 km) Turnoff east for the south entrance to Milk River's downtown businesses and the **Milk River Travel Information Center**. Open mid-May to mid-October; parking, pay phone, restrooms, picnic tables, sani-dump; 403-647-3938. The large dinosaur model on display here makes a fun photo subject.

CB 12.3 (19.8 km) **E 377.4** (607.2 km) Municipality owned Under 8 Flags Campground to east; picnic tables, dump station, campsites and hookups. The 8 flags flying over the campground represent 7 countries and the Hudson's Bay Co., all of which once laid claim to the Milk River area. ⛺

CB 12.5 (20.1 km) **E 377.2** (606.9 km) Grain elevators.

CB 12.6 (20.3 km) **E 377.1** (606.8 km) **Junction** with Secondary Road 501 east to **Writing-on-Stone Provincial Park**, 42 km/26 miles; camping, Indian petroglyphs. ⛺

CB 13.1 (21.1 km) **E 376.6** (605.9 km) **MILK RIVER** (pop. 811); restaurants, motel and truck stop east side of highway. All services. 🅱

CB 13.3 (21.4 km) **E 376.4** (605.8 km) Distance marker northbound Warner 18 km/11 miles, Raymond 55 km/34 miles, Lethbridge 84 km/52 miles.

CB 23.6 (38 km) **E 366.1** (589.1 km) **Junction** with Highway 36 north to Taber and Brooks. Access west to **WARNER** (pop. 392); gas/diesel, restaurant and RV park. Dinosaur eggs and fossilized fish and reptiles were discovered in this area in 1987. Warner is considered the gateway to the Devil's Coulee dinosaur egg site. The Devil's Coulee Dinosaur Heritage Museum is open from late-May to early-September. 🅱 ⛺

CB 23.8 (38.3 km) **E 365.9** (588.9 km) Distance marker northbound shows New Dayton 20 km/12 miles, Lethbridge 69 km/43 miles.

CB 28.6 (46 km) **E 361.1** (581.1 km) **Junction** with Secondary Road 506 West to Milk River Ridge Reservoir and campground 24 km/15 miles. ⛺

CB 28.8 (46.3 km) **E 360.9** (580.8 km) Distance marker northbound shows Stirling 25 km/16 miles, Lethbridge 52 km/32 miles.

CB 29.6 (47.6 km) **E 360.1** (579.4 km) Large double-ended turnouts both sides of highway, with litter/recycling barrels and toilets. Interpretive board memorial to Special Forces.

CB 31.8 (51.2 km) **E 357.9** (576 km) Access to Tyrrell Lake east.

CB 33 (53.1 km) **E 356.7** (574 km) **Tyrrell Lake** with fishing and boat access. 🛶

CB 36.8 (59.2 km) **E 352.9** (567.9 km) New Dayton; camping and groceries. ⛺

CB 36.9 (59.4 km) **E 352.8** (567.8 km) Distance marker northbound shows Stirling 13 km/8 miles, Lethbridge 45 km/28 miles.

CB 41 (66 km) **E 348.7** (561.2 km) **Junction** with Highway 52 west to Raymond (16 km/10 miles); Magrath (32 km/20 miles); Cardston (74 km/46 miles); and Waterton Lakes National Park (119 km/74 miles).

CB 41.1 (66.1 km) **E 348.6** (561 km) Distance marker northbound shows Stirling 6 km/4 miles, Lethbridge 39 km/24 miles.

CB 41.2 (66.3 km) **E 348.5** (560.9 km) Craddock elevators to west.

CB 46.4 (74.7 km) **E 343.3** (552.5 km) **STIRLING** (pop. 1,269), 1 km/0.6 mile west, is the oldest, best-preserved Mormon agricultural settlement in Canada. Many Mormons came to Southern Alberta at the insistence of their church. Their mission was to build settlements on the dry, windy prairie. They began the irrigation canal system that helped create the rich farmland seen today. Mormons also built the towns of Cardston, Magrath and Raymond. The "Mormon Trail" includes all 4 of these towns and is a 2–4 hour self-guided drive that features a mix of national and provincial historic sites, walkable communities and a unique cultural heritage. Stops include the Mormon Temple and **Remington–Alberta Carriage Center** in Cardston. For details see www.themormon trail.ca.

Stirling has the **Galt Historic Railway Park** with restored 1890 Victorian railway station and the **Stirling Agricultural Village National Historic Site** with Michelsen Farmstead. There is a municipal campground on 4th Avenue near the west end of town with 10 serviced sites and additional unserviced sites; showers, playground. Phone 403-756-3379. The community swimming pool and waterpark is open in summer months with water slide and kiddie pool. Pick up your walking map at the Village of Stirling office at 229 4th Ave. to enjoy a walking tour of Stirling.

CB 46.5 (74.8 km) **E 343.2** (552.3 km) Stirling elevators to east.

CB 46.9 (75.5 km) **E 342.8** (551.7 km) **Junction** with Highway 61 east to Cypress Hills. Distance marker northbound shows Lethbridge 29 km/18 miles.

CB 53.8 (86.6 km) **E 335.9** (540.5 km) **Junction** with Highway 845 north to Coaldale and Raymond; Alberta Birds of Prey Centre 17 km/11 miles via this exit. Viterra Inland Railway Terminal.

CB 54.3 (87.4 km) **E 335.4** (540 km) Distance marker northbound Lethbridge 18 km/12 miles, Calgary 249 km/155 miles.

CB 55.3 (89 km) **E 334.4** (538 km) **Junction** with Highway 508 West by elevators. Airport 12 km/7.5 miles.

CB 57.4 (92.4 km) **E 332.3** (534.8 km) Southbound-only roadside turnout with litter bins to west has information sign about irrigation.

CB 57.8 (93 km) **E 331.9** (534.1 km) Lethbridge airport to west.

CB 60 (95.6 km) **E 329.7** (530.6 km) Howe Road. RV Park and cottages to east.

CB 60.6 (97.5 km) **E 329.1** (529.6 km) Welcome to Lethbridge.

Slow for speed zones northbound.

CB 62 (99.8 km) **E 327.7** (527.3 km) Turnoff to north for 43rd Street in Lethbridge, the truck route north to Highway 3. Bypass route to Fort Macleod and Calgary.

CB 62.5 (100.6 km) **E 327.2** (526.6 km) Canadian Tire, lodging, visitor services.

CB 63.2 (101.7 km) **E 326.5** (525.4) Stoplight at **junction** of Highways 4 with 5 and Mayor Magrath Drive in Lethbridge. Highway 5 leads south to Cardston (77 km/48 miles) and Waterton Park (131 km/81 miles).

Mobile Tourism Services located at the northwest corner of Mayor Magrath and Scenic Drive, restrooms, picnic shelter, playground, dump station, and dumpster available. Supported by Tourism Lethbridge it is

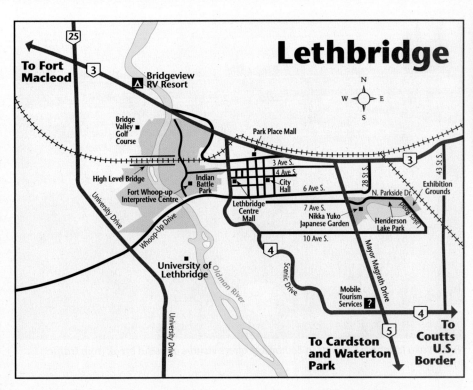

Lethbridge

open June–August. Other Mobile Tourism services are available throughout Lethbridge. Visit www.tourismlethbridge.com to find their locations.

Northbound travelers turn right at this intersection for Lethbridge services (restaurants, gas/diesel, lodging, hospital) and continuation of East Access Route log via Mayor Magrath Drive to Crowsnest Trail (Highway 3). It is 2.3 miles/3.7 km from this intersection to Highway 3 via Mayor Magrath Drive. Description of Lethbridge follows.

Northbound motorists may also continue straight through this intersection and follow the Scenic Drive route to Crowsnest Trail with easy access to visitor attractions like Fort Whoop-Up, Helen Schuler Nature Centre, Indian Battle Park, the Tourism Lethbridge Visitor Information Centre, Downtown Lethbridge and the Galt Museum; see Lethbridge map. It is 4.3 miles/6.9 km from this intersection to Highway 3 via Scenic Drive.

Log continues on page 57 for northbound travelers.

Lethbridge

CB 65.5 (105.4 km) **E 324.2** (521.7 km) Located at the junction of Highways 3, 4 and 5. **Population:** 98,198. **Elevation:** 3,048 feet/929m. **Emergency Services:** Dial 911. **Police**, 135 1st Ave. S., phone 403-327-2210; **RCMP**, 427 Stafford Dr. S., phone 403-329-5010; **Hospital:** Chinook Regional, 960–19th St. S., phone 403-388-6111.

Visitor Information: Tourism Lethbridge, 327 5th St. South, located near Galt Gardens (phone 403-394-2403 or 1-888-384-8687); open daily from 9 A.M. to 5 P.M year-round; restrooms.

Mobile Tourism Services at 2805 Scenic Dr./Highway 4, is open June–August; RV parking, restrooms, picnic shelter, playground and interpretive panels, dump station, dumpster. Email info@tourism

lethbridge.com; or visit www.lethbridge.ca, www.tourismlethbridge.com, and www.visitlethbridge.com, www.www.downtownlethbridge. **Newspaper:** *Lethbridge Herald* (daily).

Private Aircraft: Airport 4 miles/6.4 km southeast; elev. 3,047 feet/929m; length

Nikka Yuko Japanese Gardens in Lethbridge offers visitors a restful break from traffic.
(©Earl L. Brown)

6,500 feet/1,981m; paved, fuel 100, jet. FSS.

The Lethbridge region was home to 3 Indian nations: the Sik-sika (Blackfoot), Kainai (Many Leaders, now called Bloods), and Pikani (including the Ammsskaapi-piikain in Montana and Apatohsipiikani in Southern Alberta, also called Peigan). Collectively, they formed the Sow-ki'tapi (Prairie People). Because European fur traders along the North Saskatchewan River first came into contact with the Blackfoot, that tribal name came to be applied to the entire confederacy.

In 1869, the American Army decided to stop trade in alcohol with Indians on reservations across Montana. In December 1869, 2 American traders, John J. Healy and Alfred B. Hamilton, built a trading post at the junction of the St. Mary and Belly (now Oldman) rivers, near the future site of Lethbridge. The post, named Fort Hamilton, became known as Fort Whoop-Up. It was the most notorious of some 44 trading posts built in southern Alberta from 1869 to 1874. An important trade commodity "whiskey," was a concoction of 9 parts river water to 1 part pure alcohol, to which was added a plug of chewing tobacco for colour and a can of lye for more taste.

Alarmed by the activities of the whiskey traders, Prime Minister Sir John A. Macdonald formed the North West Mounted Police (NWMP), now the Royal Canadian Mounted Police, to bring law and order to the West. The NWMP reached Fort Whoop-Up on Oct. 9, 1874, and immediately put a stop to the whiskey trade.

By the late 1870s, Lethbridge had developed a steady coal market and a permanent settlement. Construction of the CPR brought more settlers to the west. Lethbridge's High Level Bridge, built by CPR in 1904, today carries freight shipments by rail west to Vancouver. The "Bridge"—with a mile-long span and 300-foot elevation—is still the longest and highest bridge of its kind in the world.

Lethbridge is Alberta's fourth largest city. It has a strong agricultural economy and is home to the University of Lethbridge and Lethbridge College. The city's ENMAX Centre, a sports and special events venue, is home to the Lethbridge Hurricanes hockey team and the Spitz Stadium is home to the Lethbridge Bulls baseball team.

Lodging, Services & Camping

As southwest Alberta's service and shopping centre, Lethbridge has several malls and a variety of retail businesses and visitor facilities. Major-chain motels/hotels (Days Inn, Holiday Inn, Best Western, Ramada, Travel Lodge, Sandman, etc.), restaurants, fast-food outlets and gas/diesel stations are primarily located on Mayor Magrath Drive. Lethbridge's shopping and culinary scene is very active and vibrant in the downtown where visitors can find international dishes, coffee houses, fine dining and a multitude of various shops to meet your shopping needs. RV Dealer, repair and service centre at Centreline RV, 4015 Major Magrath Dr. S.; 403-320-6665.

Camping at **Bridgeview RV Resort**, located on the banks of the Oldman River, with access from Highway 3; phone 403-381-2357.

Attractions

(©Judy Nadon, staff)

Fort Whoop-Up Interpretive Centre (fort.galtmuseum.com) is located 0.8 mile/1 km west of Scenic Drive (turn at 3rd Avenue) in Indian Battle Park. Fort Whoop-Up is a re-creation of the original trading post (pictured above) for trappers and Indians and NWMP fort that served this area in the late 1800s. It gained its name from brisk whiskey sales. Historical reenactments are held in summer. Open daily June 1–Oct. 1; 10 A.M. to 5 P.M. Monday–Saturday, (until 9 P.M. Thursdays); 1–5 P.M. Sundays and holidays. From Oct. 2 to May 31 open only for special events. Admission charged. Phone 403-320-3777.

Galt Museum (galtmuseum.com), features regional history and art and offers a fantastic view of the High Level Bridge. Located at 502 1st St. S., at the west end of 5th Avenue South off Scenic Drive. (For parking, use the 4th Avenue turnoff from Scenic Drive.) Phone 403-320-4258. Admission is $6/adults. Open daily, 10 A.M. to 5 P.M. Monday–Saturday (to 9 P.M. Thursdays) and Sundays and holidays 1–5 P.M.

Scenic Drive Dog Run, located 2.2 miles from the visitor centre at the Highway 4/5 junction on Scenic Drive, is one of 3 designated off-leash dog parks in Lethbridge. It is

LETHBRIDGE ADVERTISERS

part of the 200-acre Botterill Bottom Park, which includes the Coal Banks Trail. There are fine views of the University of Lethbridge from Scenic Drive.

The **Helen Schuler Nature Centre** (www. lethbridge.ca/hsnc) has self-guided trails which explore the beautiful Oldman River valley. It has interactive, hands-on exhibits for learning about local wildlife. Just off of 3rd Avenue South. Phone 403-320-3064. Open daily 10 A.M. to 6 P.M. June–August; 1–4 P.M. September–May (closed Mondays).

Nikka Yuko Japanese Gardens offers an unforgettable cultural experience combining the beauty of nature in a serene setting. From the first spring blossom to the final autumn leaf, the garden is an oasis of tranquility. Located on the corner of 9th Avenue South and Mayor Magrath Drive (Next to Henderson Lake). Limited RV and Bus Parking available. Phone 403-328-3511. Admission is $11 for adults and $7 for seniors (60-plus). Open daily 10 A.M. to 6 P.M. Special events information available on website at www.nikkayuko.com.

Henderson Lake Park on Mayor Magrath Drive includes a golf course, swimming pool, picnic area and rose gardens. Adjacent to the park, and best accessed via Mayor Magrath Drive and 9th Avenue South is the site of the Henderson Outdoor Pool. The pool is generally open from early June until Labour Day Weekend. Admission charged.

Southern Alberta Art Gallery, is located in downtown Lethbridge. This gallery offers a dynamic variety of changing exhibitions of contemporary art. It is noted as one of Canada's top ten contemporary galleries, and it has been recognized at an international level. Open year-round, Tuesday–Saturday 10 A.M. to 5 P.M.; Sunday 1–5 P.M. Admission charged, free on Sundays. Web address: www.saag.ca.

Alberta Birds of Prey Centre, 2124 16th Ave., Coaldale, is a 10-minute drive east of Lethbridge. This is a rescue and rehabilitation centre featuring hawks, falcons, eagles and owls, the majority of which have been rescued from traumatic events and rehabilitated for hopeful release to the wild. Daily flight shows (weather permitting) and tours of the facilities. Open May to September, 9:30 A.M. to 5 P.M. daily. Admission $9.50 adults, reduced price for seniors and kids. Phone 403-345-4262; www.burrowingowl. com.

East Access Route Log
(continued)

CB 65.8 (105.9 km) **E 323.9** (521.3 km) Mayor Magrath Drive/Lethbridge exit/on-ramp to Crowsnest Trail (Highway 3 West). Southbound travelers exit here for Lethbridge services. Northbound travelers merge onto Highway 3 West here.

Resume divided 4-lane highway northbound.

CROWSNEST HIGHWAY 3 WEST

CB 66 (106.2 km) **E 323.7** (520.9 km) Stafford Drive/Lethbridge exit.

CB 67 (107.8 km) **E 322.7** (519.3 km) 1st Avenue South exit to Lethbridge City Centre and Highways 4/5. (This exit southbound junctions with Scenic Drive in 1 mile.)

CB 67.6 (108.8 km) **E 322.1** (518.3 km) Oldman River bridge.

CB 67.8 (109.1 km) **E 321.9** (517.5 km) Bridge Drive/Highway 3A exit to West Lethbridge and access to **Bridgeview RV Resort**.

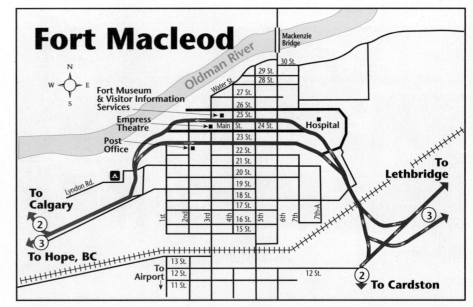

Bridgeview RV Resort. See display ad on facing page.

CB 69 (111 km) **E 320.7** (516 km) **Junction** with Highway 25 North to Park Lake Provincial Park (13 km/8 miles), Picture Butte (22 km/14 miles) and University Drive south to West Lethbridge.

CB 69.4 (111.7 km) **E 320.3** (515.5 km) Distance marker northbound shows Coalhurst 5 km/3 miles, Fort Macleod 43 km/27 miles, Calgary 211 km/131 miles.

CB 71.3 (114.7 km) **E 318.4** (512.3 km) Northbound-only roadside turnout to east with litter and recycle bins.

CB 72 (115.8 km) **E 317.7** (511.2 km) Community of **COALHURST** (pop. 2,301) just north of highway; Shell gas/diesel station, dump station and campground at the Miners Memorial Park (showers, kitchen shelter, picnic tables) $20 per night/14 sites. Call ahead, some reservations for groups are accepted and can include the entire campground; 403-381-3033.

CB 73.3 (118 km) **E 316.4** (509 km) **Junction** with Highway 509 South to Standoff and Highway 2 (49 km/30 miles).

CB 73.5 (118.3 km) **E 316.2** (508.9 km) Distance marker northbound shows Monarch 12 km/8 miles, Fort Macleod 38 km/24 miles, Calgary 216 km/134 miles.

CB 76.9 (123.7 km) **E 312.8** (503.3 km) Large turnout northbound with litter and recycling bins.

CB 78.5 (126.3 km) **E 311.2** (500.8 km) **Junction** with Highway 23 north to Vulcan and Highway 3A west to Monarch. Veer left (northbound) to continue on East Access Route to Calgary.

CB 81 (130.3 km) **E 308.7** (496.7 km) Oldman River bridge.

CB 82.4 (132.6 km) **E 307.3** (494.5 km) **Junction** with Highway 3A east to Monarch and Highway 23 north.

CB 82.5 (132.8 km) **E 307.2** (494.4 km) Distance marker northbound shows Fort Macleod 22 km/14 miles, Crowsnest Pass 99 km/62 miles and Calgary 189 km/117 miles.

CB 95.6 (153.7 km) **E 294.2** (473.5 km) **Junction** with Highway 2 South for Cardston and Waterton Lakes. Northbound travelers continue on Highway 3 for Fort Macleod businesses and historic district and Highway 2 North to Calgary. Southbound

travelers take Highway 3 East to Lethbridge.

Through the town of Fort Macleod, Highway 3 West becomes 25th Street also known as Jerry Potts Boulevard (1–way) and Highway 3 East becomes 23rd Street also known as Chief Red Crow Boulevard (1–way).

Slow for posted speed zones northbound as Highway 3 winds through Fort Macleod.

Fort Macleod

CB 95.6 (153.7 km) **E 294.2** (473.5 km) Located at the **junction** of Highways 3 and 2. **Population:** 3,117. **Elevation:** 3,300 feet/1,006m. **Emergency Services:** Dial 911. **Hospital:** Fort Macleod Health Centre, phone 403-553-5311.

Visitor Information: Visitor Information Services provided at the Fort Museum. Hours are 9 A.M. to 5 P.M. daily from early May through June; 9 A.M. to 6 P.M. daily, July to Labour Day; and 10 A.M. to 4 P.M. Wednesday–Sunday, early May and September–October. Closed November to April. Numerous events take place throughout the year. For details visit their website at fortmacleod.com/play-here/tourism for a monthly calendar showcase.

Fort Macleod has lodging, the Daisy May Campground & RV Resort, campgrounds, restaurants, fast-food, shopping facilities, laundromats, car wash and gas/diesel stations. Fort Macleod Golf & Country Club is western Canada's oldest golf course (established 1890).

The town's **Historic Main Street** is one of only 2 provincially designated historic areas in Alberta and boasts the highest concentration of Edwardian architecture in a single block in the province. The town has hosted several film and TV productions, including *Fargo S2, Interstellar, Brokeback Mountain* and *Passchendaele*. The historic **Empress Theatre** on Historic Main Street is the oldest continuously operating theatre west of Winnipeg, complete with a resident ghost fondly referred to as "Ed." The Empress offers mainstream and independent films, community theatre and live music year-round.

The **Fort Museum** of the North West

The Fort Museum in Fort Macleod features the history of the North West Mounted Police.
(©Earl L Brown)

Mounted Police, a replica of the original Fort, features the history of the North West Mounted Police, local First Nations' cultures and early pioneers. The original fort, named for Colonel J.F. Macleod, was built in 1874 and was the first outpost of the North West Mounted Police (later the Royal Canadian Mounted Police) in western Canada. The 30-acre North West Mounted Police 1884 Barracks Provincial Historic Site is at an additional site to the west of the Fort Museum. The 30-acre site preserves 3 reconstructed buildings housing period displays and artifacts.

During July and August, the museum features a local re-creation of the official RCMP Musical Ride: Youth in NWMP uniforms execute drills on horseback in a colourful display (at 10 A.M., 11:30 A.M., 2 P.M. and 3:30 P.M., weather permitting).

The museum is open 9 A.M. to 5 P.M. daily from May through June; 9 A.M. to 6 P.M. daily, July to Labour Day; and 10 A.M. to 4 P.M. Wednesday–Sunday, September to Canadian Thanksgiving (second Monday in October). The museum is closed November to April. Admission charged. For more information go to: nwmpmuseum.com.

East Access Route Log
(continued)

CB 97.4 (156.7 km) E 292.3 (470.4 km) Fort Macleod Museum parking and access to historic Main Street.

CB 97.6 (157.1 km) E 292.1 (470.1 km) Gas/diesel west, camping to east.

CB 98.1 (157.8 km) E 291.6 (469.2 km) Junction with Highway 2 North. Northbound travelers on Highway 3 West exit here for Highway 2 North to Calgary and Edmonton. View of wind turbine. There are

24 operational wind farms in Alberta and more are planned.

Southbound travelers exit to Highway 3 (Crowsnest Trail) East for Lethbridge.

Highway 3 West continues 600 miles/966 km to Hope, BC. The highway takes its name from Crowsnest Pass (elev. 4,534 feet/1,382m) located 66 miles/106 km west of here.

ALBERTA HIGHWAY 2

CB 98.3 (158.2 km) E 291.4 (469 km) Distance marker northbound shows Claresholm 37 km/23 miles, High River 110 km/68 miles and Calgary 164 km/102 miles.

CB 98.7 (158.8 km) E 291 (468.2 km) Access west to Oldman River Provincial Park and campground. 40 sites, some pull-throughs, non-potable water, pit toilets, $20 per night, open May through October. Potable water and sani-dump adjacent to the Macs Convenience Store in east Fort Macleod.

CB 99 (159.3 km) E 290.7 (467.7 km) Oldman River bridge.

Distance marker northbound shows Granum 18 km/11 miles, Claresholm 35 km/22 miles, Calgary 160 km/9 miles.

CB 99.7 (160.4 km) E 290 (466.6 km) Turnoff to the west on Highway 785 for 10 miles/16 km west to reach the UNESCO World Heritage Site Head-Smashed-In Buffalo Jump Interpretive Center. The sandstone cliff is one of the oldest, largest and best-preserved buffalo jumps in North America. Here, Plains peoples stampeded buffalo to their deaths for nearly 6,000 years.

The Interpretive Center has a series of levels describing the buffalo hunting culture. As visitors descend through the exhibits, they can visit the theatre and stop in the gift

shop on their way out. Elevators and stairs take visitors to the top of the building where they can overlook the panoramic plains. The cafe is open during the summer season. First Nations interpretive guides are available on site. Open year-round 9 A.M. to 5 P.M., May 15 to Labour Day; 10 A.M. to 5 P.M., Labour Day to May 14; closed major holidays. Admission fee as follows: $15 adults, $13 seniors, $10 youth, families $40, 6 years and younger, free.

CB 101.2 (162.8 km) E 288.5 (464.2 km) Northbound roadside turnout with litter barrels and information boards on area plants.

CB 105.2 (169.3 km) E 284.5 (457.9 km) Willow Creek.

CB 110.7 (178.1 km) E 279 (448.9 km) Junction with Highway 519 East to GRANUM (pop. 447); gas/diesel, propane, dump station, groceries and camping.

CB 110.9 (178.5 km) E 278.8 (448.7 km) Distance marker northbound shows Claresholm 18 km/11 miles, Nanton 58 km/36 miles, Calgary 142 km/88 miles.

CB 120.5 (193.9 km) E 269.2 (433.1 km) *Begin speed zone northbound.*

CB 120.8 (194.4 km) E 268.9 (432.7 km) *Begin speed zone northbound.*

CB 121.1 (195 km) E 268.6 (432.3 km) Junction with Highway 520. Turn east for Barons, AB, or west for Centennial Park Campground open May to second weekend in October. There are 28 sites with a playground, showers, spray park and sani-dump; fees are $18–$30 per night.

CB 121.2 (195 km) E 268.5 (432.1 km) Shell gas/diesel station.

CB 121.3 (195.2 km) E 268.4 (431.9 km) CLARESHOLM (pop. 3,758). Emergency Services: Dial 911.

Visitor Information: The historic Canadian Pacific railway station near the center of Claresholm served as half of the Calgary railway station from 1893 until 1910, when it was outgrown and moved to Claresholm. It now houses the Visitor Information Center and Claresholm Museum (and its other half moved to the town of High River to serve as the communities' railway station). The Museum includes a large Exhibit Hall, Claresholm's first schoolhouse, a pioneer log cabin as well as CP Rail caboose. Open daily 9:30 A.M. to 5 P.M. mid-May to Labor Day. Reduced hours in fall. See website for additional information at www.claresholmmuseum.com.

The town also has several historic buildings with a walking tour guide available at the Museum and historical murals painted on in the downtown area. You will find all visitor facilities including banks, motels (Lazy J Motel located on highway), restaurants, fast-food (A&W, DQ, Tim Hortons), gas/diesel stations, a supermarket and laundromat. The community's major employer is the health care sector.

Lazy J Motel. See display ad this page.

Claresholm also has the Appaloosa Horse Club of Canada, an 18-hole golf course and camping at Centennial Park. Open from May to second weekend in October it has 28 sites, dump station, playground, showers and spray park (see additional campground details at Milepost CB 121.1).

CB 122.1 (196.5 km) E 267.6 (430.6 km) Vehicle inspection station northbound with

an Alberta History interpretive sign, also roadside turnout with litter bins.

CB 122.6 (197.3 km) **E 267.1** (429.8 km) Distance marker northbound shows Stavely 14 km/9 miles, Nanton 40 km/26 miles, Calgary 124 km/77 miles.

CB 125.3 (201.6 km) **E 264.4** (425.4 km) Roadside turnout northbound with litter cans and historic sign about Willow Creek.

CB 130.8 (210.5 km) **E 258.9** (416.6 km) Community of Stavely to the east. All services.

CB 131 (210.8 km) **E 258.7** (416.3 km) Roadside turnout southbound with litter/recycling barrels.

CB 131.4 (211.5 km) **E 258.3** (415.7 km) Roadside turnout northbound with litter/recycling barrels and historic sign about Stavely.

CB 131.8 (212.1 km) **E 257.9** (415 km) **Junction** with Highway 527 West to Willow Creek Provincial Park.

CB 132.2 (212.8 km) **E 257.5** (414.4 km) Distance marker northbound shows Parkland 10 km/6 miles, Nanton 24 km/15 miles, Calgary 109 km/68 miles.

CB 132.4 (213 km) **E 257.3** (414 km) Southbound turnout with litter/recycling barrels.

CB 135.9 (218.7 km) **E 253.8** (408.4 km) **Junction** with Highway 529 East to Twin Valley Dam and Little Bow Provincial Park (57 km/35 miles).

CB 138 (222 km) **E 251.7** (405.1 km) Turnoff for Parkland (no services).

CB 138.8 (223.4 km) **E 250.9** (403.8 km) Distance marker northbound shows Nanton 13 km/8 miles, High River 42 km/26 miles, Calgary 100 km/62 miles.

CB 139.4 (224.3 km) **E 250.3** (402.8 km) Roadside turnout southbound with litter and recycling bins.

CB 146 (234.9 km) **E 243.7** (392.2 km) **Junction** with Highway 533 West to Chain Lakes Provincial Park (39 km/24.2 miles).

Slow for speed zone northbound entering Nanton.

CB 146.6 (235.9 km) **E 243.1** (391.1 km) **NANTON** (pop. 2,132). All visitor facilities available, including gas/diesel stations with propane, supermarket and fast-food outlets. Nanton RV Park (75 sites) is located at the junction with Highway 533 East. Nanton Golf Club 18-hole golf course is nearby.

Visitor Information: The Visitor Center located on Highway 2 North, is open May to September; www.visitnanton.com or www.nanton.ca.

Nanton's well-preserved history is on display at the Antique & Art Walk of Alberta (open daily), and along Main Street, with its restored turn-of-the-century buildings. Nanton is home to the **Bomber Command Museum of Canada**, located on Highway 2 South. The Bomber Command Museum houses an impressive display of WWII aircraft and artifacts. The centerpiece of the 26,000-square-foot museum is a 1945 Lancaster Bomber, one of the few in the world that is still intact and available to walk through. The museum is open daily from May 1 to Oct. 15. Weekends only the remainder of the year. See main website at www.bombercommandmuseum.ca for current information on special events, Merlin engine run-offs and hours of operation.

Museum of Miniatures located at the corner of Highway 2 South and 19th Street is Canadian history at 1/12 scale. Open daily May 1 to Oct. 31, 10 A.M. to 6 P.M.

Guided tours of Nanton's last 3 remaining grain elevators are available. Learn more about their history at the Canadian Grain Elevator Discovery Center. *(©Earl L. Brown)*

The Canadian Grain Elevator Discovery Center offers a popular tour; phone 403-646-1146 or visit nantongrainelevators.com; and the Nanton Agricultural Society hosts rodeo events throughout the summer www.nantonagsociety.com.

CB 147.3 (237 km) **E 242.4** (390 km) **Junction** with Highway 533 East to Vulcan and Highway 23. Turnoff east for RV park.

Fans of *Star Trek* can take a **side trip** to the small community of Vulcan (41 km/25 miles). Drive east via highways 533 E and 534 E to this unique community named after Spock's heritage. For visitor centre hours and additional information: website: www.vulcantourism.com; email: info@vulcantourism.com; or phone 403-485-2994.

CB 147.5 (237.3 km) **E 242.2** (389.8 km) Distance marker northbound shows High River 31 km/19 miles, Calgary 85 km/53 miles.

CB 148.5 (239 km) **E 241.2** (388.2 km) Mosquito Creek.

CB 153 (246.2 km) **E 236.7** (381 km) Distance marker southbound shows Nanton 8 km/5 miles, Claresholm 46 km/29 miles, Fort Macleod 89 km/55 miles.

CB 154.4 (248.5 km) **E 235.3** (378.7 km) Turn west to Cayley (3 km/1.9 miles).

CB 156.4 (251.7 km) **E 233.3** (375.5 km) **Junction** with Highway 540 West to Alberta Highway 22 ("Cowboy Trail") and access to Bar U Ranch National Historic Site (34 km/21 miles), a living history ranch preserving Canada's "old west." Open late May to early October; restaurant, gift shop, 35 historic structures.

CB 162.5 (261.5 km) **E 227.2** (365.6 km) Exit 194A to Highway 23 East and Vulcan.

CB 162.8 (262 km) **E 226.9** (365.1 km) Exit 194B west to **HIGH RIVER** (pop. 13,584); all visitor facilities. **Visitor Information:** Town of High River, phone 403-603-3101, 1-877-603-3101 or visit highriver.ca or www.choosehighriver.ca

A favorite location for the film and television industry, High River is the official home of the popular TV Series *Heartland*: Downtown features *Heartland's* "Maggie's Diner" film set. The downtown core also has spe-

cialty stores, restaurants and coffeehouses. Other attractions include historical murals, the **Museum of the Highwood** (which displays photography, movies and TV filmed in the area, and the W.O. Mitchell Room which honours the authors work), the Sheppard Family Park, an extensive walking and biking pathway system, and the 28-hole Highwood Golf & Country Club course. George Lane Park, on the Highwood River in downtown High River, offers a 57-site campground, dump station, showers, playground, ball diamond, picnic tables, and horseshoe pits; phone 403-652-2529.

Begin 5-lane divided highway northbound.

CB 162.9 (262.1 km) **E 226.8** (365 km) Distance marker northbound shows Alderside 11 km/7 miles, Calgary 66 km/41 miles.

CB 163.7 (263.4 km) **E 226** (363.7 km) Roadside turnout northbound, interpretive boards on history on Alberta oilfields; litter/recycling bins.

CB 170 (273.6 km) **E 219.7** (353.6 km) Highwood River.

CB 172 (276.8 km) **E 217.7** (350.3 km) Exit 209 to Highways 7 West/547 East to Okotoks. Don't miss the **Okotoks Erratic**, located west of town: It is the largest known glacial erratic in the world. Chinook Arch Meadery and Chinook Honey Company, to the west and just south of the erratic, has meadery tours and gift shop; phone 403-995-0830. Okotoks has 2 campgrounds: Riverbend Campground and Okotoks Lions Campground, as well as motels/hotels, shopping and restaurants.

CB 173.3 (278.9 km) **E 216.4** (348.3 km) Sheep River.

CB 173.6 (279.4 km) **E 216.1** (347.7 km) Turnoff west for campground.

CB 175.2 (281.9 km) **E 214.5** (345.2 km) Begin 6-lane divided highway northbound.

CB 180.5 (290.4 km) **E 209.2** (336.6 km) Exit 222 for Highway 2A South to Okotoks; all visitor services and Nature's Hideaway Campground east, 14 km/8.7 miles.

CB 182 (292.8 km) **E 207.7** (334.2 km)

Calgary Tower offers a dizzying view of the city's streets and skyline from 525 feet/160m.
(©David L. Ranta, staff)

Exit 225 for Deerfoot Trail or continue straight for Macleod Trail.

NOTE: Highway 2 North divides into Macleod Trail (2A) and Deerfoot Trail (2). Macleod Trail provides access to suburban malls and services, downtown Calgary and junctions with Trans-Canada Highway 1. Northbound travelers see also Stoney Trail option at Milepost CB 187.6.

Northbound travelers following this log take Deerfoot Trail for continuation of Highway 2 North to Red Deer and Edmonton, and for access to Trans-Canada Highway 1 (which leads to Banff/Lake Louise and via the Icefields Parkway to Jasper (for Icefields Parkway log, go to CANADIAN ROCKIES ROUTE on page 82).

CB 183.3 (294.9 km) **E 206.4** (332.1 km) Exit 227, golf courses, Dunbow Road, De Winton.

CB 184.7 (297.2 km) **E 205** (329.9 km) Bow River.

CB 186.4 (300 km) **E 203.3** (327.2 km) Exit 232 for Cranston Avenue and Seton Boulevard.

CB 187.6 (301.8 km) **E 202.1** (325.2 km) Exit 234 Marquis of Lorne Trail 22X/ Stoney Trail. Northbound travelers exit east to bypass Calgary via Highway 201/Stoney Trail which connects to Highway 2 north of the city (see **Milepost CB 208.1**). Part of Calgary's "Ring Road" system, the southeast, northeast and northwest sections of Stoney Trail provide 44 miles/70 km of free-flow travel on divided highway. *The southwest section was under construction in 2018.*

CB 189 (304.1 km) **E 200.7** (322.9 km) Exit 236 McKenzie Lake Boulevard and McKenzie Town Boulevard.

CB 190.1 (305.9 km) **E 199.6** (321 km) Exit 238 130 Avenue Southeast. South Trail Crossing shopping mall east off exit.

CB 191.4 (308 km) **E 198.3** (319.1 km) Exit 240 Barlow Trail North.

CB 192.4 (309.6 km) **E 197.3** (317.5 km) Exit 241 Douglasdale Boulevard/24 Street East.

CB 192.6 (310 km) **E 197.1** (317.2 km) Ivor Strong Bridge.

CB 193.3 (311.1 km) **E 196.4** (316.1 km) Exit 243 Anderson Road/Bow Bottom Trail.

CB 194.3 (312.7 km) **E 195.4** (314.5 km)

Exit 245 Southland Drive.

CB 195.4 (314.5 km) **E 194.3** (312.7 km) Exit 247 Glenmore Trail. Shopping centre to west. **Heritage Park Historical Village** west off this exit; see description on page 61 in Calgary Attractions.

CB 196.2 (315.8 km) **E 193.5** (311.4 km) Exit 248 East Glenmore Trail.

CB 198.6 (319.6 km) **E 191.1** (307.6 km) Exit 251 Peigan Trail East/Barlow Trail South.

CB 199.5 (321.1 km) **E 190.2** (306.1 km) Exit 254 Blackfoot Trail/Calgary City Centre/17th Avenue.

Description of Calgary follows. Log of East Access Route to Edmonton continues on page 62.

Calgary

CB 199.5 (321.1 km) **E 190.2** (306.1 km) Located at the confluence of the Bow and Elbow rivers, where the foothills of the Canadian Rockies meet the prairie. **Population:** 1,149,552. **Emergency Services:** Dial 911. **Hospitals:** Alberta Children's Hospital, 2888 Shaganappi Trail NW; Rockyview General Hospital, 7007–14 St. SW; Peter Lougheed Centre, 3500–26 Ave. NE; Foothills Medical Centre, 1403–29 St. NW.

Visitor Information: At the arrivals level across from baggage carousel 7–8 in Calgary International Airport (YYC); open 6 A.M. to 11 P.M. year-round. For details about what to see and do in Calgary, see visitcalgary.com, contact Tourism Calgary at 403-263-8510 (local) or toll-free in North America 1-800-661-1678, or email: info@tourismcalgary.com. Find the mobile WiFi-enabled kiosk in the summer months and speak to a counsellor by searching #askmeyyc on twitter.

Elevation: 3,736 feet/1,139m. **Climate:** Moderate 4-season climate with the most sunny days of any major Canadian city. Summer days average 72°F/22°C; fall days, 52°F/11°C; winter days, 9°F/-15°C; spring days, 42°F/9°C. **Newspapers:** *Calgary Herald* daily and *Calgary Sun* daily.

Private Aircraft: Calgary International Airport, 10.6 miles/17 km northeast of downtown Calgary; elev. 3,736 feet/1,139m; 3 runways. See Canadian Flight Supplement.

Originally established in 1875 as a fort by a contingent of the NWMP, Calgary has grown from a frontier settlement to a world-class destination. One of Alberta's 2 major population centres (the other being the provincial capital of Edmonton), Calgary uniquely mixes cosmopolitan flair and big city energy with rich western heritage and famous cultural traditions. The city boasts its own Philharmonic Orchestra and ballet, while its rich western heritage is preserved in its attractions, such as Fort Calgary (no RV parking), the Glenbow Museum, Heritage Park Historical Village and the annual Calgary Stampede. Calgary also boasts the most extensive urban pathway and bike network in North America; bike rentals available. Read under "Attractions" for additional information on these and other Calgary features.

Calgary is the gateway to the Canadian Rockies. Summer activities in the Kananaskis, Canmore, Banff and Lake Louise area include hiking, biking, kayaking, whitewater rafting, camping, horseback riding, mountain climbing, golfing, hang gliding and more. Winter activities include downhill skiing, snowboarding, cross-country skiing, dog sledding, snowshoeing and ice climbing. Calgary hosted the 1988 XV Olympic Winter Games and the former venue is now operated for use by athletes and the general public (www.winsport.ca).

Lodging & Services

There are hotels, motels and B & B's located downtown; near the airport in northeast Calgary; on Highway 2 south (Macleod Trail); on Trans-Canada Highway 1 north (16th Avenue); and on Alternate 1A (Motel Village).

Calgary's restaurants include everything from major-chain fast-food outlets to upscale restaurants serving world-famous Alberta beef and various other award-winning cuisine.

Camping

There are several campgrounds in and around the city; phone for details on facilities and season. Private campgrounds in the area include: Calaway R.V. Park & Campground, 6.2 miles/10 kms west on Trans-Canada Highway 1, phone 403-240-3822, www.calawaypark.com; Calgary West Campground, west of Winsport on Trans-Canada Highway 1, phone 1-888-562-0842, calgarycampground.com; and Mountain View Camping Ltd., phone 403-293-6640, www.calgarycamping.com. For additional camping options go to www.visitcalgary.com and click on campgrounds under the Accommodations tab.

Transportation

Air: Calgary International Airport, 20 minutes from the city centre, is Canada's fourth busiest airport and the hub for regional, domestic and international airlines.

Railroad: Passenger trains include the Rocky Mountaineer, Canada Rail Vacations and Royal Canadian Pacific.

Car Rentals: Available through Alamo, Avis, Budget, Discount Car and Truck, Driving Force, Enterprise, Hertz, National and Thrifty.

RV Rentals: Available from CanaDream

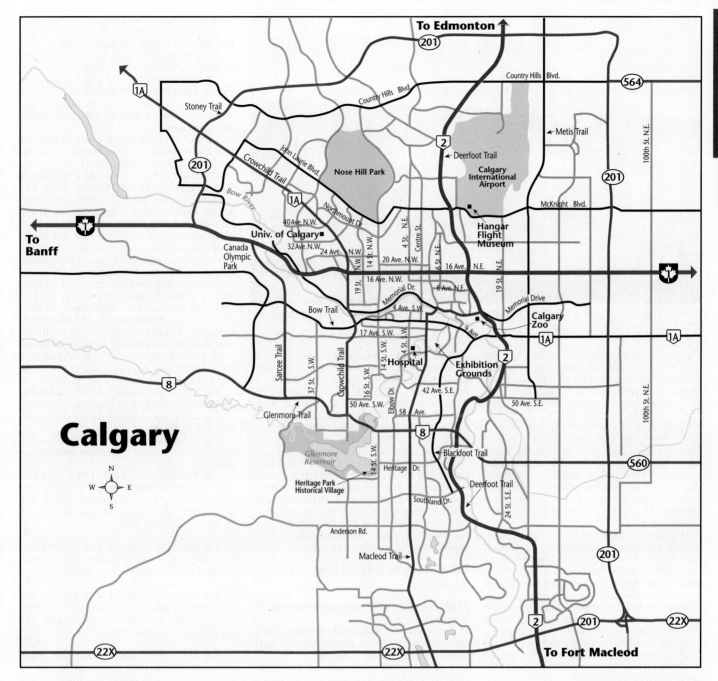

Calgary

N
W · E
S

Campers Inc. (1-800-461-7368), Candan R.V. Centre (1-800-922-6326), Fraserway RV Rentals (1-800-661-2441) and Westcoast Mountain Campers Ltd. (1-888-608-8766).

Taxi and Limousine: Service by Checker Group/Ambassador, 1-800-867-4497; Mayfair Taxi, 1-888-995-6555; Limo Lush 1-844-855-5874; and Allied Sedan & Limousine Service & Associated Cabs, 1-877-299-9555.

Bus: Calgary Transit offers bus or light rail transit (C-Train) services to nearly all parts of the city (including the airport). The C-Train offers free service in the downtown area. www.calgarytransit.com. Red Arrow busline provides service to Edmonton, Red Deer, Lethbridge and Fort McMurray; phone 1-800-232-1958; www.redarrow.ca.

Attractions

Heritage Park Historical Village, located at 1900 Heritage Dr. SW, is Canada's largest living history museum, with more than 180 historical exhibits and 127 acres of parkland. Experience the sights and sounds of life in turn-of-the-century Western Canada: An authentic steam locomotive; an antique midway; the S.S. Moyie sternwheeler; Gasoline Alley Museum, various shops, cafe and restaurant; and lively interpretive activities for the entire family. Admission fee charged. The Historical Village is open from May to October. The Gasoline Alley Museum, gift shops, Railway Cafe and Wainwright Hotel are open year-round. Heritage Park hosts special events throughout the year. Phone 403-268-8500; website: www.heritagepark.ca.

WinSport, located at 88 Canada Olympic Road SW, west from downtown Calgary on Trans-Canada Highway 1, was the site of the 1988 XV Olympic Winter Games. Today, this premier site operates as a competition, training, recreation and hospitality area designed for year-round use by athletes and the general public. Summer attractions for the general public include miniature golf, a children's activity area with climbing wall, mountain biking, wheeled bobsleigh and luge rides, and a zipline. Ride a glass eleva-tor to the highest vantage point in Calgary, stepping outside onto the deck of the 1988 Winter Olympics' biggest ski jump. The observation level also features Olympic ski jumping memorabilia. Winter facilities include skiing, snowboarding, bobsleigh and luge rides, half-pipe and cross-country skiing.

Open daily except Dec. 25. Free admission; pay per activity. For information, phone 403-247-5452 or visit their website at www.winsport.ca.

Calgary Zoo, located at 1300 Zoo Rd. NE has nearly 1,000 live animals and the Dorothy Harvie Gardens and ENMAX butterfly-filled conservatory. Journey through Destination Africa and see western lowland gorillas up close. Investigate the Canadian Wilds and Penguin Plunge, to name just a few of the attractions. Open year-round, 9 A.M. to 5 P.M. daily. For more information, phone 1-800-588-9993; or visit www.calgaryzoo.com.

Fort Calgary, located at 750–9th Ave. SE.

Alberta Highway 2/Queen Elizabeth II Highway is a busy connector route between Calgary and Edmonton. (©Kris Valencia, staff)

The Fort is undergoing $165-million upgrade and will have limited admission until the grand reopening in May 2021. For more information, visit www.fortcalgary.com.

Calgary Tower. Two 18-passenger high-speed elevators take visitors to the top of Calgary Tower (525 feet/160m) in 62 seconds. Sweeping views of city and mountains; look through glass floor at the street far below. Revolving Sky 360 Restaurant. Located in the heart of downtown at 101–9 Ave. SW. Open year-round except Christmas Day. Admission charged. For information, phone 403-266-7171 or visit www.calgarytower.com.

Calgary Stampede. The city's best-known and oldest event is the annual Calgary Stampede, "the Greatest Outdoor Show on Earth," which takes place July 5–14, 2019, at the Exhibition Grounds. The 10-day citywide celebration of Calgary's western heritage includes a parade, daily rodeo (the world's richest outdoor rodeo), Chuckwagon races, musical performances and evening Grandstand Show extravaganza.

For information and tickets, phone 1-800-661-1260, 403-261-0101 or at website: www.calgarystampede.com.

Glenbow Museum. Western Canada's largest museum traces the history of Canada's West, from its First People to the arrival of European settlers. International collections; Blackfoot Gallery, "Nitsitapi-isinni: Our Way of Life," and "Mavericks: an Incorrigible History of Alberta" (interactive exhibit). Open year-round. Admission charged. Located at 130–9 Ave. SE. For more information, phone 403-268-4100, or visit www.glenbow.org.

The **Hangar Flight Museum** was founded in 1975 by former WWII pilots and aviation enthusiasts, to preserve the history of aviation and space industry in Western Canada. Try your hand on the flight simulators, learn about the Canadian Space programs and examine the aircraft up close. The museum's aircraft collection includes a Sopwith Triplane from WWI, 5 aircraft from WWII and others. The museum is near the Calgary International Airport off McKnight Boulevard NE. Phone 403-250-3752; www.the hangarmuseum.ca.

The Royal Alberta Museum opened in its new location in October 2018. Now in Edmonton's Downtown Art District it encompasses 419,000 sq. ft. with 82,000 sq. ft. of exhibition space. Located at 9810–103A Ave. NW, the new museum aspires to "share Alberta's remarkable stories in meaningful ways." For additional details and hours, see website: royalalbertamuseum.ca.

Studio Bell, Canada's National Music Centre is a 160,000 square-foot arts hub, with exhibition and performance space. Its 5 floors honour the pioneers of Canadian music. Open Wednesday–Sunday year-round, from 10 A.M. to 5 P.M. at 850 4 St. SE. Check website for event dates and exhibition information: studiobell.ca; phone 403-543-5115.

East Access Route Log
(continued)

ALBERTA HIGHWAY 2 Queen Elizabeth II Highway

Distance from U.S.–Canada border (CB) is followed by distance from junction with Highway 16A at Edmonton (E).
Exit numbers reflect distance in kilometres from U.S. border (Carway/Port of Peigan crossing) via Highway 2.

CB 199.5 (321.1 km) **E 190.2** (306.1 km) Exit 254 Blackfoot Trail/Calgary City Centre/17th Avenue. *Description of Calgary begins on page 60.*

CB 200 (321.8 km) **E 189.7** (305.3 km) Exit 256 Memorial Drive to Calgary Zoo and City Centre.

CB 201.5 (324.3 km) **E 188.2** (302.9 km) Exit 258 to Trans-Canada Highway 1 and 16 Avenue North going east and west.

Continue north on Highway 2 for Red Deer and Edmonton (log follows).

Junction with Trans-Canada Highway 1 West to Lake Louise and the Icefields Parkway to Jasper. See "Trans-Canada Highway 1 West" log on facing page. See the CANADIAN ROCKIES ROUTE beginning on page 82 for Icefields Parkway log to Jasper.

CB 202.4 (325.7 km) **E 187.3** (301.4 km) Exit 260 to 32nd Avenue North.

CB 203.6 (327.6 km) **E 186.1** (299.5 km) Exit 261A McKnight Boulevard East; access

to Hangar Flight Museum.

CB 203.7 (327.8 km) **E 186** (299.3 km) Exit 261B McKnight Boulevard West.

CB 204.5 (329.1 km) **E 185.2** (298 km) Exit 263 for 64th Avenue North.

CB 205.5 (330.7 km) **E 184.2** (296.4 km) Exit 265 Beddington Trail West.

CB 206.9 (332.9 km) **E 182.8** (294.2 km) Exit 266 Airport Trail, Calgary International Airport to east.

CB 207.9 (334.6 km) **E 181.8** (292.6 km) Exit 268 Country Hills Boulevard; access east to Calgary International Airport.

CB 208.1 (334.9 km) **E 181.6** (292.3 km) Exit 271 Highway 201/Stoney Trail. Exit west on Stoney Trail for 14.3-mile/23-km 4-lane bypass route connecting to Trans-Canada Highway 1 west of Calgary to Banff and Icefields Parkway (take Exit 36); heavy traffic during rush hour, no easy access to traveler services on this bypass which travels through residential subdivisions.

Southbound travelers may exit east on Stoney Trail/Highway 201 to bypass Calgary and reconnect to Highway 2 south of the city (see **Milepost CB 187.6**). Part of Calgary's "Ring Road" system, the southeast, northeast and northwest sections of Stoney Trail provide 44 miles/70 km of free-flow travel on divided highway. *The southwest section was under construction summer 2018.*

CB 210.2 (338.3 km) **E 179.5** (288.9 km) Calgary northern city limits (sign).

CB 212.2 (341.5 km) **E 177.5** (285.6 km) Exit 275 to Balzac.

CB 213.5 (343.6 km) **E 176.2** (283.6 km) Northbound vehicle inspection station; pay phone.

CB 215.1 (346.2 km) **E 174.6** (281 km) Exit 282 to **AIRDRIE** (pop. 49,560); gas/diesel, lodging and restaurants to east. Fraserway RV off Kingsview Way SE for RV repairs, rentals and sales.

CB 216.2 (347.9 km) **E 173.5** (279.2 km) Exit 284 to East Airdrie Industrial; gas/diesel stations and restaurants, east off exit.

CB 218.4 (351.5 km) **E 171.3** (275.7 km) Exit 285 to Highway 567 west to city centre for lodging, gas, diesel, restaurants and shopping or east to industrial centre.

CB 223.6 (359.8 km) **E 166.1** (267.3 km) Dickson-Stephansson Stopping House on Old Calgary Trail (southbound-only) rest area and tourist information to west side, well away from the highway. Pay phones.

CB 224.3 (361 km) **E 165.4** (266.2 km) Exit 295 to West 2A Crossfield and Highway 72 to Drumheller. Alberta Highways 72 and 9 lead 60 miles/97 km east to Drumheller in the Canadian Badlands—a region characterized by scanty vegetation and intricate erosional features. Besides its fantastic scenery, the Badlands are also famous for dinosaurs, on display at the Royal Tyrrell Museum and in Drumheller. The Canadian Badlands Passion Play, presented in a 2,700-seat natural amphitheatre, takes place in July; details at www.canadianpassionplay.com.

CB 226.2 (364 km) **E 163.5** (263.1 km) Esso gas/diesel and restaurant east side of highway.

CB 230.7 (371.3 km) **E 159** (255.9 km) Exit 305 to **CROSSFIELD** (pop. 2,918); visitor services; 18-hole golf course, Farmers Market.

CB 236.6 (380.7 km) **E 153.1** (246.4 *(Continues on page 65)*

Trans-Canada Highway 1 West

Trans-Canada Highway 1 West provides access to the popular resort town of Banff.
(©Kris Valencia, staff)

An alternate route for East Access Route motorists is to take Trans-Canada Highway 1 west 115 miles/185 km from Calgary to Highway 93 North, then drive 143 miles/230 km to Jasper. From Jasper, drive 45 miles/72 km east via Yellowhead Highway 16 to the Highway 40 junction and take the Bighorn Route 204 miles/329 km to Grande Prairie, where you will rejoin the East Access Route to Dawson Creek, BC, and the start of the Alaska Highway. Total driving distance from Calgary to Grande Prairie via this route is 507 miles/816 km, versus 469 miles/755 km via Edmonton.

Trans-Canada Highway 1 is the world's longest national highway, stretching nearly 5,000 miles/8,047 km from St. Johns, NF, on the Atlantic Coast, to Victoria, BC, on Vancouver Island on the Pacific Coast. The stretch of Trans-Canada Highway 1 logged here measures 115 miles/185 km between Calgary and the start of the Icefields Parkway (Highway 93) to Jasper, and takes in Banff and Lake Louise. It also junctions with Highway 93 South to Yoho National Park and Radium Hot Springs, BC.

For Highway 93 log to Jasper and Radium Hot Springs, see the CANADIAN ROCKIES ROUTE beginning on page 82. For current road reports, visit 511.alberta.ca.

Emergency Services: Dial 911; **RCMP** in Banff, phone 403-762-2226; **RCMP** in Jasper, phone 780-852-4848.

TRANS-CANADA HIGHWAY 1 West
Distance from Calgary (C).

C 0 **Junction** of Highway 2 (Deerfoot Trail) and Trans-Canada 1 West at **Milepost CB 201.5.** Follow Trans-Canada 1 West; services and shopping first 4 miles/6.4 km. Good 2-lane highway, posted 90 kmph/55 mph.

C 8.8 (14.1 km) Traffic light. Services immediately to north include Shell and Petro-Canada gas stations, truck/carwash, Starbucks, Subway, McDonald's, Sandman/

Denny's, Wendy's.

Short access road south to site of the 1988 XV Winter Olympics. Summer activities available; visit www.winsport.ca for details.

C 9.2 (14.8 km) Exit 177 Stoney Trail North. This 14-mile/22.5-km bypass route connects to Highway 2 north of Calgary; heavy traffic during rush hour, no easy access to traveler services.

C 9.5 (15.3 km) Calgary West Campground to south along West Valley Road SW.

C 12.1 (19.5 km) Exit 172.

C 14.5 (23.3 km) Exit 169 to Springbank Range Road. Access south to Calaway Park, Western Canada's largest outdoor family amusement park, with 32 rides, live entertainment and dining. A full-service RV park is also available. Calaway Park is open daily June through August; weekends only from May 18 to June 1 and from Sept. 3 to early October.

C 19.5 (31.4 km) Exit 161B for Cochrane/Highway 22 North.

C 19.7 (31.7 km) Exit 161A/Highway 22 South for Bragg Creek and Redwood Meadows.

C 19.9 (32 km) Easy access to highway-side Petro-Canada gas station and Humpty's restaurant to north.

C 20.2 (32.5 km) Weigh station with roadside turnout to north; litter/recycling bins.

C 22.3 (35.9 km) Exit 156 for Jumpingpound Creek.

C 23 (37 km) Jumpingpound Creek.

C 30.2 (48.6 km) Exit 143 Sibbald Creek Trail/Highway 68 South.

C 32 (51.5 km) Scott Lake Hill roadside turnout to the north is long, double-ended, with litter bins for westbound traffic.

C 34.5 (55.5 km) J 223 (358.9 km) Exit

137 Bear Hill Road.

C 37.5 (60.3 km) Exit 131 for Chiniki Village to south with all visitor services. Morley Road is to north.

C 38.4 (61.8 km) Distance marker westbound shows Canmore 45 km/30 miles, Banff 66 km/41 miles.

C 41.2 (66.3 km) Exit 124, no services.

C 43.8 (70.5 km) Roadside turnouts to north and south; litter/recycling bins.

C 46 (74 km) Exit 118 to Highway 40 South for access to Barrier Lake Visitor Information Centre, 7 km/4 miles (phone 403-678-0760); Stoney Nakoda Resort/Casino, 11 km/7 miles; Kananaskis Village, Delta Lodge and Mount Kidd RV Park, 23 km/14 miles; and Boundary Ranch, 25 km/16 miles. Kananaskis Country Club Golf Course, located 26.4 km/16.4 miles south—one of the most spectacular golf courses in North America. See more details on the 36-hole course golf course at www.kananaskisgolf.com.

C 48 (77.2 km) Kananaskis River.

C 48.5 (78 km) Exit 114 to Seebe and Exshaw via Highway 1A; access to **Bow Valley Provincial Park** campgrounds (descriptions follow). Bow Valley Campground has 36 unserviced and 131 serviced (power/water) campsites that are reservation-in-advance-ONLY, open April 27–Oct. 8; camping fees $26–$40. Phone 403-673-2163 for more information; reserve by phone 1-877-537-2757. Willow Rock Campground has 90 unserviced and 34 serviced (electric) sites that can accommodate 35-plus-foot RVs; sites available first-come first-served, April 6–Oct. 21; sani-dump, firewood for sale; camping fees $26–$33.

C 49 (79 km) *CAUTION: Watch for elk next 2 km/1.2 miles westbound.*

C 54 (86.9 km) Exit 105 to **Lac Des Arcs Campground** in Bow Valley Provincial Park has 28 unserviced sites; open April 27–Sept. 4 with picnic tables, water (not guaranteed potable), toilets, firepits, firewood for sale. Camping fee $26; reserve by phone 1-877-537-2757 (reservation fee is $12).

C 54.1 (87.1 km) Distance marker westbound shows Deadmans Flats 7 km/4.3 miles, Canmore 19 km/12 miles, Banff 50 km/31 miles.

C 54.5 (87.7 km) **J 203** (326.7 km) Roadside turnout to north on river; litter/recycling bins.

C 55.5 (89.3 km) **J 202** (325.1 km) Roadside turnout to north with litter/recycling bins. Information boards on Canada geese.

C 56 (90.1 km) **J 201.5** (324.3 km) *CAUTION: Wildlife on highway.*

C 58.6 (94.3 km) Exit 98 Deadmans Flats and information board on Alberta's history. The community offers gas/diesel, lodging, groceries and restaurants. **Three Sisters Campground**, open April 13 to Nov. 18, has 36 unserviced campsites, water pump (not guaranteed potable), toilets, firewood for sale and sani-dump at nearby gas station. Camping fee is $26.

C 61 (98.2 km) Exit 93 to Canmore Nordic Centre, Bow Valley Provincial Park, Stewart Creek Golf Club 2 km/1.2 miles, Three Sisters Parkway. **Bow River Campground** (Bow Valley Provincial Park) is open April 27 to Sept. 10, has 7 unserviced and 59 serviced (electrical hookup/water) campsites with picnic tables, water, toilets, firewood

for sale and food lockers available for cycling campers. Camping fee $28–$40. No reservations.

C 62 (99.8 km) Bow River.

C 63 (101.4 km) Exit 91 for Highway 1A, Canmore. Access this exit to fast-food and restaurants (Tim Hortons, McDonald's, DQ, Boston Pizza) and lodging (Best Western, Holiday Inn). Heli-tours are south at this exit.

C 63.2 (101.7 km) *CAUTION: Elk crossing next 2 km/1.2 miles westbound.*

C 64.2 (103.3 km) Exit 89 for Canmore town centre/Silvertip Resort exit. **CANMORE** (pop. 12,317, plus approximately 5,000 seasonal residents; elev. 1,309m/4,295 feet) is a year-round resort community with full tourist facilities.

C 65.6 (105.5 km) Exit 86 for Canmore/Trans-Canada Highway 1A (Bow Valley Trail).

Access to Travel Alberta Information Centre just south of highway; RV parking, restrooms, Wapiti Campground (adjacent visitor centre) is open May 1 through Oct. 8 with 88 serviced and unserviced sites (walk-in only); camping fees are $27–$37; showers $3. Also access this exit to food, gas/diesel and lodging.

C 66.4 (106.8 km) Exit 83 to Hamlet of Harvie Heights. Lodging.

C 68 (107.8 km) East entrance gate for the national parks. Motorists staying in Jasper or Banff national parks or driving the Icefields Parkway must purchase a park pass.

C 69.4 (111.7 km) Distance marker westbound shows Banff 11 km/7 miles, Lake Louise 70 km/44 miles.

C 76 (122.3 km) Exit for Banff Avenue, Tunnel Mountain Road, Lake Minnewanka. Access to Minnewanka Lake (boat tours) and **Two Jack Lake Campground** via Minnewanka Loop Road. Open May 24 to Oct. 1, 64 sites, flush toilets, showers, firewood for sale. Camping fee is $27.40. Access via Tunnel Mountain Road (4 miles from high-

way, watch for left hand turns) to **Tunnel Mountain Campground** (pictured above). Open May 10 to Sept. 10, 618 sites (full hookup, electrical only and unserviced sites), flush toilets, showers, sani-dump, firewood. Camping fee $27.40–$38.20. Beautiful views.

C 76.5 (123.1 km) Distance marker westbound shows Banff 4 km/2.5 miles, Lake Louise 58 km/36 miles.

C 77.5 (124.7 km) Exit onto Norquay Road to **BANFF** (pop. 8,244) townsite and headquarters for Banff National Park. En route to Banff, just south off of Highway 1A on Norquay Road, there is a day-use area creek side with picnic tables, litter/recycling bins and pit toilets.

Banff National Park, established in 1885,

©Kris Valencia, staff

is the first national park designated in Canada. **Visitor Information:** Banff Visitor Centre, 224 Banff Ave., phone 403-762-1550. Banff Visitor Information Kiosk is at Banff Heritage Railway Station, 327 Railway Ave. You may purchase park passes at the visitor centres. **Elevation:** 4,540 feet/1,384m. **Emergency Services:** Dial 911. RCMP, 335 Lynx St., phone 403-762-2228; **Hospital,** Mineral Springs Hospital, 305 Lynx St., phone 403-762-2222.

This scenic resort town attracts 2.5 million visitors every year, in summer for the scenery, and in winter for the skiing at nearby Mount Norquay (also accessible via this exit), Sunshine Village and Lake Louise. Banff offers banking and currency exchange, restaurants, gas/diesel, lodging and plenty of shopping year-round. On-street parking and some parking lots designated for cars; RV parking near the hospital and at the Fenland Recreation Centre.

Attractions include the Banff Park Museum and National Historic Site; the Banff Gondola which transports visitors up Sulphur Mountain; the Fairmont Banff Springs Hotel with spa, afternoon tea, wine bar and 1888 Chop House restaurant; the hot springs at Cave & Basin National Historic Site and the Upper Hot Springs.

C 78.8 (126.8 km) Distance marker westbound shows Lake Louise 54 km/34 miles, Field 80 km/50 miles.

C 79 (127.2 km) Rest area to south for eastbound traffic has information boards, toilets and beautiful views of peaks and scenic Banff.

C 82.4 (132.6 km) Bow Valley Parkway/Highway 1A exit; access to Johnston Canyon, Castle Mountain and Protection Mountain campgrounds (waterfalls along this route). **Castle Mountain Campground** is open May 25 to Sept. 17 with 43 sites, flush toilets, firewood for sale and a camping fee of $21.50. **Protection Mountain Campground** is open May 25 to Sept. 17 with 14 sites, flush toilets and firewood for sale (not all sites have firepits/fires allowed); camping fee is $21.50.

C 82.9 (133.4 km) Distance marker westbound shows Lake Louise 48 km/30 miles, Radium Hot Springs 126 km/78 miles.

C 83 (133.6 km) Double-ended roadside turnout westbound with litter bins.

C 83.7 (134.7 km) Sunshine Road exit, Sunshine Village ski area exit; food, lodging, hiking trails and gondola rides in summer.

C 85.3 (137.3 km) Dozens of large animal overpasses along this stretch of highway allow large animals to cross the busy highway without getting hit by vehicles. The overpasses are covered in sod and made to look like natural rock. They are used by 11 species of large mammals.

C 86.1 (138.6 km) Bourgeau Lake; summer hiking trail.

C 90.2 (145.2 km) Redearth Creek; picnicking and hiking in summer. Animal overpass.

C 91.9 (147.9 km) Double-ended rest area to north for westbound traffic overlooking the river; information boards about the large animal overpasses; toilets, litter bins, kid friendly observation deck with animal cut-outs and scenic view of Castle Mountain.

C 97.3 (156.6 km) **Junction** of Trans-Canada Highway 1 with 1A (Castle Junction) with Highway 93 South to Radium Hot Springs (66 miles/106 km). Highways 1 and

93 share a common alignment next 17.5 miles/28 km westbound.

Junction with Highway 93 south to Radium Hot Springs. See CANADIAN ROCKIES ROUTE on page 82.

TRANS-CANADA HIGHWAY 1/CANADA HIGHWAY 93

C 98.5 (158.5 km) Distance marker westbound shows Lake Louise 25 km/15 miles, Field 50 km/31 miles.

C 102.5 (165 km) Taylor rest area to south accessible to both east and westbound traffic; parking, picnic tables, litter bins, toilets and hiking trail.

C 109.3 (175.9 km) Temple rest area to north for westbound traffic; viewpoint, toilets, picnic tables.

C 110.8 (178.3 km) Overflow camping/parking area to south. Free shuttle service to shore of Lake Louise daily from mid-May to early October. *Parking is extremely limited in Lake Louise village and at the lake.*

C 111.2 (179 km) Turnout to north with toilets, picnic tables and litter bins.

C 113 (181.9 km) Exit south to **LAKE LOUISE** village (description follows) via Lake Louise Drive, and north to Highway 1A (Bow River Parkway) an alternate route to Castle Junction and Banff with access to Castle Mountain, Johnston Canyon and Protection Mountain Campgrounds. Access road to Moraine Lake branches off Lake Louise Drive.

LAKE LOUISE (pop. 1,500) is a popular destination resort serving summer tourists and winter skiers; food, gas, diesel, lodging, shopping and lots of traffic in the summertime. Camping at Lake Louise Campground (turn on Fairview Drive from Lake Louise Drive); 189 RV sites, 206 tent sites. **Visitor Information:** Lake Louise Visitor Centre by Samson Mall, phone 403-522-3833; www.banfflakelouise.com.

Shopping and services 0.1 mile south from the highway. *NOTE: Parking is very limited in Lake Louise, which is why there is overflow parking on the Trans Canada Highway (see Milepost C 110.8) with shuttle service to Lake Louise.*

Both the baronial Chateau Lake Louise and the much-photographed alpine lake of the same name are located 2.5 miles/4 km from Lake Louise village via Lake Louise Drive. Be aware that you cannot see the lake from the road, and it is not unusual to drive up and be turned away because there are no places to park. You may or may not find parking along the access road (all parking lots were full when we visited on a Monday afternoon in July 2018). It is especially difficult for large RVs. NOTE: The Chateau Lake Louise parking lot is for guests only. You can try parking at Moraine Lake and take a shuttle.

C 114 (183.5 km) Exit via Slate Road for Pipestone trailhead.

C 114.8 (184.7 km) **Junction** with Highway 93 North (Icefields Parkway). *Northbound travelers exit onto Icefields Parkway/Highway 93, north to Jasper (see page 82 in the CANADIAN ROCKIES ROUTE section for log).* Trans-Canada Highway 1 continues west to Vancouver, BC.

Turn to Milepost CR 336.1
Canadian Rockies Route

(Continued from page 62)
km) Exit 315 west to Highway 581 and **CARSTAIRS** (pop. 3,442); visitor services, 2 golf courses, museum with visitor information centre. Municipal Campground with showers ($1 on timer) and potable water, $22–$27 per night; $1 for sani-dump. Firewood for sale. Phone 403-990-2059 (May through October).

CB 243.8 (392.4 km) **E 145.9** (234.8 km) Exit 326 to **DIDSBURY** (pop. 4,957) on Highway 582; visitor services available. Gas/diesel at FasGas. The Didsbury Museum is housed in a 2-storey red brick and sandstone building, with bell tower, built as a school in 1907. Free internet access available at the Didsbury Memorial Complex and the Municipal Library. Camping at the municipal Rosebud Valley Campground with 33 sites, free showers, tenting and water and power hook-up sites for $15–$30 per night; open April through October. Phone 403-335-8578.

CB 245.8 (395.6 km) **E 143.9** (231.6 km) Roadside turnout southbound with litter and recycling bins.

CB 252.9 (407 km) **E 136.8** (220.2 km) Exit 340A to Highway 27 East and to the Gopher Museum in Torrington.

CB 253.1 (407.3 km) **E 136.6** (219.8 km) Exit 340B to 27 West for Olds and Sundry. **OLDS** (pop. 7,248); visitor services. O.R. Hedges Lions Campground (45 sites) across from Centennial Park. Fee is $17–$35. Located at 5013–54 St., across from Centennial Park. Open May through Oct. 15; phone 403-556-2299.

CB 257 (413.6 km) **E 132.7** (213.6 km) Gas and food 6 km/3.7 miles to the west, southbound.

CB 257.8 (414.9 km) **E 131.9** (212.2 km) Turnout northbound with litter/recycling bins.

CB 263 (423.3 km) **E 126.7** (203.9 km) Heritage rest area southbound, Pioneer Museum and golf course. FasGas station with gas and diesel.

CB 263.1 (423.5 km) **E 126.6** (203.7 km) Exit 357 to Highway 587 West to **BOWDEN** (pop. 1,241) food, gas and lodging. Red Lodge Provincial Park west on Highway 587 (15 km/9.3 miles).

Continue west on Highway 587 then head north on Range Road 14 for Eagle Creek Farms, home of the **Bowden Sunmaze**, one of Canada's few sunflower mazes. The farm also has a corn maze, 3 acres of u-pick flowers and vegetables, and a farm store featuring organic vegetables and preserves. Admission fee charged. Open daily, 11 A.M. to 5 P.M., August and September. Limited days and hours in October. Go to sunmaze.ca for more information.

CB 268.4 (431.9 km) **E 121.3** (195.2 km) Exit 365 at the southern overpass by Innisfail. Exit east and follow signs for **RCMP Police Dog Service Training Center**. The only RCMP dog-training centre in Canada, a free 45-minute demonstration is offered to the public on Wednesdays at 2 P.M. sharp between Victoria Day (May 20, 2019) and Labour Day. *(NOTE: Demonstrations take place rain or shine and are cancelled only in the event of lightning.)* For more information email pdstc-cdcp@rcmp-grc.gc.ca.

A sunflower photographed at the Bowden Sunmaze, one of Canada's few sunflower mazes.
(©Mirjam Rand)

CB 270.9 (436 km) **E 118.8** (191.2 km) Exit 368A Highway 590 East/Big Valley; Exit 368B Highway 54 West to **INNISFAIL** (pop. 7,922). **Visitor Information:** Tourist booth at junction of Highway 54 and 50th Street (5204 50th St.), phone 403-227-1177 (town office: phone 403-227-3376).

All visitor facilities: Best Western, Boston Pizza, McDonald's west off exit. Attractions in Innisfail include the Danish Gardens, multiple museums, a Historical Village and the Discovery Wildlife Park, home to some famous bears.

Camping at the Anthony Henday Campground operated by the Innisfail Lions Club (42 serviced sites, plus 5 tent sites and group area), $15–$30. Washroom/showers, playground and kitchen shelter. Phone 403-318-3508; open May–early October.

CB 273.3 (440 km) **E 116.4** (187.3 km) Turnouts both sides with litter/recycling bins. Southbound also has interpretive signs regarding Alberta history.

CB 275.5 (443.4 km) **E 114.2** (183.7 km) U-Pick farm 1.9 km/3 km west.

CB 280.7 (451.6 km) **E 109** (175.4 km) Exit 384 to 42 West; Penhold, Pine Lake, Stephansson House Historic Site at Markerville, also Red Deer Regional Airport.

CB 282.3 (454.3 km) **E 107.4** (172.8 km) Northbound-only roadside turnout and Welcome to Red Deer.

CB 283.8 (456.7 km) **E 105.9** (170.4 km) Exit 391 to "Gasoline Alley" (first exit northbound), a tourist service area with gas/diesel stations, restaurants, fast food, lodging and retail outlets.

CB 285 (458.6 km) **E 104.7** (168.5 km) Second exit northbound, first exit southbound, to Gasoline Alley (food, gas/diesel, lodging, shopping).

CB 286.2 (460.6 km) **E 103.5** (166.7 km) Exit 394 to Penhold and Highway 2A/Gaetz Avenue *(under construction in 2018, watch for detours) Highway 2/Gaetz Avenue Interchange construction began in 2017 and is slated for completion in 2019)* to Red Deer (description follows); shopping mall and all services

to east this exit. Northbound access to Red Deer Lions Campground via Gaetz Avenue to Riverside Drive. *NOTE: Northbound traffic use exit at **Milepost CB 288.5** for Red Deer Visitor Centre; southbound traffic use Exit 397.*

Red Deer

CB 287.2 (462.1 km) **E 102.5** (164.9 km) Located 1.5 hours south of Edmonton and 6 hours from the U.S. border. **Population:** 100,418. **Emergency Services:** Dial 911 for all emergency services. **Hospital:** Red Deer Regional Hospital, phone 403-343-4422.

Visitor Information: Tourism Red Deer Visitor Center, located at 101—4200 Highway 2. Open daily year-round; phone 403-346-0180; website www.visitreddeer.com.

Red Deer has all services, including major chain motels and restaurants, retail outlets and a hospital. Collicutt Leisure Centre features a wave pool, waterslide and indoor tennis. Attractions in Red Deer include Historic Fort Normandeau; Kerry Wood Nature Centre; Bower Ponds (picnicking, paddle boats); Discovery Canyon; Heritage Ranch; Alberta Sports Hall of Fame & Museum; Heritage Square, a collection of historic buildings in a park setting; and Red Deer Museum & Art Gallery. The architecture of Douglas Cardinal's St. Mary's Church may be seen at 38th Street and Mitchell Avenue. Visit the Historical Ghosts in the downtown core and throughout the parks system. Inquire locally about special events during the summer.

Camping at **RV There Yet Campground** at Exit 405B (see description at **Milepost CB 293.7**); full-service sites, big rig friendly, open year-round. Visit website: rvthereyet camping.com.

In town at Lions Municipal Campground; open May 1–Sept. 30; 138 full and semi-services sites (12 sites with 50-amp power), washrooms, showers, laundry facilities, playgrounds, horseshoe pits. Visit www. reddeerlionscampground.com.

Reynolds-Alberta Museum in Wetaskiwin offers indoor and outdoor displays on transportation, aviation, agriculture and industry. (©Brian Stein)

East Access Route Log

(continued)

CB 288.3 (464 km) **E 101.4** (163.2 km) Southbound Exit 397 32nd Street/Fort Normandeau; access to rest area, Visitor Centre, Alberta Sports Hall of Fame & Museum and Heritage Ranch (equestrian centre).

CB 288.5 (464.3 km) **E 101.2** (162.9 km) Northbound-only exit to Tourism Red Deer Visitor Centre and Sports Hall of Fame. Open year-round; restrooms, snack shop, gift shop and sports museum. A family friendly interactive experience. The adjacent park has ample parking, a playground and picnic sites. Loop road through park accesses the Heritage Ranch equestrian centre (www.heritageranch.ca). Reservations required for trail rides, carriage or sleigh rides and kayak excursions on the Red Deer River. Cafe on site is open daily. Parking for the Waskasoo Park trail system. Roadside turnouts, both sides of highway, with litter and recycling bins.

CB 289.2 (465.4 km) **E 100.5** (161.7 km) Red Deer River.

CB 292.5 (470.7 km) **E 97.2** (157 km) Exit 401 Highway 11 West to Sylvan Lake (16 km/10 miles) and exit east to 67 Street/ Red Deer. Southbound access to Red Deer Lions Campground; 67 Street to Riverside Drive exit.

Highway 11 leads west 78 km/48 miles to the town of Rocky Mountain House and to Rocky Mountain House National Historic Park. The park preserves the sites of 4 fur trading posts that operated between 1799 and 1875. Interpretive trails and demonstrations, visitor centre with exhibits. Summer hours are weekdays 9 A.M. to 6 P.M., mid-May through August; and weekends: 10 A.M. to 6 P.M. Winter hours September to mid-May weekdays 9 A.M. to 5 P.M., and weekends: 10 A.M. to 6 P.M. Rocky Mountain House Visitor Centre; www.rockymtnhouse.com; phone 403-845-5450 or 1-800-565-3793.

CB 293.5 (472.3 km) **E 96.2** (154.8 km) Exit 405A Highway 11A, east to Red Deer.

CB 293.7 (472.6 km) **E 96** (154.5 km) Exit 405B Highway 11A West, Sylvan Lake. Many visitor attractions including camping at **RV There Yet Campground** (exit west to

traffic light and turn north on RR 275 for campground).

RV There Yet Campground, Red Deer, Alberta. Big rig friendly, pull-thrus. 50 amp. 78 full-service sites. Firepits, picnic tables. Laundromat. Free hot showers. WiFi. Pets welcome. Friendly hosts on site. Golfing adjacent. Visa/MC/Debit. Jct. Hwy 2 & Hwy 11A (exit 405), west to lights, north on RR 275 3km. 403-314-9577; rvthereyetcamping.com. [ADVERTISEMENT]

CB 294.7 (474.3 km) **E 95** (152.9 km) Southbound roadside turnout with information boards and litter/recycling barrels.

CB 295.8 (476 km) **E 93.9** (151.1 km) Blindman River.

CB 296.9 (477.8 km) **E 92.8** (149.3 km) Distance marker southbound shows Red Deer 16 km/10 miles, Calgary 157 km/98 miles.

CB 297.1 (478.1 km) **E 92.6** (149 km) Exit 412 Blackfalds/597 East, Joffre. Teepee camping, water spray park.

CB 304.4 (489.9 km) **E 85.3** (137.3 km) Exit 422A Highway 12 East to **LACOMBE** (pop. 11,707); all visitor facilities, corn maze, municipal Michener Park Campground (57 sites, May 1–Oct. 31), $18–$25. Also Aspen Beach Provincial Park. www.lacombetourism.com.

CB 304.6 (490.2 km) **E 85.1** (137 km) Exit 422B Highway 12 West to Aspen Beach Provincial Park at Gull Lake (10 km/6 miles) and Bentley.

CB 308.1 (495.8 km) **E 81.6** (131.3 km) Large, double-ended, gravel turnout southbound.

CB 309.6 (498.3 km) **E 80.1** (129 km) Exit 431 Highway 2A South, 7 km/4.3 miles east to Lacombe (all visitor facilities) and Stettler.

CB 313.3 (504.2 km) **E 76.4** (123 km) Exit 437 to Highway 2A North/East to Ponoka and Wetaskiwin.

CB 314.5 (506.1 km) **E 75.2** (121 km) Distance marker southbound shows Red Deer 43 km/27 miles, Calgary 184 km/114 miles.

CB 314.7 (506.5 km) **E 75** (120.7 km)

Exit 439 to Secondary Highway 604. Wolf Creek Golf Resort 1 km/0.6 mile to east.

CB 316.7 (509.7 km) **E 73** (117.5 km) Roadside turnout southbound with litter bins and pay phone.

CB 317.6 (511.1 km) **E 72.1** (116 km) *CAUTION: Deer crossing.*

CB 319.2 (513.7 km) **E 70.5** (113.4 km) Distance marker southbound shows Red Deer 50 km/31 miles, Calgary 191 km/119 miles.

CB 320.3 (515.5 km) **E 69.4** (111.7 km) Battle River.

CB 321.4 (517.2 km) **E 68.3** (110 km) Exit 450A Highway 53 East to **PONOKA** (pop. 6,773); all visitor facilities. Ponoka Stampede Campground. Fees $20–$30 per night; phone 403-783-5611.

CB 321.8 (517.9 km) **E 67.9** (109.3 km) Exit 450B West Rimbey. Truck museum.

CB 324.9 (522.9 km) **E 64.8** (104.3 km) Turnout northbound with litter/recycling barrels.

CB 325.9 (524.5 km) **E 63.8** (102.7 km) Turnout southbound with litter/recycling bins.

CB 328.8 (529.1 km) **E 60.9** (98 km) Exit 462 Meniak Road.

CB 329 (529.5 km) **E 60.7** (97.7 km) Distance marker southbound shows Ponoka 16 km/10 miles, Red Deer 66 km/41 miles, Calgary 207 km/129 miles.

CB 329.5 (530.3 km) **E 60.2** (96.9 km) Distance marker northbound shows Leduc 55 km/34 miles, Edmonton 89 km/55 miles.

CB 330.3 (531.6 km) **E 59.4** (95.6 km) Southbound turnout with litter/recycling barrels.

CB 332.8 (535.6 km) **E 56.9** (91.6 km) Exit 469 to Highway 611 east to Maskwacis.

CB 336.8 (542 km) **E 52.9** (85.1 km) Northbound-only access to Wetaskiwin rest area; diner, picnic tables, restrooms.

CB 341.2 (549.1 km) **E 48.5** (78.1 km) Exit 482A Highway 13 East to community of **WETASKIWIN** (pop. 12,665). Wetaskiwin provides all services, major hotels, campgrounds, restaurants and 4 museums (including the world-class **Provincial Reynolds-Alberta Museum** at 6426–40th Ave., phone 780-312-2065; reynoldsalberta museum@gov.ab.ca). The city features several exciting annual events and a fascinating historic downtown walking tour with 13 turn-of-the-century buildings including the 1907 historic courthouse which serves as the modern-day City Hall. The Manluk Centre: Wetaskiwin Regional Aquatics and Fitness, offers a state-of-the-art aquatics facility with multiple pools, waterslides and a board rider. For more information www.wetaskiwin.ca or call 780-361-4417.

CB 342 (550.3 km) **E 47.7** (76.7 km) Exit 482B Highway 13 West to Wetaskiwin, Camrose and Winfield. Access to Reynolds-Alberta Museum.

CB 345 (555.2 km) **E 43.7** (70.3 km) Distance marker southbound shows Red Deer 93 km/58 miles, Calgary 234 km/145 miles.

CB 345.2 (555.5 km) **E 43.5** (70 km) Exit 488 Correction Line Road.

CB 347.6 (559.4 km) **E 41.1** (66.1 km) Roadside turnout southbound with litter bins and recycling barrels.

CB 353.3 (568.6 km) **E 36.4** (58.6 km) Northbound-only turnout to east with litter bins and recycle bins.

CB 357.5 (575.3 km) **E 32.2** (51.8 km) Distance marker southbound shows Red

Edmonton Vicinity

(map)

To Dawson Creek
633
43
To Jasper
16
Spruce Grove
16A
Parkland Drive
Range Road 14
Stony Plain
Glowing Embers RV Park & Travel Centre
60
770
779
627
627
60
To Devon
(See Devonian Way Bypass)
633
2
28
216
16
16A
Edmonton
(see map next page)
2
216
2
14
630
628
216
21
216
21
16
16
North Saskatchewan River
To Calgary

Deer 113 km/70 miles, Calgary 215 km/134 miles.

CB 357.9 (576 km) **E 31.8** (51.2 km) Exit 508 for Glen Park and Cavanaugh; Green Valley Farms, U-pick.

CB 361.1 (581.1 km) **E 28.6** (46 km) Southbound-only truck weigh station.

CB 362.4 (583.2 km) **E 27.3** (43.9 km) Exit 516 Highway 2A South/Leduc. Access to Millet, Pigeon Lake (with music festival each August) and Mullhurst. First of 3 exits northbound for Leduc.

CB 363.1 (584.4 km) **E 26.6** (42.8 km) Exit 517 to Leduc City Centre via Highway 2A and to Highway 39 West Drayton Valley. Leduc was founded and named for the Leduc oil field. The 200-million-barrel oil field was the first of a series of oil and natural gas finds that changed the economy of Alberta.

CB 364.8 (587.1 km) **E 24.9** (40.1 km) Exit 519 to **LEDUC** (pop. 27,241); access to visitor information centre with sani-dump at 6420–50 St., motels, restaurants, fast-food, gas/diesel stations and shopping on 50th Street (Highway 2A). Leduc Lions Campground (69 sites); fees are $25–$49 daily; go south on 50th Street, then 2 km/1.2 miles east on Rolly View Road. Phone 780-986-1882.

CB 365.8 (588.7 km) **E 23.9** (38.5 km) Leduc North sector exit; 24-hour gas/diesel station with truck and tourist services.

CB 366.1 (589.2 km) **E 23.6** (38 km) Exit 522 to International Airport; access to services on Highway 2A.

CB 368.3 (592.6 km) **E 21.4** (34.4 km) Exit 525 Devon Bypass/Highway 19; gas/diesel, fast-food, east off exit. Access west to Leduc No. 1 Well Historic Site.

Junction with Highway 19 west and Edmonton Bypass route. See "Devonian Way Bypass" on page 70.

NOTE: Northbound motorists wishing to avoid heavy traffic through Edmonton may exit west on Highway 19 (Devonian Way) for Devon Bypass route. Drive 11.9 km/7.4 miles west on *Highway 19, then 22.8 km/14.2 miles north through Devon via Highway 60 to junction with Yellowhead Highway 16A west of Edmonton (see* **Milepost E 4.5** *on page 71 this section for continuation of East Access Route northbound log).* You may access **Glowing Embers RV Park** (34.8 km/21.6 miles from this turnoff) via Highways 19/60.

CB 373.2 (600.6 km) **E 16.5** (26.6 km) Welcome to Edmonton northbound sign.

CB 373.5 (601.1 km) **E 16.2** (26.1 km) The former Gateway Visitors Center is now the Edmonton police service training facility. No longer a visitor centre, it still offers a sani-dump for southbound travelers (or northbound if you detour on 23rd Avenue and head south on Highway 2.

NOTE: From here north to 23rd Avenue, traffic will be controlled by signals with 2 through lanes, one left-turn lane and one through OR left turn lane.

CB 374.8 (603.1 km) **E 14.9** (24 km) Ellerslie Road exit.

CB 375.3 (604 km) **E 14.4** (23.2 km) Left lanes provide exit for Anthony Henday/Highway 216, another bypass that avoids downtown traffic but provides easy access to businesses, including West Edmonton Mall, en route to Highway 16 westbound. Other lanes continue northbound as Gateway Boulevard.

CB 376.8 (606.3 km) **E 12.9** (20.8 km) Stoplight at 19th Avenue; big box stores to east.

CB 377.4 (607.2 km) **E 12.3** (19.8 km) Exit 539 23rd Avenue; shopping mall access.

CB 378.3 (608.7 km) **E 11.4** (18.3 km) Stoplight at 34th Avenue.

CB 379.2 (610.1 km) **E 10.5** (16.9 km) **Junction** with Whitemud Drive West/Highway 2. Continue straight ahead for downtown Edmonton (description follows). *To continue with East Access Route log, northbound travelers turn left here and follow Whitemud Drive/Highway 2 west; see map.*

CB 384 (617.9 km) **E 5.7** (9.2 km) Saskatchewan River.

CB 386 (621.1 km) **E 3.7** (6 km) Exit for **West Edmonton Mall/N 170th Street** (Highway 2). See description of West Edmonton Mall in Edmonton Attractions.

CB 387.5 (623.5 km) **E 2.2** (3.5 km) Northbound travelers exit to Anthony Henday Drive North/Highway 216.

CB 389.7 (627.2 km) **E 0 Junction** with Highway 16A West (Stony Plain Road). Dawson Creek-bound travelers follow Highway 16A West. *Log continues on page 70.*

Edmonton

CB 389.7 (627 km) **E 0** Capital of Alberta, 180 miles/290 km from Calgary; 363 miles/584 km from Dawson Creek, BC; 1,853 miles/2,982 km from Fairbanks, AK. **Population:** 877,926; area 1,328,300. **Emergency Services:** Dial 911. **Hospitals:** Grey Nuns Community Hospital, 1100 Youville Dr., phone 780-735-2000; Misericordia Community Hospital, 16940–87th Ave., phone 780-735-2611; Royal Alexandra Hospital, 10240 Kingsway Ave., phone 780-735-4111; University of Alberta Hospital, 8440–112 St., phone 780-407-8822.

Visitor Information: Contact Edmonton Tourism, phone 780-401-7696 or toll-free 1-800-463-4667, or visit www.exploreedmonton.com. Edmonton Tourism operates a visitor information center downtown at the Shaw Conference Center (9797 Jasper Ave.). Be sure to pick up Edmonton city maps and a #YEGWeekend book; a traveler to traveler endorsement that combines traditional print with the digital world to highlight Edmonton's essential experiences. **Elevation:** 2,116 feet/645m. **Climate:** Average temperatures in July range between 60–72°F/16–22°C. Average high is 73°F/23°C. In January from 0 to 16°F/-18 to -9°C with an average high of 16°F/-8°C. Average annual precipitation includes 18 inches

Edmonton

Transportation

Air: Edmonton International Airport, located approximately 11 miles/17 km south of the city centre, is the fifth busiest airport in Canada. Major airlines serving Edmonton include Air Canada, Delta/Northwest Airlines, Horizon/Alaska Airlines, WestJet, United Airlines, KLM and Icelandair. Air North offers nonstop service to Whitehorse, YT. Phone 1-800-268-7134;

Bus: Red Arrow provides service to Calgary, Red Deer Lethbridge and Fort McMurray; phone 1-800-232-1958; www.redarrow.ca.

Railroad: Edmonton is on VIA Rail's Canadian route with service to Saskatoon, Winnipeg, Toronto, Jasper and Vancouver. The Edmonton terminal is located at 12360–121 St. off the Yellowhead Highway. Phone 1-888-842-7245; www.viarail.ca.

Attractions

Alberta Legislature Building: Discover Alberta's parliamentary tradition in a free guided tour which occur every hour till 4 P.M. Tours are available 362 days of the year. The West Level 1 door is open to visitors with strollers or wheelchairs. Security scans of persons and carried items is mandatory. Visitors may also enjoy self-guided grounds tours, taking a dip in the wading pools during the summer, skating on the rink in winter, or taking in one of the many special events year-round. The Alberta Legislature Building is located at 10820–98 Ave. The Legislative Assembly Visitor Centre, just north of the Legislature building is home to the Agora Interpretive Centre, Pehonan Theatre, Borealis Gallery and Alberta Branded retail store. For more information, phone 780-427-7362; www.assembly.ab.ca.

of rain and 49 inches of snow. Edmonton is located on the 53rd latitude and enjoys 17 hours of daylight in mid-summer. Edmonton is one of the sunniest cities in Canada, with 325 days of sunshine a year. **Newspaper:** *Edmonton Sun* (daily), *Edmonton Journal* (daily), *Metro Edmonton* (daily), *Edmonton Examiner* (weekly).

Private Aircraft: Edmonton International Airport 11 miles/17 km south of the Edmonton City limits. See Canadian Flight Supplement and www.flyeia.com.

Edmonton traces its roots back to 1795, beginning as a fur-trading outpost. Just over 100 years later—during the 1897 Klondike Gold Rush—prospectors boosted Edmonton's economy when they stopped for supplies en route to Yukon. Many also made Edmonton their permanent home increasing the population to 6 times its previous size.

Today the city, which sits in the geographic centre of the province, is the hub for energy development and petrochemicals for Alberta. It has become a centre of excellence in research through the University of Alberta and the high technology industries located in the region such as the National Institute of Nanotechnology.

Historic Edmonton is seen in its magnificent Alberta Legislative building and grounds, in Fort Edmonton Park, and in walking tours of Old Strathcona. Or for a glimpse of Edmonton's commercial history, visit the Neon Sign Museum, at 104 Stret and 104 Avenue, featuring 19 restored signs from Edmonton's past. Modern-day Edmonton is reflected in the scale of West Edmonton Mall, 4th Street Promenade and the

distinctive architecture throughout the city.

The North Saskatchewan River winds through the centre of Edmonton. Flanked on both banks by swaths of green, it is the focal point of a series of parks and bikeways and the largest stretch of urban parkland in North America, 22 times the size of New York's Central Park. Located along the river's parkland is Victoria Golf Course, the oldest municipal golf course in Canada, it was first developed in 1896, pre-dating the city. William Hawrelak Park in the river valley has a lake and is home to the Heritage Amphitheatre, which hosts a number of special events. Located in Louise McKinney Park, River Valley Adventure Co. offers Segway tours through the river valley year-round. It is a great way to take in the beautiful view and learn about Edmonton's natural history. Phone 1-877-433-7347.

A city filled with sports fans, Edmonton is home to the Edmonton Oilers of the National Hockey League (NHL) and Edmonton Eskimos of the Canadian Football League (CFL).

Lodging & Services

There are more than 13,000 hotel/motel/bed & breakfast rooms in Edmonton and approximately 3,500 restaurants in the region.

RV chassis, parts service and body shop are all available here.

Camping

Camping is available at **Glowing Embers RV Park & Travel Centre** (off of 16A on Highway 60/Devonian Way) and other locations near and in the city.

©Kris Valencia, staff

West Edmonton Mall. North America's largest shopping and entertainment centre. Visitors shop at over 800 stores and services and enjoy exciting attractions like Galaxyland, the world's largest indoor amusement park, and World Waterpark, home of the world's largest indoor wave pool. The mall offers dining on Bourbon Street, bowling, billiards, mini-golf, a movie theatre, dinner theatre and nightclubs. Reserve a luxury theme room at Fantasyland Hotel or stay just across the street at West Edmonton Mall Inn.

Located between 87 and 90 avenues and 170 and 178 streets, the shopping and entertainment centre is open seven days a week. Visit wem.ca. RV parking allowed in Lot 34 or at overflow lot north of 90th at 175 St.

Art Gallery of Alberta, known for its exhibits of contemporary and historical Canadian art, the AGA maintains a collection of over 6,000 objects. It is the oldest cultural institution in Alberta and the only museum in the province solely dedicated to the exhibition and preservation of art and visual culture.

The gallery underwent a major reconstruction designed by Los Angeles architect Randall Stout. The ultra-modern structure of steel and glass is 85,000 square feet and includes a gift shop and restaurant. For current hours and exhibits phone 780-422-6223; www.youraga.ca.

Fort Edmonton Park is Canada's largest living history park. Costumed staff re-create life as it was in an 1846 Hudson's Bay trading post and Cree encampment, and as it was on the streets of 1885, 1905 and 1920. Period restaurants and retail shops are located in the park. The steam train and streetcar rides are included in the admission price. Accommodations are available in the park at Hotel Selkirk.

The park opens at 10 A.M. daily, May to September. Located at Fox Drive and Whitemud Drive. For more information, phone 780-422-5311; www.fortedmontonpark.ca.

Edmonton Valley Zoo is a great destination for travelers with children, with its birds of prey demonstrations and "Let's Talk Animals" programs, pony rides and paddle boats. The zoo has more than 100 exotic, endangered and native animals. Board the mini-train for a tour through the zoo; open daily and located at 13315 Buena Vista Rd. (87 Avenue); phone 780-442-5311; www.valleyzoo.ca.

High Level Bridge Streetcar operates spring through fall. The world's highest streetcar bridge, the High Level Bridge was built in 1912. This is a great way to travel from downtown Edmonton to Old Strathcona (one of Edmonton's trendiest neighbourhoods) while taking in beautiful views of Edmonton's river valley. Fee is $5, free for children under 6 (cash only). Access to Jasper Avenue terminal is between 109 and 110 streets just south of Jasper Ave. Website: www.edmonton-radial-railway.ab.ca/high levelbridge/.

The Ice District. A mixed-use sports and entertainment area spanning 25 acres in Edmonton's downtown, around 104th Avenue and includes a 24,000 square-foot Winter Garden attached to Roger's Place and a 77,000 square-foot public plaza, easily accessible to the arts district. There are 2,000 hotel rooms, shopping and restaurants and 5 light rail transit stations within a 5-minute walk. See more details at: icedistrict.com.

Muttart Conservatory. The 4 spectacular glass pyramids of Muttart Conservatory showcase plants from the temperate, tropical and arid climates of the world. Open daily. The conservatory has a cafe, gift shop and outdoor courtyard for programs. Perfect for family picnics, walking or biking in this beautiful river valley. Located at 9626–96A Street, phone 780-442-5311; www.muttart conservatory.ca.

The Royal Alberta Museum. This museum moved to Edmonton's Downtown Art District and opened in a new 82,000 sq. ft. space in October 2018. Located at 9810–103A Ave. NW the new museum aspires to "share Alberta's remarkable stories in meaningful ways." See website for additional details and opening hours: royalalberta museum.ca.

Sir Winston Churchill Square is an entertainment destination, providing a venue for events and festivals throughout the year. Churchill Square is located in the heart of Edmonton's vibrant downtown. The Square is bound by 99 and 100 streets and 102A and 102 avenues.

Surrounding the square are several of the attractions noted below: City Hall; the Stan-

The Alberta Legislature Building offers free guided tours daily and there is a visitor center just north of the building. The complex of buildings here make a fascinating visitor stop.
(©Earl L. Brown)

ley A. Milner Library; the Francis Winspear Centre for Music, home to the Edmonton Symphony Orchestra and the Davis Concert Organ (www.winspearcentre.com); the Citadel Theatre, presenting mainstage and special live theatre series (www.citadeltheatre.com); and the Art Gallery of Alberta.

South Edmonton Common is a massive shopping and dining open-air retail development spread over 320 acres and adjacent Anthony Henday Drive. Easily accessed, look for signage. Website: www.southedmonton common.com.

The TELUS World of Science–Edmonton is the city's space and science centre, boasting the largest planetarium dome in North America, an IMAX theatre, and 5 interactive exhibit galleries. It is located at 11211–142 St. NW; phone 780-451-3344; telusworldofscienceedmonton.ca.

Special Events. Known as "Canada's Festival City," Edmonton hosts more than

Devonian Way Bypass

This 35-km/22-mile bypass route circles the southwest edge of Edmonton, connecting Highway 2 and Highway 16 via Highway 19 and Highway 60, known as the Devonian Way. There are several stops of interest along the way.

Distance from Highway 2 and Devonian Way junction (J) is shown.

DEVONIAN WAY

J 0 Junction of Highway 2 with Highway 19 (Exit 525) at **Milepost CB 368.3.** Follow Highway 19/Devonian Way west.

J 1.4 (2.3 km) Castrol Raceway to south, Amberlea Meadows equestrian facility to north.

J 4.5 (7.2 km) Rabbit Hill Ski Resort and Shalom Waterskiing Park north 7 km/4.3 miles.

J 7.4 (11.9 km) **Junction** with Highway 60 (Edmonton truck bypass). Northbound travelers turn north on Highway 60 for Devon and Yellowhead Highway and continuation of East Access Route from Edmonton (southbound travelers turn east or left on Highway 19 for Highway 2). Drive 0.8 km/0.5 mile south from this intersection to visit **Leduc #1 Energy Discovery Centre.**

The centre has museum displays tracing the development of the energy industry in Alberta. Open year-round. Admission charged. You may visit the outdoor displays of drilling rigs for free. Phone 1-866-987-4323 for hours; www.leducnumber1.com.

The Leduc Well was brought in on Feb. 13, 1947. It was the 134th try for Imperial Oil after drilling 133 dry wells, and it was wildly successful, making Edmonton the "Oil Capital of Canada." A 174-foot/53-m derrick marks the site. There is a 20-site campground with hookups and showers in front of the Discovery Centre. Open year-round. Phone 780-987-4323. [A]

J 7.5 (12.1 km) Distance marker northbound shows Devon 3 km/2 miles, Edmonton 42 km/26 miles.

J 8.1 (13 km) Turnout to east with information boards on Alberta's History and Leduc Woodbend Oilfield.

J 8.4 (13.5 km) Traffic light in downtown **DEVON** (pop. 6,647); services east side of highway include a variety of gas stations, Boston Pizza, Rexall Pharmacy and Tim Hortons. This small, active community, branded as BikeTown Alberta, boasts several circuits for the cycling enthusiast (watch for cyclists on the highway). There are accessible and extensive trail systems throughout the town and river valley with easy access to the North Saskatchewan River, including a provincial boat launch. Visitor services including accommodations, various restaurants, fast-food outlets, gas stations, tire and lube shops and grocery stores. The Devon Lions campground has 237 sites and a day-use area (Voyageur Park). The Farmers Market is Thursday afternoons in summer and fall. The community also has a splash park, an outdoor pool, an 18-hole golf course and a conference centre. [b] [A]

J 9.5 (15.3 km) Distance marker northbound shows Edmonton 38 km/24 miles.

J 10.1 (16.3 km) Bridge over North Saskatchewan River. Exit just south of bridge to Devon Voyageur Park for picnicking and boat launch area. Toilets, litter bins and picnic tables.

J 13 (20.9 km) Entrance to **University of Alberta Botanical Gardens** east side of highway; New Aga Khan Garden, Japanese garden, alpine garden, herb garden, rose garden and other special collections gardens set in natural landscape (total of 190 acres). Tours available. Indoor display house includes a butterfly house. Concession and gift shop. Open daily from 10 A.M. to 5 P.M. June to September. Fees summer 2018: adults $15.85, senior $11.75, student $8.50, reduced rates for those under 17; family rate is $31. Phone 780-987-3054; website: botanic garden.ualberta.ca.

J 14 (22.5 km) Clifford E. Lee Nature Sanctuary, 2 km/1.2 miles to west on Woodbend Road, includes 348 acres of marshland, pine forest, meadow and aspen. Enjoy bird and wildlife viewing while walking boardwalks and trails. Wheelchair accessible with advance notice: info@cliffordelee.com. Donations accepted on site.

J 15.6 (25.1 km) Distance marker southbound shows Devon 11 km/7 miles, Leduc 34 km/21 miles.

J 16.1 (25.9 km) **Junction** with Secondary Highway 627; turn east for Edmonton, west to Stony Plain.

J 16.4 (26.4 km) Distance marker northbound shows Edmonton 30 km/19 miles.

J 18.8 (30.3 km) Traffic light; gas/diesel station to west. [b]

J 19.2 (30.9 km) RCMP station to east.

J 20.2 (32.5 km) **Junction** with Secondary Highway 628/Whitemud Drive NW, which leads east to River Cree Resort Casino (6 km/3.7 miles) and junction with Highway 216 (Anthony Henday Drive).

J 21.1 (34 km) Traffic light; business park development to west.

J 21.4 (34.4 km) Turnoff to west for 1-km/0.6-mile access road to **Glowing Embers RV Park & Travel Centre** (see display ad on page 69). [A]

J 21.6 (34.8 km) **Junction** with Yellowhead Highway 16A.

**Turn to Milepost E 4.5
East Access Route**

---

60 annual music, arts and cultural festivals throughout the year, in addition to regular theatre and symphony seasons. Among the popular events scheduled for 2019 are Ice on Whyte; the Deep Freeze: A Byzantine Winter Festival (January); Flying Canoe Voilant; Silver Skate Festival (February); Pride Festival (June); International Street Performers Festival (July); A Taste of Edmonton (July); Heritage Festival (July); Folk Music Festival (August); International Fringe Theatre Festival (August); and the Dragon Boat Festival (August). For details visit exploreedmonton.com/festivals-and-events/all.

Ukrainian Cultural Heritage Village. History is brought to life at this open-air museum where costumed role-players recreate the life of early Ukrainian pioneers that settled in east central Alberta from 1892 to 1930. Step back in time to hear real stories of hardships and triumphs in Canada's oldest and one-time largest bloc settlement of Ukrainian pioneers. Explore more than 30 relocated and restored structures including a burdei (sod house), a one-room school, grain elevator, blacksmith shop and three churches of Eastern Byzantine Rite. Special events take visitors of all ages back to east central Alberta's cultural and agricultural roots. Make your experience complete with authentic Ukrainian food. Open daily from 10 A.M. to 5 P.M., May long weekend to Labour Day. Located only 25 minutes east of Edmonton along Highway 16. For more information, phone 780-662-3640 or visit website: ukrainianvillage.ca.

Elk Island National Park. Just 35 minutes east of Edmonton on Highway 16, Elk Island protects the wilderness of the aspen parkland, one of the most endangered habitats in Canada. This beautiful oasis is home to herds of plains bison, wood bison, moose, deer and elk, and more than 250 species of birds. Astotin Lake Sandy Beach Campground provides 77 tent and vehicle/RV campsites; flush toilets, free showers. There are also Equipped Campsites where tent, sleeping pads, chairs, propane stove, cooking gear and lantern are provided. Enjoy wildlife viewing, hiking, cross country skiing, picnicking or overnight camping. Phone 780-922-5790 or visit www.pc.gc.ca/eng/pn-np/ab/elkisland/visit.aspx.

East Access Route Log
(continued from page 67)
Distance from Edmonton (E) is followed by distance from Dawson Creek (DC).

YELLOWHEAD HIGHWAY 16A WEST
E 0 DC 359.6 (578.7 km) **Junction** of Anthony Henday Drive North/Highway

216 with Highway 16A West/Stony Plain Road. NOTE: *Southbound travelers may bypass Edmonton city centre by taking Highway 216 south, skirting downtown but accessing attractions like West Edmonton Mall. You will rejoin the EAST ACCESS ROUTE at* **Milepost CB 375.3***; see page 67.*

See Vicinity map on page 67 showing Highway 16A (logged) and Highway 16 (not logged) for northbound/westbound travelers.

E 4.5 (7.2 km) **DC 355.1** (571.5 km) Exit to Devon Bypass/Highway 60. Access to **Glowing Embers RV Park** this exit is 0.6 km/0.4 mile south then west on 1-km/0.6-mile access road to RV park (watch for signs).

Glowing Embers RV Park & Travel Centre. See display ad on page 69.  [A]

NOTE: *Southbound travelers may bypass Edmonton by taking Highway 60 south, then Highway 19 east to Highway 2 (Devonian Way Bypass).*

Junction with Highway 60 south to Highway 19 east and Edmonton Bypass route. See "Devonian Way Bypass" on facing page and read log back to front.

E 4.6 (7.4 km) **DC 355** (571.3 km) Distance marker westbound shows Spruce Grove 8 km/5 miles, Stony Plain 16 km/10 miles, Jasper 316 km/196 miles.

E 9.1 (14.6 km) **DC 350.5** (564.1 km) Distance marker eastbound shows Edmonton 27 km/17 miles.

E 9.4 (15.1 km) **DC 350.2** (563.6 km) Begin Spruce Grove shopping area westbound. Century Road with Save-On-Foods.

E 10 (16.1 km) **DC 349.6** (562.6 km) Stoplight at King Street. Turn north for Spruce Grove city centre. **SPRUCE GROVE** (pop. 23,326). All visitor facilities including hotels, motels, restaurants, fast-food, gas/diesel stations, shopping malls and all emergency services. [b]

E 10.5 (16.9 km) **DC 349.1** (561.8 km) Golden Spike Road. Go south on Golden Spike Road to access the **Spruce Grove Grain Elevator and District Archives**. The Spruce Grove Grain Elevator Museum, one of Alberta's last remaining wooden grain elevators and still in working condition, was built in 1958. Elevator is visible from Highway 16A/Parkland Highway. Open Tuesday–Friday 9:30 A.M. to 3 P.M. and Saturday 9:30 A.M. to 1:30 P.M. from May to September; admission is free but donations are appreciated. Located at 120 Railway Ave., phone 780-960-4600; go to website: sprucegroveagsociety.com for event listings throughout the summer months.

E 11.1 (17.9 km) **DC 348.5** (560.9 km) Distance marker westbound shows Stony Plain 6 km/4 miles, Edson 178 km/111 miles, Jasper 338 km/210 miles.

E 11.6 (18.7 km) **DC 348** (560.1 km) Stoplight at Campsite Road intersection; shopping malls. Welcome to Spruce Grove sign for eastbound motorists. Turn south to access the Spruce Grove visitor centre and Rotary Centennial Park with picnic tables and toilets. Chamber of Commerce tourist information building at northwest edge of Rotary Park on Highway 16A, open year-round, weekends only; phone 780-962-2561.

E 12.7 (20.4 km) **DC 346.3** (557.3 km) Entering Stony Plain westbound.

E 13.3 (21.4 km) **DC 346.3** (557.3 km) Traffic light at South Park Drive; access to Stony Plain shopping mall and all services (major chain motel, fast-food outlets, supermarket, etc.). [b]

E 13.5 (21.7 km) **DC 346.1** (557 km) Distance marker eastbound shows Spruce Grove 5 km/3 miles, Edmonton 33 km/21 miles.

E 14.1 (22.7 km) **DC 345.5** (556 km) Exit to Secondary Road 779 for downtown **STONY PLAIN** (pop. 15,051). **Emergency Services:** Dial 911.

Visitor Information: Follow signs to Visitor Center at Rotary Park, 4815–44th Ave. Open weekdays in June, daily in July and August, from 8:30 A.M. to 5:30 P.M.; open weekends only in September; phone 780-963-4545. Camping at Camp n' Class RV Park 4107 50 St., Stony Plain, phone 780-963-2299. [b] [A]

Attractions in Stony Plain include 41 historic outdoor murals; 8 public art sculptures; summer festivals; Crooked Pot Gallery and Potters' Guild; Multicultural Heritage Centre; and the Stony Plain and Parkland Pioneer Museum. The Museums have seasonal hours; they are open 7 days a week through the summer. Admission is by donation for both museums. The Pioneer Museum has a historic outdoor village, an antique lamp collection, antique machinery and Legacy Street–an indoor, interactive 1930s streetscape of a small Alberta town. The Tea House on the grounds is open May to September on Fridays and Saturdays from 11 A.M. to 3 P.M. The Multicultural Heritage Centre here has a curated Public Art Gallery, historical archives, the history of Stony Plain, mural tours, two historic buildings of which one is on the list of "10 most haunted buildings in Alberta."

Established summer festivals include Summer Sessions, The Blueberry Bluegrass Festival, Stony Plain Cowboy Gathering and Farmer's Days.

E 14.6 (23.5 km) **DC 345** (555.2 km) Eastbound-only exit to service road alongside highway which accesses a car dealership, then turn right for Pioneer Museum (follow signs).

E 15.7 (25.3 km) **DC 343.9** (553.5 km) Welcome to Stony Plain eastbound sign.

E 16.6 (26.7 km) **DC 343** (552 km) Allan Beach Resort turnoff to north.

E 17.3 (27.8 km) **DC 342.3** (550.9 km) Turnoff for Hasse Lake Parkland County day-use area (10 km/6.2 miles south).

Distance marker eastbound shows Stony Plain 6 km/4 miles, Edmonton 40 km/25 miles.

E 17.8 (28.6 km) **DC 341.8** (550.1 km) Turnoff for Hubbles Lake (signed), 2 km/1.2 miles north; camping. [A]

E 19 (30.5 km) **DC 340.6** (548.1 km) Beach Corner. Esso gas station with diesel, auto repair, propane, cafe, store and liquor to north. Spring Lake to south with campground. [b] [A]

E 20.4 (32.8 km) **DC 339.2** (545.9 km) Distance marker eastbound shows Stony Plain 12 km/8 miles, Spruce Grove 17 km/11 miles Edmonton 46 km/29 miles.

E 20.6 (33.2 km) **DC 339** (545.6 km) Exit 344.

E 22.6 (36.4 km) **DC 337** (542.3 km) Distance marker eastbound shows Stony Plain 16 km/10 miles, Edmonton 50 km/31 miles.

E 23.2 (37.3 km) **DC 336.4** (541.4 km) Exit 340 for Mackenzie Highway and Alaska Highway. Grande Prairie and Whitecourt, Alberta Beach and Onoway.

Junction of Yellowhead Highway 16A with Highway 43 North. If you are continuing west for Prince George or Prince Rupert, BC, turn to **Milepost E 23.2** on page 246 the YELLOWHEAD HIGHWAY section for log of that route.

Northbound travelers turn onto Highway 43 and continue with this log for Dawson Creek, BC.

Southbound travelers take Exit 344, Highway 16A East for Edmonton and read log back to front (see map on page 67).

ALBERTA HIGHWAY 43

E 23.4 (37.7 km) **DC 336.2** (541.1 km)

The Leduc #1 Energy Discovery Center on the Devonian Way Bypass route offers outdoor exhibits that tell a fascinating story of resource development in Alberta. (©Brian Stein)

Water parks are popular along this route. This is Rotary Park in Whitecourt.
(©Earl L. Brown)

Turnout to east for northbound traffic; litter/recycling barrel and historical information sign about construction of the Alaska Highway and Alberta Beach.

E 23.7 (38.1 km) **DC 335.9** (540.6 km) Distance marker westbound shows Onoway 14 km/9 miles, Whitecourt 127 km/79 miles, Valleyview 298 km/185 miles, Grande Prairie 408 km/253 miles, Peace River 440 km/273 miles.

E 24.6 (39.6 km) **DC 335** (539.1 km) FasGas gas station to east with snack shop.

E 25 (40.2 km) **DC 334.6** (538.5 km) Welcome to Lac St. Anne County. This twinned 4-lane highway northbound is in excellent condition.

E 28.8 (46.3 km) **DC 330.8** (532.4 km) Highway 633 west 6 miles/10 km to Alberta Beach Recreation Area on Lac Ste. Anne. Facilities include a municipal campground (94 sites), open May to September.

E 29 (46.7 km) **DC 330.6** (532 km) Distance marker northbound shows Onoway 5 km/3 miles, Barhead 60 km/37 miles, Whitecourt 117 km/73 miles, Grande Prairie 398 km/247 miles.

Distance marker southbound shows Stony Plain 33 km/21 miles, Spruce Grove 38 km/24 miles, Edmonton 66 km/41 miles.

E 31.8 (51.2 km) **DC 327.8** (527.5 km) Access to **ONOWAY** (pop. 1,039) has a medical clinic, ambulance, dentist, chiropractor and veterinary clinic. Other visitor services include 2 gas/diesel with propane stations, banks and ATM machines, post office, library, grocery store, liquor store, laundromat, pharmacy, restaurants, motel, hotel, churches and car wash. The Onoway Museum is the "Old Brick School" and houses the tourist information booth. There are 15 golf courses within a 10-minute drive of Onoway. Many local lakes provide fishing, boating, canoeing, swimming and sailing. Onoway is served by Highways 43 and 37 East and by the Yellowhead Highway 16.

Sani-dump station is at the west entrance of town coming off of Highway 43 and camping is nearby at the Ruth Cust Park. Also find camping at Imrie Park 4.3 miles/7 km east of Onoway. Go fishing at **Salter Lake** 2 km/1.2 miles south of Onoway.

End improved pavement northbound, begin improved pavement southbound next 7 miles/11 km.

E 31.9 (51.3 km) **DC 327.7** (527.4 km) Distance marker northbound shows Sangudo 44 km/27 miles, Whitecourt 99 km/62 miles, Grande Prairie 383 km/238 miles.

E 33.8 (54.4 km) **DC 325.8** (524.3 km) **Junction** with Highway 37 East to Fort Saskatchewan (70 km/43 miles).

E 34 (54.7 km) **DC 325.6** (524 km) Distance marker northbound shows Gunn 7 km/4 miles, Whitecourt 105 km/65 miles.

E 34.6 (55.7 km) **DC 325** (523 km) Sturgeon River.

E 36.8 (59.2 km) **DC 322.8** (519.5 km) Distance marker southbound shows Onoway 11 km/7 miles, Edmonton 73 km/45 miles.

E 36.9 (59.4 km) **DC 322.7** (519.3 km) Distance marker northbound shows Mayerthorpe 61 km/38 miles.

E 37.7 (60.7 km) **DC 321.9** (518 km) **Junction** with Highway 33 (Grizzly Trail) north to Barrhead. Continue on Highway 43 westbound for Dawson Creek.

GUNN to south, convenience store, gas/diesel and restaurant.

E 38.3 (61.6 km) **DC 321.3** (517.1 km) Esso gas station to south. Also access to Gunn 1 km/0.6 mile, Alberta Beach 6 km/3.7 miles to the south. **Lac Ste. Anne** to south; fishing.

E 49.8 (80.1 km) **DC 309.8** (498.6 km) Exit to Highway 765 South to Darwell (26 km/16 miles) and Highway 16.

E 50 (80.5 km) **DC 309.6** (498.3 km) Distance marker northbound shows Whitecourt 81 km/50 miles, Grande Prairie 364 km/226 miles.

E 50.9 (81.9 km) **DC 308.7** (496.8 km) **Lessard Lake** Campground (50 sites); 3 km/1.9 miles south on RR 51. Open mid-

May–Sept. Fees are $27.50–$33; phone 780-284-3643; water, showers, playground, boat launch, fishing for pike and perch.

E 53.2 (85.6 km) **DC 306.4** (493.1 km) **Junction** with Highway 764 and access to Cherhill to south; food, gas, lodging.

E 60.3 (97 km) **DC 299.3** (481.7 km) Lisburn rest area to north for westbound traffic; handicap accessible toilets, litter/recycling bins.

E 63.8 (102.7 km) **DC 295.8** (476 km) Distance marker southbound shows Cherhill 17 km/11 miles, Gunn 43 km/27 miles, Edmonton 117 km/73 miles.

E 63.9 (102.8 km) **DC 295.7** (475.9 km) **Junction** with Secondary Highway 757 South and access to **SANGUDO** (pop. 398), located south of Highway 43 on the Pembina River. Sangudo is the seat of Lac Ste. Anne County and has a one-of-a-kind Grain Elevator Sundial landmark. Peppered with Heritage signage, it offers visitors glimpses into its rich past. Groomed walking trails provide picturesque, riverside strolls and throughout the community. For more information go to sangudo.net.

Visitor services include restaurants, banks, pharmacy, post office, gas/diesel stations, lodging, laundromat, car wash and liquor stores. Sangudo Riverside Campground is located on the Pembina River, adjacent a stock car race track, ball diamonds and a playground/skateboard park. The park has power hookups, showers, firewood, horseshoe pits and a dump station.

E 64.3 (103.5 km) **DC 295.3** (475.2 km) Pembina River bridge.

E 64.4 (103.6 km) **DC 295.2** (475.1 km) **Junction** with Secondary Highway 757 North.

E 66.4 (106.9 km) **DC 293.2** (471.9 km) Distance marker northbound shows Valleyview 226 km/140 miles, Grande Prairie 338 km/210 miles, Peace River 369 km/229 miles.

E 69.7 (112.2 km) **DC 289.9** (466.5 km) Second longest wooden railway trestle in the world crosses highway and Paddle River. The **C.N.R. Rochfort Bridge trestle** is 2,414 feet/736m long and was originally built in 1914.

E 70.7 (113.8 km) **DC 288.9** (464.9 km) **ROCHFORT BRIDGE.** Highway rest area at Rochfort Bridge Trading Post; gift shop, restaurant, phone, camping, museum.

E 70.9 (114.1 km) **DC 288.7** (464.6 km) Distance marker northbound shows Mayerthorpe 8 km/5 miles, Whitecourt 53 km/33 miles, Grande Prairie 333 km/207 miles.

E 73.3 (118.6 km) **DC 285.9** (460.1 km) Mayerthorpe rest area to south for eastbound traffic; toilets, litter/recycling bins.

E 75.3 (121.2 km) **DC 284.3** (457.5 km) **Junction** with Highway 22 North and access to **MAYERTHORPE** (pop. 1,398). **Emergency Services:** Dial 911. **Visitor Information:** Tourist Information Booth located at the **Fallen Four Memorial Park.** Virtual tours of the town at www.mayerthorpe.ca. There are 2 hotels/motels, 6 restaurants, grocery stores, 3 gas stations, vehicle repair, laundromat, car wash, 2 liquor stores and 2 banks. Services are located on 50th Street, the main entrance to town off of Highway 43. Camping is available south of town at the golf course.

Mayerthorpe is primarily a service centre for the surrounding agricultural district. Area farms raise everything from wild game (elk, buffalo, emu, wild boar) to cattle, pigs and sheep. Major lumber mills are located west of town. Oil and gas exploration is booming right now.

Summer recreation includes swimming at the outdoor pool, canoeing on the Pembina and McLeod rivers, golfing at the 9-hole golf course, fishing and camping. Big game hunting is popular in the fall.

Curling, hockey, snowmobiling, downhill skiing, cross-country skiing and ice fishing are the major winter sports here.

E 75.5 (121.5 km) DC 284.1 (457.2 km) Distance marker northbound shows Whitecourt 45 km/28 miles, Grande Prairie 325 km/202 miles, Peace River 335 km/208 miles, Blue Ridge 23 km/14 miles.

E 81.3 (130.8 km) DC 278.3 (447.9 km) Junction with Highway 18 East to Greencourt and Barrhead (59 km/37 miles).

Distance marker northbound shows Whitecourt 34 km/21 miles, Valleyview 204 km/127 miles, Grande Prairie 314 km/195 miles.

E 87.8 (141.3 km) DC 271.8 (437.4 km) Junction with Highway 658 North to Blue Ridge Recreation Area 13 km/8 miles; Blue Ridge Esso gas/diesel, liquor store and convenience store.

E 88.5 (142.4 km) DC 271.1 (436.3 km) Distance marker northbound shows Whitecourt 21 km/13 miles, Valleyview 194 km/121 miles, Grande Prairie 306 km/190 miles.

E 89 (143.2 km) DC 270.6 (435.5 km) Junction with Highway 751 South to Nojack on Highway 16 (61 km/38 miles).

E 89.6 (144.2 km) DC 270 (434.5 km) Distance marker northbound shows Whitecourt 19 km/12 miles, Valleyview 192 km/119 miles, Grande Prairie 304 km/189 miles.

E 99.4 (160 km) DC 260.2 (418.8 km) Distance marker northbound shows Fox Creek 89 km/55 miles, Peace River 312 km/194 miles.

E 99.9 (160.8 km) DC 259.7 (417.9 km) Roadside turnout (northbound-only) with litter bin and information boards about Whitecourt with a city map.

E 100.4 (161.6 km) DC 259.2 (417.1 km) Whitecourt & District Forest Interpretive Centre & Visitor Centre. (View description of this facility and contact information at **Milepost E 101.4**).

Access to **Whitecourt Lions Campground** (mid-April to mid-October); 72 sites, camping fee, flush toilets, showers, water, tables, free sani-dump station, firewood and firepits.

Whitecourt Lions Campground. See display ad this page.

Begin speed zone northbound through Whitecourt.

Whitecourt

E 101.4 (163.2 km) DC 258.2 (415.5 km) Located two hours from Edmonton. **Population:** 10,574. **Emergency Services:** Dial 911. **Police,** phone 780-778-5454. **Fire Department**, **phone** 780-778-2342. **Hospital:** Whitecourt Healthcare Centre at Sunset Boulevard, phone 780-778-2285. **Ambulance Service:** 780-778-4257.

Visitor Information: Tourist information in the **Forest Interpretive Center** at the east end of town just off Highway 43, across from Lion's Campground. Stop by and visit the 7,300-sq.-ft. facility with museum, the outdoor displays of equipment, the Interpretive Trail or pick up some helpful brochures on the area. Open daily in summer, weekdays in winter; ample parking for large RVs and bus tours. Sani-dump station. Phone 780-778-3433; toll-free 1-800-313-7383; www.whitecourtwoodlandtourism.com.

Elevation: 2,567 feet/782m. **Radio:** 96.7 CFXW-FM, 105.3 CIXM-FM. **Television:** 57 channels. **Newspaper:** *Whitecourt Star.*

Private Aircraft: Airport 3.1 miles/5 km west of Whitecourt; elev. 2,567 feet/782m; length 5,800 feet/1,768m; paved; fuel 80, 100, jet (24-hour, self-serve). Aircraft maintenance, 24-hour flight service station, all-weather facility.

Transportation: Air—Local charter air service available; helicopter and fixed-wing aircraft. **Bus**—Red Arrow provides daily service to Edmonton with stops at Mayerthorpe, Fox Creek, Valleyview and Grande Prairie; phone 1-800-232-1958; www.redarrow.ca.

Located at the junction of Highways 43 and 32, Whitecourt dubs itself the "Gateway to the Alaska Highway and the fabulous North." It is also known as the Snowmobile Capital of Alberta, with the Whitecourt Trailblazers Snowmobile Club grooming hundreds of miles of trails each winter. Established as a small trading, trapping and forestry centre, Whitecourt became an important stop for Alaska Highway travelers when a 106-mile section of Highway 43 connecting Whitecourt and Valleyview was completed in October 1955. This new route was 72 miles shorter than the old Edmonton to Dawson Creek route via Slave Lake.

There are 16 hotels/motels, 39 restaurants and fast-food outlets (Taco Time, Boston Pizza, McDonald's, etc.), 14 gas stations, 3 laundromats, 5 malls, 6 liquor stores and 5 banks. Most services are located on the highway or 2 blocks north in the downtown business district. There are 5 gas stations open 24 hours. Camping in town at **Whitecourt Lions Campground,** open mid-April to mid-October; pull-through sites, 30- and 50-amp hookups; phone 780-778-6782; www.whitecourtlionscampground. com. Carson Pegasus Provincial Park is at **Milepost E 108.2**. Dump stations at the Husky, behind the car wash; across from the Dairy Queen at Canadian Tire and at the Forest Interpretive Centre outside of town. This full-service community also supports a library, 11 churches, service clubs and community organizations (visitors welcome).

The Allan & Jean Millar Centre is an aquatic centre and fitness centre with indoor fieldhouse and track. Enjoy a respite from the summer heat with a stop at **Rotary Park**, which features a covered pavilion with picnic tables, and a popular man-made creek with a series of pools and drops that makes for excellent tubing. Stocked fishing pond here is cleared for skating in winter.

Other attractions include Eagle River Casino and an 18-hole public golf course.

Recreation includes fishing in area creeks, rivers and lakes (boat rentals at Carson–Pegasus Provincial Park). Swimming, tubing down McLeod River, in-line skating, tennis, walking trails, and river boating are also enjoyed in summer. In the fall, big game hunting is very popular.

Winter activities include ice fishing, snowmobiling and cross-country skiing on area trails, skating and curling, bowling and swimming at the indoor pool.

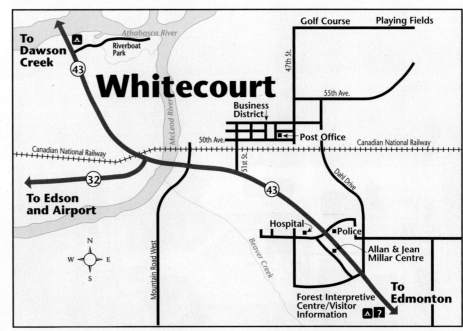

The MILEPOST® camper stops at Fox Creek's visitor information centre along Highway 43.
(©Claire Torgerson, staff)

East Access Route Log

(continued)

E 101.4 (163.2 km) DC 258.2 (415.5 km) Whitecourt Golf and Country Club and town centre to north.

E 102.6 (165.1 km) DC 257 (413.6 km) 51st Avenue North to Rotary Park.

E 103 (165.8 km) DC 256.6 (413 km) McLeod River.

E 103.3 (166.2 km) DC 256.3 (412.5 km) **Junction** with Highway 32 South (paved). Highway 32 leads 68 km/42 miles to junction with Yellowhead Highway 16 at **Milepost E 96.9** (see the YELLOWHEAD HIGHWAY section).

E 103.8 (167 km) DC 255.8 (411.7 km) Esso and Petro-Canada stations with gas/diesel, Days Inn, Tim Hortons, Subway.

E 103.9 (167.2 km) DC 255.7 (411.5 km) Turnoff to north for Sagitawah RV Park. It has 112 campsites, groceries, concession, showers and flush toilets, for $28–$35 per night; phone 780-778-3734. Riverboat Park nearby (picnicking, fishing, boat launch), both at the confluence of the **McLeod** and **Athabasca** rivers.

E 104.1 (167.5 km) DC 255.5 (411.2 km) Distance marker northbound shows Fox Creek 71 km/44 miles, Valleyview 161 km/100 miles, Grande Prairie 273 km/170, Peace River 304 km/189 miles.

E 104.3 (167.9 km) DC 255.3 (410.9 km) Athabasca River bridge.

E 106.5 (171.4 km) DC 253.1 (407.3 km) Vehicle inspection station between north- and southbound lanes, accessible to all traffic.

E 108.2 (174.1 km) DC 251.4 (404.6 km) **Junction** with Highway 32 North for Husky gas/diesel station and casino, and Eric S. Huestis Demonstration Forest, provincial parks and fishing lakes (descriptions follow). The demonstration forest has 7 km/4.3 miles of self-guided trails with information signs describing forest management and forest life-cycle.

Carson–Pegasus Provincial Park, 9.3

miles/15 km north, has 181 campsites, electrical hookups, tables, flush toilets, showers, water, dump station, firewood and playground. Boat launch, boat rentals and rainbow trout fishing are available. There are 2 lakes at the park: **McLeod (Carson) Lake**, stocked with rainbow trout and has a speed limit of 12 kmph for boaters; and **Little McLeod (Pegasus) Lake**, with northern pike and whitefish, designated electric motors and canoes only.

E 108.4 (174.5 km) DC 251.2 (404.3 km) Distance marker northbound shows Fox Creek 74 km/46 miles, Valleyview 163 km/101 miles.

E 108.7 (174.9 km) DC 250.9 (403.8 km) Alberta Newsprint Co. to south.

E 113.4 (182.5 km) DC 246.2 (396.2 km) Rest area to south for eastbound traffic; litter/recycling bins, toilets.

E 115.8 (186.4 km) DC 243.8 (392.4 km) Chickadee Creek.

E 128.2 (206.3 km) DC 231.4 (372.4 km) Rest area to north for westbound traffic; toilets and litter/recycling bins.

E 130.6 (210.2 km) DC 229 (368.5 km) Rainbow Creek.

E 132 (212.4 km) DC 227.6 (366.3 km) Improved road surface northbound for next 8 km/5 miles.

E 132.7 (213.6 km) DC 226.9 (365.2 km) Two Creeks. Improved road surface northbound for next 13 km/8 miles.

Distance marker eastbound shows Fox Creek 32 km/20 miles.

E 135.7 (218.4 km) DC 223.9 (360.3 km) Turnout to north for westbound traffic; litter/recycling bins.

E 136.5 (219.7 km) DC 223.1 (359 km) Two Creeks rest area to south for eastbound traffic; toilets, litter/recycling bins.

E 143.6 (231.1 km) DC 216 (347.6 km) Iosegun River bridge.

E 144.4 (232.4 km) DC 215.2 (346.3 km) Distance marker southbound shows Whitecourt 65 km/40 miles.

E 144.6 (232.7 km) DC 215 (346 km) **Junction** with Highway 947 South to Atha-

basca River (19 km/12 miles) and Forestry Road to Highway 16.

Distance marker northbound shows Fox Creek 16 km/10 miles.

E 146.4 (235.6 km) DC 213.2 (343.1 km) Westbound turnout litter/recycling bin.

E 151.9 (244.5 km) DC 207.7 (334.3 km) Fox Creek airport.

E 152 (244.6 km) DC 207.6 (334.1 km) Welcome to Fox Creek, northbound.

Fox Creek

E 153.6 (247.2 km) DC 206 (331.5 km) There are 2 highway exits north to Fox Creek, although travelers will find all services (gas, food, lodging, etc.) along Highway 43 as it passes through town. **Population**: 1,969. **Elevation**: 2,278 feet/853m. **Emergency Services**: Dial 911. RCMP, phone 780-622-3740. **Fire Department**, 780-622-3757. **Ambulance**, phone 780-622-5212. **Hospital**, phone 780-622-3545.

Visitor Information: The Visitor Information Center (VIC) is at the north end of town behind Winks Store and Gas Station; open 10 A.M. to 6 P.M., closed Tuesdays and Wednesdays, from late May (Victoria Day weekend) to Labour Day in September; phone 780-622-2000 or 780-622-2670. The centre is conveniently located on Don Nicolson Walking Trail for stretching legs and walking your dog and has a playground and covered picnic area. Fox Creek Nordic and Trail system, located behind the VIC, offers a bike park for practice and over 4 km of multi-use, year-round trails for biking, running, walking, snowshoeing and cross-country skiing. Fox Creek Museum, across from the VIC, features displays on area wildlife, industry and pioneer history. The museum is open in the summer and by appointment (780-622-3896 for information).

Fox Creek, a centre of oil and gas exploration and production, has all visitor facilities, including more than 330 rooms in hotels/motels, and B&Bs. Multiple gas stations with repair service. Grocery store, convenience stores, pharmacy, laundromats, liquor stores, restaurants and banks. Fox Creek has a library, ice arena, Lions Park/Splash Park, a world-class playground at Marnevic Memorial Park with a bike park adjacent. There is also a 9-hole golf course (Silver Birch Golf Club).

Camping at the Fox Creek RV Municipal Campground, located behind the tourist information centre.

Fox Creek is also a popular outdoor recreation area. Two nearby local lakes with campgrounds are popular with residents and visitors: **Iosegun Lake Provincial Park** (with 52 unserviced campsites; $25/night) and **Smoke Lake Provincial Lake** (with 47 unserviced campsites; $25/night). Smoke Lake is located 9 km/5.6 miles south of Highway 43 via good gravel roads.

East Access Route Log

(continued)

E 164.7 (265.1 km) DC 194.9 (313.7 km) *CAUTION: Moose crossing northbound next 16 km/10 miles.*

E 170.6 (274.6 km) DC 189 (304.2 km) Double-ended turnout to north is a rest area for westbound traffic; toilets, litter/recycling bins. *Improved highway surface (summer 2018) next 4 km/2.5 miles northbound.*

E 171.1 (275.4 km) **DC 188.5** (303.4 km) Double-ended turnout to south is a rest area for eastbound traffic; toilets, litter/recycling bins.

E 177.5 (285.7 km) **DC 182.1** (293.1 km) Private campground.

E 182.8 (294.2 km) **DC 176.8** (284.5 km) Distance marker southbound shows Fox Creek 47 km/29 miles, Whitecourt 129 km/80 miles, Edmonton 308 km/191 miles.

E 182.9 (294.3 km) **DC 176.7** (284.4 km) Westbound traffic must cross divided highway to reach **LITTLE SMOKY** (pop. 34). Turnoff to north on Range Road 215A for **Waskahigan River Provincial Recreation Area** (0.5 km); campground (20 sites, self-register, $20 per night), toilets, water pump (boil or bring own drinking water), fishing, tables, firepits, firewood and day-use shelter. Open mid-May–mid September.

E 183.2 (294.8 km) **DC 176.4** (283.9 km) Little Smoky River bridge.

E 183.5 (295.3 km) **DC 176.1** (283.4 km) Distance marker northbound shows Valleyview 41 km/26 miles, Grande Prairie 153 km/95 miles, Peace River 180 km/112 miles.

E 184.4 (296.8 km) **DC 175.2** (282 km) Waskahigan (House) River bridge at confluence with Smoky River.

E 193 (310.6 km) **DC 166.6** (268.1 km) Asplund Creek.

E 198.4 (319.3 km) **DC 161.2** (259.4 km) Westbound double-ended turnout to north with litter bins.

E 200.7 (323 km) **DC 158.9** (255.7 km) Tom's Creek. Adjacent oil transfer station.

E 203 (326.7 km) **DC 156.6** (252 km) **Junction** with Highway 665 West to Newalta and East to Highway 747 (24 km/15 miles).

E 203.2 (327.0 km) **DC 156.4** (251.7 km) Valleyview Riverside golf course and Potters Hand Campground with full-service sites. Open year-round; 780-524-8790.

Distance marker northbound shows Valleyview 6 km/4 miles, Grande Prairie 118 km/73 miles, Peace River 148 km/92 miles.

E 205.6 (330.9 km) **DC 154** (247.8 km) Provincial rest area and Valleyview Visitor Information Center has Alaska and Canada-wide travel information; souvenir gift shop with a good selection of books, including regional, Northern and local authors; picnic tables, potable water, free WiFi, handicap accessible flush toilets and sani-dump station. Plenty of parking and turnaround areas as well as a grassy picnic area.

The visitor center is open 10 A.M. to 6 P.M. from May 1 to October. Restrooms are open 24/7. A commemorative cairn is located at the far end of the turnaround and signifies the original Northwest Territories border.

Turn west for Valleyview airport. **Private Aircraft:** Valleyview airport; elev. 2,434 feet/742m; length, 3,300 feet/1,006m; paved; fuel. Unattended.

Valleyview

E 207.6 (334.1 km) **DC 152** (244.6 km) Approximately 3-hour drive time from Edmonton. **Population:** 1,972. **Emergency Services:** Dial 911. **RCMP,** phone 780-524-3345. **Hospital,** Valleyview General, phone 780-524-3356. **Visitor Information:**

Fields of yellow canola brighten even overcast (or smoky) days along Highway 43.
(©Kris Valencia, staff)

The Valleyview Visitor Information Center and rest stop is located southeast of Valleyview on Highway 43 at **Milepost 205.6.** It is open daily 10 A.M. to 6 P.M. from May to October; phone 780-524-2410; vic@valleyview.ca or in the off-season contact the Town Office at website: valleyview.govoffice.com; phone 780-524-5150 for information. The visitor center sells books, maps, postcards, souvenirs, snacks and refreshments. They facilitate bookings for campgrounds, hotels and transportation and provide information on Alberta, BC, Yukon and Alaska. Free WiFi and 24/7 restrooms.

Elevation: 2,247 feet/685m. **Newspaper:** *Town and Country Newspaper* (bi-weekly). **Transportation: Air**—Airport 0.7 mile/1.1 km south. **Bus**—Red Arrow provides daily service to Edmonton with stops at Mayerthorpe, Whitecourt, Fox Creek and Grande Prairie; phone 1-800-232-1958; www.redarrow.ca. **Taxi**—A2B.

Valleyview, known as the "Portal to the Peace Country" of northwestern Alberta, is located at the junction of Highways 43 and 49. From Valleyview, Highway 43 continues west to Grande Prairie and Dawson Creek. Highway 49 leads north to connect with Highway 2 east to Athabasca and north to Peace River. From Peace River, travelers may follow the Mackenzie Highway 35 to Northwest Territories (see the DEH CHO ROUTE section for details).

Originally called Red Willow when it was homesteaded in 1916, Valleyview boomed with the discovery of oil and gas in the 1950s, and services grew along with the population. Today, Valleyview's economy has diversified to include the oil and gas industry, tourism, agriculture and government services. Farming consists mainly of grain, canola, beef cattle, honey and forage production.

The community has a full range of services including banks, automatic teller machines, post office, several churches and a Public Library with internet access (open Tuesday–Saturday). The library's Art Gallery has a terrific display of more than 900 historical photos. There is a Farmers Market every Thursday in summer from 11 A.M. to 4 P.M.; located at the Memorial Hall.

All visitor facilities available, including motels, hotels, several restaurants, bowling alley, laundromat, grocery, liquor stores, clothing store and hardware stores, gift shops, spas, 2 gyms, live theatre and 2 golf courses. Valleyview municipal campground at north end of town (end of 50th Street) with pull-through sites, nightly fee of $30 power and water. Gas/diesel stations (many with major repair service, propane and 24-hour service) including the Shell station with fast food and groceries.

The area boasts many lakes and streams, abundant wildlife, and lush vegetation. Summer travelers can take advantage of the long summer days here by attending local rodeos, fairs and festivals; playing a round of golf on one of the local golf courses; visiting one of the provincial parks along Sturgeon Lake; cooling off in the outdoor swimming pool or splash park in town; or exploring the wilderness by all-terrain vehicle, horse, canoe or hiking trail.

East Access Route Log
(continued)

E 207.6 (334.1 km) **DC 152** (244.6 km) **Junction.** Highways 49/2 leads north 88 miles/142 km to the scenic community of **Peace River** and to the Mackenzie Highway 35 (13 miles/21 km west of Peace River) to Northwest Territories.

> **Junction** with Highways 49/2 north to Peace River and the Mackenzie Highway 35 to Northwest Territories. Turn to the DEH CHO ROUTE for log.

A **side trip** loop north to Peace River then south from Grimshaw to Grande Prairie via Highways 49 and 2, gives travelers a chance to take in Peace River and stop at historic Dunvegan. This side trip is 212 miles/341 km in length. Follow the logs in the DEH CHO ROUTE section. Continue west on Highway 43 for Dawson Creek.

E 208 (334.7 km) **DC 151.6** (244 km) RCMP station to east.

E 213 (342.8 km) **DC 146.6** (235.9 km) Woodpecker Creek.

Grande Prairie Visitor Center is a must stop for travelers, offering a helpful staff, brochures and maps, and museum displays. (©Earl L. Brown)

E 217 (349.2 km) **DC 142.6** (229.5 km) Calais Country Store; post office, fireworks, gas/diesel and grocery store. South access to Sturgeon Lake.

E 217.5 (350.0 km) **DC 142.1** (228.7 km) Goose Creek.

E 218.9 (352.3 km) **DC 140.7** (226.4 km) Pelican Creek.

©Kris Valencia, staff

E 219.2 (352.8 km) **DC 140.4** (226 km) Turnoff to **Sturgeon Lake** (fishing and camping) and to golf course. **Williamson Provincial Park** (pictured above) is 2 km/1.2 miles north; 67 campsites (31 with electrical hookups), boat launch, sani-dump station, day-use area. Fishing for perch, pickerel, northern pike, whitefish. Fees $27–$34; open mid-May through September.

E 222.4 (357.9 km) **DC 137.2** (220.8 km) Greenview Golf Resort; golfing, dining. Camping at Cozy Cove Campground, sani-dump.

E 224.5 (361.3 km) **DC 135.1** (217.4 km) Sturgeon Heights. Turnoff for **Youngs Point Provincial Park**, 10 km/6 miles northeast; 124 campsites (some 15- and 30-amp sites), sani-dump, coin showers, day-use area, boat launch, swimming and fishing in **Sturgeon Lake.** Camping fee $27–$34 per night, open May 1–Oct. 8. Reservations: www.reserve.albertaparks.ca or phone 1-877-537-2757 (reservation fee is $12).

E 230.9 (371.6 km) **DC 128.7** (207.1 km) Long, double-ended turnout to south for eastbound traffic; litter/recycling bins.

E 234.5 (377.4 km) **DC 125.1** (201.3 km) Crooked Creek General Store to south with gas/diesel, groceries, post office and local crafts and products from the Sturgeon Lake Native Reserve.

E 235.4 (378.8 km) **DC 124.2** (199.9 km) Distance marker northbound shows Bezanson 35 km/22 miles, Grande Prairie 69 km/43 miles.

E 237.2 (381.7 km) **DC 122.4** (197 km) Parker Creek.

E 240.2 (386.6 km) **DC 119.4** (192.2 km) Gas station to north for westbound traffic. South access to DeBolt.

E 241 (387.9 km) **DC 118.6** (190.9 km) **Junction** with Highway 736. North access to **DEBOLT** (pop. 150), a small farming community with a general store, gas/diesel station, restaurant, pub, ice cream store in summer, post office, library, and the DeBolt and District Pioneer Museum. Golf at the 9-hole Gunby Ranch Golf Course (par 3) with clubhouse that offers camping with hook-ups available from $20–$30 per night; phone 780-957-3958. The community centre has an indoor playground, fitness centre and curling rink.

E 241.2 (388.2 km) **DC 118.4** (190.5 km) Distance marker northbound shows Bezanson 25 km/16 miles, Grande Prairie 59 km/37 miles, Dawson Creek 188 km/117 miles.

CAUTION: Deer crossing.

E 247 (397.5 km) **DC 112.6** (181.2 km) **Junction** with Highway 734 South to Simonette River Provincial Recreation Area.

E 247.2 (397.8 km) **DC 112.4** (180.9 km) Distance marker northbound shows Grande Prairie 46 km/29 miles, Dawson Creek 176 km/109 miles.

E 248.5 (399.9 km) **DC 111.1** (178.8 km) Double-ended turnouts both sides of highway with litter/recycling bins; chain-up area only in winter months.

E 251.1 (404.1 km) **DC 108.5** (174.6 km) Smoky River.

Passing lane northbound begins just north of the bridge (for 3.5 km/2.2 miles).

E 254 (408.8 km) **DC 105.6** (169.9 km) Double-ended turnouts both sides of highway with litter/recycling bins; chain-up area only in winter months.

E 255.2 (410.7 km) **DC 104.4** (168 km) First westbound exit south to **BEZANSON** (pop. 85, community of 1,200). Easy access to town. General store includes post office, Tempo gas/diesel station, liquor store, grocery and propane; cafe, municipal campground (20 sites).

E 256.5 (412.8 km) **DC 103.1** (165.9 km) **Junction** with Highway 670 South and Highway 733 North to Teepee Creek (11 km/7 miles) and Wanham on Highway 49 (61 km/38 miles).

E 257 (413.6 km) **DC 102.6** (165.1 km) Second westbound exit south to Bezanson.

E 260.7 (419.6 km) **DC 98.9** (159.2 km) Kleskun Hills National Area and county operated Kleskun Campground to north 3 miles/5 km (gravel). The park features an ancient sea bottom with fossils of dinosaurs and marine life, a Native burial ground, walking trails and the preserved buildings of the Heritage Village Historic Site. There are 9 unserviced campsites here (drinking water, showers, playground, firewood). Camping fee $26; open mid-May to mid-October. Phone 780-567-3685.

E 261.8 (421.3 km) **DC 97.8** (157.4 km) Roadside turnout to north for westbound-only traffic with litter/recycling bins, information boards on the history of Alberta's Kleskun Hills.

E 266.5 (428.9 km) **DC 93.1** (149.8 km) Turnout to north for westbound-only traffic with litter/recycling bins, information boards on the history of Grande Prairie.

E 272.7 (438.9 km) **DC 86.9** (139.9 km) **Junction** with Highway 2 North to Peace River and Dunvegan (91 km/57 miles), a historic Hudson's Bay Co. post, and Grimshaw (174 km/108 miles), Mile Zero of the Mackenzie Highway, part of the Deh Cho Route to the Alaska Highway via Northwest Territories.

E 273 (439.3 km) **DC 86.6** (139.4 km) *Dawson Creek-bound travelers: Exit south for continuation of Highway 43 through Grande Prairie via 100 Street/116 Avenue/108 Street/100 Avenue (see city map on facing page); access to Visitor Centre, all services and shopping available along this route, lots of traffic. (Note that you must turn west at 116 Avenue to follow this route and skirt the downtown core.)*

*A bypass route—Highway 43X—is under construction and instead of exiting south onto 100 Street/Highway 43 here you may instead continue straight (west) on Highway 43X for about 2 miles from this junction then turn south on 116 Street (follow signs) and rejoin Highway 43/100 Avenue on the west edge of Grande Prairie (although you will miss some of the shopping, services and attractions). Highway 43X provides access to **Country Roads RV Park** for westbound travelers.*

Edmonton-bound travelers: Follow signs for Highway 43 East on-ramp.

Junction with Highway 2 to Grimshaw and the Mackenzie Highway to Northwest Territories. See the DEH CHO ROUTE for log.

Travelers bound for the Deh Cho Route via Grimshaw should exit north onto Highway 2 from here. A side trip loop north to Grimshaw then south from Peace River to Valleyview via Highways 2 and 49, gives travelers a chance to take in historic Dunvegan and Peace River. This side trip is 212 miles/341 km in length. Follow the logs in the DEH CHO ROUTE section.

Grande Prairie

E 277.4 (446.4 km) DC 82.2 (132.3 km) Traffic light at 106 Street turnoff to Grande Prairie visitor centre (look for the 40-foot-high sundial). Grande Prairie is located at the junction of Alberta Highways 43 and 2 and Highways 40 and 43. **Population:** 68,556. **Emergency Services:** Dial 911. **RCMP**, phone 780-830-5700. **Fire Department**, phone 780-538-0393. **Hospital**, Queen Elizabeth II, 10409–98th St., phone 780-538-7100.

Visitor Information: Located in the Center 2000 building, just off of the Highway 43 bypass at 11330–106 St. Look for the 40-foot-high sundial (largest in North America) at the intersection in front of the Center. An excellent information stop with year-round staff, a gift shop, free coffee, restrooms, free WiFi and a spectacular view of the city from the Center's cupola. The MILEPOST® is sold here. **Heritage Discovery Center** on the lower level (elevator available) of Center 2000 is home to Piper the animatronics dinosaur. "Welcome Wednesdays" with free snacks and refreshments, is offered to visitors every Wednesday in June, July and August. Also in summer there are Free Rotary Club bus tours of the city offered on Tuesdays, Wednesdays and Thursdays at 6:30 P.M. (registration not required). If you need to stretch your legs or walk the dog, there is access to 28 km/17 miles of trails from here that take you along Bear Creek, past playgrounds, picnic areas and bird-watching viewpoints.

Summer hours (June to September) at the Visitor Centre are 8:30 A.M. to 6:30 P.M. Winter hours: (September to May) 8:30 A.M. to 4:30 P.M. Monday–Friday and 10 A.M. to 4:30 P.M. Saturday–Sunday. Phone 780-539-7688 or toll-free 1-866-202-2202. www.gptourism.ca. Plenty of parking for all sizes of rigs at the Visitor Centre. (There is a sanidump just south of the visitor center.)

Private Aircraft: Grande Prairie Airport 3 miles/4.8 km west; elev. 2,195 feet/669m; length 6,500 feet/1,981m; paved; fuel 80, 100, jet. 24-hour flight service station.

Elevation: 2,198 feet/670m. **Radio:** 93.1 Big Country-FM, 97.7 Rock 97, 104.7 2Day FM, 98.9 Q 99, 96.3 Reach FM. **Newspaper:** Daily Herald Tribune.

Transportation: Air—Scheduled air service to Vancouver, BC, Edmonton and Calgary via Air Canada and WestJet. **Bus**—Red Arrow provides daily service to Edmonton with stops at Mayerthorpe, Whitecourt, Fox Creek and Valleyview; phone 1-800-232-1958; www.redarrow.ca

Grande Prairie is a vibrant regional center for northwestern Alberta and northeastern British Columbia. One of the fastest growing cities in Canada, Grande Prairie boasts services and facilities normally associated with larger metropolitan areas while maintaining its small-town charm and northern hospitality.

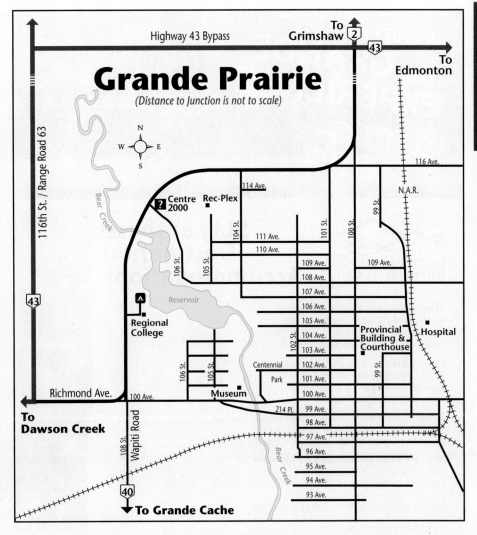

Grande Prairie
(Distance to Junction is not to scale)

Lodging & Services

Grande Prairie has all visitor facilities including major chain hotels/motels; more than 100 restaurants—from major-chain eateries and fast-food outlets (Boston Pizza, Carl's Jr., Denny's, Humpty's, Subway, Starbucks, etc.) to locally owned and operated culinary finds.

Grande Prairie is a major retail hub, with shopping malls, big box stores (Costco, Walmart, etc.) along Highway 43 and unique shops in the downtown core. Take advantage of the no provincial sales tax and stock up. **Homesteader Health Foods Ltd.** is located at 10360–111 St. Grande Prairie also offers RV/vehicle repair, generator specialists, RV dealers and more.

Camping

There are 2 campgrounds in the city.

GRANDE PRAIRIE ADVERTISERS

Bear Paw Campground .... Ph. 780-402-3800
Camp Tamarack RV Park............ Ph. 1-877-532-9998
Country Roads RV Park .... Ph. 1-866-532-6323
Grande Prairie Regional
    Tourism Assoc. .... Ph. 1-866-202-2202
Grande Prairie Visitor Centre .... Ph. 780-539-7688
Homesteader Health Ltd.............. Ph. 780-538-9970
McGoverns RV Park .... Ph. 780-532-3279
Nitehawk Wilderness RV Park
    & Campground.......................... Ph. 1-888-754-6778

Bear Paw Campground is located on South Bear Creek at 6325–100 St.; 35 sites, adjacent

BE PART OF
The **GRANDE**
EXPERIENCE
Grande
Prairie

GRANDE PRAIRIE
REGIONAL TOURISM
ASSOCIATION

REGROUP, RESTOCK
REFUEL, REPAIR then RELAX!

GPTOURISM.CA

Last Major City and Service Centre before Alaska

Grande Prairie
Region

**DESTINATION
PROPERTIES**

Stay at these Destination Accommodations

Camp Tamarack RV Park - Fully Serviced
Season: April - October   1-877-532-9998
www.camptamarckrv.com
Located on Hwy 40 South Rig Friendly

Country Roads RV Park - Fully Serviced
Season: Open Year Round   1-866-532-6323
www.countryroadsrvpark.com
Located 4.5km west on Hwy 43X

McGoverns RV Park - PW Sites - Season: May - September
1-780-532-3279   www.everygreenpark.ca
Located 5 minutes SE of Grande Prairie in Evergreen Park

Nitehawk Wilderness RV Park & Campground
Fully Serviced
Season: Open Year Round   1-888-754-6778
www.gonitehawk.com
Located South on Hwy 40 then West on Hwy 666

Bear Paw Campground - 35 PW Sites
Season: May - October   780-402-8777
www.gonitehawk.com/bear-paw-golf-course/camping-bear-paw
6325-100 Street

County Campgrounds - Bear Lake Campground - Hommy Park -
Demmitt Park - Pipestone Creek Campground - Kleskun Hill Campground
Season: May - October   www.countygp.ab.ca

So Many Reasons To Come &
Even More Reasons To Stay

REGIONAL CENTRE FOR NORTHWESTERN ALBERTA
AND NORTHEASTERN BC

81 MILES FROM MILE ZERO - ON THE ALASKA HWY

TAKE ADVANTAGE OF NO PROVINCIAL SALES TAX

RV/VEHICLE REPAIRS, NO JOB TOO BIG OR TOO SMALL
MAJOR RV DEALERS

RETAIL HUB SHOPPING MALLS, BIG BOX STORES,
COSTCO AND WALMART SUPERCENTRE

ALL MODERN AMENITIES & ACCOMMODATIONS
OVER 100 DINING OPTIONS

FOUR SEASONS PLAYGROUND & HAVEN FOR CAMPERS,
NATURE LOVERS AND OUTDOOR ENTHUSIASTS

STATE OF-THE-ART INDOOR & OUTDOOR FACILITIES

DISCOVER, DECODE, DREAM....IN THE WORLD
CLASS PHILIP J. CURRIE DINOSAUR MUSEUM

VISITOR CENTRE OPEN YEAR-ROUND, 7 DAYS A WEEK

FOR MORE INFORMATION ON OUR REGION AND FOR A FREE COPY
OF OUR VISITOR GUIDE - 1-866-202-2202 - info@gptourism.ca

par 3 golf course, bike rentals and access to bike trails. The Rotary Campground (59 sites) is located off Highway 43/108 Street; turn into the Regional College (this distinctive structure was designed by Douglas Cardinal) then make an immediate left turn. Rotary Campground has 59 sites with easy access to the Visitor Centre and scenic walking trails.

Private campgrounds near the city include: **Country Roads RV Park** (115 sites), which has an 8-acre cornfield maze, cafe and store, is located near the junction of Highways 43 and 2; **Camp Tamarack RV Park** (89 sites), located 5 miles/8.5 km south of Grande Prairie on Highway 40; **McGoverns RV Park** (77 sites) in Evergreen Park in southern outskirts of the city; and **Nitehawk Wilderness RV Park & Campground** (72+ sites), located south of Grande Prairie on Highway 40. See ads on facing page.

Attractions

Recreation facilities include the Eastlink Centre, one of the largest aquatic, fitness and adventure facilities in Canada, where you can take a surfing lesson, have something to eat, get a massage and more. There are 18-hole, 9-hole and par 3 golf courses; disc golf course; indoor/outdoor soccer; twin ice arenas; gymnastic facility; curling rink; amusement parks, tennis courts; a public library; and both public and private art galleries, including one of the largest Class A art galleries in Alberta—The Art Gallery of Grande Prairie. In summer, take your mountain bike up the chairlift at Nitehawk Adventure Park and enjoy the most vertical downhill Mountain Bike Park in Alberta. The adventure park also boasts a giant waterslide in summer, and the Aquatera Tube Zone in winter, along with skiing and snowboarding.

Muskoseepi Park, which follows the Bear Creek corridor, has: 17.4 miles/28 km of trails popular with walkers, joggers, skaters and bicyclists; lawn bowling; mini-golf; a stocked fishing pond; and a playground for children. There is a bird sanctuary at Crystal Lake. The Grande Prairie Museum is located in Muskoseepi Park; free admission. The 40-foot-high Sundial and The Heritage Discovery Center museum are located at the Visitor Information Center (Center 2000).

Annual events include the Stompede, a major rodeo held the last weekend in May; Canada Day celebrations on July 1; Street Performers Festival and Teepee Creek Rodeo in July. Horse racing all summer at Evergreen Park. Bear Creek Folk Festival in August. For a complete list of events visit Grande Prairie Regional Tourism's website at www.gptourism.ca or email info@gptourism.ca.

Area attractions in Grande Prairie County include the Philip J. Currie Dinosaur Museum, 19 km/11.8 miles west of Grande Prairie at Wembley (**Milepost E 292**); the giant beaver in Beaverlodge (**Milepost E 302.1**); the South Peace Centennial Museum just west of Beaverlodge (**Milepost E 304.7**); and the 1930s-themed town of Sexsmith just north of Grande Prairie off of Highway 2.

East Access Route Log
(continued)

E 278.3 (447.9 km) **DC 81.3** (130.8 km) Traffic light at **junction** of Highway 43/100 Avenue and 108 Street (Wapiti Road/Highway 40 South). Dawson Creek-bound motorists continue on 100 Avenue/Highway 43 West. Busy highway, multiple businesses,

A big crowd enjoys the annual Bear Creek Festival in August 2018, one of several annual events in Grande Prairie. (©Earl L. Brown)

westbound: Walmart, Staples, Home Depot, Best Buy, Petsmart, and various gas stations to name just a few. Edmonton-bound travelers turn north here to continue on 108 Street bypass then north on 100 Street, bypassing downtown Grande Prairie, to connect with Highway 43 East.

Bighorn Highway 40 connects Grande Prairie with Grande Cache (117 miles/188 km) and Yellowhead Highway 16 (203 miles/327 km). *NOTE: If you are headed south on Highway 40/Bighorn Route, fuel up in Grande Prairie, because there is no gas until Grande Cache.*

Junction with Highway 40 South. Turn to end of "Bighorn Route" log on page 251 in the YELLOWHEAD HIGHWAY section and read log back to front.

E 278.8 (448.7 km) **DC 80.8** (130 km) Traffic light at 112 Street. Home Depot, bank, liquor store and other businesses.

E 279.3 (449.5 km) **DC 80.3** (129.2 km) Traffic light at **junction** with 116 Street/Bypass Route north to Highway 43X.

E 279.8 (450.3 km) **DC 79.8** (128.4 km) Traffic light at 120 Street in Grande Prairie; Esso gas station to south.

Busy highway, multiple roadside businesses (Walmart, Home Depot, etc.) eastbound.

E 280.7 (451.7 km) **DC 78.9** (127 km) Grande Prairie airport to north.

Distance marker northbound shows Wembley 19 km/12 miles, Beaverlodge 39 km/24 miles, Hythe 54 km/34 miles, Dawson Creek 127 km/79 miles.

E 287.9 (463.3 km) **DC 71.7** (115.4 km) Legion Park campground to north on Range Road 74 (16 km west of Costco). Tenters are welcomed. $20 no hookups, tap water, firewood for donation, activity areas; phone 780-766-3663; ktzidcamp@gmail.com.

E 291.3 (468.8 km) **DC 68.3** (109.9 km)

Turn on Range Road 81, **Saskatoon Island Provincial Park** is 4 km/2.5 miles north on park road; 103 campsites (many sites can accommodate 35-foot RVs), 50 with electrical hookups, 2 wheelchair-accessible sites; shower house, toilets; campground host; dump station; boat launch for hand-launched boats only, playground. Group campsite available. Saskatoon berry picking in July. This park is a game preserve for trumpeter swans; no motorboats. Camping season early May to October 8; fees are $27–$34. Reservations: www.reserve.albertaparks.ca or phone 1-877-537-2757 (reservation fee is $12).

E 291.9 (469.8 km) **DC 67.7** (109 km) Distance marker southbound shows Grande Prairie 22 km/13 miles, Edmonton 486 km/302 miles.

E 292 (469.9 km) **DC 67.6** (108.8 km) South access to Town of Wembley and private golf course and campground. Pipestone Creek Park is 14 km/8.7 miles south.

Turnoff for the **Philip J. Currie Dinosaur Museum**, a 41,000-square-foot state-of-the-art facility right off of Highway 43 on 112 Avenue, that is located near one of the densest fossil sites in the world. The galleries are designed to bring you further into the past as you travel downwards through the exhibits, and include interactive displays, a new Alberta species never displayed before, and a view of the reconstruction process. Open year-round; go to www.dinomuseum.ca for hours and admission fees.

WEMBLEY (pop. 1,516). Visitor services include a liquor store, bank, post office, grocery store, 3 area churches, 2 schools and a daycare. A recreation complex houses the Multi-Purpose Event Centre, a Fitness Centre and a hockey rink; www.wembleyreccentre.com. There are tennis courts, a lighted football field, toboggan hill, a skateboard park and bike pump track. The library (in the Helen E. Taylor School) has 2 public-use computers with internet. For more information, visit www.wembley.ca.

A favorite photo op is the giant beaver in front of the Cultural Center in Beaverlodge.
(©Earl L. Brown)

Sunset Park Campground, located southwest end of town via 98 Avenue, has 7 campsites with electrical hookups, a non-serviced overflow area, a dump station, showers, flush toilets, firewood, picnic area, gazebo shelter, playground and a children's water park. **Pipestone Creek** Campground, 14 km/9 miles south on Range Road 82, is open for camping from May 1 to Oct. 15; 99 sites, showers, flush toilets, dump station, boat launch, firewood, fishing, playground and fossil display. Information and online reservations at www.countyofgp.ab.ca. Bird watching in area for red-winged blackbirds and yellow-headed blackbirds. Pipestone Golf Club, located near the park, is an 18-hole golf course with grass greens; www.pipestonegc.ca.

The Pipestone Creek area has received international attention due to the discovery of the world's largest Pachyrhinosaurus ("thick-nosed" horned dinosaur) bone bed. This site contains hundreds of dinosaur skeletons and is one of the best horned dinosaur bone beds found in North America.

E 292.5 (470.7 km) **DC 67.1** (108 km) Exit north to Highway 724 to La Glace on Highway 59 (28 km/17 miles) and exit south for Wembley (see entry at **Milepost E 292** for more information). Access to Anderson Wildlife Centre.

E 293.1 (471.7 km) **DC 66.5** (107 km) Distance marker northbound shows Hythe 34 km/21 miles, Dawson Creek 108 km/67 miles.

Distance marker southbound Wembley 5 km/3 miles, Grande Prairie 27 km/17 miles, Edmonton 493 km/306 miles.

E 296.1 (476.5 km) **DC 63.5** (102.2 km) Range Road 92, north to Saskatoon Mountain Recreation Area and south to Huallen.

E 298.1 (479.7 km) **DC 61.5** (99 km) Distance marker southbound shows Wembley 13 km/8 miles, Grande Prairie 35 km/22 miles, Edmonton 499 km/310 miles.

E 298.2 (479.9 km) **DC 61.4** (98.8 km) **Junction** with Highway 667 West.

E 298.3 (480.1 km) **DC 61.3** (98.7 km) Distance marker northbound shows Beaverlodge 8 km/5 miles, Hythe 24 km/15 miles, Dawson Creek 97 km/60 miles.

E 299.8 (482.5 km) **DC 59.8** (96.2 km)

End 4-lane divided highway westbound, begin 2-lane undivided highway.

CAUTION: Watch for deer. Slow for posted speed northbound through Beaverlodge.

End 2-lane undivided highway eastbound, begin 4-lane divided highway.

E 300.5 (483.6 km) **DC 59.1** (95.1 km) **Junction** with Highway 723 North to Valhalla Centre and Highway 59 (25 km/16 miles).

E 301.8 (485.7 km) **DC 57.8** (93 km) Distance marker southbound shows Wembley 19 km/12 miles, Grande Prairie 41 km/26 miles, Edmonton 513 km/319 miles.

Beaverlodge

E 302.1 (486.2 km) **DC 57.5** (92.5 km) Welcome to Beaverlodge (northbound sign). **Population:** 2,365. **Elevation:** 2,264 feet/737m. **Emergency Services:** Dial 911. **Hospital,** Beaverlodge Hospital, phone 780-354-2136. Medical and dental clinics.

Visitor Information: Located in the Beaverlodge and Area Cultural Center on the east side of Highway 43 at the east end of town next to the giant beaver statue. The Cultural Center features a gift shop with items from local artisans for sale and a tea room that makes a charming stop for tired travelers; plenty of parking, restrooms. Enjoy a free cup of tea in the Center's bright and welcoming tea room!

The 15–foot/4.6–metre–high beaver perched on a 19–foot/6–m log out in front of the Cultural Center is a favorite photo op for travelers. The large monument at the front of the Cultural Center presents 100 years of settlement history. For more information, visit www.beaverlodge.ca.

Private Aircraft: DeWit Airpark 2 miles/3.2 km south; elev. 2,289 feet/1,698m; length 3,000 feet/914m; paved; no fuel. The Beaverlodge airport is a popular stopover on the flying route to Alaska.

Home to Canada's most northerly Agricultural Research Station (open to the public), Beaverlodge serves as regional centre for grain transportation, seed cleaning and seed production. Cereal grains, such as wheat, barley and oats, are the main crops in the area. The PRT Alberta Inc., visible from the highway as you enter town, is a reforestation nursery, growing about 11 million seedlings a year.

Visitor services include 3 motels, fast-food outlets (Subway, A&W) and 3 gas stations (FasGas, Esso, Petro-Canada). There are 2 supermarkets, 2 banks, and 2 pharmacies, a post office, veterinary clinic, car wash and sporting goods store. Camping is available at the Pioneer Campground (see **Milepost E 303.4**) at the west end of town.

East Access Route Log
(continued)

E 303.4 (488.3 km) **DC 56.2** (90.4 km) Pioneer Municipal Campground located on the manicured lawn on the northeast side of Highway 43, has 29 sites that can accommodate all sizes of rigs (10 full-service sites and 9, 30-amp electrical only sites available), showers and dump station. Nice treed area; pioneer buildings. Phone 780-897-0146 or 780-354-2201 ext. 1011. Camping fees are $17–$45, weekly and monthly rates available; sani-dump fee $5.

E 303.9 (489.1 km) **DC 55.7** (89.6 km) Distance marker northbound shows Hythe 13 km/8 miles, Dawson Creek 89 km/55 miles.

E 304.6 (490.2 km) **DC 55** (88.5 km) Welcome to Beaverlodge, southbound.

E 304.7 (490.4 km) **DC 54.9** (88.4 km) **South Peace Centennial Museum** to east, watch for elk farm at entrance. This 40-acre pioneer village, is open daily in summer; phone 780-354-8869 or visit website: south peacemuseum.com. Well worth a stop! Pick up a visitor's guide and walk through the grounds, explore the buildings. Great place for a picnic if you are interested in old farm equipment, this is a "must stop:" the South Peace Centennial Museum features vintage vehicles and working steam-powered farm equipment from the early 1900s. Open daily 10 A.M. to 6 P.M., mid-May to last Sunday in August. Admission $5 per person (cash only), 6 and under, free. The annual Pioneer Day celebration, held here the third Sunday in July, attracts several thousand visitors. Camping for $10 per night (self-contained only).

E 307.1 (494.2 km) **DC 52.5** (84.5 km) **Junction** with Highway 671 West to Goodfare (13 km/8 miles). Riverbend Golf & Country Club to the east; the clubhouse is a retired NAR station. Green fees for 9-holes begin at $23; phone 780-354-2538.

Distance marker westbound shows BC Border 28 km/17 miles.

E 308.4 (496.3 km) **DC 51.2** (82.4 km) Hommy Campground is a county operated campground to west 1 km on Township Road 725. On the north bank of Beaverlodge River; very family friendly and family-oriented; enforced quiet hours and alcohol-use policy. 23 powered sites, pump water (non-potable), pit toilets, firepits, firewood and picnicking. Camping mid-May to mid-October. Fee $36. Gorgeous playground area and day-use area en route to the campground. Phone 780-354-8039.

E 311.9 (502 km) **DC 47.7** (76.8 km) **Junction** with Highway 672 west to Lymburn (16 km/10 miles) and east to Highway 2 to Sexsmith.

E 312.3 (502.6 km) DC 47.3 (76.1 km) Distance marker southbound shows Beaverlodge 20 km/12 miles, Grande Prairie 57 km/35 miles, Edmonton 521 km/324 miles.

E 312.4 (502.8 km) DC 47.2 (76 km) Welcome to Hythe. Oasis RV Park campground; phone 780-830-9684. [A]

E 312.6 (503.1 km) DC 47 (75.6 km) HYTHE (pop. 827), dubbed the "Volunteer Capital of Alberta." **Visitor Information:** Hythe Historical Information Center, located in a 1910 tack shop along the highway, has picnic tables outside on the lawn;

©Sharon Nault

photo op of **horse and buggy statue** (pictured above). Contact the Village Office at 780-356-3888 for more information or visit their website at www.hythe.ca. Hythe is an agricultural service community and retirement centre for senior citizens.

The Village has a motel, restaurant, laundromat, grocery store, bank, Esso and Husky stations with gas/diesel and food store, tire repair, car wash and shopping. Hythe Municipal Campground is on the northwest side of town adjacent to Highway 43. [B][A]

E 313.1 (503.9 km) DC 46.5 (74.8 km) Hythe Municipal Campground; 21 sites, (all with 15- and 30-amp power) flush toilets, showerhouse (inside a Northern Alberta Railroad car), drinking water, firewood, firepits, dump station and playground. It has a vintage railroad car on display. Tent sites $15; power sites $25; full-service sites $35. Some sites have 50-amp power. [A]

E 313.2 (504 km) DC 46.4 (74.7 km) Distance marker northbound shows Pouce Coupe 61 km/38 miles, Dawson Creek 67 km/42 miles.

E 313.3 (504.2 km) DC 46.3 (74.5 km) **Junction** with Highway 721 North for Hythe Motor Speedway Park and the Spring Lake Recreation Area, camping.

E 313.8 (505 km) DC 45.8 (73.7 km) Welcome to Hythe (southbound sign).

E 320.9 (516.4 km) DC 38.7 (62.3 km) Distance marker southbound shows Hythe 13 km/8 miles, Beaverlodge 28 km/17 miles, Grande Prairie 72 km/45 miles.

E 321 (516.6 km) DC 38.6 (62.1 km) **Junction** with Highway 59 east to Sexsmith on Highway 2 (63 km/39 miles).

E 331.8 (534 km) DC 27.8 (44.7 km) Demmitt Campground is a county operated campground on Highway 43; 15 sites, picnic tables, group shelter, litter/recycling bins, firepits, toilets, pull-throughs and back-ins. Open mid-May to mid-October, fee $20 per night (cash only). Phone 780-532-9727. [A]

E 332.1 (534.5 km) DC 27.5 (44.3 km) Weigh station/vehicle inspection station to south.

E 332.6 (535.3 km) DC 27 (43.5 km) FasGas gas/diesel station and convenience store to north.

E 333.9 (537.4 km) DC 25.7 (41.4 km) **Alberta–British Columbia border.** Double-ended turnout to north with litter bins.

TIME ZONE CHANGE: Alberta is on Mountain standard time. Most of British Columbia is on Pacific standard time. Both observe daylight savings time from March to November. Exceptions in BC are the Alaska Highway communities of Dawson Creek, Charlie Lake, Taylor, Fort St. John and Fort Nelson which are on Mountain standard time in winter and Pacific standard time in summer.

BC HIGHWAY 2 NORTH

E 335.1 (539.3 km) DC 24.5 (39.4 km) **Junction** with Heritage Highway 52, which leads 91 miles/146 km southwest from Highway 2 to Tumbler Ridge townsite and access to Monkman Provincial Park, site of spectacular Kinuseo Falls. Many gravel roads intersect this road, most of which are oil production pumping stations. Heritage Highway 52 loops north 59.6 miles/96 km from Tumbler Ridge to join Highway 97 just west of Dawson Creek. *(For description of Tumbler Ridge and log of Highway 52 loop north to Highway 97, see pages 139–140 in the WEST ACCESS ROUTE section.)*

Distance marker northbound shows Dawson Creek 37 km/23 miles, Fort St. John 112 km/70 miles, Chetwynd 137 km/85 miles.

E 335.7 (540.3 km) DC 23.9 (38.5 km) Tupper Creek.

E 336.4 (541.4 km) DC 23.2 (37.3 km) Distance marker northbound shows Chetwynd 135 km/84 miles, Tumbler Ridge 145 km/90 miles, Fort Nelson 489 km/304 miles.

E 337.5 (543.2 km) DC 22.1 (35.6 km) Four Mile Creek.

E 339.2 (545.9 km) D 20.4 (32.8 km) **Swan Lake Provincial Park** is 4 km/2.5 miles northeast; drive 2.3 km/1.4 miles north on gravel, then turn right and continue to park entrance. A popular local camping spot with 24 pleasant level campsites on loop road, accommodates all sizes of rigs; pump water (water quality not guaranteed for drinking, bring your own drinking water), pit toilets, large grassy picnic area and playground; camping fee $26 per night (open May to mid-October). Continue past park entrance and across bridge for access to baseball diamonds, boat launch and swimming area. Waterfowl viewing area.

Sudeten Heritage Park, turnoff to southwest, park is alongside highway. Plaque tells of immigration to this valley of displaced residents of Sudetenland in 1938–39. There are 14 campsites, picnic tables, group shelter; $18 per night, open May–October. [A]

E 340.3 (547.7 km) DC 19.3 (31.1 km) Tate Creek bridge.

E 347.4 (559.1 km) DC 12.2 (19.6 km) Double-ended turnout with litter bin to east.

E 349.2 (562 km) DC 10.4 (16.7 km) Double-ended turnout to east.

E 351.1 (565 km) DC 8.5 (13.7 km) Weigh scales to east.

E 351.3 (565.4 km) DC 8.3 (13.4 km) Bissette Creek bridge.

E 351.8 (566.2 km) DC 7.8 (12.6 km) *Slow for posted speed zone northbound through Pouce Coupe.*

E 352 (566.5 km) DC 7.6 (12.2 km) *Slow for 30 kmph/18 mph curves northbound as highway makes two 90-degree turns through Pouce Coupe.*

E 352.2 (566.8 km) DC 7.4 (11.9 km) **POUCE COUPE** (pop. 741; elev. 2,118 feet/646m). **Visitor Information:** Tourist Bureau Office located in Pouce Coupe Museum, 5006–49 Ave. (1 block south of Highway 2). Open 8 A.M. to 5 P.M., May to August. Phone 250-786-5555. Historical artifacts are displayed at the **Pouce Coupe Museum**, located in the historic NAR railroad station.

The Pouce Coupe area was first settled in 1898 by a French Canadian, Hector Tremblay, who set up a trading post in 1908. The Edson Trail, completed in 1911, brought in the main influx of settlers from Edmonton in 1912.

The village has motels, a Husky gas station and food store. [B][A]

E 352.8 (567.8 km) DC 6.8 (10.9 km) Distance marker northbound shows Dawson Creek 10 km/6 miles, Fort St. John 85 km/53 miles, Prince George 422 km/262 miles.

E 353.6 (569.1 km) DC 6 (9.7 km) End 4-lane twinning eastbound.

E 355.6 (572.3 km) DC 4 (6.4 km) Dawson Creek regional airport and Welcome to Dawson Creek sign, northbound.

E 356.1 (573.1 km) DC 3.5 (5.6 km) Distance marker southbound shows Pouce Coupe 8 km/5 miles, Grande Prairie 130 km/81 miles, Edmonton 608 km/378 miles.

E 356.4 (573.6 km) DC 3.2 (5.1 km) Traffic light. Chances Gaming Entertainment Centre; lodging.

E 357 (574.5 km) DC 2.6 (4.2 km) Traffic light. Walmart.

E 357.5 (575.3 km) DC 2.1 (3.4 km) 116th Avenue traffic light. Northern Lights Centre to west.

E 357.8 (575.6 km) DC 1.8 (2.9 km) Traffic light; Safeway, Starbucks and gas/diesel. [B]

E 358 (576.1 km) DC 1.6 (2.6 km) Traffic light. 110 Avenue; access hospital to west, Shell gas station, Dawson Mall; Safeway supermarket, Shoppers Drugmart to east. [B][+]

E 358.4 (576.8 km) DC 1.2 (1.9 km) **Junction** (roundabout) of Highways 2, 97 and 49. Follow Highway 97 north for Dawson Creek downtown and the Alaska Highway. Follow Highway 2 south for Edmonton. *This is a busy roundabout: Drive carefully.*

E 358.6 (577.1 km) DC 1 (1.6 km) Visitor Information Centre and **Dawson Creek Art Gallery** to east. **EV plug-ins** and monument for picture taking in this parking area.

Mile "O" monument is to the west on 10th Street in downtown Dawson Creek.

E 359 (578 km) DC 0.6 (1 km) Traffic light. Tim Hortons, Chevron station. [B]

E 359.2 (578.1 km) DC 0.4 (0.6 km) Traffic light. Super 8, Petro-Canada station. [B]

E 359.5 (578.6 km) DC 0.1 (0.2 km) Traffic light. Husky gas station. [B]

E 359.6 (578.7 km) DC 0 **Junction** with Highway 97 South (Hart Highway).

Turn to page 149 for the ALASKA HIGHWAY section and log of the Alaska Highway (Highway 97 North). Description of Dawson Creek begins on page 159. Turn to page 137 at the end of the WEST ACCESS ROUTE and read log back to front for log of Highway 97 South to Prince George.

Canadian Rockies Route

CONNECTS: Coeur d'Alene, ID, to Jasper, AB

Length: 479 miles   Road Surface: Paved   Season: Open all year

Entrance to Kootenay National Park, first park in the Canadian Rockies northbound on this route.
(©Kris Valencia, staff)

Distance in miles	Coeur d'Alene	Cranbrook	Radium Hot Springs	Lake Louise	Jasper
Coeur d'Alene		160	252	335	479
Cranbrook	160		92	175	319
Radium Hot Springs	252	92		83	227
Lake Louise	335	175	83		145
Jasper	479	319	227	145	

The Canadian Rockies Route begins in Coeur d'Alene, ID, and follows U.S. Highway 95 then BC Highways 3/95 and 93 north to connect with a short portion of Trans-Canada 1, before heading up the spectacular Icefields Parkway to Jasper, AB, for a total distance of 479 miles/771 km. U.S. Highway 95 runs almost the entire length of Idaho. BC Highways 95/93 take travelers through the tourist destinations of Fairmont Hot Springs, Radium Hot Springs and Kootenay National Park. Canada Highway 93 (the Icefields Parkway) is one of the most scenic drives in North America, traversing Alberta's Banff and Jasper national parks in the central Canadian Rockies.

Reservations are strongly recommended for camping and lodging along this route in summer. For campsite reservations in Canadian national parks, go to https://reservation.pc.gc.ca. Most Canadian national park campgrounds are open from May through September.

From Jasper, northbound travelers may drive 45 miles/72 km east via Yellowhead Highway 16 to the Highway 40 junction near Hinton and take the Bighorn Route 204 miles/329 km to Grande Prairie, then join the East Access Route for the 81-mile/131-km drive to Dawson Creek, BC, and the start of the Alaska Highway. Total driving distance from Jasper to Dawson Creek via this route is 330 miles/532 km. Or northbound travelers may drive 234 miles/377 km west from Jasper via Yellowhead Highway 16 to Prince George, BC, where you will join the

Major Attractions:

©Kris Valencia, staff

Radium Hot Springs, Kootenay, Jasper and Banff National Parks, Icefields Parkway

West Access Route to Dawson Creek, BC, via the 245-mile/395-km Hart Highway. Total

Canadian Rockies Route Coeur d'Alene, ID, to Jasper, AB

© 2019 The MILEPOST®

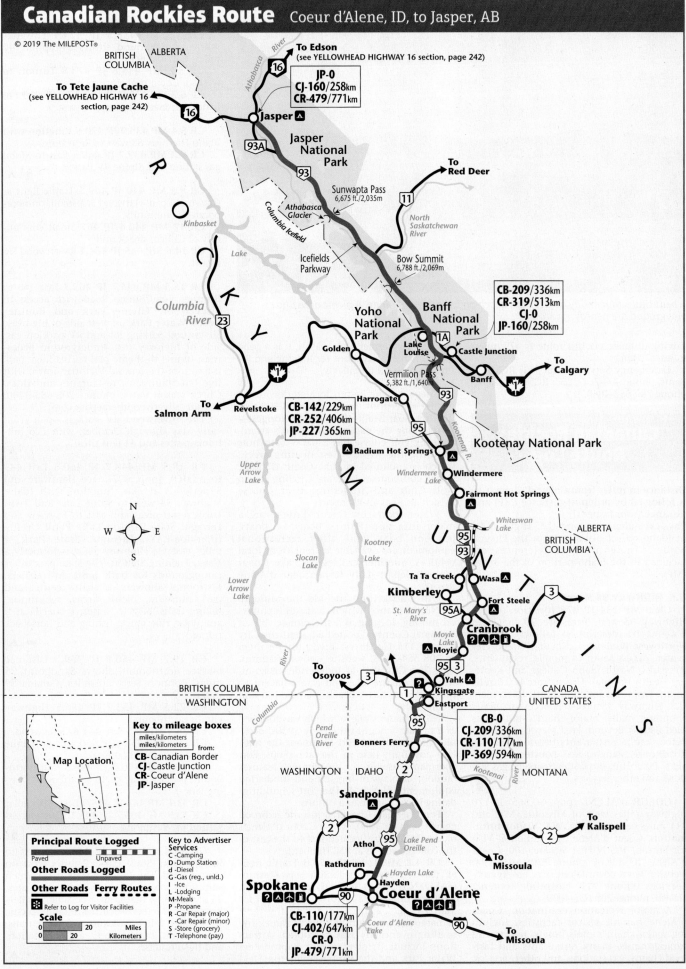

To Edson
(see YELLOWHEAD HIGHWAY 16 section, page 242)

JP-0
CJ-160/258km
CR-479/771km

To Tete Jaune Cache
(see YELLOWHEAD HIGHWAY 16 section, page 242)

BRITISH COLUMBIA | ALBERTA

Jasper

Jasper National Park

Sunwapta Pass
6,675 ft./2,035m

Athabasca River

Columbia Icefield

Athabasca Glacier

Icefields Parkway

To Red Deer

North Saskatchewan River

Bow Summit
6,788 ft./2,069m

Kinbasket Lake

Columbia River

Yoho National Park

Banff National Park

CB-209/336km
CR-319/513km
CJ-0
JP-160/258km

Golden

Lake Louise

Castle Junction

To Calgary

Vermilion Pass
5,382 ft./1,640m

Banff

To Salmon Arm

Revelstoke

Harrogate

CB-142/229km
CR-252/406km
JP-227/365km

Radium Hot Springs

Kootenay National Park

Kootenay R.

Windermere
Windermere Lake

Fairmont Hot Springs

Upper Arrow Lake

Whiteswan Lake

ALBERTA
BRITISH COLUMBIA

N
W · E
S

Kootney Lake

Slocan Lake

Lower Arrow Lake

Ta Ta Creek

Wasa

Kimberley

Fort Steele

To Osoyoos

St. Mary's River

Cranbrook

Moyie Lake

Moyie

To Missoula

Yahk

Kingsgate
Eastport

CANADA
UNITED STATES

CB-0
CJ-209/336km
CR-110/177km
JP-369/594km

BRITISH COLUMBIA
WASHINGTON

Columbia

Pend Oreille River

Bonners Ferry

WASHINGTON | IDAHO

Kootenai River | MONTANA

To Kalispell

Sandpoint

Athol

Lake Pend Oreille

To Missoula

To Kalispell

Spokane

Rathdrum

Hayden
Hayden Lake

Coeur d'Alene

Coeur d'Alene Lake

To Missoula

CB-110/177km
CJ-402/647km
CR-0
JP-479/771km

Key to mileage boxes

miles/kilometers
miles/kilometers from:
CB- Canadian Border
CJ- Castle Junction
CR- Coeur d'Alene
JP- Jasper

Map Location

Principal Route Logged
Paved — Unpaved

Other Roads Logged

Other Roads Ferry Routes

Refer to Log for Visitor Facilities

Scale
0 — 20 Miles
0 — 20 Kilometers

Key to Advertiser Services
C -Camping
D -Dump Station
d -Diesel
G -Gas (reg., unld.)
I -Ice
L -Lodging
M -Meals
P -Propane
R -Car Repair (major)
r -Car Repair (minor)
S -Store (grocery)
T -Telephone (pay)

A beautiful summer day at City Park beach on Lake Coeur d'Alene. A picnic area and playground are nearby. (©Lilly Graef)

driving distance via this route is 479 miles/miles/772 km.

Emergency Services: Dial 911; **RCMP** in Banff, phone 403-762-2226; **RCMP** in Jasper, phone 780-852-4848.

Canadian Rockies Route Log

Distance in miles from Coeur d'Alene (CR) is followed by milepost distance (MP) and distance from Jasper (JP).
Physical mileposts along U.S. Highway 95 in Idaho reflect distance from the Oregon border. These milepost references are included in the Idaho portion of the log as (MP).

U.S. HIGHWAY 95 North

CR 0 MP 134 JP 479 Junction of U.S. Highway 95 and Interstate 90 in Coeur d'Alene, ID (description follows). Exit to Northwest Boulevard, Coeur d'Alene city center. Access south to motels, restaurants, RV parks, North Idaho College and Kootenai Health hospital. Urgent care is 0.5 mile south. From this junction north to Hayden, U.S. Highway 95 provides access to many shopping malls, major-chain retail stores (Bed Bath & Beyond, Fred Meyers, Walmart, Petco, etc.), restaurants/fast-food (Texas Roadhouse, Panera, Red Lobster, McDonald's, Pizza Hut, etc.), supermarkets, gas stations and other services.

COEUR d'ALENE (pop. 50,665) is 170 highway miles west of Missoula, MT, and 311 miles east of Seattle, WA. **Visitor Information:** Coeur d'Alene Convention & Visitor Bureau, 105 N First St., Ste. 100, Coeur d'Alene, ID 83814; phone 208-664-3194; website: www.coeurdalene.org. **Emergency Services:** Phone 911. **Hospital,** Kootenai Health, phone 208-625-4000.

A major recreation destination, Coeur d'Alene has all visitor facilities, including major-chain motels/hotels, resorts and campgrounds, many restaurants and fast-food chains, gas stations, and other services.

During the summer high season, it is a good idea to make reservations for lodging and RV sites, as both fill up quickly.

Coeur d'Alene Resort, located downtown on the waterfront, has a unique 3,300-foot floating boardwalk—the world's longest—surrounding the marina. The resort's award-winning golf course has a par 3 14th hole featuring the world's first floating green, which is anchored in Lake Coeur d'Alene. Other golf courses here are Circling Raven Golf Club and Stoneridge Golf Course (which also has an RV resort).

Water sports on Coeur d'Alene are a major attraction. Fishing boats, ski boats, pontoon boats and other recreational equipment are available to rent from local vendors. Summer cruises on Lake Coeur d'Alene depart daily from Coeur d'Alene Resort.

Other attractions include the Museum of North Idaho, which features exhibits on mining, logging and the pioneer life of Kootenai County. Located adjacent the City Park at 115 Northwest Blvd.; phone them at 208-664-3448, website www.museumni.org/. The City Park at Independence Point, which is on the lake and also adjacent to the museum, has a beach, playground and picnic tables.

North Idaho College, which was founded as a private school in the early 1930s, occupies the site of old Fort Sherman, the military post built here in the late 1800s. Fort Sherman Museum, on the campus, features outdoor displays of logging and lumbering equipment, plus 3 of the fort's buildings dating back more than a century.

Fort Sherman Chapel, a historic redwood chapel built in 1880, is also Coeur d'Alene's oldest church. It is located just to the east of the college campus at 332 Hubbard.

CR 4.2 MP 434.8 JP 474.8 Traffic light at Hayden Avenue; Exxon gas station. **HAYDEN** (pop. 14,344) city center to east; food, gas, lodging. The town was named for Matt Heyden, who in 1878 won the right to name the lake during a poker game. The spelling eventually was corrupted. Attractions include Tripleplay and Raptor Reef Water Park and the Pappy Boyington Field

Museum. Hayden Lake is a popular fishing lake.

CR 4.9 MP 435.5 JP 474.1 Distance marker northbound shows Sandpoint 40 miles, Canada 99 miles.

CR 5.2 MP 435.8 JP 473.8 Turnoff to west for Coeur d'Alene airport.

CR 6.3 MP 436.9 JP 472.7 Traffic light at Lancaster; market and gas to west.

CR 8.4 MP 438.9 JP 470.6 Junction with Idaho Highway 53 west to Rathdrum.

CR 9.2 MP 439.7 JP 469.8 East to Mobil gas station and Alpine RV Park.

CR 9.5 MP 440 JP 469.5 Traffic light at Garwood Road. Garwood is a small, unincorporated community.

CR 12 MP 442.4 JP 467 Small community of Chilco, site of mill.

CR 14.6 MP 445 JP 464.4 Ravenwood RV Resort.

CR 15.3 MP 445.7 JP 463.7 Exit 446 to Brunner Road/Bunco Road with access to **Silverwood Theme Park** and **Boulder Beach Water Park** on west side of highway, Silverwood parking lot and RV park on east side of highway (use underground pedestrian tunnel to theme park). This huge park is a turn-of-the-century Victorian town, with live entertainment, restaurants and rides. Check season dates; phone 208-683-3400; website: silverwoodthemepark.com.

The Silverwood RV Park is open from early May through October, with 126 full-hookup sites and 41 tent sites.

CR 18.5 MP 448.7 JP 460.5 Exit 449 to **ATHOL** (pop. 427); Ace Hardware and Superfoods at exit. Junction with Idaho Highway 54 west to Spirit Lake and Twin Lakes resort areas and east to Bayview and Farragut State Park on **Lake Pend Oreille** (pon-doe-RAY). **Farragut State Park,** 4 miles east via Highway 54, was formerly a Naval Training Station. The state park offers campgrounds for both tents and trailers, restrooms, showers, a visitor center and park museum, picnic areas, swimming, hiking trails, bicycle routes, a boat launch and dock, rifle range, fishing and horseback riding.

CR 19.7 MP 450.9 JP 459.3 Distance marker northbound shows Sandpoint 25 miles, Bonners Ferry 58 miles, Canada 89 miles.

CR 22.5 MP 452.7 JP 456.5 Highway climbs northbound.

CR 25.4 MP 455.5 JP 453.6 Careywood.

CR 28.6 MP 458.6 JP 450.4 Begin 2-mile passing lane northbound.

CR 30.7 MP 460.7 JP 448.3 End northbound passing lane, begin southbound passing lane.

CR 33.1 MP 463 JP 445.9 Lake Cocolalla.

CR 33.9 MP 463.7 JP 445.1 Chevron gas station in Westmond.

CR 35.8 MP 465.6 JP 443.2 Turnoff to **Round Lake State Park,** 2 miles west on Dufort Road. The 142-acre state park, which surrounds a small lake, has 16 serviced sites, 35 standard (2 handicap accessible); trailers limited to 24 feet. Facilities include picnic sites, water, toilets, swimming, fishing, trails, a boat ramp, central water, a dump station, and flush toilets.

CR 38.3 MP 468.3 JP 440.7 Entering Algoma northbound, slow for speed zones.

CR 38.7 MP 468.4 JP 440.3 Farm store; entering community of **Sagle**, northbound. Turnoff to Garfield Bay Recreation Area, located 8 miles east on Lake Pend Oreille; camping. Access to Bird Aviation Museum & Invention Center (11.8 miles east via Sagle Road to Bird Ranch Road)

CR 39.1 MP 468.9 JP 439.9 Conoco gas station.

CR 39.4 MP 469.2 JP 439.6 Distance marker northbound shows Sandpoint 6 miles, Bonners Ferry 38 miles, Canada 69 miles.

CR 41.1 MP 470.8 JP 437.9 Country Inn (lodging).

CR 41.3 MP 471 JP 437.7 Turnoff on Bottle Bay Road east to Bottle Bay Resort and Marina (cabins, restaurant, bar, storage, fuel and boat launch) on Lake Pend Oreille.

CR 42.1 MP 471.8 JP 436.9 Crossing the 2-mile-long bridge that spans the mouth of the Pend Oreille River.

CR 44 MP 473.6 JP 435 Turnoff for **SANDPOINT** (pop. 8,390); all visitor services, including major chain hotels/motels and restaurants/fast-food outlets. **Visitor Information:** www.visitsandpoint.com, phone 208-263-2161.

Sandpoint is located at the north end of Lake Pend Oreille. City beach, dock and marina at the end of Bridge Street. Scenic 2-hour cruises depart the city dock from May to September; phone 208-263-4598.

A favorite shopping destination in Sandpoint is Cedar Street Bridge. This former city bridge is now a 2-story shopping area, built of tamarack logs with lots of solar windows. It houses Coldwater Creek, the mail-order giant, an espresso shop and deli.

Museums in Sandpoint include the Vintage Wheel Museum (208-263-2344) on Cedar Street and 3rd Avenue, with displays of carriages, steam engines, and automobiles dating from the early 1900s to a 1962 Rolls Royce Silver Cloud 2; admission fee charged. The Historical Society Museum (208-263-2344), at 609 S. Ella, has relics of old-time Bonner County.

CR 45.5 MP 475.1 JP 433.5 Junction with U.S. Highway 2, which shares a common alignment with U.S. Highway 95 northbound. Also junction with Idaho Highway 200, which leads east to community of Ponderay and Kootenai. Access east on Highway 200 to Sandpoint Elks 9-hole golf course, 0.5 mile.

CR 46.5 MP 476.5 JP 432.5 Traffic light: Days Inn (lodging), Bonners Mall (shopping) and McDonald's.

CR 47 MP 477 JP 432 Conoco gas station, Walmart, AutoZone, fast-food (Taco Bell, Burger King); Sandpoint Airport to west. Traffic light at Kootenai Cutoff Road; Starbucks on northwest corner. Ponderay Crossing Mall, on east side of highway.

CR 53.2 MP 483 JP 425.8 Begin 2-lane highway northbound.

CR 55.8 MP 485.6 JP 423.2 Crossing the Pack River.

CR 56.5 MP 486.3 JP 422.5 Conoco gas station with diesel, convenience store.

CR 60.1 MP 489.8 JP 418.9 Entering Elmira northbound.

CR 63.7 MP 493.3 JP 415.3 McArthur **Lake** access is on the west side of the road; scenic wildlife refuge for nesting Canadian

geese and other birds; fishing is good for bass, perch and crappie.

CR 67.3 MP 496.8 JP 411.7 Turnoff to west for Naples general store.

CR 67.6 MP 497.1 JP 411.4 Highway crosses railroad tracks.

CR 68.8 MP 498.3 JP 410.2 Turnoff for Blue Lake Resort and Cabins to west.

CR 69.3 MP 498.8 JP 409.7 Large turnout to east.

CR 70.4 MP 499.9 JP 408.6 Begin passing lane northbound.

CR 72.4 MP 501.8 JP 406.6 Turnout to west.

CR 72.6 MP 502 JP 406.4 Highway descends 6 percent downgrade northbound.

CR 73.9 MP 503.3 JP 405.1 Begin passing lane southbound as highway climbs 6 percent upgrade southbound

CR 74.7 MP 504 JP 404.3 Mirror Lake Golf Course.

CR 75 MP 504.3 JP 404 Snow Creek Recreation Area, 13 miles west.

CR 75.9 MP 505.2 JP 403.1 Bonners Ferry Ranger Station, Kaniksu National Forest (Route 4, Box 4860, Bonners Ferry, ID 83805-9764; phone 208-267-5561).

CR 76.3 MP 505.5 JP 402.7 Lodging (Best Western/Kootenai River Inn Casino& Spa), gas stations (Conoco, Chevron, etc.), fast-food (Subway, Starbucks, etc.), grocery stores (Superfoods, Safeway) are found in **BONNERS FERRY** (pop. 2,603), which also has banks, a liquor store, hospital, auto parts store and other services. *Slow for 35 mph speed zone.* Visitor Information: Chamber of Commerce; bonnersferrychamber.org, phone 208-267-5922.

Bonners Ferry is a mecca for wildlife photographers, with wildlife viewing at Kootenai National Wildlife Refuge, 5 miles west from downtown's Kootenai River bridge. (Continue another 1.5 miles to refuge headquarters on Westside Road; phone 208-267-3888; www.fws.gov/refuge/kootenai/.) The 2,764-acre refuge supports numerous species of ducks (principally mallards, goldeneyes, wigeon and pintails) during spring and fall breeding and migration periods. Some 2,500 Canada geese may be seen here in the fall.

CR 78.8 MP 508 JP 400.2 4-lane highway climbs northbound. Distance marker shows Junction with Highway 2 is 2 miles, Moyie Springs 7 miles, Canada 30 miles.

CR 81.1 MP 510.3 JP 397.9 Traffic light at junction with U.S. Highway 2 East to Kalispell (141 miles), West Glacier (169 miles) and Shelby, MT (294 miles). Exxon gas station with restaurant to east at this junction. U.S. Highways 95 and 2 share a common alignment from this junction south to Sandpoint.

CR 81.6 MP 510.8 JP 397.4 Distance marker northbound shows Customs 31 miles, Cranbrook 78 miles.

CR 81.8 MP 511 JP 397.2 Begin 2-lane highway northbound.

CR 83.3 MP 512.5 JP 395.7 Turnoff for **Smith Lake Forest Service campground**, 2.7 miles; camping, small boat launch, fishing, bird watching.

CR 92.7 MP 521.7 JP 386.3 Winter chain-up area to west.

CR 92.8 MP 521.8 JP 386.2 Junction with Idaho Highway 1, which borders the Kootenai River northwest to Canada.

CR 93.2 MP 522.2 JP 385.8 Highway

climbs northbound; southbound and northbound passing lanes over summit. Scenic overlook to west at summit.

CR 97.1 MP 526.3 JP 381.9 Winter chain-up area to east.

CR 100.9 MP 530 JP 378.1 Wildhorse Mercantile with gas to east.

CR 103.1 MP 532.2 JP 375.9 **Robinson Lake Forest Service campground**, 0.5 mile via paved access road; 10 campsites, camping fee charged, day-use area, water, pit toilets, boating, lake fishing, hiking trail. Good wading and fishing creek.

CR 103.7 MP 532.8 JP 375.3 Turnoff for Robinson Lake boat launch.

C 104.1 MP 533.1 JP 374.9 Turnout to east.

CR 105.4 MP 534.4 JP 373.6 Idyl Acres RV Park.

CR 105.8 MP 534.8 JP 373.2 Turnoff for **Meadow Creek Forest Service campground**, 10 miles via gravel road; 23 sites, camping fee, water, pit toilets.

CR 108.7 MP 537.6 JP 370.3 Moyie River bridge.

CR 108.8 MP 537.7 JP 370.2 Duty-free shop to west. Turnoff to east for **Copper Creek Forest Service campground**, 1 mile; 16 sites, water, pit toilets, hiking trails. Trail to Copper Falls (2 miles) is highly recommended; take the lower trail at fork to base of falls.

CR 109.1 MP 538 JP 369.9 *Speed zone northbound, slow to 25 mph.*

CR 109.3 MP 538.2 JP 369.7 Eastport U.S. Customs 1400 feet, Canada Customs 1900 feet (northbound sign).

CR 109.5 MP 538.4 JP 369.5 Moyie River bridge (again).

EASTPORT (pop. 64; elev. 2,580 feet), U.S. Customs and Border Protection; open 24 hours, 7 days a week; phone 208-267-3966. More information at www.usborder.com/border-crossings/id/eastport-kingsgate/.

U.S.–Canada international boundary. Crossing the Pacific–Mountain time zone line. Turn your watch back 1 hour if you are headed north; forward 1 hour if you are headed south.

CANADA HIGHWAY 95/3

Distance in miles from the Coeur d'Alene (CR) is followed by distance from Canada Border at Eastport/Kingsgate (CB), and distance from Jasper (JP) in both miles and kilometers, for northbound travelers. For southbound travelers, distance from Coeur d'Alene (CR) is followed by the physical milepost (MP) and distance from Jasper (JP).

CR 109.7 CB 0 JP 369.3 (594.3 km) Kingsgate Canada border station; open 24 hours, 7 days a week; phone (204) 983-3500. U.S.–Canada international boundary. Crossing the Pacific–Mountain time zone line. Turn your watch back 1 hour if you are headed north; forward 1 hour if you are headed south.

CR 109.9 CB 0.2 JP 369.1 (594 km) Moyie River–Kingsgate bridge.

CR 110.1 CB 0.4 JP 368.9 (593.7 km) Duty-free shop for southbound travelers.

CR 110.6 CB 0.9 JP 368.4 (592.9 km) Turnout to east on river.

CR 114.6 CB 4.9 JP 364.4 (586.4 km)

Yahk Provincial Park, 9 miles from the U.S. border at Milepost CR 119.1, offers this day-use picnic area by the river and 26 campsites in the trees. (©Lilly Graef)

Turnout to west on river.

CR 116.8 CB 7.1 JP 362.2 (582.9 km) **Junction** with Crowsnest Highway 3 west to Creston. BC Highway 95 shares a common alignment with Crowsnest Highway 3 from here north to Cranbrook.

CR 117 CB 7.3 JP 362 (582.6 km) Restaurant.

CR 117.1 CB 7.4 JP 361.9 (582.4 km) Distance marker northbound shows Yahk 3 km/2 miles, Cranbrook 71 km/44 miles.

CR 118.7 CB 9 JP 360.3 (579.8 km) Store, gas and ice cream stop .

CR 119.1 CB 9.4 JP 359.9 (579.2 km) Turnoff for **Yahk Provincial Park** on the Moyie River; 26 campsites, picnic area adjacent river (dogs and alcohol prohibited). Camping fee $21; park is open mid-May through September.

CR 119.4 CB 9.7 JP 359.6 (578.7 km) General store.

CR 119.6 CB 9.9 JP 359.4 (578.4 km) Highway crosses first the Moyie River channel then the Yahk bridge across the Moyie River.

CR 120 CB 10.3 JP 359 (577.7 km) RV park.

CR 124.2 CB 14.5 JP 354.8 (571 km) Rest area to west

CR 124.5 CB 14.8 JP 354.5 (570.5 km) Ryan Bridge across Moyie River.

CR 124.7 CB 15 JP 354.3 (570.2 km) Ryan Railroad overhead.

CR 124.8 CB 15.1 JP 354.2 (570 km) Passing lane northbound.

CR 125.3 CB 15.6 JP 353.7 (569.2 km) *CAUTION: Watch for deer.*

CR 126.9 CB 17.2 JP 352.1 (566.6 km) Turnout to east.

CR 129.3 CB 19.6 JP 349.7 (562.8 km) Double-ended turnout with litter bin.

CR 130.1 CB 20.4 JP 348.9 (561.5 km) Passing lane southbound.

CR 130.4 CB 20.7 JP 348.6 (561 km) Turnout with litter bins to west.

CR 132.4 CB 22.7 JP 346.6 (557.8 km) Turnout with litter bins to east.

Highway descends northbound.

CR 133.9 CB 24.2 JP 345.1 (555.4 km) Turnout with litter bins to east.

CR 136 CB 26.3 JP 343 (552 km) Turnout to east.

CR 138 CB 28.3 JP 341 (548.8 km) Aldridge bridge across Moyie River.

CR 138.2 CB 28.5 JP 340.8 (548.5 km) Turnoff for Eagles Nest RV Resort.

CR 139.9 CB 30.2 JP 339.1 (545.7 km) Turnout with litter bins to west.

Slow for speed zone northbound through **Moyie** (unincorporated).

CR 140.2 CB 30.5 JP 338.8 (545.2 km) General store with gas.

CR 140.3 CB 30.6 JP 338.7 (545.1 km) Turnoff for Historic Moyie Museum (1893).

CR 140.7 CB 31 JP 338.3 (544.4 km) Distance marker northbound shows Cranbrook 32 km/20 miles, Kimberley 54 km/34 miles, Fernie 137 km/85 miles.

CR 141.6 CB 31.9 JP 337.4 (543 km) Passing lane northbound.

CR 143.6 CB 33.9 JP 335.4 (539.8 km) Double-ended turnout with litter bins to east by lake.

CR 144.4 CB 34.7 JP 334.6 (538.5 km) Passing lane northbound; highway descends northbound.

CR 146.6 CB 36.9 JP 332.4 (534.9 km) Passing lane southbound; highway climbs southbound.

CR 146.8 CB 37.1 JP 332.2 (534.6 km) Bridge across channel of Moyie Lake.

CR 147.6 CB 37.9 JP 331.4 (533.3 km) Hiawatha RV Park.

CR 147.8 CB 38.1 JP 331.2 (533 km) Turnoff for **Moyie Lake Provincial Park** (0.6 mile/1 km); 111 campsites, dump station ($5), day-use area, boat launch, sandy beach. Camping fee $33. Open early May through September.

CR 148 CB 38.3 JP 331 (532.7 km) Bridge over Moyie River.

CR 149 CB 39.3 JP 330 (531.1 km) Swansea Bridge across Moyie River.

CR 150.5 CB 40.8 JP 328.5 (528.7 km) Turnout with litter bins to west.

CR 151.5 CB 41.8 JP 327.5 (527.1 km) Distance marker northbound shows Cranbrook 16 km/10 miles, Kimberley 48 km/30 miles, Fernie 117 km/73 miles.

CR 158.9 CB 49.2 JP 320.1 (515.1 km) Welcome to Cranbrook (northbound sign) at satellite visitor center; parking, picnic tables.

CR 159.2 CB 49.5 JP 319.8 (514.7 km) Elizabeth Lake Lodge.

CR 159.7 CB 50 JP 319.3 (513.9 km) Fas Gas station to west.

CR 159.9 CB 50.2 JP 319.2 (513.7 km) Prestige Rocky Mountain Resort hotel.

Cranbrook

CR 160.1 CB 50.4 JP 318.9 (513.2 km) Turnoff for downtown Cranbrook. Highways 93/3 become Van Horne Street in Cranbrook. It is approximately 50 miles/80 miles southbound to the U.S. border crossing at Kingsgate/Eastport from Cranbook.

Population: City 19,319; area 25,037. **Elevation:** 3,021 feet/921m. **Emergency Services:** Dial 911. **Hospital**, East Kootenay Regional, phone 250-426-5281.

Visitor Information: Website: cranbrook tourism.com. Visitor Information Center at 620 Van Horne St. S.; phone 250-489-5261.

Cranbrook is the main shopping and distribution center for the East Kootenays. Accommodations, services and shopping facilities are available here, either along the highway through town in in the town center. Canadian Rockies International Airport is located northwest of town on Highway 95A.

Attractions in Cranbrook include vintage railcars at Cranbrook History Center, phone 250-489-3918; cranbrookhistorycentre.com.

Canadian Rockies Route Log
(continued)

CR 160.8 CB 51.1 JP 318.2 (512.1 km) Sandman Inn, gas station, Denny's, Burger King.

CR 160.9 CB 51.2 JP 318.1 (511.9 km) Traffic light, 6th Street North; gas station.

CR 161.3 CB 51.6 JP 317.7 (511.3 km) Days Inn, Scotia Bank, Chevron, Heritage Inn, Lazy Bear Lodge, Subway, Best Western.

CR 161.5 CB 51.8 JP 317.5 (511 km) Traffic light at Victoria Avenue/Theatre Road; A&W, Husky gas station, McDonald's, Starbucks, Tim Hortons.

CR 161.6 CB 51.9 JP 317.4 (510.8 km) Tamarack Center; shopping. Distance marker northbound shows Kimberley 31 km/19 miles, Fernie 100 km/62 miles, Radium Hot Springs 142 km/88 miles.

CR 161.7 CB 52 JP 317.3 (510.6 km) Husky gas station.

CR 161.9 CB 52.2 JP 317.1 (510.3 km) Traffic light. Shell gas station, Walmart, liquor store, Super Store.

CR 162.6 CB 52.9 JP 316.4 (509.2 km) South **junction** with Highway 95A to Kimberley, a popular tourist destination and site of the Underground Mining Railway and Interpretive Center. Continue north on Highways 95/3.

CR 163.6 CB 53.9 JP 315.4 (507.6 km) Distance marker northbound shows Fernie 93 km/58 miles, Radium Hot Springs 140 km/87 miles, Lethbridge, Alberta 300 km/186 miles.

CR 163.7 CB 54 JP 315.3 (507.4 km) Turnout with litter bins to west.

CR 165 CB 55.3 JP 314 (505.3 km)

Passing lane northbound.

CR 165.1 CB 55.4 JP 313.9 (505.1 km) Turnout with litter bins to east.

CR 166.2 CB 56.5 JP 312.8 (503.4 km) **Junction** with Highway 93. Highways 95 and 3 split, with Highway 3 (Crowsnest) heading east to Alberta. Exit to Highway 93 North, which shares a common alignment with Highway 95 to Radium Hot Springs.

CANADA HIGHWAYS 95/93

CR 166.9 CB 57.2 JP 312.1 (502.3 km) Turnout with litter bins to west.

CR 167 CB 57.3 JP 312 (502.1 km) Distance marker northbound shows Invermere 123 km/76 miles, Radium Hot Springs 133 km/83 miles.

CR 170.4 CB 60.7 JP 308.6 (496.6 km) Turnoff for Fort Steele Campground.

Highway climbs southbound, passing lane.

CR 171.1 CB 61.4 JP 307.9 (495.5 km) Fort Steele Bridge crosses Kootenay River.

CR 171.2 CB 61.5 JP 307.8 (495.3 km) **Fort Steele Heritage Town**, a restored and reconstructed turn-of-the-century mining town and North West Mounted Police post; open daily year-round; hours, prices, activities, services and programs vary by season (go to fortsteele.ca). Gift shop and cafe open year-round; steam train rides, wagon rides, and Wildhorse Theatre productions in summer; heritage buildings open for viewing spring, summer, fall. Costumed park staff provide demonstrations of baking, spinning, weaving, blacksmithing and other skills while in period dress. Admission fee charged; phone 250-417-6000.

CR 171.4 CB 61.7 JP 307.6 (495 km) Fort Steele Resort & RV Park, gas station.

CR 171.9 CB 62.2 JP 307.1 (494.2 km) Distance marker northbound shows Invermere 116 km/72 miles, Radium Hot Springs 127 km/79 miles.

CR 173.7 CB 64 JP 305.3 (491.3 km) Rest area to east.

CR 177.1 CB 67.4 JP 301.9 (485.9 km) Turnout to west. Straight, mostly flat stretch of 2-lane highway continues for northbound travelers.

CR 183.2 CB 73.5 JP 295.8 (476 km) Turnoff to east for **Wasa Provincial Park** via Wasa Lake Park (loop) Drive and to community of **Wasa** (unincorporated). The provincial park is located on the east side of **Wasa Lake**; 104 campsites, dump station ($5), 4 day-use/picnic areas, excellent beaches, swimming, waterskiing, fishing, boat launch, nature trails (wheelchair accessible). Open May 1 to Sept. 30.

CR 184.9 CB 75.2 JP 294.1 (473.3 km) Gas station at second turnoff northbound to east for Wasa and Wasa Provincial Park via Wasa Lake Park (loop) Drive (see **Milepost CR 183.2** for description).

CR 185.3 CB 75.6 JP 293.7 (472.7 km) Turnout with litter bins to west.

CR 186.6 CB 76.9 JP 292.4 (470.6 km) Kootenay River bridge. Northbound travelers keep right just north of the bridge at north **junction** with Highway 95A, which leads west and south to the old mining town of **KIMBERLEY** (pop. 4,513), now nicely revamped in Bavarian style; all tourist services. In winter, Kimberley comes into its own as a destination ski resort on the slopes of North Star Mountain.

Columbia Lake viewpoint at Milepost CR 222.3. The lake is the source of the Columbia River, which flows into the Pacific Ocean at the Washington–Oregon border. (©Lilly Graef)

CR 187.1 CB 77.4 JP 291.9 (469.8 km) Distance marker northbound shows Radium Hot Springs 101 km/63 miles, Golden 206 km/128 miles, Banff 240 km/149 miles.

CR 187.4 CB 77.7 JP 291.6 (469.3 km) Wasa rest area.

CR 191.1 CB 81.4 JP 287.9 (463.3 km) Distance marker northbound shows Invermere 81 km/50 miles, Radium Hot Springs 95 km/59 miles, Golden 198 km/123 miles.

CR 194.5 CB 84.8 JP 284.5 (457.8 km) Springbrook Bridge across the Kootenay River; entering the settlement of Skookumchuck northbound.

CR 194.7 CB 85 JP 284.3 (457.5 km) RV park.

CR 194.8 CB 85.1 JP 284.2 (457.3 km) Convenience store, gas station, motel and RV park.

CR 196 CB 86.3 JP 283 (455.4 km) Turnoff for north access to **Premier Lake Provincial Park**; 61 campsites, camping fee $25, pit toilets, water pumps, boat launch suitable for small boats and trailers. Lakeside day-use area with picnic tables. Wildlife viewing, fishing. Open May 1 to Sept. 30.

CR 201.2 CB 91.5 JP 277.8 (447.1 km) Turnout with litter bin.

CR 201.5 CB 91.8 JP 277.5 (446.6 km) Distance marker northbound shows Radium Hot Springs 79 km/49 miles, Golden 182 km/113 miles, Banff 217 km/135 miles.

CR 207.6 CB 97.9 JP 271.4 (436.8 km) Turnout to west.

CR 209.5 CB 99.8 JP 269.5 (433.7 km) Turnoff for **Whiteswan Lake Provincial Park**, 11 miles/17.5 km east via Forest Service Road; 114 campsites located at 5 campgrounds, picnic areas, pit toilets, dump station ($5), fishing, swimming and boat launch. Camping fee $20–$23. Both **Alces** and **Whiteswan** lakes are stocked with rainbow trout. (Alces Lake, no powerboats, and fly-fishing only.) Lussier Hot Springs, located near the park entrance, is accessed via a short hike; change room and toilets at parking lot.

CR 211.5 CB 101.8 JP 267.5 (430.5 km)

Kootenay River bridge.

CR 211.8 CB 102.1 JP 267.2 (430 km) Restaurant, A&W, RV park.

CR 213.9 CB 104.2 JP 265.1 (426.6 km) Turnoff for **Canal Flats** (unincorporated) via loop road through town; 2.5 miles/4 km to east side of Columbia Lake is Canal Flats Provincial Park; picnic area, swimming, boat launch.

CR 214.8 CB 105.1 JP 264.2 (425.2 km) Turnout with litter bin and interpretive sign. In 1886, William Baillie-Grohman conceived a scheme to connect the Kootenay and Columbia rivers by means of a canal. (At this point, the two great rivers are separated only by 1.2 miles/2 km of flat land.) The canal and 1 lock were built, but only 2 ships made the passage. Not only was the canal too narrow and shallow, but it caused flooding of the Columbia Valley. The canal was abandoned.

CR 222.3 CB 112.6 JP 256.7 (413.1 km) Double-ended turnout to east with good view of Columbia Lake.

CR 222.5 CB 112.8 JP 256.5 (412.8 km) Rest area to east with picnic tables, litter bins and toilets; view of Columbia Lake

CR 224.1 CB 114.4 JP 254.9 (410.2 km) Turnout with litter bins.

CR 226.1 CB 116.4 JP 252.9 (407 km) Dutch Creek bridge.

CR 226.6 CB 116.9 JP 252.4 (406.2 km) Gas station and restaurant.

CR 227.8 CB 118.1 JP 251.2 (404.3 km) RV park and campground.

CR 228.1 CB 118.4 JP 250.9 (403.8 km) Columbia River bridge. Riverside Golf Course.

CR 228.9 CB 119.2 JP 250.1 (402.5 km) **Fairmont Hot Springs**, a resort community with food, gas, lodging, camping and post office. Fairmont Hot Springs Resort (250/345-6070 or 1-800-663-4979) offers lodging, an RV park, restaurants, hot mineral pools, 3 golf courses, tennis courts, and many other amenities. www.fairmonthotsprings.com.

CR 229.1 CB 119.4 JP 249.9 (402.2 km) Subway and gas station.

CR 233.8 CB 124.1 JP 245.2 (394.6 km) Distance marker northbound shows Radium Hot Springs 29 km/18 miles, Golden 131 km/81 miles, Banff 157 km/98 miles.

CR 237 CB 127.3 JP 242 (389.5 km) RV park and campground.

CR 240.1 CB 130.4 JP 238.9 (384.5 km) Entering **Windermere** northbound, a resort settlement on the east shore of Lake Windermere.

CR 240.7 CB 131 JP 238.3 (383.5 km) Gas station, restaurant.

CR 242 CB 132.3 JP 237 (381.4 km) Gas station, bowling alley.

CR 243.4 CB 133.7 JP 235.6 (379.2 km) Visitor center at **junction** with road leading 2 miles/4 km west around north end of Windermere Lake to the summer resort community of **Invermere on the Lake** and the winter ski destination **Panorama Mountain Village** (invermerepanorama.com). James Chabot Beach Provincial Park, 1 mile/2 km west, on the north shore of Windermere Lake, has picnic tables and a fine beach for swimming and water sports. Panorama Ski Resort

CR 243.7 CB 134 JP 235.3 (378.7 km) Traffic light; Tim Hortons.

CR 249.4 CB 139.7 JP 229.6 (369.5 km) Road east to **Dry Gulch Provincial Park**; 26 campsites.

CR 250 CB 140.3 JP 229 (368.5 km) Radium Hot Springs golf course.

CR 250.6 CB 140.9 JP 228.4 (367.6 km) Turnout to west with litter bin and interpretive sign.

Three more viewpoints along west side of the road next 0.4 mile northbound give good views of Rocky Mountain Trench and Columbia River. *NOTE: Safe access for viewpoints southbound traffic only.*

©Kris Valencia, staff

CR 252 CB 142.3 JP 227 (365.3 km) Entering **RADIUM HOT SPRINGS** (pop. 1,000). **Visitor Information:** Visitor Center (pictured above) on right northbound; phone 250-347-9331; tourismradium.com. This is also the turnoff for **Redstreak Campground** (Kootenay National Park); it is located 1.2 miles/2 km uphill from the visitor center. Redstreak has 232 campsites (reservations accepted), restrooms/showers, dump station, hiking trails; open mid-May to September; camping fee $27.40 to $38.20; firepits add $8.80. Winter camping available.

This resort community spreads out alongside the highway, offering an array of restaurants, motel and resort accommodations, gas stations and other services. Chief attractions include the hot mineral pool complex—Radium Hot Springs—operated by Parks Canada; river rafting on the Kootenay and Kicking Horse rivers; ziplining on Valley Zipline's 7-line course; and skiing

nearby Panorama Mountain in winter. The hot springs facility, which includes Pleiades Spa and Wellness, is open daily, year-round; phone 250-347-9485; website: hotsprings.ca.

CR 252.2 CB 142.5 JP 226.8 (365 km) Traffic light: Highway 95 continues north to Golden; Highway 93 goes east to Banff. *Northbound travelers TURN RIGHT at this light and continue on Highway 93;* southbound travelers turn left to Highways 93/95.

CANADA HIGHWAY 93

CR 253 CB 143.3 JP 226 (363.7 km) Kootenay National Park entrance gate for northbound travelers. National Park pass required for Banff, Jasper, Yoho and Kootenay; fee charged.

CR 254.1 CB 144.4 JP 224.9 (361.9 km) Radium Hot Springs; outdoor hot mineral pool, swimming pool, plunge pool, spa. Parking for cars, RVs and motorcoaches in main parking lot. Pools open daily year-round; seasonal hours posted at hotsprings. ca. The mineral water is at temperatures between 98°–104°F/37°–40°C. The water contains calcium, sulphate, magnesium, silica and bicarbonate. The springs were originally called Sinclair, but the name was changed to Radium in 1915, because of the water's relatively high radioactivity.

Northbound, the highway goes through a short tunnel known as the Iron Gates, then follows fast-flowing Sinclair Creek up to Sinclair Pass summit (elev. 4,875 feet/1,486m). This stretch of road is full of pedestrians in summer; drive with care.

CR 260.1 CB 150.4 JP 218.9 (352.3 km) Brake-check area for northbound traffic.

CR 262.6 CB 152.9 JP 216.4 (348.3 km) Viewpoint overlooking the Kootenay River valley.

CR 264.8 CB 155.1 JP 214.2 (344.7 km) Settlers Road southeast to park boundary.

CR 267.3 CB 157.6 JP 211.7 (340.7 km) Kootenay River picnic area.

CR 269.8 CB 160.1 JP 209.2 (336.6 km) McLeod Meadows picnic area. Dog Lake trailhead, 1.5 miles/2.4 km. **McLeod Meadows Campground** (Kootenay National Park) with 88 sites, kitchen shelters, dump station, flush toilets; interpretive programs. Open mid-June to mid-September. Camping fee $21.50/night; firepits add $8.80.

CR 270.7 CB 161 JP 208.3 (335.2 km) Turnout with litter bins to east.

CR 274.5 CB 164.7 JP 204.5 (329.1 km) Dolly Varden picnic area and hiking trail to west.

CR 279.7 CB 170 JP 199.3 (320.7 km) Turnout.

CR 279.8 CB 170.1 JP 199.2 (320.5 km) Kootenay River bridge at Kootenay Crossing. Warden Station. West Kootenay Trail.

CR 280.5 CB 170.8 JP 198.5 (319.4 km) Distance marker northbound shows Lake Louise 92 km/57 miles, Banff 90 km/56 miles.

CR 282.3 CB 172.6 JP 196.7 (316.5 km) Hector Gorge viewpoint. The gorge was named for Dr. James Hector, a geologist with the Palliser Expedition who explored the area in 1858.

CR 288.5 CB 178.8 JP 190.5 (306.6 km) Turnout for southbound traffic.

CR 289.5 CB 179.8 JP 189.5 (305 km) Turnout.

CR 290 CB 180.3 JP 189 (304.1 km) Turnoff for Simpson River trail.

CR 292.6 CB 182.9 JP 186.4 (300 km) **Vermilion Crossing.** Kootenay Park Lodge

(phone 250-434-9648; kootenayparklodge. com) has a small general store, 11 cabins (reservations recommended) and restaurant. Store open daily in season. Restaurant serves dinner daily, 5-8 P.M., June 1 to Sept. 16. Picnic area near river bridge. Start of Verdant and Verendrye Creek trails.

CR 297.9 CB 188.2 JP 181.1 (291.4 km) Floe Lake trailhead to west; Hawk Creek to Ball Pass, trail to east.

CR 303.2 CB 193.5 JP 175.8 (282.9 km) Turnoff for access road west across the river to Numa picnic area and trail up Numa Creek. North of the bridge, Vermilion River tumbles into picturesque falls.

CR 306.1 CB 196.4 JP 172.9 (278.2 km) Turnoff to west for Paint Pots picnic area; nature trail crosses river to area of brightly colored earth along Ochre Creek, where red and yellow clays have been stained by deposits of iron from mineral springs.

CR 307.7 CB 198 JP 171.3 (275.6 km) Turnoff to west for Marble Canyon picnic area.

CR 307.8 CB 198.1 JP 171.2 (275.5 km) Turnoff to west for **Marble Canyon Campground** (Kootenay National Park), open late June to early September; 61 sites, kitchen shelters, dump station and flush toilets. Open late June to early September. Start of 1-mile/2-km hike along rim of Marble Canyon. Camping fee $21.50; firepits add $8.80.

CR 310.1 CB 200.4 JP 168.9 (271.8 km) Trailhead parking for Stanley Glacier, 3-mile/4.8-km hike.

CR 312 CB 202.3 JP 167 (268.7 km) Banff National Park boundary. Leaving Kootenay National Park northbound.

CR 312.2 CB 202.5 JP 166.8 (268.4 km) Rest area to east.

CR 313.1 CB 203.4 JP 165.9 (267 km) Welcome to Alberta (northbound sign).

CR 313.4 CB 203.7 JP 165.6 (266.5 km) Turnout to west.

CR 314.6 CB 204.9 JP 164.4 (264.5 km) Brake-check area with litter bin for southbound motorists.

CR 315.3 CB 205.6 JP 163.7 (263.4 km) Turnoff for **Storm Mountain Lodge & Cabins**. Constructed in 1922, the cabins are historic and elegant, and the dining room is known for its fine cuisine; phone 403-762-4155; stormmountainlodge.com. The restaurant is open for breakfast, lunch and dinner daily from the beginning of June to early October. See website for restaurant and lodge operating hours/days for fall/winter/spring months.

CR 318.3 CB 208.6 JP 160.7 (258.6 km) Exit to Trans-Canada Highway 1 East for Banff and Calgary.

CR 318.4 CB 208.7 JP 160.6 (258.4 km) Avalanche gate. Large turnout.

CR 318.6 CB 208.9 JP 160.4 (258.1 km) **Castle Junction. Junction** with Trans-Canada Highway 1. Northbound travelers exit here for Trans-Canada Highway 1 West to Lake Louise and Icefields Parkway. Highways 1 and 93 share a common alignment between Castle Junction and junction with Icefields Parkway. Northbound travelers take this exit and continue with this log. *Southbound travelers exit to Highway 93 South.*

Also access at this junction to Highway 1A (Bow Valley Parkway), a scenic alternate route between Lake Louise and Banff, which also provides access to Johnston Canyon, Protection Mountain and Castle Mountain campgrounds.

Driving mileages east on Trans-Canada 1 are Banff 32 km/20 miles and Calgary is 157 km/97 miles.

CANADA HIGHWAY 93/TRANS-CANADA HIGHWAY 1

Distance from Coeur d'Alene (CR) is followed by distance from Trans-Canada Highway 1/93 Castle Junction (CJ) and distance from Jasper (JP).
Southbound, distance from Coeur d'Alene (CR) is followed by distance from the Canadian Border at Kingsgate (CB) and distance from Jasper (JP).

CR 318.6 CJ 0 JP 160.4 (258.1 km) **Castle Junction. Junction** with Trans-Canada Highway 1 and BC Highway 93 South.

CR 319.1 CJ 0.5 JP 159.9 (257.3 km) Distance marker westbound shows Lake Louise 25 km/15 miles, Field 50 km/31 miles.

CR 323.1 CJ 4.5 JP 155.9 (250.9 km) Taylor rest area to south accessible to both east and westbound traffic; parking picnic tables, litter bins, toilets and hiking trail.

CR 330.2 CJ 11.6 JP 148.8 (239.5 km) Temple rest area to north for westbound traffic; viewpoint, toilets, picnic tables.

CR 331.4 CJ 12.8 JP 147.6 (237.5 km) Overflow parking for Lake Louise to south; shuttle to Lake Louise.

CR 332.5 CJ 13.9 JP 146.5 (235.7 km) Restrooms and litter bins to north.

CR 334.6 CJ 16 JP 145.4 (234 km) Exit south to **LAKE LOUISE** village (description follows) via Lake Louise Drive, and north to Highway 1A (Bow River Parkway) an alternate route to Castle Junction and Banff with access to Castle Mountain, Johnston Canyon and Protection Mountain Campgrounds. Access road to Moraine Lake branches off Lake Louise Drive.

LAKE LOUISE (pop. 1,500) is a popular destination resort serving summer tourists and winter skiers; food, gas, diesel, lodging, shopping and lots of traffic in the summertime. Camping at **Lake Louise Campground** (Banff National Park), turn on Fairview Drive from Lake Louise Drive; 189 RV sites, 206 tent sites. **Visitor Information:** Lake Louise Visitor Center by Samson Mall, phone 403-522-3833; www.banfflakelouise.com.

Shopping and services 0.1 mile south from the highway. *NOTE: Parking is very limited in Lake Louise, which is why there is overflow parking on the Trans-Canada Highway (see **Milepost CR 331.4**) with shuttle service to Lake Louise.*

Both the baronial Chateau Lake Louise and the much-photographed alpine lake of the same name are located 2.5 miles/4 km from Lake Louise village via Lake Louise Drive. Be aware that you cannot see the lake from the road, and it is not unusual to drive up and be turned away because there are no places to park. You may or may not find parking along the access road (all parking lots were full when we visited on a Monday in July last summer). It is especially difficult for large RVs. Guests only are allowed in the Chateau Lake Louise parking lot.

CR 335.3 CJ 16.7 JP 143.7 (231.2 km) Exit for Pipestone trailhead.

CR 335.8 CJ 17.2 JP 143.2 (230.4 km) Wildlife overpass.

CR 336.1 CJ 17.5 J 142.9 (229.9 km) **Junction** of Trans–Canada Highway 1 with Highway 93 North (Icefields Parkway).

Icefields Parkway is known for its mountain and lake scenery. (©Kris Valencia, staff)

Northbound travelers exit to Highway 93 North. *Southbound travelers on this route exit east on Trans-Canada Highway 1.*

CANADA HIGHWAY 93 North (Icefields Parkway)

CR 336.5 CJ 17.9 JP 142.5 (229.3 km) Seasonal driving conditions are posted here.

CR 336.8 CJ 18.2 JP 142.2 (228.8 km) Distance marker northbound shows Saskatchewan Crossing 85 km/53 miles, Jasper 230 km/143 miles, Rocky Mountain House 250 km/155 miles.

CR 337.2 CJ 18.6 JP 141.8 (228.2 km) Northbound sign shows next gas is 53 miles/85 km at Saskatchewan Crossing, open in summer only. During winter, next gas northbound is in Jasper.

CR 338.3 CJ 19.7 JP 140.7 (226.4 km) Herbert Lake picnic area to west with litter bin and toilet. The lake is known as a "sink" because it has no visible outlet. Swimming (very narrow beach areas in tall straight pines). Good lake for tube floating.

CR 351 CJ 32.4 JP 128 (206 km) Mosquito Creek hostel on the south side of Mosquito Creek bridge. **Mosquito Creek Campground** (Banff National Park) is just to the north of the bridge and is open June 1 to Oct. 9, 32 sites, toilets, firewood for sale, potable water, picnic tables; camping fee is $17.60. Molar Pass trailhead.

CR 356.5 CJ 37.9 JP 122.5 (197.1 km) Crowfoot Glacier viewpoint to west; large paved parking area. Trailhead for Helen Lake to east (6-km/3.7-mile hike) and Dolomite Pass.

CR 357.6 CJ 39 JP 121.4 (195.4 km) Bow Lake viewpoint and picnic area to the southwest. Lake may be ice-covered into June. Turquoise-colored Bow Lake is the headwater for the Bow River.

CR 358.2 CJ 39.6 JP 120.8 (194.4 km) Turnoff for Num-ti-jah Lodge (open June to October); food, lodging and phone 403-522-2167. Num-ti-jah Lodge was built in the 1920s by pioneer guide Jimmy Simpson. The mountain above the lake was named after him. Access to Bow Glacier Falls trail.

CR 361.4 CJ 42.8 JP 117.6 (189.2 km) **Bow Summit** (elev. 2,088m/6,849 feet)—highest point on the Icefield's Parkway). Short side road west to Peyto Lake view-

point. The glacial meltwater lake, a brilliant turquoise from suspended glacial sediments, lies several hundred feet below the viewpoint. Short, steep trail from viewpoint to lakeshore. Designated bus and handicap parking.

CR 362 CJ 43.4 JP 117 (188.3 km) Turnout to east with information boards.

CR 362.2 CJ 43.6 JP 116.8 (188 km) Uphill gravel turnout to west with information boards about the geology of cirques.

CR 368.2 CJ 49.6 JP 110.8 (178.3 km) **Silverhorn Campground** (Banff National Park) to west. Open July 21 to Sept. 10; with 45 sites (first-come, first-served), suitable for large RVs; toilets, picnic tables, firepits, no water; camping fee $15.70.

CR 368.4 CJ 49.8 JP 110.6 (178 km) Double-ended paved turnout to the west.

CR 370.8 CJ 52.2 JP 108.2 (174.1 km) Viewpoint to west (brush-filled in summer 2018); litter bins.

CR 371.4 CJ 52.8 JP 107.6 (172.9 km) **Waterfowl Lake Campground** (Banff National Park) is open June 23 to Sept. 4, 116 sites, flush toilets, washing basins, sanidump, picnic tables, kitchen shelters, firewood for sale, camping fee $21.50; hiking trails to Cirque and Chephren lakes.

Northbound, the highway runs beside Waterfowl Lake.

CR 372.3 CJ 53.7 JP 106.7 (171.7 km) Turnout to west on Waterfowl Lake with litter bins.

CR 373.1 CJ 54.5 JP 105.9 (170.4 km) Turnout to west on Waterfowl Lake.

CR 376.4 CJ 57.8 JP 102.6 (165.1 km) Double-ended turnout to east.

CR 377.4 CJ 58.8 JP 101.6 (163.5 km) Turnout to west.

CR 380.3 CJ 61.7 JP 98.7 (158.8 km) Paved turnout to west and trail to Mistaya Canyon, a 10-minute walk. Here the river has worn a deep, twisting gorge into the limestone bedrock, and tumbling boulders have created potholes and a natural arch in the canyon sides.

CR 382.4 CJ 63.8 JP 96.6 (155.4 km) Saskatchewan Crossing warden station.

CR 382.5 CJ 63.9 JP 96.5 (155.3 km) Saskatchewan River bridge.

CR 383.3 CJ 64.7 JP 95.7 (154 km) Rest

area to west with litter bins, picnic tables and pit toilets; Howse Pass Lookout.

CR 383.6 CJ 65 JP 95.4 (153.5 km) Junction with Alberta Highway 11 (David Thompson Highway), which goes east to the old mining town of Nordegg, now a Provincial Historic Site; Rocky Mountain House 180 km/112 miles and Red Deer, 257 km/160 miles.

CR 383.8 CJ 65.2 JP 95.2 (153.2 km) Saskatchewan Crossing. The Crossing resort (seasonal) offers dining (restaurant, cafe, pub), lodging, service station (gas, diesel, propane, dump station) and overnight RV parking; phone 403-761-7000. The Mistaya, Howse and North Saskatchewan rivers converge here. Rest stop in front parking area has an impressive David Thompson information board, seating and "map compass." Good photo op. *Next gas northbound 153 km/95 miles.*

Distance marker northbound shows Columbia Icefields 52 km/32 miles, Jasper 153 km/95 miles.

CR 384.3 CJ 65.7 JP 94.7 (152.4 km) Trail to Glacier Lake (9 km/5.5 miles) to south. Litter bins and information boards.

CR 384.4 CJ 65.8 JP 94.6 (152.2 km) Avalanche gates.

CR 391.2 CJ 72.6 JP 87.8 (141.3 km) Rampart Creek hostel to the east.

CR 391.4 CJ 72.8 JP 87.6 (141 km) Rampart Creek Campground (Banff National Park) to west. Open June 1 to Oct. 9 with 50 sites, toilets, firewood for sale, camping fee $17.60. Some loops are suitable only for vehicles under 7.5m/25 feet.

Highway follows the North Saskatchewan River north. *CAUTION: Watch for moose.*

CR 391.9 CJ 73.3 JP 87.1 (140.2 km) Turnout to west with view.

CR 392.4 CJ 73.8 JP 86.6 (139.4 km) Turnout to west with mountain views, including Mount Amery (elev. 3,335m/10,941 feet), Mount Saskatchewan (elev. 3,342m/10,964 feet) and Cleopatra's Needle, a dolomite pinnacle also known as the Lighthouse Tower. Information board about mountains, litter bin.

CR 392.6 CJ 74 JP 86.4 (139 km) Turnout to west with mountain views. Mount Coleman viewpoint.

CR 394 CJ 75.4 JP 85 (136.8 km) Turnoff to east for Pinto Lake trailhead parking; litter bins, hiking trail information.

CR 395 CJ 76.4 JP 84 (135.2 km) Turnout to west with mountain and river views.

CR 398 CJ 79.4 JP 81 (130.3 km) Turnoff to west for access to Coleman Creek picnic area. Car, RV and tour bus friendly. Over 20 picnic tables spread out in pristine setting. Toilets, litter bins. Place to walk along river. Popular picnic spot.

CR 398.7 CJ 80.1 JP 80.3 (129.2 km) Large paved turnout to west.

CR 400.4 CJ 81.8 JP 78.6 (126.5 km) Turnout to west by North Saskatchewan River; litter bins and information board on mountains.

CR 401.4 CJ 82.8 JP 77.6 (124.9 km) Weeping Wall viewpoint to west with toilets. Water from melting snowfields high above the Cirrus Mountain cliffs finds its way through cracks in the wall and emerges as a series of graceful waterfalls.

CR 402.7 CJ 84.1 JP 76.3 (122.8 km) Turnout to west. Highway begins 3.1-mile climb northbound to "Big Bend," a steep switch-back stretch of road (*new pavement summer 2018*).

CR 403.6 CJ 85 JP 75 (120.7 km) North Saskatchewan River bridge. View Nigel Canyon from bridge.

CR 404 CJ 85.4 JP 75 (120.7 km) Turnout to west.

CR 404.9 CJ 86.3 JP 74.1 (119.2 km) Large turnout to west at Big Bend; hiking trails. Highway climbs steeply northbound; dramatic views to south.

CR 405.8 CJ 87.2 JP 73.2 (117.8 km) Turnout for long viewpoint. Great photo op of North Saskatchewan River valley. Considered the best viewpoint on this route.

CR 406.1 CJ 87.5 JP 72.9 (117.3 km) Bridal Veil Falls viewpoint to east; litter bins.

CR 406.7 CJ 88.1 JP 72.3 (116.4 km) Turnout to east at trailhead for Nigel Creek, a 7.2 km/4.5 mile 1-way (5 hours roundtrip) day hike.

CR 408 CJ 89.4 JP 71 (114.3 km) Turnout to east.

CR 409 CJ 90.4 JP 70 (112.6 km) Parker Ridge rest area with toilets and information boards to west. Trailhead for Parker Ridge trail, a popular 3-hour round-trip day hike that leads to a great view of Saskatchewan Glacier.

CR 409.5 CJ 90.9 JP 69.5 (111.8 km) Hilda Creek hostel to west.

CR 409.7 CJ 91.1 JP 69.3 (111.8 km) Rest area to east with litter bins.

CR 411.8 CJ 93.2 JP 67.2 (108.1 km) Turnout with litter bins to west at **Sunwapta Pass** (elev. 2,035m/6,676 feet), the second highest point on the Icefields Parkway. Monument and map marks the boundary between Banff and Jasper national parks.

Avalanche area northbound. Avoid stopping along this stretch of road.

Highway begins long descent southbound.

CR 412.8 CJ 94.2 JP 66.2 (106.5 km) Wilcox Creek Campground (Jasper National Park) to east, campground is in tiers with camping sites reached through loop road. Open May 30 to Sept. 17, first come, first served; with 46 sites suitable for RVs and trailers under 27 feet, sani-dump, outhouses, picnic tables, cook shelters, firepits, firewood, "Ranger Talk Theatre" is uphill in heavy timber. Camping fee $15.70/night. Trailhead for popular Wilcox Pass day hike.

CR 413.8 CJ 95.2 JP 65.2 (104.9 km) Icefield Campground (Jasper National Park) to east; tents only. Open June 5 to Oct. 14, first come, first served; with 33 sites, toilets, picnic tables, firepits. Camping fee is $15.70/night.

CR 414.5 CJ 95.9 JP 64.5 (103.8 km) Columbia Icefield Discovery Center on east side of highway features Parks Canada interpretive displays as well as information services, gift shop and restrooms. Food services include a restaurant and cafeteria. The center is open mid-April to mid-October; phone the Parks Canada desk at 780-852-6288. Tickets and shuttles for Glacier Adventure (Sno-coach tours) and Glacier Skywalk available here. Lodging is available at the Glacier View Inn, located on the top floor of the center; phone 1-866-606-6700.

Icefields Center RV Campground (Jasper National Park), open May 1 to Oct. 30, first come, first served; with 100 sites for trailers and RVs only; no water and no firepits.

CR 414.6 CJ 96 JP 64.4 (103.6 km) Athabasca Glacier trail access and parking to west via side road across highway from Glacier Center. The glaciers visible from the road are fingers of the giant Columbia Icefield, which covers 388 square km/241 square miles.

CR 414.7 CJ 96.1 JP 64.3 (103.5 km) Additional Columbia Icefield Discovery Center parking for cars and RVs to east.

CR 415.8 CJ 97.2 JP 63.2 (101.7 km) Distance marker northbound shows Jasper 102 km/63 miles.

CR 416.1 CJ 97.5 JP 62.9 (101.2 km) Slow for posted speed zone southbound.

CR 417 CJ 98.4 JP 62 (99.8 km) Slow for posted speed zones northbound.

CR 418.3 CJ 99.7 JP 60.7 (97.7 km) Glacier Skywalk to west; no public parking, no public access without a ticket. The Glacier Skywalk leads to a glass-floored observation platform 280m/918 feet above the Sunwapta Valley. Tickets and shuttle service to the Glacier Skywalk are at the Columbia Icefield Discovery Center; glacierskywalk.ca.

CR 419.1 CJ 100.5 JP 59.9 (96.4 km) Tangle Creek rest area to west. Two large parking areas with litter bins and toilets. Spectacular waterfalls just across highway—*use caution if crossing highway.*

Slow for curves northbound.

CR 420.2 CJ 1016 JP 58.8 (94.6 km) Stutfield double-ended turnout with view of glacier and mountains.

CR 420.5 CJ 101.9 JP 58.5 (94.1 km) *CAUTION: Caribou crossing next 20 kms/12 miles.*

CR 424.3 CJ 105.7 JP 54.7 (88 km) Sign and turnout east for Beauty Creek.

CR 425.5 CJ 106.9 JP 53.5 (86 km) Rest area with phone, litter bin and toilets to west at trailhead for Beauty Creek/Stanley Falls. Beauty Creek Hostel.

CR 426.6 CJ 108 JP 52.4 (84.3 km) Turnout to west with litter bin; information boards about Mushroom Peak, Endless Chain and other mountains.

CR 431.2 CJ 112.6 JP 47.8 (76.9 km) Jonas Creek Campground (Jasper National Park) to east. Open May 15 to Sept. 24, first-come, first-served; with 25 sites suitable for tents, motorhomes and trailers under 25 feet; toilets, picnic tables, firepits. Sheltered picnic area, bearproof storage boxes, potable water. Tenting sites are mostly walk-in. Camping fee is $15.70/night.

CR 434.4 CJ 115.8 JP 44.6 (71.8 km) Pobokton Creek bridge. Sunwapta station to west. Pobokton Creek trail to east. Toilets, enviro containers, telephone, garbage bins and information boards. Avalanche gates.

CR 441.4 CJ 122.8 JP 37.6 (60.5 km) Bubbling Springs picnic site to east; toilets, telephone, litter bins.

CR 445.1 CJ 126.5 JP 33.9 (54.5 km) Sunwapta Falls Rocky Mountain Lodge to west at turnoff for Sunwapta Falls. Sunwapta Falls viewpoint and picnic area is 1 km/0.6 mile west via paved road; parking, toilets, and short walk to falls at end of access road. Sunwapta Falls Rocky Mountain Lodge offers restaurant and lodging from late June into September; phone 1-888-828-5777; website: sunwapta.com.

CR 445.2 CJ 126.6 JP 33.8 (54.4 km) Distance marker northbound shows Jasper 53 km/33 miles.

CR 446.5 CJ 127.9 JP 32.5 (52.3 km) Trailhead parking to east for Buck and Osprey lakes, litter bins.

CR 447.3 CJ 128.7 JP 31.7 (51 km) **Honeymoon Lake Campground** (Jasper National Park) to east. Open May 15 to Sept. 24 (first come, first served); 35 sites suitable for tents, motorhomes and trailers under 25 feet; picnic tables, firepits, outhouses, bear proof lockers. Covered picnic table, some lakeside camping sites. Camping fee is $15.70/night. [△]

CR 447.7 CJ 129.1 JP 31.3 (50.4 km) Paved turnout with litter bins to west.

CR 450.4 CJ 131.8 JP 28.6 (46 km) Small paved turnoff with litter bins to west by riverbend.

CR 450.9 CJ 132.3 JP 28.1 (45.2 km) Small paved turnoff with litter bins to west. View of Mount Christie (elev. 3,103m/10,180 feet).

CR 453.4 CJ 134.8 JP 25.6 (41.2 km) Picnic area beside Athabasca River to south with litter bins, picnic tables, firepits and toilets.

CR 455.2 CJ 136.6 JP 23.8 (38.3 km) Turnout to west with litter bins overlooking river. View of Mount Fryatt.

Goat Lookout, a popular animal lick. Watch for motorists stopping to look at mountain goats.

CR 455.7 CJ 137.1 JP 23.3 (37.5 km) Double-ended turnout to west with litter bins and toilets. Short path to viewpoint for Mount Kerkeslin (elev. 2,956m/9,698 feet) and the Athabasca River.

CR 457.2 CJ 138.6 JP 21.8 (35.1 km) **Mount Kerkeslin Campground** (Jasper National Park) to west. Open May 15 to Sept. 30, first come, first served; with 42 sites suitable for tents, RVs and trailers under 25 feet; picnic tables, outhouses, firepits, potable water, covered picnic area, bear proof storage, firewood. Natural canoe launch and water access to Fryatt Valley. Camping fee is $15.70/night. [△]

CR 459.3 CJ 140.7 JP 19.7 (31.7 km) Athabasca hostel to east.

CR 459.7 CJ 141.1 JP 19.3 (29.1 km) **Junction** with south end of Highway 93A; a 24-km/15-mile alternate route which rejoins the main highway at **Milepost CR 474.4.** Turnoff on Highway 93A for access to **Athabasca Falls**: Follow signs 0.6 km/0.4 mile from main highway to parking area with picnic tables, garbage bins and toilets. Athabasca Falls drops just 12m/40 feet, but it is through a short, narrow canyon and the sight is worth the stop.

CR 459.9 CJ 141.3 JP 19.1 (30.7 km) Distance marker northbound shows Jasper 30 km/19 miles.

CR 461.6 CJ 143 JP 17.4 (28 km) Double-ended gravel turnout uphill to east; litter bins, toilets. Hike to Horseshoe Lake under the cliffs of Mount Hardisty.

CR 463.2 CJ 144.6 JP 15.8 (25.4 km) Large turnout with litter bins to west is mountain viewpoint for Mounts Edith Cavell and Hardisty.

CR 463.4 CJ 144.8 JP 15.6 (25.1 km) Turnout to west with litter bins; mountain viewpoint for Mounts Athabasca and Kerkeslin.

CR 469.8 CJ 151.2 JP 9.2 (14.8 km) Trailhead for Wabasso Lake, Shovel Pass and the Maligne Valley.

CR 473.1 CJ 154.5 JP 5.9 (9.5 km) Avalanche gates. Parking to east with litter bins and toilets; trailhead for Valley of the Five Lakes hike.

CR 474 CJ 155.4 JP 5 (8 km) Athabasca

Athabasca Glacier trail access and parking are on the west side of Icefields Parkway, just north of the Columbia Icefield Discovery Center. (©Lilly Graef)

River.

CR 474.1 CJ 155.5 JP 4.9 (7.9 km) Paddler parking area to east with pit toilets.

CR 474.4 CJ 155.8 JP 4.6 (7.4 km) **Junction** with Highway 93A access southwest to Marmot Basin ski area and **Wabasso Campground** (Jasper National Park). Open May 1 to Oct. 7, reservations accepted; 231 sites, best suited for tents, motorhomes and trailers under 27 feet; 51 electrical hookups; picnic tables, firepits, flush toilets. Camping fee is $21.50–$27.40/night. [△]

CR 474.8 CJ 156.2 JP 4.2 (6.7 km) **Southbound Tollgate** for Icefields Parkway. Stop here to pay toll.

CR 475.1 CJ 156.5 JP 3.9 (6.2 km) Turnout to east with area maps, information boards from the Lions Club. Welcome to Jasper (northbound sign).

CR 475.5 CJ 156.9 JP 3.5 (5.6 km) Becker's Chalets (lodging) to east.

CR 476.4 CJ 157.8 JP 2.6 (4.2 km) Turnoff to east for **Wapiti Campground** (Jasper National Park). Reservations accepted for summer season, May 2 to Oct. 6; winter season (Oct. 7 to May 1) is first-come, first-served. Campground in summer has 362 sites that can accommodate most sizes of motorhomes and trailers; 86 electrical hookups; sani-dump, showers, interpretive programs. Fees from $27.40–$32.30/night. (Winter season: 93 campsites available.) [△]

Elk (wapiti) frequent this valley in fall and winter.

CR 477 CJ 158.4 JP 2 (3.2 km) Jasper House Bungalows (lodging).

CR 477.5 CJ 158.9 JP 1.5 (2.4 km) Turnoff to west **Jasper Skytram** (description follows). *Whistlers campground, also on this side road, will be closed in 2019 for major reconstruction; it reopens in 2020.* Drive 4 km/2.5 miles west on side road for Jasper Skytram, which takes you up Whistler Mountain to the 2,285-m/7,496-ft level. Skytram parking lot will accommodate RVs; there is also a shuttle service from Jasper hotels and town center. Jasper Skytram operates late March through Nov. 1 (check seasonal operating times and rates at www.jasperskytram.com). Allow 2 hours for tram ride. At the top of

the lift is a restaurant, an interpretive area and trail to summit.

CR 477.8 CJ 159.2 JP 1.2 (1.9 km) Alternate access (93A) leads northeast to Jasper.

CR 478.2 CJ 159.6 JP 0.8 (1.3 km) Gravel turnout with litter bin to west.

Slow for speed zones northbound.

Miette River bridge.

CR 478.5 CJ 160.1 JP 0.5 (0.8 km) **Junction** of Highway 93 and Highway 16. Continue north across Highway 16 for Jasper (description follows). Turn west for Prince George and Kamloops, east for Edmonton, on Highway 16.

Junction with Yellowhead Highway 16. Turn to **Milepost E 219.9** on page 252 in the YELLOWHEAD HIGHWAY section for log of highway to Hinton or Prince George.

CR 479 CJ 160.4 JP 0 Junction of Connaught Drive/93 and Hazelton Avenue/93A in Jasper; Petro-Canada and Esso gas/diesel stations at this intersection. Next gas southbound is 153 km/95 miles from here. [⛽]

JASPER (pop. 5,235) is the townsite and park headquarters for Jasper National Park.

Visitor Information: Brochures, maps, reservations and permits at Jasper National Park Information Center, housed in the historic 1914 building. Open year-round; phone 780-852-6176. **Emergency Services:** Dial 911. RCMP, phone 780-852-4848.

Lodging available year-round, with accommodations ranging from bungalows to luxury lodges like the Fairmont Jasper Park Lodge. Jasper's compact, pedestrian-friendly town center has plenty of dining spots and shopping. Public parking for cars and RVs available along Connaught Drive.

Marmot Basin makes Jasper a popular ski area in winter. The town and park also offer a variety of summer attractions, including the nearby Skytram (shuttles from downtown hotels and town center); fishing, horseback riding, hiking, rafting, boating; and cruises on Maligne Lake.

Turn to Milepost E 219.9
Yellowhead Highway

Central Access Route

CONNECTS: Ellensburg, WA, to Yellowhead Hwy. 16 Jct., BC

Length: 596 miles   **Road Surface:** Paved   **Season:** Open all year

Wells Gray Provincial Park's waterfalls are one of the major attractions along this route. This is Spahats Falls. (©Kris Valencia, staff)

Distance in miles

	Clearwater	Ellensburg	Kamloops	Kelowna	Osoyoos	Vernon	Yellowhead 16
Clearwater		462	76	181	258	148	135
Ellensburg	462		386	281	204	314	596
Kamloops	76	386		105	182	72	210
Kelowna	181	281	105		77	33	315
Osoyoos	258	204	182	77		110	392
Vernon	148	314	72	33	110		282
Yellowhead 16	135	596	210	315	392	282	

The Central Access Route extends from Ellensburg, WA, on Interstate 90 (106 miles east of Seattle) through northcentral Washington and southcentral British Columbia to junction with Yellowhead Highway 16, at Tete Jaune Cache; a distance of 596 miles/960 km. This is a mostly 2-lane road through towns, vineyards, orchards, and pine-scented hills, past beautiful lakes offering swimming, beaches and picturesque venues for other water sports. Summers can be *very* warm. *CAUTION: Watch for deer along this route.*

From Tete Jaune Cache, travelers have 2 choices to reach Dawson Creek and the start of the Alaska Highway. One way is west on the Yellowhead Highway 16 to Prince George, then north on Highway 97 to Dawson Creek, a distance of 416 miles/669 km. The other choice is to drive east on the Yellowhead Highway 16 through the northern edge of Jasper National Park then take the Bighorn Route/Highway 40 north to Grande Prairie (this turnoff is about 5 miles west of Hinton), then Highways 43/2 to Dawson Creek, for a total driving distance of 390 miles/628 km.

The multi-lane Coquihalla Highway between Hope and Kamloops is logged as an alternate route in this section. Central Access Route travelers can catch the Coquihalla at Kamloops or west from Highway 97 south of Kelowna via Highway 97C (the Okanagan Connector). Beginning near sea

Major Attractions:

©David L. Ranta, staff

The Okanagan/Okanogan, Historic O'Keefe Ranch, Wells Gray Provincial Park

level at the confluence of the Coquihalla and Fraser rivers at Hope, it climbs for 70

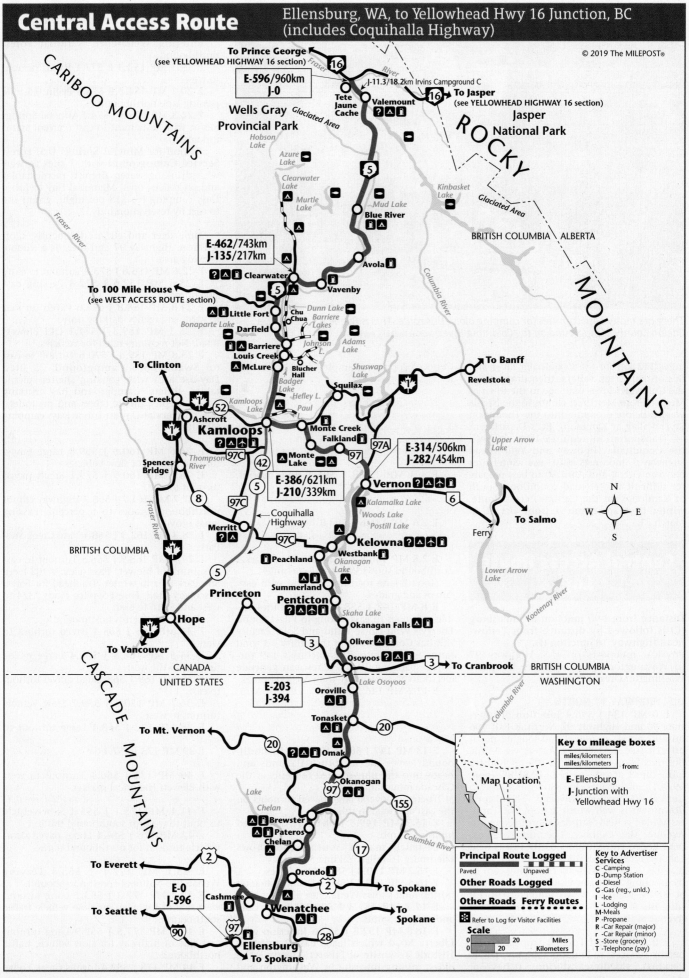

Central Access Route

Ellensburg, WA, to Yellowhead Hwy 16 Junction, BC (includes Coquihalla Highway)

© 2019 The MILEPOST®

CARIBOO MOUNTAINS

To Prince George
(see YELLOWHEAD HIGHWAY 16 section)

16

Fraser River

E-596/960km
J-0

J-11.3/18.2km Irvins Campground C

16

To Jasper
(see YELLOWHEAD HIGHWAY 16 section)

Tete Jaune Cache

Valemount

Wells Gray Provincial Park

Glaciated Area

Hobson Lake

ROCKY

Jasper National Park

Azure Lake

Clearwater Lake

5

Mud Lake

Kinbasket Lake

Glaciated Area

Murtle Lake

Blue River

BRITISH COLUMBIA \ ALBERTA

Columbia River

E-462/743km
J-135/217km

Avola

To 100 Mile House
(see WEST ACCESS ROUTE section)

Clearwater

5

Vavenby

Little Fort

Dunn Lake

Chu Chua

Barriere Lakes

Darfield

Bonaparte Lake

Barriere
Louis Creek

Johnson L.

Adams Lake

To Banff

Revelstoke

McLure

Blucher Hall

Badger Lake

Shuswap Lake

Squilax

1

To Clinton

Cache Creek

1

52

Kamloops Lake

Hefley L.

Paul L.

Monte Creek
Falkland

Upper Arrow Lake

Ashcroft

1

Kamloops

97C

Monte Lake

42

97

97A

E-314/506km
J-282/454km

Spences Bridge

Thompson River

5

E-386/621km
J-210/339km

Vernon

6

8

97C

Kalamalka Lake

Woods Lake

To Salmo

Ferry

Merritt

Coquihalla Highway

Postill Lake

97C

Kelowna

BRITISH COLUMBIA

5

Westbank

Peachland

Okanagan Lake

Lower Arrow Lake

Summerland

Princeton

Penticton

Skaha Lake

Kootenay River

Hope

Okanagan Falls

1

Oliver

3

To Vancouver

Osoyoos

3

To Cranbrook

BRITISH COLUMBIA

CANADA

CASCADE MOUNTAINS

UNITED STATES

Lake Osoyoos

WASHINGTON

E-203
J-394

Oroville

Columbia River

To Mt. Vernon

Tonasket

20

20

Omak

Okanogan

97

155

Lake Chelan

Brewster

Pateros

Chelan

17

Columbia River

To Everett

2

Orondo

To Spokane

E-0
J-596

Cashmere

2

Wenatchee

To Spokane

To Seattle

90

97

28

Ellensburg

To Spokane

Key to mileage boxes

miles/kilometers
miles/kilometers from:

E- Ellensburg
J- Junction with Yellowhead Hwy 16

Map Location

N
W   E
S

Principal Route Logged

Paved   Unpaved

Other Roads Logged

Other Roads   Ferry Routes

Refer to Log for Visitor Facilities

Scale

0   20   Miles
0   20   Kilometers

Key to Advertiser Services

C -Camping
D -Dump Station
d -Diesel
G -Gas (reg., unld.)
I -Ice
L -Lodging
M -Meals
P -Propane
R -Car Repair (major)
r -Car Repair (minor)
S -Store (grocery)
T -Telephone (pay)

There are many opportunities for camping along this route. This is Beebe Bridge Park, a Chelan County campground on the Columbia River. (©Kris Valencia, staff)

miles/112 km up the Coquihalla River and Boston Bar Creek valleys, then drops down the Coldwater River drainage to the town of Merritt. From Merritt, it climbs to the Nicola Plateau before dropping into the Thompson River Valley at Kamloops. BC's Department of Transportation requires that on both the Coquihalla Highway and Yellowhead Highway 5, motorists must use winter tires between Oct. 1 and April 30 to best prepare for difficult winter road conditions. South of Kamloops on the Central Access Route, winter tires are required from Oct. 1 to March 31.

Central Access Route Log

Distance from I-90 junction at Ellensburg (E) is followed by distance from Yellowhead Highway 16 junction (J).
Physical mileposts on U.S. Highway 97 in Washington reflect distance from the Washington-Oregon border.

U.S. HIGHWAY 97 NORTH

E 0 MP 134 J 596.4 Junction of Interstate 90 and Highway 97 North at Exit 106 on I-90. Food, gas/diesel and lodging north off exit (see next entry). Access via 4-mile Business Loop—or use Exit 109 off I-90 for more direct access—to **ELLENSBURG** (pop. 19,001); all services. Ellensburg is home to Central Washington University. The historic downtown is well worth a stop. The Farmers Market is held Saturday mornings on 4th Avenue, May–October. The annual Ellensburg Rodeo and Kittitas County Fair is held Labor Day weekend. Additional information may be found at www.myellensburg.com or by stopping in at the visitor center located at 609 N. Main St. New (summer 2018) **EV plug-ins** (a level 2 and level 3) are on 3rd Avenue at the plaza. Ⓑ

E 0.1 MP 134.1 J 596.3 Stop sign with nearby services: restaurants (Subway, IHOP, Perkins), gas/diesel stations (Chevron,

Conoco), lodging (Hampton Inn) and truck/RV wash. Ⓑ

Northbound drivers turn left (north) for Highway 97 North. NOTE: Highway 97 makes a few of these sharp turns the next 15 miles northbound, so watch for 97N signs.
Southbound drivers turn right for Interstate I-90.

E 1.3 MP 135.3 J 595.1 Roundabout. *Northbound traffic turn left for Highway 97 North. Southbound turn right for Highway 97 South.*

E 2.6 MP 136.6 J 593.8 *Northbound, turn right for Highway 97 North. Southbound, turn left for Highway 97 South.*

E 2.8 MP 136.8 J 593.6 Distance marker northbound shows Wenatchee 66 miles.
Good 2-lane road northbound with easy curves and grades.

E 8 MP 142 J 588.4 Wind turbines visible on slopes to east belong to Puget Sound Energy's Wild Horse Wind and Solar Facility (Kittitas County), one of the utility's 3 wind farms in the state. This facility's 149 turbines, spanning 10,000 acres, can generate electricity to serve more than 80,000 homes.

E 12.2 MP 146.2 J 584.2 *Turn right northbound for continuation of Highway 97 North.*
Turn left southbound for continuation of Highway 97 South (or continue straight ahead for Cle Elum).

E 13 MP 147 J 583.4 Highway 97 northbound leaves the sagebrush flatlands and heads into the pine-scented foothills of the Cascade mountains.
There are several large paved turnouts on the east and west in this area.

E 15.3 MP 149.3 J 581.1 Posted speed limit is 65 mph.
Distance marker southbound shows Ellensburg 16 miles, Yakima 55 miles.

E 16.2 MP 150.2 J 580.2 First Creek.

E 16.3 MP 150.3 J 580.1 Distance marker northbound shows Wenatchee 53 miles.

E 17.3 MP 151.3 J 579.1 Liberty Cafe and espresso stand.

E 18.8 MP 152.8 J 577.6 Junction with Liberty Road which leads east 2 miles to **Historic Townsite of Liberty**. Liberty is the oldest mining townsite in Washington and

is part of the Swauk Mining District, created in 1873. Buildings, displays and interpretive signs detail the region's history.
Entering Wenatchee National Forest northbound.

E 19.3 MP 153.3 E 577.1 Paved turnout to west.

E 20.2 MP 154.2 E 575.8 Begin 0.5 mile passing lane northbound.

E 22.3 MP 156.3 J 574.1 Mineral Springs Resort with restaurant to east (current status unknown).
Turnoff for **Mineral Springs U.S. Forest Service Campground** with 7 sites to west with drinking water, firepits, picnic tables and pit toilets; open Memorial Day to Labor Day; camping fee $18 per night, group site to east by reservation only. ▲

Mule deer and elk are frequently spotted from Highway 97 and there is a wildlife viewing area.

E 22.6 MP 156.6 J 573.8 Turnout to east.

E 23.6 MP 157.6 J 572.8 Parking east side of road.

E 24.8 MP 158.8 J 571.6 Paved turnout to west, emergency parking only.

E 25.3 MP 159.3 J 571.1 Old Blewett Road. Not recommended for vehicles.

E 25.8 MP 159.8 J 570.6 Turnoff to east for **Swauk USFS Campground**; 23 sites. Day-use area with cooking shelter, picnic tables, toilets. Campground has drinking water, firepits, picnic tables and pit toilets; open Memorial Day to Labor Day; camping fee $18. ▲

E 26.6 MP 160.6 J 569.8 Large paved turnout to east for slow vehicles.

E 26.9 MP 160.9 J 579.1 Small paved turnout to east.

E 27.7 MP 161.7 J 568.7 Highway climbs northbound; grades to 6 percent. Passing lanes provided.

E 28.3 MP 162.3 J 568.1 Pine Creek Sno-Park.

E 29.9 MP 163.9 J 566.5 Turnout to east at summit of **Blewett Pass** (elev. 4,102 feet). Sno-Park area in winter. Trailhead for Forest Discovery Trail. Forest Service roads 7324 to west and 9716 to east.
Highway descends northbound.

E 31 MP 165 J 565.4 Paved turnout to west.

E 34.5 MP 168.5 J 562.4 Large paved turnout to the west.

E 35 MP 169 J 563 Large gravel turnout to east.

E 36.7 MP 170.7 J 559.7 Slow vehicle turnout to west.

E 38 MP 172 J 558.4 Large turnout to west.

E 39 MP 173 J 557.4 *Slow for curves northbound.*

E 40 MP 174 J 556.4 Turnout to west with Blewett Historical marker.
Slow for curves northbound and southbound.

E 41.1 MP 175.1 J 555.3 Slow-vehicle turnout to west for southbound traffic.

E 42 MP 176 J 554.4 Long, paved slow-vehicle turnout for northbound traffic.
Slow for curves northbound.

E 43.1 MP 177.1 J 553.3 Leaving Wenatchee National Forest northbound.

E 43.3 MP 177.3 J 553.1 Long turnout west side of highway for slow vehicle traffic southbound.

E 43.5 MP 177.5 J 552.9 Long turnout east side of highway for slow vehicle traffic northbound.

E 44 MP 178 J 552.4 Ingalls Creek Lodge

and Christian Enrichment Center to west, retreat and group focused.

E 44.1 MP 178.1 J 552.3 Shasta RV Park to west. ⛺

E 44.5 MP 178.5 J 551.9 Old Blewett Road.

E 49.1 MP 183.1 J 547.3 Fruit stands in season.

E 50 MP 184 J 546.4 Resume posted 60 mph speed limit southbound.

E 50.5 MP 184.5 J 545.9 Distance marker southbound shows Cle Elum 47 miles, Ellensburg 51 miles, Seattle 130 miles.

E 51.1 MP 185.1 J 545.3 Junction U.S. Highways 97 and 2.

Northbound travelers turn right for continuation of Highway 97 North and access to Wenatchee. Highway 97 North shares a common alignment with Highway 2 through the Wenatchee River valley.

Southbound travelers turn left to continue on Highway 97 South to Ellensburg.

NOTE: Physical mileposts eastbound now reflect distance from Interstate 5 via Highway 2 and are included in this log.

E 51.5 MP 105.2 J 544.9 Shell gas/diesel station to west. Weigh station. Begin 4-lane divided highway northbound. ⛽

E 52.2 MP 105.9 J 544.2 Crossing the Wenatchee River.

E 52.9 MP 106.5 J 543.5 Stoplight in **Dryden**, a small, fruit-growing town. Turn-off for services; gas/diesel stations, food and groceries available. ⛽

E 53.1 MP 106.8 J 543.2 Crossing the Wenatchee River.

E 54 MP 107.7 J 542.3 Crossing the Wenatchee River.

E 55.2 MP 108.8 J 541.2 North Dryden Road. Turnoff for Peshastin Pinnacle State Park, a popular spot with rock climbers. Day use only, with pit toilets, picnic area, no water available. 1½ miles of hiking trails.

E 55.4 MP 109 J 541 Distance marker southbound shows Dryden 3 miles, Junction 97 5 miles, Leavenworth 10 miles.

E 56.5 MP 110 J 539.9 Turn on Goodwin for eastbound-only exit to Cashmere Business Loop/Aplets Way via Goodwin Road and Hay Canyon Road to west.

E 57.6 MP 111.1 J 538.8 Aplets Way and access south to downtown **CASHMERE** (pop. 3,149) via Aplets Way/North Division Street. Cashmere is probably best known as the home of Aplets & Cotlets, a confection made with apples, apricots and walnuts by Liberty Orchards.

Tour the famous Aplets & Cotlets Candy Kitchen and Country Store, located south on Aplets Way/North Division at Mission. The store is open daily, April through December, and weekdays January through March; phone 509-782-4088; www.libertyorchards.com. Tours of the candy kitchens are offered every 20 minutes and a variety of free samples are available in the store.

E 58.4 MP 112 J 538 Stoplight at Cotlets Way and Eels Road; Shell and Chevron gas/diesel stations, IGA supermarket. Access to Cashmere Historic District, visitor information, 911 Spirit of America Memorial and the Cashmere Museum/Pioneer Village via Cottage Avenue. ⛽

E 61.6 MP 115 J 534.8 Stoplight at Main Street of **Monitor**.

E 62 MP 115.5 J 534.4 Turnoff for **Wenatchee River** County Park. The park

is in a beautiful setting between river and highway with full hook-up sites, free WiFi, picnic shelter, play areas, day-use area and restrooms; firewood, ice and ice cream available on site. Open April 1–Oct. 31, fees $28–$38 per night. Tent camping not allowed. The river is open to fishing July–Oct. 15 for salmon and October–late February or early March for steelhead. 🎣⛺

E 64.7 MP 118 J 531.7 Distance markers southbound shows Cashmere 6 miles, Everett 118 miles, Seattle 145 miles, Leavenworth 18 miles, Stevens Pass 54 miles, Monroe 103 miles.

E 65.4 MP 118.7 J 531 *Northbound traffic exit and follow signs for Highway 97N/Okanogan.*

Southbound traffic follow signs for Highway 97S.

Continue straight ahead on North Wenatchee Avenue/SR 285 for access to city of **WENATCHEE** (pop. 32,701), all visitor facilities available.

E 65.7 MP 119 J 530.7 Exit right northbound for **Wenatchee Confluence State Park** (campground), Visitor Center to south.

E 65.8 MP 119.1 J 530.6 Stoplight at Easy Street. Continue straight ahead for continuation of Highway 97 North.

E 66.4 MP 119.7 J 530 Exit for Ohme Gardens, Rocky Reach Dam, Entiat and Chelan via Highway 97A, an alternate route up the west side of the Columbia River. Log of U.S. Highway 97/2 north via the east side of the Columbia River/Lake Entiat continues.

E 66.7 MP 119.9 J 529.7 Crossing the Columbia River.

E 67.6 MP 127.8 J 528.8 Junction with Washington Highway 28/Sunset Highway, which leads south 4 miles to East Wenatchee. *Northbound traffic use left lane to continue on Highway 97 North/Highway 2 East. Southbound traffic use right hand lane to turn onto Highway 97 South.*

NOTE: Physical mileposts northbound reflect an 8-mile discrepancy for Highway 2 mileages between Chelan and Douglas counties.

E 67.8 MP 128 J 528.6 Distance marker northbound shows Okanogan 87 miles. Small turnouts each side of road.

Northbound the highway passes some of the apple orchards for which the Wenatchee area is known. Hot, dry weather prevails in this region during the summer.

E 69.7 MP 130.9 J 525.5 Roundabout, turnoff for Enterprise Drive and fruit stand (in season).

E 72 MP 132.3 J 524.4 Shell gas/diesel station with propane and food-mart. ⛽

E 72.2 MP 132.5 J 524.2 Lincoln Rock State Park and **Rocky Reach Dam**. Take 97A to access the dam and visitor center. The park offers 67 RV and 27 tent sites (camping fees $25–$45 per night), several cabins, picnic areas, boat launch, sani-dump and handicap-accessible facilities. Generator use limited to 8 A.M. to 9 P.M. **Columbia River**, dammed by Rocky Reach Dam, offers fishing in summer and fall for sockeye and chinook salmon. 🎣⛺

E 75.2 MP 135.5 J 521.2 Paved turnout to west.

E 75.7 MP 136 J 520.7 Passing lane southbound next 2 miles.

E 79 MP 139.3 J 517.4 Distance marker southbound shows East Wenatchee 15, Quincy 46 miles.

E 79.4 MP 139.7 J 517 Distance marker southbound shows Wenatchee 17 miles, Cashmere 22 miles, Leavenworth 35 miles.

E 79.5 MP 213 J 516.9 Junction with U.S. Highway 2 East to Spokane and Waterville and continuation of Highway 97 North to Chelan and Okanogan. **Orondo**, an orchard town with roadside fruit and vegetable stands in season. 76 gas/diesel station to east with propane, Subway, post office. ⛽

NOTE: Mileposts northbound now reflect distance from Oregon border via Highway 97 and are included in this log.

Mileposts southbound reflect distance from Interstate 5 via U.S. Highway 2, which shares a common alignment with U.S. Highway 97 to **Milepost E 51.1.**

E 82 MP 215.5 J 514.4 Orondo River Park; pleasant grassy day-use park on a narrow stretch of land between highway and lake; coin-operated showers, picnic areas, volleyball, toilets, dock and boat launch on Lake Entiat.

E 85.4 MP 219.5 J 511 Daroga State Park. A beautiful 90-acre waterside park with 28 RV and 17 tent sites (camping fee $12–$45 per night), large playfields, swimming, picnic tables, showers, boat launch and handicap-accessible facilities. Sani-dump. Huge group camping site is located 0.6 mile south of here. ⛺

E 89 MP 223 J 507.4 Begin 0.8-mile passing lane northbound.

E 100.4 MP 234 J 496 Paved turnout to west.

E 100.9 MP 234.5 J 496.5 Distance marker southbound shows Orondo 21 miles, Wenatchee 39 miles.

E 101 MP 234.6 J 495.4 Beebe Bridge Park is operated by Chelan County and offers 46 tent/RV sites with water and electric open April 1 through October. Camping fee $25/night in off-season, $30 high season, sani-dump ($5 for non-campers), showers, playground, picnic and swimming areas, boat launch and handicap-accessible facilities. Massive day-use area. A reservation system may be in place for 2019. ⛺

E 101.2 MP 234.8 J 495.2 Columbia River bridge.

E 101.5 MP 235 J 494.9 Junction with Washington Highway 150 which leads 5 miles (winding uphill start from Highway 97) to downtown **CHELAN** (pop. 3,959), a popular vacation destination, located on one of the state's most beautiful and most heavily used lakes. Lake Chelan is the largest natural lake in Washington, the third deepest lake in the country and ninth in the world. The city offers motels, resorts, beach homes and condos for lodging; restaurants, gas stations, grocery and variety stores. The Visitor Information Center and Chamber of Commerce (www.lakechelan.com) is located at 216 Woodin Ave. in the heart of the Historic Downtown Chelan.

Don Morse City Park in Chelan has Lakeshore RV Park; beautiful shaded campground; don't expect to drive in late on a busy summer weekend and find a site, call ahead at 509-682-8023 or visit www.chelancityparks.com. There is also camping at **Chelan State Park**, one of the most popular campgrounds in Washington. Southbound from Chelan take Highway 97A south 3 miles, then turn right on South Lakeshore Road and continue 6 miles to park; 103 campsites, 18 with partial hook-ups and 17

Annual precipitation in Washington's Okanogan County is 11 to 16 inches; Puget Sound's is 32 to 35 inches. (©Kris Valencia, staff)

full hook-up sites. The sani-station/utility area is not designed for RVs longer than 30 feet will not be able to enter or use the facilities at the state park; use Lakeshore RV Park instead. [A]

E 106.6 MP 240.1 J 489.8 North **junction** with Highway 97A/Cascade Loop to Manson.

E 112.6 MP 246.1 J 483.8 Turnoff to east for Wells Dam Public Utility District. Day-use area with picnic tables, toilets, visitor information center.

E 115.2 MP 248.7 J 481.2 Sharp turn to east across railroad tracks for Starr Boat Launch to east, a large gravel parking area that includes the boat ramp, toilet and dumpster.

E 119.4 MP 253 J 477 Sign about "The China Ditch." *Begin posted speed zone northbound into Pateros.*

Distance marker southbound shows Chelan 19 miles, Entiat 39 miles, Wenatchee 57 miles.

E 119.8 MP 253.4 J 476.6 Junction with Washington Highway 153/20 to Twisp (31 miles) via the Methow River valley. Access to **Alta Lake State Park** and North Cascades Highway, located 3 miles north from here on Highway 153; 93 sites, 32 with full hook-ups and showers; $12–$45 per night. Open April through October. Reservations possible mid-April through mid-September. Boating. [A]

E 120 MP 253.6 J 476.4 Methow River bridge.

E 120.1 MP 253.7 J 476.3 Entering **PATEROS** (pop. 667) northbound; food, gas/diesel (Chevron), lodging and camping. First right as you drive northbound will take you to Riverside Park; overnight on-street parking (fee charged) adjacent the park, which has a playground and restrooms. Visitor information: www.pateros.com. [B] [A]

E 120.6 MP 254.2 J 475.8 Welcome to Pateros southbound.

E 122.5 MP 257 J 473.9 Small paved turnout to west.

E 126.4 MP 260 J 470 *Begin posted speed zone through* **BREWSTER** (pop. 2,358); motel, Columbia Cove City RV park, gas/diesel stations (Chevron, 76), fast-food (Subway, McDonald's), grocery stores, restaurants,

gift shops, tire and vehicle repair, drugstore, hardware stores, lumber yard, hospital and other services. This is a large apple and cherry processing location. Access to the Columbia River for boat launch, fishing, water sports and swimming. [B] [A]

Distance marker southbound shows Pateros 6 miles, Chelan 26 miles, Wenatchee 64 miles.

E 127.1 MP 260.4 J 469.3 Junction with Washington Highway 173 to Bridgeport and Chief Joseph Dam on the Columbia River.

E 128.1 MP 261.4 J 468.3 Railroad crossing by fruit processing buildings.

E 129.5 MP 263.8 J 466.9 Brewster Airport Anderson Field.

E 129.6 MP 264 J 466.8 Crossing Okanogan River bridge.

E 130.2 MP 264.6 J 466.2 Distance marker southbound shows Brewster 4 miles, Pateros 11 miles, Wenatchee 69 miles.

E 130.4 MP 264.8 J 466 Bridge.

E 131.8 MP 264.9 J 465.7 Junction with Washington Highway 17 South; weigh station. Several attractions on this road: Mile 0.2 for Fort Okanogan Interpretive Center, open in summer; turn off at Mile 0.5 onto Lagrange Road for a 3.5 mile drive to Gamble Sands Golf Resort with restaurant; or stay on Highway 17 S to Mile 8 for Chief Joseph Dam, Bridgeport and Bridgeport State Park, Moses Lake.

E 134.4 MP 262.3 J 463.1 Monse Bridge Road crosses to community of Monse. An astonishing number of satellites rise above the bluff, largely used as a transfer station of information from Asia to America, it also handles some FAA and DOD activity.

E 144.2 MP 277.9 J 452.2 Turnoff for Malott (unincorporated), a small community on the west side of the river with limited services. Well-known Johnny Appleseed and other early settlers planted apple trees here in the initial settlement of this area.

E 147.9 MP 281.6 J 448.5 Large turnout to west, Okanogan County Historical Society Cariboo Trail Historical Marker.

E 149.7 MP 283.3 J 446.7 Large turnout to west.

E 152.8 MP 286.4 J 444 Turnoff for Highway 97 Business Loop west to downtown Okanogan via 2nd Avenue South/Washington Highway 20. Washington High-

way 20, also called North Cascades Highway, leads to Twisp. Colville Tribal Resort & Casino is just off the highway.

E 153.2 MP 286.6 J 443.2 Distance marker northbound shows Omak 5 miles, Canadian border 50 miles, Penticton 89 miles.

E 153.5 MP 286.9 J 442.9 Exit to frontage road for downtown Okanogan via Oak Street. **OKANOGAN** (pop. 2,552) is the county seat of Okanogan County and offers all traveler services. The historic district transports visitors back to views of the early 1900s.

Okanogan Fairgrounds and RV park take Oak Street, then turn on Rodeo Trail Road. [A]

E 154.4 MP 287.9 J 442 Second turnoff northbound for Okanogan Fairgrounds and RV park to west on Rodeo Trail Road.

E 155.5 MP 290.8 J 438.9 Exxon Colville Fuels gas/diesel station to east. [B]

E 155.9 MP 291.2 J 438.5 Dayton Street. Dining, shopping, visitor information to west. Access to Omak Stampede arena. Carl Precht Memorial RV Park (open year-round, $25 RV sites, $15 tent sites) and downtown Omak to west. **OMAK** (pop. 4,792) offers food, gas/diesel and lodging. The 86th annual Omak Stampede takes place August 8–11 in 2019. East Side Park is open to self-contained campers during Stampede Weekend (fee charged). The Visitor Information Center and the Stampede Museum are inside this park. There are also 2 popular photo ops here of the nationally-acclaimed local artist Smoker Marchand's work: "Naming of the Animals" and "Spirit Horses." For more information on Omak: omakvisitorcenter.org; phone 509-826-4218. [B] [A]

Junction with Washington Highway 155 South to Grand Coulee Dam.

E 156.4 MP 291.7 J 438 Crossing highway bridge; view of Stampede Grounds.

E 156.6 MP 291.9 J 437.8 Okanogan River bridge.

E 157.1 MP 292.4 J 437.3 Omak Riverside/Engh Road intersection. Grocery Outlet, McDonald's, Walmart and Home Depot to east, shopping mall, Arby's, Dairy Queen, Pizza Hut, Taco Bell/Kentucky Fried Chicken, Burger King, Exxon and Texaco gas/diesel stations, The UPS Store, Papa Murphy's, JC Penney, Dollar tree, Rite-Aid, Big 5, Starbucks and Safeway. [B]

E 157.4 MP 292.7 J 437 Turnoff to west for Best Western, Plus Peppertree Inn, Subway, Omak Inn, Roadhouse 97 Restaurant and the Confluence Health Clinic.

Distance marker northbound shows Tonasket 22 miles, Penticton 84 miles.

E 157.9 MP 293.3 J 436.5 Turnoff to west for North 40 Outfitters and Omak Airport.

E 165.1 MP 298.7 J 431.3 RIVERSIDE (pop. 275) is a small agricultural community. Detros Western Store on Main Street.

E 165.4 MP 299.1 J 431 Turnoff to **Conconully State Park** (15 miles west); camping, swimming, boating. Fees $12 to $45. [A]

E 165.6 MP 299.3 J 430.8 *CAUTION: High kill area for deer. Watch for deer next 13 miles northbound.*

E 167 MP 300.7 J 429.4 Turnout to west. Distance marker northbound shows Tonasket 15 miles, Oroville 32 miles, Penticton 78 miles.

E 171.1 MP 304.8 J 425.3 South Pine Creek road to west for Fish Lake.

E 177 MP 310.6 J 419.4 Okanogan River bridge.

E 181.1 MP 314.3 J 415.3 *Slow for posted speed zones northbound* entering Tonasket.

Armed Forces Legacy Park Veteran's Memorial on south end of city, well worth a stop. Pets are not allowed within this park. Memorial represents all branches of the military.

E 181.2 MP 314.8 J 415.2 Junction with Highway 20 East/6th Avenue. Fast-food outlets, shopping, Exxon and Mobil gas/diesel stations. 🅱

E 181.8 MP 315.1 J 414.6 TONASKET (pop. 1,020); visitor information center (TVBRC.org). Tonasket has fast-food outlets, restaurants, espresso stands, natural food co-op, gas/diesel stations, supermarket, hardware store, RV park, banks and hospital available. 🅱➕

E 187.4 MP 321 J 409 Old Okanogan Mission Historical Marker and Indian cemetery are located behind Ellisforde's church.

E 187.8 MP 321.4 J 408.6 Ellisforde junction; small grocery. Turnoff for Spectacle Lake.

E 192.3 MP 325.9 J 404.1 Turnoff for gas station. 🅱

E 194.4 MP 328 J 402 Turnout to west with information boards about this area.

E 196.4 MP 330.5 J 400 Okanogan River bridge.

E 196.9 MP 331 J 399.5 Distance marker southbound shows Tonasket 16 miles, Okanagan 34 miles, Wenatchee 136 miles.

E 197.1 MP 331.2 J 399.3 *Slow for posted speed zone northbound* entering Oroville.

E 197.7 MP 331.8 J 398.7 OROVILLE (pop. 1,676); Depot Museum, visitor information (www.orovillewashington.org). Oroville's Main Street has restaurants, shopping, a pharmacy, 24-hour gas station, lodging. **EV plug-ins** at the Camaray Motel on Main Street. There are murals in multiple locations in town. Oroville is the last U.S. town before crossing the border into Canada. It is located at the south end of Osoyoos Lake, which straddles the international border. Wood products are a major industry here. 🅱

E 199 MP 332.6 J 397.4 Prince's Center shopping mall, gas station, at north end of Oroville. Osoyoos Veteran's Memorial Park at the south end of **Osoyoos Lake** has 86 campsites, day-use area, showers, toilets, swimming beach and a boat launch. Excellent smallmouth bass fishing. 🅱🐟🔺

E 202.5 MP 336.1 J 393.9 Gas stations with diesel. 🅱

E 202.8 MP 336.4 J 393.6 Duty-free store to west.

E 202.9 MP 336.5 J 393.5 U.S.–Canada international border, open 24 hours daily. *Have your passport and rabies certificates (for any dogs and cats that are traveling with you) ready and available for customs officers when you pull up for inspection. They were also doing agricultural inspections summer 2018. For more details on customs requirements, see Crossing the Border in the TRAVEL PLANNING section.*

CANADA HIGHWAY 97 NORTH

E 203.8 (328 km) **J 392.6** (631.8 km)

Turnoff east for s̓ẁiẁs **Provincial Park** (formerly Haynes Point) on **Osoyoos Lake.** Drive 0.5 mile (follow signs) through residential area to park entrance. Day-use area with boat launch, picnicking, swimming, waterskiing and fishing (bass and rainbow trout); 41 campsites, pit and flush toilets, tap water, hiking trail. Camping fee $32. Gates closed 11 P.M. to 7 A.M. Campground season is April to October. Campsite reservations (fee charged) accepted for mid-May to first week in September; go to www.discover camping.ca to a link for reservations. This is a very popular campground in summer and there is a maximum stay policy of 7 nights per year. 🐟🔺

E 204.3 (328.8 km) **J 392.1** (631 km) Access road leads 1.6 km/1 mile east to **OSOYOOS** (pop. 5,085) town centre; all traveler services. Saturday market is on Main Street from 9 A.M. to 2 P.M. from May–September. Gyro Beach and swimming area with picnic tables, shoreside. Beautiful Veteran's Park is just west (cross highway) of Gyro Beach.

Watch for fruit stands (seasonally) northbound.

E 205.6 (330.9 km) **J 390.8** (628.9 km) **Junction** of Highway 97 and Crowsnest Highway 3 (Princeton and Hope)/Main Street. Easy access to gas/diesel stations (Shell, Husky), fast-food outlets and shopping centres. 🅱

The Osoyoos Visitor Centre, at the northeast corner of intersection, is an interesting stop for visitors to the Okanagan region and offers information and trip planning assistance as well as an assortment of local items and gifts. ❓

E 207.3 (333.5 km) **J 389.1** (626.1 km) Winery section has 4 lanes for passing. Common tasting hours are 10 A.M. to 6 P.M.

E 209.4 (337 km) **J 387** (622.8 km) Leaving Osoyoos northbound, Highway 97 enters the Okanagan's agricultural area, with plenty of vineyards and orchards. Watch for fruit stands along the highway in season.

E 216.9 (349.1 km) **J 376.1** (605.2) Distance marker southbound Osoyoos 19 km/12 miles, Grand Forks 153 km/95 miles.

E 217.7 (350.3 km) **J 378.7** (609.4 km) One of 3 stoplights on Main Street in **OLIVER** (pop. 4,564); Oliver Place Mall. Oliver offers casual and fine dining options, fast-food outlets, gas, diesel, lodging, shopping and services. 🅱🔺

The town was named for Premier John Oliver, who encouraged irrigation here in 1919 that turned the dry sagebrush slopes into rich orchards and provided needed employment opportunities for returning WWI soldiers. Local attractions include Tuc-El-Nuit Lake (swimming, camping), Vaseux Lake (birdwatching, canoeing), golfing and a racetrack. The Okanagan River trail offers 18.8 km/11.7 miles for hiking and biking. The town's motto is "Wine Capital of Canada" and there are *many* wineries along Highway 97, most offering tasting rooms and tours (hours typically begin at 10 A.M. or later, daily).

E 218 (350.8 km) **J 378.4** (609 km) Stoplight; dining, fast-food outlets, shopping and visitor centre (located in historic CPR Building). Turnoff for Baldy Mountain Resort ski area.

E 218.6 (351.8 km) **J 377.8** (608 km)

Oliver Lions Park (day use).

E 221.6 (356.6 km) **J 374.8** (603.2 km) Turnoff to **Inkaneep Provincial Park** to west; 7 campsites, hand pump water, pit toilets, firepits, swimming, fishing. Watch for poison ivy at this park. Open June to mid-September. $18. 🐟🔺

E 222.1 (357.4 km) **J 374.3** (602.4 km) Turnoff east to Tuc-El-Nuit Lake with several camping resorts along the lake. Chevron gas station to the west with gas/diesel and propane, convenience store. Campground just below the hill, behind the gas station. 🅱🔺

E 225.5 (362.9 km) **J 370.9** (596.9 km) South end of Vaseux Lake, a federal wildlife sanctuary; resort and beach. British Columbia's largest herd of California bighorn sheep makes its home in the rocky hills and may be seen by the lake in the evenings and early mornings. Watch for dirt turnout to west on lake with access for hand-carried watercraft. *Slow for 40 kmph/for 25 mph curves northbound.*

E 227.3 (365.8 km) **J 369.1** (594 km) **Vaseux Lake Provincial Park**; 12 campsites, swimming and fishing (largemouth bass, rainbow trout and carp). No motors allowed on the lake. Open end of March to early October. Water must be boiled for drinking. Camping fee $18 per night. 🐟🔺

E 227.7 (366.4 km) **J 368.7** (593.3 km) Dirt parking area at Vaseux Wildlife Centre; interpretive panels, trails and bird blind to west.

E 229.5 (369.4 km) **J 366.8** (590.4 km) Double-ended turnout to west with information board on area.

E 230.4 (370.8 km) **J 366** (589 km) Distance marker southbound shows Oliver 22 km/14 miles, Osoyoos 43 km/27 miles.

E 231 (371.7 km) **J 365.4** (588 km) Tickleberry's (www.tickleberrys.com), a popular sweet shop featuring ice cream and other goodies, is on your right entering **OKANAGAN FALLS** (pop. 1,700). *Slow for posted speed zone through town.*

Okanagan Falls is a small resort community at the south end of Skaha Lake. It is known for beautiful beaches, award-winning wineries, summer and winter recreation opportunities, world-class rock climbing, challenging cycling and history. Food, gas/diesel (Esso) and lodging are available. The **sx\u02b7ex\u02b7nitk\u02b7 Provincial Park** (formerly Okanagan Falls) is along the Okanagan River. Open April 1 to Oct. 9, $25. These campsites are reservable for dates mid-May to Sept. 9. Reserve at: www.discovercamping.ca. This campground offers drinking water, firepits, flush and pit toilets and is wheelchair accessible. 🅱🔺

E 231.1 (371.9 km) **J 365.3** (587.9 km) Flashing traffic light: *Northbound travelers turn left to continue on Highway 97 North. Southbound travelers turn right to continue on Highway 97 South.*

E 231.2 (372.1 km) **J 365.2** (587.7 km) IGA Supermarket, Regional Library and Visitor Information Centre. Open May to October weekdays from 9 A.M. to 4:30 P.M., and Saturdays from 10 A.M. to 2 P.M. Website: www.okfalls.ca; phone 778-515-5520. Kenyon Park, Lion's Park and Christie Memorial Provincial Park offer beach access, benches, picnic tables, a spray park and walking paths one block north.

E 231.3 (372.2 km) **J 365.1** (587.5 km)

Okanagan River Trestle bridge and famous Kettle Valley River (KVR) trail network.

E 234.5 (377.4 km) **J 361.9** (582.4 km) Distance marker southbound shows Okanagan Falls 6 km/4 miles, Oliver 29 km/18 miles, Osoyoos 50 km/31 miles.

E 235 (378.2 km) **J 361.4** (581.6 km) **Junction** with Highway 3A to Keremeos and Crowsnest Highway 3 to west. Access to Dominion Radio Astrophysical Observatory, open for self-guided tours, weekdays from 10 A.M. to 5 P.M. For more information, check website www.nrc-cnrc.gc.ca/eng/solutions/facilities/drao.html or phone 250-497-2300.

Weigh station just north of this junction, on the east.

E 235.6 (379.1 km) **J 360.8** (580.5 km) Petro-Canada to east with gas/diesel, propane and convenience store. [gas icon]

E 237.3 (381.8 km) **J 359.1** (577.8 km) Double-ended turnout to east.

E 237.9 (382.9 km) **J 358.5** (576.9 km) Viewpoint to the east overlooking lake with litter bins, toilets and sign about the founding of Penticton by rancher Tom Ellis (northbound access only).

E 239.6 (385.6 km) **J 356.8** (574.2 km) Distance marker southbound shows Osoyoos 58 km/36 miles, Princeton 108 km/67 miles, Vancouver 398 km/247 miles.

E 239.8 (385.9 km) **J 356.6** (573.9 km) Wrights Beach Camp (private), open year-round. [camping icon]

E 240 (386.2 km) **J 356.4** (573.6 km) Traffic light. Public beach on south side of road at north end of Skaha Lake. Penticton airport to north.

E 240.3 (386.7 km) **J 356.1** (573.1 km) Traffic light. *Northbound turn left to continue on Highway 97 North/Skaha Lake Road which becomes Channel Parkway and bypasses Penticton city centre.* Highway 97/Channel Parkway runs beside the channel that connects Okanagan and Skaha lakes. *Southbound turn right to continue on Highway 97 South/Skaha Lake Road.*

A popular summer activity here is to float down the river on inner tubes or air mattresses from the Riverside Drive at the north end of town down to Skaha Lake. A multi-use path parallels the channel.

From this junction, continue straight on Skaha Lake Road to reach the Main Street of **PENTICTON** (pop. 32,993), a major tourist destination and the heart of the Okanagan's wine country with more than 50 wineries within 20 minutes of the city's centre. It is a retirement haven as well as a centre for fruit packing and canning. Penticton has excellent sandy beaches on 2 lakes; fine scenery, dependable hot summer weather; and complete visitor facilities. It is also famous as the venue of the Ironman Canada Triathlon, held annually in late August. [gas icon][camping icon]

E 242.2 (389.8 km) **J 354.2** (570 km) Traffic light; gas/diesel (Shell), Tim Hortons and other businesses. [gas icon]

E 243.3 (391.5 km) **J 353.1** (568.2 km) Traffic light; *Northbound travelers turn left here to continue on Highway 97 North/Eckhardt Avenue West. Southbound travelers turn right to continue on Highway 97 South.* This intersection has Penticton & Wine Country Visitor Centre, gas/diesel and fast food drive-through (Chevron). [gas icon]

E 243.5 (391.9 km) **J 352.9** (568 km)

South Okanagan Events Centre.

E 243.6 (392 km) **J 352.7** (567.8 km) Petro-Canada gas/diesel southbound. [gas icon]

E 243.7 (392.2 km) **J 352.5** (567.6 km) Ramada Inn on right southbound.

E 243.8 (392.3 km) **J 352.6** (567.4 km) Traffic light; Petro-Canada gas/diesel station northbound. [gas icon]

E 243.9 (392.5 km) **J 352.5** (567.2 km) Northbound, via Riverside Drive, Starbucks is on the right in the Riverside Mall; shopping, fast-food outlets.

See people rafting below, as you cross the channel northbound.

E 247.1 (397.7 km) **J 349.3** (562.1 km) Kickininee Provincial Park picnic area is to the east on Okanagan Lake and is accessible to northbound traffic only. It offers litter bins and picnic tables.

E 247.4 (398.1 km) **J 349** (561.6 km) Soorimpt picnic area, in Kickininee Provincial Park, to east, on Okanagan Lake; boat launch.

E 248 (399.1 km) **J 348.4** (560.7 km) Pyramid picnic area, in Kickininee Provincial Park, to east, on Okanagan Lake has tables, outhouses and litter bins.

E 249.2 (401 km) **J 347.2** (558.7 km) Sun-Oka Beach Provincial Park picnic area to east has one of the best swimming beaches in the Okanagan. Welcome to Summerland (sign).

E 249.6 (401.7 km) **J 346.8** (558.1 km) Johnson Road. Centrex gas/diesel station with propane, convenience store and U-Haul. [gas icon]

E 249.8 (401.9 km) **J 346.6** (557.7 km) Double-ended Rotary-sponsored turnout northbound with information boards on Kettle Valley Railroad.

E 252.5 (406.3 km) **J 343.9** (553.4 km) Prairie Valley Road. Medical clinic and shopping to west.

E 253.1 (407.3 km) **J 343.3** (552.5 km) Rosedale Avenue; gas, shopping. Downtown **SUMMERLAND** (pop. 11,110); all services available. **Visitor Information:** Summerland Chamber & Visitor Centre on Highway 97; www.summerlandchamber.com. [gas icon]

A colorful orchard and vineyard town, Summerland was the site of the first commercial orchard in the Okanagan, planted in 1890. A small but busy village today, with a charming mock-Tudor downtown, Summerland is still dominated by the fruit and wine industry. There are 23 wineries, cideries and breweries in the area. Summerland Sweets (www.summerlandsweets.com), on Canyon-view Road, manufactures fruit candy, jams and syrups; open year-round. Visit the beautiful Peach Orchard Beach Park to the east and downhill from Highway 97 on Peach Orchard Road. Historic Kettle Valley Railway is 6 miles/10 km west.

E 253.2 (407.4 km) **J 343.2** (552.2 km) Jones Flat Road. East to 50 Classic Cars Car Museum.

E 259.1 (417 km) **J 337.3** (542.8 km) Turnoff to **South Campground** in **Okanagan Lake Provincial Park**; 88 sites with picnic tables and 8 reservable walk-in camping sites (same price); sani-station, fishing, swimming and boat launch. A shady oasis with a great beach. Campsite reservations mid-May to first week in September (main season begins late in March through early October); go to www.discovercamping.ca for

reservations. This is a very popular campground. Camping fee $35. Winter camping fee $13. [camping icon]

E 259.8 (418 km) **J 336.6** (541.7 km) Turnoff to **North Campground** in **Okanagan Lake Provincial Park**; 80 sites with picnic tables; sani-station, fishing, swimming and boat launch. Campsite reservations mid-May to first week in September. Go to www.discovercamping.ca for reservations (fee charged). This is a very popular campground in summer. Camping fee $35. [boat icon][camping icon]

E 262.8 (422.9 km) **J 333.6** (536.9 km) Turnout to east with litter bin.

E 263.7 (424.4 km) **J 332.7** (535.4 km) Turnoff to east for Antler Beach Regional Park; picnicking and swimming beach. Northbound sign "Welcome to Peachland."

E 266 (428 km) **J 330.4** (531.7 km) Turn east at 13th Street for **PEACHLAND** (pop. 5,233), a small fruit-growing settlement with all services available.

Follow signs to Visitor Centre on Beach Avenue with plentiful beachside parking and walking path. Rest area with walking path alongside beach accesses visitor centre/museum, shops and cafes, beautiful spot to take a break in your travels. [gas icon]

E 267.6 (430.6 km) **J 328.8** (529.1 km) Gas/diesel, fast-food and market. [gas icon]

E 268.8 (432.6 km) **J 327.6** (527.2 km) Todd's RV and Camping. [camping icon]

E 269.9 (434.4 km) **J 326.5** (525.4 km) Distance marker southbound shows Peachland 6 km/4 miles, Penticton 43 km/27 miles, Osoyoos 95 km/60 miles.

E 270.7 (435.6 km) **J 325.7** (524.1 km) **Junction** with Highway 97C (Coquihalla Connector), which leads west 108 km/67 miles to Merritt at **Milepost H 71.5** on Highway 5. *See "Coquihalla Highway" log on page 102.*

E 272.8 (439 km) **J 323.6** (520.8 km) Welcome to Westbank (northbound sign); gas/diesel, all services, fast-food Dairy Queen, Boston's Pizza. **WESTBANK** (30,892) is a booming suburb of Kelowna. [gas icon]

E 273 (439.3 km) **J 323.4** (520.4 km) Brown Road. Shopping centre to south includes Shoppers Drug Mart, liquor store, bank and Starbucks.

E 273.1 (439.5 km) **J 323.3** (520.2 km) Pamela Road to west for RCMP, Visitor Information Centre, Museum and Chamber of Commerce building. Website: www.visit westside.com.

NOTE: There is only one entrance to Pamela Road for southbound travelers. To access Pamela Road from southbound lane, turn left on Old Okanagan Highway for one block, then left on 97N one block and left again onto Pamela.

E 273.3 (440.1 km) **J 322.9** (519.6 km) Gosset Road/Gellatly. McDonald's, Westbank Shopping Centre.

E 274.3 (441.4 km) **J 322.1** (518.4 km) Butt Road. Westbank Hub Centre; Home Depot, Tim Hortons, Walmart, Canadian Tire/Marks, KalTire and other businesses.

E 275.6 (443.5 km) **J 320.8** (516.3 km) Westbank Industrial turnoff.

E 276.2 (444.4 km) **J 320.2** (515.2 km) Ross Road to west. Husky gas/diesel station with propane. [gas icon]

E **278.4** (448 km) **J 318** (511.8 km) Traffic light. Esso gas/diesel, liquor store, pub.

E **279.1** (449.2 km) **J 317.3** (510.6 km) Traffic light at **junction** with Westside Road, which goes up the west side of **Okanagan Lake**. Access to **Bear Creek Provincial Park**, 7 km/4 miles from junction, with 122 campsites, camping fee $35 plus reservation fee, sani-station $5, swimming, fishing and hiking. Also access to **Fintry Provincial Park**, 25 km/16 miles north, with 100 campsites, camping fee $32 plus reservation fee. Campsite reservations are required from mid-May to mid-September; www.discover camping.ca. Gates are locked between 11 P.M. and 7 A.M.

E **280.4** (451.2 km) **J 316** (508.5 km) William Bennett Bridge crosses Okanagan Lake.

Kelowna

E **281.2** (452.5 km) **J 315.2** (507.3 km) Located on the shore of Okanagan Lake, midway between Penticton and Vernon. **Population:** 115,000. **Elevation:** 1,130 feet/ 344m. **Emergency Services:** Dial 911. **Hospital**, phone 250-862-4000. **Veterinary**, Kelowna Veterinary Hospital 250-860-2408.

Visitor Information: Tourist information centre just off Highway 97 at 544 Harvey Ave., 250-861-1515. www.tourismkelowna. com. Open Monday–Friday 9 A.M. to 5 P.M.; Saturday–Sunday and holidays 10 A.M. to 3 P.M.

The largest community in the Okanagan, Kelowna offers excellent accommodations— from luxury resorts to campgrounds—as well as many great restaurants and boutique shopping.

Settlement started here in 1859 when Oblate Missionaries Father Charles Pandosy, Father Richard and Brother Sorel founded a mission on a creek at L'Anse au Sable (Sandy Bay), built a tiny church and a school and planted apple trees and vines.

Today, Kelowna's burgeoning economy is based on fruit growing (a third of Canada's fruit exports come from this area), healthcare, tourism, manufacturing (plywood plant), construction and forestry/fishing/ mining/oil and gas. Kelowna has 19 golf courses and more than 60 parks.

Attractions include a robust wine industry; a growing craft beer scene; golfing; the largest farmers market in BC; a cultural district with museums, galleries, theatres and studios; an indoor water park; and British Columbia's first winery—Calona Vineyards Winery.

Central Access Route Log
(continued)

E **281.2** (452.5 km) **J 315.2** (507.3 km) Traffic light at city centre turnoff for Kelowna. Highway 97 North continues through Kelowna as 6-lane divided highway lined with motels, restaurants and shopping.

E **284.6** (458 km) **J 311.8** (501.8 km) Leckie Road. Safeway supermarket.

E **284.9** (458.5 km) **J 311.5** (501.3 km) Banks Road. Walmart, Holiday Inn.

E **285.2** (459 km) **J 311.2** (500.8 km) **Junction** with BC Highway 33 south to Big White Ski Area and on to Crowsnest Highway 3. Costco and Chevron gas/diesel sta-

Beautiful beaches along this corridor of British Columbia draw vacationers for swimming, sunning and relaxation. (©Claire Torgerson, staff)

tion at this intersection.

E **286.1** (460.4 km) **J 310.3** (499.4 km) Traffic light at McCurdy's Road.

E **287.7** (463 km) **J 308.7** (496.8 km) Traffic light at Sexsmith Road. Access to Kelowna Springs golf course.

E **288.8** (464.8 km) **J 307.6** (495 km) John Hindle Drive exit northbound and University Way exit southbound to University of British Columbia/Okanagan campus.

E **290.1** (466.8 km) **J 306.3** (492.9 km) Airport Way. Turnoff to east for Kelowna International Airport.

Begin 4-lane undivided highway northbound.

E **292.4** (470.5 km) **J 304** (489.2 km) Large paved turnout to east overlooking Duck Lake.

E **293.2** (471.8 km) **J 303.2** (487.9 km) Large paved turnout to east overlooking Duck Lake.

E **295.1** (474.9 km) **J 301.3** (484.9 km) Beaver Lake Road east for Save-On Foods. Glenmore Road west for Shell gas/diesel and lodging at Lake Country/Winfield.

E **295.5** (475.5 km) **J 300.9** (484.2 km) Traffic light. Fast food options to east. Petro-Canada gas/diesel station to west.

E **296.1** (476.5 km) **J 300.3** (483.3 km) Pollard Street. Petro-Canada gas/diesel station with ATM to east.

E **296.3** (477 km) **J 300.1** (482.8 km) Corner store with Husky gas/diesel station to west.

E **297.5** (478.8 km) **J 298.9** (481 km) Oceola Road. Lakewood Mall, SuperSave gas/ diesel station to east.

E **297.7** (479 km) **J 298.7** (480.7 km) Esso gas/diesel station on right northbound. *Slow for posted speed zone southbound.*

Improved 4-lane highway northbound. The narrow, 2-lane stretch of old highway along Wood Lake is under development as the multi-use "Pelmewash Parkway."

E **307.8** (495.4 km) **J 288.6** (464.5 km) Distance marker southbound shows Lake

Country 11 km/7 miles, Kelowna 44 km/27 miles, West Kelowna 52 km/32 miles.

E **308.3** (496.2 km) **J 288.1** (463.7 km) Turnoff for **Kekuli Bay Provincial Park** on Kalamalka Lake; 82 campsites and 8 walk-in sites, camping fee $32–$40, swimming, boat launch, drinking water, picnic tables, playground, showers, firepits flush and pit toilets. Open April 5 to Oct. 29. Campsite reservations accepted for mid-May to first week in September; go to www.discover camping.ca for reservations.

E **312.3** (502.6 km) **J 284.1** (457.2 km) College Way. Turnoff for **Kalamalka Lake Provincial Park picnic area**; swimming, views, boat launch and fishing.

E **313.6** (504.7 km) **J 282.8** (455.1 km) Turnoff for Vernon Jubilee Hospital to east.

E **314** (505.3 km) **J 282.4** (454.5 km) Traffic light at 25th Avenue/BC Highway 6 to Nelson in downtown Vernon. Polson Park is on your right northbound (southeast corner of intersection). Strip mall at northeast corner of intersection has a Starbucks, A&W, drugstore, Subway, Little Caesar's Pizza and Earl's Restaurant.

E **314.1** (505.5 km) **J 282.3** (454.3 km) Traffic light at 30th Avenue in downtown Vernon; shopping, dining to east.

E **314.2** (505.7 km) **J 282.2** (454.1 km) Traffic light at 32nd Avenue in downtown Vernon: Gas stations with diesel (Chevron, Esso, Husky, Shell, Petro-Canada and Super-Save); lodging at Vernon Lodge and Sandman Inn & Suites Vernon; dining at Tim Hortons along Okanagan Highway 97/32nd Street.

Vernon

E **314.2** (505.7 km) **J 282.2** (454.1 km) Vernon is located 33 miles/53 km north of Kelowna in the North Okanagan. Highway 97 cuts through town as 32nd Street, crossing 30th Avenue which is downtown Vernon's main street. **Population:**

View of historic Catholic church at O'Keefe Ranch, established in 1867. This is a heritage site that offers guided and self-guided tours of the various buildings original to this cattle ranch. (©Kris Valencia, staff)

41,671. **Elevation:** 1,824 feet/556m. **Emergency Services:** Dial 911. **Hospital:** Vernon Jubilee Hospital south edge of town on highway, phone 250-545-2211.

Visitor Information: Tourism Vernon Visitor Information at 39th Avenue; phone 250-542-1415, toll-free 1-800-665-0795; www.tourismvernon.com.

Situated between Kalamalka, Okanagan and Swan lakes, Vernon is a popular tourist destination with year-round activities and attractions suited to a wide range of ages and interests. Summer temperatures average 79°F/26°C, with a record high in July of 101.3°F/38.5°C. Winter temperatures average 23°F/-3°C.

Vernon is the Okanagan's oldest city, settled in 1867 by Luc Girouard. As head of the Okanagan Lake paddle-wheeler service, Vernon grew in importance with the construction of a branch line of the Canadian Pacific Railway. Later, irrigation made commercial agriculture possible and the area exploded.

Explore 30th Avenue, Vernon's main downtown street with shopping, ethnic and farm-to-table focused restaurants. Visit Polson Park, a green oasis lined with weeping willows and with a unique floral clock. See the historic turn-of-the-century courthouse surrounded by a flowery courtyard and waterfalls. Stop at Davison Orchards Country Village, family-owned and operated since 1933, for fresh produce, orchard tours, shopping at their gift shop or enjoying special seasonal events. Open daily from 8 A.M. to 6 P.M., May 1 to Oct. 31; www.davisonorchards.ca. You can reach Davison Orchards from Highway 97 by turning west on 30th Avenue to Bella Vista Road, then right on Davison Road. Farmers Markets are held mid-April until Canadian Thanksgiving (second Monday in October) on Mondays and Thursdays from 8 A.M. to 1 P.M., and Fridays only noon–4 P.M., from after Canadian Thanksgiving to mid-April.

The Planet Bee at 5011 Bella Vista Rd. (2.5 km/1.5 miles west off Highway 97 on 30th Avenue) has year-round mead tastings, a honey tasting bar and 2 hives with educational bee experiences. Okanagan Spirits (BCs first craft distillery) at 5204–24 St. and BX Press Cidery at 4747 E. Vernon Rd. both offer year-round tastings of locally sourced and created beverages.

There are a variety of trails including the new in September 2018, multi-use Okanagan Rail Trail which runs along the Kalamalka Lake to Kelowna. Local hiking and biking trails for all abilities are found in the 5 area provincial parks: Ellison, Kalamalka Lake, Kekuli Bay, Silver Star and Fintry. The community also hosts the largest daily groomed nordic trails (115 km/71 miles).

World-class resorts here are Sparkling Hill Resort (wellness retreats), Predator Ridge Golf Resort and SilverStar Mountain Resort. Pet-friendly gondola rides provide sightseeing options and access to summer hiking at the SilverStar Mountain Resort. A ski resort for 60 years, SilverStar is a year-round destination.

Central Access Route Log
(continued)

E 314.6 (506.4 km) **J 281.7** (453.4 km) Traffic light at 39th Avenue with Tim Hortons. Turn east for Tourism Vernon Visitor Information Centre which offers reservation services.

E 315 (506.9 km) **J 281.4** (452.9 km) Traffic light at 43rd Avenue in Vernon; Super 8, Safeway.

E 315.5 (507.7 km) **J 280.9** (452 km) **Junction** with road east to SilverStar Mountain Resort. Access to Walmart, Home Depot, Holiday Inn Express, Best Western Pacific Inn and Fairfield Inn & Suites from this intersection.

Begin 4-lane highway northbound.

E 317 (510.1 km) **J 279.4** (449.6 km) SilverStar RV Park to west; phone 250-541-2808.

▲

Slow for posted speed zones southbound.

E 319 (513.4 km) **J 277.4** (446.4 km) Weigh station centered between north- and southbound lanes.

E 320 (515 km) **J 276.4** (444.8 km) **Junction** with BC Highway 97A to Sicamous on Trans-Canada Highway 1. Northbound travelers exit here to continue with this route log via BC Highway 97 to Trans-Canada Highway 1 and Kamloops. Distance marker northbound shows Kamloops 105 km/65 miles.

Begin 2-lane highway northbound. Sections of winding road, passing lanes and uphill grades.

E 323.1 (520 km) **J 273.3** (439.8 km) **Historic O'Keefe Ranch** heritage site, a recommended stop of interest. *CAUTION: Turn-off to ranch is on a tight turn.*

Cornelius O'Keefe and his partners began a 12,000-acre cattle ranch here in 1867. A post office was established at the ranch as well as the first Catholic church, one of the oldest in the region. Today, the O'Keefe Ranch is a nonprofit 50-acre site offering guided tours of the Victorian-style O'Keefe Mansion, exhibitions in the Greenhow Museum, self-guided walking tours of the General Store, Blacksmith Shop, original Log House, artisan shops, antique farm equipment, rare breed farm and more.

O'Keefe Ranch is open daily May through October. Hours are 10 A.M. to 5 P.M. (extended hours in summer). Admission fee charged. Restaurant, gift shop, RV camping with power and water hookups, horseback tours and picnic facilities on site. Pets allowed on leash. Check website for special events, activities and summer hours: www.okeeferanch.ca.

▲

E 324.8 (522.7 km) **J 271.6** (437.1 km) Sun Valley Speedway, sprint track.

E 333.8 (537.2 km) **J 262.6** (422.6 km) Whispering Pines Cafe to west.

E 335.5 (539.6 km) **J 260.9** (419.9 km) Una rest area (eastbound-only traffic). Toilets, litter bins, picnic tables, information boards about invasive weeds.

E 341.2 (549.1 km) **J 255.2** (410.7 km) Turnoff to east for **Bolean**, **Spa** and **Arthur** lakes; rainbow trout.

🐟

E 341.7 (549.9 km) **J 254.7** (409.9 km) *Slow for posted speed zone northbound entering* **Falkland**, a small ranching community. Heritage Park and Museum. Services include a pub, coffee shop/restaurant, motel and Petro-Canada gas/diesel station.

Ⓑ

E 342.2 (550.7 km) **J 254.2** (409.1 km) Falkland Stampede Grounds. An annual 2-day stampede is held Victoria Day weekend.

Slow for posted speed zone southbound.

E 342.9 (551.8 km) **J 253.5** (408 km) Entering Falkland (southbound sign).

E 344.1 (553.7 km) **J 252.3** (406 km) Railroad tracks. Gravel turnout to east after crossing tracks.

E 350.2 (563.6 km) **J 246.2** (396.2 km) Road west to **Pinaus**, **Ladyking** and **Square** lakes, 11 km/6.6 miles; rainbow trout fishing.

🐟

E 350.6 (564.2 km) **J 245.8** (395.6 km) *Slow for S-curves and posted speed zone entering* Westwold (northbound sign).

E 352.3 (567 km) **J 244.1** (392.8 km) **Westwold** (unincorporated) Community Hall. This small farm and logging community is situated in a beautiful valley.

E 352.8 (567.8 km) **J 243.6** (392 km) Route 97 Diner.

E 353 (568.1 km) **J 243.4** (391.7 km) General store, cafe. Salmon Lake Resort turn-off.

E 353.6 (569 km) **J 242.8** (390.7 km) *CAUTION: Watch for deer, slow for curves,* leaving Westwold northbound.

E 355.6 (572.3 km) **J 240.8** (387.5 km)

Highway crosses railroad tracks, slow for curve.

E 356.2 (573.2 km) **J 240.2** (386.5 km) South end of Monte Lake. Highway winds along east shore of lake northbound; informal gravel turnouts along lake.

E 356.9 (574.4 km) **J 239.5** (385.4 km) Monte Lake (unincorporated). Monte Lake Resort to the east.

E 357.2 (575 km) **J 239.2** (384.8 km) Private RV park to east.

E 358.7 (577.3 km) **J 237.7** (382.5 km) Hillside store, SuperSave gas/diesel station, post office.

Winding 2-lane highway with 60 kmph/37 mph curves northbound. Good shoulders but no turnouts.

E 361.2 (581.3 km) **J 235.2** (378.5 km) Distance marker southbound shows Monte Lake 5 km/3 miles, Falkland 28 km/17 miles, Vernon 72 km/45 miles.

E 368.1 (592.4 km) **J 228.3** (367.4 km) Rest area and brake check area to east for northbound traffic with travel information board, toilets and litter bins.

8 percent downgrade northbound.

E 368.5 (593 km) **J 227.9** (366.8 km) Distance marker southbound shows Monte Lake 19 km/12 miles, Falkand 42 km/26 miles, Vernon 86 km/53 miles.

E 369.5 (594.6 km) **J 226.9** (365.2 km) *Northbound travelers exit left (west) here to continue on this route via Trans-Canada Highway 1 West.*

Southbound travelers use Exit 399 to continue on this route via Highway 97 to Vernon.

BC Highway 97 shares a common alignment with Trans-Canada Highway 1 west to Cache Creek. Begin 4-lane divided highway westbound on Trans-Canada 1.

TRANS-CANADA HIGHWAY 1

E 371.3 (597.5 km) **J 225.1** (362.3 km) Exit 396 Hook Road; no services. Trans-Canada Highway 1 parallels the Thompson River (seen to the north) westbound to Kamloops. Notice the eroded clay hoodoos along the river.

E 375 (603.5 km) **J 221.4** (356.3 km) Exit 391 is westbound access to Kamloops RV Park and **BC Wildlife Park** to south (eastbound motorists use Exit 390). See grizzly bears, cougars, gray wolves, moose and other rehabilitating wildlife of British Columbia. Birds of Prey show in outdoor amphitheatre during summer. Splash Water Park and train rides. Open daily, 9:30 A.M. to 5 P.M., April 30 to Oct. 8; and 9:30 A.M. to 4 P.M. March 3–April 29; weekends and holidays during winter (Oct. 9 to March 2). Admission charged.

E 377.6 (607.7 km) **J 218.8** (352.1 km) Exit 388/Kokanee Way access north; to Petro-Pass and 24-hour food, gas/diesel, RV parking.

E 380.4 (612.2 km) **J 216** (347.6 km) Stoplight at Valleyview Drive/Grand Boulevard.

E 382.9 (616.2 km) **J 213.5** (343.6 km) Stoplight at Tanager Road.

E 383.6 (617.3 km) **J 212.8** (342.5 km) Stoplight at River Road; access south to frontage road services and Thompson Drive boat launch.

E 384.1 (618.1 km) **J 212.3** (341.6 km) Stoplight at Highland Drive. Access south to frontage road and Valleyview Square shop-

ping mall.

E 384.5 (618.8 km) **J 211.9** (341 km) Stoplight at Oriole Road; access south to frontage road services (food, gas/diesel, lodging).

E 385.1 (619.7 km) **J 211.3** (340 km) Stoplight at Vicars Road; access south to frontage road services (food, gas/diesel, lodging).

E 385.6 (620.6 km) **J 210.8** (339.2 km) Exit 375 Kamloops City Centre exit for westbound motorists.

E 386 (621.2 km) **J 210.4** (338.6 km) Exit 374 to Kamloops. *Northbound, continue on Yellowhead Highway 5 to follow this log to Tete Jaune Cache on Yellowhead Highway 16.*

Highways 1, 97 and 5 share a common alignment westbound on a controlled-access freeway that bypasses the city of Kamloops. Highway 5 South (Coquihalla Highway) exits Trans-Canada Highway 1 at Exit 362 *(see end of "Coquihalla Highway" log on page 103).*

You may also continue west on Trans-Canada Highway 1/97 for 53 miles/84 km to Cache Creek and the start of Highway 97 North/Cariboo Highway *(turn to page 119 in the WEST ACCESS ROUTE section).* Trans-Canada Highway 1 west of Highway 5 South junction is a winding 2-lane highway with passing lanes. Gas in Kamloops, Savona and Cache Creek.

Kamloops

E 386 (621.2 km) **J 210.4** (338.6 km) Located at the **junction** of Trans-Canada Highway 1 and Highways 97, 5 (Coquihalla) and 5A. **Population:** 90,000. **Elevation:** 1,181 feet/360m. **Emergency Services:** Dial 911. **Police**, phone 250-828-3000. **Hospital**, phone 250-374-5111.

Visitor Information: Kamloops Visitor Centre at 1290 W. Trans-Canada Highway (Exit 368, from Highway 1) and is open daily year-round; phone 250-374-3377. Email: inquiry@tourismkamloops.com; or visit www.tourismkamloops.com.

Established by fur traders as Fort Kamloops in 1811, Kamloops is located at the confluence of the North and South Thompson rivers. Kamloops boomed with the arrival of the Canadian Pacific Railway in 1885. Today it is a bustling city with excellent shopping and tourist facilities at the crossroads of 2 major tourist routes: Trans-Canada Highway 1 and Highway 5.

Attractions include BC Wildlife Park, Kamloops Heritage Railway, Secwepemc Museum and Heritage Park, Kamloops Museum, Kamloops Courthouse Gallery, Kamloops Art Gallery, BIG Little Science Centre, Riverside Park. Music in the Park in July and August. Project X Theatre in the Park, 13 golf courses, more than 100 fishing lakes within an hour's drive, Kamloops Bike Ranch and Kenna Cartwright Park biking and hiking trails.

YELLOWHEAD HIGHWAY 5

E 386 (621.2 km) **J 210.4** (338.6 km) *Northbound travelers note: This is a busy highway with few passing lanes (although passing lane projects are ongoing). Traffic often travels above the 100 kmph/62 mph posted speed limit. Drive with care!*

Southbound travelers exit here to Kamloops city centre and Trans-Canada Highway 1 East for continuation of Central Access Route log south to Ellensburg via the Okanagan.

Travelers heading south via the Coquihalla Highway to Hope, BC, continue straight ahead and merge onto Highway 1 West, Trans-Canada Highway 1 exits Highway 5 South (Coquihalla Highway) at Exit 362 *(see "Coquihalla Highway" log on page 102).*

E 386.3 (621.6 km) **J 210.1** (338.1 km) Crossing the South Thompson River at Exit 374.

E 386.6 (622.2 km) **J 209.8** (337.6 km) East Shuswap Road. Turnoff to east for Petro Canada gas/diesel station, RCMP, golfing and access to Secwepemc Museum and Heritage Park, Harper's Trail and Sagewood wineries.

E 386.9 (622.7 km) **J 209.5** (337.2 km) Stoplight at Mount Paul Way. Silver Sage RV Park and Mount Paul Industrial Park to west.

E 389 (626 km) **J 207.4** (333.8 km) **Junction** with Paul Lake Road. Husky to east and Esso/A&W to west; gas/diesel at both. Road leads east to Harper Mountain Ski Area, mountain biking trails and **Paul Lake Provincial Park** (18 mi/11 miles) with campground; 90 sites, 47 reservable; drinking water, firepits, playground, swimming beach, hiking trails, interpretive programs, boat launch. Camping fee is $18, sani-station $5. Open mid-May to mid-September; reservable at www.discovercamping.ca. Park gate is locked from 11 P.M. to 7 A.M.

E 391.7 (630.4 km) **J 204.7** (329.4 km) Double-ended turnout to west with map of Kamloops.

E 395.3 (636.2 km) **J 201.1** (323.6 km) Rayleigh. Petro-Canada gas/diesel station to west, with restaurant.

E 397.5 (639.7 km) **J 198.9** (320 km) Tournament Capital Ranch to west has 8 slo-pitch fields and 2 full-sized rugby fields.

E 400.5 (644.5 km) **J 195.9** (315.3 km) Begin 2-lane highway northbound. Begin 4-lane highway southbound through Kamloops.

E 405.1 (651.9 km) **J 191.3** (307.8 km) Paved turnout to east.

E 407.5 (655.8 km) **J 188.9** (304 km) Truck pullout. Begin passing lane northbound.

E 411.4 (662.1 km) **J 185** (297.7 km) Pinegrove Campground and RV park.

E 412.1 (663.2 km) **J 184.3** (296.6 km) Begin 2-km/1.2-mile passing lane southbound.

E 412.9 (664.5 km) **J 183.5** (295.3 km) Fruit stand at access road west to McLure Ferry across the North Thompson River to Westsyde Road, which goes south to Kamloops and north to Barriere.

E 414.6 (667.2 km) **J 181.8** (292.6 km) Small community of **McLure**; restaurant and private RV park. Fruit stands in season. This area raises sheep and cows.

E 415.8 (669.2 km) **J 180.6** (290.6 km) Distance marker southbound shows Kamloops 50 km/31 miles.

E 416.1 (669.6 km) **J 180.3** (290.2 km) Fish Trap rest area to west with information
(Continues on page 103)

Coquihalla Highway

The Coquihalla Highway (BC Highway 5) connects Hope, at the junction of Highways 1 and 3, with Kamloops on Trans-Canada Highway 1. Created in 1986 as a more direct route to the Interior of the province, the Coquihalla may be used as an alternate route (either northbound or southbound) for both Central Access Route and West Access Route motorists.

Note that traveler services along the highway are found only in Hope, Merritt and Kamloops. There are signed exits for designated rest areas, chain-up and brake check areas, and U-turn routes.

Designated a "long combination vehicle route," the Coquihalla is a 4- to 6-lane, divided, limited access freeway with 6 to 8 percent grades. Posted speed limit is 120 kmph/75 mph and traffic moves at a brisk pace. BC's Department of Transportation requires that motorists use winter tires between Oct. 1 and April 30. This is a high mountain road (highest summit is 4,081 feet/1,244m): Expect sudden weather changes! Prepare for winter temperatures to -27°C/-17°F.

The highway may be closed in winter due to avalanche hazard; check road conditions prior to travel at www.drivebc.ca. Make sure you top off your tank. Carry winter emergency gear.

BC HIGHWAY 5

Distance from Hope (H) is followed by distance from Kamloops (K).

H 0 (0 km) **K 118** (189.9 km) **Junction** of Highway 3/Crowsnest and Trans-Canada Highway 1. Follow Highway 3 east for Coquihalla Highway access. Exit 170 to Trans-Canada Highway 1 East to Hope.

H 0.8 (1.3 km) **K 117.2** (188.6 km) Exit 171 (southbound) to Hope and Trans-Canada Highway 1 East; food, gas, lodging.

H 1.5 (2.4 km) **K 116.5** (187.5 km) Exit 173 (northbound) to Hope; food, gas, lodging.

H 4 (6.4 km) **K 114** (183.8 km) Exit 177 for Highway 3 East (Crowsnest) to Princeton. Westbound travelers continue straight for BC Highway 5/Coquihalla to Merritt and Kamloops!

H 4.3 (6.9 km) **K 113.7** (183 km) Nicolum Creek bridge.

Kilometreposts northbound reflect distance from this turnoff, not from the junction where this road log begins (4.3 miles/6.9 km south).

H 7.5 (12.1 km) **K 110.5** (178 km) Exit 183, Othello Road to Kawkawa Lake and **Coquihalla Canyon Provincial Recreation Area**; picnic area, restrooms. The former Kettle Valley Railway here has been restored as a walking trail through 3 of 5 original railroad tunnels. Restrooms at parking lot. Kawkawa Lake is a popular destination for picnics, swimming and boating. Othello Tunnels Campground with RV camping.

H 11.5 (18.5 km) **K 106.5** (171.4 km) Deneau Creek bridge.

H 13 (20.9 km) **K 105** (168.5 km) Large gravel turnout (northbound only) above Coquihalla River, east side of highway, used by fishermen.

H 13.5 (21.7 km) **K 104.5** (168.1 km) Exit 192 for Sowaqua Creek near the former Kettle Valley railway station of Jessica.

H 13.8 (22.2 km) **K 104.2** (167.7 km) Northbound only, large, paved, double-ended turnout/chain-up area.

H 14 (22.5 km) **K 104** (167.3 km) Southbound only, large, paved, double-ended turnout/chain-up area.

H 15.3 (24.6 km) **K 102.7** (165.2 km) Dewdney Creek.

H 16 (25.7 km) **K 102** (164.1 km) Exit 195 for Carolin Mine Road (an operating gold mine). Northbound travelers make U-turn to **Coquihalla River Provincial Recreation Area** located southwest of the highway; picnic tables, fishing and hiking. Entering avalanche area northbound.

H 17 (27.4 km) **K 101** (162.5 km) Ladner Creek bridge.

H 19.7 (31.7 km) **K 98.3** (158.2 km) Southbound chain-off area to west.

H 20 (32.2 km) **K 98** (157.7 km) Portia chain-up area for northbound vehicles; snow on slopes into June.

H 23.3 (37.5 km) **K 94.7** (152.4 km) Northbound large, double-ended turnout to east with litter bin.

H 23.7 (38.1 km) **K 94.3** (151.8 km) Northbound rest area to east with litter bin.

H 24 (38.6 km) **K 94** (151.3 km) From here to the summit is the most avalanche prone; 11 major avalanche tracks cross the highway alignment. Box Canyon, to west, holds the record for the deepest snowfall of the route: 15 feet in March of 1976.

H 24.5 (39.4 km) **K 93.5** (150.4 km) Northbound traffic may use Box Canyon chain-up rest area to east with litter bins and toilets.

H 25.5 (41 km) **K 92.5** (148.8 km) South portal of Great Bear snowshed, among the world's longest at nearly 300m/1,000 feet. Concrete lintels are decorated with incised figures of bears.

H 28 (45 km) **K 90** (144.8 km) Exit 217 to west to rest area/brake check area with specific lanes for trucks and passenger vehicles. Under the towering rock slab of Zopkios

Ridge; picnic site, washrooms, concession stands with food trucks.

Begin 8 percent grade southbound.

H 29 (46.6 km) **K 89** (143.2 km) **Boston Bar Creek Summit** above Romeo railway stop. Southbound double-ended chain up area to west; 6 percent decline next 17 km/11 miles.

H 30 (48.2 km) **K 88** (141.6 km) **Coquihalla Highway Summit** (elev. 1,244m/4,081 feet).

H 31.5 (50.7 km) **K 86.5** (139.2 km) Exit 221 for Falls Lake picnic area.

H 32 (51.5 km) **K 86** (138.4 km) Dry Gulch bridge.

H 33.5 (53.9 km) **K 84.5** (136 km) Rest area northbound with toilets and litter bins. Southbound passenger vehicle only, long, double-ended rest areas with toilets and litter bins.

H 35 (56.3 km) **K 83** (133.5 km) Exit 228 for Britton Creek rest area; washrooms, picnic tables in trees north of Coquihalla Lakes Lodge Road. Coquihalla Lakes Lodge to east.

H 35.5 (57.1 km) **K 82.5** (132.7 km) Coldwater River bridges, next 5 miles northbound: Bottle Top, Murray, Brookmere and Rust.

H 36 (58 km) **K 82** (132 km) Distance marker northbound shows Merritt 62 km/39 miles, Kamloops 144 km/89 miles, Kelowna 183 km/114 miles.

H 38.4 (61.8 km) **K 79.6** (128.1 km) Exit 231 southbound for Mine Creek Road; U-turn route.

H 41.5 (66.8 km) **K 76.5** (123 km) Bridge over Juliet Creek; Exit 238 north of bridge for Coldwater River Provincial Recreation Area; picnic area closed for reclamation, current status unknown, observe updated highway signage.

H 49 (78.8 km) **K 69** (111 km) Exit 250 Larson Hill, forestry access.

H 53.3 (85.8 km) **K 64.7** (104.1 km) Kingsvale Bridge. Exit 256 Coldwater Road. U-turn route.

H 54 (86.9 km) **K 64** (102.9 km) Exit to Gillis Lake and Kane Valley Road to Highway 5A south of Merritt.

H 64.8 (104.3 km) **K 53.2** (85.6 km) Distance marker southbound shows Hope 105 km/65 miles, Chilliwack 151 km/94 miles, Vancouver 260 km/162 miles.

H 65.5 (105.4 km) **K 51.5** (82.9 km) Exit 276 Comstock Road; U-turn route.

H 66.1 (106.4 km) **K 50.9** (81.9 km) Northbound, the highway descends into the dry Interior Plateau.

Distance marker northbound shows Merritt 13 km/8 miles, Kamloops 93 km/58 miles.

H 67 (107.8 km) **K 51** (82 km) Southbound sign: Next fuel 111 km/69 miles.

H 70.3 (113 km) **K 47.7** (76.8 km) Distance marker southbound shows Hope 114 km/71 miles, Chilliwack 160 km/99 miles, Vancouver 269 km/167 miles.

H 71.5 (115 km) **K 46.5** (74.8 km) Exit 286 to **MERRITT** (pop. 7,000) city centre; lodging, gas/diesel stations, Fountain Tire for vehicle repair tire repair/replace, restaurants and museums. Elev. 1,952 feet/595m. Visitor information at the Merritt Visitor Centre at the south end of the city. Merritt is called the "Country Music Capital of Canada." Merritt is also at the centre of 3 historic cattle ranches: the Nicola Ranch, the Quilchena Cattle Co. and the Douglas Lake Cattle Co., Canada's largest ranch.

The Coquihalla Highway is a truck route with a summit of 4,081 feet/1,244m.
(©Lilly Graef)

Access west via Highway 5A this exit to Merritt and junction with 97C to Logan Lake 72 km/45 miles, Ashcroft 130 km/81 miles, and Highway 8 (Nicola Highway) to Spences Bridge.

Exit east for 97C (Okanagan Connector) to Peachland 108 km/67 miles.

H 72.5 (116.6 km) **K 45.5** (73.2 km) Nicola River bridge.

H 73 (117.5 km) **K 45** (72.4 km) Exit 290 for north Merritt. Easy access west to traveler services, including food (McDonald's, Subway, KFC, DQ, Starbucks, Tim Hortons), lodging (Ramada, Super 8, Travel Lodge), gas (Petro-Canada, Shell, Chevron) and a Canadian Tire (oil changes and vehicle repair).

The Lion's Memorial Park at 2408 Voght St., has a large parking area, walking paths, picnic tables, **EV plug-ins** and restrooms. Great spot to park and walk through the charming downtown area. There is a nearby bowling green (take path over bridge to adjacent N'Kwala Park).

H 76.5 (123.1 km) **K 41.4** (66.7 km) Double-ended chain-up area with litter bins and toilets; highway north starts a long, steady climb up Clapperton Creek into the high forests of the Nicola Plateau.

Welcome to Merritt sign southbound.

H 85.9 (138.3 km) **K 32** (51.5 km) Southbound "Clapperton" chain-up and brake check area with litter bins and toilets. **Surrey Lake Summit** (formerly known as Clapperton Creek Summit) is elev. 1,445m/4,741 feet.

H 89.6 (144.2 km) **K 28.4** (45.7 km) Helmer Road Exit 315 to Helmer Lake.

H 96.5 (155.3 km) **K 21.5** (34.6 km) Begin 6 percent downhill grade for next 4.5 km/3 miles northbound.

H 101 (162.5 km) **K 17** (27.4 km) Distance marker southbound shows Merritt 48 km/30 miles, Hope 165 km/103 miles, Vancouver 316 km/196 miles.

H 102 (164.2 km) **K 16** (25.7 km) Exit 336 to Highway 97C west to Logan Lake (22 km/14 miles) and Ashcroft. Lac La Jaune Resort with lodging and dining.

H 108 (173.8 km) **K 10** (16.1 km) Highway begins 6 percent downgrade northbound as it descends from the plateau into the Thompson Valley.

H 108.6 (174.7 km) **K 9.4** (15.1 km) Roadside turnout, northbound only, with litter bins and toilet.

H 112.7 (181.4 km) **K 5.3** (8.5 km) Distance marker southbound shows Logan Lake 40 km/25 miles, Merritt 67 km/42 miles.

H 113.5 (182.6 km) **K 4.5** (7.2 km) Exit 355 for Inks Lake; U-turn route.

H 118 (189.9 km) **K 0 Junction** with Trans-Canada Highway 1 west of Kamloops. To continue northbound on the Central Access Route do not exit; Highway 5/Trans-Canada Highway 1 continues to Kamloops (see *Milepost E 386* page 101).

Travelers taking Exit 362 can join the West Access Route by heading west to Cache Creek and Prince George. Cache Creek is 53 miles/85 km west of here via Trans-Canada Highway 1. This highway is mostly a 2-lane road that winds through some spectacular high-desert country. Gas/diesel available in Kamloops, Savona and Cache Creek.

Southbound travelers on the Coquihalla Highway will find gas and other services available only in Kamloops, Merritt and Hope. Highway climbs long 6 percent grade southbound.

(Continued from page 101)
boards, picnic tables, toilets and litter bins.

E 417.3 (671.5 km) **J 179.1** (288.2 km) Large gravel turnout to west.

E 417.9 (672.5 km) **J 178.5** (287.3 km) Begin 1-km/0.6-mile passing lane northbound.

E 419.2 (674.6 km) **J 177.2** (285.2 km) Begin 1.1-km/0.7-mile passing lane southbound.

E 419.5 (675.1 km) **J 176.9** (284.7 km) Turnout with information boards at Thompson River overlook. The North Thompson River rises in the Cariboo Mountains and flows southward to meet the South Thompson at Kamloops. The route was made famous by a small group of Overlanders, led by Thomas McMicking, who turned south at Tete Jaune Cache and headed for Fort Kamloops on their way to the Cariboo goldfields in 1862. It took the party of 32 men and 1 pregnant woman with 3 children almost a month to reach the fort. The day after their arrival, Mrs. Catherine Schubert delivered her fourth child, Rose. The story of their trip is one of incredible privation and courage.

E 422.3 (679.6 km) **J 174.1** (280.2 km) **Louis Creek** (unincorporated); antique store. Still very much in evidence in this area is devastation from the 2003 Barriere-McLure wildfire. Started by a carelessly discarded cigarette, the fire destroyed the local sawmill (the largest employer in the region) and 73 homes in Barriere and Louis Creek.

E 423.9 (682.2 km) **J 172.5** (277.6 km) Turnout with litter bin to east. Welcome to Barriere northbound. *Slow for posted speed zone northbound.*

E 424 (682.3 km) **J 172.4** (277.4 km) 24-hour gas stations with gas/diesel and propane, a Subway and an RV park.

E 424.9 (683.8 km) **J 171.5** (276 km) **BARRIERE** (area pop. 5,000); Petro-Canada gas/diesel station, A&W, restaurants, motels, motel/RV park, liquor store and other services. Visitor information centre.

E 424.5 (683.1 km) **J 171.9** (276.6 km) Thompson River bridge.

E 426.2 (685.9 km) **J 170.2** (273.9 km) Welcome to Barriere southbound. Double-ended gravel turnout with litter bin. *Slow for posted speed zones southbound.*

E 426.4 (686.2 km) **J 170** (273.6 km) Crossing Thompson River.

E 427.6 (688.1 km) **J 168.8** (271.6 km) Chinook Cove Golf Club & RV Park to west.

E 431.3 (694.1 km) **J 165.1** (265.7 km) Large paved turnout to east with litter bin and view of Thompson River.

E 432.4 (695.9 km) **J 164** (263.9 km) Unincorporated community of Darfield.
CAUTION: Watch for deer.

E 436.3 (702.2 km) **J 160.1** (257.7 km) Distance marker southbound shows Barriere 16 km/10 miles, Kamloops 79 km/49 miles.

E 443.5 (713.7 km) **J 152.9** (246.1 km) Northbound sign: Welcome to Little Fort. *Slow for posted speed zone* through **LITTLE FORT** (pop. 200); Husky gas/diesel/grocery, Subway, lodging and camping.

E 443.6 (713.9 km) **J 152.8** (245.9 km) **Junction** with Highway 24, which leads west 97 km/60 miles to Highway 97 near 100 Mile House on the West Access Route. This road accesses great rainbow trout fishing in many lakes, including **Bridge** and

Sheridan lakes.

E 443.8 (714.2 km) **J 152.6** (245.6 km) Turnoff to west for creekside rest area.

E 444.1 (714.7 km) **J 152.3** (245.1 km) Distance marker northbound shows Jasper 349 km/217 miles, Prince George 518 km/322 miles.

E 444.3 (715 km) **J 152.1** (244.8 km) Southbound sign: Welcome to Little Fort. *Slow for posted speed zone.*

E 446.2 (718.1 km) **J 150.2** (241.7 km) Rivermont Motel, cafe, camping.

E 446.6 (718.7 km) **J 149.8** (241.1 km) Northbound, the highway parallels North Thompson River. Paved roadside turnout east, beside river with litter bins.

E 447.2 (719.7 km) **J 149.2** (240.1 km) Roadside turnout to east beside river.

E 453.2 (729.2 km) **J 143.2** (230.4 km) Large paved roadside turnout to east beside river; litter bin.

E 454 (730.6 km) **J 142.4** (229.2 km) Distance marker northbound shows Clearwater 16 km/10 miles, Jasper 335 km/208 miles, Prince George 512 km/318 miles.

Distance marker southbound shows Little Fort 16 km/10 miles, Kamloops 108 km/67 miles.

E 457.3 (735.9 km) **J 137.1** (220.7 km) Turnout with litter bin to east.

E 457.5 (736.3 km) **J 136.9** (220.3 km) Lacarya Golf Course & RV Park; phone 250-587-6100.

E 459.4 (739.3 km) **J 137** (220.5 km) Turnoff east for **North Thompson River Provincial Park**, 1 km/0.6 mile on good paved road. *NOTE: Possible closure.* Please check in advance of planning to use this campground. Updates to this closure will be noted at: www.env.gov.bc.ca/bcparks/explore/parkpgs/n_thm_rv/. Picnic area has oversized vehicle parking and short trails to shady sites on river. Campground has 61 campsites in trees, drinking water, pit toilets and playground. There is a sani-station ($5 fee). Fish at the mouth of the **Clearwater River**. Camping fee $23 per night (additional fee for tow vehicle). Reserve sites at www.discovercamping.ca. Hiking trail is 1.2 km/0.7 mile long.

E 460.4 (740.9 km) **J 136** (218.9 km) Clearwater River bridge. The Overlanders named this river after its crystal-clear waters that contrasted strongly with the muddy Thompson.

E 461.8 (743.2 km) **J 134.6** (216.6 km) **Junction** with Village Road at **CLEARWATER** (pop. 2,500 to 3,000). **Emergency Services:** Dial 911. **Police**, phone 250-674-2237. **Visitor Information:** Tourism Wells Gray, phone 250-674-3530 or www.wellsgray.ca. Offers lodging, restaurant, camping options and liquor store at this intersection. The village road (Old North Thompson Highway) leads west approximately 1 mile to a small business area with a gas station, liquor store, restaurant, and a bank. Access to post office to east.

E 462.4 (744.1 km) **J 134** (215.6 km) Roundabout at junction with Clearwater Valley Road to Wells Gray Provincial Park (see park description following). Grocery, pharmacy, motel, cafe, Shell gas/diesel station/A&W/Tim Hortons *NOTE: Food services close early in evening.* **Wells Gray Park Information Centre** at the northwest corner of intersection with RV parking (pictured below); open daily May-October; restrooms, gift shop; free booking service, maps and information. For more information, go to website: wellsgraypark.info or phone 250-674-3334. Clearwater Valley Resort & KOA campground is located just west of the roundabout; campsites, restaurant, hotel; phone 250-674-3909.

© Kris Valencia, staff

Wells Gray Provincial Park is a magnificent wilderness in the Cariboo Mountains, but is perhaps best known for its spectacular waterfalls, easily accessible via Clearwater Valley Road. Driving distances to the falls are: Spahats Creek Falls, at Mile 6.4/10.3 km (5-minute walk to viewpoint); Dawson Falls, at Mile 25.4/40.9 km (10-minute walk on broad trail to view); and Helmcken Falls, 26.4 miles/42.5 km to turnoff and 2.5 miles/4 km to parking area. *NOTE: Check your gas in Clearwater before driving in to see the falls; no gas available on the park road.*

This side road is narrow and paved to Helmcken Falls turnoff. The park offers canoeing, rafting, horseback riding, picnic areas, hiking trails and camping. Main camping season begins mid-May and runs into or through September. Campgrounds are: **Pyramid** (50 sites, $20/night), **Clearwater Lake** (39 sites, $23/night) and **Falls Creek** (41 sites, $23/night, sani-station $5). **Mayhood Lake** is located outside the main park corridor (32 sites, 5 double sites, $23/night).

Helmcken Falls Lodge, built in 1948, offers accommodations and dinner at Mile 21.5/34.6 km on the park access road.

E 462.7 (744.6 km) **J 133.7** (215.2 km) Business frontage road access to motel, gas/diesel station, Dairy Queen and KalTire. *Slow for speed zone southbound.*

E 465.2 (748.6 km) **J 131.2** (211.1 km) Raft River bridge.

E 465.5 (749 km) **J 130.9** (210.6 km) Stop of interest, Raft River, riparian zone with raised walkways and viewing platform to watch spawning salmon in season.

E 468.8 (754.4 km) **J 127.6** (205.3 km) Birch Island rest area downhill to east has litter bins, toilets, shaded picnic tables and view of the Thompson River valley.

E 469.5 (755.6 km) **J 126.9** (204.2 km) Birch Island campground and RV.

E 474.5 (763.6 km) **J 121.9** (196.2 km) Gravel turnout with litter bin to east.

E 475.7 (765.6 km) **J 120.7** (194.2 km) Distance marker northbound shows Avola 45 km/28 miles, Jasper 298 km/185 miles, Prince George 475 km/295 miles.

Distance marker southbound shows Clearwater 21 km/13 miles, Kamloops 145 km/90 miles.

E 477.7 (768.8 km) **J 118.7** (191 km) Road east to community of **VAVENBY**; store with gas. Vavenby is the centre of valley sheep farming.

E 485 (780.5 km) **J 111.4** (179.3 km) Distance marker northbound shows Jasper 282 km/175 miles, Prince George 454 km/282 miles.

Distance marker southbound shows Clearwater 35 km/22 miles, Kamloops 159 km/99 miles.

E 486.8 (783.4 km) **J 109.6** (176.4 km) Mad River bridge. The river gives its name to the rapids in the river below, where the weary Overlanders had to portage their rafts.

E 492.8 (793.1 km) **J 103.6** (166.7 km) Turnout with litter bins to east

E 493.5 (794.2 km) **J 102.9** (165.6 km) Roadside turnout to west.

E 495.4 (797.2 km) **J 101** (162.5 km) Turnoff to east for large rest area with litter bins, picnic tables and toilets beside Thompson River. Children's playground.

Distance marker southbound shows Clearwater 51 km/32 miles, Kamloops 175 km/109 miles.

E 495.6 (797.6 km) **J 100.8** (162.2 km) Roadside turnout to east.

E 503.2 (809.8 km) **J 93.2** (150 km) Distance marker southbound shows Clearwater 64 km/40 miles, Kamloops 188 km/117 miles.

E 503.4 (810.1 km) **J 93** (149.7 km) Roadside turnout with litter bin to east. Avola community welcome sign northbound.

Resume 100 kmph/62 mph posted speed limit southbound.

E 504 (811.1 km) **J 92.4** (148.7 km) *Slow for posted speed zone* through community of **AVOLA**; gas/diesel station and food store, restaurant and lodging.

E 504.2 (811.4 km) **J 92.2** (148.4 km) North Thompson River bridge.

E 504.6 (812.1 km) **J 91.8** (147.7 km) Roadside turnout with Avola map and litter bin to west.

Distance marker northbound Blue River 39 km/24 miles, Valemount 127 km/79 miles, Jasper 251 km/156 miles, Prince George 428 km/266 miles.

E 505.5 (813.5 km) **J 90.9** (146.3 km) Roadside turnout with litter bin to west alongside river.

E 507.6 (816.9 km) **J 88.8** (142.9 km) Tum Tum Creek.

E 513.7 (826.7 km) **J 82.7** (133.1 km) Paved Messiter chain-up (northbound traffic)/chain-off (southbound traffic) parking areas east and west sides of highway.

E 514.6 (828.1 km) **J 81.8** (131.6 km) Access road (rough, no turnarounds, not recommended for RVs or trailers) leads 3 km/2 miles to Little Hell's Gate Regional Park and view of Porte d'Enfer, or Hell's Gate canyon, below the highway. The Thompson River turns abruptly through a narrow canyon and emerges south into tempestuous whirlpools. Here the Overlanders had to abandon their rafts (after a member of the party and all the horses were drowned) and go around the rapids on foot. It took them 3 days to make the 14-km/8.5-mile walk.

E 515.4 (839.4 km) **J 81** (130.4 km) Stop-of-interest turnout to west at **Messiter Summit** (elev. 735m/2,411 feet); litter bin and toilet. Highway descends for both northbound and southbound traffic. Monashee Mountains to the east, Cariboo Mountains to the west.

E 516.1 (830.6 km) **J 80.3** (129.2 km) Gamble Creek.

E 517.2 (832.3 km) **J 79.2** (127.5 km) Paved turnout to west is Messiter chain-up area for southbound traffic.

Begin southbound passing lane 2.5-km/1.6-mile.

E 517.3 (832.5 km) **J 79.1** (127.3 km) Gravel turnout to east is Messiter chain-off area for northbound traffic.

E 521.8 (839.8 km) **J 74.6** (120.1 km) North Thompson River bridge.

E 527.5 (848.9 km) **J 68.9** (110.9 km) Distance marker southbound shows Avola 39 km/24 miles, Kamloops 229 km/142 miles.

E 527.7 (849.2 km) **J 68.7** (110.6 km) Roadside turnouts with litter bins both sides of highway. Northbound turnout on east side of highway has map of Blue River.

Slow for posted speed zone northbound.

E 528.1 (849.9 km) **J 68.3** (109.9 km) Entering Blue River northbound; Husky gas/diesel station and restaurant to east, Sandman Inn/The Grill restaurant to west.

E 528.5 (850.5 km) **J 67.9** (109.3 km) Petro-Canada gas/diesel station Rocky Mountain Deli and Glacier Mountain Lodge. **BLUE RIVER** (area pop. 300) began as a divisional point on the Canadian National Railway and is today a jumping-off point for heli-skiing, snowmobiling, backcountry skiing, hiking, canoeing and fishing in the Monashee and Cariboo mountains. Services include motels to chalet rentals, multiple restaurants, a grocery market and the Blue River Campground and RV Park. Rent canoes, bikes and camping gear for your adventure.

Turn on Angus Horne across from Petro-Canada and go 0.8 km/0.5 mile to rail tracks, then one block left for beautiful Eleanor Lake Community Park. A great picnic and swim spot. Litter bins, tables, firepits, gazebo, playground, washroom/shower house, volleyball and floating docks.

E 528.9 (851.2 km) **J 67.5** (108.6 km) **Junction** with Murtle Lake Road (gravel) which leads west 24 km/15 miles to Wells Gray Provincial Park's Murtle Lake (accessible by a 2.7-km/1.7-mile hiking trail), considered to be one of the most beautiful, canoe only, wilderness lakes in British Columbia. Also access this side road to Saddle Mountain, restaurant, motel and Blue River campground.

E 529.1 (851.5 km) **J 67.3** (108.3 km) Blue River bridge.

Slow for posted speed zone southbound.

Begin 1.3 km/0.8 mile passing lane northbound.

E 529.8 (852.6 km) **J 66.6** (107.2 km) Roadside turnout to west with litter bin and Blue River information board.

E 530.5 (853.7 km) **J 65.9** (106 km) Cedar Creek. Watch for Mud Lake Forest Service Road (north of airstrip) which leads east to River Safari jet-boat tours, phone 250-673-2309.

E 532 (856.2 km) **J 64.4** (103.6 km) Cook Creek.

E 534.5 (860.2 km) **J 61.9** (99.6 km) Whitewater Creek.

E 536.3 (862.9 km) **J 60.1** (96.7 km) Small gravel turnout to east.

E 537.5 (865 km) **J 58.9** (94.8 km) Bridge crosses Thunder River, a tributary of the Thompson River.

E 537.7 (865.3 km) **J 58.7** (94.5 km) Rest area to west by Thunder River.

E 540.6 (870 km) **J 55.8** (89.8 km) Roadside turnout with litter bin to east.

E 540.7 (870.2 km) J 55.7 (89.6 km) Bone Creek Wilderness Retreat and RV Park.

E 542.8 (873.4 km) J 53.6 (86.2 km) Miledge Creek bridge.

E 548.4 (882.5 km) J 48 (77.2 km) Chapel Creek. Passing lane begins northbound next 1.2 km/0.7 mile.

Distance marker southbound shows Blue River 34 km/21 miles, Kamloops 264 km/164 miles.

E 549 (883.5 km) J 47.4 (76.3 km) Southbound passing lane next 1.2 km/0.7 mile.

E 549.1 (884 km) J 47.1 (75.8 km) Roadside turnout with litter bin to east. View of North Thompson River.

E 553 (889.8 km) J 43.4 (69.8 km) North Thompson River Crossing, first of 3 crossings northbound.

E 554.9 (893 km) J 41.5 (66.8 km) North Thompson River crossing.

E 555.9 (894.6 km) J 40.5 (65.2 km) North Thompson River crossing.

E 556.4 (895.4 km) J 40 (64.3 km) Albreda River bridge.

E 557.5 (897.2 km) J 38.9 (62.6 km) Dominion Creek.

E 559.6 (900.6 km) J 36.8 (59.2 km) Albreda River bridge (second crossing northbound).

E 560.6 (902.2 km) J 35.8 (57.6 km) Very large gravel turnout and trailhead to west.

E 564.2 (908 km) J 32.2 (51.8 km) Paved roadside turnout with litter bin to west.

E 566.2 (911.2 km) J 30.2 (48.6 km) Trailhead parking to west with litter bins and trail information.

E 566.7 (912 km) J 29.7 (47.8 km) Large turnout to west with litter bin. Good view southbound of Albreda Glacier. Northbound, the highway enters the Rocky Mountain Trench.

E 568.4 (914.7 km) J 28 (45.1 km) Distance marker southbound shows Blue River 64 km/40 miles, Kamloops 295 km/183 miles.

E 570.8 (918.6 km) J 25.6 (41.2 km) Summit River Lodge and Campground.

E 576.7 (927.9 km) J 19.7 (31.7 km) Double-ended gravel turnout to west.

E 577.1 (928.7 km) J 19.3 (31 km) Camp Creek bridge. Passing lane southbound next 2.4 km/1.5 miles.

E 577.8 (929.9 km) J 18.6 (29.9 km) Paved parking both sides of highway with litter bins.

E 579.5 (932.6 km) J 16.9 (27.2 km) Canoe River bridge.

E 580.1 (933.6 km) J 16.3 (26.2 km) Canoe River campground.

E 581.5 (935.8 km) J 14.9 (24 km) Cedarside Regional Park. Parking area, swimming beach, picnic tables and fire pits. It has easy access.

E 581.9 (936.5 km) J 14.5 (23.3 km) Kinbasket Lake turnoff (26 km/16 miles east). Follow the East Canoe Forest Service Road (gravel) until you reach Km 21/Mile 13 and the Valemount Marina with boat launch. Three recreational campsites nearby.

E 583 (938 km) J 13.4 (21.6 km) *Slow for posted speed zone northbound entering Valemount.*

E 583.1 (938.4 km) J 13.3 (21.4 km) Best Western Valemount Inn & Suites. Robert W. Starratt Wildlife Sanctuary a Ducks Unlimited project with trails and boardwalks. Two viewing sites with observation towers. Use trail across dike.

E 583.9 (939.7 km) J 12.5 (20.1 km) Distance marker southbound shows Blue River 90 km/56 miles, Kamloops 390 km/242 miles.

E 584 (939.8 km) J 12.4 (20 km) Frontage road exit northbound to Co-op Cardlock, Tempo, Petro Canada/A&W and Esso/Tim Hortons gas/diesel stations, auto parts and supplies, post office, a Lebanese restaurant that serves donair (Canadian gyro) and burgers, a variety of shops, and hotels/motels. Shell gas/diesel station to west.

Valemount

E 584.3 (940.3 km) J 12.1 (19.5 km) Traffic light at 5th Avenue access east to downtown Valemount and Pine Road west to Shell gas station and access to Valemount Visitor Centre and Village office on Cranberry Lake Road. **Population:** 1,100. **Elevation:** 2,667 ft/800m. **Emergency Services:** Dial 911. **RCMP,** just off Highway 5 on 5th Avenue; **Health Centre** just past RCMP on 5th Avenue, phone 250-56-9138.

Visitor Information: Valemount Visitor Information Centre open year-round is just off of Highway 5 at 785 Cranberry Lake Rd.; phone 250-566-9893 or email visitorcentre@valemount.ca; website: www.visitvalemount.ca. The Centre offers free WiFi, adventure activity bookings and accommodation reservation services. It also showcases interpretive displays on the natural history of the area and the chinook salmon. The centre features a store with local arts and crafts and Valemount and BC souvenirs.

Adjacent the centre to the north is the George Hicks Park with salmon spawning viewpoints, a picnic area and a short walking trail. August is the best month for salmon viewing.

Located on Highway 5, midway between Kamloops and Prince George, Valemount has all visitor services. Drive down 5th Avenue for hotels/motels, a bank with ATM, supermarket, pharmacy, hardware store, brewery, restaurants, pub, coffee shop (The Gathering Tree), salon/spa, health food store, gift stores and car wash/recycling depot. Turn on to Main Street for the Swiss Bakery (authentic Swiss baked goods), Alpine Country Tours/Auto Parts, bike shop for repairs/rentals, and the Valemount Museum (also accessed from Dogwood). The Valemount Museum, located in a restored 1914 Railway Station, features a trapper's cabin, a model railroad and local history, including a Fallen Heroes display from the local Legion. The public library is adjacent to the museum.

Valemount is a popular service stop for motorists headed to/from Mount Robson Provincial Park and Jasper National Park. Summer activities in the Valemount area include rafting, boating, canoeing, mountain biking (bike park), hiking, fishing, horseback riding, golfing or touring on an ATV/Jeep or in a helicopter.

Winter activities include snowmobiling, dogsledding, snowshoeing, skating, and cross-country, backcountry, snowmobile or sled-assisted skiing.

Area attractions include the Robert W. Starratt Wildlife Sanctuary (locally known as the Cranberry Marsh), which has more than 90 species of birds and wildlife.

Central Access Route Log
(continued)

E 584.5 (940.6 km) J 11.9 (19.2 km) Swift Creek. George Hicks Regional Park with litter/recycling bins.

E 584.7 (941 km) J 11.7 (18.8 km) Private campgrounds both sides of highway and a bed and breakfast with cabins.

E 584.9 (941.3 km) J 11.5 (18.5 km) *Slow for posted speed zone southbound.*

E 585 (941.4 km) J 11.4 (18.3 km) Turnouts with litter bins both sides of highway. Information boards about Valemount to the west.

© Kris Valencia, staff

E 585.1 (941.6 km) J 11.3 (18.2 km) Turnoff to east for **Irvin's RV Park.** Full range of facilities for all sizes of RV rigs. Web address: www.irvinsrvpark.com.

Irvin's RV Park. See display ad on page 253 in YELLOWHEAD HIGHWAY section.

E 587.9 (946.1 km) J 8.5 (13.7 km) Railroad overpasses cross above highway.

E 588.3 (946.7 km) J 8.1 (13 km) **Mount Terry Fox Viewpoint** and rest area to west; rest area with picnic tables, toilets, recycling and litter bins. The mountain was named in 1981 for Terry Fox, a young Canadian who started an epic run across Canada on 1 leg to raise funds for cancer research. Before a recurrence of cancer took his life midway through the run, Fox raised some $25 million.

E 592.4 (953.3 km) J 4 (6.4 km) Turnoff for Jackman Flats Provincial Park picnic area to west. Unique ecosystem, several short, mostly sandy, hiking trails with some bird watching and plant identification signage.

E 595.5 (958.4 km) J 0.9 (1.4 km) Railroad crosses overhead. Begin 1.4-mile/2.3-km passing lane southbound.

E 595.9 (959 km) J 0.5 (0.8 km) Tete Jaune Cache (pronounced Tee John Cash) Access Road leads west; motel, campground, cabins, restaurant, vacation rental, B & B's and rafting. Tete Jaune is French for "yellow head." Reputedly, a fair-haired trapper regularly cached his furs here in the 18th century.

E 596.2 (959.5 km) J 0.2 (0.3 km) Fraser River bridge.

E 596.4 (959.8 km) J 0 **Junction** with Yellowhead Highway 16 and end of Highway 5. Prince George, BC, is 171 miles/275 km west from this junction; Jasper, AB, is 63 miles/101 km east and Hinton, AB, is 112 miles/180 km east from here. Dawson Creek, BC, start of the Alaska Highway, is 416 miles/669 km from here via Prince George, and it is 390 miles/628 km via Hinton and the Bighorn Route.

Junction with Yellowhead Highway 16. Turn to **Milepost E 283.2** on page 253 in the YELLOWHEAD HIGHWAY section for log of highway to Prince George.

Alaska Highway via
West Access Route

CONNECTS: Seattle, WA, to Dawson Creek, BC

Length: 807 miles   **Road Surface: Paved**   **Season: Open all year**

(See maps, pages 107-108)

Signed turnoff for Bijoux Falls Provincial Park rest area on the Hart Highway between Prince George and Dawson Creek. ©Kris Valencia, staff

Distance in miles	Cache Creek	Dawson Creek	Prince George	Seattle
Cache Creek		519	274	288
Dawson Creek	519		245	807
Prince George	274	245		562
Seattle	288	807	562	

For West Coast motorists, the West Access Route has been the most direct route to Dawson Creek, BC, and the start of the Alaska Highway since 1952, when the John Hart Highway connecting Prince George and Dawson Creek was completed. Prior to that, all Alaska Highway-bound traffic had to go through Edmonton, Alberta.

The West Access Route links Interstate 5, Trans-Canada Highway 1 and BC Highway 97. *The MILEPOST®* log of this route is divided into 4 sections: Seattle to the Canadian border crossing at Sumas via I-5 and Washington Highways 539 and 546; Trans-Canada Highway 1 from Abbotsford to Cache Creek; Highway 97, the "Cariboo Highway," from Cache Creek to Prince George; and the John Hart Highway (also Highway 97) from Prince George to Dawson Creek.

Distances via this 807-mile route between Seattle, WA, and Dawson Creek, BC, are: Seattle to Abbotsford, 118 miles; Abbotsford to Cache Creek, 170 miles; Cache Creek to Prince George, 274 miles; and Prince George to Dawson Creek, 245 miles.

The West Access Route junctions with Yellowhead Highway 16 at Prince George. This east–west highway connects Prince George with Prince Rupert, departure point for the Alaska Marine Highway System and BC Ferries. Yellowhead Highway 16 also connects Prince George, BC, with Edmonton, AB, on the East Access Route to the Alaska Highway. Turn to the YELLOWHEAD HIGHWAY 16 section for a complete log of that route.

The West Access Route offers several interesting side trips and alternate routes for northbound travelers. Also logged in this section for your consideration are: the continuation of the Interstate 5 log for those traveling from Bellingham to Vancouver; Highway 99, the "Sea to Sky Highway," a scenic, mountainous route between

Major Attractions:

Barkerville, Kinuseo Falls, WAC Bennett Dam, Fraser River · Canyon/Hell's Gate

Highest Summit:
Begbie Summit 4,042 ft.

©Courtesy BC Hydro

West Access Route

Seattle, WA, to Lac La Hache, BC (includes Sea to Sky Highway)

© 2019 The MILEPOST®

Key to mileage boxes

miles/kilometers
miles/kilometers
from:

A-Abbotsford
CC-Cache Creek
CB-Canadian Border
HB-Horseshoe Bay
J-Junction
PG-Prince George
S-Seattle

Map Location

Principal Route Logged
Paved   Unpaved

Other Roads Logged

Other Roads   Ferry Routes

Refer to Log for Visitor Facilities

Key to Advertiser Services
C -Camping
D -Dump Station
d -Diesel
G -Gas (reg., unld.)
I -Ice
L -Lodging
M -Meals
P -Propane
R -Car Repair (major)
r -Car Repair (minor)
S -Store (grocery)
T -Telephone (pay)

Scale
0   20   Miles
0   20   Kilometers

(map continues next page)

Lac La Hache

CC-82.6/132.9km Big Country Campground & RV Park CDILST

100 Mile House
N 51°38' W121°17'

Cariboo Highway →

70 Mile House
N 50°24' W121°17'
CC-25/40.2km Gold Trail RV Park and Campground CDM

Clinton

CC-19.8/32km Willow Springs Resort C

CC-0 Brookside Campsite CD
N 50°48' W121°19'

J-0
HB-192/309km

Loon Lake

Cache Creek

Lillooet

Pavilion L.

Ashcroft

A-140.6/226.3km Log Cabin Pub M

Spences Bridge

HB-63/102km
J-129/207km

Sea to Sky Highway

Pemberton

Lillooet Lake

Whistler

Lytton
N 50°13' W121°34'

Garibaldi Provincial Park

A-94/151.3km Canyon Alpine RV Park and Campground C

North Bend
Boston Bar
N 49°51' W121°26'
Hell's Gate

HB-0
J-192/309km
S-155/249km

Squamish

Britannia Beach

Harrison Lake

Yale

Horseshoe Bay

Golden Ears Provincial Park

Harrison Hot Springs

CC-120/193km
A-50/80km
N 49°22' W121°26'

Princeton

To Osoyoos

Hope

Vancouver

Mission

BRITISH COLUMBIA

Alaska State Ferry
(see Ferries in the TRAVEL PLANNING section)

Chilliwack

A-26.5/42.5km Camperland RV Resort & Cabins CLMS

CANADA
UNITED STATES

Blaine

Sumas

Abbotsford

PG-444/714km
CC-170/274km
A-0

Manning Provincial Park

WASHINGTON

Vancouver Island

S-85 Alaska Marine Highway

Bellingham

S-91/146km
CB-25/40km

S-116/187km
CB-0

To Okanogan

Victoria

North Cascades Highway

Mount Vernon

Strait of Juan de Fuca

Everett

To Wenatchee

S-0
CB-116/187km

Seattle

To Ellensburg

Lac La Hache
Canim Lake
Mahood Lake
To Tete Juane Cache
Wells Gray Provincial Park
River
Horse Lake
Bridge Lake
24
Little Fort
Green Lake
Bridge Lake
5
Bonaparte R.
Bonaparte Lake
97
North Thompson
Kamloops Lake
South Thompson River
Kamloops
Logan Lake
97C
5
5A
To Salmon Arm
97
To Osoyoos
8
Merritt
5
5A
Coquihalla Highway
(see CENTRAL ACCESS ROUTE section)
3
PG-274/440km
CC-0
A-170/274km
Nicola R.
Thompson R.
Fraser River

COAST MOUNTAINS
LILLOOET RANGE
CASCADE MOUNTAINS
Strait of Georgia
Puget Sound

7
99
5
546
539
20
5
90
2

N
W   E
S

www.themilepost.com

West Access Route

Lac La Hache, BC, to Dawson Creek, BC (includes Chilcotin Hwy., Hwy. 26 to Barkerville, Hudson's Hope Loop, Tumbler Ridge Loop)

© 2019 The MILEPOST®

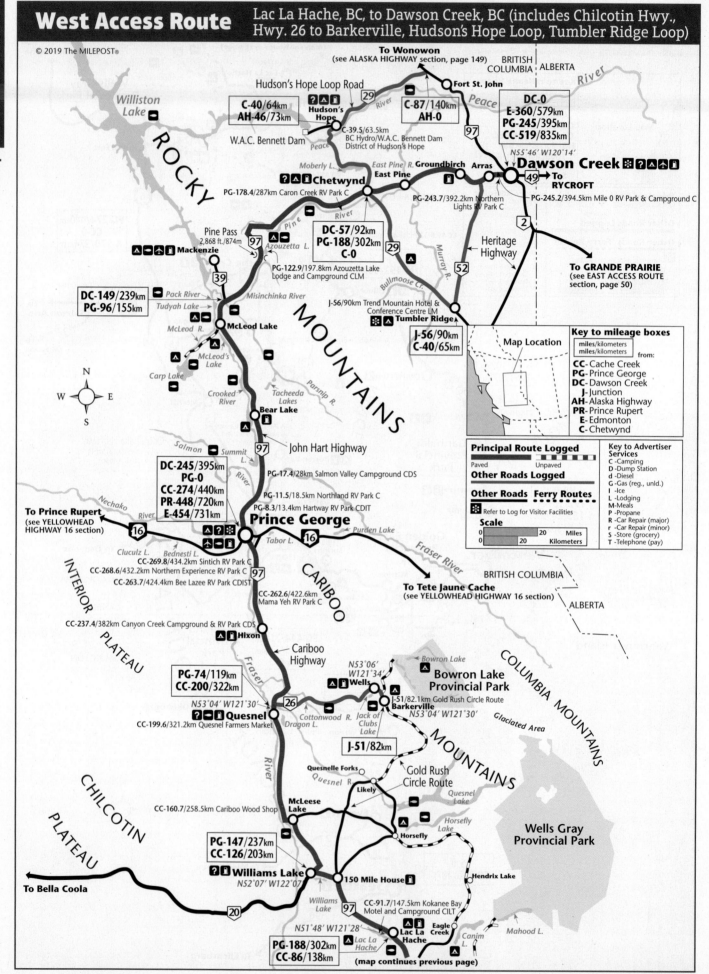

To Wonowon
(see ALASKA HIGHWAY section, page 149)

BRITISH COLUMBIA | ALBERTA

Fort St. John

Hudson's Hope Loop Road

C-40/64km
AH-46/73km
Hudson's Hope

C-87/140km
AH-0

DC-0
E-360/579km
PG-245/395km
CC-519/835km

C-39.5/63.5km
BC Hydro/W.A.C. Bennett Dam
District of Hudson's Hope

W.A.C. Bennett Dam

N55°46' W120°14'

Williston Lake

Moberly L.

East Pine R.

Groundbirch

Arras

Dawson Creek

Chetwynd

East Pine

To RYCROFT

PG-178.4/287km Caron Creek RV Park C

PG-243.7/392.2km Northern Lights RV Park C

PG-245.2/394.5km Mile 0 RV Park & Campground C

DC-57/92km
PG-188/302km
C-0

Pine Pass
2,868 ft./874m

Azouzetta L.

Heritage Highway

Mackenzie

PG-122.9/197.8km Azouzetta Lake Lodge and Campground CLM

To GRANDE PRAIRIE
(see EAST ACCESS ROUTE section, page 50)

Pack River

DC-149/239km
PG-96/155km

Misinchinka River

Tudyah Lake

McLeod R.

McLeod Lake

J-56/90km Trend Mountain Hotel & Conference Centre LM

Tumbler Ridge

J-56/90km
C-40/65km

McLeod's Lake

MOUNTAINS

Carp Lake

Crooked River

Tacheeda Lakes

Parsnip R.

Bear Lake

Summit L.

John Hart Highway

DC-245/395km
PG-0
CC-274/440km
PR-448/720km
E-454/731km

PG-17.4/28km Salmon Valley Campground CDS

Salmon River

PG-11.5/18.5km Northland RV Park C

PG-8.3/13.4km Hartway RV Park CDIT

To Prince Rupert
(see YELLOWHEAD HIGHWAY 16 section)

Prince George

Nechako River

Cluculz L.

Bednesti L.

Tabor L.

Purden Lake

Fraser River

CC-269.8/434.2km Sintich RV Park C
CC-268.6/432.2km Northern Experience RV Park C
CC-263.7/424.4km Bee Lazee RV Park CDIST

INTERIOR PLATEAU

CARIBOO

BRITISH COLUMBIA

ALBERTA

To Tete Jaune Cache
(see YELLOWHEAD HIGHWAY 16 section)

CC-262.6/422.6km Mama Yeh RV Park C

CC-237.4/382km Canyon Creek Campground & RV Park CDS

Hixon

Cariboo Highway

Bowron Lake

N53°06' W121°34'

Wells

Bowron Lake Provincial Park

PG-74/119km
CC-200/322km

J-51/82.1km Gold Rush Circle Route

Barkerville

N53°04' W121°30'

Glaciated Area

N53°04' W121°30'

Quesnel

CC-199.6/321.2km Quesnel Farmers Market

Cottonwood R.

Jack of Clubs Lake

Fraser River

J-51/82km

COLUMBIA MOUNTAINS

Quesnelle Forks

Gold Rush Circle Route

Quesnel R.

Likely

Quesnel Lake

Wells Gray Provincial Park

CC-160.7/258.5km Cariboo Wood Shop

McLeese Lake

Horsefly Lake

Horsefly

PG-147/237km
CC-126/203km

CHILCOTIN PLATEAU

To Bella Coola

Williams Lake

N52°07' W122°07'

150 Mile House

Hendrix Lake

Williams Lake

CC-91.7/147.5km Kokanee Bay Motel and Campground CILT

Eagle Creek

Canim L.

Mahood L.

N51°48' W121°28'

Lac La Hache

PG-188/302km
CC-86/138km

(map continues previous page)

Key to mileage boxes

Map Location

miles/kilometers
miles/kilometers from:

CC- Cache Creek
PG- Prince George
DC- Dawson Creek
J- Junction
AH- Alaska Highway
PR- Prince Rupert
E- Edmonton
C- Chetwynd

Principal Route Logged

Paved   Unpaved

Other Roads Logged

Other Roads   Ferry Routes

Refer to Log for Visitor Facilities

Scale
0   20   Miles
0   20   Kilometers

Key to Advertiser Services

C - Camping
D - Dump Station
d - Diesel
G - Gas (reg., unld.)
I - Ice
L - Lodging
M - Meals
P - Propane
R - Car Repair (major)
r - Car Repair (minor)
S - Store (grocery)
T - Telephone (pay)

Vancouver and the Cariboo; Highway 26 to Barkerville, a provincial historic town dating back to the 1860s; Highway 29 south to Tumbler Ridge and access to Kinuseo Falls, logged as "Tumbler Ridge Loop;" and Highway 29 north from Chetwynd to the Alaska Highway via Hudson's Hope, with access to W.A.C. Bennett Dam, which is logged as the "Hudson's Hope Loop."

West Access Route Log

This section of the log shows distance from Seattle (S) followed by distance from the Canadian border (CB) at Sumas. Physical mileposts (and exit numbers) on Interstate Highway 5 reflect distance from the Washington-Oregon border.

INTERSTATE HIGHWAY 5 NORTH

S 0 CB 116 Exit 165 northbound (165B southbound) to downtown **SEATTLE** (pop. 684,451). Seattle exits next 10 miles northbound on Interstate 5.

S 11 CB 105 Exit 176 to NE 175 St. and Highway 99, Shoreline; all services.

S 12 CB 104 Exit 177 to 244th/Lake Forest Park to east and west 4.5 miles to Edmonds and Kingston Ferry. Food, gas, diesel east off exit.

S 14 CB 102 Exit 179 220th Street; gas and diesel west off exit. Hospital 2 miles west.

S 15.5 CB 100.5 Exit 181A to Lynnwood/44th Avenue, Brier, Edmonds Community College.

S 16 CB 100 Exit 181B to Alderwood Mall Parkway to Alderwood, an indoor shopping mall with 166 stores.

S 17 CB 99 Exit 182 to **junction** with Interstate 405 South to Bellevue/Renton and to Highway 525/99 northwest to Mukilteo with access to Alderwood Mall Parkway.

S 18 CB 98 Exit 183 to 164th St. SW; Walmart, major-chain motel and fast-food outlets.

S 21 CB 95 Exit 186 to 128th St. SW/96E; 24-hour gas, diesel, food and lodging.

S 23 CB 93 Exit 188 Weigh station both sides, 24-hour truck stop, Silver Lake rest area southbound.

S 24 CB 92 Exit 189 to Everett Mall Way, Highways 527/99/526; lodging east off exit. Also access to food, gas, and diesel. Everett Mall is a major shopping destination.

S 27 CB 89 Exit 192 to Broadway/41st St., Everett city center; food, gas, diesel, lodging.

S 28 CB 88 Exit 193 Pacific Avenue/SR 529/US Hwy. 2E. Access to **EVERETT** (pop. 104,295) city center and Everett Events Center; all services.

S 29 CB 87 Exit 194 to U.S. Highway 2 East to Snohomish.

S 29.5 CB 86.5 Exit 195 northbound to Port of Everett, Marine View Drive.

S 30 CB 85 Snohomish River.

S 32 CB 83 Union Slough.

S 34 CB 82 Exit 199 to SR 528 and **MARYSVILLE** (pop. 60,785); easy on-off for food, gas, diesel, lodging both sides of freeway.

S 35 CB 81 Exit 200 to 88th St. NE/Quil Ceda Way; gas/diesel and 24-hour grocery and pharmacy east off exit. Quil Ceda Village (Walmart, Home Depot) and Tulalip Casino west off exit, with access to Seattle Premium Outlets mall.

S 37 CB 79 Exit 202 116th Street NE; State Patrol; gas stations, food and access west to Seattle Premium Outlets mall (at first major intersection to west, turn south on Quel Ceda Way for mall).

S 41 CB 75 Exit 206 to Lakewood, Smokey Point and Arlington Airport; 24-hour gas, diesel, food, shopping east off exit. Costco, Target to west. Visitor information.

S 42 CB 74 Milepost 207. Rest areas both sides of interstate. The northbound rest area has a giant arborvitae.

S 43 CB 73 Exit 208 to Silvana, Arlington, Darrington and SR 530; easy on-off to food, gas/diesel, lodging.

S 44.5 CB 71.5 Stillaguamish River. A popular fishing river it offers cutthroat trout, chinook and coho salmon, and steelhead. Summer fly-fishing only. Check state regulations before fishing.

S 45 CB 71 Exit 210 to 236th St. NE; Angel of the Winds Casino.

S 47 CB 69 Exit 212 to Stanwood, Camano Island, SRS 232W; easy access to gas/diesel and 24-hour supermarket west off exit.

S 49 CB 67 Milepost 214. Weigh station northbound.

S 50 CB 66 Exit 215 to 300th St. NW.

S 52.5 CB 63.5 Entering Skagit County northbound.

S 53 CB 63 Exit 218 to Starbird Road; no services.

S 56 CB 60 Exit 221 to Conway, LaConner (11 miles), SR 534, Lake McMurray; easy access to gas/diesel stations east and west off exit.

S 59 CB 57 Exit 224 to Old Highway 99S. Food, gas, diesel, services.

S 60 CB 56 Exit 225 to Anderson Road; easy access to gas/diesel stations east and

west off exit.

S 61 CB 55 Exit 226 to SR 536W, Kincaid Street, **MOUNT VERNON** (pop. 32,070) city center; all services.

S 62 CB 54 Exit 227 to College Way, SR 538E; easy access to food, gas/diesel, lodging and shopping just off exit.

S 63.5 CB 52.5 Skagit River.

S 64 CB 52 Exit 229 George Hopper Road; access to shopping malls.

S 65 CB 51 Exit 230 to SR20 east to Burlington, North Cascades Hwy.; west to Mount Vernon and Anacortes. Shopping, food, gas/diesel, lodging, supermarket at exit.

S 66 CB 50 Exit 231 to Bow-Edison, Chuckanut Drive/SR 11N scenic route.

S 67 CB 49 Exit 232 to Cook Road, Sedro Woolley; easy access to 24-hour gas and diesel (Shell, 76), food (DQ, Subway), lodging and camping (Burlington/Anacortes KOA). For campground, exit east to light, then turn north and follow signs 3.5 miles on North Green Road.

S 69 CB 47 Samish River.

S 71 CB 45 Exit 236 to Bow-Edison and Bow Hill Road. Exit east for The Skagit (casino with lodging, dining and entertainment). Also access this exit to Burlington KOA (follow signs east then south on North Green Road).

S 73 CB 43 Milepost 238. Bow Hill rest area to east for northbound traffic.

S 73.5 CB 42.5 Bow Hill rest area to west for southbound traffic.

S 75 CB 41 Exit 240 to Alger; easy gas and diesel east off exit.

S 76 CB 40 Entering Skagit County southbound.

S 77 CB 39 Exit 242 Nalle Road, South Lake Samish. Entering Whatcom County northbound.

Winding road northbound.

S 81 CB 35 Exit 246 to North Lake Samish and Lake Padden Recreation Area; diesel, gas and groceries west off exit.

S 85 CB 31 Exit 250 South Chuckanut Drive (Fairhaven Parkway); food, pharmacy

Expect heavy traffic on I-5 through Seattle, WA, at most times of the day. (©Sharon Nault)

I-5: Bellingham to Vancouver

WEST ACCESS ROUTE travelers may choose to continue north on Interstate 5 and cross the international border at Blaine—rather than cross at Sumas (as logged on the main West Access Route)—following Highway 99 to beautiful Vancouver, British Columbia's largest city.

From Vancouver, Alaska-bound travelers may drive the Sea to Sky Highway *(see "Sea to Sky Highway" log beginning on facing page)*. Allow about an hour-and-a-half driving time from the international border at Blaine to the start of the Sea to Sky Highway.

Another option: Take BC Ferries from either Tsawwassen or Horseshoe Bay to Vancouver Island, and drive north to Port Hardy for BC Ferries service to Prince Rupert *(see VANCOUVER ISLAND HIGHWAY section on 141)*.

NOTE: Border wait times on this route are posted on readerboards and available online at www.th.gov.bc.ca/ATIS/index.htm and www.wsdot.com/traffic/border/default.aspx.

Distance in miles from Seattle (S) is shown.

INTERSTATE 5

S 91 Exit 256A to **junction** with SR 539N/Guide-Meridian Road to Lynden and Canadian border crossing at Sumas *(see below for log)*. Exit 256B to Bellis Fair Mall Parkway. Food, gas and lodging at this exit.

S 92 Exit 257 to Northwest Avenue.

S 93 Exit 258 to Bakerview Road and Bellingham International Airport; food, lodging, gas and diesel at exit. Southbound access to Bellis Fair Mall.

S 95 Exit 260 to Slater Road, Lummi Island. Access to mini-mart with gas/diesel.

S 97 Exit 262 to Main Street/Ferndale city center. Gas and diesel.

S 98 Exit 263 to Portal Way and Ferndale; 24-hour gas and diesel to east.

S 101 Exit 266 to Custer, Grandview Road, SR 548 North.

S 102.5 Rest area.

S 105 Exit 270 to Lynden and Birch Bay; 24-hour gas and diesel at exit. Shopping mall to west. Birch Bay-Lynden Road leads 8 miles east to **junction** with SR 539 (Guide-Meridian Road).

S 109 Exit 274 to Blaine via Loomis Trail Road, Blaine Road and Peace Portal Drive; access to Semiahmoo Resort.

S 110 Exit 275 to Truck Customs (all buses and commercial vehicles) via SR 543 North 2 miles to 24-hour Customs. Access to Blaine via H Street.

S 111 Exit 276 to **BLAINE** (pop. 5,062, area 12,533) city center. This is the last exit northbound before the international border; food, gas, diesel, lodging. Visitor information available.

Freeway ends northbound.

S 111.5 U.S. Customs & Border Protection. **Peace Arch State Park**, dedicated in 1921, lies on the boundary between the U.S. and Canada. One half of the 67-foot-high Peace Arch rests in each country. Border wait times are available online at www.th.gov.bc.ca/ATIS/index.htm and www.wsdot.com/traffic/border/default.aspx.

S 112 Canada Border Services Agency.

BC HIGHWAY 99

S 112.5 Exit 2 to 8th Ave. and **junction** with Trans-Canada Highway 1 to Hope.

S 117.4 Exit 10 King George Highway, Surrey City Centre.

S 121.1 Exit 16 North Delta, New Westminster. Alternate Route 91 North to Vancouver.

S 123.5 Exit 20 Ladner, Point Roberts, Boundary Bay Airport; gas.

S 128.3 Exit 28 River Road to Tswawwassen and BC Ferries to Vancouver Island; gas, lodging.

S 129.6 Tunnel next 0.5 miles/0.8 km northbound.

S 130.4 Richmond Visitor Centre.

S 130.8 Exit 32 Steveston Highway.

S 133 Exit 36 Westminster Highway.

S 133.4 Exit 37 to Highway 91.

S 134.9 Exit 39 Bridgeport Road, Vancouver International Airport.

Entering City of Vancouver. *Freeway ends northbound. Follow signs for Whistler/BC Ferries (Horseshoe Bay) for continuation of Highway 99/Sea to Sky Highway.*

S 138.1 Turn left northbound on West 41st Street.

S 138.6 Turn right northbound on Granville Street.

S 141 Crossing Granville Bridge.

S 141.4 Exit to Seymour Street/99N at end of bridge.

S 142.2 Turn left northbound on to Georgia Street/99N.

S 143.4 Road forks northbound to Stanley Park. North to Lions Gate Bridge.

S 144.8 South end of Lions Gate Bridge.

S 145.7 North end of Lions Gate Bridge. Exit for West Vancouver/99N, BC Ferries, Horseshoe Bay.

S 146.4 Turn right northbound on Taylor Way/99/1A. *(If you miss this turn, Park Royal Shopping Centre will be on either side of Marine Drive: backtrack to Taylor Way).*

S 147 Junction with Highway 99/Trans-Canada Highway 1 West (Upper Levels Highway).

S 154.5 Exit 3 (only for traffic coming from Vancouver) on Trans-Canada Highway 1 to Horseshoe Bay/BC Ferries service to Nanaimo on Vancouver Island. Trans-Canada Highway 1 ends here, becoming the toll lanes for B.C. Ferries, then continues on Vancouver Island from Nanaimo south to Victoria.

Sea to Sky Highway/BC Highway 99 rather seamlessly begins and ends here. Distance to Squamish (27 miles/43 km), Whistler (63 miles/102 km), Pemberton 83 miles/134 km, and junction with Highway 97 near Cache Creek (192 miles/309 km).

See "Sea to Sky Highway" log on the facing page.

---

and gas west off exit. Access to Bellingham's Fairhaven shopping district and to **Bellingham Cruise Terminal**, departure point for Alaska State Ferries. Follow Fairhaven Parkway west 1.3 miles to stoplight at 12th Street; go straight 0.6 mile for ferry terminal (follow signs) or turn on 12th Street for Fairhaven shopping district.

Alaska State Ferries depart Bellingham's Cruise Terminal for Southeast Alaska year-round, with twice-weekly sailings in summer. See "Ferry Travel" in the TRAVEL PLANNING section.

S 87 CB 29 Exit 252 Samish Way, Western Washington University; access to food, gas and diesel and services west off exit.

S 88 CB 28 Exit 253 to Lakeway Drive in **BELLINGHAM** (pop. 81,862); all services. Access east off exit to Bellingham/Whatcom County Visitor Info Center; visit their website at www.bellingham.org.

S 89 CB 27 Exit 254 to State Street/Iowa Street in Bellingham. Gas and fast-food at exit.

S 90 CB 26 Exit 255 to Sunset Drive, SR 542E (Mount Baker Hwy.). Hospital west off exit. Shopping center, fast food, 24-hour gas station with diesel east off exit.

S 91 CB 25 Exit 256A to **junction** with SR 539N (Meridian St.) to Lynden and Canadian border crossing at Sumas. Exit 256B to Bellis Fair Mall Parkway. Food, gas and lodging at this exit.

The MILEPOST® West Access Route main log exits here to follow Highway 539/Guide-Meridian (12.6 miles), Highway 546 (8 miles) and Highway 9 (4.5 miles) to the international border crossing at Sumas, WA/Abbotsford-Huntingdon, BC, and the junction with Trans-Canada Highway 1 east. Highways 539/546 and 9 are fairly busy 2- to 4-lane roads through well-populated rural areas with services available in towns along the way.

Northbound travelers who wish to continue on Interstate 5 north to the border crossing at Blaine, WA, and junction with Highway 99 north to Vancouver, BC, see "I-5: Bellingham to Vancouver" log above. From Vancouver, Highway 99 continues north and east as the "Sea

to Sky Highway" to junction with the main West Access Route north of Cache Creek. Read the "Sea to Sky Highway" log beginning on the facing page.

NOTE: Border wait times on this route are posted on highway readerboards and available online at www.th.gov.bc.ca/ATIS/index.htm and www.wsdot.com/traffic/border/default.aspx.

WASHINGTON HIGHWAYS 539, 546 & 9

This section of the log shows distance from Interstate 5 junction (J) at Exit 256A followed by distance from the Canadian border (CB) at Sumas.

Physical mileposts on Highway 539 reflect distance from Interstate 5 junction.

J 0 CB 23 Exit 256 from Interstate 5 east to Guide-Meridian/Highway 539 North in Bellingham and access to Bellis Fair Mall.

J 0.1 CB 22.9 Traffic light at Telegraph Road; Denny's restaurant to south, Bellis Fair Mall to north.

J 0.2 CB 22.8 Traffic light; access north to Bellis Fair Mall via Bellis Fair Parkway; *(Continues on page 115)*

Sea to Sky Highway

The Sea to Sky Highway travels along BC Highway 99 and refers specifically to Horseshoe Bay to Whistler or Pemberton. This road log continues on to connect Vancouver, Squamish and Whistler with Lillooet and ends just outside of Cache Creek with this northern portion of road locally known as the Duffey Lake road.

Completely paved, this scenic 309-km/192-mile highway offers motorists an alternate route from the Fraser Valley to the BC Interior, connecting with Highway 97 (the Cariboo Highway) just north of Cache Creek. Driving time from Horseshoe Bay to the Highway 97 junction is about 5 hours.

Sea to Sky Highway begins as a fast-paced, winding, 4-lane road along the east shore of stunning Howe Sound. It is squeezed between the sea and the mountains in a lush, high rainfall area. The highway then climbs up into the coastal mountains with intermittent passing lanes and stretches of 4-lane highway (both divided and undivided), past popular hiking and mountain biking trails, provincial park campgrounds, fishing spots, swimming lakes and rafting rivers. Whistler, a major ski resort in winter as well as a summer destination for thousands of visitors, is located on Sea to Sky about 2-hours drive north of Vancouver.

Beyond Pemberton, the highway climbs up and over the Coast Mountains to enter the dramatically different landscape of British Columbia's Interior Plateau. *Between Pemberton and Lillooet it is strictly 2-lane with few turnouts, and there are long steep grades (9 to 11 percent) with narrow winding road and some hairpin turns.* This highway offers spectacular scenery, and has been significantly improved, but it is not always a relaxing drive. It is busy with fast-moving traffic between Vancouver and Whistler, and requires alert driving on the narrow, winding sections between Pemberton and the Highway 97 junction. For road reports, go to www.drivebc.ca, which includes web cams and also alerts motorists to special events that may affect traffic.

It is approximately 69 km/43 miles via Highway 99 from the U.S. border to the start of the Sea to Sky Highway at Horseshoe Bay.

Sea to Sky Highway Log

Distance in miles from Horseshoe Bay (HB) is followed by distance in miles from junction with Highway 97 (J).

BC HIGHWAY 99

HB 0 J 192 (309 km) Exit 3 (only for traffic coming from Vancouver) on Trans-Canada Highway 1/BC Highway 99 to Horseshoe Bay/BC Ferries service to Nanaimo on Vancouver Island. Trans-Canada Highway 1 ends here, becoming the toll lanes for BC Ferries, then continues on Vancouver Island from Nanaimo south to Victoria. Sea to Sky Highway rather seamlessly begins and ends here.

Murrin Provincial Park offers travelers picnicking, swimming and walking trails.
(©Claire Torgerson, staff)

Motorists bound for Whistler, Pemberton, Lillooet and Highway 97 junction do NOT exit here, but continue on Highway 99/Sea to Sky Highway. Intermittent passing lanes and 4-lane stretches of highway from here northeast to Pemberton on Highway 99.

IMPORTANT: Traffic on Sea to Sky Highway coming from the direction of Whistler and wishing to exit to Horseshoe Bay for BC Ferries service must proceed to Exit 4 on Trans-Canada Highway 1/BC Highway 99, then follow signs for Horseshoe Bay ferries. You end up returning to Trans-Canada Highway 1 and back-tracking to Exit 3.

For travelers leaving the ferry, get into the far right-hand lane and follow the highway around in a cloverleaf to your right to access the highway going north for Sea to Sky Highway.

HB 1.8 (2.9 km) **J 190.2** (306.1 km) Highway merges with Sea to Sky Highway 99 northbound.

HB 6.5 (10.5 km) **J 185.5** (298.5 km) Lions Bay Avenue. Village of Lions Bay. First of 3 exits.

HB 9.2 (14.8 km) **J 182.8** (294.2 km) Viewpoint to north for southwest-bound traffic only. Good view of Howe Sound, parking, litter bin and point-of-interest signs. A plaque here commemorates completion of the 2009 Sea to Sky Improvement Project.

HB 10.1 (16.3 km) **J 181.9** (292.7 km) Gravel turnout to east.

Distance marker northbound shows Squamish 28 km/17 miles, Whistler 85 km/53 miles.

HB 15.2 (24.4 km) **J 176.8** (284.5 km) **Porteau Cove Provincial Park** to west; 44 vehicle campsites and 16 walk-in sites, hot showers, reservations recommended in summer (www.discovercamping.ca), picnicking, swimming, boat launch. Popular scuba diving spot; an old ship has been sunk here to attract marine life. ▲

HB 16.6 (26.7 km) **J 175.4** (282.3 km) Turn off for Furry Creek Drive northbound-only exit. Southbound-only viewpoint of Furry Cove.

HB 17.7 (28.5 km) **J 174.3** (280.5 km) Turn off for Furry Creek Drive southbound-only exit, U-turn route.

HB 20.3 (32.7 km) **J 171.7** (276.3 km)

Traffic light at access to **BRITANNIA BEACH** (pop. about 300); restaurants, general store and shopping. From 1930 to 1935, Britannia Beach was the British Empire's largest producer of copper. Visit the BC Museum of Mining, open daily in summer. Admission charged. Highway climbs northbound.

HB 21 (33.8 km) **J 171** (275.2 km) Viewpoint with litter bin for southbound traffic.

HB 21.2 (34.1 km) **J 170.8** (274.9 km) Distance marker northbound shows Squamish 10 km/6 miles, Whistler 67 km/42 miles.

HB 22.1 (35.6 km) **J 169.9** (273.4 km) Turnoff for **Murrin Provincial Park**, a pretty day-use area with swimming, fishing, picnicking, walking trails, steep cliffs suitable for rock climbing, picturesque jewel of Browning Lake within the park and walking trail to nearby Petgill Lake outside the park.

HB 23 (37 km) **J 169** (272 km) Viewpoint to west for southbound traffic.

HB 24 (38.6 km) **J 168** (270.4 km) Pullout to east with litter bin for northbound traffic only.

HB 24.1 (38.8 km) **J 167.9** (270.2 km) Pullout with litter bin to west for southbound traffic only.

HB 24.8 (39.9 km) **J 167.2** (269 km) Traffic light; access to **Shannon Falls Provincial Park**. Very popular day-use park for hiking and picnicking. Falls plunge 1,105 feet/335m, third largest falls in BC. Good walking trails and photo opportunities.

HB 25.1 (40.5 km) **J 166.9** (268.6 km) Sea to Sky Gondola; 10-minute ride to elev. 2,904 feet/885m; suspension bridge, viewing platforms, hiking trails. Summit Lodge at top has a restaurant, bar and tea house; cafe at base camp. Gondola prices and operating hours at www.seatoskygondola.com.

HB 25.4 (40.9 km) **J 166.6** (268.1 km) Main parking area for **Stawamus Chief Provincial Park**; day-use park, campground and hiking trails. The park has 15 vehicle campsites (not suitable for RVs) and 47 walk-in campsites. Camping fee $10/person (6 years or older). Stawamus Chief is the world's second largest granite monolith (elev. 2,139 feet/652m) known internationally for its challenging rock climbing and a hiking trail for non-climbers, up the backside. ▲

HB 25.7 (41.4 km) **J 166.3** (267.6 km) Parking areas both sides of highway with litter bins; pedestrian bridge.

HB 26.4 (42.5 km) **J 165.6** (266.5 km) Traffic light at Valley Drive; Saamish Service gas/diesel station, Chances casino.

HB 26.7 (43 km) **J 165.3** (266 km) Traffic light at Clarke Drive. Parking area.

HB 26.9 (43.3 km) **J 165.1** (265.7 km) Shell gas/diesel station, fast food.

Distance marker southbound shows Horseshoe Bay 43 km/27 miles, Vancouver 64 km/40 miles.

HB 27.2 (43.7 km) **J 164.8** (265.2 km) Mamquam Blind Channel bridge.

HB 27.3 (43.9 km) **J 164.7** (265.1 km) Traffic light at Cleveland Avenue in **SQUA-MISH** (pop. 14,949); shopping mall with supermarket, Starbucks and other services; fast-food includes McDonald's and A&W. Follow Cleveland Avenue to downtown Squamish. Located at the head of Howe Sound and overlooked by Mount Garibaldi and Stawamus Chief, Squamish has all visitor services.

Visitor Information: Visitor Centre to east; **EV plug-ins.** Dubbed the Outdoor Recreation Capital of Canada, Squamish is known for its wind surfing and kite boarding at Squamish Spit, rock climbing in nearby Stawamus Chief Provincial Park and mountain biking opportunities. Excellent seasonal birding (bald eagles) from dikes in Squamish estuary and peregrine falcons nest on Stawamus Chief. Website: www.tourismsquamish. com.

The West Coast Heritage Railway Park here has Western Canada's largest collection of heritage railway equipment, including the Royal Hudson steam train in which you may ride the 3 km/1.9 mile rail route.

HB 28.3 (45.5 km) **J 160.7** (258.6 km) Traffic light at Industrial Way; food, gas/ diesel and lodging (Wendy's, Tim Hortons, Best Western, Chevron).

HB 28.6 (46 km) **J 163.4** (263 km) Traffic light at Commercial Way; Walmart access.

HB 29 (46.7 km) **J 163** (262.3 km) Turn-off for Eagle Vista RV Resort & Campground.

HB 29.2 (47 km) **J 162.8** (262 km) Manaquan River bridge.

HB 29.7 (47.8 km) **J 162.3** (261.2 km) Traffic light at Mamquam Road; Garibaldi Village shopping (food, cinema, shops), Canadian Tire. Mamquam Road leads east 10 miles/16 km to Diamond Head in Garibaldi Provincial Park, 1 of 5 park access points from the highway for this park's backcountry hiking and camping.

HB 30.1 (48.2 km) **J 161.9** (260.5 km) Traffic light at Garibaldi Way; Husky gas/ diesel, Burger King, lodging, BC liquor store, London Drugs, Boston Pizza.

Distance marker northbound shows Whistler 53 km/33 miles, Pemberton 82 km/51 miles.

HB 31.9 (51.1 km) **J 160.1** (257.6 km) Traffic light at Depot Road, access to **BRACKENDALE** (pop. about 1,000). General store, cafe and post office to west.

Brackendale is home to Brackendale Eagles Provincial Park (no visitor facilities), which has one of the largest gatherings of wintering bald eagles in the world. Visit www.env.gov.bc.ca/bcparks/explore/park-

pgs/brackendale_eagles/.

HB 33.4 (53.5 km) **J 158.6** (255.2 km) Traffic light at Squamish Valley Road (access north to Tenderfoot Hatchery on Midnight Road) and Alice Lake Road south to **Alice Lake Provincial Park**; 108 campsites amid trees with grassy areas, picnicking, swimming, canoeing, birding. Campsite reservations are highly recommended in summer ($23-for walk-in sites–$43 for vehicle sites with power).

HB 33.6 (53.8 km) **J 158.4** (254.9 km) Turnout with litter bin to west for northeast-bound traffic only, chain-up area in winter. Cheekeye Creek.

HB 36.3 (58.2 km) **J 155.7** (250.5 km) **Brohm Lake** interpretive forest with picnicking and fishing to west.

HB 37.9 (61 km) **J 154.1** (248 km) Turn-off to east for viewpoint at hilltop which overlooks valley; for northbound only traffic.

HB 38.3 (61.4 km) **J 153.7** (247.3 km) Tantalus Lookout (elev. 320m/1,050 feet) to west for southbound traffic only; parking, litter bins, viewpoint.

HB 43.6 (69.9 km) **J 148.4** (238.8 km) Gravel turnout to west, viewpoint, for southbound traffic.

HB 44 (70.8 km) **J 148** (238.2 km) Viewpoint to west for southbound traffic.

HB 44.2 (70.8 km) **J 147.8** (237.9 km) Pullout to west for southbound traffic. with litter bins and information boards.

HB 45 (72.1 km) **J 147** (236.6 km) Pull-out to north for southwest-bound traffic.

HB 45.3 (72.6 km) **J 146.7** (236.1 km) Turnout with litter bin to north for southwest-bound traffic.

HB 46 (73.7 km) **J 146** (235 km) Turnout to east with litter bin for northbound traffic. Chain-up area in winter.

HB 47.9 (76.8 km) **J 144.1** (231.9 km) Turnoff for Garibaldi Lake/Black Tusk in **Garibaldi Provincial Park** via paved road, 1.5 miles/2.5 km to trailhead parking. It is 6 miles/11 km from parking lot to Garibaldi Lake via a well-graded trail. It is 4.6 miles/7.5 km from the parking lot to Taylor Meadows. Both areas have tent spaces and pit toilets. No pets or motorized vehicles allowed in Garibaldi park.

HB 51.5 (82.6 km) **J 140.5** (226.1 km) Pull-out with litter bin and point-of-interest signs to north for southwest-bound traffic only.

HB 51.8 (83.4 km) **J 140.2** (225.6 km) **Brandywine Falls Provincial Park** to south; picnicking, fishing, hiking and biking trails. Falls are 66m/230 feet high, and well worth the 10-minute walk from the road. Good view of Daisy Lake and surrounding mountains. Access to Sea to Sky mountain bike trail.

HB 52.4 (84.3 km) **J 139.6** (224.7 km) Whistler RV Park to north.

HB 53 (85.3 km) **J 139** (223.7 km) Welcome to Whistler (sign), double-ended turnout chain-up area to east for northbound traffic.

HB 56.3 (90.3 km) **J 135.7** (218.4 km) Turnout to east for northbound traffic only.

Distance marker southbound shows Squamish 47 km/29 miles, Vancouver 111 km/69 miles.

HB 58.7 (94.3 km) **J 133.3** (214.5 km)

Junction of Alpha Lake Road and Cheaka-mus Lake Road (**Function Junction**). Cheakamus Lake Road leads 4.7 miles/7.5 km to trailhead parking for easy 1.8-mile/3-km hike to spectacular glacier-fed Cheakamus Lake in Garibaldi Provincial Park.

HB 60.5 (97.1 km) **J 131.5** (211.6 km) Traffic light at Bayshore Drive.

HB 60.9 (97.7 km) **J 131.1** (211 km) Traffic light at Lake Placid Road. Husky gas/ diesel station to east. Whistler Creek.

Northbound, Highway 99 passes a number of residential neighbourhoods— Whistler Creek, Nordic Estates, Highlands, Alta Vista, Blueberry Hill, etc.—that comprise Whistler Resort. The Valley Trail, a paved walking and cycling path, parallels the highway.

HB 62.6 (100.5 km) **J 129.4** (208.2 km) Traffic light at Blueberry Drive.

HB 63.4 (101.7 km) **J 128.6** (207 km) Traffic light at Village Gate Blvd., main entrance to **WHISTLER VILLAGE** (pop. 11,854). *Follow boulevard to public parking areas: There are several very large parking lots, although parking for RVs is somewhat limited.* Whistler is a European-style village, with cobbled streets and pedestrian-only plazas: You will have to park and get out and walk to enjoy the outdoor cafes, exclusive shops and fine restaurants. Whistler offers a variety of upscale accommodations, the most famous of which is Fairmont Chateau Whistler, a 12-storey "castle in the mountains" reminiscent of the turn-of-the-century hotels built by the Canadian Pacific Railway. **Visitor Information:** Whistler Visitor Centre at 4230 Gateway Dr., open 8 A.M. to 10 P.M. daily. www.whistler.com; phone 604-935-3357; 1-877-991-9988.

Whistler Village and adjacent Village North and Upper Village lie between 2 famous side-by-side ski hills, Whistler and Blackcomb (www.whistlerblackcomb.com). Whistler Blackcomb is consistently rated the top ski resort in North America and is the only one to offer summer skiing and snowboarding well into July (accessed via Wizard Express chairlift located at the base of Blackcomb Mountain. Whistler was the alpine venue for the 2010 Winter Olympics and Paralympic Winter Games.

In summer, Whistler boasts some of the world's best golf courses and mountain bike trails. Ride the chairlifts and gondolas for nature walking, alpine hiking, or a mountaintop picnic. Ride the PEAK 2 PEAK Gondola between Whistler and Blackcomb mountains. Access to Singing Pass hiking trail to Garibaldi Provincial Park from Whistler Village day parking area.

HB 63.8 (102.4 km) **J 128.2** (206.3 km) Traffic light at Lorimer Blvd., turnoff for Upper Whistler Village, medical clinic.

HB 64.1 (102.9 km) **J 127.9** (205.8 km) Traffic light at Nancy Greene Drive/Nesters Road. Turn east for all visitor services.

HB 64.6 (103.7 km) **J 127.4** (205 km) Traffic light at Nesters Road West/Spring Grove Way East; exit east for Riverside RV Resort.

HB 65 (104.3 km) **J 127** (204.4 km) Mons Railroad bridge overpass.

HB 65.3 (104.8 km) **J 126.7** (203.9 km) Traffic light at Nicklaus North and Cypress streets.

HB 65.8 (105.6 km) **J 126.2** (203.1 km) Traffic light at Alpine Way.

HB 65.9 (105.8 km) **J 126.1** (202.9 km)

19 Mile Creek.

HB 66.6 (106.9) **J 125.4** (201.8 km) Traffic light for Chevron gas/diesel, convenience store.

HB 67 (107.6 km) **J 125** (201.1 km) Turn-off to east with litter bins and information boards on Green Lake and waterfowl. Good bird watching and boating.

HB 70.6 (113.3 km) **J 121.4** (195.4 km) Trailhead parking for Wedgemount Lake trail in Garibaldi Provincial Park.

HB 73.4 (117.8 km) **J 118.6** (190.9 km) Shadow Lake Interpretive Forest to north.

HB 77.3 (124.1 km) **J 114.7** (184.6 km) Soo River Bridge.

Intermittent passing lanes and stretches of 4-lane highway begin southbound and continue to junction with Trans-Canada Highway 1.

HB 78.3 (125.7 km) **J 113.7** (183 km) Rutherford Creek bridge.

HB 81.4 (130.7 km) **J 110.6** (178 km) **Nairn Falls Provincial Park**; 94 campsites. An elevated 0.9 mile/1.5 km riverside trail leads to the falls which plummet 60m/197 feet into jade-coloured Green River. ▲

HB 82.4 (132.6 km) **J 109.6** (176.4 km) Turnoff east for One Mile Park, picnic tables along the water, boardwalk trail out over the water.

HB 83.2 (133.7 km) **J 108.8** (175 km) Traffic light at **PEMBERTON** (pop. 2,574); lodging, corner Husky gas/diesel station with convenience store. Petro-Canada station gas/diesel station, convenience store, lodging in several hotels/motels. The Visitor Centre is on Highway 99 (across from the Petro-Canada) with an inukshuk in its yard and picnic tables; sani-dump available; open 9 A.M. to 5 P.M. early May to late September; phone 604-894-6175. This farming village has become a bedroom community for Whistler. It is an outdoor recreation destination of its own for hiking, biking, boating, fishing and mountain adventures. Pemberton Museum features the gold rush and native culture. ▲

HB 84.6 (135.9 km) **J 107.4** (172.8 km) Lillooet River Bridge. Lillooet River flows east to Lillooet Lake. Northbound, Highway 99 winds through rural residential area, headquarters of the Lil'wat group of the Stl'atl'imx Nation. *Watch your speed!*

HB 87 (140 km) **J 105** (169 km) Distance marker northbound shows Lillooet 93 km/58 miles, Lytton 154 km/96 miles, Cache Creek 177 km/110 miles.

HB 87.2 (140.1 km) **J 104.8** (168.6 km) "T" junction. For eastbound travelers, Highway 99 turns sharply right and then begins its climb into the Cayoosh Range of the Coast Mountains. For westbound travelers, turn left for Whistler.

HB 93.2 (149.7 km) **J 98.8** (159 km) Birkenhead River. Westbound, Highway 99 winds through flatlands of the Stl'atl'imx Nation. Speed limit is 60 kmph/37 mph, narrow road, no passing, watch for horses.

HB 93.9 (150.8 km) **J 98.1** (157.9 km) Avalanche gates.

CAUTION: Steep uphill grades, narrow winding road with 20-kmph/12-mph curves, eastbound.

HB 94.1 (151.1 km) **J 97.9** (157.6 km) Lower Joffre Creek.

HB 96 (154.2 km) **J 96** (154.5 km) Large gravel turnout to west is brake-check area; there is also a runaway exit lane here.

HB 98.6 (158.4 km) **J 93.4** (150.3 km) Large gravel turnout to north.

HB 101.6 (163.2 km) **J 90.4** (145.5 km) Westbound brake-check area. *CAUTION: Steep downgrades, narrow winding road with 20-kmph/12-mph curves, westbound. Runaway truck lanes.*

Distance marker westbound shows Pemberton 30 km/19 miles, Whistler 64 km/40 miles, Vancouver 185 km/115 miles.

HB 102 (163.9 km) **J 90** (144.8 km) **Joffre Lakes Provincial Park**; 24 walk-in campsites. The 3 alpine lakes in the chain can be reached by a 3-mile/5-km trail, with an elevation gain of more than 400m/1,300 feet (4 to 6 hours round-trip.) Best view of glacier for photos is from your vehicle on the highway looking over the parking lot. ▲

HB 102.3 (164.3 km) **J 89.7** (144.4 km) *11 percent grades westbound as Highway 99 descends.*

Distance marker eastbound shows Lillooet 69 km/43 miles, Lytton 90 km/56 miles, Cache Creek 153 km/95 miles.

HB 104 (167.1 km) **J 88** (141.6 km) Bridge over Cayoosh Creek. Slow for curve. Views of Joffre Peaks.

HB 104.5 (167.9 km) **J 87.5** (140.8 km) Avalanche gates.

HB 106.7 (171.4 km) **J 85.3** (137.3 km) Large, paved and gravel shoulder parking area.

HB 109 (175.1 km) **J 83** (133.6 km) Cayoosh Creek #3 bridge (narrow, with wood-plank decking). Turnout to south at west end of bridge. Highway descends eastbound, highway climbs westbound.

HB 109.7 (176.3 km) **J 82.3** (132.4 km) Van Horlick Creek. Note transition between wet coastal forest and dry interior highland plateau.

HB 111.7 (179.5 km) **J 80.3** (129.2 km) Turnout overlooking lake.

HB 112.1 (180.1 km) **J 79.9** (128.6 km) Steep Creek on highway curve.

HB 112.4 (180.6 km) **J 79.6** (128.1 km) Priester Creek.

HB 112.6 (181 km) **J 79.4** (127.8 km) Turnout to north.

HB 113.1 (181.7 km) **J 78.9** (127 km) Large gravel turnout to north overlooking Duffey Lake.

HB 113.6 (182.5 km) **J 78.4** (126.2 km) Large gravel turnout to north overlooking Duffey Lake.

HB 113.8 (182.9 km) **J 78.2** (125.8 km) East end of Duffey Lake is marked by a massive log jam. Gravel turnout for vehicles; boat launch.

HB 115.4 (185.4 km) **J 76.6** (123.3 km) Blowdown Creek. Gravel turnout to north. Slow for 30-kmph/19-mph curves westbound.

HB 115.8 (185.9 km) **J 76.2** (122.8 km) Kane Creek, with waterfall views.

HB 116.3 (186.9 km) **J 75.7** (121.8 km) Avalanche gate. Blowdown Creek Forest Service Road.

Distance marker eastbound shows Lillooet 47 km/29 miles, Lytton 116 km/72 miles, Cache Creek 139 km/86 miles.

HB 116.6 (187.6 km) **J 75.4** (121.3 km) Gravel turnout to south.

HB 119.4 (191.9 km) **J 72.6** (116.8 km) Channel Creek bridge.

HB 121.8 (195.7 km) **J 70.2** (113 km) Cayoosh Creek bridge. Highway 99 follows Cayoosh Creek to Lillooet, crossing the creek several times via mostly narrow 1-lane bridges.

HB 122.2 (196.6 km) **J 69.8** (112.3 km) Graham River bridge.

HB 124.2 (199.6 km) **J 67.8** (109.1 km) Sharp curve and one of 2 turnoffs to south to Rogers Creek B.C. Recreation Site camping area; see description next Milepost.

Improved road surface westbound.

HB 124.6 (200.2 km) **J 67.4** (108.5 km) One of 2 turnoffs to south to **Rogers Creek B.C. Recreation Site**; 14 campsites in 2 camping areas, tables, toilets, no fee. Popular picnic stop. ▲

HB 124.8 (200.6 km) **J 67.2** (108.1 km) Cayoosh Creek bridge.

HB 125.5 (201.7 km) **J 66.5** (107 km) **Gott Creek B.C. Recreation Site**; small 4-vehicle campground with picnic tables, toilets, no fee. ▲

HB 125.6 (201.9 km) **J 66.4** (106.8 km) Gott Creek bridge.

HB 127 (204.1 km) **J 65** (104.6 km) Small gravel turnout to north.

HB 127.1 (204.3 km) **J 64.9** (104.4 km)

Watch for bicyclists on the Sea to Sky Highway. This is along scenic Green Lake between Whistler Village and Pemberton. (©Claire Torgerson, staff)

Boulder Creek 1-lane bridge.

HB 130.1 (209.1 km) **J 61.9** (99.6 km) **Cottonwood Creek B.C. Recreation Site;** 14 campsites, tables, toilets, no fee.

HB 130.4 (209.9 km) **J 61.6** (99.1 km) Gravel turnout to south.

HB 132.3 (212.68 km) **J 59.7** (96.1 km) **Cinnamon B.C. Recreation Site;** 11 campsites, tables, toilets, no fee.

HB 135.1 (217.1 km) **J 56.9** (91.6 km) Gravel turnout to north at top of 13 percent grade.

HB 136.4 (219.2 km) **J 55.6** (89.5 km) Cayoosh Creek 1-lane bridge.

HB 137.4 (220.8 km) **J 54.6** (87.9 km) Large turnout to south.

HB 137.8 (221.5 km) **J 54.2** (87.2 km) Large turnout to south.

HB 139.2 (223.7 km) **J 52.8** (85 km) Gravel turnout to south with information board on Lillooet.

CAUTION: 20-kmph/13-mph curve as highway climbs 13 percent uphill grade westbound. Narrow winding road with steep grades, no shoulder and few turnouts westbound to Pemberton.

HB 140.4 (225.7 km) **J 51.6** (83 km) Avalanche gates.

HB 140.6 (226 km) **J 51.4** (82.7) Large gravel turnout to north with scenic view of Seton Lake.

HB 141.4 (227.3 km) **J 50.6** (81.4 km) **B.C. Hydro Seton Lake Recreation Area;** scenic viewpoint overlooking jade-green Seton Lake; parking area (not much room for large RVs), picnic site and access to beach.

HB 141.8 (227.9 km) **J 50.2** (80.8 km) **B.C. Hydro Seton Lake Campground** to south.

HB 142.1 (228.4 km) **J 49.9** (80.3 km) Power Canal 1-lane, wood-plank bridge.

HB 142.3 (228.7 km) **J 49.7** (80 km) B.C. Hydro Naxwit picnic site; paved day-use area along river, information boards, walking paths, picnic tables, RV turnaround. Very nice spot.

HB 142.5 (232 km) **J 49.5** (76.7 km) Cayoosh Creek 1-lane, wood-plank bridge. *Slow for 30-kmph/19-mph curve.*

HB 143.3 (230.3 km) **J 48.7** (78.4 km) Gravel turnout to north with information board about Seton Creek Salmon Project.

Improved pavement eastbound. Fair pavement with rough patches westbound.

HB 143.8 (231.2 km) **J 48.2** (77.5 km) Lightfoot convenience store; modern facility with free coffee, picnic tables, gas/diesel. Last gas westbound for 100 km/60 miles (Pemberton).

HB 144.1 (231.6 km) **J 47.9** (77.1 km) Turnoff for golf course.

HB 144.3 (231.9 km) **J 47.7** (76.8 km) Seton River 1-lane bridge.

HB 144.4 (232.1 km) **J 47.6** (76.6 km) **Junction** with road which leads 0.5-mile up an 8 percent grade to the Main Street of Lillooet (description of town follows) and continues on to Gold Bridge (106 km). *Northbound travelers turn right for continuation of Highway 99 across the Fraser River (southbound travelers turn left). Drive up hill for downtown Lillooet and visitor services.*

Cayoosh Creek Campground is located on Highway 99 as you turn northbound to cross the Fraser River.

LILLOOET (pop. 2,324), (elev. 784

Eastbound, the highway enters the drier interior highland plateau. (©Claire Torgerson, staff)

feet/239m) is perched high above the Fraser River at its confluence with Cayoosh Creek. **Visitor Information:** www.lillooetbc.ca. Lillooet shares the highest temperature ever recorded in Canada: 111.9°F/44.4°C, in July 1941. The most recent record was 101.1°F/38.4°C on July 6, 2015. The town dates back to the Cariboo gold rush.

Stop by the excellent Lillooet Museum and take in the town's historic points of interest on a walking tour which includes a "jade walk" through town accented by examples of locally found jade. Lillooet offers travelers overnight accommodations, restaurants, a gas station with diesel and other visitor services. First Nations cultural tours, local vineyards, golf and sturgeon fishing is available. Views of the city are from multiple turnouts to the north, above the Fraser River.

The record number of wild fires in central British Columbia in 2017 caused periodic closures of Highway 99 and Highway 97 due to active fires. Residents here are not unfamiliar with wildfires: In August 2009, the Mount McLean wildfire forced a city-wide evacuation of Lillooet.

HB 144.6 (232.5 km) **J 47.4** (76.2 km) Turnout to north with point-of-interest signs and a Pelton Wheel.

HB 144.8 (232.7 km) **J 47.2** (76 km) Midspan of the Fraser River Bridge.

HB 145.3 (233.6 km) **J 46.7** (75.1 km) **Junction** of Highway 99 with Highway 12, which leads south along the Fraser River 65 km/40 miles to Lytton and Trans-Canada 1.

HB 145.6 (234 km) **J 46.4** (74.7 km) Fort Berens Estate Winery to north; tasting room.

HB 145.8 (234.6 km) **J 46.2** (74.4 km) Distance marker eastbound shows Cache Creek 86 km/53 miles, Clinton 104 km/65 miles, Kamloops 171 km/106 miles, Prince George 508 km/316 miles.

HB 146.5 (235.5 km) **J 45.5** (73.2 km) Turnoff to north for Fraser Cove Campground.

HB 147.4 (236 km) **J 44.6** (71.8 km)

Large paved turnout to north with litter bin; good view of Lillooet and Fraser River.

Slow for 50 kmph/30-mph curves westbound.

HB 147.8 (237.6 km) **J 44.2** (71.1 km) Entering Lillooet, 911 area, westbound (sign).

HB 150.3 (241.6 km) **J 41.7** (67.1 km) Large gravel turnout to north.

HB 153.7 (247.1 km) **J 38.3** (61.6 km) Fountain Flat Trading Post gas/diesel station and convenience store to north.

HB 154.6 (248.5 km) **J 37.4** (60.2 km) *Slow for 20-kmph/12-mph curve and 1-lane tunnel under railway.*

Westbound, watch for livestock; 9 percent downgrade.

HB 154.7 (249 km) **J 37.3** (60 km) Double-ended turnout to north.

HB 156.2 (251.1 km) **J 35.8** (57.6 km) *Slow for 30-kmph/19-mph curve and 1-lane tunnel under railway.* Northbound, Highway 99 leapfrogs B.C. Railway a few more times using underpasses and overpasses. You are now driving through the semi-desert benchlands of the upper Fraser River canyon.

HB 158.8 (255.3 km) **J 33.2** (53.4 km) Sallus Creek.

HB 172.1 (276.7 km) **J 19.9** (32 km) Turnout with information board on Pavilion Lake. Highway 99 follows the shoreline of Pavilion Lake for approximately 4 miles/6 km.

HB 173.8 (279.4 km) **J 18.2** (29.3 km) Distance marker westbound shows Lillooet 45 km/28 miles, Pemberton 145 km/90 miles, Whistler 179 km/111 miles, Vancouver 300 km/186 miles.

HB 174.3 (280 km) **J 17.7** (28.5 km) Crown Lake.

HB 174.6 (281 km) **J 17.4** (28 km) Turnoff to south for **Marble Canyon Provincial Park** at **Crown** and **Turquoise** lakes: 30 delightful campsites, towering yellow and red limestone cliffs, picturesque lakes. Picnicking, walking trails, swimming, fishing.

HB 177.8 (286 km) **J 14.2** (22.8 km) Graymont Pavilion Plant produces a range of lime and limestone products including high calcium quicklime and screened limestone.

HB 191.5 (308.2 km) **J 0.5** (0.8 km) Large gravel turnout to north.

HB 191.6 (308.2 km) **J 0.4** (0.6 km) Historic Hat Creek Ranch heritage site offers interpretive tours, stagecoach rides, a gift shop, licensed restaurant, camping and cabins. Admission fee charged. Open daily from 9 A.M. to 5 P.M., May through September; details at historichatcreek.ca or phone 250-457-9722.

HB 191.8 (308.4 km) **J 0.2** (0.3 km) Distance marker westbound shows Lillooet 73 km/45 miles, Pemberton 173 km/108 miles, Whistler 207 km/129 miles, Squamish 261 km/162 miles, Vancouver 328 km/204 miles.

HB 191.9 (308.8 km) **J 0.1** (0.2 km) Bonaparte River bridge.

HB 192 (309 km) **J 0 Junction** of Highway 99 with Highway 97, 7 miles/11 km north of Cache Creek.

*Turn to **Milepost CC 7** on page 120 this section for continuation of main WEST ACCESS ROUTE log.*

**Return to Milepost CC 7
West Access Route Log**

(Continued from page 110)

access south to shopping and services (Walgreens, Petco, etc.).

J 0.4 CB 22.6 Traffic light; access to lodging, shopping and other services.

J 0.6 CB 22.4 Traffic light; access to lodging, shopping and other services.

J 1 CB 22 Costco to north.

J 1.2 CB 21.8 Traffic light at East Stuart Road; shopping malls both sides of highway.

J 1.3 CB 21.7 Walmart to south.

J 2.3 CB 20.7 Entering Bellingham westbound on SR 539S.

J 3.5 CB 19.5 Traffic light at Smith Road; Chevron gas station.

J 4.5 CB 18.5 Traffic light at Axton Road.

J 5.1 CB 17.9 Traffic light at Laurel Road; 76 gas station.

J 5.8 CB 17.2 Ten Mile Creek.

J 5.9 CB 17.1 Four Mile Creek.

J 6 CB 17 Ten Mile Road roundabout; continue straight through roundabout.

J 7.6 CB 15.6 East Pole Road roundabout. Shell gas station and independent gas station. Continue straight through roundabout on SR 539N/S.

J 7.9 CB 15.1 Hidden Creek Village RV Park and Campground.

J 8.5 CB 14.5 Wiser Lake Road roundabout, continue straight through roundabout.

J 9.4 CB 13.6 Nooksack River bridges.

J 9.8 CB 13.2 River Road roundabout, continue straight through roundabout.

J 10 CB 13 Border crossing open 8 A.M. to midnight (sign) refers to Aldergrove crossing; Sumas border crossing is open 24 hours.

J 10.4 CB 12.6 Fish Trap Creek.

J 10.7 CB 12.6 Traffic light at Birch Bay-Lynden Road/Kok Road. Shopping malls and fast-food both sides of highway: Safeway supermarket, DQ, McDonald's, Burger King), Starbucks, drugstore. Continue straight ahead on SR 539N/S.

J 11 CB 12 Traffic light at Front Street access to downtown Lynden. Turnoff to east for city center. Continue straight ahead on SR 539N/S.

LYNDEN (pop. 12,104) has all services. Lynden's Dutch heritage is evident in its shops and festivals and 72-foot-high windmill in downtown (www.lynden.org).

J 11.5 CB 11.5 Traffic light at Main Street access to downtown Lynden. Turn to east for city centre, continue straight ahead on SR 539 for Sumas (north) or Bellingham (south).

J 12.6 CB 10.4 Traffic light at **junction** of Highway 539 to/from Bellingham and Highway 546. *IMPORTANT: Travelers bound for the 24-hour border crossing at Sumas turn right on SR 546/Badger Road; travelers bound for Interstate 5 turn left on SR 539 (Guide-Meridian) for Bellingham.* Northbound motorists who miss this turn will find that Highway 539 continues about 5 miles north to the border crossing at Aldergrove (open 8 A.M. to midnight), where it then continues north as BC Highway 13 for 7 miles to junction with Trans-Canada Highway 1 approximately 15 miles west of Abbotsford.

Distance marker eastbound shows Sumas 12 miles, Abbotsford 16 miles.

J 13.1 CB 9.9 Double Ditch Road.

J 13.7 CB 9.3 Benson Road. Physical Milepost 1 on SR 546 indicates distance from junction with SR 539.

Southbound on BC Highway 11 in Abbotsford, approaching the international border at Sumas, WA. Border wait times can be anywhere from 5 minutes to an hour. (©Sharon Nault)

J 14.1 CB 8.9 Depot Road roundabout: Continue straight through roundabout. Depot Road leads 1.7 miles south to Front Street in Lynden.

J 14.4 CB 8.6 Bender Road roundabout: Continue straight through roundabout.

J 14.7 CB 8.3 Milepost 2. Shell gas station.

J 15.7 CB 7.3 Milepost 3. Sign for Lynden/Bellingham KOA.

J 20.6 CB 4.4 Traffic light at **junction** of Highway 546 and Highway 9; Nooksack Valley School. *(Do NOT go south on SR 9 if you are following this log!)* Northbound travelers continue straight ahead on SR 9 for Sumas and Canadian border. *(Mileposts on SR 9 reflect distance from its junction with Highway 522 near Bothell.)*

Westbound travelers continue straight ahead on SR 546 West for SR 539 to Bellingham and Interstate 5.

J 22 CB 1 *Slow for posted speed zone northbound through Sumas.*

J 23 CB 0 SUMAS (pop. 1,232) has food, gas, lodging, shopping and services. Camping at Sumas RV Park south side of town.

U.S.–Canada international border. The Sumas, WA–Abbotsford-Huntingdon, BC, border crossing is open 24 hours daily.

Continue north on BC Highway 11 for continuation of West Access Route northbound via Trans-Canada Highway 1 East. Food, shopping and other services are located along BC Highway 11 between the border crossing at Sumas and Trans-Canada Highway 1.

J 25 CB 2 For northbound travelers, BC Highway 11 junctions with Trans-Canada Highway 1 East. Merge on to Trans-Canada Highway 1 East for Hope and continuation of West Access Route log. (BC Highway 11 continues north to downtown Abbotsford. Trans-Canada Highway 1 West continues to Vancouver.)

Southbound travelers continue south to international border crossing at Sumas, WA.

TRANS-CANADA HIGHWAY 1 EAST

This section of the log shows distance from Abbotsford (A) followed by distance from Cache Creek (CC).

A 0 CC 170 (273.6 km) Exit 92 to Abbotsford, Mission and Highway 11 south 3 miles/4.8 km to Sumas and the international border. Highway 11 north to **ABBOTSFORD** (pop. 123,864), all visitor services. Abbotsford is the "Raspberry Capital of Canada" and is the home of the Abbotsford International Airshow in August. **Visitor Information:** Use Exit 92 Sumas Way for Abbotsford Visitor Centre at 34561 Delair Rd.; phone 1-888-332-2229; website www.tourismab botsford.ca; email: info@tourismabbotsford. ca. A Circle Farm Tour brochure found at the Centre is a great self-guiding tool to use to see this area's agriculture.

Highway 11 north crosses the bridge over the Fraser River to Mission (7.2 miles/11.9 km north), and connects with Highway 7 to Harrison Hot Springs (41 miles/66 km). This 2-lane highway traverses the rural farmland on the north side of the Fraser River, rejoining Trans-Canada Highway 1 at Hope (56 miles/90 km).

A 2 (3.2 km) **CC 168** (270.3 km) Exit 95 to Whatcom Road and westbound access to rest area to south; gas/diesel, food, tourist attractions and lodging north of exit.

A 4 (6.4 km) **CC 166** (267.1 km) Exit 99 (eastbound only) to rest area with phone, picnic tables, sani-dump.

A 7.5 (12.1 km) **CC 162.5** (261.5 km) Exit 104 to small farming community of Yarrow and No. 3 Road; access to Cultus Lake Recreation Area.

A 10.2 (16.4 km) **CC 159.8** (257.1 km) Vedder Canal.

A 11 (17.7 km) **CC 159** (255.9 km) Exit 109 Yale Road West. Exit for Great Blue Heron Nature Reserve along the Vedder River. Take Yale Road West to Sumas Prairie Road and drive south to road end.

A 14.6 (23.5 km) **CC 155.4** (250 km) Exit 116 north to Lickman Road and south to Chilliwack Visitor Centre/Heritage Museum (turn left at first traffic light to Luckakuck Way for visitor centre). Many RV and automotive repair and supply stores (some with free sani-dumps) are located on Yale Road; exit north via Lickman then right on Yale.

The Chilliwack Visitor Center is open 9 A.M. to 5 P.M. daily mid-May to Labour Day in September, and 8:30 A.M. to

Bridal Veil Falls is a worthwhile side trip, with a provincial park picnic area and a private RV resort nearby. (©Claire Torgerson, staff)

4:30 P.M. weekdays rest of year; phone 1-800-567-9535; www.tourismchilliwack.com. Visitor Centre has picnic grounds and sani-dump stations ($5 fee/credit card only) open April–October. Chilliwack Heritage Park located behind the Visitor Centre.

A **15.7** (25.3 km) CC **154.3** (248.3 km) Exit 118 to Evans Road (head north for Walmart).

A **16.7** (26.9 km) CC **153.3** (246.7 km) Exit 119 to Vedder Road, eastbound access to Yale Road and **CHILLIWACK** (pop. 83,000). City centre to north; food, gas/diesel, lodging and shopping. Turn off to south for Cottonwood Mall, Safeway and other businesses. Chilliwack has hotels, motels, bed and breakfasts, restaurants, shopping malls, movie theatres, banks, gas stations with diesel and other services.

Minter Gardens, which closed in 2013 after 33 years, operates their Country Garden Store on Young Road; eastbound take Exit 119 turn right at Airport Road, then left on Young Road and continue 3.2 km/2 miles north (westbound drivers take Exit 120 on to Young Road and drive 4 km/2.5 miles north) Also access to **Chilliwack Lake Provincial Park**, **Cultus Lake Provincial Park** and Cultus Lake resort area including several campgrounds (some campsites may be reserved, open early April–early October; www.discovercamping.ca).

A **17.6** (28.3 km) CC **152.4** (245.3 km) Exit 120 westbound only to Young Road, Chilliwack.

A **18.8** (30.3 km) CC **151.2** (243.3 km) Exit 123 Prest Road north to Rosedale, south to Ryder Lake; no services.

A **22.8** (36.7 km) CC **147.2** (236.9 km) Exit 129 for Annis Road/Rosedale.

A **26.5** (42.5 km) CC **143.5** (230.9 km) Exit 135 to **junction** with Highway 9 to Agassiz and Harrison Hot Springs (14 km/8.5 miles). Eastbound access to **Bridal Veil Falls Provincial Park** ½ mile south of highway (follow blue signs); picnicking, trail to base of falls (15 minutes round-trip). Also access to waterpark, food, gas/diesel, lodging and camping. **Bridal Falls Camperland RV Resort and Cabins** (address 53730 Bridal Falls Rd., Rosedale) has full and partial hookup sites, 30- and 50-amp electrical, onsite general store, mini-golf and more; phone 604-794-7631 or visit www.htr.ca.

Bridal Falls Camperland RV Resort and Cabins. See display ad this page.

A **28.5** (45.9 km) CC **141.5** (227.7 km) Exit 138 to Popkum Road. Access to Bridal Veil Falls (follow signs).

A **33.6** (54.1 km) CC **136.4** (219.5 km) Exit 146 Herrling Island; no services.

A **36.5** (58.7 km) CC **133.5** (214.8 km) Exit 151 to Peters Road.

A **38** (61.2 km) CC **132** (212.4 km) Exit 153 to Laidlaw Road and to Jones Lake (4-wheel drive required).

A **41.5** (66.8 km) CC **128.5** (206.8 km) Westbound truck weigh scales.

A **42** (67.6 km) CC **128** (206 km) Exit 160 to Hunter Creek rest area; tables, toilet, pay phone, information kiosk.

A **44.5** (71.6 km) CC **125.5** (202 km) Exit 165 Access to Flood–Hope Road business route with access to camping, gas/diesel and Hope Regional Airpark.

A **47** (75.6 km) CC **123** (197.9 km) Exit 168 westbound access to Flood–Hope Road/ Silver Hope Creek; Flying J Travel Center to north with food, gas/diesel; gas, food and camping to south. Also access south this exit to Silver Skagit Road to provincial parks (descriptions follow).

BC Parks' directions to reach **Silver Lake Provincial Park** (25 sites): Exit highway here and follow blue park signs; turn right on to Flood-Hope Road and drive approximately 1 km then turn right on Silver Skagit Road and continue first 2 km/1.2 miles on pavement then 4 km/2.5 miles on gravel; watch for a bridge on your right at Kilometre 6; turn right and go over bridge and continue 1 km to the park. **Skagit Valley Provincial Park** with 3 campgrounds (total 142 sites) is 37 km/23 miles from Highway 1 to the park entrance then another 23 km/14.3 miles to the first and largest campground—Ross Lake Reservoir. There are no services near this park; get gas and supplies in Hope or Silver Creek before driving to Skagit Valley Provincial Park. Camping fee both parks, $18 per night, season May 1–mid-Oct. Campgrounds have pit toilets, hand pump drinking water, swimming, fishing.

A **48.5** (78 km) CC **121.5** (195.4 km) Exit 170 to Hope. *WEST ACCESS ROUTE travelers take this exit for Hope (description follows) and Trans-Canada Highway 1 East to Cache Creek. (Although you are driving north toward Cache Creek, highway directional signs indicate "East.")*

NOTE: Northbound travelers on the WEST ACCESS ROUTE may also choose to continue east on Highway 3 and take the Coquihalla Highway/Highway 5 north to Kamloops, then rejoin the main West Access Route by driving 52 miles/84 km west on Trans-Canada Highway 1 to Cache Creek. (Continue east 4 miles for start of the Coquihalla Highway.) This is an alternate route which avoids the Fraser River Canyon. (See "Coquihalla Highway" log on page 102 in the CENTRAL ACCESS ROUTE section).

©Judy Nadon, staff

A **50** (80.5 km) CC **120** (193.1 km) **HOPE** (pop. 5,985) is located on the Fraser River at the **junction** of Trans-Canada Highway 1, Highway 3 (Crowsnest Highway) and Highway 5 (Yellowhead/Coquihalla Highway). **Visitor Information:** Visitor Center and Museum (pictured above) at corner of Hudson Bay Street and Water Avenue, on right northbound as you enter town on Trans-Canada Highway 1 East; Chevron station is on north corner of Hudson Bay and Water. The visitor centre is open daily in summer 9 A.M. to 5 P.M.; in winter 10 A.M. to 4 P.M. weekdays, 9 A.M. to 5 P.M. weekends.

Hope is a convenient stop with all visitor services, including food, gas/diesel and lodging. There are 4 **EV plug-in** stations in town: a 10-port DCFast station with Tesla chargers at 830 Fraser Ave.; DCFast station at 412 Wallace St.; and Level 2 stations at the District Hall and the Recreation Centre. Camping at Telte-Yet in town on west side

of highway on Fraser River. Shopping, restaurants, town offices, public park and a number of chainsaw carvings are found on Wallace Street downtown.

A 51 (82 km) **CC 119** (191.5 km) Bridge over Fraser River.

A 51.3 (82.5 km) **CC 118.7** (191 km) Double-ended turnout to east with litter bin.

A 51.8 (83.4 km) **CC 118.2** (190.2 km) **Junction** with Highway 7 west to Harrison Hot Springs, an interesting side trip.

©Kris Valencia, staff

A 53.4 (85.9 km) **CC 116.6** (187.6 km) Shaded rest area with picnic tables, toilets, info boards, at Lake of the Woods. 10-minute walk on "Bridge Trail."

A 59.1 (95.1 km) **CC 110.9** (178.5 km) Gas/diesel station, cafe.

A 61.2 (98.5 km) **CC 108.8** (175.1 km) Esso gas station with diesel and Hope River General Store & RV Park to west. Turnoff to east for **Emory Creek Campground**; 35 level gravel sites in trees, water taps, fire rings, picnic tables, firewood ($5 per bundle), flush toilets, litter bins. Camping fee $20 per night. Open early May to mid-October. Hiking and walking trails. Gold panning and fishing in **Fraser River**.

A 64.8 (104.3 km) **CC 105.2** (169.3 km) Paved rest area to east with picnic tables, litter bins, toilets and historic signs.

Slow for posted speed zone northbound through Yale.

A 65 (104.6 km) **CC 105** (169 km) Traffic light at Albert Street in **YALE** (pop. 200); convenience store and Esso gas/diesel station. There is a tearoom east on Alberta Street and across the railroad tracks. **Emergency Services:** Dial 911. **Visitor Information:** Turn east on Albert Street then take first right onto Douglas Street for Yale Historic Site; parking, restrooms. Yale Historic Site is home to the Creighton House Museum, a recreated 1858 gold rush tent city with gold panning, and Saint John the Divine church. Pick up the free *Historic Yale Town Walking Guide* at the museum gift shop or at Barry's Trading Post.

Yale is a popular pull-out point for river rafters coming down the Fraser River from Boston Bar. Historically, Yale was the head of navigation for the Lower Fraser River and the beginning of the overland gold rush trail to British Columbia's goldfields. Saint John the Divine Church was built for the miners in 1863; it is the second oldest church in British Columbia. The Ward Tea House is located directly across the street from the church.

A 65.3 (105.1 km) **CC 104.7** (168.5 km) Yale Creek.

A 65.7 (105.7 km) **CC 104.3** (167.8 km) Yale Tunnel, first of 7 tunnels northbound through the Fraser Canyon. Turnout to east at south end of tunnel.

Hell's Gate Airtram is a breathtaking way to see the Fraser River Canyon from above.
(©Kris Valencia, staff)

Spectacular drive northbound as the highway winds through the dramatic scenery of the Fraser River Canyon. The Fraser River and canyon were named for Simon Fraser (1776–1862), the first white man to descend the river in 1808. The scenic Fraser Canyon travelers drive through today was a formidable obstacle for railroad engineers in 1881. This is the dry forest region of British Columbia, and it can be a hot drive in summer through the Fraser and Thompson river canyons.

NOTE: The next 100-km/60-miles northbound holds some challenges for today's motorists, especially driving at night or in heavy rains or high winds. There are sections of narrow, winding road high above the canyon floor, few passing lanes, truck traffic, and a few dangerous curves.

Highway signs indicate Winter Tires or Carry Chains: Oct. 1 to March 31.

A 66.6 (107.2 km) **CC 103.4** (166.4 km) Signed turnoff to east with litter bins.

A 66.7 (107.3 km) **CC 103.3** (166.3 km) *CAUTION: Dangerous curve.*

A 67.3 (108.3 km) **CC 102.7** (165.2 km) Signed turnoff to east with litter bins.

A 68.4 (110.1 km) **CC 101.6** (163.5 km) Saddle Rock Tunnel. This 480-foot/146-m tunnel was constructed in 1957-58.

A 71.1 (114.4 km) **CC 98.9** (159.1 km) Gravel turnout to east.

A 72 (115.9 km) **CC 98** (157.7 km) Sailor Bar Tunnel, nearly 984 feet/300m long. There were dozens of bar claims along the Fraser River in the 1850s bearing colourful names such as Sailor Bar.

A 73 (117.5 km) **CC 97** (156 km) Turnoff to east; avalanche gates southbound.

A 76.9 (123.7 km) **CC 93.1** (149.8 km) Signed turnoff with litter bin. Point-of-interest sign and cairn at south end of Alexandra Bridge across Fraser River. Built in 1962, Alexandra Bridge is the second largest fixed arch span in the world at more than 1,640 feet/500m in length.

A 77.5 (124.7 km) **CC 92.5** (148.9 km) **Alexandra Bridge Provincial Park**, picnic area and rest stop on west side of highway. Hiking trail down to the old Alexandra Bridge, still intact. This suspension bridge was built in 1926, replacing the original built in 1863.

A 78.3 (126.1 km) **CC 91.7** (147.6 km) Turnoff to west.

A 78.4 (126.2 km) **CC 91.6** (147.4 km) Historic Alexandra Lodge (now a private residence), one of the last surviving original roadhouse buildings on the Cariboo Waggon Road that connected Yale with the Cariboo goldfields near Barkerville. Built between 1861 and 1863 by the Royal Engineers, it replaced an earlier route to the goldfields—also called the Cariboo Waggon Road—which started from Lillooet.

A 78.7 (126.6 km) **CC 91.3** (146.8 km) Tikwalus Heritage Trail parking. This trail climbs to summit of Lake Mountain and offers views of Fraser Canyon; elevation gain is 2,493 feet/760m, round-trip distance is 8 miles/13 km.

A 79.4 (127.8 km) **CC 90.6** (145.8 km) Alexandra Tunnel.

Good views northbound of the tracks of the Canadian National and Canadian Pacific railways as they wind through the Fraser River Canyon. Construction of the CPR—Canada's first transcontinental railway—played a significant role in the history of the Fraser and Thompson river valleys. Begun in 1880, the CPR line between Kamloops and Port Moody was contracted to Andrew Onderdonk.

CAUTION: Winding road northbound to Spences Bridge.

A 81.6 (131.3 km) **CC 88.4** (142.3 km) Turnoff with litter bins to east.

A 82.4 (132.6 km) **CC 87.6** (141 km) Hell's Gate Tunnel (328 feet/100m long).

A 82.6 (132.9 km) **CC 87.4** (140.6 km) Ferrabee Tunnel (328 feet/100m long).

A 83.4 (134.2 km) **CC 86.6** (139.4 km) Turnoff with litter bins to west.

A 83.6 (134.5 km) **CC 86.4** (139 km) Northbound parking on east side of road for Hell's Gate Airtram; see description next milepost.

A 83.8 (134.8 km) **CC 86.2** (138.7 km) Southbound parking on west side of road for **Hell's Gate Airtram**. Two 25-passenger airtrams take visitors across the river to a cafe and shop complex overlooking Hell's Gate, the narrowest point on the Fraser River. There is also a steep trail down to the suspension bridge; strenuous hike. Footbridge across river to view fishways through which millions of salmon pass each year. An education center details the life cycle of

View across the Thompson River of railroad tunnels in high avalanche activity areas that allow avalanches to go over rather than close the railroad tracks. (©*Judy Nadon, staff*)

the salmon, the construction of the International Fishways and the history of Hell's Gate. For 2019 season dates or more information, phone 604-867-9277 or visit www. hellsgateairtram.com

Hell's Gate was by far the most difficult terrain for construction of both the highway and the railway. To haul supplies for the railway upstream of Hell's Gate, Andrew Onderdonk built the stern-wheel steamer *Skuzzy*. The SS *Skuzzy* made its way upstream through Hell's Gate in 1882, hauled by ropes attached to the canyon walls by bolts.

A 84.7 (136.3 km) **CC 85.3** (137.3 km) Turnout to east with litter bin. It is also a turnaround for travelers who miss the Hell's Gate parking lot or want handicap accessible parking. You have to be traveling southbound to get into the parking area in front of the Hell's Gate building.

A 85.4 (137.4 km) **CC 84.6** (136.1 km) China Bar Tunnel, built in 1960. It is almost 2,300 feet/700m long, one of the longest tunnels in North America.

A 88.4 (142.3 km) **CC 81.6** (131.3 km) Store, gas/diesel to west. Also access to Anderson Creek Campground. 0.4 mile/0.6 km down hill to west, slow for speed bumps; grassy site. Access to Tuckkwiowhum Heritage Village (Boston Bar First Nations), which recreates a Nlaka'pamax village as it would have appeared before European settlers arrived.

A 88.6 (142.6 km) **CC 81.4** (131 km) Anderson Creek.

A 89.4 (143.9 km) **CC 80.6** (129.7 km) Turnout with litter barrel to west. Avalanche gate just south.

A 90.8 (146.1 km) **CC 79.2** (127.5 km) **BOSTON BAR** (pop. 885). **Emergency Services:** Dial 911. Services include 3 gas stations, grocery, restaurants, pub and motels along the highway. Boston Bar Campground adjacent highway; full-service, gravel pull-through sites.

Boston Bar was the southern landing for the steamer *Skuzzy*, which plied the Fraser River between here and Lytton during construction of the CPR. Celebrations include May Day the 3rd weekend of May each year.

A 92 (148 km) **CC 78** (125.5 km) Turnout with litter bin to west.

A 93.1 (149.8 km) **CC 76.9** (123.7 km) Turnout with litter bin to east.

A 94 (151.3 km) **CC 76** (122.3 km) Canyon Alpine Motel and restaurant (food served 6 A.M. to 10 P.M. year-round). Also **Canyon Alpine RV Park & Campground** (description follows).

Canyon Alpine RV Park and Campground. "Big rigs and doggies our specialty!" According to our guests, we are the preferred RV camp in the Fraser Canyon. Guests resoundingly say that ours is the "best RV campground we've ever stayed at!" We as new owners are so grateful and proud. (And this year we've added a children's play area and a 2-hole putting green.) Fully-serviced, tiered sites, nestled among 90-foot evergreens, with sewer, water, power, internet access, cable TV, and free clean showers. Pull-thru's up to 72 feet. Fenced, off-leash area for doggies. Flexible check-in. Open March 1st to November 30th. Call ahead for winter camping. Hunters welcome and always open to stranded campers. Phone 604-867-9734; 1-800-644-7275; cell phone 604-897-2225; www.canyonalpinervpark. com. [ADVERTISEMENT]

A 95.2 (153.2 km) **CC 74.8** (120.4 km) The Mighty Fraser Motel, Fat Jack Diner.

A 95.9 (154.3 km) **CC 74.1** (119.2 km) Turnout with litter bins and canyon/river views to west.

A 103.7 (167 km) **CC 66.3** (106.7 km) Large gravel turnouts both sides of highway. There are several pullouts northbound on both sides of the highway as it winds through the Fraser Canyon. Litter bins to east.

CAUTION: Winding roads, grades, truck traffic and falling rock northbound. Watch for deer.

A 106.5 (171.4 km) **CC 63.5** (102.2 km) **Jackass Mountain summit**; small turnout to west with litter bins.

A 110.8 (178.3 km) **CC 59.2** (95.3 km) Turnoff to west for Siska.

A 112 (180.2 km) **CC 58** (93.3 km) Turnoff to west. View to west of Canadian National and Canadian Pacific railway crossing of the Fraser River at Siska.

A 114.6 (184.4 km) **CC 55.4** (89.2 km) Skuppah rest area (northbound only); information signs, toilets, tables, litter bins.

A 116.2 (187 km) **CC 53.8** (85.6 km) Large turnout to east.

A 117.2 (188.6 km) **CC 52.8** (85 km) **Junction** with Highway 12; Esso gas/diesel station. Access west to **Lytton** (description follows) and **Lillooet**, a historic community with plenty of adventure opportunities (*see description of Lillooet on page 114 in the "Sea to Sky Highway" log*).

LYTTON (pop. 235; elev. 656 feet/200m) is located at the confluence of the Thompson and Fraser rivers. **Emergency Services:** Dial 911. **Visitor Information:** Visitor Centre, 400 Fraser St., phone 250-455-2523. Food, gas, lodging and other services available. Lytton acts as headquarters for river raft trips on the Thompson and Fraser rivers. The community also has a Chinese History Museum (at 145 Main St.) and one of the last reaction ferries in the province. Historically, sand bars at Lytton yielded much gold, and river frontage has been set aside for recreational gold panning. Lytton shares the record high temperature for British Columbia: 111.9°F/44.4°C in July 1941.

A 118.3 (190.3 km) **CC 51.7** (83.2 km) Gravel turnout to west.

A 122 (196.3 km) **CC 48** (77.2 km) **Skihist Provincial Park** to east; 58 campsites on east side of highway with water, flush and pit toilets, telephone and dump station ($5 fee). Picnic area on west side of highway (good place to watch trains); wheelchair-accessible restrooms.

A 124.3 (200 km) **CC 45.7** (73.5 km) Turnout with litter bins to west. There are several pullouts to the west the next 6.4 miles/10.3 km northbound.

CAUTION: Sections of winding road next 4 miles/6.4 km northbound. Slow for sharp curves under railway crossings. Watch for falling rock.

A 128 (206 km) **CC 42** (67.5 km) Nicomen River.

A 130 (209.2 km) **CC 40** (64.4 km) Large gravel turnout to west with view.

A 131 (210.8 km) **CC 39** (62.8 km) Large gravel turnout to west with view, litter bin.

A 134 (216.6 km) **CC 36** (57.9 km) Turnout with picnic tables to west at entrance to **Goldpan Provincial Park**; good view of railroad tunnels. The provincial park is located alongside the **Thompson River**; open May 1-September, 14 campsites, $16/night, picnic area, hand pump water, fishing.

Turnout on highway near park entrance with good view of railroad tunnels in Thompson River canyon.

A 136.1 (219 km) **CC 33.9** (54.5 km) Northbound watch for fruit and vegetable stands in season.

A 139.3 (224.2 km) **CC 30.7** (49.4 km) **Junction** with Highway 8 to Merritt (43 miles/69 km east).

First northbound access (south access road) to **Spences Bridge**; description follows. See also Spences Bridge description at **Milepost A 140.4.**

Plaque at junction about the great landslide of 1905 reads: "Suddenly on the afternoon of August 13, 1905, the lower side of the mountain slid away. Rumbling across the valley in seconds, the slide buried alive 5 Indians and dammed the Thompson River for over 4 hours. The trapped waters swept over the nearby Indian village drowning 13 persons."

A 139.5 (224.5 km) **CC 30.5** (49.1 km)

Turnout to west with litter bin.

A 139.6 (224.6 km) **CC 30.4** (48.9 km) Thompson River bridge.

A 140.4 (226 km) **CC 29.6** (47.6 km) Turnoff for residential **SPENCES BRIDGE** (pop. 25). Spences Bridge (elev. 850 feet/259m), located at the confluence of the Thompson and Nicola rivers, is an easy half-day drive from the Washington border or the Vancouver airport.

Services here include the **Log Cabin Pub**, the Historic Packing House (now a cafe), the Inn at Spences Bridge (built in the 1860s) on Highway 18, and a grocery with tackle, supplies and fishing licenses. Camping and cabins at available, 1 block off the highway. It is the home of the largest continually operating hotel in British Columbia. Well-known for steelhead fishing, a record 30-lb., 5-oz. steelhead was caught in the Thompson River in 1984. Bighorn sheep frequent the city limits in spring and fall and seasonal produce stands provide a taste of this fertile area.

A 140.6 (226.3 km) **CC 29.4** (47.3 km) **Log Cabin Pub.** You will appreciate this unique log structure. The logs were specially selected and prepared locally, some spanning 50 feet. This pub combines the rustic charm of a turn-of-the-century roadhouse with all the amenities of a neighborhood pub. Excellent food and hospitality by your hosts John and Laurie Kingston. Visit us on the web at www.logcabinpub.com. [ADVERTISEMENT]

A 140.8 (226.6 km) **CC 29.2** (47 km) Acacia Grove R.V. Park & Cabins.

A 147 (236.5 km) **CC 23** (37 km) *Slow for narrow and winding section of highway. Road descends northbound with 60-kmph/ curves.*

A 147.8 (237.8 km) **CC 22.2** (35.7 km) Pullouts both sides of highway.

Winding upgrade southbound 60-kmph/40-mph curves.

A 149.4 (240.4 km) **CC 20.6** (33.1 km) Distance marker northbound shows Ashcroft 29 kms/18 miles, Cache Creek 32 kms/20 miles.

Winding uphill northbound with 7 percent grade.

A 152.3 (245.1 km) **CC 17.7** (28.5 km) Viewpoint to east with litter barrel overlooking Thompson River with plaque about the Canadian Northern Pacific's Last Spike reads:

"Canada's third trans-continental rail link was completed near Basque on January 23, 1915. In a simple ceremony the last spike was driven, witnessed by a small group of engineers and workmen. The line later became part of the Federal Government's consolidated Canadian Nation Railways system."

A 157.4 (253.3 km) **CC 12.6** (20.3 km) Red Hill rest area to east; information about Ashcroft, tables, toilets, litter bins, nice picnic area.

A 163.4 (263 km) **CC 6.6** (10.6 km) Stop of interest sign to east describes Ashcroft Manor Historic Site, British Columbia's oldest roadhouse, established in 1862 by C.F. and H.P. Cornwall. (Clement Cornwall became one of BC's first senators after confederation with Canada in 1871 and Lieutenant Governor of BC in 1881.) The original ranch, with its grist and saw mills, supplied Cariboo miners. The manor house was destroyed by fire in 1943, but the roadhouse survived. A gift shop is located in the old roadhouse. The Ashcroft Manor Tea Room Restaurant is located in a newer building behind the roadhouse.

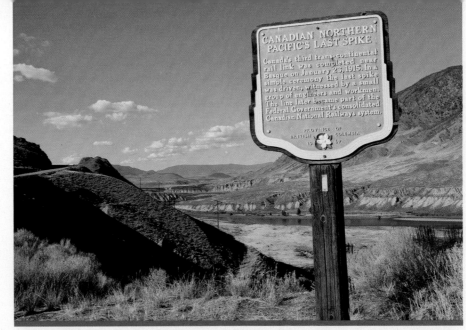

Trans-Canada Highway 1/BC Highway 97 south of Cache Creek has some winding grades. This viewpoint at Milepost A 152.3 commemorates the final spike of the railroad.
(©Kris Valencia, staff)

Summer temperatures in this dry and desert-like region typically reach the high 80s and 90s (26°C to 32°C).

A 163.6 (263.3 km) **CC 6.4** (10.3 km) Esso to east with On-the-Go Market, gas/diesel and propane at turnoff to Ashcroft.

Junction with Highway 97C to Ashcroft (description follows) and Logan Lake (39 miles/63 km east). Great viewpoint of Highland Valley Coppermine 29 miles/47 km east of here on Highway 97C (winding road with 8 to 11 percent grades).

ASHCROFT (pop. 1,700), a village on the Thompson River about 4 miles east of Highway 1, supplanted Yale as gateway to the Cariboo with the arrival of the Canadian Pacific Railway in 1885. Ashcroft Museum houses a collection of artifacts tracing the history of the region. Camping (May–Oct.) at Legacy Park on the Thompson River. **Visitor Information:** www.ashcroftbc.ca.

A 167.4 (269.4 km) **CC 2.6** (4.2 km) Second turnoff northbound for Ashcroft and **junction** with Highway 97C to Logan Lake.

Slow for speed zone northbound through Cache Creek.

Cache Creek

A 170 (273.6 km) **PG 273.6** (440.4 km) Located at the **junction** of Trans-Canada Highway 1 and Highway 97; about a 4-hour drive from the U.S. border at Sumas. **Population:** 1,050. **Emergency Services:** Dial 911. **Hospital**, in Ashcroft, phone 250-453-2211.

Visitor Information: Village of Cache Creek visitor centre at the community hall, open mid-May to mid-Sept.; village website at www.cachecreekvillage.com. Explore Gold Country is an online regional information source with details on things to do and accommodations in area communities; visit www.exploregoldcountry.com.

Elevation: 1,299 feet/396m. **Climate:** Called the Arizona of Canada, Cache Creek's climate is characterized as semi-arid, with hot, dry summers and cold, dry winters. Mean temperature in July is 85°F/30°C, with highs in the 90s°F/32°C. Mean temperature in January is 21°F/-6°C.

An oasis of traveler services in the middle of desert-like country, Cache Creek offers major chain fast-food outlets (Subway, DQ) and motels (Sandman); Husky, Petro-Canada and Chevron gas stations with diesel (Petro-Canada has propane, Chevron has an A&W), a grocery store and shopping. (Check out the 2,850 lb/1,293 kg jade boulder at the Cariboo Jade Shoppe.) Dump station in town; follows signs. Camping at **Brookside Campsite**, located east of Cache Creek on Trans-Canada Highway 1 (across from the golf course); see description following.

Brookside Campsite. 1 km east of Cache Creek on Highway 1, full (30 amp) and partial hookups, shady pull-throughs, tent sites, free WiFi, super-clean washrooms, laundry, free showers, sani-station, store, playground, heated pool, golf course adjacent, pets on leash, pay phone. *No trains!* VISA, MasterCard. Phone/fax: 250-457-6633. Email: info@brooksidecampsite.com; website: brooksidecampsite.com. [ADVERTISEMENT]

The settlement grew up around the confluence of Cache Creek and the Bonaparte River. Cache Creek became a major supply point on the Cariboo Waggon Road. Today, agriculture, logging and tourism support the community. Area soils are dry but fertile. Residents claim that with irrigation nearly anything can be grown here.

Cache Creek, Ashcroft, Williams Lake, 100 Mile House and other Highway 97 communities were severely impacted by wild fires in summer 2017, when some 1,300 fires burned more than 1.2 million hectares (or almost 3 million acres) of land in British Columbia. Fires in British Columbia's interior—including the Hanceville fire, the Central Cariboo Complex fires, the Elephant Hill fire and the Plateau fire—led to highway closures and evacuations along Highway 97, and contributed to the smoky skies over much of the Pacific Northwest in summer 2017.

West Access Route Log
(continued)

This section of the log shows distance

Clinton Museum is housed in a brick building that once served as a courthouse.
(©Kris Valencia, staff)

from Cache Creek (CC) followed by distance from Prince George (PG).

BC HIGHWAY 97 NORTH

CC 0 PG 273.6 (440.2 km) **Junction** of Trans-Canada Highway 1 and Highway 97 at Cache Creek. Southbound travelers follow Trans-Canada Highway 1 West. Northbound travelers follow Highway 97 North, the "Gold Rush Trail."

NOTE: Southbound travelers on the WEST ACCESS ROUTE may choose to drive east 52 miles/84 km on Highway 1 to Kamloops then take the Coquihalla Highway south to Highway 3, rejoining the main at Hope. Interesting drive to Kamloops through high desert country of central British Columbia; some dramatic scenery, 2- and 4-lane highway. This is an alternate route which avoids the Fraser River Canyon. (See "Coquihalla Highway" description on page 102 in the CENTRAL ACCESS ROUTE section and read log from back to front.)

NOTE: Cariboo Connector 4-Lane Upgrade between Cache Creek and Prince George has created many long 4-lane stretches of highway in addition to numerous northbound-only and southbound-only passing lanes. Expect highway improvement projects to continue into 2019.

CAUTION: Watch for deer.

CC 0.4 (0.6 km) **PG 273.2** (439.6 km) Bonaparte River.

CC 0.7 (1.1 km) **PG 272.9** (439.2 km) Gas/diesel station with propane and restaurant to east.

CC 1.2 (1.9 km) **PG 272.4** (438.3 km) Turnout with litter bin and area map to west.

CC 3.7 (6 km) **PG 269.9** (434.4 km) Bonaparte River.

CC 7 (11.3 km) **PG 266.6** (429 km) Junction with Highway 99 to Historic Hat Creek

heritage site, 0.4 mile/0.7 km west (description follows); **Marble Canyon Provincial Park**; Pavilion Lake; **Lillooet** (47 miles/76 km west); and Whistler.

Junction with Highway 99, the "Sea to Sky Highway," to Vancouver via Whistler. Southbound travelers interested in this route turn to page 112 and read description, then follow log on page 114 from back to front.

Historic Hat Creek Ranch heritage site offers interpretive tours, stagecoach rides, a gift shop, licensed restaurant, camping and cabins. Admission fee charged. Open daily from 9 A.M. to 5 P.M., May through September; details at www.historichatcreek.ca, by phone 250-457-9722 and on social media.

CC 9.5 (15.3 km) **PG 264.1** (424.9 km) Turnout to west has litter bins, views of Painted Hills and plaque about "B.X.":

"Connecting Barkerville with the outside world, the B.X. stage coaches served [the] Cariboo for over 50 years. The terminus was moved from Yale to Ashcroft after C.P.R. construction destroyed the wagon road through the Fraser Canyon. The red and yellow coaches left Ashcroft at 4 A.M., and 4 days and 280 miles later reached the end of the road at Barkerville."

CC 13.2 (21.2 km) **PG 260.4** (419 km) Turnoff for **Loon Lake**, located 16 miles/26 km east; camping, fishing, resorts.

CC 19.1 (30.9 km) **PG 254.5** (409.4 km) Large turnout with picnic table, litter bins and point-of-interest sign beside 6 Mile Lake. Nice spot.

CC 19.8 (32 km) **PG 253.8** (408.4 km) Easy access from highway to **Willow Springs Campsite**; full service pull-thru sites, tent sites on Stick Lake.

Willow Springs Campsite. See display ad this page.

CC 24.7 (39.7 km) **PG 248.9** (400.5 km) Gas station with diesel and propane. Turnoff to west for Pavilion–Clinton Road to **Downing Provincial Park** (11 miles/17 km) on popular **Kelly Lake**; 18 campsites, picnic area, swimming beach and fishing for rainbow trout. Open June–September.

Slow for speed zone northbound through Clinton.

Southbound watch for wild sheep alongside highway.

CC 25 (40.2 km) **PG 248.6** (400 km) **CLINTON** (pop. 740, area 4,000; elev. 2,911 feet/887m). **Visitor Information:** Village of Clinton, phone 250-459-2261; www.village. clinton.bc.ca. Visitor information also available in the museum.

Clinton's many antique and collectible shops do business on what was the original site of the 47 Mile Roadhouse, a gold-rush settlement on the Cariboo Wagon Road from Lillooet. Clinton boasts the oldest continuously held event of its kind in Canada, the Clinton Ball (in May the Saturday preceding Victoria Day). The ball, an annual event since 1868, is the first event of Western Heritage Week, which concludes with a 2–day rodeo. Clinton Museum, housed in a red brick building that once served as a courthouse, has fine displays of pioneer tools and items from the gold rush days. Pick up a walking tour guide of historic Clinton. Check out the fun bench in front of the Village Office (built in 1927).

Clinton has all visitor facilities, including motels, a credit union, gas/diesel stations (Shell, Petro-Canada), liquor stores, grocery stores and restaurants. Public washrooms are available in downtown and at the Reg Conn Park. Off-leash dog park located at 306 Cariboo Ave. (park rules are posted). Camping in town at **Gold Trail RV Park and Campground** (description follows). Dining at Gold Trail and at Old School's Bar & Grill located across highway from campground.

Slow for speed zone southbound through Clinton.

CC 25.8 (41.5 km) **PG 247.8** (398.8 km) Turnout with litter bins and information boards to west.

CC 30.7 (49.4 km) **PG 242.9** (390.1 km) Turnoff to west for Big Bar Lake Provincial Park (21 miles/34 km), a popular destination with area residents, offering 2 campgrounds, picnicking, swimming, playground, boat launch and rainbow trout fishing. Open mid-May through September.

CC 30.8 (49.6 km) **PG 242.8** (390.7 km) Rest area to east for northbound-traffic only. Located just north of Big Bar Lake turnoff, this large double-ended parking area has toilets, tables and litter bins.

CC 33.9 (54.5 km) **PG 239.7** (385.7 km) Turnoff for south end of loop road that leads east 2.5 miles/4 km to **Chasm Provincial Park**. There is a viewpoint and parking at the park, pit toilets, picnic area. Successive lava flows in Chasm Creek Valley formed layers in varying tones of red, brown, yellow and purple, which have been revealed in the steep canyon walls cut by erosion over the past 10 million years. Look for bighorn sheep, moose, mule deer and other animals in this area.

CC 34.7 (55.8 km) **PG 238.9** (384.4 km) Turnoff to west for **Beaver Dam Lake**, **Meadow Lakes** and other area fishing lakes or further to **Canoe** and **Dog Creek**.

CC 38.2 (61.5 km) **PG 235.4** (378.8 km) North end of Chasm Loop Road (see description at **Milepost CC 33.9**).

CC 44.4 (71.4 km) **PG 229.2** (368.8 km) Turnoff to east for Green Lake at **70 MILE HOUSE** (pop. 450, elev. 3,609 feet/100m); general store, gas station. Originally a stage stop on the Cariboo Wagon Road, 70 Mile House was named for its distance from Lillooet.

Green Lake Provincial Park to east has 3 campgrounds with 121 total sites and 66 sites that may be reserved (www.discovercamping.ca). Picnic areas, swimming, fishing, boat launch. Open May 15–Sept. 30, camping fee $18 per night, $5 for sani-station. Green Lake is a popular waterskiing lake. The area offers lodging, dining and camping.

CC 56.5 (90.9 km) **PG 217.1** (349.3 km) 8 percent grades approaching **Mount Begbie Summit** (4,042 feet/1,232m). Turn on Lookout Road for parking and picnic tables at trailhead for Mount Begbie Lookout. Built in 1923 as part of a system to detect forest fires, the tower atop Mount Begbie (elev. 4,187 feet/1,276m) is open to visitors daily in summer, 8 A.M. to 5 P.M. Panoramic views of the South Cariboo. Take the short, steep, interpretive trail up to the tower from the rest area (10 to 15 minute walk).

CC 64.3 (103.5 km) **PG 209.3** (336.8 km) **Junction** with **Highway 24** east to Little Fort on Yellowhead Highway 5 (65 miles/105 km). Travelers may use Highway 24 as a scenic paved route connecting Yellowhead Highway 5 and Highway 97. Known as "the Fishing Highway," Highway 24 provides access to resorts and fishing at 4 main lakes—Fawn, Sheridan, Bridge and Lac des Roches—as well as dozens of other area lakes. Cabins, full-service RV parks, restaurants, boat rentals and other facilities are available along Highway 24. **Bridge Lake Provincial Park** (31 miles/50 km east) has 16 campsites, a boat launch and fishing for rainbow trout, lake trout and burbot. Moondance Bay (also on Bridge Lake) offers a beautiful RV park and fishing for kokanee.

CC 67 (107.8 km) **PG 206.6** (332.5 km) Begin 6 percent downgrade northbound.

CC 67.1 (108 km) **PG 206.5** (332.3 km) Entering 100 Mile House (sign) northbound.

CC 68.1 (109.6 km) **PG 205.5** (330.7 km) Highway crosses over CN Railway tracks.

CC 68.6 (110.4 km) **PG 205** (329.9 km) *Begin posted speed zone northbound through 100 Mile House.*

CC 68.9 (110.9 km) **PG 204.7** (329.4 km) Access to Super 8 Motel and Ramada Inn via frontage road.

Highway climbs 6 percent grade southbound with passing lane.

CC 69.5 (111.8 km) **PG 204.1** (328.5 km) Traffic light at Horse Lake Road, which leads east 0.4 mile/0.6 km to the Municipal Campground; no hookups, $15 fee. Continue east on this road for **Horse Lake** (fishing for rainbow trout) and to connect with Highway 24, the "fishing highway" (see description at **Milepost CC 64.3**).

CC 69.8 (112.3 km) **PG 203.8** (328 km)

Services along busy Highway 97 at 100 Mile House include food, gas and lodging. (©Kris Valencia, staff)

Traffic light at 4th Avenue, downtown 100 Mile House; food, gas/diesel, lodging. Visitor Centre to west with giant skis.

100 Mile House

CC 70 (112.6 km) **PG 203.6** (327.6 km) Traffic light at First Avenue downtown; Coach House Square mall. 100 Mile House is located 242 miles/389 km from the international border crossing at Abbotsford-Huntingdon, BC, and Sumas, WA, or about a 5-hour drive. It is a 3½ hour drive to Prince George from 100 Mile House. **Population:** 1,200. **Elevation:** 3,050 feet/930m. **Emergency Services:** Dial 911. **Hospital**, phone 250-395-7600.

Visitor Information: At South Cariboo Visitor Center, located in the log building by 100 Mile House Marsh (a bird sanctuary at the centre of town). Look for the 39-foot-/12-m-long cross-country skis! Write Box 340, 100 Mile House, BC, V0K 2E0; phone 250-395-5353 or toll free 1-877-511-5353; visit www.SouthCaribooTourism.ca.

Visitor services in this bustling community include fast-food outlets (A&W, DQ, Subway, Tim Hortons), restaurants, motels, gas/diesel stations (Chevron, Petro-Canada, Husky), repair services, stores, a post office, 2 golf courses, a theatre, a government liquor store, supermarkets (Save-On-Foods, Safeway), banks and ATMs. Dry camping seasonally at the Municipal Campground on Horse Lake Road for small to mid-size RVs. RV sites in town at 100 Mile Motel & RV Park.

Centennial Park has picnic sites, playground and a scenic walking trail to Bridge Creek Falls, a 10-minute hike. Parking area will accommodate large RVs.

100 Mile House is the service centre for the South Cariboo, an area stretching north from Clinton to 140 Mile House, west to the Fraser River and east to Lac des Roches, with a population of approximately 24,000.

100 Mile House was established as a post house on the Cariboo Waggon Road to the goldfields. In 1930, the Marquess of Exeter established the 15,000-acre Bridge Creek

Ranch here. Today, the 100 Mile House area has 2 lumber mills and an Oriented Strand Board (OSB) plant. It is also the "handcrafted log home capital of North America," with an extensive log home industry. (Inquire at the Visitor Centre about log home sites.)

An infestation of mountain pine beetle in British Columbia's Interior has impacted forests and the timber industry in the province. Mountain pine beetles prefer mature (80 years old or more) lodgepole pine trees. Lodgepole pine forest accounts for 25 percent of the province's forestland (forestland covers two-thirds of the province). The mountain pine beetle epidemic is attributed to a number of factors, including more mature lodgepole pine, successful fire fighting, recent mild winters that have lowered normal mortality rates for beetle larvae, and trees weakened by recent drought stress. Current management emphasizes quickly removing dead trees and harvesting still salvageable timber.

West Access Route Log
(continued)

BC HIGHWAY 97 NORTH

CC 70.3 (113.1 km) **PG 203.3** (327.1 km) Traffic light at Exeter Station Road.

Highway climbs next 1.2 miles/1.9 km northbound. *CAUTION: Watch for deer.*

CC 71.5 (115.1 km) **PG 202.1** (325.2 km) Traffic light at Canim Hendrix Lake Road. Card-lock gas station under construction at this corner in summer 2018.

Highway descends next 1.2 miles/1.9 km southbound.

Junction with road east to **Ruth**, **Canim**, **Mahood** and other lakes; numerous fishing and camping resorts. Mahood Lake, 55 miles/88 km via paved and gravel roads, is located in the southwestern corner of immense Wells Grey Provincial Park. **Mahood Lake Provincial Park** campground offers camping, fishing and swimming; drinking water, playground, short, easy trails to waterfalls at Canim, Mahood and Deception Falls. Well worth the drive. See www.bcparks.com for more information.

Ducks Unlimited nesting area at north-

A 2-lane stretch of BC Highway 97/Cariboo Highway, under cloudy skies, south of Williams Lake. (©Kris Valencia, staff)

west corner of this junction; parking and trails.

CC 76.5 (123.1 km) **PG 197.1** (317.1 km) Turnoff to west for Mile 108 supermarket, Esso gas station with diesel. Once a cattle ranch, 108 Mile Ranch became a recreational community in the 1970s.

CC 76.7 (123.4 km) **PG 196.9** (316.8 km) Paved turnout with litter bins to east.

CC 76.9 (123.8 km) **PG 196.7** (316.6 km) Paved turnout with litter bins to west.

CC 78.5 (126.3 km) **PG 195.1** (313.9 km) **108 Mile Ranch Heritage Site and Rest Area** to west. This is one of the nicest rest areas along this route, with parking and restrooms adjacent the heritage site, which overlooks 108 Mile Lake. The main house/museum and historical buildings are open 10 A.M. to 5 P.M. from Memorial Day to Labour Day. Walking/biking trail around lake.

There are 13 historical buildings here, including structures from the old 108 Mile Ranch and the 105 Mile Roadhouse. Interpretive sign here explains that this site began as a post house on the Cariboo Trail in 1867. During the 1900s, it was both a horse and cattle ranch and later the land was logged during the lumber boom of the 1950s. Visit www.historicalbc.ca/main.html.

CC 82.6 (132.9 km) **PG 191** (307.3 km) **Big Country Campground & RV Park.** 3 miles south of Lac La Hache on Highway 97. Heated pool (seasonal), free showers, store, laundromat, rec room. Extra-long pull-throughs; 15-, 30- and 50-amp service; tent sites; cabins; limited cable TV; WiFi; phone. VISA, MasterCard. www.100milehouse.ca. 250-396-4181. Box 68, Lac La Hache, BC V0K 1T0. [ADVERTISEMENT]

CC 84.8 (136.4 km) **PG 188.8** (303.8 km) Long paved shoulder parking to east with litter bins.

CC 85.7 (137.9 km) **PG 187.9** (302.3 km) **LAC LA HACHE** (pop. 400; elev. 2,749 feet/838m). Also known as the "longest town in the Cariboo," the community of Lac La Hache stretches along some 11 miles of Highway 97. Lac La Hache, the body of water, is one of the most popular recreation

lakes along Highway 97. A beautiful spot. Visitor services here include lodging, Husky gas/diesel station, general store (with liquor store), cafes and lakeside resorts. Fruit stands (in season) along Highway 97.

There are many stories of how the lake got its name, but a local historian says it was named by a French–Canadian *coureur de bois* (voyageur) "because of a small ax he found on its shores." Lac La Hache is French for "Lake of the Ax." **Lac La Hache** has lake char, rainbow trout and kokanee; good fishing in summer, great ice fishing in winter. Community fishing derby in June.

CC 91.7 (147.5 km) **PG 181.9** (292.7 km) **Kokanee Bay Motel and Campground** to west (description follows), pub/restaurant, store and gas station to east.

Kokanee Bay Motel and Campground. Relaxation at its finest right on the lake-shore. Fish for kokanee and char or take a refreshing dip. We have a modern, comfortable motel, cabins. Full trailer hook-ups, grassy tenting area, hot showers, laundromat. Aquabike, boat and canoe rentals. Fishing tackle and ice. Phone 250-396-7345. Fax 250-396-4990. www.kokaneebaycariboo. com. [ADVERTISEMENT]

CC 94.5 (152.1 km) **PG 179.1** (288.2 km) **Lac La Hache Provincial Park:** Turnoff to east for campground, turnoff to west for picnic area. Provincial Park campground has 83 sites, tap water, flush and pit toilets, dump station and hiking trails. Open May 15 to Sept. 30. Sites are $15 per night, there are no hook-ups. Provincial park picnic area has boat launch, swimming, playground and excellent fishing on west side of highway. Self-guiding nature trail. Open May 15–September. Reservations at www.discovercamping.ca.

CC 97.7 (157.2 km) **PG 175.9** (283 km) Turnout to west with litter barrel.

Ribbon-like San Jose River winds through valley to the west of the highway. Canadian artist A.Y. Jackson painted in this valley.

CC 99.8 (160.6 km) **PG 173.8** (279.6 km) 130 Mile Wetlands Conservation Project

(sign). This is an important waterfowl breeding area in Canada. Watch for ducks in roadside ponds. Also good bird watching for bald eagles, osprey, great horned owls, American kestrels and pileated woodpeckers.

CAUTION: Watch for deer on highway, especially at dusk.

CC 100.6 (161.9 km) **PG 173** (278.4 km) Large turnout with litter bins to east.

CC 102.5 (164.9 km) **PG 171.1** (275.3 km) Turnout to west with litter bin and point-of-interest sign commemorating the miners, traders and adventurers who came this way to the Cariboo goldfields in the 1860s.

CC 116.4 (187.3 km) **PG 157.2** (252.9 km) Husky gas station with diesel at **150 MILE HOUSE** (pop. 1,275), which also has groceries, a pub, cafe and restaurant in the historic roadhouse. The town was named because it was 150 miles from Lillooet on the Cariboo Waggon Road. Post office was established in 1871.

CC 117.3 (188.7 km) **PG 156.3** (251.5 km) *(Begin 4-laning road construction northbound to Williams Lake summer 2018; expect continued construction and/or improved highway northbound in 2019).* **Junction** with Likely Road, which leads to Quesnel Lake and Horsefly Lake and to communities of Horsefly (35 miles/56 km) and **LIKELY** (50 miles/80 km); see description following.

Likely, BC. See display ad on page 126.

Known as the **Gold Rush Circle Route** (www.goldrushcircleroute.ca), the paved Likely Road forms a loop between Likely and Horsefly, and is also connected to Barkerville via a gravel road (summer only, can be rough) north from Likely; *see "Highway 26 to Barkerville" on page 126.*

Likely Road accesses several attractions including the 400-foot-deep Bullion Pit, Quesnel Forks and Cedar Point Provincial park. **Quesnel Forks**, located near Likely, was a gold rush town, founded in 1806, and now a historic site; visitors can explore the pioneer buildings and old cemetery. **Cedar Point Provincial Park** on Quesnel Lake is 3.7 miles/6 km from Likely; 40 campsites, picnicking, boat launch, waterskiing, swimming, fishing and outdoor mining museum. **Horsefly Lake Provincial Park** (40 miles/65 km) has a popular 23-site campground, open May 15 to Sept. 15.

CC 120.6 (194 km) **PG 153** (246.2 km) The Chief Will-Yum, gas bar with diesel, RV park to east.

CC 121.3 (195.2 km) **PG 152.3** (245.1 km) Golf course to east.

CC 122.5 (197.1 km) **PG 151.1** (243.1 km) Welcome to Williams Lake (northbound sign); turnout to east with litter bins, recycle bins, toilets, info boards.

CC 123 (197.9 km) **PG 150.6** (242.3 km) Large turnout with litter bins to west.

CC 124.6 (200.5 km) **PG 149** (239.8 km) Turnoff on frontage road for access to Super 8, Best Western and Super Save gas station with diesel.

CC 124.7 (200.7 km) **PG 148.9** (239.6 km) The **Tourism Discovery Center**, on east side of highway; motorists turn left at entrance to Center and drive around the back of the building for parking (will accommodate large RVs). Very nice facility with helpful staff offering visitor information on Williams Lake and Cariboo Chilcotin Coast, a coffee bar, gift shop, restrooms, Cariboo Chilcotin Museum, outdoor picnic area and litter bins. Pet friendly. Open year-round, 9 A.M. to 5 P.M. daily from third weekend in May to Canadian Thanksgiving weekend in October; weekdays only rest of year.

Signal Point Gaming is adjacent to the Discovery Centre. The casino has slot machines, bingo and a restaurant.

CC 126.2 (203.1 km) **PG 147.4** (237.2 km) Traffic light at Oliver Street; Chevron gas station, Denny's, A&W, Tim Hortons. Northbound travelers turn right uphill for continuation of Highway 97 north to Quesnel and Prince George. Go straight ahead on Oliver Street for Williams Lake city centre; supermarkets (Save-On-Foods/Pharmacy, Safeway), liquor store, motels, RCMP, etc.

Junction with BC Highway 20/Chilcotin Highway (description follows). For access to Williams Lake Stampede Campground, follow Highway 20 west to first right turn on Mackenzie Avenue South then follow signs to camping.

The scenic Chilcotin Highway (BC Highway 20) leads 279 miles/450 km west from Williams Lake through cattle range lands of the Fraser Plateau to Bella Coola. Highway 20 is paved and usually in good condition (check with www.drivebc.ca for current highway status). A narrow, 37-mile/60-km stretch of gravel makes a switchback descent from the top of Heckman Pass (elev. 5,000 feet/1,524m) into the Bella Coola Valley; 12 to 18 percent grades (vehicles towing fifth wheelers or travel trailers test your brakes before attempting). Attractions along Highway 20 include Bull Canyon Provincial Recreation Area; fishing and bird watching at Anahim Lake; and Tweedsmuir Provincial Park, home of Hunlen Falls (Canada's second highest waterfall). Bella Coola offers most visitor services and is served by BC Ferries. *NOTE: BC Ferries is launched seasonal direct service between Bella Coola and Port Hardy in 2018, aboard the Northern Sea Wolf. Their summer connector service between Bella Coola, Bella Bella, Shearwater and Ocean Falls continues as well. Details at bcferries.com. See log of Highway 20 at www.themilepost.com/highways/chilcotin-highway-bc-highway-20/.*

Williams Lake

CC 126.2 (203.1 km) **PG 147.4** (237.2 km) Located on the shore of Williams Lake, at the **junction** of Highways 97 and 20. Williams Lake is 74 miles/119 km south of Quesnel; 246 miles/396 km north of Hope; and 298 miles/480 km from the international border at Abbotsford-Huntingdon, BC, and Sumas, WA. **Population:** 12,000. **Elevation:** 1,922 feet/586m. **Emergency Services:** Dial 911. **Police**, phone 250-392-6211. **Hospital**, phone 250-392-4411.

Visitor Information: The Tourism Discovery Center (description follows), is open year-round, 9 A.M. to 5 P.M. daily from third weekend in May to Canadian Thanksgiving weekend in October; weekdays only the rest of year. Or contact Williams Lake Chamber of Commerce, Box 4878, Williams Lake, BC V2G 2V8; email visitors@telus.net; physical address 1660 S. Broadway, Williams Lake, BC V2G

2W4; 1-877-967-5253; website www.williamslakechamber.com or www.tourismwilliamslake.com.

The 13,000-square-foot Tourism Discovery Center, built by 3 local world-renowned log home companies, is home to the Visitor Center; coffee bar/gift store featuring unique local products; pay phones, free internet and restrooms. The Center is located at the south entrance to Williams Lake on Highway 97 and offers pull-through parking for RVs. Maps, tourist guides, interactive display featuring area history and culture, and knowledgeable staff on hand to answer questions. The Museum of the Cariboo Chilcotin is located in the Tourism Discovery Center.

Williams Lake was named for Shuswap Indian Chief Will-Yum. The town grew with the advent of the Pacific Great Eastern Railway (later British Columbia Railway) in 1919, rapidly becoming the major cattle marketing and shipping centre for the Cariboo–Chilcotin.

Williams Lake has complete visitor services, including hotels/motels, gas stations, fast-food outlets and restaurants. Boitanio Mall on Oliver Street offers shopping. The public library has free internet access on their computers. There is a bowling alley on First Avenue and a 4-screen movie theatre on Third Avenue. There are slot machines and bingo at Signal Point Gaming, which is located adjacent to the Discovery Centre just south of Williams Lake on Highway 97. Area recreation includes an 18-hole golf course, a 9-hole golf course and a par-3 golf course as well as a twin sheet arena and pool complex.

Camping at Williams Lake Stampede Campground with tenting area and RV sites (20/30- and 50-amp full service sites); phone 250-398-6718. Follow Highway 20 and take first right turn then follow signs; located at 800 Mackenzie Ave.

The famous **Williams Lake Stampede**, British Columbia's premier rodeo, is held here annually near the July 1st holiday (call the Visitor Centre for exact dates). The 4-day event draws contestants from all over Canada and the United States. The rodeo grounds are located in the city and accessed from Highway 20.

The **Station House Gallery and Gift Shop** is the oldest public building still in use in Williams Lake. Originally a train station, the structure has been repurposed into an art gallery showcasing local, regional and touring artists.

Walk the **River Valley Trail** 6.8 miles/11 km one-way from Williams Lake to the Fraser River. This multi-use path meanders through forest and grassland, offering both river and mountain views. Stop by the Info centre for more details.

At the west end of Williams Lake is **Scout Island Nature Centre**. The island is reached by a causeway, with boardwalks providing access to the marshes. A nature house is open May to August.

Explore **Xats'ull Heritage Village**, a First Nations Heritage site 21.7 miles/35.4 km north of Williams Lake on Highway 97.

West Access Route Log
(continued)

BC HIGHWAY 97 NORTH

CC 126.2 (203.1 km) **PG 147.4** (237.2 km) Traffic light at Oliver Street; Chevron gas station, Denny's, A&W, Tim Hortons. Northbound travelers turn right uphill for continuation of Highway 97 north to Quesnel and Prince George. Go straight ahead on Oliver Street for Williams Lake city centre; supermarkets (Save-On-Foods/Pharmacy, Safeway), liquor store, motels, RCMP, etc.

Junction with BC Highway 20/Chilcotin Highway *(see description at **Milepost CC 126.2**)*. For Williams Lake Stampede Campground, follow Highway 20 to first right turn (Mackenzie Avenue) then follow signs to campground at rodeo grounds.

Begin long uphill grade next 3 miles/4.8 km northbound.

CC 128.6 (206.9 km) **PG 145** (233.3 km) Traffic light at Mackenzie Ave. Welcome to Williams Lake (southbound sign).

Begin 3-mile/4.8-km descent to Williams Lake southbound.

CC 128.7 (207.1 km) **PG 144.9** (233.1 km) Southbound truck brake-check area turn-

Cowboys are a prevalent theme in Williams Lake, which hosts the famous Williams Lake Stampede each year and is also home to the Cariboo Chilcotin Museum.

(©Kris Valencia, staff)

Vendors at the Saturay Farmers Market in Quesnel sell fresh vegetables, fruits, homemade baked goods and more. (©Judy Nadon, staff)

out to west, toilets, litter bins, recycling bins.

CC 130.6 (210.1 km) **PG 143** (230 km) Double-ended turnout to east with litter bin; careful on approach northbound.

CC 132.4 (213 km) **PG 141.2** (227.2 km) Turnoff to Williams Lake airport to east.

CC 134.1 (215.8 km) **PG 139.5** (224.5 km) Race Trac gas and diesel to east, mobile home park with RV sites.

CC 136 (218.8 km) **PG 137.6** (221.4 km) Turnout with litter bin to west.

CC 137.3 (221 km) **PG 136.3** (219.3 km) Bull Mountain Road west to hiking trails.

CC 139.8 (225 km) **PG 133.8** (215.3 km) Whispering Willows Campsite.

CC 140 (225.3 km) **PG 133.6** (215 km) Deep Creek Services to west; gas, diesel.

CC 142.7 (229.6 km) **PG 130.9** (210.6 km) Large double-ended turnout to west is a rest area with toilets and litter bins.

CAUTION: Watch for deer.

CC 150.3 (241.8 km) **PG 123.3** (198.4 km) McLeese Lake recreation centre.

CC 152.5 (245.4 km) **PG 121.1** (194.9 km) *Slow for posted speed zone northbound through McLeese Lake.*

CC 152.8 (245.9 km) **PG 120.8** (194.4 km) **McLEESE LAKE** (pop. 300), a small community with general store, post office, liquor store and motels on McLeese Lake. Cafe, pub and restaurants. Farmers Market held on Sundays in summer.

McLeese Lake was named for a Fraser River steamboat skipper. **McLeese Lake**, rainbow trout to 2 lbs., troll using a flasher, worms or flatfish lure.

CC 153.1 (246.4 km) **PG 120.5** (193.9 km) **Junction** with road to Beaver Lake and to community of **LIKELY**, 53 miles/85 km. Also access to Quesnel Forks, Bullion Pit and Cedar Point Provincial Park on Quesnel Lake (camping, fishing) on the Gold Rush Circle Route; see also **Milepost CC 117.3**.

CC 153.4 (246.2 km) **PG 120.2** (193.4 km) McLeese Lake rest area to west is a small double-ended parking area with picnic tables, litter bins and restrooms overlooking McLeese Lake. Interpretive sign about pine

beetle infestation in British Columbia.

CC 155.3 (249.9 km) **PG 118.3** (190.4 km) Welcome to McLeese Lake southbound sign.

CC 157.8 (253.9 km) **PG 115.8** (186.3 km) Large double-ended turnout with litter bin to west overlooking Fraser River. Plaque about paddle-wheelers here reads:

"Down-river lay the perilous and unnavigable canyon. Up-river the Fraser was swift and strong, but sternwheelers could travel for 400 miles from Soda Creek. Men and supplies embarked here in the 1860s for the fabulous Cariboo goldfields. Later, as the GTP Railway was forged across the Province, 9 paddlewheelers formed a life-line to the north."

CC 158.6 (255.2 km) **PG 115** (185.1 km) Macallison railroad overpass.

CC 160.7 (258.5 km) **PG 112.9** (181.7 km) **Cariboo Wood Shop** to west (description follows).

Cariboo Wood Shop, a "must stop" gift shop specializing in our own quality furniture and accessories and Canadian-made gifts, local pottery and candles. And best of all: Our 20 flavours of fresh fudge. Ask for a free taste. Cappuccino, lattes and coffees, too. Easy RV access, drive-through loop. Open 7 days a week, 9 A.M. to 5 P.M. Groups welcome. www.cariboowoodshop.com. 250-747-8397. [ADVERTISEMENT]

CC 164 (263.9 km) **PG 109.6** (176.3 km) Turnout with litter bins to east.

CC 166.3 (267.6 km) **PG 107.3** (172.6 km) Watch for basalt columns to east of highway that create a formation known as the Devil's Palisades. Cliff swallows nest in the columns. Viewable northbound (south facing columns).

CC 167.1 (269 km) **PG 106.5** (171.4 km) Stone cairn at double-ended turnout with litter bins to west commemorates **Fort Alexandria**. Built in 1821, it was the last North West Co. fur-trading post established west of the Rockies. The actual site of the fort is across the river. Cairn also marks the approximate farthest point reached by Alexander Mackenzie in his descent of the Fraser in 1793.

CC 177.5 (285.6 km) **PG 96.1** (154.6 km) Rest area to west with toilets, picnic tables, litter bins and interpretive signs. Cariboo Place Campsite to east.

CC 186.2 (3299.6 km) **PG 87.4** (140.6 km) Kersley (unincorporated); general store, the Alamo motel, restaurant, RV park; gas/diesel, Fire Department.

CC 188.6 (303.5 km) **PG 85** (136.7 km) Double-ended turnout with litter bin to east.

CC 191.5 (308.2 km) **PG 80.3** (129.2 km) Begin 4-lane highway northbound to Quesnel.

CC 196 (315.4 km) **PG 77.6** (124.9 km) Traffic light. Sandman Hotel, Denny's, Walmart and gas stations (Petro-Canada, Mohawk), car wash, Starbucks. Food (A&W, Tim Hortons), gas, diesel, lodging and other South Quesnel services along highway next 1.5 miles/2.4 km northbound.

CC 196.4 (316 km) **PG 77.2** (124.2 km) Stoplight. Canadian Tire and Staples to east.

CC 196.7 (316.5 km) **PG 76.9** (123.7 km) Shell gas/diesel station, motel, supermarket via frontage road.

CC 197.3 (317.5 km) **PG 76.3** (122.8 km) Super 8 Motel and restaurant to east on Valhalla Road.

Highway descends northbound to Quesnel River. *CAUTION: Watch for deer.*

CC 198.2 (318.9 km) **PG 75.4** (121.3 km) North Star Road cloverleaf.

CC 198.8 (319.9 km) **PG 74.8** (120.4 km) Quesnel River bridge.

CC 199.4 (320.8 km) **PG 74.2** (119.4 km) Quesnel Visitor Information Center and Quesnel & District Museum and Archives on west side of highway in LeBourdais Park. The information centre is open year-round. Quesnel Museum has an excellent collection of area artifacts and is considered one of the top museums in the province.

Northbound travelers may continue straight ahead for Quesnel city centre via Carson Avenue (see map). Highway 97 North becomes Front Street at Heritage Corner. Access to shopping and services from Highway 97.

Quesnel

CC 199.6 (321.2 km) **PG 74** (119 km) Highway 97/Cariboo Highway winds through Quesnel as Carson Avenue and Front Street. **Population:** 10,561. **Elevation:** 1,555 feet/474m. **Emergency Services:** Dial 911. **RCMP**, phone 250-992-9211. **Hospital**, G.R. Baker Memorial Hospital, 543 Front St., phone 250-985-5600.

Visitor Information: At Quesnel Museum and Visitor Center on the west side of Highway 97 in LeBourdais Park. Or write Quesnel Visitor Center, 703 Carson Ave., Quesnel, BC V2J 2B6; phone 250-992-8716, toll free 1-800-992-4922. For information on BC's Central Region, contact the Cariboo Chilcotin Coast, 204-350 Barnard St., Williams Lake, BC V2G 4T9; 1-800-663-5885.

Visitor services include hotels/motels, several B&Bs, campgrounds and numerous restaurants offering everything from fast food to fine dining. There are gas stations (with diesel and propane), 2 shopping malls, 5 banks, a credit union, laundromats and car washes. Golf and a recreation centre with pool are available.

Quesnel (kwe NEL) is located at the confluence of the Fraser and Quesnel rivers. It began as a supply town for miners during

Quesnel

To Prince George
97
Bowron Ave
Quesnel River
To Williams Lake
97
Hospital
Reid St.
McLean St.
Kinchant St.
Callanan St.
St. Laurent Ave
Barlow Ave
Carson Ave
LeBourdais Park
Front St. (Hwy 97)
Fraser River
Visitor Info Centre and Museum
RCMP
Pedestrian Bridge

Barkerville is a not-to-be-missed attraction. The 51-mile drive to the historical park also takes you through the charming town of Wells. (©Judy Nadon, staff)

the Cariboo gold rush in the 1860s. The city was named after the Quesnel River, which was named by the explorer, Simon Fraser, after his clerk Jules Maurice Quesnel, a member of Simon Fraser's 1808 expedition down the Fraser River.

Explorer Alexander Mackenzie also left his mark here. Mackenzie, the first white man to cross the North American continent, left Lake Athabaska in 1793 to find a trade route to the Pacific. His journey took 72 days through 1,200 miles/2,000 km of unmapped territory. The 260-mile/420-km trail blazed by explorer Alexander Mackenzie from Quesnel has been retraced and restored in a joint federal, provincial and regional project as the Nuxalk–Carrier Route. The land trail terminates near Burnt Creek bridge on the Chilcotin Highway.

Today, forestry is the dominant economic force in Quesnel, with 2 pulp mills, a plywood plant, sawmills, planer mills and an MDF plant. Stop by the Forestry Industry Observatory on Highway 97 at the north end of town.

Quesnel Farmers Markets. Runs Saturdays, May to October, on the corner of Kinchant and Carson. 40+ vendors selling the freshest veggies, fruits, flowers, bedding plants, woodwork, herbs and much more. Homemade: everything made, baked or grown in the Cariboo. Stop by between 8:30 A.M. and 1 P.M. every Saturday. [ADVERTISEMENT]

Stop and take a walk along Quesnel's scenic **Riverfront Park** trail system, visible from Highway 97 (Front Street) in downtown Quesnel. **Heritage Corner**, at Carson and Front streets near the Quesnel footbridge, displays riveted boilers and other iron parts from the upper Fraser River's first riverboat. There is also a replica of a Cornish water wheel and a cairn commemorating the Collins Overland Telegraph. The first telegraph link in British Columbia, it connected New Westminster to Quesnel in 1865, to Barkerville in 1868 and to Yukon in 1907.

There are some interesting hoodoo formations and scenic canyon views at nearby **Pinnacles Provincial Park**, 4.4 miles/7 km west of Quesnel. It is an easy ½ mile (¾ km) walk on a well-maintained trail from the parking lot out to the viewpoint.

Billy Barker Days, a 4-day event held the third full weekend in July, commemo-rates the discovery of gold at Barkerville in 1862. Held in conjunction with the Quesnel Rodeo, Billy Barker Days is the third largest outdoor family festival in the province.

A worthwhile side trip is **Highway 26**, which intersects Highway 97 just north of town and provides access to **Barkerville Historic Town** (allow one hour for drive). A reconstructed and restored Cariboo gold rush town, Barkerville offers guided tours, stage coach rides, live theatre and the opportunity to experience an 1800s gold rush town. On the way to Barkerville, stop at Cottonwood House Historic Site. *See "Highway 26 to Barkerville" feature on page 126 for detailed log of this side trip.*

West Access Route Log
(continued)

BC HIGHWAY 97 NORTH
CC 199.8 (321.5 km) **PG 73.8** (118.8 km) Stoplight at Carson Avenue and Highway 97/Front Street; Heritage Corner.

Southbound travelers can continue straight ahead for Highway 97 South Bypass via Front Street (follow signs) or turn on Carson Avenue and drive through downtown.

CC 202 (325 km) **PG 71.6** (115.2 km) Signed turnoff for Quesnel's Forestry Industry Observatory.

CC 202.8 (326.3 km) **PG 70.8** (113.9 km) Large paved turnout to east. World's Largest Gold Pan on display here.

CC 202.9 (326.5 km) **PG 70.7** (113.8 km) Quesnel airport access and turnoff for Highway 26 to Cottonwood House Historic Site, Wells and **Barkerville Historic Town**, a major attraction.

Junction with Highway 26 to Barkerville. See "Highway 26 to Barkerville" log on page 126.

Begin a series of 6 and 7 percent grades northbound on Highway 97; moderate curves. Intermittent but frequent passing lanes with stretches of improved 4-lane highway to Prince George. *CAUTION: Watch for deer.*

CC 207 (333.1 km) **PG 66.6** (107.2 km) Turnoff to west for paved side road which leads to **10 Mile Lake Provincial Park** (0.6 mile/1 km); picnicking, camping, swimming, fishing.

CC 211 (339.5 km) **PG 62.6** (100.7 km) Cottonwood River bridge.

CC 211.2 (339.9 km) **PG 62.4** (100.4 km) Turnout with litter bin to east.

CC 212.5 (342 km) **PG 61.1** (98.3 km) Bello's railroad overpass (clearance 16.3 feet/4.96m). *Slow for curve north of overpass.*

CC 215.4 (346.6 km) **PG 58.2** (93.6 km) Short access road leads west to rest area by small lake; toilets, tables, litter bins.

CC 222.2 (357.5 km) **PG 51.4** (82.7 km) Cinema 2nd Hand; general store, groceries, fireworks, gifts and souvenirs.

CC 232.3 (373.8 km) **PG 41.3** (66.5 km) Shaded turnout with litter bin to east.

CC 237 (381.3 km) **PG 36.6** (58.9 km) *Slow for posted speed zone northbound through* **HIXON** (pop. about 500), a pleasant community on Hixon Creek with grocery store, take-out food, gas/diesel, lodging and camping; liquor outlet; community hall and post office. **Canyon Creek Campground & RV Park** is just north of here on Highway 97. Hixon is the Cariboo's most northerly community had extensive placer mining began here in the early 1900s.

CC 237.1 (381.5 km) **PG 36.5** (58.7 km) Canyon Creek bridge.

CC 237.4 (382 km) **PG 36.2** (58.2 km) **Canyon Creek Campground & RV Park** to west is a scenic, shady spot with all campground services available including large pull-through sites, full hookups, free showers, WiFi. Big rigs welcome.

Canyon Creek Campground & RV Park. See display ad on page 130.

CC 237.6 (382.4 km) **PG 36** (57.9 km) Hixon Creek bridge.

Major road construction and 4-laning was under way the next 17 miles/27 km northbound in summer 2018. Expect continued construction and/or improved highway in 2019.

CC 242.9 (390.8 km) **PG 30.7** (49.4 km) Woodpecker rest area downhill to west with toilets, tables, litter bins.

CC 249.8 (402 km) **PG 23.8** (38.3 km)

Highway 26 to Barkerville

This 51-mile/81-km paved road leads to Barkerville Historic Town in the Cariboo gold fields. Highway 26 follows the route of the original Cariboo Waggon Road. It is winding and hilly. Watch for deer. Gas is available in Wells.

Distance from Highway 97 junction (J) is shown.

J 0 Junction with Highway 97 at Milepost CC 202.9, just north of Quesnel. Turn east on Highway 26 for Barkerville. Improved road next 10.5 miles/17 km.

J 0.9 (1.4 km) Husky gas station, coffee shop, store to north.

J 16.4 (26.4 km) **Historic Cottonwood House** to south is a roadhouse complex built in 1864 to accommodate miners and stagecoach passengers on the Cariboo Waggon Road. Museum, camping, gift shop and restaurant. Open May to August daily 10 A.M. to 5 P.M.

J 26.4 (42.5 km) Robbers Roost gravel turnout to north with litter bins.

J 27.1 (43.6 km) Double-ended turnout with litter bins and historical stop of interest sign for **Blessing's Grave**. Charles Morgan Blessing was murdered in 1866 while on his way to Barkerville. His killer, James Barry, was caught when he gave Blessing's keepsake gold nugget stickpin, in the shape of a skull, to a Barkerville dance-hall girl. James Barry was the only white man hanged on Williams Creek during the gold rush.

J 38.7 (62.3 km) **Junction** with Stanley Road (1.9-mile/3-km loop) to gold-rush ghost towns of Stanley and Van Winkle.

J 40.2 (64.7 km) Devil's Canyon paved turnout to south. Begin 8 percent downgrade and avalanche zone, with no stopping for 2 km in winter.

J 44.9 (72.2 km) Double-ended paved turnout to south.

J 45.2 (72.7 km) Jack of Clubs rest area on peninsula to south; picnic tables, information signs, toilets, litter bins and boat launch. **Jack of Clubs Lake**; fishing for rainbow and lake trout and Dolly Varden.

J 46.1 (74.2 km) Double-ended lakeshore turnout with parking for Wells Visitor Centre; litter bins.

J 46.6 (75 km) Willow River bridge.

J 46.8 (75.3 km) **WELLS** (pop. 235); food, gas, lodging and camping available. Wells was built in the 1930s when the Cariboo Gold Quartz Mine, promoted and developed by Fred Wells, brought hundreds of workers to this valley. The mine closed in 1967, but the town has continued as a service centre and attraction for tourists, with its picturesque old homes and structures. Food, gas, lodging and camping and available. **Visitor Information:** Visitor Centre at west edge of town; phone 1-877-451-9355 or visit www.wellsbc.com, www.lovewellsbc.com.

District of Wells. See display ad this page.

J 47 (75.6 km) Cariboo Joy RV Park; full hookups.

J 48.6 (78.2 km) Turnout to north with litter bins and interpretive signs. **Lowhee**

(Barkerville) Campground to south; 87 sites, full hookup and electric only sites, showers, flush toilets and a playground.

J 49.8 (80.1 km) Turnout with dump station and information signs.

J 50 (80.5 km) Bowron Lake Road (gravel) leads north 0.6 mile/1 km to Forest Rose Campground and 17 miles/28 km to **Bowron Lake Provincial Park**, noted for its 72-mile/116-km canoe circuit. Forest Rose (Barkerville) Campground has 54 campsites (some pull-through), showers, flush toilets and powered sites. Bowron Lake Provincial Park: 25 sites, water, toilets, firewood, boat launch, swimming, fishing, hiking.

J 50.9 (81.9 km) Turnoff for Government Hill (Barkerville) Campground, within walking distance of the park; 23 sites (not suitable for large RVs), pit toilets, fire rings, picnic tables.

J 51 (82.1 km) Parking for cars and RVs in front of entrance to **Barkerville National Historic Site**. An admission fee is charged during summer season. You can visit Barkerville year-round, although it is best to visit between mid-May and September, when all exhibits are open and shows are held multiple times daily. **Visitor Information:** At the Reception Centre; phone toll-free 1-888-994-3332; www.barkerville.ca.

Breakfast, lunch, dinner and snacks are available at Barkerville bakeries, saloons and restaurants, and there are places to buy a latte or ice cream cone. Lodging in the park is at the St. George Hotel and at Kelly and King House bed-and-breakfasts. Camping nearby at Lowhee, Forest Rose and Government Hill campgrounds. For information or reservations, phone 1-888-994-3332, ext. 99; www.barkervillecampgrounds.ca; barkerville@barkerville.ca.

Barkerville Gold Rush Town & Park. See display ad on this page.

Barkerville was named for miner Billy Barker, who struck gold on Williams Creek. The resulting gold rush in 1862 created Barkerville. More than 130 buildings have been restored or recreated so that visitors may relive the excitement of a 19th-century gold rush town in an authentic setting. Dining, entertainment, lodging. Live musical theatre is presented daily in summer by the Theatre Royal. Costumed interpreters conduct walking tours and provide award-winning educational programming. *NOTE: No pets allowed in Barkerville with the exception of service dogs; please call 1-888-994-3332 to inquire about kennel availability. CAUTION: Temperatures can soar here in summer; do not leave pets unattended in cars unless you can be sure cool temperatures will prevail for the length of your visit.*

Travelers may continue south from Barkerville to Likely via a summer-only gravel road (inquire at Barkerville about current road conditions) on the Gold Rush Circle Route (www.goldrushcircleroute.ca), rejoining Highway 97 either at 150 Mile House (**CC Milepost 117.3**) via Likely Road or at McLeese Lake (**Milepost CC 153.1**) via Beaver Lake Road.

Return to Milepost CC 202.9
West Access Route

Stoner railroad overpass.

CC 253 (407.2 km) **PG 20.6** (33.2 km) Stone Creek bridge.

CC 253.2 (407.5 km) **PG 20.4** (32.8 km) Stone Creek RV Park.

CC 254.7 (409.9 km) **PG 18.9** (30.4 km) *Slow for curve under railroad overpass.*

CC 262.6 (422.6 km) **PG 11.4** (18.3 km) **Mama Yeh RV Park** offers huge sites, full hookups and WiFi.

Mama Yeh RV Park. See display ad on page 129.

CC 263.7 (424.4 km) **PG 9.9** (16 km) **Bee Lazee RV Park, Campground** to east (description follows).

Bee Lazee RV Park, Campground. Welcome to our lovely country setting, just minutes from Prince George. Long pull-thrus, full-service hookups, free satellite TV/WiFi. Large, clean, heated washrooms and free hot showers. Laundry. Heated pool. Tent sites. Coin RV/Car wash. Honey sales! Good Sam. Rates $25–$32. Toll-free 1-866-963-7263. Email: drone@pgon line.com. [ADVERTISEMENT]

CC 266.4 (428.6 km) **PG 7.2** (11.6 km) **"Y" junction** with bypass route to Yellowhead 16 East to Jasper and Edmonton *(see Milepost E 448.1 on page 255 in the* YELLOWHEAD HIGHWAY *section)*. Stay on Highway 97 North for Prince George and for Yellowhead Highway west to Prince Rupert.

CC 268.6 (432.2 km) **PG 5** (8 km) **Northern Experience RV Park** to west (description follows).

Northern Experience RV Park. We invite you to stay with us at our full-service RV park. Conveniently located 6 minutes from major shopping, our quiet country location provides big rig pull-throughs, 24-hour washrooms, coin-operated laundry and free WiFi. Your northern experience is our business! Phone 250-963-7577. Email: cdavis@northernexperiencerv.com. Web: www.northernexperiencerv.com. [ADVERTISEMENT]

CC 269.3 (433.3 km) **PG 4.3** (6.9 km) Stoplight at Sintich Road. Shell gas/diesel station to west. Turnoff to east for Prince George airport (3 miles/4.8 km).

CC 269.8 (434.2 km) **PG 3.8** (6.1 km) **Sintich RV Park** entrance to west via Boundary Road.

Sintich RV Park. See display ad page 131.

CC 271.4 (436.7 km) **PG 2.2** (3.5 km) Pacific Street. Husky Travel Centre to east; 24-hour gas/diesel (self-serve, cardlock), food, store, restaurant.

CC 271.6 (437 km) **PG 2** (3.2 km) Stoplight at Terminal Blvd; Shell and Super Save Gas to east; gas/diesel, convenience store, dump station.

CC 272.2 (438 km) **PG 1.1** (1.8 km) Stoplight at Railway Avenue; Co-op commercial cardlock gas station to west.

CC 272.7 (438.8 km) **PG 0.9** (1.4 km) Mid-span of Fraser River Bridge.

CC 273 (439.3 km) **PG 0.6** (1 km) Turn offs at north end of bridge for Prince George city centre via Queensway (southbound U-turn exit for Highway 97).

Northbound travelers continue straight

Highway 97 offers easy access to downtown Prince George services and attractions. (©Kris Valencia, staff)

ahead on Highway 97 North for Highway 16 West entrance to city.

CC 273.2 (439.6 km) **PG 0.4** (0.6 km) Northbound-only access to motel, restaurants and Esso station.

CC 273.4 (439.9 km) **PG 0.2** (0.3 km) Prestige Treasure Cove Hotel and Casino at the southwest corner of the Highways 16 and 97 junction, with access from both highways. RV parking available. Casino is open Sunday–Thursday 9 A.M. to 2 A.M., Friday–Saturday to 4 A.M.

CC 273.6 (440.2 km) **PG 0 Junction** of Highway 97 with Yellowhead 16 West to Prince Rupert and Yellowhead Highway 16 East/20th Avenue through downtown Prince George and to Jasper, Alberta.

Prince George services—food, gas, lodging, shopping, etc.—are located along 20th Avenue in downtown Prince George; along Trans-Canada Highway 16 West; and on frontage roads along Highway 97 the next 2 miles northbound. (*See continuation of Highway 97 North log beginning on page 133. See map of Prince George on page 132.*)

Look for "Mr. P.G." at this intersection. The 26-foot/8-metre-high statue has been a symbol of the forest industry to Prince George since it was constructed in 1960.

If you are headed west on Yellowhead Highway 16 for Prince Rupert (port-of-call for Alaska state ferries) or east for Edmonton, Alberta, turn to **Milepost PG 0** on page 255 in the YELLOWHEAD HIGHWAY 16 section for log.

Prince George

CC 273.6 (440.2 km) **PG 0 DC 245.2** (394.5 km) Located at the confluence of the Nechako and Fraser rivers, near the geographical centre of the province. **Population:** 74,003, trading area 313,556. **Emergency Services:** Dial 911. **RCMP,** phone 250-561-3300. **Fire Dept.,** phone 250-561-7664. **Poison Control Centre,** phone 1-800-567-8911. **Hospital,** University Hospital of

Northern B.C., phone 250-565-2000.

Visitor Information: The Tourism Prince George Visitor Information Center is located on the edge of downtown at 101–1300 First Ave. *(see map page 132)*. The center offers visitor information and showcases local artisans' work, loans bicycles and fishing equipment at no charge, and has a gift shop. A variety of services are available including reservations for accommodations and BC Ferries. Free WiFi and guest lounge area with computers. Phone 250-562-3700 or toll-free 1-800-668-7646; fax 250-564-9807; or visit www.tourismpg.com.

Elevation: 1,886 feet/575m. **Climate:** The inland location is tempered by the protection of mountains. The average annual frost-free period is 85 days, with 1,793 hours of bright sunshine. Dry in summer; chinooks off and on during winter which, accompanied by a western flow of air, break up the cold weather. Average summer highs 68°F/20°C, lows to 44°F/7°C. Average winter highs 38°F/3°C, lows –12°F/11°C. **Radio:** 88.7-FM CFUR, 91.5-FM CBC, 93.1-FM CFIS, 94.3-FM The Goat, 97.3-FM The Wolf, 99.3-FM The Drive, 101.3-FM The River. **Television:** 36 channels via cable. **Newspaper:** *The Citizen* (daily except Sunday and Monday).

Prince George is British Columbia's 2nd largest city (by area) and a hub for trade and travel routes in the region. Prince George is located at the junction of Yellowhead Highway 16—linking Prince Rupert on the west coast with the Interior of Canada—and Highway 97, which runs south to Vancouver and north to Dawson Creek.

In the early 1800s, Simon Fraser of the North West Trading Co. erected a post here that he named Fort George in honour of the reigning English monarch. In 1906, survey parties for the transcontinental Grand Trunk Pacific Railway (later Canadian National Railways) passed through the area, and, with the building of the railroad, a great land boom took place. The city was incorporated in 1915 under the name Prince George.

Prince George has emerged as the centre of business, education, health and culture for Northern B.C. The Prince George Forest Region is the largest in the province. The lumber industry, oil refining, mining *(Continues on page 132)*

Prince George

Welcome to Prince George, BC's northern capital.
Our lively and welcoming city offers all the amenities of a
large urban centre while being surrounded by easily accessible
nature. Take some time in Prince George to relax and prepare
for the remainder of your journey while learning what makes us
unique and why 74,000 people choose to call this place home.

Immerse yourself in the Prince George experience and give
yourself time in the city by staying at any one of our varied
accommodations. Whether you're seeking a serene campsite,
a bed and breakfast with attentive hosts, familiar rooms and
service at large hotel chains, or a unique cottage, the lodging
options in Prince George are sure to make you feel welcome.

When you arrive in Prince George, make a point of stopping
in at the Visitor Centre located at 1300 1st Avenue. The helpful
staff will make suggestions that will allow you to experience
our city in the way that suits you best. The Visitor Centre is also
stocked with information about other northern BC communities
and maps to guide the remainder of your journey.

The Visitor Centre loans out free cruiser-style bikes and fishing
equipment including rods, basic tackle, ice augers, rod holders,
and life jackets. Prince George has a few lakes within city limits
that are easy to get to, stocked with fish, and have docks to
cast your line from.

PRINCE GEORGE
British Columbia - Canada

www.TourismPG.com

Our history is a history of people in nature. We invite you to discover our unique past and how it shaped the Prince George area into the thriving and creative place that it is today. There are four key cultural attractions to explore in the Prince George area: The Exploration Place Science Centre and Museum: home to an extensive array of local knowledge, reptiles, travelling exhibits, and an award winning permanent exhibit about the Lheidli T'enneh First Nation; Central BC Railway and Forestry Museum: an expansive museum filled with relics from the early days of forestry and railway; Huble Homestead Historic Site: a living historic site on the shores of the Fraser River that includes a general store, the Huble House, First Nations' fishing camp, and more; and Two Rivers Gallery: the hub of art and creativity in northern BC, Two Rivers Gallery has two galleries, a beautiful gift shop, and a MakerLab where you're encouraged to create your own art.

CANYON CREEK CAMPGROUND & RV PARK

BC's hidden secret
Reservations recommended

- Large Pull Through Sites
- Full Amenities
- Big Rigs Welcome

TOURISM BRITISH COLUMBIA
CANADA
Approved Accommodation

P.O. Box 390 - 39035 Highway 97 South
HIXON, BRITISH COLUMBIA, CANADA
Ph: 250-998-4384
www.CanyonCreekCampground.com
rvpark@canyoncreekcampground.com

Prince George is surrounded by beautiful nature just waiting to be explored by you! We have hundreds of kilometres of trails to wander that are available to people with all types of abilities. From the accessible boardwalk at Ancient Forest/Chun T'oh Whudujut Provincial Park east of Prince George to meandering trails along the Nechako and Fraser Rivers to challenging hikes into the surrounding alpine, we have just what you're looking for. Don't want to walk the trails? The Prince George Visitor Centre has cruiser-style bikes that are suitable for pedalling around downtown or taking along some paved trails. Stop by the Visitor Centre and borrow your bike for free!

www.TourismPG.com

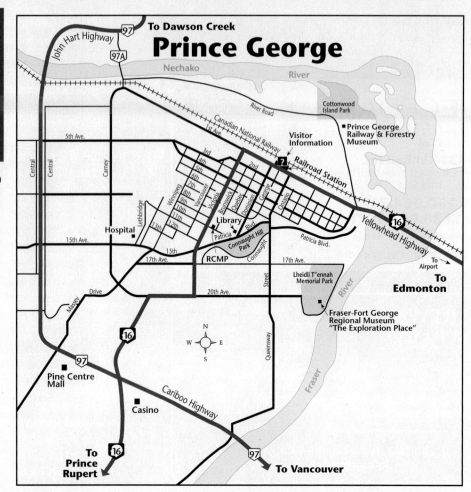

To Dawson Creek
Prince George

(Continued from page 127)
and heavy construction are the major area industries in the area. The University of Northern British Columbia, located at the top of Cranbrook Hill, opened here in the fall of 1994. It was at that time the first new university to be built in Canada in more than 25 years. It was ranked as Canada's second best small university in 2017 by *Mclean's Magazine*.

The Nechako and Fraser rivers converge here, providing a landscape that offers an array of recreation and outdoor experiences mentioned under "attractions."

Agriculture in central British Columbia is primarily a forage-livestock business, for which the climate and soils are well suited. Dairying and beef are the major livestock enterprises, with minor production in sheep, bison and poultry.

PRINCE GEORGE AREA ADVERTISERS

Bee Lazee RV Park,
  Campground .... Ph. 1-866-963-7263
Blue Cedars Campground .... Ph. 250-964-7272
Canada's Best Value Inn .... Ph. 1-800-663-3290
Canyon Creek Campground &
  RV Park .... Ph. 250-998-4384
Hartway RV Park .... Ph. 1-866-962-8848
Mama Yeh RV Park .... Ph. 1-866-961-6828
Northland RV Park .... Ph. 250-962-5010
Northern Experience RV Park ..... Ph. 250-963-7577
Salmon Valley Campground ...... Ph. 1-877-971-2224
Sintich RV Park .... Ph. 1-877-791-1152
Tourism Prince George .... Ph. 1-800-668-7646

Lodging & Services

Prince George has all visitor services with more than 30 hotels/motels, including major chains like **Canada's Best Value Inn** (phone 250-563-3671), Super 8, Ramada Plaza, Sandman, Sheraton, Coast Inn and Courtyard by Marriott; a dozen bed and breakfasts; gas stations and "big box" stores; and 200 restaurants including major chain fast-food outlets and many local restaurants in the downtown area.

Camping

The Prince George area is a great stop for campers, with RV parks located on Highways 97 and 16.

South of the city on Highway 97 are: **Sintich RV Park** (3.8 miles/6.1 km), **Northern Experience RV Park** (5 miles/8 km), **Bee Lazee RV Park** (10 miles/16 km), **MamaYeh RV Park** (11 miles/17.7 km) and **Canyon Creek Campground & RV Park** (36 miles/58 km south in Hixon).

Just north of the city on Highway 97/ Hart Highway are **Hartway RV Park** (8 miles/12.9 km), **Northland RV Park** (11.5 miles/18.5 km) and Salmon Valley Campground (17.4 miles/28 km).

West of the city via Yellowhead Highway 16 are **Blue Cedars Campground** (3.8 miles/6.1 km) on Kimball Road (turn north on the access road behind the Art Knapp store, a BC garden and home decor chain), and West Lake Campground (5.7 miles/9.2 km), watch for blue highway signs at Blackwater Road turnoff.

Transportation

Air: Prince George airport is 6.8 miles/11 km southeast of the city centre, serviced by Air Canada Regional, Central Mountain Air, Pacific Coastal Airlines and West Jet. Airport shuttle, phone 250-563-2220. Flightlink service daily from Greyhound; phone 250-564-5454.

Taxi: Emerald Taxi (250-563-3333) and Prince George Taxi (250-564-4444).

Railroad: VIA Rail's "Skeena" service connects Prince George with Prince Rupert and Jasper, AB. For schedules see website at www.viarail.ca. Train station is located at 1300 1st Ave., in the same building as the Prince George Visitor Centre.

Bus: BC Bus North provides transportation between Prince George and Prince Rupert, Valemount and Fort St. John; phone 1-844-564-7494, or visit bcbus.ca. City bus service by BC Transit, phone 250-563-0011, www.bctransit.com. Greyhound Canada ended all service in British Columbia (and also Alberta, Saskatchewan and Manitoba) at the end of October 2018.

Attractions

Two Rivers Gallery is a public gallery featuring exhibitions by local, regional and national artists. There is a particularly nice gift shop with unique, handmade arts and crafts. Located downtown in the Civic Centre Plaza at 725 Canada Games Way. Hours are 10 A.M. to 5 P.M. every day but Thursday; 10 A.M. to 9 P.M. Thursday. An admission fee is charged to visit the galleries (free on Thursdays). Phone 250-614-7800; www.tworiversgallery.ca.

The Exploration Place at 333 Becott Place, just off 20th Avenue in Lheidli T'enneh Memorial Park. Open 10 A.M. to 5 P.M. daily year-round. Galleries include Hands On Science, Demonstrations, Paleontology, Local History, a Lheidli T'enneh exhibit and Traveling Exhibitions. A good place to learn about the Northern Interior of British Columbia. Friendly staff, atrium with food service and gift shop. Phone 1-866-562-1612; www.theexplorationplace.com. Admission is charged.

The Railway and Forestry Museum, is located at 850 River Rd., next to Cottonwood Island Nature Park on the Nechako River. The museum features a dozen original railway buildings and 50 pieces of rolling stock, including 5 locomotives, a 1903 snow plow, a 1913 100-ton steam wrecking crane and a 90-foot 100-ton turntable. Items from 8 past and present railway companies are displayed. There is also a small collection of forestry, mining and agricultural machinery.

The museum is open year-round. Summer hours are 10 A.M. to 5 P.M. daily from the Victoria Day weekend in May to Labour Day weekend (May 19 to Sept. 2, 2019). Fall/winter/spring hours are 11 A.M. to 4 P.M. Wednesday to Sunday, until May 18, 2019, and then from Sept. 3, 2019 to May 18, 2020. Admission fee is charged. Phone 250-563-7351 for more information.

Fort George Park was renamed **Lheidli T'enneh Memorial Park** in 2015; it is on the original village site of the local First Nations people. The park has miles of paved walking trails along the Fraser and Nechako rivers; picnic tables, barbecue facilities; playgrounds and a spray park. A cairn here commemorates Sir Alexander Mackenzie. The park is also home to the Lheidli T'enneh cemetery. Free parking on 17th Avenue on the north side of the park, or at the Exploration Place (with room for RVs). *NOTE: This is a "No Pet Park"; pets on leash are permitted* along the Heritage River Trail only. The park is open daily year-round. Wheelchair accessible. Phone 250-562-1612.

Connaught Hill Park offers colourful flower gardens and views (somewhat obscured by trees) of the city and Fraser River Bridge. Follow Connaught Drive to the park. No parking for big rigs at this park.

Northern Lights Estate Winery is one of British Columbia's newest wineries and the most northerly in the province. Located on PG Pulpmill Road, across the Nechako River from the Heritage River Trail. Tours, tastings, food service and picnics available. Phone 250-564-1112 for information.

City Parks. There are 120 parks and 65 playgrounds, 7 nature parks, 7 athletic parks, 97 sports fields, 30 tennis courts (many of them lighted) and 66 miles/106 km of trails. Forests for the World park is a heavily treed park, located minutes from downtown, with more than 9 miles/15 km of trails through various habitats; self-guided nature walks, hiking, biking, fishing (in Shane Lake) and picnicking. The upper lookout at Shane Lake has a great view of the city. For park information and trail maps, phone 250-562-3700.

Swimming. Four Seasons Swimming Pool at the corner of 7th Avenue and Dominion Street has a pool, waterslide, diving tank and fitness centre. Open to the public from 9 A.M. to 8 P.M. Monday–Friday, and 1–5 P.M. weekends. Or check out the Aquatic Centre at 1770 George Paul Lane. It is equipped with a leisure-style wave pool, river channel and a 10-metre diving tower. Open Monday–Friday 6 A.M. to 10 P.M. and Saturdays from 10 A.M. to 9 P.M.; Sundays 10:30 A.M. to 9 P.M.

Golf Courses. Aberdeen Glen Golf Club is located just north of Prince George, 0.6 mile/1 km off Highway 97 North. Aspen Grove Golf Club is on Highway 97 South. The Prince George Golf & Curling Club is located in the heart of the city. Links of Maggie May Golf Course is located 4 miles/6.5 km from the junction of Shelley Road and Yellowhead Highway 16 East. Alder Hills Golf Club located on the east side of Prince George, 4.1 km/2.5 miles on Highway 16 East. Pine Valley Golf Course is a few minutes' drive west of Highway 97 and on Highway 16.

Summer Events: National Indigenous Peoples Day (June 21); Canada Day (July 1); Summerfest in July; BC Rivers Day in September. Details on these and other events are available from Tourism Prince George, phone 250-562-3700 or visit tourismpg.com/events.

Huble Homestead Historic Site, within the Giscome Portage Regional Park and next to the scenic Fraser River, dates from 1912. These original and reconstructed buildings are surrounded by grazing land and forest. Picnic tables, concession and gift shop. Open every day, 10 A.M. to 5 P.M., from May to September long weekend, with guided interpretive tours. Admission by donation. Located north of Prince George on Highway 97; turn east off the highway at **Milepost PG 25.4** and drive 3.7 miles/6 km on Mitchell Road. www.hublehomestead.ca.

AREA FISHING: Highways 16 and 97 are the ideal routes for the sportsman, with year-round fishing and easy access to lakes and rivers. Hunters and fishermen stop over in Prince George as the jumping-off place for some of North America's finest big game hunting and fishing.

Unique architecture of the Two Rivers Gallery, featuring local, regional and national artists.
(©Kris Valencia, staff)

The local fishery releases rainbow trout into **Ferguson Lake** and **Shane Lake** in "Forests For the World." Both lakes lie within the city limits and are stocked to encourage the development of local fishing. Both are small lakes and no motors are permitted. For more information contact Fish & Wildlife at 250-565-6145, or Tourism Prince George, phone 250-562-3700; 1-800-668-7646; www.tourismpg.com. You may purchase a fishing license online at Tourism Prince George and borrow a rod and tackle from the Visitor Centre for free.

West Access Route Log
(continued)

BC HIGHWAY 97/HART HIGHWAY
The John Hart Highway, completed in 1952, was named for the former B.C. premier who sponsored its construction. This paved highway, mostly 2-lanes, with both straight and winding stretches and some steep grades, crests the Rocky Mountains at Pine Pass.
This section of the log shows distance from Prince George (PG) followed by distance from Dawson Creek (DC).

PG 0 DC 245.2 (394.5 km) **Junction** of Highway 97 and Yellowhead Highway 16 (20th Avenue) in Prince George.

PG 0.3 (0.5 km) **DC 244.9** (394 km) Pine Centre shopping mall to west (southbound access).

PG 0.7 (1.1 km) **DC 244.5** (393.4 km) Stoplight. Turnoff for College of New Caledonia and Pine Centre shopping mall (northbound access).

PG 1.2 (1.9 km) **DC 244** (392.6 km) Stoplight at 15th Avenue; access west to fast food (McDonald's, Starbucks, etc.), bank, gas and shopping; access east to City Centre. Also access west to University of Northern British Columbia (follow signs).

PG 1.5 (2.4 km) **DC 243.7** (392.1 km) Stoplight at 10th Avenue. Access to food, gas/diesel and lodging.

PG 1.9 (3.1 km) **DC 243.3** (391.5 km) Stoplight at 5th Avenue. City Centre/Truck Route to east. Tim Hortons, Save-On-Foods,

gas/diesel to west. Also access to Spruceland shopping centre.

PG 2.3 (3.7 km) **DC 242.9** (390.8 km) John Hart Bridge over the Nechako River.

PG 4 (6.4 km) **DC 241.2** (388.2 km) Truck weigh scales to west. Husky gas station with diesel to east. Turn east onto Hoferkamp Road and follow signs for McMillan Creek Regional Park, which offers a leisurely 1 km/0.6 mile walk or longer 2.5 km/1.5 mile hike via loop trail to viewpoint overlooking Nechako River and the city of Prince George.

PG 4.2 (6.7 km) **DC 241** (387.8 km) Stoplight; Chevron gas station with diesel. Access to Aberdeen Glen Golf Club.

PG 6.2 (10 km) **DC 239** (384.6 km) Race Trac gas station to east.

PG 6.8 (10.9 km) **DC 238.4** (383.6 km) Stoplight. Restaurant to east. Petro-Pass (commercial cardlock).

PG 7.6 (12.1 km) **DC 237.6** (382.4 km) Shell gas station to west.

PG 7.7 (12.4 km) **DC 237.5** (382.2 km) Stoplight. Esso gas, station, Save-On-Foods to west; Petro-Canada (gas/diesel), Tim Hortons to east.

PG 7.9 (12.7 km) **DC 237.3** (381.9 km) West to Shoppers Drug Mart, McDonald's.

PG 8.3 (13.4 km) **DC 236.9** (381.2 km) Stoplight; gas, propane, convenience store. Also turn west here for access to **Hartway RV Park**; treed private sites, free showers, laundry, public sani-dump.

Hartway RV Park. See display ad page 131.

PG 8.8 (14.2 km) **DC 236.4** (380.4 km) **Junction** with Chief Lake Road. Husky gas/diesel station and carwash to west.

PG 9.1 (14.6 km) **DC 236.1** (380 km) *End 4-lane highway, begin 2-lane highway northbound. Begin 4-lane highway southbound.*

Distance marker northbound shows

Relive the pioneer days at Huble Homestead Historic Site; guided interpretive tours, May to September. (©Judy Nadon, staff)

Chetwynd 292 km/181 miles, Dawson Creek 394 km/244 miles.

PG 11.5 (18.5 km) **DC 233.7** (376 km) **Northland RV Park** to east; large grassy camping area, full hookups, pull-through sites.

△

Northland RV Park. See display ad on page 128.

PG 16.8 (27 km) **DC 228.4** (367.5 km) Wright Creek.

PG 17.2 (27.7 km) **DC 228** (366.9 km) Salmon River bridge (bridge completed in 2017); rest area at north end.

Highway climbs 6 percent northbound, passing lane.

PG 17.4 (28 km) **DC 227.8** (366.6 km) **Salmon Valley Campground** to east; 15-amp power and water; free hot showers, dump station, store.

Salmon Valley Campground. See display ad on page 128.

△

PG 18.8 (30.3 km) **DC 226.4** (364.3 km) Highway bridge crosses railroad.

PG 21.7 (34.9 km) **DC 223.5** (359.6 km) Turnoff to west for Goodsir Nature Park; 1.5 miles/2.4 km from highway via Old Summit Lake Road (gravel). This 160-acre park features 6 miles/10 km of nature trails, picnic tables. Open May to October, 8 A.M. to dusk; admission by donation. Adjacent owner's home; be respectful. Limited parking, bug repellent is essential.

PG 25.4 (40.9 km) **DC 219.8** (353.7 km) Paved turnout to east with litter bins and point-of-interest sign about Giscome Portage and Huble Homestead at turnoff for **Huble Homestead Historic Site**, located in Giscome Portage Regional Park, 3.7 miles/6 km east via Mitchell Road. The pioneer Huble Homestead and trading post preserves the oldest home in the region. Guided interpretive tours of original and reconstructed log buildings available May to September. Picnic areas, concession, gift shop and farm animals. Admission by donation. Phone 250-564-7033; website www.hublehomestead.ca.

PG 28.6 (46 km) **DC 216.6** (348.5 km) Paved turnout to east with point-of-interest sign.

PG 30.6 (49.2 km) **DC 214.6** (345.4 km) First of 2 turnoffs northbound to west for **Summit Lake**, a resort area popular with Prince George residents; no services. Lake char and rainbow trout fishing in the spring and fall.

🐟

PG 31.5 (50.7 km) **DC 213.7** (343.9 km) Enbridge Compressor Site.

PG 33 (53.1 km) **DC 212.2** (341.4 km) Summit Lake turnoff to west.

PG 44.4 (71.4 km) **DC 200.8** (323.1 km) *CAUTION: Slow for railroad crossing on curve.*

PG 46.3 (74.5 km) **DC 198.9** (320 km) Turnoff to west for **Crooked River (Bear Lake) Provincial Park**. Open May 12–Sept. 12. The centre of activity at this park is Bear Lake. According to BC Parks, Bear Lake's sandy beaches are some of the best in the region. 65 sites, a picnic area and shelter, flush toilets, showers, tables, firepits, dump station, playground and telephone. *No pets or alcohol allowed in day-use area.* Camping fee $22/sani-dump $5. Some sites may be reserved at www.discovercamping.ca. Powerboats are prohibited. Good fishing for rainbow trout, Dolly Varden, Rocky Mountain whitefish.

🐟 △

Highway 97 follows the Crooked River north to McLeod Lake.

PG 47.4 (76.3 km) **DC 197.8** (318.3 km) **BEAR LAKE** (pop. 300). Grizzly Inn; gas station with convenience store, hot/cold food, liquor store.

⛽

PG 56.7 (91.2 km) **DC 188.5** (303.3 km) Red Rock Creek.

PG 57.6 (92.7 km) **DC 187.6** (301.8 km) Red Rocky Lake to west.

PG 67 (107.8 km) **DC 178.2** (286.7 km) Altezega Creek.

PG 70 (112.6 km) **DC 175.2** (281.9 km) Large, double-ended, paved rest area to west beside Crooked River; litter bins, picnic tables and pit toilets.

PG 71 (114.2 km) **DC 174.2** (280.3 km) 42-Mile Creek.

PG 73.6 (118.4 km) **DC 171.6** (276.1 km) Distance marker northbound shows McLeod Lake 21 km/13 miles, Mackenzie 69 km/43 miles, Dawson Creek 291 km/181 miles.

PG 78 (125.5 km) **DC 167.2** (269 km) View northbound of sandy beach at Whisker's Point on McLeod Lake.

PG 78.7 (126.6 km) **DC 166.5** (267.9 km) **Whiskers Point Provincial Park** to west on McLeod Lake; paved loop road, 69 level gravel sites, tap water, flush toilets, boat ramp, fire rings and picnic tables. Also horseshoe pits, volleyball, playground and picnic shelter. Camping fee $22. Late May to Sept. 4. Gate is closed after Sept. 7. Self-guided nature trail loop takes 20 minutes. Boat launch, swimming and sandy beach. **McLeod Lake** has fair fishing for rainbow trout and Dolly Varden.

🐟 △

PG 85.5 (137.5 km) **DC 159.7** (256.9 km) **MCLEOD LAKE** (pop. 70), general store and post office to west. A cairn in front of the store commemorates the first European settlement west of the Rockies and the longest continuously occupied European settlement in British Columbia. The first fur trading post west of the Rockies was established here in 1805 by Simon Fraser for the North West Trading Co., and named by Fraser for Archie McLeod.

PG 86.2 (138.6 km) **DC 159** (255.8 km) Turnoff on Carp Lake Road for Tse'khene

Food & Fuel; groceries, cafe, gas, bed-and-breakfast lodging; phone 250-750-4684. For **Carp Lake Provincial Park**, continue 20 miles/32 km west via gravel road; 90 tent/RV sites on Carp Lake, 12 sites at War Lake (not suitable for long units) 3 island campsites for those with water transport. Camping fee $20, sani-dump fee is $5. Boating and excellent trout fishing.

⛽ 🐟 △

PG 86.9 (139.8 km) **DC 158.3** (254.7 km) Gravel turnout with litter bin to west, welcome to McLeod Lake southbound.

PG 89 (143.2 km) **DC 156.2** (251.3 km) Enbridge compressor station.

PG 89.7 (144.3 km) **DC 155.5** (250.2 km) Entering Mackenzie Forest District northbound.

PG 91 (146.4 km) **DC 154.2** (248.1 km) Turnoff to west for **Tudyah Lake Provincial Park**; 36 campsites with picnic tables, fire rings, pit toilets and drinking water. Day-use area with horseshoes, camping in trees for groups, boat launch, swimming and waterskiing. Open mid-May to Sept. 8 for full services, no services but open till Oct. 30. Camping fee $15. Tudyah Lake and nearby **Parsnip River** offer good fishing for rainbow trout, Dolly Varden and some grayling in summer.

🐟 △

PG 91.1 (146.6 km) **DC 154.6** (248 km) Bear Creek.

PG 91.9 (147.9 km) **DC 153.3** (246.7 km) Begin 1-mile-long passing lane northbound.

PG 95.2 (153.2 km) **DC 150** (241.4 km) Remains of Windy Point Inn were still visible in summer 2018; it burned down in February 2018.

Highway makes winding descent northbound to Parsnip River.

PG 96 (154.5 km) **DC 149.2** (240.1 km) Parsnip River Bridge; bridge replacement under construction summer 2018. This new bridge is part of the Pine Pass Expansion Project, which includes removing height/weight restrictions for industrial loads on this route.

This is the Rocky Mountain Trench, marking the western boundary of the Rocky Mountains. Northbound motorists begin gradual climb through the Misinchinka then Hart ranges of the Rocky Mountains. Passing lane northbound. Highway climbs southbound, passing lane.

PG 96.4 (155.1 km) **DC 148.8** (239.4 km) **Junction** with Highway 39; Mackenzie Junction; Petro-Canada station (250-750-4454) with cafe, gas/diesel, convenience store. Mackenzie visitor information at northeast corner of intersection.

⛽

MACKENZIE (pop. 3,700) is located 18 miles/29 km north on Highway 39 (good 2-lane paved highway). **Visitor Information:** Mackenzie Visitor Centre is located in a caboose at this junction; picnic tables, litter bins, toilets. Phone 250-997-4497 or visit www.district.mackenzie.bc.ca.

The town of Mackenzie was named after the famous explorer Sir Alexander Mackenzie, who camped near the future town site on his epic journey to the Pacific in 1793. The downtown commercial core offers all visitor services: food, gas, lodging, camping and shopping.

Mackenzie lies to the east of the south end of Williston Lake. Williston Lake is the largest man-made reservoir in North America, formed by the WAC Bennett Dam on the Peace River. The reservoir begins to freeze over during November, with total freeze-up usually occurring in mid-January.

To see Williston Lake, drive north 16.4 miles/26.4 km on Highway 39 to turnoff for BC Hydro's **Alexander Mackenzie's Landing.** It is 3.8 miles/6.1 km from this turnoff to BC Hydro's Alexander Mackenzie's Landing Campground (19 sites), and another 0.2 mile/0.3 km to Williston Lake/Alexander Mackenzie's Landing, with a beach, boat launch, picnic sites, and monument.

Other Mackenzie attractions include the World's Largest Tree Crusher, Mackenzie Nature Observatory, a 9-hole golf course, and a recreation center. Morfee Lake day-use area is 0.9 mile/1.4 km from town center via Centennial Drive, then 0.5 mile/0.8 km down a dirt and gravel access road; beach, small parking area (not suitable for large RVs). The Ernie Bodin Community Center is located on Centennial Drive and is home to the Mackenzie & District Museum (www.mackenziemuseum.ca) phone 250-997-3021 and the Mackenzie Arts Center and gallery (phone 250-997-5818). Area recreation includes hiking, mountain biking, wildlife viewing, photography, swimming, boating, canoeing, kayaking and fishing.

PG 96.6 (155.4 km) **DC 148.6** (239.1 km) Distance marker northbound shows Chetwynd 150 km/93 miles, Dawson Creek 252 km/157 miles.

PG 96.8 (155.8 km) **DC 148.4** (238.8 km) Highway crosses railroad tracks.

PG 97.1 (156.2 km) **DC 148.1** (238.3 km) *CAUTION: High mountain road with sudden weather changes (northbound sign).*

PG 100 (160.9 km) **DC 145.2** (233.6 km) Large double-ended gravel turnout to east.

PG 103.7 (166.9 km) **DC 141.5** (227.7 km) Distance marker northbound shows Chetwynd 140 km/87 miles, Dawson Creek 243 km/151 miles.

Slow for curves northbound.

PG 107.1 (172.3 km) **DC 138.1** (222.2 km) Large gravel turnout to east.

PG 109.4 (176 km) **DC 135.8** (218.5 km) Highway maintenance yard.

PG 109.6 (176.3 km) **DC 135.6** (218.2 km) Honeymoon Creek.

PG 110.7 (178.1 km) **DC 134.5** (216.4 km) Powerlines crossing highway carry electricity south from hydro dams in the Hudson's Hope area.

PG 111.6 (179.6 km) **DC 133.6** (215 km) *Slow for sharp curve across railroad tracks.*

PG 112.4 (180.9 km) **DC 132.8** (213.7 km) **Misinchinka River**, southeast of highway; fishing for grayling, whitefish and Dolly Varden.

PG 113.4 (182.5 km) **DC 131.8** (212.1 km) Rolston Creek bridge.

PG 116.3 (187.1 km) **DC 128.9** (207.4 km) Turnoff to northwest for **Bijoux Falls**

©Kris Valencia, staff

Provincial Park; fair-sized parking area with plenty of turnaround space if it is not packed with visitors, picnic tables, toilets

(wheelchair accessible). A pleasant stop to view the falls and spot Steller's jays. Good photo op. Day use only. Gravel turnout to southeast is winter chain-up area for northbound traffic.

PG 116.4 (187.3 km) **DC 128.8** (207.3 km) Large gravel turnout to southeast. *CAUTION: Abrupt pavement edge on downhill approach to turnout* is wilderness access to Pine Le Moray Provincial Park.

PG 117 (188.3 km) **DC 128.2** (206.3 km) Highway climbs 6 to 10 percent grade next 3.5 miles/5.6 km northbound to Pine Pass. Passing lane northbound.

PG 117.2 (188.6 km) **DC 128** (206 km) Highway crosses under railroad. Clearance height is 5.68m/18.6 ft.

Begin 2-km/1.2-mile passing lane northbound.

PG 119.3 (192 km) **DC 125.9** (202.6 km) Bijoux Hill chain-off turnout for northbound traffic.

PG 120.2 (193.4 km) **DC 125** (201.1 km) Northbound sign for **Pine Pass**, the highest point on the John Hart Highway. Beautiful view of the Rockies to the northeast. Good highway over pass.

Highway descends 6 to 10 percent downgrade next 3.5 miles/5.6 km southbound.

PG 120.5 (193.9 km) **DC 124.7** (200.6 km) Turnoff to Powder King ski area.

PG 120.8 (194.4 km) **DC 124.4** (200.2 km) Distance marker northbound shows Chetwynd 109 km/68 miles, Dawson Creek 211 km/131 miles.

PG 122.4 (194 km) **DC 123.5** (198.7 km) Paved turnout to east with view of picturesque **Azouzetta Lake**. Access to lake at Azouzetta Lake Lodge.

PG 122.9 (197.8 km) **DC 123** (198 km) **Azouzetta Lake Lodge and Campground** to east, phone 250-277-8245; camping, cabins, restaurant, dock, boat launch, canoe and paddleboard rentals. Beautiful lake.

Azouzetta Lake Lodge and Campground. See display ad this page.

PG 125.9 (202.6 km) **DC 119.3** (192 km) Enbridge compressor station. Highway climbs southbound, passing lane.

PG 128.1 (206.2 km) **DC 117.1** (188.4 km) Large dirt turnout to north.

PG 129.6 (208.5 km) **DC 115.6** (186 km) Highway climbs northbound; passing lane, winding road.

PG 131.8 (212.1 km) **DC 113.4** (182.5 km) Gravel turnout to northwest.

Passing lane northbound.

PG 135.2 (217.6 km) **DC 110** (177 km) Pine River transmission lines.

PG 139.8 (224.9 km) **DC 105.4** (169.6 km) Link Creek. Dirt turnout to south at east end of bridge.

PG 142 (228.5 km) **DC 103.2** (166 km) Pine River bridge.

PG 142.3 (229 km) **DC 102.9** (165.6 km) Pine River bridge.

PG 142.9 (229.9 km) **DC 102.3** (164.6 km) West Pine rest area to northwest has a large, double-ended paved parking area with picnic tables, litter bins and toilets.

PG 143.4 (230.7 km) **DC 101.8** (163.8 km) **Heart Lake** campground (**Pine Le Moray Provincial Park**) to southeast; toilets, tables, firepits and litter bins. Fishing for stocked trout.

PG 143.7 (231.2 km) **DC 101.5** (163.3 km) Bridge over West Pine River.

PG 143.8 (231.4 km) **DC 101.4** (163.2 km) B.C. Railway overpass. Height

4.92m/16.1 ft.

PG 144 (231.7 km) **DC 101.2** (162.9 km) Mount Solitude Lodge.

PG 144.6 (232.7 km) **DC 100.6** (161.9 km) Silver Sands Lodge.

PG 146.4 (235.6 km) **DC 98.8** (159 km) Cairns Creek.

PG 148.5 (238.9 km) **DC 96.7** (155.6 km) Mount LeMoray (unincorporated); no services. Highway maintenance camp.

PG 149.1 (239.9 km) **DC 96.1** (154.6 km) Lilico Creek.

PG 150 (241.4 km) **DC 95.2** (153.2 km) Martin Creek.

PG 150.7 (242.5 km) **DC 94.5** (152.1 km) Big Boulder Creek.

CAUTION: Slow for curves northbound. Watch for moose and deer in area, especially at dusk and night. Pipeline crosses road.

PG 156.5 (251.8 km) **DC 88.7** (142.7 km) Fisher Creek.

PG 157.2 (252.2 km) **DC 88** (141.6 km) Large double-ended turnout with litter bin to south beside Pine River.

PG 160.1 (257.6 km) **DC 85.1** (136.9 km) Crassier Creek bridge (under construction summer 2018) and Willow Creek Mine access. As part of the Peace Flood Recovery Project, 5 culverts along here will receive clear span bridges in 2018-19.

PG 161.9 (260.5 km) **DC 83.3** (134 km) Enbridge compressor station.

PG 169.7 (273 km) **DC 75.5** (121.5 km) Eastbound-only access to large turnout with picnic tables and litter bins to south at Jack Pine Point overlooking the beautiful Pine River valley. "Peace Foothills" information board.

Highway climbs northbound. View of the Canadian Rocky Mountain foothills to the south and west.

PG 172.6 (277.7 km) **DC 72.6** (116.8 km) Enbridge Pine River gas plant, road to east.

PG 177.6 (285.8 km) **DC 67.6** (108.8 km) Double-ended and paved turnout with litter bin to southeast.

PG 178.4 (287 km) **DC 66.8** (107.5 km) Watch for turnoff to southeast to **Caron Creek RV Park** to southeast (description follows).

Caron Creek RV Park. 7537 Highway 97S; 16 km (10 miles) west of Chetwynd. 30-amp and 15-amp fully-serviced pull-through sites, free WiFi, free hot showers. Laundromat. Discounts for seniors and all club members. Open all year-round. Email: rvpark@caroncreek.com; website www.caroncreek.com. Phone: 250-788-2522. [ADVERTISEMENT]

PG 181.6 (292.2 km) **DC 63.6** (102.3 km) *CAUTION: Slow for curve.*

PG 182 (292.2 km) **DC 63.2** (101.7 km)

It's always a fun surprise to see the newest chainsaw carvings in Chetwynd and visit old favorites around town. (©Kris Valencia, staff)

Bissette Creek bridge.

PG 183.6 (295.4 km) **DC 61.6** (99.1 km) Wildmare Creek.

PG 183.9 (296 km) **DC 61.3** (98.6 km) Private RV park to southeast.

PG 186.5 (300.1 km) **DC 58.7** (94.4 km) Paved turnout to south at Welcome to Chetwynd (northbound) sign.

Slow for posted speed zone northbound.

PG 187.1 (301 km) **DC 58.1** (93.5 km) Turnoff for Little Prairie Heritage Museum located in a 1949 post office building on Westgate Road. The museum is typically open in July and August; check with Chetwynd Visitor Center in town for current hours, phone 250-788-1943.

CAUTION: Watch for and STOP for Pedestrian Crossings entering Chetwynd eastbound!

PG 187.8 (302.2 km) **DC 57.4** (92.4 km) Turnoff to north for Chetwynd services and Visitor Center (follow signs).

Chetwynd

PG 187.9 (302.3 km) **DC 57.3** (92.2 km) Located on Highway 97 at the junction with Highway 29 north to the Alaska Highway via Hudson's Hope, and south to Tumbler Ridge. **Population:** 3,000; area 7,000. **Emergency Services:** Dial 911. **Hospital**, phone 250-788-2236.

Visitor Information: Chetwynd Visitor Center open year-round. Free internet access and information regarding free sani-dump is available for travelers at the Visitor Center. Contact the Chetwynd Visitor Center at P.O. Box 594, Chetwynd V0C 1J0; phone 250-788-1943; email tourist@gochetwynd.com; website www.gochetwynd.com.

Elevation: 2,017 feet/615m. **Radio:** Peace FM 94.5/104.1, CISN-FM 103.9, CJDC 890, CKNL 560, CBC-FM 93.5. **Television:** 7 channels (includes CBC, BCTV, ABC, CBS, CHETTV and NBC) plus pay cable.

The town, formerly known as Little Prairie, is a division point on the British Columbia Railway. The name was changed to honour the late British Columbia Minister of Railways, Ralph Chetwynd, who was instrumental in the northward extension of the province-owned railway.

Chetwynd is the "most livable small community" in British Columbia, according to one poll. Forestry, mining, natural gas processing, ranching, farming and wind energy are the main industries in Chetwynd. Chetwynd lies at the northern end of the North East Coal resource, one of the largest known coal deposits on earth. Quintette Mine, south of Chetwynd near Tumbler Ridge, the world's largest computerized open pit coal mine, was shut down in 2000 and is currently on care and maintenance. Plans to reopen the mine depend on demand for steelmaking coal, according to the Teck Resources website.

Local radio station Peace-FM 94.5/104.1 was the first community radio station in Canada to be licensed under the 1997 legislation allowing low power community stations. Peace-FM transmits to Chetwynd and Dawson Creek.

Chetwynd offers easy access to all services: several motels, fast-food outlets, restaurants, banks and bank machines, post office, laundromats, gas stations, supermarkets and a 9-hole golf course. (Heavy commercial and industrial traffic often fill up local motels and campgrounds; reserve ahead.) There are private RV parks in town and on Highway 97. The public library has free internet access.

Chainsaw sculptures. Chetwynd's collection of carvings always stops traffic. Approximately 12 new sculptures are on display each year along Highway 97. These will eventually join the more than 150 carvings displayed throughout town. Chetwynd's slogan is "Community Carved by Success." The annual International Chainsaw Carving Championship takes place in Chetwynd the second weekend of June.

Moberly Lake Provincial Park is 12 miles/19.3 km north of Chetwynd via Highway 29 north. The park has 109 campsites, beach, picnic area, playground, nature trail, boat launch and a private marina next door. Cameron Lake is 25 miles/40 km north via Highway 28 and offers camping, swimming and boating (no power boats). *(See "Hudson's Hope Loop" log on pages 137–139.)*

Tumbler Ridge side trip. Highway 97 travelers can make a loop trip south by driving 57 miles/91 km south on Highway 29 to the town of Tumbler Ridge, the site of some important recent dinosaur fossil finds. A major attraction in the area is spectacular Kinuseo Falls. (See "Tumbler Ridge Loop" on

pages 139–140.)

Chetwynd Recreation Centre has a pool with wave machine, slide, whirlpool, gym, hockey arena, curling rink, walking track, climbing wall, squash/racquetball court and weight room. Open daily, visitors welcome.

West Access Route Log
(continued)

PG 187.9 (302.3 km) **DC 57.3** (92.2 km) Traffic light at **junction** with Highway 29 North to Moberly Lake, Peace River Provincial Recreation Area, Peace Canyon Dam, Hudson's Hope and **W.A.C. Bennett Dam**. Highway 29 connects with the Alaska Highway 53.7 miles/86.4 km north of Dawson Creek. Petro-Canada gas/diesel station.

Junction with Highway 29 north to Hudson's Hope. See "Hudson's Hope Loop" log beginning on page 137.

Highway 97 climbs next 12 miles/19 km for Dawson Creek-bound motorists.

PG 188.1 (302.7 km) **DC 57.1** (91.9 km) Highway crosses railroad tracks.

PG 188.2 (302.8 km) **DC 57** (91.7 km) Traffic light. Industrial Park and airport turnoff to north. Chevron (gas/diesel), Tim Hortons, hotel to south.

PG 188.4 (303.2 km) **DC 56.8** (91.4 km) Chetwynd Recreation Centre to north.

PG 188.6 (303.5 km) **DC 56.6** (91.1 km) Centurion Creek.

PG 189.3 (304.6 km) **DC 55.9** (90 km) Westwind RV Park and Day's Inn to south.

Begin 4.4-km/2.7-mile passing lane eastbound.

PG 189.4 (304.8 km) **DC 55.8** (89.7 km) Welcome to Chetwynd (southbound sign).

PG 189.6 (305.1 km) **DC 55.6** (89.5 km) Turnoff to south for Highway 29 South to Gwillim Lake and Tumbler Ridge. Tumbler Ridge is the site of some important recent dinosaur fossil finds and is the gateway to Kinuseo Falls in Monkman Provincial Park.

Junction with Highway 29 South. See beginning of "Tumbler Ridge Loop" log beginning on page 139.

Highway climbs eastbound.

PG 192.1 (303.5 km) **DC 56.6** (91.1 km) Large paved turnout to north (westbound traffic only) with information sign. Brake-check area: Steep downgrade westbound into Chetwynd.

PG 199.2 (320.5 km) **DC 46** (74 km) Large double-ended gravel turnout to south for eastbound traffic.

PG 200.7 (323 km) **DC 44.5** (71.6 km) Wabi Hill chain-off area for eastbound traffic.

PG 205.7 (331 km) **DC 39.5** (63.6 km) East Pine (South) turnout with litter bin is a brake-check area for eastbound traffic.

Begin 6 percent downgrade with curves eastbound; passing lane. *CAUTION: Watch for deer.*

PG 207.5 (333.9 km) **DC 37.7** (60.7 km) Views of East Pine River Valley and Table Mountain.

Slow for sharp curves next 1.7 miles/2.7 km as highway descends eastbound.

PG 207.9 (334.5 km) **DC 37.3** (60 km) *Slow for 30-kmph/20-mph curve approaching East Pine River bridge eastbound.*

East Pine River rest area to south at west end of East Pine River bridge. Rest area is a large gravel parking area with litter bins located at the entrance to **East Pine Provincial Park** (0.5 mile south on gravel road). The provincial park has a boat launch which provides access to the East Pine and Murray rivers.

PG 208.1 (334.8 km) **DC 37.1** (59.7 km) East Pine River bridge.

Highway climbs 6 percent winding grade next 2.5 miles/4 km westbound. Slow for sharp curves. Passing lane. Highway climbs eastbound with passing lane.

PG 209.7 (337.4 km) **DC 45.5** (57.1 km) East Pine (unincorporated); no services.

PG 211.6 (340.5 km) **DC 33.6** (54.1 km) Rest area with toilets and litter barrel to north. Westbound use as brake-check area.

Highway descends westbound. Passing lane ends eastbound.

PG 221.4 (356.2 km) **DC 23.8** (38.3 km) Turnouts both sides of highway.

PG 222.5 (358 km) **DC 22.7** (36.5 km) **GROUNDBIRCH** (unincorporated); store, liquor outlet, gas, propane, diesel and post office.

PG 230.8 (371.4 km) **DC 14.4** (23.2 km) Progress (unincorporated); no services.

PG 237.5 (382.1 km) **DC 7.7** (12.4 km) **Junction** with Heritage Highway 52, which leads 59.6 miles/96 km south to the community of Tumbler Ridge.

From Tumbler Ridge, Heritage Highway 52 continues 92 miles/148 km east and north to connect with Highway 2 southeast of Dawson Creek.

> **Junction** with Highway 52 South. See end of "Tumbler Ridge Loop" log page 140.

PG 237.8 (382.6 km) **DC 7.4** (11.9 km) New Arras bridge across the Kiskatinaw River.

PG 238.5 (383.7 km) **DC 6.7** (10.8 km) **ARRAS** (unincorporated). The Roadhouse truck stop restaurant, open daily 5:30 A.M. to 10 P.M. Junction with Mason Road.

PG 243.2 (391.3 km) **DC 2** (3.2 km) Turnouts both sides of highway.

PG 243.7 (392.2 km) **DC 1.5** (2.4 km) **Northern Lights RV Park** entrance; full hookups, pull-throughs, laundry, WiFi.

Northern Lights RV Park. See display ad on page 161 in the ALASKA HIGHWAY section. ▲

PG 244.9 (394.1 km) **DC 0.3** (0.5 km) Traffic light. Turn north for Highway 97A/ Dangerous Goods route bypass.

PG 245 (394.2 km) **DC 0.2** (0.3 km) Entering Dawson Creek. Access north to Rotary Lake Park and back entrance to Walter Wright Pioneer Village and **Mile "O" Park & Campground.** Tubby's Car Wash & RV Park to south. ▲

Mile "O" Park & Campground/ Walter Wright Pioneer Village. See display ad on page 161 in the ALASKA HIGHWAY section.

PG 245.2 (394.5 km) **DC 0 Junction** of the John Hart Highway 97 and Alaska Highway 97. Eastbound travelers turn right for downtown Dawson Creek, left for Taylor, Fort St. John and points north on the Alaska Highway.

> Turn to ALASKA HIGHWAY section beginning on page 149 for description of Dawson Creek and log of the Alaska Highway.

Hudson's Hope Loop

The Hudson's Hope Loop (BC Highway 29) links the John Hart Highway (Highway 97) with the Alaska Highway (also Highway 97), bypassing Dawson Creek. The south end of Hudson's Hope Loop is at Chetwynd, the north end intersects the Alaska Highway at **Milepost DC 53.6** just north of Fort St. John across from Charlie Lake Provincial Park.

This 85-mile/136.8-km paved loop road provides year-round access to the town of Hudson's Hope, W.A.C. Bennett Dam, Peace Canyon Dam and Moberly Lake.

Highway 29 is a good, scenic 2-lane road with a few steep and winding sections adjacent the scenic Peace River.

HIGHWAY 29 NORTH

Distance from Chetwynd (C) is followed by distance from Alaska Highway junction (AH).

C 0 AH 85 (136.8 km) Traffic light at junction of Highways 29 and 97 at Chetwynd, **Milepost PG 187.9** on Highway 97 (Hart Highway). *See description of Chetwynd on page 136.*

C 1.2 (1.9 km) **AH 83.8** (134.9 km) Truck weigh scales to west.

C 1.5 (2.4 km) **AH 83.5** (134.4 km) Highway climbs 6 percent grade with passing lanes next 3.3 miles/5.3 km northbound.

C 2.1 (3.4 km) **AH 82.9** (133.4 km) Jackfish Road to east.

C 4.8 (7.7 km) **AH 80.2** (129.1 km) Highway descends 6 percent downgrade southbound.

C 7.7 (12.4 km) **AH 77.3** (124.4 km) Large paved turnout to west. Passing lanes southbound next 2 miles. *Watch for moose.*

C 11.7 (18.8 km) **AH 73.3** (118 km) Paved access road leads 2.2 miles/3.5 km west to **Moberly Lake Provincial Park** on south shore; 109 campsites, swimming, waterskiing, picnicking, drinking water, dump station, boat launch, $20 camping fee ($5 sani-station). This beautiful 9-mile-/15-km-long lake drains into Moberly River. Fishing for lake trout, Dolly Varden and jackfish. ➡ ▲

C 11.9 (19.2 km) **AH 73.1** (117.6 km) Moberly River bridge; parking area with litter barrel at south end.

C 12.5 (20.1 km) **AH 72.5** (116.7 km) Crow Feathers store and gas station. ⛽

C 15.4 (24.8 km) **AH 69.6** (112 km) **MOBERLY LAKE.** Store, gas and diesel (current status unknown). ⛽

C 15.6 (25.1 km) **AH 69.4** (112 km) Historic site for Moberly Lake with picnic tables, historic cairn, info panel.

C 17.8 (28.6 km) **AH 67.2** (108.1 km) Moberly Lake and District Golf Club, 0.7 mile/1.1 km east; 9 holes, grass greens, rentals, clubhouse, licensed lounge. Open May to September.

C 24.8 (39.9 km) **AH 60.2** (96.9 km) **Cameron Lake Campground** with 19 campsites; tables, toilets, playground, hiking trail, boat launch (no motorboats or power driven water sports) and swimming. No powerboats. Camping fee $20/night (firewood $5). Open May to September. ➡ ▲

C 30 (48.3 km) **AH 55** (88.5 km) Paved turnout with litter bin to east. Begin 5-mile downgrade northbound to Peace River.

C 35.2 (56.6 km) **AH 49.8** (80.1 km) Suspension bridge over Peace River; paved turnouts with litter bins at both ends of bridge have concrete totem pole sculptures. View of Peace Canyon Dam.

Begin 5-mile upgrade with passing lanes southbound.

C 35.7 (57.4 km) **AH 49.3** (79.3 km) Turnoff to west for Dinosaur Lake Campground and **B.C. Hydro Peace Canyon Dam** (0.6 mile/1 km). For more information, phone 250-783-5048 or visit bchydro.com/ peacecanyon.

Dinosaur Lake Campground, on Dinosaur Lake, has a picnic area, 16 campsites, firepits, toilets and tables; hiking trails; boat launch and swimming area. Camping fee of

HUDSON'S HOPE ADVERTISERS

BC Hydro/W.A.C. Bennett Dam....Ph. 250-783-5048
District of Hudson's Hope............Ph. 250-783-9154

Hudson's Hope Museum is housed in the former Hudson's Bay Post store, located next to St. Peter's Anglican United Church and across the road from the Visitor Center. (©Kris Valencia, staff)

son's Hope.

C 38.7 (62.3 km) **AH 46.3** (74.5 km) **King Gething Park**; small campground with 10 grassy sites, picnic tables, cookhouse, potable water, flush toilets, showers and dump station east side of highway. Wheelchair accessible. Camping fee of $20/night (firewood $5).

C 39.3 (63.2 km) **AH 45.7** (73.7 km) Gas station with diesel.

Hudson's Hope

C 39.5 (63.5 km) **AH 45.5** (73.2 km) Beattie Park Visitor Centre, on left northbound, across from Hudson's Hope Museum and St. Peter's Church. **Population:** 1,160. **Emergency Services:** Dial 911. **Medical Clinic**, phone 250-783-9991.

Visitor Information: Visitor Center in log building at Beattie Park; open May 1 to Sept. 30. Hours are 8:30 A.M. to 5 P.M. daily May through September; Visitor Center 250-783-9154 (summer) or District of Hudson's Hope Office info hotline 250-783-9901 (winter); email visitorinfo@hudsonshope.ca; website www.hudsonshope.ca.

Elevation: 1,707 feet/520m. **Climate:** Summer temperatures range from 60°F/ 16°C to 90°F/32°C, with an average of 135 frost-free days annually. Radio: CBC 940, CBC-FM 88.3, Energy 98-FM 98.5, The Bear 101.5. **Television:** Channels via satellite or fibre optic TV and internet.

$20/night (firewood $5). Open May to September.

C 37.5 (60.3 km) **AH 47.5** (76.4 km) Alwin Holland Memorial Park (0.5 mile/0.8 km east of highway) is named for the first teacher in Hudson's Hope, who willed his property, known locally as The Glen, to be used as a public park. There are 9 campsites, picnic grounds and barbecues. Camping fee of $20/night (firewood $5).

C 38.5 (62 km) **AH 46.5** (74.8 km) Turnout to east with litter bin and map of Hud-

Private Aircraft: Hudson's Hope airstrip, 3.7 miles/6 km west; elev. 2,200 feet/671m; length 5,200 feet/1,585m; asphalt.

Visitor services in Hudson's Hope include 3 hotels, 3 restaurants, 2 service stations, laundromat, a bank, post office, supermarket, convenience and hardware stores, hairdresser, gift shop and medical clinic. Camping in town at Beattie's RV Park.

The Hudson's Hope area was first visited in 1793 by Alexander Mackenzie. In 1805, a Northwest Company trading post was established here by Simon Fraser. In 1821, it, and the Hudson Bay Company combined, creating the currently named Hudson Bay Company (previously named Rocky Mountain Portage House). In 1916, after the fur-trading days were over, a major influx of settlers arrived in the area. It was the head of navigation for steamboats on the lower Peace River until 1936, the year of the last scheduled steamboat run. Area coal mines supplied Alaska Highway maintenance camps during the 1940s.

The historic log St. Peter's Anglican United Church is located next door to the Hudson's Hope Museum. The town's museum, housed in the former Hudson's Bay Post store, has several exhibits including an extensive fossil and prehistory collection; pioneer displays in on-site buildings; and an arrowhead/projectile point collection. The Museum shop offers a large selection of books, souvenirs and gift items. Admission by donation; phone 250-783-5735.

Modern development of Hudson's Hope was spurred by construction of the Peace Power project in the 1960s. Today the area's principal claim to fame is BC Hydro's 600-foot/183-m-high **W.A.C. Bennett Dam** at the upper end of the Peace River canyon, 15 miles/24 km west of Hudson's Hope. The 100-million-ton dam is one of the largest earth-fill structures in the world, and Williston Lake, behind it, is the largest body of fresh water in British Columbia. The dam provides 25 percent of British Columbia's hydroelectricity.

The not-to-be-missed W.A.C. Bennett Dam Visitor Centre is open daily from Victoria Day weekend (May 18, 2019) through Labour Day (Sept. 2, 2019) from 10 A.M. to 5 P.M. The centre offers guided tours of the dam every hour on the half-hour starting at 10:30 A.M. with the last tour leaving *promptly* at 3:30 P.M. NOTE: *Visitors must arrive at least 15 minutes before tour time.* Admission charged. For more information, and to confirm tour times, phone 250-783-5048; email bennett@bchydro.com; or visit www.bc hydro.com/bennett.

Hudson's Hope Loop Log
(continued)

C **39.6** (63.7 km) **AH 45.4** (73 km) **Junction** of Highway 29 and W.A.C. Bennett access (Canyon Drive) in Hudson's Hope; Chetwynd-bound travelers turn south here. Gas station and post office.

C **40.3** (64.8 km) **AH 44.7** (71.9 km) Turnout to north with litter bin and map.
CAUTION: Watch for deer eastbound, especially at dusk and at night.

C **43.6** (70.2 km) **AH 41.4** (66.6 km) Lynx Creek crossing followed by Lynx Creek RV campground.

C **47.3** (76.1 km) **AH 37.7** (60.7 km) Turnout to south with litter bin and view of the Peace River.

Visitor Center at Beattie Park in Hudson's Hope is open May 1 to September 30.
(©Kris Valencia, staff)

C **49.9** (80.3 km) **AH 35.1** (56.5 km) Farrell Creek bridge.
Highway climbs 10 percent grade eastbound.
C **50.2** (80.8 km) **AH 34.8** (56 km) *Highway descends 10 percent grade westbound, slow for 50-kmph/31-mph curve.*
C **55.4** (89.2 km) **AH 29.6** (47.6 km) Double-ended turnout to south long, narrow, with litter bin. View of Peace River valley.
C **56** (90.1 km) **AH 29** (46.6 km) Turnout to south with litter barrels and view of Peace River valley.
C **58.1** (93.5 km) **AH 26.9** (43.3 km) Turnoff to south to spot with litter bin.
C **63.4** (102 km) **AH 21.6** (34.7 km) Halfway River.
C **64.8** (104.3 km) **AH 20.2** (32.5 km) *Begin 10 percent upgrade eastbound.*
C **65.9** (106.1 km) **AH 19.1** (30.7 km) Rest area to south with litter bin, outhouse and picnic tables. Limited access but great view with viewing platform.
C **66** (106.2 km) **AH 19** (30.5 km) *Begin 10 percent downgrade westbound.*
C **73** (117.5 km) **AH 12** (19.3 km) Bridge over Cache Creek.
C **74** (119.1 km) **AH 11** (17.7 km) Highway begins long, winding climb eastbound.
CAUTION: Watch for deer next 5 miles/8 km westbound.
C **77** (123.9 km) **AH 8** (12.9 km) Turnout with litter bin at highest point on Highway 29 (2,750 feet/838m).
Westbound, the highway descends a 10 percent grade: *Slow for 25- to 37-mph/40- to 60-kmph curves.* Views of Peace River Plateau.
C **85** (136.8 km) **AH 0 Junction** with the Alaska Highway, 6.7 miles/10.8 km north of Fort St. John at **Milepost DC 53.6.** Distance marker westbound shows Hudson's Hope 50 miles/80 km, W.A.C. Bennett Dam 65 miles/105 km, Chetwynd 91 miles/146 km.

Return to Milepost PG 187.9
West Access Route
or Milepost DC 53.6 Alaska Highway

Tumbler Ridge Loop

Highway 97 travelers can make a loop trip by taking Highway 29 South from **Milepost PG 189.6** just east of Chetwynd, to the town of Tumbler Ridge, and returning to Highway 97 via Highway 52 North (the Heritage Highway). In addition to Tumbler Ridge's globally important paleontological significance, the major attraction in the area is spectacular Kinuseo Falls, located off of Heritage Highway 52 South via a 35 mile/56 km partially maintained gravel road. Inquire locally for directions to the falls; the turnoff is about 7 miles east of Tumbler Ridge.

Highway 29 South is a paved road that leads 55.9 miles/90 km from **Milepost PG 189.6** to the community of Tumbler Ridge. Highway 52, the Heritage Highway, is also a paved road leading 59.6 miles/96 km from Tumbler Ridge to junction with Highway 97 at **Milepost PG 237.5,** just west of Dawson Creek. Highway 52 has many rolling hills, some 8 percent grades and several S curves.

HIGHWAY 29 SOUTH
Distance from Highway 97 junction at Milepost PG 189.6 (J) is shown.

J **0 Junction** with Highway 97 at **Milepost PG 189.6.**

J **0.1** (0.2 km) Turnout with litter barrels to east. Highway 29 climbs next 2.3 miles/3.7 km southbound.

J **1.9** (3.1 km) Distance marker indicates Tumbler Ridge 55 miles/88 km; Dawson Creek 129 miles/208 km.

J **2.8** (4.5 km) Sign: Trucks check brakes, steep hill ahead.

J **3** (4.8 km) Large gravel turnouts with litter barrels both sides of highway.

J **5.5** (8.8 km) Twidwell Bend bridge over Pine River.

J **5.6** (9 km) Access road east to Long Prairie (8 miles/12.9 km).

J **6.6** (10.6 km) Highway parallels Sukunka River to west.

J **8.2** (13.2 km) Zonnebeke Creek.

J **8.5** (13.7 km) Natural Springs Resort; 9-hole golf course.

J **10.6** (17 km) Bridge over Dickebush Creek.

J **11** (17.7 km) Sanctuary Ranch.

J **13.7** (22 km) **Junction** with Sukunka Forest Road, which leads west 11 miles/17.7 km to Sukunka Falls. *NOTE: Radio-controlled road, travelers must monitor channel 151.325 MHz.*

J **13.8** (22.2 km) Highway climbs next 3 miles/4.8 km southbound.

J **16.7** (26.9 km) Turnouts both sides of highway.

J **21.6** (34.8 km) Turnout to east.

J **26.9** (43.3 km) Turnouts both sides with litter bin to east.

J **28.8** (46.3 km) Paved road leads east 1.2 miles/1.9 km to **Gwillim Lake Provincial Park,** open May 20–to Sept. 15; 49 campsites, picnic tables, hand pump water and firepits. Day-use area with playground and boat launch. Fishing for lake trout, whitefish, burbot, grayling and pike. Camping fee $16 per night, charged.

J **40.1** (64.5 km) Moose Lake, camping fishing off of Forest Road.

J 41.5 (66.7 km) Access road leads west 9 miles/14.5 km to the Bullmoose Mountain and old Bullmoose mine site (closed).

J 41.8 (67.3 km) Turnout to east. Bullmoose Marshes Wetland Interpretive Area.

J 42.1 (67.1 km) Bridge over Bullmoose Flats River.

J 46.7 (75.1 km) Turnout to east. **Phillips Way Summit**, elev. 3,695 feet/1,126m.

J 51.9 (83.5 km) Bullmoose Creek bridge.

J 53.3 (85.8 km) Wolverine River bridge. Park on the north side of the bridge between railway and highway to access trail to Wolverine Dinosaur Trackway.

J 54.9 (88.3 km) Murray River bridge.

J 55.6 (89.5 km) Flatbed Creek bridge.

J 55.7 (89.6 km) Lion's Club Flatbed Creek Campground; 43 sites, water, flush toilets, coin showers, dump station, picnic tables and playground. Flatbed Falls trail. Camping fee $20.

Tumbler Ridge

J 56.7 (91.2 km) Turnoff for community of Tumbler Ridge, located 73 miles/117 km southwest of Dawson Creek via Highways 97 and 52; 55 miles/89 km southeast of Chetwynd via Highway 29; and 91 miles/147 km southwest of BC Highway 2 via the Heritage Highway. **Population:** 2,500. **Elevation:** 2,700 feet/830m. **Emergency Services:** Dial 911. **Medical Center,** phone 250-242-4251.

Visitor Information: Visitor Center at 265 Southgate Street, phone 250-242-3123, toll-free 1-877-SAW-DINO; www.Tumbler Ridge.ca. Contact the Town Office at 250-242-4242 or Community Center at 250-242-4246; www.DistrictOfTumblerRidge.ca. By mail: District of Tumbler Ridge, P.O. Box 100, Tumbler Ridge, BC V0C 2W0; www.VisitTumblerRidge.ca.

Tumbler Ridge was incorporated April 9, 1981, making it British Columbia's newest community. The town was built in conjunction with development of the Northeast Coal resource. A very unstereotypical mining town that garners international attention in urban planning circles, it is layered in 3 tiers or benches. The primary services area is on the second or middle tier. Quintette Mine south of town was the world's largest computerized open coal pit mine until it was shut down in the fall of 2000. Conuma Coal is currently the community's largest employer, mining high-grade metallurgical coal used to make steel.

The discovery of dinosaur tracks and later bones in the Tumbler Ridge area led to British Columbia's first dinosaur dig in 2003. Exploration of Tumbler Ridge's canyons and rock exposures has turned up many remarkable discoveries, including dinosaur footprints with skin impressions. A partial Tyrannosaur skull was found in July 2017 at the Lions Campground.

Visit the **Dinosaur Discovery Gallery**, where the amazing and expanding collection of dinosaur bones and other fossils are displayed. Open May–August, daily 8 A.M. to 5 P.M.; during the rest of the year it is closed Tuesdays and Wednesdays. Visitors should check with the Visitor Center about current events and tours associated with any ongoing digs.

Tumbler Ridge was designated a Global Geopark in 2014, and is now one of more than 100 UNESCO-designated parks worldwide. It is the first Global Geopark in western North America, and the first to represent the plate tectonics that led to the formation of the Rocky Mountains. The area is noted for its geology—which spans a Precambrian to Cretaceous time range—as well as its Cretaceous dinosaur bone beds, Triassic fish and marine reptile fossils and dinosaur trackways (many of which are globally unique). A network of hiking trails lead to numerous geosites, spectacular waterfalls, dinosaur tracks, mountain summits, sedimentary rock formations, caves and canyons.

Visitor facilities include **Trend Mountain Hotel & Conference Centre** and 2 other hotels; 5 restaurants; a convenience store, retail and grocery outlets, a drugstore, hardware store, dollar store, service station, major automotive repairs, propane, and 2 car washes. Recreational facilities include a Community Centre with ice arena, climbing wall, curling rink, weight room, indoor pool, racquet and squash courts, and a library (internet access available). Outdoor facilities include tennis courts, skateboard park, ball diamonds and a 9-hole golf course.

Camping at the Lions Flatbed Creek Campground at the edge of town; 43 sites, no hookups, firewood available, a camping fee is charged; phone 250-242-1197. Monkman RV Park in town has 56 full-service sites. There are also 10 free user-maintained Recreation Site campsites in the area.

There is a 42-site provincial park campground located 37 miles/60 km south from town via a gravel road, near 213-foot/65-m **Kinuseo Falls** in Monkman Provincial Park. The campground is 1.8 miles from the viewing platform of the falls and the trail from parking lot to viewing platform extends from the lot beyond the pit toilets. If you want to climb down to the base of the falls, that trail also leads from the parking lot, NOT off of and to the right of the viewing platform trail. Both park service trails are

marked and depart from the parking lot.

©Claire Torgerson, staff

Kinuseo Falls is formed by the Murray River, which plunges 65m/213 feet over a geological fault to the river bed below. This thunderous cascade of water provides many visitors with the highlight of their trip, and the Murray River Basin is equally as scenic.

Hiking is a popular activity in Tumbler Ridge, which has nearly 50 named and maintained trails, many offering easy day hikes to scenic waterfalls. The 39-mile/63-km Monkman Pass Memorial Trail offers a 6-day trek from Kinuseo Falls to near Prince George.

HIGHWAY 52 NORTH

Highway 52 North (log follows) takes you back to Highway 97, about 12 miles/19 km from Dawson Creek. Highway 52 South loops you over to Highway 2 near the BC–Alberta border.

Distance from Tumbler Ridge (T) is shown.

T 0 Town of Tumbler Ridge.

T 2.9 (4.7 km) Small turnout to west with litter barrels. Trailhead for Quality Canyon and Quality Mouth hiking trails.

T 3.7 (6 km) Turnout to west at **Quality Falls** trailhead. This is an easy 1.5-mile/2.5-km hike through spruce forest to a picnic area and viewpoint overlooking the falls.

T 9.9 (16 km) Large turnout to west with view of Murray River Valley and Rocky Mountains.

T 10.3 (19.6 km) **Heritage Highway Summit**, elev. 4,150 foot/1,265m.

T 14.9 (24 km) **Murray Canyon Overlook** trailhead. Easy 3.7-mile/6-km hike over relatively flat terrain to the overlook. Interpretive trail guides available at trailhead and at the visitor's centre in Tumbler Ridge.

T 21.7 (35 km) Turnout to west at **Tepee Falls** trailhead. This is an easy 3.7-mile/6-km hike to a beautiful waterfall; great views of Murray River Valley.

T 29.3 (47.2 km) *Pavement breaks and dips in road; reduce speed. Slide area.*

T 33.3 (53.7 km) Large turnout to west with litter barrels.

T 35.6 (57.5 km) Salt Creek Valley.

T 41.1 (66.1 km) Large turnout to west with litter barrels.

T 43.1 (69.5 km) Brassey Creek.

T 43.3 (69.7 km) Large turnout to east with litter barrels.

T 46.1 (74.2 km) Turnout to west.

T 46.9 (75.5 km) *CAUTION: Watch for livestock.*

T 52.3 (84.3 km) *CAUTION: Watch for trucks turning at logging road.*

T 56.5 (90.9 km) Turnout to east.

T 59.6 (96 km) **Junction** with Highway 97 at **Milepost PG 237.5**.

Return to Milepost PG 237.5 or PG 189.6 West Access Route

Vancouver Island Highway

CONNECTS: Victoria to Port Hardy, BC

Length: 312 miles   **Road Surface: Paved**   **Season: Open all year**
(See map, page 142)

Victoria's lively waterfront is busy with tourists enjoying this beautiful city. ©Kris Valencia, staff

Major Attractions:

©Kris Valencia, staff

Victoria, Butchart Gardens, Whale Tours, Sea Kayaking

Highest Summit:
*Malahat Summit
1,156 ft./352m*

Most motorists begin their island visit in Victoria, located at the southern end of the island, and then drive the 312-miles/503-kms to Port Hardy, on the northeastern tip of the island, or from Nanaimo, a 246-mile/396-km drive.

Allow plenty of time for this route. A world-renowned travel destination, Vancouver Island offers travelers many attractions, enough to keep them on the island for at least several days, so plan accordingly.

Ferries from the mainland to south Vancouver Island (see map) land at Victoria (from Port Angeles, WA), Swartz Bay (from Tsawwassen, BC), Sidney (from Anacortes, WA), Nanaimo/Duke Point (from Tsawwassen, BC) and Nanaimo/Departure Bay (from Horseshoe Bay, BC). Trans-Canada Highway 1 connects Victoria and Nanaimo, and Highway 19 connects Nanaimo with the northern portion of the island and Port Hardy. *(See BC Ferries schedule in TRAVEL PLANNING section for Port Hardy sailings.)*

An additional ferry option for travel-ers coming from the south is to take the Washington Ferry from Seattle to Bainbridge Island, WA, then the Black Ball Ferry from Port Angeles, WA to Victoria, BC.

Alaska-bound travelers taking BC Ferries Inside Passage service from Port Hardy

Distance in miles	Campbell River	Duncan	Nanaimo	Port Hardy	Port McNeill	Victoria
Campbell River		128	100	147	121	166
Duncan	128		28	273	248	38
Nanaimo	100	28		246	220	66
Port Hardy	147	273	246		26	312
Port McNeill	121	248	220	26		287
Victoria	166	38	66	312	287	

Vancouver Island Highway   Victoria, BC, to Port Hardy, BC

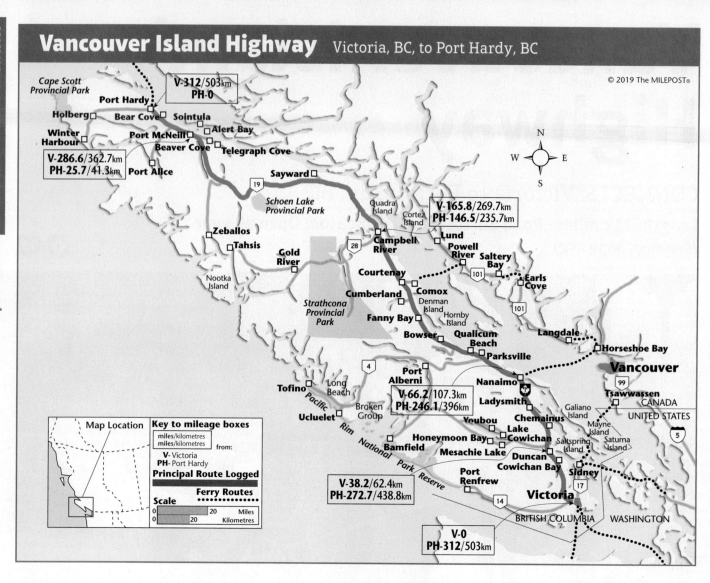

© 2019 The MILEPOST®

V-312/503km PH-0

Cape Scott Provincial Park

Port Hardy
Holberg
Bear Cove — Sointula
Winter Harbour
Port McNeill — Alert Bay
Beaver Cove
Telegraph Cove

V-286.6/362.7km PH-25.7/41.3km Port Alice

Sayward

19

Schoen Lake Provincial Park

Quadra Island
Cortez Island

V-165.8/269.7km PH-146.5/235.7km

Zeballos
Tahsis
Gold River

28

Campbell River
Lund
Powell River
Saltery Bay

Nootka Island

Courtenay
Comox
Earls Cove

Strathcona Provincial Park

Cumberland
Denman Island
Hornby Island

101

Fanny Bay

Bowser
Qualicum Beach
Langdale

Parksville
Horseshoe Bay

4

Port Alberni
Tofino
Long Beach

Nanaimo
Vancouver

99

V-66.2/107.3km PH-246.1/396km

Ladysmith
Tsawwassen
CANADA

Ucluelet
Broken Group

Youbou
Chemainus
Galiano Island
UNITED STATES

Pacific Rim National Park Reserve

Honeymoon Bay
Lake Cowichan
Mayne Island
Saturna Island

5

Bamfield
Mesachie Lake
Saltspring Island

V-38.2/62.4km PH-272.7/438.8km

Duncan
Cowichan Bay
Sidney

17

Port Renfrew

14

Victoria

V-0 PH-312/503km

BRITISH COLUMBIA   WASHINGTON

Map Location

Key to mileage boxes

miles/kilometres
miles/kilometres   from:
V- Victoria
PH- Port Hardy
Principal Route Logged

Ferry Routes ••••••••

Scale
0 ____ 20 Miles
0 ____ 20 Kilometres

---

to Prince Rupert must drive to the northeast coast of Vancouver Island. Prince Rupert, at the west end of the Yellowhead Highway, is a stop for the Alaska State Ferries sailing the Inside Passage north. *(See description of Prince Rupert beginning on page 270.)* This itinerary may also be driven in reverse for return travelers; it is a logical choice for motorists coming down the Cassiar Highway

Vancouver Island Log

Distance from Victoria (V) is followed by distance Port Hardy (PH).
Kilometreage for distance from Victoria reflects existing physical kilometreposts as noted in log.

Victoria

V 0 PH 312.3 (502.6 km) Douglas Street at Belleville in downtown Victoria. **Population:** 85,792. **Emergency Services:** Dial 911. **Hospitals:** Royal Jubilee Hospital, phone 250-370-8000; Victoria General Hospital phone 250-727-4212.

Visitor Information: www.tourismvic toria.com, www.vancouverisland.com; or

stop by the Tourism Victoria Visitor Center at 812 Wharf St., overlooking the Inner Harbor; phone 250-953-2033.

This is the capital city of British Columbia and is a major tourist destination for international travelers. As such, the city offers an extensive array of accommodations, dining experiences, shopping and sightseeing opportunities. It is a bustling city, but parking is available: View parking map at www.downtownvictoria.ca/park. RV parking is a little more challenging, although there are some parking areas that accommodate RVs. **EV plug-ins** are readily found in Victoria (www.plugshare.com); 2 are located downtown at the Victoria Conference Center at 720 Douglas St.

Climate: Moderate, with an average annual mean temperature of 10°C/50°F, and an average annual precipitation of 88 cm/34.8 inches per year.

Recommended attractions include the Legislative Buildings and the Royal British Columbia Museum. Have tea at the iconic Fairmont Empress (very popular, reserve in advance), it overlooks Victoria's Inner Harbor. Rent bikes and ride the Galloping Goose Trail. Discover the colourful floating homes of Fisherman's Wharf, the roaming peacocks in Beacon Hill Park, or the unique local shops of Lower Johnson Street (LoJo). Explore the open ocean while looking for marine wildlife on a day cruise. Take a Gray Line city tour or hop on a CVS bus

to visit the world-famous Butchart Gardens; Butchart (pronounced butch-ert) Gardens is dog-friendly and has plenty of RV parking. The indoor Victoria Butterfly Gardens (especially fun for kids) is nearby.

NOTE: Mile 0 of Trans-Canada Highway 1 is at the junction of Douglas Street and Dallas in Victoria. Head north via Douglas Street for Trans-Canada Highway 1 to Nanaimo. Head north via Blanchard Street for Highway 17 to Butchart Gardens and Schwartz Bay.

TRANS-CANADA HIGHWAY 1

V 1 (1.6 km) **PH 311.3** (501 km) Bay Street. Jiffy Lube and other auto service and repair locations.

V 1.7 (2.7 km) **PH 310.6** (499.9 km) Finlayson, east for Mayfair Shopping Centre. **EV plug-ins** at shopping mall.

V 2.1 (3.4 km) **PH 310.2** (499.2 km) Traffic light at Cloverdale; signs direct northbound traffic to turn for BC Highway 17 to Sidney/Swartz Bay ferry terminals. Trans-Canada 1 becomes Douglas Street in Victoria. Blanchard becomes Highway 17 in Victoria.

V 2.3 (3.7 km) **PH 310** (499.2 km) Traffic light at Saanich, Uptown Mall and access to Highway 17 (follow signs). Easy access to Shell gas/diesel station northbound.

V 2.5 (4 km) **PH 309.8** (498.6 km) Highway goes under Switch Bridge which is the Galloping Goose Trail crossing.

V 2.6 (4.2 km) **PH 309.7** (498.4 km) Distance marker northbound shows Duncan 58 km/36 miles, Nanaimo 109 km/68 miles.

V 3.8 (6.1 km) **PH 308.5** (496.5 km) Admirals Road west to Naval District Museum and Mackenzie Avenue to east.

V 4.8 (7.7 km) **PH 307.5** (494.8 km) Exit 8 for Helmcken Road, View Royal; hospital.

NOTE: Trans-Canada 1 between Victoria and Nanaimo has 2- and 4-lane divided and undivided highway as well as 3-lane road with intermittent north- and southbound passing lanes. Sections of highway divided by concrete barriers restrict left-hand turns. Watch for U-turn routes: these are narrow with short turning radius and may be difficult for large RVs and trailers to negotiate. Posted speed limits from 50 to 100 kmph/31 to 62 mph, with speed zones and curves as posted. Narrow road shoulders. *CAUTION: Watch for bicyclists along the highway, day and night!*

Freeway portions of highway have both exit ramps and traffic lights controlling 3-way and 4-way stops at junctions.

V 5.6 (10 km) **PH 306.7** (493.5 km) Exit 10 to View Royal, Collwood, Fort Rodd Hill, Thetis Lake.

V 6.5 (10.5 km) **PH 305.8** (492.1 km) Distance marker northbound shows Duncan 50 km/31 miles, Nanaimo 101 km/63 miles.

V 8 (14 km) **PH 304.3** (489.7 km) Exit 14 to Langford, Port Renfrew, Sooke.

V 9 (15 km) **PH 303.3** (488.1 km) Exit 15 to McCallum; Shell gas/diesel station to east, Subway.

End 4-lane divided highway, begin 2-lane highway, northbound.

V 9.3 (16 km) **PH 303** (487.6 km) Exit 16 to Leigh Road.

V 10 (16.1 km) **PH 302.3** (486.5 km) Distance marker southbound shows Victoria 16 km/10 miles.

V 10.6 (17 km) **PH 301.7** (485.5 km) Traffic light at West Shore Parkway; Shell gas/diesel station, Tim Hortons and Harley Davidson. Goldstream Provincial Park to east. Distance marker shows Duncan 45 km/28 miles, Nanaimo 95 km/59 miles. NOTE: A few physical kilometreposts northbound measure from this junction and are added to this log as landmarks.

V 11.2 (19 km) **PH 301.1** (484.5 km) Physical Kilometrepost 1 (measured from West Shore Parkway). *Slow for 60 kmph/37 mph curves northbound.* Highway climbs to Malahat Summit. Hitch-hiking and picking up hitch-hikers is illegal.

V 12.4 (21 km) **PH 299.9** (482.6 km) Goldstream day-use area with visitor information centre and picnic tables to east at end of northbound curve.

V 12.5 (21.2 km) **PH 299.8** (482.4 km) Physical Kilometrepost 3. Gravel turnout to east for northbound traffic only.

V 12.8 (20.6 km) **PH 299.5** (482 km) Southbound-only turnoff for trailhead.

V 13.5 (21.7 km) **PH 298.8** (480.9 km) Turnoff east to Goldstream Boathouse.

V 16.9 (28.5 km) **PH 295.4** (475.4 km) Physical Kilometrepost 10.

V 17.2 (28.7 km) **PH 295.1** (474.9 km) Victoria West KOA up hill to west, gas/diesel station to east. Malahat Mountain Inn is north of gas station.

V 19.2 (32 km) **PH 293.1** (471.7 km)

View from Malahat Summit viewpoint, accessible to northbound traffic only.
(©Kris Valencia, staff)

South Shawnigan Lake Road leads northwest to West Shawnigan Lake Provincial Park day-use area.

V 19.6 (31.5 km) **PH 292.7** (471.1 km) Distance marker northbound shows Mill Bay 13 km/8 miles, Nanaimo 32 km/20 miles.

V 19.7 (32.8 km) **PH 292.6** (470.9 km) Northbound-only viewpoint with toilets, information boards, litter bins to east at **Malahat Summit** (elev. 352m/1,156 feet). Easy on/off access.

V 20.9 (33.6 km) **PH 291.4** (469 km) Northbound viewpoint to east.

End 2-lane highway, begin 4-lane divided highway, northbound.

V 21.2 (35.2 km) **PH 291.1** (468.5 km) Northbound-only rest area with toilets, information boards and litter bins. Solar panels power these facilities.

V 21.6 (35.8 km) **PH 290.7** (467.8 km) Malahat Lookout viewpoint to east for northbound traffic only.

Begin 8 percent downgrade northbound.

V 22.8 (37.7 km) **PH 289.5** (465.9 km) Northbound end 2-lane highway and begin 4-lane divided highway.

Distance marker southbound shows Victoria 42 km/26 miles.

V 23.6 (39 km) **PH 288.7** (464.6 km) Exit for Bamberton, Mill Bay Road for Brentwood Ferry and **Bamberton Provincial Park** with campground, day-use area with flush toilets and picnic area, sandy beach and fishing. There are 53 sites with pit toilets, drinking water and picnic tables. Camping fee is $20/nightly in summer or $11 in winter. Summer season is early April through October with reservations available for dates mid-May to early September. Go to www.discovercamping.ca for reservations. Water and firewood are not available in winter season.

V 24.2 (38.9 km) **PH 288.1** (463.7 km) Kilometrepost 40. Distance marker northbound shows Mill Bay 5 km/3 miles, Nanaimo 74 km/46 miles.

V 26.7 (44 km) **PH 284.1** (457.2 km) Traffic light at Deloume Road; Shell gas/diesel station at southwest corner, Co-op

Gas to the northeast; fast food, South Cowichan Visitor Booth, Mill Bay Shopping Centre. Mill Bay Road to Brentwood Ferry.

V 26.9 (44.3 km) **PH 283.9** (456.9 km) Traffic light at Shawnigan Lake-Mill Bay Road junction; Pioneer Square Mall. Access for **side trip** to the **Historic Kinsol Trestle** (12 km/7.5 miles), one of 8 trestles on the Cowichan Valley Trail and one of the tallest (44m/144 feet) and longest (187m/614 feet) free-standing timber rail trestle structures in the world. To reach this trestle, head west through Shawnigan Village and turn right on Shawnigan Lake Road which becomes Renfrew Road; turn right on Gleneagles Road to reach parking lot trailhead at corner of Shelby Road. Part of the Cowichan Valley Trail, the walk to the trestle is 1.2 km/0.7 miles on a wide, gravel surface; viewpoints, benches and trash bins. Toilets at trailhead. Continue on beyond the trestle to enjoy more of this 122-km/76-mile trail.

V 27.5 (45.5 km) **PH 283.3** (455.9 km) Traffic light at Cobble Hill Road; access to Kinsol Trestle (see **Milepost V 26.9**).

V 30.2 (48.6 km) **PH 282.1** (454 km) Fisher Road. Lumberyard, bakery.

V 30.7 (49.4 km) **PH 281.6** (453.2 km) Physical Kilometrepost 50.

V 31.3 (51.1 km) **PH 281** (452.2 km) Cobble Hill Road to west, Cowichan Bay Road to east with toilets, litter bins and picnic tables, for northbound traffic only. There is a small shopping center with groceries, restaurants, medical clinic and a variety of small shops.

V 32.3 (52 km) **PH 280** (450.6 km) Distance marker northbound shows Duncan 10 km/6 miles, Lake Cowichan 41 km/26 miles, Nanaimo 61 km/38 miles.

Distance marker southbound shows Mill Bay 18 km/11 miles, Victoria 61 km/38 miles.

V 34.5 (56 km) **PH 277.8** (447.1 km) Whippletree Junction to east on frontage road; various artisan shops and restaurants, (more shops in courtyard, directly behind the front shops).

V 35.1 (57.2 km) **PH 277.2** (446.1 km)

EV plug-ins at Cowichan Visitor Center in Duncan. These electric vehicle chargers are becoming more common in British Columbia communities. (©Claire Torgerson, staff)

Traffic light at Bench Road; Co-op gas/diesel station with food mart to east.

V 37.4 (60.9 km) **PH 274.9** (442.4 km) Traffic light at Allenby/Chaster roads; Super 8 to east and safe exit to the Old Farm market.

V 37.7 (61.6 km) **PH 274.6** (441.9 km) Traffic light at Boys Road. Access to Duncan RV Park. Sun Valley Mall to west.

Duncan

V 38.2 (62.4 km) **PH 274.1** (441.1 km) Traffic light at Trunk Road/Government Street; Co-op, Petro-Canada, Shell and Mohawk gas/diesel stations; convenience stores, fast food, **EV plug-ins** in downtown near historic train station, Save-On-Foods. Turn west for downtown Duncan.
Population: 4,986. **Emergency Services:** Dial 911. **Hospital:** Cowichan District Hospital, phone 250-737-2030.

Visitor Information: Cowichan Regional Visitor Centre, 2896 Drinkwater Rd., 1-888-303-3337; www.tourismcowichan.com; adjacent the BC Forest Discovery Centre and directly off of Highway 1. **EV plug-ins** next to the Visitor Centre.

Climate: Moderate, with an average annual mean temperature of 11°C/52°F, and an average annual precipitation of 75 cm/29.5 inches per year.

Gateway to the Cowichan Valley region, Duncan has all visitor services, a post office, medical clinics, RCMP, police and churches. Shopping and services are found along Trans-Canada 1. Unique shops and artisanal shopping are in the downtown area (access west via Trunk Road/Government Street or Coronation Avenue.) Cowichan Valley Museum is located in the Duncan Train Station at 130 Canada Ave. and there are fascinating totems adjacent the museum; phone 250-746-6612; or visit www.cowichanvalleymuseum.bc.ca. City of Duncan is host to over 40 Totem Poles. Guided totem tours from June to September from the train station on Canada Avenue. Year-round self-guided totem tours.

The Duncan Farmers Market in City Square, Saturdays to 2 P.M. This is the largest year-round market on the island. It offers a wide variety of edibles, art and gifts. There is plenty of parking near the square off of Canada Avenue; www.duncanfarmersmarket.ca. There is live entertainment each week.

Major attractions in the area include wineries and several intriguing agricultural and culinary attractions, such as True Grain Bread in Cowichan Bay Village (www.truegrain.ca) and the Cowichan Valley Lavender Labyrinth (cowichanvalleylavender.com) as well as Canadas only Tea Farm (www.westholmetea.com).

Outdoor recreation includes 3 championship golf courses. Bicyclists will enjoy the Cowichan Valley Trail/Trans Canada Trail that starts at the south end of Shawnigan Lake and goes west to Cowichan Lake then east to North Cowichan and Ladysmith. Or walk the 1.2 km/0.7 mile portion to the Kinsol Trestle (see Milepost V 26.9). Lake Cowichan on Highway 18 is a popular summer recreation spot and the access of the popular Pacific Marine Circle Route.

TRANS-CANADA HIGHWAY 1
(continued)

V 38.3 (62.5 km) **PH 274** (441 km) Traffic light at Coronation; Shell gas/diesel on southeast corner. Downtown Duncan to west.

V 38.6 (63 km) **PH 273.7** (440.5 km) Traffic light at James Street; Wendy's, Boston Pizza, McDonald's, Tim Hortons, A&W and local restaurants throughout downtown Duncan to west.

V 39 (63.6 km) **PH 273.3** (439.8 km) Traffic light at Beverly Street with mall and groceries as well as a Starbucks to west.

V 39.4 (63.4 km) **PH 272.9** (439.2 km) Holmes Creek.

Distance marker northbound shows Chemainus 17 km/11 miles, Ladysmith 27 km/17 miles, Nanaimo 50 km/31 miles.

V 39.8 (64.9 km) **PH 272.5** (438.5 km) Turnout with litter bins to east.

V 40.3 (65.7 km) **PH 272** (437.7 km) Traffic light at Drinkwater Road; Cowichan

Commons, Walmart, Canadian Tire.

To east, at 2896 Drinkwater Rd., Duncan Chamber of Commerce and **Cowichan Regional Visitor Centre**, open year-round with **EV plug-ins**, free WiFi, displays of opportunities available across this region, locally focused and produced book and gift store section. The centre shares a parking lot with the **BC Forest Discovery Centre** (bcforestdiscoverycentre.com), open daily 10 A.M. to 4:30 P.M. from June 1 to Labour Day. Check website for updated dates and times and plan to ride the steam train.

V 41.2 (67.1 km) **PH 271.1** (436.3 km) **Junction** with Highway 18/Cowichan Valley Highway/Herd Road. Drive west to Lake Cowichan Recreation Area. Also access to Mount Prevost Memorial Park and Averill Creeks and Deol Estate wineries. A 55-km/34-mile road connects Lake Cowichan and Port Renfrew on Pacific Marine Circle Route. Herd Road leads 5 km/3 miles east to Raptors facilities.

V 41.6 (66.9 km) **PH 270.7** (435.6 km) Distance marker northbound shows Ladysmith 23 km/14 miles, Nanaimo 45 km/28 miles.

V 42.2 (67.9 km) **PH 270.1** (434.7 km) Weigh scale for northbound-only.

V 42.6 (69.3 km) **PH 269.7** (434 km) Traffic light at Mays Road; Chevron and Co-op Commercial Cardlock gas/diesel stations, Cowichan Exhibition Grounds to west.

V 45.5 (74 km) **PH 266.8** (429.4 km) Traffic light at Mount Sicker Road; gas/diesel station with convenience store and Russell Farm Market to west. Chevron to east (gas/diesel) and turnoff for Crofton and Salt Spring Island Ferry to east.

Distance marker southbound shows Duncan 11 km/7 miles, Lake Cowichan 33 km/21 miles, Victoria 72 km/45 miles.

V 47.8 (76.9 km) **PH 264.5** (425.7 km) Fuller Lake Road.

V 48.2 (78.4 km) **PH 264.1** (425 km) Traffic light at Henry Road; Co-op gas/diesel with convenience store at northwest corner. Exit east for **CHEMAINUS** (pop. 3,900), famous for its 44 outdoor murals and for the Boeing 737, sunk off the coast as an artificial reef for scuba divers. All services available. Chemainus Visitor Centre is at 102-9799 Waterwheel Crescent; phone 250-246-3944; chemainus.bc.ca.

V 54.4 (88.3 km) **PH 257.9** (415 km) Traffic light at North Davis Road and Chemainus Road; Co-Op gas/diesel, DQ, Save-On Foods and other services to west.

Distance marker southbound shows Chemainus 10 km/6 miles, Victoria 89 km/55 miles.

V 55.4 (89.2 km) **PH 256.9** (413.4 km) Information centre is to the west.

V 55.7 (90.4 km) **PH 256.6** (412.9 km) Traffic light at Roberts Street with Petro-Canada gas/diesel station. Drive west on Roberts Street to First Avenue and downtown **LADYSMITH** (pop. 8,376); all services. Old Town Bakery here is very popular. www.ladysmith.ca.

V 55.9 (90.7 km) **PH 256.4** (412.6 km) Shell gas/diesel station to west for southbound traffic only.

V 58 (94 km) **PH 254.3** (409.2 km) **Junction** with Oyster Sto Lo Road. Esso gas station, Microtel Inn and credit union to west and a Husky gas/diesel/convenience store with A&W and Tim Hortons to east.

V 60.2 (96.9 km) **PH 252.1** (405.7 km) Distance marker northbound Nanaimo 16 km/10 miles, Parksville 51 km/32 miles.

V 61.2 (99.3 km) **PH 251.1** (404.1 km) Spitfire Way. Nanaimo airport to east.

V 62.1 (100 km) **PH 250.2** (402.6 km) Northbound-only rest area to east; toilets, litter/recycling bins, picnic tables and a large parking area.

V 62.4 (100.5 km) **PH 249.9** (402.2 km) Nanaimo River bridge.

V 64 (103.5 km) **PH 248.3** (399.5 km) Traffic light at Morden Road; Gas & Go gas/diesel station to west.

V 65.3 (106 km) **PH 247** (397.5 km) **Duke Point Interchange**. Exit to BC Ferries/Duke Point terminal (8 km/5 miles) via Highway 19 East for ferry service to/from Tsawwassen.

V 66.2 (107.3 km) **PH 246.1** (396 km) Highway splits northbound: exit right for Highway 19 North to Parksville, Campbell River and Port Hardy; go straight for Trans-Canada Highway 1/Highway 19A (log follows) for Nanaimo city centre (description follows) and BC Ferries Departure Bay terminal for ferry service to Horseshoe Bay. *Port Hardy-bound travelers exit from Trans-Canada Highway 1 to continue north on Highway 19/ Nanaimo Parkway.* Kilometreposts northbound show distance from Duke Point.

Trans-Canada Highway 1/Highway 19A log to Nanaimo as follows. Food, gas, lodging and other services available along the highway.

Mile 0.4 Traffic light at Cedar Road.

Mile 0.7 Traffic light at Cranberry.

Mile 0.9 Traffic light at Maki Road/10th Street; South Parkway Mall to west. Chevron commercial cardlock to east. Living Forest RV Park is 0.3 mile/0.5 km east.

Mile 1.7 Petroglyph Provincial Park with hiking trail.

Mile 2.6 Traffic light at Needham; car wash to east.

Mile 2.9 Dairy Queen, gas station to west.

Mile 3 Shell gas station to east.

Mile 3.4 Esplanade/Gordon Street; Casino Nanaimo, Port Place Mall (Thrifty Foods, London Drugs, BC Liquor Store, Starbucks, restaurants).

Mile 3.7 Traffic light at Commercial. City centre.

Mile 3.8 Traffic light at Comox Road; Mr. Lube. Turn east for Maffeo Sutton Park (passenger ferry to Newcastle Island). Highway 19A/Island Highway continues as Terminal Avenue to rejoin Highway 19 just north of Exit 28/Aulds Road.

Nanaimo

Located on the east coast of Vancouver Island, Nanaimo is the third oldest city in British Columbia. **Population:** approx. 87,000. **Emergency Services:** Dial 911. **Hospital:** Nanaimo Regional General Hospital, phone 250-755-7691. Nanaimo is a transportation hub, connecting passengers and vehicles to/from the mainland via BC Ferries Tsawwassen–Duke Point service, and Horseshoe Bay–Departure Bay service, via floatplane terminals and airport.

Visitor Information: Open daily, year-round, Visitor Center at 2450 Northfield Rd., Exit 21. Downtown visitor kiosk with maps, brochures, guides and event information (May–September). Website: www.tourism nanaimo.com.

Climate: Moderate, with an average annual mean temperature of 9.5°C/49.1°F, and an average annual precipitation of 114.5 cm/45.1 inches per year.

This is a good-sized city with complete tourist facilities including major-chain hotels/motels, restaurants and retail stores. The Nanaimo Harbourfront Walkway (5 km/3 miles) is one of Nanaimo's main attractions in the downtown area. Passenger ferries also connect the downtown waterfront with Protection Island (famous for Canada's only floating pub) and Newcastle Island Marine Provincial Park with greater than 20 km/12 miles of trails. Downtown offers a great variety of different water activities from sailing cruises to snorkel gear and kayak rentals.

Nanaimo is also home of the self-guided Nanaimo Bar Trail (trail maps at Visitor Centre) that features over 35 variation of the famous Canadian dessert (including a deep-fried version). You can review a list of locations that serve these desserts at: www. tourismnanaimo.com/what-to-do/sip-and-savour/nanaimo-bar-trail. Other downtown attractions include the Nanaimo Museum at 100 Museum Way, the Old City Quarter with local shops and restaurants (www.old cityquarter.com) and the Vancouver Island Military Museum (www.vimms.ca).

Nanaimo's south area of Cedar & Yellow Point boasts a huge variety of artists, artisans, farms and food, as well as WildPlay Element Park featuring ziplines, bungy jumping, primal swing and much more. Several farmers markets run in the area from May–October.

Nanaimo has some 200-plus parks, 130 kms/81 miles of trails, and 12 off-leash dog parks (www.nanaimo.ca/recreation-parks/ parks-trails/dogs-in-parks). Nanaimo Aquatic Center (Exit 18 on Highway 19) is the largest west of Edmonton and features a wave pool, lazy river and lots of parking.

Multiple **EV plug-in** sites throughout city and downtown. Near waterfront in downtown, 2 locations: Greenlots and Vancouver Island Conference Center, both on Gordon Street.

HIGHWAY 19
(continued)

V 66.2 (14.7 km) **PH 246.1** (396 km) **Junction** of Highway 19 and Highway 19A/Trans-Canada Highway 1. Continue north on Highway 19 for Campbell River, Port McNeill and Port Hardy. Physical kilometreposts northbound show distance from Duke Point and are added to this log.

V 70 (16 km) **PH 242.3** (389.9 km) Traffic light at Exit 16 Fifth Street to east/College Drive to west.

V 71.2 (18 km) **PH 241.1** (388 km) Traffic light at Exit 18 Jingle Pot Road east to Aquatic Centre and Nanaimo City Centre, west to camping.

Northbound, the Parkway Trail (multi-use) parallels Highway 19 to Exit 28.

V 71.6 (18.6 km) **PH 240.7** (387.4 km) Millstone River.

V 73 (21 km) **PH 239.3** (385.1 km) Exit 21 Northfield Road east into Nanaimo. Turn west for Visitor Centre with picnic tables, litter bins, information and travel planning assistance.

V 75 (24 km) **PH 237.3** (381.9 km) Traffic light at Exit 24 Mostar Road east to Highway 19A/Island Highway with restaurants and lodging; Jingle Pot Road west to camping with sani-dump.

V 77.3 (28 km) **PH 235** (378.2 km) Traffic light at Exit 28 Aulds Road. Walmart/Woodgrove Centre, the island's largest shopping mall, to east.

V 77.5 (28.3 km) **PH 234.8** (378 km) Mary Ellen Drive. Northbound access east to Walmart.

V 78 (29 km) **PH 234.3** (377 km) **Junction** with Highway 19A/Island Highway southbound for downtown Nanaimo and Departure Bay ferry terminal. Victoria-bound travelers continue on Highway 19/Nanaimo Parkway southbound.

V 78.8 (30.3 km) **PH 233.5** (375.7 km) Traffic light at Ware Road to Lantzville.

V 80 (32.2 km) **PH 232.3** (373.8 km) Traffic light at Superior Road to village of Lantzville to east.

V 83.2 (37.3 km) **PH 229.1** (368.7km) Southbound-only rest area to west with picnic tables, litter/recycling bins, grassy area.

V 84.8 (39.8 km) **PH 227.5** (366.1 km) Northwest Bay Road; Petro-Canada gas/diesel station at northeast corner.

V 86.7 (42.9 km) **PH 225.6** (363km) Southbound-only access to Chevron gas/diesel station to west.

V 88.3 (45.5 km) **PH 224** (360.5 km) Exit 46 to **PARKSVILLE** and **junction** with Highway 19A North/Oceanside Route, a 2-lane highway that gives access to a string of resorts, beaches and tourist facilities between Parksville and Qualicum Beach. Attractions along here include **Rathtrevor Provincial Park** campground and beach (especially at low tide); Deep Bay Marine Field Station,

Pedestrian walkway around Nanaimo Harbor is a major attraction here.
(©David L. Ranta, staff)

Vancouver Island Visitor Center at Exit 117.
(©David L. Ranta, staff)

Milner Gardens and Woodland. Visit Second Avenue in Qualicum Beach, with local shops and no chain stores allowed; Paradise Adventure Mini-Golf & RV Park has a well-maintained and colourful miniature golf course. **EV plug-ins** at public library (100 Jensen Ave. E.) and at the waterside Parksville Community Park.

V 91.2 (50.3 km) **PH 221.1** (355.8) Exit 51 to Parksville/Coombs and Highway 4A/Port Alberni. Recommended **side trip** (description follows) to Englishman River Falls, North Island Wildlife Recovery Centre, Butterfly World & BC Orchid Garden and Old Country Market.

Exit west and follow Highway 4A north 1.5 miles and turn left (west) on Errington Road. It is approximately 5 miles/9 km to **Englishman River Falls Provincial Park.** Beautiful area of tall trees; large parking area, a multi-use trail network and 2 waterfalls. There are 105 sites with pit toilets, drinking water and picnic tables. Camping fee is $23/nightly in summer. Campground is open May through September with reservations available for dates mid-May to early September. Go to www.discovercamping.ca for reservations. Day use only in winter season.

Returning to Highway 4A, continue north 2.5 miles to Coombs to visit the very popular **Old Country Market** where you sometimes see goats c on the roofs of their farm sheds. This small complex, just south of Coombs River Bridge, has fresh fruits and vegetables and a variety of small shops that attract a big crowd, even on weekdays. Parking for cars is extensive up a narrow side street at the market; park along Highway 4A; or follow RV/bus parking signs.

From Coombs, continue north on Highway 4A 1.5 miles to junction with Highway 4; turn east and continue 1.5 miles to return to Highway 19 at Exit 60, or turn west on Highway 4 for Little Qualicum Falls/Cameron Lake, Cathedral Grove and Pacific Rim National Park.

V 96.7 (52 km) **PH 215.6** (347 km) Exit 60 to Highway 4 for **side trip** to Port Alberni, Tofino, and Pacific Rim National Park. Other major attractions west off this exit include Little Qualicum Falls (camping; day-use areas on Cameron Lake), and MacMillan Park, which contains the famous Cathedral Grove stand of Douglas fir. Exit east for Qualicum Beach and Highway 19A. **EV plug-ins** at the waterside Qualicum Beach Visitor Centre on Highway 19A.

V 101.7 (67 km) **PH 210.6** (338.9 km) Little Qualicum River.

NOTE: Signed river crossings northbound are included in this log. Creek crossings—of which there are many—are not included.

V 106.3 (74.5 km) **PH 206** (331.5 km) Exit 75 Horne Lake Road west to Spider Lake Provincial Park for swimming and hiking (9 km/5.5 miles), and Horne Lake Caves Provincial Park with day-use area (15 km/9.5 miles including gravel road). Exit east for Highway 19A/Qualicum Beach.

V 107.6 (76.6 km) **PH 204.7** (329.4 km) Big Qualicum River.

V 108.5 (78 km) **PH 203.8** (328 km) Northbound-only turnout to east.

V 111.4 (82.7 km) **PH 200.9** (323.3 km) Northbound-only paved turnout to east.

V 113.8 (86.5 km) **PH 198.5** (319.4 km) Exit 87 Cooke Creek Road to Highway 19A, Deep Bay, Fanny Bay. Drive 2 km/1 mile to Rosewall Creek Provincial Park picnic area.

V 117 (88.6 km) **PH 195.3** (314.3 km) *CAUTION: Elk crossing.*

V 121.4 (95.6 km) **PH 190.9** (307.2 km) Tsable River.

V 122.1 (100 km) **PH 190.2** (306.1 km) Exit 101 east to Buckley Bay, Union Bay and Royston. Buckley Bay ferry and junction with Highway 19A/Oceanside Route. Rest area with bike path to east.

V 130.2 (113 km) **PH 182.1** (293 km) Trent River.

V 132.6 (116.8 km) **PH 179.7** (289.2 km) Exit 117 to Cumberland, Courtenay, Royston and Comox. Hospital, police, ferry, **Vancouver Island Visitor Centre**, airport.

V 137.2 (124 km) **PH 175.1** (281.8 km) Puntledge River.

V 138.4 (126 km) **PH 173.9** (279.9 km) Browns River.

V 138.8 (126.6 km) **PH 173.5** (279.2 km) Traffic light at Exit 127 Piercy Road, Courtenay, Comox.

V 141.1 (130.3 km) **PH 171.2** (275.5 km) Exit 130 to Mount Washington Alpine Resort, Strathcona Parkway.

V 145.7 (137.4 km) **PH 166.6** (268.1 km) Tsolum River.

V 147.3 (140 km) **PH 165** (265.5 km) Large, paved, double-ended turnout both north- and southbound.

V 149.4 (143.5 km) **PH 162.9** (262.2 km) Traffic light at Exit 144 Hamm Road; Saratoga Beach, Oyster Bay and **Miracle Beach Provincial Park** (8 km/5 miles), one of Vancouver Island's most popular camping and day-use parks. Day-use area with flush toilets, beach, picnic tables and changing building. Nature trails extend from this area (NOTE: dogs are not allowed in the South Beach day-use area but are allowed in the North Beach day-use area). There are 202 campsites, flush and pit toilets, shower house, drinking water and picnic tables. Camping fee is $33/nightly in summer; $13/nightly in March and October (no services). Campground is open March through October (but no services are provided during those winter months). Sani-dump available for $5 during summer season. Reservations are available for dates mid-May to early September. Go to www.discovercamping.ca for reservations.

V 154.8 (152 km) **PH 157.5** (253.5 km) Oyster River.

V 155.5 (153.3 km) **PH 156.8** (252.3 km) Traffic light at Cranberry Road.

V 156.3 (154.5 km) **PH 156** (251 km) Little Oyster River.

V 160.2 (161.6 km) **PH 152.1** (244.8 km) Exit 161 to Jubilee Parkway and south Campbell River. Highway 19A/Oceanside Route, Visitor Information Centre to east, Campbell River airport to west.

V 164.2 (167 km) **PH 148.1** (238.3 km) Traffic light at Exit 167 Willis Road; Shell gas/diesel station to west with sani-dump and picnic tables.

Highway splits northbound: Begin 1-way Tamarac Street northbound. End 1-way Willow Street southbound.

V 165.6 (169.2 km) **PH 146.7** (236.1 km) Traffic light at 14th Avenue. Access east to Campbell River city centre.

V 165.7 (169.5 km) **PH 146.6** (235.9 km) Traffic light at 16th Avenue; Esso gas/diesel station, McDonald's. Access east to Campbell River city centre.

V 165.8 (169.7 km) **PH 146.5** (235.7 km) Traffic light at **junction** of Highway 19 with Highway 19A/Island Highway east to Campbell River (description follows). Walmart is 1.3 km/0.8 miles east on Highway 19A which continues downhill to Visitor Centre with **EV plug-ins** (2 km/1.2 miles), and Campbell River's waterfront.

Campbell River

V 165.8 (169.7 km) **PH 146.5** (235.7 km) Located on the east coast of North/Central Vancouver Island, 3.5-hour drive from Victoria and less than 2 hours north of Nanaimo. **Population:** 36,096. **Emergency Services:** Dial 911. **Hospital:** North Island Hospital, Campbell River and District, phone 250-286-7100.

Visitor Information: Campbell River Visitor Center is located in the same building as the Art Gallery in the Tyee Plaza at 1235 Shoppers Row; phone 1-877-286-5705; www.campbellriver.travel. Free parking at the center with 2 EV plug-in parking stalls.

Climate: Moderate, with an average winter temperature of 9°C/48.2°F, and an average annual precipitation of 140 cm/55 inches.

All visitor services are available including accommodations ranging from budget hotels to B&B's and vacation rentals to the world-famous Painter's Lodge. There are also several oceanside campgrounds such as the Thunderbird RV Park, phone 250-286-3344. The downtown core offers a wide variety of fine dining options and has a number of major chain stores as well as local boutiques.

Campbell River is located at the entrance to the Discovery Passage. This is a popular route for marine traffic, cruise ships, deep sea freighters and barges in transit to Alaska are a common sight. The city has a busy waterfront with multiple marinas, a fishing pier and the Rotary Seawalk which is a multi-use trail that runs 6 km/3.7 miles along the coast of Campbell River.

The waterfront Robert V. Ostler Park is several blocks from the Tyee Plaza and has beautiful gardens, totems and walkways. Continue along the harbourfront to see the Discovery Fishing Pier, Discovery Passages Aquarium (open May–August) and Maritime Heritage Centre. Pier Street Farmers Market is here on Sundays 10 A.M. to 2:30 P.M. May–September.

HIGHWAY 19
(continued)

V 165.8 (169.7 km) **PH 146.5** (235.7 km) Traffic light at **junction** of Highway 19 and Highway 28 (Gold River Highway). Access is to Parkside Campground & RV Park, 5 km/3 miles west.

V 165.9 (169.9 km) **PH 146.4** (235.5 km) Campbell River bridge.

V 166.7 (171.2 km) **PH 145.6** (234.3 km) End 4-lane highway, begin 2-lane highway, northbound. Highway 19 becomes North Island Highway: Road narrows; limited services between communities.

CAUTION: Watch for wildlife!

Highway splits southbound: Begin 1-way Willow Street southbound. End 1-way Tamarac Street northbound.

V 167.7 (173 km) **PH 144.6** (232.7 km) McDonald Road. West for Gas and Go gas/diesel and general store and markets, Friendship Inn Motel and RV Park.

V 168.8 (174.7 km) **PH 143.5** (230.9 km) Viewpoint to east.

V 170.7 (177.8 km) **PH 141.6** (227.9 km) Southbound Campbell River welcome sign.

V 172.6 (180.8 km) **PH 139.7** (224.8 km) Turnoff to east for rest area with point-of-interest sign about Seymour Narrows.

V 174.9 (184.5 km) **PH 137.4** (221.1km) Turnoff on gravel road for **Morton Lake Provincial Park**, 19 km/12 miles west; 24 lakeside campsites, day-use picnic area, swimming, canoeing/kayaking on Morton and Mohun lakes. Camping fee is $18/nightly in summer/$11 in winter (no services, winter visitors must be self-sufficient). Campground is open year-round with services mid-May through September and reservations available. Go to www.discover camping.ca for reservations.

V 176.3 (186.8 km) **PH 136** (218.9 km) Ripple Rock Recreation Hiking Trailhead to east; parking.

V 177.5 (188.7 km) **PH 134.8** (216.9 km) Turn off onto Browns Bay Road to east for Ripple Rock RV Park (7 km/4 miles), Browns Bay Resort.

V 181.5 (195 km) **PH 130.8** (210.5 km) Distance marker northbound shows Port Hardy 208 km/129 miles.

V 184.7 (200.1 km) **PH 127.6** (205.4 km) Turnoff to east for **Roberts Lake** fishing and day-use area. handicap accessible. Kilometre-post 200.

V 185.6 (201.6 km) **PH 126.7** (203.9 km) Turnoff east to Roberts Lake rest area with litter/recycling bins, picnic tables and toilets.

V 191 (210.3 km) **PH 121.3** (195.2 km) Rock Bay campground and recreation area to the east.

V 204.9 (233 km) **PH 107.4** (172.8 km) Salmon River.

V 205.7 (233.7 km) **PH 106.6** (171.6 km) Sayward Road, to Sayward Junction; convenience store and gas/diesel. Turnoff for village of Sayward (8 km/5 miles).

Distance marker southbound shows Campbell River 68 km/42 miles, Nanaimo 222 km/138 miles.

V 206.3 (234.7 km) **PH 106** (170.6 km) Long, double-ended turnout to east for Sayward Hill winter chain-up area to east for northbound traffic.

V 206.5 (235 km) **PH 105.8** (170.3 km) Sayward Hill winter chain-up area to east for northbound traffic.

Grades to 7 percent northbound. 2-lane road with some passing lanes on hills. Some patched and bumpy pavement. *CAUTION: Watch for logging trucks and for deer. Drive with headlights on at all times.*

V 208.9 (238.9 km) **PH 103.4** (166.4 km) Brake check area to west for southbound traffic descending Sayward Hill.

V 211.4 (242.8 km) **PH 100.9** (162.4 km) Keta Lake rest area to west with litter bins, picnic table and toilets.

V 217.7 (252.7 km) **PH 94.6** (152.2 km) Adam River.

V 223.4 (262 km) **PH 88.9** (143.1 km) Eve River.

V 223.5 (262.3 km) **PH 88.8** (142.9 km) Turnoff for rest area to east, well away from the highway with a circular drive, toilets and litter bins.

V 232.3 (277 km) **PH 80** (128.7 km) Long, gravel turnout to the west. Several additional gravel turnouts in a row in the next 1.5 miles/2.4 km northbound.

V 233.6 (278.1 km) **PH 78.7** (126.7 km) Distance marker northbound shows Woss 14 km/9 miles, Port McNeill 82 km/51 miles, Port Hardy 121 km/75 miles.

V 236.6 (282.9 km) **PH 75.7** (121.8 km) Southbound distance marker shows Sayward 61 km/38 miles, Campbell River 117 km/73 miles.

V 240.1 (288.5 km) **PH 72.2** (116.2 km) Turnoff west for 12 km/8 miles of rough gravel road with logging traffic to **Schoen Lake Provincial Park**. There are 9 sites with pit toilets, drinking water, picnic tables and boat launch with small day-use area. Swimmers: Heed warning signs about dangers and avoid log jams. Camping fee is $23/night. Campground is open mid-May through September with services. *NOTE: This can be an unsafe road/area in rainy weather and the campground can be closed for safety, without notice, in those conditions. The campground gates are locked due to threat of landslides from November through March.*

V 242.8 (292.7 km) **PH 69.5** (111.8 km) Hoomak Lake rest area to west with information boards about this area, toilets and litter bin; solar panels power the facility.

V 246.8 (299.2 km) **PH 65.5** (105.4 km) Woss Cutoff: road leads 1.6 km/1 mile south to community of Woss with gas/diesel station, cafe and general store. **EV plug-in** across street from gas station.

V 250.5 (305.2 km) **PH 61.8** (99.5 km) Eagles Nest roadside rest area to west with toilet and litter barrel, picnic tables.

V 251.6 (306.9 km) **PH 60.7** (97.7 km) Double-ended turnout to west. Highway climbs northbound; end passing lane.

V 252.4 (307.1 km) **PH 59.9** (96.4 km) Large, paved turnout to west.

V 252.7 (307.6 km) **PH 59.6** (95.9 km)

Large, paved turnout to west.

V 258 (317 km) **PH 54.3** (87.4 km) Double-ended brush-filled viewpoint to west alongside lake. Highway descends northbound. End uphill passing lane southbound.

V 260.3 (320.6 km) **PH 52** (83.7 km) **Junction** for Zeballos a logging town located 42 km/26 miles southwest via a gravel road.

V 272.3 (339.8 km) **PH 40** (64.4 km) Gravel turnout to west.

V 282.1 (355.3 km) **PH 30.2** (48.6 km) Turnout to east at **junction**. Paved road east leads 15 km/9 miles to **TELEGRAPH COVE** (pop. 20). This historic boardwalk village is a very picturesque community on Vancouver Island and a popular tourist destination in summer. Marine wildlife and whale watching tours depart twice daily from the May long weekend to early October with a good chance of seeing some of the over 300 fish-eating orcas known as the "Northern Residents" and inhabit Johnstone Strait in the summer months. Grizzly bear viewing tours depart daily by boat to BC mainland coastal inlets from mid-May to late September. Kayak tours and rentals are available. Stay onshore and visit the Whale Interpretive Centre with fully articulated killer whales, Dalls' porpoise, fin whale and other species. May–September daily 9 A.M. to 5 P.M. with longer hours in July and August. Admission fee. www.killerwhalecentre.org; society@kill erwhalecentre.org.

Full service RV sites and tenting is available at two campgrounds. **EV plug-in** at Telegraph Cove Resort.

V 282.5 (355.9 km) **PH 29.8** (48 km) Distance marker northbound shows Port McNeill 10 km/6 miles, Port Hardy 53 km/33 miles, Port Alice 56 km/35 miles.

V 283.2 (357.1 km) **PH 29.1** (46.8 km) Nimpkish Hatchery to west, Nimpkish River bridge; turnout with litter bins to east at north end of bridge by totems.

V 284.1 (358.7 km) **PH 28.2** (45.4 km) Hyde Creek Road. Petro-Canada gas/diesel station east of highway, car wash.

V 285 (360.1 km) **PH 27.3** (43.9 km) Port McNeill Airport Road to east.

V 286.5 (362.5 km) **PH 25.8** (41.5 km) Turnout with litter bin to east and information signs for Alert Bay.

V 286.6 (362.7 km) **PH 25.7** (41.3 km) Turnoff for Port McNeill via Campbell Way (2.6 km/1.6 miles); description follows. Petro-Canada with gas/diesel and convenience store is 0.6 km/0.4 miles from Highway 19.

Port McNeill

V 286.6 (362.7 km) **PH 25.7** (41.3 km) Located on the northeast coast of Vancouver Island on Broughton Strait. Port McNeill is 6 hours from Victoria, 4 hours from Nanaimo and 30 minutes from Port Hardy. **Population:** 2,600. **Emergency Services:** Dial 911. **Hospital:** Port McNeill Hospital, phone 250-956-4461. Conservation Officer, phone 1-877-952-7277 to report cougar or bear sightings and interactions.

Visitor Information: Port McNeill Information Center, is in the same building with the harbour manager's office at 1594 Beach Dr. (on the waterfront); phone 250-956-3881; info@portmcneillharbour.ca. Website

Port Hardy visitor center is easy to find: It's at the bottom of Main Street on the waterfront.
(©David L. Ranta, staff)

www.town.portmcneill.bc.ca. Stop in to find out about whale watching, kayak rentals or fishing.

Climate: Moderate, with an average annual mean temperature of 8°C/46.4°F, and an average annual precipitation of 174 cm/68.5 inches per year.

Port McNeill has complete tourist services. Groceries (with in-store bakery and organic items), clothing, hardware, fishing and sporting goods, and gifts are available in local stores. Many are within walking distance of the Visitor Centre. Pick up a town map at the Visitor Centre along with a list of popular local hiking and walking trails.

With its full service harbour facility, Port McNeill plays host to Inside Passage marine traffic and is also a gateway to a variety of activities, from salmon fishing to whale watching and kayaking. Campers and outdoor enthusiasts will find everything they require in this full facility community. Take BC Ferries (www.bcferries.com) to Alert Bay (www.alertbay.ca) and Sointula on Malcolm Island (www.sointulainfo.ca).

Port McNeill is home to 2 of the world's largest burls. The largest is just north of the Visitor Centre in the Community Hall parking lot. Continue past the Community Hall and turn left up-hill for Broughton RV Park. Fully serviced RV sites are $25/night in summer/high season; tent sites are $15/night and have community bear boxes for food storage; hot showers. Reservations 250-956-3224 or broughtonstrait@hotmail.com.

Special event: Orca Fest, mid-August.

HIGHWAY 19
(continued)

V 287.2 (363.6 km) **PH 25.1** (40.4km) Turnout to west with information boards on Port McNeill, Alert Bay and Alice Lake Recreational Loop.

V 292.3 (371.8 km) **PH 20** (32.1 km) Turnoff to east for Cluxewe Resort, 1.1 km/0.7 mile via gravel road; popular seaside RV Park, cabins, seasonal cafe (summer-only cafe is closed Tuesdays).

V 294.4 (374.1 km) **PH 17.9** (28.8 km) Viewpoint to east; North Vancouver Island map, litter bins.

V 297.2 (379.8 km) **PH 15.1** (24.3 km) Circular gravel rest area to east with toilets, picnic tables, partial views.

V 298.7 (382.3 km) **PH 13.6** (21.9 km) Keogh River.

V 298.9 (382.6 km) **PH 13.4** (21.6 km) **Junction** with Highway 30 which leads west 30 km/18 miles to the village of Port Alice, known as the "gateway to the Wild West Coast" for outdoor recreationists; visit www.portalice.ca. Camping available at **Marble River Provincial Park**, **Link River Regional Park** and Port Alice RV Campground.

V 308.5 (397.9 km) **PH 3.8** (6.1 km) Byng Road to Quatse Salmon Stewardship Center and Quatse River Regional Park and campground. Check website for more information: www.thesalmoncentre.org. More details at **Milepost V 309.9**.

V 309.2 (399 km) **PH 3.1** (5 km) **Junction** with Bear Cove Highway/Welcome to Port Hardy. Turnout at junction, wind farm turbine blade is on display. Highway leads east 5 km/3 miles to **BC Ferries terminal** at Bear Cove. Also access this turnoff to Wildwoods Campground (Mile 1.1), Ecoscape Cabins (Mile 1.7), Bear Cove Cottages (Mile 2.3), Bear Cove Park day-use area (Mile 2.7).

Distance marker leaving ferry terminal shows Port Hardy 10 km/6 miles, Nanaimo 387 km/240 miles, Victoria 495 km/308 miles.

NOTE: End physical kilometreposts on Highway 19. Kilometres from Victoria now reflect metric conversion of mileage. Kilometreposts continue on Bear Cove Highway and reflect distance from Duke Point ferry terminal in Nanaimo, with Kilometrepost 405 just before the ferry terminal entrance.

V 309.8 (400 km) **PH 2.5** (4 km) Port Hardy RV Resort and Campground with log cabins open year-round; phone 250-949-8111. *Because the ferry from Prince Rupert arrives late in the evening, area campground hosts generally wait up to greet campers.*

V 309.9 (400.2 km) **PH 2.4** (3.9 km) Quatse River bridge, then **junction** with

Hardy Bay Road to northeast and Coal Harbour Road to southwest. Lodging on Hardy Bay Road: Glen Lyon Inn and Quarterdeck Inn. Quatse Salmon Stewardship Center and Quatse River Regional Park and Campground are 0.5 mile/0.8 km southwest on Byng Road. Salmon Center admission $6 adults, $4 ages 5–18 and seniors, under 5 free. Family rate for up to 2 adults and 2 children is $12. Phone 250-902-0336; www.thesalmoncentre.org; info@thesalmoncentre.org.

V 310.5 (401.1 km) **PH 1.8** (2.9 km) Holberg Road to Cape Scott Provincial Park (63 km/39 miles).

V 311.8 (403.2 km) **PH 0.5** (0.8 km) 4-way stop; Continue north for accommodations. Turn east on Granville for Chevron and Esso gas/diesel stations, Thunderbird Mall (Save-On-Foods, Hardy Bay Drugstore, Subway, A&W) and Providence Inn Motel and Restaurant. Granville junctions with Market Street in downtown Port Hardy.

V 312.3 (404 km) **PH 0** Highway 19 ends/begins at **junction** with Market Street in Port Hardy; description follows.

Port Hardy

V 312.3 (404 km) **PH 0** Located on Hardy Bay on the northeast coast of Vancouver Island. **Population:** 4,500. **Emergency Services:** Dial 911. **Hospital:** Port Hardy Hospital, phone 250-902-6011. **Visitor Information:** Port Hardy & District Chamber of Commerce/Visitor Information Center (VIC), 7250 Market St. (at the bottom of Main Street); **EV plug-ins** on south side of building. Phone 250-949-7622, website www.visitporthardy.com.

Climate: Moderate, with an average annual mean temperature of 8°C/46.9°F, and an average annual precipitation of 187 cm/73.6 inches per year.

Port Hardy has all visitor services including hotels, motels, cabins, a hostel, several bed and breakfasts and campgrounds; restaurants and fast-food outlets; gas stations; marine supplies; and retail services. 24-hour ATMs inside lobbies of bank and credit union. WiFi at Cafe Guido and elsewhere (ask at Visitor Center).

Port Hardy is a base for outdoor adventures such as hiking, kayaking and fishing. The North Coast Trail is an extension of the Cape Scott Trail and is one of the longest backpacking wilderness trails on Vancouver Island. Adventure trekkers are advised to plan on 6–8 days for hiking this 58 km/36 mile trail. Water taxi and land shuttle services are available from Port Hardy to either end of the North Coast Trail. Port Hardy is also home to the award-winning Quatse Salmon Stewardship Center, a community museum, local craft shop and galleries. Additional visitor experiences include cultural tours, wildlife viewing and scenic boat tours with K'awat'si Tours are available, as well as guided day trips out to San Josef Bay. Water enthusiasts can rent stand-up paddle boards as well as surf gear (boards and suits).

There are leisurely scenic walks such as Storey's Beach, moderate hikes or more extensive hikes such as the Tex Lyon Trail. Stop into the Port Hardy Visitor Center for local maps, guides and activity recommendations.

Alaska Highway

CONNECTS: Dawson Creek, BC, to Delta Junction, AK
(includes Richardson Highway to Fairbanks)

Length: 1,390 miles   **Road Surface: Paved**   **Season: Open all year**

(See maps, pages 150-154)

`97` `1` `2`

Summit Lake, at Historic Milepost 392, is the highest summit (elev. 4,250 feet/1,295m)along the Alaska Highway. (©Sharon Nault)

Major Attractions:

©Kris Valencia, staff

*Liard Hotsprings,
Muncho Lake,
Watson Lake
Sign Post Forest,
SS Klondike, Kluane Lake*

Highest Summit:
*Summit Lake
4,250 ft./1,295m*

For many people, the Alaska Highway is a great adventure. For others, it is a long drive. But whether you fall into the first group or the second, the vastness of wilderness this pioneer road crosses will not fail to impress you. It is truly a marvelous journey across a great expanse of North America. And if you take time to stop and meet the people and see the sights along the way, it can be the trip of a lifetime.

History of The MILEPOST®

When the Alaska Highway opened for civilian traffic after WWII, it was a rugged road and facilities along the highway were few and far apart. (In 1947, there was not a single garage for 600 miles between Fort Nelson and Whitehorse, or between Whitehorse and Fairbanks.) On such a road a reliable guidebook was essential, and in 1949, William A. "Bill" Wallace published the first edition of *The MILEPOST®*.

Wallace's interest in an Alaska Highway guide began during WWII when he was working for the Interior Department's Alaska Fire Control Service at Tanacross. In 1944, Wallace published his first Alaska highway map for the agency. It was a crudely drawn sketch of Alaska's highway system on a tiny brochure marking the locations of fire stations, as well as a few other services. In 1948, Wallace formed the Alaska Research Company and published a large fold-out map.

In 1949, Wallace published the first edi- *(Continues on page 155)*

Distance in miles	Dawson Cr.	Delta Jct.	Fairbanks	Ft. Nelson	Haines Jct.	Tok	Watson Lk.	Whitehorse
Dawson Cr.		1390	1488	283	985	1282	613	895
Delta Jct.	1390		98	1107	405	108	777	495
Fairbanks	1488	98		1205	503	206	875	603
Ft. Nelson	283	1107	1205		702	999	330	612
Haines Jct.	985	405	503	702		297	372	100
Tok	1282	108	206	999	297		669	387
Watson Lk.	613	777	875	330	372	669		282
Whitehorse	895	495	603	612	100	387	282	

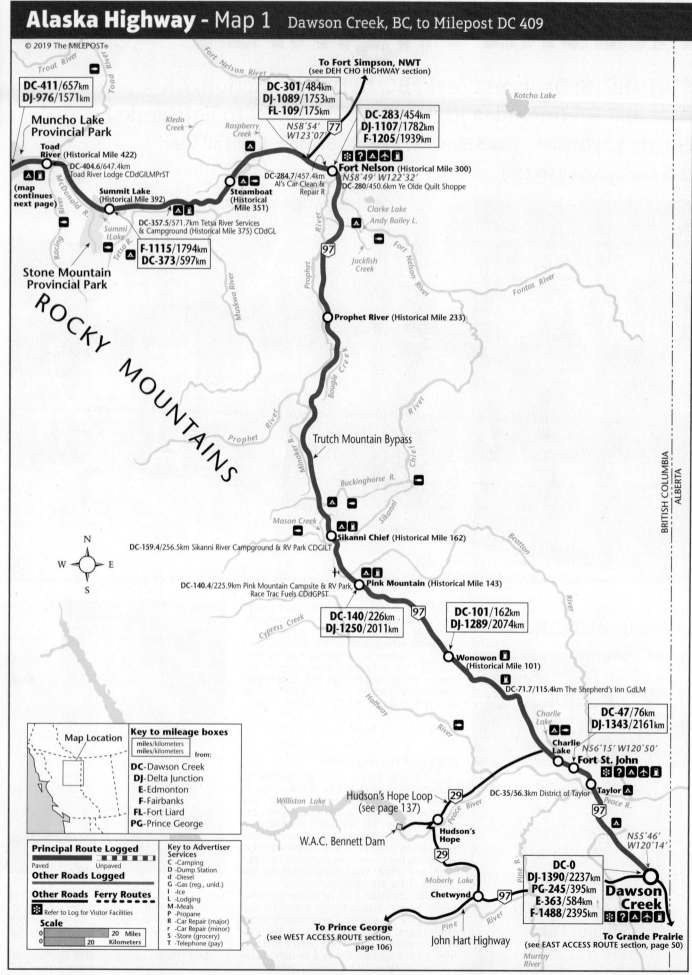

Map 1 | **ALASKA HIGHWAY**

Alaska Highway – Map 1   Dawson Creek, BC, to Milepost DC 409

© 2019 The MILEPOST®

DC-411/657km
DJ-976/1571km

Muncho Lake Provincial Park

(map continues next page)

Toad River (Historical Mile 422)
DC-404.6/647.4km
Toad River Lodge CDdGILMPrST

Summit Lake (Historical Mile 392)

Summit Lake

DC-357.5/571.7km Tetsa River Services & Campground (Historical Mile 375) CDdGL

F-1115/1794km
DC-373/597km

Stone Mountain Provincial Park

Steamboat (Historical Mile 351)

DC-284.7/457.4km
Al's Car Clean & Repair R

To Fort Simpson, NWT
(see DEH CHO HIGHWAY section)

DC-301/484km
DJ-1089/1753km
FL-109/175km

N58°54' W123°07'

77

DC-283/454km
DJ-1107/1782km
F-1205/1939km

Fort Nelson (Historical Mile 300)
N58°49' W122°32'
DC-280/450.6km Ye Olde Quilt Shoppe

97

Prophet River (Historical Mile 233)

Kotcho Lake

Clarke Lake
Andy Bailey L.

ROCKY MOUNTAINS

Trutch Mountain Bypass

Sikanni Chief (Historical Mile 162)

DC-159.4/256.5km Sikanni River Campground & RV Park CDGILT

DC-140.4/225.9km Pink Mountain Campsite & RV Park, Race Trac Fuels CDdGPST

Pink Mountain (Historical Mile 143)

DC-140/226km
DJ-1250/2011km

97

DC-101/162km
DJ-1289/2074km

Wonowon
(Historical Mile 101)

DC-71.7/115.4km The Shepherd's Inn GdLM

DC-47/76km
DJ-1343/2161km

Charlie Lake

Charlie Lake

N56°15' W120°50'

Fort St. John

BRITISH COLUMBIA | ALBERTA

Hudson's Hope Loop
(see page 137)

29

DC-35/56.3km District of Taylor

Taylor

97

N55°46' W120°14'

W.A.C. Bennett Dam

Hudson's Hope

29

Chetwynd

97

To Prince George
(see WEST ACCESS ROUTE section, page 106)

John Hart Highway

DC-0
DJ-1390/2237km
PG-245/395km
E-363/584km
F-1488/2395km

Dawson Creek

To Grande Prairie
(see EAST ACCESS ROUTE section, page 50)

Map Location

Key to mileage boxes

miles/kilometers
miles/kilometers
from:

DC-Dawson Creek
DJ-Delta Junction
E-Edmonton
F-Fairbanks
FL-Fort Liard
PG-Prince George

Principal Route Logged
Paved   Unpaved
Other Roads Logged

Other Roads   **Ferry Routes**

❄ Refer to Log for Visitor Facilities

Scale
0 ____ 20 Miles
0 ____ 20 Kilometers

Key to Advertiser Services
C -Camping
D -Dump Station
d -Diesel
G -Gas (reg., unld.)
I -Ice
L -Lodging
M -Meals
P -Propane
R -Car Repair (major)
r -Car Repair (minor)
S -Store (grocery)
T -Telephone (pay)

Map 2 ALASKA HIGHWAY

Alaska Highway - Map 2   Milepost DC 409 to Teslin, YT

© 2019 The MILEPOST®

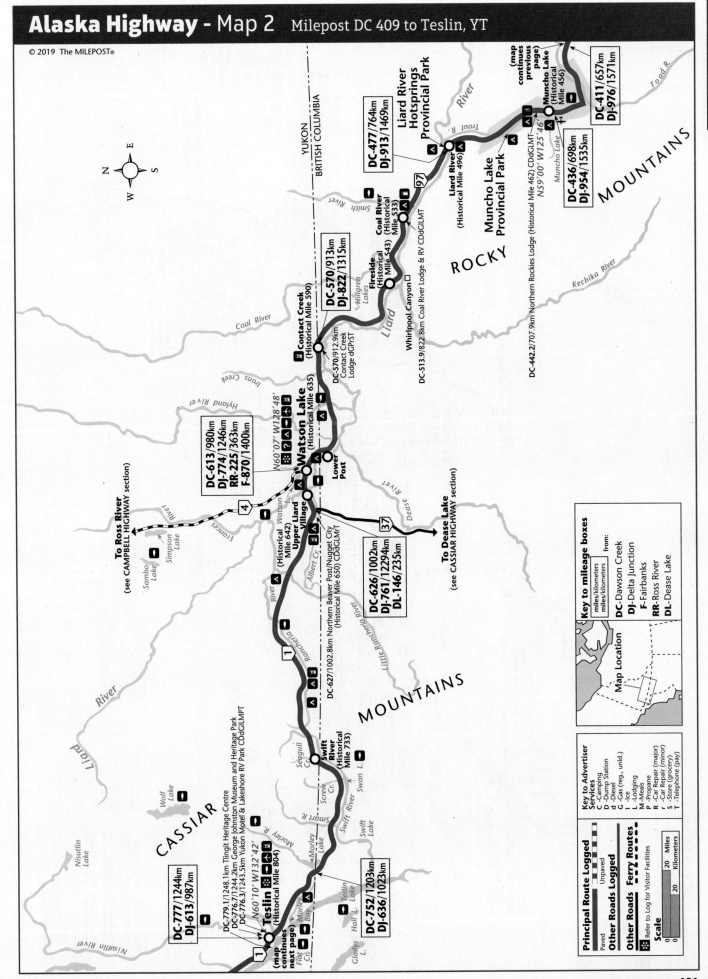

N
W E
S

YUKON
BRITISH COLUMBIA

Liard River Hotsprings Provincial Park

Liard River (Historical Mile 496)

97

DC-477/764km
DJ-913/1469km

DC-411/657km
DJ-976/1571km

(map continues previous page)

Muncho Lake (Historical Mile 456)

Muncho Lake Provincial Park

N59°00' W125°46'

DC-436/698km
DJ-954/1535km

ROCKY   MOUNTAINS

DC-442.2/707.9km Northern Rockies Lodge (Historical Mile 462) CDdGLMT

Smith River

Coal River (Historical Mile 533)

Fireside (Historical Mile 543)

Hiligren Lakes

Whirlpool Canyon

DC-513.9/822.8km Coal River Lodge & RV CDdGILMT

Liard River

DC-570/913km
DJ-822/1315km

Contact Creek (Historical Mile 590)

DC-570/912.9km Contact Creek Lodge dGPrST

Coal River

Kechika River

Irons Creek

Highland River

N60°07' W128°48'

Watson Lake (Historical Mile 635)

DC-613/980km
DJ-774/1246km
RR-225/363km
F-870/1400km

Lower Post

(Historical Watson Mile 642)

Upper Liard Village

4

DC-627/1002.8km Northern Beaver Post/Nugget City (Historical Mile 650) CDdGLMrT

To Ross River (see CAMPBELL HIGHWAY section)

Frances River

Simpson Lake

Sambo Lake

Dease River

37

To Dease Lake (see CASSIAR HIGHWAY section)

DC-626/1002km
DJ-761/12294km
DL-146/235km

Little Rancheria River

Rancheria River

Albert Cr.

1

CASSIAR   MOUNTAINS

Wolf Lake

Nisutlin Lake

Seagull Cr.

Screw Cr.

Swift River (Historical Mile 733)

Swan L.

Swift Lake

Swift River

Smart R.

Morley Lake

Morley Bay

Morley R.

DC-752/1203km
DJ-636/1023km

Teslin L.

Gladys L.

Hall L.

Teslin (Historical Mile 804)

N60°10' W132°42'

DC-779.1/1248.1km Tlingit Heritage Centre
DC-776.7/1244.2km George Johnston Museum and Heritage Park
DC-776.3/1243.5km Yukon Motel & Lakeshore RV Park CDdGILMPT

DC-777/1244km
DJ-613/987km

1

(map continues next page)

Flat Cr.

Liard River

Nisutlin River

Key to mileage boxes

	miles/kilometers from:
	miles/kilometers

DC-Dawson Creek   **DJ**-Delta Junction
F-Fairbanks   **RR**-Ross River
DL-Dease Lake

Map Location

Key to Advertiser Services

C -Camping
D -Dump Station
d -Diesel
G -Gas (reg., unld.)
I -Ice
L -Lodging
M -Meals
P -Propane
R -Car Repair (major)
r -Car Repair (minor)
S -Store (grocery)
T -Telephone (pay)

Principal Route Logged
Paved
Unpaved

Other Roads Logged

Ferry Routes

□ Refer to Log for Visitor Facilities

Scale
0   20   Miles
0   20   Kilometers

Map 3

ALASKA HIGHWAY

Alaska Highway - Map 3   Teslin, YT, to Milepost DC 1136

© 2019 The MILEPOST®

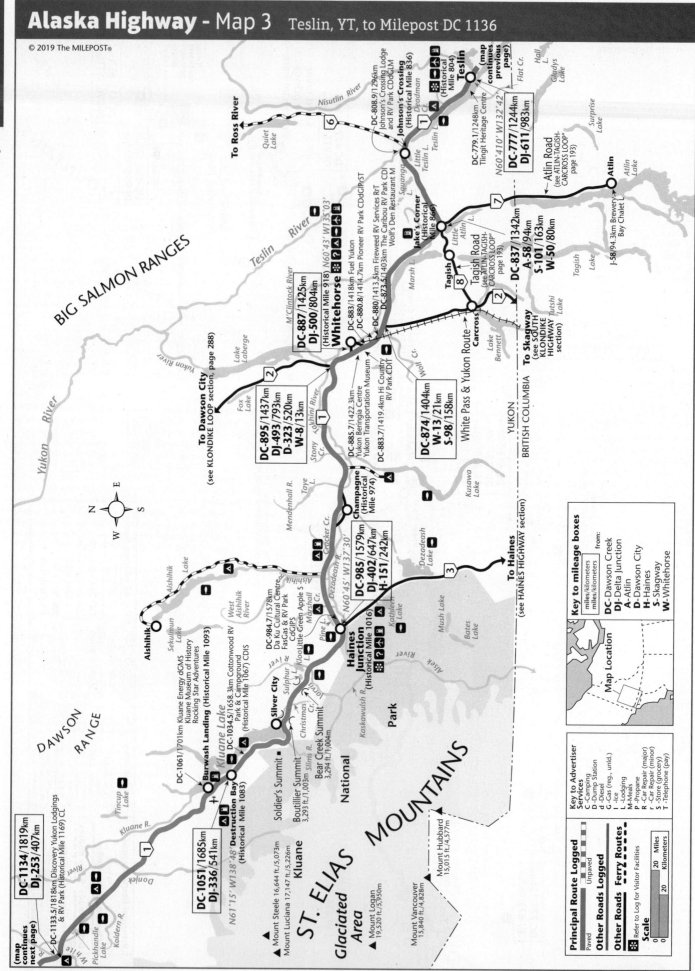

To Ross River

Nisutlin River

Quiet Lake

6

BIG SALMON RANGES

Teslin River

Lake Laberge

Yukon River

Fox Lake

To Dawson City
(see KLONDIKE LOOP section, page 288)

2

Stony Cr.

Squanga L.

Little Teslin L.

DC-808.9/1296km
Johnson's Crossing Lodge
and RV Park CDdGLM

Johnson's Crossing
(Historical Mile 836)

1

Teslin L.

Teslin
(Historical
Mile 804)

**(map
continues
previous
page)**

Flat Cr.

Hall L.

Gladys Lake

Surprise Lake

DC-779.1/1248km
Tlingit Heritage Centre

DC-777/1244km
DJ-611/983km

N60°41'0" W132°42'

Atlin Road
(see ATLIN-TAGISH-
CARCROSS LOOP"
page 193)

Atlin L.

Atlin

J-58/94.3km Brewery
Bay Chalet L.

7

DC-883/1418km Fuel Yukon
DC-880.8/1414.7km Pioneer RV Park

DC-880/1413.5km Fireweed RV Services RrT
DC-873.5/1403km The Caribou RV Park CDl
Wolf's Den Restaurant M

Jake's Corner
(Historical
Mile 866)

Little Atlin L.

Marsh L.

Tagish

8

Tagish Road
(see ATLIN-TAGISH-
CARCROSS LOOP,
page 193)

DC-837/1342km
A-58/94km
S-101/163km
W-50/80km

Tagish L.

DC-887/1425km
DJ-500/804km
Whitehorse
(Historical Mile 918)

M'Clintock River

1

Lakhini River

DC-895/1437km
DJ-493/793km
D-323/520km
W-8/13km

DC-985.7/1422.3km
Yukon Beringia Centre
Yukon Transportation Museum

DC-983.7/1419.4km Hi Country
RV Park CDlT

Wolf Cr.

White Pass & Yukon Route

Carcross

DC-874/1404km
W-13/21km
S-98/158km

Lake Bennett

Tutshi Lake

To Skagway
(see SOUTH
KLONDIKE
HIGHWAY
section)

2

To Skagway
(see SOUTH
KLONDIKE
HIGHWAY
section)

YUKON
BRITISH COLUMBIA

Taye L.

Mendenhall R.

Cracker Cr.

Champagne
(Historical
Mile 974)

Kusawa Lake

DC-985/1579km
DJ-402/647km
H-151/242km

N60°45' W137°30'

Dezadeash R.

Marshall Cr.

Pine L.

Dezadeash Lake

3

To Haines
(see HAINES HIGHWAY section)

Mush Lake

Bates Lake

DC-984.7/1578km
Da Ku Cultural Centre
FasGas & RV Park
CDdGlPS

Kloo/Little Green Apple S

Kathleen L.

**Haines
Junction**
(Historical Mile 1016)

Alsek River

Kaskawulsh R.

Park

Sulphur L.

Christmas Cr.

Jarvis R.

Slims R.

Silver City

DC-984.7/1578.m
Marshall Cr.

Aishihik

Sekulmun Lake

Aishihik Lake

West Aishihik River

Aishihik R.

DC-1061/1701km Kluane Energy dGMS
Kluane Museum of History
Rocking Star Adventures

Burwash Landing (Historical Mile 1093)

Kluane Lake

DC-1034.5/1658.3km Cottonwood RV
Park & Campground
(Historical Mile 1067) CDlS

Destruction Bay
(Historical Mile 1083)

Soldier's Summit

Boutillier Summit
3,293 ft./1,003m

Bear Creek Summit
3,294 ft./1,004m

Kluane

National

DAWSON
RANGE

Tincup Lake

Donjek River

Kluane R.

N61°15' W138°48'

DC-1051/1685km
DJ-336/541km

DC-1134/1819km
DJ-253/407km

DC-1133.5/1818km Discovery Yukon Lodgings
& RV Park (Historical Mile 1169) CL

**(map
continues
next page)**

White R.

Koidern R.

Pickhandle Lake

▲ Mount Steele 16,644 ft./5,073m
▲ Mount Luciana 17,147 ft./5,226m

▲ Mount Logan
19,520 ft./5,950m

ST. ELIAS

Glaciated
Area

MOUNTAINS

Mount Hubbard
15,015 ft./4,577m

▲ Mount Vancouver
15,840 ft./4,828m

© 2019 The MILEPOST®

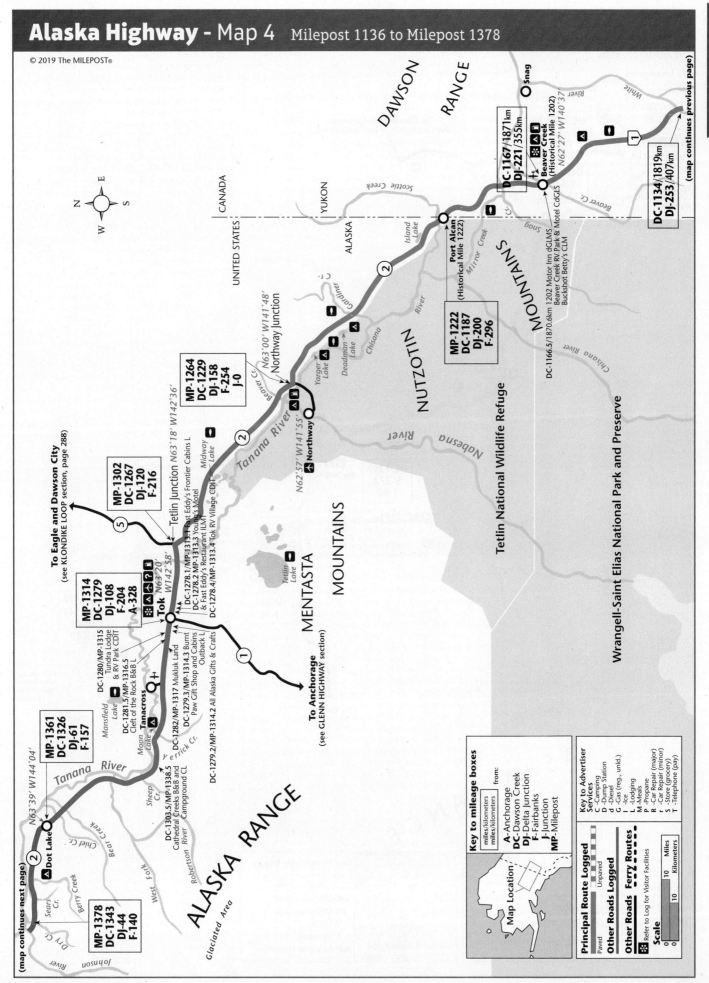

DAWSON RANGE

Snag

○ Snag

N

W — E

S

CANADA

YUKON

UNITED STATES   ALASKA

Scottie Creek

DC-1167/1871km
DJ-221/355km

Beaver Creek
(Historical Mile 1202)
N62°27' W140°37'

1

(map continues previous page)

DC-1134/1819km
DJ-253/407km

2

Island Lake

Port Alcan
(Historical Mile 1222)

Mirror Creek

DC-1166.5/1870.6km 1202 Motor Inn dGLMS
Beaver Creek RV Park & Motel CdGLS
Buckshot Betty's CLM

MP-1222
DC-1187
DJ-200
F-296

NUTZOTIN   MOUNTAINS

Gardiner Cr.

Chisana River

Chisana River

N63°00' W141°48'
Northway Junction

MP-1264
DC-1229
DJ-158
F-254
J-0

Yarger Lake

Deadman Lake

Chisana River

Nabesna River

Tetlin National Wildlife Refuge

Wrangell-Saint Elias National Park and Preserve

2

Tanana River

Midway Lake

Northway
N62°57' W141°55'

Tetlin Junction N63°18' W142°36'

Fast Eddy's Frontier Cabins L

MP-1302
DC-1267
DJ-120
F-216

To Eagle and Dawson City
(see KLONDIKE LOOP section, page 288)

5

DC-1278.1/MP-1313.1 Fast Eddy's Frontier Cabins L
DC-1278.2 MP-1313.3 Young's Motel
& Fast Eddy's Restaurant ILMT
DC-1278.4/MP-1313.4 Tok RV Village CdIT

Tetlin Lake

MENTASTA   MOUNTAINS

MP-1314
DC-1279
DJ-108
F-204
A-328

Tok
N63°20'
W142°58'

DC-1280/MP-1315
Tundra Lodge
& RV Park CDIT

DC-1281.5/MP-1316.5
Cleft of the Rock B&B L

DC-1282/MP-1317 Mukluk Land
DC-1279.3/MP-1314.3 Burnt
Paw Gift Shop and Cabins
Outback L
DC-1279.2/MP-1314.2 All Alaska Gifts & Crafts

1

To Anchorage
(see GLENN HIGHWAY section)

Mansfield Lake

Moon Lake

Tanacross

DC-1303.5/MP-1338.5
Cathedral Creeks B&B and
Campground CL

Yerrick Cr.

MP-1361
DC-1326
DJ-61
F-157

Tanana River

Sheep Cr.

Robertson River

ALASKA RANGE

Glaciated Area

N63°39' W144°04'

2

Dot Lake

Chief Creek

Bear Creek

Berry Creek

West Fork

Sears Cr.

Dry Cr.

MP-1378
DC-1343
DJ-44
F-140

Johnson River

(map continues next page)

2

Key to mileage boxes

miles/kilometers
miles/kilometers
from:

A -Anchorage
DC -Dawson Creek
DJ -Delta Junction
F -Fairbanks
J -Junction
MP -Milepost

Map Location

Key to Advertiser Services

C -Camping
D -Dump Station
d -Diesel
G -Gas (reg., unld.)
I -Ice
L -Lodging
M -Meals
P -Propane
R -Car Repair (major)
r -Car Repair (minor)
S -Store (grocery)
T -Telephone (pay)

Principal Route Logged

Paved   Unpaved

Other Roads   Ferry Routes

Refer to Log for Visitor Facilities

Scale

0   10   Miles
0   10   Kilometers

Map 5

ALASKA HIGHWAY

Alaska Highway - Map 5 Milepost 1378 to Fairbanks, AK

© 2019 The MILEPOST®

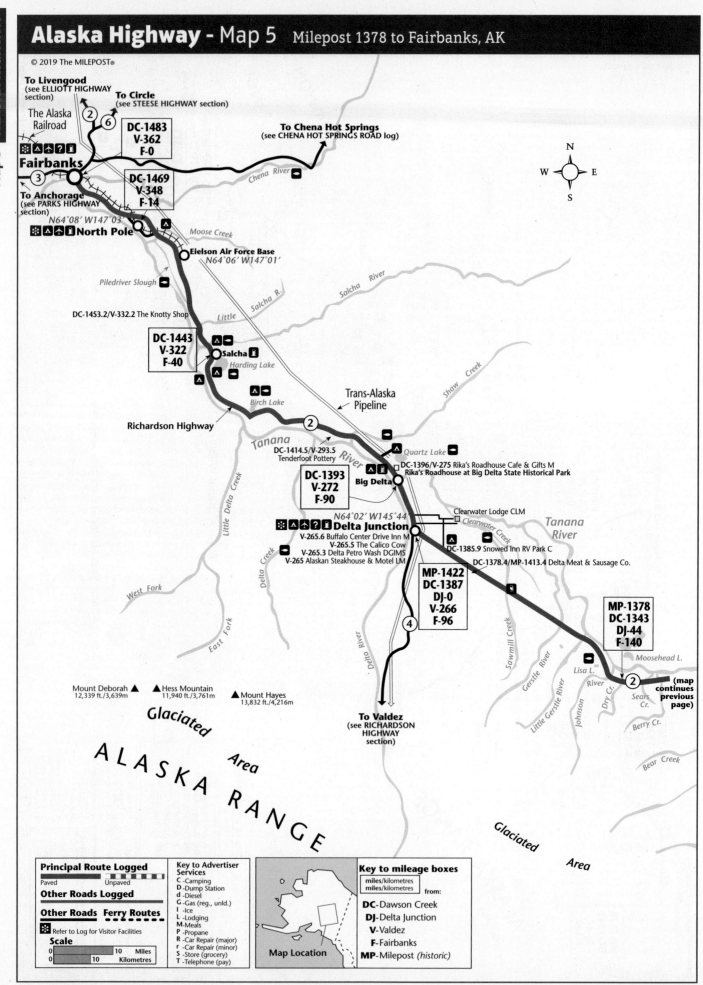

To Livengood
(see ELLIOTT HIGHWAY
section)

To Circle
(see STEESE HIGHWAY section)

2

6

The Alaska
Railroad

**DC-1483
V-362
F-0**

Fairbanks

3

To Anchorage
(see PARKS HIGHWAY
section)

**DC-1469
V-348
F-14**

To Chena Hot Springs
(see CHENA HOT SPRINGS ROAD log)

Chena River

N

W   E

S

N64°08' W147°03'

North Pole

Moose Creek

Eielson Air Force Base
N64°06' W147°01'

Piledriver Slough

DC-1453.2/V-332.2 The Knotty Shop

Little   Salcha R.

Salcha   River

Shaw Creek

**DC-1443
V-322
F-40**

Salcha

Harding Lake

Birch Lake

Trans-Alaska
Pipeline

Richardson Highway

2

Tanana

River

DC-1414.5/V-293.5
Tenderfoot Pottery

Quartz Lake

DC-1396/V-275 Rika's Roadhouse Cafe & Gifts M
Rika's Roadhouse at Big Delta State Historical Park

**DC-1393
V-272
F-90**

Big Delta

Clearwater Lodge CLM

Tanana
River

Clearwater Creek

N64°02' W145°44'

Delta Junction

V-265.6 Buffalo Center Drive Inn M
V-265.5 The Calico Cow
V-265.3 Delta Petro Wash DGIMS
V-265 Alaskan Steakhouse & Motel LM

DC-1385.9 Snowed Inn RV Park C

DC-1378.4/MP-1413.4 Delta Meat & Sausage Co.

Little Delta Creek

Delta Creek

West Fork

East Fork

Delta River

4

**MP-1422
DC-1387
DJ-0
V-266
F-96**

**MP-1378
DC-1343
DJ-44
F-140**

Moosehead L.

Lisa L.

Sawmill Creek

Gerstle River

Little Gerstle River

Johnson   River

Dry Cr.

Sears
Cr.

Berry Cr.

Bear Creek

2

(map
continues
previous
page)

Mount Deborah ▲
12,339 ft./3,639m

▲ Hess Mountain
11,940 ft./3,761m

▲ Mount Hayes
13,832 ft./4,216m

To Valdez
(see RICHARDSON
HIGHWAY
section)

Glaciated   Area

ALASKA RANGE

Glaciated
Area

Principal Route Logged

Paved   Unpaved

Other Roads Logged

Other Roads   Ferry Routes

Refer to Log for Visitor Facilities

Scale

0   10   Miles

0   10   Kilometres

**Key to Advertiser
Services**
C - Camping
D - Dump Station
d - Diesel
G - Gas (reg., unld.)
I - Ice
L - Lodging
M - Meals
P - Propane
R - Car Repair (major)
r - Car Repair (minor)
S - Store (grocery)
T - Telephone (pay)

Key to mileage boxes

miles/kilometres
miles/kilometres   from:

DC-Dawson Creek
DJ-Delta Junction
V-Valdez
F-Fairbanks
MP-Milepost *(historic)*

Map Location

(Continued from page 149)
tion of *The MILEPOST®* with help from publisher Bob Atwood. It was a 72-page saddle-stitched edition, filled with the facts and practical information Wallace had gathered during his many trips up and down the highway.

Wallace named his guidebook after the mileage location posts "that filled such a vital need along the wilderness road."

Alaska Highway facts

The Alaska Highway begins at Mile 0 in Dawson Creek, BC. The first 613 miles/987 km of the Alaska Highway are in British Columbia, where it is designated BC Highway 97 North, and travels in a northwesterly direction to the Yukon border near Watson Lake, YT (**Historical Mile 635**). From there the Alaska Highway continues as Yukon Highway 1, crossing 577 miles/929 km of Yukon to Port Alcan at the Alaska border. The Alaska Highway crosses into Alaska at **Historical Mile 1221.8**, where it becomes Alaska Route 2. From this international border, it is 200 miles to Delta Junction, AK (**Historical Mile 1422**), the official end of the Alaska Highway, and 296 miles to Fairbanks, the unofficial end of the highway at **Historical Mile 1523**.

The 96-mile stretch of highway between Delta Junction and Fairbanks is part of the Richardson Highway from Valdez, although it is designated Alaska Route 2 and treated as a natural extension of the Alaska Highway. The Richardson Highway (Alaska Route 4) was originally known as the Richardson Trail and predates construction of the Alaska Highway by some 50 years.

Construction of the Alaska Highway began March 9, 1942, and ended on October 25, 1942, when it was possible for vehicles to travel the entire length of the highway. Considered one of the great achievements of the 20th century, the pioneer road was initially built as a military necessity, in response to the bombing of Pearl Harbor and the Japanese threat to Alaska and Pacific shipping lanes. *(See "The History of the Alaska Highway" on page 158 for more details.)*

Some people still refer to the Alaska Highway as the "Alcan" Highway. ALCAN was the military's name for the pioneer road at its completion in 1942, an acronym for Alaska-Canada military highway. But it was not a popular name with many Alaskans, who were unhappy with restrictions placed on civilian traffic on the highway during the war years. The pioneer road was officially renamed the Alaska Highway in March 1943. It opened to the public in 1948.

Towns and businesses along the Alaska Highway still use their Historical Mile to identify their location, although these figures reflect historical driving distances—not actual driving distances—along the Alaska Highway.

The Alaska Highway is about 35 miles shorter today than it was in the 1940s, thanks to reconstruction and rerouting. And it continues to get shorter, as reconstruction on various sections of the road shaves off more miles. (Refer to "Mileposts and Kilometerposts" this section for more on the subject.)

Is the Alaska Highway paved?

All of the Alaska Highway is paved, although highway improvement projects often mean motorists have to drive a few miles of gravel road.

A group of motorcyclists congregate at Tetsa River Services and Campground, Historical Mile 375 on the Alaska Highway. (©Judy Nadon, staff)

New passing lanes and intersection improvement projects have been underway along the first 150 miles of the highway in British Columbia, and at Whitehorse, YT.

The most challenging and ongoing reconstruction project continues to be between Destruction Bay and the AK–YT border, where several sections of road that had previously been brought up to BST (Bituminous Surface Treatment) standard as part of the Shakwak Highway Project have developed severe frost heaves, making for a very slow and bumpy drive. Each summer road crews are out repairing damage along this length of road.

Despite the ongoing challenges of maintaining a major highway that crosses dramatically varied terrain, and that is subject to extreme temperature fluctuations, the Alaska Highway continues to improve over the years. During the 1980s, many rerouting and paving projects were completed, and by 1992—the 50th anniversary of the Alaska Highway—the last section of original gravel road was rerouted and paved.

What are road conditions like?

Road conditions on the Alaska Highway are not unlike road conditions on many secondary roads in the Lower 48 and Canada. It is the tremendous length of the highway, combined with its remoteness and the extremes of the Northern climate, that often result in surprises along this road. Historically speaking, however, the Alaska Highway has rarely been closed by any weather-related event, and even then, usually not longer than a day. (For winter road conditions, see "Driving the highway in winter," this section.)

The MILEPOST® log of the Alaska Highway reflects driving conditions as they existed when our field editors logged the road, which was summer and fall of last year. Keep in mind that any stretch of road can change dramatically—for better or for worse—in a very short time due to weather or construction.

The asphalt surfacing of the Alaska Highway ranges from poor to excellent. Much of the highway is in fair condition, with older patched pavement and a minimum of gravel breaks and chuckholes. Recently upgraded sections of road offer excellent surfacing. Relatively few stretches of road fall into the "poor" category, i.e. chuckholes, gravel breaks, deteriorated shoulders, bumps and frost heaves.

It is difficult to predict road conditions on the Alaska Highway. A hard winter or heavy rains can quickly undermine what was good roadbed, while road crews can just as quickly improve a previously substandard stretch of road.

It is also difficult to offer a summary description of 1,500-plus miles of road, but we will try.

There's a lot of straight road the first 300 miles of highway, between Dawson Creek and Fort Nelson, with grades of 6 to 9 percent.

North of Fort Nelson, the Alaska Highway crosses the Rocky Mountains. Expect about 200 miles of often narrow, winding road, interrupted by improved sections of road; grades to 10 percent, few passing lanes and wildlife on the road. This stretch of road also has some spectacular scenery, as the highway climbs first Steamboat Mountain (elev. 3,500 feet/1,067m), then Summit Pass (elev. 4,250 feet/1,295m). After Summit, the highway winds through a rocky limestone gorge high above the MacDonald River valley.

After winding along river valleys and the shore of beautiful Muncho Lake, the highway straightens out again around Liard River (**Historical Milepost 496**), with good wide road for the next 140 miles into Watson Lake, YT.

The stretch of road between Watson Lake and Whitehorse, roughly another 300 miles, is in good shape and follows easy curves through wide river valleys and along lakes.

From Whitehorse to Haines Junction, a distance of approximately 100 miles, it is straight road with poor to fair pavement, gravel breaks and frost heaves.

The next 200 driving miles, from Haines Junction to the Alaska border, consists of long straight stretches, a winding stretch of road along the shore of Kluane Lake; and a long, often bumpy, frost-heaved stretch of

Watch for wildlife along the Alaska Highway, like these Stone sheep northwest of Summit Pass near Milepost DC 376 in Stone Mountain Provincial Park. (©Sharon Nault)

road—in various stages of improvement—from Destruction Bay to the Alaska border.

From the Alaska–Yukon border to Tok, the Alaska Highway has curves and grades; it was in poor to fair condition in summer 2018. From Tok to Delta Junction, the highway is fairly straight and in fair to good condition, as was the Richardson-Alaska Highway between Delta Junction and Fairbanks. Both of these sections of road have straight stretches interrupted by easy curves.

Highway businesses and other travelers are often helpful sources of information for current road conditions. Always inquire locally about what road conditions may be like up ahead of you and—in the off-season—what facilities are available, since many businesses operate seasonally.

For daily recorded road conditions along the Alaska Highway in Alaska, phone (907) 456-7623 or go to http://511.alaska.gov/. For conditions along the Yukon portion of the Alaska Highway, phone 511 or from outside the Yukon call toll-free 1-877-456-7623, or go to www.511Yukon.ca. For conditions on the BC portion of the Alaska Highway, go to www.drivebc.ca then click on the Alaska Highway. You may view conditions on the Alaska Highway at Fort St. John by clicking on the highway cams. (Links to these agencies are also provided at www.themilepost.com; click on "Road Conditions" in the Features pull-down menu.)

Driving advice

Today's Alaska Highway is a mostly 2-lane highway that winds and rolls across the Northern wilderness. The best advice is to take your time; drive with your headlights on at all times (it is the law in Canada); keep to the right on hills and corners; use turnouts; watch for wildlife on the road; and—as you would on any highway anywhere else—drive defensively.

There are few steep grades on the Alaska Highway. Most of the 6 to 10 percent grades occur between Fort Nelson, BC, and Watson Lake, YT, where the Alaska Highway crosses the Rocky Mountains.

There are relatively few high sum-

mits on the Alaska Highway. (Summit, in the Rockies, is the highest at elev. 4,250 feet/1,295m). But keep in mind that weather may affect driving conditions in the Rockies, where it is not unusual to run into fog or sleet and snow conditions at any time of the year at higher elevations. We have experienced a hailstorm in July at Summit Lake, and snow and fog on Steamboat Mountain (**Historic Milepost 351**) in early June.

Drivers may also run into short stretches of loose gravel in areas where chip-seal repairs are under way. *IMPORTANT: Slow down for loose gravel breaks. Sudden braking or excessive speed on gravel can lead to loss of control of your vehicle, roll-overs or throwing rocks into oncoming vehicle windshields.*

Always be alert for bumps, dips and potholes in the road and for abrupt changes in highway surfacing. Many—but not all—of these surface irregularities are signed, or flagged with small, orange pennants. *Slow down if you see "Rough Road" and "Loose Gravel" signs and roadside flags.*

There are stretches of narrow, winding road without shoulders, particularly in the stretch of highway through the Rocky Mountains. Watch out for soft shoulders when pulling over to the side of the road. It is better to use formal turnouts instead of road shoulders, if possible.

Always watch for construction crews along the Alaska Highway. Travelers may be delayed briefly while waiting for a pilot car to guide them through the construction. Motorists may encounter rough driving at construction areas, and muddy roadways if there are heavy rains while the roadbed is torn up.

Avoid tickets by paying attention to posted speed limits, particularly through the small communities along the highway. Alaska State Troopers and the Royal Canadian Mounted Police (RCMP) have a "zero tolerance" policy regarding drinking and driving, aggressive driving, distracted driving (cell phone or other electronic devices) and passengers not wearing seatbelts (seatbelts are mandatory).

How far apart are services?

Gas, diesel, food and lodging are found in towns and cities along the Alaska Highway, as well as at smaller unincorporated communities, roadhouses and lodges located between the larger population centers. With the closure of several long-time roadhouses in recent years, and the seasonal nature of others, motorists can be looking at 100 to 150 miles between services on a couple stretches of highway. Pay attention to your gas tank and fill up when near a pump.

Motorists should also keep in mind that not all highway businesses are open year-round, nor are most services available 24 hours a day.

There are dozens of government and private campgrounds along the Alaska Highway; these are described at their mile location in the highway log. Most campgrounds are open from mid-May or early June to September. See also "Camping" in the TRAVEL PLANNING section.

Remember that you will be driving in 2 different countries that use 2 different currencies. Many if not most Canadian businesses will take U.S. dollars, but they will give you change in Canadian dollars. ATMs are prevalent in many cities and you can get Canadian dollars with a U.S. bank card. U.S. businesses do not take Canadian dollars. Most businesses (but not all) will take major credit cards. Be aware that credit card companies tack on a fee for foreign currency transactions. See also "Money" in the TRAVEL PLANNING section.

There are long stretches of highway without cell phone service. Service may also depend on your cell provider's coverage in Canada and the U.S.

Mileposts and Kilometerposts

Mileposts were first put up at communities and lodges along the Alaska Highway in the 1940s to help motorists know where they were in this vast wilderness. Today, those original mileposts remain a tradition with communities and businesses on the highway and are still used as mailing addresses and reference points, although the figures no longer accurately reflect driving distance.

When Canada switched to the metric system in the mid-1970s, the mileposts in British Columbia and Yukon were replaced by kilometerposts. Historian and writer Kenneth Coates recalls that as an employee of the Department of Highways, Yukon Territorial Government, he was assigned to lead a 2-person crew to remove mileposts and put up new kilometerposts in 1975.

"The job was simple enough," Coates recalls. "A driver working a day or two ahead of us marked off every two kilometers along the highway. Since he started at the BC–Yukon border and not at Dawson Creek, the distances did not quite jive. Our pick-up was stacked high with the new posts, creosoted and painted. All we had to do was dig a hole, drop in the post, prop it up and pack it down."

But "the job description did not match the work precisely," Coates continues. "As the first highway workers discovered, the Alaska Highway traverses some challenging terrain in North America: rocks, mud, muskeg, and mosquito-infested swamps. We earned our pay over the couple of weeks we spent enroute, enjoying the scenery and remarkable countryside, but exhausting ourselves with back-breaking labor. The hardest part was the abuse. People stopped to curse at us for removing the mileposts."

Kilometerposts on the British Columbia portion of the Alaska Highway were recalibrated in 1990 to reflect current driving distances rather than historical mileposts. These kilometerposts appear about every 5 kilometers on the BC portion of the highway.

Kilometerposts along the Yukon portion of the Alaska Highway have been recalibrated to the Alaska border to reflect actual driving distance. These kilometerposts are placed every 2 kilometers.

In addition to the kilometerposts in Canada, the governments of British Columbia and Yukon installed commemorative mileposts as part of the 50th anniversary celebration of the Alaska Highway in 1992. Many of these historical mile markers are accompanied by Northwest Highway System (NWHS) signs and interpretive panels.

Physical mileposts on the Alaska portion of the highway—between Port Alcan and Delta Junction—reflect historical mileposts. Thus, a discrepancy of 35 miles exists at the AK–YT border between actual driving distance and the physical milepost. (Physical mileposts on the Richardson Highway between Delta Junction and Fairbanks reflect distance from Valdez.)

Kilometerposts and mileposts may be missing on some sections of the Alaska Highway due to road construction, vandalism or because they have succumbed to the elements.

Reading the Alaska Highway log

The *MILEPOST®* log of the Alaska Highway takes into account physical mileposts and kilometerposts, historical mileposts and actual driving distance.

On the Canadian portion of the highway, *The MILEPOST®* log gives distance to the AK–YT border from Dawson Creek (DC) as actual driving distance in miles followed by kilometer distance based on the kilometerposts (*which is not necessarily a metric conversion of the first figure*). Use our mileage figure from Dawson Creek to figure correct distance between points on the Alaska Highway within Canada. Use our kilometer figure from Dawson Creek to pinpoint location in reference to physical kilometerposts on the Alaska Highway in Canada.

Traditional milepost figures in Canada are indicated in the text as **Historic Mile**. If there is a commemorative milepost the text will read **Historical Mile**.

On the Alaska portion of the highway between Port Alcan and Delta Junction, *The MILEPOST®* log gives driving distance from Dawson Creek followed by distance based on the physical mileposts. The mileposts on this section of the highway reflect traditional mileages—not actual driving distance—from Dawson Creek. Thus when you reach the AK–YT border at **Historical Mile 1221.8**, it is **Milepost DC 1189.8** (the actual driving distance from Dawson Creek) and **MP 1221.8** reflecting the physical milepost in Alaska.

On the Richardson Highway between Delta Junction and Fairbanks, driving distance from Dawson Creek is followed by distance based on the physical mileposts, which reflect distance from Valdez.

When driving the highway and reading the log, it helps to pay attention to all landmarks, not just the mileposts and kilo-

Wood bison are seen year-round along the highway between Liard Hotsprings and Watson Lake. Photograph bison from your vehicle. (©Earl Brown, staff)

meterposts. If the highway log indicates a campground is 2 miles north of a certain river crossing, then it will be 2 miles north of that river, regardless of the presence or absence of a milepost or kilometerpost.

Weather information

Since the weather frequently influences road conditions along the Alaska Highway, weather reports may be crucial to highway travelers. Current weather and regional forecasts are broadcast on local TV and radio stations; supplied to local visitor information centers, hotels, motels and lodges along the highway; posted on the internet; and available by phone.

Weather information for the Canadian portion of the Alaska Highway is available from Environment Canada. Current weather conditions and 5-day forecasts for communities throughout British Columbia, Yukon and Alberta are posted at www.weatherof fice.ec.gc.ca. A link to weather forecasts is also available at www.511yukon.ca.

Web cams along the BC Highway 97 portion of the Alaska Highway can be viewed at http://images.drivebc.ca/bchighwaycam/pub/html/www/10.html.

Travelers may get 24-hour recorded weather reports and forecasts by phone from Environment Canada. For the north Peace River region (Dawson Creek, Fort St. John, Fort Nelson, Grande Prairie and Chetwynd), phone 250-785-7669. For Whitehorse, western Yukon and northwestern British Columbia, phone 867-668-6061.

Driving the highway in winter

The Alaska Highway is open year-round, and winter drivers can expect a fair number of big rigs, along with local traffic, to be on the road. *MILEPOST®* field editor Judy Nadon, who lives on the Alaska Highway near Whitehorse, is one of those local drivers and winter is her favorite time of the year. "I think everyone should come in the winter," Judy says. "It's so beautiful. Animal

tracks are everywhere in the snow, the mountains are out of this world, and there are no bugs and no crowds!"

But it is still winter and your vehicle should be equipped to handle temperatures that routinely dip to -22°F/-30°C, with lows to -48°F/-44.5°C in the Yukon.

You will also want to be sure you can keep warm should you end up in a ditch or have a mechanical breakdown. Long-time *MILEPOST®* field editor Earl Brown, a year-round resident of Fort Nelson, BC, and a life-long Alaska Highway resident, says "I always carry an extra long set of booster cables, a tow rope, snow shovel and lots of warm clothing." He also recommends installing a block heater in your vehicle so it can be plugged in for cold weather starts. "It's a lot easier on your vehicle, and may mean the difference between starting your engine or not starting your engine the morning after an overnight stop," says Earl.

Judy agrees. "We all carry this equipment in our vehicles during winter. And just about every motel/hotel from Cache Creek, BC (on the West Access Route), north to Dawson Creek and on up the highway, has plug-ins." Also, BC requires winter tires or chains on northern highways from Oct. 1–April 30.

Road conditions in winter can be excellent, with the highway surface smoothed of potholes with graded snow. "Highway crews are generally quick to be out on the road plowing after snowfalls along the Alaska Highway," says Earl. Difficult driving conditions include fog, blowing snow, drifting snow, snow on roadway, poor visibility, freezing rain, black ice, ice glaze and icy patches. Check road conditions at 511. alaska.gov; www.511Yukon.ca; and www. drivebc.ca.

Keep your driving segments short and confined to the daytime. Driving in the dark can be dangerous for winter drivers. Animals can and do leap out on to the highway without warning, but at least in daylight you may see them in time to stop. The Alaska Highway is lightly traveled at night in the winter, so if you should break down or have an accident at night, the wait time for help could be many hours. Plan to depart at sunrise and be off the road by dark. And remember: Days are shorter in the North in winter. Here are a few more suggestions from our field editors about winter driving:

"When the road signs say to slow down for dangerous curves, Slow down!

"Be sure to travel on the top half of your fuel tank. Lots of places along the highway are only seasonal operations. There are about 120 to 150 miles between open-year-round service outlets.

"It's a good idea to check with the gas station attendant when you are filling up for what the word is about road conditions ahead.

"Phone ahead to confirm accommodations. *The MILEPOST®* log indicates those businesses that plan to be open year-round, but you don't want to be counting on staying overnight some place only to find they've decided to close for the season after all. And keep in mind there are not many businesses along the Alaska Highway that are open 24 hours a day.

"Remember that there are long stretches of highway where there is no cell phone service."

And a last piece of advice: "Plan to take a winter dip at Liard Hotsprings... It will probably be a highlight of your trip!"

Working in the extreme environment of the North, facing an urgent time line, a supply line of significant distance, and daily challenges to their engineering skills, crews still managed to punch a pioneer road through more than a thousand miles of wilderness in 8 month and 12 days. (©MILEPOST Archive Photos/Edwin Bonde)

History of the Alaska Highway

Construction of the "Alcan" Highway (ALCAN was the military acronym for the Alaska-Canada Highway) officially began on March 9, 1942. A massive mobilization of men and equipment took place in that first month following the executive order to build a military road to Alaska. The Public Roads Administration tackled the task of organizing civilian engineers and equipment. Trucks, road-building equipment, food, tents, office furniture and other supplies all had to be located and then shipped north. By June, more than 10,000 American troops had poured into the Canadian North.

The general route of the Alcan Highway determined by the War Department was along a line of existing airfields from Edmonton, AB to Fairbanks, AK, known as the Northwest Staging Route. (This chain of airfields was used to ferry more than 8,000 war planes to Russia as a part of the Lend-Lease Program.) But mapping out a general route for the Alaska Highway in Washington D.C., and actually surveying the route in the field, proved to be 2 very different things.

Some sections of the proposed route followed existing winter roads, summer pack trails and winter trap lines. Where no trails existed, reconnaissance parties scouted through river valleys and mountain passes, often struggling through waist-deep snow and climbing over "boulders as big as boxcars," according to Theodore A. Huntley, Senior Administrative Officer, Public Roads Administration, in his report, Construction of the Alaska Highway. (Read the full report, a fascinating look at the first year of construction on the Alaska Highway, at www.themilepost.com/articles/.)

Recon parties often depended on local guides to help locate possible routes for the new road. And, like the early-day explorers who preceded them, along with those who called this country home, the Alaska Highway construction crews often left their mark by naming the lakes, rivers and mountains they found along the way.

Once the route had been scouted, the survey crews would move in. "One man would set up with his compass on the staff and—utilizing the chosen bearing—locate a second man, who would proceed through the brush, waving a signal flag from the top of his staff as far as he could be seen," recalls Capt. Eschbach in Alcan Trail Blazers. "At that point, he would stick his staff in the ground, set up his compass, align it on the chosen bearing, and a third man would then move ahead of him... Leapfrogging in this manner, the unit could make as much as 8 or 10 miles on a good day."

For the soldiers and civilian workers building the Alaska Highway, it was a hard life. Working 7 days a week, they endured mosquitoes and black flies in summer and below zero temperatures in winter. And the farther away from base camp you were, the harder the living conditions. Weeks would pass with no communication between headquarters and field parties. According to Theodore A. Huntley's report, "equipment was always a critical problem. There never was enough."

In Alcan Trail Blazers, Sid Navratil describes the daily hardships for the troops. "We are working 16 hours a day, working like hell blazing a trail just ahead of the 'cats.' Our terrific chow shortage is getting everyone grumpy. The daily menu: breakfast, 3 pancakes, thin farina, coffee; lunch (when there is any), 2 biscuits size of a quarter each (and just as hard); supper, fish and potatoes... No cigarettes."

In addition to the hardships imposed by the climate, the challenging physical labor and remote location, African-American soldiers working on the Alaska Highway faced racism in various forms. Of the 7 regiments that were in place in June 1942, 3 were designated as "Negro regiments": the 93rd, 95th and 97th Engineer General Service Regiments. Long-time journalist Lael Morgan points out that "the Alaska section [of the highway] was built solely by black troops of the 97th Regiment under the command of white officers." In Heath Twichell's book, Northwest Epic, the author interviewed his father, Col. Heath Twichell Sr., who had been in command of a black unit during construction of the highway. The elder Mr. Twichell noted the "ceaseless effort" of his men, who built a timber bridge in 72 hours.

In June 1942, the Japanese invaded Attu and Kiska Islands in the Aleutians, adding a new sense of urgency to completion of the Alcan. Crews working from east and west connected at Contact Creek, YT on Sept. 15. Construction ended on Oct. 25, 1942, when it was possible for "a few vehicles to travel the entire length of the highway," as reported by Huntley, although "the road was not good enough for any considerable movement of freight." Grading and surfacing between the Donjek River and the Alaska border "were hurried and sketchy, as the ground had frozen for the winter before the construction crews met."

The official ribbon-cutting ceremony was held Nov. 20, 1942, on Soldier's Summit at Kluane Lake, YT. The Alaska Highway was opened to public traffic in 1948. The highway was named an International Historical Engineering Landmark in 1996.

Dawson Creek

DC 0 DJ 1387 (2232 km)
F 1483 (2386.5 km) **Milepost 0** of the Alaska Highway; 367 miles/591 km northwest of Edmonton, AB; 250 miles/402 km northeast of Prince George, BC; 283 miles/455 km south of Fort Nelson; and 46 miles/74 km south of Fort St. John. **Population:** 11,583, area 27,000. **Emergency Services:** Phone 911 for Police, Fire and Ambulance. Hospital, Dawson Creek & District Hospital, 31 acute care bed facility.

Visitor Information Center: At NAR (Northern Alberta Railways) Park, on Alaska Avenue at 10th Street (one block west of the traffic circle), in the red railroad station. Open year-round, 8 A.M. to 6:30 P.M. daily in summer; 10 A.M. to 4:30 P.M. Tuesday through Saturday September–Oct. 31; 10 A.M. to 4:30 P.M. weekdays November–May. Phone 250-782-9595 or toll-free 1-866-645-3022, or email info@tourismdawsoncreek. com. Trained visitor information counselors can answer questions about weather and road conditions, local events and attractions. Plenty of large vehicle parking and also **EV plug-ins** in front of the refurbished grain elevator that houses the Dawson Creek Art Gallery.

Elevation: 2,183 feet/655m. **Climate:** Average temperature in January is 8.6°F/-13°C; in July it is 60°F/15.5°C. The average annual snowfall is 72 inches with the average depth of snow in midwinter at 19.7 inches. Frost-free days total about 100, with the first frost of the year occurring about the first week of September. **Radio:** CJDC 890, Peace FM 104.1. **Television:** 49 cable channels. **Newspaper:** *The Dawson Creek Mirror* (weekly).

NOTE: Dawson Creek is on Mountain standard time (same time as Alberta) in the winter. In summer, Dawson Creek does not observe Daylight Savings Time and is therefore on Pacific standard time (same time as Prince George and Vancouver).

Private Aircraft: Dawson Creek airport, 2 SE; elev. 2,148 feet/655m; length 5,000 feet/1,524m and 2,300 feet/701m; asphalt; fuel 100, jet.

Dawson Creek (like Dawson City, in Yukon) was named for George Mercer Dawson of the Geological Survey of Canada, whose geodetic surveys of this region in 1879 helped lead to its development as an agricultural settlement. The open, level townsite is surrounded by rolling farmland, part of the government-designated Peace River Block.

The Peace River Block consists of 3.5 million acres of arable land in northeastern British Columbia, which the province gave to the Dominion Government in 1883

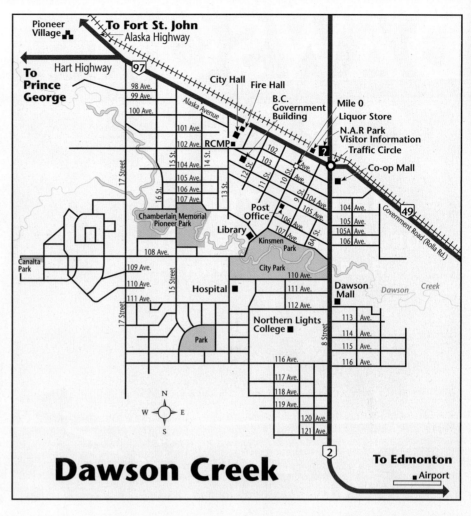

in return for financial aid toward construction of the Canadian Pacific Railway. (While a route through the Peace River country was surveyed by CPR in 1878, the railroad was eventually routed west from Calgary through Kicking Horse Pass.) The Peace River Block was held in reserve by the Dominion Government until 1920, when some of the land was opened for homesteading. The federal government restored the Peace River Block to the province of British Columbia in 1930.

Visitors may notice the fields of bright yellow flowers (in season) in the agricultural area surrounding Dawson Creek. These fields are planted with canola, a hybrid of rapeseed that is a cholesterol-free oil seed. Raw seed is processed in Alberta and Japan. The Peace River region also produces most of the province's cereal grain, along with forage, beef cattle and dairy cattle. Other agricultural industries include the production of honey, hogs, eggs and poultry. Some potato and vegetable farming is also done here.

On the British Columbia Railway line, Dawson Creek is also the hub of 4 major highways: the John Hart Highway (Highway 97 South) to Prince George; the Alaska Highway (Highway 97 North); Highway 2, which leads east to Grande Prairie, AB; and Highway 49, which leads east to Spirit River and Donnelly.

The Northern Alberta Railway reached Dawson Creek in 1931. As a railhead, Dawson Creek was an important funnel for supplies and equipment during construction of the Alaska Highway in 1942. Some 600 carloads arrived by rail within a period of five weeks in preparation for the con-

struction program, according to a report by the Public Roads Administration in 1942. A "rutted provincial road" linked Dawson Creek with Fort St. John, affording the only approach to the southern base of operations. Field headquarters were established at Fort St. John and Whitehorse. Meanwhile, men and machines continued to arrive at Dawson Creek. By May of 1942, 4,720 carloads of equipment had arrived by rail at Dawson Creek for dispersal to troops and civilian engineers to the north. *(See "The History of the Alaska Highway" on facing page.)*

With the completion of the Alaska Highway in 1942 (and opening to the public in 1948) and the John Hart Highway in 1952, Dawson Creek expanded both as a distribution center and tourist destination. Dawson Creek was also one of the major supply centers for the massive North East Coal development to the southwest of the city.

Today, significant industries in this area's economy are oil and gas exploration and servicing, agriculture, forestry and tourism.

Dawson Creek was incorporated as a city in 1958. Provincial government offices and social services for the South Peace Region are located in Dawson Creek. City Hall is located on Ben Heppner Way, named in honor of the famous opera tenor, who comes from this area. (Another well-known musician from Dawson Creek is Roy Forbes, known as "Bim," a folk music singer-songwriter.)

The city has a hospital, a public library, art gallery, a museum and the Northern Lights College (associated with the University of Northern BC in Prince George).

The 4,500-seat Encana Events Center hosts concerts and events. The Lakota Agri-Center is a state-of-the-art equestrian center.

Recreational facilities in Dawson Creek include 5 fitness centers, racquetball courts, a bowling alley, 2 ice arenas (Kin and Memorial), a curling rink and adjacent Skateboard Park, tennis courts and an outdoor gym. There are 3 area golf courses: Hillside Greens Par 3 Golf; Dawson Creek Golf & Country Club par 72; and Farmington Fairways 9-hole course at Mile 10 Alaska Highway. Ken Borek Aquatic Center is adjacent Lakota Center and Encana Events Center on Highway 2.

Downhill and nordic skiing at Bear Mountain Ski Hill. Paradise Valley Snowmobile Club maintains 300 km/186 miles of trails in winter.

There are numerous churches in Dawson Creek; check at the Visitor Center for location and hours of worship.

Lodging & Services

There are more than a dozen hotels/motels, several bed and breakfasts, and dozens of restaurants; department stores, banks, grocery stores, drug and hardware stores, antique shops and other specialty shops. Shopping is downtown in the Dawson Creek Mall or Walmart Super Store. Visitors will also find a laundromat, car and RV washes, gas stations and automotive repair shops. There are 2 liquor stores close to the Visitor Center and beer and wine in local supermarkets. Contact the Visitor Center for a complete listing of all services in the Dawson Creek area.

Enjoy free WiFi at the Visitor Center and Alaska Highway House. The only municipal dump station is at Mile "0" RV Park & Campground (although plans call for a second city dump station off 115th Ave.).

Camping

Camping in Dawson Creek at **Mile "0" RV Park & Campground** at the junction of the Hart Highway (Hwy 97) and the Alaska Highway, at **Northern Lights RV Park** and Tubbys, both on the Hart Highway. There

Staff at Tourism Dawson Creek's Visitor Center are available to answer travelers' questions.
(©Sharon Nault)

are private and provincial campgrounds north of Dawson Creek on the Alaska Highway.

Transportation

Air: Scheduled service from Dawson Creek airport to Prince George with connecting flights via Central Mountain Air. Integra Air offers daily weekday flights to Calgary. The airport is located 2 miles/3.2 km south of the Alaska Avenue traffic circle via 8th Street/Highway 2; there is a small terminal with restaurant at the airport.

Railroad: C.N. Rail provides freight service only.

Bus: Dawson Creek has a city bus transit system. BC Bus North offers service to Prince George and Fort Nelson; bcbus.ca, phone 1-844-564-7494 or 250-564-0161.

Taxi: Available.

Car Rental: Available.

Attractions

Mile 0 Post, the Alaska Highway monument. Located in downtown Dawson Creek,

This renovated grain elevator, adjacent the Visitor Center, houses the Dawson Creek Art Gallery and The Grainery Artisan & Gift Shop. (©Kris Valencia, staff)

at 10th Street and 102nd Avenue, across from the Alaska Highway House and one block from NAR Park. This colorful monument has been a favorite photo subject for Alaska Highway travelers since the original was first erected in the 1940s.

Historical Milepost 0 of the Alaska Highway is marked by a cairn and arch located at the east end of the large parking lot in NAR Park (see description following). Interpretive plaques surround the cairn, which is next to the traffic circle. The traffic circle here connects Highways 97 (Alaska), 2 (to Edmonton) and 49 (to Spirit River). The **Surveyor Statue** in the center of the traffic circle is a tribute to the engineers who arrived in Dawson Creek in 1942, to survey a route for the Alaska Highway.

Northern Alberta Railways (NAR) Park, on Alaska Avenue at 10th Street (near the traffic circle), is the site of the Visitor Center, a popular meeting place for travelers from all over the world; phone 250-782-9595. Housed in a restored railway station, the Visitor Center has a gift shop, public restrooms, free email check kiosk and the answers to all your travel questions. Pick up a free copy of the

Self-Guided Historic Walking Tour brochure. Using this as your guide, stroll the downtown core and view historic photos while reading about Dawson Creek's colorful past.

Also at the railway station is the **Dawson Creek Station Museum**, operated by the South Peace Historical Society. The museum contains pioneer artifacts and wildlife displays, including a collection of more than 50 birds' eggs from this area. Museum admission, $5 per person or $10 per family.

The **Dawson Creek Art Gallery** is housed in a renovated grain elevator, the last of Dawson Creek's heritage elevators, moved to its present location through the efforts of community organizations. Art exhibitions featuring local and regional artists are on display and there is an impressive display of historical Alaska Highway construction photos, as well as **The Grainery Artisan & Gift Shop** featuring the work of local artists and craftsmen. Open year-round, admission is by donation; www.dcartgallery.ca.

There is a **Farmers Market** located at 10300–8 St. in the big orange building, 9 A.M. to 2 P.M. February to December. Flowers

and produce (seasonally), baked goods, eggs, honey and crafts are for sale.

Walter Wright Pioneer Village contains an impressive collection of local pioneer buildings as well as recently built replicas. The entrance to the village is by way of the Mile "0" Park & Campground office (look for the beautiful flower beds at the front of the building), located just off Highway 97; plenty of parking, room for big rigs. Admission to the village is by donation.

The Alaska Highway House. Exhibits here showcase the Alaska Highway, from its inception after the bombing of Pearl Harbor and the Japanese invasion of Attu and Kiska islands in Alaska's Aleutians, through its construction in 1942–43, to its role today as a vital transportation route to the North and the driving adventure of a lifetime. Showings of the PBS documentary *"American Experience: Building the Alaska Highway."*

The Alaska Highway House is located on the corner of 10 Street and 102 Avenue in downtown Dawson Creek with the Chamber of Commerce. Hours are 9 A.M. to 5 P.M. daily in summer. Admission $5 adults, children 12 and under free. Phone 250-782-4714; www.tourismdawsoncreek.com

Dawson Creek Walking Path, a community project to restore the creek, provides a peaceful path for travelers to stretch their legs, go for a bicycle ride and take in some local scenery. The path connects Rotary Park at the junction of the Alaska and Hart highways, with Kinsmen Park on 8th Street and extends for 5 km/3 miles. Ask at the Visitor Center for directions.

Tour Dawson Creek's murals. The Historic Walking Tour brochure, available at the Visitor Center, includes details on the city's murals. Sponsored annually by the Art Gallery, South Peace Art Society and the City of Dawson Creek, the murals portray the city's history, from pioneer days through WWII and construction of the Alaska Highway.

Pick up a free Historic Walking Tour Brochure that will take you back in time through original photos and narrative text and will explain the murals you see. For details, check with the Visitor Center, phone 250-782-9595.

Side trips from Dawson Creek include Tumbler Ridge (dinosaur fossils, waterfalls and over 100 hiking trails—trail map at Tumbler Ridge Visitor Center), Chetwynd (chainsaw carvings), Hudson's Hope Loop (BC Hydro dam tours) and other destinations. An area map and information are available at the Visitor Center at NAR Park on Alaska Avenue.

Tumbler Ridge, originally built in conjunction with development of the Quintette Coal Mine, is in the middle of British Columbia's first dinosaur dig, with thousands of dinosaur bones recently uncovered. The town is also known as the gateway to spectacular Kinuseo Falls in Monkman Provincial Park. Tumbler Ridge is 72 miles/115 km from Dawson Creek by the most direct route: 11.9 miles/19.2 km west via Highway 97, then 59.6 miles/96 km south via Highway 52. Or drive to Chetwynd and drive Highway 29 South to Tumbler Ridge. *See pages 139–140 in the WEST ACCESS ROUTE for log.*

BC Hydro offers tours of one of the world's largest earthen dams at W.A.C. Bennett Dam, and a life-size Hadrosaur at Peace Canyon Dam. Both dams are accessible via the Hudson's Hope Loop; *see pages 137–139 in the WEST ACCESS ROUTE for log.*

Alaska Highway Log

Northbound: Distance from Dawson Creek (DC) is followed by distance from Delta Junction (DJ), official end of the Alaska Highway. Distance from Fairbanks (F) is given at towns and junctions. Read log: ⬇

In the Canada portion of this log, mileages from Dawson Creek are based on actual driving distance and kilometers are based on physical kilometerposts. Historical mileposts are indicated in the text as Historical Mile.

BC HIGHWAY 97 NORTH

DC 0 DJ 1387 (2232 km) **F 1483** (2386.5 km) **Junction** of Highway 97 (Alaska Avenue), Highway 2 (8th Avenue) and Highway 49 (roundabout).

DC 1.2 (1.9 km) **DJ 1385.8** (2230 km) **F 1481.8** (2384.7 km) **Junction** of the Alaska and Hart highways (both Highway 97).
Northern Lights RV Park is 1.5 miles west from this junction on Highway 97 South.

⛺

Northern Lights RV Park. See display ad on page 161.

> **Junction** of the Alaska Highway and Highway 97 South/Hart Highway to Prince George. Westbound travelers turn to page 137 for the end of the log of the WEST ACCESS ROUTE and read log back to front. Alaska-bound travelers continue with this log.

DC 1.5 (2.4 km) **DJ 1385.5** (2229.7 km) Walter Wright Pioneer Village and **Mile 0 RV Park & Campground** to west.

⛺

Mile 0 RV Park & Campground. See display ad on page 161.

DC 1.7 (2.7 km) **DJ 1385.3** (2229.4 km) **Historic Milepost 2.** Double-ended turnout to west with Northwest Highway System (NWHS) sign identifying this spot as the U.S. Army Alaska Highway Control Station in 1942–43. Also interpretive sign about Cantel Repeater Station: "843rd Signal Services Battalion of the U.S. Army Signal Corps was given the task of setting up, operating and maintaining the telephone link, called the Cantel system, between Edmonton and Fairbanks." Mile 2 was the site of 1 of 28 repeater stations built by the Army in 1942-43. The 2,850-mile/4,585-km line stretched from Dunvegan, northwest of Edmonton, AB, to Fairbanks, AK, and included a 600-mile circuit to Norman Wells. According to John Schmidt's *This Was No #@&! Picnic,* each repeater station was a small community in itself, with a crew to man the circuits 24 hours a day and tons of equipment to keep messages moving to some 1,600 army phones and teletypes. One of the world's longest open-wire toll circuits at the time, the Cantel system was the forerunner of today's communications system.

Northbound: Good pavement approximately next 284 miles/457 km (through Fort Nelson). *CAUTION: Heavy traffic, 2-lane stretches of highway with intermittent 4-lane passing to Fort St. John. Drive defensively.*

DC 1.9 (3.1 km) **DJ 1385.1** (2229 km) Distance marker northbound shows Taylor 55 km/34 miles, Fort St. John 72 km/45 miles, Fort Nelson 480 km/298 miles.

DC 2 (3.2 km) **DJ 1385** (2228.9 km) Recreation center and golf course to west.

DC 2.7 (4.3 km) **DJ 138.3** (2227.8 km) Traffic light at **junction** with Dangerous Goods Bypass route to Highway 97 South/Hart Highway. Louisiana Pacific waferboard plant to east and gas/diesel to west.

DC 2.8 (4.5 km) **DJ 1384.2** (2227.6 km) Weigh station.

DC 2.9 (4.7 km) **DJ 1384.1** (2227.5 km) Northern Alberta Railway (NAR) tracks.

DC 3.3 (5.3 km) **DC 1383.7** (2226.8 km) Turnout to east at **Historic Milepost 3.** Sign marks Curan & Briggs Ltd. Construction Camp, U.S. Army Traffic Control Center.

DC 3.4 (5.5 km) **DC 1383.6** (2226.6 km) Turnout to east at **Historic Milepost 3.** Sign marks Curan & Briggs Ltd. Construction Camp, U.S. Army Traffic Control Center.

DC 6.9 (11.1 km) **DC 1380.1** (2221 km) Leaving Dawson Creek/911 area northbound, entering Dawson Creek southbound.

DC 9.1 (14.6 km) **DJ 1377.9** (2217.4 km) Turnout to east.

DC 10 (16 km) **DJ 1377** (2216 km) Farmington Fairways golf course with restaurant and RV park.

⛺

DC 10.5 (16.9 km) **DJ 1376.5** (2215.2 km) *CAUTION: Watch for moose, next 4 km/2.5 miles northbound.*

DC 11.2 (18 km) **DJ 1375.8** (2214.1 km) Turnout to west.

DC 11.5 (18.5 km) **DJ 1375.5** (2213.6 km) Turnout to east.

DC 14.8 (24 km) **DJ 1372.2** (2208.3 km) Farmington (unincorporated).

DC 15.5 (24.9 km) **DJ 1371.5** (2207.2 km) Turnoff to east for Rolla.

DC 15.8 (25.4 km) **DJ 1371.2** (2206.7 km) Farmington store and RV park to west; gas, diesel, propane, groceries.

🅱 ⛺

DC 17.3 (27.8 km) **DJ 1369.7** (2204.3 km) Exit east for loop road to **Kiskatinaw Provincial Park.** Follow 2-lane paved road (Old Alaska Highway) 3 miles/5 km for provincial park; 28 campsites, drinking water (may not be potable), firewood, picnic tables, fire rings, toilets, garbage containers. Camping fee $18.

⛺

This interesting side road gives travelers the opportunity to drive the original old Alaska Highway and to cross the curved, wooden, **Historic Kiskatinaw River Bridge.** A sign at the bridge notes that this 531-foot/162-m-long structure is the only original timber bridge built along the Alaska Highway that is still in use today.

DC 17.5 (28.2 km) **DJ 1369.5** (2204 km) Distance marker northbound shows Taylor 29 km/18 miles, Fort St. John 47 km/29 miles, Fort Nelson 424 km/263 miles.
CAUTION: Watch for deer.

DC 18.1 (29.1 km) **DJ 1368.9** (2203 km) Distance marker southbound shows Dawson Creek 27 km/17 miles, Prince George 429 km/267 miles, Edmonton 640 km/398 miles.

DC 19.4 (31.2 km) **DJ 1367.6** (2200.9 km) Paved turnout to east.

DC 19.8 (31.9 km) **DJ 1367.2** (2200.2 km) Highway descends northbound to Kiskatinaw River.

DC 20.9 (33.6 km) **DJ 1366.1** (2198.5 km) Kiskatinaw River bridge. Turnout with picnic tables and pit toilets to east at north end of bridge.
CAUTION: Strong crosswinds on bridge. Begin 3.8-km/2.4-mile passing lane northbound.

DC 22.5 (36.2 km) **DJ 1364.5** (2195.9 km) Loop road to Kiskatinaw Provincial Park and Kiskatinaw River curved bridge (see **Milepost DC 17.3**).

DC 24.6 (39.6 km) **DJ 1362.4** (2192.5 km) Begin 4.3-km/2.6-mile 4-laning northbound.

DC 25.4 (41 km) **DJ 1361.6** (2191.2 km) NorthwesTel microwave tower to east. Alaska Highway travelers will be seeing many of these towers as they drive north. The original Cantel land line (see **Milepost DC 1.7**) between Grande Prairie, AB, and the YT–AK border was replaced by 42 microwave relay stations by Canadian National Telecommunications (now NorthwesTel) in 1963.

DC 30.2 (48.6 km) **DJ 1356.8** (2183.5 km) South Taylor Hill weigh station and truck chain-off area; very large paved turnout to west for trucks and passenger vehicles. Also, a rest area with picnic tables, toilets and litter bins.

DC 30.5 (49.1 km) **DJ 1356.5** (2183 km) South Taylor Hill lighted truck brake-check/chain-up turnout to east. Historical marker

Walter Wright Pioneer Village, adjacent Mile "0" Park & Campground, has an impressive collection of local pioneer buildings. (©Kris Valencia, staff)

about explorer Alexander Mackenzie. Also, a small lighted turnout to west.

As the highway descends to the Peace River bridge, there are views of the Peace River valley and the community of Taylor to the northeast. *CAUTION: Highway descends South Taylor Hill next 4 miles/6.4 km northbound with 6 to 10 percent grade and curves. Heavy truck traffic.*

DC 32.1 (51.6 km) **DJ 1354.9** (2180.4 km) Long gravel turnout to east for northbound traffic at **Historic Milepost 33**; view (obscured by foliage) of Peace River, bridge and Taylor.

DC 33.9 (54.6 km) **DJ 1353.1** (2177.5 km) Big Bam chain-up area to west for southbound commercial truck traffic ascending South Taylor Hill. Chain-off area to east for northbound traffic.

DC 34 (54.7 km) **DJ 1353** (2177.4 km) Turnoff to west for District of Taylor's **Peace Island Park**, 0.5 mile/0.8 km off the highway, the Peace River and on an island connected to the shore by a causeway. The park has 39 no power sites (on the island) and 60 serviced sites; gravel pads, firewood, fire rings, picnic tables, picnic shelter, toilets, potable water, playground, horseshoe pits and a boat launch. Camping fee charged. There are 4 large picnic areas and a tenting area. Convenience store located in 1 of the pioneer log buildings. Nature trail, bird watching and fishing. For reservations, phone 250-789-9295. Open May to about mid-September, weather permitting. *Boaters should use caution on the Peace River since both parks are downstream from the W.A.C. Bennett and Peace Canyon dams and water levels may fluctuate rapidly.*

DC 34.4 (55.4 km) **DJ 1352.6** (2176.7 km) **Peace River Bridge**, the longest water span on the Alaska Highway. *Metal grating bridge deck.* Bridging the Peace was one of the first goals of Alaska Highway engineers in 1942. Traffic moving north from Dawson Creek was limited by the Peace River crossing, where 2 ferries with a capacity of 10 trucks per hour were operating in May. Three different pile trestles were constructed across the Peace River, only to be washed out by high water. Work on the permanent 2,130-foot suspension bridge began in December 1942 and was completed in July 1943. One of 2 suspension bridges on the Alaska Highway, the Peace River bridge collapsed in 1957 after erosion undermined the north anchor block of the bridge. The cantilever and truss-type bridge that crosses the Peace River today was completed in 1960. Gas pipeline bridge is visible to east.

Taylor

DC 35 (56.3 km) **DJ 1352** (2175.8 km) **Historic Milepost 35**. **Population**: 1,500; **Elevation**: 1,804 feet/550m, located on the north bank of the Peace River. **Visitor Information**: The Visitor Center is on your left northbound on the Alaska Highway (make a left turn on 107th Ave.,) and on your right southbound (make a right on 103rd Ave.). Be sure to take a selfie with the Goldpanner or with the replica of Sir Alexander Mackenzie's canoe. The Visitor Center is housed in a 1932 pioneer log cabin, surrounded by beautiful gardens and a picnic area. It is open daily, 9 A.M. to 5 P.M., May 1 to Sept. 30; phone 250-789-9015.

Alaska Highway historical sign adjacent visitor center identifies Mile 35 as the first main Army camp for the 341st Engineers during construction of the Alaska Highway. Before the Peace River was bridged in 1943, the ferry from Taylor served as the major link across the river.

A hotel, motels, cafes, grocery store with liquor store, private RV park, gas/diesel station and post office are located here. The District of Taylor's popular Peace Island Park campground has a store (pictured below); turnoff at **Milepost DC 34**. Free municipal dump station located behind the Taylor Inn.

©Judy Nadon, staff

Taylor is a unique community, offering both a pleasant rural lifestyle and world-class recreational facilities, including the 18-hole, par 72 **Lone Wolf Golf Club** (home of the world's largest golf ball); RV and tent camping at **Peace Island Park Campground** (see **Milepost DC 34**); tennis courts; a motocross track; and a recreation complex with swimming pool, curling rink and District

Peace Island Park

Lone Wolf Golf Course

Gold Panning Championships

Ice Center for skating. The **World's Invitational Gold Panning Championships** are held at Peace Island Park on August long weekend.

District of Taylor. See display ad on facing page.

Alaska Highway Log
(continued)

BC HIGHWAY 97 NORTH

DC 36.3 (58.4 km) **DJ 1350.7** (2173.7 km) Railroad tracks. Taylor Curling Rink/ Swimming Pool to west. Lone Wolf Golf Course to east.

DC 37.9 (61 km) **DJ 1349.1** (2171.1 km) Turnout with litter bin to west.

DC 40.3 (64.9 km) **DJ 1346.7** (2167.2 km) Exit east for Fort St. John airport.

DC 40.9 (65.8 km) **DJ 1346.1** (2166.3 km) C.N. Railway overhead tracks.

DC 42.9 (69 km) **DJ 1344.1** (2163.1 km) Swanson Lumber Road and access to airport.

Begin divided 4-lane highway. *Slow for speed zones northbound.*

DC 44 (70.8 km) **DJ 1343** (2161.3 km) Fort St. John The Energy City (northbound sign) at East Bypass Road. Airport access.

DC 44.6 (71.7 km) **DJ 1342.4** (2160.3 km) Traffic light at 86 Street. Fresh water fill-up and dump station at northeast corner. Also access to Howard Johnson motel.

DC 45.6 (73.4 km) **DJ 1342.3** (2159.8 km) Traffic light at 92 Street; Subway, Super 8 to north. Entering Fort St. John business area northbound. A number of visitor services are located on the frontage roads (Alaska Road North and Alaska Road South) that parallel the Alaska Highway through Fort St. John.

DC 45.7 (73.5 km) **DJ 1341.3** (2158.5 km) 96 Street; access northeast to Super 8, Pomeroy Inn & Suites, Subway, Shell gas/ diesel station, Walmart pharmacy, the Totem Mall and Pomeroy Sport Center, which houses the Fort St. John Visitor Information Center.

DC 45.8 (73.7 km) **DJ 1341.2** (2158.4 km) Traffic light at 100 Street. Turn right for Safeway (with gas/diesel and propane), Starbucks, brewhouse/grill. Continue north on 100 Street for **Fort St. John North Peace Museum** and downtown Fort St. John businesses, including **Homesteader Health Foods** (right turn at 97 Avenue).

Follow 100 Street south 1.9 miles/3 km for **Peace River Lookout;** large gravel parking area with picnic tables.

DC 46.4 (74.6 km) **DJ 1340.6** (2157.4 km) Traffic light at 108 Street/109 Street. Access to gas stations and fast-food.

DC 47 (75.6 km) **DJ 1340** (2156.5 km) **Historical Mile 48.** Traffic light at 100 Avenue. Access northeast to Fort St. John City Center and airport via 100 Avenue. Chances Gaming and Pomeroy Hotel.

The Fort St. John visitor center is located inside the Pomeroy Sport Center on 96 Street.
(©Kris Valencia, staff)

Fort St. John

DC 47 (75.6 km) **DJ 1340** (2156.5 km) **Historic Milepost 47.** Dubbed the "Energetic City," Fort St. John is located approximately 236 miles/380 km south of Fort Nelson. **Population:** 21,523; area 69,000. **Emergency Services:** Dial 911. **RCMP,** phone 250-787-8100. **Hospital,** Fort St. John Hospital, 8407 112 Ave., phone 250-262-5200.

Visitor Information: The Visitor Center, is located inside the Pomeroy Sport Center at 9324 96 St. Look for "To The Rink" sculpture by Peter Vogelaar in front; it makes a good photo op. The Visitor Center offers a wide selection of brochures, a gift shop and restrooms. For information, phone 250-785-3033 or toll-free 1-877-785-6037; visitor info@fortstjohn.ca; www.fortstjohn.ca. Open year-round.

RVers are welcome to meet at the Pomeroy Sport Center's parking lot, a large lot with easy RV access and just steps from the Visitor Center. Wander over to the Visitor Center and ask about special events going on during your visit and find out what

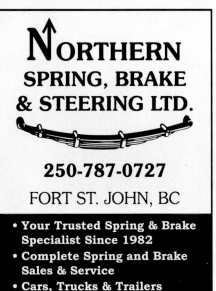

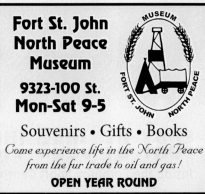

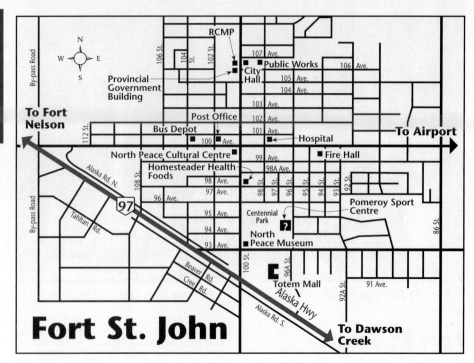

Fort St. John

attractions are within walking distance of the center.

For information on wilderness hiking and camping opportunities, contact BC Parks (Ministry of Environment), Peace Region, #400, 10003–110 Ave., Fort St. John, BC V1J 6M7, phone 250-787-3411; www.gov.bc.ca/env/ or the City of Fort St. John Visitor Center. Direct hunting and fishing queries to the Ministry of Environment, #400, 10003–110 Ave., Fort St. John, BC V1J 6M7; phone 250-787-3411. Backcountry, 10120 Alaska Rd. N., Fort St. John, V1J 1A8; phone 250-785-1461.

Elevation: 2,275 feet/693m. **Climate:** Average high temperature in July, 73°F/23°C, average low 50°F/10°C. In January, average high is 12°F/-11°C; low is -2°F/-19°C. **Radio:** CBC 88.3 FM, Sunrise Radio 92.5 FM, Energy 98.5 FM, The Moose 100.1 FM, The Bear 101.5 FM. **Television:** Cable. **Newspaper:** *Alaska Highway News* (daily), *The Northerner* (weekly), *Northeast News* (weekly)

Private Aircraft: Fort St. John airport, 3.8 E; elev. 2,280 feet/695m; length 6,900 feet/2,103m and 6,700 feet/2,042m; asphalt; fuel 100, Jet. Charlie Lake airstrip, 6.7 NW; elev. 2,680 feet/817m; length 1,800 feet/549m; gravel; fuel 100.

Fort St. John is set in the low, rolling hills of the Peace River Valley. The original Fort St. John was established as Rocky Mountain Fort in 1794, making Fort St. John the oldest European settlement in mainland British Columbia. The Peace region was homesteaded in the early 1900s. The town's early commercial development centered around a store established by settler C.M. Finch. His stepson, Clement Brooks, carried on Finch's entrepreneurship, starting several businesses in Fort St. John after WWII.

In 1942, Fort St. John became field headquarters for U.S. Army troops and civilian engineers working on construction of the Alaska Highway in the eastern sector. "Camp Alcan" at Fort St. John (along with Whitehorse, headquarters for the western sector) was the largest of the dozen or so construction camps along the highway. What had been home to 200 became a temporary base for more than 6,000. Much of the field housing, road building equipment and even office supplies were scrounged from old Civilian Conservation Corps camps and the Work Projects Administration. The Alaska Highway was opened to the traveling public in 1948, attracting vaca-

tioners and homesteaders.

In 1951, the Fort St. John No. 1 well hit gas, marking the beginning of a huge oil and gas industry in the region and making Fort St. John the oil capital of British Columbia. "Energetic City," referring to the natural energy resources and the city's potential for positive growth, became the slogan for the city. "Today, tens of thousands of oil and gas wells tap into the famous Montney formation, estimated at 271 trillion cubic feet with 100 years of production," according to *B.C. Oil & Gas Report*. Motorists will notice gas and oil patch activity along the Alaska Highway between Fort St. John and Fort Nelson, although the level of activity depends largely on the oil and gas markets.

An extension of the Pacific Great Eastern Railway, now called C.N. Rail, from Prince George in 1958 (continued to Fort Nelson in 1971), gave Fort St. John a link with the rail yards and docks at North Vancouver.

Today, Fort St. John's booming economy is based primarily on oil and gas, as well as agriculture, forestry, tourism, hydro-electric power generation (see **Milepost DC 48.2** for directions to the Site C Clean Energy Project overlook), and consumer and public services. Fort St. John is northeastern BC's shopping and service center, with boutique shops and large chain stores.

Transportation

Air: Fort St. John Regional Airport (www.fsjairport.com) is served by Air Canada, Central Mountain Air and WestJet. Daily service to Vancouver and Calgary; also service to Edmonton, Fort Nelson, Prince George and points west, Kamloops and Kelowna. **Bus:** For schedules of city transit system go to bctransit.com or phone 250-787-7433. BC Bus North service from Prince George and Fort Nelson, phone 1-844-564-7494 or 250-564-0161; bcbus.ca. **Car Rentals:** Avis, Enterprise, National and Driving Force at airport terminal. **Taxis:** Available.

Lodging & Services

Visitor services are located just off the Alaska Highway and in the city center, several blocks north of the highway. There are 17 motels/hotels in the Fort St. John area including major chains and independents. *(NOTE: Lodging fills up fast, phone ahead for reservations.)* Major chain restaurants and fast-food outlets and full-service gas stations are located on the Alaska Highway and in town.

Major chain retailers include Walmart, Shoppers Drug Mart and Canadian Tire. Shopping centers include Totem Mall on 93 Avenue, Northgate Mall on 100 Street and PC Plaza on 98A Avenue. RV and automotive services available, including **Northern Spring, Brake & Steering Ltd.** (phone 250-787-0727).

Easy access parking for RVs at the North Peace Leisure Pool on 100 Street; Totem Mall on 93 Avenue; Pomeroy SportCenter/City of Fort St. John Visitor Center on 96 Street; and the Walmart on 96 Street.

Fort St. John has supermarkets like the **Homesteader Health**; a Starbucks; 2 laundromats; pharmacies; all major Canadian banks and a Credit Union; car washes; a 12-lane bowling alley on 104 Street; a 5-plex movie theatre (Aurora Cinema Center) on 93 Avenue; and Chances Gaming Center (electronic bingo, slot machines) on Alaska Road.

Recreation facilities include the Pomeroy Sport Center and the North Peace Recreation

The Fort St. John North Peace Museum features thousands of artifacts and photos from the region as well as historic buildings. (©Kris Valencia, staff)

Center (see descriptions under Attractions).

Camping

Private campgrounds in city and north of the city on Charlie Lake at **Milepost DC 51** Alaska Highway. There is also camping at Beatton Provincial Park, 5 miles east of **Milepost DC 49.5**, and at Charlie Lake Provincial Park, **Milepost DC 53.6** Alaska Highway.

Fresh water fill-up and dump station located at the northeast corner of 86 Street and the Alaska Highway.

Attractions

Centennial Park, located on 100 Street, is home to various recreation facilities and attractions. **Rotary Spray Park**, open 10 A.M. to 9 P.M. during summer, is located here. A **Farmers Market** takes place Wednesday evenings, 5–7 P.M., and Saturdays 9 A.M. to 2 P.M. Also here are Rotary Skatepark (a second skatepark is located at the corner of 93 Street and 93 Avenue); the Rose Garden; the 8-sheet Fort St. John Curling Club in winter; a volleyball court; and swimming pool. The **North Peace Leisure Pool**, at 9505 100 St., has a lap pool, diving boards, waterslide, wave pool and fitness room; phone 250-787-8178 or 250-785-POOL.

A granite monument in Centennial Park commemorates Sir Alexander Mackenzie's stop here on his journey west to the Pacific Ocean in 1793.

The **Fort St. John North Peace Museum**, at 9323 100 St., features more than 10,000 artifacts from the region, including archeological artifacts from the fur trade items, and from the Alaska Highway, an early-day schoolroom, a dentist office and a blacksmith shop.

Historic buildings include a missionary chapel, a trapper's cabin, and the British Columbia Police Barracks. The museum's archives contain over 13,000 local photographs as well as local history books and papers, genealogical records and maps. The museum gift shop offers a good selection of local and Northwest books, DVDs, clothing, and many souvenir items.

The museum is open year-round, 9 A.M. to 5 P.M. daily except Sundays; phone 250-

787-0430.

Pioneer Pathway Walking Tour. The Energetic City revisits its past through heritage panels located in the downtown area. The panels feature historic photos and stories of Fort St. John beginning in the 1920s. Start the walking tour at the Visitor Center, where you can pick up a map.

North Peace Cultural Center, at 10015 100 Ave., houses Fort St. John Public Library (phone 250-785-3731); a 413-seat theatre which showcases musical, theatrical and other live performances throughout the year; an art gallery; and a cafe. Phone 250-785-1992; www.npcc.bc.ca.

North Peace Recreation Center, located on 96 Avenue in Centennial Park, has winter ice skating rink. A Farmers Market is held just outside of the swimming pool parking lot on Saturdays, 9 A.M. to 4 P.M., May–December. The North Peace Leisure Pool, on the other side of the recreation center, has a waterslide, wave pool, lap pool, diving boards, a sauna and steam room; phone 250-787-8178. The outdoor Rotary Spray Park is located beside the pool.

Pomeroy Sport Center, at 9324 96 St., features 2 NHL-sized ice rinks, an indoor Olympic-sized speed skating oval, a 3-lane, 380-metre-/1,247-foot-long rubberized track for community use year-round, and also houses the Fort St. John Visitor Center on the first floor. This enormous facility has extensive parking and a rainwater harvesting system that will channel rainwater from the roof to holding tanks for use in the facility's landscaping and irrigation needs. Look for the bronze "To The Rink" by Peter Vogelaar out in front.

Walking trails. Fish Creek Community Forest, adjacent to Northern Lights College, has 3 interpretive trails to learn more about the forest and forestry management. To reach the college from the Alaska Highway, follow 100 Street north 1.2 miles/2 km and turn right on the Bypass Road just before the railway tracks. Take the first left and park behind Northern Lights College. Or stop by the Visitor Center for driving directions and trail maps.

Peace River Valley view site. A wonder-

Alaska Highway monument at Charlie Lake memorializes soldiers who drowned here in 1942, during construction of the Alaska Highway. (©Kris Valencia, staff)

ful panoramic view of the Peace River valley is available from the viewpoint at the end of 100 Street southwest off the Alaska Highway (see **Milepost DC 45.8**). Follow 100 Street south 1.9 miles/3 km west from the highway to the viewpoint. There is a very large gravel parking area and picnic tables.

Trail System. More than 6 miles/10 km of paved trail loop around the perimeter of the city. Great for joggers, bicyclists and walkers. Trailheads for access to this trail are located at 100 Street and Bypass Road and at Surerus Park, 86 Street and 102 Avenue. There is also trail access from Northern Lights College.

Special Events. Hundreds of events happen in the Energetic City each year, from arts to musical performances, baseball games, ice sculpting, CKNL Tradeshow, Canada Day celebrations, Motorcycle Poker Run, North Peace Fall Fair, Annual Art Auction, and Santa Parade. The highlights in winter are the High On Ice Winter Festival during Family Day long weekend in February, which attracts professional carvers from around the world, as well as creative local artists, and the Crystal Cup Pond Hockey Challenge at Charlie Lake, also in February.

Check with the Visitor Center or visit www.fortstjohn.ca for a list of special events.

Play golf. Fort St. John's only in-town golf course is Links Golf Course, just off the Bypass Road at 86 Street; 9 holes, pro shop and lounge; phone 250-785-9995. The Lakepoint Golf Course, on Golf Course Road at Charlie Lake, has a multi-tee system, driving range, pro shop, lounge and restaurant; phone 250-785-5566. Lone Wolf Golf Club in Taylor has an 18-hole championship course, driving range, rentals, restaurant, clubhouse and pro shop; phone 250-789-3711.

W.A.C. Bennett Dam is a major attraction in the area. For an interesting **sidetrip**, drive north from Fort St. John on the Alaska Highway to **Milepost DC 53.6** and take Highway 29 west 45.4 miles/73 km to junction with the W.A.C. Bennett access road in Hudson's Hope. Highway 29 fol-

lows the original Canadian government telegraph trail of 1918. Hudson's Hope, formerly a pioneer community established in 1805 by explorer Simon Fraser, grew with construction of the W.A.C. Bennett Dam, which is located 15 miles/24 km west of town. B.C. Hydro's Peace Canyon dam is located approximately 4 miles/6.4 km south of Hudson's Hope. The new Site C dam on the Peace River—which will raise water levels along a portion of Highway 29 when it is complete—can be seen from a viewpoint west of the Alaska Highway via Road 269 (go to **Milepost DC 48.2** in the log). See "Hudson Hope Loop" log on pages 137–139.

Alaska Highway Log
(continued)

BC HIGHWAY 97 NORTH

DC 45.8 (73.7 km) **DJ 1341.2** (2158.4 km) Traffic light at 100 Street. Turn right northbound for Safeway (with gas/diesel and propane station at 100 Street entrance), Starbucks, Canadian Brewhouse & Grill. Continue north on 100 Street for **Fort St. John North Peace Museum** and downtown Fort St. John businesses, including **Homesteader Health Foods** (right turn at 97 Avenue).

Follow 100 Street south 1.9 miles/3 km for Peace River Lookout; large gravel parking area with picnic tables.

DC 46.4 (74.6 km) **DJ 1340.6** (2157.4 km) Traffic light at 108 Street/109 Street. Access to gas stations and fast-food.

DC 46.9 (75.5 km) **DJ 1340.1** (2156.6 km) Distance marker northbound shows Charlie Lake 5 km/3 miles, Wonowon 101 km/63 miles, Fort Nelson 377 km/234 miles.

DC 47 (75.6 km) **DJ 1340** (2156.5 km) **Historical Mile 48.** Traffic light at 100 Avenue. Access northeast to Fort St. John City Center.

DC 47.3 (76.1 km) **DJ 1339.7** (2156 km) Petro-Canada gas/diesel station.

DC 48.2 (77.6 km) **DJ 1338.8** (2154.5 km) Traffic light. Road 269/Business Frontage. Follow Road 269 south 3.7 miles/6 km past the Peace River Regional District landfill and watch for turnoff (marked by sign) for gated entrance to the **Site C Viewpoint.** From the viewpoint, visitors can watch Site C construction activities as BC Hydro builds a new dam on the Peace River (siteproject. com). Paved parking, interpretive signs, picnic tables, litter bins and telescopes at viewing area. The Site C Viewpoint is open year-round, 8 A.M. to 7 P.M. in summer, 9 A.M. to 4 P.M. in winter.

DC 48.6 (78.2 km) **DJ 1338.4** (2153.9 km) **Historic Milepost 49** historic sign:

Camp Alcan and the Public Roads Administration Headquarters/Okes Management Contracting Headquarters–Standard Salt & Cement Co., Coghlan Construction Co., M.G. Astleford Co., Southern Minnesota Construction Co., Art Colier, Sorenson & Volden, R.M. Smith Headquarters. "As the southern sector headquarters for the United States Military and Public Roads Administration, Fort St. John was the site of two large construction camps—pyramid tents and Quonset huts—erected in open fields just outside of town."

DC 48.8 (78.5 km) **DJ 1338.2** (2153.6 km) Welcome to Fort St. John southbound sign.

DC 49.5 (79.6 km) **DJ 1337.5** (2152.4 km) Traffic light at Road 271. Turnoff for **Beatton Provincial Park**, 5 miles/8 km east via paved road; 37 campsites, picnic shel-

ter, horseshoe pits, playground, sports field, sandy beach, swimming and boat launch. Camping fee $18. Fishing for northern pike, walleye (July best), yellow perch in **Charlie Lake.**

DC 50.5 (81.3 km) **DJ 1336.5** (2150.8 km) CAUTION: Pedestrian crossing traffic light.

DC 51 (82.4 km) **DJ 1336** (2150 km) Traffic light at Old Hope Road. Turnoff to east and follow signs to Rotary Park campground. Gas and grocery to west. Day-use area on **Charlie Lake** has parking, restrooms, a playground, lake trail, boat launch, fishing and **Alaska Highway monument** (description follows).

The Alaska Highway monument on Charlie Lake memorializes 12 American soldiers who drowned May 14, 1942, when their pontoon boat sank while crossing the lake. The soldiers, part of the 341st Engineers and the 74th Light Pontoon, were working on construction of the highway.

DC 51.3 (82.9 km) **DJ 1335.7** (2149.5 km) **Historic Milepost 52.** NWHS sign commemorates Charlie Lake, Mile 0 Army Tote Road. A major distribution camp.

DC 51.5 (83 km) **DJ 1335.6** (2149 km) Charlie Lake & Leisure RV Park to east.

DC 51.8 (83.4 km) **DJ 1335.2** (2148.7 km) End 4-lane highway, begin 3-lane highway with passing lane next 2.5 miles/4 km northbound. Begin 4-lane highway southbound.

DC 52.6 (88 km) **DJ 1334.4** (2147 km) Enbridge Charlie Lake natural gas processing facility (formerly SpectraEnergy).

DC 53.6 (86.3 km) **DJ 1333.4** (2145.8 km) Highway 29 **junction** to west. Turn west for Highway 29 to Hudson's Hope; turn east for Charlie Lake Provincial Park (see description below).

> **Junction** with Highway 29, which leads west 47 miles/76 km to Hudson's Hope and the W.A.C. Bennett Dam, then south to connect with the Hart Highway at Chetwynd. Turn to page 139 and read "Hudson's Hope Loop" log from back to front.

Turn east for **Charlie Lake Provincial Park**, just off highway; paved loop road (with speed bumps) leads through campground. There are 58 shaded sites, picnic tables, kitchen shelter with wood stove, firepits, firewood ($8), outhouses, dump station ($5), water and garbage containers. See posted restrictions on generator use. Level gravel sites, some will accommodate 2 large RVs. Camping fee $18, reservations at www. discovercamping.ca.

The provincial park has a playfield, playground, horseshoe pits, volleyball net and a 1.2-mile/2-km hiking trail down to lake. Fishing in Charlie Lake for walleye, northern pike and yellow perch. Access to the lake for vehicles and boats is from the Alaska Highway just east of the park entrance. Boat launch and picnic area at lake.

DC 53.7 (86.4 km) **DJ 1333.3** (2145.7 km) Truck weigh scales east side of highway.

DC 54.3 (87 km) **DJ 1332.7** (2145 km) End 3-lane highway, begin 2-lane highway, northbound. Intermittent passing lanes northbound to Fort Nelson.

DC 54.5 (87.7 km) **DJ 1332.5** (2144.4 km) Distance marker northbound shows Wonowon 74 km/46 miles, Fort Nelson 364 km/226 miles, Whitehorse 1342 km/834 miles.

DC 54.8 (88.2 km) DJ 1332.2 (2143.9 km) West Road.

DC 59.5 (95.8 km) DJ 1327.5 (2136.3 km) Turnouts both sides of highway. Litter bins on the east side.

DC 61.6 (99.1 km) DJ 1325.4 (2133 km) Coffee Creek RV Park to east.

DC 62.2 (100.1 km) DJ 1324.8 (2132 km) A 30-foot/9-m statue of a lumberjack marks Clarke Sawmill to west.

DC 64.8 (104 km) DJ 1322.2 (2127.8 km) Enbridge compressor station.

DC 71.7 (115.4 km) DJ 1315.3 (2116.7 km) **Historical Mile 72. The Shepherd's Inn**; popular stop with a restaurant, home-made baked goods, motel, gas/diesel.

The Shepherd's Inn. See display ad this page.

DC 72.8 (117.1 km) DJ 1314.2 (2114.9 km) **Historic Milepost 73** commemorates Beatton River Flight Strip, 1 of 4 gravel air-strips built for American military aircraft during WWII. Road to Prespetu and Buick, access to oil and gas well sites.

DC 79.1 (127.3 km) DJ 1307.9 (2104.8 km) Historical Mile 80 Rest Area to west; double-ended turnout with paved parking, heated restrooms with flush toilets, litter and recycle bins, treed picnic area with picnic tables and playground.

DC 81.4 (131 km) DJ 1305.6 (2101 km) Distance marker northbound shows Wono-won 31 km/19 miles, Fort Nelson 319 km/198 miles, Whitehorse 1297 km/806 miles.

Distance marker southbound shows Fort St. John 56 km/35 miles, Dawson Creek 131 km/81 miles.

DC 90.6 (145.8 km) DJ 1296.4 (2086.3 km) Turnoff for Inga Lake, 41 km/25 miles west; a recreation site with picnicking and camping.

DC 91.8 (147.7 km) DJ 1295.2 (2084.4 km) **Historical Mile 92.** Enbridge compres-sor station to west.

Travelers may notice natural gas explora-tion wells between Dawson Creek and Fort Nelson. Gas exploration along the Alaska Highway corridor in British Columbia and into Yukon and the Northwest Territories has been very much in evidence in recent years.

DC 94.6 (152.2 km) DJ 1292.4 (2079.8 km) Turnoff for Upper Halfway Road. This 34.5-mile/55.5-km side road (paved) leads in a southwesterly direction to area ranches.

DC 97 (155.3 km) DJ 1290 (2076 km) Large gravel turnout to east.

DC 98.7 (159 km) DJ 1288.3 (2073.3 km)

Microwave tower to east.
Slow for posted speed zone northbound.

DC 99.6 (161 km) DJ 1287.4 (2071.8 km) Motel/cabins.

DC 101 (161.7 km) DJ 1286 (2069.5 km) **WONOWON** (pop. 150), unincorporated, has an Esso gas station with diesel, general store and post office, and Chester's Chicken to west serving the traveling public. **Historic Milepost 101.** The historic sign and inter-pretive panel here commemorate the "site of the Blueberry Control Gate, a 24-hour mili-tary checkpoint operated by U.S. Army per-sonnel through the war years."

Wonowon Lodge to east is an open camp for gas-patch crews. It has a 24-hour dining room and 289 rooms in modular units. There has been considerable oil and gas exploration in recent years along the Alaska Highway north of Fort St. John, and motor-ists will notice several signed turnoffs at side roads for these camp complexes and/or oil and gas patches. Most of the camp facilities are for crews and rates run between $185–195/night. During boom times they are full, but when the oil and gas markets take a downturn, they may be shuttered or run at lower capacity.

Northbound, the Alaska Highway follows the Blueberry and Prophet river drainages north to Fort Nelson. The Blueberry River, not visible from the highway, lies a few miles east of Wonowon.

DC 102 (163.4 km) DJ 1285 (2068 km) Super 96 Camp & Hotel for gas and oil crews with 294 rooms and dining.

DC 103.5 (166.5 km) DJ 1283.5 (2065.5 km) Historic Milepost 104 marks start of Adolphson, Huseth, Layer & Welch contract during Alaska Highway construction.

DC 114.6 (183.6 km) DJ 1272.4 (2047.7 km) Paved turnout with litter bin to east.

DC 124.3 (200.5 km) DJ 1262.7 (2032.1 km) The Cut (highway goes through a small rock cut). Relatively few rock cuts were nec-essary during construction of the Alaska Highway in 1942–43. However, rock excava-tion was often made outside of the roadway to obtain gravel fill for the new roadbed.

DC 140.4 (226 km) DJ 1246.6 (2006.2 km) **Historical Mile 143. PINK MOUNTAIN** (pop. 99, area 300; elev. 3,600 feet/1,097m). Post office, Race Trac gas station (diesel, pro-pane), liquor store, groceries, and RV camp-ing to west at **Pink Mountain Campsite & R.V. Park** (description follows). Restaurant, pub, lodging and camping to east at Buffalo Inn.

Pink Mountain Campsite & R.V. Park and Race Trac Fuels. Welcome to our clean, quiet, quaint Campsite/RV Park—

Historic Mile 143—where we have some-thing to offer everyone: Gas, diesel, propane, convenience store, post office, liquor store and WiFi. Our sites are full-service and non-

service, pull-throughs and back-ins. Coin-operated showers and laundry. Sani-dump and water. We're open year-round, although camping is seasonal (winter sites can be arranged with power only). All major credit cards accepted. Please call 250-772-5133.

Relaxing by the Sikanni Chief River, 159 miles north of Dawson Creek, BC. (©Judy Nadon, staff)

Email: lory@northwestel.net. See display ad on page 169. [ADVERTISEMENT]

According to local resident Ron Tyerman, Pink Mountain gets its name from the local fall foliage, when red-barked willows give the mountain a pink colour in the morning sun. Another source attributes the pink colour of the mountain and its concentrations of feldspar.

DC 142.3 (229 km) **DJ 1244.7** (2003.1 km) Large informal gravel turnout to east.

DC 144.1 (231.9 km) **DJ 1242.9** (2002.2 km) Sasquatch Crossing Lodge; food, camping, lodging. Cardlock gas.

DC 144.7 (232.7 km) **DJ 1242.3** (1999.2 km) Beatton River bridge. The Beatton River was named for Frank Beatton, a Hudson's Bay Co. employee. The Beatton River flows into the Peace River system.

DC 145.1 (233.4 km) **DJ 1241.9** (1998.6 km) **Historic Milepost 148** double-ended gravel turnout to east with litter bins and sign commemorating **Suicide Hill**, one of the most treacherous hills on the original highway, noted for its ominous greeting: "Prepare to meet thy maker."

DC 145.5 (234 km) **DJ 1241.5** (1997.9 km) **Private Aircraft:** Sikanni Chief flight strip to east; elev. 3,258 feet/993m; length, 6,000 feet/1,829m; gravel, current status unknown. Well-known local bush pilot Jimmy "Midnight" Anderson (1926–2008) used the Sikanni Chief airstrip. This airstrip was also part of the Northwest Staging Route used during WWII.

DC 147.9 (238 km) **DJ 1239.1** (1994.1 km) Distance marker northbound shows Buckinghorse 40 km/25 miles, Fort Nelson 222 km/138 miles.

Distance marker southbound shows Wonowon 74 km/46 miles, Fort St. John 162 km/101 miles.

CAUTION: Watch for moose and deer, especially at dusk and at night.

DC 154.5 (248.6 km) **DJ 1232.5** (1983.5 km) Turnoff to west for gas and oil camps and for **Duhu Lake Provincial Park** (5.8 km/3.6 miles) with camping.

DC 156 (251 km) **DJ 1231** (1981 km) Large double-ended, gravel turnout/brake check area with litter bins to east at top of Sikanni Hill. Winter chain-up/chain removal area. Slow for 6 to 9 percent winding downgrade next 5 km/3 miles northbound to Sikanni Chief River bridge.

Section of the old Alaska Highway is visible to east; no access.

DC 159.2 (256.2 km) **DJ 1227.8** (1975.9 km) **Sikanni Chief River Bridge** (elev. 2,662 feet/811m). Steel stanchions to west are all that remain of the historic wooden Sikanni bridge, which was destroyed by arson July 10, 1992. The original timber truss bridge across the Sikanni Chief River was built in 72 hours (or 84 hours, accounts differ) on October 28, 1942, by the African American 95th Engineer General Service Regiment. It was the first permanent structure completed on the Alaska Highway. Highway construction crews rerouted much of the pioneer road built in 1942 and replaced temporary bridges with 133 steel permanent structures in 1943.

The Sikanni Chief River flows east and then north into the Fort Nelson River, which flows into the Liard River and on to the Mackenzie River, which empties into the Arctic Ocean. Check at the lodge for information on Sikanni Chief Falls (see **Milepost DC 168.5**).

Sikanni Chief River, fair fishing at mouth of tributaries in summer for grayling to 2½ lbs.; whitefish to 2 lbs.

Winding 6 to 9 percent uphill grade southbound.

DC 159.4 (256.5 km) **DJ 1227.6** (1975.6 km) **Historical Mile 162. SIKANNI CHIEF. Sikanni River Campground & RV Park** (description follows); seasonal gas, lodging and camping. Historic highway lodge location: Sikanni Chief Lodge first appeared in the 1949 edition of *The MILEPOST®.*

Sikanni River Campground & RV Park is surrounded by natural beauty and offers access to riverside camping. We have serviced and non-serviced, pull-through and back-in, sites. WiFi, coin laundry, free showers, clean washrooms, sani-dump, and a terrific playground for the kids. 3 kitchenette cabins, convenience store. Regular gas (sorry, no diesel, no propane). Open May through September. Please call 250-772-5400; website www.sikannirivercampground.ca. [ADVERTISEMENT]

Highway climbs with passing lane northbound.

DC 160 (257.5 km) **DJ 1227** (1974.6 km) Brake-check turnout to west for southbound traffic; litter bin. "Drunken Forest" on hillside to west is shallow-rooted black spruce trees growing in unstable clay-based soil that is subject to slide activity in wet weather.

DC 168.5 (270.3 km) **DJ 1218.5** (1960.9 km) Gravel road west to Sikanni Chief Falls Protected Area. Drive in 10.5 miles/16.9 km to small parking area at trailhead for 0.9-mile/1.5-km hike on well-marked trail to view the 98-foot/30-m falls. Access road has steep hills and 1-lane bridge: Do not travel this side road in wet weather. Side road is not recommended for large RVs or vehicles with trailers.

CAUTION: Watch for moose on highway northbound to Milepost DC 200, especially at dusk. Drive carefully!

DC 172.5 (277.6 km) **DJ 1214.5** (1954.5 km) Polka Dot Creek.

DC 172.7 (277.9 km) **DJ 1214.3** (1954.2 km) **Historic Milepost 175.**

DC 173.2 (278.2 km) **DJ 1213.8** (1953.4 km) Buckinghorse River bridge; access to river at north end of bridge.

DC 173.3 (278.4 km) **DJ 1213.7** (1953.2 km) Turnoff to east for **Buckinghorse River Wayside Provincial Park.** Follow the narrow gravel road 0.7 mile/1.1 km along river to camping and picnic area. Very nice spot. The park has 33 campsites, picnic tables, side-by-side camper parking, fire rings (firewood may be available), water pump, outhouses and litter bins; open May to Sept. 30, camping fee $20 CAD (self-registration). Fishing for grayling in Buckinghorse River. Swimming in downstream pools.

DC 173.4 (279 km) **DJ 1213.6** (1953 km) **Historical Mile 175.** Buckinghorse River Lodge west side of highway; seasonal 24-hour AFD public cardlock gas. The Camp complex to east.

DC 176 (282.3 km) **DJ 1211** (1948.9 km) Double-ended gravel turnout to the east with litter bins and outhouses at **Historic Milepost 191.** This is the south end of the 27-mile/43-km Trutch Mountain Bypass, completed in 1987, which rerouted the Alaska Highway around Trutch Mountain, eliminating the steep, winding climb over the mountain.

The "new" roadbed of the Alaska Highway you are driving on cuts a wide swath through the flat Minnaker River valley. The river, not visible to motorists, is west of the highway, and was named for local trapper George Minnaker. Trutch Mountain, to the east of the highway, was the second highest summit on the Alaska Highway before the highway was rerouted, with an elevation of 4,134 feet/1,260m. It was named for Joseph W. Trutch, civil engineer and first governor of British Columbia. Today, the "old road" over Trutch is narrow gravel, used by gas and oil patch crews.

DC 177.2 (284.4 km) **DJ 1209.8** (1946.9 km) Turnoff to west for Bucking Horse Sour Gas Processing Plant.

An arduous 42-mile/68-km-long all-terrain-vehicle-only trail to Redfern-Keily Provincial Park heads west from the highway near here. Restrictions apply on ATV weight and trail conditions vary. This is part of the Muskwa-Kechika Management Area and it is suggested you check with the office in Fort Nelson before attempting this trail. This remote provincial park offers 2 main hiking trails and 26 primitive campsites.

DC 182.8 (293.2 km) **DJ 1204.2** (1937.9 km) Large double-ended gravel turnout to west with litter bins and outhouse.

DC 184.5 (297 km) **DJ 1202.5** (1935 km) Distance marker northbound shows Prophet River 68 km/42 miles, Fort Nelson 156 km/97 miles.

DC 199.1 (319.5 km) **DJ 1187.9** (1911.7 km) **Historic Milepost 202.** Large gravel turnout with litter bins to west.

CAUTION: Watch for moose on highway, especially at dusk. Drive carefully!

DC 199.2 (320 km) **DJ 1187.8** (1911.5 km) Welcome to Fort Nelson Forest District (northbound sign).

DC 204.2 (328 km) **DJ 1182.8** (1903.5 km) Highway descends to **Beaver Creek**; fishing for grayling to 2½ lbs. ⬅

DC 216.6 (348.2 km) **DJ 1170.4** (1883.5 km) Distance marker southbound shows Buckinghorse River 70 km/43 miles, Fort St. John 272 km/169 miles.

DC 217.2 (349.3 km) **DJ 1169.8** (1882.5 km) Gravel side road leads west 0.4 mile/0.6 km through trembling aspen stands and mature white spruce to former Prophet River Wayside Provincial Park (no facilities or services). The park access road crosses an airstrip, originally an emergency airstrip on the Northwest Air Staging Route. This was once part of the old Alaska Highway (known as the Alcan).

The Alaska Highway roughly parallels the Prophet River from here north to the Muskwa River south of Fort Nelson.

Private Aircraft: Prophet River emergency airstrip; elev. 1,954 feet/596m; length 6,000 feet/1,829m; gravel; no services.

DC 220 (353.6 km) **DJ 1167** (1878.1 km) Welcome to Peace River Regional District (southbound sign).

DC 221.2 (355.5 km) **DJ 1165.8** (1876.1 km) Large dirt and gravel turnout to west.

DC 222.3 (357.2 km) **DJ 1164.7** (1874.3 km) Highway descends northbound to Bougie Creek bridge.

DC 223.2 (358.6 km) **DJ 1163.8** (1872.9 km) Double-ended gravel turnout with litter bin to west.

DC 226.2 (363.4 km) **DJ 1160.8** (1868.1 km) *Slow for posted speed zone northbound* through Prophet River First Nations.

DC 226.5 (363.9 km) **DJ 1160.5** (1867.6 km) **Historical Mile 232.** St. Paul's Roman Catholic Church to east.

DC 227 (364.7 km) **DJ 1160** (1866.8 km) **Historical Mile 233. PROPHET RIVER.**

Northbound: Good pavement, long straight sections of highway, to Fort Nelson.

Southbound: Good pavement, easy curves, some long 6 percent grades. ⛽

DC 227.6 (365.6 km) **DJ 1159.4** (1865.8 km) Double-ended turnout with litter bin to east at **Historic Milepost 234**, Adsette Creek Highway Realignment. This major rerouting, completed in 1992, eliminated 132 curves on the stretch of highway that originally ran between Mile 234 and Mile 275.

DC 227.7 (365.8 km) **DJ 1159.3** (1865.6 km) Adsette Creek.

DC 229.7 (371.3 km) **DJ 1157.3** (1862.4 km) Borrow Pit #1 to east.

DC 230.9 (373.2 km) **DJ 1156.1** (1860.5 km) Distance marker southbound shows Prophet River 8 km/5 miles, Fort St. John 300 km/186 miles.

DC 232.9 (374.8 km) **DJ 1154.1** (1857.3 km) Gravel turnout to west with litter bins. Good views northbound of mesa-like topography of Mount Yakatchie to north.

DC 234.1 (376.5 km) **DJ 1152.9** (1855.4 km) Distance marker northbound shows Fort Nelson 80 km/50 miles, Watson Lake 600 km/373 miles.

CAUTION: Watch for bears (grizzly and black bears) alongside the road.

DC 238.3 (383.5 km) **DJ 1148.7** (1848.6 km) Borrow Pit #2 to west; recreation site for picnicking and fishing. ⬅

DC 239.2 (385 km) **DJ 1144** (1841 km) Northbound travelers will see evidence of the Big Beaver Creek fire, which jumped the Alaska Highway here on July 8, 2015. Smoke from the fire closed the highway for about a day. The wildfire burned an estimated 8,000 hectares/19,760 acres.

DC 241.1 (388 km) **DJ 1145.9** (1844 km) Parker Creek.

DC 242.7 (390 km) **DJ 1144.3** (1841.5 km) **Historic Milepost 249.** Little Beaver Creek.

DC 243.2 (390.8 km) **DJ 1143.8** (1840.7 km) Borrow Pit #4 to east; picnicking, fishing. 🐟

DC 245.3 (394 km) **DJ 1141.7** (1837.3 km) Turnout with litter bin to west.

CAUTION: Watch for deer.

Long straight stretch of highway northbound to Fort Nelson.

DC 248.5 (400 km) **DJ 1138.5** (1832.2 km) Big Beaver Creek.

DC 258.7 (416 km) **DJ 1128.3** (1815.8 km) Borrow Pit #8 to west; single-vehicle pullout with access for fishing. 🐟

DC 260.7 (419 km) **DJ 1126.3** (1812.6 km) Long narrow double-ended turnout with litter bin to east.

DC 264.6 (425.2 km) **DJ 1122.4** (1806.3 km) Highway descends in both directions to Jackfish Creek bridge then climbs. Note the variety of trembling aspen stands and the white spruce seedlings under them.

DC 265.5 (426.5 km) **DJ 1121.5** (1804.8 km) Turnoff to east for Andy Bailey Regional Park via 6.9-mile/12-km dirt and gravel access road (keep to right at "T" at Mile 1.7 on access road). *Large RVs and trailers note: Only turn-around space on access road is approximately halfway in.* The park is located on **Andy Bailey Lake**; 14 campsites (not suitable for large RVs or trailers), picnic sites, picnic tables, fire rings, firewood, water, outhouses, litter bins, boat launch (no powerboats), swimming and fair fishing for northern pike. Camping fee $17, self-register. *Bring insect repellent!* ⬅ ⛺

DC 270.8 (435.1 km) **DJ 1116.2** (1796.3 km) Sulfur gas pipeline crosses highway overhead (7.5m/24.6 ft. height).

DC 271 (435.4 km) **DJ 1116** (1796 km) Enbridge gas processing plant to east. Sulfur pelletizing to west.

DC 276.7 (444.6 km) **DJ 1110.3** (1786.8 km) Railroad tracks.

DC 277.5 (446.2 km) **DJ 1109.5** (1785.5 km) Access to frontage road to west for commercial cardlock Husky, Shell and Petro-Pass stations. **Muskwa Heights** (unincorporated) is an industrial area with rail yard and bulk fuel outlets.

Distance marker northbound shows Fort Nelson 9 km/5.6 miles.

DC 278.1 (447.5 km) **DJ 1108.9** (1784.5 km) Truck scales to west.

DC 278.8 (448.6 km) **DJ 1108.2** (1783.4 km) **Historic Milepost 295**, Northwest Highway System sign.

DC 280 (450.6 km) **DJ 1107** (1781.5 km) Turnoff on Sikanni Road for **Ye Olde Quilt Shoppe** (follow signs). Quilters from all over the world stop here and sign the guestbook; phone 250-774-2773.

Ye Olde Quilt Shoppe. See display ad.

DC 280.9 (451.2 km) **DJ 1106.1** (1780 km) Turnoff to southwest for Muskwa River Launch access. Turnout with Muskwa-Kechika Management Area information sign.

DC 281.2 (451.7 km) **DJ 1105.8** (1779.6 km) Mid-span of the **Muskwa River** bridge, lowest point on the Alaska Highway (elev. 1,000 feet/305m); access to river, boat launch. The Muskwa River flows to the Fort Nelson River. Fair fishing at the mouth of tributaries for northern pike; some goldeye. The Fort Nelson River is too muddy for fishing. The Muskwa River valley exhibits typical river bottom balsam poplar and white spruce stands.

The Alaska Highway swings west at Fort Nelson above the Muskwa River, winding through the Canadian Rockies.

DC 282.4 (453.5 km) **DJ 1104.6** (1777.6 km) Traffic light at Syd Road/Cordova Way; Tim Hortons and gas station to southwest. Fort Nelson airport access to northeast. ⛽

NOTE: Begin posted speed zone northbound.

DC 283 (454.3 km) **DJ 1104** (1776.7 km) Entering Fort Nelson northbound. Fort Nelson's central business district extends along both sides of the Alaska Highway (see map on page 173).

Northern Rockies Regional Recreation Center houses the Visitor Center; helpful staff, maps and brochures, books and local crafts for sale. (©Kris Valencia, staff)

Fort Nelson

DC 283 (454.3 km) **DJ 1104** (1776.7 km) **F 1200** (1931 km) Located at **Historical Mile 300** of the Alaska Highway, 237 miles/381 km north of Fort St. John; 330 miles/531 km south of Watson Lake, YT. **Population:** 3,500. **Emergency Services:** RCMP, phone 250-774-2777; **Fire Department,** phone 250-774-2222; **Hospital,** phone 250-774-8100; **Ambulance,** phone 250-774-2344. Medical, dental, chiropractic and massage therapy available. *NOTE: There is no 911 service in Fort Nelson or in the Northern Rockies Regional Municipality.*

Visitor Information: The Visitor Center is located at the west end of town in the Northern Rockies Regional Recreation Center, at the corner of the Alaska Highway

and Simpson Trail, 5500 Alaska Highway. Look for the Mile 300 marker. It is open daily, 8 A.M. to 7 P.M., in summer, and weekdays, 8:30 A.M. to 4:30 P.M., the rest of the year. Inquire here about local attractions, a guide to local hiking trails, information about the Liard Highway and current events. Nice gift shop with local crafts and regional books and guides for sale. Free municipal fresh water fill-up and dump station are located adjacent the Visitor Center/Northern Rockies Recreation Center parking lot. Contact Tourism Northern Rockies at Bag Service 399, Fort Nelson, BC V0C 1R0; phone 250-774-6400; tourism@northernrockies.ca; www.tourismnorthernrockies.ca.

Another good source for local information is the Fort Nelson Heritage Museum, located across the Alaska Highway from the Visitor Center. Visit the museum for authentic displays of pioneer artifacts and to see an amazing collection of historic vehicles.

Elevation: 1,383 feet/422m. **Climate:** Winters are cold with short days. Sum-

mers are hot and the days are long. In mid-June (summer solstice), twilight continues throughout the night. The average number of frost-free days annually is 116. Last frost occurs about May 11, and the first frost Sept. 21. Average annual precipitation of 17.7 inches. **Radio:** CBC 88.3-FM, The Bear 102.3-FM. **Television:** Channel 8 and cable. **Newspaper:** *Fort Nelson News* (weekly).

Transportation: Air—Scheduled service to Prince George with connections to Edmonton, Calgary and Vancouver via Central Mountain Air. Charter service available. **Bus**—BC Bus North offers weekly bus service to Fort St. John departing Wednesdays at 8 A.M.; bcbus.ca. **Railroad**—Canadian National Railway (freight service only).

Private Aircraft: Fort Nelson airport, 3.8 ENE; elev. 1,253 feet/382m; length 6,400 feet/1,950m; asphalt; fuel 100, Jet.

Fort Nelson is located in the lee of the Rocky Mountains, surrounded by the Muskwa, Fort Nelson and Prophet rivers. The area is heavily forested with white spruce, poplar and aspen. Geographically, the town is located about 59° north latitude and 122° west longitude.

Flowing east and north, the Muskwa, Prophet and Sikanni Chief rivers converge to form the Fort Nelson River, which flows into the Liard River, then on to the Mackenzie River, which empties into the Arctic Ocean. Rivers provided the only means of transportation in both summer and winter in this isolated region until 1922, when the Godsell Trail opened, connecting Fort Nelson with Fort St. John. The Alaska Highway linked Fort Nelson with the Outside in 1942.

In the spring, the Muskwa River frequently floods the low country around Fort Nelson and can rise more than 20 feet/6m. At an elevation of 1,000 feet/305m, the Muskwa (which means "bear") is the lowest point on the Alaska Highway. There was a danger of the Muskwa River bridge washing out every June during spring runoff until 1970, when a higher bridge—with piers arranged to prevent log jams—was built.

Fort Nelson's existence was originally based on the fur trade. In the 1920s, trapping was the main business in this isolated pioneer community populated with fewer

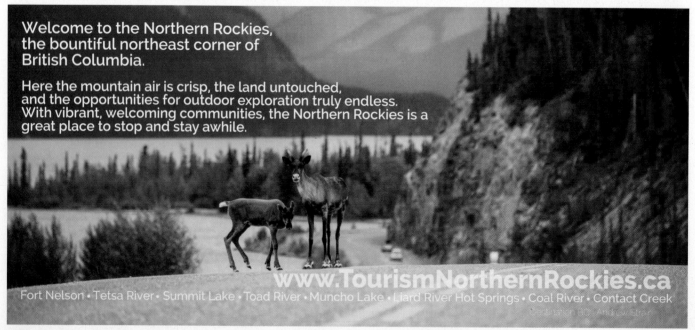

Welcome to the Northern Rockies, the bountiful northeast corner of British Columbia.

Here the mountain air is crisp, the land untouched, and the opportunities for outdoor exploration truly endless. With vibrant, welcoming communities, the Northern Rockies is a great place to stop and stay awhile.

www.TourismNorthernRockies.ca

Fort Nelson • Tetsa River • Summit Lake • Toad River • Muncho Lake • Liard River Hot Springs • Coal River • Contact Creek

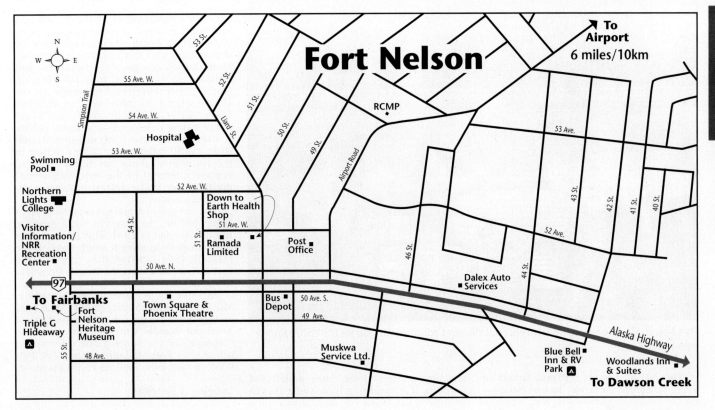

Fort Nelson

To Airport
6 miles/10km

than 200 aboriginals and a few white men. Trappers still harvest beaver, wolverine, weasel, wolf, fox, lynx, mink, muskrat and marten. Other area wildlife includes black bear, which are plentiful, some deer, caribou and a few grizzly bears. Moose remains an important food source for many residents.

Fort Nelson aboriginal people are mostly Dene, who arrived here about 1775 from the Great Slave Lake area. The Dene speak an Athabascan dialect.

Fort Nelson was first established in 1805 by the North West Fur Trading Co. The post, believed to have been located about 80 miles/129 km south of Nelson Forks, was named for Lord Horatio Nelson, the English admiral who won the Battle of Trafalgar.

A second Fort Nelson was later located south of the first fort but was destroyed by fire in 1813 after aboriginals massacred its 8 settlers. A third Fort Nelson was established in 1865 on the Fort Nelson River's west bank (1 mile from the present Fort Nelson airport) by W. Cornwallis King, a Hudson's Bay Co. clerk. This trading post was built to keep out the free traders who were filtering in from the Mackenzie River and Fort St. John areas. The free traders' higher fur prices were a threat to the Hudson's Bay Co., which in 1821 had absorbed the rival North West Fur

Trading Co. and gained a monopoly on the fur trade in Canada.

This Hudson's Bay Co. trading post was destroyed by a flood in 1890 and a fourth Fort Nelson was established on higher ground upstream and across the river, which is now known as Old Fort Nelson. The present town of Fort Nelson is the fifth site.

FORT NELSON ADVERTISERS

Fort Nelson Heritage Museum is an entertaining and educational stop for the entire family.
(©Kris Valencia, staff)

Fort Nelson saw its first mail service in 1936. Scheduled air service to Fort Nelson—by ski- and floatplane—also was begun in the 1930s by Yukon Southern Air (which was later absorbed by CPAir, now Air Canada). The Canadian government began construction of an airport in 1941 as part of the Northwest Air Staging Route, and this was followed by perhaps the biggest boom to Fort Nelson—the construction of the Alaska Highway in 1942. About 2,000 soldiers were bivouacked in Fort Nelson, which they referred to as Zero, as it was the beginning of a road to Whitehorse and another road to Fort Simpson. Later Dawson Creek became Mile 0 and Fort Nelson Mile 300.

Fort Nelson expanded in the 1940s and 1950s as people came here to work for the government or to start their own small businesses: trucking, barging, aviation, construction, garages, stores, cafes, motels and sawmills. It is surprising to consider that as recently as the 1950s Fort Nelson was still a pioneer community without power, phones, running water, refrigerators or doctors.

Fort Nelson was an unorganized territory until 1957 when it was declared an Improvement District. Fort Nelson took on village status in 1971 and town status in 1987. In 2009, the town of Fort Nelson was amalgamated with the Northern Rockies Regional District to become the Northern Rockies Regional Municipality, the first such local government in British Columbia.

Fort Nelson became a railhead in 1971 with the completion of a 250-mile extension of the Pacific Great Eastern Railway (now Canadian National Railway) from Fort St. John.

Agriculture is under development here with the establishment of the 55,000-acre McConachie Creek agricultural subdivision. Northeastern British Columbia is the only sedimentary area in the province currently producing oil and gas. Oil seeps in the Fort Nelson area were noted by early residents. Major gas discoveries were made in the 1960s—when the Clarke Lake, Yoyo/Kotcho, Beaver River and Pointed Mountain gas reserves were developed—and in the 1990s. A massive discovery of unconventional shale gas 60 miles north of Fort Nelson in the Horn River Basin has further spurred economic interest in the area, with several multi-billion dollar infrastructure investments underway.

The Enbridge natural gas processing plant at Fort Nelson, the largest in North America, was constructed in 1964. This plant purifies the gas before sending it south through the 800-mile-long pipeline that connects the Fort Nelson area with the British Columbia lower mainland.

In 1998, the BC government created the Muskwa-Kechika Management Area west of Fort Nelson. This 6.4 million hectares of Northern Rockies wilderness is called the "Serengeti of the North." The information office is in Fort St. John; phone 250-262-0065, or visit www.muskwa-kechika.com.

Lodging & Services

Fort Nelson has about a dozen hotels/motels, including the **Woodlands Inn and Suites** (see display ad), **Ramada Limited** (description follows) and **Blue Bell Inn & RV Park** (description follows). Most stores and other services are located on frontage roads just off the Alaska Highway. Dining at several local restaurants, including the **Woodlands Inn's** restaurant. There are gas stations (including 24-hour public cardlock); grocery, general merchandise and health-foods at the **Down to Earth Health Shop** (in its award-winning green building); laundromats, auto supply stores and auto repair

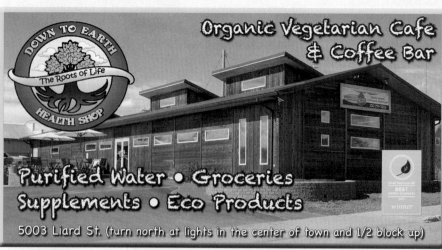
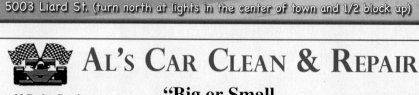

(Dalex, Muskwa Service Ltd., Al's Car Clean & Repair). See ads this section.

Blue Bell Inn & RV Park. "Your one-stop in Fort Nelson, BC," located at the south end of town. 52 recently renovated air-conditioned rooms with microwave, fridge, coffeemakers, WiFi, TV. Kitchenettes available. Convenience store with in-store ATM. Petro-Canada station with gas and diesel. Showers, laundromat, RV park. www. bluebellinn.ca; 250-774-6961. Reservations 1-800-663-5267. bluebellinn@northwestel. net. [ADVERTISEMENT]

Ramada Limited. Downtown location (behind CIBC Bank) with ample free parking. We offer 41 clean, quiet rooms with cable TV, Super Channel (VCR available), direct dial phones, high-speed internet access and free continental breakfast. Kitchenettes available. Full office services: payphone/photocopies/mail drop-off. Laundry service. Ice. 5035-51st Ave. N. 250-774-2844. Toll-free 1-866-774-2844. cyrero@gmail.com. [ADVERTISEMENT]

The post office and liquor store are on Airport Drive. There is also a liquor store attached to the Woodlands Inn and at Dan's Neighbourhood Pub. There are 2 banks, both with ATMs, and a credit union on the business frontage road along the north side of the highway. Internet access is available at the library located at Town Square and at the Visitor Center.

Camping

Triple "G" Hideaway (description follows) is located at the northwest end of town adjacent the Fort Nelson Museum; more than 130 level sites with shade trees, and an on-site restaurant (the restaurant closes Sept. 30, but the campground remains open well into October). The Blue Bell Inn has gravel RV sites adjacent their motel/gas station/convenience store at the south end of Fort Nelson.

Free municipal fresh water fill-up and dump station are located adjacent the Visitor Center/Fort Nelson Recreation Center. There is an older dump station and fresh water fill-up across the highway adjacent Fort Nelson Heritage Museum.

Triple "G" Hideaway RV Park welcomes RVers, caravans and tenters. Located next to the museum. 130-plus sites, most with full hookups. WiFi hotspot, some sites with cable, some pull-throughs. Shady. Dish and pull-outs friendly. Coin-op showers and laundry. RV pressure wash. Family restaurant and saloon. Phone 250-774-2340; fax 250-774-7903; tripleghideaway@outlook. com. See display ad on page 173. [ADVERTISEMENT]

Attractions

Welcome Visitor Program: Learn more about Fort Nelson and the Northern Rockies at the Visitor Center, located at the Northern Rockies Recreation Center across from the Fort Nelson Heritage Museum (both are at the northwest end of town alongside the Alaska Highway). Check with the Visitor Center in advance for current locations and additional information; phone 250-774-6400. Open year-round.

Fort Nelson Heritage Museum, at the west end of town and on the south side of the highway, has excellent displays of pioneer artifacts as well as what the Yukon News calls "one of the most impressive collections of antique cars in British Columbia." Marl Brown, founder and curator of the museum, keeps many of the vehicles in

Private campgrounds like Triple G Hideaway RV Park in Fort Nelson, pictured here, offer Alaska Highway travelers serviced RV sites and tent sites. (©Kris Valencia, staff)

working condition, including a 1908 Buick, which he drove to Whitehorse in June 2008.

The museum also features displays of wildlife (including a white moose) and Alaska Highway history. Outside the museum is the Chadwick Ram, a bronze sculpture by Rick Taylor. The statue commemorates the world-record Stone sheep taken in the Muskwa Valley area in 1936. If you have a connection with the history of the Alaska Highway, this is a must stop! Have your photo taken in front of the Alaska Highway Veterans and Builders Monument, which commemorates the workers who helped build the Alaska Highway in 1942.

This nonprofit museum charges a modest admission fee. Souvenirs and books are sold here.

Northern Rockies Regional Recreation Center houses Fort Nelson's visitor information, a community hall, 2 ice arenas, a curling rink, rock climbing wall, squash court, walking track, fitness and meeting rooms. It is located at 5500 Alaska Highway. The adjacent Aquatic Center, which opened in 2015, has a 6-lane 25m swimming pool, 1m and 3m diving boards, aquatic climbing wall, combined leisure/2 lane learner's pool, hot tub and 2-story water slide. There are also change rooms, a sauna and steam room. Phone information on any recreation center facilities, phone 250-774-2541. Fort Nelson's Skateboard Park is conveniently located next to the old Recreation Center on Simpson Trail.

Art Fraser Memorial Park is popular with residents and visitors alike. The park boasts 2 baseball diamonds, picnic tables and firepits, volleyball, tennis and basketball courts, playground equipment, restrooms and the Rotary Spray Park (a good place to cool off on a hot day).

A paved 3.2-mile/6-km community walking trail begins on the Simpson Trail and connects with the Alaska Highway at the east end of town.

For golfers, the Poplar Hills Golf and Country Club, just north of town on the Old Alaska Highway, is a beautiful 9-hole course with grass greens; club house, pro shop and steak frys on Friday nights; open daily.

Alaska Highway Log
(continued)

BC HIGHWAY 97 WEST

Northbound: Fair to good pavement next 327 miles/526 km between Fort Nelson and Watson Lake, YT; expect road construction. Improved highway surfacing to Liard Highway junction. Mostly winding road with both narrow and wide roadbed, some steep grades, and varying road conditions as the Alaska Highway winds through the Rocky Mountains. Not unusual to run into foggy conditions, sleet and snow at higher elevations, any time of year. Slow for icy conditions in winter.

Southbound: Good pavement, wide road, next 284 miles/457 km (to Dawson Creek). Slow for speed zone southbound through Fort Nelson.

DC 284 (456.4 km) **DJ 1103** (1775.1 km) **Historic Milepost 300,** historic sign

Leaving Fort Nelson northbound, the Alaska Highway winds towards and then through the northern Canadian Rockies. (©Kris Valencia, staff)

and interpretive panel at west end of Fort Nelson. Visitor information and free dump station on right northbound at the **Northern Rockies Regional Recreation Center. Fort Nelson Museum** is across the street on the south side of highway. **Triple "G" Hideaway RV Park** adjacent museum.

Leaving Fort Nelson northbound, the highway veers to the west and winds through the Canadian Rockies for the next 200 miles. In this densely forested region, there are many scenic vistas, where rivers meander through the wilderness to disappear in the haze of horizons 100 miles distant. Opportunities for many fine photos are offered by the beautiful scenery along this part of the highway, and travelers often see moose, bear, caribou and Stone sheep.

DC 284.7 (457.4 km) **DJ 1102.3** (1773.9 km) **Junction** with south end of Old Alaska Highway (Mile 301–308), which was bypassed in 1992. Turn here for access to **Al's Car Clean & Repair** and Poplar Hills Golf and Country Club on Radar Road via Old Alaska Highway; 9-hole golf course, driving range, clubhouse (licensed), golf club rentals, open May–Oct.

Al's Car Clean & Repair. See display ad on page 174.

DC 284.8 (457.7 km) **DJ 1102.1** (1773.6 km) Welcome to Fort Nelson (southbound sign). *Slow for posted speed zone southbound.*

Distance marker northbound shows Steamboat 75 km/47 miles, Watson Lake 520 km/323 miles, Whitehorse 973 km/605 miles.

DC 286 (459.6 km) **DJ 1101** (1771.8 km) Readerboard northbound has alerts on road conditions and road construction.

CAUTION: Watch for deer northbound. "Bison on Highway" readerboard alerts northbound travelers to presence of bison on road.

DC 291 (467.6 km) **DJ 1096** (1763.8 km) **Junction** with north end of Old Alaska Highway (Mile 308–301), Parker Lake Road.

DC 301 (483.5 km) **DJ 1086** (1747.7 km) **Junction** with Liard Highway, also known as the Liard Trail (BC Highway 77/NWT Highway 7), which leads north to Fort Liard (113 miles/181 km); the Mackenzie Highway/ NWT 1 to Fort Simpson (282 miles/454 km); and NWT Highways 1 and 3 to Yellowknife

(596 miles/959 km). Gas is available at Fort Liard, Fort Simpson and at Fort Providence on NWT 3. Inquire in Fort Nelson about current road conditions.

Junction with Liard Highway (BC Highway 77) north to Fort Liard and Mackenzie Highway to Fort Simpson and other Northwest Territories destinations. Turn to end of DEH CHO ROUTE section and read log back to front.

DC 304.1 (489.4 km) **DJ 1082.9** (1742.7 km) **Historic Milepost 320.** Start of Reese & Olson contract during construction of the Alaska Highway.

DC 308.2 (495.5 km) **DJ 1078.8** (1736.1 km) Raspberry Creek.

DC 318.4 (509.1 km) **DJ 1068.6** (1719.7 km) Kledo Creek bridge. The Kledo River is a tributary of the Muskwa River. This is a popular hunting area in the fall.

DC 318.7 (509.5 km) **DJ 1068.3** (1719.2 km) Kledo Creek wayside rest area to northeast; gravel parking with litter bin.

DC 319.5 (514 km) **DJ 1067.5** (1719 km) Sign states Muskwa (Kledo) Recreation Area to west with boat launch and picnicking. Not recommended due to narrow, unmaintained, dirt road.

DC 322.7 (516 km) **DJ 1064.3** (1712.8 km) Steamboat Creek bridge.

DC 329 (526.1 km) **DJ 1058** (1702.6 km) Double-ended gravel turnout with litter bin to southwest. Chain-up area.

Highway climbs next 6.7 miles/10.8 km northbound; winding road, 8 percent grades. *Weather (unseasonable snow, fog) at summit can cause challenging driving conditions.*

DC 332.3 (531.1 km) **DJ 1054.7** (1697.3 km) Distance marker northbound shows Summit Lake 64 km/40 miles, Watson Lake 443 km/275 miles.

DC 332.7 (531.6 km) **DJ 1054.3** (1696.7 km) **Historical Milepost 351. STEAMBOAT** (unincorporated). Steamboat Mountain Lodge (closed). A sign here marks start of Curran & Briggs Ltd. contract during construction of the Alaska Highway.

DC 333.7 (533.2 km) **DJ 1053.3** (1695.1 km) Large gravel turnout to southwest, view of Muskwa River Valley.

DC 335 (535.3 km) **DJ 1052** (1693 km)

Large gravel turnout to southwest; viewpoint for Muskwa River Valley.

DC 335.5 (536.1 km) **DJ 1051.5** (1692.2 km) Distance marker southbound shows Fort Nelson 80 km/50 miles, Fort St. John 488 km/303 miles.

Highway descends 8 percent winding downgrade next 6.7 miles/10.8 km southbound.

DC 335.7 (536.8 km) **DJ 1051.3** (1691.8 km) Large turnouts both sides of highway near **Steamboat Mountain** summit (elev. 3,500 feet/1,067m); brake-check areas with litter bins, toilet, information signs.

Rest area on southwest side of highway has a viewing platform with information panels on the Muskwa-Kechika Management Area. Views of Muskwa River Valley and Rocky Mountains to the southwest, weather permitting. Steamboat Mountain was named because of its resemblance to a steamship. *CAUTION: Watch for bears. Do not feed bears! A fed bear is a dead bear.*

Highway descends 8 percent winding downgrade next northbound, with some patched pavement.

DC 341 (545.4 km) **DJ 1046** (1683.3 km) Double-ended gravel turnout to southwest. Good view of Indian Head Mountain, a high crag resembling the classic Indian profile, as highway descends northbound

DC 341.5 (546.2 km) **DJ 1045.5** (1682.5 km) Gardner Creek (culvert), named after trapper and guide, Archie Gairdner. In Earl Brown's *Alcan Trailblazers*, about the construction of the Alaska Highway, Harry Spiegel recalls a recon trip in 1942 with Archie Gairdner:

"An old trapper by the name of Archie Gairdner, who has lived up here all his life, is the wrangler and is in charge of the string. He wears homemade moose-hide beaded moccasins, 'Kentucky-jean' pants, [and] a big beaten slouch hat. A hank of gray hair always protrudes from under his old hat and half covers his eyes. He sports a half growth of stubbly gray whiskers and smokes a crooked, big-bowled, sweet smelling pipe… Archie is 62 years old, and even though quite thin and weather-beaten, he is as straight as a spruce tree and as nimble as a boy in his teens… Archie knows this country like a book and I'm sure his knowledge of this terrain is going to be very helpful for our work."

DC 343.2 (548.9 km) **DJ 1043.8** (1679.8 km) **Teetering Rock** viewpoint (watch for hiking sign) to north; litter bin and outhouses. Teetering Rock is accessible via the 7.6-mile/12.3-km (1-way) **Teetering Rock Trail**; Steep climb, rated difficult, stay on marked trail and keep pets on leash.

DC 344.2 (550.3 km) **DJ 1042.8** (1678.2 km) Muskwa-Kechika Management Area northbound sign.

DC 344.6 (551 km) **DJ 1042.4** (1677.5 km) Mill Creek.

DC 344.7 (551.4 km) **DJ 1042.3** (1677.4 km) Turnoff to south for **Tetsa River Campground Regional Park**, a favorite local camping spot, 1.2 miles/1.9 km via gravel road. Grass tenting area, 25 level gravel sites in trees, picnic tables, fire rings, firewood, outhouses, water and bear-proof garbage containers. Camping fee $20. Reservations available by phoning 250-774-2541. Close to hiking trails and backcountry recreation. Great fishing. The Tetsa River offers Arctic grayling to 4 lbs., average 1½ lbs., flies or spin cast with lures; bull trout to 7 lbs., average 3 lbs., spin cast or flies; whitefish, small but plentiful, use flies or eggs, summer.

DC 347 (555 km) **DJ 1040** (1673.7 km) Actual driving distance between kilometerpost 555 and 560 is 2.1 kilometers.

Road conditions vary northbound from fair to good pavement and wide road to narrow winding road.

DC 357.5 (571.7 km) DJ 1029.5 (1656.8 km) **Historical Mile 375. Tetsa River Services and Campground** (description follows); gas, diesel, cabins, campground. Popular cinnamon bun stop.

Tetsa River Services and Campground. A must stop on your Alaska Highway vacation. We're third generation, family-run hosts, the Andrews, and we'll be happy to serve you our world-famous cinnamon buns (said by thousands to be the best they ever had) or homemade breads and artisan meats. Check in to our campground—country atmosphere (a creek runs through the property), with plenty of pull-through treed sites, power, fresh well-water, showers and sani-dump all included in fee. Laundromat on location. Great for tenting or stay in one of our quaint log cabins. Pets welcome. Don't miss our one-of-a-kind gift shop with many local crafts and art gallery with exclusive local artists' watercolour paintings. Reservations: tetsariverlodge@gmail.com, phone 250-774-1005. www.tetsariver.com. See display ad this page. [ADVERTISEMENT]

DC 358.9 (573.9 km) DJ 1028.1 (1654.5 km) Gravel turnout on curve overlooking the Tetsa River, one of several as the highway follows the Tetsa River westbound. The Tetsa heads near Summit Lake in the Canadian Rockies.

DC 360.3 (576.1 km) DJ 1026.7 (1652.3 km) Turnout to west with litter bin, hiking trail. Note the aspen-dominated slopes on the north side of the Tetsa River and the white spruce on the south side. Signed "riparian zones" northbound.

Narrow winding road northbound. Slow for 40-kmph/25-mph curves.

DC 362.6 (579.7 km) DJ 1024.4 (1648.5 km) Large dirt turnout to southwest.

DC 363.5 (581.1 km) DJ 1023.5 (1647.1 km) Gravel turnout to northeast.

DC 364.5 (582.7km) DJ 1022.5 (1645.5 km) Wide gravel sloping turnout to southwest.

DC 365.6 (584.6 km) DJ 1021.4 (1643.7 km) Tetsa #1 trailhead. Parking to south at east end of bridge. The 1.2-mile/2- km (1-way) trail begins across the highway and is rated as moderately easy.

Tetsa River bridge No. 1, clearance 17 feet/5.2m. *CAUTION: Metal grating on bridge deck.*

DC 365.9 (585.4 km) DJ 1021.1 (16433.2 km) Large turnout with litter bin to northeast.

DC 366.3 (585.6 km) DJ 1020.7 (1642.6 km) Beaver lodges to northeast. There are many riparian zones in this area identified by signage.

DC 367.4 (587.3 km) DJ 1019.6 (1640.8 km) Tetsa River bridge No. 2.

The high bare peaks of the central Canadian Rockies are visible ahead westbound.

NOTE: Motorists should have winter tires or carry chains Oct. 1–April 30. Commercial vehicles must carry chains.

DC 368.3 (588.7 km) DJ 1018.7 (1639.4 km) Turnout with litter bin to west.

Highway climbs northbound.

DC 369.4 (590.8 km) DJ 1017.6 (1637.6 km) Informal gravel turnout to southwest, first of 3 such turnouts next mile northbound (may be muddy in wet weather).

DC 370.8 (593.1 km) DJ 1016.2 (1635.4 km) Dunedin Trail (sign). The Dunedin Trail is described as a "challenging" 15-km/9-mile hike exploring the Dunedin River Valley.

DC 371.5 (594.2 km) DJ 1015.5 (1634.2 km) East boundary of **Stone Mountain Provincial Park.** Stone Mountain Park encompasses the Summit Pass area and extends south to include Wokkpash Protected Area. Access is via MacDonald Creek hiking trail and by 4-wheel drive from 113 Creek (see **Milepost DC 383.2**) to Wokkpash Creek trail. Contact BC Parks District Office in Fort St. John; phone 250-787-3407.

Stone sheep are frequently sighted in this area; *please reduce your speed.* Stone sheep are indigenous to the mountains of northern British Columbia and southern Yukon. Darker and somewhat slighter than the bighorn sheep found in the Rocky Mountains, they are often mistaken for mountain goats, which are not found in this area. Dall or white sheep are found in the mountains of Yukon, Alaska and Northwest Territories.

DC 372.2 (595.2 km) DJ 1014.8 (1633.1 km) **Historical Mile 390.** North Tetsa River flows under road through large culverts.

DC 372.7 (596 km) DJ 1014.3 (1632.3 km) Turnout with litter bin to north; brake-check area. Summit Ridge Trail information sign. Steep access to Tetsa River canyon.

DC 373.3 (597 km) DJ 1013.7 (1631.3 km) **Historical Mile 392. SUMMIT LAKE** (unincorporated). Summit Lake Lodge has been closed for many years. *NOTE: The Summit area is known for dramatic and sudden weather changes.* The peak behind Summit Lake is Mount St. George (elev. 7,419 feet/2,261m) in the Stone Mountain range.

CAUTION: Watch for caribou and Stone sheep along the highway. DO NOT FEED WILDLIFE. Do not stop vehicles on the highway to take photos; use shoulders or turnouts. You are now in bear country ... a fed bear is a dead bear—don't feed bears!

DC 373.5 (597.4 km) DJ 1013.5 (1631 km) Rough gravel side road leads 1.5 miles/2.5 km to **Flower Springs Lake trailhead**; 3.5-mile/5.7-km roundtrip hike to alpine lakes, flowers and waterfalls. *NOTE: Snow may remain on this side road well into summer.*

DC 373.6 (597.6 km) DJ 1013.4 (1630.9 km) **Historic Milepost 392 Summit Pass** (elev. 4,250 feet/1,295m); double-ended gravel turnout to northeast (across from campground entrance) with toilets, litter bin, point-of-interest sign and historical milepost. This is the highest summit on the Alaska Highway; there may be ice on the lake into June. A very beautiful area of bare rocky peaks (which can be snow-covered any time of the year). Information panel on Summit Peak Trail at turnout. This is a 4-mile/6.7-km roundtrip to upper viewpoint, rated moderately difficult, takes about 3½ hours to hike in, 1½ hours to hike out; be prepared for sudden weather changes.

Summit Lake (Stone Mountain) Provincial Campground to south at east end of lake; campground host, 28 level gravel sites; camping fee $18; picnic tables; water and garbage containers; information shelter; boat launch. Fair fishing for lake trout and whitefish.

DC 375.5 (600.8 km) DJ 1011.5 (1627.6 km) Double-ended turnout to northeast is brake-check area.

DC 375.9 (601.3 km) DJ 1011.1 (1627.2 km) Rocky Crest Lake. Nice spot for photos; good reflections in lake when calm.

DC 376 (601.5 km) DJ 1011 (1627 km) Large turnout to southwest is parking for Erosion Pillar Trailhead to northeast. Easy 0.6-mile/1-km hike to see erosion pillars (hoodoos).

Northbound, the highway winds through a rocky limestone gorge before descending into the wide and picturesque MacDonald River valley. *CAUTION: 8 percent grade, intermittent guardrails, winding road, wildlife on road.* Watch for safe turnouts next 2.5 miles/4 km northbound with views of the valley. Stone sheep are frequently sighted along this stretch of road. Also watch for caribou. Utilize your hazard lights to warn other travelers of wildlife on the road.

DC 376.5 (602.3 km) DJ 1010.5 (1626.2 km) Large turnout to northeast.

DC 377.7 (604 km) DJ 1009.3 (1624.3 km) The Cut Trail northbound sign and turnout to southwest. This 6-km/3.7-mile trail, rated moderately easy, follows an old section of the Alaska Highway.

DC 378.2 (605.1 km) DJ 1008.8 (1623.5 km) Baba Canyon trailhead parking to northeast. Popular hiking trail; 3.4 miles/5.5 km round trip to first viewpoint, 6.8 miles/11 km to second viewpoint, rated moderate.

CAUTION: Be alert and slow down for Stone sheep on highway!

DC 378.6 (605.7 km) DJ 108.4 (1622.8 km) **Historical Mile 397.** Rocky Mountain Lodge. If open, gas is available here.

DC 379.7 (607.4 km) DJ 1007.3 (1621 km) Large gravel turnout to southwest.

DC 380.7 (609 km) DJ 1006.3 (1619.4 km) West boundary of **Stone Mountain Provincial Park** (see description at the east boundary of the park at **Milepost DC 371.5**). *CAUTION: Watch for wildlife alongside and on the road. DO NOT FEED WILDLIFE.*

DC 381.2 (611.2 km) DJ 1005.8 (1618.6 km) Highway winds along above the wide rocky valley of MacDonald Creek. MacDonald Creek and river were named for Charlie MacDonald, a Cree Indian credited with helping Alaska Highway survey crews locate the best route for the pioneer road. MacDonald Creek offers pool fishing for Arctic grayling, bull trout and whitefish.

DC 382.6 (613.4 km) DJ 1004.4 (1616.4 km) Distance marker northbound shows Toad River 35 km/22 miles, Watson Lake 365 km/227 miles. Distance marker southbound shows Summit Lake 14 km/8 miles, Fort Nelson 162 km/101 miles.

DC 383.2 (614.4 km) DJ 1003.8 (1615.4 km) Trail access via abandoned Churchill Copper Mine Road (4-wheel drive only beyond river) to **Wokkpash Protected Area**, located 12 miles/20 km south of the highway. This remote area features extensive hoodoos (erosion pillars) in Wokkpash Gorge, and the scenic Forlorn Gorge and Stepped Lakes. Wokkpash Creek hiking trail follows Wokkpash Creek to Wokkpash Lake: 9 miles/15 km. Download trail maps at www.tourismnorthernrockies.ca/things_hikebikeride.php. Also visit www.env.gov.bc.ca/bcparks/explore/parkpgs/n_rocky/.

DC 383.3 (614.6 km) DJ 1003.7 (1615.3 km) 113 Creek. The creek was named during construction of the Alaska Highway for its distance from Mile 0 at Fort Nelson. While Dawson Creek was to become Mile 0 on the completed pioneer road, clearing crews began their work at Fort Nelson, since a rough winter road already existed between Dawson Creek and Fort Nelson. Stone Range to the northeast and Muskwa Ranges of the Rocky Mountains to the west.

DC 384.2 (615.4 km) DJ 1002.8 (1613.8 km) Side road to 115 Creek and **MacDonald Creek**; informal camping. Beaver dams nearby. Fishing for bull trout, Arctic grayling and whitefish.

DC 385.4 (616.6 km) DJ 1001.6 (1611.9 km) 115 Creek bridge. Double-ended turnout with litter bin to south at east end of bridge. Like 113 Creek, 115 Creek was named during construction of the Alaska Highway for its distance from Fort Nelson, Mile 0 for clearing crews.

DC 386.6 (618.5 km) DJ 1000.4 (1609.9 km) Turnout above MacDonald River.

DC 390.5 (624.8 km) DJ 996.5 (1603.7 km) **Historical Mile 408**; NWHS commemorative sign for "Camp 120." MacDonald River Services (closed for many years).

DC 392.5 (627.8 km) DJ 994.5 (1600.4 km) **MacDonald River** bridge, clearance 17 feet/5.2m. *CAUTION: Metal grating bridge deck.* Large, informal, narrow gravel turnout to north at east end of bridge; access to river. Fair fishing from May to July for bull trout, Arctic graying and whitefish.

Narrow road, loose gravel patches, eroded road shoulders. Highway winds through narrow valley northbound. Magnificent mountain views and photo ops for travelers.

DC 399.1 (638.6 km) DJ 987.9 (1589.8 km) Stringer Creek bridge.

DC 400.7 (641.1 km) DJ 986.3 (1587.2 km) Rest area with litter bin to north at east end of Racing River bridge (clearance 17 feet/5.2m). *CAUTION: Bridge deck is metal grate. Slow for curve at east end of bridge, posted speed limit on approach is 50-kmph/31-mph.*

The Racing River forms the boundary between the Sentinel Range and the Stone Range, both of which are composed of folded and sedimentary rock.

Note the open south-facing slopes on the north side of the river that are used as winter range by Stone sheep, elk and deer. Periodic controlled burns encourage the growth of forage grasses and shrubs, and also allow chinook winds to clear snow from grazing grounds in winter. *CAUTION: Watch for horses and wildlife on highway.* **Racing River**, Arctic grayling to 16 inches; bull trout to 2 lbs., use flies, July through September.

DC 401.2 (641.9 km) DJ 985.8 (1586.4 km) **Historical Mile 419.** Folding Mountain bed and breakfast; bed and bale pens and RV sites for those traveling with horses.

DC 404.1 (646.6 km) DJ 982.9 (1581.8 km) Welcome to Toad River (northbound sign).

DC 404.6 (647.4 km) DJ 982.4 (1581 km) **Historical Mile 422. TOAD RIVER** (unincorporated). Situated in a picturesque valley, Toad River has a highway maintenance camp, school and **Toad River Lodge**, which has been a fixture on the highway since the 1940s; description follows.

Toad River Lodge & RV Park. See display ad this page.

The historic lodge, on the southwest side of highway, has a restaurant, modern motel and cabins, gas, diesel, propane, tire repair, and RV and tent campsites nestled on Reflection Lake. Toad River Lodge is known for its collection of hats, which numbers

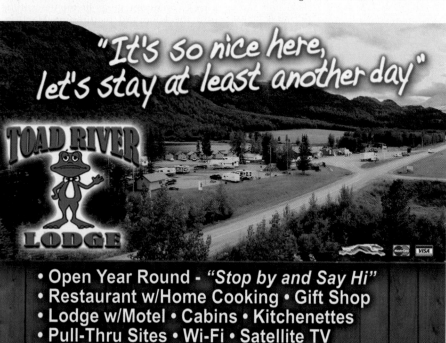

©Sharon Nault

in the thousands (a few of which are seen above). Post office and phone in lodge.

Inquire at the lodge about area wildlife viewing, fishing and hunting guide outfitters.

Private Aircraft: Toad River airstrip; elev. 2,400 feet/732m; length 3,000 feet/914m. Unattended; no fuel; prior permission to land required.

DC 405.5 (648.8 km) DJ 981.5 (1579.5 km) Double-ended turnout to south with litter bin and **Historic Milepost 422.** Sign and interpretive panel commemorate Toad River/Camp 138 Jupp Construction.

DC 406.3 (650.1 km) DJ 980.7 (1578.2 km) Turnout with dumpster.

DC 406.4 (650.3 km) DJ 980.6 (1578.1 km) Wood Creek culvert.

DC 406.9 (651.1 km) DJ 980.1 (1577.3 km) 141 Creek culvert.

DC 407.5 (652 km) DJ 979.5 (1576.3 km) **Historical Mile 426.** The Poplars; camping, cabins.

DC 408.6 (653.6 km) DJ 978.4 (1574.6 km) *Slow for 50-kmph/31-mph curve.*

DC 409.2 (654.6 km) DJ 977.8 (1573.6 km) South boundary of **Muncho Lake Provincial Park.** (The north boundary is at **Milepost DC 459.8.**) The park straddles the Alaska Highway, encompassing the alpine peaks and valleys around Muncho Lake.

DC 410.2 (656.2 km) DJ 976.8 (1572 km) Stone Mountain Safaris; lodging.

DC 410.8 (657.3 km) DJ 976.2 (1571 km) *CAUTION: Watch for caribou.*

DC 411.6 (658.5 km) DJ 975.4 (1569.7 km) Large gravel turnout with litter bin to southwest. Information panel on Folded Mountain reads:

"Originally, all of the rock of the Canadian Rockies lay flat on the shallow sea bed of the western continental shelf, where it had accumulated grain by grain for over a billion years. About 175 million years ago, the continent of North America began to move westward, overriding the Pacific floor and colliding with offshore chains of islands.

"The continental shelf was caught in the squeeze. The flat-lying layers slowly buckled into folds like those you see here. As time passed, folded mountain ranges sprang up across British Columbia. By 120 million years ago, the Rockies were showing above the sea. They grew for another 75 million years, rising faster than erosion could tear them down—likely reaching Himalayan heights. Active mountain building ended in the Canadian Rockies some 45 million years ago. The peaks have since been eroded to a small fraction of their original size."

CAUTION: Slow for 60-kmph/37-mph curve, tip-overs have occurred.

DC 412.5 (660 km) DJ 974.5 (1568.3 km) The highway follows beautiful turquoise-colored Toad River westbound, surrounded by the massive folded mountains of the Canadian Rockies. Spin or fly fishing for Arctic grayling to 16 inches; and bull trout to 10 lbs., July through September.

DC 413.4 (661.3 km) DJ 973.6 (1566.8 km) **Historic Milepost 431.**

Narrow winding road with 60-kmph/37-mph curves, patched pavement, informal gravel turnouts, northbound.

DC 415.5 (664.7 km) DJ 971.5 (1563.4 km) 150 Creek culvert.

DC 416.9 (667.1 km) DJ 970.1 (1561.2 km) 151 Creek culvert.

DC 417.6 (668.2 km) DJ 969.4 (1560 km) Gravel turnout to north with sign about flash floods (excerpt follows).

"The northern Canadian Rockies are famous for their summer downpours. When heavy rains fall on mountains largely bare of trees and other soil-holding vegetation, the water carries sand, gravel and even boulders into the gullies between the peaks. Everything

Muncho Lake is known for its beautiful deep green and blue waters. Fishermen catch Arctic grayling, whitefish and lake trout. The lake has produced a record 50-lb. lake trout.
(©Claire Torgerson, staff)

washes out onto the flat valley floors.

"This is one such deposit. It is called an alluvial fan because its outline resembles an open fan. Material carried by streams is called alluvium. This becomes distributed evenly over the fan as the stream [word obscured] sweeps back and forth, changing its position constantly."

Centennial Falls to south. (Waterfall dries up in summer, unless it is raining.)

DC 419.8 (671.7 km) DJ 967.2 (1556.5 km) **Toad River** bridge. Gravel turnout to south at west end of bridge; fishing for Arctic grayling and bull trout, July through September.

CAUTION: Watch for Stone sheep and caribou along the highway (or standing in the middle of the highway). DO NOT FEED WILDLIFE. Do not stop vehicles on the highway to take photos; use shoulders and informal gravel turnouts.

DC 421.9 (675 km) DJ 965.1 (1553.1 km) Watch for moose in boggy areas alongside road; morning or evening best.

Narrow winding road with 60-kmph/37-mph curves, patched pavement, informal gravel turnouts, southbound.

DC 422.9 (677 km) DJ 964.1 (1551.5 km) Double-ended gravel turnout to east. Winter travelers put on chains here. Distance marker northbound shows Muncho Lake 21 km/13 miles, Watson Lake 300 km/186 miles.

Highway climbs long winding grades to 7 percent next 6.5 miles/11 km northbound.

The highway swings north for Alaska-bound travelers. For Dawson Creek-bound travelers, the highway follows an easterly direction.

DC 424 (678.6 km) DJ 963 (1549.8 km) **Historic Milepost 443** at Peterson Creek No. 1 bridge. The creek was named for local trapper Pete Peterson, who helped Alaska Highway construction crews select a route through this area. Historic sign marks start of Campbell Construction Co. Ltd. contract during construction of the Alaska Highway.

DC 424.3 (679 km) DJ 962.7 (1549.3 km) Peterson Canyon trail (sign).

DC 425.2 (680.5 km) DJ 961.8 (1547.8 km) Turnout with litter bin.

DC 429.5 (687.4 km) DJ 957.5 (1540.9 km) Double-ended gravel turnout to northeast with view of Sawtooth Mountains, information shelter and litter bin. Chain removal area in winter for southbound traffic.

DC 433.7 (694.6 km) DJ 953.3 (1534.1 km) Distance marker southbound shows Toad River 45 km/28 miles, Fort Nelson 241 km/150 miles.

DC 433.8 (694.8 km) DJ 953.2 (1534 km) Double-ended gravel turnout with litter bin to east.

DC 434.1 (695 km) DJ 952.9 (1533.5 km) Muncho Creek.

DC 436 (698 km) DJ 951 (1530.4 km) **Historic Milepost 456.** A historic sign and interpretive panel mark Muncho Lake/Refueling Stop, Checkpoint during Alaska Highway construction. The highway along Muncho Lake required considerable rock excavation by the Army in 1942. Horses were used to haul away the rocks. The original route went along the top of the cliffs, which proved particularly hazardous. (Portions of this hair-raising road can be seen high above the lake; local residents use it for mountain biking.) The Army relocated the road by benching into the cliffs a few feet above lake level.

Red Rock Canyon trail.

CAUTION: Watch for Stone sheep and caribou on the highway north of here. Please DO NOT FEED WILDLIFE. Do not stop on the highway to take photos; use turnouts.

DC 436.5 (698.7 km) DJ 950.5 (1529.6 km) Entering **MUNCHO LAKE** (pop. 29) northbound. Double G Services to northeast; lodging, cafe/bakery, gas/diesel, postal service.

DC 436.9 (699.2 km) DJ 950.1 (1529 km) Gravel airstrip to west; length 1,200 feet/366m.

NOTE: Highway narrows northbound as road winds along Muncho Lake. Slow for 30-kmph/18-mph curves. No guard rails. Use roadside turnouts to take photos. Watch for falling rock.

DC 437.3 (700 km) DJ 949.7 (1528.4

km) South end of **Muncho Lake**, known for its beautiful deep green and blue waters, is 7.5 miles/12 km in length, and 1 mile/1.6 km in width; elevation is 2,680 feet/817m. "Muncho" means "big lake" in the Kaska language, and it certainly is one of the largest natural lakes in the Canadian Rockies. The colours are attributed to copper oxide leaching into the lake. Deepest point has been reported to be 730 feet/223m, although government tests have not located any point deeper than 400 feet/122m. The lake drains the Sentinel Range to the east and the Terminal Range to the west, feeding the raging Trout River in its 1,000-foot/305-m drop to the mighty Liard River. The mountains surrounding the lake are approximately 7,000 feet/2,134m high.

For fishermen, **Muncho Lake** offers Arctic grayling, whitefish to 15 inches, and lake trout. Record lake trout here is 50 lbs. Carry a current British Columbia fishing license and a copy of the current regulations.

DC 437.6 (700.5 km) **DJ 949.4** (1527.9 km) **Strawberry Flats Campground, Muncho Lake Provincial Park**; 15 sites on rocky lakeshore, picnic tables, outhouses, garbage containers. Camping fee $18. Old Alaska Highway Trail (1.2 miles/2 km). *CAUTION: Bears in area.*

DC 439.1 (702.9 km) **DJ 947.9** (1525.5 km) Large turnout on Muncho Lake.

DC 440 (704.4 km) **DJ 947** (1524 km) Double-ended gravel turnout for wildlife viewing. Also trailhead for Stones Sheep hiking trail at outwash plain here; moderately easy 4.2-km/2.6-mile round-trip hike (3 hours) up Northern drainage or 5.1-km/3.2-mile round-trip hike (3.5 hours) along southern drainage. Trail details on sign at parking area. Information panels at turnout on Stone Sheep (excerpts follow), including a map showing the geographic divide between Stone and Bighorn sheep:

"An easy way to identify male and female Stone sheep is to look at the horns. Rams (males) have large, strongly curved horns; ewes (females) have smaller, straighter horns. Sheep horns continue to grow throughout their lives and do not fall off like antlers of the deer family. The larger its horns, the more status a ram has in a herd. Stone sheep rams use their horns for battering each other during the fall mating season. Larger rams usually have the first opportunity for mating.

"Named after the American hunter-explorer, Andrew J. Stone, Stone sheep are a subspecies of the pure white Dall sheep found in the Yukon (Ovis dalli dalli). These sheep are sometimes called "thinhorn," because their horns are smaller than those of bighorn sheep found further south. Stone sheep eat grass, wildflowers and leaves of shrubs. The sheep are often seen along the roadsides licking natural and artificial accumulations of salt."

CAUTION: Watch for falling rock. Watch for caribou and sheep on highway.

DC 442.2 (707.9 km) **DJ 944.8** (1520.8 km) **Historical Mile 462**; historic highway lodge location. **Northern Rockies Lodge** (description follows) is open year-round. The lodge offers accommodations, a full-service restaurant (try their spaetzle!), gas and diesel, seasonal camping (with and without hookups) and a flying service. Inside the main lodge, the restaurant features a hand-carved map of the region, with lights reflecting the flight path of the lodge's charter service planes. Talk with the front desk about flightseeing trips Liard Air, from an afternoon of seeing the Northern Rockies to all-day fishing trips and visits to Virginia

Falls in Nahanni National Park.

©Judy Nadon, staff

Liard River Hotsprings, open year-round, is one of the major attractions along the Alaska Highway. (©Sharon Nault)

The Northern Rockies Lodge is considered by many travelers to be the best place to stay on the Alaska Highway. Clean, comfortable hotel rooms are open year-round and feature free WiFi, full ensuite washrooms and TV. With full service hotel, RV campsites, dining room, lounge and beautiful lakeshore chalets, the Northern Rockies Lodge is the most popular stop for motorcyclists, campers, families and couples alike. The one-of-a-kind log building stands four stories tall in a park-like setting between the Alcan and the shores of Muncho Lake. Unique wooden carvings in the dining room include an impressive 20-foot, hand-carved map of the region. The Northern Rockies Lodge also operates tours in the area including flightseeing, fly-in fishing and day trips to Virginia Falls in Nahanni National Park. Please visit www.nrlodge.com or call 1-800-663-5269. See display ad on facing page. [ADVERTISEMENT]

DC 442.9 (709 km) **DJ 944.1** (1519.3 km) Turnoff to west for **MacDonald Campground, Muncho Lake Provincial Park**; 15 level gravel sites, firewood, picnic tables, outhouses, boat launch, information shelter, pump water, litter bins. Camping fee $18. *CAUTION: Watch for bears in area.*

DC 443.6 (710.1 km) **DJ 943.4** (1518.4 km) **Historical Mile 463.** Muncho Lake Lodge, a historic highway lodge that had been closed for many years, was recently opened as an RV park; current status unknown.

DC 444.9 (712.2 km) **DJ 942.1** (1516.1 km) **Muncho Lake viewpoint** to southwest with **Historic Milepost 463**; large parking area, litter bins. Information panels include facts about Muncho Lake and construction of the Alaska Highway along the lake. Sign points out the location of Peterson Mountain (at the south end of lake), the Terminal Range (to the west of the lake) and the Sentinel Range (to the east). The island you see is Honeymoon Island. Memorial to Ernie Birkbeck (1939–2000), who worked as a Contractor Inspector on the Alaska Highway for 26 years. *CAUTION: Watch for Stone sheep on highway next 10 miles/16 km northbound.*

DC 447.9 (717 km) **DJ 939.1** (1511.3 km) Long double-ended gravel turnout to east at outwash plain. Boulder Canyon hiking trailhead at south end of turnout.

DC 453.3 (725.6 km) **DJ 933.7** (1502.6 km) Turnout to east.

DC 454 (726.7 km) **DJ 933** (1501.5 km) Mineral Licks Trail to west is a 5- to 10-minute loop hike to viewpoints overlooking the Trout River. Trail is slippery when wet and has steep banks; use caution when hiking and bring insect repellent. Sheep, goats, caribou and elk frequent the steep mineral-laden banks. Good photo opportunities, early morning best.

DC 455.5 (729.2 km) **DJ 931.5** (1499.1 km) Large turnout with litter bin and park information sign to west. Brake check area for northbound trucks; chain removal area in winter for southbound vehicles.

Beautiful views northbound of Trout River valley as highway descends. Watch for black bears feeding on grassy highway verge in summer. *CAUTION: 9 percent grade northbound. Watch for Stone sheep on highway next 10 miles/16 km southbound!*

Good pavement northbound, descends 9 percent grade next 2.2 miles/3.5 km.

DC 457.7 (732.7 km) **DJ 929.3** (1495.5 km) Trout River bridge. The Trout River flows into the Liard River. The Trout River offers rafting: Grade II from Muncho Lake to the bridge here; Grade III to Liard River. Inquire locally for river conditions. The **Trout River** has Arctic grayling to 18 inches and whitefish to 12 inches, May, June best; and bull trout.

The Alaska Highway follows the Trout River for several miles northbound. Highway climbs 9 percent grade next 2.2 miles/3.5 km southbound. *Chains recommended in winter.*

DC 459.8 (734.8 km) **DJ 927.2** (1492.1 km) **Historic Milepost 477.** Gravel turnout to east by Trout River. Leaving Muncho Lake Provincial Park southbound.

DC 461.6 (737.6 km) **DJ 925.4** (1489.2 km) Prochniak Creek bridge. The creek was named for a member of Company A, 648th Engineers Topographic Battalion, during construction of the Alaska Highway. North boundary of Muncho Lake Provincial Park.

DC 463.4 (740.5 km) **DJ 923.6** (1486.3 km) Large gravel turnout to southwest.

DC 464.5 (742.3 km) **DJ 922.5** (1484.6 km) Improved highway (2017) northbound.

DC 469.3 (750.3 km) **DJ 917.7** (1476.2 km) Large gravel turnout with litter bin to east.

DC 472.5 (756 km) **DJ 914.5** (1471.7 km) Washout Creek (signed).

Sweeping view of Liard River Valley as highway descends northbound. The mighty Liard River was named by French-Canadian voyageurs for the poplar ("liard") that line the banks of the lower river. The Alaska Highway parallels the Liard River from here north to Watson Lake. The river offered engineers a natural line to follow during routing and construction of the Alaska Highway in 1942.

DC 473 (756.6 km) **DJ 914** (1470.9 km) Very large gravel turnout to west.

Begin 2.1-mile/3.4 km southbound passing lane on uphill grade.

DC 475.3 (760.8 km) **DJ 911.7** (1467.2 km) **Historic Milepost 493.**

DC 476.7 (763 km) **DJ 910.3** (1464.9 km) Lower Liard River bridge (elev. 1,400 feet/427m). This is the only remaining suspension bridge on the Alaska Highway. The 1,143-foot suspension bridge was built by the American Bridge Co. and McNamara Construction Co. of Toronto in 1943.

The **Liard River** flows eastward toward the Fort Nelson River and parallels the Alaska Highway from the Lower Liard River bridge to the BC–YT border. The scenic Grand Canyon of the Liard is to the east and not visible from the highway. Many early fur traders lost their lives negotiating the wild waters of the Liard. The river offers good fishing at tributaries for bull trout, Arctic grayling, northern pike and whitefish.

DC 477.1 (763.8 km) **DJ 909.9** (1464.3 km) **Historical Mile 496.** Entering LIARD RIVER (unincorporated) northbound.

DC 477.7 (764.7 km) **DJ 909.3** (1463.3 km) Large double-ended parking area to southwest with pay phone, NWHS sign and Historic Milepost 496, across the highway from entrance to **Liard River Hotsprings Provincial Park** to the northeast (description follows).

Liard River Hotsprings has long been a favorite stop for Alaska Highway travelers. Open year-round, Liard River Hotsprings Provincial Park has a day-use area and 53 large, shaded, level gravel sites (some will accommodate 2 RVs); reservations at www.discovercamping.ca. Facilities include picnic tables, picnic shelter, water pump, garbage containers, firewood, fire rings, playground and restrooms at the hot springs with wheelchair-accessible toilet. Fees charged (cash only, as posted); camping fee includes use of hot springs pool, in effect May 1 to October; off-season rates as posted; day-use fee

Wood bison graze alongside the Alaska Highway between Liard Hotsprings area and Watson Lake. Be alert to these animals crossing the highway. Take photos from inside vehicle. (©Kris Valencia, staff)

$5/person or $10/vehicle; camping fee $26; annual adult and family hot springs pool passes available. Emergency phone at park headquarters. Park gate closes at 10 P.M. and opens at 6 A.M. *CAUTION: Beware of bears!*

A short 0.4-mile/0.6-km walk leads to pool area. Plenty of parking at trailhead. The boardwalk trail crosses a wetlands environment that supports more than 250 boreal forest plants, including 14 orchid species and 14 plants that survive at this latitude because of the hot springs. Watch for moose feeding in the wetlands. *NOTE: Watch for bears. No pets on boardwalk trail or at pools. You may want to take silver jewelry off. One reader noted that the sulphur water oxidizes it and turns it black in a few minutes.*

DC 477.8 (764.9 km) **DJ 909.2** (1463.2

km) **Historical Mile 497.** Liard Hotsprings Lodge; food, lodging, camping, gas/diesel (seasonal services, may vary).

NORTHBOUND: Watch for bison on road next 56 miles/90 km! Use extreme caution at night and in fog or poor driving conditions.

The buffalo are Wood Bison (*bison bison athabasae*). Herds are made up of cows, calves and sub adults. Mature bulls are solitary or form small groups, joining the herd during breeding season, according to Environment Yukon. *MILEPOST®* field editors have counted more than 100 bison on their seasonal drives down the highway. Do not approach bison!

SOUTHBOUND: Slow for speed zones.

DC 479 (767 km) **DJ 907.5** (1460.4 km) Mould Creek Campground; 7 RV/tent sites, 2 cabins.

DC 480 (768.3 km) **DJ 907** (1459.6 km) Mould Creek, named for trapper Tom Mould who assisted troops during construction of the Alaska Highway. Mould Creek Tower Road accesses a radio tower ad is used as a mountain bike trail of moderate difficulty; 15-km/9.3 mile round-trip, 4 hours.

DC 482.8 (772.9 km) **DJ 904.2** (1455.1 km) Teeter Creek; named for one of the surveyors with Company A, 648 Topographical Battalion, during construction of the Alaska Highway. A footpath leads up-stream; 10-minute walk to falls. Good Arctic grayling fishing.

DC 489 (783.6 km) **DJ 898** (1445.2 km) Private Aircraft: Liard River airstrip; elev. 1,400 feet/427m; length 4,000 feet/1,219m; gravel; no fuel.

DC 495 (792.3 km) **DJ 892** (1435.5 km) Historic Milepost 514. Smith River bridge, clearance 17 feet/5.2m.

DC 495.2 (792.6 km) **DJ 891.8** (1435.2 km) Access to Smith River Falls via 1.6-mile/2.6-km gravel road; not recommended for large RVs or trailers or in wet weather. Hiking trail (current status unknown) down to 2-tiered **Smith River** Falls from the parking area. Fishing in pool below falls for Arctic grayling, bull trout and whitefish; best in late summer.

DC 497.1 (795.7 km) **DJ 889.9** (1432.1 km) Historic sign here commemorates **Smith River Airport**, part of the Northwest Staging Route, located about 25 miles/40 km from the highway (accessible by 4-wheel drive only). In the early days of the Northwest Staging Route—the system of airfields used to ferry supplies and aircraft to Alaska and on to Russia during WWII—there were no aeronautical maps to guide pilots flying between Edmonton and Whitehorse. The young and relatively inexperienced pilots were given hand-drawn maps showing rivers and lakes and sent on their way with a cheery "you can't miss it!", according to the book, *Wings Over the Alaska Highway: A Photographic History of Aviation on the Alaska Highway*. This kind of navigation led to some misadventures.

DC 507.7 (812.9 km) **DJ 879.3** (1415.2 km) Double-ended turnout to west alongside Liard River.

DC 509.4 (815.6 km) **DJ 877.6** (1412.3 km) Large double-ended turnout with dumpster to west.

DC 513.5 (822 km) **DJ 873.5** (1405.7 km) Distance marker southbound shows Liard River 58 km/36 miles, Fort Nelson 365 km/227 miles.

DC 513.9 (822.8 km) **DJ 873.1** (1405 km) **Historical Mile 533. COAL RIVER.** Coal River Lodge & RV; food (good bison burgers), gas, diesel, lodging, camping and gift shop. Open May to September. Historic highway lodge location: Coal River Lodge dates back to 1949.

Coal River Lodge & RV. See display ad this page.

DC 514.2 (823.2 km) **DJ 872.8** (1404.6 km) **Historical Mile 533.2.** Coal River bridge. The Coal River flows into the Liard River south of the bridge.

DC 519.5 (831.7 km) **DJ 867.5** (1396.1 km) Turnoff to southwest for Whirlpool Canyon. Short, unpaved side road leads to small gravel parking area with litter bin, and view of Liard River rapids (not visible from the highway). Primitive campsites in trees. *NOTE: Limited turnaround space, not recommended for large vehicles or vehicles towing trailers.*

Although identified by one astute reader as Mountain Portage Rapids, Whirlpool Canyon (actually located farther downstream) is a more apt description of this location.

DC 524.2 (839.2 km) **DJ 862.8** (1388.5 km) **Historical Mile 543. FIRESIDE.** Lodge was closed in 2017; current status unknown. This community was partially destroyed by fire in the summer of 1982 by the Eg fire. The second largest fire in British Columbia history, it destroyed 400,000-plus acres. Evidence of a 2009 fire may be seen between Fireside and Liard Hot Springs. That burn jumped the highway and briefly halted traffic.

DC 524.7 (840.3 km) **DJ 862.3** (1387.7 km) Turnout above Liard River's Cranberry Rapids to west. There are additional gravel turnouts northbound not included in log.

DC 533.1 (853 km) **DJ 853.9** (1374.2 km) Turnouts with litter bins to southwest and northeast (about 0.1 mile apart) at summit overlooking the Liard River. Brake check and chain removal area for traffic. Begin 9 percent downgrade southbound.

DC 536 (857.8 km) **DJ 851** (1369.5 km) Distance marker southbound shows Fireside 14 km/8 miles, Fort Nelson 398 km/247 miles, Coal River 30 km/18 miles.

DC 550.9 (880 km) DJ 836.1 (1345.5 km) Historical Mile 570, Allen's Lookout. Very large gravel parking area to west with picnic tables, firepit and litter bin at viewpoint of Liard River. Beautiful view of river.

Legend has it that a band of outlaws took advantage of this sweeping view of the Liard River to attack and rob riverboats. A cairn near the picnic area is dedicated to the surveyors of the Alaska Highway. It shows the elevation and latitude and longitude of Allen's Lookout (N59°52'34", W127°24'21").

EXTREME CAUTION: Watch for bison next 73 miles/117 km southbound to Liard Hotsprings.

DC 557.5 (897.2 km) DJ 829.5 (1334.9 km) Welcome to Fort Nelson Forest District (southbound sign).

DC 558 (893.4 km) DJ 829 (1334.1 km) Highway swings west for Alaska-bound travelers. The Alaska Highway crosses the BC–YT border 6 times before reaching the official border at **Historic Milepost 627**.

Watch for grizzly bears feeding on grassy highway verge.

DC 560.4 (902.2 km) DJ 826.6 (1330.2 km) Scoby Creek.

DC 561 (903 km) DJ 826 (1329.3 km) Welcome to Fort Nelson Forest District (southbound sign).

DC 562.3 (905 km) DJ 824.7 (1327.2 km) Historic Milepost 585. Large gravel turnout to east; stop-of-interest. First Welcome to Yukon sign northbound.

DC 567.9 (909.4 km) DJ 819.1 (1318.2 km) Historic Milepost 588, Contact Creek. Gravel turnout to west; interpretive panel. Contact Creek was named by soldiers of the 35th Regiment from the south and the 340th Regiment from the north who met here in September 1942, completing the southern sector of the Alaska Highway. A personal reminiscence about the work of A Company 35th Combat Engineers is found in Chester Russell's *Tales of a Catskinner.*

DC 570 (912.9 km) DJ 817 (1314.8 km) Historical Mile 590. *Slow for speed zone through* **CONTACT CREEK. Contact Creek Lodge** is open year-round; snacks, gas, diesel, minor vehicle repairs, 24-hour towing and pay phone. Historic highway lodge location.

Contact Creek Lodge. See display ad on this page.

DC 571.9 (915.7 km) DJ 815.1 (1311.7 km) Cosh Creek.

DC 573.9 (918.9 km) DJ 813.1 (1308.5 km) Highway crosses Irons Creek. The original culvert here collapsed in June 2001, closing the Alaska Highway for 2 days. The culvert, which had been installed in 1998, was one of the largest in the world at 25 feet high, 135 feet long and 62 feet wide.

According to local sources, Iron Creek was named during construction of the Alaska Highway for the trucks that stopped here to put on tire irons (chains) in order to make it up the hill.

DC 575.9 (922 km) DJ 811.1 (1305.3 km) Historical Mile 596. Iron Creek Lodge (closed).

DC 585 (937.2 km) DJ 802 (1290.6 km) Historical Mile 605.9. Hyland River bridge; turnout to west at north end of bridge. The **Hyland River**, a tributary of the Liard River, was named for Frank Hyland, an early-day trader at Telegraph Creek on the Stikine River. Hyland operated trading posts

Bridges along the Alaska Highway are often narrow. It is common practice to allow wider vehicles to cross the bridge before proceeding. This is Hyland River bridge. (©Kris Valencia, staff)

throughout northern British Columbia, competing successfully with the Hudson's Bay Co. Good fishing for bull trout and Arctic grayling.

DC 598.5 (956.6 km) DJ 788.5 (1268.9 km) Mayfield Creek.

DC 598.9 (957.5 km) DJ 788.1 (1268 km) Access west to **LOWER POST** (pop. 113), a Kaska First Nations community. A sign on the highway in summer 2017 indicated an Esso gas station at Lower Post.

DC 602.8 (963.5 km) DJ 784.2 (1262 km) Turnout with litter bin to southwest.

DC 603.1 (964 km) DJ 783.9 (1261.5 km) *CAUTION: Watch for bison on highway southbound* (readerboard here in summer).

YUKON HIGHWAY 1

The Alaska Highway (Yukon Highway 1) dips back into British Columbia several times before making its final crossing into Yukon near Morley Lake.

DC 603.3 (964.5 km) DJ 783.7 (1261.2 km) Welcome to British Columbia (southbound sign) at turnout to southwest; point-of-interest signs.

DC 604.3 (966.1 km) DJ 782.7 (1259.6 km) Southbound signs: Use winter tires or carry chains beyond this point Oct. 1–April 30. Commercial vehicles must carry chains.

DC 605.4 (968 km) DJ 781.6 (1257.8 km) Distance marker northbound shows Watson Lake 12 km/7 miles, Whitehorse 457 km/284 miles.

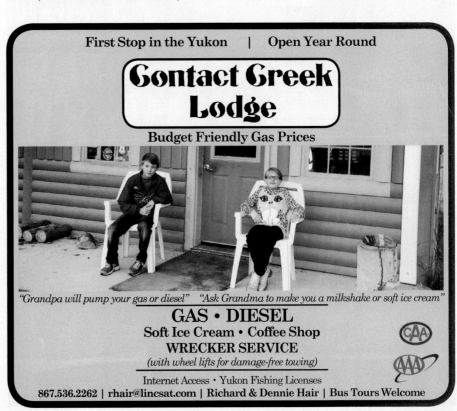

Lucky Lake makes a pleasant picnic stop, along with being a popular swimming hole.
(©Claire Torgerson, staff)

DC 605.6 (968.4 km) **DJ 781.4** (1257.5 km) Double-ended rest area to southwest; toilets.

DC 605.9 (968.9 km) **DJ 781.1** (1257 km) Distance marker southbound shows Fort Nelson 512 km/318 miles, Dawson Creek 968 km/602 miles.

DC 607 (970.6 km) **DJ 780** (1255.3 km) Long double-ended turnout to northeast with Welcome to Yukon sign. Across the

highway to the southwest is the parking lot for **Lucky Lake and Liard Canyon Recreation Site** (description follows).

Relatively shallow, Lucky Lake warms up quickly in summer, making it a popular local swimming hole. This is a very nice spot with a picnic area and adjacent ball diamond. **Lucky Lake** is stocked with rainbow trout; excellent fishing. A 1.4-mile/2.2-km hiking trail through mature pine and spruce forest down to observation platform overlooking the Liard River. Allow at least one hour for the hike. Watch for gray jays, Northern flickers and black-capped and boreal chickadees.

DC 609.5 (974.3 km) **DJ 777.5** (1251.2 km) Watson Lake 2 km/1.2 miles (northbound sign). Easy-to-miss turnoff to southwest for Watson Lake Riding Association Equestrian Center. (Look for pink metal horse southbound; look for distance sign northbound.)

The facility offers reasonably priced overnight boarding (indoor and outdoor 12x12 pens) for horses, and horse owners may camp on the grounds; phone Cheryl O'Brien at 250-536-2099 for details. The Center hosts summer classes (in gymkhana, vaulting and canoeing), boards local horses, and has a horse show in July.

DC 610.4 (976 km) **DJ 776.6** (1249.8 km) Welcome to Watson Lake (northbound sign). Entrance to weigh station.

Slow for speed zones northbound through Watson Lake.

DC 610.5 (976.3 km) **DJ 776.5** (1249.6 km) **Historical Mile 632.5**. AFD gas/diesel station.

DC 611.2 (977.5 km) **DJ 775.8** (1248.5 km) RCMP on right northbound; public pay phone, outside.

Watson Lake

DC 612.9 (980 km) **DJ 774.1** (1245.7 km) **F 870.1** (1400.3 km) **Historic Milepost 635**, "Gateway to the Yukon," located 330 miles/531 km northwest of Fort Nelson and 275 miles/443 km southeast of Whitehorse. At the **junction** of the Alaska Highway (Yukon Highway 1) and the Campbell Highway (Yukon Highway 4). **Population:** 1,563. **Emergency Services:** Dial 911. **RCMP**, phone (867) 536-5555 (if no answer call 867/667-5555). **Fire Department**, phone (867) 536-2222. **Ambulance**, phone (867) 536-4444. **Hospital**, phone (867) 536-4444.

Visitor Information: Located in the Alaska Highway Visitor Interpretive Center behind the Sign Post Forest, north of the Alaska Highway; access to the center is from

Watson Lake's Sign Post Forest, which dates back to 1942, was designated a Yukon Historic Site in August 2013. At last count (summer 2018) there were more than 88,000 signs here. Visitors are encouraged to add a sign. (©Kris Valencia, staff)

the Campbell Highway. Open daily May 1 to Sept. 30, 8 A.M. to 8 P.M.; friendly, helpful staff. Phone (867) 536-7469; fax (867) 536-2003. Pay phone with data port. Free WiFi is available at all Yukon Information Centers (VIC's). Pick up a copy of the *Watson Lake Walking Tour* brochure here.

Yukon Government campground permits are available locally. These permits are sold at stores and other vendors and are transferable. Or campers may self-register and pay at Yukon Government campgrounds.

Elevation: 2,254 feet/687m. **Climate:** Average daily temperature in January is -11°F/-24°C, in July 59°F/15°C. Record high temperature 93°F/34°C in May 1983, record low -74°F/-59°C in January 1947. Annual snowfall is 90.6 inches. Driest month is April, wettest month is September. Average date of last spring frost is June 2; average date of first fall frost is Sept. 14. **Radio:** CBC 990. **Television:** CBC and satellite.

Private Aircraft: Watson Lake airport, 6.3 miles/10.1 km north on Campbell Highway then 1.7 miles/2.7 km west; elev. 2,262 feet/689m; length 5,500 feet/1,676m and 3,530 feet/1,076m; asphalt; fuel 100, jet.

Heliport and floatplane bases also located here. Watson Lake is a major port of entry for aircraft.

Watson Lake is an important service stop on the Alaska and Campbell highways (Campbell Highway travelers, fill your gas tanks here!). The community is also a communication and distribution center for the southern Yukon; a base for trappers, hunters and fishermen; and a supply point for area mining and mineral exploration.

Watson Lake businesses are located along either side of the Alaska Highway. Watson Lake—the body of water—is not visible from the Alaska Highway, although motorists can see Wye Lake. Access to the lake, airport and hospital is via the Campbell Highway. Mount Maichen Ski Hill is about 4 miles/6.4 km out the Campbell Highway from town.

Originally known as Fish Lake, Watson Lake was renamed for Frank Watson, who settled here in 1898 with his wife, Adela Stone, of Kaska First Nations heritage. Watson, who was born in Tahoe City, California, had come north looking for gold.

Watson Lake was an important point during construction of the Alaska Highway in 1942. The airport, built in 1941, was one of the major refueling stops along the Northwest Staging Route, the system of airfields through Canada to ferry supplies to Alaska and later lend-lease aircraft to Russia. Of the nearly 8,000 aircraft ferried through Canada, 2,618 were Bell P–39 Airacobras.

The Alaska Highway helped bring both people and commerce to this once isolated settlement. A post office opened here in July

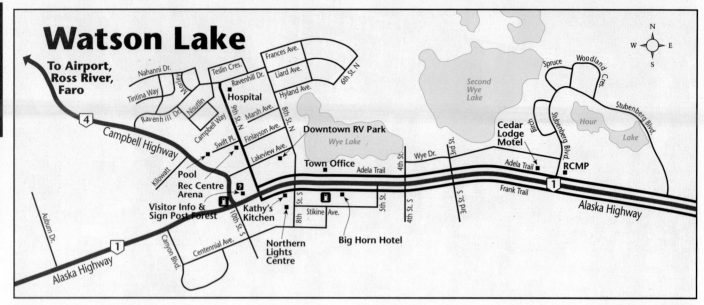

Watson Lake

To Airport, Ross River, Faro

Campbell Highway

Alaska Highway

Hospital

Downtown RV Park

Pool
Rec Centre
Arena

Visitor Info &
Sign Post Forest

Kathy's
Kitchen

Town Office

Northern
Lights
Centre

Big Horn Hotel

Cedar
Lodge
Motel

RCMP

Second
Wye Lake

Hour
Lake

Frank Trail

Alaska Highway

1942. Today, the economy of Watson Lake is based on services to mining exploration and on tourism.

Lodging & Services

Lodging choices in Watson Lake include **Big Horn Hotel** (description follows) and **Cedar Lodge Motel** (867-536-7406). Dine-in/take-out at **Kathy's Kitchen. Nugget City**, 14 miles/23 km northwest at **Milepost DC 627**, has cabins and a restaurant.

Big Horn Hotel. Centrally located on the Alaska Highway in downtown Watson Lake. Our 29 rooms are quiet, spacious, clean and boast queen-size beds; fridges; complimentary coffee; HD satellite TV. You get quality at a reasonable price. Available to you are honeymoon suites, Jacuzzi rooms, kitchenette suites. Wireless internet. We know you'll enjoy staying with us. Book ahead. Pet friendly. Phone (867) 536-2020, fax (867)

536-2021. Email info@bighornhotel.ca. See display ad on page 185. [ADVERTISEMENT]

Watson Lake has gas stations with diesel and propane; automotive and tire repair available locally. The RCMP office is east of town center on the Alaska Highway. CIBC branch open 9:30 A.M. to 5 P.M., Monday–Friday; 24-hour ATM.

Dennis Ball Memorial Swimming Pool is open in summer. Watson Lake also has a Recreation Center and a skateboard park.

Camping

Camping in Watson Lake at **Downtown R.V. Park.** Camping outside town at Watson Lake Yukon government campground, 2.4 miles/3.9 km west of the Sign Post Forest and the full-service **Nugget City RV Park**, 14 miles/23 km west.

Downtown R.V. Park (Good Sam), in the centre of town. 84 full-hookup stalls

with 20/30/50, 26 with pull-through parking; showers; laundromat. Town water. RV wash available. Satellite TV. WiFi Hot Spot. Easy walking distance to town services. Just across the street from Wye Lake Park's excellent hiking trails. Phone (867) 536-2646; atannock@hotmail.com. [ADVERTISEMENT]

Transportation

Air: Alkan Air provides charter service; yukon.alkanair.com. Helicopter charters available from Trans North Helicopters.

Bus: Scheduled service to Whitehorse via Watson Lake Shuttle & Freight Services, phone 867-536-2877. (Greyhound Canada ended its bus service along the Alaska Highway in 2018, after 70 years of serving the North.)

Attractions

The **Alaska Highway Interpretive Center**, operated by Tourism Yukon, is well worth a visit. Located behind the Sign Post Forest; turn on to the Campbell Highway then make an immediate right into their parking lot. The visitor center offers a video, an excellent presentation and displays on Yukon history and the Alaska Highway, including photographs taken in the mid-1940s showing the construction of the Alaska Highway in this area. The visitor center is open daily, 8 A.M. to 8 P.M. May through September; free admission; phone (867) 536-7469.

Stop in and pick up your free **Yukon Gold Explorers Passport** at the visitor center. Participants can use the passport as

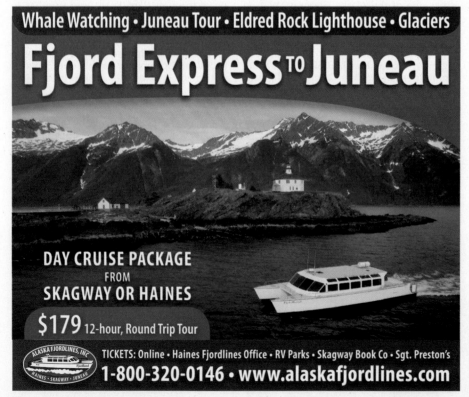

a guide to more than 30 Yukon museums and attractions. After getting your passport stamped at these locations, enter your name to win gold. The contest runs June 1 until August 31.

The Watson Lake Sign Post Forest, seen at the west end of town on the north side junction of the Alaska Highway just before its junction with the Robert Campbell Highway, was started by Carl K. Lindley (1919–2002) of Danville, IL, a U.S. Army soldier in Company D, 341st Engineers, working on the construction of the Alaska Highway in 1942. Travelers are still adding signs to the collection, which numbered more than 88,000 in 2018. Visitors are encouraged to add a sign to the Sign Post Forest. **Historic Milepost 635** is located at the Sign Post Forest. The Watson Lake Sign Post Forest was designated a Yukon Historic Site on August 30, 2013.

Northern Lights Center. The only planetarium in North America featuring the myth and science of the northern lights. Using advanced video and laser technology, the center offers presentations on the aurora borealis inside a 100-seat "Electric Sky" theatre environment. Interactive displays are also offered. Daily 2-part presentations of both *Yukon's Northern Lights* and a space-related show on the SciDome HD 360° Dome system. Total running time is 1 hour. Shows at 1, 2, 3, 6:30, 7:30 and 8:30 P.M. from May to September. Admission charged (check with the Infocenter for coupon savings on admission fee). One ticket admits you to both shows. The Center is located across the highway from the Sign Post Forest. Get your Yukon Explorer's Passport stamped here. Phone (867) 536-7827; website: www.northernlightscentre.ca.

Wye Lake Park offers a picnic area, a band shell and wheelchair-accessible restrooms. A 1.5-mile/2.5-km trail winds around First Wye Lake. Interpretive panels along the trail present information on Yukon wildflowers and local birds. The lake attracts both migrating birds (spring and fall) and resident species, such as nesting red-necked grebes. Also watch for tree swallows, violet-green swallows, mountain bluebirds and white-throated sparrows. The development of this park was initiated by a local citizens group.

St. John the Baptist Anglican Church has a memorial stained-glass window designed by Yukon artist Kathy Spalding. Titled "Our Land of Plenty," the window features a scene just north of Watson Lake off the Campbell Highway.

Lucky Lake, a few miles east of town on the Alaska Highway, is a popular local swimming hole for Watson Lake residents. Very nice spot with picnic area, waterslide, ball diamond and 1.4-mile/2.2-km hiking trail through mature pine and spruce forest down to observation platform overlooking the Liard River.

Watson Lake Community Library offers public access to the internet, email and photocopying. The library is open Tuesdays, Wednesdays and Thursdays 10 A.M. to 6 P.M., Fridays and Saturdays 12:30–4:30 P.M. Closed Sunday and Monday. Stop by and see the community quilt on display here. Phone (867) 536-7517 for more information.

The **Watson Lake Airport Terminal Building,** located 6.3 miles/10.1 km north of the Campbell Highway then 1.7 miles/2.7 km west, was built in 1942. This designated Heritage Building has an excellent display

Alaska Highway communities like Watson Lake offer year-round services. (©Kris Valencia, staff)

of historical photographs depicting the rich aviation history of this area, including early bush pilots and the WWII Lend Lease program. Get your Yukon Explorer's Passport stamped here.

Drive the Campbell Highway. This 362-mile/583-km Yukon highway connects Watson Lake to Ross River and Faro—site of the Campbell Region Interpretive Center— before junctioning with the Klondike Highway at Carmacks. Drive the first 51 miles/83 km of the highway north from Watson Lake to Simpson Lake for picnicking, fishing and camping. Or take an even shorter **side trip** out to Watson Lake Airport (8 miles/13 km out the Campbell) to see the historic terminal building. The Campbell Highway to Ross River is a narrow gravel road with short stretches of improved and widened road. Weather and heavy truck traffic may impact road conditions. *NOTE: Motorists should check with the Visitor Center in Watson Lake about current road conditions and road construction.* (Refer to CAMPBELL HIGHWAY section for highway log.)

Explore the area. Take time to fish, canoe a lake, take a wilderness trek or sightsee by helicopter. Outfitters in the area offer guided fishing trips to area lakes. Trips can be arranged by the day or by the week. Check with the visitor information center.

AREA FISHING: Watson Lake has Arctic grayling, lake trout and pike. **Hour Lake,** in Bellview subdivision (follow signs at east end of town), is stocked with rainbow trout. **Lucky Lake,** south of town on the Alaska Highway, is stocked with rainbow trout; easily fished from shore. Fly-in lakes include **Toobally Lake** and **Stewart Lake.** 🎣

Alaska Highway Log
(continued)

YUKON HIGHWAY 1

DC 612.9 (980 km) DJ 774.1 (1245.7 km) *Northbound Alaska Highway: Good pavement with some easy grades and curves to Teslin (163 miles/262 km) and Whitehorse (274 miles/441 km). Slow for gravel breaks and road construction.*

Southbound Alaska Highway: Fair to good pavement to Fort Nelson (327 miles/526 km); expect road construction. Stretches of narrow, winding road with steep grades as the Alaska

Highway winds through the Rocky Mountains. *Not unusual to run into foggy conditions, sleet and snow at higher elevations, any time of year. Slow for icy conditions in winter. British Columbia requires passenger vehicles to have winter tires on this highway from Oct. 1 to April 30. Commercial trucks must carry chains.*

Junction of the Campbell Highway (Yukon Route 4) and Alaska Highway in Watson Lake (community description begins on page 184). Tags gas station/convenience store on northwest corner, Watson Lake Sign Post Forest on northeast corner of intersection. Turn onto the Campbell Highway for access to Watson Lake's Alaska Highway Interpretive Center (entrance is first right). Also access via Campbell Highway to airport, hospital and Mount Maichen Ski Hill.

> The Campbell Highway leads north to Ross River and Faro, and junctions with the Klondike Highway to Dawson City just north of Carmacks. Turn to the CAMPBELL HIGHWAY section for log

DC 615.3 (984 km) DJ 771.7 (1241.9 km) Turnoff to north for side road to **Watson Lake Yukon government campground** and day-use area with boat launch, swimming and picnicking on Watson Lake. Drive in 3 miles/4.4 km via gravel access road (follow signs). There are 55 gravel sites—most level, 12 pull-through—on 2 loop roads; drinking water, kitchen shelters, outhouses, firepits, firewood and litter barrels. Camping permit ($12/night). ▲

DC 617.1 (986.9 km) DJ 769.9 (1239 km) Watson Lake city limits.

DC 618.5 (989 km) DJ 768.5 (1236.7 km) Watch for livestock.

DC 620 (991.3 km) DJ 767 (1234.3 km) Upper Liard River bridge. The **Liard River** heads in the St. Cyr Range in southcentral Yukon and flows southeast into British Columbia, then turns east and north to join the Mackenzie River at Fort Simpson, NWT. Fishing for Arctic grayling, lake trout, whitefish and northern pike. 🎣

DC 620.2 (991.7 km) DJ 766.8 (1234 km) **Historical Mile 642. UPPER LIARD VILLAGE,** site of Our Lady of the Yukon

Church. Upper Liard Lodge; dining.

NOTE: Slow for speed zone through Upper Liard Village.

DC 620.8 (993 km) **DJ 766.2** (1233 km) Albert Creek bridge. Turnout with litter barrel to north at east end of bridge. Turnoff to north at west end of Albert Creek bridge for Albert Creek Bird Observatory, an active bird banding station during spring and fall migrations. Top species banded include the Wilson's warbler, yellow warbler, Tennessee warbler and myrtle warbler. The public is welcome. Follow gravel and dirt track 500m to station. Open daily from about third week in April to first week in June for spring migration. www.yukonbirdobservatories.org. *NOTE: No turnaround for RVs or large vehicles.*

A sign near here marks the first tree planting project in Yukon. Approximately 200,000 white spruce seedlings were planted in the Albert Creek area in 1993.

White spruce and lodgepole pine are the 2 principal trees of Yukon, with white spruce the most common conifer. An average mature spruce can produce 8,000 cones in a good year and each cone has 140 seeds. The seed cones are about 2 inches/5 cm long and slender in shape. The pollen cones are small and pale red in color. White spruce grow straight and fast wherever adequate water is available (mature trees reach 23 to 66 feet/7m to 20m), and will grow to extreme old age without showing decay.

The lodgepole pine developed from the northern pine and can withstand extreme cold, grow at high elevations and take full advantage of the almost 24-hour summer sunlight of a short growing season.

DC 623.9 (998 km) **DJ 763.1** (1228 km) *CAUTION: Watch for Little Rancheria caribou herd.*

DC 625.5 (1001.1 km) **DJ 761.5** (1225.5 km) **Historic Milepost 649** at turnoff to north for side road (Old Alaska Highway) to **Rantin Lake**; stocked with rainbow trout, good ice fishing.

DC 626.2 (1001.6 km) **DJ 760.8** (1224.3 km) **Historical Mile 649** at intersection of Alaska and Cassiar highways. From this junction, Yellowhead Highway 16 is 450 miles south/723 km). Junction 37 Services; gas, diesel, RV park.

Junction with the Cassiar Highway, which leads south to Yellowhead Highway 16. Turn to end of CASSIAR HIGHWAY section on page 287 and read log back to front if you are headed south on the Cassiar.

©Kris Valencia, staff

DC 627 (1002.8 km) **DJ 760** (1223.1 km) **Historical Mile 650. The Northern Beaver Post/Nugget City** on the southwest side of the highway has a licensed restaurant with Yukon Brewing Co. beer; lodging in cabins; gift shop; 24-hour gas and diesel; tire repair, mechanic; dump station (fee charged for non-guests) and RV campsites with pull-throughs for big rigs. Owners Linda and Scott Goodwin also host large groups in their group dining facility.

Nugget City/The Northern Beaver Post. See display ad this page.

DC 627.3 (1003.4 km) **DJ 759.7** (1222.6 km) Large double-ended gravel rest area with litter barrels, pit toilets and map to south. No overnight camping.

DC 630 (1009.7 km) **DJ 757** (1218.2 km) Look for rock messages that are spelled out along the highway here. The rock messages were started in summer 1990 by a Fort Nelson swim team. Along with the rock messages, travelers will probably see a number of inukshuks—originally rock cairns built as landmarks by the Inuit—left by travelers.

DC 633 (1014.5 km) **DJ 754** (1213.4 km) Gravel turnout to north.

DC 637.8 (1020.5 km) **DJ 749.2** (1205.7 km) Microwave tower access road to north. *CAUTION: Caribou next 25 km.*

DC 639.8 (1023.7 km) **DJ 747.2** (1202.5 km) *CAUTION: Hill and sharp curve.*

DC 647.4 (1035.9 km) **DJ 739.6** (1190.4 km) Little Rancheria Creek bridge.

DC 650.6 (1041.3 km) **DJ 736.4** (1185.1 km) Highway descends westbound to Big Creek.

DC 651.1 (1042 km) **DJ 735.9** (1184.3 km) Big Creek bridge, clearance 17.7 feet/5.4m. Turnout at east end of bridge.

DC 651.2 (1042.2 km) **DJ 735.8** (1184.1 km) Turnoff to north at west end of Big Creek bridge for **Big Creek Yukon government campground**, adjacent highway on Big Creek; 15 sites (7 pull-through) on gravel loop road, outhouses, firewood, kitchen shelter, litter barrels, picnic tables, water pump. Camping permit ($12/night).

DC 651.3 (1042.4 km) **DJ 735.7** (1183.9 km) Watch for Little Rancheria Caribou herd southbound sign.

DC 658.5 (1059.8 km) **DJ 728.5** (1172.4 km) NorthwesTel microwave tower access road to north.

DC 664.1 (1062.7 km) **DJ 722.9** (1163.4 km) Transport rest area, a double-ended turnout with litter bins and outhouse to north on Lower Rancheria River.

DC 664.3 (1063.1 km) **DJ 722.7** (1163 km) Bridge over Lower Rancheria River. For northbound travelers, the highway closely follows the Rancheria River west from here to the Swift River. Northern bush pilot Les Cook was credited with helping find the best route for the Alaska Highway between Watson Lake and Whitehorse. Cook's Rancheria River route saved engineers hundreds of miles of highway construction.

Rancheria River, fishing for Dolly Varden and Arctic grayling.

DC 671.9 (1075.3 km) **DJ 715.1** (1150.8 km) Spencer Creek.

DC 677 (1083.7 km) **DJ 710** (1142.6 km) Turnout with litter barrel to south overlooking the Rancheria River. Trail down to river. According to R.C. Coutts, author of *Yukon: Places & Names*, the Rancheria River was named by Cassiar miners working Sayyea Creek in 1875, site of a minor gold rush at the time. Rancheria is an old Californian or Mexican miners' term in Spanish, meaning a native village or settlement. It is pronounced ran-che-REE-ah.

DC 678.5 (1086 km) **DJ 708.5** (1140.2 km) George's Gorge, culvert.

DC 683.2 (1093 km) DJ 703.8 (1132.6 km) NorthwesTel microwave tower to south.

Improved highway northbound. *Slow for loose gravel in construction areas!*

DC 687.2 (1100 km) DJ 699.8 (1126.2 km) **Historic Milepost 710.** Rancheria Lodge to south; closed. A historic highway lodge, it appeared in the first (1949) edition of *The MILEPOST®* as The Rancheria Hotel. It has operated under different owners over the years, most recently Linda and Denis Bouchard, offering travelers food, gas, camping and lodging. With the passing of both Linda and Denis in 2018, the future status of the lodge was unknown at our press time.

DC 689.2 (1103 km) DJ 697.8 (1123 km) Canyon Creek with evidence of avalanche damage.

DC 690 (1104.4 km) DJ 697 (1121.7 km) Intermittent views of the Rancheria River, which parallels the Alaska Highway.

DC 692.5 (1108.2 km) DJ 694.5 (1117.6 km) Young Creek. Named after Major Richard Henry Young of the Royal Canadian Engineers, Northwest Highway Systems.

DC 695.2 (1112.8 km) DJ 691.8 (1113.3 km) **Rancheria Falls Recreation Site** has a good gravel and boardwalk trail through boreal forest to the picturesque falls; easy 10-minute walk. Large parking area with toilets and litter bins at trailhead.

DC 696 (1114 km) DJ 691 (1112 km) Porcupine Creek.

DC 697.4 (1116.6 km) DJ 689.6 (1109.8 km) Views of the Cassiar Mountains.

DC 698.4 (1118 km) DJ 688.6 (1108.2 km) **Historical Mile 721.** Continental Divide Lodge (current status unknown).

DC 698.7 (1118.6 km) DJ 688.3 (1107.7 km) Upper Rancheria River bridge, clearance 17.7 feet/5.4m. For northbound travelers, the highway leaves the Rancheria River.

DC 699.3 (1119.6 km) DJ 687.7 (1106.7 km) **Historic Milepost 722.** Turnoff for airstrip. **Private Aircraft:** Pine Lake airstrip 3 miles/4.8 km north; deserted WWII emergency airstrip; elev. 3,250 feet/991m; length 6,000 feet/1,829m; gravel, status unknown.

DC 699.4 (1120 km) DJ 687.6 (1106.5 km) Large gravel turnout to north; outhouses, litter bins. Interpretive signs (excerpt follows) on the **Continental Divide,** which divides 2 of the largest drainage systems in North America—the Yukon River and Mackenzie River watersheds. Water draining west from this point forms the Swift River. This river drains into the Yukon River and continues a northwest journey of 3,680 kilometers (2,300 miles) to the Bering Sea (Pacific Ocean). Water that drains to the east forms the Rancheria River which flows into the Liard River then the Mackenzie River. These waters flow northward and empty into the Beaufort Sea (Arctic Ocean) after a journey of 4,200 kilometers (2,650 miles). Sign reads:

"There is a distinct difference in traditional land use patterns corresponding with this separation of river drainages. Pacific salmon migrate up the Yukon River watershed providing a reliable and relatively abundant food resource. This resource could generally support a larger and less transient human population than lands to the east."

All rivers crossed by the Alaska Highway between here and Fairbanks, AK, drain into the Yukon River system, with the exception of the Aishihik River (**Milepost DC 965.7**) and the Jarvis River (**Milepost DC 1003.5**). These 2 Yukon rivers drain into the Dezadeash River, which flows to the Pacific.

DC 702 (1124 km) DJ 685 (1102.4 km) Very large informal gravel turnout with litter

Motorists have sweeping views of the Rancheria River valley along the highway.
(©Kris Valencia, staff)

bins to south at east end of Swift River culvert; access to Swift River.

For northbound travelers, the highway now follows the Swift River west to the Morley River.

DC 705.6 (1130.4 km) DJ 681.4 (1096.6 km) Very large turnout with gravel parking area and litter bins. Sign notes no camping or overnight parking.

NOTE: Highway descends 6 to 7 percent grade next 1.1 miles/1.8 km northbound.

DC 709.1 (1136.2 km) DJ 677.9 (1090.9 km) Seagull Creek, named by members of Company D, 29th Engineers Topographic Battalion, during construction of the Alaska Highway in 1942. According to Sgt. Jim West, all of the major streams and rivers—the Morley, Swan, Swift, Rancheria and Liard—were already named when the crews came through. "However, many smaller streams had no names, so we named them." In addition to Seagull Creek, these included Hazel Creek (Upper and Lower), Log Jam Creek and Friskie Creek.

DC 709.8 (1136.7 km) DJ 677.2 (1089.8 km) **Historic Milepost 733, SWIFT RIVER;** Yukon Highway maintenance camp, no public services. The historic Swift River Lodge closed down in September 2009, and burned down in 2016. The lodge was originally a "Clyde Wann station," offering gas, rooms, meals, a general store and trailer spaces. Clyde Wann, who was born in the U.S. in 1900, came North in the 1920s and co-founded Yukon Airways and Exploration Co. After the Alaska Highway was completed, Clyde Wann built and operated—along with his wife, Helen—several highway lodges, including Swift River Lodge, Morley River Lodge, Beaver Creek Lodge and Destruction Bay Lodge. Wann also had a Chrysler franchise. In 1949, there was a maintenance camp, repeater station, cafe, store and garage here.

CAUTION: Watch for moose northbound next 25 km/16 miles.

DC 710.3 (1137.4 km) DJ 676.7 (1089 km) **Historical Mile 733.5.** Welcome to British Columbia (northbound sign), Leaving British Columbia (southbound sign).

The highway re-enters British Columbia for approximately 42 miles/68 km northbound.

DC 712.7 (1140.9 km) DJ 674.3 (1085.2

km) Partridge Creek.

DC 718.5 (1150.1 km) DJ 668.5 (1075.8 km) Screw Creek.

DC 719.6 (1152 km) DJ 667.4 (1074 km) **Historical Mile 743.** Swan Lake rest area to south; outhouse, litter bins and point-of-interest sign to south overlooking lake. The pyramid-shaped mountain to south is Simpson Peak. Access to **Swan Lake;** fishing for trout and whitefish.

DC 723.5 (1159 km) DJ 663.5 (1067.8 km) Turnoff for Swan Lake business.

DC 726 (1162 km) DJ 661 (1063.7 km) Distance marker southbound shows Watson Lake 182 km/113 miles.

DC 727.9 (1165 km) DJ 659.1 (1060.7 km) Logjam Creek culvert.

DC 735.8 (1177.4 km) DJ 651.2 (1048 km) Smart River bridge. Pull-outs at either end of bridge are posted "no camping." The **Smart River** flows south into the Cassiar Mountains in British Columbia. The river was originally called Smarch, after the Tlingit family of that name who lived and trapped in this area. The Smarch family currently includes world renowned carving artist Keith Wolfe Smarch.

DC 741.4 (1186.8 km) DJ 645.6 (1039 km) Microwave tower access road to north.

DC 744.1 (1191 km) DJ 642.9 (1034.6 km) Hazel Creek.

DC 745.2 (1192.9 km) DJ 641.8 (1032.8 km) Lower Hazel Creek.

DC 746 (1194 km) DJ 641 (1031.5 km) Rest area to north on lake; litter bins and outhouse.

DC 749 (1199.1 km) DJ 638 (1026.7 km) Andrew Creek.

DC 750.8 (1202 km) DJ 636.2 (1023.8 km) Morley Lake to north.

DC 751.2 (1202.7 km) DJ 635.8 (1023.2 km) The Alaska Highway re-enters Yukon northbound. This is the last of 7 crossings of the YT–BC border.

DC 752 (1204 km) DJ 635 (1021.9 km) Sharp turnoff on bermed access *(NOTE: RVs swing wide)* to north for Yukon government **Morley River Recreation Site.** This day-use area has a large gravel parking area (good for RVs), picnic sites with tables and firepits, firewood, kitchen shelter, water, litter bins and outhouses. Access to river; fishing.

DC 752.3 (1204.4 km) DJ 634.7 (1021.4 km) Morley River bridge. The Morley River flows into the southeast corner of Teslin Lake. The river, lake and Morley Bay (on Teslin Lake) were named for W. Morley Ogilvie, assistant to Arthur St. Cyr on the 1897 survey of the Telegraph Creek–Teslin Lake route. Good fishing near mouth of **Morley River** for northern pike 6 to 8 lbs., best June to August, use small Red Devils; Arctic grayling 3 to 5 lbs., in May and August, use small spinner; lake trout 6 to 8 lbs., June to August, use large spoon.

DC 752.9 (1205.5 km) DJ 634.1 (1020.4 km) **Historical Mile 777.7.** Morley River Lodge closed in 2005. This historic highway lodge was a Clyde Wann Station in the late 1950s called Morley River Auto Camp.

DC 757.9 (1212.2 km) DJ 629.1 (1012.4 km) Memorial cairn to south (no turnout) commemorates Alaska Highway construction worker: "In memory of Max Richardson 39163467, Corporal Co. F 340th Eng. Army of the United States; born Oct. 10, 1918, died Oct. 17, 1942. Faith is the victory."

DC 761.5 (1218.1 km) DJ 625.5 (1006.6 km) Strawberry Creek.

DC 764.1 (1223.2 km) DJ 622.9 (1002.4 km) Hays Creek.

DC 769.6 (1232 km) DJ 617.4 (993.6 km) **Historical Mile 797**. Dawson Peaks; camping.

DC 772.8 (1237.7 km) DJ 614.2 (988.4 km) Report wildfires; phone 1-888-798-FIRE (3473).

DC 774.4 (1240 km) DJ 612.6 (985.8 km) *Highway descends northbound* to Nisutlin Bay Bridge.

DC 774.8 (1240.6 km) DJ 612.2 (985.2 km) Welcome to Teslin (northbound sign).

DC 775.5 (1242 km) DJ 611.5 (984.1 km) Large double-ended rest area with litter bins, outhouse, information kiosk and view of Nisutlin Bay Bridge. Good photo op.

NOTE: Begin speed zone northbound (enforced). Watch your speed through Teslin!

DC 776 (1243 km) DJ 611 (983.3 km) **Nisutlin Bay Bridge**, second longest water span on the Alaska Highway at 1,917 feet/584m (Peace River bridge is the longest). *CAUTION: Metal grated bridge decking, slippery when wet.* The Nisutlin River forms the "bay" as it flows into Teslin Lake here. Public access to Nisutlin Bay at west end of bridge, to south. Put-in for canoeing the Nisutlin River is at Mile 42 on the South Canol Road. The Nisutlin Delta National Wildlife Area is an important waterfowl migration stopover.

Teslin Lake straddles the BC–YT border; it is 86 miles/138 km long, averages 2 miles/3.2 km across, and has an average depth of 194 feet/59m. The name is taken from the Indian name for the lake—Teslintoo ("long, narrow water").

DC 776.3 (1243.5 km) DJ 610.7 (982.8 km) **Historic Milepost 804.** Yukon Motel & Lakeshore RV Park; year-round business with restaurant, gas/diesel station, lodging, RV park (RV park is seasonal). Historic highway lodge location. Stop in and see their excellent **Yukon Wildlife Gallery**. The Teslin post office is also located here.

Yukon Motel & Lakeshore RV Park. located at north end of Nisutlin River Bridge (right side northbound). Owners: Steve, Juanita and family invite you to enjoy a fresh mouth-watering homecooked meal, presented by friendly staff, topped off with a piece of fantastic homemade pie or pastry (lots of fresh baking). Ice cream. Visit our free, museum-quality Yukon Wildlife Gallery to experience a rare look at many Northern species. Open year-round, 7 A.M. to 10 P.M. Good Sam Park; 40 pull-throughs, hookups; on the shore of beautiful Nisutlin Bay. Phone (867) 390-2575. See display ad this page. [ADVERTISEMENT]

Teslin

DC 776.5 (1244 km) DJ 610.5 (982.5 km) F 706.5 (1137 km) **Historic Milepost 804** on the Alaska Highway. Teslin is 111 miles/179 km southeast of Whitehorse, and 163 miles/263 km northwest of Watson Lake. **Population:** 450. **Emergency Services:** Dial 911. RCMP, phone (867) 390-5555 (if no answer call 867/667-5555). **Fire Department**, phone (867) 390-2222. **Teslin Health Center**, phone (867) 390-4444.

Visitor Information: Local businesses are happy to help answer visitor questions. On the web, visit www.teslin.ca.

Elevation: 2,239 feet/682.4m. **Climate:** Average temperature in January, -7°F/-22°C, in July 57°F/14°C. Annual snowfall 66.2 inches/168.2 cm. Driest month April, wettest month July. Average date of last spring frost is June 19; first fall frost Aug. 19. **Radio:** CBC 940; CHONFM 90.5; CKRW 98.7. **Television:** Channel 13.

Situated at the confluence of the Nisutlin River and Teslin Lake, Teslin began as a trading post in 1903. Today the community consists of the **Yukon Motel and Lakeshore RV Park** (restaurant, motel, RV park, gas station, post office, wildlife museum), a general store/motel/gas station, a Catholic church, health center, and library (with internet access). There is a 3-sheet regulation curling rink and a skating rink; a skateboard park, ballfield, Friendship Park and playground.

Teslin has one of the largest First Nations' populations in Yukon. Much of the community's livelihood revolves around traditional hunting, trapping and fishing. Some Tlingit (Klink-it) residents are also involved in the development of First Nations' woodworking crafts (canoes, snowshoes and sleds) and sewn art and craft items (moccasins, mitts, moose hair tufting, gun cases).

©Judy Nadon, staff

The Yukon Motel has an impressive collection of wildlife on display in its **Yukon Wildlife Gallery** (pictured above).

The Teslin area has boat rentals and charter fishing outfitters. Teslin Lake is famous for its lake trout fishing. Canoeists can fly into Wolf Lake for a 5- to 6-day trip down the Wolf River and Nisutlin River to Teslin Lake.

Don't miss the **George Johnston Museum**, located on the left side of the Alaska Highway heading north (see **Milepost DC 776.7**). Of Tlingit descent, the innovative George Johnston (1884–1972) was known for his trapping and his fine photography. His camera captured the lives of the inland Tlingit people of Teslin and Atlin between 1910 and 1940. Johnston brought the first car, a 1928 Chevrolet (on display), by paddlewheeler to roadless Teslin 13 years before the Alaska Highway was built cutting a 3-mile track for his "Teslin taxi." In winter, he hunted by car on frozen Teslin Lake. Director Carol Geddes' beautiful short film tells his unique story. Go to www.gj museum.yk.net or phone (867) 390-2550. *Big rigs can park on the side of the access road to the museum then continue out the back exit from the rear parking lot. Cars and smaller RVs please use the rear parking lot.*

Another highly recommended stop is the **Teslin Tlingit Heritage Center**, located just north of town on the southwest side of the Alaska Highway; watch for turnoff at **Milepost DC 779.1**. The center's displays feature 200 years of Inland Tlingit history and culture; open daily June to September; by appointment in winter; ample parking and turnaround area for RVs. http://teslin tlingitheritage.com.

AREA FISHING: Guided fishing trips available from Nisutlin Outfitting, located directly across from Nisutlin Trading Post. Day-use area with boat ramp at north end of Nisutlin Bay Bridge. In May and June, troll the mud line of **Teslin Lake's Nisutlin Bay** (at the confluence of the Nisutlin River and Teslin Lake), for lake trout up to 25 lbs.; Eagle Bay, casting close to shore for northern pike to 15 lbs.; **Morley Bay**, excellent fishing for lake trout at south end of the bay's mouth, good fishing at the bay's shallow east side for northern pike to 10 lbs. **Morley River**, excellent fly fishing for Arctic grayling to 4 lbs. near river mouth and upriver several miles (by boat), fish deep water.

Alaska Highway Log
(continued)

YUKON HIGHWAY 1

DC 776.7 (1244.2 km) **DJ 610.3** (982.2 km) **George Johnston Museum**, to west, displays Tlingit ceremonial robes and trade goods, a photo gallery of early Tlingit life, George Johnston's reconstructed general store and ice-highway car, and life-size subsistence trapping and hunting dioramas. Enter the rare 1942 Aeradio Range "Beam" station on site. The museum and film theatre are open daily, 9 A.M. to 5 P.M., June–September; admission charged, wheelchair accessible, gift shop. *Big rigs can park on the side of the access road to the museum then continue out the back exit from the rear parking lot. Cars and smaller RVs please use the rear parking lot.*

DC 776.8 (1244.4 km) **DJ 610.2** (982 km) Distance marker northbound shows Whitehorse 181 km/112 miles.

TESLIN ADVERTISERS

George Johnston Museum ....Ph. (867) 390-2550
Teslin Tlingit Heritage Centre....Ph. (867) 390-2532
Yukon Motel & Lakeshore
 RV Park ....Ph. (867) 390-2575

Rest area on the west side of the Nisutlin Bay bridge offers picnic area, boat launch and information about this important waterway. (©Kris Valencia, staff)

DC 777 (1244.6 km) **DJ 610** (981.7 km) Airport and police. **Historic Milepost 805. Private Aircraft:** Teslin airstrip to east; elev. 2,313 feet/705m; length 5,500 feet/1,676m; gravel; fuel 100, jet. Runway may be unusable during spring breakup.

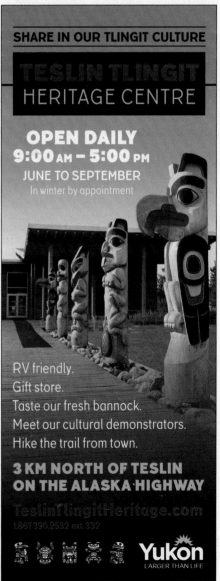

Totems and masks by master carvers are on display at the Teslin Tlingit Heritage Center.
(©Earl L. Brown)

DC 777.3 (1245.2 km) **DJ 609.7** (981.1 km) Trailhead for George Johnston Trail to east.

DC 777.5 (1245.5 km) **DJ 609.5** (980.8 km) *Slow for speed zone southbound (enforced!) Watch your speed through Teslin.*

DC 778.1 (1246.5 km) **DJ 608.9** (979.9 km) Welcome to Teslin (southbound sign).

DC 778.3 (1246.8 km) **DJ 608.7** (979.6 km) Teslin Lake Viewing Platform at **Historic Milepost 806**, west side of highway, overlooks Teslin Lake. Interpretive panels, outhouses and parking.

DC 779.1 (1248 km) **DJ 607.9** (978.3 km) Turnoff (watch for sign) to southwest for **Teslin Tlingit Heritage Center**, www.teslintlingitheritage.com. Open 9 to 5 daily, June–Sept.; by appointment in winter

The center (not visible from highway) highlights the last 200 years of Inland Tlingit history and includes displays on the lifestyles of the Tlingit people and "power of the mask." Includes Great Hall meeting place and gift shop. Ample parking and turnaround area for RVs. The 5 outdoor totems, carved by Keith Wolfe Smarch and other carvers, represent the Wolf, Eagle, Frog, Beaver and Raven clans. If you are lucky, you may get to sample some homemade bannock with wild berry jam.

Teslin Tlingit Heritage Centre. See display ad on page 191.

DC 779.5 (1248.7 km) **DJ 607.5** (977.6 km) Fox Creek.

DC 785.2 (1257.9 km) **DJ 601.8** (968.5 km) **Historical Mile 813.** Ten Mile Creek rest area to west with outhouses and litter bins at entrance to **Teslin Lake Yukon government campground**; 27 sites (some level, 6 pull-through) in trees on Teslin Lake, water pump (water must be boiled), litter bins, kitchen shelter, firewood, firepits, picnic tables. Camping permit ($12/night). Fishing. Boat launch 0.3 mile/0.5 km north.

DC 788.9 (1264 km) **DJ 598.1** (962.5 km) Lone Tree Creek.

DC 794.6 (1273.1 km) **DJ 592.4** (953.3 km) Deadman Creek.

DC 797.6 (1278 km) **DJ 589.4** (948.5 km) Timber Point Campground.

DC 800.8 (1283.5 km) **DJ 586.2** (943.4 km) Robertson Creek (not signed).

DC 801.6 (1284.4 km) **DJ 585.4** (942.1 km) Brooks' Brook at Historical Mile 829. According to R.C. Coutts in *Yukon: Places & Names,* this stream was named by African-American Army engineers, who completed this section of road in 1942, for their company officer, Lieutenant Brooks. *CAUTION: Watch for bears crossing highway here.*

DC 807.6 (1294.4 km) **DJ 579.4** (932.4 km) Distance marker southbound shows Teslin 52 km/32 miles, Watson Lake 315 km/196 miles.

DC 808.2 (1295 km) **DJ 578.8** (931.5 km) **Junction** with the South Canol Road and access to rest area with parking, outhouses, litter bin and historic sign and interpretive panel about the Canol Project. Several WWII vehicles from the Canol Project are on display here. (The old "graveyard" of WWII vehicles near here was significantly cannibalized and is no longer accessible.)

The South Canol Road is a narrow, winding gravel road which leads north 137 miles/220 km to junction with the Campbell Highway near Ross River. (The North Canol Road continues to the NWT border.)

Junction with South Canol Road (Yukon Highway 6) to Ross River and North Canol Road. See CANOL ROAD section for log of both South and North Canol Roads.

DC 808.6 (1295.6 km) **DJ 578.4** (930.8 km) **Teslin River Bridge** is the third longest water span on the highway (1,770 feet/539m). It was constructed with a very high clearance above the river to permit steamers of the British Yukon Navigation Co. to pass under it en route from Whitehorse to Teslin. River steamers ceased operation on the Teslin River in 1942. Before the construction of the Alaska Highway, all freight and supplies for Teslin traveled this water route from Whitehorse.

Distance marker northbound shows Whitehorse 130 km/81 miles.

DC 808.9 (1296.2 km) **DJ 578.1** (930.3 km) **Historic Milepost 836, JOHNSON'S CROSSING.** Motel, cafe, gas/diesel, RV park to east at north end of bridge. Johnson's Crossing is one of the original lodges on the Alaska Highway, first operated by Robert Porsild. The Porsilds later renamed it Johnson's Crossing, the local name for the Teslin River bridge.

Access to Teslin River; boat launch, no camping on riverbank. Canoeists report that the Teslin River is wide and slow, but with gravel, rocks and weeds. Adequate camping sites on numerous sand bars; boil drinking water. Abundant wildlife—muskrat, porcupine, moose, eagles and wolves—also bugs and rain. Watch for bear. The Teslin enters the Yukon River at Hootalinqua, an old steamboat landing and supply point. Roaring Bull rapids: choppy water. Pullout at Carmacks. Inquire locally about river conditions before setting out.

Teslin River, excellent Arctic grayling fishing from spring to late fall, 10 to 15 inches, use spinner or red-and-white spoons for spinning or black gnat for fly-fishing. Chinook salmon in August.

DC 809.1 (1296.4 km) **DJ 577.9** (930 km)

Access road east to the Teslin River. The Big Salmon Range, also to the east, parallels the Teslin. For Alaska-bound travelers, the highway now swings north.

DC 810.3 (1298.4 km) **DJ 576.7** (928.1 km) Turnouts both sides, with litter bins.

DC 812.8 (1302.4 km) **DJ 574.2** (924.1 km) Little Teslin Lake on west side of highway.

DC 813.8 (1304.1 km) **DJ 573.2** (922.4 km) *CAUTION: Watch for caribou (Carcross herd) next 9 km/5.6 miles northbound.*

DC 814.5 (1305.3 km) **DJ 572.5** (921.3 km) Easy-to-miss turnoff on your right northbound at **Historic Milepost 843** to Squanga Lake flightstrip, another Alaska Highway airstrip that dates back to WWII and the Northwest Staging Route.

Private Aircraft: Squanga Lake airstrip, 1 N; elev. 2,630 feet/802m; length 6,000 feet/965m; gravel, summer only, current status unknown; no services.

DC 820.4 (1314.8 km) **DJ 566.6** (911.8 km) Large gravel turnout to west at north end of Seaforth Creek bridge.

DC 821 (1315.9 km) **DJ 566** (910.9 km) Turnoff to **Squanga Lake Yukon government campground**: 16 sites, 4 pull-through, with kitchen shelter, drinking water (boil 2 minutes before use), camping permit ($12/night). Small boat launch. Fishing for northern pike, Arctic grayling, whitefish, rainbow trout and burbot.

DC 825.8 (1323.9 km) **DJ 561.2** (908.1 km) **Historic Milepost 855.**

DC 828.7 (1328.5 km) **DJ 558.3** (898.5 km) Rest area with large gravel parking area, litter bins and outhouses to northeast. Information panels. No camping allowed.

DC 836.8 (1341.5 km) **DJ 550.2** (885.4 km) **Junction** with Tagish Road at **Historic Milepost 866, JAKE'S CORNER**; gas and diesel available. Turnoff for Tagish Road to Carcross and access to Atlin Road. Distance marker shows Tagish 21 km/13 miles, Carcross 55 km/34 miles, Atlin 100 km/62 miles.

Junction with Yukon Highway 8 (Tagish Road) to Carcross and Highway 7 (Atlin Road). See "Atlin–Tagish–Carcross Scenic Loop" log on pages 193-194.

The U.S. Army Corps of Engineers set up a construction camp here in 1942, under the command of Captain Jacobson, thus giving Jake's Corner its name. However, the name is also attributed to Jake Jackson, a Teslin Indian who camped in this area on his way to Carcross. Roman "Jake" Chaykowsky (1900–1995) operated Jake's Corner Service for many years. It was known locally as The Crystal Palace, after the first lodge Chaykowsky had owned at Judas Creek, just up the road.

Distance marker southbound shows Teslin 98 km/60 miles, Watson Lake 361 km/224 miles.

DC 837.5 (1342.5 km) **DJ 549.5** (884.3 km) Entering 911 service response area northbound.

View of White Mountain southeast, named by William Ogilvie during his 1887 survey, for Thomas White, then Minister of the Interior. Yukon government introduced mountain goats to this area in 1981.

DC 843.2 (1351.8 km) **DJ 543.8** (875.1 km) Judas Creek bridge.

(Continues on page 195)

Atlin-Tagish-Carcross Scenic Loop

A sign at this Atlin marina reminds boaters that there is no cell phone service in Atlin or on Atlin Lake. (©Kris Valencia, staff)

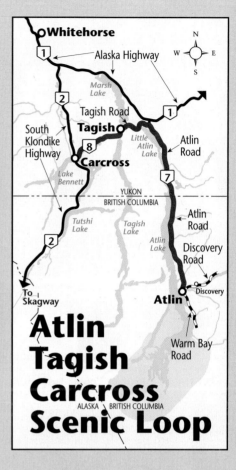

A popular **side trip** from the Alaska Highway is a visit to beautiful Atlin, BC, a 59-mile/95-km drive south from Jake's Corner (**Milepost DC 836.8** Alaska Highway) via Atlin Road. Return to the Alaska Highway by taking the all-paved "Carcross Loop," a 66-mile/106-km drive via Tagish Road to Carcross and the South Klondike Highway back to the Alaska Highway at **Milepost DC 874.4**. Total driving distance is 182 miles/293 km.

To reach Atlin Road, turn south at Jake's Corner onto Tagish Road and drive 1.1 miles/1.8 km to junction with Atlin Road (Highway 7). The 58-mile/93-km Atlin Road, built in 1949, is a good, paved 2-lane road.

Sometimes called the Shangri-la of the North, Atlin overlooks the crystal clear water of 90-mile/145-km-long Atlin Lake, elev. 3,198 feet/975m. Surrounded by spectacular mountains, Atlin Lake covers 307 square miles/798 square km and is the largest natural lake in British Columbia.

Backtrack from Atlin and take the short but scenic Tagish Road to Carcross, where you will junction with the South Klondike Highway. Drive 32 miles/52 km up the South Klondike Highway and junction with the Alaska Highway just 12 miles/19 km south of Whitehorse, and passing by the world's smallest desert and beautiful Emerald Lake. Make sure to stop by **Caribou Crossing** and see their wildlife collection.

Atlin Road Log

Distance from Tagish Road junction (J) is shown.
Physical kilometerposts show distance from Tagish Road junction.

J 0 Junction of Tagish and Atlin roads, 1 mile/1.6 km south of Jake's Corner and the Alaska Highway. *There is no cell service along Atlin Road or in the community of Atlin.*

J 2.4 (3.9 km) Large turnout to west on **Little Atlin Lake**; litter bin, boat launch. Mount Minto (elev. 6,913 feet/2,107m) to the southwest.

J 3.7 (6 km) Lodging.

J 4.8 (7.7 km) Look for sheep on White Mountain to east.

J 8 (12.9 km) Haunka Creek.

J 15.5 (24.9 km) Snafu Creek. Snafu is an army acronym for Situation Normal, All Fouled Up.

J 16.4 (26 km) Winding dirt access road leads east 0.8 mile/1.3 km to **Snafu Lake Yukon government campground**; 10 sites, camping fee, outhouses, firewood, firepits, tables, boat ramp, Arctic grayling fishing. Dirt campsites; nice lake views. Not recommended for large RVs or trailers.

J 18.4 (29.6 km) Tarfu Creek. Another army acronym: Things Are Really Fouled Up.

J 20.1 (32.3 km) Narrow, winding, dirt and gravel road leads 2.4 miles/4 km east to **Tarfu Lake Yukon government campground**; 10 campsites around a large sloping parking area; limited lake views; camping fee, drinking water, litter bins, tables, outhouses, fishing and boat launch. Not recommended for large RVs or trailers.

J 25.4 (42.4 km) Rest area with litter bin and outhouses.

J 25.6 (41.5 km) BC–YT border.

J 30.1 (50 km) Signed 7 percent grades southbound.

J 32.5 (53.9 km) Double-ended gravel turnout to east. Hitchcock Creek rest area to west.

J 36 (59.4 km) Base Camp Creek (sign); gravel turnout to west.

J 39.6 (65.1 km) Indian River.

J 49.5 (80.8 km) Davie Hall Lake.

J 51.3 (83.6 km) MacDonald Lake BC Recreation Site.

J 52.6 (85.6 km) 4th of July Creek.

J 54.1 (87.1 km) Atlin Tlingit Fuels; self-serve gas, diesel.

J 54.9 (89.4 km) **Como Lake** BC Recreation Site; stocked with rainbow trout.

J 56 (91.1 km) *Slow for speed zones southbound.*

J 57.7 (93.9 km) Turnout with litter bin and map at **junction** with Discovery Avenue. Turn west (right southbound) at stop sign and follow Discovery Avenue into Atlin (description follows). Turn east (left southbound) on Discovery Avenue, which becomes Surprise Lake Road at its junction with Warm Bay Road, to reach area attractions. **Surprise Lake Road** leads to the Atlin airport, (1.8 km/1.1 miles), dump station (3.7 km/2.3 miles), Pine Creek Falls (5.6 km/3.5 miles) public gold panning on Spruce Creek (5.8 km/3.6 miles), former townsite of Discovery (8.7 km/5.4 miles) and Surprise Lake (18 km/11 miles), 4 campsites.

Warm Bay Road (paved to Mile 5/8 km) leads 1.5 miles/2.4 km to Pine Creek campground (mid-size RVs/tents, fees posted) on the south side of Pine Creek just past bridge; beach and Monarch Mountain trails, 3.5 km/2.2 miles; Llewellyn Glacier viewpoint, 11 km/7 miles; Palmer Lake recreation site (18 km/11.2 miles), 2 campsites; Warm Bay recreation site (22 km/13.7 miles), 5 campsites; and "The Grotto" recreation site (25 km/15.5 miles), 2 small campsites.

J 57.8 (94 km) Pine Tree Restaurant (ATM), Shell gas, tire repairs.

Historic Atlin buildings provide an interesting walking tour through the community. This is Discovery Jail. (©Kris Valencia, staff)

Atlin

J 58 (94.3 km) The most northwesterly town in British Columbia, Atlin is located on the eastern shore of Atlin Lake, 60 miles/96 km south of the Alaska Highway, and 106 miles/171 km southeast of Whitehorse, YT (about a 2½-hour drive). **Population**: 350. **Emergency Services: RCMP**, phone 250-651-7511. **Ambulance**, phone 250-651-7700. **Health Centre**, Outpost Nurse, visiting physician, phone 250-651-7677.

Visitor Information: Atlin Historical Museum in 3rd Street; phone 250-651-7522 (May–September). **Elevation**: 2,240 feet/683m.

Atlin was founded in 1898. The name means "big water" in Tlingit, the language of the local Taku River Tlingit First Nation. The Atlin Lake area was one of the richest gold strikes made during the great rush to the Klondike in 1897–98. The first claims were registered here on July 30, 1898, by Fritz Miller and Kenneth McLaren.

Lodging on the waterfront at **Brewery Bay Chalet** and Atlin Mountain Inn. There are restaurants, a laundromat (with showers), gas station (propane, diesel), auto repair, grocery, government liquor store and a post office. There are no banks in Atlin, but ATMs are available. Bus tours are welcome, but phone ahead so this small community can accommodate you. Many Atlin services and attractions are open only from May to September.

Camping in town at the Norseman RV Park (follow signs). Campsites outside town on Surprise Lake and Warm Bay roads.

Atlin Arts & Music Festival takes place annually on the second weekend in July. A big crowd attends, enjoying music, art and film in a family-friendly environment. During the festival, camping is available on the festival grounds (free with an advance ticket or purchase a festival wristband). For details visit www.atlinfestival.ca.

Attractions in Atlin include the **Atlin Historical Museum**, located in Atlin's original 1-room schoolhouse at 3rd Street and Trainor Avenue. The museum has mining artifacts and photo exhibits of the Atlin gold rush. Open 10 A.M. to 1 P.M. and 2–5 P.M. daily, May–September; phone 250-651-7522. Admission charged. Historic walking tours by appointment.

Art galleries around town feature local art in a variety of mediums—from art cards to wood boxes. Stop by Festival Headquarters Gallery, Magpie's, The Orange Box, Insa's Gallery, and the Atlin Courthouse Gallery.

The MV *Tarahne* (Tah-ron) sits on the lakeshore. Built at Atlin in 1916 by White Pass & Yukon Route, she carried passengers and freight from Atlin to Scotia Bay until 1936. The restored Atlinto, a gas-powered propeller boat first launched in 1911, is also here.

Historic Atlin buildings include the Globe Theatre (1917), Kershaw's Hardware (1914), Discovery Jail (1902) and many other picturesque old structures that are now homes or businesses. More information is available from the Atlin Historical Museum.

AREA FISHING. The Atlin area is well known for its good fishing. Public boat launch on Atlin Lake, south of the MV *Tarahne*. Boat charters available. British Columbia fishing licenses are available from the government agent and at local outlets.

Tagish Road Log

After visiting Atlin, drive back out Atlin Road and follow Tagish Road to Carcross (log follows). The 34-mile/54-km paved Tagish Road connects the Alaska Highway and Atlin Road with the South Klondike Highway. Built in 1942 to lay a gas pipeline during as the Alaska Highway was constructed.

Distance from junction with Alaska Highway (J) is shown.
Kilometerposts measure east to west from Alaska Highway junction to Carcross turnoff.

J 1.1 (1.8 km) **Junction** with Atlin Road.

J 8.8 (14.2 km) Jubilee Mountain (elev. 5,950 feet/1,814m) to the south; view from top of Little Atlin Lake and Tagish River. Jubilee Mountain was named by Dr. G.M. Dawson in 1887 in honor of Queen Victoria's Jubilee.

J 12.8 (20.4 km) Tagish Trading Post; gas, oil, minor repairs, snacks, groceries and post office. Marina on north side of road at east end of Tagish bridge.

J 13 (21 km) **Tagish (Six Mile) River** bridge. West end of bridge has a day-use area with parking, picnic sites and water. Good fishing from north side of bridge on anglers' walkway for lake trout, Arctic grayling, northern pike, whitefish and cisco.

J 13.4 (21.5 km) *Slow for speed zones through* **TAGISH** (pop. 262), a small rural community in the Southern Lakes area and traditional home of the Carcross Tagish First Nation; www.tagishyukon.org. Tourist services at Six Mile River Resort (cabins, RV parking, dining) and Tagish Holiday Park (motel, coffeeshop, RV park, convenience store).

Tagish Post, originally named Fort Sifton, south of Tagish on the Tagish River, was the North West Mounted Police and Canadian customs post where duties were collected on the tons of freight carried by stampeders on their way to the Klondike goldfields in 1897–98.

J 22 (35.5 km) Turnoff for Tagish Lake Kennel, Tagish Wilderness Lodge, Southern Lakes Resort (licensed restaurant, patio).

J 29.6 (48 km) Chootla Lake.

J 31 (49.9 km) First glimpse westbound of Montana Mountain (elev. 7,230 feet/2,204m) across narrows at Carcross.

J 33.8 (54 km) C 0 **Junction** with South Klondike Highway (Yukon Highway 2). Turn left for **Carcross**, a half-mile south; gas, food, souvenirs, **Visitor Information Center** and historic sites like the *SS Tutshi* and the little locomotive *Duchess*.

Turn right (north) and continue 32 miles/51 km to junction with the Alaska Highway at **Milepost DC 874.4**. Scenic attractions along the way include **Carcross Desert** (1 mile north of this junction) and **Emerald Lake** (7 miles/11 km north).

Turn to SOUTH KLONDIKE HIGHWAY section for detailed log and description of attractions along the entire length of the South Klondike Highway.

**Return to Milepost DC 874.4
Alaska Highway**

(Continued from page 192)

DC 850 (1362.5 km) **DJ 537** (864.2 km) Turnoff for Marsh Lake Community Center; firehall and emergency service response center; pay phone.

DC 852.2 (1366.7 km) **DJ 534.8** (860.6 km) Intermittent views of beautiful **Marsh Lake** to the west for the next several miles northbound. Marsh Lake, part of the Yukon River system, is approximately 20 miles/32 km long and was named in 1883 by Lt. Frederick Schwatka, U.S. Army, for Yale professor Othniel Charles Marsh. Marsh Lake and, in particular the sandy Army Beach, is a popular recreation area for Whitehorse residents.

DC 854.4 (1370 km) **DJ 532.6** (857.1 km) **Historic Milepost 883**, Marsh Lake/Camp 4F NWHS sign. Boat launch to west.

DC 855.8 (1372.5 km) **DJ 531.2** (854.9 km) Distance marker southbound shows Teslin 132 km/82 miles, Watson Lake 395 km/245 miles.

DC 857.8 (1375.9 km) **DJ 529.2** (851.6 km) Paved shoulder parking east side of highway for commercial trucks only. Marsh Lake to west.

DC 859.9 (1379 km) **DJ 527.1** (848.3 km) **Historical Mile 890.** Turnoff to west for **Marsh Lake Recreation Site and Campground** (watch for tent/camping sign) via 0.4-mile/0.6-km gravel loop road: 41 sites, most level, some with lake views, 9 pull-through; outhouses, firewood, firepits, litter bins, picnic tables, kitchen shelter. Camping permit ($12). For group camping, follow signs near campground entrance. [A]

Day-use area includes sandy beach, change house, picnic area, playground, kitchen shelter and boat launch.

DC 860 (1379.1 km) **DJ 527** (848.2 km) Turnoff to west on Army Beach Road for **Marsh Lake Recreation Site** (watch for picnicking sign). Day-use area includes sandy beach, change house, picnic area, playground, kitchen shelter.

DC 861.1 (1381.6 km) **DJ 525.9** (846.1 km) McClintock River bridge. The river was named by Lieutenant Schwatka for Arctic explorer Sir Francis McClintock. Turnout to west at north end of bridge has boat ramp access, litter barrels and outhouse.

This boat launch is a popular put-in spot for canoe trips down the **McClintock River** to **McClintock Bay**, at the north end of Marsh Lake. The river is narrow, winding and silty, with thick brush along the shoreline, but it is a good river for boat trips, especially in late fall. McClintock Bay is a critical habitat for migrating waterfowl in spring. Good bird watching (Northern pintail, canvasback, American wigeon, common goldeneye, common merganser, American kestrels and bald eagles); best place to see mule deer in Yukon; beaver lodges in sloughs. Fish for Arctic grayling, jackfish and trout. [➾]

DC 861.3 (1381.8 km) **DJ 525.7** (846 km) Swan Haven Interpretive Center (2 miles/3.2 km from highway via good gravel road) overlooks McClintock Bay and is open in April; guided walks. Outdoor displays open all year. Best time to see swans is during migration, from late March to early May. McClintock Bay's early open water hosts some 10,000 migrating trumpeter swans, as well as tundra swans, widgeons, Canada geese, northern pintails and other birds. The annual Celebration of Swans festival is held at the center the third week of April; www.environmentyukon.gov.yk.ca/.

The Alaska Highway crosses the Yukon River south of Whitehorse. The Marsh Lake Dam rest area is at the southeast end of the bridge. (©Sharon Nault)

DC 864.3 (1388.1 km) **DJ 522.7** (841.2 km) Kettley's Canyon.

DC 867.3 (1393 km) **DJ 519.7** (836.4 km) **Historic Milepost 897. Yukon River Bridge** (elev. 2,150 feet/645m). Turnoff to north at east end of bridge for **Marsh Lake Dam** rest area; large gravel parking area, litter bins, outhouses and boat launch. Point of interest sign about Lewes Dam. Interpretive trail with signs about area history and wildlife. Viewing platform on hillside overlooks the beginning of the Yukon River (Lewes River Marsh).

Measuring nearly 2,000 miles/3,218 km, the Yukon River is the fourth or fifth longest river in North America (both the river's length and rank depend on the source). It is the principal river of both Yukon and Alaska, draining three-quarters of Yukon and a third of Alaska. It is also the "focal point of Yukon history," according to R. Coutts, in his book *Yukon: Places & Names*.

The Yukon River flows northwest from its headwaters near the Yukon–British Columbia border to Fort Yukon in Alaska. From there it turns sharply southwest across Alaska to empty into the Bering Sea at Norton Sound. Major tributaries in Yukon include the Teslin, Pelly, White and Stewart rivers; in Alaska, the Porcupine, Charley, Tanana, Innoko and Koyukuk rivers.

Hudson's Bay Company traders first explored the upper Yukon River in the 1840s. Missionaries, fur trappers and prospectors soon followed. Some 50,000 prospectors (yet another number that changes with the source) followed the Yukon River from Lake Bennett to Dawson City during the Klondike Gold Rush of 1898–1899.

DC 868 (1394 km) **DJ 519** (835.4 km) Highway climbs next 1.2 miles/1.9 km northbound. Views of Yukon River to east.

DC 873.5 (1403 km) **DJ 513.5** (826.4 km) **Historical Mile 904.** Turnoff to northeast for **The Caribou RV Park** with hookups, restrooms and showers, and RV/car wash, and for **The Wolf's Den Restaurant**, featuring Swiss specialties (call ahead for reservations); descriptions follow. [A]

The Wolf's Den Restaurant. Open daily for breakfast/lunch/dinner. Your hosts, Harry and Yvonne look forward to serving you. Enjoy our Swiss and Western cuisine—all prepared fresh: steaks, schnitzels, spaetzle, salads, pastas, fish, fondues, vegetarian dishes, and Wolf Den dessert selections. Licensed. Wir sprechen Deutsch. Reservations recommended, (867) 393-3968; info@wolfsden.ca; www.wolfsden.ca. [ADVERTISEMENT]

The Caribou RV Park. "Cozy in the Wild" but only 15 minutes from downtown, the owners welcome in 5 languages (English, German, French, Italian, Luxembourgish). Nice tent sites, or camp in the spacious pull-throughs, treed sites with 15/30 power, good drinking water, WiFi, cable TV—and enjoy the famous clean private washrooms. NEW: Convenience store with fresh-baked bread! Walking trails, sani-dump, laundromat and vehicle wash. Pets are welcome. Phone (867) 668-2961; info@caribou-rv-park.com; www.caribou-rv-park.com. See display ad this page. [ADVERTISEMENT]

The Yukon River flows through Miles Canyon, a scenic spot with walking trails. It is accessible from Schwatka Lake Road turnoff at Milepost DC 881.7. (©Sharon Nault)

DC 873.8 (1403.5 km) **DJ 513.2** (825.9 km) Empress Road. *Speed zones northbound.*

DC 874.4 (1404.4 km) **DJ 512.6** (824.9 km) **Historical Mile 905. Junction** with South Klondike Highway (Yukon Highway 2 South, also called Carcross Road), which leads 98 miles/158 km to historic Skagway, AK; 25 miles/40 km to scenic Emerald Lake; and 32 miles/52 km to Carcross. *See also "Atlin–Tagish–Carcross Scenic Loop" on pages 193–194.*

Junction with South Klondike Highway which leads south 32 miles/52 km to Carcross and 98 miles/158 km to Skagway. See SOUTH KLONDIKE HIGHWAY section for log.

Distance marker southbound shows Teslin 161 km/100 miles, Watson Lake 422 km/262 mi.

DC 874.5 (1404.6 km) **DJ 512.5** (824.7 km) Distance marker northbound shows Whitehorse City Center 22 km/14 miles, Dawson City 559 km/347 miles.

DC 874.9 (1405.2 km) **DJ 512.1** (824.1

km) Welcome to Whitehorse (northbound sign). Incorporated June 1, 1950, Whitehorse expanded in 1974 from its original 3 square miles/8 square km to 162 square miles/420 square km.

DC 876.8 (1408.2 km) **DJ 510.2** (821.1 km) **Historical Mile 906. Wolf Creek Yukon government campground** to east. An 0.8-mile/1.3-km gravel loop road leads through this campground: 40 sites, most level, 11 pull-through; kitchen shelters, water pumps, picnic tables, firepits, firewood, outhouses, litter barrels, playground; camping permit ($12). A 1.2-mile/2-km nature loop trail winds through boreal forest to an overlook of the Yukon River and returns along Wolf Creek. Interpretive brochure at trailhead and information panels at campground entrance. Fishing in **Wolf Creek** for Arctic grayling.

DC 878.3 (1410.6 km) **DJ 508.7** (818.7 km) Meadow Lakes golf course to northeast.

DC 879.3 (1412.3 km) **DJ 507.7** (817 km) Highway crosses abandoned railroad tracks of the White Pass & Yukon Route (WP&YR) narrow-gauge railroad. Although the WP&YR no longer serves Whitehorse by rail, it does offer scenic rail trips in summer out of Skagway, AK, to White Pass Summit, Lake Bennett and Carcross. (See Railroads in the TRAVEL PLANNING section for details. See also SOUTH KLONDIKE HIGHWAY section for map of rail route.)

Construction of the WP&YR began in May 1898 at the height of the Klondike Gold Rush. Completion of the railway in 1900 linked the port of Skagway, AK, with Whitehorse, YT, providing passenger and freight service for thousands of gold seekers. The WP&YR ceased operation in 1982. In 1988, WP&YR started their sightseeing rail trips between Skagway and Fraser, now a very popular tourist attraction

DC 879.6 (1412.8 km) **DJ 507.4** (816.6 km) 60° North Express commercial cardlock.

DC 879.7 (1413 km) **DJ 507.3** (816.4 km) Petro-Canada gas station with diesel to northeast.

DC 879.8 (1413.3 km) **DJ 507.2** (816.2 km) **Historic Milepost 910.** Frasier Road/East McCrae Business Park. Access to **Fireweed RV Services**; RV parts, repairs; U-Haul.

McCrae originated in 1900 as a flag stop on the newly constructed White Pass & Yukon Railway. During WWII, this area served as a major service and supply depot, a major construction camp and a recreation center.

DC 880 (1413.6 km) **DJ 507** (815.9 km) **Historical Mile 910.5. Fireweed R.V. Services** to northeast, access via frontage road; repairs, parts and accessories; U-Haul agency.

Fireweed R.V. Services Ltd. See display ad this page.

DC 880.3 (1414 km) **DJ 506.7** (815.4 km) Access via frontage road to Fireweed R.V. Services.

DC 880.8 (1414.7 km) **DJ 506.2** (814.6 km) **Historic Milepost 911** (site of Utah Construction Co. Camp). **Pioneer R.V. Park** to east; treed campsites with hookups, WiFi, showers, laundry, store, gas/diesel/propane, dump station and cabins.

Pioneer RV Park. See display ad this page.

DC 881 (1415 km) **DJ 506** (814.3 km) Turnoff for Mount Sima ski area and access to **GoNorth Yukon Car & RV Rental, RV Service & Repair and Storage**. The Mount Sima complex includes a chairlift, day-lodge and observation tower and offers typical ski area amenities in winter. The lift operates in summer for mountain biking. For details, visit www.mountsima.com.

GoNorth Yukon Car & RV Rental, RV Service & Repair and Storage. See display ad on page 202.

DC 881.3 (1415.7 km) **DJ 505.7** (813.8 km) White Pass & Yukon Route's Utah siding to east. Also site of an Army camp where thousands of soldiers were stationed during construction of the Alaska Highway.

DC 881.7 (1416.3 km) **DJ 505.3** (813.2 km) Sharp turnoff to northeast for **Miles Canyon** via Schwatka Lake Road (gated, closed October–May). Drive down hill 0.3 mile and turn right for spur road to Miles Canyon; parking area is another 0.3 mile. RVs use turnout at turn or park up hill from parking area on curve by outhouses. *Parking area at Miles Canyon will not accommodate RVs.* (The parking area is only large enough for about a dozen cars; we parked *The MILE-POST®* truck/camper there without much of a problem but if the lot had been full, turnaround space would have been tight.) Schwatka Lake Road continues another 2.7 miles from Miles Canyon spur to junction with Robert Service Way (the south access road into Whitehorse). Good viewpoint along the way of Miles Canyon and surrounding areas.

CAUTION: Watch for bicyclists, joggers and walkers on this winding, hilly side road.

Easy access from parking area to walking trails above canyon and pedestrian bridge across canyon. Popular spot with joggers, dog walkers and everyone else. *CAUTION: Steep dropoffs, supervise children and pets.*

Originally called "Grand Canyon" by early gold seekers, Miles Canyon was renamed in 1883 by Lt. Schwatka, U.S. Army, for Brigadier General Nelson A. Miles. A 1.1-mile/1.7-km trail from the bridge leads to the historic site of **Canyon City**, a gold rush settlement that existed from 1897 to 1900 as a portage point around Miles Canyon and Whitehorse Rapids. Two tramways, each several miles long, transported goods along the east and west sides of the river. Completion of the White Pass & Yukon Route in 1900 made the trams obsolete, and the settlement was abandoned. Contact the Yukon Conservation Society about their free 2-hour interpretive walks to **Canyon City** from June to late August; (867) 668-5678, www.yukonconservation.org.

Miles Canyon was an imposing challenge for miners and stampeders on their way up the Yukon to the gold fields, mainly because the narrow channel through the canyon was followed by the more daunting Whitehorse Rapids. Both Whitehorse Rapids and Squaw Rapids were eliminated by construction of the hydro-electric power plant and dam on the Yukon River at Whitehorse in 1959, which created Schwatka Lake.

DC 883 (1418 km) **DJ 504** (811 km) **Historic Mile 913.1. Fuel Yukon**; gas, diesel, snacks and souvenirs (including unique branded shirts and hats) and Midnight Sun Coffee bar.

Fuel Yukon. See display ad this section.

DC 883.5 (1419 km) **DJ 503.5** (810.3 km) City of Whitehorse rest area to east; double-ended turnout with outhouses.

One of the woolly mammoth statues alongside the Alaska Highway by the fascinating Yukon Beringia Interpretive Center, which traces the Ice Age in Yukon. *(©Kris Valencia, staff)*

DC 883.7 (1419.4 km) **DJ 503.3** (810 km) Traffic light at first Whitehorse exit northbound and access to **Hi Country RV Park. Junction** with Robert Service Way and Hamilton Boulevard; descriptions follow. *This is the first of 2 exits for Whitehorse northbound. Second exit is Two Mile Hill at* **Milepost DC 887.4**; *see description on page 207.*

Robert Service Way, the south access road to Whitehorse (right-hand turn northbound), leads downhill to Schwatka Lake Road (Mile 1.1), Robert Service Campground (Mile 1.5), Welcome to Whitehorse turnout on Yukon River (Mile 1.8), then through a roundabout and straight forward for the entrance to the *SS Klondike* sternwheeler attraction to junction with 2nd Avenue in downtown Whitehorse (Mile 2.6).

Description of Whitehorse begins on page 198.

Take Hamilton Boulevard (left-hand turn northbound) then first left-hand turn for **Hi Country R.V. Park**; full hookup sites, dump station, gift shop, cafe.

Hi Country R.V. Park. See display ad on this page.

DC 884.3 (1420.4 km) **DJ 502.7** (809 km) **Historic Milepost 914.** Whitehorse Weigh Station to southwest.

DC 885.5 (1422.1 km) **DJ 501.5** (807.1 km) First entrance northbound (for dropping off visitors only) to Yukon Beringia Center (see description next milepost). Center front door drop-off and handicap parking only.

DC 885.7 (1422.3 km) **DJ 501.3** (806.7 km) **Historical Mile 915.** Second entrance to public parking at The **Yukon Beringia Interpretive Center** with a frontage road for Yukon Beringia Center, Yukon Transportation Museum and Whitehorse Airport.

The Yukon Beringia Center traces the Ice Age in Yukon, which, unlike the rest of Canada, was for the most part ice-free. The Blue Fish Caves near Old Crow reputedly hold the earliest evidence of humans in the New World. Displays at the center trace the science and myth of an Ice Age subcontinent inhabited by great woolly mammoths, giant short-faced bears and lions. Ice Age *(Continues on page 207*

Whitehorse

Make your first stop in Whitehorse, Yukon's capital, the Yukon Visitor Information Center, located on 2nd Avenue. (©Kris Valencia, staff)

Whitehorse

DC 887.4 (1425.3 km) **DJ 499.6** (804 km) **F 603** (970 km) **Historic Milepost 918.** Located on the upper reaches of the Yukon River in Canada's subarctic at latitude 61°N. Whitehorse is 100 miles/160 km from Haines Junction; 109 miles/175 km from Skagway, AK; 244 miles/393 km from Haines, AK; and 396 miles/637 km from Tok, AK. **Population:** 26,418. **Emergency Services: RCMP, Fire Department, Ambulance,** phone 911. **Hospital,** phone (867) 393-8700.

Visitor Information: Yukon Visitor Information Center is located next to the Yukon Government Building on 2nd Avenue. RV parking is available on the Lambert Avenue side of the Visitor Center. The Center offers a 15-minute film on Yukon; daily updated information on accommodations, weather and road conditions; and printout information on attractions, restaurants and events in Whitehorse. Pick up free self-guiding maps of Historical Walking Tours of Whitehorse here and download the audio at www.heritageyukon.ca.

The Center is open daily, 8 A.M. to 8 P.M., from May 1 to Sept. 30. The rest of the year the Center is open weekdays from 8:30 A.M. to 5 P.M. and Saturdays 10 A.M. to 2 P.M. Phone (867) 667-3084, or contact a Travel Councilor with Tourism Yukon at Box 2703, Whitehorse, YT Y1A 2C6. Toll-free phone 1-800-661-0494; email vacation@gov.yk.ca; fax (867) 667-3546; website: www.travelyukon.com.

The City of Whitehorse offers year-round information that might be of interest to visitors. Call (867) 667-6401 or write City of Whitehorse at 2121 Second Ave., Whitehorse, YT Y1A 1C2. Contact the city for up-to-date information on transit, recreation

centers such as the Canada Games Center and more at www.whitehorse.ca.

Elevation: 2,316 feet/706m. **Climate:** Wide variations are the theme here with no two winters alike. The lowest recorded temperature is -62°F/-52.2°C in January 1947 and the warmest 94°F/34.4°C in June 1969. Average daily temperature in January is 14°F/-17.7°C and for July 57°F/14°C. Annual precipitation is 10.3 inches, equal parts snow and rain. On June 21, Whitehorse enjoys 21 hours of daylight and on Dec. 21 only 5 hours, 37 minutes. **Radio:** CFWH 570, CBC network with repeaters throughout territory; CBC Whitehorse; CKRW 610, local; CHON-FM 98.1; 96.1-FM The Rush; CFET-FM 106.7. **Television:** CBC–TV live, colour via ANIK satellite, Canadian network; WHTV, NADR (First Nation issues), local cable; CanCom stations via satellite, many channels. **Newspapers:** *Whitehorse Star* (weekdays); *Yukon News* (3 times a week).

Private Aircraft: Whitehorse International Airport, 3 runways; has approach over city and an abrupt escarpment; elev. 2,305 feet/703m; main runway length 9,000 feet/2,743m; surfaced; fuel 80, 100, jet fuel available. Customs clearance available.

Floatplane base on Schwatka Lake above Whitehorse Dam (take the South Access Road from Alaska Highway and turn on Robert Service Way by the railroad tracks).

Description

Whitehorse has been the capital of Yukon since 1953, and serves as the center for transportation, communications and supplies for Yukon.

The downtown business section of Whitehorse lies on the west bank of the Yukon River. The Riverdale subdivision is on the east side. The low mountains rising behind Riverdale are dominated by Canyon Mountain, known locally as Grey Mountain. McCrae, Wolf Creek, Wolf Creek North, Mary Lake, Cowley Creek, Spruce Hill, Pineridge and Fox Haven Estates are situated

at the south limits. West of downtown are Valleyview, Hillcrest and Granger subdivisions, and beyond the Canada Games Center along Hamilton Boulevard is the neighbourhood of McIntyre. North of the city are Porter Creek, Takhini and Crestview subdivisions. The Takhini area is the location of the Yukon College campus, Yukon Arts Center and Whitehorse Correctional Center. Rural Whitehorse subdivisions of Hidden Valley and MacPherson lie at the city's northern limits.

Downtown Whitehorse is flat and marked at its western limit by a rising escarpment dominated by the Whitehorse International Airport. Originally a woodcutter's lot, the airstrip was first cleared in 1920 to accommodate 4 U.S. Army planes on a test flight from New York to Nome. Access to the city is by Two-Mile Hill from the north and by Robert Service Way (South Access Road) from the south; both connect with the Alaska Highway.

In 1974, the city limits of Whitehorse were expanded from the original 2.7 square miles/6.9 square kilometers to 162 square miles/421 square kilometers, making Whitehorse at one time the largest metropolitan area in Canada. More than two-thirds of the population of Yukon live in the city. Whitehorse is the hub of a network of about 2,664 miles/4,287 km of all-weather roads serving Yukon.

History & Economy

When the White Pass & Yukon Route railway, connecting Skagway with the Yukon River, was completed in July 1900, Whitehorse came into being as the northern terminus. Here the famed river steamers connected the railhead to Dawson City, and some of these boats made the trip all the way to St. Michael, a small outfitting point on Alaska's Bering Sea coast.

Klondike stampeders landed at Whitehorse to dry out and repack their supplies after running the famous Whitehorse Rapids. (The name Whitehorse was in common use by the late 1800s; it is believed that the first miners in the area thought that the foaming rapids resembled white horses' manes and so named the river rapids.) The rapids are no longer visible since construction of the Yukon Energy Corporation's hydroelectric dam on the river. This dam created man-made Schwatka Lake, named in honour of U.S. Army Lt. Frederick Schwatka, who named many of the points along the Yukon River during his 1883 exploration of the region.

The gold rush brought stampeders and the railroad. The community grew as a transportation center and transshipment point for freight from the Skagway–Whitehorse railroad and the stern-wheelers plying the Yukon River to Dawson City. The river was the only highway until WWII, when military expediency built the Alaska Highway in 1942.

During construction of the Alaska Highway in 1942–1943, thousands of American military and civilian workers were employed in the Canadian North. It was the second boom period for Whitehorse, which was headquarters for the western sector during construction. Fort St. John was headquarters for the eastern sector. Both were the largest construction camps on the highway.

The first survey parties of U.S. Army engineers reached Whitehorse in April of 1942. By the end of August, they had constructed a pioneer road from Whitehorse west to White River, largely by following an existing winter trail between Whitehorse and Kluane Lake. November brought the final breakthrough on the western end of the highway, marking completion of the pioneer road, although when the road thawed in the spring of 1943, it was impassable in some spots. "During the spring thaw this frozen road completely disappeared and there was no traffic whatever during the summer."

In May of 1943, the total number of highway workers in Whitehorse grew from 2,500 to 3,800, with equipment and supplies arriving by rail from Skagway at a rate of about 1,800 tons per week. But it was not until mid-October that crews working south from Alaska met those working up from Whitehorse, enabling them to "permanently open the land route to Alaska that had been completely closed since the April thaw."

There was an economic lull following the war, but the new highway was then opened to civilian travel, encouraging new development. Mineral exploration and the development of new mines had a profound effect on the economy of the region, as did the steady growth of tourism. The Whitehorse Copper Mine, located a few miles south of the city in the historic Whitehorse copper belt, is now closed. The Grum Mine site north of Faro produced lead, silver and zinc concentrates for Cyprus–Anvil (1969–1982), Curragh Resources (1986–1992) and Anvil Range Mining Corp. (1994–1998). Stop by the Yukon Chamber of Mines office at 3rd and Strickland for information on mining and rockhounding in Yukon. There is an excellent Yukon mineral display at the entrance to the Visitor Information Center downtown.

Because of its accessibility, Whitehorse became capital of the Yukon (replacing Dawson City in that role) on March 31, 1953.

Lodging & Services

Whitehorse has excellent accommodations, with many modern hotels and motels downtown and along the Alaska Highway, as well as several interesting bed-and-breakfast options (see ads this section). There are also a surprising number of dining choices, from barbecue to French and Swiss/German cuisine, from family dining to fine dining. Major chain fast-food outlets and restaurants are also available in Whitehorse.

Shopping downtown on Main Street. The Yukon Center Mall on 2nd Avenue has a government liquor store, clothing store, restaurants and a Western Union. Whitehorse also has "big box" stores like Walmart, Canadian Tire and Staples; a Real Canadian Superstore at 2nd Avenue and Quartz Road; supermarkets (including **Wykes Your Independent Grocer** on Ogilvie); banks with ATMs, garages and service stations, churches, 2 movie theaters, and beauty salons. The Fireweed Farmers Market also runs on Thursdays and Saturdays between May and September in Shipyards Park. *Pedestrians and motorists note: Downtown Whitehorse is a busy place. Watch out for each other!*

The Canada Games Center/Centre Des Jeux Du Canada has an Aquatic Center, walking/running track, 3 ice surfaces, drop-in programs and fitness classes. Visit www.canadagamescentre.whitehorse.ca; phone (867) 668-4836 for information.

Postal services in Whitehorse are provided at the Shoppers' Drug Mart in the Qwanlin Center (Ogilvie and 4th) and on

Main Street at Third Avenue. The post office is located at the top of Two Mile Hill.

Best Western Gold Rush Inn boasts a convenient Main Street location in the heart of downtown Whitehorse, seconds from shopping, sightseeing and the spectacular Yukon River waterfront. The modern comfortable rooms offer the best night's sleep in the Yukon. Home to the famous Gold Pan Saloon and an Aveda spa. Free parking, free internet and coin laundry. 1-800-661-0539. See display ad on page 201. [ADVERTISEMENT]

Coast High Country Inn. Famous for our 40-foot-tall wooden Mountie, we offer a great downtown Whitehorse location, steps away from the historic Yukon River and its scenic waterfront trails. We bring together modern comfortable rooms and uniquely Yukon character. Enjoy local flavour on "The Deck"—our colourful year-round patio. Free parking, free internet and coin laundry. A/C available. (867) 667-4471. See display ad on page 201. [ADVERTISEMENT]

Camping

RV and tent camping are available at several campgrounds south of Whitehorse

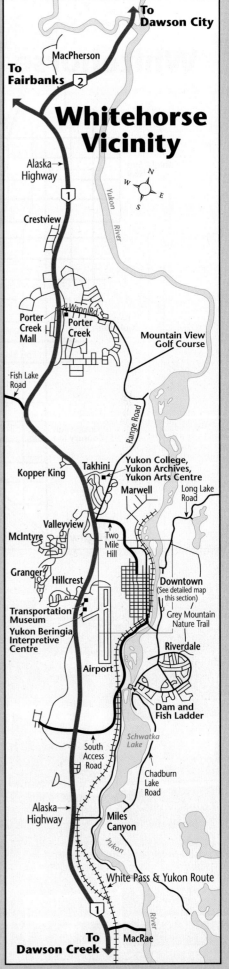

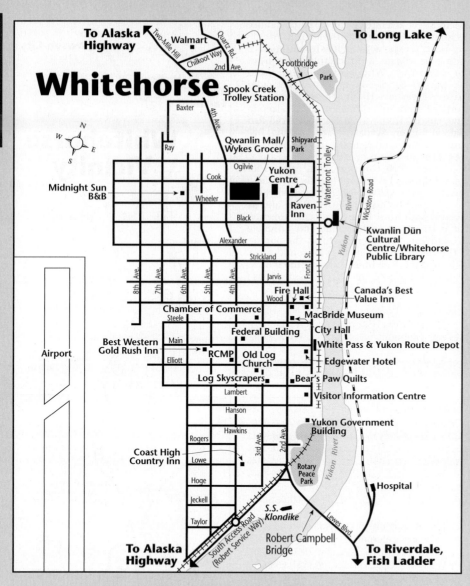

Whitehorse

To Alaska Highway

To Long Lake

Walmart
Two-Mile Hill
Quartz Rd.
Chilkoot Way
2nd. Ave.
Footbridge
Park
Spook Creek Trolley Station
Baxter
4th Ave.
Ray
Qwanlin Mall/ Wykes Grocer
Shipyard Park
Ogilvie
Cook
Yukon Centre
Midnight Sun B&B
Wheeler
Black
Raven Inn
Alexander
Kwanlin Dün Cultural Centre/Whitehorse Public Library
Strickland
Waterfront Trolley
Wickston Road
Yukon River
Front St.
Jarvis
Fire Hall
Canada's Best Value Inn
Wood
8th Ave.
7th Ave.
6th Ave.
5th Ave.
4th Ave.
Chamber of Commerce
MacBride Museum
Steele
Federal Building
City Hall
Best Western Gold Rush Inn
Main
White Pass & Yukon Route Depot
Airport
Elliott
RCMP
Old Log Church
Edgewater Hotel
Log Skyscrapers
Bear's Paw Quilts
Lambert
Visitor Information Centre
Hanson
Yukon Government Building
Hawkins
Rogers
3rd Ave.
2nd Ave.
Coast High Country Inn
Lowe
Rotary Peace Park
Hoge
Yukon River
Jeckell
Hospital
Taylor
S.S. Klondike
To Alaska Highway
South Access Road (Robert Service Way)
Robert Campbell Bridge
Lewes Blvd.
To Riverdale, Fish Ladder

on the Alaska Highway, including the following: **Hi Country RV Park (Milepost DC 883.7)**, **Pioneer RV Park (Milepost DC 880.8)**, **Caribou RV Park (Milepost DC 873.5)**, and **Wolf Creek Yukon Government Campground (Milepost DC 876.8)**. Takhini

Hot Springs on the KLONDIKE LOOP section is also a popular camping spot (half-hour drive from Whitehorse). Tent camping is available in Whitehorse at Robert Service Park on Robert Service Way.

Transportation

Air: Air Canada and WestJet to Vancouver and all points beyond. Air North to Dawson City, Old Crow, Edmonton, Calgary, Ottawa, Vancouver, Victoria, Yellowknife, Inuvik, Kelowna. Condor direct air service between Whitehorse and Frankfurt, Germany, from May through October. Alkan Air offers charters; yukon.alkanair.com. Whitehorse International Airport on the Alaska Highway just 3 km from downtown Whitehorse.

Seaplane dock on Schwatka Lake just above the Whitehorse Dam (take Robert Service Way from Alaska Highway and turn right on road by the railroad tracks to reach the base). Flightseeing tours available.

Bus: Whitehorse Transit offers service downtown and to rural subdivisions. Husky Bus runs regularly scheduled service between Dawson City and Whitehorse. Alaska/Yukon Trails offers charter service on request throughout Alaska and Yukon (including Whitehorse); www.alaskashuttle.com.

Railroad: For White Pass & Yukon Route rail trips, phone WP&YR in Skagway at 1-800-343-7373, or contact Yukon Alaska Tourist Tours at the historic WP&YR station on Front Street, phone (867) 633-5710. See "Railroads" in the TRAVEL PLANNING section.

Car, Truck, Motorhome and Camper Rentals: Go North Car & RV Rental, phone (867) 668-3222 or 1-866-236-7272.

Attractions

S.S. Klondike National Historic Site. This grand old stern-wheeler sits beside the Yukon River near the Robert Campbell bridge. There is a visitor center with gift shop and public parking at the *S.S. Klondike* National Historic Site. The site is open from Victoria Day long weekend in late May to Labour Day in September from 9:30 A.M. to 5 P.M. daily. Entry to the *S.S. Klondike* is free for self-guided tours, but check in at the visitor center before boarding: they have an excellent $2 brochure available in English, French and German. Guided tours are offered by Parks Canada for $6 per person; for additional details go to their website at www.pc.gc.ca/ssklondike.

The *S.S. Klondike* was built in 1929 by the British Yukon Navigation Company (BYNC). The vessel was the largest on the Yukon River, had a cargo capacity that was

50 percent greater than previous boats, and could carry over 300 tons. She ran aground in 1936, at the confluence of the Teslin and Yukon rivers, in a section known as Thirty Mile. Salvaged parts were used to construct a new ship—the *S.S. Klondike II* (launched in 1937)—that was almost identical to the first.

The *S.S. Klondike* carried mail, general supplies, passengers and silver lead ore along the 460-mile route between Whitehorse and Dawson City. She was retired in 1955. Donated to the Canadian government, the *S.S. Klondike* now rests on the west bank of the Yukon in Whitehorse.

For more information, phone (867) 667-4511 in summer (667-3910 in winter) or toll-free 1-800-661-0486; or visit www.pc.gc.ca/ssklondike.

The MacBride Museum of Yukon History offers a comprehensive view of the colorful characters and events that built Canada's Yukon. Discover the truth behind the Robert Service legend at Sam McGee's Original Cabin. See Engine 51, the locomotive that built the White Pass & Yukon Route Railway. Follow the Northwest Mounted Police as they establish law and order in the North. See a 7-foot grizzly in the Wild World Gallery. During the summer, the Museum offers daily tours, programs, and games. Visitors can also try their hand at gold panning.

The Museum gift shop features gold jewelry, works by local artists, historic photos and books. The MacBride Museum is located on the corner of Front and Wood streets. Open year-round. Hours are 9:30 A.M. to 5 P.M. daily from May through August; and 10 A.M. to 4 P.M. Tuesday–Saturday, September

Multi-use path along the Yukon River has benches and parks, and offers access to the *S.S. Klondike National Historic Site.* (©Kris Valencia, staff)

to mid-May. Admission is charged. For more information phone (867) 667-2709; www.macbridemuseum.com.

The MacBride Museum has a North West Mounted Police Patrol Cabin. This recreation of an early NWMP Patrol Cabin was built in 1995 as part of the 100th anniversary of the RCMP. Whitehorse became the territorial headquarters of the NWMP in 1900. The NWMP were bestowed the title "Royal" in 1904, and in 1920 became the Royal Canadian Mounted Police. The Patrol Cabin is dedicated each year to a famous figure in NWMP history. The distinctive red cloth tunic—or red serge—of the RCMP was first worn by the NWMP in 1897, but it is now worn only at formal occasions or for special programs.

The **MacBride Waterfront Trolley** is a restored 1925 trolley that offers interpretive rides featuring Whitehorse history. It operates during the summer, departing from Rotary Park, across from the *S.S. Klondike* National Historic Site, and from the Roundhouse where Wood Street connects to Front

Oversize vehicle parking available at Yukon Visitor Information Center. The visitor center also has parking passes for visitors using metered spaces for cars. (©Kris Valencia, staff)

Street. Per person fee charged.

Kwanlin Dun Cultural Center. This striking structure—adjacent the Whitehorse Public Library on Black Street at Front Street—is a place to learn about First Nations history, traditions and culture through permanent and a rotating number of temporary exhibits. It is also one of the largest meeting spaces in Whitehorse. Phone

(867) 456-5322; www.kdcc.ca.

Whitehorse Public Library is right next door to the Kwanlin Dun Cultural Center, on Black Street at Front Street. Open 10 A.M. to 9 P.M. Monday to Thursday, 10 A.M. to 6 P.M. Friday to Sunday; closed holidays. Phone (867) 667-5239.

Special Events. Whitehorse has a number of festivals and special events throughout the year.

The 31st annual **Yukon River Quest Canoe and Kayak Race** takes place June 26–30, 2019. The "Race to the Midnight Sun" begins in Whitehorse and ends in Dawson City, a 460-mile/740-km-long route that is the longest canoe and kayak race in the world. It attracts expert and novice paddlers from around the world. For more information: www.yukonriverquest.com.

July 1st is **Canada Day**, celebrated with events and entertainment for the whole family. The 21st **Yukon River Trail Marathon** is Sunday, August 4, 2019, with start/finish at Rotary Park. Registration opens in April. For details, visit www.yukonmarathon.com.

The annual running of the **Klondike Trail of '98 International Road Relay** takes place the weekend following Labour Day (Sept. 6–7, 2019). This is a 110-mile/175-km road relay from Skagway, AK, to Whitehorse,

YT; visit klondikeroadrelay.com.

Whitehorse and Fairbanks are the 2 host cities for the **Yukon Quest 1,000 Mile International Sled Dog Race** in February, with each city alternating roles as the "start" and "finish" to this great endurance race. This year (2019) the race started in Whitehorse and finished in Fairbanks. Next year (2020) it starts in Fairbanks and finishes in Whitehorse. In summer you can visit the Yukon Quest Office & Gift Shop in the White Pass Depot at Front and Main streets in downtown Whitehorse. (In Fairbanks, the Yukon Quest store and office are in the log cabin adjacent Golden Heart Plaza on First Avenue.) For more information, visit www.yukonquest.com.

Also in February is Whitehorse's big annual winter event: the **Yukon Sourdough Rendezvous Festival** at Shipyard's Park downtown (www.yukonrendezvous.com).

Waterfront Walkway. A wonderful waterfront walking trail connects the city's major parks and provides a pleasant, easy way to see the Yukon River. This paved, wheelchair-accessible path passes many of the city's major attractions and crosses the Yukon River via the Rotary Centennial Bridge. The **Waterfront Wharf**, behind the WP&YR depot, acts as a venue for various special events in the summer, including a community market

Visitors may hop-on/hop-off the bright yellow, vintage (1925) **Waterfront Trolley** at any station along its routes: Spook Creek Station (across from Walmart), Shipyards Park, Kwanlin Dun, MacBride Museum, WP&YR Depot, the Visitor Center and the *SS Klondike*. The trolley operates 10 A.M. to 6 P.M. daily in summer; fee charged.

Picnic at a park. Central to downtown and the *S.S. Klondike*, **Rotary Peace Park** is a popular picnic spot and the site of several Whitehorse special events. **Skateboard Park** is located across the river from the *S.S. Klondike*. Walk or take the trolley to **Shipyards Park**, near the foot of Ogilvie and Second Avenue; a community market takes place here on Thursdays in summer.

Old Log Church Museum. Located in the heart of downtown Whitehorse, one block off Main on Elliott Street at 3rd Avenue, the Old Log Church Museum is one of the oldest buildings in its original location in Whitehorse, built in 1900 by Rev. R.J. Bowen for the Church of England. Uncover the fascinating stories and hidden treasures of Yukon's early pioneers and missionaries. Open daily to the public from mid-May to early September; by appointment in winter. Phone (867) 668-2555; www.oldlogchurch museum.ca. Admission charged.

Yukon Beringia Interpretive Center traces the Ice Age in northern and central Yukon, which, unlike the rest of Canada, was ice-free. The Blue Fish Caves near Old Crow reputedly hold the earliest evidence of humans in North America. Displays at the Center present the science and myth of the Ice Age subcontinent of Beringia, inhabited by great woolly mammoths, giant short-faced bears and lions. Ice Age specimens include a well-preserved Ice Age Yukon horse hide and a reproduction of a scimitar cat, as well as other Ice Age mammals. The center is open daily, mid-May to late September. Open Sundays and Mondays, October to May. Phone (867) 667-8855; Fax (867) 667-8854; email beringia@gov.yk.ca; www.beringia.com. Admis-

Downtown Whitehorse has wide sidewalks and lots of shopping. (©Kris Valencia, staff)

sion fee charged.

The **Yukon Transportation Museum**, located on the Alaska Highway adjacent to the Whitehorse Airport (see **Milepost DC 885.8**), features exhibits of all forms of transportation in the North. Displays inside include the full-size replica of the *Queen of the Yukon* Ryan monoplane, sister ship to Lindbergh's *Spirit of St. Louis*; railway rolling stock; Alaska Highway vintage vehicles, dog-

sleds and stagecoaches. Also featured are the Chilkoot Trail, the Canol Highway and bush pilots of the North.

The museum includes video theatres and a gift shop with a selection of Northern books. Plenty of parking. Admission fee charged. Open daily mid-May to August 31. Phone (867) 668-4792; email info@goytm.ca; or visit www.goytm.ca.

World's largest weathervane. Located in front of the Transportation Museum on the Alaska Highway is the world's largest weathervane—a Douglas DC–3. According to Yukon pilot and aviation historian Bob Cameron, this vintage plane was originally a C-47 that was built in 1942 and flew transport missions in Asia during the war. Converted to civilian life as a DC-3 after the war (Canadian registration CF-CPY), she flew for Canadian Pacific Airlines, Connelly-Dawson Airways, Great Northern Airways and Northward Airlines from 1946 until 1970, when she blew an engine on takeoff and was then

stripped for parts and parked at the Whitehorse airport.

An airlines maintenance engineer named Joe Muff orchestrated the donation of the historic plane to the Yukon Flying club in order to restore it for permanent display at the airport. It is now owned and managed by the Yukon Transportation Museum. The restored plane was mounted on a rotating pedestal in 1981, and acts as a weathervane, pointing its nose into the wind.

Whitehorse Rapids Fishway. Located at the end of Nisutlin Drive in the Riverdale suburb. The fish ladder was built in 1959 to provide access for chinook (king) salmon and other species above the Yukon Energy Corporation hydroelectric dam. It is the longest wooden fish ladder in the world. The fish ladder is flowing from mid-July to early September during salmon-spawning season. Interpretive displays and viewing decks; open daily. Admission by donation. Open 9 A.M. to 7 P.M. daily in summer. Phone (867) 633-5965.

Tour the Yukon's oldest brewery. A popular stop in Whitehorse is the Yukon Brewing Company, located at 102 Copper Rd. They have won national and international

©Courtesy Yukon Brewing Company

recognition for their beer as well as their distinctive labels. Yukon Brewing Company's flagship brands are: Yukon Red, Yukon Gold, and Chilkoot Lager ("Beer worth freezin' for"). Open 11 A.M. to 6 P.M. daily year-round (closed major holidays). For brewery tour

Stop by and try some award winning beers from Canada's oldest brewery north of 60˚. For brewery tour info, please visit: yukonbeer.com or call 867 668 4183.

BEER WORTH FREEZIN' FOR

information and hours, phone (867) 668-4183 or visit www.yukonbeer.com.

Miles Canyon, located on the Yukon River 2 miles south of Whitehorse, was an imposing challenge for miners and stampeders on their way up the Yukon to the gold fields, mainly because the narrow channel through the canyon was followed by the more daunting Whitehorse Rapids. Both Whitehorse Rapids and Squaw Rapids were eliminated by construction of the hydroelectric power plant and dam on the Yukon River at Whitehorse in 1959, which created Schwatka Lake. Miles Canyon is also accessible by road (closed in winter): take Schwatka Lake Road off Robert Service Way (South Access Road) into Whitehorse, or turn off the Alaska Highway (see **Milepost DC 881.7**) and follow signs.

Take a hike with the Yukon Conservation Society. From late June through August, the Yukon Conservation Society (YCS) offers free guided nature walks, ranging in difficulty from easy to strenuous. Trips are 2 to 6 hours in length and informative guides explain the local flora, fauna, geology and history along the trails. Meet at the Miles Canyon bridge for their free 2-hour **Canyon City Historical Nature Hike** offered at 10 A.M. and 2 P.M. Tuesday–Saturday from early June to mid-August. Or pick up a copy of *Hikes & Bikes*, a guide to hiking and mountain biking trails in the Whitehorse area, produced by the Yukon Conservation Society. Contact Yukon Conservation Society at 302 Hawkins St.; phone (867) 668-5678; email hikes@ycs.yk.ca; www.yukonconservation.org.

The Boreal Worlds Trail starts at the end of the student parking lot at Yukon College. The trail leads through an aspen grove, past a beaver pond, and through an area dense with lichen. Free interpretive brochure available at the bookstore.

Play Golf. Mountain View Public Golf Course is accessible via the Porter Creek exit off the Alaska Highway or from Range Road; 18 holes, grass greens; greens fees. Meadow Lakes Golf and Country Club, 5 minutes south of Whitehorse at **Milepost DC 878.3**, has a 9-hole par 36 course, clubhouse, cart and club rentals; phone (867) 668-4653.

Day trips from Whitehorse. Drive north on the Alaska Highway to turnoff onto Klondike Highway 2 (the road to Dawson City) and drive just 3.6 miles/5.8 km from the junction to Takhini Hot Springs Road and for access to **Takhini Hot Springs** and **Yukon Wildlife Preserve.** Takhini Hot Springs (www.takhinihotsprings.com) offers a hot mineral pool, rental cabins, horseback riding, and camping. Yukon Wildlife Preserve (www.yukonwildlife.ca), open daily in summer, offers interpretive bus tours and self-guided walking tours of their 750-acre wildlife park. *(See page 293 in the KLONDIKE LOOP section for details on Takhini Hot Springs Road attractions.)*

Longer day trips—or overnights to allow more sightseeing time—are to Atlin, about 2½ hours 1-way by car, and Skagway, 2 hours 1-way by car. Atlin is famous for its beautiful setting. The Grotto, a natural hot springs, is also a popular destination in the Atlin area. Skagway is a historic gold rush town and port of call for both the Alaska state ferries and cruise ships. Skagway is also home to the famed White Pass & Yukon Route railway, said to be the most scenic railway in the world as it climbs through beautiful mountain terrain to White Pass

Douglas DC-3 weathervane, located in front of the Transportation Museum, is a favorite photo op. *(©Kris Valencia, staff)*

summit. Book ahead for the trip.

Scenery along the South Klondike Highway to Skagway is beautiful. Highlights include Carcross desert, the historic town of Carcross, and Emerald Lake. Tagish Road, another scenic route, connects Atlin Road with the South Klondike Highway and can be used to link these 2 side trips. *See SOUTH KLONDIKE HIGHWAY section and also "Atlin–Tagish–Carcross Scenic Loop" on pages 193–194.*

Paddle the Yukon River. Despite its immensity—the Yukon River measures nearly 2,000 miles/3,218 km—and natural hazards, such as constantly changing weather, channels, islands, sweepers and sand and gravel bars, the Yukon is generally shallow and slow moving, and paddling is relaxing. There is a boat launch at Rotary Peace Park, behind the Yukon Government Building. You may also launch at Deep Creek Campground on Lake Laberge.

Going with a group and guide is recommended for those seeking a relaxing trip.

From Whitehorse to Dawson City it is 467 miles/752 km by river and can take from 14 to 21 days to travel. Yukon River outfitters in Whitehorse are listed under Things To Do/Outdoor Activities/Canoeing & Kayaking at www.travelyukon.com. For information on Yukon River heritage sites, contact the Yukon government Heritage Branch in Whitehorse; phone 1-800-661-0408.

Sportsmen can obtain fishing and hunting regulations online from Environment Yukon at env.gov.yk.ca.

AREA FISHING: Fishing for rainbow trout, kokanee and chinook salmon in the following lakes: **Hidden Lakes** (1 and 3) and **Chadden Lake**, accessible from Chadburn Lake Road in the Riverdale subdivision; **Scout Lake**, access via Old Alaska Highway alignment from **Milepost DC 899.1** Alaska Highway; and **Long Lake**, accessible via Wickstrom Road. Nearby fly-in fishing lakes are accessible by charter plane.

THE TRUE NORTH
FUN & FREE

DAWSON CITY.ca

PERFECTLY YUKON

Photos: Hans G Pfaff, TH Archives, PR Services

Alaska Highway Log
(continued from page 197)

YUKON HIGHWAY 1

artifacts include a cast of the largest woolly mammoth skeleton ever recovered in North America. Open daily, mid-May to late Sept., 9 A.M. to 6 P.M. Winter hours: Open Sundays and Mondays, noon–5 P.M. Phone (867) 667-8855; fax (867) 667-8844; email beringia@gov.yk.ca; www.beringia.com. Admission charged.

The Yukon Beringia Centre, Yukon Transportation Museum. See display ad page 203.

DC 885.8 (1422.6 km) DJ 501.2 (806.6 km) Signed entrance to northeast for Whitehorse Airport (Erik Nielsen Whitehorse International Airport) as well as access to **DC-3 weathervane**, the **Yukon Transportation Museum** and **Yukon Beringia Interpretive Center** (*see descriptions on page 203*).

Cairns in front of the museum commemorate 18 years of service on the Alaska Highway (1946–1964) by the Corps of Royal Canadian Engineers. Near this site, the U.S. Army officially handed over the Alaska Highway to the Canadian Army on April 1, 1946.

DC 886 (1423 km) DJ 501 (806.3 km) FasGas and Airport Chalet to west. Turnoff to east for second entrance northbound to Erik Nielsen Whitehorse International Airport. The airport was built during WWII and used by both U.S. and Canadian forces. Mr. Nielsen was Yukon's longest standing member of Parliament.

DC 887.4 (1425.3 km) DJ 499.6 (804 km) **Historical Milepost 918. Two Mile Hill/ Hamilton Blvd. junction:** 4-lane highway with dedicated center turn lanes approaching traffic light. *This is the first exit southbound, second (and last) exit northbound, for downtown Whitehorse. (First exit northbound is Robert Service Way at Milepost DC 883.7; see page 197.)* Turn to northeast (right-hand turn northbound) and follow Two Mile Hill down to Whitehorse city center via 4th Avenue or 2nd Avenue (*see map page 200*). Access to Canadian Tire, Walmart, Starbucks, gas station via left-hand turn on to 2nd Avenue *or* take the "back way" which is a left-hand turn (no turn light) on to Industrial Road then a right-hand turn on Quartz Road. *CAUTION: Easy to miss overhead traffic light at Range Road. Be alert for overhead stoplights and pedestrian crosswalks in Whitehorse!*

Canada Games Center/Centre Des Jeux Du Canada is up the hill to the west.

Description of Whitehorse begins on page 198. See Vicinity map on page 199, city center map on page 200.

Fair highway surfacing northbound to Haines Junction (98 miles/158 km) with frequent frost heaves, patched pavement or damaged road surface. *Slow for gravel breaks and frost heaves northbound! Watch for horses on highway.*

DC 888.3 (1426.9 km) DJ 498.7 (802.5 km) Prospector Road. FasGas station and restaurant to southwest.

DC 888.7 (1427.4 km) DJ 498.3 (801.9 km) Easy-to-miss entrance to southwest for **Copperbelt Railway & Mining Museum**, a theme park built on the site of the early copper claims. A 2-km/1.2-mile train ride through the park introduces visitors to the early mining and railway history of the area. Free parking. Open daily 10 A.M. to 5

Copperbelt Railway & Mining Museum introduces visitors to mining and rail history on a 2-km-/1.2-mile-long train ride. (©*Judy Nadon, staff*)

P.M. (seasonal). Phone (867) 667-6355. www.yukonrails.com.

DC 889.2 (1428.3 km) DJ 497.8 (801.1 km) Fish Lake Road to west makes an interesting side trip; panoramic views from above tree line.

DC 890.1 (1429.3 km) DJ 496.9 (799.7 km) Rabbit's Foot Canyon.

DC 890.3 (1429.7 km) DJ 496.7 (799.3 km) Porter Creek subdivision.

DC 890.8 (1430.7 km) DJ 496.2 (798.5 km) Tempo gas station and a grocery store. Supermarkets are scarce northbound with only one (Little Green Apple in Haines Junction) between here and Tok on the Alaska Highway. There are several convenience stores attached to gas stations.

DC 891.1 (1431.4 km) DJ 495.9 (798.1 km) Wann Road; gas, convenience store, lodging.

DC 891.4 (1431.9 km) DJ 495.6 (797.6 km) Motel, gas, convenience store.

DC 891.8 (1432 km) DJ 495.2 (796.9 km) Historical Mile 922. Gas/diesel, propane; motel; licensed restaurant.

DC 894.1 (1436.3 km) DJ 492.9 (793.2 km) Cousins airstrip road to northeast.

DC 894.2 (1436.5 km) DJ 492.8 (793.1 km) Double-ended rest area to northeast with large gravel parking area, interpretive signs, litter bins and outhouses.

DC 894.5 (1437 km) DJ 492.5 (792.6 km) **Junction** with Klondike Highway 2 to **Takhini Hot Springs** and **Yukon Wildlife Preserve**, 10 miles/16 km; **Dawson City**, 323 miles/520 km; and the Top of the World Highway to Alaska. Dawson City is a wonderfully preserved piece of the Klondike Gold Rush and travelers should not miss visiting this iconic gold rush town. Drive Klondike Highway 2 north 323 miles/520 km from here to Dawson City and return the same way, or take the 498-mile/801 km Klondike Loop route from here or from Tetlin Junction at **Milepost DC 1266.7.**

A description of Klondike Highway 2 and the KLONDIKE LOOP section begins on page 288, with mile-by-mile logs of these routes. The

Dawson City description begins on page 302.

Junction with Klondike Highway 2 to Dawson City. See KLONDIKE LOOP section on page 288 for log of this route.

For Alaska-bound travelers, the highway now swings west.

DC 894.7 (1437.2 km) DJ 492.3 (792.3 km) Distance marker northbound shows Haines Junction 144 km/89 miles, Fairbanks 946 miles/588 miles.

Distance marker southbound shows Whitehorse City Center 12 km/7 miles, Teslin 194 km/121 miles.

DC 896.9 (1440.8 km) DJ 490.1 (788.7 km) Whitehorse city limits.

DC 897.6 (1442 km) DJ 489.4 (787.6 km) Gardner Road.

DC 897.8 (1442.3 km) DJ 489.2 (787.3 km) Husky Trail.

DC 899.1 (1443.8 km) DJ 487.9 (785.2 km) South access to 3-mile/4.8-km loop drive on Old Alaska Highway (Mile 929 to Mile 934). Access to **Scout Lake** via unmaintained road that intersects Old Alaska Highway at gravel pit, according to Yukon Environment's angler's guide. Fishing from shore for rainbow trout and small chinook salmon.

DC 901.9 (1448.2 km) DJ 485.1 (780.7 km) North access to 3-mile/4.8 km loop drive on Old Alaska Highway (Mile 934 to Mile 929).

DC 905.4 (1454.1 km) DJ 481.6 (775 km) **Historic Milepost 937.** Viewpoint turnout to north with litter bins and point-of-interest sign about the old Dawson Trail. There were at least 50 stopping places along the old Dawson Trail winter stagecoach route between Whitehorse and Dawson City, and from 1 to 3 roadhouses at each stop. At this point, the stagecoach route crossed the Takhini River. This route was discontinued in 1950 when the Mayo–Dawson Road (now Klondike Highway 2) was constructed.

DC 914 (1467.9 km) DJ 473 (761.2 km) **Takhini Salt Flats**, a series of bowl-shaped depressions where salts form on the surface as water brought up from underground springs evaporates. Although alkaline flats are not uncommon in the Yukon, this one is notable for the size of its salt crystals as well as the variety of salt-loving plants that thrive here, such as the distinctive red sea asparagus.

DC 914.7 (1468.9 km) DJ 472.3 (760.1 km) Historic Milepost 946. Takhini River bridge. According to R. Coutts in *Yukon: Places & Names*, the name Takhini derives from the Tagish Indian *tahk*, meaning mosquito, and *heena*, meaning river.

DC 916.6 (1472 km) DJ 470.4 (757 km) Distance marker southbound shows Whitehorse 50 km/30 miles, Watson Lake 496 km/308 miles.

DC 917 (1472.6 km) DJ 470 (756.4 km) Distance marker northbound shows Haines Junction 109 km/67 miles, Fairbanks 910 km/565 miles.

CAUTION: Watch for elk (Takhini Valley Elk Herd) next 20 km/12 miles northbound. Also watch for horses and other livestock grazing on open range near highway. The elk were introduced in 1951–1954 from Elk Island National Park.

DC 923.9 (1481 km) DJ 463.1 (745.3 km) Annie Ned Creek. Named for Yukon's revered native storyteller, the late Annie Ned. Ned was awarded the Order of Canada.

DC 924.5 (1484.8 km) DJ 462.5 (744.3 km) Stoney Creek.

DC 924.7 (1485.2 km) DJ 462.3 (744 km) View of Mount Bratnober, elev. 6,313 feet/1,924m. According to R. Coutts in *Yukon: Places & Names*, the mountain was named in 1897 by J.J. McArthur, Canadian government surveyor, for Henry Bratnober, who along with Jack Dalton was assisting in a cursory survey of the Dalton Trail.

DC 926 (1487 km) DJ 461 (741.9 km) Takhini Burn rest area. Turnout to south with litter bins, outhouses and viewing platform with information panels on wildlife found in the Takhini River Valley and the 1958 Takhini Burn. More than 1.5 million acres/629,058 hectares of Yukon forest lands were burned in 1958. Campfires were responsible for most of these fires.

DC 927.3 (1489.2 km) DJ 459.7 (739.8 km) Historic Milepost 960. Turnoff to south for beautiful **Kusawa Lake** via winding, hard-packed dirt/gravel road, fairly wide, that leads 14.7 miles/23 km to Kusawa (pronounced KOO-sa-wa) Lake campground; log follows. Access road is slippery when wet; short, steep stretch at Mile 8.7; watch for soft spots; and stay away from edge above river. Not recommended for large RVs or trailers. (The road was constructed by the U.S. Army in 1945 to obtain bridge timbers for Alaska Highway construction.)

©Kris Valencia, staff

Drive in 1.4 miles/3 km to Mendenhall Landing, a freight transfer point in the early 1900s for goods shipped up the Yukon and Takhini rivers. From here, goods were loaded onto wagons headed for Kluane mining operations. Today the landing is a pull-out point for canoeists. There's room to turn

around here for motorists who do not wish to continue on this side road.

At Mile 9/15 km on the side road is **Takhini River Yukon government campground**, with 13 sites, and a put-in point for canoeists.

Continue to end of road for access to **Kusawa Lake Yukon government campground** and boat launch at north end of lake. The campground has 48 sites, kitchen shelter, firepits and drinking water. Camping permit ($12). Fishing for lake trout to 20 lbs., is good to excellent; fishing also for Arctic grayling and pike.

DC 935.9 (1502.2 km) DJ 451.1 (726 km) End of 911 access area northbound.

DC 936.8 (1503.7 km) DJ 450.2 (724.5 km) Mendenhall River culvert. A tributary of the Takhini River, the Mendenhall River—like the Mendenhall Glacier outside Juneau, AK—was named for Thomas Corwin Mendenhall (1841–1924), superintendent of the U.S. Coast & Geodetic Survey.

DC 937.2 (1504.4 km) DJ 449.8 (723.9 km) Turnoff for south access road to First Nations community of **CHAMPAGNE** (population 25). There is a rest area 0.3 km/0.2 mile west on the Champagne access road. Continue southwest on access road about 8 km/5 miles for **The Long Ago Peoples Place**, a First Nations Heritage attraction that re-creates a traditional village; open May through September; phone (867) 634-7047; yukonfirstnationculture.com/.

Champagne was originally a campsite on the Dalton Trail to Dawson City, established by Jack Dalton in the late 1800s, a roadhouse and trading post were built at Champagne in 1902. It became a supply center for first the Bullion Creek gold rush and later the Burwash Creek gold rush in 1904. The origin of the name is uncertain, although one account is that Dalton's men—after successfully negotiating a herd of cattle through the first part of the trail—celebrated here with a bottle of French champagne.

Northbound, motorists are driving the Champagne Bypass, an 8.6-mile/13.9-km section of the Alaska Highway completed in 2002, which rerouted the Alaska Highway around Champagne, which was formerly **Historical Mile 974** on the Alaska Highway.

DC 945.7 (1518.2 km) DJ 441.3 (710.2 km) Turnoff for north access road to Champagne (see description above).

DC 951 (1527 km) DJ 436 (701.6 km) Distance marker southbound shows Whitehorse 108 km/67 miles, Watson Lake 564 km/350 miles.

DC 955.8 (1532.8 km) DJ 431.2 (693.9 km) First glimpse northbound of Kluane Range.

DC 957 (1534.8 km) DJ 430 (692 km) Historic Milepost 987. Cracker Creek. Former roadhouse site on old stagecoach trail. Watch for Old Man Mountain on right northbound (the rocky crags look like a face, particularly in evening light).

DC 964.7 (1546 km) DJ 422.3 (679.8 km) Historical Mile 995: Otter Falls Cutoff, **junction** with Aishihik Road; RV park, cafe, convenience store, gas/diesel, at junction.

Aishihik Road side trip leads north 26.1 miles/42.2 km to Aishihik Lake campground and 73 miles/117 km to the old Indian village of Aishihik (pronounced ay-jhee-ack; means "high place"). This is a narrow, winding gravel road, maintained for summer

travel only to the government campground at the lake. There are some steep hills and single-lane bridges. Aishihik Road is not recommended for large RVs or trailers. *CAUTION: Watch for bison on road. Be alert for bears in area.*

At Mile 17.4/28 km Viewpoint for **Otter Falls**, a double-ended turnout with litter bins and point-of-interest sign, short steep path to water. Otter Falls was once pictured on the back of the Canadian $5 bill, but in 1975 the Aishihik Power Plant diverted water from the falls. The 32-megawatt dam was built by Northern Canada Power Commission to supply power principally to the mining industry. Water is still released over the falls during the summer; flow hours are posted.

At Mile 17.5/28.2 km is Otter Falls Recreation Site, a day-use area on lake with large parking area, picnic tables, picnic shelter and outhouse.

At Mile 26.1/42.2 km is the turnoff for Aishihik Lake Yukon government campground, located at the south end of the lake; 16 sites, drinking water, picnic tables, firepits, kitchen shelter and boat launch. Camping permit ($12).

Aishihik Lake, fishing for lake trout and Arctic grayling. As with most large Yukon lakes, ice is not out until late June. Low water levels may make boat launching difficult. *WARNING: Winds can come up suddenly on this lake.* **Pole Cat Lake**, just before the Aishihik weather station; fishing for pike.

DC 965.6 (1547.5 km) DJ 421.4 (678.1 km) Historic Milepost 996. Turnoff to north at east end of Canyon Creek bridge for rest area; toilets. Interpretive signs (excerpt follows) about **Historic Canyon Creek Bridge**, a favorite photo op.

©Kris Valencia, staff

"In 1903, a gold strike in the Alsek River drainage brought a stampede of miners to the area. A wagon road was built from Whitehorse in the next year and Sam McGee and Gilbert Skelly constructed a substantial bridge over Canyon Creek. This bridge survived heavy traffic and high springs floods until the 1920s, when the government contracted the Jacquot brothers from Burwash Landing to rebuild it. In 1942, during construction of the Alaska Highway, the old bridge was dismantled and a new one built in 18 days. [Although most of the first American military bridges were of temporary pontoon and plank construction, the Canyon Creek bridge mimicked the original style.]"

The pioneer bridge was left in place when a permanent bridge was built just downriver. Restoration was done in 1986–87 and 2005.

Highway climbs northbound.

DC 965.7 (1547.7 km) DJ 421.3 (678 km) Aishihik River bridge.

DC 966.3 (1548.7 km) DJ 420.7 (677 km) View of impressive Kluane Range icefields straight ahead northbound between Kilometerposts 1550 and 1562.

DC 974.9 (1560.1 km) DJ 412.1 (663.2 km) Turnout on Marshall Creek.

An oft photographed monument affectionately named "animal cupcake" includes wildlife seen locally (top left); Our Lady of the Way church built using a discarded quonset structure (bottom left); view of junction/turn to continue on route (above). (©Kris Valencia, staff; ©Claire Torgerson, staff)

DC 976.9 (1566 km) **DJ 410.1** (660 km) Double-ended rest area to east with interpretive signs, outhouses and litter bins to northeast.

View northbound of the rugged snow-capped peaks of the Kluane Icefield Ranges and the outer portion of the St. Elias Mountains to the west. The Kluane National Park Icefield Ranges are Canada's highest and the world's largest nonpolar alpine ice field, forming the interior wilderness of the park. In clear weather, Mount Kennedy and Mount Hubbard, 2 peaks that are twice as high as the front ranges seen before you, are visible from here.

DC 979.3 (1569.8 km) **DJ 407.7** (656.1 km) Between Kilometerposts 1570 and 1572, look for the NorthwesTel microwave repeater station on top of Paint Mountain. The station was installed with the aid of helicopters and supplied by a tramline.

DC 980.8 (1572.1 km) **DJ 406.2** (653.7 km) Turnoff to north for **Pine Lake Yukon government campground and recreation area.** Day-use area with gravel parking area, sandy beach, boat launch, dock, group firepits, picnic tables, outhouses, playground and drinking water. The campground, on a 0.3-mile-loop road off the beach access road, has 42 treed sites, outhouses, firewood, litter bins, kitchen shelter, playground and drinking water. Camping permit ($12). Fishing is good for lake trout, northern pike and Arctic grayling. *CAUTION: Bears in area.*

A short nature trail winds through the boreal forest from the beach to the campground. Panels along the trail interpret the lake's aquatic habitats and marl formations. A 3.5-mile/6-km walking and biking trail begins at the campground entrance and ends at Haines Junction.

DC 982.2 (1575 km) **DJ 404.8** (651.4 km) Turnoff to north for Haines Junction airport. **Private Aircraft:** Haines Junction airstrip; elev. 2,150 feet/655m; length 5,500 feet/ 1,676m; gravel; fuel (100L). Flightseeing tours of glaciers, fly-in fishing and air char-

ters available; fixed-wing and helicopters.

Highway swings southwest approaching Haines Junction, offering a panoramic view of the Auriol Range ahead northbound.

DC 984.1 (1577.1 km) **DJ 402.9** (648.4 km) Welcome to Haines Junction sign northbound. *Slow for posted speed zone northbound through Haines Junction.*

DC 984.7 (1578 km) **DJ 402.3** (647 km) On the south side of the highway is **Da Kų Cultural Center**, which houses the Kluane National Park and Haines Junction visitor information desks; natural history displays, First Nations cultural displays, gift shop and very nice public restrooms. On the north side of the highway is: **FasGas** with 24-hour gas/diesel, convenience store and a summer RV park behind the station; and **Little Green Apple** grocery store with an ATM and a surprisingly extensive variety of grocery items to fit every taste.

Da Ku Cultural Centre. See display ad pages 210.

FasGas & RV Park. See display ad pages 211.

Little Green Apple. See display ad pages 211.

DC 985 (1578.5 km) **DJ 402** (646.9 km) **Historic Milepost 1016. Junction** of Alaska Highway and with the Haines Highway which leads 146 miles/246 km south to Haines, AK. Haines Junction wildlife monument to south, a favourite photo op. Top Spot/North 60 Petro Express; gas/diesel station with 24-hour self-serve and convenience store/espresso bar.

Top Spot/North 60 Petro Express. See display ad pages 211.

IMPORTANT: This junction can be confusing; choose your route carefully! Fairbanks- and Anchorage-bound travelers turn right (north) at this junction for continuation of Alaska Highway (Yukon 1). Haines, AK-bound motorists continue straight ahead. (Haines, AK-bound motorists note: It is a good idea to fill up with gas before leaving Haines Junction.)

Alaska Highway log continues on page 213.

Junction of Alaska Highway and Haines Highway (Haines Road). Head west on the Haines Highway (Yukon Highway 3) for port of Haines, AK. See HAINES HIGHWAY section.

Haines Junction

DC 985 (1578.5 km) **DJ 402** (646.9 km) **F 498** (801.4 km) **Historic Milepost 1016**, at the junction of the Alaska Highway (Yukon Highway 1) and the Haines Highway (Yukon Highway 3, also known as the Haines Road). Driving distance to Whitehorse, 100 miles/161 km; YT–AK border, 205 miles/330 km; Tok, 296 miles/476 km; and Haines, 151 miles/242 km. **Population:** 824. **Elevation:** 2,044 feet/623m. **Emergency Services:** Dial 911. **RCMP**, phone (867) 634-5555 or (867) 667-5555. **Fire Department**, phone (867) 634-2222. **Health Center**, phone (867) 634-4444.

Visitor Information: Available at the

HAINES JUNCTION ADVERTISERS

Welcome to the Village of

Surrounded by a beautiful and rugged landscape, Haines Junction is truly a wilderness town and offers exceptional outdoor experiences for visitors and residents alike. We invite you to stop and become immersed in the vast and spectacular wilderness year 'round, while enjoying all the amenities of home.

Winter brings Snowmobile races, hockey tournaments, bonspiels, sled dog races, family ski functions, and come MAY we ramp up the volume so you can join us as you travel through: St. Elias Lion's Club Annual Jorg Schneider Memorial Poker run; the Vancouver International Mountain Film Festival.

JUNE   Kluane Mountain Blue Grass Festival; Kluane Chilkat Intnl Bike Relay; National Parks Day; National Aboriginal Day   JULY   Canada Day Celebrations   AUGUST: Augusto! Children's Festival; Campfire Talks/ Interpretive Walks in Kluane National Park; Coffee House Fridays at The Village Bakery; Tachai Dhal Visitor Centre **SEPTEMBER Northern Nights, Kluane's Annual** Dark Sky Festival OCTOBER Hallowe'en bonfire and Fireworks   NOVEMBER Christmas Crafts Sale

DECEMBER Skate with Santa; Homecoming Hockey Tournament

Check our website www.hainesjunctionyukon.com for dates, times and details then come join the fun! We'll look forward to seeing you soon.

Haines Junction Visitors Information Centre
We can help you find your way.

Parks Canada   Parcs Canada

Da Ku Cultural Centre

YUKON
LARGER THAN LIFE

280 Alaska Highway (Milepost 1016) Haines Junction, Yukon

Hours of Operation
May – Sept   8am-8pm
7 days a week

Village of Haines Junction • Box 5339 • Haines Junction,

Haines Junction

"Gateway to Kluane"

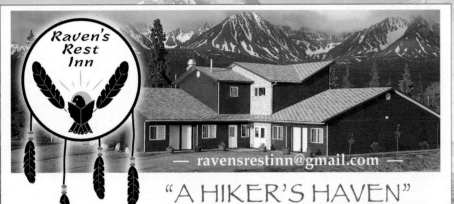

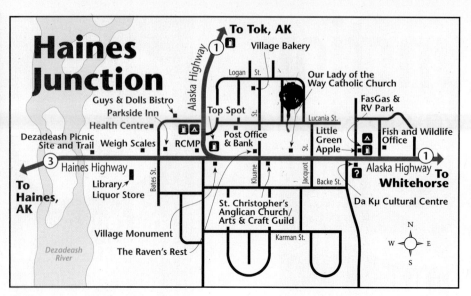

Haines Junction

Yukon Government (YTG) Visitor Information Center and at Kluane National Park and Reserve Visitor Center, both located in the Da Kų building on the Alaska Highway in Haines Junction. The center also features art by artisans throughout the territory and art from the Yukon Permanent Collection.

At the Da Kų Cultural Center, Yukon Government Tourism staff is on hand to provide Yukon travel information on events and activities, lodging, ferry information and more. Tourism Yukon is open May 1 to Sept. 30, from 8 A.M. to 6 P.M. daily (hours/days subject to change); hours are 10 A.M. to 6 P.M. during shoulder season. For more information (May–September) phone (867) 634-2345 or email vic.hainesjunction@gov.yk.ca. Year-round phone (867) 634-7250 or email: vacation@gov.yk.ca.

Also at the Da Kų Center, Kluane Park Visitor Center is open mid-May to early September, 9 A.M. to 7 P.M. daily during peak season; 9 A.M. to 5 P.M. during shoulder season (hours/days subject to change). Phone Parks Canada at (867) 634-7207 (April–October). Phone year round 1-800-661-0494 or email kluane.info@pc.gc.ca.

Private Aircraft: The airport is located on the Alaska Highway just east of town; see description at **Milepost DC 982.2. Radio:** CBC North at 106.1 FM; 103.5 FM; CKRW 98.7 FM; CHON 90.5 FM.

Haines Junction is an important stop for travelers on the Alaska and Haines highways. Services are located along both highways, and clustered around the junction. For a relatively small community, Haines Junction has a lot going on. Surrounded by a beautiful and rugged landscape, the town offers both exceptional outdoor experiences and plenty of amenities for the traveler.

Haines Junction is on the eastern boundary of Kluane (pronounced kloo-WA-nee) National Park and Reserve. The park was first suggested in 1942, and in 1943 land was set aside and designated the Kluane Game Sanctuary. A formal park region was established in 1972, and the national park and reserve boundaries were official in 1976. Kluane National Park and Reserve encompasses extensive ice fields, mountains and wilderness, and has become a world-class wilderness destination among outdoor recreation enthusiasts. Kluane National Park and Reserve, Tatshenshini–Alsek Wilderness Park, and Alaska's Glacier Bay National Park

and Wrangell–St. Elias National Park, are a joint UNESCO World Heritage Site and the largest internationally protected area in the world.

Haines Junction was established in 1942, during construction of the Alaska Highway, as an Army barracks for the U.S. Army Corps of Engineers. The engineers were to build a new branch road connecting the Alaska Highway with the port of Haines on Lynn Canal. The branch road—today's Haines Highway—was completed in 1943.

Today, Haines Junction is also the southern point of the Alaska Highway portion of the Shakwak Project, a massive reconstruction that includes approximately 300 miles/500 km of the Alaska Highway between Haines Junction and the Alaska border.

In the 1940s, civilian contractors were employed to reconstruct the Alaska Highway behind the U.S. military. Later, responsibility for the highway was passed to the Canadian Army, then Public Works Canada, and finally, Yukon Highways and Public Works.

By the 1970s, the southern sections of the Alaska Highway in Canada had been vastly improved, but the highway north of Haines Junction had received relatively little attention. Because about 85 percent of the traffic volume north of Haines Junction was of American origin, the U.S. agreed to fund reconstruction of this section of road, signing the Shakwak Agreement in 1977. The goal was to bring the road up to a modern 2-lane, 60-mph/100-kmph standard, but permafrost continues to be a major challenge for road maintenance north of Destruction Bay.

Lodging & Services

Visitor services include lodging at the **Parkside Inn, The Raven's Rest, Mount Logan Lodge** and others; gas/diesel stations (**FasGas, North 60 Petro Express,** Kluane RV); and limited garage services. Fast-food and fountain drinks at Frosty's. Dining at the **Village Bakery & Deli** and at **The Raven's Rest.** An extensive selection of international grocery items available at **Little Green Apple.** Convenience stores at **North 60 Petro Express/Top Spot** and at **FasGas.** There is an indoor heated swimming pool with showers; open daily from May to late-August, fee charged.

The James Smith Administration Build-

ing, at Kilometer 255.6 Haines Road, 0.2 mile/0.3 km south from the Alaska Highway junction, contains the government liquor store and public library. Outside the building is a dogsled sculpture—*Homeward Bound*—by local artist Bob Braun.

There is a post office, RCMP office, Lands and Forest District Office and health center. The bank, adjacent the post office, is open weekday afternoons and can provide ATM-like services via the teller; extended hours on Fridays. Internet access available at the library.

Camping

RV camping at **FasGas RV Park** (across from entrance to Da Kų Cultural Center) and Kluane RV. Pine Lake Yukon government campground is located 4.2 miles/6.7 km east of junction on the Alaska Highway. Kluane National Park has one campground, Kathleen Lake campground, located 16 miles/27 km south of town on the Haines Highway; basic facilities, first-come/first-served. Dump stations and water are available at local service stations and at the private campgrounds.

Attractions

Da Kų "Our House" Cultural Center, located along the Alaska Highway across from FasGas, features Champagne and Aishihik First Nations cultural exhibits reflecting the lifestyles and traditional identity of Southern Tutchone people. Guided tours, campfire talks, traditional artwork and cultural artifacts are also found at the center.

This center also houses the **Kluane National Park and Reserve Visitor Center,** and Tourism Yukon Information Center, information desk, interpretive exhibits, displays and a 25-minute feature film on the National Park. Check at the center for details on the park's numerous hiking trails and for a schedule of National Park led interpretive events as well as Yukon-wide travel information and planning assistance. Parks Canada at the Da Kų Cultural Center hours are 9 A.M. to 5 P.M. daily from mid-May to first week in June and for the month of September; open 9 A.M. to 7 P.M. daily from second week in June through August. It closes for the season the third week in September.

Kluane National Park activities also take place at Thachäl Dhäl Visitor Center at Sheep Mountain on the Alaska Highway; see **Milepost DC 1028.8** this section. (Kathleen Lake Campground on the Haines Highway, 16 miles/26 km west of Haines Junction, is the only established campground within Kluane National Park.) NOTE: *Backcountry travelers must register for any overnight trip into the park.* To register, please be at one of the two visitor centers a minimum of one hour before closing. Bear-resistant food canisters are mandatory on overnight hikes; a $100 deposit is required. Nightly or annual wilderness permits may be purchased.

Interpretive programs in Kluane National Park begin in June and continue through August. Fees may apply.

Contact Kluane National Park and Reserve at Box 5495, Haines Junction, YT Y0B 1L0, or phone (867) 634-7207, fax (867) 634-7208; www.parkscanada.gc.ca/kluane; kluane.info@pc.gc.ca for park-related information. For Tourism, contact Tourism Yukon VIC, Box 2032, Haines Junction, YT Y0B 1L0 or phone (867) 634-7207 (summer only), (867) 634-7250 (year-round); email vic.hainesjunction@gov.yk.ca (May–September).

The **Junction Community Market** is held on the grounds of the Da Kų Cultural Center in summer, every other Wednesday from 4–6 P.M.

The **Village Monument** is probably the most photographed spot in Haines Junction. The 24-foot-high sculpture—nicknamed "The Muffin" or "Animal Cupcake"—is located at the junction of the Haines and Alaska highways. Area wildlife is depicted in close to life-size detail on a sculpted mountain.

St. Christopher's Anglican Church. Unique, quaint, and welcoming describes St. Christopher's octagonal log church situated in the heart of Haines Junction. The current church was constructed in the early 1990s by local volunteers, replacing the old church structure established after the completion of the Alaska Highway. Visitors are welcome to explore the interior of the church for a historic tour or stroll the prayer garden and labyrinth during the spring and summer months. St. Christopher's remains a mission parish supported by the Anglican Church of Canada welcoming all to join in Sunday worship services (hours posted).

The **Arts and Craft Guild of Haines Junction** offers an exceptional selection of fine art and craft work. This includes beading, jewelry, textile arts, cards, photography, lino cut prints, original art, woodwork, books, pottery, collage and T-shirts. Items for all budgets and something for everyone. All work is locally made in the Haines Junction area. Located in the basement of the log church (St. Christopher's).

The **St. Elias Convention Center** houses a 3,000-square-foot Grand Hall, the municipal offices, a growing collection of artwork and a local history exhibit depicting significant events of the Kluane region since 1890.

Our Lady of the Way Catholic Mission is a local landmark and visitor attraction. Services are held on Sunday (check posted hours). Sign at the church reads:

"The church was built in 1954 by Father E. Morriset O.M.I., the first Catholic priest to preach the Gospel in the area. Resources were scarce and Father Morriset ingeniously converted an old quanset (sic) hut, which had been used by the American Army during construction of the Alaska Highway, into the distinctively beautiful church you see. It has the distinction of being the most photographed church in the Yukon."

Special events. (For specific dates and details, go to www.hainesjunctionyukon.com.) Spring events in May include the **St. Elias Lion's Club Annual Jorg Schneider Memorial Poker Run** and the **Vancouver International Mountain Film Festival.** Summer events begin in June with the **Kluane Mountain Bluegrass Festival** (www.yukonbluegrass.com for 2019 dates) and the **Kluane to Chilkat International Bike Relay**, scheduled around summer solstice, the third week of June. This Bike Relay draws more than 1,000 participants. Teams of 2, 4 and 8 bicyclists, as well as solo cyclists, ride in the 8-leg race, totaling 148 miles/238 km, from Haines Junction to Haines, AK. *Watch for cyclists on the highway!*

Canada Day (the anniversary of Canada's confederation) is celebrated on July 1st with a parade, barbecue, afternoon sports activities and an evening movie.

The annual **Children's Festival** takes place the second weekend in August. **Coffee House Fridays** at The Village Bakery also take place in August.

Winter brings snowmobile races, hockey tournaments, bonspiels, sled dog races, and

The Kluane Ranges are still snow-covered and trees are just leafing out in early June along the Alaska Highway in Kluane country. *(©Kris Valencia, staff)*

family ski functions. Other events include Northern Nights, Kluane's Annual Dark Sky Festival (September); Halloween bonfire and fireworks (October); Christmas Crafts Sale (November); and Skate with Santa and Homecoming Hockey Tournament (December).

Flightseeing Kluane National Park by fixed-wing aircraft or helicopter from Haines Junction is a popular way to see the spectacular mountain scenery. Check with the Visitor Center for flightseeing companies.

Tatshenshini–Alsek Wilderness Park. Created in 1993, the park protects the magnificent Tatshenshini and Alsek rivers area in Canada, where the 2 rivers join and flow (as the Alsek) to the Gulf of Alaska at Dry Bay. Known to river runners as "the Tat," the Tatshenshini is famous for its whitewater rafting, stunning scenery and wildlife. Due to a dramatic increase in river traffic in recent years, permits are required from the park agencies (the National Park Service in Alaska and B.C. Parks in Canada). For more information about the park, contact BC Parks, Tatshenshini Office, Box 5544, Haines Junction, YT Y0B 1L0; phone (867) 634-4248, fax (867) 634-2108.

The **Dezadeash River** offers a relaxed rafting experience. Picnicking and hiking trail are available at a day-use area on the river at the west edge of town on the Haines Highway.

Alaska Highway Log
(continued from page 209)

YUKON HIGHWAY 1 NORTH
Distance from Dawson Creek (DC) is followed by distance from Delta Junction (DJ). Original mileposts are indicated in the text as Historical Mile.
In the Canada portion of *The MILEPOST®* Alaska Highway log, mileages from Dawson Creek are based on actual driving distance and kilometers are based on physical kiloposts.

DC 985 (1578.5 km) **DJ 402** (646.9 km) **Junction** of the Alaska Highway (Yukon Highway 1) and the Haines Highway (Yukon Highway 3); **North 60 Petro Express/Top Spot** gas/diesel station, 24-hour self-serve

and convenience store/espresso bar.

Top Spot/North 60 Petro Express. See display ad pages 211.

Junction with the Haines Highway (Yukon Highway 3), which leads southwest 152 miles/246 km to Haines, AK. See the HAINES HIGHWAY section for log of that route.

NOTE: This junction can be confusing; choose your route carefully! Alaska-bound travelers turn right (west); Whitehorse-bound travelers turn left (east) at stop sign for continuation of Alaska Highway (Yukon Highway 1). Haines-bound motorists go south on the Haines Highway (Yukon Highway 3) to the port of Haines, AK, 152 miles/246 km from here. Haines-bound motorists note: It is a good idea to fill up with gas before leaving Haines Junction.

Next gas northbound at the Talbot Arm Motel in Destruction Bay (66 miles/106 km). Fair to good road conditions northbound to Burwash Landing (76 miles/122 km) with long stretches of improved highway, but slow down for frost heaves.

DC 985.1 (1578.9 km) **DJ 401.9** (646.8 km) Distance marker northbound shows Destruction Bay 108 kms/67 miles, Fairbanks 822 kms/510 miles. Beaver Creek is 295 kms/183 miles.

DC 985.3 (1579.3 km) **DJ 401.7** (646.4 km) Kluane RV campground; gas/diesel.

DC 985.9 (1580 km) **DJ 401.1** (645.5 km) Motel next door to Source Motors service station with 24-hour cardlock gas/diesel.

DC 988.3 (1584 km) **DJ 398.7** (641.6 km) Large paved rest area to west with litter bins and toilets.

DC 990.9 (1588 km) **DJ 396.1** (637.4 km) Beautiful views to southwest of the snow-covered Kluane Ranges as the Alaska Highway parallels the **Kluane Ranges** from Haines Junction to Koidern, presenting a nearly unbroken chain of mountains to 8,000 feet/2,438m interrupted by only a few large valleys cut by glacier-fed rivers and streams. West of the Kluane Ranges is the Duke Depression, a narrow trough separating the Kluane Ranges from the

Magnificent Kluane Lake is breathtaking from the road or from the air. (©Judy Nadon, staff)

St. Elias Mountains. Major peaks in the St. Elias (not visible from the highway) are: Mount Logan, Canada's highest peak, at 19,545 feet/5,959m; Mount St. Elias, 18,008 feet/5,489m; Mount Lucania, 17,147 feet/5,226m; King Peak, 16,971 feet/5,173m; and Mounts Wood, Vancouver, Hubbard and Steele, all over 15,000 feet/4,572m. Mount Steele (16,664 feet/5,079m) was named for Superintendent Sam Steele of the North West Mounted Police. As commanding officer of the NWMP in Yukon in 1898, Steele established permanent detachments at the summits of the White and Chilkoot passes to ensure not only that gold stampeders obeyed Canadian laws, but also had sufficient supplies to carry them through to the gold fields.

DC 991.2 (1588.5 km) Turnoff to west for **Mount Logan Lodge & Expeditions**.

Mount Logan Lodge & Expeditions. See display ad on page 211.

DC 991.4 (1589 km) **DJ 395.6** (636.6 km) Trailhead to west for Alsek Pass trail; 18 miles/29 km long, suitable for shorter day hikes, mountain bikes permitted.

DC 991.6 (1589.1 km) **DJ 395.4** (636.3 km) **Historic Milepost 1022**, Mackintosh Trading Post historic sign.

Highway makes gradual climb northbound to Bear Creek Summit.

DC 999 (1596.7 km) **DJ 388** (624.4 km) **Spruce Beetle Trail Interpretive Site** to northeast; rest area with toilets, litter bins and interpretive trail. The 1-mile/1.7-km trail is an easy loop that examines the life of the spruce bark beetle and its effect on area forests. Allow 35 to 45 minutes for walk.

Millions of acres of northern spruce forests were infested by the spruce beetle (*Dendroctonus refipennis*) during the 1990s. Damage to the tree begins when the female spruce beetle bores through the spruce bark and lays eggs in the tree's tissue layer—called the phloem—on which the larvae and adult beetles feed. The tree attempts to fight back by exuding resin at the entrance site of the attacking beetle. Trees that are under attack can be identified by this resin, as well as by accumulations of reddish-brown dust on the bark and on the ground below the tree. Dead trees may continue to host beetles.

Spruce beetles do not attack any tree species other than spruce. Small colonies of these beetles are always present in spruce forests, but under certain conditions their numbers suddenly swell to epidemic, and destructive, proportions. Many scientists blame global warming.

DC 1000.1 (1598.6 km) **DJ 386.9** (622.6 km) **Bear Creek Summit** (elev. 3,294 feet/1,004m), highest point on the Alaska Highway between Whitehorse and Fairbanks.

DC 1000.3 (1599 km) **DJ 386.7** (622.3 km) Double-ended, long turnout to west.

DC 1003.5 (1608.3 km) **DJ 383.5** (617.2 km) **Historic Milepost 1035**. Jarvis River bridge. Slow down for easy-to-miss turnout to west just north of crossing **Jarvis River**. Pretty spot for a picnic. Poor to fair fishing for Arctic grayling 8 to 16 inches all summer; Dolly Varden 8 to 10 inches, early summer.

DC 1007.2 (1614.2 km) **DJ 379.8** (611.2 km) Turnoff on short dirt and gravel access road (muddy in wet weather, potholed) to northeast for **Sulphur Lake**; canoeing, bird watching. Turnaround space at lake may be muddy and rutted in wet weather. Thousands of birds use the lake, mostly in late summer, for molting. Look for bald eagle nests along shore. Wolf pack in area.

DC 1015.7 (1628 km) **DJ 371.3** (597.5 km) Double-ended turnout to southwest with view of Kluane Range.

DC 1017.2 (1630.4 km) **DJ 369.8** (595.1 km) Christmas Creek.

Highway climbs northbound to Boutillier Summit.

DC 1019.5 (1633 km) **DJ 367.5** (591.4 km) First glimpse of Kluane Lake for northbound travelers at **Boutillier Summit** (elev. 3,293 feet/1,003m), second highest point on the highway between Whitehorse and Fairbanks.

DC 1020 (1635 km) **DJ 367** (590.6 km) **Kluane Lake Viewpoint** to east; double-ended turnout with litter bins, outhouse and interpretive signs on Kluane Lake and First Nations (excerpts follow).

"Between 300 and 400 years ago, Kaskawulsh Glacier advanced across the Slims River and closed the drainage outlet of Kluane Lake. The water level rose more than 10m/30 feet and the lake's drainage reversed. Water that had flowed south to the Gulf of Alaska carved out a new channel at the northeast end of the lake to connect with the Yukon River system. Instead of travelling 225 km/140 miles south to the Pacific Ocean, Kluane Lake waters began a journey 10 times longer: north to the Bering Sea.

"When the waters receded to their present level, the lake's drainage had been permanently altered. The highway crosses what is left of the Slims River at the south end of the lake. Looking across the lake from the highway, beaches from the former lake levels can be seen on grassy slopes up to 13m/40 feet above the present shoreline.

"The Kluane Lake area was the site of a short-lived gold rush in the early 1900s. Tagish Charlie (of Klondike fame) staked the first claim on 4th of July Creek in the summer of 1903. The North West Mounted Police followed closely behind the prospectors, setting up summer detachments in canvas tents. A permanent NWMP post was established at Silver City (see **Milepost DC 1020.5**).

"The Southern Tutchone people had a network of trails throughout the area, which became roads as the area developed. Silver City was the terminus of a trail between Whitehorse and Kluane Lake. The trail was upgraded to a wagon road in 1904 to serve area miners."

DC 1020.5 (1635.8 km) **DJ 366.5** (589.8 km) Turnoff to see the ruins of **Silver City**, located on private property. Once the site of a trading post, roadhouse and North West Mounted Police barracks, Silver City served traffic traveling the wagon road from Whitehorse to the placer goldfields of the Kluane Lake district between 1904 and 1924. The buildings begin about 2.1 miles/3.4 km in on this side road. (Large RVs park at turnaround just before road narrows and walk to ruins.)

DC 1021 (1636.6 km) **DJ 366** (589 km) Silver Creek. *NOTE: Begin chipseal multi-use trail that parallels lakeshore for next 12 miles northbound. Do not try to access this trail with vehicles. There are no turnarounds and it is not wide enough for vehicles.*

DC 1022.5 (1638.5 km) **DJ 364.5** (586.6 km) **Historical Mile 1055**. Turnoff for Kluane Lake Research Station and airstrip 0.9 mile/1.4 km east. The research station, sponsored by Arctic Institute of North America/ University of Calgary, has a small interpretive room with information on area expeditions and research.

Private Aircraft: Silver City airstrip; elev. 2,570 feet/783m; length 3,000 feet/914m; gravel; no services.

DC 1023.7 (1641 km) **DJ 363.3** (584.6 km) **Historical Mile 1056 (Historical milepost 1055)**. Kluane Camp commemorative plaque. Kluane Lake Lodge (closed down about 1990).

DC 1024 (1642.1 km) **DJ 363** (584.2 km) Large gravel turnout on south shore of **Kluane Lake**, best public access to the lakeshore for most vehicles. *CAUTION: Big rigs approach turnout with care.* This is the largest lake in Yukon, covering approximately 154 square miles/400 square km. The Ruby Range lies on the east side of the lake. Boat rentals are available at Destruction Bay and Burwash Landing. Excellent fishing for lake trout, northern pike and Arctic grayling.

Thachäl Dhäl (formerly known as Sheep Mountain) is directly ahead for northbound travelers. Thachal Dhal is Southern Tutchone and means "skin scraper mountain."

DC 1026.2 (1645.6 km) **DJ 360.8** (580.6 km) Narrow gravel access road to A'ay Chu (Slim's River) East trailhead; parking, interpretive signs.

DC 1027.8 (1647.4 km) DJ 359.2 (578.1 km) **Slims River Bridge.** *CAUTION: High winds.* The original Slims River bridge (it was replaced in 2010), built by the Canadian Army in 1955, consisted of 2 steel through truss spans on reinforced concrete piers and abutments. Slim's River (A'ay Chu), which flowed into Kluane Lake until recently, was named for a packhorse that drowned here during the 1903 Kluane gold rush.

DC 1028.8 (1649.1 km) DJ 358.2 (576.4 km) Turnoff for access road to **Thachäl Dhäl Visitor Center**; excellent interpretive programs; parking, outhouses; spotting scopes. Open mid-May to early September. Phone (867) 841-4500. Hours (subject to change) 9 A.M. to 4 P.M. daily in summer. Stop here for information on Kluane National Park and Reserve's flora and fauna.

The southern slopes of Thachäl Dhäl (formerly known as Sheep Mountain) are the primary winter and spring range and lambing area of a Dall sheep population. Rams migrate out of the area in May. Females with lambs may be seen from early May to early June. Sheep return from the alpine zone to the south-facing slopes of the mountain in late August. The face of the mountain has been designated a special preservation zone.

Check with the center for hiking trail conditions for A'ay Chu East and A'ay Chu West trails as well as a number of day hikes. *Hikers must register for overnight hikes in Kluane National Park and Reserve at either Thachäl Dhäl Visitor Center here or the Kluane National Park and Reserve Visitor Center in Haines Junction.* To register, please be at the Visitor Center 1 hour before closing time. From the Visitor Center, a number of trails are accessed via a 1.6-mile/2.6-km rough side road to trailhead parking (not recommended for motorhomes).

The small white cross on the side of Sheep Mountain marks the grave of Alexander Clark Fisher, a prospector who came into this area about 1906. The prospector's grave is accessible via the side road off the visitor center access road.

DC 1029.7 (1650.8 km) DJ 357.3 (574.8 km) Narrow, gated access to north to gravel parking area at trailhead to **Soldier's Summit, Historic Milepost 1061.** (Sharp turn at entrance may be difficult for large RVs; large vehicles may wish to park at the viewpoint across the highway; see next milepost.) Interpretive signs and litter bins at trailhead. Easy half-hour self-guided walk uphill to Soldiers Summit; beautiful view of Kluane Lake.

The Alaska Canada (ALCAN) Military Highway was officially opened with a ribbon-cutting ceremony here on blizzard Nov. 20, 1942. A red, white and blue ribbon was stretched across the road and 5 U.S. soldiers and 8 RCMP constables in dress uniform lined up facing the ribbon. The ribbon was cut by E.L. Barlett, then Alaska's voteless delegate to Congress and later Senator, and Canada's Ian MacKenzie, MP from Ottawa, while the 18th Engineers band played "God Save the King" and "The Star Spangled Banner." A plaque by the parking area was erected during the rededication ceremony held Nov. 20, 1992, commemorating the 50th anniversary of the highway.

DC 1029.8 (1650.8 km) DJ 357.2 (574.8 km) Good photo op overlooking Kluane Lake's Horseshoe Bay at viewpoint to south with large parking area and information boards (description follows).

It is an easy walk up to Soldier's Summit, from the parking lot at Milepost DC 1029.7, for an exceptional view of the Kluane Lake area. (©Kris Valencia, staff)

Information boards at this turnout on the 1903 discovery of gold on Ruby Creek which caused a gold rush in the Kluane Lake area and led to the establishment of Silver City, at one time a sizable community with a NWMP post (see **Milepost DC 1020.5**); road building around Kluane Lake as a result of the gold rush; and the Southern Tutchone name for Kluane Lake (Lu'an Man or Whitefish Lake), which along with the English name is considered a variation of the Tlingit name, Luxhani or "whitefish country." The Kluane Lake people travelled up A'ay (Slims River) to the Kaskawulsh River and Jarvis Creek on their seasonal travels to hunting and fishing grounds. Kluane Lake is a good place to fish for whitefish, trout and chum salmon but it can be quite dangerous when the wind picks up.

DC 1030.5 (1651.9 km) DJ 356.5 (573.7 km) Boat launch (signed) via gravel side road down to lake. *CAUTION: The multi-use path along Kluane Lake north and south of here can be confusing. It is NOT a frontage road. Do not access this path in vehicles: it is narrow and not intended for cars or RVs.*

DC 1034.2 (1657.8 km) DJ 352.8 (567.8 km) Williscroft Creek culvert.

DC 1034.5 (1658.3 km) DJ 352.5 (567.3 km) **Historical Mile 1067.** Turnoff on driveway towards lake for **Cottonwood RV Park and Campground** (description follows); beautiful setting.

▲

Cottonwood RV Park and Campground. Welcome to our "Wilderness Paradise." Park your RV by the lake or pitch a tent on the shore. Play mini-golf. View Dall sheep from your campsite or fish for trout and grayling. Bird watching. Hiking trails nearby. Spectacular scenery! Just 3 hours from Whitehorse, 6 hours from Tok. "A place where people stop for a day and stay another." Free WiFi. Phone (867) 841-4066;

email maryanne_glenn@cottonwoodpark.ca; website www.cottonwoodpark.ca. See display ad on page 215. [ADVERTISEMENT]

DC 1037.1 (1662.5 km) **DJ 349.9** (563.1 km) Double-ended gravel turnout to northeast. (Signed: no overnight parking or camping.)

DC 1039.3 (1666 km) **DJ 347.7** (559.5 km) **Historical Mile 1072.** Turnoff to east for **Congdon Creek Yukon government campground** on Kluane Lake. Drive in 0.4 mile/0.6 km; tenting area, 81 level sites (some pull-through) on 2 loops, one in trees and one down by the lakeshore; outhouses, kitchen shelters, litter bin, water pump, firewood, firepits, picnic tables, sandy beach, interpretive talks, playground, boat launch. Short, self-guiding interpretive trail follows shoreline of Kluane Lake. Camping permit ($12); self-registration.

The tenting area, which has room for about 8 tents (depending on their size), was enclosed with an electric fence by Yukon Parks in summer 2017, because the campground had often been closed to soft-sided camping because of the presence of bears. The enclosure is not intended for food storage: Tent campers should use the bear-proof storage bins outside the enclosure.

DC 1039.7 (1666.6 km) **DJ 347.3** (558.9 km) Congdon Creek. According to R. Coutts, *Yukon: Places & Names,* Congdon Creek is believed to have been named by a miner after Frederick Tennyson Congdon. A lawyer from Nova Scotia, Congdon came to Yukon in 1898 and held various political posts until 1911.

DC 1046 (1676.8 km) **DJ 341** (548.8 km) Nines Creek.

DC 1046.4 (1677.5 km) **DJ 340.6** (548.1 km) Mines Creek.

DC 1048.1 (1680.1 km) **DJ 338.9** (545.4 km) Bock's Creek.

DC 1049.2 (1683 km) **DJ 337.8** (542.6 km) *Slow for posted speed zones northbound through Destruction Bay.*

Destruction Bay

DC 1050.8 (1684.5 km) **DJ 336.2** (541 km) **F 432.2** (695.5 km) Talbot Arm Motel. Destruction Bay is located at **Historic Milepost 1083,** 66 miles/106 km north of Haines Junction and 116 miles/186 km south of Beaver Creek. **Population:** 55. **Emergency Services: Health clinic,** phone (867) 841-4444; **Ambulance,** phone (867) 841-3333; **Fire Department,** phone (867) 841-3331.

Restaurant, gas/diesel, tire repair, souvenirs, convenience store, motel and RV park at the Talbot Arm. Restaurant and RV sites at Destruction Bay Lodge.

Located on the shores of Kluane Lake,

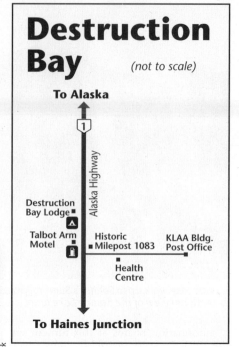

Destruction Bay
(not to scale)

To Alaska

[1] Alaska Highway

Destruction Bay Lodge ■

Talbot Arm Motel

Historic ■ Milepost 1083

KLAA Bldg. Post Office ■

Health Centre

To Haines Junction

©Sarah Strock

Destruction Bay is one of several towns that grew out of the building of the Alaska Highway. It earned its name when a storm destroyed buildings and materials here. Destruction Bay was one of the many relay stations spaced at 100-mile intervals to give truck drivers a break and a chance to repair their vehicles. A repeater station was also located here, providing telephone and telegraph service. Historic sign adjacent historic milepost. A highway maintenance camp is located here.

Boat launch, boat rentals and guided fishing tours also available locally. The Kluane Lake Fishing Derby is in July.

Next gas southbound in Haines Junction (66 miles/106 km).

Alaska Highway Log
(continued)

DC 1051.2 (1685.1 km) **DJ 335.8** (540.4 km) Rest area with litter bins and toilets.

DC 1051.3 (1685.3 km) **DJ 335.7** (540.2 km) Cluett Creek.

DC 1051.5 (1685.6 km) **DJ 335.5** (539.9 km) Distance marker northbound shows Burwash Landing 15 km/9 miles, Beaver Creek 190 km/118 miles, and Fairbanks 692 km/430 miles.

DC 1054.3 (1690.2 km) **DJ 332.7** (535.4 km) Lewis Creek.

DC 1057.5 (1695.3 km) **DJ 329.5** (530.3 km) Copper Joe Creek.

DC 1058.4 (1696.7 km) **DJ 328.6** (528.8 km) Memorial (on right northbound) began as a family tribute to Douglas ("Dougie") Richard Twiss II, Dec. 13, 1982–June 3, 2005, a Southern Tutchone man from the Champagne and Aishihik First Nations. "Follow your dreams, be kind, and always remember to enjoy every day of your life."

DC 1060.4 (1700 km) **DJ 326.6** (525.6 km) Welcome to Burwash Landing (sign northbound). Fireweed and charred trees are from June 1999 fire. The human-caused fire closed the Alaska Highway and Burwash Landing was evacuated. Some 8,000 acres were burned and 5 homes destroyed before fire crews contained the fire. Fireweed, as its name implies, is one of the first plants to

---

reestablish itself in burn areas.

NOTE: Slow for speed zones northbound through Burwash Landing.

DC 1060.9 (1700.8 km) **DJ 326.1** (524.8 km) **Kluane Museum of History** and World's Largest Gold Pan to northeast.

Burwash Landing

DC 1061 (1701 km) **DJ 326** (524.6 km) **F 422** (679 km) **Historic Milepost 1093.** Located on Kluane Lake, 10 miles/16 km north of Destruction Bay, 76 miles/122 km north of Haines Junction, and 106 miles/170 km south of Beaver Creek. **Population:** 84. **Emergency Services: Ambulance,** phone (867) 841-3333; **Fire Department,** phone (867) 841-2221.

Visitor Information: Check at the Kluane Museum of History, located on the east side of the Alaska Highway at the turnoff to Burwash Landing; open daily mid-May to mid-September; phone (867) 841-5561.

©Kris Valencia, staff

Burwash Landing has regular/premium/diesel (available 24/7) at **Kluane Energy's** above ground tank (pictured above); follow posted instructions. A cafe and grocery store are adjacent the gas station. There is also a post office, a community hall and a church. Flightseeing trips of Kluane National Park are available out of Burwash Landing. For spectacular viewing of the world's largest non-polar icefields, contact **Rocking Star Adventures** (www.rockingstar.ca).

Burwash Landing is one of the oldest settlements in Yukon. The original trading post was established in 1904 by the Jacquot brothers, Louis and Eugene, as a supply center for local miners. There are several historic structures in town, including Moose Horn Cabin (1939) and the Brewster Store (1946). The log-built structure, Our Lady of the Holy Rosary Mission, was built in 1944:

"This was the first church northwest of Whitehorse on the new Alcan Highway. Father Morrisset, then auxiliary chaplain to the U.S. Army at the road construction camps, was asked by the local residents to start a mission and day school. Land was donated by Eugene Jacquot, trading post owner. Building materials came from the Duke River camp site and included an unfinished U.S. Army mess hall and a log cabin, which form the 2 arms of the complex. The day school closed in 1952. The church opened with Christmas eve mass in 1944 and is still in use today."

The Kluane Museum of History offers wildlife exhibits with dioramas depicting natural habitat. Also displayed are Native clothing, tools and weapons, and Yukon minerals. Northern videos shown. Gift shop with locally made crafts and Northern books. Outdoor interpretive display on wildfires. Pull-through parking area accommodates vehicles up to transport truck length. World's Largest Gold Pan is on display next to the museum; good photo op. Phone (867)

Burwash Landing
(not to scale)

Kluane Lake

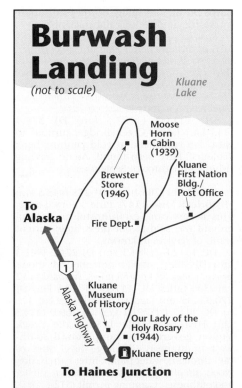

Moose Horn Cabin (1939)

Brewster Store (1946)

Kluane First Nation Bldg./ Post Office

To Alaska

Fire Dept.

1

Kluane Museum of History

Our Lady of the Holy Rosary (1944)

Kluane Energy

Alaska Highway

To Haines Junction

©Judy Nadon, staff

841-5561 for more information. Admission charged. The museum is open daily from mid-May to mid-September (hours posted).

Inquire locally about boat rentals and fishing on **Kluane Lake**. *CAUTION: Beware of high winds on Kluane Lake.*

Alaska Highway Log
(continued)

DC 1062 (1702.6 km) **DJ 325** (523 km) **Historic Milepost 1094.** Private Aircraft: Burwash Airport to north; elev. 2,643 feet/806m; length 6,000 feet/1,829m; gravel, no fuel.

Fair road conditions northbound in fall 2018, to Beaver Creek (106 miles/171 km), the Alaska border (126 miles/203 km) and Tok (218 miles/351 km), with several improved sections. But watch for frost heaves, road damage and gravel breaks. Expect some continued construction in 2019.

Fair to good road conditions southbound to Haines Junction (76 miles/122 km) with long stretches of improved highway. Slow for frost heaves.

DC 1066.3 (1709.5 km) **DJ 320.7** (516.1

View Kluane National Park glaciers from above on a charter flight with Rocking Star Adventures out of Burwash Landing. (©Judy Nadon, staff)

km) **Duke River** bridge. The Duke River flows into Kluane Lake. It was named for George Duke, an early prospector. This bridge, completed in 2009, replaced the original Duke River bridge, which was built by the Canadian Army in 1955 and consisted of 2 steel through truss spans on reinforced concrete piers and abutments. The new bridge is built to resist the stress of earthquakes. Major bridge replacement projects along this stretch of the Alaska Highway are part of the Shakwak Project, a massive reconstruction of the Alaska Highway between Haines Junction and the Alaska border.

DC 1071 (1717 km) **DJ 316** (508.5 km) Narrow bridge crosses Burwash Creek, named for Lachlin Taylor Burwash, a mining recorder at Silver City in 1903.

DC 1075.7 (1724.6 km) **DJ 311.3** (501 km) Sakiw Creek.

DC 1076.6 (1726 km) **DJ 310.4** (499.5 km) **Kluane River Overlook** rest area to northeast; information boards and observation platform overlooking Kluane River. (This overlook is at a significant distance above the valley floor, use binoculars.) Interpretive panels describe the life cycle of the chum salmon that come to spawn in this river in August and September. Watch for grizzly bears and bald eagles feeding on salmon.

DC 1077.6 (1727.6 km) **DJ 309.4** (497.9 km) Quill Creek Mine Road.

DC 1078.4 (1728.9 km) **DJ 308.6** (496.6 km) Quill Creek.

DC 1079.9 (1731.4 km) **DJ 307.1** (494.2

km) Glacier Creek.

DC 1083.4 (1737 km) **DJ 303.6** (488.6 km) **Historical Mile 1118.** Kluane Wilderness Village (closed since fall 2006, current status unknown) began as Travelers Services (Yukon) Ltd., and was later known as Mount Kennedy Motel, in about 1964–1965. By 1976 the business name appeared as Kluane Wilderness Village, owned and managed by John Trout and Joseph Frigon and later run by John and his wife, Liz, as Kluane Village. It featured a "Burl Bar" and the gift shop sold burl items fashioned by Scully. Examples of burl bowls may be seen at gift shops in Yukon and Alaska. Burls start as an irritation in the spruce. The tree sends extra sap as healant, which creates a growth or burl. Burls are either "green," harvested from live

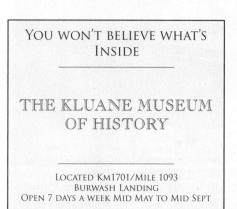

trees in the spring, or they are "dry burls," taken from dead burl trees. Burls are peeled of their bark and used in their natural form as fence posts, for example, or they may be shaped and finished into a variety of objects, such as bowls.

View of Mount Kennedy, Mount Logan and Mount Lucania.

This is the halfway mark between Whitehorse and Tok.

DC 1085.1 (1739.7 km) **DJ 301.9** (485.8 km) Swede Johnson Creek.

CAUTION: Watch for grizzly bears along the highway.

DC 1093.8 (1753.7 km) **DJ 293.2** (471.8 km) Road to NorthwesTel microwave tower.

DC 1094.9 (1755.5 km) **DJ 292.1** (470 km) Large turnout to west with view of Donjek River Valley and the Icefield Ranges of the St. Elias Mountains; litter bins, outhouses, commemorative monument and interpretive sign (excerpt follows):

"The Icefield Ranges include the highest and youngest mountains in Canada. They form the main group of peaks in the St. Elias Mountains and include Canada's highest mountain, Mount Logan, at 5,959m (19,545 feet) plus 6 other peaks over 5,000m (16,000 feet).

"In 1896, the Duke of Abruzzi, an Italian nobleman, made the first successful ascent of Mount St. Elias—the second highest mountain in Canada at 5,489m. Between 1911 and 1913, the international boundary was surveyed through the Icefield Ranges.

"The largest non-polar icefield in North America extends over most of Kluane National Park and Reserve, sending long glacial fingers into the valleys between the peaks. The ice is more than 700m (2,200 feet) thick. This icefield is the remnant of previous glaciations. The latest was the Kluane Glaciation between 29,500 and 12,500 years ago. As the glaciers melted and retreated, wind-blown silt (called loess) blanketed the newly exposed rock. The new soil supported grasses that fed bison, moose and caribou."

DC 1098.7 (1761.6 km) **DJ 288.3** (464 km) **Donjek River Bridge;** gravel access to informal parking area on river to west at north end of bridge. The wide and silty Donjek River, a major tributary of the White River. According to R. Coutts, *Yukon: Places & Names*, the Donjek was named by Charles Willard Hayes in 1891, from the Indian word for a peavine that grows in the area.

Observe No Hunting Zone Donjek River to Beaver Creek.

DC 1104.2 (1770.5 km) **DJ 282.8** (455.1 km) Small gravel turnout to west. Beaver Creek Highway Maintenance sign northbound.

Ever since the Alaska Highway was first punched through the wilderness in 10 short months in 1942, this war-time road has been under reconstruction. There never seems to be a shortage of road to straighten, culverts to fix, bridges to replace, or surfaces to level out, especially along the stretch of bumpy road between the Donjek River and the Alaska border. From the 18th Co. Engineers' pioneer road building in 1943, to the modern engineering techniques of Yukon's Dept. of Highways, this section of the Alaska Highway has presented some unique challenges.

In a 1943 report on the highway, Senior Highway Engineer R.E. Royall wrote: "By far the toughest job of grading was in building the 90 miles of road from the Donjek River in Yukon Territory to the border. Swamp ground underlain by permafrost, numerous creeks, lakes and rivers, and a thick insulating ground cover made this section difficult to penetrate for establishment of camps and conduct of work. Army forces pushed through the pioneer road late in 1942 as the ground was freezing and a limited number of vehicles went over the frozen surface during the winter. During the spring thaw (in 1943), this frozen road completely disappeared and there was no traffic whatever during the summer." Indeed, this section of road did not open until October 1943.

According to Public Works Yukon, much of the soil along the north Alaska Highway is of glacial origin and unsuitable for road embankments. "Anything that causes the permafrost to melt will cause the ice-rich soil to liquefy, and liquid soil has little strength and will settle or subside. Then if this soil refreezes during lower air temperatures, it will expand or heave." This process wreaks havoc on the drivability of the road surface by creating undulations and cracking.

Road construction has improved many sections of highway northbound to the border, but motorists should continue to watch for roadside flags indicating road damage, and slow down for bumps, dips, damaged pavement, gravel breaks and deep potholes. Expect ongoing road improvement projects in summer 2019.

DC 1111.7 (1782.5 km) **DJ 275.3** (443 km) **Edith Creek** bridge, turnout to west. Try your hand at gold panning here; "colours" have been found. Arctic grayling fishing, June through September.

DC 1112 (1783.1 km) **DJ 275** (442.5 km) **Historical Mile 1147**. Pine Valley Lodge. This bakery/cafe, cabin/hostel and campground was sold at our press time; current status of services unknown.

DC 1112.8 (1784.3 km) **DJ 274.2** (441.3 km) Distance marker northbound shows Beaver Creek 89 kms/55 miles, Fairbanks 612 kms/380 miles. **DC 1116.7** (1790.5 km) **DJ 270.3** (435 km) Koidern River bridge No. 1.

DC 1117.1 (1791.1 km) **DJ 269.9** (434.3 km) **Historical Mile 1152**. Lake Creek **Yukon government campground** southwest of highway; 28 large level sites (6 pull-through), water pump, litter barrels, firewood, firepits, picnic tables, kitchen shelter and outhouses. Camping permit ($12). ▲

DC 1123.9 (1802.1 km) **DJ 263.1** (423.4 km) **Pickhandle Lake** rest area to southwest; toilets, tables, litter bins. Information boards on Native trading routes, pond life and muskrats. Good fishing from boat for northern pike all summer; also Arctic grayling, whitefish and lingcod.

DC 1126.2 (1805.9 km) **DJ 260.8** (419.7 km) Aptly named Reflection Lake to west mirrors the Kluane Range. Watch for trumpeter swans in roadside lakes in summer. The highway parallels this range between Koidern and Haines Junction.

DC 1128.8 (1810 km) **DJ 258.2** (415.5 km) **Historical Mile 1164**. Koidern River Lodge (closed). The late Jim Cook and his wife Dorothy operated the lodge starting in 1969, selling gas, snacks, pop and souvenirs every summer.

DC 1129 (1810.2 km) **DJ 258** (415.2 km) Koidern River bridge No. 2.

DC 1132.1 (1815 km) **DJ 254.9** (410.2 km) **Historic Milepost 1167**. Remains of Bear Flats Lodge at Koidern, which operated from 1973 until it closed in 1992. During the early days of the Alaska Highway, this was a highway maintenance camp and telephone and telegraph station. A number of businesses have operated here over the years: Rover's Inn in the 1950s; Northwest Trading Post 1960s; and Koidern Gulf Services, 1970.

DC 1133.5 (1818 km) **DJ 253.5** (408 km) **Historical Mile 1169**. Discovery Yukon Lodgings and RV Park (description follows). ▲

Discovery Yukon Lodgings and RV Park. Spacious, big-rig friendly, pull-through full-service RV sites, and level grassy tent sites. Cozy cabins and queen rooms with kitchenette and private bathroom. Breakfast and evening meals available for room guests. Hot showers, WiFi hotspot, picnic area, pet-friendly. Historic military vehicle display. Meet new friends around our firepit. To book an RV spot, room or

tent site, call (867) 862-7408 or email info@ discoveryyukon.com. GPS N61°59.096 by W140°32.316. See display ad on facing page.

DC 1134.1 (1818.6 km) **DJ 252.9** (407 km) **White River** bridge. The White River, a major tributary of the Yukon River, was named by Hudson's Bay Co. explorer Robert Campbell for its white color, caused by the volcanic ash in the water.

NOTE: This river is considered very danger-ous; not recommended for boating.

DC 1140.4 (1828.5 km) **DJ 246.6** (396.8 km) **Moose Lake** to west, Arctic grayling to 18 inches, use dry flies and small spinners, midsummer. Boat needed for lake fishing; look for moose.

DC 1141.9 (1831.1 km) **DJ 245.1** (394.4 km) Distance marker northbound shows Beaver Creek 39 km/24 miles, Fairbanks 562 km/349 miles.

DC 1142.7 (1832.4 km) **DJ 244.3** (393.2 km) Sanpete Creek, named by an early prospector after Sanpete County in Utah.

DC 1145.9 (1837.5 km) **DJ 241.1** (388 km) Dry Creek No. 1.

DC 1148 (1840.8 km) **DJ 239** (384.6 km) Rest area to southwest with dramatic mountain view; outhouses, litter bins.

DC 1148.7 (1841.8 km) **DJ 238.3** (383.5 km) **Historical Mile 1184.** Dry Creek No. 2. Gravel turnout to west at south end of bridge. Dry Creek Lodge was located in this area until it burned down in the fall of 1951. Travelers transferred from the Canadian operated B.Y.N. Lines to the Alaska Coachways buses here.

Highway climbs long hill northbound.

Distance marker southbound shows Haines Junction 268 km/166 miles.

DC 1153.3 (1849.3 km) **DJ 233.7** (376.1 km) Small Lake to east. Snag Road (dirt, passable for vehicles first mile only) connects the Alaska Highway here with the abandoned airfield and Indian village at **Snag** to the northeast.

In 1947, Snag functioned as an emergency airstrip for aircraft flying from Edmonton to Anchorage and Fairbanks. Snag's claim to fame is the lowest recorded temperature in Canada: -81.4°F/-63°C on Feb. 3, 1947. (Alaska's lowest recorded temperature was -80°F/-62.8°C on January 23, 1971, at Prospect Creek, a pipeline camp 25 miles southeast of Bettles.)

DC 1153.4 (1849.6 km) **DJ 233.6** (375.9 km) **Historical Mile 1188. Snag Junction Yukon government campground**, 0.4 mile/0.6 km north on gravel loop road. There are 15 tent and vehicle sites, 3 pull-through, some overlooking lake, a kitchen shelter, outhouses, picnic tables, firewood, firepits and litter barrels. Camping permit ($12). Small-boat launch. Swimming in Small Lake.

There are several small lakes along the highway here. Watch for Trumpeter and Tundra swans resting and nesting in these ponds.

DC 1154.2 (1850.7 km) **DJ 232.8** (374.6 km) Dirt track northeast to lakes.

DC 1155.3 (1852.5 km) **DJ 231.7** (372.9 km) Dirt track north to lake.

DC 1159 (1858.4 km) **DJ 228** (366.9 km) Double-ended, gravel turnout to southwest with litter bins.

DC 1160.2 (1860.4 km) **DJ 226.8** (365 km) Enger Creek.

DC 1163 (1865) **DJ 224** (360.5 km) Vent-like structures alongside the highway here

The Yukon Government Visitor Information Center in Beaver Creek offers visitor assistance and historic photo displays. (©Kris Valencia, staff)

are part of the Alaska Highway Permafrost Research Project, which is testing specialized construction techniques. The techniques are designed to minimize melting of the permafrost by allowing cold air to penetrate the road embankment and increasing surface reflectivity. Permafrost temperatures will be monitored for the next several years to assess their effectiveness. If the designs prove to be practical and effective, they may be used more extensively along the highway. This is an international project involving Yukon Highways and Public Works, the U.S. Federal Highways Administration and other public agencies.

View of Nutzotin Mountains to northwest, Kluane Ranges to southwest. On a clear day you should be able to see the snow-clad Wrangell Mountains in the distance to the west.

DC 1165.3 (1868.6 km) **DJ 221.7** (356.8 km) Beaver Creek bridge.

Slow for speed zones northbound through Beaver Creek.

Road construction has improved many sections of highway southbound to Burwash Landing (106 miles/171 km) and Destruction Bay (116 miles/187 km), but motorists should continue to watch for roadside flags indicating road damage, and slow down for bumps, dips, damaged pavement, gravel breaks and deep potholes. Expect ongoing road improvement projects during summer.

NOTE: No cell phone service south to Burwash Landing.

Beaver Creek

DC 1166.5 (1870.6 km) **DJ 220.5** (354.8 km) **F 316.5** (509.3 km) Visitor Information Center in Beaver Creek, **Historic Milepost 1202.** Driving distance to Tok, AK, 113 miles/182 km; to Fairbanks, AK, 317 miles/509 km; to Haines Junction, YT, 184 miles/295 km; to Haines, AK, 334 miles/538 km; to Whitehorse 280 miles/450 km. **Population:** 112. **Emergency Services: RCMP**, phone (867) 862-5555. **Ambulance**, phone (867) 862-3333. **Health Centre:** phone (867) 862-4444.

Visitor Information: Yukon Government Visitor Information Center is in the

log building on the highway; open daily late May through September. Phone (867) 862-7321. The visitor center has a book on display of dried Yukon wildflowers for those interested in the flora of the territory. The center also has an Alaska Highway scrapbook with historical photos of lodges and life along the north Alaska Highway.

Private Aircraft: Beaver Creek Yukon government airstrip 1 NW; see description at **Milepost DC 1170.3. Radio:** CBC North at 93.1 FM, CHON 90.5 FM.

Food, gas, lodging and camping are available. Year-round lodging, gift shop, licensed restaurant and lounge and summer dry tent sites at **Buckshot Betty's. Beaver Creek RV Park & Motel** offers camping, motel, fuel, groceries, laundromat and gift shop. Find lodging, convenience store, cafe, gas and souvenirs at the **1202 Motor Inn.** There is a bank, open 2 days a week, located in the post office building; ATMs; and public pool beside the community club.

Beaver Creek was the site of the old Canadian customs station. Local residents were pleased to see customs relocated north of town in 1983, having long endured the flashing lights and screaming sirens set off whenever a tourist forgot to stop.

Beaver Creek is 1 of 2 sites where Alaska Highway construction crews working from opposite directions connected the highway. In October 1942, Alaska Highway construction operations were being rushed to conclusion as winter set in. Eastern and western sector construction crews (the 97th and 18th Engineers) pushed through to meet at a junction on Beaver Creek on Oct. 28, thus making it possible for the first time for vehicles to travel the entire length of the highway. East–west crews had connected at Contact Creek on Sept. 15th or 24th (depending on your source), 1942.

Yukon Centennial Gold Rush figurines and displays are located just west of How Far West Plaza (celebrating Beaver Creek's status

Beaver Creek

(not to scale)

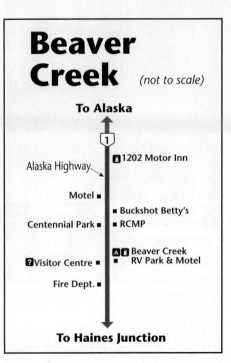

To Alaska

↑
①
Alaska Highway →
■ 1202 Motor Inn
Motel ■
■ Buckshot Betty's
Centennial Park ■
■ RCMP
▲■ Beaver Creek
RV Park & Motel
❓ Visitor Centre ■
Fire Dept. ■
↓
To Haines Junction

as most westerly Canadian community) at town center. The plaza features information on wildlife and a map of Beaver Creek.

Our Lady of Grace mission, built in 1961 from a salvaged Quonset hut left over from highway construction days, it is 1 of 3 Catholic missions on the north Alaska Highway (the others are in Burwash Landing and Haines Junction). St. Columba's Anglican Church in Beaver Creek was prefabricated in Whitehorse and built here in one week in 1975.

Alaska Highway Log
(continued)

DC 1167.9 (1872.8 km) DJ 219.1 (352.6 km) Double-ended turnout to southwest with litter bins, picnic tables and outhouses.

Northbound: Alaska border is 19 miles/31 km. Slow for gravel breaks and frost heaves. Expect road construction and/or improved highway in summer 2019. Tok is 113 miles/182 km, and is the next gas stop if Border City Lodge is not open.

Southbound: Slow for speed zone through Beaver Creek. Next gas southbound after Beaver Creek at Burwash Landing (106 miles/171 km) and Destruction Bay (116 miles/187 km).

DC 1168.4 (1873.6 km) DJ 218.6 (351.8

km) **Private Aircraft:** Beaver Creek Airport, Yukon government airstrip; elev. 2,129 feet/ 649m; length 3,740 feet/1,140m; gravel; no fuel. Airport of entry for Canada customs.

Distance marker northbound shows U.S. Customs 30 kms/18 miles..

DC 1168.5 (1873.8 km) DJ 218.5 (351.6 km) **Beaver Creek Canada Customs** station; phone (867) 862-7230. Open 24 hours a day year-round. All traffic entering Canada must stop here for clearance. Expect vigorous enforcement of customs requirements (see "Crossing the Border" in the TRAVEL PLANNING section for more details).

DC 1173.4 (1881.7 km) DJ 213.6 (343.7 km) Snag Creek.

DC 1174.6 (1883.6 km) DJ 212.4 (341.8 km) Mirror Creek. Look for nesting swans in roadside lakes in summer.

DC 1175.1 (1884.4 km) DJ 211.9 (341 km) Turnout to southwest with litter bin.

DC 1182.9 (1897 km) DJ 204.1 (328.5 km) Little Scottie Creek.

©Kris Valencia, staff

DC 1186.3 (1902.5 km) DJ 200.7 (323 km) **Historic Milepost 1221. Canada–U.S. International Border.** Rest area to south with information boards on the 141st Meridian and northern road construction. Photo op: Welcome to Alaska sign (pictured above).

The international boundary marker here makes a good photo op, as does the narrow clearing which marks the border. This is part of the 20-foot-/6-m-wide swath cut by surveyors from 1904 to 1920 along the 141st meridian (from Demarcation Point on the Arctic Ocean south 600 miles/966 km to Mount St. Elias in the Wrangell Mountains) to mark the Alaska–Canada border. This swath continues south to mark the boundary between southeastern Alaska and Canada. Portions of the swath are cleared periodically by the International Boundary Commission.

The boundary line between Alaska and Yukon was originally described in an 1825 treaty between Russia and England. The U.S. accepted this version of the boundary with its purchase of Alaska from Russia in 1867. But after gold was discovered in the Klondike in 1896, a dispute arose between the U.S. and Canada, with both claiming the seaports at the head of Lynn Canal. An international tribunal decided in favor of the U.S. in 1903.

TIME ZONE CHANGE: Alaska observes Alaska standard time, Yukon observes Pacific standard time. Alaska standard time is 1 hour earlier than Pacific standard time.

YUKON HIGHWAY 1 South
Southbound: Distance from Dawson Creek (DC) is followed by distance from Delta Junction (DJ) Read log: ↑

Road conditions southbound: Easy curves and long, fairly straight stretches. Fair pavement with possible construction to Burwash Landing. Slow for frost heaves, damaged pavement, and gravel breaks.

ALASKA ROUTE 2 North

Northbound: Distance from Dawson Creek (DC) is followed by distance from physical milepost **(MP)**, distance from Delta Junction **(DJ)** and distance from Fairbanks **(F)**. Read log:

NOTE: In the Alaska portion of The MILE-POST® Alaska Highway log, DC mileages from Dawson Creek are based on actual driving distance, and MP mileage are based on physical mileposts between Port Alcan and Delta Junction, AK, which reflect traditional distances from Dawson Creek, BC. There is a difference of 35 miles between the historic mileposts and actual driving distance.

DC 1186.4 MP 1221.4 **DJ 200.6 F 296.6**
Distance marker northbound shows Tok 93 miles, Delta Junction 200 miles, Fairbanks 298 miles, Anchorage 421 miles.

DC 1186.8 MP 1221.8 **DJ 200.2 F 296.2**
Port Alcan U.S. Customs and Border Protection station, open 24 hours daily year-round; pay phone (credit card and collect calls only) and restrooms. *All traffic entering Alaska must stop for clearance. Do not get out of your vehicle unless instructed to do so by the border protection officer or until you have cleared customs. DO NOT TAKE PHOTO-GRAPHS! Do not let pets out of vehicles.*

For details on customs requirements for returning residents and nonresidents entering the U.S., please read "Crossing the Border" in the TRAVEL PLANNING section.

Road conditions northbound: Some winding road and grades to Tok. Slow for damaged surface and gravel breaks. Possible road construction in summer.

Distance marker northbound shows Taylor Highway junction 77 miles, Fairbanks 297 miles, Anchorage 420 miles. Tok is 92 miles from here.

Distance marker southbound shows Canadian Customs 20 miles.

DC 1187.5 MP 1222.5 **DJ 199.5 F 295.5**
Purple Heart Trail Honoring Veterans' Sacrifice (northbound sign). The Alaska Highway from the border to Delta Junction was designated the "Purple Heart Trail" in May 2008, to honor veterans.

Distance marker northbound shows Tok 92 miles, Delta Junction 199 miles.

DC 1187.7 MP 1222.7 **DJ 199.3 F 295.3**
Entering Tetlin National Wildlife Refuge northbound. Established in 1980, the 730,000-acre refuge stretches south from the Alaska Highway and west from the Canadian border. Major physical features include hundreds of small lakes and 2 glacial rivers (the Nabesna and Chisana), which combine to form the Tanana River. The complex association of lakes, ponds, marshes, streams, and rivers provide for a variety of habitat favorable to numerous species of waterfowl, and the refuge has been recognized internationally as an Important Bird Area because of its habitat for migrating sandhill crane and nesting trumpeter swans. The refuge provides habitat for 126 nesting species and more than 64 migrating species. Some 42 mammals—including moose, black and grizzly bear, wolf, coyotes, beaver, red fox, lynx and caribou—are found on the refuge.

Information on the refuge is available seasonally at the Tetlin National Wildlife Refuge Visitor Center, located 6.3 miles northwest of here at **Milepost DC 1194 (physical Milepost 1229)** Alaska Highway.

For more detailed information, contact the Refuge Manager, Tetlin National Wild-

Stop at the Tetlin National Wildlife Refuge visitor center for great views and information about this area. (©Kris Valencia, staff)

life Refuge, Box 779, Tok, AK 99780; phone (907) 883-5312. Refuge headquarters is located in Tok (take the Tok Cutoff to Borealis Avenue and drive 1.3 miles north).

DC 1188.2 MP 1223.2 **DJ 198.8 F 294.8**
Distance marker northbound shows Tok 92 miles, Delta Junction 199 miles.

DC 1188.4 MP 1223.4 **DJ 198.6 F 294.6**
Scottie Creek bridge. Old cabins to southwest.

DC 1189.6 MP 1224.6 **DJ 197.4 F 293.4**
Scenic viewpoint overlooking Highway Lake. "Feathered Travelers" information board reads:

"You are traveling along the route flown by hundreds of thousands of birds each spring. Some migrate from as far as South America. They return to Alaska to raise their next generation, surrounded by food, with long days for feasting. More than 115 species of birds find an ideal nursery in Tetlin National Wildlife Refuge.

"As birds from all over Alaska return south, biologists net, band, measure and release a sample of migrating songbirds. They combine their findings with information from other banding stations in Alaska and the Yukon to track trends in songbird populations.

"About 25 species of birds live in this area all year. Chickadees store food so they can quickly replace body fat they burn off each night keeping warm. Ravens and gray jays nest while snow is on the ground. Their chicks are ready to fly when others just arrive.

"Trumpeter swans are nesting here in growing numbers, attracted to the refuge's many secluded ponds. They demand privacy for raising their cygnets and can chase away other nearby birds, including loons."

DC 1190.4 MP 1225.4 **DJ 196.6 F 292.6**
Parking area and canoe launch (not signed) for Desper Creek and access to Tetlin NWR on southwest side of highway. *NOTE: $1,000 fine for littering.*

DC 1190.5 MP 1225.5 **DJ 196.5 F 292.5**
Border City Lodge & RV Park west side of highway; current status unknown. When operating, this business offers a cafe, motel, gift shop, an RV park and gas.

Border Trading Post advertised in the 1949 edition of *The MILEPOST* as "your first opportunity to replenish your supply of American cigarettes and candy bars."

DC 1191 MP 1226 **DJ 196 F 292** Scottie Creek Services to east; current status unknown.

DC 1193 MP 1228 **DJ 194 F 290** Large double-ended paved parking area to west.

Good view to south of lakes in Chisana (Shu-SHAN-ah) River valley. The Nutzotin Mountains are to the west.

DC 1194 MP 1229 **DJ 193 F 289** Parking area to southwest for **Tetlin National Wildlife Refuge Visitor Center** adjacent highway. Great stop with viewing deck, telescopes and photo op of a cache. Exhibits inside include spring migration, Athabascan culture, nesting swans, fish camp diorama, tracks box and signs tree, science on the refuge and a topographical map model.

Interpretive programs on and demonstrations of traditional Native Athabascan culture and crafts presented daily in summer. A selection of videos may be shown on request. Audio tour tape/CD available for travelers headed toward Tok (return tape to Public Lands Information Center or Mainstreet Visitor Center in Tok). Restrooms (wheelchair accessible) are located in the building adjacent the parking lot. The visitor center is open 8 A.M. to 4:30 P.M. May 15 to Sept.15. (The center extends its hours to 6:30 P.M. when staff is available.) *NOTE: No overnight camping here.*

DC 1195 MP 1230 **DJ 192 F 288** Sign reads: Dial 511 for travel information. Cell service is not available along the highway here. When you have internet, you may check road conditions for Alaska highways at 511.alaska.gov. Yukon provides a similar service at www.511yukon.ca/.

DC 1195.7 MP 1230.7 **DJ 191.3 F 287.3**
View of Island Lake to northeast.

DC 1198.3 MP 1233.3 **DJ 188.7 F 284.7**
Long, narrow, double-ended paved turnout to northeast.

DC 1199.2 MP 1234.2 **DJ 187.8 F 283.8**
Sweetwater Creek.

DC 1199.5 MP 1234.5 **DJ 187.5 F 283.5**
Turnoff for **Seaton Roadhouse Interpretive Site and Trails** (Tetlin NWR), 0.4 to southwest via gravel road. This beautiful spot—recently developed—is a great place to get out and stretch your legs and walk the dog. There is a large parking area (good for big rigs, but no overnight RV parking); gravel hiking trails with observation decks; toilet; litter bins; and a large picnic pavilion with tables. Information boards relate history of this area, the importance of Alaska roadhouses, and tell a bit about Irene and Bill Seaton, the owners of the roadhouse that

was once located here.

Three primitive tent campsites with fire rings and benches near end of two spur trails (campers self-register).

Hikers watch for beaver, moose, wolf and bear. Old ridges of windblown glacial silt surround a small pond at site of former Seaton Roadhouse.

DC 1205 MP 1240 **DJ 182 F 278** Small parking area to southwest; trailhead parking for 1-mile hike to **Hidden Lake** in Tetlin National Wildlife Refuge. Hidden Lake is stocked with rainbow trout; use spinners, wobbling spoons, or flies (streamers and bucktails with black and red in their patterns). No overnight camping.

Much of Hidden Lake trail is a narrow boardwalk through woods and marshes. *Bring mosquito repellent!* There are life jackets and a boat with homemade paddles at the lake. Information boards on boreal forest and Tetlin Refuge. Beavers are active in this area. Beavers can swim underwater for 3 to 5 minutes and travel a half-mile before surfacing. They are most active from evening to early morning.

DC 1205.3 MP 1240.3 **DJ 181.7 F 277.7** Waist-high vertical corrugated metal culverts topped with cone-shaped "hats" seen on either side of highway were an experiment to keep ground from thawing and thus prevent frost heaves (it was unsuccessful).

DC 1208 MP 1243 **DJ 179 F 275** Good examples of sand dune road cut (and rock graffiti) typical along this stretch of highway. Westbound, the highway cuts through several of these sand dunes. The sand originally was part of the volcanic mountain range to the south. Prevailing winds moved the sand across the valley floor, forming crescent-shaped dunes now stabilized by plants. A distinct layer of volcanic ash is also found here and in the Yukon, evidence of a volcanic eruption in the St. Elias Range some 1,400 years ago.

DC 1208.7 MP 1243.7 **DJ 178.3 F 274.3** Scenic viewpoint to south on loop road is a large, paved turnout with easy access. Short walking trail along ridge to west. Tetlin Refuge information boards on fire ecology and boreal forest at turnout read:

"In a record year, more than 650 major wildfires burn across the state, half of them ignited by lightning. Although only 2 out of every 10 lightning bolts hit the ground, Interior Alaska can be struck 6,000 times daily. Without rain, lightning that strikes tinder dry fuels may ignite a wildfire.

"Quick drying, feathery mosses send fire racing along the ground in spruce forests. Fire can smolder beneath a mossy carpet several feet thick during wet weather and even throughout the winter. Where life or property is not at risk, lightning-caused fires are allowed to burn as part of the natural process of northern forest evolution.

"The Russian word taiga ('land of little sticks') best describes this boggy landscape of bottle brush trees. Black spruce grow so slowly that a tree 2 inches in diameter may be 100 years old. Where black spruce thrive, few other plants can survive. They spread their roots in the boggy, shallow soil above permanently frozen ground. Permafrost blocks water drainage and limits root growth and soil fertility.

"Black spruce invite fire. Drooping branches make a stepladder for flames to climb to the cone-laden crowns. The fire's heat opens the resin-sealed cones, spreading seeds of new life."

DC 1211.6 MP 1246.6 **DJ 175.4 F 271.4** Gardiner Creek bridge with small dirt turnout.

DC 1212.6 MP 1247.6 **DJ 174.4 F 270.4** Long, paved, double-ended turnout to north overlooks meadow.

DC 1214.3 MP 1249.3 **DJ 172.7 F 268.7** **Historic Milepost 1254** at entrance to **Deadman Lake Campground** (sharp turn to southwest). This Tetlin National Refuge campground is 1.2 miles in via a narrow, dirt and gravel access road. Camping fee by donation, 15 sites in spruce forest along half-mile loop road; firepits, toilets, picnic tables, boat ramp, information board; no reservations taken. Interpretive pavilion for evening naturalist programs during the summer season. Self-guided Taiga Trail (wheelchair friendly) with information boards at viewing deck on Deadman Lake. Maximum 14-day campground stay within a 28-day period. Scenic spot, swimming, fishing for northern pike. The lake was originally known as "Chuljuud Manh Choh," Athabascan for "Big Pike Lake."

DC 1215.3 MP 1250.3 **DJ 171.7 F 267.7** Rest area to southwest is a double-ended paved parking area with picnic tables, concrete fireplaces and view. No water or toilets.

DC 1216.3 MP 1251.3 **DJ 170.7 F 266.7** Distance marker southbound shows Canadian Border 30 miles, Haines Junction 235 miles.

DC 1217.2 MP 1252.2 **DJ 169.8 F 265.8** Uphill double-ended gravel access to scenic viewpoint on hill to southwest with Tetlin Refuge information board on insects (excerpt follows).

"Those female mosquitoes biting you need a blood meal before laying eggs. The first mosquitoes to bite in spring spent the winter as dormant adults. Others (about 30 kinds) hatch from eggs during summer. Until freeze-up, some type of mosquito is always hunting for blood. A moose may lose a pint a day to mosquitoes.

"Other biting insects include black flies (also called white sox), which cut a plug of skin and lick the blood; no-see-ums, silver-winged gnats that look like swarms of tiny mosquitoes; and deer flies, a bee-sized insect with a bite that packs a wallop. Even caribou run from them."

DC 1219 MP 1254 **DJ 168 F 264** Distance marker westbound shows Northway Junction 10 miles, Tok 60 miles.

Great view northbound from top of hill of lakes and muskeg in Chisana River valley.

DC 1221.7 MP 1256.7 **DJ 165.3 F 261.3** Turnoff to south for **Lakeview Campground** (Tetlin National Wildlife Refuge), 0.2 mile from highway via a narrow, gravel road to 11 sites on a loop road next to beautiful **Yarger Lake**; tables, firepits, wheelchair-accessible toilets, garbage container. No camping fee—by donation. Kids Don't Float life jackets. Short trail, marked by plastic ribbons, leads from back of spaces 6 and 7 to a photo blind; watch for loons. Information boards about management of Tetlin National Wildlife Refuge. *NOTE: Tight turnaround–NOT recommended for trailers, 5th wheels or RVs over 30 feet.*

Look for the Nutzotin Mountains to the south and Mentasta Mountains to the west. These 2 mountain masses form the eastern end of the Alaska Range.

DC 1228 MP 1263 **DJ 159 F 255** Beautiful views for northbound travelers (weather permitting) of Wrangell Mountains and Chisana River to the southwest. This is the land of a thousand ponds, most unnamed. Good trapping country. In early June, travelers may note numerous cottony white seeds blowing in the wind; these seeds are from willow and poplars.

DC 1228.8 MP 1263.8 **DJ 158.2 F 254.2** Distance marker southbound shows Canadian Border 42 miles, Haines Junction 247 miles.

DC 1229 MP 1264 **DJ 158 F 254** **Northway Junction:** turnoff for 9-mile-long Northway Road (paved) south across Chisana River to Northway Airport and Village (descriptions follow). Naabia Niign (at turnoff) has crafts made by residents of Northway; gas, diesel, propane; groceries; campground; shower facilities (located in store); espresso; and picnic tables. **Alaska State Troopers** east side of highway.

NORTHWAY (pop. 136) consists of 3 dispersed settlements: Northway Junction at **Milepost 1264** on the Alaska Highway, where Naabia Niign is located; Northway with the airport and post office, 7 miles south of Northway Junction; and Northway Village, 2 miles beyond the airport, which has a school and a Church of God. Historically occupied by Athabascan Indians, Northway was named to honor Chief Walter Northway. Chief Northway died in 1992; he was 117 years old.

According to the FAA website, the Northway airport "is considered a gateway to Alaska for small aircraft following the Alaska Highway because that is where they must land to clear customs unless they have enough fuel to continue on to Fairbanks or Anchorage non-stop. Most pilots do not have enough range to do that, considering that no aviation fuel is available between Whitehorse, YT and Tok, AK.

"Northway has a Flight Service Station (FSS) on the airport which provides Local Airport Advisory (LAA) service to aircraft arriving and departing. This FSS is normally open seasonally May to September. There are no services at the airport and very few services at Northway. After clearing customs, most aircraft refuel at Tok Junction Airport which is 36 nautical miles further.

"If you are flying to or from Canada and are landing in Canada, make sure you file your arrival and departure information electronically in eAPIS (Electronic Advance Passenger Information System). Some pilots assume that they do not have to call on the phone since they are filing electronically and that is not true. You are still required to call the border station to coordinate your arrival at Northway in addition to filing electronically. Check the latest Supplement Alaska for the phone number and other details."

Pilots contact the Port of Alcan/Tok office at (907) 774-2252 two hours prior to landing at Northway in order to schedule an officer onsite. Customs and border protection agents are not on the field unless they are expecting an aircraft. They drive up from the border, which takes about 1 hour. Keep in mind that you are required to stay in the aircraft until they arrive.

DC 1229.4 MP 1264.4 **DJ 157.6 F 253.6** Distance marker westbound shows Tok 50 miles, Delta Junction 158 miles, Fairbanks 254 miles, Anchorage 371 miles.

DC 1232.3 MP 1267.3 **DJ 154.7 F 250.7** Wonderful view of the Tanana River at Beaver Slide. There is a cell tower at the top of Beaver Slide. The Tanana River is the largest tributary of the Yukon River.

DC 1233 MP 1268 **DJ 154 F 250** Beaver Creek. The tea-colored water flowing in the creek is the result of tannins absorbed by the water as it flows through muskeg. This phenomenon may be observed in other northern creeks.

DC 1234 MP 1269 DJ 153 F 249 Historic Milepost 1271. Scenic viewpoint to southwest is a large paved turn-out with a Gold Rush Centennial sign about the short-lived Chisana Gold Rush and Tetlin Refuge information boards on glacial rivers and whitefish (excerpts follow).

"The 1913 gold discovery on the north side of the Wrangell Mountains triggered the last major rush of the Gold Rush era. Some 2,000 stampeders reached the Chisana diggings, but most left disappointed: only a few creeks had gold and the area was remote and expensive to supply. The boom lasted little more than a year.

"As glaciers in the Wrangell Mountains melt, they wash their grindings into the headwaters of the Nabesna (Nah-BEZ-nah) and Chisana (Shu-SHAN-ah) rivers. These waters keep scooping up more sand and silt before converging near Northway to form the fifth longest river in Alaska, the Tanana (TAN-ah-nah). The murkiest river runs clear in winter when glacial melting stops. Fish adapt by laying eggs just before freeze-up so silt doesn't smother them before hatching.

"These murky rivers have long concealed the secrets of humpback whitefish from all but local Athabascan Indians, who learned their habits to survive.

"Related to salmon and trout, humpback whitefish can live 20 years or more. They first spawn around age 5 and many reproduce annually (unlike salmon that die after spawning). Whitefish fatten in large lakes in spring. By mid-summer they migrate into the river systems and swim farther up either the Nabesna or Chisana to spawn before freeze-up. Adults return downstream for the winter. Eggs hatch in spring. Spring floods sweep newly hatched whitefish downstream, far from this area. Where they grow up is unknown. Tetlin National Wildlife Refuge protects 2 of only a few known spawning sites for humpback whitefish in Alaska."

DC 1235 MP 1271 DJ 152 F 248 Begin 6 to 7 percent grades next 2 miles northbound.

DC 1237.7 MP 1272.7 DJ 149.3 F 245.3 Large paved turnout to southwest is a scenic viewpoint with Tetlin Refuge information board on local geology. To the northwest the Tanana River flows near the highway; beyond, the Kalukna River snakes its way through plain and marshland. Mentasta Mountains are visible to the southwest.

DC 1239 MP 1274 DJ 148 F 244 Paved parking area to south (no view).

Distance marker southbound shows Northway 10 miles, Canadian Border 52 miles.

DC 1249 MP 1284 DJ 138 F 234 Distance marker westbound shows Tok 30 miles, Fairbanks 235 miles.

DC 1249.6 MP 1284.6 DJ 137.4 F 233.4 Long double-ended paved turnout to north.

DC 1251 MP 1286 DJ 136 F 232 View to southwest of 3.4-mile-long Midway Lake as Alaska Highway descends hill westbound.

DC 1254.1 MP 1289.1 DJ 132.9 F 228.9 Large paved turnout to south overlooks Midway Lake.

DC 1254.5 MP 1289.5 DJ 132.5 F 228.5 Historic Milepost 1292. Sharp turn to north for short, steep access road to paved parking area and scenic viewpoint; toilet, bear-proof litter bin. View of Midway Lake and Wrangell Mountains. Tetlin Refuge information boards on caribou and winter (excerpts follow).

"Winter on Tetlin National Wildlife Refuge arrives in early October and departs by late April. On the shortest day of the year, the sun skims the horizon from about 10 A.M. to 2:45 P.M. Freezing temperatures of -40°F, down to a record of -72°, drive away memories of summer heat. This area often takes the prize as coldest in the state. Temperatures stay below freezing about 165 days of the year.

"After snow covers their summer calving and feeding area, caribou usually trek northward across this part of Tetlin National Wildlife Refuge. They're migrating up to 200 miles in search of lichens, their major winter food. Lichens are an ancient fusion of algae and fungi. They are loaded with carbohydrates. If caribou find areas with plentiful lichens, they can maintain their weight—rare for arctic animals in winter, the lean season. Wildfires in 2004 burned about a million acres in the caribou's winter range north of the Alaska Highway, removing large areas of lichens. If the caribou behave as in the past, they may avoid those burned areas for at least 60 years until lichens regain abundance.

"Wolf packs often shadow migrating caribou herds, targeting the slow and weak. Tetlin Refuge lands are also open for subsistence hunting by Upper Tanana Athabascans and other local residents."

DC 1255.2 MP 1290.2 DJ 131.8 F 227.8 View of Midway Lake eastbound. Burn area from 1998 fire visible westbound.

DC 1256.5 MP 1291.5 DJ 130.5 F 226.5 Distance marker eastbound shows Northway Junction 34 miles, Canadian Border 70 miles, Haines Junction 275 miles.

DC 1257.4 MP 1292.4 DJ 129.6 F 225.6 Large paved parking area to south; overlooks meadow.

DC 1258.7 MP 1293.7 DJ 128.3 F 224.3 Paved parking to south.

DC 1259 MP 1294 DJ 128 F 224 Distance marker westbound shows Tok 20 miles, Fairbanks 225 miles, Anchorage 355 miles.

DC 1266.6 MP 1301.6 DJ 120.4 F 216.4 Distance marker eastbound shows Northway Junction 45 miles, Canadian Border 80 miles, Haines Junction 285 miles.

DC 1266.7 MP 1301.7 DJ 120.3 F 216.3 Historic Milepost 1306 Tetlin Junction; Alaska Route 5 (Taylor Highway) leads 66 miles to Chicken, 160 miles to Eagle and 175 miles to Dawson City, YT. *NOTE: If you are traveling to Dawson City, keep in mind that both Canada's Little Gold Creek and the U.S. Poker Creek customs stations are closed at night; you CANNOT cross the border unless customs stations are open. Customs hours are usually 8 A.M. to 8 P.M. Alaska standard time on the U.S. side, 9 A.M. to 9 P.M. Pacific standard time on the Canadian side. Customs stations are open daily in season, which is usually from about mid-May to mid-September (subject to change depending on road conditions). There are no phones at Poker Creek. Travelers are advised to check for current information at Alaska Public Lands Information Center in Tok or inquire at Port Alcan when crossing the border.*

Junction of the Alaska Highway with the Taylor Highway (Alaska Route 5) to Chicken and Eagle. The Taylor Highway junctions with Yukon Highway 9 (Top of the World Highway) to Dawson City. Turn to page 288 and read KLONDIKE LOOP introduction, then turn to page 317 and read log of Highways 5, 9 and from back to front. See also "Side Trip to Eagle" beginning on page 311.

In 1949, the Forty Mile Roadhouse located at this intersection served Alaska Highway travelers and motorists who were headed up the new Forty-Mile and Eagle Highway (now the Taylor Highway), which was still under construction with about 20 miles of road built. The roadhouse offered cabins, meals, a grocery store, and a garage with gas and oil. Ray and Mabel Scoby were listed as the proprietors of the roadhouse until 1975. The Native Village of Tetlin owned and operated the roadhouse until it closed in about 1985.

DC 1266.8 MP 1301.8 DJ 120.2 F 216.2 Turnout to south.

Distance marker westbound shows Tok 12 miles, Fairbanks 217 miles, Anchorage 347 miles.

DC 1267.9 MP 1302.9 DJ 119.1 F 215.1 Large paved turnout to south up on hill.

DC 1268 MP 1303 DJ 119 F 215 Easy-to-miss turnoff to south for short access road to rest area at east end of Tanana River Bridge; paved parking, toilets, interpretive displays (pictured below) on construction of the old and new (2010) Tanana River bridges. Viewing platform is on former abutment of the old bridge; good view (and photo op) of Tanana River and bridge.

©Kris Valencia, staff

DC 1268.6 MP 1303.6 DJ 118.4 F 214.4 Crossing the **Tanana River Bridge**; access to large paved parking with toilets and boat ramp to north at west end of bridge. The original Tanana River Bridge was built in 1943 during construction of the Alaska Highway and was one of only 5 truss bridges built in Alaska during World War II still in use (see interpretive signs at rest area to south at east end of bridge; description at **Milepost DC 1268**). Tanana (TAN-uh-naw), an Indian name, was first reported by the Western Union Telegraph Expedition of 1886. According to William Henry Dall, chief scientist of the expedition, the name means "mountain river." The Tanana is formed by the confluence of the Chisana and Nabesna rivers and flows 440 miles northwest to the Yukon River.

Northbound, the highway parallels the Tanana River to Fairbanks. The Alaska Range is to the northwest.

DC 1269.6 MP 1304.6 DJ 117.4 F 213.4 Evidence of 1990 burn from here to Tok. The Tok River fire in July 1990 burned more than 100,000 acres. The fire closed the Alaska Highway and Tok Cutoff. Tok was evacuated as firefighters' efforts to stop the fire appeared to be in vain. A "miracle wind" diverted the fire from town at the last minute.

DC 1272.8 MP 1307.8 DJ 114.2 F 210.2 Active sawmill to south.

DC 1273.5 MP 1308.5 DJ 113.5 F 209.5 Tok Weigh Station to southwest; phone.

EAST 5
DAWSON CITY.CA
182 Miles

Distinctive exterior of the Tok Visitors Center, located at the junction of the Alaska Highway and Tok Cutoff. (©Kris Valencia, staff)

DC 1273.6 MP 1308.6 **DJ 113.4 F 209.4** Small vehicle/single big-rig turnout to southwest by southbound weigh station sign.

DC 1274.2 MP 1309.2 **DJ 112.8 F 208.8** Turnoff to north just east of Tok River bridge for **Tok River State Recreation Site**; 27 campsites, some pull-through sites (vehicles to max. 60 feet); $18 per night.

Campsites are located along a good loop road beside the Tok River; campground host, tables, firepits, wheelchair-accessible toilets, litter barrels, nature trail, boat launch (can be very rough) and pay phone. Community firepits and covered picnic area. Check bulletin board for schedule of interpretive programs. Information board on WWII Lend-Lease Program, permafrost and other subjects. Camping fees posted. *CAUTION: Swift water.*

DC 1274.4 MP 1309.4 **DJ 112.6 F 208.6** Tok River bridge (clearance 15' 8"). The Tok River heads at Tok Glacier in the Alaska Range and flows 60 miles northeast into the Tanana River.

DC 1276 MP 1311 **DJ 111 F 207** Northbound travelers should have cell phone service starting here (we did).

DC 1277.2 MP 1312.2 **DJ 109.8 F 205.8** Purple Heart Trail Honoring Veterans' Sacrifice (southbound sign). The Alaska Highway from Delta Junction to the Canadian border was designated the "Purple Heart Trail" in May 2008, to honor veterans.

DC 1277.6 MP 1312.6 **DJ 109.4 F 205.4** Tok community limits. Sign southbound: "No studded tires May 1–Sept. 15." *Slow for posted speed zones (enforced) through Tok.*

DC 1277.7 MP 1312.7 **DJ 109.3 F 205.3** Tok Dog Mushers Assoc. track and buildings. Southeast end of paved bike trail.

DC 1278 MP 1313 **DJ 109 F 205** Alaskan Stoves Campground. Tok Junction airstrip (see Private Aircraft in Tok).

Southbound travelers: Driving distance from Tok to Beaver Creek is 113 miles/182 km; Haines Junction 296 miles/476 km; Haines (departure point for Alaska state ferries) 446 miles/718 km; and Whitehorse 396 miles/637 km.

DC 1278.1 MP 1313.1 **DJ 108.9 F 204.9** **Fast Eddy's Frontier Cabins** on right north-

bound; description follows.

Fast Eddy's Frontier Cabins. This is why you came to Alaska! Experience Alaska in a unique way and relax in one of our cozy cabins. Two queen beds, flat screen TV with

Direct TV–120+ channels and HD, WiFi, full modern bathrooms, coffee makers and spacious porch. Reserve early, check-in at Fast Eddy's Restaurant next door. (907) 883-4411. See display ad page 225. [ADVERTISEMENT]

DC 1278.2 MP 1313.3 **DJ 108.8 F 204.8** Iconic **Fast Eddy's Restaurant** and adjoining **Young's Motel** on right northbound; description follows.

Young's Motel and Fast Eddy's Restaurant. A touch of Alaskana in a modern setting. Affordable, clean and spacious. We cater to the independent highway traveler.

Open year-round with all the amenities: telephones, private baths, flat screen TV with 120+ channels and HD, ample parking. Nonsmoking rooms. WiFi. Check in at Fast Eddy's full-service restaurant, open summer 6 A.M. to 11 P.M.; open winter 7 A.M. to 9 P.M. Reserve early! P.O. Box 482, Tok, AK 99780. (907) 883-4411; fax (907) 883-5023; email mp@youngsenterprisesllc.

com. See display ad page 225. [ADVERTISEMENT]

DC 1278.4 MP 1313.4 **DJ 108.6 F 204.6** **Tok RV Village & Cabins** (description follows); Village Gas.

Tok RV Village & Cabins. We are your gateway to Alaska! 31-year family-owned/operated business. 161 sites, full and partial hookups, tent sites, cozy cabins, vehicle wash, cable TV, WiFi available, laundry, fishing and hunting licenses, meeting room. Very clean restroom/showers, gift shop with friendly staff to help answer your questions. 1-800-478-5878; www.tokrv.net. See display ad on page 226. [ADVERTISEMENT]

DC 1279 MP 1314 **DJ 108 F 204** Alaska Public Lands Information Center and Blue Star Memorial Highway marker.

Distance marker eastbound shows Tetlin Junction 12 miles, Canadian Border 93 miles, Haines Junction 298 miles.

DC 1279.2 MP 1314.2 **DJ 107.8 F 203.8** **Tok Junction.** Turn southwest on Tok Cutoff for Anchorage, continue northwest through intersection for Delta Junction and Richardson Highway to Fairbanks. *Northbound log continues on page 229.*

Junction of the Alaska Highway (Alaska Route 2) and the Tok Cutoff to the Glenn Highway (Alaska Route 1). It is 328 miles from Tok to Anchorage via Alaska Route 1. Turn to the GLENN HIGHWAY/TOK CUTOFF section on page 318 for log.

Tok post office adjacent **Burnt Paw Gift Shop. All Alaska Gifts** is located across from the Tok Visitor Center, adjacent Tok Memorial Park (see map page 226).

All Alaska Gifts & Crafts. Located at **Milepost 1314.2** Alaska Highway, next door to the Tok Visitor Center. Come in and enjoy free coffee with a sample of homemade fudge while looking at our life-size wildlife displays of moose, bears, sheep and wolves. We have hundreds of quality Alaska T-shirts, jewelry, Native crafts, gold nuggets and free WiFi. www.allalaskagifts.com. See display ad page 227. [ADVERTISEMENT]

ALASKA ROUTE 2 South

Southbound: Distance from Dawson Creek (DC) is followed by distance from physical milepost (MP), distance from Delta Junction (DJ) and distance from Fairbanks (F). Read log:

DC mileages are based on actual driving distance from Dawson Creek, BC, and MP mileages are based on physical mileposts between Delta Junction and the Alaska-Canada border which reflect traditional distances from Dawson Creek, BC.

Tok

DC 1279.2 MP 1314.2 **DJ 107.8 F 203.8 Historical Milepost 1314** Alaska Highway, at the junction with the Tok Cutoff (Glenn Highway). Tok is 328 miles/528 km from Anchorage, 254 miles/409 km from Valdez, 108 miles/174 km from Delta Junction, 204 miles/328 km from Fairbanks, 113 miles/182 km from Beaver Creek, YT, 294 miles/473 km from Haines Junction, YT, and 445 miles from Haines, AK. **Population:** 1,435. **Emergency Services:** Dial 911.

Alaska State Troopers, phone (907) 883-5111. **Fire Department**, phone (907) 883-5831. EMT squad and air medivac available. **Community Clinic**, on the Tok Cutoff, phone (907) 883-5855.

Visitor Information: The **Alaska Public Lands Information Center** (APLIC), located in the Troopers Building just east of the junction at **Milepost 1314**, has public restrooms and information on the Alaska Marine Highway System state ferries, fishing and hunting regulations, and recreation in state and national parks. Write P.O. Box 359, Tok, AK 99780; phone (907) 883-5667; www.alaskacenters.gov/tok.cfm.

The **Tok Visitors Center**, "**Mainstreet Thru Alaska**" is located at the junction of the Alaska Highway and Tok Cutoff; open mid-May through mid-September, hours as posted. The visitor center offers trip planning help and complete travel information on the Alaska Highway, travel in and around Alaska, as well as local information. The center also offers restrooms, WiFi current road conditions, weather forecasts, message board and numerous displays of Alaska wildlife. *(See description of the center in Attractions this section.)* Phone (907) 883-5775; www.tokalaskainfo.com.

The Alaska Dept. of Fish and Game office is located on Center Street, across from Tok Mainstreet Visitor Center at **Milepost 1314.2**. Contact ADF&G phone (907) 883-2971. Fishing licenses are available at local stores.

Elevation: 1,635 feet. **Climate:** Mean monthly temperature in January is -19° F; average low is -32°F. Mean monthly temperature in July is 59°F; average high is 72°F. Record low was -71°F (January 1965); record high, 99°F. **Radio:** FM stations are 90.5, 91.1 (KUAC-FM, University of Alaska Fairbanks), 101.5, and 104.9 (KJNP-FM, King Jesus North Pole). **Television:** Satellite channel 13. **Newspaper:** *Mukluk News* (twice monthly).

Private Aircraft: Tok Junction, 1 E; elev. 1,630 feet; length 2,510 feet; asphalt; fuel 100LL; unattended. Tok airstrip, on Tok Cutoff, 2 S; elev. 1,670 feet; length 3,000 feet; gravel; no fuel, unattended.

Description

Tok began as a construction camp on the Alcan Highway in 1942. One of the largest such camps on the pioneer road, it was called "Million Dollar Camp," a reference to the cost of equipping and maintaining it. Highway engineer C.G. Polk was sent to Fairbanks in May of 1942, to take charge of Alaska construction and start work on the road between Tok Junction and Big Delta. Work was also under way on the Gulkana–Slana–Tok Junction road (now the Tok Cutoff on the Glenn Highway to Anchorage). But on June 7, 1942, a Japanese task force invaded Attu and Kiska islands in the Aleutians, and the Alcan took priority over the Slana cutoff.

Tok Junction was also the location of the U.S. Customs and Immigration Office until 1971, when the border station was built closer to the international border.

A frequently asked question is how Tok (pronounced to rhyme with poke) got its name. A couple of theories have been put forward over the years. One believed the name Tok was derived from Tokyo Camp, the name of an Alaska Highway road construction camp that was patriotically shortened to Tok in the 1940s. Another story

was that Tok was named after a husky pup of that name, mascot to a U.S. Army's Corp battalion who were breaking trail north from Slana in 1942. Stop in at the Visitor Center for a handout on the latest historical research into Tok's name.

Because Tok is the major overland point of entry to Alaska, it is primarily a trade and service center for all types of transportation, especially for summer travelers coming up the Alaska Highway. A stopover here is a good opportunity to get the "inside scoop" on current travel information and to meet other travelers. Tok is the only town in Alaska that the highway traveler must pass through twice—once when arriving in the state and again on leaving the state. The governor proclaimed Tok "Mainstreet Alaska" in 1991. Townspeople are proud of

this designation and work hard to make visitors happy.

Tok's central business district is at the junction of the Alaska Highway and Tok Cutoff. From the junction, homes and businesses spread out along both highways on flat terrain dotted with densely timbered stands of black spruce.

Tok has 8 churches, a public library, a K–12 school and University of Alaska extension center. Local clubs include the Lions, Veterans of Foreign Wars and Chamber of Commerce.

Tok is known as the "Sled Dog Capital of Alaska" because so many of its residents are involved in some way with dogs and dog mushing, Alaska's official state sport. Judging by the number of Alaska Highway travelers cleaning their cars and RVs in Tok each

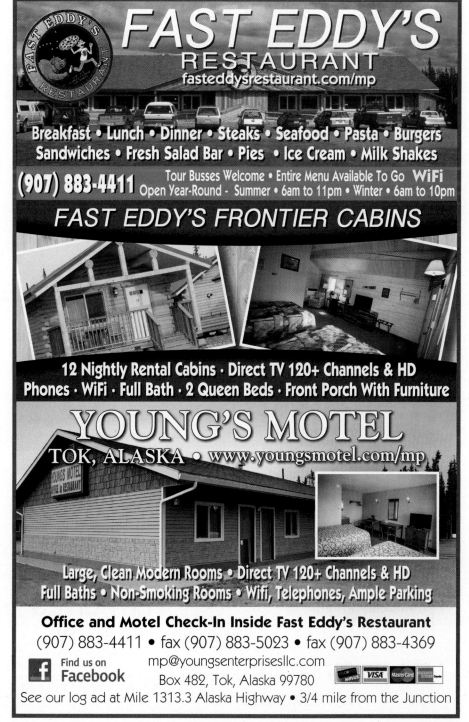

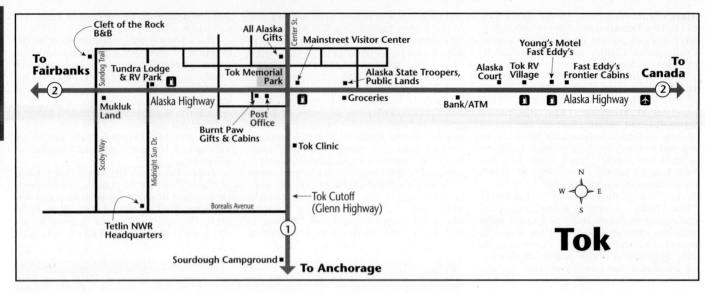

Map of Tok showing streets and points of interest including Cleft of the Rock B&B, All Alaska Gifts, Mainstreet Visitor Center, Young's Motel, Fast Eddy's, Alaska Court, Tok RV Village, Fast Eddy's Frontier Cabins, Tundra Lodge & RV Park, Tok Memorial Park, Alaska State Troopers/Public Lands, Groceries, Bank/ATM, Mukluk Land, Burnt Paw Gifts & Cabins, Post Office, Tok Clinic, Tok Cutoff (Glenn Highway), Tetlin NWR Headquarters, Borealis Avenue, Sourdough Campground. To Fairbanks, To Canada, To Anchorage.

Tok

summer, it may also qualify as the "Vehicle Washing Capital of Alaska."

Lodging & Services

Tok has all visitor services including hotels, motels, bed and breakfast, restaurants, gas stations, auto/RV repair, car washes and laundromat. Services are located along both the Alaska Highway and Tok Cutoff.

Lodging at **Burnt Paw Cabins**, **Young's Motel** and **Fast Eddy's Frontier Cabins** (see ads this section), and others. Dining at **Fast Eddy's Restaurant**.

The post office is located on the Alaska Highway just northwest of its junction with the Tok Cutoff, adjacent Burnt Paw gift shop. Fishing and hunting licenses and supplies available at local sporting goods store. Groceries, liquor and sundries available locally. Vehicle wash at **Tok RV Village**, **Tundra Lodge and RV Park** and **Sourdough Campground**.

Parking, playground and picnic shelters are available at Tok Memorial Park, across from the Tok Mainstreet Visitor Center.

Camping

There are several RV parks and campgrounds in the Tok area. See advertisements this section for **Tok RV Village** and **Tundra Lodge and RV Park** on the Alaska Highway, and **Sourdough Campground**, 2 miles south on the Tok Cutoff.

Some RVers towing cars are using Tok as a jump-off point to visit Dawson City, YT, and other destinations, leaving their big rigs at local campgrounds. Inquire locally about parking your RV at campgrounds.

Nearby state campgrounds include: Tok River State Recreation Site, 5 miles southeast of Tok on the Alaska Highway at **Milepost 1309.2**; Moon Lake State Recreation Site, 17.7 miles northwest of Tok at **Milepost 1331.9** Alaska Highway; and Eagle Trail State

Recreation Site, 16 miles southwest of Tok at **Milepost GJ 109.3** Tok Cutoff.

Transportation

Air: Charter air service available; inquire at Tok state airstrip (**Milepost 1313**). Charter flightseeing and fly-in fishing trips available. Scheduled passenger and freight service between Tok, Delta Junction and Fairbanks via 40-Mile Air.

Bus: See Bus Lines in the TRAVEL PLANNING section.

Highway: Tok is located at the junction of the Alaska Highway and Tok Cutoff (see GLENN HIGHWAY/TOK CUTOFF section). Tok has become a popular spot with RVers towing cars to park their big rigs here while they drive to Dawson City, YT, via the Taylor Highway, Boundary Spur Road and Top of the World Highway; see KLONDIKE LOOP section for details on this route.

Attractions

Tok Visitors Center, "**MainStreet Thru Alaska**," located at the junction of the Alaska Highway and Tok Cutoff, houses both the expansive Tok Mainstreet Visitors Center and the small Tok Community Public Library (staffed by volunteers), which has a separate entrance. The visitor center offers a destination-based, well-organized display of brochures from statewide attractions as well as friendly trip-planning assistance. Huge natural white spruce logs, brought in locally, support the open-beamed, cathedral ceiling of this 7,000-square-foot building. Seating and restrooms available to the public. Large picture windows frame the Alaska Range. Excellent displays of Alaska rocks, gems and fossils; gold rush history; Alaska wildlife and waterfowl; Alaska Highway memorabilia; and videos of Alaska Highway construction and other Alaska topics. Great photo ops available with the wolves mount and the dogsled display inside the center. Picnic tables are located out in front. All Alaska Gifts is located next door to the Tok Visitor

Private campgrounds in Tok include Tok RV Village (pictured here), Tundra Lodge & RV Park and Sourdough Campground. (©Kris Valencia, staff)

Center.

The **Alaska Public Lands Information Center** (APLIC), located next door to the Tok Mainstreet Visitors Center, offers trip planning information and displays of beadwork and animal and fish mounts. The standing grizzly bear mount is an especially popular attraction at the Center. APLIC staff can help you with Alaska Marine Highway ferry reservations and provide details on recreation opportunities on state and federal lands in Alaska. Free State of Alaska map.

Phone toll-free 1-888-256-6784.

Tok Memorial Park, at the Alaska Highway and Tok Cutoff intersection—across from Tok Mainstreet Visitors Center—and in front of All Alaska Gifts—has day parking, a picnic shelter and playground.

Biking: A wide paved bike trail parallels the Alaska Highway and extends from Tok southeast to the Dog Mushers Assoc. track, and northwest to Tanacross Junction. Approximate length is 13 miles. There is also a 2.4-mile bike trail along the Tok Cutoff

Sod-roofed gift shop at Burnt Paw gets mowed during the summer. (©Kris Valencia, staff)

west from Tok.

Flightseeing. 40-Mile Air offers passenger space on their twice-weekly "milk run" to Chisana for $105. A good way to see the region from the air.

Local entertainment and events. Tok RV Village offers live evening entertainment during the summer, and Sourdough Campground is the "home of the sourdough pancake toss." The Chamber of Commerce sponsors the 4th of July parade and activities, and the annual Community Flea Market, held the first Saturday in August.

Alaskan Crafts: Tok is a trade center for the Athabascan Native villages of Tanacross, Northway, Tetlin, Mentasta, Dot Lake and Eagle. Several of the Native women make

birch baskets, beaded moccasins, boots and beaded necklaces. The State of Alaska has a crafts identification program that authenticates Alaskan Native and Alaskan Craftsmen products. Examples of both may be seen at Burnt Paw and All Alaska Gifts in Tok.

Many of the moccasins and mukluks for sale in Tok are made with traditionally tanned moose hides. After scraping the hide clean, it is soaked in a soap solution. Then the moisture is taken out by constant scraping with a dull knife or scraper. The hide is then scraped again and rubbed together to soften it. Next it is often smoke-cured in rotted spruce wood smoke. The tanning process takes from a few days to a week.

Birch baskets were once used in the Native camps and villages. Traditionally, they had folded corners, held water, and were even used for cooking by dropping heated stones into the liquid in the baskets. The baskets are made by peeling the bark from the birch trees, usually in the early summer months. The bark is easiest to work with when moist and pliable. It is cut into shape and sewn together with strips of spruce root dug out of the ground and split. If the root is too dry it is soaked until it is manageable. Holes are put in the birch bark with a punch or screwdriver, and the spruce root is laced in and out. Native women dye the spruce root with food coloring, watercolors or berry juice. A few Natives also make model birch canoes and birch baby carriers.

Mukluk Land, at **Milepost 1317** Alaska Highway, has an indoor-outdoor museum, miniature golf, activities for kids, videos, educational displays. Open 2–7 P.M. daily, June to August 20. Phone (907) 883-2571; www.muklukland.net.

Sled Dog Trails and Races: Tok boasts a well-known and long-established dog mushing trail, which draws many world-class and recreational mushers. The 20.5-mile/33-km trail begins at the rustic log Tok Dog Mushers Assoc. building at **Milepost 1312.7** on the Alaska Highway. The trail is a favorite with spectators because it affords many miles of viewing from along the Alaska Highway. Racing begins in late November and extends through the end of March.

The biggest race of the season in Tok is the Race of Champions, held in late March, which also has the largest entry of any sprint race in Alaska. Begun in 1954 as a bet between 2 roadhouse proprietors, today the Race of Champions includes over 100 teams in 3 classes competing for prize money and trophies. It is considered to be the third leg of sled dog racing's "triple crown," following the Fur Rendezvous in Anchorage and the Fairbanks North American Championship. Visitors are also welcome to attend the Tok Native Assoc.'s potlatch, held the same weekend as the race.

Bill Arpino at Burnt Paw was a finisher in the 1973 Iditarod. For many years the Arpinos put on dog mushing demonstrations at their gift shop. Although the dog sled demos have ceased, Burnt Paw has a free outdoor dog team equipment display and may have sled dog puppies in the kennel adjacent the display.

Visit Dawson City, Eagle or Chicken. Leave your big rig at a campground in Tok and head north on the Taylor Highway to reach Chicken (156 miles round-trip) or Eagle (172 miles one-way). For Dawson City, YT (make sure you have your passport), it is a 187-mile drive one-way via the Taylor and

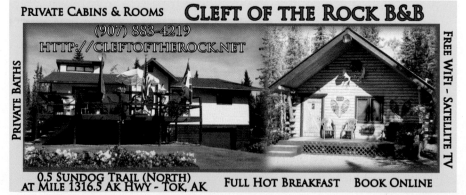

Top of the World highways. Read through the KLONDIKE LOOP introduction, then follow the log from back to front.

Moon Lake State Recreation Site at **Milepost DC 1296.9** (physical **Milepost 1331.9**) is a great place to have a picnic. If you are lucky you'll see a moose. Loons are often present at the lake. Moon Lake is a popular spot for swimming and canoeing.

AREA FISHING: There are several walk-in fishing lakes along the Alaska Highway between Tok and Delta Junction, all stocked with rainbow trout. These include: **Jan Lake** at **Milepost 1353.5**; **Lisa Lake** at **Milepost 1381**; **Craig Lake** at **Milepost 1383.7**; and **Donna Lake** and **Little Donna Lake** at **Milepost 1391.8**. Consult the ADF&G office in Delta Junction (907/895-4632) for details on fishing in these areas.

Alaska Highway Log
(continued)

ALASKA ROUTE 2 North
Northbound: Distance from Dawson Creek (DC) is followed by distance from physical milepost (MP), distance from Delta Junction (DJ) and distance from Fairbanks (F). Read log:

DC 1279.2 MP 1314.2 **DJ 107.8 F 203.8 Tok Junction.** Tok Mainstreet Visitors Center and **All Alaska Gifts.** Tok businesses (including Sourdough Campground) and a bike path extend southwest along the Tok Cutoff/Alaska Route 1. *See description of Tok beginning on page 224.*

All Alaska Gifts. See display ad on page 227.

Junction of the Alaska Highway (Alaska Route 2) and the Tok Cutoff to the Glenn Highway (Alaska Route 1). It is 328 miles from Tok to Anchorage via Alaska Route 1. See GLENN HIGHWAY/TOK CUTOFF section on page 318 for log.

Improved bike trail next 11.5 miles (to Tanacross Junction at **Milepost 1325.7**) westbound. ATV trails both sides of road to **Milepost 1323**.

DC 1279.3 MP 1314.3 **DJ 107.7 F 203.7** Tok Post Office and **Burnt Paw Gift Shop and Cabins Outback** to southwest, Tok Memorial Park to northeast.

Burnt Paw Gift Shop & Cabins Outback. See display ad on facing page.

Distance marker westbound shows Tanacross 12 miles, Delta Junction 109 miles, Fairbanks 205 miles. Sign: No studded tires May 1–Sept. 15.

Road conditions northbound: Fair to good pavement with stretches of improved surfacing, some wide straight stretches, narrow shoulders, to Delta Junction.

DC 1279.6 MP 1314.6 **DJ 107.4 F 203.4** Northbound sign: $1,000 fine for littering.

DC 1279.9 MP 1314.9 **DJ 107.1 F 203.1** Tesoro gas station; diesel.

Slow for speed zone southbound through Tok.

DC 1280 MP 1315 **DJ 107 F 203 Tundra Lodge and RV Park.** Spacious, naturally forested camping sites. Full and partial hookups; 20-, 30-, 50-amp power. Tent sites. Pull-throughs. Clean restrooms and showers included in price. Picnic tables, fire rings. Dump station. Laundromat. Vehicle wash. Ice. Cocktail lounge and meeting room. Email/DSL/WiFi Hot Spot.

tundrarvpark@gmail.com. See display ad on page 227. [ADVERTISEMENT]

DC 1280.7 MP 1315.7 **DJ 106.3 F 202.3** Midnight Sun Road. Sign: Tetlin Refuge Visitor Information 1.1 miles southwest. Tok city limits (northbound sign).

DC 1281.5 MP 1316.5 **DJ 105.5 F 201.5 Cleft of the Rock Bed and Breakfast.** See display ad on page 228.

DC 1282 MP 1317 **DJ 105 F 201 Mukluk Land.** Don't miss Tok's highlight, Mukluk Land, the home of Santa's Rocket Ship. Memorable, enjoyable and affordable for all ages. Indoor-outdoor museum, entertainment center, unique collections, dollhouse, videos, mini-golf, and much more. Open 2–7 P.M. daily, June–August 20. Admission: $5 adults, $4.50 seniors, $2 kids 3–19. Mile 1317 Alaska Highway. Phone (907) 883-2571 or (907) 505-0415; www.muklukland. net. [ADVERTISEMENT]

DC 1289.6 MP 1324.6 **DJ 97.4 F 193.4 Junction** with Old Tanacross Road (paved), marked by a colorful Smokey the Bear Fire Danger sign. Access northeast to Tanacross airstrip (0.5 mile), Alaska Dept. of Natural Resources (DNR) Tanacross Air Tanker Base 1 mile (description follows) and Tanacross Village and school 1.7 miles; or use main access at **Milepost 1325.7**. Distance marker southbound on the highway shows Tok 10 miles, Canada Border 103 miles.

The airfield at Tanacross was built in the 1930s, with assistance from local Natives, and was used by the U.S. Army in WWII as part of the Russia–America Lend Lease Program. (The Lend Lease Program sent war planes to Russia, a U.S. ally, to use in fighting Nazi Germany.) After WWII, the airfield was used for specialized arctic operations and maneuvers. The Tanacross Airfield was the sixth largest city in Alaska in 1962, housing more than 8,000 troops for "Operation Great Bear." In 1970, the Bureau of Land Management acquired the property because of the strategic location of its paved runway for refueling air tankers fighting forest fires. Alaska DNR now controls the air tanker operations at the airfield.

Private Aircraft: Tanacross airstrip; elev. 1,549 feet; 2 runways, length 5,000 feet and 5,100 feet; asphalt; unattended. *CAUTION: Forest fire aviation support may be in progress.*

DC 1289.8 MP 1324.8 **DJ 97.2 F 193.2** Distance marker westbound shows Dot Lake 37 miles, Delta Junction 99 miles, Fairbanks 195 miles.

DC 1290.6 MP 1325.6 **DJ 96.4 F 192.4** Historic Milepost 1328. Burn area next 4 miles northbound.

DC 1290.7 MP 1325.7 **DJ 96.3 F 192.3 Junction** with New Tanacross Road, the main access road north to Tanacross. Drive 1.2 miles on gravel road to "Y" intersection; turn right for airstrip (see **Milepost 1324.6**), turn left for loop road through the village of **TANACROSS** (pop. 144), a traditional Athabascan community; no visitor services.

End paved bike trail from Tok.

DC 1291 MP 1326 **DJ 96 F 192** Old burn area with stunted black spruce.

DC 1292.2 MP 1327.2 **DJ 94.8 F 190.8** Small informal turnout by small lake to southwest. Watch for swans in roadside ponds.

DC 1292.4 MP 1327.4 **DJ 94.6 F 190.6** Informal turnout to gravel parking area by pond (may be flooded in wet weather).

DC 1294 MP 1329 **DJ 93 F 189** Evidence of old burn in black spruce.

DC 1295.6 MP 1330.6 **DJ 91.4 F 187.4**

Paved parking to north with river view.

DC 1296.9 MP 1331.9 **DJ 90.1 F 186.1 Moon Lake State Recreation Site,** 0.2 mile northeast via paved access road; 17 campsites, picnic area, toilets, tables, bear-proof litter bins, water, firepits, boat launch, sandy beach (at low water). Swimming area is sometimes marked by buoys. Floatplanes use this lake. Motorized and non-motorized boating. Canoeing is especially popular on this lake. Wildlife to see includes squirrels, grey jays, loons and moose. Camping fee $15/night.

▲

DC 1298.6 MP 1333.6 **DJ 88.4 F 184.4 Historic Milepost 1339.** Yerrick Creek bridge. Turnout to south at west end of bridge.

DC 1302.6 MP 1337.6 **DJ 84.4 F 180.4** Distance marker southbound shows Tok 23 miles, Canadian border 116 miles.

DC 1303.2 MP 1338.2 **DJ 83.8 F 179.8** Highway crosses Cathedral Rapids #1 (signed).

DC 1303.5 MP 1338.5 **DJ 83.5 F 179.5** Turnoff to southwest for **Cathedral Creeks B&B and Campground** (description follows).

Cathedral Creeks B&B and Campground. An absolutely idyllic spot! This very clean and peaceful hideaway, situated

between creeks and mountains, offers campsites, rooms, and a cabin at low rates (room/cabin includes a delicious breakfast). The park-like campground features power, water, free firewood, and hot showers. Free German hospitality and WiFi! (907) 940-3176. http://www.cathedralcreeks.net. [ADVERTISEMENT]

▲

DC 1303.7 MP 1338.7 **DJ 83.3 F 179.3** Highway crosses Cathedral Rapids #2 (signed).

DC 1304 MP 1339 **DJ 83 F 179** Highway crosses Cathedral Rapids #3 (signed).

DC 1307.2 MP 1342.2 **DJ 79.8 F 175.8** Sheep Creek culvert.

DC 1309.2 MP 1344.2 **DJ 77.8 F 173.8** Distance marker westbound shows Delta Junction 80 miles, Fairbanks 175 miles.

DC 1309.5 MP 1344.5 **DJ 77.5 F 173.5** Paved parking area to northeast with picnic tables, toilets, litter bin and viewpoint. Good photo stop with view of the Alaska Range. Good place to stretch your legs. A path (wheelchair-accessible) leads 300 feet to Tanana River viewpoint; interpretive panel on "Early Hunters of the Tanana." Interpretive panel on Alaska Highway and Slim Williams at parking area reads:

"When Alaska Road Commissioner Donald MacDonald heard Clyde "Slim" Williams was mushing from Alaska to the Chicago World's Fair, he was delighted. It was perfect for promoting his idea for a highway linking Alaska with the Lower 48. He wired Slim at one of his stops asking him to place a banner on his sled and become a spokesman for the proposed road. Slim arrived at the Chicago World's Fair in September 1933, after 10 months en route. Slim Williams and his dogs gained immense popularity at the fair by giving rides to fairgoers. First Lady Eleanor Roosevelt was so impressed with her ride, she invited Slim to Washington DC to meet President Franklin D. Roosevelt."

Williams went on to ride motorcycle to Alaska in 1939. He and John Logan were novice riders who would, according to Williams "figure it out." This trip helped to promote the idea of a road to Alaska.

Distance marker southbound shows Tok Junction 30 miles, Tetlin Junction 42 miles, Canada border 123 miles.

DC 1312 MP 1347 **DJ 75 F 171 Forest Lake** trailhead (not signed); approximately 8-mile primitive ATV trail (not an easy access to this remote lake according to ADF&G). Tent platform and outhouse at the lake. Stocked with rainbow trout.

DC 1312.5 MP 1347.5 **DJ 74.5 F 170.5** Robertson River bridge. The river was named by Lt. Henry T. Allen for a member of his 1885 expedition. The Robertson River heads at the terminus of Robertson Glacier in the Alaska Range and flows 33 miles northeast to the Tanana River.

Good view of the Alaska Range to west.

Entering Game Management Unit 20D westbound, Unit 12 eastbound.

DC 1313.1 MP 1348.1 **DJ 73.9 F 169.9** Side road uphill west to public fishing access; parking. Hike in 0.3 mile for **Robertson No. 2 Lake** (not signed); rainbow trout fishing (stocked by ADF&G).

DC 1315.5 MP 1350.5 **DJ 71.5 F 167.5** Large paved and gravel turnout to southwest.

DC 1317.5 MP 1352.5 **DJ 69.5 F 165.5** Gravel turnout by pond to northeast.

Distance marker westbound shows Delta Junction 70 miles, Fairbanks 165 miles.

CAUTION: Watch for moose.

DC 1318.5 MP 1353.5 **DJ 68.5 F 164.5** Jan Lake Road to south; public fishing access. Drive in 0.5 mile/0.8 km to parking area; no overnight camping, carry out garbage. **Jan Lake** is stocked by ADF&G with rainbow trout and land-locked salmon (chinook, coho). Dot Lake Native Corp. land, limited public access.

DC 1319.2 MP 1354.2 **DJ 67.8 F 163.8** Distance marker eastbound shows Tanacross 32 miles, Tok Junction 40 miles.

DC 1321 MP 1356 **DJ 66 F 162** Large stands of aspen are seen on both sides of the highway here. Quaking aspen grow on well-drained benches, sunny south slopes and creek bottoms throughout interior Alaska. They can spread by sending up suckers from their root systems, thereby creating "clonal stands" of genetically identical trees that leaf at the same time in the spring and turn yellow at the same time in the fall.

DC 1322.3 MP 1357.3 **DJ 64.7 F 160.7** Bear Creek bridge. Paved parking area.

DC 1323.6 MP 1358.6 **DJ 63.4 F 159.4** Chief Creek bridge. Paved parking area.

CAUTION: Watch for moose.

NOTE: Slow for speed zone northbound through Dot Lake. Posted speed limit 65-mph southbound.

DC 1326 MP 1361 **DJ 61 F 157** Dot Lake School.

DC 1326.3 MP 1361.3 **DJ 60.7 F 156.7** **DOT LAKE** (pop. 13) was first homesteaded in the 1940s, and was originally a work camp called Sears City during construction of the Alaska Highway in 1942–1943.

DC 1326.5 MP 1361.5 **DJ 60.5 F 156.5** Very large paved turnout alongside Dot Lake; a nice stopping spot, lots of birds on the lake in spring and summer. **Historic Milepost 1368** here commemorates the 50th anniversary of the Northwest Highway System (1942–1992). Nearby is Dot Lake Lakeside Community Chapel, built in 1949, a wonderful old-time Alaskan church.

Dot Lake was once an Athabascan hunting camp and a spot on an Indian freight trail to the Yukon River. **DOT LAKE VILLAGE** (pop. 62), separate from the highway community, is a traditional Upper Tanana Athabascan village. It is also headquarters for the Dot Lake Native Corp.

DC 1327 MP 1362 **DJ 60 F 156** Posted speed limit 65-mph northbound.

Slow for speed zone southbound through Dot Lake.

DC 1328.5 MP 1363.5 **DJ 58.5 F 154.5** Purple Heart Trail Honoring Veterans' Sacrifice signs. The Alaska Highway from Delta Junction to the Canadian border was designated the "Purple Heart Trail" in May 2008, to honor veterans.

DC 1329.3 MP 1364.3 **DJ 57.7 F 153.7** Distance marker southbound shows Tok Junction 50 miles, Tetlin Junction 62 miles.

DC 1335.2 MP 1370.2 **DJ 51.8 F 147.8** Double-ended paved turnout to north.

DC 1335.8 MP 1370.8 **DJ 51.2 F 147.2** Entering **Tanana Valley State Forest** westbound; managed by the Dept. of Natural Resources. Established as the first unit of Alaska's state forest system in 1983, Tanana Valley State Forest encompasses 1.81 million acres and lies almost entirely within the Tanana River Basin. The forest extends 265 miles from near the Canadian border to Manley Hot Springs. Almost 90 percent of the state forest is forested, with the remainder mostly shrubland. Principal tree species are paper birch, quaking aspen, balsam poplar, black spruce, white spruce and tamarack.

DC 1336.4 MP 1371.4 **DJ 50.6 F 146.6** Berry Creek bridge. Parking area to south at west end of bridge.

DC 1336.9 MP 1371.9 **DJ 50.1 F 146.1** Distance marker westbound shows Delta Junction 50 miles, Fairbanks 145 miles.

DC 1339.3 MP 1374.3 **DJ 47.7 F 143.5** Culvert for Sears Creek. Parking area to south (no turnaround space for big rigs).

DC 1343 MP 1378 **DJ 44 F 140** Dry Creek culvert.

DC 1344 MP 1379 **DJ 43 F 139** Double-ended paved parking area to south; Alaska cotton.

DC 1345.5 MP 1380.5 **DJ 41.5 F 137.5** Johnson River bridge (clearance 15' 6"). A tributary of the Tanana River, the Johnson River was named by Lt. Henry T. Allen in 1887 for Peder Johnson, a Swedish miner and member of his party.

DC 1346 MP 1381 **DJ 41 F 137** Paved double-ended parking area to south at trailhead for 0.7-mile improved gravel trail to **Lisa Lake**; stocked with rainbow trout and land-locked coho salmon. Access to public-use cabin, available by reservation from ADF&G office in Delta Junction (907/895-4632) or Fairbanks (907/459-7228).

DC 1347.4 MP 1382.4 **DJ 39.6 F 135.6** $1,000 Fine for littering (southbound sign).

DC 1348.7 MP 1383.7 **DJ 38.3 F 134.3** **Craig Lake** public fishing access, 1.1 miles to trailhead and 0.5-mile trail to lake; stocked with rainbow trout by ADF&G.

DC 1350 MP 1385 **DJ 37 F 133** Double-ended paved parking area to north. Paved access road to Tanana River boat launch (4-wheel-drive required).

Distance marker westbound shows Delta Junction 37 miles, Fairbanks 135 miles.

Distance marker eastbound shows Tok 71 miles, Canada border 163 miles.

DC 1353.4 MP 1388.4 **DJ 33.6 F 129.6** Little Gerstle River bridge. Double-ended paved parking area to south at east end of bridge, gravel access to river to north.

DC 1356.8 MP 1391.8 **DJ 30.2 F 126.2** Large double-ended paved parking to south at trailhead for Donna Lakes public fishing access (multiple sections of the trail are muddy). Also access to public-use cabin, available by reservation from ADF&G office in Delta Junction (907/895-4632) or Fairbanks (907/459-7228). **Donna Lake** (3.5 miles) and **Little Donna Lake** (4.5 miles) are stocked with rainbow trout.

DC 1357.7 MP 1392.7 **DJ 29.3 F 125.3** Gerstle River Black Veterans Memorial Bridge. Very large dirt and gravel parking area to north at east end of bridge; access to river. (The gravel turnout to south—across the highway—is a narrow, rocky track with no turnaround space for big rigs.)

©Kris Valencia, staff

Built in 1944, the Gerstle River Bridge is 1 of 4 "steel through truss-style" bridge constructions on the Alaska Highway. It was renamed Black Veterans Memorial Bridge in 1993, to commemorate the 3,695 African American soldiers of the 93rd, 94th, 95th, 97th and 388th U.S. Army Corps of Engineers for their contribution in constructing the Alcan Highway.

The Gerstle River was named for Lewis Gerstle, president of the Alaska Commercial Co., by Lt. Henry T. Allen, whose 1885 expedition explored the Copper, Tanana and Koyukuk river regions for the U.S. Army.

DC 1358 MP 1393 **DJ 29 F 125** Turnoff to south for rest area just west of Gerstle River bridge; covered picnic table, outhouses, garbage bin, short loop road to camping spots in trees. A nice shady spot on a hot summer day. From the outhouses, drive towards the river where there is access to a large parking area. Also access via rough gravel road to a gravel bar and to another rough gravel road that goes under the bridge. Walk out on the gravel bar for breath-taking views of the bridge. *CAUTION: Possible high water on gravel bars during spring melt and heavy rains in summer.*

DC 1358.1 MP 1393.1 **DJ 28.9 F 124.9** Distance marker westbound shows Delta Junction 30 miles, Fairbanks 128 miles.

DC 1359 MP 1394 **DJ 28 F 124** Distance marker eastbound shows Tanacross 68 miles, Tok 80 miles.

DC 1366 MP 1401 **DJ 21 F 117** Double-ended paved parking area to northeast.

DC 1368.4 MP 1403.4 **DJ 18.6 F 114.6** Sawmill Creek Road to Delta barley fields. Planting is in May; harvesting in August or September. Turnout at Mile 0.6 Sawmill Creek Road (with a nice view of the Alaska Range on clear days); large RVs may have to search for turnaround space on this side road.

Distance marker southbound shows Tok 90 miles.

DC 1368.7 MP 1403.7 **DJ 18.3 F 114.3** Sawmill Creek.

DC 1369.1 MP 1404.1 **MJ 17.9 F 113.9** Silver Fox Roadhouse to north; cabins, gift shop, convenience store, wildlife display, gas/diesel.

DC 1372 MP 1407 **DJ 15 F 111** Highway passes through area of permafrost, evidenced by the stunted black spruce, also called bog spruce or swamp spruce. As elsewhere in Interior Alaska, well-drained soil and south-facing slopes support tall, dense stands of white spruce, aspen and birch, while cold wet flats, muskeg and north-facing slopes are dominated by the stunted and crooked black spruce.

On the south side of the Alaska Highway is the Delta Junction Bison Range (not visible from highway). *See more information on the Delta bison herd on page 233.*

DC 1375 MP 1410 **DJ 12 F 108** Sign: Dial 511 for Travel Information.

DC 1376.5 MP 1411.5 **DJ 10.5 F 106.5** Paved double-ended turnout to south.

DC 1378 MP 1413 **DJ 9 F 105** Distance marker westbound shows Delta Junction 10 miles, Fairbanks 105 miles.

DC 1378.2 MP 1413.2 **DJ 8.8 F 104.8** Grain storage facility to south.

DC 1378.4 MP 1413.4 **DJ 8.6 F 104.6** **Delta Meat & Sausage Co.** to south; stop in for free samples.

Delta Meat & Sausage Co. See display ad this page.

DC 1379.4 MP 1414.4 **DJ 7.6 F 103.6** Distance marker southbound shows Dot Lake 53 miles, Tok Junction 101 miles, Canada border 193 miles.

DC 1379.8 MP 1414.8 **DJ 7.2 F 103.2** Turnoff for Clearwater Road, which leads north past farmlands to **Clearwater State Recreation Site** campground and **Clearwater Lodge** (restaurant, RV park, cabins, bar). To reach the state campground and Clearwater Lodge, follow Clearwater Road 5.2 miles north to junction with Remington Road; turn right and drive 2.7 miles east for Clearwater state campground or 2.8 miles east for Clearwater Lodge; both are situated on the bank of aptly-named Clearwater Creek. The state recreation site has 15 campsites, toilets, tables, firepits, water and boat ramp (launch fee is $10). Camping fee $15/night.

Clearwater Lodge. See display ad page 232.

This side road also provides a "loop" drive back to the Alaska Highway northwest of Delta Junction. To drive the "loop" (which bypasses Delta Junction), follow Clearwater Road north and turn left on Remington Road; turn right on Souhrada; then left on Jack Warren Road, which junctions with the Richardson Highway at **Milepost V 268.3.** Total driving distance is about 15 miles via the "loop."

The **Delta–Clearwater River** (local reference; stream is actually **Clearwater Creek**, which flows northwest to the Tanana River) is a premier Arctic grayling (catch-and-release) stream. A boat is needed for best fishing. This is a beautiful, clear, spring-fed stream; Arctic grayling, whitefish and coho salmon. There is a fall (September–October) coho run.

View of Clearwater River from Clearwater Lodge. A state recreation site is located nearby.
(©Kris Valencia, staff)

DC 1380.2 MP 1415.2 **DJ 6.8 F 102.8** Distance marker westbound shows Delta Junction 7 miles, Fairbanks 102 miles.

DC 1385.2 MP 1420.2 **DJ 1.8 F 97.8** Welcome to Delta Junction (northbound sign).

DC 1385.7 MP 1420.7 **DJ 1.3 F 97.3** Alaska State Troopers, Jarvis Office Center.

DC 1385.9 MP 1420.9 **DJ 1.1 F 97.1** **Snowed Inn RV Park** to north; full-hookups, tent sites, laundry, WiFi.

Snowed Inn RV Park. See display ad page 232.

DC 1386 MP 1421 **DJ 1 F 97** Purple Heart Trail Honoring Veterans' Sacrifice (southbound sign). The Alaska Highway from Delta Junction to the Canadian border was designated the "Purple Heart Trail" in May 2008, to honor veterans.

DC 1386.3 MP 1421.3 **DJ 0.7 F 96.7** *Slow for speed zone westbound through Delta Junction.*

DC 1386.7 MP 1421.7 **DJ 0.3 F 96.3** Distance marker eastbound shows Dot Lake 61 miles, Tok 108 miles, Canada Border 201 miles.

DC 1386.9 MP 1421.9 **DJ 0.1 F 96.1** Turn on Grizzly Lane for access to Delta Junction Visitor Center parking, Sullivan Roadhouse and to connect with the Richardson Highway south to Paxson and Valdez.

DC 1387 MP 1422 **DJ 0 F 96** Junction of the Alaska and Richardson highways, referred to locally as "The Triangle." The Alaska Highway merges with the Richardson Highway, which continues northwest to Fairbanks as Alaska Route 2.

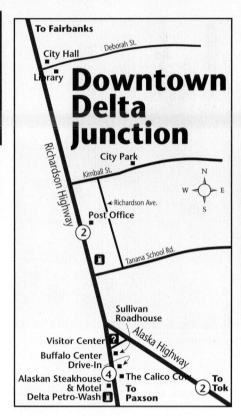

Downtown Delta Junction

To Fairbanks
City Hall
Deborah St.
Library
Richardson Highway
City Park
Kimball St.
Richardson Ave.
Post Office
(2)
Tanana School Rd.
Sullivan Roadhouse
Alaska Highway
Visitor Center
Buffalo Center Drive-In
Alaskan Steakhouse & Motel
(4)
The Calico Cow
Delta Petro-Wash
To Paxson
To Tok
(2)

Stop at the Delta Junction Visitor Center at the junction of the Richardson and Alaska highways for travel help and photo ops. *(©Kelley & Milton Barker, staff)*

Delta Junction

DC 1387 MP 1422 DJ 0 F 96 Historical Milepost 1422 Alaska Highway, physical **Milepost V 266** Richardson Highway, located at **junction** of Alaska and Richardson highways. Delta Junction is 96 miles southeast of Fairbanks, 108 miles northwest of Tok, 266 miles north of Valdez and 80 miles north of Paxson and 151 miles north of Glennallen. **Population:** 984. **Emergency Services:** Dial 911. **Alaska State Troopers**, in the Jarvis Office Center at **Milepost 1385.7**, phone (907) 895-4800. **Clinic**, Family Medical Center at **Milepost V 267.2**, phone (907) 895-5100. **Dentist**, Crossroads Family Dentistry, phone (907) 895-4274. **Chiropractor**, Arctic Chiropractic, phone (907) 895-5055.

Visitor Information: Visitor Center at junction of Alaska and Richardson highways. The visitor center is open daily from late May to late August, 9 A.M. to 7 P.M. weekdays and 10 A.M. to 5 P.M. Saturday and Sunday (hours may vary). Winter hours are 10 A.M. to 2 P.M. weekdays or by appointment. Phone (907) 895-5068. The visitor center has historical and wildlife displays (for more details, see Attractions).

Highway information, phone (907) 451-2207 or 511 or online go to 511.alaska.gov. Dept. of Fish and Game at north edge of town, **Milepost V 266.8**; phone (907) 895-4632.

Elevation: 1,180 feet. **Climate:** Mean monthly temperature in January, -15° F; in July 58°F. Record low was -66°F in January 1989; record high was 88°F in August 1990. Mean monthly precipitation in July, 2.57 inches. **Radio:** KUAC-FM 91.7 and 89.9 FM (University of Alaska, Fairbanks). **Television:** Cable and Fairbanks channels KTVF-11, KFXF-7, KUAC-9, K13XD-13.

Private Aircraft: Delta Junction (former BLM) airstrip, 1 mile north; elev. 1,150 feet; length 2,400 feet, gravel; length 1,600 feet, dirt; no fuel; unattended.

Delta Junction is the official end of the Alaska Highway. Here, the Alaska Highway (Alaska Route 2) seamlessly merges with the

Junction of the Alaska Highway (Alaska Route 2) and the Richardson Highway (Alaska Route 4). Turn to **Milepost V 265.9** in the RICHARDSON HIGHWAY section for log south to Paxson and Valdez; read log back to front.

Richardson Highway to Fairbanks. The Richardson Highway (Alaska Route 4), connecting Valdez with Fairbanks in the Interior, predates the Alaska Highway by 20 years.

Named after the nearby Delta River, Delta Junction began as a construction camp on the Richardson Highway in 1919. (It was first known as Buffalo Center because of the American bison that were transplanted here in the 1920s.) In the late 1970s, the state encouraged development of the agricultural industry in the Delta area by disposing of more than 100,000 acres of local land for farming purposes. Farms average around 500 acres, with a range of 20 to 3,000 acres.

Barley is the major feed grain grown in Delta. Other crops include oats, wheat, forage, pasture, grass seed, canola, potatoes and field peas. There are also small-scale vegetable farms, greenhouses, and livestock ranches.

According to the ADF&G, the **Delta bison herd** are plains bison, transplanted to the Delta Junction Bison Range in 1979, "in order to reduce adverse impacts of these animals on agriculture operations in the Delta area. The 90,000-acre area provides habitat and forage (especially important in winter). Money from the hunt application supports range management. The management objective is to maintain a herd size of about 360 bison at the pre-calving count. Some bison in the herd are radio collared and this helps biologists to locate animals from the ground and the air."

About 40 percent of the area's working population is employed by the federal or state government or the local school district.

Also contributing to Delta Junction's economy are the military and the trans-Alaska pipeline. Fort Greely is located 5 miles south of town on the Richardson Highway. Deactivated in 2000, Fort Greely was reactivated in 2002 as a Ground-based Midcourse Defense missile site. Alyeska Pipeline's Pump Station No. 9 is located 7 miles south of Delta Junction on the Richardson Highway.

Lodging & Services

©Kris Valencia, staff

Delta Junction offers all traveler services; see ads this section. Lodging and dining at the **Alaskan Steakhouse Motel**. Area lodging and dining at the **Lodge at Black**

Rapids (38 miles south on the Richardson Highway). Dining in town at local restaurants and at the fun **Buffalo Center Drive-In** (pictured at left). **Clearwater Lodge** on Clearwater Creek, about 10 miles east of town (see Vicinity Map), has a restaurant and a large, very nice bar. **Rika's Roadhouse Cafe and Gifts** is 9 miles northwest of town at Big Delta State Historical Park. You can stock up on bison and reindeer sausage at **Delta Meat and Sausage**, 8.6 miles southeast of town on the Alaska Highway.

There's 24-hour gas/diesel, propane, dump stations and convenience store at

Delta Petro-Wash and Buffalo Service. Delta Petro-Wash also has a coin-op laundry and a carwash with RV and automatic bays. Vehicle and RV supplies available locally. Shopping mall, post office, 2 banks with ATMs; a grocery store; **Calico Cow** quilt shop for all you traveling quilters; and several churches.

Delta's Community Center and Senior Citizens Center (no meals for seniors at this time), library and City Hall are all located on Deborah Street. The library, school, City Hall and some local businesses close when winter temperatures drop below -50°F.

The Delta Community Library, at 2291

Historic Rika's Roadhouse, 8 miles northwest of Delta Junction, dates back to 1910.
(©David L. Ranta, staff)

Deborah St., 1 block off the Richardson Highway, has 24/7 WiFi and offers free 30-minute once-daily sessions on library computers (no charge, donations encouraged). Personal laptops and covered beverages are welcome in the library, but food and cell phones are not allowed. Public fax ($2/page) and copier (25 cents/page) available. The library has handicapped parking, a bike rack, clean restrooms and a picnic area. No overnight parking/camping. Free paperback, magazine and puzzle exchange; local and state newspapers; magazines; audio books; music CDs; videos and DVDs; public review documents, IRS tax forms, PFD forms; children's programs and evening events throughout the year. A community bulletin board featuring local meetings and for-sale items is in the lobby. Library hours (subject to change) are weekdays 10 A.M. to 6 P.M. Reference questions are welcome; phone (907) 895-4102. See the Delta Library online catalog and website for current information: deltalibrarylinks.org.

Delta Junction City Hall, located at **Milepost V 266.5**, has public restrooms, local maps, an Alaska Highway historical map display and a pleasant outdoor area with gazebo and benches. City employees are well practiced in giving directions to local businesses and attractions in both Delta and along the Richardson and Alaska Highways. A small conference room is available for a nominal fee for public meetings. Check with City Hall for reservations; phone (907) 895-4656. City Hall is open 8 A.M. to 5 P.M. weekdays. Photocopy machine available, 25 cents a copy.

The Delta Junction Post Office (ZIP 99737) is located at **Milepost V 266.2** Richardson Highway. The post office is open 9:30 A.M. to 5 P.M. weekdays, and 10:30 A.M. to noon on Saturday.

Camping

Camping at **Snowed Inn RV Park** at **Milepost 1421** Alaska Highway. There are 3 public campgrounds in the area: Delta State Recreation Site campground, 1.1 miles north at **Milepost V 267** Richardson Highway; Quartz Lake Recreation Area campground, 10.7 miles north via the Richardson Highway to **Milepost V 277.7** and 2.5 miles east on a side road; and Clearwater State Recreation Site and **Clearwater Lodge** on Rem-ington Road, accessible from **Milepost 1414.8** Alaska Highway or **Milepost V 268.3** Richardson Highway *(see Delta Junction Vicinity map page 233).*

Transportation

Air: Scheduled service from Tok to Fairbanks via 40-Mile Air; Delta Junction stop on request. Local air service available.

Attractions

Delta Junction Visitor Center. Have your picture taken with Milepost 1422 in front of the visitor center that marks the highway's end or with another favorite photo op—the giant mosquito sculptures. The Chamber of Commerce visitor center has free brochures describing area businesses and attractions; restrooms; cold drinks for sale. Travelers may purchase certificates here, certifying that they have reached the end of the Alaska Highway, and shop for souvenirs in the Center's gift shop.

Indoor displays include Alaska wildlife, including a bison mount and trumpeter swans, and the history of area agriculture. Outside the visitor center, there is an interesting display of pipe used in 3 Alaska pipeline projects. For more information phone (907) 895-5068.

Enjoy free sausage samples at Delta Meat & Sausage, located 8.6 miles east of downtown (see **Milepost 1413.4**). The tasty meats and sausages for sale here are the product of a locally owned and operated family farm. Open daily in summer, 8 A.M. to 5 P.M. weekdays and 10 A.M. to 3 P.M. Saturday and Sunday. Phone (907) 895-4006.

The **Sullivan Roadhouse Historical Museum**, located across from the visitor center on the Richardson Highway, is an original log roadhouse from 1905. It has been moved twice from its original location: once by horse and once by helicopter. It is one of the last surviving roadhouses from the Valdez to Fairbanks Trail and visitors shouldn't miss seeing the interior with its intricate log ceiling. Extensive historical displays and old photographs. It is open daily in summer. Sullivan Roadhouse is staffed by local residents who also help maintain the large summer garden, fashioned after those gardens that were a standard feature of early roadhouses. A display of equipment used during construction of the Alaska Highway is located between the Sullivan Roadhouse and the Visitor Center.

Delta Junction's Farmers' Market is held behind the Sullivan Roadhouse every Saturday and Wednesday in summer. A great spot for travelers to buy fresh local produce and locally-made crafts.

Rika's Roadhouse at Big Delta State Historical Park. Located 8 miles north of town on the Richardson Highway (see description at **Milepost V 275**). Rika's Roadhouse is part of Big Delta State Historical Park. The Rika's Roadhouse complex contains a number of historic outbuildings, a garden, Rika's Roadhouse Cafe & Gifts featuring Alaskan made gifts, and restrooms. The parking area contains 23 overnight RV parking spots; camping fee $10 per vehicle. Dump station ($10 fee) on loop road. Rika's Roadhouse and Big Delta State Historical Park complex is open daily in summer. Rika's Cafe & Gifts is open daily 10 A.M. to 4 P.M. May–September.

See the Pipeline Crossing. Delta Junction is the first view of the trans-Alaska pipeline for travelers coming up the Alaska Highway from Canada. A good spot to see and photograph the pipeline is at **Milepost V 275.4** Richardson Highway, 9.5 miles north of town, at the Tanana River crossing.

Special Events: The Deltana Fair is held in late July. The fair includes a barbecue, Lions' pancake breakfast, local handicrafts, horse show, livestock display and show, games, concessions, contests and a parade. Check with the Chamber of Commerce about other special events; phone (907) 895-5068.

Tour the agriculture of the area. Take a drive on Sawmill Creek Road at **Milepost 1403.4** or Clearwater Road at **Milepost 1414.8** to see local agriculture and wild game ranches. Sawmill Creek Road goes through the heart of the grain-producing Delta Ag Project. Along Clearwater and Remington roads you may view the older farms, which produce forage crops and livestock. Tanana Loop Road and Tanana Loop Extension also go past many farms.

Pick your own vegetables and strawberries at local farms.

Bird Watching. Delta's barley fields are a popular migration stop for 150,000 to 200,000 sandhill cranes. Delta-Clearwater Creek is a good place to see spring and fall migrations of sandhill cranes, geese and other waterfowl. Sandhill cranes have a distinctive gurgling call and are also easy to spot in the sky and on the ground because they are among the tallest birds in the world: They are about 4 feet tall and have a 6-foot wingspan!

AREA FISHING: Delta–Clearwater River (local name for Clearwater Creek), Arctic grayling and whitefish; coho salmon spawn here in October. Access via Clearwater Road or Jack Warren Road.

There are 40 lakes in the Delta–Tok area that are stocked by the ADF&G. Lakes are stocked primarily with rainbow trout, Arctic grayling, Arctic char, coho and chinook salmon. Lakes are located along the road or reached by trail. **Quartz Lake**, at **Milepost V 277.7** north of Delta Junction, one of the most popular fishing lakes in the Delta area, is also the largest and most easily accessed of area lakes; angler success is excellent. Consult ADF&G offices in Delta Junction or Fairbanks.

Alaska Highway Log
(continued)

ALASKA ROUTE 2 West

Northbound: Distance from Dawson Creek (DC) is followed by distance from Valdez (V) and distance from Fairbanks (F). Read log: ↓

NOTE: Physical mileposts on the Richardson Highway reflect distance from Valdez. We continue the Alaska Highway log to Fairbanks via the Richardson Highway (also designated Route 2 on this stretch). For the log of the Richardson Highway (Route 4) south to Glennallen and Valdez, turn to **Milepost V 265.9** *in the RICHARDSON HIGHWAY section.*

DC 1387.1 V 266.1 F 95.9 Buffalo Center Service (gas, diesel, propane, tire sales, convenience store, RV dump, 24-hour card fueling) at Nistler Road. ⛽

Nistler Road leads east 6.4 miles to junction with Clearwater Road. Turn north on Clearwater and drive 0.9 mile to Remington Road, then turn right and drive 2.7 miles for Clearwater State Recreation Site or drive 2.8 miles for Clearwater Lodge.

DC 1387.3 V 266.3 F 95.7 Delta Junction post office and IGA Food Cache.

DC 1387.4 V 266.4 F 95.6 End 4-lane highway, begin 2-lane highway, northbound.

DC 1387.5 V 266.5 F 95.5 Deborah Street; access east to Delta Junction City Hall, Community Center and Library. Veterinary clinic to west.

DC 1387.6 V 266.7 F 95.3 *Slow for speed zone southbound.*

Distance marker northbound shows North Pole 82 miles, Fairbanks 95 miles.

DC 1387.8 V 266.8 F 95.2 Alaska Dept. of Fish and Game office; phone (907) 895-4632.

DC 1387.9 V 266.9 F 95.1 Rapids Road; turnoff for Delta Junction Airport.

DC 1388 V 267 F 95 Turnoff to northeast for **Delta State Recreation Site** (across the highway from Delta River): large parking area along highway (west of entrance) gives access to pleasant, wooded, day-use picnic area with grills and covered tables, excellent view of the Alaska Range. Delta River Recreation Site campground has 25 sites, water, tables, covered picnic shelter, toilets. $15 nightly fee. Campground host. ▲

DC 1388.1 V 267.1 F 94.9 Alaska Division of Forestry office.

DC 1388.2 V 267.2 F 94.8 Medical clinic to east.

DC 1389.3 V 268.3 F 93.7 Junction with Jack Warren Road (paved); see Delta Junction Vicinity map on page 233. Turnoff for **Clearwater State Recreation Site** (10.5 miles) which has 16 sites, 2 pull-throughs, toilets, tables, water and boat launch ($10 fee or annual pass); one of the state's prettiest campsites: the spring-fed **Clearwater River** is crystal clear. Camping fee $15/night or resident pass. Good fishing. **Clearwater Lodge**, just to the east of the state campground, has a restaurant, nice large porch overlooking the Clearwater River (fishing in front of lodge), a fun bar, cabins and an RV park. ◄ ▲

Driving directions: Follow Jack Warren Road 5.8 miles to a right turn where it becomes Souhrada Road; drive 1 mile then turn left on Remington Road and continue

Boat launch area at the Tanana River provides a close-up view of the pipeline bridge.
(©Kris Valencia, staff)

3.7 miles to the state campground or 3.8 miles to Clearwater Lodge. To make a loop drive, turn south on Clearwater Road and you will rejoin the Alaska Highway at **Milepost DC 1379.8** (physical Milepost 1414.8) *See Delta Junction Vicinity map on page 233.*

DC 1392.7 V 271.7 F 90.3 Tanana Loop Road (gravel). For an agricultural loop drive, follow Tanana Loop Road north 1.2 miles then turn east on Tanana Loop Extension and drive 9.1 miles to Jack Warren Road and follow Jack Warren Road 2.8 miles back to junction with the highway at **Milepost V 268.3**. There are seasonal U-pick farms along these side roads.

DC 1392.9 V 271.9 F 90.1 Big D Fire station at **BIG DELTA** (pop. 484). This unincorporated community at the junction of the Delta and Tanana rivers was originally a stop on the Valdez–Fairbanks trail. It was first known as Bates Landing, then Rika's Landing, McCarty, and finally Big Delta. Big Delta was the site of a WAMCATS telegraph station and also a work camp in 1919 during construction of the Richardson Highway. Today, agriculture, small business, and highway maintenance jobs provide employment.

DC 1395.6 V 274.6 F 87.4 Distance marker southbound shows Delta Junction 8 miles, Tok 117 miles.

DC 1396 V 275 F 87 Tesoro gas station with diesel and Tanana Trading Post on southwest side of highway. Turnoff for **Rika's Roadhouse** at **Big Delta State Historical Park** to northeast; description follows. After turning, keep to left for Rika's Roadhouse parking lot, or drive straight ahead on the paved road for a small rest area with picnic table, potable water, outhouse and dump station ($10) on loop road. Day parking for Rika's Roadhouse and 23 overnight parking spots ($20 camping fee) in Big Delta State Historical Park. ⛽ ▲ ♿

Do not miss the productive summer garden at Rika's Roadhouse. This 10-acre park is open daily from May 15 to Labor Day. Cabin rentals available. The park grounds are open until 4 P.M. A must-stop and a good place to stretch your legs. Take a walk on the banks of the Tanana River.

Rika's Roadhouse Cafe and Gifts. See display ad this page.

Rika's Roadhouse was built in 1910 by John Hajdukovich, who sold it in 1923 to Rika Wallen, a Swedish immigrant who had managed the roadhouse since 1917. Rika ran the roadhouse into the late 1940s and lived there until her death in 1969. It is now part of Big Delta State Historical Park and admission is free. This historic district was an important crossroad for prospectors, travelers, traders and the military during the early days of the 20th century. The roadhouse served travelers on the historic Valdez to Fairbanks Trail from 1913 to 1947.

Pleasant walking paths with information boards lead from the parking area through the park's grounds to the roadhouse. Historic structures open to the public include a small sod-roofed museum, a barn, Alaska Road Commission outbuilding, two WAMCATS (Washington-Alaska Military Cable and Telegraph System) buildings and the roadhouse itself. The roadhouse has interesting displays and pictures on the ground floor.

DC 1396.5 V 275.5 F 86.5 Tanana River/Big Delta bridge. Turnoff to north at east end of bridge for large, rutted dirt parking area at Alyeska Pipeline Display about **Tanana River Pipeline Bridge**. Boat launch, boat trailer parking, litter bins, portable outhouses, interpretive signs. Parking lot is a busy area in summer. *CAUTION: Fast-moving water, supervise small children and leash dogs.*

Spectacular view of the 1,200-foot-long section of pipeline suspended across the

Tanana River between 2 towers. This is the second longest of the 13 major bridges along the pipeline's 800-mile length. Information boards give pipeline history and facts, as well as details on the suspension bridge.

DC 1398.7 V 277.7 F 84.3 Turn off to east on Quartz Lake Road for **Quartz Lake State Recreation Area.** Little Lost Lake Campground at mile 2.1, has 12 pull-in or back-in campsites with picnic tables, toilet, and a large parking area with tables, litter bins and boat dock. A trail connects Lost Lake and Quartz Lake camping areas. Popular Quartz Lake campground is at mile 2.5 and has two camping areas. A pull-in type parking lot near the lake is for overnight parking with a large concrete boat launch, swimming area and boat rental concession and campground host. A forested campground nearby has many developed campsites, some long enough for big rigs. There are many picnic tables (some covered), firepits, toilets, water and garbage containers, access to Glatfelder Public Use Cabin and other trailheads. Campgrounds are $15 per night, day use $5 and boat launch $10. Quartz Lake SRA has 2 public-use cabins; 3-night maximum; $35 per night; dnr. alaska.gov/parks/cabins for details. 🏕

Quartz Lake covers 1,500 acres, more than 80 percent of which are less than 15 feet deep. Maximum depth is 40 feet. There is a boat rental concession at the lake, making this a good spot to get out on to the water. Popular fishing lake, stocked rainbow trout, Arctic char and salmon (coho and chinook). Winter ice fishery; fishing huts for rent (go to dnr.alaska.gov/parks/cabins/icehuts.htm for details). **Little Lost Lake** is stocked with rainbow trout. 🎣

DC 1401.2 V 280.2 F 81.8 Gravel turnout to south.

DC 1401.3 V 280.3 F 81.7 Begin 0.5-mile passing lane westbound.

DC 1404 V 283 F 79 81-Mile Pond (stocked with rainbow trout by ADF&G); public fishing access to east. 🎣

DC 1405 V 284 F 78 Watch for moose in roadside ponds on both sides of highway. *CAUTION: Watch for moose on highway.*

DC 1407.5 V 286.5 F 75.5 Shaw Creek Road and bridge. Popular boat launching area; gated parking area to north at east end of bridge. Shaw Creek road west side of bridge.

Good views westbound of Tanana River which parallels the highway.

DC 1408.1 V 287.1 F 74.9 Shaw Pond public fishing access to northeast. Good to excellent early spring and fall Arctic grayling fishing. 🎣

DC 1409 V 288 F 74 Scenic viewpoint at parking area (can get crowded with vehicles on nice days) to west overlooking Tanana River with panoramic view on clear days to the south of 3 great peaks of the Alaska Range: Mount Hayes (elev. 13,832 feet) almost due south; Hess Mountain (elev. 11,940 feet) to the west or right of Mount Hayes; and Mount Deborah (elev. 12,339 feet) to the west or right of Hess Mountain.

Mount Hayes is named for Charles Hayes, an early member of the U.S. Geological Survey. Mount Deborah was named in 1907 by the famous Alaskan Judge Wickersham for his wife.

DC 1410.7 V 289.7 F 72.3 South entrance to long paved double-ended parking area to north in trees.

DC 1412.8 V 291.8 F 70.2 Begin 0.7-mile passing lane westbound.

DC 1413.8 V 292.8 F 69.2 Highway descends next 1.4 miles westbound.

Distance marker northbound shows North Pole 55 miles, Fairbanks 69 miles.

DC 1414.5 V 293.5 F 69.5 Tenderfoot Pottery 0.3 mile west on Ruby Road; access and parking for a camper or mid-size RV. Studio and gallery of artist Shellie Mathews; open daily; description follows.

Tenderfoot Pottery features dinnerware, kitchenware and garden planters individually hand crafted by Shellie Mathews. All are finished with unique glazes made by Shellie and are food safe. The gallery also features a selection of fiber accessories and jewelry. Open daily from 9 A.M. to 9 P.M. Watch for signs on Richardson Highway. tenderfootpottery.com; 907-895-4039.
[ADVERTISEMENT]

DC 1414.9 V 293.9 F 68.1 Paved double-ended turnout to west with Gold Rush Centennial information boards on "Getting the Gold" (placer mining) and "Gold in the Tenderfoot" (excerpt follows):

"Two miners from the Fortymile District found gold flakes on Tenderfoot Creek in 1888. This site was too far from a supply camp, so they abandoned it. 17 years later, after gold was discovered near Fairbanks, prospector E.H. Luce found gold on Tenderfoot Creek. News of his discovery attracted about a thousand people to the area. Between 1905 and 1995, the Tenderfoot Mining District produced 120,770 ounces (3.77 tons) of placer gold. Its most productive years were 1905 to 1916."

DC 1415 V 294 F 68 Begin 1.6-mile passing lane eastbound. Highway climbs eastbound.

DC 1415.6 V 294.6 F 67.4 Fairbanks North Star Borough boundary.

DC 1416.4 V 295.4 F 66.6 Banner Creek bridge; historic placer gold stream.

DC 1416.5 V 295.5 F 66.5 Distance marker southbound shows Delta Junction 28 miles, Tok 136 miles, Valdez 300 miles.

©Kris Valencia, staff

DC 1417.3 V 296.3 F 65.7 Paved scenic viewpoint to south at top of hill has a great view (pictured above) of the braided Tanana River and the Alaska Range on a clear day.

DC 1419.2 V 298.2 F 63.8 Paved double-ended parking area to southwest; view obstructed by brush.

DC 1422 V 301 F 61 Begin 0.4-mile passing lane westbound.

DC 1422.5 V 301.5 F 60.5 East end of long double-ended turnout downhill north of highway.

DC 1422.8 V 301.8 F 60.2 West end of long double-ended turnout. East end at **Milepost V 301.5.**

DC 1423.5 V 302.5 F 59.5 Begin 0.5-mile passing lane eastbound.

DC 1425.2 V 304.2 F 57.8 Turnout to northeast.

DC 1426 V 305 F 57 Distance marker southbound shows Delta Junction 38 miles, Tok Junction 146 miles, Valdez 310 miles.

DC 1426.2 V 305.2 F 56.8 Signed turnoff to northeast on Birch Lake Road (0.2 mile) for loop road through **Birch Lake State Recreation Site;** swimming, picnicking, camping, boating, fishing, jetskiing. Lakeside picnic sites with tables, firepits, toilets and garbage on grassy day-use area. Overnight parking with campground host; 12 sites, some for tent campers; fee station; boat launch and fishing. Parking available for boat trailers. Camping fee $15, day-use $5. Fish from shore in spring, from boat in summer. Stocked with chinook salmon, Arctic char and rainbow trout. "Kids Don't Float" program life jackets. Popular buoyed swimming area. 🎣 🏕

Birch Lake Military Recreation Site (USAF Recreation Camp) is located just beyond the state recreation site on the same access road.

DC 1427 V 306 F 56 Pleasant rest area northeast side of highway on the shore of Birch Lake; toilets, parking, lakeside benches, day use only.

DC 1427.1 V 306.1 F 55.9 Lost Lake Road to south.

DC 1428 V 307 F 55 *CAUTION: Watch for moose.*

DC 1428.2 V 307.2 F 54.8 Gravel parking area at Koole Lake Trail (14.3 miles), public fishing access, to southwest.

DC 1430.3 V 309.3 F 52.7 Begin 1.1-mile passing lane westbound.

DC 1431 V 310 F 52 Large double-ended parking area to southwest.

DC 1431.7 V 310.7 F 51.3 Begin 1-mile passing lane eastbound, uphill grade.

DC 1434.1 V 313.1 F 48.9 Paved double-ended turnout to southwest on Tanana River. *(View of river was obscured by shrubs and trees in summer 2018.)* Gold Rush Centennial information boards on "Alaska's Gold Rush Era" and "Tanana Valley Gold" (excerpts follow). This was also the site of Silver Fox Lodge, the Fox Farm and the Overland Roadhouse (circa 1910) at **Historic Milepost 1471** Alaska Highway.

"Prospectors made the first significant gold discovery in Alaska at Juneau in 1880. This discovery encouraged others to look throughout Alaska and the Yukon for gold. The first strike in Alaska's Interior was along the Fortymile River in 1886. It was followed by discoveries on other Yukon River tributaries and the Kenai Peninsula. On August 16, 1896, George Carmack, Skookum Jim and Tagish Charlie made the Klondike discovery in Canada's Yukon Territory.

"The gold deposits found in 1902 north of present-day Fairbanks proved to be the richest in Alaska. Prospector Felix Pedro and trader E.T. Barnette played key roles in the discovery and initial rush. A second strike made the following summer catapulted a temporary trading post into the largest city in the territory.

"Felix Pedro, an Italian immigrant, claimed he made a rich gold strike in 1898 in the Tanana Valley foothills. While trying to find it again in 1901, he purchased supplies from E.T. Barnette's temporary trading post on the Chena River. Pedro returned to Barnette's post on July 28, 1902, to announce a new gold discovery. Barnette sent word of the strike to nearby gold camps, exaggerating its richness. Seven hundred people then stampeded to the Tanana Valley. [They] found the nearby creeks already staked, few claims being worked, and Barnette charging high prices for supplies. They considered hanging the promoters of the new camp. Before there was any blood shed, Barnette agreed to lower his prices.

"In the fall of 1903, miners on Cleary, Fairbanks and Ester creeks in the Tanana foothills announced rich gold discoveries. Another rush occurred and 1,500 people were mining in the area by Christmas. The camp Barnette named Fairbanks grew into a city of saloons and 2-story buildings."

DC 1435.8 V 314.8 F 47.2 Midway Lodge.

DC 1436 V 315 F 47 "C" Lazy Moose RV Park & Gift Shop to west. Campsites with hookups are downhill; register at gift shop or after hours, follow instructions at gate.

DC 1440.2 V 319.2 F 42.8 Harding Lake via Salcha Drive.

DC 1441.2 V 320.2 F 41.8 Distance marker northbound shows North Pole 30 miles, Fairbanks 44 miles.

DC 1442.5 V 321.5 F 40.5 Turnoff to east for **Harding Lake State Recreation Area**; drive east 1.4 miles on paved road. A terrific stop for families with small children; bring beach shoes to enjoy wading on the very shallow, rocky bottom of Harding Lake. Access lake by walking west area to west of boat launch. A drier trail is through the brush at the volleyball court. Fee station (for self-register), campground host and dump station at entrance. Grassy day-use area with picnic tables, grills, horseshoes, ballfields. There is a boat launch $10 and a 1.4 mile nature trail; 75 campsites (plus large field for group camping). Camping fee $15, day-use $5; dump station $10. Quiet hours from 11 P.M. to 6 A.M. Fishing for lake trout, Arctic char and burbot. Worth the drive! Bring your insect repellent, you may need it! Firewood from camp host or park ranger. Jet skis allowed.

DC 1443.2 V 322.2 F 39.8 SALCHA (pop. 1,048) extends along the highway for several miles. Post office (ZIP code 99714) open weekdays noon to 6 P.M., Saturday 10 A.M. to 2 P.M. Salchaket Roadhouse with food, propane and lodging on east side of highway. The village was first reported in 1898 as "Salchaket," meaning "mouth of the Salcha."

DC 1444.1 V 323.1 F 38.9 Access to **Salcha River State Recreation Site** 0.2 miles to northeast (turn at Salcha Marine), a popular boat launch with a 130-site parking area for vehicles and boat trailers; a boat ramp; picnic area; a few developed campsites and some primitive campsites; toilets and water. There may be 300 or more people here on holidays. $10 launch fee and 10-minute launch limit. Camping fee $15. Fishing for chinook and chum salmon, Arctic grayling, sheefish, northern pike and burbot. Road at end of parking area by pit toilets leads to big area of sandbar parking and informal camping on Salcha River (beware soft sand areas). Winter-use cabin available; go to dnr.alaska.gov/parks/cabins/north.htm#salcha.

DC 1444.4 V 323.4 F 38.6 Salcha River bridge (50 mph).

DC 1445 V 324 F 38 Clear Creek bridge.

DC 1445.6 V 324.6 F 37.4 Double-ended gravel turnout to northeast.

DC 1445.8 V 324.8 F 37.2 Munsons Slough bridge; fishing; Monsons Slough Road.

DC 1446.4 V 325.4 F 36.6 Salcha Elementary School to northeast.

DC 1448.7 V 327.7 F 34.3 Little Salcha River bridge.

DC 1449.3 V 328.3 F 33.7 Salcha Store and Service (ice, gas) to northeast.

DC 1450.4 V 329.4 F 32.6 Tanana River flows next to highway.

DC 1451.1 V 330.1 F 31.9 Distance marker southbound shows Delta Junction 65 miles, Tok 173 miles.

DC 1451.3 V 330.3 F 31.7 Salcha Senior Center to northeast.

DC 1451.5 V 330.5 F 31.5 Salcha Rescue; phone (907) 488-5274. For emergencies dial 911.

DC 1452.7 V 331.7 F 30.3 Salcha Fairgrounds. Fair is held the last full weekend in June.

DC 1453.1 V 332.1 F 29.9 Access east to **31-Mile Pond**; stocked with Arctic char, rainbow trout and Arctic grayling.

DC 1453.2 V 332.2 F 29.8 The Knotty Shop to west has a large and interesting selection of gifts and "Alaska's finest ice cream." Also of interest is their wildlife museum and display of ptarmigan. The burl creations out in front are popular photo ops (but please DON'T climb on burl sculptures). There are also unusual and impressive burl railings on the front porch of the shop.

©Milton & Kelley Barker, staff

The Knotty Shop. See display ad this page.

DC 1455.7 V 334.7 F 27.3 Leaving Eielson AFB southbound. Entering Eielson AFB northbound.

DC 1456.1 V 335.1 F 26.9 Access northeast to **28-Mile Pond**; stocked with rainbow trout, Arctic char and Arctic grayling.

DC 1458.5 V 337.5 F 24.5 View of Eielson AFB runway to northeast next 1.5 miles northbound. *NOTE: No stopping, no parking and no photography along this stretch of highway!* Watch for various military aircraft taking off and landing to the east.

DC 1461.5 V 340.5 F 21.5 Begin 4-lane divided freeway northbound. Begin 2-lane highway southbound.

CAUTION: Watch for heavy traffic southbound turning east into the base, 7–8 A.M., and merging northbound traffic, 3:45–5:30 P.M., weekdays. No parking, stopping, or photography!

DC 1462.3 V 341.3 F 20.7 Main entrance to **EIELSON AIR FORCE BASE** (pop. 2,867). Eielson Air Force Base occupies 63,195 acres southeast of Fairbanks, Alaska. The runway is oriented north to south and is 14,507 feet long. It was extended to its present length in the 1950s to accommodate B-36 aircraft and is the second longest runway in North America.

The 354th Fighter Wing mission is to prepare U.S. and allied aviation forces for combat, to deploy Airmen in support of global operations, and to enable the staging of forces to promote U.S. interest in the Asia-Pacific region. The 354th FW is the host unit at Eielson and is assigned to 11th Air Force headquartered at Joint Base Elmendorf-Richardson (JBER) in Anchorage, Alaska.

Eielson is home to RED FLAG-Alaska, a series of Pacific Air Forces commander-directed field training exercises for U.S.

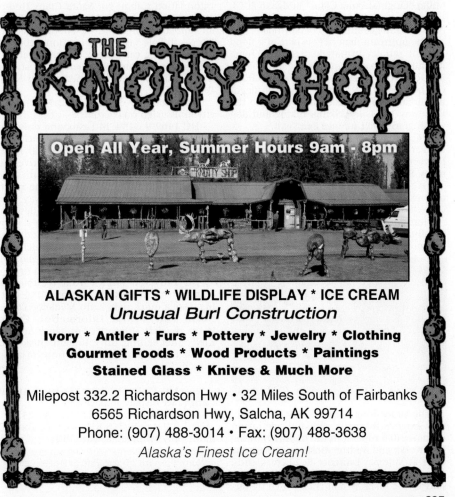

forces, providing joint offensive counter-air, interdiction, close air support, and large force employment training in a simulated combat environment.

This base was named in honor of Carl Ben Eielson, an explorer and hero who pioneered aviation in Alaska more than 80 years ago. He recognized the possibilities aviation held for Alaska's development and was the first aviator to cross the Arctic Circle and land an airplane on the North Slope. He also piloted the first flight from North America over the Arctic Ocean to Europe in 1928.

DC 1462.7 V 341.7 F 20.3 Exit to Eielson's main entrance is exit lane to north eastbound traffic.

DC 1463 V 342 F 20 North boundary of Eielson AFB.

DC 1463.7 V 242.7 F 19.3 Purple Heart Trail sign, eastbound.

DC 1464.6 V 343.6 F 18.4 Turnoff to north for Old Richardson Highway, Moose Creek Road and access to Moose Creek General Store; diesel, gas, propane. Turnoff to south for Eielson Farm Road to **Bathing Beauty Pond** and **Piledriver Slough**. Bathing Beauty Pond has a picnic area with outhouse and is stocked with rainbow trout, Arctic char and chinook salmon. Piledriver Slough has outhouses, dumpster and boat launch on Chena River.

⬛🔋 ⬛

DC 1465.6 V 344.6 F 17.4 Moose Creek.

DC 1466.4 V 345.4 F 16.6 *CAUTION: Highway crosses Alaska Railroad tracks.*

DC 1466.7 V 345.7 F 16.3 Chena Flood Channel bridge. The northbound bridge crossing was named the Nellie Miller 'Original Mrs. Claus" Bridge, and the southbound bridge crossing was named the Con Miller "Original Santa Claus" Bridge in 2013, in recognition of the Miller's many contributions to the community of North Pole.

The upstream dam here is part of a flood control project initiated after the Chena River left its banks and flooded Fairbanks in 1967. (A high water mark from this flood can be seen at the Pioneer Park train depot in Fairbanks.) For northbound access to the Floodway Lands for biking, hiking and dog walking, use the Laurence Road exit.

DC 1467.3 V 346.3 F 15.7 Distance marker westbound shows North Pole exits: Dawson Road 1 mile, Mission Road, 2.5 miles, Badger Road 2.75 miles.

DC 1467.6 V 346.6 F 15.4 Westbound-only exit north to Laurence Road for Moose Creek Dam Bikeway and Chena Lakes Recreation Area. (Eastbound traffic use Dawson-Buzby Roads eastbound-only exit at **Milepost DC 1469.**)

©Kris Valencia, staff

The 5-mile-long **Moose Creek Dam Bikeway** extends from the park-and-ride lot on Laurance (0.8 mile from the highway) to the Damworks and Visitor Kiosk on the Chena River at Mile 5.5 Laurence Road (road end). The park-and-ride lot at Mile 0.8 is at the start of the bikeway and is also used by rec-

reationists using the Floodway Lands for hiking, biking and dog walking; just walk across Laurence Road to the gravel dam crossover and down the other side to the flood plain.

Drive 2.5 miles up Laurence Road to fee station for entrance to **Chena Lakes Recreation Area**. A map of the recreation area is displayed; open year-round, day-use and camping fees charged from Memorial Day to Labor Day. Lake Park Campground is at Mile 3.6 and River Park Campground at Mile 4.9. Camping fee $12 walk-in tent site, $20 campers/RVs; $30 electric/water hookups; day-use fee $5; boat launch $10; sani-dump $10. The recreation area has 80 campsites, 92 picnic sites, pump water, toilets, firepits, picnic tables, trash bins and volleyball courts. There is a 250-acre lake with swimming beach. **Chena Lake** is stocked with coho and chinook salmon, Arctic char, and rainbow trout. Nonmotorized boats may be rented from a concessionaire. **Chena River** offers good Arctic grayling fishing and also northern pike, whitefish and burbot. The Damworks and Visitor Kiosk below the Moose Creek Dam on the Chena River, at Mile 5.5, was constructed by the Army Corps of Engineers and is run by Fairbanks North Star Borough.

⬛ ⬛

DC 1467.9 V 346.9 F 15.1 Eastbound exit for south Laurance Road. There is no access to Moose Creek Dam Bikeway or Chena Lakes Recreation Area from this exit; use Dawson-Buzby Road eastbound exit for access.

DC 1468.4 V 347.4 F 14.6 Westbound only exit for Dawson-Buzby Roads. Access to Santa Claus House and North Pole Visitor Information Cabin. For Santa Claus House, after exiting go left under overpass and take an immediate right on St. Nicholas Drive. For North Pole Visitor Information Cabin (in sod-roofed log cabin) exit, turn right at exit then make an immediate left on Mistletoe Drive and drive 0.5 mile. *See map of North Pole page 240.*

DC 1468.8 V 347.8 F 14.2 North Pole city limits (sign on overpass).

DC 1469 V 348 F 14 Eastbound-only exit to Dawson and Buzby Roads. For North Pole Visitor Information Cabin, after exit ramp make immediate left on Mistletoe Drive. Go approximately 0.5 mile and the North Pole Visitor Information Cabin is on the right. For the Moose Creek Dam Bikeway and Chena Lakes Recreation Area (see description at **Milepost DC 1467.6**), make a right turn on to Mistletoe Drive and continue until it becomes Laurence Road, which will take you to the bikeway floodplain parking lot and on to Chena Lakes Recreation Area.

DC 1469.5 V 348.5 F 13.5 Westbound-only exit north to Mission Road. After exiting, take a quick right onto Mistletoe Drive, **North Pole Visitor Information Cabin** is on the left 0.1 mile. For radio station KJNP, after exiting, drive straight ahead and turn left on a narrow road in front of a big church.

❓

North Pole Visitor Information Cabin. See display ad page 239.

KJNP Radio. See display ad page 241.

DC 1469.6 V 348.6 F 13.4 Eastbound-only traffic-only 5th Avenue exit south.

North Pole 5th Avenue Exit. See description of "North Pole" beginning on facing page.

For access to Santa Claus House, turn on to St. Nicholas Drive (first right).

DC 1470 V 349 F 13 Westbound traffic-only exit north to roundabout. Watch carefully for direction signs in roundabouts. From here you may access north to Badger Road and south to North Pole business dis-

trict via Santa Claus Lane: fast food outlets, 24-hour gas/diesel, car and truck wash, supermarket, post office, police, city hall, banks, medical clinics, indoor waterslide and swimming pool, library, playgrounds, Santa's Senior Center, parks. Also access south via Santa Claus Lane to St. Nicholas Drive (turnoff at first roundabout) to **Santa Claus House** (description follows).

Santa Claus House. Established in 1952, the Santa Claus House is home of the Original Letter from Santa. Mail your cards and letters here for an authentic North Pole postmark. Browse the gift shop and visit with Santa and his reindeer. Numerous photo opportunities. Open all year with extended summer hours, Memorial Day through Labor Day. See display ad on page 240. [ADVERTISEMENT]

To reach the North Pole Visitor Information Cabin from here, drive east on St. Nicholas to Dawson-Buzby Road, go left under the overpass, take an immediate left on Mistletoe and drive 0.5 mile. *(See map of North Pole, page 240.)*

North Pole/Badger Road Exit. See description of "North Pole" beginning on facing page.

From this exit with roundabouts, **Badger Road** loops northwest 11 miles and back to the Richardson Highway at **Milepost V 356.6**. Badger Road provides access to the following (distance from this junction shown): Nordale Road (4.6 miles), which leads 5.6 miles north to Chena Hot Springs Road. Continue on Badger Road to gas station and **Riverview RV Park** (8.4 miles); Fort Wainwright (10.1 miles); gas station (10.4 miles); and Old Richardson Highway (10.9 miles). At the end of Badger Road, Fairbanks is to the right and North Pole is straight ahead.

⬛

Riverview RV Park. See display ad on page 417 in FAIRBANKS section.

DC 1470.6 V 349.6 F 12.4 Eastbound traffic-only exit to roundabout accesses North Pole business district to south (fast-food outlets, supermarket, etc.) and Badger Road to north (Tesoro station). Turn on St. Nicholas Road for **Santa Claus House**. For access to the North Pole Visitor Information Cabin, continue eastbound on the Richardson Highway to the Buzby-Dawson exit.

⬛

DC 1471.1 V 350.1 F 11.9 Peridot Lane exit to north and south (for east and westbound traffic). Family diner to north.

DC 1471.5 V 350.5 F 11.5 Alaska Railroad crossing. Entering North Pole city limits (eastbound).

DC 1472.3 V 351.3 F 10.7 Distance marker westbound shows Fairbanks 11 miles, Fox 22 miles, Circle 169 miles.

DC 1476 V 355 F 7 Sign: $1,000 fine for littering (eastbound).

DC 1477.6 V 356.6 F 5.4 Badger Road interchange westbound. This 11-mile road loops back to the Richardson Highway at **Milepost V 349.5**, providing access to Old Richardson Highway (0.2 mile from this junction); gas station (0.7 mile); Fort Wainwright (1 mile); **Riverview RV Park** and gas station (2.7 miles); and Nordale Road (6.4 miles), which leads 5.6 miles north to Chena Hot Springs Road. At Mile 2.3 Nordale Road there is a boat launch on the Chena River with paved parking area, outhouses and dumpster. ▲

DC 1478.6 V 357.6 F 4.4 Eastbound exit to Badger Road and **Riverview RV Park.** ▲

DC 1480.2 V 359.2 F 2.8 Railroad crossing.

DC 1480.6 V 359.6 F 2.4 Westbound traffic use south lane to exit for Old Richardson Highway and South Cushman Street.

DC 1481.2 V 360.2 F 1.8 Distance marker eastbound shows North Pole 11 miles, Delta Junction 98 miles, Tok Junction 202 miles, Anchorage 440 miles.

Eastbound exit for Lakeview Drive. This area subject to fog (signed).

DC 1481.5 V 360.5 F 1.5 Eastbound exit for Lakeview Drive. This area subject to fog (signed).

DC 1481.6 V 360.6 F 1.4 Westbound exit (next right northbound) for Mitchell Expressway, which **junctions** with Parks Highway (Alaska Route 3) to Denali Park, Nenana and Anchorage.

Begin 4-lane divided freeway eastbound (Alaska Route 2 South).

Turn to end of PARKS HIGHWAY section on page 407 and read log back to front for log from Fairbanks south to Anchorage.

DC 1482.2 V 361.2 F 0.8 Welcome to Fairbanks sign and flowers, westbound. Eastbound traffic exit to Mitchell Expressway to junction with Parks Highway (Alaska Route 3) to Denali Park, Nenana and Anchorage.

DC 1482.5 V 361.5 F 0.5 Eastbound traffic exit to South Cushman.

DC 1483 V 362 F 0 FAIRBANKS. Junction with Airport Way and Steese Expressway northbound; downtown Fairbanks to west (take Airport Way and turn north on Cushman Street for downtown); Fort Wainwright Main Gate (Gaffney Road) to east.

Turn to FAIRBANKS section beginning on page 408 for description of city and maps.

ALASKA ROUTE 2 East

Southbound: Distance from Dawson Creek (DC) is followed by distance from Valdez (V) and distance from Fairbanks (F). Read log: ↑

Southbound travelers note: The Alaska Highway (Route 2) officially ends at Delta Junction, and the Richardson Highway (Route 4) connects the 96 miles between Delta Junction and Fairbanks as Route 2. Physical mileposts on this stretch of highway reflect distance from Valdez.

www.themilepost.com

North Pole

Meet Santa's reindeer up-close and personal at the Antler Academy of Flying & Reindeer Games in North Pole. *(©Kris Valencia, staff)*

North Pole

DC 1470 V 349 F 13 North Pole is on the Richardson Highway, approximately 14 miles southeast of Fairbanks. **Population:** 2,138. **Emergency Services:** Dial 911. **Police**, phone (907) 488-6902. **Alaska State Troopers** (Fairbanks), phone (907) 451-5100. **Fire Dept./Ambulance**, phone (907) 488-2232.

Visitor Information: North Pole Visitor Information Cabin (VIC), operated by the North Pole Chamber of Commerce, located across the Richardson Highway from the Santa Claus House at 2550 Mistletoe Dr.; phone (907) 488-2242; email info@northpolechamber.us; website www.northpolechamber.us. The VIC offers friendly traveler assistance, locally made arts and crafts, souvenirs, coffee/tea/cocoa and candy canes. It is also a geocache locations. Take Mission Road or Dawson exit off the Richardson Highway. Open Monday–Saturday from 10 A.M. to 6 P.M., Sundays 12:45 P.M.–6 P.M. from Memorial Day to Labor Day.

Elevation: 483 feet. **Radio:** KJNP-AM 1170, KJNP-FM 100.3, **Television:** KJNP-Ch 4; also Fairbanks radio and television stations.

Private Aircraft: Bradley Sky Ranch, 1 NW; elev. 483 feet; length 4,100 feet; gravel; fuel 100.

North Pole has all traveler services, including many fine restaurants, fast-food outlets, gas stations, supermarkets, pharmacies and other services. The post office is on Santa Claus Lane. **Hotel North** Pole, which has a special "Santa Suite" available, offers lodging year-round; it is located at the far northwest end of the North Pole Plaza park-

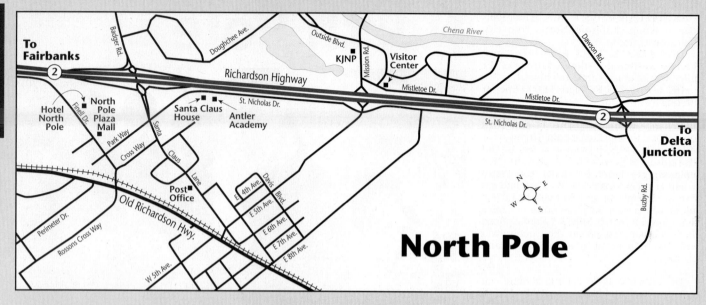

North Pole

ing lot; phone (907) 488-4800. North Pole has a wonderful library, located at 656 NPHS Blvd. (near the high school); phone (907) 488-6101; https://fnsblibrary.org/np/.

Full-service camping at **Riverview RV Park**, located on Badger Road (turnoff at **Milepost V 356.6** on the Richardson Highway). North Pole Public Park, on on 5th Avenue, has tent sites in the trees. Dump station available at North Pole Plaza.

North Pole is the home of many Fairbanks commuters but is also one of 2 energy production centers in Alaska. Almost half of Alaska Railroad's freight revenue has been

from hauling petroleum products made in North Pole. The North Pole area Petro Star Refinery produces heating fuel, jet fuel, asphalt and other petroleum products. Eielson AFB and Fort Wainwright military bases are nearby.

North Pole had its beginnings in 1944, when Bon V. and Bernice Davis homesteaded this area. Dahl and Gaske Development Co. bought the Davis homestead, subdivided it and named it North Pole, hoping to attract a toy manufacturer who could advertise products as being made in North Pole. The city incorporated in 1953

and developed as a theme city: "Where the spirit of Christmas lives year round." The city's light poles are painted to look like candy canes.

Local landmark and long-time visitor attraction **Santa Claus House** was started by Con and Nellie Miller in 1952. A merchant and fur buyer from Fairbanks, Con had been donning an old red Santa suit and entertaining village children at Christmas since arriving in the territory. Building the Santa Claus House in North Pole proved an inspired next step, as over the years it has garnered international attention.

Antler Academy (of Flying & Reindeer Games), or "Antler Academy" for short, is an exciting new reindeer-themed attraction located in the red barn right next door to Santa Claus House in North Pole. You can feed and interact with Santa's reindeer, learn some of the history and mythology surrounding them, and even have your photo taken with "the reindeer team." Open to families, though group sizes and the number of children per group are limited for the safety of both the reindeer and visitors. Visitors are welcome to view the reindeer through the fence at any time of the year, at no cost, however, the "in the pen experience" is available during the summer season only, Memorial Day to Labor Day, for an admission fee. For more information, contact Santa Claus House, 1-800-588-4078 or www.santaclaushouse.com.

Special Events: There's a big summer festival weekend celebration with carnival rides, food booths, arts and crafts booths, and a parade. Every third Friday of the month, celebrate local artists at the Third Friday Art Show at the North Pole Grange. North Pole has an annual Winter Carnival the first weekend of December with fireworks display, candle and tree lighting ceremonies, food and craft booths and other activities. Starting in December, Christmas In Ice (www.christmasinice.org) is a 6-week winter ice park located next to Santa Claus House in North Pole, featuring Christmas-themed ice art competition pieces, ice slides, kids' crafts, ice sculpture demonstrations and more.

Radio station KJNP (King Jesus North Pole), operated by Calvary's Northern Lights Mission, broadcasts music and religious pro-

It is Christmas year-round in North Pole, home of the Santa Claus House. (©Kris Valencia, staff)

grams on 1170 AM and 100.3 FM radio and on TV Channel 4. The station was started in October 1967, by the late Don and Gen Nelson. The inspiration for the station came one Christmas when weather kept the couple from flying out to their ministry among rural villages. Instead, they broadcast their Christmas message from Fairbanks, and received such an overwhelming response that they started a regular program called "Far North Gospel Song and Hymn Time." Visitors are welcome between 9 A.M. and 6 P.M. Monday–Friday. Large group tours

may be arranged by calling (907) 488-2216. KJNP is located on Mission Road, about 0.6 mile northeast of the Richardson Highway, near the VIC, (turn left in front of the large church). The missionary project includes a dozen hand-hewn, sod-roofed homes and other buildings constructed of spruce logs.

NORTH POLE ADVERTISERS

Yellowhead Highway 16

CONNECTS: Edmonton, AB to Prince Rupert, BC

Length: 902 miles   Road Surface: Paved   Season: Open all year

(See maps, page 243-245)

Watch for wildlife along the Yellowhead Highway, but give them plenty of room.
(©Sharon Nault)

(See maps, page 243-245)

Distance in miles	Edmonton	Jasper	Prince George	Prince Rupert	Terrace
Edmonton		220	454	902	810
Jasper	220		234	682	590
Prince George	454	234		448	356
Prince Rupert	902	682	448		92
Terrace	810	590	356	92	

Prince George to Prince Rupert, BC, a distance of 448 miles/721 km, for a total of 902 miles/1,452 km. Prince Rupert is a port for BC and Alaska state ferries.

This is a major east–west route, providing access to a number of attractions in Alberta and British Columbia. Yellowhead Highway 16 is also a very scenic highway, passing through mountains, forest and farmland. Visitor services are readily available in towns along the way, with camping available at both private campgrounds and provincial parks. (It is illegal to overnight in rest areas.)

British Columbia requires that passenger vehicles have winter tires between Oct. 1 and April 30 on the Yellowhead Highway west to Terrace, and from Oct. 1 to March 31 from Terrace to Prince Rupert.

Yellowhead Highway 16 is a paved trans-Canada highway that extends from Winnipeg, Manitoba, to Prince Rupert, BC. (The highway connecting Masset and Queen Charlotte on Graham Island is also designated Yellowhead Highway 16.) *The MILEPOST®* logs Yellowhead Highway 16 in 2 parts: from Edmonton, AB, to Prince George, BC, a distance of 454 miles/731 km, and from

Yellowhead Highway 16 Log

Westbound: The log shows distance from Edmonton (E) followed by distance from Prince George (PG). Read log: ↓

(Continues on page 246)

Major Attractions:

©Claire Torgerson, staff

Canadian Rockies/ Jasper National Park, Mt. Robson, 'Ksan, Fort St. James

Highest Summit:
Obed Summit 3,819 ft.

Yellowhead Highway 16

Edmonton, AB to Prince George, BC (includes Bighorn Hwy.)

© 2019 The MILEPOST®

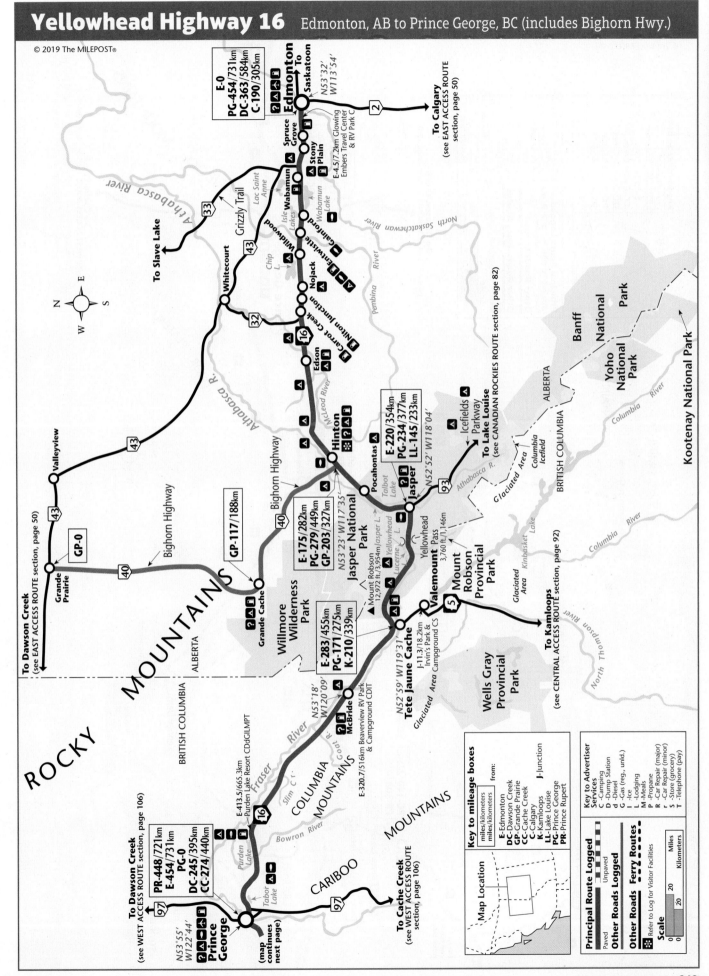

E-0
PG-454/731km
DC-363/584km
C-190/305km

To Edmonton
Saskatoon

To Calgary
(see EAST ACCESS ROUTE
section, page 50)

Spruce Grove
Stony Plain
E-4.5/7.2km Glowing
Embers Travel Center
& RV Park C

Isle Wabamun
Lakes
Wabamun
Lake

Lac Saint Anne

Grizzly Trail

To Slave Lake

Athabasca River

Wildwood
Carrot Creek
Entwistle
Niton Junction
Nojack

Chip L.

North Saskatchewan River

Pembina River

Whitecourt

Edson

McLeod River

Hinton

Pocahontas

Talbot Lake

Jasper

E-220/354km
PG-234/377km
LL-145/233km

N52°52' W118°04'

Icefields
Parkway

To Lake Louise
(see CANADIAN ROCKIES ROUTE section, page 82)

Columbia
Icefield

Glaciated Area

Columbia River

ALBERTA
BRITISH COLUMBIA

Banff
National
Park

Yoho
National
Park

Kootenay National Park

Valleyview

Bighorn Highway

Athabasca R.

GP-0

Grande
Prairie

GP-117/188km

E-175/282km
PG-279/449km
GP-203/327km

N53°23' W117°35'
Jasper National
Park

▲Mount Robson
12,972 ft./3,954m

Jasper L.

Lucerne L.

Yellowhead Pass
3,760 ft./1,146m

93

Grande Cache

Willmore
Wilderness
Park

E-283/455km
PG-171/275km
K-210/339km

N53°18'
W120°09'

McBride

Mount Robson
Provincial Park

Valemount

5

To Kamloops
(see CENTRAL ACCESS ROUTE section, page 92)

Wells Gray
Provincial
Park

Kinbasket Lake

North Thompson River

Columbia River

ROCKY
MOUNTAINS

ALBERTA
BRITISH COLUMBIA

Fraser River

Beaverview RV Park
& Campground CDIT
E-320.7/516km

Goat R.

Slim Cr.

J-11.3/18.2km
Irvin's Park &
Campground CS

Tete Jaune Cache

N52°59' W119°31'

Glaciated Area

To Dawson Creek
(see EAST ACCESS ROUTE section, page 50)

43

40

COLUMBIA
MOUNTAINS

E-413.5/665.3km
Purden Lake Resort CDdGILMPT

16

Fraser River

Bowron River

CARIBOO
MOUNTAINS

To Dawson Creek
(see WEST ACCESS ROUTE section, page 106)

PR-448/721km
E-454/731km
PG-0
DC-245/395km
CC-274/440km

N53°55'
W122°44'
Prince
George

(map
continues
next page)

97

Purden
Lake

Tabor
Lake

97

To Cache Creek
(see WEST ACCESS ROUTE section, page 106)

Key to mileage boxes

miles/kilometers
miles/kilometers from:

E-Edmonton	
DC-Dawson Creek	
GP-Grande Prairie	
CC-Cache Creek	
C-Calgary	
K-Kamloops	
LL-Lake Louise	
PG-Prince George	
PR-Prince Rupert	**J**-Junction

Key to Advertiser Services

C -Camping
D -Dump Station
d -Diesel
G -Gas (reg., unld.)
I -Ice
L -Lodging
M -Meals
P -Propane
R -Car Repair (major)
r -Car Repair (minor)
S -Store (grocery)
T -Telephone (pay)

Map Location

Principal Route Logged

Paved
Unpaved

Other Roads Logged

Other Roads — — —
Ferry Routes · · · · ·

Refer to Log for Visitor Facilities

Scale

Miles
Kilometers
0   20
0   20

Yellowhead Highway 16 Prince George, BC, to Topley, BC

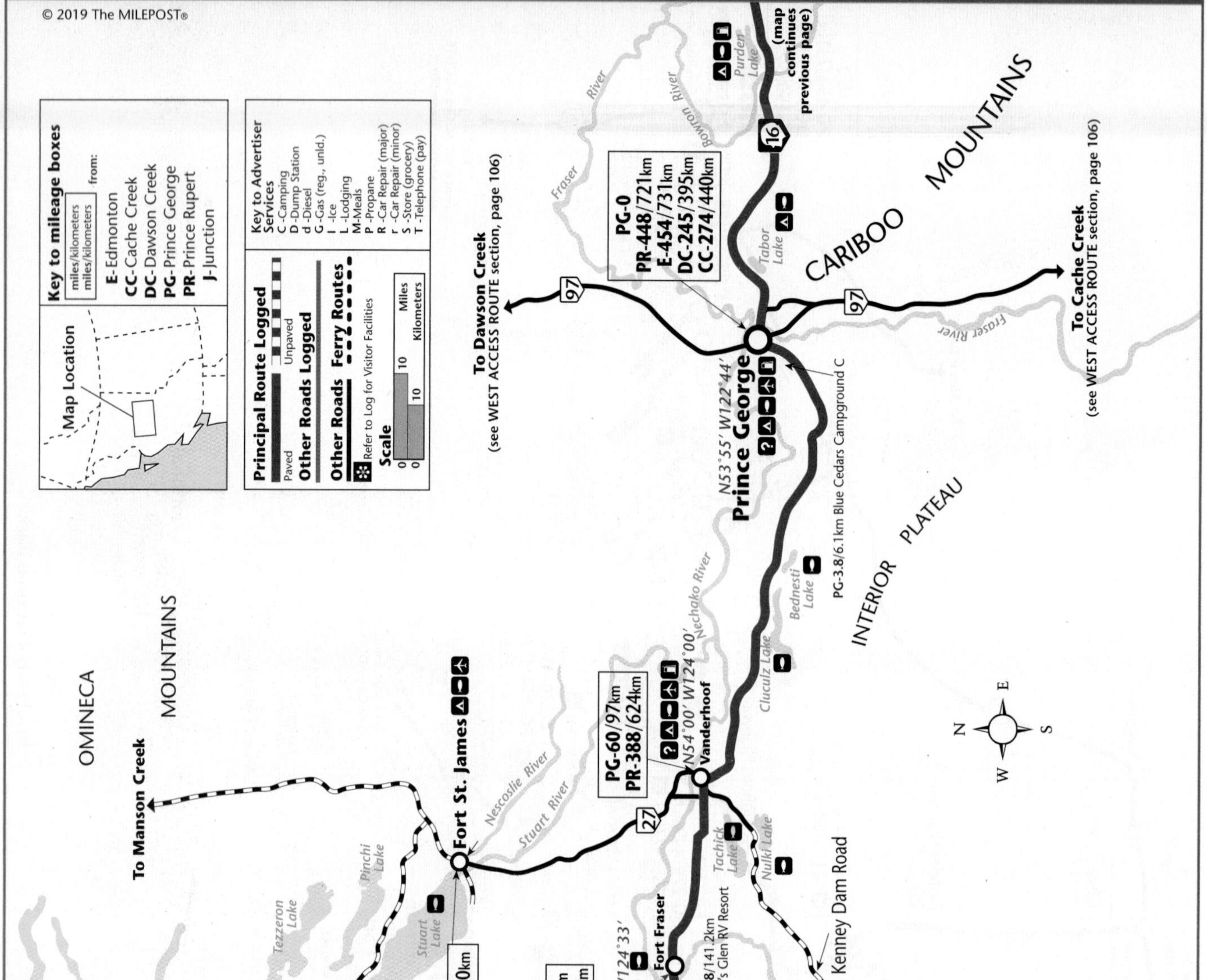

© 2019 The MILEPOST®

Key to mileage boxes

miles/kilometers from:
miles/kilometers

E-Edmonton
CC-Cache Creek
DC-Dawson Creek
PG-Prince George
PR-Prince Rupert
J-Junction

Key to Advertiser Services

C -Camping
D -Dump Station
d -Diesel
G -Gas (reg., unld.)
I -Ice
L -Lodging
M-Meals
P -Propane
R -Car Repair (major)
r -Car Repair (minor)
S -Store (grocery)
T -Telephone (pay)

Map Location

Principal Route Logged
Paved — Unpaved
Other Roads Logged
Other Roads **Ferry Routes**

Refer to Log for Visitor Facilities

Scale
0 | 10 Miles
0 | 10 Kilometers

CARIBOO MOUNTAINS

(map continues previous page)

Purden Lake

16

Bowron River

River

Fraser

PG-0
PR-448/721km
E-454/731km
DC-245/395km
CC-274/440km

Tabor Lake

97

To Dawson Creek
(see WEST ACCESS ROUTE section, page 106)

97

Fraser River

To Cache Creek
(see WEST ACCESS ROUTE section, page 106)

N53°55' W122°44'
Prince George

PG-3.8/6.1km Blue Cedars Campground C

INTERIOR PLATEAU

Bednesti Lake

Cluculz Lake

OMINECA MOUNTAINS

To Manson Creek

Nechako River
N54°00' W124°00'

Vanderhoof

PG-60/97km
PR-388/624km

Tezzeron Lake

Pinchi Lake

Tachie River

Tachie

Stuart Lake

Nesacoslie River

Stuart River

Fort St. James

J-37/60km

27

Tachick Lake

Nulki Lake

Kenney Dam Road

Trembleur Lake

Taltapin Lake

PG-96/154km
PR-352/566km

N54°03' W124°33'
Fraser L.
Fort Fraser

PG-88/141.2km
Piper's Glen RV Resort CDL

Nechako River

Knewstubb Lake

N54°03' W124°47'
Fraser Lake

Endako

Stellako R.

Kenney Dam

Cheslatta Lake

Natalkuz Lake

16

PG-140/225km
PR-308/496km

Burns Lake

Pinkut Lake

Tchesinkut Lake

35

Ferry

Uncha Lake

Takysie Lake

Francois Lake Road

Francois Lake

Ootsa Lake

Babine Lake

J-31/51km
Granisle

J-24/39km

Topley Landing

PG-171/275km
PR-277/445km

N54°30' W126°17'
Topley

Rose Lake

Decker Lake

N54°13' W125°45'
Burns Lake

PG-140.1/225.2km Regional District of Bulkley Nechako Yam and Sew On

(map continues next page)

Tweedsmuir Provincial Park

N
W — E
S

Yellowhead Highway 16 Topley, BC, to Prince Rupert, BC

© 2019 The MILEPOST®

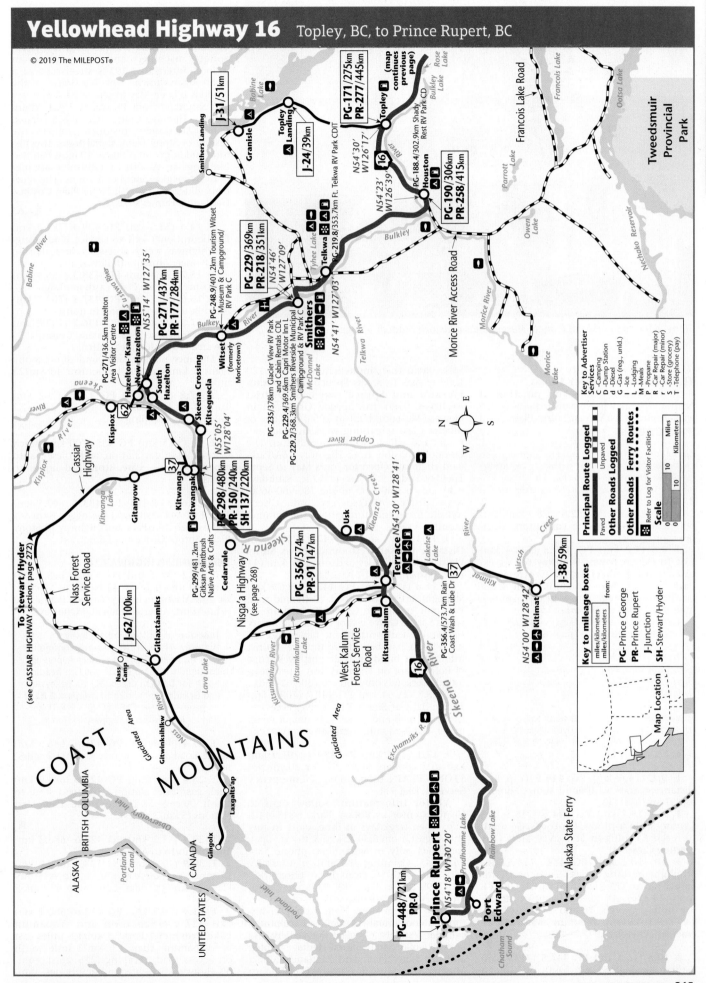

PG-171/275km
PR-277/445km
Topley (map continues previous page)

J-31/51km

J-24/39km

Topley Landing

Granisle

Smithers Landing

Babine Lake

Rose Lake
Bulkley Rest RV Park CDT

PG-188.4/302.9km Shady Rest RV Park CD

N54°30' W126°17'

16

PG-190/306km
PR-258/415km
Houston

N54°23' W126°39'

Francois Lake Road

Francois Lake

Tweedsmuir Provincial Park

PG-219.8/353.7km Ft. Telkwa RV Park CDIT

PG-229/369km
PR-218/351km

Telkwa

N54°46' W127°09'

Bulkley

Owen Lake

Parrott Lake

Nechako Reservoir

Ootsa Lake

PG-248.9/401.2km Tourism Witset
Museum & Campground/ RV Park C

PG-271/437km
PR-177/284km

Babine River

Skeena River

PG-271/436.5km Hazelton Area Visitor Centre

Hazelton-'Ksan

Kuswka River

N55°14' W127°35'

New Hazelton

South Hazelton

Witset (formerly Moricetown)

Bulkley River

PG-235/378km Glacier View RV Park and Cabin Rentals CDL
PG-229.4/369.6km Capri Motor Inn L
PG-229.2/368.3km Smithers Riverside Municipal Campground & RV Park C

Smithers

N54°41' W127°03'

McDonnel Lake

Tyhee Lake

Telkwa River

Morice River Access Road

Morice River

Morice Lake

Skeena Crossing

Kitseguecla

N55°05' W128°04'

Kispiox

62

Kispiox River

Gitanyow

Cassiar Highway

Kitwanga Lake

37

Kitwanga

Gitwangak

PG-298/480km
PR-150/240km
SH-137/220km

Copper River

Kitsumkalum River

Kleanza Creek

Hirsch Creek

PG-299/481.2km Gitksan Paintbrush Native Arts & Crafts

Cedarvale

Skeena R.

Usk

N54°30' W128°41'

PG-356/574km
PR-91/147km

Terrace

Lakelse Lake

37

J-38/59km

Kitimat

N54°00' W128°42'

To Stewart/Hyder (see CASSIAR HIGHWAY section, page 272)

Nass Forest Service Road

J-62/100km

Gitlaxt'aamiks

Nisga'a Highway (see page 268)

Kitsumkalum

Kitsumkalum Lake

West Kalum Forest Service Road

Skeena River

16

PG-356.4/573.7km Rain Coast Wash & Lube Dr

Nass Camp

Gitwinksihlkw

Nass River

Glaciated Area

Lava Lake

Kitsumkalum River

COAST MOUNTAINS

Glaciated Area

Laxgalts'ap

Exchamsiks R.

Glaciated Area

ALASKA
UNITED STATES

BRITISH COLUMBIA
CANADA

Observatory Inlet

Portland Canal

Gingolx

Portland Inlet

Prudhomme Lake

Rainbow Lake

PG-448/721km
PR-0

Prince Rupert

N54°18' W130°20'

Port Edward

Chatham Sound

Alaska State Ferry

Key to Advertiser Services

- C –Camping
- D –Dump Station
- D –Diesel
- G –Gas (reg., unld.)
- I –Ice
- L –Lodging
- M –Meals
- P –Propane
- R –Car Repair (major)
- r –Car Repair (minor)
- S –Store (grocery)
- T –Telephone (pay)

Principal Route Logged
Paved   Unpaved
Other Roads Logged   **Ferry Routes** ·····
Refer to Log for Visitor Facilities

Scale
Miles
Kilometers
0   10
0   10

Key to mileage boxes

miles/kilometers
miles/kilometers   from:

PG-Prince George
PR-Prince Rupert
J-Junction
SH-Stewart/Hyder

Map Location

N
W   E
S

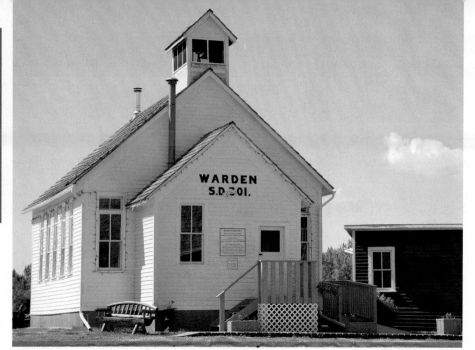

Stony Plain and Parkland Pioneer Museum has a historic outdoor village.
(©Kris Valencia, staff)

(Continued from page 242)

YELLOWHEAD HIGHWAY 16A

E 0 PG 454 (730.6 km) **Junction** of Anthony Henday Drive North/Highway 216 with Highway 16A West/Stony Plain Road *(see map page 67).*

NOTE: Southbound travelers may bypass Edmonton city center by taking Highway 216 south, skirting downtown but accessing attractions like the West Edmonton Mall. You will join the EAST ACCESS ROUTE at Milepost CB 375.3; see page 67.

E 1.2 (1.9 km) **PG 452.8** (728.7 km) Eastbound sign: Welcome to Edmonton, Alberta's capital city.

E 4.5 (7.2 km) **PG 449.5** (723.4 km) Exit to Devon Bypass/Highway 60. Access to **Glowing Embers Travel Centre & RV Park** this exit: drive 0.6 km/0.4 mile south on Highway 60 then turn west on 1-km/0.6-mile access road to RV park.

Glowing Embers Travel Centre & RV Park. See display ad page 69.

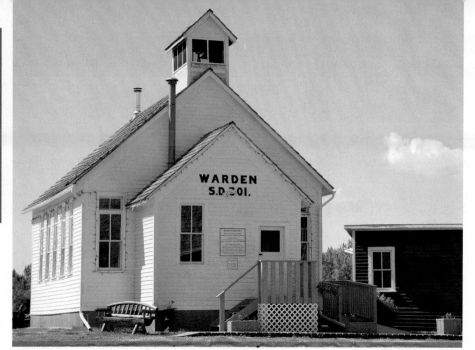

NOTE: Southbound travelers may bypass Edmonton by taking Highway 60 south, then Highway 19 east to Highway 2 (Devonian Way Bypass).

Junction with Highway 60 south to Highway 19 east and Edmonton Bypass route. See "Devonian Way Bypass" on page 70 and read log back to front.

E 9.1 (14.6 km) **PG 444.9** (716 km) Distance marker eastbound shows Edmonton 27 km/17 miles.

E 9.4 (15.1 km) **PG 444.6** (715.5 km) Century Road with Save-On-Foods. Go south to reach **EV plug-in** at Peavey Mart (161 Century Crossing).

E 10 (16.1 km) **PG 444** (714.5 km) Stoplight at King Street. Turn north for Spruce Grove city center. **SPRUCE GROVE** (pop. 23,326). All visitor facilities including hotels, motels, restaurants, fast-food, gas/diesel stations, shopping malls and all emergency services.

E 10.5 (16.9 km) **PG 443.5** (713.7 km) Golden Spike Road. Go south on Golden Spike Road then immediately east to 120 Railway Ave. to access **Spruce Grove Grain Elevator and Spruce Grove & District Archives.** Tour the Spruce Grove Grain Elevator Museum, built in 1958, it is one of Alberta's last remaining wooden grain elevators and still in working condition. The Elevator is visible from Highway 16A/Parkland Highway. Open for tours May to Sept., Tuesday–Friday 9:30 A.M. to 3 P.M., Saturdays 9:30 A.M. to 1:30 P.M.; phone 780-960-4600; www.sprucegroveagsociety.com. Check website for events throughout the summer months.

E 11.1 (17.9 km) **PG 442.9** (712.8 km) Distance marker westbound shows Stony Plain 6 km/4 miles, Edson 178 km/111 miles, Jasper 338 km/210 miles.

E 11.6 (18.7 km) **PG 442.4** (711.9 km) Stoplight at Campsite Road. Eastbound sign: Welcome to Spruce Grove. Turn south to access Spruce Grove visitor center and Rotary Centennial Park with picnic tables and toilets. The Chamber of Commerce tourist information building is at northwest edge of Rotary Park on Highway 16A, open year-round, weekends only; phone 780-962-2561.

E 13.3 (21.64 km) **PG 440.7** (709.2 km) Traffic light at South Park Drive; access to shopping mall and all services (major chain motel, fast-food outlets, supermarket).

E 14.1 (22.7 km) **PG 439.9** (707.9 km) Exit to Secondary Road 779 for downtown **STONY PLAIN** (pop. 15,051). **Emergency Services:** Dial 911.

Visitor Information: Follow signs to Visitor Center at Rotary Park, 4815–44th Ave. Open weekdays in June, daily in July and August, from 8:30 A.M. to 5:30 P.M.; open weekends only in September; phone 780-963-4545. Camping at Camp n' Class RV Park 4107–50th St., Stony Plain, phone 780-963-2299 and at Lions RV Park and Campground, phone 780-963-4505.

Attractions in Stony Plain include 41 historic outdoor murals; 8 public art sculptures; summer festivals; Crooked Pot Gallery and Potters' Guild; Multicultural Heritage Center; and the Stony Plain and Parkland Pioneer Museum. The Museums have seasonal hours; they are open 7 days a week through the summer. Admission is by donation for both museums. The Pioneer Museum has a historic outdoor village, an antique lamp collection, antique machinery and Legacy Street—an indoor, interactive 1930s streetscape of a small Alberta town. The Tea House on the grounds is open May to September on Fridays and Saturdays from 11 A.M. to 3 P.M. Multi-cultural Heritage Center here has a curated Public Art Gallery, historical archives, the history of Stony Plain, mural tours, two historic buildings and is one of 10 most haunted buildings in Alberta. Established summer festivals include Summer Sessions, The Blueberry Bluegrass Festival, Stony Plain Cowboy Gathering, Farmer's Days.

E 14.6 (23.5 km) **PG 439.4** (707.1 km) Eastbound-only exit to service road alongside highway which accesses a car dealership and Pioneer Museum (follow signs).

E 15.7 (25.3 km) **PG 438.3** (705.4 km) Welcome to Stony Plain eastbound sign.

E 16.6 (26.7 km) **PG 437.4** (703.9 km) Allan Beach Resort turnoff to north.

E 17.3 (27.8 km) **PG 436.7** (702.8 km) Turnoff for Hasse Lake Parkland County day-use area (10 km/6 miles south).

Distance marker eastbound shows Stony Plain 6 km/4 miles, Edmonton 40 km/25 miles.

E 17.8 (28.6 km) **PG 436.2** (702 km) Turnoff for Hubbles Lake (signed), 2 km/1.2 miles north; camping.

E 19 (30.5 km) **PG 435** (700 km) Beach Corner. Esso gas station with diesel, auto repair, propane, cafe, store and liquor to north.

E 20.6 (33.2 km) **PG 433.4** (697.5 km) Take Exit 344 eastbound for logged route via Yellowhead 16A/Parkland Highway to Stony Plain, Spruce Grove and Edmonton.

YELLOWHEAD HIGHWAY 16

E 23.2 (37.3 km) **PG 430.8** (693.3 km) Exit 340 for Highway 43 North to Mackenzie and Alaska highways. Grande Prairie and Whitecourt, Alberta Beach and Onoway.

Junction of Yellowhead Highway 16 with Highway 43 North. If you are continuing west for Prince George or Prince Rupert, BC, continue with this log. If you are heading north for Dawson Creek, BC, via Valleyview and Grande Prairie, turn to **Milepost E 23.2** on page 71 of the EAST ACCESS ROUTE section for log of Alberta Highway 43 North.

E 27.4 (44.1 km) **PG 426.6** (686.5 km) Range Road 31, golf course (2 km/1.2 miles) north.

E 28.4 (45.7 km) **PG 425.6** (684.9 km) Shell gas/diesel station with food store to south. Access to Duffield and Paul First Nations (5 km/3 miles).

E 29.4 (47.3 km) **PG 424.6** (683.3 km) Turnoff north to Alberta Beach.

E 30.9 (49.7 km) **PG 423.1** (680.9 km) Distance marker eastbound shows Stony Plain 29 km/18 miles, Edmonton 63 km/39 miles.

E 31.4 (50.5 km) **PG 422.6** (680.1 km) Exit 327 for Kapasiwin and **Wabamun Lake Provincial Park**, 3 km/1.8 miles east of Wabamun, then 1.6 km/1 mile south on access road; camping (276 sites), coin-op showers, hookups, public phones, sani-dump $3, picnicking, fishing, boating and swimming. A golf course is adjacent campground. Camping fees $29 (unserviced), $36 (power). Reservations 1-877-537-2757 or reserve.albertaparks.ca. May–October.

E 33.4 (53.8 km) **PG 420.6** (676.9 km) Overpass; exit for village of **WABAMUN** (pop. 682); **Emergencies:** Dial 911. Services include gas, propane, hardware store, convenience store, car wash, laundromat, library, liquor store, groceries, bank, dump station, 3 hotels/motels, 1 bed and breakfast and post office. Wabamun Waterfront Park has a cooking area, shelter, water spray park, tables, boat launch, litter bins, washroom/changing rooms and flush toilets. Total of 6 city parks. World's largest dragonfly statue greets visitors as they enter Wabamun.

E 36.6 (58.9 km) **PG 417.4** (671.7 km) Shell gas/diesel station to the south side with snack shop.

E 38.7 (62.3 km) **PG 415.3** (668.4 km) **Junction** 765 North to Darwell.

Distance marker eastbound shows Stony Plain 40 km/25 miles, Spruce Grove 48 km/30 miles, Edmonton 69 km/43 miles.

E 41.4 (66.6 km) **PG 412.6** (664 km) To the south and away from highway, **FALLIS** (pop. 190); store.

E 44.9 (72.3 km) **PG 409.1** (658.4 km) Exit 306 for Highway 759 to the south for Tomahawk, Coco-Moco day-use area and Seba Beach; Isle Lake to north with RV Park (3 km/1.5 miles).

E 46.2 (74.4 km) **PG 407.8** (656.3 km) Entering **GAINFORD** (pop. 205); cafe, hotel and post office. Public park with 8 campsites.

E 50.1 (80.6 km) **PG 403.9** (650 km) **Junction** with 757 North for Magnolia and Sangudo. Views of trestle bridge.

Distance marker eastbound shows Gainford 5 km/3 miles, Stony Plain 58 km/36 miles, Edmonton 85 km/53 miles.

E 55.5 (89.3 km) **PG 398.5** (641.3 km) Exit 289 to 16A West to Entwistle and Highway 22 South to Dayton Valley.

Exit north for **ENTWISTLE** (pop. 453) town center; food, lodging, store. Exit south for easy access eastbound to all visitor services. Esso gas/diesel station to south, restaurants, fast food and shopping. Camping at **Pembina River Provincial Park**, 3.1 km/1.9 miles north, near Pembina River gorge; 134 campsites, tables, showers, flush toilets, water and dump station. Camping fee $26–$33. Reservations 1-877-537-2757; website reserve.albertaparks.ca/. Open May 18–Oct. 10 for fishing, swimming and playground.

E 56.2 (90.4 km) **PG 397.8** (640.2 km) Pembina River bridge. Exit to **EVANSBURG** (pop. 795), gas/diesel station, restaurants, grocery store, lodging, recreation center.

E 60.5 (97.4 km) **PG 393.5** (633.3 km) **Junction** with 22 North to Mayerthorpe (bypass Edmonton).

E 62.1 (99.9 km) **PG 391.9** (630.7 km) **Junction** with 16A East to north.

E 66 (106.2 km) **PG 388** (624.4 km) Exit to Chip Lake and **WILDWOOD** (pop. 273). Post office, hotel, gas/diesel station, restaurants, library and shops. Campground

at **Chip Lake** (9 km/5.6 miles north, and 10.5 km/6.5 miles west of Wildwood) with 22 sites, $20 fee, tables, firewood, pullthroughs, pit toilets, water, fishing, swimming, boat launch. Chip Lake Park is 20 km/12.4 miles to north.

E 75.8 (122 km) **PG 378.2** (608.7 km) Eastbound-only access to Nojack rest area with picnic tables, toilets and litter bins.

E 81.5 (131.2 km) **PG 372.5** (599.5 km) **Nojack Provincial Recreation Area** and campground to north; day-use area with shelter, water/pump (boil water for drinking), 24 sites, open May 10–Oct. 30, camping fee $15.

E 87.7 (141.1 km) **PG 366.3** (589.5 km) Lobstick River.

E 88.4 (142.3 km) **PG 365.6** (588.4 km) **NITON JUNCTION** (pop. 38). Esso and Shell gas/diesel stations, restaurant, lodging, Subway and A&W, convenience store to north. Hidden Grove RV Campground and RV Park. Community offers a rest area with garden area with picnic tables and gazebo; dog walking, no toilets.

E 92.2 (148.4 km) **PG 361.8** (582.3 km) **CARROT CREEK**; gas/diesel station with convenience store, liquor store and, post office to south. Store hours: 9:30 A.M. to 9 P.M. Monday–Friday; 11 A.M. to 8 P.M. Saturday–Sunday. Fewer hours in winter.

E 96.9 (155.9 km) **PG 357.1** (574.7 km) **Junction** with Highway 32 North which leads 67.6 km/42 miles north to Peers, Whitecourt and Highway 43.

E 98.8 (159 km) **PG 355.2** (571.6 km) Westbound traffic weigh station, with litter barrel and toilets.

E 101.3 (163 km) **PG 352.7** (567.6 km) Turnoff for Minnow Lake Provincial Recreation Area 26 km/16 miles south and **Wolf Lake West Provincial Recreation Area** with campground, located 53 km/33 miles south on gravel road; 36 campsites, pit toilets, boat launch, water pumps, firewood. Open May–Oct. 13. Camping fee $22. Reservation phone 780-723-0738.

E 104.6 (168.3 km) **PG 349.4** (562.3 km) Westbound access (and second entrance eastbound) to the Edson rest area to south. (For westbound travelers, a connecting road between the twinning lanes allows westbound access to this rest area to the south).

E 104.9 (168.8 km) **PG 349.1** (561.8 km) Eastbound turnoff for Edson rest area to south. Nice large facility off highway with flush toilets, water, tables, shelter, phone and sani-dump.

E 105.9 (170.4 km) **PG 348.1** (560.2 km) Rosevear Road; eastbound access to Edson rest area. Turn north on Rosevear Road to the Rosevear Ferry that departs from here. One of the few remaining Alberta ferries, it runs from May–October and has been in operation for more than 70 years.

E 107.9 (173.6 km) **PG 346.1** (557 km) Wild Rose Campground 5 km/3.1 miles north.

E 110.1 (177.2 km) **PG 343.9** (553.4 km) East of Edson RV Resort to south.

E 113.2 (182.1 km) **PG 340.8** (548.4 km) McLeod River.

E 114 (183.5 km) **PG 340** (547.2 km) **Junction** with Highway 748 north and Shell

gas/diesel station.

E 115 (185 km) **PG 339** (545.5 km) Welcome to Edson sign westbound. Edson RV Campground and Edson Golf Course, 18-hole golf course and driving range; and Moose Meadows 18-hole golf course and driving range 2 km further south.

E 116.6 (187.6 km) **PG 337.4** (543 km) Gas/diesel station, motel, fast-food and Lions Park Campground to the north at east end of Edson.

Begin speed zone westbound through Edson. Highway 16 splits westbound, with 1-way westbound and eastbound lanes forming the main avenues of Edson.

Edson

E 116.6 (187.6 km) **PG 337.4** (543 km) Highway 16 westbound and eastbound lanes form the main avenues of Edson, with services located along the highway and cross-streets. **Population:** 8,646. **Emergency Services:** Dial 911. **Hospital:** Edson Healthcare Center 780-723-3331.

Visitor Information: At Galloway Station Museum and Travel Center, easily accessible from Yellowhead Highway 16; RV parking, coffee bar, free WiFi, restrooms. Open year round, daily in summer and Monday–Saturdays in winter; 223–55th St. For more information on Edson, go to websites: gallowaystationmuseum.com or www.edson.ca.

Edson is a large highway community with all services, including many motels, gas stations and truck stops, restaurants and major chain fast-food outlets. Edson's economy is based on coal mining, forestry, oil, natural gas and manufacturing. Oil and gas workers may fill up local hotel and motel rooms, so reserve ahead.

Recreational facilities include Kinsmen Spray Park, indoor pool, curling and ice rinks, 18-hole golf course, skateboard park, movie theater and library. Camping at Lions Park Campground and Willmore Park 6 km south of town. Sani-dump on 1st Avenue between 56th and 57th streets.

Yellowhead Highway 16 Log
(continued)

E 118.3 (190.3 km) **PG 335.7** (540.2 km) Edson airport.

E 118.7 (191 km) **PG 335.3** (539.6 km) Turn off on 63rd Street south for Willmore Park, 6 km/3.7 miles; 41 unserviced campsites, potable water, firepits, free firewood, self-register. Boat launch, fishing and swimming on the **McLeod River**, hiking trails, day-use areas with picnic tables, camping fee $17.

E 120 (193.1 km) **PG 334** (537.5 km) Sign: Welcome to Edson. Begin 4-lane divided highway westbound.

E 123.1 (198.1 km) **PG 330.9** (532.5 km) **Junction** with Highway 47 South.

E 125.3 (201.7 km) **PG 328.7** (529 km) Sundance Creek.

E 127.5 (205.2 km) **PG 326.5** (525.4 km) **Hornbeck Creek Campground and Recreation Area** to north; 32 campsites, picnic area, water pump (may not be potable), pit toilets, firewood. Open May 1–Sept. 30,

Popular William A. Switzer Provincial Park day-use area is a short drive north from Yellowhead Highway 16 on the Bighorn Route. (©Sharon Nault)

camping fee $20.

E 140.9 (226.8 km) **PG 313.1** (503.9 km) Eastbound-only turnout with litter bins.

E 141.4 (227.6 km) **PG 312.6** (503.1 km) Westbound-only roadside turnout with picnic tables, pit toilets and litter/recycling bins; generous, paved parking area.

E 148.9 (239.6 km) **PG 305.1** (491 km) **Obed Lake Campground and Provincial Park** to north; 7 campsites, day-use area, water pump (may not be potable), firewood, pit toilets, boat launch, fishing, beach area. Open May 1–Oct. 31; camping fee $11.

E 157.3 (253.1 km) **PG 296.7** (477.5 km) **Obed Summit**, highest elevation on the Yellowhead Highway at 1,164m/3,819 feet.

E 158.6 (255.2 km) **PG 295.4** (475.4 km) Westbound roadside turnout; generous parking area, picnic tables, toilets and litter bins. Good view of the Rockies from here.

E 167.7 (269.8 km) **PG 286.3** (460.7 km) Welcome to Hinton sign westbound.

Distance marker eastbound shows Edson 81 km/50 miles, Edmonton 274 km/170 miles.

E 168.8 (271.6 km) **PG 285.2** (459 km) Lakeview Inns & Suites, restaurants, Holiday Inn, Esso gas/diesel station.

E 169.6 (272.9 km) **PG 284.4** (457.7 km) Turnoff for Day's Inn and Super 8 to north.

E 170.4 (274.2 km) **PG 283.6** (456.4 km) View of Hinton industrial area. *Begin speed zone westbound through Hinton.*

Hinton

E 170.9 (275 km) **PG 283.1** (455.6 km) Stoplight in downtown Hinton. Hinton is a 3-hour drive from Edmonton and just east of the Bighorn Highway 40 junction. **Population:** 9,882. **Emergency Services:** Dial 911. **Hospital:** Hinton Healthcare Center 780-865-3333.

Visitor Information: Information Center is open daily May–October, 9 A.M. to 7 P.M.; November–April, Monday–Friday 9 A.M. to 5 P.M.; phone 1-877-446-8666. Or contact Town of Hinton, phone 780-865-6000; www.hinton.ca.

A major service stop on Yellowhead Highway 16, Hinton has all visitor facilities, including major chain hotels/motels, restaurant and fast-food outlets; gas stations; RV parts and services; Safeway supermarket; shopping centers and shopping mall; dental offices, RCMP post, bowling alley, curling rink, golf course and recreation complex with indoor pool. Big box stores include Walmart and Canadian Tire. Hinton is only 28 km/17.5 miles east of Jasper National Park gate, 6.4 km/4 miles east of the Bighorn Highway, 80 km/50 miles west of Edson and 287 km/178 miles west of Edmonton.

Campgrounds are available in Hinton. There are also several campgrounds within William A. Switzer Provincial Park along Highway 40 North *(see "Bighorn Route" log on page 249)*.

The Hinton Center (Aboriginal Center) has a city campground on Switzer Drive. Follow signs which lead through downtown.

Hinton began in the 1900s as a construction camp for railroad, coal mining and logging crews. The community grew dramatically after construction of the pulp mill in 1955. Major industry in community and surrounding area includes coal mining, forestry, oil and gas and tourism. Hinton's latest attraction is the 1.9 mile/3 km Beaver Boardwalk, winding through wetlands and offering views of an actively used beaver pond. The Hinton Mountain Bike Park and trails offer outdoor adventure and fun for all ages and skill levels. Ask for directions and a map at the Visitor Information Center.

Yellowhead Highway 16 Log
(continued)

E 171.6 (276.1 km) **PG 282.4** (454.5 km) Second stoplight westbound in Hinton; access to Husky truck stop with gas/diesel, Boston Pizza, Subway, Tim Hortons and other services.

E 172.3 (277.2 km) **PG 281.7** (453.3 km) Hinton golf club and Gateway RV Park.

E 172.6 (277.7 km) **PG 281.4** (452.9 km) Stoplight. Access to Parks West Mall; Walmart, Canadian Tire, Safeway, White Wolf Inn and McDonald's. *Begin speed zone eastbound through Hinton.*

E 173.8 (279.6 km) **PG 280.2** (450.9 km) **Junction** with Bighorn Highway 40 South to Cadomin.

E 175 (281.6 km) **PG 279** (449 km) **Junction** with Bighorn Highway 40 North (paved) which leads 86 miles/139 km to Grande Cache and 203 miles/327 km to Grande Prairie.

Junction with Bighorn Highway 40 to Grande Cache and Grande Prairie. See "Bighorn Route" log beginning on facing page.

End divided 4-lane highway, begin 2-lane highway with passing lanes westbound. Begin divided 4-lane highway eastbound.

Distance marker eastbound shows Hinton 2 km/1 mile, Edson 95 km/59 miles, Edmonton 288 km/179 miles.

E 176.2 (283.5 km) **PG 277.8** (447.1 km) Turnoff for Hinton/Jasper KOA.

E 178.1 (286.6 km) **PG 275.9** (444 km) Jasper-Hinton airport.

E 179.5 (288.8 km) **PG 274.5** (441.8 km) Maskuta Creek. Private campground.

E 180.9 (291.1 km) **PG 273.1** (439.5 km) Weigh scales to south doubles as a vehicle inspection station for watercraft/invasive species.

E 182 (292.8 km) **PG 272** (437.7 km) Turnoff for **Wildhorse Lake Provincial Recreation Area**, 5 km/3.1 miles north; day-use area and 19 unserviced vehicle sites and 3 walk-in tent sites at **Wildhorse Lake Campground**, 10 unserviced sites at nearby **Kinky Lake Campground**; camping fee $23; water pump (may not be potable), pit toilets, firewood, hiking, fishing, boat launch/pier. Open May 1–Oct. 31. Reservation phone 780-865-2154.

E 184.4 (296.7 km) **PG 269.6** (433.9 km) Jasper East Cabins and Jasper Gates Campground and Cabins.

E 185.1 (297.9 km) **PG 268.9** (432.8 km) Folding Mountain rest area turnout to north with toilets, litter bins and information boards about Alberta's history.

E 185.9 (299.1 km) **PG 268.1** (431.5 km) Food and lodging to north.

E 186.9 (300.7 km) **PG 267.1** (429.8 km) *CAUTION: Watch for bighorn sheep on and alongside the highway.*

E 187.6 (310.8 km) **PG 266.4** (428.7 km) **Jasper National Park, East Entrance.** Park fees are charged on a per-person basis and must be paid by all visitors using facilities in Rocky Mountain national parks. No charge for motorists passing through park on Highway 16. Public phones. **RCMP** phone number for Jasper 780-542-4848.

Alberta's Jasper National Park is part of the Canadian Rocky Mountains World Heritage Site. It is the largest of Canada's Rocky Mountain parks, covering 4,200 square miles/10,878 square kms. It adjoins Banff National Park to the south. Visitors can sightsee this spectacular mountain scenery from Highway 93 (see turnoff to Icefields Parkway at **Milepost E 219.9**).

Highway 16 has restricted speed zones through the park. Drive carefully and watch for wildlife. NOTE: It is illegal to feed, touch, disturb or hunt wildlife in the national park. All plants and natural objects are also protected and must not be removed or destroyed.

E 192 (308.9 km) **PG 262** (421.6 km) Pocahontas Cabins on highway; turnoff to south for **POCAHONTAS** (2 km/1.2 miles) *(Continues on page 251)*

Bighorn Route

The Bighorn Highway (Alberta Highway 40, "The Road to Alaska") is a 203-mile/327-km route connecting Yellowhead Highway 16 and Highway 43. It is a 2-lane paved highway with moderate grades and curves. Older damaged 2-lane road (no shoulder) alternate with improved surfacing with shoulders and passing lanes on the southern half of the road. *A major road improvement project south of Grande Cache was underway in summer 2018.* Truck traffic can get heavier the closer you get to Grande Prairie. Watch for logging activity signs as well as signs noting reforestation projects within the first 45 miles/72 km of the road. Passing lanes are frequently provided for uphill stretches. This road has areas of narrow shoulders; turnout only in designated locations. The 3 major communities along this route—Hinton (on Yellowhead 16), Grande Cache (on Highway 40), and Grande Prairie (on Highway 43)—have all visitor facilities. For emergencies along this route dial 911. Speed limit is 100 kmph/62 mph.

ALBERTA HIGHWAY 40

Northbound: Distance from Yellowhead Highway 16 junction (Y) is followed by the distance from Grande Prairie (GP). Read log: ⬇

Y 0 GP 203.4 (327.3 km) **Junction** with Yellowhead Highway 16 at **Milepost E 175,** just west of Hinton. Next gas northbound 141 km/88 miles.

Y 0.1 (0.2 km) **GP 203.3** (327.2 km) Distance marker northbound shows Muskeg 113 km/70 miles, Grande Cache 142 km/88 miles, Grande Prairie 325 km/202 miles.

Y 0.6 (1 km) **GP 202.8** (326.4 km) Private campground to east. ⛺

Y 2.2 (3.5 km) **GP 201.2** (323.8 km) Community of **ENTRANCE** (pop. 15) to west. Railroad crossing overpass.

Y 3.1 (5 km) **GP 200.3** (322.4 km) Athabasca River bridge.

Y 3.7 (6 km) **GP 199.7** (321.4 km) Access road west to community of Brule (16 km/10 miles). Hinton airfield to east.

Y 4.4 (7.1 km) **GP 199** (320.3 km) Entrance Ranch to east; trail rides. Northbound passing lane begins.

Y 6.4 (10.3 km) **GP 197** (317 km) Northbound passing lane ends.

Y 7.3 (11.7 km) **GP 196.1** (315.6 km) *CAUTION: Logging trucks crossing* (sign) and southbound, leaving William A. Switzer Provincial Park.

Y 8.3 (13.4 km) **GP 195.1** (314 km) Hinton Lookout Nordic Center (1 km/0.6 miles).

Y 8.9 (14.3 km) **GP 194.5** (313 km) Turnout to east with litter bins and information boards with a map of the William A. Switzer Provincial Park showing designated campgrounds.

Y 9.7 (15.6 km) **GP 193.7** (311.7 km) Access road leads 3 km/1.9 miles east, downhill to **Jarvis Lake** open year-round, camping fee $26; and **Pine Bay** (group) campgrounds open May 18–Oct. 3, camping fee $24. Day-use areas popular with locals. Picnic area along large sandy beach. Roped off swimming area. Telephone, toilets, unpotable water, boat launch. ⛺

Y 9.8 (15.8 km) **GP 193.6** (311.6 km) Distance marker northbound shows Muskeg 90 km/56 miles, Grande Cache 119 km/74 miles, Grande Prairie 302 km/188 miles.

Y 12.4 (20 km) **GP 191** (307.4 km) Jarvis Creek.

Y 12.6 (20.3 km) **GP 190.8** (307.1 km) **William A. Switzer Provincial Park** at **Kelley's Bathtub** day-use area to the west, offers a seasonal visitor center April 1–May 30 (Monday 10 A.M. to 3 P.M.; Thursday–Saturday 1–8 P.M.; Sunday 10 A.M. to 5 P.M.; closed Tuesday, Wednesday); June 1–Aug. 31 (Monday 10 A.M. to 3 P.M.; Tuesday, Wednesday and Sunday 10 A.M. to 4:30 P.M.; Thursday and Saturday 10 A.M. to 8 P.M.); large parking area with toilets, public phone, swimming and hiking trail. Jarvis Lake at **Milepost Y 9.7** is the preferred swimming location in the area. Trail around the perimeter of Kelly's Bathtub takes 20+ minutes.

Y 13.9 (22.4 km) **GP 189.5** (305 km) Winter Creek.

Y 15.1 (24.3 km) **GP 188.3** (303 km) Side road to east leads 2 km/1.2 miles to Cache Lake and 4 km/2.4 to Graveyard Lake. **Cache Lake Campground** has 14 sites, open May 17–Sept. 4; sewer hookups, water pump, picnic tables, shelter, children's playground, camping fee $26. **Graveyard Lake Campground** has 12 sites, open May 17–Sept. 4, sewer hookups, water available at Cache Lake campground; fee $26. ⛺

Y 16.6 (26.7 km) **GP 186.8** (300.6 km) Access road 1.7 miles east to **Gregg Lake Campground** and day-use area; 164 sites open May 17–Sept. 4, sewer hookups, tap water, picnic tables, picnic shelter, firepits, playground, fish-cleaning stand, sani-dump, beach, hiking trails, boat launch, dock, public phone. Camping fee based on site chosen $26–$40. Winter camping may be available (weather, road maintenance permitting). Day use hours are 7 A.M. to 11 P.M. ⛺

Y 17.4 (28 km) **GP 186** (299.3 km) Roadside turnout with litter/recycling bins. Distance marker southbound shows Hinton 31 km/19 miles.

Y 17.8 (28.6 km) **GP 185.6** (298.7 km) Hay River Road. Distance marker north-

bound shows Muskeg 77 km/48 miles, Grande Cache 106 km/66 miles, Grande Prairie 289 km/180 miles.

Y 18 (29 km) **GP 185.4** (298.4 km) Turnout to west with litter bins and information sign about **William A. Switzer Provincial Park** for southbound travelers.

Y 23.6 (38 km) **GP 179.8** (289.4 km) Wild Hay River bridge.

Y 25.3 (40.7 km) **GP 178.1** (286.6 km) Willmore Wilderness Park and side road to west leads 51.5 km/32 miles to **Rock Lake Provincial Recreation Area** with campground on Rock Lake; 93 sites, sewer hookups, water pump, tables, shelter, trails, boat launch, camping fee of $15. 🚣 ⛺

Y 32.6 (52.4 km) **GP 170.8** (274.9 km) Distance marker northbound shows Muskeg 53 km/33 miles, Grande Cache 82 km/51 miles, Grande Prairie 265 km/165 miles.

Y 36.4 (58.6 km) **GP 167** (268.8 km) Railroad crossing (sign).

Y 39.9 (64.2 km) **GP 163.5** (263.1 km) Little Berland River.

Y 42.5 (68.4 km) **GP 160.9** (258.9 km) Fox Creek.

Y 46.2 (74.4 km) **GP 157.2** (253 km) *CAUTION: Wild game on road next 32 kms/20 miles northbound.*

Y 47.2 (76 km) **GP 156.2** (251.4 km) Wildlife sanctuary next 40 km/25 miles northbound. No hunting within 365 m/400 yards of the road.

Y 47.7 (76.8 km) **GP 155.7** (250.6 km) Berland River bridge. Big Berland Provincial Recreation Area's **Big Berland Campground** near the river is at the north end of bridge then to the west (2 km/1.2 miles). Keep to the left when the road forks. It is adjacent railroad tracks. Open May 17–Sept. 4, it has 18 sites, water pump, picnic tables, shelter, camping fee $28. No firewood available in 2018. Information boards on Cariboo Country. Informal turnout with camping to east. ⛺

Y 48.8 (78.6 km) **GP 154.6** (248.8 km) Distance marker northbound shows Muskeg 27 km/17 miles, Grande Cache 56 km/35 miles, Grande Prairie 239 km/149 miles.

Y 48.9 (78.7 km) **GP 154.5** (248.6 km) Cabin Creek.

Grande Cache Tourism and Interpretive Center makes a great stop just short of the half-way mark northbound on the Bighorn Route. (©*Kris Valencia, staff*)

Bighorn Route
(continued)

Y 49.3 (79.3 km) **GP 154.1** (248 km) Welcome to Yellowhead County, southbound.

Y 52.1 (83.8 km) **GP 151.3** (243.5 km) Hendrickson Creek.

Y 53.3 (85.8 km) **GP 150.1** (241.6 km) Welcome to the Municipal District of Greenview.

Y 55.3 (89 km) **GP 148.1** (238.3 km) Wildlife Sanctuary.

Y 56.4 (90.8 km) **GP 147** (236.6 km) Shand Creek.

Y 58.4 (94 km) **GP 145** (233.4 km) Improved highway with wide shoulders next 5 miles/8 km northbound.

Y 60.3 (97 km) **GP 143.1** (230.3 km) Burleigh Creek.

Y 63.4 (102 km) **GP 140** (225.3 km) Roadside turnout to west with litter bins. Improved highway with wide shoulders, southbound.

Y 64.2 (103.3 km) **GP 139.2** (224 km) **Pierre Grey's Lakes Provincial Recreation Area** 3 km/1.8 miles to east; 83 campsites (some suitable for long rigs) in heavily wooded area and some lakeside sites; pump water, picnic tables, shelter, playground, fireplaces, firewood (for sale), hiking trails, boat launch, fishing, camping fee $26–$33 (power). Open May 17–Oct. 2. Office is staffed by Parks Canada in July and August.

Y 65.6 (105.6 km) **GP 137.8** (221.8 km) Muskeg (pop. approximately 12).

Y 65.8 (105.9 km) **GP 137.6** (221.4 km) Lone Teepee Creek.

Y 65.9 (106.1 km) **GP 137.5** (221.3 km) Roadside gravel turnout to east off of highway with information boards about Cariboo Country.

Y 66.1 (106.4 km) **GP 137.3** (221 km) Long, paved roadside turnout with litter bin to east.

Y 66.6 (107.2 km) **GP 136.8** (220.2 km) Distance marker northbound shows Grande Cache 27 km/17 miles, Grande Prairie 210 km/131 miles. Southbound distance marker shows Hinton 115 km/72 miles.

Major road construction underway next 26 km/16 miles northbound in summer 2018. Expect improved highway in summer 2019, as well as creek crossings, turnouts and access to recreation not included in current log.

Y 74.4 (119.7 km) **GP 129** (207.6 km) Access road to Grande Cache airport.

Y 83.1 (133.7 km) **GP 120.3** (193.6 km) **Grande Cache Lake** to south; beautiful beach and picnic area, swimming, boat launch and fishing. Easy access for RVs.

Y 85.1 (137 km) **GP 118.3** (190.4 km) **Victor Lake** to south; canoeing, fishing.

Y 86.4 (139 km) **GP 117** (188.3 km) Northbound passing lane.

Grande Cache

Y 86.5 (139.2 km) **GP 116.9** (188.1 km) Entering Grande Cache northbound; visitor information and interpretive center east side of highway. Grande Cache is 132 miles/212 km northwest of Jasper, Alberta. **Popula-**

Grande Cache visitor center features natural history displays and a gift shop inside, picnic area outside. (©Kris Valencia, staff)

tion: 3,300. **Elevation:** 4,200 feet/1,280m. **Emergency Services:** Dial 911; **Health Complex,** phone 780-827-3701.

Visitor Information: Grande Cache Tourism and Interpretive Center is located at 9701 100th St. (Highway 40) at the south entrance into town. Summer hours July and August are 9 A.M. to 6 P.M. daily; winter hours 10 A.M. to 5 P.M. daily; shoulder season hours may vary, phone ahead to double check 780-827-3300 or 1-888-827-3790; email: tourism @grandecache.ca; www.grandecache.ca. They offer hiking guide books, exhibits, displays spanning history from dinosaur tracks, ice age to mining and trapping. The facility includes a gift shop area with locally-made items and books. A small art gallery looks out onto panoramic views of the Rocky Mountains. The large parking allows large RVs to pull through. Pleasant picnic area with outdoor displays and adjacent parking.

Private Aircraft: Grande Cache airport is closed.

Grande Cache was established in 1969 in conjunction with resource development by McIntyre Porcupine Coal Ltd. In 1980 a sawmill was built by British Columbia Forest Products Ltd. and in 1984 a medium security correctional center opened.

Historically, the location was used as a staging area for fur trappers and Natives prior to their departure to trap lines in the valleys and mountain ranges now known as Willmore Wilderness Park. Upon their return, they stored large caches of furs while waiting for transportation opportunities to trading posts. A "cache" is basically a cabin on stilts, and the origin of the town's name. Translated from French, it is pronounced "cash" and means "large storage place."

Visitor facilities include 4 motels, 2

hotels, several B & B's and lodging houses, restaurants, 2 banks and 1 credit union, 2 real estate agencies, 1 laundromat, 2 service stations (Esso and Fas-Gas) and 1 car wash. Shopping facilities include several small shopping centers, a supermarket, and 2 department stores. WiFi and public-use computers available at municipal library.

Grande Cache has been dubbed the "ATV Capital of Alberta;" inquire locally about trails. *MILEPOST®* readers have commented on the great swimming pool available at the Grande Cache Recreation Center for a reasonable admission fee. The $26-million facility features wave and lane pools (lap swim hours available), saunas, fitness rooms, a curling rink and skating rink.

Grande Cache Golf and Country Club, located in the northeast part of town, has 9 holes, clubhouse and pro shop. Golfers enjoy mountain views from course.

Camp at the Grande Cache Municipal Campground at the north end of town (take golf course turnoff); 77 serviced sites, full and partial hookups, washroom facilities, showers, public phone, laundromat, fee $26–$32, open May 20 to Oct. 12th. Phone 780-827-2404.

No services northbound, next 182 km/113 miles.

Bighorn Route Log
(continued)

Y 86.9 (139.9 km) **GP 116.5** (187.5 km) Turnoff to east for golf course and Grande Cache Municipal Campground. Town center to west.

Y 89.3 (143.7 km) **GP 114.1** (183.6 km) Turnoff for **Smoky River South Provincial Recreation Area**; Group Campground 5 units/per night $170. 22 sites in campground (extra sites are $24), water pump, firewood, firepits, tables, pit toilets, boat launch. May-October. Fishing for Arctic grayling, Dolly Varden, whitefish.

Y 89.8 (144.5 km) **GP 113.6** (182.8 km) Smoky River bridge (wood deck).

Long, straight, uphill and downhill grades (to 7 percent) next 137 km/85 miles northbound.

Y 90.2 (145.2 km) **GP 113.2** (182.1 km) Watch for occasional frost heaves next 18 miles/29 km northbound. Distance marker northbound shows Grande Prairie 181 km/112 miles.

Y 90.4 (145.5 km) **GP 113** (181.9 km) Turnoff for **Sulphur Gates Campground and Provincial Recreation Area** (6.4 km/4 miles south); 14 sites, boil water for drinking, camping fee $26, open year-round.

Y 90.8 (146.1 km) **GP 112.6** (181.2 km) Trail access to Willmore Wilderness Park. Horse staging area for entering Willmore Wilderness Park. May–October. Sulphur Gates Provincial Area (7 km/4.3 miles).

Y 91.9 (147.9 km) **GP 111.5** (179.4 km) Roadside turnout to west with litter bin.

Y 93.2 (150 km) **GP 110.2** (177.3 km) User-maintained camping area both sides of highway. Wooded area with firepits. No charge (signed).

Y 94 (151.3 km) **GP 109.4** (176.1 km) Twin Falls hiking trail to the west.

Y 98.8 (159 km) **GP 104.6** (168.3 km) Northbound, the highway parallels the Northern Alberta Resource Railroad and the Smoky River.

Y 98.9 (159.2 km) **GP 104.5** (168.2 km) Alberta Power H.R. Milner Generating Station, Grande Cache Coal Corp. with smokestacks (closed down in 2017). Turnout to east for views. Litter/recycling bins.

Y 104.8 (168.7 km) **GP 98.6** (158.7 km) Turnoff east across the tracks to **Sheep Creek Provincial Recreation Area**; 6 sites, self-register, camping fee $26; shaded picnic tables, water pump, firepits, litter bins, outhouses, hiking trails, equestrian trails and gravel parking. Back-in for Smoky River boat launch. May 16-Sept. 4. Fine ($287) for harvesting wood for fires. *CAUTION: Watch for bears.* [A]

Y 105.3 (169.5 km) **GP 98.1** (157.9 km) Sheep Creek.

Y 106 (170.6 km) **GP 97.4** (156.7 km) Sheep Creek Road.

Y 108.2 (174.1 km) **GP 95.2** (153.2 km) Wanyandie Road to east. NOTE: Highway climbs series of uphill grades to 7 percent northbound. Watch for occasional frost heaves next 18 miles/29 km southbound.

Y 113.9 (183.3 km) **GP 89.5** (144 km) Roadside turnout to east; litter bin.

Y 114.8 (184.8 km) **GP 88.6** (142.6 km) Roadside turnout to west; litter bin.

Y 116.9 (188.1 km) **GP 86.5** (139.2 km) Prairie Creek Road.

Y 122.8 (197.6 km) **GP 80.6** (129.7 km) **Southview Provincial Recreation** day-use area to east close to the road with easy in and out for all sized rigs. Picnic tables, firepits, firewood, litter and recycle bins and pit toilets.

Y 126.4 (203.4 km) **GP 77** (123.9 km) *CAUTION: Logging trucks on roads next 60 km/37 miles.*

Y 128.1 (206.2 km) **GP 75.3** (121.2 km) 16th base line sign marks north-south hunting boundary.

Y 133.1 (214.2 km) **GP 70.3** (113.1 km) *CAUTION: Use lower gears, steep descent northbound.*

Y 137.7 (221.6 km) **GP 65.7** (105.7 km) Roadside turnout with litter bin to east. Long, winding descent northbound.

Y 143 (230.1 km) **GP 60.4** (97.2 km) Kakwa River bridge.

Y 143.3 (230.6 km) **GP 60.1** (96.7 km) **Kakwa River Provincial Recreation Area** to east has 8 pleasant campsites, picnic tables, firewood, firepits, water pump (water quality not guaranteed), outhouses, recycling bins, parking area. User maintained, no fee. Garbage should be carried out by users. Open May to September. Fish for Arctic grayling. [⬅][A]

Y 145.9 (234.8 km) **GP 57.5** (92.5 km) Paved turnout to west.

Y 151.2 (243.3 km) **GP 52.2** (84 km) *CAUTION: Logging trucks entering road.*

Y 156.7 (252.2 km) **GP 46.7** (75.2 km) Access road leads east 6 km/3.6 miles to **Musreau Lake Provincial Recreation Area** campground and day-use area; 50 picnic sites, 69 campsites, fee $27, picnic tables, firewood, firepits, water pump, litter bins, pit toilets, equestrian trails, swimming, boat launch and fishing. Open mid-May- to mid-October. [⬅][A]

NOTE: Very muddy when wet.

Y 160 (257.5 km) **GP 43.4** (69.8 km) Rest area to east with recycle bin.

Y 160.3 (257 km) **GP 43.1** (69.4 km) 7 percent descent northbound, trucks use lower gears.

Y 161.4 (259.7 km) **GP 42** (67.6 km) Cutbank River bridge. Food trailer (fry stand) in 2018. Large paved turnout to east with garbage bins near access to user-maintained campground, no fee. [A]

Y 162.5 (261.5 km) **GP 40.9** (65.8 km) Elk Creek.

Y 169.2 (272.3 km) **GP 34.2** (55 km) Paved roadside turnout to west with litter/recycling bin.

Y 177.6 (285.8 km) **GP 25.8** (41.5 km) Big Mountain Creek.

Y 179.5 (288.9 km) **GP 23.9** (38.5 km) Bald Mountain Creek.

Y 183.4 (295.2 km) **GP 20** (32.2 km) **Big Mountain Creek Provincial Park** (6 km east), open year-round, group campground; 4 informal sites with firepits and pit toilets, will hold 5–25 units; $100 per night/site. Landfill to the west. [A]

Y 185.9 (299.2 km) **GP 17.5** (28.2 km) Turnoff west for Grovedale (11 km/7 miles).

Y 188.1 (302.7 km) **GP 15.3** (24.6 km) Bent Pipe Creek.

Y 190.9 (307.2 km) **GP 12.5** (20.1 km) Norbord O.S.B. Plant to east.

Y 195.9 (315.3 km) **GP 7.5** (12.1 km) **Junction** with Highway 666 which leads southwest to O'Brien Provincial Park day-use area; Dunes Golf and also access to **Nitehawk Ski Area** (5 km/3 miles off highway) which has a full-service RV park in summer with sani-dump, showers, laundry adjacent ski lodge/lounge. WiFi at lodge. [A]

Y 196.3 (315.9 km) **GP 7.1** (11.4 km) *CAUTION: Watch for frost heaves* just before the Wapiti River bridge.

Y 197.6 (318 km) **GP 5.8** (9.3 km) Sign: Entering Grande Prairie, northbound.

Y 197.9 (318.5 km) **GP 5.5** (8.9 km) Turnoff to east for **Camp Tamarack RV Park**; full service sites, sani-dump, propane, showers, laundry. [A]

Y 199.4 (320.8 km) **GP 4** (6.5 km) Turn east on Township Road 668 for **McGovern's RV Park**, 77 sites in Evergreen Park. [A]

Y 200.6 (322.8 km) **GP 2.8** (4.5 km) Distance marker southbound shows Grande Cache 180 km/112 miles, Hinton 327 km/203 miles.

Y 200.8 (323.2 km) **GP 2.6** (4.2 km) Dunvegan Gardens (greenhouse and gift shop) to west.

Y 201.4 (324.1 km) **GP 2** (3.2 km) **Junction** with Township Road 712. Go east to the Community Knowledge Campus and the Eastlink Center (aquatics recreation center).

Y 203.4 (327.3 km) **GP 0** Grande Prairie, junction of 100th Avenue and Highway 43.

Junction with Highway 43. Turn to page 77 for description of Grande Prairie and page 79 for continuation of EAST ACCESS ROUTE log to Dawson Creek, BC, and Mile 0 of the Alaska Highway.

ALBERTA HIGHWAY 40

Southbound: Distance from Yellowhead Highway 16 junction (Y) is followed by the distance from Grande Prairie (GP). Read log: [↑]

**Turn to Milepost E 278.3
East Access Route or Milepost E 175
Yellowhead Highway**

(Continued from page 248) and Miette Hot Springs Road to Jasper National Park's **Pocahontas Campground**, 1 km/0.6 mile, with 140 unserviced sites (best for tents and less than 25' RVs), picnic tables, potable water, flush toilets, firepits, firewood, public phone, trails, food lockers, recycling, interpretive programs; open mid-May to early-September, camping fee $21.50. Miette Hot Springs Pool is located 17 km/11 miles from the highway via this side road. There are 2 manmade pools fed by sulfur hot springs; bathing suit and towel rentals available. Beautiful setting. Open May to early-October, fee adult $7.05, discounted for children and seniors; website www.pc.gc.ca/hotsprings. [A]

E 195 (313.8 km) **PG 259** (416.8 km) Turnout to south with cairn, litter bin and pit toilet. Mineral lick here is frequented by goats and sheep. Watch for wildlife, especially at dawn and dusk.

E 195.4 (314.4 km) **PG 258.6** (416.1 km) Park area with litter bin by Rocky River. View of Pyramid Mountain.

E 195.9 (315.2 km) **PG 258.1** (415.4 km) First Rocky River crossing westbound.

E 197 (317 km) **PG 257** (413.6 km) Roadside turnout to north with litter bin.

E 197.3 (317.5 km) **PG 256.7** (413.1 km) Second Rocky River crossing westbound.

E 197.6 (317.9 km) **PG 256.4** (412.6 km) Rest area to north with toilets and litter bin; trailhead information boards.

E 199.7 (321.3 km) **PG 254.3** (409.2 km) Roadside turnout to south by Talbot Lake; litter bin, pit toilet, boat launch and day-use area.

E 201.5 (324.2 km) **PG 252.5** (406.3 km) Roadside turnout to south, lakeside with litter bin.

E 204 (328.3 km) **PG 250** (402.3 km) Roadside turnout to south with litter bin.

E 205.2 (330.2 km) **PG 248.8** (400.4 km) *CAUTION: Watch for elk westbound.*

E 205.5 (330.7 km) **PG 248.5** (399.9 km) Roadside turnout to south with litter bin.

E 205.8 (331.1 km) **PG 248.2** (399.4 km) *CAUTION: Watch for sheep on roadway.* Turn off at roadside turnout to south for photography and to get out of the way of traffic.

E 206.2 (331.8 km) **PG 247.8** (398.8 km) First of 2, 1-lane bridges eastbound (0.5 mile apart) that cross the Athabasca River.

Slow for 50 kmph/31 mph speed zone eastbound for 1-lane bridges.

E 207.1 (333.2 km) **PG 246.9** (397.3 km) "The Palisades" mountain view to north.

E 208.2 (335 km) **PG 245.8** (395.6 km) Snaring River bridge.

E 209.8 (337.6 km) **PG 244.2** (393 km) Jasper airfield to south.

E 211.4 (340.1 km) **PG 242.6** (390.4 km) **Snaring River Campground** to north 5 km/3 miles best for rigs under 27 feet. 63 unserviced sites, picnic tables, firepits, firewood, pit toilets, potable water, food lockers; fee $15.70; open mid-May to mid-September. Palisades Center nearby offers educational programs and opportunities. [A]

E 212.1 (341.3 km) **PG 241.9** (389.3 km) Palisades Picnic Area with pit toilets to the south.

E 213.2 (343 km) **PG 240.8** (387.4 km) Mount Edith Cavell and Colin Range turnout to south with litter bins.

E 213.9 (344.2 km) **PG 240.1** (386.4 km) Turnout to north with information boards.

E 215.1 (346.1 km) **PG 238.9** (384.5 km)

Beautiful Maligne Lake, just east of Jasper, has scheduled boat tours and boat rentals.
(©Mirjam Rand)

Distance marker eastbound shows Hinton 75 km/47 miles, Edmonton 365 km/227 miles.

E 215.2 (346.2 km) PG 238.8 (384.4 km) Large, paved roadside turnout to south with litter bin.

E 215.6 (346.9 km) PG 238.4 (383.6 km) Turnout to north with Lion's Club welcome and information boards.

E 216.1 (347.7 km) PG 237.9 (382.9 km) Access road south to Jasper Park Lodge (lodging, restaurant, golf), scenic Maligne Canyon (11.5 km/7 miles) and Maligne Lake (48 km/30 miles). Glacier-fed **Maligne Lake** is one of Jasper's premier attractions; scheduled boat tours, reserve ahead in Jasper, shuttles available. www.malignelake.com.

E 216.6 (348.6 km) PG 237.4 (382 km) Turnout to south with litter barrel.

E 217.3 (349.7 km) PG 236.7 (380.9 km) Pine Bungalows to south.

E 218.6 (351.8 km) PG 235.4 (378.8 km) Turnout to south with litter barrel; mountain viewpoint.

E 219.1 (352.6 km) PG 234.9 (378 km) **Junction** with Highway 93A.

E 219.9 (353.9 km) PG 234.1 (376.7 km) Stoplight at **junction** with Highway 93.

Turnoff to north for **JASPER** (pop. 5,236), townsite and park headquarters for Jasper National Park. **Emergencies:** Dial 911. RCMP 780-542-4848.

Visitor Information: Jasper National Park Information Center, housed in the historic 1914 building that originally housed park administration offices, offers maps, brochures, permits and visitor information. Open year-round, phone 780-852-6176, email pnj.jnp@pc.gc.ca.

Food, gas/diesel (at Petro-Canada and Esso) and lodging available year-round, with accommodations ranging from bungalows to luxury lodges like Jasper Park Lodge. A popular ski area in winter, Jasper also offers a variety of summer attractions, including fishing, hiking, horseback riding, rafting, boating, and boat tours on Maligne Lake. To reach the scenic Pyramid Lake area from town, follow Connaught Drive and turn right onto Cedar Avenue, which becomes Pyramid Lake

Road shortly after passing the Recreation Center.

Turnoff to south for scenic Highway 93 (Icefields Parkway) to Columbia Icefield, Lake Louise, Banff and Trans-Canada Highway 1 to Calgary.

Junction with Highway 93 (Icefields Parkway) south. Turn to the end of CANADIAN ROCKIES ROUTE on page 91 and read log back to front.

NOTE: Next gas stop westbound at Mount Robson Visitor Center, 53 miles/85 km.

E 220.4 (354.7 km) PG 233.6 (375.9 km) Roadside turnout to south with information board and litter/recycling bins.

E 220.5 (354.8 km) PG 233.5 (375.8 km) Miette River bridge.

E 221.7 (356.8 km) PG 232.3 (373.8 km) Small turnout to north with litter bin.

E 222.3 (357.7 km) PG 231.7 (372.9 km) Roadside turnout to north with litter bin.

E 225.6 (363 km) PG 228.4 (367.6 km) Paved turnout to north on Miette River with toilet, litter bins and information board about Yellowhead Pass.

E 226.7 (364.8 km) PG 227.3 (365.8 km) Meadow Creek bridge.

E 226.8 (364.9 km) PG 227.2 (365.6 km) Trailhead parking with litter bin to north at west end of bridge for Virl Lake, Dorothy Lake and Christine Lake.

E 229.5 (369.3 km) PG 224.5 (361.3 km) Clairvaux Creek.

E 232.6 (374.3 km) PG 221.4 (356.3 km) *Begin speed zone for park entrance westbound.*

E 232.9 (374.7 km) PG 221.1 (355.8 km) **Jasper National Park, West Entrance** for eastbound travelers. Park fee must be paid by all visitors using facilities in Rocky Mountain national parks. No charge for motorists passing through park on Highway 16. Pay phone.

E 235.5 (379 km) PG 218.5 (351.6 km) **Yellowhead Pass** (elev. 1,146m/3,760 feet), Alberta–British Columbia border and east entrance to **Mount Robson Provincial Park**.

This park is designated a UNESCO World Heritage Site. Very nice rest area to north on picturesque Portal Lake; picnic tables, pit toilets, information board, hiking trail and point-of-interest sign on Yellowhead Pass:

"Named after 'Tete Jaune,' blond fur trader at Jasper House, this low pass was favoured by Sandford Fleming in his railway surveys of the 1870s. Rejected by the CPR, the route was later used by the Grand Trunk Pacific and the Canadian Northern Pacific; the union of these helped form the CN. Today's highway traces the route of this historic pathway through the Rockies."

TIME ZONE CHANGE: Alberta observes Mountain standard time. Most of British Columbia observes Pacific standard time, which is 1 hour earlier than Mountain standard time. Both observe daylight savings time.

British Columbia requires that passenger vehicles have winter tires and that commercial vehicles carry chains driving west on Highway 16 to Terrace, BC between Oct. 1–April 30, for safe travel on this highway. This regulation is enforceable and may result in fines or by being turned back from your route, if you are not in compliance.

E 235.7 (379.2 km) PG 218.3 (351.3 km) Large turnout to south with litter bin and toilets.

Distance marker westbound shows McBride 60 km/37 miles, Prince George 357 km/222 miles, Kamloops 419 km/260 miles.

E 235.8 (379.5 km) PG 218.2 (351.1 km) Turnout to north with toilets.

E 238.8 (384.2 km) PG 215.2 (346.3 km) Long, double-ended turnout to north with litter bin and toilet.

E 239.1 (384.8 km) PG 214.9 (345.8 km) Long, double-ended turnout with historic site to north.

E 239.7 (385.7 km) PG 214.3 (344.9 km) Turnoff downhill to north for **Yellowhead Lake**; 2 picnic tables, toilets, litter bins, boat launch and fishing. Mount Fitzwilliam viewpoint.

E 241.3 (388.3 km) PG 212.7 (342.3 km) Mount Fitzwilliam to south.

E 241.5 (388.6 km) PG 212.5 (342 km) **Mount Robson Provincial Park's Lucerne Campground** to north; open May 15–Sept. 15 (weather permitting); 36 sites, picnic tables, hand water pump, pit toilets, swimming, horseshoe pits; camping fee $22.

E 242.8 (390.7 km) PG 211.2 (339.9 km) Fraser Crossing trailhead to south; small parking area with litter bins and information sign. This trail is described as difficult and not well marked.

E 242.9 (390.8 km) PG 211.1 (339.8 km) Fraser River bridge No. 1.

E 244.8 (393.9 km) PG 209.2 (336.7 km) Ghita Creek.

E 245.9 (395.7 km) PG 208.1 (334.9 km) Fraser River bridge No. 2.

E 248.8 (400.4 km) PG 205.2 (330.2 km) Sleeper Mountain to south (sign)

E 249.7 (401.8 km) PG 204.3 (328.8 km) Grant Brook Creek. Mount Mowat to north (sign). *CAUTION: Watch for black bears.*

E 252.6 (406.5 km) PG 201.4 (324.1 km) Moose River bridge.

E 253 (407.1 km) PG 201 (323.5 km) Mount George Graham view to north (sign).

E 254.7 (409.8 km) PG 199.3 (320.7 km) Nice rest area to south at east end of **Moose Lake**; information board, litter bin, pit toilet and boat launch, fishing.

E 255.5 (411.2 km) PG 198.5 (319.4 km) Railroad bridge.

E 257.3 (414.1 km) **PG 196.7** (316.6 km)
CAUTION: Moose next 30 km/19 miles westbound.

Distance marker westbound shows Mount Robson 24 km/15 miles, Prince George 322 km/200 miles, Kamloops 383 km/238 miles.

E 258.2 (415.5 km) **PG 195.8** (315.1 km) Emerald Ridge view to south (sign).

E 259.3 (417.2 km) **PG 194.7** (313.3 km) Roadside turnout with litter bin to north.

E 263.8 (424.5 km) **PG 190.2** (306.1 km) Large paved turnout to south with litter bins. Avalanche gates.

E 267.8 (431 km) **PG 186.2** (299.7 km) Paved turnout to south.

E 268.4 (431.9 km) **PG 185.6** (298.7 km) Begin long 5 to 6 percent downhill grade westbound. Slow for curves. End eastbound passing lane.

E 270.3 (434.9 km) **PG 183.7** (295.6 km) Turnout to south. Begin passing lane eastbound. Watch for falling rocks.

E 271.8 (437.3 km) **PG 182.2** (293.2 km) **Overlander Falls** rest area to south; pit toilets, litter bins. Trail leads downhill to Overlander Falls viewpoint; allow about 45 minutes round-trip according to the sign. *CAUTION: Steep drop-offs, supervise children and keep pets on leashed.*

E 272.7 (438.8 km) **PG 181.3** (291.7 km) Viewpoint of **Mount Robson** (elev. 3,954m/12,972 feet), highest peak in the Canadian Rockies. Turnoff to north for the **Mount Robson Visitor Center** with small museum on ground floor, restrooms, gift shop, WiFi, picnic tables and litter bins; open daily in summer 8 A.M. to 7 P.M. Next door there is a gas/diesel station and cafe. Berg Lake trailhead. This stop offers an incredible view of Mount Robson weather permitting.

Mount Robson Provincial Park's Robson Meadows Campground south of highway, open May 15–Sept. 30 (weather permitting) with 125 treed sites, (some wheelchair accessible), sani-station, showers, pay phone, interpretive programs, tables, flush toilets, water and horseshoe pits; group camping; camping fee $28.

E 273.7 (440.5 km) **PG 180.3** (290.2 km) **Mount Robson Provincial Park's Robson River Campground** to north, open May 15–Sept. 15 with 19 sites (some wheelchair-accessible), tables, pit toilets, showers, water and horseshoe pits; camping fee $28.

E 274.2 (441.3 km) **PG 179.8** (289.4 km) Robson River bridge. Look for Indian paintbrush *(Castilleja miniata)* June through August.

E 274.4 (441.6 km) **PG 179.6** (289 km) West entrance to **Mount Robson Provincial Park**. Avalanche gates. Turnout with litter bin and statue to south.

E 274.5 (441.8 km) **PG 179.5** (288.9 km) Turnout to south. Avalanche gates.

E 275.6 (443.5 km) **PG 178.4** (287.1 km) Swift Current Creek.

E 276 (444.2 km) **PG 178** (286.4 km) Double-ended gravel turnout to east.

E 276.9 (445.6 km) **PG 177.1** (285 km) Distance marker westbound shows McBride 76 km/47 miles, Prince George 280 km/174 miles.

E 277.1 (445.9 km) **PG 176.9** (284.7 km) Distance marker westbound shows Tete Jaune Cache 13 km/8 miles, Valemount 33 km/21 miles, Kamloops 352 km/219 miles.

E 277.8 (447.1 km) **PG 176.2** (283.6 km)

Turn off at Milepost E 272.7 for the Mount Robson visitor center and an incredible view of this mountain (weather permitting). (©Claire Torgerson, staff)

Robson Shadows Campground and Mount Robson Lodge to south.

E 278.8 (448.7 km) **PG 175.2** (282 km) **Mount Terry Fox** rest area to south, accessible both east- and westbound; picnic tables, restrooms, phone and viewing telescope. The information board here points out the location of Mount Terry Fox in the Selwyn Range of the Rocky Mountains. Named in 1981 it honors cancer victim Terry Fox who raised some $25 million for cancer research during his attempt to run across Canada prior to succumbing to his disease.

E 280.7 (451.7 km) **PG 173.3** (278.9 km) Turnout to north with Yellowhead Highway information board.

E 280.9 (452.1 km) **PG 173.1** (278.6 km) **Rearguard Falls Provincial Park** picnic area, to south. Easy 5-minute walk downhill to falls viewpoint. *(CAUTION: Steep drop-offs, supervise children; pets must be leashed.)* Upper limit of 1,300-km/800-mile migration of Pacific salmon; look for chinook salmon in late summer. Plan at least a half-hour to enjoy this amazing natural attraction.

E 282.2 (454.2 km) **PG 171.8** (276.5 km) Turnout with litter bin to south overlooking Fraser River. Avalanche gates.

E 282.7 (455 km) **PG 171.3** (275.7 km) Weigh scales to south.

E 283 (455.4 km) **PG 171** (275.2 km) Tete Jaune Cache rest area to south; double-ended turnout with picnic tables, litter bin and toilets.

E 283.2 (455.8 km) **PG 170.8** (274.9 km) **Junction** with Yellowhead Highway 5 south which leads 20 km/12 miles to **VALEMOUNT** (all services); camping at **Irvin's Park & Campground**; www.irvinsrvpark.com.

Irvin's Park & Campground. See display ad this page.

Junction with Yellowhead Highway 5 South to Valemount (20 km/12 miles), Wells Gray Provincial Park (216 km/134 miles) and Kamloops (339 km/210 miles). Southbound travelers turn to page 105 in the CENTRAL ACCESS ROUTE and read log back to front.

E 283.5 (456.2 km) **PG 170.5** (274.3 km) Tete Jaune Lodge to south; cabins, motel, restaurant, campground (seasonal) and rafting.

E 287.1 (461.9 km) **PG 166.9** (268.5 km) Spittal Creek Interpretive Forest to north; hiking trails, tables, litter bins and toilets.

E 292 (469.8 km) **PG 162** (260.7 km) Terracanna Resort to south; food, lodging.

E 292.9 (471.3 km) **PG 161.1** (259.2 km) Small River rest area to north on loop road (good RV access); picnic tables, toilets and litter bins.

E 294.7 (474.3 km) **PG 159.3** (256.4 km) Horsey Creek.

E 297.5 (478.7 km) **PG 156.5** (251.8 km) Horsey Creek bridge.

E 304 (489.1 km) **PG 150** (241.4 km) Turnoff to south for settlement of Dunster; gas only, open until 5 P.M.

E 304.3 (489.7 km) **PG 149.7** (240.9 km) Distance marker westbound shows McBride 30 km/19 miles, Prince George 241 km/150 miles.

Distance markers eastbound shows Tete Jaune Cache 37 km/23 miles, Valemount 55 km/34 miles, Kamloops 377 km/234 miles, Alberta Border 112 km/70 miles, Jasper 138 km/86 miles.

E 307.8 (495.3 km) **PG 146.2** (235.2 km) Holliday Creek.

E 308.3 (496.1 km) **PG 145.7** (234.4 km) Baker Creek rest area to south with picnic tables, litter bin and toilets.

E 313.2 (504 km) **PG 140.8** (226.6 km)

Private campgrounds along this route provide RV sites with hookups. This is Beaverview RV Park & Campground near McBride. (©Judy Nadon, staff)

Mountainview Chalets and RV Resort to north. △

E 315 (506.8 km) **PG 139** (223.7 km) Beaver River Falls to north, hiking trail to falls is 0.3 mile/0.5 km.

E 315.2 (507.3 km) **PG 138.8** (223.4 km) Turn north on Holmes forest service road and go 1 km to Beaver River Campground. Campground has 10 sites on the Beaver River and is operated by the McBride community. Services are limited to tables and pit toilets. △

E 315.3 (507.3 km) **PG 138.7** (223.2 km) Holmes River bridge.

E 320.7 (516 km) **PG 133.3** (214.5 km) **Beaverview RV Park & Campground**; very nice campground with grassy pull-through sites, hookups, laundry and sani-station. McBride Park, across from the RV park, has hiking trails. △

Beaverview RV Park & Campground. See display ad this page.
Entering speed zones westbound to McBride.

E 321.2 (516.9 km) **PG 132.8** (213.7 km) Fraser River bridge.

Watch for turnoff to Regional Park to north on west side of bridge; picnic tables, gazebos, toilets, litter bins.

E 321.6 (517.5 km) **PG 132.4** (213 km) Turnout to north with welcome sign, information boards and litter bin.

Entering McBride westbound. *Begin speed zone. Next gas westbound is 146 km/91 miles from here at Purden Lake Resort (summer only).*

McBride

E 322.1 (518.3 km) **PG 131.9** (212.2 km) Turn off Highway 16 on Bridge Road to south for McBride town center. **Population:** 616. **Elevation:** 2,350 feet/722m. **Emergency Services:** Dial 911. **Hospital:** McBride and District Hospital 250-569-2251.

Visitor Information: In the Robson Valley Visitor Center at the historic train station (0.6 mile/1 km south of main highway at First Avenue and Main Street); open daily, 9 A.M. to 5 P.M., June to September; 10 A.M. to 4 P.M., October to May. Phone 250-569-3366; toll-free 1-866-569-3366; visitmcbride.ca. This historic train station also houses a cafe and the **Whistle Stop Gallery** which features local art.

Located in the Robson Valley by the Fraser River, the village of McBride was established in 1913 as a divisional point on the railroad and was named for Richard McBride, then premier of British Columbia. Forest products, agriculture and tourism are the mainstays of the local economy. **The Valley Museum and Archives**, at 241 Dominion St., displays local history as well as current artists; www.valleymuseum.ca.

McBride has all visitor facilities, including hotels/motels (Sandman Inn), bed and breakfasts, cabin rentals, supermarket, convenience/video stores, clothing stores, art gallery, several restaurants, a pharmacy, hospital and 2 gas/diesel stations (1 with sani-dump, 1 co-op card lock, propane at JNR Auto Services). Full-service camping at **Beaverview RV Park & Campground**.

Yellowhead Highway 16 Log
(continued)

E 322.7 (519.3 km) **PG 131.3** (211.3 km) First turnoff eastbound to McBride (see description at main access, **Milepost E 322.1**); pub. The visitor center is 0.8 km/0.5 mile south.

E 322.9 (519.5 km) **PG 131.1** (210.9 km) Roadside turnout to south with litter bin. *Begin speed zone eastbound entering McBride.*

E 325.3 (523.4 km) **PG 128.7** (207.1 km)

Dore River bridge.

E 327 (526.2 km) **PG 127** (204.4 km) Large paved turnout to south.

E 330.6 (532 km) **PG 123.4** (198.6 km) Private campground and bed-and-breakfast to north. △

E 330.8 (532.3 km) **PG 123.2** (198.2 km) Macintosh Creek.

E 332.2 (534.5 km) **PG 121.8** (196 km) Clyde Creek.

E 337.3 (542.8 km) **PG 116.7** (187.8 km) West Twin chain-up/chain-off areas; narrow paved turnouts both sides of highway, litter bins.

E 339.3 (546 km) **PG 114.7** (184.6 km) West Twin Provincial Park (westbound sign).

E 340.4 (547.7 km) **PG 113.6** (182.8 km) West Twin Creek bridge.

E 341.8 (550 km) **PG 112.2** (180.6 km) West Twin chain-up/chain-off turnouts both sides of highway, litter bins.

E 345.5 (556 km) **PG 108.5** (174.6 km) Goat River East chain-up/chain-off gravel turnouts both sides of highway; litter bin to south.

E 347.3 (558.8 km) **PG 106.7** (171.7 km) Goat River bridge. Paved rest area to north at west end of bridge *(NOTE: Not recommended for large RVs or trailers due to limited turnaround space);* tables, toilets and litter bins.

Winding upgrades eastbound and westbound from Goat River bridge.

E 349.7 (562.8 km) **PG 104.3** (167.8 km) Western boundary of West Twin Provincial Park (sign).

E 350.1 (563.4 km) **PG 103.9** (167.2 km) Goat River West chain-up/chain-off gravel turnouts both sides of highway.

E 351.2 (565.1 km) **PG 102.8** (165.4 km) Turnoff for LaSalle Lake Recreation Site and campground (operated by the city of McBride) to south; 20 campsites, tables, pit toilets, a boat launch and beach. There is plenty of room for big rigs. △

E 353.6 (568.9 km) **PG 100.4** (161.5 km) Snowshoe Creek. Watch for bears browsing highway verge.

E 364.5 (586.5 km) **PG 89.5** (144 km) Ptarmigan Creek bridge.

E 367.6 (591.5 km) **PG 86.4** (139 km) Double-ended turnout to north with litter bin.

E 371.9 (598.4 km) **PG 82.1** (132.1 km) Winding 6 percent downgrade next mile westbound.

E 373 (600.2 km) **PG 81** (130.3 km) Dome Creek.

Begin winding 6 percent upgrade next mile eastbound.

E 377.3 (607.1 km) **PG 76.7** (123.4 km) Slim Creek rest area to south with information kiosk, tables, large playground, litter bins and wheelchair-accessible toilets. *CAUTION: Watch for bears.*

E 378.1 (608.4 km) **PG 75.9** (122.1 km) Slim Creek bridge.

E 379.7 (611.1 km) **PG 74.3** (119.6 km) Leaving Slim Creek Provincial Park westbound.

E 379.9 (611.4 km) **PG 74.1** (119.2 km) Turnout to north.

E 381.3 (613.6 km) **PG 72.7** (117 km) **Ancient Rainforest Trail**. Trailhead parking to south. Walk through a fascinating ancient forest. Bring plenty of bug repellent.

E 384.6 (618.9 km) **PG 69.4** (111.7 km) Driscol Trail to south.

E 391.8 (630.4 km) **PG 62.2** (100.1 km) Roadside turnout to north with litter bin.

E 396 (637.2 km) **PG 58** (93.3 km) Turn south on Hungary Creek Forest Service Road 13 km/8 miles to Grizzly Den Trailhead and 15.6 km/9.7 miles to Raven Lake Trailhead.

E 396.4 (637.9 km) **PG 57.6** (92.7 km) Sugarbowl Grizzly Den Provincial Park (westbound sign).

E 398.6 (641.5 km) **PG 55.4** (89.2 km) Viking Ridge Trailhead to south.

E 401.8 (646.6 km) **PG 52.2** (84 km) Sugarbowl chain-off area eastbound.

E 402.3 (647.4 km) **PG 51.7** (83.2 km) Sugarbowl Trailhead to south.

E 403.1 (648.7 km) **PG 50.9** (81.9 km) Sugarbowl Grizzly Den Provincial Park (eastbound sign).

E 403.6 (649.5 km) **PG 50.4** (81.1 km) Turnout out to south; Sugarbowl chain-up area eastbound.

E 405 (651.8 km) **PG 49** (78.9 km) Double-ended turnout to north with litter bin.

E 412.5 (663.7 km) **PG 41.5** (66.8 km) Ski Hill Road to Purden Mountain ski area.

E 413.5 (665.3 km) **PG 40.5** (65.2 km) **Purden Lake Resort** to north (description follows); cafe, fuel (May-September), phone, lodging and camping.

Purden Lake Resort. Lakefront RV park with marina and sandy beach; full hookups; sani-dump; hot coin shower; laundry; playground. Restaurant, fuel station (unleaded, diesel, propane) 60 kms/40 miles east of Prince George, 145 kms/90 miles west of McBride. P.O. Box 1239, Prince George, BC V2L 4V3. Phone 250-565-7777, www. purden.com. [ADVERTISEMENT]

NOTE: Next gas eastbound is 146 km/91 miles from here (McBride).

E 415.1 (667.9 km) **PG 38.9** (61.8 km) Turnoff for **Purden Lake Provincial Park**, 3 km/1.9 miles north; 78 campsites, day-use area with 48 picnic tables, water, pit and flush toilets, dump station $5, firewood, litter and recycling bins, playground and horseshoe pits. Sandy beach, change houses, swimming, walking trails, paddling, waterskiing and boat launch. Fish for rainbow trout and burbot. Camping fee $22; sani-dump $5. No highway noise. Some campsites reserveable: www.discovercamping.ca. Open May–mid-September.

E 417 (671 km) **PG 37** (59.5 km) Bowron River bridge.

E 417.1 (671.1 km) **PG 36.9** (59.4 km) Sharp turn to north for narrow access road to rest area at west end of Bowron River bridge; toilets, tables and litter bins. Entrance on curve; use care.

E 417.9 (672.5 km) **PG 36.1** (58.1 km) Turnouts both sides of highway; litter bins.

E 424.2 (682.5 km) **PG 29.8** (47.9 km) Vama Vama Creek.

E 427.2 (687.4 km) **PG 26.8** (43.1 km) Wansa Creek.

E 430.3 (692.4 km) **PG 23.7** (38.1 km) Willow River bridge.

E 430.5 (692.7 km) **PG 23.5** (37.8 km) Sharp turn to north at west end of Willow River bridge for narrow access road to Willow River rest area; tables, litter bins, toilets and nature trail. The 1.9-km/1.2-mile-long Willow River Forest Interpretation Trail is an easy 45-minute walk.

E 432.8 (696.4 km) **PG 21.2** (34.1 km) Bowes Creek.

E 432.9 (696.5 km) **PG 21.1** (33.9 km) Double-ended turnout to north with litter bins and information board on forest fire and moose habitat. Circle trail to moose

observation site.

E 435.3 (700.5 km) **PG 18.7** (30.1 km) Tabor Mountain cross-country recreation trails to south.

E 436.7 (702.7 km) **PG 17.3** (27.8 km) Large turnout to north with litter bin.

E 438.5 (706 km) **PG 15.2** (24.5 km) Tabor Mountain ski hill to south.

E 438.8 (706 km) **PG 15.2** (24.5 km) Turnout to north with litter bin.

Distance marker westbound shows Prince George 23 km/14 miles.

E 439.5 (707.2 km) **PG 14.5** (23.3 km) Begin 7 percent downgrade on curve westbound.

E 448.1 (721 km) **PG 5.9** (9.5 km) **Junction** with bypass route to Highway 97 South. *(Travelers using this bypass will join Highway 97 at Milepost CC 266.4 in 6.2 miles/10 km; turn to page 127 in the WEST ACCESS ROUTE section and read log back to front.)*

E 448.7 (722 km) **PG 5.3** (8.5 km) Petro-Canada gas/diesel station.

E 449.1 (722.6 km) **PG 4.9** (7.9 km) View of Prince George westbound from small turnout as Highway 16 descends to the Fraser River.

E 450.7 (725.3 km) **PG 3.3** (5.3 km) Fraser River bridge.

E 451 (725.7 km) **PG 3** (4.8 km) Welcome to Prince George (westbound sign).

E 451.9 (727.1 km) **PG 2.1** (3.4 km) **Prince George Downtown Visitor Center** (free WiFi; bicycles and fishing rods for loan) on First Avenue; phone 250-562-3700.

E 452 (727.3 km) **PG 2** (3.2 km) Stoplight. Highway 16/Victoria Street westbound through downtown Prince George.

E 453 (728.9 km) **PG 1** (1.6 km) Highway 16/Victoria Street **junctions** with 20th Avenue in **PRINCE GEORGE** (pop. 74,000); *see description of Prince George beginning on page 127 in the WEST ACCESS ROUTE section.* Turn west on 20th to continue on Highway 16 West. Turn east on 20th Avenue for Fort George Park.

E 454 (730.5 km) **PG 0 Junction** of Highway 16 and Highway 97. Continue west on Yellowhead Highway 16 for Prince Rupert

(log follows after junction box).

Eastbound: The log shows distance from Edmonton (E) followed by distance from Prince George (PG). Read log:

Junction with Highway 97 south to Cache Creek and north to Dawson Creek and the beginning of the Alaska Highway. Turn to page 133 in the WEST ACCESS ROUTE section for the log of Highway 97 North. Turn to page 127 for Highway 97 South and read log back to front.

Westbound: The log shows distance from Prince George (PG) followed by distance from Prince Rupert (PR). Read log:

NOTE: Physical kilometerposts along Highway 16 between Prince George and Prince Rupert reflect distance from Prince Rupert.

PG 0 PR 447.7 (720.5 km) **Junction** of Highways 16 and 97 (20th Avenue/Central Avenue/Cariboo Highway) in Prince George.

From Prince George to Prince Rupert, Highway 16 is a 2-lane highway with 3-lane passing stretches. Fairly straight, with no high summits, the highway follows the valleys of the Nechako, Bulkley and Skeena rivers, paralleling the Canadian National Railway route. There are few services between towns.

PG 0.5 (0.8 km) **PR 447.2** (719.7 km) Stoplight. Ferry Avenue; access to Canadian Superstore, restaurants, golf and curling club.

PG 0.7 (1.1 km) **PR 447** (719.4 km) Stoplight. Vance Avenue; no services.

PG 1.1 (1.8 km) **PR 446.6** (718.7 km) Stoplight. Access to Costco, Boston Pizza, gas/diesel station and other services.

PG 2.1 (3.5 km) **PR 445.6** (717 km) Stoplight. Domano Boulevard; access south to gas/diesel stations (Esso, Chevron), Canadian Tire, Walmart, Starbucks, bank, DQ, KFC, Shoppers Drugmart, Save-On supermarket and other shopping and services.

PG 2.4 (3.9 km) **PR 445.3** (716.6 km) Eastbound-only and westbound-only exits to Southbridge Avenue; Walmart, fast-food, Esso

Prince George Downtown Visitor Center on First Avenue has free WiFi and helpful staff to answer any travel questions. (©Sharon Nault)

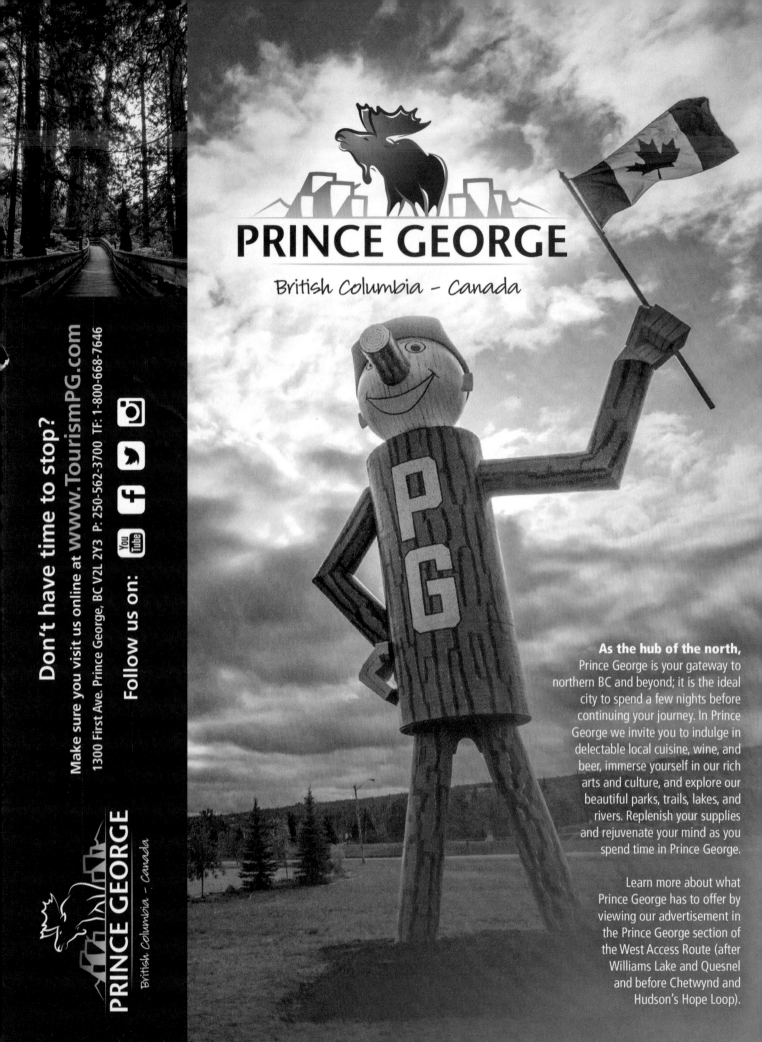

gas/diesel station and Canadian Tire.

PG 3.1 (5 km) **PR 444.6** (715.5 km) Stoplight. Westgate Avenue.

PG 3.8 (6.1 km) **PR 443.9** (714.4 km) Bon Voyage Motor Inn and strip mall with Esso gas/diesel and liquor store to south. Turnoff to north on Kimball Road for **Blue Cedars Campground**; it is a short distance from the Art Knapp store plant and home decor chain fronting the highway.

Blue Cedars Campground. See display ad on page 131 in the WEST ACCESS ROUTE section.

PG 4.7 (7.6 km) **PR 443** (712.9 km) Stoplight. Shell gas/diesel station and convenience store to north. Yellowhead Golf Course to south.

Begin 4-lane highway eastbound. Begin 2-lane highway westbound. Expect intermittent passing lanes and some 7 percent grades.

PG 5.7 (9.2 km) **PR 442** (711.3 km) Blackwater Road. Turnoff for private campground (12 km/7.5 miles) and West Lake Provincial Park 14 km/8.7 miles south; day-use area with picnic shelter, swimming beach, fishing and boat launch (above water exhaust motors prohibited).

PG 9.2 (14.8 km) **PR 438.5** (705.7 km) Petro-Canada gas/diesel, store to north.

PG 12.5 (20.1 km) **PR 435.2** (700.4 km) Chilako River.

PG 38.7 (62.3 km) **PR 409** (659 km) Cluculz rest area to south with flush toilets (summer only), picnic tables and litter bins.

PG 39.1 (62.9 km) **PR 408.6** (657.6 km) Resort to north; camping, gas/diesel.

PG 58.9 (94.8 km) **PR 388.8** (626 km) Sign: "Welcome to Vanderhoof." Double-ended rest stop with litter bins, picnic tables, toilets and area info map.

PG 59.9 (96.4 km) **PR 387.8** (624.1 km) Stoplight; car and truck wash.

PG 60.1 (96.7 km) **PR 387.6** (623.8 km) Stoplight. Tim Hortons restaurant, gas/diesel bar and supermarket to south.

Vanderhoof

PG 60.2 (96.9 km) **PR 387.5** (623.6 km) Stoplight at Burrard Avenue; A&W Husky, Chevron with gas/diesel. Turn north on Burrard for downtown Vanderhoof businesses. **Population:** approx. 5,000; area 12,000. **Elevation:** 2,225 feet/668m. **Emergency Services:** Dial 911. **Hospital:** St. John Hospital, phone 250-567-2211.

Visitor Information: The Vanderhoof Museum & Visitor Center is at 478 First St. West. Summer hours (May–September), daily 10 A.M. to 6 P.M.; phone 250-567-3374; www.vanderhoof.ca. You may pick up hiking maps at this location and tour the museum.

Vanderhoof is the geographical center of British Columbia and on your way to and from the northwest coast of B.C. The town was named for Chicago publisher Herbert Vanderhoof, who was associated with the Grand Trunk Railway. Today, Vanderhoof is the supply and distribution center for area agriculture, forestry and mining and is a great stop for shopping, history, and beautiful scenery.

All visitor services are available in Vanderhoof, including food (Tim Hortons, Subway, A&W, etc.), WiFi, public library, pubs, gas/diesel and lodging.

Summer recreation includes a tennis court, fishing lakes, an 18-hole golf course, outdoor running track, spray park, mountain bike park, hunting opportunities, farm tours and the Sturgeon Hatchery. Riverside Park (from Yellowhead Highway 16, go 0.7 mile/1.1 km north on Burrard Avenue then turn left before bridge) is a scenic spot to take a break: nature trails, playground, bird-watching perch overlooking Nechako River Migratory Bird Sanctuary.

Camping is available for a fee (with services) at Riverside Park and the Rotary Campground which is at the west edge of town.

Vanderhoof Heritage Museum at 478 1st St., on Highway 16 at **Milepost PG 60.6**, is a wonderful place to learn about the area's history. Relocated pioneer structures furnished with period artifacts recall the early days of the Nechako Valley.

The Migratory Bird Sanctuary, located on the Nechako River, is a major migratory stopping place for thousands of Canada Geese. Other migratory species seen here include trumpeter swans, Northern pintails and sandpipers.

Yellowhead Highway 16 Log

(continued)

PG 60.4 (97.2 km) **PR 387.3** (623.3 km) Junction with Kenney Dam access road.

PG 60.6 (97.5 km) **PR 387.1** (623 km) Vanderhoof Heritage Museum to south; good photo stop.

Distance marker westbound shows Fort Fraser 37 km/23 miles, Terrace 477 km/296 miles, Prince Rupert 621 km/386 miles.

PG 64.7 (104.1 km) **PR 383** (616.4 km) Junction with Highway 27 (2-lanes, paved), which leads north 60 km/37 miles to the town and the historic site known as Fort St. James (descriptions follow).

The community of **FORT ST. JAMES** (pop. 4,757 which includes surrounding small communities) is located on the shores of 59-mile-/95-km-long Stuart Lake, southernmost in a 3-lake chain which provides hundreds of miles of boating and fishing. Fort St. James has a health clinic, Stuart Lake General Hospital (phone 250-996-8201), RCMP detachment, accommodations, restaurants, a Subway, grocery stores, gas/diesel stations, liquor store, banks, pharmacy, laundromat and shopping. Cottonwood Park at north end of town on Stuart Lake has a large parking area, washrooms, beach, walking path on lake, sani-dump, playground and camping area.

The Fort St. James **Visitor Information Center** has internet access, wheelchair access and picnic tables and is at the entrance to town on Douglas Avenue at Kwah Road (at the turnoff to Fort St. James National Historic Site) and is open 9 A.M. to 5 P.M. daily, May through September; 9 A.M. to 5 P.M.; website: fortstjames.ca.

Downtown offers a 2 km/1.2 mile self-guided interpretive walk, exploring the community's past from fur trade post to a bastion of bush-plane aviation.

Visiting golfers are welcomed at Stuart Lake Golf Club. Annual summer events here include the Canada Day celebrations July 1, Stuart Lake Fishing Derby early July, Night Market and Caledonia Days mid-August and Music on the Mountain Festival in late August.

Fort St. James National Historic Site is a completely restored Hudson's Bay Company post, located on the shores of Stuart Lake. Plenty of parking; enter through the historic site's visitor center. Fort St. James was an economic powerhouse of trade and commerce in the 19th century, and today is the largest existing group of original wooden buildings representing the fur trade in Canada; depicting the relationship between fur traders and the Carrier First Nations. Costumed interpreters provide a first-hand look at how people lived, loved, ate, worked and died more than a century ago. Check out the Daily Adventure programs; the lake shore restaurant; and Sunday afternoon teas (must reserve for tea and sells out early in the year); and varied special events during

Vanderhoof's Ferland Park has a children's playground, Kinsmen Spray Park (in summer), and picnic tables. (©Judy Nadon, staff)

the operating summer season. The site is open 9 A.M. to 5 P.M. daily, open June 1 to Labor Day. Admission is charged. Well worth the drive! Phone 250-996-7191. Website: www.pc.gc.ca/eng/lhn-nhs/bc/stjames/index.aspx.

PG 83.1 (133.6 km) **PR 364.6** (586.9 km) Turnout to south with litter bin and view of Nechako River. The Grand Trunk Pacific Railway was completed near this site in 1914. The railroad (later the Canadian National) linked Prince Rupert, a deep-water port, with interior British Columbia. Entering Lakes District. This high country has over 300 freshwater lakes.

PG 83.7 (134.6 km) **PR 364** (585.9 km) *Begin speed zone through* **FORT FRASER** (pop. 950); 24-hour Petro-Canada truck stop with gas/diesel, propane, convenience store, restaurant, and showers; lodging. **Visitor Information:** In railroad car to south. Named for Simon Fraser, who established a trading post here in 1806. Now a supply center for surrounding farms and sawmills. The last spike of the Grand Trunk Railway was driven here, April 7, 1914.

PG 84.5 (135.9 km) **PR 363.2** (585.6 km) Nechako River bridge. Turnout to south with parking, litter bins and access to **Nechako River**; fishing for rainbow trout and Dolly Varden, June to fall. At the east end of Fraser Lake, the Nautley River—less than a mile long—drains into the Nechako River.

PG 85.9 (138 km) **PR 361.8** (582.5 km) Nautley Road leads north to **Beaumont Provincial Park**, on **Fraser Lake**, north side of highway; site of original Fort Fraser. Boat launch, swimming, hiking, fishing, 49 campsites, and 5 walk-in tenting sites with beach access. Sites include picnic tables and firewood. Campground has flush and pit toilets, water, playground, horseshoe pits, sanidump ($5). Fishing for rainbow and lake trout and burbot. Open mid-May to mid-September. Fee $22. Go to www.discovercamping.ca for online reservations.

PG 86.5 (138.8 km) **PR 361.2** (581.7 km) *CAUTION: Narrow bridge.*

PG 88 (141.2 km) **PR 359.7** (580 km) **Piper's Glen RV Resort** to north (description follows).

Piper's Glen RV Resort. It's just viewtiful! Overlooking Fraser Lake with lake view sites and housekeeping cabins. Long pull-throughs, full and partial hookups, tent sites. Free showers, firepits, sani-dump, WiFi. Pet friendly. Good fishing with rainbow trout and char, lake access, dock. Phone 250-690-7565; email pipersglen@uniserve.com; website www.pipersglenresort.com. [ADVERTISEMENT]

PG 89.5 (143.5 km) **PR 358.2** (577 km) Dry William Lake rest area to south on lake; shade trees, large parking area, picnic tables, toilets and litter bins. Information sign about Cheslatta Trail.

PG 92.7 (148.6 km) **PR 355** (571.9 km) Fraser Lake sawmill to north.

PG 93 (149.1 km) **PR 354.7** (571.4 km) Lejac Gas Bar (with diesel) to south.

Views of Fraser Lake (body of water) to north for westbound travelers.

PG 95.8 (153.7 km) **PR 351.9** (566.8 km) Welcome to Fraser Lake (westbound sign).

PG 96.2 (154.3 km) **PR 351.5** (566.2 km) *Begin speed zone westbound through* **FRASER LAKE** (pop. 1,354; elev. 2,200 feet/670m); visitor center and police station to north. **Visitor Information:** Fraser Lake Museum and Visitor Center in log building; www.fraserlake.ca. Small, lakeside community with all facilities. Known for white swans, outdoor recreation and great fishing. Fraser Lake, good fishing for rainbow trout to 8 lbs., May to October; kokanee to 1 lb., use flashers, willow leaf, flashers with worms, flatfish or spinners, August and September; char to 30 lbs., use large flatfish or spoon, June and July. A prominent landmark here is Mouse Mountain which has several hiking trails and a stunning summit view. Fraser Lake was developed by Endako Mines Ltd. in 1964; named after the explorer Simon Fraser. Endako Mines Ltd. was Canada's largest molybdenum mine until production slowed in 2015. Forestry and agriculture are the main industries for this area.

PG 96.5 (154.7 km) **PR 351.2** (565.8 km) Stoplight. Shopping center, Chevron gas/diesel station, motels and medical clinic. The lakeside White Swan Park has 11 free RV sites; boat launch, wharf, picnic/BBQ shelter, swimming area with sandy beach, waterfront trails and a new playground. Next to the library is Kin Park with a playground, water park, picnic tables and change rooms with washroom.

PG 98.6 (158.1 km) **PR 349.1** (562.4 km) **Junction** with main access road south to scenic Francois Lake; also accessible via roads from Burns Lake to Houston. Francois Lake Road (chip seal surfacing) leads south 11 km/7 miles to the east end of Francois Lake (where the Stellako River flows from the lake) and back to Highway 16 at Endako. *(It does not link up to the Francois Lake Ferry, south of Burns Lake.)* Golf course, Stellako Lodge, Nithi Resort, Francois Lake Resort and other resorts offering camping, cabins and boats, are located on this scenic rural road through the Glenannan area.

Francois Lake, good fishing for rainbow trout to 5 lbs., May to October; kokanee to 0.75 lb., use flashers, willow leaf, flashers with worms, flatfish or spinners, August and September; char to 30 lbs., use large flatfish or spoon, June and July. **Stellako River** is world renown for fly-fishing with rainbow trout over 5 lbs., all summer; whitefish averaging 1 lb., year-round.

PG 98.7 (158.3 km) **PR 349** (562.2 km) Stellako River bridge.

PG 99.8 (160.1 km) **PR 347.9** (560.4 km) Esso gas/diesel station with convenience store to north.

PG 104.8 (168.1 km) **PR 342.9** (552.4 km) **ENDAKO** (pop. 150), a small highway community; roadhouse.

PG 107.4 (172.3 km) **PR 340.3** (548.2 km) Endako River bridge and railroad bridge.

PG 111 (178.1 km) **PR 336.7** (542.4 km) Savory rest area is a large double-ended turnout with picnic tables and litter bins to north beside Watkins Creek.

PG 119.6 (191.8 km) **PR 328.1** (528.7 km) Winding 7 percent downgrade next mile westbound. *CAUTION: Watch for moose.*

PG 123.2 (197.7 km) **PR 324.5** (522.8 km) Double-ended paved turnout to south with litter bin and toilet.

PG 126.1 (203 km) **PR 321.6** (517.6 km) Turnoff on Augier Road (gravel) for 4.5 km/2.8 miles to Co-Op Lake Campground operated by Burns Lake. It offers 6 campsites with one group site, tables, toilets, boat launch. No fee.

PG 127.8 (205.2 km) **PR 319.9** (515.3 km) Turnoff for Babine Forest Products to south.

PG 128.5 (206.5 km) **PR 319.2** (514 km) Views of Burns Lake (body of water) to south.

PG 129.8 (208.5 km) **PR 317.9** (512 km) Homeside Antique Place to south.

PG 132.1 (212.3 km) **PR 315.6** (508.2 km) Rest area to south is a large double-ended turnout with toilet, tables, litter bins and **Tintagel Cairn**. The central stone in this cairn once formed part of the Norman walls of Tintagel Castle, reputed birthplace of King Arthur.

PG 135.8 (218 km) **PR 312.9** (502.5 km) Private campground.

PG 139.5 (224 km) **PR 308.2** (496.5 km) Stoplight at **junction** with Highway 35 South (Francois Lake Drive); lodging, fast-food, shopping and supermarket at junction.

Scenic Highway 35 (paved) leads south 16 km/10 miles to campground on **Tchesinkut Lake**, and 29 km/18 miles to **Francois Lake Ferry** landing. This free ferry, with a capacity of 52 vehicles, makes at least one 15-minute crossings from the north and south shores each hour (see schedule at www2.gov.bc.ca/gov/content/transportation/passenger-travel/water-travel/inland-ferries/francois-lake-ferry).

From the south shore of Francois Lake, Highway 35 continues to **Takysie Lake** and **Ootsa Lake**, with access to a number of other fishing lakes. Another of the Yellowhead's popular fishing areas with a variety of family-owned camping and cabin resorts.

PG 139.7 (224.3 km) **PR 308** (496.2 km) Gas bar with gas/diesel.

PG 139.8 (224.5 km) **PR 307.9** (496 km) Chevron gas/diesel station. Westbound, Highway 16 winds through the town of Burns Lake (description follows).

Begin speed zone through Burns Lake.

Burns Lake

PG 140.1 (225.2 km) **PR 307.6** (495.3 km) Burns Lake Heritage Center and Museum. **Population:** 2,726; area 10,000. **Elevation:** 2,300 feet/707m. **Emergency Services:** Dial 911. **RCMP:** 250-692-7171; **Hospital:** Lakes District Hospital and Health Center 250-692-2400; **Ambulance:** 1-800-461-9911.

Visitor Information: The Burns Lake Visitor Center, housed in the Old Forestry Home, built in 1919 and located at 540 Highway 16. Open daily in summer from 8 A.M. to 5 P.M. Monday–Friday and open weekends (hours vary). Open weekdays 9 A.M. to 4 P.M. in winter. Website: www.burnslakechamber.com or VisitBurnsLake.ca. Free WiFi is available inside or out of the center; walking/biking trail takes off from parking lot. RVs use the larger parking area across the highway at the College of New Caledonia. The Lakes District Museum holds community artifacts since the turn of the century. Take the Heritage Buildings walking circle tour for standing history within the village.

Climate: Average temperature in summer, 68°F/20°C; in winter, 12.9°F/-10.6°C. **Radio:** CFLD 760 AM, CJFW-5 92.9 FM, CBXB 99.1 FM. **Newspaper:** *Lakes District News.* **Transportation: Railroad**–VIA Rail; **Bus**–Bus North; website: bcbus.ca and BC Transit, phone 250-624-3343; website: bctransit.com.

The Village of Burns Lake had its modest beginnings in 1911, as the site of railway construction. Forestry is the mainstay of the economy, along with ranching and tourism.

Burns Lake has 5 motels, 2 bed and breakfasts, a laundromat, library with internet access, food (Subway, A&W, etc.), a shopping center and specialty stores like **Yarn and Sew On** with quilting, knitting, crocheting and other sewing supplies. **EV plug-ins** at downtown parking lot at 313 Highway 16 West and Burns Lake Husky at 613 Highway 16 West.

The world-class Burns Lake Bike Park has more than 80 km/50 miles of trails for all ages and skill levels, a 4-cross track and pump track. Boer Mountain Recreation Area and campground draws skilled riders with numerous trails of all levels. It offers 12 campsites surrounding Kager Lake, 2.8 km/1 mile from Burns Lake which has swimming and a day-use area. No fee; operated by the Burns Lake Mountain Biking Association. Kager Lake campground nearby offers 15 sites on the lake with tables, toilets, boat launch, dock and multi-use paths. No fee; operated by Lakes Outdoor Recreation Society.

Camping is available at the municipal campground at Spirit Square Park, 2 blocks off Highway 16 on Highway 35; washrooms, playground, picnic tables and swimming area. Canoe, kayak and skateboard rental in summer. Skateboard park, playground and free outdoor exercise equipment nearby. Private lakeside campgrounds are located south of town.

From Burns Lake, a side road leads north to Babine Lake, the longest natural lake in the province and one of British Columbia's most important salmon-producing lakes.

Regional District of Bulkley Nechako. See display ad this page.

Yarn and Sew On. See display ad this page.

Forestry remains a mainstay of the economy along the highway here. Watch for logging trucks. (©Judy Nadon, staff)

Yellowhead Highway 16 Log
(continued)

PG 140.6 (226 km) **PR 307.1** (494.5 km) Car wash, Napa Auto Parts.

PG 140.7 (226.2 km) **PR 307** (494.3 km) Sunshine Inn.

PG 141.1 (226.8 km) **PR 306.6** (493.7 km) Turnout with map and information sign to south.

PG 145 (233.3 km) **PR 302.7** (487.2 km) **DECKER LAKE** Trading Post; above-ground gas tank, ice, pop, fireworks.

PG 150.9 (242.8 km) **PR 296.8** (477.7 km) Palling rest area to south is a large double-ended turnout with picnic tables, toilets, litter bins and a map.

PG 153.2 (246.5 km) **PR 294.5** (475 km) Baker airport to south.

PG 161.7 (260.2 km) **PR 286** (460.3 km) Duncan Lake gas.

PG 164.7 (265.2 km) **PR 283** (456.5 km) **Six Mile Summit** (elev. 840m/2,756 feet) to west. China Nose Mountain, with steep west-facing cliff, is visible to the south.

PG 165 (265.4 km) **PR 282.7** (456 km) Double-ended turnout to north with brake check, toilet and litter bins. Chain-off turnout to south with litter bin.

Long, 7 percent downgrade westbound.

PG 166.5 (267.9 km) **PR 281.2** (452.6

BURNS LAKE ADVERTISERS

Regional District of
  Bulkley Nechako..........................Ph. 250-692-3773
Yarn and Sew On...........................Ph. 250-692-0080

Stuart Lake, Fraser Lake, Francois, Babine (seen here) and other lakes offer camping, fishing and boating opportunities. (©Judy Nadon, staff)

km) Turnout to south with litter bin. Eastbound chain-up area in winter for Six Mile Hill.

Long, 7 percent uphill grade with 1.9 km/1.2 mile passing lane eastbound.

PG 171 (275.1 km) **PR 276.7** (445.4 km) Turnout to north with litter bins, map of **TOPLEY** (pop. 300); food, gas, lodging. Topley General Store has a grocery and take-out food.

PG 171.1 (275.3 km) **PR 276.6** (445.2 km) **Junction** with Highway 118, a beautiful drive to Granisle and Red Bluff Provincial Park on **Babine Lake**, the longest natural lake in BC. From the highway junction at Topley, mileages on this paved side road are as follows: Mile 24.4/39.3 km, turnoff to **TOPLEY LANDING** and access to fishing lodges; Mile 28.8/46.3 km, world's longest manmade spawning channel at **Fulton River**, sockeye salmon run late August to mid-October; Mile 28/45.1 km, **Red Bluff Provincial Park** with camping, picnicking, boat launch, swimming and fishing (go to www.discovercamping.ca for online reservations); Mile 30.6/49 km, Lions Beach Park with camping, picnicking, playground, boat launch, swimming and fishing; Mile 31.4/50.5 km, **GRANISLE** (pop. 352); gas, restaurant, lodging, marina and boat launch. Consult with the helpful staff at Granisle Information Center and Museum (www.granisle.

ca). Take time to walk through Memorial Park, with its panoramic views and lovely gardens.

At this same junction, go south on Sunset Lake Road to Sunset Lake Campground. This 8-site campground has a beach, playground, toilets, fishing. No fee.

PG 171.8 (277.2 km) **PR 275.9** (445 km) Large double-ended rest area to south with map of Babine Lake, toilets and litter bins.

PG 179.7 (289.9 km) **PR 268.8** (431.6 km) Turnout to north with litter bin.

PG 188.4 (302.9 km) **PR 259.3** (417.6 km) Well-maintained **Shady Rest RV Park** to south; hookups, tent sites, laundry.

Shady Rest RV Park. See display ad this page.

PG 189.1 (304 km) **PR 258.6** (416.5 km) Houston Railway bridge. Bulkley River bridge. *Begin speed zone westbound through Houston.*

PG 189.7 (305 km) **PR 258** (415.5 km) A&W, Subway and police to south, **Houston Visitor Center** to north. The visitor center has Canada's Largest Fly Rod, restrooms, a picnic area, parking, **EV plug-in**, historic structures and access to Steelhead Park walking trail. Steelhead Park has a dog run.

PG 189.8 (305.2 km) **PR 257.9** (415.3 km) Stoplight. Shopping mall to south.

Houston

PG 190 (305.5 km) **PR 257.7** (415 km) Stoplight: Petro-Canada gas station/7-11. Houston is located mid-way between Burns Lake and Smithers on Highway 16. **Population:** 2,993. **Emergency Services:** Dial 911. **Police:** phone 250-845-2204; **Ambulance:** phone 250-845-2900; **Fire Department:** phone 250-845-2250; **Clinic:** Houston Health Center phone 250-845-2294.

Visitor Information: The Visitor Center is located on Highway 16 across from the mall and next to Steelhead Park (look for the giant fly rod); open year-round. Write Houston Visitor Center, 3289 Highway 16, (P.O. Box 396) Houston, BC V0J 1Z0, or phone 250-845-7640 or www.houstonchamber.ca; email info@houstonchamber.ca. Large parking area with plenty of room for RVs and buses.

Canada's Largest Fly Fishing Rod is on display at the Visitor Center. The 60-foot-long anodized aluminum fly rod was designed by a local avid fly fisherman and built by local volunteers. (The 21-inch fly is a fluorescent "Skykomish Sunrise.") The Houston & District Chamber of Commerce, located on Highway 16, features the Hungry Hill Grizzly Bear. The park also has a steelhead fountain made by local artist, Frank Eberman.

Elevation: 1,972 feet/601m. **Climate:** Average temperature in summer, 71°F/21°C; in winter, 19°F/-7°C. **Radio:** The Moose CHBV-FM 106.5, The Mix CJFW-FM 105.5. **Newspaper:** *The Houston Today.* **Transportation:** Railroad–VIA Rail. **Bus**–Bus North; website: bcbus.ca.

Houston has all visitor facilities, including motels, campgrounds, restaurants, fastfood (Subway, A&W, etc.), gas stations, a shopping center and a golf course. The Leisure Facility has a lap pool, leisure pool, fitness room, hot tub and steam room.

Established in the early 1900s, Houston was a tie-cutting center during construction of the Grand Trunk Pacific Railway in 1912. It was named for Prince Rupert newspaperman John Houston, the former mayor of Nelson, BC. Logging continued to support the local economy with the rapid growth of mills and planer mills in the 1940s and 1950s. Houston was incorporated as a village in 1957.

The main industry in Houston today is still forest products. There is one large sawmill here, Canadian Forest Products Ltd.

Mining is also an industry here. The Equity Silver Mine operated from 1980 to 1994. The Huckleberry Copper Mine, southwest of Houston, went into production in 1997. This open pit mine has an estimated life of 16 to 25 years, extracting copper as well as molybdenum, silver and gold.

Hunting, canoeing, hiking, snowmobiling and sportfishing are major attractions here. Special events include a Winter Festival in February, Pleasant Valley Days in May, Canada Day celebrations in July and Light Up in November.

Yellowhead Highway 16 Log
(continued)

PG 190 (305.5 km) **PR 257.7** (415 km)

Stoplight. Esso gas/diesel station with 7-11 convenience store.

PG 192.6 (310 km) **PR 255.1** (411.2 km) **Junction** with the Morice River access road which extends 84 km/52 miles south to Morice Lake. Approximately 32 km/20 miles along the Morice River Road you can turn east on a gravel road which leads past Owen Lake and Nadina River Road to Francois Lake. From Francois Lake ferry landing Highway 35 leads north to Burns Lake.

The 2 famous salmon and steelhead rivers, **Morice** and **Bulkley**, unite near Houston, and it is possible to fish scores of pools all along the Morice River. Fishing for resident rainbow trout, cutthroat and Dolly Varden; steelhead and salmon (chinook, coho) in season.

NOTE: Special requirements apply to fishing these rivers; check with Fish and Game office, online or in print (regulation booklets readily available in stores).

PG 193 (310.7 km) **PR 254.7** (409.8 km) Bulkley River bridge; rest area to north at west end of bridge with tables, litter bins and toilets.

Highway climbs 8 percent hill next 2.4 km/1.5 miles westbound. *CAUTION: Watch for moose.*

PG 200.5 (322 km) **PR 247.2** (398.5 km) **Hungry Hill Summit** (elev. 844m/2,769 feet). To the north are the snowcapped peaks of the Babine Mountains, to the west is the Hudson Bay Range.

PG 203.3 (327.7 km) **PR 244.4** (393.8 km) Rest area to north with large paved parking area with picnic tables, toilets and litter bins.

PG 217.1 (349.4 km) **PR 230.6** (372.3 km) Bulkley View rest area to south; large double-ended turnout with picnic tables, toilet and litter bins with view of Bulkley River. Overland Telegraph marker, information boards.

PG 219.8 (353.7 km) **PR 227.9** (366.8 km) **Ft. Telkwa RV Park** to south.

Ft. Telkwa R.V. Park. See display ad this page.

Highway descends 7 percent winding downgrade westbound into Telkwa. *Begin speed zone through town.*

Telkwa

PG 220.4 (354.5 km) **PR 227.3** (366 km) Telkwa Museum to south; post office adjacent to the west of the museum. Telkwa (name means "meeting of the water") is located at the confluence of the Telkwa and Bulkley rivers. **Population:** 1,400. **Elevation:** 1,710 feet/520m. **Emergency Services:** Dial 911. **Hospital:** nearest hospital is 9 miles west in Smithers phone 250-847-2611.

Visitor Information: Visitor Infocenter at the Telkwa Museum and the Village of Telkwa office. Visit www.telkwa.com for more information.

Transportation: Railroad–VIA Rail. **Bus**–Bus North; website: bcbus.ca; Rider Express; phone, 833-583-3636; website; riderexpress.ca.

Telkwa is a charming village with a convenience store, laundromat, post office, a service station that includes a laundromat and cafe, pottery store, Telkwa Museum, gift

This old-time schoolroom is one of the historic displays at Telkwa Museum. (©Judy Nadon, staff)

shop, ice cream parlor, furniture and clothing warehouse store and a coffee shop. Fishing and hunting information, licenses and supplies available at the general store. Riverside and lakeside lodging available.

Camping at **Ft. Telkwa RV Park** (250-846-5012) with free RV pressure wash, WiFi and 30/50 amp service on the east edge of town and **Tyhee Lake Provincial Campground**, outside the village.

Eddy Park, on the western edge of town along the Bulkley River, is a good spot for picnicking (look for the wishing well); litter bin, washrooms, gazebo and riverside walk. St. Stephen's Anglican Church (now Mount Zion Lutheran) was built in 1910 and the bell and English gate added in 1921. Other Heritage buildings date back to 1908. Historic walking tour brochures are available at the museum or village office or online at www.telkwa.com/html/history.htm. Walking trail to historic townsite of Aldermere and to Tyhee Lake Provincial Park.

The annual Kinsman Barbecue is held over Labor Day weekend. This event features a major northern baseball tournament, kids games, live music, contests, a demolition derby, and barbecue.

Yellowhead Highway 16 Log
(continued)

PG 220.7 (355 km) **PR 227** (365.5 km) Turnoff for **Tyhee Lake Provincial Park**, 1 km/0.6 mile north; open mid-May to mid-September; 59 campsites with playground, pit toilets, picnic tables, firepits, showers, drinking water; 26 day-use picnic tables, hiking trails, wildlife viewing platform, fishing, swimming, boat launch. Camping fee $27, sani-dump $5; go to www.discover camping.ca for online reservations.

Also turnoff here on the Telkwa High Road, which intersects with Babine Lake access road (gravel), which leads 46 miles/74 km north to Smithers Landing (very, very

rough road, not recommended for trailers or RVs) on Babine Lake and 56 miles/90 km to Granisle.

Tyhee Lake, rainbow and lake trout to 2 lbs., June through August; Kamloops trout to 2 lbs. **Babine River**, steelhead to 40 lbs., late fall. **Telkwa River**, coho to 24 lbs., spring to fall.

PG 221.1 (355.6 km) **PR 226.6** (364.9 km) Race Trac gas/diesel station to north.

PG 225.5 (362.7 km) **PR 222.2** (357.8 km) Second turnoff westbound to north for Babine Lake/Smithers Landing (very rough road not recommended for trailers or RVs).

PG 227.2 (366.1 km) **PR 220.5** (354.4 km) Smithers Par 3 RV & Golf to south.

PG 227.5 (366.6 km) **PR 220.2** (353.9 km) Turnoff to north for Driftwood Canyon Provincial Park (11 km/6.8 miles); day-use area with picnic tables, toilets, firepits, hiking trails. Recognized as one of the world's most significant fossil beds.

PG 227.6 (366.8 km) **PR 220.1** (353.7

km) Bridge over Bulkley River.

PG 227.8 (367 km) PR 219.9 (353.5 km) Turnout to north; litter bin, picnic tables, area map, Welcome to Smithers sign.

PG 228 (367.3 km) PR 219.7 (353.2 km) Stoplight. Forest District Office to north.

PG 228.6 (367.9 km) PR 219.1 (352.6 km) Stoplight. Grocery store to north (includes bulk foods). Access south to Canadian Tire, Hudson Bay Lodge and RCMP via frontage road.

PG 228.9 (368.8 km) PR 218.8 (351.7 km) Stoplight. Access to RCMP and Chandler Park to south via frontage road.

PG 229.2 (368.3 km) PR 218.5 (351.2 km) King Street stoplight; Safeway, gas/diesel stations. Westbound turn right (north) for **Smithers Riverside Municipal Campground & RV Park.**

Smithers

PG 229.3 (369 km) PR 218.4 (350.5 km) Main Street stoplight in Smithers. Turn south for downtown shopping; turn north for Fire Department and Riverside Park. **Population:** 5,504; area 20,000. **Emergency Services:** Dial 911. **Police,** phone 250-847-3233. **Hospital** and **Poison Center** phone 250-847-2611. **Ambulance,** phone 250-847-8808.

Visitor Information: The **Smithers Visitor Center and Chamber of Commerce** are located behind the railcar, across from the Bulkley Valley Museum. The museum has developed a self-guided walking tour called the Smithers Culture Crawl and includes historic buildings and museum exhibits on display in downtown businesses. Open year-round, the Visitor Center has detailed information and maps on area services and recreation. Contact P.O. Box 2379, Smithers, BC V0J 2N0; phone 1-800-542-6673; email info@tourismsmithers.com; www.tourism smithers.com and www.smitherschamber. com.

Elevation: 1,636 feet/496m. **Climate:** Relatively warmer and drier than mountainous areas to the west; average temperature in July is 58°F/14°C, in January 14°F/-10°C; annual precipitation, 13 inches. **Radio:** The Moose AM 870 and FM 106.5, CJFW-FM 92.9 or 105.5, CFNR FM-95.1, CBC-FM 97.5, 88.1 and CICK FM-93.9. **Television:** Channels 5, 13, satellite and cable. **Newspaper:** *Interior News* (weekly).

Transportation: Air—Scheduled service via Air Canada (Jazz) and Central Mountain Air. **Railroad**—VIA Rail. **Bus**—BC Bus North; website: bcbus.ca; BC Transit, phone 250-624-3343; website: bctransit.com. **Car Rentals**—Available.

Sitting amidst rugged mountains, the downtown shopping area has alpine-themed storefronts and buildings murals. (There

Smithers has a charming downtown area for shopping and dining. Traveler services are also found along Yellowhead Highway 16. (©Michael Robb)

is even an alpenhorn statue at the head of Main Street.) Main Street offers a wide array of unique boutiques, shops and restaurants.

Incorporated as a village in 1921, Smithers officially became a town in Canada's centennial year, 1967, but the original site was chosen in 1913 by construction crews working on the Grand Trunk Pacific Railway. The town was named for one-time chairman of the railway A.W. Smithers. Today it is a distribution and supply center for farms, mills and mines in the area.

Smithers is the largest town in the Bulkley Valley and the site of Hudson Bay Mountain, a popular ski area in winter. Summer activities here include many outdoor opportunities including jet boat tours, heli-excursions and remote "glamping" (glamorous camping). There are two 18-hole golf courses with rentals and clubhouse: Smithers Golf & RV east of town, and Smithers Golf & Country Club west of town, with its championship course.

All visitor services including accommodations at **Capri Motor Inn**, restaurants, gas stations, supermarkets and a fun downtown shopping district. The government liquor store is located on Highway 16 in the Smithers Shopping Center. **EV plug-in** at Smithers city parking lot at 3749 Second Ave.

Camping at **Smithers Riverside Municipal Campground & RV Park**; security, free firewood, showers and flush toilets, water and electrical hookups, potable water, cookhouse and picnic area. Located at Riverside Park on the Bulkley River; turn north on Main Street and watch for signs. **Glacier View RV Park and Cabin Rentals** is located 8 km/5 miles west of town.

Special events include the Bulkley Valley Fall Fair—one of the largest agricultural exhibitions in the province—held the last weekend in August each year. The Midsummer Music Festival (first weekend in July) features local, regional and national artists and the Telkwa Barbecue and Demolition Derby is the longest running, consecutive event in British Columbia.

Smithers offers a number of scenic drives. Hudson Bay Mountain (elev. 8,700 feet/2,652m) is a 14-mile/23-km drive from Highway 16; the plateau above timberline at the ski area is a good spot for summer hikes.

Fossil enthusiasts should drive to Driftwood Canyon Provincial Park; turn off Highway 16 just east of the Bulkley River bridge (travelers are advised to stop first at the Visitor Center in town for a map and directions). A display at the park illustrates the fossils, such as metasequoia, a type of redwood which occurs in the shale formation. BC Parks asks visitors to refrain from removing any fossils.

Beautiful spots not to be missed are Twin Falls and Glacier Gulch. Drive west on Highway 16 to Lake Kathlyn Road turnoff; follow this paved road south to Glacier Gulch Road and then continue 1.1 miles/1.8 km on pavement and 1.5 miles/2.4 km on narrow gravel road to a day-use-only parking area. Hike along the creek to the right for 15 minutes for spectacular views. *NOTE: Rocks are slippery when wet.*

In the winter months, Smithers boasts one of the largest ski hills in northern British Columbia at 5,413 feet/1,650m. Hudson Bay Mountain's ski area's triple chair and 2 T-bars have a 1,750-feet/533-m vertical rise, with dozens of ski runs. A list of lake and river fishing spots in the area, with informa-

tion on boat launches and boat rentals, is available from the Visitor Center, Box 2379, Smithers, BC V0J 2N0; phone 250-847-5072 or 1-800-542-6673. 🐟

Yellowhead Highway 16 Log
(continued)

PG 229.4 (369.6 km) **PR 218.3** (350.9 km) Stoplight at Queen Street in Smithers; access to **Capri Motor Inn**, Sandman Inn, Dairy Queen and Tim Hortons.

PG 229.9 (370.4 km) **PR 217.8** (350.1 km) Stoplight at Bulkley Drive and Toronto Street in Smithers; fast-food and lodging.

PG 230.5 (371.4 km) **PR 217.2** (349.1 km) Smithers Golf and Country Club.

PG 231.7 (373.2 km) **PR 216** (347.3 km) First turnoff westbound for Lake Kathlyn (Loop) Road, which leads 1.4 miles/2.3 km (paved) to junction with Glacier Gulch Road, which leads 2.6 miles/4.2 km (last 1.5 miles/2.4 km narrow gravel) to **Twin Falls**

BC Recreation Site picnic area; large parking area with toilet, picnic tables in trees and trails to Twin Falls and Glacier Gulch. 2 campsites for tenting. Narrow, unpaved access road has limited visibility. 🏕️

PG 232.7 (374.9 km) **PR 215** (345.6 km) Turnoff to north for Smithers airport.

PG 233.6 (376.3 km) **PR 214.1** (344.2 km) Lake Kathlyn Jct. Road, connects with Lake Kathlyn Road.

PG 234 (377 km) **PR 213.7** (343.5 km) Last turnoff westbound for Lake Kathlyn (Loop) Road to south, which junctions with Glacier Gulch Road to Twin Falls BC Recreation Site, 5.8 km/3.6 miles south (see **Milepost PG 231.7**).

PG 235 (378 km) **PR 212.7** (342.6 km) Turnoff to north for access to **Glacier View RV Park and Cabin Rentals**; full hookups, cabins and cottages, WiFi, showers, laundromat, dishwashing room, sani-dump. 🏕️

TOURISM WITSET

Located on Highway 16, 30 km west of Smithers

Walter Joseph Photo

MUSEUM · TOURS · CAMPGROUND/RV

Glacier View RV Park and Cabin Rentals. See display ad on page 263.

PG 235.1 (378.4 km) **PR 212.6** (341.1 km) Hudson Bay rest area with picnic tables, litter bins and a wildlife museum. Beautiful view of Hudson Bay Mountain.

PG 243.1 (391.5 km) **PR 204.6** (329 km) Trout Creek bridge.

PG 243.2 (391.8 km) **PR 204.5** (328.7 km) Soaring Spirits Camp organic produce stand. Camp teaches organic farming principles to Thai and North American students.

PG 248.5 (400.7 km) **PR 199.2** (319.8 km) Narrow single-vehicle turnout to north with historic sign and litter bins.

PG 248.7 (400.9 km) **PR 199** (319.6 km) Stop-of-interest: Gravel parking area to north with view of Bulkley River and **Widzin Kwah (formerly Moricetown) Canyon**; picnic tables, litter bins, good photo stop.

PG 248.9 (401.2 km) **PR 198.8** (319.3 km) Telkwa High Road is a short side road on the north side of the highway leading to parking and benches overlooking **Widzin Kwah Canyon and Falls** on the Bulkley River and to **Widzin Kwah Canyon House Museum** and **Tourism Witset RV Park and Campground**. For centuries, this canyon and falls has been a famous First Nations' fishing spot. Aboriginal people may still be seen here netting salmon July through September. 🏕️

Tourism Witset (formerly Moricetown Canyon) invites you to stay in our outstanding completely renovated RV Park and Campground. Large full-service pull-thru 50/amp sites, fully-accessible washrooms, WiFi, laundry and a marvelous new playground. Visit our Widzin Kwah Canyon House Museum and Gift Shop and take part in our Witsuwit'en cultural tours and events. Call 1-800-881-1218 or visit our website www.tourismwitset.com. See display ad on this page. [ADVERTISEMENT]

PG 249.2 (401.5 km) **PR 198.5** (319 km) **Junction** with Beaver Road, Esso gas/diesel station entering **WITSET** (formerly Moricetown, pop. 815; elev. 1,341 feet/409m). ⛽

Witset is a First Nations reserve and village, and the oldest settlement in the province. Traditionally, the First Nations' people (Wet'suwet'en) took advantage of the narrow canyon to trap salmon. The centuries-old settlement ('Kyah Wiget) was once named after Father A.G. Morice, a Roman Catholic missionary. Born in France, Father Morice came to British Columbia in 1880 and worked with the aboriginals of northern British Columbia from 1885 to 1904. He achieved world recognition for his writings in anthropology, ethnology and history.

PG 259 (417.3 km) **PR 188.7** (304 km) Small paved turnout with litter bin to north.

PG 259.9 (418.8 km) **PR 187.8** (302.9 km) Paved turnout with litter bin to north.

PG 260.8 (420.2 km) **PR 186.9** (301.3 km) Paved turnout to north with litter bin and view of Bulkley River.

PG 261.6 (421.5 km) **PR 186.1** (299.8 km) Paved shoulder parking to north.

PG 269.3 (433.9 km) **PR 178.4** (287.6 km) Turnoff for **Ross Lake** Provincial Park picnic area, 2 km/1.2 miles north; 25 picnic sites and firepits, pit toilets, boat launch (electric motors only), swimming beach, hiking trail. Fish for stocked rainbow and eastern brook trout. 🐟

PG 270.7 (436.1 km) **PR 177** (284.4 km) Turnout to north with map of New Hazelton. Entering New Hazelton westbound (description follows). *Begin speed zone westbound through town.*

New Hazelton

PG 271 (436.5 km) **PR 176.7** (284 km) Stoplight. Food, gas and lodging along highway. **Population** (of The Hazeltons): 6,500. **Emergency Services:** Dial 911. **Police,** phone 250-842-5244. **Hospital:** Wrinch Memorial Hospital 250-842-5211.

©Judy Nadon, staff

Visitor Information: New Hazelton Area Visitor Center in 2-story log building at the junction; museum, local artisan display, restrooms, free sani-dump, potable water, picnic tables. Look for the 3 statues representing the gold rush packer Cataline, the Northwest miner, and the Upper Skeena logger. Phone 250-842-6071 in summer; 250-842-6571 October to May; websites www.newhazelton. ca and www.hazeltontourism.ca.

Elevation: 1,150 feet/351m. **Radio:** CBC 1170. **Transportation: Railroad**–VIA Rail. **Bus**–BC Transit, phone 250-624-3343; website: bctransit.com.

The first of 3 communities westbound sharing the name Hazelton (the others are Hazelton and South Hazelton), known collectively as The Hazeltons. Lodging at Cataline Motel and RV Park, Robber's Roost Motel, 28 Inn, and **Bulkley Valley Motel** (description follows).

Bulkley Valley Motel. In the heart of New Hazelton on Highway 16 at 4444–10th Avenue. Clean, quiet, renovated rooms, new LED TVs, new duvets and covers, high-speed Internet, in-room A/C, private 4-piece bath, cable TV, coffee, phone, microwave, minifridge. Full kitchenettes available. From $89. Call 1-888-988-1144 or 1-250-842-8727. [ADVERTISEMENT]

Camping in South Hazelton at Cataline RV Park (year-round); Seeley Lake Provincial Park or Anderson Flats Provincial Park mid-May to mid-September (weather permitting); 'Ksan Campground on River Road in Hazelton; and at Bulkley Canyon Ranch.

Other services include a Royal Bank of Canada and a credit union, a laundromat with showers, and 3 gas stations. Shopping facilities include a bakery, two grocery stores, hardware/automotive stores and a department store. ATMs are located in the Chevron station in New Hazelton; at Bulkley Valley Credit Union off of Highway 16, at the Royal Bank and at the Gitanmaax Food and Fuel gas station on Highway 62 leading to Old Hazelton; and the Esso Station in Kispiox. There are several restaurants and cafes in the area.

Attractions in this area include Historic Old Hazelton, the replica First Nations'

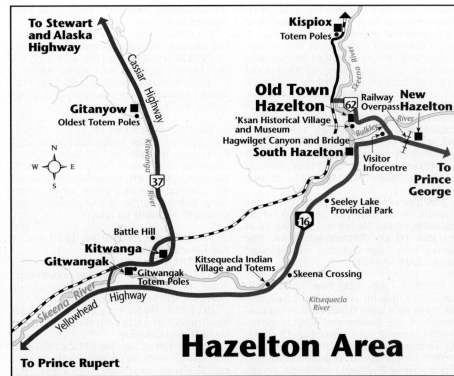

Hazelton Area

village of 'Ksan, and various outdoor recreation opportunities such as hiking, rafting, and sport fishing on the Bulkley, Skeena and Kispiox rivers. The Roché de Boulé mountain range, which includes Hagwilget Peak, elev. 8,000 feet/2,438m, towers behind the town.

From May through early fall, a Country Market and Farmer's Market is held on Sundays from 10 A.M. to 2 P.M. at The Hazeltons Visitor Center on Highway 16, featuring locally grown produce and handmade goods.

The Hagwilget Canyon of the Bulkley River is one of the most photographed places in Canada. A 1-lane bridge spans the canyon on the road to Hazelton, one of the highest suspension bridges in Canada (spans 460 feet and is 262 feet above the river).

HAZELTON. Situated at the confluence of the Skeena and Bulkley rivers, Hazelton developed at "The Forks" as an integral shipping point on the Skeena, and a wintering place for miners and prospectors. Thomas Hankin established a Hudson's Bay Co. trading post here in 1868. The name Hazelton comes from the numerous hazelnut bushes growing on the flats.

Cataline, a famous pioneer packer and traveler, is buried near here in an unmarked grave in the Gitanmaax Cemetery. Jean Caux (his real name) was a Basque who, from 1852 to 1912, used loaded mules to supply mining and construction camps from Yale and Ashcroft to Hazelton, where he often wintered. Hazelton was founded in 1866, some years before the arrival of the railroad and highways, and functioned as an important part of the existing shipping route. Supplies for nearby trading posts, and the Omineca goldfields, were moved by riverboat from the coast to Hazelton, and from

there over trails into the backcountry. Some of the Yukon gold rushers passed through Hazelton on their way to the Klondike, and pack trains made the trip from Hazelton to Telegraph Creek over the old Telegraph Trail as early as 1874.

Reconstructed to look much like it did in the 1890s, look for the antique machinery placed throughout the town. The history of the Hazelton area can be traced by car on the self-guided Hands of History tour. Pick up a brochure from the Information Center showing the location of the 19 historic sites on the driving tour. Pioneer Day is the second Saturday in August, and celebrates the historic spirit of the community.

'KSAN Historical Village and Museum, a replica Gitxsan village, is 4.5 miles/7.2 km from Highway 16. It is a reconstruction of a traditional Gitxsan Village, which had stood in this location for centuries. It is located at the confluence of the Bulkley and Skeena

rivers. There are 7 traditionally styled cedar longhouses, as well as an assortment of totem poles and dugout canoes.

For a nominal charge from May to September, you can join a guided tour of three longhouses. Performances of traditional song and dance are presented every Wednesday evening during July and August in the Wolf House. Admission to grounds is by donation and children under 6 are free. Guided tours are $15/adults, $10/students and seniors. Open daily from May to October, hours are posted. In the winter, the gift shop hours are 10 A.M. to 4:30 P.M., Monday to Friday. Phone 1-250-842-5544 or visit www.ksan.org.

The 'Ksan Campground, adjacent to the museum, is a full-service campground on the banks of the Skeena and Bulkley rivers operated by the Gitanmaax Band. The season runs May–October; campground phone, 250-842-5940.

KISPIOX (pop. 825) First Nations village and 3 fishing resorts are 9 miles/15 km north on a good paved road at the confluence of the Skeena and Kispiox rivers. Kispiox is noted for its stand of 15 standing totems close to the river. There is a market garden (fresh vegetables) located approximately 7 miles/11 km north on the Kispiox Road (about 2 miles/3.2 km before the Kispiox totem poles). Camping, accommodations and fishing are available at various lodges and campgrounds located in the valley. The valley hosts the Kispiox Rodeo, an annual event since 1952, the first weekend of June and an annual music festival is held the last weekend in July

Fishing: Skeena River, Dolly Varden to 5 lbs.; spring salmon, mid-July to mid-August; coho 4 to 12 lbs., Aug. 15 through September; steelhead to 20 lbs., July through November. Kispiox River is famous for its trophy-sized steelhead. Check regulations, restrictions may apply. Season is mid-June to late September for salmon, trout and steelhead. Excellent fly-fishing waters.

Yellowhead Highway 16 Log
(continued)

PG 271.2 (436.9 km) PR 176.5 (283.6 km) Railroad bridge.

PG 271.3 (437.1 km) PR 176.4 (283.4 km) Hazelton Visitor Center at junction with Highway 62, which leads north to Old Town (Historic) Hazelton, 'Ksan Village, Museum and Campground and Kispiox Valley.

PG 271.8 (437.9 km) PR 175.9 (282.6 km) Narrow double-ended turnout to south

with Hazelton information sign and map (eastbound access).

PG 273.2 (440.1 km) PR 174.5 (280.4 km) Mission Creek (railroad underpass).

PG 273.6 (440.7 km) PR 174.1 (279.8 km) Turnoff to north for Cataline Motel & RV Park. Side road continues through residential area of South Hazelton and loops back to the highway.

PG 276.7 (444.5 km) PR 171 (275.1 km) Turnoff to south for Seeley Lake Provincial Park; open mid-May to mid-September. 20 campsites with firepits, picnic tables, drinking water, pit toilets, firewood, camping fee $20. Day-use area with picnic tables, swimming. Fish for cutthroat and rainbow trout, electric motors only on lake.

PG 287.2 (462.7 km) PR 160.5 (257.8 km) River bridge.

PG 287.6 (463.2 km) PR 161.1 (257.3 km) KITSEGUECLA, First Nation's village. Totem poles throughout village are classic examples, still in original locations.

PG 287.8 (463.6 km) PR 160.9 (256.9 km) Turnout to south with historical plaque about Skeena Crossing.

PG 298 (480.2 km) PR 149.7 (240.3 km) Gas station with diesel and a cafe at Cassiar Highway junction. Gitwangak, 0.2 mile/0.4 km north, has historic totems, St. Paul's Church and bell tower (with bell from 1893). Camping at Cassiar RV Park 2.5 miles/4 km north.

Junction with Cassiar Highway (BC Highway 37) north to the Alaska Highway, with access to Stewart, BC/Hyder, AK. See CASSIAR HIGHWAY section on page 272.

Westbound, the Yellowhead Highway offers good views of Seven Sisters peaks; the highest is 9,140 feet/2,786m.

©Judy Nadon, staff

PG 299 (481.2 km) PR 148.7 (239.4 km) Gitksan Paintbrush Native Arts & Crafts. See display ad this page.

PG 303.2 (488.6 km) PR 144.5 (231.9 km) Boulder Creek bridge.

PG 303.5 (489.2 km) PR 144.4 (231.4 km) Double-ended rest area with parking for large vehicles; toilets, litter bins and picnic tables.

PG 307.6 (495.6 km) PR 140.1 (224.9 km) Paved turnout to north with litter bin.

PG 308 (496.3 km) PR 139.7 (224.2 km) Gull Creek with hiking trail across from it.

PG 309.2 (498.2 km) PR 138.5 (222.3 km) Hand of History sign about "Holy City."

PG 312.5 (503.5 km) PR 135.2 (217 km) Paved turnout to north with litter bin overlooking the Skeena River.

PG 315.3 (507.9 km) PR 132.4 (212.6 km) Flint Creek.

PG 319.1 (513.9 km) PR 128.6 (208.4 km) Turnout to north with litter bin along river and historical plaque about Skeena

River Boats:

From 1889, stern-wheelers and smaller craft fought their way through the Coast Mountains, churning past such awesome places as 'The Devil's Elbow' and 'The Hornet's Nest.' Men and supplies were freighted upstream, furs and gold downstream. A quarter century of colour and excitement began to fade in 1912, as the Grand Trunk Pacific neared completion.

PG 336.3 (541.1 km) PR 111.6 (181.4 km) Sanderson rest area on Skeena River with double-ended access; large, pleasant area with water pump, picnic tables, toilets, recycling and litter bins.

NOTE: Steep cliffs, supervise children.

PG 343.4 (552.4 km) PR 105.5 (170 km) Tiny chapel to south serves small community of USK. The nondenominational chapel is a replica of the pioneer church that stood in Usk on the other side of the river until 1936, when the Skeena River flooded, sweeping away the village and the church. The only item from the church to survive was the Bible, which was found floating atop a small pine table.

PG 345.2 (555.6 km) PR 102.4 (165 km) Side road leads 0.5 mile/0.8 km south to Kleanza Creek Provincial Park; Open mid-May to mid-September, 34 campsites, 25 picnic sites, fishing, drinking water, pit toilets, firewood, wheelchair access. Camping fee $20. Gate closed between 11 P.M. and 7 A.M. No pets in day-use area, designated creekside pet area is near site #1. Reserve at website: discovercamping.ca.

PG 345.4 (555.9 km) PR 102.3 (164.7 km) Kleanza Creek bridge. Salmon habitat.

PG 346.9 (558.3 km) PR 100.8 (162.3 km) Paved turnout to north.

PG 350.5 (564.1 km) PR 97.2 (156.4 km) Copper (Zymoetz) River bridge, can be fished from Highway 16 or follow local maps. Coho to 10 lbs., use tee-spinners in July; steelhead to 20 lbs., check locally for season and restrictions.

PG 351.3 (565.5 km) PR 96.4 (155 km) Double-ended turnout to north with tourist information sign and area map.

PG 352.2 (566.8 km) PR 95.5 (153.7 km) Turnoff on frontage road for access to motel and RV park.

PG 353.9 (569.6 km) PR 93.8 (150.9 km) Chevron gas/diesel station and Northern Motor Inn to south.

PG 354.3 (570.2 km) PR 93.4 (150.3 km) Esso and Petro-Canada gas/diesel and propane at Old Lakelse Lake Road south to Furlong Bay.

PG 354.7 (570.8 km) PR 93 (149.7 km) 4-way stop at junction with Highway 37 South, which leads 59 km/38 miles on a nice side trip to Kitimat (description follows). This side road is a good 2-lane paved highway with multiple passing lanes. Northwest Regional Airport is located at Mile 3/Km 4.8. Lakelse Lake Provincial Park recreation sites along the road are: Grunchy Beach and sockeye salmon viewing trail at Mile 7.8/Km 12.5; picnic grounds at Mile 8.6/Km 13.8; and the Furlong Bay unit at Mile 11.3/Km 18, which has 156 vehicle and tent campsites (50 with hookups). Open mid-May to mid-September. Camping fee $28–$34. The park has picnic tables, firepits, drinking water, wheelchair access, firewood, nature trails, swimming, sandy beach, pit and flush toilets, showers, playground, sani-dump

($5), boat launch, interpretive programs and fishing for Dolly Varden. Reserve at www. discovercamping.ca.

KITIMAT (pop. 8,131) is a major deep sea port and site of the Rio Tinto BC Works aluminum smelter. Originally planned and built in the early 1950s, when the B.C. government encouraged Alcan (Aluminum Co. of Canada) to establish a smelter here, the plant underwent a $4.8 billion modernization (in 2014–2015) designed to increase production capacity and reduce greenhouse gases.

Visitor's Information: Visitor Center at 2109 Forest Ave. Kitimat, BC V8C 2G7. Phone 250-632-6294 or 1-800-664-6554; www.tourismkitimat.ca.

Kitimat is a popular fishing spot. Fishermen line the banks of the Kitimat River in May for the steelhead run. The chinook salmon run follows in June and July and coho fill the river in late August and into September.

Many scenic hiking trails are available including those to view the Giant Spruce Tree and Moore Creek waterfalls. The Kitimat Museum and Archives is located at 293 City Center; phone 250-632-8950. Open June–August, Monday–Saturday 10 AM. to 5 P.M.; September–May, weekdays 10 A.M. to 4 P.M. and Saturday noon–4 P.M. Another attraction is Kitamaat Village, the original aboriginal settlement area.

Camping at Radley Park; 36 sites electrical hookups, showers, fishing, toilets, playground and sani-dump station. Phone 250-632-8955 for details.

PG 354.9 (571.1 km) PR 92.8 (149.4 km) First bridge westbound over the Skeena River. "Skeena" means "River of the mist" in First Nation's language.

PG 355.2 (571.7 km) PR 92.5 (148.8 km) **Ferry Island Municipal Campground**; 103 sites, half with electrical hookups; water taps throughout, covered picnic shelters, barbecues, coin-op showers, Kids' Park, a fishing sandbar and walking trails with carvings in the trees done by local artists. Fee $20–$28. Phone 250-615-9657 (summer only).

PG 355.3 (571.9 km) PR 92.4 (148.6 km) Second bridge westbound over the Skeena River.

PG 355.6 (572.4 km) PR 92.1 (148.1 km) Stoplight. Access to Walmart to south.

PG 355.7 (572.5 km) PR 92 (148 km) Terrace Visitor Center to south. Sani-dump behind Visitor Center.

PG 355.8 (572.6 km) PR 91.9 (147.9 km) Stoplight at Kalum Street. Tim Hortons to south, liquor store to north.

PG 355.9 (572.8 km) PR 91.8 (147.7 km) A&W.

PG 356 (572.9 km) PR 91.7 (147.6 km) Pedestrian stoplight. Esso station to north. Napa Auto Parts/Fountain Tire to south.

PG 356.2 (573.4 km) PR 91.5 (147.1 km) Stoplight. Go west on Keith Street for **Rain Coast Wash & Lube**. *Westbound (Prince Rupert-bound) travelers turn right and cross Sande Overpass. Eastbound (Prince George-bound) travelers turn left (no stoplight) and continue on Highway 16/Keith Street.*

Rain Coast Wash & Lube. See display ad this page.

PG 356.4 (573.7 km) PR 91.3 (146.8 km) Stoplight at Highway 16 and Sande.

Westbound travelers turn left for continuation of Highway 16 to Prince Rupert, or turn right for Terrace city center. Eastbound travelers turn left over Sande Overpass for continuation of Highway 16 to Prince George or go straight ahead for downtown Terrace.

Terrace

PG 356.4 (573.7 km) PR 91.3 (146.8 km) Located along Yellowhead Highway 16, a 1½ hour's drive east of Prince Rupert. **Population:** 11,320; area 18,581. **Emergency Services:** Dial 911. **Police,** phone 250-635-4911. **Fire Department,** 250-638-8121. **Ambulance,** 250-638-1102. **Hospital,** 250-635-2211.

Visitor Information: Visitor Center located in the log building on Highway 16 with sani-dump. Open daily in summer, 9 A.M. to 5 P.M.; weekdays in winter, 10:30 A.M. to 2:30 P.M. www.visitterrace.com.

Elevation: 220 feet/67m. **Climate:** Average annual mean temperature of 6.1°C/43°F, and an average annual precipitation of 129.5 cm/51 inches per year. **Radio:** CFNR 92.1 FM, CJFW 103.1 FM, EZ Rock CFTK 590 AM, **Television:** CFTK-TV Channel 7. **Newspaper:** *Terrace Standard* (weekly).

Logging was the major industry in Terrace for decades. For a time, the community was known as the "cedar pole capital of the world," and the world's largest cedar pole (162 feet/50m) was cut here. The economy has since diversified, and Terrace remains a commercial hub, with major-chain motels, restaurants, fast-food outlets, and "big box" stores like Walmart (no camping permitted) and Canadian Tire. There are 18 motels/hotels and several shopping centers. Wash your rigs and dogs at the **Rain Coast Wash and Lube**. The government liquor store is at 3250 Eby St. Secured RV storage can be found at Queensway Mini Storage; phone 250-638-0204 for more information. Find **EV plug-ins** at 4741 Lakelse Ave., at Skeena Mall and at City Hall at 3215 Eby St.

The community has a library and art gallery, an aquatic center with 2 saunas and full-sized and child-sized indoor swimming pools, tennis courts, a golf course, bingo parlor, casino, bowling alley, fitness cen-

ters, skateboard park, Bike Skills Park, 2 ice arenas, racquetball court, archery and shooting range, curling club, ski hill, a local brewery and theater.

The Grand Trunk Pathway parallels highway 16 across from the Sandman Inn/Denny's and Sherwood Mountain Brewery. With hanging flower baskets, benches, and historic and cultural information boards, a railcar, monuments and more, it is a great place to stretch your legs and have an ice cream at the Chill Shop.

Terrace has several private campgrounds. There is a public campground located at Ferry Island (see **Milepost PG 355.2**). Lakelse Lake Provincial Park campground at Furlong Bay, located at Mile 11.3/Km 18 on Highway 37 South (see **Milepost PG 354.7**). Kleanza Creek Provincial Park campground is located on Highway 16 West at **Milepost PG 345.2**.

Heritage Park Museum, a collection of original log buildings chosen to represent both the different aspects of pioneer life as well as various log building techniques, is well worth a visit. Guided tours available, admission charged. The structures include the Kalum Hotel, Dix's Dance Hall, Hampton Barn, Johnstone Cabin, trapper's cabin, miner's cabin, lineman's cabin, Conroy Homestead cabin. These restored cabins house over 4,000 artifacts. To get to the park, follow Kalum Street/Skeena View north. Open daily May–August 10 A.M. to 6 P.M. and by appointment the rest of the year. Phone 250-635-4546; website: heritagepark museum.com.

Another historic building, the George Little House, was the homestead of the founder of Terrace. It is now home to the VIA Rail Depot downtown.

Special events in Terrace include the annual National Aboriginal Days celebration held June 21. In August, Riverboat Days, held the BC Day long weekend through to the following weekend to include the Downtown Street Fest.

Sportfishing in the **Skeena, Copper, Kalum, Nass, Tseax, Kitimat** and **Lakelse rivers**. Cutthroat, Dolly Varden and rainbow trout are found in all lakes and streams; salmon (coho and chinook) from May to late autumn. Chinook average 40 to 70 lbs.; coho 14 to 20 lbs. Check locally for season and restrictions on steelhead. Information

Nisga'a Highway

More than 300 cultural treasures of the Nisga'a First Nation are displayed at Nisga'a Museum near Laxgalts'ap. (©Mike Coachman)

The Nisga'a Highway makes an interesting **side trip**, providing access to 4 First Nation villages as well as a variety of interesting attractions. Pick up the self-guided auto tour of this route at the Terrace Visitor Center. This route is paved, with the exception of a few short gravel breaks north of Lava Lake.

The first major attraction along the Nisga'a Highway is **Anhluut'ukwsim Lamihl Angwinga'asanskwhl Provincial Park** (formerly Nisga'a Memorial Lava Beds). There is an information kiosk on the Nisga'a lava beds at Mile 42.4, near the southern boundary of the park (at the south end of Lava Lake), and another at Mile 48.9, as the highway narrows and begins winding its way through the lava beds. The lava flow is thought to be the most recent volcanic eruption in Canada (approximately 250 years ago). It covers an area about 6 miles/10 km long and 1.8 miles/3 km wide and was created by a volcano less than 361 feet/100m high. The eruption produced little ash or cinder, but large quantities of basalt. The eruption destroyed 2 villages and killed more than 2,000 people.

The **Nisga'a Lava Beds and Area Visitor Center** is located 59 miles/95 km north of the Yellowhead Highway junction. The Visitor Center is open Saturday–Sunday 10 A.M. to 5 P.M. to June 26, then Tuesdays–Sundays 10 A.M. to 5 P.M. to Sept. 4. The **Nisga'a Campground**, adjacent the visitor center, is open May 8–Oct. 15 and has 16 campsites, picnic tables, pump water, firepits, pit toilets, a day-use area, hiking trails, fishing on **Tseax River**; camping fee $20. Lava bed tours available. For more information on tours, campground and visitor center, visit Nass Valley Tours at: www.nass113.com/. There is a grocery store, gas station, restaurant, health services and bed and breakfasts in the area.

GITLAXT'AAMIKS (pop. 806), formerly New Aiyansh, is accessible via a 5-km/3-mile access road from Mile 58.7 Nisga'a Highway. Located in the beautiful Nass Valley, this is the central village of the Nisga'a Nation. Residents maintain a rich cultural tradition. The Nisga'a Treaty was the first modern-day treaty in British Columbia. It has a lodge, bed and breakfast, grocery/restaurant/gas station and a health center (phone 250-633-2298).

Beyond Gitlaxt'aamiks, 7 miles/11 km to the northeast, is **NASS CAMP**, a logging community with motel rooms, RV sani-dump and a restaurant. A rough and narrow logging road (not suitable for low-clearance vehicles) connects Nass Camp with Cassiar Highway 37 at Cranberry Junction, 48 km/30 miles east of Nass Camp.

Turnoff at Mile 63.1 Nisga'a Highway for access to **GITWINKSIHLKW** (pop. 201), formerly Canyon City, via a 1.3-mile/2.1-km access road. There is a suspension bridge over the Nass River in Gitwinksihlkw. The village has a bed and breakfast, store and a health center (phone 250-633-2298).

Between Gitwinksihlkw and Laxgalts'ap, watch for signage to **Hlgu Isgwit Hot Springs**, located on the south side of the highway, just east of the Ksi Ansit aagan (Ansedegen Creek). Boardwalk access to spring-fed tubs; the trailhead is near a rest area. Changing rooms are available.

At Mile 78.6 Nisga'a Highway, there is a turnoff for **Mill Bay**, reached via a 29-km/17-mile gravel spur road.

LAXGALTS'AP (pop. 474), formerly Greenville, is at Mile 86.2 Nisga'a Highway. Services include 2 small stores, a cafe, bed and breakfast, church, school and health center (phone 250-621-3274).

The **Nisga'a Museum** (nisgaamuseum. ca), located just west of Laxgalts'ap, contains more than 300 cultural treasures of the Nisga'a First Nations.

The Nisga'a highway ends at Mile 167.9 km/104 miles from the Yellowhead Highway junction at **GINGOLX** (pop. 341), formerly Kincolith, with bed and breakfasts, a cafe, 2 small stores and a health center (phone 250-326-2345). Gingolx has had road access only since 2003. It is known for salmon fishing and an annual crab fest in early July.

Emergency Services: Call the **RCMP** for emergencies 250-633-2222.

> **Return to Milepost PG 357.5**
> **Yellowhead Highway**

and fishing licenses are available from BC Government Access Center, 3220 Eby St., Terrace; phone 250-638-6515, and at sporting goods stores.

Yellowhead Highway 16 Log
(continued)

PG 356.6 (574 km) **PR 91.1** (146.5 km) Stoplight at Eby Street. Access north to Skeena Mall, Husky gas/diesel station.

PG 356.7 (574 km) **PR 91** (146.4 km) Sandman, Denny's.

PG 356.9 (574.4 km) **PR 90.8** (146.1 km) Shell gas/diesel station, Boston Pizza.

PG 357 (574.5 km) **PR 90.7** (146 km) Stoplight at Kenney Street. End 4-lane highway, begin 2-lane highway, westbound.

PG 357.2 (574.8 km) **PR 90.5** (145.6 km) Canadian Tire to north (2 entrances).

PG 357.5 (575.3 km) **PR 90.2** (145.2 km) **Junction** with Nisga'a Highway (BC Highway 113) which leads north for a nice **side trip** to 4 Nisga'a villages: **Gitlaxt'aamiks**, formerly New Aiyansh, a 60-mile/97-km drive; **Gitwinksihlkw**, formerly Canyon City, 64 miles/103 km; **Laxgalts'ap**, formerly Greenville, at Mile 86.2; and **Ginglox**, formerly Kincolith, at Mile 167.9.

> **Junction** with Nisga'a Highway (BC Highway 113) to north. See "Nisga'a Highway" sidebar on this page.

PG 358.4 (576.8 km) **PR 89.3** (143.7 km) Lodging (some with restaurants and with RV parks along highway here), includes (from east to west) Mumford's Lodging, Wild Duck Motel, Reel Inn, Rainbow Inn and Kalum Motel.

PG 359 (577.7 km) **PR 88.7** (142.7 km) Entrance to Fishermen's Memorial Park and Boat Launch to south on Kalum River; parking for cars and boat trailers, outhouses, picnic table.

PG 359.1 (578.1 km) **PR 88.6** (142.4 km) Kalum River bridge.

PG 359.2 (578.1 km) **PR 88.5** (142.4 km) Kitsumkalum Tempo gas/diesel station, convenience store and car wash to north. *(NOTE: Last gas westbound until Prince Rupert.)* Kitsumkalum RV Park & Boat Launch to south; gravel lot, picnic tables, outhouse, firepits, camping fee $10.

PG 359.7 (578.7 km) **PR 88** (141.6 km) Wide shoulder parking south side of highway.

PG 360 (579.3 km) **PR 87.7** (141.1 km) Small paved turnout to south.

PG 360.2 (579.7 km) **PR 87.5** (140.8 km) Small double-ended turnout to south with litter bin and picnic tables. Good view of river.

PG 362.6 (583.4 km) **PR 85.1** (136.1 km) Zymacord River bridge.

PG 363.1 (584.1 km) **PR 84.6** (135.4 km) Begin 2.1-km/1.3-mile passing lane westbound.

PG 363.3 (584.4 km) **PR 84.4** (135.1 km) Yellow Cedar Lodge to south.

PG 363.6 (584.9 km) **PR 84.1** (134.6 km) Pioneer Fishing Lodge to north.

PG 365.7 (588.4 km) **PR 82** (132.1 km) Paved parking to south.

PG 370.9 (596.8 km) **PR 76.8** (122.7 km) Shames River, small gravel parking area to east.

PG 371.1 (597.1 km) **PR 76.6** (123.4 km)

Shames Mountain Ski Area 13 km/8 miles north via good gravel road; summer hiking blueberry picking in August.

PG 374.1 (601.8 km) **PR 73.6** (118.7 km) Distance marker eastbound shows Terrace 29 km/18 miles, Kitimat 90 km/56 miles, Prince George 603 miles/375 miles.

PG 375.6 (604.2 km) **PR 72.1** (116.3 km) Esker railroad overhead.

PG 376.9 (606.6 km) **PR 70.8** (114 km) Exstew rest area to south adjacent river; double-ended turnout with picnic tables, toilets.

PG 377.1 (606.9 km) **PR 70.6** (113.6 km) Avalanche gates.

PG 378 (608.1 km) **PR 69.7** (112.4 km) Exstew River highway and railroad bridges.

PG 382 (614.8 km) **PR 65.7** (105.7 km) Boat launch to south.

PG 382.7 (615.8 km) **PR 65** (104.7 km) *CAUTION: Slow for 40 kmph/25 mph curve as highway turns sharply across railroad tracks. Prepare to stop when lights flash.*

PG 384.1 (618 km) **PR 63.6** (102.5 km) Road narrows at "Carwash Rock."

PG 389.3 (626.5 km) **PR 58.4** (94 km) **Exchamsiks River** Provincial Park picnic area to north; 2 day-use areas with 20 picnic sites, hiking trails and pit toilets among old-growth Sitka spruce. Open year-round and very popular with fishermen. Good salmon fishing in Exchamsiks River. Boat launch. No overnighting here.

PG 389.5 (626.8 km) **PR 58.2** (93.7 km) Exchamsiks River bridge.

PG 389.8 (627.3 km) **PR 57.9** (93.2 km) Turnoff to north for boat launch on Exchamsiks River; toilets, tables, litter bin.

PG 392.3 (631.1 km) **PR 55.4** (89.4 km) Kasiks Wilderness Resort to north; lodging and camping.

PG 394.3 (634.5 km) **PR 53.4** (85.9 km) Kasiks railway overhead.

PG 394.7 (636.2 km) **PR 53** (85.3 km) Kasiks River bridge.

PG 398.2 (640.8 km) **PR 49.5** (79.5 km) Small paved turnout to south. Short, steep, rocky access to gravel bars of Skeena River; high clearance, 4WD vehicle only, drive at your own risk!

PG 399.7 (643.2 km) **PR 48** (77.4 km) Snowbound Creek. Gravel turnout to south at west end of bridge.

PG 401.4 (646 km) **PR 46.3** (74.7 km) Informal parking to south at west end of Kwinsta East Creek.

PG 404.6 (651.1 km) **PR 43.1** (69.4 km) Kwinsta River.

PG 409.1 (658.3 km) **PR 38.6** (62.2 km) Telegraph Point rest area to south on bank of Skeena River; small paved, double-ended turnout with outhouses, picnic tables, litter bins. Watch for seals and sea lions in spring and during salmon season.

PG 413.2 (664.9 km) **PR 34.5** (55.6 km) Paved turnout to south overlooking the Skeena River.

PG 415.4 (668.5 km) **PR 32.3** (52 km) Basalt Creek rest area to south just west of Basalt Creek bridge; picnic tables, toilet, litter bins, recycle, and good view of Skeena River. *Limited turnaround space for large RVs.*

PG 416.2 (669.6 km) **PR 31.5** (50.9 km) Khyex River bridge.

PG 418.7 (673.6 km) **PR 29** (46.9 km) Distance marker eastbound shows Terrace 100 km/62 miles, Kitimat 160 km/99 miles, Prince George 637 km/396.

PG 420.1 (675.8 km) **PR 27.6** (44.7 km) Boat launch parking to south on Skeena River.

PG 422.5 (680 km) **PR 25.2** (39.8 km) Watch for pictograph, visible from the road for eastbound traffic only. It was rediscovered in the early 1950s by Dan Lippett of Prince Rupert. Look below 3 powerline poles at railway grade level; small white sign on rock face. There is no turnout here.

PG 423 (680.5 km) **PR 24.7** (40 km) Small double-ended viewpoint of Skeena River to south with limited entrance space; picnic tables, litter bins, historical plaque about the Skeena River:

"'K-Shian' The Skeena, 'river of mists', makes a major cleft through the Coast Mountains. To Coastal Tsimshian Indians and Interior tribes it was vital to trade and travel. In later years, Port Essington, near the river's mouth, became the main port on this swift, treacherous waterway—a route serving pioneers from the 1860s to 1914 when the railway was built."

Highway leaves Skeena River westbound. Beautiful views of Skeena River eastbound.

PG 424.4 (682.8 km) **PR 23.3** (37.7 km) Large double-ended turnout with litter bin to north adjacent Green River Forest Road. Chain-up area in winter.

PG 424.6 (683 km) **PR 23.1** (37.5 km) McNeil River.

PG 424.9 (683.3 km) **PR 22.8** (37.2 km) Begin 1.3-km/0.8-mile passing lane westbound.

PG 427.6 (688 km) **PR 20.1** (32.5 km) Large turnout at top of **Rainbow Summit**, elev. 161m/528 feet.

PG 429.3 (690.7 km) **PR 18.4** (29.8 km) Large paved turnout to north.

PG 429.7 (691.5 km) **PR 18** (29 km) Viewpoint to south; gravel parking area.

PG 430 (692 km) **PR 17.7** (28.5 km) Boat launch (sign). Avalanche gates.

PG 431.9 (695 km) **PR 15.8** (25.5 km) Begin 0.8-km/0.5 mile passing lane eastbound.

PG 432.5 (696 km) **PR 15.2** (24.5 km) Turnoff for **Prudhomme Lake Provincial Park**; 24 small- to medium-sized campsites, (10 sites may be reserved, go to website: www.discovercamping.ca), potable water, pit toilets, fishing; camping fee $20. Open mid-May to mid-September. Kayak and/or canoe rentals are available in season. Gravel access road from highway to lake to north just east of park entrance.

PG 432.9 (696.5 km) **PR 14.8** (24 km) Paved turnout to north with litter bin.

PG 433.2 (697 km) **PR 14.5** (23.5 km) Diana Creek crossing.

PG 433.4 (697.3 km) **PR 14.3** (23.2 km) Turnoff for **Diana Lake Provincial Park Picnic Area**, 2.4 km/1.5 miles south via single-lane gravel road (use turnouts). Day use only facility, open mid-May to mid-September. Grassy picnic area on lakeshore with picnic tables, kitchen shelter, grills, wheelchair access, pit toilets, garbage cans and hiking trails. Plenty of parking. The only freshwater swimming beach in the Prince Rupert area. Fish viewing in August and September at Diana Creek on the way in to the lake. Fishing for all species of salmon and Dolly Varden.

PG 438.1 (705 km) **PR 9.6** (15.5 km) Turnout with litter bin to south. Distance marker eastbound shows Terrace 132 km/82 miles, Kitimat 194 km/121 miles, Prince George 703 km/437 miles.

PG 438.2 (705.2 km) **PR 9.5** (15.3 km) **Junction.** Turnoff to south for **North Pacific Historic Fishing Village and Museum** (6.3

miles). The historic North Pacific Cannery at **PORT EDWARD**, built in 1889, is the oldest cannery village on the north coast.

©Judy Nadon, staff

It is a 6.3-mile drive from the main highway to the cannery via a paved road that narrows to no shoulders; surface has many frost heaves, best taken slowly. *NOTE: There is a sharp downhill turn into the parking lot.* Join a guided tour or explore on your own. Admission charged. Open May through September, guided tours at 11 A.M., 1 P.M. and 3 P.M. Cafe hours are from 11 A.M. to 3 P.M. Get updates to information by phone 250-628-3538 or at www.northpacificcannery.ca.

PG 438.3 (705.3 km) **PR 9.4** (15.2 km) Galloway Rapids bridge.

PG 438.6 (705.8 km) **PR 9.1** (14.7 km) Viewpoint to south with parking, litter bin, picnic tables.

PG 440.4 (708.5 km) **PR 7.3** (12 km) Oliver Lake rest area to south adjacent highway; picnic tables, litter bins, grills. Oliver Lake Dwarf Forest Nature Walk.

PG 442.1 (711.5 km) **PR 5.6** (9 km) Welcome to Prince Rupert (westbound sign). Westbound turnoff for Butze Rapids viewpoint (1.9 km/1.2 miles) and trail. The current flowing over these rapids changes direction with the tide. The phenomenon is called a reversing tidal rapid, and the effect is most dramatic an hour after low tide. Easy, fairly level hiking on well-maintained, chip-covered interpretive trail (used as a loop it is 5.4 km/3.3 miles and takes about 1.5 hours).

PG 442.5 (712 km) **PR 5.2** (8.6 km) Distance marker eastbound shows Port Edward 11 km/7 miles, Terrace 139 km/86 miles, Stewart 710 km/441 miles.

PG 442.7 (712.4 km) **PR 5** (8.1 km) Turnoff for Prince Rupert industrial park. Petro-Canada gas/diesel station with propane, convenience store and sani-dump ($3).

PG 445.2 (716.1 km) **PR 2.5** (4.4 km) Stop sign on McBride at 5th Avenue.

PG 445.5 (717 km) **PR 2.2** (3.5 km) Stoplight on McBride and 3rd Avenue. Turnoff to right for Cow Bay and Visitor Center.

PG 445.6 (717.1 km) **PR 2.1** (3.4 km) Westbound travelers turn onto 2nd Avenue from McBride and continue straight 2.1 miles/3.4 km for ferry terminal.

Eastbound travelers turn onto McBride from 2nd Avenue for continuation of Yellowhead Highway 16E. Safeway supermarket (with Starbucks), gas/diesel stations, shopping and other services are located on 2nd Avenue West in downtown Prince Rupert.

PG 447 (719.4 km) **PR 0.7** (1.1 km) Entrance to Prince Rupert RV Campground on right westbound, on left eastbound.

PG 447.6 (720.3 km) **PR 0.1** (0.2 km) Welcome to Prince Rupert (eastbound sign).

PG 447.7 (720.5 km) **PR 0** Ferry terminal for BC Ferries and Alaska state ferries. Airport ferry terminal. End of Highway 16 on mainland; Highway 16 continues on Graham Island in Haida Gwaii (formerly the Queen Charlotte Islands), west of Prince Rupert.

Eastbound: The log shows distance from Prince George (PG) followed by distance from Edmonton (E). Read log: ⬆

Eastbound Travelers NOTE: British Columbia requires passenger vehicles have winter tires and that commercial vehicles carry chains from Oct. 1 to March 31 east to Terrace and from Oct. 1 to April 30 beyond Terrace. This regulation is enforced; non-compliance may result in fines or you can be turned back.

Prince Rupert

PG 447.7 (720.5 km) PR 0 Located on Kaien Island near the mouth of the Skeena River, 90 miles/145 km by air or water (6-hour ferry ride) south of Ketchikan, AK. **Population:** 13,392; area 21,000. **Emergency Services:** Dial 911. **RCMP,** 250-624-2136; **Hospital:** Prince Rupert Regional, 250-624-2171.

Visitor Information: Prince Rupert Visitor Information Center located at 200-215 Cow Bay Rd.; open daily in summer. Phone toll-free 1-800-667-1994 or 250-624-5637; website: visitprincerupert.com.

Elevation: Sea level. **Climate:** Temperate with mild winters. Annual precipitation 95.4 inches. **Radio:** CHTK 99.1 FM, CBC 860 AM; CJFW 101.9 FM, CFNR 98.1 FM. **Television:** 64 channels, cable. **Newspaper:** *The Northern View* (published weekly).

Prince Rupert, "Gateway to Alaska," was surveyed prior to 1905 by the Grand Trunk Pacific Railway (later Canadian National Railways) as the terminus for Canada's second transcontinental railroad.

Twelve thousand miles/19,300 km of survey lines were studied before a final route along the Skeena River was chosen. Some 833 miles/1,340 km had to be blasted from solid rock, 50 men drowned and costs rose to $105,000 a mile (the final cost of $300 million was comparable to Panama Canal construction) before the last spike was driven near Fraser Lake on April 7, 1914. Financial problems continued to plague the company, forcing it to amalgamate to become part of the Canadian National Railways system in 1923.

Charles M. Hays, president of the company, was an enthusiastic promoter of the new terminus, which was named by competition from 12,000 entries. While "Port Rupert" had been submitted by two contestants, "Prince Rupert" (from Miss Eleanor M. Macdonald of Winnipeg) called to mind the dashing soldier–explorer, cousin to Charles II of England and first governor of the Hudson's Bay Co., who had traded on the coast rivers for years. Three first prizes of $250 were awarded and Prince Rupert was officially named in 1906.

Prince Rupert's proposed port and adjacent waters were surveyed by G. Blanchard Dodge of the hydrographic branch of the Marine Dept. in 1906, and in May the little steamer Constance carried settlers from the village of Metlakatla to clear the first ground on Kaien Island. Its post office opened November 23,

1906, and Prince Rupert, with a tent-town population of 200, began an association with communities on the Queen Charlotte Islands, with Stewart, and with Hazelton, 200 miles/322 km up the Skeena River.

Incorporated as a city March 10, 1910, Prince Rupert attracted settlers responding to the enthusiasm of Hays, with his dreams of a population of 50,000 and world markets supplied by his railroad. Both the city and the railway suffered a great loss when Charles M. Hays went down with the Titanic in April 1912. Even so, work went ahead on the Grand Trunk Pacific. Two years later the first train arrived at Prince Rupert, linking the western port with the rest of Canada. Since then, the city has progressed through 2 world wars, economic ups and downs and periods of growth and expansion, not only as a busy port but also as a visitor center.

During WWII, more than a million tons of freight and 73,000 people, both military and civilian, passed through Prince Rupert on their way to military operations in Alaska and the South Pacific.

In 1951, construction of wood processing facilities on Watson Island increased the economic and industrial potential of the area. The facilities, which included a pulp mill and kraft mill, operated until 2001.

With the start of the Alaska State Ferry System in 1963, and the British Columbia Ferry System in 1966, Prince Rupert's place as an important visitor center and terminal point for highway, rail and marine transportation was assured.

Prince Rupert is the second major deep-sea port on Canada's west coast, exporting grain, lumber and other resources to Europe and Asia. Prince Rupert has also become a major coal and grain port with facilities on Ridley Island. Other industries include fishing and fish processing, and the manufacture of forest products.

Lodging & Services

More than a dozen hotels and motels accommodate the influx of ferry passengers each summer. Many restaurants feature fresh local seafood in season.

Walmart, local shops and shopping centers are available. Government liquor store is at the corner of 2nd Avenue and Highway 16. There are 5 main banks and a laundromat. Tim Hortons (open 4 A.M. to 1 A.M.), McDonald's and Subway located here as well as several local cafes and coffee shops in the Cow Bay area. The Safeway on Second Avenue has a Starbucks (open 7 A.M. to 10 P.M.).

The Jim Ciccone Civic Center, located at 1000 McBride St., has squash, basketball and badminton; ice skating and rollerskating rinks (summer only); phone 250-624-9000 for more information and hours. Earl Mah Aquatic Center next door has an indoor swimming pool, tot pool, weight room, saunas, showers, whirlpool, slides and diving boards. Access for persons with disabilities. Phone 250-624-9000 for operating hours and more information. Admission charged.

The golf course includes 18-hole course, resident pro, equipment rental, clubhouse and restaurant. Entrance on 9th Avenue West.

Camping

Prince Rupert RV Campground on Highway 16, between downtown and the ferry terminal, has 77 campsites with full hookups, unserviced tent sites, restrooms, hot showers, WiFi and laundry; phone 250-627-

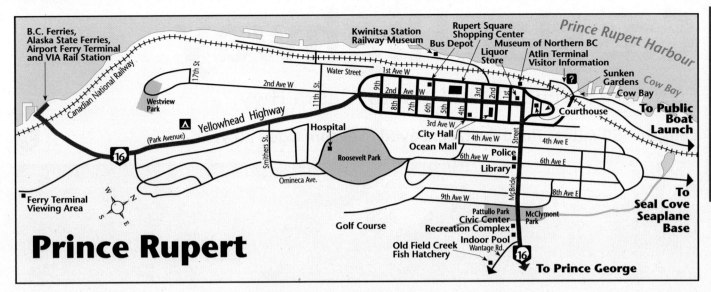

Prince Rupert

1000. Campground host opens for late arrivals on the BC Ferries run from Port Hardy.

There are 24 campsites at Prudhomme Lake Provincial Park (10 sites may be reserved, go to www.discovercamping.ca), at **Milepost PG 432.5** Yellowhead Highway 16, located 15.2 miles/24.5 km east from the ferry terminal. Open mid-May to mid-September. Camping fee $20.

Transportation

Air: North Pacific Seaplanes and Inland Air Charter to outlying villages and Queen Charlotte Islands; Air Canada and Hawkair offer daily service to Vancouver.

Prince Rupert airport is located on Digby Island. A city-operated ferry/bus shuttle is provided for passengers with airline tickets. The airport shuttle leaves from the Highliner Plaza Hotel and Conference Center. Check website for shuttle times: website: ypr.ca/travellers/commercial-airlines/. If you are not flying commercially, look under tab "Private Aircraft & Charters."

There is a seaplane base at Seal Cove with airline and helicopter charter services.

Ferries: British Columbia Ferry System (BC Ferries), terminal phone 1-888-223-8778, provides vehicle and passenger service from Prince Rupert to Port Hardy, and between Prince Rupert and Skidegate in the Queen Charlotte Islands.

Alaska State Ferry phone 907-465-3941 or 1-800-642-0066, provides year-round vehicle and passenger service to southeastern Alaska. NOTE: Allow extra time to clear U.S. or Canadian Customs when arriving or departing by ferry.

Car Rentals: National Car Rental, phone 250-624-5318.

Taxi: Skeena Taxi, phone 250-624-2185. Prince Rupert taxi cabs are powered by LNG (liquefied natural gas).

Railroad: VIA Rail service to Prince George and Jasper. VIA Rail station is located at the BC Ferries terminal. (Ticket sales available on board train, online or over the phone, but not at this terminal.) Phone from Canada or the U.S. 1-888-842-7245; or www.viarail.ca.

Bus: BC Transit, phone 250-624-3343; website: bctransit.com/prince-rupert. First Canada ULC busline, phone 250-624-6400. Charter sightseeing tours available.

RV Storage: Secured, covered storage at Queensway Mini Storage in Terrace; phone 250-638-0204.

Attractions

Totem Pole Tour. Scattered throughout the city are 18 large cedar totem poles, each with its own story. Most are reproductions by Native craftsmen of the original Tsimshian (SHIM-shian) poles from the mainland and the Haida (HI-duh) carvings from the Queen Charlotte Islands. The originals are now in the British Columbia Provincial Museum in Victoria. Several totem poles may be seen at Totem Park near the hospital.

City Parks. Mariner's Park, overlooking the harbor, has memorials to those who have been lost at sea. Roosevelt Park honors Prince Rupert's wartime history. Service Park overlooks downtown Prince Rupert. Sunken Gardens, located behind the Provincial Courthouse, is a public garden planted in the excavations for an earlier court building. City maps are available at the Visitor Center, located at 200–215 Cow Bay Rd.

©Judy Nadon, staff

Cow Bay. Located along the waterfront northeast of downtown, this revitalized area boasts the Visitor Center, numerous boutiques, seafood restaurants, cafes, a popular pub and a bed-and-breakfast. The ambience is historic (antique phone booths, old-fashioned lamp posts), but the theme is bovine, with businesses and buildings bearing cow names or cow colors (the black and white Holstein pattern is popular).

Kwinitsa Station Railway Museum. Built in 1911, Kwinitsa Station is one of the few surviving stations of the nearly 400 built along the Grand Trunk Pacific Railway line. In 1985 the station was moved to the Prince Rupert waterfront park. Restored rooms, exhibits and videos tell the story of early Prince Rupert and the role the railroad played in the city's development. June–August 9 A.M. to noon, and 1–5 P.M. daily. Admission charged. Phone for additional information 250-624-3207.

Prince Rupert Fire Museum. This small museum is located at the fire hall on 1st Avenue, just south of the Museum of Northern British Columbia. The museum houses a rebuilt 1925 R.E.O. Speedwagon fire engine. Phone 250-624-2211.

The Museum of Northern British Columbia, is situated in an award-winning Chatham Village Longhouse, displays an outstanding collection of artifacts depicting the settlement history of British Columbia's north coast. Traveling art collections are displayed in the gallery. Located at 1st Avenue and McBride Street. Hours are 9 A.M. to 5 P.M. daily June–September and 9 A.M. to 5 P.M. Tuesday–Saturday, October–May. Phone 250-624-3207. Admission charged; website: museumofnorthernbc.com. A postal collection depository is located out front.

Special Events. Seafest is a 3-day celebration, June 7–June 9, which includes a parade, games, music and memorial service. June 21 is National Aboriginal Day and July 1 is Canada Day. The All Native Basketball Tournament, held in February, is the largest event of its kind in Canada.

North Pacific Cannery National Historic Site at Port Edward is located east of Prince Rupert on the Yellowhead Highway (turnoff at **Milepost PG 438.2**), then 6.3-mile drive south via paved road. Built in 1889, North Pacific Cannery is the oldest and most intact salmon cannery remaining on the West Coast of North America. Open May through September; www.northpacificcannery.ca.

Visit Haida Gwaii (formerly the Queen Charlotte Islands). BC Ferry service is available between Prince Rupert and Skidegate on Graham Island, largest of the 150 islands and islets that form the Haida Gwaii. More information at www.gohaidagwaii.ca.

Go Fishing. For information on bait, locations, regulations and licensing, contact local sporting goods stores or the Visitor Center. This area abounds in all species of salmon, steelhead, crab and shrimp. Public boat launch facility is located at Rushbrook Public Floats at the north end of the waterfront. There is a parking fee. Public floats are also available at Fairview, past the Alaska State Ferry terminal, near the breakwater.

The Cassiar Highway offers a side trip to Stewart, BC, and Hyder, AK, via Highway 37A. Attractions include Salmon Glacier, seen here. (©Judy Nadon, staff)

Distance in miles	Alaska Hwy.	Dease Lake	Iskut	Jade City	Stewart/Hyder	Yellowhead Hwy.	Watson Lake
Alaska Hwy.		146	198	75	393	450	13
Dease Lake	146		52	71	247	304	159
Iskut	198	52		123	195	252	211
Jade City	75	71	123		318	375	88
Stewart/Hyder	393	247	195	318		139	406
Yellowhead Hwy.	450	304	252	375	139		463
Watson Lake	13	159	211	88	406	463	

and service stops, outstanding scenery and good wildlife viewing. Watch for black bears with cubs along the highway (especially in spring); caribou at Gnat Pass (spring and fall); and Stone sheep south of Good Hope Lake.

The Cassiar Highway junctions with Yellowhead Highway 16 at the Skeena River bridge (see **Milepost PG 298** in the YELLOWHEAD HIGHWAY 16 section) and travels north to junction with the Alaska Highway 13.3 miles/21.4 km west of Watson Lake, YT (see **Milepost DC 626.2** in the ALASKA HIGHWAY section). The Cassiar route offers a savings of about 130 miles/210 km over the all-Alaska Highway route.

The Cassiar provides access to Stewart, BC, and Hyder, AK, via 40-mile-/64-km-long Highway 37A from Meziadin Junction at **Milepost J 97**; and to Telegraph Creek, via a 71-mile/113-km side road from Dease Lake junction at **Milepost J 303.9**. See detailed road logs and community descriptions this section.

The Cassiar Highway is generally narrower than most 2-lane highways, with little or no shoulder. It has easy curves and some long straight stretches. *Drive with your headlights on at all times.* Although not particularly hilly, there are a few 8 percent grades and two switchback-style turns. There are no centerlines or shoulder line markings on the

Major Attractions:

©Kris Valencia, staff

Hyder, AK/Stewart, BC, Salmon and Bear Glaciers, Grand Canyon of the Stikine/ Telegraph Creek Road

Highest Summit: Gnat Pass 4,072 ft.

The Cassiar Highway (BC Highway 37), completed in 1972, is an all-season road that connects the Yellowhead Highway in British Columbia with the Alaska Highway in Yukon, and also provides access to the communities of Stewart, BC, and Hyder, AK, via Highway 37A.

The 450-mile-/724-km-long Cassiar Highway is a scenic route with sufficient fuel

Cassiar Highway

Yellowhead Highway Junction to Alaska Highway Junction
(includes Stewart-Hyder Access Rd. and Telegraph Creek Rd.)

© 2019 The MILEPOST®

Map Location

Key to mileage boxes
miles/kilometers
miles/kilometers
from:
J- Yellowhead Hwy. Jct.
AH- Alaska Highway Jct.
M- Meziadin Junction
D- Dease Lake Junction
PG- Prince George
PR- Prince Rupert
WL- Watson Lake
T- Teslin

To Teslin
(see ALASKA HIGHWAY section, page 149)

To Ross River
(see CAMPBELL HIGHWAY section)

Watson Cr.

N60°07' W128°48'

Watson Lake

YUKON
BRITISH COLUMBIA

To Fort Nelson
(see ALASKA HIGHWAY section, page 149)

Liard River

Albert Cr.
Cormier Cr.
Blue River
French Cr.
Dease River

AH-0
J-450/724km
WL-13/21km
T-150/241km

Baking Powder Creek

Boya Lake

AH-75/121km
J-375/602km

Centreville
Cassiar
Good Hope Lake
Good Hope Lake

J-369.6/594km Vines & Puppies Hideaway L

Jade City

Vines L.

Cotton Lake

Cottonwood R.
Pine Tree Lake
Joe Irwin Lake

CASSIAR

Beady Creek

Dease Lake

AH-146/235km
D-0
J-304/489km

J-310/498.2km Waters Edge Campground C

Tasto Creek

J-303.9/488.5km Arctic Divide Lodge L
Northway Motor Inn LM
The Shack M

Dease Lake
N56°06' W129°18'

J-298.1/479.2km Dease Lake Tanzilla Campground C

Tanzilla River
Tahltan R.
Tuya R.
Stikine R.

Gnat Pass Summit
(4,072 ft./1,241m)

J-254.1/408.5km Mountain Shadow RV Park & Campground CDLT

D-69/110km

Telegraph Creek
N57°53' W131°09'

D-69/109.7km Hyland Creek B&B L

Morchuea L.
N57°36' W130°07'

Iskut

AH-198/318km
J-253/406km

Glenora

Kluachon L.
Eddontenajon Lake

J-250.4/402.5km Red Goat Lodge CL

Mount Edziza
9,143 ft./2,787m

Tatogga L.

J-242.7/390.1km Tatogga Lake Resort CdGLM

Kinaskan L.

Spatsizi Wilderness Provincial Park

Natadesleen Lake

Mount Edziza Provincial Park

SKEENA MOUNTAINS

MOUNTAINS

COAST
Glaciated
MOUNTAINS

Stikine River

Area

Thomas Creek
Devil Creek

Bob Quinn L.
Ningunsaw R.

Nass River

AH-295/475km
J-155/249km

Ningunsaw Summit
(1,530 ft./4661m)
Snowbank Creek

J-155/249km
Bell 2 Lodge CdGLMPrT

Iskut River

Bell 2

BRITISH COLUMBIA
ALASKA

Bell 1

Wrangell
N56°05' W132°04'

Bell-Irving R.

AH-353/568km
M-0
J-97/156km

Bowser Lake

N56°06' W129°18'

Mount Bell-Irving
5,148 ft./1,569m

Meziadin Junction

AH-403/648km
J-47/76km

Alaska State Ferry

Premier
Salmon River

M-36.9/59.4km
Bear River RV Park CT

Meziadin L.

Meziadin R.

Prince of Wales Island

Hyder
N55°54' W130°00'

Stewart

M-40/65km

N55°56' W129°59'

Nass Forest Service Road

Nass River
Skeena R.

Alice Arm

Ketchikan

N55°04' W131°06'

Portland Canal
Observatory Inlet
Portland Inlet

Gitlaxt'aamiks

Dragon L.

Gitanyow
N55°05' W128°04'

J-2.5/4km Cassiar RV Park CDT

Hazelton
New Hazelton

South Hazelton

Kitwanga

Kitseguecla

Nisga'a Highway

Lava Lake

Gingolx

Nass R.

Kitsumkalum Lake

AH-450/724km
J-0
PG-298/479km
PR-150/241km

To Prince George
(see YELLOWHEAD HIGHWAY 16 section, page 242)

UNITED STATES
CANADA

West Kalum Forest Service Road

Skeena R.

Terrace

Dixon Entrance

Prince Rupert

Principal Route Logged
Paved   Unpaved

Other Roads Logged

Other Roads   Ferry Routes

Refer to Log for Visitor Facilities

Scale
0   20   Miles
0   20   Kilometers

Key to Advertiser Services
C - Camping
D - Dump Station
d - Diesel
G - Gas (reg., unld.)
I - Ice
L - Lodging
M - Meals
P - Propane
R - Car Repair (major)
r - Car Repair (minor)
S - Store (grocery)
T - Telephone (pay)

The Cassiar offers frequent campgrounds for travelers. This is Cassiar RV Park.
(©Judy Nadon, staff)

northern half of the highway.

The paved or hard surface sealed road surfacing is good from the Yellowhead Highway junction to the Alaska Highway junction. Road improvement projects are under way each summer: Slow down for construction zones.

British Columbia requires that passenger vehicles have winter tires and that commercial vehicles carry chains between Oct.

1–April 30, for safe travel on this highway. This regulation is enforceable and may result in fines or by being turned back from your route, if you are not in compliance. While the highway is generally clear of snow by May, spring travelers may see ice on lakes and snow on the side of the road at higher elevations into June. You can view webcams and check current road and weather conditions by visiting www.drivebc.ca. Watch

for logging and freight trucks on the Cassiar Highway. *Exercise extreme caution when passing or, when being passed, reduce speed and allow trucks adequate clearance.*

Food, gas and lodging are available along the Cassiar Highway, although distances between services average 60 to 100 miles. Gas is available at both ends of the highway and at: Gitanyow, Meziadin Junction, Stewart, Bell 2 Lodge, Tatogga Lake Resort (seasonal), Iskut, Dease Lake and Good Hope Lake (seasonal). Service may be limited on weekend days and most locations don't offer 24-hour self-service. Plan to get fuel during typical business hours so you don't find yourself waiting for the station to open before your early morning departure.

Be sure your vehicle is mechanically sound with good tires and carry a spare. It is a good idea to carry extra fuel in the off-season. Check the highway log for exact distances between services and inquire locally about possible seasonal closures of services. In case of emergency, motorists are advised to flag down trucks to radio for help. *Cell phone service is generally not available on the Cassiar.*

Minor vehicle repair may be available in communities and at highway businesses, but the nearest major repair is in Watson Lake, YT, for northbound travelers, and Terrace, BC, for southbound travelers. Vehicle parts may have to be ordered from Whitehorse, YT, Smithers or Prince George, BC.

Camp at private campgrounds or in the provincial park campgrounds. There are several private campgrounds, provincial parks, and rustic recreation sites. *It is illegal to camp overnight in turnouts and rest areas unless otherwise posted; camping or parking in gravel pits is also illegal.*

Cassiar Highway Log

Northbound: Distance from junction with the Yellowhead Highway (J) is followed by distance from Alaska Highway (AH). Read log: ↓

BC HIGHWAY 37 North

J 0 AH 450.1 (723.7 km) Gas/diesel station on Yellowhead Highway 16.

Junction with the Yellowhead Highway, **Milepost PG 298**. Turn to page 266 in the YELLOWHEAD HIGHWAY section and continue with log to Prince Rupert or read log back to front to continue to Prince George.

J 0.1 (0.2 km) **AH 450** (723.5 km) Bridge across Skeena River from Yellowhead Highway 16 to Cassiar Highway.

J 0.2 (0.3 km) **AH 449.9** (723.4 km) Turn east on Bridge Street to view totem poles of **GITWANGAK** (pop. 430). The Native reserve of Gitwangak was renamed after sharing the name Kitwanga with the adjacent white settlement. Gitwangak has some of the finest authentic totem poles in the area. Also here is St. Paul's Anglican Church (the bell tower standing beside the church houses the original bell from the 1893 bell tower).

J 0.3 (0.5 km) **AH 449.8** (723.2 km) Distance marker northbound shows Stewart 217 km/134 miles, Dease Lake 489 km/303 miles, Alaska Highway junction 724 km/450 miles.

J 1.7 (2.7 km) **AH 448.4** (721.6 km) Begin 0.4-mile/0.6-km passing lane northbound.

Discover British Columbia's
STEWART CASSIAR
TRAVEL THE GREAT NORTHERN CIRCLE TOUR!
HWY 37
STEWARTCASSIARHIGHWAY.COM

This is the only truck lane on the Cassiar Highway.

J 2.5 (4 km) **AH 447.6** (719.7 km) Turnoff to west for **Cassiar RV Park** with RV supplies, public phone and full-service sites May–September.

Cassiar RV Park. See display ad this page.

Kitwanga River Salmon Enumeration floating fence, located near the river's mouth, directs fish through visual boxes, where they can be identified and counted. Good opportunity to watch the life cycle of the Pacific salmon. The Kitwanga River, a tributary of the Skeena River, supports ocean runs of steelhead and all 5 Pacific salmon, with pinks accounting for some 97 percent of the returning stock. Most of the salmon returning to the Kitwanga spawn during the late summer and early fall in the upper sections of the river.

J 2.7 (4.3 km) **AH 447.4** (719.4 km) South end of 1.5-mile/2.4-km Kitwanga Loop; post office about halfway around the loop. This access road leads to **KITWANGA** (included in Gitwangak census), Centennial Park and Gitwangak Battle Hill (description follows).

Kitwanga is at the crossroads of the old upper Skeena "grease trail" trade. The "grease" was eulachon (candlefish) oil, which was a trading staple among tribes of the Coast and Interior. The grease trails are believed to have extended north to the Bering Sea.

A paved turnout with litter barrel and sign on the Kitwanga access road mark Gitwangak Battle Hill National Historic Site, where a wooden fortress and palisade once crowned the large, rounded hill. Seven interpretive panels along the stairway and boardwalk to Battle Hill explain the history of the site. The hill offers great views of the river below and the Seven Sisters peaks to the south. This was the first major western Canadian Native site commemorated by Parks Canada.

J 4.4 (7 km) **AH 445.6** (717.1 km) North end of 1.5-mile/2.4-km loop access road (Kitwanga North Road) to Kitwanga; see description preceding milepost. At 0.7 km from this turnoff is the National Historic Site of Battle Hill.

J 5.5 (9 km) **AH 444.6** (714.7 km) Tea Lake Forest Service Road to east.

The mountain chain of Seven Sisters is visible to southwest (weather permitting) the next few miles northbound.

J 12.6 (20.3 km) **AH 437.5** (703.4 km) Turnout with litter bin to west.

J 13.1 (21 km) **AH 437** (702.7 km) South access to **GITANYOW** (pop. 434), formerly Kitwancool (1.4 miles/2.3 km from highway), is a small First Nations village; gas/diesel bar with convenience store (basic automotive supplies, groceries, snacks, fast-food style hot items). Gitanyow has one of the largest concentrations of standing totem poles in northwestern British Columbia.

J 16.2 (26 km) **AH 433.9** (697.7 km) North access to Gitanyow.

J 18.9 (30.3 km) **AH 431.2** (693.4 km) Bridge over Moonlit Creek.

J 19.1 (30.6 km) **AH 431** (693.1 km) Turnoff to east for Moonlit rest area below highway; tables, toilets, litter barrels.

J 21.2 (34 km) **AH 428.9** (689.7 km) Distance marker northbound shows Meziadin Junction 121 km/75 miles, Stewart 183

Gitwangak Battle Hill, located just off Highway 37 on the Kitwanga Loop, is a national historic site. An interesting stop and a place to stretch your legs. (©Judy Nadon, staff)

km/114 miles, Dease Lake 454 km/282 miles.

J 26.4 (42.4 km) **AH 423.7** (681.3 km) Kitwancool Forest Service Road.

J 28.4 (45.6 km) **AH 421.7** (678.1 km) Entering Nass Wildlife Management Area northbound.

J 39.2 (63 km) **AH 410.9** (660.7 km) **Cranberry River** bridge No. 1. A favorite salmon stream in summer; consult fishing regulations.

J 45.7 (73.4 km) **AH 404.4** (650.3 km) Distance marker northbound shows Meziadin Junction 83 km/52 miles, Stewart 144 km/89 miles, Dease Lake 415 km/258 miles.

J 45.9 (73.7 km) **AH 404.2** (650 km) Distance marker southbound shows Kitwanga 74 km/46 miles, Terrace 167 km/104 miles, Smithers 180 km/112 miles.

J 46.9 (74.7 km) **AH 403.2** (649 km) Turnout to west.

J 47.3 (76 km) **AH 402.8** (647.7 km) **Cranberry Junction**. Highway 37 junctions with Nass Forest Service Road, which leads west 30 miles/48 km to Nass Forest Service Camp and beyond to **GITLAXT'AAMIKS** (formerly New Aiyansh) (pop. 737) and the Nisga'a Highway. Nass Forest Service Road is rough and narrow; not recommended for low-clearance vehicles and not maintained regularly. You may encounter blown-down trees blocking the road.

J 47.6 (76.5 km) **AH 402.5** (647.2 km) Cranberry River bridge No. 2. *CAUTION: Watch for bears.*

J 48.1 (77.3 km) **AH 402** (646.4 km) Mitten Forest Service Road.

J 50.6 (81.3 km) **AH 399.5** (642.4 km) **Bonus Lake Recreation Site** to west is user-maintained with 3 campsites, tables and toilets; and dock for small boats and canoes.

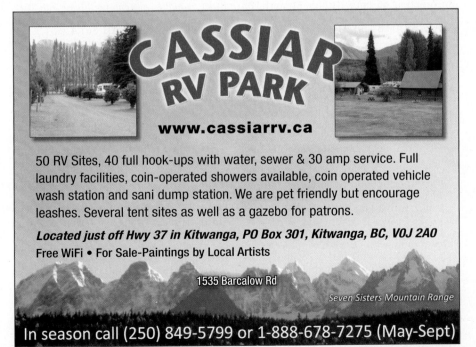

Bear Glacier is a major attraction along Highway 37A to Stewart and Hyder. This turnout offers a great photo op of the glacier. (©Judy Nadon, staff)

J 50.7 (81.4 km) **AH 399.4** (642.3 km) Derrick Creek.

J 51.8 (83.2 km) **AH 398.3** (640.5 km) **Derrick Lake Recreation Site** to the east via 5.7 km/3.5 miles of rough forest service road. User-maintained, no fee, with 4 campsites, tables, toilets; boat launch for canoes, trout fishing.

J 53.5 (86 km) **AH 396.6** (637.7 km) BC Hydro power line crosses and parallels highway. Completed in 1990, this line links Stewart to the BC Hydro power grid. Previously, Stewart's power was generated by diesel fuel. Also in evidence northbound is BC Hydro's Northwest Transmission Line.

J 55 (88.4 km) **AH 395.1** (635.3 km) Entering Kalum Forest District northbound. Watch for signs telling dates of logging activity and observe patterns of regrowth.

J 56.1 (90 km) **AH 394** (633.7 km) Distance marker northbound shows Meziadin Junction 66 km/41 miles, Stewart 127 km/79 miles, Dease Lake 398 km/247 miles.

J 62.8 (100.8 km) **AH 387.3** (622.9 km) Grizzly culvert.

J 64.6 (103.7 km) **AH 385.5** (620 km) Paved turnout to west.

J 66.9 (107.4 km) **AH 383.2** (616.3 km) Brown Bear Creek culvert.

J 68.3 (109.8 km) **AH 381.8** (613.9 km) Brown Bear Forest Service Road leads east 10 km/6 miles to **Jigsaw Lake Recreation Site** with 4 user-maintained campsites with tables and toilets, canoeing, boating and fishing.

Views northbound (weather permitting) of the Coast Mountains to the northwest.

J 68.7 (110.3 km) **AH 381.4** (613.4 km) Van Dyke culvert.

J 70.8 (113.7 km) **AH 379.2** (610 km) Paved turnout with litter bin to west.

J 74 (118.7 km) **AH 376** (605 km) Distance marker northbound shows Meziadin Junction 38 km/24 miles, Stewart 99 km/62 miles, Dease Lake 370 km/230 miles.

J 75.4 (121 km) **AH 374.7** (602.7 km) Kitwaneliks Creek.

J 77.5 (124.5 km) **AH 372.6** (599.2 km) Brown Bear rest area and parking to west

with litter bin and toilets.

CAUTION: Watch for black bears grazing alongside the highway.

Distance marker southbound shows Kitwanga 125 km/78 miles, Terrace 218 km/135 miles, Smithers 231 km/144 miles.

J 79.4 (127.5 km) **AH 370.7** (596.2 km) Paved turnout to west.

J 80.7 (129.7 km) **AH 369.4** (594 km) Wolverine Creek culvert.

J 82.6 (132.7 km) **AH 367.5** (591 km) Moore Creek.

J 85.8 (137.7 km) **AH 364.3** (586 km) Paved turnout to west.

J 86.1 (138.2 km) **AH 364** (585.5 km) Ellsworth culvert.

J 86.7 (139 km) **AH 363.4** (584.7 km) Ellsworth industrial camp to east; no public services. *Watch for speed zones and construction next 2 miles/3.2 km summer of 2019.*

J 88.4 (141.9 km) **AH 361.7** (581.8 km) *Slow for 50 kmph/31 mph curve as highway makes winding descent northbound to Nass River.*

J 88.7 (142.4 km) **AH 361.4** (581.3 km) Paved Nass rest area with picnic tables, toilets, litter bins and information signs to east (open seasonally).

J 88.8 (142.6 km) **AH 361.3** (581.1 km) **Nass River bridge**; *under construction fall of 2018 through fall of 2019. Watch for speed zones and construction workers.* The gorge is almost 400 feet/122m wide; main span of bridge is 187 feet/57m. Bridge decking is 130 feet/40m above the riverbed. Plaque at north end of bridge commemorates bridge opening in 1972 that joined roads to form Highway 37 *(this area will be closed for reconstruction through fall 2019).*

J 94.1 (151.1 km) **AH 356** (572.6 km) Tintina Creek. Along with Hanna Creek, this stream produces 40 percent of the sockeye salmon spawning in the Meziadin Lake watershed.

J 95.2 (153.1 km) **AH 354.8** (570.6 km) Large informal gravel turnout to west.

J 95.5 (153.4 km) **AH 354.6** (570.3 km) Bridge over Hanna Creek South.

J 96.5 (155.3 km) **AH 353.4** (568.4 km) Turnoff for the lovely **Meziadin Lake Provincial Park** downhill to west; 66 campsites

(many on lake), day-use area with picnic tables and shelter, convenience store with public phone, information shelter (water pump adjacent), pit toilets, some wheelchair access, pay phone, WiFi, swimming, firewood, recycling, bear-proof garbage containers, boat launch. Open mid-May to mid-September (weather permitting). Camping fee $22, $27 with power, $90 a week (limited sites), pay campground host. Some sites reservable; www.discovercamping.ca. Lake tours and glacier tours offered here. *CAUTION: Watch for bears. The hills around the lake are prime bear habitat.*

Meziadin Lake (pronounced Mezy-AD-in) has good fishing for rainbow trout, mountain whitefish and Dolly Varden. Best fishing at mouths of small streams draining into the lake. Four species of salmon spawn in the lake. This is 1 of only 3 areas in the province where salmon spawn in the bays and inlets of a lake.

J 97 (156.1 km) **AH 352.9** (567.9 km) **Meziadin Junction: Junction** of Cassiar Highway 37 with Highway 37A (Stewart-Hyder Access Road, a highly recommended **side trip**). Cafe, convenience store, lodging, sani-dump ($15) and gas/diesel station at Meziadin Gasbar. Stop sign for traffic northbound on Highway 37. No stop for southbound traffic on Highway 37. Highway 37A leads west 38 miles/61 km to Stewart, BC, and 41 miles/66 km west to Hyder, AK; food, gas, lodging and camping are available at these communities. Turnout with litter bin and map to north at start of Highway 37A.

This junction can be confusing. Choose your route carefully. Northbound travelers turn right to continue on the Cassiar Highway to Alaska Highway. Southbound travelers turn left to continue on Cassiar Highway to Yellowhead Highway 16.

Junction with BC Highway 37A west to Stewart, BC, and Hyder, AK. See "Stewart, BC–Hyder, AK, Access Road" log beginning on facing page.

Check your fuel (northbound sign): Next gas westbound (by turning onto Highway 37A is in Stewart 65 km/40 miles), or northbound on Highway 37 at Bell 2 Lodge 93 km/58 miles from here.

J 97.7 (156.8 km) **AH 352.4** (566.9 km) Distance marker northbound shows Iskut 260 km/162 miles, Dease Lake 333 km/207 miles, Alaska Highway 569 km/353 miles.

J 102.1 (164 km) **AH 348** (559.7 km) Hanna Creek North, small gravel turnout just north of bridge, *wood-decked bridge, slippery when wet.*

J 105.4 (169.3 km) **AH 344.7** (554.2 km) Large double-ended turnout to west with litter bins. Southbound brake-check area with grade profile.

J 117.1 (182.7 km) **AH 333** (541 km) Slow for downhill curve northbound approaching Bell I Crossing.

J 117.3 (188 km) **AH 332.8** (535.7 km) Bell I Crossing: Bell-Irving River bridge #2. *CAUTION: metal grating.*

J 117.4 (188.1 km) **AH 332.7** (535.6 km) Double-ended paved turnout at north end of bridge to Bell I rest area with picnic tables, toilets, litter bin and information signs.

Highway climbs long curve northbound to Kilometerpost 190.

J 119.4 (191.4 km) **AH 330.7** (532.3 km)
(Continues on page 279)

Stewart–Hyder Access Road (Highway 37A)

This 2-lane paved spur road (good surface with centerline, narrow to no shoulder) junctions with the Cassiar Highway at **Milepost J 97** and leads west 40.4 miles/65 km to Stewart, BC, and on to Hyder, AK. Food, gas/diesel, lodging and camping are available at these 2 communities. There are several excellent dining options.

Highway 37A winds through scenic Bear Creek Canyon into the magnificent Coast Range mountains, snow-topped for much of the summer, with waterfalls cascading down the mountainsides.

Major attractions in the Stewart–Hyder area include Bear Glacier at **Milepost M 15.2**, Fish Creek bear viewing area (located beyond Hyder) and Salmon Glacier beyond that. The road is paved through Hyder all the way to the Fish Creek Observation Site.

HIGHWAY 37A

Distance is measured from Meziadin Lake Junction (M) to the international border (B) at Hyder, AK.
Physical kilometerposts reflect distance from international border.

M 0 B 40.4 (65 km) Junction of Highway 37A with Cassiar Highway (Highway 37) at **Meziadin Junction** (see **Milepost J 97**). Turnout to north with litter bin and signs.

M 1 (3 km) B 39.4 (62 km) Turnout to south.

M 2.7 (4.3 km) B 37.7 (60.6 km) Avalanche gates.

M 3.3 (5.3 km) B 37.1 (59 km) Informal gravel turnout to south.

M 7.6 (12.2 km) B 32.8 (52.8 km) Surprise Creek bridge.

M 8 (12.8 km) B 32.4 (52.1 km) Large turnout to north. Chain up area for Windy Hill.

M 10.1 (16.2 km) B 30.3 (48.8 km) Large gravel turnout to south.

M 10.3 (16.6 km) B 30.1 (48.4 km) Large gravel turnout to north.

M 10.6 (17 km) B 29.8 (48 km) Turnout to south.

M 11.3 (18.2 km) B 29.1 (46.8 km) Windy Point bridge.

M 12 (19.3 km) B 28.4 (45.8 km) Entrance bridge.

M 12.7 (20.4 km) B 27.7 (44.6 km) Cornice Creek bridge.

M 13.3 (21.4 km) B 27.1 (43.6 km) Strohn Creek bridge. Small turnouts to each side of bridge.

M 13.7 (22 km) B 26.7 (43.2 km) Large gravel turnout to north.

M 15.2 (24.5 km) B 25.2 (40.5 km) Multiple turnouts *(CAUTION: No guardrails)* along lake at the terminus of **Bear Glacier**. Morning light is best for photography. At one time the glacier reached this side of the valley. The old highway can be seen hundreds of feet above the present road.

*CAUTION: This is an active slide area (next 2 km/1.2 km). Do not stop along the road, use turnout at **Milepost M 15.9**. Be aware of the edges of turnouts across from the glacier, they may be eroding from the lake.*

M 15.9 (25.6 km) B 24.5 (39.4 km) Large gravel turnout to south with litter bin.

M 18.2 (29.3 km) B 22.2 (35.7 km) Gravel turnout north end of Cullen River bridge.

M 20.5 (33 km) B 19.9 (32 km) Rufus Creek culvert.

M 21.3 (34.2 km) B 19.1 (30.8 km) Argyle Creek culvert. Turnout to south.

M 22.7 (36.5 km) B 17.7 (28.5 km) Entering narrow, scenic, steep-walled Bear River Canyon westbound. River rushes alongside road to the south. Leaving Bear River Canyon eastbound. *Watch for rocks on road.*

M 23.7 (38 km) B 16.8 (26.9 km) Entering Bear Creek Canyon eastbound. Distance marker eastbound shows Meziadin Junction 38 km/24 miles, Kitwanga 195 km/121 miles, Dease Lake 372 km/231 miles.

M 24.3 (39 km) B 16.1 (26 km) Large gravel turnout with litter bin to north and American Creek Trailhead with parking.

M 24.6 (39.6 km) B 15.8 (25.6 km) Bear River bridge #2.

M 28.8 (46.3 km) B 11.6 (19 km) Clements Creek bridge.

M 29.3 (47.2 km) B 11.1 (17.8 km) Large paved turnout with litter bins south side. Avalanche gates.

M 29.7 (47.8 km) B 10.7 (17.2 km) Road to south leads 1 km to **Clements Lake Recreation Site**; 5 sites, tables, pit toilets, small rigs or tenting only, picnicking, canoeing, swimming and a floating dock. Open May–October. No fee, user maintained. ▲

M 29.9 (48 km) B 10.5 (17 km) Bitter Creek bridge.

M 32.2 (51.8 km) B 8.2 (13.2 km) Wards Pass cemetery. The straight stretch of road along here is the former railbed from Stewart.

M 36.4 (58.6 km) B 4 (6.4 km) Avalanche gate for eastbound traffic.
Slow for speed zone through Stewart.

M 36.7 (59.1 km) B 3.7 (6 km) Bear River bridge #1.

Distance marker eastbound shows Meziadin Junction 58 km/36 miles, Kitwanga 212 km/132 miles, Dease Lake 398 km/247 miles.

M 36.9 (59.4 km) B 3.5 (5.6 km) Welcome to Stewart sign westbound; turnout to north. Turn south for **Bear River RV Park**. ▲

Bear River RV Park. See display ad this page.

M 37.7 (60.7 km) B 2.7 (4.4 km) 10th Avenue, **Stewart Mountain Lodge and B&B**

Stewart's colorful main street includes cafes, lodging, grocery/stores and the visitor center.
(©Judy Nadon, staff)

Stewart–Hyder Access Road
(Continued)

House Austria.

Stewart Mountain Lodge and B&B House Austria. See display ad this page.

M 37.9 (61 km) **B 2.5** (4 km) Stop sign. Highway joins main street of Stewart (description follows).

M 38 (61.2 km) **B 2.4** (3.9 km) RCMP, 8th Avenue. Rainy Creek Municipal Campground is 0.4 mile north.

M 38.2 (61.5 km) **B 2.2** (3.5 km) Stop sign for westbound traffic. Highway 37A/Conway Street joins main street (5th Avenue) of Stewart; description follows. Route continues to the right.

Full-service, Petro-Canada gas/diesel station with propane to south.

M 38.5 (61.9 km) **B 1.9** (3.1 km) Stewart Visitor Center, access to estuary via boardwalk nature trail, parking, toilets.

M 38.6 (62.1 km) **B 1.8** (2.9 km) Playground.

M 39.8 (64.1 km) **B 0.6** (1 km) Portland Canal Stewart Yacht Club.

M 39.9 (64.2 km) **B 0.5** (0.8 km) Salty Dog dock.

M 40.4 (65 km) **B 0** (0 km) **U.S.–Canada International Border.** Entering Hyder, AK (description follows). Canadian Customs at Hyder–Stewart Border Crossing is open 8 A.M. to 12 A.M. daily, open to cross at night but must phone in (instructions and phone number at location). There is no U.S. Customs station here. You will need a passport.

NOTE: Stewart and Hyder observe Pacific standard time, although the post office in Hyder, AK, operates on Alaska standard time because it is a federal building.

Stewart BC/Hyder AK

M 40.4 (65 km) **B 0** (0 km) **Stewart** is at the head of Portland Canal on the AK–BC border. **Hyder** is 2.3 miles/3.7 km beyond Stewart. **Population:** Stewart 400; Hyder 100. **Emergency Services:** Dial 911, EMS personnel and Medivac helicopter available. **Stewart Health Center,** phone 250-631-2221 or 250-631-2614; *NOTE: Emergencies that require overnight stays must be sent to/transported to the hospital in Terrace, BC.* **RCMP** detachment in Stewart, phone 250-636-2233.

Visitor Information: Stewart Visitor Center, located in Chamber of Commerce Building on 5th Avenue; phone 250-636-9224, Seasonal operation (approx. mid-May to mid-September). The visitor center is staffed with friendly representatives who can help you plan your time in Stewart/Hyder.

This location is a good resource with a number of helpful brochures on sightseeing and recreational opportunities in the area, including 1 on local hiking trails. District of Stewart: www.districtofstewart.com; phone 250-636-2251

Elevation: Sea level. **Climate:** Maritime, with warm winters and cool rainy summers. Summer temperatures range from 50°F/11°C to 68°F/20°C; winter temperatures range from 25°F/-4°C to 43°F/6°C. Average temperature in January is 27°F/-3°C; in July, 67°F/19°C. Reported record high 89°F/32°C, record low -18°F/-28°C. Slightly less summer rain than other Northwest communities, but heavy snowfall in winter. **Radio:** CBC 1415. **Television:** Cable, 15 channels.

Private Aircraft: Stewart airport, on 5th Avenue; elev. 10 feet/3m; length 3,900 feet/1,189m; asphalt; fuel 80, 100. Also, seaplane dock for aircraft.

Description

Stewart and Hyder are on a spur of the Cassiar Highway, at the head of Portland Canal, a narrow saltwater fjord approximately 90 miles/145 km long. The fjord forms a natural boundary between Alaska and Canada. Stewart has a deep harbor and boasts of being Canada's most northerly ice-free port.

Prior to the influx of the white man, Nass River Indians knew the head of Portland Canal as Skam-A-Kounst, meaning safe place, probably referring to the place as a retreat from conflict with the coastal Haidas. The Nass came here annually to hunt birds and pick berries. Little evidence of their presence remains.

In 1896, Captain D.D. Gaillard (after whom the Gaillard Cut in the Panama Canal was later named) explored Portland Canal for the U.S. Army Corps of Engineers. Two years after Gaillard's visit, the first prospectors and settlers arrived. Among them was D.J. Raine, for whom a creek and mountain in the area were named. The Stewart brothers arrived in 1902 and in 1905 Robert M. Stewart, the first postmaster, named the town Stewart. Hyder was first called Portland City. It was then renamed Hyder, after Canadian mining engineer Frederick B. Hyder, when the U.S. Postal Authority told residents there were already too many cities named Portland.

Gold and silver mining dominated the early economy. Hyder boomed with the discovery of rich silver veins in the upper Salmon River basin in 1917–1918. Hundreds of pilings, which supported structures during this boom period, are visible on the tidal flats at Hyder.

Hyder became an access and supply point for the mines, while Stewart served as the center for Canadian mining activity. Mining continues with Pretium's Brucejack

mine and the IDM's Red Mountain Gold Mine is in final development stages. The economy is driven by forestry, mining and tourism. Several movies and commercials have been filmed in the area. Films include *"Bear Island"* (1978), John Carpenter's *"The Thing"* (1981), *"The Ice Man"* (1982), *"Leaving Normal"* (1991) and *"Insomnia"* (2002).

Lodging & Services

Stewart: Lodging at the Ripley Creek Inn, the **Stewart Mountain Lodge and B&B House Austria** and the King Edward Hotel. Groceries at Harbour Light General Store (free WiFi) and Lucky Dollar Foods/Bobs Mercantile. There are three churches, a Petro-Canada station (gas/diesel, propane), hardware store, post office, BC liquor store, museum, and small shops. Camping at **Bear River RV Park** (beautiful spot by Bear River) and Rainey Creek Municipal Campground in town. Dining at the Bitter Creek Cafe, Silverado Pizza, Temptations Bakery, and at the Rookery/Toaster Museum Cafe (breakfast/lunch only). Fishing and sightseeing charters on Portland Canal available. The area is well known for winter activities such as snowmobiling and heliskiing. Cellular service is available within Stewart town limits.

Ripley Creek Inn is Stewart's top-rated hotel accommodation. Located on the edge of the estuary and surrounded by mountains, the inn is a collection of historic buildings brought together offering a "modern and rustic" theme. Nine buildings with a total of 37 rooms, all with antique furniture, have the modern conveniences of a microwave, fridge, coffee-maker and WiFi. www.ripleycreekinn.com. Phone 250-636-2344. And we're on Facebook. [ADVERTISEMENT]

Hyder: A post office, 2 motels and 2 general stores. Dining at Seafood Express, Glacier Inn and Grandview Inn. Camping at Camp Run-A-Muck RV Park.

Transportation

Private Boats: Public dock and boat launch available. A private dock in Stewart accommodates yachts.

Attractions

Stewart Museum, operated by the Stewart Historical Society is located in the Service BC/Courthouse building 703 Brightwell St. Open 10 A.M. to 4 P.M., May 1 to Sept. 1; remainder of the year by appointment. Glimpse into Stewart's past and present as you wander through the 2 floors of this unique museum: mining room, wildlife exhibit, special collections, archival material, movie room. Take in the featured documentary film on Stewart's early history, *Mountain of Gold.* Gift shop on site. Guided group tours of historic buildings in town may be arranged by contacting the museum. Phone 250-636-2229 or email info@stewartbcmuseum.ca.

Historic Buildings: In Stewart, the former fire hall at 6th and Columbia streets built in 1910; Raineys Cabin at Rainey Creek Park; the Empress Hotel on 4th Street; and

St. Mark's Church (built in 1910) on 9th Street at Columbia. On the border at Eagle Point is the stone storehouse built by Captain D.D. Gaillard of the U.S. Army Corps of Engineers in 1896. This is the oldest masonry building in Alaska. Originally 4 of these buildings were built to hold exploration supplies. This one was subsequently used as a cobbler shop and jail. Storehouses Nos. 3 and 4 are included on the (U.S.) National Register of Historic Places.

Estuary Boardwalk. Stroll down the boardwalk adjacent the visitor center for a spectacular view of Portland Canal. Information boards explain flora and fauna.

Special Events: Canada Day celebrations begin July 1 in Stewart and then on to Hyder on July 4th as these border towns celebrate "International Days." Parades, pancake breakfast, fireworks and special events take place over these 4 days. Bear Arts Festival is held the 2nd weekend in August each year.

Fish Creek Wildlife Observation Area. From the international border, follow paved road through Hyder (keep to right at T junction) and continue on Salmon River Road. The first parking area and pay station is about 4.3 miles/6.9 km from the border. RVs use second parking lot. This U.S. Forest Service day-use recreation area allows visitors to observe brown (grizzly) and black bears as they fish for salmon in the shallow waters of Fish Creek and Marx Creek. Best viewing times for bears are early morning and evenings, from mid-July through early September. Viewing is from a gated boardwalk that overlooks the creek; please observe rules posted at entrance. $5 per person fee (under 16 years of age free).

Salmon Glacier. Continue on Granduc Road past the Fish Creek viewing area for views of Salmon Glacier from viewpoints along the road. Pavement ends and gravel begins just past Fish Creek's second parking lot by Titan Trailhead. Granduc Road, built to connect Stewart with mining interests to the north, offers spectacular views of Salmon Glacier (weather permitting) and surrounding area. Premier Mines viewpoint at Mile 14 (distance measured from international border); Toe of Salmon Glacier viewpoint (Mile 16); Salmon Glacier Summit viewpoint (Mile 21.7). Road continues to Granduc Mine (private property). *CAUTION: Narrow, winding, steep gravel road with potholes and possible road construction. Dusty in dry weather, muddy in wet. Watch for mine traffic. Pick up a brochure at the Stewart Visitor Center.*

AREA FISHING: Portland Canal, salmon to 50 lbs., use herring, spring and late fall; coho to 12 lbs. in fall, fly-fishing. (NOTE: Alaska or British Columbia fishing license required, depending on whether you fish U.S. or Canadian waters in Portland Canal.) Excellent fishing for salmon and Dolly Varden at mouth of **Salmon River.** Up the Salmon River road from Hyder, **Fish Creek** has Dolly Varden 2 to 3 lbs., use salmon eggs and lures, best in summer. Fish Creek is a spawning ground for some of the world's largest chum salmon, mid-summer to fall; it is illegal to harvest chum salmon in fresh water in British Columbia. It is legal to harvest them from both salt and fresh water in Alaska. Check local fishing regulations as they do change from year to year.

Return to Milepost J 97 Cassiar Highway

(Continued from page 276) Spruce Creek bridge.

J 120.8 (193.7 km) **AH 329.3** (530 km) Distance marker northbound shows Dease Lake 294 km/183 miles, Alaska Highway 530 km/329 miles.

J 121.9 (195.3 km) **AH 328.2** (528.4 km) Informal gravel turnout to east.

J 124.8 (200 km) **AH 325.3** (523.7 km) Bell-Irving River to west.

J 126.3 (202.6 km) **AH 323.8** (521.1 km) Cousins Creek culvert. Turnout to east.

J 127.9 (205.2 km) **AH 322.2** (518.5 km) Ritchie Creek bridge. *Wood-decked bridge; slippery when wet.*

J 130.1 (209 km) **AH 320** (514.7 km) Gravel turnout to west.

J 131.7 (211.3 km) **AH 318.4** (512.4 km) Taft Creek bridge. *Wood-decked bridge; slippery when wet.* Gravel turnout to west at north end of bridge.

J 133.4 (214 km) **AH 316.7** (509.7 km) Signed pullout to west is a large gravel turnout with litter bin.

J 134.3 (215.5 km) **AH 315.8** (508.2 km) Signed access to Brucejack Project (no public access), a high-grade gold excavation project in the Valley of the Kings.

J 137 (220 km) **AH 313.1** (503.7 km) Distance marker southbound shows Meziadin Junction 64 km/40 miles, Stewart 126 km/78 miles, Kitwanga 221 km/137 miles.

Large gravel turnout to west.

J 137.3 (220.5 km) **AH 312.8** (503.2 km) Deltaic Creek bridge. Entering Tahltan Territory northbound (sign).

J 138.1 (221.6 km) **AH 312** (502.1 km) Distance marker northbound shows Iskut 197 km/122 miles, Dease Lake 270 km/168 miles, Alaska Highway 506 km/314 miles.

J 142.8 (229.2 km) **AH 307.3** (494.5 km) Glacier Creek.

J 145 (232.7 km) **AH 305.1** (491 km) Skowill Creek bridge.

J 149.5 (239.8 km) **AH 300.6** (483.9 km) Oweegee Creek, with informal double-ended gravel turnout to east at south end.

J 153.6 (246.8 km) **AH 296.5** (476.9 km) Mehan Lake rest area to east. Gravel parking area with information signs, picnic tables, litter bins, toilets, cartop boat launch. Fly fish or troll for small rainbow trout.

J 155 (249 km) **AH 295.1** (474.7 km) **Bell 2 Lodge**; food, gas, lodging, tent and RV

Bell 2 Lodge at Milepost J 155 offers year-round accommodations, dining, and gas. RV sites are available here in summer.
(©Kris Valencia, staff)

camping (description follows).

Bell 2 Lodge. Year-Round: Great food and snacks, comfy accommodation and a gas station make Bell 2 Lodge the ideal stopover to and from the Yukon/Alaska. Log chalets come with ensuite bathrooms and wood burning stoves. Other amenities include showers, laundry, basic satellite Internet and telephone. Open mid-May to mid-September: Serviced and non-serviced big-rig friendly RV sites, plus tenting spots. Reservations: 1-888-499-4354, bell2lodge.com. See display ad on this page. [ADVERTISEMENT]

J 155.2 (249.3 km) **AH 294.9** (474.4 km) **Bell II Crossing.** Bridge crosses Bell-Irving River. *CAUTION: metal grating.*

J 158.3 (254 km) **AH 291.8** (469.7 km) Informal gravel turnout to west on curve by pond; watch for swans. Beautiful mountain views.

Helicopters are a common sight along the Cassiar, used for both tourist activities (these are Bell 2 Lodge helicopters) and for mining and construction. (©Judy Nadon, staff)

J 160.2 (257.2 km) **AH 289.9** (466.5 km) Distance marker southbound shows Meziadin Junction 103 km/64 miles, Stewart 164 km/102 miles, Kitwanga 260 km/162 miles.

J 160.7 (257.9 km) **AH 289.4** (465.8 km) Snowbank Creek bridge.

J 162.9 (261.6 km) **AH 287.2** (462.1 km) Double-ended turnout to Red Flats rest area on east side of highway; picnic tables, toilets and avalanche information signs. Memorial plaque dedicated to highway avalanche technicians killed in a slide here. The avalanche chutes are clearly visible on mountain slopes to the west in summer.

CAUTION: Avalanche area northbound to Ningunsaw Pass; no stopping in winter or spring.

J 163.2 (262.1 km) **AH 286.9** (461.6 km) Redflat Creek.

J 165.7 (266.1 km) **AH 284.4** (457.6 km) Revision Creek.

J 166.7 (267.7 km) **AH 283.4** (456 km) Fan Creek.

J 168.2 (270 km) **AH 281.9** (453.7 km) Beaver Pond Avalanche Area next 2 km/1.2 miles northbound.

J 171.2 (274.8 km) **AH 278.9** (448.9 km) **Ningunsaw Summit** (sign), elev. 466m/1,530 feet. Nass–Stikine water divide. Creeks northbound feed into the Ningunsaw River, which parallels the highway. The Ningunsaw is a tributary of the Stikine watershed.

J 171.3 (274.9 km) **AH 278.8** (448.8 km) Distance marker northbound shows Bob Quinn Lake 27 km/17 miles, Dease Lake 215 km/134 miles, Alaska Highway 451 km/280 miles.

J 171.5 (275.3 km) **AH 278.6** (448.4 km) Beaver Pond Creek bridge.

J 171.8 (275.8 km) **AH 278.3** (447.9 km) Liz Creek.

J 174.3 (280 km) **AH 275.8** (443.7 km) Alger Creek. Highway parallels Ninginsaw River northbound.

Avalanche chutes visible to west next 2 km south.

J 176.3 (283.1 km) **AH 273.8** (440.6 km) Bend Creek (sign).

J 177.2 (284.7 km) **AH 272.9** (439 km) Gamma Creek (sign).

J 178.5 (286.8 km) **AH 271.6** (436.9 km)

Ogilvie Creek.

J 179.4 (288 km) **AH 270.7** (435.7 km) Gravel turnout to west with point-of-interest sign about Yukon Telegraph line:

"Born of the Klondike Gold Rush of 1898, the 1,900-mile Dominion Telegraph Line linked Dawson City with Vancouver via the CPR wires through Ashcroft. Built in 1899–1901, the line blazed a route across the vast northern section of the Province but gave way to radio communications in the 1930s. Today, some of the trail and cabins used by the isolated telegraphers still serve wilderness travellers."

J 179.6 (288.4 km) **AH 270.5** (435.3 km) Echo Lake (signed) to west. Flooded telegraph cabins were once visible in the lake below. Good view of Coast Mountains to west. Spectacular cliffs seen to the east are part of the Skeena Mountains (Bowser Basin).

J 182.4 (292.9 km) **AH 267.7** (430.8 km) Avalanche gates.

J 182.6 (293.5 km) **AH 267.5** (430.2 km) Bob Quinn Forest Service Road. Turnoff to west for Northwest Projects AltaGas.

J 183.2 (294.2 km) **AH 266.9** (429.5 km) **Little Bob Quinn Lake** (sign). Rainbow trout and Dolly Varden, summer and fall. Access to Bob Quinn Lake at **Milepost J 185.1**.

J 184 (295.5 km) **AH 266.1** (428.2 km) Bob Quinn paved rest area with litter bins, picnic tables and toilet next to Bob Quinn Lake airport (sign). This was once a staging site for supplies headed for the Stikine/Iskut goldfields. Today it is often used as a staging area for various highway and resource development projects along the Cassiar Highway.

J 185 (297.1 km) **AH 265.1** (426.6 km) Bob Quinn highway maintenance camp; helicopter base.

Distance marker northbound shows Iskut 109 km/68 miles, Dease Lake 192 km/119 miles, Alaska Highway 428 km/266 miles.

Distance marker southbound shows Meziadin Junction 147 km/91 miles, Stewart 209 km/130 miles, Kitwanga 304 km/189 miles.

J 188.7 (303.2 km) **AH 261.4** (420.5 km) Turnouts with litter bins on both sides of highway.

J 192 (308.5 km) **AH 258.1** (415.2 km)

Devil Creek bridge (metal grating). Large turnout to west at north end of bridge.

J 192.8 (309.8 km) **AH 257.3** (413.9 km) Large paved turnout to west.

J 195.4 (314 km) **AH 254.7** (409.7 km) Thomas Creek.

Highway passes through Iskut burn, where fire destroyed 78,000 acres in 1958. This is also one of British Columbia's largest huckleberry patches.

Northbound, the vegetation begins to change to northern boreal white and black spruce. This zone has cold, long winters and low forest productivity. Look for trembling aspen and lodgepole pine.

Southbound, the vegetation changes to cedar–hemlock forest of the interior zone. Cool wet winters and long dry summers produce a variety of tree species including western hemlock and red cedar, hybrid white spruce and subalpine fir. Vegetation becomes more lush the farther south you drive on the highway.

Report wildfires; phone 1-800-663-5555.

J 198.1 (318.5 km) **AH 252** (405.2 km) Large paved turnout to west.

J 199.2 (320 km) **AH 250.9** (403.7 km) Slate Creek.

J 200.3 (321.8 km) **AH 249.8** (401.9 km) Double-ended gravel turnout to east.

J 201.6 (323.9 km) **AH 248.5** (399.8 km) Durham Creek.

J 205.5 (330 km) **AH 244.6** (393.7 km) South Burrage double-ended turnout to east is brake-check area for northbound traffic. Double-ended turnout to west is chain-off area for southbound traffic. Litter bins.

Distance marker northbound shows Iskut 75 km/47 miles, Dease Lake 158 km/98 miles, Alaska Highway 394 km/245 miles.

J 207 (332.7 km) **AH 243.1** (391 km) Downgrade to 8 percent and winding descent northbound to **Burrage River** bridge. Note picturesque rock pinnacles upstream (to east) in Burrage River. Paved parking spot to west just north of bridge.

Begin 2.6-mile/4.2-km uphill grade to 8 percent northbound. *CAUTION: Narrow, winding road, no shoulders, steep drop-offs.*

J 207.5 (333.4 km) **AH 242.6** (390.3 km) Paved turnout to west with view of Iskut River as the highway winds along the hillside above the river; guardrails.

J 208.8 (335.2 km) **AH 241.3** (388.5 km) Paved turnout to west with view of Iskut River; good photo op (weather permitting).

J 209.8 (336.9 km) **AH 240.3** (386.8 km) Burrage Hill. Southbound brake-check area to west; litter bin, grade profile shows 8 percent grades, next 2.6 miles/4.2 km. Chain removal area for northbound traffic in winter.

J 212.3 (341.1 km) **AH 237.8** (382.6 km) Gravel turnout to west.

J 215 (345.5 km) **AH 235.1** (378.2 km) Eastman Creek rest area to west; picnic tables, toilet, litter bins, and information sign with map. The creek was named for George Eastman (of Eastman Kodak fame), who hunted big game in this area before the highway was built.

J 218 (350.2 km) **AH 232.1** (373.5 km) Rescue Creek bridge. *Narrow 2-lane wood-decked bridge; slippery when wet.*

J 220 (353.5 km) **AH 230.1** (370.2 km) Willow Creek bridge. *Narrow 2-lane wood-decked bridge; slippery when wet.*

J 221 (355.6 km) **AH 229.1** (369 km) Gravel turnout to east.

J 222.4 (357.7 km) **AH 227.7** (366 km) Trailhead with toilet and parking area.

J 224.6 (360.8 km) **AH 225.5** (362.9 km) Unmaintained (soft spots, abrupt edge) double-ended gravel turnout to west.

J 225 (361.8 km) **AH 225.1** (361.9 km) Halfway point on the Cassiar Highway.

J 227.1 (365 km) **AH 223** (358.7 km) Turnoff to west for **Kinaskan Provincial Park**. This park has a campground with 50 sites, open mid-May to mid-September (weather permitting), camping fee ($20/night per site), pit toilets, drinking water, and firewood. Picnic and day-use area with gravel parking for large vehicles, tables and firepits; some handicap-accessible facilities. Swimming, boat launch and rainbow fishing (July and August) on **Kinaskan Lake**. Trailhead for 15-mile/24-km hike to Mowdade Lake in Mount Edziza Provincial Park.

Distance marker southbound shows Meziadin Junction 214 km/133 miles, Stewart 276 km/172 miles, Kitwanga 371 km/231 miles.

J 229 (368.1 km) **AH 221.1** (355.6 km) Distance marker northbound shows Iskut 35 km/22 miles, Dease Lake 118 km/73 miles, Alaska Highway 354 km/220 miles.

J 230.2 (370 km) **AH 219.9** (353.7 km) First of 3 logged turnouts to west, some with views of Kinaskan Lake, the next 2 miles northbound.

J 231.2 (372.1 km) **AH 218.9** (352.3 km) Turnout with litter bin to west.

J 232.1 (373 km) **AH 218** (350.7 km) Turnout with litter bin to west. *CAUTION: Watch for bears.*

J 233.8 (375.8 km) **AH 216.3** (347.9 km) Turnout with litter bin to west.

J 234.4 (376.8 km) **AH 215.7** (346.9 km) Todagin Guest Ranch.

J 235.2 (378.1 km) **AH 214.9** (345.6 km) Gravel turnout to east.

J 235.5 (378.5 km) **AH 214.6** (345.2 km) Todagin River bridge.

J 240.5 (386.4 km) **AH 209.6** (337.3 km) Distance marker northbound shows Iskut 19 km/12 miles, Dease Lake 102 km/63 miles, Alaska Highway 338 km/210 miles.

Distance marker southbound shows Meziadin Junction 232 km/144 miles, Stewart 294 km/183 miles, Kitwanga 389 km/242 miles.

J 242.7 (390.1 km) **AH 207.4** (333.6 km) **Tatogga Lake Resort**; food, wildlife mounts (pictured below), gas/diesel, camping, lodging (open May–October).

©Sharon Nault

Tatogga Lake Resort. See display ad this page.

Driving south you will see frequent Northwest Transmission Line (NTL) service roads. Construction of the 287-kilo-volt transmission line. The line will eventually extend north to Dease Lake, providing power to the mining sector and local communities currently relying on diesel generators. The 344-km/214-mile transmission line extends from the Skeena Substa-

tion near Terrace to Bob Quinn Lake on this highway.

J 244.6 (393.1 km) **AH 205.5** (330.6 km) Highway narrows for 1.25 miles/2 km northbound. No centerline, no shoulders, bumpy road as highway winds along Eddontenajon Lake northbound. Guardrails.

J 246.8 (396.8 km) **AH 203.3** (326.9 km) Rest area to west beside **Eddontenajon Lake** (Ed-don-TEN-ajon); picnic tables, litter bins and toilet. It is unlawful to camp overnight at turnouts. There is also a boat launch for vehicles with high clearance, at the south access to this rest area. Please be careful with refuse and dump only in appropriate and approved locations.

Spatsizi trailhead to east in Spatsizi Plateau Wilderness Park access. Trailhead for Didene Portage (128 km), Eaglenest Trail (49 km), McEwan Trail (28 km). Lake breaks up in late May; freeze-up is early November. Rainbow trout fishing July and August.

J 250.4 (402.5 km) **AH 199.7** (321.1 km) **Red Goat Lodge** with year-round rooms and seasonal lakeside camping.

Red Goat Lodge. See display ad this page.

J 251.9 (404.5 km) **AH 198.2** (319.2 km) Iskut (unincorporated), northbound sign.

Slow for speed zone northbound through Iskut.

J 252.2 (405.3 km) **AH 197.9** (318.4 km) Zetu Creek.

Iskut

J 252.5 (406 km) **AH 197.6** (317.7 km) Kluachon Center Store at Iskut, a small First Nations community on the Cassiar Highway. **Population:** 295. **Emergency Services: Health Clinic:** Phone 250-234-3511. **RCMP:** (detachment is in Dease Lake) Phone 250-771-4111. **Private Aircraft:** Eddontenajon airstrip, 0.6 mile/1 km north of Iskut; elev. 3,100 feet/945m; length 3,000 feet/914m; gravel; fuel available.

Kluachon Center Store on east side of

highway has gas/diesel, a grocery, hardware supplies and houses the post office; open 7 days a week in summer. Camping and cabins at **Mountain Shadow RV Park** (www.mtshadowrvpark.com), which also offers seaplane sightseeing tours to Mount Edziza, Grand Canyon of the Stikine and Spatsizi Plateau; fishing, hiking, wildlife viewing. Camping and cabins just south of town at **Red Goat Lodge** at **Milepost J 250.4**.

Cassiar Highway Log
(continued)

J 253.1 (407 km) **AH 197** (316.7 km) Entering Iskut southbound. *Slow for speed zone southbound.*

Check fuel sign northbound. Next gas 82 km/51 miles (Dease Lake).

Highway climbs northbound. No centerline, no shoulders.

J 254.1 (408.5 km) **AH 196** (315.2 km) **Mountain Shadow RV Park & Campground** 0.5-mile/0.8 km downhill to west.

The Cassiar Highway just north of Iskut. View of Eddontenajon Lake in distance.
(©Judy Nadon, staff)

Sign warns motorcyclists to be cautious crossing metal-decked Stikine River bridge.
(©Sharon Nault)

Cabins are also available. There is a short nature walk to **Kluachon Lake**; excellent fishing and wildlife viewing.

Mountain Shadow RV Park & Campground. See display ad this page.

J 257.6 (414 km) **AH 192.5** (309.7 km) Bear Paw Resort to west.

J 258.4 (415.5 km) **AH 191.7** (308.2 km) Trapper's Gift Shop.

J 260.1 (418.2 km) **AH 190** (305.5 km) Tsaybahe Creek; private homestead.

J 263.1 (423 km) **AH 187** (300.7 km) Double-ended Morchuea Lake rest area to west with toilets, picnic tables, litter bins, map and distance chart.

Panoramic views of Skeena and Cassiar mountains.

From here southbound, the dormant volcano of Mount Edziza (elev. 9,143 feet/2,787m) and its adjunct cinder cone can be seen to the southwest. The park, not accessible by road, is a rugged wilderness with a glacier, cinder cones, craters and lava flows.

J 264.3 (425 km) **AH 185.8** (298.7 km) Turnoff to west for **Morchuea Lake Recreation Site**; 8 campsites with tables, pit toilets and boat launch. Large enough access for large RVs and trailers, overflow area for groups. No fee at this user maintained site.

J 266.5 (428.4 km) **AH 183.6** (295.3 km) Stikine River Provincial Park boundary (northbound sign).

J 267.3 (429.7 km) **AH 182.8** (294 km) South Stikine Hill brake-check area. Double-ended turnout to east for northbound-only trucks; litter bin and grade profile information sign. *Highway descends to Stikine River northbound. Long, winding, downgrades to 8 percent. No centerline, no shoulders. Abrupt dropoffs to 5 feet from road shoulder. Slow for gravel breaks and curves.*

J 270.8 (435.3 km) **AH 179.3** (288.4 km) *CAUTION: Slow for 30-kmph/18-mph hairpin curve (sign).*

J 271.7 (436.8 km) **AH 178.4** (286.9 km) Turnout to east with litter bin.

J 272.1 (437.4 km) **AH 178** (286.3 km) Stikine River bridge (metal grate decking). The Stikine River flows 330 miles northwest then south from British Columbia to the Eastern Passage in Alaska, 2 miles north of Wrangell. Stikine is a Tlingit Indian name meaning "Great River." The Stikine River was first reported in 1799 by Capt. Rowan, of the whaling ship Eliza out of Boston, Mass.

Highway climbs northbound. Watch for livestock and wildlife and avalanche areas. Long, winding upgrades to 8 percent next 4.6 miles/7.4 km southbound.

J 273.9 (440.3 km) **AH 176.2** (283.4 km) Distance marker northbound shows Dease Lake 49 km/30 miles, Alaska Highway 285 km/177 miles, Watson Lake 308 km/191 miles.

J 275.4 (442.6 km) **AH 174.7** (281.1 km) Distance marker southbound shows Meziadin 288 km/179 miles, Stewart 350 km/217 miles, Kitwanga 445 km/277 miles.

J 276 (443.7 km) **AH 174.1** (280 km) Brake check to west for southbound traffic with litter bin and grade profile information sign. Stikine River Provincial Park boundary sign southbound.

CAUTION: Abrupt dropoffs to 5 feet from road shoulder.

Downhill grades to 7 percent next 3.8 miles southbound as highway descends to Stikine River.

J 281.7 (452.7 km) **AH 168.4** (271 km) Large turnout with litter bin to east at Tees Creek.

J 284.7 (457.7 km) **AH 165.4** (266 km) Paved turnout to east.

Long scar across Gnat Pass valley to east was grading preparation for BC Railway's proposed Dease Lake extension from Prince George. Construction was halted in 1977. Grade is visible for several miles northbound.

J 287 (461.4 km) **AH 163.1** (262.3 km) Narrow dirt access road east to **Upper Gnat Lake** with informal camping adjacent lake. Rainbow trout fishing.

J 288.6 (464 km) **AH 161.5** (259.7 km) Turnout to east with litter bin at **Lower Gnat Lake**. Rainbow trout fishing.

J 290.6 (467.1 km) **AH 159.5** (256.4 km) Large turnout with litter bin to east.

J 291.2 (468.2 km) **AH 158.9** (255.5 km) Gravel turnout to west.

J 291.5 (468.5 km) **AH 158.6** (255.2 km) Highest point on the Cassiar, **Gnat Pass Summit**, elev. 1,241m/4,072 feet. Watch for caribou in spring.

J 294.5 (473.4 km) **AH 155.6** (250.3 km) Begin long downgrade to 6 percent northbound as highway descends to the Tanzilla River.

J 298.1 (479.2 km) **AH 152** (244.5 km) **Tanzilla River** bridge. Turnout to east at north end of bridge with picnic tables and outhouses. Entrance to **Dease Lake Lions Tanzilla Campground** at north end of narrow wooden bridge. Best for small rigs. Fishing for Arctic grayling, June and July; use flies.

Dease Lake Lions Tanzilla Campground. 15 natural wooded RV sites plus tenting on Tanzilla River, adjacent to Highway 37. Facilities: Picnic tables, firepits, overnight or day use, no hookups, non-flush toilets. Fees: $10 per night. Bring your own firewood. Voluntary donation for day use.
[ADVERTISEMENT]

J 298.7 (480.2 km) **AH 151.4** (243.5 km) Turnout with litter bin to west on Tanzilla River. Nice picnic spot.

J 299.3 (481.1 km) **AH 150.8** (242.6 km) Dalby Creek.

J 302.7 (486.6 km) **AH 147.4** (237.1 km) Welcome to Dease Lake (sign) northbound; see description at **Milepost J 303.9.**

Slow for speed zone northbound through Dease Lake.

J 303.3 (487.6 km) **AH 146.8** (236.1 km) Dease Lake RV Park.

J 303.6 (488.1 km) **AH 146.5** (235.6 km) Ministry of Transportation & Service BC to east; Northern Lights College campus to west.

J 303.8 (488.4 km) **AH 146.3** (235.3 km) Turnout to east at Arctic Pacific Crossroads sign, marking divide between Pacific and Arctic ocean watersheds.

Arctic Divide Lodge to east and RCMP to west. (**Northway Motor Inn** is next left northbound.)

J 303.9 (488.5 km) **AH 146.2** (235.2 km) Petro-Canada/Super A grocery store at **junction** with Telegraph Creek Road; gas/diesel, full grocery with deli and liquor store. *Weekend hours vary here; get gas during regular business hours to avoid delays.*

NOTE: Next fuel southbound 52 miles/82 km at Iskut. Next reliable fuel northbound 146 miles/235 km at Alaska Highway junction.

Junction with Telegraph Creek Road. See "Telegraph Creek Road" log on page 284.

Dease Lake

J 303.9 (488.5 km) **AH 146.2** (235.2 km) Located at the **junction** of the Cassiar Highway and Telegraph Creek Road. **Population:** 450. **Emergency Services: Stikine Health Center** 250-771-4444; **RCMP** detachment 250-771-4111.

Private Aircraft: Dease Lake airstrip, 1.5 miles/2.4 km south; elev. 2,600 feet/792m; length 6,000 feet/1,829m; asphalt; fuel JP4, 100. No commercial flights available.

Dease Lake has all visitor services including gas/groceries; accommodations at **Northway Motor Inn** and **Arctic Divide Lodge**; dining at the Northway Motor Inn and at **The Shack**. Descriptions follow.

Arctic Divide Lodge. Very popular accommodation! New owners offer "home-away-from-home" atmosphere. Newly-renovated log lodge. Motel/kitchenettes available, pet-friendly. Plug-ins, parking for all size vehicles. Great breakfast included. Fast WiFi. Popular for motorbike travelers. Very clean, extremely friendly, and safe. Come enjoy our wood heated lobby. Open year-round. www.arcticdivide.ca or 250-771-3119. [ADVERTISEMENT]

Northway Motor Inn, rated number 1 place to stay on TripAdvisor. Located a ½ block off Highway 37, which makes for a quiet stay. The Northway is a modern hotel, with many upgrades. The WiFi is the fastest you will find anywhere. The hotel is spectacularly clean and you can be assured of a great night's sleep. New in 2018 is a cozy, dine-in licensed restaurant serving some of the best pizza you will find anywhere. Delicious! Kitchenettes are available and some rooms are pet friendly. This is a popular hotel and it's a good idea to book ahead in the summer months. Toll free 1-866-888-2588. www.northwaymotorinn.com. See display ad this page. [ADVERTISEMENT]

The Shack. We're just a block off the highway on Boulder Street. Enjoy our large selection of fish and seafood, 6 kinds of burgers (including bison, venison, vegetarian), quesadillas and wraps, ice cream, sundaes and shakes. Sit at our picnic tables or take your order with you on the road. Open 11:30 A.M. to 9:30 P.M. daily except Sundays. Open May through October. Call 250-771-3317. [ADVERTISEMENT]

Camping in town at Dease Lake RV. Camping south of town at **Dease Lake**

The community of Dease Lakec offers travelers all services: lodging, dining, camping, gas and groceries. (©Sharon Nault)

Lions Tanzilla Campground, and north of town at **Water's Edge Campground**.

A Hudson's Bay Co. post was established by Robert Campbell here in 1838, but abandoned a year later. The lake was named in 1834 by John McLeod of the Hudson's Bay Co. for Chief Factor Peter Warren Dease. Laketon, across the lake, was a center for boat building during the Cassiar gold rush of 1872–1880. In 1874, William Moore, following an old Indian trail, cut a trail from Telegraph Creek on the Stikine River to the gold rush settlement on Dease Lake. This trail became Telegraph Creek Road, which was used in 1941 to haul supplies for construction of the Alaska Highway and Watson Lake Airport to Dease Lake. The supplies were then ferried down the Dease River.

Today, Dease Lake is a government center and supply point for the district. Northern Lights College (University of Northern British Columbia) has a campus here. It is also a popular point from which to fly-in, hike-in, or pack-in to Mount Edziza and Spatsizi wilderness parks.

Cassiar Highway Log
(continued)

J 303.9 (488.5 km) **AH 146.2** (235.2 km) Petro-Canada/Super A grocery store at **junc-** **tion** with Telegraph Creek Road; gas/diesel, full grocery with deli and liquor store. *Weekend hours vary here; get gas during regular business hours to avoid delays.* Turnoff to west for **side trip** to Telegraph Creek, via spectacular Telegraph Creek Road.

Junction with Telegraph Creek Road. See "Telegraph Creek Road" log on page 284.

NOTE: Next reliable fuel northbound 146 miles/235 km at Alaska Highway junction. Good Hope Lake, 85 miles/137 km, may also supply fuel (seasonally); call ahead if you are counting on this fuel stop: phone 250-239-3000.

Next fuel southbound 52 miles/82 km at
(Continues on page 285)

DEASE LAKE ADVERTISERS

Telegraph Creek Road

The sometimes steep and winding gravel of Telegraph Creek Road is not for everyone or for every rig, but this side trip offers dramatic views of the Grand Canyon of the Stikine River.
(©David L. Ranta, staff)

Built in 1922, Telegraph Creek Road (Highway 51) was the first road into this remote area of northern British Columbia, long the domain of the Tahltan First Nations people. Robert Campbell was the first European in the area in 1838.

Settlement of the region grew with the discovery of gold on the Stikine River in 1861. Efforts to establish a transatlantic telegraph line also brought attention to the Telegraph Creek area in the 1860s. The Cassiar (1873–1876) and Klondike (1897–1898) gold rushes contributed to the growth of both Telegraph Creek and Glenora, 12 miles/20 km downriver, according to writer Rana Nelson.

The scenery along portions of this road is remarkable, with views of the Grand Canyon of the Stikine River and Mount Edziza. Historic Telegraph Creek at road's end has many turn-of-the-century buildings from the gold rush days.

In summer 2018, the Alkali Lake Wildfire caused an evacuation of Telegraph Creek and road closure. Many homes in the Telegraph Creek community were destroyed and reconstruction had begun in fall 2018.

Telegraph Creek Road is a narrow gravel road with several sets of steep switchbacks. Drive carefully and carry a spare tire. This road is not recommended for trailers or large RVs. Check road conditions at the highway maintenance camp or RCMP office in Dease Lake at 250-771-4111, before starting the 70-mile/112.7-km drive to Telegraph Creek. Allow a minimum of 2 hours driving time with good conditions. Gas up in Dease Lake.

BC HIGHWAY 51/TELEGRAPH CREEK ROAD
Distance is shown from Dease Lake junction (D) on the Cassiar Highway.
Kilometerposts show distance from Dease Lake.

D 0 Dease Lake. **Junction** at **Milepost J 303.9** Cassiar Highway; Petro-Canada gas station. *NOTE: Fill your gas tank before leaving Dease Lake!*

D 0.9 (1.4 km) **T junction:** Turn left for Telegraph Creek, turn right for boat launch/floatplane base.

D 1.4 (2.3 km) Entrance to airport.

D 3.1 (5 km) Pavement ends, gravel begins westbound.

D 5 (8 km) Entering Tanzilla Plateau. *Road narrows, some winding 8 percent grades, some washboard.*

D 7.2 (11.6 km) Tatcho Creek (Eightmile) 1-lane bridge.

D 15.7 (25.3 km) 16 Mile Creek.

D 17 (27.3 km) Augustchilde Creek, 1-lane bridge.

D 18.8 (30 km) 19 Mile Creek.

D 18.9 (30.2 km) Turnout to south with litter bin.

D 20 (32.3 km) 22 Mile Creek.

D 20.5 (33 km) Turnout to north.

D 20.7 (33.3 km) Glimpse of Tanzilla River to south.

D 32 (51.3 km) Moose Horn swamp.

D 36.9 (58.9 km) Stikine River Provincial Park boundary.

D 37 (59 km) Short walk uphill for good views and photographs.

D 38 (60.6 km) Turnout with litter bin to north. Excellent view of Mount Edziza on clear days.

D 42.5 (67.8 km) Sign reads: *Steep Mountain Highway next 70 km/43.5 miles. Grades to 20 percent.*

D 42.9 (68.4 km) Avalanche gate.

D 46.1 (74.2 km) Turnout with litter barrels to south.

Begin steep downgrades to 18 percent and 30-kmph/19-mph curves westbound. Sections of the road are single lane; be prepared to stop and yield to oncoming traffic.

D 47.7 (76 km) Tuya River 1-lane bridge.

D 47.9 (76.3 km) Turnout with litter bin.

D 49.4 (78.7 km) *CAUTION: Watch for horses on road!*

D 49.6 (79 km) Old section of Telegraph Creek Road intersects newer road.

D 51.8 (83.4 km) Small turnout with litter barrels; excellent viewpoint. Day's Ranch.

D 52.1 (82.9 km) Large turnout with litter bin and view.

CAUTION: 20 percent downhill grade for approximately 0.6 mile/1 km as narrow road/single lane with switchbacks down hillside.

D 55.4 (89.7 km) Turnoff for short loop road through rest area with picnic tables, pit toilet, litter bin and view.

D 56.1 (90.3 km) Road runs through lava beds, on narrow promontory about 150 feet/51m wide, dropping 400 feet/122m on each side to Tahltan and Stikine rivers. Excellent views of the **Grand Canyon** of the Stikine and **Tahltan Canyon** can be seen by walking a short distance across lava beds to promontory point. Best views of the river canyon are by flightseeing trip. The Stikine River canyon is only 8 feet/2.4m wide at its narrowest point.

D 57.5 (91.3 km) Point-of-interest sign at bottom of hill; reads:

"The Stikine River at the Tahltan has always been the lifeblood of the Tahltan Nation. Each year the Tahltan returned to the Stikine when the salmon were running as the fish it provided was a main food source. One fishing method involved using a gaff (long pole with a large hook at one end) to catch the salmon, which were dried in smokehouses. The Tahltan has been a main gathering place for meetings, potlatches and other ceremonial traditions."

D 57.6 (91.5 km) Tahltan River 1-lane bridge.

D 58 (92.1 km) *CAUTION: Begin section of very narrow road/single lane on ledge rising steeply up the wall of the Stikine Canyon next 3 miles/4.8 km, rising to 400 feet/122m above the river.*

D 58.6 (93 km) Turnout with view of the Grand Canyon of the Stikine and Tahltan Canyon. The Stikine River canyon is only 8 feet/2.4m wide at its narrowest point.

D 60.5 (97.4 km) Old Tahltan Native community above road. Private property: No trespassing! Former home of Tahltan bear dogs. Aggressive and smart, the little black and white dogs were used to hunt bears. Only 12 to 16 inches at the shoulder, weighing 10 to 18 lbs., they had short hair, oversize ears and a shaving-brush tail. The breed was recognized by the Canadian Kennel Club in the 1940s, but is believed to have died out, although debate continues whether or not representatives of this aboriginal American dog may indeed survive. A similar breed—the Karelian Bear Dog from northern Europe—has been growing in popularity with Northern dog owners.

D 61.5 (98 km) Nine Mile Ranch.

D 64.3 (102.1 km) Turnout with view of the Grand Canyon of the Stikine. Good photo op.

D 68.9 (111 km) Bridge over Telegraph Creek canyon. Steep winding descent into old town.

D 69 (109.7 km) TELEGRAPH CREEK (pop. 200; elev. 1,100 feet/335m). **Emergency Services:** RCMP detachment phone 250-235-3111; **Nursing station** phone 250-235-3211. **Tahltan Band Office**, phone 250-235-3151. There is lodging at the **Hyland**

Creek B&B (description follows). Residents make their living working for the Tahltan First Nations; doing construction work, mining, logging and tourism. Wildfires destroyed 27 structures in the Telegraph Creek area in summer 2018, representing 30 to 45 percent of the buildings in this community.

Hyland Creek Bed and Breakfast. Our exquisite handcrafted cabin is nestled on a spectacular property with incredible mountain views just 5 minutes past Telegraph Creek on the Glenora Road. Although off-grid, there is power, water, full bathroom, kitchenette, TV (DVD player only) and WiFi. A home-cooked breakfast is included with your stay. We can accommodate large (10 people) or small groups, or rent the entire cabin for yourself! We're open year-round and are pet friendly. River boat tours can be arranged. www.hyland creek.ca. Phone 250-235-3295 or email us at info@hylandcreek.ca. [ADVERTISEMENT]

D 70.3 (111.9 km) Keep left westbound for historic Telegraph Creek. Steep, narrow winding descent as road passes gold-rush era buildings to cross 1-lane bridge across Telegraph Creek.

D 70.4 (112.1 km) Y **junction** turnoff for Glenora Road (to left) and historic Telegraph Creek (to right). Glenora Road leads 12 miles/19.3-km to former townsite of Glenora, now indistinguishable from the forest which has taken over. This is Tahltan land and the site of a seasonal fish camp. Glenora was the limit of larger riverboat navigation on the Stikine and the site of an attempted railroad route to the Yukon.

D 70.9 (112.7 km) Vance Creek 1-lane bridge.

D 71 (112.9 km) T-junction: turn right for **Historic Telegraph Creek**, head of navigation on the lower Stikine during the gold rush heyday and once a telegraph communication terminal. An estimated 5,000 stampeders set off from Telegraph Creek to attempt the Stikine–Teslin Trail to the goldfields in Atlin and the Klondike. The prospectors brought with them diseases that devastated the Tahltan population.

The scenic view along the main street bordering the river has scarcely changed since gold rush days. Historic St. Aidan's Anglican Church is located here. Residents were evacuated during the 2018 wildfire, but the buildings in historic Telegraph Creek survived the fire.

D 71.1 (113 km) The 1898 Hudson's Bay Co. post, a Heritage Building, houses the Stikine RiverSong Lodge & Cafe, which is owned by the Tahltan Band. Please call ahead to determine what services may be offered here summer 2019. Open May through September. Phone 250-235-3004.

Return to Milepost J 303.9
Cassiar Highway

The Cassiar Highway is a popular route thanks to its scenery and wildlife. This is a view along the northern half of the highway. (©Kris Valencia, staff)

(Continued from page 283)
Iskut.

J 304.1 (488.9 km) **AH 146** (234.8 km) Distance marker northbound shows Good Hope Lake 137 km/85 miles, Alaska Highway 234 km/145 miles, Watson Lake, YT, 257 km/160 miles.

Distance marker southbound shows Meziadin Junction 334 km/208 miles, Stewart 399 km/248 miles, Kitwanga 491 km/305 miles.

J 304.2 (489.1 km) **AH 145.9** (234.6 km) Stikine Health Center, Ambulance and Fire Department to west.

J 304.7 (489.7 km) **AH 145.4** (234 km) Hotel Creek.

J 304.9 (490 km) **AH 145.2** (233.7 km) No centerline, road narrows, poor to fair surfacing northbound.

J 306.7 (492.9 km) **AH 143.4** (230.8 km) Tahltan Floatplane Base to west.

J 307.1 (493.6 km) **AH 143** (230.1 km) Welcome to Dease Lake (sign) southbound.

Slow for speed zone southbound through Dease Lake.

J 310 (498.2 km) **AH 140.1** (225.5 km) **Water's Edge Campground** (description follows) to west on Dease Lake.

Water's Edge Campground. A beautiful wilderness campground situated on the shores of Dease Lake, 10 km/6 miles north of the townsite on Highway 37. Cabin rentals, RVs, campers, tents and cyclists welcome. Boat launch, firepits, picnic tables. Firewood available. Limited WiFi. Fish from our boat launch. Your hosts: Chuck and Grace Phillips. Phone 250-771-3392. Email cwphillips99@hotmail.com; or website www.watersedgecampground.ca. [ADVERTISEMENT]

J 312 (501.3 km) **AH 138.1** (222.4 km) Turnout with litter bin to west. Views of Dease Lake to west.

J 312.7 (502.6 km) **AH 137.4** (221.1 km) Serpentine Creek.

J 313 (502.9 km) **AH 137.1** (220.8 km) Highway climbs northbound.

CAUTION: Slow for narrow, winding road, with soft shoulders.

J 316.6 (508.7 km) **AH 133.5** (215 km) There are several informal gravel turnouts to west with some views of Dease Lake along this stretch of highway.

J 317.4 (510 km) **AH 132.7** (213.5 km) Winding 8 percent downgrade northbound (sign).

J 319 (512.4 km) **AH 131.1** (211.3 km) Large gravel turnout to west with litter bin overlooking Dease Lake.

Narrow winding road next 7 km/4.3 miles northbound (sign).

J 319.4 (513.4 km) **AH 130.7** (210.3 km) Halfmoon Creek.

J 320.5 (515 km) **AH 129.6** (208.6 km) 7 percent downgrade northbound (sign).

J 322 (517.6 km) **AH 128.1** (206.1 km) Rabid Grizzly rest area to west with picnic tables, travel information signs, litter bins and toilets. View of Dease Lake.

Distance marker northbound shows Good Hope Lake 108 km/67 miles, Alaska Highway 205 km/127 miles, Watson Lake 228 km/142 miles.

J 322.6 (518.5 km) **AH 127.5** (205.2 km) The site of the ghost town Laketon lies across the lake. Laketon was the administrative center for the district during the Cassiar gold rush (1872–1880). Boat building was a major activity along the lake during the gold rush years, with miners heading up various creeks and rivers off the lake in search of gold.

J 322.9 (519 km) **AH 127.2** (204.7 km) Gravel turnout to west, bottom of the hill, north end of lake.

J 323.5 (520 km) **AH 126.6** (203.7 km) Watch for black bear and moose along the highway.

J 325.4 (522.7 km) **AH 124.7** (201 km) Paved turnout to west with litter bin.

J 327.4 (526.6 km) **AH 122.7** (197.1 km) Black Creek.

J 329.6 (529.7 km) **AH 120.5** (194 km) Turnoff to west for narrow gravel road (steep) to **Sawmill Point Recreation Site** on Dease Lake; 10 sites; tables, firepits, pit toilets; boat launch. Fishing for lake trout, use spoons, plugs, spinners, June–October, deep trolling in summer, spin casting in fall. Trailers and RVs should use caution. No camping fees at this user maintained site.

J 330.6 (531.4 km) **AH 119.5** (192.3 km) Dorothy Creek. Road widens northbound.

J 331.3 (532.5 km) **AH 118.8** (191.2 km)

Jade City makes an interesting stop for travelers, with its jade-cutting demonstrations and an extensive selection of raw jade and jade products. (©Kris Valencia, staff)

Distance marker southbound shows Dease Lake 44 km/27 miles, Stewart 440 km/273 miles, Kitwanga 535 km/332 miles.

J 333.5 (536 km) **AH 116.6** (187.7 km) Beady Creek.

Entering the Cassiar Mountains northbound.

J 335 (538.4 km) **AH 115.1** (185.3 km) Turnout to west with litter bin overlooking the **Dease River**; pretty spot. The Dease River parallels the highway. Arctic grayling, Dolly Varden and lake trout; northern pike, May through September.

Marshy areas to west; good moose pasture. *CAUTION: Watch for wildlife on road, especially at dawn and dusk.*

J 336.7 (541.1 km) **AH 113.4** (182.6 km) Large gravel turnout (watch for potholes) to west with litter bins.

J 337.8 (542.9 km) **AH 112.3** (180.8 km) Packer Tom Creek, named for a well-known First Nations man who lived in this area.

J 339.4 (545.5 km) **AH 110.7** (178.2 km) Elbow Lake (signed) to west.

J 345.2 (554.8 km) **AH 104.9** (168.9 km) Pyramid Creek.

J 345.6 (555.3 km) **AH 104.5** (168.2 km) Dease River Crossing; current status unknown. Distance marker southbound shows Dease Lake 67 km/42 miles, Stewart 467 km/290 miles, Kitwanga 558 km/347 miles.

J 345.7 (555.5 km) **AH 104.4** (168 km) Dease River 2-lane concrete bridge.

J 346 (556 km) **AH 104.1** (167.7 km) Distance marker northbound shows Good Hope Lake 70 km/43 miles, Alaska Highway 167 km/104 miles, Watson Lake 190 km/118 miles.

J 347.3 (558.1 km) **AH 102.8** (165.6 km) Beale Creek.

J 348.5 (560 km) **AH 101.6** (163.7 km) Northbound, the highway travels in easy curves and straight stretches along a wide, flat valley floor.

Southbound, the highway begins a series of long, winding grades with some straightaways.

J 350.7 (563.5 km) **AH 99.4** (160.2 km) Gravel turnout to east with litter barrel. Foliage blocks view of Pine Tree Lake.

J 351.3 (564.5 km) **AH 98.8** (159.2 km) Long paved shoulder parking to east with litter barrel beside **Pine Tree Lake**. Good Arctic grayling and lake char fishing.

J 352.1 (566 km) **AH 98** (157.7 km) Kamlah Creek.

J 354.1 (569 km) **AH 96** (154.7 km) Distance marker southbound shows Dease Lake 84 km/52 miles, Stewart 480 km/298 miles, Kitwanga 575 km/357 miles.

J 354.7 (572 km) **AH 95.4** (151.7 km) Evidence of old burn.

J 356.5 (572.9 km) **AH 93.6** (150.8 km) Cotton Lake (sign).

J 357.1 (573.9 km) **AH 93** (149.8 km) Gravel turnout with litter barrel to east.

J 359.9 (578.7 km) **AH 90.2** (145 km) Northbound Cottonwood River rest area 0.4 mile/0.6 km west via old highway on south side of the **Cottonwood River**. Fishing for Arctic grayling and whitefish. Early summer runs of Dolly Varden.

J 360.1 (579 km) **AH 90** (144.8 km) Cottonwood River bridge.

J 360.7 (580 km) **AH 89.4** (144 km) Southbound Cottonwood River rest area No. 2 is 0.5 mile/0.8 km west on old highway adjacent river; pit toilet, picnic tables, informal camping, litter bins. Slow for potholes on rest area access road, area is not well-suited for large rigs.

J 367.2 (590 km) **AH 82.9** (133.7 km) Large turnout to west beside **Simmons Lake**; information kiosk and small beach. Fishing for lake trout.

J 368.7 (592.4 km) **AH 81.4** (131.3 km) Gravel turnout to west, access to Twin Lakes.

J 368.8 (592.6 km) **AH 81.3** (131.1 km) Road runs on causeway between Twin Lakes.

J 369.3 (593.4 km) **AH 80.8** (130.3 km) **Vines Lake**, named for bush pilot Lionel Vines; fishing for lake trout. Ice on lake to late May or early June.

J 369.6 (594 km) **AH 80.5** (129.7 km) **Vines and Puppies Hideaway** with lakefront accommodations.

Vines & Puppies Hideaway. See display ad this page.

J 370.5 (595.5 km) **AH 79.6** (128.2 km) Limestone Creek.

J 370.8 (596 km) **AH 79.3** (127.7 km) Lang Lake to east.

Views of Needlepoint Mountain southbound.

J 374.5 (601.8 km) **AH 75.6** (121.9 km) Trout Line Creek.

J 374.7 (602.1 km) **AH 75.4** (121.5 km) South entrance to Jade City on west side of highway (description follows).

Jade City

J 374.9 (602.4 km) **AH 75.2** (121.3 km) Jade City is located 71 miles/114 km north of Dease Lake. **Population:** approx. 50. **Visitor Information:** The Cassiar Mountain Jade Store acts as the information center for this area.

Jade City is not a city but a highway community made up of one jade business that specializes in jade products—there is an extensive selection of gifts in their store. They offer free jade-cutting demonstrations. A small motel offers lodging and RVs may overnight in the parking area adjacent the store.

Jade City earned its name as a commercial outlet for jade mined from the nearby mountains. Cassiar Highway travelers have come to know this spot as the place to stop and buy jade. There are several major jade mines in the Cassiar region. The mines in the Cassiar Mountain Range, produce about 1 million pounds of jade each year, and half of that is exported.

Cassiar Highway Log
(continued)

J 374.9 (602.4 km) **AH 75.2** (121.3 km) North entrance to Jade City on west side of highway.

J 375.7 (603.7 km) **AH 74.4** (120 km) Distance marker southbound shows Dease Lake 116 km/72 miles, Stewart 512 km/318 miles, Kitwanga 607 km/377 miles.

J 376 (604.2 km) **AH 74.1** (119.2 km) Junction with Cassiar Road, which leads west 6.2 miles/10 km to the former Cassiar Asbestos Mine and Cassiar townsite. Much of the world's high-grade chrysotile asbestos came from here. The mine closed in March 1992, and the townsite was dismantled and sold off then reclaimed by BC Chrysotile Corp. No services available.

Distance marker northbound shows Good Hope Lake 21 km/13 miles, Alaska Highway 120 km/74 miles, Watson Lake 143 km/89 miles.

J 376.2 (604.5 km) **AH 73.9** (118.9 km) Large turnout to east with litter bin.

J 376.7 (605.3 km) **AH 73.4** (118.1 km) Gravel turnout to east.

J 377.1 (606.1 km) **AH 73** (117.6 km) McDame Creek.

J 380.5 (611.6 km) **AH 69.6** (112.1 km) No. 3 North Fork Creek.

J 380.7 (611.9 km) **AH 69.4** (111.8 km)

Large gravel turnout to west at avalanche gates.

J 381.6 (613.5 km) **AH 68.5** (110.2 km) Turnout to east overlooking Holloway Bar Project. Sign: 90-m/295-foot drop to river. Keep back from the banks while enjoying the view.

J 381.9 (613.9 km) **AH 68.2** (109.8 km) No. 2 North Fork Creek.

J 382.6 (614.8 km) **AH 67.5** (108.9 km) Gravel turnout to east.

J 384.6 (618 km) **AH 65.5** (105.7 km) Turnout to east with litter bin and historic plaque about Cassiar gold.

"The gold rush town of Centreville was located in this area. Named for its central location between Sylvester's Landing (later McDame Post) at the junction of McDame Creek with the Dease River, and Quartzrock Creek, the upstream limit of pay gravel on McDame Creek, the town had a population of 3,000. A miner named Alfred Freeman washed out the biggest all-gold (no quartz) nugget ever found in British Columbia on a claim near Centreville in 1877; it weighed 72 ounces. Active mining in area."

J 384.7 (618.2 km) **AH 65.4** (105.5 km) No. 1 North Fork Creek.

J 387.7 (623.4 km) **AH 62.4** (100.3 km) Distance marker southbound shows Dease Lake 137 km/85 miles, Stewart 537 km/334 miles, Kitwanga 628 km/390 miles.

J 388.9 (625.3 km) **AH 61.2** (98.5 km) Sign identifies Good Hope Lake.

J 389.5 (626.3 km) **AH 60.6** (97.4 km) **GOOD HOPE LAKE** (pop. approx. 75). Home to Dease River First Nations people. Dease River First Nation Store and Fuel with gas and diesel (above-ground tank), Canada Post and laundry facilities; scheduled open Monday–Friday 9 A.M. to 5 P.M. This has not been a reliable source for fuel for highway travelers. Call ahead if you are counting on this fuel stop: 250-239-3000.

Road narrows, no centerline, winding road northbound.

J 390.3 (627.7 km) **AH 59.8** (96 km) Turnout with litter bin on Aeroplane Lake (no access southbound).

J 391.2 (629 km) **AH 58.9** (94.7 km) Dry Creek.

J 393 (631.6 km) **AH 57.1** (92.1 km) Aptly named Mud Lake to east.

J 397.2 (638.7 km) **AH 52.9** (85 km) Turnout with litter barrels to east at entrance to **Tā Ch'il ā Provincial Park** (formerly **Boya Lake**). The provincial park is 1.2 miles/2 km east of highway via a good paved access road. There are 44 campsites (some on lake, some in woods) along 2 loops, with picnic tables and grills. Litter bins, pit toilets, some wheelchair-accessible facilities, picnic area at lakeshore, boat launch, drinking water, firewood and swimming. A very scenic spot, the park has 2 short walking trails (1.5 km/0.9 mile) with interpretive panels. Campground attendant. Open mid-May through September (weather permitting). Camping fee $20. Canoe rentals, fish for lake char, whitefish and burbot.

J 397.3 (638.9 km) **AH 52.8** (84.8 km) Distance marker northbound shows Alaska Highway 86 km/53 miles, Watson Lake 109 km/68 miles, Whitehorse 509 km/367 miles.

J 400.3 (644.3 km) **AH 49.1** (79 km) Charlie Chief Creek.

J 402.3 (647.4 km) **AH 47.4** (76.3 km) Beaver Dam Creek.

J 403.2 (648.9 km) **AH 46.5** (74.8 km) Beaver Dam rest area to west has a very large gravel parking area, picnic tables in trees, litter bins and toilets. Distance information

sign and information sign regarding wildfires that burned through the area to the north in 2010 and 2012.

Leaving Cassiar Mountains, entering Yukon Plateau, northbound. The Horseranch Range may be seen on the eastern horizon. These mountains date back to the Cambrian period, or earlier, and are the oldest in northern British Columbia.

J 406.1 (653 km) **AH 44** (70.7 km) Baking Powder Creek.

J 414.5 (665.9 km) **AH 35.6** (57.8 km) Turnoff to east for **French Creek Recreation Site**, which offers 4 semi-open campsites with tables and pit toilets, access to fishing in Dease River and French Creek. Not recommended for larger vehicles, limited access. User maintained, no fees.

J 414.9 (667.1 km) **AH 35.2** (56.6 km) French Creek 2-lane concrete bridge.

Distance marker northbound shows Alaska Highway 57 km/35 miles, Watson Lake 80 km/50 miles, Whitehorse 476 km/296 miles.

J 416 (668.4 km) **AH 34.1** (55.3 km) Distance marker southbound shows Good Hope Lake 43 km/27 miles, Stewart 580 km/360 miles, Kitwanga 671 km/417 miles.

J 421.2 (676.8 km) **AH 28.9** (46.9 km) Highway descends both directions to 28-Mile Creek. Cassiar Mountains to south.

J 424 (681.3 km) **AH 26.1** (42.4 km) Wheeler Creek (signed) to west.

J 426.7 (685.7 km) **AH 23.4** (38 km) Blue River South Forest Service Road to east.

J 430.1 (691.4 km) **AH 20** (32.3 km) Blue River 2-lane concrete bridge.

J 430.6 (691.8 km) **AH 19.5** (31.9 km) Narrow winding road with some straight stretches, hilly with grades to 8 percent, no centerline, no shoulders, next 20 miles northbound. Keep to right on hills and blind corners.

Distance marker northbound shows Alaska Highway 33 km/20 miles, Watson Lake 56 km/35 miles, Whitehorse 537 km/333 miles.

J 433.6 (697.1 km) **AH 16.5** (26.6 km) Turnout with litter bin on grassy point at **Blue Lakes**. Another small picnic area is at the south end of the lake with picnic table, trash barrel and small gravel turnout. Fish for pike and Arctic grayling.

Evidence of wildfires. The Tisigar Lake fire in 2011 closed the highway. If you see flames or smoke phone *5555 on cell or 1-800-663-5555.

J 435.4 (700 km) **AH 14.7** (23.7 km) Mud Hill Creek. Highway climbs steeply, northbound.

J 436.8 (702.3 km) **AH 13.3** (21.4 km) Large turnout to west.

J 444.1 (714 km) **AH 6** (9.7 km) Cormier Creek.

Highway climbs northbound.

J 447.1 (718.7 km) **AH 3** (5 km) Dirt turnout at High Lake to east. Pretty spot, informal campsite.

J 447.9 (720 km) **AH 2.2** (3.5 km) Sign: Leaving British Columbia (northbound).

J 448 (720.3 km) **AH 2.1** (3.4 km) **BC–YT Border**, 60th parallel. "Welcome to Yukon" (northbound sign), "Welcome to British Columbia" (southbound sign). Rest area with information sign, pit toilet and litter bin. See webcam live views at this website: images.drivebc.ca/bchighwaycam/pub/html/www/353.html.

Seatbelt use required by law in Yukon

Beautiful Boya Lake—now Ta Ch'il a Provincial Park—offers camping, swimming and fishing just 1.2 miles/2 km east of the highway. (©Judy Nadon, staff)

(northbound sign) and British Columbia (southbound sign). *Drive with headlights on at all times both directions.*

Narrow winding road with some straight stretches, hilly with grades to 8 percent, no centerline, no shoulders, next 20 miles southbound. Keep to right on hills and blind corners. Distance marker southbound shows Good Hope Lake 97 km/60 miles, Stewart 634 km/394 miles, Kitwanga 725 km/451 miles.

J 449.4 (722.6 km) **AH 0.7** (1.1 km) **Albert Creek** offers good Arctic grayling fishing. Yukon fishing license required.

J 449.8 (723.4 km) **AH 0.1** (0.3 km) Distance marker southbound shows Dease Lake 235 km/146 miles, Kitwanga 723 km/449 miles.

J 450.1 (723.7 km) **AH 0 Junction** of the Cassiar Highway and Alaska Highway; Junction 37 Services (gas/diesel). Watson Lake, 13.3 miles/21.4 km southeast, is the nearest major community. **Nugget City** (gas/diesel, lodging, restaurant, gift shop, mechanic, camping) is located less than a mile west of here on the Alaska Highway.

Distance marker on the Alaska Highway shows Teslin 241 km/150 miles, Whitehorse 424 km/263 miles.

Turn to **Milepost DC 626.2** on page 188 in the ALASKA HIGHWAY section for log of Alaska Highway from this junction.

BC HIGHWAY 37 South

Southbound: Distance from junction with the Yellowhead Highway (J) is followed by distance from Alaska Highway (AH). Read log:

Southbound travelers note: British Columbia requires passenger vehicles have winter tires and that commercial vehicles carry chains between Oct. 1–April 30 on the Cassiar Highway. This regulation is enforced. Seatbelt use also required by law. Drive with headlights on at all times.

Klondike Loop

Klondike, Top of the World and Taylor Highways
Includes Silver Trail

CONNECTS: Alaska Hwy. in YT to Alaska Hwy. in AK

Length: 498 miles **Road Surface:** Pavement, Seal Coat & Gravel
Season: Hwy. 2 open all year, Hwys. 9 and 5 closed in winter

(See maps, pages 289–290)

 2 9 5 11

Five Finger Rapids on the Yukon River was named for the 5 channels, or fingers, formed by the rock pillars. (©Sharon Nault)

Distance in miles	AK Hwy YT Jct.	Carmacks	Chicken	Dawson City	Eagle	Tetlin Jct. AK	Whitehorse
AK Hwy YT Jct.		102	432	323	467	498	10
Carmacks	102		330	221	365	396	112
Chicken	432	330		109	95	66	442
Dawson City	323	221	109		144	175	333
Eagle	467	365	95	144		161	477
Tetlin Jct. AK	498	396	66	175	161		508
Whitehorse	10	112	442	333	477	508	

YT. Although about a hundred miles longer than taking the more direct all-Alaska Highway route between Whitehorse and Tok, the Klondike Loop is a popular choice for travelers because it takes them by way of historic Dawson City, the Top of the World Highway with its top-of-the-world views, and the Taylor Highway through Fortymile country to the colorful community of Chicken, AK.

The Klondike Loop is logged from its turnoff at **Milepost DC 894.5** Alaska Highway (just north of Whitehorse) to its junction at **Milepost DC 1266.7** Alaska Highway (just south of Tok).

The first section of the "loop" for motorists traveling northbound is the 323-mile/520-km-long stretch of Yukon Highway 2, the North Klondike Highway (also called the "Mayo Road"), from its junction with the Alaska Highway north of Whitehorse to Dawson City. The second stretch is the 79-mile/127-km Top of the World Highway (Yukon Highway 9 and Boundary Spur Road in Alaska), which connects Dawson City in Yukon with the Taylor Highway at Jack Wade Junction in Alaska.

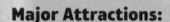
Major Attractions:

*Dawson City, YT,
Eagle, AK,
Mayo's Binet House,
Keno City Mining Museum,
Chicken, AK*

©Kelley & Milton Barker, staff

Together, the Klondike Highway, Top of the World Highway and Taylor Highway form the "Klondike Loop," a 498-mile/801-km route that takes Alaska Highway travelers through Dawson City,

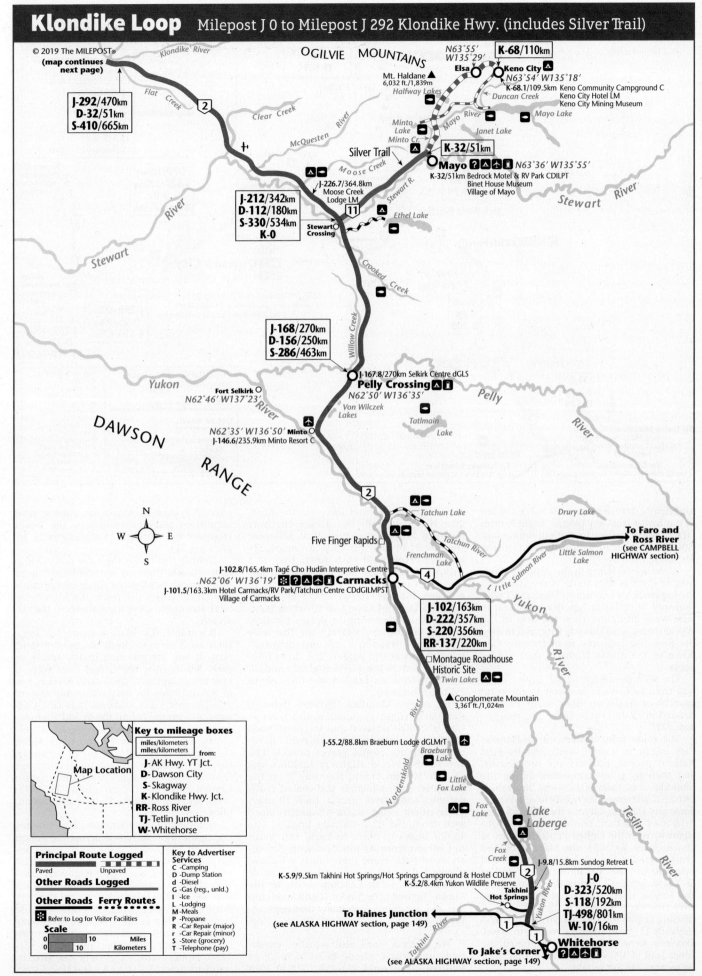

Klondike Loop
Milepost J 0 to Milepost J 292 Klondike Hwy. (includes Silver Trail)

© 2019 The MILEPOST®
(map continues
next page)

OGILVIE MOUNTAINS

N63°55'
W135°29'

K-68/110km

Elsa

Keno City

N63°54' W135°18'

Mt. Haldane ▲
6,032 ft./1,839m

K-68.1/109.5km Keno Community Campground C
Keno City Hotel LM
Keno City Mining Museum

Klondike River

Flat Creek

2

J-292/470km
D-32/51km
S-410/665km

Clear Creek

McQuesten

River

Halfway Lakes

Duncan Creek

Mayo Lake

Minto
Lake

Mayo River

Janet Lake

Minto Cr.

K-32/51km

Silver Trail

Moose Creek

Mayo

N63°36' W135°55'

K-32/51km Bedrock Motel & RV Park CDILPT
Binet House Museum
Village of Mayo

J-226.7/364.8km
Moose Creek
Lodge LM

J-212/342km
D-112/180km
S-330/534km
K-0

11

Stewart R.

Stewart
Crossing

Ethel Lake

Stewart River

River

Stewart

Crooked Creek

J-168/270km
D-156/250km
S-286/463km

Willow Creek

J-167.8/270km Selkirk Centre dGLS

Yukon

Fort Selkirk

N62°46' W137°23'

Pelly Crossing

N62°50' W136°35'

Pelly

River

River

Von Wilczek
Lakes

Tatlmain
Lake

DAWSON

N62°35' W136°50' Minto
J-146.6/235.9km Minto Resort C

RANGE

2

Tatchun Lake

Drury Lake

Five Finger Rapids

Frenchman
Lake

Tatchun River

Little Salmon
Lake

To Faro and
Ross River
(see CAMPBELL
HIGHWAY section)

J-102.8/165.4km Tagé Cho Hudän Interpretive Centre

N62°06' W136°19' Carmacks

J-101.5/163.3km Hotel Carmacks/RV Park/Tatchun Centre CDdGILMPST
Village of Carmacks

4

Little Salmon River

Yukon

River

J-102/163km
D-222/357km
S-220/356km
RR-137/220km

□ Montague Roadhouse
Historic Site

Twin Lakes

▲ Conglomerate Mountain
3,361 ft./1,024m

River

J-55.2/88.8km Braeburn Lodge dGLMrT

Braeburn
Lake

Nordenskiold

Little
Fox Lake

Fox Lake

Lake
Laberge

Teslin

Fox
Creek

River

J-9.8/15.8km Sundog Retreat L

K-5.9/9.5km Takhini Hot Springs/Hot Springs Campground & Hostel CDLMT
K-5.2/8.4km Yukon Wildlife Preserve

Takhini
Hot Springs

2

J-0
D-323/520km
S-118/192km
TJ-498/801km
W-10/16km

To Haines Junction
(see ALASKA HIGHWAY section, page 149)

1

Yukon River

Takhini River

1

Whitehorse

To Jake's Corner
(see ALASKA HIGHWAY section, page 149)

Key to mileage boxes

miles/kilometers
miles/kilometers
from:

J- AK Hwy. YT Jct.
D- Dawson City
S- Skagway
K- Klondike Hwy. Jct.
RR- Ross River
TJ- Tetlin Junction
W- Whitehorse

Map Location

Principal Route Logged

Paved   Unpaved

Other Roads Logged

Other Roads   Ferry Routes

⊠ Refer to Log for Visitor Facilities

Scale

0   10   Miles
0   10   Kilometers

N
W   E
S

Key to Advertiser Services

C - Camping
D - Dump Station
d - Diesel
G - Gas (reg., unld.)
I - Ice
L - Lodging
M - Meals
P - Propane
R - Car Repair (major)
r - Car Repair (minor)
S - Store (grocery)
T - Telephone (pay)

Klondike Loop
Milepost J 292 to Tetlin Junction, Alaska Highway (includes Top of the World and Taylor highways)

© 2019 The MILEPOST®

Key to mileage boxes

miles/kilometers
miles/kilometers from:

J-AK Hwy. YT Jct.
D-Dawson City
E-Eagle
T-Taylor Hwy. Jct.
TJ-Tetlin Jct.
S-Skagway

Map Location

N64°47' W141°12' Eagle
TJ-160.5 Falcon Inn B&B L

E-0
TJ-161

Taylor Highway

American Cr.

King Solomon Cr.

Columbia Cr.

North Fork

Middle Fork

Alder Cr.

O'Brien Cr.

Liberty Fork

Fortymile River

Yukon River

Clinton Creek

T-79/127km
J-323/520km
D-0
S-442/715km

To Inuvik
(see DEMPSTER HIGHWAY section)

Rock Cr.

North Klondike R.

T-0
TJ-96
E-65
D-79

Steele Creek Dome
4,015 ft./1,224m

U.S. Poker Creek
Canada Little Gold Creek

Boundary

Top of the World Highway

Free Ferry

Dawson City
N64°04' W139°25'

J-319.5/514.2km
Chief Isaac
Mechanical R

Klondike River

(map continues previous page)

Flat Creek

Jack Wade Junction

Chicken
N64°04' W141°56'

Boundary Spur Road

Road Closed in Winter

Sixtymile

Sixtymile River

Yukon R.

J-321.4/517.2km Dawson City RV Park CDdGIPrST
J-321.3/517.1km Bonanza Gold Motel & RV Park CDLMT
J-321.2/516.9km Claim 33 Gold Panning

J-298/480km
D-25/40km
S-416/675km

J-292/470km
D-32/51km
S-410/665km

Road not maintained in winter

TJ-66
E-94
D-109

South Fork

Walker Fork

Liberty Creek

Logging Cabin Creek

Mosquito Fork

West Fork

Taylor Highway

Mount Fairplay
5,541 ft./1,689m

Dennison Fork

East Fork

ALASKA
YUKON

UNITED STATES
CANADA

TJ-0
E-161
D-175

Tanana River

To Delta Junction
(see ALASKA HIGHWAY section, page 149)

Tok

To Glennallen
(see GLENN HIGHWAY section, page 318)

Fourmile Lake

Tetlin Junction N63°18' W142°36'

To Haines Junction
(see ALASKA HIGHWAY section, page 149)

Principal Route Logged
Paved   Unpaved

Other Roads Logged

Other Roads

Refer to Log for Visitor Facilities

Scale
0   20 Miles
0   20 Kilometers

Key to Advertiser Services
C -Camping
D -Dump Station
d -Diesel
G -Gas (reg., unld.)
I -Ice
L -Lodging
M -Meals
P -Propane
R -Car Repair (major)
r -Car Repair (minor)
S -Store (grocery)
T -Telephone (pay)

And finally, travelers drive 96 miles/154 km of the Taylor Highway (Alaska Route 5) from Jack Wade Junction to the community of Chicken and on to Tetlin Junction on the Alaska Highway.

If you are traveling in the opposite direction of the log, this route is reversed (and the log reads back to front): Drive the Taylor Highway from Tetlin Junction near Tok to Jack Wade Junction; then the Top of the World Highway to Dawson City; and finally, the Klondike Highway from Dawson City down to the Alaska Highway near Whitehorse.

The 65-mile stretch of the Taylor Highway from Jack Wade Junction to the community of Eagle on the Yukon River is covered in "Side Trip to Eagle" *(beginning on page 311).*

The route from Whitehorse to Dawson City began as a trail, used first by First Nations people, trappers and prospectors, and then by gold stampeders during the Klondike Gold Rush of 1897–98. Steamships provided passenger service between Whitehorse and Dawson City via the Yukon River.

A road was built connecting the Alaska Highway with the United Keno Hill Mine at Elsa in 1950. By 1955, the Mayo Road had been upgraded for automobile traffic and extended to Dawson City. In 1960, the last of 3 steel bridges crossing the Yukon, Pelly and Stewart rivers, was completed. The only ferry crossing remaining is the Yukon River crossing at Dawson City. Mayo Road (Yukon Highway 11) from Stewart Crossing to Mayo, Elsa and Keno City was redesignated the Silver Trail in 1985 *(see the "Silver Trail" road log on page 298 this section).*

It is about a 6-hour drive via the Klondike Highway from the Alaska Highway north of Whitehorse (turnoff at **Milepost DC 894.5**) to Dawson City, a remarkably well-preserved gold rush town that is a national historic site and the major attraction on the Klondike Loop. Allow 3 to 4 hours for the 109-mile/175-km drive between Dawson City and Chicken (next service stop), factoring in delays for slow driving conditions, waiting for the ferry crossing at Dawson City and negotiating customs at the border. The drive from Chicken back to the Alaska Highway and on to Tok is 78 miles/126 km and takes about 1½ hours nonstop.

All of the Klondike Highway between the Alaska Highway junction and Dawson City is asphalt-surfaced and in fair to good condition, with some damaged pavement and occasional gravel breaks. The Top of the World Highway includes the 66-mile/106-km Yukon Highway 9 on the Canadian side, which is seal-coated (with potholes and gravel breaks), then 13 miles of pavement along Alaska's Boundary Road west from the U.S.–Canada border. The Taylor Highway north to Eagle and south to Chicken from its junction with Boundary Road (Jack Wade Junction) is a narrow, winding, dirt and gravel road with little or no shoulder. From Chicken south to the Alaska Highway, the Taylor Highway is chip seal and pavement with many damaged sections. *Drive with your headlights on at all times and yield to oncoming large vehicles on curves.*

For current road and weather conditions in Canada, phone 867-456-7623, or toll-free in Yukon 1-877-456-7623 or visit www.511yukon.ca. Check on current road conditions and construction on the Taylor Highway by visiting 511.alaska.gov or by phoning 511.

Neither the Taylor Highway nor the Top of the World Highway are maintained from mid-October to May and the arrival of snow effectively closes the roads for winter. Do NOT attempt to drive these routes in the off-season.

If you intend to make the complete loop, there are 3 items to check on ahead of time. First, if you are traveling in the spring or early fall, be sure the *George Black* ferry is operating. Typically, the Yukon River is free of ice and open for ferry traffic mid-May to mid-October. Also, confirm that U.S. Customs is open on Top of the World Highway so that you can cross into Alaska. Third, check on current road conditions along the Top of the World and Taylor highways. Good contacts for current information on these 3 items are the Visitor Information Center in Dawson City, phone 867-993-5566, and the Klondike Visitors Association, phone 867-993-5575.

Completing the Klondike Loop requires taking the short ferry ride across the Yukon River on the *George Black* ferry that connects the Klondike Highway at Dawson City with the Top of the World Highway. Travelers should be aware that in summer there may be a wait as long as 3 hours for the ferry during peak hours. Also, U.S. and Canada customs on Top of the World are open daily in summer only (mid-May to late September, depending on weather) phone 703-921-7750. Hours were 9 A.M. to 9 P.M. (Pacific standard time), 8 A.M. to 8 P.M. (Alaska standard time) in summer 2018. There are no restrooms, services or currency exchanges available at the border and no public phone.

Emergency Services: Dial 911, or, on Yukon Highway 2 from **Milepost J 0** to **J 55.2** (Whitehorse to Braeburn Lodge), phone Whitehorse Ambulance at 911 or 867-667-3333; RCMP at 867-667-5555. From **Milepost J 55.2** to **J 167.8** (Braeburn Lodge to Pelly Crossing), phone Carmacks Medical Emergency 867- 863-4444 or RCMP 867-863-5555. From **Milepost J 167.8** to **J 240.2** (Pelly Crossing to McQuesten River bridge), phone Mayo Medical Emergency 867-996-4444 or RCMP 867-996-5555. From **Milepost J 240.2** to **J 323.4** (McQuesten River bridge to Dawson City) and on Yukon Highway 9 from **Milepost D 0** to **D 65.7** (Dawson City to Alaska border), phone Dawson City Medical Emergency 867-993-4444 or RCMP 867-993-5555. From **Milepost D 65.7** to **D 79.2** (Alaska border to Taylor Highway), phone Tok Area EMS at 911 or Alaska State Troopers at 907-883-5111.

Klondike Loop Log

Lake Laberge is a 40-mile-/64-km-long lake formed by a widening of the Yukon River. Boaters should be aware that storms can blow up quickly on this lake. (©Judy Nadon, staff)

Northbound: This section of the log shows distance from junction with the Alaska Highway (J) followed by distance from Dawson City (D) and distance from Skagway (S). Read log:

NOTE: Physical kilometerposts, on right hand side northbound, reflect distance from Skagway. In this log, distance from Skagway in miles reflects driving distance. Distance in kilometers reflects the physical kilometerpost and is not an accurate conversion of the mileage.

YUKON HIGHWAY 2

J 0 D 323.4 (520.3 km) **S 118.1** (190 km) Turnoff for Yukon Highway 2/Klondike Highway to Dawson City (323 miles/520 km) with continuation via Top of the World and Taylor highways to Chicken (432 miles/695 km from here) and then south to **junction** with the Alaska Highway at **Milepost DC 1266.7** (a total of 498 miles/801 km).

Junction with the Alaska Highway at **Milepost DC 894.5.** It is 7.1 miles/11.7 km southeast on the Alaska Highway from here to the Two Mile Hill exit to downtown Whitehorse. Turn to page 207 in the ALASKA HIGHWAY section.

J 0.5 (0.8 km) **D 322.9** (519.6 km) **S 118.6** (190.8 km) Distance marker northbound shows Carmacks 164 km/102 miles, Mayo 395 km/245 miles.

J 1.1 (1.8 km) **D 321.8** (517.8 km) **119.7** (192.6 km) Couch Road to the west, B&B.

J 2.2 (3.5 km) **D 321.2** (516.9 km) **S 120.3** (195.5 km) Takhini River bridge. The Takhini flows into the Yukon River. The name is Tagish Indian, *tahk* meaning mosquito and *heena* meaning river, according to R. Coutts in *Yukon: Places & Names*.

Leaving Whitehorse city limits northbound.

J 3.6 (5.8 km) **D 319.8** (514.6 km) **S 121.7** (195.8 km) Gas, grocery and licensed cafe at **junction** with Takhini Hot Springs Road, a fun **side trip** with access to **Yukon Wildlife Preserve**, **Takhini Hot Springs** and

Hot Springs Campground and Hostel.

Junction with Takhini Hot Springs Road. See road log on page 293.

J 7.6 (12.2 km) **D 315.8** (508.2 km) **S 125.7** (202.3 km) Whitehorse rodeo grounds to west.

J 9.8 (15.8 km) **D 313.6** (504.6 km) **S 127.9** (205.8 km) Turn right on Policeman Point Road for **Sundog Retreat**; pet-friendly cabins, phone 867-633-4183; sundogretreat. com.

Sundog Retreat. See display ad on page 200 in the ALASKA HIGHWAY section.

J 12.5 (20.1 km) **D 310.9** (500.3 km) **S 130.6** (212 km) Horse Creek.

J 20 (32.2 km) **D 303.4** (488.3 km) **S 138.1** (224 km) Deep Creek.

J 20.3 (32.7 km) **D 303.1** (487.8 km) **S 138.4** (224.6 km) Turnoff for Deep Creek Road to **Lake Laberge Yukon government campground.** Drive in 1.8 miles/2.9 km on (paved road with gravel breaks) past residential area; keep to left at fork with Deep Creek South Road. The campground is on the shores of Lake Laberge next to Deep Creek. *NOTE: Unmarked roads in this area are residential driveways. Please do not park in front of these roads.*

Lake Laberge Yukon government campground has 16 sites, open May 12–Oct. 1; camping permit ($12), group camping area, kitchen shelter, water (may be non-potable), firewood, pit toilets, recycling and garbage bins, swimming beach, boat launch, and fishing for lake trout, grayling and northern pike. Information boards highlight the 30-mile Heritage River.

The Yukon River widens to form this 40-mile-/64-km-long lake. Lake Laberge was made famous by Robert W. Service with the lines: "The Northern Lights have seen queer sights. But the queerest they ever did see, was that night on the marge of Lake Lebarge I cremated Sam McGee," (from his poem "The Cremation of Sam McGee").

According to Yukon Renewable Resources, Lake Laberge is the only place in the Yukon where cormorants are seen. Loons and other water birds are commonly seen here.

CAUTION: Storms can blow up quickly and without warning on Lake Laberge, as on other northern lakes. Canoes and small craft stay to the west side of the lake, where the shoreline offers safe refuges. The east side of the lake is lined with high rocky bluffs, and there are few places to pull out. Small craft should not navigate the middle of the lake.

J 21.2 (34.1 km) **D 302.2** (486.3 km) **S 139.3** (226 km) Northbound the highway enters the Miners Range, plateau country of the Yukon, an immense wilderness of forested dome-shaped mountains and high ridges, dotted with lakes and traversed by tributaries of the Yukon River. To the west, Pilot Mountain in the Miners Range (elev. 6,739 feet/2,054m) is visible.

J 22.6 (36.4 km) **D 300.8** (484.1 km) **S 140.7** (228.4 km) **Fox Creek** bridge; grayling, excellent in June and July.

J 23.3 (37.5 km) **D 300.1** (483 km) **S 141.4** (229.5 km) Distance marker northbound shows Carmacks 125 km/78 miles, Dawson City 486 km/302 miles.

J 28.6 (46 km) **D 294.8** (474.4 km) **S 146.7** (238 km) Highway now follows the east shoreline of Fox Lake northbound. Fox Lake is a waterfowl stop during spring and fall migrations. Some waterfowl can be seen in spring (lake ice stays late), and large numbers of birds, especially swans, are present in fall. Muskrats also feed here: muskrat "push-ups" can be seen dotting the frozen surface of the lake in the winter and spring.

J 29.2 (47 km) **D 294.2** (473.5 km) **S 147.3** (239 km) Turnout to west on Fox Lake.

Information sign here reads: "In 1883, U.S. Army Lt. Frederick Schwatka completed a survey of the entire length of the Yukon River. One of many geographical features that he named was Fox Lake, which he called Richthofen Lake, after geographer Freiherr Von Richthofen. Known locally as Fox Lake, the name was adopted in 1957.

Takhini Hot Springs Road

Takhini Hot Springs Road turns off the Klondike Highway/Yukon 2 just 3.6 miles/5.8 km northeast of the Alaska Highway. This straight, paved road leads west 6 miles/10 kms to Takhini Hot Springs, the Hot Springs Campground and Hostel and the Yukon Wildlife Preserve. Speed limit is 55 mph/90 kmph, but be alert for traffic from the many private residence driveways along the highway.

Distance is measured from the junction with Klondike Highway (K).

Takhini Hot Springs Road

K 0 Junction with Klondike Highway; gas/diesel, grocery and licensed cafe.

K 1.1 (1.8 km) Boreal Road to east, access to Miner's Ridge residential subdivision.

K 5.2 (8.4 km) **Yukon Wildlife Preserve** offers interpretive bus tours and self-guided walking tours on their 700-acre wildlife park. Mountain goats, woodland caribou, moose, elk, wood bison, musk oxen, mule deer, and mountain sheep roam in their natural habitats. Phone 867-456-7300; www.yukonwildlife.ca. Open daily May to early September and Friday–Sunday the rest of the year.

Yukon Wildlife Preserve. See display ad on facing page.

K 5.6 (9 km) Country Cabins Bed & Breakfast to east.

K 5.7 (9.2 km) Takhini River Road cutoff, access to Eldorado Elk Farm and Boarding Kennels (1.1 miles/1.7 km) and Takhini River Lodge (4.6 miles/7.4 km).

K 5.8 (9.3 km) Bean North Coffee Roasters cafe to east.

K 5.9 (9.5 km) **Takhini Hot Springs and Hot Springs Campground & Hostel.** There is nothing better than a soak in naturally hot mineral pools. Open year-round. Phone 867-456-8000. www.takhinihotsprings.com. Wooded campground and hostel; description follows.

Hot Springs Campground and Hostel. Welcome to our forested campground and newly-built hostel. The Yukon's first Klondike-themed escape rooms are also located on the property escape@yukon

Takhini Hot Springs is a year-round destination. They hold a Hair Freezing Contest in winter. (©Courtesy Takhini Hot Springs)

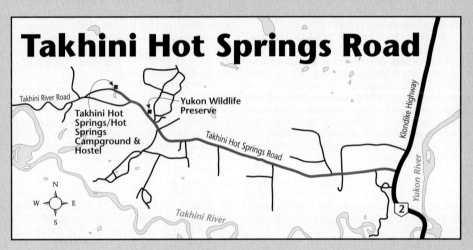

escapegames.com; www.yukonescapegames. com. We're open year-round, and offer wooded campsites: 15/30 and 50-amp, pull-through sites, WiFi, firepits, picnic tables. Indoor toilets and coin-operated showers in campground office. Sani-dump and water available summer only. The 20-bed hostel is wheelchair-accessible, has a self-catering kitchen, WiFi, showers, games/TV area. We're only a 2-minute walk from the hot springs, where our guests receive a 20

percent discount off admission. For reservations, contact 867-456-8004. Email camp@yukoncampground.com. www.yukoncampground.com. See display ad on page 292. [ADVERTISEMENT]

Takhini Hot Springs. See display ad on facing page.

K 6.2 (10 km) Crêperie and cafe.

**Return to Milepost J 3.6
Klondike Highway**

The Miners Range to the west was named by geologist/explorer George Mercer Dawson in 1887 'for the miners met by us along the river.'"

J 34.5 (55.5 km) **D 288.9** (464.9 km) **S 152.6** (247.7 km) Turnoff west for **Fox Lake Yukon government campground**; 43 campsites, open May 11 to Sept. 30; camping permit ($12), kitchen shelter, playground, water (may not be potable), pit toilets and boat launch. Good fishing for lake trout and burbot from the shore at the campground; excellent grayling year-round.

J 40.1 (64.5 km) **D 283.3** (455.9 km) **S 158.2** (256.6 km) Burn area northbound is from a major forest fire in this area in summer 1998. Burn year signs mark several

of these wildfires northbound.

J 43.2 (69.5 km) **D 280.2** (450.9 km) **S 161.3** (261.8 km) **Little Fox Lake** (northbound sign). Check current harvest recommendation for small resident population of lake trout before fishing.

J 49.5 (79.6 km) **D 273.9** (440.8 km) **S 167.6** (272 km) **Fox Lake Burn** rest area to west; large, double-ended parking area with outhouses and litter bins. Short trail through burn area to viewpoint; excellent information boards about the 1998 fire. *CAUTION: Steep drop-off at end of trail: Supervise children and pets.*

J 51.8 (83.4 km) **D 271.6** (437.1 km) **S 169.9** (275.5 km) *CAUTION: Watch for elk next 50 km/31 miles northbound (sign).* According to Renewable Resources Wildlife

Viewing Program, about 50 elk live here year-round. They are most commonly seen in winter and spring. Look for their distinctive white rumps on the exposed south-facing slopes. Elk are a protected species in Yukon. Grizzly bears feed on roadside vegetation (and also elk) in this area in spring and summer.

J 55.2 (88.8 km) **D 268.2** (431.6 km) **S 173.3** (280.8 km) **Braeburn Lodge** to west; food, gas, diesel, lodging and minor car repairs. A Braeburn Lodge cinnamon bun will feed 4 people. The lodge is also an official checkpoint for the 1,000-mile Yukon Quest International Sled Dog Race.

Braeburn Lodge. See display ad page 294.

Private Aircraft: Braeburn airstrip to

east, dubbed Cinnamon Bun Strip; elev. 2,350 feet/716m; length 3,000 feet/914m; dirt strip; wind sock.

J 65.6 (105.6 km) **D 257.8** (414.9 km) **S 183.7** (298 km) Paved pull-through turnout on east side of highway is a rest area and photo stop with information sign about Conglomerate Mountain (elev. 3,361 feet/1,024m). Sign reads:

"The Laberge Series was formed at the leading edge of volcanic mud flows some 185 million years ago (Early Jurassic). These flows solidified into sheets several kilometres long and about 1 km wide and 100m thick. This particular series of sheets stretches from Atlin, BC, to north of Carmacks, a distance of about 350 km. Other conglomerates of this series form Five Finger Rapids."

Several outcroppings of conglomerate may be found in the immediate area. Conglomerate, also called "Puddingstone" because of its appearance, consists of pebbles welded into solid masses of varying size by a natural cement. Composition of the cementing material varies, as does the size and composition of the pebbles.

J 71.3 (114.7 km) **D 252.1** (405.7 km) **S 189.4** (307 km) Turnouts on both sides of highway between Twin Lakes. These 2 small lakes, 1 on either side of the road, are known for their beauty and color.

J 71.9 (115.7 km) **D 251.5** (404.7 km) **S 190** (308 km) Turnoff to west for **Twin Lakes Yukon government campground**; 26 sites, open May 11 to Sept. 30; camping permit ($12); picnic tables, water (may not be potable), firewood, garbage bins, pit toilets, boat launch. Lake is stocked. Large parking area with informational panels on the Nordenskiold River. Enjoyable fishing for lake trout, grayling and pike. Good swimming for the hardy!

J 72.1 (116 km) **D 251.3** (404.4 km) **S 190.2** (308.4 km) Distance marker northbound shows Carmacks 48 km/30 miles, Mayo 280 km/174 miles, Dawson City 405 km/252 miles.

J 79.6 (128.1 km) **D 243.8** (392.3 km)

S 197.7 (320.5 km) Northbound motorist will note layers of volcanic ash in banks alongside highway. About 1,250 years ago a layer of white volcanic ash coated a third of the southern Yukon, or some 125,000 square miles/323,725 square km, and it is still quite visible along many roadcuts. This distinct line conveniently provides a division used by archaeologists for dating artifacts: Materials found below this major stratigraphic marker are considered to have been deposited before A.D. 700, while those found above the ash layer are postdated A.D. 700. It has been theorized that the ash may have been deposited during a single violent volcanic eruption from a source now buried under the Klutlan Glacier in the St. Elias Mountains in eastern Alaska.

J 80.6 (129.7 km) **D 242.8** (390.7 km) **S 198.7** (322.4 km) **Montague Roadhouse Historic Site** to east; dirt parking area, picnic tables, litter bins and outhouses. The remains of this old roadhouse make a great photo op. Montague House was a typical early-day roadhouse, offering lodging and meals to travelers on the stagecoach route between Whitehorse and Dawson City. A total of 52 stopping places along this route were listed in the Jan. 16, 1901, edition of the *Whitehorse Star* under "On the Winter Trail between Whitehorse and Dawson Good Accommodations for Travellers." Montague House was listed at Mile 99.

J 89.2 (143.5 km) **D 234.2** (376.9 km) **S 213.1** (336 km) Watch for waterfowl in ponds along highway. Wetlands to west are part of the Nordenskiold River (Tsalnjik Chu) system. Waterfowl stage here during spring and fall migrations. Watch for trumpeter swans and ruddy ducks. Other area wildlife include beaver, muskrat, moose, mink and fox.

The **Nodenskiold River** was named by Lt. Frederick Schwatka, U.S. Army, for Swedish arctic explorer Erik Nordenskiold. This river, which parallels the highway for several miles, flows into the Yukon River at Carmacks. Good grayling and pike fishing all summer.

J 93.3 (150.1 km) **D 230.1** (370.3 km) **S 211.4** (345.4 km) Turnout to east at Mineral Trail; information sign about agate deposits.

J 99.3 (159.8 km) **D 224.1** (360.6 km)

S 217.4 (352.3 km) Entering village of Carmacks (northbound sign).

J 100.6 (161.9 km) **D 222.8** (358.6 km) **S 218.7** (354.4 km) Rest area to east; double-ended turnout with litter bins, outhouses and information boards. The **Carmacks Visitor Information Center** here has pamphlets, maps and information. The Welcome to Carmacks loon mosaic seen here was designed by artists Chris Schearbarth, Brian Tom and Clarence Washpan and constructed by members of Little Salmon Carmacks First Nations.

Carmacks

J 101.5 (163.3 km) **D 221.9** (357 km) **S 219.6** (355.8 km) Located on the banks of the Yukon River, Carmacks is the only highway crossing of the Yukon River between Whitehorse and Dawson City. **Population:** 539. **Emergency Services:** Dial 911. **Village Office**, phone 867-863-6271.

Visitor Information: Located in the Old Telegraph Station, which also contains a mini-museum and a display of area geology. Phone the Visitor Information Center at 867-863-6330 (summers only). Or contact the **Village of Carmacks**, Box 113, Carmacks, YT Y0B 1C0; phone 867-863-6271; website www.carmacks.ca.

Private Aircraft: Carmacks airstrip; elev. 1,770 feet/539m; length 5,200 feet/1,585m; gravel; no fuel.

Traveler facilities at the **Hotel Carmacks/ RV Park** include hotel accommodations and RV parking with hookups, and the Gold Panner Restaurant and Gold Dust Lounge (wonderful ambience). Hotel Carmacks also has a laundromat for RV and hotel guests to use. **Tatchun Centre**, part of the hotel complex, has a wide selection of groceries and souvenirs, as well as gas and diesel.

Baked goods, ice cream and a post office available locally. *NOTE: For those traveling with dogs, be aware that unaltered dogs run loose through town.*

Carmacks was once an important stop for Yukon River steamers traveling between Dawson City and Whitehorse, and it continues as a supply point today for modern river travelers. Carmacks has survived—

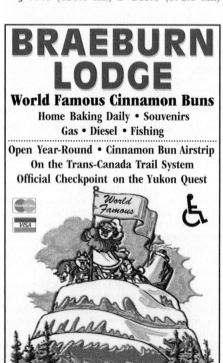

while other river ports have not—as a service center for highway traffic and mining interests. Carmacks was also a major stopping point on the old Whitehorse to Dawson Trail. Today it is a checkpoint on the Yukon Quest sled dog race and Yukon Ultra Marathon in February, and the Yukon River Quest in summer. Restored pioneer structures in Carmacks include the Carmacks Roadhouse and the Hazel Brown cabin.

Carmacks was named for George Carmack, who established a trading post here in the 1890s. Carmack had come North in 1885, hoping to strike it rich. He spent the next 10 years prospecting without success. In 1896, when the trading post went bankrupt, Carmack moved his family to Fortymile, where he could fish to eat and cut timber to sell. That summer, Carmack's remarkable persistence paid off—he unearthed a 5-dollar pan of coarse gold, during a time when a 10-cent pan was considered a good find. That same winter, he extracted more than a ton of gold from the creek, which he renamed Bonanza Creek, and its tributary, Eldorado. When word of Carmack's discovery reached the outside world the following spring, it set off the Klondike Gold Rush.

Visit the **Tagé Cho Hudän Interpretive Center** just north of the Yukon River bridge at **Milepost J 102.8**. It offers guided tours of Northern Tutchone culture with exhibits that include beaded slippers, a dug-out canoe, traditional garments and many other items. Indoor and outdoor exhibits. Phone 867-863-5831 for hours.

Enjoy the 1.2-mile/2-km interpretive boardwalk stroll alongside the Yukon River in Carmacks. Wheelchair accessible. There's a beautiful view of the countryside and Tantalus Butte; gazebo and park at end of trail.

For rock hounds, there are 5 agate trails in the area, which can double as good, short hiking trails. Abundant fishing in area rivers and lakes: salmon, grayling, northern pike, lake and rainbow trout and whitefish. 🐟

Klondike Loop Log

(continued)

J 102.1 (164.3 km) **D 221.3** (356.1 km) **S 220.2** (356.8 km) **Yukon River** bridge. Turnout and parking area at south end of bridge; 2.3-mile-/3.7-km-long trail to Coal Mine Lake.

J 102.8 (165.4 km) **D 220.6** (355 km) **S 220.9** (358 km) Northern Tutchone Trading Post with post office at north end of Yukon River bridge. The Northern Tutchone First Nations **Tagé Cho Hudän Interpretive Center** features archaeological displays on Native life in a series of indoor and outdoor exhibits, and marked interpretive trails. The center also features a mammoth snare diorama and has some arts and crafts.

J 103.5 (166.5 km) **D 219.9** (353.8 km) **S 221.6** (359.1 km) Turnoff to east for Campbell Highway, which leads south to Faro and Heritage Yukon's Campbell Region Interpretive Center (110 miles/177 km), Ross River (144 miles/232 km) and Watson Lake (373 miles/600 km). The Coal Mine (camping, cabins, food) located at this junction,

caters to river travelers; canoe rentals. 🅰️

Junction with Campbell Highway (Yukon Highway 4). Turn to end of CAMPBELL HIGHWAY section and read log back to front.

Highway climbs northbound.

J 104.4 (168 km) **D 219** (352.4 km) **S 222.5** (360.6 km) Turnout to west with litter bins, information sign and view of Yukon River Valley.

J 116.3 (187.2 km) **D 207.1** (333.3 km) **S 234.4** (380 km) **Five Finger Rapids Recreation Site** to west; large double-ended parking area to west with picnic tables, hiking trails, pit toilets, litter bins and viewing platform. Five Finger Rapids was named by early miners for the 5 channels, or fingers, formed by the rock pillars. They are a navigational

Carmacks Roadhouse (seen here) is on the historical walking tour; pick up a brochure at the Visitor Information Center. (©Sharon Nault)

CARMACKS ADVERTISERS

Hotel Carmacks/RV Park..............Ph. (867) 863-5221
Tatchun Centre.............................Ph. (867) 863-6171
Village of Carmacks.....................Ph. (867) 863-6271

Big Jonathon House in Pelly Crossing houses the Selkirk Heritage Center, featuring First Nations history and crafts. (©Judy Nadon, staff)

hazard. The safest passage is through the nearest, or east, passage. Stairs (219 steps) and a 0.6-mile/1-km trail lead down to a closer view of the rapids. Area flora includes prairie crocus, kinnikinnick, common juniper and sage. Watch for white-crowned sparrows and American tree sparrows. Information boards along stairway.

Information board at turnout on the Wood Cutters Range, the low hills in front of you, which were named "to honor the wood cutters who, between 1898 and 1955, worked tirelessly to stockpile wood for the fleet of sternwheelers on the Yukon River and its tributaries."

J 117.8 (189.6 km) **D 205.6** (330.9 km) **S 235.9** (382.2 km) Tatchun Creek bridge.

J 117.9 (189.7 km) **D 205.5** (330.7 km) **S 236** (382.4 km) Turnoff to east for **Tatchun Creek Yukon government campground**; 12 sites (4 pull-through), camping permit ($12), kitchen shelter, firewood, picnic tables, pit toilets and water (may not be potable). Good fishing for grayling, May 18–September 9; fish for salmon, July through August.

Highway climbs; passing lane northbound.

J 118.5 (190.5 km) **D 205** (329.9 km) **S 236.5** (383.5 km) Turnoff to east for Frenchman Lake Road (narrow, gravel) which leads to 3 campgrounds, each open May 18–Sept. 9; camping permit $12. Travel 5.2 miles/8.4 km to **Tatchun Lake Yukon government campground**; 20 campsites, boat launch. If road conditions allow, it is 20.7 miles/33.3 km to **Nunatuk Yukon government campground** (15 sites) and 26 miles/41.7 km to **Frenchman Lake Yukon government campground** (10 sites) before it junctions with the Campbell Highway. See **Milepost WL 337.5** in the CAMPBELL HIGHWAY section.

J 125.5 (202 km) **D 197.9** (318.5 km) **S 243.6** (394.8 km) **Yukon Crossing Viewpoint** to west; large, double-ended, gravel turnout with litter bins and toilets. Good photo stop overlooking the Yukon River. Welcome to Beringa interpretive sign reads:

"Beringa is the land mass stretching from Eastern Siberia through Alaska to the Yukon. If you could stand here 15,000 years ago near the end of the last glaciation, the vista would be of a dusty, treeless steppe at the edge of the ice sheet."

J 130.8 (210.5 km) **D 192.6** (310 km) **S 248.9** (403.5 km) McGregor Creek.

J 134.7 (216.8 km) **D 188.7** (303.7 km) **S 252.8** (409.7 km) Distance marker northbound shows Pelly Crossing 55 km/34 miles, Dawson City 308 km/191 miles.

J 142.6 (229.5 km) **D 180.8** (291 km) **S 260.7** (422.5 km) McCabe Creek. Double-ended gravel turnout to west at north end of bridge. *CAUTION: Watch for grizzly bears.*

J 146.6 (235.9 km) **D 176.8** (283.5 km) **S 264.7** (428.6 km) Access to **Minto Resort** (description follows). The resort hosts tour groups for lunch in a riverside pavilion and offers camping and a small convenience store to the general public, catering to both vehicle traffic and river traffic.

Minto Resort. Located on the Old Dawson Trail, half a kilometer off the Klondike Highway, Minto Resort is open from mid-May to mid-September. This beautiful location situated on the banks of the scenic Yukon River is a regular tour bus lunch stop. Minto also offers a rustic campground with pull-through RV sites, washhouse with bathrooms, showers and laundry, and a small convenience store. We welcome highway travelers, river travelers and anyone looking for a calm place to stop and take a break from their journey. Upgrades to full service RV sites, WiFi, cabins, boat launch, new kitchen and bathrooms will be undertaken during the next 2 years, so please stop in and see what we have to offer, as it is constantly improving! Visit our website at www. selkirkdevcorp.com and click on Minto Resort link. For reservations, email minto resort@selkirkdevcorp.com. [ADVERTISEMENT]

Fort Selkirk is located 25 river miles/40 km from Minto. The fort was established by Robert Campbell in 1848, for the Hudson's Bay Co. In 1852, the fort was destroyed by Chilkat Indians, who had dominated the fur trade of central Yukon, trading here with the Northern Tutchone people (Selkirk First Nations), who used the area as a seasonal home and exchanged furs for the Chilkat's coastal goods, until the arrival of the Hudson's Bay Co. The site was occupied sporadically over the years by traders, missionaries and the RCMP up until the 1950s. About 40 buildings—dating from 1892 to 1940—still stand in good repair; for details, go to www. tc.gov.yk.ca/publications/Fort_Selkirk.pdf. Fort Selkirk was designated a Yukon Historic Site in August 2010.

Fort Selkirk is accessibly only by river, most visitors arrive by canoe on their way from Whitehorse to Dawson City. There are no boat tours to Fort Selkirk currently available.

J 147.3 (237 km) **D 176.1** (283.4 km) **S 265.4** (429.9 km) Minto Road, a short loop road, leads west to Minto Mine (copper-gold) and the former riverboat landing and trading post of **MINTO**. **Private Aircraft:** Minto airstrip; elev. 1,550 feet/472m; length 5,000 feet/1,524m; gravel.

J 154 (247.8 km) **D 169.4** (272.6 km) **S 272.1** (440.6 km) Side road east to Lhútsäw Lake (Von Wilczek Lakes), an important wetland for ducks.

J 158.8 (255.5 km) **D 164.6** (264.9 km) **S 276.9** (448.2 km) Narrow dirt side road leads east 0.2 mile/0.3 km to small turnaround at Rock Island Lake (Tthi Ndu Mun Lake). Water lilies and other rare aquatic wildflowers bloom here in the shallows. American coots nest in the area.

J 161.3 (259.6 km) **D 162.1** (260.9 km) **S 279.4** (449.7 km) Forest Fire 1969 (sign).

J 162 (260.7 km) **D 161.4** (259.7 km) **S 280.5** (453.5 km) Meadow Lake to west is an athalassic or inland salt lake; note white salt deposits along the lakeshore. Look for American coots and horned grebes.

J 163.1 (262.5 km) **D 160.3** (258 km) **S 281.2** (455.7 km) Distance marker northbound shows Pelly Crossing 8 km/5 miles, Mayo 136 km/85 miles, Dawson City 261 km/162 miles. Wild strawberries (in season) along the highway.

J 166 (267.1 km) **D 157.4** (253.3 km) **S 284.1** (460.4 km) Highway descends northbound to Pelly Crossing. *Slow for speed zone through Pelly Crossing.*

Distance marker southbound shows Carmacks 100 km/62 miles, Whitehorse 277 km/172 miles.

Pelly Crossing

J 167.8 (270 km) **D 155.6** (250.4 km) **S 285.9** (463.1 km) Located on the banks of the Pelly River, halfway between Whitehorse and Dawson City. **Population:** 296. **Emergency Services:** Dial 911. **Radio:** CBC North 106.1 FM.

Private Aircraft: Pelly Airstrip, elev. 1,870 feet/570m; length 3,000 feet/914m; gravel; no services.

Selkirk Center has 24-hour cardlock gas/diesel, a grocery store, motel rooms, laundry, showers, bank and post office. The **Selkirk Heritage Center**, a replica of the **Big Jonathon House** at Fort Selkirk, is located next to the grocery store. The center offers self-guided tours of First Nations heritage, including beadwork displays, and crafts are for sale. The large, inspiring murals at Big Jonathon House were painted by local artists. Open mid-May to mid-September, daily 9 A.M. to 7 P.M.; closed Saturdays.

Selkirk Center. See display ad on facing page.

Pelly Crossing became a settlement when

the Klondike Highway was put through in 1950. A ferry transported people and vehicles across the Pelly River, where the road eventually continued to Dawson City. Most inhabitants of Pelly Crossing came from historic Fort Selkirk, now a national historic site.

This Selkirk First Nation community attracted residents from Minto when the highway to Dawson City was built. There is a school, curling rink, baseball field, swimming pool, church, youth center and laundromat. The local economy is based on hunting, trapping, fishing and guiding. The Selkirk First Nation has erected information boards near the bridge on the history and culture of the Selkirk people.

Klondike Loop Log
(continued)

J 168 (270.3 km) **D 155.4** (250.1 km) **S 286.1** (463.7 km) Pelly River bridge.

Slow for frost heaves and rough pavement northbound.

J 168.8 (271.6 km) **D 154.6** (248.8 km) **S 286.9** (465 km) Turnout to east: view of Pelly Crossing and river valley; monument and information boards (excerpts follow).

"In the 1950s a road was constructed north from Whitehorse, and Pelly Crossing was established as a ferry crossing and highway construction camp. With the completion of the road, the paddlewheelers stopped running the rivers and Fort Selkirk was virtually abandoned. The Selkirk First Nation first moved to Minto and finally settled at Pelly Crossing. Their Final Claims and Self-Government Agreements were signed at Minto in 1997. The Selkirk First Nation Council administers the community of Pelly Crossing.

"Robert Campbell was a Hudson's Bay Co. clerk at Fort Halkett, on the Liard River, in May 1840. After receiving instructions to explore the upper Liard River, he and 7 travelling companions paddled north to Frances Lake, traveled overland past Finlayson Lake and, on reaching the Pelly River, built a raft and poled a short distance downstream. Pelly Banks Post was constructed at the head of the Pelly River in 1842-43 and Campbell spent the next 2 winters there.

"In the winter of 1847-48, Campbell established Fort Selkirk at the mouth of the Pelly River."

The Pelly River was named by Robert Campbell in 1840 for Sir John Henry Pelly, governor of the Hudson's Bay Co. The Pelly heads near the Northwest Territories border and flows approximately 375 miles/603 km to the Yukon River.

J 169.7 (273 km) **D 153.7** (247.3 km) **S 287.8** (466.5 km) **Private Aircraft:** Airstrip to east; elev. 1,870 feet/570m; length 3,000 feet/914m; gravel. No services.

J 172.1 (277 km) **D 151.3** (243.5 km) **S 290.2** (470.4 km) Slow for frost heaves northbound.

J 177.9 (286.3 km) **D 145.5** (234.2 km) **S 296** (479.5 km) Double-ended turnout to east.

J 182.2 (293.2 km) **D 141.2** (227.2 km) **S 300.3** (486.4 km) Willow (Du Dettho) Creek culvert.

J 193.2 (310.9 km) **D 130.2** (209.5 km) **S 311.3** (505.4 km) Distance marker northbound shows Stewart Crossing 30 km/48 miles, Mayo 85 km/53 miles, Dawson City 210 km/130 miles.

J 195.3 (314.3 km) **D 128.1** (206.2 km) **S 313.4** (508 km) Turnout with litter bins to east. Winding descent begins for northbound traffic.

Distance marker southbound shows Pelly Crossing 40 km/25 miles, Carmacks 146 km/91 miles, Whitehorse 322 km/200 miles.

J 203.7 (327.8 km) **D 119.7** (192.6 km) **S 321.8** (519.7 km) Crooked Creek bridge.

(NOTE: Wood bridge decking can be slippery when wet.) Large turnout with litter bin to west at north end of bridge. Pike; grayling, use flies, summer best.

Southern boundary of Ddhaw Gro Special Management Area (formerly McArthur Wildlife Sanctuary). Grey Hunter Peak and surrounding hillsides support many species of wildlife, including Fannin sheep.

J 205 (329.9 km) **D 118.4** (190.5 km) **S 323.1** (523.7 km) Double-ended turnout with litter bin to east at turnoff for **Ethel Lake Yukon government campground**. Drive in 16.6 miles/26.7 km on narrow and winding side road (not recommended for large RVs) for campground; 10 sites, boat launch, fishing. Open May 18 to Sept. 9, camping permit $12.

J 211.6 (340.5 km) **D 111.8** (179.9 km) **S 329.7** (534 km) Stewart Crossing; gas/diesel. Silver Trail Information Center to west. Highway maintenance camp.

In 1886 **STEWART CROSSING** was the site of a trading post established by Arthur Harper, Alfred Mayo and Jack McQuesten to support gold mining in the area. Later a roadhouse was built here as part of the Whitehorse to Dawson overland stage route. Stewart Crossing also functioned as a fuel stop for riverboats and during the 1930s was a transfer point for the silver ore barges from Mayo. Harper, Mayo and McQuesten are 3 prominent names in Yukon history. Harper, an Irish immigrant, was one of the first white men to prospect in the Yukon, although he never struck it rich. Mayo, a native of Maine, explored, prospected and traded in the Yukon until his death in 1924. McQuesten, like Harper, worked his way north from the California goldfields and is often referred to as the "Father of the Yukon." A founding member of the Yukon order of Pioneers, Jack Leroy Napoleon McQuesten ended his trading and prospecting days in 1898 when he moved to California. He died in 1909 while in Seattle for the Alaska–Yukon–Pacific Exposition.

J 212.1 (341.3 km) **D 111.3** (179.1 km) **S 330.2** (535 km) Stewart River bridge. The Stewart River flows into the Yukon River upstream from Dawson City.

J 212.2 (341.5 km) **D 111.2** (179 km) **S 330.3** (535.2 km) Stop sign at north end of Stewart River bridge at **junction** with Yukon Highway 11 east for **side trip** to Mayo and Keno City. (Northbound travelers turn right

for Keno City, left to continue to Dawson City.

Junction with the Silver Trail (Yukon Highway 11) to Mayo, Elsa and Keno City. See the "Silver Trail" log beginning on page 298.

View to southwest of Stewart River and mountains as highway climbs northbound.

Slow for frost heaves and damaged road northbound.

J 218.5 (351.6 km) **D 104.9** (168.8 km) **S 336.6** (545.4 km) Dry Creek.

J 222 (357.3 km) **D 101.4** (163.2 km) **S 340.1** (551 km) Double-ended dirt turnout to south is Stewart River viewpoint; pit toilet, picnic tables, information boards. A major tributary of the Yukon River, the Stewart River was named for James G. Stewart, an assistant to Robert Campbell of the Hudson's Bay Co. In 1849, Stewart was the first European to discover the river.

J 224 (360.5 km) **D 99.4** (160 km) **S 342.1** (554.2 km) Distance marker northbound shows Dempster Highway 121 km/75 miles, Dawson City 161 km/100 miles.

J 226.7 (364.8 km) **D 96.7** (155.6 km) **S 344.8** (558.5 km) **Moose Creek Lodge.** A must for Yukon travelers! The historic log building has a restaurant offering excellent food and legendary pastries; souvenir shop; and books. Cozy rustic guest cabins, operated as B&B with hearty breakfasts. Open daily 8 A.M. to 6 P.M., mid-May through mid-September. Groups, caravans, motorcycles welcome. Reservations recommended. www.moosecreek–lodge.com. Phone 867-996-2550. [ADVERTISEMENT]

J 226.9 (365.1 km) **D 96.5** (155.3 km) **S 346** (556.8 km) Moose Creek bridge.

J 227.1 (365.5 km) **D 96.3** (155 km) **S 346.2** (559.3 km) Turnoff to west for **Moose Creek Yukon government campground** adjacent Moose Creek and Stewart River; good picnic spot; 36 sites (4 pull-throughs), kitchen shelter, playground, playfield, picnic tables, firepits, firewood, water (may not be potable), garbage and recycling bins, bear proof lockers, pit toilets. Open May 18–Sept. 19, camping fee $12. Short trail to **Stewart River** is a 30-minute walk through boreal forest along Moose Creek. Good grayling fishing and good birdwatching.

Highway climbs northbound.

J 240.2 (386.6 km) **D 83.2** (133.9 km) **S 358.3** (580.2 km) McQuesten River bridge, a tributary of the Stewart River, named for
(Continues on page 300)

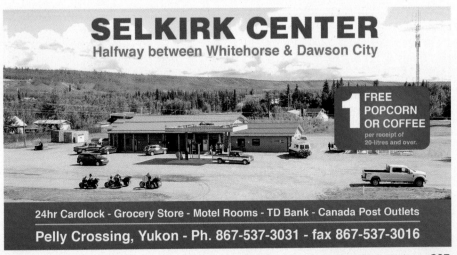

Silver Trail

The unique community of Keno City is located at the end of the Silver Trail. (©Judy Nadon staff)

Silver Trail leads northeast from **Milepost J 212.2** Klondike Highway to Mayo, Elsa and Keno City, a favorite destination for Yukoners. It is approximately 140 miles/225 km round-trip to Keno City and an easy day trip for motorists. If you have a Yukon Explorer's Passport, the Binet House Museum in Mayo and the Keno City Mining Museum in Keno City are considered two of the most exclusive passport stamps.

The road is asphalt-surfaced to Mayo, and well-maintained gravel from Mayo to Keno City. *IMPORTANT: Gas is available only at Stewart Crossing and Mayo; there is no fuel in Keno City.*

The Silver Trail to Mayo follows the Stewart River through what has been one of the richest silver mining regions in Canada. The Silver Trail region encompasses the traditional lands of the First Nation of Nacho Nyäk Dun.

YUKON HIGHWAY 11

Distance is measured from the junction with the Klondike Highway (K).

K 0 Silver Trail (Stewart Crossing). The Silver Trail leads northeast from **Milepost J 212.2** on the Klondike Highway.

K 4 (6.4 km) View of Stewart River to the south. Highway follows river eastbound, view often obscured by trees.

K 6.4 (10.3 km) Devil's Elbow trail; parking and turnaround area at end of side road to south. Narrow interpretive trail leads back across Silver Trail and up steep bank to view-

ing platform; 30 minutes round-trip, bring mosquito repellent.

K 11.9 (19.1 km) Large double-ended turnout with litter bin and information boards overlooking the Stewart River.

K 19.5 (31.3 km) Double-ended turnout and rescue shelter.

K 27.4 (44.1 km) Double-ended rest area with pit toilets and litter bin.

K 30.9 (49.7 km) McIntyre Park municipal campground (entrance prior to bridge westbound) on banks of the Mayo River west side of bridge; 5 picnic sites and a shelter; free camping and wood provided. ▲

Mayo River bridge. Good fishing from bridge for grayling. ⌐

K 31.5 (50.7 km) **Junction** with access road to Mayo (description follows); AFD Petroleum public cardlock gas/diesel station. Turn south for Mayo, keep north for road to Elsa and Keno City. ⛽

Mayo

K 31.5 (50.7 km) Located on the bank of the Stewart River near its confluence with the Mayo River. **Population:** 450. **Emergency Services:** Dial 911.

Visitor Information: Visit the **Binet House Interpretive Center/Museum** (pictured below); open 10 A.M. to 6 P.M. daily mid-May to mid-September; phone 867-996-2926; 867-996-2317; email mayo@northwestel.net; website: www.villageofmayo.ca. Visit the Binet House Museum to see exhibits about the geology and history of the area or shop their gift shop. Get your Yukon Explorer's Passport stamped here. Pick up a free copy of the excellent *Mayo Historical Buildings Walking Tour* booklet.

Elevation: 1,650 feet/503m. **Climate:**

©Kris Valencia, staff

Residents claim it's the coldest and hottest spot in Yukon. Record low, -80°F/-62.2°C (February 1947); record high, 97°F/36.1°C (June 1969). **Radio:** CBC 1230 AM; CHON 90.5 FM; CKRW (RUSH) 98.7 FM. **Television:** CBC Anik, Channel 7; Shaw or Bell Satellite TV. **Transportation:** Air North (www.flyairnorth.com) serves Mayo with scheduled flights on Tuesday, Wednesday and Thursday. Alkan Air floatplane service, located on the Stewart River at Mayo,

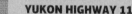

offers drop-off service to the rivers of central Yukon, including the Peel River Watershed, and provides campsites and hot showers for river paddlers at their Stewart River property. Charter helicopter service available.

Private Aircraft: Mayo airstrip, 4 miles/6.5 km north; elev. 1,653 feet/504m; length 4,850 feet/1,478m; gravel; fuel 100, Jet B.

Mayo has most traveler facilities, including food, gas and lodging. Lodging and camping at **Bedrock Motel and RV Park.** Groceries at the TGP store along the riverfront. Post office, liquor store and library located in the Government of Yukon Territory Administration Building (high-speed internet available in the Binet House Museum, the library and at Yukon College). Bank service available at Mayo Firehall Tuesday to Friday 10:30 A.M. to 3 P.M. There are 2 churches in the area. Depending on your provider, there should be cell service available in this community.

Mayo began as a river settlement and port in 1902–1903 after gold was discovered in the area. It was also known as Mayo Landing. River traffic increased with silver-lead ore shipments from Keno Hill silver mines to Whitehorse. Today, Mayo is a service center for mineral exploration in the area. Yukon Energy Corporation operates a hydroelectric project here.

There is a viewing deck with interpretive signs overlooking the Stewart River. Canoeists can put in at Mayo on the Stewart River for a paddle to Stewart Crossing or Dawson City.

Silver Trail Log
(continued)

K 31.5 (50.7 km) **Junction** with access road to Mayo; AFD gas station.

K 32.1 (51.6 km) **Bedrock Motel & RV Park.** See display ad on facing.

K 32.4 (52.1 km) Mayo airport, built in 1928 by the Treadwell–Yukon Mining Co.

K 34.5 (55.5 km) Side road (closed to public) to Mayo hydro dam, built in 1951 and completed in 1952. A walking trail departs from this location.

K 35.3 (56.8 km) Turnoff to west for **Five Mile Lake Yukon government campground**; 20 sites (open May 18–Sept. 9, camping fee $12), kitchen shelter, picnic tables, pit toilets, firepits, hiking trail and swimming.

K 35.5 (57.1 km) Five Mile Lake day-use area with playground. Pavement ends, gravel begins, northbound.

K 37.2 (59.9 km) Wareham Lake to west, created by the Mayo River power project.

K 39.8 (64 km) Minto bridge; marshy area, good birdwatching. Parking to west with interpretive signs, hiking trails, toilets, garbage bins. Minto Farm to east.

K 42.3 (68.5 km) **Junction** of Yukon Highway 11 with Minto Lake Road and Duncan Creek/Mayo Lake Road. Continue on Yukon Highway 11 for Keno City.

For **Minto Lake** drive 12 miles/19 km west on Minto Lake Road; good fishing for lake trout and grayling. Also access to Highet Creek.

The 25-mile/40-km Duncan Creek Road to the east was the original Silver Trail used by Treadwell–Yukon during the 1930s to haul silver-lead ore from Keno City into Mayo. It is now a back road into Keno City

and to Mayo Lake. *NOTE: Inquire in Mayo or Keno City about road conditions on this side road before driving.*

K 47.3 (76 km) Watch for turnoff for Mount Haldane trail; follow gravel road 2 miles/3.2 km to trailhead. This 4-mile-/6.4-km-long walking trail leads to the summit of **Mount Haldane,** elev. 6,023 feet/1,836m, and offers sweeping views of the McQuesten River valley, the Elsa mine and the Village of Mayo. Hikers in good physical condition can make the round-trip in approximately 6 hours. Inquire locally for current trail conditions. The switched-back trail is visible on the south face of Mount Haldane. The trail was cut by a mining company in the 1970s and brushed out in recent years.

K 47.5 (76.4 km) Turnout with information boards by Halfway Lake.

K 47.7 (76.7 km) Entrance to Silver Trail Inn and RV Park.

K 48.4 (77.7 km) Mount Haldane Lions survival shelter.

K 53.8 (86.5 km) South McQuesten River Road.

K 59.3 (95.4 km) Main gate to **ELSA.** This active mining and reclamation site is owned and operated Alexco Resources. There is no visitor access, although buildings at Elsa are visible from the road and there are turnoffs to these structures. Information sign here reads:

"In 1924, prospector Charlie Brefalt staked a silver claim here on Galena Hill and named it after his sister, Elsa. It proved to be a major discovery and eventually produced millions of ounces of silver. Other properties in the area, such as the Silver King and Calumet, also developed into major mines. By the 1930s, the town of Elsa had taken shape and it gradually became the major community serving the mines. Since, 1948, Elsa has been home to United Keno Hill Mines, which at one time was the world's fourth largest producer of silver concentrates."

K 59.5 (95.7 km) Watch for a plaque commemorating American engineer Livingston Wernecke, who came to the Keno Hill area in 1919 to investigate the silver-lead ore discoveries for Treadwell-Yukon Mining Co.

K 63 (101.4 km) Side road leads north to Hanson Lakes and McQuesten Lake (9.2 miles/14.8 km). Galena Hill to east.

Keno City

K 68.1 (109.5 km) Historic frontier town nestled in the mountains at the end of the Silver Trail. **Population:** 20. **Emergency Services:** Dial 911. **Nursing Station:** Mayo Health Center, phone 867-996-4444. **Visitor Information:** At the **Keno City Mining Museum.**

Enormously rich discoveries of silver made Keno City a boom town in the 1920s. Today, Keno City is home to an eclectic mix of oldtimers, miners, and artists (the town

was featured in a *New York Times* article, Oct. 15, 2017). Visitor services in Keno City include hotel accommodations at the historic **Keno City Hotel;** accommodations at the Silver Moon Bunkhouse; and dining at Keno City Snack Bar and The Sourdough Cafe & Tavern. Showers and laundromat adjacent Community Center.

Keno Community Campground, in town next to Lightning Creek, has secluded RV sites, water, firewood, firepits and pit toilets.

High-grade silver-lead ore was first discovered near Keno Hill area in 1903. Mining was underway in 1913 and the first mill was constructed on Keno Hill in 1925. **Keno City Mining Museum,** located in Jackson Hall, is a Heritage Yukon site. Featured at the museum are tools and equipment used in the early days of mining (larger equipment is housed in the building which is across from the museum); a large photography collection; and artifacts of everyday life in the Yukon's isolated mining towns. Museum hours (subject to change) are 10 A.M. to 6 P.M. daily from May 20, 2019 (Victoria Day, 3-day weekend) to mid-September. Have your Yukon Passport stamped here.

Next door to the museum, the Alpine Interpretive Center has displays on area fauna, such as butterflies, marmots and pikas.

Good hiking and biking trails criss-cross the area, leading to historic mine sites, scenic valleys and alpine meadows. The trails vary in distance from a half-mile/1 km to 12 miles/20 kms, and range from easy to strenuous. There is also fishing and canoeing on area lakes and guided hunting.

A popular side trip is walking or driving the winding Signpost Road 6.5 miles/10.5 km to the top of **Keno Hill,** elev. 6,065 feet/1,849m. Panoramic views of the valley and mountain ranges. *IMPORTANT: Inquire locally about road conditions before driving Keno Hill Road to the summit, or Duncan Creek Road back to Mayo.*

Return to Milepost J 212.2
Klondike Loop

Bonanza Creek Road offers access to the magnificent Dredge No. 4 (seen here), as well as gold panning sites and historical stops (©Kris Valencia, staff)

(Continued from page 297)
Jack (Leroy Napoleon) McQuesten.

J 244.8 (394 km) **D 78.6** (126.5 km) **S 364.3** (587.8 km) Partridge Creek Farm.

J 246.6 (396.9 km) **D 76.8** (123.6 km) **S 364.7** (590.7 km) **Private Aircraft:** McQuesten airstrip 1.2 miles/1.9 km west; elev. 1,500 feet/457m; length 5,000 feet/1,524m; gravel and turf. No services.

J 254.6 (409.8 km) **D 68.7** (110.6 km) **S 375.1** (603.7 km) Distance marker northbound shows Dempster Highway Jct. 71 km/44 miles, Dawson City 111 km/69 miles.

J 260.9 (419.9 km) **D 62.5** (100.6 km) **S 379** (614 km) Beaver Dam Creek.

J 263.2 (423.5 km) **D 60.2** (96.9 km) **S 381.3** (617.7 km) Willow Creek.

J 266.1 (428.2 km) **D 57.3** (92.2 km) **S 384.2** (621 km) Gravel Lake rest area; large parking area with litter bins, outhouses and information boards. Gravel Lake is an important wetland for migratory birds in spring and fall. Because of its location on the Tintina Trench corridor, unusual birds are sometimes seen here, including ruddy ducks, black scoters and the most northerly sightings of American coots.

J 270 (434.3 km) **D 53.6** (86.2 km) **S 389.6** (627 km) Meadow Creek.

Slow for frost heaves and damaged road northbound.

J 274.1 (441.1 km) **D 49.5** (79.7 km) **S 393.7** (639.7 km) Causeway crosses over marshy area. Slow for damaged road.

J 276.7 (445.3 km) **D 46.7** (75.2 km)

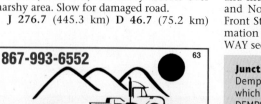

S 394.8 (638 km) Begin 6 to 8 percent winding downhill grade northbound.

J 277.5 (446.6 km) **D 45.9** (73.9 km) **S 395.6** (639.7 km) Stone Boat Swamp.

J 285.6 (459.6 km) **D 37.8** (60.8 km) **S 403.7** (652.4 km) Distance marker northbound shows Dempster Highway 21 km/13 miles, Dawson City 61 km/38 miles.

J 286.3 (460.7 km) **D 37.1** (59.7 km) **S 404.4** (655.2 km) Tintina Trench rest area to east; large gravel turnout with litter bins, pit toilets and information panels. The Tintina Trench, which extends hundreds of miles across Yukon and Alaska, is the largest fault in North America and 1 of 2 major bird migration corridors in the Yukon (the other is the Shakwak Trench).

J 291.9 (469.7 km) **D 31.5** (50.7 km) **S 410** (664.4 km) Flat Creek bridge.

J 294.4 (473.8 km) **D 29** (46.7 km) **S 412.5** (664.5 km) Viewpoint to east with historic sign about Klondike River and information board on Dempster Highway. Highway follows Klondike River northbound.

J 298.3 (480 km) **D 25.1** (40.4 km) **S 416.4** (674.6 km) **Junction** with Dempster Highway at Dempster Corner. AFD public cardlock gas/diesel station.

The Dempster Highway leads northeast from here 456 miles/734 km to Inuvik, NWT. Services are available on the Dempster only at Eagle Plains Hotel, Fort McPherson and Inuvik. Stop by the Dempster Highway and Northwest Territories Info Center on Front Street in Dawson City for more information and refer to the DEMPSTER HIGHWAY section in this book.

Junction of Klondike Highway and the Dempster Highway (Yukon Highway 5), which leads northeast to Inuvik, NWT. See DEMPSTER HIGHWAY section for log of that road.

J 298.8 (480.9 km) **D 24.6** (39.6 km) **S 416.9** (675.5 km) Distance marker northbound shows Dawson City 40 km/25 miles.

J 304.1 (489.4 km) **D 19.3** (31.1 km) **S 422.2** (683.9 km) Goring Creek.

J 308.1 (495.8 km) **D 18.9** (30.4 km) **S 426.2** (690.5 km) *Slow for speed zone northbound through* Henderson's Corner residential area.

J 310.5 (499.7 km) **D 12.9** (20.8 km) **S 428.6** (694 km) Rock Creek.

J 311.7 (501.6 km) **D 11.7** (18.8 km) **S 429.8** (696.7 km) Turnoff to northeast for **Klondike River Yukon government campground**, located on Rock Creek next to the Klondike River; 35 sites (2 pull-through), kitchen shelter, picnic tables, firepits, firewood, bear-proof lockers, pit toilets, garbage and recycling bins, water (may not be potable), playground. Open May 18 to Sept. 9, camping permit, $12. A 1.7 km/1 mile interpretive trail/boardwalk leads to the river. Flora includes Labrador tea, highbush cranberry, prickly rose, Arctic bearberry and horsetails.

J 313.3 (504.2 km) **D 10.1** (16.2 km) **S 431.4** (697.5 km) Dawson City airport to southwest.

J 314 (505.3 km) **D 9.4** (15.1 km) **S 432.1** (700.2 km) Viewpoint and Hunker Creek Road to west. Hunker Creek Road (gravel) connects with Upper Bonanza Creek Road, which makes a 60-mile/96-km loop back to the Klondike Highway via Bonanza Creek Road. Upper Bonanza Creek Road is a narrow, gravel, mountain road that is *not suitable for RVs or trailers. The climb is a challenge for an average car.*

Albert Hunker staked the first claim on Hunker Creek Sept. 11, 1896. George Carmack made the big discovery on Bonanza Creek on Aug. 17, 1896. Hunker Creek is 16 miles/26 km long, of which 13 miles/21 km was dredged between 1906 and 1966.

J 315.3 (507.4 km) **D 8.1** (13 km) **S 434.2** (702.1 km) Gas/diesel station.

J 315.6 (507.9 km) **D 7.8** (12.5 km) **S 433.9** (702.4 km) Bear Creek Road leads to subdivision.

J 315.9 (508.4 km) **D 7.5** (12.1 km) **S 434** (703 km) Distance marker northbound shows Dawson City 11 km/7 miles.

J 316.2 (508.9 km) **D 7.2** (11.6 km) **S 434.3** (703.8 km) Turnout to east with historic sign about the Yukon Ditch and tailings. The Yukon Ditch, built by Yukon Gold Co., was a ditch, flume and pipe system that carried water from the Ogilvie Mountains to the hydraulic mining operations on Bonanza Creek. It operated from 1909 until the 1930s. The tailings (mounds of gravel and rock) from hydraulic mining operations line both sides of the highway.

J 318.1 (511.9 km) **D 5.3** (8.5 km) **S 436.2** (706 km) Dawson City's welcome kiosk.

J 319.5 (514.2 km) **D 4.2** (6.7 km) **S 437.6** (709.2 km) Callison subdivision. Access to ERS fuel station, 0.3 mile west; with gas/diesel and propane, and **Chief Isaac Mechanical** truck and vehicle repair.

Chief Isaac Mechanical. See display ad this page.

J 321.2 (516.9 km) **D 2.2** (3.5 km) **S 439.3** (711.6 km) **Junction** with **Bonanza Creek Road.** This wonderful **side trip** should not be missed! Bonanza Creek Road provides access to **Claim 33 Gold Panning,** Dredge No. 4, Discovery Claim National Historic and Interpretive Site and Free Claim No. 6 gold panning site; mileages and descriptions follow. Information boards along Bonanza Creek Road highlight the history of mining in this area.

Mile 1.7/2.7 km Pavement ends, gravel begins, southbound.

Mile 6/9.6 km: Learn to gold pan at

Claim 33 or pick up a book about the gold rush (*Gold Diggers: Striking It Rich in the Klondike* by Charlotte Gray is a great read).

Claim 33 Gold Panning. Learn to pan for gold (guaranteed) at Historic Claim 33—one of the original claims staked on Bonanza Creek. Wander around artifacts that will transport you back to the heyday of the Klondike Gold Rush. Souvenir shop and gold

jewelry from the Klondike. Tour groups welcome. Open mid-May–mid-September. Km 10/Mile 6 Bonanza Rd. Phone 867-993-6626. claim33@northwestel.net. www.claim33.vpweb.ca. [ADVERTISEMENT]

Mile 7.4/11.9 km **Dredge No. 4** is the largest wooden hull, bucket-line dredge in North America. Built in 1912, it was one of 2 dozen dredges that worked this area. There is an information kiosk at the site and guided tours are offered.

Mile 8.6/13.8 km Road forks southbound: Take center fork.

©Kris Valencia, staff

Mile 8.8/14.2 km Double-ended turnout with parking, toilets, litter bins and picnic tables at **Discovery Claim National Historic Site.** Excellent walking paths with benches and information boards (pictured above). Discovery Claim was the first gold claim on Bonanza Creek and the one that started the Klondike Stampede of 1898.

Mile 9.4/15.1 km Klondike Visitor Association's free attraction, **Claim No. 6** on Bonanza Creek. You can pan for gold for free at any time; bring your own gold pan. Information boards, picnic tables, litter bins and parking.

Mile 9.5/15.3 km Large rutted turnaround and outhouses.

Bonanza Creek Road is maintained to about Mile 11/18 km. It connects with Upper Bonanza Creek Road (narrow, winding, unmaintained gravel), which forms a 60-mile/96-km loop that climbs to an elevation of 4,000 feet before descending back to the Klondike Highway at **Milepost J 314** via Hunker Creek Road. *Upper Bonanza Creek Road is not recommended for RVs or trailers.*

J 321.3 (517.1 km) D 2.1 (3.4 km) S 439.4 (711.9 km) Napa and AFD gas/diesel station to northeast, **Bonanza Gold Motel & RV Park** to southwest.

Bonanza Gold Motel & RV Park. See display ad on this page.

J 321.4 (517.2 km) D 2 (3.32 km) S 439.5

The Commissioner's Residence housed 6 Yukon Commissioners between 1901 and 1916, including George and Martha Black. (©Kris Valencia, staff)

(712 km) **Dawson City RV Park & Campground** and gas station (gas/diesel and propane), tire repair, convenience store with grocery items, books and souvenirs.

Dawson City RV Park & Campground. See display ad on page 302.

J 321.5 (517.4 km) D 1.9 (3.1 km) S 439.6 (712.4 km) Klondike River bridge.

J 322 (518.2 km) D 1.4 (2.3 km) S 440.1 (713.4 km) Take Dome Road (chip-sealed) to north for a 4.5 miles/7.2 km **side trip** to **Midnight Dome** (elev. 2,911 feet/887m). This offers a wonderful viewpoint of Dawson City, the Yukon and Klondike rivers, Bonanza Creek and the Ogilvie Mountains.

J 322.7 (519.3 km) D 0.7 (1.1 km) S 440.8 (714.6 km) RCMP detachment post.

J 322.9 (519.6 km) D 0.5 (0.8 km) S 440.4 (713.9 km) Double-ended turnout with picnic tables by Yukon River walk.

Across the street is the Commissioner's Residence; costumed interpreter on site.

J 323.3 (520.2 km) D 0.1 S 441.4 (715.2 km) **Dawson City Visitor Information Center** on Front St. at King St. *Description of Dawson City begins on page 302.*

J 323.4 (520.3 km) D 0 S 441.5 (715.4 km) Staging area for *George Black* passenger/vehicle ferry across Yukon River to/from Top of the World Highway. *Log of Klondike Loop continues on page 308.*

Southbound: This section of the log shows distance from junction with the Alaska Highway in Yukon (J) followed by distance from Dawson City (D) and distance from Skagway (S). Read log:

Physical kilometerposts southbound reflect distance from Skagway. Distance from Skagway in miles reflects driving distance.

View from the Dome of Dawson City, situated on the Yukon River at its confluence with the Klondike River. (©Kris Valencia, staff)

Dawson City

J 323.4 (520.3 km) **D 0**
S 441.5 (715.4 km)
Located 165 miles/266 km south of the Arctic Circle, 333 miles/536 km north of Whitehorse and 187 miles from Tok, AK. Situated on the Yukon River at its confluence with the Klondike River. Landmark for river travelers is Moosehide Slide. **Population:** 1,879. **Emergency Services:** Dial 911. **Hospital,** Dawson City Community Hospital, 501 Sixth Ave., phone 867-993-4444.

Visitor Information: The Visitor Information Center, operated by Yukon Government and Parks Canada, is located at the corner of Front and King Street. Open daily, 8 A.M. to 8 P.M., May to September; phone 867-993-5566; website DawsonCity.ca. (From October to April, the Klondike Visitors Association on the second floor is available to answer visitor questions.)

Housed in a replica of the 1897 Alaska Commercial Co. store, the Visitor Center provides tour and accommodation information; a Dawson City street map; and a schedule of summer programs available.

Watch Dawson City historical movies and see the model railway of the historic Klondike Mines railway. Parks Canada walking tours are available daily from mid-May to late September, with a costumed guide or as a self-guided audio tour (fee charged). Tickets for walking tours/audio may be purchased at the Visitor Center's Parks Canada information desk; phone 867-993-7210.

Dawson City has lots to do and see. If you want to take it all in, plan a stay for 3 days or more to cover most of the attractions. Check out Dawson City on Facebook (Dawson City, Yukon), Instagram (@Visit DawsonCity) and Twitter (@DawsonCity Yukon) for inspiration before your visit.

The Dempster Highway and Northwest Territories Information Center is located in the B.Y.N. (British Yukon Navigation) Building on Front Street (across from the Dawson City Visitor Information Center); open daily 9 A.M. to 7 P.M. in summer. Information on Tombstone Territorial Park, the Northwest Territories and the Dempster Highway. Phone 867-993-6167, fax 867-993-6334.

Elevation: 1,050 feet/320m. **Climate:** There are 20.9 hours of daylight June 21, 3.8 hours of daylight on Dec. 21. Mean high in July, 72°F/22.2°C. Mean low in January, -30.5°F/ -34.7°C. First fall frost end of August, last spring frost end of May. Annual snowfall 59.8 inches. **Radio:** CBC 560 AM; CBC-2 104.9 FM; CHON 90.5 FM; local community broadcasts Thursday to Sunday on CFYT 106.9 FM. **Television:** Cable & Satellite **Newspaper:** *Klondike Sun* (bi-weekly).

Private Aircraft: 11 miles/17.7 km south. Runway 02-20; elev. 1,215 feet/370m; length 5,005 feet/1,526m; taxiway and apron are paved, airstrip is gravel; 100LL, Jet A. Customs available; call 867-993-5338. Flightseeing trips and air charters available.

Description

For millennia, the Han-speaking Tr'ondëk Hwëch'in lived and traveled in a vast area extending from the Yukon River valley into the neighboring mountains. At the heart of their home was Tr'ochëk, a large fish camp at the confluence of the Klondike and Yukon Rivers, adjacent to what is now Dawson City. With the discovery of gold on a Klondike River tributary (Rabbit Creek, now named Bonanza Creek) in 1896, the Tr'ondëk Hwëch'in were displaced by the influx of gold seekers and the boom town built to serve them. The Tr'ondëk Hwëch'in moved their camp to Moosehide Village, downstream from Dawson City.

Most of the prospectors who staked claims on Klondike creeks were already in the North before the big strike, many working claims in the Forty Mile area north of Dawson City. The stampeders coming North in the great gold rush the following year found most of the gold-bearing streams already staked.

Dawson City was Yukon's first capital, when the Yukon became a separate territory in 1898. But by 1953, Whitehorse—on the railway and the highway, and with a large airport—was so much the hub of activity that the federal government moved the capital from Dawson City, along with 800 civil servants. Some recompense was offered in the form of a road linking Whitehorse with the mining at Mayo and Dawson City. With its completion, White Pass trucks replaced White Pass river steamers.

New government buildings were built in Dawson, including a fire hall. In 1962 the federal government reconstructed the Palace Grand Theatre for a gold rush festival that featured the Broadway musical Foxy, with Bert Lahr, who played the cowardly lion in the classic Wizard of Oz. A museum was established in the Administration Building and tours and entertainments were begun.

Dawson City was declared a National Historic Site of Canada in the early 1960s and has been nominated for UNESCO World Heritage Site status (under the name Tr'ondek-Klondike). Many buildings here have been restored, some reconstructed and others stabilized. Parks Canada offers a range of interpretive programs for visitors to this historic town.

In 1998, 100 years after the gold rush, the Tr'ondëk Hwëch'in negotiated the return of self-governance. The Tr'ochëk fish camp has been designated a Tr'ondëk Hwëch'in Heritage Site as well as a National Historic Site of Canada. Visitors may explore the traditional and contemporary life of the Tr'ondëk Hwëch'in at the Dänojà Zho Cultural Center, across from the Visitor Information Center. The center is open May to August and by special request during the off-season.

Lodging & Services

Accustomed to a summer influx of visitors, Dawson has modern hotels and motels (rates average $125 and up), bed and breakfasts and hostels. Dawson City accommodations fill up early in summer and for special events, so make reservations in advance. There are many places to eat in Dawson City, from ice cream shops and coffee houses to fine dining. Many if not most of the hotels also have dining rooms and pubs and saloons. *See advertisements this section and the list of Dawson City Advertisers on page 306.*

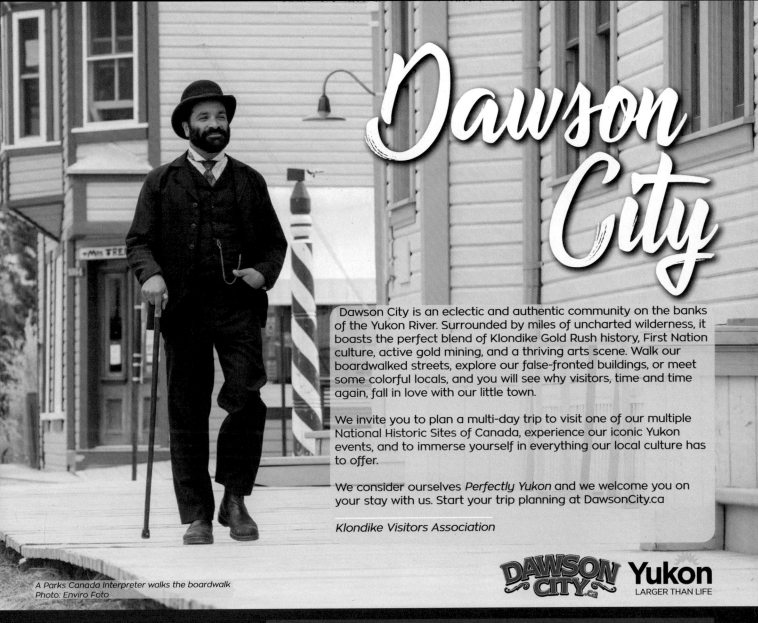

Dawson City

Dawson City is an eclectic and authentic community on the banks of the Yukon River. Surrounded by miles of uncharted wilderness, it boasts the perfect blend of Klondike Gold Rush history, First Nation culture, active gold mining, and a thriving arts scene. Walk our boardwalked streets, explore our false-fronted buildings, or meet some colorful locals, and you will see why visitors, time and time again, fall in love with our little town.

We invite you to plan a multi-day trip to visit one of our multiple National Historic Sites of Canada, experience our iconic Yukon events, and to immerse yourself in everything our local culture has to offer.

We consider ourselves *Perfectly Yukon* and we welcome you on your stay with us. Start your trip planning at DawsonCity.ca

Klondike Visitors Association

A Parks Canada Interpreter walks the boardwalk
Photo: Enviro Foto

DAWSON CITY.ca   **Yukon** LARGER THAN LIFE

WIDE OPEN SPACES

Three unique northern drives to make you feel like the King of the Road

Dawson City is at the junction of three amazing roads, each offering its own iconic opportunity to see the North:

DEMPSTER HIGHWAY

The only highway in Canada with access to the Arctic Ocean. This bucket-list gravel route features spectacular vistas, over 450 miles of pristine wilderness while crossing two of Canada's Territories. A must do for any modern-day adventurer!

Highlights: Arctic Circle/Ocean, Tombstone Park

TOP OF THE WORLD

Connecting the Yukon to Alaska between mid-May & late-September, this road dares to be different. Travellers snake along the top of a mountain ridge while eperiencing breathtaking rolling scenery and unexpected flora and fauna.

Highlights: Chicken, AK, George Black Ferry

NORTH KLONDIKE HIGHWAY

For over 300 miles, this road follows the route of the Gold Rush Stampeders of 1897-98. Take your time and meander along the mighty Yukon River, passing by historical and environmental wonders.

Highlights: Tintina Trench, Five Finger Rapids

The Dempster Highway in fall
Photo: Julien Schroeder

☑ SOURDOUGH CHALLENGE

Want a true-Yukon experience? Complete this Dawson City to-do list and they'll be calling you a Sourdough in no-time!

- [ ] **Find some gold!**
  (By panning or at one of our local shops)
- [ ] **Learn to say "Hello" in Hän**
  (Dänojà Zho Cultural Centre has you covered!)
- [ ] **Get Local!**
  (Eat local, shop local, meet a local)
- [ ] **Attend one of our exciting events!**
  (We host the most!)
- [ ] **Dare to kiss the Sourtoe Cocktail**
  (We bet it's not as bad as you think!)
- [ ] **Take your picture atop the Dome**
  (No flash required!)
- [ ] **Hit a "Jackpot" at Gerties**
  (By gambling or enjoying a cancan show!)
- [ ] **Find 10 heritage sites or buildings**
  (There are over forty around Dawson)
- [ ] **See the magic of our Northern skies**
  (Catch Northern lights or the iconic midnight sun)
- [ ] **Recite a quote on *Authors on Eighth***
  (There are stranger things done in the midnight sun...)

DAWSON CITY.ca

Parks Canada's SS Keno, National Historic Site of Canada
Photo: Rolling Van Creative

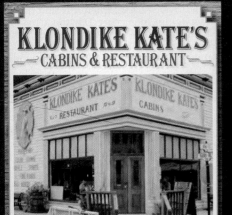

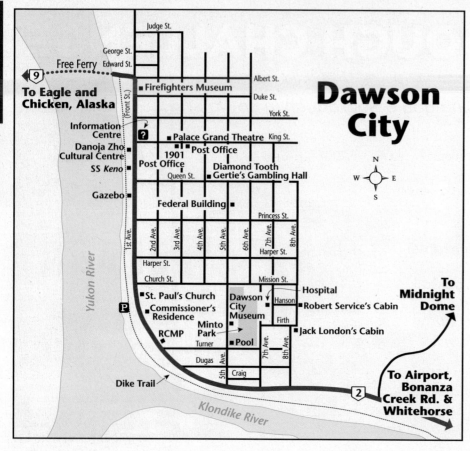

Dawson City

9 To Eagle and Chicken, Alaska

Free Ferry

Judge St.
George St.
Edward St.
(Front St.)

Firefighters Museum

Information Centre
Danoja Zho Cultural Centre
SS Keno
Gazebo

? Palace Grand Theatre

1901 Post Office
Post Office
Diamond Tooth Gertie's Gambling Hall

Federal Building

Albert St.
Duke St.
York St.
King St.
Queen St.

Princess St.

Harper St.
Church St.

1st Ave.
2nd Ave.
3rd Ave.
4th Ave.
5th Ave.
6th Ave.
7th Ave.
8th Ave.
Harper St.

Mission St.

St. Paul's Church
Commissioner's Residence
RCMP
Minto Park
Pool
Turner
Dugas
Craig

Dawson City Museum
Hanson
Firth

Hospital
Robert Service's Cabin
Jack London's Cabin

To Midnight Dome

To Airport, Bonanza Creek Rd. & Whitehorse

Dike Trail
Yukon River
Klondike River

N W E S

Camping

Private RV parks in Dawson: **Gold Rush Campground & RV Park**, downtown at 4th and York; and **Bonanza Gold RV Park** and **Dawson City R.V. Park and Campground**, located just east of downtown on the Klondike Highway. See ads this section.

There are 2 Yukon government (YTG) campgrounds in the Dawson area. Yukon River YTG campground is across the Yukon River (by ferry) from town, adjacent to the west-side ferry approach. Klondike River YTG campground is 15 minutes southeast of town near the airport.

Gold Rush Campground & RV Park. 4th Avenue and York Street. Dawson City's only downtown RV park. 82 sites: 23 with 15-amp/water, 7 with 15-amp/water/sewer, 42 with 30-amp/water/sewer. 18 pull-throughs, 12 unserviced. Free WiFi. Public showers. Laundromat, dump station. Your hosts, Pat and Dianne Brooks. Discover Yukon hospitality. Toll-free 1-866-330-5006 (within Canada). Phone 867-993-5247; Email goldrushcampground@shaw.ca. Fax 867-993-6047. See display on page 304. [ADVERTISEMENT]

Transportation

Air: Dawson City airport is 11.5 miles/18.5 km southeast of the city. Air North connects Dawson City with Whitehorse (daily service), and with Inuvik, NWT, and Old Crow. Charter services available from Great River Air & Alkan Air. Charter and flightseeing tours available. Airport shuttle service available from most downtown hotels and bed and breakfasts. Husky Bus/Klondike Experience (867-993-3821) also offers airport shuttles during the summer.

Ferry: The Yukon government operates the free *George Black* ferry, to cross the Yukon River from about late May to mid-October. Season dates for the ferry depend on spring break-up and fall freeze-up.

The *George Black* ferry makes the short (6 to 7 minutes on average) trip across the Yukon River 24 hours a day (except for Wednesdays, 5–7 A.M., when it is shut down for servicing), departing Dawson City on demand. It carries vehicles and passengers across to connect to the Top of the World Highway (Yukon Highway 9). To avoid long

---

Truck/auto repair at **Chief Isaac Mechanical**; phone 867-993-6552.

There is a CIBC Bank/ATM at Second Avenue and Queen. There are 2 laundromats (with showers), grocery store with bakery, a deli/grocery store, general stores, souvenir shops, churches, art galleries, an art school, post office, government offices, government liquor store, massage therapists, doctor services, hair salon and swimming pool. Many Dawson City merchants honor the Fair Exchange Policy, and offer an exchange rate within 4 percent of the bank rate.

Bonanza Gold Motel & RV Park. 1 mile south of city centre at the entrance to Bonanza Creek Road. Motel with deluxe accommodations, kitchenettes, standard

rooms with air conditioners or fans. Cable TV, WiFi. Bonanza Gold RV Park: full-service sites 15/30/50 amp; Cable TV, WiFi. RV/car wash. Laundromat. Toll-free 1-888-993-6789. Long-term-stay packages available. Email bonanzagold.dawson@gmail.com; website www.bonanzagold.ca. See display ad on page 301. [ADVERTISEMENT]

Sandy McClintock, Registered Massage Therapist offers relaxation and stress management. Deep tissue therapy will ease away the miles. Or sit down for a complete hair style and full esthetics in the Hair Cabaret. Open 7 days a week, the corner of Queen/Second streets. Call today for an appointment 867-993-5222. haircabaret@gmail.com. [ADVERTISEMENT]

DAWSON CITY ADVERTISERS

waits, don't cross during peak traffic times (7–11 A.M. and 4–7 P.M.) and ask the Visitor Center about scheduled caravan departures. Shut off all propane appliances and follow directions from ferry personnel when loading/unloading. Tour bus traffic has priority 6–9 A.M. and 5–9 P.M.; fuel truck traffic has priority 7 P.M. to 6 A.M. Phone 867-993-5441, fax 867-993-5321 for more information.

Bus: Alaska/Yukon Trails offers Fairbanks–Dawson City–Whitehorse van service in summer; www.alaskashuttle.com. The Klondike Experience/Husky Bus offers regular van service Whitehorse–Dawson City, daily tours and backcountry packages to Tombstone Territorial Park in summer (klondikeexperience.com).

Attractions

Dawson City has a lot of things to do for a small town. Visit DawsonCity.ca to see it all, or stop by the Visitor Information Center to pick up a current list of available activities.

Palace Grand Theatre. This magnificently reconstructed theatre is part of the Dawson Historical Complex National Historic Site. Arizona Charlie Meadows opened the Palace Grand in 1899, and today's visitors, sitting in the curtained boxes around the balcony, will succumb to the charm of this beautiful theatre. Go to DawsonCity.ca or check with the Visitor Information Center between May and September, for up-to-date tour information. Admission fee charged.

Commissioner's Residence. Located on Front Street and part of the Dawson Historical Complex National Historic Site, this was the official residence of the Yukon's federal government representative—the Commissioner of the Yukon—from 1900 to 1916. Throughout the decades it also served as a hospital and as the home of one of the Yukon's most intriguing and influential women, Martha Louise Black, who walked to Dawson City via the Trail of '98 and stayed to become the First Lady of the Yukon. The award-winning program *The Mountie, the Maid and the Miner*, is performed here daily during peak season. Up-to-date tour information at the Visitor Information Center, May to September. Admission fee charged.

Visit the Escape Room at the Commissioner's Residence and solve a murder mystery in under an hour, one that was investigated by the North West Mounted Police more than 100 years ago. This interactive program is a unique way to experience history. Pre-booking required at the Visitor Information Center, May to September. Details at www.pc.gc.ca/en/lhn-nhs/yt/klondike/activ/eva-esc.

Dänojà Zho Cultural Center offers a relaxed and friendly atmosphere to explore the story of the original people of the Klondike: the Tr'ondek Hwëch'in. The cultural center is a symbol of the Tr-ondeck Hwech'in people's history, perseverance, pride and hope. It rose from the desire to make a strong presence in the traditional territory of the Tr'ondek Hwëch'in that would not be bound to the "gold rush" era, but would speak to the strength of the Tr'ondek Hwëch'in. There are 2 gallery exhibitions, guided tours, special events and film presentations. The gift shop boasts the largest selection of beaded moccasins in the Yukon and specializes in unique jewelry, First Nation gifts, art and books. Located on Front Street across from the Dawson City Visitor Center. Open mid-May to mid-September.

Tour Dawson City's Palace Grand Theatre, once known as the "prettiest little theatre north of San Francisco." (©Kris Valencia, staff)

Adult admission is $7; tickets are valid for 2 days.

Dawson City Firefighter's Museum. In the City of Dawson Administration Building, this museum features historic steam engines and trucks; some dating back to the late 19th century. Admission Fee charged. Open May to September, or by special appointment with City of Dawson Fire Chief; phone 867-993-7400.

Dawson City Museum, on 5th Avenue in the Old Territorial Administration Building, is a National Historic Site. The museum features the Kings of the Klondike and City Life Galleries, First Nation and pre-gold rush exhibits. The film "City of Gold" is shown daily. Visitor programs throughout the day; check with the front desk.

The museum has a gift shop, wheelchair ramp, resource library, genealogy service and an extensive photography collection. A building adjacent the Territorial Administration Building contains the museum's collection of narrow-gauge locomotives, including a Vauclain-type Baldwin engine, the last one in existence in Canada. Open daily from 10 A.M. to 6 P.M., May long weekend until Labor Day in September; call for visits October to May. Admission fee charged. Phone 867-993-5291 or email: info@dawsonmuseum.ca.

Diamond Tooth Gerties Gambling Hall, at the corner of Fourth Avenue and Queen Street, open daily 7 P.M. to 2 A.M., from May 10, 2019 (opening night) to late September; 3 shows nightly. Opens at 2 P.M. Saturdays and Sundays in summer (mid-June to Labor Day). Admission fee charged. The casino has Klondike gambling tables (specially licensed in Yukon), more than 60 slot machines, bar service and nightly cancan-style shows. Don't drink or gamble? Then enjoy a soft drink and watch the performance by Diamond Tooth Gertie and her Gold Rush Gals. Persons under 19 not admitted. Gerties hosts weekly poker tournaments. For more information phone 867-993-5575 or visit Diamond ToothGerties.ca.

Downtown Walking Tour. The Then & Now town tour leaves the Visitor Information Center daily in summer. The 1½-hour guided walk highlights the history of Dawson City through the eyes of past and current residents. A self-guided audio tour is also available in English, French and German. Fee charged.

Farmers and Artists Market. Dawson City hosts a weekly market on the Waterfront Park, from May to September that features artisans, growers, and merchants. Saturday's 11 A.M. to 5 P.M.

Jack London Museum at the corner of 8th Avenue and Firth Street, a Yukon Heritage attraction. Jack London was the author of The Call of the Wild and White Fang. The museum features a log cabin built with half of the original logs from the cabin where London stayed in 1897. (The other half of the original logs were used to build a second replica cabin located in Jack London Square in Oakland, CA.) Also at the site are a cache and a museum with a collection of photos tracing London's journey to the Klondike during the Gold Rush. Open daily, 11 A.M. to 6 P.M. in summer; interpretive talks are offered, $5 per person.

Klondike Institute of Art and Culture. Operates artistic and cultural programming, exhibitions and events. Visit the ODD Gallery, which features special exhibits, or see what upcoming events or programming they have, by visiting www.KIAC.ca.

Join the Sourtoe Cocktail Club, which dares you to down a shot featuring a real human toe at the bottom of the glass. Located at the Sourdough Saloon in the Downtown Hotel at 2nd and Queen. "You can drink it fast, you can drink it slow, but your lips have got to touch the toe." **Pierre Berton Residence**, located on 8th Avenue, was the childhood home of the late Canadian author. Now used as a writers' retreat, tours of the home are not available, but you may visit the grounds and read the information boards placed outside by the Klondike Visitors Association.

The Robert Service Cabin, part of the Dawson Historical Complex National Historic Site, sits on the hillside on 8th Avenue. The bank clerk who became the "Bard of the Yukon" lived in this cozy cabin, which has been restored by Parks Canada. Daily programs by a costumed guide include the recitation of some of Service's most memorable poems, including "The Shooting of Dan McGrew" and "The Cremation of Sam McGee." Open daily. Admission fee charged. (Robert Service's typewriter is on display at

SS Keno National Historic Site preserves the 130-foot riverboat that once plied the Yukon River. It is one of only 2 historic riverboats that survive in the Yukon. (©Kris Valencia, staff)

the Visitor Information Center.)

SS *Keno* National Historic Site. For thousands of years, First Nations' people traveled the Yukon River by birch bark canoe, raft and moosehide boat to fish and trade. By 1866, the first steamboats were operating on the lower Yukon River, providing winter supplies to early trading posts. This 130-foot riverboat was built in Whitehorse in 1922 by the British Navigation Company. The smallest of the fleet, she was used to transport silver-lead ore for 29 years from the Mayo District on the Stewart River. The SS *Keno* is one of only 2 historic riverboats that survive in the Yukon (the other is the SS *Klondike* in Whitehorse), and was the last steamer to rum the Yukon River when she sailed from Whitehorse in 1960 to her present berth on the riverbank next to the old CIBC bank. Open daily for visits, with costumed staff and an interpretive display by Parks Canada.

Special Events. Dawson City hosts a number of unique celebrations during the year. Following is a round-up of events. For current information inquire at the Visitor Information Center or visit https://dawson city.ca/events/.

June's long days are celebrated with many events. The **Commissioner's Tea** at the Commissioner's Residence takes place in early June, with the **Klondike Ball** held the same day in the evening; email commiss ioner@gov.yk.ca or visit www.commissioner. gov.yk.ca/news/ball.htm for 2019 date. The **Midnight Sun Golf Tournament** is held at Dawson City Golf Course in June; email dawsongolf@hotmail.ca for details. **Aboriginal Day Celebration**, June 21, 2019, at the Zho Cultural Center offers an array of activities, celebrating the Tr'ondëk Hwëch'in way of life. The **D2D (Dust to Dawson) Motorcycle Ride** (not a rally), June 20–21 2019, an annual event since 1992, invites motorcycle enthusiasts from around the world to gather in Dawson City for motorcycle games and fun.

July begins with **Canada Day Celebrations** July 1st. The **Yukon River Quest** (www.yukonriverquest.com), a canoe and kayak race from Whitehorse to Dawson City, takes place June 26–30, 2019. The **Yukon Gold Panning Championship** is scheduled

for the afternoon of July 6, 2019.

Then it's the 41st annual **Dawson City Music Fest** (www.dcmf.com), held July 19–21, 2019, featuring entertainers and artists from Canada and around the world. **Air North Midnight Dome Race** takes place July 20, 2019, coinciding with the Music Fest.

If you are in Dawson City Aug. 15–19, 2019, be sure to join the **Discovery Days Celebrations**, including a fun run, golf tournament, mud bog, arts festival and other events. **Discovery Day** (third Monday in August) is a Yukon holiday commemorating the Klondike gold discovery of Aug. 17, 1896. The **Great Klondike International Outhouse Race**, scheduled for Sept. 1, 2019, is a race of decorated outhouses on wheels over a 3-km course through the streets of Dawson City.

Hiking and walking trails. The popular Waterfront Trail follows the dike along the Yukon River and has viewpoints, information boards and benches. The Ninth Avenue Trail is a well-maintained and scenic trail that loops around the town, an easy hike that takes 30 to 40 minutes, it also accesses multiple other trails such as the Crocus Bluff Trail. The Orchid trail on Sunnydale Road, just off the Top of the World Highway, is a short hike to see wild orchids; it overlooks Sternwheel Slough. The Visitor Information Center on Front Street has maps and detailed guides to many trails in the region.

Bonanza Creek Road, which junctions with the Klondike Highway 2.2 miles/3.5 km south of downtown just east of Kilometerpost 712 *(see description at* **Milepost J 321.2** *on pages 300-301)*, is a not-to-be-missed attraction. This inconspicuous, mostly gravel road traverses one of the richest gold mining areas in North America. While evidence of the thousands of gold diggers who transformed this valley during the gold rush of 1898-99 has been erased by time, there remain miles of tailings and significant locations and sites, such as Dredge No. 4 National Historic Site, Discovery Claim National Historic Site and Free Claim No. 6 (bring your own gold pan).

The grand old **Dredge No. 4 National Historic Site** was built in 1912 for the Canadian Klondike Mining Co.'s Boyle

Concession in the Klondike River Valley. Dredge No. 4 was pulled from the muck of Bonanza Creek in 1992, exactly as the last shift had left it 32 years before. It is the largest wooden hulled bucket line gold dredge in North America. This impressive machine represents the pinnacle of the insatiable quest for gold that transformed not just the landscape but Yukon society. Guided tours available; tickets on-site or at the tour providers kiosk on Front Street in Dawson City. Download Parks Canada's Explora Dredge No 4 (Google Play).

Discovery Claim National Historic Site was originally staked on Aug. 17, 1896, and is the site of the gold discovery that sparked the Klondike Gold Rush. A 0.6-mile/1-km walking trail with information boards describe the story of the discovery and the evolution of mining techniques. An interpretive trail brochure is available at the Parks Canada information desk at the Visitor Information Center in town. This site is always open; free admission.

Gold panning is a major attraction for many visitors. There are several mining operations set up to permit you to actually pan for your own "colors." Two on Bonanza Creek Road include **Claim 33**, at Mile 6/Km 10, and the Klondike Visitors Association's public panning area at the **Free Claim No. 6** above Discovery Claim, 13 miles/21 km from Dawson City on Bonanza Creek Road. *(Bonanza Creek Road continues up into the hills past private gold claims and connects with Hunker Creek Road; this portion of the road is not suitable for RVs or trailers.)* Check with the Visitor Information Center or visit DawsonCity.ca.

See the Midnight Sun: If you are in Dawson City on June 21, be sure to make it to the top of the Dome by midnight, when the sun barely dips behind the 6,000-foot/1,829-m Ogilvie Mountains to the north—the picture of a lifetime. There's quite a local celebration on the Dome on June 21, so for those who don't like crowds, a visit before or after summer solstice will also afford fine views and photos.

Klondike Loop Log
(continued from page 301)

TOP OF THE WORLD HIGHWAY

The **Top of the World Highway** (Yukon Highway 9 and Boundary Spur Road) connects Dawson City with the Taylor Highway (Alaska Route 5). Its top-of-the-world views make it a favorite with many travelers.

The *George Black* ferry crosses the Yukon River from Dawson City to Top of the World Highway daily from about mid-May to mid-October. However, whether or not Customs is open at the border also determines the viability of this route and Customs has closed in September.

Yukon Highway 9 and Alaska Route 5 are not maintained from mid-October to April, and the arrival of snow effectively closes the roads for winter.

CAUTION: Allow plenty of time for this drive. This is a narrow, winding road with some steep grades and few guardrails. Watch for soft shoulders. Slow down on loose gravel and washboard. The maximum posted speed limit is 50-mph/80-kmph. DRIVE WITH YOUR HEADLIGHTS ON!

IMPORTANT: Driving time westbound to the international border is at least 1 hour and 30 minutes (or more, depending on road conditions). Alaska Customs closes at 8 P.M. Alaska

standard time (which is 9 P.M. Pacific standard time). Make sure you allow enough time to arrive at the border when the Customs station is open.

The Canadian portion of Top of the World Highway (Yukon Highway 9) has been seal-coated, but paved sections are frequently interrupted by gravel breaks. Potholes are prevalent after wet weather.

Top of the World Highway winds above the timberline for many miles. The lack of fuel for warmth and shelter made this a perilous trip for the early sourdoughs.

On the Alaska side, Boundary Road is paved from the U.S.-Canada border to Jack Wade Junction (**junction** with the Taylor Highway). *NOTE: No shoulders, abrupt edge, on Boundary Road.* Additional improvement projects may be under way on the Taylor Highway, which is a winding dirt and gravel road from Jack Wade Junction south to Chicken and north to Eagle. For current road conditions visit 511.alaska.gov or phone 511. Also check with the Dawson City Visitor Information Center for current road and weather conditions; phone 867-993-5566.

The Alaska Highway is 175 miles/281 km from Dawson City via Yukon Highway 9 and Alaska Route 5.

NOTE: From Dawson City next gas stop westbound on the Klondike Loop is Chicken (108 miles/174 km) or Tok (187 miles/300 km).

YUKON HIGHWAY 9

Westbound: This section of the log shows distance from Dawson City (D) followed by distance from Tetlin Junction on the Alaska Highway (TJ). Read log: ↓

Physical kilometerposts show distance from Dawson City.

D 0 TJ 175 (127.1 km) Ferry landing for free *George Black* ferry that carries passengers and vehicles across the Yukon River between Dawson City and Top of the World Highway from about mid-May to mid-October (depending on break-up and freeze-up). The ferry trip across the river is just a few minutes, but the wait time can be as long as 3 hours during peak periods. *NOTE: The boarding process is not intuitive. Watch "Slow/Stop" signals from ferry personnel: If they point the Slow sign at your line, proceed to ferry. If they wave you back, it was not your turn. You do not necessarily board in the order you lined up!*

Driving distances for Alaska-bound travelers on the Klondike Loop: Chicken 108 miles/174 km, Tok 187 miles/300 km.

D 0.2 (0.3 km) **TJ 174.8** (281.3 km) Turnoff to north for **Yukon River government campground** on riverbank opposite Dawson City. Very nice wooded campground with 102 sites, including 20 pull-through sites, open May 11 to Sept. 30, camping permit $12. 2 kitchen shelters, playground, picnic tables, pit toilets, firepits, garbage and recycling bins, bear proof lockers and water (may not be potable). Free firewood available for use at campground only. Walk down to the river and head downstream, watching for remains of old stern-wheelers in the brush near shore. This campground is also a put-in and take-out spot for Yukon River travelers. Deck overlooks the Yukon River. A family of peregrine falcons nests in the cliffs across the river during the summer. ▲

Highway climbs next 8.7 miles/14 km westbound. Views of Dawson City and the Yukon and Klondike rivers.

The George Black ferry takes passengers and vehicles across the Yukon River between Dawson City and the Top of the World Highway to Alaska. (©Kris Valencia, staff)

D 2.3 (3.7 km) **TJ 172.7** (277.9 km) Access via 3.2-mile/5.1-km Sunnydale Road (gravel) to Dawson City Golf Course.

D 6.2 (10 km) **TJ 168.8** (271.6 km) *Begin variable road conditions westbound to international border with good chip seal surfacing, sections of potholes and damaged pavement, gravel breaks and washboard.*

D 8.9 (14.3 km) **TJ 166.1** (267.3 km) Double-ended turnout to large rest area with toilets, picnic tables, litter barrels. A short path leads to a viewing platform overlooking the Yukon River Valley. There are information boards about the Fortymile caribou herd and the history of the people of this area. Welcome to Dawson City information kiosk.

D 11.6 (18.6 km) **TJ 163.4** (263 km) Large turnout to north with good view.

D 18.2 (29.3 km) **TJ 156.8** (252.3 km) Double-ended gravel turnout to south.

D 24.8 (40 km) **TJ 150.2** (241.7 km) Large gravel turnout to north with view.

D 31.8 (51.2 km) **TJ 143.2** (230.5 km) Informal campsite to south near rock outcropping; large turnaround space, good views and hiking. Watch for grouse. ▲

D 34.2 (55.2 km) **TJ 138.9** (225 km) Gravel turnout to south.

D 34.7 (56 km) **TJ 140.3** (225.8 km) Main outcropping of Castle Rock; lesser formations are also found along this stretch. Centuries of erosion have created these formations.

D 36.8 (59.2 km) **TJ 138.2** (222.4 km) **Junction** with Clinton Creek Road, which leads north to the former settlement of Clinton Creek. Cassiar Asbestos Corp. Ltd. operated the Clinton Creek mine there from 1967 to 1978, when all of the available asbestos had been mined. Generally in fair condition for the first 33 miles/53 km to the Clinton Creek bridge. There are no facilities or services available along the road. The confluence of the Yukon and Fortymile rivers is 3 miles/4.8 km below the former townsite of Clinton Creek. Clinton Creek bridge is an access point on the Fortymile River National Wild, Scenic & Recreation River system. The Fortymile River offers intermediate and

advanced canoeists over 100 miles/160 km of challenging water.

Yukon River, near Clinton Creek, grayling to 3 lbs. in April; chum salmon to 12 lbs. in August; chinook salmon to 40 lbs., July and August. **Fortymile River**, near Clinton Creek, grayling to 3 lbs. during spring breakup and fall freezeup; inconnu (sheefish) to 10 lbs. in July and August. ➘

Distance marker westbound shows U.S. border 43 km/27 miles.

D 38.1 (61.3 km) **TJ 136.9** (220.3 km) Large turnout to north with sweeping views.

D 53.9 (86.7 km) **TJ 121.1** (194.9 km) Turnoff to south for 60 Mile Road to old mine workings at Sixtymile.

D 54.2 (87.8 km) **TJ 120.8** (194.4 km) Rest area with pit toilet and litter bins, adjacent old sod-roofed cabin. This was originally a supply and stopping place for the McCormick Transportation Co.

D 60.6 (98 km) **TJ 114.4** (184.1 km) Turnout to north. Gravel stockpile.

D 62.5 (100.6 km) **TJ 112.5** (181 km) Large gravel turnout to south with litter bin. Information sign about Top of the World Highway viewpoint:

"Yukon Highway 9 began as a pack trail out of Dawson City shortly after the gold rush. It serviced Sixtymile and neighbouring gold creeks. The trail was gradually improved and came to be known as Ridge Road.

"In the 1930s, the road was extended to the border and from there to Jack Wade and Chicken, connecting these Alaskan communities to Dawson City in Canada. In the late 1940s, Alaska's Taylor Highway gave all these communities road access to the outside world by way of the newly completed Alaska Highway."

D 64.7 (104.5 km) **TJ 110.3** (177.5 km) Double-ended rest area to south, good view of Customs buildings. Just across the highway, short hike to cairn, excellent viewpoint. Highest point on Top of the World Highway (elev. 1,376m/4,515 feet).

D 65.7 (105.7 km) **TJ 109.3** (175.9 km) **U.S.–Canada Border** (elev. 4,127 feet/1,258m). **U.S. Poker Creek and Canada Little Gold Creek Customs.** This joint facility opened in 2001–2002, replacing the construction trailer (now gone) that housed Canadian customs, and the log structure

Top of the World Highway offers top-of-the-world views for motorists driving to or from Dawson City, YT, and the Taylor Highway in Alaska. *(©Kris Valencia, staff)*

that housed U.S. customs, viewed on your right westbound after going through customs. *All traffic entering Alaska or Canada must stop here.* Road is gated after hours.

IMPORTANT: U.S. and Canada customs are open from about May 15 to late September or October, depending on weather. In summer 2018, customs was open daily, 9 A.M. to 9 P.M. (Pacific standard time) on the Canadian side; 8 A.M. to 8 P.M. (Alaska standard time) on the U.S. side. Customs hours of operation subject to change; there is no phone at the border, so check with the RCMP or Visitor Information Center in Dawson City. Serious fines are levied for crossing the border without clearing customs! There are no services or currency exchanges available here. See also "Crossing the Border" in the TRAVEL PLANNING section.

TIME ZONE CHANGE: Alaska observes Alaska standard time; Yukon observes Pacific standard time. Alaska standard time is 1 hour earlier than Pacific standard time.

Paved road with no shoulder next 13.6 miles/21.9 km westbound. Downhill grades next 4 miles/6.4 km westbound. NOTE: Physical mileposts westbound show distance from Jack Wade Junction.

BOUNDARY SPUR ROAD

D 65.9 TJ 109.1 Westbound travelers watch for mining activity in the valley to south next 3 miles.

Distance marker westbound shows Boundary 4 miles, Chicken 43 miles, Eagle 77 miles.

D 66.3 TJ 108.7 Davis Dome Wayside (BLM). Double-ended paved turnout to north with scenic viewing platform, pit toilets (not recommended). Beautiful views. Information board about Fortymile River Region. Welcome to Alaska sign.

D 67.1 TJ 107.9 *Steep approach* to large, double-ended paved turnout to north with interpretive sign about the Fortymile caribou herd.

D 69.6 TJ 105.4 BOUNDARY. Boundary Roadhouse, (closed) dates from about 1926, and was one of the first roadhouses in Alaska. It served miners in the Walker Creek drainage, according to writer Ray Bonnell,

who researched this area. The roadhouse dates from about 1926, while the mining camp was first established in the 1890s. A post office served the area from 1940 until 1956.

Jack Corbett owned and operated Boundary Roadhouse for many years. More recently it has operated sporadically under various owners. It has been closed the last several years and the store burned down in 2012. The original roadhouse was still standing in summer 2018.

D 69.7 TJ 105.3 Access road south to Boundary airstrip; elev. 2,940 feet/896m; length 2,100 feet/640m; dirt and gravel; fuel 80; unattended.

D 72.3 TJ 102.7 Paved shoulder parking to south.

D 79.5 TJ 95.5 Jack Wade Junction. First junction westbound: Keep right westbound at Y-junction for Eagle. Keep left westbound for Taylor Highway to Chicken *(see map this page).* CAUTION: *Westbound traffic* YIELD *at merge.*

NOTE: *The road to Eagle is quite challenging and not recommended for large RVs or trailers. If you have a tow vehicle, consider parking your rig at Walker Fork BLM campground or at an RV park in Chicken, and driving your car to Eagle. See "Side Trip to Eagle" facing page.*

Distance marker southbound shows Chicken 28 miles, Tok 96 miles. The Taylor Highway extends 64 miles north from Jack Wade Junction to the community of Eagle on the Yukon River.

See "Side Trip to Eagle" log beginning on facing page.

Eastbound: This section of the log shows distance from Dawson City (D) followed by distance from Tetlin Junction on the Alaska Highway (TJ). Read log: ↑

Eastbound travelers note: Boundary Spur Road is paved to the U.S.-Canada border, with physical mileposts reflecting distance from Jack Wade Junction. From the border to Dawson City, Top of the World Highway (Yukon Highway 9) is paved but frequently interrupted by

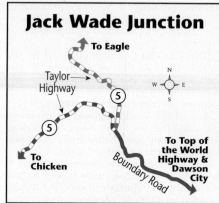

gravel breaks, washboard and potholes. Physical kilometerposts eastbound on the Canadian portion of Top of the World Highway shows distance from Dawson City.

TAYLOR HIGHWAY ALASKA ROUTE 5

Southbound: This section of the log shows distance from Tetlin Junction on the Alaska Highway (TJ) followed by distance from Eagle (E) and distance from Dawson City (D). Read log: ↓

Physical mileposts on the Taylor Highway (which are sporadic) reflect distance from Tetlin Junction. NOTE: *Sections of rough road, soft shoulders, hairpin curves, steep drop-offs and narrow road south to Chicken. Do not risk a tip over by putting a wheel into the soft shoulder! Stop for oncoming traffic at narrow spots.*

TJ 95.5 E 65 D 79.5 Jack Wade Junction. Eastbound travelers keep right at Y-junction for Top of the World Highway east to Dawson City, YT. Keep to left for continuation of Taylor Highway north to Eagle *(see map this page).* The road to Eagle is quite challenging and not recommended for large RVs or trailers. If you have a tow vehicle, consider parking your rig at Walker Fork BLM campground or at an RV park in Chicken, and driving your car to Eagle.

Distance marker northbound shows Eagle 64 miles, Boundary 9 miles, Dawson City 75 miles.

TJ 95.2 E 65.3 D 79.8 Pavement ends, dirt and gravel begin westbound (summer 2018).

Eastbound to Dawson City, YT: Paved road to U.S.-Canada border. From border to Dawson City on Top of the World Highway (Yukon Highway 9) paved sections are frequently interrupted by gravel breaks, washboard and potholes.

TJ 92 E 68.5 D 83 Federal Subsistence Hunting Area boundary.

Highway straightens as the Taylor Highway follows Jack Wade Creek next 7 miles southbound.

Steep climb on narrow road northbound as highway ascends Jack Wade Hill. Limited passing room, soft shoulders and long drop-offs make this a dangerous stretch. This area is particularly dangerous in wet weather. If in doubt, STOP for oncoming traffic: Do not risk a tip over by putting a wheel into the soft shoulder!

TJ 91.5 E 69 D 83.5 Active mining visible from road.

TJ 90 E 70.5 D 85 Double-ended dirt turnout.

TJ 89 E 71.5 D 86 Nice turnout to east above creek.

TJ 88.7 E 71.8 D 86.3 Big gravel turnout
(Continues on page 313)

Side Trip to Eagle

At Jack Wade Junction, Klondike Loop travelers either turn south on the Taylor Highway (if they have just entered Alaska) or veer east to Dawson City (if they are leaving Alaska). But there is another option: They can head north on the Taylor Highway for a **side trip** to visit Eagle. Located at the end of the Taylor Highway on the Yukon River, Eagle has an impressive history for a small town at the end of a gravel road. Highlights on the Taylor Highway to Eagle are the top-of-the-world views and the likelihood you will see caribou along this road.

The Taylor Highway from Jack Wade Junction to Eagle is similar to the highway between Chicken and Jack Wade Junction: *Narrow, winding, gravel, no shoulders or soft shoulders, steep dropoffs.* There are numerous single-vehicle turnouts to allow traffic to pull over for oncoming vehicles on narrow road and approaching sharp curves. *This section of the Taylor Highway is not recommended for large RVs. If you have a tow vehicle, consider leaving your big rig in Chicken or at the Walker Fork BLM Campground.*

It is 65 miles one-way from Jack Wade Junction to Eagle. *Expect your highway speeds to be between 30- and 35-mph (and often, much slower). Be alert for oncoming traffic on blind hills and curves!* There are no services until you reach Eagle. Most Eagle businesses are open 9 A.M. to 5 P.M. daily in summer. Call ahead for lodging. Camping is available at the BLM campground, just past Fort Egbert.

The Taylor Highway is not maintained in winter, with seasonal maintenance ending about mid-October. Crews begin plowing snow and ice from the highway in early April but it takes weeks of clearing before it is ready for traffic. Current road conditions are available at 511.alaska.gov.

NOTE: Please double-check your spare tire and ALL tire changing equipment to ensure you have what you need if you get a flat. Make sure that your jack is appropriate for the weight you are carrying and that all tire irons are at hand. Motorcyclists should use extra caution on all bridge decks.

ALASKA ROUTE 5

Distance from Tetlin Junction (TJ) is followed by distance from Eagle (E).

Mileposts along this route reflect distance from Tetlin Junction on the Alaska Highway.

TJ 95.5 E 65 Jack Wade Junction. Continue north on the Taylor Highway (Alaska Route 5) for Eagle.

TJ 96 E 64.5 Continue 9 miles on a scenic wilderness road. Many photo ops and top of the world views. Watch for caribou.

TJ 96.1 E 64.4 Large gravel turnout to west.

TJ 98.8 E 61.7 Small informal camping area to west, overlooking valley.

TJ 103 E 57.5 Turnout to east.

TJ 105 E 55.5 Downhill grade next 7 miles northbound (sign) as road begins spectacular descent from Polly Summit to the valley of the Fortymile River, so named because its mouth was 40 miles below Fort Reliance, an old trading post near the confluence of the Yukon and Klondike rivers.

TJ 105.2 E 55.3 Very popular turnout on

American Summit area offers spectacular views along the Taylor Highway to Eagle.
(©Sharon Nault)

"Polly Summit." Check brakes and tires here. Primitive campsites near the road and back in the brush.

TJ 109.5 E 52 Entering subsistence hunting northern boundary

TJ 109.8 E 52.7 Turnout to east on curve.

TJ 112.5 E 48 BLM wayside at south end of Fortymile River Bridge (*wood decking, slippery when wet*). Information board, life jackets, handicap-accessible outhouse, picnic tables down a brushy trail to river. No camping. Fortymile Mining District (sign); active mining in area.

Bumpy road to steep and difficult to access boat launch across road from wayside. Access to the Fortymile River National Wild, Scenic & Recreation River system.

There are private homes at the north end of the bridge.

TJ 113.1 E 47.4 O'Brien Creek DOT/PF state highway maintenance camp. Remains closed by budget cuts.

TJ 113.2 E 47.3 O'Brien Creek bridge.

CAUTION: Watch for small aircraft using road as runway.

TJ 114.7 E 45.8 *Road narrows to 1-lane northbound for a short stretch. Watch for falling rock and steep drop-off next 1.5 miles northbound.* Highway parallels O'Brien Creek to Liberty Fork.

TJ 117.2 E 43.3 Alder Creek bridge, river access southwest side.

TJ 119.3 E 41.2 Narrow section of road northbound. Watch for oncoming traffic

TJ 122 E 38.5 *CAUTION: Slow down for hairpin curves northbound.* Great view to south of Fortymile River Canyon.

TJ 124.5 E 36 Columbia Creek bridge.

TJ 125.5 E 35 Old O'Brien Creek Lodge (private property, closed).

TJ 129.9 E 30.6 Large gravel turnout to west.

TJ 131.5 E 29 King Solomon Creek bridge. (The creek has a tributary named Queen of Sheba.) Leaving Federal Subsistence Hunting Area.

TJ 133.6 E 26.9 Large gravel turnout east doubles as a gravel storage area for road maintenance.

TJ 134.7 E 25.8 Gravel turnout to informal camping area, great views of valley.

TJ 135.6 E 24.9 Large primitive camping area to west by landmark boulder, south of

Solomon Creek.

TJ 135.7 E 24.8 North Fork King Solomon Creek bridge. *Road narrows northbound; watch for soft shoulders. Begin slow ascent to American Summit.*

TJ 138 E 22.5 Expansive view of 2004 burn area (*see description of Taylor Complex fire at Milepost TJ 3.4 on page 317*).

TJ 142.6 E 18 American Summit liquor store and snack shop (closed). There are turnouts with views north and south of here that are suitable for overnighting for small, self contained RVs.

TJ 143.2 E 17.4 Turnout to east at **American Summit**. Top of the world views. Highway begins winding descent northbound to Yukon River.

TJ 143.5 E 17 Large gravel turnout to west with expansive views of valley.

TJ 149.1 E 11.4 Discovery Fork Creek bridge.

TJ 151.6 E 8.9 Bridge No. 1 over American Creek.

TJ 152.5 E 8 Bridge No. 2 over American Creek. Spacious turnout to east at south end of bridge. Turnout to west at north end of bridge.

TJ 153.2 E 7.3 Small turnout to east where spring water is piped to side of road.

TJ 159.3 E 1.2 Telegraph Hill Services; gas/diesel and tire repair. Telegraph Hill is visible from the road. *Begin speed zone into Eagle.*

TJ 159.7 E 0.8 Jewelry store.

TJ 160.3 E 0.2 Turnoff for **Eagle BLM campground** and Fort Egbert.

TJ 160.4 E 0.1 Eagle Library. Library also serves as an information center. Times are posted. Usually open late afternoons and evening hours only and on weekdays.

Eagle

TJ 160.5 E 0 Front Street at the end of Taylor highway. **Population:** 86. **Emergency Services:** Dial 911. Alaska State Troopers (in Northway), phone 907-778-2245; Eagle EMS/Ambulance, phone 907-547-2300; Eagle Village Health Clinic, phone 907-547-2243.

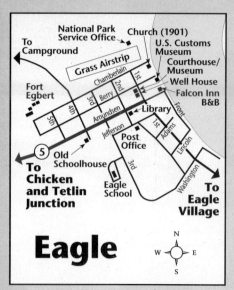

Eagle

©Sharon Nault

Visitor Information: The **National Park Service and BLM Visitor Center**, located at the end of the grass airstrip, offers informal talks and interpretive programs; information on Yukon–Charley Rivers National Preserve and Fort Egbert; reference materials; books and other items for sale; and public restrooms. Visitor center hours are 8 A.M. to 5 P.M. daily in summer (mid-June through Labor Day weekend) and weekdays 8 A.M. to 4 P.M. the rest of September. Closed in winter. Write Box 167, Eagle, AK 99738; phone 907-547-2233.

Elevation: 820 feet. **Climate:** Mean monthly temperature in July 59°F; in January -13°F. Record low -71°F in January 1952; record high 95°F in July 1925. July also has the greatest mean number of days (21) with temperatures above 70°F. Mean precipitation in July, 1.94 inches; in December, 10.1 inches. Record snow depth 42 inches in April 1948. **Radio:** KEAA-LP 97.9 FM, Eagle's own radio station, is broadcast from the school. Residents bring in their favorite tunes, which results in some interesting lineups: a Hank Williams song followed by Led Zeplin followed by Tony Bennett.

Transportation: By road via the Taylor Highway (closed by snow October to April); air taxi, scheduled air service, by river, in summer; dog team and snow machine in winter. U.S. customs available for persons entering Alaska via floating the Yukon River or by air in summer.

Private Aircraft: Eagle airstrip, 1.2 miles east on First Avenue, then 0.3 miles on airport access road; elev. 880 feet; length 4,500 feet; gravel; unattended. Float planes land on the Yukon River.

Eagle is located on the south bank of the Yukon River below Eagle Bluff (elev. 1000 feet/305m). This small community was once the supply and transportation center for miners working the upper Yukon and its tributaries. Francois Mercier established his Belle Isle trading post here in 1880. Eagle was founded in 1897 and became the commercial, military and judicial center for the Upper Yukon. By 1898, Eagle's population was 1,700.

Fort Egbert was established in 1899 adjacent to the city, and became a key communications center for Alaska when the 1,506-mile-long Washington-Alaska Military Cable and Telegraph System (WAMCATS) was completed in June 1903.

On July 15, 1900, Judge James Wickersham arrived to establish the first federal court in the Interior of Alaska. In 1901, Eagle became the first incorporated city in the Interior of Alaska.

In 1905, Roald Amundsen trekked to Eagle to announce to the world the completion of the first successful Northwest Passage Sailing. A monument to him stands at the Amundsen Memorial Park in town.

By 1910, Eagle's population had dwindled to 178, as gold strikes in Fairbanks and Nome lured away many residents. With the conversion of telegraph communication to wireless, most of the U.S. Army left Fort Egbert in 1911.

Historic structures in town include: the Wickersham Courthouse, built in 1901 for Judge James Wickersham; the church (1901); the Waterfront Customs House (1900); the schoolhouse (1903); and the Improved Order of Red Men Lodge (1904).

Historically an important riverboat landing, today Eagle is a popular stop for Yukon River travelers. Breakup on the Yukon is in May; freeze-up in October.

During spring breakup in 2009, Eagle's waterfront suffered extensive damage when a Yukon River ice jam forced ice and water inland, moving some buildings off their foundations and destroying others. Signs around town show water levels from the 2009 flood. A 2013 ice jam during breakup also caused damage and loss. Video of this devastating event can be viewed at the National Park Service Information Center.

Eagle Village (pop. 67), a traditional Han Kutchin (Athabascan) community with a subsistence lifestyle, located 3 miles east of Eagle (follow First Ave. out of town); no visitor facilities. Village residents relocated away from the river due to erosion and seasonal flooding on the Yukon River.

Lodging, Camping & Services

Located on the waterfront, the new Riverside Hotel has an ATM, restaurant, and accommodations; phone (907) 547-7000. Eagle River Trading Co is on First Avenue, phone (907) 547-2220; grocery store, laundromat, gas, diesel and propane sales.

The charming **Falcon Inn Bed and Breakfast** offers rooms with views of the river; (www.falconinnlodgelogcabins.com). Motel rooms are in high demand: Please reserve in advance of your arrival.

Falcon Inn Bed and Breakfast. On the banks of the Yukon River we have 5 cozy, clean and comfortable rooms. Relax in one of our two common areas or just enjoy the view of the river from the deck. After a full breakfast, take a tour of the Eagle Historical Society which start less than a block from our front door. (907) 547-2254. falconinn@gmail.com. [ADVERTISEMENT]

As in other small Northern communities, not all local businesses take credit cards and some food staples can be expensive here.

Eagle's well-house, hand-dug in 1903, provides water for about 70 percent of Eagle's residents. Three diesel generators provide the community's power. Public phones are located in an old red telephone booth, across from the well-house. Satellite TV and internet available.

Camping at the well-maintained **Eagle BLM Campground** just outside town (take 4th Avenue to Fort Egbert and follow signs 0.7 mile from the main road—watch for sand dunes along the way). The BLM campground has 18 very nice sites in a beautiful forest setting; raised tent platforms, handicapped camping site, some recycling, public drinking water at nearby well-house in town, free firewood to paying campers, garbage containers, outhouses, $10 camping fee, $5 for Federal Senior or Access pass holders (cash or check). Look for abundant mushrooms after a rain.

Attractions

Eagle Historical Society Museum and Walking Tour. Meet at the Wickersham Courthouse which houses the museum. Usually guided by a resident of Eagle, the guided tour leaves daily at 9 A.M. in summer. This tour is a favorite of one of our field editors who says it is "Alaska's Best Little Tour!" The guided tour includes the museum, courthouse as well as other interesting buildings. It is a wonderful look at Interior Alaska history, from early exploration and the military presence here to the lifestyle of gold miners and trappers and the communities "local color." Contact Eagle Historical Society and Museums to make sure times haven't changed: phone/fax 907-547-2325, 547-2244 or 547-2297; www.eaglehistoricalsociety.com.

Eagle Library, on Amundsen and 2nd, is a unique place with WiFi, a woodstove and an outhouse out back. Comfortable chairs and a homey atmosphere make this a fun place to visit.

Fort Egbert, a National Historic Landmark, is comprised of 5 of the 45 original structures that were stabilized and restored by the BLM between 1974 and 1979. The BLM and Eagle Historical Society and Museums manage the Fort Egbert National Historic Landmark, which includes: the Quartermaster Storehouse (1899), the Mule Barn (1900), the Water Wagon Shed, the Granary (1903), and the NCO quarters (1900). The Storehouse has an interpretive exhibit and photo display showing the reconstruction. Check out the Jeffery (or Nash) Quad Truck built circa 1914, 1 of 2 still running in the U.S.

BLM daily walking tours visit the many museums in Eagle (Memorial Day through Labor Day). Tour takes about 2 hours and begins at 9 A.M. at the Courthouse Museum. Fees are $7/per person. Special tours are available by contacting office in advance. An additional cost of $10 is due for special tours. Phone 907-547-2233.

Yukon-Charley Rivers National Preserve is a popular attraction for those who wish to float the Yukon River. River runners travel the 175 miles of the Yukon River between Eagle and Circle through the preserve. Eagle Bluff, the prominent geological structure to the west of the waterfront, is a landmark for Yukon River travelers. Its rusty color results from oxidation of iron in the greenstone. The Yukon River float trip through the preserve takes from 5 to 10 days. It is suitable for canoes, kayaks or rafts. Details at the National Park Service visitor center in Eagle.

**Return to Milepost TJ 95.5
Klondike Loop**

(Continued from page 310)
to west. Highway climbs above creek northbound.

TJ 88.1 E 72.4 D 86.9 Nice gravel turnout to east by creek.

TJ 87.3 E 73.2 D 87.7 Turnout by creek.
Mining operations may be under way along here in summer. *Do not trespass on mining claims.*

TJ 84 E 76.5 D 91 Turnout to east for BLM wayside to increase access to this recreational gold panning area.

TJ 83.5 E 77 D 91.5 Large turnout to west is a public gold panning area; posted "no camping."

There are several informal turnouts next 1.5 miles northbound.

TJ 82 E 78.5 D 93 Crossing Walker Fork bridge.
Turnoff to west at north end of bridge for **Walker Fork BLM Campground**; use campground as a day-use area if one is needed. People often leave their oversized rigs here to drive to Eagle in their tow vehicle. Old road grader on display at campground entrance parking area, where there is an information board with BLM brochures on area attractions. The campground has 20 level sites (13 pull-throughs and 7 back-ins) on loop road; 2 tent platforms; 1 covered site for bicyclists and motorcyclists; 1 handicap sites with wheelchair accessible platforms; picnic tables; free firewood to paying campers; firepits, grills, pit toilets, litter bins. Drinking water from water tank is hauled in from Fairbanks. Camping fee is $10 per night, discount with America the Beautiful, Senior or Access pass; 10-day limit. Check the campground information board or talk with the campground host about where you can pan for gold on the river. You may not use motorized equipment such as suction dredges, pumps, etc. The gold panning area is across the highway on Jack Wade Creek. It begins ¼ mile upstream from campground and continues downstream for a total of 3 miles (to approximately **Milepost TJ 85**).

CAUTION: Southbound, expect stretches of narrow, winding road with hairpin curves and little or no road shoulder and no guardrails. This is a very dangerous area to be passing and driving big rigs. Do NOT pull over too far or the soft shoulder may give way.

Highway straightens as the Taylor Highway follows Jack Wade Creek next 7 miles northbound.

TJ 80 E 80.5 D 95 Highway descends next 2 miles northbound to Walker Fork. Physical Milepost 80 is 0.8 mile off from where it should be located.

TJ 78 E 82.5 D 97 Views of South Fork and Walker Fork of the Fortymile River to west northbound between **Mileposts TJ 78** and **82**. *CAUTION: Approximately 1,000 foot drop-offs, no guardrails, soft shoulders. If you are "towing" watch where the back wheels of your tow vehicle are on any tight curves.*

MILEPOST® field editor Sharon Nault says, "some of the following stretches of road, northbound, are unique and spectacular!" Locals call it "the goat trail." Between the South Fork Fortymile River bridge and the Walker Fork bridge, the Taylor Highway winds along the side of the mountain like a narrow shelf, with vertical drops to the valley far, far below.

TJ 76.8 E 83.7 D 98.2 Dirt turnout on *20-mph curve*. View of oxbow lakes in South Fork valley.

TJ 75.3 E 85.2 D 99.7 South Fortymile River bridge.

TJ 75.2 E 85.3 D 99.8 Turnoff to west for **South Fork River Wayside**. This BLM Wayside has a large turnaround area to the west on the south side of the bridge, for big rigs; 2 pit toilets; nice covered picnic area overlooking the river; cooking grills; dumpster; boat access; and information board about the Fortymile Gold Rush. Life preservers available. Most popular river put-in and access point. Dirt road leads south to the launch then becomes a private road used by miners.

TJ 74.5 E 86 D 100.5 South Fork DOT/PF state highway maintenance station. Large level parking area (do not block gate). Access to South Fork Fortymile River across road from parking area.

TJ 72 E 88.5 D 103 Entering Federal Subsistence Hunting Area. Good views of South Fork Fortymile River.

TJ 70 E 90.5 D 105 Large dirt turnout; do not use if it has rained.

CAUTION: Expect stretches of narrow, winding road with hairpin 20- to 30-mph curves and little or no road shoulder and no guardrails northbound. This is a very dangerous area to be passing and driving big rigs. Do NOT pull over too far on the soft shoulder.

TJ 68.9 E 91.6 D 106.1 Lost Chicken Creek. Site of Lost Chicken Hill Mine, established in 1895. Mining was underway in this area several years before the Klondike Gold Rush of 1897–1898. The first major placer gold strike was in 1886 at Franklin Gulch, a tributary of the Fortymile. Hydraulic mining operations in the creek. It is privately owned and mined.

TJ 68.1 E 92.4 D 106.9 BLM Chicken field station to west (not a public facility); information and emergency communications. Across the road from the field station, on the east side of the highway, is a turnout with trailhead for **Mosquito Fork Dredge Hiking Trail.**

Park at turnout on west side of road to hike this well-marked trail to an overlook with a bench and a view of the Mosquito Fork Dredge (also known as the Cowden Dredge, owned by the Alaska Gold Company). It is a 20- to 40-minute walk to the overlook; moderate downhill climb with a short, steep, stepped section near the end. Allow more time for uphill return. Well-maintained trail, but tree roots make for uneven walking surface. If you are short on time (or energy), it is only a 5-minute walk from the road to an overlook with a bench and a great view of the Chicken Creek area. (There are 3 benches, including the one at the last overlook.)

Good view from highway for southbound travelers of Chicken town and airstrip.

TJ 67.1 E 93.4 D 107.9 Chicken Creek bridge. *New (2018) pavement southbound to Milepost TJ 64.3.*

TJ 66.9 E 93.6 D 108.1 Turnoff to **The Goldpanner/Chicken Creek RV Park**; food, gas/diesel, store, camping.

Actual driving distance between physical Mileposts 67 and 66 is 0.6 mile.

TJ 66.4 E 94.1 D 108.6 Junction with Chicken Airport Road east to **Downtown Chicken** and **Chicken Gold Camp**; food, gas/diesel, stores, camping.

Chicken

TJ 66.4 E 94.1 D 108.6 Chicken is located 80 miles from Tok, AK, 94 miles from Eagle and 108 miles/174 km from Dawson City, YT. **Population:** 23 in summer, 7 in winter. **Emergency Services:** Dial 911 or 907-883-5111. **Private Aircraft:** Chicken airstrip, 0.8 mile east of highway (N 64° 04′ W 141° 56′); elev. 1,640 feet; length 2,500 feet; gravel; maintained year-round. Use channel 122.8 Unicom when landing in Chicken; it is a surprisingly busy airport.

Commercial Chicken consists of 3 businesses, each with their own unique attraction for travelers, and each worth a visit: **Downtown Chicken** and **Chicken Gold Camp**, are both just off the highway (turn on Chicken Airport Road), and the **Town of Chicken/The Gold Panner/Chicken Creek RV Park** is located on the highway at the Chicken Creek bridge.

Although remote, Chicken is getting

Pedro Dredge No. 4, located at Chicken Gold Camp, is a good example of the floating dredges that were used in Alaska and Yukon to excavate for gold from the early 1900s to the 1950s.
(©Kris Valencia, staff)

Colorful Downtown Chicken is yet another favorite photo op in Chicken.
(©Kelley & Milton Barker, staff)

more and more traffic each year as the Klondike Loop continues to grow in popularity with motorists driving to and from Alaska. It is not unusual to see quite a diverse group of travelers enjoying this scenic little spot on the highway. For local businesses, it is something of a challenge to provide services to this growing number of travelers. There is no city water, sewer or electric service in Chicken. There is no cell service in this area.

Generators and pit toilets are utilized here, with residents providing their own water for drinking and showers, and generating their own electricity, including the 20- and 30-amp service for RVers at the RV parks. There is a sani-dump station.

Chicken was supposedly named by early miners who wanted to name their camp ptarmigan, but were unable to spell it and settled instead for chicken, the common

name in the North for ptarmigan. As the result of this choice, Chicken, Alaska is the place to find all manner of chicken items. An active gold mining town, most of the gold items for sale in Chicken are locally mined in the Fortymile Mining District. Chicken is also well-known as the home of the late Anne Hobbs Purdy, whose story is told in the book *Tisha* (by Anne Purdy and Robert Specht).

Lodging, Camping & Services

The post office is located to the south, just off the highway, at the top of the hill before entering Chicken (see description at **Milepost TJ 66.3**). Phone (via satellite or computer), internet (with WiFi), and email are available. Traveler services here (available from about mid-May to mid-September) include cafes, lodging, RV Parks, gift shops, gas/diesel/propane, recreational mining, historic tours, liquor stores and saloons. These are provided by the town's 3 major summer businesses: **Chicken Gold Camp** owned and operated by 40-year residents Mike and Lou Busby and their family; **Downtown Chicken**, owned by Susan Wiren, a pioneering-style woman who says "after 20 plus years, I enjoy running these businesses and greeting guests more each year!"; and the **Town of Chicken**, which includes The Gold Panner and Chicken Creek RV Park, owned by Bronk Jorgenson. *See map on facing page for locations.* See also ads this section and descriptions following.

Chicken Gold Camp & Outpost, a first class, rustic retreat includes a clean RV Park with 20 and 30 amp pull-thrus, back-ins, dry sites, wooded tent sites, private

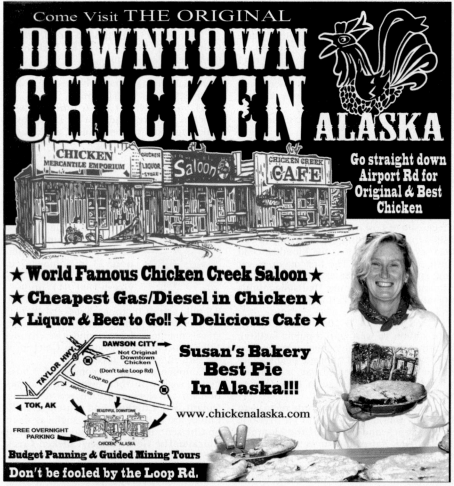

cabins, showers, free WiFi, one of Alaska's finest gift stores showcasing Alaska-made gifts and a cafe offering fresh, gourmet entrees. The Busbys, who built and run the business, have lived in Chicken for over 40 years and are passionate about the area. They give a fantastic tour of the historic Pedro Dredge and museum. Interested in gold? The Camp provides access to their gold claims with guides, equipment and transportation. Stake your own mini-claim and keep the gold you find! Gold panning is also available in the campground. The cafe serves world famous fresh baked scones, cookies, hearty homemade soups, delicious grilled Italian sandwiches, Alaskan hand-roasted espresso, local micro-brewed beer, wine and wood-fired pizza. Dine inside or out on the decks. Take your picture with "Eggee", the giant metal chicken. Alaskan hospitality at its best! Located on the left side of Airport Road with big rig/bus access and parking. ChickenRVpark@gmail.com. See display ad on this page. [ADVERTISEMENT]

Downtown Chicken is the original and a rare treat for those with the courage to stray just a few hundred yards from the beaten path. Turn on the road to Chicken's airport and look for the Big Orange Chicken on the right! Don't be fooled by cafe signs on the left. We are often imitated, but never equaled. Our Chicken Creek Cafe is famous for its bakery, chicken pot pie, and homemade chicken soup. Everything is made daily from scratch, with love. The Mercantile abounds with original items designed by owner Susan Wiren. Find good times at the legendary Chicken Creek Saloon. Beer, wine and liquor to go available at Chicken Liquor. Free camping for tents and RV'ers. Overnight rentals; wall tents $25, cabin for 2, $75, and a very private cabin that sleeps 4 w/incredible view $95 nightly, are also available. Email Chicken Sue all year at swiren@gci.net for info and reservations. Also visit our website at www.chickenalaska.com. See display ad on facing page. [ADVERTISEMENT]

Town of Chicken. Town of Chicken. Welcome to the Town of Chicken, a family-owned travel destination for the entire family. The pet friendly Chicken Creek RV Park features 20- and 30-amp sites with dump station, showers, and water fill-up at no extra cost. The Park also features beautiful creekside cabins and the only ensuite style hotel rooms on the Taylor Highway complete with private bath, Wi-Fi, and satellite TV. Visit the Goldpanner Gift Store for your unique Chicken keepsakes, custom T-shirts, free coffee, and free Wi-Fi. The Goldpanner also offers twice a day walking tours of the historic and original town featuring Tisha's schoolhouse. Eat at the Chicken Burger Barn and enjoy gourmet burgers, halibut, and chicken! Suffering from Gold Fever? Nothing will cure that like some free gold panning along Alaska's richest creek. You will find what you are looking for along the banks of Chicken Creek. Look for the Town of Chicken signs and turn at the bridge. www.townofchicken.com. See display ad on facing page. [ADVERTISEMENT]

Attractions

Tour Historic Chicken. The tin roofs of the old townsite may be seen from the road. The Historic Chicken tour includes the only remaining roadhouse (built in 1899) on the Taylor Highway, complete with a huge cookstove; Tisha's schoolhouse; the old John Powers Store, a former roadhouse; and a dozen or so other structures dating back to the early 1900s. This historic area—on the National Register of Historic Places—is located on private property; inquire at the Town of Chicken/The Goldpanner RV Park about guided tours.

Look for gold. A big attraction here is looking for gold, whether it's gold panning in a trough or in the creek, or going out on a real claim for some recreational gold mining. Each of the businesses now offers gold panning opportunities and gold pans to use onsite. Chicken Gold Camp also offers rec-

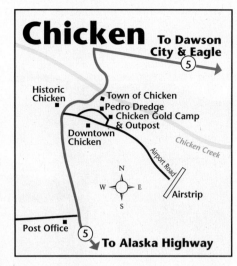

The Taylor Highway south from Chicken to the Alaska Highway is in fair condition with some gravel breaks and damaged pavement. There are 2.8 miles of new (2018) pavement entering Chicken. (©Sharon Nault)

reational mining on a claim; bring your own sluices and highbankers or use what is there.

Gold Dredges were used in Alaska and Yukon from the turn-of-the-century to the 1950s. Parts of the old Jack Wade Dredge are on display across from the post office at **Milepost TJ 66.3**, and there are views of the old Mosquito Fork Dredge from hiking trail at **Milepost TJ 68.1**.

The dredges were land-locked floating machines, digging ponds that allowed them to float across the area to be mined. The dredges operated 24 hours a day, from late April or early May and ending in November. The dredge most common in the North was the bucket-line dredge, which used a continuous line of buckets (called the "digging ladder") to scrape the bottom and edge of the pond. The buckets carried the mud and rock to a screening area, where the heavier metal particles were separated from the rest of the material.

Pedro Dredge No. 4 is located at Chicken Gold Camp on Airport Road in Chicken. This dredge operated on Chicken Creek between 1959 and 1967, after mining Pedro Creek outside Fairbanks from 1938 until 1959. Mike Busby and Bernie Karl (of Chena Hot Springs Resort) purchased the dredge and moved it and other mining equipment down to Chicken in 1998 as a tourist attraction. It was put on the National Register of Historic Places in 2006.

To reach Pedro Dredge (visible from the highway), turn on Chicken Airport Road at **Milepost TJ 66.4** then turn left on loop road for a large parking area with covered picnic tables adjacent the dredge. For more information on the dredge and/or tours, turn in at the Chicken Gold Camp off this road (www.chickengold.com).

There are 3 unusual "Chicken" photo ops in Chicken, AK. The very large and colorful chickens that sit outside the Gold Panner Gift Shop, the huge orange chicken at the entrance to Downtown Chicken and an impressive landmark, the giant chicken statue at Chicken Gold Camp. The 18-by-12 foot chicken was built of recycled high school lockers in Homer, AK, and transported to Chicken by truck (averaging 20 mph).

A small suspension bridge from the Gold Panner Gift Store and RV Park has drawn the curiosity of many visitors. Cross with care to the other side of Chicken Creek.

The annual **Chickenstock Music Festival** draws a big crowd. The festival takes place in June Go to https://www.facebook.com/ChickenstockMusicFest/ or www.chickenstockmusicfest.com for 2019 dates.

Klondike Loop Log
(continued)

TJ 66.4 E 94.1 D 108.6 Junction with Chicken Airport Road; signs here point you in the direction of Chicken's 3 major businesses.

NOTE: Gas/diesel available in Chicken. Next gas for northbound travelers is in Eagle (94 miles from here and off the direct route to Dawson City) or in Dawson City (108 miles). Next fuel for southbound travelers is in Tok (78 miles).

TJ 66.3 E 94.2 D 108.7 Chicken post office (ZIP code 99732), and community hall, located up hill to west of road; large turnaround area for big rigs above the post office, do not park along the highway. A minor attraction in itself, the post office was established in 1903 along with the mining camp. The post office is open weekdays (hours as posted). The mail plane arrives twice a week (Tuesday and Friday).

A few pieces of the Jack Wade Dredge are displayed here with information boards. The original dredge (pictured above) was located near **Milepost TJ 86** of the Taylor Highway. The dredge was dismantled by the BLM in September 2007. According to the *Fairbanks Daily News Miner,* BLM officials said the

deteriorating condition of the old dredge made it a safety hazard. The Jack Wade Dredge was one of the first bucketline dredges in the Fortymile mining district. It was freighted up the Fortymile River from Dawson City, YT, in the winter of 1906–1907, and operated at its former location from 1935 to 1941.

TJ 66 E 94.5 D 109 Chicken Community (northbound sign).

Actual driving distance between physical milepost 66 and 67 is 0.6 miles.

TJ 65.2 E 95.3 D 109.8 Federal Subsistence Hunting Area boundary. Small turnout to east with view of Mosquito Fork.

TJ 64.3 E 96.2 D 110.7 Bridge over Mosquito Fork of the Fortymile River. **BLM Mosquito Fork Wayside** to west at north end of bridge. Day-use area with parking, 3 picnic tables, elevated cooking grill, handicap-accessible pit toilet and information boards. This is a nice picnic spot overlooking the river. Signed: No overnight parking.

The Mosquito Fork and Dennison Fork converge east of this bridge to form the 33-mile-long South Fork Fortymile River. The South Fork Fortymile crosses under the Taylor Highway at **Milepost TJ 75.3**.

Mix of loose gravel and damaged pavement southbound to Alaska Highway. New (2018) pavement northbound to Chicken.

TJ 63.7 E 96.8 D 111.3 Federal Subsistence Hunting Area boundary.

TJ 58.9 E 101.6 D 116.1 Scenic viewpoint at turnout to east.

TJ 57 E 103.5 D 118 Gravel pit turnouts with gravel piles, both sides of road with expansive views.

TJ 56.9 E 103.6 D 118.1 Gravel pit turnouts both sides of road.

TJ 55.2 E 105.3 D 119.8 Highway descends northbound to Mosquito Fork of the Fortymile River.

TJ 55.1 E 105.4 D 119.9 Large turnout.

TJ 52 E 108.5 D 123 *CAUTION: Watch for moose.*

TJ 50.4 E 110.1 D 124.6 Highway descends both directions to cross Taylor Creek bridge. Trail to Taylor and Kechumstuk mountains, used in hunting season west side, south of bridge.

NOTE: Slow for loose gravel and gravel breaks.

TJ 49.2 E 111.3 D 125.8 Bridge over **West Fork** of the **Dennison River.** Access point for Fortymile River National Wild, Scenic & Recreation River system; day-use area with large parking area, no facilities, boat launch to west at south end of bridge. Fishing for grayling.

Mix of loose gravel and damaged pavement next 15 miles northbound.

TJ 49 E 111.5 D 126 Turnoff to west for **West Fork BLM Campground**, a public campground and picnic area. The campground access road forks: Right fork leads to an open wooded camping area with 7 pull-throughs, firepits and grills, picnic tables, well maintained handicap-accessible outhouse, and picnic area with shelters, pit toilet and view; left fork leads to individual campsites on loop road.

Camping area on left fork has 26 total level sites in trees (some pull-throughs, 18 back-in and 1 with an accessible tent platform); 1 covered site for bicyclists and motorcyclists; drinking water near site 13 (hauled in from Fairbanks); outstandingly clean, handicap-accessible pit toilets; tables, firepits, litter bin; free firewood (for campground use only, ask host for location); and campground hosts. Some of the sites overlook Johna's Lake (named for former campground host Don Marshall's dog), where moose and beaver are often spotted. Watch for peregrine falcons, gray jays, snowshoe hare and lots of squirrels. Dumpster at campground entrance used for all trash. $10 camping fee charged (cash or check); discount for America the Beautiful, Senior and Access pass (U.S. residents only). Bicyclists and motorcycles may use the gazebo for shelter, first come first served. *Bring your mosquito repellent!*

TJ 48.3 E 112.2 D 126.7 Federal Subsistence Hunting Area boundary.

TJ 47.5 E 113 D 127.5 Redundant sign northbound: Rough road next 4 miles.

TJ 44.5 E 116 D 130.5 Federal Subsistence Hunting Area boundary.

TJ 43 E 117.5 D 132 Unmarked turnoff to west south side of bridge for narrow gravel access road to **Logging Cabin Creek BLM Picnic Area.** *Slow for steep entrance* to small parking area (no turnaround space for big rigs); pleasant picnic spot overlooking creek with a picnic table and information board. No overnight parking.

Logging Cabin Creek bridge. Logging Cabin Creek flows into the West Fork Dennison Fork.

TJ 39.3 E 121.2 D 135.7 Double-ended gravel turnout to east on curve.

TJ 37.6 E 122.9 D 137.4 View of Mount Fairplay southbound.

TJ 35.9 E 124.6 D 139.1 Unmaintained double-ended turnout to east.

TJ 35.1 E 125.4 D 139.9 Federal Subsistence Hunting Area boundary. In these areas, local residents have an expanded season for subsistence hunts of moose and caribou. There are several of these signs along the Taylor Highway.

TJ 35 E 125.5 D 140 South entrance to **Mount Fairplay Wayside,** a large double-ended turnout to east with information boards on Taylor Highway, Fortymile River, caribou, moose. Viewing platform with good view of Mount Fairplay (elev. 5,541 feet). Brochures regarding the Fortymile area are typically available at notice board; pit toilets (wheelchair accessible) and a picnic table. Look for the small root-covered trail that leads to open area with good views.

Entering **Fortymile Mining District** northbound. The second-oldest mining district in Alaska, it first yielded gold in 1886. Claims were filed in both Canada and Alaska due to boundary uncertainties.

This is the south end of the BLM's Fortymile River National Wild, Scenic & Recreation River, the second longest designated wild and scenic river in the nation.

TJ 34.5 E 126 D 140.5 Southbound, the highway begins long, winding 5 to 7 percent uphill and downhill grades for the next 25 miles. Highway begins 9 percent downgrade northbound.

TJ 34.4 E 126.1 D 140.6 Large double-ended gravel turnout to west with panoramic views of the Alaska Range and the many stream valleys that form the Fortymile River. Good photo op.

TJ 30.2 E 130.3 D 144.8 Gravel turnout to west.

TJ 28.4 E 132.1 D 146.6 Large gravel turnout to west with good view of Alaska Range on clear days. Gravel pit to east.

TJ 28 E 132.5 D 147 Sign: 9 percent downgrade southbound.

TJ 22.2 E 138.3 D 152.8 Double-ended paved parking area to east (information boards on Fortymile region, Mount Fairplay, the Taylor Highway and the Fortymile caribou herd were missing in summer 2018).

TJ 21 E 139.5 D 154 Great view from very large, flat, gravel turnout to west, may have gravel stockpile for road maintenance.

TJ 17.8 E 142.7 D 157.2 The quixotic nature of wildfire is demonstrated the next mile northbound, as you see burn evidence on only one side of the highway, then evidence of fire on both sides of the road.

Informal grassy turnouts along the Taylor are popular parking spots for berry pickers in August. Various plants including blueberries, wildflowers (such as fireweed) and mushrooms flourish in burn areas along the Taylor Highway.

TJ 16 E 144.5 D 159 Watch for Northern hawk owls, one of the only owls to hunt during the day. These owls like to sit atop charred trees in the burn area.

TJ 15.6 E 144.9 D 159.4 Double-ended parking area to east.

View straight ahead northbound of Mount Fairplay.

TJ 14 E 146.5 D 161 Highway travels through area ravaged by 2004 Taylor Complex fire. Brilliant displays of fireweed (*Epilobium angustifolium*) cover areas recently burned. A common wildflower along the roads of the North (it is the territorial flower of the Yukon), fireweed is named for its ability to flourish in burn areas. Another unique characteristic is its flower display. When it blooms in late June, the lowest flowers on the stem bloom first. As summer passes, it begins losing flowers from the top of the stem down. Fireweed can grow to 6 feet and is usually bright pink in color, although it also occurs in pale pink and white. In fall, leaves are a blaze of bright orange and reds. Here, fireweed has given way to brush and other plants that fill in as the years pass after a fire.

TJ 12.4 E 148.1 D 162.6 Large double-ended parking area on viewpoint to east.

Northbound road sign reads: $1,000 fine for littering.

Northbound, the Taylor Highway winds along ridges and over hills overlooking several streams that eventually converge to form the Fortymile River. To the west of the highway, Logging Cabin Creek flows into the West Fork Dennison Fork, which crosses under the Taylor Highway at **Milepost TJ 49.2** on its 53-mile journey northeast to join the Dennison Fork. The Dennison Fork, mostly out-of-sight to the east of the highway, flows 60 miles northeast to join Mosquito Fork and form the 33-mile-long South Fork Fortymile River.

The North Fork Fortymile River heads at Independence and Slate creeks, flowing southeast 44 miles to join the South Fork and form the Fortymile River. The Fortymile River flows northeast 60 miles to the Yukon River in Canada.

TJ 10.7 E 149.8 D 164.3 Gravel pit stockpile to west.

TJ 10.5 E 150 D 164.5 Entering Tok Management Area, Tanana State Forest, southbound.

TJ 10.1 E 150.4 D 164.9 Narrow double-ended parking area to east on viewpoint.

TJ 9.4 E 151.1 D 165.6 Entering Game Management Subunit 12 southbound; entering GMU 20E northbound. Caribou hunting by permit only (sign).

TJ 6 E 154.5 D 169 Gravel turnout to east.

Northbound, the highway begins long, winding, 5 to 7 percent uphill and downhill grades for the next 25 miles as it ascends to Mount Fairplay's summit.

CAUTION: Slow for sections of frost heaves, soft spots, loose gravel and deteriorated pavement northbound. Many but not all, are marked by orange flags.

TJ 5.7 E 154.8 D 169.3 Entering Tanana State Forest northbound.

TJ 5 E 155.5 D 170 Highway descends 7 percent grade northbound.

TJ 4.4 E 156.1 D 170.6 Large double-ended parking area to east.

A 0.7-mile trail leads to **Four Mile Lake;** rainbow trout, sheefish.

TJ 3.4 E 157.1 D 171.6 The Taylor Complex Fires in 2004 burned 1.3 million acres. You can still see evidence of the fire damage from this 2004 wildfire along the Taylor Highway. Wildfires are common in Alaska from April or May through the summer months (depending on rainfall), with lightning the most common cause. The total number of fires in 2004 was 707, a not unusually high number in what was a very hot and dry summer for most of the state. But the total acreage burned for the year was nearly 6.6 million acres, the largest number of acres lost to wildfire in recorded Alaska history.

TJ 2.6 E 157.9 D 172.4 Double-ended paved parking area to west.

TJ 2.5 E 158 D 172.5 Highway descends 5 percent grade northbound.

TJ 1 E 159.5 D 174 Note stabilized sand dunes (and rock graffiti) next several miles northbound.

TJ 0.8 E 159.7 D 174.2 Double-ended turnout to east. Sign for caribou hunters.

TJ 0.2 E 160.3 D 174.8 Next services (food, gas/diesel, camping) northbound 67 miles (sign) at Chicken. Nearest services to this Tetlin Junction for southbound motorists are in Tok, 12 miles northwest on the Alaska Highway.

TJ 0 E 160.5 D 175 Tetlin Junction. Forty Mile Roadhouse, closed since about 1985 *(see page 223 in the ALASKA HIGHWAY section for more information on this historic landmark).*

Junction with the Alaska Highway, 12 miles southeast of Tok. Turn to **Milepost DC 1266.7** on page 223 in the ALASKA HIGHWAY section for log of that route.

TAYLOR HIGHWAY ALASKA ROUTE 5

Northbound: This section of the log shows distance from Tetlin Junction on the Alaska Highway in Alaska (TJ) followed by distance from Eagle (E) and distance from Dawson City (D). Read log:

Physical mileposts on the Taylor Highway (which are sporadic) reflect distance from this junction.

For those traveling north from the Alaska Highway here, the Taylor Highway begins a long, winding climb (up and down grades, 5 to 7 percent) out of the Tanana River valley. Distance marker northbound shows Chicken 66 miles, Boundary 104 miles, Customs 109 miles, Eagle 160 miles.

Dawson City-bound motorists cross the international border. U.S. and Canada Customs open mid-May to mid-September. Hours in summer 2018 were 8 A.M. to 8 P.M. Alaska standard time, 9 A.M. to 9 P.M. Pacific standard time.

Glenn Highway Tok Cutoff

CONNECTS: Tok to Anchorage, AK

Length: 328 miles   **Road Surface:** Paved   **Season:** Open all year

(See maps, page 319–320)

Mount Drum dominates the horizon eastbound on the Glenn Highway at Milepost A 177. (©Kelley & Milton Barker, staff)

Distance in miles	Anchorage	Glennallen	Palmer	Tok	Valdez
Anchorage		189	42	328	304
Glennallen	189		147	139	115
Palmer	42	147		286	262
Tok	328	139	286		254
Valdez	304	115	262	254	

The Glenn Highway/Tok Cutoff (Alaska Route 1) is the principal access route from the Alaska Highway west to Anchorage, a distance of 328 miles. This paved all-weather route includes the 125-mile Tok Cutoff, between Tok and the Richardson Highway junction; a 14-mile link via the Richardson Highway; and the 189-mile Glenn Highway, between the Richardson Highway and Anchorage. The 139-mile stretch of the Glenn Highway between Anchorage and Eureka Summit was declared a National Scenic Byway in 2002.

It is a full day's drive between Tok and Anchorage, although there are enough attractions along the way to recommend making this at least a 2- or 3-day drive. The speed limit varies, from 35 mph through communities to 65 mph on the relatively straight stretch of improved road between **Mileposts A 91** and **A 185** along the Glenn Highway. Current road conditions and weather at 511.alaska.gov.

Road conditions are fair along the Tok Cutoff and good along the Glenn Highway, where several sections of highway have been improved in recent years. Motorists can expect about 25 miles of winding road—and future road improvement projects—on the Glenn Highway from **Milepost A 91** (Purinton Creek) to **Milepost A 66** (near Sutton).

Major Attractions:

©Kris Valencia, staff

Alaska State Fair, Matanuska Glacier, Independence Mine

Highest Summit:
Eureka Summit 3,322 ft.

Glenn Highway
Tok Cutoff (GJ-125 to GJ-0) to Milepost A 160

© 2019 The MILEPOST®

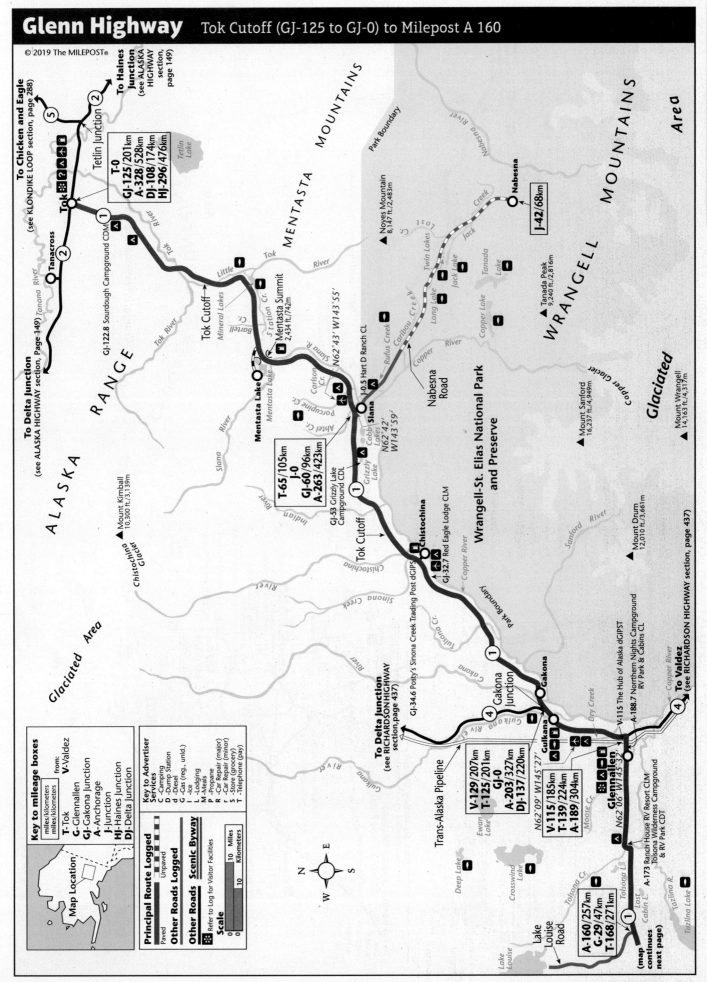

To Haines Junction
(see ALASKA HIGHWAY section, page 149)

To Chicken and Eagle
(see KLONDIKE LOOP section, page 149)

Tetlin Junction

T-0
GJ-125/201km
A-328/528km
DJ-108/174km
HJ-296/476km

Tok

Tanacross

To Delta Junction
(see ALASKA HIGHWAY section, Page 149) Tanana River

GJ-122.8 Sourdough Campground CDM

ALASKA RANGE

▲ Mount Kimball 10,300 ft./3,139m

Chistochina Glacier

Glaciated Area

Tok River

Little Tok River

Mineral Lakes

Tok Cutoff

Mentasta Summit 2,434 ft./742m

Station Cr.
Bartell Cr.

MENTASTA MOUNTAINS

Tok River

Slana R.

N62°43' W143°55'

J-0.5 Hart D Ranch CL

Mentasta Lake

Mentasta Lake

Carlson Cr.
Porcupine Cr.
Ahtel Cr.

Slana
N62 42'
W143 59'

J-0
T-65/105km
GJ-60/96km
A-263/423km

GJ-53 Grizzly Lake Campground CDL

Cobb Lakes
Grizzly Lake

Slana River

Indian River

Tok Cutoff

Chistochina

GJ-32.7 Red Eagle Lodge CLM

Chistochina River

Sinona Creek

GJ-34.6 Posty's Sinona Creek Trading Post dGIPS

To Delta Junction
(see RICHARDSON HIGHWAY section, page 437)

Trans-Alaska Pipeline

Tulsona Cr.

Gakona River

Gakona Junction

Gakona

GJ-0
V-129/207km
T-125/201km
A-203/327km
DJ-137/220km

N62°09' W145°27'

V-115/185km
T-139/224km
A-189/304km

Gulkana

Gulkana River

Glennallen
N62 06'W145 32'

A-173 Ranch House RV Resort CLM
Tolsona Wilderness Campground & RV Park CDT

V-115 The Hub of Alaska dGIPST

A-188.7 Northern Nights Campground RV Park & Cabins CL

To Valdez
(see RICHARDSON HIGHWAY section, page 437)

Nabesna

J-42/68km

▲ Noyes Mountain 8,147 ft./2,483m

Nabesna River

Park Boundary

Lost Creek

Jack Creek

Twin Lakes

Long Lake
Jack Lake
Tanada Lake
Copper Lake

Caribou Creek

Rufus Creek

Copper River

▲ Tanada Peak 9,240 ft./2,816m

WRANGELL MOUNTAINS

Nabesna Road

Wrangell-St. Elias National Park and Preserve

Glaciated Area

▲ Mount Sanford 16,237 ft./4,949m

Sanford River

Copper Glacier

▲ Mount Drum 12,010 ft./3,661m

Park Boundary

Copper River

Dry Creek

Copper River

▲ Mount Wrangell 14,163 ft./4,317m

Deep Lake
Ewan Lake
Crosswind Lake

Moose Cr.
Tolsona Cr.
Tolsona L.

Lost Cabin L.

Tazlina R.
Tazlina Lake

Lake Louise Road

Lake Louise

Lake Louise Road
A-160/257km
G-29/47km
T-168/271km

(map continues next page)

Key to mileage boxes
miles/kilometers from:
- **V**-Valdez
- **T**-Tok
- **G**-Glennallen
- **GJ**-Gakona Junction
- **A**-Anchorage
- **J**-Junction
- **HJ**-Haines Junction
- **DJ**-Delta Junction

Map Location

Key to Advertiser Services
- **C** -Camping
- **D** -Dump Station
- **d** -Diesel
- **G** -Gas (reg., unld.)
- **I** -Ice
- **L** -Lodging
- **M** -Meals
- **P** -Propane
- **R** -Car Repair (major)
- **r** -Car Repair (minor)
- **S** -Store (grocery)
- **T** -Telephone (pay)

Principal Route Logged
Paved ▬▬▬ Unpaved ▭▭▭

Other Roads Logged
Other Roads ▬▬▬ Scenic Byway ▣▣▣

Refer to Log for Visitor Facilities

Scale
0 — 10 Miles
0 — 10 Kilometers

N E S W

Glenn Highway Milepost A 160 to Anchorage, AK

© 2019 The MILEPOST®

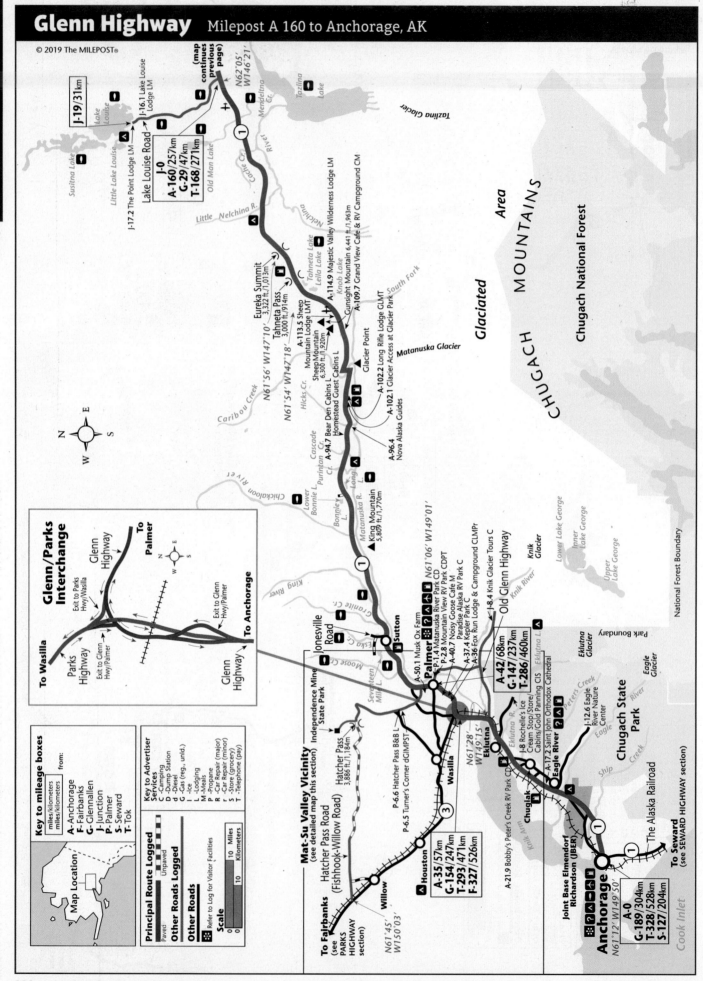

J-19/31km

J-0
A-160/257km
G-29/47km
T-168/271km

Lake Louise Road
J-17.2 The Point Lodge LM
J-16.1 Lake Louise Lodge LM

N62°05'
W146°21'

(map continues previous page)

Tazlina Lake

Mendelta Cr.

Tazlina Glacier

Little Nelchina R.

Cache Cr.

Old Man Lake

Susitna Lake
Little Lake Louise
Lake Louise

Eureka Summit
3,322 ft./1,013m
N61°56' W147°10'
Tahneta Pass
3,000 ft./914m
Tahneta Lake
Leila Lake
Knob Lake

A-114.9 Majestic Valley Wilderness Lodge LM
A-113.5 Sheep Mountain Lodge LMT
Gunsight Mountain 6,441 ft./1,963m
A-109.7 Grand View Cafe & RV Campground CM

Sheep Mountain
6,300 ft./1,920m
N61°54' W147°18'
A-102.2 Long Rifle Lodge GLMT
Glacier Point
A-102.1 Glacier Access at Glacier Park
Bear Den Cabins L
A-94.7 Homestead Guest Cabins L
A-96.4 Nova Alaska Guides

South Fork

Matanuska Glacier

Hicks Cr.
Caribou Creek
Cascade Cr.
Purintan Cr.

Chickaloon River

Lower Bonnie L.
Bonnie L.
Long L.

King Mountain 5,809 ft./1,770m

Matanuska R.

CHUGACH MOUNTAINS
Glaciated Area

Chugach National Forest

Glenn/Parks Interchange

To Palmer
Glenn Highway
Exit to Parks Hwy/Wasilla
Parks Highway
To Wasilla
Exit to Glenn Hwy/Palmer
Exit to Glenn Hwy/Palmer
Glenn Highway
To Anchorage

Mat-Su Valley Vicinity
(see detailed map this section)

Independence Mine State Park
Hatcher Pass 3,886 ft./1,184m

Jonesville Road
Sutton
Eska Cr.
Granite Cr.
King River
Seventeen Mile L.
Moose Cr.

A-50.1 Musk Ox Farm
Palmer N61°06' W149°01'
P-1.4 Matanuska River Park CD
P-2.8 Mountain View RV Park CDPT
P-40.7 Noisy Goose Cafe M
Paradise Alaska RV Park C
A-37.4 Kepler Park C
A-36 Fox Run Lodge & Campground CLMPr
I-8.4 Knik Glacier Tours C
Old Glenn Highway

Knik Glacier
Knik River
Eklutna R.
Eklutna L.

Lower Lake George
Inner Lake George
Upper Lake George

National Forest Boundary
Park Boundary

A-42/68km
G-147/237km
T-286/460km

A-21.9 Bobby's Peter's Creek RV Park CD
I-8 Rochelle's Ice Cream Stop/Store/Cabins/Gold Panning CIS
Eagle River N61°28' W149°15'
A-17.2 Saint John Orthodox Cathedral
J-12.6 Eagle River Nature Center

Eklutna
Chugiak

Knik Arm
Eagle River

Eklutna Glacier
Eagle Glacier

Chugach State Park

Ship Cr.
Peters Creek

Joint Base Elmendorf Richardson (JBER)
Saint John Orthodox Cathedral

The Alaska Railroad

To Seward
(see SEWARD HIGHWAY section)

Anchorage
A-0
G-189/304km
T-328/528km
S-127/204km
N61°12' W149°50'

Cook Inlet

Hatcher Pass Road
(Fishhook-Willow Road)
P-6.6 Hatcher Pass B&B L
P-6.5 Turner's Corner dGlMPST

Wasilla

Houston
A-35/57km
G-154/247km
T-293/471km
F-327/526km

Willow

To Fairbanks
(see PARKS HIGHWAY section)
N61°45'
W150°03'

Key to mileage boxes
miles/kilometers from:
A- Anchorage
F- Fairbanks
G- Glennallen
J- Junction
P- Palmer
S- Seward
T- Tok

Key to Advertiser Services
C - Camping
D - Dump Station
d - Diesel
G - Gas (reg., unld.)
I - Ice
L - Lodging
M - Meals
P - Propane
R - Car Repair (major)
r - Car Repair (minor)
S - Store (grocery)
T - Telephone (pay)

Map Location

Principal Route Logged
Paved
Unpaved
Other Roads Logged
Other Roads
Refer to Log for Visitor Facilities

Scale
0   10 Miles
0   10 Kilometers

Five side roads are logged in this section: the Nabesna Road, which provides access to Wrangell–St. Elias National Park and Preserve lands; Lake Louise Road to Lake Louise State Recreation Area; Hatcher Pass Road, connecting the Glenn and Parks highways to Independence Mine State Historical Park; the Old Glenn Highway, an alternate route between Palmer and Anchorage, that offers camping, fishing and Knik Glacier access via airboat; and Eagle River Road to the Eagle River Nature Center.

Emergency Services: Dial 911.

Glenn Highway Tok Cutoff Log

Westbound: Distance from junction with the Richardson Highway at Gakona Junction (GJ) is followed by distance from Anchorage (A) and distance from Tok (T). Read log: ⬇️

Physical mileposts show distance from Gakona Junction.

ALASKA ROUTE 1

GJ 125 A 328 T 0 TOK; Junction of Alaska Highway and Tok Cutoff. Distance marker eastbound shows Fairbanks 208 miles, Canadian border 90 miles. Tok Visitor Center at southeast corner of intersection. *(See Tok map page 226.)* Paved bike path begins south side of highway. Improved highway westbound to **Milepost GJ 109.**

> **Junction** of the Tok Cutoff (Alaska Route 1) and the Alaska Highway (Alaska Route 2) in Tok. Turn to page 224 in the ALASKA HIGHWAY section for description of Tok and log of the Alaska Highway southeast to the Canadian border or northwest to Delta Junction.

Distance marker westbound shows Glennallen 141 miles, Valdez 254 miles, Anchorage 328 miles.

GJ 124 A 327 T 1 Actual driving distance between physical Mileposts 124 and 125 at Tok junction is 0.5 miles.

GJ 123.5 A 326.5 T 1.5 Turnoff to north on Borealis Avenue for **Tetlin National Wildlife Refuge Headquarters** (1.3 miles northwest). The Tetlin NWR office is open 8 A.M. to 4:30 P.M., May 15 to Sept. 15; parking, information boards, a good display of Alaska's owls, brochures on the refuge, information on campgrounds, and import/export permits for hunters. The visitor center for Tetlin National Wildlife Refuge is located at physical **Milepost 1229** Alaska Highway *(see description on page 221).*

Slow for speed zone eastbound entering Tok.

GJ 122.8 A 325.8 T 2.2 Sourdough Campground to west has wooded sites and is home to the Sourdough Pancake Toss. 🅰️

Sourdough Campground. See display ad on page 226 in the ALASKA HIGHWAY section.

GJ 122.6 A 325.6 T 2.4 Private Aircraft: Tok airstrip to southeast; elev. 1,670 feet; length 1,700 feet; gravel; unattended. No services. Private airfield across the highway.

GJ 116.6 A 319.6 T 8.4 Paved turnout at westbound boundary sign for Tok Management Area, **Tanana Valley State Forest.** End of the 8.5 mile paved bike trail coming from Tok.

Tok is a popular full-service stop at the junction of the Alaska Highway and Tok Cutoff.
(©Kris Valencia, staff)

Established as the first unit of Alaska's state forest system in 1983, **Tanana Valley State Forest** encompasses 1.81 million acres and lies almost entirely within the Tanana River Basin. The forest extends 265 miles from near the Canadian border to Manley Hot Springs. Almost 90 percent of the state forest is forested. Principal tree species are paper birch, quaking aspen, balsam poplar, black spruce, white spruce and tamarack. Almost 7 percent of the forest is shrubland, chiefly willow. The forest is managed by the Dept. of Natural Resources.

GJ 114 A 317 T 11 Distance marker eastbound shows Tok 10 miles, Canadian Border 100 miles.

GJ 112 A 315 T 13 Large turnout to southeast.

GJ 111 A 314 T 14 Distance marker westbound shows Nabesna Junction 53 miles, Glennallen 128 miles, Anchorage 315 miles.

GJ 110 A 313 T 15 Highway straightens eastbound.

GJ 109.3 A 312.3 T 15.7 Clearwater Creek bridge.

GJ 109.2 A 312.2 T 15.8 Turnoff to north for **Eagle Trail State Recreation Site** at west end of Clearwater Creek bridge. Gravel access to creek to south.

Eagle Trail SRS has 35 campsites in nicely wooded area, 15-day limit, 2 picnic sites, water, toilets, firepits, picnic shelters. Camping fee $20/night. After entering campground, big rigs should take second right for pull-throughs and park-alongs. Information boards at trailhead for Valdez to Eagle Trail (Old Slana Highway and WAMCATS); 1-mile nature trail or 2.5-mile trail to overview of Tok River Valley. Operated by concessionaire CWL Enterprises, phone (907) 505-0319. 🅰️

GJ 106 A 309 T 19 Mountain views westbound as the highway passes through the Alaska Range. The Mentasta Mountains are to the southeast.

GJ 104.4 A 307.4 T 20.6 Paved shoulder parking to north. **Tok Overflow** runs under highway in culvert; fish for Arctic grayling and Dolly Varden. 🐟

GJ 104 A 307 T 21 Actual driving distance between physical milepost 103 and 104 is 1.4 miles.

CAUTION: Watch for moose.

GJ 103.8 A 306.8 T 21.2 Bridge over Tok

River, side road north to riverbank and boat launch. The Tok River heads at Tok Glacier in the Alaska Range and flows northeast 60 miles to the Tanana River. Tok-bound travelers are in the Tok River Valley, although the river is out of sight to the southeast most of the time.

GJ 103.5 A 306.5 T 21.5 Paved shoulder parking to north. Tok Overflow; fish for Arctic grayling and Dolly Varden. 🐟

GJ 99.5 A 302.5 T 25.5 Turnout to north. Wild roses in summer with vitamin C-rich rose hips in the fall.

GJ 98.5 A 301.5 T 26.5 Turnoff to southeast on Old Tok Cutoff Road.

GJ 98.2 A 301.2 T 26.8 Bridge over **Little Tok River**, which parallels highway. Narrow, sloping access road to south at west end of bridge. The Little Tok River heads in the Mentasta Mountains to the south and flows north 32 miles to the Tok River.

Slow for gravel breaks, mild frost heaves, bumps and patched road westbound.

GJ 95.4 A 298.4 T 29.6 Turnout to southeast; surrounded by mountains on the edge of a deep valley. Views to north and northeast.

GJ 91 A 294 T 34 Little Tok River bridge (weight limit 20 tons); good fishing for Arctic grayling, 12 to 14 inches, use small spinner. Large turnout. 🐟

Distance marker shows Slana 34 miles, Glennallen 109 miles.

GJ 90.1 A 293.1 T 34.9 Paved turnout.

GJ 89 A 299 T 36 Between **Milepost GJ 89** and **GJ 86** watch for moose and trumpeter swans (see **Milepost GJ 77.9**) in wetlands along Lower Station Creek to the southeast. The creek provides excellent moose habitat and a breeding place for waterfowl. The creek flows into **Mineral Lake** and makes a pleasant canoe trip. It offers good fishing for northern pike and Arctic grayling. 🐟

GJ 88.2 A 291.2 T 36.8 Large informal gravel turnout to northwest.

GJ 85.7 A 288.7 T 39.3 Small turnout to north.

GJ 84.5 A 287.5 T 40.5 *CAUTION: Slow for road damage.*

GJ 83.2 A 286.2 T 41.8 Bridge over Bartell Creek. Just beyond is the divide between

The Tok Cutoff heads southwest from Tok across the Mentasta Mountains.

(©Kris Valencia, staff)

the drainage of the Tanana River, tributary of the Yukon River system flowing into the Bering Sea, and the Copper River system, emptying into the Pacific near Cordova.

GJ 82.9 A 285.9 T 42.1 Distance marker eastbound shows Tok Junction 40 miles, Canada Border 136 miles.

GJ 81.5 A 284.5 T 43.5 Gravel turnout to south.

GJ 81 A 284 T 44 Access road leads north 7 miles to **MENTASTA LAKE** (pop. 121), unincorporated. This is a primarily Athabascan community with a subsistence-based lifestyle; no visitor services.

The Mentasta area was particularly hard hit by a 7.9 earthquake that jolted the Interior and Southcentral regions of the state in November 2002. Centered about 80 miles south of Fairbanks, it was the strongest quake ever recorded along the Denali Fault. (The Denali Fault runs in a great arc from Southeast Alaska through Canada, then re-enters Alaska, slicing Denali National Park in half.) The Tok Cut-Off, Richardson and Glenn highways all sustained damage.

GJ 79.2 A 282.2 T 45.8 Mentasta Summit (elev. 2,434 feet). The U.S. Army Signal Corps established a telegraph station here in 1902. The Mentasta Mountains rise to about 6,000 feet on either side of the highway. The 40-mile-long, 25-mile-wide Mentasta Range is bounded on the north by the Alaska Range. Watch for Dall sheep on mountainsides.

Boundary between Game Management Units 12 and 13C and Sportfish Management Units 8 and 2.

GJ 78.1 A 281.1 T 46.9 Mentasta Lodge to southeast; cafe, motel, gas, diesel and propane.

NOTE: Next gas westbound is at Posty's in Chistochina, 43 miles from here. There is no gas available on the Nabesna Road.

GJ 77.9 A 280.9 T 47.1 Large gravel turnout to northwest by large pond; watch for waterfowl.

Watch for trumpeter swans in the spring and fall in bodies of water along northern highways. Eighty percent of the world's population of trumpeter swans (the largest of the 7 types of swans found worldwide) nest in Alaska, although they are far outnumbered by the smaller tundra swans. Other than the size difference, the 2 swans are similar in appearance, although tundra swans have a bright yellow mark on their otherwise black bills, while trumpeter swans have all-black bills.

From both east and west of Gakona Junction, the highway becomes a patchwork of good highway going bad (frost heaves, damaged pavement), and improved sections of highway. Watch for and slow down for frost heaves and gravel breaks!

GJ 76.3 A 279.3 T 48.7 Bridge over Mable Creek. Mastodon flowers (marsh flea-bane) in late July; very large (to 4 feet) with showy seed heads.

GJ 75.8 A 278.8 T 49.2 Bridge over Slana Slough.

CAUTION: Watch for moose.

GJ 75.5 A 278.5 T 49.5 Bridge over **Slana River**. Double-ended rest area with picnic table and outhouse to south just west of bridge. This river flows from its source glaciers some 55 miles to the Copper River.

GJ 73.9 A 276.9 T 51.1 Large gravel turnout to south is scenic viewpoint of Mentasta Mountains, with view of Slana River and possible swan sightings.

GJ 72.3 A 275.3 T 52.7 Distance marker westbound shows Nabesna Junction 13 miles, Glennallen 88 miles.

GJ 69 A 272 T 56 Large gravel turnout to north. Views westbound (weather permitting) of snow-covered **Mount Sanford**, elev. 16,237 feet, to south. Mount Sanford is in the Wrangell Mountains and it is 1 of Alaska's 10 highest peaks.

GJ 67.9 A 270.9 T 57.1 Carlson Creek bridge.

GJ 65 A 267 T 59 *CAUTION: Watch for multiple pavement breaks between* **Milepost GJ 65** *and* **GJ 66.**

GJ 65.5 A 268.5 T 59.5 Paved turnout overlooking Slana River to south (by mail boxes) is a scenic viewpoint; road leads down to riverbank. Magnificent views (weather permitting) of the Wrangell Mountains. Dominant peak is snow-covered Mount Sanford.

Highway parallels Slana River westbound.

GJ 64.2 A 267.2 T 60.8 Sharp turn to north at east end of Porcupine Creek bridge for **Porcupine Creek State Recreation Site,** 0.2 mile from highway. Thickly forested area with 12 campsites on loop road, 3-day limit, $20 nightly fee per vehicle, water pump (boil water), firepits, outhouses, picnic tables and good fishing for Dolly Varden and Arctic grayling. Hiking trails up Porcupine Creek to Carlson Lake and Bear Valley (trails are poorly marked, carry topo map). Lowbush cranberries in fall. Watch for moose. Concessionaire is Hart D Ranch, phone (907) 822-3973. ⬅️ ⛺

GJ 64.1 A 267.1 T 60.9 Bridge over Porcupine Creek.

GJ 63 A 266 T 62 Scenic viewpoint to southeast with view of Wrangell Mountains. The dominant peak to the southwest is Mount Sanford, a dormant volcano; the pinnacles of Capital Mountain can be seen against its lower slopes to the west. Mount Jarvis (elev. 13,421 feet) is visible due south, with the jagged buttresses of Tanada Peak (elev. 9,240 feet) to its left.

Sign here about Noyes Mountain, elev. 8,147 feet (view obscured by brush), which was named for U.S. Army Brig. Gen. John Rutherford Noyes, a one-time commissioner of roads in the Territory of Alaska. Appointed adjutant general of the Alaska National Guard in 1953, he died in 1956 from injuries and frostbite after his plane crashed near Nome.

GJ 62.7 A 265.7 T 62.3 Duffy's Roadhouse (closed for many years). **Private Aircraft:** Duffy's Tavern/Slana (private) airstrip, N62°43.48' W143°55.23'; elev. 2,420 feet; 1,200 feet, gravel; unattended.

GJ 62 A 265 T 63 Parking area and informal camping site. Begin 7 percent downhill grade next 1.7 miles westbound.

GJ 61 A 264 T 64 Midway Service to northwest; grocery store, cabins rentals, tent camping. ⛺

Begin 7 percent uphill grade next 1.7 miles eastbound.

GJ 60.8 A 263.8 T 64.2 Bridge over **Ahtell Creek**; Arctic grayling fishing (no bait, single-hook, artificial lures only in Copper River drainage streams). Watch for salmon spawning late June through July. (*This stream is closed to chinook salmon fishing*). Gravel parking area at end of bridge across from midway service. This stream drains a mountain area of igneous rock, where several gold and silver-lead claims are located. ⬅️

GJ 60 A 263 T 65 Distance marker eastbound shows Tok 66 miles, Tetlin Junction 78 miles, Canada Border 158 miles.

GJ 59.8 A 262.8 T 65.2 Junction with Nabesna Road. Turnoff to south for Nabesna Road; post office, pay phone, private camping, lodging and art gallery (open year-round) at Mary Frances DeHart's **Hart D Ranch**, Mile 0.5 Nabesna Road. Wrangell-St. Elias National Park ranger station is located just 0.2 mile south of here.

Hart D Ranch See display ad on facing page.

There is no gas available on Nabesna Road. Nearest gas is at Mentasta Lodge (18 miles east) or Posty's (25 miles west). ⛺

Junction with Nabesna Road. See the "Nabesna Road" log beginning on facing page.

Begin long 6 percent uphill grade westbound.

(Continues on page 324)

Nabesna Road

The 42-mile Nabesna Road leads southeast from **Milepost GJ 59.8** on the Tok Cutoff to the northern area of Wrangell–St. Elias National Park and Preserve and is 1 of only 2 road accesses to the park (the other is McCarthy Road). Take time to drive out to Dead Dog Hill Wayside at **Milepost J 17.8** or Rock Lake Wayside at **Milepost J 21.8**: The scenery is worth the trip.

Stop at the ranger station at **Milepost J 0.2** for details on activities within the park, off-road vehicle permits (required) and current road conditions. Cabin permits may be done over the phone at (907) 822-7253 or by email WRST_Tweet@nps.gov.

Visitor services available on Nabesna Road include lodging and camping at **Hart D Ranch (Milepost J 0.5)**, owned and operated by artist and sculptor Mary Frances DeHart. Gas, groceries and food are not available on this road. The nearest gas and food are on the Tok Cutoff at either Mentasta Lodge 18 miles east at **Milepost GJ 78.1**, or Posty's, 25 miles west at **Milepost GJ 34.6**. Midway Service at **Milepost GJ 61** has groceries.

There are several developed waysides with outhouses, picnic tables, firepits and litter bins as well as primitive campsites and established campgrounds on Nabesna Road. The area offers good fishing and hunting in season. Horses are permitted on all trails. Wildlife to watch for: black and brown bears, wolves, caribou, moose, ptarmigan, trumpeter swans and other birds.

The first 16 miles of road are paved/chip sealed, the remainder is dirt and gravel. Carry a good spare tire. *Sudden changes in creek water levels possible and can make this route impassable in spring or during heavy rains, requiring high clearance or 4-wheel-drive vehicle.* The dirt and gravel portion of the road can be slick in wet weather: Watch for soft shoulders and soft spots in turnouts. Cell phone service is sporadic on Nabesna Road.

This is not a road for big rigs; smaller RVs are fine. If you have a tow vehicle, you can drop your RV or trailer at Hart D Ranch, drive the road, then return for an overnight.

Distance is measured from the junction with the Tok Cutoff (J).
Driving distance is based on physical mileposts on the Nabesna Road.

J 0 Junction with the Tok Cutoff at Milepost GJ 59.8.
J 0.2 Turnoff to right southbound for access to Slana Ranger Station (parking, visitor information, restrooms) and Slana DOT Maintenance Station, phone (907) 822-3301. Not a through road, limited parking; big rigs can usually turn around just beyond the station.

The ranger station has information on road conditions and activities in Wrangell–St. Elias National Park & Preserve; issues ATV permits; provides backcountry trip planning assistance and bear-proof containers (free with deposit); and has hunting information and subsistence permits available. Ask about summer ranger programs for visitors. USGS maps and natural history books for sale. Open 8 A.M. to 5 P.M. daily, Memorial Day through September; by appointment rest of

Nabesna Road provides access to the northern Wrangell-St. Elias National Park & Reserve. The first 16 miles of road are paved, the remainder is gravel. (©David L. Ranta, staff)

year. Phone (907) 822-7401.
J 0.5 Slana post office (with antique glass fronted boxes), open Monday, Wednesday, Friday, 8:30 A.M. to 1 P.M. Pay phone station at entrance to **Hart D Ranch** complex; lodging (year-round) and RV park. This picturesque ranch is the home and studio of sculptor Mary Frances DeHart. DeHart also raises Affenpinscher dogs. Call ahead in winter months.

Hart D Ranch. See display ad this page.
J 1.1 Slana elementary school. **SLANA** (pop. 139; unincorporated), once an Indian village on the north bank of the Slana River, now refers to this general area, much of which was homesteaded in the 1980s. Slana once boasted a popular roadhouse, now a private home.
J 1.6 Slana River bridge. Boundary between Game Management Units 11 and 13C. Private property, no roadside parking, next few miles southbound.
J 3.8 Entering Wrangell–St. Elias National Park & Preserve ahead southbound, National Preserve boundary.
J 3.9 Four Mile Road. Huck's Hobbit Hostel B&B (phone ahead, 907/822-3196).
J 4.6 Double-ended gravel turnout.
J 5.4 Signs mark Wrangell–St. Elias National Park lands to southwest, National

Preserve lands to northeast.
J 6.1 Pleasant primitive campsite to east with picnic table and firepit on bank of **Rufus Creek**. Fishing for Dolly Varden to 8 inches, June to October. Watch for bears, especially during berry season.
J 7 Road crosses Rufus Creek culvert; small turnout. Private homes.
J 7.9 Large rough turnout to west, can be muddy in wet weather.
J 8.8 Rough gravel turnout to south.
J 8.9 Large open parking area to south; informal camping.
J 9.2 Dirt turnout to east.
J 11.1 Large gravel parking area to west.
J 11.2 Suslota Lake trail to east; trailhead parking at **Milepost 11.1**. This trail can be very wet. It is used primarily by ATVs and is not recommended for hiking. Blueberries, cranberries and Labrador tea.
J 11.9 Creek culvert. Watch for owls (great horned, northern hawk, short-eared and boreal) in tall trees in this area.
CAUTION: Watch for gravel breaks and patched roadway.
J 12.2 Parking to west at **Copper Lake** trailhead; picnic table, primitive campsite. Good trail for short day hikes, with recent gravel work done on first 3 miles of trail, to Tanada Creek bridge. Plan on 2-day strenu-

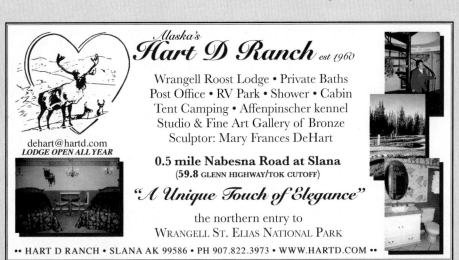

ous hike (stream crossings) to reach Copper Lake (16.7 miles). Fishing for lake trout, Arctic grayling, burbot.

J 12.8 Large informal dirt and gravel parking area with sloping approach to east. Watch for moose.

J 13.4 Dirt turnout to east.

J 16 Pavement/chip seal ends, gravel begins, southbound.

J 16.6 Kettle Lake Wayside; primitive campsite to south; picnic table, firepit. Unusual and no doubt often photographed sign southbound stating "Toilet 1 mile." Beautiful views of Kettle Lake, Mount Sanford, Capital Mountain, Mount Wrangell, Mount Zanetti and Tanada Peak in the Wrangell Mountains to the southwest.

©Kris Valencia, staff

J 17.8 Dead Dog Hill Wayside (pictured above) has camping, picnic table, vaulted toilet, litter bin. Look for trumpeter swans on lake just east of this rest area. Great view of Noyes Mountain (elev. 8,147 feet) in the Mentasta Mountains to the north.

J 18.3 Caribou Creek culvert.

J 18.9 Signed gravel parking area to east for Caribou Creek trail, which is 1,500-feet up the road (see next milepost).

J 19.2 Caribou Creek trail; park at **Milepost J 18.9.** This is a multi-use trail for first 3 miles to Caribou Creek public-use cabin (reservation required, phone Wrangell-St. Elias Visitor Center in Copper Center at 907/822-7253). Good hiking with views of the Wrangell Mountains and the Copper River valley.

J 20.6 Large, primitive, double-ended parking area to east.

J 21.1 Rock Creek culvert.

J 21.8 Rock Lake Wayside to west; camping, picnic table, vaulted toilet, litter bin. Great views of Mount Sanford and Tanada Peak to the south.

Trail to east for Viking Lodge public-use cabin (reservation required, phone Slana Ranger Station at 907/822-7401). No ATVs allowed on trail.

J 22.4 Long Lake (signed); Arctic grayling fishing.

J 22.8 Small turnout at dip in road is protected from the wind.

J 23.4 Single-vehicle turnout to east.

J 23.9 Tanada Lake trailhead parking to west. Trail at Mile 24.5 can be very wet; not recommended for hiking. Fishing for Arctic grayling and lake trout.

J 24.7 Watershed divide (elev. 3,320 feet) between streams draining into the Copper River watershed and into the Gulf of Alaska, and those entering the Yukon River watershed which drains into the Bering Sea. Boundary between Sportfish Areas C and K, and Game Management Areas 11 and 12.

J 24.9 Local homes and lodge. Glimpse of Tanada Lake beneath Tanada Peak to the south.

J 25.3 Little Jack Creek culvert.

J 27.8 Kendesnii Campground gravel loop road to 10 campsites; free, first-come, first-served, picnic tables, information boards, 2 vaulted toilets, litter bin. **Twin Lakes** is a good place to observe waterfowl (this is a major gathering place for swans in the fall). Fishing for lake trout and Arctic grayling 10 to 18 inches, mid-May to October, flies or small spinner. Wildflowers in June include Lapland rosebay, lupine and mountain avens.

J 28 Lodge, current status unknown.

Watch for a small resident caribou herd on Sugarloaf Mountain to the south. The larger Nelchina caribou herd migrates through here in October, according to the Fredericks who own the lodge and have said that the caribou usually stay until April and are a popular attraction, with sightseers coming in by snow machine to see the herd.

J 29 Trail Creek culvert.

J 29.8 Trail Creek trailhead.

J 30.7 Lost Creek crossing.

J 31 Small creek crossing.

J 31.2 Lost Creek trailhead and parking, a multi-use trail with access to Big Grayling Lake, Soda Creek, Platinum Creek, Mineral Springs and Soda Lake. Inquire at Slana Ranger Station for ATV permits and private property boundaries in area.

J 31.6 Chalk Creek culvert.

J 33.3 Radiator Creek culvert.

J 35.3 Jack Creek 1-lane bridge and a small rest area (big rigs check turnaround space before entering) to west. Pretty camping spot with picnic tables, vaulted toilet, litter bin. Arctic grayling fishing.

J 36 *Road narrows southbound, soft spots in road after rain.* Timbers from old corduroy road visible in roadbed.

J 36.2 Skookum Volcano trail (hiking only).

J 36.4 Rock and gravel cover former creek crossing. *These crossings can be rough, with large rocks.*

J 37.9 Rock and gravel cover former creek crossing.

J 39.6 Rock and gravel cover former creek crossing.

J 40 Reeve's Field trailhead. This trail was constructed during WWII to connect Nabesna Road with a large airstrip near the Nabesna River. The airstrip (which has washed out) and trail were named for aviation pioneer Bob Reeve.

J 40.2 *Begin long uphill climb southbound.*

J 40.6 State maintenance ends. Begin 10 mph speed limit.

J 40.8 Leaving Wrangell-St. Elias National Park and Preserve southbound.

J 42 End of Nabesna Road; Public access permitted only on dirt road, Private property adjacent to road. Do not park on private airstrip.

At Mile 0.2 beyond this there is a parking area and any further travel is on foot or by bicycle. At Mile 0.5 there is the Rambler Mine Trail; strenuous trail leads south uphill 1 mile to abandoned mine ruins. Do not take or disturb mine debris. Do not enter mine shafts or structures, as they are dangerous with potential to collapse.

Return to Milepost GJ 59.8
Tok Cutoff

(Continued from page 322)

GJ 59.4 A 262.4 T 65.6 Distance marker westbound shows Glennallen 76 miles; Valdez 189 miles; Anchorage 263 miles.

GJ 58.7 A 261.7 T 66.3 Begin long 6 percent down grade eastbound.

GJ 56.5 A 259.5 T 68.5 Double-ended turnout to south is a scenic viewpoint overlooking Cobb Lakes, a chain of 3 lakes. Red raspberries in season. Watch for moose in ponds. View to the south and southwest of Tanada Peak (9,240 feet); Mount Sanford (16,237 feet), center; Mount Blackburn (16,390 feet); and Mount Drum (12,010 feet). Gold Rush Centennial sign about Lt. Henry T. Allen's expedition of 1885.

Begin long 6 percent downgrade eastbound.

GJ 55.2 A 258.2 T 69.8 Tanada Peak viewpoint; long, large double-ended paved turnout to south.

CAUTION: Watch for horses on road.

GJ 53 A 256 T 72 Turnoff to south for **Grizzly Lake Campground;** lodging, RV park, trail rides. Owned by long-time Alaskans Doc and Phoebe Taylor, and by their daughter, Cathy, and her husband Jim Knighten. Grizzly Lake Campground is situated in a beautiful wilderness setting with wonderful views.

Grizzly Lake Campground. See display ad on this page.

GJ 46 A 249 T 79 Westbound, Mount Drum (12,010 feet) is directly ahead; Mount Sanford (16,237 feet) is to the left of Mount Drum. Views are weather permitting.

GJ 43.8 A 246.8 T 81.2 Bridge over **Indian River.** Watch for salmon spawning in late June through July. This river is closed to chinook salmon fishing.

GJ 43.7 A 246.7 T 81.3 Rest area to south at west end of Indian River bridge; toilet, garbage bins, access to gravel bars in river, canoe launch; big rigs should use extra care and scope out the location prior to entering.

GJ 40.1 A 243.1 T 84.9 Gravel turnout to south.

GJ 39 A 242 T 86 Views of the Copper River Valley and Wrangell Mountains. Looking south, peak on left is Mount Sanford and on right is Mount Drum.

GJ 38.7 A 241.7 T 86.3 Gravel shoulder parking to north.

GJ 37 A 240 T 88 Chistochina (sign westbound).

GJ 35.5 A 238.5 T 89.5 Chistochina River bridge.

GJ 35.2 A 238.2 T 89.8 Turnoff to north at west end of bridge for 0.1-mile drive in to a very spacious, flat, paved, parking area with outhouse. Access to Chistochina River trailhead allows access to approximately 40 miles of trails in hills north of the highway, according to the BLM. Used during hunting season by ATV and large track vehicles; trails may be muddy in wet weather. For permits or more information, phone Ahtna, Inc. in Glennallen at (907) 822-3476. Sign reads:

"This is a 50-foot-wide ANCSA 17(b) easement. Please respect the private property you have the privilege of driving through. Travel off this easement is considered trespassing. Brown Carsonite markers appear every half-mile. Allowed: Foot traffic, dog sleds, animals, snow-machines, 2- and 3-wheeled vehicles, track vehicles, 4-wheel-drive vehicles. Prohibited: Camping on easement, hunting on easement, travel off easement, fishing from easement, blocking easement."

The Chistochina River heads in the Chistochina Glacier in the Alaska Range and flows south 48 miles to the Copper River, which is just south of the highway here. The Tok Cut-Off parallels the Copper River from here southeast to the Richardson Highway.

GJ 34.6 A 237.6 T 90.4 Posty's Sinona Creek Trading Post to north is open daily year-round; food, gas/diesel, gifts, laundry and showers, fishing/hunting licenses.

Posty's Sinona Creek Trading Post. See display ad this page.

NOTE: Next gas eastbound is at Mentasta Lodge, 43 miles from here.

GJ 34.5 A 237.5 T 90.5 Bridge over Sinona Creek. Sinona is said to mean "place of the many burls," and there are indeed many burls on area spruce trees. Paved bike path begins and extends 1.6 miles westbound alongside highway.

GJ 33 A 236 T 92 Distance marker westbound shows Glennallen 49 miles, Valdez 155 miles, Anchorage 227 miles.

Distance marker eastbound shows Tok 90 miles, Canadian border 180 miles.

GJ 32.9 A 235.9 T 92.1 Chistochina school. Road access to **CHISTOCHINA** (pop. 88, unincorporated), a traditional Copper River Athabascan Indian village with subsistence lifestyle.

Private Aircraft: Chistochina airstrip, adjacent south; elev. 1,850 feet; length 2,060 feet; turf and gravel; unmaintained, unattended.

GJ 32.8 A 235.8 T 92.2 Site of old Chistochina Lodge to southeast which burned down in 1999. Built in the early 1900s, the original roadhouse served sled traffic on the Valdez to Eagle Trail. Paved bike path ends. Begin improved highway westbound.

GJ 32.7 A 235.7 T 92.3 Turnoff for historic **Red Eagle Lodge** (description follows); cabins, camping, fishing.

Red Eagle Lodge. Fly-in or drive-in. Experience "Real Alaska" at a 1920s Roadhouse site along the old Valdez to Eagle

Viewpoint at Milepost GJ 1 overlooks the valley of the Copper and Gakona rivers.
(©Kris Valencia, staff)

Trail. Themed authentic homestead cabins feature rustic luxury. The historic cabins' ambience is enhanced with queen beds (down bedding), wood-burning stoves, braided rugs, handcrafted quilts, antiques. Newly scribed 30x50-foot log bathhouse equipped with washers/dryers. Experience "glamourous camping" in a platform wall tent. Watch wildlife in comfort from a porch swing/rocker. Enjoy spectacular views of Mount Sanford on the bike path (bicycles provided). In the evening, relax in the warmth of a campfire cookout. Start your day with a special breakfast served by owners at the lodge, Richard and Judy Dennis. www.redeaglelodge.com. Phone (907) 822-5299. See display ad this page.
[ADVERTISEMENT]

GJ 31.4 A 234.4 T 93.6 Paved turnout to north.

GJ 31 A 234 T 94 Chistochina (eastbound sign).

GJ 30.1 A 233.1 T 94.9 Small paved turnouts both sides of highway. End improved highway westbound.

GJ 28.2 A 231.2 T 96.8 Long double-ended paved parking area to south (no view) with a marker on the Alaska Road Commission. The ARC was established in 1905, the same year the first automobile arrived in Alaska at Skagway. The ARC operated for 51 years, building roads, airfields, trails and other transportation facilities. It was replaced in 1956 by the Bureau of Public Roads (referred to by some Alaskans at the time as the Bureau of Parallel Ruts). In 1960, the Bureau of Public Roads was replaced by the Dept. of Public Works.

GJ 25 A 228 T 100 Large rest area with paved double-ended parking area to south; toilets, litter bins, picnic tables and firepits in treed area. The Copper River—out of sight to the south—heads on the north side of the Wrangell Mountains and flows 250 miles to the Gulf of Alaska. Gold Rush Centennial sign in woods near parking area about gold prospecting.

GJ 22.9 A 225.9 T 102.1 Small turnout (no turnaround) above Copper River; view of river and mountains.

GJ 22 A 225 T 103 Views to southeast of the Wrangell Mountains: Mount Sanford on the left, Mount Drum on the right. Highway

Mount Sanford, at elev. 16,237 feet, is a prominent peak in the Wrangell Mountains, and can be seen from the Tok Cutoff in most weather. (©*Kris Valencia, staff*)

climbs 7 percent grade next mile westbound.

GJ 21 A 224 T 104 Highway descends 7 percent grade between next mile eastbound.

GJ 20.9 A 223.9 T 104.1 Shoulder parking to southeast.

GJ 20 A 223 T 105 Concentrations of black spruce occur in several areas along the Tok Cutoff/Glenn Highway. Note the black spruce in this area, recognizable by their stunted size and often crooked shape, topped by fat, shrubby clusters of branches. Look for thick, ball-shaped tangles of spruce branches, twigs and needles close to the trunk of the tree which are called Witch's broom. Witch's broom is caused by a fungus. Black spruce is generally found in poorly drained areas, such as wetlands and permafrost, where white spruce will not grow.

Gray jays are abundant in this area. Of the family *Corvidae*, gray jays are also called "camp robbers" for their propensity to make off with any food left out on picnic tables or elsewhere in camp.

GJ 18.2 A 221.2 T 106.8 Large informal gravel turnout to northwest.

GJ 17.6 A 220.6 T 107.4 Tulsona Creek bridge. Good Arctic grayling fishing. Walk down the old Tok Cutoff here for access to the creek away from the road.

GJ 14.2 A 217.2 T 110.8 Highway descends long grade eastbound. Views of river and mountains (Mount Sanford and Mount Drum).

GJ 13 A 216 T 112 Gravel shoulder turnout to north.

GJ 12.1 A 215.1 T 112.9 Distance marker westbound shows Glennallen 26 miles, Valdez 144 miles, Anchorage 206 miles.

GJ 11.7 A 214.7 T 113.3 Gravel shoulder turnout to southeast. Look for yellow pond lily (*Nuphar polysepalum*) in pond north side of highway.

GJ 11.3 A 214.3 T 113.7 HAARP (High Frequency Active Auroral Research Program) to north of highway. Owned by the University of Alaska Fairbanks, the facility states its goal is "to conduct fundamental study of the physical processes at work in the very highest portions of our atmosphere, called the thermosphere and ionosphere. This research falls into two categories (1) active, which requires the use of the Ionospheric Research

Instrument and (2) passive, which only uses monitoring instruments." Principal elements include an HF transmitter and antenna array and UHF ionospheric radar. There are no visitor tours due to lack of staffing but there is an annual open house in August. Check website for details and next event date: www.gi.alaska.edu/haarp/haarp-open-house.

GJ 9.4 A 212.4 T 115.6 Large paved turnout.

GJ 6.5 A 209.5 T 118.5 Small paved turnout to south. Views (weather permitting) to south of Mount Sanford and Mount Drum as highway descends westbound to Gakona River. Begin uphill grade eastbound.

GJ 4.6 A 207.6 T 120.4 Red Igloo Cabins to south.

GJ 4.2 A 207.2 T 120.8 Gakona Alaska RV Park and Cabins to south.

GJ 2.6 A 205.6 T 122.4 Post office to south serves **GAKONA** (pop. 181). Originally an Ahtna Athabascan wood and fish camp, it became a permanent village. This unincorporated community is located at the confluence of the Gakona and Copper rivers. (Gakona is Athabascan for rabbit.)

GJ 2 A 205 T 123 Gakona Lodge & Trading Post; lodging, restaurant (open for dinner only). Listed on the National Register of Historical Places, the lodge was built in 1929.

GJ 1.8 A 204.8 T 123.2 Gakona River bridge. The river flows 64 miles south from Gakona Glacier in the Alaska Range to join the Copper River here. Entering Game Management Unit 13B westbound and 13C eastbound.

GJ 1 A 204 T 124 Paved viewpoint to south overlooks the valley of the Gakona and Copper rivers; picnic table. View of Mount Drum and Mount Sanford. Good photo op in clear weather. Ahtna heritage sign. Gold Rush Centennial sign about Washington-Alaska Military Cable and Telegraph System (WAMCATS). The 1,506-mile line was completed in 1903 and obsolete by the late 1920s with the advent of radio technology. Highway descends eastbound.

GJ 0.2 A 203.2 T 124.8 Gakona (sign eastbound); see description at **Milepost GJ 2.6.**

GJ 0.1 A 203.1 T 124.9 Distance marker

eastbound shows Tok Junction 123 miles, Canadian border 213 miles.

From here east to Tok, the highway is a patchwork of new, improved highway and good highway going bad. Slow for frost heaves, gravel breaks and damaged road. Physical mileposts eastbound to Tok show distance from Gakona Junction.

GJ 0 A 203 T 125 Gakona Junction. Stop sign westbound at **junction** of Tok Cutoff (Alaska Route 1) with Richardson Highway (Alaska Route 4). The 2 roads share a common alignment for the next 14 miles south. Westbound travelers: Turn south on the Richardson Highway for Glennallen and Valdez or turn north here on the Richardson Highway for Delta Junction and Fairbanks.

Paxson- or Delta Junction-bound travelers turn to **Milepost V 128.5** on page 447 in the RICHARDSON HIGHWAY section for log of Alaska Route 4 North.

NOTE: *This junction can be confusing; see map on page 328.*

ALASKA ROUTE 1 (Tok Cutoff)

Eastbound: Distance from junction with the Richardson Highway at Gakona Junction (GJ) is followed by distance from Anchorage (A) and distance from Tok (T). Read log: ↑

ALASKA ROUTE 4

Southbound: Distance from Valdez (V) is followed by distance from Anchorage (A) and distance from Tok (T). Read log: ↓

Physical mileposts for the next 14 miles southbound give distance from Valdez, so distance from Valdez is given first.

V 129 A 203 T 125 Gakona Junction; Stop 'n Shop Grocery, ECO gas station, charter fishing services.

Distance marker southbound shows Glennallen 16 miles, Valdez 129 miles, Anchorage 196 miles.

Distance marker northbound shows Paxson 56 miles, Delta Junction 137 miles; Fairbanks 235 miles.

V 128 A 202 T 126 Highway descends long hill next 1.2 miles southbound to Gulkana River.

V 126.9 A 200.9 T 127.1 Access road east to village of **GULKANA** (pop. 108) on the east bank of the Gulkana River at its confluence with the Copper River. Established as a telegraph station in 1903 and named "Kulkana" after the river. Most of the Gulkana River frontage in this area is owned by Ahtna, Inc. and closed to the public for hunting and trapping. However, land use permits may be purchased from Ahtna for fishing and boating access on Ahtna lands. Ahtna land use permits can be purchased online at www.ahtna-inc.com/land-permit; in person at the corporate headquarters office in Glennallen (Monday–Friday from 8 A.M. to 5 P.M.); phone at (907) 822-3476.

V 126.8 A 200.8 T 127.2 Gulkana River bridge. Very popular fishing spot in season. *Watch for pedestrians.* Public access to river south of bridge; see **Milepost V 126.5.** *No public access to river at north end of bridge.* The Gulkana River flows more than 90 miles to the Copper River. Entering Game Management Unit 13B northbound, 13A southbound.

Highway climbs next 1.2 miles northbound.

V 126.5 A 200.5 T 127.5 Paved access road east 0.4 mile to large gravel parking area with litter bins, portable toilet, and access to rough gravel road to second large parking area and boat launch on **Gulkana River**; day use along river, with overnight parking allowed as signed. This is a very busy area when the fish are in. *NOTE: Access roads can be in rough shape.*

Fish in the **Gulkana River** for Arctic grayling all year; chinook June to mid-July; sockeye salmon late July to late August. Click "Fishing Reports" at www.sf.adfg. state.ak.us/statewide/sf_home.cfm and go to Interior region then Upper Copper/Upper Susitna Management Area. Be familiar with current fishing regulations and closures.

V 126 A 200 T 128 Large paved turnout to west.

V 121.9 A 195.9 T 132.1 Glennallen regional landfill to west.

V 118.1 A 192.1 T 135.9 Private Aircraft: Gulkana Airport to east; elev. 1,579 feet; length 5,000 feet; asphalt; fuel 100LL.

V 118 A 192 T 136 Short gravel access road leads west to **Dry Creek State Recreation Site**; 50 wooded campsites on loop roads accommodate all sizes of RVs; drive-in, pull-through or walk-in. Open May 15 to Sept. 15. Clean pit toilets, potable water, fire rings, tent pads, no hookups, picnic tables. Quiet hours strictly enforced. Camping fee $20 (self-registration); day use fee $5. Camping limited to 15 days. Pets on leash are welcome. Hiking trails and fishing. No ATVs.

V 116.6 A 190.6 T 137.4 Bush Bottle Bin to east with ATM, sporting licenses and gear, liquor and grocery.

V 115.2 A 189.2 T 138.8 Distance marker northbound shows Paxson 71 miles, Tok 139 miles, Fairbanks 251 miles. Canada Border 256 miles from this point.

V 115 A 189 T 139 Junction of Glenn and Richardson highways; 24-hour gas, diesel, and convenience grocery at **The Hub of Alaska** (open year-round). Greater Copper Valley Chamber of Commerce Visitor Center, open daily in summer. The aptly named The Hub of Alaska is on the northwest corner of this intersection; a busy place in summer. **Ahtna, Inc.'s** Corporate Headquarters is on the east side of the Richardson Highway at this intersection. Anchorage-bound travelers turn west.

The Hub of Alaska. See display ad this page.

Ahtna Inc. See display ad on page 330.

Junction of the Richardson Highway (Alaska Route 4) and Glenn Highway (Alaska Route 1). Turn to **Milepost V 115** on page 446 in the RICHARDSON HIGHWAY section for log of highway south to Valdez.

ALASKA ROUTE 4
Northbound: Distance from Valdez (V) is followed by distance from Anchorage (A) and distance from Tok (T). Read log: ↑

ALASKA ROUTE 1
Westbound: Distance from Anchorage (A) is followed by distance from Glenn–Richardson highway junction (G) at Glennallen and distance from Tok (T). Read log: ↓

Enjoy the natural history displays at the Greater Copper Valley Visitor Center located at The Hub of Alaska. (©Serine Reeves)

Physical mileposts westbound reflect distance from Anchorage.

A 189 G 0 T 139 Junction of the Glenn and Richardson Highways; 24-hour gas, diesel, and convenience grocery at **The Hub of Alaska** (open year-round). Greater Copper Valley Visitor Center, open daily in summer, 9:30 A.M. to 6:30 P.M. Eastbound travelers turn left for Tok and right for Valdez. Seasonal food truck and espresso drive-thru adjacent The Hub.

Distance marker westbound shows Glennallen 2 miles, Palmer 141 miles, Anchorage 189 miles.

Slow for speed zone westbound through Glennallen.

A 188.9 G 0.1 T 139.1 One of 2 entrances to **The Hub of Alaska** and to food truck and drive-thru espresso place (very

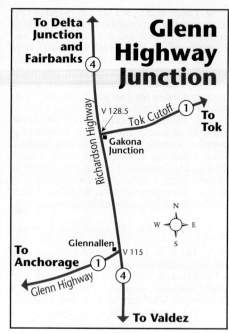

Glennallen is a busy, full-service town at the junction of the Glenn and Richardson highways. (©Sharon Nault)

good). The Hub is open year-round with 24-hour gas/diesel and store.

A 2.8-mile bike trail begins on the north side of the Glenn Highway westbound.

Sign westbound for "State Trooper Bruce A. Heck Memorial Corridor." See memorial plaque at **Milepost A 120.2.**

A 188.8 G 0.2 T 139.2 Sparks General Store with groceries, gas and Radio Shack to south.

A 188.7 G 0.3 T 139.3 Northern Nights Campground and RV Park & Cabins to north (description follows).

Northern Nights Campground RV Park & Cabins, located at **Milepost 188.7.** Offering RV spaces, tent sites and fully-furnished, not dry cabins. Open mid-May through September, weather permitting. Full-hookup sites plus pull-throughs. Shower house, restroom and laundry, and free WiFi. Free dessert night M-W-F from mid-June through mid-August. northernnightscampground.com; (907) 822-3199. [ADVERTISEMENT]

A 188.6 G 0.4 T 139.4 Copper Valley Telecom to north.

A 188.5 G 0.5 T 139.5 Glennallen Community Chapel to north.

A 187.5 G 1.5 T 140.5 Wells Fargo Bank and Department of Motor Vehicles to north, cafe to south with burgers and fries.

A 187.1 G 1.9 T 140.9 Copper Valley IGA to north is an impressively well-stocked supermarket. First National Bank is adjacent to supermarket. Glennallen Fuels to south offers gas, diesel, propane, towing, auto repair and tires.

Glennallen

A 187 G 2 T 141 Downtown Glennallen (post office); located 2 miles west of the junction of the Glenn and Richardson highways. Distance marker shows Palmer 138 miles, Wasilla 151 miles, Anchorage 187 miles, Valdez 117 miles. **Population:** 465. **Emergency Services:** Dial 911. **Alaska State Troopers, Milepost A 187,** phone (907) 822-3263. **Clinic,** and pharmacy, Cross Road Medical Center at **Milepost A 186.7;** urgent care available; phone (907) 822-3203.

Visitor Information: The Greater Copper Valley Chamber of Commerce Visitor Center is located at the junction of the Glenn and Richardson highways, **Milepost A 189;** open daily in summer 9:30 A.M. to 6:30 P.M.; phone (907) 822-5555 or www.traveltoalaska.com. The Alaska Dept. of Fish and Game office is located at **Milepost A 186.3** on the Glenn Highway, open weekdays 8 A.M. to 5 P.M.; phone (907) 822-3309.

Elevation: 1,460 feet. **Climate:** Mean monthly temperature in January, -10°F; in July, 56°F. Record low was -61°F in January 1975; record high, 90°F in June 1969. Mean precipitation in July, 1.53 inches. Mean precipitation (snow/sleet) in December, 11.4 inches. **Radio:** KCAM 790, KCAM-FM 88.7, KOOL 107.1, KUAC-FM 92.1, KXGA-FM 90.5 (community public radio). **Television:** KYUK (Bethel) and Wrangell Mountain TV Club via satellite; Public Broadcasting System.

Private Aircraft: Gulkana airstrip, northeast of Glennallen at **Milepost A 192.1;** elev. 1,579 feet; length 5,000 feet; asphalt; fuel 100LL. Parking with tie downs.

The name Glennallen is derived from the combined last names of Capt. Edwin F. Glenn and Lt. Henry T. Allen, both leaders in the early exploration of the Copper River region.

Four prominent peaks of the majestic Wrangell Mountains are to the east; from left they are Mounts Sanford, Drum, Wrangell and Blackburn. The best views are on crisp winter days at sunset.

Glennallen businesses are located for several miles along the Glenn Highway west from the junction of the Glenn and Richardson highways. About two-thirds of the area's residents are employed by trade/service firms; the balance hold various government positions.

Offices for the Bureau of Land Management, the Alaska State Troopers and Dept. of Fish and Game are located here. Glennallen is the location of Prince William Sound Community College.

There is a substantial Native population in the area, and the Alaska Native-owned Ahtna, Inc. has its corporate headquarters in Glennallen at the junction of the Glenn and Richardson highways. Ahtna, Inc. is owned by more than 2,000 shareholders, the majority of whom are of Ahtna Athabascan descent. A premiere Alaskan-owned business, Ahtna, Inc. is guided by its vision statement: "Our Culture Unites Us; Our Land Sustains Us; Our People are Prosperous." The use of Ahtna lands for recreation and other activities requires a land use permit which can be purchased online at www.ahtna-inc.com/land-permit; in person at the corporate headquarters office in Glennallen (Monday–Friday from 8 A.M. to 5 P.M.); or by phone at (907) 822-3476. To learn more about the Ahtna family of companies visit www.ahtna-inc.com.

Also headquartered here is KCAM radio, which broadcasts area road condition reports and also airs personal messages during the popular "Caribou Clatters."

Glennallen is a fly-in base for several guides and outfitters. Summer recreation in Glennallen includes flightseeing, hunting, fishing and river rafting in summer; snow-machining and dog sledding in winter. ATVs are popular; rentals available locally.

Transportation

Air: Gulkana airport, northeast of Glennallen at **Milepost V 118.1** on the Richardson Highway.

Bus/Van: Summer service to McCarthy with Kennicott Shuttle (www.kennicottshuttle.com); phone (907) 822-5292. Soaring Eagle Transit (www.gulkanacouncil.org) serves the Copper River Basin, Valdez and Anchorage; phone (907) 822-4545.

Lodging & Services

Glennallen has all visitor services. Lodging and dining in town at the **Caribou Hotel,** with adjacent gift shop and fuel complex (description follows). **Northern Nights Campground RV Park and Cabins** at **Milepost A 188.7** has dry cabins and **Ranch House Resort,** west of town at **Milepost A 173,** has dry cabins, restaurant and bar. Groceries, espresso, deli and bakery at **Copper Valley IGA.** Services include a

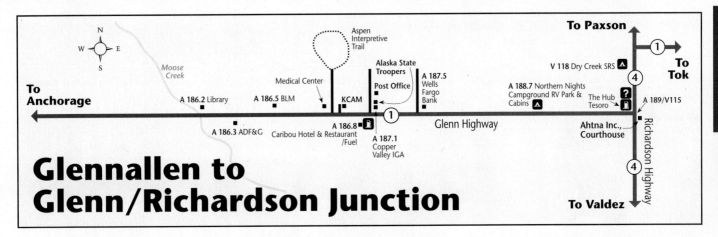

Glennallen to Glenn/Richardson Junction

Wells Fargo Bank with ATM, First National Bank Alaska with ATM, a dentist, several churches, a chiropractic center, a laundromat, gas stations and major auto repair. WiFi access at the Hub of Alaska, the Caribou Hotel and Copper Valley Community Library.

New Caribou Hotel, Restaurant, Gift Shop & Glennallen Fuel Complex. Caribou Hotel with 55 new rooms, whirlpool bath and suites available. Alaska decor, satellite TV, fax lines. Fireweed Grill at the Caribou Hotel is completely remodeled with seating for 135, with private dining room for tour buses. Daily specials, homemade soups, pies and pastries. Caribou Gift Shop in a quaint Alaska log cabin full of gifts, souvenirs, handmade items, jewelry, furs, knives, T-shirts and sweatshirts. Glennallen Fuel Service Station carries quality fuel and tire products, diesel, Cooper tires and propane. PO Box 329, Glennallen, AK 99588. Mile 186.5 Glenn Highway. Hotel reservations phone (907) 822-3302. Restaurant reservations phone (907) 822-4222. Service Station phone (907) 822-3303. www.caribouhotel.com; email info@caribouhotel.com. See display ad this page. [ADVERTISEMENT]

Camping

Camping in town at **Northern Nights Campground RV Park & Cabins** (Milepost A 188.7). Area camping at Dry Creek State Recreation Site, 3 miles north of the Glenn-Richardson Junction on the Richardson Highway, and at **Tolsona Wilderness Campground and RV Park** and at **Ranch House Resort**, both 14 miles west at Milepost A 173 Glenn Highway and **Sailors Campground** located at **Milepost V 129.5** of the Richardson Highway offers RV and tent campsites with Gulkana River access (north of Glennallen 14 miles).

GLENNALLEN ADVERTISERS

Ahtna, Inc. ....Ph. (907) 822-3476
Caribou Hotel, Restaurant
  and Fuel Complex, The ....Ph. (907) 822-3302
Copper Valley IGA ....Ph. (907) 822-3334
Hub of Alaska, The ....Ph. (907) 822-3555
Northern Nights Campground
  RV Park & Cabins ....Ph. (907) 822-3199
Ranch House RV Resort
  & Cabins ....Ph. (907) 822-5634
Tolsona Wilderness
  Campground & RV Park ....Ph. (907) 822-3900

Attractions

Aspen Interpretive Trail is a 1-mile walk through 3 boreal forest ecosystems: aspen/white spruce forest, black spruce forest and sedge meadow. Information signs about area plants and animals were developed by local students. Trailhead parking is on Co-op Road (turn north off the Glenn Highway just

east of the BLM office).

Glennallen is the service center for the Copper River Basin. It is also the starting point and finish line for the **Copper Basin 300 Dog Sled Race** (www.cb300. com). Called by some "the toughest 300 miles in Alaska," the race is held the second Saturday in January. One of the first races of

EXPLORE FOR YOURSELF

The traditional homeland of the Ahtna Athabascan people includes **MILLIONS OF ACRES OF PRISTINE WILDERNESS TO EXPLORE** with breathtaking scenic vistas around every corner.

Sailors Campground located at MP 129.5 of the Richardson Highway offers developed RV & tent campsites with Gulkana River access. *Family camping at its best – salmon fishing at its finest.*

Hilltop Campground located at MP 3 McCarthy Road offers wonderful views of the Copper and Chitina Rivers. *12 RV camping and tent pads located within the Wrangell St. Elias National Park.*

WELCOME to the Ahtna Region

Ahtna
An Alaska Native Corporation

ahtna-inc.com

THE LAND IS THE HEART & SOUL OF OUR PEOPLE

Please remember that Ahtna lands are private lands. We welcome you and hope you have a safe and wonderful stay; we only ask that you respect this land as it is our home. To access our lands, a Land Use Permit is required at all times: **permits.ahtna-inc.com**

the season, the Copper Basin is a qualifier for the Iditarod, attracting a variety of participants, from top mushers to first-time rookies. The race travels through Chistochina, over to Paxson, down to Sourdough, Lake Louise and Tolsona before returning to Glennallen.

Summer special events include a parade and salmon bake on the **4th of July** and an arts and crafts fair on the July 4th weekend.

Glennallen is the gateway to the Wrangell Mountains. The **Wrangell-St. Elias National Park Visitor Center** is about 10 miles south of Glennallen on the Richardson Highway and well worth a visit. The National Park visitor center offers interpretive programs during the summer.

Lake Louise, 27 miles west on the Glenn Highway and 16 miles north on Lake Louise Road, is a popular recreation area for fishing (Arctic grayling, lake trout and burbot) in summer and snow machining in winter. Lakeside resorts offer food, lodging and boat rentals. **Lake Louise State Recreation Area** offers camping and a boat launch.

AREA FISHING: Arctic grayling fishing and good chinook and sockeye salmon fishing (June and July) in the **Gulkana River** at the Gulkana River bridge on the Richardson Highway, a 14-mile drive from Glennallen.

According to the ADF&G, 25 lakes in the Glennallen area are stocked with Arctic grayling, rainbow trout and coho salmon. A complete list of lakes, locations and species is available at the visitor center at the Glenn-Rich junction, or from the ADF&G office at **Milepost A 186.3** and online at www.adfg. alaska.gov/index.cfm?adfg=fishregulations. no_sportfish. Locally, there is good Arctic grayling fishing in **Moose Creek; Tolsona Creek** to the east at **Milepost GJ 17.6,** and to the west at **Tolsona Creek, Milepost A 172.9;** and at **Lake Louise.**

Fly-in lakes include: **Crosswind Lake,** large lake trout, whitefish and Arctic grayling, early June to early July; **Deep Lake,** all summer for lake trout to 30 inches; **High Lake,** lake trout to 22 inches, June and early July; **Tebay Lakes** and **Summit Lake,** excellent rainbow trout fishing, 12 to 15 inches, all summer; **Jan Lake,** 12- to 14-inch coho salmon, June, spinners; also rainbow trout; **Hanagita Lake,** excellent Arctic grayling fishing all summer; and **Minnesota Lake,** lake trout to 30 inches, all summer.

Glenn Highway Log
(continued)

A 187 G 2 T 141 KCAM radio station to north, AM 790, FM 88.7.

A 186.9 G 2.1 T 141.1 Distance marker westbound shows Palmer 138 miles, Wasilla 151, Anchorage 187 miles. Aspen Hiking Trailhead to north.

A 186.8 G 2.2 T 141.2 Napa Auto Parts to south.

Distance marker eastbound shows Valdez 117, Tok Junction 141, Fairbanks 253.

A 186.7 G 2.3 T 141.3 Cross Road Medical Center clinic (EMS, 24-hour emergency room) to north has a pharmacy and clinic. Phone (907) 822-3203.

A 186.5 G 2.5 T 141.5 Bureau of Land Management Glennallen Field Office to north; phone (907) 822-3217.

A 186.3 G 2.7 T 141.7 Alaska Dept. of Fish and Game to south; phone (907) 822-3309.

A 186.2 G 2.8 T 141.8 Copper Valley Library to north.

A 186.1 G 2.9 T 141.9 Moose Creek cul-

vert, parking to north; good Arctic grayling fishing.

Beginning of a 2.8-mile bike trail north side of highway going eastbound.

A 185.5 G 3.5 T 142.5 Large paved turnout to north.

A 185.4 G 3.6 T 142.6 *Slow for speed zone eastbound through Glennallen.*

A 185 G 4 T 143 True Value Hardware store to north.

A 184 G 5 T 144 Fishers Fuel to north.

A 182.2 G 6.8 T 145.8 Basin Liquors to south has some interesting topiary done in native shrubs like willow and birch.

A 176.7 G 12.3 T 151.3 Paved historical viewpoint to south with view southeast across the Copper River valley to Mount Drum. Northeast of Mount Drum is Mount Sanford, and southeast is Mount Wrangell (elev. 14,163 feet), the only active volcano in the Wrangell Mountains.

Tolsona (westbound sign), an unincorporated community located along about a 16-mile stretch of the Glenn Highway.

A 176.5 G 12.5 T 151.5 Distance marker eastbound shows Glennallen 10 miles, Tok 152 miles.

A 174.8 G 14.2 T 153.2 Double-ended paved turnout to south. Great views (on clear days) of Mount Drum directly ahead for eastbound travelers.

A 173 G 16 T 155 Turnoff to north for **Tolsona Wilderness Campground and RV Park** (now with yurt rentals) and for the **Ranch House RV Resort** with restaurant and bar, cabins and RV Park (see descriptions following). Beautiful area.

Ranch House RV Resort, built in the early 50's, is one of the oldest roadhouses still in operation. Built before the Glenn Highway was paved, the original builders used sled dog teams to haul logs and supplies to this historic landmark. Enjoy grayling and trout fishing in the Tolsona Creek which surrounds the property. The current roadhouse offers a mix of Alaskan history with some modern updates. There are full RV hookups, pull-through sites, dry cabin rentals, tent sites, and tavern and liquor store. Phone: (907) 822-5634. Website: alaska ranchhouselodge.com. See display ad this page. [ADVERTISEMENT]

Tolsona Wilderness Campground & RV Park. AAA approved, Good Sam Park. This beautiful campground, located three-quarters of a mile north of the highway, is surrounded on 3 sides by untouched wilderness. All 80 campsites are situated beside sparkling Tolsona Creek and are complete with table and fireplace. It is a full-service campground with tent sites, restrooms, dump station, hot showers, laundromat, water and electric hookups for RVs. Free Wi-Fi. Hiking trail and public phone. Open seasonally. Phone (907) 822-3900. Email: camp@tolsonacampground.com. Website: www.tolsonacampground.com. See display ad on page 332. [ADVERTISEMENT]

A 172.9 G 16.1 T 155.1 Turnout to south at east end of Tolsona Creek bridge; parking for walk-in use (no overnight camping). Fishing for Arctic grayling to 16 inches, use mosquito flies in still, clear pools behind obstructions, June, through August. Best fishing 1.5 miles upstream from highway.

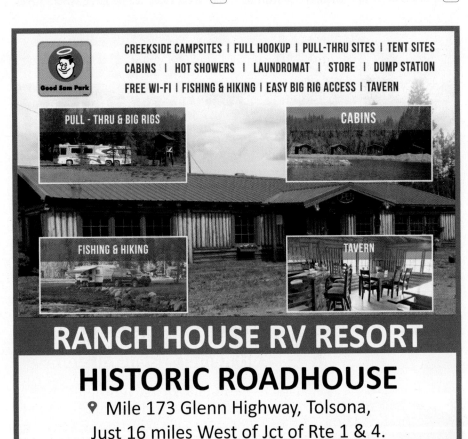

Moose cow and her calves graze on lush summer grasses. Calves are born mid-May to early June. Twins are common but triplets are not. (©Kelley & Milton Barker, staff)

A 170.5 G 18.5 T 157.5 Turnoff to north on Tolsona Lake Road for **Tolsona** and **Moose** lakes; Lee's air taxi, public parking along road and near lodge (closed). Fish for Arctic grayling and stocked rainbow trout. Check with the ADF&G office in Glennallen for details.

Good views eastbound on the Glenn Highway (weather permitting) of Mount Drum (center peak); Mount Sanford (to left of Drum); and Mount Wrangell (to right of Drum).

A 170 G 19 T 158 Crosswind Lake trail. This is a 14-mile winter snowmachine trail for access to the lake. According to the ADF&G, the lake supports Arctic grayling, burbot, lake trout, sockeye salmon and whitefish. The trail is too boggy for summer use.

A 169.3 G 19.7 T 158.7 Paved double-ended parking area to south. Long narrow **Mae West Lake**, fed by Little Woods Creek,

is less than a mile from the highway. Arctic grayling fishing.

A 168 G 21 T 160 Soup Lake to north (view obscured by trees).

A 166.9 G 22.1 T 161.1 Distance marker westbound shows Lake Louise Junction 7 miles, Sutton 106 miles, Palmer 119 miles.

A 165.9 G 23.1 T 162.1 Paved double-ended turnout to south and hiking trail to **Lost Cabin Lake** to north; fish for Arctic grayling and burbot.

Tolsona Mountain (elev. 2,974 feet), a prominent ridge just north of highway, is a landmark for miles in both directions. This area is popular with berry pickers in late summer and early fall.

A 164 G 25 T 164 Halfway point between Tok and Anchorage. Glimpse of Tazlina Glacier and lake in the distance to south.

A 162.3 G 26.7 T 165.7 Paved turnout to south.

A 162 G 27 T 166 Gravel turnout to north at signed public fishing access to **Tex Smith Lake**; stocked with rainbow trout.

A 161 G 28 T 167 Westbound, note the changes in vegetation as the highway passes through various transition zones. Well-drained soil and south-facing slopes support tall, dense stands of white spruce, aspen and birch, while cold wet flats, muskeg and north-facing slopes are dominated by the stunted and crooked black spruce.

A 160 G 29 T 168 Eastbound sign for TOLSONA (area pop. 29), an unincorporated community located along about a 16-mile stretch of the Glenn Highway.

A 159.8 G 29.2 T 168.2 Turnoff to north for Lake Louise Road (see description this section).

Junction with 19.3-mile Lake Louise Road (paved) to lodges and State Recreation Area on Lake Louise. See "Lake Louise Road" log on facing page.

A 159.6 G 29.4 T 168.4 **Little Junction Lake** signed public fishing access to south (0.5-mile hike) Arctic grayling.

A 157.9 G 31.1 T 170.1 *SLOW for dips*
(Continues on page 334)

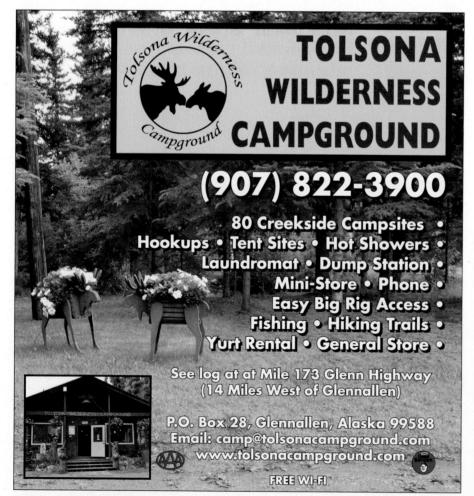
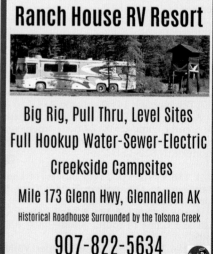

Lake Louise Road

This paved road (turnoff is 27 miles west of Glennallen) leads north 19.3 miles from **Milepost A 159.8** Glenn Highway to **LAKE LOUISE** (pop. 53), known for its fishing (lake trout and Arctic grayling) and its lakeside lodges and campgrounds. Dining, boat rentals, boat tours and fishing charters are available at the lodges. Excellent cross-country skiing and snowmachining in winter. Good views of Tazlina Glacier and berry picking (in season) along Lake Louise Road. Posted speed limit is 45 mph (road has many frost heaves, use caution); maintained year-round.

LAKE LOUISE ROAD

Distance is measured from the junction with the Glenn Highway (J).

J 0 Junction with Glenn Highway at **Milepost A 159.8.** *Slow for frost heaves and damaged pavement. Watch for caribou next 20 miles. Watch for snow machines in winter.*

J 0.2 Junction Lake to east; Arctic grayling fishing (stocked by ADF&G).

J 1 Large gravel turnout to west.

J 1.2 Double-ended turnout to west with view of Tazlina Glacier. Just north is the road west to **Little Crater Lake** and **Crater Lake**, stocked with rainbow trout by ADF&G.

J 5.1 Old Road Lake and Round Lake public access to east (.25 mile via narrow, gravel, potholed road); stocked by ADF&G with rainbow trout.

J 6.6 Mendeltna Creek to west 5 miles to public access via rough gravel road (4-wheel-drive access only); Arctic grayling fishing.

J 7 Gravel parking area across from 0.1-mile trail east to **Forgotten Lake**; Arctic grayling fishing public access.

J 9.4 Paved shoulder parking to west. First view of Lake Louise northbound.

J 10 View of pothole lakes.

J 10.2 Long narrow turnout adjacent highway on the west.

J 10.5 Highway descends hill northbound. Good view on clear days of the Alaska Range and Susitna River valley.

J 11.5 Small dirt parking to east. Side road leads west then north to **Caribou Lake**; Arctic grayling fishing. Turnout to east by **Elbow Lake**; Arctic grayling fishing.

J 13.9 Large gravel parking area to east.

J 14 Boundary of Matanuska-Susitna Borough. Welcome Lake Louise Community (sign).

J 14.9 Gravel turnout to east.

J 15.3 Waste transfer site to east.

J 15.8 Signed gravel shoulder parking to east.

J 15.9 North and **South Jans Lakes** to east (7 miles; trail access); rainbow trout. Turnout area for parking and trail access.

J 16.1 Turnoff for **Lake Louise Lodge** on Lake Louise to east (0.8 miles); lodging, dining, boat tours and water taxi services. It is closed late fall through mid-February, then open for winter visitors (as well as all

Lake Louise Road is a gateway to fishing and boating opportunities in summer, cross-country skiing and snowmachining in winter. (©Serine Reeves)

summer long). Call ahead for confirmation.

Lake Louise Lodge. See display ad page 333.

J 16.5 Turn east for Evergreen Lodge and Wolverine Lodge.

J 16.8 Conner Lake public access to west; Arctic grayling fishing.

J 17 Snow machine crossing.

J 17.2 Gravel side road leads northeast to **The Point Lodge** (0.8 miles) and **Lake Louise State Recreation Area.** Drive 0.3 miles to "T"; turn west and continue 0.5 mile for **The Point Lodge** to the west and to the east for Lake Louise Campground; turn east at "T" for Army Point Campground (0.7 mile).

The Point Lodge. See display ad page 333.

©Milton & Kelley Barker, staff

Army Point Campground and Lake Louise Campground (Lake Louise State Recreation Area) have 67 campsites on loop roads, firepits, water pumps (boil water), toilets (wheelchair accessible), covered picnic tables, picnic shelter, walking trail. Camping fee $20/night per vehicle; boat launch $15 at Lake Louise Campground; daily parking $7. Hosts noted "They always have sites available, even on holiday weekends." Swimming in Lake Louise (no lifeguard, Kid's Don't Float lifejackets are at the boat launch area). Popular winter ski trail and snowmachine access. No ATVs.

J 18 *Slow for gravel breaks northbound.* View of Lake Louise to northeast.

J 18.3 Private Aircraft: Lake Louise airport, N62°17.62' W146°34.77'; elev. 2,450 feet; length 7,000 feet; gravel; unattended. Lake Louise seaplane base, N62°16.97', W146°31.13'. Attended daylight hours in summer.

J 19.2 Lake Louise rest area to east at road end has picnic tables, fireplaces, toilets.

J 19.3 Road ends. Large parking area to west and boat launch to **Dinty Lake** (west) and **Lake Louise** boat launch (east).

Arctic grayling and lake trout fishing good year-round, best spring through July, then again in the fall; early season use herring or whitefish bait, cast from boat; later (warmer water) troll with #16 red-and-white spoon, silver Alaska plug or large silver flatfish; for Arctic grayling, casting flies or small spinners, June, July and August; in winter jig for lake trout. Check ADF&G regulations. **Susitna Lake** can be reached by boat across Lake Louise (narrow channel; watch for signs); burbot, lake trout and Arctic grayling fishing. *Both lakes can be rough with winds increasing suddenly; under-powered boats not recommended.*

Return to Milepost A 159.8
Glenn Highway

(Continued from page 332)
and damaged road.

A 157 G 32 T 171 Distance marker westbound shows Palmer 109 miles, Anchorage 157 miles.

Distance marker eastbound shows Glennallen 31 miles, Tok 173 miles.

A 156.4 G 32.6 T 171.6 Good view (weather permitting) to south of **Tazlina Glacier**, which feeds into 20-mile-long Tazlina Lake, at the head of the Tazlina River, a tributary of the Copper River.

A 156.3 G 32.7 T 171.7 Gravel turnout. **Buffalo Lake** public fishing access to north; stocked with rainbow trout.

A 156 G 33 T 172 Tazlina airstrip to north; elev. 2,450 feet; length 1,200 feet; gravel. Not recommended for use. Tazlina Glacier Lodge to south (closed in 2018).

A 155.8 G 33.2 T 172.2 Arizona Lake public fishing access to south; Arctic grayling.

A 155.6 G 33.4 T 172.4 Large paved turnout to south.

A 155.4 G 33.6 T 172.6 Begin long downhill grade westbound.

A 155.3 G 33.7 T 172.7 Gergie Lake public fishing access to south (1¼ mile); fish for rainbow trout (stocked).

A 154 G 35 T 174 MENDELTNA (pop. 39). The big part of this unincorporated community was lost when the historic Mendeltna Creek Lodge, located at **Milepost A 153**, burned down on December 10, 2017. The area was originally a stop used by Natives traveling from Lake Tyone to Tazlina Lake. Gold brought prospectors into the area in the late 1800s.

A 152.7 G 36.3 T 175.3 Mendeltna Creek bridge; spawning salmon in August. Fish for Arctic grayling and whitefish, May to November, use spinners and flies. This creek is closed to all salmon fishing. Good fishing north to **Old Man Lake**; *CAUTION: Watch for bears.*

RV campground.

A 152.6 G 36.6 T 175.4 Paved double-ended rest area to north with handicap accessible toilet, litter bin and picnic table. Interpretive sign on Bendiilna', Lake Flows Creek, and the interconnectivity of creeks and rivers.

A 151.4 G 37.6 T 176.6 "Mendeltna" sign eastbound; see description at **Milepost A 154**.

A 151 G 38 T 177 Distance marker eastbound shows Glennallen 37 miles, Tok 179 miles.

A 150.4 G 38.6 T 177.6 Westbound sign for **NELCHINA** (pop. 66). This unincorporated community consists of approximately 33 homes.

A 150 G 39 T 178 Distance marker westbound shows Sutton 89 miles, Palmer 103 miles. Eastbound view of Mount Sanford and Mount Drum straight ahead.

A 149 G 40 T 179 Grizzly Country Store and Towing. **Ryan Lake** access to south; rainbow trout, stocked by ADF&G.

A 143.3 G 45.7 T 184.7 Nelchina Lodge has WiFi for customers.

A 142.6 G 46.4 T 185.4 Distance marker eastbound shows Lake Louise Junction 17 miles, Glennallen 47 miles, Tok 189 miles.

A 141.2 G 47.8 T 186.8 Nelchina state highway maintenance station, phone (907) 822-3714.

A 140 G 49 T 188 Large gravel turnout to north.

A 138.5 G 50.5 T 189.5 Highway descends to Little Nelchina River westbound. *Trucks use low gear on downhill westbound.*

"Nelchina" sign eastbound (see description at **Milepost A 150.4**).

A 137.6 G 51.4 T 190.4 Former Little Nelchina State Recreation Site (no sign) 0.3 mile north from highway; unmaintained campsites on very pot-holed loop road, no fee, no drinking water, firepits, outhouse, boat launch. No ATVs. Watch for moose and bear. Fish for Arctic grayling.

A 137.5 G 51.5 T 190.5 Little Nelchina River bridge.

A 137.3 G 51.7 T 190.7 Boundary of Matanuska–Susitna Borough (sign). A borough is a unit of regional government in Alaska, much like counties in the rest of the U.S. There are currently 16 boroughs in the state, along with several areas outside the existing boroughs.

A 135.9 G 53.1 T 192.1 Paved turnout to north.

A 135.1 G 53.9 T 192.9 Slide Mountain Cabins and RV Park to north.

A 134.1 G 54.9 T 193.9 Begin 1.1-mile truck lane westbound.

A 133 G 56 T 195 Double-ended paved turnout to north. John Lake trailhead (unsigned).

Highway descends eastbound.

Watch for caribou.

A 132.8 G 56.2 T 195.2 Huge gravel parking area to south used by ATVers, hikers and hunters.

A 132 G 57 T 196 Great views (weather permitting) to southwest of Nelchina Glacier. View of snow-covered Mount Drum eastbound.

Bent poles along highway are snow poles to guide snow plows during winter.

A 130.5 G 58.5 T 197.5 Large gravel parking area to north used by hunters, ATVers and hikers. Old Man Creek trailhead (Old Man Creek 2 miles; Crooked Creek 9 miles; Nelchina Town 14.5 miles). Established trails west from here to Palmer are part of the Chickaloon-Knik-Nelchina trail system.

A 129.5 G 59.5 T 198.5 Eureka Summit (elev. 3,322 feet), highest point on the Glenn Highway. Unobstructed views to south of the Chugach Mountains. Nelchina Glacier winds downward through a cleft in the mountains. To the northwest are the peaks of the Talkeetnas, and to the west the highway descends through river valleys which separate these 2 mountain ranges. This is the divide of 3 major river systems: Susitna, Matanuska and Copper.

A 129.4 G 59.6 T 198.6 Paved double-ended turnout to south with Gold Rush Centennial sign about Captain Edwin F. Glenn, who passed near here on his way from Cook Inlet to the Tanana River in 1898. Glenn led one of 3 teams, the Cook Inlet Exploring Expedition. His orders were to locate the most practical route from Prince William Sound through Cook Inlet to the Tanana River. The Glenn Highway is named in his honor.

A 128.5 G 60.5 T 199.5 Distance marker eastbound shows Glennallen 58 miles, Valdez 179 miles, Tok 198 miles.

A 128.3 G 60.7 T 199.7 Tesoro with food, gas, diesel, lodging, bar and liquor store at the Eureka Lodge. The first lodge on the Glenn Highway, opened by Paul Waverly in 1937.

A 128 G 61 T 200 Gunsight Mountain (elev. 6,441 feet) is visible to the west for the next few miles to those approaching from Glennallen. The notch or "gunsight" is plain if one looks closely. Eastbound views (weather permitting) of snow-covered Mount Sanford, Mount Drum, Mount Wrangell and Mount Blackburn.

State Trooper Bruce A. Heck Memorial Corridor (sign); see **Milepost A 120.2**.

A 127 G 62 T 201 *CAUTION: Watch for caribou.* The Nelchina caribou herd travels through here October through November.

A 126.4 G 62.6 T 201.6 Watch for turnoff to south, to Chickaloon-Knik-Nelchina Trail System. (Eureka Creek 1.5 miles, Goober Lake 8 miles, Nelchina River 9 miles), gravel trailhead parking.

A 123.4 G 65.6 T 204.6 Belanger Pass trailhead to north via Marten Road. Marten Road (rutted dirt) leads north 1.5 miles through private homesteads and then forks: keep to left at fork for Belanger Pass trail. According to the DOT, this 8-mile trail terminates at Caribou Creek Trail. It is part of a network of ATV trails and mining roads around Syncline Mountain in the Talkeetna Mountains to the north.

A 122.7 G 66.3 T 205.3 Tahneta Lake to south has "good spring fishing" according to the ADF&G.

A 122.1 G 66.9 T 205.9 Large double-ended gravel parking to north.

A 122 G 67 T 206 Tahneta Pass (elev. 3,000 feet).

A 121.4 G 67.6 T 206.6 Signed trailhead to north; small parking area. According to DOT, this 1-mile-long trail loops around a small lake north of Leila Lake. **Leila Lake:** Arctic grayling 8 to 14 inches abundant through summer, best fishing June and July; burbot, success spotty for 12 to 18 inches in fall and winter; whitefish.

A 120.3 G 68.7 T 207.7 Gravel pit parking to north. Gunsight Mountain Ski Hill (abandoned). The hexagonal Chalet St. Christopher and a rope tow were built here in the 1960s.

A 120.2 G 68.8 T 207.8 Paved double-ended scenic viewpoint to south (lots of potholes in summer 2018). The largest lake is Leila Lake; in the distance is Tahneta Lake. A monument here honoring Trooper Bruce A. Heck reads:

"On a cold winter night, on January 10, 1997, Alaska State Trooper Bruce Heck gave his life in the line of duty near this location. While on duty in the area of Mile 157.9 of the Glenn Highway, Trooper Heck attempted to arrest a suspect who had run into the woods after wrecking a stolen taxicab. In sub-zero temperatures and deep snow, a struggle ensued where the suspect overpowered Trooper Heck and took his life. The suspect, who was arrested by other officers who arrived on scene shortly thereafter, was convicted and sentenced to life in prison. In 1999, the Alaska State Legislature designated the Glenn Highway from Mile 128 to Mile 189 as the Trooper Bruce A. Heck Memorial Corridor so that his sacrifice will not be forgotten. This monument is placed in remembrance of Trooper Heck's selfless act of giving his life while protecting the citizens of Alaska."

A 118.8 G 70.2 T 209.2 Long, double-ended turnout to south with beautiful view of Chugach Mountains (weather permitting) and Knob Lake. The landmark "knob" (elev. 3,000 feet), topped by microwave tower, marks entrance to Chickaloon Pass

for small planes. This turnout is a popular birder gathering spot in the spring, when raptors pass through on their way to western Alaska nesting sites. The migration of golden eagles, gyrfalcons, kestrels, hawks and other raptors usually takes place during a 2- to 4-week window beginning in early April. The Anchorage Audubon Society holds an annual Raptor Tailgate Party and Census during April.

A 118.5 G 70.5 T 209.5 Trailhead Access Road rest area to north; large parking area with outhouses, picnic tables, viewing telescope and Gold Rush Centennial and Alaska State Park signs. Nice stop, good views.

A 118.4 G 70.6 T 209.6 Alascom Road leads 3.3 miles south. Narrow gravel road in fair condition. There are no turnarounds for large vehicles and small turnouts along the road are used as informal campsites. Public access to **North** and **South Knob lakes**; stocked with rainbow trout. Road up to tower signed No Trespassing.

A 118.3 G 70.7 T 209.7 Trail Creek.

A 118.2 G 70.8 T 209.8 Begin 0.2-mile truck lane westbound.

A 117.4 G 71.6 T 210.6 Begin 0.6-mile truck lane eastbound.

A 117.3 G 71.7 T 210.7 Double-ended paved turnout to south with view of Chugach Mountains. Signed Camp Creek Trailhead for skiing, snow machining and hiking.

CAUTION: Slow for frost heaves and damaged road.

A 117.1 G 71.9 T 210.9 Camp Creek.

A 116.4 G 72.6 T 211.6 Rough road with frost heaves and steep downgrade next 1 mile, westbound.

A 116 G 73 T 212 Begin 0.9-mile truck lane eastbound.

A 115.5 G 73.5 T 212.5 Paved double-ended turnout to south with view.

A 115.3 G 73.7 T 212.7 Rough road next 1 mile eastbound.

A 115 G 74 T 213 Double-ended paved turnout to north.

A 114.9 G 74.1 T 213.1 Turnoff to south for **Majestic Valley Lodge** (description follows), a lodge offering rooms, cabins and fine dining with advance reservations.

Majestic Valley Wilderness Lodge is a hand-crafted log lodge offering rooms and cabins with private baths. 100-person capacity dining room and lounge with spectacular mountain views serves unforgettable meals *(advance reservation required)*. Relax on the covered porch with a cup of coffee or a

Iconic views of Lions Head (Glacier Point) begin at Milepost A 114.8 westbound on the Glenn Highway. (©Milton & Kelley Barker, staff)

glass of wine. Miles of hiking, skiing or snow machining trails make this a pristine destination. Hike in the Dall Sheep Reserve, just steps out your door, or view wildlife, take a glacier trek, or go river rafting. 8-person hot tub. Free wireless internet access and TV in lodge rooms. Phone (907) 746-2930; website www.majesticvalleylodge.com. See display ad on this page. [ADVERTISEMENT]

A 114.8 G 74.2 T 213.2 For Anchorage-bound travelers a vista of incomparable beauty as the highway descends westbound in a long straightaway toward **Glacier Point, also known as the Lions Head**, an oddly formed rocky dome.

A 114.2 G 74.8 T 213.8 Shoulder parking to north.

A 113.6 G 75.4 T 214.4 Begin 1.4-mile truck lane eastbound.

A 113.5 G 75.5 T 214.5 Turnoff for **Sheep Mountain Lodge** (description follows), located on the north side of the highway; restaurant, lodging, camping, pay phone. The lodge also maintains a hiking trail system.

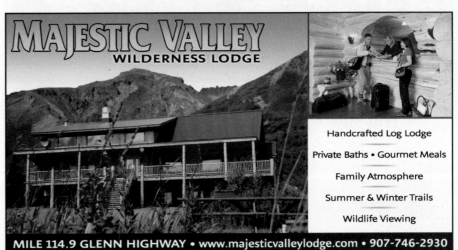

The Fireweed 400 round-trip bike race to Valdez, scheduled for July 12–13, 2019, is the largest and longest event of its kind in Alaska and it begins and ends at Sheep Mountain Lodge. There are also 50-, 100-, 200- and 300-mile races starting at the lodge the same time. For details and registration, visit www.fireweed400.com.

Sheep Mountain Lodge. Our charming log lodge, established in 1946, has been serving travelers for half a century. We're famous for our wholesome homemade food, fresh baked breads, pastries and made from scratch desserts and espresso. Fresh Alaskan salmon and halibut. Our comfortable guest cabins, all with private bathrooms, boast spectacular mountain views. RV hookups, full bar with Alaskan beers on tap and Alaskan gifts. Stretch your legs on our well-marked trail system, offering easy strolls and challenging ascents. Trail maps available at the lodge. Watch Dall sheep through our telescope and relax in the hot tub after a day of traveling or hiking. Toll-free phone 1-877-645-5121. Phone (907) 745-5121. Internet: www.sheepmountain.com. See display ad on this page. [ADVERTISEMENT]

Wonderful views to north of **Sheep Mountain** (elev. 6,300 feet). Sheep are often seen high up these slopes. In the 1930s trapper Ed Ueeck, known as the man from Sheep Mountain, was concerned that construction of the Glenn Highway would lead to overhunting of area sheep. His efforts led to the designation of the Sheep Mountain Closed Area, where sheep hunting is illegal.

A 113 G 76 T 215 Turnoff on Sheep Mountain Airport Road for Sheep Mountain airstrip to north. **Private Aircraft:** Sheep Mountain airstrip; elev. 2,750 feet; length 2,300 feet; gravel/dirt; unattended.

A 112.8 G 76.2 T 215.2 Double-ended paved turnout to south with picnic table; good photo op of Sheep Mountain to north and Chugach Mountains to south. Interpretive signs on Sheep Mountain gypsum and Dall sheep.

A 112.1 G 76.9 T 215.9 Gypsum Creek (sign).

A 111.6 G 77.4 T 216.4 Begin 1-mile truck lane eastbound.

A 111 G 78 T 217 Distance marker westbound shows Palmer 63 miles, Anchorage 104 miles.

Distance marker eastbound shows Glennallen 77, Valdez 194, Tok 218.

A 110.5 G 78.5 T 217.5 Begin 0.5-mile truck lane eastbound.

A 109.7 G 79.3 T 218.3 Aptly named **Grand View Cafe and RV Campground** (description follows) to south has homestyle dining in log lodge, pull-through RV sites and wide-open glacier views.

Grand View Cafe & RV Campground. Matanuska Glacier, Dall sheep, an ancient volcano; spectacular sights surrounding this scenic stop. Log cafe serves homestyle meals, brick oven pizza, espresso, beer and wine. Please check our website for cafe hours. Repeatedly praised for cleanliness and friendliness, and centrally located between Palmer and Glennallen. Full service pull-thru RV sites, Cable TV and cell reception. Ten minutes to Glacier Access, by car. Summer only (907) 746-4480. Winter email: info@grandviewrv.com; www.grandviewrv.com. See display ad on this page. [ADVERTISEMENT]

Good views westbound of Matanuska Glacier.

A 109 G 80 T 219 Begin 6 to 8 percent downgrade westbound.

A 108.1 G 80.9 T 219.9 Paved shoulder parking on north side of highway.

A 107.7 G 81.3 T 220.3 Large paved scenic viewpoint to south (posted no overnight parking/camping). Fortress Ridge (elev. 5,000 feet) to the north.

A 106.9 G 82.1 T 221.1 Caribou Creek bridge. There are 26 creeks named Caribou Creek in the *Dictionary of Alaska Place Names*. This Caribou Creek heads at a glacier terminus in the Talkeetna Mountains and

flows 35 miles southeast to the Matanuska River. Sheep Mountain reserve boundary.

A 106.2 G 82.8 T 221.8 Begin 0.7-mile passing lane westbound. Highway climbs 7 percent uphill grade westbound.

A 106 G 83 T 222 Caribou Creek State Recreational Mining Area: gold panning, mineral prospecting or mining using light portable field equipment (e.g. hand-operated pick, backpack power drill, etc.) is allowed in these designated areas on state lands without mining claims. Go to http://dnr.alaska.gov/mlw/factsht and click on Caribou Creek Recreational Mining Area.

Watch for sharp turnoff to a *small* gravel parking area on hillside. According to the Alaska Dept. of Natural Resources, a *very* steep trail leads down to the creek from the parking lot. Only pedestrian traffic is permitted on the trail (no ATVs).

A 104.7 G 84.3 T 223.3 Begin 0.8-mile passing lane eastbound.

A 104.4 G 84.6 T 223.6 Paved shoulder parking both sides of highway.

A 104 G 85 T 224 Access to Glacier View Elementary School, which overlooks Matanuska Glacier.

A 103.3 G 85.7 T 224.7 Shoulder parking to south with view of Matanuska Glacier.

A 102.2 G 86.8 T 225.8 Long Rifle Lodge to south; open year-round 9 A.M. to 8 P.M., offers breakfast, lunch and dinner, gas, gifts and lodging overlooking Matanuska Glacier. Pay at lodge. Dumpster to north.

Long Rifle Lodge. See display ad on this page.

A 102.1 G 86.9 T 225.9 Access to Matanuska Glacier to south via steep side road to **Glacier Access at Glacier Park**; admission charged. Camping available, inquire at Wickersham Trading Post.

Glacier Access at Glacier Park. Join us for a great, fun-filled day exploring Matanuska Glacier, the largest glacier accessible by personal vehicle. We offer a recommended guided hike with Matanuska Glacier Adventures to take you onto the white ice. This is a real Alaskan, real world experience and lots of adventure. No reservations required May through September. Gift shop and snacks. Access at Mile 102 Glenn Highway (6500 S. Glacier Park Rd., Sutton, AK 99674). Two-hour drive from Anchorage. Attention: From Anchorage, you must drive through Palmer NOT Wasilla. Confusing interchange at Mile 34 Glenn Highway. You must exit the Glenn Highway

Matanuska Glacier SRS at Milepost 101 offers photo ops of the glacier from a distance. Stop at Glacier Park, Milepost A 102.1, for up-close views. *(©Kris Valencia, staff)*

at Mile 34 to stay on the Glenn Highway. 1-888-253-4480. See display ad on this page.

A 101.5 G 87.5 T 226.5 Paved shoulder parking to south with good view of Matanuska Glacier across from a popular rock message wall on the road cut.

A 101 G 88 T 227 Matanuska Glacier State Recreation Site to south; campground and rest area with scenic viewpoint. Campground (to right after turning off the Glenn Highway) has 12 campsites on a gravel loop road, water pump, toilets, $20 nightly fee with self-registration; 14-day limit. Log cabin available for nightly rental. Access road continues straight ahead and loops through rest area. Managed by Long Rifle Lodge, phone (907) 745-5151.

The rest area has a large paved parking area (will accommodate large RVs), picnic tables, telescopes, toilets, litter bin, interpretive shelter and scenic viewpoint with excellent views of Matanuska Glacier. Day parking $5, overnight parking in rest area, $10 (pay at campground). Edge Nature Trail, a 20-minute walk through boreal forest to glacier viewing platforms with interpretive signs. This fairly easy trail is a good place to stretch your legs (and walk your pet) but it does have moderate inclines and an uneven walking surface.

Matanuska Glacier heads in the Chugach Mountains and trends northwest 27 miles. Some 18,000 years ago the glacier reached all the way to the Palmer area. The glacier's average width is 2 miles; at its terminus it is 4 miles wide. The glacier has remained fairly stable the past 400 years. At the glacier terminus meltwater drains into a stream that flows into the Matanuska River.

Distance marker westbound shows Sutton 42 miles, Palmer 53 miles, Anchorage 94 miles.

A 100 G 89 T 228 *CAUTION: Watch for moose.*

A 99.6 G 89.4 T 228.4 Matanuska Lodge B&B.

A summertime float on the Matanuska River. (©Milton & Kelley Barker, staff)

A 99.3 G 89.7 T 228.7 Paved double-ended turnout to north is a scenic viewpoint with view of Matanuska Glacier.

A 98.9 G 90.1 T 229.1 Glacier View Adventures to south; zip line and ATV tours. Restaurant with pizza, ice cream and espresso.

A 98.6 G 90.4 T 229.4 Begin 0.6-mile passing lane westbound.

A 98.5 G 90.5 T 229.5 Glacier View Bible Church to north.

A 98.3 G 90.7 T 229.7 Paved shoulder parking to south, view.

A 97.5 G 91.5 T 230.5 Pinochle Circle to north. Distance marker eastbound shows Glennallen 90 miles, Valdez 207 miles, Tok 226 miles.

A 97 G 92 T 231 Begin 1.6-mile passing lane eastbound.

A 96.6 G 92.4 T 231.4 Glenn Highway alignment passes through an enormous road cut. Crews moved over 2.4 million cubic yards of material and finished blasting through this solid rock hill in 2008, as part of the Hicks Creek Road Project, which rerouted this stretch of the Glenn Highway.

A 96.4 G 92.6 T 231.6 Trailhead Road to north, paved turnout to south. Trailhead Road is entrance for **Nova River Runners** facility for Matanuska River rafting and glacier hiking.

Nova River Runners. See display ad on this page.

A 96.3 G 92.7 T 231.7 Bridge over Hicks Creek. Hicks Creek was named by Captain Glenn in 1898 for H.H. Hicks, the guide of his expedition. Anthracite Ridge to the north.

A 96.2 G 92.8 T 231.8 Large paved parking area to north. Begin 4.2-mile passing lane westbound.

A 96.1 G 92.9 T 231.9 Matanuska Road to south.

A 95 G 94 T 233 Large paved turnout southwest of this milepost.

Distance marker eastbound shows Glennallen 92 miles, Valdez 209 miles, Tok 243 miles.

A 94.8 G 94.2 T 233.2 Enormous paved parking area to south; scenic viewpoint overlooking Matanuska River.

A 94.7 G 94.3 T 233.3 Victory Road to north; access to **Bear Den Cabins** and **Homestead Guest Cabins** (descriptions follow).

Bear Den Cabins. Experience the old Alaska charm. The Den, a quaint haven in the community for over 40 years, has 2 bedrooms, large living room, full kitchen, full bath, washer/dryer, deck/grill. Our Cub Cabin is a small rustic dry log cabin with log outhouse. Great place to relax with your family while exploring the Glacierview area. Open year-round. vrbo.com/705477; vrbo.com/778175; (907) 745-2395. beardencabins95@gmail.com. [ADVERTISEMENT]

Homestead Guest Cabins. Cozy hand-crafted log cabins available year-round; located off the highway in a quiet, peaceful setting, just minutes away from the Matanuska Glacier and close to hiking, 4-wheeler and snow machine trails. Cabins are furnished with full kitchens and private baths. Owners are friendly, helpful and long-time Alaskans. Phone (907) 745-4514; www.homesteadcabinsak.com. [ADVERTISEMENT]

A 93.6 G 95.4 T 234.4 Distance marker westbound shows Palmer 46 miles, Anchorage 87 miles.

A 92 G 97 T 236 Begin 1.8-mile passing lane and improved highway eastbound. There are 2 gravel turnouts to south within the next mile westbound.

A 90.8 G 98.2 T 237.2 Purinton Creek Trailhead (sign); large gravel parking area to north with dumpster.

CAUTION: Narrow, winding road westbound next 25 miles; no passing lanes, very few turnouts, 7 percent grades, slow for 35 mph curves. For current road construction projects, go to 511.alaska.gov.

A 89 G 100 T 239 Puritan Creek bridge (sign); small turnout to north at west end of bridge. Stream heads on Anthracite Ridge and flows into the Matanuska River.

CAUTION: Watch for moose.

A 88.7 G 100.3 T 239.3 Small gravel turnout to south.

A 88.2 G 100.8 T 239.8 Gravel turnout to south.

A 88 G 101 T 240 Small gravel turnout to south.

A 87.8 G 101.2 T 240.2 Small turnout to south.

A 87.6 G 101.4 T 240.4 Single-vehicle access to south at west end of **Weiner Lake** (stocked by ADF&G); public fishing access is a large, paved/gravel signed parking area. Fish for rainbow trout and Arctic grayling.

A 87.4 G 101.6 T 240.6 Gravel turnout to north.

A 87.2 G 101.8 T 240.8 End slide area eastbound. Begin slide area westbound.

CAUTION: 35 mph speed limit on winding road as highway descends hillside next 1.7 miles westbound; soft dirt shoulder to south with steep dropoffs and no guardrails. Views of Long Lake.

A 85.5 G 103.5 T 242.5 Begin slide area eastbound.

A 85.4 G 103.6 T 242.6 Long Lake State Recreation Site; parking and boat launch. Long Lake is a favorite fishing spot for Anchorage residents. Stocked by ADF&G with rainbow trout and Arctic char. Fair for Arctic grayling to 18 inches, and native lake trout, spring through fall; fish deeper as the water warms in summer. Fair ice fishing in winter for burbot, average 12 inches.

CAUTION: Highway winds up hillside next 1.7 miles eastbound. Falling rock, soft dirt shoulder to south with steep dropoffs and no guardrails.

A 84.4 G 104.6 T 243.6 Gravel turnout to south. End slide area westbound. Begin steep downgrade and slide area eastbound.

A 84.1 G 104.9 T 243.9 Large parking area to south.

Great views of Matanuska River and Chugach Mountains to south as highway makes winding descent eastbound.

A 83.3 G 105.7 T 244.7 Narrow gravel road leads north to **Ravine Lake** and **Lower Bonnie Lake** (day use only). Watch for potholes at entrance of road. *(This steep and winding side road is signed as unsafe and closed to motorhomes, large vehicles or trailers; not recommended for any vehicle during rainy season.)* Drive in 0.8 mile on side road to reach Ravine Lake; fish from shore or float tube for rainbow trout. Lower Bonnie Lake is a 2-mile drive from the highway. ADF&G public access at Lower Bonnie Lake; good fishing for native rainbow trout and Arctic grayling. No camping or fires.

A 83 G 106 T 245 Views westbound of distinctive pyramid shape of King Mountain (elev. 5,809 feet) to the southeast.

A 81.2 G 107.8 T 246.8 Distance marker westbound shows Chickaloon 5 miles.

A 80.8 G 108.2 T 247.2 Eastern boundary of Matanuska Valley Moose Range. Turnout to south.

CAUTION: Watch for moose.

A 80.1 G 108.9 T 247.9 Distance marker eastbound shows Glennallen 107 miles, Tok 224 miles, Valdez 243 miles.

Expansive views of King Mountain and Matanuska River.

A 79.2 G 109.8 T 248.8 Gravel turnout to south; steep downgrade begins 0.2 mile westbound.

A 78.5 G 110.5 T 249.5 Paved turnout with views to south.

A 78.3 G 110.7 T 249.7 Signed parking to south.

A 78.1 G 110.9 T 249.9 Gravel turnout to south at east end of Chickaloon River bridge. *(This area was under construction in summer 2018.)* Boundary between Game Management Units 13 and 14. Entering Subunit 14A westbound.

A 78 G 111 T 250 Turnoff to north for Chickaloon Branch Road at west end of Chickaloon River bridge. No trespassing and private property signs are posted along this road (state road maintenance ends 1.2 miles from highway). Gravel parking area and rafting put-in/take-out under bridge.

A 77.5 G 111.5 T 250.5 Signed shoulder parking to south.

The Glenn Highway closely parallels the

Matanuska River westbound to Palmer. Nova River Runners offers scenic floats and whitewater trips on the river (see **Milepost A 96.4**). The Matanuska River is formed by its East and South forks and flows southwest 75 miles to the Knik Arm of Cook Inlet.

A 77.3 G 111.7 T 250.7 Small gravel turnout to north.

A 77.2 G 111.8 T 250.8 Signed gravel parking to south along river.

A 77 G 112 T 251 Slide area next 1.1 miles eastbound.

A 76.8 G 112.2 T 251.2 CHICKALOON (pop. 245) is an unincorporated community, established around 1916 as the terminus of an Alaska Railroad spur. It currently serves as a stop for river rafters.

A 76.6 G 112.4 T 251.4 End slide area eastbound. View of King Mountain to the southeast.

A 76.4 G 112.6 T 251.6 King Mountain State Recreation Site to south. Pleasant campground on the banks of the Matanuska River (*Danger: Swift current*); 22 campsites, picnic shelter, campground host, fireplaces, picnic tables, water, toilets. Camping fee $25/night; 7-day limit. Daily parking fee $7. Reservations via concessionaire Great Holiday Campgrounds; (907) 240-9797. [▲]

Post office to north. Chickaloon (sign) eastbound.

A 76.2 G 112.8 T 251.8 Distance marker westbound shows Palmer 29, Anchorage 70.

A 76 G 113 T 252 Single-vehicle gravel turnouts to south on Matanuska River. Driving distance between physical Mileposts 76 and 75 is 0.5 mile.

A 74.5 G 114.5 T 253.5 Signed parking areas to south along Matanuska River.

A 73.2 G 115.8 T 254.8 Paved turnout to north.

A 72.9 G 116.1 T 255.1 Fish Lake Road leads north 3 miles through a rural residential area; views of Castle Mountain. Limited public fishing access to **Ida Lake** via Gronvold Drive (0.2 mile north from highway, then left on Ida to Oline Circle); steep walk down to narrow shoreline. [🐟]

A 71.8 G 117.2 T 256.2 Gravel turnout to north.

A 71 G 118 T 257 Signed parking areas to south along Matanuska River.

A 70 G 119 T 258 Pinnacle Mountain RV Park to north. [▲]

A 68.4 G 120.6 T 259.6 Paved and gravel shoulder parking (signed) to south along Matanuska River next 0.5 mile westbound and turnouts both sides of highway next 1 mile, eastbound.

A 68 G 121 T 260 Begin slide area eastbound (sign). Pinnacle Mountain (elev. 4,541 feet) rises directly southeast of the highway, easy to identify by its unusual top. Cottonwoods and aspen along the highway. Talkeetna Mountains to the north.

A 66.6 G 122.4 T 261.4 Gravel turnout to south on river.

A 66.5 G 122.5 T 261.5 Gravel turnout to north and access to river at east end of **King River** bridge. Early summer is best for for Dolly Varden fishing; use eggs. [🐟]

A 66.3 G 122.7 T 261.7 Turnoff to north just west of King River bridge for access road to river (no turnaround) and access to King River Trail (multi-use public access; ATVs 15 mph) with parking on loop road. Turnoff to south for improved gravel access road

to King River at confluence with Matanuska River; informal camping.

CAUTION: Narrow, winding road eastbound next 25 miles; no passing lanes, very few turnouts, 7 percent grades, 35 mph curves. For current road construction projects go to 511.alaska.gov.

A 66.1 G 122.9 T 261.9 Begin 2.2-mile passing lane and improved highway westbound.

A 66 G 123 T 262 Distance marker westbound shows Sutton 5 miles.

A 64.3 G 124.7 T 263.7 Distance marker eastbound shows Glennallen 123 miles, Valdez 240 miles, Tok 259 miles.

A 64.1 G 124.9 T 263.9 Begin 1.3-mile passing lane eastbound.

A 62.7 G 126.3 T 265.3 Large, paved double-ended parking area south along **Matanuska River**. Dwarf fireweed and sweet pea in June. Fishing. [🐟]

A 62.4 G 126.6 T 265.6 Granite Creek bridge; beautiful stream. Fish for small Dolly Varden, spring or early summer, use flies or single eggs. [🐟]

Paved bike path begins westbound on the north side of the highway and extends to Sutton.

Slow for speed zone westbound.

A 61.6 G 127.4 T 266.4 Turnoff on Chickaloon Way to north for Sutton post office (ZIP code 99674), **Sutton Library** (description follows) and entrance to **Alpine Historical Park**, an open-air museum featuring the concrete foundation of the Sutton Coal Washery (1920–22) and historic mining equipment from the Wishbone Hill Coal Mining Company. Admission is free, but donations are greatly appreciated. The park and visitor center are open Memorial Day through Labor Day, from 9 A.M. to 7 P.M. The park is home to the Coal Miner's Hall of Fame, Athabaskan house and an indoor Road Builders exhibit of photographs and narrative recalling construction of the Glenn Highway. Additional features include a huge playground, picnic tables, firepits, grill, toilets, garden and exercise pavilion.

The Sutton Library is located at 11301 N. Chickaloon Way. This wonderful library— a center for community activities—was designed by Architect Andrew Simaski to resemble a coal washery. Funds for the $2.4 million structure were raised thanks to an enthusiastic local fundraising effort and grants.

A 61.2 G 127.8 T 266.8 Granite Peak Washeteria to north.

A 61 G 128 T 267 SUTTON-ALPINE (area pop. 967). This small highway community has a fire station with emergency phone, a bar, liquor store (left door of the Alpine Inn building), general store and cafe. The modern Sutton Library hosts an Art & Farm Market on Saturdays in summer.

Sutton was established as a railroad siding in about 1918 for the once-flourishing coal industry at Jonesville Mine, which operated on and off from 1920 until 1959. A post office was established at Sutton in 1948. Underground and surface coal mining in the Jonesville area on Wishbone Hill north of Sutton dates back to the early 1900s. The Sutton General Store has photos of the old mine.

Jonesville Road leads north through Sutton residential area. Pavement ends at Mile 1.3. Access to **Slipper Lake** west from Mile 1.5 stocked with rainbow trout (just before physical milepost 2). State mainte-

nance ends and road deteriorates at Mile 1.9. Road (in very poor condition) continues to **Coyote Lake** and access to Granite Peak; 4-wheel-drive, high-clearance vehicle recommended. Coyote Lake has some fair rainbow trout fishing and is also a popular spot to hunt fossils. [🐟]

A 60.8 G 128.2 T 267.2 Eska Creek bridge.

A 60.7 G 128.3 T 267.3 C'eyiits' Hwnax (Life House Community Health Center) to north open 8 A.M. to 5 P.M. weekdays. (907) 631-7665. [✚]

Distance marker westbound shows Palmer 13 miles, Anchorage 54 miles.

A 60.6 G 128.4 T 267.4 Begin 2.8-mile passing lane and improved highway westbound.

Slow for speed zone eastbound.

A 60.4 G 128.6 T 267.6 Long, narrow, paved double-ended turnout to south.

A 60.1 G 128.9 T 267.9 Long, narrow, paved double-ended turnout to south.

A 59.6 G 129.4 T 268.4 Tesoro gas/diesel station to south; laundry, showers. Hilltop Premium Green cannabis dispensary is here. Please review "What you need to know about using Marijauna in Alaska" and "Get the Facts about Marijauna and Driving" at http://dhss.alaska.gov/dph/Director/Pages/marijuana/law.aspx if you are unfamiliar with Alaska laws. [⛽]

Begin steep downgrade eastbound.

A 58.5 G 130.5 T 269.5 Paved viewpoint to south (views obstructed by brush summer 2017).

A 57.8 G 131.2 T 270.2 58–Mile Road leads north 1 mile to Palmer Correctional Center. Access to **Seventeenmile Lake**: drive 0.5 mile north and turn east; continue 2.4 miles through rural residential area, keeping to right at forks, to reach lake. Day-use area parking (no camping). Fish for small Arctic grayling, stocked rainbow trout and char. Private property in area. [🐟]

A 56.8 G 132.2 T 271.2 Western boundary of Matanuska Valley Moose Range.

A 55.9 G 133.1 T 272.1 Begin 2.1-mile passing lane eastbound.

A 54.6 G 134.4 T 273.4 Bridge over **Moose Creek**. Fish for Dolly Varden in summer; use eggs. Rest area with informal camping. Entrance is at the bottom of hill and on curve, use caution turning here. [🐟]

A 54.5 G 134.5 T 273.5 Turnout to north for Moose Creek Campground. Take 0.3-mile gravel loop for sites that offer firepits and tables. Campground has toilets, trash cans and 2 picnic pavilions (half-day pavilion use $20, full-day use $30). Information boards. Camping fee $10, payable at entrance. Chickaloon Village Traditional Council, phone (907) 745-0749. [▲]

A 53 G 136 T 275 Buffalo Mine Road to north. Access to Wishbone Lake 4-wheel-drive trail.

A 50.9 G 138.1 T 277.1 Harold Stephan Fire Station.

A 50.7 G 138.3 T 277.3 Farm Loop Road to north, a 3-mile loop road connecting with Fishhook-Willow Road.

A 50.4 G 138.6 T 277.6 Distance marker eastbound shows Glennallen 137 miles, Valdez 254 miles, Tok 273 miles.

A 50.1 G 138.9 T 277.9 Sharp turn north

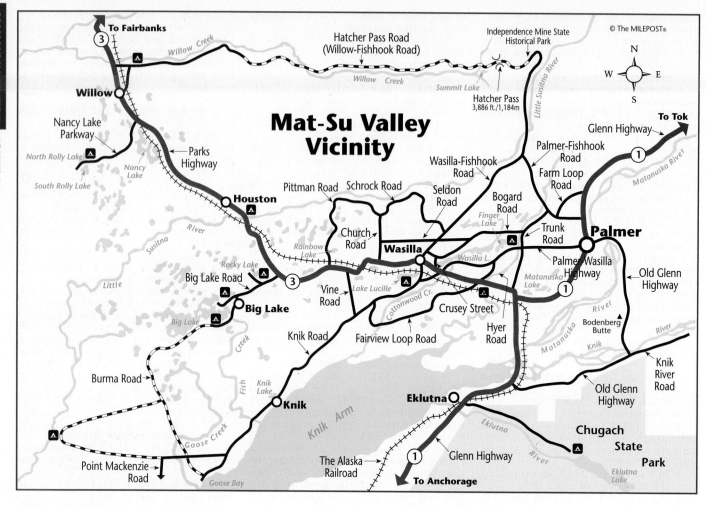

Mat-Su Valley Vicinity

on Archie Road (watch for signs before turn-off) for the **Musk Ox Farm** (just 0.2 miles north) a great place to see these magnificent, ancient animals.

The Musk Ox Farm. Experience this unique agricultural project where prehistoric musk oxen are raised for their ultra-fine underwool, qiviut. All qiviut fiber is gently hand-combed in the springtime from these majestic creatures. Let our interpretive guides lead you through our chutes while surrounded by over 80 musk oxen with breathtaking views of the Chugach and Talkeetna mountains. Open Mother's Day through mid-September, 10 A.M. to 6 P.M. Winter by appointment. Museum, fine qiviut garments, & yarns. Large pull-through parking lot for any sized rig. 12850 E. Archie Rd., Palmer. www.muskoxfarm.org. (907) 745-4151. See display ad this page.

[ADVERTISEMENT]

MUSK OX FARM
12850 ARCHIE RD · PALMER
www.muskoxfarm.org · (907) 745-4151 · info@muskoxfarm.org

Begin 3-lane highway westbound. Begin 2-lane highway eastbound.

A 49.9 G 139.1 T 278.1 Paved double-ended turnout to south with Gold Rush Centennial sign.

A 49.5 G 139.5 T 278.5 Junction with Palmer-Fishhook Road; access to Fishhook Golf Course and Hatcher Pass Road for **side trip** to **Independence Mine State Historical Park** (19 miles).

Junction with Hatcher Pass (Palmer-Fishhook) Road which connects with the Parks Highway at **Milepost A 71.2** north of Willow. See "Hatcher Pass Road" log beginning on page 341.

A 49.1 G 139.9 T 278.9 Cedar Hills subdivision to north. Entering Palmer, which extends to **Milepost A 41**. (Actual driving distance between physical milepost 49 and 42 is 1 mile.)
Slow for speed zone westbound.

A 42 G 147 T 286 Traffic light at West Arctic Avenue/Old Glenn Highway; Fred Meyer gas station with diesel and propane to south. First of several turnoffs south to downtown Palmer. West Arctic becomes the Old Glenn Highway. Access to Palmer High School to north.

Junction with Old Glenn Highway, an alternate route that rejoins the Glenn Highway at **Milepost A 29.6**. Turn to page 347 for the Old Glenn Highway log and read log back to front if you are heading south on the Old Glenn Highway from this junction.

Palmer

A 42 G 147 T 286 In the Matanuska Valley northeast of Anchorage. **Population:** 6,296. **Emergency Services:** Dial 911. **Alaska State Troopers**, phone (907) 745-2131. **City Police**, phone (907) 745-4811. **Fire Department**, phone (907) 745-3709. **Hospital**, Mat-Su Regional Medical Center, phone (907) 861-6000.

Visitor Information: The Palmer Visitors Center & Museum are located in the log cabin at 723 S. Valley Way at East Fireweed Avenue. A great place to pick up brochures, get a cup of coffee, chat with local tour guides (by appointment) and learn about local history. Pick up a walking tour map of historic Palmer and check the outdoor kiosk for visitor information. Open daily 9 A.M. to 6 P.M. May 1 to Sept. 30. Restrooms and pay phone. Website: www.palmermuseum.org.

Be sure to visit the Matanuska Valley Agricultural Showcase Gardens, adjacent the visitor center, featuring exotic flowers and giant vegetables. Or contact the Palmer Visitors Center and Museum, 723 S. Valley Way, Palmer, AK 99645; phone (907) 746-7668.

Elevation: 240 feet. **Climate:** Temperatures range from 4° to 21°F in January and December, with a mean monthly snowfall of 8 to 10 inches. Record low was -40°F in January 1975. Temperatures range from
(Continues on page 343)

Hatcher Pass Road

A highly recommended summer **side trip** to scenic alpine country and the historic Independence Mine, this 49-mile-long road loops over Hatcher Pass (elev. 3,886 feet) between the Glenn Highway and the Parks Highway *(see Mat-Su Valley Vicinity map on facing page)*. Independence Mine opens for visitors the first Saturday in June (depending on snow) and closes after Labor Day. You can visit Independence Mine at any time, but when the visitor center is closed, the access road is gated, so you will have a 1-mile walk from the lower parking area up to the mine complex.

Hatcher Pass Road is both an old-time Alaska road—narrow, bumpy, dirt and gravel—and a modern paved route complete with scenic turnouts for the tourists. It is improved paved road to **Milepost P 17.2** from the Palmer side, and for the first 10 miles from the Willow side. Much of the gravel stretch is steep, narrow, switch-backed road with potholes and washboards. You can make a 170-mile loop drive from Anchorage by driving 49 miles out the Glenn Highway to the turnoff at Palmer (take Palmer-Fishhook which becomes Hatcher Pass Road), then driving the 49-mile Hatcher Pass Road to junction with the Parks Highway and the 71-mile drive back to Anchorage. If you want to limit both the mileage and the mountain driving, just backtrack from Independence Mine to Palmer and the Glenn Highway to Anchorage for a 132-mile round-trip (although it would be a shame not to continue just 2 miles west beyond the turnoff for Independence Mine to take in the view from Summit Lake State Recreation Site).

Popular summer activities along this road include hiking, biking, paragliding, gold panning and berry picking. For current status/conditions at Hatcher Pass trailheads and parks, visit http://dnr.alaska.gov/parks/asp/curevnts.htm.

Hatcher Pass is a popular winter sports area for snow machining and cross-country skiing. Chains or 4-wheel drive required in winter. Both Gold Mint and Fishhook trailheads are used by snowmachines in winter. Hatcher Pass Road is maintained in winter from the Palmer side to the historical park and Hatcher Pass Lodge. However, Gold Cord Road (the access road to the historical park) is not plowed and the 15.2-mile stretch of Hatcher Pass Road from **Milepost P 17.2 to P 32.4** is also unmaintained in winter and may be closed and gated from late September well into June, depending on snow. *This route is never recommended for motorhomes or vehicles with trailers due to steep grades and sharp switchbacks.*

Distance from junction with the Glenn Highway at Palmer (P) is followed by distance from junction with the Parks Highway at Willow (W).

P 0 W 49.1 Junction of Hatcher Pass Road/Palmer-Fishhook Road with the Glenn Highway at **Milepost A 49.5.**

P 0.1 W 49 Palmer Fishhook Golf Course.

P 1.4 W 47.7 Junction with Farm Loop Road.

P 2.4 W 46.7 Junction with Trunk Road.

P 3.2 W 45.9 Wasilla Creek.

Independence Mine is a major attraction on Hatcher Pass Road.
(©Kris Valencia, staff)

P 6.5 W 42.6 Turner's Corner. Gateway to Hatcher Pass. Jim Turner welcomes you to scenic Hatcher Pass. We have 3 grades of gasoline, diesel, propane, grocery store, liquor store, cafe, soft-serve ice cream, ice, showers, laundromat, ATM, air, water. Stop by the Yellow Store—Turner's Corner. VISA, MasterCard, Discover, AMEX accepted. [ADVERTISEMENT]

P 6.6 W 42.5 Hatcher Pass Bed & Breakfast. Experience our authentic Alaskan log cabins and chalets located at the base of beautiful Hatcher Pass. Comfortable, sparkling clean, private, and equipped with all the modern conveniences. Breakfast is included in the privacy of your own cabin. Come enjoy a peaceful getaway! Phone (907) 745-6788, fax (907) 745-6787. Website www.hatcherpassbb.com. [ADVERTISEMENT]

P 6.8 W 42.3 Junction with Wasilla-Fishhook Road (Wasilla 11 miles); continue on Willow-Fishhook Road for Hatcher Pass.

P 7.1 W 43 Junction with Edgerton-Parks Road and access to **Government Peak Recreation Area** at Hatcher Pass. The signage and name are a bit confusing, as you keep driving straight (northbound) for Hatcher Pass. Edgerton-Parks does not lead to Hatcher Pass or the Parks Highway; instead, this side road dead ends about 2 miles west of here but provides access to Government Peak Recreation Area. Drive west 0.9 mile on Edgerton-Parks Road then turn north on Mountain Trails Drive and continue 0.9 mile to the day-use area. The trailhead has a huge parking lot and a chalet used as a warming hut in winter and also available as a rental for private functions. The park access road is gated (gate closes at 10 P.M.). The park has an extensive trail system for cross-country skiing and fat tire biking in winter, and hiking and mountain biking in summer, as well as equestrian trails.

P 7.8 W 41.3 Hatcher Pass Management Area boundary northbound. Recreational activities allowed within this public use area include (unless posted as prohibited): hiking, picnicking, berry picking, camping, skiing, snow machining, snow board-

ing, fishing, grazing, hunting and trapping. ATVs and dirt bikes are prohibited on roadway. Please respect private property. No discharge of weapons within ¼ mile of roadway. Recreational mining is allowed within the boundaries of the public use area except on land with valid active mining claims. The Dept. of Natural Resources suggests recreational miners use the parking areas along the Little Susitna River or the Gold Mint Trail, which runs north along the Little Susitna River from the trailhead parking lot. Gold panning is also allowed in the Independence Mine State Historical Park, but consult with park personnel before panning.

P 8.4 W 40.7 Little Susitna River bridge.

P 8.5 W 40.6 Large double-ended paved scenic overlook with interpretive signs (pictured below) is at north end of bridge.

©Kris Valencia, staff

Road parallels Little Susitna River next 5 miles northbound. This gold-bearing stream heads at Mint Glacier in the Talkeetna Mountains and flows 110 miles to Cook Inlet.

P 8.6 W 40.5 Avalanche gate. Winding road climbs northbound past signed private property.

P 8.9 W 40.1 Parking on loop turnout to east, across from rock cut; view of Little Susitna River obscured by trees.

P 9.2 W 39.9 Shoulder parking along Little Susitna River.

P 9.4 W 39.7 Shoulder parking area.

P 9.5 W 39.6 This area open to recreational gold mining (sign).

P 10.3 W 38.8 Gravel parking area to east.

P 10.6 W 38.5 Gravel turnout to west

at gated gravel alpine access road. The bulletin board here has notices posted about Skeetawk, which is an alpine ski area run by Hatcher Alpine Xperience (HAX), a non-profit working towards developing alpine sports at Hatcher Pass, with a triple chairlift to be installed in 2019; www.skeetawk.com. A notice posted here in summer 2018 read: "Visitors are welcome to hike, snowshoe, ski, sled, snowboard, paraglide and generally enjoy the mountain even if the gate is locked. Please park here if that's the case. Please be kind to each other and respectful of Hatcher Alpine Experience equipment when visiting. Thanks!"

P 10.8 W 38.3 Government Peak riverside picnic and camping area; outhouse, tables; $5 day-use fee, $15 camping fee.

P 11.3 W 37.8 Paved parking area.

P 11.9 W 37.2 Paved parking area. Popular sledding hill in winter and terminus of the Mile 16 Bike Trail.

P 12.6 W 36.5 Paved turnout.

P 13 W 36.1 Small parking area. *Slow for damaged road.*

P 13.3 W 35.8 Small gravel turnout with good mountain view.

P 13.8 W 35.3 Milepost 14. Little trace remains of Motherlode Lodge, which burned down in April 2015. The lodge was built in 1942, and named the Little Susitna Roadhouse. Before its demise, the Motherlode Lodge served as a bed-and-breakfast and a banquet facility for a number of years. Property on either side of the road here is posted as private, no parking; use the parking area at Gold Mint Trailhead (just ahead and to the right for northbound drivers; description follows).

The signed Gold Mint Trailhead has a large parking area, restrooms, picnicking and car camping. Day-use fee $5; camping fee $15. Gold Mint is a very popular trail with hikers and mountain bikers in summer. It is 8 miles one-way to Mint Glacier. Gold Mint Trail is 1 of 2 snowmachine trailheads on the east side of the pass in winter (the other is Fishhook Trailhead).

Avalanche gate. Hatcher Pass Road makes a sharp turn and begins climb to Hatcher Pass via a series of switchbacks. Posted speed limit 35 mph. No parking or stopping on road (use turnouts).

P 14.1 W 35 Narrow, double-ended gravel turnout.

P 14.6 W 34.5 Gravel parking area ($5 fee) to south (good viewpoint) and turnoff for Archangel Valley Road to north. The side road after Archangel Creek bridge is unmaintained and very rough. Limited parking for the Reed Lakes Trail is available just before the bridge. Carpool if possible and follow all posted signs regarding parking. The road leads 4 miles up Archangel Valley and ends at Fern Mine (private property, do not trespass). Access to Reed Lakes Trail (9-mile hike round-trip) from this side road. Not recommended for RVs. Archangel Road is a groomed, multi-use trail in winter.

P 14.9 W 34.2 Gravel turnout with view.

P 16 W 33.1 Large paved parking area (signed) with sweeping view. Upper trailhead for the Mile 16 Bike Trail, a 2-mile downhill mountain bike trail that ends at **Milepost P 11.9.** The bike trail (not signed) starts at the east end of the parking lot; it is reportedly steep with technical turns.

P 16.1 W 33 Gravel turnout.

P 16.4 W 32.7 Fishhook Trailhead; large paved parking area, outhouse, car camping; parking fee $5. Popular with paragliders in summer. Snowmachine access to Marmot Mountain, Gold Mint Trailhead/Archangel Road Trail, and 18-mile Hatcher Pass Trail, which follows unplowed road up and over the pass toward Willow.

P 16.6 W 32.5 Gravel shoulder parking. There are a couple more gravel turnouts next half-mile westbound.

P 17.2 W 31.9 Hatcher Pass Road makes a *sharp* turn. For **Independence Mine State Historical Park** (description follows) turn north on Gold Cord Road (paved). Hatcher Pass Lodge, offering lodging in cabins and dining at their cafe (reduced hours after Labor Day), is just north of the junction. Just past the lodge's driveway is the park's lower Independence Bowl parking lot; toilets and fee station for parking ($5). The upper parking lot for Independence Mine is 1.2 miles from turnoff and also has public toilets, a $5 fee per vehicle for day-use parking, and a $3 per person admission fee at the historical park.

©MILEPOST staff photo

The 271-acre Independence Mine State Historical Park includes several buildings and old mining machinery. Restoration of the buildings is ongoing. Park visitor center (wheelchair accessible) is housed in what was originally the mine manager's home, built in 1939. Alaska Pacific Consolidated Mine Co., one of the largest gold producers in the Willow Creek mining district, operated here from 1938 through 1941. The Gold Cord Mine buildings (private property) are visible on the hill above and to the north of Independence Mine. Gold Cord Lake Trail (1.7 miles round-trip) is a good hike for families and all fitness levels.

The park usually opens the second week in June (depending on snow), with free guided tours of the building complex beginning later in the month. Visitors can take a free self-guided tour of the park at any time, but remember that when the park is closed the access road is gated, so expect a 1-mile walk to the mine complex from the lower parking lot. The park's visitor center is open in summer. For current season dates, visitor center hours and guided tour times in summer, visit http://dnr.alaska.gov/parks/asp/curevnts.htm.

P 17.2 W 31.9 Gates. Winter road closure for westbound traffic from late September to July.

Pavement ends, steep, winding gravel begins westbound.

P 18.3 W 30.8 Summit Lake State Recreation Site boundary westbound; no camping or ground fires permitted. Turnout.

P 18.9 W 30.2 Hatcher Pass Summit (elev. 3,886 feet); parking area, April Bowl Trailhead (2.2 miles round-trip).

Steep, winding descent eastbound.

P 19.3 W 29.8 Parking area at **Summit Lake State Recreation Site.** Summit Lake is the headwaters of Willow Creek. Visitors can walk around the lake or up to bluff for scenic views to west. Good view to northeast of "Nixon's Nose," a launch point for paragliders. Elevation about 3,800 feet.

Westbound, the road descends following Willow Creek from here to the Parks Highway. *CAUTION: Steep, narrow, winding road westbound as highway descends.*

P 20.5 W 28.6 Summit Lake State Recreation Site boundary eastbound; no camping or ground fires permitted.

Gates. Winter road closure for eastbound traffic from October to July.

P 20.6 W 28.5 Junction with Upper Willow Creek Valley Road (road deadends).

P 23.1 W 25.9 Pullout above valley.

P 23.2 W 25.8 Lucky Shot Gold Mine road to north, rough.

P 23.8 W 25.3 Craigie Creek Road (rough) leads to old mine sites. Remains of historic Lucky Shot (on left) and War Baby (on right) mines visible on hillside to north.

P 25.5 W 23.6 Large gravel pullouts both sides for ATV's and informal campsites.

P 26.2 W 22.9 *Road narrows and begins more steep grades eastbound; watch for potholes and rough road.*

P 27.2 W 21.9 Small turnout; good view of beaver ponds and terraced beaver dams. Watch for more beaver dams and lodges along here.

P 28.2 W 20.9 Pullout above creek.

P 30.3 W 18.8 Leaving Hatcher Pass Management Area westbound.

P 30.5 W 18.6 Pullout by river.

P 31.9 W 17.2 Dave Churchill Memorial Trail; popular snowmachine trail in winter. Access to informal camping on gravel bars.

P 32.4 W 16.7 No winter maintenance beyond this point (eastbound sign).

P 33.5 W 15.6 Informal turnouts along road eastbound allow access to scenic Willow Creek.

P 34.2 W 14.9 Little Willow Creek bridge. Turnout to north at east end of bridge; snowmachine access to Willow Mountain trail in winter.

P 34.5 W 14.6 Turnout to north with view of Willow Creek.

P 35.7 W 13.4 Twelvemile Lake (no public access).

P 38.9 W 10.2 *Gravel ends, pavement begins, westbound.*

Pavement ends, narrow gravel road begins eastbound. Watch for potholes.

P 39.2 W 9.9 Public Safety Building to north; *Emergency Phone 911.*

P 41.7 W 7.4 Coyote Gardens (private). The gardens at this private home are open one weekend a year in July as a fundraiser for the Willow Garden Club and the Alaska Botanical Garden in Anchorage.

P 47.7 W 1.4 Deception Creek public fishing access.

P 47.8 W 1.3 Deception Creek bridge; turnout at east end.

P 47.9 W 1.2 Junction with Willow Station Road south to Willow to rejoin the Parks Highway at **Milepost A 69.6.**

P 48.5 W 0.6 Road crosses railroad tracks. Turnoff to south for North Country RV Park.

P 49.1 W 0 Junction of Fishhook-Willow Road (Hatcher Pass Road) with the Parks Highway at **Milepost A 71.2,** 29 miles north of Wasilla.

**Return to Milepost A 49.5
Glenn Highway or
Milepost A 71.2 Parks Highway**

(Continued from page 340)
44° to 68°F in June and July, with a mean monthly precipitation of 2 inches. Record high was 89°F in June 1969. Mean annual rainfall is 15.5 inches, with 50.7 inches of snow. **Radio:** KJLP 88.9; Anchorage stations; KMBQ 99.7 (Wasilla). **Television:** Anchorage channels and cable. **Newspaper:** *The Frontiersman* (3 times weekly).

Private Aircraft: Palmer Municipal Airport, 1 nm SE; elev. 232 feet; length 6,000 feet and 3,616 feet; asphalt; fuel 100LL, Jet. FSS and full services.

Description

This appealing community is both a bit of pioneer Alaska as well as a modern-day commercial center for the Matanuska and Susitna valleys (collectively referred to as the Mat–Su Valley). Palmer is home to Mat-Su College (University of Alaska) and also home to the state's only accredited resident 4-year Bible college. The Alaska Bible College is at 248 E. Elmwood Ave.; (907) 745-3201.

Palmer was established about 1916 as a railway station on the Matanuska branch of the Alaska Railroad. Before that, the area had long been used by Athabascan Indians and, starting in 1890, the site of a trading post run by George Palmer.

In 1935, Palmer became the site of one of the most unusual experiments in American history: the Matanuska Valley Colony. The Federal Emergency Relief Administration, one of the many New Deal relief agencies created during Franklin Roosevelt's first year in office, planned an agricultural colony in Alaska to utilize the great agricultural potential in the Matanuska Valley, and to get some American farm families—struck by first the dust bowl, then the Great Depression—off the dole. Social workers picked 203 families, mostly from the northern counties of Michigan, Wisconsin and Minnesota, to join the colony, because it was thought that the many hardy farmers of Scandinavian descent in those 3 states would have a natural advantage over other ethnic groups.

The colonists arrived in Palmer in the early summer of 1935, and though the failure rate was high, many of their descendants still live in the Matanuska Valley. Palmer gradually became the unofficial capital of the Matanuska Valley, acting as headquarters for a farmers' cooperative marketing organization and as the business and social center for the state's most productive farming region.

Palmer is Alaska's only community that developed primarily from an agricultural economy. The growing season averages 100

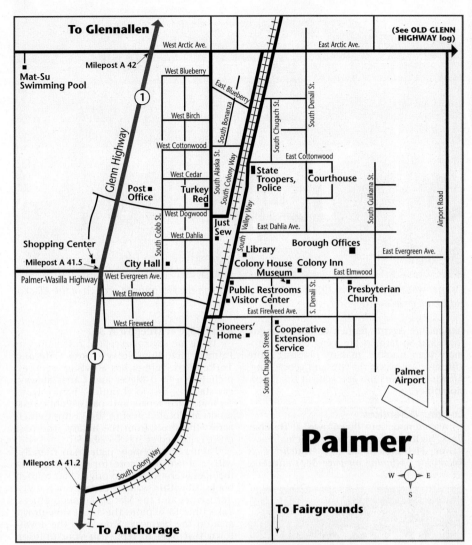

to 118 days annually, and the unique microclimate produces amazing giant vegetables, many of which are displayed at the annual Alaska State Fair in Palmer. Buy locally-grown produce at farmers markets/stores.

The University of Alaska Fairbanks has a district Cooperative Extension Service Office at 809 S. Chugach St. According to District

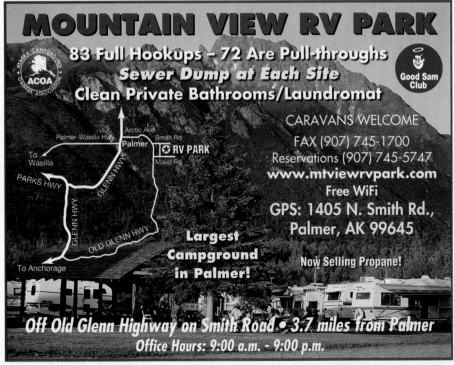

Palmer was established in 1916 as a railway station on the Matanuska branch of the Alaska Railroad. (©Serine Reeves)

Agriculture Agent Stephen C. Brown, many local Mat-Su farmers are using GPS to automate their tractors, making planting more efficient. An expert on GPS and geocaching, Brown maintains the geocache at the Extension office.

Lodging & Services

Accommodations downtown, at **Hatcher Pass B&B** out on scenic Hatcher Pass/Palmer-Fishhook Road *(see "Hatcher Pass Road" log beginning on page 341)* and **Fox Run Lodge** at **Milepost A 36**.

There are several excellent restaurants in Palmer, including **Noisy Goose Cafe** and **Turkey Red**. Palmer has all visitor services, including a Fred Meyer and Carrs/Safeway, gas stations, fast-food outlets, banks, laundromat, auto repair and parts. Public restrooms are located next to the Visitor Center, across the street from the library. The post office is located at 500 S. Cobb St.

Palmer is extremely pedestrian friendly, with a downtown core for shopping that includes everything from original art to used books, all within walking distance of the Visitor Center and the Mat-Su Borough offices. Take time to explore the small downtown area off the highway. Stop in at the downtown **Just Sew** to replenish your quilting supplies.

Camping

Mountain View RV Park is located 3 miles from downtown Palmer via the Old Glenn Highway. The Mat–Su Borough operates the 86-site **Matanuska River Park**, located 1 mile from town on the Old Glenn Highway *(see log of Old Glenn on page 347 this section)*. Finger Lake State Recreation

Site campground is accessible from **Milepost P 4** Palmer-Wasilla Highway. **Paradise Alaska RV Park** is located at 16199 E. Outer Springer Loop; take Inner Springer Loop at either **Milepost A 40.7 or A 39.5**. **Kepler Park** at **Milepost A 37.4** and **Fox Run Lodge & Campground** is at **Milepost A 36** several miles further west of Palmer on the Glenn Highway.

Transportation

Air: No scheduled service, but the local airport has a number of charter operators.

Bus: Mat-Su Community Transit connects Palmer, Wasilla, Eagle River and Anchorage.

Railroad: Round-trip passenger service from Anchorage to South Palmer Station during the Alaska State Fair in August. Contact the Alaska Railroad for current schedule; (907) 265-2494, alaskarailroad.com.

Attractions

A Must Stop: The Palmer Visitor Information Center and Palmer Museum of History & Art, inside the log building just off the "main drag" (at 723 S. Valley Way between East Fireweed and East Elmwood). Charming exhibits on the early history of Palmer until 1935, videos, helpful staff. Outside is the fabulous Mat-Su Valley agricultural showcase gardens. Restrooms outside on East Elmwood. Phone (907) 746-7668.

The **Palmer Library**, across the street from the visitor center, has a paperback and magazine exchange. Out in front of the library is a monument dedicated to the families of the Matanuska Colony. From the library, enjoy a stroll along the greenbelt's multi-use path with interpretive stops along the way.

Farmers Markets. Friday Flings, a weekly farmers market featuring Alaska-grown produce, flowers and crafts, is held across from the visitor center every Friday, 10 A.M. to 5 P.M., from about mid-May to mid-August. **Colony Farmers Market** takes place at Palmer Depot on Mondays from noon to 7 P.M. in summer.

Annual events include **Palmer Colony Days** in June, a festival commemorating the colonists of the Matanuska farming community; craft fair, farmer's market, carnival rides, fun run, parade. The annual **Alaska Highland Games** and **Gathering of the Clans** takes place the last Saturday in June at the Alaska State Fairgrounds in Palmer. This event features Scottish music, dancing, food and events (hammer toss, caber and stone throw). For details and dates, visit www.alaskascottish.org.

The **Palmer Pride Picnic**, held the fourth Friday in July, is a free picnic hosted by the City of Palmer and Greater Palmer Chamber of Commerce. A **Midsummer Art and Garden Faire**, held in early July, celebrates the fruits and vegetables of summer in Alaska and showcases the work of many local artists, chefs and gardeners.

In August, a great downtown parade kicks off the first weekend of the **Alaska State Fair**. As Alaska's largest event, the fair is a mix of giant vegetables, entertainment, food booths, carnival and midway rides, roving performers, farm animals, pony rides, pig races and more. The fair takes place August 22 to Sept. 2, in 2019. This is a very popular event: Be prepared for lots of traffic! Visit www.alaskastatefair.org or phone (907) 745-4827 for more information.

The second weekend in December **is Colony Christmas**, an old-fashioned, family-oriented Christmas celebration with a winter parade, fireworks, several craft fairs, cookie contest, sleigh rides, reindeer petting, and a gingerbread house competition.

For more information on Palmer events, phone The Greater Palmer Chamber of Commerce at (907) 745-2880.

Colony House Museum is a historic little house at 316 E. Elmwood Ave., just south from the Visitor Center, that was built in the 1930s. The house represents modification of one of 4 basic house plans available to Matanuska Valley Colonists. The Colony House was moved to its present location and restored and furnished by members of Palmer's pioneer community. Open 10 A.M. to 4 P.M. May 1 to Aug. 31.

The restored **Colony Inn,** at 325 E. Elmwood Ave., which now serves as a hotel, was built as a teacher's dormitory for the Matanuska Colony project and is a lovely reminder of the elegance of this bygone era.

The United Protestant Church in Palmer—the **Church of a Thousand Logs**—also dates from Matanuska Colony days and is one of the oldest churches in Alaska still holding services. It is included in the National Register of Historic Places. Another historic building on the National Registry is the downtown **Palmer Depot,** one of the few remaining central buildings from the Matanuska Colony, and Palmer's Community Center.

Drive the Old Glenn Highway. An alternate route bypassing part of the Glenn Highway, the Old Glenn Highway also accesses recreation sites and businesses. **Knik Glacier Tours,** 10 miles south via the Old Glenn then 8.4 miles up Knik River Road, transports visitors to the face of Knik Glacier. *See the "Old Glenn Highway" log on page 347 this section.*

Play Golf. Known for its scenery and one-of-a-kind setting, the award-winning Palmer Municipal Golf Course has 18 holes (par 72, USGA rated), gas golf carts and clubs, driving range, pro shop, practice green and bar, RV parking and a snack bar. A favorite for locals and visitors alike, it is one of the first Alaska courses to open in spring (as early as mid-April some years). Located across the street from the airport off the Old Glenn Highway. Phone (907) 745-4653.

The unique Fishhook Golf Course on Palmer-Fishhook Road (see Hatcher Pass Road log this section), is a 9-hole course set in a former horse pasture. Though it's a short course, it's more challenging than it looks. Cart rentals, a driving range and a small pro shop with snacks. Phone (907) 745-7274.

Go to a Mat-Su Miners Game. The Mat-Su Miners, based in Palmer, are one of 5 collegiate teams in the Alaska Baseball League (www.alaskabaseballleague.org) with players recruited from major colleges. The other league teams are the Anchorage Bucs, the Anchorage Glacier Pilots, the Peninsula Oilers and Chugiak-Eagle River Chinooks. Miners' home games are at Hermon Bros. Field: turn off the Glenn Highway at the Alaska State Fairgrounds main parking lot and continue to the far end of the lot to the ballpark's main gate. Baseball schedules are published in the local newspapers or visit www.matsuminers.org.

Don't miss the Musk Ox Farm. Located east of Palmer (turnoff the Glenn Highway at **Milepost A 50.1**; *see page 340*), this is a

great place to learn about and see the shaggy prehistoric musk-oxen up-close. A native cooperative uses the fine wool (qiviut) to knit beautiful and warm wares. Hunted to near extinction in Alaska in 1865, the species was reintroduced in the 1930s. May to September; fee charged, gift shop onsite.

Hike or bike area trails. Hiking trails south of Palmer on the Old Glenn Highway (see log this section) include: Matanuska Peak, turnoff 3 miles south of Palmer (**Milepost J 15.6**); Lazy Mountain, 2.4 miles from Palmer (**Milepost J 16**); Bodenburg Butte, (the West Butte Trail) 6 miles from Palmer (**Milepost J 12.6**); and **Pioneer Ridge-Austin Helmers Trail** from Knik River Road, 10 miles south of Palmer (**Milepost J 8.6**). The **Crevasse Moraine** trail system is accessible from **Milepost P 1.9** Palmer-Wasilla Highway.

Go Swimming: The 80-foot swimming pool is open to the public weekdays (closed weekends). Fees charged, showers available. The pool is located at Palmer High School on West Arctic Avenue; phone (907) 745-5091.

Enjoy Water Sports. On the Glenn Highway, visit Kepler-Bradley Lakes, accessible from the family-run Kepler Park at **Milepost A 37.4**, which offers camping, day use, boat rentals and a small store. Kepler-Bradley Lakes is also accessible from the state recreation area at **Milepost A 36.1**. Fishing, boating, waterskiing, and other water sports are popular in summer at Finger Lake. Drive west on Palmer-Wasilla Highway 4 miles, then go north on Trunk Road 1 mile to Bogard Road; turn west and drive 0.7 mile to **Finger Lake State Recreation Site**. A scenic spot with camping, picnic tables, water and boat launch. Life jackets provided.

Visit Scenic Hatcher Pass. From **Milepost A 49.5** near Palmer, Hatcher Pass Road/Palmer-Fishhook Road provides access to the beautiful Hatcher Pass Recreation Area and Independence Mine State Historical Park. Well worth the 20-mile drive for the scenery, the hiking trails and berry picking (in season). *See "Hatcher Pass Road" log on pages 341–342.*

See the Matanuska Glacier: Drive 60 miles east on the Glenn Highway from Palmer to visit this spectacular 27-mile-long glacier, one of the few you can drive to and explore on foot. Access to the foot of the glacier is through Glacier Park at **Milepost A 102**; admission charged. If you're not interested in getting close, you can see the glacier from the highway at multiple turnouts along the road, or from Matanuska Glacier State Recreation Site at **Milepost A 101**.

Glenn Highway Log
(continued)

A 41.6 G 147.4 T 286.4 Traffic light at Dogwood Avenue to south. Access to Palmer post office, city hall, banks and downtown.

Don't miss the Musk Ox Farm on Archie Road; turnoff at Milepost A 50.1.

(©Serine Reeves)

A 41.5 G 147.5 T 286.5 Traffic light at **junction** with Palmer–Wasilla Highway and Evergreen Avenue. Urgent Care, Chevron gas station and fast-food to south on West Evergreen; Carrs/Safeway with gas, Fred Meyer's, and McDonald's to north on Palmer-Wasilla Highway. The 10-mile Palmer-Wasilla Highway connects Palmer on the Glenn Highway with Wasilla on the Parks Highway. It is a busy road with a number of businesses and residential subdivisions.

A 41.3 G 147.7 T 286.7 Tesoro gas/diesel station with propane and ATM. Oil/lube shop and auto parts store to south.

A 41.2 G 147.8 T 286.8 First access eastbound to Palmer business district via South Colony Way.

A 41.1 G 147.9 T 286.9 Commercial Drive.

A 40.7 G 148.3 T 287.3 Inner Springer Loop (east end) to south. **Noisy Goose Cafe** to north; an Alaskan family-friendly restaurant serving breakfast all day. For **Paradise Alaska RV Park** head south to golf course then right on outer Spring Loop.

Noisy Goose Cafe. See display ad on facing page.

Paradise Alaska RV Park. Palmer's newest camping site. Located across from the Palmer Golf Course and surrounded by mountains. Our park is 1.5 miles from the Alaska State Fairgrounds; 1.7 miles from downtown and a short 45 min. from Anchorage. The perfect place to use as home

The Alaska State Fair is scheduled for August 22 to September 2, 2019, at the Palmer Fairgrounds. (©Kris Valencia, staff)

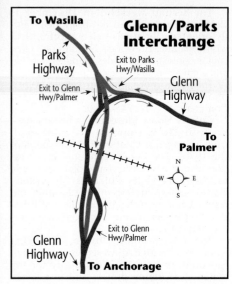

base to visit the beautiful Mat-Su Valley. Website: www.paradisealaska.com/rvpark. html. Phone (907) 775-6359. See display ad on page 345. [ADVERTISEMENT]

A 40.2 G 148.8 T 287.8 Main entrance to Fairgrounds (site of Alaska State Fair) and Hermon Bros. Field (home of the Mat–Su Miners baseball team). The Alaska State Fair is held the end of August through the first week in September. *Slow for special traffic patterns during fair and obey speed limits!* South Palmer Train Station, south side of highway, offers fair train service; www.alaskarailroad.com/ride-a-train/event-trains/fair-train.

A 39.5 G 149.5 T 288.5 Inner Springer Loop (west end). **Paradise Alaska RV Park** to south at 16199 E. Outer Springer Loop.

A 39.2 G 149.8 T 288.8 Outer Springer Loop to south. Short, steep trail to **Meiers Lake**; Arctic grayling and rainbow trout fishing.

A 37.4 G 151.6 T 290.6 Slow down for Kepler Drive turnoff on north side of highway for **Kepler Park** (description follows): camping, boat rentals, fishing.

Kepler Park. Family-owned and operated with a family atmosphere. Camping, day-use, boating, fishing on 2 beautiful lakes stocked annually. Pedal boat, rowboat, canoe rentals. Small store with concessions, bait, tackle. Short distance to local conveniences and other attractions. Open May 1 to September 15. Phone (907) 745-3053. Website www.keplerpark.us. [ADVERTISEMENT]

A 37.2 G 151.8 T 290.8 Echo Lake public parking and fishing access to south; 4-vehicle parking and short trail to lake (visible from parking area). Fish for landlocked salmon and rainbow trout (stocked).

A 36.1 G 152.9 T 291.9 Entrance to **Matanuska Lakes** (formerly called Kepler–Bradley Lakes) **State Recreation Area** to north; day-use area on Matanuska Lake; water, toilets, parking, picnic tables, hiking trails and fishing. Small tent camping area. ADF&G stocks lakes (Kepler, Bradley, Matanuska, Canoe, Irene, Long, Claire and Victor lakes) with rainbow trout, Arctic char, Arctic grayling and landlocked salmon. Wheelchair-accessible trail to lake.

Distance marker eastbound shows Palmer 5 miles, Glennallen 145 miles, Tok 281 miles.

A 36 G 153 T 292 Fox Run Lodge and Campground (description follows) to north; full-hookup sites, restaurant, hotel rooms.

Fox Run Lodge & Campground features a variety of services for travelers, including meals by reservation in the dining room or on the deck. Also, RV and tent sites, private lakefront hotel rooms, art gallery, studios, massage therapy, efficiencies, dorm-style cabins, WiFi, laundry, showers, propane, swimming, hiking, fishing, boat rentals. See display ad on this page. [ADVERTISEMENT]

A 35.8 G 153.2 T 292.2 Glenn–Parks Interchange (*see illustration on this page*). Westbound exit for Wasilla/Parks Highway (Alaska Route 3). Also access this exit

to Matanuska-Susitna Visitor Center and Mat-Su Regional Medical Center (use Trunk Road exit off the Parks Highway).

Junction of the Glenn Highway (Alaska Route 1) with the Parks Highway (Alaska Route 3) to Denali Park and Fairbanks. See the PARKS HIGHWAY section on page 377 for log.

A 35.3 G 153.7 T 292.7 Right lane ends northbound, right lane begins southbound.

A 34 G 155 T 294 Palmer/Glenn Highway 2-lane exit for northbound traffic continuing east on the Glenn Highway (Alaska Route 1). Wasilla/Parks Highway traffic continues straight ahead.

Anchorage-bound Glenn Highway traffic merges with westbound traffic from Parks Highway.

A 33.5 G 155.5 T 294.5 Palmer Hay Flats State Game Refuge (southbound sign) supports migrating waterfowl and shorebirds, plus a variety of other wildlife. In winter, large numbers of moose can congregate on the flats in view of the highway. The refuge can be accessed at the Knik River Access/Reflections Lake trail (see **Milepost A 30.6**).

CAUTION: Watch for moose and bear crossing the highway.

A 31.5 G 157.5 T 296.5 Bridge over the Matanuska River, which is fed by the Matanuska Glacier.

A 30.8 G 158.2 T 297.5 Sgt. James Bond-steel Bridge of Honor crosses Knik River. The **Knik River** comes down from the Knik Glacier to the east and splits into several branches as it approaches Knik Arm. Knik Arm is a 3-mile-wide estuary that extends 40 miles southwest to Cook Inlet.

Matanuska–Susitna Borough boundary.

A 30.6 G 158.4 T 297.4 Knik River Access. **Reflections Lake** 1.1-mile loop trail around lake is ADA accessible, with boardwalk over the wetlands, benches overlooking the lake for bird watching, a covered pavilion, a kiosk with interpretive panels, restrooms and a 35-foot steel Wildlife Viewing and Interpretive Tower. Wildflowers, nesting waterfowl, beaver activity and other wildlife are abundant here. The lake is stocked with trout. Come for a free Family Fun Days event, details at www.palmerhayflats.org.

A 30.3 G 158.7 T 297.7 Knik River bridge.

Old Glenn Highway

The Old Glenn Highway is a moderately busy 18.4-mile, paved, 2-lane road with 45 mph curves. It is used by local residential traffic and as an alternate route to the Glenn Highway, with which it junctions at **Milepost A 29.6** and **Milepost A 42** (in Palmer). This road also provides access to campgrounds, the Knik River and businesses offering ATV and boat tours to Knik Glacier. The Bodenburg Butte area—accessible via a loop road—has original Matanuska Colony farms and 3 popular local attractions: the Reindeer Farm, Pyrah's Peak U-pick Farm and Bodenburg Butte hiking trails.

Distance from south junction with the Glenn Highway (J) is followed by distance from Palmer (P).

J 0 P 18.4 Exit from Glenn Highway at Milepost A 29.6.

J 0.5 P 17.9 Bridge over railroad tracks.

J 3.7 P 14.7 Eklutna Tailrace ADF&G day-use area and public fishing access (pictured below); handicap accessible. Open May to October 1; good early summer and fall fishing for chinook (mid to late June is best) and coho (August) (stocked). Nice spot. Won the 2018 #1 position on the national "Top 10 Mom-Approved Places to fish and boat" as voted on at website: TakeMeFishing. org.

There is a large gravel parking area *(drive slowly; access road and parking area may be potholed)* with restrooms and dumpster; fish-cleaning table; bridge/walkway (extends from here to paved turnout at **Milepost J 4** by power plant). No fee.

©Kris Valencia, staff

J 4 P 14.4 Small paved parking area with outhouses to west for walk-in only access to Eklutna Tailrace fishing (connects with main area at **Milepost 3.7**). Across the road is the Eklutna Power Plant (Alaska Power Administration), which uses water from Eklutna Lake to provide power to Anchorage and the Mat-Su Valley.

J 6 P 12.4 Goat Creek bridge.

J 6.9 P 11.5 Winter avalanche area next 1.5 miles, do not stop. Road parallels Knik River.

J 8.5 P 9.9 Paved turnout to west with view of Knik River.

J 8.6 P 9.8 Junction with **Knik River Road**, an 11-mile-long paved road that is bordered by private property. **Pioneer Falls** (a waterfall) at Mile 1.2 *(CAUTION: Black bears)*; public access to Knik River at Mile 1.4; Pioneer Ridge-Austin Helmers trailhead at Mile 3.9 (4.5-mile-hike 1-way, difficult, great views); and a view of Knik Glacier at about Mile 7.2 (the glacier is best viewed from the river). **Knik Glacier Tours** at Mile

8.7 (description follows) offers camping and daily airboat trips to Knik Glacier. Knik River Road deadends 11.1 miles east of the Old Glenn Highway at Knik River Lodge. ▲

Knik Glacier Tours, Mile 8.4 Knik River Road. Your gateway to Knik Glacier. Tours depart daily to our wilderness camp at the face of this spectacular glacier. Campground surrounded by breathtaking scenery. Park has great hiking trails with good opportunities to see local wildlife. RV and tent sites free with glacier tour. Reservations phone (907) 745-1577. Website: www.knik glacier.com. [ADVERTISEMENT]

J 8.7 P 9.7 Knik River bridge. Entering Game Management Subunit 14A eastbound. Pedestrian bridge adjacent highway bridge (formerly the old highway). .

J 9 P 9.4 Gravel access west to riverbank for vehicles and pedestrian bridge to east at north end of Knik River bridge.

J 10.4 P 8 Turnoff to east on Sullivan Avenue for Alaska Raceway Park (raceak. com), 0.8 mile east. Drive east on Sullivan Ave. 1 mile for Jim Creek public-use area; large parking area, toilets, access to exceptional fishing and to ORV trailhead. Jim Creek is part of the Knik River Public-Use Area, which was created partly in response to chronic vandalims at Jim Creek. ➡

J 11.5 P 6.9 Green Store and Cafe to east at junction with Bodenburg Loop Road (description follows) and Plumley Road. The Green Store has a liquor store, convenience store items and gas pump, but the cafe is closed. ⛽

This intersection is the South **junction** with the 5.8-mile-long Bodenburg Loop Road, which leads west from here to: the "Old" Bodenburg Butte trailhead (0.6 mile to small fee parking area on private land), the steeper of 1 of the 2 trails up the Butte (for the other trail see North Junction with Bodenburg Loop at **Milepost J 12.6**); the Reindeer Farm (0.8 mile), a commercial reindeer farm offering tours (phone ahead (907) 745-4000 or book online at www.rein deerfarm.com); and Pyrah's Pioneer Peak Farm (2.8 miles), a popular U-pick destination; pppfarm.net. Bodenburg Butte Road rejoins the Old Glenn Highway opposite Back Acres Road at **Milepost J 12.6.**

J 11.8 P 6.6 BUTTE (pop. 3,409); fire and ambulance service station #21; emergency phone 911. Fire permits May 1 to Sept. 30.

J 12.6 P 5.8 Junction with Back Acres Road and north end of 5.8-mile Bodenburg Butte Loop Road (south end at **Milepost J 11.5**). Turn here to hike Bodenburg Butte via the borough-maintained West Butte Trail. Drive 0.5 mile to Mothershead Lane—a dirt road leading to parking lot with toilets. The trailhead is another couple hundred yards further. The 1.5 mile hike takes you up to 700 feet in elevation; great views from the top. Bodenburg Butte is a geological formation known as a monodnock (residual mountain) on a peneplain. It is also a popular destination for local hikers, offering 360° views from the top. For other attractions along Bodenburg Loop, see description at **Milepost J 11.5.**

J 14.7 P 3.7 Maud Road, access east to shooting range (Knik River Public-Use Area; rules posted).

J 15.6 P 2.8 Junction with Smith Road. Access to **Mountain View RV Park** (0.8 mile) and Matanuska Peak Trail (1.5

miles). Matanuska Peak Trail climbs 5,670 feet in 4.1 miles; rated moderate to difficult.

Mountain View RV Park. See display ad on page 343. ▲

J 16 P 2.4 Clark–Wolverine Road; access to Lazy Mountain Recreation Area. For recreation area, drive east 0.8 mile to "T"; turn right on Huntley Road at T and drive 0.9 mile; then take right fork downhill 0.2 mile to trailhead parking for popular 2.5-mile summit hike.

J 16.6 P 1.8 Paved loop road down to Matanuska River photo viewpoint and gravel riverbank, a popular gathering spot.

J 16.8 P 1.6 George Palmer Memorial Bridge crosses the Matanuska River. Photo viewpoint to east at north end of bridge on old alignment; access to pedestrian bridge and trail.

J 17.4 P 1 Matanuska River Park (Mat-Su Borough Parks & Recreation) with camping and day-use areas. The Palmer Bike Park is adjacent the playground and picnic area. It has a popular pump track on nearly 2 acres with some jumps and short wooden boardwalk sections.

Matanuska River Park. See display ad this page. ▲

J 17.6 P 0.8 Airport Road leads west to Palmer municipal airport and to Palmer Golf Course.

J 17.9 P 0.5 *Slow for speed zone entering downtown Palmer.*

J 18.2 P 0.2 Valley Way; go west for Palmer city center.

J 18.3 P 0.1 Traffic light at Alaska Street; go west for Palmer city center.

J 18.4 P 0 Junction of Old Glenn Highway (West Arctic Avenue) with **Milepost A 42** Glenn Highway at Palmer. *Description of Palmer begins on page 340.* Fred Meyer gas station with diesel and propane. ⓑ

Return to Milepost A 42 or A 29.6 Glenn Highway

A 29.6 G 159.4 T 298.4 Exit to the Old Glenn Highway overpass to Eklutna Tailrace day-use area (3.7 miles), Knik River, **Knik Glacier Tours**, Mountain View RV Park, Matanuska River Park and Palmer (see log).

Junction with Old Glenn Highway. See "Old Glenn Highway" log on page 347.

A 27.3 G 161.7 T 300.7 The highway crosses a swampy area known locally as Eklutna Flats. These flats are a protected wildflower area (picking flowers is strictly prohibited). Look for wild iris, shooting star, chocolate lily and wild rose in early June.

A 26.1 G 162.9 T 301.9 Exit for **Eklutna Lake Road** and Eklutna Historical Park (descriptions follow). *NOTE: Eklutna overpass, clearance 15'10"; overheight trucks MUST USE EXIT.*

©Kris Valencia, staff

Exit west for Eklutna Village Clinic, **Eklutna Historical Park** (description follows) and the residential community of **EKLUTNA** (pop. 70), a Dena'ina Athabascan village. It is the earliest indigenous people to live in the Knik Arm area. Eklutna Historical Park, just west of the highway, includes the Eklutna Heritage Museum, St. Nicholas Russian Orthodox Church, a hand-built Siberian prayer chapel and traditional spirit houses or grave houses. Admission fee charged (pay at gift shop). Guided tours available on demand, weekdays 10 A.M. to 5 P.M. (closed holidays) from mid-May to mid-September; phone (907) 764-7233, www.eklutnahistoricalpark.org. Parking area has limited turnaround space; no big rigs with tow vehicles.

Every other year (next in 2020), Eklutna celebrates an open potlatch/powwow which welcomes non-Natives to this alcohol-free celebration.

From the overpass, follow signs east about a half-mile to Eklutna Lake Road (paved), which leads 9.5 miles to **Eklutna Lake Recreation Area** in Chugach State Park. Use caution along this road due to unstable shoulders and steep dropoffs. The last 7 miles of Eklutna Lake Road are very narrow and winding with no shoul-

ders, although there are a few turnarounds (including one at Rochelle's, contrary to the sign at Mile 2) and the pavement was in good condition in 2018. **Rochelle's Ice Cream Stop** (description follows) at Mile 8.

©Kris Valencia, staff

Rochelle's Ice Cream Stop/Store/ Cabins/Gold Panning located 1½ miles from Eklutna Lake in Chugach State Park wildlife viewing area. Best milkshakes, old fashioned banana splits, espresso, fishing licenses, ice, groceries, picnic supplies, Eklutna Lake posters/postcards. Shower/laundry available. Phone (907) 688-6201, 1-800-764-6201; website: goalaskan.com.

Public-use cabins are available for rent. Reservations may be made online for the cabin; go to www.reserveamerica.com. For picnic pavilion or group campsite reservations, phone the Dept. of Natural Resources at (907) 269-8400. For Serenity Falls Hut go to dnr.alaska.gov/parks/cabins/anch.htm.

Eklutna Lake is the largest lake in Chugach State Park, measuring approximately 7 miles long by a mile wide. The lake is used to generate hydro-electric power at the Eklutna Plant, and is also a drinking water source for Anchorage. Fed by Eklutna Glacier, Eklutna Lake offers fair fishing for Dolly Varden and rainbow trout. Boats are limited to electric trolling motors and non-motorized boats permitted. No boat ramp. *CAUTION: High winds can make this lake dangerous for boaters.* Interpretive displays on wildlife and a viewing telescope are located at the trailhead.

The Lakeside trailhead parking lot at Eklutna Lake accommodates 80 cars and offers easy access to the lake. It also acts as a boat launch for hand-carried boats. The Lakeside trail—popular with hikers and bicyclists—follows Eklutna Lake shoreline and gives access to Eklutna Glacier (12.7 miles).

A 25.2 G 163.8 T 302.8 Thunderbird Falls exit for northbound traffic only. From exit drive 0.4 mile (follow signs) to small trailhead parking lot just before Eklutna River bridge (bridge closed to motor vehicles). **Thunderbird Falls** is a 2-mile round-trip hike from the trailhead. This easy family walk is along a wide, scenic trail, but supervise children because there are steep cliffs just off the trail. The trail forks, with the right fork leading to a viewing platform, and the left fork leading down a steep path to Thunderbird Creek. The falls are just upstream. $5 parking fee. *CAUTION: Do NOT venture beyond the end of the trail to climb the cliffs overhanging the falls! Watch for bears.*

A 24.5 G 164.5 T 303.5 Southbound-only exit to Edmonds Lake residential area and Mirror Lake Municipal Park; boating, swimming, fishing, picnic shelters, picnic tables, grills, outhouses, volleyball court, play field, beach, swings. **Mirror Lake**, located at the foot of Mount Eklutna, is stocked with rainbow trout and landlocked

chinook salmon.

A 23.6 G 165.4 T 304.4 Northbound-only exit to **Mirror Lake Municipal Park** (see description above), located immediately off this exit; frontage road deadends at parking area on lake (ice fishing in winter). Return to freeway via access to Edmonds Lake.

A 22.8 G 166.2 T 305.2 North Peters Creek overpass (clearance 17'0"). Exit to North Peters Creek Business Loop (use next exit at **Milepost A 21.9** for more direct access to services).

A 22 G 167 T 306 Southbound exit to PETERS CREEK. Take Voyles Boulevard west to Old Glenn Highway/Bill Stephens Drive for access to local businesses. Services this exit include gas stations, grocery, body repair shop, restaurant and **Bobby's Peter's Creek RV Park**.

Bobby's Peter's Creek RV Park. See display ad this page.

A 21.5 G 167.5 T 306.5 Northbound exit to Peters Creek; (see description of businesses at previous milepost).

A 20.9 G 168.1 T 306.9 Chugiak North Birchwood Loop Road overpass; exits both sides of highway. Turn east for community of **CHUGIAK** (pop. 5,484) on the Old Glenn Highway. Chugiak has a post office, senior center, convenience store with gas, diesel, showers and laundromat. Loretta French Municipal Park offers ballfields, an equestrian center, and an archery range and model airplane field for club members. It is also home to the Chugiak-Eagle River Chinooks ABL baseball team (www.cerchinooks.com).

Private Aircraft: Birchwood Airport; elev. sea level; 2 runways, paved and gravel.

Bicycles and pedestrians may use the multi-use path alongside the Glenn Highway between Chugiak and East Anchorage. Pedestrians are not allowed on the Glenn Highway between Chugiak and the Parks Highway junction, although bicyclists may use the shoulders along this segment.

A 17.2 G 171.8 T 310.8 Chugiak South Birchwood Loop Road underpass exits both sides of highway. Access west to Chugiak High School (indoor swimming pool, public hours); Park and Ride Lot; and summer hiking trails/winter ski trails from Beach Lake Chalet. Also access to Beach Lake Municipal Park (0.8 mile west, turn left and follow narrow, winding, mostly paved road 2 miles); fishing, swimming and canoeing in summer at Beach Lake; dog mushing trails in winter (Chugiak Dog Mushing Assoc. is headquartered here).

Exit east for **St. John Orthodox Cathedral** (description follows); drive 0.6 mile east on Birchwood Loop; turn right on Old Glenn Highway and drive 0.2 mile; turn on Monastery Drive and drive 0.3 mile to cathedral.

Saint John Orthodox Cathedral. Take a peaceful break from your travels. Visit this unique, geodesic-dome cathedral with

St. Sergius of Radonezh Chapel on the grounds of Saint John Orthodox Cathedral in Eagle River. (©Serine Reeves)

birch ceiling and beautiful icons. Or hike to St. Sergius Chapel. Visitors are welcome at our services: Saturday Vespers, 7:15 P.M.; Sunday Divine Liturgy, 10 A.M. Bookstore. Monastery Drive off Old Glenn. (907) 696-2002. www.stjohnalaska.org. [ADVERTISEMENT]

A 15.5 G 173.5 T 312.5 North Eagle River overpass (clearance 16'3"). Exit to North Eagle River, Terrace Lane. Follow signs to Old Glenn Highway junction (0.2 mile) for Providence Health & Services/Urgent Care, Fred Meyer gas/diesel/propane and Spenard Builders Supply. Turn right at light on Old Glenn Highway for other businesses in downtown Eagle River (you'll rejoin the Glenn Highway at **Milepost A 13.4**). Turn left on Old Glenn Highway and drive 0.5 mile north and turn off on to Harry McDonald Road for the Harry J. McDonald Memorial Center (0.4 mile uphill) with Olympic-sized ice rink and indoor jogging track.

A 14 G 175 T 314 Highway narrows from 3 to 2 lanes northbound.

A 13.4 G 175.6 T 314.6 South Eagle River overpass. Clearance is 18'8", according to an article in the *Anchorage Daily News* about an 18-wheeler carrying a modular building that hit this overpass in March 2018, closing the southbound lanes of the Glenn Highway for a period of time. Exit east to community of Eagle River via Artillery Road; all visitor services (description follows). Also access to Eagle River Road to Eagle River Nature Center in Chugach State Park *(see Eagle River Road log on page 350).*

Eagle River

A 13.4 G 175.6 T 314.6 Population: 24,000; area 35,000. **Emergency Services:** Dial 911. **Police,** Anchorage Police Dept., phone (907) 786-8500. **Alaska State Troopers,** phone (907) 269-5511. **Urgent Care,** (in Provi-

dence building), phone (907) 694-7223; open daily 8 A.M. to 8 P.M., walk-ins welcome.

Visitor Information: Contact the Chugiak-Eagle River Chamber of Commerce, P.O. Box 770353, Eagle River, AK 99577; phone (907) 694-4702; or visit www.cer.org. You can also visit the Chamber office in the Eagle River Town Center, 12001 Business Blvd., Suite 108. **Newspaper:** *Alaska Star* (www.alaskastar.com, weekly).

The Chugiak–Eagle River area was homesteaded after WWII when the new Glenn Highway opened this rural area northeast of Anchorage. Today, Eagle River is a fast-growing residential area with a full range of businesses, most located along the Old Glenn Highway east off the Glenn Highway.

The Chugiak-Eagle River area has more than 20 churches, including the very unique **Saint John Orthodox Cathedral** (see **Milepost A 17.2**) with its geodesic dome.

Visitor services include fast-food restaurants, supermarkets, banks, laundromat, post office, gas/diesel stations, oil and lube shop and shopping centers. Ice skating, hockey and speed skating at the Harry J. McDonald Memorial Center located a half-mile north of the Fred Meyer store via the Old Glenn Highway and 0.4 mile uphill on Harry McDonald Road. The nearest public campground is Eagle River Campground; take Hiland exit, then follow signs on frontage road (see **Milepost A 11.6**).

There is a summer **Farmers Market** on Tuesdays, 3–7 P.M., at the VFW Post parking lot.

The 34th annual **Bear Paw Festival**, scheduled for July 10–14, 2019, features the Teddy Bear Picnic and Family Fun Day, the Bear Paw Royalty Pageant and Running with the Bears, a 300-yard fun run—"because after 300 yards it isn't fun anymore." There's

also a classic car show, Slippery Salmon Olympics, Human Foosball Tournament, fabulous food and the Grand Parade. Phone (907) 694-4702 or visit www.bearpawfestival.org for more information.

Eagle River Nature Center at Mile 12.6 Eagle River Road has natural history displays and self-guiding nature trails. Guided nature hikes are offered in summer and there are nature programs scheduled year-round. Visit www.ernc.org or phone (907) 694-2108 for current information. *See "Eagle River Road" log on page 350 for details.*

Eagle River Nature Center is also the finish line for the **Crow Pass Crossing**, an annual 22.5-mile trail race held late in July. This mountain race follows the Crow Pass

Mile 12 Eagle River Road
Eagle River
Alaska

907-694-2108
Trails, programs, & hike-to yurts & cabin.

FRIENDS OF **EAGLE RIVER NATURE CENTER**
www.ernc.org

Eagle River Road

Eagle River Road leads 12.6 miles east to Eagle River Nature Center, a geat destination with indoor natural history displays, outdoor nature trails and year-round nature programs.

(©Kris Valencia, staff)

Eagle River Road leads 12.6 miles east from downtown Eagle River to Eagle River Nature Center in Chugach State Park. It is a paved 2-lane road, with local traffic, accessible from the Glenn Highway via Artillery Road from the Eagle River exit at **Milepost A 13.4**, or from Eagle River Loop road, which exits at **Milepost A 11.6**.

NOTE: Watch for driveway traffic, school bus stops, pedestrians and moose. Slow traffic use turnouts.

Distance from junction (J) with Old Glenn Highway is shown.

J 0 Junction with Old Glenn Highway. Eagle Center houses UAA Eagle River Campus and a Key Bank.

J 0.2 Fire station to west.

J 0.3 Junction with VFW Road which connects with Eagle River Loop (1.5 miles) and also accesses Eagle River state campground (drive 1 mile on VFW Road then turn on Hesterberg and follow signs to campground). 🅰

J 1.6 Junction with Eagle River Loop Road.

J 1.7 Walmart.

J 2.3 End bike route from Eagle River.

J 3.3 P&M Gardens greenhouses.

J 7.8 Mile 7.4 North Fork Put-In. Short, bumpy, gravel road south to **North Fork Eagle River** access for kayaks, rafts and canoes; large gravel parking area, outhouse. Day-use area only, no camping. No fires; carry out trash. Hiking trail from parking area to main stem of river. The Eagle River offers Class II, III and IV float trips. Fish for rainbow trout, Dolly Varden and a limited chinook salmon fishery. Cross-country skiing and snowmachining in winter. Check with Chugach State Park ranger for information on river conditions; phone (907) 345-5014. 🔁

J 9 Signed paved parking to south. Moose Pond access for Eagle River floats.

J 9.1 Signed paved fee parking to south.

J 9.3 Signed paved parking to south. Fill site for Fire Department.

J 10.5 Chugach State Park 2 miles (sign).

J 11.4 Small paved turnout to north.

J 12.6 Eagle River Nature Center operated by the nonprofit Friends of Eagle River Nature Center to provide educational and recreational opportunities for Chugach State Park visitors. The Nature Center has brochures, natural history displays, a cozy sitting area and year-round nature programs; latrine and public phone outside building, restrooms by entrance to parking lot. Beautiful views of the Chugach Mountains, particularly from the viewing decks on the Rodak Nature Trail. Walk the nature trails at your own pace, or join one of the free guided nature walks offered 1:30–2:30 P.M. Tuesday–Sunday from June 1 to August 31. Pets must be on leash on the Rodak and Albert Loop trails.

The center is open year-round from 10 A.M. to 5 P.M.; Tuesday through Sunday (June–August) Wednesday through Sunday May & September and Friday through Sunday (October–April). Trails are always accessible but check for bear and wildlife warnings posted at building and trailhead. A rustic cabin and 3 yurts—each located within 2 miles of the Nature Center—are available for rent ($75/night) and may be reserved up to a year in advance online. Contact the center for current activities schedule and trail conditions. Phone (907) 694-2108, or visit their website at www.ernc.org. Parking ($5 fee). The main parking lot can fill quickly on busy days. Limited parking area for RVs and vehicles with trailers. *NOTE: The overflow parking is off limits for RVs or vehicles with trailers (too steep and no space to turn around.)*

This is also the trailhead for the Historic Iditarod–Crow Pass Trail and the finish line for the Crow Pass Crossing, an annual 22.5-mile trail race held the third Saturday in July. This mountain race follows the Crow Pass trail from Girdwood to Eagle River. Visit www.healthyfutures.org for more information.

Eagle River Nature Center. See display ad on page 349.

Return to Milepost A 13.4 Glenn Highway

trail from Girdwood to Eagle River. Visit www.healthyfutures.org for registration information.

The 4.5-mile Eagle River Loop *(see map on page 349)* provides access to Eagle River residential and business areas. Alaska State Parks maintains a day-use area and river access at Mile 1.5 Eagle River Loop (eastbound access only). Boaters are advised that a permit is required for boating the Eagle River on Fort Richardson Military Reservation.

Glenn Highway Log
(continued)

A 12.8 G 176.2 T 315.2 Eagle River bridge.

A 11.6 G 177.4 T 316.4 Hiland Road/ Eagle River Loop overpass (clearance 16' 2" southbound, 16' 4" northbound); north- and southbound exits for Anchorage Municipal Landfill (to west), state correctional center and state campground to east via VFW Road (description follows), and east to Eagle River Loop road.

The 4.5-mile Eagle River Loop/Veterans Memorial Highway provides access to: Hiland Road for **South Fork Valley trailhead** in Chugach State Park (6-mile trail to Eagle and Symphony lakes, spectacular view of surrounding peaks); Alaska State Parks Briggs Bridge day-use area (1.5 miles from exit, eastbound access only); Eagle River Road junction, 2.5 miles from exit (see Eagle River Road log this page); and connects to Old Glenn Highway in downtown Eagle River. 🅰

For **Eagle River Campground** (Chugach State Park), exit east at Eagle River Loop Road and immediately turn north on VFW Road (parallels Glenn Highway). Although a 2018 sign indicated 1.4 miles to campground you actually drive a half-mile and then turn on Hesterberg Road and follow signs 0.6 mile to campground entrance. There are 57 campsites, walk-in tent camping, 4-day camping limit, picnic shelter (may be reserved in advance), dump station, pay phones, flush toilets and drinking water. Camping fee is $20/night. Day-use fee $5. Dump station $5. Operated by concessionaire; phone (907) 746-4644. VFW Road extends 1.5 miles north from Eagle River Loop Road to Eagle River Road.

A 10.6 G 178.4 T 317.4 Truck weigh stations on both sides of highway; pay phones. Trooper Hans Roelle Memorial Weigh Station eastbound only.

The last 9 miles of the Glenn Highway into Anchorage has been designated the **Veterans' Memorial Parkway.**

A 7.5 G 181.5 T 320.5 Exit to Richardson Gate for **Joint Base Elmendorf-Richardson** or **JBER** (pronounced "J-Bear"); description follows. Also southbound exit for Arctic Valley Road (see description at **Milepost A 6.1**).

NOTE: Visitor Control Center at this gate 24/7. Visitor/vehicle passes required to get on base. Visitors must have current vehicle registration or rental car agreement; current driver's license; name, location and phone number of sponsor on base. Other restrictions may apply; check with gate personnel.

JBER is home to Air Force, Army, Alaska Army and Air National Guard, Marine Corps and Navy detachments, Air Force Reserve and U.S. Coast Guard units. **Fort Richardson** was first established as the home of "America's Arctic Warriors," a name originating in 1867 when Brevet Major General

Jefferson C. Davis assumed command of the Military District of Alaska and instituted the motto Arctic Tough and the salute Arctic Warriors. The major units under USARAK (U.S. Army Alaska) are the 1st Stryker Brigade Combat Team. The 4th Brigade Combat Team, the 25th Infantry Division, (based at Fort Wainwright); and the 4th Infantry Brigade Combat Team (Airborne), 25th Infantry Division, at JBER. There is a National Cemetery on JBER, however getting on base is difficult and generally not an opportunity available to the general public. *CAUTION: Watch for moose next 7 miles northbound.*

A 6.1 G 182.9 T 321.9 Northbound only exit to Arctic Valley Road (description follows) and access to JBER's Richardson Gate by driving 1 mile north via frontage road, (Arctic Valley Gate on west side of highway here is an exit-only gate for the base.) Follow Arctic Valley Road 1 mile east for Moose Run Golf Course; 36-holes (Hill Course and Creek Course), driving range, rental carts and clubs, clubhouse. Open to the public. Phone (907) 428-0056 for tee times; www.mooserungolfcourse.com. Season is May–October.

Arctic Valley Road/Ski Bowl Road leads 7 miles from junction with frontage road to Arctic Valley Alpenglow in Chugach State Park; hiking, alpine wildflowers and berry picking in summer, weekend skiing in winter. (The Anchorage Ski Club operates a T-bar and 2 chairlifts.) Pavement ends at Mile 1.6; wide gravel road to end; some steep grades and washboard; posted 25 to 30 mph. Military gate at Mile 1.7 is closed from 10 P.M. to 6 A.M. (Much of the land along the road is part of JBER and there are often training exercises going on in the area.) Best view of the Richardson side of JBER and Anchorage from turnout at Mile 4.2. Emergency phones at Mile 3.7 and 6.3. Trailhead for Arctic to Indian trail (Chugach State Park) at Mile 6.3. Views of Arctic Valley from road are obscured by foliage. Fee parking, toilets and summer hiking at Arctic Valley Alpenglow ski area, Mile 7. Trailhead for Rendezvous Peak Trail: "The hike to the saddle (elev. 3,468 feet) is a relatively gentle climb, and the added push to Rendezvous Peak (elev. 4,050 feet) is well worth the spectacular scenery that awaits." Allow 2 to 5 hours for the 3.5-mile round trip.

A 6 G 183 T 322 Ship Creek.

A 5 G 184 T 323 Actual driving distance between physical mileposts 5 and 6 is only 0.5 mile.

A 4.2 G 184.8 T 323.8 Muldoon Road overpass; exit north for **Alaska Native Heritage Center** (description follows), Tikahtnu Commons Shopping Center (includes Regal Stadium 16 & IMAX theatre) Target, DoD/VA Joint Venture Hospital, U.S. Air Force Hospital (base access required) and Bartlett High School. Entrance (Muldoon Gate) to Joint Base Elmendorf-Richardson (JBER) is on Provider Drive.

Exit south on Muldoon for food, gas/diesel, shopping, lodging and **Centennial Park municipal campground** (description follows). Muldoon connects with the New Seward Highway via Tudor Road. There is a bicycle trail alongside the Glenn Highway from Muldoon Road to Mirror Lake at **Milepost A 23.6**.

Alaska Native Heritage Center is a premier cultural center sharing the rich heritage of Alaska's 11 major cultural groups. Six

Hiking in Arctic Valley's Alpenglow ski area offers spectacular views of the Chugach Mountain Range. (©Serine Reeves)

traditional village sites are along a walking path around a 2-acre lake. Cultural presentations, food and crafts inside the Welcoming House. Free shuttle service from several downtown locations in Anchorage (check website). Open mid-May to mid-September. Admission fee. Phone (907) 330-8000; www.alaskanative.net.

©Courtesy Alaska Native Heritage Center

Alaska Native Heritage Center. See display ad on page 365.

Centennial Campground is open May 25 to Sept. 4. It accommodates large and small RVs with 88 RV/campsites, which includes 21 electric sites, 2 group sites, and 6 pull-through sites. To reach Centennial Campground, take Muldoon Road south to first left onto Boundary, take the next left and follow the signs. For more details, phone (907) 343-6986; www.muni.org/Departments/parks/Pages/Camping.aspx. Private security at night.

Centennial Campground. See display ad on page 358.

A 3.4 G 185.6 T 324.6 Turpin Road (eastbound exit only).

A 3.1 G 185.9 T 324.9 Distance marker eastbound shows Eagle River 10 miles, Palmer 38 miles, Wasilla 39 miles.

A 2.7 G 186.3 T 325.3 Boniface Parkway overpass. Exit south on Boniface Parkway for services (food, gas, shopping) and Russian Jack Springs City Park (entrance on DeBarr). Exit north for JBER Boniface Gate via Vandenberg; 24/7; Visitor Center open 6 A.M. to 9 P.M. weekdays.

A 1.7 G 187.3 T 326.3 Bragaw Street overpass. Exit north on Bragaw for Alaska

Museum of Science & Nature.

A 1.2 G 187.8 T 326.8 Traffic light. Turn north on Mountain View Drive and take first or second right for access for Glenn Square Shopping Center (visible from freeway just east of exit). Glenn Square has several dining options. Major stores include Bass Pro Shops, Petco, Michael's and food outlets.

Turn south on Airport Heights Drive for access to Northway Mall, Carrs Grocery and gas/diesel, Merrill Field and Alaska Regional Hospital.

Slow for speed zone westbound.

A 1 G 188 T 327 Traffic light at Reeve Boulevard intersection; access to Merrill Field.

A 0.6 G 188.4 T 327.4 Traffic light at Concrete and Wilbur intersection.

A 0.4 G 188.6 T 327.6 Welcome to Anchorage sign for westbound travelers.

A 0.2 G 188.8 T 327.8 Glenn Highway forks and becomes 5th Avenue one-way westbound to downtown Anchorage. Coming from downtown Anchorage, 6th Avenue (one-way eastbound) ends here. A Blue Star Memorial Highway marker is located at this 'Y.' The Blue Star Memorial Highway program began in 1945 in cooperation with the National Council of State Garden Clubs as a way to honor the armed forces of the United States. Blue Star Memorials are found on highways in every state, each marker sponsored and maintained by a local garden club.

A 0.1 G 188.9 T 327.9 Traffic light at Karluk Street intersection.

A 0 G 189 T 328 Junction with Ingra Street (1-way northbound) is followed by **junction** with Gambell Street (1-way southbound) for westbound drivers. For the Seward Highway to the Kenai Peninsula (see SEWARD HIGHWAY section), turn south on Gambell Street, which becomes the New Seward Highway. See ANCHORAGE section following for description of city.

ALASKA ROUTE 1

Easttbound: Distance from Anchorage (A) is followed by distance from Glenn–Richardson highway junction (G) at Glennallen and distance from Tok (T). Read log:

Anchorage

(See maps, pages 354, 356 and 364)

Aerial view of downtown Anchorage highrises and south to Northern Lights Boulevard. To the north, mountains are left to right, Mount Foraker, Mount Hunter and Denali. (©Ken Graham/Courtesy Visit Anchorage)

Alaska's largest city, Anchorage is in the heart of the state's southcentral gulf coast. Located on the upper shores of Cook Inlet, at 61° north latitude and 150° west longitude, the Anchorage bowl is on a low-lying alluvial plain bordered by mountains, water and dense forests of spruce, birch and aspen.

Distance in miles	Anchorage	Denali NP	Fairbanks	Homer	Seward	Tok	Valdez
Anchorage		237	362	233	127	328	304
Denali NP	237		125	470	364	565	541
Fairbanks	362	125		595	489	206	366
Homer	233	470	595		180	561	537
Seward	127	364	489	180		455	431
Tok	328	565	206	561	455		254
Valdez	304	541	366	537	431	254	

Cook Inlet's Turnagain Arm and Knik Arm define the broad peninsula that is the city's home, and the rugged Chugach Mountains form a striking eastern backdrop. More than half the state's population lives in Anchorage and the neighboring Matanuska-Susitna borough, which includes Palmer and Wasilla. Anchorage is situated 362 miles south of Fairbanks via the Parks Highway; 328 miles from Tok via the Glenn Highway/Tok Cutoff; 304 miles from Valdez, southern terminus of the trans-Alaska pipeline, via the Glenn and Richardson highways; 2,459 driving miles via the West Access Route, Alaska Highway and Glenn Highway/Tok Cutoff from Seattle; 1,644 nautical miles, and approximately 3–3.5 hours flying time from Seattle. Prior to the opening of Russia's Far East to air traffic and refueling, Anchorage was named the "Air Crossroads of the World," and today is still a major air logistics center and cargo carrier for Asia, Europe and North America. In terms of nonstop air mileages, Anchorage is the following distance from each of these cities: Amsterdam, 4,475; Chicago, 2,839; Copenhagen, 4,313; Hamburg, 4,430; Honolulu, 2,780; London, 4,487; Paris, 4,683; San Francisco, 2,015; Seattle, 1,445; Tokyo, 3,460.

Population: 297,483 (Alaska Dept. of Labor). **Emergency Services:** Dial 911.

Anchorage Police Department (APD) Headquarters, 4501 Elmore Rd.; main phone (907) 786-8900. **Anchorage Emergency Conditions Line**, recording, phone (907) 343-4701. **Alaska State Troopers, Dept. of Public Safety**, 5700 E. Tudor Rd., main phone (907) 269-5511. **U.S. Coast Guard**, Sector Anchorage Command Center, phone (907) 428-4100. **Hospitals:** Alaska Regional Hospital, phone (907) 276-1131; Alaska Native Medical Center, phone (907) 563-2662; Providence Alaska Medical Center, (907) 562-2211; Joint Base Elmendorf-Richardson Medical Care (907) 580-2778. **Suicide and Crisis and Psych Intervention**, (907) 563-3200. **Rape and Assault**, (907) 276-7273. **Child Abuse**, 1-800-478-4444. **Abused Women's Aid in Crisis**, (907) 272-0100. **Pet Emergency**, (907) 519-6588. **Road Conditions**, statewide, phone 511, outside Alaska 1-866-282-7577; or visit 511.alaska.gov.

Visitor Information: Visit Anchorage operates 2 information centers at the corner of 4th Avenue and F Street: The Log Cabin Visitor Information Center, which fronts 4th Avenue, and directly behind it—and part of the old City Hall building—a modern walk-in Visitor Information Center. Both offer free brochures and maps. The centers are open daily, year-round (except for major holidays); phone (907) 257-2363. Hours mid-May to mid-September are 8 A.M. to 7 P.M.; from mid-September to mid-May, hours are 9 A.M. to 4 P.M.

A third visitor information center is located in the South Terminal of Ted Stevens Anchorage International Airport. For current and upcoming events, things to do and other travel planning help, and to order a free guide to Anchorage, visit www.anchorage.net.

The **Anchorage Alaska Public Lands Information Center (AAPLIC)**, 605 W. 4th Ave., Suite 105 in the historic Old Federal Building, has extensive displays and information on outdoor recreation lands in Alaska *(see detailed description on page 366)*. NOTE: You will need to go through security for entrance to the Old Federal Building. AAPLIC phone is (907) 644-3678. www.alaskacenters.gov/anchorage.cfm.

The **Department of Natural Resources Public Information Center**, 550 W. 7th Ave., Ste. 1260, is open weekdays from 10 A.M. to 5 P.M. with information on state parks and recreational mining. Phone (907) 269-8400; website: www.dnr.alaska.gov/commis/pic.

Other contacts for information about the city include the Municipality of Anchorage at www.muni.org, Anchorage Downtown Partnership at www.anchoragedowntown.org, or the Anchorage Chamber of Commerce at anchoragechamber.org.

Elevation: Sea level. **Climate:** Anchorage's climate resembles the Rocky Mountain area, tempered by proximity to the Pacific Ocean. Shielded from excess ocean moisture by the Kenai Mountains to the south,

the city has an annual average of only 15.9 inches of precipitation. Winter snowfall averages about 74.5 inches per year, with snow from October to April. Winter of 2014–15 broke the record low at 25.1 inches, while 2011–12 broke the record high, at 134.5 inches of snow.

Anchorage is in a transition zone between the moderating influence of the Pacific and the extreme temperatures of Interior Alaska. The average temperature in January (coldest month) is 14°F; in July (warmest month), 58°F. A record 41 days of 70°F temperatures or higher was set in 2004. The record high was 85°F in June 1969. The record low was -34°F in February 1975.

The 100–120 day growing season extends from late May to early September. Anchorage has a daily maximum of 19 hours, 22 minutes of daylight in summer (functional daylight is 22 hours), and a minimum of 5 hours, 28 minutes in winter (functional daylight of almost 8 hours).

Radio: AM stations: KTZN 550 (The Zone, Sports Radio); KHAR 590 (Sports); KENI 650 (News, Talk, Sports); KBYR 700 (News, Talk, Sports); KFQD 750 (News, Talk); KUDO 1080 (Business, News, Talk). FM stations: KNIK 87.7 (The Breeze); KRUA 88.1 (The Edge, UAA); KAKL 88.5 (KLOV Christian Radio); KATB 89.3 (Christian Radio); KNBA 90.3 (Public Radio, Alaska Native owned); KSKA 91.1 (National Public Radio); KAFC 93.7 (Christian Radio); KFAT 92.9 (Hip-hop and R&B); KZND 94.7 (Rock); KEAG 97.3 (KOOL FM, Oldies); KLEF 98.1 (Classical Music); KYMG 98.9 (Magic, Adult Contemporary); KBFX 100.5 (The Fox, Pure Rock); KGOT 101.3 (The Mix, 80s, 90s, Top

40); KDBZ 102.1 (The Buzz, Easy Listening); KMXS 103.1 (Contemporary); KBRJ 104.1 (KBEAR, Country Favorites); KMVN 105.7 (Adult Contemporary); KWHL 106.5 (Modern Rock); KASH 107.5 (New Country). **Television:** Broadcast channels are Channel 2 KTUU (NBC); Channel 4 KTBY (Fox); Channel 5 KYES (Anchorage's only locally owned TV station, a UPN affiliate); Channel 7 KAKM (PBS); Channel 11 KTVA (CBS); and Channel 13 KYUR (ABC). Cable channels available by satellite and pay cable television service.

Newspapers: *Anchorage Daily News* (Sunday–Friday); *Alaska Journal of Commerce* (weekly); *Anchorage Press* (weekly); *Arctic Warrior* (weekly); *Alaska Star* (weekly).

Private Aircraft: Anchorage airports provide facilities and services to accommodate all types of aircraft. Consult *Supplement Alaska*, and related aviation guides and charts for Ted Stevens Anchorage International, Merrill Field and Lake Hood seaplane and airstrip.

Description

Covering 1,961 square miles (1,697 square miles of land, 264 of water), Anchorage lies between the Chugach Mountains on the east and Knik Arm of Cook Inlet on the west. The surrounding mountain ranges— the Chugach, the Kenais, the Talkeetnas, the icy peaks of the Tordrillo Mountains across Cook Inlet, the dramatic peaks of the Alaska Range (with Denali visible on the northern horizon, weather permitting) and the Aleutian Range surround the city in scenic splendor. Perched within the edge of Alaska's vast, varied expanse of forests, mountains,

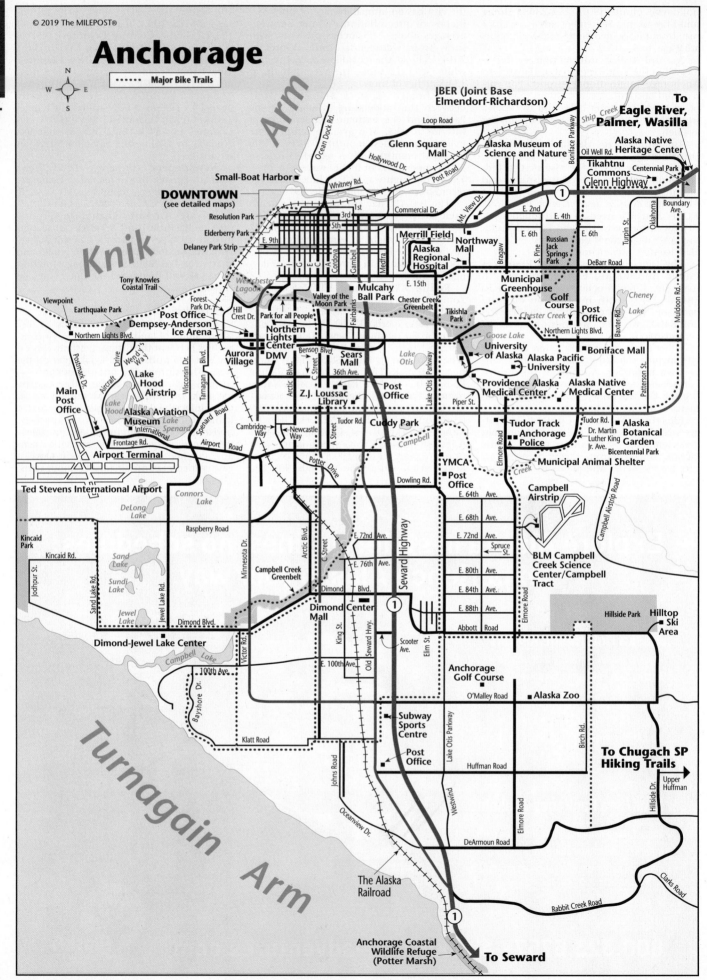

Anchorage

· · · · · Major Bike Trails

N W E S

© 2019 The MILEPOST®

Knik Arm

Turnagain Arm

JBER (Joint Base Elmendorf-Richardson)

To Eagle River, Palmer, Wasilla

Ship Creek

Loop Road

Glenn Square Mall

Hollywood Dr.

Alaska Museum of Science and Nature

Alaska Native Heritage Center

Ocean Dock Rd.

Post Road

Oil Well Rd.

Boniface Parkway

Tikahtnu Commons

Centennial Park

Glenn Highway (1)

Whitney Rd.

Small-Boat Harbor

DOWNTOWN (see detailed maps)

1st

Commercial Dr.

E. 2nd

E. 4th

Boundary Ave.

Resolution Park

3rd

5th

Mt. View Dr.

E. 6th

Russian Jack Springs Park

E. 6th

Turpin St.

Oklahoma

Elderberry Park

Delaney Park Strip

E. 9th

Cordova

Gambell

Medfra

Merrill Field

Northway Mall

Bragaw

S. Pine

DeBarr Road

Muldoon Rd.

Alaska Regional Hospital

E. 15th

Municipal Greenhouse

Cheney Lake

Westchester Lagoon

Mulcahy Ball Park

Chester Creek Greenbelt

Golf Course

Post Office

Baxter Rd.

Tony Knowles Coastal Trail

Viewpoint

Earthquake Park

Forest Park Dr.

Post Office

Dempsey-Anderson Ice Arena

Hill Crest Dr.

Park for all People

Valley of the Moon Park

Tikishla Park

Chester Creek

Goose Lake

University of Alaska

Alaska Pacific University

Boniface Mall

Patterson St.

Northern Lights Blvd.

Northern Lights Center DMV

Benson Blvd.

Fairbanks

Lake Otis

Lake Otis Parkway

Providence Alaska Medical Center

Alaska Native Medical Center

Northern Lights Blvd.

Aircraft Drive

Wisconsin Dr.

Aurora Village

C Street

Sears Mall

36th Ave.

Post Office

Piper St.

Main Post Office

Lake Hood Airstrip

Alaska Aviation Museum

Lake Hood

Lake Spenard

Tarnagan Blvd.

Arctic Blvd.

Z.J. Loussac Library

Tudor Rd.

Cuddy Park

Tudor Track

Anchorage Police

Tudor Rd.

Dr. Martin Luther King Jr. Ave.

Alaska Botanical Garden

Postmark Dr.

Wendy's Way

Spenard Road

Cambridge Way

Newcastle Way

A Street

Campbell Creek

Bicentennial Park

Elmore Road

International

Frontage Rd.

Airport Road

Potter Drive

YMCA Post Office

Municipal Animal Shelter

Airport Terminal

Ted Stevens International Airport

Connors Lake

Dowling Rd.

E. 64th Ave.

Campbell Airstrip

Campbell Airstrip Road

DeLong Lake

E. 68th Ave.

Kincaid Park

Kincaid Rd.

Raspberry Road

Minnesota Dr.

Arctic Blvd.

C Street

E. 72nd Ave.

E. 72nd Ave.

Spruce St.

BLM Campbell Creek Science Center/Campbell Tract

Jodhpur St.

Sand Lake Rd.

Sand Lake

Sundi Lake

E. 76th Ave.

E. 80th Ave.

Jewel Lake Rd.

Jewel Lake

Campbell Creek Greenbelt

Dimond Blvd.

E. 84th Ave.

Seward Highway

E. 88th Ave.

Hillside Park

Hilltop Ski Area

Dimond-Jewel Lake Center

Dimond Blvd.

Victor Rd.

Dimond Center Mall

King St.

Abbott Road

Elmore Road

Campbell Lake

Bayshore Dr.

100th Ave.

E. 100th Ave.

Old Seward Hwy.

Scooter Ave.

Elim St.

Anchorage Golf Course

Hillside Dr.

Klatt Road

Subway Sports Centre

Post Office

Johns Road

Oceanview Dr.

Lake Otis Parkway

O'Malley Road

Alaska Zoo

Birch Rd.

To Chugach SP Hiking Trails

Upper Huffman

Huffman Road

Westwind

Elmore Road

Clarks Road

The Alaska Railroad

DeArmoun Road

Rabbit Creek Road

(1)

Anchorage Coastal Wildlife Refuge (Potter Marsh)

To Seward

rivers, taiga and tundra, the city offers abundant wilderness experiences in every direction.

Anchorage began as an anchorage on Ship Creek in 1915, staging ground for construction of a railroad to the Interior. Today, it is Alaska's largest city and its railroad and port remain crucial to the transportation of goods and resources. Some 90 percent of the merchandise goods for 85 percent of Alaska's population come through the Port of Anchorage.

Earthquakes are a fact of life in Alaska, where they occur every 15 minutes somewhere in the state. Most go undetected by residents, with the exception of the 1964 Good Friday Earthquake, magnitude 9.2, which caused tremendous damage to Anchorage, and the Point Mackenzie Earthquake, on Nov. 30, 2018, a magnitude 7.0 earthquake, which caused considerable damage in Anchorage, Eagle River and the Mat-Su Valley.

Anchorage was voted one of the "10 Happiest Cities in America" by *National Geographic*, October 2017, and "Best City for Making the Most of Summer" by *Outside Magazine*, July 2017. Anchorage is also a 5-time winner in the "100 Best Communities for Young People," based on its community programs for youth, focus on education and youth community involvement.

Anchorage's extensive award-winning trail system is one of the best in the country, encompassing 135 miles (217 km) of paved trails and 300 miles (482 km) of unpaved and wilderness trails, offering endless opportunities for activities such as running, walking, rollerblading, biking, hiking, horseback

There is a population of nearly 250 black bears within the Anchorage city limits.
(©Donna Dewhurst)

riding, roller-skiing, skiing and skijoring. *Bicycling Magazine* noted that "Anchorage's trail system is one of the best in the U.S."

Within the city limits of Anchorage there are an estimated 1,500 moose, nearly 250 black bears and almost 60 brown bears. With all that Anchorage has to offer, and its wild attractions, it is no wonder that the city brand is Big Wild Life, encompassing the components of work, life and play.

Anchorage is noted for the profusion of flowers and hanging baskets that decorate homes and businesses during summer months: parks, street medians and lampposts are vibrantly colored with millions of flower blossoms, dubbing it the City of Flowers. In winter, Anchorage is transformed into the City of Lights. Residents are encouraged to follow the lead of municipal agencies in displaying strings of miniature white lights on homes, trees and office buildings to brighten the entire city.

Anchorage City Center

© 2019 The MILEPOST®

Whitney Rd.

Ship Creek

Post Road

Old Federal Building (Alaska Public Lands Info Center)

Ship Creek Salmon Viewing

E. Ship Creek Ave.

Alaska Railroad Depot

The Alaska Railroad

Knik Arm

Nesbett Courthouse

W. 1st
E. 1st
E. 2nd

W. 2nd

Christensen Dr.

Oscar Anderson House

Resolution Park

W. 3rd
E. 2nd Ct.
E. 3rd

Sunshine Plaza
4th Avenue Market

Pioneer Schoolhouse

E. 4th

Mile 0 Glenn Highway

Elderberry Park

State Court Bldg.

Log Cabin Visitor Center

W. 4th
Fire
A Street

W. 5th
Old City Hall
Egan Center
E. 5th

5th Ave. Mall
Alaska Center for the Performing Arts
W. 6th
E. 6th

Denali St.
Eagle St.

Downtown Transit Center
City Hall
W. 7th
Anchorage Museum
E. 7th

Hostel
W. 8th
Dena'ina Convention Center
Federal Bldg.
City Cemetery
E. 8th

O St.

Gambell St.

E. 9th

W. 9th
Delaney Park Strip

W. 10th
Barrow St.
Cordova St.
Denali St.
Eagle St.
Fairbanks St.
E. 10th

P Street
N Street
M Street
L Street
K Street
I Street
H Street
G Street
F Street
E Street
D Street
C Street

W. 11th
E. 11th
Hyder St.
Ingra St.
Juneau St.
Karluk St.
Latouche St.
Medfra St.
Nelchina St.
Orca St.

W. 12th
E. 12th

W. 13th
W. 14th
B Street
A Street
E. 13th

Inlet Pl.
W. 15th
E. 14th
Gambell St.

Virginia Ct.
L Street
Coffey Ln.
W. 16th
W. 15th Ter.
Avenues West
Avenues East
E. 15th Ter.
E. 15th

George M. Sullivan Sports Arena
Begin/End New Seward Highway
McHugh Ln.

E. 16th
Mulcahy Ball Park
Ben Boeke Arena
E. 16th Ter.

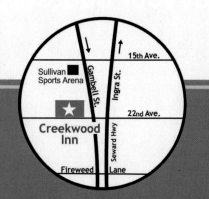

Two premier convention facilities (www.anchorageconventioncenters.com) form the downtown Anchorage convention district: The William A. Egan Civic & Convention Center on 5th Avenue, and the Dena'ina Civic and Convention Center, which occupies an entire city block on 7th Avenue, between F and G streets. The Dena'ina, named after the Athabascan people who first populated southcentral Alaska, features works of art from local and national artists, all incorporating the relationship between Alaska's indigenous peoples and the land. At

The Alaska Center for the Performing Arts ("the PAC") hosts Broadway musicals and local theater, concerts, the symphony, opera and other events. (©Frank Flavin/Courtesy Visit Anchorage)

200,000-square-feet, Dena'ina is the largest civic center in Alaska.

Ice-free sidewalks and covered walkways connect the 2 convention centers and a third public building—the Alaska Center for the Performing Arts. The PAC is a 176,000-square-foot structure with 4 theaters that host the city's symphony, opera, an extensive concert schedule and other events. The PAC (www.myalaskacenter.com) is located on beautiful Town Square Park between 5th and 6th avenues.

The Anchorage Museum on C Street, between 6th and 7th avenues, is another important public building that is both a major visitor attraction and an integral part of the city's cultural life. *See page 366 in "Downtown Anchorage" section for detailed information on the museum.*

Remember: You are in bear and moose country! Anchorage shares its streets, yards, greenbelts and trails with these wild animals, and it is not uncommon to see either a bear or moose crossing the road or foraging along a trail. Moose are particularly agitated by dogs. The ADF&G advises: "Give moose an extremely wide berth if you have a dog with you and do not let your dog chase a moose."

Lodging & Services

There are more than 8,000 motel and hotel rooms in the Anchorage area, with prices for a double room ranging from $50 to $300 and up. Reservations are a must. Bed-and-breakfast accommodations are also available in more than 250 private residences; prices range from about $60–$200.

Comfortable, low-cost hostel accommodations are in multiple locations in downtown and in midtown.

Camping

Anchorage has several private campgrounds: **Anchorage Ship Creek RV Park**, near downtown; **Creekwood Inn RV Park**, on New Seward Highway in midtown Anchorage; and **Golden Nugget RV Park** on Debarr Road in East Anchorage, across from the Debarr Road Costco. *(See their advertise-*

ments, referenced under "Campgrounds" on this page, for more details).

Anchorage has one public campground: **Centennial Campground**, open late-May to early September, and well suited for large RVs. It is operated by the Municipality of Anchorage and has 88 campsites, 22 RV-only sites with electric ($35/night) and 66 campsites without electricity ($25/night), 2 group sites and 6 drive-through sites; maximum 14 day stay.

Chugach State Park campgrounds located near Anchorage on the Glenn Highway are Eagle River at **Milepost A 11.6** and Eklutna Lake, access via Eklutna Lake Road from **Milepost A 26.1.**

Ted Stevens International Airport sees 5 million passengers each year and is a major air logistics center and cargo carrier for Asia, Europe and North America. (©Donna Dewhurst)

Transportation

Air: Twelve international and domestic air carriers and several intra-state airlines serve Ted Stevens Anchorage International Airport, located west of Minnesota Drive (take L Street south from downtown and follow signs). More than 240 flights arrive daily, with over 5 million passengers using the airport each year. The rental car center at the airport makes renting and returning a car safe, easy and warm.

Cruise Ship: The primary cruise ship ports are in Seward and Whittier with few traveling to dock in Anchorage (port depth is only 35'). From Seward and Whittier, passengers travel to Anchorage either by the Alaska Railroad or by motorcoach. See "Cruising" in the TRAVEL PLANNING section.

Ferry: The nearest ferry port to Anchorage is Whittier, on Prince William Sound, served by the Alaska Marine Highway System with service to Cordova and Valdez. Whittier is accessible from Anchorage via the Seward Highway and Whittier Access Road (see SEWARD HIGHWAY section). See "Ferry Travel" in the TRAVEL PLANNING section.

Railroad: The Alaska Railroad offers daily passenger service aboard 3 trains during the summer. Service includes daily round-trip service between Anchorage, Girdwood and Seward; northbound service to Wasilla, Talkeetna, Denali National Park and Fairbanks; and service from Anchorage, Girdwood, and Portage to Whittier, where passengers can connect to Prince William Sound cruises, Spencer Glacier Whistle Stop and scenic Grandview Valley. Reduced service in winter, when service between Anchorage and Fairbanks is available on weekends and select mid-week dates. Special event trains year-round; check website. Phone toll free 1-800-544-0552 or (907) 265-2494; email reservations@akrr.com; www.AlaskaRailroad.

com. The Alaska Railroad Depot is located on First Avenue, within easy walking distance of downtown.

Bus: Local service via People Mover, serving most of the Anchorage bowl from Peters Creek to Oceanview. Passes, schedules and tokens available at the Downtown Transit Center at 6th Avenue and H Street, ZJ Loussac Library, Muldoon Library and Chugiak-Eagle River Library in Eagle River. For bus route information, phone the RideLine at (907) 343-6543, or visit www.peoplemover.org.

For more options in bus service to other communities, see "Bus Lines" in the TRAVEL PLANNING section.

Anchorage Trolley Tours, (907) 276-5603, offers sightseeing service that departs from the Log Cabin Visitor Center.

Additional businesses offer shuttle services from downtown to their locations: Alaska Native Heritage Center, the Ulu Factory, and the Alaska Zoo. There is also a shuttle to Flattop trail hiking. (See information on each of these attractions for details regarding their shuttle services.)

The Bear Square, (907) 277-4545, offers Segway tours of downtown Anchorage and Lake Hood.

Taxi: Alaska Yellow Cab, (907) 222-2222; Anchorage Checker Cab, (907) 644-4444. Uber and Lyft are available via their apps.

Car and Camper Rentals: There are dozens of car rental agencies located at the airport and downtown, as well as several RV rental agencies (see advertisements this section).

Parking (cars and RVs): Diamond Parking Service (www.diamondparking.com) manages 33 surface lots in Anchorage with daily and monthly parking; fees average $5 for 0-2 hours. EasyPark (Anchorage Community Development Authority) manages all on-street metered parking for downtown Anchorage as well as more than a dozen lots and garages. For location and rates for parking, visit www.easyparkalaska.com. EasyPark office located at 440 B St.; phone (907) 276-PARK (7275). After Hours or Security (907) 297-4471; email info@easypark alaska.com.

Highway: Anchorage can be reached via the Glenn Highway and the Seward Highway. See GLENN HIGHWAY and SEWARD HIGHWAY sections for details.

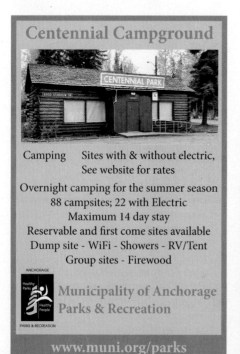

The Z.J. Loussac Library on Denali Street at 36th Avenue, opened in 1986. It is adjacent the popular Cuddy Family Park. (©Kris Valencia, staff)

Attractions

(See Downtown section beginning on page 364 for details on such attractions as the Anchorage Museum, Alaska Center for Performing Arts, etc.)

Enjoy the Parks. Anchorage parks are rich in the range of activities they offer, with something for everyone's taste, from small "pocket parks" perfect for relaxing or picnicking to vast tracts set aside for skiing,

hiking and bicycling. According to the Parks & Recreation website (www.muni.org/departments/parks/pages/default.aspx) they have "10,946 acres of municipal parkland; 223 parks with 82 playgrounds; 250 miles of trails and greenbelts linking neighborhoods with surrounding natural open spaces and wildlife habitat (135 miles of paved trails); 110 athletic fields; 5 pools; and 11 recreation facilities." For information on park facilities and group reservations to use municipal park picnic facilities, phone (907) 343-4355 or email parks@muni.org.

Parks & Recreation also offers several facilities to rent for indoor functions: meetings, parties, weddings, receptions, seminars and special events. These include Lidia Selkregg Chalet at Russian Jack Springs Park and Kincaid Outdoor Center in Kincaid Park.

A few of Anchorage's parks and trails are listed below:

Kincaid Park: It is not unusual to run into a moose or see a bear at 1,500-acre Kincaid Park. Located southwest of the airport, this park's rugged trails are popular in summer with mountain bikers, runners and disc golfers. In winter, the trails are groomed for cross-country skiers. To reach the Kincaid Outdoor Center, follow Raspberry Road west from Minnesota Drive to the park entrance. The park road winds uphill (past trailheads) to end at a large parking area in front of the Center, which houses an information desk, tables, restrooms and vending machines. The Center has limited hours; park gates lock at 10 P.M. daily. Kincaid is also accessible via the Tony Knowles Coastal Trail, which follows the shoreline from West 2nd Avenue, downtown, 11 miles to the Kincaid Outdoor Center.

Russian Jack Springs: One of the city's oldest parks, with land transferred from the Bureau of Land Management in 1948, Russian Jack Springs has a lot to offer. Facilities at the park include Selkregg Chalet, the Mann Leiser Memorial Greenhouse within the Municipal Greenhouse Complex, Cartee and RJS Softball Complexes, soccer fields, the Girl Scouts Day Camp, tennis courts, picnic/playground areas, the 9-hole Russian Jack Springs golf course, disc golf and 9 miles of bike/ski trails.

Valley of the Moon Park: A great park for parents looking for a playground to keep their children entertained, Valley of the Moon Park is located on Arctic Boulevard/E Street in the Chester Creek Greenbelt. This park has parking, restrooms, a large grassy area and picnic tables.

Earthquake Park: Set aside to commemorate the 1964 Good Friday Earthquake, Earthquake Park offers views as well as interpretive displays about the quake (evidence of the 9.2 earthquake has been obscured over time). A paved path leads from the parking lot to the earthquake exhibit and Knik Arm overlook. From the New Seward Highway, drive west (toward the water) on Northern Lights Boulevard for 3.5 miles to reach Earthquake Park.

Point Woronzof: The best park views of Cook Inlet (Knik Arm) and the Alaska Range are at Point Woronzof. Drive west on Northern Lights Boulevard, which becomes Point Woronzof Road at Postmark Drive. (Postmark Drive leads one mile south to Anchorage post office and airport.) A viewpoint at this intersection offers parking and view of downtown Anchorage, Cook Inlet, Denali and Mount Foraker (on clear days). Follow Point Woronzof Road 1 mile

to Point Woronzof, a favorite spot to watch the sunset, with fine views of the inlet and mountains. Point Woronzof can also be reached via the Tony Knowles Coastal Trail.

Off Leash Dog Parks. Designated areas of University Lake Park, Far North Bicentennial Park (North Gasline Trail), Russian Jack Park, Connors Bog, Arctic Benson Park in Midtown and South Anchorage Sports Park are off-leash dog parks. Areas are marked, and dog owners may let their dogs play unleashed, as long as Parks & Recreation and Animal Control regulations are followed. For information and maps, visit www.muni.org/Departments/parks/Pages/DogParks.aspx.

Sea Services Veterans Memorial Park, at the mouth of Ship Creek, is a good place to see the Anchorage waterfront, with its huge cargo cranes off-loading supplies from container ships. The park is dedicated to veterans of the Navy, Marine Corps, Coast Guard and Merchant Marine. The monument consists of a huge anchor and chain weighing 22,500 pounds upon a raised mound. The park also offers good whale watching when belugas are in the inlet. From downtown, take E Street and West 2nd down the hill to merge with North C Street. Continue across the second set of railroad tracks and turn left. The access road follows Ship Creek out to the small-boat dry dock harbor and the park.

Tour Anchorage by Bicycle or On Foot: The municipality has an impressive and ever-expanding pedestrian and bike trail system (135 miles of paved trails, many lit for winter use). The 11-mile-long **Tony Knowles Coastal Trail** begins downtown, runs through Earthquake Park, then wraps around the airport (it is not uncommon to encounter moose along this route). The Tony Knowles trail ends at Kincaid Park, with its roller-coaster terrain that serves cross-country skiers in winter and mountain bikers in summer. Tony Knowles Coastal Trail also connects with the **Ship Creek Trail,** which parallels Ship Creek from North C Street 2.5-miles east. The eastern end of the trail is at the William Jack Hernandez Sport Fish Hatchery is at the intersection of Reeve Boulevard and North Post Road.

For cyclists and joggers looking for a pleasant ride or run through the trees, the **Lanie Fleischer Chester Creek Trail** fills the bill. The 4-mile trail stretches from Westchester Lagoon, at 15th Avenue and U Street, to Goose Lake, a favorite summer swimming beach (accessible from UAA Drive). Chester Creek trail is accessible from all of the parks along its length, including Tikishla (in the Airport Heights area), Valley of the Moon Park (Arctic Boulevard/E Street) and Westchester Lagoon, where it junctions with the Coastal Bike Trail.

Campbell Creek Greenbelt paved trail system begins at Dimond Boulevard, between Minnesota Drive and Jewel Lake Road, and follows Campbell Creek northeast to Elmore Road. Taku Lake/Campbell Park, located off King Street, offers fishing access (stocked) and picnic tables. Peter Roberts of Downtown Bicycle Rental says that bicyclists can combine the Coastal Trail, Ship Creek, Chester Creek and Campbell Creek greenbelt trails, creating a 36-mile circuit with "very little road riding." Their website's Trails/Routes drop-down menu at www.alaska-bike-rentals.com/Home.aspx has information on the city's major bike trails as well as Kincaid Park.

Chugach State Park also offers a multi-tude of options for bicyclists (and even more for hikers)—from leisurely rides on easy gravel roads to gnarly mountainside single track. A few of the most popular area bike trails include Bird to Gird, a paved 7-mile trail that parallels the Seward Highway along Turnagain Arm; Eklutna Lakeside Trail, a 13-mile dirt trail along Eklutna Lake; and the Powerline Trail, an 11-mile dirt trail in Chugach State Park. Chugach Parks trail maps are available at the Alaska Anchorage Public Lands Information Center at 605 W. 4th Ave., Ste. 105.

Free Anchorage bike maps are available at the Visit Anchorage's Visitor Information Center on 4th Avenue and F Street and at Downtown Bicycle Rental (W. 4th Avenue and C Street). See also www.trailsofanch orage.com/Maps/TrailWatchMap.pdf.

The Tour of Anchorage bike race takes place in summer. For more information on this event and other local bike races, visit www.arcticbike.org, the website for the non-profit Arctic Bicycle Club, which promotes bicycling safety, education and sporting activities in Anchorage.

Take in a Free Film. The Alaska Anchorage Public Lands Information Center, located in the historic Old Federal Building on 4th Avenue and F Street, offers a schedule of films about Alaska in their theater. Phone (907) 644-3678 or visit www.alaskacenters.gov/anchorage.cfm.

Additional Alaska film options (for fee) include downtown's Alaska Experience Theatre for films about Alaska's 1964 Earth-

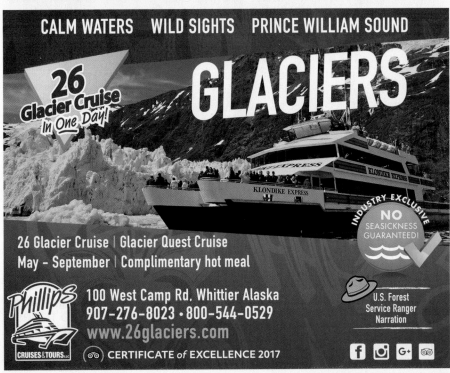

quake and the Alaska Center for Performing Arts for a film on the Aurora Borealis. In midtown, explore the University of Alaska Anchorage Planetarium. Travel from outside the galaxy to inside a molecule, and many exotic places in between via the Planetarium, live shows and full-dome films. Also at this site, the Alaska-filmed show "River of Bears" which brings you (seemingly) face-to-face with brown bears in Alaska's McNeil River State Game Sanctuary. Learn more at uaa.alaska.edu/planetarium.

Visit the Alaska Native Heritage Center. Located just 10 minutes east of downtown, the Heritage Center allows visitors the opportunity to experience a sample of Alaska's Native cultures in one facility. Located on 26 wooded acres on Heritage Center Drive (take the North Muldoon Road exit off the Glenn Highway), the center includes the 26,000-square-foot Welcome House, 6 traditional village settings, a 2-acre lake and walking trails.

Many of the programs and exhibits celebrating Alaska Native culture take place indoors in the Welcome House. Visitors experience Alaska Native culture first-hand through engaging storytelling, authentic Native song and dance, artist demonstrations and interactive Native Games demonstrations in the Gathering Place. A 95-seat theater offers a film introduction to Native history and culture. Heritage Gifts provides a wonderful shopping opportunity for Native arts and crafts. An outdoor walk around Tiulana Lake takes visitors to 6 different regions, each representing one of Alaska's 6 Native cultures: Athabascan, Yupik/Cupik, Inupiaq, Unangax, Alutiiq and Tlingit/Haida/Eyak/Tsimshian. Demonstrations of traditional techniques for fishing, hunting and constructing dwellings, take place in summer.

Heritage Center hours are from 9 A.M. to 5 P.M. daily mid-May through early September. Summer rates: adults, $24.95; children (7–16), $16.95; military/seniors (62 or older), $21.15; also family admission rates. Ask for Alaska resident rates. Only open for special events in winter (October–April), reduced rates. Phone (907) 330-8000; toll free 1-800-315-6608; www.alaskanative.net.

The Alaska Culture Pass (alaskaculturepass.net) gives you admission to the Alaska Native Heritage Center and the Anchorage Museum for $32. This includes shuttle service between the two locations. Group rates available for 20 or more people. For facility rental availability, call (907) 330-8013.

Running events: Anchorage also has its share of 5Ks, 10Ks, marathons and triathlons. The Heart Run, held April 20, 2019, kicks off the summer running season. Two popular women's runs are the Women's Gold Nugget Triathlon in mid-May and the Alaska Run for Women in June. Many Anchorage residents celebrate Summer Solstice by running in the Mayor's Marathon, half-marathon or 5-miler (June 22, 2019). The Anchorage RunFest, which features a children's run, 5K race, half and full marathons as well as a team marathon relay, takes place Aug. 17–18, 2019.

Information on running events can be found at www.anchoragerunningclub.org. Anchorage Parks & Recreation's complete schedule of city and statewide running events is at www.muni.org/Departments/parks/Pages/RunnersCalendar.aspx.

Watch Small Planes. Drive out to Merrill Field, Lake Hood or Lake Spenard for an afternoon of airplane watching.

While at Merrill Field, named for early Alaska aviator, Russell Hyde Merrill, you can see more than 1,100 takeoffs and landings on a summer day. Follow 15th Avenue East to light at Lake Otis Parkway, and turn north on Merrill Field Drive. This route takes you under the approach to one of the runways. Merrill Field is also accessible off the Glenn Highway and from Airport Heights Drive (across from Northway Mall). For more information, visit www.muni.org/departments/merrill_field/pages/default.aspx.

Lake Hood is the world's largest and busiest seaplane base, with approximately 500 takeoffs and landings on a peak summer day. Easy access to lakes Hood and Spenard off International Airport Road: Heading west from Minnesota, turn right on Spenard then left on Aviation Drive, which follows the shore of Lake Spenard and dead-ends at the Dept. of Transportation parking lot. From here you are looking at the channel connecting lakes Hood and Spenard, which is used by floatplanes shuttling between the 2 lakes or for take-offs and landings. From the Department of Transportation building, get back onto International Airport Road going west (towards the airport) then exit for the Aviation Museum on Lake Hood (see description following).

Alaska Aviation Museum, 4721 Aircraft Dr., is located on the south shore of Lake Hood and a short walk or shuttle bus ride to or from Ted Stevens International Airport. The museum features historic Alaskan aircraft and bush pilot exhibits, military aircraft and exhibits, restoration hangar, flight simulator, WWII theater and gift store. Enjoy a panoramic view of Lake Hood, the busiest seaplane base in the world from the old Merrill Field Tower cab. Summer hours are 10 A.M. to 6 P.M. daily beginning April 15. Winter hours are Oct. 1–April 14, 10 A.M. to 5 P.M. Tuesday–Saturday, Sunday noon–5 P.M.; closed Mondays. Phone (907) 248-5325. Admission: Adults $15, Seniors 65+ and Military, $12 children 5 to 12 $8, under 5 free. Group and tour rates available. Wheelchair accessible. Website: www.alaskaairmuseum.org; phone (907) 248-5325.

The Alaska Botanical Garden is located at 4601 Campbell Airstrip Rd. off Tudor Road in East Anchorage. As a living museum, the Alaska Botanical Garden showcases native Alaska plants and hardy perennials (standouts include Himalayan blue poppies and a Gold Medal peony collection), as well as wildflowers, herbs and alpine plants. Explore the half-mile paved loop and seven display gardens on your own with a self-guided trail map, or request a guided tour (by appointment only June–August, please call ahead).

A half-mile paved loop trail with benches along the way provides easy walking through the boreal spruce and birch forest to visit the various themed gardens. A power scooter is available for use on the main paved trail. This is an outdoor facility, please dress accordingly. Signs identify many of the plants in our permanent collection. There is a retail nursery and gift shop near the garden entrance. A 2 mile nature trail offers views of Campbell Creek and the Chugach Mountains.

The admission fee can be paid by cash or credit card. Parking is free. Picnics are allowed in the plaza only. Dog walking is only permitted along the outside of the

perimeter fence. Please use caution, you are in bear and moose country.

Popular special events include the Annual Plant Sale in May, Beer Garden in July, Wine in the Woods in August, and Holiday Lights in December. Call or go to website for more information on admission rates and hours, special events, and guided tours: www.alaskabg.org, phone (907) 770-3692; email garden@alaskabg.org; and on facebook.

BLM's Campbell Tract Trails and Campbell Creek Science Center. The 730-acre Campbell Tract in East Anchorage provides more than 12 miles of non-motorized trails that are very popular for walking, biking, dog walking, dog mushing, cross-country skiing, snowshoeing and horseback riding. Campbell Tract abuts Far North Bicentennial Park, with several trails crossing from BLM land on to the parkland. The Campbell Tract trail system is managed by the Bureau of Land Management (BLM), as is the Campbell Creek Science Center, which is located off Elmore Road at 5600 Science Center Dr. The gate at the beginning of Science Center Drive closes at 6 P.M. and opens at 7 A.M. on weekdays; it remains closed throughout the weekend. Gate hours are extended for evening and special weekend events. Directions for the Science Center and Smokejumper trailhead: From New Seward Highway exit east on Dowling Road and drive 1.6 miles to Elmore; turn right (south) on Elmore and drive 0.6 miles and make a left-hand turn east on to BLM Road (this turn is just past light at 68th Avenue). You will pass Smokejumper trailhead parking area near the entrance; continue left at the fork in the road for the Science Center. The Campbell Creek Science Center is open weekdays, from 7:30 A.M. to 5:30 P.M. in summer, and from 8 A.M. to 4 P.M. in winter.

Campbell Creek Science Center offers regularly scheduled public lectures, classes and outdoor programs for children, adults and families: Check their website at www.blm.gov/ccsc for current events. Customized field trips for preschool, K-12 students and adults are also available by prior arrangement: phone (907) 267-1247 or email sciencecenter@blm.gov. The Science Center has classrooms for their environmental education programs, and meeting rooms are available for rent for natural resource meetings and events. The reception area, located at the East (main) entrance to the Science Center, has brochures and trail maps. The gardens at this entrance feature Alaska native plants and there is a plaque dedicated to Verna Pratt, author of *Field Guide to Alaskan Wildflowers*.

Trail maps are posted at the Campbell Tract trailheads. Smokejumper trailhead is located just off Elmore Road on BLM Road, before the Science Center Drive gate. You can walk the 1-mile paved road to the Center when the gate is closed, or walk Moose Track Trail, which parallels the road. Parking and a path to the Science Center (follow the salmon!) are located at the end of Science Center Drive, 1.1 miles from the Elmore Road entrance. The Science Center parking lot also acts as a trailhead parking lot (during open gate hours) for access to Campbell Airstrip Trail and Salmon Run Trail. Other trailheads are the Abbott Loop Trailhead at Abbott Loop Community Park, 1.4 miles south on Elmore Road from Dowling; the Campbell Airstrip trailhead at Mile 1 on Campbell Airstrip Road off Tudor; and

Anchorage is home to the world's largest and busiest seaplane base, Lake Hood.
(©Kelley & Milton Barker, staff)

South and North Bivouac (Far North Bicentennial Park) trailheads at Mile 2.3 Campbell Airstrip Road. (Campbell Airstrip Road—also the location of the Alaska Botanical Garden—is 3.2 miles east of the New Seward Highway via Tudor Road.)

Alaska Heritage Museum at Wells Fargo, on Northern Lights Boulevard and C Street, has an excellent collection of over 900 Alaska Native artifacts, ivory carvings and hand-woven baskets on display. Started by the National Bank of Alaska, and purchased by Wells Fargo along with the bank- *(Continues on page 367)*

Downtown Anchorage

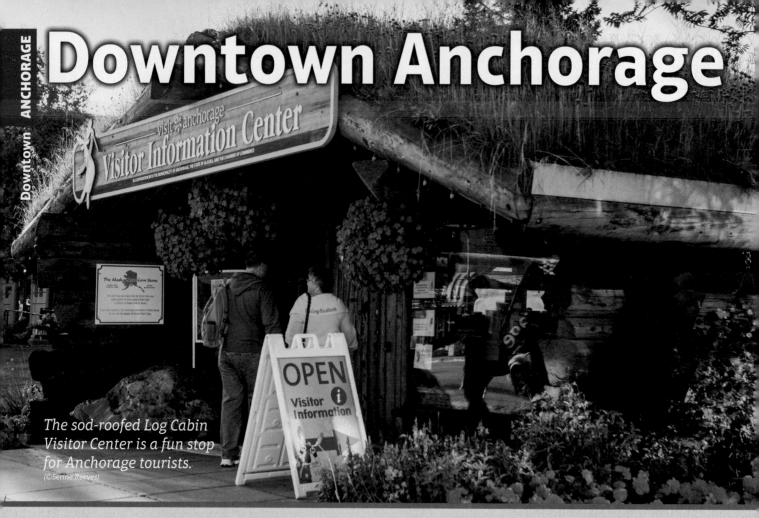

The sod-roofed Log Cabin Visitor Center is a fun stop for Anchorage tourists.
(©Serine Reeves)

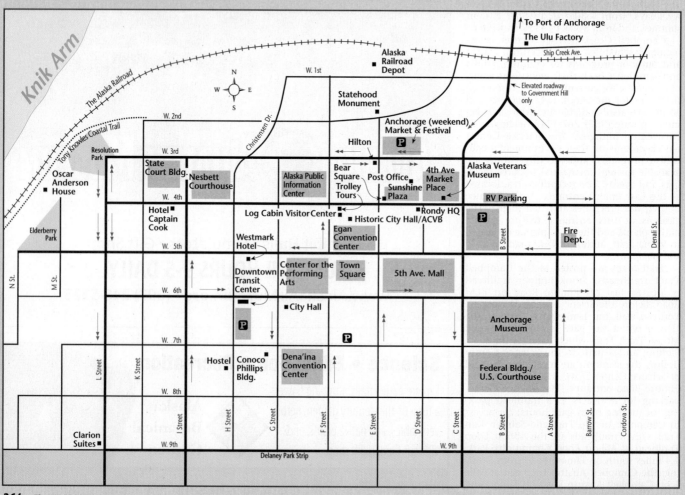

To Port of Anchorage

The Ulu Factory

Ship Creek Ave.

Knik Arm

The Alaska Railroad

Tony Knowles Coastal Trail

W. 1st

Alaska Railroad Depot

Elevated roadway to Government Hill only

N
W — E
S

W. 2nd

Christensen Dr.

Statehood Monument

Anchorage (weekend) Market & Festival

W. 3rd

Resolution Park

Hilton

P

Oscar Anderson House

State Court Bldg.

Nesbett Courthouse

Alaska Public Information Center

Bear Square Trolley Tours

Post Office

Sunshine Plaza

4th Ave Market Place

Alaska Veterans Museum

W. 4th

RV Parking

Elderberry Park

Hotel Captain Cook

Log Cabin Visitor Center

Historic City Hall/ACVB

Rondy HQ

P

B Street

Fire Dept.

Denali St.

N St.

M St.

Westmark Hotel

Egan Convention Center

W. 5th

Downtown Transit Center

Center for the Performing Arts

Town Square

5th Ave. Mall

W. 6th

P

City Hall

Anchorage Museum

W. 7th

P

L Street

K Street

Hostel

Conoco Phillips Bldg.

Dena'ina Convention Center

Federal Bldg./ U.S. Courthouse

W. 8th

I Street

H Street

G Street

F Street

E Street

D Street

C Street

B Street

A Street

Barrow St.

Cordova St.

Clarion Suites

W. 9th

W. 9th

Delaney Park Strip

The best way to begin your exploration of downtown Anchorage is with a stop at the **Log Cabin Visitor Information Center** and adjacent **Downtown Visitor Information Center**, located on 4th Avenue and F Street. The picturesque Log Cabin visitor center is a favorite meeting place and popular photo subject with its sod roof and flowers. The downtown visitor information center (through the metal arch sculpture behind the Log Cabin) is housed in a modern addition to the city's historic City Hall. Pick up brochures and a free copy of Visit Anchorage's *Official Guide to Anchorage* here. Phone (907) 257-2363; or visit www.anchorage.net.

Visit the Ulu Factory. The ulu, or Eskimo woman's knife, is an all-purpose, traditional tool with a flat, fan-shaped blade that is used for cutting and scraping. A very popular and useful souvenir. At the Ulu Factory on West Ship Creek Avenue, visitors can learn the history of the ulu knife and see a demonstration. Free trolley rides to and from the factory from the Log Cabin Visitor Center downtown. Phone (907) 276-3119 or 1-800-488-5592; www.theULUfactory.com.

©Kris Valencia, staff

Downtown City Parks. Peratrovich Park at 4th Avenue and E Street (pictured above) hosts the popular "Music in the Park" series. The concerts feature local groups playing everything from jazz to country, usually every Wednesday from noon–1 P.M. in summer; check locally for a current schedule or online at www.AnchorageDowntown.org.

Elderberry Park, at the west end of 5th Avenue, faces Knik Arm and accesses the popular Coastal Trail, which begins at the end of West 2nd Avenue. Resolution Park,

This is the Oscar Anderson House. Built in 1915, it is now a museum that offers a glimpse of early Anchorage history. (©Serine Reeves)

at 3rd Avenue and L Street (no parking adjacent to this park, it is directly off of L Street), displays a statue of Capt. James Cook overlooking the Knik Arm of the inlet which bears his name.

Delaney Park Strip, from A to P streets between 9th and 10th avenues, has rose gardens, Veterans memorial, ball fields, tennis courts and Engine No. 556 at 9th and E Street, a historic locomotive (fenced off). Delaney Park Strip also hosts a number of special events throughout the year.

Oscar Anderson House Museum is located at the west end of 5th Avenue, 420 M St., in Elderberry Park. It is one of the city's first privately built wood-frame houses and Anchorage's only historic house museum. Built in 1915, it was home to Oscar Anderson, a Swedish immigrant and early Anchorage pioneer and businessman (the 18th person to arrive in what became Anchorage). Now on the National Register of Historic Places, it has been beautifully restored and is well worth a visit. Call ahead in summer for hours of operation (2017 hours were Tuesday–Sunday noon–4 P.M.). Swedish Christmas tours, first 2 weekends in December. With advance arrangements group tours (maximum 10 participants) may be possible. Phone (907) 929-9870 or visit www.aahp-online.net/oscar-anderson-house-museum.html.

Anchorage Trolley Tours. Make the most of your stay in Anchorage by hopping aboard Anchorage's favorite trolley. Visit historic spots, watch floatplanes depart from Lake Hood, view the breathtaking mountains, and don't forget the camera for the many photo opportunities. Learn about Anchorage's past and present with tips on the best places for shopping, dining and entertainment. Phone (907) 276-5603; www.anchoragetrolley.com/sales@anchoragetrolley.com. [ADVERTISEMENT]

Enjoy the Flowers. Numerous hanging baskets transform the core area of down-

The Anchorage Museum, open year-round, houses exhibits that explore the art, history and science of Alaska. (©Courtesy Visit Anchorage/Ashley Heimbigner)

town Anchorage, and thematic arrangements highlight the well-maintained flower beds lining the city's walkways. The Centennial Rose Garden is the centerpiece of the Delaney Park Strip at 9th and N streets, and the downtown area at the Town Square municipal park, located between 5th and 6th avenues along E Street, next door to the **Alaska Center for the Performing Arts**, offers the city's most spectacular flower displays in summer.

See the **"Whaling Wall,"** a 400-foot-long mural of beluga and bowhead whales by artist Wyland (JC Penney wall on 5th Ave.)

The Anchorage Museum, located at the corner of 6th Avenue and C Street, has something for everyone. Three permanent exhibitions explore the art, history and science of Alaska and the North: The 10,000-square-foot Smithsonian Arctic Studies Center provides a look at Alaska Native culture through its exhibition Living Our Cultures, Sharing Our Heritage: The First Peoples of Alaska. More than 600 objects on loan from the Smithsonian's National Museum of Natural History and the National Museum of the American Indian pro-

vide a look at Alaska Native cultures. The 12,000-square-foot Alaska exhibition, is organized into 13 themes and presents the story of Alaska through multiple voices and perspectives. The Art of the North galleries in the museum's 31,000-square-foot wing, which also opened in September, features landscapes, portraits, sculptures, photographs and video that reveal the land, people and culture of Alaska and the Circumpolar North.

An additional four galleries house rotating exhibitions. Films, talks and performances take place in the 230-seat auditorium. The atrium provides comfortable seating, a variety of artist installations and a cafe for sandwiches, snacks and beverages. The full-service Muse restaurant, located off the lobby, serves fresh fare in a modern setting. The Museum Store offers Alaska Native art and craft, fine art and jewelry by Alaska artists and books on local and state history.

Families may want to start in the Discovery Center, which offers a hands-on Alaska science center with more than 60 exhibits, live animals and a planetarium. For the very young (ages 5 and younger), TOTE Kid-

Space offers a variety of tactile experiences. The 39-seat Thomas Planetarium presents astronomy, nature and wildlife films, and music and light shows using 3-D graphics, surround sound and a full-dome screen.

The museum offers docent-guided tours daily in summer (included with general admission) that focus on Alaska history, art, indigenous cultures and more. Check tour hours at www.anchoragemuseum.org/visit/tours. Regular museum admission is $18 for adults; $12 for seniors/students/military; $7 for ages 3-12; and free for those 2 and younger. The Culture Pass, available mid-May through mid-September, provides admission (and shuttle) to both the Anchorage Museum and the Alaska Native Heritage Center for $32 (see ad on page 365).

Summer museum hours (May 1 through Sept. 30) are 9 A.M. to 6 P.M. daily. Winter hours (Oct. 1 through April 30) are 10 A.M. to 6 P.M. Tuesday through Saturday; noon to 6 P.M. Sunday; and closed Monday and Thanksgiving, Christmas and New Year's day. The museum is open late for Polar Nights from October through April with half-price or free admission from 6–9 P.M. Wheelchair accessible. Lockers available. Phone (907) 929-9200 for recorded information; www.anchoragemuseum.org.

Enjoy "Lunch on the Lawn" at the Anchorage Museum at 6th Avenue and C Street. From 11:30 A.M. to 1:30 P.M. on Tuesdays June–August bring your lunch (or buy one at nearby food trucks or restaurants) and enjoy free entertainment and activities.

The **Old Federal Building** at 605 West 4th Ave. at F Street (pictured below) is listed on the National Register of Historic Places and currently houses the Anchorage Alaska Public Lands Information Center (description follows) in the east wing.

Built in 1940, this Federal Building served as the city's Federal Court and main post office until the 1970s, when Federal courts and offices moved to the new federal building on West 7th and C Street, although, the refurbished court room in the west wing has been home to the federal bankruptcy court since 1988. When court is not in session—look for the "Open to the Public" sign displayed by the front door facing 4th Avenue—visitors are welcome in the Historic Court Room, which has a Depression-era mural by artist Arthur Kerrick, and visit the small conference room across the hall with its displays of old photos and a history of bankruptcy information panel.

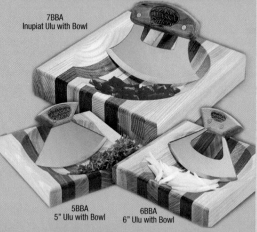

©Serine Reeves

Anchorage Alaska Public Lands Information Center (AAPLIC), located in the historic Old Federal Building (pictured above) on 4th Avenue at F Street, offers a wide variety of exhibits, movies, special programs and information on all of Alaska's state and federal parks, forests, wildlife refuges and other public lands. Natural history and cultural exhibits and a self-help trip-planning area are available. Center staff provides additional assistance, maps, brochures and current travel information. Federal passes (annual, military, senior and access) and state park day-use annual passes are available.

Rangers, authors and other special guest speakers present programs at 2 P.M. daily in the summer; call for current schedule. Free ranger-led 45-minute walking tours, offered at 3:15 P.M. daily during the summer, explore the public lands of Alaska with stops at downtown statues. Museum scavenger hunts and Junior Ranger books are popular activities enjoyed by young and old alike. The center is staffed year-round. Summer hours (Memorial Day to Labor Day) are 9 A.M. to 5 P.M. daily (building doors close at 5 P.M.); winter hours may vary, call ahead.

This is a secured facility and screening is required before entering. For information, phone (907) 644-3678 or 1-866-869-6887; write the center at 605 W. 4th Ave., Ste. 105, Anchorage, AK 99501; or visit the website at www.alaskacenters.gov/anchorage.cfm.

Alaska Veterans Museum, shares the stories of our Veterans, military members and families through exhibits, artifacts and many recorded oral histories. All branches of the military and services are represented. Exhibits range from the Civil War to modern era conflicts. Permanent exhibits feature Alaska's unique involvement in America's military history; traveling exhibits honor individuals or showcase artifact collections. 333 W. 4th Ave. Ste. 227. Phone (907) 677-8802, website: www.alaskaveterans.org for current hours of operation.

Alaska State Trooper Museum. This unique museum presents the history of law enforcement in the Territory and State of Alaska, with displays of photos and exhibits of historic police equipment. Gifts and memorabilia are available for purchase. Admission free. Hours are 10 A.M. to 4 P.M. weekdays and noon to 4 P.M. Saturdays. 245 W. 5th Ave., between B and C streets. Phone (907) 279-5050 or 1-800-770-5050; foast@gci.net; www.alaskatroopermuseum.com.

Visit the Anchorage Market & Festival. This popular outdoor market operates 10 A.M. to 6 P.M. Saturday and 10 A.M. to 5 P.M. Sunday, from mid-May through mid-September. Held in the parking lot at 3rd Avenue between C and E streets, there is no admission fee. About 200 booths sell a variety of Alaskan-made and Alaska-grown products as well as handmade and imported home and novelty items of all types. Choose from over 30 food booths and enjoy live entertainment. It is fun for the whole family. Phone (907) 272-5634, or visit www.anchoragemarkets.com.

Anchorage Fire Department Museum, located in the headquarters building at 4th Avenue and A Street, has a vintage 1921 American LaFrance pumper, the department's first fire truck. Check out the equipment and technology and learn about the history of the Anchorage Fire Department. Hours are Monday–Friday 7:30 A.M. to 4:30 P.M. For more information, call (907) 267-4936.

Alaska Statehood Monument. Located at the corner of 2nd Avenue and E Street (just a block downhill from the Hilton) at the Ship Creek Overlook. A plaque and bronze bust of President Eisenhower commemorate the Alaska Statehood Act that made Alaska the 49th state on January 3, 1959.

First Friday Art Walk. Anchorage's numerous art galleries offer special exhibits and honor the artists at late afternoon/evening receptions from 5–8 P.M. on the first Friday of each month. For detailed information about the artists and locations of the galleries, consult the entertainment and arts sections of the local newspapers or www.anchoragedowntown.org.

See a Historic Schoolhouse. The Pioneer Schoolhouse at 3rd Avenue and Eagle Street is a 2-story memorial to the late Ben Crawford, an Anchorage banker. On the National Register of Historic Places, this was the first school in Anchorage. Views from the exterior only, the interior is not open to the public.

©Ken Graham/Visit Anchorage

Ship Creek Salmon Viewing. From downtown, either walk down the hill from the Hilton toward the train station or stroll down Christensen Street (with its fish fence and fine views of the inlet) past the train station, to reach the Ship Creek area. There is a paved path that begins adjacent The Bridge Seafood Restaurant (behind the Ulu Factory and Comfort Inn) that follows Ship Creek to a pedestrian bridge across the creek. Visitors can watch the salmon—as well as the fishermen—from spots along either bank, from the viewing platform or from the dam. Watch for chinook from early June until mid-July, coho in late-July through August. Salmon viewing can also be found at the William Jack Hernandez Sport Fish Hatchery.

(Continued from page 363)
ing system in 2002, the collection continues to keep Alaska art in the state and to share Alaska history and culture with residents and visitors. Sydney Laurence, Eustace Ziegler and Fred Machetanz are among featured artists. A 46 oz. gold nugget found near Ruby, AK, is part of the Alaskan mining history collection. Free admission. Open weekdays year-round: noon–4 P.M. Off-hour tours are welcome and can be arranged by calling (907) 265-2834 or check out www.wellsfargohistory.com/museums/anchorage. Wheelchair accessible.

Other Alaska Native art displays and gift shops are located at the Alaska Native Medical Center and in the Anchorage Museum.

Z. J. Loussac Public Library, located at 36th Avenue and Denali Street (3600 Denali St.), is the headquarters for the Anchorage Public Library system. Its unique architecture makes it a local landmark, as does its Carl Nesjar Memorial Fountain and statue of William H. Seward. The library hosts various dynamic events, programs and classes throughout the year, from the musical "Live at the Library" to summer reading programs for kids, teens, and adults. Loussac Library has an extensive collection of books related to Alaska history and culture as well as rich and diverse online resources. Hours are Monday–Thursday 10 A.M. to 9 P.M., Friday and Saturday 10 A.M. to 6 P.M. and Sunday 1–5 P.M. For information, phone (907) 343-2975 or visit www.anchoragelibrary.org.

Adjacent to the library is **Cuddy Family Park,** with playground, benches, paths, a pond and a large open field used for kite flying and other summer fun. An ice-skating oval and ice rink are featured in winter.

The Alaska Museum of Science and Nature, located at 201 N. Bragaw St., 2 blocks north of the Glenn Highway, offers hands-on exploration of Alaska's unique geological, ecological and cultural history. Learn about Ice Age Alaska, Alaska's current dinosaur finds, and sea monsters (plesiosaurs and mosasaurs) from the Age of Dinosaurs; see rocks and gems, birds and marine mammals of Alaska. Open Thursday–Saturday 10 A.M. to 4 P.M. Admission fee: Adults $8; children 3–12 years $6; senior/military $7; school groups $5. For more information, call (907) 274-2400, or visit www.alaskamuseum.org.

Take a Tour: Tour operators offer local and area sightseeing tours. These range from a 1-hour narrated trolley tour of Anchorage to full-day tours of area attractions such as Portage Glacier and Alyeska Resort. Flightseeing tours provide an up-close view of Denali and a bird's-eye view of bears and other wildlife. Two-day or longer excursions by motorcoach, rail, ferry and air to nearby attractions such as Prince William Sound or remote areas are available. *See list of Tours & Transportation advertisers on page 357.*

Portage Glacier Cruise. See one of Alaska's most popular attractions, up close from the deck of the MV *Ptarmigan.* This Gray Line of Alaska cruise takes you right to the face of the imposing 10-story-high Portage Glacier, an incredible experience! Cruise departs 4 times daily; tour including cruise and transportation departs Anchorage once daily. Cruise + Transportation tour is $89.95 per person; cruise only price is $39 per person. Visit graylinealaska.com or call 1-800-544-2206 to book. [ADVERTISEMENT]

Tour a Campus: Two colleges are located in Anchorage: the University of Alaska

Anchorage at 3211 Providence Dr., and Alaska Pacific (formerly Alaska Methodist) University at 4101 University Dr.

Alaska Pacific University (APU) is the state's only private 4-year university. APU's first students were enrolled in the fall of 1960. The university offers liberal-arts-based educational programs for all ages. The APU campus is located on 170 forested acres, featuring the 3-tiered Atwood Fountain, Waldron Carillon Bell Tower and the Jim Mahaffey Trail System for skiers, runners, hikers and mountain bikers. Phone 1-800-252-7528 for tours or information about university programs, or visit www.alaskapacific.edu/visit.

The University of Alaska Anchorage (UAA) is the largest university in the state, with a main campus in the heart of Anchorage and satellite campuses in Homer, Kodiak, Palmer, Soldotna and Valdez. Founded as Anchorage Community College in 1954, it has undergone explosive growth in recent years. Expansion and development continue as UAA attracts a larger and more diverse student base. The 5,000-seat Alaska Airlines Center hosts UAA sports, concerts and community events.

Check out Farmers Markets. The Center Market is held year-round each Wednesday and Friday 10 A.M. to 6 P.M. and Saturdays from 10 A.M. to 4 P.M. at the Mall at Sears, on Benson Boulevard and Denali Street. Through summer months: Anchorage Farmers Market, Saturdays 9 A.M. to 2 P.M. on 15th Avenue and Cordova Street. Downtown's Anchorage Market & Festival, Saturdays 10 A.M. to 6 P.M. and Sundays 10 A.M. to 5 P.M. at 3rd Avenue and E Street. South Anchorage Farmers Market 9 A.M. to 2 P.M. Saturdays at the Subway/Cellular One Sports Center (May–September) and also 10 A.M. to 4 P.M. Wednesdays in parking lot south of Dimond Center Mall (July–September). Spenard Farmers Market 9 A.M. to 2 P.M. Saturdays at 2555 Spenard Rd.

Visit the Alaska Zoo, located on 20 wooded acres along O'Malley Road in South Anchorage, 2 miles east of the Seward Highway. The zoo provides homes for more than 100 orphaned and injured animals from both Arctic and subarctic climates, making it the most complete collection of animals in the state of Alaska. Resident zoo species include brown bears, moose, Dall sheep, river otters, black bears, fox, musk-oxen, bald eagles, wolverines, wolves and more. The polar bear exhibit features an underwater viewing area and waterfalls. The zoo is also home to many non-native and cold climate species including Bactrian camels, Amur tigers, snow leopards, and Tibetan yaks.

Services include a gift shop and coffee shop. Free round-trip summer shuttle service (May 15–Sept. 20) from downtown Anchorage at 4th Avenue and F Street (go to website for times and details). Summer zoo hours are from 9 A.M. to 9 P.M. daily, June, July & August. Tuesday evenings in the summer include educational programs beginning at 7 P.M. Daily, behind-the-scenes "Discovery" tours are offered during summer months. Winter hours are from 10 A.M. to 4 P.M. (or dusk) daily (closed on Thanksgiving and Christmas days). Last entry daily is 30 minutes before posted closing time.

The zoo offers educational camps, programs and public events year-round. "Zoo Lights," a fun display of lighted animal silhouettes with movement and sound, takes place during the holidays and with evening hours Thursday-Sunday starting after Thanksgiving. Zoo Lights entry fee including admission to the zoo is $7 for annual zoo members, $9 for non-members. A full schedule with dates and times is posted online.

Zoo admission is $15 for non-resident adults, $13 for resident adults, $10 seniors and military with ID, $7 children 3–17, 2 years and younger are free. Please note that prices are subject to change without notice. Check the website for all of the latest information on hours, prices, programs and events; www.alaskazoo.org, phone (907) 346-3242.

Hike Chugach Park. Chugach State Park's 500,000-acre wonderland borders the edge of the Anchorage bowl. Whether it is a leisurely afternoon stroll or a strenuous, weekend-long backpack trip, the Chugach Mountains offer wilderness opportunities for everyone.

The park is open year-round and there are a number of easy-to-access trailheads from Girdwood to Eagle River. An online and print park trail map is available. For the online version, go to www.dnr.alaska.gov/parks/aspunits/index.htm and click link to access park map. For additional hiking trail information stop by the Alaska Public Lands Information Center on 4th Avenue in downtown Anchorage (phone 907/644-3661) or phone the Department of Natural Resources at (907) 269-8400.

The most popular and accessible day hikes in Anchorage are located in the park's Hillside Trail System with its 3 trailheads—Glen Alps, Prospect Heights and Upper Huffman—all accessed via residential areas on the Anchorage Hillside. All trailhead parking lots have a $5/day parking fee. Weather conditions can change rapidly in Chugach Park—always bring extra clothing, water and proper footwear. Bears and moose frequent the area, so make noise.

Hillside trails, known for their panoramic views of the city and surrounding mountains and valleys, include Powerline—and the most popular hiking trail in the state—Flattop. On a sunny summer day, it

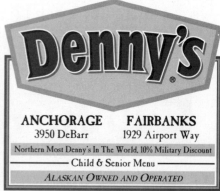

sometimes seems that half of Anchorage is out hiking to the top of Flattop Mountain. The parking lot can fill to overflowing, so get there early. There is also a shuttle (fee) between downtown and Flattop in the summer; phone (907) 279-3334 or visit www.hike-anchorage-alaska.com for details.

The 3.5-mile (round trip) trail up Flattop takes anywhere from 2 to 5 hours and offers spectacular views of the Anchorage bowl, Cook Inlet and the Alaska Range. As popular as it is, it is imperative to be cautious while climbing. Accidents and rescues are not uncommon. Above all, stay on the path.

Flattop Mountain (elev. 3,510 feet), and Powerline trail are accessed from the Glen Alps trailhead. From the New Seward Highway, turn east on O'Malley Road. At Hillside Drive go right (south) for 1 mile, then turn left (east) at Upper Huffman Road. Go uphill 0.7 mile and turn right (south) on Toilsome Hill Drive (4-wheel drive vehicles and chains are advised in winter). Toilsome will switchback uphill for another 1.3 miles, becoming Glen Alps Road. Look for the Glen Alps parking lot on the left.

Powerline trail is an old gravel roadway that heads up the South Fork Campbell Creek Valley from Glen Alps parking lot. Hikers and bikers enjoy the 12-mile trail for its rolling terrain and relatively flat surface. A number of trails branch off from the Powerline trail to access surrounding peaks.

Visit the Greenhouses: The municipality maintains the extensive Mann Leiser greenhouses and horticulture complex at Russian Jack Park, 1321 Lidia Selkregg Lane, where myriad plantings supply local parks—like downtown's Town Square—with flowers. The horticulture section of Anchorage Parks & Recreation is responsible for planting and maintaining the city's 461 flowerbeds and baskets with more than 76,000 annual flowers at 81 sites, as well as trees and shrubs and turf throughout Anchorage.

Visitors to the greenhouse enjoy the displays of tropical plants, the fish pond and the aviary where finches, cockatiels and tropical birds enliven an attractive area popular for small weddings and volunteer-guided educational tours. Open daily year-round, 8 A.M. to 3 P.M., (closed holidays). Phone (907) 343-4717; www.muni.org/Departments/parks/Pages/Greenhouse.aspx.

Watch the Tide Come In: With frequent tidal ranges of 30 feet within 6 hours, and some approaching 40 feet, one of Anchorage's best nature shows is the action of the tides in both the Knik and Turnagain arms of upper Cook Inlet. Vantage points along Knik Arm are Earthquake Park, Elderberry Park (west end of 5th Avenue), Resolution Park (near corner of 3rd Avenue and L Street) and the Anchorage small-boat harbor.

Turnagain Arm has one of the highest tides in North America, rising to a maximum height of 42 feet. There are good views of Turnagain Arm from the Seward Highway, starting about 12 miles south of Anchorage. Good overlooks for Turnagain tides are Beluga Point at **Milepost S 110.3** Seward Highway, 16.7 miles south of Anchorage; and Bird Point at **Milepost S 96.5**, 30.5 miles south of Anchorage. With careful timing you might see a bore tide, an interesting phenomenon rarely seen elsewhere. A bore tide is a foaming wall of tidal water, up to 6 feet in height, formed by a flood tide surging into the constricted inlet of Knik and Turnagain arms.

CAUTION: In most places, the mud flats of

Hikers enjoy the view of Cook Inlet from the Turnagain Arm Trail in Chugach State Park.
(©Courtesy of Visit Anchorage/Jody O. Photos)

Knik and Turnagain arms are like quicksand. Do not go wading!

Play Golf: What better way to enjoy the midnight sun than on a golf course? Anchorage offers unique opportunities for golfing enthusiasts, from short, par-3 courses to 36-hole links.

The Russian Jack Springs Golf Course, located in Russian Jack Springs Park, is run by Anchorage Parks & Recreation. It is a 9-hole course that features artificial greens, wooded fairways and beautiful scenery just 15 minute drive from downtown Anchorage. For additional information or tee times call (907) 343-6992.

The Anchorage Golf Course is an 18-hole, par 72 course located about 15 minutes from downtown Anchorage. Tee times begin as early as 5 A.M., and golfers can play until after midnight on long summer days. It offers a pro shop, lessons, a driving range and putting green, restaurant, snack bar, pull carts, electric carts, club rentals and club repair. Open May–October depending on weather. For more information, call the pro shop at (907) 522-3363 or visit anchorage golfcourse.com.

Moose Run is a 36-hole, military-run facility accessed via Arctic Valley Road off of the Glenn Highway. Moose Run has a driving range, clubhouse, and plenty of wildlife viewing opportunities on its 2 courses: Moose Run Hill Course and Moose Run Creek Course. The Creek Course has been ranked #49 in a list of America's 50 Toughest Golf Courses. And the Hill Course has been named in *Golf Digest's* 2015 "Best in State." Website: www.mooserungolfcourse.com.

Tanglewood Lakes Golf Club maintains a 9-hole, par-3 course with a chalet for parties at 11801 Brayton Dr.; phone (907) 345-4600 for greens fees. Tanglewood also has a golf "dome" with an indoor driving range. Located on the east side of the New Seward Highway between Huffman and O'Malley exits (use 1-way frontage road north from the Huffman exit). Website: www.foxhollowak.com. Alaska's golf season lasts from May to September, depending on the weather.

Play Disc Golf: Disc golf is played with a plastic flying disc instead of clubs and a ball, and the "hole" is a metal basket mounted on a pole. Players throw their discs into the baskets and the low score wins. A round of disc golf takes only 1 to 2 hours, can be played year-round and is usually free. Anchorage has many established courses. One of the most popular is at Kincaid Park, which has a grass/dirt, 18-basket, par 54 course that begins near the park's chalet. Visit www.facebook.com/ADGA907 for courses and dates of local tournaments and other events.

Play Tennis: The Municipality of Anchorage maintains 37 tennis courts. In addition, private clubs offer year-round indoor courts.

Watch Birds: Excellent bird-watching opportunities are abundant within the city limits. Westchester Lagoon and lakes Hood and Spenard, for example, are teeming with seaplanes but also, during the summer, are nesting areas for grebes and arctic loons. Also seen are sandhill cranes, widgeons, arctic terns, mew gulls, green-winged teals and sandpipers.

Large flocks of Canada geese nest and raise their young here during the summer. It is not unusual to see traffic at a standstill as a pair of geese, followed by a tandem procession of goslings, cross the street.

Another birding spot is **Potter Marsh**, at the southern end of the Anchorage Coastal Wildlife Refuge and a 15-minute drive south from downtown Anchorage via the Seward Highway (turnoff at **Milepost S 117.6**). Viewing boardwalks extend over the marshland offering close-up photo opportunities. Early July evenings are best, according to local bird watchers. Forests surrounding Anchorage also are good for warblers, juncos, robins, white-crowned sparrows, varied thrushes and other species.

See a Baseball Game: Every summer the Alaska Baseball League hosts some of the nation's top college players (among past notables are Tom Seaver and 1998 home-run king Mark McGwire). Aaron Judge, a 2011 Glacier Pilot, was a 2017 addition to the Yankees. The ABL includes the Anchorage Glacier Pilots, Anchorage Bucs, Chugiak-Eagle River Chinooks, Peninsula Oilers, and the Mat–Su Miners. Anchorage games are played at Mulcahy Stadium, Cordova Street and E. 16th Avenue. Check local newspapers for schedules or phone the Anchorage Bucs, (907) 561-2827, www.anchoragebucs.com; or the Glacier Pilots, (907) 274-5687, www.glacierpilots.com.

Watch Salmon: Chinook, coho, pink and a few chum salmon swim up Ship Creek and can be seen at the Ship Creek Viewing Area (see description in Downtown Anchorage attractions) and near the Alaska Department of Fish and Game's William Jack Hernandez Sport Fish Hatchery on Reeve Boulevard. Watch for chinook from early June until mid-July and for other species from mid-August until September. Salmon can also be viewed in Campbell Creek, which runs through the middle of Anchorage. Watch for spawning chinook in late July and coho in August from the boardwalks at Folker Street off Tudor Road. Another excellent viewing spot is the Potter Marsh Nature Trail, June through August.

Watch an Equestrian Event: The William Clark Chamberlin Equestrian Center at 3900 Abbott Rd (1.8 miles east of Dimond exit off the New Seward Highway on Abbott Road) hosts a variety of equestrian events every weekend from late May through late September. This public facility is open from 10 A.M. to 10 P.M. daily. Phone (907) 522-1552; www.anchoragehorsecouncil.net. The Eaton Equestrian Centre at 5801 Moose Meadow Lane on the hillside offers riding lessons and special events. Phone (907) 346-3745 for more information or www.eatonequestrian.com.

Charter a Plane: Dozens of air taxi operators are based in Anchorage. Fixed-wheel planes or floatplanes (skis in winter) may be chartered for flightseeing trips to Denali and Prince William Sound, for fly-in hunting and fishing, wildlife and glacier viewing, photo safaris or just for transportation. Scheduled flightseeing trips by helicopter are also available. See advertisements in this section, and inquire locally. Weather is a factor when traveling by aircraft in Alaska. Be prepared to change plans if the weather is bad. Check the FAA website at http://avcams.faa.gov for weather conditions and flight information.

River Running: Guided rafting tours in the region include trips on the Matanuska near Palmer, Sixmile near Hope, and the Kenai River on the Kenai Peninsula. Also on the Kenai Peninsula are the Swanson River and Swan Lake canoe trails, located within Kenai National Wildlife Refuge.

Nancy Lake State Recreation Area, 67 miles north of Anchorage, offers a popular canoe trail system which includes public-use cabins and camping for overnight trips. Closer to Anchorage, Matanuska Lakes State Recreation Area, at **Milepost A 36.1** Glenn Highway, also offers canoeing. Check with advertisers in *The MILEPOST®* about guided river trips: Nova River Runners at www.nov-alaska.com, offers a good example of what's available along the Glenn and Seward highways and there are multiple raft trip providers in Denali National Park.

Go Boating: Cook Inlet waters around Anchorage are only for the experienced because of powerful bore tides, unpredictable weather, dangerous mud flats and icy, silt-filled waters.

Cruises on larger boats are available from Whittier into Prince William Sound, from the Homer Spit into Kachemak Bay and Cook Inlet, and from Seward into Resurrection Bay and Kenai Fjords National Park. Kayak and canoe rentals are readily available in those locations.

Go Swimming: Anchorage has an indoor waterpark, located east off the O'Malley exit on the New Seward Highway. The YMCA, at 5353 Lake Otis Pkwy., has a swimming pool; phone (907) 563-3211; www.ymcaalaska.org. The University of Alaska Anchorage pool is located in the Wells Fargo Sports Complex on Providence Drive; phone (907) 786-1231; uaa.alaska.edu/recreation/sports-complex/pool.

The municipality operates 6 swimming pools located in local high schools; public hours vary: Service Pool on Abbott Road; Bartlett Pool on Muldoon Road; West High

Pool (pool and water slide) on Hillcrest Drive; East High Pool at Northern Lights Boulevard and East 24th Avenue; Dimond High Pool at 2909 W. 88th Ave.; and Chugiak Pool at 16525 S. Birchwood Loop.

For more information on aquatics at Anchorage pools, contact the Anchorage Parks & Recreation Dept.; phone (907) 343-4402 or visit www.muni.org/Departments/parks/Pages/Pools.aspx.

There are 2 municipal beaches in Anchorage, located at Jewel Lake and Goose Lake, with supervised swim areas. Lifeguards are on duty from mid-May to mid-August, noon–9 P.M. daily. The lakes are prone to "swimmer's itch" in the mid to late summer months. For more information on Anchorage lakes, go to www.muni.org/Departments/parks/Pages/Lakes.aspx.

CAUTION: Do not consider swimming in Cook Inlet! Quicksand-like mud, swift tides and icy water make these waters extremely dangerous!

Saltwater Charter Boats: Sightseeing and fishing charters are available on the Kenai Peninsula at Whittier, Seward, Ninilchik and Homer. Peak times for saltwater fishing for salmon and halibut are June and July. May and August can also be excellent fishing, depending on the weather.

Freshwater Charter Boats: There are a wide variety of river and lake fishing charters available throughout Southcentral, from Cantwell to Homer. River seasons run from the May chinook salmon fishery through the September coho salmon fishery. Some lake charters run year-round for ice fishing.

Winter Attractions: The premier winter festival of North America is "Rondy," more formally known as the Anchorage Fur Rendezvous (Feb. 22–March 3, 2019). This 12-day-long celebration dates from 1935, when it began primarily as a winter sports tournament, fur auction and community celebration. Today there are more than 90 events, including Native arts and crafts market, a parade, carnival, fireworks, wacky

Potter Marsh, less than 10 miles south of the city on the Seward Highway, offers excellent wildlife viewing from its boardwalks. (©Donna Dewhurst)

fun competitions, snow sculpting contest, fur auctions, Native blanket toss and ice sports. Highlights include the annual Running of the Reindeer, Miners and Trappers Pardi-gras and the World Championship Open Sled Dog Races in downtown Anchorage, depending on seasonal snow accumulation. Visit Rondy headquarters at 4th Avenue and D Street. For event dates, visit www.furrondy.net.

The Iditarod Trail Sled Dog Race® has a ceremonial start on 4th Avenue in downtown Anchorage on the first Saturday in March. Mushers finish at the Campbell Airstrip. The racers then pack up and head to Willow, 70 miles north of Anchorage on the Parks Highway, for the official re-start of the race the following day (Sunday). For more

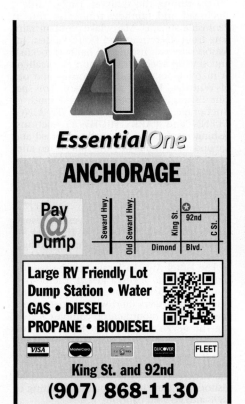

information, phone (907) 376-5155; www. iditarod.com.

Anchorage accommodates a wide range of winter activities, from outdoor ice skating to downhill skiing. Alyeska Resort, Alaska's largest ski area, with an international reputation for its facilities, is a 45-mile drive south from Anchorage. Numerous past Olympi-

ans including Tommy Moe, Hillary Lindh and Rosie Fletcher got their start at Alyeska. Closer to downtown, Hilltop Ski Area, on the hillside in south Anchorage, offers lighted slopes for beginner to intermediate. Arctic Valley Ski Area off the Arctic Valley exit from the Glenn Highway has a popular tubing park, several chairs and intermediate

level ski runs and is also popular with back-country skiers.

Cross-country skiing is big in Anchorage, with a network of trails at Kincaid, Russian Jack and Hillside Park. The Tour of Anchorage ski marathon (first Sunday in March), North America's longest running and largest citizen's racing and touring series, offers a 50k, 40k, or 25k route across town. For more information, visit www.anchoragenordicski.com/tour_of_anchorage.html.

Go Fishing: The Alaska Dept. of Fish and Game annually stocks more than 22 lakes and 3 streams in the Anchorage area with rainbow trout, chinook salmon, coho salmon and Arctic char. These fish are raised at the William Jack Hernandez Sport Fish Hatchery in Anchorage. The Hatchery is located at 941 North Reeve Blvd. The public is welcome to visit the hatchery and the Ship Creek Fisheries Center during normal operating hours. All stocked lakes are open to the public. In addition, salmon-viewing is available in local streams. For more information on hatcheries and stocking, visit www.adfg.alaska.gov/index.cfm?adfg=fishingSportStockingHatcheries.williamjackhernandez.

Chinook, coho and pink salmon can be caught in Ship Creek in downtown Anchorage; coho, pink and chum salmon are available in Bird Creek, just north of Girdwood on the Seward Highway, from mid-July through August. Coho salmon fisheries are found in Campbell Creek and Ship Creek in Anchorage and also Bird Creek. The Alaska Department of Fish and Game office here is located at 333 Raspberry Rd., Anchorage, AK 99518; phone (907) 267-2218 for sport fishing information.

The Ship Creek Slam'n Salm'n Derby, a benefit for the Downtown Soup Kitchen, takes place June 8–15, 2019 (www.anchorage.net/events/salmon-derby).

Many excellent fishing spots are within a day's drive of Anchorage. The Kenai Peninsula offers streams where chinook, sockeye, coho, pink and chum salmon may be caught during the summer. Dolly Varden, steelhead and rainbow trout also run in Peninsula streams. Many lakes contain rainbow trout, lake trout and Dolly Varden. In-season saltwater fishing for halibut, rockfish and several species of salmon is excellent at many spots along the Peninsula and out of Whittier, Homer and Seward. For specific fishing spots both north and south of Anchorage, see the SEWARD, STERLING, GLENN and PARKS HIGHWAY sections. Fishing regulations are strictly enforced and are updated annually by the state, often after *The MILEPOST®* deadline, so it is wise to check current regulations for various Alaska regions at www.adfg.alaska.gov/index.cfm?adfg=fishregulations.main.

Day Trip Ideas: Visit Alyeska Resort. Drive south on the Seward Highway to **Milepost S 90** (37 miles from Anchorage) and turn off on the Alyeska Highway. Here, at The Hotel Alyeska located at the base of Mount Alyeska, Alyeska Resort, the 60-passenger Alyeska Aerial Tramway carries summer sightseers (and winter skiers) from the hotel to a mountaintop complex featuring the Seven Glaciers and Bore Tide restaurants. In summer, make it an adventure and hike back down. The Crow Creek Mine Road, off of the Alyeska Highway, accesses the **Crow Creek Mine historic site**. Today visitors can view historic buildings dating to 1898 and go gold panning.

Portage Glacier and Whittier. Drive south on the Seward Highway to **Milepost S 78.9** (48.1 miles from Anchorage) to junction with the access road east to Portage Glacier (5.4 miles from the highway) and Whittier (11.4 miles from the highway). At Portage Glacier, the Begich, Boggs Visitor Center (open summer months) offers interactive interpretive displays, films and other programs on the natural history of this area, regular showings of films of interest and Forest Service naturalists are available to answer your questions. **Portage Glacier Cruises** offers daily sightseeing trips on Portage Lake from mid-May to mid-September.

Continue east to Whittier. At Mile 7, traffic enters the Anton Anderson Memorial Tunnel, at 13,300 feet the longest highway tunnel in North America. It takes a vehicle 6.5 minutes to travel through this tunnel which was formerly dedicated to train travel. There is a toll charged and travel is one-way in the tunnel. Openings are for 15 minutes each hour from either side. Vehicles must wait in the staging area before entering the tunnel. See "Whittier/Portage Glacier Access Road" in the SEWARD HIGHWAY section.

Returning to the Seward Highway for the drive back to Anchorage, stop by the Alaska Wildlife Conservation Center, just north of the junction (on the west side of the road) at **Milepost S 79**, for a walk/drive-through tour of this wildlife park. The non-profit center is home to moose, bears, caribou, bison, elk, Sitka black-tailed deer and other wildlife.

Ride the Railroad. Reserve a seat on the Alaska Railroad's summer scheduled *Denali Star* train for a morning trip to Talkeetna. Enjoy a few hours of sightseeing, dining and shopping in this charming Alaska village. Visit unique museums and historic sites, take a jetboat trip on the Susitna River or enjoy spectacular views of Denali on a flightseeing trip around North America's highest mountain before returning to Anchorage by train in the late afternoon.

Or head south aboard an early morning departure of the *Coastal Classic Train*, arriving to Seward in time for a glacier and whale-watching cruise in Kenai Fjords National Park. The return rail journey departs for Anchorage in the early evening,

Portage Lake is a 53-mile drive south of Anchorage. The Begich, Boggs Visitor Center here (not pictured) focuses on the Chugach National Forest. (©Kris Valencia, staff)

allowing for a full day of exploring coastline.

In summer and early fall, the *Glacier Discovery* offers a multitude of day trips: disembark in Whittier to cruise Prince William Sound, go for a guided hike or raft excursion at the Spencer Glacier Whistle Stop, or simply stay on board and watch Alaska's remote landscapes unfold on the journey to Grandview. You will be back in Anchorage by evening. Phone (907) 265-2494 or 1-800-544-0552 for reservations or online at www.alaskarailroad.com.

Explore the Mat-Su Valley. Wasilla and Palmer are the portals to Alaska's famous Mat-Su Valley. For a day-long circle tour of this area, drive north on the Glenn Highway to **Milepost A 29.6** and take the Old Glenn Highway to downtown Palmer for lunch and shopping. Visit the Colony House Museum, a restored 1930s home originally occupied by Matanuska Valley colonists. Palmer Visitor Center is home to the Palmer Museum and a Showcase Garden.

Head back down the Glenn to the Glenn/

Parks Interchange and turn northwest on the Parks Highway for Wasilla. Local history is also featured at the Wasilla's Museum and Visitor Center at 323 N. Main St. in downtown Wasilla. Follow Main Street across the Parks Highway to Knik Road and drive west 2.1 miles for the Iditarod Trail Sled Dog Race® Headquarters and Visitor Center. The center has dog "cart" rides offered, films on dog mushing and Iditarod souvenirs. Continue down Knik Road to Mile 13.9 for the Knik Museum Mushers' Hall of Fame for more Iditarod Race history.

Mat-Su attractions to add to your itinerary include the Museum of Alaska Transportation & Industry at **Milepost A 47** Parks Highway; Big Lake, turnoff at **Milepost A 52.3** Parks Highway; Independence Mine on Hatcher Pass Road; the Musk Ox Farm at **Milepost A 50.1** Glenn Highway; and Matanuska Glacier, from the state recreation site at **Milepost A 101** Glenn Highway or from Glacier Park at **Milepost A 102.1**. *See Mat-Su Vicinity Map on page 340 or page 378.*

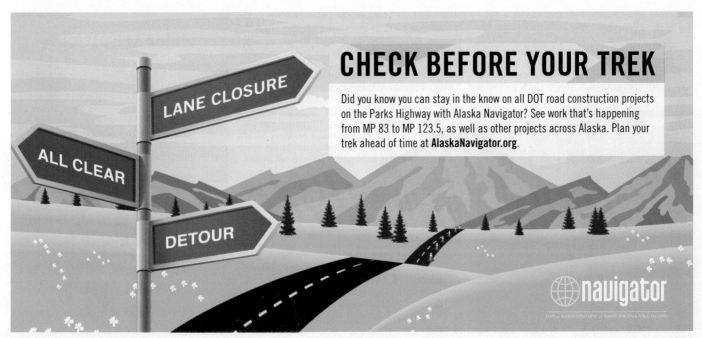

Parks Highway

CONNECTS: Anchorage to Fairbanks, AK

Length: 362 miles   **Road Surface:** Paved   **Season:** Open all year

(See maps, pages 375–376)

Motorists enjoy spectacular mountain views at Milepost A 224 of the Parks Highway. (©Serine Reeves)

The Parks Highway was called the Anchorage–Fairbanks Highway after its completion in 1971, then renamed the George Parks Highway in July 1975, in honor of George A. Parks (1883–1984), the territorial governor from 1925 to 1933.

Still officially the George Parks Highway, it is more commonly referred to as the "Parks" Highway. Designated Alaska Route 3, the Parks Highway junctions with the Glenn Highway (Alaska Route 1) 35 miles from Anchorage and leads 327 miles north to Fairbanks. Together, these highways connect 2 of Alaska's largest population centers.

Designated a National Scenic Byway in 2009, the George Parks Highway passes through some of the grandest scenery that Alaska has to offer. Highest summit on the Parks Highway is at Broad Pass (see **Milepost A 195**), at approximately 2,400 feet. Motorists can see current weather conditions at Broad Pass by checking the website: avcams.faa.gov for the FAA videocam at Summit airport. The Parks Highway between **Milepost A 132** and Fairbanks is an Alaska Scenic Byway.

The Parks Highway junctions with the Denali Highway (Alaska Route 8) at Cantwell at **Milepost A 210**. The entrance to Denali National Park is located at **Milepost A 237.4** on the Parks Highway, approximately 27 miles north of Cantwell and 125 miles south of Fairbanks.

Distance in miles

	Anchorage	Denali Park	Fairbanks	Talkeetna	Wasilla
Anchorage		237	362	113	42
Denali Park	237		125	153	195
Fairbanks	362	125		278	320
Talkeetna	113	153	278		71
Wasilla	42	195	320	71	

Major Attractions:

Alaska Veterans Memorial, Denali National Park, Mat-Su Valley

Highest Summit:
Broad Pass 2,400 ft.

©Kris Valencia, staff

Parks Highway Anchorage, AK, to Milepost A 169

© 2019 The MILEPOST®

Denali National Park and Preserve

(map continues next page)

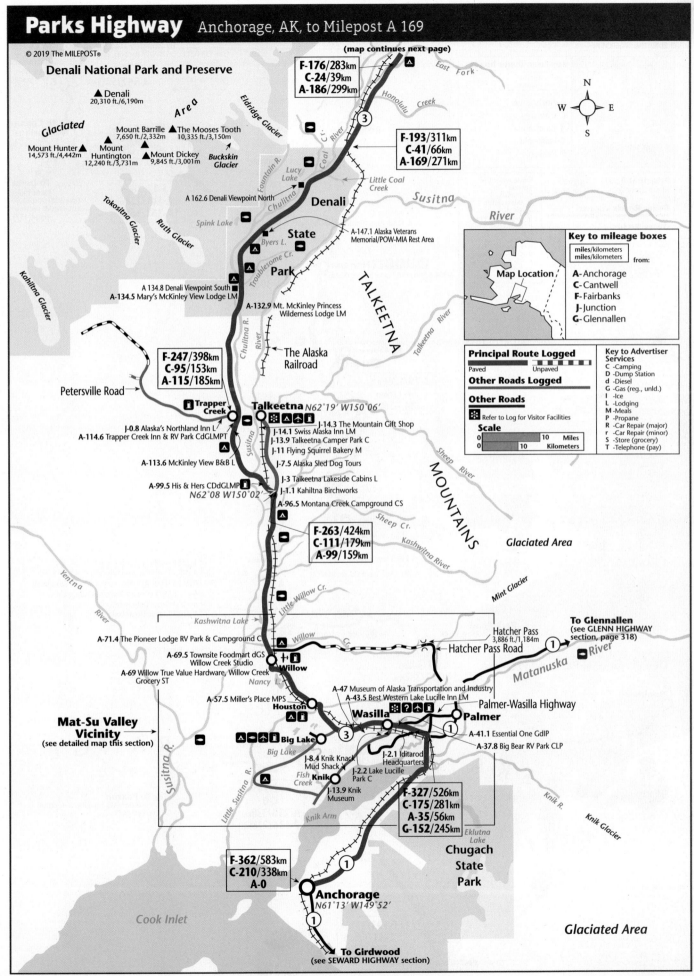

▲ Denali
20,310 ft./6,190m

Glaciated *Area*

Mount Barrille ▲ ▲ The Mooses Tooth
7,650 ft./2,332m   10,335 ft./3,150m

Mount Hunter ▲   ▲ Mount Dickey   *Buckskin*
14,573 ft./4,442m   ▲ Mount   9,845 ft./3,001m   *Glacier*
        Huntington
        12,240 ft./3,731m

F-176/283km
C-24/39km
A-186/299km

F-193/311km
C-41/66km
A-169/271km

A 162.6 Denali Viewpoint North

Denali

A-147.1 Alaska Veterans Memorial/POW-MIA Rest Area

State

Park

A 134.8 Denali Viewpoint South
A-134.5 Mary's McKinley View Lodge LM

A-132.9 Mt. McKinley Princess Wilderness Lodge LM

The Alaska Railroad

F-247/398km
C-95/153km
A-115/185km

Petersville Road →

Trapper Creek   **Talkeetna** N62°19' W150°06'

J-0.8 Alaska's Northland Inn L
A-114.6 Trapper Creek Inn & RV Park CdGLMPT

J-14.3 The Mountain Gift Shop
J-14.1 Swiss Alaska Inn LM
J-13.9 Talkeetna Camper Park C
J-11 Flying Squirrel Bakery M

A-113.6 McKinley View B&B L

J-7.5 Alaska Sled Dog Tours

A-99.5 His & Hers CDdGLMP
N62°08 W150°02'

J-3 Talkeetna Lakeside Cabins L
J-1.1 Kahiltna Birchworks

A-96.5 Montana Creek Campground CS

F-263/424km
C-111/179km
A-99/159km

MOUNTAINS

Glaciated Area

A-71.4 The Pioneer Lodge RV Park & Campground C

Hatcher Pass
3,886 ft./1,184m

Hatcher Pass Road

To Glennallen
(see GLENN HIGHWAY section, page 318)

A-69.5 Townsite Foodmart dGS
Willow Creek Studio
A-69 Willow True Value Hardware, Willow Creek
Grocery ST

Willow

A-57.5 Miller's Place MPS

A-47 Museum of Alaska Transportation and Industry
A-43.5 Best Western Lake Lucille Inn LM

Palmer-Wasilla Highway

Houston

Wasilla   **Palmer**

**Mat-Su Valley
Vicinity**
(see detailed map this section)

A-41.1 Essential One GdIP
A-37.8 Big Bear RV Park CLP

Big Lake

J-8.4 Knik Knack
Mud Shack

J-2.1 Iditarod
Headquarters

J-2.2 Lake Lucille
Park C

Knik

J-13.9 Knik
Museum

F-327/526km
C-175/281km
A-35/56km
G-152/245km

**Chugach
State
Park**

F-362/583km
C-210/338km
A-0

Anchorage
N61°13' W149°52'

Cook Inlet

To Girdwood
(see SEWARD HIGHWAY section)

Glaciated Area

Key to mileage boxes

Map Location

miles/kilometers
miles/kilometers

from:

A - Anchorage
C - Cantwell
F - Fairbanks
J - Junction
G - Glennallen

Principal Route Logged

Paved   Unpaved

Other Roads Logged

Other Roads

⊞ Refer to Log for Visitor Facilities

Key to Advertiser Services

C - Camping
D - Dump Station
d - Diesel
G - Gas (reg., unld.)
I - Ice
L - Lodging
M - Meals
P - Propane
R - Car Repair (major)
r - Car Repair (minor)
S - Store (grocery)
T - Telephone (pay)

Scale

0   10   Miles
0   10   Kilometers

Parks Highway Milepost A 169 to Fairbanks, AK

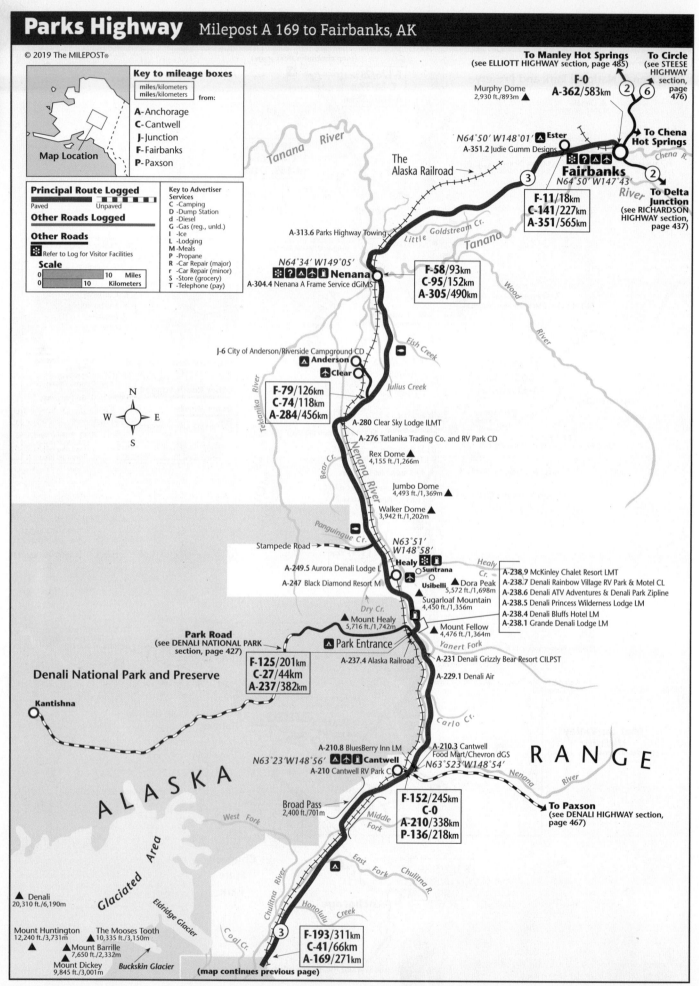

© 2019 The MILEPOST®

Key to mileage boxes

miles/kilometers
miles/kilometers
from:

A-Anchorage
C-Cantwell
J-Junction
F-Fairbanks
P-Paxson

Map Location

Principal Route Logged

Paved   Unpaved

Other Roads Logged

Other Roads

❋ Refer to Log for Visitor Facilities

Key to Advertiser Services

C - Camping
D - Dump Station
d - Diesel
G - Gas (reg., unld.)
I - Ice
L - Lodging
M - Meals
P - Propane
R - Car Repair (major)
r - Car Repair (minor)
S - Store (grocery)
T - Telephone (pay)

Scale

0   10 Miles
0   10 Kilometers

N
W   E
S

To Manley Hot Springs
(see ELLIOTT HIGHWAY section, page 485)

To Circle
(see STEESE HIGHWAY section, page 476)

Murphy Dome
2,930 ft./893m ▲

F-0
A-362/583km

N64°50′ W148°01′ ▲ Ester
A-351.2 Judie Gumm Designs

Fairbanks
N64°50′ W147°43′

To Chena Hot Springs

Chena R.

F-11/18km
C-141/227km
A-351/565km

To Delta Junction
(see RICHARDSON HIGHWAY section, page 437)

Tanana River

The Alaska Railroad

A-313.6 Parks Highway Towing

Little   Goldstream Cr.

Tanana

Wood River

N64°34′ W149°05′ **Nenana** ❋?▲🏕🏔🏚
A-304.4 Nenana A Frame Service dGiMST

F-58/93km
C-95/152km
A-305/490km

J-6 City of Anderson/Riverside Campground CD
🏕 **Anderson**
✈ **Clear**

Fish Creek

Julius Creek

F-79/126km
C-74/118km
A-284/456km

A-280 Clear Sky Lodge ILMT
A-276 Tatlanika Trading Co. and RV Park CD

Teklanika River

Bear Cr.

Nenana River

Rex Dome ▲
4,155 ft./1,266m

Jumbo Dome ▲
4,493 ft./1,369m

Walker Dome ▲
3,942 ft./1,202m

Panguingue Cr.

Stampede Road →

N63°51′ W148°58′

Healy ❋?🏔
○ **Suntrana**
A-249.5 Aurora Denali Lodge L   Healy Cr.
🏕
A-247 Black Diamond Resort M   ▲ **Usibelli** Dora Peak ▲
                                         5,572 ft./1,698m

Sugarloaf Mountain ▲
4,450 ft./1,356m

A-238.9 McKinley Chalet Resort LMT
A-238.7 Denali Rainbow Village RV Park & Motel CL
A-238.6 Denali ATV Adventures & Denali Park Zipline
A-238.5 Denali Princess Wilderness Lodge LM
A-238.4 Denali Bluffs Hotel LM
A-238.1 Grande Denali Lodge LM

Dry Cr.

Mount Healy ▲
5,716 ft./1,742m

▲ Mount Fellow
4,476 ft./1,364m

Park Road
(see DENALI NATIONAL PARK section, page 427)

🏚 **Park Entrance**

Yanert Fork

A-237.4 Alaska Railroad

A-231 Denali Grizzly Bear Resort CILPST

A-229.1 Denali Air

F-125/201km
C-27/44km
A-237/382km

Denali National Park and Preserve

Kantishna ○

Carlo Cr.

R A N G E

Nenana   River

A-210.8 BluesBerry Inn LM
N63°23′W148°56′ 🏕🏔🏚 **Cantwell**
A-210 Cantwell RV Park C

A-210.3 Cantwell Food Mart/Chevron dGS
N63°523′W148°54′

To Paxson
(see DENALI HIGHWAY section, page 467)

A L A S K A

Broad Pass
2,400 ft./701m

West Fork

Middle Fork

F-152/245km
C-0
A-210/338km
P-136/218km

East Fork   Chulitna R.

🏕

Chulitna River

Glaciated Area

Eldridge Glacier

Denali ▲
20,310 ft./6,190m

Mount Huntington ▲
12,240 ft./3,731m

The Mooses Tooth ▲
10,335 ft./3,150m

Mount Barrille ▲
7,650 ft./2,332m

Mount Dickey ▲
9,845 ft./3,001m

Buckskin Glacier

Coal Cr.

Honolulu Creek

③

F-193/311km
C-41/66km
A-169/271km

(map continues previous page)

The Parks Highway is a good 2-lane paved road with passing lanes on improved sections and 4-lane stretches through towns. Expect moderate S-curves. Heavy foliage may reduce sight distance: Pass with care. *CAUTION: Drive with headlights on at all times. Watch for moose. Watch for local cross traffic. Check highway conditions in winter.*

The Parks Highway provides the most direct highway access to Denali National Park and Preserve (formerly Mount McKinley National Park) from either Anchorage or Fairbanks. At 20,310 feet, Denali—formerly Mount McKinley—is visible from the highway, weather permitting. Some of the best Denali viewpoints include Denali Viewpoint South, at **Milepost A 134.8**, with a large parking area, interpretive boards and viewing scopes. There is also an excellent Denali viewpoint on the Talkeetna Spur Road, 12.9 miles from **Milepost A 98.7**.

Emergency medical services: Phone 911. Alaska State Trooper posts in Anchorage, Wasilla, Cantwell, Healy, Nenana and Fairbanks. Hospitals in Anchorage and Fairbanks and at junction of Glenn and Parks Highway (Mat-Su Regional Medical Center). Ambulance/Fire/EMS in Anchorage, Chugiak, Wasilla, Cantwell, Healy, Nenana, Anderson/Clear, Ester, Fairbanks.

Parks Highway Log

Northbound: Distance from Anchorage (A) is followed by distance from Cantwell (C) and distance from Fairbanks (F). Read log: ⬇

Mileposts along the Parks Highway indicate distance from Anchorage.

ALASKA ROUTE 1

A 0 C 210 F 362 ANCHORAGE. Follow the Glenn Highway (Alaska Route 1) north 35 miles to junction with the Parks Highway. *(Turn to the end of the GLENN HIGHWAY section on page 351 and read log back to front from Anchorage to junction with the Parks Highway).*

A 34 C 176 F 328 Exit east to Palmer via Glenn Highway for northbound traffic.

> **Junction** of the Parks Highway (Alaska Route 3) with the Glenn Highway (Alaska Route 1) to Glennallen and the Tok Cutoff. Turn to **Milepost A 34** on page 346 in the GLENN HIGHWAY section for log of that route.

A 35 C 175 F 327 Glenn-Parks Interchange: Northbound sign on overpass indicates Glenn Highway (Alaska Route 1) ends and Parks Highway (Alaska Route 3) begins. This massive interchange has obscured the start of the Parks Highway, since the interchange provides 2 lanes for continuous flow north–south traffic while those eastbound on the Glenn Highway (Route 1) headed to Palmer must exit.

ALASKA ROUTE 3

A 35.4 C 174.6 F 326.6 Southbound exit for Glenn Highway (Route 1) east to Palmer and Glennallen.

A 35.5 C 174.5 F 326.5 Trunk Road exit northbound; access to Mat–Su Regional Medical Center (visible from the highway on hill to east); see description at **Milepost A 36.1.**

A 36.1 C 173.9 F 325.9 Trunk Road overpass; use north- and southbound exits to access **Mat-Su Regional Medical Center** to east. Exit west and follow frontage road north to S. Church Street for access to **Big Bear RV Park** (see description at **Milepost A 37.8**).

➕ ⛺

Trunk Road leads northeast 0.2 mile to roundabout access to a very large Park and Ride parking lot with interpretive sign. Continue 0.7 mile to E. Duchess Drive with access to University of Alaska Fairbanks' Matanuska Experiment Farm; no tours, but you can observe the community gardens. Also access via Trunk Road to Mat-Su College and the Glenn Massay Theater (1.8 miles); Palmer-Wasilla Highway (2.9 miles); Bogard Road roundabout (3.8 miles) with access to Finger Lake State Recreation Site to west; and Palmer-Fishhook Road (6 miles). Turn south for Palmer and north for Hatcher Pass.

A 36.4 C 173.6 F 325.6 Trunk Road southbound exit; access to Mat–Su Regional Medical Center (visible from the highway on hill to east); see description at **Milepost A 36.1.**

A 36.9 C 173.1 F 325.1 Distance marker northbound shows Wasilla 7 miles, Denali National Park 201 miles, Fairbanks 319 miles.

A 37.5 C 172.5 F 324.5 Fairview Loop/Hyer Road northbound exit. See description at **Milepost A 37.8.**

A 37.8 C 172.2 F 324.2 Fairview Loop/Hyer Road underpass: use north- and southbound exits to access gas station/foodmart. Denali Harley–Davidson Shop east off exit. Exit west and follow frontage road south to Church Street for access to **Big Bear RV Park.**

⛽ ⛺

Big Bear RV Park. See display ad this page.

Also use this exit to Palmer Hay Flats State Game Refuge from Fairview Loop (description at **Milepost J 4.1** Knik–Goose Bay Road. *See log page 379*).

A 38.2 C 171.8 F 323.8 Fairview Loop/

Hyer Road southbound exit. See description at **Milepost A 37.8.**

A 39 C 171 F 323 Northbound exit to Seward Meridian Road; see description at **Milepost A 39.3.**

A 39.3 C 170.7 F 322.7 Seward Meridian Road overpass: use north- and southbound exits. Exit west on Seward Meridian Parkway South for Seward Meridian Plaza shopping mall and Walmart. (Wasilla's Walmart is the largest Walmart in the state and, as reported by Anchorage's newspaper, has sold more duct tape than any other Walmart in the world.) Drive 0.4 mile west to T junction and turn right for access to The Valley Cinema and XTreme Fun Center.

A 39.6 C 170.4 F 322.4 Southbound exit to Seward Meridian Road; see description at **Milepost A 39.3.**

A 40.1 C 169.9 F 321.9 Wasilla Veterinary Clinic, Kendall Ford, Alaskan View Motel.

A 40.4 C 169.6 F 321.6 Traffic light at Hermon Road; access to Lowes, liquor store

Glenn/Parks Interchange

To Wasilla
Parks Highway
Exit to Parks Hwy/Wasilla
Exit to Glenn Hwy/Palmer
Glenn Highway
To Palmer
Exit to Glenn Hwy/Palmer
Glenn Highway
To Anchorage

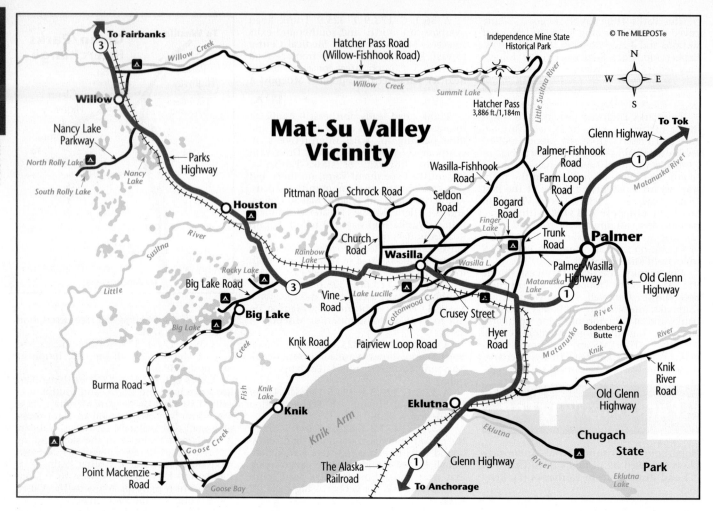

Independence Mine State
Historical Park

© The MILEPOST®

To Fairbanks

Willow Creek

Hatcher Pass Road
(Willow-Fishhook Road)

Willow Creek

Summit Lake

Hatcher Pass
3,886 ft./1,184m

Little Susitna River

Glenn Highway   To Tok

**Mat-Su Valley
Vicinity**

Willow

Nancy Lake
Parkway

North Rolly Lake

Nancy
Lake

South Rolly Lake

Parks
Highway

Palmer-Fishhook
Road

Farm Loop
Road

Pittman Road   Schrock Road

Wasilla-Fishhook
Road

Seldon
Road

Bogard
Road

Finger
Lake

Matanuska
River

Trunk
Road

Palmer

Houston

Church
Road

Wasilla

Wasilla L.

Palmer-Wasilla
Highway

Old Glenn
Highway

Susitna River

Rainbow
Lake

Rocky Lake

Lake Lucille

Cottonwood Cr.

Matanuska
Lake

Bodenberg
Butte

Matanuska   River

Big Lake Road

Big Lake

Big Lake

Vine
Road

Crusey Street

Hyer
Road

Knik
River
Road

Knik Road

Fairview Loop Road

Old Glenn
Highway

Burma Road

Fish Creek

Knik
Lake

Knik

Eklutna

Chugach
State
Park

Point Mackenzie
Road

Goose Creek

Knik Arm

The Alaska
Railroad

Glenn Highway

Eklutna River

Eklutna
Lake

Goose Bay

To Anchorage

---

and other businesses.

A **40.5** C 169.5 F 321.5 Pilgrims Baptist Church.

A **40.7** C 169.3 F 321.3 Sun Mountain

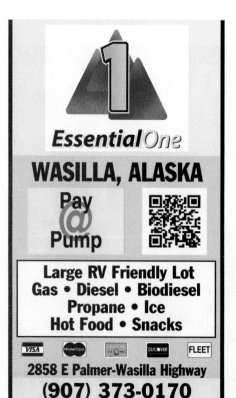

Avenue. Sportsman's Warehouse to northeast, shopping center.

A **40.8** C 169.2 F 321.2 Creekside Plaza.

A **41** C 169 F 321 Wasilla Police, fast-food, family dining.

A **41.1** C 168.9 F 320.9 Traffic light at **junction** with Palmer-Wasilla Highway. Access east to Target, Starbucks, fast-food (Taco Bell, KFC, etc.), Walgreens, Fred Meyer, Petco, Tesoro and **Essential One** gas stations. **Essential One** at 2858 E. Palmer-Wasilla Highway is RV friendly with gas, diesel, biodiesel, propane, ice and food.

Essential One. See display ad this page.

The 10-mile Palmer-Wasilla Highway connects Wasilla on the Parks Highway with Palmer on the Glenn Highway. It is a very busy road.

Palmer–Wasilla Highway extension to west connects with Glenwood Avenue to Knik–Goose Bay Road.

A **41.8** C 168.2 F 320.2 Northbound access to Newcomb Wasilla Lake Park; limited parking, picnic shelter, restrooms, playground and swimming beach, rainbow trout fishing. Monument to George Parks. Kids flotation devices available here through the "Kids Don't Float" program.

A **41.9** C 168.1 F 320.1 Crusey Street intersection; McDonald's and Midas. Southbound access to Wasilla Lake. Turn east on Crusey Street for Bogard Road access to Finger Lake State Recreation Site (7.1 miles).

A **42** C 168 F 320 Carrs/Safeway Mall to east; Carrs/Safeway supermarket and other shops.

Yenlo Street; Subway, access to Carrs/Safeway.

A **42.1** C 167.9 F 319.9 North Boundary Street; gas station. Access to **Gold Rush Jewelers** and **Last Frontier Brewing Co.**

A **42.2** C **167.8** F **319.8 Junction** with Knik-Goose Bay Road to south, Main Street to north; gas station. Historic Alaska Railroad Depot south side of highway (see Wasilla Attractions). Main Street leads 1 block north to the visitor center and museum, 2 blocks to the post office. Take the Wasilla-Fishhook Road 0.4 mile north to the relocated **Veterans Monument**, a 20-ton granite boulder with a bronze plaque and inscription, and **Veterans Wall of Honor**— intended to resemble the Vietnam Wall in Washington D.C. (see more information under Attractions).

Iditarod Trail Headquarters. See display ad on page 379.

Junction with Knik-Goose Bay Road and access to Lake Lucille Park, Iditarod Trail Sled Dog Race Headquarters and other attractions. See "Knik-Goose Bay Road" log on page 379.

Main Street becomes Wasilla–Fishhook Road and leads northeast 10 miles to junction with Hatcher Pass Road to Independence Mine State Historical Park; see the map located above. (Hatcher Pass Road is logged on pages 341–342 in the GLENN HIGHWAY section.)

(Continues on page 381)

www.themilepost.com

Knik–Goose Bay Road

Knik-Goose Bay Road leads southwest from the Parks Highway in Wasilla, providing access to Goose Bay State Game Refuge and to Point Mackenzie Road. Point Mackenzie Road accesses the popular Little Susitna River Public-use Facility in Susitna Flats State Game Refuge. *CAUTION: Drive carefully! This road is a Highway Safety Corridor due to its high accident rate.* There are quite a few subdivisions along this road; expect heavy traffic during commuting hours.

The first 15 miles of Knik-Goose Bay Road have been designated the Joe Redington Sr. Memorial Trail; Joe was instrumental in organizing the Iditarod Trail Sled Dog Race. (Stop by the Iditarod Trail headquarters at **Milepost J 2.1** for more on the history of this major Alaska sporting event.)

KNIK-GOOSE BAY ROAD

Distance from the junction (J) with Parks Highway.

J 0 Junction with Parks Highway at **Milepost A 42.2**, Main Street, Wasilla.

J 0.1 Historic Railroad Depot. *CAUTION: Road crosses railroad tracks.*

J 0.2 City center Wasilla mall.

J 0.5 Benteh Nuutah Valley Native Primary Care Center.

J 0.7 Traffic light at **junction** with the

Don't miss your chance to visit the Iditarod Trail Sled Dog Race™ Headquarters at Milepost J 2.1 Knik-Goose Bay Road. (©Serine Reeves)

Palmer-Wasilla Highway which connects with the Parks Highway at **Milepost A 41.1**.

J 1.5 Subway sandwich shop. Knik Tire and Auto Center.

J 1.9 Smith Ballfields. RV parking $20. Tent camping $10.

J 2.1 Main entrance for **Iditarod Sled Dog Race™ Headquarters** and visitor center. The center has historical displays

and films on sled dog racing and mushers, as well as a souvenir shop with Iditarod memorabilia. Dog team cart rides in summer. Sled dog puppies are sometimes on view. Open 8 A.M. to 7 P.M., daily in mid-May to mid-September, weekdays 8 A.M. until 5 P.M. the rest of the year.

Iditarod Trail Headquarters. See display ad this page.

J 2.2 Turnoff on Endeavor Street for **Lake**

Lake Lucille Park offers 59 campsites nestled in a heavily wooded area.
(©Serine Reeves)

Lucille Park (Mat–Su Borough) campground and day-use area, located 0.6 mile north via gravel road. There are 59 campsites (2 pull-throughs; 16 sites with electric) in a heavily wooded area on a gravel loop road; picnic pavilions; campground host; water; firewood, firepits, restrooms. Camping fee $10 (hookup sites $25). Fishing for landlocked coho salmon. Short boardwalk walking trail to lake. Open mid-May 15 through September, weather permitting. 14-day maximum stay. Phone (907) 373-9010.

J 4.1 Tesoro gas station, liquor and grocery at junction with Fairview Loop Road, which loops 11 miles back to the Parks Highway and also accesses Palmer Hay Flats

State Game Refuge (description follows).

Palmer Hay Flats State Game Refuge is a 45-square-mile area of forests, wetlands, lakes, creeks and tidal sloughs that supports migrating waterfowl and shorebirds plus a variety of other wildlife. Accessed by driving 1.9 miles on Fairview Loop from this junction to where the road makes a 90-degree turn and intersects with Hayfield Road. Follow Hayfield Road 1.3 miles to the signed turnoff for Palmer Hay Flats refuge. Improved gravel access road leads from Hayfield Road 0.3 mile to Scout Ridge trailhead with covered observation deck with panoramic views, and forested walking trail. Another 0.3 mile along the access road leads to second trailhead at Cottonwood Creek with restrooms and wetlands trail. The lower 1 mile of Cottonwood Creek is open to salmon fishing (primarily sockeye and coho, not chinook) on weekends only from 5 A.M. to 10 P.M. (closed April 14–June 15). Other activities include fall waterfowl hunting (limited ATV trail use generally allowed), bird watching, photography, hiking, trapping, cross-country skiing and snow machining. More information at www.adfg.state.ak.us and www.palmerhayflats.org.

J 6 Three Bears Alaska warehouse-style shopping. Shell Gas.

J 6.8 Traffic light at **junction** with Vine Road, which leads 3.4 miles to the Parks Highway. Vine Road also junctions with Hollywood Road, which leads 6.5 miles to connect with Big Lake Road.

J 7 Central Mat-Su Fire Department Station No. 62.

J 7.9 Gas station at turnoff for Settlers Bay residential area; Settlers Bay Lodge & Village Center (restaurant). Access to 18-hole Settlers Bay golf course (follow signs); settlersbay.com. Paved bike path ends. Mat-Su Urgent Care at 5851 South Knik Goose Bay Rd.; phone (907) 864-1300.

J 8.4 Turn on Carmel Road for **Knik Knack Mud Shack**.

Knik Knack Mud Shack. See display ad this page.

J 12.6 Joe Redington Sr. Memorial Trail (sign).

J 13 Entering Knik Historic District (sign). KNIK–FAIRVIEW, formerly known as Knik (pop. 14,923) has a bar, pay phone, liquor store, gas station and private campground on Knik Lake. Knik was a checkpoint on the Iditarod Trail Sled Dog Race™ route. It's been called the "Dog Mushing Center of the World" in reference to the many dog mushers that have lived in this area.

J 13.9 Double-ended turnout to northwest (watch for "Old Knik" sign); **Knik Museum** (description follows) and public fishing access to **Knik Lake** (stocked with rainbow trout; 5 hp motors only). Short, steep, narrow gravel access road to museum and lake. Interpretive signs. A traditional Athabascan graveyard with fenced graves and spirit houses is located behind Knik Museum. On sacred ground, visitors may view it from the Iditarod Trail.

Knik Museum. Once a village and trade center for Native Alaskans, it became a trailhead for winter dog sled and summer wagon trails and grew to a large town in the early 1900s. Open May 1 to Oct. 30, Wednes-

day–Sunday, 1–6 P.M. Admission $3. Winter tours by appointment, weather permitting. Annual picnic July 15, 2018. Phone (907) 376-7755; www.wkhsociety.org. [ADVERTISEMENT]

J 14.5 Double-ended scenic overlook to south.

J 16 Fish Creek bridge.

J 17.2 Point Mackenzie Road junction. *Turn here for access to Little Susitna River Public-Use Site (Point Mackenzie Road log follows). Continue straight ahead for Goose Bay.*

J 18.4 Tug Bar and Goose Bay Inn; liquor store, ATM, camping, cabin and cabin rentals.

J 19.5 Turnoff northwest leads 1.2 miles (keep to left at "Y") via very steep, deeply rutted, winding access road (*recommended for 4WD only*). Wetlands and foot trail 4 miles to right, Knik Arm and foot trail 1/2 mile to left. Good waterfowl hunting in the fall; no developed public-use facilities.

J 19.7 Goose Bay airport. Large gravel parking lot. No shooting within 1/2 mile of all refuge access points (signed).

POINT MACKENZIE ROAD

Distance from Mile J 17.2 Knik-Goose Bay Road (K) is followed by distance from Parks Highway junction (J).

K 0 J 17.2 Junction with Knik Goose Bay Road.

K 3.4 J 20.6 Central Mat-Su Fire Department Station 64, Mat-Su EMS; *Emergency phone.*

K 6.8 J 24.2 Mat-Su Transfer Station.

K 7.4 J 24.6 'T' junction: turn left on paved road for Goose Creek Correctional Center (4 miles) and Port Mackenzie (13.5 miles), proposed site of Knik Arm bridge to Anchorage. Turn right at this junction for Susitna Flats State Game Refuge, 5.2 miles (continue with this road log).

K 7.6 J 24.8 Junction with Burma Road, (gravel) 8.5 miles to Big Lake Road.

K 8.6 J 25.8 South Farmers road leads 0.5 mile to **Carpenter Lake** public fishing access.

K 9.4 J 26.6 Port MacKenzie Rail Extension Segment. The rail extension involves 32 miles of new rail line extending from Port MacKenzie to the ARRC mainline just south of Houston.

K 9.5 J 26.7 S. Guernsey Road; access to Point MacKenzie Correctional Farm (0.6 mile), Farmer and Barley lakes.

K 10 J 27 Little Susitna River trailhead.

K 10.2 J 27.4 Road forks; keep to right for Little Susitna.

K 12 J 29.2 Entering Susitna Flats State Game Refuge (sign).

K 12.7 J 29.9 My Creek Trailhead. Day-use area. Parking $7.

K 13.1 J 30.3 Entrance/fee station for **Little Susitna River Public-Use Facility** at River Mile 28.5 in the Susitna Flats State Game Refuge (N 61°26.229' W 150°10.453'). Continue on access road for Little Susitna River campground and boat launch; 83 parking spaces, 40 campsites, picnic tables, litter bins, outhouses, firewood $8, boat ramps, dump station $10, water, toilets. Daily parking $7; boat launch, $15 (includes parking); overnight camping, $15. Popular boat launch site for fishermen after salmon on the Little Susitna. Phone (907) 745-3975.

Return to Milepost A 42.2 Parks Highway

Wasilla

(Continued from page 378)

A 42.2 C 167.8 F 319.8
Located between Wasilla and Lucille lakes in the Matanuska-Susitna Valley, about 45 minute drive from Anchorage, 12.5 miles from Palmer, 71 miles from Talkeetna, and 195 miles from Denali National Park entrance.

Population: 9,200. **Emergency Services:** Phone 911 for Police, Fire and Ambulance. **Alaska State Troopers,** Mat-Su West Post, phone (907) 373-8300. **City Police,** Milepost A 41, phone (907) 352-5401. **Medical/ Hospital,** Mat-Su Regional Urgent Care, 950 E. Bogard Rd., Wasilla; phone (907) 352-2880. Mat-Su Regional Medical Center and Providence Matanuska Health Care are located off the Parks Highway northeast of Trunk Road.

Visitor Information: Available at the **Wasilla Museum & Visitor Center** on Main Street, just off the Parks Highway. Museum visitors enjoy exhibits, learn local history and walk through historic homes and buildings. The museum, housed in what was originally the community hall, was established in 1967 as Wasilla's first museum. The museum building and 1917 schoolhouse are listed on the National Register of Historic Places. The historic town, located behind the museum, has 8 historic buildings. The museum is open year-round; summer hours are Tuesday–Friday, from 9 A.M. to 5 P.M. Admission charged but Fridays are always free. Phone (907) 373-9071; www. cityofwasilla.com/museum.

Radio and **Television** via Anchorage stations; KMBQ 99.7 FM, Classic Country 100.9 FM, Hometown radio 1430 AM, KJHA (King Jesus Houston Alaska) 88.7 FM, Hatcher Pass Radio 95.5 FM. **Newspapers:** *The Frontiersman* (Tuesday, Friday, Sunday). **Transportation: Air**—Charter service available. **Railroad**—Alaska Railroad stops at the historic depot (visible on south side of Parks Highway), located at 415 E. Railroad Ave. The depot is not staffed by the Alaska Railroad and "is often closed and locked at train arrival/departure times." **Bus**—Mat-Su Community Transit, service between Mat-Su locations and Anchorage; phone (907) 376-5000. **Rental Cars**—Enterprise Rent-A-Car (907)

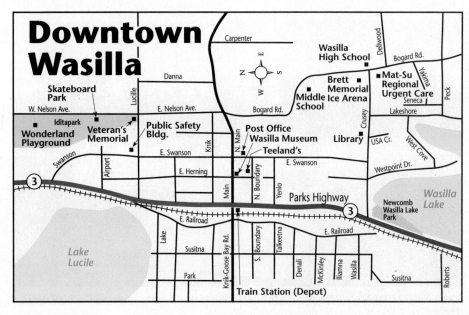

Downtown Wasilla

373-2080. **Taxis**—A Cab (907) 775-6622; Alaska Cab (907) 357-2727.

Private Aircraft: Wasilla municipal airport, 1.6 miles southwest from S. Clapp St. and Parks Highway intersection; elev. 348 feet; length 3,700 feet; asphalt; unattended. Wasilla Lake seaplane base, 5.7 miles northeast; elev. 330 feet. Numerous private airstrips and lakes in vicinity.

One of the Matanuska–Susitna Valley's pioneer communities, Wasilla began as a station on the Alaska Railroad about 1917. With the railroad, and a government land auction bringing in new settlement, Wasilla became a supply staging point for gold mines in the Willow Creek Mining District.

With the advent of a farm-based economy in the 1930s and 40s—precipitated by the Matanuska Valley Colony project— Palmer replaced Wasilla as the regional ser-

vice and supply center. Palmer remained the commercial hub of the Mat-Su Valley until the 1970s, when the new Glenn Highway bypassed downtown Palmer, and the

WASILLA ADVERTISERS

Scenic Finger Lake State Recreation Site offers a boat launch and campsites (no hookups).
(©Serine Reeves)

Anchorage–Fairbanks Highway (now Parks Highway) was completed. The new highway, coupled with the pipeline boom, brought both people and traffic to Wasilla.

Today, Wasilla is the business and financial center for the Mat-Su Valley, with major chain retail stores, small businesses, fast-food restaurants and auto dealerships along the Parks Highway in Wasilla. New residential subdivisions have sprung up along Wasilla's back roads in this fastest-growing area in the state. Wasilla celebrated its Centennial in 2017.

Lodging & Services

All visitor facilities available. Accommodations at **Best Western Lake Lucille Inn** (description follows), **Hillside Cabins**, and other hotels/motels. Dining at **The Last Frontier Brewing Company** on N. Boundary St. Wasilla has banks, a post office, gas/diesel stations, major-chain retail stores, fast-food restaurants and supermarkets.

Best Western Lake Lucille Inn. Conveniently located on the way to Denali, only 45 miles from Anchorage. The Valley's premier hotel has a superb location on beautiful Lake Lucille with breathtaking views of the Chugach Mountains. Amenities: Free hot breakfast and WiFi internet, laundry, fitness room and sauna. 1-800-897-1776; www.BestWesternLakeLucilleInn.com. See display ad on page 381. [ADVERTISEMENT]

A great stop for families traveling with active children is Iditapark on Nelson Avenue, with a playground, skateboard park, BMX track, basketball, volleyball, 3 picnic pavilions and tennis courts. Indoor entertainment in Wasilla includes movies at the 12-screen Valley Cinema. The Brett Memorial Ice Arena, at E. Bogard Road and N. Crusey Street, has ice skating. The city's Curtis D. Menard Memorial Sports Complex, at 1001 S. Clapp St., is a premier indoor sports facility with NHL-size ice arena, indoor artificial turf courts and walking track; phone (907) 357-9100.

Camping

There are several RV parks on the Parks Highway, including the **Big Bear RV Park**. Public campgrounds in the Wasilla area include **Lake Lucille Park** on Knik-Goose Bay Road and Little Susitna River public-use facility off Point Mackenzie Road (see Knik-Goose Bay Road log on page 379); and Finger Lake State Recreation Site is located on E. Bogard Road. See descriptions following.

Lake Lucille Park. Nestled among 80 acres of pure nature! Open May 15th–Sept. 30th. 59 campsites for tents and RVs in heavily wooded area on gravel loop road; picnic pavilions, campground host, firewood, firepits, restrooms. 16 spaces electrical hookups available, $30. Camping fee $15 (2 tent/2 vehicle limit per site). Take Knik-Goose Bay Road 2.3 miles southwest, turn on Endeavor Street (just beyond Iditarod headquarters parking lot), drive 0.6 mile on a gravel access road. (907) 373-9010

or http://cityofwasilla.com/departments-divisions/parks-and-recreation/lake-lucille-park/camping-rv-parking. [ADVERTISEMENT]

Little Susitna River public use facility is located off Point Mackenzie Road, 30 miles from the Parks Highway. There are 83 parking spaces, 40 campsites, campsite host, boat ramps, dump station, water, tables, toilets. Daily parking, $7; boat launch, $15 (includes parking); overnight camping, $15; dump station, $10; firewood, $8. See *Milepost K 13.1 in "Knik–Goose Bay Road" log on page 380.*

Finger Lake State Recreation Site is located at on E. Bogard Road 5 miles from the Trunk Road Overpass at **Mile A 36.1** on the Parks Highway. Scenic spot with 24 campsites, RVs up to 60 feet, 2 group campsites, campground host, wheelchair-accessible toilets, picnic tables, firepits, water, canoe trail, swimming beach and boat launch, $25–$30 camping fee, $15 boat launch fee, $5 day parking fee, 7-day limit. Life preservers available for children through the "Kids Don't Float" program. Visit reserveamerica.com or call (907) 745-3975.

Attractions

Wasilla Museum & Visitor Center at 391 N. Main St., Wasilla. Exhibits, historic building tours and events year-round. Open Tuesdays–Fridays, 9 A.M. to 5 P.M. Admission charged. Fridays are always free. For more information, visit www.cityofwasilla.com/museum; www.facebook.com/wasillamuseum; or call (907) 373-9071. [ADVERTISEMENT]

The 28-acre **Iditapark** on W. Nelson Avenue includes Wonderland playground, a skateboard park, tennis, volleyball and basketball courts, and ample parking. A Farmers Market is held at Iditapark on Wednesday's during the summer, 10 A.M. to 6 P.M. Crafts, food and Mat-Su Valley vegetables for sale.

Iditarod Trail Sled Dog Race™ headquarters is located just west of the Parks Highway in Wasilla at 2100 S. Knik-Goose Bay Rd. The internationally known 1,000-mile Iditarod Trail Sled Dog Race™ to Nome takes place the first Saturday in March with the start in Anchorage, followed by the re-start in Willow. The headquarters, open year-round, has historical displays on the Iditarod, videos, summer cart rides with an Iditarod musher and dog team, and a gift shop with unique souvenirs. Open daily in summer 9 A.M. to 7 P.M., weekdays in winter 8 A.M. to 5 P.M. Large tours are welcome (calls in advance appreciated), phone (907) 376-5155, ext. 108. Circular drive for buses and motorhomes. No admission fee. Fee charged for rides on wheeled cart pulled by dogs.

The 2018 champion, Joar Leifseth Ulsom, finished the race in 9 days, 12 hours. Find out more about "The Last Great Race on Earth®" at Iditarod headquarters or online. Website: www.iditarod.com.

Knik Museum, at Mile 13.9 Knik-Goose Bay Road, has dog mushing equipment, musher's portraits and historical displays of the Iditarod Trail. The museum is open May 1 to Oct. 30 (dependent on the weather), Wednesday–Sunday, 1–6 P.M. Admission $3. Open in winter by appointment. Website www.wkhsociety.org; phone (907) 376-7755.

Wasilla's 1917 Alaska Railroad Depot is also on the National Register of Historic Places. Restored by the local Lions Clubs and the Greater Wasilla Chamber of Commerce and Visitors Center, the depot now houses the Greater Wasilla Chamber of Commerce and is located on the south side of the Parks

Highway on Knik-Goose Bay Road. A sign there reads:

"Construction of the depot began 1916 as part of a national goal for the Alaska Railroad to open access to the interior of Alaska. This site marks the R.R. junction with the important Carle Trail (now known as Knik Rd./Main St./Fishhook Rd.) that was the main supply route between the tidewater trade center of Knik and the gold mines of the Willow Creek (Hatcher Pass) area. By drastically improving the lines of supply to miners and settlers in this region, this junction both created the new town of Wasilla and hastened the demise of Knik. For many years this depot was the major 'Outside' communication point for the surrounding district, via trains, the telegraph, and later one railroad system telephone. (On a regional basis, electricity did not become available to local farms and homes until 1942, and telephone until 1957.)"

Visit the Veteran's Monument and Veteran's Wall of Honor. Take the Wasilla-Fishhook Road 0.4 mile north to the Veterans Monument, a 20-ton granite boulder with a bronze plaque and inscription, which honors all veterans of the U.S. armed forces. Also here is the Veterans Wall of Honor—intended to resemble the Vietnam Wall in Washington D.C.—consisting of black granite panels inscribed with the names of veterans, living or deceased, who have either received an honorable discharge or are presently serving in the military. The names of the only 2 Alaskan MIAs (Marine E4 Thomas E. Anderson and Navy E3 Howard M. Koslosky) from the Vietnam War appear on the Wasilla Wall of Honor.

Museum of Alaska Transportation and Industry, located a few miles west of Wasilla at **Milepost A 47,** has 20 acres of historic aircraft, railroad equipment, old farm machinery, mining and military equipment and a 1937 Colony Barn. Gift shop, clean restrooms and gallery for your enjoyment. New exhibits and events are being added all the time. www.museumofalaska.org; phone (907) 376-1211. Open 10 A.M. to 5 P.M. daily from Mother's Day through Labor Day.

The restored **Herning-Teeland-Mead Building,** which now houses Krazy Moose Subs and Salads, was built in 1918. Located on E. Herning Avenue adjacent to the Wasilla Museum & Visitor Center on Main Street, it is on the National Register of Historic Sites.

Play Golf. The well-maintained, 18-hole Settlers Bay Golf Course is a par 71 course, located off Knik-Goose Bay Road (see log this section), offers stunning views of the Mat-Su Valley and Chugach mountains. The course has several challenging holes. Cart rentals, driving range, putting green, pro shop and dining are also available. Visit www.settlersbay.org or phone (907) 376-5466 for information.

Sleepy Hollow Golf Course, a 9-hole, par 27 course, is located 7 miles north of Wasilla at 2721 Sleepy Hollow Circle. Driving range, putting green, pull carts, rental clubs. The longest hole is 200 yards. Hours are 9 A.M. to 9 P.M. Tuesday–Sunday, May–September. For more information and driving directions, phone (907) 376-5948.

AREA FISHING: Check the ADF&G website for sport fishing updates for Mat-Su Valley (Palmer/Matanuska-Susitna Valley) lakes and streams at www.sf.adfg.state.ak.us. Also check with local fishing guides.

Mat-Su Valley lakes are stocked with rainbow trout, landlocked salmon, Arctic grayling, Arctic char, or some combination of these fish. A list of stocked lakes is available from ADF&G at www.adfg.alaska.gov/index.cfm?adfg=fishingSportStockingHatcheries.lakesdatabase.

Chinook salmon begin to move into the clear water streams of the **Susitna River** drainage in early June. Highest catch rates in early June are usually from **Deshka River** and the **Little Susitna River.** The Little Susitna River produces fair to good catches of chinook salmon through June, with most of the fishing occurring from the Little Susitna Public-Use Facility *(see "Knik Goose Bay Road" log pages 379-380)* upstream to the Parks Highway. By late June, fishing is good near the Parks Highway bridges. As June wears on, chinook fishing improves in the Parks Highway streams. **Willow Creek** and the other Parks Highway roadside streams are open to chinook fishing from Jan. 1 through the third Monday in June, and then on weekends only until the season closes on July 13. A weekend is Saturday, Sunday, and Monday. *NOTE: Check sport fishing regulations carefully for seasons and restrictions.*

Parks Highway Log
(continued from page 378)

(continued from page 378)

A 42.5 C 167.5 F 319.5 Stoplight at Lucille Street. View of Lake Lucille to south.

A 42.7 C 167.3 F 319.3 Frontier Mall to north.

A 42.8 C 167.2 F 319.2 Shopping center to north.

A 43 C 167 F 319 Stoplight at Weber Drive. Access to Iditapark. Gas/diesel station.

A 43.2 C 166.8 F 318.8 Westside Center.

A 43.5 C 166.5 F 318.5 Lucus Road; Hallea Lane access to Lake Lucille; access to **Best Western Lake Lucille Inn** to south. Bike route begins northbound.

Best Western Lake Lucille Inn. See display ad on page 381.

A 44 C 166 F 318 Traffic light at Deskas Street.

Welcome to Wasilla (southbound sign).

A 44.5 C 165.5 F 317.5 Traffic light at Church Road/S. Clapp Street. Access north to Bumpus ball fields from Church Road. Take S. Clapp Street ¼ mile to Curtis D.

Menard Sports Complex; ice rink, turf court and running track. Open to public. Menard Market here on weekends in summer from 10 A.M. to 5 P.M.

CAUTION: Moose Danger Zone. Watch for moose next 12.7 miles northbound. Begin Highway Traffic Safety Corridor northbound to Milepost A 53: Traffic fines double.

A 45.2 C 164.8 F 316.8 Distance marker northbound shows Cantwell 164 miles, Denali National Park 192 miles, Fairbanks 309 miles.

A 45.4 C 164.6 F 316.6 Wasilla city limits.

A 46.5 C 163.5 F 315.5 Railroad overpass.

A 47 C 163 F 315 Turnoff to south on West Museum Drive for Wasilla municipal airport and the **Museum of Alaska Transportation and Industry.** The museum, located approximately 1 mile from the highway (follow signs), makes a nice stop for travelers. Historic aircraft, railroad equipment, old farm machinery, mining and military equipment are displayed in a 20-acre park-like setting. RV parking and turnaround. Open daily, 10 A.M. to 5 P.M., from Mother's Day to Labor Day. www.museumofalaska.org; (907) 376-1211.

Museum of Alaska Transportation and Industry. See display ad on page 382.

A 47.3 C 162.7 F 314.7 Distance marker northbound shows Big Lake Junction 5 miles, Houston 10 miles.

A 47.7 C 162.3 F 314.3 Stoplight at Vine Road. Shell Gas Station with diesel to south. (Vine Road connects with Knik-Goose Bay Road.)

A 48.6 C 161.4 F 313.4 Stoplight at junction with Sylvan Road and Pittman Road. Tesoro2Go, cafe and access to Meadow Lakes City Center to south. Alaska State Troopers/Mat-Su West Post (emergency phone) is to the north at 527 Pittman Rd., next to Three Bears. Hours are 8 A.M. to 4:30 P.M.; phone (907) 373-8300. If you require assistance after hours, phone (907) 352-5401 (Mat-Com Dispatch).

The 18-hole Settlers Bay Golf Course offers views of the Mat-Su Valley and Chugach Mountains. (©Serine Reeves)

Voted "Best in the Valley for ice cream and customer service," Miller's Place is a favorite local stop. (©Kris Valencia, staff)

A 48.7 C 161.3 F 313.3 Holiday gas station with diesel/Subway to north; Meadow Lakes Road access to Seymour, Lalen, Visnaw lakes.

A 48.8 C 161.2 F 313.2 *NOTE: Construction expected in 2019 to widen the highway to a 4-lane divided thoroughfare from* **Milepost** *A 48.8 to past the Big Lake junction at* **Milepost** *A 53. For details visit www.parkshighway44-52.info.*

A 49 C 161 F 312.8 4-lane highway becomes 2-lane northbound.

A 51 C 159 F 311 VCA Big Lake Animal Hospital.

A 51.5 C 158.5 F 310.5 Fisher's Fuel Inc. Tesoro gas/diesel station to west.

A 52.2 C 157.8 F 309.8 Southbound distance marker shows Wasilla 10 miles, Anchorage 52 miles.

A 52.3 C 157.7 F 309.7 Junction with Big Lake Road (a traffic light is planned for this intersection); Meadowood Mall. Mall stores include Top Drawer, a giant thrift store with everything from antiques to 99-cent clothing; Lumberyard Deli (good burgers); Church Alive; a garden supply store; and a hair salon. Napa auto parts adjacent.

Big Lake Road leads west to Big Lake recreation area (camping, boating).

> **Junction** with Big Lake Road. See "Big Lake Road" log on page 385.

Houston city limits. Houston is the only place in the Mat-Su Borough where it is legal to sell fireworks, so there are usually several fireworks outlets near the Big Lake Road junction. Fireworks are illegal in Anchorage.

A 52.7 C 157.3 F 309.3 Distance marker northbound shows Cantwell 157 miles, Denali National Park 184 miles, Fairbanks 302 miles.

A 53 C 157 F 309 *End highway construction northbound (see* **Milepost** *A 48.8).*

A 53.2 C 156.8 F 308.8 Turnoff for Houston High School.

A 54 C 156 F 308 Begin 1.4 mile passing lane northbound.

A 54.8 C 155.2 F 307.2 Bike route begins northbound, east side of highway.

A 56.1 C 153.9 F 305.9 Miller's Reach Road. Alaska's most destructive wildfire began here in June 1996. The Big Lake wildfire burned some 37,500 acres and 433 buildings and homes.

A 56.3 C 153.7 F 305.7 Alaska Railroad overpass.

A 56.6 C 153.4 F 305.4 King Arthur Drive; public access to Bear Paw, Prator and Loon lakes to east. Views of Pioneer Peak southbound.

A 56.8 C 153.2 F 305.2 *CAUTION: Moose Danger Zone. Watch for moose next 12.7 miles southbound.*

Improved highway northbound.

A 56.9 C 153.1 F 305.1 Paved double-ended turnouts with parking spaces on both sides of highway.

A 57 C 153 F 305 Highway bridge and pedestrian bridge cross the Little Susitna River; a very popular fishing and camping area. Parking areas both sides of highway with pedestrian access to Little Susitna River.

The **Little Susitna River** has a tremendous chinook salmon run and one of the largest coho salmon runs in southcentral Alaska. Chinook salmon to 30 lbs., mid-May through late June on lower river, mid-June through season close in mid-July on upper river; use large red spinners. Coho to 15 lbs., mid-July through mid-August on lower river, early August through early September on upper river. Also sockeye salmon to 10 lbs., mid-July through early August. Charter boats nearby. This river heads in the Talkeetna Mountains to the northeast and flows 110 miles into Upper Cook Inlet.

A 57.3 C 152.7 F 304.7 Turnoff to east on Armstrong Road for Houston City Hall with picnic tables and litter bins, William A. Philo Public Safety Bldg. *(emergency phone)* and City of Houston-operated **Little Susitna River Campground** (follow signs). Dump station ($10) at entrance to campground is open May through October. The campground has 86 sites (many wide, level gravel sites); picnic tables, firepits; restrooms, water pump, playground, large picnic pavilion; $15/per vehicle camping fee; extra vehicles $5.

A 57.5 C 152.5 F 304.5 HOUSTON (pop. 1,588). West side of highway: Groceries, snacks and beverages, ice cream, propane, post office, laundry at the popular **Miller's Place** (description follows); RV camping at nearby park. East side of highway: Three Bears convenience store, gas/diesel, dump station.

Houston is a popular fishing center for anglers on the Little Susitna River. Fishing charter operators and marine service are located here. Emergency phone at **Milepost A 57.3** William A. Philo Public Safety Building. Originally Houston siding on the Alaska Railroad, the area was homesteaded in the 1950s and incorporated as a city in 1966.

A Founder's Day celebration is held in August. This annual event features a barbecue dinner, fireworks and entertainment.

Radio station KJHA (King Jesus Houston Alaska) 88.7 FM went on the air in Houston on July 8, 1998, broadcasting by satellite from North Pole.

A 58.3 C 151.7 F 303.7 Begin 2.4-mile passing lane northbound. *CAUTION: Watch for moose next 5 miles northbound.*

A 59.1 C 150.9 F 302.9 Zero Lake Road. 0.4 miles to Multi-use area for "children at play, logging trucks, sled dog teams, snowmobiles, cross country skiers, hikers, recreational hunters and four-wheelers." Houston Willow Creek Sled Trailhead with picnic shelter, litter bins, toilets, and large parking area. Day use parking is $5. Overnight parking is $10.

A 60.1 C 149.9 F 301.9 Gold Miners Lodge to east; cabins, canoe rentals, cafe. Liquor sales.

A 61 C 149 F 301 Houston city limits northbound.

A 61.1 C 148.9 F 300.9 Welcome to Willow northbound.

A 62.1 C 147.9 F 299.9 Begin 1.4-mile passing lane southbound.

A 62.4 C 147.6 F 299.6 Begin 1.5-mile passing lane northbound.

A 64.7 C 145.3 F 297.3 Allen Road to east. Turnoff for Iditarod kennel tours and bed-and-breakfast lodging.

A 66.3 C 143.7 F 295.7 White's Crossing highway bridge crosses Alaska Railroad tracks.

A 66.5 C 143.5 F 295.5 Turnoff to west for **Nancy Lake State Recreation Site**; turn left (south) on Buckingham Palace Road and drive 0.3 miles; 30 campsites, picnic tables, firepits, benches, water, campground host, toilets, boat launch, "Kid Don't Float" lifejackets, horseshoe pits, camping fee $20/night. Day use parking, $5. This is the easiest public access to Nancy Lake, which offers 4 public-use cabins accessible by land or canoe (see also Nancy Lake Parkway access

Big Lake Road

Big Lake Road is a paved 2-lane road providing access to homes and recreation areas on Big Lake. It is an extremely busy road. Posted speed limit is 45- to 55-mph; slow for curves and speed zones. *Pass with care!* There is a bike trail along Big Lake Road.

Big Lake has been a resort destination for Alaskans since the 1940s. The area has grown in recent years—along with the rest of the Mat-Su Valley—and now has a number of residential subdivisions and the traffic that accompanies population growth. Watch for ATVs in summer and snow machines in winter along Big Lake Road.

Summer recreation at Big Lake includes swimming, camping, boating, fishing and jet skiing. Public access to the lake is provided by 2 state recreation sites: Big Lake North and Big Lake South. Winter sports include snowmachining, cross-country skiing and ice fishing.

For more information on state recreation sites, phone the regional Alaska State Parks office at (907) 317-9094; or visit their website at www.greatholidaycampgrounds.com.

BIG LAKE ROAD
Distance is measured from the junction (J) with the Parks Highway, Milepost A 52.3.

J 0 Junction with Parks Highway; Meadowood Mall. Mall stores include Top Drawer, a giant thrift store with everything from antiques to 99-cent clothing; Lumberyard Deli (good burgers); Church Alive; a garden supply store and a hair salon. Napa auto parts store adjacent.

J 0.2 Begin bike route westbound.

J 1.3 Turnoff to north for Houston High School and senior center.

Willow, birch and aspen trees have replaced the spruce forest that fueled the June 1996 Miller's Reach Fire, which burned more than 37,0000 acres and destroyed 433 buildings and homes.

J 3.3 Junction with Beaver Lake Road; access to Rocky Lake SRS and Martin Buser's Happy Trails Kennel. Drive 0.5 mile north (follow signs) tor Rocky Street for **Rocky Lake State Recreation Site**; day use parking ($5/day), 12 campsites with picnic tables and firepits ($20–30/night) on a bumpy, gravel loop road, outhouses, dumpster, firepits, water pump and boat launch ($15 fee) *NOTE: Rocky Lake is closed to jet skis, jet boats and airboats.* Life preservers available for children through the "Kids Don't Float" program. Not recommended for large RVs. www.greatholidaycampgrounds.com.

J 3.5 Tesoro 24-hour gas/diesel station, store, firewood, ice, propane, ATM. Welcome to Alaska's Year-Round Playground sign here has map of Big Lake. Big Lake is

Big Lake is very popular for recreational boating and jet skiing. (©Sharon Leighow, staff)

connected with smaller lakes by dredged waterways. It is possible to boat for several miles. Fish in **Big Lake** include Dolly Varden, rainbow trout, sockeye and coho salmon, burbot and Arctic char.

J 3.6 Roundabout with exits to Big Lake Road and North Shore Drive. **BIG LAKE** (pop. 3,350) post office (ZIP code 99652); liquor store, laundromat. **Visitor information:** Big Lake Chamber of Commerce, P.O. Box 520067, Big Lake, AK 99652; phone (907) 892-6109, www.biglakechamber.org.

Take North Shore Drive (paved) 1.5 miles to end at **Big Lake North State Recreation Site**; 60 overnight parking spaces ($20–$25/night), walk-in tent sites, campground host, pay phone, picnicking, shelters, water, outhouses, dumpsters, camp store, day-use fee $7, boat launch $15. Located on the lake; good views of the Alaska Range and Denali on a clear day. Life preservers are available for children to use through the statewide "Kids Don't Float" program.

Exit left on Big Lake Road from roundabout.

J 3.8 Edward "Bud" Beech Firehall/West Lake Fire Dept. *Emergency phone.*

J 3.9 Big Lake Library to north with shared parking for the Jordan Lake Park with viewing platform, picnic area and litter bins.

J 4 East Lake Mall; grocery store, 2 restaurants, liquor store, credit union, gift shop and other businesses. Big Lake Chamber of Commerce Visitor Center is located in a cabin at the corner of this parking lot. Junction with Hollywood Road, which connects to Knik Road via Vine. Bus stop.

J 4.1 Three Bears grocery and Shell Gas Station. Transfer station.

J 4.2 Doc Rockers RV Park, laundromat

and showers.

J 4.5 Big Lake Elementary school.

J 4.6 Private Aircraft: Big Lake airport; elev. 150 feet; length 2,400 feet; gravel; fuel 100LL.

J 4.8 Airport Motel and Hangar Lounge to north. Current status unknown.

J 4.9 Jay Nolfi Fish Creek Park (Mat-Su Borough), a popular day-use area with access to Fish Creek, salmon spawning observation deck, picnic area, swimming, pavilion, restroom, playground, parking and open lawn area. End bike lane. Bridge over Fish Creek.

J 5.2 Big Lake South State Recreation Site; gravel parking area (potholes); day-use and overnight camping with 20 campsites ($20/night), firepits, outhouses, water, dumpsters, parking, fishing and boat ramp. "Kids Don't Float" life preservers. Day-use $7 fee, boat launch $15.

J 5.4 Turnoff for Big Lake Power Sports and Marine.

J 5.5 Resort and restaurant.

J 6.4 Road becomes West Susitna Parkway westbound. Turn right to continue on South Big Lake Road.

J 8.2 Big Lake Boat Launch; day-use area with paved parking ($5 fee), restrooms, fishing and boat launch ($15 fee).

J 8.8 Big Lake Road rejoins West Susitna Parkway at Burma Road junction. Burma Road is a winding dirt road that leads 8.5 miles south to junction with Point Mackenzie Road. West Susitna Parkway continues several miles as a gravel road through a rural residential area. Big Lake Road ends.

Return to Milepost A 52.3 Parks Highway

at **Milepost A 67.3**). Reserve cabins at www.reserveamerica.com.

A 67 C 143 F 295 Distance marker southbound shows Wasilla 25 miles, Anchorage 67 miles.

A 67.3 C 142.7 F 294.7 Turnoff to west on Nancy Lake Parkway (paved) for **Nancy Lake State Recreation Area**; very popular canoeing area with canoe trails, public-use

cabins, hiking trails, fishing, picnicking and camping in summer; skiing, snowmachining and dog mushing in winter. Access to lakes, cabins and canoe trails from trailheads along Parkway (description follows). Ice is usually off area lakes by mid-May.

Nancy Lake Parkway mileages: **Mile 0.7** Long Lake Road; **Mile 1.3** entrance station and park ranger; **Mile 1.6** trail to

Nancy Lake canoe launch; **Mile 1.8** trailhead parking and summer trail to Nancy Lake public-use cabins 1, 2, 3 and 4; **Mile 2.1** ski trailhead parking with fee station and toilets and winter gates (gate closes in October, date determined by snowfall, as it is unmaintained); Access allowed beyond this gate closure for skiers, dog mushers, snow machines as a multi-use trail; **Mile 2.6** Bald Lake trailhead; **Mile 4.8** Tanaina Lake

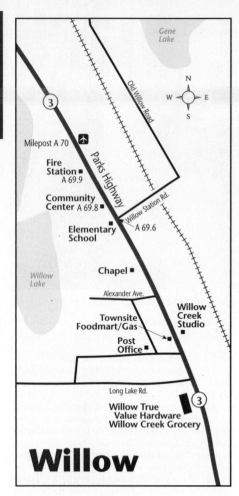

Willow

(paved parking lot with toilets, canoe trailhead); **Mile 5.1** Rhein Lake trailhead; **Mile 5.6** East Redshirt Lake Trail; **Mile 5.9** North Rolly Lake trailhead; **Mile 6.1** South Rolly Overlook (picnic area with covered tables, firepits, toilets, litter bins, RV parking); **Mile 6.5** road ends at Red Shirt Lake trailhead parking and entrance to South Rolly Lake Campground. The campground has 98 sites, firepits, toilets, water, canoe rental and boat launch (trolling motors only); firewood for sale. Camping fee $20–$25/night; $15 boat launch fee; $5 day-use parking fee. **South Rolly Lake** has a small population of rainbow trout that average 12 to 14 inches.

To plan a multi-lake/multi-cabin canoe trip, see the general information brochure at dnr.alaska.gov/Assets/uploads/DNRPublic/parks/brochures/nancylake.pdf. Cabin fact sheet at dnr.alaska.gov/Assets/uploads/DNRPublic/parks/cabins/nancylkfs.pdf.

The 14 public-use cabins are $45–$70 a night, and they sleep 4–8. Make sure to bring sleeping pads (the wood sleeping platforms are hard) and bug spray (lots of mosquitoes). Also consider a sleeping mask in the summer: There are no shades on the windows and it stays light until quite late on summer nights. Reserve cabins at www.reserveamerica.com.

A 67.6 C 142.4 F 294.4 End passing lane southbound.

NOTE: Driving distance between Mileposts 68 and 70 is 1.8 miles.

A 68.6 C 141.4 F 293.4 *Slow for posted speed zone northbound through Willow.*

Begin passing lane southbound.

A 68.8 C 141.2 F 293.2 Newman's Hilltop Tesoro west side of highway. Weekly Willow Farmers Market on Fridays in summer, east side of highway.

A 69 C 141 F 293 **Willow Creek Grocery** and **Willow True Value Hardware** store on west side of highway. Willow extends about 2.5 miles north along the Parks Highway.

Willow True Value Hardware and Willow Creek Grocery. See display ad this page.

A 69.2 C 140.8 F 292.8 Long Lake Road; access to Sunshine Community Health Center open daily 9 A.M. to 5 P.M., located 0.5 mile west; phone (907) 495-4100. Paved turnout to east.

A 69.3 C 140.7 F 292.7 Beluga Road access to Heart of Willow Medical Clinic (phone 907/495-4362) and mini-mall.

Willow

A 69.5 C 140.5 F 292.5 Pop. 2,102. **Emergency Services:** Fire Dept., phone (907) 495-6728. **Radio:** KTNA 88.9 FM. **Townsite Foodmart** to west, open 24 hours, has gas, diesel, deli, liquor store, fishing licenses and supplies, pay phone. Alexander Avenue; access west to Willow Post Office. **Willow Creek Studio** on the east side of the road makes an interesting stop with its variety of arts, crafts and gifts.

Willow had its start about 1897, when gold was discovered in the area. In the early 1940s, mining in the nearby Talkeetna Mountains slacked off, leaving Willow a virtual ghost town. The community made a comeback upon completion of the Parks Highway in 1972. In 1976, Alaska voters selected the Willow area for their new capital site. However, funding for the capital move from Juneau to Willow was defeated in the November 1982 election.

The Willow Area Community Organization sponsors an annual Winter Carnival the last weekend in January and the first weekend in February. The Iditarod Restart takes place on Willow Lake, the day after the ceremonial start of the race in Anchorage on the first Saturday in March. The Iditarod Restart crosses Willow Lake and it is exciting to line up with thousands of other race fans and cheer on the mushers. There is very limited parking in Willow for the Iditarod Restart, and you can park and ride at one of the organized sites offering shuttle bus service: Lakefront Anchorage Hotel, Wasilla High School, Houston High School and Curtis D. Menard Memorial Sports Center on S. Clapp Street. And get an early start: traffic on the Parks Highway can be at a standstill.

Willow has a well-established winter trail system, popular with snow machines and recreational mushers.

The Big Susitna River and Deshka River

WILLOW ADVERTISERS

on the west and the Willow Creek tributaries flowing from the east make for fantastic area fishing. Four of the 5 species of pacific salmon are available here along with rainbow trout and Arctic grayling.

Parks Highway Log
(continued)

A 69.6 C 140.4 F 292.4 Willow Elementary School to west. Willow Station Road (paved) leads east to Willow Trading Post (restaurant) and continues north to junction with the Willow-Fishhook Road to Hatcher Pass or return to Parks Highway (see **Milepost A 71.2**).

Views of Denali northbound, weather permitting.

A 69.8 C 140.2 F 292.2 Willow Community Center Circle to west with access to Willow Library and Willow Community Center on Willow Lake. Library hours vary; phone (907) 861-7655. The community center has a large parking area, commercial kitchen, covered picnic pavilion, grills, playground, basketball court and boat launch. Available for rent to groups, 500-person capacity; phone (907) 495-6633.

A 69.9 C 140.1 F 292.1 Fire station to west. *Emergency phone.*

A 70 C 140 F 292 Willow Airport Road to east. **Private Aircraft:** Willow airport; elev. 221 feet; length 4,400 feet; gravel; fuel 100LL. Unattended.

A 70.1 C 139.9 F 291.9 *Slow for posted speed zone southbound through Willow.*

A 70.8 C 139.2 F 291.2 **Junction** with Willow Creek Parkway (paved); access to Susitna River from Willow Creek SRA (3.8 miles) and Deshka Landing (7.2 miles), descriptions follow.

Follow Willow Creek Parkway west to **Willow Creek State Recreation Area** entrance/fee station; camping $15 per night, parking $5 per day. Paved parking for side-by-side camping with firepits and tables, litter bins, water and toilets. Day-use parking area is gravel. Campground host, walking paths, interpretive displays, walk to creek. Fishing for coho, pink, chum and chinook salmon. It is ¼-mile to confluence with the Susitna River. Willow Creek is the 4th busiest chinook salmon fishing area in the state. Current fishing conditions posted at fee station.

Access to **Deshka Landing** boat launch facility: At Mile 2 Willow Creek Parkway; turn left on N. Crystal Lake Road and continue 5.2 miles on paved road, turn left on Mishap Avenue to Gomer Lane to Deshka Landing Road. Concessionaire-operated facility at Deshka Landing is open daily 9 A.M. to 6 P.M. in summer; phone (907) 495-3374, www.deshkalanding.com. Fees charged for boat launch and parking. Fishing for salmon and rainbow trout.

The **Susitna River** begins at Susitna Glacier in the Alaska Range to the northeast and flows west then south for 260 miles to Cook Inlet. The **Deshka River**, a tributary of the Susitna River about 6 miles downstream from Deshka Landing, is one of southcentral Alaska's best chinook salmon fisheries. According to the ADF&G, the chinook salmon run is from late May through late June on the lower river, and early June through season close in mid-July on the upper river; peak fishing at the mouth of the Deshka River is usually June 13–20. The Deshka River is open to the retention of chinook salmon for the first 19 miles, which

Beautiful Little Willow Creek area begins just 15 miles east of the Parks Highway on Willow-Fishhook (Hatcher Pass) Road. (©MILEPOST Staff photo)

is indicated by a marker at Chijuk Creek. Coho salmon run from mid-July through early August on the lower river, and late July through early September on the upper river.

Also signed public fishing access to **Little Lonely Lake** on Crystal Lake Road and to **Vera Lake** on Deshka Landing Road.

A 71.2 C 138.8 F 290.8 **Junction** with Willow–Fishhook (Hatcher Pass) Road; espresso stand at northeast corner in summer. This 49-mile side road connects with the Glenn Highway at Palmer. Summit Lake State Recreation Site is 30 miles from here. Independence Mine State Historical Park is 32 miles from here on the east side of Hatcher Pass (usually snow-free by mid-June).

> **Junction** with Willow–Fishhook (Hatcher Pass) Road. See "Hatcher Pass Road" log on in the GLENN HIGHWAY section. Turn to page 342 and read log back to front.

Distance marker northbound shows Cantwell 138 miles, Denali National Park 166 miles, Fairbanks 283 miles.

Bike trail ends northbound, begins southbound.

A 71.4 C 138.6 F 290.6 Willow Creek bridge. The **Pioneer Lodge RV Park & Campground** (description follows) to west on south side of bridge; camping, dining, boat launch. Excellent chinook salmon fishing in **Willow Creek**; also coho and rainbow trout. Inquire at resort for information. Entering Game Management Subunit 14B northbound, 14A southbound.

A 72.1 C 137.9 F 289.9 Large turnout to west. Begin 1.7-mile northbound passing lane.

A 73.5 C 136.5 F 288.5 Evidence of the Sockeye Fire, which destroyed 55 homes in the area in June 2015. The evacuation area during the fire extended from **Milepost A 63** to **Milepost A 78** of the Parks Highway.

A 74.7 C 135.3 F 287.3 Bridge over **Little Willow Creek**. Parking to west, pedestrian access to east. Fishing for salmon and trout; *check regulations booklet carefully!*

A 75.2 C 134.8 F 286.8 Capital City Speedway to west.

A 76.4 C 133.6 F 285.6 Large paved parking area with interpretive signs to west by scenic **Kashwitna Lake**; signed public fishing access. Kashwitna Lake is stocked with rainbow trout. Floatplanes land on lake. Private floatplane base on east shore. Good camera viewpoints of lake and Denali (formerly Mount McKinley).

Begin 0.9-mile southbound passing lane.

A 76.9 C 133.1 F 285.1 Begin 1.5-mile northbound passing lane.

A 81 C 129 F 281 Begin 2-mile southbound passing lane.

A 81.2 C 128.8 F 280.8 Paved parking area to west; **Grey's Creek** fishing access. *CAUTION: Watch for moose.*

A 81.5 C 128.5 F 280.5 Begin 1.1-mile northbound passing lane.

A 82.4 C 127.6 F 279.6 Distance marker southbound shows Wasilla 40 miles, Anchorage 83 miles.

A 82.5 C 127.5 F 279.5 E. Susitna Landing Drive to **Susitna Landing Access Facility**, Public Boat Launch; 1 mile west via gravel road. Concessionaire operated RV park and boat launch on ADF&G land. The boat launch is on the **Kashwitna River**, just upstream of the **Susitna River**, and provides access to both rivers. Fees charged for camping, boat launch, daily parking and firewood. Wheelchair-accessible restrooms, showers, and bank fishing. Winter snow machine and ski access.

Take the Talkeetna Spur Road to this Denali viewpoint at Mile J 12.9. This side road terminates at Main Street in Talkeetna, a fun stop for visitors to Alaska. (©Serine Reeves)

A 83.2 C 126.8 F 278.8 Bridge over the Kashwitna River. A pedestrian bridge also crosses this river. The Kashwitna River heads in the Talkeetna Mountains and flows westward to the Susitna River. Parking to the west on north side of bridge.

Views of Denali northbound (weather permitting).

A 83.5 C 126.5 F 278.5 Distance marker northbound shows Cantwell 126 miles, Denali Park 153 miles, Fairbanks 271 miles.

A 84 C 126 F 278 Large paved parking area to west.

A 84.1 C 125.9 F 277.9 E. Susitna Shores Road to west. Drive 0.4 mile for **Caswell Creek** public access (walk-in); chinook, coho, pink and rainbow trout. 14-day camping limit. Portable toilets.

A 85.1 C 124.9 F 276.9 Caswell Creek (sign).

A 86 C 124 F 276 Resolute Drive. Turnoff to west for **Sheep Creek Slough** public fishing access. Drive 1.3 miles west to large gravel parking area, toilets and trail to mouth of creek. Fishing for chinook, coho, pink and rainbow trout. 14-day camping limit.

A 88 C 122 F 274 Sheep Creek Lodge.

A 88.5 C 121.5 F 273.5 Bridge over **Sheep Creek**. Narrow access to creek to west at north end of bridge. Pedestrian bridge crosses creek; pedestrian tunnel under highway. Fishing for salmon and trout.

A 89 C 121 F 273 Slow vehicle turnouts both sides of highway.

A 90 C 120 F 272 Road construction begins northbound.

A 90.8 C 119.2 F 270.2 Mat-Su Valley RV Park 0.1 mile east.

A 91.5 C 118.5 F 270 Railroad overpass.

A 93.4 C 116.6 F 268.6 Goose Creek culvert (unsigned); small, gravel turnouts to east and west. Fishing.

A 93.5 C 116.5 F 268.5 Distance marker northbound shows Talkeetna Road Junction 5 miles.

A 95 C 115 F 267 Road construction begins southbound.

A 95.2 C 114.8 F 266.8 Gravel turnout to east.

A 96.1 C 113.9 F 265.9 Montana Creek shoulder parking to east.

A 96.2 C 113.8 F 265.8 Montana Creek Road. **MONTANA CREEK** (pop. about 500) was settled by homesteaders in the 1950s. **Radio:** KTNA 88.9-FM.

A 96.5 C 113.5 F 265.5 **Montana Creek Campground**, east side of highway, has camping, short-term fee parking for fisher-

men, general store with fishing supplies, rental gear, snacks, beverages; firewood available for campers. **Montana Creek State Recreation Site** west side of highway; camping. Pedestrian tunnel under highway and pedestrian bridge adjacent highway bridge across Montana Creek. Public access trail to mouth of Montana Creek on the Susitna River. Excellent chinook salmon fishing, also coho, pink (even-numbered years), Arctic grayling, rainbow trout and Dolly Varden.

Montana Creek Campground. See display ad this page.

A 96.6 C 113.4 F 265.4 Montana Creek bridge.

A 97.4 C 112.6 F 264.6 Large gravel turnout to east.

A 98.2 C 111.8 F 263.8 Distance marker southbound shows Wasilla 56 miles, Anchorage 98 miles.

A 98.4 C 111.6 F 263.6 Montana Creek Baptist Church to east. Turnoff to west for Senior Center and for Su Valley Jr/Sr High School, the first high school in Alaska to receive certification as a LEED (Leadership in Energy and Environmental Design) building. There is a 3.1-mile trail for running in summer, cross-country skiing in winter.

Distance marker southbound shows Wasilla 56 miles, Anchorage 98 miles.

A 98.6 C 111.4 F 263.4 Cubby's Market to east; groceries, deli, liquor store.

A 98.7 C 111.3 F 263.3 Talkeetna Y. **Junction** with paved spur road to Talkeetna.

Junction with Talkeetna Spur Road, which leads 14 miles northeast to Talkeetna. See "Talkeetna Spur Road" beginning on facing page for log of road; description of Talkeetna begins on page 391.

A 98.8 C 111.2 F 263.2 Public Safety Building on west side of highway; *emergency phone.* Tesoro gas station east side of highway, north of Talkeetna "Y", has convenience store, Subway (in log building), ATM, gas, diesel, propane and showers (for a fee), RV hookups.

A 99.3 C 110.7 F 262.7 **North Friend (Montana) Lake** to east, **South Friend (Montana) Lake** to west. Public access to Little Montana Lake (stocked with rainbow trout) from gravel parking area to west.

Distance marker northbound shows Cantwell 111 miles, Denali National Park 138 miles, Fairbanks 256 miles.

A 99.5 C 110.5 F 262.5 **His & Hers Lakeview Lounge & Restaurant**; food, gas/diesel station, RV park to east overlooking lake (detailed description follows).

His & Hers. Restaurant, lounge, RV sites. Enjoy lakeview dining; lunch and dinner. "Our bread pudding is famous statewide." Lakeside camping; pull-throughs, 30-amp RV sites, RV dump, laundry, showers. Caravans and tours welcome (please call in advance, 48-hour notice). Phone (907) 733-2415. [ADVERTISEMENT]

A 100.5 C 109.5 F 261.5 Railroad overpass.

A 102.2 C 107.8 F 259.8 Large, paved turnout to east.

A 102.6 C 107.4 F 259.4 Sunshine Creek Road to east; transfer station. Access east to Sunshine Creek via 0.6-mile narrow, uneven, potholed, single-lane, dirt road to **Sun-**
(Continues on page 394)

Talkeetna Spur Road

Talkeetna has a lively street scene in summer, with lots of visitors and lots of shops, restaurants and tourist services. (©Claire Torgerson, staff)

The Talkeetna Spur Road turns off the Parks Highway at **Milepost A 98.7** and leads north 14 miles to dead end at the community of Talkeetna. This is a good, paved side road with a paved non-motorized trail along the west side of the road.

Talkeetna is a unique blend of old-time Alaska small town and modern tourist destination. It is an aviation and supply base for Denali climbing expeditions. Talkeetna has restaurants, lodging, shops, excellent museums, fishing, zip lining, flightseeing, river and railroad tours.

TALKEETNA SPUR ROAD
Distance from Parks Highway junction (J) at Milepost A 98.7 is shown.

J 0 Junction with the Parks. Tesoro to west. Brown Bear coffee hut to east.

Distance marker shows Talkeetna 14 miles. "For weather tune to 88.9" sign.
J 0.2 Moores Hardware. Mat Valley Federal Credit Union, CarQuest to west.
J 1.1 Kahiltna Birchworks. See display ad this page.

J 1.8 Denali Brewing Company with tasting room to the south. Food trucks in parking lot, daily in summer.
J 3 Talkeetna Lakeside Cabins. See display ad this page.
J 3.1 E. Yoder Road (paved for first 2 miles). Go east 2.6 miles on Yoder Road for informal access to gravel bars at Montana Creek bridge and Historic Luthman Trail that leads 4.5 miles to Montana Creek

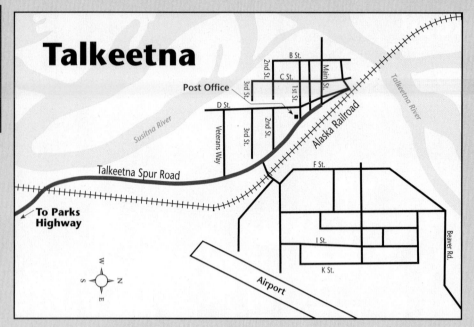

Talkeetna

(Map labels: 2nd St., B St., C St., Main St., 3rd St., 1st St., Post Office, D St., Susitna River, Veterans Way, 3rd St., 2nd St., Talkeetna River, Alaska Railroad, Talkeetna Spur Road, To Parks Highway, F St., I St., K St., Beaver Rd., Airport)

waterfall.

J 3.5 Talkeetna Baptist Church.

J 4.2 Sunshine Community Health Center to west; phone (907) 733-2273.

J 5.2 Answer Creek.

J 7.7 Birch Creek Blvd. Access to **Alaska Sled Dog Tours** (see description following).

Alaska Sled Dog Tours. Mush your own team of friendly sled dogs on our custom carts at the homestead of Iditarod Champion Dallas Seavey. Play with the retired legends and cuddle future champions in our 2-acre playpen as our experienced guides share how our dogs live, play and train. Visit www.AKsleddogtours.com or call (907) 947-4210 for reservations. Tours available year-round. [ADVERTISEMENT]

J 9 Alaska Bush Floatplane Service. Paved turnout and Fish Lake to east.

J 10.4 Crowley Fields gas, diesel.

J 10.8 Whigmi Road. Talkeetna Lakes Park and Whigmi Trailhead with access to 5-loop trail system. Portable toilet, fishing, kayaking, canoeing, packrafting, biking, skiing and hiking. Parking is $5/day, $40/year. No tires, camping, snowmachining, ATVs or horses. with Tigger Lake public fishing access via 0.3-mile dirt road to short trail to lake. Stocked with rainbow trout.

J 11 Flying Squirrel Bakery Cafe. Visit this unique cafe with creative deli-style menu and artisan breads baked in a wood-fired brick oven. Featuring local and Alaska grown ingredients. Organic Alaska-roasted espresso, WiFi. 3 miles from Talkeetna—no tour bus crowds; trees out the windows; open year-round. Phone (907) 733-6887. www.flyingsquirrelcafe.com. See display ad on page 389. [ADVERTISEMENT]

J 11.8 Talkeenta transfer station.

J 12 Comsat Road (paved) leads east 0.1 miles to Talkeetna Lake Park and Comsat Trailhead, with access to five-loop trail system. Outhouse, litter bins, fishing, kayaking, canoeing, packrafting, biking, skiing, and hiking. Parking is $5 per day, $40 per year. No tires, camping, snowmobiles, ATVs, or horses. Christiansen Lake Road off Comsat Road has public fishing access.

J 12.2 Double-ended gravel turnout to the west.

J 12.3 Talkeetna Public Library and Community Center to east. Hours Monday–Saturday 11 A.M. to 6 P.M. excellent Alaska section and free internet/Wi-Fi. Phone (907) 861-7645.

J 12.4 Double-ended gravel turnout to the east.

J 12.5 Talkeetna Alaskan Lodge; accommodations, restaurant, viewing deck, shuttle. *Slow for posted speed zones northbound.*

J 12.9 Large paved double-ended turnout with interpretive sign and viewpoint to west. Splendid views of Denali, Mount Foraker and the Alaska Range above the Susitna River. A must stop photo stop. *Watch for bicyclists; do not park on bike trail!*

J 13.4 *CAUTION: Alaska Railroad crossing.*

J 13.5 Turnoff for Alaska Railroad Depot.

J 13.7 Talkeetna Camper Park. See display ad this page.

J 14.1 Second Street leads to state airport (K2 Aviation, Talkeetna Air Taxi), Talkeetna Hostel, St. Bernard's Catholic Church, Climbers' Memorial (at cemetery), **Swiss Alaska Inn, Mahay's Jetboat Adventures** and public boat launch. Northern Susitna Institute to west.

J 14.3 Talkeetna Post Office (ZIP code 99676).

Mountain Gift Shop. Come shop this fun place with Denali and moose theme items. Moose "nugget" novelties are our specialty. Also license plate signs; kids' plush moose/bear toys; wind chimes; numerous

sale T-shirts, hats; Alaska snacks and candy. Open May–September. (907) 733-1686/2710. See display ad on this page. [ADVERTISEMENT]

J 14.4 Main Street, Talkeetna. "Welcome to Beautiful Downtown Talkeetna" sign and Talkeetna's Village Park. *IMPORTANT NOTE ABOUT PARKING: This small village was platted in 1918, without RVs in mind. The roads and alleys are narrow and parking is at a premium. To make your visit more enjoyable, please park before Main Street and walk into town. Parking options for RVs include the Northern Susitna Institute ($5/day), only 150 yards before Main Street on the Talkeetna Spur, and the Talkeetna Elementary School, free parking when school is not in session from June 1 to about August 12. And if you are staying at one of the 2 RV campgrounds (one on the east side of the railroad tracks near the boat launch and the other, Talkeetna Camper Park, at Mile J 13.7 on the Talkeetna Spur) leave your RV at your site and walk to town center. RVs with tow vehicles should avoid driving down Main Street as the street deadends with little room to turn around.*

Talkeetna

J 14.4 Located on a spur road, 14 miles north of **Milepost A 98.7** Parks Highway, at the confluence of the Talkeetna, Susitna and Chulitna rivers. **Population:** 876. **Emergency Services: Fire Department** and **Ambulance**, Dial 911. Sunshine Community Health Center (walk-ins welcome), at Mile 4.2 Talkeetna Spur Road, phone (907) 733-2273.

Visitor Information: Stop by the Talkeetna Historical Society Museum, which acts as an unofficial visitor center. The Historical Society has created a free downtown walking tour app, available on Android or iTunes. Look for "Talkeetna Historic Downtown Walking Tour" and download the free app then download the tour.

Walter Harper Talkeetna Ranger Station is on B Street; open all year. Information on Denali National Park and climbing in the Alaska Range; reference library, mountaineering orientation program for climbers and a free film throughout the day. Contact the rangers at P.O. Box 588, Talkeetna, AK 99676; phone (907) 733-2231; www.nps.gov/dena/.

Talkeetna Chamber of Commerce, P.O. Box 334, Talkeetna, AK 99676; www.talkeetnachamber.org; info@talkeetnachamber.org.

Elevation: 346 feet. **Radio:** KSKA-FM (PBS) 91.1-FM and local station KTNA 88.9-FM, which broadcasts to communities throughout the Upper Susitna Valley. **Television:** Channels 2, 4, 5, 7, 13.

Private Aircraft: Talkeetna State Airport, adjacent east; elev. 358 feet; length 3,500 feet; paved; fuel 100LL, Jet B (call out).

Talkeetna began as a trading post in 1896, and grew as a riverboat supply base following the Susitna River gold rush in 1910. The population boomed during construction of the Alaska Railroad, when Talkeetna was headquarters for the Alaska Engineering Commission in charge of railroad construction, but declined following completion of the project. Talkeetna has several historic buildings and is on the National Register of Historic Places.

Few other locations are blessed with such

Walter Harper Talkeetna Ranger Station is open year-round, providing information on climbing in the Alaska Range. (©Claire Torgerson, staff)

fortunate geography, with breathtaking views of Denali and the Alaska Range. This spectacular setting combines with a highly creative citizenry, imaginative shops and businesses, and the mystique of the mountain-climbing community.

Talkeetna is the jumping-off point for most climbing expeditions to Denali (formerly Mount McKinley). Most expeditions use the West Buttress route, pioneered by Bradford Washburn. Specially equipped ski-wheel aircraft fly climbers to Kahiltna Glacier to start the climb from about 7,200 feet to the summit of the South Peak (elev. 20,310 feet). Several air services based in Talkeetna specialize in the glacier landings necessary to ferry climbers and their equipment to and from the mountain. The climb

Talkeetna Camper Park is on the Spur Road close to downtown. (©Claire Torgerson, staff)

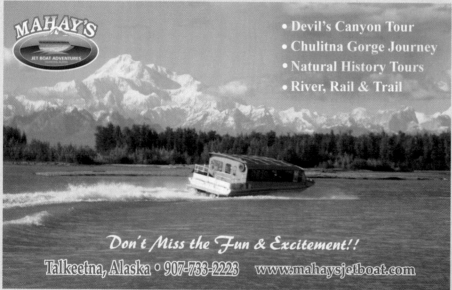
via the West Buttress route usually takes 18 to 20 days. Flightseeing the mountain is also popular.

Lodging & Services

For such a small community, Talkeetna offers some wonderful dining and accommodations. It has 8 motels/hotels, 2 hostels, many bed and breakfasts, gorgeous log cabins, and rooms at the roadhouse; see ads this section. Talkeetna restaurants include family style at the **Talkeetna Roadhouse**, gourmet pizza and Italian tinged options at the **Mountain High Pizza Pie**, fantastic breakfasts and gluten free/fresh baking at **Flying Squirrel Bakery and Cafe** and so many other choices, including dining at the **Swiss Alaska Inn**. Gas is available at Mile 10.4 on the Spur Road. Bike rentals available at south edge of town. The general store carries groceries, deli items, beer and wine and other items. There are a number of locally owned and operated gift shops and galleries; descriptions follow.

Talkeetna Roadhouse. Located on Main Street in "beautiful downtown Talkeetna" the Frank Lee cabin, circa 1917, has been in operation as a full-service roadhouse since 1944. Now famous for breakfasts—featuring a 1902 sourdough starter—as well as cinnamon rolls, daily breads, pies, cookies, savory pasties, reindeer chili and a simple menu of meals all made from scratch, served at big tables where folks sit family-style. Overnight accommodations in co-ed hostel-style Bunk Room, private rooms and cabins. Open year-round. Phone (907) 733-1351. See display ad on page 391. [ADVERTISEMENT]

Camping

RV camping at **Talkeetna Camper Park** at **Milepost J 13.7** Talkeetna Spur Road; phone (907) 733-2693. Tent camping only at Talkeetna River Park at the end of Main Street; fee charged. Camping is also available at the ADF&G concessionaire-operated public boat launch in East Talkeetna near the Swiss Alaska Inn. Turn off at airport and follow posted signs for directions to private campground.

Transportation

Air: There are several air taxi services in Talkeetna. Charter service, flightseeing and glacier landings are available. See ads this section.

©Claire Torgerson, staff

Talkeetna state airport has a 3,500-foot paved runway. Local flying services have offices downtown and at the airport.

Railroad: The Alaska Railroad provides daily passenger service on its Anchorage–Talkeetna-Denali Park–Fairbanks service. Flag-stop service between Talkeetna and Hurricane (see Attractions this section). Railroad Depot is located at **Milepost J 13.5** Talkeetna Spur Road; open daily 10 A.M. to 5 P.M., mid-May to mid-September. Get your parking permit and tickets at the Depot; passenger parking is at the far end of the parking lot. Leave parking permit on your dash while you're on the train.

Highway: At the end of a 14-mile-long spur road off the Parks Highway.

Van service: Sunshine Transit operates a van between downtown and the Talkeetna Y on weekdays from 8:30 A.M. to 7 P.M.; Saturdays 10 A.M. to 5 P.M. with stops along the way; $1 one-way.

Taxi: Talkeetna Taxi (907) 355-8294.

Attractions

The **Talkeetna Historical Society Museum** is located 1 block off Main Street opposite the Sheldon Community Arts Hanger. The original 1-room schoolhouse, built in 1936, exhibits historical items, local art and a display on the late Don Sheldon, famous Alaskan bush pilot. The original Railroad Depot building has a 20-minute video on the history of the Alaska Railroad; also read about the history of Curry, AK, and gold mining in the region. The Railroad Section House has an impressive 12-foot-by-12-foot scale model of Denali (formerly Mount McKinley) with photographs by Bradford Washburn. A mountaineering display features pioneer and recent climbs of Denali. Ask about scheduled lectures held here in summer. The Ole Dahl cabin and the Harry Robb cabin, both early trapper/miners' cabins located on the museum grounds, are furnished with period items. Admission prices (subject to change) are: $5 general/$4 seniors and military; kids 10 and under free. Family rate is $15. Pick up a free walking tour map of Talkeetna's historic sites here. Museum buildings open 10 A.M. to 6 P.M. daily, first of May to end of September; open weekends in winter. Mailing address: P.O. Box 76, Talkeetna, AK 99676. Phone (907) 733-2487; website www.talkeetnahistorical society.org.

Take a **Mahay's Jetboat Adventure** up Susitna River, Talkeetna River, to Devil's Canyon, and Chulitna River; phone (907) 733-2223. **Phantom Tri-River Charters** offers 5- to 8-hour fishing charters; phone (907) 733-2400. Commercial float trips and raft tours offer another popular way of exploring the roadless wilderness. Talkeetna is located at the confluence of the Susitna, Talkeetna and Chulitna Rivers.

Flightsee Denali. Local flying services (K2 Aviation, Talkeetna Air Taxi) offer flightseeing trips of Denali along with glacier landings on the mountain. This is a very popular activity in Talkeenta. Contact the air services by visiting their local offices or going online (see ads this section).

©Claire Torgerson, staff

Ride the **Hurricane Turn Train**. The Alaska Railroad's flag-stop train between the Talkeetna depot and Hurricane makes an interesting day trip. Used by people who live in the Bush, as well as hunters, hikers, and fishermen, the 115-mile round-trip route parallels the Susitna River and traverses Indian

Talkeetna's rivers provide whitewater trips, like Mahay's Jet Boat Adventures (seen here), or a relaxing fishing charter with Phantom Tri-River Charters. (©Claire Torgerson, staff)

River Canyon. The train stops for anyone wanting to be picked up for a ride into town or to be dropped off in the wilderness between Talkeetna and Hurricane, so it may run late depending on the number of stops. The train runs Thursday through Monday in summer; www.alaskarailroad.com. Tickets may be purchased at the depot (**Milepost J 13.5**); 1-800-544-0552 or (907) 265-2494.

Special Events. 4th of July barbecue and parade. Winterfest in December features a month of special events and competitions, of which the best known are the Bachelor Auction and the Wilderness Woman's Contest, both held the first Saturday in December. The Talkeetna Bachelor Auction raises funds for local charities by auctioning off bachelors for cash. For more information, www.talkeetnabachelors.com.

Fishing. The Susitna River basin offers many top fishing trout and salmon streams and lakes, either accessible by road, charter plane or riverboat.

Access to the banks of the Susitna River is via an unsigned gravel access at Milepost A 104.6, on the north side of the Susitna River bridge. (©Serine Reeves)

(Continued from page 388)

shine Creek stream access (Mat-Su Borough; phone 907/861-8578); public parking, toilets, litter bin. Fishing for rainbow trout and seasonal salmon runs.

A 103.9 C 106.1 F 258.1 Distance marker southbound shows Talkeetna Road Junction 5 miles.

A 104.2 C 105.8 F 257.8 Bridge over Susitna River. Entering Game Management Unit 16A, northbound, Unit 14B southbound.

A 104.6 C 105.4 F 257.4 Unsigned gravel road to west at north end of bridge accesses gravel bars on Susitna River.

A 104.8 C 105.2 F 257.2 Large gravel turnout to west.

A 105.7 C 104.3 F 256.3 Rabideux Creek (northbound sign); watch for signed public fishing access.

A 107.8 C 102.2 F 254.2 View of Denali (weather permitting) for northbound travelers.

A 108 C 102 F 254 CAUTION: Watch for moose.

A 109.9 C 100.1 F 252.1 Distance marker northbound shows Trapper Creek 5 miles.

A 113.2 C 96.8 F 248.8 Trapper Creek Welcomes You (sign).

A 113.6 C 96.4 F 248.4 **McKinley View B&B.** See display ad this page.

A 114.1 C 95.9 F 247.9 Devonshire Drive to Emergency Services Bldg. with outside emergency phone (0.1 mile). Trapper Creek Public Library (0.2 mile); open Monday, Wednesday, Thursday and Saturday, free internet and computer stations, Alaskana section and book exchange for travelers.

A 114.6 C 95.4 F 247.4 **Trapper Creek Inn & RV Park** on east side of highway; 24-hour gas and diesel, cafe, store, laundry, showers, general store, camping and lodging (see detailed description following). NOTE: Check your gas gauge; next gas northbound is in Cantwell, 95 miles from Trapper Creek.

Trapper Creek Inn & RV Park. See

display ad this page.

A 114.8 C 95.2 F 247.2 TRAPPER CREEK (pop. 426) at the **junction** of the Parks Highway and Petersville Road; food, gas and lodging at **Trapper Creek Inn & RV Park.** Lodging also on Petersville Road at **Alaska's Northland Inn** (see description at turnoff). **Emergency Services:** Dial 911. Trapper Creek has a post office (ZIP code 99683) and a library. The library, located at 8901 E. Devonshire Dr., is open Mondays, Wednesdays, Thursdays and Saturdays; free internet and computer stations (time limit may apply), Alaskana section and book exchange for travelers. The community holds a Fireweed Festival in July.

A 114.9 C 95.1 F 247.1 Petersville Road turnoff to west. Miners built the Petersville Road in the 1920s, and federal homesteading began here in 1948. Today, a cluster of businesses around this junction serve Parks Highway travelers and make up the community of Trapper Creek. Accommodations along Petersville Road at **Alaska's Northland Inn.**

> **Junction** with Petersville Road, which leads west 18.7 miles. See "Petersville Road" log on facing page.

A 115.4 C 94.6 F 246.6 Wal Mikes. Distance marker northbound shows Cantwell 94 miles, Denali National Park 122 miles, Fairbanks 239 miles.

A 115.5 C 94.5 F 246.5 Trapper Creek Trading Post east side of highway.

A 115.6 C 94.4 F 246.4 Highway crosses Trapper Creek.

Excellent views of Denali (weather permitting) northbound.

A 118 C 92 F 244 View of Denali northbound (weather permitting).

A 119.6 C 90.4 F 242.4 Distance marker southbound shows Trapper Creek 5 miles, Wasilla 78 miles, Anchorage 120 miles.

A 121.1 C 88.9 F 240.9 Chulitna highway maintenance camp to west.

A 121.5 C 88.5 F 240.5 Paved loop to east with parking areas and outhouses; access to Chulitna Bluffs scenic view and East-West Express winter trails.

A 122 C 88. F 240 Coffee hut to west.

A 123.8 C 86.2 F 238.2 Large paved turnout to west.

A 126.6 C 83.4 F 235.4 Large paved parking area to east.

A 127.1 C 82.9 F 234.9 Large gravel turnout to west.

A 132.2 C 77.8 F 229.8 South boundary of **Denali State Park.** Adjacent to the southern border of Denali National Park and Preserve, this 324,420-acre parkland borders the Parks Highway between the Talkeetna Mountains and the Alaska Range. The park's 4 campgrounds, 4 viewpoints and 5 trailheads are located along the Parks Highway between here and **Milepost A 168.5.**

The park's outstanding features are the 30-mile spines of Curry and Kesugi ridges. Small lakes and unspoiled tundra cover the

(Continues on page 396)

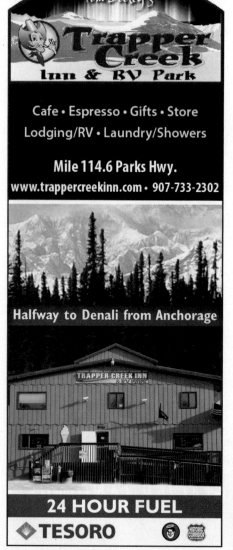

Petersville Road

Petersville Road leads west and north from Trapper Creek at **Milepost A 114.9** on the Parks Highway through a homestead area notable for its mountain views and its bed and breakfasts. The Trapper Creek/Petersville Road area is a logical and convenient stop for travelers, particularly those headed for Denali National Park.

Built as a mining road, today Petersville Road is very popular with 4-wheelers in summer and snowmachines in winter *(please respect private property)*. The MILEPOST® logs the first 18.7 miles of Petersville Road to Peters Creek access. Inquire locally for current road conditions beyond Forks.

PETERSVILLE ROAD

Distance from junction with the Parks Highway (J) is shown.

J 0 Junction with Parks Highway at **Milepost A 114.9**, Trapper Creek (description begins on page 394).

J 0.1 Turnouts both sides of the road. Distance marker that shows Moose Creek 7 miles, Peters Creek 19 miles.

J 0.6 Historic Donaldson 59er Cabin to south. Gold Rush Centennial sign:

"In 1906, prospectors ascended the Susitna River and discovered gold in several creeks in the Cache Creek–Dutch Hills area. News of the discoveries set off a rush the following year. Miners later developed an easier route to their claims that included travel by boat from Cook Inlet up the Susitna and Yentna rivers to a supply point called McDougall. Hiking and using packhorses, they continued up the McDougall Trail crossing rushing streams, swampy bogs and rugged mountains. In winter, travel was easier over firm, frozen ground with the use of dog and hand sleds.

"Miners improved the 50-mile McDougall Trail, but in places it was hard to follow. In 1917, packer Richard Feltham lost his way in the swamps near Hungryman Camp. After 6 days, a search party found him near his horse. 'Evidences of the struggle of the man to find his way were pitiful to see,' according to one of his rescuers. Feltham had blazed marks on trees in a futile effort to find what other miners considered 'a most obscure trail.' Feltham died several hours after he was found.

"Miners in the area petitioned the government for help in the construction of a 'dirt road that will guarantee to get us home in safety ... and won't leave us somewhere to perish, as it did Dick Feltham.' After crews started building a railroad through the area, miner Henry Bamburg blazed a trail from the mines to the new railstop called Talkeetna. In 1918, the Alaska Road Commission began improving the trail, which is now the Petersville Road that passes in front of the Trapper Creek Museum."

J 0.8 Alaska's Northland Inn. See display ad on this page.

J 2.6 Trapper Creek elementary school to south; ski trails, ballfield, playground, basketball court, picnic tables.

J 6.2 *CAUTION: Dog team crossing (westbound sign).*

J 6.3 Oil Well Road.

J 6.8 *Slow for posted speed zone westbound.*

J 7.2 Moose Creek.

J 7.8 Gravel turnout to north.

J 8 Gravel turnout to south.

J 9.5 Large turnout to south. Pavement ends, gravel begins westbound. Observe posted speed limit. Watch for potholes and slow for washboard.

J 10.7 Gate Lake. Public access fishing, stocked by ADF&G. Turnouts on both

Watch for off-road vehicle (ORV) traffic on Petersville Road. This side road accesses Peters Creek, a popular fishing spot adjacent the ORV bridge to Dollar Creek Trailhead.

(©Kris Valencia, staff)

sides of the road. Look for cotton grass in summer. There are 14 species of cotton grass in Alaska.

J 11.6 Turnouts on both sides of road.

J 11.8 Turnout to south. Begin 7 percent downhill grade westbound.

J 12.2 *Large potholes in road, summer 2018.*

J 12.4 Gravel turnouts on both sides of road.

J 12.9 Large turnouts both sides of road.

J 13.5 Turnouts both sides of road. Downgrade westbound slow to 25-mph.

J 13.7 Large gravel parking area is staging area for ATVs in summer and snow machines in winter. Outhouse. Road closed beyond this point, June 2018.

CAUTION: Begin steep downhill westbound; slow for sharp curve. Watch for ATVs!

J 13.9 Kroto Creek bridge. Road narrows westbound. Slow for rough road (washboard and potholes). Muddy road in spring or during heavy rains.

J 14.4 Turnout with view.

J 15.2 Parking at ORV trailhead.

J 15.3 Parking.

J 15.7 Parking at ORV trailhead.

J 16.4 Small ORV parking area.

J 17.3 Parking at Shulin Lake ORV trailhead.

J 17.4 Parking at Kenay Lake ORV trailhead.

J 18.7 Petersville Road forks: Right fork is continuation of Petersville Road *(high clearance 4-wheel drive vehicles only beyond Forks Roadhouse)* and leads to Petersville Recreational Mining Area. Left fork leads 0.2 mile to Peters Creek (descriptions follow).

This site was a supply depot for gold miners in the Petersville Hills and Susitna Valley in the early 1900s. In the early 1930s, the Forks Roadhouse was constructed here; it carried mining supplies and had a saloon. The roadhouse operated for some 80 years until it burned down in April 2012.

Take the left fork for informal camping (no facilities) on Mat-Su Borough public land at **Peters Creek**. Beautiful spot. Fishing for salmon and trout; bridge across Peters Creek is Dollar Creek Trailhead: ORVs only, no cars on bridge or trail.

Take right fork for Petersville Road to former mining camp of Petersville and downstream boundary of Petersville Recreational Mining Area (about 11 miles). Peters Creek must be forded to reach the upper end of the Recreational Mining Area. Petersville Road ends about 18 miles beyond the Forks. This stretch of road is usually not passable until late June.

Recreational gold panning, mineral prospecting and mining using light portable field equipment are allowed without any permit from the Dept. of Natural Resources (DNR). Mining in fish-bearing bodies of water using suction dredges requires a permit from Dept. of Fish & Game Division of Habitat; phone (907) 267-2821. Or phone the Division of Mining, Land & Water in Anchorage at (907) 269-8600. Visit http://dnr.alaska.gov/mlw/factsht/mine_fs/petersvi.pdf for Petersville Recreational Mining Area information.

Return to Milepost A 114.9 Parks Highway

View Denali (weather permitting) from the Denali Viewpoint South at Milepost A 134.8, a good spot to stop and take a break along the Parks Highway. (©Kris Valencia, staff)

(*Continued from page 394*)

ridge lands, whose heights overlook the heart of the Alaska Range, the spires of the Tokosha Mountains, glaciers, gorges and the vast, braided Chulitna River. The Kesugi Ridge hike has been rated a "must do" trail by national backpacking magazines. Hardwood forests along the highway and alpine tundra above tree line are home to myriad wildlife, including brown/grizzly and black bears.

A 132.8 C 77.2 F 229.2 Middle of the **Chulitna River** bridge. Fishing for Arctic grayling and rainbow trout.

Entering Game Management Subunit 13-E, leaving unit 16A, northbound.

A 132.9 C 77.1 F 229.1 Intersection with McKinley View Drive at north end of bridge. Turn east uphill and follow paved road 0.5 mile for turnout with view and 1.3 miles for **Mt. McKinley Princess Wilderness Lodge**; restaurants (open to public), lodging, packaged tours, beautiful view from the deck of the Alaska Range.

Mt. McKinley Princess Wilderness Lodge. See display ad on this page.

A 133 C 77 F 229 Narrow dirt driveway to west and Alaska Nature Guides.

A 134.5 C 75.5 F 227.5 Mary's McKinley View Lodge ("last cafe for 75 miles"); longtime restaurant and accommodations on an original homestead. Spectacular view of Denali (formerly Mount McKinley) from dining room. Description follows.

Mary's McKinley View Lodge. Located on Mary Carey's original homestead. Spectacular view of McKinley from every room, especially the glass-walled restaurant. Mary, famous for Alaskan books, homesteaded before the state park was created. She fought for highway completion to share her magnificent view with travelers. Now a movie is being filmed about her life. Enjoy dining, browse the gift shop, get a personally autographed children's book from Mary's daughter, Jean Richardson, or spend a pleasant night in the modern rooms. Call (907) 733-1555. See display ad this page.
[ADVERTISEMENT]

A 134.8 C 75.2 F 227.2 Double-ended entrance west to **Denali Viewpoint South** (Denali State Park); paved and landscaped day-use parking area; scenic viewpoint, viewing scopes, interpretive boards; 9 campsites with firepits and picnic tables ($15/night); toilets, water pump; and 800-foot-long uphill trail to overlook. Parking area accommodates RVs.

From here northbound for many miles there are views (weather permitting) of glaciers on the southern slopes of the Alaska Range to the west. Ruth, Buckskin and Eldridge glaciers are the most conspicuous. Flightseeing trips offer close-up views of Denali, Don Sheldon Amphitheater, Ruth Glacier, the Great Gorge and Moose's Tooth.

Ruth Glacier extends 31 miles southeast through the Great Gorge, nicknamed the Grand Canyon of Alaska for its towering 5,000-foot peaks that rise up on both sides of the glacier. The gorge opens into Don Sheldon Amphitheater at the head of Ruth Glacier, where the Don Sheldon mountain house sits. Donald E. Sheldon (1921–75) was a well-known bush pilot who helped map, patrol, and aid search and rescue efforts in this area.

View of 20,310-foot Denali on a clear day. Peaks to be sighted, south to north, along the next 20 miles to the west are: Mount Hunter (elev. 14,573 feet); Mount Huntington (elev. 12,240 feet); Mount Barrille (elev. 7,650 feet); and Mount Dickey (elev. 9,845 feet).

A 135.6 C 74.4 F 226.4 Access road

to east leads uphill to **K'esugi Ken Campground** (Denali State Park). Interpretive pavilion (1.3 miles from highway); day-use area (1.4 miles from highway) with toilet, picnic tables, oversize parking for big rigs, Moose Flats Loop Trail and Curry Ridge Trail; and entrance to the K'esugi Ken Campground (1.5 miles from highway). Day use parking fee is $5. The campground has 43 treed, gravel, back-in RV sites with picnic tables, firepits and electrical hook-ups, located along a paved loop road. There are 10 tent sites with food storage lockers; 3 public-use cabins; a picnic shelter; water, group campsite; ranger contact station. Camping fees from $20 to $35 per night. Firewood for sale. Walking and skiing trails; hiking trail to alpine lake on Curry Ridge. In summer, Wednesday–Sunday 3 P.M. guided interpretive walk at Moose Flat Loop Trailhead and a 7 P.M. campground program at interpretive center. ⬛🅰

A 137.2 C 72.8 F 224.8 Lower Troublesome Creek (Denali State Park) campground and trailhead to west; large parking area, shelter. There are 20 campsites in trees with tables and firepits and 32 parking spaces (for camper use between 6 P.M. and 9 A.M.); $15 camping fee/night. Day-use area with sheltered picnic sites, toilets, water and litter barrels; $5 day-use fee. There is a 0.7-mile trail to the Chulitna River from the parking lot. Short gravel trail on north side of parking area to Troublesome Creek. 🅰

A 137.4 C 76.6 F 224.6 Troublesome Creek bridge. **Troublesome Creek** is usually a clear runoff stream, not silted by glaciers. The stream heads in a lake and flows to the Chulitna River. Fishing for rainbow trout, Arctic grayling and salmon (chinook fishing prohibited), June to September. 🐟

A 137.6 C 72.4 F 224.4 Upper Troublesome Creek Trailhead to east is a 15.2-mile trail to Byers Lake Campground (see **Milepost A 147**). The trail, rated as difficult, climbs to the Kesugi Ridge; expansive views. Check for postings on current trail conditions before heading out. *CAUTION: Watch for bears.*

A 139.8 C 70.2 F 222.2 Small paved turnout to west. Distance marker southbound shows Wasilla 98 miles, Anchorage 140 miles.

A 143.1 C 65.3 F 218.9 Double-ended gravel turnout to east.

A 143.9 C 66.1 F 218.1 Bridge over Byers Creek.

A 144 C 66 F 218 Byers Creek Lodge to west. Cabin rentals.

A 145.6 C 64.4 F 214.4 Paved turnout to west.

A 147 C 63 F 215 Turnoff for **Byers Lake Campground** (Denali State Park) to east via paved road. Drive downhill 0.3 miles for day-use parking area with picnic tables and firepits. Access road continues east to additional day-use parking with toilets (0.4 miles from highway), dumpsters, parking, toilets, water pump, boat launch, and campground loop road (0.6 mile from highway). Byers Lake Cabin #1 is also located on this access road. Byers Lake Cabins #2 and #3 are a half-mile walk or 1.7 miles from the road in winter. For details and availability, go to http://dnr.alaska.gov/parks/cabins/matsu.htm or www.reserveamerica.com.

The campground has 73 sites with and dump station/$10 fee, campground

Turnoff at Milepost A 135.6 for K'esugi Ken Campground in Denali State Park, seen here. Also access this turnoff to interpretive programs and hiking trails. (©Serine Reeves)

host, camping fee/$20, picnic tables, firepits, water, toilets. Walking trails connect campground with Veterans Memorial (see **Milepost A 147.1**). **Byers Lake** (no outboard motors permitted) has fishing for Arctic grayling, burbot, rainbow trout, lake trout and whitefish. *CAUTION: Bears, keep clean camp.* ⬛♿🅰

Byers Lake Trailhead is on campground loop road. Hiking distances are: Byers Creek bridge 1 mile; Cascade 1.6 mile; Lakeshore Campground (a remote campsite) 1.8 miles; Tarn Point 4.2 miles; Troublesome Creek Trailhead 15 miles.

A 147.1 C 62.9 F 214.9 South end of **Medal of Honor Loop to Alaska Veterans Memorial/POW–MIA Rest Area** to east; large parking areas for vehicles and big rigs; picnic tables, drinking water; visitor information center, interpretive kiosk, viewing scopes; toilets, garbage containers; pet walk. Wheelchair accessible. A popular picnic stop. Stretch your legs on the short trail down to Byers Lake Campground that begins at the upper (big rig) parking area. The visitor center/store is open Thursday–Sunday 8 a.m. to 5 p.m. Memorial Day–Labor Day weekends. Camping is permitted at this rest area only "after 8 P.M. if Byers Lake Campground is full and you must pay the $15 camping fee at the campground."

The **Alaska Veterans Memorial** adjacent the rest area, consists of an alcove and a semicircle of five 20-foot-tall concrete panels, one for each branch of service and each with a large star on the upper part and inscriptions on the lower part.

Panels and plaques also memorialize the Alaska National Guard; the Merchant

Marine; the Submariners, victims of the Air Force C-47 crash on nearby Kesugi Ridge in February 1954, and other memorials. Three flag poles stand at the site: the center pole flying the American flag; the pole to the right the Alaska flag, and the pole to the left the flags of the POW-MIA.

The memorial was erected in 1983 and dedicated in 1984 by Governor Bill Sheffield, a veteran, and other civilian and military leaders. The Byers Lake site was selected because it was centrally located between Alaska's 2 largest cities, Anchorage and Fairbanks, and there is a wonderful view of Denali from the entrance to the memorial.

The memorial reads: "We dedicate this quiet place to the remembrance of the veterans of Alaska who have served their country at home and throughout the world. We honor their heroism and dedication."

A 147.5 C 62.5 F 214.5 North entrance to Denali State Park's Alaska Veterans Memorial/POW–MIA Rest Area to east via Medal of Honor Loop.

A 156 C 54 F 206 Distance marker northbound shows Cantwell 54 miles, Denali National Park 81 miles, Fairbanks 199 miles.

A 156.1 C 53.9 F 205.9 Paved turnout to east. Gravel turnout to west.

A 156.5 C 53.5 F 205.5 Ermine Hill Trailhead (Denali State Park) to east; trail is 3 miles one-way.

A 159.3 C 50.7 F 202.7 Large gravel turnout to west.

A 159.8 C 50.2 F 202.2 Distance marker southbound shows Wasilla 118 miles, Anchorage 160 miles.

A 161 C 49 F 201 Large gravel shoulder parking east side of highway.

A 162.4 C 47.6 F 199.6 Large paved turnout to west; Denali viewpoint.

A 162.6 C 47.4 F 199.4 Denali View North Campground (Denali State Park) to west. Large, open, paved parking area with day-use parking and 20 side-by-side spaces for overnight parking with firepits and picnic tables; also long pull-through sites for large RV rigs with tow vehicles. Walk-in tent sites behind fee station. Camping fee is $15/night per vehicle. Outhouse (wheelchair accessible), water, litter bins, interpretive kiosks, spotting scope, nature trail. Overlooks Chulitna River. Views (weather permitting) of Denali, Moose's Tooth, Mount

©Kris Valencia, staff

Capturing scenery at Broad Pass from turnout at Milepost A 201. The pass is the lowest summit along the North American mountain system at elev. 2,400 feet. (©Serine Reeves)

Huntington and Alaska Range peaks above Hidden River valley.

A 162.8 C 47.2 F 199.2 Paved turnout to east.

A 163.1 C 46.9 F 198.9 Large double-ended paved turnout to west.

A 163.3 C 46.7 F 198.7 Little Coal Creek bridge. Rainbow trout, Arctic grayling and salmon, July through September.

A 163.8 C 46.2 F 198.2 Turnoff to east for Little Coal Creek Trailhead (Denali State Park) with toilets; $5 parking fee. Trail offers access (1½-hour hike) to alpine country. It is a 27-mile hike to Byers Lake via Kesugi Ridge.

A 165.5 C 44.5 F 196.5 Paved turnouts on both sides of highway by creek. Good berry picking in the fall.

A 168.5 C 41.5 F 193.5 Denali State Park boundary (leaving park northbound, entering park southbound). See park description at **Milepost A 132.2.**

CAUTION: Winding hilly road northbound, foliage obscures sight line, pass with care.

A 169 C 41 F 193 *CAUTION: Railroad crossing.* A solar panel here helps to power the warning signals.

A 170 C 40 F 192 Long paved turnout to west side of highway.

A 173 C 37 F 189 Paved turnout to west.

A 173.9 C 36.1 F 188.1 Shoulder parking west side of highway, just south of bridge.

A 174 C 36 F 188 Hurricane Gulch Bridge. Paved parking area to west at north end of bridge. The 550-foot deck of the bridge is 260 feet above Hurricane Creek, not as high as the railroad bridge that spans the gulch.

A 176 C 34 F 186 Small paved turnout to east.

Slow for curves as highway descends long grade northbound to Honolulu Creek.

A 176.5 C 33.5 F 185.5 Narrow, double-ended turnout on curve to west with uphill grade.

A 177.8 C 32.2 F 184.2 Small paved turnout to east.

A 178 C 32 F 184 Honolulu Creek bridge. Rough gravel access to creek to west at north end of bridge.

Highway begins ascent northbound to Broad Pass, the gap in the Alaska Range crossed by both the railroad and highway.

A 179.5 C 30.5 F 182.5 Paved turnout to west by **Mile 180 Lake**; public fishing access; stocked with Arctic grayling.

A 180 C 30 F 182 Narrow double-ended turnout to west by Mile 180 Lake.

A 183.2 C 26.8 F 178.8 Double-ended paved turnout to west below highway. Look to the west across the Chulitna River for dramatic view of the Alaska Range (weather permitting).

A 184.5 C 25.5 F 177.5 Paved turnout to west.

A 185.1 C 24.9 F 176.9 Bridge over East Fork Chulitna River.

A 185.6 C 24.4 F 176.4 East Fork Chulitna Wayside (not signed) to east; 0.5-mile paved loop to rest area and overnight parking with picnic tables, concrete firepits, picnic shelter, toilets. Popular stop for RVers. This wayside is located in a bend of the East Fork Chulitna River amid a healthy growth of Alaska spruce and birch.

A 186.3 C 23.7 F 175.7 Single-vehicle turnout to east. View from highway of eroded bluffs to east.

Winding upgrade northbound, slow for 50-mph curve.

A 187.5 C 22.5 F 175.5 Paved/gravel double-ended turnout to west.

A 188.7 C 21.3 F 174.3 Igloo City. This local landmark first advertised in the 1973 edition of *The MILEPOST®* as Tesoro Igloo Service, "scheduled for completion in 1973," promising a hotel, restaurant, gift shop, fuel, tires and towing. The hotel never happened. In the 1976 edition, it advertised as Igloo Service, offering gas and diesel. Under new ownership in 1999, it appeared as Igloo City Resort, offering 24-hour gas and diesel, snacks and gifts. It closed in 2005.

A 191.1 C 18.9 F 170.9 Large paved turnout to west.

A 192 C 18 F 170 NOTE: *Ahtna, Inc. lands border much of the Parks Highway northbound to* **Milepost A 230.** *Ahtna, Inc. lands are open to entry by permit only; for more information and links to online permits go to www.ahtnainc.com/land-permit.*

A 193.7 C 16.3 F 168.3 View northbound from highway railroad overpass of old highway alignment below which crossed the railroad tracks. It was replaced when reconstruction on this section of highway

was completed in 2016.

A 194.5 C 15.5 F 167.5 Middle Fork Chulitna River bridge.

A 195 C 15 F 167 Entering **Broad Pass** northbound. Broad Pass is one of the most beautiful areas on the Parks Highway. A mountain valley, bare in some places, dotted with scrub spruce in others, and surrounded by mountain peaks, it provides a top-of-the-world feeling for the traveler, although it is one of the lowest summits along the North American mountain system. Named in 1898 by George Eldridge and Robert Muldrow, the 2,400-foot pass, sometimes called Caribou Pass, marks the divide between the drainage of rivers and streams that empty into Cook Inlet and those headed to the Yukon River.

A 196 C 14 F 166 Large gravel and pavement turnout to east; watch for potholes. Good mountain views.

A 197.9 C 12.1 F 164.1 Begin 2.1-mile passing lane northbound.

A 199 C 11 F 163 Summit Lake (1.3 miles long) to east.

A 200 C 10 F 162 Begin 2.1-mile passing lane southbound.

A 201 C 9 F 161 Large paved parking area to east with mountain view. Denali (formerly known as Mount McKinley) is visible to the southwest on clear days.

A 201.3 C 8.7 F 160.7 Broad Pass summit (not signed), 2,400 feet. Summit airport and abandoned weather service station to west (no camping sign). An FAA Flight Service Station was commissioned here in May 1940 and closed in 1972. FAA remote weather reporting service and video camera here (go to http://avcams.faa.gov and click on Summit).

Private Aircraft: Summit state airport; elev. 2,409 feet; length 3,800 feet; gravel; unmaintained.

A 202 C 8 F 160 Small green-roofed white cabins at south end of Mirror Lake to east are privately owned; no road access.

A 202.1 C 7.9 F 159.9 Boundary of Matanuska–Susitna and Denali boroughs. Alaska is unique among the 50 states in that much of the state (but not all of it) is organized into local forms of government called boroughs, similar to counties in other states. There are 16 boroughs in Alaska.

A 203.2 C 6.8 F 158.8 Alaska Railroad overpass.

A 203.5 C 6.5 F 158.5 Large paved parking area with view of Denali (weather permitting).

A 206.8 C 3.2 F 155.2 Watch for caribou.

A 208 C 2 F 154 Paved viewpoint to west at south end of Pass Creek bridge. Blueberries in season. *Slow for road damage next 1 mile northbound.*

A 208.7 C 1.3 F 153.3 *Slow for posted speed zones northbound.*

A 209 C 1 F 153 Distance marker northbound shows Denali Highway 1 mile. *Slow for road damage next 1 mile southbound.*

A 209.4 C 0.6 F 152.6 Welcome to Cantwell (northbound sign).

A 209.6 C 0.4 F 152.4 Bridge over Jack River. Cleared area on southeast side is Private Property. Do not enter.

A 209.9 C 0.1 F 152.1 USA gas station with convenience store to west.

A 210 C 0 F 152 Junction of Parks and Denali highways at Cantwell (description follows). Turn west for **Cantwell RV Park** (0.3 mile), the Alaska Railroad siding, Cantwell Cafe (1.9 miles). Turn east for Cantwell School (0.1 mile) and Backwoods

Lodge (0.2 mile), State Troopers Office (0.5 mile).

Junction of the Parks Highway (Alaska Route 3) and the Denali Highway (Alaska Route 8). Turn east for Denali Highway to Paxson (134 miles). For eastbound travel on the Denali Highway turn to the end of the DENALI HIGHWAY section on page 475 and read log back to front.

Cantwell

A 210 C 0 F 152 Located at **junction** with the Denali Highway, 21 miles south of entrance to Denali National Park. **Population:** 183. **Emergency Services:** Dial 911. **Alaska State Troopers,** business phone (907) 768-2202. **Fire Department,** phone (907) 768-2162. **Clinic,** Cantwell Clinic, phone (907) 768-2122.

Elevation: 2,190 feet. **Private Aircraft:** Cantwell airport, adjacent north; elev. 2,190 feet; length 2,100 feet; gravel; fuel 100LL.

Cantwell began as an Alaska Railroad flag stop and continues as a work station for the railroad. The village was named for the Cantwell River, the original name of the Nenana River, named by Lt. Allen in 1885 for Lt. John C. Cantwell of the Revenue-Cutter Service, Kobuk River area explorer.

Cantwell visitor services include the **Cantwell Food Mart/Chevron** and USA gas stations/convenience stores; **Cantwell RV Park** and **BluesBerry Inn.** Tire repair and some groceries are available. Cantwell businesses are located both at the intersection of the Denali and Parks highways and west of the Parks Highway on the access road to "old" downtown Cantwell at Mile 1.7.

NOTE: Next gas southbound on the Parks Highway is at Trapper Creek, 95 miles from here. First gas stop eastbound on the Denali Highway is at Clearwater Mountain Lodge, 52 miles from here. First restaurant eastbound on the Denali Highway is Maclaren River Lodge, 92 miles from here; see the DENALI HIGH-

WAY section for details.

Cantwell provides services (gas stations/convenience stores, campground, lodging, flying service) for both Parks Highway travelers and Denali Highway travelers. A good view of Denali (weather permitting) in the Cantwell area is from a turnout 1 mile east on the Denali Highway.

Berry pickers, hikers, hunters and other outdoor recreationists visiting the Cantwell area should inquire locally about land status before venturing off-road. Ahtna Inc. lands border much of the Parks Highway between **Milepost A 192** and **A 230**, including Cantwell and permits are required. Go to www.ahtna-inc.com/land-permit.

Parks Highway Log
(continued)

A 210.1 C 0.1 F 151.9 Cantwell post office (ZIP 99729), west side of highway; open 10:30 A.M. to 4 P.M., Monday–Friday, and 9:30 A.M. to 1 P.M. on Saturdays.

A 210.3 C 0.3 F 151.7 Cantwell Food **Mart** to east with Chevron station with gas/diesel, convenience store, ATM and snacks.

Cantwell Foodmart/Chevron. See display ad on this page.

Slow for posted speed zone southbound.

A 210.8 C 0.8 F 151.2 BluesBerry Inn. Family-friendly log cabin motel in beautiful Cantwell. 16 affordable rooms; most rooms have private bath/shower, many have TV, all have WiFi (from $80+T dry cabins, $120+T rooms with bath or shower). Big multiple day discounts available. Wild blueberry country! MP 210.8, west on (unmarked) Matlock Drive 0.1 mile. GPS: Intersection Matlock Drive and Gore Road, Cantwell 99729 or coordinates N63.40052 W 148.89336. Reservations (907) 768-2415; www.bluesberryinn.com. See display ad this page. [ADVERTISEMENT]

A 211.6 C 1.6 F 150.4 Double-ended paved parking area to west.

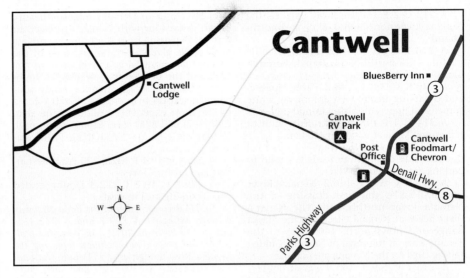

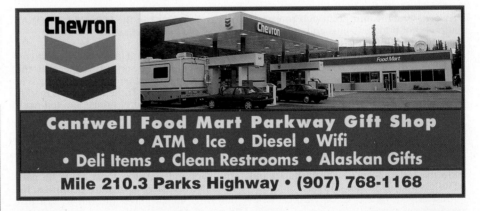

CANTWELL ADVERTISERS

A 212 C 2 F 150 Highway parallels the Nenana River northbound. Slide area northbound.

A 213.1 C 3.1 F 148.9 Begin 1.7-mile passing lane northbound. Denali Borough Transfer Station to west.

A 213.8 C 3.8 F 148.2 Paved double-ended parking area to west among tall white spruce and fireweed starting in mid-July.

A 214 C 4 F 148 Views northbound of Limestone Mine at base of mountain.

A 215.4 C 5.4 F 146.6 Gravel access road on west side of highway leads 0.4 mile to parking area at Nenana River.

A 215.8 C 5.8 F 146.2 Nenana River bridge. This is the first crossing of the Nenana River northbound. The Nenana River heads at Nenana Glacier in the Alaska Range and flows north 140 miles to the Tanana River at the town of Nenana. Guided rafting trips on the Nenana are popular.

A 216.1 C 5.9 F 145.9 Paved double-ended parking area on rise to west. Good spot for photos of Panorama Mountain (elev. 5,778 feet), the prominent peak in the Alaska Range visible to the east.

Entering Game Management Unit 20A and leaving unit 13E northbound.

A 218.5 C 8.5 F 143.5 Paved double-ended parking area to west with beautiful view of Nenana River. Frost heaves next two miles southbound.

A 218.9 C 8.9 F 143.1 Begin 0.4-mile slide area northbound.

A 219.8 C 9.8 F 142.2 Double-ended paved parking area to west.

A 220.5 C 10.5 F 141.5 South end of long, paved, double-ended parking area to west on old highway alignment along the Nenana River. North end at **Milepost A 220.8**. Good place to view rafters.

A 222 C 12 F 140 Snow poles beside roadway guide snowplows in winter.

A 222.2 C 12.2 F 139.8 Paved double-ended turnout to west beside Nenana River.

A 223.9 C 13.9 F 138.1 Carlo Creek Lodge to west.

A 224 C 14 F 138 Bridge over Carlo Creek. Restaurant and pizza pub to east at south end of bridge. Cabins and cafe to east at north end. Hostel to west.

A 224.9 C 14.9 F 137.1 Large informal gravel parking area to west (no overnight camping). Mountain views southbound.

A 226 C 16 F 136 Fang Mountain (elev. 6,736 feet) to west. Erosion pillars on hillside ahead northbound.

A 228 C 18 F 134 Gravel parking area to east is trailhead for public access across Ahtna, Inc. private lands to BLM public lands for "travel by foot, dogsled, animals, snow machines, 2- and 3-wheel vehicles and ATVs less than 3,000 lbs. GVW.

A 228.9 C 18.9 F 133.1 Husky Homestead.

A 229 C 19 F 133 Denali Cabins to east; food, lodging, tours.

A 229.1 C 19.1 F 132.8 Denali Air,

Inc. Fly closer to Denali's majestic beauty on an aerial tour with Denali's pioneer air service! Departing from our exclusive private airstrip, we give you the most views of the spectacular mountains and glaciers in the Park and the best odds of seeing the highest mountain in North America. Enjoy your window seat on twin engine aircraft piloted by the most experienced pilots in the area. Call (907) 683-2261. See display ad on page 434 in the DENALI NATIONAL PARK section. [ADVERTISEMENT]

A 229.4 C 19.4 F 132.6 229 Parks Restaurant and tavern to west.

A 229.7 C 19.7 F 132.3 Double-ended paved parking area to west.

NOTE: Reconstruction of the Parks Highway between **Milepost A 229.7** *and* **A 232.3,** *is expected to begin in 2019. The proposed project (at our press time) includes: replacing the Nenana River bridge; a new Denali National Park & Preserve wayside; new turn lanes; bicycle and pedestrian facilities from* **Milepost A 231** *to the wayside; pedestrian underpasses at the* **Milepost A 231** *intersection and the north bridge abutment; and trail connections and re-routing of Triple Lakes and Oxbow trails.*

A 230 C 20 F 132 NOTE: Ahtna, Inc. lands border much of the Parks Highway southbound to **Milepost A 192.** Ahtna, Inc. lands are open to entry by permit only; for more information and links to online permits go to www.ahtna-inc.com/land-permit.

A 230.5 C 20.5 F 131.5 Highway descends 6 percent grade northbound.

A 231 C 21 F 131 Turnoff for **Denali Grizzly Bear Resort** to west; description follows. Turnoff to east for **Denali Park Village**; lodging, dining, Cabin Nite Theater.

Denali Grizzly Bear. Toll-free 1-866-583-2696. Denali Park. Variety of Alaskan accommodations, pioneer family owned and operated. New Cedar hotel, rooms with private decks on river, TV, WiFi($) and other amenities. Charming, affordable cabins, private, with spectacular views. For camping, wooded RV sites and riverside tent. Only 6 miles south of Denali Visitor Center. See display ad page 432 in the DENALI NATIONAL PARK section. [ADVERTISEMENT]

▲

A 231.1 C 21.1 F 130.9 Nenana River Bridge. This is the second bridge over the Nenana River northbound (first crossing is at **Milepost A 215.8**). Triple Lakes Trail marker to west at north end of bridge; limited roadside parking.

A 231.3 C 21.3 F 130.7 Northbound sign marks boundary of Denali National Park and Preserve. From here north for 6.8 miles the Parks Highway is within the boundaries of the park and travelers must abide by park rules. No discharge of firearms permitted. No hunting. Rough gravel turnout to east just north of sign.

A 231.7 C 21.7 F 130.3 Distance marker northbound shows Denali National Park 6 miles.

A 232.4 C 22.4 F 129.6 Improved highway northbound.

A 232.7 C 22.7 F 129.3 Begin 2-mile passing lane northbound.

A 234.1 C 24.1 F 127.9 Double-ended scenic viewpoint up hill to east; no camping. Mount Fellows (elev. 4,476 feet), to the east, makes an excellent camera subject with its constantly changing shadows. Exceptionally beautiful in the evening. To the southeast stands Pyramid Peak (elev. 5,201 feet).

A 234.6 C 24.6 F 127.4 Begin 1.7-mile passing lane southbound.

A 235 C 25 F 127 *CAUTION: Railroad crossing.* Solar panels and wind generators provide power for crossing signals.

A 236.7 C 26.7 F 125.3 Alaska Railroad overpass. Highway begins 6 percent downgrade northbound.

A 237.3 C 27.3 F 124.7 Riley Creek bridge.

Distance marker southbound shows Cantwell 27 miles, Wasilla 196 miles, Anchorage 237 miles.

A 237.4 C 27.4 F 124.6 Denali National Park and Preserve entrance. Turnoff to west on Park Road for access to Denali National Park and Preserve.

©Kris Valencia, staff

Park sign (pictured above) just west of this junction is a popular photo op.

Drive 0.4 mile west on Park Road for turnoff to Riley Creek Mercantile (open 7 A.M. to 10 P.M. in summer; you may register for campsites at the store) and Riley Creek Campground. Drive 0.7 mile west for turnoff to Wilderness Access Center (hub for park buses and camping permits). Drive 1.4 miles west for access to Denali Visitor Center Campus and **Alaska Railroad** Depot. Drive 1.5 miles for Murie Science and Learning Center (and acting visitor center in winter).

Alaska Railroad. See display ad on facing page.

Junction with 92-mile-long Park Road, which provides access to visitor services and attractions in Denali National Park. See DENALI NATIONAL PARK section on page 427 for Park Road log and details on park entrance fee, campgrounds, transportation and activities in the park.

Begin paved pedestrian path on west side of Parks Highway, which leads north along the highway to Denali Park commercial area.

Begin posted speed zone northbound.

A 237.7 C 27.7 F 124.4 Turnout to west by Denali National Park southbound.

A 238 C 28 F 124 Third bridge northbound over the Nenana River. Access to east to Glacier Way. Access to west for double-ended **Mile 238 Rest Area**; parking, toilets, interpretive signs, picnic tables and access to the pedestrian path. *CAUTION: Supervise children; pets must be on a leash. It is a long drop to the river from the rest area.* The rest area is also the access point for Nenana River rafting companies and a great spot to watch riverrunners start down the Class III and IV whitewater section of the Nenana. The pedestrian path and pedestrian bridge across the Nenana River are used by walkers and bicyclists heading south to the park or north to the commercial area.

Begin Denali Park commercial area northbound. This mile-long strip of seasonal services *(see map page 402)* is called the Nenana River Canyon, and it is where most park visitors and many highway travelers stop in summer. For residents, **DENALI PARK** (pop. 145 in summer) refers to the area along the

Parks Highway from about Carlo Creek, 13 miles south of the Park entrance, to the Nenana River Canyon, 3 miles north of the Park entrance. A variety of services is offered, including river running and ATV bookings; gift shops, accommodations, restaurants; groceries/liquor store; and a gas station. Most businesses are open in summer only.

A 238.1 C 28.1 F 123.9 Kingfisher Creek. North entrance to Mile 238 Rest Area (see description at **Milepost A 238**) to west. Grande Drive to east to **Grande Denali Lodge**.

Grande Denali Lodge. Panoramic views from our perch on Sugarloaf Mountain. Enjoy our fireside lobby, dine at award-winning Alpenglow Restaurant, or grab a bite at Peak Spirits. 160 guest rooms, 6 cozy cabins, private meeting room. Rooms have WiFi, Keurig coffee maker, A/C, fridge. Tour desk, free shuttle, on-site laundry. 1-855-683-8600. [ADVERTISEMENT]

A 238.4 C 28.4 F 123.6 Bluffs Road to east to **Denali Bluffs Hotel**; description follows. Market and liquor store.

Denali Bluffs Hotel. Nestled into Sugarloaf Mountain, with views of Denali National Park! Enjoy hearty BBQ at Mountaineer Grill and Bar or tasty treats at Perky Moose Cafe. 112 Hillside and 64 Riverview rooms. All have WiFi, coffee maker and fridge; RiverView rooms have verandas and A/C. Tour desk, free shuttle, on-site laundry. 1-855-683-8600. [ADVERTISEMENT]

A 238.5 C 28.5 F 123.5 The huge **Denali Princess Wilderness Lodge** complex begins on the west side of the highway; description follows. Parking to east for restaurant.

Denali Princess Wilderness Lodge. Riverside accommodations overlooking the Nenana River and Denali National Park.

One mile from the park entrance and visitor center. The area's best dining, optional excursions for purchase and shuttle service to the rail depot and visitor center. Rail packages from Anchorage or Fairbanks. Reservations 1-800-426-0500; Princesslodges.com. See display ad on page 431 in the DENALI NATIONAL PARK section. [ADVERTISEMENT]

A 238.6 C 28.6 F 123.4 Traffic light at Denali Drive. More of **Denali Princess Wilderness Lodge** to west. Park Mart gas and convenience store to east. South entrance to **Denali Rainbow Village RV Park and Motel**. Local seasonal businesses are housed in the row of log cabins that make up a mall on the east side of the highway here, such as **Denali ATV Adventures** and **Denali Park Zipline** (description follows).

Denali ATV and Denali Park Zipline Denali's two must-do activities: Four unique, guided 2½–4 hour ATV tours on single or 2–6 passenger side-by-side units or a thrilling 3-hour zipline tour through the boreal forest and over the tundra! 7 ziplines and 6 suspension bridges. On the Boardwalk near Tesoro Gas. (907) 683-4ATV or 683-

Seasonal businesses occupy log cabin complex on the east side of the Parks Highway in Denali Park service area in summer. (©David L. Ranta, staff)

2ZIP. www.DenaliATV.com or www.DenaliZipline.com. [ADVERTISEMENT]

A 238.7 C 28.7 F 122.9 Sourdough Road. Access east to **Denali Rainbow Village RV Park and Motel**, located behind the Boardwalk Mall *(see map on page 402);* large motel rooms, 55 RV sites with hookups. Canyon Clinic urgent care to the west.

Denali Rainbow Village RV Park and Motel. See display ad on page 433 in the DENALI NATIONAL PARK section.

A 238.9 C 28.9 F 123.1 Traffic light at Canyon Drive. Turnoff to west for **McKinley Chalet Resort** (lodging, dining, tour desk), which hosts the popular Music of Denali Dinner Theatre; description follows. Turnoff to east for several local businesses, including rafting outfitter and Prospectors Historic Pizzeria. Also access east to DOT **Nenana Canyon Viewpoint**, which is also the end

of the pedestrian/bike path that extends into Denali Park.

McKinley Chalet Resort. Situated in the heart of the Denali Canyon, one mile from the park entrance and visitor center,

the McKinley Chalet Resort features modern amenities, comfortable accommodations, inviting dining options, the Denali Square

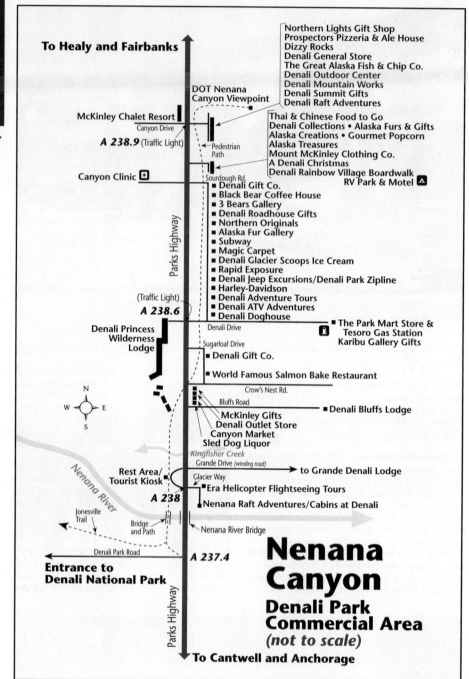

To Healy and Fairbanks

Northern Lights Gift Shop
Prospectors Pizzeria & Ale House
Dizzy Rocks
Denali General Store
The Great Alaska Fish & Chip Co.
Denali Outdoor Center
Denali Mountain Works
Denali Summit Gifts
Denali Raft Adventures

DOT Nenana
Canyon Viewpoint

McKinley Chalet Resort
Canyon Drive
A 238.9 (Traffic Light)

Pedestrian
Path

Thai & Chinese Food to Go
Denali Collections • Alaska Furs & Gifts
Alaska Creations • Gourmet Popcorn
Alaska Treasures
Mount McKinley Clothing Co.
A Denali Christmas
Denali Rainbow Village Boardwalk
RV Park & Motel

Canyon Clinic

Sourdough Rd.
■ Denali Gift Co.
■ Black Bear Coffee House
■ 3 Bears Gallery
■ Denali Roadhouse Gifts
■ Northern Originals
■ Alaska Fur Gallery
■ Subway
■ Magic Carpet
■ Denali Glacier Scoops Ice Cream
■ Rapid Exposure
■ Denali Jeep Excursions/Denali Park Zipline
■ Harley-Davidson
■ Denali Adventure Tours
■ Denali ATV Adventures
■ Denali Doghouse

(Traffic Light)
A 238.6

Denali Princess
Wilderness
Lodge

Denali Drive

■ The Park Mart Store &
Tesoro Gas Station
Karibu Gallery Gifts

Sugarloaf Drive
■ Denali Gift Co.

■ World Famous Salmon Bake Restaurant

Crow's Nest Rd.

Bluffs Road
McKinley Gifts
Denali Outlet Store
Canyon Market
Sled Dog Liquor

■ Denali Bluffs Lodge

Kingfisher Creek
Grande Drive *(winding road)*   → to Grande Denali Lodge

Rest Area/
Tourist Kiosk
Glacier Way
■ Era Helicopter Flightseeing Tours
A 238
■ Nenana Raft Adventures/Cabins at Denali

N
W   E
S

Nenana River

Jonesville
Trail
Bridge
and Path
Nenana River Bridge

Denali Park Road
A 237.4

**Entrance to
Denali National Park**

Parks Highway

Nenana Canyon

Denali Park Commercial Area
(not to scale)

To Cantwell and Anchorage

---

entertainment complex and a vast selection of optional tours! See display ad on page 431 in the DENALI NATIONAL PARK section. [ADVERTISEMENT]

A 239 C 29 F 123 Entering Nenana River Canyon northbound. Slide area begins northbound.

A 239.8 C 29.8 F 122.2 Slide area begins southbound.

A 240 C 30 F 122 Bridge over Iceworm Gulch. Iceworm Creek.

A 240.1 C 30.1 F 121.9 Hornet Creek.

A 240.2 C 30.2 F 121.8 Double-ended turnout to west.

A 240.7 C 30.7 F 121.3 Long double-ended turnout to west.

A 241.2 C 31.2 F 120.8 Fox Creek.

A 241.7 C 31.7 F 120.3 Large gravel turnout to west, posted no camping.

A 242.2 C 32.2 F 119.8 Double-ended paved turnout to west. Signed "no camping" to east.

A 242.3 C 32.3 F 119.7 Dragonfly Creek.

A 242.7 C 32.7 F 119.3 Double-ended turnout to west.

A 242.8 C 32.8 F 119.2 Moody Bridge across Nenana River. *CAUTION: Windy area next mile northbound.* This 4th bridge northbound over the Nenana River is 174 feet from the bottom of the canyon.

A 243.5 C 33.5 F 118.5 Bridge over Bison Gulch. Sharp turn at north end to east for paved viewpoint; no camping. Hiking trail across highway goes up mountain to west.

A 244 C 34 F 118 Begin improved highway northbound.

A 244.6 C 34.6 F 117.4 Antler Creek.

A 245.1 C 35.1 F 116.9 Denali RV Park and Motel.

A 245.4 C 35.4 F 116.6 Begin 1.2-mile passing lane northbound.

A 246.8 C 36.8 F 115.2 Paved turnout to east.

A 247 C 37 F 115 Junction with Otto Lake Road, to the west, with access to Black

---

Diamond Resort (description in side road log following). This area is a fast-growing tourist destination of its own, providing food, lodging, activities and entertainment just outside the bustle of the park. Log of this side road is as follows:

Mile 0.1 Denali Park Hotel turnoff.

Mile 0.6 Denali Outdoor Center to south rents bikes, canoes and kayaks, and offers camping, cabins and river trips.

Mile 0.7 Lion's Club Park to south on Otto Lake offers playground, picnic tables, picnic shelter, lifejackets and boat launch. No fires or camping allowed. Swim at your own risk.

Mile 0.8 **Black Diamond Resort** (restaurant, tours) with 9-hole golf course and, clubhouse; description follows.

Black Diamond Resort. Black Diamond offers an amazing variety of unique backcountry adventures for all ages. ATV Tours are available with backcountry dining or try our treasure hunt ATV Tour with geocache and outdoor dining. We also offer horse-drawn covered wagon rides and a unique 9-hole golf course high in the mountains of Alaska. After a day of adventure, enjoy a freshly prepared meal at Black Diamond Restaurant. www.blackdiamond tourco.com; blackdiamondresortco@gmail. com; (907) 683-4653 or winter number (907) 683-4500. [ADVERTISEMENT]

Mile 1 Denali Lakeview Inn and Denali ATV.

A 247.3 C 37.3 F 114.7 Highway descends long downhill grade to Healy northbound.

A 247.9 C 37.9 F 114.1 Begin 0.7-mile passing lane southbound.

A 248 C 38 F 114 Healy (northbound sign).

A 248.1 C 38.1 F 113.9 White Moose Lodge to west; lodging.

A 248.2 C 38.2 F 113.8 Alaska Family Pharmacy. *Slow for posted speed zone northbound.*

A 248.4 C 38.4 F 113.6 49th State Brewing Co. to east; indoor/outdoor restaurant/ bar. Site of the replica bus from the movie *Into the Wild.*

A 248.5 C 38.5 F 113.5 Tri-Valley Gas and Midnight Sun RV and Campground.

A 248.6 C 38.6 F 113.4 Three Bears store with grocery, gas and Ace Hardware. Paved turnout to east.

Healy

A 248.7 C 38.7 F 113.3 Located along the Parks Highway at Healy Road. **Population:** 1,027. **Emergency Services:** Dial 911. **Alaska State Troopers,** phone (907) 683-2232. **Fire Department,** phone (907) 683-2223/2222. **Clinic,** Interior Community Health Center, located on 2nd floor of Tri–Valley Community Center at Mile 0.5 Healy Spur Road, phone (907) 683-2211 (weekdays 9 A.M. to 5 P.M.).

Visitor Information: Available at the Chamber of Commerce log building at Mile 0.4 Healy Spur Road from 10:30 A.M. to 5 P.M. June 1–Labor Day. Phone (907) 683-4636; www.denalichamber.com. Stop in and get the scoop on the area from friendly and knowledgeable volunteers.

Elevation: 1,294 feet. Radio: KUAC-FM 101.7 (from Fairbanks). Private Aircraft: Healy River airstrip 2.1 miles east of Parks Highway via Healy Spur Road; length 2,920 feet; asphalt; unattended. 8 tie-downs available. McKinley flightseeing tours and glacier landings are offered in summer.

Visitor services in Healy include lodging in town on Healy Spur Road and on the Parks Highway at **Aurora Denali Lodge.** Gas/diesel/propane, deli/market and campsites at Tri-Valley Gas and Midnight Sun RV Park; gas, groceries, hardware at Three Bears. Call **Parks Highway Towing** for towing and roadside assistance, phone (907) 832-5583. The Healy post office is located on Coal Street. Play golf, enjoy fine dining or book a backcountry tour with **Black Diamond Resort** on Otto Lake Road.

Usibelli Coal Mine, Inc. is a fourth generation family owned business. Joe Usibelli Jr. is President of the corporation while his father, Joe Usibelli, is Chairman of the Board of Directors. Joe Sr.'s father Emil Usibelli, founded the company in Healy in 1943, and it remains headquartered here today. The mine produces approximately 1-million tons of subbituminous coal annually. Laboratory testing proves the sulfur content of UCM coal is among the lowest of any coal produced in the world. Other environmental benefits of the coal include high calcium content and excellent performance in equipment designed to reduce gas emissions and provide an efficient, clean energy source.

Coal is supplied to 5 Interior Alaska electrical power plants including: Fort Wainwright (U.S. Army); Eielson Air Force Base; Golden Valley Electric Association's Healy Units 1 and 2; Aurora Energy, a wholesale supplier of electricity and provider of district heat in Fairbanks; and the University of Alaska Fairbanks.

The 49th State Brewing Company at **Milepost A 248.4** has an indoor restaurant/bar and an outdoor beer garden where the bus from the movie *Into the Wild* is on display. The bus is an exact replica of the Fairbanks City Transit System Bus 142 that Christopher McCandless used as his wilderness home until his death. Inside are photos from the movie.

Parks Highway Log
(continued)

A 249 C 39 F 113 Suntrana Road to east; access to Tri–Valley School. Healy post office is located on Coal Street (left off Suntrana).

A 249.2 C 39.2 F 112.8 Tesoro; gas, diesel, propane.

A 249.3 C 39.3 F 112.7 Dry Creek bridge No. 1.

A 249.5 C 39.5 F 112.5 Aurora Denali Lodge. Meticulously kept family-owned inn. 28 large rooms, all non-smoking, feature queen beds, private baths, free WiFi, TVs, phones and homey Alaskan decor. We serve breakfast and pack lunches ($13) for our summer guests. Our peaceful location is a 12 mile drive from Denali Park entrance. Phone 1-800-683-4501 from U.S. or (907) 683-4500 from Canada. www.auroradenalilodge.com. [ADVERTISEMENT]

A 249.8 C 39.8 F 112.2 Dry Creek bridge No. 2.

A 250 C 40 F 112 Begin 0.9-mile passing lane northbound.

A 250.9 C 40.9 F 111.1 Begin 0.7-mile passing lane southbound.

A 251.1 C 41.1 F 110.9 Junction with Lignite Road to east and Stampede Road to west. **Stampede Road** (paved/gravel) leads west 8 miles and accesses some beautiful, treeless, highland country on the north side of Denali. Camping, hunting and shooting prohibited. *Please drive slowly.*

Mile 0 Stampede Road.

Mile 4.0 Horse outfitters.

Mile 4.1 Coffee house, gift shop, sled dog expeditions and lodge.

Mile 4.4 Paved turnout. Gravel begins westbound. Large rigs are advised not to travel beyond this point.

Mile 5.2 Large gravel turnout to north.

Mile 7.1 Touring company.

Mile 8 Stampede Road ends for vehicle traffic; large turnaround. Narrow gravel ATV road continues.

If you have read *Into the Wild*, locals advise it is a long hike in from the end of Stampede Road and you have to cross the Savage and Teklanika Rivers. *River crossings can be dangerous during high water and drownings have occurred.* Inquire locally for current status of the bus, the trail and the rivers before proceeding. The bus from the movie is located at the 49th State Brewing Co. in Healy. For details on the McCandless Foundation visit: chrispurpose.org.

A 252.5 C 42.5 F 109.5 Bridge over Panguingue Creek. Gravel turnout to west at south end of bridge. Fishing for Arctic grayling.

A 254.4 C 44.4 F 107.6 *NOTE: Improved highway with northbound and southbound passing lanes alternates with old pavement and 2-lane highway northbound to Nenana (next 50 miles).*

A 259.3 C 49.3 F 102.7 Paved turnout to east by mail boxes. Views of Rex Dome to the northeast. Walker Dome, Jumbo Dome and Liberty Bell mining area to the east.

Distance marker southbound shows Denali Park 22 miles, Cantwell 52 miles, Anchorage 262 miles.

A 260.7 C 50.7 F 101.3 Slide area next 0.3 mile northbound.

A 261 C 51 F 101 Dirt turnout to east at Parks **261 Pond** public fishing access; rainbow trout.

A 262.7 C 52.7 F 99.3 Paved turnout to east.

A 264.3 C 54.3 F 97.7 Paved turnout to west.

A 269 C 59 F 93 June Creek rest area and picnic spot to east with tables, bear-proof trash cans and toilets. Short trail on south side of parking area leads to covered picnic pavilion in woods.

A 269.3 C 59.3 F 92.7 Paved turnout to east.

A 269.4 C 59.4 F 92.6 Bridge over Bear Creek.

A 269.8 C 59.8 F 92.2 Distance marker northbound shows Nenana 34 miles, Fairbanks 85 miles.

HEALY AREA ADVERTISERS

Stop by the Nenana visitor center, located at the turnoff to Nenana's main street, and see a replica of the Ice Classic tripod. (©Kris Valencia, staff)

A 271.4 C 61.4 F 90.6 Paved turnout to west.

A 275.6 C 65.6 F 86.4 Entering Game Management Unit 20A northbound, 20C southbound.

A 275.8 C 65.8 F 86.2 Jack Coghill/ Nenana River Bridge. Scenic spot; northbound travelers can see **Tatlanika Trading Co. RV Park** (description next milepost) campsites on the north bank of the river.

A 276 C 66 F 86 Tatlanika Trading Co. and RV Park. Wilderness setting along the Nenana River. Tent sites and riverfront RV parking, 20- and 30-amp hookups, dump station, clean restrooms, showers, laundry and potable water. 10 acres of grass for walking dogs, and trails. 39 miles from Denali National Park on the Nenana River. Our gift shop features a gathering of handmade art/crafts/artifacts from various villages. See over 50 mounts including world-class polar bear, along with relics and antiques from Alaska's colorful past in a museum atmosphere. Many historical and educational displays. Visitor information. Refreshments, snacks, ice cream and free coffee. This is a must stop. See display ad on page 432 in the DENALI NATIONAL PARK section. [ADVERTISEMENT]

A 280 C 70 F 82 Clear Sky Lodge to west, open year-round; dining (known for its steaks and burgers), WiFi, liquor store, ice.

Clear Sky Lodge. See display ad this page.

A 282.5 C 72.5 F 79.5 *CAUTION: Moose Danger Zone next 22 miles northbound. Watch for moose!*

A 283.5 C 73.5 F 78.5 Junction with Clear Road (paved) west 1.9 miles to Clear Air Force Station gate and 6 miles to **Anderson** (description follows), home to the Anderson Family Music Festival (July 26–28, 2019).

Clear AFB is a military installation (ballistic missile early warning site); sign at turnoff states it is unlawful to enter without permission. However, you can drive into Anderson without permission. The turnoff for Anderson is 1.2 miles west of the Parks Highway before you get to Clear AFS.

ANDERSON (pop. 536), named for homesteader Arthur Anderson, was settled in the late 1950s and was incorporated in 1962. **Visitor Information:** Contact the City Office at (907) 582-2500 or email coaclerk@ mtaonline.net. **Emergency Services:** Anderson Fire Dept./EMS Ambulance, phone 911. The community has a City Hall/Post Office, DMV, church, a seasonal restaurant, bed and breakfast, softball fields and shooting range.

Anderson's **Riverside Park** campground (a 6.3-mile drive from the highway) has 40 sites on the Nenana River. A real "get-away from it all" area it is especially good for travelers with pets. Lots of wide open spaces for game playing. Rustic camping is $20, electric hookups $25 and dump station $10. Restrooms/showers, picnic tables, litter bins and pavilion. Drive straight through Anderson toward the river to reach the park.

Riverside Park/City of Anderson. See display ad this page.

A 283.6 C 73.6 F 78.4 Distance marker northbound shows Nenana 20 miles, Fairbanks 71 miles.

A 285.7 C 75.7 F 76.3 Julius Creek.

A 286.3 C 76.3 F 75.7 View (weather permitting) of Denali southbound.

A 286.7 C 76.7 F 75.3 Mile 287 Rest Area on east side of highway; nice double-ended paved turnout with outhouses, litter bins and picnic tables.

A 288.3 C 78.3 F 73.7 Leaving Denali Borough northbound.

A 288.5 C 78.5 F 73.5 Fireweed Roadhouse (for sale in 2018).

A 296.7 C 86.7 F 65.3 Bridge over **Fish Creek.** Gravel access to creek at south end of bridge to west; Arctic grayling fishing.

A 301.3 C 91.3 F 60.7 Nenana city limits.

A 303 C 93 F 59 *Slow for posted speed zone northbound.*

A 303.6 C 93.6 F 58.4 Gravel pullout to east by lake; look for nesting grebe in summer.

A 303.7 C 93.7 F 58.3 Nenana Airport Road.

A 304.3 C 94.3 F 57.7 Alaska State Troopers and courthouse to west.

A 304.4 C 94.4 F 57.6 Nenana A-Frame Service Chevron gas station with diesel and food mart to west.

Nenana A-Frame Service. See display ad on facing page.

A 304.5 C 94.5 F 57.5 Entering Nenana (description follows) northbound at **junction** with A Street access to downtown. The

Alaskan Gallery Visitors Center and Gift Shop is located at the "V" fork between the Parks Highway and A Street; visitor information, Nenana Ice Classic ticket information, restrooms.

NOTE: Improved highway with southbound and northbound passing lanes alternates with old pavement and 2-lane highway next 50 miles southbound to Milepost A 254.4. CAUTION: Moose Danger Zone next 22 miles southbound. Watch for moose!

Nenana

A 304.5 C 94.5 F 57.5 Located at the confluence of the Tanana and Nenana rivers. **Population: 553. Emergency Services:** Dial 911. **Fire Department,** VFD/EMS, phone (907) 832-5600. **Clinic,** Nenana Native Clinic, phone (907) 832-5247, or Fairbanks hospitals. **Police,** Alaska State Troopers (907) 451-5100.

Visitor Information: In the sod-roofed log cabin at the junction of the highway and A Street. Open weekdays 9:30 A.M. to 5 P.M., Memorial Day weekend to mid-September; phone (907) 832-9720; www.alaskan.gallery. Picnic tables and restrooms are beside the restored *Taku Chief,* located behind the visitor information center. This little tugboat plied the waters of the Tanana, Yukon and Koyukuk rivers for many years.

Elevation: 400 feet. **Climate:** Nenana has an extreme temperature range, with an average daily maximum in summer of 65 to 70° F; daily minimum in winter is well below 0° F. **Radio:** KIAM 630–AM, KIAM–FM 89.9. **Transportation:** Air—Nenana maintains an FAA-approved airport.

Private Aircraft: Nenana Municipal Airport, 0.9 mile south; elev. 362 feet; length 4,600 feet; asphalt; fuel 100LL, Jet B. Floatplane and ski-plane strip.

Nenana has food, gas/diesel at **Nenana A-Frame Service,** lodging, an RV park, auto repair shop, radio station, several churches, a library, restaurants, a cultural center (with a large number of Alaska Native made items for sale), a laundromat, a seniors' social center and senior housing units. Coghill's General Merchandise built in 1916 has served the community for more than 90 years. The **Rough Woods Inn & Cafe** (food and lodging) reflects the woodworking skill of Larry Coy and the cooking talent of Ruth Coy, both pioneer Alaskan homesteaders.

The town was first known as Tortella, a white man's interpretation of the Athabascan word *Toghottele.* A 1902 map indicates a village spelled Tortilli on the north bank

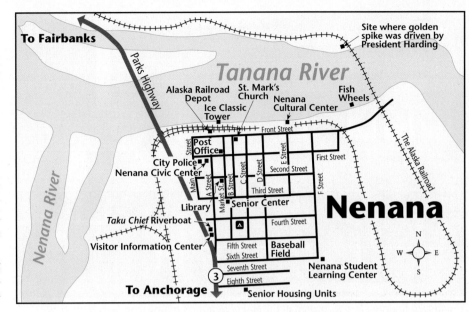

of the Tanana River, on the side of the hill still known as Tortella. In the same year Jim Duke built a roadhouse and trading post, supplying river travelers with goods and lodging. The settlement became known as Nenana, an Athabascan word meaning, "a good place to camp between the rivers." The town thrived as a trading center for Natives of the region and travelers on the vast network of interior rivers.

Nenana boomed during the early 1920s as a construction base for the Alaska Railroad. On July 15, 1923, Pres. Warren G. Harding drove the golden spike at Nenana signifying the completion of the railroad.

Today, Nenana has one company, Ruby Marine, for the tug boat and barges that provide goods to numerous villages. Tons of fuel, freight and supplies move from the docks north of Nenana from late May through September each year. Because the rivers are shallow and silt-laden, the barges move about 12 mph downstream and 5 mph upstream.

Nenana is perhaps best known for the **Nenana Ice Classic,** an annual event that awards cash prizes to the lucky winners who guess the exact minute of the ice breakup on the Tanana River. The contest has been a spring highlight since 1917.

Ice Classic tickets are sold statewide from Feb. 1st through April 5th. In Nenana, tickets may be purchased at the Ice Classic Office on Riverfront Street and at various local businesses from Memorial Day weekend through April 5th. In other Alaska communities, try the local supermarket (e.g. Carrs/Safeway, Fred Meyer), VFW and

American Legion posts, bars, restaurants and other businesses. (For a complete list of ticket sale locations in Alaska, go to www.nenanaakiceclassic.com.) Completed tickets with name, address, date, and time sections filled out, are deposited into Nenana Ice Classic cans located at the ticket sales location. Due to Alaska Gaming regulations, they do not mail blank tickets out-of-state. In order to participate from outside Alaska, mail your list of guesses along with $2.50 per guess (no cash or credit cards) to the Nenana Ice Classic, Box 272, Nenana 99760. They fill out the tickets for you. If you would like copies of your completed entries, include a self-addressed stamped envelope.

Ice Classic festivities begin the first weekend in March with Tripod Weekend, the tripod raising festival, and culminate at breakup time in late April or May. When the surging ice on the Tanana River dislodges the tripod, a line attached to the tripod trips a clock located in a tower on the bank of the Tanana River, thus recording the official breakup time. Summer visitors can see the watch tower and this year's winning time at

NENANA ADVERTISERS

The Alaska Railroad Depot, located at the end of Nenana's main street, was built in 1923 and houses the state's Railroad Museum. (©Kris Valencia, staff)

the Ice Classic office on Front Street.

One block from the railroad depot is **St. Mark's Episcopal Church**. This little log building, built in 1905, is always open to the public. It is graced with hand-hewn pews and a raised altar decorated with Native beaded moosehide frontal and dossal hangings.

The **Alfred Star Nenana Cultural Center and Gift Shop** is located near the end of C Street and open Monday–Saturday May until mid-September. Learn about the history of the Natives in Nenana and the surrounding area as well as the city's early history. Come in and see the many historical items on display. This shop has become well-known for its large selection of exceptional Native crafts and other hand-crafted items that are for sale. View the Tanana River and bridges from front porch, phone (907) 832-5527.

The **Alaska Railroad Depot**, located at the end of Main Street, is on the National Register of Historic Places. Built in 1923 and renovated in 1988, the depot houses the state's Alaska Railroad Museum, open 8 A.M. to 5 P.M. Monday–Saturday.

The **Nenana Public Library** offers the highway traveler computers and internet access, fax and copy machines. Hours vary. 2nd Avenue and Market Street. Phone (907) 832-5812.

Parks Highway Log
(continued)

A 305 C 95 F 57 The north end of the **Alaska Native Veterans' Honor Bridge** across the Tanana River. Sharp turn to west at north end of bridge through narrow entrance for turnout (*not recommended for RVs or trailers*).

This steel through-truss style bridge was built in 1966–67. It was dedicated on Aug. 5, 2000, to commemorate Alaska Natives who have served in U.S. Armed Forces. The bridge spans the Tanana River just upstream of the confluence of the Nenana River. There is no other bridge downstream of this one all the way to the mouth of the Yukon River in Norton Sound. The second, shorter bridge northbound is the Shirley Demientieff Memorial Bridge. Long, narrow turnout to west at north end of bridge.

The Tanana is formed by the joining of the Chisana and the Nabesna rivers near

Northway and flows 440 miles westward to the Yukon River. From the bridge, watch for freight-laden river barges bound for the Yukon River.

Entering Game Management Unit 20B northbound, 20A southbound.

A 305.9 C 95.9 F 56.1 Large double-ended gravel turnout to east, small turnout to west.

A 306 C 96 F 56 *Begin posted speed zone southbound.*

A 308.3 C 98.3 F 53.7 Highway overpass passes over the railroad tracks.

A 308.9 C 98.9 F 53.1 Large, paved double-ended turnout to west. View obstructed by foliage.

A 309.1 C 99.1 F 52.9 Monderosa Drive to west. Access to Monderosa Grill with classic car collection.

A 312 C 102 F 52 Distance marker northbound shows Ester 39 miles, Fairbanks 44 miles.

A 313.6 C 103.6 E 48.4 Parks Highway Towing to west; 24-hour towing, jump starts, tire changes, lock services, phone (907) 832-5583.

A 314.6 C 104.6 F 47.4 Mile 314 Rest Area to west; paved double-ended turnout with outhouses, litter bins and picnic tables.

A 314.7 C 104.7 F 47.3 Bridge over Little Goldstream Creek.

A 315 C 105 F 47 Highway begins a series of long winding grades with intermittent passing lanes next 38 miles northbound. Patched pavement.

A 318.7 C 108.7 F 43.3 Paved double-ended scenic viewpoint to north. Beautiful view overlooking bogs, small lakes, and creeks between Parks and Elliott highways. The Tanana River is on both sides of the highway here. It follows a horseshoe-shaped course, the top of the closed end being the bridge at Nenana.

A 322 C 112 F 40 Distance marker southbound shows Nenana 17 miles, Clear 43 miles, Anchorage 322 miles.

A 324.5 C 114.5 F 37.5 West end of 0.2-mile-long dirt loop road to viewpoint to south (obscured by brush) of the Alaska Range (Purvis Lookout). East end of loop road at **Milepost A 324.7.**

A 325 C 117 F 37 Gravel turnout to north.

A 325.6 C 115.6 F 36.4 Entering Fair-

banks North Star Borough northbound and communications tower.

A 328 C 118 F 34 Skinny Dick's Halfway Inn to west; bar and gift shop.

A 331.6 C 121.6 F 30.4 West end of 0.3-mile-long double-ended parking area to south along old highway alignment. East end at **Milepost A 331.9.**

A 335.6 C 125.6 F 26.4 West end of 0.4-mile-long double-ended gravel parking area to north along old highway alignment. East end at **Milepost A 336.**

A 338 C 128 F 23 This stretch of highway is often called Skyline Drive; views to west.

A 338.5 C 128.5 F 23.5 Expansive views to southeast of Tanana River. Look for Murphy Dome (elev. 2,930 feet), with white communication installations on summit, to northeast.

A 341 C 131 F 21 West end of long double-ended dirt scenic viewpoint to south. East end at **Milepost A 341.2.**

A 342.5 C 132.5 F 19.5 Old Nenana Highway to west.

A 344.3 C 134.3 F 17.7 Viewpoint to southeast with view of Tanana River; good photo opportunity. A plaque mounted on a boulder honors George Alexander Parks (1883–1984), territorial governor of Alaska from 1925 to 1933, and the man for whom the George Parks Highway is named. On a clear day, the Alaska Range is visible from this viewpoint.

A 349 C 139 F 13 Cripple Creek Road to south, Parks Ridge Road to north.

A 349.2 C 139.2 F 12.8 Highway climbs southbound. This is the first in a series of long winding grades with intermittent passing lanes next 38 miles southbound.

A 349.8 C 139.8 F 12.2 Alder Creek.

A 351.2 C 141.2 F 10.8 Turnoff to west for **Ester** via Old Nenana Highway to Village Road (first right by Ester Post Office). Ester is home to **Judie Gumm Designs** (description follows). Fire station and Ester Community Park playground to west.

Junction with side road west to Ester; see "Ester" description on facing page.

Judie Gumm Designs. Noted for her silver sculptural interpretations of Northern images, Judie Gumm's work has been featured in many national publications. Priced moderately, easy to pack, her jewelry makes a perfect remembrance of your adventure North. Ester turnoff (**Milepost A 351.2**). In Ester, just follow her studio signs. Weekdays 10 A.M. to 6 P.M. and Saturday noon–5 P.M. RV parking available across from the Golden Eagle Saloon. See display ad on facing page.
[ADVERTISEMENT]

A 352.2 C 142.2 F 9.8 Gold Hill Road. The U.S. Smelting, Refining and Mining Co. mined some 126,000 ounces of gold from Gold Hill between 1953 and 1957.

Bike path begins northbound.

A 353.5 C 143.5 F 8.5 Tesoro gas station, beer and wine store and food drive-through on north side of the highway.

A 353.8 C 143.8 F 8.2 Ursa Major Distillery.

A 355.2 C 145.2 F 6.8 Little Shot Road to south; Ester Transfer site, public dumpster.

A 355.7 C 145.7 F 6.3 Turnoff to north for Sheep Creek Road to Ester Dome Road and access to Ester Dome single-track bike trail.

A 356 C 146 F 6 Distance marker southbound shows Ester 5 miles, Nenana 53 miles, Anchorage 357 miles.

Begin 4-lane divided highway eastbound.

Begin 2-lane highway westbound.

A 356.8 C 146.8 F 5.2 Geist Road/Chena Pump Road Exit. Access to **University of Alaska/Museum of the North** (2.5 miles north from highway via Geist Road and Fairbanks Street).

A 357.7 C 147.7 F 4.3 Bridge over Chena River.

A 357.8 C 147.8 F 4.2 West Airport Way exit to Fairbanks International Airport and access to **Riverboat Discovery**.

A 358 C 148 F 4 East Airport Way exit to **River's Edge RV Park** and **River's Edge Resort** (turn left at Sportsmans Way and left onto Boat Street); lodging, camping, dining. Also access to Fred Meyer, fast-food outlets and other shopping and services on Airport Way. From Airport Way, turn north on University Avenue for University of Alaska Fairbanks and the Museum of the North. [A]

Parks Highway (Alaska Route 3) continues through Fairbanks as the Mitchell Expressway.

A 359 C 149 F 3 Stoplight at University Avenue. Turn north on University Avenue for University of Alaska and **Museum of the North**. For **Chena River State Recreation Site** with camping, picnic areas and boat launch, turn east on Airport Way, turn north on Washington Avenue, left on Geraghty Avenue and right into campground. [A]

A 360 C 150 F 2 Peger Road South exit for eastbound traffic.

A 360.3 C 150.3 F 1.7 Stoplight at intersection with Peger Road; access to North Peger Road. North for access to **Pioneer Park**, Alaska's only Pioneer Theme Park. Free admission and a fun stop for history and entertainment *(see description page 420)*. Camping is allowed in the park's parking lot; self-register as per posted instructions. [A]

A 361.2 C 151.2 F 0.8 Stoplight at Lathrop Street intersection.

A 362 C 152 F 0 First visible milepost westbound, last milepost eastbound. Turn north for Cushman Street to Fairbanks City Center. Turn south for Van Horn Road access; lots of car dealers and auto service centers on South Cushman (GMC/Chevrolet/Buick, Chrysler/Dodge/Jeep/Ram). Turn left on Van Horn Road for Crowley Petroleum (propane supplies), turn right for H&H Service.

See FAIRBANKS section beginning on page 408 for description of city.

The Parks Highway divides eastbound about 0.3 miles from here, merging with the Steese Expressway to Fox (Alaska Route 2 North) and the Richardson Highway to Delta Junction (Alaska Route 2 South).

Junction with Richardson Highway (Alaska Route 2 South) and Steese Highway (Alaska Route 2 North). Turn to end of the ALASKA HIGHWAY section on page 239 and read log back to front for log of Alaska Route 2 South. Turn to the STEESE HIGHWAY section on page 476 for log of Alaska Route 2 North.

Southbound: Distance from Anchorage (A) is followed by **distance from Cantwell (C)** and **distance from Fairbanks (F)**. Read log: [↑]

Mileposts along the Parks Highway indicate distance from Anchorage.

Ester

Jewelry designer Judie Gumm is known for her sculptural silver jewelry inspired by Northern themes. (©Serine Reeves)

Located 0.6 mile west of **Milepost A 351.2** Parks Highway via Old Nenana Highway to Village Road. **Population:** 2,041. **Emergency Services:** Dial 911. **Fire Department**, phone (907) 479-6858. **Radio:** KCBF 820-AM. Post office is on Village Road at Old Nenana Highway. Nearest Visitor Center is in Fairbanks. **Newspaper:** *Ester Republic* www.esterrepublic.com.

Ester is an appealing combination of historic and contemporary Alaska, with its old buildings and mining artifacts, and its cutting edge artists, all located in a beautiful setting.

A tent camp of miners in 1906, the Fairbanks Exploration Company built Ester Camp 30 years later to support a large-scale gold dredge operation. After 20 years of operation, the mine was shutdown, but it reopened in 1958 as a summer visitor attraction. The Ester Gold Camp complex, which includes the Malemute Saloon and historic Bunkhouse, was a major tourist attraction for many years; it closed in 2008.

Ester Community Park, located just past the turnoff from the Parks Highway onto the Old Nenana Highway, has a children's playground. Fresh produce may be available for purchase at the farmer's market held at the park in summer.

As you turn into Ester, look across from the post office in the woods for a small gazebo, the perfect spot for a picnic or to watch the world go by. And check out the popular Golden Eagle Saloon, the biggest business in town and a favorite gathering spot for Esterites, as Ester's eclectic population refers to themselves (Esteroids are newcomers). Ester holds a Duct Tape Ball and 4th of July celebration. The post office is open weekdays, 10 A.M. to 1 P.M. and 1:30–5 P.M., and Saturdays, 10–11 A.M.

Several artists make their home in Ester. **Judie Gumm Designs** is on Main Street; follow signs to her house/shop. Parking and turnaround space at her shop is very limited; RV parking is available across from the Golden Eagle Saloon. Her studio is open weekdays from 10 A.M. to 6 P.M. and on Saturdays from noon to 5 P.M.

Judie Gumm Designs. See display ad this page.

Return to Milepost A 351.2 Parks Highway

Fairbanks

(See maps, pages 415 and 416)

The authentic Old Chena Indian Village is one of Riverboat Discovery's tour stops.
(©Donna Dewhurst)

Distance in miles

	Fairbanks	Anchorage	Deanli NP	Homer	Seward	Tok	Valdez
Fairbanks		360	125	595	489	204	366
Anchorage	360		237	233	127	328	304
Denali NP	125	237		470	364	565	541
Homer	595	233	470		180	561	537
Seward	489	127	364	180		455	431
Tok	204	328	565	561	455		254
Valdez	366	304	541	537	431	254	

Located in the heart of Alaska's Interior, Fairbanks is approximately 1,488 driving miles north of Dawson Creek, BC, the start of the Alaska Highway (traditional milepost distance is 1,523 miles); 96 miles from Delta Junction (official end of the Alaska Highway); approximately 360 miles from Anchorage via the Parks Highway; and 2,305 miles from Seattle.

Population: Fairbanks city, 31,957; Fairbanks North Star Borough, 98,957. **Emergency Services:** Dial 911. **Alaska State Troopers,** phone (907) 451-5100; **Police,**

phone (907) 450-6500; **Hospitals,** Fairbanks Memorial, phone (907) 452-8181; Chief Andrew Isaac Health Center (907) 451-6682; Bassett Army Community Hospital, Fort Wainwright, phone (907) 361-5172; Eielson Clinic, Eielson AFB, phone (907) 377-1847; **Pet Emergency** (907) 479-2700, 8 Bonnie Ave., open 24-hours on holidays and weekends.

Visitor Information: Explore Fairbanks Visitors Center is located at 101 Dunkel St., inside the **Morris Thompson Cultural and Visitors Center**. This facility is a truly marvelous place, with visitor information and trip-planning help from a knowledgeable staff, and an interpretive exhibit gallery featuring displays on the land, seasons and people of Fairbanks, Interior Alaska and the Arctic. It also includes a theater, public restrooms and ample visitor parking. Open daily: 8 A.M. to 9 P.M. in summer; 8 A.M. to 5 P.M. in winter. Closed Thanksgiving, Christmas and New Year's Day. Phone (907) 456-5774 or 1-800-327-5774; website www.explorefairbanks.com. Inquire about activities, tours and attractions in Fairbanks and the surrounding area. Audio guides are available in English, Japanese and German for self-guided walking tours. Free WiFi and public computer access (no printer).

Step back in time at the Gould Cabin, in front of the visitor center. Built in 1905, this is one of the few pioneer structures in Fairbanks to remain on its original site.

Visitor information is also available at the Fairbanks International Airport in the

baggage claim area, at Pioneer Park and at the Alaska Railroad depot.

The **Alaska Public Lands Information Center,** located at 101 Dunkel St., inside the Morris Thompson Cultural and Visitors Center, offers free information and trip-planning assistance for recreational opportunities in the state. The center also offers films, lectures, an Alaska Geographic bookstore, free activities for children and free brochures and pamphlets on natural history, cultural artifacts and public lands in Alaska. The exhibit area is open daily in summer, 8 A.M. to 9 P.M.; and the information desk is staffed daily from 8 A.M. to 6 P.M. Winter hours are 8 A.M. to 5 P.M. Phone (907) 459-3730, or toll-free 1-866-869-6887; www.alaskacenters.gov/fairbanks.cfm.

Elevation: 439 feet at Fairbanks International Airport. **Climate:** January temperatures range from 18°F to -22°F. The lowest temperature ever recorded was -66°F in December 1961. July temperatures average 62°F, with a record high of 99°F in July 1919. Fairbanks experiences 70 days of light from May 17 through July 27 as the sun never goes far enough below the horizon for the sky to get dark, a phenomenon known as the midnight sun. In June and early July daylight lasts more than 21 hours (the other hours have twilight). Annual precipitation is 8.4 inches, with an annual average snowfall of 58.5 inches. The record for snowfall is 147.3 inches, set in the winter of 1991. **Radio:** CHET-FM, KFAR-AM, KCBF-AM, KAKQ-FM, KFBX-AM, KIAK-FM, KJNP-

Information signs in downtown Fairbanks acquaint visitors with the history and attractions of this Interior city. (©Kris Valencia, staff)

AM/FM (North Pole), KKED-FM, KSUA-FM, KUWL-FM, KXLR-FM, KWLF-FM, KYSC-FM, KUAC-FM 89.9. **Television:** Channels 2, 4, 7, 9, 11, 13 and cable. **Newspapers:** *Fairbanks Daily News–Miner.*

Private Aircraft: Consult the *Alaska Supplement* for information on Eielson AFB, Fairbanks International, Fairbanks International Seaplane, Chena Marina Air Field and Fort Wainwright Army Base. Or phone the Fairbanks Flight Service Station at (907) 474-0137. For recorded information on special use airspace for central Alaska, phone 1-800-758-8723.

History & Economy

In 1901, Captain E.T. Barnette set out from St. Michael on the stern-wheeler *Lavelle Young*, traveling up the Yukon River with supplies for his trading post, which he proposed to set up at Tanana Crossing (Tanacross), the halfway point on the Valdez–Eagle trail. But the stern-wheeler could not navigate the fast-moving, shallow Tanana River beyond the mouth of the Chena River. The stern-wheeler's captain dropped off Barnette on the Chena near the present site of First Avenue and Cushman Street. A year later, Felix Pedro, an Italian prospector, discovered gold about 16 miles north of Barnette's temporary trading post, and, alert to the possibilities, Barnette abandoned his original plan to continue on to Tanana Crossing.

In September 1902, Barnette convinced the 25 or so miners in the area to use the name "Fairbanks" for the town that he expected would grow up around his trading post. The name had been suggested that summer by District Court Judge James Wickersham, who admired Charles W. Fairbanks, the senior senator from Indiana. The senator later became vice president of the United States under Theodore Roosevelt.

The town grew, largely due to Barnette's promotion of gold prospects and discoveries in the area, and in 1903 Judge Wickersham moved the headquarters of his Third Judicial District Court (a district which encompassed 300,000 square miles) from Eagle to Fairbanks.

Thanks to Wickersham, the town gained government offices and a jail. Thanks to Barnette, it gained a post office and a branch of the Northern Commercial Company, a large Alaska trading firm based in San Francisco. In addition, after Barnette became the first mayor of Fairbanks in 1903, the town acquired telephone service, set up fire protection, passed sanitation ordinances and contracted for electric lights and steam heat. In 1904, Barnette started a bank. The town of "Fairbanks" first appeared in the U.S. Census in 1910 with a population of 3,541.

Alaska embarked on a unique route to gain statehood. In November of 1955, 55 delegates from around Alaska convened in College, just outside of Fairbanks, to create a state constitution. Part of the constitution, known as the Alaska-Tennessee Plan, called for an unusual approach to achieving statehood. Under the plan, Alaskans elected two U.S. Senators and one U.S. Congressman to lobby for admission. By 1957, Senators Ernest Gruening and William A. Egan joined Rep. Ralph J. Rivers in Washington, D.C. to convince America that Alaska was ready to be a state. Their efforts were rewarded on June 30, 1958 when the U.S. Senate finally approved the Alaska statehood bill. On January 3, 1959, President Eisenhower signed a proclamation naming Alaska as the 49th state.

Today, the city's economy is linked to its role as a service and supply point for Interior and Arctic industrial activities as well as the federal and state government spending. Fairbanks played a key role during construction of the Trans-Alaska Oil Pipeline in the 1970s. The Dalton Highway (formerly the North Slope Haul Road) to Prudhoe Bay begins about 84 miles north of town. Extractive industries such as oil and mining continue to play a major role in the economy.

The University of Alaska Fairbanks is the second largest employer in the city and boosts the economy by attracting students and research dollars. Trade and service industries such as retail sales and tourism round out the economic diversity.

Government employment contributes significantly to the Fairbanks economy. More than 30 percent of employment

---

FAIRBANKS ADVERTISERS

in Fairbanks is through the government, including military jobs at Fort Wainwright and Eielson Air Force Base.

Fort Wainwright (www.wainwright. army.mil) was the first Army airfield in Alaska, established in 1938, and named Ladd Field, in honor of Maj. Arthur Ladd, an Air Corps pilot killed in a crash in 1935. The first Air Corps Cold Weather Detachment arrived April 1940. The men tested clothing and equipment during the bitter cold winters until World War II. Ladd Field became a transfer point for the Lend Lease Program, in which the U. S. delivered nearly 8,000 aircraft to Russia.

The Army assumed control of Ladd Air Force Base in January 1961, renaming it Fort Jonathan M. Wainwright, in honor of the Medal of Honor recipient who led forces on Bataan and Corregidor. The fort currently employs over 15,000 soldiers and civilians. Fort Wainwright is home to the 1st Stryker Brigade Combat Team, 25th Infantry Division, 1st Battalion, 52nd Aviation Regiment and the 1st Attack Reconnaissance Battalion, 25th Aviation Regiment.

Eielson Air Force Base (www.eielson. af.mil), located 26 miles southeast of Fairbanks on the Richardson Highway, was constructed in 1944. Originally a satellite base to Ladd Army Air Field (now Fort Wainwright) and called Mile Post 26 Airfield, it served as a storage site for the Lend-Lease aircraft program during WWII. (A statue honoring this program is located in Griffin Park.) Closed after WWII, the base reopened about a year later.

In 1948, the base was renamed Eielson Air Force Base in honor of aviation pioneer Carl Ben Eielson. Eielson pioneered aviation in Alaska in the 1920s, realizing the possibilities aviation held for Alaska's development. He was the first aviator to cross the Arctic Circle and land an airplane on the North Slope. He also piloted the first flight from North America over the Arctic Ocean to Europe in 1928. He died in 1929 in a plane crash, along with his mechanic, Earl Borland, while trying to rescue personnel and furs from a cargo ship trapped in the ice off the coast of Siberia.

Eielson AFB is home to RED FLAG-Alaska, a series of Pacific Air Forces commander-directed field training exercises for U.S. and allied forces, providing joint offensive counter-air, interdiction, close air support, and large force employment training in a simulated combat environment. Eielson was also recently selected to receive 2 squadrons of F-35A Lightning II 5th-generation fighter aircraft in 2020, making it the first F-35A operational base in the Pacific Air Forces' Area of Responsibility.

The modern Morris Thompson Cultural and Visitors Center is a great place to browse brochures, talk to local experts and explore an interpretive exhibit gallery. (©Kris Valencia, staff)

Eielson is the farthest-north U.S. Air Force Base. It has more than 67,000 square miles of military training space in the Joint Pacific Alaska Range Complex, making it the largest instrumented air, ground, and electronic training range in the world.

Description

Alaska's third largest city and the administrative center of the Interior, Fairbanks is a blend of old and new: Modern full-service hotels, shopping centers and malls stand beside log cabins and historic buildings.

Fairbanks lies in the forested Tanana Valley on the banks of the Chena River. Good views of the valley are available from Chena Ridge Road and the university campus to the west and Farmers Loop Road to the north.

The city is bounded on the north, east and west by low rolling hills of birch and white spruce. To the south are the Alaska Range and Denali National Park, about a 2½-hour drive via the Parks Highway. The Steese and Elliott highways lead north to the White Mountains.

Lodging & Services

Fairbanks has all visitor services. Reservations are suggested for all Fairbanks accommodations during summer. Shopping ranges from unique Northern art galleries to major chain stores like Walmart, Fred Meyer and Costco. There is a Regal 16/IMAX Theater at Airport Way and Lathrop. There are more than 100 restaurants, including favorites like **The Cookie Jar** and **The Turtle Club**. Several hotels and motels also offer fine dining experiences, like **Fairbanks Princess Riverside Lodge**, **Chena's Alaskan Grill** at River's Edge, **Zach's** at Sophie Station Suites and the **Red Lantern** at the Westmark. Vehicle/RV services available in various locations (see ads this section). Noel Wien Public Library at 1215 Cowles St. has many services and lots of parking.

Abbey Archway Inn. Located centrally to major attractions, lodging includes rooms, condos and apartments. Most have private Jacuzzis, and many have fireplaces and kitchens. All come with TV/DVDs, free wireless internet and free breakfasts. Laundry facilities. Great northern lights viewing.

The Riverwalk offers benches from which to observe the Chena River. (©Kris Valencia, staff)

www.abbeyarchwayinn.com. 4316 Birch Lane, Fairbanks. Phone (907) 479-7300. [ADVERTISEMENT]

Ah, Rose Marie Downtown Bed and Breakfast. Wow! Two quaint, cozy 1930's homes near old downtown restaurants, shops, galleries & Visitors Center. Full breakfasts. Families, groups welcomed. Extraordinary hospitality. Hosts John, son Chris. Guidebook recommended. (Est. 1989.) Year round, $65–$120. 302 Cowles St., Fairbanks, AK 99701. Phone (907) 456-2040; ahrosemarie@yahoo.com; www.Ahrosemarie.com. [ADVERTISEMENT]

Fairbanks Inn & Suites is right across from the University entrance, with lots of extras: full kitchens with stove/oven, dishes, private balconies, coin-op washers/dryers, cable TV with 200 channels, free WiFi and pet friendly units upon request. Call (907) 479-7100, 700 Loftus, Fairbanks. www.fairbanksinn.net. [ADVERTISEMENT]

Camping

There are several excellent RV parks in the Fairbanks area: **River's Edge RV Park**, on Boat Street off of East Airport Way; **Tanana Valley RV Park & Campground**, off of College Road at the State Fairgrounds, **Fairbanks RV Park and Campground** at **Chena River State Recreation Site**, north on Washington Drive to Geraghty Avenue from Airport Way (follow signs); **Riverview RV Park**, east of the city on Badger Road; and **Northern Moosed RV Park**, 12 miles north of Fairbanks on the Elliott Highway near Fox.

Overnight camping at Pioneer Park parking lot for self-contained RVs, 5-night limit, potable water, $12 nightly fee (fill out form and deposit with payment in drop box).

Public campgrounds are located on Chena Hot Springs Road northeast of the city *(see log on pages 425–426 for details)*.

Northern Moosed RV Park & Campground. Easy access, full hookups, water, 30 Amp electricity, sewer; dump station, bathrooms, laundry, showers. Base your travel through Alaska here. Close to general store, gas, restaurants. From Fairbanks follow Alaska Route 2 north 12 miles to Fox. Located at 0.2 mile on Elliott Highway just past the weigh station. Open mid-May–September. Phone (907) 451-0984. [ADVERTISEMENT]

Transportation

Air: International, domestic and intra-Alaska carriers serve Fairbanks International Airport, accessible via the West Airport Way exit off the Parks Highway (Alaska Route 3). Alaska Airlines, Delta Air Lines and Ravn Alaska operate year-round while Air North, Condor and United Airlines operate seasonally from May to September. Various Asian charter operators serve Fairbanks during Aurora season from August through April.

Fairbanks' aurora borealis monument is located on the road leaving Fairbanks International Airport. The *Solar Borealis* sculpture is faced with material which disperses sunlight into a rainbow of colors.

Air charter services are available in Fairbanks for flightseeing; fly-in fishing, hunting and hiking, and additional intra-Alaska travel to rural communities; see ads this section.

Railroad: Alaska Railroad passenger depot at 1031 Alaska Railroad Depot Rd., 2 miles from downtown. Depot is open daily 6:30 A.M. to 3 P.M. from mid-May to mid-September. Open limited hours for arrival/departure days only in winter. Daily passenger service in summer between Fairbanks and Anchorage with stopovers at Denali National Park. Weekend service only in winter; mid-week winter service is available end of December and February through March. Phone (907) 265-2494; 1-800-544-0552; or go to www.alaskarailroad.com.

Bus: Metropolitan Area Commuter System (MACS), Monday through Saturday (limited schedule on Saturdays); no service on Sundays and 6 major holidays. Drivers do not carry change so exact change or tokens must be used. Purchase a day pass and ride all day. Seniors ride free. MACS serves most major hotels, tourist attractions and shopping venues. Downtown Transit Center located at 501 Cushman St.; (907) 459-1011; www.fnsb.us/transportation.

Dalton Highway Express twice-weekly van service between Fairbanks and Deadhorse from June through August; phone (907) 474-3555.

Tours: Local and area fly and/or drive tours are available from several companies. **Northern Alaska Tour Company** offers Arctic Circle Adventure, Barrow Adventure and Arctic Circle Air Adventure tours, phone 1-800-474-1986.

Taxi: More than 20 cab companies, Uber and Lyft available via app.

Car and Camper Rentals: Several companies rent cars, campers and trailers.

Attractions

Get Acquainted: A good place to start is the **Explore Fairbanks Visitor Information Center** at 101 Dunkel St. (downtown Fairbanks), inside the **Morris Thompson Cultural and Visitors Center**, adjacent to Griffin Park, where you will find free brochures, maps and tips on what to see and how to get there. Information and audio tapes for self-guided walking tours. Free internet access for 10-minute periods. Phone (907) 456-5774 or 1-800-327-5774. For a recording of current daily events phone (907) 456-4636, email info@explorefairbanks.com or go to www.explorefairbanks.com/events.

Meet a Real Alaskan–Schedule a Golden Heart Greeter. Golden Heart

Period fashion captures the spirit of the times at Fountainhead Antique Auto Museum which pairs vintage clothing with classic cars. (©Kris Valencia, staff)

Greeter is a free service where visitors are matched, based on interests, with friendly, helpful, local Alaskan residents who want to share their insights and enthusiasm for Fairbanks. Greeters, who are not commercial tour guides but volunteers from different walks of life, welcome travelers and help them get more from their stay. A typical visit is 1–2 hours in a public place such as a coffee house, hotel lobby or some other agreed-upon location. Schedule a greeter by email at: goldenheartgreeter@explorefairbanks.com or by calling (907) 456-5774. A minimum of 1 week's notice is needed.

Golden Heart Plaza, is the site of the 18-foot bronze monument, "Unknown First Family." The statue, by sculptor Malcolm Alexander, and park were dedicated in July 1986 to celebrate Fairbanks' history and heritage.

The plaza is a venue for free summer concerts; Tuesdays and Fridays at noon or Wednesday evenings, enjoy an hour-long concert by varied performers. Phone (907) 456-1984 or visit festivalfairbanks.info for more information.

A pedestrian bridge crosses the Chena River at Golden Heart Plaza, providing safe, scenic access for foot traffic to a wonderful riverwalk that connects to the Morris Thompson Cultural and Visitors Center via an antler arch. The riverwalk provides convenient benches and fine views of river activities.

Visit the Fountainhead Antique Auto Museum, one of the top attractions in Fairbanks, located at Wedgewood Resort. This collection showcases more than 70 historically significant automobiles produced in the United States prior to World War II, including the first car in the Territory of Alaska, built in 1905, a rare 1921 Heine-Velox Sporting Victoria, and an unusual Fordson Snow Devil. For a complete list, go to www.fountainheadmuseum.com.

Each vehicle illustrates an important development in early American automotive history, from early steam, electric and hybrid cars, to the first American production car with front-wheel drive. Almost every car displayed at the museum is maintained in operating condition. Historical Alaskan photographs line the walls and a fabulous vintage fashion collection follows the cars through time. Wedgewood Resort is located at 212 Wedgewood Dr.; phone (907) 456-3642.

Tour the **Ruth Burnett Sport Fish Hatchery**. Downtown at Wilbur Street and

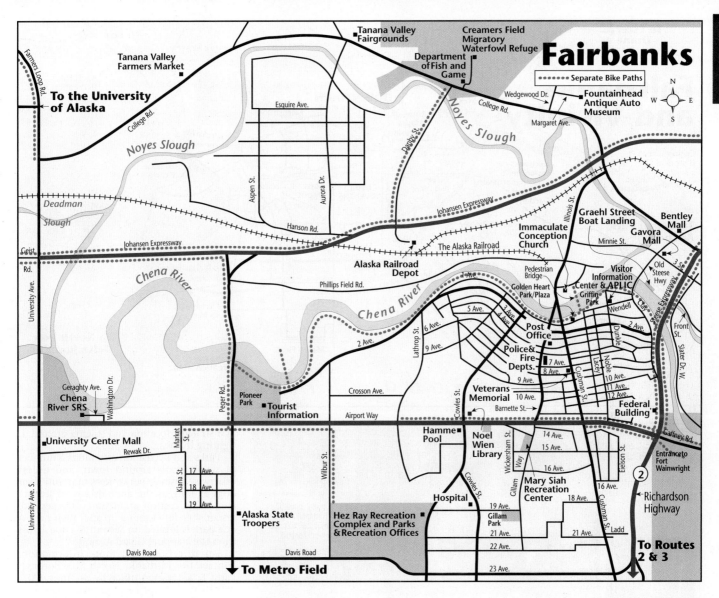

Fairbanks

········ Separate Bike Paths

Tanana Valley Fairgrounds

Creamers Field Migratory Waterfowl Refuge

Department of Fish and Game

Tanana Valley Farmers Market

Wedgewood Dr.

College Rd.

Fountainhead Antique Auto Museum

Margaret Ave.

To the University of Alaska

College Rd.

Esquire Ave.

Noyes Slough

Noyes Slough

Aspen St.

Aurora Dr.

Darby St.

Illinois St.

Deadman Slough

Johansen Expressway

Hanson Rd.

The Alaska Railroad

Immaculate Conception Church

Graehl Street Boat Landing

Minnie St.

Bentley Mall

Gavora Mall

Geist Rd.

Johansen Expressway

Chena River

Alaska Railroad Depot

Phillips Field Rd.

Chena River

1 Ave.

Pedestrian Bridge

Golden Heart Park/Plaza

Visitor Information Center & APLIC

Griffin Park

Old Steese Hwy

3 St.

University Ave.

5 Ave.

3 Ave.

4 Ave.

Wendell

Steese Expressway

2 Ave.

Front St.

Slater Dr. E.

6 Ave.

Post Office

Dunkle

Geraghty Ave.

Washington Dr.

Chena River SRS

Lathrop St.

2 Ave.

9 Ave.

Police & Fire Depts.

7 Ave.

8 Ave.

Cushman St.

Noble

Lacey

10 Ave.

11 Ave.

12 Ave.

Federal Building

Slater Dr. W.

Peger Rd.

Pioneer Park

Tourist Information

Crosson Ave.

Cowles St.

Veterans Memorial

Barnette St.

9 Ave.

10 Ave.

Gaffney Rd.

Airport Way

Hamme Pool

Noel Wien Library

14 Ave.

15 Ave.

Wickersham St.

Entrance to Fort Wainwright

University Center Mall

Market St.

Rewak Dr.

16 Ave.

Gillam Way

Mary Siah Recreation Center

Eielson St.

2

University Ave. S.

Kiana St.

17 Ave.

18 Ave.

19 Ave.

Wilbur St.

Hospital

Cowles St.

19 Ave.

Gillam Park

16 Ave.

18 Ave.

16 Ave.

Cushman St.

Richardson Highway

Ladd

Alaska State Troopers

Hez Ray Recreation Complex and Parks & Recreation Offices

21 Ave.

21 Ave.

Davis Road

Davis Road

22 Ave.

To Routes 2 & 3

To Metro Field

23 Ave.

Hilton Avenue, this hatchery welcomes visitors with a 5,000 gallon aquarium filled with hatchery-raised fish. See the methods and results here, where tens of thousands of fish grow each year to stock local lakes and rivers.

Tour the University of Alaska Fairbanks. The 2,250-acre campus sits on a ridge overlooking Fairbanks and the Alaska Range, giving UAF the best view in town. The campus has all the amenities of a small town, including a radio and TV station, medical clinic, museum, concert hall, theater, and its own police and fire departments.

UAF boasts a world-class faculty and a unique blend of nearly 9,000 students from around the world. It serves 180 communities statewide through in-person and distance delivery of instruction, public service and research. It is America's only Arctic university, a Land, Sea and Space Grant institution and an international center for Arctic research. Scientific facilities operated by UAF include a 261-foot oceanography ship, a research rocket launch range, centers that track earthquakes and volcanoes, a ground station to collect satellite remote-sensing data and an antenna array for studying the upper atmosphere.

Free 1½-hour tours of campus begin at Signers' Hall at 10 A.M. and 2:30 P.M. week-

days (except holidays) year-round. Separate tours of several campus facilities are offered in the summer. For details, go online to www.uaf.edu/visituaf. Arrange customized campus visits for prospective students by phoning the Admissions Office at (907) 474-7500 or 1-800-478-1823; emailing admissions@uaf.edu; or by completing a form found at www.uaf.edu/admissions/visit.

Summer Sessions and Lifelong Learning hosts many weekly events throughout the summer, including special lectures and concerts. Visit www.uaf.edu/summer or phone (907) 474-7021 for details.

Public Parks. Fairbanks has more than 100 public parks that make good stops for a picnic. Graehl Park has a boat launch and is a good place to watch river traffic.

Griffin Park, also on the river, has the **WWII Lend–Lease Monument**, a memorial erected in 2006. This statue honors WWII Russian and American pilots as well as Women Airline Service Pilots. The monument commemorates Alaska's importance

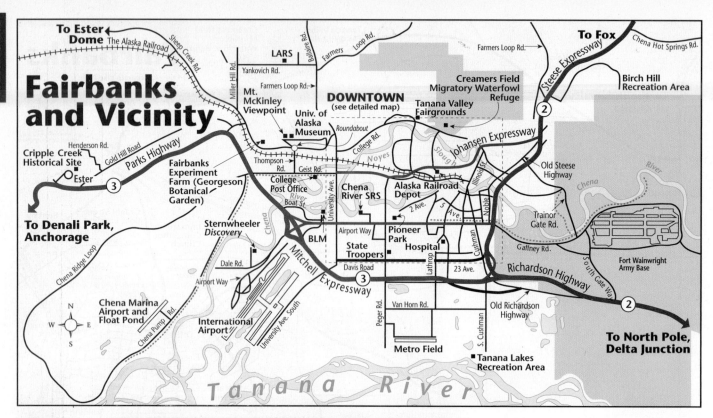

Fairbanks and Vicinity

To Ester Dome The Alaska Railroad
Sheep Creek Rd.
To Fox
Chena Hot Springs Rd.
Farmers Loop Rd.
LARS
Yankovich Rd.
Farmers Loop Rd.
Creamers Field Migratory Waterfowl Refuge
Steese Expressway
Birch Hill Recreation Area
Mt. McKinley Viewpoint
DOWNTOWN (see detailed map)
Tanana Valley Fairgrounds
Univ. of Alaska Museum
Roundabout
Johansen Expressway
Cripple Creek Historical Site
Henderson Rd.
Gold Hill Road
Parks Highway
College Rd.
Noyes
Slough
Old Steese Highway
Chena
River
Ester
Fairbanks Experiment Farm (Georgeson Botanical Garden)
Thompson Rd.
Geist Rd.
College Post Office
River Boat St.
University Ave.
Chena River SRS
Alaska Railroad Depot
2 Ave.
Illinois St.
Noble
Trainor Gate Rd.
To Denali Park, Anchorage
Chena Ridge Loop
Sternwheeler Discovery
BLM
Airport Way
Pioneer Park
S. Ave.
Gaffney Rd.
Fort Wainwright Army Base
State Troopers
Hospital
Lathrop
Cushman
Richardson Highway
Dale Rd.
Davis Road
23 Ave.
South Gate Way
Chena Marina Airport and Float Pond
Airport Way
Mitchell Expressway
Peger Rd.
Van Horn Rd.
Old Richardson Highway
S. Cushman
International Airport
Chena Pump Rd.
University Ave. South
Metro Field
To North Pole, Delta Junction
Tanana Lakes Recreation Area
N W E S

Tanana River

as a strategic location and staging ground in fighting this war.

Parks and Recreation also offers a number of scenic trails around town, and unless otherwise posted, pet owners may run their dogs as long as the animals are on leashes and under control at all times. Owners are responsible for cleaning up after their pets. A dog park is located on Second Avenue across from the National Guard Armory.

For directions and more information, contact the Fairbanks North Star Borough Parks & Recreation office by phoning (907) 459-1070 or visit www.co.fairbanks.ak.us/pr.

The University of Alaska Museum of the North, Alaska's most distinctive architectural landmark, is a "must-see" for Fairbanks visitors and a world-class facility. The museum exhibits are the best introduction to Alaska's diverse wildlife, people, land, and the research made possible by the more than 1.5 million objects in its collections help advance scientific discovery.

Highlights from the Gallery of Alaska include the state's largest public display of gold; Blue Babe, an ancient steppe bison mummy radiocarbon dated at more than 50,000 years-old; and extensive displays of Alaska wildlife and Alaska Native cultures. The Rose Berry Alaska Art Gallery presents 2,000 years of Alaska art, with ancient ivory carvings, coiled grass baskets and other Alaska Native works displayed alongside both historical and contemporary paintings and sculptures. The Family Room offers a sitting area with puzzles and games for children and families. Visitors can explore multimedia resources, along with books and art, in this space. "The Place Where You Go to Listen" draws on wind patterns, cycles of day and night, seismic activity and the electromagnetic activity of the aurora to create an ever-changing sound and light experience.

The museum is situated on the West Ridge of the UAF campus, overlooking Geist Road. The museum has a store and cafe.

Summer hours (June–Aug. 31) are 9 A.M. to 7 P.M. daily. Winter hours (Sept. 1–May 31) are 9 A.M. to 5 P.M. Monday–Saturday, closed Sundays, Thanksgiving, Christmas and New Year's Day. Admission is charged; children 4 and under free. For more information, phone (907) 474-7505; email ua-museum@alaska.edu; or visit www.uaf.edu/museum.

Georgeson Botanical Garden, on the UAF campus, is open to the public June 1 through Labor Day, from 8 A.M. to 8 P.M. daily. Colorful displays feature many varieties of flowers in season and a kiosk offers information on northern horticulture. The garden hosts a variety of free events throughout the summer. Requested donation is $5 per person. *NOTE: No pets please, in the garden or on nearby lawn.* The garden is part of the Fairbanks Experiment Farm, originally a federal experiment station established in 1906, and is operated by UAF's School of Natural Resources and Extension. It is located at 117 W. Tanana Dr., on the west end of campus. Phone (907) 474-7222 or visit www.georgesonbotanical garden.org for more details.

Noel Wien Public Library. The library is a great place to read and catch up on email, especially on a rainy day. Located at the corner of Airport Way and Cowles Street, the library has a large parking area adjacent a park strip. Inside, services include WiFi, computers, scanning and printing. The library holds several weekly events for children. Hours are 10 A.M. to 9 P.M. Monday to Wednesday, 10 A.M. to 6 P.M. Thursday and Friday, and 10 A.M. to 5 P.M. on Saturday; closed Sundays. Address is 1215 Cowles St.; phone (907) 459-1020; website: fnsblibrary.org.

Noel Wien Public Library, at the corner of Airport Way and Cowles Street, offers residents and travelers an inviting place to read. (©Melissa Harter)

The Alaska Public Lands Information Center, downtown at 101 Dunkel St., in the Morris Thompson Cultural and Visitors Center, offers free information and trip-planning assistance for recreational opportunities in the state. The center also offers films, lectures, an Alaska Geographic bookstore and free brochures and pamphlets on natural history, cultural artifacts and public lands in Alaska. The exhibit area is open daily in summer, 8 A.M. to 9 P.M.; and the information desk is staffed daily, 8 A.M. to 6 P.M. Winter hours are 8 A.M. to 5 P.M. Phone (907) 459-3730 or toll-free 1-866-869-6887; www.alaskacenters.gov/fairbanks.cfm.

Special Events. Major events are listed below. For a listing of all current events, phone (907) 456-4636 or visit www.explore fairbanks.com/events.

The **Midnight Sun Festival**, scheduled

Rubber Duckie Race on the Chena River is just one of many events during the annual Golden Days celebration, held the third weekend in July. (©Courtesy Explore Fairbanks/Katelin Delaney)

for June 23, 2019, celebrates summer solstice with a street fair. Vendors occupy the city's streets on the longest day of the year. Details at www.downtownfairbanks.com.

Baseball. Summer visitors can take in a semi-pro baseball game at Growden Park (2nd Avenue and Wilbur Street), where the Alaska Goldpanners take on other Alaska teams several times each week, typically at 7 P.M. in the summer months. Check the local newspaper for game schedule.

The annual **Midnight Sun Baseball Game** begins at 10:30 P.M. on or near summer solstice and is played at Growden Park without artificial lights. A very popular annual event. Tickets and 2019 date available at www.goldpanners.com.

World Eskimo-Indian Olympics. Since 1961 this annual event pits athletes against each other in unique sporting events. The ear-pull, one-legged jump and other competitions continue the Native tradition of competing for athletic prowess as well as preparing for occasions of extremes. Each event is significant to Native life and tradition. A Native dance festival, traditional regalia contest and one of the largest Native arts and crafts markets in the state also take place during these Olympics. Visit www.weio.org or phone (907) 452-6646 for more information. The event is held at the Carlson Center July 17–20, 2019.

Golden Days, when Fairbanksans turn out in turn-of-the-century dress and celebrate the gold rush, is scheduled for July 13–21, 2019. Golden Days starts off with a Felix Pedro look-alike taking his gold to the bank and includes a Grand Parade and rededication of the Pedro Monument at Milepost 16.6 of the Steese Highway (Alaska Route 6), honoring the man who started it all when he discovered gold in the Tanana Hills. Other events include the Rubber Duckie Race; a downtown street fair featuring food and crafts booths; a comedy night with Grizzly Alaskan Contests; a barbecue cookoff; and a River Regatta of homemade vessels. For additional information, phone (907) 452-1105; www.fairbankschamber.org.

Fairbanks Summer Arts Festival provides workshops and performances taught by internationally acclaimed artists for all levels in music, dance, theatre, culinary, literary, healing and visual arts. July 14–28, 2019. For details phone (907) 474-8869 or visit www.fsaf.org.

The Tanana Valley Fair began in 1924, making it Alaska's oldest fair. It takes place August 2–10, 2019, and features agricultural exhibits, arts and crafts, food booths, carnival rides, many vendors, and lots of entertainment. For more information, phone (907) 452-3750 or visit www.tananavalleyfair.org.

Tanana Valley Farmers Market takes place Wednesdays and Sundays, from May to September, at 2600 College Rd., adjacent the state fairgrounds. The market features Alaska-grown produce and plants and Made in Alaska/Silver Hand arts and crafts. Information at www.tvfmarket.com.

Enjoy the Chena River from shore. From the Morris Thompson Cultural and

Visitors Center, walk through the world's "Farthest North Antler Arch" (made up of over 100 caribou and moose antlers collected from all over Interior Alaska) and take the River Walk along the Chena River to Golden Heart Plaza. From Cushman Street the River Walk extends more than 1.5 miles to Pioneer Park.

Chena River State Recreation Site offers a boat launch and a picnic area with tables and great river views. From Airport Way take Washington Drive north to Geraghty and follow signs to the park.

Cruise the Chena River. Fairbanks is situated on the Chena River, near its confluence with the Tanana River, and the river is a popular form of transportation for both residents and visitors alike.

CanoeAlaska, located at "Paddler's Cove" on Peger Road (behind Pioneer Park), has canoes and kayaks for rent and both pick-up and drop-off service available. For more information and reservations, phone (907) 457-2453. Paddlers may launch from "Paddler's Cove" and travel downstream to the Chena Pump House, or they can launch from Nordale Road (*see Milepost J 6.3 in "Chena Hot Springs Road" log on page 425*) for a longer trip.

Most visitors explore the river aboard the Riverboat *Discovery* (see description following).

Take the Riverboat *Discovery* Cruise. This family-owned, Fairbanks attraction began in 1950 and today is justifiably one of the city's most popular destinations, both with visitors and Alaskans. Cruises depart daily at 9 A.M. and 2 P.M., mid-May to mid-September, for a half-day cruise on the

Chena and Tanana rivers. Enjoy informative narration about Native culture; view Susan Butcher's sled dogs in action; see a bush pilot demonstration; walk through the Old Chena Indian Village; and just enjoy a pleasant few hours on the water. Snacks onboard, plus complimentary donuts and coffee.

To get to the dock, exit south off the Parks Highway on Airport Way to Dale Road and follow signs. For information on rates, additional cruise times, etc., contact Riverboat Discovery, 1975 Discovery Dr., Fairbanks, AK 99709; email reservations@riverboatdiscovery.com; phone (907) 479-6673 or 1-866-479-6673; or visit their website at www.riverboatdiscovery.com.

Visit Historic Churches. Saint Matthew's Episcopal Church, 1029 1st Ave., was originally built in 1904, but burned in 1947 and was rebuilt the following year. Of special interest is the church's intricately carved altar, made in 1906 of Interior Alaska birch and saved from the fire, and the church's 12 stained glass windows, 9 of which trace the historical events of the church and Fairbanks. Immaculate Conception Church, on the Chena River at the Barnette Street bridge, was drawn by horses to its present location in the winter of 1911 from its original site at 1st Avenue and Dunkel Street.

Ride Bikes. The city has an extensive network of bike trails (multi-use paths). Best choices for day touring around Fairbanks include the bike trail from Pioneer Park to 1st Avenue downtown, and Airport Way/ Boat Street west to Chena Pump Road or Geist Road. Pick up a "Bikeways" map for Fairbanks and vicinity at the Morris Thompson Cultural and Visitor Center.

Meet reindeer and musk-oxen at UAF's Large Animal Research Station (LARS). Tours and naturalist programs are offered during the summer. (©Kris Valencia, staff)

CanoeAlaska rents bikes at their shop near Pioneer Park. (Their website, canoe-alaska.com/fairbanks-bike-rentals, has bike ride itineraries.) They also offer a bike and canoe package: paddle the Chena River then

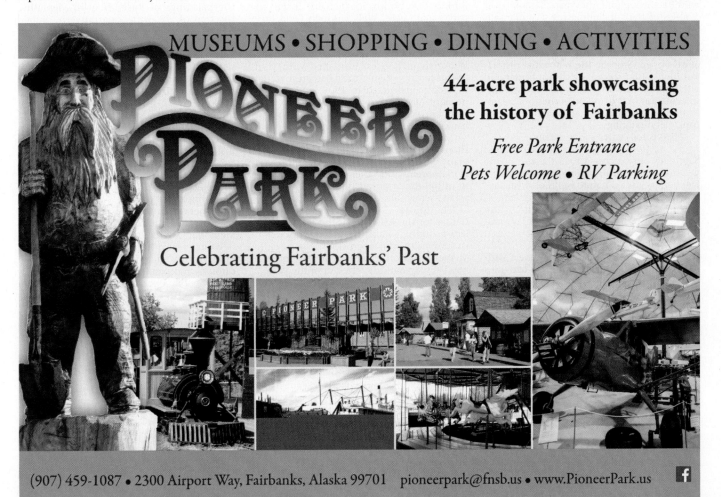

bicycle back to Barnette Landing.

Another program, FairBikes, is a bike-share system charging $5 an hour or an annual membership program. FairBikes has bike racks at various locations; look for the red bikes with yellow tires.

For year-round organized rides, there's the Fairbanks Cycle Club. Membership information and a monthly calendar of rides at www.fairbankscycleclub.org. For information on the Ester Dome Singletrack Loops, accessed via Sheep Creek Road to Ester Dome Road west of Fairbanks, check with the cycle club or Goldstream Sports (goldstreamsports.com). Goldstream Sports also has fat bike rentals.

Farmhouse Visitor Center, Creamer's Field Migratory Waterfowl Refuge. 1300 College Road. Visitor Center hours 9:30 A.M. to 5 P.M., May 14–Sept. 15, noon–4 P.M. Saturdays, Sept. 17–May 12. Trails open year-round. Free guided nature walks and events throughout the year. Call for schedule. Phone (907) 452-5162; director@friendsofcreamersfield.org or visit www.friendsofcreamersfield.org. [ADVERTISEMENT]

Watch Birds at Creamer's Field. Follow the flocks of waterfowl to Creamer's Field Migratory Waterfowl Refuge at 1300 College Rd. Located 1 mile from downtown Fairbanks, on the site of the historic Creamer's Dairy Farm, this 2,000-acre refuge managed by the Alaska Dept. of Fish and Game offers opportunities to observe large concentrations of ducks, swans, geese, shorebirds, sandhill cranes and other birds during the spring and fall migrations, and resident wildlife throughout the year. Explore over 5 miles of trails including the 1½-mile self-guided Boreal Forest Trail that features winding boardwalks through a boreal forest. Entrance to the Refuge is free and trails are always open. Stop by the renovated historic farmhouse that serves as a visitor center and gift shop to find the trail and viewing area information, maps and brochures on Creamer's Field and get information about the historic dairy buildings.

The visitor center is open daily, 9:30 A.M. to 5 P.M., from mid-May to mid-September; Saturdays only, noon–4 P.M., the rest of the year. The non-profit Friends of Creamer's Field offers guided nature walks on weekdays and Saturdays at 10 A.M. and on Wednesday evenings at 7 P.M. during June, July and August, and at noon on Tuesdays and Thursdays during September–November and March–May.

Friends of Creamer's Field partners with ADF&G to host refuge events and activities throughout the year. The Tanana Valley

Sandhill Crane Festival is scheduled for August 23–25, 2019. For additional information and a full calendar of events at Creamer's Field, phone (907) 452-5162 or visit www.friendsofcreamersfield.org.

Wedgewood Wildlife Sanctuary is a 75-acre private preserve providing habitat for wildlife of Interior Alaska. Two trails stretch through boreal forest with access to views of beaver lodges, interpretive signs, benches that line the trails, and an observation deck. These trails are accessed by entering the Wedgewood parking area between the McKinley and Laurel buildings. From College Road, take Margaret Avenue to Wedgewood Drive to reach the resort.

Visit Pioneer Park. This is a must-see, enjoyable attraction for visitors. It is a pleasant stop especially for those with children, with its historic buildings, small shops, food, entertainment, picnic areas, playgrounds, disc golf and train rides. The park is open year-round, although most attractions within the park are open only from Memorial Day to Labor Day. Attractions are usually staffed from noon–8 P.M. Admission to the park is free, with a nominal charge for some activities. For more information about Pioneer Park, phone (907) 459-1087.

To drive to Pioneer Park (at Airport Way and Peger Road), take Airport Way to Wilbur, turn north onto Wilbur, then immediately west onto access road, which leads into the Pioneer Park parking lot.

The 44-acre historic park was created in 1967 as the Alaska Centennial Park to commemorate the 100th anniversary of U.S. territorial status and provide a taste of Alaska history. Visitors may begin their visit at the information booth, located just inside the park's main gate. Walk through Gold Rush Town, a narrow, winding street of authentic old buildings that once graced downtown Fairbanks: the Kitty Hensley and Judge Wickersham houses, furnished with turn-of-the-century items; the First Presbyterian Church, constructed in 1904; and the Pioneers of Alaska Museum, dedicated to those who braved frontier life to establish Fairbanks.

Many of the pioneer buildings house shops selling food and crafts. You will find many Made in Alaska items, including artwork, jewelry and other merchandise. There is an old-time portrait photographer—a fun way to remember your trip to Fairbanks.

The top level of the Alaska Centennial Center for the Arts houses the Bear Art Gallery featuring rotating contemporary exhibits and paintings; open noon–8 P.M. daily, Memorial Day through Labor Day; noon–6 P.M. Tuesday–Saturday the rest of the year.

The **Pioneer Air Museum**, located

behind the Alaska Centennial Center for the Arts, chronicles the rich and adventurous history of Bush aviation in the Interior of Alaska from 1913 to present day. Many unique displays for the aviation enthusiast, including a Will Rogers and Wiley Post exhibit. The Air Museum is open daily, noon–8 P.M., from Memorial Day to Labor Day. Admission is $4 for adults, 12 years and under are free if accompanied by an adult. Phone (907) 451-0037 for details.

Pioneer Park is home to the SS *Nenana*, a national historic landmark. Known as the "Last Lady of the River," she is the largest stern-wheeler ever built west of the Mississippi. (Visit friendsofssnenana.com to find out about efforts to renovate her.) On display inside is a 300-foot diorama of life along the Tanana and Yukon rivers in the early 1900s. Explore the old stern-wheeler on your own, or take a formal tour, offered daily in summer from noon–8 P.M.

The popular Alaska Salmon Bake is located in Mining Valley at Pioneer Park. Mining Valley features displays of gold mining equipment from the gold rush days. The Salmon Bake provides both outdoor and heated indoor seating area and is open daily for dinner, 5–9 P.M., from mid-May to mid-September. Salmon, cod and prime rib are served, rain or shine.

The show season at Pioneer Park runs from mid-May through mid-September. The Palace Theatre & Saloon features the musical comedy review, "Golden Heart Revue," about early and present-day life in Fairbanks. Nightly performances at 8:15 P.M.

The Big Stampede show in Gold Rush Town is a theater in the round, presenting the paintings of Rusty Heurlin, depicting the trail of '98, with a narrative by Ruben Gaines.

The Crooked Creek & Whiskey Island Railroad, a narrow-gauge train, takes passengers for a 12-minute guided ride around the park. Learn about the history of the park from one of the well-trained staff onboard. Ride fee is $2 for adults, $1 for children under 12 years and seniors.

The Tanana Valley Railroad Museum holds displays of Interior Alaskan railroad history as well as the historic Engine #1, a 8.5 ton, 36" gauge, H.K. Porter, coal fired and built in 1899. The first locomotive to this area, it is currently the farthest north operating steam engine. Volunteers restored and operate the engine several times each season. Museum hours noon–8 P.M. daily, Memorial Day–Labor Day.

Other recreational activities available at Pioneer Park include disc golf, an antique carousel and picnic areas with covered shelters. A public dock is located on the Chena

River at the rear of the park, and visitors can rent canoes, kayaks and bicycles at Canoe-Alaska. CanoeAlaska rents bikes at their shop near Pioneer Park. They also offer a bike and canoe package: paddle the Chena River then cycle back to Barnette Landing. *See more details under "Ride Bikes" on page 419.*

Visitors are welcome to take part in square, round and contra dances year-round at the Farthest North Square and Round Dance Center. Phone (907) 452-5699 evenings for calendar of events.

Visit the Fairbanks Children's Museum. This interactive museum environment is designed for children to explore multi-sensory, hands-on, active and child-centered activities. Open Tuesday-Saturday, 10 A.M. to 5 P.M. and Sundays 11 A.M. to 5 P.M. General admission is $8. Adults must be accompanied by a child, and children must be accompanied by a supervisor over the age of 16. The museum is located at 302 Cushman St.; phone (907) 374-6873; website www.fairbankschildrensmuseum.com.

Running Reindeer Ranch. A unique opportunity to see reindeer in their pen or walk with the reindeer through boreal forest. Jane Atkinson and daughter Robin offer tours to help support the feeding and care of the reindeer. Reservations required (RunningReindeer.com).

The Robert G. White Large Animal Research Station (LARS), operated by UAF, allows visitors a close-up view of musk-oxen, caribou and reindeer. Public tours are offered June through August (closed 4th of July weekend). Tour times are posted in the parking lot at LARS and also on the LARS website at www.muskoxuaf.org or phone (907) 474-5724 for information. Tour is via a ¼-mile walking tour. Admission is $10 for adults, $6 for students, $9 for senior citizens (over 65) and for military; children 5 and under free. To reach LARS from Geist Road, drive north 2 miles on University Avenue (it becomes Farmers Loop Road north of College), turn left on Ballaine Road, then make a left-hand turn on Yankovich Road and drive 1.2 miles west to LARS, which will be on your right.

Take a Day Trip to Chena Hot Springs (125 miles round trip). Drive 5 miles north from Fairbanks via the Steese Expressway and exit east on Chena Hot Springs Road. This good, all-weather paved road leads 57 miles east to Chena Hot Springs, a private resort (open daily year-round). It offers indoor and outdoor natural mineral hot springs pools. See the Aurora Ice Museum, the world's only year-round ice museum and ice bar. The resort has a restaurant, lodging, camping and recreational activities. *(See "Chena Hot Springs Road" pages 425–426.)*

Visit North Pole and Chena Lake Recreation Area. Head down Highway 2 (Richardson Highway) to North Pole, 13 miles from downtown Fairbanks, and get a head start on your Christmas shopping *(see description of North Pole on pages 239–241).* Drive another 2 miles east of North Pole for Chena Lake Recreation Area. Operated by the Fairbanks North Star Borough Parks and Rec-

The interior of Wickersham House in Pioneer Park offers a glimpse of life in Fairbanks at the turn-of-the-century. *(©Kris Valencia, staff)*

reation Department, this recreation area is built around the Chena Flood Control Project constructed by the Army Corps of Engineers. Drive 5.5 miles from the highway on the main road along Moose Creek Dike to the visitor kiosk below the dam site. You can also bike out to the dam on the 5-mile-long Moose Creek Dam Bikeway. From the Main Road, turn on Lake Park Road for 250-acre Chena Lake. There are campsites, walking trails, a swimming beach, play area, picnic tables, shelters, kayak and canoe rentals, fishing dock and boat ramp. Chena Lake Bike Trail begins at Chena Lake swim beach and intersects with the Moose Creek Dam Bikeway. Camping fees and a per vehicle

day-use fee are charged between Memorial Day and Labor Day. For more information about Chena Lake Recreation Area, phone (907) 488-1655.

View Peaks of the Alaska Range: Enjoy Fairbanks' best views of the Tanana Valley and the high peaks the Alaska Range through the Alaska Range Viewing Window in the UAF Museum of the North. Weather permitting, you may see: Mount Hayes (elev. 13,832 feet); Hess Mountain (elev. 11,940 feet); Mount Deborah (elev. 12,339 feet);

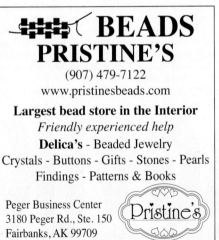

Trans-Alaska Pipeline viewpoint is just 8 miles from Fairbanks on the Steese Expressway.
(©Serine Reeves)

and Denali (elev. 20,310 feet).

Gold, gold, gold. Head out the Steese Expressway to **Milepost F 8.4** and do some gold panning with **Gold Daughters**, or tour their gold mining machinery museum *(see display ad on page 420)*. Then continue to **Milepost F 9.5**, turn on Goldstream Road and then turn left onto Old Steese Highway North to see the historic **Gold Dredge 8**, a 5-deck, 250-foot dredge built in 1928. Tours of the dredge and gold panning are available. *(See ads this section for contact details.)*

At **Milepost F 28.6** on the Steese Highway, across from Chatanika Lodge, there's an old gold dredge that operated from the 1920s until 1962. It is the second largest stacker dredge in Alaska. The dredge is on private land but is easily viewed from the highway; do not trespass. After these stops, you can either return to Fairbanks to make this an easy 50-mile round trip, or extend your drive 100 miles to see more of gold mining history.

Farther out on the Steese Highway, at **Milepost F 57.3**, is the Davidson Ditch Historical Site. This large pipe was built in 1925 by the Fairbanks Exploration Co. to carry water to float gold dredges. The 83-mile-long ditch begins at **Milepost F 64** Steese Highway and ends near Fox. If you are feeling adventurous, U.S. Creek Road (steep, gravel) winds up and over the hills from the Davidson Ditch site 7 miles to Nome Creek Gold Panning Area in the White Mountains National Recreation Area.

See the STEESE HIGHWAY section for a detailed log of this road.

Gold Dredge 8. Your adventure at Gold Dredge 8 begins with a ride on a replica of the Tanana Valley Railroad through the gold fields of Interior Alaska. Before you board our train, enjoy a close-up view of the TransAlaska pipeline and informational displays about the pipeline. Aboard the train our conductor and local miners provide lively commentary about the history of mining in Alaska. The train ride takes you to Gold Dredge 8 where you will see first hand how the dredge worked the gold fields. Once the train arrives at the camp, you will receive a poke sack filled with pay dirt, and get a chance to pan for gold. You will find gold—we guarantee it! After you pan for gold, explore the dredge and feel the history come alive. This tour is interesting and entertaining

for the whole family. Travel professionals describe this tour as "the best 2 hours you will spend in the State." Tours depart daily and reservations are recommended. Contact Gold Dredge 8 at (907) 479-6673, reservations@golddredge8.com, www.golddredge8.com. 1803 Old Steese Highway North, Fairbanks, AK 99712. See display ad on page 409. [ADVERTISEMENT]

See the Pipeline. For a good look at the Trans-Alaska Oil Pipeline System (TAPS)—the oil pipeline—and a taste of the Dalton Highway, consider this long day trip. Drive out the Steese Expressway from Fairbanks, stopping first at the TAPS viewpoint just outside Fairbanks at **Milepost F 8.4**. You can walk along a portion of the pipeline and see a "pig"—a device used to collect data and clean the pipeline walls. Excellent opportunity for pipeline photos.

Drive north a few more miles to the end of the Steese Expressway and then continue north on the Elliott Highway 73 miles to the junction with the Dalton Highway. The Elliott Highway is paved to the Dalton Highway junction. Turn off onto the Dalton Highway and drive 56 miles north to the Yukon River bridge (Yukon Crossing). The pipeline parallels the route much of the way, although there is no public access, so you will get good views but no close-ups until you reach the BLM visitor center at Yukon Crossing.

From Yukon Crossing it is another 60 miles to the **Arctic Circle BLM Wayside**, adding 120 miles to the already 280-mile trip. The Arctic Circle wayside has an interpretive display and picnic area, at N 66°33' W 150°48'. At this latitude, the sun does not set on summer solstice (June 20 or 21) and it does not rise on winter solstice (December 21 or 22). There is a BLM campground about 0.5 mile up a gravel road behind this wayside.

See the ELLIOTT HIGHWAY and the DALTON HIGHWAY sections for details.

Play Tennis: There are 6 outdoor asphalt courts at the Dan Ramras Community Tennis Courts off Airport Way on Schaible Street (due east of Lathrop High School). No fees or reservations. For more information, phone the Fairbanks Tennis Association at (907) 455-4301.

Birch Hill Recreation Area, located in the hills of Fairbanks, is a world class multi-use recreational facility. More than 30 kilometers of trails are great for hiking, biking, and running, but it is also a quiet, peaceful place for a picnic. One of its most popular summer attractions is its 18-hole disc golf course, free of charge. The ski chalet is a great spot to rent for weddings, reunions and other group events. Birch Hill trails are popular with cross-country skiers in winter. Phone (907) 457-4488 for more information.

Tanana Lakes Recreation Area. Located on South Cushman Street, the 750-acre recreation area is free to enjoy and offers an outdoor shooting range, miles of trails, birdwatching locations, a reservable picnic area, a huge sand beach with entry to Tanana Lake, motorized boat launch accessing Tanana River, a non-motorized boat launch to paddle or SUP around Tanana Lake.

Go Swimming. Fairbanks North Star Borough Parks and Recreation Dept. offers 3 pools that are open to the public. Mary Siah Recreation Center, at 805 14th Ave., also offers a sauna, whirlpool and fitness equipment; phone (907) 459-1082 or (907) 459-1081 for recorded information. Hamme Pool, at 901 Airport Way, also offers diving boards and lap lanes; phone (907) 459-1085. Wescott Pool, at 300 E. 8th in North Pole, offers lap lanes and a water slide; phone (907) 488-9401.

Play Golf: Fairbanks Golf Course, located on Farmers Loop Road, is the oldest operating course in Interior Alaska. It has 9 holes on a 3,132-yard course; phone (907) 479-6555 or visit www.fairbanksgolfcourse.com for details. North Star Golf Club, located north of downtown on the Old Steese Highway, offers a regulation 18-hole course, open to the public; phone (907) 457-4653; website www.northstargolf.com. The 18-hole Chena Bend Golf Course, located on Fort Wainwright, is open to the public; phone (907) 353-6223.

Go Fishing: There are several streams and lakes within driving distance of Fairbanks, and local fishing guides are available. **Chena Lake**, about 20 miles southeast of the city via the Richardson Highway at Chena Lake Recreation Area, is stocked with rainbow trout, chinook and coho salmon, Arctic grayling and Arctic char. The **Chena River** and its tributaries offer fishing for Arctic grayling, whitefish, northern pike and burbot. The Chena River flows through Fairbanks. Arctic grayling fishing in the upper Chena is very good, with some large fish. Arctic grayling fishing in the Chena is restricted to catch-and-release year-round. Chena Hot Springs Road off the Steese Highway provides access to fisheries in the Chena River State Recreation Area *(see log of "Chena Hot Springs Road" on pages 425-426).* The Steese Highway also offers access to the **Chatanika River**. Special regulations apply in these waters for Arctic grayling, northern pike and salmon fishing. ADF&G Division of Sport Fish office phone (907) 459-7228.

Air taxi operators and guides in Fairbanks offer short trips from the city for rainbow trout, Arctic grayling, northern pike and lake trout fishing in lakes and streams of the Tanana and Yukon river drainages. Some operators have camps set up for overnight trips while others specialize in day trips. The air taxi operators usually provide a boat and motor for their angling visitors. Rates are reasonable and vary according to the distance from town and type of facilities offered.

Winter in Fairbanks. Although winter temperatures in Fairbanks can dip well below zero, the city has a number of big attractions that draw thousands of visitors and residents alike outdoors, even on the coldest days.

The **World Ice Art Championships** (www.icealaska.com) hosts an international field of artists who come to sculpt art from ice, beginning mid-February and extend-

Just outside Fairbanks (away from city lights) is prime aurora watching territory from fall into spring. Check local aurora forecasts for atmospheric activity. (©Mike Fisher)

ing through March. The event begins with huge blocks of ice that are then transformed by skilled competitors into life-sized reindeer, dragons, airplanes, chariots, knights on horseback and other imaginative works of art. When completed, the colossal sculptures are on exhibit at the venue and may be viewed during the day or at night, when colorful illumination adds a magical quality

to the creations.

Aurora Borealis. Another major winter event (that also spans the spring and fall) brings visitors from the States as well as from overseas to Fairbanks for the opportunity to experience the aurora borealis or northern lights. The best time to see the northern lights is August–April after dark, when skies are clear. In Fairbanks, the aurora is seen

Winter view of the SS Nenana in Pioneer Park. A fund-raising effort is underway to renovate the 'Last Lady of the River.' (©Courtesy Explore Fairbanks/Sherman Hogue)

on at least 8 out of 10 clear, dark nights in winter. While the mystery of the aurora has been solved by science, its beauty continues to amaze and captivate viewers.

Great viewing opportunities can be found at nearly any high viewpoint in Fairbanks at night or out at the Chena Hot Springs Resort. Far from the city lights, natural viewing is possible by just stepping outside or even while enjoying the hot springs

from this location. Daily forecasts of auroral activity over Alaska are found at www. gi.alaska.edu/AuroraForecast.

Sled Dog Racing. A big winter attraction in Fairbanks is sled dog racing. The Alaska Dog Mushers Assoc. (www.alaskadogmushers.com) holds a series of sprint races from December through March. The championship race season kicks off in February with the Midnight Sun Gold Run in mid-Febru-

ary. March events include the Annamaet Limited North American Championship scheduled for March 8–10, 2019, with 2-dog skijor and 4-, 6- and 8-dog races over various distances. The race season is crowned by the GCI Open North American Championship Sled Dog Race (20/20/27.6 miles), March 15–17, 2019. First run in 1946, the Open is the oldest continuously run sled dog race of any kind in the world.

The Mushers Hall and Jeff Studdert Race Grounds are located at 925 Farmers Loop Rd., where visitors can watch dog teams train and race. For more information and a complete schedule of races and events, visit www.alaskadogmushers.com or phone (907) 457-6874.

Fairbanks and Whitehorse, YT, are the 2 host cities for the **Yukon Quest 1,000-Mile International Dog Race**, held in February, with each city alternating roles as the "start" and "finish" to this great endurance race. The annual race starts in Fairbanks and finishes in Whitehorse in 2020. In summer, visit the Yukon Quest store and office in the log cabin adjacent Golden Heart Plaza on 1st Avenue in Fairbanks. (The Yukon Quest office in Whitehorse is inside the White Pass & Yukon Route Depot at Front and Main street downtown.) For more information on the race, visit www.yukonquest.com.

The annual **Iron Dog** (www.irondog. org) race takes place each February. Two-man snowmachine teams race from Big Lake to Nome with a finish in Fairbanks on the Chena River. This popular event is the world's longest and toughest snowmobile race in which racers cross 2,000 miles of Alaska wilderness.

Chena Hot Springs Road

Head out the Steese Expressway from Fairbanks to **Milepost F 4.6** to junction with Chena Hot Springs Road. This good, all-weather paved road (posted 55 mph) leads east through Chena River State Recreation Area, an exceptional year-round recreation area for picnicking and camping (at Rosehip, Tors and Red Squirrel); hiking the popular Angel Rocks and Granite Tors trails); canoeing the river from various put-in points; fishing the popular Arctic grayling fishery (river is catch-and-release only); and wildlife viewing, particularly moose.

The Chena is popular with paddlers, but should not be underestimated: The river is cold and the current very strong. Watch for river-wide logjams and sweepers. Secure your gear in waterproof containers. Suggested paddles are **Milepost J 37.9** to J 27 (First Bridge to Rosehip Campground); J 39.4 to J 37.9 (Second Bridge to First Bridge); J 44 to J 39.4 (Third Bridge to Second Bridge); and J 48.9 to J 44 (Fourth Bridge to Third Bridge). Allow about an hour on the river for each road mile traveled.

For links to maps and other information on the recreation area, visit dnr.alaska.gov/parks/units/chena.

The road ends at Chena Hot Springs Resort, a major Fairbanks attraction known for its innovative uses of geothermal energy and for its famous Aurora Ice Museum. Chena Hot Springs Resort is open daily year-round with modern accommodations, hotsprings pools (indoor and outdoor), RV parking, and camping, dining, horseback riding and many other activities in summer and winter.

There are numerous unsigned, narrow dirt tracts leading off Chena Hot Springs Road, some to public-use river access and others to private property. Watch for posted private property signs before exploring these side roads.

NOTE: Picnicking and camping on the gravel bars of the Chena River is one of the great pleasures of this side trip. However, in spring or during heavy rains, be aware that flooding can occur on the Chena River and plan accordingly when choosing your recreation sites.

CHENA HOT SPRINGS ROAD

Distance is measured from junction with the Old Steese Highway (J).

J 0 Junction of Chena Hot Springs Road with Old Steese Highway at Curry's Corner (groceries and gas to south; post office to south), 0.2 mile west of the Steese Expressway. Access to North Star Golf Club (0.8 mile) via Old Steese Highway north to Golf Club Road.

J 0.1 Junction of Chena Hot Springs Road at **Milepost F 4.6** Steese Expressway. The 4-lane road travels east, up and down hills and through a busy residential area the next 4 miles. The Chena River Recreation Area begins 26 miles from here. Four-lane highway travels up and down hills through busy rural residential area next 4 miles. *CAUTION: Watch for frost heaves eastbound to Milepost J 20.8.*

J 1.6 *CAUTION: Watch for moose.*

J 3 Hot Springs Gas station to south; propane, liquor, groceries.

J 4 Road narrows to 2 lanes eastbound, begin 4-lane highway westbound. *Eastbound travelers note: Numerous private drives and local roads cross Chena Hot Springs Road. Pass with care! Slow for damaged road.*

J 6.3 Junction with Nordale Road, which leads south 5.7 miles to Badger Road, which junctions with the Richardson Highway. From this turnoff it is 3.2 miles south to the Chena River public boat launch on Nordale Road.

J 8.4 Paved double-ended turnout to south. *NOTE: No shooting area (posted along the road in several places).*

J 11.8 Bridge over Little Chena River. Water gauging station in middle of bridge. This Army Corps of Engineers flood control project, completed in 1979, was designed to prevent floods such as the one which devastated Fairbanks in 1967.

J 15.9 Two Rivers Lodge restaurant to north.

J 17.4 Trail Crossing (signed). Watch for trail crossings eastbound.

J 18.3 Junction with Two Rivers Road to elementary school and Two Rivers Recreation Area (skiing, hiking, transfer site and nature trails).

J 20 Highway crosses Jenny M. Creek. *CAUTION: Watch for moose.*

J 20.1 Double-ended paved parking area to south followed by a trail crossing.

J 20.5 Watch for horses.

J 23.4 Pleasant Valley Store to south; gas (last chance to buy gas), diesel, propane, groceries, liquor, firewood and ice, and **TWO RIVERS** post office (ZIP 99716).

This unincorporated community (pop. 703) is home to a number of dog mushers, including 5-time Iditarod champ Rick Swenson. There is an extensive system of mushing trails in the area (motorists will notice the "trail crossing" signs along the road), and the Yukon Quest trail runs through the middle of Two Rivers. Mushers often camp in the big field near store. Picnic tables here for use.

Public mail drop at east end of store and post office.

J 23.9 Laundromat and showers, beauty shop. Long grassy strip with picnic tables for the public.

J 25 Mile 25 Pond; gravel access road leads short distance to pond stocked with Arctic grayling and rainbow trout. Large gravel parking area to north.

J 26.1 Entering the 254,000-acre **Chena River State Recreation Area**. No shooting except at target range at **Milepost J 36.4**. For more information on Chena River State Recreation Area contact the Alaska State Parks in Fairbanks, phone (907) 451-2695, or visit the Alaska Public Lands Information Center in downtown Fairbanks. Reservations are required, and fees are charged for public-use cabins within Chena River SRA. There are many single-vehicle turnouts along the road within the recreation area. Arctic grayling fishing on the Chena River is catch-and-release only.

J 26.5 Flat Creek. Large paved parking area with ATV ramp to north; no overnight parking. Winter trail for snow machines. Information signs.

Chena Hot Springs Road offers wildlife viewing, fishing, paddling and just plain old relaxing on riverbanks. It ends at the wonderful Chena Hot Springs Resort.

(©Kris Valencia, staff)

J 26.7 Flat Creek Slough. Large parking area with loop road to boat launch ($5 fee). Toilets here, life jackets for loan.

J 27 Turnoff to south for **Rosehip State Campground**. Rest area on paved shoulder by campground entrance; toilets and information signs. Campground has 37 level, shaded sites, picnic tables, firepits, toilets, water. Large gravel pads are pull-in or back-in, no pull-throughs. Some hold 2 units. An easy 0.7-mile loop road makes this a good campground for large RVs and trailers. Spacious, grassy tent areas. Beautiful site. Nightly camping fee $15; firewood $5. Carry out your trash if there are no bins. Beautifully situated on the **Chena River**. Drive back into park for a well-marked nature trail, which starts by the river. Day-use area has covered picnic tables and firepits. Canoe and raft launch area. This is the **Mile 27 River Access** canoe and rafting exit point.

J 27.5 Small gravel turnout to south.

J 27.8 Mile 28 River Access to south 0.6 mile. *NOTE: This river access is too steep for large RVs.* Large parking area turn-around; outhouse. Canoe and raft exit point. Two adequate primitive camping spots on the road. Access to gravel bar parking at end. Popular sunbathing spot.

J 28 Watch for moose in Slough Lake next 0.6 mile.

J 28.5 River Access (signed Gravel Bar River Access; may require high-clearance vehicle) leads south 0.7 mile to canoe launch, outhouse, parking.

J 29.5 Compeau trailhead parking to north; multi-use year-round trail provides access to Colorado public-use cabin and views of Chena River Valley, Alaska Range and White Mountains. Hodgins Slough (unsigned) turnout to south. Unloading ramp and information boards.

J 30 Twin Bears Camp (available to rent for group camping). Public access to lake when camp is not in use. Stocked with Arctic grayling and rainbow trout.

J 31.4 Mile 31.4 River Access, 0.2 mile to loop turnaround and canoe launch; undeveloped, no sandbar access. Also trailhead for South Fork winter trail to Nugget Fork Cabin. When these roads have not been recently graded, potholes can be a serious issue.

J 31.7 Turnoff to north for gravel parking at Colorado Creek trailhead for winter trail to Colorado Creek public-use cabin (summer access via Compeau Trailhead) and for Lower Stiles Creek. Bring mosquito repellent. Water pump and outhouse. Bear-proof trash cans, ATV ramp and good turnaround area. Well-marked trailhead with information boards.

J 32.2 Gated access road to Chena River Cabin (public-use) to south; by reservation only (www.reserveamerica.com).

J 33.9 Highway crosses Four Mile Creek. Watch for moose grazing here.

J 35.8 Scenic viewpoint to south; paved parking, interpretive signs about tamaracks and tors. Tors are isolated pinnacles of granite, exposed by erosion and sculpted by "frost wedging," that jut up from the surrounding landscape.

J 36.4 Turnoff to north for Stiles Creek Trailhead and shooting range (follow signs); large gravel parking area with outhouse; weapons discharge notice posted; informal camping around pond. Designated areas for ATV use. Take road to right for shooting range, road to left for pond campsites.

Mist Creek trailhead south of highway; 6-mile hike, experienced hikers only, provides year-round access to Nugget Creek cabin.

J 37.7 Mile 37.7 River Access. Turnoff to south on dirt road, turn left at fork and continue past outhouse for access to river, launch area and informal camping on gravel bar. NOTE: Small turnaround area on dirt road, larger turnaround on gravel bar (if bar is unchanged). *When camping on gravel bars, be aware of changing water levels due to snowmelt in spring or heavy rainfall in summer!*

J 37.9 First bridge over the North Fork Chena River.

J 38.2 Mile 38.2 River Access. Side road to spacious gravel parking area along river. Primitive camping. Plenty of turnaround space. Room for many units. Also, wide road on top of levee between pond and river. This area is built up and above the river. There are no gravel bars or sloping river access.

J 39.1 Small paved turnout to south.

J 39.4 Second bridge over North Fork Chena River. Turnoff to north just east of bridge for double-ended loop road through **Tors Trailhead State Campground** (loop road exits back on to Chena Hot Springs Road at **Mile 39.7**). Campground has 24 large sites (good for large RVs) among tall birch and spruce trees, water, toilets, tables, firepits, firewood; pay $15 nightly camping fee at fee station. Carry out trash if no bins are available.

Beautiful riverside day-use picnic area, toilets, firepits and some cement slabs and large paved parking area adjacent camping area. Day-use fee $5. This is the parking area for the Granite Tors Trail which begins at the west end of the bridge and to the south across Chena Hot Springs Road. Interpretive signs at kiosk about Granite Tors Trail and tors, climbing and hiking safety. Hikers allow 6–10 hours roundtrip for this 15-mile loop. Expect and dress for sudden and extreme weather changes.

J 39.6 Mile 39.6 River Access; good, brushy 0.2-mile side road (take the right fork) leads south to Chena River primitive camping area with pit toilet and a riverbank of flat rocks ideal for sunbathing. Easy small boat launch. Be alert for changes caused by flooding.

J 39.7 Parking and toilet at Tors Trailhead Campground Road exit to north.

J 41.6 Long gravel parking area to south by stream.

J 42 Double-ended paved parking area to south. Watch for muskrats and beaver in ponds here.

J 42.6 Gated access to Hunt Memorial Cabin to south. Reservation only access.

J 42.8 Red Squirrel Campground; good gravel road leads north to pleasant picnic area on grassy area by pond. This is a good campground for tenters; 12 campsites; 2 covered picnic areas, firepits, outhouses and water. Carry out trash if no bins available. Camping fee $15/vehicle. No motorized boats. *CAUTION: Watch for moose.*

J 42.9 Gravel turnout to south overlooking river.

J 43 Side road leads south to **Mile 43 River Access.**

J 44 Third bridge over North Fork Chena River. **Mile 44 River Access.** Gravel parking area with toilets to north, outhouse, canoe and raft launch, primitive camping near river. Sign here lists approximate times for float trips to different locations down the river. Fishing.

J 45.5 Mile 45.5 Pond. Public fishing access to south via gravel road. Firepit grill, picnic table, primitive camping, turnaround space. Pond is stocked with Arctic grayling and rainbow trout. Beavers may be active in pond.

J 45.7 Bridge across North Fork Chena River (signed).

J 46 Small paved turnout to south.

J 46.7 Double-ended paved turnout to south.

J 47.7 North Fork public-use cabin to north. By reservation only, gated road.

J 47.9 Public fishing access to 47.9-Mile Ponds 0.1 mile south via good gravel road. There are 2 beautiful ponds, with 6 camping spots with firepits and picnic tables. Pond is stocked with Arctic grayling and rainbow trout; picnic tables, outhouse, informal campsites around pond. Bring firewood, carry out trash.

J 48.9 Fourth bridge over North Fork Chena River. Turnoff to south at west end of bridge for Angel Rocks trail.

Loop road leads south through parking and picnic area for Angel Rocks Trailhead, one of the best developed public-use sites on Chena Hot Springs Road. (Good place for a picnic, even if you do not intend to hike the trail!) There is a large cement pad with picnic tables, firepits and grills, outhouse. Carry out trash if there are no bins. Angel Rocks trail is a 3.5-mile loop trail to spectacular rock outcroppings; moderately difficult hike (elevation gain of 900 ft.). Details regarding an additional 8½-mile-hike on Chena Hot Springs Trail are at the trailhead. Fishing; information boards about wildfires, trails and rock formations; no overnight camping; parking fee $5 (fine for not paying this is $60).

J 49.1 Good gravel side road leads 0.2 mile north to a loop turnaround at Lower Chena Dome Trailhead; parking, pump water and toilets. This 30-mile loop trail is a strenuous hike that circles the Angel Creek drainage. Bring mosquito repellent!

J 49.7 Angel Creek Lodge to north. *Watch for horses along road.*

J 49.9 Bridge over Angel Creek. Small turnout to north.

J 50.5 Turnoff to north for Upper Chena Dome and Angel Creek Trailhead; parking area to north adjacent road; toilets, bear-proof garbage cans and registration kiosk. Bring mosquito repellent!

J 50.6 Leaving Chena River SRA eastbound. No shooting in areas along the highway (watch for signs).

J 52.3 Bridge over West Fork Chena River. Access to riverbank to south at west end of bridge.

J 53.3 Large, paved double-ended turnout to the northwest; loading ramp for ATVs.

J 55.4 North Fork Chena River bridge.

J 56.6 Entrance to **Chena Hot Springs Resort** (description follows); home of the **Aurora Ice Museum** and ice-carved appletini glasses (between 12,000 and 15,000 of these unique glasses are carved each year). Chena Hot Springs Resort offers camping, lodging, indoor and outdoor hot springs pools, hydroponic gardens and advanced thermal energy innovations. Bernie and Connie Karl, owners, annually host a renewable fair here and there are many activities year-round. Wonderful flower displays in summer, internationally known aurora watching site in winter.

Chena Hot Springs Resort. Rustic Alaskan year-round 100+ year old hot springs resort. 60 scenic miles from Fairbanks. 1,940 pristine acres of wilderness, 80 lodge rooms and 8 dry cabins, full ser-

vice restaurant and bar, natural hot springs (ages 18+). Indoor family pool, RV park, summer and winter activities. Feel the chill of 25 degrees in our year-round Aurora Ice Museum. Sip an appletini in an ice carved martini glass at the Aurora Ice Bar, your souvenir to take with you! Daily tours: 11 A.M., 1 P.M., 3 P.M., 5 P.M. and 7 P.M. Free daily 2 P.M. and 4 P.M. Geothermal Energy Tours showcasing Chena's renewable energy projects. Winter aurora viewing and summer packages too! (907) 451-8104. Website: chenahotsprings.com. See display ad on page 416. [ADVERTISEMENT]

Denali National Park

Includes log of Park Road

(See map, page 428)

Denali, elev. 20,310 feet, is the highest peak in North America and the centerpiece of Denali National Park and Preserve.
(©Donna Dewhurst)

Denali National Park and Preserve was established in 1917 as Mount McKinley National Park. It was designated a park and preserve—and renamed Denali—in 1980. The mountain was officially renamed Denali in 2015. The Park entrance is 237 highway miles north of Anchorage and 125 miles south of Fairbanks via the Parks Highway.

The Park is open all year, although visitor access varies with the change of seasons. Opening and closing dates for the 92-mile-long Park Road are dependent on snow.

The Park Road is open to the public to Mile 30 (Teklanika rest area) from late-April until the shuttle buses start running in mid-May. From mid-May to mid-September, the Visitor Transportation System (comprised of shuttle buses and tour buses) provides transportation into the Park beyond Mile 15. (The first 15 miles of the Park Road are open to all vehicles during the summer.) The Park Road is also open to the public to Mile 30 from mid-September until the first major snow-

storm (usually in October). From October until mid-February, the Park Road is maintained only to Park Headquarters at Mile 3.4. Beyond Mile 3.4, the road is unplowed and access to the Park is by skis, snowshoes or dog sleds, depending on snow cover. The road opens to Mile 12.8 (Mountain Vista rest area) in mid-February; this is a trial program to provide increased access for winter visitors. Each September, after the shuttle buses stop running for the season, the park hosts its 5-day Road Lottery event (with one of those days set aside for active duty military serving in Alaska). Lottery winners are eligible for a 1-day permit to drive their private vehicles the length of the Park Road (or as far as it is passable). For details go to www.nps.gov/dena/planyourvisit/road-lottery.htm.

Most campgrounds, dining and shuttle bus service within the Park, are available only from mid-May to mid-September. (Riley Creek Campground, near the park entrance area, is open year-round; no running water in winter.) Opening dates for

facilities and activities for the summer season are announced in the spring by the Park Service and depend mainly on snow

Distance in miles	Denali NP	Anchorage	Fairbanks	Homer	Seward	Tok	Valdez
Denali NP		237	125	470	364	565	541
Anchorage	237		362	233	127	328	304
Fairbanks	125	362		595	489	206	366
Homer	470	233	595		180	561	537
Seward	364	127	489	180		455	431
Tok	565	328	206	561	455		254
Valdez	541	304	366	537	431	254	

Denali National Park and Preserve

© 2019 The MILEPOST®

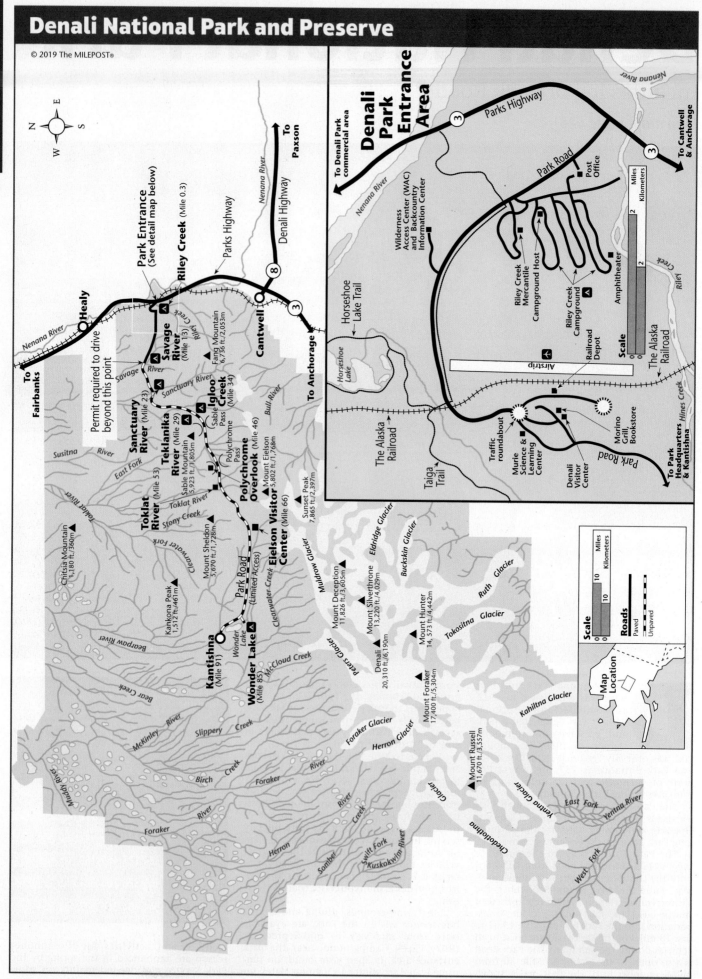

Denali Park Entrance Area

Parks Highway

To Denali Park commercial area

Wilderness Access Center (WAC) and Backcountry Information Center

Horseshoe Lake Trail

Horseshoe Lake

The Alaska Railroad

Taiga Trail

Park Road

Post Office

Riley Creek Mercantile

Campground Host

Riley Creek Campground

Amphitheater

Airstrip

Railroad Depot

The Alaska Railroad

Traffic roundabout

Murie Science & Learning Center

Denali Visitor Center

Morino Grill, Bookstore

To Park Headquarters & Kantishna

Hines Creek

Riley Creek

To Cantwell & Anchorage

Scale

Miles

Kilometers

0 | 2

0 | 2

N E W S

To Paxson

Denali Highway

Nenana River

Parks Highway

Park Entrance (See detail map below)

Riley Creek (Mile 0.3)

Healy

Nenana River

To Fairbanks

Permit required to drive beyond this point

Savage River (Mile 13)

Savage River

Fang Mountain 6,736 ft./2,053m

Cantwell

To Anchorage

Sanctuary River (Mile 23)

Sanctuary River

Sable Mountain

Igloo Creek (Mile 34)

Sable Pass

Teklanika River (Mile 29) 2,923 ft./1,805m

Polychrome Pass

Bull River

Susitna River

East Fork

Toklat River (Mile 53)

Sable Mountain 5,923 ft./1,805m

Toklat River

Stony Creek

Clearwater Fork

Polychrome Overlook (Mile 46)

Mount Eielson 5,802 ft./1,768m

Eielson Visitor Center (Mile 66)

Sunset Peak 7,865 ft./2,397m

Chitsia Mountain 1,180 ft./360m

Kankona Peak 1,512 ft./461m

Mount Sheldon 5,670 ft./1,728m

Clearwater Creek

Park Road (Limited Access)

Muldrow Glacier

Mount Deception 11,826 ft./3,605m

Mount Silverthrone 13,220 ft./4,029m

Eldridge Glacier

Buckskin Glacier

Ruth Glacier

Toklat River

Bearpaw River

Kantishna (Mile 91)

Wonder Lake

Wonder Lake (Mile 85)

McCloud Creek

Denali 20,310 ft./6,190m

Mount Hunter 14,573 ft./4,442m

Tokositna Glacier

Peters Glacier

McKinley River

Slippery Creek

Birch Creek

Bear Creek

Foraker River

River

Mount Foraker 17,400 ft./5,304m

Foraker Glacier

Herron Glacier

Kahiltna Glacier

Muddy River

Foraker

Herron

River

Creek

Swift Fork

Kuskokwim River

Sombet

River

Glacier

Mount Russell 11,670 ft./3,557m

Chedotlothna Glacier

Yentna Glacier

East Fork

Ventna River

West Fork

Scale

Miles

Kilometers

0 | 10

0 | 10

Roads

Paved

Unpaved

Map Location

conditions in May.

For general rules and regulation, and regulations governing the use of aircraft, firearms, snow machines and motorboats in the park additions and in the national preserve units, and for all other questions, write Denali National Park and Preserve, P.O. Box 9, Denali Park, AK 99755; phone (907) 683-9532, website: www.nps.gov/dena.

At approximately 6 million acres, most visitors will see only a fraction of the Park from the 92-mile-long Park Road, which was constructed between 1923 and 1938. The crown jewel of the Park is Denali (formerly Mount McKinley), North America's highest mountain, elev. 20,310 feet.

On a clear day, Denali is visible from Anchorage and many points along the Parks Highway. However, summer's often overcast or rainy weather frequently obscures the mountain, allowing summertime visitors only about a 30 to 40 percent chance of seeing "the mountain" even inside the Park.

First mention of "the mountain" was in 1794, when English explorer Capt. George Vancouver spotted "a stupendous snow mountain" from Cook Inlet. Early Russian explorers and traders called the peak *Bolshaia Gora*, or "Big Mountain." The Athabascan Indians of the region called it Denali, "the High One." In 1896 a prospector, William A. Dickey, named the mountain for presidential nominee William McKinley of Ohio, although McKinley had no connection with Alaska. Protests that the mountain be returned to its original name, Denali, ensued almost at once. But it was not until the Alaska National Interest Lands Conservation Act of 1980 changed the park's status and name that the Alaska Board of Geographic Names changed the mountain's name back to Denali. The U.S. Board of Geographic Names, however, continued to show the mountain as McKinley until the 2015 name change at the federal level. The 1980 legislation also enlarged the park from 2 million acres to its present 6 million acres to protect Denali on all sides and to preserve the habitat of area wildlife.

The history of climbs on Denali is as intriguing as its names. In 1903, Judge James Wickersham and party climbed to an estimated 10,000 feet, while the Dr. Frederick A. Cook party reached the 11,000-foot level in 1903. Cook returned to the mountain 3 years later and claimed to have reached the summit. Cook's vague description of his ascent route and a questionable summit photo led many to doubt his claim. (The exhaustive research of McKinley expert Bradford Washburn has proven the exaggeration of Cook's claim.)

The 1910 Sourdough Party, which included Tom Lloyd, Charles McGonagall, Pete Anderson and Billy Taylor, claimed they had reached both summits (north and south peaks), but could not provide any photographic evidence. However, the spruce pole they left behind on the north peak was witnessed in 1913.

The first ascent of the true summit of Denali was made in June 1913 by the Rev. Hudson Stuck, Episcopal archdeacon of Yukon, Walter Harper, Harry Karstens (co-leader) and Robert Tatum. Harper, an Athabascan, was the first person to set foot on the higher south peak. (Harper drowned in 1918, along with more than 300 other passengers and crew, when the SS *Princess Sophia* sank near Juneau.) Harry Karstens went on to become the first superintendent

Riley Creek Mercantile is a hub of activity with groceries, laundromat, showers and campground reservation services. (©Kris Valenica, staff)

of Mount McKinley National Park.

Out of respect for the Native people, Stuck refused to refer to the mountain as McKinley. He recorded the story of their achievement in his book, *The Ascent of Denali*.

Today, more than a thousand people attempt to climb Denali each year between April and mid-July, most flying in to base camp at 7,200 feet on the Kahiltna Glacier. In a typical season, slightly more than half the climbers attempting to summit Denali succeed.

Geographic features in the park bear the names of early explorers: Eldridge and Muldrow glaciers, after George Eldridge and Robert Muldrow of the U.S. Geographic Service who determined the peak's altitude in 1898; Wickersham Wall; Karstens Ridge; Harper Icefall; and Mount Carpe and Mount Koven, named for Allen Carpe and Theodore Koven, both killed in a 1932 climb.

Climate and Landscape: Typical summer weather in the Park is cool, wet and windy. Visitors should bring clothing for temperatures that range from 40°F to 80°F. Rain gear, a light coat, sturdy walking shoes or boots and insect repellent are essential. Winter weather is cold and clear, with temperatures sometimes dropping to -50°F at park headquarters. In the lowlands, snow seldom accumulates to more than 3 feet.

Timberline in the Park is at 2,700 feet. Below timberline are vast areas of taiga, a term of Russian origin that describes scant tree growth. Together with the subarctic tundra, the landscape of Denali National Park and Preserve supports more than 750 species of trees, shrubs, herbs and flowering plants. Major species of the taiga are white spruce in dry areas; dry tundra covers the upper ridges and rocky slopes above the tree line from about 3,500 to 7,500 feet. In the wet tundra black spruce is common, intermingled with aspen, paper birch and balsam poplar. Wet tundra features willow and dwarf birch, often with horsetails, sedges and grasses along pothole ponds.

Denali's subarctic ecosystem helped it gain International Biosphere Reserve status in 1976. Outstanding features of the park include the Outer Range, Savage River Canyon, Wonder Lake, Sanctuary River,

Muldrow Glacier and the Kantishna Hills. The Outer Range, located just north of the central Alaska Range, is composed of some of Alaska's oldest rocks, called Bison Gulch schist, which can be clearly seen in the Savage River Canyon.

Caribou calving grounds are located near the headwaters of the Sanctuary River, which passes through the Outer Range between Mount Wright and Primrose Ridge. Muldrow Glacier, the largest glacier on the north side of the Alaska Range, is 32 miles long and descends 16,000 feet from near Denali's summit.

Wonder Lake, 2.6 miles long and 280 feet deep, hosts many migrating species and is a summer home for loons, Arctic terns and other birds. Wonder Lake is at Mile 84.4 on the Park Road. Nearby Reflection Lake offers a peerless reflection of Denali.

The Kantishna Hills were first mined in 1905 when the town of Eureka boomed with gold seekers. In 1980 the Kantishna area was included in the Park. From the Park entrance

DENALI PARK AREA ADVERTISERS

Denali Visitor Center is a great place to learn more about the Park's natural history and find out about ranger-led events taking place. (©Serine Reeves)

at **Milepost A 237.4** of the Parks Highway, the 92-mile Park Road traverses Denali National Park and Preserve to private land holdings in Kantishna.

Visitor Information

The Park's visitor centers are your source for on-site information about camping, backcountry travel, the Park shuttle bus system and daily ranger-led hikes, walks and interpretive programs. For more information, contact Denali National Park and Preserve, P.O. Box 9, Denali Park, AK 99755; phone (907) 683-9532, website: www.nps.gov/dena. The visitor centers located within the Park are:

The **Denali Visitor Center** is accessed from the roundabout at Mile 1.4 and from Mile 1.6 on the Park Road. It is open 8 A.M. to 5 P.M. from mid-May to mid-September. Here you can chat with a park ranger, watch a film at the Karstens Theatre or learn more about the Park's natural history in the exhibit hall. This is the main visitor center for the Park, and the complex includes the Backcountry Information Center, focused on helping backcountry hikers, Denali Bookstore (operated by Alaska Geographic) and the Morino Grill (cafeteria-style dining and espresso bar). The bus stop at the Visitor Center is where you catch the shuttle bus for the Sled Dog Demonstration (follow signs).

Wilderness Access Center (WAC)/Denali Bus Depot is accessed from Mile 0.7 Park Road. The WAC acts as the park's transportation hub, where visitors can make reservations for shuttle or bus tours; reserve or check-in for campsites in the Park; and pick up visitor brochures on various subjects. There is a small gift shop and a coffee bar with snacks in the WAC. The WAC is open from mid-May to mid-September. Hours are 5 A.M. to 4 P.M. for bus loading, 7 A.M. to 7 P.M. for the reservation desk; phone (907) 683-9278.

Murie Science & Learning Center, at Mile 1.5 of the Park Road, is used as a winter visitor center from mid-September until mid-May. It is open year-round daily from 9 A.M. to 4:30 P.M.

Eielson Visitor Center, at Mile 66 on the Park Road, is an excellent Denali viewpoint.

Eielson is open daily from 9 A.M. to 5:30 P.M., June 1 until mid-September. (Hours are subject to change.)

Entrance Fees: Visitors to the Park pay an entrance fee for each person 16 years of age and older. The entrance fee is $15. The America the Beautiful, Access and Senior interagency passes and Denali Annual Pass can be applied to the fee; information about these passes may be obtained at the Denali Visitor Center. Entrance fees are collected at the time of booking tour or shuttle tickets. With reserved campsites, entrance fees are collected when you pick up your camping permit at either Riley Creek Mercantile or the WAC.

Advance Reservations: 65 percent of the Park's shuttle bus seats, and 100 percent of Riley Creek, Savage River, Teklanika River and Wonder Lake campsites, are available for advance reservations. Park shuttle bus tickets and Park campsites may be reserved online, by mail, by phone or in person at the Wilderness Access Center. Riley Creek Mercantile, at Mile 0.3 Park Road, also has shuttle bus and tour bus ticket sales and campground reservations and check-in. The Mercantile is open 7 A.M. to 10 P.M. in summer; phone (907) 683-9246.

You may make reservations for shuttles and campgrounds in person up to 2 days in advance and by phone or internet up to 1 day in advance of your visit. There is a fee charged for each campsite change or to cancel a reservation 24 hours or more prior to check-in. Cancellations within 24 hours of scheduled arrival are non-changeable and non-refundable. In addition to entrance and camping fees, there is a $6 fee charged for each campground reservation.

For online reservations visit www.reservedenali.com; go to Check Rates on the menu bar and fill in your travel dates and what you want to reserve (shuttle, tour, campsite). Wait for the system to check availability then select an available date; rates and details will follow. For reservations by phone, call toll-free 1-800-622-7275 (nationwide), or for international calls, phone (907) 272-7275. Prepaid, reserved shuttle bus tickets may be picked up at the Wilderness Access Center shuttle desk. Any unclaimed, prepaid tickets

for buses departing before 7 A.M. will be in the possession of the bus driver; however, the drivers do not sell tickets.

Backcountry Permits: Day hikers do not need special permits. Backcountry permits are required for overnight visits. Permits are issued 1 day in advance of backcountry trip; reservations are not accepted. Backcountry permits are available at the Backcountry Information Center (BIC) in summer and at the Murie Science and Learning Center in the winter. The BIC, located in the Denali Visitor Center, is open daily from 9 A.M. to 5 P.M. during the summer. (The permitting process takes about an hour, so arrive no later than 4 P.M.) Information on obtaining a backcountry permit is also available on the Park website at www.nps.gov/dena/planyourvisit/permits.htm.

Denali's backcountry consists of 85 units, in which a limited number of visitors are allowed per night. Check the quota board at the Backcountry Information Center for unit availability. Backpackers must confirm that their desired unit is not closed. *NOTE: Large groups may be divided if units are too full.*

Backpackers must carry bear-resistant food containers (BRFC's). These are available for pick-up at the Backcountry Information Center or Park Headquarters, and must be returned at the end of your trip. Camping gear should include a gasoline or propane stove, rain gear and a tent or waterproof shelter. Water should be boiled or treated. A camper bus pass must be purchased in order to reach most backcountry camping units.

Fishing Licenses: Not required in the wilderness area; state law is applicable on all other lands. Specified limits for each person per day should be carefully observed. Fishing is poor because most rivers are silted and ponds are shallow.

Mountaineering: Climbing Denali requires extensive planning. Registration is mandatory for all climbs on Denali and Foraker and mountaineers are required to purchase a permit ($370/person age 25 or older, $270 age 24 or younger) prior to climbing these peaks. *Permit applications must be received at least 60 days prior to the start of the expedition.*

The National Park Service maintains a ranger station in Talkeetna that is staffed full-time year-round (limited hours in winter). Rangers there can provide all necessary information on climbing Denali, Foraker and other Alaska Range peaks. Contact the Walter Harper Talkeetna Ranger Station at P.O. Box 588, Talkeetna, AK 99676; phone (907) 733-2231; or visit www.nps.gov/dena/planyourvisit/mountaineering.htm.

Pets: Pets are not allowed in the backcountry. They are allowed in parking lots, on roads, in campsites and on designated trails in park entrance areas.

Special Permits: Each year the Park issues permits to a limited number of individuals, selected by lottery, to drive their vehicles through the Park on one chosen day, Friday to Monday, on the second weekend after Labor Day. It is not unusual for these late-season visitors to have their tour curtailed by early snows within the Park. Road lottery applications are accepted online during the month of May. A fee is charged for each entry application and each entry must be completed online before the end of the month. If selected, an additional fee will be charged to the same credit card. For more details on the road lottery, visit www.nps.gov/dena/planyourvisit/road-lottery.htm or phone (907) 683-9532.

For information concerning special permits for the Professional Photographer Program, the Artist-in-Residence Program and Commercial Filming, call (907) 683-9532.

Emergency Services: Call 911 or contact state troopers at (907) 451-5100. For healthcare, go to Canyon Clinic, an urgent care clinic on the Sourdough Road, just north of Princess Lodge.

Lodging & Services

North of the park entrance about a mile on the Parks Highway is a commercial district with numerous hotels, restaurants, RV parks, a gas station with convenience store, assorted shops and commercial outfitters. Lodges, cabins, campgrounds and restaurants are also found along the Parks Highway south and north of the park entrance, from Cantwell to Healy; see pages 398–403 in the PARKS HIGHWAY section. There are several wilderness lodges inside the Park in the Kantishna area, at the far western edge of the Park.

The Riley Creek Mercantile at Riley Creek Campground is stocked with a limited selection of groceries, beer, wine and sundries. Firewood, showers and laundry facilities are also available at the Mercantile. If the Mercantile doesn't have what you need, try stores located in the Nenana Canyon commercial area on the Parks Highway.

No food or drink service is available in the Park west of the Visitor Center Campus (turnoff at Mile 1.4 Park Road), which has the Morino Grill and an espresso bar (doors open 8 A.M. to 5 P.M.). Adjacent the Morino Grill is the Alaska Geographic

Stop at the Wilderness Access Center (WAC) to check-in or reserve a campsite or a shuttle or bus tour. Park staff are on hand to answer your questions. (©Kris Valencia, staff)

Bookstore, open 8 A.M. to 6 P.M. There are restrooms with outside entrances at the Visitor Center.

Denali Park Village. DenaliPark Village.com. Located just 7 miles from the entrance of Denali National Park, Denali Park Village embraces the natural beauty and rich history of Alaska. Spread across 20 acres, the property offers 338 guest rooms between the Lodge at Denali Park Village and The Cabins at Denali Park Village and is home to Cabin Nite Dinner Theatre, park tours, dining options and a marketplace, designed to be reminiscent of a historic mining town complete with individually themed gift shops. 1-800-276-7234. [ADVERTISEMENT]

Denali Rainbow Village. Good Sam RV Park, 1 mile north of Denali Park entrance. Large motel rooms with kitchens and queen beds available. 55 RV sites with full or partial hook-up, pull-thru, WiFi, cable TV, showers, laundry and dump station. Mall

with services and activities. (907) 683-7777. See display ad on page 433. [ADVERTISEMENT]

Transportation

Highway: Access via the Parks Highway from Anchorage or Fairbanks. The entrance to Denali National Park is at **Milepost A 237.4** Parks Highway, 237 miles north of Anchorage; 28 miles north of Cantwell and 125 miles south of Fairbanks. See PARKS HIGHWAY section beginning on page 374.

The 92-mile Park Road *(log begins on page 435)* provides access to Denali National Park's campgrounds and the Kantishna area, where some privately owned, backcountry lodges are located. The Park Road is closed to private vehicles beyond Mile 15 (Savage River checkpoint). The exception is for campers with vehicles staying overnight at

The Alaska Railroad's Denali Star train stops at Denali train depot daily in summer from both Anchorage and Fairbanks.
(©Serine Reeves)

Teklanika River Campground at Mile 29.1. You must have camping reservations for Teklanika (also accessed by bus) and there is a 3-night minimum stay requirement. The other 3 campgrounds beyond the checkpoint are tents only and accessible only via the shuttle bus system.

Air: Charter flights are available from many nearby locations, and flightseeing tours are offered by operators from the Park area or out of Talkeetna, Anchorage or Fairbanks. A round-trip air tour of the Park from Anchorage takes 3 to 4 hours.

Private Aircraft: Denali Park airstrip; elev. 1,720 feet; length 3,000 feet; gravel; unattended.

Aviation information for private pilots is available at www.nps.gov/dena/planyour visit/pilotinformation.htm. Review before flying this airspace.

Talkeetna Air Taxi. Explore Denali and the National Park with Talkeetna Air Taxi as your flightseeing guide. Experience

an ice age world among sculpted peaks and land on spectacular glaciers with our amazing tours. Call (907) 733-2218 for a free brochure and see our web cam at www.talkeetnaair.com for live views of Denali. See display ad on page 393 in the PARKS HIGHWAY section. [ADVERTISEMENT]

Railroad: The Alaska Railroad's *Denali Star* train offers daily service between Anchorage, Denali Park and Fairbanks during the summer. The train trip to Denali Park takes approximately 4 hours from Fairbanks, 7½ hours from Anchorage. The **Alaska Railroad** offers standard coach service and premium glass-domed GoldStar railcars for booking. Phone reservations at (907) 265-2494 or toll-free at 1-800-544-0552 or visit www.alaskarailroad.com. See also "Railroads" in the TRAVEL PLANNING section.

Details on private dome rail service and booking available at www.alaskatrain.com.

The turnoff for the Denali Park Depot is located 1.4 miles west of the Parks Highway via the Park Road, within walking distance of the Denali Visitor Center Campus.

Bus: Daily bus service to the Park is available from Anchorage and Fairbanks (see "Bus Lines" in the TRAVEL PLANNING section); see also Shuttle Buses and Tours, following.

Shuttle Buses and Bus Tours: Visitors

have the choice of taking the Park shuttle buses or one of the concessionaire-operated narrated bus tours in summer. Both tour buses and shuttle buses use the Park Road and both charge fees. For reservation information for shuttle buses and bus tours, phone 1-800-622-7275, visit www.reserve denali.com or www.nps.gov/dena/planyour visit/visiting-denali.htm.

The Visitor Transportation System (VTS) was established in 1972 to protect the natural resources of Denali National Park. The green VTS buses depart the Wilderness Access Center (WAC) throughout the day between 5:15 A.M. and 4 P.M. for Toklat River (3 hours 1-way), Eielson Visitor Center (4 hours 1-way), and Wonder Lake (5½ hours 1-way). Some shuttle buses operate exclusively in the entrance area, shuttling visitors between the WAC, Riley Creek Campground, railroad depot, Denali Visitor Center Campus, Horseshoe Lake Trailhead, Park Headquarters, the sled dog demonstrations, Mountain Vista rest area and out to the Savage River area at Mile 14.9.

Travelers accessing Park campgrounds or hiking trails, or looking for a no-frills sightseeing trip, use the shuttle buses. The VTS buses are school bus-style; they are not luxurious. You must bring your own food and beverages (or purchase them at the WAC before you take off—limited to snacks and beverages). There are rest stops no more than 2 hours apart that allow you to stretch your legs, use the restrooms and photograph the view (weather permitting). You can disembark the shuttle bus anytime to hike, photograph or spend time in an area of interest by asking the bus driver to let you off. When you are ready to re-board, flag down the next bus that comes by and—when space is available—you can continue along the bus route.

The 6-, 8- and 11-hour round-trip shuttle bus trips can be exhilarating and exhausting at the same time. Consider carefully your ability to endure narrow, cliff-side roads (no guardrails, buses passing each other on a narrow road); endless searching of a terrain that may be empty of wildlife that day; and a ground-speed of 35-mph or less. Children may become bored on these tours, since the wildlife viewing is uncertain, infrequent and typically at quite a distance, at the best of times. Planning ahead to get off the bus and do your own hike, then catch a bus on its return route, is a great way to maximize the VTS-style travel experience. (NOTE: Do *not* wait until the last bus of the day to catch a return ride or you may be disappointed. If you are in a group, be willing to split up.)

The VTS shuttle buses do not offer narration, although many of the Park bus drivers are long-term navigators of the Park Road, quite knowledgeable about the area, and happy to answer questions. These drivers are entirely English speaking.

The shuttle buses do stop for wildlife viewing and photography (from inside the bus, telephoto lens and binoculars are helpful). Brown bears, wolves, fox, caribou and moose sometimes walk the road. Wheelchair-accessible buses are available.

The concessionaire-operated bus tours operate from late May or early June to mid-September, with morning and afternoon departures from the WAC. The Denali Natural History Tour (4–5 hours) goes to Teklanika River at Mile 30 on the Park Road. The Tundra Wilderness Tour travels either 61 miles to Stony Hill Overlook (7–8 hours) or 53 miles to Toklat River rest area (6–7 hours,

Boarding the shuttle bus at the Wilderness Access Center. The green buses depart throughout the day during summer and provide service throughout the Park. (©Kris Valencia, staff)

offered during shoulder season only). The Kantishna Experience (11–12 hours) has 2 morning departures and travels to the end of the Park Road and back.

The bus tours use an upgraded bus, similar in style to a motorcoach; are narrated by the driver/naturalist; and may include a boxed lunch, snacks and beverages. Check details at www.reservedenali.com under Tours & Shuttles. Wheelchair-accessible buses are available on request when you make your reservation, and all stops are wheelchair accessible.

Bicycles: There is no policy restricting bicycle access on the Park Road, although bicyclists must stay on the road. Bicyclists wishing to camp in the Park must either camp in one of the campgrounds or, if they are camping in the backcountry, must park their bikes in one of the campgrounds. Eielson, Toklat and Wonder Lake buses have bike racks. Only 2 bikes can be accommodated, so reserve ahead.

Camping

Denali National Park has 6 campgrounds *(see chart on page 435)* located along the Park Road: Riley Creek (**Mile J 0.3**), Savage River (**Mile J 12.9**), Sanctuary River (**Mile J 22.6**), Teklanika River (**Mile J 29.1**), Igloo Creek (**Mile J 34**) and Wonder Lake (**Mile J 84.4**). Riley Creek and Savage River are accessible by personal vehicle at any time. Wonder Lake, Igloo Creek and Sanctuary River are

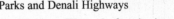

The Park Kennels is a favorite stop. There is time to visit with the dogs before seeing the sled dog demonstration. This is a free activity and takes about an hour. (©Kris Valencia, staff)

tents only (no vehicles) and access is by shuttle bus. Teklanika River Campground is for both tents and RVs. Camping fees range from $15 to $30 a night, not including the $6 reservation fee. Group camping is available at Savage River for $46 a night. Reservations are recommended *(see Advance Reservations on page 430)*. For reservations visit www.reservedenali.com; call toll-free 1-800-622-7275.

Riley Creek Campground is the largest campground in the Park, with 146 campsites located along 3 gravel loops. Campsite assignment at Riley Creek is based on vehicle size. Generator hours are 8–10 A.M. and 4–8 P.M. Maximum 8 people per site. Maximum 3 tents per site, use designated pads. Check-in/-out time is 11 A.M. Riley Creek is the campground most convenient to services, located in the park entrance area adjacent Riley Creek Mercantile, which carries grocery items and firewood and also has laundry/shower facilities and a dump station and water fill-up.

Teklanika River (or "Tek") Campground is open to tent and RV camping. A minimum 3-night stay is required by visitors who choose to drive their personal vehicle to the campground (restricted to one round-trip only). Tent campers or visits of less than 3 nights must use the transit system to access the campground. The Tek shuttle bus pass is for campers based at Teklanika River Campground and ensures a bus seat farther into the Park. On the first complete day of a visitor's stay, the Tek Pass is good for a confirmed space on any available shuttle (green) bus. During the remainder of the stay, the pass allows space available seating on any shuttle bus.

There are no RV hookups in Park campgrounds. Visitors may camp a total of 14 days per year. Riley Creek is the only Park campground open year-round (no running water in winter) and the only campground with a dump station and water-fill. The other campgrounds are open from mid-May to mid-September, depending on the weather. *NOTE: Campgrounds may be closed to tent camping or all camping due to wildlife activity.* You can reserve campsites ahead of time (see "Advance Reservations" this section) or check with the Wilderness Access Center (WAC) upon arrival for current campsite availability. The WAC is open 7 A.M. to 7 P.M. in summer; phone (907) 683-9274. You can also register for campground sites at the Riley Creek Mercantile, which is open from 7 A.M. to 10 P.M. in summer; phone (907) 683-9246.

Also keep in mind that private campgrounds are located outside the Park along the Parks Highway. The nearest to the Park entrance is **Denali Rainbow Village** in the Nenana Canyon commercial area.

Attractions

Free Sled Dog Demonstrations are held at the Park Kennels. Board the free dog demo bus at the Denali Visitor Center and catch the morning program or one of the afternoon demonstrations. Demonstrations are usually offered at 10 A.M., 2 P.M., and 4 P.M.; check schedule at the visitor center for current show times and bus schedule. You may also drive out to the kennel, although parking is limited and RVs will have a hard time finding a spot. Kennel visitors can photograph and pet the sled dogs before attending the formal demonstration from the adjacent platform seating.

The dog sled demonstration includes a talk by park rangers about the dogs, their role in the park and the history of the kennel. The demonstration and free time to visit the dogs adds up to about an hour. *NOTE: Arrive on time for the shows. Latecomers will find this sign blocking their entry: "Dog demonstration in progress. Please wait out of sight near the buses until 45 minutes past the hour before entering the kennels area."*

The kennels are open to visitors throughout the day—*except* during the sled dog demonstrations—9 A.M. to 5 P.M. Donations are accepted to help support the kennel. If you'd like to contribute to supporting the kennels, throw some money in the "donation dog."

Wildlife viewing is probably second only to mountain viewing as the goal for visitors in Denali. The Park is home to one amphibian (the wood frog) and 39 species of mammals which, among many others, include: caribou, grizzly bear, wolf, wolverine, moose, Dall sheep, red fox, lynx, ground squirrel, snowshoe hare and vole. About 169 species of birds have been recorded in the park. Year-round residents include the great horned owl, raven, and white-tailed rock and willow ptarmigan. The majority of species, however, visit the Park only during summer. Some of these summer visitors include: sandhill cranes, long-tailed ducks, sandpipers, plovers, gulls, buffleheads and goldeneyes. Golden eagles are a common sight throughout the Park. Feeding of any wildlife is prohibited.

Hiking in Denali National Park is cross-country: There are few established trails in the backcountry. For the day-hiker or the visitor with only a short amount of time, however, there are several trails in the front-country/entrance area from Mile 1 to Mile 15 (Savage River) that are accessible by car, shuttle bus, on foot or by bike. These trails range from easy to strenuous and provide opportunities to experience the wildlife and grandeur of Denali. Check the Daily Ranger Program Schedule at the visitor center for time and location of ranger-guided hikes. A board is at the entrance each day with updated information offered on it or check website: www.nps.gov/dena/planyour

Campground	Spaces	Tent	RVs	Pit toilets	Flush toilets	Tap water	Fee
Igloo Creek	7	•		•			$15
Riley Creek	147	•	•	•	•	•	$15-30
Savage River	33	•	•	•	•	•	$24-30
Sanctuary	6	•		•			$15
Teklanika River	53	•	•		•	•	$25
Wonder Lake	28	•		•	•	•	$16

Savage Alpine trailhead at Mile 14.9, across the river from the vehicle checkpoint, has picnic tables, vault toilets, interpretive signs and a great view of the river. (©Serine Reeves)

visit/walks-and-hikes.htm. Private guided excursions are available. These 3- to 4-hour guided hikes are available from mid-May to mid-September and include area hotel pickup.

Murie Science and Learning Center specializes in educational programs that foster stewardship for national parks. These programs include field seminars, teacher trainings and youth camps. Visitors can stop by the Center's main building and explore an array of exhibits on science and research, purchase books and enjoy comfortable seating and views. The Center is open year-round. For more information on educational programs, visit www.nps.gov/rlc/murie/index.htm. For general inquiries, phone (907) 683-6432.

Planning park activities. How much you can see and enjoy in Denali depends a lot on your schedule. A half-day visit might include watching the 18-minute film *Heartbeats of Denali* at the Denali Visitor Center or riding the Savage River shuttle bus to Mile 15. You can get off the bus at any location, do a short hike, then reboard the Savage River shuttle bus coming out of the Park, all for free. (The visitor centers will have suggestions on short hikes you can take.) Denali is visible in the distance, weather permitting, from about Mile 10 on the Park Road.

If you have a full day, take a bus farther out into the Park; get off and hike or just sit and enjoy the wilderness; join a ranger for a Discovery Hike or Guided Walk (schedules and locations at Eielson and Denali visitor centers); plan your own hike (topo maps, guide books and knowledgeable staff can assist you with trip planning).

If you have a few days, visit Wonder Lake and hike the McKinley Bar Trail or do another Discovery Hike; attend a ranger-led program; experience adventure activities outside the Park such as river-rafting, flight-seeing and horseback riding.

During Denali summers when there are between 18 and 21 hours of daylight, recreational opportunities such as hiking, gold panning and other activities extend into late evening hours. Evenings are ideal for flightseeing adventures or for an easy hike around Horseshoe Lake near the DVC. Visitors staying in the Nenana Canyon commercial area just north of the Park entrance will enjoy a fun and energetic show—along with family-style dining—at the Music of Denali Dinner Theatre, presented nightly at McKinley Chalet Resort. Those staying south of the park entrance can enjoy the Alaska Cabin Nite Dinner Theatre at the Denali Park Village.

Winter visits. The Park is accessible in winter beyond Mile 3.4 Park Road by skis,

snowshoes, skijor or dog sled. Winter attractions include observing wildlife, viewing the aurora borealis and seeing the Park's impressive wintertime landscape. The Park Service is plowing the Park Road to Mile 12.8 (Mountain Vista rest area) as a trial program to enhance winter recreational opportunities starting in February. Visit the Denali Chamber of Commerce for information on winter lodging at www.denalichamber.com or phone (907) 683-4636.

The annual Winterfest Celebration is a community-wide celebration offering snowshoe walks, sled dog rides, ski and skijoring events, avalanche safety awareness clinics, stargazing, winter ecology programs and more. Information is available at Park Headquarters, phone (907) 683-9532.

Park Road Log

Distance from the junction (J) with Parks Highway is shown.

PARK ROAD LOG

J 0 Junction with the Parks Highway (Alaska Route 3) at **Milepost A 237.4**; turn west onto the Park Road (the Park Road is paved for the first 15 miles). There is a parking lot to right off the Parks Highway at this junction with access to Denali National Park and Preserve sign, a popular photo op, and a gravel walking trail along the Park Road to Mile 1.4. No cell phone service beyond about Mile 5 westbound.

NOTE: The Park Road was designed for scenic enjoyment, not for high speed. Maximum speed is 35 mph and lower limits are posted. Several walking paths cross the Park Road. Watch for pedestrians.

J 0.2 Turnoff for **post office** parking and access to Riley Creek Campground (see description next milepost).

J 0.3 Turnoff for **Riley Creek Mercantile** and **Riley Creek Campground**. The Mercantile is open 7 A.M. to 10 P.M. in summer; phone (907) 683-9246. The Mercantile has shuttle bus and tour ticket sales and campground reservations and check-in; conve-

nience store style groceries, alcohol and other merchandise; and a public phone, showers, laundry facilities and firewood for sale. Make sure you get all necessary supplies before proceeding to campgrounds west of here on the Park Road.

Riley Creek Campground has 147 sites along 3 gravel loops. ("Bear" loop is open year-round for camping.) Walking trails to the Mercantile and to an amphitheater. A campground host, flush toilets and water pumps are available in summer. Trash bins. Nightly camping fee is $24–$30 for RVs (depends on length), and $15 for walk-in tent sites. (During the off-season, only a vault toilet is provided.) ▲

J 0.7 Turnoff for **Wilderness Access Center (WAC)** 0.2 mile to parking area. The WAC is the transportation hub of the Park and has shuttle bus tickets, camping permits and restrooms. The WAC is open from mid-May to mid-September. Hours are 5 A.M. to 4 P.M. for bus loading, 7 A.M. to 7 P.M. for the reservation desk; phone (907) 683-9274.

J 1.1 Alaska Railroad crossing. Horseshoe Lake Trailhead parking. More than 200 hikers use this trail each day in peak season and ranger-led hikes are available. Built in 1940, the trail was rebuilt and expanded in 2014 and now circles the entire lake and is around 3 miles in length. Bus stop.

J 1.4 Traffic roundabout provides access to **Visitor Center Campus** (Denali Visitor Center, Backcountry Information Center, Morino Grill, Bookstore), the **Alaska Railroad Depot** and continuation of Park Road. *NOTE: No commercial traffic allowed without permit beyond this point.*

Overnight hiking permits are available from the Backcountry Information Center (BIC), which is located in the Denali Visitor Center. The BIC is open daily from 9 A.M. to 5 P.M. during the summer.

J 1.5 Murie Science and Learning Center dedicated to ongoing scientific park research, and science-based education programs.

J 1.6 Turnoff for Visitor Center Campus.

J 3.3 Rock Creek bridge, elev. 2,030 feet.

J 3.4 Park Headquarters: Denali National Park and Preserve administration. The **Park**

Eielson Visitor Center at Mile 66 on the Park Road offers sweeping vistas. (©Serine Reeves)

Kennels are also located here, just west of the HQ building (follow the barking). Limited parking, no large sites for RVs. Sled dog demonstrations are given at 10 A.M., 2 P.M. and 4 P.M.; be on time, latecomers are not allowed to enter during the demonstration. Access by shuttle bus from Denali Visitor Center; check schedule at the visitor center for bus and demonstration times. Visitors can tour the kennels before the formal program, which includes a demonstration and explanation of the role of sled dogs in the Park. The demonstration is free but donations are accepted to help support the kennel. A fun stop and perfect for visitors of all ages.

Park Headquarters: Denali National Park and Preserve administration. Report emergencies to the rangers. *NOTE: There are no public phones west of this point. Watch out for dog walkers to Mile 7 westbound.*

J 5.5 Paved viewpoint. There are numerous small turnouts along the Park Road. Denali is first visible about Mile 10 (weather permitting).

Cell phone service stopped working here for The MILEPOST® field editor.

J 7.3 Paved turnout to south.

Watch out for dog walkers eastbound to Mile 3.4.

J 10.2 Paved turnout to north.

J 10.7 Paved turnout to south with mountain view.

J 11.9 Paved turnout to south with interpretive sign.

J 12.8 Mountain Vista rest area to south; parking, restrooms, picnic areas, walking trails. This is a great stop for motorists, with plenty of parking that also accommodates RVs. The Mountain Vista Loop, rated easy, leads a short distance to a picnic area and mountain view and has interpretive signage. A short connecting trail leads to Savage River Campground. This rest area is also the trailhead for the longer Savage Alpine Trail to the Savage River (4 miles). Bus stop.

J 12.9 Savage River Campground (elev. 2,780 feet); 32 campsites (8-person max. per site); 3 group tent sites (9–20 people/site); reservations required. $24–$30 per night, $46 group site fee per night.

J 13.1 Savage Cabin Trailhead; parking, outhouses, litter bins. This ¼-mile interpretive loop trail is wheelchair accessible.

J 14.4 Paved turnout to south with vista of Savage River.

J 14.9 Turnoff for parking and trailhead for the Savage Alpine Trail; picnic tables by river, outhouse, litter and recycling bins, limited parking (not recommended for RVs). The Savage Alpine Trail is a strenuous day hike with walk through spruce and cottonwood, up alpine meadows and across a high alpine pass in rock fields. Considered moderate to difficult (it climbs 1,500 feet in 2 miles).

J 15 Bridge over the Savage River. Pavement ends, gravel begins, westbound.

Savage River check station west side of bridge. Permit or shuttle bus ticket required beyond this point. *Road travel permits for motorists with campsite reservations at Teklanika River Campground are issued at the Denali Visitor Center. In early May and late September, the road may be open to all vehicles to Mile 30 (weather permitting).*

J 17.3 Primrose Ridge. Viewpoint of the Alaska Range with restrooms.

J 21.3 Hogan Creek bridge (unmarked)

J 22.6 Sanctuary Campground (elev. 2,468 feet); 7 tent sites, $15 per night. Reserve in person at the WAC or Riley Creek Mercantile no more than 2 days in advance.

J 22.7 Sanctuary River bridge, elev. 2,940 feet. Look for wolves crossing riverbed.

J 29.1 Teklanika River Campground (elev. 2,580 feet); 53 tent/RV sites; camping fee $25 per night; no trailers or towed vehicles except for 5th wheels. There is no sani-dump here but there is a water filling station. Online reservation requires 3-night minimum; to reserve shorter stay, phone 1-866-761-6629.

J 30.2 Teklanika rest area with vault toilets and viewing deck overlooking Teklanika River.

J 31.2 Bridge over Teklanika River. Wolves may be seen crossing this riverbed.

J 34 Igloo Creek Campground (tent camping only), 7 walk-in sites, camping fee

$15/night, vault toilets, water taken from creek. Reserve in-person 2 days in advance at the WAC. Igloo Creek bridge. Grizzlies are often seen in the area.

J 37.2 Views of Cathedral Mountain to south, Igloo Mountain to north.

NOTE: The area within 1 mile of each side of the Park Road from Milepost J 38.3 to J 42.9 is closed to all off-road foot travel as a special wildlife protection area. These closures vary from year to year, place to place. Watch for signs.

J 39.1 Sable Pass (elev. 3,900 feet).

J 43.4 Bridge over East Fork River, elev. 3,055. Views of Polychrome Mountain, the Alaska Range and several glaciers are visible along the East Fork from open country south of the road.

J 45.9 Summit of **Polychrome Pass** (elev. 3,700 feet); rest stop. The broad valley of the Toklat River is visible below to the south. Good hiking in alpine tundra above the road.

J 47 Wide valley views.

J 53.1 Bridge over the Toklat River. The Toklat and all other rivers crossed by the Park Road drain into the Tanana River, a tributary of the Yukon River.

J 53.4 Toklat River rest area; bookstore, vault toilets, viewing telescopes.

J 58.3 Summit of **Highway Pass** (elev. 3,980 feet). This is the highest point on the Park Road.

J 61 Stony Hill Overlook (elev. 3,890 feet). This is the most photographed view of Denali and the Alaska Range on clear days.

J 62 Viewpoint.

J 64.5 Thorofare Pass (elev. 3,950 feet).

J 66 Eielson Visitor Center has an energy efficient design, with solar panels and microhydroelectric generator. Excellent Denali viewpoint. On clear days the north and south peaks of Denali are visible to the southwest. The impressive glacier, which drops from the mountain and spreads out over the valley floor at this point, is the Muldrow.

For several miles beyond the visitor center the road cut drops about 300 feet to the valley, paralleling the McKinley River.

J 84.4 Access road leads left, westbound, to **Wonder Lake Campground** (elev. 2,090 feet); 28 tent sites, $16 per site; campground access by shuttle bus only. An excellent Denali viewpoint. This is the closest the Park Road gets to Denali: You are now within 27 miles of North America's highest peak.

J 85.2 Reflection Pond, a kettle lake formed by a glacier.

J 86.5 Wonder Lake ranger station.

J 89 Moose Creek bridge. North Face Lodge and Camp Denali; accommodations, meals and activities.

J 91 KANTISHNA (pop. 110 in summer, 0 in winter; elev. 1,750 feet). Established in 1905 as a mining camp at the junction of Eureka and Moose creeks. Some of the area around Kantishna is private property and there may be active mining on area creeks in summer. Kantishna Roadhouse (www.kantishnaroadhouse.com), a full-service backcountry lodge, is located here.

Private Aircraft: Kantishna airstrip, 1.3 miles northwest; elev. 1,575 feet; length 1,850 feet; gravel; unattended, no regular maintenance.

J 92 Denali Backcountry Lodge, at end of Park Road; accommodations, meals and activities.

Richardson Highway

CONNECTS: Valdez to Fairbanks, AK

Length: 366 miles   **Road Surface:** Paved   **Season:** Open all year

(See maps, pages 438–439)

4

Motorcyclists stop for a break and a photo at one of the many beautiful turnouts along this route. (©Sharon Nault)

Major Attractions:

© Kris Valencia, staff

Trans-Alaska Pipeline, Worthington & Gulkana Glaciers, Rika's Roadhouse

Highest Summit:
Isabel Pass 3,280 ft.

The Richardson Highway extends 366 miles from Valdez on Prince William Sound to Fairbanks in the Interior of Alaska. This is an exceptionally beautiful route—much of the highway is designated an Alaska Scenic Byway—with magnificent views of the Chugach Mountains and Alaska Range, and some of the best glacier viewing in Alaska. Popular Worthington Glacier State Recreation Site has a trail that leads to the Worthington glacier.

The Richardson is a wide, paved, mostly 2-lane highway in fair to good condition, with some long sections of frost heaves and patched pavement. Updated road conditions are available online at 511.alaska.gov or by dialing 511.

The Richardson Highway (Alaska Route 4) junctions with 7 other highways: the Edgerton Highway (Alaska Route 10) at **Milepost V 82.5**; the Glenn Highway (Alaska Route 1) at **Milepost V 115** at Glennallen; the Tok Cut-Off (Alaska Route 1) at **Milepost V 128.5** Gakona Junction; the Denali Highway (Alaska Route 8) at **Milepost V 185.5** at Paxson; the Alaska Highway (Alaska Route 2) at **Milepost V 266**, Delta Junction (where the Richardson Highway becomes Alaska Route 2 between Delta Junction and Fairbanks); and with the Parks Highway (Alaska Route 3) and the Steese Expressway/Steese Highway (Alaska Routes 2/6) at its end in Fairbanks.

In Valdez, the Richardson Highway junctions with the Alaska Marine Highway's southcentral ferry system. Ferry service to Cordova and Whittier is available from Valdez; see the heading "Ferry Travel" in the TRAVEL PLANNING section.

The Richardson Highway offers good views of the trans-Alaska pipeline. The trans-Alaska pipeline carries oil 800 miles from Prudhoe Bay on the Arctic Ocean to the pipeline terminus at Port Valdez. There are formal viewpoints with information boards at **Milepost V 215.9** (Denali Fault), **Milepost V 243.5**, and the Tanana River Pipeline Crossing at **Milepost V 275.5**.

The Richardson Highway was Alaska's first road, known to gold seekers in 1898 as the Valdez to Eagle Trail. Gold stamped-

Distance in miles	Delta Jct.	Fairbanks	Glennallen	Paxson	Valdez
Delta Jct.		96	151	80	270
Fairbanks	96		247	177	366
Glennallen	151	247		71	119
Paxson	80	177	71		190
Valdez	270	366	119	190	

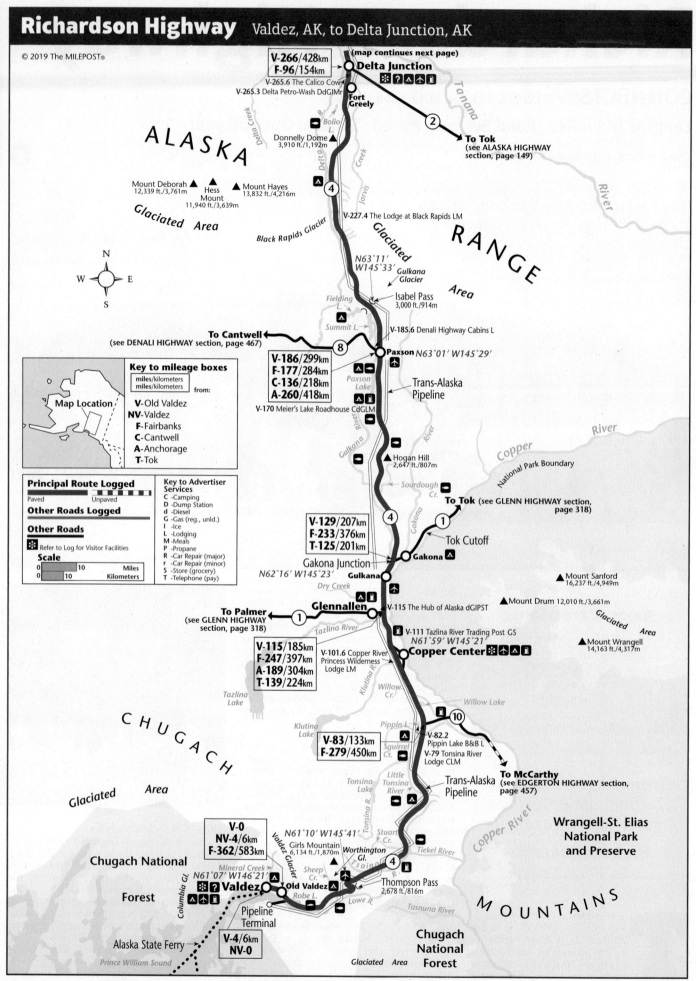

Richardson Highway Valdez, AK, to Delta Junction, AK

© 2019 The MILEPOST®

V-266/428km
F-96/154km

(map continues next page)

Delta Junction
V-265.6 The Calico Cow
V-265.3 Delta Petro-Wash DdGIMr
Fort Greely

A L A S K A

Delta Creek

Bolio L.

Donnelly Dome 3,910 ft./1,192m

2

4

To Tok
(see ALASKA HIGHWAY section, page 149)

Mount Deborah 12,339 ft./3,761m
Hess Mount 11,940 ft./3,639m
Mount Hayes 13,832 ft./4,216m

Jarvis Creek

Delta R.

River

Glaciated Area

V-227.4 The Lodge at Black Rapids LM

Black Rapids Glacier

Glaciated

R A N G E

N63°11' W145°33'
Gulkana Glacier

Isabel Pass 3,000 ft./914m

Fielding L.

Summit L.

V-185.6 Denali Highway Cabins L

To Cantwell
(see DENALI HIGHWAY section, page 467)

8

V-186/299km
F-177/284km
C-136/218km
A-260/418km

Paxson N63°01' W145°29'

Trans-Alaska Pipeline

Paxson Lake

V-170 Meier's Lake Roadhouse CdGLM

Area

River

Copper River

National Park Boundary

Hogan Hill 2,647 ft./807m

Sourdough Cr.

Gakona River

To Tok (see GLENN HIGHWAY section, page 318)

4

1

V-129/207km
F-233/376km
T-125/201km

Tok Cutoff

Gakona Junction
N62°16' W145°23'

Gakona

Gulkana

Mount Sanford 16,237 ft./4,949m

Mount Drum 12,010 ft./3,661m

Dry Creek

Glennallen
V-115 The Hub of Alaska dGIPST

Glaciated Area

To Palmer
(see GLENN HIGHWAY section, page 318)

1

Tazlina River

V-111 Tazlina River Trading Post GS
N61°59' W145°21'

Mount Wrangell 14,163 ft./4,317m

V-115/185km
F-247/397km
A-189/304km
T-139/224km

V-101.6 Copper River Princess Wilderness Lodge LM

Copper Center

Tazlina Lake

Klutina R.

Willow Cr.

Willow Lake

Klutina Lake

Pippin L.

10

C H U G A C H

Squirrel Cr.

V-82.2 Pippin Lake B&B L
V-79 Tonsina River Lodge CLM

V-83/133km
F-279/450km

To McCarthy
(see EDGERTON HIGHWAY section, page 457)

Little Tonsina River

Trans-Alaska Pipeline

Tonsina Lake

Tonsina R.

Wrangell-St. Elias National Park and Preserve

Glaciated   Area

N61°10' W145°41'

V-0
NV-4/6km
F-362/583km

Girls Mountain 6,134 ft./1,870m

Stuart Cr.

Copper River

Chugach National

Valdez Glacier

Mineral Creek

Worthington Gl.

Sheep Cr.

Tiekel River

4

N61°07' W146°21'
Valdez

Old Valdez

Robe L.

Lowe R.

Thompson Pass 2,678 ft./816m

Tasnuna River

M O U N T A I N S

Forest

Pipeline Terminal

Chugach National Forest

Alaska State Ferry

V-4/6km
NV-0

Columbia Gl.

Prince William Sound

Glaciated   Area

Key to mileage boxes

miles/kilometers
miles/kilometers   from:

V-Old Valdez
NV-Valdez
F-Fairbanks
C-Cantwell
A-Anchorage
T-Tok

Map Location

Principal Route Logged
Paved   Unpaved

Other Roads Logged

Other Roads

Refer to Log for Visitor Facilities

Scale
0   10   Miles
0   10   Kilometers

Key to Advertiser Services
C -Camping
D -Dump Station
d -Diesel
G -Gas (reg., unld.)
I -Ice
L -Lodging
M -Meals
P -Propane
R -Car Repair (major)
r -Car Repair (minor)
S -Store (grocery)
T -Telephone (pay)

Richardson Highway   Delta Junction, AK to Fairbanks, AK

© 2019 The MILEPOST®

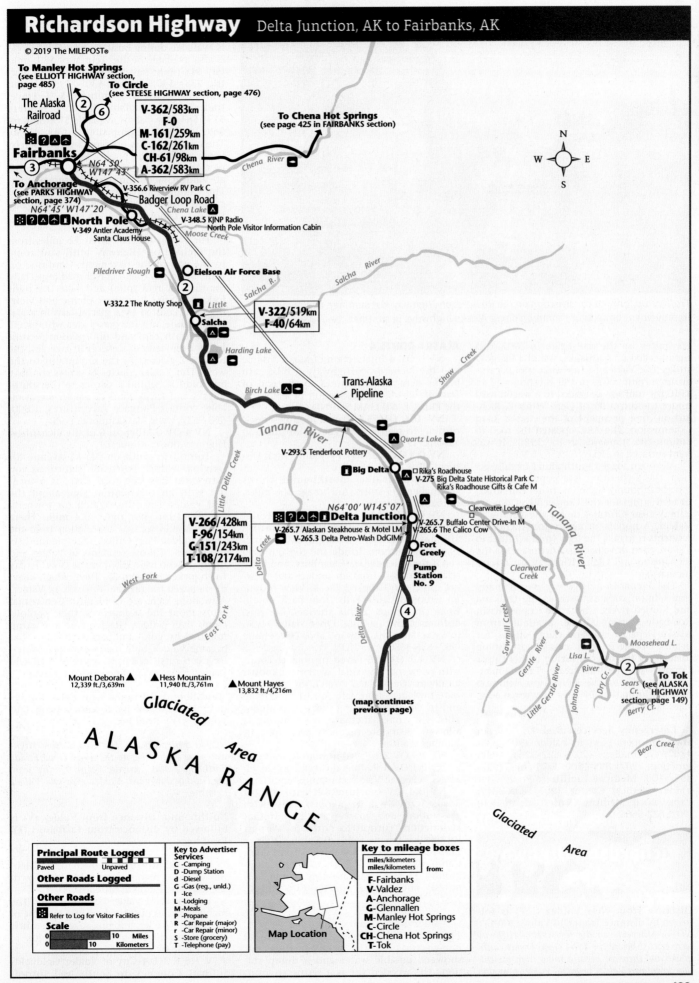

To Manley Hot Springs
(see ELLIOTT HIGHWAY section, page 485)

To Circle
(see STEESE HIGHWAY section, page 476)

The Alaska Railroad

To Chena Hot Springs
(see page 425 in FAIRBANKS section)

```
V-362/583km
F-0
M-161/259km
C-162/261km
CH-61/98km
A-362/583km
```

Chena River

Fairbanks

N64°50'
W147°43'

To Anchorage
(see PARKS HIGHWAY section, page 374)

N64°45' W147°20'

North Pole

V-356.6 Riverview RV Park C
Badger Loop Road
Chena Lake

V-348.5 KJNP Radio
North Pole Visitor Information Cabin

V-349 Antler Academy
Santa Claus House

Moose Creek

Piledriver Slough

Eielson Air Force Base

V-332.2 The Knotty Shop

Little Salcha R.

Salcha

Salcha River

```
V-322/519km
F-40/64km
```

Harding Lake

Birch Lake

Trans-Alaska Pipeline

Tanana River

Shaw Creek

V-293.5 Tenderfoot Pottery

Quartz Lake

Big Delta

Rika's Roadhouse
V-275 Big Delta State Historical Park C
Rika's Roadhouse Gifts & Cafe M

N64°00' W145°07'

Delta Junction

Clearwater Lodge CM

```
V-266/428km
F-96/154km
G-151/243km
T-108/2174km
```

V-265.7 Alaskan Steakhouse & Motel LM
V-265.3 Delta Petro-Wash DdGlMr

V-265.7 Buffalo Center Drive-In M
V-265.6 The Calico Cow

Fort Greely

Pump Station No. 9

Tanana River

Clearwater Creek

Little Delta Creek

Delta River

West Fork

East Fork

Sowmill Creek

Gerstle River

Little Gerstle River

Johnson River

Dry Cr.

Lisa L.

Moosehead L.

To Tok
(see ALASKA HIGHWAY section, page 149)

Sears Cr.

Berry Cr.

Bear Creek

Mount Deborah ▲
12,339 ft./3,639m

▲ Hess Mountain
11,940 ft./3,761m

▲ Mount Hayes
13,832 ft./4,216m

(map continues previous page)

Glaciated Area

ALASKA RANGE

Glaciated Area

Key / Legend

Principal Route Logged
Paved   Unpaved

Other Roads Logged

Other Roads

Refer to Log for Visitor Facilities

Scale
0   10 Miles
0   10 Kilometers

Key to Advertiser Services
C -Camping
D -Dump Station
d -Diesel
G -Gas (reg., unld.)
I -Ice
L -Lodging
M -Meals
P -Propane
R -Car Repair (major)
r -Car Repair (minor)
S -Store (grocery)
T -Telephone (pay)

Key to mileage boxes
miles/kilometers
miles/kilometers   from:
F-Fairbanks
V-Valdez
A-Anchorage
G-Glennallen
M-Manley Hot Springs
C-Circle
CH-Chena Hot Springs
T-Tok

Map Location

Traffic stop for road construction on the Richardson Highway last summer. Highway improvement projects are common along Alaska highways in summer. (©Kris Valencia, staff)

ers started up the trail again in 1902, this time headed for Fairbanks, site of a big gold strike. The Valdez to Fairbanks trail became an important route to the Interior, and in 1910 the trail was upgraded to a wagon road under the direction of Gen. Wilds P. Richardson, first president of the Alaska Road Commission. The ARC updated the road to automobile standards in the 1920s. It was hard-surfaced in 1957.

Although logged northbound in this section, the Richardson is a popular corridor for southbound travelers from Fairbanks, headed either for the Copper River dip-net fishery near Chitina, or for the fishing at Valdez. A popular itinerary for Anchorage residents is to take the ferry from Whittier to Valdez, then drive back to Anchorage via the Richardson and Glenn Highway (or reverse itinerary).

The Richardson Highway passes many fine salmon streams, such as the Gulkana and Klutina rivers. Check the Copper Basin Roadside Fishing Guide, available from Alaska Dept. of Fish and Game offices, for details. On the internet, check sport fishing updates for the Interior region (either Upper Copper/Upper Susitna Area or Tanana management areas for the Richardson Highway) under Information By Area at www.sf.adfg. state.ak.us/statewide/sf_home.cfm.

Emergency Services: Dial 911. **Alaska State Troopers** posts in Valdez, (907) 835-4307; Glennallen, (907) 822-3263; Delta Junction, (907) 895-4800; Fairbanks, (907) 451-5100. **Medical Facilities:** Providence Valdez Medical Center, (907) 835-2249; Cross Road Medical Center Glennallen, (907) 822-5686.

Richardson Highway Log

Distance from New Valdez (NV) is followed by distance from Old Valdez (OV).
NOTE: Mileposts on the Richardson Highway were erected before the 1964 Good Friday earthquake and therefore begin 4 miles from present-day downtown Valdez near Old Valdez townsite.

ALASKA ROUTE 4

NV 0 OV 4 Intersection of Meals Avenue and the Richardson Highway. A bike path begins here and continues to the end of Dayville Road. See description of Valdez in the PRINCE WILLIAM SOUND section.

NV 0.4 OV 3.6 Paved double-ended turnout to north with Valdez information gazebo.

NV 0.5 OV 3.5 DOT/PF Southcentral District Office.

Distance marker northbound shows Glennallen 117 miles, Anchorage 306 miles, Fairbanks 355 miles.

NV 0.9 OV 3.1 Chugach National Forest Service's **Crooked Creek Information Site** has an outside viewing deck to watch spawning salmon. Inside the log building you'll find friendly staff, exhibits, and a TV relaying images from an underwater viewing camera in Crooked Creek. View beautiful Crooked Creek Falls from back porch. Great photo ops. Picnic shelters, fire pits, outhouses and parking. Open daily 9 A.M. to 6 P.M. Memorial Day to Labor Day. Phone (907) 835-4680. *CAUTION: Watch for bears!*

NV 1.2 OV 2.8 Paved turnout to south with view of intertidal wetlands known locally as "Duck Flats." Watch for migrating waterfowl here from late April to mid-May and in October. Nesting birds in summer. This is a game sanctuary; no shooting is allowed. Bears are regularly seen here in summer months.

NV 1.9 OV 2.1 Paved turnout to south.

NV 2.1 OV 1.9 Mineral Creek Loop Road; access to Port of Valdez container terminal.

NV 3.4 OV 0.6 Junction with Airport Road; **Acres Kwik Trip** (open daily) with gas station, deli, market and laundromat at junction. Turnoff to north for Airport Park/Senior League Field (0.8 mile); **Valdez Pioneer Airport** and Valdez Airport Man Camp (0.9 mile); Valdez Glacier Campground (2.3 miles); shooting range (2.6 miles); and Valdez Glacier (3.6 miles). Descriptions follow.

Valdez Glacier Campground has 94 sites, 11 with 20/30/50 amp electric pads and 10 non-electric pads. The facility provides hot showers, potable water and a dump station. The wooded site is a serine environ-

ment with fire pits, grills, dumpsters, and covered picnic areas. There are 73 standard tent camping sites and a campground host is available during business hours. Firewood is also available onsite. Tent sites $20, military $15 (must have I.D.); RV pad with electric $35 – $40, military $30 - $35, RV pad without electric $25, military $20. Travel trailer rentals available $89–$94, military $79– $84. Dry Cabins available $79, military $69. Pavilion camping site starting at $50. The campground is operated by Fort Greely, but is open to the public. Reservations can be made by calling (907) 873-4795 or online at ValdezGlacierCampground@gmail.com. The campground host can be reached by calling (907) 297-8524. Open Memorial Day through Labor Day. *CAUTION: Beware of bears, and watch for eagles!*

For Valdez Glacier, drive 3.6 miles from the Richardson Highway until you come to the end of the pavement. Continue on wide, but often rough gravel road (especially for the last half mile) and take the right fork to Glacier View Park picnic and viewing area. Located by a glacial lake in a glacial moraine, this is a grassy area with picnic tables, trash cans and information boards. Interesting views of icebergs in lake and the tops of 2 glaciers in the mountains to the west. The Valdez glacier is across the lake and hidden behind a corner to the south. Kayaks and kayak tours to glacier are available; contact **Pangaea Adventures**, 1-800-660-9637, www.AlaskaSummer.com.

NV 4 OV 0 Milepost 0 of the Richardson Highway (log continues).

Turnoff to south on Alaska Avenue for **Original Valdez Townsite** (signed) as you turn onto this side road there is a turnout with an information sign about the Old Valdez Townsite. Watch for townsite memorial on your right, 0.4 mile. There are 2 plaques set in a foundation from the "old" Valdez Post Office. One plaque lists the names of those residents of Valdez and Chenega who were killed in the Good Friday Earthquake on March 27, 1964, which heavily damaged the original townsite of Valdez. Also along here are Gold Rush Centennial signs about the stampeders, their perilous climb over Valdez Glacier, and the camp founded by gold stampeders in 1897 that became Valdez. Side road continues (watch for deep ruts) to empty waterfront of Old Valdez; views of pipeline marine terminal.

Southbound: Distance from New Valdez (NV) is followed by distance from Old Valdez (OV). Read log:

NOTE: Mileposts on the Richardson Highway were erected before the 1964 Good Friday Earthquake and therefore begin 4 miles from present-day downtown Valdez near Old Valdez townsite.

Northbound: Distance from Valdez (V) is followed by distance from Fairbanks (F). Read log:

V 0 F 362 Mile 0 of the Richardson Highway at access road to Original Valdez Townsite (see description at **Milepost NV 4**).

V 0.9 F 361.1 Valdez Glacier Stream. The highway passes over the terminal moraine of the Valdez Glacier, bridging several channels and streams flowing from the melting ice.

V 1 F 361 Physical Milepost 1.

V 1.6 F 360.4 City of Valdez Goldfields Softball Complex to south and turnoff for local swimming hole and Early Valdez Cemetery (signed). For cemetery, follow well-maintained Walter Day Memorial Drive (gravel) south 0.6 mile; turn right on narrow, rocky access road (signed Pioneer Cemetery) and continue 0.2 mile to cemetery. Graves date from 1897 to 1916; information boards. There is a firepit gathering place with picnic tables at the entrance.

V 1.7 F 360.3 Ball parks and playground.

V 2 F 360 Valdez KOA (formerly Bear Creek Cabins & RV Park). Cabins and full-service RV sites; laundry, dump station and other amenities. Phone (907) 835-2723. ⬛A

V 2.4 F 359.6 Valdez Memorial Cemetery to south along a loop road.

V 2.6 F 359.4 Double-ended paved turnout to south.

V 2.8 F 359.2 Turnoff to south for popular **Dayville Road**, an excellent option for RVers and fishermen. This is a wide, paved, improved side road (with bike trail) that leads to shoreside camping at Allison Point, picnicking, fishing and scenic views along Port Valdez, the 13-mile-long estuary at the head of Valdez Arm. Look for seals, sea lions, birds and bears (especially when salmon are spawning). Berry picking in season. *CAUTION: Watch for bears.*

Dayville Road is open to the public to Mile 5.4, where a guardhouse restricts public access to the Alyeska Pipeline Terminal complex. *NOTE: There is NO public access to the marine terminal and there are NO public tours of the terminal.* The Solomon Gulch Fish Hatchery and large parking area are located at Mile 3.8. There are some dramatic views and photo opportunities from the bridge here of the Solomon Gulch Falls and dam site (Copper Valley Electric cogeneration project). The hatchery is open daily throughout summer and visitors can take self-guided walking tours outside the hatchery to a viewing platform and along the ponds and hatchery building. Mile 4.5 marks the beginning of camping areas (with water, bear proof dumpsters, outhouses). There is a wonderful array of wildlife viewing opportunities, steps away from your campsite. RV camping (52 sites) $20, walk-in tent sites $15 and day-use fees charged (main campground registration area is at Mile 5). At Mile 4.7 is the trailhead for John Hunter Memorial Trail. Trail begins with steep climb up hill to the east of the road. Pink and coho salmon fishing from shore in season at **Allison Point** at Mile 4.8. Handicapped fishing platform is located here. *CAUTION: Watch for bears!* ⬛⬛

V 3 F 359 Weigh station to south (closed).

V 3.3 F 358.7 Rough, paved side road leads 0.5 mile north to **Robe Lake**; parking and boat launch area at lake. Robe Lake is popular with jet skiers. Salmon fishing in season. *CAUTION: Watch for bears!* ⬛

V 4 F 358 Long gravel turnout to southeast along **Lowe River**; Dolly Varden, sockeye salmon (fly-fishing only, mid-May to mid-June). ⬛

V 5.1 F 356.9 Salmonberry Ski Hill to north.

V 6 F 356 Cummings Way north for Robe Lake.

V 8 F 354 Watch for horses on the road.

V 9.3 F 352.7 Signed: Emil Wegner Memorial Corridor (in honor of a local long-

Keystone Canyon photo ops include Bridal Veil Falls (seen here) and nearby Horsetail Falls.
(©Milton & Kelley Barker, staff)

time mail carrier), "headlights on for safety."

V 11.6 F 350.4 Paved turnout to southeast. Avalanche gates. Road closures are not uncommon here in winter. In December 2017, 76 inches of snow fell during 5 days and then was topped by 45 inches of snowfall in Thompson Pass in one night; all of this caused an avalanche that closed the highway between **Milepost V 12** and **V 55** for several days. Until the road was cleared completely, the only access to Valdez was by ferry or by plane.

V 11.8 F 350.2 Turnoff to west for Pack Trail of 1899. Paved 0.7-mile loop road to access trail. Loop road leads to creek and small turnout at 0.3 mile and trailhead at 0.4 mile; parking best at north end of loop at **Milepost V 12.4.**

V 12.8 F 349.2 Lowe River emerges from **Keystone Canyon**. The canyon was named by Captain William Ralph Abercrombie, presumably for Pennsylvania, the Keystone State. In 1884, Abercrombie had been selected to lead an exploring expedition up the Copper River to the Yukon River. Although unsuccessful in his attempt to ascend the Copper River, he did survey the Copper River Delta and a route to Port Valdez. He returned in 1898 and again in 1899, carrying out further explorations of the area (see **Milepost V 13.9**). The Lowe River is named for Lt. Percival Lowe, a member of his expedition. Glacier melt imparts the slate-gray color to the river.

V 13.5 F 348.5 Horsetail Falls; large paved turnout to west.

CAUTION: Watch for pedestrians.

V 13.9 F 348.1 Large paved turnout to west across from **Bridal Veil Falls**.

This is also the trailhead for the **Valdez Goat Trail** (begins near the south end of turnout to west); hike to scenic overlook (¼ mile), trail end is 2 miles. This is a restored section of the Trans-Alaska Military Pack-train Trail through Keystone Canyon that led to the first glacier-free land route from Valdez to the Interior. The first gold rush trail led over the treacherous Valdez Glacier, then northeast to Eagle and the Yukon River route to the Klondike goldfields. Captain W.R. Abercrombie and the U.S. Army Copper River Exploring Expedition of 1899

rerouted the trail through Keystone Canyon and over Thompson Pass, thus avoiding the glacier.

As the Klondike Gold Rush waned, the military kept the trail open to connect Fort Liscum in Valdez with Fort Egbert in Eagle. In 1903, the U.S. Army Signal Corps laid the trans-Alaska telegraph line along this route.

V 14.9 F 347.1 Lowe River bridge No. 1 (first of 3 bridges northbound); turnout to east at north end of bridge. View of Huddleston Falls.

V 15 F 347 Large paved turnout at **Old Railroad Tunnel** with sign that reads:

"This tunnel was hand cut into the solid rock of Keystone Canyon and is all that is left of the railroad era when 9 companies fought to take advantage of the short route from the coast to the copper country. However, a feud interrupted progress. A gun battle was fought and the tunnel was never finished. The Iron Trail by Rex Beach describes these events and this area."

NOTE: You can walk into this tunnel.

V 15.3 F 346.7 Turnout to east at south end of Lowe River bridge No. 2. Horse and Sled Trail (sign) reads:

"On the far side, just above the water, are the remains of the old sled trail used in the early days. It was cut out of the rock, just wide enough for 2 horses abreast. 200 feet above can be seen the old goat trail. This road was used until 1945."

V 15.4 F 346.6 Two bridges make up what is called Lowe River bridges No. 2, built in 1980, replaced previous highway route through the long tunnel visible beside highway.

V 15.6 F 346.4 Sloping entrance to informal gravel turnout to east.

V 15.7 F 346.3 Leaving Keystone Canyon northbound, entering Keystone Canyon southbound.

V 16 F 346 Turnout down off the road to rock quarry to east.

V 16.3 F 345.7 Lowe River bridge No. 3.

V 16.4 F 345.6 Turnout to southeast.

V 18.1 F 343.9 Large paved turnouts both sides of highway; *emergency phone* and trailhead at turnout to west. Good stop for northbound travelers before heading up the long grade to Thompson Pass. Welcome to Valdez sign, southbound.

V 18.6 F 343.4 Sheep Creek bridge.

V 18.8 F 343.2 *Gates here are used for road*

This photo of Worthington Glacier was taken in summer 2009. Compare it to today's view of the glacier and see if you notice any recession in the last 10 years. (©Sharon Nault)

closures. *Truck lane begins northbound as highway climbs next 7.5 miles to Thompson Pass; few turnouts, steep grade. Narrow outside lane northbound, hemmed in by guardrail, makes for a really tight squeeze when big rigs are passing. Large vehicles USE CAUTION when passing.*

This was one of the most difficult sections of pipeline construction, requiring heavy blasting of solid rock for several miles. The pipeline runs underground.

V 18.9 F 343.1 Paved turnout to east at Heiden View. Beautiful mountain view. Do not block pipeline road access.

V 19.6 F 342.4 Sign: access to trail of '98.

V 21.5 F 340.5 Large paved turnout to east with scenic view.

V 22.3 F 339.7 Snow poles along highway guide snow plows in winter.

V 23 F 339 Large wide gravel parking area east side of highway.

V 23.4 F 338.6 Paved turnout to east. Photo of mountains and glaciers.

V 23.5 F 338.5 Access to **Thompson Lake** (formerly Summit Lake No. 1) to west makes a nice stop; parking area and lake access, grayling and rainbow trout fishing.

V 23.7 F 338.3 Paved turnout to east.

V 24.1 F 337.9 Paved road leads south 0.8 mile to **Blueberry Lake State Recreation Site**; 25 campsites, 4 picnic shelters, 25 picnic sites, (lakeshore area sites with covered picnic tables), toilets, firepits, water, no RV size limit, camping fee $20/night, 15 day camping limit, campground host. Firewood is sometimes available. Tucked into an alpine setting between tall mountain peaks, this is one of Alaska's most beautifully situated campgrounds. Access trail beside campsite #9 for a hike up above the brush to alpine terrain; beautiful 360° views. Berry picking in season. Blueberry Lake offers grayling and rainbow trout fishing.

V 24.4 F 337.6 Large paved turnout to west.

V 25.5 F 336.5 Large paved turnout to west. Rough access road out to promontory; terrific view of Lowe River far in the valley below. Great place to stretch your legs and get top-of-the-world views. Bare-bone peaks of the Chugach Mountains rise above the highway. Thompson Pass ahead northbound.

Marshall Pass is to the east. During the winter of 1907, the A.J. Meals Co. freighted the 70-ton river steamer *Chitina* (or *Chittyna*) from Valdez over Marshall Pass and down the Tasnuna River to the Copper River. The ship was moved piece by piece on huge horse-drawn freight sleds and assembled at the mouth of the Tasnuna. The 110-foot-long ship navigated 170 miles of the Copper and Chitina rivers above Abercrombie Rapids, moving supplies for construction crews of the Copper River & Northwestern Railway. Much of the equipment for the Kennecott mill and tram was moved by this vessel.

V 25.7 F 336.3 Excellent 2-level viewpoint parking area to south. Lower level has very steep entrance. You can walk down to the lower level for a great view of the mountains and Lowe River valley far below. Artists often come here to paint this scene. Access to Trail of '98.

V 25.9 F 336.1 Thompson Pass (elev. 2,678 feet) at head of Ptarmigan Creek. Beautiful alpine area. End northbound truck lane. Begin 7.5-mile steep descent southbound.

Thompson Pass, named by Captain Abercrombie in 1899, is comparatively low elevation but above timberline. Wildflower lovers will be well repaid for rambling over the rocks in this area: tiny alpine plants may be in bloom, such as Aleutian heather and mountain harebell.

The National Climatic Center credits snowfall extremes in Alaska to the Thompson Pass station, where record measurements are: 974.5 inches for season (1952–53); 298 inches for month (February 1953); and 62 inches for 24-hour period (December 1955). Snow poles along the highway mark the road edge for snow plows.

Private Aircraft: Thompson Pass airstrip; elev. 2,080 feet; length 2,500 feet; turf, gravel; unattended.

V 26 F 336 Paved turnout to east. Good views of 27 Mile Glacier to north.
Slow for damaged road.

V 26.8 F 335.2 Thompson Pass highway maintenance station, phone (907) 835-5363; closed in summer by budget cuts.

V 27.5 F 334.5 Entrance to parking area to east overlooking **Worthington Lake**; rainbow trout fishing.

V 28.9 F 333.1 Parking to north by stream.

V 29 F 333 Worthington Glacier State Recreation Site. The entrance to the glacier is about 0.3 mile south of physical milepost 29. There is a paved parking area on the Richardson Highway at the entrance road and next to this a paved access road which leads 0.4 mile up hill to large paved parking area (pull-through sites for large vehicles), shelter, viewing telescopes, information boards and restrooms. (Pay phone at a rest area with information boards, located near highway entrance.) No camping. Pets on leash. Gold Rush Centennial sign about Thompson Pass at bottom of hill near highway.

According to state park rangers, this is the most visited site in the Copper River Basin. Views of Worthington Glacier, which heads on Girls Mountain (elev. 6,134 feet), from the parking area and from paved path which leads to glacier viewpoints with benches and information boards. This is a National Natural Landmark. *WARNING: Do not approach any glacier from below due to falling ice and rock. Do not walk on any glacier unless you are experienced in and equipped for crevasse rescues. Trail closures may occur due to unstable glacial ice.*

V 29.1 F 332.9 Paved parking area to west; good photo op of Worthington Glacier. Great blueberry picking in the fall.

V 30.1 F 331.9 Large paved turnouts both sides of highway. Excellent spot for photos of Worthington Glacier.

V 32.4 F 329.6 Highway parallels Tsaina River northbound. Long climb up to Thompson Pass for southbound motorists; views of Worthington Glacier.

V 34.5 F 327.5 Double-ended turnout to west. Tsaina Lodge to east.

The mountains in this area are the site for many winter activities like extreme skiing. Helicopter businesses offer backcountry adventures and tours.

V 35 F 327 Improved highway southbound to **Milepost V 24** in summer 2018.

V 37 F 325 Entering BLM public lands northbound, leaving BLM public lands southbound.

V 37.3 F 324.7 Tsaina River bridge at scenic Devil's Elbow. Large paved turnout to east at south end of bridge. Deep gorge visible from each side of bridge.

V 37.8 F 324.2 *Begin avalanche area northbound: Do not stop (in winter).*

V 40.7 F 322.3 Large gravel turnout to west at crest of hill with beautiful mountain views close to river. Highway descends next 1.5 miles northbound.

V 42.1 F 319.9 Small gravel turnout to west.

V 43 F 319 Large double-ended turnout to west, sheltered by brush and a rock wall.

V 45.5 F 316.5 Stuart Creek bridge. Paved, large turnout north end of bridge.

V 45.6 F 316.4 Large paved and gravel turnout to the east. Rendezvous Lodge and tavern, heli-camp for winter sports (usually open February–March for heli-skiing and dinner).

V 45.7 F 316.3 Welcome to Copper River Valley (northbound sign).

V 46.8 F 315.2 Tiekel River bridge; small Dolly Varden. Small turnout to west at north end of bridge.

V 47.8 F 314.2 View of Mount Billy Mitchell directly ahead of entrance to large paved rest area to west. Drive to end of access road for loop road through treed area near Tiekel River. Outhouses, 4 covered picnic sites with room to pitch tents under and rock fire rings, no dumpsters or water. Historical sign about Mount Billy Mitchell. There is an old log cabin near this entrance.

Lieutenant William "Billy" Mitchell (1879–1936) was a member of the U.S. Army Signal Corps, which in 1903 completed the trans-Alaska telegraph line (Washington–Alaska Military Cable and Telegraph System) to connect all the military posts in Alaska. The 2,000 miles/3,200 km of telegraph wire included the main line between Fort Egbert in Eagle and Fort Liscum at Valdez, and a branch line down the Tanana River to Fort Gibson and on to Fort St. Michael near the mouth of the Yukon and then to Nome. Mitchell was years later to become the "prophet of American military air power" with his idea that "He who holds Alaska will hold the world as far as defending the North American continent." He received the Medal of Honor posthumously for his foresight.

V 50.4 F 311.6 Very small turnout to west.

V 50.6 F 311.4 Bridge over Tiekel River. Look for lupine in June, dwarf fireweed along the Tiekel River in July. Dead spruce trees in this area were killed by beetles. The old Tiekel River Lodge was northeast of here. There are private cabins in this area.

V 54.1 F 307.9 Large paved turnout to east.

V 54.5 F 307.5 *CAUTION: Watch for moose.*

V 55.1 F 306.9 Large paved/gravel turnout to east.

V 56 F 306 Tiekel River Lodge, closed summer 2018; current status unknown.

V 56.2 F 305.8 Large paved turnout to east alongside Tiekel River.

V 57 F 305 Southbound, the Emil Wegner Memorial Corridor is named for long-time local mail carrier. Watch for beaver dams.

V 60 F 302 Large paved turnout to east; access to Tiekel River. Highway parallels **Tiekel River**, visible to the east southbound; fishing for small Dolly Varden is especially fun with a fly rod.

V 61.6 F 300.4 This area used to be covered with moose ponds that were also home to numerous beavers. Heavy rainfall in 2009 flooded the area. Placer mining to the east.

V 62 F 300 Ernestine Station (DOT/PF highway maintenance) to west, phone (907) 822-3312.

V 62.2 F 299.8 Entering Upper Copper/Upper Susitna Sport Fish Management Area northbound.

V 63.6 F 298.4 Views of pipeline from highway to east; no turnouts.

V 64.6 F 297.4 Pump Station 12 to east; no public access. Begun in March 1975 and completed in 1977, pipeline construction employed some 30,000 workers at its peak and was the largest and most expensive privately funded construction project ever undertaken. These boom years, known as "pipeline days," also brought lasting changes

State recreation sites like Squirrel Creek typically offer basic campsites with tables and firepits as well as day-use areas for picnicking. (©Sharon Nault)

to Alaska's landscape and economy.

Today, the pipeline is owned and operated by Alyeska Pipeline Service Company, a consortium of oil companies that includes BP, ConocoPhillips, Exxon/Mobil and Unocal.

The 48-inch-diameter pipeline winds through 3 major mountain ranges, with its highest point (elev. 4,739 feet) at Atigun Pass in the Brooks Range, 170 miles south of Prudhoe Bay. Along the Richardson Highway, the pipeline crests the Alaska Range at (elev. 3,420 feet) Isabel Pass, before descending into the Copper River basin. It crosses the Chugach Mountains at Thompson Pass and descends through the Keystone Canyon to Valdez, where it is fed by gravity into tanks or directly into waiting oil tankers at the marine terminal.

V 65 F 297 Little Tonsina River; fishing for Dolly Varden and Arctic grayling (bait and treble hooks allowed). Fishing for chinook salmon is prohibited.

V 65.1 F 296.9 Unmarked road to the west. Former Little Tonsina River State Recreation Site to west on short loop road through pleasant wooded area; no services or facilities. Pull-in parking areas, good picnic spots. Day use only. Good berry picking in fall.

V 65.3 F 296.7 For weather information, turn to AM-790 on your radio. This area of highway has long stretches of gentle frost heaves and annoying rough expansion joints.

V 71 F 291 Paved/gravel double-ended turnout to east.

V 72 F 290 Double-ended paved and gravel turnout to west with view across valley of trans-Alaska pipeline following base of mountains.

Leaving BLM public lands northbound. Entering BLM public lands southbound.

CAUTION: Slow for frost heaves in highway.

V 73 F 289 Tonsina Controlled Use Area: Closed to motorized vehicles and pack animals, July 26 to Sept. 30.

V 74.4 F 287.6 Double-ended paved turnout to west is a beautiful place to stop and take a break. According to our ADF&G source, there is a side pipeline access road here, just past the turnout, that allows access

to the **Little Tonsina River** and its confluence with the **Tonsina River**. There is good fishing for Dolly Varden, grayling, sockeye and coho (mid-September to October). Fishing for chinook salmon is prohibited.

V 76.3 F 285.7 Watch for moose in pond to west.

V 79 F 283 Tonsina River Lodge to east. Open year-round. Closed Tuesdays in winter. Lodging, RV hookups, laundry, landing strip for small airplanes, bar and restaurant that specializes in Russian Cuisine.

Tonsina River Lodge. See display ad this page.

Distance marker northbound shows Copper Center 21 miles, Glennallen 36 miles.

V 79.2 F 282.8 Bridge over Tonsina River, which rises in Tonsina Lake to the southwest.

V 79.3 F 282.7 Paved turnout to east.

V 79.4 F 282.6 Squirrel Creek State Recreation Site to east at south end of Squirrel Creek bridge; 25 treed, pleasant, shaded campsites with tables and firepits on the bank of Squirrel Creek and near a pond. Some pull-through spaces suitable for large rigs with tow vehicles; camping fee $20 night; bear-proof trash cans, outhouses, potable water (Signed: boiling suggested) and firepits. Pets on leash. Day-use fee $7. Close to Tonsina River Lodge and the Ton-

Public fishing access to roadside lakes and streams is usually posted, as it is here at Pippin Lake, Milepost V 83. (©Sharon Nault)

sina River. Large turnaround area for big rigs at the end of campground road. Fishing for rainbow trout and grayling in pond, and grayling in creek. Fishing for sockeye and chinook salmon in Tonsina River (bait and treble hooks). Open May 15–Sept. 30.

V 79.5 F 282.5 Squirrel Creek.

V 79.7 F 282.3 Tonsina Hill northbound. Begin 1.2-mile passing lane and 8 percent upgrade northbound. Turnout to east at top of hill.

V 81 F 281 End passing lane northbound. Begin 8 percent downgrade southbound.

Distance marker southbound Valdez 81 miles.

V 82.2 F 279.8 Pippin Lake Bed and Breakfast. See display ad this page.

V 82.5 F 279.5 Junction with the Edgerton Highway to Chitina (33 miles) and end of McCarthy Road (92 miles) with access to Kennicott/McCarthy and Wrangell-St. Elias National Park. **Kenny Lake Mercantile & RV Park**, 7.2 miles east from here on the Edgerton Highway, has gas/diesel, propane and store.

Junction with the Edgerton Highway (Alaska Route 10) east to Chitina and McCarthy Road to Kennicott/McCarthy area. See EDGERTON HIGHWAY section on page 457 for log of that route.

V 82.6 F 279.4 Gift shop to west with snacks, Alaska Native crafts, fishing licenses and other items open Monday–Saturday 11 A.M. to 6 P.M.

V 83 F 279 Paved turnout to west; public fishing access to **Pippin Lake**. Stocked with rainbow trout.

V 83.7 F 278.3 Highway descends hill next 3 miles northbound.

V 87.7 F 274.3 Large paved double-ended turnout to east at scenic Willow Lake Viewpoint; viewing platforms with telescopes; information sign identifies peaks in the Wrangell Mountains to east. (There is no public access to this lake and has no fish.)

On a clear day this lake mirrors the Wrangell Mountains to the east, which lie within Wrangell–St. Elias National Park and Preserve. From left to right they are: Mount Drum, with the smaller Snider Peak on its south flank; Mount Sanford; Mount Wrangell, with the pyramid-shaped Mount Zanetti on its northwest flank; and Mount Blackburn. Gold Rush Centennial information board at turnout about copper mining in the Wrangell Mountains.

V 88.5 F 273.5 Alyeska Pipeline gravel loop road to parking area to west; pedestrian access to pipeline, information sign. Good photo op of pipeline.

V 90.8 F 271.2 Paved turnout to west by Willow Creek culvert.

V 91 F 271 Old Edgerton Highway access to Kenny Lake, east.

V 92.7 F 269.3 Grizzly Pizza restaurant.

V 100.2 F 261.8 South **junction** with **Old Richardson Highway** loop road through Copper Center; well worth a stop. Access to airstrip Mile 0.1, camping, lake tours, whitewater rafting, fishing charters, tackle, groceries, liquor and gas at Mile 0.5 on this loop. From Mile 0.5, turn on the inner Loop Road and go 0.4 mile for Old Town Copper Center Inn & Restaurant (food, beer/wine, lodging); garage and museum/visitor center in adjacent historic buildings.

See the "Copper Center Loop" feature on facing page for description of Copper Center and attractions along the Old Richardson Highway.

V 100.6 F 261.4 Gravel side road (Slemsec Way) east to private RV park.

V 101.1 F 260.9 Klutina River bridge. Access to river to the southeast of bridge, *poor turnaround area for big rigs.* Excellent fishing in the **Klutina River** for sockeye and chinook salmon. Also grayling and Dolly Varden. Chinook to 65 lbs., average 35-45 lbs.; from July 1 to Aug. 10, peaking in late July. Sockeye have two runs, mid-June and again mid-July.

Check sportfishing conditions online under Information By Area at www.sf.adfg. state.ak.us/statewide/sf_home.cfm; go to Interior region, Upper Copper/Upper Susitna Management Area. Also, check out the How-To video on fishing Klutina River sockeye salmon at www.adfg.alaska.gov/index. cfm?adfg=fishingSport.howto_videos. Be familiar with current fishing regulations and closures. *NOTE: Most riverfront property is privately owned. Inquire locally about river access.*

V 101.6 F 260.4 Brenwick-Craig Road west for **Copper River Princess Wilderness Lodge**; drive 0.9 mile uphill and turn left at Princess sign, just before end of pavement. For access to Klutina Lake Road, continue straight on gravel to T junction, then turn left 1.4 miles from highway. Turn east off highway to access Old Richardson Highway and Copper Center via Brenwick–Craig Road.

Good views of Copper Center, the Klutina River and the Wrangell Mountains are available from the viewing platform near the front of the Copper River Princess Wilderness Lodge. The casual visitor can also dine at the Princess Lodge and restaurant then walk out along Klutina Lake Road for bird's-eye views of the Klutina River.

Klutina Lake Road. Visitors planning to drive Klutina Lake Road should contact Ahtna, Inc. in Glennallen for allowable use, road conditions and possible usage fees and necessary permits. Ahtna, Inc. land use permits can be purchased online at www. ahtna-inc.com/land-permit; in person at the corporate headquarters office in Glennallen (weekdays from 8 A.M. to 5 P.M.); or by phone at (907) 822-3476. To learn more about the Ahtna family of companies visit www.ahtna-inc.com.

Copper River Princess Wilderness Lodge. See display ad on facing page.

V 106.1 F 255.9 North junction with Old Richardson Highway loop road 5.6 miles through Copper Center (for fastest access to main business area, turn off at **Milepost V 100.2**, 5 miles south of here). Copper Center is well worth a stop. From this junction it is 1.9 miles to the Copper River Native Association's Headquarters; 4.5 miles to the post office and the gallery of Copper Valley artist Jean Rene; and 4.7 miles to the loop road that takes you to the George I. Ashby Museum adjacent the Old Town Copper Center Restaurant and Inn. Access to Klutina River charter services and food, gas and lodging in Copper Center. (From the loop road you can get to the Copper River Princess Wilderness Lodge by turning west on *(Continues on page 446)*

Copper Center Loop

Copper Center

V 100.2 F 261.8 Located on the Old Richardson Highway; 105 miles north of Valdez via the Richardson Highway; 200 miles from Anchorage. **Population:** 312, unincorporated. **Emergency Services:** Dial 911. **Elevation:** 1,000 feet.

Private Aircraft: Copper Center NR 2 airstrip, 1 S; elev. 1,150 feet; length 2,200 feet; gravel; unattended.

A historical marker at **Milepost V 101.9** Old Richardson Highway reads:

"Founded in 1896 as a government agriculture experiment station, Copper Center was the first white settlement in this area. The Trail of '98 from Valdez over the glaciers came down from the mountains and joined here with the Eagle Trail to Forty Mile and Dawson. 300 miners, destitute and lonely, spent the winter here. Many suffered with scurvy and died. Soon after the turn of the century, the Washington–Alaska Military Cable and Telegraph System, known as WAMCATS, the forerunner of the Alaska communications system, operated telegraph service here between Valdez and Fairbanks."

A post office was established here in 1901, the same year as the telegraph station. Copper Center became the principal settlement and supply center in the Nelchina–Susitna region.

Copper Center was first called Kluti-Kaah by the Ahtna Native people. Visit the Ahtna Cultural Center at **Milepost V 106.6** to learn more about Ahtna history.

Copper Center has a post office. Dining and lodging at the **Copper River Princess Wilderness Lodge** (access via side road west from **Milepost V 101.6** and at Old Town Copper Center Inn & Restaurant (formerly Copper Center Lodge; see description in following paragraph). A grocery, gas & liquor store is open daily; unleaded gas/propane available. The nearest public campground is Squirrel Creek State Recreation Site, located on the Richardson Highway at **Milepost V 79.4.** Try local fishing charter services in Copper Center for campsites as well.

The landmark Copper Center Lodge, located on the inner loop road, burned down on May 20, 2012. Built in 1932, Copper Center Lodge had its beginning as the Holman Hotel, and was known as the Blix Roadhouse during the gold rush days of 1897–1898. It was the first lodging place in the Copper River Valley. Rebuilt in 2013–2014, it is now called Old Town Copper Center Inn & Restaurant. The historic Copper Center garage across the street offers auto repair by appointment.

Visitor information available at the **George I. Ashby Memorial Museum and Trail of '98 Museum Annex,** housed in historical cabins located adjacent the Old Town Copper Center Inn. These buildings were spared by the 2012 fire. Operated by the Copper Valley Historical Society, the museum is open daily 11 A.M. to 5 P.M. from June 1–September 15; season and hours may vary. Website: www.oldtowncoppercenter. com. Early Russian religious articles, Athabascan baskets, telegraph equipment and minerals, copper and gold mining memorabilia,

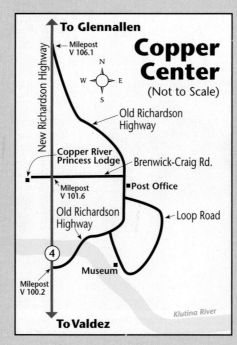

and trapping articles from early-day Copper Valley are on display. Gift shop with locally made items. Free admission, but donations are appreciated! Information boards outside the museum reveal local history.

For a good viewpoint of Copper Center, the Klutina River and the Wrangell Mountains, drive up the hill to the Copper River Princess Wilderness Lodge. The view from the observation point in front of the lodge offers fine views on a clear day of the surrounding area and mountains.

Copper Center is located on the **Klutina River,** 1 mile from its confluence with the Copper River. Fishing charters, tackle, riverboat service, jet-boat adventure tours, hunting and fishing guides are available locally. There is a short trail to the Klutina behind the George I. Ashby Memorial Museum; ask permission at the Old Town Copper Center Inn. The Klutina River is popular for its sockeye salmon run from June to early August, and its chinook salmon run, which peaks in mid-July. Check current fishing regulations.

Trail of '98 Museum Annex in Copper Center is housed in a historic cabin that survived the 2012 fire. (©David L. Ranta, staff)

A favorite photo subject is the Copper Center City Hall, an old outhouse located next to Jean Rene' Studio Gallery near the post office. Businessman Bill Wyatt of Valdez tacked the sign on this structure years ago as a joke, and owners Bob and Jeanie Sunder let it stay. Photographers should respectfully avoid parking in or blocking the Sunders private drive.

The first church in the Copper River region, the Chapel on the Hill, was built here in 1942 by Vince Joy and U.S. Army volunteers stationed in the area. Mr. Joy built other churches and a Bible college in the area over the years. The log Chapel on the Hill was disassembled in 2010–2011 and reassembled on private property visible from the road. Please do not trespass on private property.

Return to Milepost V 100.2 or V 106.1 Richardson Highway

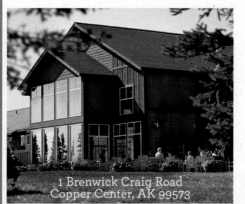

Turnoff at Milepost V 106.6 for Wrangell-St. Elias National Park and Preserve Visitor Center and adjacent Ahtna Cultural Center. (©David L. Ranta, staff)

(Continued from page 444)
Brenwick-Craig Road.)

See the "Copper Center Loop" feature on page 445 for description of Copper Center and attractions along the Old Richardson Highway.

V 106.6 F 255.4 Turnoff to east for 0.2 mile access road to **Wrangell-St. Elias National Park and Preserve Visitor Center and Ahtna Cultural Center**; parking and information panels at entrance. (These gates are closed from 6 P.M. to 9 A.M.)

Field editor Sharon Paul Nault says this is "a great facility and a 'must stop' for travelers." Take the half-mile Boreal Forest Valdez Trail Loop through the balsam poplar, quaking aspen and white spruce trees; interpretive programs usually available in summer. *Crown of the Continent*—a 22-minute movie about the park—is shown in the theater building on the hour or upon request from 9 A.M. to 5 P.M. There is also a Junior Ranger Program for kids.

The visitor center has a large parking area that accommodates buses and RVs; indoor restrooms; drinking water, benches, picnic tables and bear proof trash cans. Bottled water is for sale and hot drinks are available (for a donation) at the Visitor Center. Free WiFi, information boards, a bookstore/gift shop (topographic maps are available for sale here), fireplace with comfortable couch and chairs, and park staff to answer questions on the park and the Copper River Valley region are housed in one building. The park's museum is nearby in a separate building with exhibit hall. Ranger programs are offered daily. Beautiful view of the Wrangell Mountains from a short interpretive trail behind the center.

The Visitor Center is open daily, 9 A.M. to 6 P.M., from early May through September. It is closed October and April. Phone (907) 822-7205; website www.nps.gov/wrst/index.htm. Winter travelers are welcomed in winter months at the Administration Building nearby, but should call ahead. Phone (907) 822-5234.

Also stop by the Ahtna Cultural Center, located in the visitor center complex. It is open weekdays in summer, 9:30 A.M. to 4:30 P.M. The center has a big fish wheel and log cache on display outside and indoor displays of Native history and culture.

V 109.2 F 252.8 Long downhill northbound.

V 110 F 252 Tazlina DOT station and Dept. of Natural Resources office. Report forest fires here or phone (907) 822-5534.

Begin long uphill southbound.

V 110.6 F 251.4 Rest area to east at south end of Tazlina River bridge; large paved parking area, handicap accessible toilets and picnic shelters, dumpster. *CAUTION: Riverbank may be hazardous during high water. Respect hazard signs and barricades.*

V 110.8 F 251.2 Tazlina River bridge. *Tazlina* is Athabascan for "swift water." The river flows east from Tazlina Glacier into the Copper River. Fishing for sockeye, rainbow trout and burbot (no bait, single hook only except for burbot sets).

V 110.9 F 251.1 School Road once led to a Catholic boarding school attended by many who live in the **TAZLINA** (pop. 260) area. There is no sign of the school remaining.

Begin 0.8 mile bike path northbound.

V 111 F 251 Tazlina River Trading Post to east; groceries, liquor and gas, hardware, sporting goods, hunting and fishing licenses. Readers of *The MILEPOST®* have commented that this store has an amazing variety and selection of items. (907) 822-3277.

Tazlina River Trading Post. See display ad this page.

V 111.6 F 250.4 Robert Marshall Building to east.

V 111.7 F 250.3 Paved turnout before

Copperville Road to east. Developed during pipeline construction, this area has a church, private homes and Glennallen fire station. Bike path ends northbound.

Highway climbs Simpson Hill northbound; views to east of Wrangell Mountains. Mount Drum dominates the skyline to east in clear weather.

V 112.3 F 249.7 Steep downgrade southbound to Tazlina River.

V 112.6 F 249.4 The Simpson Hill overlook has a long paved parking area east side of highway. A wide, paved access road leads south to large paved turnaround area and excellent viewpoint. On a clear day, the Wrangell Mountains are in view. Sign at viewpoint with an identification diagram of the Wrangell Mountains: Mount Sanford (elev. 16,237 feet); Mount Drum (elev. 12,010 feet); Mount Wrangell (elev. 14,163 feet); and Mount Blackburn (elev. 16,390 feet). From Glennallen, it appears as if Mount Drum is the tallest peak, but it is 4,000 feet shorter than Mount Sanford.

Visitor information for Wrangell–St. Elias National Park is available at **Milepost V 106.6** Richardson Highway.

V 115 F 247 Junction of Richardson and Glenn highways. **The Hub of Alaska** and **Copper Valley Visitor Information** are located at the northwest corner of the intersection; 24-hour gas and diesel, convenience grocery, pay phone, food trucks in summer. The Copper Valley visitor information center is a large facility with friendly staff, many exhibits (including a full-sized bear mount), a telephone and gift shop. Open 9 A.M. to 7 P.M. Local hiking trails, fishing and other pertinent information found here. *Next gas is 55 miles north at Milepost V 170!*

The Hub of Alaska. See display ad on page 327 in the GLENN HIGHWAY section.

Courthouse and Ahtna, Inc. Corporate Headquarters on east side of highway. The town of **GLENNALLEN** extends west along the Glenn Highway from here; **Cross Road Medical Center** (open 24 hours) is located 2.3 miles west on Glenn Highway; phone (907) 822-5686. **Alaska State Troopers** 2 miles west; phone (907) 822-3263. *(See description of Glennallen on pages 328–331 in the GLENN HIGHWAY section.)*

Distance marker southbound shows Copper Center 14 miles, Valdez 115 miles.

Junction of the Richardson Highway (Alaska Route 4) with the Glenn Highway (Alaska Route 1) to Anchorage (189 miles west from here). Anchorage-bound travelers turn to **Milepost A 189** on page 331 in the GLENN HIGHWAY section for log of that route.

Valdez (turn south)) or Fairbanks (turn north) bound travelers continue with this log as indicated by arrows.

Southbound read log:

Distance from Valdez (V) is followed by distance from Fairbanks (F).

Northbound read log:

For the next 14 miles northbound the Richardson and Glenn highways share a common alignment. They split at **Milepost V 128.5**.

Distance marker northbound shows

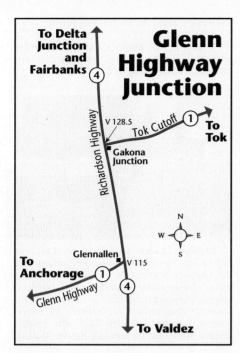

Glenn Highway Junction

To Delta Junction and Fairbanks — (4)

Richardson Highway

V 128.5
Tok Cutoff — (1) To Tok

Gakona Junction

N / W–E / S

Glennallen
V 115

To Anchorage — (1)

Glenn Highway — (4)

To Valdez

Scenic little lake along the Richardson Highway. Private, public and Native corporation lands are found along this highway. (©Kris Valencia, staff)

Paxson 71 miles, Tok 139 miles, Fairbanks 251 miles, Canada Border 256 miles. Delta Junction is 151 miles.

V 116.8 F 245.2 Ice/beer/liquor store to east.

V 118 F 244 Dry Creek State Recreation Site to west via short, potholed access road offers 50 wooded campsites, drive-in, long pull-throughs, walk-ins, picnic tables, firepits, dumpster, toilets, water, room for big rigs, no ATVs. Pets on leash. Bring mosquito repellant. Camping fee $15 per night; day-use fee $5. Open May 15–Sept. 15. [A]

V 118.1 F 243.9 Private Aircraft: Gulkana airport to east; elev. 1,579 feet; length 5,000 feet; asphalt; fuel 100LL.

V 121.8 F 240.2 Sanitary landfill to west.

V 126 F 236 Very large paved turnout to west.

V 126.5 F 235.5 Paved road east 0.4 mile to large parking area, outhouses, dumpster and boat launch on **Gulkana River**. This is a very busy area when the fish are in. Fishing in the Gulkana River for Arctic grayling all year; chinook June to mid-July; sockeye salmon late July to late September. Click on www.adfg.alaska.gov/sf/sfpublic/Fishing Reports and go to Interior region then Upper Copper/Upper Susitna Management Area. Check current fishing regulations. [fish]

V 126.8 F 235.2 Gulkana River bridge. Very popular fishing spot in season for sockeye, chinook and Arctic grayling. *Watch for pedestrians.* Public access to river south of bridge; see **Milepost V 126.5**. *No public access to river at north end of bridge.* The Gulkana River flows 60 miles from Gulkana Glacier in the Alaska Range to the Copper River. Entering Game Management Unit 13B northbound, 13A southbound. [fish]

Highway climbs next 1.2 miles northbound.

V 126.9 F 235.1 Access road east to village of **GULKANA** (pop. 108) on the east bank of the Gulkana River at its confluence with the Copper River. Established as a telegraph station in 1903 and named "Kulkana" after the river.

Most of the Gulkana River frontage in

this area is owned by Ahtna, Inc. Ahtna lands are closed to the public for hunting and trapping. However, land use permits may be purchased from Ahtna for fishing and boating access on Ahtna lands; www.ahtna-inc.com/land-permit.

V 128 F 234 Highway descends long hill next 1.2 miles southbound to Gulkana River.

V 128.5 F 233.5 Gakona Junction; Gakona ECO gas station (1 pump/unleaded, pay inside, seasonal) and grocery. [gas]

This is the **junction** of Richardson Highway (Alaska Route 4) and Tok Cutoff (Alaska Route 1). The 2 roads share a common alignment for the next 14 miles southbound. Turn east on Alaska Route 1 for Tok. Continue north on Alaska Route 4 for Paxson and Delta Junction. Continue south on Route 4 for Valdez and turnoff for Glennallen and Alaska Route 1 (Glenn Highway) to Anchorage.

> **Junction** of the Richardson Highway with Tok Cutoff to Tok (125 miles east from here). Tok-bound travelers turn to **Milepost GJ 0** on page 326 in the GLENN HIGHWAY/TOK CUTOFF section and read log back to front.

Valdez (turn south) or Fairbanks (turn north) bound travelers continue with this log as indicated by arrows.

Southbound read log: [up arrow]

Distance from Valdez (V) is followed by distance from Fairbanks (F).

Northbound read log: [down arrow]

An important note for northbound travelers: Gas/diesel is available along the Richardson Highway between Glennallen and Delta Junction only at Meier's Lake Roadhouse at **Milepost V 170**. Meier's Lake offers gas/diesel 8 A.M. to 8 P.M. daily, year-round. You can fill up in Glennallen at The Hub (see **Milepost V 115**).

Distance marker northbound shows Paxson 56 miles, Delta Junction 137 miles; Fairbanks 235 miles. Distance marker southbound shows Glennallen 16 miles, Valdez 129 miles, Anchorage 196 miles. Improved highway southbound.

V 128.9 F 233.1 Gulkana River Ranch. Rough road next 18 miles north (sign). Expect bumpy patched pavement and dips northbound to **Milepost V 149**.

V 129.5 F 232.5 Turnoff to west for BLM public easement and **Ahtna, Inc.'s Sailors Campground** with RV and tent camping and Gulkana River access. BLM trail at highway turnoff accesses public lands for foot traffic, dog sleds, pack animals, snowmobiles, 2- or 3-wheel vehicles, ATVs less than 3,000 lbs. GVW. Wide, gravel road goes straight downhill 0.4 mile to Ahtna, Inc. river access and fee box; sign lists all permits and fees, payable in a pay station. Fees (subject to change) $125/annual use, $25/day use camping near river in forested area (www.ahtna-inc.com/permits). Keep to the right to get up the ridge to the campground, self-register using recreation fee permit envelopes. **Gulkana River**; fishing for rainbow trout, Arctic grayling, chinook and sockeye salmon. Check fishing regulations carefully before fishing. *NOTE: The Gulkana River is open to the public, but much of the land along the river here is owned by Ahtna, Inc. and recreation permits are required to use or cross Ahtna lands. Land use permits can be purchased online at www.ahtna-inc.com/land-permit; in person at the corporate headquarters office in Glennallen (weekdays from 8 A.M. to 5 P.M.); or by phone at (907) 822-3476.* [fish] [A]

Ahtna, Inc. See display ad on page 330 in the GLENN HIGHWAY section.

V 130 F 232 Paved parking area to west.

V 132 F 230 Gulkana River Fishing and Camping Park. [A]

V 132.2 F 229.8 Paved parking area to west.

V 135.8 F 226.2 Paved parking to east.

V 136.8 F 225.2 Turnoff with access to west (signed "BLM Gulkana River Trail") is a gravel side road that leads 0.3 mile to Ahtna, Inc.'s **Poplar Grove/Gulkana River** public fishing access trail (portage boat to launch over narrow trail to river) and informal camping in dirt parking lot area. Recreation fee box is at entrance to access road with signs about Ahtna, Inc. fees and regulations; $25/day use (individual), $125/annual camping per group or vehicle (summer 2018 rates); seasonal passes available, go to:

ahtna-inc.com/permits. Also access to BLM Gulkana River trail. 🛶

V 138.1 F 223.9 Poplar Grove Creek culvert.

V 139.4 F 222.6 Paved parking to west. *CAUTION: Damaged pavement, gravel breaks, road construction (summer 2018) to Milepost V 144.*

V 140.6 F 221.4 Paved parking to east. Glimpse of the Alaska Range northbound on a clear day. Southbound view of the Wrangell Mountains, dominated by—from east to west—Mount Sanford (elev. 16,237 feet), Mount Wrangell (elev. 14,163 feet) and Mount Drum (elev. 12,010 feet).

V 141.4 F 220.6 Paved double-ended scenic viewpoint to west. BLM trail (1-mile) to Gulkana River. 🐟

V 145 F 217 Distance marker northbound shows Paxson 40 miles, Delta Junction 120 miles.

Watch for roadside ponds with water lilies. The Yellow Pond Lily (*Nuphar polysepalum*) is common in shallow ponds in Alaska: large floating leaves, bright yellow blooms.

V 146.4 F 215.6 Entering Federal Subsistence Hunting Area northbound, leaving southbound.

V 147 F 215 Double-ended scenic viewpoint to west of Alaska Range and pipeline northbound, weather and foliage permitting.

V 147.5 F 214.5 BLM Sourdough Creek Campground to west across Sourdough Creek bridge. Follow signs for boat launch and grassy day-use area or camping area. Good for large RVs with tow vehicles. There are 42 level sites on a gravel loop with raised tent platforms and designated handicapped sites, covered picnic tables, (a trail with information boards is near here and takes you to Sourdough Creek and around the campground), grills, outhouses, information boards, potable water, firewood may be available; campground host. Camping fee $12 in summer 2018, current fees posted; $6 for walk-in camping. America the Beautiful, Senior or Access pass gives a half price discount. Walk-in tenting areas with outhouse and bear-proof cans and food storage.

For boaters, there is the "Kids Don't Float" life jacket program in effect at **Gulkana River** boat launch. Large parking area, grills, benches, outhouse, picnic area. Guided fishing trips available. Dump station for boaters is behind the outhouse (there is no RV sani-dump), recycling for aluminum. *CAUTION: Watch for bears.*

The Gulkana River is part of the National Wild and Scenic Rivers System managed by the BLM. A popular float trip for experienced canoeists begins at Paxson Lake and ends at Sourdough Campground. See description at **Milepost V 175**.

Gulkana River above Sourdough Creek, grayling 9 to 21 inches (same as Sourdough Creek below), rainbow trout 10 to 24 inches, spinners, June through September; sockeye salmon 8 to 25 lbs. and chinook salmon up to 62 lbs., use streamer flies or spinners, mid-June through mid-July. **Sourdough Creek**, grayling 10 to 20 inches, use single yellow eggs or corn, fish deep early May through first week in June, use spinners or flies mid-June until freezeup. 🐟

Improved road surface next 11 miles northbound.

V 147.6 F 214.4 Sourdough Creek.

V 147.7 F 214.3 Historic Sourdough Roadhouse; closed in 2018. A sign in their window said they were still offering car shuttles (for a fee) for river runners. Built in 1903 (or 1906, depending on your source) it was once one of the busiest roadhouses along the old Valdez-Fairbanks Trail and it was a major station on Ed Orr's Valdez-Fairbanks Stage Line. It burned down in 1992 and was rebuilt in 1993. All that is left of the original roadhouse are the 2 cabins that remain.

V 149 F 213 Large paved turnout to west.

V 151.2 F 210.8 Double-ended gravel turnout to west.

Improved highway with rumblestrips begins northbound. Motorcyclists use care. In good condition in summer 2018.

V 153.2 F 208.8 Wide paved parking area to west.

V 153.5 F 208.5 Huge paved turnout to east.

V 153.9 F 208.1 Distance marker northbound shows Paxson 32 miles, Delta Junction 112 miles, Fairbanks 206 miles.

V 154 F 208 $1000 fine for littering (sign).

V 156 F 204 Paved turnout to west with view.

V 156.8 F 204.2 Large turnout to west with great views of pothole lakes.

V 157 F 204 As the highway winds through the thickly treed and brush covered foothills of the Alaska Range, over a crest called Hogan Hill (elev. 2,647 feet), there are magnificent views of 3 mountain ranges (on a clear day): the Alaska Range through which the highway leads, the Wrangell Mountains to the southeast and the Chugach Mountains to the southwest.

Good views of pothole lakes to west. The headwaters of the Susitna River converge on the platform to the west. The Susitna empties into Cook Inlet west of Anchorage.

Good long-range viewpoints from highway. Moose and other wildlife may be spotted from here (use binoculars).

V 158.8 F 202.2 Road narrows (no shoulder), end improved highway northbound.

V 159 F 202 Northbound highway travels through wilderness, with few good turnouts. Plan ahead to stop at **Milepost V 169.4** gravel pit if you need a large area to stop. Do not block APL access roads.

V 160.3 F 201.6 Big wilderness views as highway descends northbound.

V 160.6 F 201.4 Haggard Creek BLM trailhead parking to west (can be muddy); Arctic grayling fishing. Gulkana River 7 miles to west. 🐟

V 160.9 F 201.5 Narrow gravel access to Haggard Creek.

V 161.5 F 200.5 Wilderness views as road descends southbound.

V 162.2 F 199.8 Long, narrow, sloping, double-ended gravel turnout to east (muddy in wet weather), very uneven.

V 166.4 F 195.6 June and **Nita Lakes** BLM trail; 1 mile to west, take trail west for 0.5 miles to first fishing access. 🐟

V 168.1 F 193.9 Gillespie Lake BLM trailhead and small (bumpy) parking area to west. Walk up creek 0.4 mile to lake; Arctic grayling fishing. 🐟

V 169.4 F 192.6 Large gravel pit to west used as turnout. Turnout to west. Gravel road to Middle Fork BLM trail to **Meier's Lake** and Middle Fork Gulkana River at north corner of gravel pit turnout. Meier's

Lake offers good Arctic grayling fishing. 🛶

V 170 F 192 Meier's Lake Roadhouse with gas/diesel, dining, lodging and dry camping; open 8 A.M. to 8 P.M. daily. 🅱️ ⛺

©Kris Valencia, staff

Meier's Lake Roadhouse. Last gas before the Denali Highway. Restaurant and bar features homemade foods. Bakery items made fresh daily. Hand-packed burgers, soups, pancakes, biscuits and gravy from scratch. Homemade ice cream! 14 motel rooms, cabins, laundry facilities, convenience store. Come see our Native Alaskan museum room. Grayling fishing out back. Phone: (907) 822-3151. Email: meiers.lake. roadhouse2016@gmail.com. [ADVERTISEMENT]

There is a long, narrow, gravel parking area just north of the lodge on the west side of the highway, one of the few turnouts along Meier's Lake. Walk down short road by lodge to lake. Good place to spot trumpeter swans, loons, lesser scaups and other waterfowl. Watch for resident bald eagles. Birds are especially abundant in fall (and the fall colors are beautiful). Also watch for otters in the lake. Watch for caribou in the fall.

V 171.6 F 190.4 Gravel turnout to west with sloping entrance.

V 171.7 F 190.3 Large gravel turnout to west.

V 172.9 F 190.1 Access to **Dick Lake** to east. Big gravel park and turnaround area, primitive road leads down to lake, no turnaround on this road. Good grayling fishing in summer. View of trans-Alaska pipeline across the lake. Good spot for photos. Primitive camping. Leaving Federal Subsistence Hunting area northbound. 🛶

V 173 F 189 Dick Lake access by taking a steep narrow dirt track east up hill (long units will drag). Nice primitive camping/ parking area with 2 trails down to lake. Hand-carried boats may be launched here. Turnaround area. View of Alaska Range from lake. ⛺

V 173.2 F 188.8 Rough access to Dick Lake, east.

V 174.4 F 187.6 Improved highway begins northbound. Damaged road southbound.

V 175 F 187 Turnoff to west for **BLM Paxson Lake Campground** and the Gulkana National Wild and Scenic River. Wide gravel access road (with great views of Paxson Lake) leads downhill 1.4 miles for access to camping and boat launch. Good for large RVs with tow vehicles. Special handicap accessible spaces. We had good cell phone reception here (AT&T) summer 2018.

Large camping area near lakeshore has 50 campsites (40 RV, some pull-throughs, 10 walk-in tent sites), 14-day limit, outhouses, water, tables, firepits, free dump station, recycling bins, information boards about river travel, and firewood may be available (for fee). Camping fee $12; $6 for walk-in campsites, bear-proof food locker storage for tenters available. America the Beautiful and Senior passes offer half price discount. Concrete boat launch and parking area for 80 vehicles. Child-sized life jackets here as part of the "Kids Don't Float" program. View of Alaska Range on a clear day. Bring mosquito repellent.

Fishing in **Paxson Lake** for lake trout and Arctic grayling. Paxson Lake is closed to all salmon fishing. Boaters are required to register before launching; registration box is located outside cabin at boat launch and offers information for boaters. *CAUTION: Watch for bears.*

This is the launch site for floating the Gulkana River to the BLM Sourdough Creek Campground at **Milepost V 147.5**. Total distance is about 50 miles and 4 days travel, according to the BLM, which manages this national wild river. While portions of the river are placid, the Gulkana does have Class II and III rapids, with a gradient of 38 feet/mile in one section. Canyon Rapids may be Class IV depending on water levels (there is a portage). *Recommended for experienced boaters only.* For further information on floating the Gulkana, contact the BLM at (907) 822-3217; or www.blm.gov/alaska.

V 176.9 F 185.1 Turnout to west.

V 177 F 185 Turnout to east.

V 178.5 F 183.5 Turnout to west.

V 178.7 F 183.3 Long turnout to west with view of Paxon Lake.

V 179 F 183 Hufman Creek. Turnout to east.

V 180 F 182 Large paved turnout to west by lake.

V 180.2 F 181.8 Double-ended gravel turnout to west near lake.

V 182.2 F 179.8 Large gravel turnout. Sign here reads: No bait allowed, only unbaited single hook, artificial lures are permitted in Paxson and Summit lakes. Southbound views of Paxson Lake.

V 183.1 F 178.9 Paved turnout to west.

V 184 F 178 Good view of Gulkana River. Old highway alignment east beyond this milepost, provides a good turnout for informal camping.

V 184.3 F 177.7 *CAUTION: Slow for dips.*

V 184.7 F 177.3 One Mile Creek bridge. Paxson Mountain to west; good example of a lateral moraine created by Gulkana Glacier (visible).

V 185.2 F 176.8 AT&T building to east.

V 185.4 F 176.6 Entering Paxson Closed Area southbound (see description at **Milepost V 182.2**). Distance marker northbound.

V 185.5 F 176.5 PAXSON (pop. 15) at the **junction** of the Richardson Highway (Alaska Route 4) and the Denali Highway (Alaska Route 8). Paxson began in 1906 when Alvin Paxson established a roadhouse at Mile 192. He later built a larger roadhouse at Mile 191. The current Paxson Lodge closed in late 2013 and remained closed and for sale in 2018. **Private Aircraft:** Paxson airstrip, adjacent south; elev. 2,653 feet; length 2,800 feet; gravel; emergency fuel; attended.

If you are at this junction on a sunny day it is a shame not to drive the 21 paved miles west on the Denali Highway for a quick side trip to enjoy the scenery.

Denali Highway Cabins offers very nice log cabin lodging as well as kayak and electric bike rentals; access at **Milepost V 185.6**.

Gas available at Meiers Lake Roadhouse

Kids Don't Float life jacket loaner board at Paxson Lake. This safety program, supported by multiple state and federal agencies, began in Homer in 1996. *(©Kris Valencia, staff)*

(907/822-3151), 15 miles south at **Milepost V 170**, or at Tangle River Inn, 20 miles west on the Denali Highway (call first: 907/822-3970).

Distance marker southbound shows Glennallen 74 miles, Valdez 186 miles.

> **Junction** with Denali Highway (Alaska Route 8) to Cantwell and the Parks Highway. See DENALI HIGHWAY section on page 467 for log.

Glennallen (turn south) or Delta Junction (turn north) bound travelers continue with this log as indicated by arrows.

Southbound read log:

Distance from Valdez (V) is followed by distance from Fairbanks (F).

Northbound read log:

V 185.6 F 176.4 Access west to **Denali Highway Cabins**; year-round lodging, electric bicycle rentals, kayak rentals, hiking.

Denali Highway Cabins. See display ad this page.

V 185.8 F 176.2 Ruins of old Paxson Roadhouse (private property) east side of highway. Paxson Station DOT highway maintenance to west.

V 188 F 174 Gulkana Hatchery to west (not open to public). *The MILEPOST®* had to brake for an otter crossing the road here last summer!

V 188.4 F 173.6 Long paved double-ended rest area with outhouse to east across from Gulkana River. Alvin J. Paxson's Timberline Tent Roadhouse established near here in 1906. The Gulkana River flows south to the Copper River.

V 189.5 F 172.5 Long, very narrow paved double-ended turnout to west.

V 190.4 F 171.6 Paved parking area by **Gulkana River Salmon Spawning Viewpoint** to west; views of pipeline, picnic table, toilets, viewing platform and information board about spawning sockeye salmon. Large screen box protects dumpster from bears attracted by spawning salmon. Good photo op. *Fishing for salmon prohibited.* Public fishing access to **Fish Lake** (2-mile

hike); trailhead across highway from turnout. Fish Lake offers grayling fishing.

V 191 F 171 Welcome to Copper River Valley sign southbound. Snow poles along highway.

V 191.1 F 170.9 South end of beautiful Summit Lake. Former Water's Edge to west.

V 192.2 F 169.8 Gravel turnout on **Summit Lake** with public access boat launch. Posted fishing regulations: "no bait,

Rainbow Ridge is a popular photo subject thanks to its varicolored talus slopes.
(©Kelley & Milton Barker, staff)

single-hook artificial lures only on Paxson and Summit lakes April 16 to Oct. 31." Fishing for lake trout, grayling, burbot and sockeye salmon.

Summit Lake, 7 miles long, is named for its location near the water divide between the Delta and Gulkana rivers. The Gulkana River flows into the Copper River, which flows into Prince William Sound. The Delta River is part of the Yukon River drainage.

V 192.6 F 169.4 Large gravel turnout to west on Summit Lake. Highway winds along shore of Summit Lake northbound.

V 193 F 169 Small informal turnouts along Summit Lake next few miles northbound.

V 195 F 167 SUMMIT LAKE; elev. 3,210 feet (above the timber line). There are a number of homes in this alpine valley on the east side of Summit Lake. Magnificent Gulkana Glacier comes into view for northbound travelers.

Summit Lake hosts the **Annual Arctic Man Ski & Sno-Go Classic**, scheduled for April 9–14, 2019. The main event involves 2-member teams—a downhill skier and a snow machine driver. The skiers start at elev. 5,800 feet and drop 1,700 feet in less than 2 miles to the bottom of a narrow canyon, where they must catch the tow rope from their partner on the snowmachine, who then tows them 2¼ miles uphill (at speeds up to 86-mph), before they separate and the skier finishes the race by going over the side of a second mountain and dropping 1,200 feet to the finish line. Details on the event are found at www.arcticman.com. Arctic Man draws thousands of spectators. During the event, you may camp at the designated parking area off the Richardson Highway.

V 196 F 166 North end of Summit Lake.

V 196.8 F 165.2 Gunn Creek bridge. Access roads both sides of highway.

V 197 F 165 View of pingo to south. Pingos are dome-shaped, ice-cored hills that form in areas of permafrost.

V 197.5 F 164.5 Wide gravel road to east leads past old Isabel Pipeline camp site (no evidence remains of the camp) toward the base of **Gulkana Glacier**. Primitive camping begins at Mile 1.2. Best glacier views are at first campsites. If any areas look as if they

could be used as airstrips, they might! Park on the edges. Remarkable scenery and photo op.

V 197.7 F 164.3 Summit of **Isabel Pass** (elev. 3,280 feet). View of Gulkana Glacier from gravel parking area to east. Gold Rush Centennial information board about women in the gold rush, including Isabelle Barnette, for whom Isabel Pass is named. Memorial monument honoring Gen. Wilds P. Richardson, for whom the highway is named. Gulkana Glacier, perched on 8,000-foot Icefall Peak, feeds streams that drain into both Prince William Sound and the Yukon River.

V 197.8 F 164.2 Large gravel turnout to east.

V 198.2 F 163.8 Gravel turnout to west.

V 198.5 F 163.5 Gravel parking area to west with view.

V 199.9 F 162.1 Large gravel parking area to west.

V 200.4 F 161.6 Wide, rough and sometimes rocky gravel side road (*drive slowly!*) leads west 2 miles to **Fielding Lake State Recreation Area**. Several primitive campsites on the way in. State campground is situated in a pleasant area above tree line; no water, no camping fee, picnic tables, bear proof garbage cans, pit toilets, large parking areas and boat launch. (No overnight parking allowed at boat launch.) Loop turnaround. (*Hunting camps and private cabins adjacent recreation area; respect private property signs.*) Fielding Lake public-use cabin available for rent; sleeps 6, 3-night maximum; visit dnr.alaska.gov/parks/cabins/index.htm. Fishing for lake trout, grayling, burbot. No bait allowed, closed to fishing for burbot and lake trout the month of September. Look for moose in pond.

V 201 F 161 Snow poles along highway help plow drivers identify the roadbed in bad snowstorms.

V 201.4 F 160.6 Phelan Creek bridge. Gulkana Glacier is the headwaters of Phelan Creek and flows 16 miles to the Delta River.

V 202.4 F 159.6 McCallum Creek bridge, highway follows Phelan Creek northbound. Gulkana Glacier is the headwaters for Phelan Creek, which flows northwest to the Delta River. Entrance to turnout to south of the bridge, on east side of highway. Historically,

the glacial-colored stream emptied into Summit Lake but was diverted into Phelan Creek, which makes Summit Lake a clear water lake today. There is a turnout to the east, south of the McCallum bridge.

Views northbound of Rainbow Ridge and Rainbow Mountain (see description at **Milepost V 206**).

V 203.1 F 158.9 Entering Federal Subsistence Lands northbound, leaving subsistence lands southbound.

V 203.9 F 158.1 Double-ended paved area to east. Water piped from hillside is potable (reportedly).

V 204.6 F 157.4 Large gravel parking area to west. Good photo op northbound of pipeline going up over hill.

V 206 F 156 Double-ended paved scenic viewpoint. Good photo op. Good view southbound of **Rainbow Ridge** and Rainbow Mountain. This 6,000-foot-high ridge extends northwest 8 miles from McCallum Creek. The highest point on the ridge is 6,700-foot Rainbow Mountain. The last mountain of Rainbow Ridge, Mount Naidine, was named for Naidine Johnson, owner/operator of Tangle River Inn at **Milepost P 20** on the Denali Highway. Popular photo subjects, the mountain and ridge were named for their varicolored talus slopes. The reds and greens are volcanic rock; the yellows and pastels are siltstone and sandstone.

V 206.3 F 155.7 Distance marker northbound shows Delta Junction 60 miles, Fairbanks 155 miles.

V 207 F 155 Large gravel turnout to west.

V 207.2 F 154.8 Begin rock slide and avalanche area next 5 miles northbound, end slide area southbound.

V 208.1 F 153.9 Gravel turnout to west overlooking creek.

V 208.5 F 153.5 Gravel turnout to west overlooking creek.

V 209 F 153 Gravel shoulder parking to east. Leaving Federal Subsistence Lands northbound, entering subsistence lands southbound.

V 209.6 F 152.4 Shoulder parking, sharp dropoff to river; views.

CAUTION: Falling rock. Watch for rough patches of road northbound to Milepost V 220.

V 210 F 152 Good view southbound of aptly named Rainbow Ridge and Mountain (see description at **Milepost V 206**).

V 211.5 F 150.5 Huge gravel parking area to west. Dikes in place for flood control.

V 212.3 F 149.7 Wide gravel shoulders and turnouts to west beside Phelan Creek are found along the highway north and south of here. Road to the west leads to a take-out point for Delta River float that begins at Tangle Lakes Campground on the Denali Highway and is marked for river travelers along this stretch of the Richardson Highway. Take-out point changes due to river channeling. A turnout here takes you to parking down by the river.

Experienced kayakers or whitewater rafters may also float 18 miles downstream from here past Black Rapids Glacier.

V 213.2 F 148.8 Gravel shoulder parking to west.

V 213.6 F 148.4 Rock slide and avalanche area ends northbound, begins southbound.

V 214 F 148 Double-ended paved turnout to east.

V 214.3 F 147.7 Entering Federal Subsistence Lands northbound, leaving subsistence lands southbound.

V 215.2 F 146.8 Miller Creek bridge;

turnouts both sides of bridge. Pipeline crosses creek next to bridge.

V 215.9 F 146.1 Large gravel parking area to west with information board is **Denali Fault/Pipeline Visitor Viewing Area**; good stop for pipeline photos. Information boards at viewing area give pipeline history and facts, and detail design solutions used to make the pipeline earthquake-proof. The zigzag pattern often seen in the aboveground sections allows for pipe expansion or contraction due to temperature changes or movement caused by other forces, such as earthquakes. *Do not climb on pipe.*

The pipeline has an earthquake detection system. Ground accelerometers at pump stations measure earth movement, and computers identify critical supports, valves and other items to check after a quake. The pipeline's design was tested in November 2002 by a tremendous 7.9 earthquake and again that damaged several areas of roadway.

V 216.2 F 145.7 Leaving Federal Subsistence Lands northbound, entering subsistence lands southbound.

Distance marker northbound shows Delta Junction 50 miles, Fairbanks 149 miles.

V 216.7 F 145.3 Lower Miller Creek bridge. Gravel turnout to west at south end. Pipeline crosses the river above ground alongside the bridge to the west.

V 217 F 145 Gravel turnout. Do not block pipeline access road. Good view of pipeline from turnout.

V 217.2 F 144.8 Castner Creek; turnouts at both ends of bridge.

V 218.2 F 143.8 Trims Camp. Trims Station (DOT/PF highway maintenance) to west, phone (907) 895-6275.

V 218.8 F 143.2 Trims Creek bridge. Wildflowers in the area include lupine, sweet pea and fireweed. Watch for caribou on slopes. Parking to the northwest.

V 219.1 F 142.9 Access road west to Pump Station No. 10.

V 219.8 F 142.2 Michael Creek bridge; turnouts both ends.

Southbound drivers have a spectacular view of Pump Station No. 10 and the surrounding mountains.

V 220.6 F 141.7 Gravel viewpoint to west with view to the south of pump station 10, mountains and glaciers.

V 220.7 F 141.3 Flood Creek bridge; parking to east at north end of bridge.

V 222.5 F 139.5 Gravel turnout to west, view of flood control dikes on river. Several narrow tracts lead to the river dike along here.

V 223 F 139 Whistler Creek bridge. Turnout to east at north end of bridge. Highway has frost heaves and is patched in many places.

V 223.8 F 138.2 Boulder Creek bridge. Parking to east at north end of bridge.

V 224.5 F 137.5 Lower Suzy Q Creek bridge; parking to east, both ends of bridge.

V 224.7 F 137.3 Entering Federal Subsistence Lands southbound. Leaving Federal Subsistence Lands northbound.

V 224.8 F 137.2 Upper Suzy Q Creek bridge. Gravel turnout to east at north end of bridge.

V 225.2 F 136.8 Large gravel turnout to east. Watch for lush growths of cow parsnip along roadside in summer.

V 225.4 F 136.6 Double-ended scenic paved viewpoint with picnic table to west. Information board on area bison. East of this scenic viewpoint the slopes often have Dall sheep on them.

Historical marker here identifies the terminal moraine of Black Rapids Glacier to the west. Currently a retreating glacier with little ice visible, this glacier was nicknamed the Galloping Glacier when it advanced more than 3 miles during the winter of 1936–1937. Rapids Lake Trail begins across the highway from the historical sign (0.3 mile to lake). Rapids Lake is stocked with rainbow trout by the ADF&G. Look for wild sweet pea blooming in June. ◄

V 226.2 F 135.8 Long gravel shoulder parking.

V 226.4 F 135.6 Falls Creek bridge. Turnout to west.

V 226.5 F 135.5 Camp Terry Creek. Boundary between Game Management Units 20D and 13.

V 226.7 F 135.3 Black Rapids U.S. Army training site at Fall Creek.

V 226.9 F 135.1 Gunny Sack Creek.

V 227 F 135 Gravel shoulder parking to west.

©Sharon Nault

V 227.4 F 134.6 The old **Black Rapids Roadhouse** (pictured above), on the east side of the highway, was established about 1902 and is one of the last remaining roadhouses on the historic Valdez–Fairbanks Trail (today's Richardson Highway). Restoration efforts have stabilized the old roadhouse. The beautiful new lodge up on the hill offers lodging and meals.

The Lodge at Black Rapids. A 10-room, timber framed lodge, in the heart of the Alaska Range. Hand-crafted rooms with 2 stone fireplaces and panoramic views for northern lights viewing or to dine by in the full-service restaurant. Open year-round. Call for reservations at (907) 388-8391. www.lodgeatblackrapids.com. See display ad on this page. [ADVERTISEMENT]

V 228.3 F 133.7 One Mile Creek bridge.

V 229.7 F 132.3 Paved shoulder parking west side of highway, access to river.

V 230.3 F 131.7 Paved turnout to west.

Good view from highway south of this turnout of Delta River. The Delta River heads at Tangle Lakes and flows 80 miles north to the Tanana River.

V 230.9 F 131.1 Turnout to west.

V 231 F 131 Darling Creek. View of braided Delta River to west. The wind can really whip up the dust along the riverbed.

V 231.6 F 130.4 Gravel parking area to west, nice mountain views.

V 232.1 F 129.9 Gravel turnout to west.

V 233.3 F 128.7 Bear Creek bridge. Small gravel turnout with access to creek to west south of bridge.

V 234.2 F 127.8 Double ended gravel turnout to east, pipeline access road.

V 234.5 F 127.5 Large paved turnout to west.

V 234.7 F 127.3 Improved highway and bridge at Ruby Creek; large parking area to west at north end of bridge.

V 236 F 126 Distance marker south-

bound shows Paxson 51 miles, Glennallen 121 miles, Valdez 236 miles.

V 238 F 124 Gravel turnout to west provides access to a narrow, deeply rutted, gravel loop road which leads through **Donnelly Creek State Recreation Site**; enter via the second road on left northbound (first side road on left northbound is end of the loop road and provides best access to large parking areas for big rigs; camping fee required). There are 12 treed campsites along the loop road; tables, firepits, outhouses, water pump and garbage containers. Camping fee $15/night. A large dike built to keep the river from flooding here provides a good place to walk. Blueberries in season. ▲

V 238.2 F 122.8 Gravel parking to east above pond.

V 239.2 F 122.8 Gravel turnout to east.

V 240.3 F 121.7 Gravel turnout to west.

V 241.3 F 120.7 Large paved turnout to west at top of hill; good photo op of Delta River to west, top of Donnelly Dome to east. Southbound views of braided Delta River.

Highway makes long winding descent southbound to **Milepost V 238**.

V 242.1 F 119.9 Easy-to-miss, narrow dirt turnoff for Coal Mine Road to east, marked by a small sign on tree at small dirt turnout. This road is for 4-wheel-drive vehicles only. It leads east to 8 small fishing lakes, most stocked with rainbow trout, Arctic char, Arctic grayling and chinook salmon. Lakes are **Coal Mine #5** and **Backdown** lakes (trailhead at Mile 1.6); Last Lake (Mile 1.9) **Brodie Lake** (Mile 2.1); **Paul's Pond** (Mile 2.6); **Rangeview Lake** (Mile 2.7); **Dick's Pond** (Mile 4.1); and **Ken's Pond** (Mile 4.7). Coal Mine #5 and Ken's Pond have public use cabins available by reservation through the ADF&G offices in Delta Junction and Fairbanks.

The ADF&G says: "A nice place to try on a bright sunny day with little or no wind, offering a beautiful view of hanging glaciers and snow-capped mountains. Fish from shore or by float tube or small canoe or even just wading out from shore will increase your effectiveness. Try dry flies or spinners (0 to 1) for best luck." ◄

V 242.8 F 119.2 Public fishing access from Dome Road to west for **Weasel Lake**; stocked with rainbow trout. Recreation Access Permit (RAP) required. ◄

V 243.5 F 118.5 Pipeline Viewpoint to east with information boards with pipeline facts and an overview of Alaska animals. Good photo stop. The trans-Alaska pipeline snakes along the ground and over the horizon. Because of varying soil condi-

Delta Junction Visitor Center makes a fun and informative stop, with its outside displays, helpful staff and natural history displays inside the center. (©Steven Miley)

tions along its route, the pipeline is both above and below ground. Where the warm oil would cause icy soil to thaw and erode, the pipeline goes above ground. Where the frozen ground is mostly well-drained gravel or solid rock, and thawing is not a problem, the line is underground.

V 243.8 F 118.2 Gravel side road to lake.

V 243.9 F 118.1 Paved double-ended scenic viewpoint to east. A spectacular view (on a clear day) to the southwest of 3 of the highest peaks of the Alaska Range. From west to south they are: Mount Deborah (elev. 12,339 feet); Hess Mountain (elev. 11,940 feet), center foreground; and Mount Hayes (elev. 13,832 feet).

V 244.3 F 117.7 Rough informal dirt turnout (dips from road).

V 244.4 F 117.6 Public fishing access to east to **Donnelly Lake**; stocked with rainbow trout. 3 turnouts next mile, northbound.

V 244.6 F 117.4 Double-ended rough gravel turnout to east.

V 245.6 F 116.4 Informal gravel turnout to east.

V 245.9 F 116.1 Distance marker northbound shows Delta Junction 20 miles, Fairbanks 118 miles.

V 247.3 F 114.7 From here northbound the road extends straight for 4.8 miles. Good view southbound of Donnelly Dome. *NOTE: No shoulders, drive carefully.*

Donnelly Dome to west (elev. 3,910 feet), was first named Delta Dome. For years the mountain has been used to predict the weather: "The first snow on the top of the Donnelly Dome means snow in Delta Junction within 2 weeks." Great view southbound of the Alaska Range.

CAUTION: Watch for moose and caribou (especially in August).

V 247.5 F 114.5 Bumpy gravel track leads east to an area where some people boondock (dry camp). Walk road before driving in.

V 248.7 F 113.3 U.S. Army Donnelly Training Area.

V 249.5 F 112.5 Distance marker southbound shows Paxson 65 miles, Glennallen 139 miles.

V 249.6 F 112.4 Turnoff to west for Dome Road, which crosses U.S. Army Military Reservation Donnelly Training Area. This is a restricted access area: "When flag is flying, military training is being conducted in this area and this area is off limits." For entry at other times, contact Range Control, Monday–Friday, 7:30 A.M. to 4:30 P.M. at (907) 873-4714.

V 252.8 F 109.2 Paved, double-ended turnout to west.

V 255 F 107 Dial 511 for travel information.

V 256 F 106 Fort Greely Ridge Road and old Richardson Highway to west. Access to Ghost, Nickel, "J" and Chet lakes; Recreation Access Permit (RAP) required.

V 257.1 F 104.9 Improved road surface northbound to Delta Junction.

V 257.6 F 104.4 Meadows Road to west; access to 10 fishing lakes, Recreation Access Permit (RAP) required.

V 258.3 F 103.7 Alyeska Pipeline (Delta Region Raw Maintenance and Oil Spill Response Base) Pump Station No. 9 to east; no tours. This station is at Pipeline Mile 548.71, with the Prudhoe Bay station being Mile 0. The pipeline was designed with 12 pump stations, although Pump Station 11 was never built. Information board at pump station entrance.

V 258.7 F 103.3 South boundary of Fort Greely.

V 260.9 F 101.1 Distance marker southbound shows Paxson 76 miles, Glennallen 150 miles.

V 261.1 F 100.9 FORT GREELY (restricted area) main gate is flanked by 2 tanks on exhibit. Fort Greely was established in in 1942 when an advance detail of 15 men arrived in the Big Delta Area to establish an Army Air Corps Base. These first Army units set up camp on June 30, 1942 at what was to become Station 17, Alaskan Wing, Air Transport Command. Throughout World War II, the post was a rest and refueling spot for American pilots ferrying aircraft to Ladd Army Airfield (now Fort Wainwright) for the Lend Lease Program.

In 1948, Fort Greely was activated as a staging area for the U.S. Army's first post-WWII cold weather training maneuver —"Exercise Yukon"—which led to the estab-

lishment of the Northern Warfare Training Center. Cold weather field tests of Army equipment began at Fort Greely's Cold Regions Test Center in 1949.

The Fort Greely area has temperature extremes ranging from –69°F to 91°F. Fort Greely was named for A.W. Greely, an arctic explorer and author of *Three Years of Arctic Service*. In 1995, the installation underwent Base Realignment and Closure (BRAC) and was warm based in 1997. In 2001, it was partially removed from the BRAC list and reactivated as a ballistic missile defense site in 2002. The missile defense complex is operated by the Alaska National Guard, which maintains 40 interceptors. The 65-foot-long, 3-stage interceptors travel at a max speed of 17,000 mph.

Watch for heavy traffic between Fort Greely and Delta Junction.

Distance marker northbound shows Delta Junction, 5 miles.

V 261.6 F 100.4 Wills Range Road to west. **V 262.1 F 99.9** An ATV trail begins near Delta and comes out at Fort Greely.

V 262.5 F 99.5 Double-ended paved rest area to west with litter bins, toilets, picnic tables, scenic view. Gold Rush Centennial sign about the Richardson Highway and interpretive sign on the Denali Fault. Area subject to high winds.

"The Denali Fault runs in a great arc from Southeast Alaska through Canada, then re-enters Alaska, slicing Denali National Park in half. The great fault passes just south of here, allowing the spectacular Alaska Range to tower above its surroundings."

A 7.9 earthquake jolted the Interior and Southcentral regions in November 2002. The quake was centered about 80 miles south of Fairbanks. The Richardson Highway, Tok Cut-off and Glenn Highway all sustained damage.

V 264.8 F 97.2 Jarvis Creek bridge.

V 264.9 F 97.1 Leaving Fort Greely Military Reservation northbound, entering Fort Greely Military Reservation and Donnelly Training Center southbound.

V 265.1 F 96.9 "Welcome to Delta Junction" sign northbound. *Begin speed zone northbound. CAUTION: High wind area.*

V 265.3 F 96.7 Delta Petro-Wash. 24-hour gas station and convenience store with free RV dump station, potable water and air for tires. Clear away the road dust

at the carwash with RV and automatic bays. Coin-op laundry. Try one of our famous breakfast burritos! 5 A.M. to 10:30 A.M. Hot food to go, coffee and large selection of cold drinks. Daily lunch specials, call ahead for pizza to go (5 A.M. to 8 P.M.). Ice, ATM, automotive supplies, Alaska gifts and free WiFi. More information at Facebook @Delta PetroWash, or by calling (907) 895-5073. [ADVERTISEMENT]

NOTE: Southbound travelers will find gas/diesel available at Meier's Lake Roadhouse, **Milepost V 170.** *For travelers accustomed to services along this route, note that long-time businesses Paxson Lodge and Sourdough Roadhouse have closed.*

V 265.6 F 96.4 The Calico Cow quilting

shop to east; Alaska fabrics, classes, patterns, books.

The Calico Cow. See display ad on page 232 in the ALASKA HIGHWAY section.

V 265.7 F 96.3 The Alaska Steakhouse & Motel is to the west with lodging and dining. **Buffalo Center Drive-in** to east adjacent **Sullivan Roadhouse Museum**, which is across Grizzly Lane from the Visitor Center on the east side of Richardson Highway. Open daily in the summer, this original 1906 Roadhouse has historical displays and photographs, a garden and it displays Alaska Highway road-building equipment. A Farmers Market is held behind the Roadhouse on Saturdays and Wednesdays, 10 A.M. to 5 P.M., from mid-May to September.

The Alaskan Steakhouse & Motel. See display ad page 233 in the ALASKA HIGHWAY section.

Buffalo Center Drive-in. See display ad page 232 in the ALASKA HIGHWAY section.

NOTE: Turn east on Grizzly Lane for access to Alaska Highway eastbound (to Tok) and for Delta Junction visitor center parking. Continue straight ahead northbound for access to Alaska Highway westbound (to Fairbanks); see next entry at **Milepost V 265.9**.

V 265.8 F 96.2 Delta Junction Visitor Information Center, on the east side of the Richardson Highway and south side of the Alaska Highway, sits at what is locally referred to as The Triangle. The center has historical and wildlife displays and information on local sights and services, brochures and restrooms. End of Alaska Highway monument and pipeline display outside.

V 265.9 F 96.1 Stop sign northbound marks end of Alaska Route 4. The Richardson Highway continues to Fairbanks as Alaska Route 2. CAUTION: Northbound traffic crosses oncoming traffic traveling eastbound on Highway 2, and must merge with westbound Alaska Highway traffic.

Junction of the Richardson and Alaska highways in DELTA JUNCTION. Turn to page 232 in the ALASKA HIGHWAY section for description of Delta Junction and log of Alaska Highway to Tok.

Glennallen (turn south) or Fairbanks (turn north) bound travelers continue with this log as indicated by arrows.

Southbound read log: ⬆

Distance from Valdez (V) is followed by distance from Fairbanks (F).

Northbound read log: ⬇

V 266.1 F 95.9 Buffalo Center Service (gas/diesel, 24-hour, propane, convenience store, RV dump) at Nistler Road. Nistler Road leads east 6.4 miles to junction with Clearwater Road. Turn north on Clearwater and drive 0.9 mile to Remington Road, then turn right and drive 2.7 miles for Clearwater State Recreation Site and **Clearwater Lodge**.

V 266.3 F 95.7 Delta Junction post office and IGA Food Cache.

V 266.4 F 95.6 End 4-lane highway, begin 2-lane highway, northbound.

V 266.5 F 95.5 Deborah Street; access to Delta Junction City Hall; Community Center and Library; veterinary clinic to west.

V 266.7 F 95.3 Distance marker northbound shows North Pole 82 miles, Fairbanks

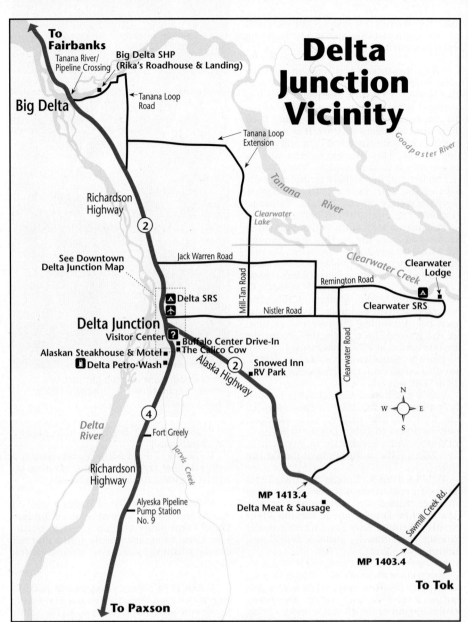

95 miles. Begin speed zone southbound.

V 266.8 F 95.2 Alaska Dept. of Fish and Game office; phone (907) 895-4632.

V 266.9 F 95.1 Rapids Road; turnoff for Delta Junction Airport.

V 267 F 95 Turnoff to northeast for **Delta State Recreation Site** (across the highway from Delta River); large parking area along highway (west of entrance) gives access to day-use picnic area with grills and covered tables. Excellent view of the Alaska Range. The campground has 25 sites, water, tables, covered picnic shelter, toilets, $15 nightly fee. Campground host.

V 267.2 F 94.8 Family Medical Center to east on Service Street.

V 268.3 F 93.7 Turnoff for **Clearwater State Recreation Site** (10.5 miles) which has 16 sites, 2 pull-throughs, toilets, tables, water and boat launch ($10 fee or annual pass); one of the state's prettiest campsites: the spring-fed Clearwater River is crystal clear. Camping fee $15/night or resident pass. Good fishing. **Clearwater Lodge**, just to the east of the state campground, has a restaurant, nice large porch overlooking the Clearwater River (fishing in front of lodge), a fun bar, cabins and an RV park.

Driving directions: follow Jack Warren Road 5.8 miles to a right turn where it becomes Souhrada Road; drive 1 mile then turn left on Remington Road and continue 3.7 miles to the state campground or 3.8 miles to Clearwater Lodge.

Clearwater Lodge. See display ad in ALASKA HIGHWAY section page 232.

V 271.7 F 90.3 Tanana Loop Road (gravel).

V 272 F 90 BIG DELTA (pop. 484) Big D Fire Station. This unincorporated community at the junction of the Delta and Tanana rivers was originally a stop on the Valdez–Fairbanks trail. It was first known as Bates Landing, then Rika's Landing, McCarty Station and finally Big Delta. Big Delta was the site of a WAMCATS telegraph station and also a work camp in 1919 during construction of the Richardson Highway.

V 275 F 87 Tesoro gas station with diesel and Tanana Trading Post on southwest side of highway. Turnoff to northeast for **Big Delta State Historical Park**. After turning, keep to left for Rika's Roadhouse parking lot, or drive straight ahead on the paved road for a small rest area with picnic table, potable water, outhouse and dump station on loop road. Day parking for Rika's Roadhouse and 23 overnight parking spots; $10 camping fee/$10 dump fee.

Rika's Roadhouse was built in 1910 by John Hajdukovich, who sold it in 1923 to Rika Wallen, a Swedish immigrant who had managed the roadhouse since 1917. Rika ran the roadhouse into the late 1940s and lived there until her death in 1969. It is now part of Big Delta State Historical Park and admission is free. This historic district was an important crossroad for prospectors, travelers, traders and the military during the early days of the 20th century. The roadhouse served travelers on the historic Valdez-to-Fairbanks Trail from 1913 to 1947.

Pleasant walking paths with information boards lead from the parking area through the park's grounds to the roadhouse. Historic structures open to the public include a small sod-roofed museum, a barn, Alaska Road Commission outbuilding, two WAMCATS (Washington-Alaska Military Cable and Telegraph System) buildings. The roadhouse itself has interesting displays and pictures on the ground floor. View the productive summer garden at Rika's Roadhouse.

Rika's Roadhouse Cafe & Gifts. See display ad on page 235 in the ALASKA HIGHWAY section.

Rika's Roadhouse Cafe & Gifts is open daily from May 13, 2019 to Labor Day 10 A.M. to 4 P.M. The park grounds are open daily mid-May to Labor Day until 6 P.M. A must-stop and a good place to stretch your legs. Take a walk on the banks of the Tanana River.

V 275.5 F 86.5 Tanana River/Big Delta bridge. Turnoff to north at east end of bridge for large, rutted dirt parking area at Alyeska Pipeline Display about **Tanana River Pipeline Bridge**. Boat launch, boat trailer parking, litter barrels, portable outhouses, interpretive signs. *CAUTION: Fast-moving water, supervise small children and leash dogs.*

Spectacular view of the 1,200-foot-long section of pipeline suspended across the Tanana River between 2 towers. This is the second longest of the 13 major bridges along the pipeline's 800-mile length. Information boards give pipeline history and facts, as well as details on the suspension bridge.

V 277.7 F 84.3 Turn off to east on Quartz Lake Road for **Quartz Lake State Recreation Area**. Little Lost Lake Campground at mile 2.1, has 12 pull-in or back-in campsites with picnic tables, toilet, and a large parking area with tables, litter bins and boat dock. Excellent fishing for rainbow trout, Arctic char, chinook and landlocked coho salmon stocked by ADF&G. A trail connects Little Lost Lake and Quartz Lake camping areas. Popular Quartz Lake campground is at mile 2.5 and has 2 camping areas. A pull-in type parking lot near the lake for overnight parking with a large concrete boat launch, swimming area and boat rental concession and campground host. A forested campground nearby has many developed campsites, some long enough for big rigs. There are many picnic tables (some covered), firepits, toilets, water and garbage containers, access to Glatfelder Public Use Cabin and other trailheads. Campgrounds are $15 per night, day use $5 and boat launch $10. Quartz Lake SRA has 2 public-use cabins; 3-night maximum; visit dnr.alaska.gov/parks/cabins for details. **Little Lost Lake** is stocked with rainbow trout.

V 280.2 F 81.8 Gravel turnout to south.

Rika's Roadhouse offers a glimpse of pioneer life in Alaska in the early 1900s.
(©David L. Ranta, staff)

V 280.3 F 81.7 Begin 0.5-mile passing lane westbound.

V 283 F 79 81-Mile Pond (stocked with rainbow trout and Arctic grayling by ADF&G); public fishing access to east.

V 287.1 F 74.9 Gated parking area to north and south at east end of bridge. **Shaw Pond** public fishing access to northeast. Good to excellent early spring and fall grayling fishing; subject to closure (check locally).

V 288 F 74 Scenic viewpoint at parking area to west overlooking Tanana River with panoramic view (on clear days) to the south of 3 great peaks of the Alaska Range: Mount Hayes (elev. 13,832 feet) almost due south; Hess Mountain (elev. 11,940 feet) to the west or right of Mount Hayes; and Mount Deborah (elev. 12,339 feet) to the west or right of Hess Mountain.

V 289.7 F 72.3 South end of long paved double-ended parking area to north in trees.

V 291.8 F 70.2 Begin 0.7-mile passing lane westbound.

V 292.8 F 69.2 Highway descends next 1.4 miles northbound.

Distance marker northbound shows North Pole 55 miles, Fairbanks 69 miles.

V 293.5 F 68.5 Tenderfoot Pottery 0.3 mile west on Ruby Road. The studio and gallery of artist Shellie Mathews is open 9 A.M. to 9 P.M. daily; access for camper or mid-sized RV; tenderfootpottery.com or phone (907) 895-4039.

V 293.9 F 68.1 Paved double-ended turnout to west with Gold Rush Centennial information boards on "Getting the Gold" (placer mining) and "Gold in the Tenderfoot."

V 294 F 68 Begin 1.6-mile passing lane eastbound. Highway climbs miles eastbound.

V 294.6 F 67.4 Fairbanks North Star Borough boundary.

V 295.4 F 66.6 Banner Creek bridge; this

is a historic placer gold stream.

V 295.5 F 66.5 Distance marker southbound shows Delta Junction 28 miles, Tok 136 miles, Valdez 300 miles.

V 296.3 F 65.7 Paved scenic viewpoint to south at top of hill has great view of Tanana River and the Alaska Range (on a clear day).

V 298.2 F 63.8 Paved double-ended parking area to southwest, view obstructed by brush.

V 301.5 F 60.5 East end of long double-ended turnout downhill north of highway.

V 301.8 F 60.2 West end of long double-ended turnout. East end at **Milepost V 301.5**.

V 302.5 F 59.5 Begin 0.5-mile passing lane eastbound.

V 304.2 F 57.8 Turnout to northeast.

V 305 F 57 Distance marker southbound shows Delta Junction 38 miles, Tok 146 miles, Valdez 310 miles.

V 305.2 F 56.8 Birch Lake State Recreation Site; (0.2 mile) to northeast on Birch Lake Road. Swimming, picnicking, camping, boating, fishing, jetskiing. Lakeside picnic sites with tables, firepits, water pump, toilets and dumpster. Grassy day-use area. Campground host; small area with sites for tent campers and pull-in, parking lot type overnight spaces for RVs; fee station; boat launch. Parking available for boat trailers. Overnight fee $15, day-use $5. Fish from shore in spring, from boat in summer. Stocked with chinook salmon, Arctic char and rainbow trout. "Kids Don't Float" program life jackets. Popular buoyed swimming area.

Birch Lake Military Recreation Site (USAF Recreation Camp) is located just beyond the state recreation site on the same access road.

V 306 F 56 Pleasant rest area northeast side of highway on the shore of Birch Lake; toilets, parking, lakeside benches; day use only.

V 307.2 F 54.8 Gravel parking area at Koole Lake Trail (14.3 miles), public fishing access, to southwest, winter only trail crosses the Tanana River.

V 309.3 F 52.7 Begin 1.1-mile passing lane westbound.

V 310 F 52 Large double-ended parking area to southwest.

V 310.7 F 51.3 Begin 1-mile passing lane eastbound, uphill grade.

V 313.1 F 48.9 Paved double-ended turnout to southwest on Tanana River. (*View of river was obscured by shrubs and trees, summer 2018*). Gold Rush Centennial information boards on "Alaska's Gold Rush Era" and "Tanana Valley Gold."

V 314.8 F 47.2 Midway Lodge.

V 315 F 47 "C" Lazy Moose RV Park & Gift Shop to west. Campsites with hookups are downhill; register at gift shop or after hours follow instructions at gate.

V 317.8 F 44.2 The parking area to south is signed "You are on a Purple Heart Highway."

V 319.3 F 42.7 Signed access road to Harding Lake (best access is at **Milepost V 321.5**).

V 320.2 F 41.8 Distance marker northbound shows North Pole 30 miles, Fairbanks 44 miles.

V 321.5 F 40.5 Turnoff to east on Harding Drive for **Harding Lake State Recreation Area**; drive east 1.4 miles on paved road. A terrific stop for families with small

children; bring beach shoes to enjoy wading on the very shallow, rocky bottom of Harding Lake. Access lake by walking wet area to west of boat launch. A drier trail is through the brush at the volleyball court. Fee station, campground host and dump station at entrance. Grassy day-use area with picnic tables, grills, horseshoes, ballfields. There is a boat launch $10 and a 1.4 mile nature trail; 75 campsites (plus large field for group camping). Camping fee is $15, day use $5, sanidump $10. Quiet hours from 11 P.M. to 6 A.M. Fishing for lake trout, Arctic char and burbot. Worth the drive! Bring your insect repellent, you may need it! Firewood from camp host or park ranger. Jet skis allowed.

V 322.2 F 39.8 SALCHA (pop. 1,048) extends along the highway for several miles. Post office (ZIP code 99714) open weekdays noon to 6 P.M., Saturday 10 A.M. to 2 P.M. Salchaket Roadhouse with food, propane and lodging on east side of highway. The village was first reported in 1898 as "Salchaket," meaning "mouth of the Salcha."

V 323.1 F 38.9 Access to **Salcha River State Recreation Site** 0.2 miles to northeast (turn at Salcha Marine) a popular boat launch with a 130-site parking area for vehicles and boat trailers; a boat ramp; picnic area; a few developed campsites and some primitive campsites; toilets and water. There may be 300 or more people here on holidays. $10 launch fee and 10-minute launch limit. Camping fee $15. Fishing for chinook and chum salmon, grayling, northern pike and burbot. Road at end of parking area by pit toilets leads to big area of sandbar parking and informal camping on Salcha River (beware soft sand areas). Winter-use cabin available; go to dnr.alaska.gov/parks/cabins/north.htm#salcha.

V 323.4 F 38.6 Salcha River bridge (*slow to 50 mph*).

V 324 F 38 Clear Creek bridge.

V 324.6 F 37.4 Double-ended gravel turnout to northeast.

V 324.8 F 37.2 Munsons Slough bridge; fishing; Monsons Slough Road.

V 327.7 F 34.3 Little Salcha River bridge.

V 328.3 F 33.7 Salcha Store and Service (ice, gas) to northeast.

V 332.1 F 29.9 Access east to **31-Mile Pond**; stocked with Arctic char, rainbow trout and Arctic grayling.

V 332.2 F 29.8 The Knotty Shop to west; gifts and wildlife display. The burl creations out in front are popular photo ops (please DON'T climb on these).

The Knotty Shop. Stop and be impressed by a truly unique Alaskan gift shop and wildlife museum. From the unusual burl construction to the Alaskan wildlife displayed in a natural setting to the handcrafted Alaskan gifts. Don't miss the opportunity to stop and browse. See display ad on page 237 in the ALASKA HIGHWAY section. [ADVERTISEMENT]

V 335.1 F 26.9 Access northeast to **28-Mile Pond**; stocked with rainbow trout, Arctic char and Arctic grayling.

V 340.5 F 21.5 Begin 4-lane divided freeway northbound. Begin 2-lane highway southbound.

CAUTION: Watch for heavy traffic southbound turning east into the base, 7–8 A.M., and

View of the Alaska Range from the Richardson Highway. The patched pavement evident in this photo is common along this highway. (©Milton & Kelley Barker, staff)

merging northbound traffic, 3:45–5:30 P.M., weekdays. No parking, no stopping, no photography!

V 341.3 F 20.7 Main entrance to **EIELSON AIR FORCE BASE** (pop. 2,867). Eielson Air Force Base occupies more than 63,195 acres southeast of Fairbanks, Alaska. The runway is oriented north to south and is 14,507 feet long. It was extended to its present length in the 1950s to accommodate B-36 aircraft and is the second longest runway in North America.

The 354th Fighter Wing mission is to prepare U.S. and allied aviation forces for combat, to deploy Airmen in support of global operations, and to enable the staging of forces to promote U.S. interest in the Asia-Pacific region. The 354th FW is the host unit at Eielson and is assigned to 11th Air Force headquartered at Joint Base Elmendorf-Richardson (JBER) in Anchorage, Alaska.

Eielson is home to RED FLAG-Alaska, a series of Pacific Air Forces commander-directed field training exercises for U.S. and allied forces, providing joint offensive counter-air, interdiction, close air support, and large force employment training in a simulated combat environment.

This base was named in honor of Carl Ben Eielson, an explorer and hero who pioneered aviation in Alaska more than 80 years ago. He recognized the possibilities aviation held for Alaska's development and was the first aviator to cross the Arctic Circle and land an airplane on the North Slope. He also piloted the first flight from North America over the Arctic Ocean to Europe in 1928. Visit the Pioneer Air Museum at Pioneer Park in Fairbanks for more on Eielson.

V 343.6 F 18.4 Turnoff to north for Old Richardson Highway, Moose Creek Road and access to Moose Creek General Store; diesel, gas, propane. Turnoff to south for Eielson Farm Road to **Bathing Beauty Pond** and Piledriver Slough. Bathing Beauty Pond has a picnic area and is stocked with rainbow trout, Arctic char and chinook salmon. Piledriver Slough has outhouses, dumpster and boat launch on Chena River.

V 344.6 F 17.4 Moose Creek.

V 345.4 F 16.6 *CAUTION: Highway crosses*

Alaska Railroad tracks.

V 345.7 F 16.3 Chena Flood Channel bridge. Upstream dam is part of flood control project initiated after the Chena River left its banks and flooded Fairbanks in 1967. (A high water mark from this flood can be seen at the Pioneer Park train depot in Fairbanks.) For northbound access to the Floodway Lands for biking, hiking and dog walking, use the Laurence Road exit.

V 346.6 F 15.4 Westbound-only exit north to Laurence Road for Moose Creek Dam Bikeway and Chena Lakes Recreation Area. (Eastbound traffic use Dawson-Buzby Roads exit at **Milepost V 348**).

The 5-mile-long **Moose Creek Dam Bikeway** extends from the park-and-ride lot on Laurance Road (0.8 mile from the highway) to the Damworks and Visitor Kiosk on the Chena River at Mile 5.5 Laurence Road (road end). The park-and-ride lot at Mile 0.8 is at the start of the bikeway and is also used by recreationists using the **Floodway Lands** for hiking, biking and dog walking; just walk across the road to the gravel dam crossover and down the other side to the flood plain.

Drive 2.5 miles up Laurence Road to fee station for entrance to **Chena Lakes Recreation Area**. A map of the recreation area is displayed; open year-round, day-use and camping fees charged from Memorial Day to Labor Day. Lake Park Campground is at Mile 3.6 and River Park Campground at Mile 4.9. Camping fee $12 walk-in tent site; $20 campers/RVs; $30 electric/water hookups; day-use fee $5; boat launch $10; sani-dump $10. The recreation area has 80 campsites, 92 picnic sites, pump water, toilets, firepits, picnic tables, trash bins and volleyball courts. There is a 250-acre lake with swimming beach. **Chena Lake** is stocked with cohos, Arctic char, chinook salmon and rainbow trout. Nonmotorized boats may be rented from a concessionaire. **Chena River** offers good Arctic grayling fishing and also northern pike, whitefish and burbot. The Damworks and Visitor Kiosk below the Moose Creek Dam on the Chena River, at Mile 5.5, was constructed by the Army Corps of Engineers and is run by Fairbanks North Star Borough.

The MILEPOST® truck at North Pole's gigantic Santa. This town is a delightful stop for visitors of all ages. (©Kris Valencia, staff)

V 347.4 F 14.6 Westbound only exit for Dawson-Buzby Roads. Access to **Antler Academy**, **Santa Claus House** and **North Pole Visitor Information Cabin**. For Santa Claus House and Antler Academy, exit then go left under overpass and take a right on St. Nicholas Drive. For North Pole Visitor Information Cabin (in sod-roofed log cabin) exit, turn right and make an immediate left on Mistletoe Drive and drive 0.5 mile. (*See map of North Pole map on page 240.*)

Antler Academy. See display ad on page 241 in the ALASKA HIGHWAY section.

Santa Claus House. See display ad on page 240 in the ALASKA HIGHWAY section.

V 347.8 F 14.2 North Pole city limits (sign on overpass).

V 348 F 14 Eastbound-only exit to Dawson and Buzby Roads. For Santa Claus House, after exiting, turn right immediately onto St. Nicholas Drive. For **North Pole Visitor Information Cabin** after exit ramp proceed under the overpass and make immediate left on Mistletoe Drive. Continue approximately 0.5 mile and the North Pole Visitor Information Cabin is on the right. For the Moose Creek Dam Bikeway and Chena Lakes Recreation Area (see description at **Milepost DC 1467.6**) make a right turn on to Mistletoe Drive and continue until it becomes Laurence Road, which will take you to the bikeway/floodplain parking lot and on to Chena Lakes recreation area.

V 348.5 F 13.5 Westbound-only exit north to Mission Road. After exiting, take a quick right onto Mistletoe Drive, **North Pole Visitor Information Cabin** is on the left 0.1 mile. For radio station **KJNP**, after exiting, drive straight ahead and turn left on a narrow road in front of a big church. (*See

description in North Pole attractions on page 240).

North Pole Visitor Information Cabin. See display ad on page 239 in the ALASKA HIGHWAY section.

KJNP Radio. See display ad on page 241 in the ALASKA HIGHWAY section.

V 348.6 F 13.4 Eastbound traffic-only at 5th Avenue, exit south. For access to Santa Claus House, turn onto St. Nicholas Drive (first right).

For a complete description of North Pole businesses and attractions, see "North Pole" feature on pages 239–241 in the ALASKA HIGHWAY section.

V 349 F 13 Westbound traffic-only exit north to roundabout (watch carefully for direction signs in roundabouts). Access north to Badger Road and south to **NORTH POLE** (pop. 2,138) business district via Santa Claus Lane: fast-food outlets, 24-hour gas/diesel, car and truck wash, supermarket, post office, police, city hall, banks, medical clinics, indoor waterslide and swimming pool, library, playgrounds, and senior center. **Hotel North Pole** (at west end of Safeway parking lot) has a special Santa room.

Also access south via Santa Claus Lane to St. Nicholas Drive turnoff to famous **Santa Claus House**. Established in 1952, this is a favorite stop for many visitors, as is the adjacent **Antler Academy**, where visitors can meet Santa's reindeer. To reach the **North Pole Visitor Information Cabin** from here, drive east on St. Nicholas to Dawson-Buzby Road, go left under the overpass, take an immediate left on Mistletoe and drive 0.5 mile.

From this exit, Badger Road loops north-

west 11 miles and back to the Richardson Highway at **Milepost V 356.6**. Badger Road provides access to the following (distance from this junction shown): Nordale Road (4.6 miles), which leads 5.6 miles to Chena Hot Springs Road. Continue on Badger Road to gas station and **Riverview RV Park** (8.4 miles); Fort Wainwright (10.1 miles); gas station (10.4 miles); and Old Richardson Highway (10.9 miles). At the end of Badger Road, access to Fairbanks is to the right and North Pole is straight ahead.

V 349.6 F 12.4 Eastbound traffic-only exit to roundabout accesses North Pole business district to south (fast-food outlets, supermarket, etc.) and Badger Road to north (Tesoro station). Turn on St. Nicholas Road for Santa Claus House. For access to the North Pole Visitor Information Cabin, continue eastbound on the Richardson Highway to the Buzby-Dawson exit.

V 350.1 F 11.9 Peridot Lane exit to north and south (for east and westbound traffic). Family diner to north.

V 350.5 F 11.5 Alaska Railroad crossing. Entering North Pole city limits (eastbound).

V 356.6 F 5.4 Exit for westbound traffic for Badger Road interchange. This 11-mile road loops back to the Richardson Highway at **Milepost V 349**, providing access to Old Richardson Highway (0.2 mile from this junction); gas station (0.7 mile); Fort Wainwright (1 mile); **Riverview RV Park** and gas station (2.7 mile); Nordale Road (6.4 mile), which extends 5.6 miles north to Chena Hot Springs Road.

Riverview RV Park. See display ad page 417 in the FAIRBANKS section.

V 357.6 F 4.4 Exit for eastbound traffic for Badger Road interchange (see description previous milepost); access to **Riverview RV Park**.

V 359.6 F 2.4 Westbound traffic use south lane to exit for Old Richardson Highway and South Cushman Street.

V 360.6 F 1.4 Westbound exit (next right northbound) for Mitchell Expressway which **junctions** with Alaska Route 3 (Parks Highway to Denali Park, Nenana and Anchorage).

Begin 4-lane divided freeway eastbound on Alaska Route 2 South.

Turn to end of PARKS HIGHWAY section on page 407 and read log back to front for log of that highway from Fairbanks south to Anchorage.

V 361.2 F 0.8 Welcome to Fairbanks sign, garden display, westbound. Eastbound traffic exit to Mitchell Expressway which **junctions** with Route 3, Parks Highway to Nenana, Denali National Park and Anchorage.

V 361.5 F 0.5 Eastbound traffic exit to South Cushman.

V 362 F 0 FAIRBANKS. Junction with Airport Way and Steese Expressway northbound; downtown Fairbanks to west (take Airport Way and turn north on Cushman Street for downtown); Fort Wainwright Main Gate (Gaffney Road) to east.

Turn to FAIRBANKS section beginning on page 408 for description of city and maps.

Southbound: Distance from Valdez (V) is followed by distance from Fairbanks (F). Read log:

Edgerton Highway McCarthy Road

CONNECTS: Richardson Highway Junction to McCarthy, AK

Length: 93 miles   Road Surface: 51% Paved, 49% Gravel

Season: McCarthy Road not maintained in winter

View from top of Kennecott Mill of Kennicott and the moraine of Kennicott Glacier. (©Serine Reeves)

Major Attractions:

©Serine Reeves

Copper River, Kennicott/McCarthy, Wrangell-St. Elias National Park & Preserve

The Edgerton Highway (Alaska Route 10) is a scenic, improved paved road leading 33.6 miles east from its junction with the Richardson Highway (Alaska Route 4) to the small town of Chitina, gateway to the McCarthy Road. The mostly gravel McCarthy Road leads 58.8 miles east from Chitina, across the Copper River, and dead-ends at the Kennicott River. From the end of the road, travelers must walk or take a shuttle to McCarthy (0.6 mile from footbridge) and Kennicott (5 miles from footbridge). Total driving distance from the Richardson Highway turnoff to the end of the McCarthy Road is 93 miles. The McCarthy Road is not recommended for large RVs or trailers beyond the Chitina–McCarthy bridge across the Copper River.

NOTE: *Gas and diesel are available at Kenny Lake Mercantile at* **Milepost J 7.2** *Edgerton Highway. Gas only is available 24/7 at* **Milepost J 33.** *Neither gas nor diesel is available east of Chitina.*

This corner of Alaska draws an increasing number of visitors each year, and with good reason. Chitina has several picturesque

Distance in miles	Anchorage	Chitina	Fairbanks	Glennallen	McCarthy	Valdez
Anchorage		255	362	187	314	308
Chitina	255		313	67	60	120
Fairbanks	362	313		249	372	366
Glennallen	187	67	249		127	119
McCarthy	314	60	372	127		179
Valdez	308	120	366	119	179	

old buildings and a growing number of services. The town of McCarthy retains many of its original structures and all of its original flavor. Nearby Kennicott offers solitude and scenery, including the massive moraine

Edgerton Highway/McCarthy Road Richardson Highway to McCarthy, AK

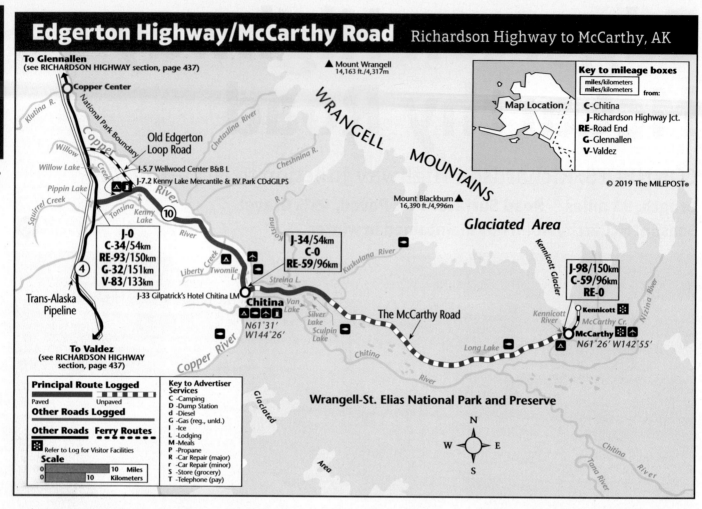

of Kennicott and Root glaciers and the historic Kennecott Mine mill and concentrator. All of this is surrounded by the wilderness of Wrangell–St. Elias National Park and Preserve.

Food, lodging and 2 full-service RV parks are available along the Edgerton Highway to Chitina. There is paid parking and camping at the end of the McCarthy Road. Food, lodging and outdoor tour providers are available in the McCarthy/Kennicott area. See the road logs this section for more detailed information. *(NOTE: Some businesses do not take credit cards.)*

Named for U.S. Army Major Glenn Edgerton of the Alaska Territorial Road Commission, the Edgerton Highway—known locally as the Edgerton Cutoff—provides access to homesteads in the Kenny Lake area and to the salmon dip-net fishery on the Copper River at Chitina. A popular seasonal activity for many Alaskans, details on the Copper River personal use dip-net fishery are posted at the ADF&G website (www.adfg.state. ak.us). Updates are also available by phone in summer at (907) 267-2511 in Anchorage; (907) 459-7382 in Fairbanks; or (907) 822-5224 in Glennallen.

The McCarthy Road follows the right-of-way of the old Copper River & Northwestern Railway. Begun in 1907, the CR&NW (also referred to as the "can't run and never will") was built to carry copper ore from the Kennecott Mines to Cordova. It took 4 years to complete the railway. The railway and mine ceased operation in 1938. The McCarthy–Kennicott Historical Museum, housed in the red historic railway depot, has historical artifacts and photos.

The McCarthy Road is recommended for those who like adventurous driving. Passenger cars, pickups, vans, campers and a few smaller RVs regularly traverse the McCarthy Road in the summer and early fall. For those who don't like adventurous driving, Wrangell Mountain Air provides twice daily air service to McCarthy/Kennicott from Chitina. Or let Kennicott Shuttle (www.kennicottshuttle.com) or Wrangell St. Elias Tours (www.alaskayukontravel.com) do the driving for you.

Take your time on the McCarthy Road. We recommend slow speeds (5 to 10-mph) on sections of rough road, and no more than the posted speed limit—35-mph—on improved gravel and chipseal. Watch for sharp rocks, railroad spikes, no shoulders, narrow sections of road, soft spots, washboard, potholes and a few "roller coaster" curves. Motorists with large vehicles or trailers should exercise caution, especially in wet weather.

Flat tires are not uncommon on the McCarthy Road: Carry a spare. Tire repair is available in Chitina.

The National Park Service ranger station in Chitina has information on current road conditions and also on backcountry travel in Wrangell–St. Elias National Park and Preserve. The ranger station and is open in summer, early May to early September (Memorial Day to Labor Day), days open are subject to staffing, from 10 A.M. to 4:30 P.M. Call the ranger station for days of operation at (907) 823-2205.

There is no vehicle access to McCarthy/Kennicott for visitors; motorists must park and cross the Kennicott River via the foot-

bridge that also accommodates bicycles. It is a little more than a half-mile walk from the footbridge to the town of McCarthy. It is 5 miles from the footbridge to Kennicott. Local businesses offer shuttle van service between the footbridge, McCarthy and Kennicott. If you arrive after shuttles have quit for the day, try calling local businesses from the free phone at the end of the bridge to ask about a ride.

Emergency Services: Dial 911. The nearest medical assistance is at the Cross Road Medical Center in Glennallen (907) 822-3203; the nearest Alaska State Trooper post is in Glennallen (907) 822-3263.

Edgerton Highway Log

Distance from junction with Richardson Highway (J) is followed by distance from McCarthy Road junction at Chitina (C).

ALASKA ROUTE 10 EAST

J 0 C 33.6 **Junction.** The Edgerton Highway leads east from the Richardson Highway. Downhill grade next 4 miles eastbound. View from the top of this hill is of 7.2 miles of straight highway going east. Fine for littering, $1000.

Junction of the Edgerton Highway (Alaska Route 10) and the Richardson Highway (Alaska Route 4). Turn to **Milepost V 82.5** on page 444 in the RICHARDSON HIGHWAY section for log of Route 4.

Distance marker eastbound shows Chitina 33 miles, McCarthy 94 miles.

Excellent views of Wrangell Mountains as highway descends 1 mile eastbound into Copper Valley. Most prominent are Mount Drum (elev. 12,010 feet) to the northeast, and Mount Wrangell (elev. 14,163 feet) and Mount Blackburn (elev. 16,390 feet), straight ahead.

J 1.6 C 32 Turnout to south, photo op of mountains.

J 1.7 C 31.9 Paved turnout to south.

J 4.5 C 29.1 Begin bike path eastbound. Do not park on this path even though it resembles a parking area at this point.

J 5.1 C 28.5 Kenny Lake Fire Station to south on Alpine Way.

J 5.2 C 28.4 Kenny Lake School, to south, has about 109 students in grades K–12.

J 5.3 C 28.3 Willow Creek. Paved turnout to the north.

J 5.7 C 27.9 Wellwood Center Bed and Breakfast, phone (907) 822-3418, www.wellwoodcenter.com.

Wellwood Center Bed & Breakfast. See display ad this page.

J 7.2 C 26.4 Kenny Lake Mercantile & RV Park to north with general store, fishing licenses, dipnet permits, gas, diesel, propane, laundromat, showers, hotel, camping and dump station. Popular stop for tourists and locals alike. Open daily 7 A.M. to 10 P.M., gas is NOT 24-hour self-serve, so plan ahead.

Kenny Lake Mercantile & RV Park. See display ad this page.

J 7.3 C 26.3 Intersection with old Edgerton Highway. End bike path eastbound. Begin bike path westbound.

Eastbound, watch for a colorful yurt made by Alaska's "Yurt Lady."

J 7.4 C 26.2 Kenny Lake Community League Hall and fairgrounds. **KENNY LAKE** (pop. 284) is an unincorporated agricultural community located along the Edgerton Highway between about Mile 1 and Mile 17.

Radio: KCAM (Glennallen).

The Kenny Lake Fair, held on a Friday evening and Saturday in August, is a fun family event with games, food and crafts booths and local entertainment. The Kenny Lake Fair was first held in 1973 as part of the school carnival. Proceeds from the fair benefit the local school scholarship fund.

J 7.7 C 25.9 Long double-ended paved turnout to south in trees beside lake.

J 9.2 C 24.4 Kenny Lake Community Chapel to south.

J 9.5 C 24.1 Golden Spruce Cabins to north; food, espresso, lodging.

J 10.3 C 23.3 Wengers Country Store to south; groceries, propane, ATM, dipnet permits.

J 11 C 22.6 Libby's Farm to south.

J 12.3 C 21.3 Paved parking area to south for Tonsina River Trail. Well-marked 2-mile (round trip) BLM trail leads south through woods to a picnic site overlooking the Tonsina River. Rated easy. Private property borders this trail.

Liberty Falls State Recreation Site at Milepost J 23.6 makes a nice stop for a picnic.
(©Milton & Kelley Barker, staff)

J 12.5 C 21.1 Paved parking area to north; Copper River trailhead at west end of turnout. This BLM trail is 7 miles round-trip and recommended as a good trail for bird watchers. The trail is fairly flat and marshy, winding through dense vegetation to end at the Copper River. Use caution along the Copper River: it is very swift and cold.

J 12.9 C 20.7 Turnoff to south for access to Tonsina Native Arts & Crafts.

J 14.9 C 18.7 Farming area; most fields are planted in hay. Also watch for Tibetan yaks grazing in a field south of the road along here. Herd belongs to Circle F Ranch.

J 15 C 18 Paved turnout to south, great for viewing yaks.

J 17.6 C 16 Steep (8 percent) downhill grade next 1 mile eastbound. Views of the Copper River and bluffs to north.
CAUTION: Watch for falling rock on road from cliffs.

J 19.3 C 14.3 Tonsina River bridge. Turnout with river access. Both black and grizzly bears pass under this bridge in the dense brush below the road.

J 20.1 C 13.5 Small gravel turnout to north.

J 20.4 C 13.2 Small gravel turnout to north.

J 20.5 C 13.1 Highway climbs steep 1.3-mile hill eastbound. Watch for fallen rock, road damage and frost heaves. Maximum speed 25-mph.

J 21.5 C 12.1 Paved viewpoint to north with sweeping view of Copper River.

View of Wrangell Mountains to north

on clear day (Mount Blackburn and Mount Wrangell are nearest). Bison roam above the bluffs across the river. Begin steep 1.3-mile downhill grade westbound.

J 21.8 C 11.8 Begin long gradual descent eastbound with winding downhill (and uphill) grades.

J 23.3 C 10.3 Liberty Falls Creek BLM trailhead to south. This trail does not provide views of falls. Go to the recreation site, 0.3 miles east, for best view of falls.

J 23.6 C 10 Liberty Creek bridge (8-ton load limit). Entrance to **Liberty Falls State Recreation Site**, just south of the highway on the banks of rushing Liberty Creek. *(NOTE: Steep, narrow, brushy loop road through recreation site. Of the 2 entrance roads, the one to the east is better.)*

Great view of this picturesque waterfall from the bridge across Liberty Creek on loop road through site. This is a great place to stop for a rest and picnic. Only the very sure-footed should attempt to hike the trail up to the falls. Single-track on eroding bank, no handholds or safety measures in place. Secluded location provides a quiet camping spot for tenters, cars, vans and small RVs. This recreation site has 10 campsites (4 tent platforms), toilets, water pump, picnic tables and firepits with grills. Camping fee $20; (if you don't register within 30 minutes, rate increases to $25) day-use fee $5.

CAUTION: Slow for frost heaves eastbound.

J 28.4 C 5.2 Wide, paved side road leads 0.1 mile to Chitina Tribal Community

Historic downtown Chitina includes the restored and renovated 1914 building—on left—that houses Gilpatrick's Hotel Chitina. *(©Milton & Kelley Barker, staff)*

Health Clinic (open to public) and Wrangell View RV park (with full hook-ups; it is a popular drop-off spot for RVers flying in to McCarthy from the nearby airport); 0.2 mile to Chitina DOT/PF maintenance station, phone (907) 823-2218; and 0.4 mile north to busy Chitina Airport. **Private Aircraft:** Chitina airport, elev. 556 feet; length 2,800 feet; gravel; unattended. Small parking area at top of hill overlooking airport.

Wrangell Mountain Air provides commuter service to McCarthy from here for those who prefer flying to driving to McCarthy; phone 1-800-478-1160, www.Wrangell MountainAir.com.

Watch for community fishwheels on the Copper River in the airport area. Interesting to watch and photograph. Signage from ADF&G states it is illegal to walk on the fishwheel platforms or touch the fish if you don't hold the permit for the wheel.

J 29.5 C 4.1 Small gravel turnout by Three Mile Lake to north.

J 29.7 C 3.9 Paved turnout to north by **Three Mile Lake**; good grayling and rainbow trout fishing (stocked by ADF&G). Frequented by moose.

J 30.7 C 2.9 Large paved parking area to south at east end of **Two Mile Lake**; good grayling and rainbow trout fishing (stocked by ADF&G).

J 31.7 C 1.9 One Mile Lake (also called First Lake). Access road at east end of lake. One Mile Lake cabin rentals (nightly or long term). Paid RV parking available with toilet, no hookups.

J 32 C 1.6 Begin 1.5-mile bike path eastbound. Slow for frost heaves next mile eastbound.

J 33 C 0.6 Chitina post office. Spirit Mountain gas station (no diesel), open 24/7.

Chitina

J 33 C 0.6 Chitina is located 120 miles northeast of Valdez, and 66 miles southeast of Glennallen. **Population:** 97. **Emergency Services:** Dial 911 for all emergency services. **Copper River EMS,** phone (907) 822-3671; **Chitina Clinic,** phone (907) 823-2213; **Copper Center Clinic,** phone (907) 822-3541; **Cross Road Medical Center** in Glennallen, phone (907) 822-3203; **Chitina Volunteer Fire Department,** phone (907) 823-2263 or 823-2250; **Alaska State Troopers** in Glennallen, phone (907) 822-3263.

Visitor Information: The Wrangell–St. Elias National Park and Preserve Chitina Ranger Station is housed in the cozy, historic Ed S. Orr Cabin (1910). It is operated by Park Rangers and it has limited hours. The Alaska Geographic Bookstore is also here. Stop by here for road conditions, and information about local trails, nearby fishwheels and fishing the Copper River. Audio tour CDs are available here for the drive to McCarthy (you return it as you leave). Phone (907) 823-2205. Visitors may also stop by the Park's main visitor center and park headquarters located at **Milepost V 106.6** Richardson Highway, 9 miles south of Glennallen; open April–October; phone (907) 822-7250; website www.nps.gov/wrst.

Climate: Temperature extremes from

-58°F to 91°F; average snowfall 52 inches, annual precipitation 12 inches. **Newspaper:** *Copper River Record* (bi-weekly).

Chitina (pronounced CHIT-na) sprang to life almost overnight with the arrival of the Copper River & Northwestern Railway on Sept. 11, 1910. The railroad was built to haul ore from Kennecott Copper Mines at McCarthy to Cordova for shipment south to Seattle, and Chitina became a supply town for both the railway and mine. Chitina's population numbered in the thousands at a time when Anchorage was just a tent city.

Chitina also became the main freight route for goods and materials moving into the Interior via the Richardson trail, (now the Richardson Highway) and a tourist stop. Tourists would arrive in Chitina by rail from Cordova or by stagecoach and later motorcar shuttle from Valdez and Fairbanks via the Richardson Trail.

When the mine closed in 1938, Chitina became a ghost town almost overnight. In the 1950s and 1970s, ghosts were painted on several of the abandoned buildings.

Today, several original buildings remain and some have been restored, such as Gilpatrick's Hotel and Chitina Saloon and the neighboring building long-used by Spirit Mountain Artworks (current status unknown).

Chitina is the gateway to the McCarthy Road and Wrangell–St. Elias National Park and it is also Alaska's "Dip-Netting Capital." Alaskans come by the hundreds to participate in the seasonal dip-net salmon fishery on the Copper River, and almost as many non-Alaskans come to watch. Motorists stop in Chitina to eat, rest, hike, bike, fish, picnic or spend the night.

Gilpatrick's Hotel Chitina and Saloon, open daily May 1 to Oct. 1, offers rooms with private baths, a full-service restaurant and a garden pub; phone (907) 823-2244 in summer, or www.hotelchitina.com.

Gilpatrick's Hotel Chitina and Saloon. See display ad this page.

Wrangell View grocery store is in a small cabin at the end of Chitina Lake, just before the start of McCarthy Road. Fresh drinking water is available for 50 cents at the hard-to-find city well. To get to the well from Main Street, turn at the Chitina Emporium and watch for right turn at "Chitina Public Well" sign (across from the fire station). Continue to rear of red building.

The big attraction—the **Copper River** dip-net salmon fishery—coincides with the seasonal salmon run (sockeye, chinook or coho). *(NOTE: This fishery is open to Alaska residents only.)* Fishermen are allowed to dipnet between O'Brien Creek and Haley Creek, with Wood Canyon offering the best results. Vehicle access to Copper River via O'Brien Creek Road (see **Milepost J 33.4**). Charter operations in Chitina ferry fishermen from a site upstream of O'Brien Creek to fishing spots on the river. The dip-net fishery for salmon runs June through September (depending on harvest levels), with scheduled opening dates and hours announced throughout the season. *CAUTION: The Copper River is a cold, swift and powerful river; exercise extreme caution.* Special regulations and permits apply. Check with ADF&G recorded information line in Anchorage at (907) 267-2511; in Fairbanks at (907) 459-7382; and in the Glennallen area at (907) 822-5224. Local residents ask that you clean your fish in the river, not in the lake.

Edgerton Highway Log
(continued)

J 33.4 C 0.2 Junction with **O'Brien Creek Road**, a paved potholed road leading 2.8 miles to a large parking area at O'Brien Creek bridge; access to gravel bars and the Copper River. (Sign says: "End of the Copper River Highway.") This side road provides access to the Chitina subdistrict personal use dip-net salmon fishery on the Copper River between O'Brien Creek and Haley Creek. (Check with ADF&G for season, regulations, public access points and other permit details.) *WARNING: The Copper River is extremely swift and can be hazardous; fishermen have been swept away.*

Lots of primitive camping spots along O'Brien Creek Road, most high above the **Copper River.** Two of the best are at Mile 1.8 and Mile 2.1; portable toilets and trash cans along the road. *(Steep fine for littering!)* Steep descent to the O'Brien Creek parking area begins at Mile 2.6. Also access to 10 Mile (RT) trail, easy to moderate, from O'Brien to Haley Creek. Trail follows railbed of 1911 CR&NW Railway. Stay on trail, privately-owned land all around.

J 33.5 C 0.1 Chitina Wayside; day use only (no overnight parking), state-maintained rest area with large paved parking lot, public restrooms, phone, covered picnic table. Across the road is Chitina Lake (also called Town Lake).

End 1.5-mile bike path eastbound.

J 33.6 C 0 Junction with McCarthy Road (log follows).

McCarthy Road Log

The McCarthy Road was built along the old Copper River & Northwestern railway bed. Watch for old rails and railroad ties embedded in the road or lying along the roadside. The McCarthy Road ends at the Kennicott River, 58.8 miles east of Chitina and a little over half-a-mile west of the town of McCarthy. It is a mainly gravel road with some sections of chip seal.

Despite the narrow road and steep drop-offs found along the first 3 miles of road, much of the McCarthy Road rolls along on relatively flat landscape. Don't power around corners on the narrow, winding sections, you might meet someone on the curve. Flying rocks can damage windshields, so follow the 35-mph speed limit.

Field editor Sharon Nault encourages motorists to "drive slowly over potholed and washboard sections and watch for sharp rocks." Be sure to carry a fully inflated spare, not a doughnut tire! Flats are more apt to happen after recent road grading, when small nails and spikes are churned up.

Keep in mind that much of the land along the McCarthy Road is privately held. Use only signed public access points for off-road activities. Local residents have asked that visitors please help protect water sources from contamination and that they carry out their garbage.

Cell phone coverage has been sporadic on the McCarthy Road. Verizon and AT&T have worked in the Kennicott/McCarthy area for our field editors.

NOTE: No gas/diesel or tire repair available east of Chitina.

View of the Copper River shows the braided appearance of silt and gravel channels created by this much-loved salmon producing river. (©Milton & Kelley Barker, staff)

Distance from Chitina (C) is followed by distance from road end (RE).

ALASKA ROUTE 10 EAST

C 0 RE 58.8 McCarthy Road begins at rock cut made to accommodate the CR&NW railroad. No road maintenance east of here between Oct. 15 and May 15. Informal turnouts with views next mile.

C 1.1 RE 57.7 Crossing the **Copper River (Chitina–McCarthy) Bridge.** Construction of this 1,378-foot steel span, designed for year-round use, cost $3.5 million. It re-established access across the river into the McCarthy–Kennicott area when it was completed in 1971.

View from bridge of fishwheels on the Copper River. Dip netting and fishwheels are permitted upstream of the bridge as part of the Glennallen subdistrict subsistence salmon fishery permit. Fishwheels are not allowed downstream of the bridge in the Chitina permit area. Watch for bears and eagles.

C 1.5 RE 57.3 Turnoff to southeast for campground with 17-plus campsites in trees, some picnic tables, firepits and toilets. (Fresh water in Chitina at city well).

Turnoff to northwest for well-marked easement (consider your vehicle's clearance!) across Ahtna, Inc. land to popular informal camping and parking on gravel bars alongside **Copper River**; portable toilets. No camping fee on public land. Camping fee on Ahtna, Inc. lands, $25/day use and $125/annual use. Map shows public easement. Fishing for sockeye and chinook salmon; tag return box located here. Watch for bears. When dipnetting and the fishwheels are in full swing, there is a lot of activity here. Look for both bald and golden eagles.

NOTE: Hunting, fishing and trapping for any purpose is strictly forbidden on property of Ahtna, Inc. Fees are posted for day-use, for camping and seasonal use on Native lands.

Signs on road read: "Entering Wrangell-St. Elias National Park Preserve Boundary 21.5 miles," and "Much of the land along the road is privately owned. For land ownership information, contact Ahtna, Inc. at (907/822-3476), Chitina Village Corp. Inc.

(907/823-2223), or the National Park Service (907/822-7250)."

Pavement ends, gravel begins eastbound. *CAUTION: Watch for rocks on road; rock slides and soft spots in wet weather. Narrow winding road with steep drop-offs, no guardrails. Drive at slow speeds with caution; use turnouts.*

C 1.6 RE 57.2 Entering Game Management Unit 11 eastbound, GMU 13D westbound.

C 2.9 RE 55.9 Ahtna, Inc.'s Hilltop Campground. Drive 0.2 mile up to small hilltop for camping. Wonderful views of the Copper and Chitina Rivers with 12 RV camping and tent pads located within the Wrangell St. Elias National Park.

Frost heaves eastbound next 5 miles.

C 3 RE 55.8 Chip seal begins eastbound at physical Milepost C 3.

C 4 RE 54.8 Occasional gravel turnouts next mile eastbound. Expansive view of Chitina River.

C 5.2 RE 53.6 Two turnouts with view of Chitina River to south.

C 7.8 RE 51 Gravel turnout to south.

C 8.9 RE 49.9 Gravel turnout to south.

C 10.1 RE 48.7 Public fishing access via 0.3-mile trail north to **Strelna Lake**; rainbow trout and coho salmon (stocked by ADF&G). *(Please respect private property adjacent trail.)*

C 10.8 RE 48 Turnout to north for parking and signed pedestrian public fishing access (walk-in only) to **Silver Lake** and **Van Lake** to the south; good rainbow trout fishing.

NOTE: Please stay within 10-foot public fishing access easement across private land. ADF&G phone (907) 822-3309.

C 11 RE 47.8 Watch for water lilies, ducks, swans, beaver and moose in ponds.

C 12 RE 46.8 Sculpin Lake signed public fishing access to south; pedestrian access only. *Please respect private property.* Good rainbow trout fishing (stocked by ADF&G).

C 12.5 RE 46.3 Beaver lodge to the north in large pond.

C 14.3 RE 44.5 Airstrip to south.

C 14.4 RE 44.4 Gravel road to north and access to Nugget Creek Trailhead and Dixie Pass Trailhead.

Pedestrian bridge at the end of the McCarthy Road provides access across the Kennicott River. (©Danny Reeves)

C 15.8 RE 43 Entering Wrangell-St. Elias National Park and Preserve eastbound.

C 16.8 RE 42 Long gravel turnout at Strelna Creek culvert.

C 16.9 RE 41.9 Three turnouts with views of Kuskulana River and bridge; good photo op.

C 17.2 RE 41.6 Kuskulana Bridge, mid-span. *NOTE: 1-lane bridge, YIELD TO ONCOMING TRAFFIC.* This former railroad bridge (built in 1910) is 775 feet long and 238 feet above the river. It is a narrow (14.5 feet), 3-span steel truss railway bridge, rehabilitated with wood decking and guardrails.

NOTE: Chip seal ends at bridge. Eastbound, road conditions depend on grading schedule and weather, and range from good to poor accordingly. Watch for potholes, washboard and wet or soft spots.

Wayside at southeast end of Kuskulana Bridge has a picnic table, bear-proof litter bins, an outhouse, interpretive signs. Additional parking at gravel pit (adjacent east). As you approach the bridge going to McCarthy a steep access road leads down to parking and primitive camping near the river. *CAUTION: Underneath the bridge, the banks above the canyon are unstable and extremely dangerous. DO NOT STAND TOO CLOSE TO THE EDGE!*

C 17.9 RE 40.9 Primitive campsite to south with small parking area. △

C 19.7 RE 39.1 National Park to north, National Preserve to south sign eastbound.

C 20.4 RE 38.4 View opens up eastbound as road crosses large, marshy meadow.

C 22.1 RE 36.7 Road prone to flooding from nearby creek.

C 23.9 RE 35.3 Turnout to south.

C 25 RE 33.8 Lou's Lake to north; coho salmon and Arctic grayling fishing. Watch for swans that are frequently seen here and look for the beaver lodge that is built on the south side of this small lake. Also look for mastodon flowers, also called marsh fleabane, along here. ➹

C 25.6 RE 33.2 Preserve/Park signs.

C 26.5 RE 32.3 Alaska Halfway House B&B (sign) was closed in summer 2018. Chokosna Trading Post was open in 2018, with intermittent hours. Chokosna Trading Post offers cold drinks, fresh coffee, snacks, camping gear and tire repair supplies.

C 26.7 RE 32.1 Private property to west, airstrip entrance to east.

C 26.8 RE 32 Chokosna River bridge.

C 27.1 RE 31.5 Turnout to south.

C 27.3 RE 31.3 Entering Park & Preserve (sign) eastbound, small turnout.

C 29 RE 29.8 *Steep grades both directions down to* Gilahina River bridge (1-lane). Large gravel parking area to south at west end of bridge; tables, outhouse, litter bin. A National Park Service footpath on the other side of the road leads a short way up and under the old wooden Gilahina Trestle, which can be seen from the road.

C 29.5 RE 29.3 Large gravel turnout to south.

C 30.3 RE 28.5 Turnout to south.

C 30.5 RE 28.3 Turnout to south.

C 33.1 RE 25.7 Turnout to north.

C 34.6 RE 24.2 Turnout to north toward high mountains for Crystalline Hills trailhead. Beautiful mountain views in this area. Trail is moderate, 2–3 hours, 2½ mile loop. Stays mostly in forest but you can leave the trail for views of Moose Lake and the Chitina River Valley.

C 34.8 RE 24 Entering Wrangell-St. Elias National Park & Preserve (westbound sign).

C 35.3 RE 23.5 Sloping access south to lake; primitive camping.

C 35.6 RE 23.2 Leaving Wrangell-St. Elias National Park & Preserve (westbound sign). Marshy lowland area prone to potholes and flooding.

C 36.3 RE 22.5 Large turnout.

C 39.4 RE 19.4 Large turnout to south.

C 41.2 RE 17.6 Culvert crossing; *slow for roller coaster dip in road.*

C 41.4 RE 17.4 TJ's Rock and Roll Camping (closed).

C 42.8 RE 16 Small turnout with view (beyond the brush).

C 43 RE 15.8 Road follows high ridge; steep drop-off to south and no shoulder. Small turnouts.

C 44.1 RE 14.7 Lakina (pronounced "lack-in-aw") River 1-lane bridge; maximum height 13'2". Access to river from large turnout to north, at west end of bridge.

C 44.3 RE 14.5 Espresso, ice cream, gift stand. Salmon spawning ground are open.

C 44.5 RE 14.3 Long Lake Wildlife Refuge sign; shooting prohibited (eastbound sign).

Road narrows eastbound as it follows shoreline of Long Lake.

C 45.1 RE 13.7 Sign identifies entrance to Collins Estate (1961), a well-known wilderness home. Private property extends along the roadside.

C 45.2 RE 13.6 Airstrip to the north.

C 45.8 RE 13 Small turnout to north with access to **Long Lake**; a beautiful spot. Fishing for lake trout, coho, grayling, Dolly Varden, burbot. Salmon spawning lake; 10 hp boat motor restriction. ➹

C 47.8 RE 11 Large gravel turnout (used for road maintenance gravel storage in 2017).

C 48.5 RE 10.3 Small turnout to south.

C 50 RE 8.8 Large gravel turnouts used for gravel storage on both sides of road at physical milepost 51. Man-made rock structures, similar to the "inukshuks" or cairns made by the Inuit, sometimes show up here in summer.

C 51.9 RE 6.9 *CAUTION: Creek has overflown the road (caused by beaver dam). Be alert.*

C 52.2 RE 6.6 Turnouts to south here and at **Milepost C 52.3.**

C 53.5 RE 5.3 *Slow for dip* as road crosses culvert. Large turnout to south.

CC 55 RE 3.8 Alaska State Forestry Wayside; large rest area with outhouses, covered picnic area, 2 tables, firepits, bear-proof litter bins and information boards.

CC 56 RE 2.8 *Slow for dip* as road crosses Swift Creek. Parking areas to north.

C 56.7 RE 2.1 Currant Ridge Cabins offers cabins and private guest house with full bath.

C 57.4 RE 1.4 Small turnout to south. Road travels along Fireweed Mountain. *CAUTION: Road narrows, begin slide area, eastbound. Steep drop-off, slow speeds advised. Use turnouts to yield to oncoming traffic.*

C 57.8 RE 1 Turnout with National Preserve sign.

C 58.1 RE 0.7 Small turnout to south.

C 58.4 RE 0.4 Turnoff to north for National Park Service McCarthy Ranger Station, an unstaffed information kiosk. Public toilets near kiosk. Trailhead for West Kennicott Glacier Trail (signed).

C 58.5 RE 0.3 McCarthy B&B, Glacier View Campground; camping, food, bike rentals. Glacier View is the first of 3 parking areas (fee) available eastbound. Note signs and posted fees indicating paid day-use and long-term parking areas. Visiting motorists use one of the posted parking areas along here unless you are certain you can legally park in a "free" spot (unlikely). △

C 58.6 RE 0.2 Visitor Information cabin and second of 3 parking areas (fee) to north.

C 58.7 RE 0.1 Kennicott River Lodge cabins and hostel.

C 58.8 RE 0 Entrance to Base Camp, last parking area (fee); camping (fee charged) available; potable water. (There is no garbage service; please carry out your trash.) The McCarthy Road ends here, at the Kennicott River; a pedestrian footbridge spans the river's main channel to provide access to the road on the other side of the river that leads to the town of McCarthy (0.6 mile) and the old mining town of Kennicott (5 miles). Pedestrians and bicycles use this footbridge. Luggage carts are available at the pedestrian bridge.

Before the state constructed the footbridge across the Kennicott River in 1997, travelers had to haul themselves across the river on a hand-pulled, open-platform cable tram. *CAUTION: Do not attempt to wade across this glacial river; strong currents and cold water make it extremely treacherous.*

The Kennicott River flows from Kennicott Glacier to the Nizina River. *There is no vehicle access for visitors across the river.* (Residents pay an annual fee to use a restricted service bridge downstream.)

Walk or bicycle 0.6 mile to the town of McCarthy. The historic mining community of Kennicott is 5 miles from the footbridge. The lodges and flying services run shuttles throughout the day between the bridge, McCarthy and Kennicott (schedule posted on notice board by footbridge); cost is $5 one-way between McCarthy and Kennicott and $2–$3 one-way for shuttle from footbridge into McCarthy.

Use the courtesy phone by the bridge to call businesses in McCarthy and Kennicott (if you are staying at one of the lodges, they will provide van service).

Public phones are located at the west end of the footbridge; on the front of McCarthy Lodge; on the road below Kennicott Glacier Lodge (behind menu); and at the National Park Service Kennicott Visitor Center at the historic Blackburn School. Local calls are free. For long-distance use a credit card, phone card or call collect.

NOTE: Be aware that—local leash laws not withstanding—there are *many* loose local dogs in the McCarthy/Kennicott area. If you bring your dog it would be a very good idea to keep your dog leashed.

McCarthy/Kennicott

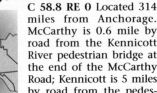

C 58.8 RE 0 Located 314 miles from Anchorage. McCarthy is 0.6 mile by road from the Kennicott River pedestrian bridge at the end of the McCarthy Road; Kennicott is 5 miles by road from the pedestrian bridge. **Population:** 34. **Emergency Services:** McCarthy EMS (907) 554-1240; Chitina Health Clinic, phone (907) 823-2213; Copper Center Clinic, phone (907) 822-3541; Cross Road Medical Center in Glennallen, phone (907) 822-3203; Alaska State Troopers in Glennallen, phone (907) 822-3263.

Elevation: 1,531 feet. **Climate:** McCarthy lies in the continental climate zone. Minimum and maximum daily temperatures range from -24°F to 90°F; maximum measured snow depth 24 inches; annual precipitation 12 inches. **Radio:** KXKM-FM 89.7 (public radio,) KIAM-FM 94.3 (religious).

Private Aircraft: McCarthy NR 2, 1 NE; elev. 1,531 feet; length 3,500 feet; gravel; unattended, unmaintained. This is a busy

MCCARTHY/KENNICOTT ADVERTISERS

Copper Oar....................................Ph. 1-800-523-4453
Kennicott Glacier Lodge............Ph. 1-800-582-5128
Kennicott Wilderness Guides.....Ph. (907) 554-4444
Ma Johnson's Historic Hotel......Ph. (907) 554-4402
McCarthy Lodge ....Ph. (907) 554-4402
St. Elias Alpine Guides ....Ph. 1-888-933-5427
Wrangell Mountain Air..............Ph. 1-800-478-1160

Visitors gather at Wrangell Mountain Air office in McCarthy. The air service provides a variety of fly-in adventure trips. (©Milton & Kelley Barker, staff)

airstrip in summer.

The 2 settlements in this area, McCarthy and Kennicott, both originated with the establishment of the Kennecott Mines

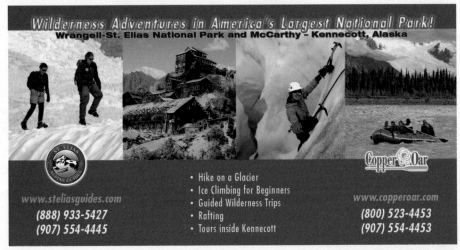

The National Park Service continues to renovate Kennicott structures and has created several interpretive displays for visitors. (©Milton & Kelley Barker, staff)

Company in 1906. (The mining company is spelled with an "e" while the glacier, river and community are spelled with an "i" after naturalist Robert Kennicott.)

The mining town of Kennicott, perched on the side of Bonanza Ridge above the wide and rocky Kennicott Glacier moraine, housed the mine offices, homes, a hospital, school and a movie theatre. Today, the 14-story Kennecott Mine mill and concentrator building towers over the narrow gravel road through "town," which includes historic structures like the old hospital and assay office, the restored recreation center, some private buildings and Kennicott Glacier Lodge. Restoration of several buildings is ongoing.

McCarthy, 5 miles away, sprang up to provide the miners with more housing, saloons, a newspaper, stores, hotels, restaurants and a red-light district. A number of these pioneer structures have been restored or rebuilt and now house a variety of businesses that serve the influx of summer visitors and the small year-round population of homesteaders.

There are no central water, sewer or electrical systems in McCarthy/Kennicott. Generators provide power and water is pumped from wells or hauled by hand. Outhouses and septic systems are used. There are no state schools or health clinics (the nearest clinic is in Chitina). There are no post offices in McCarthy/Kennicott. The mail plane arrives twice-weekly from Glennallen. Cell phone service is iffy.

The area's remoteness, historic buildings and magnificent scenery draw an increasing number of visitors every year. Food, lodging and guide and flying services are provided by the local businesses that operate here in summer *(see ads this section).*

Lodging & Services

There are a surprising number of fine dining and comfortable accommodations in this remote area. McCarthy has the **McCarthy Lodge** (fine dining), the **Golden Saloon** (casual dining) and **Ma Johnson's Historic Hotel** (description follows), as well as McCarthy Center Store (a grocery store that also serves ice cream) and the Roadside Pota-

tohead (meals and espresso). Bicycles are available for rent locally. McCarthy public restrooms are near the museum and behind the McCarthy Center Store.

Accommodations and services in Kennicott include the **Kennicott Glacier Lodge**, which offers lodging and dining (ask about their daily meal specials and their annual Labor Day barbecue); descriptions follow. Casual dining at the Meatza Wagon food truck with sandwiches and cold drinks.

Built in 1971, the historic Blackburn School (first building on the left at the entrance to Kennicott) houses the National Park Service. Here you may purchase books, souvenirs, some outdoor gear and the facility acts as the National Park Service Visitor Center. The restored General Store (formerly used as the visitor center) is open for viewing but has no visitor services.

McCarthy Lodge & Ma Johnson's Historic Hotel. Our "Living Museum Hotel" won a coveted spot in National Geographic's "129 Hotels We Love To Stay At." New York Magazine's Grubstreet.com rated us the #1 destination restaurant in Alaska. Featured in Sunset magazine's Food Lovers issue. Food & Wine rated us "one of 5 new summer destinations." Outstanding wine list. Visit www. McCarthyLodge.com. (907) 554-4402. See display ad on this page. [ADVERTISEMENT]

Kennicott Glacier Lodge, in the middle of Wrangell-St. Elias National Park, offers the area's finest accommodations and dining. Family owned and operated for 30 years, Kennicott Glacier Lodge provides 43 clean, comfortable guest rooms, 3 common rooms, and a spacious dining room. From the 180-foot front porch you get a panoramic view of the Wrangell Mountains, Chugach Mountains and Kennicott Glacier. The South Wing features 20 guest rooms, each with private bathrooms: a unique luxury in a remote lodge. The homemade food, served family-style, has been called "wilderness gourmet." Activities at this destination lodge include alpine and glacier hiking, flightseeing, historical and nature tours, and rafting. Open May 25 to Sept. 8, 2019. Phone 1-800-582-5128. www.Kennicott Lodge.com. See display ad facing page. [ADVERTISEMENT]

Camping

Camping is available on the west side of the pedestrian bridge at Base Camp parking lot and Glacier View Campground. There is no free camping on the parking area side of the footbridge at the end of the McCarthy Road. A fee of $20 (subject to change) is charged for camping on private land in this area.

There are no designated campgrounds within the surrounding McCarthy area; wilderness camping only, the nearest being a 1.5-mile hike out of Kennicott. Check with the National Park Service about camping in the Kennicott area. Mandatory bear-resistant containers are loaned with deposit. (Earth Sacks do not meet the requirements here and are illegal.)

Transportation

Transportation: Air—Charter service to and from airstrip near McCarthy. **Wrangell Mountain Air** also offers 3 scheduled flights daily between Chitina and McCarthy, phone (907) 554-4411. The airstrip is reached via a wide road north from McCarthy. Shuttle service available. Good photo opportunities for shots of surrounding mountains from the airstrip.

Shuttle—Summer shuttle service between McCarthy and Kennicott via Wrangell Mountain Bus from Wrangell Mountain Air office; fare is $5/adults, $2/dogs; phone (907) 554-4411. The McCarthy–Kennicott shuttle runs on the half-hour during the high season only and every hour or every 2 hours in May, early June and September. There is also a shuttle for $2–$3 that covers the 0.6 mile distance between the footbridge and McCarthy. Local lodges also run shuttles for guests only.

Attractions

The **McCarthy–Kennicott Historical Museum** is located in the red historic railway depot and has historical artifacts and photos from the early mining days. It is open daily (hours vary) Memorial Day weekend through Labor Day and is staffed by volunteers. A self-guided Historical Walking Tour of McCarthy is on sale at the museum. A short walking trail takes off across from the museum to an old railroad turnaround.

Take a guided tour of Kennicott. The National Park Service offers free tours of the town and its more accessible mine buildings. St. Elias Alpine Guides offers a tour that takes you inside the mill building for a unique and unforgettable look where the copper was processed. The mill tour is more strenuous than the town tour, but both tours offer a fascinating look at this area's history. Do not miss these tours!

Slide presentations and other programs are presented by the National Park Service at Kennicott in summer. Also ask to see the 15-minute *Kennecott Mill* movie, shown upon request. Lectures and talks are presented by Park Rangers throughout the day on a variety of subjects. Check the schedule posted outside the park visitor center, which is located in the historic Blackburn School (built in 1917).

A popular day hike from Kennicott is the **Root Glacier Trail**. The easy to moderate 3-mile round trip takes you from Kennecott Mill Town along the lateral moraine of the Kennicott and Root Glaciers to the toe of the glacier. Allow 2 to 6 hours to hike. Also makes a good mountain bike trip, according to the Park Service. The Bonanza Mine hike is a longer and more strenuous hike (9 miles round-trip with 3,800-foot elevation gain) that splits off of the Root Glacier trail about 0.5 mile from Visitor Center. Another that splits off the same trail is the Jumbo Mine trail. It is a 10-mile, 3,300-foot elevation gain route to Jumbo Mine. Check with Park personnel about other area hikes.

Wrangell Mountain Center, located in one of the oldest buildings in McCarthy, exists to foster understanding, appreciation and stewardship of wildlands and mountain culture in Alaska through scientific and artistic inquiry in the Wrangell Mountains. The bulletin board has information on lectures, demonstrations, and workshops.

Also check other bulletin boards in McCarthy and Kennicott to find out about local summer events and activities.

Guided hikes, flightseeing, ice climbing, river rafting, fly-in and/or hike-in backpacking, mountaineering and other outdoor activities are offered by area outfitters. Outfitters usually offer scheduled trips to accommodate independent travelers and small tour groups, but also customize both dates and trips to satisfy individual needs. Contact: **Kennicott Wilderness Guides** (www.kennicottguides.com); **St. Elias Alpine Guides** (www.steliasguides.com); **Wrangell Mountain Air** (www.WrangellMountainAir.com); and **Copper Oar** (www.copperoar.com).

Kennicott Wilderness Guides. We are a small group of dedicated, knowledgeable guides enthusiastic about the beauty and diversity of their home. Join KWG, the most experienced guides of the area, for a day on the glacier, paddle in a glacial lake or hike around the historic Kennicott Valley. Located on Mainstreet Kennicott. Contact www.kennicottguides.com or (907) 554-4444. [ADVERTISEMENT]

St. Elias Alpine Guides offers full and half day hikes on nearby glaciers with professional guides. Those looking for unique Alaskan adventure can try ice climbing with a full day beginner lesson. Historic tours inside the Kennecott mill building available daily. Call for information and reservations. Phone 1-888-933-5427 or (907) 554-4445. www.steliasguides.com. See display ad on page 463. [ADVERTISEMENT]

Wrangell Mountain Air provides 3 scheduled flights daily between Chitina and McCarthy–Kennicott as an alternative to driving the McCarthy Road. Just park your car or RV at the Chitina Airport and enjoy a spectacular flight with world-class vistas of 16,000-foot peaks, 25-mile-long glaciers and massive icefalls. Day trips and overnight lodging available. Guided Kennicott Tours, glacier hikes, ice climbing and river rafting are just some of the unique experiences you will find in the area. Wrangell Mountain Air specializes in flightseeing tours of the Park, fly-in backpacking and rafting trips as well as day hiking. Aircraft are high wing for unobstructed viewing and equipped with intercoms and individual headsets for each passenger. Call toll-free for reservations and information, 1-800-478-1160 or (907) 554-4411. Email: info@WrangellMountainAir.com. Visit our website at www.WrangellMountainAir.com. See display ad on page 463. [ADVERTISEMENT]

Wrangell–St. Elias National Park and Preserve

Kennecott Mill structures are designated a National Historic Landmark. (©Serine Reeves)

Wrangell-St. Elias National Park and Preserve is the largest unit in the National Park system, encompassing 13.2 million acres of wild lands and 9.7 million acres of designated Wilderness. Formed by the Wrangell, St. Elias, Chugach and Alaska mountain ranges, the park contains the greatest collection of peaks over 16,000 feet on the continent, including Mount St. Elias (elev. 18,029 feet), the second tallest peak in the United States. Major peaks in the park include Mount Wrangell (elev. 14,163 feet, an active volcano), Mount Blackburn (elev. 16,390 feet), Mount Sanford (elev. 16,237 feet) and Mount Drum (elev. 12,010 feet).

The park also contains the largest concentration of glaciers on the continent. One of these, Malaspina Glacier, is North America's largest piedmont glacier, a type formed when 2 or more glaciers flow from confined valleys to form a broad fan- or lobe-shaped ice mass. Malaspina Glacier covers an area of about 1,500 square miles—larger than the state of Rhode Island. It has been designated a National Natural Landmark. Hubbard Glacier, which flows out of the St. Elias Mountains into Disenchantment Bay, is one of the most active glaciers in North America. It is advancing in spite of global climate change.

Also located in the park are Chitistone and Nizina canyons. Both have been described as exceeding the scale of Yosemite Valley in California, with an even greater variety of geological wonders. There is a spectacular, 300-foot waterfall in upper Chitistone Canyon, and the lower canyon has sheer walls rising 4,000 feet above the river.

Although the scale of the park seems overwhelming, for motorists the choices of how to visit Wrangell-St. Elias are relatively few. Road access to the northern section of the park and preserve is from Slana on the Tok Cutoff via the 43-mile Nabesna Road. The major road access to the west side of Wrangell-St. Elias is via the Edgerton Highway/McCarthy Road.

The Kennecott area is one of the major centers of activity in the park, perhaps because it contains one of the park's best known attractions: the huge complex of barn-red buildings that make up the Kennecott mill town, now a National Historic Landmark. The mill was built in 1907 by Kennecott Copper Corporation (an early day misspelling made the mining company Kennecott, while the glacier, river and city is Kennicott).

The National Park Service purchased many of the mill structures (although several are still privately owned), and work is under way to rehabilitate and stabilize the site. There is variable access to the buildings: not all structures are open due to concerns for visitor safety. Narrated tours of the mill are available from St. Elias Alpine Guides. The National Park Service conducts daily summer ranger programs at the Kennecott Visitor Center and offers daily programs in the recreation hall in Kennecott.

The Kennecott mines, including 70 miles of subterranean tunnels, are up near the ridge top (behind present-day Kennicott Glacier Lodge), and were connected to the mill by aerial trams. The mine operated from 1911 until 1938. *WARNING: Do not enter or attempt to enter any mine in the park.*

While copper mining inspired some of the early prospectors to travel to the land that is now Wrangell-St. Elias National Park and Preserve, it was the discovery of gold in Chisana (pronounced Shooshana) that began the last great gold rush in Alaska. In 1913, thousands of stampeders made the treacherous journey through rugged country by whatever means possible to reach the newfound mining district. Chisana soon became known as "the largest log cabin town in the world." It was a short boom, lasting only a few years, but an important part of the history of this area.

Recreational opportunities in Wrangell-St. Elias include hunting, fishing, expedition mountaineering, backpacking/hiking, cross-country skiing, rafting/kayaking and wildlife observation. All hunting, fishing and trapping must be done in accordance with state and federal laws and regulations.

Navigable rivers in the park include the Copper and Chitina rivers. It is also possible to float several other streams in the park, such as the Nabesna and Kennicott rivers. Several guides and outfitters offer a variety of trips in the park and preserve.

Other than a handful of improved trails, hikers follow unimproved backcountry routes consisting of mining trails, historic routes, streambeds, shorelines, game trails and open country. For many hikers, hiring the services of a local guide will make the trip safer and more enjoyable. In general, the areas above tree line afford the easiest hiking and best views. These areas are often accessed by charter plane to one of the many "bush" landing strips in the park. Contact the park for current information on summer and winter use of ATVs or snow machines on park and preserve lands.

The Park Service cautions that visitors to the Wrangell-St. Elias backcountry must be self-sufficient; sources of assistance are frequently many miles away. Wilderness travel and survival skills are essential.

There are 14 public-use cabins located within Wrangell-St. Elias. All cabins are in remote locations and require hikers/campers to make appropriate plans for backcountry travel. Most cabins are available on a first-come, first-served basis, however there are currently 4 cabins that require advance reservations. Go to the park's public-use cabin page at www.nps.gov/wrst/planyourvisit/backcountry-cabins.htm to learn more about these cabins and to make a reservation.

There are a few designated campgrounds within the park/preserve; most opportunities are wilderness camping. No permits are necessary for camping or backpacking although voluntary registration is requested.

Visitor Information: The Kennecott Visitor Center is located in the historic Blackburn School in Kennicott, built in 1917. Open daily in summer; books, souvenirs and other items for sale. Slide presentations, a film, and other programs are presented here by the National Park Service. Phone (907) 554-1105.

The main Wrangell-St. Elias National Park and Preserve Visitor Center complex is located at **Milepost V 106.6** on the Richardson Highway. The visitor center, theater and exhibit hall are open daily in summer. Call ahead for hours; phone (907) 822-7250.

Park information is available intermittently at the historic Chitina Ranger Station in Chitina, and at the McCarthy Ranger information station kiosk at **Milepost C 58.4** McCarthy Road. Phone (907) 823-2205.

At the northern end of the park, information is available daily during the summer (closed in winter) at the Slana Ranger Station at Mile 0.2 Nabesna Road, just south of the Tok Cutoff; phone (907) 822-7401.

For more information, contact Wrangell-St. Elias National Park and Preserve, Park Headquarters, P.O. Box 439, Copper Center, AK 99573; phone (907) 822-5234; email wrst_tweet@nps.gov; or visit their website at www.nps.gov/wrst for additional details and information on recreational opportunities and various aspects of the park.

Denali Highway

CONNECTS: Paxson to Cantwell, AK

Length: 134 miles   **Road Surface:** 15% Paved, 85% Gravel   **Season:** Closed in winter

(See map, page 468)

Paddling the Maclaren River on the Denali Highway.
(©Milton & Kelley Barker, staff)

Major Attractions:

© Sharon Nault

*Tangle Lakes–Delta River Canoe Trail,
Maclaren Summit Trail,
Susitna & Maclaren Rivers,
Alaska Range*

Highest Summit:
*Maclaren Summit
4,086 ft.*

The 134-mile-long Denali Highway links Paxson at **Milepost V 185.5** on the Richardson Highway to Cantwell at **Milepost A 210** on the Parks Highway. When the Denali Highway opened in 1957, it was the only road link to Denali National Park and Preserve (then Mount McKinley National Park) until the completion of the Parks Highway in 1972. "If you want real wilderness scenery—vast tundra-covered valleys where caribou roam beneath breathtaking snow-covered mountains—then this highway is for you," says *MILEPOST®* field editor Sharon Nault.

Gas is available on the Denali Highway at Tangle River Inn, **Milepost P 20**, and at Clearwater Mountain Lodge, **Milepost P 82.2**. Gas is available at the west end of the Denali Highway in Cantwell, on the Parks Highway. Gas is not available in Paxson, at the east end of the Denali Highway on the Richardson Highway. The nearest gas on the Richardson Highway is 15 miles south of Paxson at Meier's Lake Roadhouse or 71 miles south in Glennallen, at The Hub. Gas is also available at Delta Petro-Wash in Delta Junction, 80 miles north.

The first 21 miles of the Denali Highway from Paxson and the first 3 miles from Cantwell are paved (speed limit is 50 mph). The remaining 110 miles are gravel. On a sunny day, Richardson Highway travelers should not miss a side trip on the Denali Highway, even if it is only the first 21 miles of pavement, the views are amazing.

Summer road conditions on the gravel portion of the Denali Highway vary, depending on how recently there has been highway maintenance, weather and the opinion of the driver. Trenching along the highway makes for rough access to many of the turnouts. But if you slow down for the rough spots, this road is very drivable.

Road surfacing beyond the paved sec-

Distance in miles	Cantwell	Delta Junction	Denali Park	Paxson
Cantwell		214	27	134
Delta Junction	214		241	80
Denali Park	27	241		161
Paxson	134	80	161	

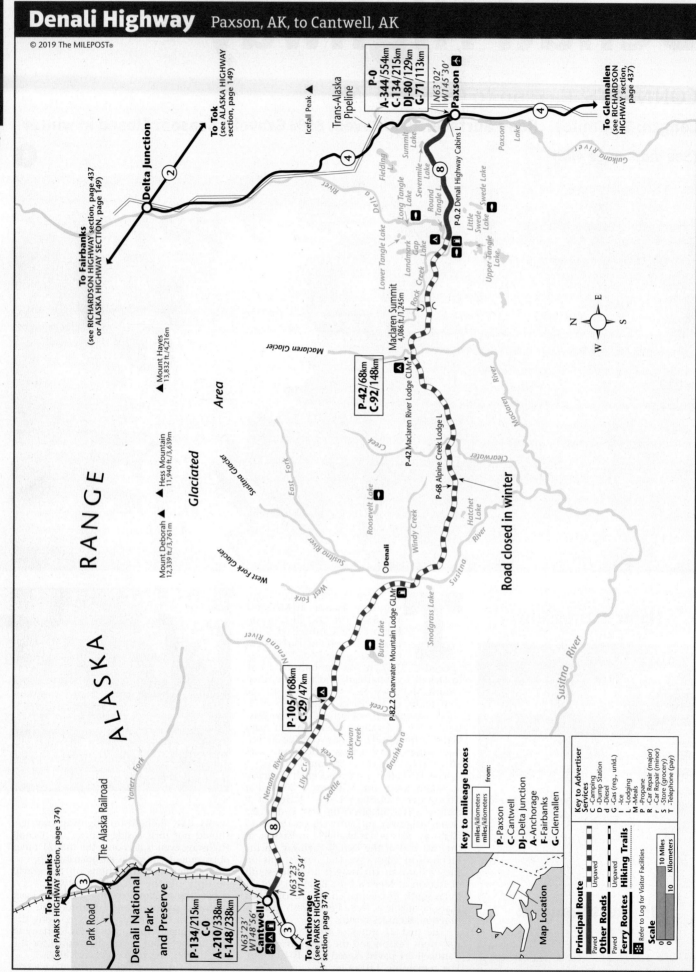

Denali Highway Paxson, AK, to Cantwell, AK

© 2019 The MILEPOST®

To Tok
(see ALASKA HIGHWAY
section, page 149)

Icefall Peak ▲

Trans-Alaska
Pipeline

P-0
A-344/554km
C-134/215km
DJ-80/129km
G-71/113km

N63°02'
W145°30'

Paxson ✈

To Glennallen
(see RICHARDSON
HIGHWAY section,
page 437)

Delta Junction

To Fairbanks
(see RICHARDSON HIGHWAY section, page 437
or ALASKA HIGHWAY SECTION, page 149)

8

P-0.2 Denali Highway Cabins L

Summit
Lake

Fielding
L

Sevenmile
Lake

Round
Tangle L

Little
Swede
Lake

Swede
Lake

Paxson
Lake

Guilkana River

Long Tangle
Lake

Upper Tangle
Lake

Lower Tangle Lake

Landmark
Lake

Rock Creek Lake

▲ Mount Hayes
13,832 ft./4,216m

Glaciated

Area

Maclaren Glacier

Maclaren Summit
4,086 ft./1,245m

P-42/68km
C-92/148km

P-42 Maclaren River Lodge CLMr

Maclaren River

▲ Hess Mountain
11,940 ft./3,639m

Mount Deborah ▲
12,339 ft./3,761m

Susitna Glacier

R A N G E

Clearwater

P-68 Alpine Creek Lodge L

Road closed in winter

East Fork

Susitna River

Roosevelt Lake

West Fork Glacier

Denali

Windy Creek

Hatchet
Lake

Susitna River

Susitna River

A L A S K A

West Fork

Snodgrass Lake

Butte Lake

Nenana River

P-82.2 Clearwater Mountain Lodge CLMr

P-105/168km
C-29/47km

Yanert Fork

Lily Cr.

Seattle
Creek

Stixkwan Creek

Brushkn a

The Alaska Railroad

To Fairbanks
(see PARKS HIGHWAY section, page 374)

3

Park Road

Denali National
Park and Preserve

P-134/215km
C-0
A-210/338km
F-148/238km

N63°23'
W148°56'

Cantwell

N63°23'
W148°54'

3

To Anchorage
(see PARKS HIGHWAY
section, page 374)

N
W ─── E
S

Key to mileage boxes

miles/kilometers
miles/kilometers   **from:**

P-Paxson
C-Cantwell
DJ-Delta Junction
A-Anchorage
F-Fairbanks
G-Glennallen

**Key to Advertiser
Services**

C -Camping
D -Dump Station
d -Diesel
G -Gas (reg., unld.)
I -Ice
L -Lodging
M-Meals
P -Propane
R -Car Repair (major)
r -Car Repair (minor)
S -Store (grocery)
T -Telephone (pay)

Principal Route
Paved   Unpaved
Other Roads
Paved   Unpaved
Ferry Routes   **Hiking Trails**
🅰 Refer to Log for Visitor Facilities

Map Location

Scale
0   10 Miles
0   10 Kilometers

www.themilepost.com

tions normally ranges from good gravel to rough and rocky. Stretches of washboard and potholes can develop quickly after days of rain. It can also be a dusty drive for motorists—and a very dusty ride for bicyclists—in dry weather. Road may be oiled to help to keep dust down. All types of vehicles and bicyclists share this road. The recommended speed of travel is 30 mph on gravel portions of the road, with slower speeds in areas with sharp rocks. Remember to decrease speed when approaching oncoming traffic to avoid rock chips from flying rocks.

For updated road information, phone 511 in state, toll-free 1-866-282-7577 out of state, or 511.alaska.gov.

The highway becomes narrower and more winding west of Maclaren Summit (elev. 4,086 feet). This is the second highest highway pass in the state, and represents the only significant grade on the highway. (It is also a great spot for a hike.)

The Denali Highway has been a favorite destination for many Alaskans over the years. Long-standing businesses and newer businesses along the highway that attest to this road's enduring popularity with travelers from east to west are: Audie and Jenny's **Denali Highway Cabins** at Paxson; the Tangle River Inn at **Milepost P 20**; Alan and Susie Echols' **Maclaren River Lodge** at **Milepost P 42**; **Alpine Creek Lodge** at **Milepost P 68** and the Kelley's **Clearwater Mountain Lodge** at **Milepost P 82.2**.

The Denali Highway provides access to the Delta River canoe trail at Tangle Lakes, headwaters of the Delta Wild and Scenic River, and to dozens of off road vehicle (ORV) trails. During the fall hunting season, the many small turnouts along the Denali Highway are packed with cars, campers and ORVs. For detailed information on ORV use on public lands or canoeing the Delta River, contact the Bureau of Land Management (BLM) field office in Glennallen, phone (907) 822-3217, or visit www.blm.gov/alaska for more information.

Birders will find Smith's Longspur, harlequin ducks, gyrfalcons, arctic warblers and more than 100 other species along the Denali Highway.

The Denali Highway is unmaintained and closed to vehicle traffic in winter, but draws a significant snow machine crowd. When snow covered, the Denali Highway becomes a winter destination of hundreds of snow machiners who travel out to lodges along the highway. Seasonal road maintenance ends Oct. 15. The Alaska Dept. of Transportation & Public Facilities reminds drivers that travel on an unmaintained highway during the winter is extremely risky and drifts can claim vehicles and lives. Crews begin opening the highway in early May, which involves 8 personnel working for 3 weeks from both Cantwell and Paxson.

Emergency Services: Dial 911. Nearest Alaska State Troopers from the Parks Highway entrance are at Cantwell, phone (907) 768-2205 or from Richardson Highway, the Glennallen Alaska State Trooper post at (907) 822-3263. Glennallen Cross Road Medical Clinic (907) 822-3203.

NOTE: Cell phone service is spotty on the Denali Highway to Milepost P 31, and then no service on the highway until Milepost P 128.2, just a few miles from the Parks Highway. Calling from lodges can be expensive via radio phone.

The Alaska Range captured with a zoom lens from viewpoint at Milepost P 94.5.
(©Sharon Nault)

Denali Highway Log

Westbound: Distance from Paxson (P) is followed by distance from junction with the Parks Highway at Cantwell (C). Read log: ⬇

ALASKA ROUTE 8

P 0 C 134.4 PAXSON (pop. 10; unincorporated) began in 1906 when Alvin Paxson established a roadhouse at Mile 192. He later built a larger roadhouse at Mile 191; the ruins can be seen on the east side of the highway at **Milepost V 185.8** Richardson Highway. The modern Paxson Lodge, a local landmark, has been closed since December 2013.

Lodging is available at **Denali Highway Cabins**, see description at **Milepost P 0.2**.

> **Junction** of the Richardson Highway (Alaska Route 4) with the Denali Highway (Alaska Route 8). Turn to **Milepost V 185.5** on page 449 in the RICHARDSON HIGHWAY section for log.

Private Aircraft: Paxson airstrip, adjacent south; elev. 2,653 feet; length 2,800 feet; gravel.

P 0.2 C 134.2 Gulkana River bridge. Side road to north at east end of bridge leads to **Denali Highway Cabins**; bed and breakfast open year-round, very nice cabins, dining hall, gift shop, electric bicycle rentals. Phone (907) 987-0977. Stop by and meet Aurora and Borealis, Jenny and Audie's well-known Alaska malemute dogs.

Denali Highway Cabins. See display ad on page 449 in RICHARDSON HIGHWAY section.

P 0.3 C 134.1 Active gravel pit to south; informal camping. Spawning red salmon in season. (This portion of the Gulkana River is closed to salmon fishing.) Look for "harleys" (harlequin ducks), arctic terns and other birds. Trail to Mud Lake.

Distance marker shows Tangle Lakes 21 miles, Cantwell 136 miles, Denali Park 164 miles.

P 0.4 C 134 Entering Paxson Closed Area (sign) westbound. The area south of the Denali Highway and east of the Richardson Highway is closed to the taking of all big game; see **Milepost P 4.4**.

P 0.7 C 133.7 Large paved turnout to south.

P 1.5 C 132.9 Large paved turnout to south.

P 2.1 C 132.3 Large paved turnout on hilltop to south. Westbound travelers may note the change in vegetation from spruce forest to alpine tundra.

P 3.4 C 131 Paved turnout to south. Several more turnouts next 3 miles westbound with views of Summit Lake to the north, Gakona Glacier to the northeast, Icefall Peak and Gulkana Glacier west of Icefall Peak, all in the **Alaska Range**. The 650-mile-long range, which extends across southcentral Alaska from the Canadian border southwest to Iliamna Lake, also contains Denali, the highest peak in North America.

Good views of trans-Alaska pipeline for Paxson-bound travelers.

P 4 C 130.4 Paved turnout to north. Views to east next 3 miles westbound of Mounts Sanford, Wrangell and Drum in the Wrangell Mountains; see viewpoint at **Milepost P 12.7**.

P 4.4 C 130 Large paved viewpoint to the north. Leaving Paxson Closed Area westbound. Closed to big game hunting, this area was set aside in 1958 to provide wildlife viewing adjacent the junction of the Richardson and Denali Highways. Beaver, moose and waterfowl are commonly seen. Moose are most common in winter because of the elevation and vegetation.

P 5 C 129.4 Large paved turnout to north.

P 5.7 C 128.7 Large paved turnout to north.

P 5.9 C 128.5 Gravel side road to north to large gravel parking area and primitive camping. ⛺

P 6.2 C 128.2 Paved turnout to south.

P 6.4 C 128 Side road to north leads 0.1 mile to small lake and 0.5 mile down to **Sevenmile Lake** to gravel parking area, informal camping, primitive firepits and good lake trout fishing (bait and treble hooks allowed). Primitive boat launch. 🚤 ⛺

P 6.7 C 127.7 Large paved turnout to south.

P 7 C 127.4 Paved rest area to the north. Informative stop with truly great views. Vehicle, bus and RV parking. This area offers viewing benches, picnic tables, pit toilet, bear proof garbage cans. Stunning view (on clear days) of Alaska Range and Sevenmile Lake and, in the distance, of Summit Lake and Gulkana Glacier. Interpretive sign with diagram of the Alaska Range and the names of the peaks. Other signs titled "Fish on the Denali" and "Trauma Under the Ice."

P 7.2 C 127.2 Large paved turnout to north. Highway climbs westbound.

P 7.8 C 126.6 Large paved turnout to north with view of Denali Highway.

P 8.3 C 126.1 Federal Subsistence area boundary. Paved turnout to north.

P 9.5 C 124.9 Paved turnout overlooking Ten Mile Lake. Primitive camping area with narrow, difficult gravel roads ahead.

P 10 C 124.4 Sloping, paved turnout to south on curve; overlooks Ten Mile Lake; good Arctic grayling fishing and some rainbow trout fishing (catch and release only). Narrow gravel road access south to primitive camping in gravel pit. Beaver dams on both sides of highway.

P 10.5 C 123.9 Paved turnout overlooking Ten Mile Lake to south at the top of an extensive glacial outwash plain dotted with kettle ponds; known locally as Hungry Hollow. These are examples of kettle lakes, formed by melting chunks of buried glacier. Highway begins to climb hill westbound.

P 10.6 C 123.8 Very rough, narrow, gravel road leads 0.3 mile south to **Octopus Lake**; limited parking, informal camping, fishing for lake trout, Arctic grayling, whitefish.

P 11 C 123.4 Excellent view of Octopus Lake. Federal Subsistence Hunting area (westbound sign).

P 11.1 C 123.3 Paved turnout to south. Look for blueberries in season. Treeless tundra to the north.

Watch for frost heaves and soft shoulders next 5.2 miles westbound.

P 11.5 C 122.9 Paved turnout to south.

Views of Hungry Hollow continue westbound.

P 12.1 C 122.3 Paved turnout to south with sweeping views of the tundra and lakes.

P 12.6 C 121.8 Gravel double-ended turnout to south with primitive camping.

P 12.7 C 121.7 Paved turnout to south is Wrangell Mountain viewpoint. BLM information sign on Denali Highway campgrounds, trailheads, points of interest and services can be found here. BLM brochures on the area are usually available at a box next to the sign.

The Wrangell Mountains are about 78 air miles southeast of here. The prominent peak on the left is Mount Sanford (elev. 16,237 feet); Mount Drum (elev. 12,010 feet) is on the right; and Mount Wrangell (elev. 14,163 feet) is in the center. Mount Wrangell is the northernmost active volcano on the Pacific Rim.

Adjacent gravel turnout provides room for primitive camping.

Slow for frost heaves, potholes, gravel patches to Milepost P 17.

P 13.6 C 120.8 Lake locally referred to as Cottongrass Lake. Beaver lodge near road.

P 14 C 120.4 Paved turnout to **14 Mile Lake**. Area offers primitive camping, and fishing for lake and rainbow trout (ADF&G stocked lake). The lake is 2.5 miles north of the highway and is in the valley to the west of Ridge Trail. ADF&G has a GPS trail route to access this lake.

P 14.1 C 120.3 Paved turnout; small visible lakes to north. Hikers often begin the 14 Mile Lake hike from here.

P 14.6 C. 119.8 Paved turnout to north.

Highway begins descent westbound to Tangle Lakes area. Frost heaves. Rough road, both sides of the turnout.

P 15.4 C 119 Large paved turnout to south with view of Swede lakes area to southwest.

P 16.2 C 118.2 Entering the **BLM Tangle Lakes Archaeological District** (sign to south) westbound. Within this 226,000-acre area, more than 500 archaeological sites chronicle man's seasonal reliance on the local natural resources. For more than 10,000 years, hunter-gatherers have dug roots, picked berries, fished and hunted big game (primarily caribou) in this area. You may hike along the same high, gravel ridges once used by prehistoric people and used today by modern hunters, anglers and berry pickers. To protect cultural resources, ORV travel is restricted to designated trails from this point to **Milepost P 38**.

P 16.6 C 117.8 Unmarked access road south to the beginning of the **Swede Lake Trail**; leads 0.3 mile into a large parking area with pit toilet and loading dock. Little Swede Lake 3 miles (take right fork), Big Swede Lake 4 miles. This trail connects with the Middle Fork Gulkana River branch trail (access to Dickey Lake and Meier Lake trail) and the Alphabet Hills trail. **Big Swede Lake** has excellent fishing for lake trout, Arctic grayling, whitefish and burbot. **Little Swede Lake** is excellent for lake trout. Inquire at Tangle River Inn for directions and trail information.

P 16.7 C 117.7 Paved turnout and gravel pit to south. Trucks entering the roadway here. Long gravel turnout to north is referred to by locals as "the one with the big rock in it," a landmark because of area fishing lakes. At the east end of this turnout, a trail leads to an unnamed but good fishing lake. At the west end of the turnout, alongside the road, is a shallow lake that has a visible beaver lodge and fish when water levels are high. Primitive camping. For fishing questions and local lakes, ask Jack Johnson at Tangle River Inn.

P 17.1 C 117.3 Paved turnout to north. Trailhead for **Rusty Lake** leads 0.75 mile to lake. Registration box at head of the trail. Fishing for lake trout and Arctic grayling.

P 17.6 C 116.8 Paved turnouts both sides of highway. Good berry picking in fall.

P 18.1 C 116.3 Gravel turnouts by small lakes both sides of highway. Beaver lodge to south.

P 18.3 C 116.1 Entrance to private hunting camp to south.

P 18.6 C 115.8 Paved turnout to north with view.

P 19.3 C 115.1 Paved turnout to south. A hiker registration box and trailhead are located here in the brush on south side of highway. The trail provides access to Swede Mountain and views of the Tangle Lakes and Alaska Range. Federal Subsistence area boundary. Delta U.S. Department of Interior Wild and Scenic River (sign).

P 20 C 114.4 Tangle River Inn to south, a long-time, family operated business; good food, gas, lodging and bar. Pet-friendly. Canoe and fishing gear rentals available featuring custom tied flies with proceeds donated to Wounded Warriors. This is an interesting stop with friendly and knowledgeable staff. Open mid-May through the end of September.

Jack Johnson homesteaded this area in 1953. The BLM honored his wife, Naidine Johnson, by naming a mountain after her in 2003 (see the plaque and the map showing the location of Mount Naidine).

P 20.1 C 114.3 Large paved turnout to north, just below the highway and west of the Tangle River Inn, overlooks Round Tangle Lake. *NOTE: Some turnouts in area posted No Parking.* This lake is one of a series of long, narrow lakes connected by the Tangle River that form the headwaters of the Delta River. The name Tangle is a descriptive term for the maze of lakes and feeder streams contained in this drainage system.

View to north of Alaska Range.

P 20.5 C 113.9 Paved turnout to north. Primitive gravel campsite below the turnout.

P 21 C 113.4 The Nelchina caribou herd travels through this area usually at the end of August or early in September, although hundreds have been spotted along the Denali Highway as early as late July.

P 21.1 C 113.3 Pavement ends. Hard chipseal begins.

P 21.3 C 113.1 One-lane bridge over Tangle River. Turnoff to north for access road (5-mph speed limit, watch for falling rocks) to **BLM Tangle Lakes Campground**, 0.5 mile north from highway. Information sign and campground map on access road. Campground fee $12/night in 2018, walk-in $6, rates subject to change and half-price discount for America the Beautiful, Senior and Access pass holders. There are 45 vehicle campsites (suitable for all sizes of rigs), walk-in raised tent sites and a group camping area. Facilities include: pit toilets, tables, firepits with grills, potable water, aluminum-can recycling, bear-proof garbage cans, numerous hiking trails, parking for boat trailers and cement boat launch, Kids Don't Float life jackets. Firewood may be available ($5). Information board gives instructions on what to do if you catch a tagged fish. This is a favorite place to camp for many Alaskans. Good berry picking in season. Walk the high ridges for wonderful views. Watch for mink, squirrels, ptarmigan, eagles, swans, caribou and moose along the Tangle River. Popular fishing spot for Arctic grayling and lake trout.

Easy access to boat launch for **Delta River Canoe Trail**, which goes north through Tangle Lakes to the Delta River. Self-register for river trips. The 2- to 3-day float to the takeout point on the Richardson Highway requires 1 portage. The Delta River Canoe Trail is managed by the BLM.

P 21.5 C 112.9 **BLM Delta Wild and Scenic River Wayside** and boat launch to south, day use only, no camping (strictly enforced); picnic tables, firepits with grills, garbage cans, pit toilets, potable water, Kids Don't Float life jackets, boat launch area, no fee. Two turnaround loops for easy-flow traffic in narrowed areas. Launch point for Upper Tangle Lakes canoe trail, which goes south through Tangle Lakes (portages required) to Dickey Lake, then follows the Middle Fork to the main Gulkana River. For details, contact the BLM at (907) 822-3217. Register here for river trips. Interpretive signs on water, wildlife and willows.

Watershed divide. The Gulkana River joins the Copper River, which flows into Prince William Sound. The Delta River joins the Tanana River, which flows into the Yukon River. The Yukon flows into the Bering Sea.

The Tangle Lakes system north and south of the highway **Long Tangle, Round Tangle, Upper Tangle** and **Lower Tangle Lake**) offers good Arctic grayling and lake trout fishing. Fishing begins as soon as the ice goes out, usually in early June, and continues into September. Troll shelf edges for lake trout.

P 22 C 112.4 Tangle Lakes Lodge offers cabin and canoe rentals and pizza.

P 22.3 C 112.1 Federal Subsistence area boundary.

P 23 C 111.4 Several primitive roadside campsites next 1.4 miles westbound (to Rock Creek bridge).

P 24.4 C 110 Gravel turnout to south. Landmark Gap Trailhead visible to north, Rock Creek bridge to west.

Distance marker westbound shows Cantwell 110 miles.

P 24.5 C 109.9 Landmark Gap, the cut in the mountains to the north, is visible from the highway. It is used by caribou during migration. This is a favorite trail for hikers too. A side road leads north to well-marked, improved Landmark Gap Trailhead. Primitive camping up rocky road onto a hill to the north. The trail leads 4 miles north to the south end of **Landmark Gap Lake**; Arctic grayling and lake trout fishing. According to the State of Alaska, Department of Natural Resources, this trail is suitable for mountain bikes and hiking.

P 24.7 C 109.7 Rock Creek 1-lane bridge; turnout and informal camping to north at west end of bridge. Arctic grayling fishing. Parking and creek access to north at both ends of bridge.

P 24.8 C 109.6 Landmark Gap South ORV Trail is signed to the southwest of highway; parking. The trail leads to the Oscar Lake area (11 miles).

Double-ended gravel parking to south just west of trailhead.

P 25 C 109.4 Short, rough gravel road up hill to north. Great primitive campsite with 360-degree view overlooks Landmark Pass and Rock Creek.

P 25.4 C 109 Rough gravel turnout to south for informal campsite and expansive views.

P 26 C 108.4 Side road to north to primitive campsite.

P 27.4 C 107 Gravel begins westbound, chipseal surface eastbound.

P 27.7 C 106.7 Gravel turnout to north.

P 28.1 C 106.3 Gravel turnout to north, overlooking lake and ponds.

P 29.3 C 105.1 Informal campsite beside small lake to south. Watch for grouse and caribou. Unmarked primitive roads to north and south.

P 30 C 104.4 Downhill dirt access to north to primitive camping area.

P 30.5 C 103.9 Gravel turnouts to north

Maclaren Summit at Milepost P 36.7 is the second highest highway pass in Alaska.
(©Sharon Nault)

and south on high, sometimes windy, overlook for Glacier Lake ORV Trail, which leads north 3 miles to **Glacier Lake**; lake trout and Arctic grayling fishing. Registration box at head of the trail. Trail is suitable for mountain biking and hiking. 360 degree views of Alaska Range. Rock Creek to the north runs parallel to the highway in valley below.

Highway winds along steep-sided esker westbound. An esker is a ridge made of silt, sand, gravel, rocks and boulders carried by a stream beneath a glacier. When the glacier melts an elongated rise of these substances remains. The Denali Highway has some of the best examples of eskers found in North America.

P 30.7 C 103.7 Steep downhill gravel turnout to north overlooking lake and ponds.

P 31.4 C 103 Very rough, double-ended rock turnout to north. In spite of this, people camp here for the view (primitive). Cell phone, via Verizon, worked here in 2018.

P 32.1 C 102.3 Gravel turnout to south and turnout to north (can have a pond in wet weather) with dramatic view of Amphitheater Mountains above High Valley. Glacier Lake is visible in the gap in these mountains. Glacier Gap trailhead; multi-purpose trail. East side of parking lot runs to Glacier Gap Lake and out to 7 Mile Lake. Trail to 7 Mile Lake is 9 miles (local trail-builder labeled the lake "spectacular").

P 33.6 C 100.8 Parking area (often used by highway department for storage) and informal camping to south. Small turnout to north. Locals claim that there are 20 to 30 caribou that range near here, year-round.

P 34.5 C 99.9 Dramatic high peaks of the Alaska Range visible to north, weather permitting.

P 35.2 C 99.2 Turnout to north. Views to the northwest of lakes on the western rim of "High Valley." Below the plunging rim to the west is the valley of the Maclaren River. The Amphitheatre Mountains parallel the highway to the northwest. Wildflowers here include various heaths, frigid shooting star, dwarf fireweed.

P 36 C 98.4 Thirtysix Mile Lake ½-mile hike north; lake trout and Arctic grayling.

P 36.3 C 98.1 Small rough turnout to south (turns down steeply to south). This area gets muddy in wet weather.

P 36.4 C 98 Sloping entrance for turnout to north with excellent views.

P 36.7 C 97.7 Maclaren Summit (elev. 4,086 feet). Second highest highway pass in Alaska (after 4,800-foot Atigun Pass on the Dalton Highway). From here you can look to the west where the Denali Highway enters the notch at **Milepost P 44.8**. For westbound travelers the highway drops down beneath the rim of the High Valley Mesa to the Maclaren River. Oscar Lake ORV Trail to south leads approximately 7 miles to Oscar Lake. Good parking area to south for both this and the Maclaren Summit ORV Trailhead on north side of road. The trailhead sign says it is about 2 miles; it is 1½ miles to a fork, bear left for best views. Trail continues if you are looking for a longer hike. Wonderful photo ops in this area.

The Alaska Dept. of Natural Resources recommends this 3-mile trail for mountain biking and hiking. Black currant berries and blueberries in season. Good views of the Alaska Range. Watch for swans, moose and other wildlife here. Registration boards with map.

P 36.8 C 97.6 Maclaren Summit elevation sign (elev. 4,086 feet). Small turnout to west with view of river valley, Mount Hayes (elev. 13,382 feet) and the Alaska Range. (There are several good view turnouts around Maclaren Summit.) As you descend your view is of Mount Hayes with Maclaren Glacier beneath, Eureka Glacier is to the east of Maclaren.

P 37 C 97.4 Rocky turnout with view of valley to west. Northbound traffic watch for soft muddy section west side of road.

P 37.6 C 96.8 Leaving Tangle Lakes Archaeological District westbound; see description at **Milepost P 16.2**. Turnout to southwest.

P 38 C 96.4 Large gravel turnout to southwest with views of valley and mountains.

P 38.4 C 96 Small turnouts to west, views.

Guide waits with gear for his party of hikers at Maclaren River Lodge. The lodge is also a jump-off point for jet boat rides. (©Sharon Nault)

P 38.8 C 95.6 Beaver lodges in lakes on both sides of highway in 2018.

P 39.7 C 94.7 Sevenmile Lake ORV Trail to north (watch for sign about 200 feet from road); 6.5-miles-long, brushy, parallels Boulder Creek, crosses peat bog. This is often very muddy in summer. Cow parsnip along the highway. Clearwater Creek Controlled Use Area (sign).

P 40 C 94.4 Distance marker eastbound shows Paxson 40 miles.

P 40.2 C 94.2 Double-ended gravel turnout to south with firepit.

P 40.5 C 93.9 Entering Mat-Su Borough (westbound sign)

P 40.6 C 93.8 Tangle Lakes Archaeological District (westbound sign)

P 40.8 C 93 Pond with sloughing bank to the south with marshy bottom. Areas here have been carbon-dated to 10,500 years ago.

P 40.9 C 93.5 Well used trail to south.

P 41.2 C 93.2 Turnout and parking to south. Entrance to airstrip that serves this area.

P 41.3 C 93 Double-ended turnout and dirt track to south.

P 41.4 C 92.4 Rough turnout to north.

P 41.9 C 92.5 Denali Highway Tours and Cabins.

P 42 C 92.4 Maclaren River Bridge, a 364-foot multiple span crossing this tributary of the Susitna River; parking. Turnout with picnic area and firepit to north at east end of bridge; great views of Maclaren Glacier. Maclaren River Lodge at west end of bridge (description follows).

Maclaren River Lodge to south on west side of bridge; good food, dry RV parking, pet-friendly, cabins, camping, tire repair, gas, boat launch, scenic boat trips. Gift shop specializing in furs. Easy hiking and good fishing. Friendly staff and family-oriented activities. Ask about canoe trips and remote camps in summer, especially the one near Maclaren Glacier (access by jet boat). Maclaren River Lodge is a popular snow machine destination in winter and provides a rustic, real-Alaska experience. It is surrounded by 100 miles of groomed snow machine trails extending out from the lodge. Groups book in advance. Open February 1 through October 1.

Maclaren River Lodge. See display ad this page.

P 43.3 C 91.1 Maclaren River Road to north leads 14 miles to Maclaren Glacier; mountain biking. Small parking area near entrance. It is a 4 mile rugged dirt road to the river crossing which can be deep and treacherous.

The Maclaren River rises in the glaciers surrounding Mount Hayes. For the next 60 miles westbound, the highest peaks of this portion of the mighty Alaska Range are visible, weather permitting, to the north. From east to west: Mount Hayes, Hess Mountain (elev. 11,940 feet) and Mount Deborah (elev. 12,339 feet). Mount Hayes, first climbed in August 1941, is named after Charles Hayes, an early member of the U.S. Geological Survey. Mount Deborah, first climbed in August 1954, was named in 1907 by Judge Wickersham after his wife.

Clearwater Creek Controlled Use Area to north (sign).

P 43.8 C 90.6 Short gravel road to north offers private primitive camping. Deep dip at entrance.

P 44.4 C 90 Distance marker westbound shows Cantwell 90 miles.

P 44.8 C 89.6 Westbound, the highway enters **Crazy Notch**, a long gap in the glacial moraine cut by a glacial stream that geologists state is 12,000–13,000 years old. From Crazy Notch to **Milepost P 56** there are many primitive campsites and side roads.

P 46 C 89.4 Eastbound, highway enters Crazy Notch (see description above).

P 46.2 C 88.2 Long gravel turnout to north.

P 46.4 C 88 Unsigned roads in this area lead to lake north of the highway. Watch for swans, hawks and redpolls. Fishing for Arctic grayling in lake and outlet stream.

P 46.6 C 87.8 Side road to informal camping above lake to north.

P 47.1 C 87.3 Side road to north.

P 48 C 86.4 Highway begins traveling on top of an esker westbound, providing great views. Watch for wildlife. Excellent Arctic grayling fishing in **Crooked Creek**, which parallels the highway.

P 48.5 C 85.9 Informal campsite by small lake to south. Turnouts both sides of road. Trail leads to mountain to the south.

P 49 C 85.4 The highway follows an esker between 4 lakes. (See **Milepost P 58** for description of eskers.) Watch for ducks, geese, grebes and shorebirds in lakes, as well as bald eagles, moose, caribou, beaver and fox in the vicinity. Look for a pingo (earth-covered ice hill) at lakeshore.

P 49.4 C 85 Turnout to north with primitive firepit. Next 0.6 mile, watch for sections of chipseal on road.

P 49.5 C 84.9 Turnout to north overlooks 50 Mile Lake. Interpretive plaque on glacial topography and wildlife. Watch for moose to south.

P 49.6 C 84.8 Primitive road to north leads down to lake and informal camping. Used in fall by hunters.

P 50.9 C 83.5 Small turnout to southwest with view.

P 51.5 C 82.9 Rugged dirt road to north to informal campsites. Moore's hunting camp (private) to south. Trail and overlook to north. Beaver lodge in pond to south.

P 53.2 C 81.2 Gravel road to north.

P 53.6 C 80.8 Gravel track to south.

P 55.3 C 79.1 Large primitive camping area to south.

P 55.7 C 78.7 Clearwater Creek 1-lane bridge. Wayside with pit toilet east side of bridge; informal camping, 2 firepits, 2 picnic tables, Arctic grayling fishing. Large turnouts both sides of bridge. (West side turnout has launch area.) Clearwater Creek Trail South begins here. See map at registration booth. Caribou have been seen in this area in early August.

P 56.1 C 78.3 Primitive campsite to north.

P 56.4 C 78 Primitive campsite to north.

P 57.2 C 77.2 Double-ended turnout to north on top of small esker; muddy when wet.

P 58 C 76.4 Road winds atop an esker flanked by kames and kettle lakes; great views below, watch for moose, birds, other wildlife. Eskers are ridges of silt, sand and gravel carried by inner glacial streams and left behind when the glacier receded. The eskers along Denali Highway are some of the best examples in North America. Eskers are great places to take a walk.

P 58.9 C 75.5 Small gravel turnout to north.

P 59.1 C 75.3 Long, sloped, uneven and deeply pitted turnout to north. Look for patches of blueberries in season on top of esker.

P 59.3 C 75.1 Small rough turnout with view to north

P 59.4 C 75 Long gravel turnout to north.

P 59.8 C 74.6 Begin climb up esker for westbound traffic. Leave esker for eastbound traffic.

P 60 C 74.4 Large, primitive camping area to south with ATV trail, just east of milepost.

P 61.5 C 72.9 Small, rough gravel viewpoint up hill to south.

P 61.9 C 72.5 Narrow side road to south leads ¼ mile to informal camping.

P 62.5 C 71.9 Rough informal camping with firepits to south.

P 63 C 71.4 Single-vehicle turnout to north by Sarah Lake.

P 63.7 C 70.7 Rough double-ended turnout up hill to south, informal camping spot. Good view.

P 64 C 70.4 Road descends westbound into Susitna River valley; good view of river ahead as you drive down the hill to the west. Small turnout to south.

P 64.4 C 70 Small turnout to south.

Distance marker westbound shows Cantwell 70 miles.

P 64.9 C 69.5 Rough turnout to south with view; room for large RV.

P 65.5 68.9 Primitive campsite up hill to north.

P 66 C 68.4 Dirt turnout to north.

P 66.7 C 67.7 Small, steep, rocky double-ended turnout with view to south.

P 67.2 C 67.2 Small turnout with view to south.

P 67.9 C 66.5 Turnout to south. Rough road eastbound.

P 68 C 66.4 Alpine Creek Lodge offers good food, bar, lodging and free coffee. Old-time Alaska lodge atmosphere, beautiful views from lodge. This lodge is the destination for hundreds of snow machiners in winter. Visitors reported seeing caribou, grizzly and moose tracks after a trail ride here in summer 2017. There are 2 uphill driveway entrances to the north. Park at the first level and walk up, or drive all the way up and then to the left going by the back of the lodge to use the large parking area on the side. They have 3 RV spots for dry camping. Pet-friendly.

Alpine Creek Lodge. See display ad this page.

P 69.5 C 65.9 Road winds around Clearwater Mountains westbound.

P 69.8 C 64.6 Small turnout to south with view.

P 71 C 63.4 Road winds through brush on side of mountain. Watch for caribou.

P 72.6 C 61.8 Short gravel road (0.5 mile) to turnaround with primitive camping, firepit.

P 72.7 C 61.7 Highway travels by 2 lakes. Clearwater Mountains to north.

NOTE: There are many small tracks leading off the highway through the brush, often to good primitive campsites. Travelers are advised to check these out prior to pulling into them to ensure access for your rig. These can offer great camping opportunities.

P 73.6 C 60.8 Access road leads north to large lake. Good turnaround area, primitive campsites on hill above the lake. Brushy trail to water.

P 74.9 C 59.5 Small turnout with view to south. Informal camping.

P 77.3 C 57.1 Airfield to north.

P 77.7 C 56.7 The privately-owned Old Susitna Lodge, next to lake northeast of highway, has been closed and privately owned for business for many years. *Please respect private property.*

For northbound traffic, old mining trails are visible to the side of the 5,556-foot mountain straight ahead, part of the Alaska Range, near Windy Creek.

P 78.2 C 56.2 Road to north into very large gravel pit.

P 78.4 C 56 Narrow road to south goes to end of esker. Walk out to view.

P 78.5 C 55.9 Expansive view of Susitna River and bridge.

P 79.1 C 55.3 Valdez Creek Road leads 11.5 miles north to the former mining camp of Denali. *NOTE: The first few miles of this side road have several informal camping areas that have been used as primitive mining camps. Travel may not be recommended due to road damage and washouts.* Denali was first established in 1907 after the 1903 discovery of gold in the Clearwater Mountains. The Valdez Creek Mine operated at this site until closing in 1995, producing 495,000 oz. of gold. Area mining equipment was donated to the Museum of Transportation and Industry, located at **Milepost A 47** Parks Highway. Do not trespass on mining claims.

Fair fishing reported in **Roosevelt Lake** and area creeks. Watch for bears.

Clearwater Creek Controlled Use Area (sign).

P 79.2 C 55.2 Wide entrance to road to north to very large gravel pit.

P 79.4 C 55 Susitna River boat launch at northeast end of bridge. May be rough due to earlier flooding. The bank can drop

View of Denali country, and a woodpile for winter, at Alpine Creek Lodge.
(©Milton & Kelley Barker, staff)

off steeply depending on water levels. It is possible to launch with a boat trailer but advisable to have some help. Very limited parking, with most available space needed for launching. Parking at **Milepost P 79.1** (Valdez Creek Road), and at **Mileposts P 80** and **P 80.3** (heavily used).

P 79.5 C 54.9 Susitna River bridge (1-lane, wood deck), a combination multiple span and deck truss, 1,036 feet long. Butte Creek trailhead.

CAUTION: Bridge is slippery when wet. Slow for rough edges at both ends of bridge.

The Susitna River heads at Susitna Glacier in the Alaska Range (between Mounts Hess and Hayes) and flows southwest 260 miles to Cook Inlet. Downstream through Devil's Canyon, it is considered unfloatable. The river's Tanaina Indian name, said to mean "sandy river," first appeared in 1847 on a Russian chart. Blueberry picking west end of bridge in fall.

Entering Game Management Unit 13E westbound, leaving unit 13B eastbound.

P 80 C 54.4 Gravel pit; parking to south, room for large RVs.

Distance marker eastbound shows Paxson 80 miles.

P 80.3 C 54.1 Large parking areas both sides of highway (used by hunters in season; watch for ATVs on road). There are some good, level places up roads here for primitive camping.

P 80.4 C 54 Double-ended turnout to south.

P 81.1 C 53.3 Road north to lake is private property. Please do not trespass.

©Milton & Kelley Barker, staff

P 82.2 C 52.2 Historical Milepost 82. Clearwater Mountain Lodge to south; a B&B with multiple tour options, large meeting room, baked goodies, The Sluice Box bar, food, gas and tire repair. Phone (907)

203-1057. Open February through the end of September.

Clearwater Mountain Lodge. See display ad this page.

P 82.8 C 51.6 Large turnout to north with firepit.

P 82.9 C 51.5 Large gravel turnout with primitive camping.

P 84 C 50.4 Large Lake to the south; Arctic grayling fishing. Watch for moose here (especially on autumn mornings).

P 84.4 C 50 Distance marker westbound shows Cantwell 50 miles.

P 84.6 C 49.8 View of lake (0.5 mile) and the Alaska Range westbound. Blueberries in season along highway.

P 85.2 C 49.2 Turnout to north. There are numerous informal campsites heavily used by hunters and campers the next 10 miles westbound.

P 87 C 47.4 Turnout to north. Primitive gravel camping area to north. Pothole-type lake to south. View of Valdez Creek mining area across Susitna River to south.

P 87.6 C 46.8 Turnout and side road to south.

P 87.9 C 46.5 Side road to south leads to primitive parking and trail that goes up and over mountain to south. (Trail can be used by ORVs.)

P 88.2 C 46.2 Turnout to south, primitive camping with firepit. Good view of Alaska Range.

P 88.4 C 46 Large double-ended turnout to north into a rough gravel area. One of the best views of the Alaska Range on this highway. Primitive camping area with firepits. Views of Mounts Deborah, Hess and Hayes.

P 88.7 C 45.7 Lake next to highway to north.

P 89.3 C 45.1 Double-ended turnout to north with firepits and mountain and valley views.

P 90 C 44.4 Large dirt turnouts with views to north and small turnout to south.

P 90.1 C 44.3 Dirt turnout to south with view overlooking lake and mountains to the north.

P 90.5 C 43.9 Pond to south fed by small stream. A major water drainage divide occurs near here. East of the divide, the tributary river system of the Susitna flows south to Cook Inlet. West of the divide, the Nenana River system flows north to the Yukon River, which empties into the Bering Sea.

P 91.2 C 43.2 Dirt turnout to north.

P 91.7 C 42.7 Rough dirt side road leads north to informal campsite.

P 92.2 C 42.2 Turnout to north.

P 92.7 C 41.7 Rough brush-lined road to north leads to informal camping, firepit, view.

P 92.9 C 41.5 Large turnout with mountain view (may be used for gravel storage).

P 93.4 C 41 Large primitive camping area to north with good mountain and valley views. Landmark is a rustic 2-story building in the distance. ORV trail to south.

P 93.5 C 40.9 Informal campsite to north.

P 93.7 C 40.7 Small sloped turnout to north with views and informal camping.

P 94 C 40.4 Butte Lake ORV Trail leads 5 miles south to lake; well-used road to trailhead. Best fishing June through September. Lake trout, troll with red-and-white spoons or Arctic grayling remains; Arctic grayling, small flies or spinners.

P 94.1 C 40.3 Rough turnout with big view to north.

P 94.5 C 39.9 Short road through brush to north leads to parking area above pond, can accommodate big rigs; expansive views; primitive campsites, firepits. Information board on earthquakes and schematic identifying peaks of Alaska Range. Beautiful vista includes Monahan Flat and Alaska Range to the north. This is a favorite viewpoint for many Alaskans. The ORV trail below this parking area travels 12 miles north to the West Fork Glacier, below Mount Deborah. Decent hiking but can be rough and muddy. Look for caribou here late in July.

Begin steep downhill westbound.

P 95 C 39.4 Bridge over Canyon Creek. Turnout to south at east end of bridge; sloped turnout to north at west end of bridge.

P 95.7 C 38.7 Sloping turnout to north with view; watch for soft spots. ORV trail to south.

P 95.8 C 38.6 Large dirt turnout to north. Watch for soft ruts.

P 96 C 38.4 Turnout and overlook to north. Primitive firepit and fairly level parking. Looking north up the face of this glacier, Mount Deborah is the peak on the left; Mount Hess is the peak nearest it.

P 96.3 C 38.1 Rough turnout to north with good view.

P 96.5 C 37.9 Parking both sides of highway (very steep access to north) and access to "the Knob" viewpoint; expansive views of valley, mountains and West Fork Glacier. A favorite spot for hunters, hikers and photographers; may be accessible with 4-wheel-drive vehicles. This viewpoint is surrounded by an amphitheater of mountains. A trail leads south across the road from the viewpoint and goes up over the top of the hill to the south.

P 97.2 C 37.2 Side road leads south to viewless, sheltered parking area. From the highway, the Alaska Range is to the north, Mount Deborah, is to the right and behind it is Hess Mountain. Further to the right, the highest, with 2 knobs is Mount Hayes; to the left are the lower peaks of the Alaska Range and Nenana Mountain.

P 97.8 C 35.6 Rough 4-wheel drive road leads north to campsite; stunning view of Alaska Range and lake below on a clear day.

P 98 C 36.4 Wide access road to north leads to large sparsely forested viewpoint of Alaska Range. Primitive campsites on rugged road with loop turnaround. Transition zone: leaving alpine terrain westbound as landscape becomes more heavily forested with spruce trees.

P 98.9 C 35.5 Sloping dirt turnout to north with firepit.

P 99 C 34.4 Sloping turnout to south.

P 99.5 C 33.9 Private lodge to south (status unknown).

P 100 C 33.4 Distance marker eastbound shows Paxson 100 miles.

P 100.6 C 33.8 Steep access road to north with primitive campsite.

P 100.8 C 33.6 Primitive camping area to north with view of the Alaska Range to north.

P 102.2 C 32.2 Turnout to north, pond to south.

P 102.9 C 31.5 Large turnout to north and several small turnouts with terrific views on a clear day.

P 103.3 C 31.1 Long narrow turnout to north on top of esker; 360° view.

P 103.4 C 31 Several view turnouts along

this esker. Blueberries in season. Good view of Alaska Range, weather permitting. Watch for caribou, moose, marmot and swans. Nice place for a walk.

P 104 C 30.4 Dirt turnout; also side road leading south.

P 104.5 C 29.9 Distance marker westbound shows Cantwell 30 miles.

P 104.6 C 29.8 Brushkana River bridge (narrow) and **BLM Brushkana Creek Campground** to north at west end of bridge. Well-maintained, thickly forested campground; information board and campground map at entrance; turnaround area at fee box. Camping fee $12/night (summer 2018; fee subject to change); America the Beautiful, Senior and Access pass for half-price discount. There are 22 sites for both RVs and tents (some tent sites have raised, grass-covered platforms) beside river, most sites are in trees; tables, picnic shelter, firepits, pit toilets, bear-proof litter bins, aluminum can recycling, and potable water. Firewood sometimes available. Nice day-use area with picnic shelter and tables, right on the river. Very good fishing for Arctic grayling. Access to BLM Brushkana Creek trail (2 miles).

Distance marker westbound shows Cantwell 30 miles.

P 104.7 C 29.7 Sloped dirt turnout to north.

P 105.5 C 28.9 Dirt road to south.

P 106.2 C 28.2 Primitive dirt road to south.

P 106.9 C 27.5 Canyon Creek, Arctic grayling fishing (was barely a trickle in 2018). Side road to north.

P 107.4 C 27 Stixkwan Creek flows under highway in culvert. Small level turnout to north above creek. There are many unexplored side roads in this area. *CAUTION: This corner has no shoulder and slopes to the north.*

P 109.2 C 25.2 Gravel turnout to south. Well-used side road to north.

P 110.4 C 24 Road to gravel pit to north.

P 110.6 C 23.8 Steep downgrade westbound next 0.7 mile to Seattle Creek; trucks use low gear.

P 111.3 C 23.1 Seattle Creek bridge. Fishing for Arctic grayling and Dolly Varden. Long narrow gravel access to north on east side of bridge with parking area. Watch for moose and porcupine.

P 111.7 C 22.7 Turnout to north with nice view.

P 112 C 22.4 Rough turnout to north, trail to south.

P 112.2 C 22.2 Lily Creek. Side road to north leads out along bluff and then down to informal camping area on Lily Creek.

P 112.5 C 21.9 Turnout with firepit and trail to south.

P 113.5 C 20.9 Matanuska–Susitna Borough boundary eastbound and Denali Borough westbound. Road improves for 5 miles westbound.

P 113.6 C 20.8 Turnout with view to north; trail to south. View to east of the Alaska Range and extensive rolling hills and valleys grazed by caribou.

P 115 C 19.4 Long rough turnout to north. Side road to south.

P 115.8 C 18.6 Short turnout and trail to south. Good views as highway begins descent westbound to Nenana River.

P 116 C 18.4 Turnout to north, view of Nenana River obscured by brush. Just west is

Water pump at BLM campground on the Denali Highway. (©Sharon Nault)

a large turnout to north with BLM information board on the Denali Highway and view of Nenana River.

Steep downgrade westbound.

The Denali Highway now parallels the Nenana River westbound. The Nenana River heads in Nenana Glacier and flows into the Tanana River, a tributary of the Yukon River. The Nenana is popular with professional river rafters—particularly the stretch of river along the Parks Highway near the Denali Park entrance—but it is not good for fishing, due to heavy glacial silt.

P 116.8 C 17.6 Begin steep grade uphill next 0.8 mile eastbound.

P116.9 C 17.5 Small road to south offers primitive camping. Not for RVs.

P 117 C 17.4 Begin improved highway westbound.

P 117.7 C 16.7 Informal campsite in a small hollow to the north of the highway. There is river access here (in disrepair), but respect posted private property near this area. Westbound motorists are leaving BLM public lands.

P 118 C 16.4 *Ahtna, Inc. lands border highway to Parks Highway junction. Ahtna lands are open to entry by permit only; for more information and links to online permits go to www.ahtna-inc.com/land-permit.*

P 118.2 C 16.2 Long, narrow double-ended turnout to south.

P 118.3 C 16.1 Turnout to north on Nenana River at Mile 16 Put-In for Nenana River Users, and large parking area to south, just east of put-in. A small boat can be put over the bank here. *NOTE: The boat launch access has been in poor shape in the past due to flooding. CAUTION: Watch for grizzly bears and fast flowing water; river bank has drop-offs.*

P 118.7 C 15.7 Large stream runs through culvert under highway. Parking area and gravel pit to south. Posted: Private property.

P 119 C 15.4 Large level turnout and gravel track to south.

P 120 C 14.4 *CAUTION: Watch for moose.* Distance marker eastbound shows Paxson 120 miles.

P 121.2 C 13.2 Gravel turnout to south.

P 121.5 C 12.9 Large turnout at gravel pit to north.

P 121.8 C 12.6 Beautiful big stream runs under road in culvert.

P 122.1 C 12.3 Small sloping gravel turnout with view to north.

P 122.9 C 11.5 Large level turnout to north. Views westbound of Denali (weather permitting).

P 124.3 C 10.1 Parking area to north. Turnout overlooking pond to south; primitive camping.

Distance marker westbound shows Cantwell 10 miles.

P 124.4 C 10 Small gravel turnout to south. Look for large beaver dam.

P 126.2 C 8.2 Turnout to south with parking and lake access. Primitive camping with firepit. Information board with map. Joe Lake, about 0.5 mile long, is south of highway and is sometimes used by air services. **Jerry Lake** is about 0.2 mile north of the highway; Arctic grayling.

P 126.5 C 7.9 Turnout to south on Joe Lake (can flood).

P 127.2 C 7.2 Small turnout to north.

P 128.8 C 5.6 Fish Creek. Access to creek and turnout to south.

Beautiful view (weather permitting) of Talkeetna Mountains to the south and Denali to the southwest.

P 128.9 C 5.5 Fish Creek bridge. Road is chipseal surfaced westbound.

P 130 C 4.4 Road improves westbound. Cell service begins westbound in 2018.

P 130.5 C 3.9 Large gravel turnouts on both sides of highway.

P 131.4 C 3 Very large turnout to north. Popular parking spot for snow machiners in winter.

P 131.7 C 2.7 *Large turnout is for school buses, snow plows and road graders only.*

P 131.8 C 2.6 Gravel ends, pavement begins, westbound. Pavement ends, gravel begins, eastbound. Watch for potholes, washboard and washouts eastbound.

P 132.5 C 1.9 CAUTION: Steep drop-off to north.

P 132.7 C 1.7 Large gravel turnout to north.

P 133 C 1.4 Power station to north.

P 133.4 C 1 Large turnout to south with photo op of Denali on a clear day (brush may obscure view).

P 133.8 C 0.6 Cantwell Station DOT highway maintenance camp.

P 134 C 0.4 Alaska State Trooper Post to north. Phone (907) 768-2205.

P 134.4 C 0 CANTWELL at **junction** of the Denali Highway (Route 8) and the Parks Highway (Route 3). **Cantwell RV Park** is straight ahead westbound. Turn north on Parks Highway for **Cantwell Food Mart/ Chevron** gas/diesel station, **BluesBerry Inn** lodging, Denali National Park and Fairbanks. Turn south on highway for gas station/ convenience store, Talkeetna, Wasilla and Anchorage. *See description pages 398–399 in the PARKS HIGHWAY section.*

Junction of Denali Highway and Parks Highway at Cantwell. Turn to **Milepost A 210** on page 398 in the PARKS HIGHWAY section for log.

Eastbound: Distance from junction with the Richardson Highway at Paxson (P) is followed by distance from Cantwell (C). Read log:

*NOTE: Ahtna, Inc. lands border highway eastbound to **Milepost P 118**, permit required; www.ahtna-inc.com/land-permit.*

Steese Highway

CONNECTS: Fairbanks to Circle, AK

Length: 161 miles   **Road Surface:** 50% Paved, 50% Gravel   **Season:** Open all year

The Steese Highway offers beautiful summit views and alpine hiking. (©Sharon Nault)

Distance in miles	Central	Chena Hot Springs	Circle	Fairbanks
Central		180	34	128
Chena Hot Springs	180		213	61
Circle	34	213		161
Fairbanks	128	61	161	

The Steese Highway connects Fairbanks to Circle, a small settlement 161 miles to the northeast on the Yukon River, 50 miles south of the Arctic Circle. The Steese Highway is designated a Scenic Byway and the scenery alone makes this a worthwhile drive. It is especially colorful in late August and early September when the leaves turn. Acres of fireweed have filled up burned areas and offer bright splashes of color in the summer and fall. The Steese Highway offers beautiful summit views, hiking, berry picking, wildlife and camping.

The first 81 miles of the Steese Highway is good paved road while the next 45 miles is wide gravel road to the community of Central at **Milepost F 127.7**, where there is a 1.5-mile stretch of paved road. The final 33 miles, from Central to Circle, is winding gravel road, in fair to good condition. Road conditions depend on grading schedules; this road can develop washboard and soft spots. It is normally quite drivable and usually has little traffic, *but use caution on blind curves and be alert for oncoming traffic: some drivers take it too fast!*

The Steese Highway was completed in 1927 and named for Gen. James G. Steese, U.S. Army, former president of the Alaska Road Commission. It provided access to the Central Mining District, and remains an important route to the Yukon River. At 2,000 miles, the Yukon is Alaska's largest river. It heads in Canada, then flows west into Norton Sound on the Bering Sea.

The Steese Highway is open year-round. Check with the Dept. of Transportation in Fairbanks regarding winter road conditions, as the road may be closed due to weather. Phone 511 in Alaska or go to 511.Alaska.gov.

Gas and diesel are available at the Tesoro at **Milepost F 11** Steese Expressway, in Central and at the **H.C. Company Store** in Circle, **Milepost F 161.2**.

Major Attractions:

©Sharon Nault

Davidson Ditch, Gold Dredges/Gold Panning, Pipeline Viewpoint, Nome Creek Valley, Yukon River

Highest Summit:
Eagle Summit 3,685 ft.

Steese Highway Fairbanks, AK to Circle, AK

© 2019 The MILEPOST®

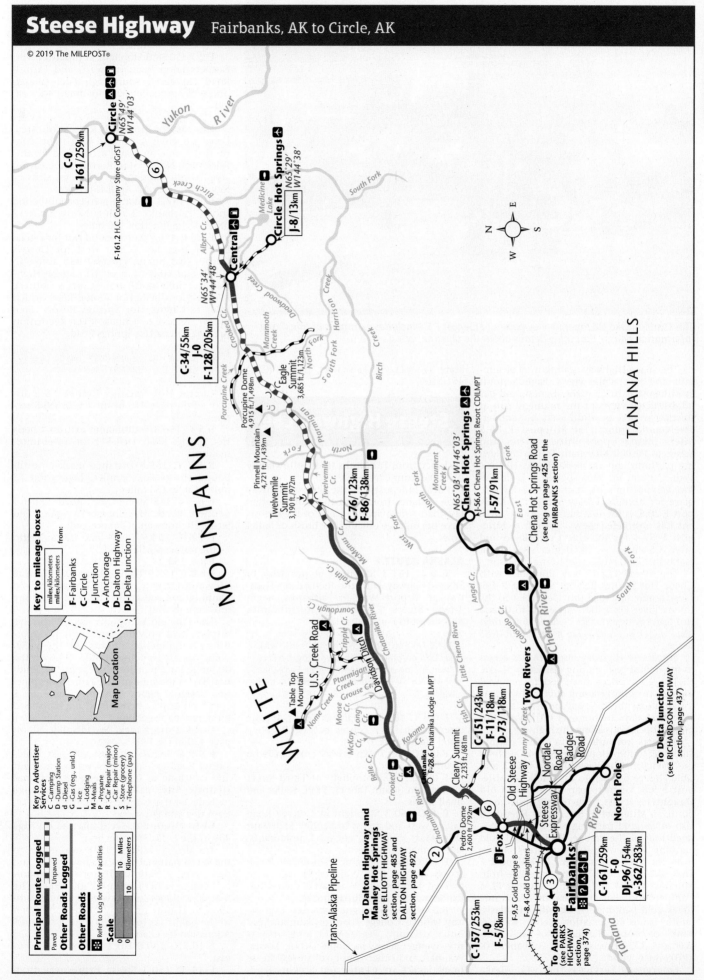

Key to mileage boxes

miles/kilometers
miles/kilometers

from:

F-Fairbanks
C-Circle
J-Junction
A-Anchorage
D-Dalton Highway
DJ-Delta Junction

Map Location

Key to Advertiser Services

C -Camping
D -Dump Station
d -Diesel
G -Gas (reg., unld.)
I -Ice
L -Lodging
M -Meals
P -Propane
R -Car Repair (major)
r -Car Repair (minor)
S -Store (grocery)
T -Telephone (pay)

Principal Route Logged

Paved
Unpaved

Other Roads Logged

Other Roads

✦ Refer to Log for Visitor Facilities

Scale
0   10   Miles
0   10   Kilometers

Circle N65°49', W144°03'

C-0
F-161/259km

F-161.2 H.C. Company Store dGrST

Yukon River

Birch Creek

6

Circle Hot Springs N65°29', W144°38'

Central N65°34', W144°48'

J-8/13km

Medicine Lake

Albert Cr.

Albert Cr.

South Fork

C-34/55km
J-0
F-128/205km

Crooked Cr.

Porcupine Creek

Mammoth Creek

Deadwood Creek

North Fork

Harrison Creek

South Fork

Birch

Eagle Summit 3,685 ft./1,123m

Porcupine Dome 4,915 ft./1,498m

Pinnell Mountain 4,721 ft./1,439m

Ptarmigan Cr.

North Fork

Twelvemile Summit 3,190 ft./972m

C-76/123km
F-86/138km

WHITE

MOUNTAINS

McManus Cr.

Faith Cr.

Table Top Mountain

U.S. Creek Road

Nome Creek

Sourdough Cr.

Cripple Cr.

Ptarmigan Creek
Grouse Cr.
Moose Cr.
Long Cr.
McKay Cr.

Davidson Ditch

Chatanika River

Kokomo Cr.

Chatanika
F-28.6 Chatanika Lodge ILMPT

Belle Cr.
Crooked Cr.

Chatanika River

Pedro Dome 2,600 ft./792m

2

Fox

F-9.5 Gold Dredge 8
F-8.4 Gold Daughters

C-157/253km
J-0
F-5/8km

Trans-Alaska Pipeline

To Dalton Highway and Manley Hot Springs (see ELLIOTT HIGHWAY section, page 485 and DALTON HIGHWAY section, page 492)

To Anchorage (see PARKS HIGHWAY section, page 374)

Cleary Summit 2,233 ft./681m

C-151/243km
F-11/18km
D-73/118km

Fish Cr.

Little Chena River

Monument Creek

North Fork

West Fork

East Fork

Angel Cr.

Colorado Cr.

Chena Hot Springs N65°03', W146°03'

J-56.6 Chena Hot Springs Resort CDILMPT

J-57/91km

Chena Hot Springs Road (see log on page 425 in the FAIRBANKS section)

Two Rivers
Jenny M Creek

Chena River

South Fork

TANANA HILLS

N

E

W

S

Old Steese Highway

Steese Expressway

Nordale Road

Badger Road

North Pole

Tanana River

Fairbanks
C-161/259km
F-0
DJ-96/154km
A-362/583km

6

3

To Delta Junction (see RICHARDSON HIGHWAY section, page 437)

The Trans-Alaska Oil Pipeline viewpoint at Milepost F 8.4 includes examples of "pigs" and information boards that relay details about the pipeline. (©David L. Ranta, staff)

The Steese Highway is a highway of summits and spectacular views. Eagle Summit at **Milepost F 107.1** is the highest, and has unobstructed views of the midnight sun at solstice as well as wildflowers in summer. Twelvemile Summit at **Milepost F 85.5** offers biking opportunities, views and access to Pinnell Mountain Trail with viewing platform and Circle–Fairbanks Historic Trail. Caribou are often spotted at Eagle and Twelvemile summits in the fall, a favorite place for hunters. Cleary Summit at **Milepost F 20.5**, is the first summit on the route but has obstructed views. Turnoff at **Milepost F 57.4** for the U.S. Creek Road and drive 3.5 miles for 360-degree views from platform. Good blueberry picking in season.

The Steese Expressway junctions with Chena Hot Springs Road at **Milepost F 4.6**. This 56-mile side road provides access to the Chena River Recreation Area and to Chena Hot Springs Resort. *(See "Chena Hot Springs Road" log on pages 425–426 in the FAIRBANKS section.)*

The Steese Highway also provides access to the richest gold mining district in Alaska. Higher gold prices have led to renewed interest in mining along this highway. As a sign along the highway puts it: "the old Gold Rush days are not over yet!" Watch for mining operations along the highway.

Artifacts from the region's early mining days are found along the Steese, such as the Davidson Ditch at **Milepost F 57.3** and Gold Dredge 8 (open to the public) at **Milepost F 9.5**. Learn to pan for gold at **Gold Daughters**, across from the pipeline viewpoint at **Milepost F 8.4**. **Gold Dredge 8** also offers gold panning along with a narrated tour of the dredge. Recreational gold panning is allowed at Pedro Creek, across from the Pedro Monument at **Milepost F 16.6**, at Nome Creek Valley, accessible from **Milepost F 57.4** and at Cripple Creek BLM Campground. For information on Nome Creek gold panning, check with the Alaska Public Lands Information Center in Fairbanks, or contact the Bureau of Land Management, 222 University Ave., Fairbanks, AK 99709-3816; phone (907) 474-2200.

Emergency Services: Dial 911. Alaska State Troopers in Fairbanks, phone (907) 451-5100.

Steese Highway Log

Distance from Fairbanks (F) is followed by distance from Circle (C).
Physical mileposts on the Steese Highway show distance from Fairbanks, but are often less than a mile apart. Several of these posts have the mileage obscured by brush or bullet holes.

ALASKA ROUTE 2

F 0 C 161.3 Stoplight at **junction** of Steese Highway with the Richardson Highway at Airport Way in Fairbanks. Begin 4-lane Steese Expressway northbound. Access east to Fort Wainwright.

Turn to end of RICHARDSON HIGHWAY section on page 456 and read log back to front for log of that highway from Fairbanks south to Delta Junction, Glennallen and Valdez.

F 0.3 C 161 Stoplight at Tenth Avenue intersection; city center access, Regency Hotel and dentist to west.

F 0.6 C 160.7 Expressway crosses Chena River.

F 0.8 C 160.5 Stoplight at Third Street intersection; Joann Fabrics, VFW, FedEx and small shops.

F 1 C 160.3 Stoplight at College Road exit to west and access to Bentley Mall with OfficeMax; shopping, fast food, restaurants, laundromat, carwash.

F 1.3 C 160 Stoplight. Trainor Gate Road; access east to Fort Wainwright and west to Fred Meyers and Walmart Supercenter. Expressway crosses railroad tracks.

F 2 C 159.3 Stoplight. Johansen Expressway west to College Road for Fountainhead Auto Museum, Peger Road and University Avenue; access to Home Depot, Lowes, Walmart and other "big box" stores; Steese Immediate Care Center and Seekins Ford.

City Lights Boulevard to east.

F 2.1 C 159.2 Distance marker northbound shows Fox 8 miles, Livengood 76 miles, Circle 156 miles.

F 2.7 C 158.6 Stoplight at **junction** with Farmers Loop Road (to west) and Fairhill Road (to east); Sourdough Fuel (diesel, unleaded, propane) with foodmart to west.

Exit east for **Birch Hill Recreation Area**. Drive 1.8 miles to 'T' and turn right; continue 0.3 mile on gravel access road for this Fairbanks North Star Borough recreation area. Nordic skiing only (no dogs, sleds or foot traffic) Oct. 15–April 15; chalet.

F 4 C 157.3 Distance marker southbound shows Fairbanks 2 miles, North Pole 17 miles, Delta Junction 100 miles.

F 4.6 C 156.7 Northbound exit for Chena Hot Springs Road. Exit west for Curry's Corner (gas pump, grocery) and access to North Star Golf Club on Old Steese Highway (0.7 mile north from Curry's Corner). Exit east for Chena Hot Springs Road, which leads to **Chena Hot Springs Resort** (56.6 miles). Access to Chena River Recreation Area via Chena Hot Springs Road.

See "Chena Hot Springs Road" log on pages 425–426 in the FAIRBANKS section.

Chena Hot Springs Resort. See display ad on page 416 in the FAIRBANKS section.

F 5 C 156.3 Southbound exit for Chena Hot Springs Road. Dial 511 for travel information.

F 5.7 C 155.6 Distance marker northbound shows Fox 5 miles, Livengood 72 miles, Circle 153 miles.

F 6.3 C 155 Steele Creek Road. Exit for Bennett Road, Hagelbarger Avenue, Old Steese Highway and Gilmore Trail.

F 7.8 C 153.5 End 4-lane traffic, begin 2-lane traffic, northbound.

F 8 C 153.3 *CAUTION: Watch for moose.*

F 8.4 C 152.9 Trans–Alaska Oil Pipeline Viewpoint to east and **Gold Daughters** gold panning and self-guided tours of a mining museum, to west.

The Pipeline Viewpoint has interpretive displays and provides an excellent opportunity for pipeline photos. At the viewpoint you are standing at Mile 449.6 on the 800-mile-long pipeline that begins at Prudhoe Bay. A monument here remembers pipeline designer James A. Maple. There are 2 "pigs" on display here. "Pigs" are tools used for maintenance of pipes.

Gold Daughters. See display ad on page 420 in the FAIRBANKS section.

F 9.5 C 151.8 Exit west and take Goldstream Road to Old Steese Hwy. N., turn left and continue to **Gold Dredge 8 National Historic Site**; daily tours of the dredge include gold panning, gold rush history, train ride and gift shop.

Gold Dredge 8. See display ad on page 409 in the FAIRBANKS section.

The dredge, built in 1928, was added to the list of national historic sites in 1984 and designated a National Historical Mechanical Engineering Landmark in 1986. The 5-deck, 250-foot-long dredge operated until 1959; it is now privately owned and open to the public for tours daily during summer. Admission fee charged.

F 10.7 C 150.6 Fox's Den drive-thru to east.

F 11 C 150.3 Steese Expressway from

Fairbanks ends at **junction** of Steese and Elliott Highways (Alaska Routes 6 and 2); Tesoro to southwest has gas, diesel, propane, groceries. Weigh station to northeast.

Access west to **FOX** (pop. 439), established as a mining camp before 1905 and named for nearby Fox Creek, has Fox General Store; Silver Gulch Brewery, Fox Gardens & Gift Shop, the Howling Dog Saloon, and the Turtle Club restaurant, at Mile 0.5 Old Steese Highway North (great prime rib).

The Turtle Club. See display ad on page 415 in the FAIRBANKS section.

Turn east for continuation of Steese Highway, now Alaska Route 6 (log follows). Distance marker shows Chatanika 17 miles, Central 118 miles, Circle 152 miles. *NOTE: Next gas on Steese Highway is 117 miles from here.*

Junction with Elliott Highway (Alaska Route 2) which continues northwest to the Dalton Highway and Manley Hot Springs. See ELLIOTT HIGHWAY section on page 487 for log.

ALASKA ROUTE 6

Distance from Fairbanks (F) is followed by distance from Circle (C).

Physical mileposts on the Steese Highway show distance from Fairbanks, but are often less than a mile apart. Several posts have the mileage obscured by brush or bullet holes.

F 11.1 C 150.2 Distance marker eastbound shows Chatanika 17 miles, Central 118 miles, Circle 152 miles.

F 11.9 C 149.4 Tailings (gravel and boulders of dredged streambeds alongside highway) from early mining activity which yielded millions of dollars in gold.

F 13.5 C 147.8 Gated entrance to NOAA/NESDIS Command and Data Acquisition Station at Gilmore Creek to east. This facility tracks and commands multiple NOAA polar orbiting, environmental satellites (circle earth at 520 miles above its surface). Tours are not available.

A log cabin visitor's center with handicapped access is conveniently located at the entrance. The station's mission and history is explained on information boards inside the cabin. No restrooms are available.

F 14.2 C 147.1 Some homes and businesses in this area are built on land that was leveled from old tailings. *CAUTION: Watch for moose.*

F 16.4 C 144.9 West entrance to south to **Felix Pedro Creek** large parking area. *Use caution negotiating abrupt drop from highway into parking lot.*

Recreational gold panning is allowed on the creek, across from the monument. This is the **Discovery Claim**, owned by Igloo No. 4, Pioneers of Alaska. Recreational gold panning only (no mechanical devices). A sign here reads: "Good Panning and Good Luck!" Pedro and Gilmore creeks join just downstream of the panning area to form Goldstream.

F 16.6 C 144.7 Felix Pedro Monument and Wayside. Large, paved parking area with pedestrian ramp (wheelchair-accessible) to monument; picnic shelter over benches, and (wheelchair-accessible) toilet; bearproof trash cans. Nice place for a walk with paved walkway lined by information boards, an overlook of the Steese Highway and free gold panning. This loop trail ends at the lower parking lot.

Felix Pedro Monument at Milepost F 16.6 commemorates the prospector who discovered gold in July 1902, starting a gold rush that led to the founding of Fairbanks. (©Sharon Nault)

Felix Pedro was the prospector who discovered gold in July 1902 and started the rush that resulted in the founding of Fairbanks. Information signs here provide interesting facts, figures and photographs about gold discoveries in this area. Approximately $1.8 million in gold was taken from the Fairbanks mining district 1903–1910. Gold at that time was $17.73 an ounce.

Winding ascent (6 to 8 percent grades) northbound next 3.5 miles to Cleary Summit.

F 17.5 C 143.8 Large paved parking area to southeast.

F 19.6 C 141.7 Very large paved turnout to southeast.

F 19.7 C 141.6 Twin Creek Road. Signed: No public access.

F 20 C 141.3 Twin Creeks Road, Fort Knox Gold Mine to east (no public access) is Alaska's largest operating gold mine. It has produced nearly 3.5 million ounces of gold since beginning production late in 1996.

True North Road is to the north.

F 20.5 C 140.8 Cleary Summit (elev. 2,233 feet). The summit was named for early prospector Frank Cleary. Fairbanks Creek Road. Turn south and then east for large, elevated, double ended parking area close to the highway. Viewpoint of valley to east may be obscured by brush. Side road leads east 0.1 mile to Mount Aurora Skiland access road (0.8 mile up access road). Circle to Fairbanks Historic Trail is 3.4 miles from Steese Highway. Turnaround area and sign at trailhead. Fish Creek Road has good views of area.

F 20.9 C 140.4 Long double-ended turnout to east. Venturing beyond the parking surface is considered trespassing.

F 21.5 C 139.8 Highway descends steep winding 7 percent grade northbound.

F 28 C 133.3 Sharp turn up hill to southeast for historical Chatanika Gold Camp, the Old F.E. (Fairbanks Exploration Co.) Camp; closed and for sale (status summer 2018). The camp was built in 1925 to support gold dredging operations in the valley. Between 1926 and 1957, the F.E. Co. removed an estimated $70 million in gold. The gold camp is on the National Register of Historic Places.

F 28.6 C 132.7 Chatanika Lodge to east, owned by Ron and Shirley Franklin, provides food and lodging; it is a favorite of Fairbanks' locals. Old gold dredge across highway. Description follows.

Chatanika Lodge. See display ad this page.

Originally a trading post for miners beginning in the late 1930s, Chatanika Lodge burned down in 1974 and was then rebuilt and expanded to offer food, lodging and entertainment. The lodge is decorated with Alaska artifacts, including a 1955 T-Bird inside the lodge. The lodge hosts many special events throughout the year.

The old gold dredge across the highway from Chatanika Lodge, behind the tailings on the west side of the road, operated from the 1920s until 1962. It is the second largest stacker dredge in Alaska. There was a fire on the dredge in 2013, but it is still there and an interesting site. To see this old gold dredge, follow the trail across the highway from the lodge to dredge viewpoints; absolutely No Trespassing on the dredge! *(Dredge*

Public fishing access at Mile 36.6 Pond. There are several of these stocked ponds along the Steese Highway with parking for fishermen and picnickers. (©Kris Valencia, staff)

is private property; a short walk on a rocky path across from lodge lends better viewing but you must not get on the dredge itself.)

F 29.5 C 131.8 Access west to **29.5 Mile Pond** (stocked) public fishing access; rainbow trout and Arctic grayling.

Turnoff to south for Neal Brown Road to Poker Flat Research Range, operated by the Geophysical Institute, University of Alaska Fairbanks. It is the largest land-based rocket research range in the world, the only high-latitude rocket range in the United States and the only one owned by a university. Poker Flat launches scientific sounding rockets and performs satellite tracking. Tours are offered at 2 P.M. on the first and third Thursdays of the month during summer. Phone (907) 474-5823 or visit www.pfrr.alaska.edu.

F 31.6 C 129.7 Public fishing access to **31.6 Mile Pond** to north; pond very close to road is stocked with rainbow trout and Arctic grayling.

F 32.1 C 129.2 Originally an eagle and then an osprey nest (according to some local residents) on top of the power pole. Please do not use drones to take photos of birds.

F 32.3 C 129 Captain Creek bridge, no turnouts.

F 33.5 C 127.8 Public fishing access to **33.5 Mile Pond** to north very close to road. Stocked with rainbow trout and Arctic grayling.

F 34 C 127.3 Double-ended turnout to south on pond.

F 34.6 C 126.7 Pleasant parking area by **Mile 34.6 Pond** public fishing access to south (stocked); rainbow trout and Arctic grayling. *NOTE: Do not trespass on nearby private property.*

F 34.8 C 126.5 Double-ended paved turnout to north. River makes big horseshoe bend by turnout.

Highway parallels the Chatanika River northbound.

F 35.8 C 125.5 Public fishing access to **Mile 35.8 Pond** to south (stocked); very small turnaround area. Rainbow trout and

Arctic grayling.

F 36.3 C 125 Paved turnout to south.

F 36.6 C 124.7 Public fishing access to **Mile 36.6 Pond** to north; stocked with rainbow trout and Arctic grayling; 3 good primitive campsites by pond.

F 37.3 C 124 Kokomo Creek bridge.

F 39 C 122.3 Chatanika River bridge. **Upper Chatanika River State Recreation Site**, turnoff to north at east of the bridge, is a beautiful forested campground with river access and rocky beach. Registration at campground entrance. There are 24 sites with firepits and a gravel parking area with toilets; water pump at the entrance; carry out your trash. Leveling blocks needed for some sites. Camping fee $15/night. Firewood may be available for sale. Plentiful wild roses in June. **Chatanika River**, Arctic grayling 8 to 20 inches, use flies or spinners, May to September. Gravel access road to boat launch area on gravel bars, can get flooded, check status before using road. Bring your mosquito repellent. This is an access point to the Chatanika River canoe trail. See **Milepost F 60** for information on canoeing this river.

F 40.4 C 120.9 Crooked Creek bridge.

F 41.4 C 119.9 Belle Creek bridge. Private homes in area.

F 42.5 C 118.8 McKay Creek Trailhead; double-ended paved turnout to north with unloading ramp for snow machines. Second level parking above turnout has trailhead, information board and sled dog unloading

area. *Do not block private road.*

McKay Creek Trail is 17.5 miles long. It climbs steeply for 5.5 miles to ridge top at boundary of White Mountains National Recreation Area. The first 8 miles are suitable for summer use, (hiking, 4-wheeling and ORV) according to the BLM. Winter use from Oct. 15–April 30. This trail intersects with the Lower Nome Creek Trail. Information sign boards. Groomed trails for dog mushing, skiing, snowshoes and snowmachining in winter. For trail conditions visit www.blm. gov/visit/white-mountains.

F 42.6 C 118.7 McKay Creek bridge.

F 43 C 118.3 Highway travels through burn area.

F 43.9 C 117.4 Sloping double-ended paved turnout to northwest.

F 45.5 C 115.8 Long Creek bridge. Long Creek Trading Post to north at east end of bridge; cafe (current status unknown). This area began as a hunting camp, and it continues to be a very popular hunting destination. Fishing (and gold panning) in **Long Creek**; Arctic grayling 8 to 14 inches, use spinners or flies, May to September.

F 48.2 C 113.1 Large double-ended turnout to southeast. View of Chatanika River valley from turnout (foliage has obscured river valley views from highway). Evidence of 2004 Taylor Complex fires. The fires came very close to buildings at Long Creek and fire damaged parts of the Davidson Ditch.

F 50.2 C 111.1 Long, narrow, sloping loose gravel parking area; view.

F 55.9 C 105.4 Paved turnout to southeast and access to road that leads to valley floor.

F 56.7 104.6 Double-ended turnout to southeast.

F 57.3 C 104 Access to **Davidson Ditch** historical site. Turn north and drive 0.1 mile to large turnaround area for close-up views of this historic water pipeline. Information signs here explain the pipe was built in 1925 by the Fairbanks Exploration Co. to carry water to float gold dredges. The 83-mile-long ditch, designed and engineered by J.B. Lippincott, begins near **Milepost F 64** on the Steese Highway and ends near Fox. A system of ditches and inverted siphons, the pipeline was capable of carrying 56,100 gallons per minute. After the dredges closed, the water was used for power until 1967, when a flood destroyed a bridge and flattened almost 1,000 feet of pipe.

F 57.4 C 103.9 Junction with **U.S. Creek Road**. Spacious, level wayside at turnoff with outhouse, paved parking, loading ramp for ATVs and helpful information boards with map. You are entering BLM White Mountains National Recreation Area northbound. This 1-million-acre recreation area offers campgrounds, hiking trails, gold panning spots, ATV trails, floatable rivers, recreation cabins and winter trails. Free electronic maps that are GPS capable can be downloaded at www.blm.gov/maps/georeferenced-PDFs. Access is from the Steese and Elliott highways.

U.S. Creek Road winds up and over the hills to the north for 7 miles to junction with Nome Creek Road (descriptions of both roads and recreation areas follow). *NOTE: For status on road conditions and more information on area, check with BLM in Fairbanks, phone (907) 474-2200.*

The 6.9-mile U.S. Creek Road is a wide gravel road suitable for any vehicle. The first

3.5 miles to the summit have physical mile-posts, 6 turnouts and blueberries in season. At Mile 3.5 there is a viewing platform, a picnic area and information boards. Well worth the drive. Road descends north from summit for 3.4 miles to junction with Nome Creek Road. Nome Creek Valley Wayside, at Mile 6.8, has bear-proof trash cans, an out-house, and information boards with a map of Nome Creek Valley and instructions of where it is legal to pan for gold. Gold pan-ning in Nome Creek Valley is allowed with non-motorized tools, such as gold pans, rocker boxes, sluice boxes, picks and shovels.

After crossing Nome Creek bridge, U.S. Creek Road junctions with Nome Creek Road, which provides access to camp-grounds in the Nome Creek Valley. Turn west on Nome Creek Road for Ophir Creek BLM Campground (12 miles), turn east for Quartz Creek Trailhead (3.2 miles) and Mount Prindle BLM Campground (4 miles); descriptions follow.

The 4-mile-long road to Mount Prindle BLM Campground is good gravel, narrow, with some wide spots. Quartz Creek Trail-head at Mile 3.2 has a large parking area, loading dock and trail registration. **Mount Prindle BLM Campground** at Mile 4 has 13 sites, outhouses, water pump, picnic tables, firepits and bear-proof trash cans; $6/night fee (half-off for America the Beautiful, Senior and Access pass holders).

The 12-mile-long road to Ophir Creek is narrow, hard-packed dirt and gravel. Heavy rains can create muddy areas and water-filled trenches in the road. (During a heavy rain one summer, *MILEPOST®* field editors Sharon and J.V. drove this road in their Road Trek—which has relatively low clear-ance—and found it "quite driveable.") At Mile 1.3 there is parking, information boards and view of mining area. At Mile 3.2 Moose Creek Road junction. At Mile 8.4 is Table-top Mountain trailhead parking with infor-mation boards and trail registration. At Mile 12, **Ophir Creek BLM Campground** has 20 sites on 2 loop roads in a pleasant forested area; outhouses, water pump, bear-proof trash cans, picnic tables, firepits with grills, information boards. $6/night camping fee (America the Beautiful, Senior and Access Pass holders receive half-off discount).

Beaver Creek Wild and Scenic River put-in is 0.3 mile beyond the campground; information boards, bear-proof trash cans, outhouse and registration.

F 58 C 103.3 Large, paved, double-ended turnout to southeast overlooking river and mountains.

F 58.2 C 103.1 Sign: Alaska Highway 6 East.

F 59 C 102.3 Very large double-ended paved parking area, flat and wide, to south-east.

F 60 C 101.3 Turnoff to east for **Cripple Creek BLM Campground**, day-use area and boat launch. Drive straight in for camp-ground which has 6 tent-only sites and 12 regular campsites (some sites will accommo-date larger units); 10-day limit; crank water pumps (boil water), firepits, outhouses, bear-proof dumpsters, picnic tables; nature trail and information boards. Camping fee $6 (half-off for America the Beautiful, Senior and Access pass holders); $3 for walk-ins.

Take gravel road to left at entrance for forested day-use area with outhouses, trash cans and launch. Nature trail leads to the remnants of an old trapper's cabin. The road from this day-use area to the river is

4-wheel-drive only. Recreational gold pan-ning permitted. The Chatanika River winds around this campground. Bring mosquito repellent!

Berry picking is a favorite summer activity for Alaskans and visitors alike. *(©Sharon Nault)*

Cripple Creek bridge is the uppermost access point to the Chatanika River canoe trail. Follow 0.2 mile side road near camp-ground entrance to canoe launch site; park-ing area, outhouses. *CAUTION: This canoe trail may not be navigable at low water.* The Chatanika River is a clear-water Class II stream. The Steese Highway parallels the river for approximately 28 miles and there are many access points to the highway downstream from the Cripple Creek bridge. No major obstacles on this canoe trail, but watch for overhanging trees. Downstream pullout points are Perhaps Creek, Long Creek and Chatanika Campground.

F 60.2 C 101.1 Entrance to Old Steese Highway to north; evidence of old burn.

F 62.2 C 99.1 Sloping, double-ended gravel turnout to south. *CAUTION: Watch for moose.*

F 63.3 C 98 View of historic David-son Ditch pipeline to north (see **Milepost F 57.3**). Highway continues through burn area.

F 63.8 C 97.5 Entrance to Old Steese Highway to north.

F 64.8 C 96.5 View of Davidson Ditch to south below the road is accessed via a dead-end, limited turnaround road.

F 65 C 96.3 Large parking area on hill with good view to south (partially obscured by brush) of Chatanika River valley, David-son Ditch pipe and extensive burn area from 2004 Taylor Complex fire.

Southbound highway sign: Alaska 6 S.W.

F 65.5 C 95.8 Sourdough Creek bridge, private home.

F 65.8 C 95.7 Sourdough Creek Road; sign states "use this road at your own risk."

F 66.6 C 94.7 *CAUTION: Watch for moose.*

F 68 C 93.3 Long gravel turnout to south.

F 68.5 C 92.8 Gated gravel pit road.

F 69 C 92.3 Faith Creek bridge. Active mining near here.

Highway climbs 6 to 7 percent grade next

2 miles northbound.

F 70 C 91.3 Distance marker southbound shows Fox 70 miles, Fairbanks 79 miles.

F 71.6 C 90.7 Large gravel turnout to southeast.

F 75.1 C 86.2 Distance marker north-bound shows Central 50 miles, Circle 84 miles.

Views of wide open country and working mines below highway.

F 79.1 C 82.2 Road widens with long narrow gravel parking area next 500 feet. View down to McManus Creek.

F 80.1 C 81.2 Montana Creek state high-way maintenance station to northeast. Long double-ended turnout to south. Montana Creek runs under road and into McManus Creek to the east. McManus Dome (elev. 4,184 feet) to west.

F 81.2 C 80.1 Road closure gates (for hazardous road conditions, including ava-lanches). Turnout to southeast.

F 81.3 C 80 Pavement ends, gravel begins, northbound.

Highway begins ascent to Twelvemile Summit. Speed limit is 50 mph.

F 81.6 C 79.7 Steep entrance to gravel parking, south below road.

F 83 C 78.3 Scalloped waves of soil on hillsides are called solifluction lobes, caused by saturated soil and frequent freeze-thaw cycles.

CAUTION: Slow down for 30-mph hairpin curve.

F 84.4 C 76.9 Guardrails and yellow poles are for additional safety and naviga-tion in winter for snowplows.

F 84.5 C 76.8 Small dirt turnout to southeast.

F 84.7 C 76.6 Highway rises above tree line northbound.

F 85 C 76.3 *CAUTION: Slow down for 35-mph curve.*

F 85.5 C 75.8 Parking area to south with outhouse, trash cans and viewing platform. The registry for Pinnell Mountain Trail (see description below) is at this parking area. The trailhead is across the Steese Highway and to the north.

An access road leads 0.5 mile south to

Eagle Summit, highest of the 3 summits on the Steese Highway, offers hiking and spectacular views. (©Sharon Nault)

Twelvemile Summit (elev. 3,190 feet), which is on the divide of the Yukon and Tanana river drainages. The Circle Fairbanks Historic Trail begins 0.3 mile in on this side road. An access road winds around a gravel pit pond to a viewpoint with turnaround space and room for informal camping. This is a favorite parking area for hunters. Blueberry picking in season. Caribou in the fall. Sweeping views in every direction.

Pinnell Mountain National Recreation Trail, also accessible from Eagle Summit at **Milepost F 107.1**, was named in honor of Robert Pinnell, who was fatally injured in 1952 while climbing nearby Porcupine Dome. This 27-mile-long hiking trail—marked by rock cairns—winds through alpine terrain, along mountain ridges and through high passes. Highest elevation is 4,721 feet. Shelter cabins at Mile 10.7 and Mile 17.7. Views of the White Mountains, Tanana Hills, Brooks Range and Alaska Range from vantage points along the trail. Wildlife includes willow ptarmigan, hoary marmot, rock pika, moose, grizzly bear, wolf and caribou. Mid-May through July is the prime time for wildflowers, with flowers peaking in mid-June. Carry drinking water and insect repellent at all times.

Contact the Bureau of Land Management, 222 University Ave., Fairbanks, AK 99709-3816; phone (907) 474-2200.

This is caribou country; from here to beyond Eagle Summit (**Milepost F 108**), watch for migrating herds of caribou from late July through May. Wildflowers carpet the alpine tundra slopes.

The boundary between Game Management Units 25C and 20B, and marks Fairbanks–North Star Borough limits.

Distance marker northbound shows Central 40 miles, Circle 74 miles.

Highway descends 6 percent grade next 2.5 miles northbound.

F 86.6 C 74.7 Small dirt turnout to southeast.

F 88.6 C 72.7 Reed Creek bridge.

F 90.6 C 70.7 Large gravel turnout to southeast. Lichen-covered slopes (much loved by caribou) to the south.

F 92 C 69.3 Highway parallels Twelvemile Creek in valley below.

F 93.4 C 67.9 North Fork Twelve Mile Creek bridge. Nice picnic spot to the north on the east side of the bridge.

F 94 C 67.3 Turnoff for Upper Birch Creek Wayside: Follow gravel road 0.2 mile down to Twelve Mile Creek access and then another 0.2 mile to the wayside, located on the north fork of Birch Creek. Wayside has a very large, level parking area near creek posted "no camping allowed"; information boards with maps; outhouse, garbage cans; registration kiosk; and canoe launch. Birch Creek is a Wild and Scenic River: this is the main put-in point for Birch Creek float trips—a 110 mile river float to the take out at Steese Highway **Milepost F 140.4**.

Extensive mining in area. **Birch Creek**, Arctic grayling to 12 inches; use flies, June to October.

F 95.1 C 66.2 Evidence of recent gold mining operations to south below this stretch of highway.

IMPORTANT: Do not trespass. Do not approach mining equipment without permission.

F 95.8 C 65.5 Willow Creek bridge. Cotton grass grows along roadside.

F 97.6 C 63.7 Bear Creek bridge. Private home to south.

F 98.8 C 62.5 To the south, Butte Creek comes out of the mountains and down to the valley near the road.

F 99 C 62.3 Highway travels along Fish Creek to the south. Active mining below road.

Sections of the Steese Highway are used as a MOA (Military Operations Area), referring to military flight training that takes place in this airspace. Operation Red Flag is the largest series of flying exercises executed in Alaska using mostly F16s out of Eielson Air Force Base. Do not be surprised if you see some unusual flying in the sky above you. It is probably Red Flag.

F 99.6 C 61.7 Fish Creek bridge; cabins and mining road.

F 100.8 C 60.5 Informal gravel parking along Ptarmigan Creek.

F 101.4 C 59.9 Site of old 101 Lodge. Cabins in this area have served as checkpoint on the Yukon Quest International Sled Dog Race, which follows the Steese Highway between Circle and Milepost 94. See the trail map at www.yukonquest.com/race-central/yukon-quest-trail/yukon-quest-trail-map.

Weather gates may close if road conditions are hazardous over the summit.

Ptarmigan Creek bridge (elev. 2,398 feet). Highway climbs to summit northbound. Alpine meadows carpeted with wildflowers in spring and summer for next 9 miles. Good view to east of mining activity down in valleys.

F 102 C 59.3 Road ascends towards Eagle Summit eastbound.

F 103.5 C 57.8 Highway travels above tree line for eastbound traffic. Active mining in the valley below to the south.

F 103.6 C 57.6 Mining road to south, drops over side and down to active mining claims.

F 104.5 C 56.8 Old mining buildings below to south. Gold has been mined here since 1903.

F 105 C 56.3 Snow poles mark road edge.

F 105.4 C 55.9 Large gravel turnout with view to north of the highway. Ptarmigan in area.

F 107.1 C 54.2 Eagle Summit Wayside. Large parking area, 360° views, wheelchair-accessible toilet, bear-proof litter container, emergency shelter, information boards and weather station. Eagle Summit trailhead for Pinnell Mountain Trail; see description at **Milepost F 85.5**. The short loop trail near the Pinnell trailhead has information boards and leads to a viewing platform. The tundra here is covered with lichen, believed to be some of the world's oldest living things. Lichens are prime food for caribou.

Eagle Summit is a favorite spot for local residents to observe summer solstice (weather permitting) on June 21. Possibly some of the best wildflower viewing on Alaska's highway system is here, including: dwarf forget-me-nots, alpine rhododendron or rosebay, rock jasmine, alpine azalea, arctic bell heather, mountain avens, Jacob's ladder, anemones, wallflowers, Labrador tea, lupine, oxytropes, gentians and louseworts. The museum in Central has a photographic display of Eagle Summit alpine flowers.

F 107.3 C 54 Eagle Summit (elev. 3,685 feet). This is the third and highest of 3 summits (which include Cleary and Twelvemile) along the Steese Highway.

F 108 C 53.3 Westbound Eagle Summit sign.

F 109.5 C 51.8 Large parking area to south; trail leads to top of hill across road. Highway begins 7-mile-long descent northbound, edges tree line.

F 111.4 C 50.9 Parking area on curve to east. Acres of fireweed cover forest fire burn areas along Steese Highway.

F 113.7 C 48.6 Views (some obscured by brush) of "Gold Rich" Independence, Mastodon, and Mammoth creeks, all flowing into narrow valley below the road. As some of the names reveal, miners have discovered many bones from prehistoric animals while digging for gold on these creeks.

F 114.2 C 47.1 Avalanche gates. Parking area to east above the Mastodon, Mammoth, Miller and Independence creeks area (view is somewhat obscured by foliage). Prospectors were finding gold on these creeks 2 years before the Klondike gold rush. Active mining still takes place in this area.

The historic Miller House, which began in 1896 as a cabin built by prospector Fritz Miller, was located in the valley below the road. Miller House was originally a stopover on the sled trail between Circle City and Fairbanks. With the completion of the Steese Highway, it became a year-round roadhouse, offering meals, gas, groceries, a post office and rental cabins, operating until 1970. Items taken from here are now in Central's Museum. The Miller House burned down some years ago.

F 114.3 C 47 Mining road to the south leads down to the creeks and passes close to the location of the old Miller House. No state maintenance on this road, not recommended for travel.

F 116.3 C 45 Mammoth Creek bridge, water from Independence and Mastodon creeks. Near here, fossil remains of many species of pre-glacial Alaska mammals have been excavated and may be seen at the University of Alaska Museum of the North in Fairbanks and at the museum in Central. Active mining to north.

F 117 C 44.3 Highway crosses over Stack Pup Creek. From here the highway gradually descends to Central.

F 117.5 C 43.8 Parking area to north. The stunted trees you see are an indication of permafrost in this area.

F 119.1 C 42.2 Bedrock Creek. Access to creek that flows into Crooked Creek.

F 120 C 41.3 Partial views (obscured by foliage) of large mining operation to north below highway, next mile eastbound. Watch for old tailing piles in the Crooked Creek/Albert Creek area.

F 121 C 40.3 Sawpit Creek bridge.

F 122.5 C 38.8 Road north has pond-side parking.

F 125.3 C 36 Boulder Creek bridge.

F 126 C 35.3 Lupine and wild roses bloom along the road in June.

F 126.7 C 34.6 Begin 1.5-mile stretch of paved highway northbound. *Slow for speed zone northbound.*

F 127.5 C 33.8 Central post office (ZIP code 99730), postcards for sale.

©David L. Ranta, staff

F 127.6 C 33.7 The **Circle District Historical Society Museum**, open during the summer months, has displays covering the history of the Circle Mining District and its people. Also here are a photo display of wildflowers, fossilized remains of pre-glacial mammals, a minerals display, library and archives, gift shop and visitor information. A large barn beside the museum (which also serves as a community center) has displays of mining equipment, household items, antique toys and dogsleds. A large covered wagon offers photo op.

Public restrooms are located beyond the museum building on the left side and are open 7 days a week. $1 donation requested; members free. Museum is open Friday to Monday, noon to 5 P.M., Memorial Day–Labor Day.

The Yukon Quest Sled Dog Race™ stops at Central Corner each February. (©David L. Ranta, staff)

Central

F 127.7 C 33.6 Junction of Steese Highway and Circle Hot Springs Road. **Population:** 86. **Emergency Services:** Nearest medical clinic is in Circle, (33 miles east) Circle Health Clinic (907) 773-7425. **Elevation:** 965 feet. **Climate:** Subarctic, characterized by seasonal extremes of temperature. Winters are long and harsh, and summers warm and short. The average high temperature during July ranges from 65 to 72°F. The average low temperature during January is well below zero. Extended periods of -50 to -60°F are common. Extreme temperatures have been measured, ranging from a low of -71 to a high of 97 °F. Annual precipitation averages 6.5 inches, and annual snowfall averages 43.4 inches.

Services include gas, propane, food, lodging, WiFi and bar at Central Corner; open all year, phone (907) 520-5600. Gas, diesel, snacks and small gift shop with local crafts available at Mile 0.3 Circle Hot Springs Road (see side road log following).

Central, formerly called Central House, is situated on Crooked Creek and is the central point in the huge Circle Mining District, one of the oldest and still one of the most active districts in the state. Central is an unincorporated community in the Yukon-Koyukuk Census Area. There is no school in Central.

The annual Circle Mining District Picnic for local miners and their families is held in August in the museum's display barn. A Farmers Market is held at the Circle District Historical Society Museum (see **Milepost F 127.6**) on Saturdays during the summer.

The caribou migration path has taken them right through town.

Circle Hot Springs Road accesses local businesses, including a gas station. The road ends at Circle Hot Springs Lodge, which closed (current status unknown). Side road log follows:

Mile 0.3 Gas, diesel, oil products, tire and minor repairs.

Mile 0.8 Cemetery Road accesses Central Community Christian Church; 0.3 mile to cemetery (1-lane road).

Mile 2.7 Dead Wood Creek.

Mile 4.7 Ketchem Creek Road (unsigned), a 1-lane dirt and gravel road which leads to private mining claims and rock formations (keep right at forks in road) continues 3+ miles.

Mile 5.7 Ketchum Creek, former BLM campground; unmaintained, current status unknown. *CAUTION: Can be very muddy. Access is on southwest side of bridge.*

Mile 7.3 Dave's Tire Repair.

Mile 8.1 Nugget Gulch to west.

Mile 8.2 Circle Hot Springs Resort (closed, caretaker in residence; no trespassing). The hot springs were used as a gathering place by area Athabascans before the gold rush. Local prospectors used the springs as early as the 1890s. Cassius Monohan homesteaded the site in 1905, selling out to Frank Leach in 1909. Leach built the airstrip, on which Noel Wien landed in 1924. (Wien pioneered many flight routes between Alaska communities.) Leach also built a 3-story hotel, which formed the core of the resort complex.

Steese Highway Log
(continued)

F 127.8 C 33.5 Bridge (1-lane) over Crooked Creek. Remains of Central House roadhouse on north side of bridge is covered in brush.

Distance marker northbound shows Circle 33 miles.

F 128.1 C 33.2 Central DOT/PF highway maintenance station (closed).

F 128.2 C 33.1 Pavement ends, gravel begins, northbound. *CAUTION: Sections of road have blind curves. Watch for some soft shoulders, loose gravel areas and soft spots. Subject to rough and rocky surfacing; washboard between gradings.*

F 128.4 C 32.9 Private Aircraft: Road to south leads to Central Airport; state-maintained airstrip, adjacent north; elev. 932 feet; length 2,782 feet; gravel; unattended.

F 130.5 C 30.8 Pond frequented by a variety of ducks and lots of cattails. Road proceeds east through miles of burned trees.

F 131 C 29.3 Albert Creek bridge, creek

The Steese Highway ends at the Yukon River in Circle, a popular stop for river traffic.
(©David L. Ranta, staff)

access to north at east end of bridge.

F 138 C 23.3 Primitive road leads north to Crazy Hills area. Limited view through trees from highway to faraway cabin.

F 140.4 C 20.9 Lower Birch Creek Wayside (BLM) to east. Drive 0.1 mile via wide gravel road to a large parking area with outhouse, bear-proof garbage containers and boaters' registration kiosk. The parking area is posted "no camping allowed." A primitive trail extends from the parking area to the river. Most boaters floating Birch Creek Wild and Scenic River from the Upper Birch Creek Wayside at Steese Highway Milepost F 94 take out here. Boaters can also put in here and float down to Birch Creek bridge at **Milepost 147.2.** Information board with maps. Fishing for northern pike and Arctic grayling.

F 141 C 20.3 *CAUTION: Blind curves next few miles northbound. Drive carefully!*

F 141.2 C 20.1 Small turnout to south. Gravel pit parking to north.

FRIENDLY SERVICE
at the END of the HIGHWAY

H.C. COMPANY STORE

• CIRCLE CITY •

Unleaded Gas • Diesel Fuel • AV Gas
Oil Products • Tire Repair

GROCERIES • SNACKS
COLD POP   PHONE

We accept Visa & Mastercard

OPEN DAILY YEAR AROUND

Dick and Earla Hutchinson, Proprietors

Phone: (907) 773-1222 • Fax: (907) 773-1200
www.ptialaska.net/~hutch/aurora.html

F 141.7 C 19.6 Taller trees in area, indicates absence of permafrost.

F 142.8 C 18.5 Gravel turnout to south.

F 144.4 C 16.9 Road travels through large open burned area.

F 145.1 C 16.2 Birch Creek and small turnout to south.

F 146.3 C 15 Riprap along Birch Creek protects highway from erosion. Wide parking space to north with good open view of Birch Creek.

F 146.9 C 14.4 Birch Creek Boat Launch. Large parking area, concrete boat ramp, Kids Don't Float lifejackets, information board with map of Birch Creek and area; bear-proof trash cans. No camping allowed in the parking area.

F 147.2 C 14.1 Bridge (1-lane) over Birch Creek; clearance 13 feet, 11 inches.

F 147.6 C 13.7 Large, weed-covered turnout to south. Watch for mud.

F 148.6 C 12.7 Turnout in gravel pit to northeast.

F 150 C 12.3 *CAUTION: Many blind corners. Be alert for speeding drivers.*

F 150.6 C 11.7 *SLOW for dangerous curve; unstable bank.*

F 152.7 C 9.6 Single-vehicle turnout to south with view.

F 155.5 C 5.8 *CAUTION: 2 hairpin curves northbound. No shoulder and sloping road.*

F 156.6 C 4.7 Gravel pit turnout north, small turnout to south.

F 157.5 C 3.8 Turnout to south on curve.

F 158.4 C 2.9 *Slow for speed zone, watch for children.*
This area is a graveyard to cars that came to Circle and never left.

F 159.5 C 1.8 Historic Alaska Native cemetery to east. (Private, do not stop.)

F 161 C 0.3 Circle post office (ZIP code 99733). *Speed zone through town.*

F 161.1 C 0.2 Private Aircraft: Circle City state-maintained airstrip, adjacent west; elev. 610 feet; length 3,000 feet; gravel; fuel 100LL.

F 161.2 C 0.1 H.C. Company Store, the business hub of Circle, is operated by Dick Hutchinson, who with his late wife, Earla, a former teacher, opened this store many years

ago. Unleaded and diesel, tire repair, groceries, and snacks available; open year-round. Inside the store, water levels are marked off for the 7 times the store has flooded. Old-time phone booth in front. Washeteria to east.

H.C. Company Store. See display ad this page.

Circle

F 161.3 C 0 Steese Highway ends. Old "Welcome to Circle City" sign makes a good photo op. Large unmaintained parking area on Yukon River; boat launch, picnic tables, trash cans, overnight parking allowed. This is a good place to sit and watch river traffic. Information boards on the Yukon National Wildlife Refuge. From here, you are looking at one channel of the mighty Yukon River and are centrally located in this small town. **Population:** 108. **Emergency Services: Clinic,** Circle Health Clinic, phone (907) 773-7425. **Elevation:** 596 feet. **Climate:** Mean monthly temperature in July 61.4°F, in January -10.6°F. Record high 91°F July 1977, record low -69°F in February 1991. Snow from October through April. Monthly precipitation in summer averages 1.45 inches.

Located on the banks of the Yukon River, 50 miles south of the Arctic Circle, Circle City was the largest gold mining town on the Yukon River, before the Klondike Gold Rush of 1898 created Dawson City, YT. The town began as a supply point to the new gold diggings on Birch Creek in 1893, and grew as a hub for Interior gold camps.

The town was named Circle City because the early miners thought it was located on the Arctic Circle. Today, Circle serves a small local population and visitors coming in by highway or by river. Circle School (Pre-K through 12) has 26 students and 2 teachers. A large hotel in Circle remains unfinished; current status unknown. There's a lot of summer river traffic here. Inquire locally about guided river trips and air service.

Gas, diesel, groceries, snacks and sundries are available at the **H.C. Company Store.** This store is the only place in town with food for sale: there were no restaurants or coffee shops in Circle, summer 2018.

When the Yukon River flooded most recently on May 18, 2013, 45 inches of water covered the H.C. Company Store. During the Interior's summer fires in 2009, some 300 firefighters camped out in Circle.

The 2-story log Rasmusson House (privately owned), built circa 1909, is a favorite subject for artists and photographers. The old Pioneer Cemetery, with its markers dating back to the 1800s, is also an interesting spot to visit. To get there, walk west to the gravel road that goes to the right just before the Yukon River parking lot. Keep to the left fork by private homes. To the right, behind some trees, you can see the old Army Wireless Building built in 1908. Continuing on to the cemetery you will have to cross through a private front yard *(please be respectful of private property)* to get to the trail. Walk straight ahead on the trail, which goes through densely wooded trees (many mosquitoes), for about 10 minutes. The path is to the left of the graves, which are scattered among the trees.

Elliott Highway

CONNECTS: Fox to Manley Hot Springs, AK

Length: 150 miles   **Road Surface:** 50% Paved, 50% Gravel   **Season:** Open all year

(See map, page 486)

(See map, page 486)

2

The MILEPOST truck at a turnout near Milepost FX 60 on the Elliott Highway to Manley Hot Springs.
(©David Ranta, staff)

Major Attractions:

©Sharon Nault

Manley Roadhouse, Minto Lakes

The Elliott Highway extends 150 miles from its junction with the Steese Highway at Fox (11 miles north of Fairbanks) to Manley Hot Springs, a small settlement with a natural hot springs, near the Tanana River. The Elliott Highway is open year-round and also pro-vides access to the village of Minto which, accounts for much of the traffic on the road, and to the Dalton Highway to Prudhoe Bay which, along with Livengood creates most of the truck traffic on the Elliott. The highway was named for Malcolm Elliott, Alaska Road Commission president from 1927 to 1932.

This is a great drive to a pocket of pio-neer Alaska. West from its junction with the Dalton Highway—where the pavement ends—the gravel portion of the Elliott High-way travels the ridges and hills to Manley Hot Springs.

The paved section of the Elliott High-way (the first 73.1 miles of road) is in fair to good condition. Despite improvements made in recent years, this is not a highway for relaxed driving. Be alert for frost heaves, grooves and cracks in the pavement, and sloughing shoulders. *Drive with care!*

The remaining 76.9 miles—from the Dalton Highway junction to Manley—are mostly gravel, with sections of improved and/or chip-sealed road, sections under con-struction, and some stretches of rough road with sharp rocks embedded in the surface (hard on tires). Road conditions depend on weather and maintenance. The gravel por-tion of the highway is subject to potholes and ruts in wet weather. Be sure to carry a good spare and prepare to travel at slow speeds in these conditions. Gravel road may be treated with calcium chloride for dust control in dry weather which can be very slick when wet. Wash your vehicle after travel to prevent corrosion.

Despite the sometimes challenging road conditions, the panoramic views make this a worthwhile drive, as does the opportunity to see wildlife and pick berries.

From Fox to the Dalton Highway junc-tion, the Elliott Highway is a series of long upgrades and downgrades, with equally long and beautiful vistas as the road winds through the White Mountains. Watch for

Distance in miles	Dalton Hwy	Fairbanks	Manley	Minto
Dalton Hwy		84	77	47
Fairbanks	84		161	131
Manley	77	161		51
Minto	47	131	51	

Elliott Highway

Fox, AK, to Manley Hot Springs, AK

© 2019 The MILEPOST®

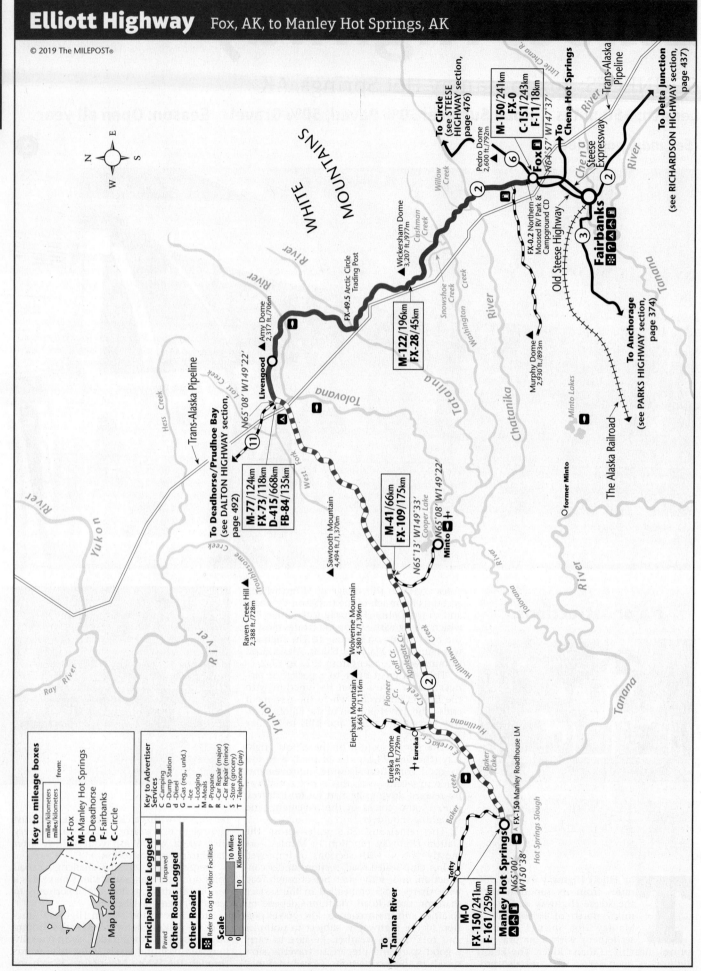

To Circle
(see STEESE
HIGHWAY section,
page 476)

M-150/241km
FX-0
C-151/243km
F-11/18km

To Chena Hot Springs

Trans-Alaska Pipeline

Pedro Dome
2,600 ft./792m

Fox

N64°57' W147°37'

To Delta Junction
(see RICHARDSON HIGHWAY section,
page 437)

To Anchorage
(see PARKS HIGHWAY section,
page 374)

Steese
Expressway

Fairbanks

N65°57' W147°37'

FX-0.2 Northern
Moosed RV Park &
Campground CD

Old Steese Highway

The Alaska Railroad

Murphy Dome
2,930 ft./893m

Minto Lakes

former Minto

Little Chena R.

Chena River

Chena River

Tanana River

WHITE MOUNTAINS

Willow Creek

Wickersham Dome
3,207 ft./977m

Cushman Creek

Snowshoe Creek

Washington Creek

Tatalina River

Chatanika River

FX-49.5 Arctic Circle
Trading Post

M-122/196km
FX-28/45km

Amy Dome
2,317 ft./706m

Livengood

N65°08' W149°22'

Tolovana River

Trans-Alaska Pipeline

Hess Creek

Lost Creek

West Fork

To Deadhorse/Prudhoe Bay
(see DALTON HIGHWAY section,
page 492)

M-77/124km
FX-73/118km
D-415/668km
FB-84/135km

Sawtooth Mountain
4,494 ft./1,370m

Minto

N65°13' W149°33'

Cooper Lake

M-41/66km
FX-109/175km

N65°08' W149°22'

Raven Creek Hill
2,388 ft./728m

Troublesome Creek

Ray River

Yukon River

Wolverine Mountain
4,580 ft./1,396m

Elephant Mountain
3,661 ft./1,116m

Pioneer Cr.

Goff Cr.

Applegate Cr.

Eureka Cr.

Hutlinana

Hutlinana Creek

Baker Creek

Baker Lake

Eureka Dome
2,393 ft./729m

Eureka

FX-150 Manley Roadhouse LM

Manley Hot Springs

N65°00' W150°38'

Hot Springs Slough

Tofty

To Tanana River

M-0
FX-150/241km
F-161/259km

Key to mileage boxes

miles/kilometers
miles/kilometers

from:

FX-Fox
M-Manley Hot Springs
D-Deadhorse
F-Fairbanks
C-Circle

Map Location

Key to Advertiser Services

C -Camping
D -Dump Station
d -Diesel
G -Gas (reg., unld.)
I -Ice
L -Lodging
M -Meals
P -Propane
R -Car Repair (major)
r -Car Repair (minor)
S -Store (grocery)
T -Telephone (pay)

Principal Route Logged

Paved ▬▬▬ Unpaved

Other Roads Logged

Other Roads

Refer to Log for Visitor Facilities

Scale

0   10 Miles
0   10 Kilometers

large trucks on the Elliott Highway between Fairbanks and the Dalton Highway junction. From the Dalton Highway junction to Manley, the road is narrow and winding, with some steep grades, blind hills and curves.

Gas, diesel and propane are available at Tesoro at **Milepost FX 0**, Hilltop Truckstop at **Milepost FX 5.5** and in Manley at the end of the road. If you are headed up the Dalton Highway, the first gas/diesel and propane stop on that highway is at the Yukon River crossing, **Milepost J 56** (56 miles north of junction with the Elliott Highway, 129 miles from Fox or 140 miles from Fairbanks).

The Elliott Highway provides access to 2 trailheads in the White Mountains National Recreation Area. These trails lead to recreation cabins. For more information and cabin registration, visit www.recreation.gov or www.blm.gov/visit/white-mountains or stop by the BLM office at 222 University Ave., Fairbanks, AK 99709-3816, phone (907) 474-2200 or 1-800-437-7021; or the Alaska Public Lands Information Center, 101 Dunkel St., Ste. 110, Fairbanks, AK 99701; Phone (907) 459-3730; or visit www.alaskacenters.gov/visitors-centers/fairbanks.

Emergency Services: Dial 911. Between Fox and Manley Hot Springs, Alaska State Trooper phone (907) 451-5100 or use CB channel 19.

Elliott Highway Log

Distance from Fox (FX) is followed by distance from Manley Hot Springs (M).
NOTE: To determine distance from Fairbanks, just add 11 miles to the distance from Fox figure given in the log. The Elliott Highway ends at physical milepost 153 on the banks of the Tanana River, just beyond the settlement of Manley Hot Springs.

ALASKA ROUTE 2

FX 0 M 150 Steese Expressway from Fairbanks ends at **junction** of Steese and Elliott Highways (Alaska Routes 6 and 2); Tesoro to west is a great travel stop with gas, diesel, propane and groceries. Weigh station at northeast corner of intersection.

Junction with Steese Highway (Alaska Route 6) which leads 161 miles to Circle. Turn to **Milepost F 11** on page 479 of the STEESE HIGHWAY section for log of that route.

Access west to **FOX** (pop. 439), which was established as a mining camp before 1905 and named for nearby Fox Creek. Silver Gulch Brewery is 0.1 mile to the west (restaurant, tours); the Howling Dog Saloon is across the road from Silver Gulch; Fox Gardens and Gift Shop is north of Silver Gulch on Old Elliott Highway and the local favorite for great prime rib, the **Turtle Club** restaurant, is located at Mile 0.5 Old Steese Highway North.

Turtle Club. See display ad on page 415 in the FAIRBANKS section.

FX 0.1 M 149.9 Distance marker northbound shows Livengood 67 miles, Manley 154 miles. Watch for frost heaves next 12 miles northbound.

FX 0.2 M 149.8 Easy access to **Northern Moosed RV Park & Campground**; full hookups with 30-amp power, dump station,

Olnes Pond day-use and camping area at Milepost FX 10.6 is in the Lower Chatanika River State Recreation Site. (©David L. Ranta, staff)

laundry and showers. Open May to September. Phone (907) 451-0984.

FX 0.3 M 149.7 Double-ended paved turnout to west at Fox Spring; fresh well water tap called "the most popular watering hole in Interior Alaska" by writer Dermot Cole. The Dept. of Transportation and Public Facilities has maintained the well since 1966. The "natural spring" costs $20K–$50K annually to maintain and may need to be re-drilled as the water table has receded. Friends of Fox Spring is partnering with the DOT to pay for annual maintenance (current status unknown).

Northbound, highway begins climb toward hilltop.

FX 1.3 M 148.7 Eldorado Gold Mine Road (unmarked) to west.

FX 3.3 M 146.7 Old Murphy Dome Road (current status unknown) leads west around Murphy Dome to Murphy Dome Road.

FX 3.4 M 146.6 Silver Fox Mine Road to east.

FX 5.5 M 144.5 Hilltop Truckstop (3 entrances); 24-hour gas, diesel, propane, restaurant, phone, ATM and groceries. Truckers' dining room.

NOTE: Next services northbound are at Yukon Crossing on the Dalton Highway, 124 miles from here, or at Manley, 145 miles.

FX 7.4 M 142.6 Views to northeast of Pedro Dome and Dome Creek. Buildings of Dome and Eldorado camps are in the valley below to the east (best view is southbound).

CAUTION: Lots of truck traffic here.

FX 8 M 142 Slow for frost heaves and pavement cracks next mile northbound.

FX 9.2 M 140.8 Sign reads "Entering Olnes City (pop. 1)." Olnes was a railroad station on the Tanana Valley Railroad and a mining camp. Old tailings and abandoned cabins.

FX 10.6 M 140.4 Turnoff for **Lower Chatanika River State Recreation Site** at Olnes Pond, 1 mile southwest of highway via wide gravel access road (subject to potholes); camping, firepits, cooking shelter, outhouses, trash bins; fishing, swimming; carry out your trash; 15-day limit, $15 camping, $5 daily parking. Very popular with ATVers (speed limit enforced), local families and campers visiting Fairbanks. Gravel

road loops around the pond; campsites are in the trees and in open grassy areas. Pond is stocked with rainbow trout and Arctic grayling by the ADF&G. Camper rules posted and enforced. No motorized watercraft on pond. Access to Chatanika River.

FX 11 M 139 Chatanika River bridge.

FX 11.1 M 138.9 Turnoff to south at north end of bridge; take first left for parking area, loop turnaround, outhouse, dumpster and boat launch. Continue on main side road to access **Lower Chatanika River Whitefish Campground**; riverside campsites with tables and firepits; grassy picnic area with covered tables and a firepit surrounded by benches. $15 camping fee, $5 daily parking, $10 boat launch fee.

FX 11.4 M 138.6 Haystack Drive to north.

FX 13 M 137 Willow Creek bridge.

FX 15 M 135 Himalaya Road.

FX 17.2 M 132.8 Begin long sweeping downgrade westbound into deep valley.

FX 18.4 M 131.6 Washington Creek bridge. Access to creek at southeast end of bridge.

FX 18.9 M 131.1 Small turnout to south with sign that reads:

"Located here is an experimental trenching site that is part of a project studying the feasibility to construct a natural gas pipeline to transport gas from Alaska's North Slope to market. The technical trenching trials were conducted here to determine the efficiency and economics of various methods of trenching in permafrost. This site, which is 1 of 3, was chosen because it is composed of discontinuous permafrost in silt. The other sites, which contain continuous permafrost, are located in the Prudhoe Bay area. The trenching trial was completed in spring 2002. The site will be monitored for 10 years to evaluate the amount of fill subsidence and to study the success of several methods of revegetation."

FX 20.1 M 129.9 Paved double-ended parking area to southeast near gravel pit.

FX 23.4 M 126.6 Large double-ended parking area on curve to southwest.

FX 24.2 M 126.8 Long double-ended turnout on Old Elliott Highway alignment to northeast on curve.

NOTE: Although these old highway alignments make good pullouts for rest stops or overnights, motorists are reminded that they are not maintained. These sections of old highway can be narrow and rough, with potholes, bumps, or overgrown brush; you may not be able to drive completely around the loop. The MILEPOST® has NOT driven all of these old alignments.

FX 25 M 125 Long double-ended turnout on Old Elliott Highway alignment to northeast on curve.

FX 27.6 M 122.4 Passing BLM's White Mountains National Recreation Area northbound. Large double-ended parking area to south on curve. (Cell phones sometimes work here, depending on provider.) Turnoff to north for large parking area with outhouse, bear-proof garbage cans, ATV loading/unloading dock and access to 2 trails (descriptions follow).

Wickersham Creek Trail (winter-use) is 20 miles long, ATVs permitted as far as Lee's Cabin. White Mountain Summit Trail (year-round) is 20 miles long and accesses Borealis–LeFevre BLM cabin (reservation required). In summer, access to the cabin involves wading or floating across Beaver Creek Wild and Scenic River. Ski loop trail junction is at Mile 2; there is a small public use shelter available first-come, first-served, Beaver Creek and Borealis/LeFevre Cabin at Mile 20. Be sure to register before hiking; sign-up sheets in metal boxes at trailheads. Blueberries in season; no ATVs allowed on this trail.

Much of the 1-million-acre White Mountains NRA is primarily a winter-use area. There is good summer hiking on upper trails, but lower trails are often very wet.

The Elliott Highway winds around the base of Wickersham Dome (elev. 3,207 feet). Views of the White Mountains, a range of white limestone mountains (elev. 5,000 feet).

Entering Livengood/Tolovana Mining District northbound, Fairbanks Mining District southbound. Begin long descent to Washington and Willow creeks.

FX 28 M 122 Distance marker northbound shows Manley 125 miles, Dalton Highway 46 miles. Distance marker southbound shows Fox 26 miles, Fairbanks 36 miles.

FX 28.8 M 121.2 Paved double-ended parking area to south. Watch for Sled Dog Rocks on horizon northbound.

FX 29.3 M 120.7 Long double-ended turnout on Old Elliott Highway alignment to northeast.

FX 29.6 M 120.4 Paved turnout to south. Spring water piped to road. (A sign here warns that the spring water is not tested for purity and it should be boiled or chemically treated before drinking.)

FX 30.4 M 119.6 Double-ended turnout on Old Elliott Highway alignment to southwest. Fairbanks–North Star Borough boundary.

FX 31 M 119 Long double-ended road, Old Elliott Highway alignment to northeast on curve.

FX 32 M 118 Large turnout to southwest; partial view. Good view of Sled Dog Rocks next mile southbound.

FX 32.6 M 117.4 Begin long 6 percent downgrade next 4.4 miles northbound to Globe Creek.

FX 34.4 M 115.6 First clear view of pipeline to west. Highway travels through 2015 burn area.

FX 35 M 115 Slow for patched and cracked pavement and frost heaves next mile, northbound.

FX 36.4 M 113.6 Large paved double-ended turnout to north with mountain views.

FX 36.8 M 113.2 Small gravel turnout to north.

FX 37 M 113 Globe Creek bridge. Small parking area at west end of bridge with sloping access. **Grapefruit Rocks**—2 large outcrops—are visible ahead, northbound. Grapefruit Rocks is a popular rock-climbing spot; hike in from turnout at **Milepost FX 39**.

Slow for frost heaves west of bridge.

FX 38 M 112 Highway climbs westbound.

FX 39 M 111 Side road to northeast deadends at a small turnaround. According to the Alaska Public Lands Information Center (APLIC), access to Upper Grapefruit Rocks is from here; follow trail leading up above road. Beautiful views. Trail is steep and exposed to hot sun; bring water, insect repellent and sunscreen. Popular climbing features at Grapefruit Rocks are the Morning Wall and Falcon Rock.

Highway descends southbound. View of Globe Creek canyon. Rocks are visible to southbound traffic.

FX 39.3 M 111.7 Double-ended turnout to south. According to APLIC, Lower Grapefruit Rocks is accessible from this turnout by following the 4-wheel drive trail leading west from the turnout to a clearing with a firepit. Hike is an easy ¼ mile, but trail can be muddy and mosquitoes can be bad.

FX 40.5 M 109.5 Double-ended paved turnout to north, scenic view. *Avoid the large, low drain embedded in part of parking area.*

FX 41.2 M 108.8 Access to Old Elliott Highway alignment to north.

FX 41.6 M 108.4 Small paved turnouts both sides of highway.

FX 41.9 M 108.1 Small paved turnouts both sides of highway.

FX 42.8 M 107.2 Pipeline pump station No. 7 to west (not visible from road). No services.

FX 43 M 107 Begin long downgrade northbound.

FX 43.1 M 106.9 Turnout to northeast.

FX 44.4 M 105.6 Views of trans-Alaska pipeline to northwest. Ascending long grade southbound.

FX 44.7 M 105.3 Paved and gravel parking area to east at Tatalina River bridge. Walk to old wood-decked bridge upstream from parking area beside river. Primitive

campsite above river. The Tatalina is a tributary of the Chatanika. Tatalina is the Athabascan name for this 60-mile-long stream.

FX 47.1 M 102.9 Gravel turnout to east. View obstructed by brush.

FX 47.4 M 102.6 Turnout to west into active gravel pit.

FX 48 M 102 Steep gravel side road to south.

Slow for patched pavement and frost heaves northbound.

FX 49.5 M 100.5 "Welcome to Joy, AK" (sign). **JOY** has a small population of people and quite a few dogs. Joy was named for the late Joy Griffin, who homesteaded this land with her husband, Norman "Dick" Griffin. Joy wrote a popular book, *Home Sweet Homestead* (now out-of-print), about her experiences.

Arctic Circle Trading Post to east was built by the Carlson's, who settled here with their 23 children (18 of whom were adopted). Drawings and books by Nancy Carlson (*Joy Abounds*) and daughter Cherie Carlson Curtis (*The Homestead Kid*) are for sale. The sign may still read Wildwood General Store, but it has been Arctic Circle Trading Post since 1997. The trading post has free coffee and Arctic Circle Crossing certificates, as well as gifts, snacks and Arctic Circle memorabilia for sale. Learn about auroras here on Northern Alaska Tour Company's Homestead Aurora tour in August. Posted by the door is a sign that reads: "Not a single mosquito at Joy ... they are all married with large families."

The Arctic Circle Trading Post. See display ad this page.

FX 51.4 M 98.6 The Hit and Run snack shack to east down side road with interesting signs.

FX 51.9 M 98.1 Large parking area to north on curve at top of hill.

Glimpses—through thick brush—of White Mountains to northeast and the Elliott Highway descending slopes of Bridge Creek valley ahead. Bridge Creek flows into the Tolovana River. Steep winding downgrades northbound.

FX 52 M 98 Slow for dangerous sections of patched frost heaves and pavement cracks that make for a rocky drive between **Mileposts FX 52 and FX 55**.

FX 56.9 M 93.1 Distance marker northbound shows Dalton Highway 14 miles, Manley 93 miles.

FX 57 M 93 Slow for frost heaves next mile northbound.

FX 57.1 M 92.9 Turnoff to east at south end of Tolovana River bridge for Colorado Creek trailhead and cabin access to the White Mountains National Recreation Area. Large parking area with outhouse, with ATV loading dock and access to the Colorado Creek trail. Colorado Creek trail (recommended for winter use) leads 15 miles to Colorado Creek Cabin and connects with Windy Creek trail; for current trail conditions visit www.blm.gov/visit/white-mountains.

If access road to old wayside across highway is signed "closed," do NOT stay there. A local referred to this area by saying "People who come to Alaska think that bears are the danger when really it is the creeks and rivers." Do not park on the sandbars or low areas near water in wet weather, flooding can happen quickly. Fishing here in the **Tolovana River** for small Arctic grayling to 11 inches and northern pike.

Slow for frost heaves next 4 miles northbound.

FX 58 M 92 Northbound highway winds around Amy Dome (elev. 2,317 feet) to east. The Tolovana River flows in the valley to the southwest, paralleling the road.

FX 59.4 M 91.6 Turnoff on sloping road to small primitive camping area near riverbank; not recommended for large RVs.

FX 60 M 90 Parking area with view to south. Grouse have been seen here.

Slow for frost heaves and patched pavement next mile northbound.

FX 61 M 89 Begin long upgrade westbound.

FX 62 M 88 *CAUTION: Uneven highway surface, patched and frost heaved road persists northbound.*

FX 62.3 M 87.7 Watch for unsigned gravel road to northeast which winds uphill 0.3 mile to the Fred Blixt BLM public use cabin (reservation required). According to the BLM, the original cabin was built in 1935 by Fred Blixt, a Swedish trapper and prospector who built several such cabins in the Livengood area. The original cabin burned down in 1991 and was replaced in 1992. The cabin is 12-by-16 feet and constructed with 2-sided logs. For more information and cabin registration, visit www.recreation.gov or www.blm.gov/visit/white-mountains or stop by the BLM office at 222 University Ave., Fairbanks, AK 99709-3816, phone (907) 474-2200 or 1-800-437-7021; or the Alaska Public Lands Information Center, 101 Dunkel St., Ste. 110, Fairbanks, AK 99701; Phone (907) 459-3730; or visit www.alaskacenters.gov/visitors-centers/fairbanks.

FX 65 M 85 Good eastbound view of highway unspooling in 3 long folds across the hills ahead. Highway is in fair to good condition from here to Livengood junction.

FX 65.5 M 84.5 North Country Mercantile (closed to general public).

FX 68.5 M 81.5 Highway begins descent westbound to Livengood.

FX 70.1 M 79.9 Livengood Creek bridge. Money Knob to northeast.

FX 71 M 79 Wide gravel access road leads 2 miles to Livengood state highway maintenance station; no visitor services. Bridge at Mile 0.8, turnouts at north and south ends. Yield to trucks and heavy equipment on all Livengood roads. Overnight parking beside Elliott Highway at double-ended turnout near this intersection. Blueberries in season.

LIVENGOOD (pop. 11), unincorporated, consists of 34 homes on 265 square miles of land. Nathaniel R. Hudson and Jay Livengood discovered gold on Livengood Creek in July 1914, and by 1915 there was a mining camp and a post office. Between 1915 and 1920, the claim yielded some $9.5 million in gold. Large-scale mining attempts in the late 1930s and in the 1940s failed. The post office was discontinued in 1957. A mining corporation acquired much of the gold-rich Livengood Bench. Active mining may be underway. *No trespassing on mining claims.*

Over the course of the summer, be alert to increased truck traffic on the Elliott Highway between Livengood and Manley Hot Springs, as summer highway maintenance projects get under way.

FX 71.1 M 78.9 Large paved double-ended turnout to south. Overnight parking allowed (big rigs often stop here, so pull over far enough to allow them to drive through turnout). Practice "Leave No Trace" camping and take your trash with you. Ⓐ

Painted gold pan and other collectibles on display at Arctic Circle Trading Post (formerly Wildwood General Store) at Milepost FX 49.5. (©Sharon Nault)

FX 71.3 M 78.7 Large gravel pit/storage area to north.

FX 73 M 77 Distance marker westbound shows Minto 40 miles, Manley 80 miles, Yukon River 56 miles.

FX 73.1 M 76.9 Road forks at **junction** of Elliott and Dalton Highways. This is a popular photo op for the Dalton Highway sign, but there is very little parking, so watch out for each other. (There is a newer sign at Milepost 1.1 Dalton Highway.)

TURN SOUTHWEST HERE to continue on Elliott Highway to Minto and Manley Hot Springs (log follows). Turn north for Dalton Highway to Yukon River Bridge, Coldfoot, Arctic Circle and Deadhorse/Prudhoe Bay.

Junction with Dalton Highway (Alaska Route 11). See DALTON HIGHWAY section on page 492 for log.

NOTE: Pavement ends, gravel begins, westbound to Manley. Slow for sections of road where sharp rocks are embedded in the road surface. Gravel is treated with calcium chloride to control dust. Road conditions depend on grading and weather. Road narrows (no shoulders).

FX 74.3 M 76.7 Former Livengood pipeline camp to northwest.

FX 74.7 M 75.3 West Fork Tolovana River bridge. River access at both ends of bridge; Arctic grayling to 15 inches, use spinners or flies. Small boat launch west of bridge with long parking area (subject to flooding during periods of heavy rain); picnicking, overnight parking. 🐟

Travelers may notice an abundance of dragonflies along the Elliott Highway. Their main food is mosquitoes. The Four-Spot Skimmer Dragonfly was adopted as the state insect in 1995.

Highway traverses area of thick spruce, alder and brush.

FX 78 M 72 Thaw pipes in culverts use steam to melt ice that would dam flowing water during freezing temperatures.

FX 78.6 M 71.4 Double-ended turnout on old road alignment. Wild iris in spring.

FX 79.1 M 70.9 Turnout to south; level parking in former gravel pit.

FX 79.8 M 70.2 Low hills to north form Cascaden Ridge.

FX 79.9 M 70.1 Sloping access to parking area to south.

FX 82.5 M 67.5 *Slow for steep, blind hill westbound.* Large turnout to south at top of hill.

Slow for rough road with washboard and potholes, few turnouts, westbound.

FX 83 M 67 The burned areas both sides of the road are from the Applegate fire of June 1, 2010. Evidence of this fire continues on towards Manley.

FX 85.4 M 64.6 Turnouts on both sides of road. Highway crosses unnamed stream.

FX 86.4 M 63.6 Small turnout to southwest with view. Highway climbs westbound, usually offering a somewhat smoother ride at higher elevation; no guard rails. Applegate burn in evidence.

FX 88.5 M 61.5 Looking south through dense trees toward the Tolovana River valley, travelers may glimpse Tolovana Hot Springs Dome (elev. 2,386 feet).

FX 89.6 M 60.4 Road begins a long ascent of Ptarmigan Hill westbound. Fireweed and foxtail grow alongside the road in summer. Road is slippery in wet weather.

FX 91.2 M 58.8 Turnout. Distance marker westbound shows Minto 29 miles, Manley 61 miles.

Bird watchers note: Local resident Frank Gertler relayed to field editor Sharon Nault that there are 4 kinds of grouse in this area in addition to ptarmigan: spruce hens, willow grouse, sharp-tailed and blue grouse.

FX 92 M 58 Sweeping views to southeast and northwest as highway straddles a ridge westbound.

FX 92.6 M 57.4 Turnout to south.

FX 93 M 57 Large viewpoint turnout to south with loading platform. Trailhead for Tolovana Hot Springs. The moderate to strenuous 10-mile hike crosses over Tolovana Hot Springs Dome (spectacular views). The trail continues past the springs to the Tolovana River Valley, where canoeing and fishing are available. Tolovana Hot Springs may also be reached by air taxi from Fairbanks. The Hot Springs has 3 hot tubs and cabins. For reservations (required), phone (907) 455-6706 or visit their website at www.tolovanahotsprings.com. The trail

Minto residents beach their boats on the shores of Tolovana River. (©Sharon Nault)

and cabins are heavily used in winter by locals traveling on skis, snowshoes and by snow machine.

FX 93.5 M 56.5 View of beautiful Minto Flats (on a clear weather day).

FX 94 M 56 Long narrow turnout with great view near top of Ptarmigan Hill. Good vantage point to view Minto Flats, Tanana River and foothills of the Alaska Range to south. The White Mountains are to the northeast and Sawtooth Mountain is to the northwest.

Between about **Milepost FX 93** and **FX 108**, the Elliott Highway is subject to high winds in winter and drifting snow often causes temporary road closures. Summer drivers may notice that the roadside brush is cleared far from the road shoulders along here; road maintenance workers do this to minimize winter snow drifts.

FX 95 M 55 Highway travels through an area of stunted black spruce. If the trees are tilted, it is probably a result of permafrost. Despite their small stature, the trees you see are 50 to 100 years old. Slow for rocks sticking up out of the road surface.

FX 96.3 M 53.7 Eastbound traffic climbs Ptarmigan Hill; turnout. Alaska cotton in June. Rough road. *CAUTION: Watch for moose.*

FX 97.8 M 52.2 Small turnout to south with panoramic view. The mountains to the north are (from east to west): Sawtooth (elev. 4,494 feet); Wolverine (elev. 4,580 feet); and Elephant (elev. 3,661 feet). To the south are Tolovana River Flats and Cooper Lake.

FX 98.3 M 51.7 Small gravel turnout to south with view. Start looking for blueberries in season along the highway westbound.

FX 100.1 M 49.9 The highway along here can be muddy in wet weather as potholes fill with rain.

FX 101.3 M 48.7 Large turnout to north.

Watch for sharp rocks in road, especially between **Mileposts FX 102** and **FX 104.**

FX 103.5 M 46.5 Good blueberry picking in August along here. Check beyond cleared roadside sections.

FX 105.8 M 44.2 Highway climbs to summit westbound.

FX 106.4 M 43.6 Turnout with view of Sawtooth Mountains to north is a good spot

to stop; information board with map.

Highway continues westbound along edge of mountain.

FX 109.2 M 40.8 Distance marker westbound shows Minto 11 miles, Manley 43 miles.

FX 109.3 M 40.7 Junction with 10.5-mile paved access road to village of **MINTO** (pop. 212). Minto Road's pavement has deteriorated in places; turnout areas at Mile 4.6, Mile 7.4 and Mile 8.1 (cemetery); airport at Mile 9.6. *Respect 10-mph speed limit through village.* Minto is located on the west bank of the Tolovana River. Enjoy sweeping views of Tolovana River, creeks, ponds, lakes and the huge area that is Minto Flats. Groceries, gas, diesel, propane and lodging are available. Minto has a health clinic, a senior center and a school. Inquire about van service to Manley Hot Springs and Fairbanks at Minto View Lodge. Minto is a "dry" village: The sale or importation of alcohol is banned. There are hefty fines and possible jail time for offenders.

Minto residents are mainly Tanana Athabascans. The Minto Band originally built permanent cabins at Old Minto on the Tanana River. The village was relocated to its present location, 40 miles north of the old site, in 1969 due to repeated flooding and erosion. The present site had been used as a fall and winter camp since the early 1900s.

The climate here is extreme: the average daily maximum temperature during July is in the low 70s; the average daily minimum in January is well below zero, with extended periods of –40°F and very strong wind chill factors. Average annual precipitation is 12 inches, with 50 inches of snowfall.

Most of the year-round employment is with the school, clinic or village council. Many residents work during summers, fire fighting for the BLM. Some residents trap or make birch-bark baskets and beaded skin and fur items. Subsistence is an important part of the local economy. Salmon, whitefish, moose, bear, small game, waterfowl and berries are utilized. Several families have seasonal fishing/hunting camps and trapping areas on the Tanana River.

Minto Flats is one of the most popular duck hunting spots in Alaska, according

to the ADF&G. **Minto Lakes** refers to all lakes in this lowland area. Accessible only by plane or boat; best to fly in. Pike to 36 inches; use spinners, jigs, bait, red-and-white spoons, good all summer. Also burbot, sheefish and whitefish.

Private Aircraft: Minto Al Wright Airport 1 mile east; elev. 500 feet; length 3,400 feet; gravel; unattended. No fuel or services.

FX 119.5 M 30.5 Highest point on the Elliott Highway, turnout at top of hill with view (if not obscured by brush) of **Eureka Dome** (elev. 2,393 feet) to north. Highway descends east- and westbound.

FX 121.5 M 28.5 *CAUTION: Watch for moose.*

FX 122.7 M 27.3 Large parking area to north at top of 6 Mile Hill. Beautiful view of Elephant Mountain and the Applegate burn area (2010).

Highway makes long curve and begins descent of 6 Mile Hill westbound. Slow for potholes and road damage.

FX 128.8 M 21.2 Hutlinana Creek bridge. Small turnouts both sides of road.

FX 129.1 M 20.9 Long turnout to south.

FX 130.5 M 19.5 Junction with Eureka and Rampart Road (11.8 miles) to north; unmaintained. *NOTE: No trespassing on active or inactive mining claims in this area.* A trail leads to the former mining camp of Eureka, at the junction of Pioneer and Eureka creeks, 3 miles south of Eureka Dome. Manley 19 miles (signed).

Winter dog and snowmachine trails cross highway ahead.

FX 131.3 M 18.7 Junction with Old Elliott Highway loop. The 2010 Applegate fire jumped back and forth across the highway along here.

FX 132.1 M 17.9 Junction with Old Elliott Highway loop. Sign: "Watch for children at play."

FX 133.3 FX 16.7 Old physical milepost 134. Evidence of a 2015 burn that jumped the highway several times between **Milepost FX 134** and **FX 136.**

FX 136.1 M 13.9 Baker Creek bridge. Fishing for Arctic grayling 8 to 14 inches, use flies, black gnats, mosquitoes, May-September.

CAUTION: Watch for moose.

FX 136.7 M 13.3 Pavement ends westbound, begin narrow gravel road with some rocky spots. This 12.3-mile stretch of highway into Manley winds through extremely dense trees and brush. Turnouts at **Milepost FX 138.6, FX 140.1** and **FX 142.8.**

FX 145.1 M 4.9 Turnout to north at gravel pit.

FX 146.8 M 3.2 Sign reads: "No Shooting in Residential Areas."

FX 148.3 M 1.7 Walter Woods Tribal Hall and Recreational Park. This is a tribal hall used for potlatches and meetings. Clinic and washeteria to north; laundromat, restrooms, showers (well-marked with signage). MVC Offices, Village Express Public Transit Maintenance Facility and Hot Springs Market (convenience store).

FX 149 M 1 Pavement begins, gravel ends, westbound. Community well house to north (move silver-colored switch to activate potable water). Please do not take more than 100 gallons per day.

"Welcome to Manley Hot Springs" sign.

FX 149.1 M 0.9 DOT station to south.

FX 149.2 M 0.8 Junction with Tofty–Tanana Road. This 35-mile-long side road ends 6 miles upstream (and on the opposite bank) from the village of **TANANA** (pop. 224). The 20 miles of new road connected with the pre-existing 15-mile-long Tofty Road—which was also improved—in 2016, to connect the Elliott Highway to the banks of the Tanana River, helping reduce freight and transportation costs for Tanana residents. The old Tofty Road had originally accessed the gold mining area of Tofty, founded in 1908 by pioneer prospector A.F. Tofty. The new dirt and gravel road has some narrow sections and is not recommended for RVs. Parking at the Tanana River is restricted to Tanana residents. Much of the land along the route is owned by Tozitna Ltd., Tanana's Native corporation.

FX 149.7 M 0.3 Turn uphill for private hot springs, owned by long-time resident Gladys Dart. The hot springs—contained in 4 concrete baths inside the Dart greenhouse—are used by locals and visitors alike. No changing rooms; donations welcome, 1-hour limit. Instructions for reservations are sometimes posted at greenhouse entrance or call ahead from the Manley Roadhouse.

©David L. Ranta, staff

Gladys Dart School National Historic Site is located on the road to the hot springs. Established in 1958, it was named for Gladys (owner of the hot springs), who taught there until her retirement in 1986. *NOTE: Do NOT drive big rigs up to the greenhouse. Park along highway (or in Manley) and walk up. Or you may park in front of the old school near the greenhouse.*

Manley Hot Springs

FX 150 M 0 1-lane bridge over Hot Springs Slough (yield to oncoming traffic). Manley Hot Springs is located on Hot Springs Slough, 3 miles north of the Tanana River and 161 miles from Fairbanks via the Elliott Highway. **Population: 127. Emergency Services:** Dial 911. **Clinic,** phone (907) 672-3333; **Alaska State Troopers,** in Fairbanks, phone (907) 451-5100.

Elevation: 270 feet. **Climate:** Mean temperature in July is 59°F, in January -10.4°F. Record high 93°F in June 1969, record low -70°F in January 1934. Precipitation in summer averages 2.53 inches a month. Snow from October through April, with traces in September and May. **Transportation:** Air taxi service.

Private Aircraft: Manley Hot Springs civil airstrip (open year-round), adjacent southwest; elev. 275 feet; 3,400-feet long, 60-feet wide; gravel; unattended, turbine fuel may be available.

A pocket of "Pioneer Alaska." J.F. Karshner homesteaded here in 1902, about the same time the U.S. Army Signal Corps established a telegraph station nearby. The

A 1-lane bridge crosses Hot Springs Slough on the way into Manley Hot Springs.

(©Sharon Nault)

location soon became known as Baker Hot Springs, after nearby Baker Creek, and later was known simply as Hot Springs. Frank Manley built the 4-story Resort Hotel here in 1907. The population peaked at about 1,000 in 1910, as the village became a trading center for nearby Eureka and Tofty mining districts. In 1913, the hotel burned down. By 1950, the population was down to 29 as mining waned. The settlement's name was changed to Manley Hot Springs in 1957.

Today, Manley Hot Springs is a quiet settlement with gardening, hunting and fishing helping to sustain many residents. There are now about 50 year-round homes in Manley. Manley was also home of Iditarod musher, the late Joee Redington Jr., the son of the founder of the Iditarod and an Iditarod musher himself, who ran the Iditarod Kennels just outside town with his wife Pam. He raised sprint dogs for racing until his death in 2017.

Manley Roadhouse dates back to 1903. Its great room is a flashback in history with cozy furniture, original piano, local artifacts and pictures as well as a large mammoth bone hanging over the entrance to the dining room. The roadhouse offers meals, a bar and overnight accommodations; phone (907) 672-3161. The abandoned Northern Commercial Co. is down the road from Manley Roadhouse.

Manley Roadhouse. Come visit one of Alaska's oldest original roadhouses from the gold rush era. See the many prehistoric and Alaskana artifacts on display. New rooms with private baths added 1997. Private cabins. The Manley Roadhouse is a great place to meet local miners, dog mushers, trappers or fishermen. We specialize in traditional Alaska home-style hospitality, fresh-baked pies, giant cinnamon rolls and good food. Largest liquor selection in Alaska. Stop by and see us. See display ad this page. [ADVERTISEMENT]

The Manley Trading Post (grocery, post office) and a gas station with propane are located a short drive beyond Manley Roadhouse by the old airstrip (now a tie-down area for planes). Continue on for the airport.

Residents have long been enjoying the

square cement tubs at the hot springs at **Milepost FX 149.7**, thanks to the generosity of owner Gladys Dart. The hot springs water is soft, containing some chloride and carbonate but no sulfur. Visitors are asked to be respectful of the pools and greenhouse plants. Call ahead for specific times to go (stays are limited to 1 hour).

There is a big annual 4th of July celebration here, featuring a community feed and boat races on the slough.

Tent camping, picnic area and playground beside lodge. Tent/RV sites, picnic tables, firepits, outhouse and boat launch across street. Pay $5 camping fee at the roadhouse. Showers are available at the roadhouse for a fee. The washeteria at **Milepost FX 148.3** has showers and a laundry.

Hot Springs Slough flows into the Tanana River. Fishing for pike 18 to 36 inches, use spinning and trolling lures, May through September.

The Elliott Highway ends 3 miles past Manley Roadhouse at **Milepost FX 153** on the banks of the **Tanana River**. There is a large parking area, an outhouse, and benches to sit on and watch the river traffic. Chinook, coho and chum salmon from 7 to 40 lbs., June 15 to Sept. 30. Subsistence fishwheels and nets are used. Fishing charter services are available locally.

CAUTION: Areas of the bluff are sloughing off into the river.

Dalton Highway

CONNECTS: Elliott Hwy. to Deadhorse/Prudhoe Bay, AK

Length: 415 miles   **Road Surface: 25% Paved, 75% Gravel**

Season: Open all year   **Steepest Grade: 12 percent**

Caribou cross the Dalton Highway on the North Slope.
(© Steven Miley)

Distance in miles	Coldfoot	Deadhorse	Fairbanks	Wiseman
Coldfoot		240	259	14
Deadhorse	240		499	226
Fairbanks	259	499		273
Wiseman	14	226	273	

The 415-mile Dalton Highway begins at **Milepost FX 73.1** on the Elliott Highway, 84 miles from Fairbanks, and ends at Deadhorse/Prudhoe Bay on the Beaufort Sea coast. The highway follows the Trans-Alaska pipeline, up hills and down, through forested valleys, over the Brooks Range at Atigun Pass, and across the treeless North Slope.

The Dalton Highway is unique in its scenic beauty, wildlife and recreational opportunities, but it is also one of Alaska's most remote, dangerous and challenging roads. Driving distance (round-trip) between Fairbanks and Deadhorse is approximately 1,000 miles. Allow at least 3 days for the trip. The Dalton is open all year and can be driven in winter.

The Dalton is still called "the Haul Road" by many, a name that dates back to its days as an access road during construction of the Trans-Alaska Pipeline System (TAPS) as well as its continued use today by freight haulers providing supplies to Alaska's oil field. All types of vehicles—from motorcycles to passenger cars to freight haulers—drive the Dalton Highway each year. Not everyone, however, is meant for this drive. We encourage you to read the entire log of this highway before you decide to set out on this adventure so you are prepared for Dalton Highway road conditions. *Recreational travelers must remember this is an industrial road and remember to always give freight haulers the space and respect they deserve.* Free electronic maps that are GPS capable can be downloaded at www.blm.gov/maps/geo referenced-PDFs.

The Dalton is a favorite drive of *MILEPOST®* field editor Sharon Nault, but she is realistic about its challenges: "Hit a pothole or frost heave going too fast and you

Major Attractions:

(©David L. Ranta, staff)

Trans-Alaska Pipeline,
Arctic Circle,
Yukon River Crossing,
Arctic Ocean

Highest Summit:
Atigun Pass 4,800 ft.

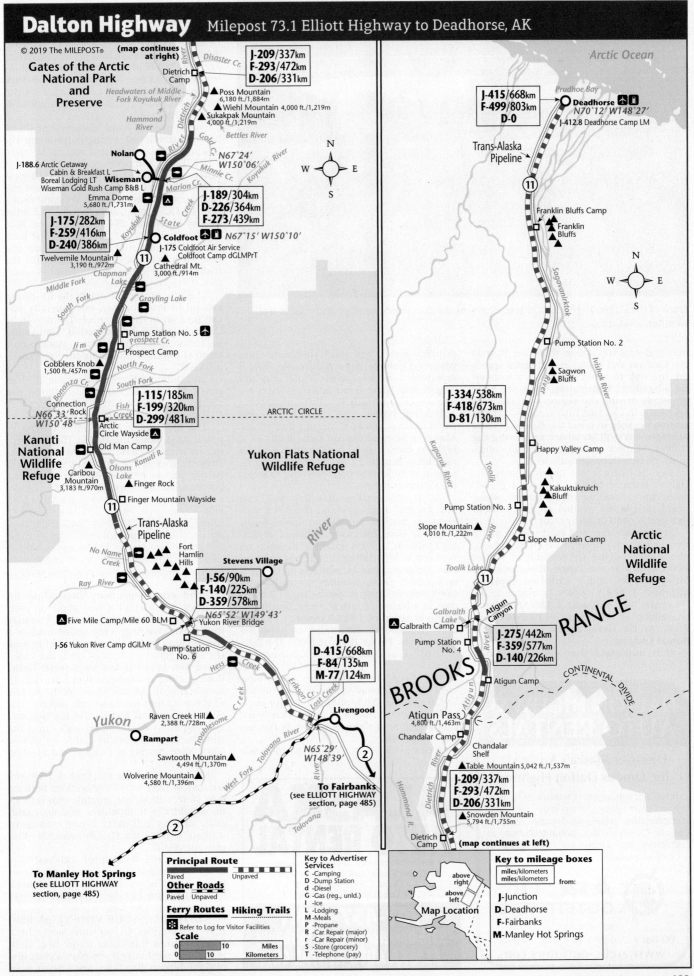

Much of the Dalton Highway is gravel, which means dust in dry weather and mud in wet weather. (©Michael K. Robb)

may end your trip sooner than you planned on. Caution and slower than normal speeds are the way to assure you have a wonderful adventure. Fortunately, there are a lot of people driving the Dalton who will stop and help if you run into trouble." At the same time, keep in mind the Bureau of Land Management's (BLM) advice on driving the Dalton: "Expect and prepare for all conditions. Prepare to be self-sufficient."

Despite many recent improvements, the Dalton remains about 75 percent gravel, with tire-puncturing rocks, bumpy washboard, dust in dry weather, slippery mud in wet weather and dangerous curves.

Services are few and far between along the Dalton Highway. Gas/diesel, food, phone and lodging are available at **Yukon River Camp** at the Yukon River crossing; **Milepost J 56**, and at **Coldfoot Camp** at **Milepost J 174.8** (open year-round). In Wiseman (see **Milepost J 188.6**), lodging is available at **Wiseman Gold Rush Camp B&B**, **Arctic Getaway Cabin B&B** and **Boreal Lodging**.

It is important that you bring along drinking water, and refill your water jugs whenever potable water is available. This is especially true for bicyclists: Water may add weight, but there is no drinking water for *long* stretches of road. Bicyclists should bring a filtration system with them, but be prepared for mosquitoes at streams and ponds. Also keep in mind that on some stretches of highway there may be no shoulders and the road berm may be 15 feet above the tundra, making it difficult to both park and to access the stream or pond.

At Deadhorse/Prudhoe Bay you can buy gas and diesel fuel and there is a general store that has snacks and drinks, but it is best to shop for groceries before departing Fairbanks. Food is usually available at oil field hotels with dining facilities, but accommodations may not be available to the general public: These facilities normally cater to oil field workers, so phone ahead 3 to 10 days in advance of arrival. Only **Deadhorse Camp** at **Milepost J 412.8** caters to tourists: they offer rooms and dining to pre-registered guests. Phone them at (907) 474-3565 or 1-877-474-3565, www.deadhorsecamp.com.

IMPORTANT: If you plan on driving the Dalton Highway to Deadhorse/Prudhoe Bay in summer 2019, phone ahead for overnight accommodations to assure that space is available. *See Lodging & Services in Prudhoe Bay on page 508.*

Access to the Arctic Ocean is possible only

through the authorized tour operators: Northern Alaska Tour Company multi-day trip (1-800-474-1986; www.northernalaska.com) or via Deadhorse Camp (1-877-474-3565; at www.deadhorsecamp.com/arctic-ocean-shuttle). Photo I.D. and 24-hour advance reservations are required for this tour. Stop and check with Arctic Interagency Visitor Center in Coldfoot for current details on the Arctic Ocean tours offered in Prudhoe Bay.

The Bureau of Land Management (BLM) has one developed campground along the Dalton Highway (Marion Creek at Milepost J 179.7) and 3 undeveloped no fee sites: At **Milepost 60 BLM Campground** (**Milepost J 60.5**); Arctic Circle, on the hill above the picnic area at Arctic Circle Wayside (**Milepost J 115.5**); and Galbraith Lake, 4.3 miles west of **Milepost J 274.7**. Camping on BLM lands is limited to 14 days at any one location. Coldfoot Camp has RV hookups and tent sites. Informal campsites alongside the road are noted in the log. *NOTE: It is illegal to park or camp on pipeline access roads (enforced).*

There is no formal overnight RV campground in Prudhoe Bay, but generally you can find an overnight space. Try the Arctic Oilfield Hotel or Tesoro station. Tent camping is discouraged due to bears. Many people camp at informal sites along the Sagavanirktok River.

Sani-dump stations are available at **Milepost J 60.5** (no fee) and at Deadhorse (fee charged, inquire at NANA office). *Please do NOT dump holding tanks along the road.*

The BLM manages 2.1 million acres of public land along the Dalton Highway. For information, contact the BLM's Fairbanks District Office at 222 University Ave. in Fairbanks; phone (907) 474-2200; www.blm.gov/visit/dalton-highway.

NOTE: Cell phone service is limited to a 15 mile area around Coldfoot (for those with GCI coverage) and the Deadhorse area. Land lines are available at Yukon River Camp, in Coldfoot and Wiseman, but have a calling card or credit card with you or plan to call collect (calls between Coldfoot and Wiseman are considered local/free).

Road conditions vary depending on weather, maintenance and time of year. On recently rehabilitated sections, you may find good pavement, chip-sealed road or a combination of rough gravel and chip seal. On some gravel sections of road, the washboard can be so severe your teeth rattle. Road grading and construction can result in long berms of dirt and gravel in the middle of the road that interfere with driving. The posted speed limit for most of the highway is 50-mph. Avoid throwing rocks into the windshields of oncoming traffic by *slowing down when passing or being passed by other vehicles!*

Many stretches of the Dalton Highway are narrow road with some sections built up 6 to 15 feet above the ground, with little or no shoulder, soft shoulders, and no guardrails, making roll-overs a not infrequent mishap. Driving the Dalton demands extra concentration!

Motorcyclists: Be alert for potholes! Slow down for bridges: approaches are often potholed; bridge edges can be sharp; and metal bridge decking can be very slick in wet weather.

NEVER STOP YOUR VEHICLE on hills, curves or bridges. If you must stop, check your rear-view mirror for traffic first, then pull to the right only if you have a clear line of sight in both directions, and turn on your

direction signals. When you do pull over for a photo or for whatever reason, be very wary of soft shoulders; use turnouts instead.

There are several steep (10 to 12 percent) grades on the Dalton Highway. *Drive with your headlights on at all times. Keep headlights and taillights clean so that you are visible in dust, fog and snow.*

Watch for ruts and sharp rocks; dusty driving conditions in dry weather; potholes and soft spots in wet weather; and trucks and road maintenance equipment at all times. The volume of truck traffic hauling materials between Fairbanks and Prudhoe Bay varies, but *always watch for trucks and give them the right-of-way.* Pull off at the nearest turnout and let faster-moving trucks pass. Slow down and pull over to the side of the road when meeting oncoming trucks. *Use caution when pulling over to the side of the road. Soft shoulders and abrupt drop-offs at the edge of the roadway have caused tipovers.*

NOTE: *CB radios are strongly recommended to monitor road conditions and truck traffic. Use channel 19.*

Check current road conditions and for road construction projects at 511.alaska.gov.

Flat tires are a common occurrence on this road. The BLM recommends that travelers carry at least 2 full-sized spare tires mounted on rims. *MILEPOST®* field editors Sharon Nault and J.V. Teague have helped many people with flat tires along Alaska's roads, and they suggest a tire-changing runthrough before leaving home. They also recommend carrying an extra set of lug nuts and to ensure your tire iron is the correct size. Driver Jack Wiles reminds travelers that the Dalton can be very muddy. He suggests bringing a tarp or carpet to kneel on, a board or platform to set the jack on, and to carry spare tires inside of your vehicle so they don't get caked with mud. He also recommends bringing a small bucket to collect water and a squeegee to clean the back window, license plate and tail lights.

Towing fees by private wrecker service can be costly. If you belong to an auto or RV club with road service, inquire about coverage on the Dalton Highway before you depart. Alaska Dept. of Transportation maintenance stations along the highway do not provide vehicle services or gas. Calcium chloride is used on unpaved sections of road to control dust; it is corrosive to vehicles and slippery when wet.

Rental car agencies, such as **Arctic Outfitters** and **Alaska Auto Rental** in Fairbanks, may offer a limited number of vehicles that are allowed for travel on the Dalton Highway. Renters are responsible for towing and vehicle damage while traveling on this and other gravel roads. See display ads this

The MILEPOST® camper gets gas at Deadhorse—it is an unusual experience—the pumps come out of the wall of a building. *(©David L. Ranta, staff)*

section for details.

For those who don't want to drive themselves, commercial tours are available from **Dalton Highway Express** (www.daltonhighwayexpress.com) and **Northern Alaska Tour Company's Arctic Ocean Adventure** (www.northernalaska.com). See display ads this section for details.

If you would like a flightseeing option, **Coldfoot Air Service**, located in Coldfoot and Fairbanks, provides flightseeing to the Gates of the Arctic and Kobuk National Parks and the Arctic National Wildlife Refuge. Phone (907) 687-3993; www.coldfootair.com. See display ad this section for details.

The highway is named for James William Dalton, an arctic engineer involved in early oil exploration efforts on the North Slope. It was built as a haul road between the Yukon River and Prudhoe Bay during construction of the trans-Alaska pipeline, and was originally called the North Slope Haul Road. Construction of the road began April 29, 1974, and was completed 5 months later. The road is 28 feet wide with 3 to 6 feet of gravel surfacing. Some sections of road are underlain with plastic foam insulation to prevent thawing of the permafrost.

Construction of the 800-mile-long pipeline between Prudhoe Bay and Valdez began April 29, 1974, and ended June 20, 1977. It cost $8 billion to build. The 48-inch-diameter pipeline, of which slightly more than half is above ground, has 6 operating pump stations. The operations control center is in Valdez. Design, construction and operation of the pipeline are managed by Alyeska Pipeline Service Company. For more information, contact Alyeska Pipeline Service Co.;

A favorite photo op and stop for motorists along the Dalton is this sign at Milepost J 1.1.
(©David Ranta, staff)

phone (907) 787-8700.

Alyeska pump stations do not provide any public services. Although former pipeline camp names are noted on our strip map, these camps have been removed.

Commonly spotted wildlife along the Dalton Highway include grizzly bear, moose, caribou, Dall sheep, musk-ox and the ubiquitous Arctic ground squirrel. Some 158 bird species have been recorded in the diverse habitats along this road, from northern boreal forest to the tundra of the North Slope and Arctic coastal plain.

Mosquitoes are prevalent along the Dalton Highway. Bring mosquito nets and/or spray!

All waters between the Yukon River bridge and Dietrich River are part of the Yukon River drainage, and most are tributaries of the Koyukuk River, a large tributary of the Yukon River. Fishing for Arctic grayling can be good in rivers accessible by foot from the highway. The large rivers also support burbot, salmon, northern pike and several species of whitefish. Small Dolly Varden are at higher elevations in streams north of Coldfoot. Fishing for salmon is closed within 5 miles either side of the highway in the trans-Alaska pipeline corridor. According to the Dept. of Fish and Game, anglers should expect high, turbid water conditions throughout much of June as the snowpack melts in the Brooks Range, with the best fishing occurring during July and August. 🐟

Fishing regulations are available online or at ADF&G offices or from the Arctic Interagency Visitor Center in Coldfoot, Yukon Crossing Visitor Contact Station or any license vendors.

Report wildlife violations to Fish & Wildlife Service or the State Trooper at Coldfoot.

Emergency Services: Contact the Alaska State Troopers Fairbanks dispatch office at (907) 451-5100 or 1-800-811-0911, via CB radio, Channel 19, or contact any state highway maintenance camp along the highway. DOT maintenance camp personnel are not medically trained, but they will assist travelers in contacting the proper authorities to get medical attention in the event of an accident or medical emergency.

Dalton Highway Log

Distance from junction with Elliott Highway (J) is followed by distance from Fairbanks (F) and Deadhorse/Prudhoe Bay (D).

ALASKA ROUTE 11

J 0 F 84 D 415 Dalton Highway begins at Elliott Highway junction (N65°29', W148°39'). Sign at start of Dalton Highway: "Heavy Industrial Traffic. All vehicles drive with headlights on. Speed 50 mph next 416 miles."

CAUTION: Steep grades and frequent narrow road northbound. Watch for trucks (give them plenty of room!) and road construction. Use your rear-view mirrors continuously. The first 20 miles of the Dalton Highway require extra driver alertness and give first-time travelers a taste of the challenges on this road. (Reconstruction of 7½ miles of highway from the Elliott Highway junction is under study.) Plan to stop at **Milepost J 1.1** for a photo op with the Dalton Highway sign, then take a break at **Milepost J 20.6** if you need one.

Junction with Elliott Highway to Fairbanks and Manley Hot Springs. Turn to **Milepost FX 73.1** on page 489 in the ELLIOTT HIGHWAY section for log of that route.

Distance marker southbound shows Fairbanks 81 miles, Minto 48 miles, Manley 80 miles.

J 0.1 F 84.1 D 414.9 Gravel begins, pavement ends, northbound. Calcium chloride treated road surface conditions vary from very smooth to some washboard to rough gravel first 18.5 miles northbound. Sign: "Remember to drive with headlights on next 425 miles."

Road climbs through permafrost stunted trees.

J 1.1 F 85.1 D 413.9 Big gravel turnout at Dalton Highway sign; good photo op.

Distance marker northbound shows Yukon River 56 miles, Coldfoot 175 miles, Deadhorse 414 miles.

J 1.4 F 85.4 D 413.6 Steep downhill grade next 1.5 miles northbound.

J 3 F 87 D 412 Turnout to west.

J 3.2 F 87.2 D 411.8 Northbound, top of short, steep grade, steep downhill ahead.

J 4 F 88 D 411 Small turnout to south as highway descends "Five Mile Hill" into the Lost Creek valley. *This is a steep, curving stretch of road; there have been accidents here. Shift to low gears and remember to watch out for big trucks and stay out of their way.*

J 4.8 F 88 D 410.2 Pipeline is visible stretching across the ridge of the distant hill.

J 5.6 F 89.6 D 409.4 Turnout to west on south side with access to Lost Creek which flows under the highway in culverts and on into the west fork of the Tolovana River. Physical mileposts may be obscured by brush.

J 5.7 F 89.7 D 409.3 APL (Alyeska pipeline) access road; no public admittance. There are many of these pipeline access roads along the highway; most are signed with the milepost on the pipeline. Because they are so numerous, most APL pipeline access roads are not included in *The MILEPOST®* log unless they occur along with another feature. Most of these access roads are closed to the public for security and safety concerns. Do not block APL access roads.

J 6.1 F 90.1 D 408.9 Large gravel turnout to west is on a curve and top of hill.

J 6.6 F 90.6 D 408.4 Small dirt turnout to west. Muddy when wet.

J 7.7 F 91.7 D 407.3 Turnout to east; muddy when wet.

J 8.3 F 92.5 D 406.7 Large turnout at side road to east. Some side roads along the Dalton lead to private mining claims.

J 9.4 F 93.4 D 405.6 Good view of pipeline as highway descends northbound. Entering Game Management Unit 20F northbound.

Steep and winding 9 percent downgrades next 3.6 miles northbound. Some soft shoulders and narrowed shoulders.

J 11 F 95 D 404 Turnout to west.

J 12 F 96 D 403 Large turnout near huge culvert.

J 13.7 F 97.7 D 401.3 Small turnout to west.

J 15.9 F 99.9 D 399.1 Turnouts both sides of highway.

J 17.4 F 101.4 D 397.6 Gravel turnout to west.

J 18.5 F 102.5 D 396.5 Pavement begins northbound. Panoramic views. Well-used side road to west.

J 20.6 F 104.6 D 394.4 Long parking area west side of road with sweeping view of mountains and the valley where Hess Creek is flowing en route to the Yukon River. Interpretive panels on the 2003 Erickson Creek Fire and the 1991 Hess Creek Fire. Views of old Dalton Highway below.

J 21.3 F 105.3 D 393.7 Active gravel pit to east.

J 21.4 F 105.4 D 393.6 Large signed parking area to west.

J 21.8 F 105.8 D 393.2 Small gravel parking area to east.

J 22.2 F 106.2 D 392.8 Steep downhill grade next 2.4 miles northbound as highway descends to Hess Creek.

J 23 F 107 D 392 Pavement ends, begin 14-mile stretch of calcium chloride treated gravel northbound; road conditions will vary depending on the weather.

J 23.7 F 107.7 D 391.3 Hess Creek bridge; turnout to west at south end. Whitefish and Arctic grayling fishing at bridge. *Bring your mosquito repellent!* Hess Creek, known for its colorful mining history, is the largest stream between the Elliott Highway junction and the Yukon River bridge. ☞

J 24.5 F 108.5 D 390.5 Turnout to west by rock face.

J 25.1 F 109.1 D 389.9 Double-ended gravel turnout to east.

J 25.5 F 109.5 D 389.5 Small turnout. Pipeline nearby. Highway descends southbound to Hess Creek and valley. Evidence of lightning-caused forest fires. Distance marker northbound shows Yukon River 31 miles, Coldfoot 150 miles, Deadhorse 389 miles.

J 26.4 F 110.4 D 388.6 Turnout at side road to west.

J 26.6 F 110.6 D 388.4 Pipeline, about 250 feet away, parallels highway; good photo op. APL access road; there is room to park, but do not block the road.

J 27.5 F 111.5 D 387.5 Highway passes lush open spaces, dotted with dead trees from old burn and, in season, covered with fireweed.

J 28.2 F 112.2 D 386.8 Large turnout to west. State monitors CB Channel 19 (sign).

Downgrade northbound, *slow for 40-mph curves. Drive with headlights on at all times.*

J 28.6 F 112.6 D 386.4 Pipeline parallels road.

J 29.6 F 113.6 D 385.4 Begin steep grade southbound.

J 29.8 F 113.8 D 385.2 Double-ended gravel turnout to east (do not use in wet weather).

J 32.6 F 116.6 D 382.4 Double-ended turnout to east in front of rock face.

J 33.3 F 117.3 D 381.7 Turnouts both sides of road. Gravel pit.

Crosses along the highway are memorials to those who have died in accidents on this road.

J 33.8 F 117.8 D 381.2 APL pipeline access road. Goalpost-like structures, called "headache bars," guard against vehicles large enough to run into and damage the pipeline.

J 35.5 F 119.5 D 379.5 Gravel turnout to east is muddy when wet.

J 36.6 F 120.6 D 378.4 Begin 12.5-mile stretch of improved wide paved road northbound. Surfacing is fair, with areas of frost heaves.

J 37 F 121 D 378 Small turnout to west.

J 38.1 F 122.1 D 376.9 Mile 38 Dalton Highway Crossing: Pipeline goes under road. Good photo opportunity. APL access road; do not block road.

J 40.7 F 124.7 D 374.3 Spacious paved parking area to east with view of highway. Many trucks stop overnight here.

J 42 F 126 D 373 View of Dalton Highway as it snakes up a hillside northbound provides a good photo op.

J 46 F 130 D 369 "Top of the world" scenery comes into view for northbound travelers.

J 46.6 F 130.6 D 368.4 Small paved turnouts both sides of highway.

J 47.3 F 131.3 D 367.7 Paved turnout to west.

J 49.2 F 133.2 D 365.8 End 12.5-mile stretch of paved road, begin narrow, calcium-chloride treated road, northbound. Very small gravel turnouts both sides of road.

J 50.4 F 134.4 D 364.6 Side road to east with access to pond, no turnaround.

J 51.1 F 135.1 D 363.9 Wide private side

BLM Yukon Crossing Visitor Contact Station is across the highway from Yukon River Camp.
(©Sharon Nault)

road with 2 entrances leads east 5.4 miles to Yukon River.

J 53 F 137 D 362 Views of the Yukon River and Yukon River Bridge as road descends next mile northbound. The Yukon River is the longest river in Alaska; it flows 1,979 miles from Canada to the Bering Sea. Fort Hamlin Hills are beyond the river.

Steep downhill grade next mile northbound.

J 53.8 F 137.8 D 361.2 Pump Station No. 6 (also an "oil spill response base") to west. Alyeska pump stations monitor the pipeline's oil flow on its journey from Prudhoe Bay to Valdez. No public facilities.

J 54.2 F 138.2 D 360.8 Highway passes over pipeline. *CAUTION: Do NOT stop or park here.*

J 54.5 F 138.5 D 360.5 Turnout to west at side road to small knoll. APL access road to east.

J 55.1 F 139.1 D 359.9 Distance marker northbound shows Arctic Circle 60 miles, Coldfoot 120 miles, Deadhorse 360 miles.

J 55.3 F 139.3 D 359.7 Gravel ends, pavement begins, northbound.

J 55.4 F 139.4 D 359.6 APL access to east and very small turnout to west just south of **Yukon River Bridge**. *Bicyclists and motorcyclists: Wood decking on bridge, may be very slippery when wet.* Formally known as the E.L. Patton Bridge, named for the president of the Alyeska Pipeline Service Co. after his death in 1982, the wood-decked Yukon River Bridge, completed in 1975 (upgraded in 1999), is 2,290 feet long and has a 6 percent grade. This is the largest privately funded construction project in U.S. history led by Edward L. Patton.

J 56 F 140 D 359 Turnoff to east and drive under pipeline for **BLM Yukon Crossing Visitor Contact Station**; parking, pit toilets, observation decks, interpretive panels. The center, staffed by volunteers, is open from 10 A.M. to 6 P.M. daily in summer. Information on road conditions and Arctic Circle Crossing certificates available here. Short trail to Yukon River observation decks with information boards and excellent view of Yukon River Bridge (great photo op). Wildflowers include wild calla lily, lady's slipper, round leaf and green bog orchids.

Exit west for **Yukon River Camp** with

gas, diesel, propane, The Noodle House restaurant with Chinese-style soups and baguette sandwiches, lodging, gift shop and phone; see description below. The phone only works with a phone card, toll-free numbers or collect calls. Phone cards are sold at the Camp. Flightseeing tours and bus tours can be arranged from here. Check out the boarded up window at the Camp with a picture of a bear on it. The window was broken one winter by a bear (there's a scrapbook on the incident at the front desk). Tours for Northern Lights viewing are very popular here in winter. Also inquire here about overnight parking in their large parking areas. Local resident Dorothy Towson often sells crafts from a shed in the parking lot.

Yukon River Camp. Rustic lodging, fuel and Arctic Circle Gifts along the Yukon River. The Noodle House at Yukon River Camp serves Bahn Mi sandwiches, homemade noodle soups, and fresh salads. Packages available including transportation, tours and lodging. Convenient location just on the north side of the Yukon River Bridge. (907) 474-3557. See display ad this page. [ADVERTISEMENT]

Finger Mountain BLM Wayside is a good place to stretch your legs and explore intriguing rock formations. *(©Sharon Nault)*

NOTE: Next gas stop northbound is at Coldfoot, 119 miles from here.

Follow the access road between Yukon River Camp buildings and the river west for public boat launch, trailer parking, pit toilets and garbage containers; no overnight camping allowed.

IMPORTANT: Travelers headed for Deadhorse/Prudhoe Bay call ahead to confirm availability of accommodations; see Lodging & Services on page 508 or check with the Visitor Contact Station here. And remember that 24-hour advance reservations are required for Prudhoe Bay's Arctic Ocean tour; phone (907) 474-3565 or 1-877-474-3565.

J 56.1 F 140.1 D 358.9 Very large double-ended turnout to west with bear-proof trash cans and toilet. Access to Yukon River Camp.

State law prohibits the use of motorized vehicles (including ATVs) within 5 miles of either side of the Dalton Highway from the Yukon River north to Deadhorse/Prudhoe Bay. Only persons with valid mining claims may use ORVs on certain trails to access their claims.

Hunters note: The Alaska Dept. of Fish & Game allows bow hunting only (NO firearms) within the 5-mile corridor adjacent highway from Yukon River to Deadhorse/Prudhoe Bay.

J 59.5 F 143.5 D 355.5 Note the change in vegetation northbound, as the highway passes through boreal forests, boggy lowlands and tundra. Tall, dense forests of white spruce and birch, like these, are found in well-drained soil without permafrost, usually on south-facing slopes.

J 60.1 F 144.1 D 354.9 Northbound sign indicates "Next services 120 miles" (Coldfoot). A good reminder for travelers to stop for gas at Yukon River Camp and to get drinking water at the Milepost 60 BLM Campground stand pipe.

J 60.3 F 144.3 D 354.7 Turnoff to west is first of 2 entrances northbound to the Hot Spot Cafe. Mammoth remains were discovered near the Hot Spot Cafe during highway construction.

J 60.5 F 144.5 D 354.5 Milepost 60 BLM Campground via loop road. The BLM campground is located near an artesian well. The water site with the large hose is for truckers. A potable water fill-up with a short hose is available at the dump station, which is around the corner from the truckers' well.

(Next potable water fill-up is available at Coldfoot, **Milepost J 174.8.**) The campground is set in a flat gravel parking area with picnic tables, firepits, bear-proof trash containers and interpretive panels. A campground host may be in residence. Firewood for campground-use only may be available. NO vehicle washing. *CAUTION: Watch for bears in area!*

J 60.7 F 144.7 D 354.3 Highway crosses pipeline. Old Five Mile Airstrip (not in use).

J 61.8 F 145.8 D 353.2 Seven Mile Station DOT highway maintenance to east; no services. APL access road to west.

Calcium chloride treated road surface northbound to **Milepost J 90**; road surface conditions may vary from very smooth to washboard, can be slick in wet weather.

J 62.1 F 146.1 D 352.9 Watch for thaw pipes along the road here. They are used to infuse steam heat into culverts during winter.

J 63.6 F 147.6 D 351.4 Turnout to west near creek below road. Creek is often used by DOT to fill water truck.

J 66.8 F 150.8 D 348.2 Long, double-ended turnout to west at bottom of hill; muddy when wet, use caution.

Highway climbs northbound and southbound.

J 67.6 F 151.6 D 347.4 Turnouts both sides of road. *Highway descends steeply northbound with sharp curve at bottom of hill.* Thaw pipe to east on curve.

J 69.1 F 153.1 D 345.9 Long, double-ended turnout (not level) to west.

J 69.4 F 153.4 D 345.6 Good view northbound of buried pipeline going up hill.

J 70.1 F 154.1 D 344.9 Turnout to west.

J 70.7 F 154.7 D 344.3 Steep descent northbound.

J 72.5 F 156.5 D 342.5 Sloping turnouts both sides of highway at south end of Fort Hamlin Hills Creek bridge. Water trucks often use the sloping turnout to east.

J 73.3 F 157.3 D 341.7 Very small turnout to west; muddy when wet.

J 73.4 F 157.4 D 341.6 Begin steep 0.5-mile ascent of Sand Hill (signed) northbound.

J 74.9 F 158.9 D 340.1 Large turnouts both sides of highway at top of hill; muddy when wet. This is a brake check area.

Begin steep descent northbound followed by steep ascent, dubbed the "Roller Coaster."

J 75.7 F 159.7 D 339.3 *"Roller Coaster" begins southbound.*

J 77 F 161 D 338 Stunted, low-growing black spruce in this area indicate permafrost (permanently frozen soil) near the surface, or poorly drained soil.

J 78.3 F 162.3 D 336.7 Turnout to west.

J 79 F 163 D 336 Narrow bridge over **No Name Creek** (signed), also called North Fork of the Ray River or Joshua Creek. Small turnout to east near creek; fishing for burbot, Arctic grayling and whitefish.

J 81.6 F 165.6 D 333.4 Fort Hamlin Hills are visible to the southeast. Tree line on surrounding hills is about 2,000 feet. Highway travels through old burn area.

J 82 F 166 D 333 Views of Castle Mountain to northeast.

J 85.3 F 169.3 D 329.7 This section of the highway passes close to the pipeline.

J 86.6 F 170.6 D 328.4 Side road (will accommodate most rigs, but drive slowly) leads west 1 mile to scenic **86-Mile Overlook** located in an interesting mountainside gravel pit: Observation deck provides expansive views of pipeline and sweeping views to the south. Interpretive panels about the 8.6-million-acre Yukon Flats National Wildlife Refuge. Nice view of tors to northeast, Yukon Flats Wildlife Refuge to east and Fort Hamlin Hills to southeast. Loop turnaround through pit.

Tors are high, isolated pinnacles of jointed granite jutting up from the tundra and are a residual feature of erosion.

APL access road to east.

J 87.2 F 171.2 D 327.8 Begin long, steep ascent up imposing Mackey Hill next 1.5 miles northbound; slippery in wet weather. *Drive defensively.*

J 88.5 F 172.5 D 326.5 It is possible to pull over here, but do not block pipeline access road. Begin steep 0.5-mile descent of Mackey Hill northbound.

Entering Game Management Unit 25D northbound, Unit 20F southbound.

J 89.3 F 173.3 D 325.7 Narrow pullout to east.

J 90.1 F 174.1 D 324.9 Begin paved road northbound, but watch for potholes, frost heaves, patched pavement to Arctic Circle Wayside at **Milepost J 115.5.**

Begin calcium chloride treated road surface southbound to **Milepost J 61.8.**

J 90.2 F 174.2 D 324.8 Long paved parking areas on both sides of highway at crest of hill. These are used by truckers for rest or to check on their loads so give them lots of room to pull in if you stop here. Good photo op of road and pipeline to the north. Note the zigzag design which allows the pipeline to flex, accommodating temperature changes. The small green structure over the buried pipe is a radio-controlled valve used to shut down oil flow when necessary.

Highway descends northbound to Dall Creek. Drive with headlights on at all times (sign).

J 91.1 F 175.1 D 323.9 Dall Creek culvert. Sloping access to creek on east side of highway, used by water trucks.

Highway climbs steeply next mile northbound near pipeline.

J 94.1 F 178.1 D 320.9 Turnout to west at side road to former gravel pit road. Sweeping view of portion of highway and pipeline. Watch for deep potholes on this stretch of road.

J 95 F 179 D 320 The vegetation changes noticeably northbound as the highway crosses an area of alpine tundra for about the next 5 miles. Lichens and white mountain avens dominate the well-drained rocky ridges, while the more saturated soils alongside the road are covered by dense stands of dwarf shrubs. Beautiful views. Finger Rock (elev. 1,875 feet) stands out on horizon ahead for northbound traffic.

J 96 F 180 D 319 Good view northbound of **Finger Rock**, a tor, east of the road. Tors are visible for the next several miles northbound and date back to the cretaceous period nearly 110 million years ago. Prehistoric hunting sites are also numerous in this region. *Please do not collect or disturb artifacts.*

J 97 F 181 D 318 Pull-in/back-out parking pad to east.

J 97.9 F 181.9 D 317.1 Distance marker southbound on Finger Mountain shows Yukon River 42 miles, Fox 166 miles, Fairbanks 176 miles.

J 98.1 F 182.1 D 316.9 Turnoff to east at crest of hill for **Finger Mountain BLM Wayside**. Rest area with 2 pit toilets, parking, and interpretive trail around interesting rock formations. No camping. Interpretive trail leads to nearby rock formations. A longer hike over rough (no trail) terrain takes you to **Finger Rock**.

A must stop, this wayside offers good opportunities for picnicking, photography, berry picking in season (blueberries, lowbush cranberries), wildflower viewing and hiking. Also great for bird watching and seeing Arctic ground squirrels.

Olsens Lake, Kanuti Flats, Kanuti River drainage and site of former Old Man Camp are visible ahead northbound as the road descends and passes through several miles of valley bottom. Excellent mountain views.

Highway descends steeply next 1.7 miles northbound. Challenging road surface northbound.

J 98.3 F 182.3 D 316.7 Large roadside turnout parallel to and just above the wayside offers expansive views in all directions. Steep descent northbound.

J 99.5 F 183.5 D 315.5 Pipeline access road to east. Room to park (do not block access road); access through thick brush to nearby rock formations. Steep descent for northbound traffic to **Milepost J 100**.

J 100.6 F 184.6 D 314.4 Buried pipeline passes under road. Highway offers sweeping 360 degree views northbound. Green thaw pipes seen along the highway can be filled with steam to thaw culverts when needed.

J 102.3 F 186.3 D 312.7 Cluster of buildings (private property).

J 103.5 F 187.5 D 311.5 View of Caribou Mountain to west.

J 104.1 F 188.1 D 310.9 Distance marker northbound shows Coldfoot 71 miles, Deadhorse 311 miles.

J 105.7 F 189.7 D 309.3 Large parking area to east at south end of **Kanuti River** bridge; cement ramp to river, fishing for burbot, whitefish, northern pike and Arctic grayling. The size of the area draining into this river is that of the state of Delaware. Good pipeline photo op. 🐟

J 106 F 190 D 307 Primitive access road just south of milepost leads east to runway.

J 107 F 191 D 308 Level parking area below road to east at site of Old Man Camp, a former pipeline construction camp; no structures remain. Big views.

J 107.4 F 191.4 D 307.6 Sloping turnout

to east. *CAUTION: Watch for bears. A fed bear is a dead bear. Do not feed bears!*

J 108.3 F 192.3 D 306.7 Buried pipeline passes under highway. APL access road.

J 109.8 F 193.8 D 193.8 D 305.2 Beaver Slide sign. Highway descends 9 percent gravel grade next 2 miles northbound. Calcium-chloride treated surface may be slippery when wet.

J 112.2 F 196.2 D 302.8 Turnout at pipeline access road. Moose and bear frequent willow thickets here.

J 114 F 198 D 301 Turnouts at both ends of **Fish Creek** bridge. Bumpy, sandy access down to creek to west at north end of bridge. Fishing for Arctic grayling 12–18 inches. Nice spot. 🐟

J 115.5 F 199.5 D 299.5 Well-signed turnoff to east for loop road to **Arctic Circle BLM Wayside** with picnic tables scattered through pristine woods, grills, pit toilets and litter barrels. Interpretive display on observation deck. The road to campground is at the north end of wayside. (No camping allowed in wayside area.)

The Arctic Circle sign, with a big blue earth and Latitude 66°33' on it, is a popular photo op with travelers. At this latitude (N 66°33' W 150° 48'), the sun does not set on summer solstice (June 20 or 21) and it does not rise on winter solstice (December 21 or 22). A third of Alaska lies within the Arctic Circle, the only true polar region in the state.

For overnight camping, follow a good gravel side road at the north end of the wayside, 0.5 mile uphill for the camping area (if you reach the red Alyeska access gate, you have driven too far). This camping area is on a loop road, located on higher ground and still under development. It has a few picnic tables, a pit toilet and bear-proof garbage containers scattered among the brush and young alder trees. No camping fee. Bring mosquito repellent! *CAUTION: Watch for bears.* Many people enjoy staying here so they can say "we spent the night in the Arctic Circle!" 🏕

Distance marker northbound shows Coldfoot 60 miles, Deadhorse 300 miles.

Distance marker southbound shows Arctic Circle 1 mile, Yukon 60 miles, Fairbanks 194 miles.

J 115.6 F 199.6 D 299.4 North entrance to Arctic Circle BLM Wayside and camping area (0.5 mile). Long turnout with pit toilet and garbage container on highway.

Slow for potholes and frost heaves northbound to **Milepost J 124**. Northbound traffic begins steep and winding 0.7-mile descent followed by 2-mile upgrade.

Drive with headlights on and monitor your rearview mirror.

J 118 F 202 D 297 Wide pipeline access road to east, closed to the public: Do NOT block this road.

Dalton Highway travels along a ridge, above timberline.

J 120.7 F 204.7 D 294.3 Connection Rock (may be buried in brush) is marked by a sign (but there's no place to park). North and south road-building crews linked up here.

Steep descent northbound is a 9 percent grade.

J 121.1 F 205.1 D 293.9 Side road to west leads down to creek.

J 122.3 F 206.3 D 292.7 Long double-ended turnout at APL access road to east.

J 124 F 208 D 291 Look for wolves, they frequent this area.

J 124.7 F 208.7 D 290.3 South Fork Bonanza Creek bridge; burbot, Arctic grayling, whitefish. *Extremely steep* access south to small area near creek. Gold panning is permitted downstream on Bonanza Creek or upstream for 2.5 miles. Suction dredging is prohibited on federal lands along the highway. For more information, pick up the BLM brochure *"Panning for Gold along the Dalton Highway."* 🐟

J 125.7 F 209.7 D 289.3 North Fork Bonanza Creek bridge (narrow). Access to creek to east at south end of bridge; small, informal campsite on sloping ground. Fishing for burbot, Arctic grayling, whitefish. 🐟

J 126.5 F 210.5 D 288.5 Northbound, the highway climbs steep curve up Paradise Hill. Many truckers have lost their loads coming around this sloping curve too fast. Blueberries and lowbush cranberries in season on hillside. Rock tors to the east.

J 127.7 F 211.7 D 287.3 Large sloping turnout to east. This area is lush with lichens and the small plants that dominate the alpine tundra.

J 129 F 213 D 286 Begin long, steep, ascent next 2 miles northbound.

J 130 F 214 D 285 Highway travels through burn area.

J 131.2 F 215.2 D 283.8 Small turnout to west.

J 131.5 F 215.5 D 283.5 Stunning view of wide vistas and Pump Station No. 5 to north. Best photo op at **Milepost J 132.1**.

J 132.1 F 216.1 D 282.9 Gobblers Knob Wayside (elev. 1,500 feet). Large turnout with bear-proof litter barrels and pit toilet. Observation deck with interpretive panels about Haul Road construction ("the last 358 miles of road were completed in just 154 days"), includes an old photo of the first treacherous road built over Atigun Pass.

A map here helps travelers name the mountains seen from here: the Jack White Range, Pope Creek Dome (the dominant peak to the northwest), Prospect Creek drainage, Pump Station No. 5, Jim River drainage, South Fork Koyukuk drainage and the Brooks Range on the northern horizon.

Truckers often overnight at the very large gravel pit parking area across the road from wayside. Blueberry picking in early June.

Begin long, steep descents.

J 135 F 219 D 280 Narrow bridge over **Prospect Creek**; Arctic grayling, whitefish and northern pike. Active gold mining area. Gold panning is permitted downstream on Prospect Creek or upstream for 1.5 miles. 🐟

J 135.7 F 219.7 D 279.3 Turnout to east. Panoramic view to north of Pump Station No. 5. Access west to site of **PROSPECT CAMP**, which holds the record for lowest officially recorded temperature in Alaska (-80°F/-62°C, Jan. 23, 1971). Motorized vehicles prohibited beyond the old camp. 🏕

J 136 F 220 D 278 Watch for deteriorating pavement northbound to Grayling Lake, **Milepost J 150.2**.

J 137.1 F 221.1 D 277.9 APL access road at Mile 274.7 on the pipeline at **Pump Station No. 5** to east. Pump station No. 5 is not actually a pump station, but a "drain down" or pressure relief station to slow the gravity-fed flow of oil descending from Atigun Pass in the Brooks Range. Glacial moraine marks

Most travelers stop in at Coldfoot Camp for food, gas, and/or lodging. Stay awhile and go flightseeing with Coldfoot Air Service. (©Sharon Nault)

the southern boundary of Brooks Range glaciers during the most recent ice age.

Private Aircraft: Airstrip sign; length 5,000 feet; lighted runway. This airstrip is used as a BLM fire fighting staging area.

J 138.1 F 222.1 D 276.9 Jim River Station (DOT/PF highway maintenance) to west; "No services" (sign).

NOTE: Drive with headlights on at all times.

J 140.1 F 224.1 D 274.9 Small turnout (single-vehicle campsite) to east at south end of **Jim River No. 1** bridge. Stand of unusually large spruce trees for this far north. Fishing for burbot, Arctic grayling, northern pike, whitefish. Fishing for salmon is prohibited within 5 miles of highway from the Yukon River north. *CAUTION: Watch for bears who arrive for the fall salmon run.*

J 141 F 225 D 274 Small turnout to west at south end of **Jim River No. 2** bridge; fishing.

J 141.8 F 225.8 D 273.2 Douglas Creek wood-decked bridge. Thaw pipes to east, north of bridge. Good view of pipeline as it parallels highway. Active beaver pond below highway to west; beaver dams and lodges are visible.

J 144.1 F 228.1 D 270.9 Large parking area at APL access road to east at south end of **Jim River No. 3** bridge crossing the river's main channel. Room for primitive camping. Fishing. Chinook and chum salmon swim from the Bering Sea, 1,040 miles against swift currents, to arrive at the Jim River to spawn. Parking area and river access at north end of bridge. APL access.

J 145.5 F 229.5 D 269.5 Small vehicle turnout. Pipeline passes under road.

J 150.2 F 234.2 D 264.8 **Grayling Lake Wayside** to east; parking, pit toilet and bear-proof garbage cans. Pleasant gravel walking path. Beautiful view of pipeline, highway and lake. Interpretive display on early hunters who used the area. Ducks, loons, bears and moose may be seen here.

Fair to good pavement northbound to Coldfoot at **Milepost J 174.8**.

J 150.8 F 234.8 D 264.2 Turnout to east. Access to Grayling Lake. Place to launch canoe or small, light boats. *NOTE: Float-*

planes use lake. Small primitive camping area.

J 153.3 F 237.3 D 261.7 Northbound, the highway traverses a scenic pass (elev. approximately 1,340 feet) that is used by wildlife. *CAUTION: Watch for moose.*

J 154.1 F 238.1 D 260.9 Access road uphill to gravel pit visible from highway.

J 155.1 F239.1 D 259.9 Turnouts both sides of road. Good photo op for vistas of South Fork Koyukuk River, pipeline and highway.

Sign: Bow hunting only area.

J 156.1 F 240.1 D 258.9 Large parking area with pit toilet and litter barrels to east at south end of **South Fork Koyukuk River** bridge. This large river flows past Allakaket, Hughes and Huslia before draining into the Yukon River near Koyukuk. Primitive campsite to west at south end of bridge. Fishing for Arctic grayling, whitefish. Fishing for salmon prohibited within 5 miles of the highway from the Yukon River north.

North from this bridge, the highway sweeps uphill in a steep curve. You are passing through the foothills of the Brooks Range. There is active gold mining beyond the hills to the west. Many side roads off the Dalton Highway lead to these private claims (motorized vehicle access restricted to claim holders).

J 157.4 F 241.4 D 257.6 Large gravel turnout to east.

J 158.8 F 242.8 D 256.2 Turnout to east. An abundance of Alaska cottongrass here in summer.

J 159.1 F 243.1 D 255.9 Bridge over pipeline; large-animal crossing over pipeline to the west.

Pipeline parallels highway northbound.

J 159.4 F 243.4 D 255.6 Gravel pit access road. Large turnout area to west below highway.

J 160 F 244 D 255 Good view of Chapman Lake west of road as highway descends steeply northbound. Side road visible to west leads to active mining claims, motorized access restricted to claim holders.

J 161.1 F 245.1 D 253.9 Long gravel parking area to west at turnoff to well-used side road.

J 164.6 F 248.6 D 250.4 Example of sag bend to east. This is a short section of buried

pipeline that allows large animals to cross.

J 165.2 F 249.2 D 249.8 Two turnouts to west, one is on lake. Good view/photo op of pipeline which is close to the road here.

J 165.7 F 249.7 D 249.3 Large gravel turnout at scenic overlook to west.

J 166.4 F 250.4 D 248.6 Large, fairly level, double-ended turnout to west. Pipeline goes under road and emerges close to road at **Milepost J 167.8**.

J 168 F 252 D 247 View of Cathedral Mountain to northeast, Twelvemile Mountain to east.

J 168.6 F 252.6 D 246.4 Small turnout to west.

J 169.5 F 253.5 D 245.5 Begin steep 0.5-mile descent northbound, followed by ascent of steep hill.

J 170.7 F 254.7 D 244.3 Distance marker northbound shows Deadhorse 244 miles.

J 171.7 F 255.7 D 243.3 View northbound of pipeline and Coldfoot Airport in the distance below the road next to the Middle Fork Koyukuk River.

J 172.6 F 256.6 D 242.4 Small, flat turnout to west. Side road to east.

Steep downgrade northbound.

J 173 F 257 D 242 Entering public lands (sign) northbound. Steep descent, southbound. Road to west is a pipeline road which goes along a lake sometimes used by floatplanes.

J 173.7 F 257.7 D 241.3 Turnout to west. *CAUTION: Watch for moose.*

J 174.3 F 258.3 D 240.7 Road follows pipeline to west. *Slow for speed zone northbound.*

Coldfoot

J 174.8 F 258.8 D 240.2 First signed turnoff northbound for half-mile loop road which leads east to **COLDFOOT** (pop. 8; elev. approximately 1,086 feet); food, gas, lodging, camping, tire and minor vehicle repair, post office (open 1:30–6 P.M., Monday, Wednesday, Friday), and airport. **Emergency Services:** Alaska State Troopers, phone (907) 678-5211. (Phone at Coldfoot Camp.) Also signed turnoff for the **Arctic Interagency Visitor Center** to west. See descriptions following.

Visitor Information: The award-winning **Arctic Interagency Visitor Center** (AIVC), operated by the BLM, USFWS and National Park Service, is a "must stop" for visitors, providing travel information, topographic maps, natural history exhibits, a bookstore, evening programs at 8 P.M. daily (7 P.M. after Labor Day) about the region, hunting and fishing information, bear-proof container loans, helpful staff, trip-planning assistance, backcountry registration and clean restrooms. Impressive boulder display of native rocks at entrance. You can listen to recorded oral history given by area residents or watch films on permafrost, the aurora borealis and many other topics.

Interesting short trails near here—listed in Trail Map and Guide pamphlet—offer scenic viewpoints and an opportunity to stretch your legs or walk the dog. Field editor Sharon Nault calls this location "a haven for weary travelers." Open 11 A.M. to 10 P.M. from late May through the second week of September. After Labor Day hours are noon–8 P.M.; phone (907) 678-5209 (summer only); www.blm.gov/visit/dalton-highway.

Kanuti's Winter Visitor Center, located inside the USFWS Kanuti National Wildlife Refuge Coldfoot Field Office, opened in February 2016. It is the only winter visitor contact station on the Dalton Highway and an important resource where visitors and community members alike can learn about nearby federal public lands and local area services, hear weather and aurora updates, view educational films, use the resource library, enjoy interpretive offerings and more. Renovations, including an expanded visitor area, are underway. Call the Kanuti NWR Fairbanks office at (907) 456-0329 or 1-877-220-1853 for more information.

Coldfoot Camp (local phone 907/474-3500) offers food, lodging and 24-hour fuel. The "trucker's table" at the restaurant is a good place to get news on the highway. Personal messages for travelers are posted on the log behind the counter in the restaurant. This is also one of the few places to get potable water along the highway, so fill your water jugs. Gift shop, bar, pay phone (takes phone cards, sold here if you need one; calls to Wiseman are free), laundromat with showers, fuel facility with gas and diesel (pay at restaurant before you pump and remember your pump number); 24-hour clerk (food service ends at midnight); tire repair, and air for tires, minor vehicle repair; and RV park with hookups. Post office is adjacent to restaurant. Tenters can camp for free in the grassy areas here; check with the front desk.

You can book many different kinds of tours here. **Coldfoot Air Service** provides flightseeing to the Gates of the Arctic and Kobuk National Parks and the Arctic National Wildlife Refuge. Phone (907) 687-3993; www.coldfootair.com. There is a 4,000-foot runway maintained by the state (see Private Aircraft at **Milepost J 175**).

Coldfoot is a former mining camp, located at the mouth of Slate Creek on the east bank of the Middle Fork Koyukuk River. A post office was established here in 1902, when Coldfoot consisted of "one gambling hole, 2 roadhouses, 2 stores and 7 saloons."

The name Coldfoot was first reported in 1933 by Robert Marshall, a forester who made a reconnaissance map of the northern Koyukuk Region. "In the summer of 1900, one of the waves of green stampeders got as far up the Koyukuk as this point, then got cold feet, turned around, and departed."

Mining activity later moved upstream to Nolan and Wiseman creeks.

Coldfoot experienced another short boom during the 1970s, when it became a construction camp for the trans-Alaska pipeline. In 1995, when the highway opened to the public, all the way to Deadhorse, Coldfoot became an important service stop for travelers and a gateway to the Brooks Range.

NOTE: Travelers headed to Deadhorse/Prudhoe Bay should call ahead about the availability of hotel rooms (3 or more days in advance) and for space on the Arctic Ocean tours (requires 24-hour advance security clearance with ID required). Visit www.deadhorsecamp.com/arctic-ocean-shuttle or phone (907) 474-3565 or 1-877-474-3565; tours depart from Deadhorse Camp at **Milepost J 412.8**.

NOTE: Next gas/diesel northbound is 240 miles from here at Deadhorse/Prudhoe Bay. Cell service provided by GCI in a 15 mile area around Coldfoot.

Improved pavement northbound to **Milepost J 209.3**. Drive with headlights on!

Dalton Highway Log
(continued)

J 175 F 259 D 240 Coldfoot Airport, Alaska State Troopers and Dept. of Transportation to west. Second turnoff (for northbound traffic) to east for loop road to Coldfoot; post office, food, gas/diesel, lodging, RV hookups, potable water and tire repair at Coldfoot Camp (see preceding description).

Private Aircraft: Coldfoot airport to west, N67°15.13', W150°12.23'; elev. 1,042 feet; length 4,000 feet, gravel; runway sur-

COLDFOOT ADVERTISERS

Wiseman is a historic mining town. Check out the Wiseman Historical Museum for a look at local history and old mining equipment. (©Michael K. Robb)

face soft and muddy after rain, packed snow on runway during winter. Unattended.

J 175.1 F 259.1 D 239.9 Narrow bridge over Slate Creek. Gold bearing gravel was discovered here in 1899. A 23 oz. nugget came from here in 1940.

J 175.5 F 259.5 D 239.5 *Slow for speed zone southbound.*

J 179.7 F 263.7 D 235.3 Turnoff to east for **Marion Creek BLM Campground;** 27 sites on gravel loop road, $8 camping fee (half price with America the Beautiful, Senior or Access passes), tables, grills, firepits, toilets, bear-proof litter and food containers, information kiosk, 3 raised tent pads and 11 pull-through RV sites. Wheelchair-accessible. A campground host ("meet the farthest north public campground host in America") is present from Memorial Day to Labor Day. No satellite TV or cell phone reception available and no hookups. If water pump is working, potable water is available here. *CAUTION: Bears in area, store food*

safely. Bear-proof locker at trailhead at back of campground.

This is a popular spot to park RVs and drive tow vehicles to Prudhoe Bay. *It is strongly recommended that you have overnight accommodations arranged before you get to Prudhoe Bay (see Lodging & Services page 508).*

Marion Creek Falls trailhead (signed) is a 1- to 2-hour 2-mile hike upstream to waterfall (much of it follows a mining road). Good berry picking (blueberries, lowbush cranberries) in season. Inquire with campground host for more details.

J 179.8 F 263.8 D 235.2 Marion Creek.

J 185 F 269 D 230 Kalhabuk Mountain to west.

J 186.2 F 270.2 D 228.8 Large paved parking area to east.

J 186.7 F 270.7 D 228.3 Fairly level paved parking areas both sides of highway.

J 187.2 F 271.2 D 227.8 Parking areas to west at south end of **Minnie Creek** bridge (narrow); fishing for Arctic grayling. This is a placer gold creek.

J 188.3 F 272.3 D 226.7 Distance marker southbound shows Coldfoot 13 miles, Fairbanks 267 miles.

J 188.4 F 272.4 D 226.6 Distance marker northbound shows Wiseman 3 miles, Dietrich 22 miles, Deadhorse 227 miles.

J 188.5 F 272.5 D 226.5 Middle Fork Koyukuk River No. 1 crossing (narrow bridge); turnout. Arctic grayling, burbot.

J 188.6 F 272.6 D 226.4 Turnoff for **Wiseman** (description follows); good photo op of pipeline at turnoff. The access road (improved, narrow in spots) leads 1.5 miles south to **junction** with road to Nolan, then continues 0.8 mile south along the Koyukuk River to Wiseman.

The road to **NOLAN** is narrow dirt and gravel, ranging from good to very poor (obey road signs). It leads 5.5 miles west to Nolan Creek Gold placer mine. There is a signed turnaround area before you reach the mine: *Do not proceed on to mine property without permission.* The mine is owned by Silverado Gold Mines Ltd..

Located 2.3 miles south of the Dalton Highway via a side road. **Population:** 13. Wiseman is a historic mining town on the Koyukuk River established in 1905. The heyday of Wiseman came in about 1910, after gold seekers abandoned Coldfoot. This is still an active mining area. A 150 oz. gold nugget was found in the Hammond River.

Visitor services are limited. Accommodations at **Arctic Getaway Cabin & Breakfast, Boreal Lodging** and **Wiseman Gold Rush Camp B&B.** Wiseman Gold Rush Camp B&B is located near the museum; office is in the little green house. Continue on access road across bridge for Arctic Getaway Cabin & Breakfast (in the historic Pioneer Hall Igloo No. 8), road continues to the antler decorated entrance of Boreal Lodging with coffee and gifts in large log shop. There is a good-sized turnaround area at the entrance to Boreal Lodging.

There is no formal campground here, but camping in turnouts is accepted off of Wiseman Road. There is river access and informal camping at sandbars by the Wiseman Road turnoff at the Middle Fork of the Koyukuk River bridge. *CAUTION: Be aware that sand bars do flood at high water.*

For the public phone, go about 60 feet past the green house, phone "booth" is on the left side of the road before corner. Coldfoot or Wiseman calls are local and free (do not dial area code), outside calls require a calling card. Payphone number is (907) 678-9320.

Boreal Lodging sells coffee, cold drinks, snacks, limited groceries and gifts—some locally made.

The non-denominational Kalhabuk Memorial Chapel (on access road past the lodges) is a small, cozy log cabin, always open and a favorite stop for visitors. Sunday services are at 11 A.M., visitors welcome. Access road continues to airstrip.

Several interesting historic buildings are found in Wiseman. Visitors can park by the post office (not in service), located in an original log cabin, and walk around this picturesque settlement. *(All the structures are privately owned and most are residences; be respectful while taking photos!)*

The **Wiseman Historical Museum,** located in the historic Carl Frank Cabin (behind the small green house), contains old miner's journals, hotel registers and historical photos. It is open only for guided tours; contact Northern Alaska Tour Company *(see ad on page 497 or inquire at Coldfoot Camp).* The Koyukuk Miners Museum is located on the road surrounded by mining equipment and across from the small, bright green house. (If there is someone in the little green house with the flags, ask if "Clutch" Lounsbury is available to let you into his miners' museum.) The old Pingel Roadhouse sits near the river to the east of the museum and is privately owned. Inquire locally about access to the museum.

At pullout near the entrance to Wiseman, follow sign for trail to the old Wiseman cemetery. It is about a 20-minute walk to the cemetery; bring mosquito repellent!

The American Legion Arctic Post #9, the farthest north post in the world, sponsors the **Miners Picnic on 4th of July**; music, food and miners; public welcome.

This is one of the best areas to watch the aurora borealis with near guaranteed, exceptional viewing during equinox months (March 21 and September 21) each year.

Dalton Highway Log
(continued)

J 189 F 273 D 226 The improved stretch of highway along here is built on a high gravel base above the river; *no shoulders, drive carefully!* Spur (finger) dikes keep the river away from the highway and pipeline during high water. Some dikes may be parked on but there is no room to turn around so you must back out.

J 190.6 F 274.6 D 224.4 Narrow bridge over Hammond River. Rough bridge decking. Gold mining area upstream. Some of the largest gold nuggets ever found in Alaska have been found on the Hammond River.

J 190.9 F 274.9 D 224.1 Middle Fork Koyukuk River No. 2 crossing. Narrow bridge; rough bridge decking. View of "guide banks," another example of river training structures.

J 192.7 F 276.7 D 222.3 Link Up (signed), where 2 sections of road constructed by different crews were joined when the Dalton Highway was completed in 1974.

J 194 F 278 D 221 First view northbound of Sukakpak Mountain (elev. 4,000 feet). Northbound travelers will have many photo ops of this distinctive mountain. Sukakpak Mountain is sometimes said to mark a traditional boundary between Eskimo and Athabascan Alaska Native territories. It rises 3,000 feet above the road. Wiehl Mountain (elev. 5,765 feet) is east of Sukakpak.

J 195 F 279 D 220 Wide side road leads to large, level, open space; primitive camping. Grassy hills are result of reseeding project.

J 196 F 280 D 219 Pipeline close to road is mounted on sliding shoes to allow flexing. It takes about a week for oil in pipeline to travel from Prudhoe Bay to Valdez.

J 197 F 281 D 218 Gold Creek bridge. From 1900–1970 more than 330,000 oz. of placer gold was produced in the upper Koyukuk and Chandalar mining districts. Many miners and active mines in area. Do not trespass on private claims.

J 197.5 F 281.5 D 217.5 Linda Creek in culvert. Private mining claims on creek.

J 197.6 F 281.6 D 217.4 Large paved turnout to east and view of Wiehl Mountain. Side road to gold mining area; motorized vehicle access restricted except for holders of valid mining claims.

J 200 F 284 D 215 View of the Middle Fork Koyukuk River, a typical braided river exhibiting frequent changes of the streambed during high water.

J 203.1 F 287.1 D 211.9 Paved parking area to east. View of ponds and Sukakpak Mountain.

J 203.4 F 287.4 D 211.6 Paved parking area to west.

J 203.7 F 287.7 D 211.3 Large parking area to east. Turnouts next 0.6 mile northbound with view of palsas, the short mounds of earth visible between the road and Sukakpak Mountain, which are formed by ice beneath the soil pushing the vegetative mat and soil upward.

J 204 F 288 D 211 Paved parking area to west.

J 204.3 F 288.3 D 210.7 Middle Fork Koyukuk River No. 3 bridge. Large parking area with toilets to east at north end of bridge offers good access to riverbank. Primitive camping. Beautiful views of imposing Sukakpak Mountain. The pressures on the limestone have changed much of the mountain into marble. Note veins of copper, quartz, crystalline and cinnabar in mountainside.

J 204.5 F 288.5 D 210.5 Middle Fork Koyukuk River No. 4 crossing. Narrow bridge; rough bridge decking. Parking to east at south end of bridge, river access.

J 205.2 F 289.2 D 209.8 Long, paved turnout to west (do not block pipeline access road). Good view of north side of Sukakpak Mountain.

J 206 F 290 D 209 View of Dillon Mountain (elev. 4,820 feet) just east of highway.

J 207 F 291 D 208 Dietrich River bridge. Halfway mark on the Dalton Highway. Turnouts at both ends of bridge. Fishing for burbot, Arctic grayling, whitefish and Dolly Varden. The Dietrich River flows south to join Bettles River, forming the Middle Fork Koyukuk River.

The dominant mountain nearest the highway looking south is Dillon Mountain. This mostly limestone mountain was named for JT Dillon, an Alaskan geologist who spent his life studying the Brooks Range.

J 207.4 F 291.4 D 207.6 Turnout to east.

J 208.5 F 292.5 D 206.5 $1,000 fine for littering (sign).

J 209.2 F 293.2 D 205.8 Distance marker northbound shows Dietrich 1 mile (to west), Deadhorse 205 miles. Dietrich is a former pipeline construction camp (dismantled, no public access).

J 209.3 F 293.3 D 205.7 Turnout to east. Pavement ends, gravel begins, northbound. Gravel surfacing ranges from poor to good depending on maintenance schedule. Improved, widened surface northbound to **Milepost J 222.3**.

J 209.4 F 293.4 D 205.6 Distance marker southbound shows Coldfoot 35 miles, Fairbanks 289 miles.

J 210.9 F 294.9 D 204.1 Very large turnout to east with old loading dock at back of parking area. This is the former Disaster Creek checkpoint from when travel on the highway north of here was restricted to permit holders.

J 211.8 F 295.8 D 203.2 Pipeline goes under road twice between here and just north of **Milepost J 212**. In 1985, a 270-foot-long section of pipe here had to be raised up after the ice-ledge it was on, settled 15 feet.

Road is very slick when wet.

J 213 F 297 D 202 Many large and small streams flow under the highway the next 14 miles northbound. Some of these streams continue to flow during winter below a frozen surface. Tall piping on some creek culverts are "thaw pipes," which help keep ice from blocking culverts in winter.

This is an area of wilderness vistas: river views, quiet valleys, spectacular mountains. Great photo op (weather permitting).

J 213.5 F 297.5 D 201.5 Creek flows under road in culvert.

J 213.7 F 297.7 D 201.3 Turnout to west.

J 216.2 F 300.2 D 198.8 Snowden Creek culvert. Panorama of Dietrich River valley and Brooks Range north and west of the road. View of mountain spires to east.

J 217.5 F 301.5 D 197.5 Small primitive parking area to east down by creek. Unusual mountain formations above. Rock spire to east is part of **Snowden Mountain** (elev. 5,794 feet). *NOTE: There are no established hiking trails off the Dalton Highway within the Brooks Range.*

J 219.8 F 303.8 D 195.2 Gravel pit access road to west.

J 219.9 F 303.9 D 195.1 Highway crosses creek in culvert; turnout. Pipeline goes underground in valley to west. Watch for large white patches of snow in creeks even in July and August.

J 221.1 F 305.1 D 193.9 Highway crosses large stream. Parking area to east.

Fall colors line the edge of the Dalton Highway at one of 4 crossings of the Koyukuk River.
(©Michael K. Robb)

Bicyclists descend the long, winding grade from Atigun Pass, elev. 4,800 feet, highest highway pass in Alaska. (©Sharon Nault)

J 221.7 F 305.7 D 193.3 Quarry to east has black marble with white calcite veins. The rock is used as rip-rap on road and river embankments.

J 222.2 F 306.2 D 192.8 Parking to west below road, near river.

J 222.6 F 306.6 D 192.4 Large gravel stockpile to west on the Dietrich River. Castellated mountains to east.

J 223 F 307 D 192 North of Snowden Mountain there are several distinctive peaks that are unnamed. Watch for grizzly bears in area. Cubs are born in the den when the mother is hibernating. During hibernation—which can last 7 months in the far north—the adult bears do not eat, drink, defecate or urinate. Newborn cubs will nurse on their lactating mother.

J 224 F 308 D 191 Turnout at gravel pit to east.

J 224.3 F 308.3 D 190.7 Narrow parking area. Streams flows under road in culvert.

J 225.4 F 309.4 D 189.6 Narrow, double-ended turnout to west on wide braided section of Dietrich River. Also turnout to east.

J 225.7 F 309.7 D 189.3 Turnouts on both sides of highway.

J 225.9 F 309.9 D 189.1 Room to park at APL access road (do NOT block road). Pipeline remote valve just west of road. The arch-shaped concrete "saddle weights" keep pipe-line buried in areas of possible flooding. They may be stored here until needed.

J 226.7 F 310.7 D 188.3 Turnout to west.

J 227.3 F 311.3 D 187.7 Bridge over Nutirwik Creek (*CAUTION: This bridge decking can be very slippery when wet*); creek is a tributary of the Dietrich River. Narrow shoulder parking on west side of highway south of bridge. View of Table Mountain to northeast.

J 228 F 312 D 187 Highway parallels Dietrich River. Physical Milepost 228 in the water on west side of road (all others have been on the east side of road).

J 228.9 F 312.9 D 186.1 Double-ended turnout (subject to flooding) to east; view of pipeline valve to east.

J 230.9 F 314.9 D 184.1 Turnout to west overlooking Dietrich River, which can be a vivid glacial blue depending on the light; good photo op.

J 231.3 F 315.3 D 183.7 Small turnouts (good in dry weather only) on both sides of highway.

J 232.5 F 316.5 D 182.5 Turnout to the east near creek which flows through a culvert beneath the highway.

J 232.7 F 316.7 D 182.3 Gravel turnout (muddy when wet) to west.

J 234.4 F 318.4 D 180.6 View to east of pipeline emerging from underground.

J 234.8 F 318.8 D 180.2 Northbound sign reads: Entering North Slope Borough—the world's largest municipality (in land area). Unlike the rest of the United States, which is organized into counties, Alaska's unit of regional government is the borough. Each borough has independent, incorporated communities within its boundaries. North Slope Borough offices are located in Utqiagvik (formerly known as Barrow).

J 235.1 F 319.1 D 179.9 Turnout to east.

J 235.2 F 319.2 D 179.8 A spruce tree once stood here and was the farthest north spruce tree along the Dalton. It was cut down by vandals. The dead tree was put in storage at the Coldfoot Visitor Center. There are now at least 3 other spruce trees growing to the north of here.

J 235.4 F 319.4 D 179.6 Very large turnout with bear-proof litter barrel, interpretive panels on northern treeline and tundra, and a pit toilet. Truck chain-up area in winter. *NOTE: Turnouts along here can be very muddy in wet weather; bring your mud boots!*

Road climbs to Chandalar Shelf. Treeline here is at 2,500 feet (in contrast, Alberta's treeline is at 7,500 feet, Colorado is at 12,000 feet and Ecuador, near the equator is 19,000 feet).

Begin 2-mile-long 10 percent uphill grade northbound. *Give trucks plenty of room. Do not stop on road. Dirt road surface can be slippery in wet weather, be sure to slow down. Watch for soft spots.*

J 236.8 F 320.8 D 178.2 Turnout to west up steep hill to flat area, a favorite stop for small tour vans; good photo ops. This turnout makes a great informal campsite for 1 or 2 small RVs, but it is a poor choice for big rigs because of small turnaround space.

Steep descent southbound.

J 237.1 F 321.1 D 177.9 Turnoff to east

for large parking area at summit of **Chandalar Shelf**, great views. Headwaters of the Chandalar River are to the east. Table Mountain (elev. 5,042 feet) is 5 miles south. Evidence of a glacial moraine lies on the shelf left by a glacier that extended over the side and down into the Dietrich Valley.

J 238.8 F 322.8 D 176.2 *SLOW (sign)*. Aircraft control gate.

J 239.3 F 323.3 D 175.7 SLOW DOWN (northbound sign) alerts motorists to intersection with access roads west to Chandalar Station (DOT/PF highway maintenance); no visitor services are available at the station. Use CB Channel 19 for emergencies.

Chandalar Camp, the former pipeline construction camp, was located just south of here.

J 239.5 F 323.5 D 175.5 Airstrip entrance. Bridge over river to east, primitive camping. No camping near runway.

J 239.9 F 323.9 D 175.1 Distance marker northbound shows Galbraith 34 miles, Deadhorse 173 miles.

Distance marker southbound shows Dietrich 32 miles, Coldfoot 67 miles, Fairbanks 321 miles.

J 240.6 F 324.6 D 174.4 Turnout to east. Watch for arctic ground squirrels, a food staple of foxes, golden eagles, wolves, weasels, wolverines and grizzly bears. These squirrels dig extensive burrows and are at home on well-drained tundra. The ultimate hibernators, their bodies are designed to withstand cold temperatures underground.

J 242.1 F 326.1 D 172.9 Small turnout to east. Atigun Pass (sign). Avalanche gun emplacement. *CAUTION: Watch for open metal covers on the ground.*

J 242.2 F 326.2 D 172.8 West Fork of the North Fork Chandalar River bridge; turnout to west. The scalloped waves of soil seen to the north on the hillside are formed when meltwater saturates the thawed surface soil then flows down the hill. These are called solifluction lobes.

Begin long, steep (12 percent), winding, uphill grade northbound to Atigun Pass. Winter avalanche area. Slide area next 5 miles northbound.

The pipeline is to the east in a buried, insulated concrete cribbing to protect it from rock slides and avalanches, and to keep the ground from thawing. Construction in this area was extremely complex, difficult and dangerous.

J 242.6 F 326.6 D 172.4 Rough gravel turnout overlooks valley below; spectacular views.

J 243.4 F 327.4 D 171.6 Turnout with great view of Slide Path 11 (signed), one of several areas where rock and debris have crashed down and across the road. These slide paths are signed and numbered on Atigun Pass.

J 244.1 F 328.1 D 170.9 Turnout to east at Slide Path 23. Look for wolves and for Dall sheep on rocky slopes below. The pipeline is buried in the narrow deep valley far below the highway. *CAUTION: Watch for falling rock.*

J 244.3 F 328.3 D 170.7 Evidence of a 2012 slide at Slide Path 25.

J 244.5 F 328.5 D 170.5 Narrow turnout to east.

J 244.7 F 328.7 D 170.3 "Avalanche Safety Zone" (sign). Very large turnout at top of **Atigun Pass**, elev. 4,800 feet, in the Brooks Range, highest highway pass in Alaska and where the highway crosses the Continental Divide. A Wyoming gauge to

DALTON HIGHWAY

measure precipitation is located here. Nice example of a cirque, an amphitheater-shaped bowl or depression caused by glacial erosion, in mountain east of road. Endicott Mountains are to the west, Philip Smith Mountains to the east. James Dalton Mountain is ahead and to the left, northbound. Avalanche safety area (sign) to east.

CAUTION: Watch for Dall sheep. The sheep congregate on and near the highway to lick the calcium chloride put on the roads for dust reduction. Dall sheep range throughout Alaska's major mountain ranges. The only white, wild sheep in the world, Dall sheep have honey-colored or dark brown horns. Rams have heavy, curled horns. Ewes and immature sheep of both sexes have thinner, almost straight horns, which causes some viewers to mistake them for mountain goats. The white-coated mountain goats have a black muzzle, a long beard, slender black horns and a more squarish body than Dall sheep. Mountain goats are generally confined to Southeast and southcentral Alaska.

J 245 F 329 D 170 Many mountains in this area exceed 7,000 feet in elevation.

J 245.4 F 329.4 D 169.6 Long, sloping, trenched parking area west side of highway may be difficult to access for northbound traffic. Short gravel side road east to large gravel parking area. Avalanche gun emplacements along highway.

J 246.6 F 330.6 D 168.4 Sloping turnout to west.

J 246.8 F 330.8 D 168.2 Very large, fairly flat, turnout to east. Avalanche gun emplacement. Pipeline is under road.

Begin long, steep (12 percent), winding, uphill grade southbound to Atigun Pass. Winter avalanche area. Slide area next 5 miles southbound.

J 248.4 F 332.4 D 166.6 Large gravel turnouts both sides of highway. Big views of valley below. Look for bears.

J 249.4 F 333.4 D 165.6 Gravel turnout to west where creek runs through 3 culverts. Room for primitive camping.

Permafrost to the north of Atigun Pass is called continuous and is found everywhere. Its thickness increases on the north side of the pass. Permafrost to south is discontinuous (spotty, decreases in thickness). The North Slope receives about 5 inches of rainfall annually (less than half that of Tucson, AZ), although the permafrost prevents the water from being absorbed by the soil.

J 249.7 F 333.7 D 165.3 Road closure gates used to stop traffic in extreme weather or emergency conditions. Very small parking area by APL access road (do not block) that leads east to staging area.

J 250 F 334 D 165 Long gravel turnout to east, large sloping gravel turnout to west. Large cleared area below road used for various kinds of camps.

NOTE: There are 2 physical Milepost 250's here. The MILEPOST® measures distance from the one farthest south.

J 251.5 F 335.5 D 163.5 Several turnouts next 0.2 mile northbound provide opportunities for photos.

J 252.9 F 336.9 D 163.1 Large parking area to west below road just south of Atigun River bridge No. 1.

J 253 F 337 D 162 Atigun River bridge No. 1. Watch for potholes at bridge ends; can be slippery when wet. Active gravel pit to east at north end of bridge.

CAUTION: Watch for oncoming truck traffic in rearview mirrors and pull over when possible.

Mileage sign at Galbraith Camp. The former pipeline camp offers an unimproved camping area. (©Steven Miley)

J 256 F 340 D 159 Great photo opportunity of pipeline, mountains and highway. Long straight section with pipeline beside it. Calcium chloride on highway, northbound. From Atigun Valley northward, you may see some unusual songbirds such as the Northern wheatear, yellow wagtail, Smith's longspur and bluethroat. Some of these birds winter as far away as Africa and Asia.

J 257.5 F 341.5 D 157.5 "Check valves" on pipeline keep oil from flowing backwards in the event of a leak. Expansive views of pipeline, valley and James Dalton Mountain to south.

J 258.5 F 342.5 D 156.5 Trevor Creek bridge may be slippery when wet. Turnout to west at south end of bridge.

J 258.6 F 342.6 D 156.4 Turnout to west. Good spot to park and hike up to rocks. *CAUTION: Grizzly bears in area.*

J 260.7 F 344.7 D 154.3 Gravel pit access road to east up hill.

J 260.8 F 344.8 D 154.2 Large turnout to west; view of check valve.

J 261.4 F 345.4 D 153.6 Turnout west close to pipeline road entrance.

J 262 F 346 D 153 View northbound of Pump Station No. 4 in the distance; see description at **Milepost J 269.2.**

Watch for potholes and pavement breaks in this area.

J 263.2 F 347.2 D 151.8 Small turnout to east and APL access to west. View to east of interesting rock formations on mountains.

J 264 F 348 D 151 Views of pipeline in the distance as it zigzags toward Pump Station 4. Lots of arctic ground squirrels in this area. Bears eat arctic ground squirrels.

J 265.1 F 349.1 D 149.9 Roche Moutonee [sic] Creek (signed) wood-decked bridge. (Correct spelling is Roche Moutonnee, French for a glacially scoured rock ridge in the shape of a sheep's back. The formation is located several miles upstream.) Turnout to west at north end of bridge.

J 266.8 F 350.8 D 148.2 Very small turnout to west.

J 267.1 F 351.1 D 147.9 Turnout to west.

J 267.5 F 351.5 D 147.5 Bridge over Holden Creek. Creek access road to west at north end of bridge.

J 269.2 F 353.2 D 145.8 Entrance to

Pump Station No. 4. This station has the highest elevation of all the pipeline stations (elev. 2,760 feet), and is also a launching and receiving station for special measuring and cleaning devices called "pigs." A scraper pig consists of spring-mounted scraper blades and/or brushes on a central body which moves through the pipe, cleaning accumulated wax from interior walls and monitoring conditions inside the pipe. There are "dumb" pigs and "smart" pigs. Dumb pigs clean out wax deposits in the line. Smart pigs scan the pipeline to check welds, wall thickness and other properties to help insure the integrity of the piping and identify maintenance needs. **Tea Lake** off road; fishing for Arctic grayling and burbot.

J 269.4 F 353.4 D 145.6 Highway bridge over pipeline. Tea Lake Outfall culvert (signed).

J 270 F 354 D 145 Second signed Tea Lake Outfall culvert northbound.

J 270.4 F 354.4 D 144.6 Bow Hunting Only (sign).

J 270.9 F 354.9 D 144.1 Atigun River bridge No. 2. Large parking area to west, south of bridge, with large cement boat launch ramps to the north, west side of bridge.

J 272 F 356 D 143 View of Galbraith Lake and Galbraith Camp. Galbraith Lake is a remnant of a huge glacial lake that filled the valley in the last ice age. It was named by USGS geologists in 1951 for Bart Galbraith, a bush pilot who was lost while flying in the area.

J 273.6 F 357.6 D 141.4 Improved highway next 15 miles northbound.

J 274.1 F 358.1 D 140.9 Wide gravel turnout to east.

J 274.6 F 358.6 D 140.4 Distance marker northbound shows Galbraith 1 mile, Deadhorse 139 miles.

J 274.7 F 358.7 D 140.3 Improved gravel road leads 4.3 miles west to **GALBRAITH CAMP.** This access road passes an active airstrip, several buildings and the Arctic National Wildlife Refuge Administrative Cabin (at Mile 2.1), which is open to the public *only in an emergency.* Continue

2.2 miles beyond the cabin, past gravel pit, for **Galbraith Lake BLM Campground**. This campground is in a wide tundra-covered valley ringed by mountains. The clear waters of Camp Creek run down its south boundary. It is a large campground with well-spaced, unimproved sites, some picnic tables, a pit toilet, litter barrels and bear-proof containers for tent campers. A road leads to many primitive camping areas in the tall brush. Nice wildflower display in season, good bird watching and lots of arctic ground squirrels. Interpretive panels on Galbraith's archaeological sites, survival skills of plants, arctic butterflies, mosquitoes and much more. A favorite spot for many Alaskans. *Bring mosquito repellent!* Plenty of hiking/walking opportunities.

▲

J 274.9 F 358.9 D 140.1 Distance marker southbound shows Galbraith 7 miles, Coldfoot 92 miles, Fairbanks 346 miles.

J 276.5 F 360.5 D 138.5 Island Lake to west.

J 281.5 F 365.5 D 133.5 Gravel turnouts both sides of highway.

J 281.6 F 365.6 D 133.4 Narrow double-ended gravel turnout to west.

J 281.7 F 365.7 D 133.3 View of Toolik Field Station. *CAUTION: Watch for caribou.*

J 282.1 F 366.1 D 132.9 Gravel turnout to east.

J 282.4 F 366.4 D 132.6 Small turnout at pipeline road turnoff; do not block road.

J 284.1 F 368.1 D 130.9 Gravel turnout to east.

J 284.3 F 368.3 D 130.7 Side road west to Toolik Lake, originally a pipeline construction camp, now the site of **Toolik Field Station**. Run by the Institute of Arctic Biology of the University of Alaska Fairbanks, the field station conducts research on Arctic ecology and the effects of climate change. No public facilities or services available. Scientists from around the world come here to study an intact arctic ecosystem.

This area is designated as a Research Natural Area (RNA) by the BLM. The public may fish and hunt on this land but overnight camping is not permitted anywhere in the RNA including the highway between **Mileposts J 278** and **J 293.**

J 286.2 F 370.2 D 128.8 Turnout to east at high point in road. Excellent photo stop; 360° view. View of Toolik Lake and Field Station. View of Brooks Range south and east. Philip Smith Mountains to west. Panoramic views of incredible beauty.

Bow hunting only area (sign).

J 288.4 F 372.4 D 126.6 Highway descends northbound to Kuparuk Creek bridge.

J 288.9 F 372.9 D 126.1 Kuparuk Creek bridge. Access east to creek at both ends of bridge. Informal camping; do not block pipeline access road. Watch for caribou here.

North to Deadhorse, the highway surface alternates between smooth, calcium chloride-treated road and a rough, hard gravel that offers a bumpier ride.

J 289.3 F 373.3 D 125.7 Small parking on east side. Highway crosses over pipeline. Short buried section of pipeline to north is called a sag bend and allows for wildlife crossing. Watch for caribou northbound.

J 290.3 F 374.3 D 124.7 Turnout to east with 360-degree view. Steep downgrade followed by long upgrade northbound. APL access.

J 290.6 F 374.6 D 124.4 Imnavait Creek culvert.

J 291.3 F 375.3 D 123.7 Toolik River culvert.

J 291.5 F 375.5 D 123.5 Shoulder narrows northbound (sign).

J 294.3 F 378.3 D 120.7 Sag bend in pipeline to west.

J 294.5 F 378.5 D 120.5 We often see our first caribou northbound here in summer. *CAUTION: Watch for caribou crossing the highway.*

J 297.5 F 381.5 D 117.5 Snow poles ("delineators") mark roadway for truckers during whiteouts from blowing snow or during dense fog.

J 297.8 F 381.8 D 117.2 Oksrukukuyik (or locally "Oks," pronounced *ox*) Creek. Road travels over 2 huge culverts. Two large sloping turnouts to the east at south and north ends of bridge.

J 298.2 F 382.2 D 116.8 Small turnouts both sides of highway at top of hill. First view northbound of Sagavanirktok ("the Sag") River valley. Slope Mountain (elev. 4,010 feet) to west. Watch for Dall sheep. Many blind hills, keep to right.

J 300 F 384 D 115 Northern boundary of BLM-managed land. Land north of here is managed by the Alaska Dept. of Natural Resources.

J 301 F 385 D 114 Slope Mountain to west, good place to glass for Dall sheep and birds. Parking to west by APL access road (do not block traffic).

Northbound traffic sign "Only state hunting regulations apply." Entering public lands.

J 303 F 387 D 112 *CAUTION: No shoulder along this stretch of highway.*

J 304 F 388 D 111 Sagavanirktok "Sag" River visible in the distance for northbound travelers.

J 305.5 F 389.5 D 109.5 Distance marker northbound shows Slope Mountain Camp 1 mile, Deadhorse 110 miles. Pipeline goes underground.

J 305.6 F 389.6 D 109.4 Sag River Station DOT highway maintenance. Slope Mountain Camp No. 1, a former pipeline construction camp, (now dismantled) 1 mile east. APL access.

J 305.7 F 389.7 D 109.3 Distance marker southbound shows Coldfoot 131 miles, Fairbanks 385 miles.

J 306.3 F 390.3 D 108.7 Small rough turnout to west. *There are dozens of these single-vehicle pullouts along the highway from here to Deadhorse. Use them rather than stop in the middle of or on the side of the road.*

J 307 F 391 D 108 Exceptionally brilliant fireweed seen to the west (in season) continues along the highway for many miles northbound.

J 309 F 393 D 106 Highway parallels Sagavanirktok River northbound.

J 309.5 F 393.5 D 105.5 Long turnout to west.

J 311.9 F 395.9 D 103.1 Entrance to **Pump Station No. 3**; mobile construction camp facility.

J 312 F 396 D 103 Highway parallels Sag River. Watch for caribou.

CAUTION: Highway northbound built on high gravel base; no shoulders, abrupt drop-offs to tundra and few turnouts.

J 313.8 F 397.8 D 101.2 Sam Schuyler Memorial Bridge crosses Oksrukukuyik Creek.

J 314 F 398 D 101 Highway shoulders narrow (even more) northbound.

J 314.3 F 398.3 D 100.7 Narrow gravel side road to east is a popular informal campsite for hunters during bow hunting season.

J 318.1 F 402.1 D 96.9 Wide gravel parking at turnoff to east for side road to river (do not block road) and primitive campsites; no turnaround areas for big rigs at river.

CAUTION: Steep, blind hills northbound. Watch for oncoming traffic on hills. Trucks will need to gather speed to crest hills. NOTE: Oil Spill Hill (coming up) and Ice Cut at **Milepost J 325** are 2 dangerous spots where CB radio users should call out ahead of the curve: "northbound 4-wheeler" or "southbound 4-wheeler" at "[name the curve]." (To truckers, anything not a big rig—such as cars, pickup trucks, vans, campers—is a "4-wheeler." Large RVs should identify themselves as "large RV.")

J 319.6 F 403.6 D 95.4 Turnout to east at Oil Spill Hill. Steep downhill grade.

J 320 F 404 D 95 The long range of hills east of the road are the Kakuktukruich Bluffs. Nice views northbound of the Sagavanirktok ("Sag") River.

J 320.6 F 404.6 D 94.4 Gustafson Gulch culverts.

J 320.8 F 404.8 D 94.2 Short side road east to Sag River; primitive campsite, limited turnaround space, do not block road.

J 322.7 F 406.7 D 92.3 Small single-vehicle pullout to east.

J 323 F 407 D 92 *Due to heavy truck traffic, stretches of the road are treated with calcium chloride north to Deadhorse. Wash your vehicles after driving the Dalton.*

J 224.9 F 408.9 D 90.1 Side road east to popular primitive campsite.

"Ice Cut" (sign) signals steep grade northbound.

J 325.2 F 409.2 D 89.8 Turnout to east at former storage yard.

J 325.5 F 409.5 D 89.5 Small turnout to east on ledge in middle of "Ice Cut" grade; popular spot with bow hunters after caribou because of its view. There are also turnouts at the bottom and at the top of this grade. Pipeline road access to large gravel area near river.

NOTE: Stay out of the way of northbound trucks accelerating for the steep climb.

J 325.8 F 409.8 D 89.2 Very large flat turnout to east with big views of pipeline to west and Sagavanirktok (Sag) River to east.

J 326.2 F 410.2 D 88.8 Pipeline crosses under bridge. APL access.

Highway can become soft and muddy along this section in wet weather.

J 327 F 411 D 87 Watch for grizzly bears digging for roots and other food around the pipeline supports.

J 328.8 F 412.8 D 86.2 Small, rocky, sloping turnout by creek to west.

J 330.7 F 414.7 D 84.3 Steep downhill (both directions) to Dan Creek bridge. Sloping turnout to east at north end of bridge; check before entering.

J 332.9 F 416.9 D 82.1 Turnout to east.

J 334.4 F 418.4 D 80.6 **Happy Valley**, former pipeline construction camp. No public facilities. Private crew camp occupies main buildings. Busy airstrip in summer and during hunting season, when an Alaska State Trooper may be present. Private guiding operations also work out of here.

Watch for caribou northbound.

J 337.7 F 421.7 D 77.3 Begin improved section of pavement with yellow lines, northbound.

J 339.8 F 423.8 D 75.2 Distance marker northbound shows Deadhorse 74 miles.

Distance marker southbound shows Slope Mountain Camp 36 miles, Coldfoot 166 miles, Fairbanks 420 miles.

J 345.5 F 429.5 D 79.5 Birdwatchers note: Peregrine falcons, gyrfalcons and rough-legged hawks have been seen in this area.

This section of highway can be thick with wildflowers in summer.

J 346.5 F 430.5 D 68.5 Ungated gravel road leads east to river.

J 347.8 F 431.8 D 67.2 Sag River Overlook. Long, narrow, sloping parking area to west. Gravel path beside road leads up to observation deck with interpretive displays. Good birdwatching in spring, bring your binoculars.

J 348.8 F 432.8 D 667.2 Small sloping gravel turnout to east.

J 350.5 F 434.5 D 64.5 View of Sagwon Bluffs to the east.

J 352 F 436 D 63 Steep downgrade to creek crossing followed by slow rolling ascent northbound. View at creek crossing of unusual rock formation in the tundra.

J 353.2 F 437.2 D 62.8 Side road west to gravel pit.

J 354.6 F 438.6 D 60.4 Last Chance Wayside to west at crest of hill. Large gravel parking area (watch for potholes), pit toilet and garbage container.

Panoramic views from wayside (weather permitting) of Arctic coastal plain; look for musk-oxen. Follow short dirt road uphill from wayside for primitive campsites. *HUNTERS PLEASE NOTE: Do not dump gut piles in trash containers. State hunting regulations require game be field dressed out of sight of roads and trails. And the seasonal workers who haul out the trash will appreciate it!*

Porcupine and Central Arctic caribou herds migrate through this area on their way to and from their calving grounds.

Migratory birds from around the world nest and breed on the Arctic coastal plain. Bird watchers come to view the king eiders, spectacled eiders, Canada geese, snow geese, tundra swans, jaegers, snowy owls and a variety of other species seen here in the spring.

Road widens as highway descends northbound.

J 355 F 439 D 60 Long, narrow turnout to east with expansive panoramic view. A favorite stop for truckers.

Highway widens northbound.

J 356.5 F 440.5 D 58.5 Metal poles mark road edge, a great help in winter when blowing snow obscures road. The small brown object far out on the tundra to the west draws lots of attention each year, but it is 2 barrels, not a bear!

J 357.2 F 441.2 D 57.8 Pavement ends, gravel begins, northbound.

J 359 F 443 D 56 Pump Station No. 2 to the east. Begin long, straight stretch northbound.

J 360.2 F 444.2 D 54.8 Small gravel turnout to east.

J 362 F 446 D 53 *CAUTION: The worst winter weather conditions on the Dalton Highway are experienced the next 38 miles northbound. Blowing snow may obscure visibility and block road.*

Improved highway northbound. *Drive with headlights on.*

J 365.1 F 449.1 D 49.9 Large level turnout to west. Watch for waterfowl, especially swans, geese and ducks, in large lakes along highway.

J 366.6 F 450.6 D 48.4 Gravel side road to primitive campsites. Used by commercial hunting guide during caribou season; do not

Dalton Highway travelers have a good chance of seeing musk-oxen on the North Slope.
(©Steven Miley)

block road.

J 367.8 F 451.8 D 47.2 Lake Desiree turnout to the west. Floatplanes sometimes land at this lake.

J 369.6 F 453.6 D 45.4 Distance marker southbound shows Coldfoot 196 miles, Fairbanks 450 miles.

J 370.9 F 454.9 D 44.1 Narrow side road to primitive campsite; do not block road.

J 375 F 459 D 40 To the east (not visible from road), the Ivishak River empties into the Sagavanirktok River on its journey to the Arctic Ocean.

J 376 F 460 D 39 The small hill seen on the horizon, about 3 miles west of the road, is a pingo (this one is named "Percy Pingo"). Pingos often form from the bed of a spring-fed lake that has been covered by vegetation. Freezing of the water can raise the surface several hundred feet above the surrounding terrain.

J 377.3 F 461.3 D 37.7 Large, extra nice turnout to east is viewpoint for distant Franklin Bluffs (bring binoculars). There is a large, flat, storage area at this turnout.

J 379 F 463 D 36 Improved surfacing to **Milepost J 414.**

J 383 F 467 D 32 Buried pipeline and Franklin Bluffs to the east, and a pingo to the west.

J 384 F 468 D 31 Dalton Highway snakes its way northbound across the flat coastal plain. Watch for golden eagles, ducks, Arctic fox, snowy owl, jaegers, swans, bears and caribou.

J 386.1 F 470.1 D 28.9 Large gravel turnout to east; good spot for photos of Franklin Bluffs. Oxidized iron minerals give these bluffs their colors. The white patches are usually snow.

J 388.6 F 472.6 D 26.4 Turnout to east. Musk-oxen are often seen along here between the road and the river.

J 394 F 478 D 21 Gravel visible to west in the tundra was deposited by flood waters from the Sagavanirktok River in May 2015. The flood was attributed to a "perfect storm" of events: heavy summer rains followed by extensive freezing in winter that trapped the water in place, then a rapid spring thaw due to record warm temperatures in this region.

The unprecedented flooding between **Mileposts J 392** and **J 414** caused an 18-day closure of the Dalton Highway, created a lake around Deadhorse, and cost an estimated $15.5 million in repairs. The improvements include sturdier embankments, new culverts and fish passages.

J 394.7 F 478.7 D 20.3 Distance marker northbound shows Deadhorse 20 miles.

J 395.3 F 479.3 D 19.7 Turnout to east, Caren Pond to west.

J 395.9 F 479.9 D 19.1 Watch for musk-oxen along the Sagavanirktok ("Sag") River.

J 400.9 F 484.9 D 14.1 Rough turnout to east.

J 405 F 489 D 10 Large gravel turnout to east; look for caribou and other wildlife.

J 406.3 F 490.3 D 8.7 Gravel access road leads east toward Sag River.

J 407 F 491 D 8 Popular local fishing spot and informal camping area used by travelers (tents and RVs) along the **Sagavanirktok (Sag) River**. There are primitive firepits. Bring firewood; carry trash out. ➡

J 408 F 492 D 7 Small turnout to east.

J 408.7 F 492.7 D 6.3 Turnout to west.

J 411.1 F 495.1 D 3.9 Narrow gravel side road to east.

J 411.5 F 495.5 D 3.5 Access road to gravel pit, followed by access road to Bill Meyer Lake.

J 412.8 F 496.8 D 2.2 Deadhorse Camp offers rooms and dining for overnight guests; phone ahead for reservations. Gift shop. The Arctic Ocean Shuttle leaves from Deadhorse Camp; make reservations at least 24-hours in advance. Phone (907) 474-3565 or 1-877-474-3565; www.deadhorsecamp.com.

Deadhorse Camp. See display ad page 509.

J 413.8 F 497.8 D 1.2 Double-ended turnout by Sag River.

J 414.1 F 498.1 D 0.9 Large turnout on curve. Free maps of Deadhorse are usually available in a box here *(please secure lid after taking a map)*. Be sure to pick one up, they are very useful. Lake Olivia is the small lake north of the highway as you drive into town. Watch for birds, bears and caribou.

After driving 415 miles through wilderness, the industrial landscape of Deadhorse on the horizon is something of a surprise.

(©Sharon Nault)

Deadhorse/Prudhoe Bay

J 415 F 499 D 0 Stop sign: End of Dalton Highway. Business signs will point you in the direction of various services in Deadhorse/Prudhoe Bay. Behind the signs is Lake Colleen, an important body of water in Prudhoe Bay because it provides water for the camps. What look like small cabins across the lake are actually oil wells. Since Deadhorse/Prudhoe Bay in no way resembles a traditional town, it is hard to know where you are within it especially when it is foggy. Best bet is to follow signs to any of the businesses mentioned in *The MILEPOST®*, since they serve the traveling public. The road does not go through to the Arctic Ocean. If you want to see the Arctic Ocean you must book a tour. It is reached via a secured area and unavailable to the public outside of a tour provider (inquire about a tour before arriving and allow 24 hours for security clearance).

Population: 2,174. (Oil crews can inundate this community, which is why hotels often run at 100 percent capacity.) *NOTE: Cell phone service is available in Deadhorse/ Prudhoe Bay and for about the first 14 miles south on the Dalton Highway, then there is no service until Coldfoot and near Fairbanks. Tune in to radio station 1610 AM for weather information.*

Visitor Information: Deadhorse Camp at Milepost J 412.8 caters to the traveling public and runs the Arctic Ocean Shuttle; phone (907) 474-3565. Other businesses here are designed for industrial services, not tourism. See "Lodging and Services" for additional information.

Private Aircraft: Deadhorse Airport, N70°11.69' W148°27.91'; elev. 65 feet; length 6,500 feet, asphalt; fuel NC-100, B, mogas. A 5,000 foot private gravel airstrip is owned and maintained by ConocoPhillips Alaska, Inc. A state-owned heliport is located here.

Climate: Arctic, with temperatures ranging from -56°F in winter to 78°F in summer. Precipitation averages 5 inches; snowfall 20 inches. **Radio:** KCDS 88.1 FM. **Transportation:** Scheduled jet service to Deadhorse/ Prudhoe Bay from Anchorage, Fairbanks and Barrow. (Flying time from Anchorage is 1 hour, 45 minutes.) Packaged tours of the North Slope area are available from Anchorage and Fairbanks. Air taxi service is available at Deadhorse Airport.

The industrial complex that is Deadhorse is clustered around or near Lake Colleen, on Prudhoe Bay, on the Beaufort Sea Coast, Arctic Ocean. Prudhoe Bay is ranked third in the nation in reserves and output. It has produced more than 12.5 billion barrels of oil since production began. Kuparuk, 40 miles west of Prudhoe Bay, is ranked sixth in the nation.

Most buildings in Deadhorse are modular, pre-fab-type construction. Some are set on refrigerated concrete slabs that do not melt the permafrost. Other buildings are constructed on pilings. Virtually all the businesses here are engaged in oil field or pipeline support activities, such as drilling, construction, maintenance, telecommunications, warehousing and transportation. Oil field employees work a rotation, such as 2 weeks on the job, then 2 weeks off. Workers typically work 7 days a week, 10 to 12 hours each day.

According to Deborah Bernard in an article in the *Prudhoe Bay Journal*, there is more than one version of how Deadhorse got its name, but basically it was named after Deadhorse Haulers, a company hired to do the gravel work at the Prudhoe Bay airstrip. (How the company came to be called Deadhorse Haulers is another story.) Everybody began calling the airstrip "Deadhorse," and the name stuck—too well for those who prefer the name Prudhoe Bay. Some people were surprised when Prudhoe Bay got its own ZIP code on June 3, 1982, and was listed as "Deadhorse, AK 99734," rather than Prudhoe Bay. It was later changed back to Prudhoe Bay, AK 99734.

Transportation

Air: Alaska Airlines.

Bus: Scheduled van service between Fairbanks and Deadhorse via Dalton Highway Express. Phone (907) 474-3555.

Lodging & Services

Visitor accommodations and meals (call ahead) are available for Northern Alaska Tour Co. guests at **Deadhorse Camp**, located south of Deadhorse at **Milepost 412.8**, phone (907) 474-3565, toll-free 1-877-474-3565, www.deadhorsecamp.com.

Other facilities that may have rooms for visitors, but cater primarily to oil field workers, are: Prudhoe Bay Hotel (907/659-2449), Arctic Oilfield Hotel (907/685-0500) and Aurora Hotel (907/670-0600). Call in advance to inquire about space. Also ask about purchasing meals at their cafeterias. Cafeteria hours are generally: Breakfast 5:30–8 A.M., lunch noon–1 P.M., dinner 5–8 P.M., with self-serve snacks available for purchase in-between.

Many of the visitor services available in Deadhorse are found at Brooks Range Supply (phone 907/659-2550). They are located in the building with the "Welcome to Deadhorse, Alaska, end of the Dalton Highway" sign (fun photo op), which houses the Napa Store, Prudhoe Bay General Store (open daily 6 A.M. to 9 P.M.), and the post office (open 1–3 P.M. and 7–9 P.M. daily). Check out the post office bulletin board for local happenings. The "Colville Mini-Mall" carries industrial supplies and sundries. Propane bottle refills may be available.

Alcohol, ammunition and weapons are not available in Deadhorse.

There is no bank in Deadhorse, but ATMs are available. Credit cards and traveler's checks are generally accepted, but Fish and Game licenses and postage must be paid for in cash.

Regular, unleaded gas and No. 1 diesel are available at NANA (Chevron) or the Deadhorse/Prudhoe Bay Tesoro Station. Tesoro is a 24-hour self-serve station; an attendant is available and cash accepted from 7 A.M. to 6 P.M. Pay prior to pumping. Credit card machines on fueling island are available after hours. Public restrooms are located inside the Tesoro office by the station. At NANA, the pumps are kept in barrels, and you can pay at a machine inside. NANA also has a dump station; $15 fee with fill-up, $25 dump station only.

Tire and vehicle repairs are available at Prudhoe Bay Fleet Service, Jacobs Engineering Group Fleet Services, NANA and at GBR. Local auto parts and hardware store has an assortment of supplies. Warranty work for Ford and Dodge is available in Deadhorse.

Public access beyond Deadhorse is restricted. For security reasons, travel north of Deadhorse, including visits to the Arctic Ocean, is limited to commercial tours. Tour information is available at the hotels or call Northern Alaska Tour Company at (907) 474-8600 or 1-800-474-1986.

Camping

There is no formal overnight RV campground but usually you can find an overnight space. Try the Arctic Oilfield Hotel or Tesoro station. Tent camping is generally discouraged due to bears. Many people camp just outside town on the Dalton Highway at turnouts along the Sagavanirktok River.

CAUTION: Beware of bears in the area. The Prudhoe Bay/Deadhorse area has been overrun with grizzly bears in summers past. Polar bears have been known to wander into town. Use caution when camping or walking around. Also be alert for caribou in road: They have the right-of-way.

Attractions

Take the Arctic Ocean Shuttle from Deadhorse Camp on an oil field tour. The tour takes you by the largest natural gas processing plant in the world and the largest drilling rig tower in the world (named "Liberty"). Take a dip in the Arctic Ocean and become a part of the Polar Bear Club; certificates are available for those who go into the water. Tour bus drivers bring towels and blankets.

You must reserve space on this tour 24-hours in advance and carry identification. Inquire about additional restrictions. For tour information and reservations, phone (907) 474-3565 or 1-877-474-3565.

Wildlife watching is always an attraction here. It is not unusual to see a number of caribou in Prudhoe Bay. Caribou congregate on the coast after calving in late June and July. Be careful not to drive into restricted areas near Deadhorse and Prudhoe Bay entrance.

Bring your binoculars! Bird life is abundant on the North Slope. Birders will enjoy a unique opportunity to see breeding colors on species that are normally only in remote areas, such as the king, common and spectacled eider, pomarine jaeger, parasitic jaeger, Sabine's gull and many more. Drive around Deadhorse roads slowly and scan ponds and wetlands for wildlife from late May to late June.

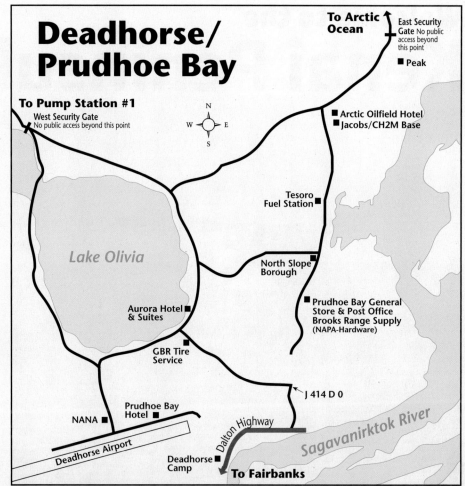

Welcome to the
Kenai Peninsula

Kite flying is popular on Kenai Peninsula beaches. (©Donna Dewhurst)

The Kenai Peninsula, south of Anchorage, has been labeled the playground of southcentral Alaska. It is a favorite destination for Alaskans and visitors from Outside, who are drawn by its incomparable scenery and variety of fishing opportunities on the Kenai, Russian and Kasilof rivers, and in Resurrection Bay, Kachemak Bay and Cook Inlet.

The Seward Highway provides access to the Kenai Peninsula from Anchorage. Completed in 1951, the Seward Highway (Alaska Routes 1 and 9) winds along the north shore of Turnagain Arm, crossing the isthmus that separates the Kenai Peninsula from the rest of southcentral Alaska some 52 miles south of Anchorage. Without the "Welcome to the Kenai Peninsula" sign at **Milepost S 75**, motorists probably would never notice they had crossed onto a peninsula, having left behind the urban setting of Anchorage just 45 miles up the Seward Highway.

Along that 52-mile stretch of the Seward Highway between Anchorage and the Kenai Peninsula, motorists enjoy panoramic vistas of the Chugach and Kenai mountain ranges and Turnagain Arm.

Turnagain Arm is a 48-mile-long estuary stretching from the mouth of the Placer River to the head of Cook Inlet. It was named "River Turnagain" by Captain James Cook in 1778, when he discovered it had no eastern outlet. The name was adopted by Captain George Vancouver, who surveyed the area in 1794, as Turnagain Arm.

That stretch of the Seward Highway also junctions with the Alyeska Highway to the Alyeska Resort and recreation area, and with the Portage Glacier/Whittier Access Road. The Alyeska Highway leads to Girdwood, a community of nearly 2,000, and home of the world-class ski resort at Mount Alyeska. The Portage Glacier/Whittier Access Road leads to the Anton Anderson tunnel, originally a railroad tunnel now doubles as road access to the formerly isolated port of Whittier. Portage Glacier, a popular tourist destination, has the Begich-Boggs Visitor Center and boat trip to view Portage Glacier.

Once the Seward Highway crosses on to the Kenai Peninsula, it first climbs to Turnagain Pass, a stunning alpine area that is a favorite winter recreation area as well as a summer viewpoint. Beyond Turnagain Pass at **Milepost S 56.3**, the Seward Highway junctions with the 18-mile Hope Highway, which leads to the historic mining town of Hope on the south shore of Turnagain Arm.

The Seward Highway ends at the picturesque town of Seward on Resurrection Bay, gateway to Kenai Fjords National Park.

The Sterling Highway is the other major highway on the Kenai Peninsula. The Sterling Highway begins at its junction with the Seward Highway at **Milepost S 37**, Tern Lake Junction, 90 miles south of Anchorage. (It is at this junction that the Seward Highway becomes Alaska Route 9.) From here, the Sterling Highway (Alaska Route 1) travels 57 miles west to Cook Inlet, before turning south and following the west coast of the Kenai Peninsula 85 miles to the scenic town of Homer on Kachemak Bay. (This stretch of highway offers magnificent views across Cook Inlet of 3 active volcanoes: Redoubt, Iliamna and Augustine.) Across from Homer are the settlements of Halibut Cove and Seldovia, both accessible by boat.

The Sterling Highway provides access to the communities of Cooper Landing, Soldotna, Kenai (via the Kenai Spur Road), Kasilof, Clam Gulch, Ninilchik and Anchor Point. The Sterling Highway also provides access to the world-famous Kenai River and Russian River, Kasilof River and Anchor River, considered to be some of Alaska's most popular fishing rivers.

Hiking and canoeing are 2 equally well-known pursuits on the Kenai Peninsula, and the Sterling Highway provides access to the popular Resurrection North Pass Trail and to canoe trails in the Kenai National Wildlife Refuge.

Detailed information about the attractions of the Kenai Peninsula, including the geography, history, communities, wildlife, fishing, camping and other recreation will be found in the SEWARD HIGHWAY section beginning on page 511, and in the STERLING HIGHWAY section beginning on page 538.

Seward Highway

CONNECTS: Anchorage to Seward, AK

Length: 127 miles **Road Surface: Paved** **Season: Open all year**

(See map, page 512)

(See map, page 512)

1 **9**

The Seward Highway has several popular hiking trails, including Turnagain Arm Trail with its glorious views. (©Donna Dewhurst)

Major Attractions:

©Claire Torgerson, staff

Alaska SeaLife Center, Portage and Exit Glaciers, Mount Alyeska, Kenai Fjords National Park

Highest Summit:
Turnagain Pass 1,015 ft.

The 127-mile-long Seward Highway connects Anchorage with the community of Seward on the east coast of the Kenai Peninsula (driving time about 3 hours). The Seward Highway's outstanding scenic, historic and recreational resources have given it a triple designation: National Forest Scenic Byway, All-American Road and Alaska Scenic Byway.

The Seward Highway also provides access to Girdwood and Alyeska Ski Resort via the Alyeska Highway from **Milepost S 90**; to Whittier and to Portage Glacier via the Whittier/Portage Road from **Milepost S 78.9**; to Hope via the Hope Highway from **Milepost S 56.3**; and to the Sterling Highway from **Milepost S 37** (Tern Lake Junction), 90 miles south of Anchorage. The Sterling Highway leads to Soldotna, Kenai and Homer *(see log of that route beginning on page 538).*

The Seward Highway is open all year. Physical mileposts along this route reflect distance from Seward (Mile 0). There are no gas stations on the Seward Highway between **Milepost S 90** (Girdwood turnoff) and Seward.

The first 9 miles of the highway are referred to as the "New" Seward Highway, a major Anchorage thoroughfare (4-lane divided freeway) connecting South Anchorage with downtown. South of Anchorage, the Seward Highway is a paved, 2-lane highway with passing lanes.

Leaving Anchorage, the Seward Highway follows the north shore of Turnagain Arm through Chugach State Park and Chugach National Forest and offers a panoramic view of the south shore and the Kenai Mountains on the Kenai Peninsula. The Kenai Peninsula is just that—a peninsula, measuring 150 miles long and 70 miles wide, extending southwest from Turnagain Arm and Passage Canal. It is bounded to the east by the Gulf of Alaska, and to the west by Cook Inlet. The Seward Highway crosses the isthmus that separates the Kenai Peninsula from the rest

Distance in miles	Alyeska	Anchorage	Hope	Seward	Whittier
Alyeska		42	56	95	28
Anchorage	42		88	127	60
Hope	56	88		75	52
Seward	95	127	75		91
Whittier	28	60	52	91	

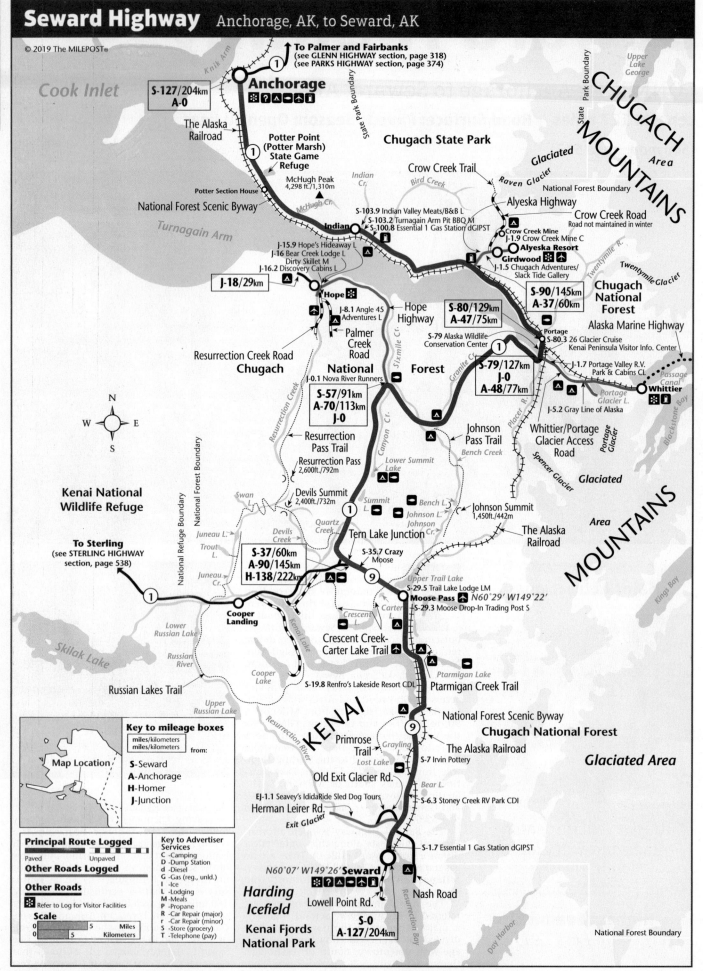

Seward Highway
Anchorage, AK, to Seward, AK

© 2019 The MILEPOST®

Cook Inlet

To Palmer and Fairbanks
(see GLENN HIGHWAY section, page 318)
(see PARKS HIGHWAY section, page 374)

1 **Anchorage**

S-127/204km
A-0

The Alaska Railroad

Potter Point
(Potter Marsh)
State Game
Refuge

Potter Section House

McHugh Peak
4,298 ft./1,310m

National Forest Scenic Byway

Turnagain Arm

Chugach State Park

Indian Cr.

Bird Creek

Crow Creek Trail

Raven Glacier

Glaciated

CHUGACH MOUNTAINS
Area

Upper Lake George

National Forest Boundary

S-103.9 Indian Valley Meats/B&B L
S-103.2 Turnagain Arm Pit BBQ M
S-100.8 Essential 1 Gas Station dGIPST

Indian

McHugh Cr.

Alyeska Highway

Crow Creek Road
Road not maintained in winter

Crow Creek Mine
J-1.9 Crow Creek Mine C

Alyeska Resort

Girdwood
J-1.5 Chugach Adventures/
Slack Tide Gallery

Chugach National Forest

Twentymile R.

Twentymile Glacier

J-15.9 Hope's Hideaway L
J-16 Bear Creek Lodge L
Dirty Skillet M
J-16.2 Discovery Cabins L

J-18/29km

Hope

J-8.1 Angle 45
Adventures L

Palmer
Creek
Road

Resurrection Creek Road

Chugach

National

Forest

Hope
Highway

Sixmile Cr.

S-80/129km
A-47/75km

S-79 Alaska Wildlife
Conservation Center

Granite Cr.

Portage
S-80.3 26 Glacier Cruise
Kenai Peninsula Visitor Info. Center

Alaska Marine Highway

S-90/145km
A-37/60km

J-1.7 Portage Valley R.V.
Park & Cabins CL

Passage Canal

Whittier

Blackstone Bay

J-0.1 Nova River Runners

S-57/91km
A-70/113km
J-0

Resurrection
Pass Trail

Resurrection Pass
2,600ft./792m

Devils Summit
2,400ft./732m

Resurrection Creek

Canyon Cr.

Lower Summit Lake

Johnson Pass Trail

Bench Creek

Placer R.

S-79/127km
J-0
A-48/77km

Johnson Pass Trail

J-5.2 Gray Line of Alaska

Whittier/Portage
Glacier Access
Road

Portage Glacier L.

Portage Glacier

Spencer Glacier

Glaciated

Kenai National Wildlife Refuge

National Refuge Boundary

National Forest Boundary

Swan Lake

Juneau L.

Devils Creek

Trout L.

Juneau L.

Quartz Creek

Summit L.

Bench L.

Johnson L.
Johnson Cr.

Johnson Summit
1,450ft./442m

Area

MOUNTAINS

Kings Bay

S-37/60km
A-90/145km
H-138/222km

To Sterling
(see STERLING HIGHWAY
section, page 538)

Tern Lake Junction

S-35.7 Crazy
Moose

9

Upper Trail Lake
S-29.5 Trail Lake Lodge LM

Moose Pass N60°29' W149°22'
S-29.3 Moose Drop-In Trading Post S

1 **Cooper Landing**

Lower Russian Lake

Kenai Lake

Russian River

Cooper Lake

Crescent L.

Carter L.

Crescent Creek-
Carter Lake Trail

KENAI

Russian Lakes Trail

Skilak Lake

Upper Russian Lake

Resurrection River

S-19.8 Renfro's Lakeside Resort CDL

Ptarmigan Lake

Ptarmigan Creek Trail

National Forest Scenic Byway

Chugach National Forest

Glaciated Area

Primrose Trail

Grayling L.

Lost Lake

9

The Alaska Railroad

S-7 Irvin Pottery

Old Exit Glacier Rd.

Bear L.

EJ-1.1 Seavey's IdidaRide Sled Dog Tours

Herman Leirer Rd.

Exit Glacier

S-6.3 Stoney Creek RV Park CDI

Harding Icefield

N60°07' W149°26' **Seward**

Lowell Point Rd.

S-1.7 Essential 1 Gas Station dGIPST

Nash Road

Kenai Fjords National Park

S-0
A-127/204km

Resurrection Bay

Day Harbor

National Forest Boundary

Key to mileage boxes

miles/kilometers
miles/kilometers from:

S-Seward
A-Anchorage
H-Homer
J-Junction

Map Location

Principal Route Logged

Paved   Unpaved

Other Roads Logged

Other Roads

Refer to Log for Visitor Facilities

Scale

0   5 Miles
0   5 Kilometers

Key to Advertiser Services

C -Camping
D -Dump Station
d -Diesel
G -Gas (reg., unld.)
I   -Ice
L -Lodging
M -Meals
P -Propane
R -Car Repair (major)
r   -Car Repair (minor)
S -Store (grocery)
T -Telephone (pay)

of southcentral Alaska at **Milepost S 75**, 52 miles south of Anchorage.

Bike trails along the Seward Highway include a 3-mile trail between Indian and Bird; a 6-mile trail between Girdwood and Bird Point; and an 8-mile bike trail (the Sixmile Trail) between the Hope Highway junction and the Johnson Pass Trailhead. There are also a number of trailheads along the Seward Highway for both Chugach State Park and Chugach National Forest hiking trails.

Emergency medical services: Phone 911. Hospitals in Anchorage and Seward and in Soldotna (on the Sterling Highway). Alaska State Troopers in Anchorage (907) 269-5511, Crown Point (Moose Pass), (907) 288-3346; and Cooper Landing (on the Sterling Highway), (907) 595-1233. Emergency call boxes are located at Turnagain Pass (**Milepost S 68.5**); at **Milepost J 0.1** on the Hope Highway near junction (**S 56.3**); Summit Lake Lodge (**S 45.8**); and at the Sterling Highway junction.

NOTE: Cell phone service is sporadic between Anchorage and Seward.

Seward Highway Log

Distance from Seward (S) is followed by distance from Anchorage (A).
Physical mileposts show distance from Seward.

ALASKA ROUTE 1

S 127 A 0 Gambell Street and 10th Avenue in Anchorage. The New Seward Highway (Gambell Street southbound, Ingra northbound) connects with the Glenn Highway in Anchorage via 5th Avenue (westbound) and 6th Avenue (eastbound). *(See map on page 354 in the ANCHORAGE section.)* Follow Gambell Street south.

S 126.8 A 0.2 Traffic light at 13th Avenue.

S 126.7 A 0.3 Traffic light at 15th Avenue. Access east to Merrill Field and the Alaska Regional Hospital.

S 126.6 A 0.4 Access southbound to Sullivan sports arena, Ben Boeke ice rinks and baseball stadium.

S 126 A 1 Traffic light at Fireweed Lane. Gas/diesel, shopping and services to west.

S 125.8 A 1.2 Traffic light at Northern Lights Boulevard (one-way westbound). Access west to Walgreens at northwest corner, and former Sears Mall at southwest corner. Sears Mall was the first shopping mall in Anchorage. Sears closed in April 2018, and the mall is to be renamed Midtown Mall. It has a Carr's/Safeway, REI, Nordstrom Rack and other stores. Fred Meyer and gas stations east side of highway (southbound traffic use Benson Boulevard for access).

S 125.7 A 1.3 Traffic light at Benson Boulevard (one-way eastbound). Fred Meyer access.

S 125.4 A 1.6 Southbound access only to Old Seward Highway and 36th Ave. businesses; popular Moose's Tooth Pizza to west.

S 125.3 A 1.7 Traffic light at 36th Avenue. The Providence Hospital and University of Alaska Anchorage (UAA) campuses are 2 miles east. Z.J. Loussac Library, Midtown post office, Century 16 Cinema, fast-

food and other services to the west.

Begin 4- to 6-lane freeway and 65-mph speed limit southbound. Begin 4-lane divided highway and *45-mph speed limit northbound.*

S 124.7 A 2.3 Tudor Road overpass. Exit west for gas/diesel station, Dairy Queen, Home Depot, IHOP, Lowes and other businesses. Exit east for Anchorage Police, Municipal Animal Shelter, shopping and services.

S 124.4 A 2.6 Highway crosses Campbell Creek; Campbell Creek Greenbelt. Chugach Mountains are to the east.

S 123.7 A 3.3 Dowling Road underpass; exits east and west to businesses. Roundabouts at both Dowling off ramps: Exiting motorists are reminded to yield to traffic already in the circle; to follow the counterclockwise traffic pattern in the circle without stopping; and to use turn signals when exiting the circle. Access to Anchorage recycling center to west.

S 122.6 A 4.4 Southbound-only exit for 76th Avenue; access west to Old Seward Highway, gas and other services; access east to Lore Road and highway return via northbound on-ramp.

S 122.2 A 4.8 Dimond Boulevard overpass; exits on both sides of highway. Access west to Dimond Center Mall (shopping, dining, theater), Starbucks (drive-thru), 24-hour gas stations, fast-food, restaurants, strip malls, and Costco. Gas stations and supermarkets, restaurants to east.

S 121.8 A 5.2 Scooter Avenue southbound exit only. Access to south end of shopping area with banks, Petco, Michael's, liquor store, Sportsman's Warehouse, OfficeMax, Texas Roadhouse, Taco Bell, etc.).

S 120.7 A 6.3 O'Malley Road underpass; exits north and southbound. Turn east on O'Malley Road and drive 2 miles to reach the **Alaska Zoo**. Continue east on O'Malley for Chugach State Park Upper Hillside hiking trails (follow signs), which include the popular **Flattop Mountain** trail. Large structure visible on east side of this exit is Alaska's only indoor waterpark.

Turn west for Minnesota Drive to Ted Stevens Anchorage International Airport.

S 119.7 A 7.3 Huffman Road underpass; exits both sides of highway to roundabouts. Exit west for gas/diesel station, 24-hour supermarket, pharmacy, fast-food outlets and other services. South Anchorage residential area. The large inflated dome on the east side of the highway near this exit is an indoor golf driving range with 9-hole outdoor course; access via 1-way frontage road north on east side of freeway.

S 118.8 A 8.2 DeArmoun Road southbound exit only. (Northbound access to DeArmoun is via Rabbit Creek exit, then north on Old Seward Highway.)

S 118.1 A 8.9 Exit to Rabbit Creek Road (east), Old Seward Highway (west); access to South Anchorage subdivisions. The picturesque Chapel by the Sea overlooks Turnagain Arm. The church is often photographed because of its unique setting.

View of Turnagain Arm and Mount Spurr southbound. Seward Highway Scenic Byway sign southbound.

S 117.6 A 9.4 Turnoff to east at 154th for **Potter Marsh** access road which leads east 0.2 mile to a large paved parking area (pictured below) that is gated from 10 P.M. to 6 A.M., with bus/RV parking, restroom and access to boardwalk viewing. This is a great place to take a walk and see wildlife; description follows. Turnoff to west for **Rabbit Creek Rifle Range** (ADF&G); description follows.

Boardwalks provide wonderful bird viewing opportunities at Potter Marsh, part of the Anchorage Coastal Wildlife Refuge. *(©Kris Valencia, staff)*

©Kris Valencia, staff

Potter Marsh (Anchorage Coastal Wildlife Refuge) is a very popular spot for bird watching. From the parking lot, an extensive boardwalk with interpretive signs crosses the

The Alaska Railroad parallels the Seward Highway between Anchorage and Seward. This is at Beluga Point scenic viewpoint at Milepost S 110.3 (©Kris Valencia, staff)

marsh, a refuge and nesting area for waterfowl, including Arctic terns, Canada geese, trumpeter swans, gulls and many small birds. Muskrats, foxes and other small animals are often seen here. Bring binoculars. The 564-acre marsh was created during construction of the Alaska Railroad when an embankment was built to support the railroad tracks and the resulting pond was filled with fresh water by area creeks.

Rabbit Creek Rifle Range is open to the public; summer and winter hours posted on gate or phone (907) 345-7831 for recorded information on hours. Center-fire range, handgun range, rim-fire range, and archery range. Visit www.adfg.alaska.gov/index. cfm?adfg=anchoragerange.main for more information.

Begin 2-lane highway southbound. *Pass with care! Drive with headlights on at all times.*

Begin 4-lane highway northbound.

CAUTION: High accident rate on Seward Highway southbound due to heavy traffic, variable weather conditions, speeding and unsafe passing. Be alert to shared passing lanes. Delay of 5 vehicles or more is illegal; use slow vehicle turnouts.

Designated Highway Safety Corridor next 30.5 miles southbound. This designation is given to provide extra enforcement of speed limits and passing zones and discourage aggressive driving behavior in high accident areas. Traffic fines double in these zones. Highway Traffic Safety Corridor ends at Milepost S 90 then begins again at Milepost S 87.

For avalanche conditions along the Seward Highway in winter, phone 511 or visit 511.alaska.gov.

S 117.3 A 9.7 Distance marker southbound shows Girdwood 27 miles, Seward 115 miles, Homer 211 miles.

S 116 A 11 Potter Marsh turnout east side of highway.

S 115.4 A 11.6 Junction with Old Seward Highway; access to Potter Valley Road east to Potter Creek subdivision. Large double-ended turnout by mail boxes; access to Potter Marsh bench. Old Seward Highway connects with Rabbit Creek Road.

The natural gas pipeline from the Kenai Peninsula emerges from beneath Turn-

again Arm here and follows the roadway to Anchorage.

WARNING: When the tide is out, the sand in Turnagain Arm might look inviting. DO NOT go out on it. Some of it is quicksand. You could become trapped in the mud and not be rescued before the tide covers you.

S 115.2 A 11.8 Entering Chugach State Park southbound. Turnoff to west (use second entrance southbound) for **Chugach State Park Headquarters**, housed in the Potter Section House; parking, outhouse. The historic structure was once home to a small crew of Alaska Railroad workers who maintained the tracks between Seward and Anchorage in the days of coal- and steam-powered locomotives.

Chugach State Park offers exceptional outdoor recreational opportunities year-round, including hiking, biking, fishing, camping, kayaking, rafting, climbing, ATV and snow machine riding, skiing, hunting and trapping.

Maps and information on Chugach State Park, as well as parking passes in the headquarters building. Open Monday–Friday 10 A.M. to 4:30 P.M. (closed for lunch noon to 1 P.M.); phone (907) 345-5014 or visit dnr. alaska.gov/parks/units/chugach/.

S 115.1 A 11.9 Turnoff to east for **Potter Creek Viewpoint and Trail** (Chugach State Park). Small parking area overlooking marsh with interpretive signs about wetlands and the railroad's role in creating these accidental marshes. Also an interpretive sign about the feeding habits of moose.

Drive up the hill via 2-lane paved road for large parking area (fee area), viewing platform with telescopes, interpretive signs and hiking trails.

This is the Potter Creek Trailhead for **Turnagain Arm Trail**. From here to McHugh Creek Picnic Area (at **Milepost S 111.9** on the Seward Highway) it is 3.3 miles, making it a good choice for a family hike. One-way walking time is about 1½ hours. Turnagain Arm trail continues to Rainbow (7.5 miles) and to Windy Corner (9.4 miles) at **Milepost S 106.7** Seward Highway; see trail information signs. Turnagain Arm Trail parallels the Seward Highway and

offers good views of Turnagain Arm. Rated as easy, with 250- to 700-foot elevation gains from the parking areas to the generally level trail on the hillside above the 4 trailheads.

S 114.7 A 12.3 Weigh station to east.

S 114.5 A 12.5 Double-ended gravel turnout to east (posted no camping).

S 113.4 A 13.6 Gravel turnout to east.

S 113.3 A 13.7 Slow vehicle turnout to west for southbound traffic. *Delay of 5 vehicles illegal; must use turnouts.*

S 113.1 A 13.9 The first of several informal gravel turnouts used by rock climbers on the east side of the highway. *NOTE: Please do NOT go near the railroad tracks. Fencing is in place because hikers refused to leave the railroad tracks. This land is the property of the Alaska Railroad and is closed to the public. Use turnouts for photography and designated trails for exploration.*

S 113 A 14 Informal gravel turnout to east at McHugh boulder area used by rock climbers. The cliffs are part of the base of McHugh Peak (elev. 4,298 feet).

S 111.9 A 15.1 Easy-to-miss turnoff to east for **McHugh Creek Picnic Area**, uphill via paved side road. (Access road not recommended for vehicles over 24-feet.) This state wayside on the flank of McHugh Peak has 3 parking levels, each with outhouses. There is a $5 day-use fee (after a 30-minute grace period). Exceptional picnic overlook on second level with tables, grills and viewing platform with telescopes. Good view of Turnagain Arm. Access to McHugh Creek trailhead from third parking level. McHugh Creek trail connects to Turnagain Arm Trail. *CAUTION: Bears in area.*

S 111.6 A 15.4 Informal turnout to east used by rock climbers. Posted "no camping."

S 110.3 A 16.7 Beluga Point scenic viewpoint and photo stop to west is a large paved double-ended turnout with a commanding view of Turnagain Arm. A good place to see bore tides and beluga whales. (The only all-white whales, belugas are easy to identify.) Telescopes and interpretive signs on beluga whales, bore tides, mountain goats, and Captain Cook. Some say the bore tide is more impressive from Bird Point at **Milepost S 96.5**.

Turnagain Arm is known for having one of the world's remarkably high tides, with a diurnal range of more than 33 feet. A bore tide is an abrupt rise of tidal water just after low tide, moving rapidly landward, formed by a flood tide surging into a constricted inlet such as Turnagain Arm. This foaming wall of water may reach a height of 6 feet and is very dangerous to small craft. To see a bore tide, check the Anchorage-area tide tables for low tide, then add approximately 2 hours and 15 minutes to the Anchorage low tide for the bore to reach points between 32 miles and 37 miles south of Anchorage on the Seward Highway. Visitors should watch for bore tides from Beluga Point south to Girdwood.

An easterly extension of Cook Inlet, Turnagain Arm was called Return by the Russians. Captain Cook, seeking the fabled Northwest Passage in 1778, called it Turnagain River, and Captain Vancouver, doing a more thorough job of surveying in 1794, gave it the present name of Turnagain Arm.

WARNING: Do not go out on the mud flats at low tide. The glacial silt and water can create a dangerous quicksand.

S 110.1 A 16.9 Gravel turnout to east used by rock climbers.

S 109.8 A 17.2 Slow vehicle turnout to

west for southbound traffic. Watch for falling rocks.

S 109.2 A 17.8 Small paved turnout to west. Fresh water spigot out of rock wall across highway. (*A dangerous spot to cross the highway on foot: lots of fast-moving traffic.*)

S 108.7 A 18.3 Paved double-ended viewpoint to west; view of Kenai Mountains, Turnagain Arm.

S 108.3 A 18.7 Rainbow trailhead (Turnagain Arm Trail) parking east side of highway; posted no camping.

S 108.2 A 18.8 Paved turnout to west.

S 108.1 A 18.9 Gravel parking east side of highway.

S 107.7 A 19.3 Turnout to west with Gold Rush Centennial signs "Hope Survives Gold Fever" and "Stampeders Flood the Arm."

S 106.9 A 20.1 Scenic viewpoint to west; popular rock climbing face, Goat's Head Soup begins here. Trail begins left of the big tree. Double-ended paved turnout. Popular spot to watch for Dall sheep on steep hillsides above highway (bring binoculars). *Do not feed wildlife. CAUTION: Watch for slowing traffic and watch for pedestrians on highway.*

S 106.7 A 20.3 Windy Corner Trail. Trailhead to Turnagain Arm Trail east side of highway; parking.

S 106.6 A 20.4 Paved shoulder parking to west.

S 105.7 A 21.3 Falls Creek Trailhead parking east side of highway. Moderate 1.5-mile hike along creek.

S 104.5 A 22.5 Very small single-vehicle turnout to east under rock overhang by small waterfall.

S 104.2 A 22.8 Very small single-vehicle turnout to east.

S 104.1 A 22.9 Paved turnout to west.

S 104 A 23 Indian Valley Mine National Historic Site.

S 103.9 A 23.1 Indian Road (paved) leads to **Indian Valley Meats.**

Indian Valley Meats. Reindeer sausage and much more from this federally inspected processor of exotic game and fish. Fish boxes ready for shipping, gift packs with game jerky, smoked salmon and much more. Come visit our gift shop. Great buys! In business 40 years. Tour the stunning grounds, featuring flowers, rock walls, B&B. Just ½ mile up Indian Road. See display ad on this page. [ADVERTISEMENT]

S 103.8 A 23.2 INDIAN (sign). Indian was first listed as a flag stop on the timetables of The Alaska Railroad in 1922. Its name is derived from the nearby creek.

S 103.4 A 23.6 Indian House restaurant.

S 103.2 A 23.8 Turnagain Arm Pit BBQ. Also in Midtown Anchorage. Open 7 days 11 A.M. to 9 P.M. Authentic southern "Q" on the shores of Turnagain Arm with

the 'most stellar view of any BBQ place in the world.' Low'n'slow pit-smoked brisket, pulled pork, ribs, beans'n'slaw, fried okra, real sweet tea and more! Serving Alaska's best BBQ along with fresh lettuce and herbs grown year round in our hydroponic farm. Beer'n'wine. Find us on Facebook; www.turnagainarmpitBBQ.com; (907) 653-1953. Dine-in, take-out, drive-thru. We cater 'Northern Exposure to Southern Smoke.' Voted best BBQ 6 years and running. [ADVERTISEMENT]

S 103.1 A 23.9 Bridge over **Indian Creek**; Chugach State Park parking to west with outhouse, interpretive signs and telescope. Begin 3-mile-long Indian to Bird bike trail south to Bird Creek campground. Indian Creek is heavily fished for pink salmon, sea-run Dolly Varden, few coho salmon and rainbow trout. No camping or overnight parking.

S 103 A 24 Bar and motel to east.

S 102.8 A 24.2 Valley Bible Chalet.

S 102.1 A 24.9 Bird Ridge Trailhead parking east side of highway; $5 day-use fee. This is a steep 2.5-mile hike (moderate to difficult). *CAUTION: Bears in area.*

S 101.6 A 25.4 Bird Creek access (Chugach State Park) to east. Large paved parking area with toilets just north of Bird Creek; $5 day-use fee. **Bird Creek** is a very popular fishing spot. Coho salmon run from late July through mid-August. Pink salmon (even-numbered years), from early July through mid-August. Check with ADF&G for current information on salmon runs and fishing regulations.

S 101.4 A 25.6 Bird Creek.

S 101.3 A 25.7 Turnoff to east for additional **Bird Creek/Chugach State Park** parking. No fee parking on dirt surfaced lot just inside turnoff adjacent highway. Follow paved road up hill to another large parking area that doubles as a campground and

day-use parking. Vault toilets, information boards, view telescope, picnic tables, toilet, firepits, and 20 overflow campsites; $20 fee. Stairway at far end takes you to steep trail access to highway, walking path and creekside.

S 100.8 A 26.2 Essential 1 Gas Station to east with gas/diesel, propane, ice and grocery. Bird Creek campground.

Essential 1 Gas Station. See display ad this page.

Turnoff on short access road to west for **Bird Creek Campground and Day-Use Area, Chugach State Park.** Campground (turn right at end of access road) has 28 level campsites in trees, firepits, pay phone, covered picnic tables, toilets and water. Firewood may be available. Camping fee $20 per night. Parking and walk-in access to Beluga public-use cabin from campground. Turn left at end of access road for day-use area; parking, toilets, interpretive signs. Access to the paved 13.3-mile Bird to Gird bike path; rated easy and multi-use for walking, biking and winter skiing Day-use parking fee is $5.

WARNING: Do not go out on the mud flats at low tide. The glacial silt and water can create a dangerous quicksand.

S 100.7 A 26.3 Bird Ridge Motel & RV Park to east; lodging and RV park.

S 100 A 27 Art gallery to east in large log cabin structure. Paved parking area to west, adjacent bike trail.

S 99.9 A 27.1 Avalanche gates.

S 99.3 A 27.7 Paved parking area to west with view across Bird Flats on Turnagain Arm to the cut in the mountains where Sixmile Creek drains into the arm (the old mining settlement of Sunrise was located there). The town of Hope is to the southwest. The peak visible across Turnagain Arm between here and Girdwood is Mount Alpenglow in the Kenai Mountain Range.

S 99.1 A 27.9 Double-ended paved turn-

Scenic viewpoints along the Seward Highway have interpretive signs on the wildlife, history and natural history of the area. (©Kris Valencia, staff)

out to west with plaque is dedicated to workers caught in an avalanche while clearing the road. In February 2000, Mr. Brookman of the Alaska Railroad lost his life while 2 others injured in the avalanche survived.

Prior to highway reconstruction in 2004–2005, the 9-mile corridor from here south to the Girdwood turnoff was known as "avalanche alley."

S 98.8 A 28.2 Begin passing lane, resume 65 mph speed limit, southbound.

End passing lane.

S 97.7 A 29.3 End passing lane southbound.

S 97.2 A 29.8 Begin passing lane northbound.

S 96.5 A 30.5 Southbound turn lane for **Bird Point Scenic Overlook** (Chugach State Park) to west. Very nice rest area with restrooms and a large parking lot. Day-use fee $5 after 30-minute grace period. Wheelchair-friendly walkway to sheltered viewpoint; benches, telescopes, information boards and an excellent view of Turnagain Arm. This is one of the best places along the arm to stop for a breather and enjoy the scenery.

Beluga whales are often spotted from Bird Point. Look for the sculptures of these white whales with their backs rising out of the pavement at the end of the parking area. The sculptures are designed to reflect how belugas appear when swimming in the water. Some say this is the best vantage point to view the bore tide.

Access from overlook parking area to the Bird Point to Girdwood ("Bird to Gird") Trail. This 6-mile bike trail goes over Bird Hill on the old Seward Highway alignment. The trail has information displays, viewpoints and telescopes along the way.

S 95.6 A 31.4 Begin passing lane southbound. *CAUTION: Watch for 2 directional passing lanes.*

S 95.3 A 31.7 Double-ended scenic turnout to west overlooking Turnagain Arm. Gold Rush Centennial signs about Sunrise City, a gold rush camp established in 1895 at the mouth of Sixmile Creek, and the Crow Creek Boys, a partnership of stampeders formed in 1896 to mine gold on Crow Creek near present-day Girdwood. ("The boys" sold out to 2 Nome mining engineers in the early 1900s, and Crow Creek mine

went on to become one of the largest gold producing mines on Turnagain Arm.) Interpretive signs on Turnagain Arm.

S 94.1 A 32.9 Scenic turnout to west with interpretive signs on belugas, hooligan and whales.

S 93.6 A 33.4 End passing lane southbound.

S 93.3 A 33.7 Double-ended scenic turnout to west overlooking Turnagain Arm with interpretive signs on beluga whales, tides, mudflats and bore tides.

S 92.7 A 34.3 End passing lane northbound.

S 92.5 A 34.5 Double-ended scenic turnout to west overlooking Turnagain Arm with interpretive signs on the 1964 earthquake, Portage Pass and Trails, Rails and Blacktop.

S 92.2 A 34.8 Large double-ended paved turnout to east. Watch for Dall sheep.

S 91.5 A 35.5 Double-ended paved scenic turnout to west overlooking Turnagain Arm with interpretive signs on glaciers.

S 91 A 36 Distance marker northbound shows Anchorage 36 miles.

S 90.5 A 36.5 Bridge crosses Tidewater Slough.

S 90.4 A 36.6 Leaving Chugach State Park southbound, entering the state park northbound.

The 1964 Good Friday earthquake caused land to sink in the Turnagain Arm area, particularly apparent from here to **Milepost S 74.** As a result, many trees had their root systems invaded by salt water, as seen by the stands of dead spruce trees along here. Good bird watching, including bald eagles, Arctic terns and sandhill cranes.

S 90.2 A 36.8 Toadstool Drive. Welcome to Girdwood sign southbound. Turnoff for Girdwood Railroad Station to east. Girdwood DOT maintenance station; parking, access to Bird to Gird bike trail.

End avalanche area southbound.

Begin passing lane northbound. Watch for 2-directional passing lanes.

S 90 A 37 Girdwood Junction. Girdwood Station Mall here has a 24-hour Tesoro station (gas/diesel, sani-dump station and water) with a convenience store. Also ice cream shop, bakery and dining options. ⓑ

This intersection of the Seward Highway

and Alyeska Highway is "old" Girdwood. After the 1964 earthquake, Girdwood moved up the access road 2.1 miles to the New Girdwood townsite (see "Alyeska Highway" log on page 517).

Junction with 3-mile Alyeska Highway to Crow Creek Mine, Girdwood and Alyeska Recreation Area. Worth the drive! See "Alyeska Highway" log beginning on the facing page.

NOTE: *Next gas available southbound on the Seward Highway is at* **Milepost S 1.7** *(approximately 88 miles); next gas available northbound at* **Milepost S 100.8** *(10.8 miles from here); next gas available westbound on Sterling Highway is the Sunrise Inn at* **Milepost S 44.9,** *in Cooper Landing, approximately 60 miles from here.*

S 89.8 A 37.2 Glacier Creek bridge.

Wonderful views southbound of the glaciated Kenai Mountains.

S 89.5 A 37.5 Resume 65-mph speed limit southbound. *Begin 55-mph speed zone northbound.*

S 89.1 A 37.9 Virgin Creek bridge. View of 3 hanging glaciers to east.

S 88.8 A 38.2 Distance marker southbound shows Seward 87 miles, Homer 183 miles.

S 88.2 A 38.8 Gravel road leads west to pond.

S 87.4 A 39.6 Abrupt turn west to rough gravel turnout at avalanche gun emplacement. Turnout to east.

Distance marker southbound shows Portage Glacier Road Junction 9 miles, Whittier 20 miles.

S 87 A 40 IMPORTANT NOTE: *Highway Safety Corridor next 30.5 miles northbound. This designation is given to provide extra enforcement of speed limits, passing zones and discourage aggressive driving behavior in high accident areas. Traffic fines double in these zones.*

S 86 A 41 Small parking area with Chugach National Forest boundary sign.

Watch for belugas on incoming tides and bald eagles on mud flats at low tide.

S 84.1 A 42.9 Peterson Creek. View of Blueberry Mountain. Watch for waterfalls on mountainsides east of the highway between **Mileposts S 84** and **S 83.**

S 82 A 45 Good view of Spencer Glacier, directly ahead southbound. The Alaska Railroad offers excursions to Spencer Glacier in summer. Bartlett and Trail glaciers to the south of Spencer Glacier (Discovery Glacier train trip). Pavement has rough surfaced areas next few miles.

S 81.1 A 45.9 Slow for pedestrians and parked cars along this stretch of highway during hooligan fishing.

S 81 A 46 Turnoff to east for gravel side road leading 0.3 mile to dead end at Twentymile River between railroad and highway bridges.

Distance marker northbound shows Girdwood 9 miles, Anchorage 46 miles.

S 80.7 A 46.3 Parking and boat launch to west at north end of **Twentymile River Bridge** (rough surface). Watch for dipnetters in the spring fishing for hooligan (also known as eulachon or candlefish), a species of smelt. Dipnetting for hooligan is open only to Alaska residents who hold a valid Alaska sportfishing license. Alaska residents under the age of 18 do not need to purchase a sportfishing license to participate.

The Twentymile River flows out of Twen-
(Continues on page 520)

Alyeska Highway

The 3-mile Alyeska Highway provides access to Crow Creek Road and the historic Crow Creek Mine, Girdwood, Alyeska Resort ski area and The Hotel Alyeska. There are many restaurants, gift shops and accommodations in the Girdwood area. Major attractions include the Alyeska Aerial Tramway and rainforest hiking trails. Well worth the drive.

There is a bike trail along this highway connecting with the Bird to Gird trail (from Bird Creek) and extending to Hotel Alyeska. **Distance is measured from junction with Seward Highway (J).**

J 0 Girdwood Junction. Girdwood Station Mall here has a 24-hour Tesoro station (sani-dump station and water) with a convenience store. Also an ice cream shop, bakery and dining options.

J 0.2 Bridge over Alaska Railroad tracks.

Paved bike trail to Alyeska Resort begins. This is also the south end of the Bird to Gird bike trail from Bird Point at **Milepost S 96.5** on the Seward Highway.

J 0.3 Forest Station Road. **Chugach National Forest Glacier Ranger District** office (P.O. Box 129, Girdwood, AK 99587; phone 907/783-3242). Open 8 A.M. to 5 P.M. weekdays in summer; closed holidays. Maps and information available here.

J 0.7 Local transfer station to right. Access to fishing on **Glacier Creek**.

J 1.5 Chugach Adventures (tours) and **Slack Tide Gallery** (art and gifts store) on north side of road; description follows.

Chugach Adventures. Outfitter guide service offering rafting, kayak, glacier & train tours. Top day tour from the AK Railroad *Glacier Discovery* train, visit Spencer Glacier today. Visit www.AlaskanRafting.com for more information. (907) 783-1860. **Slack Tide Gallery.** Boutique offers locally made art, gifts, jewelry and more. Open 9 A.M. to 5 P.M. every day in summer. (907) 783-1860.

[ADVERTISEMENT]

©Claire Torgerson, staff

J 1.9 Junction with **Crow Creek Road** (not maintained in winter) which leads to: the Double Musky Inn (dining) at Mile 0.3; Iditarod Trail parking at Mile 1.4 and at Mile 2.5; parking for Glacier Creek hand-tram/Winner Creek Trail at Mile 2.7; and **Crow Creek Mine National Historic Site** (pictured above) at Mile 3. Explore the old mining structures at picturesque Crow Creek Mine, open daily May to September. Crow Creek Mine offers gold panning and also has

View from atop Alyeska Mountain at Alyeska Resort. Take the tram to the top for the view, for dining, or for the hike down in summer. (©David L. Ranta, staff)

an RV/tent campground. Great spot.

Crow Creek Mine. See display ad on this page.

Beyond Crow Creek Mine, the road narrows and continues to the trailhead for Crow Pass Trail at Mile 6. (This road is not recommended for large RVs beyond Crow Creek Mine at Mile 3. Also, watch for children playing along Crow Creek Road in residential areas.) There is a large parking area at the Crow Pass trailhead; gorgeous view, 2 picnic tables, toilet. Winner Creek and Crow Pass trails are part of the Iditarod National Historic Trail. Stop at Glacier Ranger District office at **Milepost J 0.3** on the Alyeska Highway for more detailed information on area hiking trails.

J 2 California Creek bridge.

Girdwood

J 2.1 Located at the **junction** of Alyeska Highway, Hightower Road and Egloff Drive. **Population:** about 2,710. **Emergency Services:** EMS and **Fire Dept.**, phone 911 or (907) 783-2511 or (907) 269-5711. **Medical Clinic: Girdwood Clinic**, across from the post office at the corner of Hightower and Lindblad, has a family nurse practitioner and is open Tuesday–Saturday, 10 A.M. to 6 P.M.; phone (907) 783-1355.

Visitor Information: There is no visitor center in Girdwood, but the Girdwood Chamber of Commerce publishes a free map of local businesses, or visit www.girdwoodchamber.com for more information. **Radio:** KEUL 88.9. **Newspaper:** *Glacier City Gazette,*

bi-monthly.

The town was named after Col. James Girdwood, who established a mining operation near here in 1901. Today, Girdwood has a substantial year-round community and a flourishing seasonal population, thanks to its appeal as both a winter and summer resort destination. The downtown area has a lovely town park with beautiful landscaping, lights and seating, and its parks and trails share borders with the Chugach State Park and Chugach National Forest. Cooperatively they manage miles of trails that range from paved to rustic single-track. The city of Girdwood has 10 parks in 120 acres of parkland.

Lodging & Services

Girdwood offers bed-and-breakfast accommodations as well as home and condo rentals. The nearest major hotel is Alyeska Resort's Hotel Alyeska, a 2-mile drive from downtown Girdwood. Girdwood's Alyeska Hostel, located at 227 Alta Dr., has dormitory bunks, private rooms and cabins; phone (907) 783-2222 or visit www.alyeskahostel.com. There are several restaurants in the Girdwood area. Girdwood has a grocery, laundromat, vacation rental offices, a school (K through 8), library and fire hall. Girdwood Post Office is located at 118 Lindblad Ave.; open weekdays 9 A.M. to noon. and 1–5 P.M., Saturdays 10 A.M. to noon. Flightseeing services at Girdwood airport.

Alyeska Highway at Girdwood, looking towards Alyeska Resort and the T-junction at Arlberg Avenue. (©Kris Valencia, staff)

Camping

The only campground with RV sites in the Girdwood area is at Crow Creek Mine, Mile 3 on Crow Creek Road. There's tent camping (18 walk-in sites) available just past the ballfield on Egloff Drive; maximum stay 14 nights/$10 per night; drinking water behind city hall, 1 block away. In the summer, overnight RV parking is available at the Alyeska Resort Daylodge parking area (turn off at **Milepost J 2.9** Alyeska Highway). Fee is $10/night, no hookups.

Attractions

Crow Creek Mine. A historic site dating to 1896 that offers a glimpse into the Alaska Gold Rush past as well as a chance to pan for gold. Call ahead for privately guided tours.

Open daily May–September. Call for winter activities. RVs and tenters welcomed; WiFi available. Phone (907) 229-3105.

Girdwood Lions Park, known locally as Forest Fairgrounds, is at the corner of Hightower Road, Egloff Drive and Alyeska Highway. There is a Little Bears Playground, baseball field and 18-hole disc golf course.

The annual **Girdwood Forest Fair** takes place at the community park. This popular summer crafts fair, which draws thousands of visitors features crafts, food and entertainment. No admission fee. Go to www.girdwoodforestfair.com for 2019 dates and more details.

The annual **Girdwood Fungus Fair** takes place in September. Check 2019 dates and learn more about this mycological event at www.fungusfair.com.

The Alyeska Blueberry Festival takes place in August at The Hotel Alyeska. The outdoor festival celebrates blueberry season and features live music and food vendors.

A popular skiing event at Alyeska in April is the **Spring Carnival and Slush Cup**, known as the "biggest beach party this side of Hawaii." Skiers in costume ski downhill then try to jump across a 100-foot-long pond of ice cold water.

Hiking trails in the area include Winner Creek Gorge Trail and Upper Winner Creek Trail. Both of these Chugach National Forest trails begin near the Alyeska Aerial Tramway ticket office. The Winner Creek trail is a good one to experience Girdwood's rain forest and a good day hike for the entire family. The 2.5-mile-long trail is a pleasant hike with no severe ups or downs and a maximum elevation gain of only 260 feet.

Wooden planking keeps hikers above most soggy spots. The trail leads through a tall

©Kris Valencia, staff

spruce and hemlock forest to the picturesque gorge where Winner Creek cascades through a small cleft in the rocks. Upper Winner Creek Trail climbs 5.5 miles beyond Winner Creek gorge and is a good overnight hike.

Alyeska Highway Log
(continued)

J 2.2 Glacier Creek bridge.

J 2.5 Donner Drive access to Girdwood airstrip (follow signs); flightseeing.

Private Aircraft: Girdwood airstrip; elev. 150 feet; length 2,100 feet; gravel; unattended.

J 2.6 Timberline Drive to residential area of Girdwood. Trailhead parking at end of road for Virgin Creek Falls hike.

J 2.9 Alyeska Highway ends at **junction** with Arlberg Avenue, which forks; turn south (right) for Alyeska Daylodge; overnight RV parking in summer, ski school and rentals in winter. Turn north (left) and continue with this log for the Hotel Alyeska and tram at **Milepost J 4.1**.

Alyeska Resort, Alaska's largest ski area, is a popular year-round destination that includes The Hotel Alyeska and the award-winning Seven Glaciers restaurant, as well as the ski area. Ski season is generally from late-November to April. Facilities include the 60-passenger aerial tramway, which operates year-round and departs from The Hotel Alyeska (see description at **Milepost J 4.1**); 2 high-speed detachable quads, 2 fixed-grip quads, 2 double chair lifts and 2 Magic Carpets. Night skiing is available during holiday periods in December, and Thursday through Saturday, January through March. Ski school, ski rental shop and sports shops are available. Phone (907) 754-7669 for more information.

Summer activities include sightseeing, hiking, mountain biking, berry picking and flightseeing. The Alyeska Mountain Run is held in August, the final stop for the Alaska Mountain Runners Grand Prix series.

J 3 Olympic Mountain Loop; access to dining at The Bake Shop and Jack Sprat restaurant.

J 3.2 Gravel turnout by Moose Meadows; watch for moose, bears and other wildlife.

J 3.9 Entrance to the Hotel Alyeska; follow signs for parking and shuttle bus to hotel and tram.

J 4.1 Turn left for public parking, with shuttle service to **Alyeska Resort's** Hotel

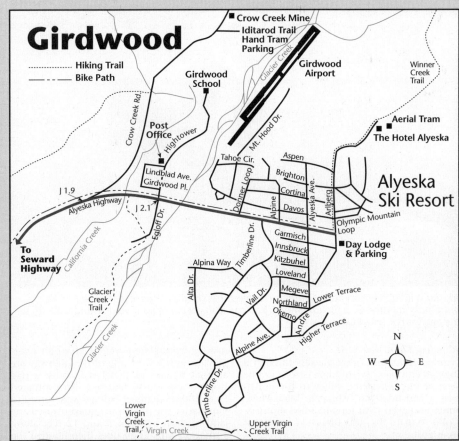

©David L. Ranta, staff

The **Alyeska Aerial Tramway** transports visitors to the 2,300-foot level of Mount Alyeska (the mountain's summit is at 3,939 feet) and a mountaintop complex featuring fine dining at Seven Glaciers restaurant and casual dining at the Bore Tide Deli (check for food service hours before departing base). The resort is offering a $39 special that includes the tram ride and lunch at their mountaintop complex.

The 60-passenger enclosed tram is a great sightseeing choice for anyone, especially those who have difficulty walking or negotiating stairs. There is a passenger drop-off right in front of the tram, and there is elevator access to the tram level at both the

Alyeska and Aerial Tramway terminal (descriptions follow); turn right for passenger drop-off only (no parking) at tramway terminal. Continue straight ahead 0.3 mile for trailhead parking for the multi-use (summer) and ski-only (winter) 5K Nordic Loop at the end of Arlberg Avenue.

The 301-room **Hotel Alyeska** features 5 dining venues, a full-service spa, 3 retail shops and a fitness center with indoor swimming pool, sauna, whirlpool and exercise room. For information phone (907) 754-2111 or 1-800-880-3880; www.alyeskaresort.com.

bottom of the mountain and the top. Panoramic views from the top of surrounding glaciers, Turnagain Arm and the Chugach Mountains. The Roundhouse Museum here features Alyeska history; open daily in summer, 10 A.M. to 7 P.M.

Hikers can use the **North Face Trail** to reach the top of Mount Alyeska. The challenging but scenic, 2.2-mile trail takes 1 to 1½ hours to hike, climbing 2,300 feet. Stop to catch your breath and enjoy the stunning views above tree line. The trail begins near the tram terminal at the resort. Hikers can get a free tram ride back down the mountain.

The tram operates daily in summer (beginning late May) from 9:30 A.M. to 9:30 P.M. Tram cars depart about every 10 to 15 minutes. Purchase tickets at the ticket windows at the foot of the tram. Check current schedule and rates by phoning (907) 754-2275. It is closed for 2 weeks in May and mid-October to mid-November for annual maintenance.

For hikers and bikers (cyclists walk bikes first 0.3 mile), **Winner Creek Trail** begins directly above the tram's lower terminal. Continue 1.2 miles to junction with the Upper Winner Creek Trail. Stay on Lower Winner Creek Trail until you reach the hand-tram across Glacier Creek. Hikers can make the 7.7-mile Girdwood Valley Loop rail by crossing Glacier Creek via the hand-tram to Crow Creek Road, walking down Crow Creek Road to the Alyeska Highway and returning via the bike path back to the resort parking lot. Check bulletin board at Winner Creek trailhead for bear alerts.

Alyeska Resort/Dine & Ride Special. See display ad on facing page.

Return to Milepost S 90 Seward Highway

Alaska Wildlife Conservation Center is a drive-through wildlife park featuring Alaska mammals (a musk-ox is pictured here). You can also get out of your vehicle and walk up to the enclosures. (©David L.Ranta, staff)

(Continued from page 516)

tymile Glacier and other glaciers through a long green valley. Twentymile Glacier can be seen at the end of the valley to the northeast. Good hooligan fishing in May. These smelt are taken with long-handled dip nets. Coho 4 to 10 lbs., use attraction lures, best in August.

S 80.5 A 46.5 Parking to east.

S 80.3 A 46.7 First turnoff southbound to Alaska Railroad parking area and **Kenai Peninsula Visitor Information Center** on east side of highway. This is the former Whittier shuttle vehicle loading area. Prior to the completion of the road to Whittier, the shuttle was the only means of overland transportation to Whittier. The Alaska Railroad currently offers day trips on the *Glacier Discovery Train* to Grandview and Spencer Glacier from their Portage facility. Kenai Peninsula Information Center here has information and discounts on glacier and wildlife cruises as well as the hundreds of other attractions and services on the Kenai Peninsula. Description follows.

Kenai Peninsula Visitor Information Center. First turnoff southbound to gift shop and reservation service for lodging, tours and other activities. Discounts on glacier and wildlife cruises. Open 7 days a week from 9 A.M. to 6 P.M., Memorial Day through Labor Day. Phone (907) 783-3001. Alaska Railroad tickets available, daily departures from Portage. [ADVERTISEMENT]

26 Glacier Cruise. Voted "Best Glacier & Wildlife Cruise by residents. See tidewater glaciers, otters and kittiwakes! Our *26 Glacier Cruise* and *Glacier Quest Cruise* explore glacier carved fjords, view magnificent mountains and watch for playful wildlife. Travel aboard stable catamarans with large picture windows, reserved heated seating, outdoor viewing decks, complimentary hot meal and full service bar/snacks for purchase. Narration provided by a U.S. Forest Service Ranger. Only 63 miles south of Anchorage, this is one Alaska experience you won't want to miss! Sharing the Sound for 60+ years. Daily May–September. (907) 276-8023. www.26glaciers.com. See display ad page 523. [ADVERTISEMENT]

S 80.1 A 46.9 Deteriorating buildings and rusting truck barely visible through overgrowth on the west side of the highway are all that remain of **PORTAGE**, once a flag stop on the Alaska Railroad. An estimated 50 to 100 residents of Portage were forced to move after the 1964 earthquake caused the land to drop between 6 and 12 feet along Turnagain Arm. High tides then flooded the area with salt water. (The dead trees you see along the highway here were killed by salt water.)

Leaving Game Management Unit 14C, entering unit 7, southbound.

S 80 A 47 Second turnoff southbound to former railroad loading area and Kenai Peninsula Visitor Information Center (reservation service for lodging, tours and other activities).

S 79.4 A 47.6 Portage Creek No. 2 bridge. Parking to west at south end of bridge. This gray-colored creek carries the silt-laden glacial meltwater from Portage Glacier and Portage Lake to Turnagain Arm. Mud flats in Turnagain Arm are created by silt from the creek settling close to shore.

S 79 A 48 Turnoff to west just north of Portage Creek No. 1 bridge for **Alaska Wildlife Conservation Center**. This 140-acre drive-through animal park is a major attraction and well worth the stop. Dedicated to the rehabilitation of orphaned and injured animals, AWCC works year-round with state and federal agencies, providing wildlife emergency treatment, rescue and care. Bear viewing is particularly popular here, with up-close looks at both adult and juvenile brown bears. A bear enclosure with an elevated walkway provides a unique viewing experience. Along with bears, the center features eagles, owls, caribou, moose, musk-oxen, elk, Sitka black-tailed deer, and bison. Wood bison have been extinct in Alaska for more than 100 years. AWCC assisted with the state's bison program with care and growth of a bison herd, and then delivery. In 2015, 130 animals were delivered to northwestern Alaska to form Alaska's first wood bison herd.

A log lodge houses the AWCC gift shop and a snackbar operates on the lodge deck during the summer months. Phone (907) 783-2025 for current hours and fees.

Alaska Wildlife Conservation Center. See display ad on page 361 in the ANCHORAGE section.

Portage Creek No. 1 bridge.

S 78.9 A 48.1 Turnoff for Whittier and Portage Glacier. Access to **Portage Valley R.V. Park & Cabins** at Milepost J 1.7 on Whittier/Portage Glacier Road. Large gravel turnout to east.

Junction with Whittier/Portage Glacier Access Road, which leads 5.4 miles to Portage Glacier and 11.4 miles to Whittier. See "Whittier/Portage Glacier Access Road" log beginning on facing page.

S 78.4 A 48.6 Placer River bridge (rough surface). Parking and river access east side of highway at south end of bridge; gravel launch is put-in point for kayakers paddling up the Placer River.

Fishing for coho, from late July or early August, run usually peaks in late August or early September. Tide comes in quickly, be alert!

Between Placer River and Ingram Creek, there is an excellent view on clear days of Skookum Glacier to the northeast. To the north across Turnagain Arm is Twentymile Glacier. Arctic terns and waterfowl are often seen in the slough here.

S 77.9 A 49.1 Placer River overflow bridge has rough surface. Paved turnout to east at south end of bridge.

Begin 55-mph speed zone northbound.

S 77.8 A 49.2 Distance marker southbound shows Seward 76 miles, Homer 172 miles.

S 76.5 A 50.5 Look for swans in ponds to the east.

S 76 A 51 Improved highway next few miles.

S 75.6 A 51.4 Distance marker northbound shows Portage 4 miles, Whittier 15 miles.

S 75.5 A 51.5 Paved double-ended Scenic Byway turnouts both sides of highway.

Road access to **Ingram Creek** to east, turnout; fishing.

S 75.2 A 51.8 Bridge over Ingram Creek.

CAUTION: The Seward Highway from Ingram Creek through Turnagain Pass to Summit Lake has a high number of traffic accidents due to speeding and unsafe passing. DRIVE CAREFULLY!

S 75 A 52 Paved turnout to west; Welcome to the Kenai Peninsula sign. The Seward Highway has now crossed the isthmus that separates the Kenai Peninsula from the rest of southcentral Alaska.

Highway climbs next 6.5 miles southbound to Turnagain Pass.

S 74.9 A 52.1 Begin 5.7-mile southbound passing lane.

S 74.5 A 52.5 Long paved double-ended turnout to east for northbound traffic.

S 72.5 A 54.5 Double-ended paved turnout to east for northbound traffic.

S 71.4 A 55.6 Long paved double-ended turnout to west for southbound traffic.

S 71.2 A 55.8 Double-ended paved turnout to west for southbound traffic.

S 70.9 A 56.1 Large paved turnout to east for northbound traffic.

S 68.8 A 58.2 Southbound passing lane ends. Begin 1.4-mile divided highway southbound. End divided highway northbound.

Wide shoulder to east next 0.2 mile northbound for slow vehicles.

(Continues on page 525)

Whittier/Portage Glacier Access Road

This **side trip** allows access to Portage Glacier, 5.4 miles from the Seward Highway, which along with the Begich, Boggs Visitor Center is a major attraction for visitors, and to Whittier (11.4 miles), gateway to Prince William Sound. It also provides access to hiking trails and the Gray Line boat ride to the face of Portage Glacier.

The stretch of road between Portage Glacier and Whittier was the culmination of a 3-year project to connect that community to the road system. Opened in June 2000, the road branches off the older Portage Glacier Highway. Prior to construction of the Whittier spur road, Whittier was accessible overland only by train.

The Whittier vehicle access spur required the modification of the 2.5-mile-long Anton Anderson Memorial Tunnel to handle both railroad and vehicle traffic. The Anton Anderson tunnel is 1-lane, and cars and trains take turns traveling through it. In summer, the tunnel is open daily 5:30 A.M. to 11:15 P.M., allowing 15-minute alternating directional use for vehicle traffic every half-hour except during scheduled passenger trains. Vehicles must wait in the staging areas on either end of the tunnel when the train is using the tunnel. It is recommended that motorists arrive at least 5 minutes before the scheduled tunnel opening. *NOTE: It is especially important that motorists with ferry or cruise ship reservations out of Whittier time their arrival to allow for the tunnel opening as well as for ferry or cruise ship check-in.*

Tunnel tolls are charged according to vehicle class and are round-trip. Tolls are as follows: Motorcycles and passenger vehicles and RVs (less than 28 feet) not pulling trailers, $13; RVs 28 feet or greater not pulling trailers/towing vehicles, or less than 28 feet pulling a trailer, $22; RVs 28 feet or greater pulling a trailer/towing vehicles, $38. Tolls are paid by eastbound motorists at the Bear Valley staging area. Tolls are not charged for vehicles traveling westbound from Whittier to Portage. *NOTE: Bicycles and pedestrians are NOT permitted in the tunnel.*

For current tolls and more tunnel information phone (907) 566-2244 from Anchorage; toll-free (877) 611-2586; or visit www.tunnel.alaska.gov.

Distance is measured from junction with the Seward Highway (J).

J 0 Junction with Seward Highway at Milepost S 78.9. *CAUTION: Alaska Railroad crossing.*

J 1.2 Moose Flats Day-Use Area; picnic tables, hiking trails, beautiful ponds with accessible docks and outhouses. RV pull-through parking spaces and litter bins. The "Wetland Walk" is a ¼-mile gravel and boardwalk trail with interpretive displays. The longer Trail of Blue Ice extends 5 miles to Portage Lake and the Begich, Boggs Visitor Center. The trail is level and perfect for easy hiking, biking and cross-country skiing. Non-motorized use only.

J 1.4 Alder Pond Day-Use Area/Lower Explorer Pond to south; parking, picnic tables, outhouse, garbage bin. Hiking trails to fishing docks; trout fishing, paddling and primitive camping.

Whittier Access Road provides access to Chugach National Forest recreation areas, Portage Glacier and the Anton Anderson tunnel. (©Kris Valencia, staff)

J 1.7 Portage Valley R.V. Park & Cabins. See display ad this page.

J 2.4 Explorer Glacier Viewing Area; double-ended paved turnout. Access to Trail of Blue Ice, picnic tables, interpretive kiosk.

J 3 Five Fingers Campground and trailhead/walk-in campsites. Gravel parking area with access to Trail of Blue Ice and rustic campsites.

J 3.2 Tangle Pond access to east. Trout fishing.

J 3.6 Turnout to north with creek access.

J 3.7 Black Bear USFS Campground; 13 sites designed for tents and pop-up campers (no RVs). First-come, first-served only. Campfire rings, bear-proof dumpster, bear-proof food lockers, water pump, picnic tables and outhouses. No hookups, no dump station. Camping fee $18. Pleasant spruce tree wooded area. Easy access to the Trail of Blue Ice from here.

J 4.1 Williwaw Fish Viewing Platform. Spawning sockeye, chum and pink salmon can be viewed from late July to mid-September. Trailhead for the Williwaw Nature Trail is located to the right of the platform. This trail connects to the Trail of Blue Ice and connects back to the Fish Viewing Platform to create a 2-mile loop. Williwaw Creek is closed to all salmon fishing.

J 4.3 Williwaw USFS Campground, beautiful campground south of road below Middle Glacier; 59 fully accessible paved campsites designed for RV and tent camping; some pull-throughs; campground host; campfire rings, bear-proof dumpster, bear-proof food containers, water pump, picnic tables and outhouses. No hookups, no dump station. Camping fee $18 single, $28 double. Some sites may be reserved, the rest are first-come, first served. (For reservations, phone 1-877-444-6777 or visit www.recreation.gov; $9 online reservation fee,

$10 for call center reservation.)

CAUTION: Unexploded artillery shells from avalanche mitigation may be found in various locations in Portage Valley. While extremely rare, if you do find one, mark its location 10 feet away with a rock pile or bright cloth. Report it to the Alaska State Troopers in Anchorage; (907) 269-5511.

J 4.5 Parking near river, picnic table.

J 5.2 Road forks: right fork leads to Portage Glacier Day Lodge; 0.2 mile to Begich, Boggs Visitor Center at Portage Lake; 1.2 miles to Byron Glacier trailhead and 1.5 miles to **Portage Glacier Cruises** (descriptions follow). Left fork leads to Whittier (continue with this log).

Since 1986, the **Begich, Boggs Visitor Center** at **Portage Lake** has focused on the Chugach National Forest and its rich natu-

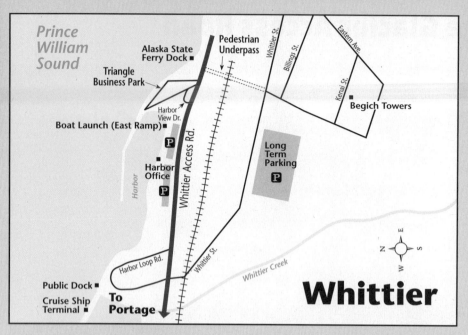

Whittier

Prince William Sound

Alaska State Ferry Dock
Triangle Business Park
Pedestrian Underpass
Whittier St.
Billings St.
Eastern Ave.
Kenai St.
Begich Towers
Harbor View Dr.
Boat Launch (East Ramp)
Harbor
Whittier Access Rd.
Long Term Parking
Harbor Office
Harbor Loop Rd.
Public Dock
Whittier St.
Whittier Creek
Cruise Ship Terminal
To Portage

ral and cultural history. U.S. Forest Service interpreters are available to answer questions and to present programs. Main exhibit rooms are arranged so visitors have a sense of walking up Portage Valley, through Portage Pass and down into Prince William Sound. Visitors may also enter the "Alaskans and Their Stories" room, where they can read or listen to stories about real people who lived in this area. The "Wild Side" room focuses on animals that live in the Chugach National Forest. Displays include a life-sized moose and calf as well as a life-sized model of Smokey Bear. The Visitor Center includes a 200-seat theater that shows the award-winning *Retreat and Renewal.* The center is named for congressmen Nick Begich of Alaska and Hale Boggs of Louisiana, both of whom died in a plane crash in 1972.

The Visitor Center is open daily, 9 A.M. to 6 P.M., from Memorial Day weekend to mid-September. For more information phone (907) 783-2326 (May–Sept.) or (907) 783-3242 (Oct.–April). Admission fee $5 adults, 15 and under free.

At lakefront parking lot of Portage Lake, look for the trailhead for the "Trail of Blue Ice" which leads 5 miles, semi-paralleling the road, back to the Moose Flats Day-Use area. It is for non-motorized use only and is a lovely walk or bike ride.

Just past the Portage Glacier Day Lodge is Byron Glacier Road which leads to Byron Glacier Trail. Trailhead is 0.6 mile down the road, second parking lot on the right. This 0.8-mile trail makes a good family outing, according to the Forest Service, with a flat, well-maintained path to the glacier viewpoint, followed by a rocky path with small stream crossings to the snowfields below Byron Glacier. Avalanche danger can exist in the early part of the summer.

Drive past the trailhead 0.3 mile for *M/V Ptarmigan* boat dock and passenger waiting area. Portage Glacier Cruises offers daily sightseeing trips on Portage Lake at 10:30 A.M., noon, 1:30, 3 and 4:30 P.M., from mid-May to mid-September. Portage Glacier has retreated dramatically in recent years. In the early 1990s, the glacier was within view of the visitor center, but in recent years it has retreated around the corner of Byron Peak's northeast ridge. This cruise is the only way

to get an up-close view of Portage Glacier. A U.S. Forest interpreter is onboard the vessel.

Gray Line of Alaska Portage Glacier Cruise. See display ad this page.

J 5.3 Crossing Portage Creek, then entering 450-foot tunnel under Begich Peak.

J 6 Placer Creek.

J 6.1 Large paved parking area provides views of Begich, Boggs Visitor Center, Portage Lake, Byron Glacier and floating icebergs possible in spring and early summer. Sign about tunnel tolls.

There are several excellent spots in the area to observe salmon spawning (August and September) in Portage Creek and its tributaries.

J 6.7 Toll booths at **Bear Valley staging area**. The 8-lane staging area controls vehicle traffic entering the **Anton Anderson Memorial Tunnel**. The tunnel uses a computerized traffic-control system that regulates both rail and highway traffic. Each vehicle class is metered into the tunnel at different time intervals, with commercial trucks entering the tunnel last. The speed limit in the tunnel is 25-mph. It takes 6.5 minutes for a vehicle to travel through the tunnel. The tunnel's ventilation system combines jet and portal fans. It is the longest highway tunnel and longest combined highway/railroad tunnel in North America at 13,200 feet.

NOTE: Motorcycles need to be particularly cautious of the slick surface inside the tunnel and avoid getting near or crossing the steel railways.

The Anton Anderson Memorial Tunnel through Maynard Mountain was built in 1941–43 as part of the Whittier Cutoff, a 12.4-mile-long railway line constructed to safeguard the flow of military supplies from the port of Whittier. The tunnel was named in 1976 for the chief engineer of that project—Anton Anderson. The railway line includes a second tunnel between Bear Valley and Portage that is 4,910 feet long.

J 6.8 Entering Anton Anderson Memorial Tunnel eastbound.

J 9.6 Exiting Anton Anderson Memorial Tunnel eastbound.

J 10 Whittier staging area for westbound tunnel traffic.

J 10.1 Rest area, pay phone and interpretive signs to south. Turn north on gravel road to airstrip and drive 0.3 mile (slow for potholes) to City of Whittier Campground; large, flat gravel area for tents and RVs with nice view, toilets, $20/night (self-pay kiosk or pay at Harbormaster's in town). ▲

J 10.2 Watch for Portage Pass (Chugach National Forest) trail sign to south; follow gravel access road to trailhead. This 2-mile trail (4 miles round-trip) has a 750-foot elevation gain (strenuous) to top of pass, then levels out and descends to Portage Lake. Only established trail with a view of Portage Glacier.

J 11.1 Whittier Street. Access to paid parking lot and Whittier businesses.

Whittier

J 11.4 Located at the head of Passage Canal on Prince William Sound, 59.5 miles southeast of Anchorage. **Population:** 253. **Emergency Services:** Dial 911 or City Police, Fire Dept. and Ambulance, phone (907) 472-2340. **Clinic:**

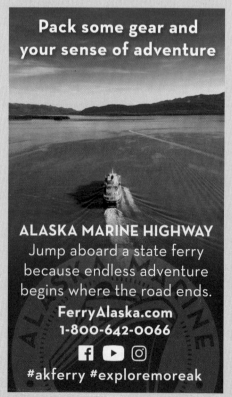

Whittier Health Clinic, phone (907) 472-2303. **Harbormaster:** phone (907) 472-2330.

Visitor Information: Stop by the Harbormaster's office or ask at local businesses. Visit the Greater Whittier Chamber of Commerce website at www.whittieralaskachamber.org or the City of Whittier website at www.whittieralaska.gov. The U.S. Forest Service yurt, located at the West Boat Launch Ramp, has information on kayaking and camping in Prince William Sound. **Elevation:** 30 feet. **Climate:** Normal daily temperature for July is 56°F; for January, 25°F. Maximum temperature is 84°F and minimum is -29°F. Mean annual precipitation is 174 inches, including 260 inches of snow. Winter winds can reach speeds of 60-mph and greater.

Private Aircraft: Airstrip adjacent northwest; elev. 30 feet; length 1,100 feet; gravel; no fuel; unattended. *CAUTION: Bird activity in area.* Runway condition not monitored, visual inspection recommended prior to landing. No winter maintenance.

Named after the poet John Greenleaf Whittier, the community of Whittier is nestled at the base of mountains that line Passage Canal, a fjord that extends eastward into Prince William Sound. Passage Canal (also known as Portage Bay, Passage Arm and Passage Channel) leads to a portage between Prince William Sound and Cook Inlet. It was named by Capt. Vancouver in 1794.

Whittier was created by the U.S. Army during WWII as a port and petroleum delivery center tied to bases farther north by the Alaska Railroad and later a pipeline. The railroad spur from Portage was completed in 1943, and Whittier became the primary debarkation point for cargo, troops and dependents of the Alaska Command. Construction of the huge buildings that dominate Whittier began in 1948, and the Port of Whittier, strategically valuable for its ice-free deep-water port, remained activated until 1960, at which time the population was 1,200. The city of Whittier was incorporated in 1969.

The 14-story Begich Towers, formerly the Hodge Building, houses more than half of Whittier's population and the City Offices. Now a condominium, the building was used by the U.S. Army for family housing and civilian bachelor quarters. The building was renamed in honor of U.S. Rep. Nick Begich of Alaska, who, along with Rep. Hale Boggs of Louisiana, disappeared in a small plane in this area in 1972. The Buckner Building, completed in 1953, once the largest building in Alaska, was called the "city under one roof."

Whittier Manor was built in the early 1950s by private developers as rental units for civilian employees and soldiers who were ineligible for family housing elsewhere.

Most visitor services can be found in Whittier: kayak rentals, wildlife cruises, gift shops and espresso. Take time to visit the museum, buy an ice cream cone or lunch on fish and chips.
(©Kris Valencia, staff)

In early 1964, the building was bought by another group of developers and became a condominium, which now houses the remainder of Whittier's population.

Since military and government activities ceased, the economy of Whittier rests largely on the fishing industry (commercial and sportfishing), the port and increasingly on tourism. The Alaska State Ferry docks here as do Prince William Sound tour boats and cruise ships. Whittier is also a popular harbor with Anchorage boat owners.

Lodging & Services

Lodging at The Inn at Whittier, Anchor Inn and bed-and-breakfast. Dining at hotels and at cafes on the Triangle. **Lazy Otter Charters & Cafe** (description follows) offers espresso, ice cream, snacks and boxed lunches. Anchor Inn has a laundromat. Check the Chamber of Commerce website for more information at www.whittieralaska chamber.org.

Lazy Otter Charters and Cafe. One stop shop for your Prince William Sound adventure. Offering customized glacier and wildlife tours. The day is tailored to your desires and offers exclusive departures and beach landings. Visit this whimsical and charming charter office/cafe on the harbor. Serving espresso, baked goods and soft serve ice cream. You must try the world famous salmon spread. www.lazyottercharters.com. [ADVERTISEMENT]

Many of the waterfront businesses—restaurants, shops and tours—located along Harbor View Drive and "the Triangle," are seasonal, operating only during the summer months.

NOTE: Parking is at a premium in Whittier in the summer. Look for signed 2-hour free public parking. 24-hour parking permits are required for the long-term lot; purchase permit from the Harbormaster or at the boat

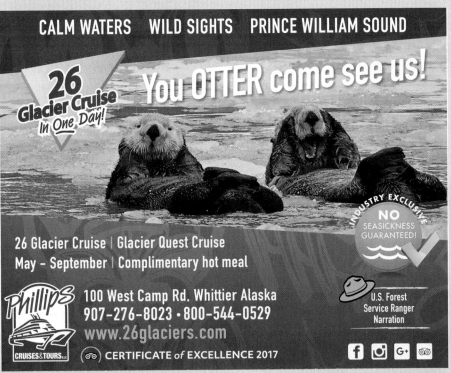

Shoreside fishing near the Alaska Marine Highway ferry dock in Whittier.
(©Kris Valencia, staff)

via the gravel airstrip road, which is just east of the tunnel line-up area.

Transportation

Ferry: Cross-Sound service to Valdez and Cordova via **Alaska Marine Highway** phone 1-800-642-0066 or Whittier Terminal, phone (907) 472-2378.

Railroad: Alaska Railroad passenger service from Anchorage. There is no Alaska Railroad depot in Whittier. The *Glacier Discovery Train* loads and off-loads passengers in the white tented area across from the cruise ship terminal and the marina. Visit www.alaskarailroad.com.

Cruise Ship: Princess Cruises and Norwegian Cruiseline call at Whittier.

Highway: Accessible via an 11-mile side road from Seward Highway.

Boat Charters: Available.

Bus: Shuttle service between Anchorage and Whittier. (907) 360-5501; www.whittierbus.com. Cruise ship and tour boat operators may also arrange bus transportation for clients.

Rental Cars: Avis car rentals available at the Harbor Store seasonally (May to September), phone (907) 440-2847.

Attractions

The beauty of Prince William Sound is Whittier's primary attraction. Arrive by cruise ship, or take a tour boat or ferry across the Sound, launch a motorboat or paddle a kayak into the Sound. Several USFS cabins

launch kiosk at the east end of the harbor. RVs park at campground and walk.

The Harbormaster's office has showers and a public restroom.

Whittier offers gas/diesel, marine services, repairs, and supply store, boat launch and lift, freight services, dry storage and self-storage units. The Harbor Store (907/440-2847) has groceries, fishing supplies, ATM, Avis Car Rental (open May–September, only). Card gas available at harbor.

Camping

City of Whittier campground is accessed

are located in this area for rentals (www. recreation.gov). The second biggest attraction is in Whittier's harbor. Sightseeing cruises departing from Whittier include **26 Glacier Cruises**.

Area hiking trails. Follow Whittier Street 0.5 mile to Eastern Avenue; cross Eastern and drive 0.3 mile up Blackstone Road, then turn right on Salmon Run Road just past the Buckner Building. Salmon Run Road (narrow, dirt) leads 0.4 mile to **Horsetail Falls Trail**, a 1-mile planked trail to platform with view of Whittier and Passage Canal. Or follow Salmon Run Road 0.2 mile and turn left on a second narrow dirt road for 0.4 mile to Smitty's Cove, Lu Young Park picnic area and access to Emerald Cove and Shotgun Cove trails beyond.

For the 2-mile-long **Portage Pass Trail**, turnoff on the Chugach National Forest access road just east of the tunnel. The first 0.75 miles of this trail—to the pass at 750 feet elevation—is well maintained. It continues another mile as a primitive route to Portage Lake.

©Kris Valencia, staff

The Whittier Army Port Historic District Walking Tour is located in the original townsite area on the south side of the rail yard. It can be accessed from the waterfront area of town via a pedestrian tunnel that runs under the rail yard. The entrance to the tunnel is located across the street from the Alaska Ferry Terminal. Whittier's history as a Cold War Army Port is recounted on signs affixed to the large concrete buildings that have survived for 60-70 years, including **Begich Towers** (pictured above). Walking tour map with a short history of Whittier is located at the P-12 Motor Pool building across the street from the pedestrian tunnel.

A Tribute to Alaska's Legends/Prince William Sound Museum, located at the Anchor Inn in downtown Whittier, has 25 exhibits within the 1200 sq. ft museum. Some exhibits highlight the town's history. Other exhibits cover the Anton Anderson Memorial Tunnel, the Alaska Railroad, the Alaska Steamship Co., the battle of Attu and Kiska in the Aleutians, Cold War military flights—"The Eagle and the Bear"—guarding Alaska's coastline, and heroic rescue and survival stories, including the sinking of the S.S. *Yukon* in 1946. An outstanding museum experience. Open 9 A.M. to 7 P.M. daily in summer; admission fee $5.

Annual events in Whittier include an old-fashioned Fourth of July Celebration with a parade and barbecue. Fireworks at midnight on July 3rd. Whittier Fish Derby, for halibut and salmon, takes place May 1 to Sept. 15. For more details visit www.whittier alaskafishderby.org.

Return to Milepost S 78.9
Seward Highway

(Continued from page 520)

S 68.5 A 58.5 Turnagain Pass Recreation Area (elev. 1,015 ft). Parking area west side of highway with restrooms (southbound lane). Paved loop walking path. *Emergency phone.* U-turn lane.

Turnagain Pass Recreation Area is a favorite winter recreation area for snow machiners (west side of highway) and cross-country skiers (east side of highway). Snow depths here frequently exceed 12 feet. Patches of snow here into June.

S 68 A 59 Parking area east side of highway with restrooms and picnic tables for northbound traffic. A ¼-mile trail crosses Lyon Creek and ends at a remote picnic site; a ski trail (not developed for summer use) continues up to Center Ridge. U-turn lane.

S 67.7 A 59.3 Lyon Creek bridge.

The highway traverses an area of mountain meadows and park like stands of spruce, hemlock, birch and aspen interlaced with glacier-fed streams. The many flowers seen in surrounding alpine meadows here include lupine, wild geranium, yellow and purple violets, mountain helio-trope, lousewort and paintbrush.

S 67.5 A 59.5 End divided highway southbound, begin 1.4-mile divided highway northbound.

S 67.4 A 59.6 Gravel access to west to informal camping.

S 66.8 A 60.2 Paved double-ended turnout to east.

S 66 A 61 Gravel turnout to east.

S 65.4 A 61.6 Bertha Creek (signed). Turnoff to west for **Bertha Creek USFS Campground**; 12 sites in nicely wooded area by creek; hand-pumped water, toilets, firepits, tables, garbage containers, firewood $5; camping fee $18. Waterfall access from site #6. Small bear-proof food lockers are located at the campground. △

S 65.3 A 61.7 Paved turnout to west.

S 65.1 A 61.9 Begin passing lane southbound. End passing lane northbound.

S 64.7 A 62.3 Spokane Creek (signed).

S 64 A 63 Pete's Creek. End passing lane southbound.

S 63.9 A 63.1 Begin passing lane northbound.

S 63.7 A 63.3 Access road to large parking area with toilets at **Johnson Pass Trailhead**. This is the north trailhead of the 23-mile-long Chugach National Forest trail. Rated easy, this is a good, fairly level trail which follows a portion of the Old Iditarod trail which went from Seward to Nome (see **Milepost S 32.6**). Johnson Pass trail leads to **Bench Lake**, which has Arctic grayling, and **Johnson Lake**, which has rainbow trout. Both lakes are about halfway in on trail. ✏

North end of **Sixmile Trail**, an 8-mile-long paved bike trail along Sixmile Creek's east fork to the Hope Highway Cutoff at **Milepost S 56.3**.

CAUTION: Watch for moose next 4 miles southbound.

S 63.3 A 63.7 Granite Creek bridge. Halfway point on highway between Anchorage and Seward. Paved bike trail on east side of highway.

S 62.7 A 64.3 Begin passing lane southbound. End passing lane northbound.

S 62.6 A 64.4 Granite Creek USFS Campground, 0.8 mile east of highway via narrow, winding gravel road (expect potholes), keep right at fork. There are 17 back-in sites located on a loop road; some sites are

beside creek and some sites will accommodate large RVs. This campground has water, toilets, dumpsters, tables, firepits, firewood (fee charged), campground host, $18 camping fee. Campsite reservations at www.recreation.gov or phone 1-877-444-6777. Scenic setting (cottonwood and spruce forest) with mountain views. Fishing for small Dolly Varden. Interpretive sign about how beetles kill spruce trees. ✏ △

S 62.2 A 64.8 Granite Creek recreation area to east; gated, undeveloped, closed to public.

S 61.8 A 65.2 Begin passing lane northbound. End passing lane southbound.

S 61.5 A 65.5 East Fork Sixmile Creek bridge.

S 61.3 A 65.7 *CAUTION: Watch for moose next 4 miles southbound* (sign).

S 61.1 A 65.9 Silvertip Creek (sign).

S 61 A 66 Begin passing lane southbound. End passing lane northbound.

S 60.4 A 66.6 End passing lane southbound. Begin passing lane northbound.

S 59 A 68 Paved parking area to west with interpretive sign about moose. Staging area for raft trips on **Sixmile Creek** to take-out near Sunrise on the Hope Highway. *CAUTION: Sixmile Creek has Class IV and V rapids; consult with local river runner outfitters (several are located on the Hope Highway) before attempting to paddle this creek.*

Excellent place to photograph this glacial stream. The Sixmile bike trail and walking path leads south to the Hope Highway junction and north to Johnson Pass trailhead.

S 58.8 A 68.2 North end of double-ended turnout on old highway alignment to west.

S 58.6 A 68.4 South end of double-ended turnout on old highway alignment to west.

S 57.7 A 69.3 Scenic viewpoint to west; parking area. Steep climb down through trees overlooks Sixmile Creek canyon. Access to Sixmile Trail (bike trail).

S 56.8 A 70.2 Parking and trailhead to east. Bike trail on west side of highway.

Distance marker southbound shows Seward 54 miles, Homer 150 miles.

Distance marker northbound shows Whittier 33 miles, Girdwood 33 miles, Anchorage 70 miles.

S 56.7 A 70.3 Canyon Creek rest area to west with large paved parking area and restrooms overlooks confluence of Canyon and Sixmile creeks; interpretive signs, access to Sixmile Trail (bike trail).

S 56.5 A 70.5 Canyon Creek bridge; view of old Canyon Creek bridge.

S 56.3 A 70.7 Hope Cutoff. Southbound turn lane for Hope Highway. Rest area and access to Sixmile Trail (bike trail) at Mile 0.1 Hope Highway. *Emergency phone* at Mile 0.1 Hope Highway.

Junction with Hope Highway to historic community of Hope. See "Hope Highway" log beginning on page 526.

Begin passing lane southbound.

S 55.8 A 71.2 Distance marker southbound shows Seward 54 miles, Homer 150 miles.

S 55.3 A 71.7 Scenic viewpoint (long, slow-vehicle shoulder parking) east side of highway. Distance marker northbound shows Hope Junction 1 mile.

S 54.7 A 72.3 Double-ended paved parking area to east.

S 53.5 A 73.5 Parking area to east with *(Continues on page 528)*

Hope Highway

Many of Hope's historic pioneer building are still in use, often repurposed as businesses.

(©Milton & Kelley Barker, staff)

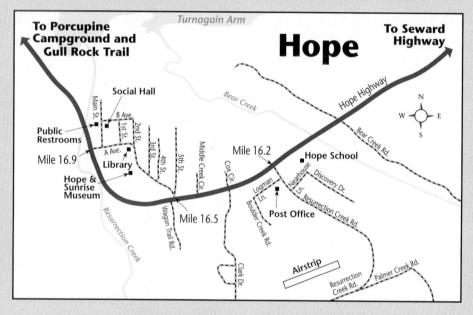

The paved 17.8-mile Hope Highway leads northwest from **Milepost S 56.3** on the Seward Highway to the historic community of Hope on the south side of Turnagain Arm and provides access to the Resurrection Creek area. This is a good 2-lane road with a posted speed limit of 50-mph and some 35- to 40-mph curves.

There are a number of scenic highlights along this road, including glimpses of Turnagain Arm; the picturesque historic town of Hope; the spectacular high country off Palmer Creek Road; and Resurrection Pass Trail. Nova River Runners offers various length Class IV and V whitewater trips from the beginning of this road.

Hope makes a good 1- or 2-day trip from Anchorage.

Distance is measured from junction with the Seward Highway (J).

HOPE HIGHWAY

J 0 Junction with Seward Highway at **Milepost S 56.3**.

J 0.1 Rest area with outhouse, parking and access to Canyon Creek pedestrian bridge; *emergency phone*. **Nova River Runner** departure point for **Sixmile Creek** trips.

Nova River Runners. See display ad on facing page.

CAUTION: Sixmile Creek has Class IV and V rapids; consult with local river runner outfitters before attempting to paddle this creek. Rafting outfitters generally require participants to demonstrate that they have the ability to swim across the river before signing on for this trip.

This is also the south end of the Sixmile Trail, an 8-mile-long bike trail along Sixmile Creek's east fork to the Johnson Pass trailhead at **Milepost S 63.7** Seward Highway.

J 0.2 Silvertip highway maintenance station.

J 0.7 Narrow, paved double-ended turnout to north.

J 2.2 Paved turnout to north, overlooking creek.

J 3.3 Paved turnout to north. Narrow, pothole-filled dirt track leads to informal campsite.

J 3.5 Small gravel turnout to north.

J 3.9 Large paved turnout to north.

J 4.4 Paved double-ended turnout to north.

J 4.9 Small gravel turnout to north.

J 5.8 Small gravel turnout to north.

J 6.4 Small gravel turnout to north by stream.

J 7.6 Chugach Outdoor Center.

J 8.1 Driftboat fishing and cabin rentals at **Angle 45 Adventures**.

Angle 45 Adventures. See display ad on facing page.

J 10 Paved turnout to north with brush-obstructed view of Turnagain Arm.

J 11.1 Large paved turnout to north with view of Turnagain Arm.

J 11.7 Large double ended paved turnout to north.

J 13 Very narrow dirt track loops down to scenic cove on Turnagain Arm.

J 15 "Welcome to Hope" sign followed by several 35-mph signs to remind motorists to reduce their speed in town. *NOTE: Slow for 35-mph speed zone; watch for pedestrians.*

J 15.5 Waste transfer station to south. This is the best place for RVers to drop their garbage. Recycling available.

J 15.6 Fire Department to south.

J 15.7 Bear Creek Road to south.

J 15.8 Grocery, laundry, showers, hotel rooms, cabin and RV park on the north at Coldwater Lodge & Market.

J 15.9 Hope's Hideaway. Find comfort and adventure in Hope! Two 3-bedroom cottages, each equipped with a kitchen and a private bathroom. Perfect for families and groups in need of a base camp for a series of day trips. Conveniently located off the Hope Highway and within steps of espresso. Phone (907) 764-1910; email info@hopeshideaway.com; website www.hopeshideaway.com. [ADVERTISEMENT]

J 16 Bear Creek Lodge. See display ad on facing page.

Dirty Skillet. See display ad on facing page.

J 16.2 Junction with **Resurrection Creek Road** (see description below). Access to Hope School, post office and Discovery Cabins. Take first left on Nearhouse Lane, then right on Discovery Drive for **Discovery Cabins** (description follows). Post office is across from the Nearhouse Lane junction.

Discovery Cabins. 5 rustic log cabins on a bluff overlooking Bear Creek, each with its own private deck. Main lodge features 2 baths, washer/dryer, and full kitchen with big deck, all shared. $95 per night double-occupancy. Pet-friendly cabins available. Text or phone (907) 301-0399; discovery cabins@yahoo.com; www.discoverycabins.com. [ADVERTISEMENT]

Resurrection Creek Road continues to Hope airstrip (0.9 miles from highway), the USFS trailhead (4 miles from highway) for **Resurrection Pass North Trailhead** and to a recreational mining area (with several primitive camping spots). The 38-mile-long Resurrection Pass Trail climbs from an elevation of 400 feet at the north trailhead to Resurrection Pass at 2,600 feet, before descending to the south trailhead at **Milepost S 53.2** on the Sterling Highway.

Palmer Creek Road junctions with Resurrection Creek Road 0.6 mile south of the Hope Highway. Palmer Creek Road provides access into Chugach National Forest. The road is winding and gravel, not recommended for RVs or vehicles with trailers, and leads 7 miles to Coeur d'Alene USFS Campground (6 walk-in tent sites, primitive). No fee. *CAUTION: Watch for bears.*

J 16.5 First turnoff northbound for Hope via gravel loop road. Cafe on this corner. *There is a 15-mph speed limit through Hope's Historic District.*

Hope

J 16.5 Located on Turnagain Arm at the mouth of Resurrection Creek, 87 miles from Anchorage. **Population:** 190. **Visitor Information:** Hope Chamber of Commerce, P.O. Box 89, Hope, AK 99605; visit their website at www.hopealaska.info. The staff at the Hope and Sunrise Community Library and the Hope and Sunrise Historical and Mining Museum—both open noon to 4 P.M. every afternoon in the summer—may provide visitor information. Public restrooms are across from the Hope Social Hall.

Private aircraft: Hope airstrip 1 mile SE; elev. 200 feet; length 2,000 feet; gravel.

Hope has a post office, library, museum, cafes, B&Bs, a lodge and cabins, and food and espresso stops (see ads this section). Camping at Seaview RV Park & Campground (907/782-3300) on Main Street. *No overnight vehicle camping on downtown streets and no tent camping on the tidal flats.* Porcupine USFS Campground, at the end of the Hope Highway, offers very pleasant campsites—some with views of Turnagain Arm—surrounded by lush foliage.

NOTE: There are 4 bear-proof trash cans in town for small trash. RV campers are asked to please use the recycling and trash receptacles at the transfer station just outside town at **Milepost J 15.5** *as the quantity left at these downtown locations can overwhelm the volunteers who empty these cans. Pets on leash at all times; use pet poop disposal containers provided downtown.*

Visitor services are found along the highway from **Milepost J 15.5** to road end, and along the loop road through "downtown" Hope. Check for gas availability with Pioneer Liquor & Gas at **Milepost J 17.6**; phone (907) 782-3418.

This picturesque community was a frenzy of gold rush activity in 1896. Miners named their mining camp on Resurrection Creek Hope City, after young prospector Percy Hope. But the gold rush here was short-lived. By 1899, many of the miners had joined the gold

rush to the Klondike. Hope City persisted, and it is now the best preserved gold rush community in southcentral Alaska. Hope's historic district includes the 1896 store (now the Seaview Cafe & Bar) and the 1902 log Social Hall, which still hosts community events (public restrooms are across from the hall). The **Hope and Sunrise Historical and Mining Museum** has an extensive collection of gold mining equipment that is displayed both indoors and outside on the museum grounds. NOTE: *The historic district has narrow streets; please park only on the designated side of the streets so that emergency vehicles can get through.*

Today, Hope is a quiet, friendly oasis, popular with hikers, campers, bicyclists, bird watchers and recreational gold miners. The community is dedicated to keeping the streets and creekside clean and asks visitors to "please do your part and leave nothing behind and respect the 15-mph speed limit throughout the historic district."

Special events here include the annual 2-day **Wagon Trail Festival** (weekend of the third Sunday in July), which features a 5K run, pancake breakfast and cake walk at the Hope Social Hall.

At **Milepost J 17.7** Hope Highway, just before Porcupine USFS Campground, a short road to the south leads to the trailhead for **Gull Rock Trail.**

Hope Highway Log
(continued)

J 16.9 Second turnoff northbound for Hope via dirt loop road. Access to Seaview Cafe and Bar.

Resume 35-mph speed zone on Hope Highway or slow to 15-mph speed limit through Hope's Historic District.

J 17 Resurrection Creek bridge.

J 17.6 Pioneer Liquor & Gas, call ahead to see if they have gas; (907) 242-0204. 🅖

J 17.7 Gull Rock Trail, turn south off of the Hope Highway prior to the entrance to the campground. This 5.7-mile trail is rated easy, and is a relatively flat trail through lush vegetation that ends at Gull Rock overlooking Turnagain Arm. Allow 2- to 3-hours to hike one way. Trail has lots of tree roots and some muddy spots.

J 17.8 Hope Highway ends.

Begin an 0.8-mile loop road leads through **Porcupine USFS Campground** providing access to campsites. Very pleasant campground set in lush vegetation with a few sites overlooking Turnagain Arm. There are 34 paved sites, tables, tent spaces, campground host, outhouses, firewood, firepits, dumpster, drinking water. Open May 25–late September. Camping fee $18; fee for firewood. 🅰

Return to Milepost S 56.3
Seward Highway

(Continued from page 525)

Gold Rush Centennial signs about hydraulic mining and Wible's mining camp on Canyon Creek.

S 53.3 A 73.7 End passing lane southbound.

S 52.6 A 74.4 Large, paved slow vehicle turnout to east.

S 52.4 A 74.6 Sign northbound reads: Delay of 5 vehicles illegal, must use turnouts.

Begin passing lane southbound as highway climbs 7 percent grade.

S 51.4 A 75.6 Double-ended scenic viewpoint to east.

Begin 7 percent downgrade northbound.

S 51.2 A 75.8 Distance marker northbound shows Hope Junction 5 miles.

S 50.6 A 76.4 Scenic viewpoint to east.

S 50.3 A 76.7 End passing lane southbound.

S 48.7 A 78.3 Begin passing lane southbound.

S 48.5 A 78.5 End passing lane southbound.

S 48 A 79 Turnout for Alaska Mountain Huts (non-profit organization). Hike-in or ski-in to the Manitoba Cabin, 0.7 mile from the turnout. This fully refurbished 1936-built cabin is a rustic, backcountry destination. Cabin has a wood stove, propane stove/oven, kitchen space and solar lights. Nearby there are two insulated heated yurts that each sleep 8. Travelers need to bring sleeping bags and food. For reservations call or go online: (907) 306-3908; www.alaska huts.org.

S 47.9 A 79.1 Large paved parking area to east.

S 47.7 A 79.3 Double-ended parking area to east at north end of Lower Summit Lake with access to path and footbridge.

S 47.3 A 79.7 Double-ended turnout to east is a slow vehicle turnout for northbound traffic at the south end of Lower Summit Lake. A favorite photo stop for its lush growth of beautiful wildflowers in summer.

Upper and Lower Summit lakes, good spring and fall fishing for landlocked Dolly Varden (goldenfins) and rainbow trout. 🐟

S 46 A 81 Colorado Creek bridge. Turnoff to east at south end of bridge for **Tenderfoot Creek USFS Campground,** located 0.6 mile from highway via gravel access road. There are 35 sites (some pull-throughs, no hookups) located along a loop road. Beautiful setting on the east side of **Upper Summit Lake;** great for canoes, kayaks and small fishing boats. A favorite campground for many Alaskans. There are tables, firepits, bear-proof dumpsters, water, toilets (wheelchair accessible), and a boat launch. Firewood available (fee charged). Campground host. Camping fee $18. Campsite reservations at www.recreation.gov or phone 1-877-444-6777. Lake fishing for Arctic char and stocked rainbow trout. Also access to Colorado Creek at back of campground. 🐟🅰

S 45.8 A 81.2 Summit Lake Lodge east side of highway; food and lodging. Closed in winter. *Emergency phone* located on pole next to lodge sign.

S 45.7 A 81.3 Winter avalanche area begins southbound. Avalanche gates.

S 45.4 A 81.6 Turnout to east overlooking Upper Summit Lake.

S 44.5 A 82.5 Double-ended paved turnout to east at south end of Upper Summit

Lake.

S 43.9 A 83.1 Gravel turnout to east.

S 43.8 A 83.2 Winter avalanche area begins northbound. Avalanche gates.

S 43.7 A 83.3 Slow vehicle turnout east.

S 42.4 A 84.6 End passing lane northbound.

S 42.2 A 84.8 Quartz Creek.

S 41.5 A 85.5 Begin passing lane northbound.

S 39.6 A 87.4 Avalanche gates.

S 39.5 A 87.5 Devils Creek Trail; trailhead parking to west; toilet. This 10-mile (one-way) USFS trail (rated more difficult) starts at an elevation of 1,000 feet and follows Devils Creek to Devils Pass (elev. 2,400 feet), continuing on to Devils Pass Lake and Resurrection Pass North and South trails. Hiking time to Devils Pass is about 5 to 6 hours.

Camping options are at Mile 2.3 the Beaver Pond tent site, or at Mile 5.3 for a campsite or the Devils Pass public-use cabin (must be reserved in advance). Avalanche danger begins at Mile 3 in winter and winter use is not recommended beyond this point. Not open to snow machine use. Closed to horses April–June.

S 39.4 A 87.6 Distance marker northbound shows Anchorage 88 miles, Whittier 50 miles, Girdwood 50 miles.

S 39.2 A 87.8 End passing lane northbound.

S 39 A 88 Begin passing lane northbound.

S 38.5 A 88.5 Small paved turnout overlooking Jerome Lake.

S 38.4 A 88.6 Paved double-ended Scenic Byway turnout to west adjacent **Jerome Lake;** interpretive signs and public fishing access. Lake is stocked; rainbow trout and Arctic char to 22 inches, use salmon egg clusters, year-round. 🐟

S 38.1 A 88.9 End passing lane northbound.

S 37.7 A 89.3 First exit (southbound-traffic only) to west for Sterling Highway (Alaska Route 1). Continue straight ahead on Alaska Route 9 for second Sterling Highway exit at Tern Lake and for continuation of Seward Highway.

First **junction** southbound with Sterling Highway to Soldotna, Homer and other Sterling Highway communities. Turn to the STERLING HIGHWAY on page 538 for log.

S 37.2 A 89.8 Paved double-ended turnout to west overlooks Tern Lake. Access to Tern Lake is from the Sterling Highway; use Tern Lake Junction turnoff (next turnoff southbound).

S 37 A 90 Tern Lake Junction. Main junction of Seward and Sterling highways. Turn off to west (2-way traffic) on Sterling Highway for access to Tern Lake and **Tern Lake USFS Wildlife Viewing Area.** This is a good spot to see nesting birds, mountain goats, sheep and occasionally moose and bear. Tern Lake is a prime bird-watching area in summer. 👀

Tern Lake Junction: Second turnoff southbound and first northbound of the Seward Highway with the Sterling Highway (Alaska Route 1) to Soldotna, Kenai and Homer. Turn to **Milepost S 37** on page 538 in the STERLING HIGHWAY section for log.

Seward-bound travelers continue straight ahead southbound on Alaska Route 9 for Seward (continue with this log).

Begin 1-mile passing lane northbound.

ALASKA ROUTE 9

S 36.5 A 90.5 Distance marker southbound shows Moose Pass 7 miles, Seward 34 miles.

S 36.4 A 90.6 Avalanche gates.

S 36 A 91 Lakeside lodging.

S 35.7 A 91.3 Crazy Moose to east (on left southbound); description follows.

Crazy Moose. Wide circle driveway for motorhomes. Bring your camera for a souvenir photo with "The Moose!" Like no other shop in Alaska. Two artists, husband and wife, inspired by Alaska, creating heirlooms on site. Russ and Melissa's creations, once sold in fine art galleries and shops around the state, are now available exclusively at Crazy Moose. If coming from Seward, get ready to turn after Milepost 35. Seasonal restroom. www.crazymoosealaska.com.
[ADVERTISEMENT]

S 33.1 A 93.9 Carter Lake USFS trailhead No. 4 to west; parking and a toilet. Trail starts at an elevation of 500 feet and climbs 986 feet to **Carter Lake** (stocked with rainbow trout). Trail is 2 miles long, good, but steep; rated more difficult with a hiking time of 2 hours. Good access to sheep and mountain goat country. Excellent snowmachining area in winter.

S 32.6 A 94.4 Johnson Pass USFS south trailhead with parking area, toilet. North trailhead at Milepost S 63.7.

S 32.4 A 94.6 Turnout to west; short trail to stream where spawning salmon may be seen in August.

CAUTION: Be bear aware. This is a high-use area for bears in salmon spawning season.

S 32.1 A 94.9 Cook Inlet Aquaculture Association. **Trail Lake Fish Hatchery** on Moose Creek; this hatchery raises sockeye and coho salmon and has juveniles and smaller (no adults). Display room (in winter, if this is locked, just come to the office and they will open it for you). Open 8 A.M. to 5 P.M. daily, year-round. Guided tours available if requested in advance or self-guided visitor center exhibits whenever facility is open. Phone (907) 288-3688.

NOTE: There is no public restroom here but there is a pit toilet at the Johnson Pass South trailhead, 0.5 mile north of here.

S 31.7 A 95.3 Double-ended turnout to east on Upper Trail Lake; picnic table.

S 30.3 A 96.7 *Begin 45-mph speed zone southbound. Resume 55-mph speed limit northbound.*

S 29.7 A 97.3 Turnout east side of highway with view of Trail Lake.

S 29.6 A 97.4 *Begin 35-mph speed zone southbound. PLEASE DRIVE SLOWLY THROUGH TOWN!*
Begin 45-mph speed zone northbound.

S 29.5 A 97.5 Moose Pass DOT Highway maintenance station. Avalanche phone (907) 478-7675.

S 29.4 A 97.6 Gravel turnout to east, no views.

Groceries and waterwheel west side of highway and **Trail Lake Lodge** (description follows) motel and restaurant to east at turnoff.

Trail Lake Lodge. Located between the Kenai River and Resurrection Bay, nestled in the heart of the Chugach Range. Trail Lake Lodge offers a perfect jumping off point for

Slow down and stop in Moose Pass for roasted moose nuts, a great hamburger or an overnight stay. (©Kris Valenia, staff)

your outdoor activities. We offer affordable lodging, restaurant with all of your Alaskan favorites, all-inclusive adventure packages, day fishing trips and live music. www.trail lakelodge.com. (907) 288-3101. [ADVERTISEMENT]

Junction with loop road leads east past Moose Pass school to post office.

Moose Pass

S 29.3 A 97.7 Located on the shore of Upper Trail Lake, 98 miles from Anchorage. **Population:** 226. **Emergency Services:** Volunteer Fire Dept./EMS, phone 911; Seward General Hospital or Central Peninsula Hospital in Soldotna by highway or helicopter. Alaska State Trooper Post (907) 288-3346.

Visitor Information: Moose Pass Chamber of Commerce, www.moosepassalaska.com.

Moose Pass has food, lodging, camping, a general store and fishing guide businesses. This is a charming mountain village located on the shores of scenic Upper Trail Lake. A post office and highway maintenance station are located here.

Moose Drop-in Trading Post. Home of Morris the Talking Moose. We specialize in great fudge, roasted moose nuts and hot coffee. We make our own fudge on site. We also sell handcrafted items created by Native Alaskans and local artists, hand-painted ornaments, treasure boxes, Alaskan photography and souvenirs. (907) 288-2453. www. MooseDropinTradingPost.com. [ADVERTISEMENT]

Moose Pass began as a construction camp on the Alaska Railroad in 1912. Local resident Ed Estes attributed the name Moose Pass to a 1904 observation by Nate White of the first moose recorded in this area. Another version holds that "in 1903, a mail carrier driving a team of dogs had considerable trouble gaining the right-of-way from a giant moose." A post office was established in 1928 and first postmistress Leora (Estes) Roycroft officially named the town Moose Pass.

Moose Pass has a 1.3-mile-long paved bike trail which winds along Trail Lake from the Moose Pass ball diamond to the McFadden house on the south. Gravel turnout by lake.

The main street of town is the site of the Annual Moose Pass Summer Festival, a community-sponsored event which takes place the weekend nearest summer solstice (June 21). The festival features a triathlon, arts and crafts booths, a barbecue and other events.

The large waterwheel on the west side of the road is a local landmark, as is the sign posted there for so many years: "Moose Pass is a peaceful little town. If you have an ax to grind, do it here." The wheel continues to turn a lathe that may be used to sharpen tools.

This is a third-generation waterwheel, rebuilt by Jeff Estes with the help of local craftsmen in 2003, in memory of his father, Ed Estes. This waterwheel replaces one built by Ed Estes in 1976, which in turn was a replica of a waterwheel built by his stepfather, Frank Roycroft, that was used to cut lumber for the family's homestead.

Seward Highway Log
(continued)

S 28.5 A 98.5 *Begin 35-mph speed zone northbound. Begin 45-mph speed zone southbound.*

S 28.3 A 98.7 Moose Pass (sign) northbound.

S 27.5 A 99.5 *Begin 45-mph speed zone northbound. Resume 55-mph speed limit southbound.*

S 25.8 A 101.2 Gravel turnout to west. The timbered slopes of Madson Mountain (elev. 5,269 feet) to the west. Crescent Lake lies just west of Madson. Lower Trail Lake is on the east side of the highway. Grant Lake lies just east of Lower Trail Lake.

S 25.4 A 101.6 One-lane bridge over Trail River.

Trail to east at south end of bridge leads 1.5 miles to **Vagt Lake**; stocked with rainbow trout.

S 24.2 A 102.8 Side road leads 1.2 miles to **Trail River USFS Campground**; 91 camp-

The turnout at Milepost S 12.3 is a good spot to stretch your legs and enjoy the scenery.
(©Claire Torgerson, staff)

sites, some pull-throughs, good for all size rigs. Campground host. Group camping available; large covered pavilion. Park and walk to picnic tables on shore of Kenai Lake. Camping fee $18. Campsite reservations at www.recreation.gov or phone 1-877-444-6777. Shelter, volleyball net, playground. Good spot for mushrooming and berry picking in August.

Lower Trail River, lake and rainbow trout and Arctic char, July, August and September, small spinners. Access via Lower Trail River campground road. **Trail River**, Dolly Varden and rainbow trout. Closed to fishing mid-April to mid-June; use of bait prohibited year-round.

S 23.5 A 103.5 *CAUTION: Railroad crossing.* USFS Kenai Lake work center (no information services available). Report forest fires here. Alaska State Troopers to west.

Private Aircraft: Lawing landing strip; elev. 475 feet; length 2,200 feet; gravel; unattended.

S 23.3 A 103.7 Gravel turnout to west. Turnoff for **Ptarmigan Creek USFS Campground**; 16 back-in sites, water, toilets, tables, firepits and dumpsters. Campground host. Camping fee $18. Campsite reservations at www.recreation.gov or phone 1-877-444-6777. Fair to good fishing in creek and in **Ptarmigan Lake** (hike-in, see trail information following) for Dolly Varden. Viewing platform to see spawning salmon in Ptarmigan Creek, best in August and September.

Water and picnic area at trailhead for Ptarmigan Creek USFS trail, which begins at the campground (elev. 500 feet) and leads 3.5 miles to Ptarmigan Lake (elev. 755 feet). Trail is steep in spots; round-trip hiking time 5 hours. Good chance of seeing sheep, goats, moose and bears. Carry insect repellent. Trail is poor for winter use due to avalanche hazard.

S 23.1 A 103.9 Ptarmigan Creek bridge; narrow bridge, slow for curves on approach.

S 23 A 104 Turnoff for Alaska Nellie's Homestead. The late Nellie Neal-Lawing arrived in Alaska in 1915. She was the first woman to get a governmental grant to open a roadhouse. Her colorful life included cooking for the railroad workers and big game hunting and guiding. (There is no sign of the roadhouse today.)

S 22.7 A 104.3 Gravel turnout to east. Paved shoulder parking west side of highway provides scenic viewpoint overlooking Kenai Lake. This lake (elev. 436 feet) extends 24 miles from the head of the Kenai River on the west to the mouth of Snow River on the east. A sign here explains how glacier meltwater gives the lake its distinctive color.

Winter avalanche area next 3 miles southbound.

S 21.8 A 105.2 Small gravel turnout to west with obstructed views of Kenai Lake.

S 21.4 A 105.6 Small gravel turnout to west overlooking Kenai Lake (view obscured by brush).

S 20 A 107 Victor Creek bridge. Victor Creek USFS trail No. 23 on north side of bridge is a 2¼-mile hike with good view of mountains. Elevation gain of 1,100 ft.

S 19.8 A 107.2 Renfro's Lakeside Retreat to west has an RV park with full hookups and lakeside guest cabins (description follows). *Turnoff is between 0.1 and 0.2 mile south of Victor Creek bridge and physical Milepost S 20, and 1.3 miles north of physical Milepost S 18.*

Renfro's Lakeside Retreat. Fully furnished modern log cabins (with kitchens and baths) on Kenai Lake, surrounded by Kenai Mountains. Breathtaking views. Picnic area, playground, pedal boats, fishing, firepits, laundry. Full hookup RV park, WiFi, free showers. 20 minutes to Seward. Web: www.renfroslakesideretreat.com. Email: renfroslakesideretreat@gmail.com. Phone (907) 288-5059. [ADVERTISEMENT]

S 18 A 109 Driving distance between physical Milepost 18 and Milepost 20 is 1.2 miles.

S 17.5 A 109.5 Bridge over center channel of Snow River. This river has 2 forks that flow into Kenai Lake.

S 17 A 110 Distance marker northbound shows Kenai 68 miles, Homer 151 miles, Anchorage 110 miles.

S 16.9 A 110.1 Bridge over south chan-

nel of **Snow River**. Easy-to-miss turnoff for Primrose Road at south end of bridge that leads west 1 mile to **Primrose USFS Campground**. (*Campground access road leads past private homes: Drive carefully!*) The campground, overlooking Kenai Lake, has 7 sites best suited for small rigs and tents. There are pit toilets, bear-proof food storage containers, dumpsters, tables, firepits, boat ramp, potable water, $18 camping fee. Popular salmon fishing spot with busy creek use in July–August.

Primrose trail (6.5 miles long) starts from the campground and connects with Lost Creek trail (7 miles). High alpine hike to Lost Lake, stocked with rainbow trout.

S 16.8 A 110.2 Begin 1.1-mile passing lane southbound.

S 16.6 A 110.4 Distance marker southbound shows Seward 17 miles.

S 15.8 A 111.2 Snow River Hostel. (907) 440-1907 (call between 6 P.M. and 10 P.M. Alaska Time). http://snowriverhostel.org/.

S 15.7 A 111.3 End passing lane southbound.

S 15.5 A 111.5 Large gravel turnout to east.

S 14.7 A 112.3 Paved parking at boardwalk viewpoint overlooking Lily Pad Lake to east. Watch for moose in lake and swans nesting nearby.

S 14 A 113 View to east of railroad bridge.

S 13.3 A 113.7 Begin passing lane southbound.

S 13.2 A 113.8 Large paved parking area to east. Grayling Lake USFS trailhead parking to west. Grayling Lake trail is rated easy. Allow 1 hour each way for the 1.6-mile hike. It connects with trails to Meridian, Long and Leech lakes. Good spot for photos of Snow River valley. Watch for moose. **Grayling Lake**, 6- to 12-inch grayling, use flies, May to October. **Meridian** and **Long** lakes are stocked with rainbow trout.

S 12.3 A 114.7 Scenic viewpoint to east is a very large paved parking area with interpretive signs on Chugach culture and the Native Claims Settlement Act.

S 12 A 115 End passing lane northbound.

S 11.3 A 115.7 Golden Fin Lake trailhead parking to west. This is a 0.6-mile hike on a very wet trail: wear rubber footwear. Fishing at Golden Fin Lake for Arctic char averaging 8 inches. Ski trails in winter.

S 10.6 A 116.4 Large paved turnout to east.

S 10 A 117 Driving distance between physical Mileposts 10 and 11 is 0.8 mile.

S 8.8 A 118.2 Begin 3.2-mile passing lane as highway climbs next 3 miles northbound.

S 8.2 A 118.8 Large paved turnout to east. Entering Chugach National Forest (sign) northbound.

S 7 A 120 Turnoff to west on Timber Lane for **Irvin Pottery**. Description follows.

Irvin Pottery, just outside Seward, is a delightfully unique home pottery, operated by Tom and Sharon Irvin. They offer fine, hand-crafted, functional, wheel-thrown and hand-built stoneware pottery with original and colorful hand painted glaze designs. Dishwasher safe and non-toxic. Turn on Que Sera Drive, follow signs to pottery. 14527 Rain Forest Circle, Seward, AK 99664; irvpots@gmail.com; www.irvinpottery.com; (907) 224-3534. [ADVERTISEMENT]

S 6.6 A 120.4 Junction with Bear Lake Road to **Bear Creek Weir** (0.6 miles west), a popular viewing spot for sockeye salmon in late spring/early summer and coho salmon in late summer/fall. There is also a resident population of dipper birds. The salmon pass through the weir on their 7-mile journey from Resurrection Bay to their spawning grounds in nearby Bear Lake. Cook Inlet Hatchery releases smolt here increasing the potential of productive return salmon runs. The weir is operated by Cook Inlet Aquaculture Assoc. (www.ciaanet.org). *CAUTION: Be bear aware. Where there are salmon, there are bears.*

Bear Lake trail runs from Bear Lake 7.5 miles north to near railroad bridge, **Milepost S 14**. Moderate, best in June–October.

S 6.5 A 120.5 Bear Creek.

S 6.3 A 120.7 Stoney Creek Avenue, crosses railroad tracks. Access to **Stoney Creek RV Park** (description follows).

Stoney Creek RV Park. Seward's only luxury RV park, located on 15 acres of pristine creekside property, and built to accommodate travelers who enjoy cleanliness, friendliness, and full utility services at their individual sites, including water, power, sewer, satellite TV. We also have clean hot showers and laundry facilities. Phone, DSL and WiFi, and shuttle to town available. Please see our display ad map (Mile 6.3) for directions. You may email us at info@stoneycreekrvpark.com. Phone toll free 1-877-437-6366. See display ad on this page.
[ADVERTISEMENT]

S 5.9 A 121.1 Salmon Creek. Good fishing in stream begins Aug. 1st for sea-run Dolly Varden averaging 10 inches; use of bait prohibited Sept. 16–Dec. 31.

S 5.5 A 121.5 Lodging and hostel.
Seward Highway Scenic Byway (northbound sign).

S 5.2 A 121.8 Turnoff to west for Lost Lake subdivision and access to Lost Lake

USFS Trail. For trailhead, drive west 0.2 mile and turn left on Heather Lee Lane; drive 0.2 mile and turn right on Hayden Berlin Road; rough and narrow road winds uphill and deadends at trailhead.

S 5.1 A 121.9 Bear Creek volunteer fire department to west. *Emergency phone.*

S 5 A 122 Large double-ended turnout to west.

S 4.1 A 122.9 Distance marker northbound shows Soldotna 91 miles, Anchorage 123 miles, Homer 165 miles.

S 3.8 A 123.2 Clear Creek bridge.

S 3.7 A 123.3 Turnoff to west for Exit Glacier in Kenai Fjords National Park, located 8.4 miles west via Herman Leirer Road. Lodging and attractions are located on Exit Glacier Road and Old Exit Glacier Road. A scenic drive.

Junction with Herman Leirer Road to Exit Glacier. See "Exit Glacier" on page 532.

S 3.2 A 123.8 Turnoff for paved Nash Road which leads east to paved turnouts and views of Resurrection Bay and Seward (after Mile 3) and to **Spring Creek Campground** (City of Seward) campground at Mile 5.1. Spring Creek has a large gravel parking area, outhouse, dumpster and access to water; fish from shore. Camping fee charged; no hookups. Just past Spring Creek Campground, Nash Road enters an industrial area; no thru traffic.

S 3 A 124 Resurrection River bridge; first of 3 bridges southbound crossing 3 channels of the river. This river flows from the Harding Icefield into Resurrection Bay just north-

east of Seward.
Seward city limits.

S 2.9 A 124.1 Resurrection River bridge No. 2.

S 2.8 A 124.2 Resurrection River bridge No. 3.

S 2.7 A 124.3 Turnoff to east just south of bridge for Seward airport.

S 2.5 A 124.5 Hemlock Street. Turnoff for **Forest Acres Municipal Campground** just off highway; wooded sites on gravel loop; flush toilets, firepits, picnic tables, 14-day limit. Camping fee: $10/tent, $15/RV, no power or water hookups available here.

Begin 45-mph speed zone entering Seward.

S 2.3 A 124.7 Sea Lion Avenue for access to a vacation/camping facility for active and retired military and access to Seward Middle and Seward Elementary schools.

S 2 A 125 Seward Chamber of Commerce and Convention and Visitors Bureau Visitor Center west side of highway. Stop in with questions and see their 11-foot, 1,400-lb. Alaska brown bear mount. Open daily Memorial Day through Labor Day, weekdays the rest of the year; phone (907) 224-8051; www.seward.com.

S 1.9 A 125.1 Safeway supermarket, Starbucks.

S 1.7 A 125.3 Grocery and **Essential 1 gas station** to west; gas, diesel, propane, car/boat/RV wash, convenience store; phone (907) 224-8041.

Essential 1. See display ad on this page.
S 1.6 A 125.4 Shell gas station with gas/
(Continues on page 533)

Exit Glacier

View of Exit Glacier from access road.

(©Claire Torgerson, staff)

Turn west on Herman Leirer Road (paved, 45-mph posted speed limit) at **Milepost S 3.7** Seward Highway and drive 8.4 miles to reach Exit Glacier in Kenai Fjords National Park. Close-up views of Exit Glacier and Resurrection River, as well as access to local attractions, make this a worthwhile side trip.

Lodging, dining and camping are located along Herman Leirer Road and on Old Exit Glacier Road (gravel), which loops off the main access road just west of the Seward Highway (logs follow for both roads).

HERMAN LEIRER ROAD

Distance from junction (J) with the Seward Highway is shown.

J 0 Junction with the Seward Highway at Milepost S 3.7.

J 0.1 Junction with Old Exit Glacier Road loop (see log following). Distance marker says Exit Glacier 8.6, Kenai Fjords National Park 7.2, Resurrection River Trail.

J 0.5 Seward Windsong Lodge.

J 0.6 Resurrection Roadhouse Restaurant.

J 1.2 Large paved parking area to south.

J 1.3 Junction with Old Exit Glacier Road loop (see log following) 0.5-mile access to Ididaride Sled Dog Tours.

J 1.4 Winter gates; no road maintenance beyond this point generally November to mid-May. Exact closure dates based on snow and ice conditions. In winter, the road is closed to passenger vehicles but open to winter recreationists.

Entering **Exit Glacier Road Special Use Area** (Alaska Dept. of Natural Resources) westbound; recreational tent and small RV camping at designated off-road pullouts next 2.2 miles westbound; 8-day limit, outhouses, pack out garbage.

J 3.1 Small paved pullout to south overlooking river.

J 3.6 Chugach National Forest (sign). Large turnouts both sides of road.

J 4.6 Bridge.

J 4.7 Long paved shoulder parking area to north.

J 6.3 Small turnouts both sides of road.

J 6.7 Parking area and scenic viewpoint of Exit Glacier; good photo op.

J 6.9 Trailhead parking with toilet for **Resurrection River Trail** (Chugach National Forest). This 16-mile trail ties in with the Russian Lakes trail and is part of the 75-mile Hope-to-Seward route. *CAUTION: Black and brown bears also use this trail.*

J 7 Resurrection River bridge.

J 7.2 Welcome to **Kenai Fjords National Park's Exit Glacier** (sign). Shortly hereafter, watch for numbered signs alongside the roadway noting year when Exit Glacier extended to this location. The year 1815 is the first noted as you continue up this road.

J 8.1 Turnoff for free walk-in tent campground with 12 sites (first come, first served).

J 8.4 Parking area. Easy walk on paved path to Exit Glacier Nature Center; adjacent handicap-accessible restrooms and picnic area. *NOTE: Pets must be on leash in parking lot and are not allowed outside the parking lot area. Overnight parking is prohibited in the parking area, but there is free camping at turnouts along Herman Leirer Road (see* **Milepost J 1.4**).

Exit Glacier Nature Center is open seasonally, with displays, Alaska Geographic bookstore, and park information. Exit Glacier is 2.5 miles long and descends 2,400 feet from the Harding Icefield. Continue on paved path 0.4 mile past Nature Center to fork: Harding Icefield Trail (4.1 miles, one-way, strenuous) heads uphill; Trail to Edge of the Glacier (moderate uphill on dirt, gravel and rock) leads another 0.6 mile to views of Exit Glacier (worth the effort). You can see the glacier midway on the 1-mile-long accessible trail to Glacier View, which loops back to the Exit Glacier Nature Center. *CAUTION: Falling ice possible at edges of glacier; stay behind warning signs. Watch for moose and bears on trails.*

Summer activities include daily ranger guided walks, pavilion talks, and junior ranger activities. A public-use cabin is available in winter. Phone the park office in Seward at (907) 422-0500; for recorded information phone (907) 422-0573; or visit www.nps.gov/kefj.

OLD EXIT GLACIER ROAD

Distance is measured from the east junction (EJ) and west junction (WJ) with Exit Glacier Road.

EJ 0 WJ 1.6 Junction with Exit Glacier Road at Mile 0.1.

EJ 0.5 WJ 1.1 Clear Creek.

EJ 1.1 WJ 0.5 Seavey's IdidaRide Sled Dog Tours. Mitch Seavey, the 2004, 2013 and 2017 Iditarod winner, and his family (son Dallas won the Iditarod in 2012, 2014, 2015 and 2016) introduce visitors to their sled dog business on Old Exit Glacier Road homestead. Guests can take a dog sled ride on a wheeled sled; pet irresistible sled dog puppies, check out the arctic gear worn at 50 below temperatures, and hear fascinating stories about dogs and dog mushing.

Seavey's IdidaRide Sled Dog Tours. See display ad this page.

EJ 1.5 WJ 0.1 Entering Glacier Road Special Use Area; 8-day camping limit.

EJ 1.6 WJ 0 Junction with Exit Glacier Road at Mile 1.3.

Return to Milepost S 3.7 Seward Highway

Fishing from shore is easily accessible on Resurrection Bay in Seward. (©Kris Valencia, staff)

(Continued from page 531)
diesel and 3 Bears Grocery store.

S 1.4 A 125.6 Phoenix Road to west. Port Avenue to east, access to cruise ship dock. Train station to east (access is from **Milepost S 2**).

Slow for 35-mph speed zone southbound.

S 1.3 A 125.7 Dairy Hill Lane to west. Large parking area to west at **Benny Benson Memorial**. In 1926, as a seventh-grader, Benny Benson entered a contest to design the Alaska flag. His winning design—8 gold stars (representing the Big Dipper and the North Star) on a field of blue—earned him a $1,000 scholarship.

S 1.2 A 125.8 North Harbor Street; Chevron gas/diesel station.

S 1.1 A 125.9 South Harbor Street; access to Seward Boat Harbor, Harbormaster office, Kenai Fjords National Park Visitor Center and boardwalk (see details in Seward Lodging & Services and Attractions).

S 1 A 126 Van Buren Street.

S 0.6 A 126.4 Monroe Street. Mount Marathon Trail is at the end of Monroe (see information signs at the trailhead).

S 0.4 A 126.6 Madison Street. Post office 2 blocks east. Hostel.

S 0.3 A 126.7 Jefferson Street. Seward Senior Center. Hospital at Jefferson and First. City Hall is one block east. Mount Marathon Race Trail is at the end of Jefferson; continue past hospital and one block up Lowell Canyon Road. For hiking Mount Marathon outside of the race, please go to the end of Monroe Street.

S 0.2 A 126.8 Adams Street.

S 0 A 127 Mile 0 of the Seward Highway (3rd Avenue) at Railway Avenue, which becomes Lowell Point Road. Alaska SeaLife Center is located on the bay at the end of 4th Avenue (one block south of here on Railway Avenue).

Seward

S 0 A 127 Located on Resurrection Bay, east coast of Kenai Peninsula; 127 miles south of Anchorage by road, or 35 minutes by air. **Population:** 2,740. **Emergency Services:** Dial 911. **State Troopers**, phone (907) 288-3346. **Hospital**, Providence Seward Medical Center, 1st Avenue and Jefferson Street, phone (907) 224-5205. **Maritime Search and Rescue**, phone (800) 478-5555.

Visitor Information: Available at the Seward Chamber of Commerce–Convention and Visitors Bureau Visitor Center at Milepost S 2 Seward Highway. Open daily Memorial Day through Labor Day, weekdays the rest of the year; phone (907) 224-8051; www.seward.com.

Kenai Fjords National Park Visitor Center, 1212 4th Ave. (in the Small Boat Harbor). The Visitor Center is open 9 A.M. to 7 P.M. daily in summer with a park film, information, and a bookstore. Phone the park office at (907) 422-0500 or the Visitor Information recorded information line at (907) 422-0573. Or write P.O. Box 1727, Seward, AK 99664; web site www.nps.gov/kefj.

Elevation: Sea level. **Climate:** Average daily maximum temperature in July, 62°F; average daily minimum in January, 18°F. Average annual precipitation, 67 inches (received 15.05 inches on Oct. 10, 1986 a record year and gained the record of highest rainfall anywhere in Alaska); average snowfall, 80 inches. **Radio:** KSKA-FM 88.1, KPEN 102.3, KPFN 105.9, KSWD 950, KWVE 104.9. **Television:** Several channels by cable. **Newspaper:** *Seward Journal* (weekly) *Seward Phoenix Log* (weekly). **Private Aircraft:** Seward airport, 2 NE; elev. 22 feet; length 4,200 feet; asphalt; fuel 100LL, jet.

Seward—known as the "Gateway to Kenai Fjords National Park" has been voted an All-America City 3 different times—is a picturesque community nestled between high mountain ranges on a small rise stretching from Resurrection Bay to the foot of Mount Marathon. Thick groves of cottonwood and scattered spruce groves are found in the immediate vicinity of the city, with

Shop Seward's downtown shopping area along 4th Avenue then walk the waterfront path down to the Seward Harbor. (©Kris Valencia, staff)

stands of spruce and alder growing on the surrounding mountainsides.

Historically, Seward was an important transportation hub for Alaska's mining, exploration, fishing and trapping industries. The town was established in 1903 by railroad surveyors as an ocean terminal and supply center. The Iditarod trail was surveyed in 1910 as a mail route between Seward and Nome. It was used until 1924, when it was replaced by the airplane. (The 938-mile-long trail—now a National Historic Trail—is probably best known for the Iditarod Trail Sled Dog Race that is run each March between Willow and Nome.)

The city was named for William H. Seward, U.S. Secretary of State under president Andrew Johnson. Seward was wounded the same night Lincoln was assassinated, by a co-conspirator, Lewis Powell. Seward was instrumental in arranging the purchase of Alaska from Russia in 1867.

Resurrection Bay, a year-round ice-free harbor, made Seward an important cargo and fishing port as well as a strategic military post during WWII. Resurrection Bay was named in 1792 by Russian fur trader and explorer Alexander Baranof. While sailing from Kodiak to Yakutat he found unexpected shelter in this bay from a storm and named the bay Resurrection because it was the Russian Sunday of the Resurrection (Easter).

Seward's economic base includes tourism, a coal terminal, marine research, fisheries and government offices. The Alaska Vocational Technical Center is located here. The Alaska SeaLife Center, a marine educational center, is also here (see Attractions this section for more details).

Lodging & Services

Seward has all visitor facilities, including hotels, motels, hostels, bed and breakfasts, cafes and restaurants, post office, grocery stores, pharmacy (inside the Safeway grocery store), a library/museum (see Attractions this section), travel agencies, gift shops, gas stations, bars, laundromats, churches and a summer market.

The Harbor Master Building has public restrooms, pay showers, drinking water fountain and mailbox. Weather information is also available here. Phone the Harbormaster at (907) 224-3138 or VHF channel 17.

Public restrooms and pay showers on Ballaine Boulevard along the ocean between the boat harbor and downtown. There are well-marked day-use picnic areas with ocean views and covered tables along Ballaine Boulevard, just south of the harbor, and at Adams Street.

For hostel accommodations, phone Moby Dick Hostel at (907) 224-7072; website: www.mobydickhostel.com.

Harbor 360 Hotel. Seward's premier waterfront hotel located directly on the waterfront of the Seward Small Boat Harbor. Hotel features 360-degree views, pool and hot tub, free breakfast and convenient location. Glacier and wildlife cruises depart from dock directly behind hotel. Open year-round. 1-888-514-8687 or (907) 865-6224; harbor360hotel.com. [ADVERTISEMENT]

Camping

Waterfront Park Municipal Campground (City of Seward) provides designated tent and RV camping along the waterfront between the Seward Boat Harbor and historic downtown, with most camping areas located along Ballaine Boulevard. Camping fee charged, no reservations for individuals (the city does accept reservations for caravan groups of 10 units or more). Campers should pick a numbered site then register and pay at nearest automated pay station (most are located at camping area entrances). Display printed permit at site or on vehicle dash so it can be read from the outside. There are restrooms with coin-operated showers; 99 sites offer water and electric hookups; 22 tent-only sites; over 150 dry RV sites; dump station $5. No public consumption of alcohol. Pets on leash. Camping fees for high season (June 1 to Sept. 30) area: tent site (maximum 2 tents), $10; dry RV site, $20; RV sites with water and electric (50/30/20 amp), $40. Major credit cards and cash are accepted (no checks). See more information at www.cityofseward.us under Visitors>Parks>Campgrounds or phone the City of Seward at (907) 224-4055.

Camping along the Seward Highway includes the luxurious **Stoney Creek** RV Park with full hookups and all amenities, located at **Milepost S 6.3**; the wooded **Forest Acres Municipal Campground** at **Milepost S 2.5** (no hookups); and the municipal **Spring Creek Campground** (no hookups), located 5.1 miles east of **Milepost 3.2** on Nash Road, with fees of $20/RV, $10/tent, $5/parking (July 1 through Sept. 30 or as posted).

Transportation

Air: Seward airport is reached by turning east on Airport Road at **Milepost S 2.7** on the Seward Highway. There is no scheduled service into Anchorage. Flightsee with Marathon Helicopters; fly-in fishing and backcountry drop-offs are also available, ask locally or at the visitor's center.

Railroad: Seward is Mile 0 of the Alaska Railroad. The Alaska Railroad connects Seward to Anchorage and Fairbanks. Depot at 410 Port Ave., open daily 10 A.M. to 6 P.M. from mid-May to mid-Sept.

Bus: Scheduled service to Anchorage.

Taxi: Service available.

Car Rental: Hertz, phone (907) 224-4378.

Highway: Seward is Mile 0 of the Seward Highway. The 127-mile Seward Highway (Alaska Routes 9 and 1) connects Seward with Anchorage.

Cruise Ships: Seward is port of call for several cruiselines, including Holland America, Celebrity, Norwegian Cruise Lines, Royal Caribbean, Silversea and Regent Seven Seas.

Charter Boats: Check at the Seward Boat Harbor and see advertisements this section.

Private Boats: Contact the Harbormaster; phone (907) 224-3138.

Attractions

Walking Tour of Seward encompasses more than 30 attractions including homes and businesses that date back to the early 1900s; some are still being used, while others have been restored as historic sites. A brochure containing details on all the attractions of the tour is available at the visitor center or online at www.seward.com. The complete tour covers about 2 miles and takes 1 to 2 hours, depending upon how much time you wish to spend browsing. Walking the bike path along the water is your best bet at spotting sea otters in the bay.

Murals. Seward was named the "Mural Capital of Alaska" in 2008 by Gov. Sarah Palin at the completion of the town's 12th colorful outdoor mural. Don't miss these outdoor artworks created by the Seward Mural Society. The murals are designed by Alaskan artists, including Jon Van Zyle, Tom Missel, Gail Niebrugge, Susan Swiderski, Dot Bardarson and Barbara LaVallee.

Each artist's design is projected on to sheets of Alumalite and traced with pens, then each outlined shape is assigned a number corresponding to a paint color. Society members and volunteers fill in the colors.

The Alaska SeaLife Center is the only facility in Alaska that combines a public aquarium with marine research, public education and wildlife rescue and rehabilitation. The Center is situated on Resurrection Bay at Mile 0 of the scenic Seward Highway. Visitors to this "window to the sea" can have close encounters with puffins, octopuses, sea lions and other marine life while learning from the staff of educators and studying Alaska's rich seas and diverse sea life. The Alaska SeaLife Center has nearly 2,000 invertebrates, fish, seabirds, and marine mammals on exhibit—approximately 177 different species—and offers a variety of tours and encounters for all ages.

Behind the Scenes tours and puffin, octopus, and marine mammal encounters are a few of the options for enhancing visitors' experiences. Call ahead or ask the ticketing staff for schedules, pricing and details. Open daily year-round. Admission fee charged. Age restrictions apply on some tours. Call toll-free 1-888-378-2525 or online at www. alaskasealife.org.

©Sharon Nault

Seward Community Library & Museum are combined in a strikingly modern building at 239 6th Ave., on the corner of Sixth and Adams. The Seward Community Library & Museum acts as a community center with the facilities and resources to offer continuing education, community enrichment, live entertainment and the continued preservation of Seward's heritage.

The library offers more than 30,000 volumes, including recorded books, music, computer CDs and DVDs, and digital content for download. Free WiFi, 4 public access computers and 5 laptops for use in the building. The museum contains thousands of objects, photographs and archives that represent the history of Seward. Special programs are offered for visitors and local residents. The community rooms are available for scheduled use. For current hours and other information, phone (907) 224-4082.

Visit the Seward Boat Harbor. This busy municipal harbor, built after the 1964 earthquake, is home port to fishing boats, a number of sailboats, charter boats, sea kayak expeditions and sightseeing boats. This is where you board for day cruises out to Kenai Fjords National Park (*see description on page 537*), with outfits like Major Marine Tours or stop by the Adventure Center to book a Kenai Fjords or Fox Island guided kayak trip with Sunny Cove Sea Kayaking (descriptions follow).

Around 5 P.M. on most summer evenings, you can watch charter boats return to dock with their clients. For those who are not fishing, it is a chance to see what was caught that day as charters bring in their fish to weigh, display and clean. The harbor is also home to sea otters, harbor seals and bald eagles—watch for them!

Major Marine Tours. Wildlife and glacier cruises into the Kenai Fjords National Park and Prince William Sound. See whales, otters, puffins, and more. Cruises hosted by park rangers and offer junior ranger programs for kids. Large boats feature reserved table seating inside heated cabins. Freshly prepared salmon and prime rib meal served onboard. Daily departures from Seward and Whittier, March through October. 1-800-764-7300 or (907) 274-7300; www.major marine.com. See display ad on page 537.
[ADVERTISEMENT]

Sunny Cove Sea Kayaking. Kayak along the cliffs and coves of Fox Island. Watch otters, harbor seals and eagles along the coastline of Resurrection Bay or paddle amongst bergy bits and calving glaciers in Kenai Fjords National Park. Our guides provide an educational and fun eco-friendly tour. No experience necessary. Phone (907) 224-4426 or visit www.sunnycove.com.
[ADVERTISEMENT]

St. Peter's Episcopal Church, at the corner of 2nd Avenue and Adams Street, was built in 1906. It is considered the oldest

Protestant church on the Kenai Peninsula. In 1925, Dutch artist Jan Van Emple was commissioned to paint the Resurrection, for which Alaskans were used as models and Resurrection Bay as the background. Obtain key to church from the Seward Museum.

Mount Marathon Race®. Good things rarely come out of a bar bet, but 2 Sourdoughs wagered whether Mount Marathon could be climbed in under an hour and Seward's annual Fourth of July endurance race was born. The first year of the official race is uncertain with records that indicate that it was either 1912 or 1915. This run to the top of Mount Marathon (elev. 3,022 feet) and back down is a grueling test for athletes. The descent is so steep that it's part run, part jump and part slide. The race attracts competitors from all over, and thou-

Waterfront path between the Alaska Sealife Center and Seward Boat Harbor is perfect for walking, jogging, biking and dog walking. *(©Kris Valencia, staff)*

sands of spectators line the route each year.

The race start is in downtown Seward at 4th and Adams. Spectators congregate along 4th Avenue, where there is always food, music and lots of excitement. The crowd then follows the racers as they make their way up 4th Avenue then to the end of Jefferson and up Lowell Canyon Road. The race finish at 4th and Washington is marked by medics standing by to bandage cuts, scrapes and bruises. This race shares the claim as the second oldest footrace in America; entries are limited and fill up months in advance. Details on the race and sign-up information found at http://mmr.seward.com.

Hikers wanting to try climbing Mount Marathon can find the trailhead at **Milepost S 0.6** on Monroe Street.

Drive Lowell Point Road. This winding gravel road, narrow in places (with potholes, unless recently graded), hugs the shore of Resurrection Bay on its way to Lowell Point, 3 miles from downtown Seward. Many visitors just walk out the first 0.2 mile to see the gushing Lowell Creek waterfall cascade down under a bridge. Lowell Point Road accesses beachcombing, hiking, camping, boating and historical sites. Also access to **Sunny Cove Sea Kayaking** office where clients meet up with their guides for the Resurrection Bay Tour. *Large vehicles and RVs use extra care when meeting oncoming traffic on Lowell Point Road. Watch for fallen rocks on road.*

At Mile 1.8 is the turnoff for Silver Derby Campground & RV Park. At Mile 2.3, turn right on Pinnacle View Road and continue 0.2 mile for entrance to **Lowell Point State Recreation Site**. The 2-tiered parking area accommodates cars and small RVs only (no trailers or big rigs). The Caines Head (Coastal) Trail leaves from this recreation site and accesses sites within Caines Head State Recreation Area. Fort McGilray, an abandoned WWII fort at Caines Head, is a 7.4-mile hike (1-way). Tonsina Point is 2.1 miles 1-way. Hiking this trail beyond Tonsina Point requires advance planning due to tides; for details visit dnr.alaska.gov/parks/units/caineshd.htm.

Continue on Pinnacle View Road (past the Lowell Point SRS turnoff) for Lowell Point State Recreation Area; beach parking lot and access to a narrow stretch of rocky shore for beachcombing. Pinnacle View Road ends at Beach Drive, and Beach Drive loops back to Border Avenue. (Lowell Point Road becomes Border Avenue). Miller's Landing (camping, cabins, boat rentals) is located at the end of Border Avenue at Beach Road.

Fishing tournaments add to the excitement and fun of fishing out of Seward. The Annual Halibut Tournament® begins at 6 A.M. June 1 and ends at 8 P.M. June 30. The Annual Seward Silver Salmon Derby® in August is one of the oldest and largest sporting events in Alaska (since 1956). Record derby catch to date is a 22.24-lb. salmon caught by Shirley Baysinger of Cooper Landing, AK. For more details, phone (907) 224-8051, email events@seward.com, or go to Seward.com.

AREA FISHING: Charter and rental boats are available. Public boat launch. Fishing in Resurrection Bay, coho salmon to 22 lbs., use herring, troll or cast, July to October; chinook salmon to 45 lbs., May to August; also bottom fish, flounder, halibut to 300 lbs. and cod. Use jig-weighted spoons and large red spinners for year-round fishing for these species.

SEWARD ADVERTISERS

Seward Harbor is a hub of activity in summer with daily departures of boat tours to Kenai Fjords National Park.
(©Kris Valencia, staff)

Kenai Fjords National Park was formed when glaciers flowed down to the sea from the Harding Icefield and then retreated, leaving behind fjords, the deeply carved glacial valleys filled with sea water. These fjords characterize the park's coastline.

Substantial populations of marine mammals inhabit or migrate through the park's coastal waters, including sea otters, Steller sea lions, Dall porpoises and whales. Icebergs from calving glaciers provide ideal refuge for harbor seals, and the rugged coastline provides habitat for more than 100,000 nesting birds.

The park's scenic coastline and coastal wildlife is most commonly viewed by private kayak tours (Lowell Point Road), or by day-cruises that depart from Seward's Small Boat Harbor daily in summer (see advertisements this section).

Two public-use cabins are located in the park at Holgate Arm and Aialik Bay. The cabins are available for use in summer (Memorial Day weekend through Labor Day) by reservation only. Reservations are available at www.recreation.gov or phone 1-877-444-6777. The park's website has descriptions of the cabins; go to www.nps.gov/kefj/planyourvisit/lodging.htm.

Kayakers and boaters may camp on the beaches but must be aware ahead of time of land status. Some 42,000 acres of coastline are owned by Native corporations. Public camping is available by permit only from the Native corporations. For more information about Native lands and permits, phone (907) 284-2212. Maps indicating land ownership are available from the park visitor center.

NOTE: Private boaters should consult with the Harbormaster in Seward for detailed information on boating conditions.

Another dominant feature of the 699,983-acre Kenai Fjords National Park is the Harding Icefield, a 695-square-mile vestige of the last ice age. Harding Icefield can be reached by a strenuous all-day hike (8.2 miles round trip, 3,500-foot elevation gain) from the base of Exit Glacier or by a charter flightseeing trip out of Seward.

Exit Glacier is the most accessible of the park's glaciers. Turn at **Milepost S 3.7** on the Seward Highway and follow Herman Leirer Road to the Nature Center parking area. **Exit Glacier Nature Center** is open daily from Memorial Day weekend through Labor Day, from 9 A.M. to 8 P.M. The center offers interpretive programs, exhibits and has a bookstore.

Several trails in the Exit Glacier area afford excellent views of the ice and surrounding mountains. A 1-mile trail leads from the parking lot to the glacier. The 8.2-mile round trip Harding Icefield Trail is a spectacular day hike. Make sure to heed safety signs as you approach the glacier, since glacier ice is unstable, unpredictable and *very dangerous*.

Ranger-led nature walks are available in summer at 10 A.M., 2 P.M. and 4 P.M. There is also a picnic area and 12 walk-in campsites at Exit Glacier. Visitor information is available at the Exit Glacier Nature Center; open summer only. Exit Glacier is accessible in winter by skis, dogsled or snow machine. One public-use cabin is available in winter by permit. Call (907) 422-0500 for additional information on Exit Glacier's winter-only Willow Cabin.

Videos, exhibits and information on Kenai Fjords National Park and organized activities at the park are available at the park visitor center on 4th Avenue in the Seward Boat Harbor area next to the Harbormaster's office. The center is open daily Memorial Day weekend–Labor Day from 9 A.M. to 7 P.M. Shoulder season hours are 9 A.M. to 5 P.M. The center is closed in winter.

You may write to Kenai Fjords National Park via the address: Box 1727, Seward, AK 99664, or phone the park office at (907) 442-0500. There is also Visitor Information available via recorded message at (907) 422-0573 and additional information for visitors at their website at www.nps.gov/kefj.

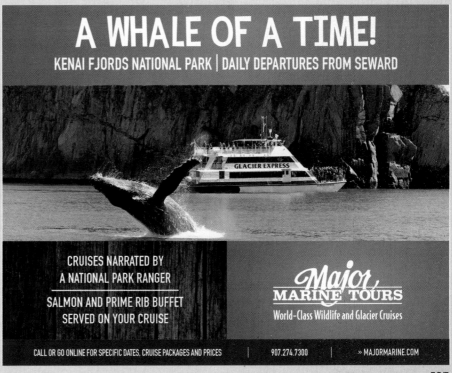

Sterling Highway

CONNECTS: Seward Highway to Homer, AK

Length: 142 miles   **Road Surface:** Paved   **Season:** Open all year

(See maps, pages 539–540)

1

From rest area at top of Homer Hill, Milepost S 169.6 Sterling Highway, a sweeping view of Kachemak Bay and Cook Inlet. (©Kris Valencia, staff)

Distance in miles	Anchorage	Homer	Kenai	Seward	Soldotna
Anchorage		226	158	127	147
Homer	226		90	173	79
Kenai	158	90		105	11
Seward	127	173	105		94
Soldotna	147	79	11	94	

The Sterling Highway (Alaska Route 1) begins 90 miles south of Anchorage at its junction with the Seward Highway at Tern Lake and ends 142 miles later at the end of Homer Spit in Homer. Several major Kenai Peninsula side roads junction with the Sterling Highway and are also logged in this text including: Skilak Lake (Loop) Road, Swanson River Road, Kenai Spur Highway, Kalifornsky Beach Road, Funny River Road, Cohoe Loop Road and Anchor River (Beach) Road.

The Sterling Highway, open year-round, is a paved, mostly 2-lane highway, with some passing lanes and some short sections of 4-lane highway. It passes through Chugach National Forest and Kenai National Wildlife Refuge. The Kenai Mountains are home to Dall sheep, mountain goats, black and brown bears and caribou. The many lakes, rivers and streams of the Kenai Peninsula are well-known for their sport fishing.

From Soldotna south, the Sterling Highway follows the west coast of the Peninsula along Cook Inlet. There are beautiful views of the volcanic peaks of Spurr, Redoubt, and Iliamna in the Chigmit Mountains across Cook Inlet.

The Sterling Highway opened in the fall of 1950, connecting the small communities and scattered homesteads on the west side of the Kenai Peninsula with the road to Seward on the east side. The Sterling Highway was named in honor of Hawley Sterling, an engineer of the Alaska Road Commission.

Emergency Services: Dial 911 or use CB channels 9, 11 or 19. Hospitals are located in Seward, Soldotna and Homer. Alaska State

(Continues on page 541)

Major Attractions:

©Kris Valencia, staff

Russian Orthodox Churches, Homer Spit Kenai River, Kenai National Wildlife Refuge

Sterling Highway Tern Lake Junction to Soldotna, AK

© 2019 The MILEPOST®

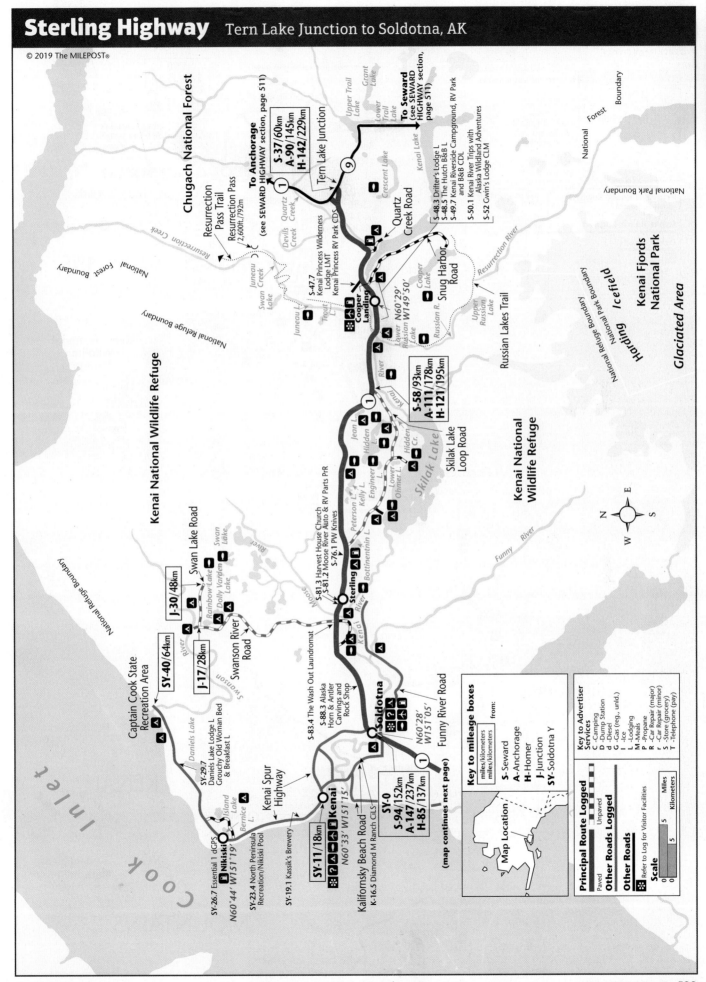

Chugach National Forest

Resurrection Pass Trail
Resurrection Pass 2,600ft/792m

To Anchorage
(see SEWARD HIGHWAY section, page 511)

S-37/60km
A-90/145km
H-142/229km

Tern Lake Junction

To Seward
(see SEWARD HIGHWAY section, page 511)

Upper Trail Lake
Lower Trail Lake
Grant Lake
Kenai Lake

Quartz Creek Road

S-48.3 Drifter's Lodge L
S-48.5 The Hutch B&B CDL and B&B CDL
S-49.7 Kenai Riverside Campground, RV Park and Alaska Wildland Adventures
S-50.1 Kenai River Trips with Alaska Wildland Adventures
S-52 Gwin's Lodge CLM

Crescent Lake

Devils Creek
Quartz Creek

S-47.7 Kenai Princess Wilderness Lodge LMT
Kenai Princess RV Park CDS

Resurrection River

Cooper Landing   N60°29' W149°50'

Snug Harbor Road

Lower Russian Lake
Upper Russian Lake

Russian R.

Russian Lakes Trail

Kenai Fjords National Park

Harding Icefield

Glaciated Area

Kenai National Wildlife Refuge

National Refuge Boundary
National Park Boundary

National Forest Boundary

National Forest Boundary

National Refuge Boundary

Resurrection Creek

Juneau Creek
Swan Lake
Juneau L.
Trout L.

Kenai River

S-58/93km
A-111/178km
H-121/195km

Skilak Lake Loop Road

Jean L.
Hidden L.
Peterson L.
Kelly L.
Engineer L.
Lower Ohmer L.
Hidden Cr.

Skilak Lake

Kenai National Wildlife Refuge

Funny River

Funny River Road

Swan Lake Road
J-30/48km

Rainbow Lake
Dolly Varden Lake
Swan Lake

SY-40/64km

J-17/28km

Swanson River Road

Swanson River

Moose River

S-81.3 Harvest House Church
S-81.2 Moose River Auto & RV Parts PrR
S-76.1 PW Knives

Sterling
Bottinentnin L.

Kenai River

S-83.4 The Wash Out Laundromat
S-88.3 Alaska Horn & Antler Carvings and Rock Shop

Captain Cook State Recreation Area

Daniels Lake
SY-29.7 Daniels Lake Lodge L
Grouchy Old Woman Bed & Breakfast L

Kenai Spur Highway

Island Lake
Bernice L.

SY-26.7 Essential 1 dGPS
Nikiski   N60°44' W151°19'

SY-23.4 North Peninsula Recreation/Nikiski Pool

SY-19.1 Kassik's Brewery

Kenai   N60°33' W151°15'

SY-11/18km

K-16.5 Diamond M Ranch CILS
Kaliformsky Beach Road

Soldotna   N60°28' W151°05'

SY-0
S-94/152km
A-147/237km
H-85/137km

(map continues next page)

Key to mileage boxes
miles/kilometers
miles/kilometers
from:
S-Seward
A-Anchorage
H-Homer
J-Junction
SY-Soldotna Y

Key to Advertiser Services
C -Camping
D -Dump Station
d -Diesel
G -Gas (reg., unld.)
I -Ice
L -Lodging
M -Meals
P -Propane
R -Car Repair (major)
r -Car Repair (minor)
S -Store (grocery)
T -Telephone (pay)

Map Location

Principal Route Logged
Paved
Unpaved
Other Roads Logged
Other Roads
Refer to Log for Visitor Facilities

Scale
Miles
Kilometers

N E S W

Cook Inlet

Sterling Highway Soldotna, AK, to Homer, AK

© 2019 The MILEPOST®

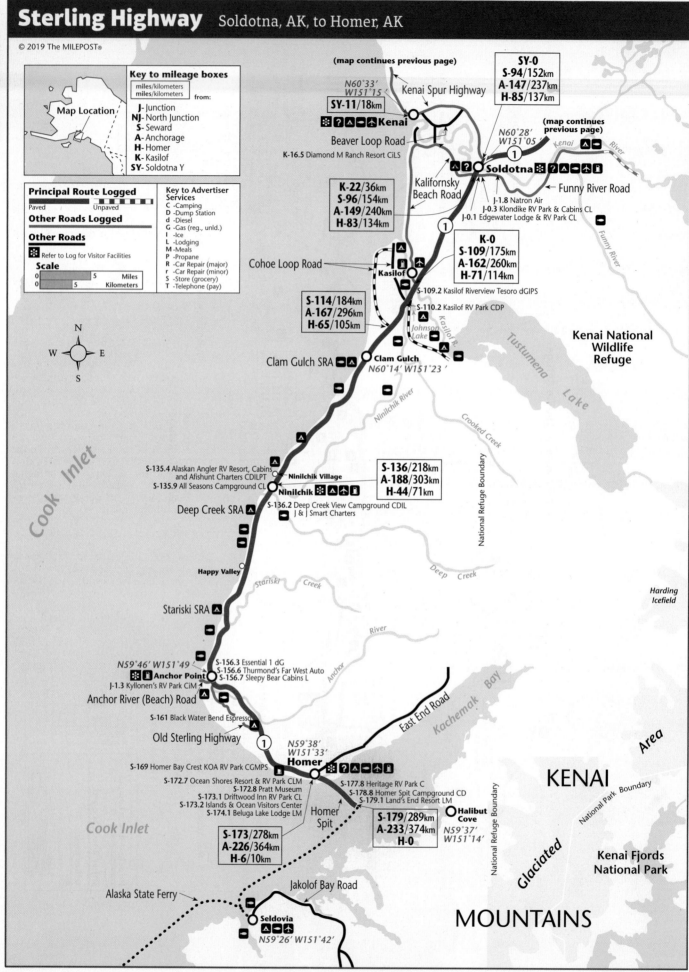

Key to mileage boxes

miles/kilometers
miles/kilometers from:

J- Junction
NJ- North Junction
S- Seward
A- Anchorage
H- Homer
K- Kasilof
SY- Soldotna Y

Map Location

Principal Route Logged
Paved   Unpaved

Other Roads Logged

Other Roads

❄ Refer to Log for Visitor Facilities

Scale
0   5   Miles
0   5   Kilometers

Key to Advertiser Services
C -Camping
D -Dump Station
d -Diesel
G -Gas (reg., unld.)
I -Ice
L -Lodging
M -Meals
P -Propane
R -Car Repair (major)
r -Car Repair (minor)
S -Store (grocery)
T -Telephone (pay)

(map continues previous page)

N60°33' W151°15'

Kenai Spur Highway

SY-11/18km

Kenai

Beaver Loop Road

K-16.5 Diamond M Ranch Resort CiLS

SY-0
S-94/152km
A-147/237km
H-85/137km

(map continues previous page)

N60°28' W151°05'

Kenai River

1

Soldotna

K-22/36km
S-96/154km
A-149/240km
H-83/134km

Kalifornsky Beach Road

Funny River Road

J-1.8 Natron Air
J-0.3 Klondike RV Park & Cabins CL
J-0.1 Edgewater Lodge & RV Park CL

1

K-0
S-109/175km
A-162/260km
H-71/114km

Cohoe Loop Road

Kasilof

S-109.2 Kasilof Riverview Tesoro dGIPS

Funny River

S-114/184km
A-167/296km
H-65/105km

S-110.2 Kasilof RV Park CDP

Johnson Lake

Kasilof R.

Kenai National Wildlife Refuge

Tustumena Lake

Clam Gulch SRA

Clam Gulch
N60°14' W151°23'

Ninilchik River

Crooked Creek

National Refuge Boundary

S-135.4 Alaskan Angler RV Resort, Cabins
and Afishunt Charters CDILPT
Ninilchik Village
S-135.9 All Seasons Campground CL

Ninilchik

S-136/218km
A-188/303km
H-44/71km

Deep Creek SRA

S-136.2 Deep Creek View Campground CDIL
J & J Smart Charters

Cook Inlet

Happy Valley

Starlski Creek

Deep Creek

Harding Icefield

Stariski SRA

River

Anchor

S-156.3 Essential 1 dG
S-156.6 Thurmond's Far West Auto
Anchor Point
S-156.7 Sleepy Bear Cabins L
N59°46' W151°49'
J-1.3 Kyllonen's RV Park CiM

Anchor River (Beach) Road

S-161 Black Water Bend Espresso

Old Sterling Highway

East End Road

Kachemak Bay

1

N59°38' W151°33'

S-169 Homer Bay Crest KOA RV Park CGMPS

Homer

S-172.7 Ocean Shores Resort & RV Park CLM
S-172.8 Pratt Museum
S-173.1 Driftwood Inn RV Park CL
S-173.2 Islands & Ocean Visitors Center
S-174.1 Beluga Lake Lodge LM

S-177.8 Heritage RV Park C
S-178.8 Homer Spit Campground CD
S-179.1 Land's End Resort LM

KENAI

Homer Spit

Halibut Cove

S-173/278km
A-226/364km
H-6/10km

S-179/289km
A-233/374km
H-0

N59°37' W151°14'

Cook Inlet

National Refuge Boundary

National Park Boundary

Glaciated

Kenai Fjords National Park

Alaska State Ferry

Jakolof Bay Road

MOUNTAINS

Seldovia

N59°26' W151°42'

(Continued from page 538)
Trooper Post locations are in Cooper Landing, phone (907) 595-1233; Soldotna, (907) 262-4453; Anchor Point, (907) 235-8239; Ninilchik, (907) 567-3660.

Sterling Highway Log

Distance from Seward (S) is followed by distance from Anchorage (A) and distance from highway end on Homer Spit (H). Physical mileposts show distance from Seward.

ALASKA ROUTE 1

S 37 A 90 H 142.1 Tern Lake Junction, the T-intersection of the Sterling Highway with the Seward Highway. Two-way traffic.

> **Junction** with Seward Highway (Alaska Route 9) to Seward and Anchorage. Turn to **Milepost S 37** on page 528 in the SEWARD HIGHWAY section for log.

Turnout to south for **Tern Lake Wildlife Viewing Area**; parking areas along lake. Watch for Arctic terns in spring and trumpeter swans in the fall. Bears are occasionally spotted on the small islands in Tern Lake. Begin Alaska Scenic Byway westbound.

S 37.3 A 90.3 H 141.8 Turnoff to south for **USFS Tern Lake Picnic Area**; toilet and salmon viewing platform. Gravel trail leads to secluded picnic sites in forest with tables and firepits (no overnight camping). Access to Old Sterling Highway (signed).

Begin 1.7-mile passing lane westbound.
CAUTION: Watch for moose and bear.

S 37.5 A 90.5 H 141.6 One-way southbound traffic from Seward Highway merges with westbound Sterling Highway traffic here.

Eastbound sign—"Hospital 38 miles"—refers to Providence Seward Medical Center, which is approximately 38 miles south and the nearest hospital in case of emergency. Cooper Landing, 11 miles west, has a volunteer ambulance. Central Peninsula Hospital in Soldotna is 58 miles west of here.

S 38 A 91 H 141.1 Distance marker westbound shows Soldotna 57 miles, Kenai 60 miles, Homer 131 miles.

S 38.5 A 91.5 H 140.6 Distance marker westbound shows Cooper Landing 6 miles.

S 39.6 A 92.6 H 139.5 Dave's Creek (sign). Dave's Creek flows west into Quartz Creek.

S 40 A 93 H 139.1 Begin 0.5-mile passing lane westbound.

S 40.2 A 93.2 H 138.9 Turnout to north. Avalanche gates.

S 40.8 A 93.8 H 138.3 Quartz Creek. This stream empties into Kenai Lake.

S 41.9 A 94.9 H 137.2 Small paved turnout to south. Distance marker eastbound shows Seward Highway 5 miles.

S 42.5 A 95.1 H 137 Large paved double-ended scenic viewpoint to south with information boards.

S 42.8 A 95.8 H 136.3 Small turnout to south.

S 43 A 96 H 136.1 Small turnout to south.

Begin 1-mile passing lane westbound.

S 43.5 A 96.5 H 135.6 Small paved turnout to south.

S 43.7 A 96.7 H 135.4 Small paved turnout to south.

S 44 A 97 H 135.1 Solid waste transfer to south; easy access loop road, hours posted.

S 44.5 A 97.5 H 134.4 Small gravel turnout to north.
CAUTION: Watch for horses.

S 44.9 A 97.9 H 134.2 Sunrise Inn to south; cafe, bar, motel, regular gas (pre-pay in cafe/bar), RV Park. **Junction** with **Quartz Creek Road** (description follows), which leads south to Quartz Creek day-use area (0.2 mile) and **Quartz Creek Campground** (0.5 mile) on **Kenai Lake**. The campground has 45 sites (will accommodate large RVs), some pull-thrus, tables, firepits, firewood ($6), flush toilets, dump station ($8), camping fee; reservations, www.recreation.gov.

Quartz Creek Road continues south from Quartz Creek day-use area and campground on Kenai Lake to a fork in the road at Mile 1.1: keep left for Crescent Creek campground and trailhead (2.8 miles). The campground has 9 level sites on a gravel loop in a heavily wooded area, toilet, firepits, tables, water pump, bear-proof food box. The Crescent Creek trail leads 6.2 miles to **Crescent Lake**; stocked with grayling.

If you keep right at the fork at Mile 1.1, drive 0.3 mile to second fork and keep right again; then continue 0.2 mile past private homes to road end at Kenai Lake and picnic area.

CAUTION: Slow for turning traffic. Highway narrows, winding road, westbound. Begin posted speed zone; no passing zone westbound. Begin 0.5-mile passing lane eastbound.

Distance marker eastbound shows Seward 43 miles, Anchorage 98 miles.

S 45 A 98 H 134.1 Kenai Lake. Westbound travelers are entering one of Alaska's best-known lake and river fishing regions. Kenai Lake drainage—all lakes and tributaries—are closed to salmon fishing. *NOTE: The diversity of fishing conditions and frequent sport fish regulation changes on all Kenai waters make it advisable to consult the local ADF&G for fishing news and regulation updates or online at www.adfg.alaska.gov.*

See the Upper Kenai River map on page 543 and the Lower Kenai River map on pages 556–557 for reference.

The proposed Sterling Highway Milepost 45–60 Project will construct 5.5 miles of new alignment. The proposed Cooper Landing Bypass Environmental Impact Statement was signed in March 2018, bringing to close one of the longest active environmental documents in the U.S. Started nearly 40 years ago, the project has been particularly challenging to develop due to its proximity to the Kenai River, Kenai Lake, Kenai National Wildlife Refuge and Resurrection Pass trail, as well as its rugged terrain, nearby historic and cultural resources sites, and limited right-of-way, according to the Alaska Dept. of Transportation and Public Facilities. A construction schedule had not yet been decided at our press time.

S 45.6 A 98.6 H 133.5 Large paved turnout to south; view of Kenai Lake through trees. Watch for Dall sheep on mountainside above highway.

S 47 A 100 H 132.1 Small paved turnout to south.

S 47.1 A 100.1 H 132 Small paved turnout to south.

S 47.2 A 100.2 H 131.9 View of Kenai Lake. Restaurant to south.

S 47.4 A 100.4 H 131.7 *CAUTION: Slow for posted speed zone westbound through Cooper Landing. Heavily congested area with many driveways fronting the highway. Narrow road, no passing. Drive with care.*

S 47.5 A 100.5 H 131.6 Wildman's to north, open year-round; convenience store, laundromat and showers, restrooms, espresso, ice cream shop, liquor store, food service and shuttle service.

S 47.7 A 100.7 H 131.4 Turnoff to north on paved Bean Creek Road and drive 1.9 miles for **Kenai Princess Wilderness Lodge** and **Kenai Princess RV Park** (description follows). Beautiful setting! View of Kenai River from lodge, outside dining on deck overlooking river. Also Kenai River view from paved turnout at Mile 1.1.

Kenai Princess Lodge. See display ad on this page.

Kenai Princess RV Park. A stunning wilderness setting on the Kenai River. Premier RV accommodations with water, septic, TV hookup and power at each site. General store, laundry, showers. Dining, lounge and free wireless at Kenai Princess Lodge. Mile 47.7 Sterling Highway, 17225 Frontier Circle, Cooper Landing, AK 99572. Mid-May through mid-September. $45 per night.

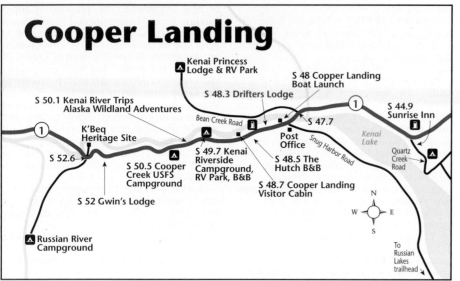

Cooper Landing

S 47.8 A 100.8 H 131.3 Bridge over Kenai River at mouth of **Kenai Lake**. The pedestrian walkway on the bridge is accessible from the Cooper Landing boat launch facility at **Milepost S 48**: It is a good spot for photos of the river.

Kenai Lake serves as the headwaters of the Kenai River Special Management Area (KRSMA), established in 1984 to protect this unique resource. The 105-mile-long KRSMA stretches from Kenai Lake almost to the city of Kenai. The highway travels alongside the Kenai River for the next 10 miles westbound.

S 47.9 A 100.9 H 131.2 Junction with **Snug Harbor Road** (description follows), which leads 12.1 miles south to Cooper Lake. Volunteer fire department to north. Alaska State Trooper station.

From the Sterling Highway, Snug Harbor Road leads 0.1 mile south to the post office and continues past St. John Neumann Catholic Church to pavement end at Mile 1.8. (Road conditions on the gravel portion of Snug Harbor Road depend on grading.) *Watch for children at Mile 4*. Primitive road leads to shore of Kenai Lake (check before driving) at Mile 5.7. Gravel road continues along Kenai Lake to Mile 8.2, then begins a long ascent to a mountain valley. At Mile

8.9 is a winter recreation parking area for snow machine access to Chugach National Forest; outhouse. At Mile 10.8 is the **Rainbow Lake** trailhead; ¼-mile hike to lake stocked with rainbow trout. The road reaches the **Russian Lakes** trailhead at Mile 11.3. (*NOTE: Large vehicles use trailhead turnouts to turn around; there is limited to no room at end of road.*)

The 23-mile-long Russian Lakes trail is open to hikers and mountain bikes in summer, cross-country skiers in winter (check seasons for horses and snow machines); permits required for public-use cabins on trail. Reserve at www.recreation. gov or call 1-877-444-6777. Primitive ATV trail to Cooper Lake at Mile 11.8.

Snug Harbor Road ends at a gate at Mile 12.1 by Cooper Lake. Beautiful Cooper Lake offers informal camping. There is very limited turnaround space here and the short access road to the lake may be in poor condition.

S 48 A 101 H 131.1 Turnoff to north on King Salmon Drive for access road to **Cooper Landing State Recreation Site** Boat Launch Facility, adjacent to the Kenai River Bridge. Pleasant rest area/day-use facility adjacent boat launch has toilets, walkways along Kenai River, information boards and telescopes. $5 parking fee after 30-minute grace period. The state boat launch has a concrete boat ramp. $10 launch fee.

Upper Kenai River, from **Kenai Lake** to **Skilak Lake**, including Skilak Lake within a half mile of the Kenai River inlet, special regulations apply. For current recorded fishing forecast, phone (907) 267-2502 in Anchorage or (907) 262-2737 in Soldotna. Coho salmon 5 to 15 lbs., July 1–Oct. 31; pink salmon 3 to 7 lbs., July–August; sockeye salmon 3 to 12 lbs., June 11–mid-August; rainbow trout and Dolly Varden June 11–October. *IMPORTANT: Be familiar with current sport fish regulations and closures. Dates given here are subject to change!*

S 48.2 A 101.2 H 130.9 Grocery, hardware and tackle shop.
Slow for posted speed zone westbound.

S 48.3 A 101.3 H 130.8 Turn north for **Drifters Lodge** (description follows).

Drifters Lodge. Fishing–Rafting–Cabins. Guided rafting/scenic floats (good for all ages) easy 2-hour and 3-hour adventures leave 4 times daily. Certified fishing guides for salmon or trout, half- or full-day, kids to experts. Professional equipment included. Guided walk-in, fly-in drift/power boat. Call (907) 595-5555 now. www. dri[f]terslodge.com; info@drifterslodge.com. [ADVERTISEMENT]

Cooper Landing

S 48.4 A 101.4 H 130.7 Cooper Landing is located at the west end of Kenai Lake. **Population:** 250. **Emergency Services:** Dial 911. Nearest hospital is Central Peninsula in Soldotna (50-mile drive west of here) or Providence Seward Medical Center in Seward (48-mile drive east then south).

Visitor Information: Cooper Landing Chamber of Commerce operates in a building adjacent the museum at **Milepost S 48.7** that is operated by volunteers. Open daily in

Upper Kenai River

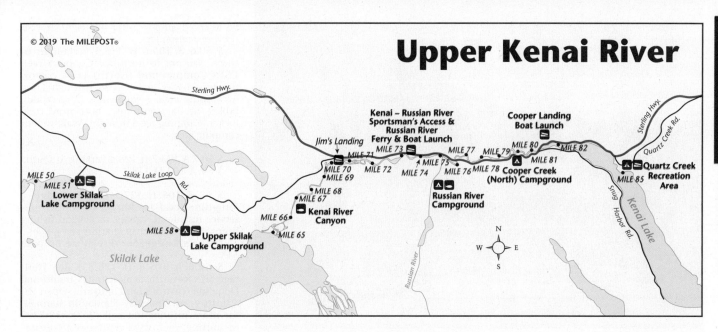

© 2019 The MILEPOST®

summer; email info@cooperlandingchamber.com.

Private Aircraft: State-owned Quartz Creek airstrip, 3 W; elev. 450 feet; length 2,200 feet; gravel; unattended. Floatplanes land at Cooper Lake.

Cooper Landing stretches along several miles of the Sterling Highway (see map). All visitor facilities are available in Cooper Landing including food, lodging, camping and a grocery. Gas at Grizzly Ridge (**Milepost S 48.5**) and Sunrise Inn (**Milepost S 44.9**). The post office is located on Snug Harbor Road, **Milepost S 47.9** Sterling Highway. The Cooper Landing Library is located at Mile 0.8 Bean Creek Road.

Cooper Landing was named for Joseph Cooper, a miner who discovered gold here in 1894. A school and post office opened in the 1920s to serve the miners and their families living in the area. Cooper Landing was connected to Kenai by road in 1948, and to Anchorage in 1951. Cooper Landing is a popular destination in summer thanks to its outdoor recreational activities. It is known for its fishing on the Upper Kenai River (see map above), scenic rafting trips, hiking and biking.

Cooper Landing Museum, located at **Milepost S 48.7,** is a fun stop for the whole family. The museum features a fully articulated brown bear skeleton. Look for the museum complex on the north side of the highway, housed in the pioneer school and post office buildings.

Sterling Highway Log
(continued)

S 48.4 A 101.4 H 130.7 *CAUTION: Slow*

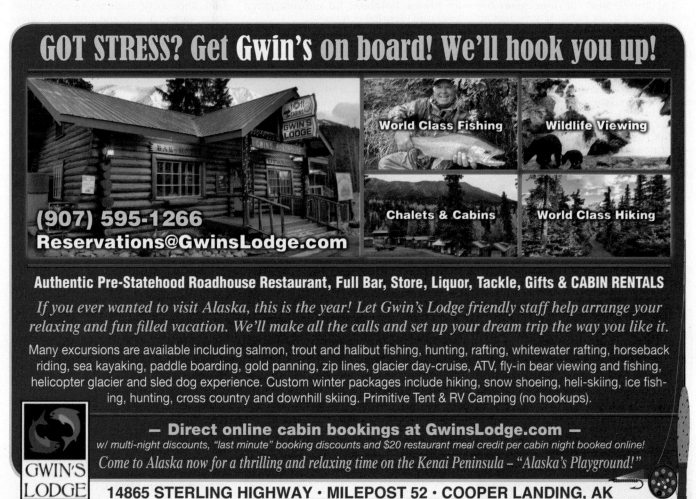

Cooper Landing State Recreation Site boat launch on the Kenai River. Turn off the highway at Milepost S 48 for this day-use area. (©Kris Valencia, staff)

for posted speed zone westbound. Heavily congested area next 4 miles, with many driveways fronting the highway. Narrow road, no passing.

S 48.5 A 101.5 H 130.6 Lodging at **The Hutch Bed & Breakfast** (description follows). Grizzly Ridge (formerly Hamilton's); gas/diesel, convenience store, camping.

The Hutch B&B. 12 clean, smoke-free rooms with private baths at very reasonable rates. Plus new 2-bedroom cabin. Continental breakfast served until 10 A.M. WiFi. Common area TV/VCR. View mountain goats, Dall sheep and Kenai River from our covered decks. Our parking area accommodates boat trailers and large vehicles. Look for the "Bunny Trail" sign. Phone (907) 595-1270, fax (907) 595-1829. See display ad on page 542. [ADVERTISEMENT]

S 48.7 A 101.7 H 130.4 Cooper Landing Museum and **Chamber of Commerce** on the north side of the highway, housed in the pioneer school and post office buildings. The museum features area history and a brown bear skeleton. A great stop!

S 49.7 A 102.7 H 129.4 Turn north for **Kenai Riverside Campground, RV Park and B&B** (description follows).

Kenai Riverside Campground, RV Park and B&B. On the banks of the Kenai River, in Cooper Landing. Open, level RV sites, most with partial hookups (20/30 amps plus water). Dry sites. B&B rooms and tent campsites available. Showers and dump station. Guest discounts on guided fishing and rafting trips. Visa/MasterCard; phone 1-888-KENAIRV (888-536-2478); info@ kenaiRV.com; www.kenaiRV.com/mp. See display ad this page. [ADVERTISEMENT]

S 50.1 A 103.1 H 129 Turnoff to north for **Alaska Wildland Adventures:** Kenai River trips (description follows).

Kenai River Trips with Alaska Wildland Adventures (AWA). Rafting and fishing day trips on the Kenai River since 1977. Join a scenic natural history float, a full-day Kenai Canyon raft trip, or fish with our friendly, professional guides for the Kenai River's world-famous salmon and rainbow trout. Gear provided; four raft departures daily. Located in Cooper Landing; look for the blue sign! Overnight cabin rentals with private bath available. Save $5 with this ad! 1-800-478-4100; info@alaskariver trips.com; www.alaskarivertrips.com/mp. See display ad on page 542. [ADVERTISEMENT]

S 50.5 A 103.5 H 128.6 Bridge over Cooper Creek.

Cooper Creek USFS Campground (South). Huge cottonwood trees mark the entrance to wooded camping area to south (Loop B): 23 large, level sites on good gravel road; tables, water, firepits, firewood, outhouses; campground host. Camping fee is $18 single, $28 double. Campsites may be reserved, phone 1-877-444-6777 or visit www.recreation.gov.

S 50.6 A 103.6 H 128.5 Restaurant to south. Turnoff to north for **Cooper Creek USFS Campground (North)** via a narrow 0.2-mile 1-way gravel road through Loop A camping area; 7 small sites (2 riverside), tables, firepits, outhouse, bear-proof food locker. Camping fee $18/night. Walk-in tent camping area.

S 50.7 A 103.7 H 128.4 Parking to south.

S 51 A 104 H 128.1 *Slow for posted speed zone eastbound.*

S 52 A 105 H 127.1 Gwin's Lodge, a long-time local landmark, to south; full-service restaurant, cabins, tackle and fishing licenses, gift shop, river charters and guides.

Gwin's Lodge. See display ad on page 543.

S 52.6 A 105.6 H 126.5 K'Beq Heritage Site to north demonstrates traditional Dena'ina customs and culture. Open 10 A.M. to 4 P.M. Thursday–Sunday in summer; for more information call (907) 335-7290 or online at www.kenaitze.org/culture/ kbeq-cultural-site/.

Turnoff to south for **USFS Russian River Campground** access road *(CAUTION: Slow for bumps and dips in road).* Fee station at Mile 0.2 and parking area; Upper Russian Lake and Russian Falls trailhead parking at Mile 1.1 (see trail descriptions following); dump station at Mile 1.3; Park Manager at Mile 1.6; camping and day-use sites to Mile 1.9; Lower Russian Lake trailhead parking at Mile 2.6. The Russian River Campground is often full during the summer, particularly during the Russian River sockeye salmon runs. Arrive early! There are 84 sites, toilets, water, tables, firepits and firewood. Camping fees (subject to change): $18 single RV occupancy, $28 double RV occupancy, $11 12-hour day-use parking, $8 dump station. Concessionaire-operated. Reserve campsites by phoning 1-877-444-6777 or visit www. recreation.gov.

The **Russian River**: Closed to all fishing May 2 through June 10. Bait prohibited at all times in Russian River drainage. Check regulations for limits and other restrictions. Sockeye salmon run starts mid-June. Second run begins July 20–25 and lasts about 3 weeks. Coho salmon to 15 lbs., run begins mid-August. *NOTE: Please do not clean fish at the river or in the campground; use Kenai River cleaning stations located near the ferry crossing. CAUTION: Bears in this area will get into belongings. Keep your backpack on or near. Do not leave food in your pack. Do not leave your cleaned fish lying around. Do NOT approach bears. There have been attacks in this area.*

Lower Russian Lakes Trail: elev. 500 feet; hiking time 1½ hours; good trail first 3 miles; spur trail to Russian River Falls viewing platform. A good place to view jumping salmon from mid-June–end of July, and a nice family hike. Handicap accessible trail. There are pathways and metal stairways to access the river's edge. Stay out of the green fenced areas. This area is under bank restoration. **Upper Russian Lake:** elev. 690 feet, 12 miles. Trail continues to Cooper Lake at end of Snug Harbor Road (see **Milepost S 47.9**). Public-use cabins along trail (reserve at www.recreation.gov/1-877-444-6777. Winter use: good snowmobiling to lower lake only, avalanche danger beyond.

S 53 A 106 H 126.1 Bridge over Kenai

COOPER LANDING ADVERTISERS

Alaska Wildland Adventures	Ph. 1-800-478-4100
Drifters Lodge	Ph. (907) 595-5555
Gwin's Lodge	Ph. (907) 595-1266
Hutch B&B, The	Ph. (907) 595-1270
Kenai Princess Lodge	Ph. 1-800-426-0500
Kenai Princess RV Park	Ph. (907) 595-1425
Kenai Riverside Campground, RV Park and B & B	Ph. 1-888-536-2478
Kenai River Trips	Ph. 1-800-478-4100

River. Cooper Landing (eastbound sign). Watch for bears and moose from bridge.

S 53.2 A 106.2 H 125.9 Wide shoulder parking to north. Gravel road leads north to **Resurrection Pass Trailhead**, large parking area with toilet and registration kiosk. This 38-mile-long USFS trail climbs to Resurrection Pass (elev. 2,600 feet) and descends to the north with trailhead near Hope on Turnagain Arm.

S 53.6 A 106.6 H 125.5 Turnout to south with 1,100-foot-long woodchip trail along Kenai River was established in 1992 to preserve, protect and interpret Kenaitze Indian Tribe cultural and natural resources in this area. Fishing access and parking (no RVs or trailers).

S 53.8 A 106.8 H 125.3 Turnout to south connects with Kenaitze woodchip trail along Kenai River.

Distance marker westbound shows Soldotna 41 miles, Kenai 44 miles, Homer 115 miles.

S 54.6 A 107.6 H 124.5 Small gravel parking area to south at Chugach National Forest boundary sign.

S 54.8 A 107.8 H 124.3 Small parking area to south is used by motorists who do not want to pay the daily fee at Sportsman's Landing.

S 54.9 A 107.9 H 124.2 Kenai and Russian River Access/Sportsman's Access Site (ADF&G)/Kenai and Russian River Ferry entrance to south; 180-space parking lot *(minimum 24-hour parking fee charged)*, scenic overlook, picnic tables, boat launch, toilets and access to bank fishing and ferry. Privately operated 26-person Russian River Ferry crosses the Kenai River to opposite bank and to the mouth of the Russian River for fishermen. Early sockeye salmon run usually arrives by June 15 on the Russian River. The second run usually arrives in mid-July and is the larger of the 2 runs. *CAUTION: Bears frequently walk the riverbanks. Call out if you see a bear.*

Fees (subject to change): 24-hour parking, vehicle under 20 feet, $11.25; vehicle over 20 feet, $14.25; ferry $10.25 adults, $5.15 children 3-11 years; boat launch $11.25. America the Beautiful, Senior and Access pass discounts may apply. During salmon season this recreation area is heavily used.

S 55 A 108 H 124.1 Entering Kenai National Wildlife Refuge westbound, administered by the USF&WS; contains more than 1.97 million acres of land set aside to preserve the moose, bear, sheep and other wildlife found here. Leaving Game Management Unit 7, entering Game Management Unit 15 westbound.

Distance marker eastbound shows Cooper Landing 7 miles, Seward 54 miles, Anchorage 108 miles.

NOTE: Actual driving distance between physical mileposts 55 and 58 is 3.6 miles.

S 55.5 A 108.5 H 123.6 Parking area to south; Kenai River access.

S 56.4 A 109.4 H 122.7 Double-ended parking area to south; Kenai River access.

S 56.8 A 109.8 H 122.3 Double-ended parking area to south; Kenai River access.

S 57.2 A 110.2 H 121.9 Fuller Lakes trailhead (well marked); parking to north. Steep hike with scenic views. No camping at trailhead. **Lower Fuller Lake**, Arctic grayling; **Upper Fuller Lake**, Dolly Varden.

S 57.9 A 110.9 H 121.2 Large gravel

Bears like fish too, so be alert for bears wherever you are fishing on the Kenai Peninsula.
(©Steven Miley)

parking area to north for Jim's Landing boat trailer overflow parking; water pump, toilets. No overnight camping.

S 58 A 111 H 121.1 East **junction** with Skilak Lake Road which loops southwest through Skilak Wildlife Recreation Area (Kenai National Wildlife Refuge) to rejoin the Sterling Highway at **Milepost S 75.3.**

Junction with Skilak Lake Road. See "Skilak Lake Road" log on page 546.

*CAUTION: Moose Danger Zone next 21 miles westbound to **Milepost S 79**. This stretch of highway crosses the Kenai National Wildlife Refuge and has one of the highest moose-vehicle collision rates in the state.*

Actual driving distance between physical mileposts 58 and 59 is 1.2 miles.

S 60 A 110 A 119.1 Large double-ended turnout to north (abrupt pavement edge). Easy-to-miss turnoff (not signed) down hill to south leads to **Jean Lake Campground**; 3 sites, picnic area; boat launch, rainbow trout fishing. (Big rigs: Check access before driving down to Jean Lake.)

S 60.6 A 113.6 H 118.5 Gravel turnout to south overlooking lake (view obscured by foliage).

S 61.4 A 114.4 H 117.7 Double-ended trailhead parking area to south for **Skyline Trail**, which leads north into the Mystery Hills; steep climb, good views.

S 62.6 A 115.6 H 116.5 Large gravel parking area (watch for potholes) to north. Hideout Hill to the south.

S 64 A 117 H 115.1 Mystery Creek Access Road (gated) to north. This road provides access to the Mystery Hills area; ATVs prohibited. For seasonal opening dates, contact Kenai NWR at (907) 260-2820.

S 65 A 118 H 114.1 Highway straightens westbound and descends into old Kenai Burn.

CAUTION: High speed traffic on straightaway westbound. Be alert to passing traffic.

Straightaway ends eastbound, begin winding road as highway descends toward

the Kenai River.

S 68.8 A 121.8 H 110.3 Turnoff to south for Petersen Lake (0.4 mile, turn right at fork) and Kelly Lake (0.6 mile, go straight) Kenai NWR public campgrounds. Both have 3 lakeside gravel overnight parking sites (free), picnic tables, firepits, toilets and water; carry out trash. **Kelly** and **Petersen** lakes have rainbow trout population. Boat launch at Kelly Lake. Access to Seven Lakes trail.

S 70.7 A 123.7 H 108.4 Egumen Lake trailhead parking area to south (trailhead is east of parking area). Half-mile marshy trail to **Egumen Lake** (lake not visible from highway); good rainbow trout population.

S 71.3 A 124.3 H 107.8 Parking areas both sides of highway. Entrance to **Watson Lake Kenai NWR Campground** (free); 0.4-mile drive from highway to small campground with 3 sites, toilets, picnic tables, fire grates, water; carry out your trash. Steep boat launch (suitable for canoes or hand-carried boats). East Fork Moose River trailhead. **Watson Lake**, rainbow trout.

S 72.9 A 125.9 H 106.2 Paved double-ended turnout to south, lake to north.

S 74.6 A 127.6 H 104.5 Distance marker eastbound shows Seward 75 miles, Anchorage 128 miles.

S 75.3 A 128.3 H 103.8 West **junction** with Skilak Lake Road, which loops southeast through Skilak Wildlife Recreation Area (Kenai National Wildlife Refuge) to rejoin the Sterling Highway at **Milepost S 58.**

Junction with Skilak Lake Road. See "Skilak Lake Road" log on page 546.

S 76 A 129 H 103.1 Entering Kenai National Wildlife Refuge lands eastbound.

S 76.1 A 129.1 H 103 PW Knives, knife shop to south sells custom handmade knives as well as factory knives. Find your fillet knife here. Plenty of parking. Open 9 A.M. to
(Continues on page 547)

Skilak Lake Road

Hidden Lake at EJ 3.5 has a campground, a picnic area and boat launch. (©Kris Valencia, staff)

Originally part of the first Sterling Highway that opened in 1950, the 19-mile Skilak Lake Road is a good gravel road that loops off the Sterling Highway at **Milepost S 58**, and travels through the Skilak Wildlife Recreation Area to campgrounds, trails and fishing spots before rejoining the Sterling Highway at **Milepost S 75.3**. *NOTE: Do not leave valuables in unattended boats or vehicles.*

CAUTION: Skilak Lake Road travels through prime brown bear habitat. The Kenai National Wildlife Refuge cautions hikers to be prepared for the possibility of encountering a bear.

Distance from east junction (EJ) with Sterling Highway at Milepost S 58 is followed by distance from west junction (WJ) with Sterling Highway at Milepost S 75.3.

EJ 0 WJ 19 Junction with Sterling Highway at **Milepost S 58**.

EJ 0.1 WJ 18.9 Double-ended turnout to west across from turnoff to Jim's Landing day-use area, 0.2 mile from road on Kenai River; toilets, tables, firepits, water, boat launch, parking area.

Pavement ends westbound.

NOTE: The Kenai River downstream from Jim's Landing is considered Class II and Class III whitewater and for experienced boaters only. Wear a personal flotation device. The Kenai River is non-motorized to Skilak Lake. Motors may be used on Skilak Lake to travel to Upper Skilak Lake Campground boat ramp. There is no road access to the Kenai River between Jim's Landing and Upper Skilak Lake Campground: be prepared to travel the entire distance by boat. Use caution when crossing Skilak Lake, as winds from Skilak Glacier frequently create dangerous boating conditions. Be prepared to wait overnight at river mouth until winds abate.

EJ 0.6 WJ 17.9 East entrance to Upper Kenai River Trail; trailhead parking, map and trail chart. Hike in ½ mile for scenic view of Kenai Canyon. Oversized vehicle parking.

EJ 1.9 WJ 17.1 Hideout trailhead; parking.

EJ 2.3 WJ 16.7 West entrance to Kenai River Trail; trailhead parking.

EJ 2.4 WJ 16.6 Pothole Lake Overlook, brush obscures view. Interpretive sign on bear awareness and bald eagles.

EJ 3.5 WJ 15.5 Hidden Lake Campground, 0.8 mile down paved road, has 44 campsites. Exceptionally nice lakeshore camping and picnic area on paved Lake Loop with 6 campsites, picnic pavilions, information boards, wheelchair-accessible toilets, tables, water, firepits, firewood and boat launch. Ridge Loop, on the hill behind the Lake Loop, has 12 campsites and paths leading down to the lake. Skyview Loop has 26 secluded campsites. Dump station on entrance road. Campground host. Campfire programs on evenings in summer at amphitheater. Camping fee $10 per vehicles. Boat trailer parking area. ▲

Hidden Lake, lake trout average 16 inches and sockeyes 9 inches, year-round, best from May 15 to July 1, use spoon, red-and-white or weighted, by trolling, casting and jigging. This lake is a favorite among local ice fishermen from late December through March. ➥

EJ 4.5 WJ 14.5 Parking area and interpretive sign at Hidden Creek trailhead; 3 mile round-trip hike to beach on Skilak Lake.

EJ 5.1 WJ 13.9 Hidden Creek Scenic Overlook with sweeping view of one arm of Skilak Lake.

EJ 5.4 WJ 13.6 Gravel parking area (no

facilities) at Skilak Lookout trailhead; 5 mile round-trip hike.

EJ 6 WJ 13 Parking area at Bear Mountain trailhead; 2 mile round-trip hike (moderate, steep) to scenic view of Skilak Lake and probable wildlife sightings.

EJ 6.8 WJ 12.2 Turnout with overlook (steep drop-off, no guardrails).

EJ 7.6 WJ 11.4 Parking for Upper Ohmer Lake public-use cabin. Located ¼-mile hike from here, this popular cabin must be reserved in advance. Cost is $45 per night. Phone 1-877-444-6777 or www.recreation. gov.

EJ 8.4 WJ 10.6 Upper Skilak Lake Campground, drive 1.8 miles along Lower Ohmer Lake; wide, paved 0.2-mile loop road through well-maintained campground (good for big rigs). There are 25 campsites (some sites on lakeshore), tables, toilets, firepits, water, and boat launch with boat trailer parking. Campground host. Large day-use picnic area with covered tables. Camping fee $10/vehicle, $5/tent site (walk-in). Access to 1.5-mile-long Vista Trail from campground. ▲

EJ 8.6 WJ 10.4 Lower Ohmer Lake Campground side road to parking area on lake; 5 campsites, no camping fee; toilet, boat launch, firepits, tables. ▲

Lower Ohmer Lake, rainbow trout 14 to 16 inches, year-round. **Skilak Lake** offers rainbow trout and Dolly Varden. Sockeye salmon enter lake in mid-July. ➥

EJ 9.3 WJ 9.7 Turnout overlooking Engineer Lake.

EJ 9.4 WJ 9.6 A 0.4-mile side road (narrow in places) leads to Engineer Lake; boat launch and Seven Lakes trailhead (4.4-mile hike to campground at Kelly Lake).

EJ 11.7 WJ 7.3 Large, paved, double-ended parking area to south with dump stations and toilets.

EJ 13.7 WJ 5.3 Wide gravel 1-mile side road leads south to **Lower Skilak Lake Campground**; 14 campsites, no fee, tables, toilets, firepits, picnic areas and boat launch for Skilak Lake and Kenai River fishing. *CAUTION: Skilak Lake is cold; winds are fierce and unpredictable. Wear life jackets!* ▲

Kenai River from **Skilak Lake** to Soldotna. Consult sport fishing regulations for legal tackle, limits and seasons. Chinook 20 to 80 lbs., use spinners, excellent fishing June to August; sockeyes 6 to 12 lbs., many, but hard to catch, use flies, best from July 15 to Aug. 10; pinks 4 to 8 lbs., abundant fish on even years Aug. 1 to Sept. 1, spoons; cohos 6 to 15 lbs., use spoons, Aug. 15 to Nov. 1; rainbow trout, Dolly Varden 15 to 20 inches, June–September, use spinners, winged bobber, small-weighted spoon. ➥

EJ 18.5 WJ 0.5 Bottenintnin Lake; well-marked side road leads 0.3 mile to large parking area (good turnaround) on lakeshore; no facilities, carry out trash. This is a shallow lake: No sport fish, but nice for recreational canoeing. Watch for loons and grebes.

EJ 18.9 WJ 0.1 Turnout with hunting information sign. *Pavement ends eastbound.*

EJ 19 WJ 0 Junction with Sterling Highway at **Milepost S 75.3**.

Return to Milepost S 58 or S 75.3 Sterling Highway

(Continued from page 545)
6 P.M. daily.

PW Knives. See display ad this page.

S 79 A 132 H 100.1 *Slow for posted speed zone westbound. CAUTION: Moose Danger Zone next 21 miles eastbound to* **Milepost S 58.**

S 79.2 A 132.2 H 99.9 Kenai Keys Road.

S 79.8 A 132.8 H 99.3 Begin 4-lane divided highway westbound. Begin 2-lane undivided highway with little or no shoulder and few turnouts eastbound to Cooper Landing.

S 80.3 A 133.3 H 98.8 Turnoff to south for lodging, camping, fishing packages, boat rentals, Kenai River access and Bing's Landing State Recreation Site (description follows).

Bing's Landing State Recreation Site (0.5 mile from highway to campground turnoff) is a large campground in a forest setting, accommodating rigs of all sizes. There are 36 tent/RV campsites, tables, water, firepits, toilets (wheelchair accessible) and dumpster. Campground host. Picnic area, boat launch. New (2018) day-use parking and fishing access at the Bings Backline, located on the right just before the boat launch area. Day-use fee is $5, credit cards accepted. Camping fee $15/night, 7-day limit from June 1 to August 15, 15-day limit all other times; boat launch $15. Toilets and fee box. This is a very busy place when the fish are in.

S 80.5 A 133.5 H 98.6 Welcome to Sterling (westbound sign). *Slow for posted speed zone westbound.*

S 80.6 A 133.6 H 98.5 Very large double-ended paved parking area to south.

Sterling

S 81 A 134 H 98.1 Most Sterling businesses are located along a 4-lane stretch of the Sterling Highway. The community is situated at the confluence of the Moose and Kenai rivers. **Population:** 6,011. **Emergency Services:** Dial 911. **Hospital,** Central Peninsula in Soldotna, phone (907) 714-4404. **Elevation:** 150 feet. **Climate:** Average winter temperatures from 4°F to 22°F; summer temperatures from 46°F to 65°F. Annual precipitation 20 inches.

This unincorporated community serves the summer influx of Kenai River sport fishermen, campers and canoeists paddling the Moose and Swanson rivers. Businesses with a Sterling mailing address extend from the Bing's Landing turnoff at **Milepost S 80.3** west to **Milepost S 84.9** on the Sterling Highway.

Traveler services include dining, auto and RV parts and repair at **Moose River Auto & RV Parks (Milepost S 81.2)**, gas/diesel and sani-dump at Cook's Corner (**Milepost S 81.5**); the **Wash Out Laundromat at Milepost S 83.4** (Swanson River Road); gift and hardware/automotive supply stores. Accommodations available in Sterling and camping at private businesses and Bing's Landing State Recreation Site at **Milepost S 80.3**. This campground has 36 tent/RV campsites.

The name Sterling was formalized in 1954 when a post office was established. The Sterling post office is at **Milepost S 81.3.** Sterling has one school. **Harvest House Church** at **Milepost S 81.3.** Moose River Raft Race and Sterling Days are held in July.

Sod-roofed log cabin at entrance to Izaak Walton State Recreation Site, with camping, picnic area and boat launch at confluence of Kenai and Moose rivers. (©Kris Valencia, staff)

Sterling Highway Log
(continued)

S 81.2 A 134.2 H 97.9 Moose River Auto & RV Parts open Tuesday–Saturday, April to October has parts and propane.

Moose River Auto & RV Parts. See display ad this page.

S 81.3 A 134.3 H 97.8 Sterling post office (ZIP code 99672) to south. Also access to **Harvest House Church** (description follows) off Otter Trail.

Harvest House Church, 10 A.M. Sundays, off Otter Trail. All welcomed in an accepting atmosphere. Jesus said, "...So that they may receive forgiveness of sins and a place among those who are set apart by faith in Me," Acts 26:18. Call Art at (907) 252-7250 for directions. [ADVERTISEMENT]

S 81.5 A 134.5 H 97.6 Gas/diesel station with propane, ATM, food, sani-dump, fishing gear and licenses.

S 81.7 A 134.7 H 97.4 Turnoff to south at east end of bridge for **Izaak Walton State Recreation Site**, located at the confluence of the Kenai and Moose rivers. Turn on access road by picturesque sod-roofed log cabin. Day-use area with parking by river, 31 campsites on loop road; tables, toilets, water and dumpster. Campground host. Camping fee $15/night, 7-day limit; day-use parking fee $5 after 30-minute grace period; boat launch $15.

STERLING ADVERTISERS

Good access to **Kenai River** for fishermen.

S 81.9 A 134.9 H 97.3 Bridge over Moose River; 0.3 mile of fishing down to confluence with Kenai River. *CAUTION: Drive carefully during fishing season when fishermen walk along bridge and highway.* Reds here in June. Big summer run of sockeyes follows into August; cohos into October. **Kenai** and **Moose rivers** (confluence), Dolly Varden and rainbow trout, salmon (chinook, sockeye, pink, coho). June 15 through October for trout; year-round for Dolly Varden. Chinook salmon from May through July, pink salmon in August and coho salmon from August through October. Always check ADF&G sport fish regulation booklet or call (907) 262-9368 for updates.

This is one terminus of the Swan Lake canoe trail *(see "Swanson River Road" log on page 549 for information on canoe trail).*

S 82.5 A 135.5 H 96.6 Lodging.

S 82.7 A 135.7 H 96.4 Truck weigh station; senior center to south.

Camping at Swiftwater Park Municipal Campground in Soldotna. *(Kris Valencia, staff)*

Highway narrows to 2 lanes westbound. Begin divided 4-lane highway eastbound.

S 83.4 A 136.4 H 95.7 Junction with Scout Lake Loop Road south to Morgan's Landing State Recreation Site (see details at **Milepost S 84.9**) and **junction** with Swanson River Road to north. Access via Swanson River Road north to **The Wash Out Laundromat** (0.1 mile) and Swan Lake Road (Mile 17). Access to camping and canoe trails.

Junction with Swanson River Road. See "Swanson River Road" on page 549.

The Wash Out Laundromat. See display ad this page.

S 83.5 A 136.5 H 95.6 Central Emergency Services to north.

S 84 A 137 H 95.1 Lodging, camping and canoe rentals.

S 84.9 A 137.9 H 94.2 Turnoff to south for Scout Lake Loop Road (4.3-mile paved road) which leads to Scout Lake day-use area and Morgan's Landing State Recreation Area and Campground (descriptions follow) before rejoining the Sterling Highway at **Milepost S 83.4**. *Begin speed zone for Highway Safety Corridor westbound to Soldotna for Sterling Highway traffic. Fines double in these zones.*

Scout Lake State Recreation Site (0.1 mile south) has toilets and a covered picnic shelter. Scout Lake has good fishing for stocked rainbow trout and grayling.

Drive 1.5 miles south on Scout Lake Loop Road and turn right on Lou Morgan Road (paved, winding road; use caution), then drive 2.4 miles for **Morgan's Landing State Recreation Area**; day-use parking area, 39 campsites, 10 pull-through sites, some double sites in park-like setting, picnic tables; toilets and water; $15 camping fee, 7-day limit; $5 day-use fee. Kenai Peninsula State Parks Headquarters is located at Morgan's Landing.

Morgan's Landing SRA offers good access to bank fishing on the **Kenai River**. Fishing for chinook salmon, mid-June through July, average 30 lbs. Sockeye salmon average 8 lbs., use flies in July–August; coho salmon to 15 lbs., August–September, use lure; pink salmon average 4 lbs. with lure, best in July, mainly even-numbered years; rainbow trout and Dolly Varden, use lures, June–August.

S 87.5 A 140.5 H 91.6 Robinson Loop Road to north, Tustumena Loop Road to south.

S 88.3 A 141.3 H 90.8 Plenty of parking at the **Alaska Horn & Antler Carvings and Rock Shop.**

Alaska Horn & Antler Carvings and Rock Shop. Free Mammoth Ivory! That's right! Stop in! Receive one piece of mammoth ivory when you visit us. Horn, antlers, bone, stone, ivory, raw products, gift items, jewelry and fine art. Watch Tom carve. Then head over next door to Two Rusty Ravens—vintage gift shop, scrimshaw pocket knives, Made in Alaska™ jewelry, watercolors by Tom's #1 Wifey, collectible license plates, Alaskan ornaments, decals, and smiles galore! Large pull-through driveway, Mile 88.3 Sterling Highway. Phone (907) 262-9759. [ADVERTISEMENT]

S 88.7 A 141.7 H 90.4 West Drive to south. Public fishing access and boat launch on **Longmere Lake**; stocked with rainbow trout and cohos.

CAUTION: Moose Danger Zone next 6 miles westbound.

S 91.3 A 144.3 H 87.8 Gas/diesel station with grocery and liquor store to south.

S 91.8 A 144.8 H 87.3 Harley Davidson shop to south. Soldotna city limits (sign).

S 92.1 A 145.1 H 87 Distance marker eastbound shows Sterling 10 miles, Seward 90 miles, Anchorage 145 miles.

S 92.2 A 145.2 H 86.9 Car wash, State Division of Forest, Land and Water Management (with fire danger indicator sign) and Soldotna Animal Hospital (phone 907/260-7851) to south along highway. For pet emergency/after hours, phone (907) 398-3838.

S 93.4 A 146.4 H 85.7 Begin 4-lane highway and *slow for posted speed zone westbound through Soldotna.*

*NOTE: Begin posted speed zone for **Highway Safety Corridor** eastbound to **Milepost S 84.9**. Fines double in these zones.*

S 93.7 A 146.7 H 85.4 Kleeb Loop (east end) to north with access to Whistle Hill; waffles and lattes in restored railcar, gift shop, restaurant.

S 93.8 A 146.8 H 85.3 St. Elias Brewery to south (just to the east of Fred Meyer); turn on side street. Kleeb Loop (west end) to north to Whistle Hill dining and gift shop.

S 93.9 A 146.9 H 85.2 Entrance to Fred Meyer to south. *(Westbound traffic use entrance at next light.)*

S 94 A 147 H 85.1 Traffic light at Devin Drive. Turnoff to south for Fred Meyer, gas/diesel station and fast-food. Overnight RV parking permitted in Fred Meyer parking lot; there's a dump station and freshwater fill-up on the west side of the parking lot (facing Petco). Also access to Petco and East Redoubt Avenue. (This is the easiest access for westbound traffic to East Redoubt Avenue and Swiftwater Park; see description next milepost.)

S 94.1 A 147.1 H 85 East Redoubt Avenue; Holiday gas station, Auto Fix. Access **Swiftwater Park Municipal Campground** (0.4 mile from highway); and Moose Range Meadows Fishing Access (3.7 miles); descriptions follow.

Follow East Redoubt 0.4 miles south to turnoff for **Swiftwater Park Municipal Campground**, then another 0.4 mile west to park entrance; 40 campsites (some pull-throughs) along a loop road above the **Kenai River**; tables, firepits, firewood ($6), dump station ($20), litter bins, toilets, boat launch (fee). Camping $21–$26; day-use fee $8; boat launch fee; cash or check only; season passes available at the Soldotna Parks and Rec. office or Centennial Campground. Excellent fishing access to Kenai River.

For **Moose Range Meadows Public Fishing Access**, continue on East Redoubt Avenue—which turns into Keystone Drive—3.7 miles to the fishing access on the north bank of the Kenai. This Kenai NWR Kenai River public fishing access is open July 1 to Sept. 30; gravel parking area, toilets, no camping. Fishing platforms and boardwalks *(Continued on page 550)*

Swanson River Road

Swanson River Road leads north from **Milepost S 83.4** to what *Alaska* magazine calls "a world-class canoe trail system." Located within the David Spencer Wilderness Unit of Kenai National Wildlife Refuge, the system consists of 2 canoe trails: the 60-mile Swan Lake route, connecting 30 lakes; and the 80-mile Swanson River route, linking 40 lakes. Trips can range anywhere from 1 to 7 days. Swanson River has a few more long portages than Swan Lake, but both are well worth a side trip.

Swanson River Road connects canoeists with the Swanson River route at 2 places: Swanson River Landing, 17.5 miles north of the Sterling Highway, and Paddle Lake at Mile 12 Swan Lake Road, entrance to the Swan Lake canoe trail.

Basic canoe skills are required to successfully negotiate these canoe trails. Sudden winds pose the greatest danger on lake crossings, so it is recommended that canoeists stick to the shoreline rather than cutting straight across the lakes. The most physically demanding part of a canoe trip on these trails are the portages, from short watery canals to one-mile long portage trails, though none are too grueling if you pack light as you would for backpacking.

Canoe Lake #1 and #2 as well as some of the other lakes close to the Swan Lake trailhead are great for day trips. For the weekend traveler, just a day's paddle gets you to the heart of the trail system on more isolated Gavia Lake, with camping and other recreation. Those who have a little more time (five days) can do the popular loop trail from the put in on Swan Lake Road to the Moose River bridge outside of Sterling.

There are established campsites along the lakeshores though travelers must keep in mind that this is wilderness camping, and the sites are primitive. Minimal-impact camping and recreation are also the rule, leave all areas just as you found them.

The canoe trails offer fishing, hiking, sightseeing, wildlife viewing and bird watching (200 species in this area). Bring binoculars and camera.

Stop by or contact the Kenai National Wildlife Refuge Visitor Center on Ski Hill Road, in Soldotna; phone (907) 260-2820, or go online to: www.fws.gov/refuge/Kenai/visit/visitor_activities/canoe.html for more information. Locally, canoe rentals and river shuttles are available at Alaska Canoe & RV Park, **Milepost S 84** Sterling Highway.

CAUTION: Do not leave valuables in vehicles at canoe trailheads. Drive with headlights on at all times. Watch for truck traffic at all times.

Swanson River Road is a fairly wide and level winding gravel road. Although well-maintained, be prepared for washboards. Posted speed limit is 35-mph.

Distance from junction with the Sterling Highway (J) is shown.

SWANSON RIVER ROAD

J 0 Junction with Sterling Highway at **Milepost S 83.4**. Sterling Baptist Church.

J 0.1 The Wash Out Laundromat.

J 0.4 Jana House Hostel & RV park.

J 0.6 Robinson Loop Road; rejoins Sterling Highway at **Milepost S 87.5**.

Pavement ends, gravel begins, northbound.

J 3.5 Turnout.

J 4.4 Entering Kenai National Wildlife Refuge. Turnout with interpretive signs.

J 7.8 Mosquito Lake, turnout; ½-mile trail to lake. Rainbow trout.

J 8.6 Turnout.

J 9 Silver Lake trailhead parking; 1-mile hike to lake. Rainbow trout and Arctic char. Arctic char are most easily caught in spring when the surface water is still cool. Once summer temperatures warm the surface, the char descend to deeper waters and are much harder to catch.

J 10.4 Forest Lakes parking; 0.3-mile trail to lake. Rainbow trout; best fished from canoe or raft.

J 12.8 Small turnout by **Weed Lake** trail; rainbow trout.

J 13 Drake and **Skookum** lakes trailhead parking (not signed), registration kiosk; 2-mile trail. Rainbow trout and Arctic char (spring).

J 13.7 Parking and access to Breeze Lake.

J 13.9 Dolly Varden Lake Campground; 12 sites, no camping fee, water, toilets, boat launch, carry out your trash. *NOTE: 0.5-mile loop road to campground is narrow and very bumpy; RVs check turnaround space before driving in.* Beautiful camping area. Some campsites overlook lake. Fishing for Dolly Varden and rainbow trout; best in late August and September.

J 14.5 Continue straight ahead northbound for Swanson River Landing. Southbound stop sign at oil field access road to west (gated; closed to private vehicles). The Swanson River Road was originally built as an access road to the Swanson River oil field. Richfield Oil Co. and Standard Oil established the first oil well—Swanson River Unit No. 1—in September 1957. Because the well was located on Kenai National Moose Range land administered by the U.S. Fish & Wildlife Service, the well was capped as soon as it was completed. It was not until late 1958 that then Interior Secretary Fred Seaton opened the northern half of the range to oil drilling and production. (Kenai National Moose Range became Kenai National Wildlife Refuge in 1980.) Other companies also began drilling in the area, and in 1959, Unocal discovered a major natural gas field near the Swanson River oil field. Current oil and gas field operator is Hilcorp, Alaska.

J 15.4 Rainbow Lake Campground has 3 campsites on lakeshore, outhouse, water, boat launch. No camping fee. Carry out your trash. Fishing for Dolly Varden and rainbow trout. *CAUTION: Steep road; difficult turnaround. Large RVs check visually before driving in.*

J 17 Junction with **Swan Lake Road**, which leads east 12 miles and deadends at Paddle Lake access. Driving distance from this junction to facilities and lakes on Swan Lake Road are as follows: Mile 3 **Fish Lake Campground** (2 campsites, outhouse, tables); Mile 3.5 Canoe Lake (Swan Lake Canoe Route west entrance); Mile 6.1 Merganser Lakes, parking, outhouse, picnic table; Mile 8 Nest Lake parking area; Mile 9.5 Portage Lake (Swan Lake Canoe Route east entrance), 15-minute parking only, outhouse, registration kiosk; Mile 10.1 double-ended pullout with parking; Mile 11.5 gravel turnout; Mile 12 End Swan Lake Road, begin 0.5-mile access road to Paddle Lake (entrance to Swanson River Canoe Route), parking, outhouse, registration kiosk.

J 17.3 Swanson River Landing Campground; 4 sites with toilets, tables, firepits, outhouse. No potable water, carry out your trash. No camping fee; 14-day limit.

J 17.5 Swanson River Landing at end of Swanson River Road; gravel parking area, boat launch, fishing. This is the terminus of the Swanson River canoe route, which begins at Paddle Lake at the end of Swan Lake Road.

Return to Milepost S 83.4 Sterling Highway

A partially boardwalked trail with lake access along Swanson River Road. *(©Michael K. Robb)*

Soldotna has several fish walks along the Kenai River, including this one at Soldotna Creek Park. (©Kris Valencia, staff)

(Continued from page 548)

along a 3-mile stretch of river in this area. Moose Range Meadows is subject to fishing closures.

S 94.2 A 147.2 H 84.9 Traffic light near Walgreens drugstore to south via Mullen Drive. Westbound travelers continue straight on Sterling Highway for Soldotna businesses along a 1.5-mile stretch of highway and continuation of highway to Homer.

Turn north on Kenai Spur Highway for more Soldotna businesses, the city of Kenai, Nikiski and Captain Cook State Park.

Junction with Kenai Spur Highway to city of Kenai. See "Kenai Spur Highway" log on page 558.

CAUTION: Moose Danger Zone next 6 miles eastbound.

S 94.4 A 147.4 H 84.7 Entrance to **Soldotna Creek Park** (day use only) to south; benches overlooking the river, playground, picnic tables and restrooms. Many fun events are held at this park in summer, with weekly concerts, vendor markets and special events. Good family fun, nice crowd.

Follow trail down hill to extensive fish walks along the Kenai River. Massive ice flows sometimes devastate these fish walks in winter, and they have to be repaired or rebuilt in spring for summer use. It is also the site of the annual Kenai River Festival, Frozen River Fest and Soldotna's Progress Days.

Traffic light at Birch Street; gas station, and second access to Soldotna Creek Park.

S 95.1 A 148.1 H 84 Traffic light at Binkley Street; access to fire station, police station, post office. Subway, Kaladi Brothers, Peninsula Center Mall, Sportsman's Warehouse and 24-hour Safeway with Starbucks.

Sterling Highway log to Homer continues on page 557.

Soldotna

S 95.2 A 148.2 H 83.9 On the western Kenai Peninsula, the city stretches over a mile southwest along the Sterling Highway and northwest along the Kenai Spur Highway. **Population:** 4,376; Kenai Peninsula Borough 57,212. **Emergency Services:** Dial 911. **Alaska State Troopers** at Mile 22 Kalifornsky Beach Road just off Sterling Highway, phone (907) 262-4453. **City Police**, phone (907) 262-4455. **Fire Department**, phone (907) 262-4792. **Ambulance**, phone (907) 714-4444. **Hospital**, Central Peninsula, phone (907) 714-4404. **Veterinarians:** Soldotna Animal Hospital (907) 260-7851 or for after hours pet emergency phone (907) 398-3838, Twin Cities Veterinary (907) 262-4581.

Visitor Information: The Soldotna Visitor Information Center is located in downtown Soldotna on the Sterling Highway south of Kenai River's David Douthit–Veterans Memorial bridge. Fish walk access to Kenai River. The center is open daily 9 A.M. to 7 P.M. mid-May to mid-September; 9 A.M. to 5 P.M. Monday–Friday mid-September to mid-May. A free visitors guide is available from the Soldotna Chamber of Commerce, phone (907) 262-9814, or www.visit soldotna.com.

Elevation: 115 feet. **Climate:** Average daily temperature in July, 63°F to 68°F; January, 19°F to 23°F. Annual precipitation, approximately 18 inches. **Radio:** KGTL-AM 620, KBBI-AM 890, KSRM-AM 920, KSLD-AM 1140, KDLL-FM 91.9, KBAY-FM 93.3, KKIS-FM 96.5, KWHQ-FM 100.1, KPEN-FM 101.7, KWAVE-FM 103.5 and KFSE-FM 106.9. **Television:** Network channels 2 (NBC), 4 (FOX), 7 (PBS), 11 (CBS), and 13 (ABC) from Anchorage, and cable channels. **Newspapers:** *Peninsula Clarion* (daily); *The Dispatch* (weekly).

Private Aircraft: Soldotna airstrip 1 mile SE on Funny River Road; elev. 107 feet; length 5,000 feet; asphalt; fuel 100LL; unattended.

The town of Soldotna was established in the 1940s because of its strategic location at the Sterling–Kenai Spur Highway junction. (Visitors may see the homestead cabin, which became Soldotna's first post office in 1949, at its original location on the Kenai Spur Highway at Corral Avenue.)

Soldotna was incorporated as a first-class city in 1967 and became a home-rule city in 2016. It has become the retail, governmental and medical hub of the Peninsula. Kenai Peninsula Borough headquarters and state offices of the Departments of Highways, Public Safety, Fish and Game, and Forest, Land and Water Management are located here. Central Peninsula Hospital in Soldotna serves the Soldotna and Kenai areas. Soldotna is also headquarters for the Kenai Peninsula Borough School District. University of Alaska–Kenai Peninsula College is also located in Soldotna.

While the best unobstructed views of the volcanic mountains across Cook Inlet are from either the Kenai Spur Highway north of Soldotna or the Sterling Highway south of Soldotna, there are frequent views of Mount Redoubt from Soldotna city streets. Mount Redoubt (elev. 10,197 feet) most recently erupting in March 2009, after a 20-year nap. For the current status of the volcano, visit the Alaska Volcano Observatory at www.avo.alaska.edu/index.php.

Soldotna gets very busy during fishing season. Popular fishing rivers in the area include the Kasilof River and the Kenai River. For those fishermen who want a more remote fishing spot—or for visitors who want to see wildlife and glaciers—Natron Air

Alaska's Kenai River City
SOLDOTNA

The Kenai River was recently named by CNN Travel as one of the **World's 15 best rivers for travelers.**

CNN Travel

Soldotna is the perfect place to experience all The Kenai, Alaska's Playground, has to offer. With over 200 riverside campsites, a mile of elevated river boardwalk, 50 sets of river access stairs and 724 acres of park land along the banks of the world-famous Kenai River, the City of Soldotna truly is Alaska's Kenai River City. All of this is right out your door when you stay in the heart of our vibrant downtown.

2017 © Jenny Neyman

Stay in one of our campgrounds or fabulous accommodations. Play in our parks or on our trails. You'll be within walking distance of shopping, restaurants, breweries, year-round events, and great entertainment options during your visit to Soldotna.

Start planning your trip!
Contact us today for your free Soldotna Visitor Guide.

907.262.9814 | www.visitsoldotna.com
44790 Sterling Highway, Soldotna, AK

Soldotna
CHAMBER OF COMMERCE

Learn more about the City of Soldotna, including our great parks and amenities at
www.Soldotna.org

Soldotna's Visitor Center is at the south end of David Douthit-Veterans Memorial Bridge.
(©Kris Valencia, staff)

offers fly-in fishing trips for rainbow trout, grayling, salmon and Dolly Varden.

Lodging & Services

All facilities are available, including supermarkets, banks, hotels/motels, bed-and-breakfasts, cabin rentals and lodges, restaurants and fast-food. Joyce K. Carver library at 235 N. Binkley St. Sports complex on K-Beach Road. Outdoor gear is available at **Alaska WildGear Clothing Company.**

Alaska WildGear Clothing Company. Conveniently located in Soldotna at 44624 Sterling Highway near the Kobuk Street intersection, just 2 city blocks from the Kenai River. Alaska WildGear Clothing Company (famous for their "Angry" king salmon logo) is your one stop shop for raingear, jackets, hoodies, T-shirts and headwear from the top Alaska brands: Alaska WildGear, Octopus Ink, Salmon Sisters, Alaska Chicks, and Mountains & Mermaids.

We feature quality technical gear to protect you from the elements on your fishing trip or excursion. Soldotna's best selection of printed T-shirts, hoodies, sweatshirts and headwear with the best images and logos from your favorite Alaska brands. Summer hours: Monday–Friday 10 A.M. to 6 P.M., and Sunday 11 A.M. to 5 P.M. Phone (907) 420-0855. Alaska WildGear was established in 2006, as a way to share our love of the state with locals and the many visitors. We look forward to meeting you. See display ad this page. [ADVERTISEMENT]

Edgewater Lodge & RV Park, located right on the Kenai River, across from the Soldotna Visitor Center. 15 spacious riverfront rooms with private baths, 60 full and partial hookups, WiFi, laundry, showers, grassy sites, bank fishing and fish cleaning facilities. Walk to stores and restaurants. Reservations and information: Phone (907) 262-7733; email: edgewaterlodge@sunriseresorts.com; website www.sunriseresorts.com. 48798 Funny River Rd., Soldotna, AK 99669. See display ad on page 554. [ADVERTISEMENT]

Camping

There are private campgrounds located in and near Soldotna; see ads this section. Fred Meyer allows overnight RV parking in signed areas; free dump station and water fill-up at west end of parking lot (facing Petco).

There are 2 City of Soldotna campgrounds: Swiftwater and Centennial. Campsites for both tents and RVs (no hookups). These campgrounds are heavily used; first-come, first-served. Camping fees higher during July 7–31 peak time; cash or check only; register at entrance.

For Swiftwater Campground, turn off the Sterling Highway on to East Redoubt Street, by the Holiday gas station (see **Milepost S 94.1** Sterling Highway), and drive 0.4 mile to campground turnoff; 40-plus campsites (some pull-throughs); tables, firepits, firewood, dump station ($20), litter barrels, toilets, boat launch (fees vary). Steep stairway down to Kenai River fish walk.

Centennial Park Campground is 0.1 mile from the Sterling Highway just south of the Kenai River bridge on Kalifornsky Beach Road (turn west at **Milepost S 96.1**) on the banks of the Kenai River; 176 campsites, tables, firepits, firewood provided, water, handicap accessible fishing area, restrooms, dump station ($20), boat launch (fees vary). Fishing from fish walk. Overflow camping is available for self-contained RVs at Soldotna Regional Sports Complex.

Transportation

Air: Soldotna airport is south of Soldotna at Mile 2 Funny River Road. Turn off the Sterling Highway at **Milepost S 96.1**, just after crossing Kenai River bridge. Charters available from Natron Air, phone (907) 262-8440.

The Kenai airport, 10.6 miles from Soldotna, has daily service to Anchorage. Drive north from Sterling Highway via Kenai Spur Highway and turn right on Airport Way.

Local: Taxi service; motorhome, auto, van and pickup rentals; vehicle leasing; and boat rentals and charters are available.

Highway: Accessible via the Sterling and Seward highways (Alaska Routes 9 and 1), 148 miles from Anchorage.

Attractions

Fish walks. Several public fish walks have been constructed in the Soldotna area in order to make the popular Kenai River more accessible to the public. Although this beautiful river cuts right through the center of town, public access is limited by private land ownership along the riverbank, as well as the nature of the river itself. The wide, swift Kenai River does not have an easily accessible, gently sloping riverbank. The fish walks allow the city to put people on the riverbank without degrading the environment.

Map: Soldotna-Kenai Vicinity

To Nikiski and Captain Cook State Recreation Area

Kenai Airport

Airport Way

MILEPOST SY-6.4

Kenai Spur Highway

Visitor Information Center

MILEPOST SY-10.8

Kenai

Beaver Loop Road

Kenai

Bridge Access Road

Cannery Rd.

K-16.5 Diamond M Ranch Resort

Ciechanski Rd.

To Sterling, Anchorage, and Seward

Sterling Highway

MILEPOST S-94.2

Kenai Peninsula College

Soldotna

1

Kalifornsky (K-Beach) Road

Kalifornsky Beach Road

Cook Inlet

Visitor Information Center

Soldotna Airport

MILEPOST S-96

Funny River Road

River

1

N
W   E
S

Cohoe

South Cohoe Loop Road

North Cohoe Loop Road

Kasilof River

Kasilof

MILEPOST S-108.6

To Homer

Sterling Highway

Soldotna-Kenai Vicinity

Fish walks are located at the following locations: Centennial and Swiftwater campgrounds; Rotary Park, at the Soldotna Visitor Center (by the Kenai River bridge);

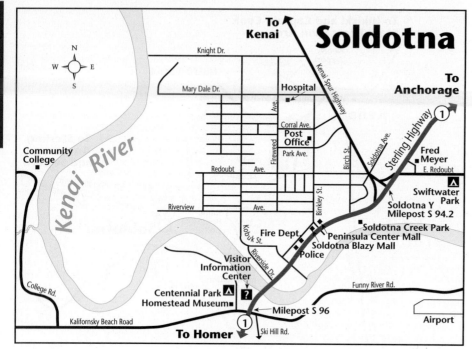

To Kenai

Soldotna

To Anchorage

To Homer

Milepost S 96

Airport

behind the Donald E. Gilman River Center on Funny River Road; and at Soldotna Creek Park, located off the Sterling Highway in the center of town; and the USFWS fish walks—Upper and Lower Moose Range Meadows—at Mile 3.5 and Mile 6 East Redoubt Street.

Swiftwater Park, the Soldotna city campground down East Redoubt Street (turn by the Fred Meyer) has the most extensive fish walk, with 200 feet of riverfront fish walk. Swiftwater Campground and Rotary Park and the Soldotna Visitor Center have handicap accessible river access with assistance. There are handicap-only fishing platforms at East Redoubt, Centennial, Swiftwater and Soldotna Creek parks.

Soldotna's Homestead Museum, located off K-Beach Road on Centennial Park Road,

features an indoor wildlife display and an outdoor collection of early homestead cabins. Soldotna's first homesteaders arrived in 1947. How they lived is revealed in a collection of handmade utensils and pioneer artifacts on display in the former Chamber of Commerce log tourist center. Slikok Valley School, the last of the Territorial log schools, built in 1958, is maintained in its original state. Damon Hall, a large building constructed for the Alaska Centennial, features an outstanding collection of wildlife mounts. An interesting display of Alaska Native artifacts are also displayed in Damon Hall. Fishing has been a mainstay, beginning with the first settlers, and boats are part of the museum's collection as well. A profusion of Alaska wildflowers line the pathways between the historic log buildings. The museum is open May 15–Sept. 15, 10 A.M. to 4 P.M., Tuesday through Saturday; Sunday noon–4 P.M. Visit www.soldotnamuseum.com.

Visit Soldotna Municipal Airport. Located on Funny River Road, 1.8 miles east of its intersection with the Sterling Highway, the airport is home to flying services like **Natron Air**; (907/262-8440), which offer bear viewing, fly-out hunting and fishing, and flightseeing.

Up on a 20-foot pedestal by the airport entrance gate is a Starduster SA 100 single-engine, single seat, open cockpit biplane. Built by local residents in the early 1960s, the plane was used for aerobatics at Alaska air shows until the 1990s. It was retired to this spot in 2001 as a remembrance of early Soldotna area aviators.

Natron Air. How about an unforgettable flight over breathtaking sights for the most lasting memory of your Alaskan experience? Natron Air is the charter for you. If you're an avid fisherman, you know the success of fly-out fishing trips generally exceeds that of road accessible waters and Natron Air knows the hot spots. See bears in their natu-

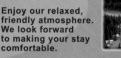

SOLDOTNA ADVERTISERS

Accommodations
Diamond M Ranch Resort........... Ph. (907) 283-9424
Edgewater Lodge & RV Park...... Ph. (907) 262-7733
Klondike RV Park & Cottages ...Ph. 1-800-980-6035

Auto & RV Services & Rentals & Gas
Alaska Recreational RV Parts....Ph. (907) 262-2700
Essential One .... Ph. (907) 262-2250

Campgrounds
Diamond M Ranch Resort........... Ph. (907) 283-9424
Edgewater RV Park...................... Ph. (907) 262-7733
Klondike RV Park.......................... Ph. (907) 262-6035

Fishing Guides, Charters & Lodges
Edgewater Lodge & RV Park...... Ph. (907) 262-7733
Natron Air .... Ph. (907) 262-8440

Shopping
Alaska Wildgear Clothing Co. .....Ph. (907) 420-0855

Tours & Transportation
Natron Air .... Ph. (907) 262-8440

Visitor Information
Soldotna Chamber of
Commerce.................................Ph. (907) 262-9814

ral habitat in an area of unsurpassed beauty. Watch the bears grazing, chasing and catching salmon or clamming along with other wildlife viewing. Natron Air will give you these opportunities at an affordable price. 1.8 miles from the Sterling Hwy on Funny River Road. Tim and Janet Pope say: "We have fun and we want to share it with you." Call today to book your activities! www. NatronAir.com. (907) 262-8440. See display ad on this page. [ADVERTISEMENT]

Join in Local Celebrations. From June through August, **Music in the Park** takes place every Wednesday evening at Soldotna Creek Park. Sponsored by the Chamber of Commerce, local and national bands take the stage, a beer garden serves local brews, and the Wednesday Market vendors stay open late for shopping and eating. A family fun evening with a good crowd.

Soldotna's big summer event is **Progress Days**, held the 4th weekend in July at Soldotna Creek Park (July 26–28, 2019). Started in 1957 to commemorate the completion of the natural gas line, Progress Days has grown into one of the peninsula's biggest annual attractions. The main event is the parade down Marydale Drive to Binkley Street, which begins 11 A.M. Saturday morning. Other activities include a Community BBQ Friday night at the Homestead Museum, a rodeo, music, food and crafts vendors, and a free community barbecue hosted by the City of Soldotna on Sunday afternoon.

Kenai Watershed Forum's annual **Kenai River Festival** (June 7–9, 2019), held at Soldotna Creek Park, focuses on the recreational, economic and educational importance of the Kenai River watershed. This summer event features free activities and educational displays for children and adults alike, including live music, food and crafts booths, and the 5K and 10-mile Run for the River. Live music, food and crafts booths. For more information visit www.kenaiwater shed.org.

In August, enjoy the annual **Kenai Peninsula Beer Festival**, held at the Soldotna Regional Sports Complex on K-Beach Road. Breweries from around the state make their way to Soldotna for this event. Local brewers include St. Elias Brewing Company (it is located is on the Sterling Highway just east of the Fred Meyer), Kenai River Brewery (located off Homestead Lane behind Walgreens), and **Kassik's Brewery** *(see description on page 562)*, located at **Milepost SY 19.1** Kenai Spur Highway.

In January, the **Peninsula Winter Games** take place in Soldotna. Activities include a hockey tournament, free games and food for the kids, a fireworks display and the Native Youth Olympics.

The fourth Saturday in January is the start of the **Tustumena 200 Sled Dog Race**. The T-200 is a qualifier for the Iditarod and Yukon Quest, so mushers from around the world head to the Kenai Peninsula to participate. The race starts at Freddie's Roadhouse (Mile 16 Oilwell Road) then heads into the Caribou Hills and to Homer, and ends back at the roadhouse. There are several accessible checkpoints from which to view the race. For more information visit www.Tustumena200.com.

Frozen River Fest is held Feb. 16, 2019. Join the community for this winter beer festival in Soldotna Creek Park. Event updates at www.facebook.com/FrozenRiverFest or www.visitsoldotna.com

Play Golf. Area courses include the

Kenai National Wildlife Refuge Visitor Center features exhibits that focus on the refuge's wildlife and their habitats. *(©Kris Valencia, staff)*

no frills but fun Bird Homestead Golf Course at Mile 11.8 Funny River Road; the 18-hole **Kenai Golf Course**, at **Milepost SY 9.4** Kenai Spur Highway, with pro shop, driving range, carts and club rentals; and Birch Ridge Golf Course, just east of Soldotna.

Kenai National Wildlife Refuge Visitor Center, located at the top of Ski Hill Road (south turnoff at **Milepost S 98**) and also accessible from Funny River Road, hosts some 25,000 visitors annually. This modern center features exhibits that focus on the Refuge's wildlife and their habitats. Don't miss the relief map that highlights salmon migration on the Kenai Peninsula. Free wildlife films, ranger-led programs, special events and activities throughout the year. Phone (907) 260-2820 or visit www.fws.gov/refuge/kenai/ for more information. The visitor

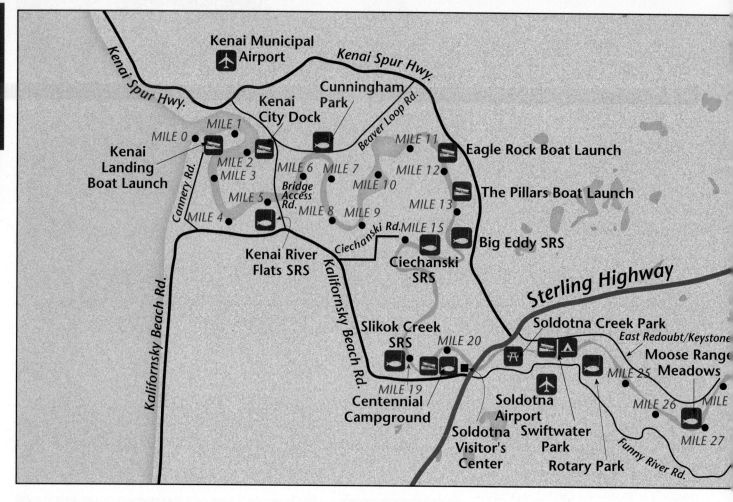

Map labels:

Kenai Spur Hwy.

Kenai Municipal Airport

Kenai Spur Hwy.

Cunningham Park

Kenai City Dock

Beaver Loop Rd.

MILE 11

Eagle Rock Boat Launch

MILE 0   MILE 1

Kenai Landing Boat Launch

MILE 2   MILE 6   MILE 7   MILE 12

MILE 3   Bridge Access Rd.   MILE 10   MILE 13

The Pillars Boat Launch

Cannery Rd.

MILE 5   MILE 8   MILE 9

MILE 4   Ciechanski Rd. MILE 15

Big Eddy SRS

Kenai River Flats SRS

Ciechanski SRS

Sterling Highway

Kalifornsky Beach Rd.

Kalifornsky Beach Rd.

Slikok Creek SRS   MILE 20

Soldotna Creek Park

East Redoubt/Keystone

Moose Range Meadows

MILE 25

MILE 19   Centennial Campground   Soldotna Airport   Swiftwater Park   MILE 26   MILE

Soldotna Visitor's Center   Rotary Park   Funny River Rd.   MILE 27

---

center is open daily, 9 A.M. to 5 P.M., June through August; Tuesday–Saturday 10 A.M. to 5 P.M. the rest of the year. No admission fee. The visitor center has restrooms and an Alaska Geographic bookstore.

There is a ¼-mile-long and a ¾-mile-long Keen-Eye Nature Trail, both leading to an observation platform on Headquarters Lake. (The shorter trail is wheelchair accessible with assistance.) For those looking for a longer hike, try the 2.2-mile (round-trip) Centennial Trail. The Elwell Lodge Guest Cabin, built in the 1940s on Upper Russian Lake, was dismantled, moved here and restored in 2014.

Information is available on outdoor recreation throughout the refuge, including hiking, camping, canoeing and wildlife

viewing. Complete information on Kenai Peninsula canoe trails (the 80-mile Swanson River route and the 60-mile Swan Lake route) is available at the visitor center or contact the Kenai National Wildlife Refuge at (907) 260-2820; www.fws.gov/refuge/kenai/.

The refuge was created in 1941 when President Franklin D. Roosevelt set aside 1.73 million acres of land (then designated the Kenai National Moose Range) to assure that the large numbers of moose, Dall sheep and other wild game would remain for people to enjoy. With the passage of the Alaska National Interest Lands Conservation Act in 1980, the acreage was increased to 1.92 million acres and renamed Kenai National Wildlife Refuge.

Fly to West Cook Inlet. Just across the water from the west coast of the Kenai Peninsula, the West Cook Inlet area offers great bear viewing and bird watching. Most of these activities take place at the 2 lodges—Silver Salmon Creek Lodge (silver salmoncreek.com) and Homestead Lodge (alaskawildlife.com)—located on a 160-acre parcel of private land within Lake Clark National Park. The lodges accommodate both overnight guests and day trippers. For day visitors, excursions are typically 4-hours or full day tours.

Bears are a major attraction here. From mid-June through mid-September, brown bears may be seen fishing Silver Salmon Creek; prowling the tide line, looking for anything edible that might have washed up onshore; and foraging or sleeping in the huge grassy meadow that lies between the beach and the lodges.

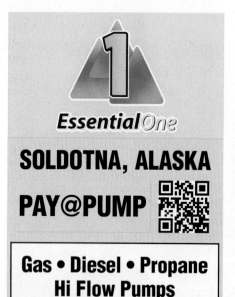

Lower Kenai River

© 2019 The MILEPOST®

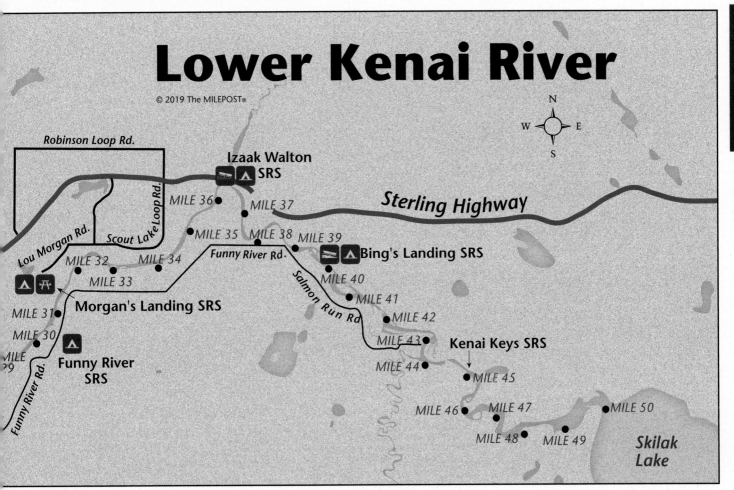

Izaak Walton SRS

Sterling Highway

MILE 36

MILE 37

MILE 35

MILE 38

MILE 39

Funny River Rd.

Bing's Landing SRS

Robinson Loop Rd.

Scout Lake Loop Rd.

Lou Morgan Rd.

MILE 32

MILE 34

MILE 33

Morgan's Landing SRS

MILE 31

MILE 30

MILE 29

Funny River Rd.

Funny River SRS

Salmon Run Rd.

MILE 40

MILE 41

MILE 42

MILE 43

Kenai Keys SRS

MILE 44

MILE 45

MILE 46

MILE 47

MILE 50

MILE 48

MILE 49

Skilak Lake

Transportation to West Cook Inlet lodges from Soldotna is via a 30-minute flight with Natron Air; stop by their office at the Soldotna Airport on Funny River Road or phone (907) 262-8440; www.natronair.com.

Fish the Kenai River. Soldotna is one of Alaska's best-known sport-fishing headquarters. The largest chinook salmon ever caught here was in 1985, at 97 lbs., 4 oz. hooked by Les Anderson, a local (see the skin mount of Les's fish and the carving of Les and his fish at the Soldotna Visitor Center). The early run of chinook begins about May 15, with the peak of the run typically occurring between June 12 and 20. The late run enters the river about July 1, peaking between July 23 and 31; season closes July 31. Always check ADF&G regulation booklet or call (907) 262-9368 Soldotna, for updates. The first run of sockeye enter the river during early June and is present in small numbers throughout the month; the second run enters about July 15 and is present through early August. In even years, pinks are present from early through mid-August. The early coho run arrives in early August, peaks in mid-August, and is over by the end of the month. Late run cohos enter the Kenai in early September, peak in mid- to late September, and continue to enter the river through October. Dolly Varden and trophy rainbow trout can be caught all summer.

Sterling Highway Log
(continued from page 550)

S 95.4 A 148.4 H 83.7 Traffic light at Kobuk Street, Lovers Lane; access to Kaladi Brothers (espresso), Soldotna High School.

S 95.6 A 148.6 H 83.5 David Douthit–Veterans Memorial Bridge across the Kenai River. Entering Game Management Unit 15B, southbound.

S 95.9 A 148.9 H 83.2 Soldotna Visitor Center and Soldotna Chamber of Commerce to west at south end of Kenai River bridge; visitor information, displays including the record 97 lb. chinook salmon and rainbow trout. Restrooms, good parking, good turnaround. Access to Homestead Museum by walking/bike path. Access to fish walk on Kenai River. Entering Game Management Unit 15A northbound.

S 96 A 149 H 83.1 Traffic light at **junction** of Funny River Road and Kalifornsky (K-Beach) Road. Funny River Road to east accesses Soldotna businesses, the airport and state recreation site; also access to Kenai National Wildlife Refuge Visitor Center (see description in Soldotna Attractions) via 0.8-mile gravel portion of Ski Hill Road, first right-hand turn on Funny River Road; there is a second access to Ski Hill Road and the visitor center at **Milepost S 98**. Kalifornsky (K-Beach) Road to west accesses Centennial Park Campground (description follows) and Soldotna Homestead Museum (see "Kalifornsky Beach Road" log); also access to Alaska State Troopers, ADF&G, **Diamond M Ranch Resort** and other businesses. K-Beach Road also provides access to Kenai River Flats SRS and to Kenai via the Bridge Access Road (see map on page 553).

Junction with Kalifornsky (K-Beach) Road and with Funny River Road. See "Funny River Road" log on this page; see "Kalifornsky Beach Road" log on page 565.

Centennial Park Campground and Homestead Museum, 0.1 mile west, on the banks of the Kenai River; 126 campsites (some on river), day-use areas, tables, firepits, firewood provided, water, restrooms, dump station. Large parking area at boat launch. This is a popular riverbank fishing site.

S 97.2 A 150.2 H 81.9 Distance marker southbound shows Kasilof 12 miles, Homer 73 miles.

S 98 A 151 H 81.1 Skyview Middle School to west. Ski Hill Road to east *(turnoff is easy to miss)* leads 1 mile (paved) to **Kenai National Wildlife Refuge Visitor Center.** The building has wildlife exhibits, nature trails, free wildlife films, restrooms, a small gift shop, and information on canoeing, hiking and camping in the refuge. Activities and events are scheduled throughout the year at this wonderful visitor center. Open daily, 9 A.M. to 5 P.M., Memorial Day through Labor Day; open Tuesday to Saturday, 10 A.M. to 5 P.M., from September through May. Inquire here about the 15 public-use cabins available to rent within the refuge, or go to kenai.fws.gov/cabin.htm for details. Ski Hill Road loops 0.8 mile back to Funny River Road.

Skyview Middle School has the popular **Tsalteshi Trails System** (built by volunteers), with nearly 9 miles of loop trails for walking, running and skiing. (The first 3.5 miles of trail are lit in winter.) Parking by hockey rink at back of the school; trailhead behind rink. Running and skiing events are held here.

(Continues on page 564)

Kenai Spur Highway

The Kenai Spur Highway at Willow Street in Kenai. That is Mount Redoubt peeking out in the far background. (©Kris Valencia, staff)

The Kenai Spur Highway junctions with the Sterling Highway at the **Milepost S 94.2** and leads north through Soldotna 10 miles to the city of Kenai. It ends at Captain Cook State Recreation Area, 39 miles north of Soldotna. This is an excellent 2- to 4-lane paved highway with posted speed limits from 35- to 55-mph. A multi-use pathway runs along the west side of the highway.

Distance from Soldotna Y (SY) is shown.

SY 0 Junction with Sterling Highway at **Milepost S 94.2** in **Soldotna** *(see description page 554).*

SY 0.6 Soldotna City Hall.

SY 1 Marydale Avenue. Central Peninsula General Hospital 0.4 mile west. 24-hour gas station east side of highway.

SY 1.9 Big Eddy Road to west; 6-hour public parking (1.4 miles); access to fishing guides and private boat launches (1.8 miles).

SY 2.1 Cheechako Drive. Access to Stewart's Landing off Fish Trap Court (0.25 mile); private parking and boat launch on Kenai River.

SY 2.3 Sports Lake Road, access to public fishing.

SY 2.8 Distance marker northbound shows Kenai 1 mile, Nikiski 24 miles.
CAUTION: Moose crossing.

SY 3.3 Small chapel to east is privately owned and rented out for receptions.

SY 4.2 Silver Salmon Drive (paved and gravel) leads 0.5 mile west to The Pillars Boat Launch (Alaska State Park) on the **Kenai River**; large gravel parking area, water, toilets, boat ramp, fee station. Bank angling not permitted. Fees: $20/launch, $5/day use. Closed October–May.

SY 5.3 Turnoff to west on Eagle Rock Place for Eagle Rock Boat Launch (Alaska State Parks).

SY 6.4 Twin City Raceway to east, a popular venue for motocross races. This intersection is also the south **junction** with 3.7-mile

Beaver Loop Road to west, which connects with the Bridge Access Road (see description at **Milepost SY 10.8**). Also access via Beaver Loop Road to **Cunningham Park** (2.7 miles), which has public access to the **Kenai River**, a trail, fish walk and restrooms; one of the more popular bank fishing spots during peak salmon runs.

SY 8 Begin divided 4-lane highway, *slow for posted speed zone, northbound.* Begin 2-lane highway southbound.

SY 9.4 Traffic light at Tinker Lane. Access to Peninsula Oilers baseball park, **Kenai Golf Course** (18 holes, open 7 A.M. to 10 P.M., daylight permitting, May–September, 907/283-7500) and Kenai Eagle Disc Golf Course.

SY 9.7 Kenai Central High School.

SY 9.8 Challenger Learning Center of Alaska, a science, math and technology space center for Alaska youth; day programs for youth and residential camps. Visit www.akchallenger.org.

SY 10.1 Welcome to Kenai sign.
Slow for posted speed zone northbound.

SY 10.2 Traffic light and access east to Walmart and Daubenspeck Family Park. The community park has a small beach, restrooms and parking. The lake is used for ice skating in winter.

SY 10.4 Traffic light at **junction** with Airport Way and Walker Lane. Access east to Home Depot and Kenai airport, access west to Aspen Suites.

SY 10.6 Kenai Plaza shopping; Home Depot, Carrs/Safeway.

SY 10.8 Traffic light at **junction** with south end of Main Street Loop in Kenai to east and Bridge Access Road to west (description follows); Holiday gas station, and Arby's. Continue straight ahead on Kenai Spur Highway for Kenai Visitor and Cultural Center.

Bridge Access Road leads west to Beaver Loop Road **junction** (1.3 miles); City of Kenai public dock and boat ramp (1.6 miles

west, 0.4 mile north); turnoff for Kenai Flats viewing platform (2.2 miles); Warren Ames Bridge (2.6 miles); **Kenai Flats State Recreation Site** (2.8 miles; 6-hour parking, picnic tables, information signs, bird watching); and **junction** with Kalifornsky Road (3.3 miles); *see "Kalifornsky Beach Road" log on page 565 and area map on page 553.*

SY 11 Leif Hansen Memorial Park. The Kenai City Clock and Merchant Marine Memorial are located in the park. The memorial is dedicated to "American WWII Merchant Marine Veterans, all Mariners, present and future."

SY 11.2 Junction with Willow Street in Kenai; Chevron and Tesoro gas/diesel stations.

SY 11.5 Traffic light at **junction** with north end of Main Street Loop. **Kenai Visitor and Cultural Center** to west (see description in Kenai under Visitor Information and under Attractions). The visitor center is a good place to park (especially for RVs) then walk west to Holy Assumption of Virgin Mary Russian Orthodox Church and the St. Nicholas Chapel in Kenai's Old Town and the Kenai Fine Arts Center at 816 Cook Ave. Open year-round, Wednesday–Saturday, noon–5 P.M. Extended hours May–August. Phone (907) 283-7040; www.kenaifinearts.com. *(See Attractions on pages 561–562).* Log continues on page 562.

CAUTION: Left-hand turn for northbound traffic wishing to access the Visitor Center and Old Town crosses 2 busy southbound lanes. Watch for oncoming cars!

Kenai

SY 11.5 Junction of the Kenai Spur Highway with Kenai's Main Street. Kenai is 159 driving miles from Anchorage (about a 3-hour drive) and 89 miles from Homer. **Population:** 7,098. **Emergency Services:** Dial 911. **Alaska State Troopers** (in Soldotna), phone (907) 262-4453. **Kenai City Police**, phone (907) 283-7879 or 283-7980. **Fire Department** and **Ambulance**, dial 911. **Hospital** (in Soldotna) Central Peninsula Hospital, phone (907) 714-4404. Medical and dental centers in Kenai. **Maritime Search and Rescue**, dial 0 for Zenith 5555, toll free. **Veterinarian**, phone (907) 283-4148.

Traffic light at junction with north end of Main Street Loop. Kenai Visitor and Cultural Center to west. The visitor center is a good place to park (especially for RVs) then walk west to Holy Assumption of Virgin Mary Russian Orthodox Church and the St. Nicholas Chapel in Kenai's Old Town.

CAUTION: Left-hand turn for northbound traffic wishing to access the Visitor Center and Old Town crosses 2 busy southbound lanes. Watch for oncoming cars!

Visitor Information: Kenai Visitors & Cultural Center, located at **Milepost SY 11.5** Kenai Spur Highway, provides brochures, free WiFi, reservation assistance, directions, recommendations, maps and other visitor information. Very nice restrooms. Write the Kenai Chamber of Commerce & Visitor Center, 11471 Kenai Spur Highway, Kenai, AK 99611; phone (907) 283-1991, email info@visitkenai.com; website www.visitkenai.com, kenaichamber.org.

The visitor center offers seasonal art shows, wildlife displays, historical and cultural exhibits (pictured below), special

©Kris Valencia, staff

visitor programs and, during the summer months, an outdoor Saturday market 10 A.M. to 5 P.M. The historic Moose Meat John's Cabin is located across the parking lot from the Kenai Visitors & Cultural Center.

Elevation: 93 feet. **Climate:** Average daily maximum temperature in July, 64°F; January temperatures range from 11° to -19°F. Lowest recorded temperature in Kenai was -48°F. Average annual precipitation, 18.16 inches (68.7 inches of snowfall). **Radio:** KDLL-FM 91.9, KBAY-FM 93.3, KKIS-FM 96.5, KWHQ-FM 100.1, KPEN-FM 102, K-WAVE-FM 105, KGTL 620, KSRM 920, KSLD 1140. **Television:** Several channels and cable. **Newspaper:** *Peninsula Clarion* (daily).

Private Aircraft: Kenai Municipal Airport is the principal airport on the Kenai Peninsula. It is accessible from Willow Street or Airport Way. There is a terminal building with ticket counter and baggage handling for commuter airlines, and a large parking lot. Elev. 92 feet; length 7,575 feet; grooved and paved; fuel 100LL and Jet A; attended. A 2,000-foot gravel runway is also available. There is an adjacent floatplane basin with a 4,600-foot water runway; camping spots and slips are available.

Kenai is situated on a low rise overlooking the mouth of the Kenai River where it empties into Cook Inlet. The area affords majestic views across Cook Inlet of 3 major volcanic peaks in the Chigmit Mountains: Mount Spurr (elev. 11,100 feet), the largest, which last erupted in 1992; Mount Iliamna (elev. 10,016 feet), identified by the 3 smaller peaks on its left; and Mount Redoubt (elev. 10,197 feet), which was identified by its very regular cone shape until it erupted in December 1989. Mount Redoubt erupted again in 2009. Both eruptions had significant impact on the aviation and oil industries, as well as the people of the Kenai Peninsula.

There are good views of Spurr, Iliamna and Redoubt from various points along the Kenai Spur Highway. In Kenai, walk out to the bluff viewpoints on Mission Avenue in Historic Old Town Kenai. There is a public beach access at the end of Spruce Drive, turnoff at **Milepost SY 11.7** Kenai Spur Highway, or try the scenic viewpoint 0.4 mile west on South Forest Drive from **Milepost SY 11.9** Kenai Spur Highway.

Kenai is the largest city on the Kenai Peninsula. Prior to Russian Alaska, Kenai was a Dena'ina Native community. The Dena'ina people fished, hunted, trapped, farmed and traded with neighboring tribes here. In 1791 it became the second permanent settlement established by the Russians in Alaska, when a fortified post called Fort St. Nicholas, or St. Nicholas Redoubt, was built near here

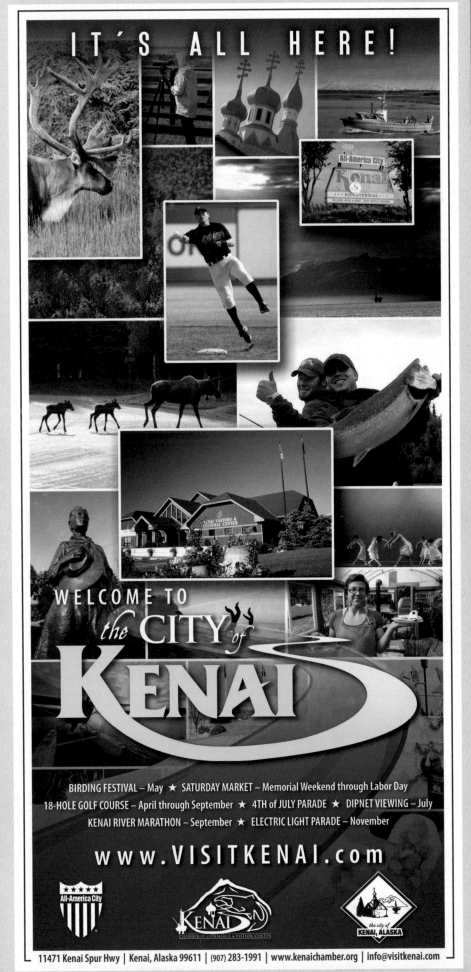

Holy Assumption of the Virgin Mary Russian Orthodox Church in Old Town Kenai.
(©Kris Valencia, staff)

by Russian fur traders. In 1797, at the Battle of Kenai, the Dena'ina defeated the Russian settlement of 150 men. In subsequent years, the post remained a minor trading post. In 1848, the first Alaska gold discovery was made on the Russian River. In 1869 the U.S. Army established Fort Kenai (Kenay). The first fish canneries were established in the 1880s. A post office was authorized in 1899.

Oil exploration began in the mid-1950s, with the first major discovery in this area, the Swanson River oil reserves, 20 miles/32.2 km northeast of Kenai in 1957. Two years later, natural gas was discovered in the Kalifornsky Beach area 6 miles/9.6 km south of the city of Kenai. Extensive exploration offshore in upper Cook Inlet has established

that Cook Inlet's middle-ground shoals contain one of the major oil and gas fields in the world.

The industrial complex on the North Kenai Road is the site of the Andeavor (formerly Tesoro) refinery which transforms Cook Inlet oil into fuel and propane. The Agrium plant here produced ammonia and urea for fertilizer until it shutdown in 2008. Also located here is the ConocoPhillips LNG plant. Shuttered now, the plant is up for sale.

Offshore in Cook Inlet are numerous drilling platforms, all with underwater pipelines bringing the oil to the shipping docks on both sides of Cook Inlet for loading onto tankers.

Lodging & Services

Kenai has all shopping facilities and conveniences including a Walmart. Several motels and hotels and about a dozen restaurants and drive-ins are located in Kenai. Favorites include the **Burger Bus** (behind the visitor center) and **Charlotte's** on South Willow, open 7 A.M. to 3 P.M. weekdays in summer 2018.

Medical and dental clinics, banks, laundromats, theaters, pharmacies, supermarkets, and numerous gift and specialty shops are located on and off the highway and in the shopping malls. Local artists are featured at the Kenai Fine Arts Center on Cook Street.

Tanglewood Bed & Breakfast. Fish king salmon from our backyard, on lower Kenai River. View moose, caribou, bears, wolves, eagles, ducks, seals, beluga whales on regular basis. Rooms $100. Common room with fireplace. Fully equipped private suite with Jacuzzi, $150. Full breakfast. Laundry facilities. (907) 283-6771. Open year-round. Life-long Alaskans. See display ad this page. [ADVERTISEMENT]

Kenai Recreation Center on Caviar Street has showers, sauna, weight room, racquetball courts and gym; phone (907) 283-7926 for hours. Indoor swimming and a waterslide are available at the **Nikiski Pool** (see **Milepost SY 23.4** Kenai Spur Highway); phone (907) 776-8800.

The Unity Bike Trail along the Kenai Spur Highway is popular with runners and bicyclists. The mile markers along the Unity trail were put up by local resident Terrence Carlson as part of an Eagle Scout project.

The Kenai Senior Center, accessible from **Milepost SY 11.2** Kenai Spur Highway, is located on the bluff overlooking the Kenai River flats. The center provides a variety of services to seniors, including a computer room, internet access, arts and crafts classes, exercise program, and no-host dinners. Visitors are welcome.

Camping

Private RV parks include **Beluga Lookout Lodge & RV Park** in Kenai and **Diamond M Ranch Resort** on K-Beach Road (descriptions follow). Public campgrounds are available north of Kenai on the Kenai Spur Highway in Captain Cook State Recreation Area (see highway log). Dump stations located at several local service stations and city dock.

Beluga Lookout Lodge & RV Park, 3 blocks from Visitors Center in Historic Old Town Kenai. Overlooking the mouth of the Kenai River, spectacular views of Cook Inlet and Kenai beach, Mount Redoubt, Beluga whales. Book bear viewing and fishing charters. Historic Russian Orthodox Church next door. Lodge rooms, cabins, gift shop, private

showers and bathrooms, laundry. 65 full hookups, free WiFi, free TV, pull-throughs, 20-30-50-amps. Caravans welcome. Phone (907) 283-5999; Fax (907) 283-4939; reservations at www.belugalookout.com. Email belugarv@belugalookout.com. See display ad on facing page. [ADVERTISEMENT]

Diamond M Ranch Resort overlooks the Kenai River, Cook Inlet and Alaskan Mountain Range. Lodging includes suites and cabins. RV sites include full hookup, 50-amp, super-size and pull-thrus. A popular destination with WiFi, showers, laundry, fire pits, picnic tables, socials, hiking, biking, hayride farm tour, charters, cruises, rafting, fly out bear viewing and fishing. Located between Kenai and Soldotna. www.diamondmranchresort.com. (907) 283-9424. See display ad on page 553. [ADVERTISEMENT]

Transportation

Air: Kenai Municipal Airport is served by Ravn Aviation (www.flyravn.com) and Grant Aviation (www.flygrant.com), both of which offer scheduled passenger service to Ted Stevens International Airport in Anchorage and numerous other destinations throughout Alaska. It is a 25-minute flight from Kenai to Anchorage (about 60 miles) and there are more than a dozen flights a day to choose from.

Local: Limousine and taxi service is available as well as car rentals, vehicle leasing, boat rentals and charters.

Highway: On the Kenai Spur Highway, 11 miles north of Soldotna.

Attractions

The **Kenai Visitor and Cultural Center**, located at **Milepost SY 11.5** Kenai Spur Highway, features excellent cultural and wildlife displays, seasonal art shows, Alaska-themed movies, books and reference materials, maps, and apparel. The Visitor Center is headquarters for the annual Kenai Birding Festival, held each May. The Kenai Visitor and Cultural Center also sponsors a Saturday market from May through September that features Alaskan produce, products, crafts and gift items. For more information/calendar of events, visit www.kenaichamber.org.

Already Read Books. 506 Attla, Kenai. Phone (907) 335-2665. One block off Willow Street between cinema and rec center at Caviar Street in the purple building. Featuring a grand selection of already read books; paperback and hardcover. Find an escape from the splendor of Alaska in our mélange of books. Use the exchange policy to replenish your books for the trip "home." [ADVERTISEMENT]

Kenai Community Library is centrally located at 163 Main St. Loop, adjacent the Fire Station and City Hall. The library has a large collection of Alaskana for history buffs, as well as books, periodicals, CDs, DVDs and audio books. A non-resident library card is available to visitors and summer residents with a local mailing address. WiFi hot spot with free internet access. Mini laptops may be checked out for use in the library. Phone (907) 283-4378 or go to www.kenailibrary.org for library hours, programs and other information.

Kenai Fine Arts Center. Go south on Main Street 2 blocks and left on Cook Avenue (816 Cook Ave.). Stop by and enjoy its exhibits and locally made items in the gift shop. Art exhibits change monthly and 1st Thursday show opening receptions are from 5–7 P.M. with refreshments and presen-

tation by exhibiting artists. Next door is a working pottery studio (not open to public). See the historic jail cell in the back of the building. Plenty of parking and turnaround for big rigs. Open Wednesday–Saturday year-round, noon–5 P.M. Extended hours May–August. Phone (907) 283-7040; www.kenaifinearts.com.

Old Town Kenai self-guided walking tour takes in Fort Kenay, the Russian Parish House Rectory, Russian Orthodox church and chapel (see descriptions following). Park at the Visitor Center, pick up a walking tour brochure there, then walk down Overland Street toward Cook Inlet. Meeks Trail leads down to the beach from Alaska Way.

Fort Kenay was the first American military installation in the area, established in 1868. More than 100 men were stationed here in the 1½ years it officially served to protect American citizens in the area. A replica of the fort's barracks building was constructed as an Alaska Purchase Centennial project by Kenai residents in 1967. This was the site of the original Russian schoolhouse which was torn down in 1956.

Parish House Rectory, constructed in 1881, directly east of Fort Kenay, is considered to be the oldest building on the Kenai Peninsula. Of the 4 rectories contracted by the Russian Orthodox Church in Alaska it is the only one still remaining. Restored

in 1998–99, the rectory continues to house priests who serve the church. Hand-hewn logs, joined with square-notched corners, are covered by wood shingle siding and painted the original colors.

Holy Assumption of the Virgin Mary Russian Orthodox Church, across from the rectory, is one of the oldest Russian Orthodox churches in Alaska and a National Historic Landmark. The original church was founded in 1846 by a Russian monk, Father Nicholai. The present church was built in 1895 with a $400 grant from the Russian Synod. With its 3 onion-shaped domes it is considered one of the finest examples of a Russian Orthodox church built on a vessel or quadrilateral floor plan. Icons from Russia and an 1847 Russian edition of the Holy Gospel—with enameled icons of Matthew, Mark, Luke and John on the cover—are displayed. Regular church services are held here. Please call ahead for tours. Phone (907) 283-4122. Donations are welcomed.

St. Nicholas Chapel was built in 1906 as a memorial to Father Nicholai and his helper, Makary Ivanov, on the site of the original church, which was inside the northwest corner of the Russian trading post of Fort St. Nicholas. The 2 men were honored for their distribution of the first smallpox vaccine in the territory.

Play golf at Kenai Golf Course. Golfers

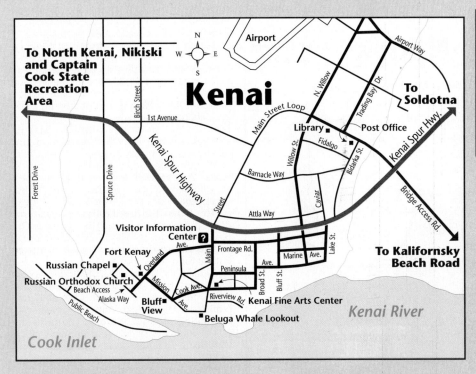

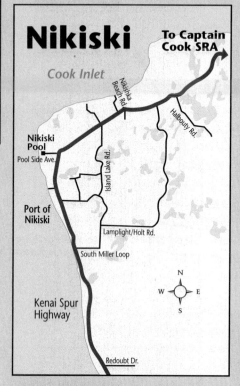

Nikiski

To Captain Cook SRA

Cook Inlet

Nikiski Pool

Pool Side Ave.

Port of Nikiski

Nikiska Beach Rd.

Halbouty Rd.

Island Lake Rd.

Lamplight/Holt Rd.

South Miller Loop

Kenai Spur Highway

Redoubt Dr.

N W E S

---

will enjoy the 18-hole course, pro shop, driving range, cart and club rentals. From **Milepost SY 9.4** Kenai Spur Highway, turn on Tinker, then make a left on Lawton. Phone (907) 283-7500.

Watch A Baseball Game. Kenai is the home of the Kenai Peninsula Oilers. It is one of 5 teams that make up the Alaska Baseball League. The other teams include the Anchorage Bucs, Anchorage Glacier Pilots, Chugiak-Eagle River Chinooks and the Mat-Su Miners.

Some fine semipro baseball is played at Coral Seymour Memorial Ball Park in Kenai. For current game schedule, phone (907) 283-7133 or visit their website at www.oilersbaseball.com.

Volcano and Whale Watching. The Kenai River beach at the west end of Spruce Street and Erick Hansen Scout Park at the end of Upland Street, offer good views of Kenai's fish-processing industry and Cook Inlet volcanoes, including Mount Redoubt, which last erupted in 2009. Also look for beluga whales, the only all-white whale, in the spring and fall.

Visit Kassik's Brewery. This North Kenai brewery features 10 quality ales on tap, including their signature brews, Moose Point Porter and Caribou Kilt Scotch Ale. Samples and tours available. From Mile 19.1 Kenai Spur Highway, turn right on Miller Loop, right on Holt-Lamplight, then left on Spruce Haven. Phone (907) 776-4055; www.kassiksbrew.com.

Kenai Parks and Recreation maintain facilities popular with both visitors and residents. Leif Hansen Memorial Park in downtown Kenai on the highway is perhaps the premier location in town for viewing flowers. The park also has a gazebo, water fountain, benches and drinking fountain. Erik Hansen Scout Park, at the end of Upland Street in Old Town Kenai, features benches and a great view of Cook Inlet. The Kenai Eagle 18-hole Disc Golf Course on Tinker Lane, behind the Peninsula Oilers baseball field, is free and open year-round. Kenai

Skate Board Park, located on Coral Street, is designed for skaters and BMX riders.

North Peninsula Recreation. Stop to play at the waterslide in the indoor **Nikiski Pool,** located 12 miles north of downtown Kenai at **Milepost SY 23.4** on the Kenai Spur Highway.

Kenai River Flats is a must stop for birders. Siberian snow geese and other waterfowl stop to feed on this saltwater marsh in the spring. Kenai Flats State Recreation Site on the Bridge Access Road at the west end of Warren Ames Bridge; parking and picnic tables. A boardwalk and viewing telescope for wildlife-watchers is located on the Bridge Access Road east of the Warren Ames Bridge.

The **Kenai Birding Festival** is a natural fit for this bird–filled area. This annual event is usually held in May. Visit www.kenaipeninsula.org/kenai-peninsula-birding-festival for more information.

Kenai City Dock. Take the Bridge Access Road west from Kenai Spur Highway 1.6 miles then turn off for the City of Kenai public dock and boat launch. A busy and fascinating place in summer, the port has 2 boat launches, a 170-foot concrete dock with floats, 3 cranes, gas and diesel fuel, restrooms and parking. Trailered boats may be launched from May to September. Parking and launch fees charged.

Kenai Spur Highway Log
(continued)

SY 11.9 Spruce Drive. Follow Spruce Drive west for huge parking area on flat area near beach; restrooms. A very busy spot during dip netting season. An access road for cars and trucks only from the parking lot to a drop-off/pick-up area on the beach is used to transport fishing and camping gear.

SY 12.1 Traffic light at Forest Drive. Access west to Handicapable Park; playground, toilets. This large forested park has trails and picnic tables (some covered).

Scenic viewpoint with parking at end of Forest Drive overlooks Cook Inlet and has stairway access to beach.

End 4-lane highway, begin 2-lane highway, northbound.

SY 12.8 Kenai Sports Complex; ball fields.

SY 13 Mount Spurr is directly ahead northbound.

SY 17.8 Nikiski Fire Station No. 1.

SY 19 Views through trees of Mount Redoubt to west and Mount Spurr to north.

CAUTION: Watch for moose next 2 miles northbound.

SY 19.1 South Miller Loop. **Kassik's Brewery** (description follows), a 1.6-mile drive through rural North Kenai, the brewery was established in 2004 and has won 4 World Beer Championships and a World Beer Cup. Open daily in summer (May–August) and 6 days a week the rest of the year.

Kassik's Brewery. Award-winning brewery featuring 10 styles on tap. Samples and tours available. Directions: Mile 19.1 Kenai Spur Highway, right on Miller Loop, right on Holt-Lamplight, left on Spruce Haven. RV turnaround. For more information call (907) 776-4055 or visit www.kassiksbrew.com. [ADVERTISEMENT]

SY 20.5 Tesoro gas station and 2Go Store to west.

SY 21 Agrium Kenai Nitrogen Operations plant. This petrochemical facility produced nitrogen-based agriculture products urea and

ammonia. This plant has been closed since 2008.

SY 21.4 Andeavor LNG export terminal.

SY 22.2 Tesoro Road to Andeavor Refinery. This refinery was built in 1969 and refines about 72,000 barrels of oil a day. The crude oil—of which 67 percent comes from Alaska's North Slope, 20 percent from Cook Inlet, and 13 percent from foreign sources—is turned into propane, gasoline, jet fuel, diesel fuel and fuel oil, among other products.

SY 23.4 Turnoff to west on Poolside Avenue and drive 0.3 mile for **North Peninsula Recreation's Nikiski Pool,** housed in the copper-domed building seen from the highway. Great place to take a break from driving and get in some laps. Kids love the 136' water slide. The Nikiski Pool has lap lanes, kiddie swim area with "Rainbrella" and "Bubble Beach," a hot tub, restrooms with showers and lockers, visitor observation area, weight room, racquetball and volleyball courts, outdoor picnic area, playground, skateboard park and hiking trails (3-mile handicap accessible, fitness stations along the way). The Jason Peterson Memorial Ice Rink is located behind the pool facility. Courtesy RV parking (must be self–contained). Phone (907) 776-8800 for pool hours; www.northpenrec.com.

North Peninsula Recreation/Nikiski Pool. See display ad below.

SY 25.8 Island Lake Road. Senior Center to east.

SY 26.7 NIKISKI (pop. 4,616). **Emergency Services,** Dial 911. **Fire Dept.,** Nikiski Fire Station No. 2. Hospital in Soldotna. **Radio:** KXBA-FM 93.3. Grocery; 2 restaurants; **Essential 1** station (pictured below) with gas/diesel, propane, ice; bar/liquor store/motel; and a post office.

©Kris Valencia, staff

Essential 1. See display ad this page.

Nikiski, also known as "North Kenai" or "The North Road," was homesteaded in the 1940s and grew with the discovery of oil on the Kenai Peninsula in 1957. By 1964, oil-related industries here included Unocal, ConocoPhillips LNG, Chevron and Tesoro. Commercial fishing is still a source of income for some residents.

SY 26.8 Nikishka Beach Road leads west to Nikiski High School (0.3 mile); Halliburton facility, beach access, Arness Dock, built on a base of WWII Liberty ships (still visible) at road end (0.8 mile). Good view of Nikishka Bay, Mount Spurr and Alaska Range.

SY 28.7 Holt/Lamplight Road to south (also known as the Nikiski Bypass, it rejoins the Kenai Spur Highway near Kassik's Brewery).

SY 29.7 Halbouty Road; access to **Grouchy Old Woman B&B** and **Daniels Lake Lodge** (2.1 miles).

Daniels Lake Lodge. See display ad

this page.

Grouchy Old Woman B&B. See display ad this page.

SY 32.3 Turnout to west opposite Twin Lakes.

SY 35.6 Entering **Captain Cook State Recreation Area** northbound. No hunting with firearms (sign).

SY 35.9 Bishop Creek day-use area (Captain Cook SRA) 0.1 mile to west; parking ($5 fee), water, picnic tables, firepits. A 0.2-mile walk through lush forest to beach and creek access, viewpoint and outhouses. A great walk. Spawning sockeye salmon in creek in July and August, cohos August to September. Closed to all salmon fishing.

SY 36.5 Stormy Lake day-use area (Captain Cook SRA), 0.5 mile east via gravel road.

SY 36.7 Stormy Lake Overlook, a large paved turnout to east with view of lake.

SY 36.9 One-way 0.3-mile loop road provides access to 2 covered picnic tables located on brushy bluff with view of Stormy Lake.

SY 37.8 Stormy Lake boat launch, 0.2 mile east.

SY 38.6 Turnoff on wide gravel road for Swanson River canoe landing area; 0.6 mile east to parking, picnic tables and toilets, river access. *No turnaround area at river access for vehicles over 35-feet long.* This is the end of the Swanson River canoe trail system.

SY 38.7 Clint Starnes Memorial Bridge crosses **Swanson River**; parking next to bridge. *Watch for fishermen on bridge.* View of Mount Spurr. Fishing for coho and sockeye salmon, and rainbow trout.

SY 39 Highway ends; trailer parking. **Discovery Campground** (0.4 mile west) and

Day-use area at end of Kenai Spur Highway offers beautiful views and beach access.
(©Kris Valencia, staff)

Picnic Area (0.5 mile) via gravel access road. Campground has 53 campsites, hiking trail, water, fireside programs in season. Camping fee $15/night. Day-use picnic area (keep to right at second fork) has gravel parking area, tables and toilets on bluff overlooking ocean. Day-use fee $5. Stupendous views of Mount Spurr across Cook Inlet. *CAUTION: Steep, high cliffs. Supervise children and pets!*

Spur access road to beach (4-wheel drive vehicles only); signed as "unsafe due to high tides and loose sand." ATVs are allowed in designated areas only.

Return to Milepost S 96
Sterling Highway

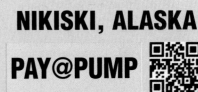
Kenai was made a Russian settlement in 1791.

Funny River Road

Funny River Road branches east off the Sterling Highway at **Milepost S 96**, providing access to rural residential areas, lodges and a state recreation site. There is no Kenai River crossing on this road. It is paved with little or no shoulder. Speed limit is 45-mph with 30-mph curves.

Distance from junction with the Sterling Highway is shown (J).

FUNNY RIVER ROAD

J 0 Junction with Sterling Highway. Immediate right turn (in front of Spenard Builders Supply) is to Ski Hill Road, which leads 0.8 mile to access to Kenai National Wildlife Refuge visitor center.

J 0.1 Edgewater Lodge & RV Park to north; phone (907) 262-7733.

Edgewater Lodge & RV Park. See display ad on page 554.

J 0.2 Access to Klondike RV Park & Cottages (description follows).

Klondike RV Park & Cottages. 35 sites with full hookups, rigs to 60-feet. Most sites are 25 feet wide. Free WiFi, showers, restrooms. Laundromat on site. Located 1 block off the Kenai River in Soldotna, Alaska. We have cottages for rent. Four W Woodall rating. (907) 262-6035 or 1-800-980-6035. See display ad on page 554.

[ADVERTISEMENT]

J 1.6 Donald E. Gilman River Center to north is a multi-agency permitting, information and education center for Kenai Peninsula watersheds. Fishing access to Kenai River behind center via staircases and a handicap accessible ramp; open to public May 15–Oct. 1; no parking for RVs or campers. Absolutely NO overnight stays (enforced).

J 1.8 Entrance to Soldotna Municipal Airport (electronic gate) and access to **Natron Air**; bear viewing, fly-out hunting and fishing, phone (907) 262-8440.

Natron Air. See display ad shown on page 555.

Private Aircraft: Soldotna airstrip 1 SE on Funny River Road; elev. 107 feet; length 5,000 feet; asphalt; fuel 100LL, Jet A; unattended. Privately-operated hangar facilities and fuel service. Temporary tie down spaces available.

Up on a 20-foot pedestal by the entrance gate is a Starduster SA 100 single-engine, single seat, open cockpit biplane. Built by local residents in the early 1960s, the plane was used for aerobatics at Alaska air shows until the 1990s. It was retired to this spot in 2001 as a remembrance of early Soldotna area aviators.

J 2.4 Watch for gravel parking to north, just past east end of airport, for Rotary Park access to Kenai River; ¾-mile trail to river (handicap-accessible with assistance), restrooms, day-use fee charged.

J 2.9 Entering Kenai National Wildlife Refuge lands eastbound; small paved turnout.

J 3.8 Mann Road to north leads to Salmonberry Lodge.

J 3.9 Small paved turnout to south.

Parking at Funny River State Recreation Site. (©Kris Valencia, staff)

Slow for 30-mph curves.

J 6.5 Paved turnout to south.

J 6.7 Paved parking to south; marked trailhead for horse trail.

J 8.8 Paved turnout to south.

J 9.4 Small paved parking to north.

J 9.6 Fire Danger sign.

J 9.9 Solid waste facility; dumpsters.

J 10.1 Scenic viewpoint on curve to north; view of Kenai River through trees.

J 10.8 Welcome to Funny River (sign).

J 11.1 Funny River bridge.

J 11.2 Funny River State Recreation Site 0.2 mile to north; access road dead-ends at small turnaround area. This state park accommodates about 6 RVs and also has tent sites; $15 camping fee, 7-day limit; outhouse, drinking water, tables; pack out trash; campground host. Open May–September. Day-use parking on one side of access road (signed). Fills up quickly mid-July when fishing season starts. Short trail to **Kenai River** fish walk.

J 11.7 Turnoff on access road south to Bird Homestead 9-hole golf course.

J 11.9 Log Cabin Liquor, open daily; groceries, ice, fishing licenses.

J 12.5 Turnoff for Funny River Community Center (0.1 mile) via Pioneer Access Road. The community center has an annual festival the weekend after Soldotna's Progress Days.

J 14 Rabbit Run Road to Brown's Lake Road. Public boat launch at Brown's Lake, very popular place for swimming and waterskiing in summer. Good bird watching in early morning. Limited turnaround space for RVs. *All property around Brown's Lake is private; no trespassing.*

J 16.2 Lake Road to Brown's Lake.

J 16.9 Central Emergency Services, Funny River Station.

J 17 Funny River Road ends at large gravel turnaround with many mailboxes. Junction with Salmon Run Drive and Moonshine Drive.

Return to Milepost S 96 Sterling Highway

(Continued from page 557)

S 98.3 A 151.3 H 80.8 Arc Lake to east; dirt and gravel parking area, picnic table, unmaintained. Easy boat launch for canoes, kayaks. Watch for eagles in summer.

S 98.5 A 151.5 H 80.6 Landfill to east; good place to recycle or get rid of larger items.

CAUTION: Moose Danger Zone next 10 miles southbound.

S 100 A 153 H 79.1 Three Guys No Wood gallery to south. Stop in to see works of art made from wood, gallery has birch bowls to mixed-wood hardwood platters and much more. www.threeguysnowood.com.

S 102 A 155 H 77.1 Gas/diesel station with propane and convenience store.

S 103 A 156 H 76.1 *IMPORTANT: Begin intermittent slow-vehicle lanes for southbound and northbound passing. A number of these very short passing lanes have been added to the busy 2-lane highway between Soldotna and Homer. Do NOT use slow-vehicle lanes as parking areas. Park only in designated (signed) parking areas. Parking areas are included in our log; these short passing lanes are typically not, but they are well-signed for motorists. The delay of more than 5 vehicles is illegal.*

S 107 A 160 H 72.1 Rogue Lake public fishing access to east. Decanter Inn.

S 108.6 A 161.6 H 70.5 South junction with Kalifornsky Beach (K-Beach) Road.

K-Beach Road is a 22-mile loop road that rejoins the Sterling Highway at **Milepost S 96**. Kasilof post office is 0.1 mile west of here on K-Beach Road; Kasilof Regional Historical Museum is 0.5 miles west; and beach access is 4.8 miles (via Kasilof Beach Road).

Junction with Kalifornsky (K-Beach) Road. See "Kalifornsky Beach Road" log on this page 565.

S 109 A 162 H 70.1 Kasilof Mercantile east side of road. **KASILOF** (pop. 532) was originally a settlement established in 1786 by the Russians as St. George. A Kenaitze Indian village grew up around the site, but no longer exists. The current population of Kasilof is spread out over a 90-square-mile area. Income is derived from fishing and fish processing.

S 109.2 A 162.2 H 69.9 Kasilof Riverview Tesoro to west with 24-hour gas/diesel, groceries, liquor store, espresso and tackle.

Kasilof Riverview Tesoro. See display ad on facing page.

S 109.3 A 162.3 H 69.8 Bridge over Kasilof River, which drains Tustumena Lake. Entering Game Management Subunit 15C southbound, 15B northbound.

S 109.5 A 162.5 H 69.6 Turnoff for **Kasilof River State Recreation Site** (to east) on Spetz Road; day-use area on a knoll above the river. Picnic tables and firepits in forested area above parking; wheelchair-accessible toilets, water and interpretive trails. This is a popular boat launch for drift boaters fishing for chinook salmon late May through July. Parking $5 after 30-minute grace period. Boat launch fee $10.

The **Kasilof River** is a powerful glacial river that drains Tustumena Lake, the Kenai Peninsula's largest lake. It flows 17 miles northwest to Cook Inlet. Although silty, very rocky and shallow in places, the Kasilof River is popular for its sport fishing, whitewater kayaking, canoeing and wildlife viewing opportunities.

Most of the sport fishing on the Kasilof River takes places between the Sterling Highway bridge at **Milepost S 109.3** and the river's confluence with Crooked Creek. The Crooked Creek area is one of the most productive bank fishing spots on the Kenai Peninsula for chinook salmon fishing, and is popular late in the season for coho salmon fishing. Fishing access is from Crooked Creek State Recreation Site (see **Milepost S 111** Sterling Highway for directions and description).

Access to the upper Kasilof River and Tustumena Lake is from the Slackwater Boat Launch on Tustumena Lake Road (see description at **Milepost S 110.2** Sterling Highway).

During periods of low water, navigating the Kasilof River in a powerboat is nearly impossible. During high water, the swift current makes boating conditions hazardous. *Special restrictions apply to both boating and fishing on the Kasilof River, so check the ADF&G regulation booklet carefully.* The sockeye salmon dip-net fishery here is open to Alaska residents only

S 110 A 163 H 69.1 Tustumena Elementary School to east.

Distance marker northbound shows Soldotna 14 miles, Kenai 25 miles and Anchorage 162 miles.

S 110.1 A 163.1 H 69 Central Emergency Services, Kasilof Station, west side of highway.

S 110.2 A 163.2 H 68.9 Abram Avenue. Turn east on Abram for access to **Johnson Lake Recreation Area**, **Tustumena Lake** and **Kasilof RV Park**; directions and descriptions follow.

Kasilof RV Park. See display ad on page 566.

Drive 0.1 mile on Abram then turn right and drive 0.3 mile on Johnson Lake Road for Johnson Lake Recreation Area day-use site; toilets, picnic tables and trash container in a pleasant woodsy setting.

Continue to the left past the day-use area to the big metal "T" which marks the beginning of Tustumena Lake Road. Johnson Lake Recreation Area Campground is at Mile 0.1 of Tustumena Lake Road (descriptions follow).

Kalifornsky Beach Road

Also called K–Beach Road, Kalifornsky Beach Road leads west from the Sterling Highway at Soldotna, following the shore of Cook Inlet south to Kasilof. K-Beach Road also provides access to Kenai via the Bridge Access Road.

Distance from the north junction at Milepost S 96 Sterling Highway at Soldotna (S) is followed by distance from south junction at Milepost S 108.6 Sterling Highway at Kasilof (K).

S 0 K 22.2 North **junction** with Sterling Highway at **Milepost S 96**. K-Beach Road mileposts reflect mileage from Kasilof.

S 0.1 K 22.1 Turnoff for **Homestead Museum** and **Centennial Park Municipal Campground**. This huge municipal campground, located on the banks of the **Kenai River**, is a popular spot for day use fishing and the parking lot fills up fast when the fish are in. First-come, first-served camping; 176 sites, tables, firepits, firewood, water, restrooms, dump station, pay phones, boat launch and fish walk. Camping fees $21–$26; $8 parking/day-use. Access to Angler's Trail (signed), a footpath for fishermen.

Homestead Museum is a fun and interesting stop for the whole family with historic log cabins like Slikok Valley School (pictured above); *see full description on page 554.* Open mid-May to mid-September, 10 A.M. to 4 P.M. Tuesday–Saturday, and noon–4 P.M. Sundays. Closed Mondays.

©Kris Valencia, staff

S 0.2 K 22 Alaska State Troopers.

S 0.4 K 21.8 Gehrke Field, rodeo grounds.

S 0.6 K 21.6 Soldotna Sports Center on Sports Center Road; phone (907) 262-3151. The Center has showers available for $3. The parking lot is used for overflow camping from Swiftwater Campground during July.

S 0.8 K 21.4 West Endicott Drive access 0.5 mile to the **Slikok Creek** unit of the Kenai River Special Management Area. Parking and trail access to mouth of Slikok Creek, **Kenai River** public fishing access. Day use fee charged. Public toilets available.

S 1.6 K 20.6 College Loop Road to Kenai Peninsula College (1.3 miles north).

S 2.7 K 19.5 Harvard Avenue. K-Beach center. ADF&G office, wildlife troopers; stop in here for current sport fishing information.

S 2.9 K 19.3 Poppy Lane intersection; gas station, espresso.

Access to Kenai Peninsula College (1.3 mile north). At the college, the Boyd Shaffer nature trail begins directly behind the Clayton Brockel building. Trail access to **Slikok Creek State Recreation Area**, a **Kenai River** public fishing access; watch for

sign marking trailhead.

S 3.5 K 18.7 Red Diamond Center; theatre, restaurants, motel, grocery and other stores. **Essential One** gas/diesel, propane.

Essential One. See display ad on page 556.

S 4.7 K 17.5 Ciechanski Road; access to **Ciechanski State Recreation Site** (2.4 miles) on the Kenai River (River Mile 15.5). This small site's primary purpose is to provide restroom access for boaters. There is a small, 12-hour public parking area (no camping), outhouse and dock walk, which offers a good view of the river, but no bank access to river and no fishing from the dock.

S 5.5 K 16.5 Turnoff for **Diamond M Ranch Resort**. Large RV park with lodging and many activities. Centrally located on the Kenai Peninsula, Diamond M is a popular vacation destination with great fishing on the Kenai River. Visit www.diamondmranch.com for more information.

Diamond M Ranch Resort. See display ad on page 553 this section.

S 6 K 16.2 Traffic light at **junction** with Bridge Access Road. Turn here for access to **Kenai River Flats State Recreation Site** (0.5 mile), 6-hour parking, picnic tables, information signs, bird watching; **Warren Ames Bridge** (0.7 mile); Kenai Flats boardwalk viewing telescope (1.1 miles); City of Kenai public dock (1.6 miles); Beaver Loop Road junction (1.9 miles); and Kenai Spur Highway (3.3 miles) at city of Kenai.

Bike route ends, road narrows, northbound.

S 8.3 K 13.7 Cannery Road leads 1.2 miles to public beach access at the mouth of the Kenai River.

S 10 K 12.2 Central Emergency Services (fire station).

S 17.4 K 4.8 Kasilof Beach Road leads 0.9 mile to unimproved grassy dunes bordering mud flats at mouth of Kasilof River; pleasant, primitive and busy day-use and overnight area during salmon runs. No public access beyond cannery gate. Respect private property.

S 20.1 K 2.1 Private aircraft; Kasilof airstrip, 2N; elev. 125 feet; length 2,400 feet; gravel; unattended.

S 21.8 K 0.4 Kasilof Regional Historical Museum is a park of historic buildings and displays showcasing Kasilof's development beginning in the 1890s. The main museum, with displays of Native culture, fox farming, homesteading, trapping and fishing history of the area, is housed in the McLane Building. This structure was originally built for a fish cannery hospital in the 1890s and converted to the Kasilof Territorial school from 1937 to the 1950s. Seven additional historical cabins date back to early Kasilof days and each have a story. Also on view are outbuildings, machinery and old boats. The historical park, with interpretive signs, is always accessible. Staffed part-time with friendly and knowledgeable volunteers. Paved parking, free admission, picnic tables. No facilities when closed. Open Memorial Day through Labor Day, daily 1–4 P.M. For information, or to schedule a tour the rest of the year, phone (907) 262-299.

S 22.1 K 0.1 Kasilof Post Office.

S 22.2 K 0 Junction with Sterling Highway at Kasilof, **Milepost S 108.6**.

Return to Milepost S 96 or S 108.6 Sterling Highway

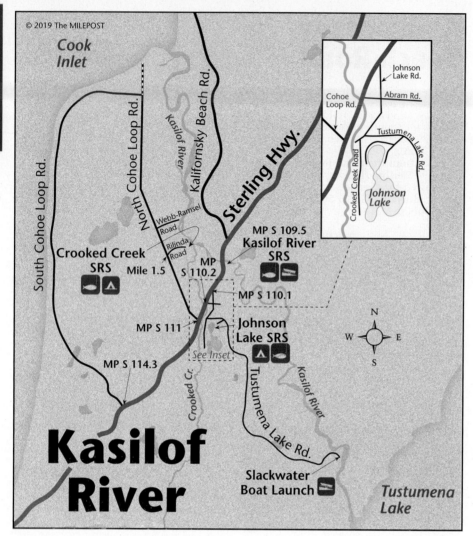

© 2019 The MILEPOST

Cook Inlet

South Cohoe Loop Rd.

North Cohoe Loop Rd.

Kasilof River

Kalifornsky Beach Rd.

Sterling Hwy.

Webb-Ramsel Road

Rilinda Road

Crooked Creek SRS   Mile 1.5

MP S 110.2

MP S 109.5
Kasilof River SRS

MP S 110.1

MP S 111

Johnson Lake SRS

MP S 114.3

See Inset

Crooked Cr.

Kasilof River

Tustumena Lake Rd.

Slackwater Boat Launch

Tustumena Lake

Kasilof River

N W E S

Inset: Johnson Lake Rd., Cohoe Loop Rd., Abram Rd., Tustumena Lake Rd., Crooked Creek Road, Johnson Lake

Turn to the right at the day-use area and drive 0.1 mile, then turn on Crooked Creek Road and continue 0.5 for **Kasilof RV Park** (description follows).

Kasilof RV Park offers a quiet, relaxing atmosphere in a park-like setting with green areas and trees separating campsites. We have very clean restrooms and showers and are central to all Peninsula activities. We are an extended-stay campground, no nightly camping. Located ½-mile south on Crooked Creek Road at the end of Johnson Lake Road east off Milepost 110.4 on Sterling Highway. Lat/Lon 60°17.41 N - 151°16.30 W. Visit us at www.kasilofrvpark.com or call us at (907) 262-3704 for a reservation. See display ad this page. [ADVERTISEMENT]

Tustumena Lake Road is a 6-mile paved and gravel road (gravel portion can be rough) that begins at the large metal T on Johnson Lake Road and ends at the Kasilof River. Road log is as follows:

Mile 0.1 **Johnson Lake State Recreation Area Campground**; 50 sites (some pull-throughs) in forested area on lake; tables, firepits, toilets, water, dumpster, launch for non-motorized boats. **Johnson Lake** is stocked with rainbow trout. Swimming. Campground host. Camping fee $15. (There is also a group campsite here for no more than 6 vehicles, 30 people, $120/night, 4-night stay limit.)

Mile 2.9 Pavement ends, gravel begins.

Mile 3.8 Access to **Centennial Lake** public fishing access; large parking area, no facilities (carry out garbage). Swimming, canoeing, and fishing for landlocked salmon and rainbow (stocked).

Mile 6 Road ends at Slackwater Boat Launch on the Kasilof River which provides access to Tustumena Lake (description follows). Large parking area and toilets, primitive campsites (no fees).

Tustumena Lake, which is upriver from the boat launch, is 6 miles wide and 25 miles long, accounting for more than 60,000 acres of Kenai National Wildlife Refuge. For fishing regulations, refer to the ADF&G regulations booklet or go online for statewide and regional regulations at www.sf.adfg.state.ak.us. *WARNING: Tustumena Lake is subject to sudden and severe winds. Water tem-*

peratures rarely exceed 45°F. Be prepared. Fatalities have occurred. Strong winds coming off Tustumena Glacier and the Harding Icefield can change boating conditions from calm water to 3- to 6-foot waves without warning. The silty waters create zero visibility obscuring submerged rocks and logs. Weather systems in Cook Inlet and the Gulf of Alaska can also bring high winds. Boaters unfamiliar with operating in these conditions should not venture out on lake.

S 110.5 A 163.5 H 68.6 Double-ended paved turnout to west.

S 110.6 A 163.6 H 68.5 Tustumena Lodge to west.

S 111 A 164 H 68.1 Junction with Cohoe Loop Road to west (description follows). Paved parking to east is access to ADF&Gs **Crooked Creek Weir** fish viewing area with educational kiosks and 2 viewing platforms overlooking the creek. Restored by Kenai Watershed Forum and partners, this is a good spot for fish viewing and bird watching.

This is the north **junction** with 15.3-mile **Cohoe Loop Road**, which rejoins the Sterling Highway at **Milepost S 114.3**. Use this turnoff for most direct access to **Crooked Creek State Recreation Site** and Kasilof Beach. For the state recreation site, drive west 1.5 miles from this junction then turn on Rilinda Road and continue straight 0.4 miles on access road to "Y" intersection (keep to left). Crooked Creek SRS has a large parking lot which accommodates 79 vehicles with side-by-side overnight parking; 36 day-use sites, toilets, well water, tent sites, campground host and trails along the Kasilof River for fishermen. Mike Heinicke memorial bench here is named for a long-time park host. Camping fee $15/night, day-use fee $5/vehicle.

For Kasilof Beach, drive 5.6 miles west from this junction and follow gravel road 0.7 mile to parking/camping area and beach access. Outhouses and dumpsters at site. Beach access for 4-wheel-drive vehicles only. Set-netting in season, check regulations carefully. This beach can be packed with people and vehicles, allowing little or no turn-around room for a big rig.

S 112.3 A 165.3 H 66.8 Slow vehicle turnout for southbound traffic.

S 113.3 A 166.3 H 65.8 Distance marker southbound shows Clam Gulch 5 miles, Homer 57 miles.

S 114.3 A 167.3 H 64.8 South **junction** with 15.3-mile Cohoe Loop Road which loops back to the Sterling Highway at **Milepost S 111**. For Crooked Creek State Recreation Site, use north junction with Cohoe Loop Road (see **Milepost S 111**).

S 116.5 A 169.5 H 62.6 Slow vehicle turnouts for southbound and northbound traffic.

S 117.3 A 170.3 H 61.8 Large gravel parking to east for Clam Shell Trailhead (Caribou Hills Cabin Hoppers).

S 117.4 A 170.4 H 61.7 Clam Gulch State Recreation Area, 0.5 mile west from highway via dirt access road; picnic tables, picnic shelter, toilets, water, 116 side-by-side overnight parking spaces, campground host, $15 nightly camping fee, $5 day-use fee. Long stairway leads from mid-campground down to beach. *CAUTION: High ocean bluffs are dangerous.* Short, steep access road to beach (recommended for 4-wheel-drive vehicles only); deep, loose sand at beach.

The panoramic view of Mount Redoubt, Mount Iliamna and Mount Spurr across Cook Inlet and the expanse of beach are well worth the short side trip to Clam Gulch SRA. There was no clamming on Cook Inlet's eastside beaches in 2018, and this may also be the case in 2019. According to the ADF&G, "From 2009–2015, eastside Cook Inlet razor clams experienced poor recruitment of juvenile sized razor clams and a high natural mortality rate of mature sized razor clams, which both resulted in a significant decline in abundance leading to the closure of the fishery." The closure effects beaches from the tip of Homer Spit to the mouth of the Kenai River.

S 118.2 A 171.2 H 61 CLAM GULCH (pop. 167); post office, established in 1950, Bakers Clam Shell Lodge, which had been closed since 2011, burned down in 2017.

S 119.6 A 172.6 H 59.5 Clam Gulch Lodge.

S 122.9 A 175.9 H 56.2 Double-ended paved parking area to west (no view).

S 124.9 A 177.9 H 54.2 Double-ended paved scenic viewpoint to west.

S 126.8 A 179.8 H 52.3 Double-ended turnout to west (no view).

S 127 A 180 H 52.1 Double-ended paved scenic viewpoint to west. Interpretive sign at viewpoint about the "ring of fire": Mount Iliamna, elev. 10,016 feet, 52 miles away; Mount Redoubt, elev. 10,197 feet, 54 miles away; Mount Augustine, elev. 4,025 feet, 83 miles to the south; and Mount Spurr, elev. 11,100 feet, 85 miles to the north. Mount Augustine has erupted several times, most recently in 2006. Mount Spurr last erupted on March 22, 2009, resulting in ash fall as far away as Anchorage. Visit the Alaska Volcano Observatory at www.avo.alaska.edu/index.php for details on Alaska's volcanoes.

S 130.6 A 183.6 H 48.5 Distance marker southbound shows Ninilchik 5 miles, Homer 40 miles.

S 132.2 A 185.2 H 46.9 Fishing charter and campground. [A]

S 133.4 A 186.4 H 45.7 Distance marker northbound shows Soldotna 36 miles, Kenai 48 miles, Anchorage 184 miles.

S 134.1 A 187.1 H 45 Welcome to Ninilchik (southbound sign).

S 134.2 A 187.2 H 44.9 *Slow for posted speed zone southbound.*

S 134.5 A 187.5 H 44.6 Turnoff to east for **Ninilchik River State Recreation Site Campground**; 39 campsites set among birch and spruce trees on 2 gravel loop roads (upper and lower loops); campground host; picnic tables, grills, water, outhouses; $15 camping fee. Trail to Ninilchik River; fishing for chinook and coho salmon, steelhead and Dolly Varden (seasonal restrictions apply, consult ADF&G booklet). [fish][A]

S 134.6 A 187.6 H 44.5 *CAUTION: Slow for 35-mph curve (southbound sign).* Turnoff to west on gravel Orthodox Road which leads 0.4 mile west to **Holy Transfiguration of Our Lord Russian Orthodox Church** (not visible from highway), one of the most popular tourist sites on the Kenai Peninsula. Limited parking and turnaround space in front of church. *(NOTE: Large RVs will have difficulty turning around in the parking area, as a pair of our MILEPOST® readers—one driving a motorhome with tow vehicle, the other a 5th-wheeler—discovered!)*

Beautiful views and photo-ops of Cook Inlet, Ninilchik Village and church ceme-

Picturesque Ninilchik Village offers fishing, beach walking and fantastic eagle watching in summer. (©Kris Valencia, staff)

tery (especially when fireweed is in bloom). A small American Legion cemetery and Leo Steik Veterans Memorial Wall are also located here. *NOTE: This is an active church. Please respect church services and activities.*

S 134.9 A 187.9 H 44.2 Ninilchik River Scenic Overlook and Campground (Ninilchik SRA) to east. This is a 2-tiered paved parking area with walking trail (hike or to fish) above river; toilets, picnic tables, interpretive signs, barbecues, garbage, water pump; $15 camping fee, $5 day-use fee. [fish][A]

S 135.1 A 188.1 H 44 Ninilchik River bridge. At south end of bridge turn west on Mission Avenue for **NINILCHIK VILLAGE**, at the mouth of the Ninilchik River. Drive west on Mission Avenue 0.2 mile to Y: Turn right for Ninilchik Village (designated parking area by river, gift shop, homes); road deadends at turnaround, or continue left at Y on Mission Road to Park Beach access and frontage road. Turn right to the tidal harbor and dock (0.6 mile) and the mouth of Ninilchik River (0.7 mile).

The parking area above the Ninilchik River by the old blue fishing boat (signed the "Bob Chenier Fishermen's Memorial") is a popular fishing spot on the river and good beach walking area. Crowded when the fish are in. Fantastic eagle watching from beach frontage road. [fish][A]

Ninilchik Village was settled at the turn of the 19th century and is the "old" village. (The "new" Ninilchik is located on the Sterling Highway.) The village has several old dovetailed log buildings. A trail leads up to the green and white Russian Orthodox Church on the hill (please do not walk through private property) or drive to the church via Orthodox Avenue (see **Milepost S 134.6**).

S 135.4 A 188.4 H 43.7 Turnoff for Kingsley Road access to **Alaskan Angler RV Resort & Cabins and Afishunt Charters** (0.1 mile), see description following; Ninilchik Post Office (0.2 mile); Emergency Services (0.2 mile); Senior Center on Aspen Street (0.3 mile); and junction with Oilwell

Road (0.6 mile), see description at **Milepost S 135.9**. [fish][A]

Alaskan Angler RV Resort & Cabins and Afishunt Charters. See display ad on page 568.

DOT/PF road maintenance station to east.

S 135.5 A 188.5 H 43.6 Inlet View Lodge to east. **Ninilchik View State Campground** to west has dump station ($5 fee) by entrance; 12 campsites with tables on narrow gravel loop road; toilets, drinking water fill-up and litter disposal available. Best for smaller camping units. Camping fee $15/night. View of Ninilchik Village from bluff at campground. Long stepped path leads down to beach and village. Watch for eagles. [fish][A]

S 135.7 A 188.7 H 43.4 Ninilchik School (grades K–12) to west.

S 135.8 A 188.8 H 43.3 First entrance southbound to cluster of businesses on west side of highway which include **Afishunt Charters**, Ninilchik General Store (groceries, liquor), and Rosco's (pizza, burgers).

S 135.9 A 188.9 H 44.2 Junction with Oilwell Road; Tesoro gas/diesel station. Oilwell Road leads approximately 18 miles to the Caribou Hills. The first 5 miles include fishing charters, rental cabins, B&Bs, a cafe, RV Parks, residential areas and the Ninilchik airport; **All Seasons Campground** (Mile 3.1), description follows. Pavement ends, gravel begins, at Mile 5.8. The gravel portion of the road has some steep, winding sections; beautiful views across Cook Inlet on clear days. Freddies Roadhouse at Mile 16 serves food, beer and wine; Caribou Hills trail access at Mile 18; road deadends at turnaround at Mile 18.5. [B][fish][A]

Ninilchik businesses are located alongside the Sterling Highway and on Kingsley and Oilwell roads. (©Kris Valencia, staff)

Ninilchik

S 135.9 A 188.9 H 44.2 Ninilchik (pronounced Ni-NILL-chick) is located between **Mileposts S 119** and **S 144** on the Sterling Highway, with a number of businesses located between the Ninilchik River (at **Milepost S 135.1**) and Deep Creek (at **Milepost S 137.3**). **Population:** 860. **Emergency Services:** Dial 911. **Medical Clinic,** Ninilchik Health Clinic on Kingsley Road, phone (907) 567-3970.

Visitor Information: Ninilchik Chamber of Commerce; website: www.ninilchikchamber.com; email: ninilchikchamber@gmail.com

Private Aircraft: Ninilchik airstrip, 3 SE; elev. 276 feet; length 2,400 feet; dirt and gravel; unattended.

Ninilchik is a year-round destination, with seasonal access to Cook Inlet beaches via two State Recreation Areas for salt and fresh water sport fishing, and is a seasonal port for the commercial fishing fleet, The Caribou Hills offer wintertime snow machine, cross country ski and mushing trails and summer ATV trails.

Lodging & Services

Include grocery and liquor stores, a local artists gift shop, a gas station, many B&B and cabin rentals, dining at several restaurants, guided fishing charters and custom fish processing, campgrounds and RV parks are located along several miles of the Sterling Highway or just off the highway on Oilwell Road. Ninilchik has an active senior center, a library, and a swimming pool at Ninilchik High School.

The original village of Ninilchik (signed Ninilchik Village) is reached via Mission Avenue (see description at **Milepost S 135.1**), which follows the Ninilchik River to Cook Inlet.

The **Ninilchik Chamber of Commerce Clam Scramble**, a 5K run from river to river over a beach natural obstacle course, is hosted every year by the Ninilchik Chamber of Commerce and Ninilchik Emergency Services (NES) on the biggest low tide Saturday near the June 21 Summer Solstice. The event celebrates the stunning view of Solstice over Cook Inlet and helps raise public awareness of the area's great beaches and natural resource issues while benefiting NES and the Chamber's promotion of Ninilchik.

The Kenai Peninsula Fairgrounds is

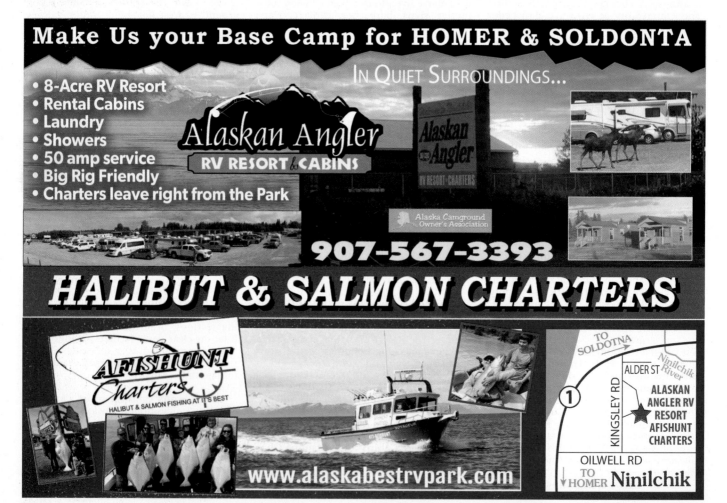

home to **Salmonfest**, held annually on the first weekend of August. Thousands of festival goers and musicians converge here for a 3-day celebration of our Salmon heritage with music. This event raises funds to support the legal defense of our natural resources against industrial development threats.

The annual **Kenai Peninsula Fair** is held here the third weekend in August. Dubbed the "biggest little fair in Alaska," it features the Peninsula Rodeo, a parade, horse show, 4H livestock competition and sale, exhibits ranging from vegetable produce to arts and crafts, a midway of carnival rides, food and craft vendors, live music and entertainment throughout this 3 day weekend event. Visit www.ninilchikchamberofcommerce.com/events/ for monthly events.

AREA FISHING: With the opening of the tractor boat launch every 1st of May at Deep Creek Beach, the Ninilchik sport fishing season officially starts, and makes Ninilchik the first lower peninsula gateway access to the saltwater fishing grounds in Cook Inlet. Ninilchik is well known as one of the oldest fishing villages on Cook Inlet, and in more recent decades, as home to world class halibut and salmon sport fishing. Record-sized fish of both species are caught here and a large fleet of guided fishing charters provide opportunity for residents and visitors to harvest this resource.

On Memorial Day weekend, Ninilchik has been referred to as the "third largest city" in Alaska, as thousands of residents of Alaska's interior arrive for the opening of the local freshwater rivers for a 3 weekend long chinook salmon season and for the opportunity for holiday recreation on the beaches in two local State recreation areas. Each month of the summer and fall offers windows of opportunity to fish for all species of salmon as well as Dolly Varden and Steelhead in the rivers here. Check local sport fishing regulations. Steelhead fishing in Ninilchik River and Deep Creek starting in mid-August through October is a not-so-well-kept local secret and well worth the effort. The halibut fishery off Ninilchik has produced some of the largest trophy halibut found in Cook Inlet, including a 466-lb. unofficial world record sport-caught halibut.

Sterling Highway Log
(continued)

S 136 A 189 H 43.1 Access west side of highway to Ninilchik businesses.

S 136.2 A 189.2 H 42.9 to west, description follows; and **Kenai Peninsula Fairgrounds** to east, site of the Kenai Peninsula 4th of July Rodeo, Salmonfest, and the Fair (see city description for additional details on events).

J&J Smart Charters. See display ad on this page.

Deep Creek View Campground. Million dollar view! Family-owned camp-

Deep Creek State Recreation Area, 0.3 mile west of the Sterling Highway, is a favorite spot with unobscured views of Mount Redoubt and Mount Iliamna. (©Kris Valencia, staff)

ground located on the bluff overlooking Cook Inlet, with an incredible view of snow-covered volcanoes, eagles soaring, and spectacular sunsets. Grassy tent camping areas; electrical hookups, dump station, shower building, and cabins with private baths. Book Alaska halibut fishing charters available now with J&J Smart Charters. Fish safely in the 28-foot Alumaweld and 30-foot ABC boats with hard-top cabins and marine head. Professional vacuum sealing, freezing, and shipping of your catch. Don't miss your Alaskan experience! Call now, toll-free number 1-888-HALIBUT (1-888-425-4288) www.smartcharters.com. See display ad on this page. [ADVERTISEMENT]

S 136.7 A 189.7 H 42.4 Bridge over Deep Creek. Recreation sites to the east on either side of Deep Creek: **Deep Creek North** and **Deep Creek South**. Deep Creek North offers camping. Deep Creek South is day use only. Both have restrooms, water, interpretive kiosks, tables and fireplaces. $15 camping fee; $5 day-use fee.

Freshwater fishing in **Deep Creek** for chinook salmon up to 40 lbs., use spinners with red bead lures, Memorial Day weekend and the 3 weekends following; Dolly Varden in July and August; coho salmon to 15 lbs., August and September; steelhead to 15 lbs., late September through October. No bait fishing permitted after Aug.

31. Mouth of Deep Creek access from **Deep Creek State Recreation Area** turnoff at **Milepost S 137.3**. NOTE: Sport fishing openings/closings can change based on Emergency Orders.

S 137.3 A 190.3 H 41.8 Turnoff to west for Deep Creek Access Road (Wayside Drive) to Deep Creek State Recreation Area (description follows). Drive 0.3 mile via steep paved road for Deep Creek SRA. A private RV park is just west of highway.

Deep Creek State Recreation Area, on the beach at the mouth of Deep Creek, is a favorite with Alaskans and tourists alike. Drive by busy boat launch area to large day-use parking area adjacent: $5 fee after 30-minute grace period. Additional gravel parking area adjacent day-use parking has 80 overnight campsites, some by the beach, others in a flat camping area surrounded by beach grasses; water, tables, dumpsters, restrooms, firepits, campground host. Camping fee $15/night per vehicle.

Anglers try to intercept chinook salmon in the salt water before the salmon reach their spawning rivers. The Deep Creek beach tractor-launch service is an Alaska State Parks concession operated by a private contractor to provide a safe, fee-based means of launching and retrieving boats up to 33' into Cook Inlet. There are only a few hours on either side of a high tide to float them

A path through a private field leads from the large turnout at Milepost S 142.5 to cliff-side view of Mount Redoubt and Mount Iliamna. (©Kris Valencia, staff)

without use of the tractor-launch. The cost of putting in and retrieving a boat is about $75.

Good bird watching in wetlands behind beach. Watch for bald eagles. The beaches here are lined with coal, which falls from the exposed seams of high cliffs.

Most visitors enjoy watching boats coming and going with their catches. Park in designated areas and keep yourself and your rig out of the busy launching area.

CAUTION: Extreme tides, cold water and bad weather can make boating here hazardous. Carry all required and recommended USCG safety equipment. There are seasonal checks by U.S. Coast Guard for personal flotation devices, boating safety. Although the mouth of Deep Creek affords boaters good protection, low tides may prevent return; check tide tables.

S 137.6 A 190.6 H 41.5 *Slow for posted speed zone northbound.*

S 138.5 A 191.5 H 40.6 Solid waste transfer station; dumpsters to west.

S 142.5 A 195.5 H 36.6 Slow vehicle lane for southbound traffic and a large paved turnout to west. This is one of the best photo viewpoints across Cook Inlet of Mount Iliamna (on the right) and Mount Redoubt (on the left); information sign. Mount Redoubt had a major eruption in December 1989. The eruptions continued through April 1990, then subsided to steam plumes. Beginning again in early 2009, Mount Redoubt was quite active on and off during the spring and summer, shutting down air traffic multiple times due to volcanic activity or the imminent threat of another eruption. Late September of 2009 the mountain was no longer actively perking and it was declared "all-clear."

S 143.7 A 196.7 H 35.4 Happy Valley Creek (sign).

S 145.2 A 198.2 H 33.9 Happy Valley Store to west.

S 148 A 201 H 31.1 Double-ended paved turnout to west; view of Mount Iliamna.

S 150.8 A 203.8 H 28.3 Stariski Creek bridge. Parking to west at north end of bridge. Access to **Stariski Creek** fish walk; public fishing access. Clean off boats to avoid spreading invasive species.

Begin Scenic Byway southbound, which extends to Homer Spit.

S 151.3 A 204.3 H 27.8 Slow vehicle turnout for southbound traffic.

S 151.5 A 204.5 H 27.6 Distance marker southbound shows Anchor Point 5 miles, Homer 20 miles.

S 151.9 A 204.9 H 27.2 Turnoff to west for **Stariski State Recreation Site**; 16 campsites in tall trees on gravel loop road; $12 nightly fee; toilets (wheelchair accessible) and well water. Small campground with outstanding views of Iliamna and Redoubt. This is a good place to stop for a picnic or to take a break. *CAUTION: Eroding bluff; supervise children.*

S 152.6 A 205.6 H 26.5 Short (0.4 mile) but extremely steep road access west to **Whiskey Gulch Beach.** At the bottom of this side road there is a small camping area to the right and a larger camping area to the left. There is an outhouse, but carry out your trash. *Do not trespass on private land.* Sign reads: "Whiskey Gulch Access Road is narrow and has a blind 90 degree turn at the top of the hill. The road is maintained as a 4-wheel drive vehicle access road only. The road to the beach is very steep and difficult to climb, even in 4-wheel drive. Two-week camping limit."

S 154.1 A 207.1 H 25 Gift shop.

S 155.7 A 208.7 H 23.4 Anchor Point welcome sign southbound.

CAUTION: Watch for black bears and watch for moose.

Distance marker northbound shows Soldotna 58 miles, Kenai 69 miles, Anchorage 206 miles.

S 156 A 209 H 23.1 *Slow for posted speed zone southbound.*

S 156.3 A 209.3 H 22.8 Grocery to west; 24-hour gas station to east.

Anchor Point

S 156.6 A 209.6 H 22.5 Anchor Point post office. Anchor Point is located on the Sterling Highway, 61 miles south of Soldotna. **Population:** 2,043. **Emergency Services:** Dial 911. **Alaska State Troopers,** at **Milepost S 156.8,** phone (907) 235-8239. **SVT Medical Clinic** on the Anchor River Inn property, phone (907) 226-2238.

Visitor Information: Anchor Point Chamber of Commerce, at **Milepost S 156.9;** phone (907) 235-2600; www.anchorpointchamber.org; info@anchorpointchamber.org. Located in the small brown building on west side of highway just south of the Alaska State Trooper's office.

Anchor Point is a full-service community with a Chamber of Commerce, post office and a variety of businesses. Lodging at **Sleepy Bear Cabins** on North Fork Road. There are coffees and treats at the drive-thru **Black Water Bend Espresso**; gas and diesel at the **Essential 1** and at **Thurmond's Far West Auto,** which also has a convenience store, propane, ice and bait; fishing charters, cafe, and camping at **Kyllonen's RV Park.** Also groceries, laundries and gift shops can

Anchor Point

To Soldotna

Visitor Information Center

Milo Fritz Road

North Fork Road

School

School Street

North Fork

To Russian Village

Anchor River

Sterling Highway

1

Anchor River (Beach) Road

Old Sterling Highway

South Fork

N W E S

To Homer

This tractor service launches and retrieves boats off the beach at the end of Anchor River Road. It is fascinating to watch. (©Kris Valencia, staff)

be found along the highway and area roads. Churches, a library, senior citizen center and VFW are among the many organizations here.

Anchor Point was originally named "Laida" by Captain James Cook in the summer of 1778, when the *Resolution* and *Discovery* sailed into Cook Inlet looking for the Northwest Passage. It was later renamed Anchor Point by early homesteaders to commemorate the loss of an anchor off the point by Captain Cook. A post office was established here in 1949.

Anchor Point is the home of the "Most Westerly Highway in North America." Take your photo with the sign located at the end of Anchor River (Beach) Road.

In addition to fishing, local attractions include beachcombing, golf and hiking. The Russian village of Nikolaevsk is located 9 miles from downtown Anchor Point and has a picturesque Russian church.

Special events in Anchor Point include Snow Rondi (last weekend in February); Saltwater King Tournament (Mother's Day weekend); Memorial Weekend Family Fun Festival; Kids All-American Fishing Derby (June); and 4th of July celebration.

The Anchor Point area is noted for its excellent seasonal chinook and coho salmon, steelhead and rainbow trout fishing opportunities. There is bank fishing along the Anchor River for chinook and coho salmon, rainbow trout and steelhead and Dolly Varden, or fishermen can access salt water by using the tractor launch on the beach. Fishing begins the weekend prior to Memorial Day weekend in Anchor Point on the Anchor River for chinook salmon and continues for the next 5 weekends. July 1, the Anchor River reopens with Dolly Varden, followed by coho salmon, which

runs into the steelhead fishery that continues until freezeup. The Cook Inlet fishery consists of all 5 species of salmon, halibut and a variety of rockfish.

Sterling Highway Log
(continued)

S 156.7 A 209.7 H 22.4 Junction with Milo Fritz Avenue to west and North Fork Road to east (description follows). Milo Fritz Avenue leads the Fire station at Mile 0.1; the VFW and library at Mile 0.2; the senior center at Mile 0.3; Anchor River Lodge at Mile 0.7; and continues to private homes (no turnaround areas).

North Fork Road to east is a 10.2-mile paved road as follows:

Mile 0.1 **Sleepy Bear Cabins**; lodging, fishing charter.

Mile 0.5 Anchor River.

Mile 9.4 Anchor Point Volunteer Fire Station No. 2.

Mile 9.5 **NIKOLAEVSK** (pop. 287), a settlement of "Russian Old Believers," who purchased land here in 1967. According to the Dept. of Community & Economic Development: "The community includes Russian Orthodox Old-Rite (Russian Old Believers) and some non-Russians, living in 3 distinct settlements. The Old Believers in this area lead a family-oriented, self-sufficient lifestyle. They use modern utilities, and food sources are from gardening, small livestock, fishing and hunting. Families are typically very large (8 to 12 children). Traditional clothing is worn, Russian is the first language, and the church dictates that males do

not shave."

Mile 9.9 Post Office.

Mile 10.1 Russian Orthodox Church.

Mile 10.2 Pavement ends, gravel road continues through private property.

S 156.8 A 209.8 H 22.3 Alaska State Troopers.

S 156.9 A 209.9 H 22.2 Anchor Point Chamber of Commerce to west.

S 157.1 A 210.1 H 22 Junction of Sterling Highway and Old Sterling Highway; take Old Sterling Highway to Anchor River Inn and **Anchor River (Beach) Road;** fishing and camping. Old Sterling Highway (paved) rejoins the Sterling Highway at **Milepost S 164.8.** Take Anchor River (Beach) Road 1.3 miles to **Kyllonen's RV Park** for camping, charters, gift shop and cafe.

Kyllonen's RV Park. See display ad this page.

> **Junction** with Old Sterling Highway and access to Anchor River (Beach) Road. See "Anchor River (Beach) Road" log on page 572.

Blue Star Memorial Highway marker at turnoff.

S 157.2 A 210.2 H 21.9 Anchor River bridge.

S 157.5 A 210.5 H 21.6 Welcome to Anchor Point (northbound) sign.

S 158.5 A 211.5 H 20.6 Distance marker

Anchor River (Beach) Road

Fishermen try their luck at the Anchor River Coho-Chinook day-use area. (©Kris Valencia, staff)

Turn off the Sterling Highway at **Milepost S 157.1** on to the Old Sterling Highway and continue past the Anchor River Inn and across the Anchor River bridge. Just beyond the bridge, turn on Anchor River (Beach) Road, a 1.2-mile spur road providing access to the popular Anchor River Recreation Area for camping and fishing. Anchor River Road ends at the most westerly point in North American accessible by a continuous road system. Worthwhile side trip.

Check current sport fishing regulations for the Anchor River. Special restrictions apply to chinook salmon.

Distance from junction (J) is shown.

J 0 Junction of Old Sterling Highway and Sterling Highway at **Milepost S 157.1**. Anchor River Inn: motel, restaurant, lounge, convenience store and gift shop.

J 0.3 Anchor River bridge, also known as "the erector set bridge." Clearance 13' 2".

J 0.4 Road forks: Turn right (west) for Anchor River (Beach) Road. Left fork is Old Sterling Highway, which continues south through rural residential area and rejoins Sterling Highway at **Milepost S 164.8**.

At this junction is the first of 5 recreation sites in Anchor River State Recreation Area: Coho-Chinook day-use area (**Anchor River State Recreation Area**) on river; parking area, toilets, dumpster, $5 day-use fee.

J 0.6 Coho Campground (Anchor River SRA); gravel parking area, toilets, tent sites in trees, picnic tables; $15 camping fee, $5 day-use fee. Side-by-side parking.

J 0.8 Cuffel Ditlon Road to **Steelhead Campground** (Anchor River SRA); numbered side-by-side day-use parking area, picnic tables, grills, grassy tent camping area in trees. Picnic tables, toilets, no water; $15 camping fee, $5 day-use fee.

J 1.1 Slidehole Campground (Anchor River SRA); 30 treed campsites on loop road, day-use parking area, $15 camping fee, $5 day-use fee, tables, firepits, water, toilets, special senior/wheelchair camping area, large day-use parking lot, trail access to river. Camp host may sell firewood.

J 1.3 Kyllonen's RV Park. Full hookups, fire rings, picnic tables and WiFi at every campsite. Showers, restrooms and laundry available to guests 24-hours. Gift shop, fish-cleaning station, ice, charters and fishing licenses. Gorgeous ocean and volcano views, a quick walk to photograph eagles at the beach as well as world-class fishing on the Anchor River. A relaxing getaway just 15 minutes from Homer. See display ad on page 571. [ADVERTISEMENT]

J 1.5 Halibut Campground (Anchor River SRA); day-use parking and picnic sites, 20 campsites on gravel loop, toilets, water. $12 camping fee, $5 day-use fee.

Loop road accesses beach. Parking with outhouse and covered viewing area by campground entrance: benches, telescopes, display boards. Gold Rush Centennial sign on mining on this beach in the 1890s. Beautiful view of Aleutian Range. Sign here marks the most westerly point on the North American continent accessible by continuous road system. N 59°46' W 151°52'.

J 1.6 Road dead-ends on shore of Cook Inlet; viewing deck, telescopes, beach access, paved parking, 12-hour limit, fee. Private tractor boat launch service. Tractors allow boats to launch at just about any tide. Fascinating to watch boats use the tractor service. Drive on beach at your own risk (soft sand).

Return to Milepost S 157.1 Sterling Highway

southbound shows Homer 14 miles.

S 161 A 214 H 18.1 Black Water Bend Espresso to west (description follows), Norman Lowell Road to east leads to the gallery of longtime Alaskan homesteader Norman Lowell, a well-known Alaska artist. Open May 1–Sept. 15.

Black Water Bend Espresso. Not your average drip! Double entrances, easy access for big rigs to get your favorite coffee, latte, decaf, smoothie, tea, juice, sugar-free drink, goodies. Something for everyone, treats for your dog. Look for big sign and pink barn. 3:30 A.M. to 10 P.M. Call ahead for faster service. blackwaterbend@horizonsatellite.com; phone (907) 235-6884. [ADVERTISEMENT]

S 161.4 A 214.4 H 17.7 Gravel turnout to east by Anchor River.

S 161.9 A 214.9 H 17.2 Distance marker northbound shows Anchor Point 5 miles.

S 164.3 A 217.3 H 14.8 North Fork (Loop) Road.

S 164.8 A 217.8 H 14.3 Junction with Old Sterling Highway (paved) which leads 8 miles northwest to connect with Anchor River (Beach) Road.

S 168.2 A 221.2 H 10.9 *Slow for posted speed zone southbound on curve.*

S 169 A 222 H 10.1 Tesoro gas/diesel station with 24-hour service; convenience store, propane, restaurant; and **Homer Bay Crest KOA RV Park** (description follows).

Homer Bay Crest KOA RV Park. A peaceful retreat from the crowds. Overlooking Kachemak Bay and Cook Inlet. All of our spacious sites have 50-amp power with full hookups and free WiFi. Restrooms, laundry, showers, picnic tables, campfire rings. Big rig friendly, pull-throughs. Tesoro station, convenience store with propane and restaurant with great food. Milepost 169. (907) 435-7995. Make reservations online at http://koa.com. [ADVERTISEMENT]

Begin 4-lane highway southbound. Begin 2-lane highway northbound. Distance marker northbound shows Soldotna 71 miles, Kenai 82 miles, and Anchorage 219 miles. Homer DOT/PF highway maintenance station east side of highway.

S 169.6 A 222.6 H 9.5 Popular rest area at top of Homer Hill has a large paved parking area and a spectacular view of Kachemak Bay, Homer Spit, glaciers, mountains and the oceans. Telescopes, wheelchair accessible restrooms, litter bins, benches and great flower displays in summer by local garden club. A great photo stop. Gold Rush Centennial interpretive sign.

Begin 6 percent downgrade southbound.

S 170.3 A 223.3 H 8.8 Expansive views of Homer Spit and Kachemak Bay as highway descends "Homer Hill."

S 171.9 A 224.9 H 7.2 West Hill Road; connects to Skyline Drive and East Hill Road for scenic drive along Homer Bluff.

S 172 A 225 H 7.1 Last physical milepost southbound on Sterling Highway.

S 172.1 A 225.1 H 7 West Homer Elementary School to east.

Slow for posted speed zone southbound.

S 172.4 A 225.4 H 6.7 St. Augustine Episcopal Church.

S 172.5 A 225.5 H 6.6 Best Western to west. Homer Middle School to east.

S 172.7 A 225.7 H 6.4 Ocean Shores Resort & RV Park See display ad on page 574.

S 172.8 A 225.8 H 6.3 Junction with Pioneer Avenue; auto parts store, Fat Olives restaurant and a liquor store. Turn on Pioneer for downtown **HOMER** (*description begins on this page*). Drive 0.2 mile on Pioneer Avenue and turn left on Bartlett Avenue for the **Pratt Museum** (*see description and display ad on page 577*). Pioneer Avenue continues to Homer businesses, the police and fire department, the connects with East End Road.

S 173 A 226 H 6.1 Homer Chamber of Commerce Visitor Center to the west.

S 173.1 A 226.1 H 6 Junction with Main Street; auto parts store. Turn east to connect with Pioneer Avenue to downtown Homer. Turn west then turn on W. Bunnell Avenue for **Driftwood Inn, Charters & RV Park.** Turn on E. Bunnell Avenue, then right on Beluga Avenue, for **Bishop's Beach Park**; public beach access, parking, picnic tables and Beluga Slough trailhead.

S 173.2 A 226.2 H 5.9 Islands & Ocean Visitor Center. to the west. The center is open daily from 9 A.M. to 5 P.M., Memorial Day through Labor Day; Tuesday through Saturday from noon to 5 P.M. the rest of the year. Admission is free. This facility allows visitors to "virtually visit" Alaska Maritime National Wildlife Refuge, which encompasses the remote Alaska coastline through interactive exhibit. Ample parking, restrooms, bookstore, wheelchair accessible. **Beluga Slough Trail** access. Inquire inside about naturalist-led walks. The center plays host to the annual Kachemak Bay Shorebird Festival in May.

S 173.3 A 226.3 H 5.8 Chevron station with store (RV supplies) at Poopdeck St.

S 173.4 A 226.4 H 5.7 Safeway Center with Starbucks, Wells Fargo Bank.

S 173.5 A 226.5 H 5.6 Heath Street. Homer post office (ZIP code 99603) northeast side of highway. Homer Animal Shelter is down side street to west.

S 173.6 A 226.6 H 5.5 Entrance to dump station; fee charged.

S 173.7 A 226.7 H 5.4 Traffic light at Lake Street; McDonald's. Access to Pioneer Avenue business area and Lakeside Center, Ulmers True Value Hardware and pharmacy.

S 174 A 227 H 5.1 Causeway crosses Beluga Lake; view of floatplane bases.

S 174.1 A 227.1 H 5 Turnoff for **Beluga Lake Lodge** (dining, lodging).

S 174.2 A 227.2 H 4.9 Farmers Market takes place here Wednesdays 3–6 P.M. and Saturdays 10 A.M. to 3 P.M. in summer.

S 174.4 A 227.4 H 4.7 Douglas Place. Access to Alaska Dept. of Fish and Game office at 3298 Douglas Place (behind Alaska Tire Co.). Stop by for a current copy of area sport fishing regulations.

S 174.6 A 227.6 H 4.5 Airport (FAA) Road to Homer Airport terminal and Beluga Wetlands Wildlife Observation deck across from airport.

S 174.8 A 227.8 H 4.3 Junction with Kachemak Drive; access to air charter services. Start of the **Homer Spit Walking Trail**; trailhead parking here for access to this pedestrian/bike trail along Homer Spit. This trail offers a fabulous ride along Homer Spit, with 2 viewpoints overlooking Mud Bay with telescopes and information boards. A favorite with birders.

Lighthouse Village and restaurant to north. Sterling Highway crosses onto Homer Spit (see description in Homer Attractions).

S 175.3 A 228.3 H 3.8 Mariner Beach Park; public parking for beach access and

The Homer Spit is popular for camping, beachcombing, kite flying and strolls on the beach.
(©Kris Valencia, staff)

for camping (RVs and tents); picnic tables, firepits, outhouse, fee charged. Self-register or stop at the Camp Fee Office here. Favorite kite flying spot.

S 176.4 A 229.4 H 2.7 Highway passes weathered, beached vessel that resembles a pirate ship and serves as a private home. Good view of old boats and buoys from pedestrian/bike path. Private property, be respectful and stay on path.

S 176.9 A 229.9 H 2.2 Kevin Bell Arena (Homer ice rink). Ice hockey is very popular in Homer (and in Alaska!).

S 177.7 A 230.7 H 1.4 Heritage RV Park with 24-hour office, private beach. See description under "Camping" in Homer.

S 177.9 A 230.9 H 1.2 Nick Dudiak Fishing Lagoon; public parking, restrooms, accessible for people with disabilities. Fee Office to north for Homer Spit public camping permits. The City of Homer provides spaces for beach camping and limited RV parking (no hookups); phone (907) 235-1583.

S 178 A 231 H 1.1 Fishing Hole public campground (fee charged, self-register); restrooms, dump station, potable water, dumpster, picnic tables. Fish cleaning station. Homer's Pier One Theatre is here.

S 178.1 A 231.1 H 1 Freight Dock Road. Access to public boat ramp, boat trailer parking, Harbor Master Office and deep-water dock. *The Time Bandit* and other vessels from the *Deadliest Catch* TV series may be docked here.

S 178.2 A 231.2 H 0.9 Public parking, restrooms for Ramp 5. From here to the end of the Homer Spit Road it can get pretty congested, with vehicles and pedestrians. Boat Harbor parking area has 7-day limit, no camping. Boardwalk shopping and dining to west.

Slow for posted speed limit.

S 178.3 A 231.3 H 0.8 Homer Chamber of Commerce Spit Office; derby tickets, maps, information, restrooms.

S 178.5 A 231.5 H 0.6 Fee parking and public restrooms; Ramp 2.

S 178.6 A 231.6 H 0.5 Famous Salty Dawg Saloon & Lighthouse, built in 1898.

S 178.7 A 231.7 H 0.4 Often photographed **Seafarer's Memorial**, a monument to those who have been lost at sea. Memorial Bell, picnic tables and benches. Take Fish Dock Road (opposite memorial) to Coal Point Park, a small park with a harbor view.

S 178.8 A 231.8 H 0.3 Homer Spit Campground has beachside campsites with power hookup, showers and laundry; see description under "Camping" in Homer.

S 178.9 A 231.9 H 0.2 Ice Dock Road to U.S. Coast Guard dock; intersects with Fish Dock Road. Small park overlooks harbor.

S 179 A 232 H 0.1 Alaska State Ferry Homer Terminal.

S 179.1 A 232.1 H 0 Sterling Highway ends at **Land's End Resort** at the tip of Homer Spit; *see description on page 576*. Parking area by beach. Beach fishing. Walk on beach around the front of the Land's End Resort to see the memorial bench dedicated to Jean Keene, the "Eagle Lady."

NOTE: It is illegal to feed eagles, crows, gulls and ravens in Homer.

Homer

S 179.1 A 232.1 H 0 Located on the southwestern Kenai Peninsula on the north shore of Kachemak Bay; 226 miles by highway or 40 minutes by jet aircraft from Anchorage. **Population:** 5,252. **Emergency Services:** Dial 911. **City Police,** phone (907) 235-3150. **Fire Department** and **Ambulance,** phone (907) 235-3155. **Animal Control,** phone (907) 235-3141. **Port/ Harbor,** phone (907) 235-3160. **Coast Guard,** phone (907) 235-4288. **Hospital,** South Peninsula Hospital, phone (907) 235-8101. **Veterinary Clinic,** phone (907) 235-8960.

Visitor Information: Chamber of Commerce Visitor Center is located on the Sterling Highway (Homer Bypass) between

The iconic Salty Dawg Saloon on the Homer Spit is a favorite stop and photo op for visitors.
(©Kris Valencia, staff)

Pioneer and Main Street as you drive into town. The center offers personalized travel information, free maps, WiFi, picnic tables, restrooms and information on activities and lodging. Open year-round, daily in summer. Contact the Homer Chamber of Commerce, 201 Sterling Highway, Homer 99603; phone during business hours (907) 235-7740; website www.homeralaska.org. To find out about local concerts, art shows and other arts events in Homer, phone the Homer Council of the Arts at (907) 235-4288; or check out the *Homer News & Homer Tribune*, (Thursdays); www.homernews.com.

The Alaska Maritime National Wildlife Refuge's **Islands & Ocean Visitor Center**, located on the Sterling Highway, is a state of the art interpretive and educational facility that offers ranger-led walks and activities, hosts family nature programs and provides information on area wildlife hotspots. Explore, experience and discover the national treasure. Open daily from 9 A.M. to 5 P.M., Memorial Day–Labor Day. Winter hours Tuesday–Saturday noon to P.M. Admission is free. For more information, phone (907) 235-6961, email: alaskamaritime@fws.gov or visit www.fws.gov/refuge/Alaska–Maritime/.

The Pratt Museum is open daily 10 A.M. to 6 P.M. from mid-May to mid-September; open noon to 5 P.M. Tuesday through Saturday from mid-September to mid-May. Contact the Pratt Museum, 3779 Bartlett St., Homer 99603. Phone (907) 235-8635; email info@prattmuseum.org; www.prattmuseum.org.

Elevation: Sea level to 800 feet. **Climate:** Winter temperatures occasionally fall below zero, but seldom colder. The Kenai Mountains north and east protect Homer from severe cold, and Cook Inlet provides warming air currents. The highest temperature recorded is 81°F. Average annual precipitation is 27.9 inches. Prevailing winds are from the northeast, averaging 6.5 mph/10.5 kmph.

Radio: KGTL-AM 620, KWVV 103.5/104.9/106.3, MBN-FM 107.1/96.7/95.3, KBBI-AM 890, KMJG-FM 88.9; KPEN-FM 99.3/100.9/102.3, KWHQ-FM 98.3. **Television:** KTUU, KTBY, KTVA, KAKM, KIMO. **Newspaper:** *Homer News* (weekly), *Homer Tribune* (weekly).

Private Aircraft: Homer airport on Airport Road; elev. 78 feet; length 7,400 feet; asphalt; fuel 100LL, Jet A; attended. Terminal building. Homer was established on the north shore of Kachemak Bay at Homer Spit in 1895, and named for local prospector Homer Pennock. A post office was established here in 1896.

Kachemak, the Russian name for the bay, means "high cliffs on the water." Another interpretation of the name suggests it means "smoky bay" and is derived from the smoke which once rose from the smoldering coal seams jutting from the clay bluffs of the upper north shore of Kachemak Bay and the cliffs near Anchor Point. In the early days, many of the exposed coal seams were slowly burning from causes unknown. Today the erosion of these bluffs drops huge fragments of lignite and bituminous coal on the beaches, creating a plentiful supply of winter fuel for the residents. There are an estimated 400,000,000 tons of coal deposit in the immediate vicinity of Homer.

A coal mine was operating at Homer's Bluff Point in the late 1800s, and a railroad carried the coal out to the end of Homer

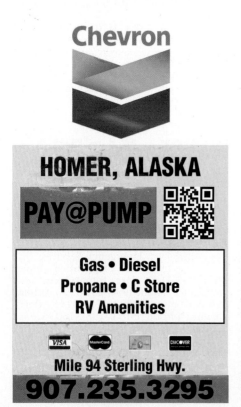
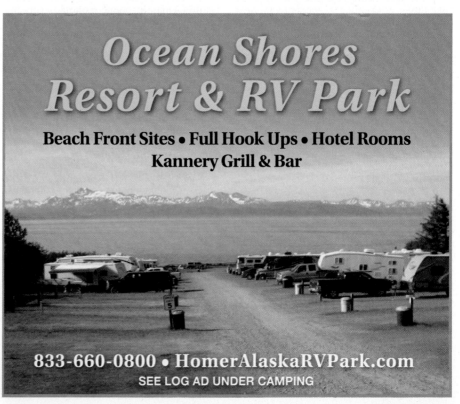

Spit. (The railroad was abandoned in 1907.) Gold seekers debarked at Homer, bound for the goldfields at Hope and Sunrise. Coal mining operations ceased around the time of WWI, but settlers continued to trickle into the area, some to homestead, others to work in the canneries built to process Cook Inlet fish.

Jutting out for 4.5 miles from the Homer shore is the **Homer Spit**, a long, narrow bar of gravel. The road along the backbone of the Spit is part of the Sterling Highway, which is the main road through Homer. Adjacent the road is a multi-use bike and walking path that spans the length of the spit. The Spit has had quite a history, and it continues to be a center of activity for the town. In 1964, after the earthquake, the Spit sank 4 to 6 feet, requiring several buildings to be moved to higher ground.

Today, Homer Spit is the site of a major dock facility for boat loading, unloading, servicing and refrigerating. The deep-water dock can accommodate 340-foot vessels and 30-foot drafts, making it accessible to cruise and cargo ships. The Pioneer Dock can accommodate ships up to 800 feet. Homer is home port to the Alaska Marine Highway ferry MV *Tustumena* (transportation to Aleutian Islands and Kodiak Island) and U.S. Coast Guard vessels. The small-boat harbor on the Spit has a 5-lane load/launch ramp. Also in the small-boat harbor area are the harbormaster's office, canneries, parking/camping areas, charter services, small shops, live theater, galleries, restaurants, motels and bed and breakfasts.

Rising behind downtown are bluffs which level off at about 1,200 feet to form the southern rim of the western plateau of the Kenai Peninsula. These slopes provide a colorful backdrop from the bay, tinted in green and pastel shades by wildflowers from June to September, and in golds and yellows in the fall. The slopes are also prime residential real estate, thanks to their view of magnificent Kachemak Bay.

Homer's picturesque setting, mild climate, arts, dining and great fishing (especially for halibut) attract thousands of visitors each year. In addition to its tourist industry and role as a trade center, Homer's commercial fishing industry is an important part of its economy. Homer calls itself the "Halibut Fishing Capital of the World." Manufacturing and seafood processing, government offices, trades and construction are other key industries.

Homer is host to a large artist community. Potters, sculptors, painters and jewelers practice their crafts and sell their goods in local shops, farmers markets and galleries. The local theater group provides live performances year-round.

Homer has 8 schools. Homer High School has the complete skeleton of a sperm whale hanging from the ceiling of the school's lobby. A local fisherman found the dead whale washed up on Chugach Island in 1998. It was recovered and the skeleton preserved through the efforts of the U.S. Coast Guard, the Pratt Museum and the high school students.

Lodging & Services

USA Today Travel chose Homer as the "most picturesque small town in Alaska," November 2015 and *Budget Travel* chose Homer as 1 of the "top 10 coolest small towns" in 2006. Homer has hundreds of small businesses offering a wide variety of goods and services. Choose from accommodations at many hotels, lodges, vacation rentals, cabins and bed and breakfasts; see

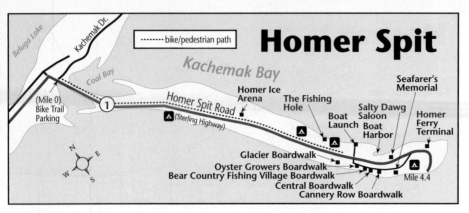

Homer Spit

Kachemak Bay

bike/pedestrian path

Beluga Lake

Kachemak Dr.

Coal Bay

(Mile 0)
Bike Trail
Parking

Homer Spit Road

(Sterling Highway)

Homer Ice
Arena

The Fishing
Hole

Boat
Launch

Salty Dawg
Saloon

Boat
Harbor

Seafarer's
Memorial

Homer
Ferry
Terminal

Glacier Boardwalk
Oyster Growers Boardwalk
Bear Country Fishing Village Boardwalk
Central Boardwalk
Cannery Row Boardwalk

Mile 4.4

descriptions following. Camping at private and municipal campgrounds (see "Camping" this section). Dozens of restaurants offer everything from cafes to fine dining. Reservations are advised for both lodging and camping in summer.

Homer has a post office, library, museum, laundromats, gas stations with propane and dump stations (one on the Homer Spit near the fishing lagoon and one across from the post office), banks, churches, a hospital and airport terminal. There are many fishing charter services, boat repair and storage facilities, marine fuel at Homer marina; bait, tackle and sporting goods stores; and art galleries, gift shops and groceries. Homer Spit has long-term parking and camping.

The Beluga Lake Lodge is a cozy vintage property that is lovingly being remodeled and updated. We choose to keep some of its charm and intricacies. One of the most beautiful locations in Homer, overlooking Beluga Lake and estuary. There you can witness abundant wildlife and floatplane activity. With a variety of room styles, our 35 units can accommodate most needs, from families to singles. All are nonsmoking and have free WiFi, private baths, free local phone, cable TV. Some have full kitchens while others have a micro/fridge combo. The Bar and Grill is fast becoming famous for some of the best gourmet burgers and

seafood in the area. The lodge is centrally located near the airport, beachcombing, and nearby fishing charters, flight-viewing and bear-viewing tours, galleries and shopping. www.belugalakelodging.com. (907) 235-5995, 888-795-6343. Located at 204 Ocean Drive Loop. [ADVERTISEMENT]

Driftwood Inn, Charters and RV Park. Offering rooms with king-size beds. Charming, newly refurbished, historic beachfront inn, lodge and cottage with 27 rooms and full-hookup RV park. Both have spectacular views overlooking beautiful Kachemak Bay, mountains, glaciers. Quiet in-town location. Immaculately clean, charming rooms. Free coffee, tea, local information. Comfortable common areas with TV, fireplace, library, microwave, refrigerator, barbecue, shellfish cooker, fish cleaning area, freezer, picnic and laundry facilities. Central highspeed internet access, WiFi free. Economy breakfast available in lobby. We are a smoke-free facility. Halibut and salmon charters available year-round with experienced captains and lifelong Alaskans. The RV park has 20-/30-/50-amp electric, water, sewer, clean, comfortable laundry and shower room for RV guests. Friendly, knowledgeable staff, specializes in helping make your stay in Homer the best possible. Reasonable, seasonal rates. Pet friendly. Open year-round. Owned by 5th generation

Alaskans. Write, call for brochure. 135 W. Bunnell Ave., MP, Homer, AK 99603. (907) 235-8019. Email: driftwoodinn@alaskan. com. Website: www.thedriftwoodinn.com. See display ad on this page. [ADVERTISEMENT]

Land's End. Just the beginning of your Alaskan adventure. Surrounded by majestic views of Kachemak Bay and nestled at the end of the Homer Spit, Land's End is Homer's premier destination for waterfront lodging. Dine in the Chart Room Restaurant or relax and soak in the view from your private deck. Take a short stroll to the harbor for world-class fishing or shop until you drop with the boardwalk stores. We are also home to 2,900 square feet of conference/event space with an ocean front view. Reservations: (907) 235-0400; Lands-End-Resort. com. [ADVERTISEMENT]

Camping

©Kris Valencia, staff

Homer is a popular camping spot, with several private RV parks (descriptions follow; see also ads this section). There are 2 City of Homer public campgrounds (Mariner Beach and Fishing Hole) and 2 tenting areas on Homer Spit. Daily camping fees are $24 for RVs, $15 for tents; no reservations; no hook-

---

HOMER ADVERTISERS

Accommodations
Beluga Lake Lodge ....Ph. (907) 235-5995
Driftwood Inn & RV Park.............Ph. (907) 235-8019
Lands End Resort.........................Ph. (907) 235-0400
Ocean Shores Resort &
  RV Park ....Ph. 1-833-660-0800

Attractions, Activities & Entertainment
Homer Trolley Tour.....................Ph. (907) 299-6210
Islands and Ocean
  Visitor Center ....Ph. (907) 235-6545
Pratt Museum ....Ph. (907) 235-8635

Campgrounds
Driftwood Inn & RV Park.............Ph. (907) 235-8019
Heritage RV Park.........................Ph. (907) 226-4500
Homer Bay Crest KOA RV Park..Ph. (907) 435-7995
Homer Spit Campground ....Ph. (907) 235-8206
Ocean Shores RV Park..............Ph. 1-833-660-0800

Fishing Charters
Bob's Trophy Charters...............Ph. 1-800-770-6400
Driftwood Inn Charters ....Ph. (907) 235-8019

Shopping and Services
Chevron ....Ph. (907) 235-3295
NOMAR® (Northern Marine
  Canvas Products)......................Ph. (907) 235-8363

Visitor Information
Homer Chamber of
  Commerce..................................Ph. (907) 235-7740

ups; 14-day limit; self-register or check in with the Camp Fee Office at Mariner Beach Park; phone (907) 235-1583. Karen Hornaday Hillside Park, a City of Homer campground, is accessed via Bartlett and Fairview avenues (follow signs). Located behind the ball fields, in a densely treed and brushy hillside, the park has 31 campsites, restrooms, water, picnic tables, firepits, trash cans and a playground, but no campground host. Camping fee is $24/day for RVs, $15 for tents. No reservations, no hookups; only small RVs. Information available at visitor center. Weekly rates, 2–week limit.

Homer offers 2 municipal RV dump sites: on Homer Spit at Fishing Hole, near the lagoon, and across from the post office along the Sterling Highway.

Heritage RV Park. A full-service RV park located on the Homer Spit, adjacent to the "Fishing Hole." All spacious sites include hookups; 50 amp electric, septic, city water, Satellite TV and free WiFi. Laundry room with free showers for guests. Beachfront sites are directly on the water for wonderful beachcombing, clamming, eagle-watching and fishing. Local Alaskan art store and coffee cafe in the common building. Enjoy the bike trail, charters and all of Homer's recreation opportunities on the Homer Spit! See display ad on page 575. [ADVERTISEMENT]

Homer Spit Campground, where the land ends and the sea begins, on beautiful Kachemak Bay. RV beach camping. Showers, electric to full hookups, pull throughs, dump station, laundromat, WiFi and gift shop. Family owned and operated for over 40 years. (907) 235-8206. homerspitcamp ground@gci.net. See display ad on page 576. [ADVERTISEMENT]

Ocean Shores RV Park (Good Sam), 455 Sterling Highway, next to Kannery Grill and Bar on right coming into Homer. Big rigs welcome. Spectacular view of Kachemak Bay, beachfront setting. Large pull-through spaces in a terraced park. WiFi available at site. Full/partial hookups, super clean restrooms, free showers, laundry, TV, picnic area. Easy walking distance to downtown Homer. Discounted fishing charter rates for guests and booking reservations assistance. Reservations at email mbarling1965@gmail. com. See display ad page 574. [ADVERTISEMENT]

Transportation

Air: Regularly scheduled air service to Anchorage. Several charter services also operate out of Homer; inquire locally.

Ferry: The Alaska State ferry system connects Homer with Seldovia and Kodiak. The Alaska Marine Highway System ferry terminal is located at the Pioneer Dock on Homer Spit; phone (907) 235-8449. Information,

End of Homer Spit in front of Land's End Resort. Public parking is available at several spots along the 4-mile-long Homer Spit; pay attention to parking restrictions. (©Kris Valencia, staff)

reservations and ticketing, phone 1-800-642-0066, (907) 235-8449. Schedules are online at www.ferryalaska.com.

Water taxis, catamarans and day-tour boats offer passenger service to Seldovia and to Halibut Cove from Homer Spit.

Car Rental cars and Taxi: Available.

Charter Boats: See ads this section.

Private Boats: Transient moorage available; 5-lane Load and Launch Ramp (fee charged). Harbor Office at 4311 Freight Dock Rd., Ramp 7; phone (907) 235-3160.

Attractions

The Pratt Museum, located off Pioneer Avenue at 3779 Bartlett St., is a must-stop for visitors interested in the arts, science and culture of the area. *Kachemak Bay, an Exploration of People and Place*, displays artifacts from the first Native people here, thousands of years ago, to those of homesteaders of the 1930s and 1940s. Audio exhibits, films, lectures and interactive exhibits also introduce visitors to the region.

Aquariums and a tide pool tank show live Kachemak Bay sea creatures. Fish feedings are Tuesdays and Fridays at 4 P.M. throughout the year. Alaska birds and land and sea mammals, including the complete skeletons of a Bering Sea beaked whale and a beluga whale, are on display.

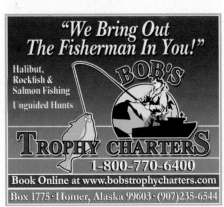
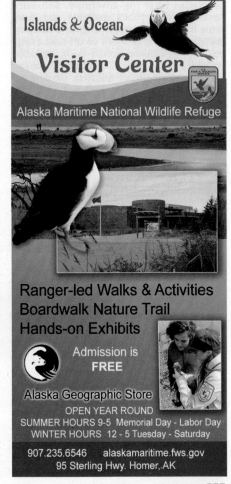
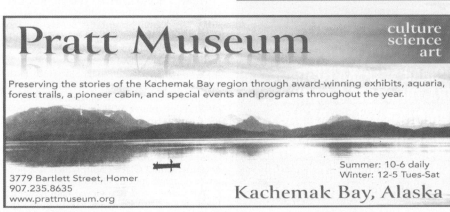

A popular attraction at the museum is the Sea Bird Cam, showing live images via remote video camera of the seabird rookery at Gull Island, located 8 miles away in Kachemak Bay. Between May and September, visitors may manipulate the camera for a close-up view of common murres, kittiwakes, puffins, cormorants and glaucous-winged gulls in their natural habitat.

Summer visitors may take a self-guided tour through the outdoor Botanical Garden and on the Forest Ecology Trail. The Harrington Cabin features objects and artifacts from years gone by, when homesteaders lived off the land and sea.

Admission is charged. Under renovation in 2018, the museum will reopen in May 2019. Summer hours (mid-May to mid-September) are 10 A.M. to 6 P.M. daily. Winter hours are noon to 5 P.M., Tuesday through Saturday. Phone (907) 235-8635; website www.prattmuseum.org.

Homer Trolley Tour. Sit back and enjoy the ride on our narrated Trolley tour of Homer. We pick up at RV parks, hotels, along the Spit and through Old Town. We stop at downtown galleries, Pratt Museum, Islands & Ocean Visitors Center and more. Hop on and hop off with a $15 All Day pass. For information and schedules, visit us online at www.homertrolley.com. Groups welcome/special events. Call (907) 299-6210. [ADVERTISEMENT]

Bishop's Beach is accessible by car from the Sterling Highway (Homer Bypass) at Main Street. Parking, public access to the beach, picnic tables and the trailhead for the award-winning Beluga Slough Pedestrian Trail are located at Bishop's Beach. It is possible to walk several miles along the coastline in either direction from Bishop's Beach. *CAUTION: Check tide tables.* (A walking path connects the beach with the Alaska Islands and Ocean Visitor Center.)

Homer Spit. Visitors and residents naturally gravitate toward this bustling strip of land jutting out into Kachemak Bay. Highlights include a 4.5-mile biking/walking trail from the parking area at Kachemak Drive. Watch for eagles on the mud flats from the trail's viewing platforms.

The **Seafarer's Memorial** (pictured below) at **Milepost S 179**, is a Spit landmark dedicated to those who have lost their lives at sea. There is a parking area adjacent the

©Kris Valencia, staff

memorial. Another Spit landmark and favorite photo subject is the **Salty Dawg Saloon**. Originally a cabin, built in 1897, it also served as Homer's first post office (among other things). It was connected to an adjacent structure (built in 1909) and opened as the Salty Dawg Saloon in 1957.

Fishing charter services and a variety of shops and restaurants are housed in the Spit's unique boardwalk structures. The Spit also offers camping and accommodations. The Homer Boat Harbor and State Ferry Terminal are located on the Spit.

The Homer Farmers Market is held on Ocean Drive (Sterling Highway, between Beluga Lake and the Spit) across from the Washboard, every Saturday, 10 A.M. to 3 P.M., beginning the last weekend in May, and Wednesdays, 2–5 P.M., beginning the last weekend in May through the last Saturday of September. Locally grown produce, flowers, seafood, prepared foods, and hand crafted items. Music, chef at the market demonstrations, and more. No pets or smoking. Visit www.homerfarmersmarket.org or phone (907) 299-7540 for more information.

Islands & Ocean Visitor Center, located at **Milepost S 173.2** Sterling Highway, is a state-of-the-art interpretive and educational facility for the Alaska Maritime National Wildlife Refuge. This facility allows visitors to "virtually visit" the remote Alaska coastline through interactive exhibits that capture the islands, rocky coastline, seabirds and marine mammals in hands-on exhibits and informational videos.

Ample parking, restrooms, bookstore, wheelchair accessible. Access to Beluga Slough trail. Ask about naturalist-led walks and activities. The Center is open daily from 9 A.M. to 5 P.M., Memorial Day through Labor Day; Tuesday–Saturday from noon to 5 P.M. the rest of the year. Admission is free. The Center is also the main meeting place for the annual Kachemak Bay Shorebird Festival held in May (see description below).

The Kachemak Bay Shorebird Festival celebrates the arrival of over 100,000 migrating shorebirds to the tidal flats of Kachemak Bay. The 27th annual festival is May 9–12, 2019. Festival highlights include keynote speakers from the ornithology world, offers guided bird walks and workshops for beginning and advanced birders. It hosts Junior Birder activities for kids. This wonderful event promotes awareness of this critical shorebird habitat that provides a feeding and resting place for at least 20 species of shorebirds on the last leg of their journey from Hawaii and Central and South America to the fertile breeding grounds of the Arctic. Sponsored by Friends of Alaska National Wildlife Refuges and U.S. Fish & Wildlife Service, with Alaska Islands & Ocean Visitor Center as festival headquarters. For more information visit www.kachemakshorebird.org.

Beluga Wetlands Wildlife Observation Deck. Turnoff at **Milepost S 174.6**, Airport (FAA) Road. More than 100 bird species visit this ADF&G site. Interpretive signs and boardwalk. Locals also pick berries, ski, hike and view wildlife here.

The Historic Homer Theatre (http://homertheatre.com), located at 106 West Pioneer Ave., is the longest running movie house in Alaska. The theater shows current films and is also home to the Homer Documentary Film Festival in late September.

See a play. Homer's community theater—Pier One Theatre—presents weekend performances of plays, dance concerts and a variety of other shows, from Memorial Day to Labor Day (typical play nights are Thursday–Sunday). Pier One, which started in 1973, is located in a converted city warehouse on Homer Spit. Phone (907) 235-7333.

Take a scenic drive. The glaciers that spill down from the Harding Icefield straddling the Kenai Mountains across the bay create an ever-changing panorama visible from most points in Homer. The most spectacular and largest of these glaciers is Grewingk Glacier in Kachemak Bay State Park, visible to the east directly across Kachemak Bay from Homer. The glacier was named by Alaska explorer William H. Dall in 1880 for Constantin Grewingk, a German geologist who had published a work on the geology and volcanism of Alaska. The Grewingk Glacier has a long gravel bar at its terminal moraine, called Glacier Spit, which is a popular excursion spot by charter plane or boat.

For glacier and bay views, take East End Road to East Hill Road and continue up the

hill to junction with Skyline Drive; turn left on Skyline and follow it to West Hill Road, which heads downhill to junction with the Sterling Highway at **Milepost S 171.9**. Or just continue out busy East End Road, which accesses Bear Creek Winery (turnoff at Mile 3). Good Kachemak Bay views begin about Mile 12, although both routes lack formal viewpoints.

Go Kayaking or Paddle Boarding. Try Homer Spit outfitters like True North Adventures for guided kayak trips and rentals. They also offer SUPing (Stand Up Paddle-boarding) trips, rentals and instruction.

Charter Boats and water taxis operating out of the boat harbor on Homer Spit offer sightseeing and fishing trips and drop-off service for kayakers and wilderness hikers. Homer is one of Alaska's largest charter fishing areas (most charters are for halibut fishing). Charter operators provide gear, bait and expert knowledge of the area. Several sightseeing boats operate off the Homer Spit, taking visitors to view the bird rookery on Gull Island, and providing transportation to Halibut Cove, Seldovia and Tutka Bay Wilderness Lodge (for cooking classes and lodging). Sightseeing/wildlife viewing boat trips are generally available from Memorial Day to Labor Day.

Bear Viewing. Homer is often referred to as the "bear viewing capital of Alaska." It is the main base for visitors flying across Cook Inlet to bear viewing areas at **McNeil River State Game Sanctuary** and **Katmai National Park**, as well as areas within Lake Clark National Park. Local air services offer bear viewing, as well as custom charters, flightseeing, fly-in fishing and hiking.

Visits to the **McNeil River** game sanctuary are on a permit basis; a drawing is held in March each year. (Permits are not required for Katmai or Lake Clark visits.) Applications for McNeil River permits are available from the Alaska Dept. of Fish and Game online at www.adfg.alaska.gov/index. cfm?adfg=viewingpermits.mcneil_apply; or phone (907) 267-2100.

©Sharon Nault

Visit Halibut Cove. Located 7 miles southeast of Homer on the east shore of Kachemak Bay. A day trip to Halibut Cove via the *Danny J* ferry (which includes cruising Gull Island), then a meal at the Saltry Restaurant, is a top attraction.

©Sharon Nault

Visit Seldovia. Located 16 miles from Homer on Seldovia Bay, Seldovia is con-

Taking an early morning fishing charter? This is what Homer Harbor looks like at 4 A.M. in early September. (©David Ranta, staff)

nected to Homer by the Alaska Marine Highway ferry system and several private water taxis, catamarans and tour boats that depart Homer Spit in summer. Seldovia has retained much of its old Alaska charm and traditions (the historic boardwalk dates from 1931).

Seldovia has most visitor facilities, including hotels, B&Bs, a general store, a whole-foods store, restaurants, coffee shops, liquor store and gift stores. Favorite activities here are kayaking and bird watching.

The Center for Alaskan Coastal Studies in Homer is an outdoor education nonprofit organization that offers a variety of opportunities for people of all ages and abilities to connect with the nature of Alaska year-round on guided explorations that range from 1 hour to multi-day stays at 3 sites on Kachemak Bay: Carl E. Wynn Nature Center, Peterson Bay Field Station, and at the Center's yurt on Homer Spit. Phone (907) 235-6668, stop by their headquarters at 708 Smokey Bay Way in Homer, or visit www. akcoastalstudies.org for details.

Kachemak Bay State Park is located on the south shore of the bay and accessible by float plane or private water taxis from Homer. It is one of Alaska's most popular parks for sea kayaking, hiking, fishing and beachcombing. The park's coves, bay, valleys and mountains provide a great variety of recreational opportunities, including: more than 80 miles of trails (see website for trail descriptions: www.dnr.state.ak.us/parks/ units/kbay/kbaytrs.htm); campsites at Glacier Spit, Halibut Cove Lagoon, China Poot Lake and additional backcountry locations; 5 public-use cabins; and excellent kayaking, clamming, tide pooling and beachcombing opportunities. For cabin information visit dnr.alaska.gov/parks/cabins/kenai or reserve at www.reserveamerica.com.

The Kachemak Bay Water Trail is a 125-mile route that extends from the Homer Spit, east along Kachemak Bay to the head of the bay, and further along the southern side of the bay to the City of Seldovia. The water route passes by public and private land, diverse habitat from intertidal areas to alpine trails, and spectacular wildlife viewing opportunities. www.kachemakbaywatertrail.org.

Fish the Annual Homer Jackpot Halibut Derby, sponsored by the Homer Chamber of Commerce, runs from May 15 to Sept.

15. $10 tickets are available for purchase at 28 locations in Homer and at the Chamber Derby Shack on the spit. The state's largest cash halibut derby provides around 100 tagged fish and final jackpot prize. The derby also has a $50,000 and $10,000 prize drawing for a tagged fish. Tickets are available at the Jackpot Halibut Derby headquarters on Homer Spit, at the Chamber of Commerce and Visitor Information Center and from some local businesses. Phone (907) 235-7740; www.homerhalibutderby.com.

AREA FISHING: The Kachemak Bay and Cook Inlet area is one of Alaska's most popular spots for halibut fishing, with catches often weighing 100 to 200 lbs. (typical catch is in the 20–30 lb. range). Guides and charters are available locally.

Halibut up to 350 lbs. are fished from June through September; fish the bottom with herring. Year-round trolling for chinook salmon is popular; use small herring or artificial lures. Chinook salmon may also be taken during late May and June in area streams. Pink salmon (4 to 5 lbs.) may be caught in July and August; use winged bobbers, small weighted spoons and spinners. Similar tackle or fresh roe will catch coho salmon weighing 6 to 8 lbs. in August and September. Dolly Varden are taken throughout the area April to October; try single eggs, small spinners, spoons or wet flies. Steelhead and rainbow trout are available in local streams, but are catch and release only.

Fishermen have had great success in recent years casting from the shore of Homer Spit for chinook salmon. The Nick Dudiak Fishing Lagoon (named by the City of Homer for a state fisheries biologist who resided in Homer from 1977–2005, and referred to as the Fishing Lagoon or Spit Lagoon) on the Homer Spit supports a large run of hatchery-produced chinook and coho salmon beginning in late May and continuing to September. Chinook salmon range from 12 to 25 lbs. The fishery is open 7 days a week in season. Limited RV parking (fee charged). Fish cleaning tables nearby and can be a good place to view eagles as fishermen clean their catches.

Regulations vary depending on species and area fished, consult the ADF&G sport fish regulations booklet before fishing.

Kodiak

View of Chiniak Bay from pullout on the Chiniak Highway, 2 miles south of the city of Kodiak. (©Kris Valencia, staff)

The Kodiak Island Archipelago lies in the Gulf of Alaska, southwest of Cook Inlet and the Kenai Peninsula. The city of Kodiak is located near the northeastern tip of Kodiak Island, at the north end of Chiniak Bay. By air it is 55 minutes from Anchorage. By ferry from Homer it is 9 to 10 hours. **Population:** 6,124 (city), 13,563 (Kodiak Island Borough). **Emergency Services:** Dial 911. **Alaska State Troopers**, phone (907) 486-4121. **Police**, phone (907) 486-8000. **Fire Department**, phone (907) 486-8040. **Harbor:** phone (907) 486-8080. **Hospital**, Providence Kodiak Island Medical Center, Rezanof Drive, phone (907) 486-3281. **Coast Guard**, phone (907) 487-5170. **Crime Stoppers**, phone (907) 486-3113.

Visitor Information: Located at 100 E. Marine Way, Ste. 200, Kodiak, AK 99615. Hours are 8 A.M. to 5 P.M. Monday through Friday year-round, with additional weekend hours in summer. A very helpful place to stop: Knowledgeable staff will answer questions, help arrange tours and charters, and make sure you don't miss anything on Kodiak Island. Free maps, brochures, and hunting/fishing information available here. Good view from visitor center of *The Starr of Kodiak*, a WWII Liberty ship now used as a cannery. Contact Discover Kodiak: phone (907) 486-4782 or 1-800-789-4782; email: visit@kodiak.org; www.kodiak.org.

Elevation: Sea level. **Climate:** Average daily temperature in July is 57°F; in January 30°F. September, October and January are the wettest months in Kodiak, with each month averaging more than 6 inches of precipitation. **Radio:** KVOK-AM 560, KMXT-FM 100.1 (public station, website: www.KMXT.org), KRXX-FM 101.1 (Hot 101.1), KPEN-FM 102.7 (country), KWAV 104.9 (rock). **Television:** Local channel KMXT 9, and via cable and satellite. **Newspapers:** *The Kodiak Daily Mirror* (weekdays only).

Private Aircraft: Kodiak state airport, 4.8 miles southwest; elev. 73 feet; length 7,500 feet; asphalt; fuel 100LL, Jet A-1. Kodiak Municipal Airport, 2 miles northeast; elev. 139 feet; length 2,500 feet; paved; unattended. Trident Basin seaplane base, on east side of Near Island, unattended, floats for 14 aircraft; fuel. Trident Basin has AV gas, (credit card or prepay).

Gravel airstrips at Akhiok, length 3,320 feet; Karluk, length 2,000 feet; Larsen Bay, length 2,700 feet; Old Harbor, length 2,750 feet; Ouzinkie, length 3,300 feet; and Port Lions, length 2,200 feet.

Kodiak Island, home of the oldest permanent European settlement in Alaska, is known as Alaska's Emerald Island. It is the largest island in Alaska and the second largest island in the United States (after Hawaii), with an area of 3,588 square miles and about 87 miles of road (see logs this section). The Kodiak Island Borough includes some 200 islands, the largest being Kodiak (about 100 miles long), followed in size by Afognak, Sitkalidak, Sitkinak, Raspberry, Tugi-

dak, Shuyak, Uganik, Chirikof, Marmot and Spruce islands. The borough has an unincorporated townsite called **ALENEVA** (pop. 24) on Afognak Island.

The 6 incorporated cities in the Kodiak Island Borough are: **KODIAK** (pop. 5,952), with all visitor services (see Visitor Services, Transportation and Attractions this section); **AKHIOK** (pop. 88) at Alitak Bay on the south side of Kodiak Island, 80 miles southwest of Kodiak; **LARSEN BAY** (pop. 86)

Major Attractions:

Fort Abercrombie SHP, The Baranov Museum, Kodiak NWR

©Kris Valencia, staff

on the northwest coast of Kodiak Island, 62 miles southwest of Kodiak; **OLD HARBOR** (pop. 214) on the southeast side of Kodiak Island, 54 miles from Kodiak; **OUZINKIE** (pop. 146) on the west coast of Spruce Island; and **PORT LIONS** (pop. 175) on Settler's Cove on the northeast coast of Kodiak Island, served by state ferry to/from Kodiak and Homer.

The **KODIAK COAST GUARD STATION** (pop. 1,303) is on the west side of Kodiak Island, south of Kodiak.

KARLUK (pop. 29), on the west coast of Kodiak Island, 75 air miles from Kodiak, is an incorporated Native Village.

Kodiak Island was originally inhabited by the Alutiiq people, who were maritime hunters and fishermen. More than 7,000 years later, the Alutiiq people still call Kodiak home.

In 1763, the island was discovered by Stephen Glotov, a Russian explorer. The name Kodiak, of which there are several variations, was first used in English by Captain Cook in 1778. It is derived from the Alutiiq word for island, qikertaq. Kodiak was Russian Alaska's first capital city, until the capital was moved to Sitka in 1804.

Kodiak's turbulent past includes natural disasters such as the 1912 eruption of Novarupta Volcano, on the nearby Alaska Peninsula, and tsunamis resulting from the 1964 earthquake. The Novarupta eruption covered northern parts of the archipelago with a black cloud of ash. When the cloud dissipated, Kodiak was buried under 18 inches of drifting ash.

On Good Friday in 1964, the greatest earthquake ever recorded in North America (8.6 on the Richter scale, Mw 9.2) shook the Kodiak area. The tsunami that followed virtually leveled downtown Kodiak, destroying the fishing fleet, processing plants, canneries and 158 homes. Giant waves also destroyed 3 Alutiiq villages.

Alaska completed a strategically important defense triangle with Panama and Hawaii across the Pacific Ocean, referred to as "Plan Orange" in a 1936 defense plan. Federal funds were allocated for military facilities on Kodiak, due to its ice-free harbor and milder climate. Construction of the Kodiak Naval Operating Base began in 1939. The Japanese attack on Pearl Harbor in December of 1941, then Dutch Harbor in June 1942, prompted construction of coastal defense outposts by the army. Fort Abercrombie, now a state historical park and a national historic landmark, was one of the first secret radar installations in Alaska. Cement bunkers still remain for exploration by the curious. The Coast Guard occupies the old Kodiak Naval Station.

Coast Guard Base Kodiak is the largest Coast Guard base in the country. It supports several tenant commands in Kodiak and remote units throughout western Alaska.

The base is home to Air Station Kodiak, which operates HC-130 Hercules airplanes, MH-60 Jayhawk and HH-65 Dolphin helicopters. Cutters that call Kodiak home are the 378-foot Coast Guard Cutter *Munro* (WHEC-724), 270-foot Cutter *Alex Haley* (WMEC-39) and the 225-foot Cutter *SPAR* (WLB-206). Cutters are designed as multi-mission platforms to carry out the Coast Guard's many safety, security and stewardship roles, some of which include enforcing federal laws at sea, conducting search and rescue operations and protecting homeland security.

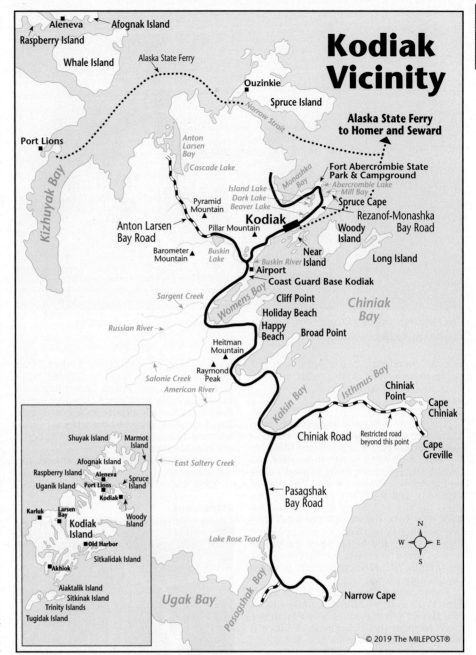

Kodiak Vicinity

© 2019 The MILEPOST®

A 12-foot star, situated halfway up the side of Old Woman Mountain overlooking the base, was rebuilt and rededicated in 1981 in memory of military personnel who have lost their lives while engaged in operations from Kodiak. Originally erected in the 1950s, the star is lit every year between Thanksgiving and Christmas.

St. Paul and St. Herman harbors are homeports to 800 local fishing boats and serve several hundred outside vessels each year. Commercial fishing is the backbone of Kodiak's economy. Kodiak is one of the largest commercial fishing ports in the U.S. Some 1,000 commercial fishing vessels use the harbor each year, delivering salmon, shrimp, herring, halibut and whitefish, plus king, tanner and Dungeness crab to the 11 processing companies in Kodiak. Cannery tours are available with pre-scheduling. Kodiak's famous seafood is pre-marketed, with almost all of the commercially caught seafood exported. Kodiak is also an important cargo port and transshipment center. Container ships stop twice weekly.

Kodiak is internationally recognized for its efforts to use 95 percent renewable energy by 2020. After surpassing the goal, Kodiak's model has been implemented worldwide. Using hydroelectric generators, a 6.5 ton flywheel and 6 wind turbines, the system has allowed Kodiak to move away from the use of diesel fuel.

Lodging & Services

There are hotels, motels and bed-and-breakfast accommodations in the downtown area as well as near the airport. Contact the Visitor Center for names. A variety of restaurants offer a range of menus and prices and the Kodiak Island Brewing Co. serves locally brewed beer. Shopping is readily available for gifts, general merchandise and sporting goods. There is a movie theater and 750-seat performing arts center.

Choose from more than 30 remote fly-in hunting and fishing lodges in the Kodiak area; roadhouses on the island road system; public-use cabins available within Kodiak National Wildlife Refuge, Shuyak Island and

The Holy Resurrection Russian Orthodox Cathedral is a prominent landmark in downtown Kodiak. (©Kris Valencia, staff)

Afognak Island state parks; and private wilderness camps and cabin rentals available throughout the Kodiak area.

Camping

There are 3 state campgrounds: Fort Abercrombie State Historical Park, north of town (*see Milepost K 3.8 Rezanof–Monashka Bay Road, page 584*); Buskin River State Recreation Site, south of town, a good choice for big rigs (*see Milepost K 4.1 Chiniak Road, page 585*); and Pasagshak River State Recreation Site (*see Milepost J 8.8 Pasagshak Bay Road, page 587*). There is also Leave No Trace free camping along rivers, on beaches above high-tide line, and beside roads (be sure to park so that you do not interfere with traffic). Inquire locally about permits from the Leisnoi Native Corp.

Dump stations are located at the Petro-Express station on Mill Bay Road and St. Paul Harbor spit in front of Alaska Fresh Seafoods (contact the harbormaster's office at 403 Marine Way, phone 907/486-8080).

Transportation

Air: Scheduled service to Kodiak via Ravn Airlines and Alaska Airlines. On island, charter services offer flightseeing, bear viewing, fishing and hunting transport.

Ferry: The Alaska Marine Highway System serves Kodiak from Homer (9–10 hour ferry ride). Kodiak is also the port of departure for Aleutian Chain trips in summer. Phone (907) 486-3800. See Southwest and Aleutian Chain schedules at www.ferryalaska.com. For additional details on the ferry system, see "Ferry Travel" in the TRAVEL PLANNING section.

Cruise Ships: Cruise ships planning to make Kodiak a port of call in 2019 include Holland America's *Westerdam* and *Maasdam*, Azumara's *Azamara Quest,* Regent Seven Seas' *Mariner*, Seabourn's *Sojurn*, Silverseas' *Silver Muse*. Windstar's *Star Legend*, Crystal Cruises' *Symphony*, Viking's *Orion*. All ships arrive between May and September.

Highways: There are 4 roads on Kodiak Island (see logs this section). The 11-mile Rezanof–Monashka Bay Road leads from downtown Kodiak north to Fort Abercrombie and Monashka Bay. Chiniak Highway leads 42.8 miles south from Kodiak along the island's eastern shore to Chiniak Point and Chiniak Creek. Anton Larsen Bay Road leads 11.7 miles from junction with Chiniak Road near Kodiak airport to Anton Larsen Bay. Pasagshak Bay Road branches off Chiniak Road and leads 16.4 miles to Fossil Beach at Pasagshak Point.

Car Rental: Available at the airport and downtown.

Taxi: Kodiak Island Taxi (907) 486-2515.

Attractions

The **Baranov Museum** (pictured above), operated by the Kodiak Historical Society, is located at 101 Marine Way, Kodiak 99615; phone (907) 486-5920. The museum is open in summer, 10 A.M. to 4 P.M. Monday through Saturday; Labor Day to late May, 10 A.M. to 3 P.M. Tuesday through Saturday. Special openings upon request. The building is the oldest in Alaska, built in 1805–1808 as a warehouse by the Russian American Company. It is the oldest Russian-built structure in the United States. Purchased by the Alaska Commercial Co. around 1867, it was sold to a prominent Kodiak businessman, W.J. Erskine, in 1911; the Erskine family lived there for more than 30 years. In 1962, it was declared a National Historic Landmark, and opened as a museum in 1967.

Many items from the Alutiiq, Russian and American eras are on display, in the 3 exhibit rooms, with an emphasis on the last 200 years of Kodiak's history. In the gift shop, work by local artists and crafters and Russian art and handiwork, including nesting dolls, are for sale. Admission is $5 per adult, children under 12 free; phone (907)

486-5920; email: info@baranovmuseum.org; or visit their website at www.baranovmuseum.org.

Kodiak National Wildlife Refuge Visitor Center, located at 402 Center Ave., is operated by the U.S. Fish & Wildlife Service and features unique and detailed sculptures of Alaskan animals found in Kodiak, such as Kodiak brown bears. A very unique display of a fully articulated gray whale skeleton can also be seen there. Other exhibits depict salmon life-history, birds commonly found in Kodiak, and "A Bear's Supermarket," where you can learn about all of the wild foods that sustain Kodiak's iconic brown bears. There are various hands-on interactive displays, a bookstore and gift shop operated by the non-profit Alaska Geographic, public talks and films about Kodiak's wildlife and the Kodiak National Wildlife Refuge. For more information call 1-888-592-6942 or (907) 487-2626, or go to their website at www.fws.gov/refuge/kodiak/.

The **Alutiiq Museum** and **Archaeological Repository** in downtown Kodiak interprets the history of Kodiak's Native people. The museum houses and displays artifacts from archaeological sites around Kodiak Island as well as historic items, Native clothing and contemporary Alutiiq artwork. Visitors can watch short videos on Alutiiq traditions and try hands-on activities in a children's corner. The museum store features local and Native-made artwork, jewelry and books. Located at 215 Mission Rd., First Floor; phone 1-844-425-8844; website www.alutiiqmuseum.org; email info@alutiiqmuseum.org. Museum hours are 10 A.M. to 4 P.M. Tuesday–Friday; noon to 4 P.M. Saturday. Admission fees: $7 adult, children 16 and under, free.

Holy Resurrection Russian Orthodox Cathedral, at 410 Mission Rd. is a prominent landmark in downtown Kodiak and listed on the National Register of Historic Places. The church was founded in 1794 but has burned down 3 times since then. The current structure dates back to the 1940s. The church interior provides a visual feast which visitors are encouraged to photograph. The public is invited to visit the church and attend services. Vespers is held Saturdays at 6 P.M. and Sunday services at 9 A.M. Phone (907) 486-5532. Donations are appreciated. The All Saints of Alaska log chapel, a scale replica of the original Holy Resurrection church building, is located nearby on the grounds of St. Herman Theological Seminary on Mission Road.

Visit Kodiak's Harbors. Kodiak offers a full range of dockage, boat yard and marine services for commercial fishing, cargo, passenger, and recreational vessels. The City of Kodiak's Harbor Department operates 2 marinas: St. Paul Harbor downtown and St. Herman Harbor on Near Island.

The 2 harbors provide protected moorage for 650 vessels up to 150 feet in length. Large vessels, including the state ferry, cruise ships and cargo vessels are moored at the 3 deepwater piers. Call or visit the Harbormaster's office for more information. Harbor staff may be reached 24 hours per day, 7 days per week on VHF channel 12 or 16. The office is open 8 A.M. to 5 P.M. Monday through Friday in the winter. During the summer months, the office is open 7 days per week.

Kodiak Public Library at 612 Egan Way is a good spot to spend some time on a rainy day. The library has computers, internet access, magazines, newspapers and 70,000-plus books. Open Monday 12:30–9 P.M.; Tuesday–Thursday, 10 A.M. to 9 P.M.; Friday 10 A.M. to 7 P.M.; Saturday–Sunday 1–5 P.M. Phone (907) 486-8686.

WWII gun emplacements are found at Fort Abercrombie State Historical Park. This park is a fascinating stop for history buffs. (©Kris Valencia, staff)

Fort Abercrombie State Historical Park is located north of Kodiak city on scenic Miller Point. WWII gun emplacements, concrete bunkers (as pictured above) and building foundations are scattered along the high bluffs and in the forested area of the park. The park also offers picnicking, hiking trails and camping (primarily for tent campers) in a setting of lush rainforest, wildflowers, seabirds and eagles. In summer, look for the massive orange salmonberry (tastes like a raspberry). Whales and other marine wildlife are often seen from the overlooks and cliff side trails. Self-guided historical walking tour maps of Fort Abercrombie are posted in multiple areas of the park or pick up a brochure at the Kodiak Military History Museum or the park's headquarters at 1400 Abercrombie Dr.; phone (907) 486-6339. Day-use parking fee at Fort Abercrombie is $5 per day per vehicle, or purchase a $50 annual Alaska State Parks pass; phone the Kodiak District State Park office for details, (907) 486-6339.

Naturalist programs may be offered at various times from June through August at Fort Abercrombie State Historical Park. Programs may include plant lore, outdoor photography, sea kayaking, tidepool exploration and more. For more information on park facilities and program times and dates, phone the State Park office at (907) 486-6339 or www.dnr.state.ak.us/parks/units/kodiak.

Make your first stop at the **Kodiak Military History Museum**, located inside the Ready Ammo bunker on the bluff by Miller Point. The museum features displays of WWII memorabilia, including relics from the Aleutian campaign. The bunker that houses the museum has a roof that is 5 feet of steel reinforced concrete; bronze door hinges to prevent sparks; and light fixtures designed to prevent exploding bulbs from hitting anything explosive. Try the old short-wave radio, telephones and typewriter. Interesting for kids and adults. Museum hours (subject to change) are usually Friday–Monday 1–4 P.M. in June, July and August; 1–4 P.M. Saturday and Sunday in May and September; 1–4 P.M. Memorial Day; and anytime for WWII vets or groups with advance notice. Winter closures due to unplowed roads. For current hours and group tours, phone (907) 486-7015; or visit their website at www.kadiak.org/museum/museum.html.

Shuyak Island State Park encompasses 47,000 acres and is located 54 air miles north of Kodiak. Access by boat or floatplane only. Hunting, fishing and kayaking are the major recreational activities. Four public-use cabins are available at $80 per night. Cabins are 12 feet by 20 feet and sleep up to 8 people. Afognak Island State Park has two additional public-use cabins on interior island lakes, access via floatplane only, for $60 per night and now has a saltwater cabin on the north side of the island in Discovery Bay for $80 per night. Reservations accepted up to 6 months (to the day) in advance for non-residents with a full nonrefundable payment and 7 months (to the day) for Alaska residents. Call (907) 486-6339 or www.dnr.state.ak.us/parks/units/kodiak/shuyak.htm.

Go for a Hike. Hiking trails around the Kodiak area provide access to alpine areas, lakes, coastal rainforests and beaches. Waterproof hiking/birding trail guides available for $12 at the visitors center, phone (907) 486-4782, and at other locations around the city. Pay attention to notes regarding footwear and clothing, tides, bears, trailhead access and weather conditions.

Picnic and camp on the beach. There are some outstandingly beautiful, unpopulated beaches along Chiniak Road and Pasagshak Road *(see logs this section)*. Excellent beachcombing. Watch for Sitka black-tailed deer and fox. Be cautious of the bison herds along Pasagshak Road.

Kodiak Fisheries Research Center at 301 Research Court, houses the National Marine Fisheries Service and Alaska Dept. of Fish and Game. The Interpretive Center is dedicated to enriching public knowledge of the Kodiak Island Archipelago ecosystems. The Aquarium and Touch Tank are open to the public; beaked whale skeleton on display. Admission is free. Open 8 A.M. to 4:30 P.M. Monday–Saturday from Memorial Day to Labor Day and weekdays only in winter 8 A.M. to 4:30 P.M. To get there, cross the Fred Zharoff Bridge to Near Island, turn on Tri-dent Way, then take second left to science building. Phone (907) 481-1800.

Go Mountain Biking or Surfing. Kodiak is known for its premier mountain biking, attracting racers and enthusiasts from around the country. It is also known for its accessible surf breaks at Cape Chiniak and Pasagshak Bay.

Visit a brewery. Visitors may taste test local beer at the Kodiak Island Brewing Co., located at 117 Lower Mill Bay Rd. Phone (907) 486-2537; www.kodiakbrewery.com.

Bear Valley Golf Course. The 9-hole Bear Valley Golf Course is located on Anton Larsen Bay Road. Owned and operated by the U.S. Coast Guard, the course has a driving range, putting green and pro shop. The course is open to the public from May until mid-October, depending on weather. The pro shop carries golf clothing, items and rental equipment, and snack bar. Hours of operation vary according to weather and daylight hours. Phone (907) 487-5323.

Drive up Pillar Mountain. The 2.2-mile winding gravel road up Pillar Mountain dead ends at the wind turbines. Fabulous island and ocean views on this drive. To get there, take Mill Bay Road to Birch; follow Birch to Maple; head up Maple until it becomes Pillar Mountain Road.

Special Events. ComFish Alaska, the nation's largest commercial fishing annual trade show, takes place the end of March. The Whalefest Kodiak, held each April, celebrates the return of migrating whales. Whale sightings are reported daily and arts performances are scheduled throughout the festival; visit www.whalefestkodiak.org.

The Kodiak King Crab Festival, May

Rezanof-Monashka Bay Road

Mill Bay Beach Park is a popular spot, especially on a sunny day, with easy beach access.
(©Kris Valencia, staff)

Distance is measured from Y junction of Rezanof Drive and Marine Way in downtown Kodiak (K).

K 0 Y junction of Rezanof Drive with Center Street and Lower Mill Bay Road.

Lower Mill Bay Road accesses the library and post office; Kodiak Police Dept. (1.6 miles); Kodiak College (1.9 miles); Petro gas station (2 miles); fast food, Safeway with Starbucks, Oaken Keg, Alaska USA bank, postal services and pharmacy (2.1 miles); Walmart (2.2 miles); and junction with Rezanof Drive (2.7 miles) at **Milepost Y 2.9.**

©Kris Valencia, staff

K 0.3 Entrance to Near Island bridge. Head across the bridge for Northend Park (trails, beach access, picnic areas);

St. Herman Harbor (pictured at left); Kodiak Fisheries Research Center; ADF&G; UAF Kodiak Seafood & Marine Science Center; Rotary Park; and Trident Basin seaplane base.

K 0.5 Kodiak High School, Home of the Bears.

K 1.4 Providence Kodiak Island Medical Center.

K 1.9 Turn on Benny Benson Drive for Kodiak College; Benny Benson **junction** with Mill Bay Road.

Begin paved trail, which parallels main road to Fort Abercrombie State Historic Park. Excellent for walking, jogging and bicycling.

K 2.9 Junction with Mill Bay Road; turn on to Mill Bay Road for Walmart, Safeway and other businesses.

K 3.1 Gas station.

K 3.3 First of 2 turnouts/parking areas for Mill Bay Beach Park, a popular spot on scenic **Mill Bay** with easy beach access, picnic tables, beaches, barbecue grates. Good ocean fishing for hatchery coho from beach.

K 3.5 Bayside Fire Department.

K 3.8 Drive in 0.2 mile to **Fort Abercrombie State Historical Park**; day use

parking fee is $5 per vehicle per day or an annual parking decal. Follow signs for campground (0.5 mile from Rezanof Drive to fee box); 3 small, unlevel walk-in campsites and a 5-site campground for small RVs or tents on the Monashka Bay side of the park; 7-night limit; $15/night; water, toilets; bayside picnic shelter; campground host; stocked rainbow trout fishing, swimming, picnicking and beach access at Lake Gertrude; view of bay and beach. The park also has an extensive system of hiking trails. Trailhead for Lake Gertrude is at Mile 0.4 on the access road. No off-road biking. Naturalist programs June through August. Just beyond the park entrance is the Alaska State Parks ranger station, (907) 486-6339, open Monday–Friday 9 A.M. to 4 P.M. with intermittent weekend hours; public restrooms, park information; www.dnr.state.ak.us/parks/units/kodiak/ftaber.htm.

A big attraction at Fort Abercrombie State Historical Park is the Kodiak Military History Museum, housed in the War Ready Ammo bunker *(see detailed description of park and museum on page 583).*

K 6.1 Kodiak Island Borough baler/landfill facility. Recycling center. Good place to watch for eagles.

K 6.8 Turnoff for VFW Post 7056 with RV sites with electrical hookups; phone (907) 486-3195. Access to Kodiak Island Sportsman's Assoc. indoor shooting range, (907) 486-8566, www.kisaorg.com.

K 7.5 Pillar Creek bridge and Pillar Creek Hatchery.

K 7.9 Parking and gravel access to Pillar Beach, a beautiful black-sand beach at mouth of creek. Scenic picnic area. Dolly Varden pink and coho salmon; fishing allowed downstream from Monashka Bay Road.

K 9 Scenic overlook and panoramic views of Monashka Bay and Monashka Mountain.

K 10.2 Turnout and parking; North Sister trailhead.

K 10.9 Bridge over Monashka Creek.

K 11 Road ends; large turnaround parking area. Paths lead through narrow band of trees to secluded **Monashka Bay** beach. Large, sweeping band of sandy beach. Excellent for picnics. Picnic tables, improved beach access. Fishing off beach for Dolly Varden, pinks, coho and stocked chinook; check current ADF&G regulations.

To the north of parking area is trailhead for **Termination Point Trail**, a beautiful 5-mile hike on a loop trail along meadows, ocean bluffs and dense Sitka spruce forest. *NOTE: Leisnoi Tribal Corp. user permit required to hike Termination Point Trail; go online to https://leisnoi.com/land-resources/permits.*

23–27, 2019, celebrates the history of Kodiak's crab industry with parades, carnival booths and midway, races and tournaments, blessing of the fleet, Kodiak Seafood Cook-off, concerts and art shows; visit www.kodiakchamber.org.

The Pillar Mountain Running Race is a 9.2-mile mountain race from the Harbormaster Building; phone (907) 486-8665 for dates. The Kodiak Kids' Pink Salmon Jamboree takes place in mid-August. And Kodiak's State Fair and Rodeo are held Labor Day weekend at the fairgrounds in Women's Bay.

Join the St. Herman's Pilgrimage, which takes place annually August 7–9. Pilgrims travel to Monk's Lagoon at Spruce Island where St. Herman lived and originally was buried. Father Herman, arrived in Kodiak in 1794 and was the first saint of the Russian Orthodox Church in North America, canonized in Kodiak in 1970. A schedule of services during the Pilgrimage is available upon request; phone (907) 486-3854 or visit website: doaoca.org.

See Kodiak by Kayak. One of the best ways to experience Kodiak's beautiful coast-

line, and view marine mammals and seabirds, is from a kayak. Day kayak tours around the nearby islands are available for all skill levels, or schedule an extended tour. Ask at the visitor center for recommendations and names of area providers.

Kodiak National Wildlife Refuge encompasses 1.9 million acres on Kodiak, Uganik, Afognak and Ban Islands. The Refuge was established in 1941 to preserve the natural habitat of the famed Kodiak brown bear and other wildlife. Biologists (Continues on page 586)

Chiniak Highway

Distance from Kodiak's U.S. post office building (K).

NOTE: The post office on Lower Mill Bay Road is 1 mile from Milepost 1 on Chiniak Highway.

K 0 Kodiak post office building on Mill Bay Road.

K 0.2 The Y **junction** of Rezanof Drive, Lower Mill Bay Road and Center Street.

K 0.3 Marine Way.

K 0.9 Fishermen's Terminal, Port of Kodiak, Pier No. 2. Matson shipping terminal adjacent.

K 2.2 Gibson Cove. Large, double-ended turnout with telescopes and benches at Deadman's Curve; panoramic view of Kodiak, Chiniak Bay and nearby islands. Interpretive sign about Kodiak's role as a coastal defense outpost during WWII. The bunker on the hill across the highway was 1 of 12 constructed on Kodiak. Manned with 12 to 18 soldiers, each bunker was equipped with nightscopes and positioned to guard a segment of coastline.

K 2.7 Small pullout.

K 3.3 Steep access to small pullout.

K 3.6 Boy Scout Lake, paved turnout and parking. Fishing for rainbow trout. Hiking trail to WWII relics.

K 3.7 Paved turnout.

K 4.1 Gravel access road to **Buskin River State Recreation Site** (Alaska State Parks) campground, overflow parking and day-use area near beach (1-mile drive from Chiniak Highway).

The campground has 15 RV campsites with a 14-night limit at $15/night, picnic tables, firepits with grills, covered picnic area, bear-proof food containers, toilets, drinking water, trails and beach access. Campground host onsite June–August. Fishing along Buskin River and on beach area at river's mouth for sockeye, coho and pinks, Dolly Varden and rainbow trout. Parking; handicap accessible fishing platform. For details contact Alaska State Parks.

K 4.8 Junction with **Anton Larsen Bay Road** *(see log on page 587),* just north of the Buskin River bridge.

K 4.9 Kodiak airport turnoff.

K 6.3 Entrance to U.S. Coast Guard station.

K 6.6 Turnout on Women's Bay with picnic tables, boat launch. Interesting interpretive signs give a historic overview of Kodiak Naval Operating Base, the Naval Air Station and the submarine base.

Buskin River State Recreation Site has treed campsites and access to fantastic salmon fishing. *(©Kris Valencia, staff)*

Chiniak Highway continues around Women's Bay. USCG cutters tie up at pier across the bay.

K 7.2 Large shipping and container operation and log storage area.

K 9 Turnoff to Kodiak Island Fairgrounds and Kodiak Island Raceway. Excellent bird watching on tide flats; park at entrance to gravel road across from fairgrounds.

K 9.8 Sargent Creek bridge. Good fishing for pinks in August.

K 10 Russian River bridge; parking area. Good fishing for pinks, Dolly Varden in August, coho in September. Access to Sargent Creek and Bell's Flats roads.

K 10.4 Grocery, liquor, gas and diesel.

K 10.5 Java Flats restaurant and Russian River Roadhouse.

K 10.8 Rendezvous Bar and Grill.

K 11.3 Small pullout.

K 11.4 Four-wheeler trail and trailhead to 2,300-foot Kashevaroff Mountain. Gradual incline, great views in alpine country, lowbush cranberries in fall. *CAUTION: Watch for bears.*

K 11.5 Small pullout.

K 11.7 Salonie Creek; small parking area. Pinks (early August), chums, coho, Dolly Varden, stocked chinook.

K 12.1 Salonie Creek Rifle Range turnoff.

K 12.2 Large turnout with bay access.

K 12.5 Begin climb up Marine Hill. Kashevaroff trailhead; wildflowers, cranberries in fall. *NOTE: This area can be a very hazardous section of road in winter when icy.*

K 13.3 Turnout with panoramic view of Mary Island, Women's Bay, Bell's Flats, Kodiak. Mountain goats visible with binoculars in spring and fall in mountains behind Bell's Flats.

K 14.1 Pullout at **Heitman Lake** trailhead. Beautiful views. Lake is stocked with rainbow trout.

K 14.3 Turnout to **Dragon Fly Lake**.

View of Long Island and Cliff Point. Lake is stocked with rainbow trout.

K 14.9 Dirt road and trailhead to **Horseshoe Lake**. Trail continues past second grove of spruce trees down to lake. Lake is stocked with rainbow trout.

K 15.6 Turnout at top of hill on ocean side of highway

K 16.7 USCG communications facility; *emergency phone.*

K 18.7 Undeveloped picnic area in grove of trees along beach of Middle Bay; easy access to beach. Watch for livestock.

K 19.2 Small Creek bridge.

K 19.7 Salt Creek bridge. Excellent bird watching on tideflats to left.

K 20.5 American River bridge. Turnout at **American River. Saltery River** access road (very rugged, recommended for 4WD only); excellent fishing for pinks, chums, coho, stocked chinook and Dolly Varden; Saltery fished for sockeye, pinks, chums, coho, rainbow trout and Dolly Varden.

K 20.6 Unimproved road (barely passable even for 4-wheel-drive) to Saltery Cove. Primitive camping.

K 20.7 Felton Creek bridge. Fish for pinks and coho.

K 22.8 Foot access to gravel beach; nice picnic site.

K 24.2 Pullout and access to Mayflower Lake.

K 24.3 Gravel turnouts for Mayflower Beach public access. Beachcombing, picnicking, hiking.

K 25.1 Double-ended pullout with view of beach.

K 25.2 Narrow double-ended turnout with view of beach.

K 27.4 Gravel turnout with spectacular view of Kalsin Bay and highway winding along coastline.

K 27.8 Improved pullout.

K 27.9 Improved pullout. Steep road drops down to head of Kalsin Bay.

Horses at junction of Chiniak Highway and Pasagshak Bay Road hustle drivers for treats.
(©Kris Valencia, staff)

K 28.2 Improved pullout.

K 28.6 Turnoff of access to west side of **Kalsin Beach** and **Olds River** mouth. Excellent fishing for pinks, chum, coho, stocked chinook and Dolly Varden. Goats often seen in hills in fall and spring.

K 29 Deadman Creek bridge.

K 29.7 Turnout at **Olds River**. Excellent fishing for pinks, chum, coho, chinook and Dolly Varden.

K 30.2 Kalsin River (creek) bridge.

K 30.4 Junction: Turn left for Chiniak, right for Pasagshak Bay Road (*see Pasagshak Bay Road log on page 587*). Cattle and horses range freely in this area. The horses will come right up to the car window as if expecting a treat. *CAUTION: Watch for cattle and horses on road.*

K 30.7 Kalsin Pond; excellent fall coho fishing.

K 30.9 Turnoff for access to mouth of **Olds River** and beach. Excellent fishing for pinks, chum, coho, stocked chinook and Dolly Varden.

K 31.3 Highway maintenance station.
K 31.4 *Pavement ends, gravel begins.*

K 31.5 Karl Armstrong Campground.

K 31.8 Picnic area beside Kalsin Bay. Nice beach.

K 32.1 Road to unimproved picnic area. Gravel beach. Fishing for pinks and Dolly Varden.

K 32.9 Myrtle Creek bridge just past turnoff; picnic site.

K 33 Access to Myrtle Beach.

K 34.6 Thumbs Up Cove; old pier.

K 34.7 Chiniak post office. Window hours Tuesday and Thursday 4–6 P.M., Saturday noon to 2 P.M. Hunting and fishing licenses sold here. Visitor information.

K 35.6 Brookers Lagoon. Access to gravel beach. Excellent birding for waterfowl, eagles and shorebirds.

K 36.9 Roslyn River bridge.

K 37.4 Access to mouth of Roslyn River. Fishing for pinks, coho and Dolly Varden.

K 39.3 Access to a beautiful point overlooking the sea; site of WWII installations. Good place for photos. Sea otters in kelp beds year-round.

K 39.5 Twin Creeks Beach, dark sand and rolling breakers. Good place for beach walking, tide pooling. Watch for sea otters in kelp beds. Look for 3 WWII bunkers on the cliffs above the beach.

K 40.1 Twin Creeks. Good pink fishing in August, coho fishing in fall.

K 40.5 Silver Beach.
K 40.6 Pony Lake.
K 40.7 Small turnout by beach.
K 40.8 Beach access road.

K 41.1 Chiniak wayside, a borough park; benches, beautiful setting.

Chiniak school, playground and ballfield. Baseball diamond, play area, picnic tables. Chiniak residents are on the power grid, but they get their water from wells or cisterns. The now closed Road's End Restaurant is used for community potlucks.

K 41.2 Turnoff onto King Crab Way. Location of Tsunami Evacuation Center and public library.

K 41.9 Whale watching for gray whales in April.

Beyond this point the cliff is eroded right to the edge of the road. Exercise extreme caution while driving this stretch.

©Sharon Nault

K 42.1 Chiniak Point, seen in the distance, is also known as Cape Chiniak. It is the southernmost point of land at the entrance to Chiniak Bay. (Capt. Cook named the point Cape Greville in 1778, but that name is now applied to the point of land 2 miles southeast of here.) Watch for unmaintained roads leading toward the point. Hike up the bluff to WWII bunker. Fantastic views from here. Watch for whales, sea lions, seals and puffins. Wonderful secluded beach; primitive camping.

State road maintenance ends here. Unmaintained road continues as public easement across Leisnoi Native Corp. land. Public access is limited beyond Chiniak Creek.

K 42.6 Public road ends at **Chiniak Creek** culvert. Pink fishing in mid-summer; coho fishing in fall. View of Chiniak Point. Turnaround point.

(Continued from page 584)
estimate that more than 3,500 bears inhabit the Kodiak Archipelago. Most bears enter dens by November and remain there until April. Bears are readily observable on the Refuge in June through August, when they congregate along streams to feed on salmon. Visitors to the Refuge typically go to fish, observe and photograph wildlife, backpack, kayak, camp and hunt. There are primitive public-use cabins available for rent (reservations must be made in advance at www.recreation.gov. *NOTE: The Refuge is accessible only by floatplane or boat.* More information is available at the Kodiak Refuge Visitor Center located in downtown Kodiak at the corner of Center Avenue and Mission Road, or on its website at www.fws.gov/refuge/kodiak/. If you need to speak to someone directly you can call 1-888-408-3514 or (907) 487-2600.

AREA FISHING: Kodiak Island is in the center of a fine marine and freshwater sport fishery and possesses some excellent fishing for rainbow, steelhead, halibut, Dolly Varden and 5 species of Pacific salmon. Visiting fishermen will have to charter a boat or aircraft to reach remote lakes, rivers and bays, but the island road system offers many good salmon streams in season. Roads access sockeye salmon fisheries in the Buskin and Pasagshak rivers. Introduced chinook runs are available at the American, Olds and Salonie rivers. Pinks and coho are found in virtually all road accessible streams including the **Buskin**, **Saltery**, **Salonie**, **American**, **Olds** and **Pasagshak** rivers, and **Monashka**, **Pillar**, **Russian**, **Roslyn**, **Sargent** and **Chiniak** creeks.

Afognak and Raspberry islands, both approximately 30 air miles northeast of Kodiak, offer excellent remote hunting and fishing. Both islands are brown bear country. Hikers and fishermen should make noise and stay in the open, use bear-proof food containers, and discard fish waste in rivers. If you take a dog, make sure it is under control. Dogs can create dangerous situations with bears.

CAUTION: A paralytic shellfish poisoning alert is in effect for all Kodiak Island beaches. This toxin is extremely poisonous. There are no approved beaches for clamming on Kodiak Island. For more current information, call the Dept. of Environmental Conservation in Anchorage at (907) 269-7501.

Pasagshak Bay Road

Pasagshak Bay Road leads to the Pacific Spaceport Complex Alaska, a commercial rocket launching facility. (©Sharon Nault)

Distance is measured from junction with Chiniak Road (J).

J 0 Junction at **Milepost K 30.4** Chiniak Road for Pasagshak Bay.

CAUTION: Watch for cattle and horses on road. Horses may come right up to your car window.

J 3.7 Turnout to picnic area in trees.

J 4.7 Turnouts at top of Pasagshak Pass; scenic views.

J 5.3 Turnout.

Road makes a winding descent southbound.

J 6.8 Road crosses **Lake Rose Tead** on causeway. Good fishing in Lake Rose Tead for coho and in river from here to ocean, fish for sockeye in July. Good place to view spawning salmon and eagles late summer through fall.

J 7 Combined barn and single aircraft hangar to right. Remnant of Joe Zentner Ranch, established in the 1940s.

J 7.9 Turnout with dumpster.

J 8.7 Entering Pasagshak River State Recreation Site.

J 8.8 Begin **Pasagshak River State Recreation Site** next half-mile to mouth of Pasagshak River; 6 tent sites (park on left side of road and walk down to sites on river) and 3 RV sites located in main parking lot; additional turnouts on road for day-use parking. This recreation site has some picnic tables, firepits, well water, bear resistant trash bins, outhouse; campground host; fishing and beach access; $15/night camping fee, $5 day-use fee, or annual $50 State Parks decal, contact Kodiak District State Park office for more

information, (907) 486-6339.

J 9 Gravel parking area, outhouse.

J 9.2 Access to traditional gravel boat launch ramp and mooring area. Four-wheel-drive vehicles recommended to use launch ramp.

J 9.4 Hairpin turn as highway climbs.

J 9.5 Small turnout with view of Pasagshak Bay.

J 10.3 Cattle Guard crossing and beginning of Kodiak Cattle Co. grazing lease. Public land—hunting, fishing, hiking, but keep vehicle on road.

CAUTION: Watch for free-roaming cattle and bison. Bison sometimes block the road. Stop and wait; they will eventually move. Sounding your horn is not advised. Do not approach bison on foot.

J 11.3 Road to beach access.

J 11.6 Bear Paw Ranch Youth Camp.

J 12.1 Road access to beach; big breakers when surf is up. Primitive camping, carry out trash.

J 13.1 Welcome to the Pacific Spaceport Complex Alaska (PSCA), a low-earth-orbit launch facility of the Alaska Aerospace Development Corporation (AADC). The complex is the nation's first commercial aerospace launch facility on non-federally-funded land. There are no scheduled visitor tours.

J 14.1 PSCA's Integration Processing Facility (IPF), rebuilt in 2016 due to damage sustained during a 2014 launch.

J 15.1 Large turnout.

J 15.2 Road ends 1,000 feet (sign). **Fossil Beach** road branches off to the right: Steep road in poor condition descends to beach; consider parking at top of road, walking down. *Be certain of your ability to drive back up before descending the hill. Cliffs are extremely unstable. Watch for falling rock.*

J 16.2 Twin Lakes to east; stocked rainbow trout.

J 16.4 Road ends at Fossil Cliffs; parking, limited turnaround area. Fossils embedded in cliffs are visible along Fossil Beach to left and right (low tide only). Beautiful vistas and views of WWII observation bunkers on Narrow Cape to the left.

Anton Larsen Bay Road

Distance is measured from the turnoff (T) at Milepost K 4.8 Chiniak Road.
NOTE: Road may be closed in winter.

T 0 Turnoff for Anton Larsen Bay Road at **Milepost K 4.8** Chiniak Highway, just north of the Buskin River bridge.

T 0.6 Buskin River bridge No. 6. Parking area accesses fishing along river. (There are several turnouts along the road in this area.) Side road leads to good fishing holes.

T 1.5 Buskin River bridge No. 7. Turnoff before crossing bridge to access river and outlet of **Buskin Lake**. Good fishing for Dolly Varden, steelhead and salmon.

T 2.9 USCG **Bear Valley Golf Course**; clubhouse, snack bar, driving range, 9-holes, open to the public, May until mid-October, depending on weather, phone (907) 487-5323.

Pavement ends, gravel begins.

T 3.5 Begin slow ascent northbound.

T 4.1 *Road narrows northbound,*

T 5.7 Buskin Valley Winter Recreation Area; parking. Popular sledding, skiing, snowboarding spot. Summer trailhead to top of 2,400-foot Pyramid Mountain. Trail follows ridgeline. Great vistas from top.

T 6.6 Gradual descent with switchbacks northbound. Slow down. View of valley and mountains to west.

T 6.8 First view of Anton Larsen Bay.

T 7.2 *Road descends northbound, 15-mph switchback. Slow down!*

T 7.5 Red Cloud Creek bridge. Trailhead parking for Shariton Mountain (3.7 miles).

T 8.5 Residential area. *Slow down for potholes!*

T 9.3 Head of scenic Anton Larsen Bay.

T 10.3 Anton Larsen Boat Ramp; concrete small-boat launch. Ample parking.

T 10.4 Anton Larsen Bay public dock.

T 11.7 Road ends; limited parking and turnaround space. Footpath continues beyond this point to access beach via public easement.

Prince William Sound

Includes Valdez and Cordova and the Copper River Highway

(Whittier is on page 522 in the SEWARD HIGHWAY section)

Sightsee glaciers in Prince William Sound by cruise tour, by plane or by helicopter. This is Harvard Glacier. (©Bill Rome)

Major Attractions:

©Bill Rome

Glacier Viewing, Fishing, Sea Kayaking, Hiking & Wildlife Viewing

Southcentral Alaska's Prince William Sound is an area famous for both scenery and wildlife. Dotted with islands, this 70-mile-wide gulf extends 30 miles north and west from the Gulf of Alaska to the Kenai Peninsula. It is bordered on the southeast by Montague and Hinchinbrook islands, which form Hinchinbrook Entrance,

the 10-mile-long water passage from the Gulf of Alaska to Prince William Sound. To the north, the sound is edged by a glaciated coastline and the Chugach Mountains.

The most prominent glacial feature in the glacier-ringed Prince William Sound is the Columbia Glacier, one of the largest and most magnificent of the tidewater glaciers along the Alaska coast. Columbia Glacier is also the second fastest moving glacier in the world. It travels about 80 feet per day and discharges 2 cubic miles of ice into the Sound annually. It has receded more than 12 miles since 1986. The glacier is currently 34 miles in length, 3 miles wide and more than 3,000 feet thick in some places. It is the greatest glacial contributor in North America. Visitors to Prince William Sound see its tidewater terminus 6 miles away. How close you get to the glacier's face depends on iceberg production: the more icebergs, the greater the danger.

The glacier was named by the Harriman Alaska expedition in 1899 for Columbia University in New York City. The glacier's source is Mount Einstein (elev. 11,552 feet) in the Chugach Mountains. Columbia Glacier is off of College Fjord and is part of what is known as the "College Glaciers." Neighboring glaciers include Harvard and Yale.

There are several ways to explore Prince William Sound. From Anchorage, drive (or take the Alaska Railroad) south on the Seward Highway 47 miles and take the

Whittier/Portage Glacier Access Road 11.4 miles east to Whittier on Prince William Sound. From Whittier, you may take the Alaska Marine Highway ferry system (drive-on or passenger-only) across the Sound to Valdez or Cordova and return the same route. *(See details on Whittier and a log of the access road, on pages 521–525 in the SEWARD HIGHWAY section; see also "Ferry Travel" in the TRAVEL PLANNING section.)*

Embark on a ferry/drive combo of the Sound by driving 304 miles from Anchorage to Valdez via the Glenn and Richardson highways (see GLENN HIGHWAY and RICHARDSON HIGHWAY sections). From Valdez, take the Alaska Marine Highway ferry to Cordova, then to Whittier, to complete the loop back to Anchorage.

Glacier cruises and kayaking adventure companies tour Prince William Sound from each port *(see advertisers this section and across the Sound in Whittier on pages 522–525).*

All-inclusive tours of Prince William Sound are also available out of Anchorage. Depending on itinerary and transportation, you may return to Anchorage the same day or overnight along the way.

However you choose to see Prince William Sound, it is spectacular! On a clear day, you are surrounded by a pristine wilderness of snow-capped mountains, glaciers and emerald-hued islands. And don't forget to watch for wildlife: Humpback whales and porpoises are star attractions.

Valdez

Valdez harbor is home port for many fishing charters, tour boats and kayak rentals.
(©Kelley & Milton Barker, staff)

Located on Port Valdez (pronounced val-DEEZ), an estuary off Valdez Arm in Prince William Sound. Valdez is 115 air miles and 304 highway miles from Anchorage and 366 highway miles from Fairbanks. Valdez is the southern terminus of both the Richardson Highway and the trans-Alaska pipeline. **Population:** 4,011.

Emergency Services: Dial 911. **Hospital,** Providence Valdez Medical Center, phone (907) 835-2249. **U.S. Coast Guard Search and Rescue,** (907) 835-7206. **Oil Spills,** 1-800-478-9300. **Harbormaster,** phone (907) 835-4981; www.ci.valdez.ak.us/harbor/. **Police,** (907) 835-4560; **Alaska State Troopers,** phone (907) 835-4307.

Visitor Information: The **Valdez Convention and Visitors Bureau** is located at 309 Fairbanks Dr. Open Monday–Friday, 8 A.M. to 5 P.M., year-round; phone (907) 835-2984; email info@valdezalaska.org; www.valdezalaska.org.

Elevation: Sea level. **Climate:** Record high was 90°F in June 2013; record low -23°F in February 1968. Normal daily maximum in January, 27°F; daily minimum 17°F. Normal daily maximum in July, 62°F; daily minimum 48°F. Average snowfall in Valdez from October to May is 326.3 inches, or about 27 feet. (By comparison, Anchorage aver-

ages about 6 feet in that period.) New snowfall records were set in January 1990, with snowfall for one day at 47½ inches. Record monthly snowfall is 180 inches in February 1996. Record rainfall in one day on Oct. 8th, 2013, 1.81 inches. Windy (often to 40-mph) in late fall. **Radio:** KCHU AM 770, KVAK AM 1230 and KVAK-FM 93.3. **Television:** Many channels via cable and satellite. **Newspaper:** *Valdez Star* (weekly).

Private Aircraft: Valdez, 3 miles east; elev. 120 feet; length 6,500 feet; asphalt; fuel 100LL, Jet B; attended. The airport terminal building has the Puddle Jumpers Saloon (beer, coffee, grill hamburgers).

Located on a majestic fjord, where the 5,000-foot-tall Chugach Mountains rise from Prince William Sound, Valdez is often called Alaska's "Little Switzerland." The city is on the north shore of Port Valdez, an estuary named by Spanish explorer Don Salvador Fidalgo in 1790 in honor of Antonio Valdes y Basan, a Spanish naval officer.

Valdez was established in 1897–98 as a port of entry for gold seekers bound for the Klondike goldfields. Thousands of stampeders arrived in Valdez to follow the All American Route to the Eagle mining district in Alaska's Interior, and from there up the Yukon River to Dawson City and to the Klondike. The Valdez trail was an especially dangerous route; the first leg of it led over Valdez Glacier, where the early stampeders faced dangerous crevasses, snowblindness and exhaustion.

On the heels of the gold rush, copper discoveries north of Valdez in the early 1900s brought more conflict and development to Valdez. A proposed railroad from tidewater to the rich Kennecott copper mines near McCarthy began a bitter rivalry between Valdez and Cordova for the railway line. The Copper River & Northwestern Railway eventually went to Cordova, but not before Valdez had started its own railroad north. The Valdez railroad did not get far, the only trace of its existence is an old hand-drilled railway tunnel at **Milepost V 15** on the Richardson Highway.

The original gold rush trail out of Valdez was modified into a sled and wagon road in the early 1900s. It was routed through Thompson Pass (rather than over the Valdez Glacier) by Captain Abercrombie of the U.S. Army, who was commissioned to connect Fort Liscum (a military post established in 1900 near the present-day location of the Alyeska Marine Pipeline Terminal) with Fort Egbert in Eagle. Colonel Wilds P. Richardson of the Alaska Road Commission further developed the wagon road, building the first automobile road from Valdez to Fairbanks that was completed in the early 1920s.

Until 1964, Valdez was located about 4 miles east of its present location, closer to Valdez Glacier. The 1964 Good Friday earthquake, the most destructive earthquake ever to hit southcentral Alaska, measured 9.2 on the Richter scale and was centered in Prince

(Continues on page 591)

Captain Fred shares his knowledge and enthusiasm aboard the *"Limousine of Prince William Sound"* on the most entertaining glacier/ wildlife cruise in Alaska...

...it's simply the BEST!

For more information:
P.O. Box 1832
Valdez, AK 99686
907.835.5141

Lu-Lu Belle
Glacier Wildlife Cruises

Reservations Hotline
1.800.411.0090
www.lulubelletours.com

Glacier Wildlife Cruises/Lu-Lu Belle. The motor yacht Lu-Lu Belle is probably the cleanest, plushest tour vessel you will ever see! This is an adult oriented cruise, and yes they will allow quiet, well behaved kids; however unruly unattended children will be sold to pirates. When you come aboard and see all the teak, mahogany and oriental rugs, you will understand why Captain Fred Rodolf asks you not to smoke and to wipe your feet before boarding. The Lu-Lu Belle has wide walk-around decks, thus assuring everyone ample opportunity for unobstructed viewing and photography.

Captain Fred is a born entertainer; he will personally guide and narrate every cruise. He has logged over 4,951 Columbia Glacier Cruises since 1979—that is more than anyone in Alaska. He is also known to be a "bit of a character".

The Columbia Glacier Wildlife Cruise of Prince William Sound is awesome! Wildlife seen on the cruises will vary throughout the season as the Lu-Lu Belle cruises from Valdez to the Columbia glacier on the calm protected waters of the Sound.

Boarding time is 10:30 am each day from

May thru August. The length of the cruise can vary from 7 to ? hours. Please don't watch the clock because the crew does not. In this world of mass merchandising what a refreshing experience to enjoy a day aboard the wonderfully unique Lu-Lu Belle with Alaska's ever popular and entertaining Captain Rodolf. This up close and personal tour is event oriented not schedule oriented. The iceberg conditions at the Columbia Glacier are always changing. There is no way to predict how long it will take to get to the glacier face, but if any boat can make it all the way to the face, it will be the Lu-Lu Belle! Experience spectacular calving events, see for yourself as the ice falls into the sea causing thunderous explosions and massive plumes of spray. They will stay at the glacier for at least 1 hour to make sure you have a chance to record some of those amazing events.

The cost is $145.00 per person (with a cash discount price of $140.00)*. On Sunday mornings from 8:00 to 9:00am, the Lu-Lu Belle becomes the "Chapel of the Sea"—everyone is welcome, no charge.

On the cruises the crew prepares

fresh baked goodies in the galley, all at reasonable prices. Gracious hospitality on a beautiful yacht are reasons why people refer to the Lu-Lu Belle as the "Limousine of Prince William Sound".

Join Captain and crew for an extra-special day and find out why Captain Fred refers to Switzerland as the "Valdez of Europe". They know that the best advertisement is their happy guests. Phone (800) 411-0090 or (907) 835-5141.

Pre-season bookings will be locked in at this price. During the season, a fuel surcharge may be added.

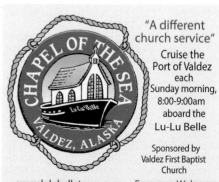

"A different church service"
Cruise the Port of Valdez each Sunday morning, 8:00-9:00am aboard the Lu-Lu Belle

Sponsored by Valdez First Baptist Church

www.lulubelletours.com   Everyone Welcome

(Continued from page 589)

William Sound. The quake did not destroy Valdez but the series of local waves caused by massive underwater landslides swept over and engulfed the Valdez wharf taking 33 people with it. Seismic action shook the downtown and residential areas. Though much damage was sustained, only the waterfront was destroyed. After the quake, the Army Corps of Engineers determined the town should be relocated. By late August 1964, relocation was underway. The last residents remaining at "old" Valdez moved to the new town in 1968.

Since its days as a port of entry for gold seekers, Valdez has been an important gateway to Interior Alaska. As the most northerly ice-free port in the Western Hemisphere, and connected by the Richardson High-

VALDEZ

Acres Kwik Trip	Ph. (907) 835-3278
Bayside RV Park	Ph. 1-888-835-4425
Bear Paw RV Park	Ph. (907) 835-2530
Chapel of the Sea (Lu-Lu Belle)	Ph. (907) 835-5141
Downtown B&B Inn	Ph. 1-800-478-2791
Eagle's Rest RV Park & Cabins	Ph. 1-800-553-7275
Easy Freeze, Inc.	Ph. (907) 835-4208
Lu-Lu Belle Glacier Wildlife Cruises	Ph. 1-800-411-0090
Pangaea Adventures	Ph. 1-800-660-9637
Stan Stephens Glacier & Wildlife Cruises	Ph. 1-866-867-1297
Valdez KOA	Ph. (907) 835-2723

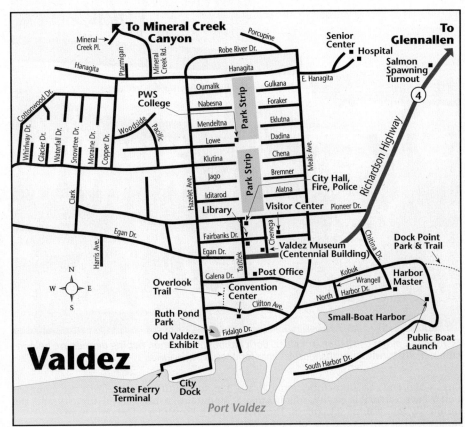

Valdez

way to the Alaska Highway system, Valdez offers the shortest link to much of interior Alaska for seaborne cargo. Construction of the trans-Alaska pipeline began in 1974 and was completed in 1977. The 800-mile-long pipeline begins at Prudhoe Bay on the Arctic

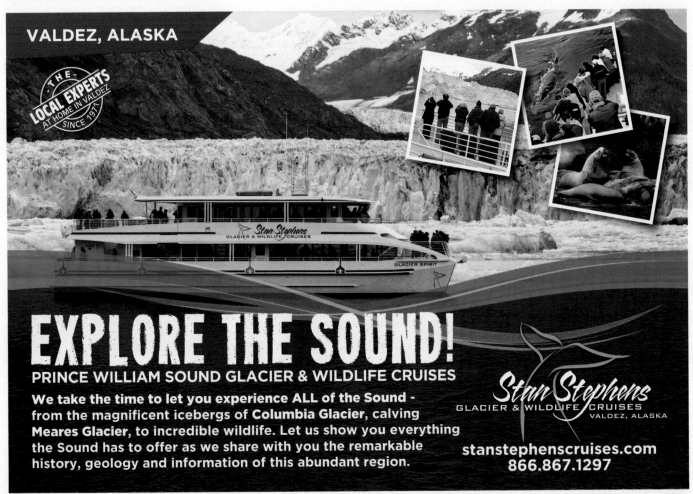

Fishing is a major attraction in Valdez. Both halibut and salmon fishing derbies are held in summer; visit www.valdezfishderbies.com for details. (©Sharon Nault)

Ocean and ends at the marine terminal at Port Valdez, where it is gravity fed into tanks or directly into waiting oil tankers. The first tanker load of oil shipped out of Valdez on August 1, 1977. In March 1989, national attention was focused on Valdez and the pipeline when the oil tanker *Exxon Valdez* ran aground on Bligh Reef (some 25 miles from Valdez) and resulted in an 11-million-gallon oil spill. Although the oil did not reach Valdez, it was marked as the largest oil spill in North American history at that time.

Valdez's economy depends on the oil industry, the Prince William Sound fishery, government and tourism. The city limits of Valdez comprise an area of 274 square miles and include all surrounding mountains to timberline. Valdez has long been known for its beautiful setting, with the Chugach Mountains rising behind the city and the colorful small-boat harbor in front.

Lodging & Services

Valdez has motel/hotel facilities and several bed and breakfasts *(see display ads this section)*. Summer lodging and campsite reservations are advised.

Services here include restaurants, sporting goods stores, liquor store, gift shops and gas stations (1 in town on Pioneer near Eagle's Rest RV Park, the other 2 on the highway and on Airport Road). There is a supermarket on Meals Avenue that is open 4:30 A.M. to midnight, daily in summer, and the Food Cache on Egan Drive has bulk grocery items.

Downtown B & B Inn. Motel accommodations, 113 Galena Dr. Centrally located near small boat harbor, museum, ferry terminal, downtown shopping. View rooms, private and shared baths, coin-op laundry, TV and phones in rooms. Wheelchair accessible. Deluxe continental breakfast May 15–Sept. 15. Reasonable rates. Single, double, family rooms. Phone 1-800-478-2791 or (907) 835-2791. Email: 1n2rs@alaska.net. Free WiFi. www.valdezdowntowninn.com. See display ad on this page. [ADVERTISEMENT]

Camping

Private RV parks in and around Valdez offer hookups, dump stations and other amenities (see ads and descriptions following). The Tesoro station has a dump station

Bayside RV Park is located in town and within walking distance to everything. Full, partial and no hookups with hot unmetered showers, laundromat, cable TV, free WiFi, huge community firepit and a beautiful view of the mountains, glaciers and wildlife. Rated #1 on Trip Advisor. Call 1-888-835-4425 for reservations. Email: bayside1@cvinternet.net. www.baysiderv.com. See display ad page 594. [ADVERTISEMENT]

Bear Paw R.V. Park, centrally located on scenic North Harbor Drive overlooking the boat harbor, puts you within easy walking distance of museum, shops, restaurants, entertainment, charter boats—no need to unhook and drive to grocery stores or points of interest. Full, partial or no hookups; immaculate private restrooms with hot, unmetered showers. Dump station and coin-operated launderette with irons and ironing boards available for guests. Also available, for adults only: waterfront full-hookup RV sites with cable TV, guest lounge, computer modem access line. Very nice, quiet wooded adult tent sites, some platforms, among the salmonberries on Porcupine Hill. Tables, fire pits. Campfire wood for sale. Let us book your glacier tour with Stan Stephens Cruises at the reservations desk in our spacious office lounge. Don't miss the Bear Paw Trading Post Gift Shop. Advance reservations recommended: (907) 835-2530. (Bear Paw does fill up!) The coffee pot is always on at Bear Paw. Let us know if you're coming in on the evening ferry and we'll be there to help you get parked. Email: bearpaw@valdezak.net. Internet: www.bearpawrvpark.com. See display ad on page 595. [ADVERTISEMENT]

Eagle's Rest RV Park, the friendliest RV park in downtown Valdez, offers you Good Sam Park service with a smile. Let our helpful staff take care of all your bookings on cruises, tours and charters. Enjoy

the beautiful panoramic view of our mountains and glaciers right from your RV! We will let you know where the hottest fishing spots are or the quietest walking trails. Fish-cleaning table is available. We also have 19 fully furnished rental cabins. Parking with us puts you within walking distance of our museums, gift shops, grocery store and banks. Shuttle service is available for glacier cruises. No charge to wash your RV at your site. Phone us for reservations, 1-800-

553-7275 or (907) 835-2373. Email: info@ eaglesrestrv.com. Internet: www.eaglesrestrv. com. Stay with us and leave feeling like part of the family. See display ad on this page.

[ADVERTISEMENT]

Valdez Glacier Campground has 94 sites, 11 with 20/30/50 amp electric pads and 10 non-electric pads. The facility provides hot showers, potable water and a dump station. The wooded site is a serine environment with fire pits, grills, dumpsters, and covered picnic areas. There are 73 standard tent camping sites and a campground host is available during business hours. Firewood is also available onsite. Tent sites $20, military $15 (must have I.D.); RV pad with electric $35–$40, military $30–$35; RV pad without electric $25, military $20. Travel trailer rentals available $89–$94, military $79–$84.

Dry cabins available $79, military $69. Pavilion camping site starting at $50. The campground is operated by Fort Greely, but is open to the public. Reservations can be made by calling 907-873-4795 or online at ValdezGlacierCampground@gmail.com. The campground host can be reached by calling 907-297-8524. Open Memorial Day through Labor Day. *CAUTION: Beware of bears, and watch for eagles!*

There is also RV/tent camping for $15/ night along Dayville Road on Allison Point. The turnoff for Dayville Road is 7 miles east of downtown *(see description of Dayville Road on page 596).* Bears are prevalent on Dayville Road. *CAUTION: Beware of bears.* Use signed overnight RV parking areas only. Day-use only parking is also available. There are no off-road parking areas available within

Valdez: All camping must be done within an RV Park or Campground for the safety of everyone visiting Valdez.

Transportation

Air: Daily scheduled service via Ravn Alaska airlines. Several air taxi services operate out of Valdez. There are no scheduled flights from Valdez to Cordova.

Ferry: Scheduled **Alaska Marine Highway** ferry from Whittier and Cordova. Phone 1-800-642-0067 (Juneau office). Advance reservations are a must! Visit www. ferryalaska.com.

Taxi: One local taxi service, Valdez Yellow Cab (907) 835-2500.

Car Rental: One company offers car rentals available at airport terminal: Valdez U-Drive (907) 835-4402 (one-way drop-off

Explore the Valdez waterfront promenade, with its view of the busy harbor. Across the street are a variety of businesses. (©Milton & Kelley Barker, staff)

not available).

Highway: The Richardson Highway extends north from Valdez to the Glenn Highway and the Alaska Highway. See the RICHARDSON HIGHWAY section.

Attractions

Explore the Valdez waterfront. The waterfront in Valdez is set up to accommodate fishermen and visitors out for a stroll. Restaurants, shops, boat and kayak rentals line one side of North Harbor Drive, while across the street the public promenade offers fine views of—and access to—the small boat harbor where you may see fishermen clean their catch.

Walk east along the promenade (which has picnic tables and public restrooms) to Dock Point Park, located past the boat launch where Kobuk Drive curves around the harbor. Dock Point Park has covered picnic tables, a restroom and a 1-mile trail with scenic overlooks of the Port of Valdez. The combination gravel and boardwalk trail provides easy access for people of all ability levels. NOTE: Kobuk Drive curves around the harbor and passes the Peter Pan cannery and its fresh seafood market.

Walk west on North Harbor Drive to Fidalgo Drive and continue to Ruth Pond Park on the corner of Hazelet Avenue and Fidalgo Drive. There are picnic tables and a trail at Ruth Pond. Across the street is the Valdez Museum Annex, which houses the Remembering Old Valdez Exhibit (see description this section). A memorial bench by a standing plaque here at the corner of Hazelet and Meals, commemorates the Copper River Gold Rush History.

Walk up Hazelet Avenue and turn up the hill on Clifton Avenue (towards the Valdez Convention & Civic Center). Overlook Trail branches off this street, affording fine views of downtown Valdez. Continue on Clifton Avenue to return to North Harbor Drive.

Visit Museums. Valdez has 3 outstanding museums, each offering a unique experience (descriptions follow).

Valdez Museum & Historical Archives, located in downtown Valdez at 217 Egan Dr., features artifacts and stories from 1898 to the present. Interpretive exhibits explain the impact of the gold rush, the 1907 railroad speculation boom, and the construction of the trans-Alaska oil pipeline. "A

Moving Experience" commemorates the 1964 earthquake. Learn about the cultural heritage of the region's Native peoples, the Ahtna, Alutiiq and Eyak. Do not miss the exhibit about the 1989 *Exxon Valdez* Oil Spill. View the fully restored 1907 Ahrens steam fire engine and see regional art here. Open daily, 9 A.M. to 5 P.M. May–September; noon–5 P.M. Tuesday–Sunday in winter.

The Remembering Old Valdez Exhibit/ Museum Annex, near the waterfront at 436 South Hazelet Ave. (next to the port and near the ferry terminal), commemorates the devastating 1964 Good Friday Earthquake, and marks the transition from the Historic Old Town Valdez to the Valdez of today. The original town site is remembered in a 1:20 scale replica as it appeared in 1963. This detailed model includes over 400 buildings and 60 city blocks that recall the thriving community that existed before the 9.2 quake. The documentary on the earthquake is a must-see for visitors. Also for viewing is the video, *Between the Glacier and the Sea*. The Museum Annex is open daily, 9 A.M. to 5 P.M., May to September; by appointment only in winter. Phone (907) 835-2764, or visit www.valdezmuseum.org.

The Maxine and Jesse Whitney Museum at Prince William Sound College, 303 Lowe St., (go north on Hazelet, right at the first college sign) is a real gem among Alaska museums. This huge collection in a state-of-the-art facility, features an amazing array of Alaska animal mounts, including 2 full-sized polar bears, black bear and grizzly bears, musk ox, moose and more, Native dolls, an Eskimo kayak, prehistoric artifacts (check out the arrowheads in drawers) and a one-of-a-kind collection of Native carved ivory, including the Paul Kulik Transportation Collection. Admission fee is by donation. For more information and details on summer hours and programs, phone (907) 834-1690; www.MJWhitneymuseum.org. Museum hours are posted locally.

Valdez Consortium Library, located at 212 Fairbanks St., (same block as the Valdez Museum, has an extensive Alaska Historical & Archive section, as well as many Alaska videos which can be viewed at the library. It also features a paperback exchange (a trade is appreciated but not required) and a variety of current newspapers and magazines. The library has public computers, laptops, WiFi and a photocopier. Wheelchair accessible. Drinking fountains, restrooms, telephone with 3-minute limit. Open Monday and Friday 10 A.M. to 6 P.M., Tuesday–Thursday 10 A.M. to 8 P.M., Saturday noon to 5 P.M. and Sunday 1–5 P.M. Website: www.ci.valdez. ak.us/library.

Take a boat tour to see Columbia Glacier, second largest tidewater glacier in North America, Shoup Glacier, Meares Glacier and other Prince William Sound attractions. See ads in this section.

Stan Stephens Glacier & Wildlife Cruises. Explore the fjords and passageways of Prince William Sound with Stan Stephens Glacier & Wildlife Cruises. The Stephens family and crew invite you to travel the calm waters of the Sound to Columbia Glacier or Meares Glacier. Stan Stephens Cruises, the only Valdez-based cruise company operated by Alaskans, has shared the wonders of their home with travelers since 1971. A day spent on the water with Stan Stephens is a complete Alaskan experience! They will take the time to let you view magnificent icebergs at Columbia Glacier; calving at Meares Glacier; orca or humpback whales, sea lions, sea otters, seals, puffins, bald eagles, kittiwakes, cormorants, porpoise, goats or bears. You will also learn about the history of the Sound including commercial fishing, oil shipping and early explorers. Stan Stephens Cruises offers 2 departures: a 6-hour Columbia Glacier Cruise or an 8.5-hour Meares Glacier Excursion. Travelers of all ages, families and special groups are welcome and encouraged. Staying in an RV park? Complimentary park to dock transfers are offered. For more information please contact Stan Stephens Cruises toll free at 1-866-867-1297 or online at www.stanstephenscruises.com. See display ad on page 591. [ADVERTISEMENT]

Prince William Sound College is located at 303 Lowe St. (The school's student housing is located on Pioneer Street.) Access from the college parking lot to park strip and Barney Meyring Park, with children's play area and picnic tables. Look for the 2 huge wooden carvings by artist Peter Toth on campus. One is at the college proper on Lowe Street and the other is in front of the student housing on Pioneer Street. Both are dedicated to Native Americans. Toth has carved 67 statues honoring Native Americans and donated them to towns in each of the 50 states. Referred to as "Whispering Giants," the 20- to 40-foot-high monuments are found on the grounds of museums, parks, libraries and other public places in North America.

Visit Old Valdez. The original, pre-earthquake site of Valdez is located 4 miles from downtown via the Richardson Highway (watch for signed turnoff). Information sign about Old Valdez town site at Mile 0.1 mile on access road. A memorial at Mile 0.4 has 2 plaques that are set in a foundation from "old" Valdez. One plaque lists the names of those residents of Valdez and Chenega who were killed in Good Friday earthquake on March 27, 1964.

Go Fishing. Fish from the wharf for salmon or come to see salmon get reeled in. This is a good place to take a picture of the Valdez pipeline terminal. (The wharf parking lot is just across from the Remembering Old Valdez/Museum Annex.) There is also shore fishing at Allison Point on Dayville Road.

Go Hiking. A popular short day hike is to Gold Creek, 3.5 miles from Valdez. Other area hikes include Keystone Canyon (2.6 miles), Dock Point Trail (1 mile) and Solomon Gulch Trail (3.8 miles). A 10-mile hike along Valdez Arm to Shoup Bay State Marine Park starts at the Mineral Creek trailhead in town.

Go Sea Kayaking. Pangaea Adventures offers guided sea kayaking tours at the small boat harbor. This is an ideal way to explore Prince William Sound. Guided trips range from an afternoon paddle around Port Valdez to glacier day tours and camping tours and are suitable for all levels of experience. See ad on this page or go to: www. alaskasummer.com.

Visit Crooked Creek Information Site, the Chugach National Forest salmon spawning viewing stream. Drive out the Richardson Highway about a mile from downtown to the log building on Crooked Creek. The center is open Memorial Day weekend to Labor Day; outhouses, spacious parking area.

Outdoor viewing platform to watch spawning pinks and chum (mid-July to early September). Indoor science center features fish cam, hands-on exhibits and friendly staff. Good view of Crooked Creek Falls from back deck. A great stop.

Across the highway from the viewing area are intertidal wetlands known locally as "Duck Flats." Watch for migrating waterfowl here from late April to mid-May and in October. Nesting birds in summer. This is a game sanctuary; no shooting is allowed. Good spot for photos.

Drive Dayville Road. Dayville Road is 6.8 miles from Valdez via the Richardson Highway. Drive this 5.2-mile-long side road for opportunities to enjoy wild Alaska without venturing far from your vehicle.

This is a wide, paved, improved side road with a bike trail that leads to shoreside camping, picnicking, fishing and scenic views along Port Valdez, the 13-mile-long estuary at the head of Valdez Arm. There are many roadside benches and signed parking for day use. Look for seals, sea lions, birds, bears (especially when spawning salmon are returning to the Solomon Gulch Fish Hatchery in the fall). Berry picking in season.

See Milepost V 2.8 on page 441 in the RICHARDSON HIGHWAY section for a detailed description of Dayville Road.

The **Solomon Gulch Fish Hatchery** and large parking area are located at Mile 3.8. There are some dramatic views and photo opportunities from the bridge here of the Solomon Gulch Falls and dam site (Copper Valley Electric co-generation project). Walkways at the fish hatchery go to a viewing platform and along the ponds and hatchery building, more information signs. *CAUTION: Be bear aware in this area.*

Dayville Road is open to the public to Mile 5.2, where a guardhouse restricts public access to the Alyeska Pipeline Terminal complex. *NOTE: There is NO public access to the marine terminal and there are NO public tours of the terminal.*

See Waterfalls. From downtown Valdez, drive out the Richardson Highway 17.5 miles to see **Horsetail Falls**. A short distance

beyond Horsetail Falls is **Bridal Veil Falls**. Both are favorite photo stops. There are also waterfalls visible from town.

State marine parks in the Valdez area include Shoup Bay, Jack Bay and Sawmill Bay. Accessible mainly by water, these parks offer cabins or tent platforms and fire rings. They are popular with fishermen and sea kayakers. Website: dnr.alaska.gov/parks/units/pwssmp/smpvald.htm.

Public-Use Cabins. McAllister Creek, Moraine and Kittiwake public-use cabins are located within Shoup Bay State Marine Park. Check the fact sheet at: dnr.alaska.gov/parks/cabins/pws. Jack Bay USFS cabin is located at the east end of Jack Bay off of Valdez Narrows. Access is by floatplane (15 minutes from Valdez) or boat (20 miles from Valdez). Cabin reservations can be made by calling 1-877-444-6777 or visit www.recreation.gov. See water taxi options available at: www.alaskasummer.com/pages/watertaxi-princewilliamsound-valdez.html.

The Mayday Fly-in & Air Show, every Mother's Day weekend in May, celebrates the history of bush flying in Alaska. View bush pilot competitions, aerial acrobatics and airplane exhibits, go for rides or just climb aboard and see how it feels to be behind a yoke. Find more information at: www.valdezflyin.com/.

Fish a Derby. The Halibut Derby takes place May 18–Sept. 1, 2019 and the Halibut Hulabaloo is the second week of June. Other annual fishing derbies include the Kids' Pink Salmon Derby (July 20, 2019); Silver Salmon Derby (July 20–Sept. 1, 2019); and the Women's Silver Salmon Derby (August 10, 2019). Silver Big Prize Fridays are July 26 and August 30, 2019. Derby awards are on Sept.1, 2019. If you're going fishing, don't miss the payout, buy a derby ticket. Visit www.valdezfishderbies.com.

Valdez Gold Rush Days, this celebration is an annual event that includes a parade, contests, game night, city-wide wine walk, town fish fry and much more. During Gold Rush Days, cancan girls peruse local establishments and the "Hoosegow" jail is pulled through town by "deputies" who arrest citizens without beards. The jail is on display in a yard across from the museum the rest of the year. Scheduled for July 31–August 4, 2019; find more information at www.valdezgoldrushdays.org.

Winter Sports. Valdez's proximity to Thompson Pass has made it a desirable winter destination for adventurous extreme skiers, snow machiners and snowboarders and various snowboarding championship competitions take place here. Check with the Valdez Convention and Visitors Bureau for a list of winter events and outfitters at www.valdezalaska.org.

AREA FISHING: Valdez Arm supports the largest sport fishery in Prince William Sound. Important species include pinks and coho, halibut, rockfish and Dolly Varden. Charter boats are available in Valdez. Favorite shoreside public fishing spots are Valdez city dock and **Allison Point**. Allison Point is located on Dayville Road; turnoff is 4.8 miles east of downtown via the Richardson Highway. The Allison Point fishery, created by the Solomon Gulch Hatchery, has one of the largest pink salmon fisheries in the state and produces a major coho salmon return annually. Pinks from mid-June through late July; coho from mid-July through late August.

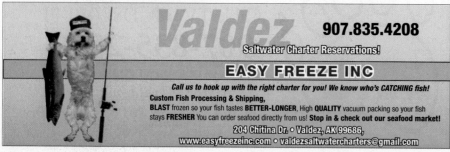

Cordova

Cordova's small boat harbor is one of Alaska's largest single-basin harbors. (©Sharon Nault)

Located on the southeast shore of Orca Inlet on the east side of Prince William Sound. Cordova is accessible only by plane, boat and ferry. **Population:** 2,386. **Emergency Services:** Dial 911. **Alaska State Troopers**, phone (907) 424-3184. **Police**, phone (907) 424-6100. **Hospital**, Cordova Community Medical Center, phone (907) 424-8000. Ilanka Health Center, phone (907) 424-3622.

Visitor Information: Available in 3 places: The Chamber of Commerce, 404 1st St.; phone (907) 424-7260; email office@cordovachamber.com; www.cordovachamber.com. The Cordova Center at 601 First St., houses city offices, the library and museum, theatre and meeting spaces. And lastly at the Chugach National Forest Cordova Ranger District office located at 612 2nd St. This white, multi-storied federal building was built in 1925, and once housed the post office, jail and courthouse. Natural history displays are on the 2nd and 3rd floors. U.S. Forest Service personnel can provide information on trails, cabins and other activity options on national forest lands. Open weekdays from 8 A.M. to 5 P.M. Phone (907) 424-7661; www.fs.usda.gov/chugach/.

Elevation: Sea level to 400 feet. **Climate:** Average temperature in July is 65°F, in January 21°F. Average annual precipitation is 167 inches. During the winter of 2011–2012, Cordova had over 220 inches of snow, the largest amount since the record-breaking winter of 1998–1999, when almost 200 inches fell. Prevailing winds are easterly at about 4 knots. **Radio:** KLAM-AM 1450 (country), KCHU-FM 88.1 (Community Public Radio), KCDV-FM 100.9 (The Eagle). **Television:** Cable. **Newspaper:** *The Cordova*

Times (weekly).

Private Aircraft: Merle K. "Mudhole" Smith Airport, Mile 12.1 Copper River Highway; elev. 42 feet; length 7,500 feet; asphalt; attended. It has an EMAS arrestor bed safety feature made of crushable, lightweight concrete and is 1 of 63 airports nationwide to feature this technology. Aircraft that overrun the runway sink into this bed and stop.

Cordova Municipal (city airfield), 0.9 mile east; elev. 12 feet; length 1,900 feet; gravel; fuel 100, 100LL available for private sales when Cordova Air is open. Eyak Lake seaplane base, 0.9 mile east, adjacent to city field.

The Cordova area was first inhabited by the Eyak tribe. European fishermen came to ply the surrounding fish-rich waters, and by 1889 there was a busy fish camp and cannery site on Odiak Pond.

The town had its origin as the railroad terminus and ocean shipping port for the copper ore shipped by rail from the Kennecott mine up the Copper River. The town was named Cordova by Michael J. Heney, builder of the Copper River & Northwest Railway. The name of the town was derived from the adjacent water—Puerto Cordova—so named by Spanish explorer Don Salvador Fidalgo in 1790. A post office was established here in 1906. The townsite was moved from Eyak Lake to the shore of Orca Inlet in 1908. The first trainload of copper ore from Kennecott arrived on April 8, 1911.

Cordova was incorporated in 1909. The mines closed in 1938 but the town continued to prosper due to the fishing industry. The gulf and sound waters held amazing quantities in multiple fisheries and Cordova's economy thrived. The *Exxon Valdez* oil spill in 1989 devastated the herring fishery and other fisheries in the area. The recovery has been long and slow. Reports show that of 73 herring permit holders, only 2 fished in 2016 (last available record). Other fisher-

ies such as black cod and salmon have had a better recovery rate. The fishing fleet can be seen at Cordova harbor, also the home port of the USCG cutter *Sycamore*. Salmon runs begin in early May and continue to September, with chinook, sockeye and coho taken from the Copper River area, sockeye, chums and pinks from Prince William Sound. Black cod, halibut and shrimp seasons run during the winter/spring months.

Lodging & Services

Accommodations year-round at **The Reluctant Fisherman Inn** and **Prince William Motel**. Advance reservations are recommended.

Cordova has several dining choices, Chinese, Filipino fusion, cafes, espresso shacks and food trucks, Baja Taco and Harborside Pizza (wood-fired oven pizza) behind AC Value Center shopping. Cordova also has a Harbormaster's office, a laundromat, 2 supermarkets, several other stores and gift shops. There are 2 banks in town: First National Bank of Alaska and Wells Fargo (both banks have 24-hour ATM).

There are free of charge **EV plug-ins** in downtown at the Cordova Center (2 in the lower parking area and 2 in the upper area). Short-term and long-term parking available in designated areas in the harbor area. For information phone (907) 424-6200. *NOTE: Do NOT park on the street within 20 feet of a crosswalk, you may receive a ticket.*

The small boat harbor has 711 slips. Contact the Harbormaster for reservation information prior to arrival. The Harbormaster's office on Nicholoff Way has free tide books and other information as well as a courtesy phone, book swap, restrooms, showers and drinking fountains. The office is open 8 A.M. to 5 P.M. weekdays; phone (907) 424-6400 or visit their website at www.cityofcordova.net. Sani-dump for RVers is right behind this building. Follow the signs. There are also oil

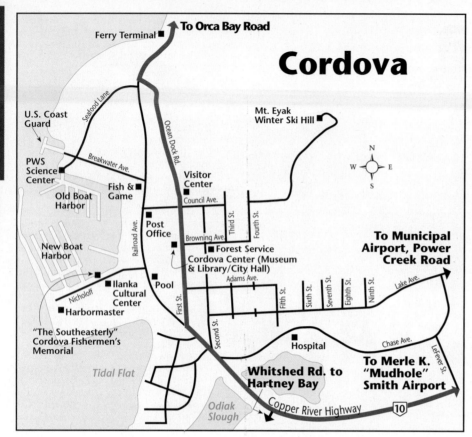

Cordova

A/C Market (on Nicholoff Way) and at the Airport.

Look for the beautiful Russian Orthodox church with blue roof and onion-dome, one of many churches in this community and representative of the many commercial fishing families here of Russian descent.

The Hollis-Henrichs Park has a platform for picnickers with a large grassy field for running kids and pets, and a path and boardwalk over Odiak Pond featuring a small gazebo and a playground for kids. Public restrooms adjacent park. This park is on Chase Avenue, between the Copper River Highway and the Cordova Community Health Center and Hospital. The Noel Pallas Children's Memorial Playground (fondly referred to as the "Tot Lot" by locals) is a great place for kids to play, located adjacent to the baseball field near the Cordova Jr/Sr High School. Bathrooms are near ball field.

Camping

Odiak Camper Park on Whitshed Road is a flat gravel parking lot style site with showerhouse/toilets and 24 RV spaces that have electric hookups. These sites are often reserved for a month at a time by commercial fishermen and it can be difficult to obtain a reservation.

Shelter Cove Campground and overnight RV parking is 0.6 mile out Orca Road (flat gravel area for RVs), 3 private sites for RV or tent. These include tent platforms in woods. Private site is $20 per day. Econo RV parking (parking lot) is $11 per day. If you arrive after hours, you may park in available Econo parking and pay the following morning at Bidarki Recreation Center. This campground is adjacent a salmon run pond and stream, and just across the highway from Orca Bay.

NOTE: All campsite reservations are made at the Parks and Recreation Department administrative office located in the Bidarki Recreation Center, downtown at 103 Council Rd. Phone (907) 424-7282.

No reservations are needed at Forest Service campsites along the Copper River Highway and there are no fees charged. These sites are available on a first come, first served basis with limited facilities, so plan ahead to get water. Established camping sites are provided in two locations: at Alaganik Slough Recreation Area (four gravel tent pads, see Attractions) and One-Eyed Pond Recreation Site (3 raised tent platforms constructed in 2018, see Attractions). Camping/parking is also allowed, for one night only, at turnouts between Mile 13 and Mile 26 on the Copper River Highway.

NOTE: The Childs Glacier Recreation Area, an 11-site campground at Mile 48 Copper River Highway with spectacular views of two nearby

---

receptacles for used oil drop off.

The Cordova Library, in the Cordova Center at 601 First St., is open in summer, Tuesday through Thursday, from 10 A.M. to 8 P.M.; Friday from 10 A.M. to 6 P.M.; Saturday and Sunday from noon–5 P.M.; closed Monday. The library offers free internet access via PC computers and WiFi, phone (907) 424-6667; website www.cordovalibrary.org.

The Bidarki Recreation Center has a weight room, showers, sauna and exercise facility. It is located at 2nd and Council. Open 10 A.M. to 6 P.M., Monday–Friday (pass holders can access the facility 5 A.M. to 10 P.M. 7 days a week. Rent Skater's Cabin, on Eyak Lake for $25/night, through the Recreation Center. *All campsite reservations are*

made at the Parks and Recreation Department administrative office located in the Bidarki Recreation Center office. Phone (907) 424-7282.

Bob Korn Memorial Swimming Pool is located on Railroad Avenue, next to the police station at the head of Nicholoff. The heated indoor pool offers lap swim, family swim, exercise classes and lessons. Open year-round. Phone (907) 424-7200 for pool hours and programs. Admission is charged. Showers are available with paid admission.

The U.S. Forest Service maintains 16 public-use cabins in the Cordova District. Phone 1-877-444-6777, or visit www.recreation.gov, for details and reservations.

Courtesy phones and restrooms are at the Cordova Center, the Harbormaster's Office, the Alaska Marine Highway Ferry Office, the

glaciers and the historic Million Dollar Bridge, is closed to vehicle access indefinitely due to bridge failure at Mile 36 on the Copper River Highway. Additional road damage occurred in 2018, washing out part of the road at Mile 44. However, the recreation area is open to the public if you can get there. Day trips are popular and overnight camping is available for $10 per night. Phone the Cordova Ranger District for details at (907) 424-7661. CAUTION: Watch for bears.

There are several primitive camping areas available on Chugach National Forest Land on the Copper River Highway outside of town. First come, first serve. No reservations required. For more details visit cordovachamber.com/hiking.

The Harbormaster's office on Nicholoff Way has an RV sani-dump located behind it and showers are available in the facility for a fee.

Transportation

Air: Scheduled service via Alaska Airlines. Local charter service with Cordova Air Service at (907) 424-3289 and Alaska Wilderness Outfitters at (907) 424-5552. Merle K. "Mudhole" Smith Airport at Mile 12 on the Copper River Highway. Merle K. "Mudhole" Smith was a legendary Alaska bush pilot who flew for Cordova Air Service for many years. He later served as president of the air service, which merged with Alaska Airlines in 1968.

Ferry: The Alaska Marine Highway system connects Cordova with Valdez and Whittier. Phone (907) 424-7333 or 1-800-642-0066. For current ferry schedules visit www.ferryalaska.com.

Taxis: Cordova Taxi (907) 253-5151. For airport shuttle, call Chinook Auto Rentals (907) 424-5279 ($10 per person shuttle pickup at the airport).

Car Rentals: Available via Chinook Auto Rentals (907) 424-5279.

Highways: The Alaska state highway system does not connect to Cordova. The 49-mile Copper River Highway leads east from Cordova and ends just beyond the Million Dollar Bridge. The highway currently is closed to traffic at **Milepost C 35.8** *(see "Copper River Highway" log on page 601).*

Private Boats: Cordova has a "new" and an "old" boat harbor with 727-slips serving recreational boaters as well as the commercial fishing fleet. Contact the Harbormaster's office at (907) 424-6400 or on VHF Channel 16.

Attractions

Take a walking tour. A self-guided walking tour map of Cordova historic sites, prepared by the Cordova Historical Society, is available at the Visitor Center as well as the Cordova Museum. Although much of early Cordova was destroyed by fire, several picturesque old structures and historic sites remain. Take a trip back in time with the Cordova Historical Museum's guide to the first 13 miles of the Copper River Highway sharing the history of the Copper River and Northwest Railway, the building of the airport and relaying the history of bridge names.

Cordova Fishermen's Memorial, *The Southeasterly,* is located on Nicholoff Way overlooking the New Harbor. Created by local sculptor Joan Bugbee Jackson, this is a favorite photo subject for visitors and is a reminder of the dangers this fishing fleet faces each day.

Ilanka Cultural Center, located across

Alaganik Slough Recreation Area, Milepost C 16.8 Copper River Highway, is a good place to see trumpeter swans. (©Sharon Nault)

from the Fishermen's Memorial, features contemporary artwork as well as artifacts of the local Eyak tribe. Native Art classes are taught throughout the year; call ahead for schedule. On site gift shop has authentic handicrafts and unique and beautiful items for purchase. Open 10 A.M. to 5 P.M., Monday through Friday. Phone (907) 424-7903; www.ilankaculturalcenter.com.

The Cordova Center, at 601 First St., overlooking the South Harbor, houses the museum, library, city hall and a 200-seat theatre. The Center is easy to find: It's just across from the Alaskan Hotel, or uphill from the Southeasterly Monument that is adjacent the South Harbor.

Cordova Historical Museum, part of the Cordova Center, offers an excellent overview of the area's history, tracing "the tracks of Cordova's past through industrial and cultural exhibits, displays and interpretation."

The museum, opened in 2017 with new exhibits and two art galleries featuring original work by Alaskan artists Sydney Laurence, Eustace Ziegler and Jules Dahlager. Donations suggested for those 12 and older. Open 10 A.M. to 5 P.M. Tuesday through Friday, 10 A.M. to 5 P.M. Saturdays from noon–5:00 P.M. Phone (907) 424-6665 or visit www.cordovamuseum.org. The Cordova Historical Society operates a museum store featuring local history books made in Alaska crafts and jewelry.

Watch Birds. The Copper River Delta is one of the most important stopover places in the Western Hemisphere for one of the largest shorebird migrations in the world. As many as 5 million shorebirds rest and feed here during spring migration. Birders can view up to 31 different species. Birders planning to visit in the spring should consider timing their arrival to coincide with the Copper River Delta Shorebird Festival May 2–5, 2019; website:coppershorebird.com.

Hartney Bay and Alaganik Slough are the most popular of several bird-watching areas. Drive out Whitshed Road 5.5 miles to road end to reach Hartney Bay, an estuary on the edge of Orca Inlet and a great place to see shorebirds. The USFS recreation area at Alaganik Slough is 16.8 miles from down-

town, but worth the drive to see trumpeter swans and dusky Canada geese up-close. The slough is part of the 300,000-acre Copper River Delta mudflats which was uplifted up to 15 feet during the 1964 earthquake. There are 4 camping sites along the Alaganik River, a boat launch and a boardwalk with interpretive signs, viewing blind and elevated platform over the slough for bird watchers.

Visit the USCGC *Sycamore.* While there are no formal tours of the *Sycamore,* if the cutter is in port and the crew is not busy, you may be able to get on board. Inquire at the Quarterdeck shack on the North Fill Dock, just off of Seafood Lane or the "T" Pier.

Go Boating. Cordova is ideally situated for exploring Prince William Sound. Visit the harbor area, or search for outfitters online at: cordovachamber.com to charter a jet boat for fishing or sightseeing.

Disc Golf. The Cordova Disc Golf Course is accessed from a small parking area near Mile 0.2 Whitshed Road. There is a small City of Cordova Water Dept. structure on one side of the parking area and a barricaded access road on the other. Take the gravel access road—a somewhat steep walk—to a small water tower with a trail leading around to the left. Continue on the trail up another somewhat steep section until it flattens out, revealing meadows on the hiker's left and a "Meals Reservoir" sign. This is the entrance to the Cordova Disc Golf Course. The course consists of 9 holes that are scattered through the meadows.

Continue on the trail, past the disc golf course, for Cordova Reservoir. While using this area for recreation, please be sensitive to your watershed impacts. Remember this is the City's drinking water and anything you leave on the ground or in the water will have an effect on the water.

Overflow parking is available at the multi-purpose field next to Odiak Camper Park at Mile 0.5 Whitshed Road. This is also the location of a disc golf practice tee. Discs are available for purchase at local stores.

Mount Eyak Ski Area. Ski hill is usually open for skiing early December to the end of April, depending on snow conditions. Brought here from Sun Valley, Idaho, the single chair lift rises 800 feet/244m up Mount Eyak and overlooks the town and harbor from 1,200 feet. Walk up or drive your own vehicle. A hiking trail from the base of the mountain to the top of the chair lift and beyond connects with the USFS Crater Lake Trail.

Winter schedule is Wednesday, Saturday, Sunday and holidays, 9 A.M. to dusk. To reach the ski area, take 1st Avenue and turn on Browning, then left on 4th Avenue, right on Council, left on 6th up to the ski area (about 1 mile from Main Street). Phone (907) 424-7766 for further information. www.mteyak.org.

Walk or Drive Orca Bay Road. Pleasant evenings bring locals out to walk along Orca Bay Road. It is also a favorite with dog-walkers. The 2.1-mile-long road is right on the shores of the bay (no sandy beach) and ends at a lodge. Shelter Cove Campground at Mile 0.6 has pit toilets and is adjacent a salmon run pond/stream. (Read more about this campground under Camping.) There is a busy fish cleaning station, located adjacent the road at Mile 0.7 that attracts seals, sea otters and birds.

Drive Power Creek Road (signed Lake Avenue). This is a scenic drive along the shore of Lake Eyak past waterfalls and through massive, moss-covered trees to the trailhead for USFS Power Creek Trail (description follows). Check with the USFS office in town for trail status, (907) 424-7661. Enjoy berry picking, fish viewing and fishing for Dolly Varden along this road.

From 2nd Avenue in downtown Cordova, drive out Lake Avenue 0.6 mile to Nirvana Park on Lake Eyak. Built in 1930–1935, the park once contained whimsical sculptures (photographs of them are at the museum in town). Continue out past the municipal airport. An old airplane hangar here is thought to be the oldest in Alaska.

At Mile 1.7 is City of Cordova's Skaters Cabin (rent from Bidarki Recreation Center—includes vault toilet, trash receptacles, covered deck, wood stove, outdoor fire pit, swim-out floating dock). Pavement ends and a gravel road continues from this site. Just across from Skaters Cabin is USFS Crater Lake Trail. The 2.4-mile trail climbs to 1,500 feet past excellent views to an alpine lake with fishing for rainbow trout. *CAUTION: Watch for bears.*

Self-contained RV or tent camping is allowed in turnouts beyond Mile 1.7 for one night with no fee (see signs). Practice "leave no trace" camping. No facilities are available—pack in and pack out in consideration of the next visitor.

At Mile 2.5 a sign notes: "road narrows next 4 miles" (not recommended for big rigs past this point) as Power Creek Road winds toward the head of the lake at Mile 5.7. The road ends at Mile 7.3 at Power Creek Trailhead and a turnaround area. This 4.2 mile trail accesses both the USFS public-use cabin in Power Creek Basin and a ridge trail that connects with Crater Lake Trail, creating a 12-mile loop. This difficult hike offers spectacular scenery with waterfalls, hanging glaciers and views of Power Creek Basin (called "surprise valley" by locals), the Chugach Range and Prince William Sound. Excellent berry picking. *CAUTION: Watch for bears.*

©Sharon Nault

Drive the Copper River Highway. Although closed indefinitely to all vehicle traffic beyond **Milepost C 35.8**, the Copper River Highway still offers accessible hiking hiking trails, fishing spots and bird watching opportunities. (*See "Copper River Highway" on facing page.*) Two of the highway's major attractions—the **Million Dollar Bridge** (pictured above) and **Childs Glacier**, both at road's end—are no longer accessible by vehicle.

Childs Glacier Recreation Area is open to the public but closed to vehicle access indefinitely due to the failure of Bridge 339 on the Copper River Highway. Prior to the 2018 washout of the road near **Milepost C 45**, Orca Adventure Lodge (www.orca adventurelodge.com), Riverside Inn (www.riversideinncordova.com) and Childs Glacier Lodge (www.childsglacierlodge.com) offered transportation and tours to Childs Glacier

via shuttle van and boat. Check websites for current information or contact Cordova Ranger District at (907) 424-7661.

Take a hike. A popular family hike for locals and visitors is the Haystack Trail at **Milepost C 19.1** Copper River Highway. This 0.8-mile trail leads up stairs and along boardwalks through lush spruce-hemlock forest to a spot overlooking the Copper River Delta, providing wonderful views with benches to sit on and relax. Moose are often spotted from here. In 2018 a new Agents of Discovery augmented reality mobile game (app) mission was developed at this site featuring nature-based educational challenges during the hike. Phone the Cordova Ranger District for details at (907) 424-7661. Be sure to wear waterproof boots as the trail is often muddy in areas without boardwalks. *CAUTION: Watch for bears.*

Another popular hike is the USFS Heney Ridge Trail at Mile 5.1 Whitshed Road. A 3.5-mile long hike one-way, the first 2 miles are moderately easy and offer good views of Hartney Bay. The last mile is a steep climb up to the ridge, where on a clear day you are treated to spectacular views of Prince William Sound and the Gulf of Alaska. Be sure to wear waterproof boots with good traction on most trails in Cordova. *CAUTION: Watch for bears.*

Stop by the USFS office on 2nd Street for current trail conditions and more details on over 40 miles of nearby hiking trails. Phone (907) 424-7661.

Have a picnic. Take advantage of rare blue-bird days in Cordova. Sheridan Glacier Recreation Site at Mile 13.7 provides a nice starting-off point for picnicking beside a river, or pack your lunch less than a mile to Sheridan Lake, where icebergs from the glacier change the landscape year-round. At 18 Mile Recreation Site and One-Eyed Pond, three hardened picnic sites near the creek include pit toilets and bear-proof garbage cans with three raised tent platforms along a ¼ mile trail around One-Eyed Pond. There are two picnic sites with fire rings at 22 Mile Recreation Site on the Alaganik River along with a covered pavilion. This site is popular for fishing and boating up to McKinley Lake Cabin and includes interpretive displays of Native Alaskan history in the area.

Special Events. The **Copper River Delta Shorebird Festival** is scheduled for May 2–5, 2019. Many birder activities, speakers, workshops and community events are scheduled throughout the festival. Details at www.copershorebird.com.

An **Old Time Downtown 4th of July Celebration** draws hundreds of residents and visitors to First Street each year to enjoy and participate in activities, like the Kelp box derby—always popular with young and old alike—a race of homemade soapbox-style racers. Moose Kids games for children ages 3 to 12 include races, an egg toss, and other competitions for prizes. The highlight of the day is the free wild red salmon barbeque potluck feast served up hot from the grills by volunteers. Community members provide side dishes and desserts and the local seafood processors such as Trident Seafoods and Copper River Seafoods generously donate fresh Copper River and Prince William Sound wild sockeye salmon for everyone's enjoyment.

Cordova's **Copper River Salmon Jam** takes place July 12–13, 2019, at Mount Eyak Ski Hill, and features the live music, free kids' fun and educational activities, an artisan market, the Taste of Cordova wild food

cook-off, and the Alaska Salmon Runs, a series of road races that includes the King Salmon Marathon, the Sockeye Half-Marathon, Coho 10K, Humpy 5K and the Smolt 1-mile fun run/walk; website: salmonjam. org.

In 1961, a few Cordovans created the Iceworm Festival to break up the winter blahs. Today, the **Iceworm Festival** is Cordova's most popular winter event, held annually the first full weekend of every February. The highlight of the week-long festival is the 100-foot-long "iceworm" that winds its way through the streets of Cordova during the parade. Other activities include the survival suit race, variety show, a talent show, food and crafts fairs, and the selection of Miss Iceworm, who then represents Cordova at the Fur Rendezvous festival in Anchorage.

Cordova Fungus Festival celebrates the bounty of Cordova's harvest season with guided mushroom foraging forays, expert speakers, art and crafting events, free kids' activities and a Wild Harvest Feast dinner featuring a visiting guest chef and highlighted with wild mushrooms and Copper River coho salmon. The weekend festival usually occurs near the end of August or beginning of September. Find the exact dates and more information at cordovafungusfest.com.

AREA FISHING: According to the ADF&G, "Saltwater fishing in **Orca Inlet** and adjacent eastern **Prince William Sound** is readily accessible from Cordova. Species include halibut, rockfish and 5 species of salmon. Trolling for salmon is best for chinook in the winter and spring, and coho in the summer and fall. Boat charters are available locally. Road-accessible fishing opportunities exist for salmon in saltwater at **Fleming Spit/Lagoon**, near the ferry terminal off Orca Bay Road. Strong runs of hatchery-enhanced chinook (in the spring) and coho (August and September) return to this terminal fishery.

©Sharon Nault

"Road-accessible freshwater fishing is also good in the Cordova Area. **Eyak River** supports strong returns of sockeye during June and July and coho in August and September. The area at the outlet of the lake, where the road crosses, is fly-fishing only. Several streams along the Copper River Highway between Eyak Lake and the Million Dollar Bridge also support runs of sockeye and coho. These streams include **Clear Creek**, **Alaganik Slough**, **Eighteen-mile Creek**, **Ibeck Creek** and **Twenty-mile Creek**. In addition, cutthroat trout and Dolly Varden are present in most of these streams. Lake fishing for sockeye, Dolly Varden and cutthroat trout is available in **McKinley Lake**, **Power Creek** and the **Pipeline Lake** system. Fly-out fishing from Cordova is also popular for salmon, Dolly Varden and cutthroat trout. Charter operators are available locally."

Copper River Highway

Designated a Scenic Byway in 2011, the Copper River Highway originally led 48.6 miles northeast from Cordova to the Childs Glacier Recreation Area and the Million Dollar Bridge. But currently it is *CLOSED INDEFINITELY* to vehicle traffic beyond **Milepost C 35.8.** due to bridge failure. In 2018, the road also washed away near **Milepost C 45** due to heavy rains. Tour companies stepped in after the bridge failure to ferry people across the river then drive them to Childs Glacier. With the second washout, plans changed and future tours are on hold; inquire locally for current status.

You can still drive out to the recreation areas located in the first 35 miles of good gravel road. There are multiple USFS hiking trails and interpretive stops to enjoy as well as camping opportunities (see log).

The Copper River Highway is built along the abandoned railbed of the Copper River & Northwestern Railway, completed in 1911, which connected the port of Cordova with the Kennecott Copper Mines near Kennicott and McCarthy. The mine and railway ceased operation in 1938. Construction began on the highway in 1945. It was to extend to Chitina (on the Edgerton Highway), but progress was halted by the 1964 Good Friday earthquake, which knocked the north span of the Million Dollar Bridge into the Copper River. The bridge was officially re-opened to traffic in 2005, although travel beyond the bridge is restricted to ATVs.

Distance is measured from Cordova (C).
NOTE: This is an abbreviated highway log showing some of the highlights along the Copper River Highway.

ALASKA ROUTE 10

C 0 Junction of Ferry Terminal Road and Orca Road in Cordova. This is the location of the Alaska Marine Highway ferry terminal.

C 1 Turn north for Hollis-Henrichs Park. Take the boardwalk to the gazebo, picnic tables, pit toilets. Continue south on Ocean Dock Road and turn east on Council Avenue for Prince William Motel located on 2nd and Council.

C 1.3 Turn south for **Whitshed Road.** At Mile 0.1 is access to Reservoir Trail and Cordova Disc Golf Course. Reservoir Trail is good for snowshoeing in the winter and a beautiful hike in the summer. Be respectful of watershed and leave no waste. At Mile 0.5 is Odiak Municipal Campground (24 sites, limited tenting area). Reserve in advance at the Bidarki Recreation Center. Commercial fishing fleet families reserve these spaces for month-long stays. After passing physical milepost 5, watch for trailhead. Park by bridge in boat launch area. At Mile 5.1 is USFS Heney Ridge Trailhead parking (3.5-mile hike one way); *CAUTION: Watch for bears.* At Mile 5.6 is Hartney Bay, a popular birdwatching spot for the spring shorebird migration. Fish from **Hartney Bay** bridge.

C 5.6 Paved turnout at **Eyak Lake** to north. Marie Smith Jones Bridge over Eyak River; access to USFS Eyak River Trail. Good fly fishing for salmon in season. The 2.2-mile trail, much of which is boardwalk over muskeg, is popular with fishermen. This is a good spot to see waterfowl feeding near the outlet of Eyak Lake. Watch for trumpeter

swans. Although most trumpeter swans fly south for the winter, as many as 100 will winter at the outlet to Eyak Lake where the water remains ice-free.

C 5.9 USFS **Eyak River** Boating Site. Boat launch, fishing and pit toilet.

C 6.8 The Riverside Inn & Child's Glacier Tours.

C 9.3 USFS Sand Trail ATV route leads 12 miles through Scott Valley to the base of Scott Glacier.

C 10.7 Large paved turnout with bear-proof litter barrel to south. U.S. Forest Service pavilion with 8 interpretive plaques about Copper River Delta/Chugach National Forest areas and wetlands. View of slough to south, Scott and Sheridan glaciers to north. The Copper River Delta is the largest continuous wetland on the west coast of North America.

C 12 Cordova Airport to south. Access north 2.5 miles via narrow road to USFS Lake Elsner Trailhead; pit toilet and bear-proof garbage can; fishing. Camping and day use permits available for **Cabin Lake** Recreation Area through The Eyak Corporation. Call (907) 424-7161.

C 13.6 Access road leads 4 miles to the terminus of Sheridan Glacier. Easy walking trail to good views of glacier. Pit toilets, bear proof garbage cans. Also trailhead for USFS Sheridan Mountain Trail (2.9 miles long one-way; difficult). The glacier was named by U.S. Army explorer Capt. Abercrombie for Gen. Philip H. Sheridan of Civil War fame. *CAUTION: Watch for bears.*

C 16.8 Turnoff for Alaganik Slough Road (narrow, maintained gravel, but potholed) to **Chugach National Forest Alaganik Slough Recreation Area.** Drive 3 miles for interpretive signs, 4 campsites for tent/RV camping, picnic tables, firepits, pit toilets, bear-proof garbage, boat launch (with "Kids Don't Float" signage and life jackets). No potable water. No fee area. Limited to 3 consecutive days in 7-day period. Large turnaround suitable for all rigs. Interpretive boardwalk with viewing blind and elevated viewing platform for birders and wildlife watchers to enjoy the slough. Fishing for Dolly Varden, sockeye (July) and coho (August–September). *CAUTION: Be bear aware. Bring mosquito repellent.*

Trumpeter swans, one of the largest of all North American waterfowl (6- to 8-foot wingspan), may be seen in ponds. Alaska harbors more than 80 percent of the world's trumpeters, and more than 7 percent of the world's trumpeter population breeds in the Copper River Delta (according to USFS).

C 18.7 Turnout to north access to USFS Muskeg Meander Ski Trail (3.1 miles one-way) and Fox Farm Trail (length 0.8 mile one-way). Muskeg Meander trail offers a beautiful view of the Copper River Delta. Recommended for winter use only. This is the only cross-country ski trail in the district. Watch for swans in summer in nearby slough. The Fox Farm Trail, much of which is boardwalk over muskeg, is popular with coho salmon fisherman and meets up with the Haystack Trail.

C 19.1 USFS Haystack Trail and trailhead parking to south. Uphill climb for 0.8 mile on stairs and boardwalks, leads to delta overlook with benches. This family friendly hike goes through lush spruce-hemlock forest; waterproof boots recommended.

C 21.3 USFS **Pipeline Lakes** Trail to north, trailhead parking to south. The 1.8-

mile trail was originally built as a water pipeline route to supply locomotives on the CR&NW railway. Segments of the pipeline are still visible. Trail joins McKinley Lake Trail. Lake fishing.

C 21.5 USFS **McKinley Lake** Trail to north; easy 2.2-mile hike with excellent fishing for sockeye, Dolly Varden and cutthroat. Access to USFS public-use cabins: McKinley Trail Cabin (100 yards from highway) and McKinley Lake Cabin (2.4 mile hike in from highway; also accessible by boat via Alaganik Slough). Trail is a local favorite, originally built in 1917. Cabins must be reserved in advance at recreation.gov or through US Forest Service Cordova Ranger District.

C 22.1 USFS 22 Mile Recreation Area. Entrance to **Alaganik Slough** with boat launch area, picnic tables, firepits, pit toilets, bear-proof garbage, covered tables, wildflowers, fishing access to south at west side of bridge. Also boat access to **McKinley Lake,** well-loved by locals. Signed No Camping. Interpretive signs note that this is a "cultural crossroads." Look for river otters in slough.

C 24.8 Side road leads north 1 mile to USFS Saddlebag Glacier Trail and trailhead parking area. Tent camping and RV parking. Undeveloped campsite #1 is at Mile 0.6, undeveloped campsite #2 is at Mile 0.7. Both campsites are 0.1 mile off access road, neither has much space for an RV to turn around. Be prepared to back out to access road. No fee camping and there are no facilities provided; pack in and pack out.

This is an easy 3-mile trail to Saddlebag Lake and the best trail in the district for mountain biking. Stunning turquoise water and a view of Saddlebag Glacier in spring; look for goats on surrounding mountains. *CAUTION: Watch for bears and keep pets leashed, stay on trail (area is used for winter trapping).*

C 35.8 *ROAD CLOSED TO ALL TRAFFIC BEYOND THIS POINT. Bridge is washed out ahead. For access to Childs Glacier Recreation Area, contact one of the vendors listed in the Camping section.*

C 36.1 Bridge No. 339 is one of 11 bridges crossing the Copper River Delta. Naturally occurring changes to the flow of water between channels across the delta led to a dramatic increase in 2011, in the amount of water running under this bridge. Based upon the channel configurations at the time of this bridge's construction in 1977, bridge designers estimated that water under the bridge would flow at 18,500 cubic feet per second (cfs). U.S. Geological Survey (USGS) hydrologists measured the water flow in excess of 85,000 cfs and closed the bridge in August 2011; soon thereafter, it washed out. *A new washout occurred at Milepost C 45 in summer of 2018.*

C 48.3 U.S. Forest Service **Childs Glacier Recreation Area** has a large covered viewing platform for watching the 300-foot face of Childs Glacier. There are information boards, a hiking trail, 11 large sites, picnic tables, bear proof garbage cans, 2 vault toilets and a water pump. Camping fee $10/night.

C 48.6 The Million Dollar Bridge. Constructed from 1909 to 1910 for $1.4 million, the 1,550-foot-long steel truss bridge spans the Copper River. It was the longest steel bridge on the Copper River & Northwestern Railway. The bridge was added to the National Register of Historic Places in 2000.

Southeast Alaska

Southeast Alaska port cities, like Ketchikan (pictured here), are served by the Alaska Marine Highway System. Major port cities also host more than a million cruise ship passengers each year. (©Michael K. Robb)

Southeast Alaska, referred to by Alaskans simply as "Southeast," is Alaska's Panhandle. It stretches from Dixon Entrance at the U.S.–Canada border south of Ketchikan to Icy Bay, northwest of Yakutat. Comprised of a narrow strip of mainland backed up against the Coast Mountains and Canada, and hundreds of islands of the Alexander Archipelago, Southeast forms the all-water route to Alaska known as the Inside Passage.

The Alaska Marine Highway ferries move people and vehicles between communities in Southeast and connect Southeast Alaska via the Inside Passage to Prince Rupert, BC, and Bellingham, WA, and to southcentral Alaska via Cross-Gulf sailings between Juneau and Whittier. (See "Ferry Travel" in the TRAVEL PLANNING section.)

The port communities of Haines and Skagway offer road connections to the Alaska Highway via the Haines Highway and South Klondike Highway 2. *(See HAINES HIGHWAY on page 651 and SOUTH KLONDIKE HIGHWAY on page 656.)*

A region where industry, transportation, recreation and community planning are dictated by its unique topography, Southeast also offers unique attractions for visitors. Enjoy Russian (Sitka) and Tlingit (Haines) dance performances; colorful saloons like the Red Onion (Skagway); sportfishing throughout; and sightseeing and/or whale watching cruises of Glacier Bay, Misty Fiords, LeConte Glacier, the Stikine River and Tracy Arm. Bear viewing (at Anan and Pack creeks) is also a top attraction. See "Attractions" within each of the following community descriptions.

The region is accessible by air, land or sea. Jet service is available to Juneau, Ketchikan, Wrangell, Petersburg, Sitka and Gustavus. Smaller communities are served by local commuter aircraft.

Cruise ships are a popular way to visit Southeast, with hundreds of sailings and varied itineraries to choose between. (See "Cruising to Alaska" in the TRAVEL PLANNING section.)

Southeast Alaska lies between 54°40' and 60° north latitude, the same as Scotland and southern Sweden. The region measures about 125 by 400 miles, with 60 percent consisting of islands covered with spruce, hemlock and cedar forests characteristic of moist coastal climates. The largest island in the region is Prince of Wales Island (third largest island in the U.S.). Prince of Wales Island also has the most extensive road system in Southeast Alaska. The Inter-Island Ferry Authority offers daily, year-round passenger and vehicle service between Ketchikan and Hollis on Prince of Wales Island (see "Ferry Travel" in the TRAVEL PLANNING section).

The majority of Southeast Alaska lies within Tongass National Forest, the largest national forest in the United States.

Some 71,000 people live along the Inside Passage. Slightly less than 20 percent of the region's population is Alaska Native: Tlingit (KLINK-it) Indian, Haida (HI-duh) and Tsimshian (SHIM-shian). Alaska's Natives occupied this region long before Vitus Bering arrived in Alaska in 1741.

Russia controlled Alaska from the turn of the 19th century until October 18, 1867, when Alaska was transferred to the U.S. As the Russian capital of Alaska, Sitka was the center of Russia's fur-trading empire and a port of international trade, controlling trading posts from California to the Aleutians.

In 1867, the United States, under President Andrew Johnson, purchased Alaska from Russia for $7.2 million. The American flag was raised at Sitka on Oct. 18, 1867. As the Russian population moved out, and the fur trade declined, so did interest in Southeast Alaska. But it was rekindled by the salmon industry as canneries were established, the first at Klawock in 1878. Salmon canning peaked in the late 1930s then declined from overfishing.

The first significant white populations arrived because of gold. Thousands of gold seekers traveled through the Inside Passage in 1898 to Skagway and on to Canada's Klondike (sparking interest in the rest of Alaska). The largest gold ore mine of its day, the Treadwell near Juneau, began operation in 1884.

Juneau became Alaska's capital in 1906, and Southeast remained Alaska's dominant region until WWII, when military activity and the Alaska Highway shifted emphasis to Anchorage and Fairbanks.

Additional population growth came to Southeast with new timber harvesting in the 1950s. Increased government activities, as a result of Alaska statehood in 1959, brought even more people. Fishing is an ongoing industry in Southeast.

The Inside Passage is the last stronghold of the American bald eagle. More than 20,000 eagles reside in the region, and sightings are frequent. Humpback and killer whales, porpoises, sea lions and seals are often observed from ferries, cruise ships and charter boats. Bear viewing opportunities are offered at Pack Creek on Admiralty Island, Anan Creek near Wrangell, Fish Creek near Hyder and Herring Cove near Ketchikan.

Ketchikan

Creek Steet, in downtown Ketchikan's historic district, is a popular destination with visitors. (©David L. Ranta, staff)

Located on the southwest coast of Revillagigedo Island, Ketchikan is 235 miles south of Juneau and 90 miles north of Prince Rupert, BC. Ketchikan and Saxman are the only communities on Revillagigedo Island. **Population:** Ketchikan city, 8,313; Ketchikan Gateway Borough, 13,856. **Emergency Services:** Phone 911 for all emergency services. **Alaska State Troopers**, at **Milepost K 7.3** North Tongass Highway, phone (907) 225-5118. **City Police**, phone (907) 225-6631. **Coast Guard**, Base Ketchikan, 1300 Stedman St., phone (907) 228-0340; or Juneau, phone (907) 463-2000. **Hospital**, PeaceHealth Ketchikan Medical Center, 3100 Tongass Ave., phone (907) 225-5171. **Veterinarian:** Stonetree Veterinary Clinic, phone (907) 247-6051; Island to Island Veterinary Clinic, phone (907) 313-7911.

Visitor Information: Maps and trip planning help available at Ketchikan Visitors Bureau, located off Front Street at Mission Street adjacent "The Rock" statues and the famous rain gauge. The visitor center is open daily, May through September, from 8 A.M. to 5 P.M. and weekdays from October through April. There are two other visitor center locations, one at cruise ship Berth 3 (open when cruise ships are in port in summer) and one at Berth 2 (open in winter). SPOT GPS locators available year-round for hiking. Write them at 50 Front St., Suite 203, Ketchikan 99901; phone (907) 225-6166 or 1-800-770-3300; email: info@ visit-ketchikan.com; website www.visit-ketchikan.com.

Revillagigedo Island is located in Tongass National Forest. Maps, brochures, trip planning assistance and general information on recreational opportunities in Tongass National Forest and other federal lands in Alaska are available at the **Southeast Alaska Discovery Center**, 50 Main St., Ketchikan, AK 99901; phone (907) 228-6220, fax (907) 228-6234; or visit www.alaskacenters.gov/ketchikan.cfm.

The Ketchikan-Misty Fiords U.S. Forest Service Ranger District encompasses 3.2 million acres of Tongass National Forest land in Southeast Alaska, maintaining 60 miles of trails, 2 campgrounds, and 30 public-use cabins (most accessible by floatplane or boat). The district office is located at 3031 Tongass Ave.; open 8 A.M. to 4:30 P.M. weekdays; phone (907) 225-2148; www.fs.usda.gov/tongass/. Cabins and campsites can be reserved through the National Recreation Reservation Service (NRRS); phone toll-free 1-877-444-6777 or visit www.recreation.gov.

Elevation: Sea level. **Climate:** Rainy. Yearly average rainfall is 162 inches and snowfall is 36.9 inches. Average summer temperature is 55°F and average winter temperature is 31°F. **Radio:** KTKN-AM 930, KRBD-FM 105.3, KGTW-FM 106.7, KFMJ-FM 99.9. **Television:** KUBD, KTOO and 43 cable channels. **Newspapers:** *Ketchikan Daily News* (daily); *The Local Paper* (weekly).

Private Aircraft: Ketchikan International Airport on Gravina Island; elev. 88 feet; length 7,500 feet; asphalt; fuel 100LL, A. Ketchikan Harbor seaplane base downtown; fuel 80, 100, A.

Ketchikan is located on the southwest side of Revillagigedo (ruh-vee-uh-guh-GAY-

Major Attractions:

Saxman Totem Park, Totem Bight, Creek Street, Misty Fiords National Monument

doh) Island, on Tongass Narrows opposite Gravina Island. One interpretation of the name Ketchikan is derived from a Tlingit name, Kitschk-Hin, which translates to "spread wings of a prostrate eagle." Ketchikan Creek flows through the town, emptying into Tongass Narrows. Before Ketchikan was settled, the area at the mouth of the creek was a Tlingit Indian fish camp. Settlement began with interest in both mining and fishing. The first salmon cannery established in 1886, operated under the name of Tongass Packing Co. It burned down in August 1889. Gold was discovered nearby in

Downtown Ketchikan

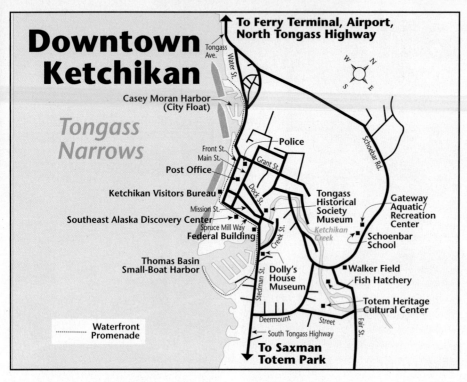

Tongass Narrows

To Ferry Terminal, Airport, North Tongass Highway

Casey Moran Harbor (City Float)

Police

Front St.
Main St.
Post Office
Ketchikan Visitors Bureau
Mission St.
Southeast Alaska Discovery Center
Spruce Mill Way
Federal Building

Grant St.
Dock St.
Creek St.

Tongass Historical Society Museum

Ketchikan Creek

Schoenbar Rd.

Gateway Aquatic/ Recreation Center

Schoenbar School

Thomas Basin Small-Boat Harbor

Dolly's House Museum

Walker Field Fish Hatchery

Stedman St.

Totem Heritage Cultural Center

Deermount Street
South Tongass Highway

Fair St.

To Saxman Totem Park

Waterfront Promenade

1898. Ketchikan was incorporated in 1900.

As mining waned, the fishing industry began to grow. By the 1930s, more than a dozen salmon canneries had been built. During the peak years of the canned salmon industry, Ketchikan earned the title of "Salmon Capital of the World." But overfishing caused a drastic decline in salmon by the 1940s. Today, Southeast Alaska accounts for slightly more than half the pink salmon harvested in Alaska. Trident Seafood Corporation, a shore-based cannery in Ketchikan, produces canned salmon, operating from early July through September.

As fishing reached a low point, the timber industry expanded. The first sawmill was built in 1898 at Dolomi on Prince of Wales Island to cut timber for the Dolomi Mine. It was dismantled and moved to Ketchikan and rebuilt in 1903. A large pulp mill was built northwest of town in 1953 at Ward Cove. It closed in 1997.

Tourism is an extremely important industry here. Ketchikan is first port-of-call in Alaska for cruise ships. It is also the first Alaska port-of-call for Alaska Marine Highway's northbound Inside Passage sailings from Bellingham, WA, and from Prince Rupert, BC. (British Columbia's Prince Rupert is 6 hours away by ferry.) The Inter-Island Ferry Authority's MV *Stikine* and MV *Prince of Wales* connect Ketchikan with Prince of Wales Island.

Ketchikan is a linear waterfront city, with much of its 3-mile-long business district suspended above water on pilings driven into the bottom of Tongass Narrows. Its homes cling to the steep wooded hillside, many reached by "staircase streets"—lengths of wooden stairs rather than paved road. All of Ketchikan's original streets and walkways were built as wooden trestles because of the steep and rocky terrain.

Ketchikan is an easy town to explore on foot or by tour bus. The waterfront is the center of the city, and most attractions are within walking distance of where the cruise ships dock. Pick up a walking tour map at one of the 3 Visitors Bureau locations

(locations noted in Visitor Information at the start of this section). Tour highlights include: St. John's Episcopal Church; the Grant Street Trestle, on the National Register of Historic Places; the Ketchikan Creek Fish Ladder; and other landmarks. You may also book tours at the Visitors Bureau.

The area supports 5 public grade schools, 4 parochial grade schools, a junior high school, 2 high schools and the University of Alaska Southeast campus.

Lodging & Services

Accommodations at Best Western Plus Landing Hotel (907/225-5166; www.landinghotel.com), Cape Fox Lodge (907/225-8001; www.capefoxlodge.com), Gilmore Hotel (907/225-9423; www.gilmorehotel.com), Inn at Creek Street & New York Hotel (907/225-0246; www.thenewyorkhotel.com), and Super 8 Motel (1-800-800-8000; www.super8.com).

Shopping downtown and at Plaza Mall on Tongass Avenue (North Tongass Highway). There 2 laundromats with showers, a bookstore on Stedman Street, supermarkets, fast-food outlets, banks, many gift shops and a variety of other shops and services. Many local businesses downtown offer free WiFi. Ketchikan also has a Walmart, 4 miles north of downtown off the Tongass Highway.

Dining downtown and on the road system (see North and South Tongass Highway logs this section).

Ketchikan Hostel is located downtown in the United Methodist Church at Grant and Main streets. Open June 1 to August 31. Check-in time is 7–9 A.M. and 6–11 P.M. (will open for late ferry arrivals; phone from terminal as soon as you arrive). Reservations recommended. Phone (907) 225-3319 (summer); email ketchikanhostel@gmail.com.

The Ketchikan Library offers free WiFi, restrooms, plug-ins for personal computers, public computers available for 30 minute intervals (with I.D.). Here, mountain views and comfortable chairs offer a charming rest stop for travelers. Hours are 10 A.M. to 8 P.M.

Monday–Wednesday, 10 A.M. to 6 P.M. Thursday–Saturday and 1–5 P.M. Sunday. Located at 1110 Copper Ridge Lane. Access the Library at the south end of Berth 4 (along the waterfront promenade). Phone (907) 225-3331.

Ketchikan's 35,000-square-foot Gateway Aquatic Center connects to the existing Recreation Center and offers visitors a place to swim laps, take a sauna and work out, all for a $6 admission fee. The Aquatic Center has an 8-lane main competition pool; 1-meter and 3-meter diving boards; a separate warm-water pool with walk-in entry; 2 slides, including a twisty one called the "Tongass Tornado;" sauna; locker rooms and family changing rooms with showers; fitness and weight room. Located at 601 Schoenbar Rd.; phone (907) 228-6650; ak-ketchikangatewayborough.civicplus.com/200/Gateway-Aquatic-Center.

Camping

There are 3 public campgrounds in the Ketchikan vicinity: Signal Creek and Last Chance, U.S. Forest Service campgrounds at Ward Lake Recreation Area, approximately 10 miles north of downtown; and Settlers Cove State Recreation Site, 18 miles north of the city via North Tongass Highway (*see highway log this section*). Advance reservations can be made for designated sites at the Forest Service campgrounds through the NRRS; phone toll-free 1-877-444-6777 or visit www.recreation.gov.

The only private RV park with hookups is Clover Pass Resort at **Milepost K 14.2** North Tongass Highway, phone 1-800-410-2234.

The Walmart at **Milepost K 4** North Tongass Highway may allow overnight camping in their parking lot for self-contained RVs; check with store.

A dump station is located at Ketchikan Street Department Warehouse, **Milepost K 2.5** North Tongass Highway. It is available weekdays from 8 A.M. to 4:30 P.M. Ask inside the building to have the potable water turned on; you must bring your own hose.

Transportation

Air: Daily scheduled jet service is provided from the Ketchikan International Airport by Alaska Airlines to other Southeast cities, Anchorage and Seattle, WA. Commuter and charter service is available to other Southeastern communities via Pacific Airways, Promech Air, Southeast Aviation and Taquan Air.

Airport terminal, across Tongass Narrows on Gravina Island, is reached via shuttle ferry (5-minute ride one way) departing at half-hour intervals from the airport parking area on Tongass Avenue (North Tongass Highway), 2.8 miles from downtown.

Ferry: Two ferry systems operate out of Ketchikan—the Alaska Marine Highway System and the Inter-Island Ferry Authority. Alaska Marine Highway vessels connect Ketchikan with all mainline southeastern Alaska port cities, Prince Rupert, BC, and Bellingham, WA, and the Cross-Gulf ferry. The Alaska state ferry system also provides service between Ketchikan and Metlakatla (1 hr. 15 min.). For schedules, fares and reservations, visit www.ferryalaska.com.

The Alaska Marine Highway Terminal is located 2.3 miles north of downtown Ketchikan on Tongass Avenue (North Tongass Highway). The terminal building has a large waiting room, vending machines, restrooms, public phones and brochure racks; phone

(907) 225-6182. Toll-free reservations phone 1-800-642-0066. Taxicabs meet most ferry arrivals. Bus schedules are available in the terminal building and there is a bus stop nearby.

The Inter-Island Ferry Authority's MV *Stikine* or MV *Prince of Wales* provide daily passenger and vehicle service of 3 hours between Ketchikan and Hollis/Clark Bay on Prince of Wales Island. Check with the IFA reservation desk located inside the Alaska Marine Highway terminal building; phone (907) 225-4838. For current information and reservations visit www.interislandferry.com. See also "Ferry Travel" in the TRAVEL PLANNING section.

Bus: The free, downtown loop, Salmon Run shuttle service has a decorated bus that travels a 20-minute circuit between popular destinations from May to September. The Silver Line bus provides service from the ferry terminal and airport south to downtown and north to Walmart. The Silver Line bus also serves Saxman Totem Park south of the city and north of the city to Totem Bight State Park. Contact Ketchikan Gateway Borough Transportation Services with questions, phone (907) 225-8726; www.borough. ketchikan.ak.us/145/Transit.

Parking: There is 2-hour on-street parking available. When *The MILEPOST®* visited Ketchikan, we had no problem parking either our truck/camper or Class B motorhome on Front Street (north of the promenade), but there are no parking lots downtown to accommodate large RVs. It is best to find big-rig parking away from downtown and ride the buses or rent a car.

Car Rental: Available from Alaska Car Rental on Tongass Avenue, phone (907) 225-5000; First City Rental, phone (907) 225-7368; Budget Rent-a-Car, phone (907) 225-6003; Alaska Smart Rentals, phone (907) 225-1753.

Taxi: Sourdough Taxi Co., Alaska Cab and Yellow Taxi, phone (907) 225-5555. Taxicabs meet ferry arrivals and airport arrivals at the Ketchikan-side terminal areas.

Highways: North Tongass and South Tongass highway (see logs this section).

Cruise Ships: Ketchikan is first port-of-call for many cruise ships to Alaska. There are anywhere from 1 to 5 ships docked at Ketchikan on any given day in summer. See "Cruising to Alaska" in the TRAVEL PLANNING section.

Tour Boats: Harbor cruises/city tours with the amphibious Ketchikan Duck Tours. Day cruises to Misty Fiords with Allen Marine Tours. Fishing charters galore.

Private Boats: Moorage space in Ketchikan is limited; all private boats should contact the harbormaster's office just prior to arrival by phoning (907) 228-5632 or use VHF 73 or 16.

Attractions

Enjoy the Waterfront Promenade. This unique walkway provides a pedestrian path along Ketchikan's busy shoreline, with plenty of photo viewpoints, helpful signage, historical markers, unique benches for sitting to enjoy the view, and colorful art. The completed section of the Waterfront Promenade starts at Tongass Avenue near cruise ship Berth 4, and continues past Casey Moran Harbor, Berth 3, and the Ketchikan Visitor Bureau's Visitor Annex (with public restrooms) down past "The Rock" statues to the Downtown Visitors Bureau on the concrete docks at Berth 2. The promenade

"The Rock" sculpture and the city's visitor center are on Ketchikan's waterfront, which also has a wonderful promenade for enjoying all the harbor activity. (©Kris Valencia, staff)

continues past the Salmon Landing market, behind the Great Alaskan Lumberjack Show, to the Federal Building. Additional platforms extend out into Thomas Basin for scenic views and fishing.

Cape Fox Hill Funicular, located at the back of Creek Street, was constructed in 1990. This automated cable car traverses a 70 percent incline, rising 130 vertical feet from Creek Street to the top of Cape Fox Hill and the lobby of the Cape Fox Lodge. The hotel has an extensive collection of Native art and a restaurant. (Cape Fox Lodge is also accessible by road.)

The funicular operates daily from 7 A.M. to 11 P.M. It works very much like an elevator: just press the call button to summon the funicular. When the doors open, get inside and push the Up button to go up or the Down button to go down. A modest fee is charged to ride the funicular, but your ticket is good for all day. (The funicular is free if you are dining at Cape Fox Lodge.)

From the top, you may return to Creek Street by following Married Man's Trail (boardwalk and stairs) back down the hill through the trees. Great views and good photo ops of downtown from this trail

City Park is a beautiful park offering a pleasant and convenient rest stop for walking tourists and a popular outdoor area for Ketchikan residents. The park's small ponds were once used as holding ponds for Ketchikan's first hatchery. The generically named City Park is located along Park Avenue. Hiking access to the park via a footbridge from Totem Heritage Center.

Whale Park, conveniently located between the cruise ship docks and Creek Street on Mill Street, is shaped like a whale. A very small park, it is a popular rest stop and has the Chief Kyan Totem Pole (carved by Israel Shotridge) and the historic Knox Brothers Clock.

Saxman Totem Park, located 2.3 miles south of downtown via South Tongass Highway, has 21 totems and a clan house that may be enjoyed year-round. Independent travelers can see the totems on their own or take a tour—available May through

September—to include a short video introducing the culture and history of Saxman, a visit to the Beaver Clan House, where visitors are welcomed by song and dance by the Cape Fox Dance group, a guided tour of the totems and a visit to the Village Carving Center. Details at www.capefoxtours.com or email info@capefoxtours.com. If you are arriving in Ketchikan by cruise ship, make tour reservations through the shore excursion office aboard ship.

Great Alaskan Lumberjack Show. The 1-hour show features events such as buck sawing, axe throwing, power sawing, springboard chop, logrolling duels, and a 50-foot tree climb. Covered grandstand seating. Located 1 block off cruise ship docks near Salmon Landing Market. Shows performed 3 to 5 times daily, May through September; call or stop by for times. Phone toll-free 1-888-320-9049 or (907) 225-9050; www. lumberjacksports.com or www.capefoxtours. com.

Totem poles, a major attraction in Ketchikan, are scattered around the city. Major collections are found at the Totem Heritage Center, Saxman and Totem Bight (see detailed descriptions this section).

Southeast Alaska Discovery Center, located at 50 Main St., is 1 of 4 Alaska Public Lands Information Centers (APLICs) in the state (the others are located in Fairbanks, Anchorage and Tok). The Discovery Center, like the other APLICs, offers trip planning assistance, information on Alaska public lands, and a well-stocked Alaska Geographic Association bookstore and gift

©Kris Valencia, staff

Totem Bight State Historical Park (above), about 10 miles north of downtown, is 1 of 2 major totem parks here, along with Saxman Totem Park, 2 miles south of town. (©Kris Valencia, staff)

shop. In addition, the Discovery Center has interpretive exhibits on Native traditions, rainforest, ecosystems, wildlife, natural resources and art. Rangers provide scheduled interpretive programs, the 200-seat theatre presents 8 multi-media programs, there is a Junior Ranger program, scavenger hunt, Agents of Discovery app, and a rotating art gallery that hosts the Alaska Hummingbird Festival art show.

The Discovery Center is open year-round: weekdays from 8 A.M. to 4 P.M., May 1 to Sept. 30 (closed Memorial Day, July 4th and Labor Day); open Fridays in winter. Admission fee $5, 15 years and under free. Phone (907) 228-6220 or visit www.alaskacenters. gov/ketchikan.cfm.

Totem Heritage Center, at 601 Deermount St., houses 33 totem poles and fragments retrieved from deserted Tlingit and Haida Indian villages. This national landmark collection comprises the largest exhibit of original totems in the United States. Facilities include craft exhibits, a full range of classes (a few for children) and the formal Native Arts Study Program and reference library. Outside the center are 2 poles by Tlingit carver (and National Living Treasure), Nathan Jackson.

Guided tours during summer months. Admission fee charged. Summer hours are 8 A.M. to 5 P.M. daily. Winter hours (October to April) are 1–5 P.M. Monday through Friday. Phone (907) 225-5900.

Totem Bight State Historical Park, located at **Milepost K 9.9** North Tongass Highway, contains an excellent model of a Tlingit community house and 14 totems in a beautiful wooded setting. The park began as a Civilian Conservation Corps (CCC) project in 1938, when a U.S. Forest Service program aimed at salvaging abandoned totem poles by hiring skilled Native carvers and young, unskilled apprentices to reconstruct or copy the poles. Alaskan architect Linn Forrest designed the model Native village, which was originally called Mud Bight. The name was changed to Totem Bight and title to the land transferred to the state in 1959. It was added to the National Register of Historic Places in 1970.

The community house, or clan house, is representative of those found in early 19th century Indian villages. Totems reflect Haida and Tlingit cultures.

Creek Street, a boardwalk street on pilings that spans Ketchikan Creek near the Stedman Street bridge, was once Ketchikan's

©Kris Valencia, staff

"red-light district," where Black Mary, Dolly, Frenchie and others plied their trade for over half a century until 1954. At one time nearly 20 houses lined the far side of Ketchikan Creek. Today, the remaining old houses have been restored and, along with newer structures, house a variety of shops. Dolly's House, a former brothel, is open during the summer months (admission charged, $10).

In late July, watch for salmon in Ketchikan Creek. Besides shopping and seeing the creek, visitors can take a ride on the Cape Fox Hill Funicular.

Tours, tours, and more tours. From narrated trolley rides and historical sightseeing cruises to tours by airplane and amphibious boat, Ketchikan has an abundance of tour opportunities, many tailored for the thousands of cruise ship passengers spending the day here. Stop by Ketchikan Visitors Bureau's tour center, located on the cruise ship docks at 131 Front St., where a couple dozen vendors are on hand, and offer everything from fishing charters, sightseeing cruises, to zipline tours.

Misty Fiords National Monument. Located east of Ketchikan, Misty Fiords National Monument encompasses 2.3 million acres of wilderness and is known for its spectacular scenery. Taking its name from

the almost constant precipitation characteristic of the area, Misty Fiords is covered with dense forests of Sitka spruce, western hemlock and cedar, which grow on nearly vertical slopes from sea level to mountain tops. Dramatic waterfalls cascade into glacially carved fjords. The monument is bisected by the 100-mile-long Behm Canal, extraordinary among natural canals for its length and depth. New Eddystone Rock, a 237-foot volcanic plug, rises straight out of Behm Canal and is visible for miles.

The monument is accessible by boat or by floatplane from Ketchikan. Tours of Misty Fiords by floatplane and by boat are available out of Ketchikan. Some cruise ships include Behm Canal and Rudyerd Bay in their itineraries. Rudyerd Bay is also a popular destination for sea kayakers.

For more information on the monument, stop by the Southeast Alaska Discovery Center on Main Street in Ketchikan, phone (907) 228-6220, or the U.S. Forest Service office at 3031 Tongass Ave., phone (907) 225-2148; www.fs.usda.gov/tongass/.

Arts, entertainment and events. The Main Street Gallery, at 330 Main St., hosts exhibits year-round and displays a wide variety of mediums from local and national artists, as well as traveling exhibits. The Main Street Gallery is also home to the Ketchikan Area Arts & Humanities Council, a sponsor of such events as the Blueberry Festival and the Alaska Hummingbird Festival. See their events calendar at www.ketchikanarts.org/arts-calendar/event-calendar.html.

First City Players, located in the old Fireside/Elks Building at 335 Main St., offers plays and events year-round; check their schedule. In July, enjoy one of 6 performances of the rollicking Fish Pirate's Daughter, Ketchikan's original musical melodrama; includes crab or salmon dinner.

The annual Gigglefeet Dance Festival takes place in early August. Celebrating the joy and diversity of dance, Gigglefeet performances feature choreographers and dancers of many different schools of training, varied ages and cultures. For more information, contact First City Players box office by phone (907) 225-4792; email info@firstcityplayers.org; www.firstcityplayers.org.

The Tongass Historical Museum is located on Dock Street near the entrance to Creek Street, in downtown Ketchikan. Summer season (May 1–Sept. 30) hours are 8 A.M. to 5 P.M. daily. Winter (Oct. 1–April 30) hours are 1–5 P.M. Tuesday to Saturday (closed Sunday and Monday). Look for the Raven Stealing the Sun totem pole that stands at the entrance. Salmon viewing platforms nearby. The museum's new (2018) permanent exhibit explores the ideas and industries that have shaped Ketchikan and surrounding area. For more information, phone (907) 225-5600 or visit www.KetchikanMuseums.org. Admission fee $6 for adults, $5 for seniors, kids and military free.

Hiking trails, for all levels of ability, are accessible by road in the Ketchikan area. Pick up the free Ketchikan Area Trails Guide at the U.S. Forest Service office at **Milepost K 2** North Tongass Highway. Several U.S. Forest Service trails are accessible from Revilla Road north of Ketchikan (see **Milepost 7** North Tongass Highway). These include Ward Lake Nature Trail, an easy 1.3-mile path around Ward Lake, and the more difficult 2.4-mile Perseverance Lake Trail, which begins just past the entrance to 3 C's

Group Campground on Ward Lake Road.

The Deer Mountain U.S. Forest Service Trail is a strenuous hike that offers rewarding views. The 2.75-mile, 2,600-foot ascent to the summit gives trekkers scenic overlooks at Miles 1 and 2 for ocean and island views. Also access via left fork to Deer Mountain shelter (first-come, first-served, no fee) and 10.5-mile Silvis Lakes traverse.

The Whitman Trail begins at **Milepost K 8.6** South Tongass Highway and follows Whitman Creek to Whitman Lake.

Picnic areas. Drive out to Settlers Cove State Recreation Site at **Milepost K 18.2** North Tongass Highway. **Settlers Cove** has a day-use area with picnic tables. From the picnic area take the Lower Lunch Falls Loop, a ¼-mile boardwalk trail through lush forest that also provides access to the rocky beach.

Other picnic areas accessible from the North Tongass Highway are Refuge Cove State Recreation Site at **Milepost K 8.7**, and picnic facilities along Ward Lake Road (turnoff at **Milepost K 7** and go to Mile 1.3 Revilla Road for Ward Lake access).

View of Tongass Narrows and beach access at Rotary Beach Recreation Area, **Milepost K 3.5** South Tongass Highway.

Charter a boat, take a cruise tour. Many vessels operate out of Ketchikan for half-day, all-day or overnight sightseeing or fishing trips and transport to U.S. Forest Service public-use cabins and outlying communities. Cruises are offered to see whales, glaciers, birds and other wildlife. Stop by the Ketchikan Visitors Bureau for help in choosing one.

Go sea kayaking. Circumnavigation of Revillagigedo Island is about a 150-mile trip. The east coast of Revillagigedo Island lies within Misty Fiords National Monument Wilderness. Popular kayaking destinations within the monument include Rudyerd Bay, Punchbowl Cove and Walker Cove. For trip-planning help, stop by the Southeast Alaska Discovery Center on Main Street, phone (907) 228-6220, or the U.S. Forest Service office at 3031 Tongass Ave., phone (907) 225-2148; www.fs.usda.gov/tongass/.

Charter planes operate from the airport and from the waterfront on floats and are available for fly-in fishing, bear viewing, service to lodges and smaller communities and flightseeing, including Misty Fiords.

Annual King Salmon Derby is held in May and June. For derby dates, rules and past derby winners, visit website: ketchikankingsalmonderby.com.

Fishing lodges and resorts in the area offer sportfishing for steelhead, salmon, halibut, trout, lingcod and red snapper. Resorts near Ketchikan include Yes Bay Lodge. There are also several fishing lodges on nearby Prince of Wales Island. For details, go to www.visit–ketchikan.com.

AREA FISHING: Check with the Alaska Dept. of Fish and Game at 2030 Sea Level Dr., Ste. 205, or phone (907) 225-5195 for details on fishing in the Ketchikan area. Good fishing spots range from Mountain Point, a 5-mile drive from Ketchikan on South Tongass Highway, to streams, lakes, bays, and inlets 50 miles away by boat or by air. Half-day and longer charters and skiff rentals available out of Ketchikan. Species include salmon, halibut, steelhead, Dolly Varden, cutthroat and rainbow trout, Arctic grayling, eastern brook trout, lingcod, rockfish, and shellfish: Dungeness crab and shrimp.

South Tongass Highway

Saxman Totem Park is just over 2 miles from Ketchikan on the South Tongass Highway.
(©Kris Valencia, staff)

The 13-mile-long South Tongass Highway provides access to Saxman Totem Park, Rotary Beach Park, Mountain Point and Hole in the Wall harbors, and George Inlet. Posted speed limits from 25- to 50-mph. **Distance from downtown Ketchikan (K) is shown.**

K 0 Stedman Street and Totem Way intersection.

K 0.1 Ketchikan Creek bridge (pictured below with fishermen). Begin intermittent bike path southbound. *Watch for bicyclists!*

K 0.3 Deermount Street; liquor/grocery store.

K 0.9 U.S. Coast Guard Station Ketchikan, established in 1989.

K 2.3 Turnoff for Totem Row Road up to **Saxman Totem Park**. (If you drive up this road, you'll be directed to the pay parking area; see Bear Clan Street next milepost.) *See description of Saxman Totem Park on page 605.* SAXMAN (pop. 434) was founded in 1896 by Tlingit Alaska Natives and named after a Presbyterian missionary who served the Tlingit people.

K 2.4 Vehicles turn on Bear Clan Street for Saxman Totem Park parking lot. Also provides access to local eatery. Note decaying old totems lying on the ground at the parking lot/entrance.

K 2.6 Dog Salmon Street access to local eatery to east, Petro-Express gas station and convenience store to west.

K 3.5 First of 2 parking areas for **Rotary Beach Recreation Area**; picnic shelter, tables, firepits, litter bins and beach access.

K 5.2 Large gravel parking area with view.

K 5.5 Mountain Point Public Boat Launch; restrooms, litter bins, large parking area. Access to good salmon fishing from shore in July and August.

K 7.5 Hole in the Wall Harbor and bar.

K 8.1 Wood Road, access to Alaska Rainforest Sanctuary and Alaska Canopy Tours (0.2 mile); www.alaskarainforest.com. The canopy (zipline) and rainforest tours are offered as day shore excursions for cruise ship passengers. Independent travelers should phone (907) 225-5503 regarding availability and booking.

K 8.3 Herring Cove bridge. Road at the south end of bridge leads to small parking and viewing area (pictured above) just prior to a private hatchery. Watch for bears during salmon runs.

K 8.4 Whitman Creek Trailhead parking.

K 8.7 Whitman Creek.

K 8.9 Single-vehicle paved turnout and gravel turnout (no view).

K 9.8 Small paved turnout, no view.

K 10.2 Beaver Falls; small turnout to view waterfall.

K 10.9 Paved turnout, no view.

K 11.4 Emergency parking only.

K 11.9 George Inlet Lodge; scenic spot. The lodge serves lunch mainly to cruise ship passengers; inquire about availability to general public. Limited parking, lots of stairs.

K 12.1 Single-vehicle paved turnout.

K 12.9 Paved road ends. Gravel road continues across bridge to parking area (potholes) at Beaver Falls Hydroelectric Project.

North Tongass Highway

From downtown Ketchikan, North Tongass Highway leads 18.4 miles northwest along Tongass Narrows, then north along Clover Passage to deadend at Settlers Cove State Recreation Site.
Distance from downtown Ketchikan (K) is shown.

K 0 Ketchikan Visitors Bureau on the cruise ship docks at Front and Mission streets. Follow Front Street north.

K 0.3 Tiny Eagle Park here is dominated by Tlingit master carver Nathan Jackson's **Thundering Wings** (pictured below). If

©Kris Valencia, staff

you are lucky you might see Mr. Jackson at Saxman on a tour. Front Street becomes Tongass Avenue northbound after passing through the Ketchikan Tunnel (built in 1954).

K 1.1 Sea Level Drive; access to Super 8, pizza place.

K 1.2 Washington Street traffic light. The Plaza shopping mall, McDonald's and Super 8 to west.

K 1.3 Jefferson Street traffic light; entrance west to Safeway/gas station.

K 1.7 Bar Harbor boat basin to west.

K 2 Ketchikan Ranger Station/Misty Fiords National Monument to west.

K 2.1 PeaceHealth Ketchikan Medical Center.

K 2.2 Carlanna Lake Road; PeaceHealth Ketchikan Medical Center to east.

K 2.3 Entrance to **Ketchikan Ferry Terminal** for the Alaska Marine Highway to west; Best Western on east side of highway. Ferry terminal building has seating area, restrooms, vending machines and brochure racks. The Inter-Island Ferry Authority (IFA) ticket desk with service to Hollis is located inside the ferry terminal. The ferry loading dock is to the south of the terminal building. Once daily departures from Ketchikan at 3:30 P.M. arrive in Hollis at 6:30 P.M.

Tongass Avenue becomes North Tongass Highway northbound.

K 2.4 Main branch post office to west adjacent ferry terminal; grocery/liquor store to east.

K 2.5 Dump station to west.

K 2.6 Carlanna Creek and bridge.

K 2.8 Entrance to Ketchikan International Airport parking and airport ferry shuttle service. Airport terminal is across Tongass Narrows on Gravina Island.

K 3.1 Viewpoint to west.

K 4 Don King Road; Wells Fargo bank to east and access to Walmart.

K 5.5 Small, double-ended, viewpoint to west overlooking Tongass Narrows; float-

plane dock.

K 5.7 Ketchikan city limits.

K 6 Cannery Creek and bridge.

K 6.6 View northbound of Ward Cove Cannery and Ketchikan Pulp Mill. The cannery was built in 1912 and purchased in 1928 by Wards Cove Packing Co. The pulp mill was built in 1953 and closed in 1997.

K 6.7 Ward Lake Road, open to hikers and bikers only. Road access to Ward Lake Recreation Area is from Revilla Road at **Milepost K 7**.

K 6.9 Ward Creek and bridge.

K 7 Junction with 6.7-mile Revilla Road to USFS **Ward Lake Recreation Area**, Harriet Hunt Road and Brown Mountain Road (log of road follows).

©Kris Valencia, staff

Mile 1.3 Revilla Road: Turn off for paved Ward Lake Road to **Ward Lake** day-use area (0.6 mile) and Signal Creek campground (1 mile). The day-use area (pictured above) has paved parking, 3 picnic shelters, and a 1.3-mile nature trail around Ward Lake. There are single-vehicle picnic sites located along Ward Lake Road between the day-use area and road end at Signal Creek Campground. Also on this stretch of road is parking for Perseverance Lake Trail. *Watch for black bears.* Three C's Group Campground, adjacent Perseverance Lake Trail, is open for overflow camping only. **Signal Creek Campground** has 24 gravel sites (2 are drive-in) with tables, firepits, campground host; water and pit toilets; and a $10 camping fee. Phone 1-877-444-6777 for reservations. Access to Ward Lake Trail.

Mile 2.3 Revilla Road: Turn off for **Last Chance Campground**, with 19 gravel sites, drive-in camping units, 17 are wheelchair accessible, tables, pit toilets, water, $10 camping fee. Phone 1-877-444-6777 for reservations.

Mile 2.4 Revilla Road: Pavement ends and gravel begins. Turn on Connell Lake Road for trailhead to 2.1-mile-long Connell Lake Trail.

Mile 6.5 Revilla Road: Turnoff for Harriett Hunt Road, which leads 2.4 miles to Harriet Hunt Lake Recreation Area; parking, pit toilets and fishing.

Mile 6.6 Revilla Road: Road dead ends just past turnoff for Brown Mountain Road (gravel). Brown Mountain Road ends at Dude Mountain Trail, which is a 1.5-mile-long, difficult ascent to the 2,848-foot peak.

K 7.2 WARD COVE. Post office, gas station and Ward Cove Market.

K 7.3 Alaska State Troopers Ketchikan Post, phone (907) 225-5118.

K 8.7 Turnoff for Refuge Cove State Recreation Site to west; 14 picnic sites.

K 9.9 Totem Bight Road is exit for **Totem Bight State Historical Park**; entrance is just north of here. There is a parking area, restrooms, bookstore and phones. A short trail leads through the woods to Totem Bight

community house and totem park. A striking setting. Don't miss this!

The park's totems are either restored originals or duplicates carved by Natives as part of a U.S. Forest Service program begun in 1938 using Civilian Conservation Corps (CCC) funds.

The park's clan house or community house is representative of those found in many early 19th century Native Alaska villages in Southeast.

K 10.1 Double-ended paved turnout with view.

K 10.8 Grocery store, gas station.

K 11.7 Whipple Creek.

K 11.9 Gas station and convenience store. Pond Reef Road.

K 12.2 South Higgins Point Road winds 1.2 miles west through residential area to deadend at Higgins Point.

K 12.9 Paved viewpoint to west overlooks **Guard Islands lighthouse.** This light marks the easterly entrance to Tongass Narrows/Clarence Strait. It was established in 1904; first lit in 1924; and automated in 1969. Present optic is solar powered. It is an active navigation aid.

K 14.2 Junction with North Point Higgins Road. Turn west and take first right (Knudson Cove Road), then left at sign for **Knudson Cove Marina**; public boat launch, restaurant, propane station. Knudson Cove Road rejoins North Tongass Highway at **Milepost K 14.7**. North Point Higgins Road provides access to Clover Pass Resort, 0.6 mile west; RV sites, marina.

K 14.7 Knudson Cove Road west to marina (0.3 mile from highway).

K 15.4 Paved turnout at Settlers Cove trailhead.

K 16 *CAUTION: Watch for deer.*

K 16.1 First Waterfall Creek.

K 16.6 Double-ended paved turnout. Turnoff for Salmon Falls Resort.

K 16.7 Second Waterfall Creek.

K 17.1 Paved turnout, no view.

K 17.5 Paved turnout, no view.

K 18.2 Turnoff on Settlers Cove Road for **Settlers Cove State Recreation Site**, which has a 14-site campground ($15 camping fee) and a day-use parking area; picnic area with tables, water, picnic shelters, pit toilets, campground host, hiking trails (descriptions follow). Access to good gravel beach. Open May 1–Sept. 30. Campers register at fee station. Site is gated from 10 P.M. to 6 A.M.

©Kris Valencia, staff

The ¼ mile Lower Lunch Falls Loop Trail is a scenic boardwalk and gravel hike through spruce-hemlock forest with access to rocky beach. This trail is wheelchair accessible only to the bridge over Lunch Creek, where you may see spawning pink salmon in August. The upper trail follows Lunch Creek for 3.5 miles.

K 18.4 Road ends; trailhead parking.

Prince of Wales Island

Prince of Wales Island abounds with scenic vistas. This is Sandy Beach on the island's east coast. (©Kris Valencia, staff)

Visitor Information: Prince of Wales Chamber of Commerce, P.O. Box 490, Klawock, AK 99925; phone (907) 755-2626; email info@princeofwalescoc.org; www.princeofwalescoc.org. The **U.S. Forest Service** has offices in Craig, phone (907) 826-3271, and in Thorne Bay, phone (907) 828-3304; www.fs.usda.gov/tongass.

Prince of Wales Island is the third largest island under the American flag (Kodiak is second, the Big Island of Hawaii is first), measuring roughly 135 miles north to south by 45 miles east to west. A mountainous, heavily forested island with a cool, moist, maritime climate, the island is best known for its world-class fishing and for having the most extensive road system in Southeast Alaska.

Designated a State Scenic Byway in 2010, the island road system, with over 400 miles of paved road, offers visitors a unique driving experience. The scenery is anything but repetitive, as the roads travel through old-growth forest and clear-cut areas, with mountain views and views of coastline and offshore islands.

Wildlife viewing opportunities abound—from bald eagles to bears. It is not uncommon to have to brake for black bears or Sitka black-tailed deer crossing the road.

The road system connects 9 communities and also provides access to hiking trails; roadside fishing streams (sockeye, pink and coho salmon, cutthroat, rainbow trout and Dolly Varden); and some unique geological attractions.

Most of the island is within **Tongass National Forest**, the largest national forest in the nation comprised of 16.9 million acres, 13.7 million acres of which are either wilderness or National Monuments. Timber harvest is allowed on less than one half of one percent per year. On Prince of Wales Island, the Forest Service manages 5 designated wilderness areas, as well as public-use cabins, campgrounds, hiking trails and canoe trails.

It is estimated that there are thousands of caves on the island. The major geological attraction on the island is **El Capitan Cave**, located 75 miles from Craig via the North Prince of Wales Road.

With more than 13,000 feet of passageways, El Capitan Cave is the largest known cave in Alaska. A steep staircase trail (more than 365 steps) leads up to the cave entrance. The cave is accessible only by guided tour offered by the Forest Service. These free tours are offered Thursdays through Sundays from Memorial Day to mid-August (when the students who lead the tours return to school) or until Labor Day weekend (if docents are available). To book a tour, phone the Thorne Bay Ranger District at (907) 828-3304 at least 2 days in advance. Tours last about 2 hours and tour groups are limited to 6 people. For safety reasons, no children under age 7 are allowed on the tour. Wear warm clothes and boots. The U.S. Forest Service provides flashlights and safety helmets with headlamps.

Four miles south of the turnoff for El Capitan is the Beaver Falls Karst Trail. This 1-mile

Major Attractions:

El Capitan Cave, Totem Parks, Sport Fishing

©Kris Valencia, staff

boardwalk trail crosses ancient muskegs and cathedral forests, and displays many karst features, such as sinkholes, deep vertical pits, lost rivers and collapsed channels.

Historically, salmon and timber have been the economic mainstays of Prince of Wales Island. One of Alaska's first canneries was built at Klawock in 1878, and some 25 more canneries were eventually built on the

island to process salmon.

Annual events on the island include the International Marathon in May. The 26.2-mile marathon begins and ends at the high school in Craig. This annual event takes place the Saturday preceding Memorial Day. For fishermen there are salmon derbies in Thorne Bay (May–July) and Craig–Klawock (June–August).

Many of the island's communities began as logging camps. Today, timber harvests on the island are only a fraction of what they once were. Motorists get a close-up look at the effects of logging as they drive the island's roads. Clear-cut areas, in various stages of regrowth, alternate with old-growth forest as you travel from one end of the island to the other. Watch for logging truck traffic throughout the island.

A major attraction here is the world-class saltwater sportfishing that abounds immediately offshore and throughout the many smaller islands surrounding Prince of Wales Island. Most communities have boat ramps. Visiting fishermen may also charter with a local operator. Lodges providing guided fishing charters and packages include: **Fireweed Lodge**, Log Cabin Resort, Kingfisher Charters & Lodge, Shelter Cove, SureStrike, Catch-a-King, Steamboat Bay Resort and Alaska's Waterfall Resort. Visit the Prince of Wales Chamber of Commerce website at www.princeofwalescoc.org. *(See ads this section.)*

Ocean fishing for salmon is best in July and early August for chinooks, August and September for coho, July, August and September for pinks, and August and September for chum. Halibut to 100 lbs., 50-lb. chinook salmon and 15-lb. coho salmon are not considered uncommon during the sport season, usually May through August due to the weather and fish migration patterns. Abundant bottom fish, including lingcod, halibut and red snapper, reside throughout these waters year-round.

Communities

Of the 9 communities connected by the island road system, Coffman Cove, Craig, Hydaburg, Kasaan, Klawock, Thorne Bay and Whale Pass have city status *(these communities are described in more detail in this section on pages 612–615)*. The smaller communities of Hollis and Naukati and Whale Pass are described in the road logs.

PORT PROTECTION (pop. 42), **POINT BAKER** (pop. 16), and **EDNA BAY** are 3 communities not on the island road system. Located on the northern tip of Prince of Wales Island, these 3 small fishing villages are accessible by floatplane and skiff.

Lodging & Services

Accommodations on the island range

Prince of Wales Island

© 2019 The MILEPOST®

Map Location

Scale

0		10Miles
0	10	Kilometers

Logged Roads

paved

unpaved

Other Roads

paved

unpaved

Ferry Routes

00 Forest Road   00 Forest Hwy

Refer to Log for Visitor Facilities

To Petersburg

To LeConte Bay

Stikine LeConte Wilderness

Stikine River

BRITISH COLUMBIA

ALASKA

Mitkof Island

Crystal Lake

Kupreanof Island

South Mitkof/ Banana Point

Wrangell

Virginia Lake

Glaciated Area

Alaska Marine Highway

Woronkofski Island

Zimovia Highway

Wrangell Island

N
W   E
S

Pt. Barrien

Strait Island

Sumner Strait

Port Protection

Pt. Baker

Red Bay

Pt. Colpoys

Zarembo Island

Chichagof Pass

Stikine Strait

Zimovia Strait

Thoms Lake

Marten Lake

Harding River

Labouchere Bay

North Prince of Wales Road

Salmon Bay Lake

Calaer Bay

Kashevarof Islands

Etolin Island

Bradfield Canal

Anan Bay

Anan Lake

Anan Bear Observatory

Barrier Islands

Shakan Bay

El Capitan Cave

Twin Island Lake's

27

Neck Lake

25

Whale Pass

Kashevarof

Passage

South Etolin Wilderness

Deer Island

Lake McDonald

Kosciusko Island

El Capitan Passage

43

Prince

Coffman Cove

Coffman Cove Road

3030

Luck Lake

30

Clarence

Spacious Bay

North Prince of Wales Road

44

Naukati

of

Sandy Beach Road

Alaska Marine Highway

Ernest Sound

Sea Otter Sound

Tuxekan

Tuxekan Island

Thorne

30

Narrow Pt.

Cleveland Peninsula

Heceta Island

North Prince of Wales Road

43

Wales

Thorne Bay Road

Thorne Bay

River

30

Maurelle Islands Wilderness

Big Salt Lake Road

Control Lake Junction

Island

Karta River Wilderness

Salmon Lake

Karta Bay

Strait

Kasaan

Behm Canal

Naha Bay

Noyes Island

San Fernando Island

San Alberto Bay

Klawock

Craig-Klawock- Hollis Highway

Kasaan Bay

North Tongass Highway

Revilla Rd.

Lulu Island

Klawock Lake

Hollis

Clark Bay Ferry Terminal

Grindall Island

Outside Islands Wilderness

San Juan Bautista Island

Craig

Hydaburg Road

Inter-Island Ferry Authority

Vallenar Bay

Baker Island

Bucareli Bay

Trocadero Bay

Waterfall

Soda Bay

Chasina Pt.

Ketchikan

South Tongass Highway

To Prince Rupert

Suemez Island

Cholmondelev Sound

Gravina Island

Windy Pt.

Cape Bartolome

Hydaburg

Nichols Passage

Dolomi

Quarry

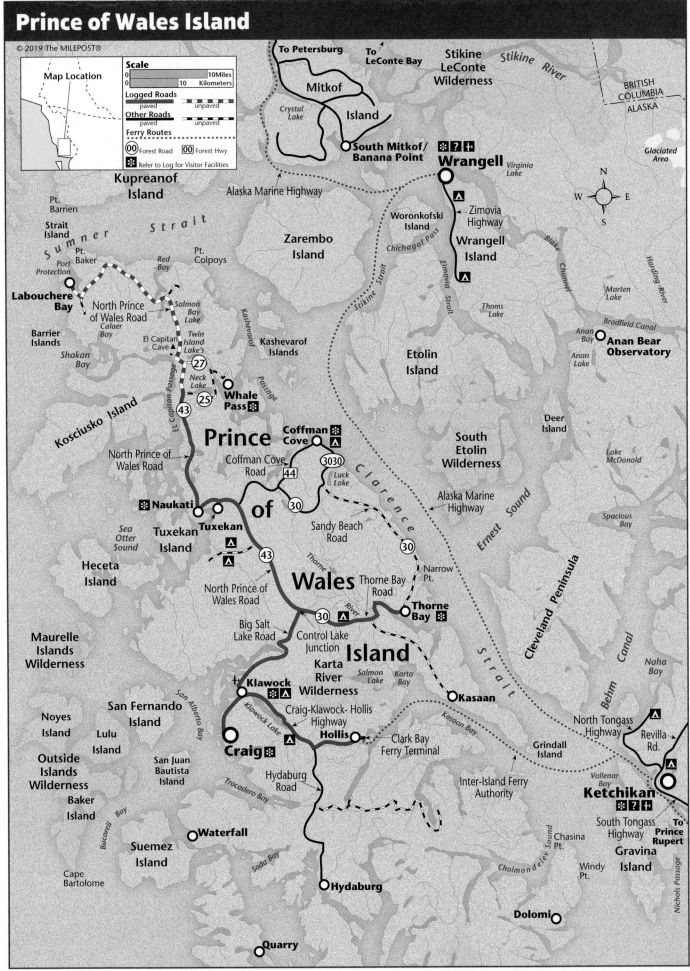

Watch for deer—and also black bears—on the Prince of Wales Island road system.
(©Michael K. Robb)

from lodges, cabins and bed-and-breakfasts to guest houses and apartments. If you are dining out, Craig has the widest selection of eateries, from pizza to bakery/cafes to food trucks. Shopping and other services are also found mainly in Craig and in neighboring Klawock. WiFi can be found at libraries in Craig, Coffman Cove, Thorne Bay and Whale Pass; and for customers at Papa's Pizza in Craig.

Fireweed Lodge (www.fireweedlodge.com) is located in Klawock on the Craig–Klawock–Hollis Highway; the entrance is across the street from St. John's By the Sea Catholic Church. Fireweed Lodge has a dining room and arranges fishing charters. **Klawock River Inn** (www.klawockriverinn.com) also on the Klawock-Hollis Highway, offers modern rooms with WiFi. **Southeast Alaska Getaway** in Hollis is a rustic cabin for up to 5 guests (phone 817/907-1038).

For a complete list of lodges and other businesses on the island, visit the **Prince of Wales Chamber of Commerce** website at www.princeofwalescoc.org. (See ads on page 610.)

Camping

Log Cabin RV Park & Resort in Klawock has waterside camping; reserve ahead. There is an RV park in Thorne Bay, across from the USFS office on Sandy Beach Road.

There are 2 U.S. Forest Service campgrounds on the island—Eagle's Nest on Thorne Bay Road and Harris River on the Craig–Klawock–Hollis Highway. Camping fee at both is $8. Campground sites are available on a first-come, first-served basis. If you are in a group and wish to book adjacent sites ahead of time, this may be possible; please call the Craig Ranger District at (907) 826-3271. Several undeveloped dispersed campsites are accessible via the island road system; see www.fs.usda.gov/tongass/.

There are 17 USFS cabins (accessible by plane, boat or on foot) and 2, 3-sided shelters (free) available for public use; reservations and a fee are required ($20–$45 a night, per cabin). Online reservations are available; visit www.fs.usda.gov/tongass/.

Transportation

Air: Daily scheduled service from Ketchikan available. All communities on the island are served by floatplane. Wheel planes land at Klawock Airport. Alaska Seaplanes (www.flyalaskaseaplanes.com), phone 1-800-354-2479; Taquan Air (www.taquanair.com); phone 1-800-770-8800. Island Air Express, phone 1-888-387-8989. Pacific Airways, phone 1-877-360-3500.

Ferry: Year-round, daily passenger and vehicle service via **Inter–Island Ferry Authority**. The IFA's MV *Stikine* or MV *Prince of Wales* connect Ketchikan and with the Hollis Ferry Terminal at Clark Bay, which is 23 miles from Klawock and 30 miles from Craig via the Craig-Klawock-Hollis Highway (see road log on page 614). Ferry crossing time is about 3 hours. For reservations, phone 1-866-308-4848; online at www.interislandferry.com. In Ketchikan, stop by the IFA ticket counter inside the Alaska Marine Highway terminal, or phone (907) 225-4838.

Car rentals: Hollis Adventure Rentals (www.harentals.com), phone (907) 530-7040; Rainforest Auto Rentals, phone (907) 826-2277; Wesley Rentals, at Klawock Airport, phone (907) 617-8837.

Highways: The island's road system (an Alaska Scenic Byway) is logged in this section as the Craig–Klawock–Hollis Highway (paved), connecting the IFA Ferry Landing at Hollis/Clark Bay with downtown Craig; Big Salt Lake Road (paved), connecting Klawock to the Control Lake junction; Thorne Bay Road (paved), connecting Control Lake Junction with the community of Thorne Bay; and North Prince of Wales Road/FH 43, from Control Lake Junction to road end at Labouchere Bay (improved pavement and narrow gravel). See map and road logs this section.

NOTE: The Island's roads are relatively narrow and winding, with some grades. Road conditions vary, from rough gravel U.S. Forest Service Roads to improved, paved highway. They do an excellent job with frequent distance markers. Cell phone service is fair, at best, on the island.

Drive with headlights on at all times and obey posted speed limits! Be alert for oncoming traffic on hills and corners, and watch for logging trucks, deer and bears.

Coffman Cove

Located 55 miles north of Klawock, a 2-hour drive from Hollis/ferry terminal. Coffman Cove is the only community on the north end of Prince of Wales Island that is accessible by paved road. It is also connected to Thorne Bay by the narrow, scenic Sandy Beach Road. **Population:** 198. **Emergency Services:** Coffman Cove Fire/EMS, phone 911. **Coffman Cove Clinic:** Part-time hours, phone (907) 329-2051.

Visitor Information: For information on this community, contact the City of Coffman Cove, phone (907) 329-2233, or visit their website at www.ccalaska.com.

Coffman Cove has a public library. Other tourist services include: the Riggin Shack, a small general merchandise and grocery store; the Doghouse Saloon and Liquor store; and AK-49 Cafe, which serves burgers, sandwiches and more. R&R Fuels has gas/diesel/propane. Accommodations include fishing lodges and cabin rentals. Cove Connect has WiFi available in the bay and downtown.

Coffman Cove has a post office on the corner of Loggers Lane and Kodiak Drive (open 1–3:30 P.M. weekdays except Tuesdays when it is open from 5–7:30 P.M.). There are 2 public docks with transient moorage available, fish cleaning tables, boat launch, public phone and restrooms here. The Harbormaster's phone is (907) 329-2233.

Seaside Park has telescopes and covered tables for picnicking; narrow entrance/parking area.

Area wildlife includes black bears, Sitka black-tailed deer, whales, herons, Steller sea lions and incredible bird watching while you enjoy hiking, kayaking, fishing or boating. Guided ocean charters are available locally.

Special Events. The King Salmon Derby is scheduled for May 1 through August 31. The Silver Salmon Tournament takes place July 3rd. The 9th annual "By the Sea" Arts & Seafood Festival will be held Friday and Saturday, August 9–10, in 2019; visit www.artsandseafoodfestival.com. For more information on these events, contact the City of Coffman Cove, phone (907) 329-2233; or visit www.ccalaska.com/events/ for dates and times.

Craig

Located 31 miles from Clark Bay ferry terminal and 7 miles from Klawock, on the western shore of Prince of Wales Island. **Population:** 1,241. **Emergency Services:** Craig EMS, phone 911. **Police,** phone 911 or (907) 826-3330. **Alaska State Troopers,** phone (907) 826-2918. **Clinic,** Peace-Health Medical Group, phone (907) 826-3257; Craig Public Health Center, phone (907) 826-3433. **Dentist,** Southeast Dental Centers, phone (907) 826-2273. **Hospital,** in Ketchikan.

Visitor Information: See website at

www.craigak.com.

Named for founder Craig Millar, who established a saltery and cold storage facility here in the early 1900s, Craig was incorporated in 1922. Today, it is the largest city on the island and offers most services. There are half a-dozen places to eat, from pizza places to bakery/cafes; 2 banks; supermarket and liquor stores; gas stations, propane, towing and auto repair; and several gift shops featuring local handmade and cultural crafts. If you have difficulty locating something specific, ask a local. Many businesses are tucked away in hard-to-find places.

Accommodations are available at Shelter Cove Lodge, Catch-A-King Lodge, Sunnahae Hotel and at numerous bed-and-breakfasts. The nearest campground is Log Cabin Resort in Klawock. There is an RV dump station located on Cold Storage Road, behind the Alaska Commercial Company grocery/liquor store on the highway.

Craig has 2 boat harbors, North Cove and South Cove, located on either side of the causeway crossed by the Craig–Klawock–Hollis Highway where it merges with Water Street. The harbor is a nice place for visitors to stroll, take in the local atmosphere and watch for bald eagles along the waterfront. Craig also has a seaplane float, fuel dock, city dock and float, 2 fish-buying docks and a historic cannery dock. The Craig harbormaster's office, which offers public showers and restrooms, is located on the corner close to South Cove; phone (907) 826-3404, VHF Channel 16.

Craig is the home port of many commercial fishing and charter sportfishing boats that fish for halibut, coho and chinook salmon, lingcod and red snapper (yelloweye).

Hydaburg

Located 36 miles from Hollis. Population: 405. **Emergency Services:** Phone 911. **Clinic,** Alma Cook Medical Center, phone (907) 285-3462.

Hydaburg was founded in 1911, and combined the populations of 3 Haida villages: Sukkwan, Howkan and Klinkwan. President William Howard Taft established an Indian reservation on the surrounding land in 1912, but, at the residents' request, most of the land was restored to its former status as part of Tongass National Forest in 1926. Hydaburg was incorporated in 1927, 3 years after its people became U.S. citizens. Hydaburg is the most populous community of Haidas in the U.S.

Hydaburg has an excellent collection of restored Haida totems. A totem park is in front of the Hydaburg School. Native carvers restored and replicated totems brought in from the traditional Haida villages on southern Prince of Wales Island. The totem restoration project was founded in the late 1930s by the Civilian Conservation Corps. The Hydaburg Totem Park Restoration Project was completed in 2015.

Haida Corp. provides lodging for visitors. Haida Fuels provides fuel and gas. Alaska Commercial Company provides groceries and sundry items, Tongass Federal Credit Union has a micro-site, and DD's Kitchen is the local eatery.

The Small Boat Harbor offers transient, monthly and annual moorage. Amenities include: skiff haul-out, grid, boat launch, fish cleaning station, water and electricity.

Kasaan

Located at the head of Kasaan Bay. **Population: 89. Emergency, Services:** Phone 911. Alaska State Troopers, in Craig, phone (907) 826-2918. Village Public Safety Officer (VPSO) and Volunteer Fire Dept. in Kasaan. Kasaan gets its name from the Tlingit word meaning "pretty town." According to the Alaska Dept. of Commerce, this historic Haida community was originally Tlingit territory, until Haidas "migrated north from Haida Gwaii (formerly the Queen Charlotte Islands) in the early 1700s and established the village now known as Old Kasaan. Between 1892 and 1900, the Copper Queen mine, camp, sawmill, post office, and general store were built by a group of businessmen on Kasaan Bay, and the Haida people relocated to this new village. The copper mine went bankrupt after 4 years, but in 1902 the first salmon cannery was constructed." The cannery operated sporadically until 1953.

"Chief Son-i-Hat built the Whale House during the 1880s, a traditional clan house

which became the focus of the new Kasaan Totem Park. Many of the totems left from the old village site were moved to the park in 1938. Kavilco, Inc., the local village corporation, purchased the old cannery buildings and property in 1974. Organized Village of Kasaan, a federally recognized tribe, was formed in Kasaan in 1938. The City of Kasaan was incorporated in 1976."

This historic Haida village is located at the end of a 17-mile gravel road off of the road to Thorne Bay. Cabin rentals, a cafe and tours are available; phone (907) 617-3386, visit kasaan.org.

Klawock

Located 23 miles from Clark Bay ferry terminal. **Population: 799. Emergency Services:** Phone 911 for all emergencies. **City Police,** phone (907) 755-2777; **Clinic,** SEARHC Alicia Roberts Medical Center, phone (907) 755-4800. **Private Aircraft:** Klawock airstrip, 2 miles northeast; elev. 50 feet; length 5,000 feet; lighted and paved.

Visitor Information: The Prince of Wales Chamber of Commerce and Visitor Center is located in the Klawock-Heenya Mall; phone (907) 755-2626; email info@princeofwalescoc.org; visit www.princeofwalescoc.org.

Klawock was originally a Tlingit Indian summer fishing village; a trading post and salmon saltery were established here in 1868. Ten years later, a salmon cannery was built, one of several cannery operations in the area. Over the years, the population of Klawock, like other Southeast communities, grew and then declined with the salmon harvest. The local economy is still dependent on fishing, along with timber harvesting and sawmilling. A fish hatchery is
(Continues on page 615)

Chief Son-i-Hat Whale House is part of Kasaan Totem Park. Guided Tribal Tours that focus on Haida culture can be arranged. (©Michael K. Robb)

Craig–Klawock–Hollis Highway

This paved highway (SR 924) begins at the Hollis Ferry Terminal at Clark Bay and leads 31 miles west through Klawock then south to Craig, taking motorists through the temperate rainforest environment typical of Southeast Alaska. It is a 2-lane road with good surfacing and narrow shoulders. Posted speed is 50-mph with some 35- to 40-mph curves and speed zones through communities. *CAUTION: Watch for deer.*

Distance from Craig (C) is followed by distance from Hollis Ferry Terminal at Clark Bay (F). Physical mileposts reflect distance from Craig.

C 31 F 0 Entrance to **Inter-Island Ferry Authority Hollis Terminal** at Clark Bay; phone (907) 530-4848 or 1-866-308-4848. There is a large paved turnout area, terminal parking spaces (14-day limit), and a fenced loading area for vehicles. If you are catching an early ferry, you may ask permission at the terminal to stay in your self-contained rig outside the terminal loading area. Otherwise the nearest campground is Harris River USFS Campground, 11.3 miles from here.

C 29.8 F 1.2 Turnoff to south for **HOLLIS** (pop. 109); boat launch ramp and harbor. Hollis served as a Ketchikan Pulp Co. logging camp and base for timber operations on Prince of Wales Island until 1962, when the camp moved to Thorne Bay. Reserve lodging at the **Southeast Alaska Getaway** in Hollis at a rustic cabin for up to 5 guests (phone 817/907-1038; *see ad on page 610*).

C 28.9 F 2.1 Hollis Fire Department.

C 28.5 F 2.5 Maybeso Creek bridge; small parking areas either end of bridge. Fish include cutthroat; Dolly Varden; pinks and cohos; steelhead run begins in mid-April. Pools offer the best fishing. Walking is good along the streambed but more difficult along the bank. *CAUTION: Watch for bears.*

C 27.1 F 3.9 Gravel turnout with interpretive signs about Hollis.

C 26.4 F 4.6 Large paved turnout with 2 picnic tables, interpretive signs, nice water view (pictured above).

C 24.3 F 6.7 Paved turnout.

C 22.5 F 8.5 Access to Harris River interpretive area and Harris River Trailhead parking. Large turnouts. Harris River fishing for cutthroat; steelhead run mid-April; salmon and Dolly Varden run beginning in mid-July. Easy walking on the gravel bars in the middle of 1.3-mile-long river.

C 20.5 F 10.5 Junction with Hydaburg Road which leads south 23 miles to the City of Hydaburg (see description on facing page). Mileposts along this road indicate distance from Hydaburg, not from this junction. Hydaburg Road also provides access to One

Duck Trailhead (Mile 20), Cable Creek with fish viewing (Mile 13.3), side road to access 12 Mile Cabin, Dog Salmon Fishpass and Polk Inlet with Estuary (Mile 12.5). This side road is very narrow and not meant for large RVs. Dog Salmon Fishpass provides an excellent opportunity to watch Alaska's salmon swim up the waterfall or the fish ladder. Bear viewing is excellent during the salmon run from mid-July through mid-September. Facilities at the site include a table, firepit, viewing platform and interpretive signs.

C 20 F 11 Side road to USFS trailhead for 3-mile-long Twenty Mile Spur Trail.

C 19.7 F 11.3 Turnoff for **Harris River USFS Campground and Picnic Area**. 14 campsites on gravel loop road (best suited for small to mid-sized RVs); level tent sites, firepits, tables, outhouse, bear-proof garbage and water. Camping fee $8. Muskeg nature trail. Very nice walk-in picnic area with tables, water, firepits, toilets and group shelter. A pedestrian bridge across the Harris River offers river views. Park at campground entrance and follow gravel path to picnic area.

C 19.6 F 11.4 Harris River bridge.

C 19.1 F 11.8 Paved turnout.

C 18.7 F 12.3 Large paved turnout.

C 17.1 F 13.9 Paved turnout.

C 14.9 F 16.1 Paved turnout and access to Klawock Lake; posted no camping.

C 12 F 19 Paved turnout. Three Mile Creek.

C 10.9 F 20.1 Paved turnout.

C 9.7 F 21.3 Paved turnout. Half-mile Creek.

C 9.1 F 21.9 Paved turnout.

C 9 F 22 Prince of Wales Hatchery.

C 8.3 F 22.7 Klawock city limit. *(See description of Klawock on page 613.)*

C 7.4 F 23.5 Entrance to Klawock-Heenya mall at **junction** with Boundary Road; large supermarket, with Western Union, liquor store and deli; credit union, post office, eye clinic, beauty salon. **Prince of Wales Island Chamber of Commerce** office inside mall has visitor information. Gas station with diesel and propane; 24-hour card service. Rivals Cafe. Tlingit Longhouse to the east with carving shed.

Junction with Boundary Road (which quickly becomes Big Salt Lake Road); leads 16.2 miles to Control Lake Junction, where it intersects with Thorne Bay Road and North Prince of Wales Road. See "Big Salt Lake Road" log on page 615.

C 7.3 F 23.7 Junction with Big Salt Lake Road. Black Bear Market/Petro Express with gas and propane, tackle, hunting and fishing licenses. Access Log Cabin RV Park & Resort, a popular resort with RV sites and cabins on Saltwater Beach.

C 7.2 F 23.8 Alaska Court System, Hemlock Road.

C 7.1 F 23.9 Turnoff for **Fireweed Lodge**; motel rooms, family-style dining and fishing charters available.

Fireweed Lodge. See display ad on page 610.

Across the street from Fireweed Lodge is

St. John's By the Sea Catholic Church. It was designed and built with local lumber and materials by the local parish. The stained-glass windows were designed and built by local artists. Visitors are welcome to view the church.

C 7 F 24 Turn west on Anchorage Street to access Dan Snider Park with picnic area, the city boat ramp and harbor. Continue on loop road to Bayview Boulevard and Church Street to see **Klawock Totem Park**. Also access via Klawock Street to city park, ballfields and boat launch. **Klawock River Inn** is on the highway just past this turn-off.

Klawock River Inn. See display ad on page 610.

C 6.8 F 24.2 Bayview Boulevard loops west to Klawock Totem Park (turn on Union Street).

C 6.6 F 24.4 Klawock River bridge spans tidal estuary where river meets saltwater; no fishing. Good eagle viewing at Klawock River estuary during salmon season.

Alicia Roberts Medical Center. *Slow for posted speed zone entering Klawock.*

C 6 F 25 Viking Sawmill.

C 4.9 F 26.1 Turnout, no view.

C 4.1 F 26.9 Turnout with view.

C 4 F 27 Craig city limit.

C 3.7 F 27.3 Turnout with scenic view of Klawock Inlet and San Alberto Bay.

C 1.8 F 29.2 Welcome to Craig (sign). J.T. Brown Street with access to False Island leads to Petro Marine dock, Silver Bay Seafoods, public docks, and boat ramp. Car wash, auto repair, and boat storage facility.

C 1.7 F 29.3 Craig High School.

C 1.1 F 29.9 *Slow for posted speed zone entering Craig.*

C 0.6 F 30.4 Napa Auto Parts. Port Bagial Boulevard access to large hardware store/lumberyard.

C 0.5 F 30.5 Craig post office (ZIP 99921), Wells Fargo, and Annie Betty's bakery/cafe, with drive-thru.

C 0.4 F 30.6 Cold Storage Road. Alaska Commercial Company supermarket/liquor store. Strip mall has outdoor clothing retailer, Papa's Pizza, Whale Tail Pharmacy, Bread Box Bakery/Cafe, gift shop, Alaska State Troopers, Alaska Dept. Fish & Game office, State DHSS offices, VFW Post 26.

Turn north on Cold Storage Road for dump station, on right in gravel area.

C 0.3 F 30.7 North and South Cove harbors are located on either side of the highway here. Harbormaster's Office, restrooms, public showers.

C 0.2 F 30.8 U.S. Forest Service to south on 9th Street.

C 0 F 31 Intersection of Third, Front and Water streets; J.T. Brown store. Gravel parking area (2-hour and 8-hour parking).

Take the boardwalk/path to Ward Cove Mess Hall to see a display of debris deposited on Prince of Wales Island beaches by the 2011 Japanese tsunami.

(Continued from page 613)
located on Klawock Lake near the site of a former salmon hatchery (1897–1917).

The Prince of Wales Chamber of Commerce is located in the mall, an Alaska Commercial Company supermarket with deli, Western Union, and liquor store; optometry clinic, beauty salon, credit union and many other businesses are located here. Gas, diesel and propane are available. Black Bear Grocery and Tackle is located on Big Salt Lake Road. Accommodations and family-style dining at **Fireweed Lodge**, located along the main highway, near the Big Salt Road junction; phone (907) 755-2930. **Klawock River Inn** (www.klawockriverinn.com) also on the Klawock-Hollis Highway, offers modern rooms with WiFi. Cabins and full-hookup RV sites are at the Log Cabin RV Park & Resort, phone 1-800-544-2205.

A major attraction in Klawock is the **Totem Park**, which contains 21 masterfully carved replicas of the original totem poles that once stood in Tuxekan, the old winter village of the Keenya Kwaan people. The poles were relocated here in 1938–40 as a Civilian Conservation Corps project. A totem dedicated to U.S. Veterans was erected in 2018. The Long House, named Gaani Ax Adi, is located along the main highway in downtown Klawock near the carving shed.

Recreation here includes good fishing for salmon and steelhead in Klawock River, and saltwater halibut fishing. ⊖

Thorne Bay   🅱 ⊖ ➕ 🅰

Located on the east coast of Prince of Wales Island, 57 miles from the Clark Bay ferry terminal, and 34 miles from Klawock. **Population:** 530. **Emergency Services:** Phone 911. *NOTE: Some cell carriers require dialing (907) 828-3399 from a cell phone to get the local 911 dispatchers.* **Village Public Safety Officer (VPSO)**, phone (907) 204-0247. **Alaska State Troopers**, in Craig, phone (907) 826-2918. **Medical,** SEARHC Alicia Roberts Clinic in Klawock, phone (907) 755-4800, or PeaceHealth in Craig, phone (907) 826 3257.

Visitor Information: City of Thorne Bay, P.O. Box 19110, Thorne Bay, AK 99919; phone (907) 828-3380, email reception@thornebay-ak.gov; website www.thornebay-ak.gov. To contact the U.S. Forest Service office in Thorne Bay, phone (907) 828-3304. Or contact the Prince of Wales Island Chamber of Commerce; phone (907) 755-2626; email info@princeofwalescoc.org; or visit www.princeofwalescoc.org.

Thorne Bay began as a floating logging camp for Ketchikan Pulp Co. (KPC) in 1962. Float homes were moved onto land forming a community that incorporated in 1982, making it one of Alaska's newer cities. It was connected to the island road system in 1974.

When timber was big in the 1960s and 1970s, Thorne Bay was the largest logging camp in North America, with more than 600 residents, mostly men, living under a camp boss. When Ketchikan Pulp Co. completed its final timber sales in 2001 and closed down operations Thorne Bay's population dropped by half.

Thorne Bay is home to hunting and fishing lodges, Southeast Island School Dis-

Big Salt Lake Road

Big Salt Lake Road (SR 929) begins as Boundary Road in Klawock at **Milepost C 7.4** on the Craig–Klawock–Hollis Highway (SR 924) and extends 16.2 miles to junction with Thorne Bay Road and North Prince of Wales Road (FR 43) at Control Lake Junction. It is an improved paved road with posted speed limits to 50 mph.
Distance from junction with Craig–Klawock–Hollis Highway at Klawock (K) is followed by distance from Thorne Bay (T). Physical mileposts reflect distance from Klawock. *CAUTION: Watch for deer.*

K 0 T 33 Junction with Craig–Klawock–Hollis Highway at Klawock. Shopping mall with supermarket, liquor store, post office and Prince of Wales Chamber of Commerce.

> **Junction** with "Craig–Klawock–Hollis Highway" (SR 924) at **Milepost C 7.4** on that highway; see log on page 614.

K 0.5 T 32.5 Boundary Road becomes Big Salt Lake Road at **junction** with old Big Salt

©Kris Valencia, staff

Lake Road. Turnoff for Log Cabin RV Park & Resort; lodging, camping, boat rentals. 🅰

K 1.4 T 31.6 Bennett Creek.
K 2.3 T 30.7 Turnoff for Klawock Airport (0.6 mile). Parking is limited.
Private Aircraft: Klawock airstrip; elev. 80 feet; length 5,000 feet; lighted and paved.
K 3.8 T 29.2 Little Salt Creek. Big Salt Lake Road climbs eastbound. Beautiful views of islands and inlets but no turnouts for photo ops. *CAUTION: Watch for deer.*
K 5.3 T 27.7 Duke Creek (sign).
K 8.3 T 24.7 Turnout and gravel access to **Big Salt Lake**. An estuary, Big Salt Lake extends northeast 8 miles off Klawak and Shinaku inlets on the west coast of Prince of Wales Island. This saltwater body is protected by small islands that are visible from several spots along Big Salt Lake Road. Be aware of strong currents when boating on

this tidal lake. Across from Big Salt Lake you will see the remains of a Vietnam era DC-3 aircraft that crashed in 1968 with no loss of life while being transported from McCord Air Force Base to Southeast Asia via Anchorage.
K 9.3 T 23.7 Parking at west end of **Black Bear Creek** bridge. Fishing for cutthroat, Dolly Varden, sockeye, pink, chum and coho salmon. ⊖

K 9.7 T 23.3 Paved turnout, no view.
K 10.2 T 22.8 Paved turnout. Second growth forest management (Sealaska sign).

©Kris Valencia, staff

K 10.5 T 22.5 Paved turnout with views of Big Salt Lake. Many such views are available but there's no place to park along this good paved, winding road.
K 12 T 21 Steelhead Creek bridge. Fishing for cutthroat, Dolly Varden, steelhead, pink, chum and coho salmon. ⊖

K 13 T 20 Entering Tongass National Forest land eastbound.
K 16 T 17 Control Lake; rainbow and cutthroat trout; Dolly Varden; steelhead (spring and fall run); pink and coho salmon; good sockeye salmon stream in August. U.S. Forest Service public-use cabin with skiff. ⊖

K 16.5 T 16.5 Control Lake Junction. Large parking areas both sides of highway.

> **Junction** of Big Salt Lake Road (SR 929) with Thorne Bay Road (FH 42/30) and North Prince of Wales Road (FH 43/20). See road logs this section.

Distance marker for northbound traffic shows Naukati 26 miles, Coffman Cove 30 miles, Whale Pass 48 miles, Labouchere Bay 81 miles.
Distance marker for eastbound traffic shows Thorne Bay 18 miles, Kasaan 28 miles.
Distance marker westbound shows Klawock 17 miles, Craig 24 miles, Hollis 40 miles.

trict offices, the Thorne Bay Ranger District Headquarters, several local specialty lumber mills, Southeast Road Builders and the barge terminal that serves all of Prince of Wales Island.

Thorne Bay has a grocery store, liquor store and hardware store; general merchandise, boat fuel, convenience store, gas, diesel and post office at The Port. AK-49 Cafe is a great stop for lunch or dinner (eat-in or takeout). The Tackle Shack and Floatel offers fishing and hunting licenses. Lodging is available at numerous lodges and a couple

of B&Bs. The Thorne Bay RV Park offers nightly and weekly RV sites with hookups. Public restrooms and showers and moorage are available at the Harbor Facility.

Sandy Beach Road (gravel) winds north along the east coast of Prince of Wales Island from Thorne Bay to Coffman Cove, a total driving distance of 37 miles. There are a number of ocean views along the way to the beautiful **Sandy Beach USFS Day-Use Site** at Mile 7. Sandy Beach is named for its long stretch of fine, soft sand and it is a favorite spot with local families.

Thorne Bay Road

Thorne Bay harbor has moorage, a boat launch, fuel, restrooms and showers. (©Kris Valencia, staff)

Thorne Bay Road is a paved road with easy curves, no steep grades and posted speed limits to 50-mph. It extends 17.2 miles from Control Lake Junction to the community of Thorne Bay.

Driving distance from Control Lake Junction (CJ) is followed by distance from Thorne Bay (T).

CJ 0 T 17.2 Control Lake Junction.

Junction with Big Salt Lake Road at **Milepost K 16.5** and Mile 0 of the North Prince of Wales Road (FH 43). See Big Salt Lake Road log on page 615 and the North Prince of Wales Road (FH 43) log on page 617.

CJ 1.2 T 17 Control Creek.

CJ 1.8 T 15.4 Eagle's Nest USFS campground on a 0.6-mile paved road; 12 sites on level, gravel pads *(NOTE: parking spurs are narrow and perpendicular to the campground road, large RVs may be difficult to back in)*; $8 camping fee (self-serve); walk-in tent sites; potable water, tables, firepits, garbage, outhouses. Sites are on a first-come, first-served basis, but phone the Craig Ranger District at (907) 826-3271 regarding reservations. A wheelchair-accessible boardwalk trail offers views of spawning salmon. Also watch for waterfowl in spring and summer, bald eagles year-round. Trail to **Balls Lake** picnic area. Access to **Control Creek**; fishing for cutthroat, Dolly Varden, sockeye, pink and coho salmon.

CJ 2 T 15.2 Balls Lake USFS picnic area and trail; paved parking area for 10 cars, vault toilet, no potable water, litter bin. Follow gravel trail about 150 feet from parking area to picnic shelter with 2 tables and fire ring. Trailhead for Balls Lake Trail by picnic shelter; trail is 2.2 miles around lake, 0.5 mile to Eagle's Nest Campground.

CJ 4.8 T 12.4 Rio Roberts Creek; cutthroat, pink and coho salmon fishing.

CJ 5.2 T 12 Newlunberry Creek (narrow bridge).

CJ 6.9 T 10.3 Rio Beaver Creek (narrow bridge).

CJ 9.9 T 7.3 Paved turnout.

CJ 11.1 T 6.1 Goose Creek bridge (signed "narrow bridge"); turnout at east end. Excellent spawning stream. Pink salmon run mid-August; cutthroat and coho salmon.

CJ 11.2 T 6 Junction with narrow gravel road (can be rough and washboarded) which leads 17 miles southeast to the historic Haida village of **KASAAN** (pop. 89), which was connected to the road system in 1996. Kasaan has a post office, school and boat docks. The main visitor attraction here is the totem park (access via dirt trail, about a ½-mile hike). The last remaining Haida long house in the United States is here. *See description of Kasaan on page 613.*

CJ 11.3 T 5.9 Double-ended paved turnout.

CJ 12.4 T 4.8 Single-vehicle paved turnout.

CJ 12.7 T 4.5 Thorne River (signed "narrow bridge"). Fish for cutthroat, Dolly Varden, steelhead, rainbow trout and sockeye, pink, chum and coho salmon.

Slow for 30-mph curve.

CJ 13 T 4.2 Paved turnout.

CJ 13.2 T 4 Paved turnout.

CJ 13.3 T 3.9 Falls Creek bridge (narrow bridge); parking.

CJ 13.6 T 3.6 Loop road access to parking for **Gravelly Creek USFS picnic area**; picnic area on the bank of Thorne River at the mouth of Gravelly Creek; tables, fire rings, vault toilet and open-sided shelter.

Pink salmon run in August and September. *CAUTION: Watch for bears.*

CJ 13.9 T 3.3 Gravelly Creek bridge.

CJ 14.2 T 3 Physical Milepost 3.

CJ 15.2 T 2 Paved turnout.

CJ 16.7 T 0.5 *Slow for speed zone entering Thorne Bay.*

CJ 16.8 T 0.4 Junction of Thorne Bay Road (to the right) and Sandy Beach Road (straight ahead); description follows. Thorne Bay Ranger Station and the **Municipal RV Park** are located 0.2 mile from here. **Sandy Beach USFS Picnic Ground**, at Mile 7 Sandy Beach Road, has picnic tables, firepits, toilets and shelters; wildlife watching; tidepooling; and beautiful driftwood beach setting. Camping is allowed in designated area at Sandy Beach.

Sandy Beach Road (FR 30) follows the east coast of Prince of Wales Island 28 miles north from Thorne Bay to Luck Lake Junction, where FR 3030 leads 9 miles north to Coffman Cove and FH 30 leads 10 miles to junction with FH 23. Driving distance from Thorne Bay to Coffman Cove is 37 miles. It is a scenic drive with mountain views and views of Clarence Strait (water views begin about Mile 6.1 from Thorne Bay).

CAUTION: Sandy Beach Road is a 1-lane, sometimes narrow, winding gravel road with steep grades (not suited for large RVs). There are no services or facilities along the road. Mileposts reflect distance from Control Lake Junction.

CJ 17.1 T 0.1 Paved turnout, Welcome to Thorne Bay sign, picnic tables, litter bins. U.S. Forest Service Thorne Bay Ranger District headquarters.

CJ 17.2 T 0 Thorne Bay Road continues as Shoreline Drive through **THORNE BAY**. Access to The Port (store, gas and diesel), AK-49 Cafe, library/city hall, and to harbor with public restrooms and showers. *See description of Thorne Bay on page 615.*

North Prince of Wales Road/FH 43

North Prince of Wales Road (Forest Highway/FH 43), the "island highway," leads north 78 miles from Control Lake Junction to Labouchere Bay on the northwest corner of the island. This road provides paved access to Coffman Cove, Naukati, Whale Pass, Cavern Lake, El Capitan Cave and Beaver Falls Karst Trail. This is an interesting drive through old-growth forest and clearcut areas, with a good chance of seeing deer and black bear.

Distance from Control Lake Junction (CJ) is followed by the physical milepost (MP). Physical mileposts reflect distance from Thorne Bay to the Coffman Cove turnoff. Beyond that, physical mileposts reflect distance from Hydaburg. Watch for logging trucks and logging operations.

CJ 0 MP 16.8 Control Lake Junction. Large paved turnout on left northbound. Improved wide paved road next 40 miles northbound.

Junction with Big Salt Lake Road and Thorne Bay Road; see logs this section.

CJ 3.7 MP 20.5 Turnout at 787-foot summit on highway.

CJ 9.8 MP 26.5 Double-ended paved turnout to west.

CJ 10.6 MP 27.6 Signed side road leads 5 miles west to Staney Creek (public-use) Cabin. Nightly fee $35–$50. Reserve at www.recreation.gov or phone 1-877-444-6777. Half-mile hike to cabin from parking area on boardwalk. Cutthroat and rainbow trout, Dolly Varden, 4 species of salmon. Ducks, geese along Staney Creek and tidal flats. Bald eagles, gulls and other shore birds in tidal zone. Black bear, Sitka black-tailed deer.

CJ 14.3 MP 31 Large gravel turnout.

CJ 15.2 MP 31.9 Large paved turnout. **Junction** with **Coffman Cove Road** which leads northeast to Coffman Cove *(see description on page 612)*. Paved, widened and improved road with moderate grades and curves. *CAUTION: Watch for deer!* Mileposts on Coffman Cove Road read backwards from the junction: first milepost is Milepost 19 at Mile 0.6 from junction. Immediately past the junction are fossils exposed in the cut rock. Stops along the road include: Log Jam Creek (Mile 4.5/MP 15.8); Honker Divide Canoe Trail (Mile 9/MP 10.7); Hatchery Creek Falls (Mile 11/MP 8.8); junctions at Mile 9.4/MP 10.4 with FR 30 to Luck Lake (19 miles) and Thorne Bay (37 miles) via Sandy Beach Road; Sweetwater Lake trail/cabin access at Mile 13.2/MP 6.7. Stop sign at T junction at Mile 20: Turn left for Coffman Cove, turn right for Luck Lake (5 miles).

Physical mileposts (MP) northbound now show distance from Hydaburg.

CJ 17.4 MP 70.6 Turnouts both sides of road.

CJ 18.6 MP 71.8 Naukati Creek.

CJ 19.7 MP 72.9 Turnout.

CJ 21.6 MP 74.8 Yatuk Creek.

CJ 23.5 MP 76.7 Junction with improved access road west to Naukati (pronounced KNOCK-eh-tee). **NAUKATI BAY** (pop. 115)

was established as a mining camp and then a logging camp for Ketchikan Pulp Co. Today, it has a number of single-family homes located along a labyrinthian road system with many children playing and loose dogs. Naukati's post office, liquor, groceries, gas, propane and diesel available at the Naukati Connection; free RV parking on the waterfront. The boat ramp at Naukati provides access to Tuxekan Narrows and Sea Otter Sound. There is a school and a floatplane dock. In summer, Naukati hosts the popular "mud bogs," a competition involving large trucks and lots of mud. For more information, go to www.naukatibay.com.

CJ 23.6 MP 76.8 Distance marker northbound shows Naukati 3 miles, Whale Pass 25 miles, El Capitan 27 miles.

CJ 26.3 MP 79.5 Clam Creek.

CJ 26.6 MP 79.8 Clam Creek No. 2.

CJ 26.7 MP 79.9 Sarkar Lake to east, a beautiful spot; paved parking, picnic shelter, litter and recycle bins, firepit with benches, outhouse, boat launch, fishing for cutthroat, Dolly Varden and salmon. Sitka black-tailed deer, black bear, otter, mink, beaver and marten in area. This scenic lake is part of the Sarkar Lake Canoe Loop, a 15-mile trail covering 7 lakes, with Sarkar Lake as the terminus. USFS public-use cabin at east end of lake. Skiff here is for registered cabin users only; cabin reservations phone 1-877-444-6777 or go to www.recreation.gov.

CJ 28.3 MP 80.3 Turnout at Sarkar Rapids (Sarkar Lake outlet to salt water); recycle bins. Sockeye salmon in July. Parking south side of bridge; walk down trail. *CAUTION: Watch for bears.*

CJ 28.7 MP 80.7 Deweyville trailhead parking.

Signed 7 to 9 percent downgrades northbound; winding road, easy curves. Intermittent shoulder parking.

CJ 30.6 MP 82.6 Tunga Creek.

CJ 33.9 MP 85.9 Chum Creek.

CJ 39.4 MP 91.4 Junction with gravel access road east 8 miles to the community of Whale Pass and connects with FR 27, which loops back to the highway. About 1 mile east of here is 3-mile-long Neck Lake.

WHALE PASS (pop. 39) was the site of a floating logging camp on Whale Passage. The camp moved out in the early 1980s, but new residents moved in with a state land sale. There is a small grocery store and gas pump (no diesel, irregular hours). Accommodations

at Alaska's Fish Tales Lodge. There is also a school, post office and floatplane dock. WiFi available at community library.

CJ 39.5 MP 91.5 Paved road ends, gravel begins, northbound; no turnaround spot. Road narrows northbound.

CJ 45.5 MP 100.6 Beaver Falls Karst Trail to east; parking, outhouse. This 1-mile boardwalk trail crosses ancient muskegs and cathedral forests, and displays many karst features, such as sinkholes, deep vertical pits, lost rivers and collapsed channels.

CJ 47.5 MP 102.6 Junction with FR 27 which leads east past **Twin Island Lake** to **Whale Pass** (7 miles) and **Exchange Cove** (16 miles). FR 27 junctions with FR 25, that loops back to the island highway at **Milepost CJ 39.4**. There is a parking area and short trail down to **Cavern Lake Cave** overlook 3.4 miles east of here on FR 27. This unusual geological feature is at the lake outlet, where Cavern Lake drains first into a cave, then exits out of a cavern several hundred feet downstream.

CJ 49.9 MP 105 Junction with FR 15 that leads west 1 mile to **El Capitan Cave**. A steep staircase trail (more than 365 steps) leads up to the cave entrance. The Forest Service offers free guided cave tours throughout the summer; phone the Thorne Bay ranger district at (907) 828-3304 for tour times, reservations and other information (must reserve at least 2 days in advance). Open visitation only to the locked gate a short distance within the cave; guided tours only beyond the gate.

CJ 70.6 MP 126.5 Memorial Beach picnic area 1.7 miles north via FR 2086; follow signs to parking area. A short trail leads to picnic tables, pit toilet, memorial plaque and beach. Camping is allowed at the trailhead and on the beach.

This site is a memorial to 12 victims of a 1978 air crash. Good view of Sumner Strait and Kupreanof Island. According to the ADF&G, Memorial Beach is a good spot to look for humpback and killer whales in the strait, harbor seals and Steller sea lions closer to shore. Summer birds include pelagic cormorants, rhinoceros auklets, buffleheads, storm petrels and pigeon guillemots.

CJ 77.6 MP 133.8 Labouchere Bay (sign). Wide sand and rock area covered with debris from the sea. Road circles to right for skiff launch to Port Protection (very rough access).

Sarkar Lake rest area at Mile CJ 26.7 has a picnic area and a firepit. (©Kris Valencia, staff)

Wrangell

The community of Wrangell is located on the shore of Zimovia Strait. (©David L. Ranta, staff)

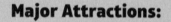

Major Attractions:

©Sharon Nault

Chief Shakes Island, Nemo Point, Anan bears, Stikine River

Located at northwest tip of Wrangell Island on Zimovia Strait; 6 miles southwest of the mouth of the Stikine River Delta; 3 hours by ferry or 32 air miles southeast of Petersburg, the closest major community; and 6 hours by ferry or 85 air miles north of Ketchikan. **Population: 2,448. Emergency Services:** Phone 911 **Police,** phone (907) 874-3304. **Alaska State Troopers,** phone (907) 874-3215. **Fire Department** and **Ambulance,** phone (907) 874-3223. **Maritime Search and Rescue,** contact the Coast Guard at 1-800-478-5555. **Hospital,** Wrangell Medical Center, 310 Bennett St., just off Zimovia Highway, phone (907) 874-7000.

Visitor Information: Stop by the visitor information desk at the James and Elsie Nolan Center on Campbell Drive. The Nolan Center also houses the Wrangell Museum. Short videos are shown on request at the small theatre in the Nolan Center (inquire at visitor information counter or in the museum gift shop). Phone 1-800-367-9745 or (907) 874-3699; www.wrangell.com; wrangell@wrangell.com.

Visitor information is also available at a kiosk in the Stikine Inn (managed seasonally by the Chamber of Commerce).

The U.S. Forest Service maintains several recreation sites and trails along the Wrangell Island road system, as well as remote public-use cabins. Contact the USFS office in Wrangell, 525 Bennett St., phone (907) 874-2323; www.fs.usda.gov/tongass/.

Elevation: Sea level. **Climate:** Mild and moist with slightly less rain than other Southeast communities. Mean annual precipitation is 79.2 inches, with 63.9 inches of snow. Record monthly precipitation, 20.43 inches in October 1961. Average daily maximum temperature in June is 61°F; in July 64°F. Daily minimum in January is 23°F. **Radio:** KSTK-FM 101.7. **Television:** Cable and satellite. **Newspaper:** *Wrangell Sentinel* (weekly).

Private Aircraft: Wrangell airport, adjacent northeast; elev. 44 feet; length 6,000 feet; paved; fuel 100LL, A.

Wrangell is the only Alaska city to have existed under 4 nations and 3 flags—the Stikine Tlingits, the Russians, Great Britain and the United States. Wrangell began in 1834 as a Russian stockade called Redoubt St. Dionysius, built to prevent the Hudson's Bay Co. from fur trading up the rich Stikine River to the northeast. The Russians leased Wrangell Island and the mainland of southeastern Alaska to Hudson's Bay Co. in 1840. Under the British, the stockade was called Fort Stikine.

The post remained under the British flag until Alaska was purchased by the United States in 1867. A year later, the Americans established a military post here, naming it Fort Wrangell after the island, which was named by the Russians after Baron von Wrangel, a governor of the Russian–American Co.

Its strategic location near the mouth of the Stikine River made Wrangell an important supply point not only for fur traders but also for gold seekers following the river route to the goldfields. Today, Wrangell serves as a hub for goods, services and transportation for outlying fishing villages, remote settlement areas and logging camps. The town depended largely on fishing until Japanese interests arrived in the mid-1950s and established a mill (now Silver Bay Logging). Fishing remains one of Wrangell's largest industries and active seafood processing operations are on the waterfront.

Lodging & Services

Accommodations at the **Stikine Inn**

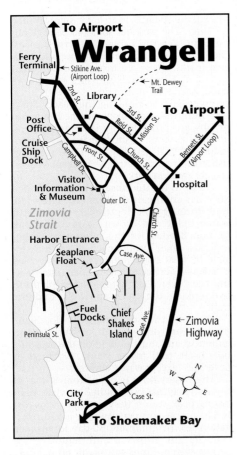

Wrangell

To Airport
Ferry Terminal
Stikine Ave. (Airport Loop)
2nd St.
Library
Mt. Dewey Trail
Post Office
3rd St.
Reid St.
Mission St.
To Airport
Cruise Ship Dock
Campbell Dr.
Front St.
Church St.
Bennett St. (Airport Loop)
Visitor Information & Museum
Outer Dr.
Hospital
Zimovia Strait
Harbor Entrance
Seaplane Float
Church St.
Case Ave.
Fuel Docks
Chief Shakes Island
Case Ave.
Zimovia Highway
Peninsula St.
City Park
Case St.
To Shoemaker Bay

The James and Elsie Nolan Center on Campbell Drive houses the visitor center and Wrangell Museum. *(©David L. Ranta, staff)*

(1-888-874-3388; www.stikineinnak.com); *see ads this page.* The Wrangell Hostel, open June through August, is located in the Presbyterian church; phone (907) 874-3534.

Meals at the Stikine Inn, Marine Pizza, and 2 cafes. Wrangell has 2 supermarkets; gas stations; hardware, marine, sporting goods and auto parts stores; banks; a laundromat; clothing stores and gift shops.

The Nolan Center serves as the local movie theater, showing current feature films on most weekends.

Breakaway Adventures offer scheduled and custom-designed trips to the Anan Bear and Wildlife Observatory as well as to the Stikine River and nearby glaciers. Rent boats and canoes from them for complete flexibility in plans.

Irene Ingle Public Library, just up from the ferry terminal on Second Street, has internet, computers, a copy machine, paperback exchange and public restrooms. Open Monday and Friday 10 A.M. to noon and 1–5 P.M.; Tuesday–Thursday 1–7 P.M.; and Saturday 9 A.M. to 5 P.M. Closed Sunday. Access free public WiFi outside the library, 24/7.

Camping

The city-owned **Shoemaker RV Park and Campground** provides tent and RV camp-

ing at Shoemaker Bay Recreation Area, **Milepost 4.5** Zimovia Highway. There are 6 tent sites located adjacent to the creek and park area. RV sites are located in the harbor with some overflow sites in the harbor parking lot. There is a total of 25 RV spaces: 16 with electricity in the north parking area, and the 9 harbor parking lot sites with no hookups. Potable water, dump station and restrooms adjacent harbor parking lot sites. Camping fees are $20/night for non-hookup sites, $30/night for sites with hookups. 10-day limit for RVs, 5-day limit for tent campers. Phone (907) 874-2444; www.wrangell.com/recreation/shoemaker-rv-park.

Tent camping only at City Park, located at **Milepost 1.7** Zimovia Highway. There are restrooms, tables and firepits. Tent camping is restricted to 48 hours; no tents in picnic shelters. Because overnight parking is prohibited at the city park, tent sites are restricted to bicyclists or walk-ins. Nice views during the day off of this park's loop for travelers.

Nemo Point USFS Recreation Area, 13.6 miles south of town via the Zimovia Highway, has 4 recreation sites for tent campers and RVs with dramatic views of Zimovia Strait. No fees, no reservations. Steep and narrow gravel access road to sites; NOT good for large RVs. An information board at Mile 0.5 on the access road has site maps and information about site accessibility, summer weekly interpretive programs and other campground activities.

Another option is staying at Wrangell's USFS public-use cabin. The cabin fee is $45/night plus a $9 reservation fee. The

One of many displays at the very comprehensive survey of culture and history in the Wrangell Museum. (©David L. Ranta, staff)

Middle Ridge Cabin is located 19 miles from Wrangell. Cabin is at 1,500 feet elevation and access may be limited seasonally because of snow. For details, contact the Forest Service office in Wrangell, phone (907) 874-2323; www.fs.usda.gov/tongass/. Cabin reservations at www.recreation.gov or phone 1-877-444-6777.

Transportation

Air: Daily scheduled jet service is provided by Alaska Airlines to other Southeast cities with through service to Seattle and Anchorage. Charter services available.

The airport terminal is 1.1 miles from the ferry terminal via Evergreen Avenue or 1.1 miles from Zimovia Highway via Bennett Street. Taxi to town or check with local hotels about courtesy van service.

Ferry: Alaska Marine Highway serves Wrangell. The ferry terminal is at the end of Second/Church streets. Walk or take a taxi from the ferry terminal to town. Terminal facilities include ticket office, waiting room and vehicle waiting area; phone (907) 874-3711. Reservations phone 1-800-642-0066. Visit www.ferryalaska.com for tariffs and schedules.

Car Rental: Available at the airport from Practical Rent-A-Car (907) 874-3975.

Taxi: Clearwater Cab, phone (907) 660-7778.

Highways: Zimovia Highway (see log this section). Logging roads have opened up most of Wrangell Island to motorists. Check with the USFS office at 525 Bennett St. for a copy of the Motor Vehicles Use Map. Write USDA Forest Service, Wrangell Ranger District, Box 51, Wrangell, AK 99929; phone (907) 874-2323.

Private Boats: Transient moorage downtown on Reliance Float near Shakes Tribal House, and at Mile 1.4 Zimovia Highway at Heritage Harbor. If you are traveling to Wrangell by boat, contact harbor master for tie-up space, phone (907) 874-3736 or 874-3051 or radio VHF Ch. 16.

Attractions

Wrangell Museum, in the Nolan Center at 296 Campbell Dr., features exhibits highlighting Wrangell's diverse history. Exhibit areas focus on Native culture; fur trade and exploration; the military; mining, fishing, timber; and 20th century topics. The oldest known Tlingit house posts in Southeast Alaska are on display, along with a spruce root and cedar bark basket collection. Museum hours are 10 A.M. to 5 P.M. Monday–Saturday from April 1 to Sept. 30; noon to 5 P.M. Friday and Saturday in winter. Phone (907) 874-3770; email museum@wrangell.com. Admission charged (children 6 and under free). Current movies are shown Friday–Sunday at the theater in Nolan Center.

Chief Shakes Island and Tribal House, in the middle of Wrangell Harbor, is reached by boardwalk. Constructed in 1940, by the Civilian Conservation Corp, it is a replica of the original 19th century Tribal House. The Tribal House was reconstructed in 2012, using local carvers and re-dedicated in 2013. The Tribal House is open when cruise ships are in port during the summer or by appointment. Phone (907) 305-0404 for details. Admission is charged.

St. Rose of Lima Catholic Church is a 0.2-mile walk from the Ferry Terminal up Second/Church streets. This picturesque church is the oldest Roman Catholic parish in Alaska, founded May 2, 1879.

Just beyond is the First Presbyterian Church, which has a red neon cross, 1 of 2 in the world that serve as navigational aids. This was the first church in Wrangell and is one of the oldest Protestant churches in Alaska (founded in 1877 and built in 1879). In summer it doubles as the Wrangell Hostel.

Muskeg Meadows Golf Course is a USGA regulation 9-hole golf course with a 250-yard driving range, putting green and pro-shop. Opening tournament in May coincides with the Stikine River Birding Festival. Muskeg Meadows hosts tournaments almost every weekend during the summer. For details, phone (907) 874-4653; www.wrangellalaskagolf.com.

Petroglyph Beach State Historic Park is located a half-mile from the ferry terminal via Stikine Avenue (watch for sign; limited parking). The park has some 40 petroglyphs (ancient designs carved into rock faces) that may be found between low and high tide marks. These are thought to be Tlingit in origin. A boardwalk provides access from cul-de-sac to an observation deck with interpretive signs overlooking the beach. Stairs lead from the deck to the beach. The petroglyphs are protected by state and federal antiquities laws: Visitors may only photograph the real petroglyphs. Make rubbings using the replica petroglyphs displayed on the observation deck.

Anan Wildlife Observatory is located 30 miles southeast of Wrangell. From late June through mid-September, visitors can watch black and brown bears catch pink salmon headed for the salmon spawning grounds. Anan (pronounced an-an) is accessible by boat or floatplane plane only. The U.S. Forest Service manages Anan, maintaining the covered deck/observation platform overlooking the creek and falls, and the trail.

Visitors to Anan, arriving by floatplane or boat, are dropped off at the "lagoon entrance" and must walk in on the half-mile boardwalk trail (some stairs). No food or beverages (except water) allowed.

The observatory is open from 8 A.M. to 6 P.M. A day pass is required to visit Anan during peak season (July 5–August 25); cost is $10 per person per day plus a $10 reservation fee. (A minimum 30-day in advance cancellation allows a full refund.) The permit system limits visitors to 60 per day. If you visit the observatory with a guide or outfitter, the permit may be included in the cost of the trip. The Forest Service office in Wrangell has more information about the permit system and a list of guides and outfitters permitted to transport visitors to Anan; phone (907) 874-2323. Purchase permits online at www.recreation.gov. 🅜

The Stikine River Delta lies north of Wrangell within the Stikine–LeConte Wilderness and is accessible only by boat or plane. The Stikine is the fastest free flowing, navigable river in North America, and can be rafted, canoed or run by skiff or jetboat. Floatplane and jetboat charters for both sightseeing and drop-offs at put-in sites for river runners, are available in Wrangell.

The Stikine River plays host to a stunning migration of birds each spring, according to the Alaska Dept. of Fish and Game. The second highest concentration of bald eagles in the world occurs on the Stikine during the annual spring run of eulachon. Grasses and sedges on the Stikine Flats at the mouth of the river attract up to 10,000 snow geese each year. The Stikine River Delta is a critical refueling stop for millions of shorebirds during their annual migration. These birds feed on tiny invertebrates and small fish before continuing on to their Arctic breeding grounds. Great bird watching, but like all migratory bird watching, timing is everything and the birds have their own schedule. **The Stikine River Birding Festival** celebrates spring and the arrival of the birds in late spring. Check with the local visitor's bureau or Forest Service office when planning a birding trip. 🅜

LeConte Glacier, also within the Stikine-LeConte Wilderness, is at the head of LeConte Bay, just north of the Stikine River Delta. It is the southernmost tidewater glacier in North America. Charter trips for sightseeing LeConte Glacier are available locally.

Garnet Ledge, a rocky outcrop on the south bank of the Stikine River Delta at Garnet Creek, is 7.5 miles from Wrangell Harbor, reached at high tide by small boat. Garnet, a semiprecious stone, can be found embedded in the ledge here. The garnet ledge is on land deeded to the Presbytery of Alaska from the Southeast Council of the Boy Scouts of America (who had previously acquired the land from the late Fred Hanford, former mayor of Wrangell). Garnets are sold by children at the docks when ships and ferries are in port. Anyone who is not a child from Wrangell must get a permit to dig garnets. Contact the Presbyterian Church in Wrangell.

Hiking Trails. There are several popular trails close to town. The Mount Dewey Trail begins at Third Street and leads to the top of 400-foot Mount Dewey, overlooking the downtown area and Zimovia Strait. Volunteer Park Trails are located off Bennett Street behind the elementary school, near the Little League ballfields. This is an easy loop walk through muskeg, shrub forests and old-growth forest.

Rainbow Falls is a popular local trail that begins across from the Shoemaker Bay Recreation Area at **Milepost 4.6** Zimovia Highway. It is a steep 0.7-mile trail to a scenic waterfall. Institute Creek trail intersects with Rainbow Falls trail at Mile 0.6 and leads 2.7 miles to viewpoint and shelter overlooking Shoemaker Bay and Zimovia Strait. Institute Creek Trail also intersects with Wrangell High Country trail, which leads to 2 high-elevation shelters.

Nemo Point USFS Recreation Area, 13.6 miles south of town via the Zimovia Highway, offers dramatic views of Zimovia Strait from campsites and overlooks. From the end of the Zimovia Highway and from the Nemo Point road there is access to the island's extensive forest road system. These narrow logging roads provide access to lakes, trails and campsites. Favorite destinations for locals include Earl West Cove recreation site; Highbush Lake; and Thoms and Long lakes (both walk-in).

USFS cabins in the surrounding area are a major attraction here. There are 23 USFS public-use cabins scattered throughout the region that are accessible by air or by boat. The U.S. Forest Service office is open 8 A.M. to 4:30 P.M. weekdays; 525 Bennett St., phone (907) 874-2323; or visit www.fs.usda.gov/tongass/.

AREA FISHING: Pats Lake and **Highbush Lake** are accessible by road. **Thoms Lake** and **Long Lake** are accessible via road and trail. Fly in to **Kunk Lake, Anan Lake, Marten Lake, Virginia Lake, Eagle Lake** and **Salmon Bay** (on Prince of Wales Island). **Stikine River** near Wrangell (closed to freshwater chinook salmon fishing), Dolly Varden to 22 inches, and cutthroat to 18 inches, best in midsummer to fall; spring steelhead to 12 lbs., coho salmon 8 to 12 lbs., September and October.

Saltwater fishing near Wrangell for chinook salmon, 10 to 30 lbs., best in May and June. There are bait, minimum size and other restrictions (see current sportfishing regulations). Stop by the Dept. of Fish and Game at 215 Front St. for details. Wrangell Salmon Derby runs from mid-May to mid-June; occasional chinook to 50-plus lbs. ⬅

Zimovia Highway

Zimovia Highway leads 13.8 miles south of the ferry terminal where it connects with the island's Forest Service road system. A paved walking and biking path parallels the Zimovia Highway to Mile 5.2.
Distance from ferry terminal is shown.

0 Alaska Marine Highway ferry terminal at end of Second Street, which becomes Church Street then Zimovia Highway. Paved bike path to Mile 5.2 Zimovia Highway.

0.1 Wrangell Public Library.

0.2 Rose of Lima Catholic Church

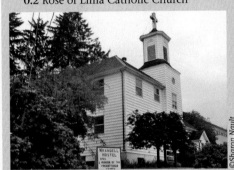

©Sharon Nault

0.3 Wrangell Hostel is housed at the First Presbyterian Church in summer.

0.4 Wrangell High School/Middle School.

0.5 Church Street/Wrangell Avenue junctions with Bennett Street and Zimovia Highway. Access to Wrangell Medical Center. Bennett Street (Airport Loop) leads north to the airport and back around to the ferry terminal.

0.6 Public Safety Building, fire station.

1.4 Heritage Harbor; transient moorage and commercial fishing vessels.

1.7 Loop road along shore accesses City Park; picnic area with shelters, firepits, restrooms, litter barrels. Tent camping only; 48-hour limit. ⛺

2 Turnout with public parking and beach access to west. Watch for bald eagles, shorebirds and great blue herons in Zimovia Strait.

3.3 Gravel turnouts.

4.6 Shoemaker Bay Recreation Area has 2 adjacent lots that make up the **Shoemaker RV Park & Campground**. 16 sites with electric hook-ups. Sites are along shoreline, some with views. Very few level sites. Restrooms are in the Shoemaker Harbor Parking Lot. Pay area is small green box near big white sign. Envelopes are in green box, fill them out and put into brown tube with slit for registration; $30/night camping fee. While staying in the RV park, you have free use of the city pool, gym and showers. ⛺

Shoemaker RV Park & Campgrounds. See display ad on page 619.

4.7 Shoemaker Bay Harbor. The parking lot here has 9 sites (no hook-ups/$20) and 6 tent sites. Pull in grassy area between painted log stumps. Pay area is small green box near big white sign. Envelopes are in green box, fill them out and put into brown tube with slit for registration. Parking tip: be watchful of sinking in grassy areas if it is wet. Restrooms, dump station. ⛺

Trailhead for **Rainbow Falls/Institute Creek/High Country trails** on east side of Zimovia Highway across from harbor entrance.

4.8 Tennis court, horseshoe pits and children's playground.

4.9 Institute Creek. Watch for spawning chum in July.

5 Paved turnout with beach access.

5.2 Shoemaker Bay Loop road. Bike path ends.

5.8 Shoemaker Bay Loop road.

6.7 Scenic turnout.

7.6 Turnout.

8.2 Turnout; access to **8 Mile Beach** (aka Agate Beach) tide permitting. This undeveloped recreation area has a beautiful beach.

8.8 Small paved turnout.

10.6 Turnoff to FR 6259 which leads 0.4 mile to **Pat's Lake**; watch for migrating trumpeter swans in early spring. One-mile trail from lake to estuary at mouth of Pat's Creek. Picnic and camping areas on short spur at turnoff. ⛺

11 Pat's Creek. The estuary at the mouth of Pat's Creek is a good place to watch spawning pinks, late July to early August. A 1-mile trail follows the creek from the estuary to Pat's Lake. Watch for American dippers, Sitka black-tailed deer and the occasional black bear along the trail. 🏃

13.3 McCormack Creek bridge. Small, active sawmill east side of road.

©Sharon Nault

13.6 Turnoff for **Nemo Point Recreation Area**. Steep and narrow gravel access road to sites; not recommended for large RVs. An information board at Mile 0.5 on the access road has site maps and information about site accessibility, summer weekly interpretive programs and other campground activities. Access road continues to Yunshookuh Campsite (Mile 0.7), 3 Sisters Overlook/Campsite (Mile 1.5), Anita Bay Overlook/Campsite (Mile 2.3) and Highline Campsite (Mile 3.5). Fantastic views of Zimovia Strait and north Etolin Island. Picnic tables, firewood, fire grills and outhouses each site. Access road continues for miles to remote campsites (no fee sites available) and lakes along the Wrangell Island forest road system. Highbush Lake, Thoms Lake and Long Lake have skiffs for public use. Check with USFS office in Wrangell for more information. ⬅⛺

13.8 Two-lane paved road ends just beyond Tongass National Forest sign. *Large vehicles use turnaround at "Road Narrows" sign.* One-lane gravel FR 6265 begins and connects with other Forest Roads. A map showing island roads with recreation sites and trails is available from the USFS office in Wrangell.

Watch for logging trucks and other heavy equipment.

Petersburg

Iconic Sons of Norway Hall is on the National Register of Historic Places. *(©David L. Ranta, staff)*

Major Attractions:

©Sharon Nault

Norwegian Heritage, Le Conte Glacier, Whale Watching

Located on the northern tip of Mitkof Island at the northern end of Wrangell Narrows, midway between Juneau and Ketchikan. **Population:** 3,147. **Emergency Services: Borough Police, Fire Department and Ambulance,** phone 911. **Alaska State Troopers,** phone (907) 225-5118. **Hospital and**

Clinic, Petersburg Medical Center, 2nd and Fram St., phone (907) 772-4291. **Poison Control** (statewide), phone 1-800-222-1222. **Maritime Search and Rescue**: Contact the Coast Guard at 1-800-478-5555. Harbormaster, phone (907) 772-4688, or VHF Channel 16/9.

Visitor Information: The Petersburg Visitor Information Center is located in a historic ranger station at 1st and Fram streets. The 24-foot by 28-foot wooden structure holds a surprising amount of information, including an interactive marine mammal kiosk. The center is open all year. Hours are Monday–Friday 9 A.M. to 5 P.M.; Saturday 11 A.M. to 4 P.M.; Sunday noon to 4 P.M., May 13 to Sept. 8; Monday–Friday from 10 A.M. to 2 P.M., Sept. 9–30 and April 1–May 12; and 10 A.M. to 2 P.M., Mondays, Wednesdays and Fridays only from Oct. 1–March 31. Write Petersburg Visitor Information Center, Box 649, Petersburg AK 99833; phone (907) 772-4636; www.petersburg.org.

Clausen Museum, 2nd and Fram streets, phone (907) 772-3598. Alaska Dept. of Fish and Game, State Office Building, Sing Lee Alley; open 8 A.M. to 4:30 P.M., Monday through Friday, phone (907) 772-3801. Area maps and general information on U.S. Forest Service lands available at the Petersburg Ranger District office in the Federal Building downtown, open weekdays 8 A.M. to 5 P.M. and at the Visitor Center.

Elevation: Sea level. **Climate:** Average daily maximum temperature in July,

64°F; daily minimum in January, 20°F. All-time high, 84°F in 1933; record low, -19°F in 1947. Mean annual precipitation, 110 inches; mostly as rain. **Radio:** KFSK-FM 100.9. **Television:** Alaska Rural Communication Service, Channel 15; KTOO (PBS) Channel 10 and cable channels. Newspaper: *Petersburg Pilot* (weekly/Thursday).

Private Aircraft: James A. Johnson Airport (PSG), 1 mile southeast; elev. 107 feet; length 6,000 feet; asphalt; fuel 100, A. Seaplane base 0.5 mile from downtown.

Petersburg boasts the largest home-based fishing fleet in Alaska and is also well known for its shrimp, crab, salmon, herring and other fish products. Many families here depend on the fishing industry for their livelihood.

The town grew up around a sawmill, dock and salmon cannery built in 1897-99 by Peter Buschmann, after whom the town was named. The post office was established in 1900. Buschmann was followed by other Norwegian immigrants who came to fish and work in the cannery and sawmill. Since then the cannery has operated continuously (with rebuilding, expansion and different owners) and is now known as Petersburg Fisheries Inc., a division of Icicle Seafoods Inc. Petersburg Fisheries shares the waterfront with two other canneries, other cold storage plants and several other fish processing facilities.

The Borough Hall and the Federal Building are both located downtown. Nearby, at the corner of Nordic and Haugen, are 2 healing totem poles, one commemorating the Eagle Clan and the other, the Raven Clan. The poles were carved by Sitka carver Tommy Joseph.

Lodging & Services

Lodging downtown at 2 hotels/motels and several bed and-breakfasts; visit www.petersburg.org for listings. Dining downtown at Coastal Cold Storage and Deli, The Salty Pantry, Papa Bear's, Inga's Galley, Helse, and El Rincon. The 5-block-long downtown commercial area on Main Street (Nordic Drive) and old town Sing Lee Alley has a grocery store; 2 coffee shops, 2 hardwares, marine and fishing supply stores; drugstore; bookstore, a travel agency (**Viking Travel Inc**.); banks (Wells Fargo and First Bank); a liquor store, 2 bars; fresh fish market; gift shops, art galleries; and clothing stores specializing in both Alaska and Norwegian items. Auto repair, towing, gas and diesel at the corner of 2nd and Haugen. Additional vehicle and marine fuel can be found at the corner of South Nordic Drive and Dock Street.

Petersburg has a post office and 13 churches. The spacious Hammer and Wikan grocery/deli is located a half-mile from downtown on Haugen Drive.

The public library is located at the corner of South 2nd and Haugen Drive. The community gym, activities and pool complex is within the Petersburg School District Campus. A community gym with racquetball courts, climbing wall and weight room is located between the high school and elementary school on Charles W. Street off 3rd street. The Petersburg Aquatic Center, with 2 pools and water slide, is located at the school and offers frequent open swims. Parks and recreation also offer kayak, snowshoe and cross-country ski rentals. Phone Petersburg Parks and Recreation at (907) 772-3392. Additional parking lot, RV dump station and facility entrance located at 500 N. 3rd St., off Wrangell Avenue.

Camping

Enjoy RV campsites with hookups and a general store at **The Trees RV Park**, Mile 10.2 Mitkof Highway. The nearest public campground is Ohmer Creek USFS Campground (unmaintained), at Mile 21.4 Mitkof Highway, with 10 sites (RVs to 35 feet). There are 20 campsites at the upgraded Green's Camp Campground on Sumner Strait, Mile 26.1 Mitkof Highway. (See Mitkof Highway log on page 625 for details.)

Transportation

Air: Daily scheduled jet service by Alaska Airlines, (907) 772-4255, to major Southeast cities and Seattle, WA, with connections to Anchorage and Fairbanks. Daily connections to Juneau and Ketchikan by Island Air Express; 1-888-387-8989. Other local air services include Pacific Wing (907) 772-4258 and Nordic Air (907) 518-0244.

The airport is located 1 mile from the Federal Building on Haugen Drive. It has a ticket counter and waiting room. Hotel cour-

Canneries, cold storage and fish processing plants dominate the waterfront here.
(©Sharon Nault)

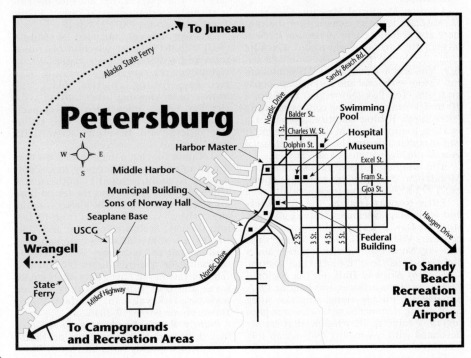

tesy van and taxi service available.

Ferry: Alaska Marine Highway ferries dock at the ferry terminal at **Milepost 0.8** Mitkof Highway. It is not too long a walk to downtown from the ferry terminal unless you arrive late at night and it is raining or you have a lot of luggage. Terminal facilities include ticket office, waiting room and vehicle waiting area; phone (907) 772-3855. Reservations 1-800-642-0066. Visit www.ferryalaska.com for tariffs and schedules.

Car Rental: Allstar Car Rentals at Scandia House Hotel (907) 772-4281; UHaul at Petersburg Motors (907) 772-3223.

Taxi: Island Cab (907) 518-1279; City Cab (907) 772-2489. Highways: The 34-mile Mitkof Highway (see log this section); 21-mile Three Lakes Loop Road; and Sandy Beach Road.

Cruise Ships: Cruise ships dock at Petersburg's South Harbor, Petro Marine dock and at the Drive Down Float.

Private Boats: There are 3 boat harbors that can accommodate up to a 200 ft vessel. Transient vessels check in with harbormaster; VHF Channel 16/9, or phone (907) 772-4688.

LeConte Glacier is a major area attractions. Tour boats may be chartered out of Petersburg to view the glacier. (©Sharon Nault)

Attractions

Clausen Memorial Museum, 203 Fram St., displays artifacts representing the cannery and fisheries, items reflecting its Norwegian heritage, a world-record 126.5-lb. chinook salmon, the Cape Decision light station lens and a Tlingit canoe. The museum has a store with local and regional art, books and gifts. The Fisk (Norwegian for fish), a 10-foot bronze sculpture commemorating Petersburg's fishing tradition, stands in a working fountain in front of the museum. It was completed during the Alaska centennial year of 1967 by sculptor Carson Boysen.

The museum is open 10 A.M. to 5 P.M., Monday to Saturday in summer. Phone (907) 772-3598 for more information.

Little Norway Festival, the third weekend each May, celebrates Norwegian Constitution Day. It features old-country dress, contests, Vikings Valkyries, a Viking ship, dancing, Norwegian pastries, a parade and a Norwegian "fish feed" for locals and visitors.

Sons of Norway Hall, on the National Register of Historic Places, was built in 1912. Situated on pilings along Sing Lee Alley overlooking Hammer Slough (a favorite photography subject), its window shutters are decorated with rosemaling (Norwegian tole painting).

Fisherman's Memorial Park, next to the Sons of Norway Hall, commemorates those townspeople lost at sea. The Viking ship Valhalla, next to the memorial, is another favorite photo subject.

Whale Watching. Of the estimated 6,000 humpback whales in the North Pacific, approximately 2,000 feed in Southeast Alaska during the summer, and nearly half of those enter Frederick Sound.

A whale watching cruise tour out of Petersburg provides consistent and often spectacular whale viewing. These whale watching trips start in May and continue through the summer, with July and August the prime viewing time for humpbacks. Hundreds of humpbacks congregate in Frederick Sound and lower Stephen's Passage. Other large marine mammals to see are killer whales, Dall's porpoises, harbor seals and Steller sea lions. Bird watching on these trips includes marbled murrelets, scoters and pigeon guillemots. Charters generally take 6–14 people per trip; advance booking is strongly recommended. Contact Viking Travel, Inc., phone (907) 772-3818.

Viking Travel, Inc. 101 N. Nordic, (907) 772-3818. Great selection of cruises, tours and activities all over Alaska. Whale-watching, sea kayaking, LeConte Glacier Bay, fishing charters, black and brown bear viewing, river rafting, Glacier Bay tours. Independent travel packages for all Alaska. Ferry and airline reservations and ticketing. www.Alaska FerryVacations.com. [ADVERTISEMENT]

LeConte Glacier, a major area attraction, lies 25 miles east of Petersburg in LeConte Bay. It is the continent's southernmost active tidewater glacier and the fastest flowing glacier in the world. The glacier continually "calves," creating icefalls from its face into the bay. Seals are common and killer whales are sometimes seen. Helicopters, small aircraft and boats may be chartered in Petersburg (or Wrangell) to see LeConte Glacier. Tongass Kayak Adventures offers guided kayak and boat trips to LeConte Glacier; www.tongasskayak.com. Contact Viking Travel, phone (907) 772-3818.

Sandy Beach Road. Make a 4.5-mile loop drive beginning downtown on Nordic Drive, which quickly turns into Sandy Beach Road. First stop (and also an easy 0.1-mile walk from downtown) is Eagle's Roost Park, which has picnic tables and usually a couple of eagles roosting in the trees.

Continue on Sandy Beach Road 1.4 miles to Outlook Park, renovated in 2015, this park is tucked in between waterfront homes, with a picnic table and easy access to beach. Outlook has a small parking area, shelter and 2 spotting scopes. Look for humpback whales in Frederick Sound from June through September.

Continue 1.1 miles beyond Outlook Park to Sandy Beach Park, which offers picnic tables, 3 shelters, firepits, playground, volleyball court and a sandy beach. Parking is a little more generous at Sandy Beach Park, where there are roadside spaces and a gravel parking lot (not recommended for RVs). This park is located at the junction with Haugen Drive, which takes you 1.7 miles back to downtown Petersburg.

Across from Sandy Beach Park, the Raven Trail features about a mile of wheelchair-accessible path heading up towards Raven's Roost Cabin. At the top of the mile-long trail is a beautiful view of Frederick Sound, with benches to sit on.

U.S. Forest Service public-use cabins, canoe/kayaking routes and hiking trails may be accessed from Petersburg, which is the administrative center for the Stikine Area of Tongass National Forest. For information, stop by the USFS office in the Federal Building, or write the Petersburg Ranger District, P.O. Box 1328, Petersburg, AK 99833; phone (907) 772-3871; www.fs.usda.gov/tongass/.

The Visitor Center also has a kiosk with information on forest service cabins, trails and other recreation in the Tongass.

Take a drive. The 34-mile-long Mitkof Highway and 21-mile Three Lakes Loop Road may only add up to 55 miles of road system, but there are quite a few interesting spots to stop along these routes.

Watch for Sitka black-tailed deer along the road system, especially in June and July when does bring their fawns to feed on lush roadside plants. Fawns sometimes bed down right on the road, so be alert while driving.

The boardwalk trail (handicap-accessible) at Blind River Rapids, **Milepost 14.2** Mitkof Highway, is not only a popular destination for fishermen, it also offers a close-up view of muskeg. Muskeg covers 10 percent of Alaska.

Salmon migration and spawning may be observed July through September at Falls Creek bridge and fish ladder, see **Milepost 10.7** Mitkof Highway.

Three Lakes Loop Road makes a nice side trip and an opportunity to experience a temperate rainforest. Stop in at the Visitor Center for a map of this area. This narrow, winding gravel road loops off the Mitkof Highway between **Mileposts 10.6** and **20.4,** providing access to boardwalk trails. Spectacular view of the mainland from LeConte Glacier Overlook. Rental cars are not allowed on Three Lakes Loop Road.

And make sure to stop for a picnic at one of Mitkof Highway's 2 scenic picnic sites. Man-Made Hole at **Milepost 19.7** is a beautiful spot, with a handicap-accessible boardwalk trail, picnic tables and shelter. Blind Slough, at **Milepost 17.2,** is adjacent the Crystal Lake Fish Hatchery.

The Crystal Lake Fish Hatchery produces coho and chinook salmon for local waters. No tours, but hatchery personnel will answer questions. Visitors welcome Monday through Friday from 8 A.M. to 4 P.M., and Saturday and Sunday from 8 A.M. to 2 P.M.

AREA FISHING: Salmon, steelhead, cutthroat and Dolly Varden fishing at Falls Creek, Blind Slough and Blind River Rapids (see log of Mitkof Highway this page). Salmon can be caught in the harbor area and Scow Bay area. (Rapid tidal currents in front of the town necessitate the use of an outboard motor.) Dolly Varden can be caught from the beach north of town and from downtown docks. Petersburg Creek, directly across Wrangell Narrows from downtown within Petersburg Creek–Duncan Salt Chuck Wilderness Area, also offers good fishing. Contact the Sport Fish Division of the Alaska Dept. of Fish and Game in Petersburg at (907) 772-5231 for more information. Petersburg King Salmon Derby takes place Memorial Day weekend. Check with the Visitor Information Center for details.

Mitkof Highway

The major road on Mitkof Island, Mitkof Highway leads 33.8 miles south from downtown Petersburg to the Stikine River Delta at the south end of the island. The highway is paved to **Milepost 25**; wide gravel to road end. Walking/biking path along waterfront to Mile 1.8, paved shoulder to Mile 2.8. *CAUTION: Watch for deer.*

Distance from downtown Petersburg is shown.

0 Federal Building and totem poles at Nordic Drive and Haugen.

0.1 Bridge over Hammer Slough, an intertidal estuary.

0.4 South Harbor parking with a small viewing area, benches and information boards about humpback whales.

0.8 Alaska Marine Highway ferry terminal, office and waiting area on right.

1 Bike path next 1.7 miles southbound.

2.9 RV campground on Scowbay Loop Road; hookups.

5 Three small turnouts between Mile 5 and 6.

6.1 Large paved turnout with view.

7.4 Twin Creek.

©David L. Ranta, staff

10.2 The Trees RV Park and General Store. See display ad on page 623.

10.6 Junction with **Three Lakes Loop Road.** This 21-mile-long, hilly, narrow, winding gravel road (not recommended for large RVs) loops from **Milepost 10.6** to **Milepost 20.4** Mitkof Highway. (Locals use the entrance at **Milepost 20.4** to reach hiking trails on this side road.) There are no services available along the road, but there are boardwalk hiking trails to 3 lakes: Sand, Hill and Crane. Rowboats available for public-use at the lakes.

Distance marker at junction shows Sand Lake Trail 13.9 miles, Hill Lake Trail 14.3 miles, Crane Lake Trail 14.7 miles. The turnoff for LeConte Glacier Overlook, a picnic site with a spectacular view of the mainland, is located 12.1 miles from this junction on Three Lakes Loop Road. The Visitor Center has maps of this area.

10.7 Falls Creek and new viewing platforms that overlook the fish ladder. "This is a fantastically beautiful place, well-worth the stop, even if there are no fish present" according to our contributing editor, Sharon Nault. See steelhead, April and May; pinks below falls in August; cohos, August and September; Dolly Varden and cutthroat late summer and fall. No fishing within 300 feet of fish ladder. *CAUTION: Watch for bears.*

10.9 Turnoff for Papke's Landing boat launch (0.5 mile).

The Mitkof Highway rewards drivers who continue to its end with views like this one.
(©David L. Ranta, staff)

14 Entering Tongass National Forest.

14.2 Blind River Rapids very large parking area and ¼-mile trail; outhouse. Boardwalk trail through muskeg meadow (pictured below) to Blind River Rapids fishing area. Wheelchair-accessible boardwalk loop. Hatchery steelhead, mid-April to mid-May; chinook, June to late July; pinks, July and August; coho, mid-August to October. Also Dolly Varden and cutthroat trout.

©David L. Ranta, staff

16.1 Blind Slough Trumpeter Swan Observatory. Covered platform with interpretive signs; bring binoculars or spotting scope for best viewing. Hundreds of trumpeter swans stop to feed and rest here between mid-October and December before resuming their southern migration. Up to 75 swans spend the winter here each year. Also watch for mergansers, mallards, geese and bald eagles in summer. A flock of about 20 trumpeter swans winter here.

17.2 Turnoff for short road to Blind Slough Picnic Area and fish hatchery. A large picnic area with many nice tables, large shelter and pit toilets; no overnight camping. This is a very popular place for locals. Swimming and grassy areas, short walk over bridge to hatchery. Area is closed at 10 P.M. **Crystal Lake Fish Hatchery** is open for visiting, but no tours (360) 928-7181. Fishing in Blind Slough for cutthroat and Dolly Varden in summer; coho, mid-August to mid-September; chinook, June and July. Check with ADF&G for current regulations;

phone (907) 772-3801.

19.7 Turnoff on short loop road for **Man-Made Hole** picnic area with tables, firepits, toilets, swimming and trail. Beautiful spot. Fishing for cutthroat and Dolly Varden year-round; best summer/fall.

20.4 Junction with 21-mile-long **Three Lakes Loop Road** (see description at **Milepost 10.6**). Distance marker at junction shows Crane Lake Trail 6.3 miles, Hill Lake Trail 6.7 miles, Sand Lake Trail 7.2 miles. The turnoff for LeConte Glacier Overlook, a picnic site with a spectacular view of the mainland, is 8.3 miles from this junction.

21.2 Ohmer Creek nature trail, 1½-mile loop; first 0.3 mile is barrier-free.

21.4 Katelyn Ohmer Markley Bridge crosses Ohmer Creek. **Ohmer Creek USFS Campground**, 10 unmaintained sites in trees on half-mile loop road; tables, firepits. Open spring to fall. Accommodates RVs to 35 feet. Trout fishing July and August; pinks August to September.

22.7 Leaving Tongass National Forest.

24.2 Site of Blind Slough USFS Log Transfer Facility, huge parking area. Fishing from skiff for coho, mid-August to mid-September. Fishing from shore for chinook. Popular kayaking spot.

26.1 Access to Green's Camp campground on Sumner Strait.

28 Wilson Creek recreation area (not signed); picnic table, grills, toilet, parking.

28.6 Banana Point dock/boat launch; 0.2-mile access road to concrete boat ramp, toilet, gravel loop, parking.

29.3 Pavement ends, gravel begins. Highway continues along Sumner Straight.

31 Stikine River mud flats, visible at low tide. Part of the Stikine River Delta, where Dry Strait meets Sumner Strait.

32.9 Blaquerie Point Boat Launch (Borough of Petersburg) to access Stikine River; large parking area, picnic tables, toilet, firepits, garbage service.

33.8 Road ends with turn-around.

Sitka

Sitka, located on the west coast of Baranof Island, was capital of Russian Alaska in 1808. ©David L. Ranta, staff

Major Attractions:

©Kris Valencia, staff

Sitka National Historic Park, Baranof Castle Hill State Historic Site, Sitka Summer Music Festival

Located on the west side of Baranof Island, 95 air miles southwest of Juneau, 185 air miles northwest of Ketchikan; 2.5 hours flying time from Seattle, WA. **Population:** 9,084. **Emergency Services: Alaska State Troopers, City Police, Fire Department, and Ambulance,** phone 911. **Hospitals:** Sitka Community, 209 Moller Ave., phone (907) 747-3241; SEARHC Mount Edgecumbe, 222 Tongass Dr., phone (907) 966-2411. **Maritime Search and Rescue,** phone the Coast Guard at (907) 463-2000 or the operations center for Sitka at (907) 966-5447.

Visitor Information: Year-round visitor information center is located at 104 Lake St; phone (907) 747-8604; www.visitsitka. org. Summer information desk—open when cruise ships are in port—is located at Harrigan Centennial Hall, 330 Harbor Dr.

USDA Forest Service information at the Sitka Ranger District, 2108 Halibut Point Rd., Sitka, AK 99835; phone (907) 747-6671; email r10_sitka_rd@fs.fed.us; www. fs.usda.gov/tongass/. For information on Sitka National Historical Park, write 106 Metlakatla St., Sitka, AK 99835; phone (907) 747-0110; website: www.nps.gov/sitk.

Elevation: Sea level. **Climate:** Average daily temperature in July, 56°F; in January, 34°F. Annual precipitation, 86 inches. **Radio:** KIFW-AM 1230, KSBZ-FM 103.1, KCAW-FM 104.7/90.1. **Television:** Cable channels, satellite service and KTNL-CBS. **Newspaper:** *Daily Sitka Sentinel* (daily).

Private Aircraft: Sitka's "Rocky Guitierrez" airport on Japonski Island; elev. 21 feet; length 6,500 feet; asphalt; A1. Sitka Seaplane base adjacent to the west.

Sitka's beauty is renowned and it draws thousands of visitors each year. Facing the Pacific Ocean, Sitka is protected by smaller islands like Kruzof Island, where 3,201-foot Mount Edgecumbe, a dormant volcano, is situated. O'Connell Bridge connects Sitka with Japonski Island. The 1,255-foot-long bridge was the first cable-stayed, girder-span bridge in the United States, dedicated Aug. 19, 1972.

Originally occupied by Tlingits, Alexander Baranof, chief manager of the Russian–American Co. (headquartered in Kodiak) built a trading post and fort (Redoubt St. Michael's) north of Sitka in 1799. The Tlingits burned down the fort in 1802. Baranof returned in 1804 for the Battle of Sitka, which was the last major armed conflict between the Native population and the Russians. By 1808, Sitka was capital of Russian Alaska; Baranof was governor (1799–1818). Remnants of Sitka's Russian past are found throughout the community. Artifacts from its Tlingit Alaska Native heritage are on view at Sheldon Jackson Museum and Sitka National Historical Park.

Salmon was the mainstay of the economy from the late 1800s until the 1950s, when a pulp mill was established at nearby Silver Bay and operated from 1960 to 1993.

History-rich Sitka has many important historic sites, meaningful in Alaska's history. The first American flag raised in Alaska, after the U.S. purchased Alaska from the Russians in 1867, was raised in Sitka at what is now Castle Hill State Historical Site. (Secretary of State William H. Seward signed the Alaska purchase treaty on March 30, 1867; Seward's Day is an observed Alaska holiday on the last Monday in March. Russia transferred Alaska to the U.S. on October 18, 1867, now Alaska Day, an observed state holiday.)

Sitka's natural beauty attracted the attention of Hollywood when it was named as the hometown of a character in the movie "The Proposal." However, Sitka's location proved too expensive for the producers to actually film here. The film was shot in Boston and Rockport, MA, and the snow-capped peaks were added digitally. Plus the eagle that grabbed the dog was an Australian Wedged-tailed Eagle, not a Bald Eagle.

Healthcare, government and commercial fishing are among the economic mainstays here. Herring eggs, or roe, are one of many fisheries in Sitka. The herring move into the waters of Sitka Sound between late February and early April to spawn along the beaches, laying egg clusters on rocks, pilings and kelp.

Lodging & Services

Accommodations at hotels/motels, including the Longliner Lodge and Suites, Westmark Sitka Hotel, Totem Square Hotel & Marina, Sitka Hotel, Aspen Hotel and Super 8. Also inns, lodges and many bed-and-breakfasts. For more on accommodations go to www.sitka.org.

Dining choices include fast-food (Subway and McDonald's) to make-a-reservation-worthy Mediterranean fare (at Ludvig's Bistro & Wine Bar). A favorite coffee shop is The Highliner Coffee Cafe. Try local beer at the Baranof Island Brewing Co., 1209 Sawmill Creek Rd., open daily.

Sitka International Hostel, at 109 Jeff Davis St. a short walk from downtown, is open year-round. Phone (907) 747-8661 or visit sitkahostel.com.

Services in Sitka's downtown area include restaurants, drugstore, clothing and grocery stores (grocery store also at **Milepost 0.6** Halibut Point Road), and gift shops. Laundry may be done at the Super 8 as they allow the public to use their facilities. There are 2 additional laundromats within 1.5 miles from downtown. Shopping and services are also available along Sawmill and Halibut Point roads. A dump station is located at the city's Wastewater Treatment Plant on Japonski Island.

The Sitka Library is conveniently located near Harrigan Centennial Hall at the waterfront. Tables with plug-ins for electronics, nice views, restrooms and helpful staff make this a good stop for visitors.

Camping

RV camping in the Sitka area at the Sitka Sportsmans RV Park, located a block from the ferry terminal on Halibut Point Road. It is open year-round with 16 full-service ocean front sites; phone (907) 623-7740; www. rvsitka.com. The municipal Sealing Cove RV Park, adjacent to Sealing Cove Boat Harbor on Japonski Island, is open April 1–Sept. 30; first-come, first-served.

The U.S. Forest Service's Starrigavan Recreation Area is at **Milepost 7.1** Halibut Point Road *(see description in Halibut Point Road log on page 629)*. This recreation facility is gated at night; access varies depending on daylight hours. If you are arriving late evening or early morning, contact the Sitka Ranger District during business hours for gate schedule; phone (907) 747-6671. For Starrigavan campsite reservations (May through September) phone 1-877-444-6777 or go to www. recreation.gov.

Transportation

Air: Year-round scheduled jet service on Alaska Airlines. Delta offers seasonal service. Regional service via Harris Air and Alaska Seaplanes. Charter service also available. The airport is on Japonski Island, across O'Connell Bridge, 1.7 miles from downtown. Van and taxi service available to downtown hotels and accommodations.

Ferry: Sitka is served by the Alaska Marine Highway. Ferry terminal is located at **Milepost 7** Halibut Point Road; phone (907) 747-8737 when ferry is in port. Reservations phone 1-800-642-0066; www.ferryalaska. com. Ferry shuttle service in summer for daytime arrivals, phone (907) 747-5800 (phone ahead if arriving after 10 P.M.).

Bus: The Ride (ridesitka.com) offers weekday service from 6:30 A.M. to 7:30 P.M. in town. Purchase tickets on the bus or at Sitka Tribal Enterprises (456 Katlian St.), Old Harbor Books (201 Lincoln St.) or Sea Mart Grocery (1867 Halibut Point Rd.); phone The Ride Hotline at (907) 747-7103.

Car Rental: Avis Rent-a-Car at the airport. Sitka Car Rental offers pickup service.

Taxi: Baranof Taxi, Hank's Cabs, Sunset Cab, 738-Taxi and Cummins Taxi.

Highways: The 7.1-mile-long Halibut Point Road provides access to many businesses, the Alaska Marine Highway ferry terminal and Starrigavan Recreation Area *(see log on page 629)*. Sawmill Creek Road leads 5.5 miles south from Lake Street to Sawmill Cove Industrial Park

Cruise Ships: Cruise ships either anchor in Sitka Sound, and passengers are lightered to shore to the Crescent Harbor visitors' dock and O'Connell Bridge visitors' dock, or they anchor at the Old Sitka Dock, 5 miles from downtown by the ferry terminal.

Private Boats: Transient moorage available at Eliason and ANB Harbors. Contact Harbormaster (907) 747-3439 or Channel 16 VHS.

Attractions

Walking tour of Sitka. Historic landmarks and contemporary shops are all within walking distance in downtown Sitka. One of the city's most noticeable landmarks, **St. Michael's Cathedral**, is located in the center of Lincoln Street downtown. Originally built in 1844–48, then rebuilt after it burned down in 1966, this is the focal point of Sitka's history as the capital of Russian Alaska and a favorite photo op. Another popular stop is the Russian Bishop's

House across from Crescent Harbor, built in 1842. Tours are available at Russian Bishop's House from National Park Service rangers.

©David L. Ranta, staff

The **Sitka Pioneers' Home** at Lincoln and Katlian streets was built in 1934 on the former Russian Parade Ground. Pioneers' Homes are also located in Fairbanks, Palmer, Anchorage, Ketchikan and Juneau. These state-supported homes offer housing and care for Alaskans who are at least 65 years old. The Sitka Pioneers' Home has a gift shop on the first floor featuring handicrafts made by residents. The Prospector, a 13½-foot clay and bronze statue in front of the Pioneers' Home, was sculpted by Alonzo Victor Lewis and dedicated on Alaska Day in 1949. The model for the statue was real pioneer William "Skagway Bill" Fonda.

Building 29 (Tilson Bldg.), at 206 Lincoln St., is a National Historic Landmark. Built in 1835 of spruce logs, with sawdust insulation, it is one of the only surviving structures in Sitka—along with the Russian Bishop's House—from Alaska's Russian era.

The **Alaska Native Brotherhood (ANB) Hall** on Katlian Street is another landmark. Built in 1914, it serves as a Tlingit community center and houses Sitka's Farmers

Sitka

Map labels:
To Sandy Beach, Harbor Mountain, Halibut Point Wayside, Ferry Terminal, Old Sitka and Starrigavan Campground
Kimsham St.
Wachusetts St.
Peterson Ave.
Brady St.
Cascade St.
Sitka High School
Verstovia St.
A St.
Charles
Sirstad St.
Lake St.
Peterson St.
Monastery St.
Hospital
Moller
Siginaka
Ballfield
Lakeview St.
Crabapple
Swan Lake
Osprey St.
Round-about
Merrill St.
Geodetic Way
DeGroff St.
Sitka National Cemetery
State Trooper Academy
Indian River Rd.
Thomsen Harbor
Andrews St.
Katlian St.
Hemlock
Saint Peter's by-the-Sea
Biorka St.
Etolin St.
Sheldon Jackson College
Indian
River
Sitka Harbor
Erler St.
Russian Cemetery
Baranof St.
Finn Alley
Firn Alley
Lincoln St.
Alaska Raptor Rehabilitation Center
Sawmill Creek Rd.
Post Office
To Airport
ANB Harbor
Block House
Seward St.
Lake St.
Sheldon Jackson Museum
Jarvis St.
Sealing Cove Harbor
Pioneers' Home
St. Michael's Cathedral
Russian Bishop's House
Blarney Stone
Metlakatla St.
Admiralty St.
Totem Square
Harbor Dr.
Crescent Harbor
Shelter
Japonski Island
Harbor Dr.
O'Connell Bridge
Castle Hill
Harrigan Centennial Hall Isabel Miller Museum
Sitka National Historical Park Visitor Center
Russian Memorial
To Fortress of The Bear
Fritz Island
Turning Island
Sitka Sound
Sitka National Historical Park
Site of Fort
Mitchell Rock

Old-growth forest and totems make a walk through Sitka National Historical Park a unique and memorable experience. (©Michael K. Robb)

Market during the summer growing season.

Castle Hill (Baranof Castle Hill State Historic Site) is where Alaska changed hands from Russia to the United States on Oct. 18, 1867. Graduated walkway is located on south side by the bridge (look for sign) or stairs on north side off of Lincoln Street. Good photo op of the harbor and town.

Totem Square, has a double-headed eagle totem that reflects Sitka's Russian heritage. This park is a grassy, open area with benches. The **Russian Blockhouse**, located behind the Pioneers' Home, is a replica of the blockhouse that was part of the stockade wall that separated Russian and Tlingit sections of Sitka after the Tlingits moved back to the area approximately 20 years after the 1804 battle.

Sitka Lutheran Church contains artifacts from the original 1843 Finnish Lutheran Church, including a Kessler Organ. Free tours by volunteers on limited days from mid-May to mid-September. Princess Maksoutoff, first wife of Alaska's last Russian governor, Dimitri Maksoutoff, is buried in the Lutheran cemetery.

Crescent Harbor Park (pictured above) runs between Lincoln Street and Crescent Harbor. The park strip offers the Sitka Sea Walk, with benches, picnic shelters, basketball and tennis courts, a playground and views of Crescent Harbor. Many of Sitka's special events are held at the largest picnic shelter. Ramps below the shelter are often used for tour boat pick-ups.

The **Sitka Summer Music Festival**, is an annual event featuring the best in chamber music performed by world-famous artists. Scheduled for June 4–30, 2019, chamber

music concerts are presented Friday and Saturday evenings in Harrigan Centennial Hall, with additional concerts and special events taking place during the festival. Advance tickets are a good idea; the concerts are popular. *Children under 6 years not admitted.* Contact Sitka Summer Music Festival, P.O. Box 3333, Sitka, AK 99835; phone (907) 747-6774; www.alaskaclassics.org.

The **Harrigan Centennial Hall**, built in 1967 and recently renovated, hosts the Summer Music Festival and houses the Sitka Historical Museum (description follows). It is located on Harbor Drive along the waterfront. This location has a summer information desk run by Visit Sitka (open only when cruise ships are docked) and it provides free maps and visitor information.

Sitka History Museum provides a great overview of Sitka's rich Tlingit, Russian and American past through displays, photographs and artifacts and is a great first-stop to orient visitors to Sitka. The new main gallery opened in 2018 and the museum also includes a gift shop featuring a selection of historical books about Sitka, locally created Tlingit art and other gifts, including handmade wooden Russian Matryoshka nesting dolls. Free city maps, available at the museum, guide visitors to Sitka's Historic Sites. The museum is located at 330 Harbor Dr., inside Harrigan Centennial Hall. Open daily from 9 A.M. to 4 P.M. most days in summer; www.sitkahistory.org.

The **Naa Kahidi Native Dancers** perform regularly during the summer at the Sheet'ka Kwaan Naa Kahidi Tribal Community House at 200 Katlian St. The tribal house is built in the style of a Tlingit clan house and boasts the largest hand-carved house screen in the Pacific Northwest, as well as large, carved exterior house panels. For dance performance schedule, go to www.sitkatours.com or phone (907) 747-7137.

The **New Archangel Dancers** are a group of local women who perform authentic Russian dances in traditional costumes. When large cruise ships are in port, the dancers are usually performing at Harrigan Centennial Hall auditorium at 330 Harbor Dr. For dance performance schedule, call the Russian Dance Hotline at (907) 747-5516; website:

www.newarchangeldancers.com.

Alaska Day. Oct. 18 commemorates the transfer of Alaska from Russia to the United States. The Alaska Day Festival, featuring a period costume ball and a parade, takes place in Sitka the week prior.

Sheldon Jackson Museum, 104 College Dr., on the Sheldon Jackson College campus. The museum contains some of the finest Native arts and crafts found in Alaska. Built in 1897 and occupied since, it is the first concrete building built in Alaska. The majority of artifacts were collected between 1888 and 1899. The museum has an Alaska Native Artist Residency Program in summer and early fall, and visitors can watch these Alaska Native artists at work as well as talk with them about their work.

Open in summer (mid-May to mid-September), 9 A.M. to 4:30 P.M. Tuesday through Saturday; closed holidays. Summer admission fee to the museum is $7/adults, $6/seniors (65 years and older), free for under 18 years. Winter hours are 10 A.M. to 4 P.M. Tuesday through Saturday; closed holidays. Winter admission fee is $5, 18 and under free. Phone (907) 747-8981, or visit www.museums.alaska.gov.

Walk around the Sheldon Jackson Campus, a Historic Landmark that was transferred to Sitka Fine Arts Camp in 2011. This vibrant year-round arts program sponsors classes and camps for all ages. Check with their office for various entertainment events or visit www.fineartscamp.org.

Sitka Sound Science Center, at 834 Lincoln St., is located on the waterfront on the way to the Sitka National Historic Park. The Science Center operates an educational fish hatchery and the Molly Ahlgren Aquarium, where touch tanks provide an up-close view of the organisms found in an outer coast tide pool. A special fish tank features an observation bubble for children to crawl into and enjoy a different view of fish.

The Science Center welcomes visitors in the summer Monday through Saturday, 9 A.M. to 4 P.M. (limited hours/days in winter). Tours of the hatchery are available; call for tour times. Admission fee charged. The Center also offers regular natural history lectures on topics such as commercial fisheries, fish, wildlife and forest ecology. Phone (907) 747-8878, or visit www.sitkascience.org.

Visit the **Alaska Raptor Center**, located on Raptor Way, 0.7 mile south on Sawmill Creek Road from downtown. This unique facility treats injured eagles, hawks, owls and other birds. The Raptor Center is open daily in summer. Tour the outside displays and enjoy views of eagles inside the building through one-way glass. Informative guides are on site. Large group tours may be possible with advanced notice. Summer hours are typically 8 A.M. to 4 P.M. daily; call for winter hours. Phone (907) 747-8662; www.alaskaraptor.org. Admission $13 for adults, $6 for children.

Sitka National Historical Park reflects both the community's rich Southeast Alaska Native heritage and its Russian-American past. Its Visitor Center is open daily in summer 8 A.M. to 5 P.M. The 113-acre park consists of 2 units—the Fort Site, located at the end of Lincoln Street, a half-mile from town, and the Russian Bishop's House, located on Lincoln Street near Crescent Harbor. Built by the Russian–American Co. in 1842 for the first Russian Orthodox bishop to reside in Alaska, the house was occupied by the church until 1969, and was

©Kris Valencia, staff

Halibut Point Road

Halibut Point Road (paved) leads northwest from Lake Street to dead end just beyond the entrance to Starrigavan Recreation Area.
Distance from Lake Street is shown.

0 Traffic circle for Lake Street and Sawmill Road.

0.6 Stoplight at Katlian; Lakeside Center, AC Company. Moller Field ballpark.

0.7 Beachfront Turnaround Park, has a skatepark, dog park, large paved parking area (below road) and beach access.

0.8 Emergency entrance to Sitka Community Hospital, McDonald's, laundromat and True Value Hardware.

1.6 Seamart Grocery to west.

1.7 Pioneer Park to west with picnic area; parking, beach access via trails.

1.8 Paved turnout; picnic shelter, beach access via trails.

2 Cascade Creek bridge.

2.2 Sandy Beach; good swimming (cold water), parking, restrooms. View of Mount Edgecumbe.

2.7 Gravel turnout overlooking water.

3.1 Turnoff for Harbor Mountain Bypass/Kramer Avenue; wide and paved for 0.25 mile, then wide gravel road to Mile 1 where road narrows at gate; steep, narrow, winding gravel road 5 miles to picnic area and viewpoint, (from here it is not suitable for RVs, travel trailers or pick-up campers as per Sitka Ranger District); 5.6 miles to **Harbor Mountain Ridge Trailhead**.

4.2 Halibut Point State Recreation Site; parking areas, swimming beach, picnic shelters, tables, firepits and toilets. Turn on Granite Creek Road for golf course (0.5 mile).

5.6 Cove Marina next to Alaska Wildlife Protection Office and Dock.

6.4 Sportsmans RV Park and oceanfront campground.

▲

6.5 No Name Creek. Entrance to Alaska Marine Highway ferry terminal. Turn right when leaving Ferry Dock for Sportsmans RV Park and Sitka; turn left for USFS Starrigaven Recreation Area.

6.8 Old Sitka State Historical Site; boat launch, parking. Forest and Muskeg trail-

Sandy Beach on a sunny summer's day, with Mount Edgecumbe in the background.
(©Kris Valencia, staff)

head for ¾-mile, barrier free hike.

6.9 Old Sitka State Historical Site; commemorative plaque, interpretive signs. This was the site of Fort Archangel Michael, the first Russian settlement in the area in 1799. In 1802, in a surprise attack, the Tlingit Indians of the area destroyed the fort and killed most of its occupants, driving the Russians out until Baranof's successful return in 1804.

7 Starrigavan Creek. Spawning pink salmon in August and September. Estuary Life trailhead north side of creek; parking. **The Estuary Life Trail** is a barrier-free ¼-mile boardwalk trail around the estuary where the saltwater Starrigavan Bay meets the freshwater Starrigavan Creek. Excellent birding for great blue herons, bald eagles, common mergansers, belted kingfishers, canvasbacks, mallards, buffleheads and many other birds.

7.1 USFS Starrigavan Recreation Area. Popular year-round recreation area includes 23 individual campsites, 2 double family sites and Starrigavan Creek Cabin in the "Estuary Loop;" 3 hike-in campsites overlooking Starrigavan Bay in the "Bayside Loop" (parking in service area); and 6 hike-in campsites in the "Backpacker Loop" (hikers and bikers only).

Camp host, ADA accessible sites, garbage service, message board, picnic tables, toilets. Camping fees $12–$16 for individual sites, $30 for double family sites, $75 for Starrigavan Creek Cabin. Some campsites are first-come, first-served, other campsites and cabins may be reserved up to 4 days in advance by phoning 1-877-444-6777 or online at www.recreation.gov.

Bayside Loop to west leads to Starrigavan Picnic Area, with 4 picnic sites and 2 group shelters; access to and views of Starrigavan Bay. Also access to Mosquito Cove Trail, a 1.3-mile loop that passes through spruce-hemlock forest and along shoreline.

This recreation facility is gated at night; late evening or early morning new arrivals contact the Sitka Ranger District during business hours for gate schedule; phone (907) 747-6671, email r10_sitka_rd@fed.us. For Starrigavan campsite reservations (May through September) phone 1-877-444-6777 or go to www.recreation.gov. There is a year-round host at the entrance to the Bayside Loop. Off-season vehicle access restricted when there is snow or ice on roadway.

⬅ ▲

Halibut Point Road ends just beyond the entrances to Starrigavan Recreation Area.

---

added to Sitka National Historical Park in 1973. Open summer 9 A.M. to 5 P.M. Request Russian Bishop's House tours in winter.

A free self-guiding trail leads through the park to the fort site. The National Park Service conducts guided walks in summer; check for schedule. The park's totem pole collection includes original pieces collected in 1901–03, and copies made of the originals that were lost to time and the elements. There are also modern carved poles erected in honor of various people and events, including the Park's Centennial in 2010. The park grounds and trails are open daily, 6 A.M. to 10 P.M., in summer; 6 A.M. to 8 P.M. in winter. Hiking through the rainforest in this park is considered to be one of the most memorable experiences of a visit to Sitka.

The park's Visitor Center houses an exhibit of Tlingit and Russian artifacts. The building is open 8 A.M. to 5 P.M., daily in

summer. Phone (907) 747-0110.

Fortress of the Bear, at Mile 5.6 Sawmill Creek Road in the Sawmill Cove Industrial Park, is a non-profit education and rescue center for orphaned brown bear cubs. Open 9 A.M. to 5 P.M. daily May through September; call for information October through April (when bears are hibernating). Admission fee $15/adults, $5/children ages 8–18, free for age 7 and under; phone (907) 747-3032; http://fortressofthebear.org/.

Drive Sawmill Creek Road. From its junction at the traffic circle at Lake and Erler streets, Sawmill Creek Road leads 0.4 mile on to Sitka National Cemetery and 0.6 mile to Indian River. At Mile 0.8, Raptor Way provides access to the Alaska Raptor Center. At Mile 0.9 is the parking lot for Sitka National Historical Park trails and for the Visitor Center. At Mile 3.5 is parking for the 1.8-mile Thimbleberry Lake-Heart Lake trail.

Whale Park Wayside at Mile 3.8 has covered picnic tables and viewing platform overlooking Silver Bay. Paved road ends just past the Fortress of the Bear at Mile 5.6. Gravel road continues to Herring Cove Trailhead at Mile 7.3.

AREA FISHING: Sitka holds an annual salmon derby Memorial Day weekend and the weekend following. Contact the Sitka Sportsman's Assoc.; phone (907) 747-6790. Saltwater fishing charters available locally. Good fly-fishing at Baranof Island lakes and rivers. Try Sawmill Creek and Starrigavan River on the road system; Katlian River, 11 miles northeast of Sitka by boat; or remote waters such as Rezanof Lake, 40 air miles southeast of Sitka. USFS public-use cabins are at some lakes. Stop by the Dept. of Fish and Game office at 304 Lake St. for details; phone (907) 747-5355.

⬅

Juneau

View of downtown Juneau and Gastineau Channel from Goldbelt Mount Roberts Tramway. (©Michael K. Robb)

Major Attractions:

©Kris Valencia, staff

Mendenhall Glacier, Mount Roberts Tramway, Tracy Arm

Located on Gastineau Channel, 95 miles northeast of Sitka. **Population:** Borough 33,064. **Emergency, Services:** Phone 911 for all emergencies. **Police**, phone (907) 586-0600. **Fire Department**, phone (907) 586-5322. **Alaska State Troopers**, phone (907) 465-4000. **Hospital**, Bartlett Regional, 3260 Hospital Dr., phone (907) 796-8900. **Maritime Search and Rescue**, Coast Guard, (907) 463-2000 or 1-800-478-5555.

Visitor Information: Travel Juneau, phone (907) 586-2201 or 1-888-581-2201; Website: www.traveljuneau.com; Email: info@traveljuneau.com. Visitor information centers are operated year-round, in the Juneau airport lower terminal and at the Auke Bay ferry terminal. The downtown visitor centers are open 8 A.M. to 5 P.M. from May through September, and when cruise ships are in port. A kiosk-type center is at Marine Park near the library, and the other is the large blue building at the cruise ship terminal at Dock D, on South Franklin Street.

U.S. Forest Service information on camping, trails and cabins is available from the Juneau Ranger District, 8510 Mendenhall Loop Rd., Juneau, AK 99801; phone (907) 586-8800. For Tongass National Forest information online: www.fs.usda.gov/tongass.

Elevation: Sea level. Climate: Mild and wet. Juneau averages 222 days of precipitation a year, with September and October the wettest months and April through June the driest. The monthly rainfall record for July is 10.36 inches (1997). Average daily maximum temperature in July, 64°F; daily minimum in January, 19°F. Highest recorded temperature, 90°F in July 1975; the lowest was -22°F in January 1968 and 1972. Average annual precipitation, 56.5 inches (airport), 92 inches (downtown); 103 inches of snow annually. Snow on ground intermittently from mid-November to mid-April. Prevailing winds are east-southeasterly. **Radio:** KBJZ-FM 94.1, KJNO-AM 630, KINY-AM 800, KXLL-FM 100.7, KRNN-FM 102.7, KTOO-FM 104.3, KTKU-FM 105.1, KSUP-FM 106.3, KVIM-FM 92.7. **Television:** KJUD Channel 8 (ABC); KATH Channel 15 (NBC); KTNL Channel 14 (CBS); KTOO Channel 10 (PBS). **Newspapers:** *Juneau Empire* (daily) and *Capi-*

tal City Weekly (weekly).

Private Aircraft: Juneau International Airport, 9 miles northwest; elev. 18 feet; length 8,456 feet; asphalt; fuel 100LL, Jet A. Juneau harbor seaplane base, due east; restricted use, no fuel. International seaplane base, 7 miles northwest; 5,000 feet by 450 feet, avgas, Jet A. For more information, phone the Juneau Flight Service Station at (907) 586-7382.

History and Economy

In 1880, nearly 20 years before the great gold rushes to the Klondike and to Nome, 2 prospectors named Joe Juneau and Richard Harris found "color" in what is now called Gold Creek, a small, clear stream that runs through the center of present-day Juneau. Local history states that it was a Tlingit, Chief Kowee, who showed Joe Juneau where to find gold in Gold Creek. What the prospectors found led to the discovery of one of the largest lodes of gold quartz in the world. Juneau (called Harrisburg the first year) quickly boomed into a gold rush town as claims and mines sprang up in the area.

In 1881, Pierre "French Pete" Erussard discovered gold on Douglas Island, across Gastineau Channel from Juneau. A year later, John Treadwell bought the claims and in 1887 he formed Alaska Treadwell Gold Mining Company. In 36 years of operation, Treadwell produced an estimated $66 million in gold. A cave-in and flood closed the mine in 1917. The Alaska–Gastineau Mine, operated by Bart Thane in 1911, had a 2-mile shaft through Mount Roberts to the Perseverance Mine near Gold Creek. The Alaska–Juneau (A–J) Mine was constructed on a mountain slope south of Juneau and back into the heart of Mount Roberts. It operated until 1944, when it was declared a nonessential wartime activity after producing over $80 million in gold. Post–WWII wage and price inflation and the fixed price of gold prevented its reopening.

Congress first provided civil government for Alaska in 1884. Alaska was governed by a succession of presidential appointees, first as the District of Alaska, then as the Territory of Alaska. Between 1867 (when the United States purchased Alaska from Russia) and 1884, the military had jurisdiction over the District of Alaska, except for a 3-year period (1877–79) when Alaska was put under control of the U.S. Treasury Dept. and governed by U.S. Collector of Customs.

By 1900, Juneau had eclipsed Sitka—capital of Russian Alaska and then the Territory of Alaska—as the center of power in Southeast. A Civil Code for Alaska, passed by Congress under the Carter Act in 1900, provided the Territory with 3 judicial districts, one of which was Juneau, and moved the seat of government from Sitka to Juneau.

In 1974, Alaskans voted to move the capital from Juneau to a site closer to Anchorage. In 1976, Alaska voters selected a new capital site near Willow, but funding for the capital move—an estimated $2.8 billion—was defeated in November 1982.

Prior to the arrival of the Russians, explorers, prospectors, miners and other settlers, this was Tlingit land. Described as having one of the most sophisticated social structures and intricate societies of any indigenous people in the world, the Tlingit are 1 of the 2 major Alaska Native groups in Southeast. The other major group, the Haidas, have a different language although their lifestyle, history and tradition are similar to the Tlingit, as is the lifestyle of the Tsimshians, a First Nations group from Canada that settled on Annette Island.

It was a Tlingit, William Paul Sr., who was instrumental in bringing about the Alaska Native Claims Settlement Act of 1971. One of the first Tlingits to receive a college degree and the first Alaska Native to win a seat in the territorial legislature, Paul originally brought suit against the U.S. government in the 1930s for lands taken from the Tlingits and Haidas. Forty-four million acres and nearly a billion dollars were involved in the Alaska Native Claims Settlement Act. In addition to cash and land settlements, the act established 12 regional corporations and a system of local village corporations. The intent of the corporate structuring was to create a revenue-producing entity that would assure a financial future for all Alaska Natives.

The local corporation formed for the Juneau area was Goldbelt, Inc. Currently, Goldbelt, Inc. has some 3,600 Tlingit and Haida shareholders. Many shareholders are employed in Goldbelt's businesses, which include Goldbelt Mount Roberts Tramway.

Education, health services, tourism and mining are the largest employers in Juneau's private sector, while government (federal, state and local) comprises an estimated half of the total basic industry.

Description

Juneau, often called "a little San Francisco," is nestled at the foot of Mount Juneau (elev. 3,576 feet) with Mount Roberts (elev. 3,819 feet) rising immediately to the east on the approach up Gastineau Channel. The residential community of Douglas, on Douglas Island, is south of Juneau and connected by a bridge. Neighboring residential areas around the airport, Mendenhall Valley and Auke Bay lie north of Juneau on the mainland.

Shopping is in the downtown area and at suburban malls in the airport and Mendenhall Valley areas.

Juneau's skyline is dominated by several government buildings, including the Federal Building (1962), the massive State Office Building (1974), the State Court Building (1975) and the older brick and marble-columned Capitol Building (1931). The Sealaska Plaza is headquarters for Sealaska Corp., 1 of the 12 regional Native corporations formed after congressional passage of the Alaska Native Claims Settlement Act in 1971.

The Juneau area supports 35 churches, 2 high schools, 2 middle schools, 7 elementary schools, 2 charter/community schools and a University of Alaska Southeast campus at Auke Lake. There are 3 municipal libraries and the state library.

The area is governed by the unified city

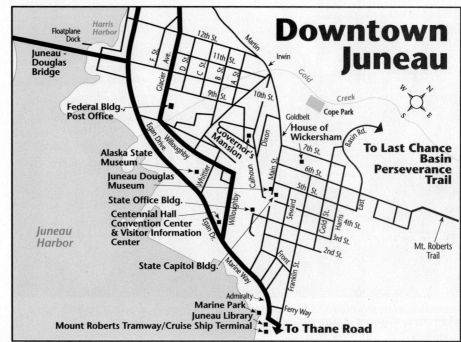

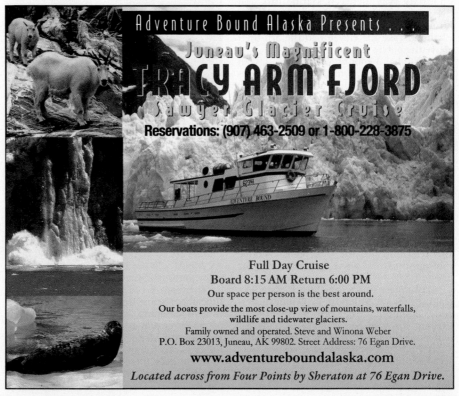
JUNEAU ADVERTISERS

Glacier Nalu Campground..........Ph. (907) 789-1990
Goldbelt Mt. Roberts Tramway..Ph. (907) 463-3412
Macaulay Salmon Hatchery........Ph. (907) 463-4810
Tracy Arm Fjord–
  Adventure Bound ....Ph. (907) 463-2509

Juneau's historic downtown has narrow but pedestrian-friendly streets. It's a lively scene when cruise ships are in port. (©Kris Valencia, staff)

and borough of Juneau, which encompasses 3,250 square miles. It is the first unified government in the state, combining the former separate and overlapping jurisdictions of the cities of Douglas and Juneau and the greater Juneau borough.

Lodging & Services

Juneau has a variety of hotels, motels, bed-and-breakfasts and vacation rentals downtown and in the airport area. The Juneau International Hostel is located at 614 Harris St.; phone (907) 586-9559; www.juneauhostel.net.

Juneau offers a wide variety of dining spots and plenty of shopping. Watch for sidewalk food vendors downtown in summer. A unique service that will be appreciated by spa lovers is Glacier Salt Cave.

Juneau Library, at South Franklin and Admiralty Way, between Marine Park and the cruise ship terminal, has a wonderful view of Juneau, Douglas and Gastineau Channel. Take the elevator to the 5th floor above the public parking garage.

Juneau has 3 craft breweries. The Alaskan Brewing Company, and 2 breweries downtown: Barnaby Brewing and Devil's Club Brewery.

Juneau has **EV plug-in** charging stations for electric cars available at the Alaska State Museum, Eagle Beach, Savikko Park and in the Downtown Library Structure.

Camping

Juneau has no place for overnight RV parking except at organized campgrounds. If you are parked overnight anywhere but a campground, you will probably be asked to move. Campsite reservations for Alaska State Parks can be made through www.reserveamerica.com, and for U.S. Forest Service campgrounds at www.recreation.gov or phone 1-877-444-6777.

Alaska State Park's Eagle Beach State Recreation Area, at **Milepost 27.6** Juneau Veteran's Memorial Highway, has overnight parking for vehicles and gravel pads for tenters. Park host on site, $15 camping fee, 7-day limit. An extensive trail system here accesses the beach and river.

Savikko Park, owned by the City & Borough of Juneau, in Douglas has 3 sites for fully self-contained RVs. No hookups or other services are available. $10 camping fee, 3-day limit; obtain permit and directions on weekdays at Harbormaster's office at 1600 Harbor Way, phone (907) 586-5255.

The City and Borough of Juneau operates a 24-hour dump station at Jackie Renninger Park, 2400 Mendenhall Loop Rd., next to the skateboard park; phone (907) 790-2525.

Glacier Nalu Campground is located 2.2 miles east of the Glacier Highway via the Mendenhall Loop Road turnoff at **Milepost 12.1**; description follows. It is a very convenient location that also provides reservation services for local tours and a shuttle service for RVers.

Glacier Nalu Campground, formerly known as Spruce Meadow RV Park, is a beautiful 12.5 acre property located in Juneau,

Alaska. We have full service RV sites, deluxe camping & standard tenting sites. Spaces have 30-amp, free WiFi and cable TV, sparkling clean restrooms and showers, laundry facility, local tours can be booked on site. Located on bus route 3.7 miles from ferry terminal, 4 miles to Mendenhall Glacier, 14 miles to downtown Juneau. Reservations are highly recommended. Reserve online or by phone. 10200 Mendenhall Loop Rd., Juneau, AK 99801. Phone (907) 789-1990; website www.juneaurv.com. [ADVERTISEMENT]

There are 2 USFS campgrounds north of Juneau accessible from the Glacier Highway/Juneau Veterans' Memorial Highway *(see log on pages 636–637)*: Auke Village Campground and Mendenhall Lake Campground (descriptions follow). You can camp at both campgrounds for a combined 14 calendar days per year. USFS Campground Rangers are available 7 A.M. to 10 P.M. at both camp-

grounds and can also be reached by phone at (907) 209-8998 or (907) 209-4191 during operating dates.

Auke Village Campground is located in the Auke Village Recreation Area (see **Milepost 14.7** Glacier Highway). It has 11 basic sites (no hookups), with potable drinking water, $10 camping fee, $10 reservation fee, pit toilets, picnic tables and firepits. Accommodates RVs to 40 feet. Open 24/7 from May 1 to September 30. A good camping choice for late ferry arrivals

Mendenhall Lake Campground has a total of 69 sites; 9 sites have electric, water and sewer; 9 sites have electric and water; and 7 sites are located in a separate walk-in area for backpackers. RVs to 60 feet. Picnic tables, firepits, water, flush toilets and hot showers available. There is a dump station. Open 24/7 from May 15 to September 15; phone (907) 586-8800. Campground host on site. Camping fees are $10 to $28 per night plus $10 reservation fee.

To reach Mendenhall Lake Campground from the Ferry Terminal, exit the roundabout at **Milepost 12.1** Glacier Highway at Auke Bay to Back Loop Road. Drive 2.5 miles to Montana Creek Road and turn onto it; continue 0.7 mile (keep to right when Montana Creek Road becomes Skaters Cabin Road) to the fancy rock-faced entry to the campground. Continue past the campground entrance to reach Skater's Cabin Picnic Site. This natural stone picnic shelter—built in 1936 by the Civilian Conservation Corps—has a spectacular view of the glacier. Skater's Cabin is available first-come, first-served or by reservation for groups; phone (907) 586-8800. From the city, you take the Glacier Highway to **Milepost 9.3**.

Transportation

Air: Juneau International Airport is northwest of downtown via Glacier Highway. Airport terminal contains ticket counters, waiting area, gift shop, rental cars, restaurant, lounge and visitor information center. Phone (907) 789-7821.

The city express bus inbound, stops at the airport weekdays from 7:11 A.M. to 6:11 P.M. Taxi service to downtown is also available. Courtesy vans to some hotels.

Alaska Airlines serves Juneau daily from Anchorage (90-minute flight) and other Alaska cities, and from Seattle, WA (2-hour flight). Delta Airlines has a once-daily flight to/from Seattle from late May through late August. Scheduled commuter service to Haines, Skagway, Sitka, Angoon and other points via various air services.

Charter air service is available for hunting, fishing, flightseeing and transportation to other communities. Flightseeing by helicopter is very popular in Juneau, and several helicopter services operate here.

Ferry: Juneau is served by Alaska Marine Highway ferries. For schedules, fares and reservations visit www.ferryalaska.com. The state ferries dock at the Auke Bay Terminal at **Milepost 13.8** Glacier Highway; phone (907) 465-8853; or go to www.ferryalaska.com. The main reservation center is located at 6858 Glacier Highway (7 miles from downtown Juneau) and is open Monday–Friday, 7:30 A.M. to 4:30 P.M.; phone (907) 465-3941 or 1-800-642-0066. There is a ticket counter at the Auke Bay terminal. It is open only when a vessel is arriving or departing.

Taxi: Service is available from Auke Bay terminal to downtown Juneau. There is also a bus stop 1.5 miles toward town from the ferry terminal.

Bus: Capital Transit, (907) 789-6901, www.juneaucapitaltransit.org. Route map and schedule available at the visitor information center or can be downloaded from their website. Use exact fare ($2 adult, $1 ages 6–18); drivers do not make change.

Parking: Parking in the core downtown area is metered and is closely monitored. On-street parking available with 2 hours (consecutive) free parking. Public parking at the Downtown Library (Marine Park Garage) is available Monday through Friday 4 P.M. to 8 A.M. and all weekend; and North Franklin Lot at corner of Franklin Street and Second Street.

Juneau streets are narrow and it is difficult—if not impossible—to find a legal spot to park a large RV. Leave your RV at the campground and use your tow vehicle, arrange for a rental car, or park outside city and bus or taxi in to town.

Highways: Glacier Highway begins in downtown Juneau and leads 43 miles north past Echo Cove; see "Glacier Highway/ Juneau Veterans' Memorial Highway" this section. Other major roads are Douglas and North Douglas highways.

Cruise Ships: Juneau is southeast Alaska's most frequent port of call.

Car Rental: Car rental agencies located at the airport (reserve ahead of time because of the great demand for cars). Avis (907) 789-9450; Hertz (907) 789-9494; Budget, (907) 790-1086; National/Alamo (907) 789-9814; and Juneau Rental Car (will drop-off vehicle), phone (907) 957-7530.

Boats: Charter boats are available for fishing, sightseeing and transportation. Kayak rentals available. The visitor information center can provide a list of charter operators. Transient moorage is available downtown at Harris and Douglas floats and at Auke Bay. Most boaters use Auke Bay. For more information, call the Juneau harbormaster at (907) 586-5255.

Bicycles: Bike rentals available downtown through Cycle Alaska. Designated bike routes to Douglas, Mendenhall Glacier and Auke Bay. The Mendenhall Glacier route starts at the intersection of 12th Street and Glacier Avenue; total biking distance is 15 miles. Bike-route map and information available at visitor information centers.

Attractions

Juneau walking tour. It is easy to explore downtown Juneau on foot and is preferable to driving. The streets are narrow and congested with pedestrians and traffic. Walking tour maps of Juneau are available at all visitor information centers. Descriptive signs are posted at many locations, identifying significant sites in the downtown historic district.

Downtown landmarks to look for include the Ed Way bronze sculpture, "Hard Rock Miners," located at Marine Park. Marine Park is located at the foot of Seward Street, and has tables, benches, an information kiosk and free WiFi during summer months. Another bronze sculpture commemorates "Patsy Ann," a bull terrier that during the 1930s and 1940s would meet arriving vessels at Juneau's dock.

USS *Juneau* Memorial, located on the waterfront, immediately north of the South Franklin Dock, commemorates the sinking of the USS *Juneau* during WWII. All but 10 of the crew of 700 lost their lives (including

Marine Park (seen here) and the Mount Roberts Tramway/Cruise Ship Terminal are 2 of the busiest spots on Juneau's waterfront. (©David L. Ranta, staff)

the 5 Sullivan brothers) when the ship was torpedoed the night of Nov. 13, 1942.

Overstreet Park is on the downtown seawalk at the ends of West 8th and 9th streets. The park features a full size humpback whale fountain, restrooms, picnic shelter, benches, tables, interpretive signs and paved walkways.

Goldbelt Mount Roberts Tramway. One of Juneau's top attractions, the Goldbelt Mount Roberts Tramway brings spectacular views within easy reach of visitors. Two 60-passenger aerial trams transport visitors from Juneau's downtown waterfront to a modern mountaintop complex at the 1,800-foot level of Mount Roberts. Observation platform with panoramic view of the city, harbor and surrounding mountains. The mountaintop complex includes a theater, restaurant, bar, gift shop, and access to alpine walking trails. The tram ticket and a hand stamp allow you to ride the tram all day long if you wish. The tram operates daily, from May through September; phone (907) 463-3412.

State Capitol Building. 120 E. 4th St. Congress authorized construction of the Federal and Territorial Building in 1911, but the $1 million structure was not started until 1929, after local citizens and businesses pitched in by buying some of the lots needed for the building site and deeding them over to the federal government. Completed in 1931, today the Capitol building houses the offices of the State Legislature, the Governor, and the Lieutenant Governor. Because it was originally designed as an office building for the Territory, it is one

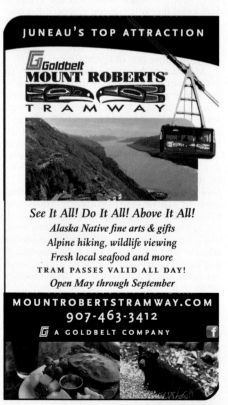

Learn more about one of Alaska's biggest resources—salmon—by visiting the Macaulay Salmon Hatchery on Gastineau Channel. (©Kris Valencia, staff)

of the few capitols in the U.S. that does not have a dome.

When the Legislature is in Session (mid-January to mid-April), the Capitol is open to the public 7 days a week from 7 A.M. to 9 P.M. When the Legislature is not in Session, the Capitol is open to the public from 7 A.M. to 5 P.M., Monday through Friday, closed Saturday and Sunday. Self-guided tours are available from the capitol lobby in summer. Details and links to brochure at website: w3.legis.state.ak.us/pages/capitol.php.

The **Juneau-Douglas City Museum** explores the rich and diverse community of the greater Juneau-Douglas area through exhibits focusing on its history, art and culture. The museum is housed in the Veterans Memorial Building (on the National Register of Historic Places), at the corner of 4th and Main streets, across from the Alaska State Capitol Building. Look for the totem poles flanking either side of the building.

Museum highlights include a rare 500- to 700-year-old basketry-style fish trap; exhibits on Aak-w and T-aaku Kwaan history; digital stories about statehood, Juneau cultures and state government; a hands-on Mining and Drilling gallery; and the video Juneau: City Built on Gold. Temporary exhibits of local art, culture and history change seasonally. The gift shop features books, Juneau memorabilia, and crafts by local artists as well as trail guides and maps of the region. Guided Historic Downtown Walking Tours are offered May through September.

For museum hours and admission fees, visit www.juneau.org/library/museum or phone (907) 586-3572. The City Museum is a Blue Star Museum: No admission charge for active-duty military and their families between Memorial Day and Labor Day.

The Alaska State Museum has been a major cultural highlight of Juneau for more than 100 years. Located in the Father Andrew P. Kashevaroff Building at 395 Whittier St., along with the Alaska State Library and Alaska State Archives, the museum features superbly curated exhibits on Native culture, maritime history, WWII in Alaska, Russian America and more. There are 2 temporary galleries in which the museum rotates a robust schedule of contemporary art, photography and other special exhibits. There is also a Discovery Room/Kids Area for children; Science on a Sphere; kayak display; history of fishing display and more. The museum is open daily May through September, and Tuesday–Saturday during the winter.

DIPAC's Macaulay Salmon Hatchery. Visitors get a chance to see adult and young salmon up-close and personal while listening to an educational commentary led by an experienced guide. Beautiful views on outside deck of Gastineau Channel. The hatchery incubates, rears and releases 3 species of Pacific salmon (chinook, chum and coho). Adult salmon return is from late June through early October. Inside the Ladd Macaulay Visitor Center, see more than 100 species of Southeast Alaska's marine life in one of the state's largest saltwater aquarium displays. Summer hours: 10 A.M. to 6 P.M., weekdays, 10 A.M. to 5 P.M. weekends. By appointment in the winter. Admission is charged. Located at 2697 Channel Dr., about 4 miles from downtown; turn at **Milepost 3.8** Glacier Highway (see road log on page 636). Phone (907) 463-4810; www.dipac.net.

Mendenhall Glacier Visitor Center. Located about 13 miles from downtown Juneau, spectacular Mendenhall Glacier and the adjacent U.S. Forest Service visitor center are a major attraction in Juneau. The visitor center offers a hands-on exhibit hall, a theater, an observatory and short interpretive presentations during the summer season. Remote cams offer live viewing of a salmon stream and beaver den.

From downtown Juneau, drive out Glacier Highway/Egan Drive and turn right at **Milepost 9.3** (Mendenhall Loop Road), then drive straight 3.4 miles to Mendenhall Glacier parking area. From the Alaska Marine Highway ferry terminal in Auke Bay, drive toward downtown Juneau on Glacier Highway and turn left at Milepost 9.3. There are 2 public parking areas. (Charter and tour buses use assigned parking area.) Paved walking path switchbacks uphill to the visitor center (elevator available). There are also

short trails down to the lake, along a salmon stream, through the forest, and along the lake to Nugget Falls. Trailheads for 2 longer trails—East Glacier and remote Nugget Creek—originate from the visitor center.

NOTE: No food or flavored beverages outside in summer due to bear activity.

The visitor center is open daily, May to September, from 8 A.M. to 7:30 P.M. Day-use fee of $5 (15 years and under free) is charged for certain outdoor areas and the visitor center in summer. Federal lands passes are accepted. From October to March the visitor center is open Friday–Sunday, 10 A.M. to 4 P.M. The visitor center is closed for winter holidays and in April. The grounds are open year-round 6 A.M. to midnight. From October to April no fee is charged. For more information, phone (907) 789-0097 or visit www.mendenhallglacier.net. Find them on Facebook at U.S. Forest Service-Mendenhall Glacier Visitor Center.

Tracy Arm. Located 50 miles southeast of Juneau, Tracy Arm and adjoining Endicott Arm are the major features of the Tracy Arm–Fords Terror Wilderness Area. Both Tracy and Endicott arms are long, deep and narrow fjords that extend more than 30 miles into the heavily glaciated Coast Mountain Range. Active tidewater glaciers at the head of these fjords calve icebergs into the fjords. Fords Terror, off of Endicott Arm, is an area of sheer rock walls enclosing a narrow entrance into a small fjord. The fjord was named in 1889 for a crewmember of a naval vessel who rowed into the narrow canyon at slack tide and was caught in turbulent icy currents for 6 terrifying hours when the tide changed.

Access to this wilderness area is primarily by boat or floatplane from Juneau. Some large and small cruise ships and charter boats include Tracy Arm and Endicott Arm in their itineraries. It is also a popular destination for sea kayakers.

Tracy Arm Fjord–Adventure Bound, Alaska's greatest combination of mountains, wildlife, icebergs and tidewater glaciers. Tracy Arm could be called "cascade fjord" because of its many waterfalls or "icy fjord" because it is the home of Alaska's largest icebergs. Best viewed from our boats. Juneau's favorite because the Weber family doesn't overcrowd and they take the time to enjoy it all. For comfort, viewing time, elbow room and personal attention, this is the quality cruise that you are looking for. Street address: 76 Egan Dr. Mailing address: P.O. Box 23013, Juneau, AK 99802. Reservations: Phone (907) 463-2509, 1-800-228-3875; www.adventureboundalaska.com. See display ad on page 631. [ADVERTISEMENT]

Juneau Arts & Culture Center, operated by the Juneau Arts & Humanities Council, provides a location for concerts and events, a rotating gallery, and a lobby gift shop featuring the work of local artists. Located at the corner of Whittier Street and Egan Drive; phone (907) 586-2787; https://jahc.org. Open 9 A.M. to 6 p.M. daily in summer; call and go online for winter schedule.

St. Nicholas Orthodox Church, 5th and Gold streets, a tiny structure built in 1894, is now the oldest original Russian Orthodox church in southeast Alaska. Visitors are welcome to Sunday services; open daily for visitation.

The Governor's House at 716 Calhoun Ave., has been home to Alaska's chief executives since it was completed in 1913. The 2½-story structure, containing 12,900 square feet of floor space, took nearly a year to build. Public tours are not available.

Walter Soboleff Center, the Sealaska Heritage Institute building at 105 South Seward St., is named after Dr. Walter Soboleff, a Tlingit scholar, esteemed elder and translator who specialized in traditional oratory and storytelling. The facility serves as a cultural center and research facility. Admission fee charged to view cultural exhibit and clan house.

Wickersham State Historic Site. A steep climb up to 7th Street takes visitors to the historic home of Alaska's Judge James Wickersham. Wickersham was the first judge of the Third Judicial District of Alaska, arriving in Eagle, AK, from Tacoma, WA, in 1900. He served seven terms as Alaska's Delegate to Congress where he introduced bills to make Denali a National Park, to finance the first Alaska university, and to have home rule in the state. He also introduced a bill resulting in a $35,000,000 appropriation to build the Alaska Railroad, as well as the first bill for statehood. House of Wickersham, located at the corner of 7th Street and Seward (at 213 7th St.), contains the judge's collection of artifacts gathered during his extensive travels throughout his 300,000-square-mile district. Phone (907) 586-9001 for information. Open mid-May to late-September, Sunday to Thursday, from 10 A.M. to 5 P.M. May be open daily in July and August.

Glacier Gardens Rainforest Adventure. Access Glacier Gardens at the Fred Meyer exit (**Milepost 7.9** Glacier Highway), then turn right and continue to 7600 Glacier Highway. What was once a landslide-scarred hillside has been transformed into a fantastic garden featuring thousands of plants and unique floral creations. Huge hanging baskets of petunia, begonia, and geranium flowers cascade from the Visitor Center's rafters, which also houses a gift shop and cafe. Outside, upside-down tree stumps act as whimsical flower pots. The tour includes a narrated trip by motorized carts through Tongass National Forest up to a viewpoint on Thunder Mountain. Open 9 A.M. to 6 P.M. daily, May to September. Phone (907) 790-3377; visit www.glaciergardens.com. *NOTE: There is no on-street parking; use parking lot. RVs use bus entrance for RV parking.*

Last Chance Mining Museum is the only historic mining building open to the public from Juneau's Gold Rush era. On display are historic mining tools and equipment and the world's largest Ingersoll-Rand air compressor. Drive or walk to the end of Basin Road to reach the museum, which is located in the Compressor Building of the historic Alaska–Juneau Mine. Basin Road ends 1 mile from East Street; park at Perseverance Trailhead and follow trail uphill to the museum. The museum is open daily, 9:30 A.M. to 12:30 P.M. and 3:30–6:30 P.M.; admission fee $5. Open from mid-May to mid-September. The museum is operated by the non-profit Gastineau Channel Historical Society; phone (907) 586-5338. Renee Hughes can answer any questions you may have. Basin Road offers good views of Mount Juneau waterfall and also accesses the Perseverance Trail. *NOTE: Basin Road is very narrow in spots and popular with joggers, walkers and dogs. Drive carefully.*

Go Hiking. Downtown Juneau offers several beautiful trails that are very popular with locals, with trailheads off Basin Road. The **Flume Trail** is an easy, level boardwalk trail above Gold Creek that begins at 0.4 mile

Basin Road, sharing parking with the Basin Road trailhead. A walker can return via the Flume trail or loop through Juneau neighborhoods and Cope Park back to Basin Road.

The **Mount Roberts Trail** is an accessible, moderately difficult hike with several options and side routes. Access to Mount Roberts Trail is from the trailhead at Mile 0.4 Basin Road. The trail can also be accessed at the 1,800-foot level by taking the Mount Roberts Tram–the base of the tram is located on South Franklin Street downtown. Options include a 20-minute hike from the Basin Road trailhead to an observation point above town; a 1½-hour hike to the Mount Roberts Tram mountain complex; the Gold Ridge side trail about 2 miles up; Gastineau Peak, a ridgeline, about 3 miles up, and the Mount Roberts summit at 3,819 feet, a 5-hour hike about 4 miles up.

Mount Roberts hikers may purchase down-only tram tickets in the shop or bar at the Goldbelt Mount Roberts Tramway mountaintop complex at 1,800 ft. Or spend $10 or more in the restaurant or gift shop and use their receipt as a ticket.

Hike the Perseverance Trail. This scenic and popular trail, which begins at the end of Basin Road, is a wonderful hike and popular with local walkers and joggers. It follows what is said to be the first road in Alaska. Originally called the Johnson Road, it provided access to gold mining operations in the Gold Creek Valley, including Perseverance Mine and the Alaska-Juneau mine. Ruins and artifacts from the old mining operations are still scattered throughout the valley. Beautiful scenery, wide rocky trail that doesn't get muddy in wet weather, 3½ miles long, junctions with several other trails.

©Kris Valencia, staff

Take a Drive. Glacier Highway/Juneau Veterans' Memorial Highway provides access to a number of attractions, including: Mendenhall Glacier; Auke Village and Lena Beach picnic areas; Eagle Beach (pictured above) recreation areas; the Shrine of St. Therese, a complex that includes the famous stone chapel and the stations of the cross; Jensen-Olson Arboretum; and numerous hiking trails. This is a truly scenic route with great views and the possibility of spotting humpback whales and other marine animals from shore. *(See the "Glacier Highway/Juneau Veterans' Memorial Highway" log beginning on page 636.)*

Thane Road begins just south of downtown Juneau and extends 5.8 miles along Gastineau Channel. Sheep Creek Trailhead is at Mile 4.

Douglas Island Highlights. Take Juneau-Douglas Bridge across Gastineau Channel. Third Street/South Douglas Highway leads 2.3 miles to the city of Douglas and accesses the popular **Sandy Beach recreation area**; parking, beach access, nice views of Gastineau Channel. The scenic North Douglas Highway follows the island's shoreline 11.4

miles to False Outer Point, affording nice oceans views. Also access to the Eaglecrest Ski Area, North Douglas Boat Harbor, Rainforest Trail and Outer Loop Trail. Eaglecrest has a zipline; phone (907) 523-2920; www.alaskazip.com.

Brown Bear Viewing at Pack Creek. The Stan Price State Wildlife Sanctuary at the mouth of Pack Creek, on Admiralty Island, 28 air miles/30 minutes south of Juneau, is a well-known bear-viewing area cooperatively managed by the Alaska Dept. of Fish and Game and U.S. Forest Service. Bears, particularly sows and cubs, can be viewed and photographed feeding on sedges in early summer and salmon from early July through August. Bears can be viewed from 2 locations: at the end of a gravel spit near the mouth of the creek, and about a mile upstream from the spit from a viewing tower overlooking the creek. Visitors will hike alongside a guide on a maintained trail between the spit and tower. All visitors are also provided with a detailed orientation.

Permits are required to visit Pack Creek from June 1 through Sept. 10, and the viewing area is open daily 9 A.M. to 9 P.M. Permits become available Feb. 1 each year. During peak season—July 5 through August 25—only 24 visitors are allowed per day with 12 permits available through commercial guides and 12 available to independent visitors. Peak season permits cost $50 a day for adults, $25 a day for seniors/children. Peak season permits are *only* available by advanced reservation. Shoulder seasons are June 1–July 4 and Aug. 26–Sept. 10; cost is $20 per day for adults, $10 for seniors/children. It may be possible to get a last minute reservation during shoulder seasons.

Commercial tours arrange flights for clients. Independent visitors will need to charter their own floatplane. For those with permits, Pack Creek can also be accessed by boat or kayak. Camping is not permitted in the viewing area, but primitive camping (no facilities) is allowed on nearby Windfall Island. To apply for Pack Creek permits visit www.recreation.gov or call toll-free 1-877-444-6777. See links at www.adfg.alaska.gov/index.cfm?adfg=stanprice.main.

AREA FISHING: Good Dolly Varden fishing available along most saltwater shorelines in Juneau area, especially from mid-May through June. Dolly Varden regulations along the Juneau road system are 2 fish daily and 2 in possession with no size restrictions, Cutthroat and rainbow trout limits (in combination) are 2 fish daily and 2 in possession, 14-inch minimum and 22-inch maximum. Chinook salmon fishing best from mid-May to mid-June; chinook salmon regulations are updated yearly so check online or phone for current requirements. Pink and chum salmon are available June through August; coho salmon best August to mid-September. Marine boat angling for salmon and other species including halibut and rockfish available from Juneau, Auke Bay, Tee Harbor and Amalga Harbor to access **Favorite** and **Saginaw channels**, **Chatham Strait** and **Stephens Passage**. USFS public-use cabins available near Juneau; reserve online at www.reserveamerica.com. For up-to-date angling information in the Juneau area, contact the ADF&G, Division of Sport Fish, Area Management Biologist, P.O. Box 110024, Juneau, AK 99811; phone (907) 465-4270; www.state.ak.us/adfg.

Glacier Highway/Juneau Veterans' Memorial Highway

From downtown Juneau, head northwest along South Franklin Street which becomes Marine Way, then Egan Drive (named for William A. Egan, first governor of the State of Alaska). Egan Drive then becomes Glacier Highway at **Milepost 9.3**, then Juneau Veterans' Memorial Highway from **Milepost 12.3** to road end, 43 miles north of Juneau. This is a scenic drive along Favorite Channel.

Distance from downtown Juneau cruise-ship terminal is shown.

0 Cruise ship terminal, Goldbelt Mount Roberts Tramway terminal; South Franklin Street.

1.1 Stoplight at junction with Tenth Street to east and Douglas Highway west to Douglas Island via the Juneau–Douglas Bridge. Access to Sandy Beach Recreation Area and North and South Douglas Highways.

1.2 Turnoff for Harris boat harbor.

1.4 Harbormaster's office.

1.6 Turnoff for Aurora boat harbor.

2.8 Northbound access east to Glacier Highway, which loops south through residential area.

3.8 Stoplight at Channel Drive. Turnoff to east for Bartlett Memorial Hospital, Alaska Native Health Center and access via Glacier Highway north to Twin Lakes Picnic Area. Turnoff to west for Channel Drive and access to **DIPAC's Macaulay Salmon Hatchery** visitor center, city park with restroom, parking and fishing access adjacent.

DIPAC's Macaulay Salmon Hatchery. See display ad page 633.

5.3 Stoplight. Vanderbilt Hill Road; police.

6 Mendenhall Wetlands State Game Refuge. Great place to see eagles and waterfowl. Viewpoint, southbound only.

6.2 Northbound exit east to Glacier Highway, Walmart and Switzer Creek.

7.9 Exit east from Egan Drive to Yandukin for access to Fred Meyer shopping center with gas station and bank. *Southbound motorists use CAUTION turning east on to Yandukin Drive across northbound traffic!* Also access east to Glacier Gardens Rainforest Adventure *(see description on page 635)*, located less than a half-mile from Fred Meyer via Glacier Highway; bike trail.

8.7 Stoplight at junction with Glacier Highway; access west to Juneau International Airport, Super 8, McDonald's, Nugget shopping mall with Office Max, Petco, Sportsmans Warehouse, etc. The 1-mile Glacier Highway Loop to east rejoins Egan Drive at **Milepost 9.3**.

9.3 Stoplight. Glacier Highway becomes Egan Drive, **South junction** with **Mendenhall Loop Road**. Turn west for airport. Turn east for Mendenhall Mall and post office (0.1 mile east of junction, take Mall Road). To reach Mendenhall Glacier from this junction, drive east 3.4 miles to parking area. **Mendenhall Glacier Visitor Center** is open daily in summer *(see description on page 634)*.

Mendenhall Loop Road is a paved 6-mile loop that rejoins Glacier Highway at **Milepost 12.1**. To reach **Mendenhall Lake** USFS Campground, drive east 2.1 miles to where

road makes a 90 degree turn. Turn on Montana Creek Road and continue 0.4 mile, keeping to right where road then becomes Skater Cabin Road. Look for large rock and sign at campground entrance.

9.5 Stoplight. Riverside Drive; access to Mendenhall Mall, post office.

9.6 Vintage Boulevard. (northbound exit only); access to post office, Safeway, gas station and Mendenhall Mall.

9.8 Mendenhall River and Brotherhood Bridge. The bridge was named in honor of the Alaska Native Brotherhood; bronze plaques symbolize the Raven and Eagle clans.

Begin 2-lane highway northbound. Begin 4-lane highway southbound.

10 Mendenhall Glacier Viewpoint to east via Wild Meadow Lane; parking area and trailhead for Kaxdegoowu Heen Dei/Clear Water Creek Trail (Mendenhall River Greenbelt). This popular paved trail extends 0.9 mile to Montana Creek, 2.1 miles to River Road parking lot. Wheelchair-accessible.

10.4 Alaska State Troopers Post to west.

10.6 Engineer's Cutoff to west through residential area. Mendenhall Peninsula Road branches south off Engineer's Cutoff; signed public access to Mendenhall Wetlands State Game Refuge (2.1 miles).

11.4 Large paved parking area to east with toilet and boat launch on Auke Lake. Good view of Mendenhall Glacier reflected in the lake. This is one of the most photographed spots in Alaska. The 3-mile **Auke Lake Trail** offers forest and water views. A popular choice for hikers of all abilities, it also offers wildlife viewing opportunities and good birdwatching. Wheelchair accessible but may need assistance in some areas. Sockeye, pink and coho salmon spawn in Auke Lake system July to September.

11.5 Turnoff to east for Auke Lake Way to **Chapel-by-the-Lake**, a Presbyterian congregation with 2 sanctuaries. The smaller log structure perched above Auke Lake is one of the most photographed churches in Southeast Alaska. Fritz Cove Road to west leads 2.6 miles through residential area and deadends at Smuggler's Cove; weekend parking for kayakers.

12.1 Roundabout for **North junction** with **Mendenhall Back Loop Road**; DeHart's Store here has a gas station, convenience store, liquor store and deli. The 6-mile Mendenhall Loop Road rejoins Glacier Highway at **Milepost 9.3**. From this junction it is: 0.1 mile to University of Alaska Southeast campus; 2.1 miles to **Glacier Nalu Campground**; 2.5 miles to Montana Creek Road where you turn and travel 0.4 more miles to access **Mendenhall Lake USFS Campground**, West Glacier trailhead and Montana Creek trailhead; and 5.4 miles to Mendenhall Glacier visitor center. Also access to USFS Juneau Ranger District office. *See Juneau Vicinity map this page.*

12.2 Large paved parking area to west for Auke Bay small-boat harbor.

12.3 Glacier Highway becomes Juneau

Veterans' Memorial Highway northbound.

12.4 AUKE BAY (pop. 5,316); post office (99821), gas, RV station, Fishermen's Bend Marina, bait, fuel.

12.6 Spaulding Meadows Trailhead to east; 4-mile hike through muskeg meadow (5 to 6 hours round trip). Popular cross-country ski route in winter. Also access to **Auke Nu Trail**; junction is 0.8 mile up then 2.6 miles to USFS John Muir cabin. Overnight reservations through www.recreation.gov and open to day use 10 A.M. to 5 P.M. Propane heat provided.

12.8 Waydelich Creek and bridge.

13.4 Stabler's Point Rock Quarry (no stopping).

13.8 Alaska State Ferry Auke Bay Terminal. Follow signs for parking area. Check-in at ticket counter *BEFORE* entering loading lanes. Restrooms, vending machines, pay phones and visitor information inside terminal.

NOTE: If you are arriving in Juneau by ferry, you will turn right onto the highway upon leaving the ferry terminal for Mendenhall Glacier or downtown Juneau (read this road log backwards from here). Mendenhall Loop Road, which leads to Glacier Nalu Campground and Mendenhall Lake USFS Campground, is signed at the roundabout and exits the Glacier Highway across from DeHart's Store at **Milepost 12.1**. (Additional directions at 12.1 Glacier Highway.) You will turn left on the highway if you are headed for Auke Village recreation area or other destinations northwest of here on Juneau Veterans' Memorial Highway continue with this road log.

14.7 Exit west for 2-mile loop road through **Auke Village Recreation Area**. Located along this side road are staircases to beachside picnic shelters and Auke Village USFS campground, with 11 campsites, tables, firepits, water spigots, flush and pit toilets; camping fee $10, plus $10 reservation fee. America the Beautiful, Senior or Access pass cardholder discounts.

15 Drive with headlights on at all times.

15.8 Aant'Iyeik Park uphill to east with baseball fields and disc golf course.

16.2 South end of Point Lena Loop Road and north end of **Auke Village Loop Road** (0.1 mile west) to Auke Village Recreation Area (see description at **Milepost 14.7**).

16.8 North end of Point Lena Loop Road.

16.9 Turnoff to west for **Lena Beach USFS Picnic Area** (pit toilets, picnic shelters, tables, firepits).

18 Tee Harbor–Point Stevens turnoff. Paved road leads 0.3 mile west to public parking area and a private marina.

18.3 Distance marker northbound shows Amalga Harbor 6 miles, Echo Cove 22 miles.

18.9 Inspiration Point. Turnouts to west here and at **Milepost 19** with views of the Chilkat Range, Tee Harbor and Shelter Island across Favorite Channel. Once a bread-and-butter commercial fishing area, hence the name "The Breadline," it is now a popular sportfishing area.

21.8 Breadline Bluff Trail; paved parking area to west. This is an old cannery trail that leads 3 miles from Amalga to Tee Harbor, following a bluff above the rocky shore of Favorite Channel. The south trailhead is located off Cohen Drive.

22.5 Turnoff for **Shrine of St. Therese**, a complex that includes gardens, Stations of the Cross, a labyrinth, lodge, cabins, a gift shop, restrooms and the famous stone chapel. Park at first or "upper" lot and follow signs downhill to the complex. (There is handicap parking and passenger off-loading at the bottom of the hill for anyone with physical challenges.) Or park at lower lot overlooking channel and follow signed gravel path to the complex. *Pets on leash.*

The Shrine of St. Therese, built in honor of St. Therese of Lisieux ("The Little Flower"), Patron Saint of Alaska, began with construction of a retreat house in 1933. It was to be followed by construction of a log chapel on Crow Island (later renamed Shrine Island), a tiny island located about 400 feet from the mainland shore. A causeway was built out to the island. The chapel is located in a quiet glade. It was built in 1938 using natural stone.

The lodge and cabins can be rented by "groups or persons who respect the spirit of the shrine." Phone (907) 586-2227, ext. 24 for more information. The complex is open 8 A.M. to 10 P.M., May to September and provides beautiful, secluded views and walks through quiet forest gardens along the bay.

22.6 Large gravel turnout to west.

22.8 Paved turnout to west with view of channel. The small island on which the Shrine of St. Therese is situated is directly in front of you to the south.

23.2 Jensen-Olsen Arboretum open Wednesday–Sunday, year-round. Small parking area is Point Caroline trailhead parking.

23.5 Paved trailhead parking area east side of highway for Peterson Lake trail; 4.3-mile hike through gravel trail then through muskeg (planked) and forest to the USFS Peterson Lake cabin. Reservations at www.recreation.gov, open to day users from 10 A.M. to 5 P.M. Propane heat provided. Rated more difficult; estimated round-trip hike 5 to 7 hours.

23.8 Peterson Creek bridge. View spawning salmon here in late summer and early fall. Salmon and trout fishing opportunities available. *CAUTION: Bears in area. NOTE: Juneau area road system freshwater special regulations apply. Cutthroat and rainbow trout limits (in combination) are 2 daily, 2 in possession, 14-inch minimum, 22-inch maximum. Dolly Varden limits are 2 daily, 2 in possession, no size limit. Steelhead catch-and-release fishing only; all steelhead must be released immediately. Consult the Southeast Alaska Sport Fishing Regulation Summary for all other species and area regulations.*

24.4 Turnoff to west for Amalga Harbor; boat launch (permit required to launch).

26.7 Windfall Lake Trail, 3.2 miles long, begins at turnoff for Herbert River Road (gated), just before Herbert River bridge; trailhead parking beside highway.

26.8 Herbert River bridge.

26.9 Paved trailhead parking area on east side of highway for Herbert Glacier trail; 4.9-mile hike that ends at Herbert Glacier. Rated easy; 5 to 6 hours round-trip.

27.1 Entering Eagle Beach State Recreation Area northbound.

27.2 Eagle River bridge. Paved parking to east at north end of bridge for Amalga trailhead to east; Eagle River Trail to west. The trail leads 5.5 miles to USFS Eagle Glacier cabin and continues another 1.2 miles to Eagle Glacier. Rated most difficult; round-trip 10 to 12 hours; rubber boots recommended. The Eagle River trail connects with network of walking trails from Eagle Beach SRA. Overnight reservations for the cabin can be made at www.recreation.gov and open to day users 10 A.M. to 5 P.M. Propane heat provided.

27.6 Roadside parking west side of highway at entrance to **Eagle Beach State Recreation Area**; large paved parking area, restrooms, extensive trail system accesses beach and river; picnic sites; interpretive signs; viewing scopes; campsites; handicap accessible; 3 rentable cabins on site. Open all year. Day use and camping fee charged.

28.1 Entrance to Eagle Beach USFS Picnic Area (day use only); picnic shelter, picnic tables, toilets, park host. View of Chilkat Range across Lynn Canal. Good bird watching, also watch for whales.

28.2 Scenic viewpoint to west.

28.8 Scenic viewpoint to west.

29 Paved road, steep downhill, to small parking area on beach.

30.4 Gravel turnout, no view.

31.1 Paved turnout with view.

32.2 Paved turnout to west with view of Benjamin Island to southwest; just beyond it is Sentinel Island lighthouse. Visible to the northwest is North Island and northwest of it is Vanderbilt Reef, site of a great sea disaster. The SS *Princess Sophia*, carrying 288 passengers and 61 crew, ran aground on Vanderbilt Reef early in the morning of Oct. 24, 1918. All aboard perished when a combination of stormy seas and a high tide forced the *Princess Sophia* off the reef and she sank early in the evening of Oct. 25. Walter Harper, who in 1913 was the first person to stand on the summit of Mount McKinley, was among the *Princess Sophia's* casualties. Vanderbilt Reef is now marked by a navigation light.

33.6 End improved highway, begin older bumpy surfacing. Road narrows. Northbound, watch for parking areas with beach access.

34.1 Large gravel turnout.

35.1 Sunshine Cove public beach access (signed); parking, toilets. Watch for parking with beach access along here.

37 Gravel parking to west, North Bridget Cove, beach access.

38 Point Bridget trailhead to west; 3.5-mile hike to Point Bridget (7 hours round-trip); panoramic view of Lynn Canal and Chilkat Mountains. The 2,850-acre Point Bridget State Park offers meadows, forests, rocky beaches, salmon streams and a trail system. Popular area for cross-country skiing in winter. Firepit fires allowed on beach.

38.8 Cowee Creek bridge; fishing. Large parking area to west at north end of bridge.

39.8 Turnoff to west on paved spur road 0.2 mile for Echo Cove city boat launch ramp on Berners Bay; outhouse, parking, camping. Berners Bay, 37 miles northwest of Juneau by water, is a popular destination for Juneau paddlers.

Chip-seal road with reflectors continues north almost 3 miles with signs indicating National Forest Land boundaries.

42.7 Road ends at large gravel turnaround. The Juneau Access Improvements Project (juneauaccess.alaska.gov) to extend this road north for 50 miles, was officially closed in July 2018 by the Federal Highway Administration.

Built in 1938, the Shrine of St. Therese (patron Saint of Alaska) at Milepost 22.5 is a favorite stop for many. (©David L. Ranta, staff)

Gustavus

Gustavus lies at the mouth of the Salmon River, and offers visitors many photo ops.
(©David L. Ranta, staff)

Gateway to Glacier Bay National Park and Preserve, the small community of Gustavus is located at the mouth of the Salmon River, on the north shore of Icy Strait, 48 miles northwest of Juneau. It is 10 miles by road from Gustavus to Bartlett Cove within the park. **Population:** 544. **Emergency Services:** Phone 911. **Clinic:** Gustavus Community Clinic, phone (907) 697-3008.

Visitor Information: Gustavus Visitors Assoc., phone (907) 500-5143; or visit www.gustavusak.com. Also www.nps.gov/glba/planyourvisit/index.htm.

Private Aircraft: Gustavus airport, adjacent northeast; elev. 36 feet; length 6,700 feet; asphalt.

Surrounded by Glacier Bay National Park, Gustavus has a panoramic view of the majestic Fairweather Mountains and the Chilkat Range. Gustavus offers expansive sandy beaches, open land and forest. It is a small community with fishing, whale watching, kayaking, hiking, photography and flightseeing opportunities.

Homesteaded in 1914 as a small agricultural community, the area was once named Strawberry Point because of its abundant wild strawberries.

Today, residents work in seasonal tourism, create and sell arts and crafts, work for the National Park Service, fish (commercial and subsistence) and in various other local trades.

Gustavus was incorporated as a city on April 1, 2004. It retains the charm of a small, remote settlement where people wave at strangers, ride bikes to get around, volunteer within the community and appreciate the area's wildlife and natural beauty.

Lodging & Services

Accommodations in Gustavus range from full-service lodges and inns to vacation homes and bed-and-breakfasts. **Annie Mae Lodge** and other lodges serve meals for guests and often feature local seafood. (Drop-in customers check for space-available meal reservations.) **Glacier Bay Lodge**, located at Bartlett Cove, has a restaurant.

Shop for locally-made treasures created by an amazing number of talented local artists. Painters, potters, sculptors, jewelers and woodcarvers fill local galleries, studios and shops with their unique work.

Gustavus has a post office; library with internet access; 4 churches; a pre-school and childcare program and a K–12 school; a general store with groceries and hardware; cafe; liquor store; 2 coffee shops; a natural foods store (with a deli); and fish-processing/retail store. Fishing supplies and licenses may be purchased locally.

GUSTAVUS ADVERTISERS

Annie Mae Lodge, The ....Ph. 1-800-478-2346
Bud's Rent-A-Car...........................Ph. (907) 697-2403
Glacier Bay Lodge & Tours.......Ph. 1-888-229-8687
Gustavus Visitors
  Association ....Ph. (907) 500-5143

Glacier Bay Lodge, located at Bartlett Cove, has a restaurant and lounge, and also operates the day boat trip into Glacier Bay. Bartlett Cove offers 1 of the 2 campgrounds in the Gustavus area—walk-in, tenting only.

Annie Mae Lodge in Gustavus at Glacier Bay. Beautiful full service lodge on the Good River. Boasting gourmet food, beer, wine, Glacier Bay tours, fishing, whale watching, kayaking, courtesy van, bikes and much more. We offer an experience of a lifetime while carrying on the tradition of country hospitality in frontier Alaska. Your true Alaskan experience is waiting for you here. Box 55, Gustavus, AK 99826. Phone 1-800-478-2346 or (907) 697-2346, fax (907) 697-2211. Email: reservations@anniemae. com. www.anniemae.com. See display ad on this page. [ADVERTISEMENT]

Transportation

Ferry: Alaska Marine Highway ferry ervice. Check current schedules at www. ferryalaska.com.

Air: Alaska Airlines daily jet flights from Juneau to Gustavus airport in summer. 2 year-round air taxis. Scheduled and charter service from Juneau, Sitka, Haines and Skagway to the Gustavus airport. Bus service between the airport and Bartlett Cove is available for arriving jet flights as is taxi service. Courtesy van service is available from many of the local accommodations.

Roads: Gustavus has less than 20 miles of paved roads.

Taxi: TLC Taxi, phone (907) 697-2239; Strawberry Taxi & Tours, (907) 697-2155.

Rental Cars: Bud's Rent-A-Car, phone (907) 697-2403.

Boat Service: A catamaran day-boat tour of Glacier Bay National Park, operated by the park concession, departs from Bartlett Cove daily in summer. Saltwater charter boats are available in Gustavus for sightseeing/whale watching or fishing.

Attractions

Besides its proximity to the national park, Gustavus offers a truly unique southeast Alaska experience. Cruise ships do not stop here, so independent travelers can experience Alaska without the crowds. The Gustavus shoreline offers 18 miles of wild sandy beach, ideal for **beachwalking**. Guests and locals alike enjoy exploring Icy Strait, Point Adolphus, the Outer Coast, Glacier Bay and Pleasant Island.

The Glacier Bay National Park Visitor Center and the **Huna Tribal House** in Bartlett Cove are open daily Memorial Day weekend–Labor Day weekend. Attractions include an outdoor exhibit of a 3,729-lb whale skeleton, park information, films, exhibits and trip planning. Join a park ranger for daily guided walks, hikes and evening presentations. Check the schedules posted in town and at the Glacier Bay Lodge.

The Nature Conservancy supports the Gustavus Forelands Preserve. Here you will find the Nagoonberry Loop trail, an easy 2.2 mile loop through forests and meadows to the Gustavus beach.

The gas station is a local attraction: the **Gustavus Dray**, a pre-WWII replica of a Mobil gas station that has a working 1937 Wayne 60 gas pump, a gift shop and a petroleum museum.

Sea kayaking companies provide kayak rentals and guided tours. These tours range in length from a few hours to many weeks.

Local **charter boats**—sometimes called

The Gustavus dray is a pre-WWII working replica with a 1937 gas pump. (©David L. Ranta, staff)

"6 packs" because they carry about 6 passengers—are available for sportfishing (salmon, halibut), sightseeing Icy Strait and Glacier Bay, and whale watching. Whale sightings are almost guaranteed at nearby Point Adolphus.

The Gustavus area is very flat and **bike riding** is a popular way to get around. (There's a paved road in town.) Most inns offer bicycles for use by guests.

Glacier Bay

Boat tours of Glacier Bay are a must for visitors. (©David L. Ranta, staff)

One of southeastern Alaska's most dramatic attractions, Glacier Bay has been called "a picture of icy wildness unspeakably pure and sublime" (John Muir, 1879). A national park and preserve, Glacier Bay is best viewed from the water, either from a cruise ship, a tour boat or charter out of Gustavus—the nearest community. The only land route to Glacier Bay National Park is a 10-mile road connecting the small community of Gustavus to Bartlett Cove, site of the park's ranger station, walk-in campground (no vehicle parking or RV services), visitor center, Glacier Bay Lodge and the concessionaire-operated tour boat. There are no entrance fees or user fees at Glacier Bay and no vehicle campgrounds or recreational vehicle services (no sani-dump, no hookups, no parking) available.

(©David L. Ranta, staff)

Visitor Information: Glacier Bay National Park and Preserve, P.O. Box 140, Gustavus, AK 99826; phone (907) 697-2230, fax (907) 697-2654; www.nps.gov/glba.

Glacier Bay Visitor Center, located on the second floor of Glacier Bay Lodge has exhibits, an information desk (pictured above), bookstore and auditorium. Open daily from late May through early September. Park rangers present evening programs, show educational videos and lead walks and hikes. Junior Ranger program for kids.

Emergency Services: In Gustavus dial 911. Inside park, phone (907) 697-2651. KWM20 Bartlett Cove on marine band 16.

With passage of the Alaska National Interest Lands Conservation Act in December 1980, Glacier Bay National Monument, established in 1925 by Pres. Calvin Coolidge, became a national park. More than a half-million acres were added to the park/preserve to protect fish and wildlife habitat and wilderness. The 3.3 million acre park includes Mount Fairweather, the highest peak in Southeast Alaska, located in the Fairweather Range of the St. Elias Mountains.

Originally, 4 Huna Tlingit clans occupied territories in and around Glacier Bay using its abundance of fish, wildlife and plants. Glacier Bay remains their spiritual homeland through stories, songs and dances. Tribal members continue traditional harvest activities and various cultural programs in the park today. Dedicated in 2016, the Huna Tribal House is the first permanent clan house in Glacier Bay since Tlingit villages were destroyed by an advancing glacier over 250 years ago.

When the English naval explorer Capt. George Vancouver sailed through the ice-choked waters of Icy Strait in 1794, Glacier Bay was little more than a dent in the coastline. Across the head of this seemingly minor inlet stood a towering wall of ice marking the seaward terminus of an immense glacier that completely filled the broad, deep basin of what is now Glacier Bay. To the north, ice extended more than 100 miles into the St. Elias Mountains, covering the intervening valleys with a 4,000-foot-deep mantle of ice.

During the century following Vancouver's explorations, the glacier retreated some 40 miles back into the bay, permitting a spruce–hemlock forest to gradually fill the land. By 1916, the Grand Pacific Glacier, which once occupied the entire bay, had

receded some 65 miles from the position observed by Vancouver in 1794. Nowhere else in the world have glaciers been observed to recede at such a rapid pace.

Today, few of the many tributary glaciers that once supplied the huge ice sheet extend to the sea. Glacier Bay National Park includes 7 active tidewater glaciers, including several on the remote and seldom-visited western edge of the park along the Gulf of Alaska and Lituya Bay. Icebergs, cracked off from near-vertical ice cliffs, dot the waters of upper Glacier Bay.

Glacier Bay's rich marine waters are a sanctuary for endangered humpback whales. Special vessel regulations apply and the National Park Service limits the number of vessels from June to August. Check with the National Park Service for current regulations.

Glacier Bay is home to a wide variety of wildlife both marine and terrestrial. Look for mountain goats on steep cliffs in the mid- to upper bay. Moose are common in Gustavus, Bartlett Cove and the lower bay where they browse the grasses and willows around the bay, but they are relative newcomers: moose weren't seen here until the late 1960s. Small mammals include porcupine, coyotes, river otters and red squirrels. Boaters may see harbor seals, sea lions, harbor porpoise and sea otters.

The park is home to brown/grizzly bears and black bears. One unique variation specific to this area is the "glacier" bear. It is a black bear that is a blue-gray color with long guard hairs that are yellow or white and blend in with a backdrop of glaciers. Visitors are cautioned to practice bear safety, especially when fishing, hiking or camping in the backcountry. Bear spray is recommended.

Fishing in Glacier Bay and Icy Straits for coho and pink salmon, Dolly Varden and halibut. Charter fishing trips are available from Gustavus.

Lodging & Services

Glacier Bay Lodge, located at Bartlett Cove, is the only accommodation within the national park, although nearby Gustavus *(description begins on page 638)* has a number of lodges, inns, and bed and breakfasts. For information on Glacier Bay Lodge and excursion boat cruises offered from the lodge, visit www.visitglacierbay.com.

Glacier Bay Lodge & Tours. See display ad on page 639.

There is a Visitor Information Station staffed with park rangers for boaters and campers; restrooms and picnic shelter located near the lodge by the public-use dock in Bartlett Cove. Open May through September; phone (907) 697-2627.

Camping

There is a walk-in only campground, open year-round at Bartlett Cove with 33 tent sites, 14-day limit, a warming hut, and firewood may be available; open year-round. No RV services of any kind—such as dump stations or hookups—are available anywhere in Gustavus or Glacier Bay National Park. Overnight parking is available but no camping is allowed in the parked vehicle.

Wilderness camping is available throughout the park; many campers/kayakers use the drop-off service from the park's concession-operated tour boat. Campers must obtain a free permit and attend a camper orientation (presented multiple times daily at the Visitor Information Station). Bear-resis-

Glacier Bay National Park and Preserve

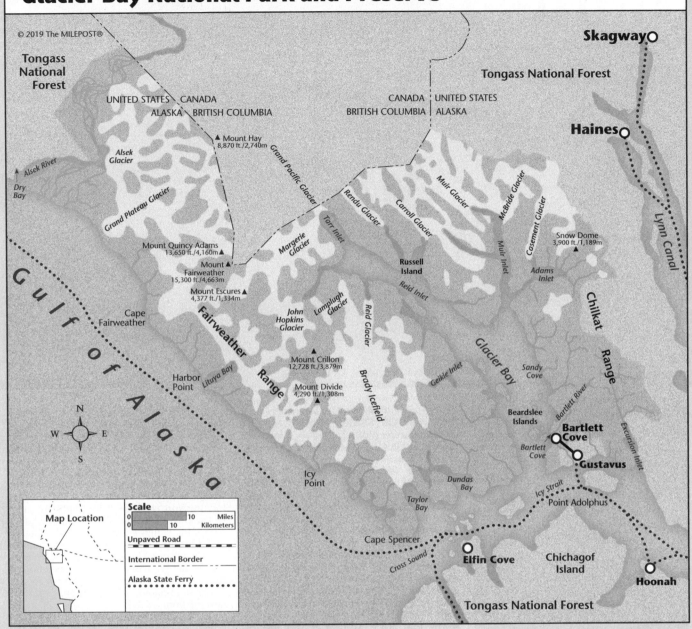

© 2019 The MILEPOST®

Tongass National Forest

Skagway

Tongass National Forest

Haines

UNITED STATES | CANADA
ALASKA | BRITISH COLUMBIA

CANADA | UNITED STATES
BRITISH COLUMBIA | ALASKA

▲ Mount Hay
8,870 ft./2,740m

Alsek Glacier

Grand Pacific Glacier

Rendu Glacier

Muir Glacier

McBride Glacier

Casement Glacier

Snow Dome
3,900 ft./1,189m ▲

Alsek River

Grand Plateau Glacier

Margerie Glacier

Tarr Inlet

Carroll Glacier

Muir Inlet

Adams Inlet

Dry Bay

Mount Quincy Adams
13,650 ft./4,160m ▲

Mount ▲
Fairweather
15,300 ft./4,663m

Mount Escures ▲
4,377 ft./1,334m

Lamplugh Glacier

John Hopkins Glacier

Reid Glacier

Russell Island

Reid Inlet

Cape Fairweather

Fairweather Range

Lituya Bay

Harbor Point

▲ Mount Crillon
12,728 ft./3,879m

Mount Divide
4,290 ft./1,308m ▲

Brady Icefield

Geikie Inlet

Glacier Bay

Sandy Cove

Bartlett River

Beardslee Islands

Bartlett Cove

Bartlett Cove

Gustavus

Excursion Inlet

Chilkat Range

Lynn Canal

Icy Point

Dundas Bay

Taylor Bay

Icy Strait

Point Adolphus

Cape Spencer

Cross Sound

Elfin Cove

Chichagof Island

Hoonah

Tongass National Forest

Gulf of Alaska

Map Location

Scale
0 — 10 Miles
0 — 10 Kilometers

Unpaved Road
International Border
Alaska State Ferry

---

tant food canisters, available at no charge, are required for back-country camping.

Transportation

Air: Scheduled Alaska Airlines and Juneau-based charter air service to Glacier Bay lands at Gustavus airport. All wilderness/non-motorized waters are closed to aircraft landing from May 1 to Sept. 15. For air service information, go to www.gustavusak.com.

Ferry: Alaska Marine Highway has regularly scheduled sailings between Juneau and Gustavus year-round. www.ferryalaska. com. *NOTE: There are no vehicle friendly campgrounds or services for recreational vehicles in Gustavus or Glacier Bay National Park and Gustavus has less than 20 miles of paved roads.*

Boat Service: Excursion boats operated by Glacier Bay Lodge concessionaire depart from Bartlett Cove. Charter boats are available in Gustavus for sightseeing, whale watching or fishing. Overnight cruise tours and scheduled day trips by catamaran are available from Juneau.

Cruise Ships: Thousands of park visitors experience the beauty of Glacier Bay from the decks of cruise ships and a number of cruise lines visit Glacier Bay as part of longer itineraries.

Private Boats: Glacier Bay National Park is about 100 miles from Juneau by boat. Park rangers at Bartlett Cove are available to assist visitors who wish to tour Glacier Bay in private boats or by kayak. Kayak rentals and daily guided kayak trips from Glacier Bay Sea Kayaks (907) 697-2257, www.glacierbaysea kayaks.com. Multi-day guided kayak trips are available through Spirit Walker Expeditions Gustavus, www.seakayakalaska.com; Alaska Discovery in Juneau, phone 1-888-831-7526, www.mtsobek.com; and Alaska Mountain Guides in Haines, phone 1-800-766-3396, http://alaskamountainguides.com.

Permits are required for private marine motorized vessels from June 1 through August 31; permits are free and good for 7 consecutive days. Permits must be obtained prior to entry into Glacier Bay and Bartlett Cove. Phone (907) 697-2627 or call KWM20 Bartlett Cove on marine band 16 to confirm permits are available. Advance application is strongly advised. Private Vessel Entry Permit applications are available online at www. nps.gov/glba/planyourvisit/boat.htm. Boat permit applications must be made no more than 60 days in advance of your requested date of entry.

Fuel dock at Bartlett Cove (phone lodge or contact on marine band 16 for hours). Anchor out in designated areas at Bartlett Cove. The Park Service identifies possible anchorages on their website, in the park newspaper, The Fairweather, and during every boater orientation.

CAUTION BOATERS: No attempt should be made to navigate Glacier Bay without appropriate charts, tide tables and local knowledge. Floating ice is a special hazard. Because of the danger from waves caused by falling ice, small craft should not approach closer than 0.25 mile from tidewater glacier fronts.

Haines

Tent camping at Portage Cove in Haines. One of only 2 Southeast Alaska ports connected to the Alaska Highway system, Haines is a popular point of entry. (©David L. Ranta, staff)

Major Attractions:

©Kris Valencia, staff

Fort Seward, Museums, Welcome Totems, Alaska Chilkat Bald Eagle Preserve

Located on Portage Cove, Chilkoot Inlet, on the upper arm of Lynn Canal, 80 air miles northwest of Juneau; 150 road miles southeast of Haines Junction, YT, via the Haines Highway. NOTE: Haines is only 15 miles by water from Skagway, but it is 355 miles by road! (Alaska Marine Highway ferry service year-round; more frequent passenger-only fast ferry available seasonally.) **Population:** Haines Borough 2,530. **Emergency Services: Alaska State Troopers**, phone (907) 766-2552. **Police, Fire Department** and **Ambulance,**

emergency only phone 911; business phone: (907) 766-6430. **SEARHC Haines Medical Clinic**, phone (907) 766-6300. **Maritime Search and Rescue**, contact the Coast Guard at 1-800-478-5555.

Visitor Information: Haines Visitor Center, 122 Second Ave. S., Box 530, Haines, AK 99827; phone (907) 766-6418; email hcvb@haines.ak.us; www.visithaines.com. Open 8 A.M. to 5 P.M. weekdays, 9 A.M. to 4 P.M. weekends, June–September. Open 8 A.M. to 5 P.M. weekdays, October–May. Free brochures for all of Alaska and Yukon. Ask at the Visitor Center for WiFi locations. **Elevation:** Sea level. Climate: Average daily maximum temperature in July, 66°F; average daily minimum in January, 16°F. Extreme high summer temperature, 98°F; extreme winter low, -18°F; average annual precipitation, 59 inches. **Radio:** KHNS-FM 102.3. **Television:** 35 cable channels. **Newspaper:** *Chilkat Valley News* (weekly).

Private Aircraft: Haines airport, 4 miles west; elev. 16 feet; length 3,000 feet; asphalt; fuel 100; unattended.

Haines is a small town that hosts a large number of visitors each summer. As a gateway to the Alaska Highway for Inside Passage travelers, Haines has become an important service stop. Its spectacular scenery, outdoor recreation and laid-back lifestyle have also made Haines a popular destination. At least part of the community's appeal lies in its small town friendliness, captured in local writer Heather Lende's books, *If You Lived Here, I'd Know Your Name* and *Find The Good.*

The original Indian name for Haines was *Dtehshuh*, meaning "end of the trail," referring to where Chilkat and Chilkoot Indians met and traded with Russian and American ships at the end of the peninsula. It was also their portage route for transporting canoes from the Chilkat River to Portage Cove and Lynn Canal.

In 1879 missionary S. Hall Young and naturalist John Muir came to the village of Yandustuky (near today's airport) to determine the location of a Presbyterian mission and school. The site chosen was on the narrow portage between the Chilkat River and Lynn Canal. The following year, George Dickinson established a trading post for the Northwest Trading Company, next to the mission site. His wife Sarah began a school for Tlingit children. By 1881, Eugene and Caroline Willard arrived to establish Chilkat Mission. The mission and town were named for Francina E. Haines, secretary of the Presbyterian Women's Executive Society of Home Missions, who raised funds for the new mission.

In 1882 the Haines post office was established. The Dalton Trail, which crossed the Chilkat mountain pass to the Klondike goldfields in the Yukon, started at Pyramid Harbor Cannery across the Chilkat River from Haines. The town became an important outlet for the Porcupine Mining District, producing thousands of dollars' worth of placer gold at the turn of the century.

Just to the south of Haines city center is Fort Seward on Portage Cove. Named Fort William H. Seward, in honor of the secretary of state who negotiated the purchase of Alaska from Russia in 1867, this was established as the first permanent Army post in the territory. The first troops arrived in 1904 from Camp Skagway. In 1922, the fort was renamed Chilkoot Barracks, after the

HAINES ADVERTISERS

mountain pass and the Indian tribe on the Chilkoot River.

Chilkoot Barracks was deactivated in 1946 and sold in 1947 to a group of enterprising U.S. veterans who had designs of creating a business cooperative on the site. Their original plans were never fully realized, but most stayed on, creating the city of Port Chilkoot by converting some of the buildings into homes and businesses.

In 1970, Port Chilkoot merged with Haines to become a single municipality, the City of Haines. Two years later, the post was designated a national historic site and became officially known, again, as Fort William H. Seward (although the underlying land is still owned by the Chilkoot Company). In 2002, the City of Haines was consolidated with the Borough of Haines to form Haines Borough.

Fishing and gold mining were the initial industries of the Haines area. Today, halibut and gill-net salmon fishing and tourism are the basis of the economy. Haines is an important port on the Alaska Marine Highway System as the southern terminus of the Haines Highway, 1 of the 2 year-round roads linking southeastern Alaska with the Alaska Highway in Canada.

Lodging & Services

For a small town, Haines is very much a full-service community. Accommodations at 5 hotels/motels, including **The Captain's Choice Motel** (907/766-3111); the historic **Hotel Halsingland** (phone 1-800-542-6363); and Eagle's Nest Motel (phone 1-800-354-6009); the Aspen Suites Hotel (phone 907/766-2211); and The Inn at Haines (phone 907/766-2970). Find cabins, lodges and B&Bs at www.visithaines.com/lodging.

Haines has hardware stores, grocery stores (Howser's IGA Supermarket, Olerud's Market Center); restaurants, cafes and taverns; automotive repair, a car wash; laundries, a post office and First National Bank, Alaska. ATMs available at bank and businesses. Mountain Market & Cafe, on Third Avenue and the Haines Highway, is a natural foods market with a deli/cafe and full espresso bar (and it is open daily if you need a latte for that early morning ferry line).

There are several gift shops and galleries, many featuring the work of local artisans. Art galleries, museums and businesses host First Friday events year round from 5–7 P.M.

Port Chilkoot Distillery is a micro distillery using local herbs and wild plants in their blends of whiskey, vodka, gin and other spirits; tasting room, tours, gifts; on Blacksmith Drive at Fort Seward; phone (907) 766-3434.

The Haines Senior Center invites seniors to come and have lunch. They are open 8 A.M. to 2 P.M. Monday–Thursday. Call in advance (907) 766-2383. The award-winning Haines public library offers internet access. Swimming available at Haines Pool adjacent the high school.

Camping

RV parks in Haines include **Haines Hitch-up RV Park** (description follows) and **Oceanside RV Park** (see ads on this page).

Haines Hitch-Up RV Park offers easy access to 92 full hook-up, spacious, grassy, level sites. Pull-through, cable TV and 50 amp sites available. Laundromat, free immaculate restrooms and free (Ltd.) WiFi. Tour tickets and information. Located at the junction of the Haines Highway and Main Street. 851 Main St., Haines, AK 99827.

Reserve online at www.hitchuprv.com or call (907) 766-2882. See display ad on this page. [ADVERTISEMENT]

There are 4 state campgrounds in the Haines area: Portage Cove State Recreation Site on the waterfront, with 9 walk-in tent sites; Chilkat State Park, located 7 miles south of Haines on Mud Bay Road (then another 2 miles on the Chilkat State Park Road), which has 32 tent/RV sites and 3 waterfront tent sites; Chilkoot Lake State Recreation Site, 10 miles from downtown Haines via Lutak Road, with 32 sites; and Mosquito Lake State Recreation Site at **Milepost H 27.2**, with a small, primitive camping area and no outhouse.

Transportation

Air: Haines airport is 3.5 miles from downtown. Alaska Seaplanes (www.flyalaskaseaplanes.com) offers daily scheduled service to and from Juneau, Skagway and other southeast Alaska communities. There are also 2 charter services. Some motels offer courtesy car pickup from the [...]

Car Rental: At **Captain's [...]** phone (907) 766-3111.

Highways: The Haines Hi[...] nects Haines, AK, with Haines Ju[...] It is maintained year-round. U.S. C[...] open 7 A.M. to 11 P.M. (Alaska standa[...] See HAINES HIGHWAY section page 65[...]

The 10-mile Lutak Road leads t[...] Alaska Marine Highway terminal [...] Chilkoot Lake SRS. The 7-mile Mud [...] Road accesses Chilkat State Park.

Bus: Visitor Shuttle Bus when cruise ship[...] are in port offer free loop rides around city on regular intervals (approximately every 15 minutes).

Ferries: Alaska Marine Highway vessels provide year-round service to Haines; visit www.ferryalaska.com for schedule. Ferry terminal on Lutak Road, 4.5 miles from downtown Haines; phone (907) 766-2111. NOTE: There is no WiFi in the ferry terminal or on the ferries. There is only sporadic cell phone service on Lutak Road.

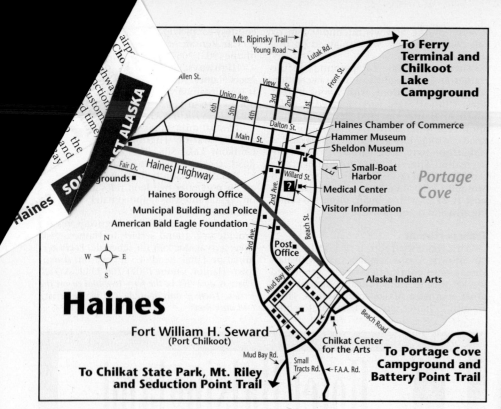

Haines

Fort William H. Seward
(Port Chilkoot)

To Chilkat State Park, Mt. Riley
and Seduction Point Trail

Flag"—once lived in these quarters. Look for historic and interpretive signs.

Alaska Indian Arts. This nonprofit organization, located in the restored hospital at Fort Seward, is part of the walking tour. It is dedicated to the revival of Tlingit Indian art. See displays of Native art. Local craftsmen carve totem poles and work with silver and stone. Visitors hours 9 A.M. to 5 P.M. weekdays, year-round. Phone (907) 766-2160; www.alaskaindianarts.com.

See the Welcome Totems located at the Y on the Haines Highway. These poles were created by carvers of Alaska Indian Arts Inc. and are read from bottom to top. *The Raven* pole is symbolic of Raven, as founder of the world and all his great powers. The second figure is *The Whale*, representing Alaska and its great size. The bottom figure is the head of *The Bear*, which shows great strength. *The Eagle* pole tells of its feeding grounds (the Haines area is noted for eagles). The bottom figure is *The Brown Bear*, which feeds on salmon and is a symbol of strength. *The Eagle Chief*, head of the Eagle clan, is the third figure, and the top figure is *The Salmon Chief*, who provides the late run of salmon to the feeding grounds.

©Kris Valencia, staff

Haines Sheldon Museum is located on the old Haines Mission property at the end of Main Street, on the corner of Main and First, with a view of the boat harbor. The main gallery features the sesquicentennial exhibit "Everything from Afar Drifts Ashore," focusing on the 50 years from 1850 to 1900, when the protected Tlingit land, Jilkaat Aani, transitioned into the multi-national Chilkat Mission and then the city of Haines. The exhibit includes Chilkat blankets, spruce root baskets, Tlingit carvings, Russian trunks, the Eldred Rock Lighthouse lens, Jack Dalton's sawed-off shotgun and historic photographs. A changing exhibit gallery shows local art and history. The children's interactive gal-

Alaska Fjordlines offers a day cruise to Juneau in summer; phone 1-800-320-0146 or (907) 766-3395. Includes bus tour of Juneau and Mendenhall Glacier plus free time for shopping and sightseeing.

Haines–Skagway Fast Ferry provides passenger-only service (seasonally) between Skagway and Haines 1-888-766-2103.

Cruise Ships: Several cruise ships call in Haines.

Private Boats: Transient moorage is available at Letnikof Cove and at the small-boat harbor downtown. Contact the harbormaster, phone (907) 766-2448.

Attractions

Take the walking tour of historic Fort William H. Seward. The walking tour includes 13 wayside interpretive history panels, beginning at the Cruise Ship Dock and Picture Point, and the open-air sculpture garden in the barracks foundation ruins, with 16 sculptures by Haines artists there and at other locations.

Historic buildings of the post include the former cable office; warehouses and barracks; fire hall; the guard house (jail); contractor's office; plumber's quarters; the post exchange (now a lodge); gymnasium; movie house; the mule stables; and "Soapsuds Alley," the housing for noncommissioned officers whose wives did laundry for the soldiers. The former headquarters building, fronted by a cannon and a totem depicting a bear and an eagle, is now a private residence.

Officers' Row at the "Top O' the Hill" is now restored homes and apartments. Hotel Halsingland occupies the commanding officers quarters. Elinor Dusenbury, who later wrote the music for the state song—"Alaska's

lery features a clan house, fish camp and boat.

The museum is open daily in summer 9 A.M. to 5 P.M. Monday–Saturday and 1–4 P.M. Sunday. Open Monday–Saturday 1–4 P.M. in winter. Admission fee $10; children 12 and under free. Museum store is in the entrance lobby. Research archives are on the lower level. Phone (907) 766-2366; www.sheldon museum.org.

The Hammer Museum on Main Street. This unique museum is dedicated to preserving the history of man's first tool and is a tribute to working men and women everywhere. The hammer tells the story of man's progress and ingenuity from ancient times to modern day. With over 2,000 hammers and related objects on display, this museum has something for every age. The hammers range from a hammer used in the building of the third pyramid at Giza to a hammer used to remove manhole covers. The museum can be easily found by the 20-foot-high hammer in front. It is just up the street from the boat harbor. Open Monday–Friday May to mid-September 10 A.M. to 5 P.M. and Saturdays from 10 A.M. to 2 P.M. Admission fee $5, kids under 12 free when accompanied by adult. Website: www.hammer museum.org.

The American Bald Eagle Foundation is a natural history museum and live raptor center, located on the Haines Highway at 2nd Avenue. The museum showcases wildlife found in the Chilkat Valley with more than 200 taxidermied specimens and multiple interactive displays. Visitors may also observe 10 raptors living in the outdoor raptor center. Call ahead for daily program schedule; phone (907) 766-3094; website www.baldeagles.org.

Alaska Chilkat Bald Eagle Preserve is the annual gathering site of more than 3,500 bald eagles from mid-October through December with the Bald Eagle Festival in November each year (www.baldeagle festival.org). The 48,000-acre preserve was established in 1982 to protect and perpetuate one of the world's greatest concentration of bald eagles and their critical habitat. The main eagle viewing area lies along the Chilkat River flats between **Milepost H 18** and **H 24** of the Haines Highway. There is a walkway and viewing platform system that spans between the parking lots at Mile 19 and 21 and includes interpretive displays. The eagles are drawn here by the late run of salmon, mostly chum and some coho. For more information, contact Alaska State Parks, phone (907) 766-2292, or www.dnr. state.ak.us/parks/units/eagleprv.htm.

Special Events. The **Annual Great Alaska Craft Beer and Home Brew Festival,** held at Dalton City May 24–25, 2019, features a gourmet beer banquet and a microbrew tasting.

The **Kluane to Chilkat Bike Relay** (June 15, 2019) starts in Haines Junction, YT, and finishes 152 miles later in downtown Haines, AK. The free Community King Salmon Barbecue follows the bike race at "Dalton City" on the Haines Fairgrounds.

The **51st Annual Southeast Alaska State Fair** takes place July 25–28, 2019. It features 4 days of fun for all ages. Live music on 3 stages, exhibits, a children's carnival, rides, games, races, dancing, a regional talent show and wearable art review, and the famous Logging Show and Fishermen's Rodeo. With tasty fair food, lots of vendors and exciting events, this fair has something for the whole family. Details at www.seakfair.org.

The **Alaska Bald Eagle Festival**, Nov. 6–9, 2019, celebrates the winter gathering of eagles near Haines. Visit their website at www.baldeagles.org.

Dalton City is a replica of the gold rush town and was built for the "White Fang" Disney film set. It is located at the Haines fairgrounds. The former movie set houses a cafe with Southern food and several shops, and hosts special events like the Homebrew Festival as well as the Southeast Alaska State Fair.

Drive out Beach Road. This waterfront road begins at the cruise ship dock and accesses Portage Cove State Recreation Site (at Mile 0.5), which has 9 walk-in campsites, day-use parking and a short trail to a scenic overlook. Beach Road ends at Mile 1.5 at Battery Point Trail, one of the most popular day hikes in the area. This short, easy hike on a well-maintained trail follows the shoreline to a pleasant beach and provides access to Mount Riley trail (see Hike Area Trails).

Drive out Mud Bay Road. This scenic side road is logged as follows: Mile 2.4, Mount Riley Trail and parking area; Mile 3.4, roadside spring water; Mile 3.7, large paved view turnout along water; Mile 4.5, large parking area, boat harbor, launch, outhouse and views of **Haines Packing Co.**; Mile 4.8, entrance to Haines Packing Co. with interpretive signs, free self-guided tour, gift shop; Mile 6.1, turnoff on gravel road which leads to **Chilkat State Park and Campground**. For the state park, turn right and continue 1.2 miles to park entrance, then a half-mile further for fee station. The campground has 35 sites, picnic sites, beach access, a boat launch and a 7-mile (one-way) hiking trail to Seduction Point at the southern tip of the Chilkat Peninsula. For more information, contact Alaska State Parks, phone (907) 766-2292; website: dnr.alaska.gov/parks/asp units/southeast/chilkatsp.htm.

If you continue past the campground, in a half-mile you arrive at a shoreline picnic area with spectacular views, grill-style firepits, tables, picnic shelter and pit toilets. This is a favorite wedding venue for local residents. There are beautiful views of Rainbow and Davidson glaciers across Chilkat Inlet.

©Kris Valencia, staff

Drive out Lutak Road. This road begins at the intersection of Main Street and Second Avenue (which becomes Lutak Road). At Mile 0.7, Picture Point picnic area with covered pavilion, grill-style firepit, toilets, bear-proof trash bin, picnic tables and a picture-perfect view of the Chilkat Inlet and Haines. At Mile 3.1 there is a popular picnic area with beach access; small parking, tables, grill-style firepits, bear-proof trash bins, pit toilets. The Alaska Marine Highway terminal is located at Mile 4 Lutak Road. Continue north past the ferry terminal to road end at Chilkoot Lake Road and turn left. The road parallels the Chilkoot River for about a mile before it ends at a parking area on beautiful Chilkoot Lake. It is about 10 miles from

downtown Haines to **Chilk**[...] **Recreation Site**, which has [...] and 32-site campground. For [...] tion, contact Alaska State Parks, [...] 766-2292; website: dnr.alaska.[...] aspunits/southeast/chilkootlksrs.ht[...]

The ADF&G operates a fish wei[...] Chilkoot River between June and S[...] ber to count the sockeye salmon retu[...] to Chilkoot Lake and the river. This are[...] good for fish and wildlife viewing. Due [...] bear activity during salmon runs, there a[...] areas along the road that restrict driver[...] from stopping and getting out of their cars. *CAUTION: Be bear aware!*

Hike Area Trails. Stop at the visitor information center for a free copy of the pamphlet, *Haines is for Hikers* (www.visit haines.com/sites/default/files/Haines%20 is%20for%20Hikers.pdf), which contains trail descriptions and maps. Or contact Alaska State Parks at (907) 766-2292.

Mount Ripinsky trail is a strenuous all-day hike—recommended for experienced hikers only—with spectacular views from the summit of mountains and tidal waters. Battery Point trail leads about 1.2 miles to Kelgaya Point overlooking Lynn Canal along relatively flat ground. Mount Riley (elev. 1,760 feet) has 3 routes to the summit. The steepest and most widely used trail starts at Mile 3 Mud Bay Road and climbs 2.8 miles to the summit and, according to our Park Ranger source, this trail may also be accessed from 0.9 mile of the Battery Point Trail.

Visit Jilkaat Kwaan Cultural Heritage Center at Klukwan, approximately 22 miles from Haines via the Haines Highway. A carving shed, smokehouse, replica clan house and various state-of-the-art exhibits introduce you to the Tlingit culture. Open mid-May to September. Stop by anytime for a self-guided tour or phone ahead for guided tour, (907) 767-5485; jilkaatkwaanheritage center.org

Kroschel Wildlife Center is about 28 miles from Haines (take the Haines Highway to **Milepost H 27.2**, turn on Mosquito Lake Road and continue to Mile 1.8). Shows are about 2 hours and include a guided walk on an easy trail. Access to over 15 species of Alaska wildlife. Open May 15–Sept. 15. Independent visitors must reserve tour space ahead of visit. For details, call (907) 767-5464 or visit www.kroschelfilms.com.

Go Flightseeing. Local air charter operators offer flightseeing trips for spectacular close-up views of glaciers, ice fields, mountain peaks and bald eagles. The heart of Glacier Bay is just west of Haines.

Take a Tour. Charter boat operators in Haines offer fishing, sightseeing and photography trips. Local tour companies offer bicycle tours, guided hiking, bus tours and nature walks.

AREA FISHING: Good fishing May–June for chinook in **Chilkat Inlet**. Halibut best June–September in **Chilkat, Lutak** and **Chilkoot inlets**. Dolly Varden fishing good in all lakes and clear water rivers, and along marine shorelines from early spring to late fall. Great pink fishing in August along the marine shoreline of **Lutak Inlet** and in the **Chilkoot River**. Sockeye in the **Chilkoot River**, late June through August. Coho in the **Chilkoot River** and **Chilkat River,** mid-September through October. Cutthroat trout year-round at **Chilkoot Lake** and **Mosquito Lake**. Contact the Alaska Dept. of Fish and Game at (907) 766-3638.

gway

...reet in Skagway has ...storic structures housing ...y of businesses. *(©Kris Valencia, staff)*

Major Attractions:

©Kris Valencia, staff

Klondike Gold Rush National Historical Park, White Pass & Yukon Route Railway

Located on the north end of Taiya Inlet on Lynn Canal, 90 air miles northwest of Juneau; 108 road miles south of Whitehorse, YT. The northern terminus of the Alaska Marine Highway Southeast ferry system and southern terminus of the South Klondike Highway, which connects with the Alaska Highway. *NOTE: Although Skagway is only 15 miles by water from Haines, it is 355*

miles by road! *(Alaska Marine Highway ferries and more frequent passenger-only fast ferry are available.)* **Population:** 1,036. **Emergency Services:** Phone 911 for all emergencies. **Police**, phone (907) 983-2232. **Fire Department**, phone (907) 983-2450. **Clinic**, Dahl Memorial, phone (907) 983-2255. **Maritime Search and Rescue**, contact the Coast Guard at 1-800-478-5555. **U.S. Customs** located at Mile 6.8 Klondike Highway 2; phone (907) 983-2325.

Visitor Information: The Visitor Center is located in Arctic Brotherhood Hall between 2nd and 3rd on Broadway. Open daily early May–late September; only Monday–Friday during winter. They offer information on area attractions and accommodations, walking and trail maps. Contact the Skagway Convention and Visitors Bureau, Box 1029, Skagway, AK 99840; email skagwayinfo@skagway.org; phone (907) 983-2854; www.skagway.com.

Klondike Gold Rush National Historical Park Visitor Center is located in the restored railroad depot at 2nd Avenue and Broadway. Open daily in summer; exhibits and films on the history of the area and information on hiking the Chilkoot Trail. Write Klondike Gold Rush NHP, Box 517, Skagway, AK 99840; phone (907) 983-9200; www.nps.gov/klgo. Public restrooms are located in a small building at the east end of 6th Street and at the small boat harbor. The Klondike Gold Rush National Historical Park, Arctic Brotherhood Hall, Skagway Museum and the Railroad Depot provide public restrooms as do many other buildings and businesses throughout town.

Elevation: Sea level. **Climate:** Average daily temperature in summer, 57°F; in winter, 23°F. Average annual precipitation is 26.16 inches. **Radio:** KHNS-FM 91.9. **Televi-**sion: KTOO and ARCS. **Newspaper:** *Skagway News* (bimonthly).

Private Aircraft: Skagway airport, adjacent west; elev. 44 feet; length 3,550 feet; asphalt; fuel 100LL; attended.

The name Skagway (originally spelled Skaguay) is said to mean "stiffly wind rippled water" in Tlingit. It is the oldest incorporated city in Alaska (incorporated in 1900). Skagway is also a year-round port and 1 of the 2 gateway cities to the Alaska Highway in Southeast Alaska: Klondike Highway 2 connects Skagway with the Alaska Highway. (The other is Haines, connected to the Alaska Highway via the Haines Highway.)

Skagway owes its birth to the Klondike Gold Rush. Skagway, and neighboring Dyea, boomed as thousands of gold seekers arrived to follow the White Pass and Chilkoot trails to the Yukon goldfields.

In July 1897, the first boatloads of stampeders bound for the Klondike landed at Skagway and Dyea. By October 1897, according to a North West Mounted Police report, Skagway had grown "from a concourse of tents to a fair-sized town, with well-laid-out streets and numerous frame buildings, stores, saloons, gambling houses, dance houses and a population of about 20,000." Less than a year later it was reported that "Skagway was little better than a hell on earth." Customs office records for 1898 show that in the month of February alone 5,000 people landed at Skagway and Dyea.

By the summer of 1899 the stampede was all but over. The newly built White Pass & Yukon Route railway reached Lake Bennett, supplanting the Chilkoot Trail from Dyea. Dyea became a ghost town. Its post office closed in 1902, and by 1903 its population consisted of 1 settler. Skagway's population dwindled to 500. But Skagway persisted, both as a port and as terminus of the White Pass & Yukon Route railway, which connected the town to Whitehorse, YT, in 1900. Throughout most of the twentieth century the railroad transported regular shipments of ore and freight to and from Skagway's port. Cruise ships, and later the Alaska State Ferry System, brought tourism and business to Skagway. Scheduled state ferry service to southeastern Alaska began in 1963.

Today, tourism is Skagway's main economic base, with Klondike Gold Rush National Historical Park, and the White Pass and Yukon Route railway, Skagway's major visitor attractions. Within Skagway's downtown historical district, false-fronted buildings and boardwalks dating from gold rush days line the streets. The National Park Service, the Municipality and local residents have succeeded in preserving Skagway's gold rush atmosphere.

Lodging & Services

Skagway offers a variety of accommodations, from hotels to bed and breakfasts like At the White House B&B, to lodges and log cabins. There are several restaurants and cafes and an espresso/smoothie shop. Red Onion Saloon and Skagway Brewing Co. also serve food. **Poppies Restaurant** at Jewell **Gardens**, Mile 2 South Klondike Highway, serves a daily lunch, and features organic produce from their gardens.

Skagway has grocery and natural foods stores, a Harley Davidson store, international dry goods store and hardware store; clothing stores; many gift and novelty shops offering Alaska and gold rush souvenirs, photos, books, furs and ivory. The **Skaguay News Depot** on Broadway carries a great selection of local books and out-of-town newspapers. Skagway has a post office and a bank (Wells Fargo) with an ATM.

Gas stations in town include Family Fuel on 2nd and State, and Corner Fuel at 4th and Main, both with 24-hour fuel. There's also a laundromat, store and ATM at Family Fuel. There is a laundromat for guests at Garden City RV Park on State Street.

Camping

RV camping at Garden City RV Park at 15th and 17th on State Street in town, and Pullen Creek RV Park on the waterfront. Dyea Campground at the Chilkoot Trail trailhead has 22 campsites and there's camping at Dyea Flats, but the narrow winding road is not recommended for RVs over 25 feet.

The nearest campground on the 98-mile South Klondike Highway is Conrad Yukon Government Campground, about 56 miles from Skagway.

Transportation

Air: Alaska Seaplanes (www.flyalaska seaplanes.com) offers daily scheduled service to and from Juneau, Haines and other southeast Alaska communities. Flightseeing tours offered by Temsco Helicopters, phone (907) 983-2900, www.temscoair.com. Transportation to and from the airport is provided by the flight services and local hotels.

Bus: Bus/van service to Whitehorse, YT (summer only). The S.M.A.R.T. Bus provides shuttle service in town and to/from the ferry and cruise ship pier, (907) 983-2743. $2 for one-way, $5 for all day pass.

Car Rental: Avis phone (907) 983-2247.

Highway: Klondike Highway 2, open daily year-round, when border crossing is

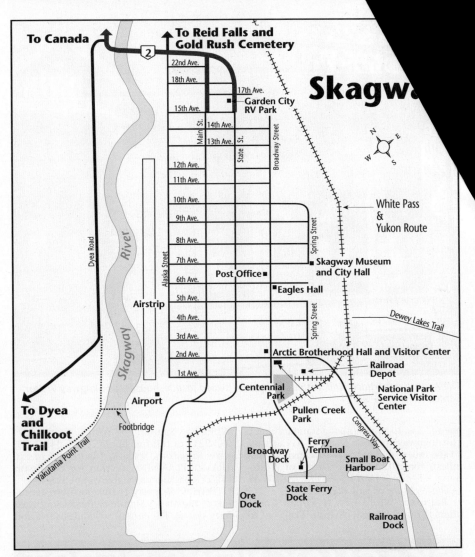

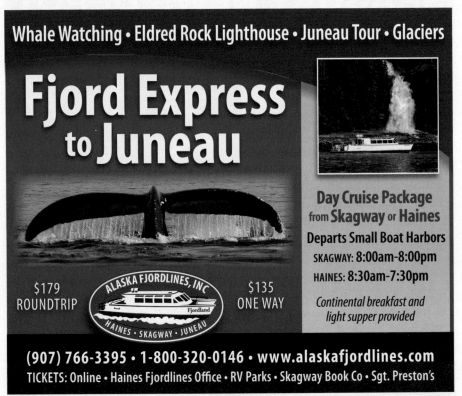

Skagway owes its birth to the Klondike Gold Rush and the stampeders who began to arrive in 1897.

The Arctic Brotherhood Hall, with its unique driftwood facade, houses the Skagway Visitor Center. (©Kris Valencia, staff)

open (7 A.M. to 11 P.M. Alaska standard time). This highway connects Skagway to Carcross, YT (66 miles), and to the Alaska Highway (98 miles), about 12 miles southeast of Whitehorse, YT. (*See SOUTH KLONDIKE HIGHWAY section beginning on page 656.*)

Railroad: White Pass & Yukon Route offers 3-hour excursions from Skagway to White Pass Summit and return. Phone (907) 983-2217 or toll-free phone 1-800-343-7373; www.wpyr.com. See also "Railroads" in the TRAVEL PLANNING section for details on WP&YR packages available out of Skagway.

Ferries: Skagway is the northern terminus of the Alaska Marine Highway Southeast ferry system. For current schedules, fares and reservations, visit www.ferryalaska.com. The ferry terminal is at the end of Broadway on the waterfront (see city map this section); restrooms. Ferry terminal office hours vary and are usually posted on the front door. Phone (907) 983-2229. It is an easy walk into town, but some hotel and motel vans do meet ferries.

Private passenger ferry service is available. **Alaska Fjordlines Express** service between Skagway and Juneau; phone (907) 766-3395 or 1-800-320-0146, or visit www.alaskafjordlines.com. Haines–Skagway Fast Ferry provides passenger-only, seasonal service between Skagway and Haines 1-888-766-2103. This is not the same as the Alaska Marine Highway ferries.

Cruise Ships: Skagway is a regular port of call for Princess, Holland America, Norwegian Cruise Lines, Regent Seven Seas, Silversea, Oceania, Celebrity Cruises, Disney Cruise Line and Royal Caribbean.

Private Boats: Transient moorage is available at the Skagway small-boat harbor. Contact the harbormaster at (907) 983-2628. Space for cruisers up to 100 feet; gas, diesel fuel and water available.

Attractions

The Arctic Brotherhood Hall, located on Broadway between 2nd and 3rd avenues, houses the Skagway Visitor Center. The Arctic Brotherhood Hall's facade has more than 8,833 pieces of driftwood sticks arranged in a mosaic pattern, with the Brotherhood's AB letters and symbols, a gold pan with nuggets.

Klondike Gold Rush National Historical Park Visitor Center is located in the restored railroad depot on 2nd Avenue and Broadway. Visitor center hours: 8:30 A.M. to 5:30 P.M. daily from May through September. The visitor center offers free daily guided walking tours of the Skagway Historic District, ranger talks on a variety of topics, and a free 30-minute film, shown multiple times each day in the visitor center theatre. There are also public restrooms here.

Klondike Gold Rush National Historical Park was established by Congress in 1976 to preserve and interpret the history of the Klondike Gold Rush of 1897–98. It is the nation's only International Historical Park, with units in Seattle, Skagway, British Columbia and Yukon. The U.S. units of the park, managed by the National Park Service, consists of over a dozen buildings in Skagway's historic downtown; a 17-mile-long corridor that is the former townsite of Dyea and the U.S. side of the Chilkoot Trail; a 5-mile-long corridor of land that is part of the White Pass Trail; and a visitor center in Seattle, WA. The Skagway unit is the most-visited national park site in Alaska. For information, phone (907) 983-9200; www.nps.gov/klgo/.

Jewell Gardens & Glassworks, at the

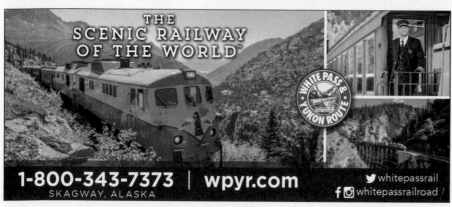

historic Clark Farm at Milepost 2 on the South Klondike Highway, is Skagway's showcase garden. An easy drive or bike ride from town, Jewell Gardens also has a glass-blowing studio where glass blowing is demonstrated for visitors; a gift shop featuring glasswork; a G-scale railroad; and a restaurant that serves lunches (daily) featuring local produce. Phone (907) 983-2111.

Hike the Chilkoot Trail. This 33-mile trail begins on the Dyea Road and climbs over Chilkoot Pass (elev. 3,739 feet) and into Canada to Lake Bennett, following the historic route of the gold seekers of 1897–98. The original stampeders took an average of 3 months to transport the required "ton of goods" (a year's worth of supplies and equipment) over the Pass. Today's adventurers take 3 to 5 days to hike the Chilkoot Trail.

The Trail Center, located on Broadway between the 5th and 6th avenues, has Chilkoot Trail permits and information on Chilkoot Trail fees and customs requirements, regulations, camping, weather, required equipment and current trail conditions. The Trail Center is open 8 A.M. to 5 P.M. daily, June to September; phone (907) 983-9234. Ranger talks are also scheduled at Sheep Camp. Information on hiking the Chilkoot Trail is available online at www.nps.gov/klgo, with links to the Parks Canada website (www.pc.gc.ca/chilkoot) for information and reservations on the Canadian side, or phone (867) 667-3910, toll-free 1-800-661-0486.

Skagway parks. Centennial Park, at the foot of Broadway, has the **Rotary Snowplow #1,** the city's Centennial Statue, benches, and native flora. Nearby Pullen Creek Park has a covered picnic shelter, a footbridge and a small dock. Watch for pinks in August, coho in September (Pullen Creek and pond are closed to fishing Sept. 15–Nov. 30). The Mollie Walsh Park is at the end of 6th Avenue and has an elaborate children's playing area (picnic tables nearby for adults).

McCabe College Building/City Hall is the first granite building constructed in Alaska. It was built by the Methodist Church as a school in 1899–1900 to be known as McCabe College, but public-school laws were passed that made the enterprise impractical, and it was sold to the federal government. Today it houses City Hall and the Skagway Museum.

The Skagway Museum, in the McCabe College Building/City Hall, is one block east of Broadway on Spring Street at 7th Avenue. The museum's primary focus is to help preserve Alaska historical material and to display Alaska pioneer life. On display is a Tlingit canoe, a Portland Cutter sleigh, kayaks and an Alaska Native Heritage collection of baskets, beadwork and carvings. Also exhibited are tools, supplies and gambling equipment used in the Klondike Gold Rush of 1898. The museum is open daily, May through September, from 9 A.M. to 5 P.M. Monday–Saturday; 1 P.M. to 4 P.M. Sunday. Admission $2 adults, $1 students, children under 12 free. Call for winter hours. Phone (907) 983-2420.

Corrington Museum of Alaska History, 3rd and Broadway, offers exhibits featuring scenes from Alaska history, each hand-engraved (scrimshawed) on a walrus tusk. Open in summer; worthwhile and free of charge.

The Days of '98 Show, the longest run-

White Pass & Yukon Route Railway offers daily scenic train trips out of Skagway in summer. (©Kris Valencia, staff)

ning show in the North, is held in Alaska's oldest Eagles aerie, F.O.E. #25 (established 1899), at 6th Avenue and Broadway. This lively 1-hour musical/drama is based on historical records and centers on con man Soapy Smith's reign over Skagway during the days of the Klondike Gold Rush. Shows are performed up to 4 times daily, May to September. 2019 is their 96th season. Phone (907) 983-2545; www.thedaysof98show.com.

Drive Dyea Road. This narrow, winding, gravel road offers spectacular scenery for those driving appropriate vehicles. The road begins at **Milepost S 2.5** South Klond-

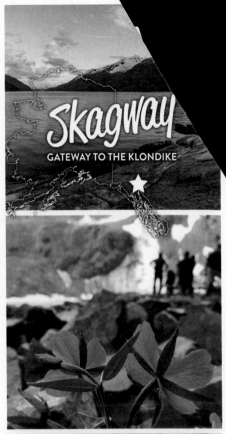

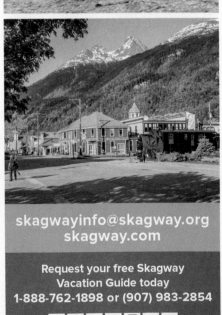

Scenic gravel section of Dyea Road winds along Taiya Inlet. (©Kris Valencia, staff)

Dyea Road begins at **Milepost S 2.5** on the South Klondike Highway and leads about 8 miles to the old Dyea Townsite (not much there) and then ends at beautiful Dyea Flats Recreation Area.

Dyea Road is a narrow, winding, gravel road beyond Mile 1.4 and is not recommended for motorhomes or trailers. **Distance from junction (J) with the South Klondike Highway is shown.**

J 0 Junction with the South Klondike Highway, 2.5 miles from Skagway. (See SOUTH KLONDIKE HIGHWAY section.)

J 0.6 Shoulder parking at old cemetery.

J 1.4 Scenic overlook with view of Skagway, Taiya Inlet and the Skagway River; paved parking, outhouse.

J 1.7 Pavement ends, gravel begins. *Road narrows; use caution on blind curves.* There are many small turnouts to use when passing oncoming vehicles.

J 1.9 Skyline trailhead, parking south side of road. This trail leads to top of AB Mountain (elev. 5,000 feet).

J 3.4 Turnout with interpretive signs and good view.

J 4.1 *Sharp switchback.*

J 4.8 *Road narrows.*

J 5.1 Turnout with interpretive signs on transportation and Dyea. View of the old pilings: the docks of Dyea used to stretch from the trees to beyond the pilings to deep water.

J 6.2 Gravel ends, pavement begins.

J 6.5 Parking area with interpretive signs and water access for river rafters.

J 6.7 Klondike Gold Rush Dyea Campground, unstaffed Ranger Station, Chilkoot Trail trailhead and overnight parking. Campground has 22 campsites, pit toilets, picnic tables and grills at each site; walk-in sites have bear proof food containers; bear proof trash and recycling containers located near ranger station. Campground host during peak months; $10 camping fee. Discount offered for America the Beautiful, Senior or Access pass holders. ▲

J 6.8 Chilkoot Trail Outpost, lodging; www.chilkoottrailoutpost.com.

J 7.2 Chilkoot Trail trailhead; no over-night parking here. Taiya River 1-lane bridge; height 11'2".

J 7.3 Turn here at the signed turnoff immediately after the Taiya River bridge for Klondike Gold Rush National Historical Park's Dyea Historic Town Site, Slide Cemetery and Dyea Flats; descriptions follow. Dyea Road continues straight ahead for about a mile and deadends for most vehicles at Ward Creek bridge.

Drive 0.7 mile west on this side road and turn north (right) for the 0.3-mile access road to **Slide Cemetery** parking lot. The cemetery contains the graves of people killed in the Palm Sunday avalanche, April 3, 1898, on the Chilkoot Trail.

Drive 0.7 mile west on this side road and turn south (left) and continue 0.3 mile for **Historic Dyea Town Site**; limited parking, toilets, trash and recycling. Interpretive signs provide Dyea history on a 1 mile trail following the historic street grid. During the Klondike Gold Rush of 1898–99, Dyea was the jump-off point to the Klondike gold fields via Chilkoot Pass. Now covered with wild iris, fireweed and lupine in summer, little trace remains of Dyea and the buildings that housed up to 8,000 people and 150 businesses—from attorneys to undertakers—at the height of the gold rush.

©Kris Valencia, staff

Continue past the Dyea Town Site another 0.3 mile, crossing Nelson Slough bridge, for **Dyea Flats** multi-use recreation area; fishing, hiking, ATV use, and a city-owned campground. Beautiful area. See the information kiosk (pictured above) at the big gravel turnaround for rules and activities. ▲

ike Highway and leads to the Chilkoot Trail trailhead and the old Dyea Townsite. The National Park Service offers walking tours of this historic site in summer (check schedule at the park visitor center in town). There are fine views of Skagway, Taiya Inlet and the Skagway River from Dyea Road. *(See "Dyea Road" log on this page.)*

Tour by train, helicopter, bike, jeep, ferry or car. Ride mountain bikes down from White Pass Summit to Skagway, or drive up the Klondike Highway. See glaciers from the air or fly out to dog sled camp. Take a ride on the historic White Pass & Yukon Route railway. Take the fast ferry over to Haines and explore Lynn Canal.

Gold Rush Cemetery is 1.9 miles from downtown and makes a nice walk. Go north on State Street, then follow signs to the cemetery. "Bad guy" Soapy Smith and "good guy" Frank Reid are buried here. Both men died in a gunfight in July 1898. (Their story is brought to life in the Days of '98 Show.) It is a short hike from Reid's grave to scenic **Lower Reid Falls.**

Special Events: The Buckwheat Ski Classic (March 23, 2019) is a cross-country ski race held on the 4th Saturday in March on the Log Cabin Ski Trails. buckwheatskiclassic.com.

Skagway's Independence Day Celebration on the 4th of July is an old-fashioned family fun day, with races, contests and events like the Slow Bike Race, a pie eating contest, horseshoe tournament and egg toss.

The **Klondike International Road Relay** is September 8–9, 2019; race registration at http://klondikeroadrelay.com.

Pullen Creek Stream Walk. A pleasant pedestrian trail along the creek with interpretive signs about salmon.

AREA FISHING: Obtain a fishing license through local charter operators or at the Skagway Hardware store on Fourth and Broadway. Local charter boat operators offer chinook salmon fishing trips. The Alaska Dept. of Fish and Game, Sport Fish Division, recommends the following areas and species:

Fish the shore of **Skagway Harbor, Long Bay** and **Taiya Inlet,** May through August, for Dolly Varden. Also try the Taiya River by the steel bridge in Dyea when the water is clear in early spring or fall; use red and white spoons or salmon eggs.

Try fishing in saltwater, downtown Skagway, June–August. Pinks are plentiful at **Pullen Creek** in August (odd-numbered years). Coho, pink and chum salmon near the steel bridge on the Taiya River, in September and October. Trolling in the marine areas for chinook is good but high winds are often dangerous for small boats. A steep trail near town will take you to Dewey lakes, which were stocked with Colorado brook trout in the 1920s. **Lower Dewey Lake,** half-hour to 1-hour hike; heavily wooded shoreline. The brook trout are plentiful and grow to 16 inches but are well fed, so fishing can be frustrating. **Upper Dewey Lake,** a steep 2½-hour to 4-hour hike to above tree line, is full of hungry brook trout to 11 inches. Use salmon eggs or size #10 or #12 artificial flies. **Lost Lake** is reached via a rough trail near Dyea (ask locals for directions). The lake lies at about elev. 1,300 feet and has a good population of rainbow trout. Use small spinners or spoons.

For more information contact the Alaska Dept. of Fish and Game office in Haines; phone (907) 766-3638. ➥

Haines Highway

CONNECTS: Haines, AK, to Haines Junction, YT

Length: 146 miles   **Road Surface: Paved**   **Season: Open all year**

(See map, page 652)

The Haines Highway offers motorists remarkable mountain scenery. (©Sharon Nault)

The 146-mile/235-km Haines Highway connects Haines, AK, at the head of Lynn Canal, with Haines Junction, YT, on the Alaska Highway. Open year-round, and usually snow-free by late May, it is a good, 2-lane paved highway. Driving time is 3–4 hours.

Noted for its grand views of glaciated mountains and the variety of its scenery—from coastal forests to alpine tundra—the Haines Highway was awarded National Scenic Byway status in 2009.

The Haines Highway winds through the Chilkat River flats outside Haines before beginning a long climb up to Chilkat Pass (elev. 3,510 feet), where it crosses a wide alpine valley before descending to Haines Junction via a series of long, easy grades. It accesses the Chilkat Bald Eagle Preserve; skirts Tatshenshini–Alsek Wilderness Provincial Park; and follows the eastern border of Kluane National Park Reserve.

Part of what is now the Haines Highway was originally a "grease trail" used by the coastal Chilkat Indians trading eulachon oil for furs from the Interior. In the late 1880s, Jack Dalton developed a packhorse trail to the Klondike goldfields along the old trading route. The present road was built in 1943 as a military access highway during WWII to provide an alternate route from tide-water into Yukon.

IMPORTANT: U.S. customs is open 7 A.M. to 11 P.M. (Alaska standard time), while Canada customs is open at the same time, but due to the time zone difference, hours are 8 A.M. to midnight (Pacific standard time). You cannot drive south to Haines or north to Haines Junction at any time of the night that this border is closed. Phone (907) 767-5511 for changes in U.S. and Canadian customs hours in 2019. Fuel up before leaving Haines, AK, or Haines Junction, YT.

A valid Alaska fishing license is required for fishing along the highway between Haines and the international border at **Milepost H 40.4**. The highway then crosses the northern tip of British Columbia into Yukon. You must have valid fishing licenses for both British Columbia and Yukon if you fish these areas, and a national park fishing license if you fish waters in Kluane National Park.

Check road conditions by phoning (867) 456-7623 for daily recorded report or visit 511Yukon.ca or 511.alaska.gov. Flashing lights at the Haines Junction weigh scales indicate hazardous winter road conditions (travel not recommended). In Haines Junction, the maintenance station (867/634-2227) may have details on conditions.

Emergency Services: Between Haines and the U.S.–Canada border, dial 911. Alaska State Troopers in Haines at (907) 766-2552. Between the U.S.–Canada border and Haines Junction, phone the RCMP at (867) 634-5555.

Distance in miles	Beaver Creek	Haines	Haines Jct.	Tok	Whitehorse
Beaver Creek		329	184	113	283
Haines	329		146	443	246
Haines Jct.	184	146		297	100
Tok	113	443	297		396
Whitehorse	283	246	100	396	

Haines Highway Log

Northbound: Distance from Haines (H) is followed by distance from Haines Junction (HJ). Read log: ↓

ALASKA ROUTE 7

H 0 HJ 146.2 HAINES *(see description on*

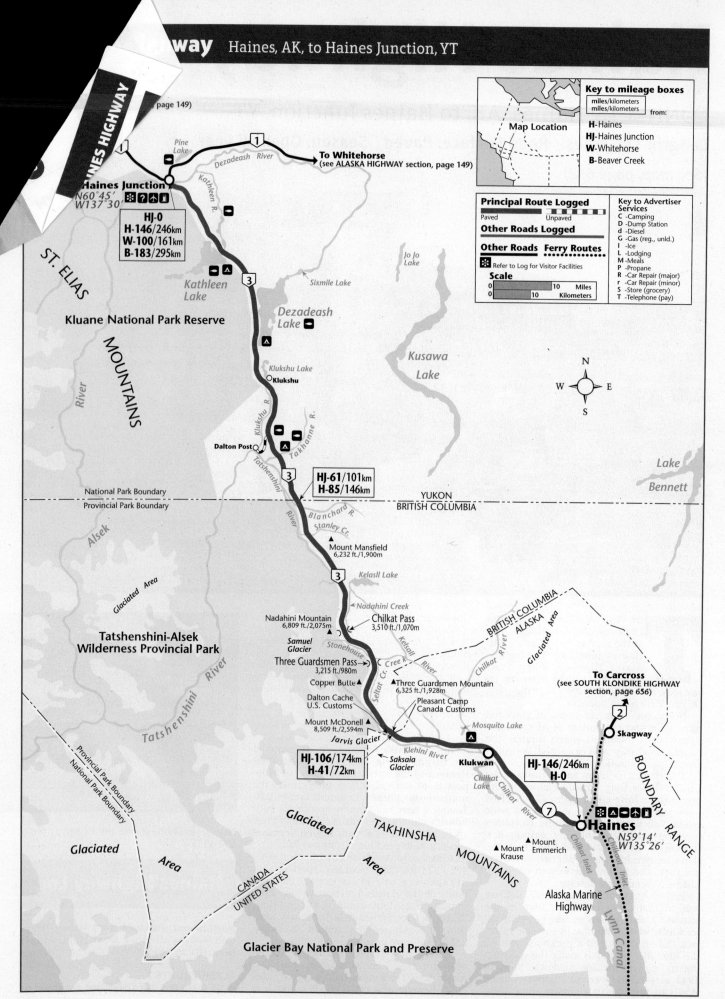

(page 149)

To Whitehorse
(see ALASKA HIGHWAY section, page 149)

Pine Lake

1

Dezadeash River

Kathleen R.

Haines Junction
N60°45'
W137°30'

HJ-0
H-146/246km
W-100/161km
B-183/295km

3

ST. ELIAS

Kathleen Lake

Kluane National Park Reserve

MOUNTAINS

River

Sixmile Lake

Jo Jo Lake

Dezadeash Lake

Kusawa Lake

Klukshu Lake

○ Klukshu

Klukshu R.

Takhanne R.

Dalton Post ○

Tatshenshini

3

HJ-61/101km
H-85/146km

National Park Boundary
Provincial Park Boundary

YUKON
BRITISH COLUMBIA

Alsek

River

Blanchard R.

Stanley Cr.

Lake Bennett

▲ Mount Mansfield
6,232 ft./1,900m

Glaciated Area

3

Kelasll Lake

Tatshenshini-Alsek Wilderness Provincial Park

← Nadahini Creek

Nadahini Mountain
6,809 ft./2,075m

Chilkat Pass
3,510 ft./1,070m

BRITISH COLUMBIA
ALASKA

Tatshenshini

Samuel Glacier

Stonehouse

Three Guardsmen Pass
3,215 ft./980m

C. Creek

Kelsall River

Chilkat River

Glaciated Area

River

Copper Butte ▲

▲ Three Guardsmen Mountain
6,325 ft./1,928m

To Carcross
(see SOUTH KLONDIKE HIGHWAY
section, page 656)

2

Dalton Cache U.S. Customs

**Pleasant Camp
Canada Customs**

Mosquito Lake

Mount McDonell ▲
8,509 ft./2,594m

Jarvis Glacier

HJ-106/174km
H-41/72km

← *Saksaia Glacier*

Klehini River

Klukwan ○

○ **Skagway**

HJ-146/246km
H-0

BOUNDARY

Glaciated

Chilkat Lake

Chilkat River

7

Haines
N59°14'
W135°26'

RANGE

TAKHINSHA

▲ Mount Emmerich

Glaciated

Area

CANADA
UNITED STATES

Area

▲ Mount Krause

MOUNTAINS

Alaska Marine Highway

Chilkoot Inlet

Chilkat Inlet

Lynn Canal

Glacier Bay National Park and Preserve

pages 642–645); all visitor services. **Junction** of Haines Highway, Front Street and Mud Bay Road.

H 1 HJ 145.2 Haines Hitch-Up RV Park; full-service sites, laundromat. Entrance is on Main Street. Fair Drive leads to Dalton City/ Southeast Alaska Fairgrounds.

©David L. Ranta, staff

Haines Hitch-Up RV Park. See display ad on page 644 in SOUTHEAST ALASKA section.

H 1.2 HJ 145 Junction of Haines Highway and Main Street, a "Y" intersection for southbound motorists and location of 2 welcome totem poles. Tesoro gas/diesel station to east on Main Street. Main Street accesses downtown area of Haines and deadends at Front Street by the Small Boat Harbor; *see map on page 643.*

H 3.5 HJ 142.7 Private Aircraft: Haines airport; elev. 16 feet; length 4,000 feet; asphalt; fuel 100; unattended.

H 3.7 HJ 142.5 Long, double-ended rest area with pit toilets to the west.

H 4.3 HJ 141.9 There are several gravel turnouts along the Chilkat River the next 10 miles northbound that are used for camping, picnicking and fishing. Watch for fishwheels on river.

The Haines Highway winds through the Chilkat River Valley for the next 18 miles northbound. The Chilkat River heads at Chilkat Glacier in British Columbia's Coast Mountains and flows 52 miles to Chilkat Inlet on Lynn Canal.

H 6.9 HJ 139.3 7-Mile trailhead (Mount Ripinski).

Magnificent views to the southwest of Takhinsha Mountains across Chilkat River. This range extends north from the Chilkat Range. Prominent peaks are Mount Krause (elev. 6,183 feet) and Mount Emmerich (elev. 6,405 feet) in the Chilkat Range. Glacier Bay National Park and Preserve is on the other side.

H 8.3 HJ 137.9 Entering **Alaska Chilkat Bald Eagle Preserve** northbound. *NOTE: Please use turnouts.* Established in 1982, the 48,000-acre preserve is the seasonal home to more than 3,000 bald eagles, which gather each year to feed on the late run of chum salmon. Eagle-viewing area begins at **Milepost H 19.3;** best viewing is mid-October to January. Eagles build nests in trees along the shoreline. Nests are added to each year and can be up to 7 feet across. (Nests the size of pickup trucks have fallen out of trees.) Nesting eagles also have a backup nest. Eagles lay their eggs in April; the eaglets fledge in August.

Watch for trumpeter swans along the Haines Highway.

H 14.3 HJ 131.9 Double-ended, narrow gravel turnout with pit toilet and boat launch by the **Chilkat River.** There are several informal turnouts along the Chilkat

River next 10 miles southbound that are used for camping, picnicking and fishing. Watch for fishwheels on river.

H 19.3 HJ 126.9 Council Grounds Chilkat Bald Eagle Preserve viewing area; parking, interpretive signs, pit toilets. Access to paved pedestrian path along river. Begin eagle viewing area (northbound) on Chilkat River flats. The annual Haines **Alaska Bald Eagle Festival** is held in November; visit www.baldeagles.org for details on the 2019 festival. Of the more than 40,000 bald eagles in Alaska, most are found in Southeast. Eagles build nests in trees along the shoreline. Best viewing is mid-October to January. *CAUTION: No stopping on highway; use turnouts!*

H 20.1 HJ 126.1 Paved turnout by river; access to paved pedestrian path to viewpoints. Another small turnout is 0.3 miles north of here.

H 20.6 HJ 125.6 Council Grounds Chilkat Bald Eagle Preserve viewing area; paved parking area with pit toilet and interpretive sign. Access to paved pedestrian path to viewpoints.

H 21.5 HJ 124.7 Turnoff via paved access road for Chilkat Indian village of **KLUKWAN** (pop. 95). The name Klukwan is taken from the Tlingit phrase *Tlakw Aan* which means "Eternal Village." Klukwan offers visitors both interpretive and self-guided tours that provide an introduction to its Native Heritage at their **Jilkaat Kwaan Cultural Heritage and Bald Eagle Preserve Visitor Center.** The Heritage Center is a complex of buildings that include a carving shed, smokehouse, replica clan house and a state-of-the-art museum-type facility. Highlights with this facility include the world famous Whale House exhibit and a gift shop which features locally made arts and crafts. Open mid-May through first week of September. Phone (907) 767-5485 to arrange a guided tour or stop in any time for a self-guided tour. Check their website for current days and hours of operation: jilkaatkwaan heritagecenter.org.

H 23.8 HJ 122.4 Chilkat River bridge. Highway now follows Klehini River northbound. *CAUTION: Watch for moose.*

H 26.2 HJ 120 Porcupine Crossing; side road leads west across Klehini River.

H 26.7 HJ 119.5 Klehini River scenic viewpoint; paved parking area, picnic shelter/tables, interpretive signs, viewing scopes.

H 27.2 HJ 119 Turnoff on Mosquito Lake Road for Kroschel Wildlife Center at Mile 1.8 and camping at the Mosquito Lake State Recreation Site, at Mile 2.4.

The Wildlife Center provides access to over 15 species of Alaska wildlife; open May 15–Sept. 15 for scheduled tours, phone (907) 767-5464. Keep to right at road fork (Mile 2.1), then watch for easy-to-miss, narrow, gravel road leading down to **Mosquito Lake State Recreation Site.** There is a dock and boat launch. The recreation site has a small day-use area, primitive campsites in the trees along a narrow road (best for small RVs or vans); firepits; no pit toilets. Beautiful spot. Pack it in, pack it out; bring insect repellent. There is a large turnaround area here.

H 28.8 HJ 117.4 Muncaster Creek bridge.

H 31 HJ 115.2 Scenic viewpoint; double-ended parking area to west overlooking the Klehini River. The Klehini heads in a glacier on Nadahini Mountain in Canada and flows 42 miles to the Chilkat River.

Leaving Alaska Chilkat Bald Eagle Preserve northbound.

H 31.6 HJ 114.6 Little Boulder Creek bridge.

H 33.1 HJ 113.1 33 Mile Roadhouse; food, gas/diesel, cabins, laundromat, beer.

H 33.8 HJ 112.4 Big Boulder Creek bridge.

H 35.5 HJ 110.7 Paved, level turnout to east with interpretive signs about wetlands and a good view of the Saksaia Glacier to west. Note finger dikes along the river, which help prevent erosion.

H 35.6 HJ 110.6 Paved parking area to west with interpretive signs about gold seekers and Tlingits. View of Saksaia Glacier.

H 40.2 HJ 106 Port of Entry: Dalton Cache U.S. Customs and Border Protection.

The Chilkat River has a number of fishwheels on it that rotate from the river's current and scoop fish up, trapping them for pick-up by the fishwheel's owner. (©Kris Valencia, staff)

There is still snow at higher elevations along the Haines Highway in mid-May.

(©Kris Valencia, staff)

All travelers entering the United States MUST STOP. *U.S. customs is open daily from 7 A.M. to 11 P.M. (Alaska standard time). Southbound travelers cannot drive south to Haines if the customs station is closed.* Phone (907) 767-5511. Restrooms, large parking area. The historic Dalton Trading Post (behind customs station) was originally the men's quarters for the NWMP Dalton Detachment in 1898. The international boundary line was redefined in 1900, and the structure ended up on the U.S. side.

H 40.4 HJ 105.8 U.S.–Canada border. *TIME ZONE CHANGE: Canada observes Pacific standard time. Pacific standard time is 1 hour later than Alaska standard time.*

Northbound travelers: Kilometers logged on the Canadian portion of this highway reflect physical kilometerposts and are not a metric conversion of the mileage figure.

Southbound travelers: Driving distances from Haines, in miles, are based on the physical mileposts along this route.

H 40.6 (72 km) **HJ 105.6** (174 km) **Pleasant Camp Canada Customs and Immigration office.** All travelers entering Canada MUST STOP here. *Canada customs is open daily from 8 A.M. to midnight (Pacific standard time). You cannot drive north into Canada if the customs station is closed.* No public facilities. *NOTE: $500 fine for littering.*

H 40.7 (72.2 km) **HJ 105.5** (173.8 km) Granite Creek.

H 42.5 (75 km) **HJ 103.7** (171 km) Large gravel turnout to west.

H 42.6 (75.2 km) **HJ 103.6** (170.8 km) Northbound sign: Tatshenshini-Alsek Park.

Southbound sign: Steep Hill. Customs 3 km, be prepared to stop.

H 43.6 (76.9 km) **HJ 102.6** (169.1 km) Tatshenshini-Alsek Park (northbound sign).

H 44.5 (78.2 km) **HJ 101.7** (167.8 km) Five Mile Creek.

H 46.8 (82.2 km) **HJ 99.4** (163.8 km) Distance marker northbound shows Haines Junction 174 km/108 miles.

H 48.4 (84.8 km) **HJ 97.8** (161.2 km) Fuchs Creek.

H 49 (85.4 km) **HJ 97.2** (160.6 km) Gravel turnout to west.

H 49.9 (87.3 km) **HJ 96.3** (158.7 km) Dou-ble-ended turnout to west with interpretive sign about Haines Road and **Historic Milepost 48.** Beautiful views of glaciated mountains as highway descends southbound.

H 50 (87.5 km) **HJ 96.2** (158.5 km) Highway crosses Seltat Creek. Three Guardsmen Mountain to east.

H 50.6 (88.4 km) **HJ 95.6** (157.6 km) Marinka's Hill.

H 51.3 (89.2 km) **HJ 94.9** (156.8 km) Small gravel turnout to west with trailhead for Marinka's Hill.

H 51.5 (89.8 km) **HJ 94.7** (156.2 km) Steep hill next 18 kms/11 miles southbound; check brakes.

H 51.7 (90.2 km) **HJ 94.5** (155.8 km) Gravel shoulder parking by northbound sign: Shakwak Highway Improvement Project next 25 km/16 miles.

H 52.6 (91.6 km) **HJ 93.6** (154.4 km) South end of Three Guardsmen Lake. Glave Peak (elev. 6,325 feet/1,928m), part of Three Guardsmen Mountain, rises directly behind the lake.

H 55.1 (96 km) **HJ 91.1** (150 km) Stonehouse Creek. The tall poles along the highway indicate the edge of the road for snowplows.

H 55.4 (96.5 km) **HJ 90.8** (149.5 km) Clear Creek.

H 56 (97.6 km) **HJ 90.2** (148.4 km) Distance marker northbound shows Haines Junction 149 km/92 miles, Whitehorse 308 km/191 miles, Fairbanks 981 km/610 miles.

(©Kris Valencia, staff)

H 59 (102.4 km) **HJ 87.2** (144 km) Paved viewpoint to west at **Haines Highway Summit** (elev. 3,510 feet/1,070m), **Chilkat**

Pass. The wind blows almost constantly on the summit and causes drifting snow and road closures in winter. Snow until late May. This is avalanche terrain and fatal accidents have occurred here.

The Chilkat Pass was one of the few mountain passes offering access into the Yukon from the coast. The Chilkat and the Chilkoot passes were tenaciously guarded by Tlingit Indians. These southern Yukon Indians did not want their lucrative fur-trading business with the coastal Indians and Russians jeopardized. The gold rush of 1898, that brought thousands of white people inland, forever altered the lives of the Interior Natives.

H 59.7 (103.5 km) **HJ 86.5** (142.5 km) Large paved viewpoint to west.

H 61.7 (106 km) **HJ 84.5** (140 km) Large gravel rest area with pit toilet to west.

H 62.5 (108 km) **HJ 84** (135.2 km) Pit toilet and warming shelter.

H 63.2 (109.3 km) **HJ 83** (136.7 km) Braided Nadahini River.

H 66.8 (115 km) **HJ 79.4** (131 km) Wind sock at airstrip.

Private Aircraft: Mule Creek airstrip, elev. 2,900 feet/884m; length 4,000 feet/1,219m; gravel/turf. No services.

H 67.8 (116.5 km) **HJ 78.4** (129.5 km) Mule Creek. **Historical Mile 75.** Mule Creek Highway Maintenance Station with pit toilet.

H 72.2 (124 km) **HJ 74** (122 km) Goat Creek bridge.

H 74.2 (127.2 km) **HJ 72** (118.8 km) Holum Creek.

H 76.3 (130.9 km) **HJ 69.9** (115.1 km) Twin Lakes (northbound sign). Watch for trumpeter swans.

H 76.6 (131.3 km) **HJ 69.6** (114.7 km) Twin Lakes (southbound sign).

H 78.2 (134 km) **HJ 68** (112 km) Large paved parking area to west is viewpoint for Tatshenshini–Alsek Wilderness Provincial Park. The Tatshenshini and Alsek rivers are famous for their river rafting opportunities.

H 78.6 (134.5 km) **HJ 67.6** (111.5 km) Mansfield Creek.

H 79.8 (136.5 km) **HJ 66.4** (109.5 km) Stoney Creek.

H 84.3 (144 km) **HJ 61.9** (102.1 km) Informal gravel turnout to west, by pond. Beautiful mountain scenery opens up for southbound travelers as the highway crosses a wide alpine valley.

H 84.8 (144.8 km) **HJ 61.4** (101.2 km) Blanchard River bridge. This is the put-in point for whitewater rafting on the Blanchard River. (Turnoff for rafting outfitter to west just north of bridge.) The Blanchard River crosses the Yukon–BC boundary and joins the Tatshenshini River near Dalton Post.

H 85.2 (145.5 km) **HJ 61** (100.5 km) Welcome to Kluane Country/Welcome to Yukon (northbound signs). Welcome to British Columbia (southbound sign); small turnout with litter bin to east. BC–YT border. Drive with headlights on.

NOTE: In Yukon, maximum speed is 50-kmph/31-mph wherever equipment is working. Also, using radar detection is illegal.

H 85.9 (146.6 km) **HJ 60.3** (99.4 km) Distance marker northbound shows Haines Junction 100 km/62 miles, Whitehorse 259 km/161 miles, Fairbanks 922 km/573 miles.

H 88.3 (150.6 km) **HJ 57.9** (95.4 km) Large gravel viewpoint to west.

H 93.5 (159 km) **HJ 52.7** (87 km) Turnoff for Yukon government **Million Dollar**

Falls Campground (1.8 mile/3 km west); 34 campsites (many level), kitchen shelters, firewood, camping fee $12, playground, pit toilets, drinking water (boil water), bear proof lockers, litter bins and recycling, hiking trails, wheelchair accessible. Short boardwalk trail with several stretches of stairs (total of 46 steps with resting spots on landings) leading to viewing platform of scenic falls and rapids. Well worth the effort!

Good fishing below **Takhanne Falls** for grayling, Dolly Varden, rainbow trout and salmon. **Takhanne River**, excellent king salmon fishing in early July. *CAUTION: The Takhanne, Blanchard, Tatshenshini and Klukshu rivers are grizzly feeding areas. Exercise extreme caution when fishing or exploring in these areas.*

H 93.6 (159.2 km) **HJ 52.6** (86.8 km) Takhanne River bridge.

H 93.7 (159.4 km) **HJ 52.5** (86.6 km) Short gravel access road west to informal turnout by Takhanne River. Nice spot. Highway climbs steep grade next 1.7 miles/2.7 km northbound.

H 95.4 (162 km) **HJ 50.8** (84 km) Large paved rest area; photo viewpoint of Kluane Range with viewing platform, litter bins and pit toilet. Interpretive signs reveal details of early exploration in this area. Highway descends steep grade next 1.7 miles/2.7 km southbound.

H 96.7 (164.1 km) **HJ 49.5** (81.9 km) Turnoff to west (not signed) for Dalton Post. Narrow, winding, dirt and gravel road with some washboard, deep ruts and a short but very steep downhill section. *Not suitable for RVs.* Road forks at Mile 3.2; follow right fork 0.2 mile for Shawshee/Dalton Post day-use area; large gravel parking area, pit toilets, litter bins. The **Klukshu River** system hosts seasonal runs of king, red and silver salmon. Interpretive signs on salmon. Fishing restrictions posted. *CAUTION: Watch for bears.*

H 101 (171 km) **HJ 45.2** (75 km) Motheral Creek.

H 102.1 (173 km) **HJ 44.1** (73 km) Large turnout to west.

H 102.7 (174.2 km) **HJ 43.5** (71.8 km) Vand Creek.

H 107.3 (181.9 km) **HJ 38.9** (64.1 km) Klukshu Creek. Paved turnout to east at south end of creek crossing. *CAUTION: Watch for bears.*

H 108.1 (183.2 km) **HJ 38.1** (62.8 km) Historic Milepost 118 at turnoff for **KLUKSHU**, a First Nations village, located 0.6 mile/1 km off the highway via a good gravel road. This summer fish camp and village on the banks of the Klukshu River is a handful of log cabins, meat caches and traditional fish traps and fish drying racks.

Klukshu is on the old Dalton Trail and offers good photo opportunities. Information signs on First Nations heritage and traditional fish drying and fishing techniques. Crafts for sale at small shop (if locked, inquire locally).

H 109.2 (185 km) **HJ 37** (59.5 km) Gribbles Gulch.

H 110.3 (186.8 km) **HJ 35.9** (57.7 km) Parking and interpretive signs at St. Elias Lake trailhead (Kluane National Park trail). Posted no overnight camping or parking. Trail winds through subalpine meadow; 4.5 miles/7.2 km round-trip.

H 112.7 (190.7 km) **HJ 33.5** (53.9 km) Flying Squirrel Creek.

H 113.4 (192 km) **HJ 32.8** (52.8 km)

Moe's Yukon Ranch; cabins and hostel. Phone (867) 634-2666.

H 113.8 (192.6 km) **HJ 32.4** (52.1 km) Historic Milepost 125. Old Dezadeash Lodge; interpretive sign. Mush Lake Road behind lodge is an old mining road; ski trail in winter.

H 114.5 (194 km) **HJ 31.7** (52 km) Large, long paved turnout along Dezadeash Lake. There are good views of this large lake for several miles along the highway. Dezadeash Lake (pronounced DEZ-dee-ash). Posted no camping or overnight parking. Interpretive sign about the lake's "Warmer Waters" (excerpt follows):

"Dezadeash is a large shallow bathtub averaging 4 meters (13 feet) deep. The surface temperature can climb to 18°C (64°F) and higher in summer. Lake trout prefer water temperature that ranges between 8° and 12°C (46° and 54°F). During hot summer days, Dezadeash lake trout find themselves under much more stress than their counterparts who swim the frigid depths of nearby Kathleen Lake, where surface water is rarely warmer than 11°C (52°F)."

Dezadeash Lake offers trolling, also fly-fishing along shore at feeder streams, for northern pike, lake trout and grayling. *CAUTION: Storms may come up quickly.*

H 115.6 (195.7 km) **HJ 30.6** (50.3 km) Entrance to a sometimes rut-filled loop road for Yukon government **Dezadeash Lake Campground**, a very scenic spot on the lake is down below the highway; 20 campsites (no pull-throughs), camping fee $12, kitchen shelter, picnic area, bear proof lockers, litter bins, pit toilets and boat launch.

H 117.7 (199 km) **HJ 28.5** (47 km) Distance marker northbound shows Haines Junction 47 km/29 miles, Whitehorse 206 km/128 miles, Fairbanks 819 km/509 miles.

H 119.6 (202.3 km) **HJ 26.6** (43.7 km) Parking area and viewpoint. Rock Glacier Trail to west; short 0.5-mile/0.8-km self-guiding trail, partially boardwalk. Interesting walk with some steep sections.

H 122.5 (207 km) **HJ 23.7** (39 km) Dalton Trail Lodge offers accommodations, gourmet meals and fishing/hiking/outdoor adventure packages, phone (867)634-2099.

©Kris Valencia, staff

H 130.2 (219.7 km) **HJ 16** (26.3 km) Turnoff to west and drive downhill 0.7 mile/1.1 km via good gravel road to picnic area on Kathleen Lake (pictured above); parking, outhouses, water, picnic tables. The 53-mile/85-km Cottonwood Loop and Kings Throne trailhead nearby.

Access at Mile 0.5 on this side road to **Kathleen Lake Campground**, the only established campground within Kluane National Park; 39 campsites and a kitchen area; day-use area with picnic tables, restrooms, water; boat launch at lake; campfire programs by park staff. Campsites are first come, first served. 2 group sites can be reserved in advance. 5 oTENTik sites (permanent tent cabins) can be booked in advance by phoning

(867)634-7250. Camping fee $15.70; group sites (6-person minimum) $4.90 per person. Firewood $8.80 per site.

Kathleen Lake, nearly 400 feet/122m deep, offers fishing for lake trout and grayling year-round. *NOTE: National Park fishing license required.*

H 130.5 (220.2 km) **HJ 15.7** (25.8 km) Historic Milepost 142. Kathleen Lake Lodge (closed in 2017, current status unknown).

H 131.1 (221 km) **HJ 15.1** (25 km) Kathleen River bridge. Gravel turnout to east has information boards and provides access to the **Kathleen River**. Easy half-day paddle to **Lower Kathleen** and **Rainbow** lakes. Fishing for rainbow trout, June–September; grayling, July–August; lake trout in September.

H 134.4 (226.5 km) **HJ 11.8** (19.5 km) Huge paved turnout to west with far-off view of Kathleen Lake; good photo op. Interpretive sign regarding this UNESCO World Heritage Site. This is the largest internationally protected land mass on earth and includes Glacier Bay and Wrangell-St. Elias national parks, Kluane National Park and Tatshenshini-Alsek Provincial Park.

H 138.4 (233.2 km) **HJ 7.8** (12.8 km) Quill Creek, gravel access. *CAUTION: Watch for moose and bears.*

H 142 (239 km) **HJ 4.2** (7 km) Parking area and interpretive sign to west at Auriol Trailhead (4.5 mile/15 km loop trail); skiing/hiking.

H 143.7 (242 km) **HJ 2.5** (4 km) Welcome to Haines Junction (sign) and rest area to east with litter bins, pit toilets and view to north of Haines Junction and Shakwak Valley.

H 145.4 (244.7) **HJ 0.8** (1.3 km) *Slow for posted speed zones northbound into Haines Junction.*

H 145.8 (245.4 km) **HJ 0.4** (0.6 km) Dezadeash River bridge. Dezadeash Trail to north at east side of bridge; easy walk along river's edge (2.2 miles/3.5 km).

H 145.9 (245.6 km) **HJ 0.3** (0.4 km) Truck weigh scales. Large unsigned parking area behind the weigh scales building. Pit toilets, litter bins, river access for canoes and rafts, picnic table and river trailhead.

H 146.2 (246 km) **HJ 0 HAINES JUNCTION**; all services and RCMP. Visitor Center is 0.8 miles/1.3 km north on the Alaska Highway. *See description in ALASKA HIGHWAY section on pages 209–213.*

"Buckle Up, Lights On" sign: Headlights on at all times, seatbelt use required by law. In winter, watch for snowplows on road.

Junction of the Haines Highway (Yukon Highway 3) and Alaska Highway (Yukon Highway 1) at Haines Junction. Turn to **Milepost DC 985** on page 209 in the ALASKA HIGHWAY section for highway log. Whitehorse-bound travelers read log back to front, Alaska-bound travelers read log front to back.

Southbound: Distance from Haines (H) is followed by distance from Haines Junction (HJ). Read log:

Kilometers logged on the Canadian portion of this highway reflect physical kilometerposts and are not a metric conversion of the mileage figure. Driving distances in the Alaska portion of the log are based on physical mileposts.

South Klondike Highway

CONNECTS: Skagway, AK, to Alaska Hwy., YT

Length: 98 miles   Road Surface: Paved   Season: Open all year

Highest Summit: White Pass 3,292 feet

Bove Island and Tagish Lake viewpoint at Milepost S 58.7
(©Kris Valencia, staff)

Distance in miles	Alaska Hwy. Jct.	Atlin	Carcross	Skagway	Whitehorse
Alaska Hwy. Jct.		125	32	98	12
Atlin	125		92	158	81
Carcross	32	92		65	45
Skagway	98	158	65		110
Whitehorse	12	81	45	110	

The 98-mile/158-km-long South Klondike Highway (also known as the Skagway–Carcross Road) connects Skagway, AK, with the Alaska Highway at **Milepost DC 874.4**, 12 miles/19 km south of downtown Whitehorse. The highway between Skagway and Carcross (referred to locally as the Skagway Road) was built in 1978, and formally dedicated on May 23, 1981. The highway connecting Carcross with the Alaska Highway (referred to locally as the Carcross Road) was built by the U.S. Army in late 1942, to lay a gas pipeline from Skagway to Whitehorse. (The North Klondike Highway turns off the Alaska Highway north of Whitehorse and leads to Dawson City; see the KLONDIKE LOOP section.)

The South Klondike Highway offers some spectacular scenery and adds only about 60 miles/100 km to the trip for Alaska-bound motorists compared to the Haines Highway route. Like the Haines Highway, it crosses from Alaska into British Columbia, then into Yukon. (Driving distance from Haines to Tok, AK, is 415 miles/670 km; driving distance from Skagway to Tok is 475 miles/760 km. Add 328 miles/528 km to Anchorage; 206 miles/332 km to Fairbanks.)

The South Klondike Highway is a 2-lane, asphalt-surfaced road, open year-round. There is a steep (11 percent grade) 11.5-mile/18.5-km stretch between Skagway and White Pass. For daily recorded road condition report, phone (907) 983-2333 or (867) 456-7623; or visit 511Yukon.ca or 511.alaska.gov.

IMPORTANT: U.S. Customs station is open daily year-round, 7 A.M. to 11 P.M. (Alaska standard time); Canadian Customs station is open 8 A.M. to midnight (Pacific standard time). You cannot cross the border during hours that customs is closed. For U.S. border information, phone (907) 983-2325. For Canada border information, phone (867) 821-4111. Avalanches and severe storms can cause temporary closures on this road in winter.

The South Klondike Highway is 1 of 2 highways connecting ferry travelers with the Alaska Highway; the other is the Haines Highway out of Haines (see HAINES HIGHWAY section).

Emergency Services: Between Skagway and Log Cabin, dial 911. Between Log Cabin and Annie Lake Road, phone the **RCMP** at (867) 821-5555 or the **Carcross Ambulance** at (867) 821-4444. Between Annie Lake Road

South Klondike Highway
Skagway, AK, to Alaska Highway Jct.

© 2019 The MILEPOST®

To Carmacks
(see KLONDIKE LOOP section, page 288)

To Haines Junction
(see ALASKA HIGHWAY section, page 149)

N60°43' W135°03'
Whitehorse
S-98/158km
AH-0
W-12/19km

Kookatsoon Lake

Cowley

Cowley Lake

Robinson

Two Horse Cr.

Bear Cr.

Lewes Cr.

South Klondike Highway

The Alaska Highway

Marsh Lake

To Johnson's Crossing
(see ALASKA HIGHWAY section, page 149)

Jake's Corner

Needle Mountain

Watson River

Lewes L.

Annie

Mount Gillam

Watson R.

Wheaton R.

Spirit L.

Carcross Desert

Crag Lake

Chootla Lake

Nares Lake

Carcross
N60°11' W134°43'

AH-33/52km
S-65/106km

Montana Mountain
7,280 ft./2,219m

Windy Arm

Bove Island

Lime Mountain
5,225 ft./1,593m

N60°18' W134°16'
Tagish

Tagish River

Tagish Road

Tagish Road

Little Atlin Lake

Atlin Road
(see ATLIN-TAGISH-CARCROSS SCENIC LOOP, pages 193-194)

Snafu Lake

Lubbock River

Snafu Creek

Tarfu Lake

Tarfu River

YUKON
BRITISH COLUMBIA

YUKON
BRITISH COLUMBIA

Lake Bennett

Mount Racine

Mount Conrad

AH-47/75km
S-52/83km

Tutshi Lake

Jack Peak
7,050 ft./2,149m

Tagish Lake

Toku Arm

Mount Minto
6,913 ft./2,107m

Hitchcock Creek

Indian Lake

Gladys Lake

White Pass & Yukon Route

Bennett

Chilkoot Trail

Log Cabin

CANADA
UNITED STATES

South Klondike Highway

Tutshi R.

Indian Creek

Atlin Lake

Taku Arm

McDonald Lake

Fourth of July Cr.

Surprise Lake

Fraser

Chilkoot Pass
3,739 ft./1,140m

Glaciated Area

Bernard Lake
Summit Lake
N59°43' W135°03'

AH-83/134km
S-14/23km

White Pass
3,292 ft./1,003m

White Pass Fork

White Pass & Yukon Route

Scotia

N59°35' W133°43'
Atlin

Discovery

Discovery Road

Pine Creek

Spruce Creek

Dyea Road

S-2 Jewell Gardens
& Glassworks M

AH-98/158km
S-0

Goat Lake

Skagway River

N59°27' W135°18'
Skagway

BRITISH COLUMBIA
ALASKA

Lutak Inlet

To Haines Junction
(see HAINES HIGHWAY section, page 651)

McKee Creek

Warm Bay Road

Palmer

Birch Mountain
6,755 ft./2,060m

Teresa Island

Wilson Creek

O'Donnel River

Haines

Lynn Canal

Chilkat Inlet

Chilkoot Inlet

Taiya Inlet

Alaska Marine Highway

COAST MOUNTAINS RANGES

BOUNDARY

Glaciated Area

Atlin Provincial Park

Llewellyn Glacier

Map Location

Key to mileage boxes
miles/kilometers
miles/kilometers from:
S-Skagway
AH-Alaska Highway
W-Whitehorse

Principal Route Logged
Paved — Unpaved
Other Roads Logged
Other Roads — **Ferry Routes**
Refer to Log for Visitor Facilities

Scale
0 — 10 Miles
0 — 10 Kilometers

Key to Advertiser Services
C -Camping
D -Dump Station
d -Diesel
G -Gas (reg., unld.)
I -Ice
L -Lodging
M -Meals
P -Propane
R -Car Repair (major)
r -Car Repair (minor)
S -Store (grocery)
T -Telephone (pay)

N
W E
S

The William Henry Moore suspension bridge honors a man who is credited with helping to settle the town of Skagway. The bridge crosses a 110-foot gorge. (©Kris Valencia, staff)

and the Alaska Highway, dial 911 for the **Whitehorse Ambulance**.

South Klondike Highway Log

Northbound: Distance from Skagway (S) is followed by distance from Alaska Highway (AH). Read log: ⬇

Mileposts in Alaska and kilometerposts in Canada reflect distance from Skagway. Kilometer distance from Skagway in the Canadian portion of the log reflects physical kilometerposts and is not necessarily a metric conversion of the mileage figure.

ALASKA ROUTE 98

S 0 AH 97.7 Alaska Marine Highway System ferry terminal at the foot of Broadway Street in downtown **SKAGWAY** *(see description of Skagway beginning on page 646).*

Distance marker northbound shows U.S.–Canada border 15 miles/24 km, Carcross 66 miles/106 km, Whitehorse 113 miles/180 km.

S 0.5 AH 97.2 Turn left northbound on Second Avenue for Family Fuel gas station at corner of 2nd and State; 24-hour pump with credit card; store, laundromat, ATM. ⛽

NOTE: Continue north on State Street, which turns into Klondike Highway 2. You can drive up Broadway Street to 15th and then access State Street, but when cruise ships are in town, Broadway is crowded with pedestrians.

S 1.2 AH 96.5 Garden City RV Park at 16th Street and State Street.

S 1.7 AH 96 Welcome to Skagway sign southbound; Klondike Highway becomes State Street in Skagway *(see map on page 647)*. WP&YR railway maintenance shops. Turnoff on signed gravel side road for Gold Rush Cemetery (0.6 mile), the final resting place of "bad guy" Soapy Smith and "good guy" Frank Reid (both men died in a gunfight in July 1898). It is only a short hike from Frank Reid's grave to Reid Falls.

S 1.8 AH 95.9 Skagway River highway bridges. Pat Moore Bridge for bicyclists and pedestrians.

S 2 AH 95.7 Jewell Gardens & Glassworks has a glass-blowing studio, a gift shop, G-scale railroad and a restaurant open for lunch daily; phone (907) 983-2111. A highly recommended stop.

Jewell Gardens & Glassworks. See display ad on page 649.

S 2.5 AH 95.2 Junction with Dyea Road. This narrow, winding, 8-mile mostly gravel road leads to the Chilkoot Trail, Dyea townsite, Slide Cemetery and Dyea Flats recreation area. Not recommended for large motorhomes past the Mile 1.4 overlook. There are fine views of Skagway, Taiya Inlet and the Skagway River from this road. *(See "Dyea Road" log on page 650 for details.)* Campground at Chilkoot Trailhead and camping at Dyea Flats. ⛺

S 2.8 AH 94.9 Highway maintenance camp and avalanche gate.

S 3 AH 94.7 *Highway begins steep 11.5-mile/18.5-km ascent northbound from sea level to elev. 3,290 feet/1,003m at White Pass; 11 percent grade.*

There are interpretive viewpoints (logged) and several pullouts with amazing waterfall views along this stretch of road.

S 5 AH 92.7 Large turnout to east with view across canyon of White Pass & Yukon Route railway tracks and bridge. The narrow-gauge WP&YR railway was completed in 1900.

S 5.5 AH 92.2 Turnout to west with historical information signs about Brackett

Wagon Road and WP&YR.

S 6.8 AH 90.9 Port of Entry Skagway: U.S. Customs and Border Protection, open daily year-round 7 A.M. to 11 P.M. Alaska standard time. Phone (907) 983-3144 for border crossing (customs); or phone (907) 983-2325. *All travelers entering the United States must stop. Have identification ready. See "Crossing the Border" in the TRAVEL PLANNING section.*

Southbound view of glacier above customs station.

S 7.4 AH 90.3 Paved shoulder parking alongside highway.

S 7.7 AH 90 Paved viewpoint with interpretive sign about Goat Lake hydroelectric project; good photo stop for **Pitchfork Falls**, visible across the canyon.

The 4,000-kilowatt Goat Lake hydroelectric project was licensed on July 15, 1996, to provide electricity to Skagway. A 15-mile-long underwater cable connected Haines to the grid in 1998. Water is piped from Goat Lake reservoir down to the powerhouse next to the Skagway River.

S 8.2 AH 89.5 Paved turnout with good view. Watch for bicyclists on road in summer. In winter, snow poles along the highway guide snow plows and traffic over White Pass and avalanche gates come down during road closures due to avalanches or hazardous driving conditions.

NOTE: Avalanche areas are posted northbound. Do not stop in avalanche areas.

S 8.6 AH 89.1 Shoulder parking with views next 0.2 mile northbound.

S 9.1 AH 88.6 Paved turnout to east with historical interest signs about White Pass City and Deadhorse Trail.

S 9.8 AH 87.9 Truck emergency runout ramp to west for large transport units that may lose air brakes on steep descent southbound. *It is illegal to park here.*

S 10 AH 87.7 Turnout at Bridal Veil Waterfall.

S 10.8 AH 86.9 Large informal gravel turnout to east.

S 11.1 AH 86.6 William Henry Moore Bridge. This unique suspension bridge spans a 110-foot-wide gorge over Moore Creek, 180 feet below. Just north of the bridge to the west is a large waterfall. The bridge is named for Capt. William Moore, a riverboat captain and pilot, prospector, packer and trader, who played an important role in settling the town of Skagway. Moore helped pioneer this route over White Pass into Yukon and was among the first to realize the potential of a railroad across the pass.

This bridge is scheduled to be replaced. Construction of the new bridge started in May 2017, but completion has been moved to fall 2019, from its originally scheduled completion date of Aug. 31, 2018.

The current bridge is considered too narrow to meet current highway standards. As reported in the *Skagway News*, "the sizes of trucks making the trip in and out of Skagway have increased since the bridge was constructed," and the larger trucks are putting "more stress on the bridge than was expected when it was built." When completed, the new bridge will carry vehicle traffic and the old bridge will be open for pedestrians.

S 11.5 AH 86.2 Large paved parking areas to east with interpretive signs on Klondike Highway and migration corridor. Good photo op of Skagway River gorge, William Moore Bridge and waterfalls.

S 12 AH 85.7 Truck emergency runout

ramp to west. There are vehicle turnouts on both sides of the highway as you approach White Pass northbound.

S 13 AH 84.7 Gravel turnout to west with view (weather permitting) toward summit of White Pass.

S 13.2 AH 84.5 Paved turnout to west.

S 14.3 AH 83.4 White Pass Summit (elev. 3,292 feet/1,003m). Paved turnout to west with interpretive sign. Skagway cycling tours often start their downhill trips from here.

CAUTION: Southbound traffic begins steep 11.5-mile/18.5-km descent to Skagway; 11 percent grade.

Thousands of gold seekers poured into Canada over the Chilkoot and White passes on their way to Dawson City. An initial contingent of North West Mounted Police, led by Inspector Charles Constantine, had come over the Chilkoot Pass in 1894—well before the gold rush—to establish law among the miners at Dawson City. But in 1898, the Canadian government sent reinforcements, led by Superintendent Samuel Steele.

Upon his arrival at the foot of Chilkoot Pass in February of 1898, Steele found thousands of men waiting to pack their supplies over the pass. He immediately stationed permanent detachments at the summits of Chilkoot and White passes, both to maintain law and order and to assert Canadian sovereignty at these 2 international borders.

After witnessing the desperate condition of many men arriving in the Klondike, Steele set a minimum requirement of a year's supply of food and equipment—"one ton of goods"—for any miner entering Canada.

S 14.5 AH 83.2 Paved turnout to west offers good photo op of Welcome to Alaska sign (pictured below) and an inukshuk erected by the Kiwanis.

©Kris Valencia, staff

S 14.7 (24.3 km) AH 83 (132.9 km) U.S.–Canada/AK–BC border. Welcome to Canada (northbound sign) and Welcome to USA (southbound sign). Avalanche gate. Turnout to west offers view of International Boundary Monument, located atop the rock wall to the southeast (across from avalanche gate). Plaque reads:

"This unfortified boundary line between the Dominion of Canada and the United States of America should quicken the remembrance of the more than century old friendship between these countries, a lesson of peace to all nations."

TIME ZONE CHANGE: Alaska observes Alaska standard time; British Columbia and Yukon observe Pacific standard time.

NOTE: Drive with headlights on at all times. Seatbelt use required by law.

WINTER DRIVERS NOTE: Snow plows working when lights flashing. Avalanche areas are posted northbound. Do not stop in avalanche areas.

BC HIGHWAY 2

S 15 (24.5 km) AH 82.7 (133.1 km) Gravel turnout to west offers best view of International Border Falls, on rocky hillside to west.

Distance marker northbound shows Canada Customs 12 km/7 miles, Whitehorse 156 km/97 miles.

S 15.4 (25 km) AH 82.3 (132.4 km) Large gravel turnout to east with toilets, litter bins and avalanche sign. Good turnout for views of subalpine landscape and Summit Lake.

Northbound, the highway winds through the rocky valley of Summit Lake (visible to east). The subalpine landscape of stunted trees and lakes between the U.S. border and Log Cabin, often referred to as a "moonscape," represents a transition zone between the treed lower elevations and the true alpine above tree line. The small, twisted alpine firs (also known as "mopheads") are shaped by a combination of heavy snow burying their lower branches and icy winds sculpting their upper branches.

S 17 (27.3 km) AH 80.7 (128.7 km) Multiple gravel turnouts both sides, next 4 miles.

S 17.7 (29 km) AH 80 (128.7 km) Huge gravel turnout and a great access for climbing rocks and getting photos of Summit Lake and the unique landscape. Multiple pullouts next 4 miles/6.4 km northbound.

S 22 (36 km) AH 75.7 (121.8 km) Large gravel turnout to the east.

S 22.5 (36.5 km) AH 75.2 (121 km) Canada Border Services at **FRASER** (elev. 2,400 feet/732m). Open daily year-round 8 A.M. to midnight (Pacific standard time). Phone (867) 821-4111. *All travelers entering Canada must stop. Have proper ID for all travelers, including children. Review "Crossing the Border" information in the TRAVEL PLANNING section.*

The red building to the east is the last water tower remaining from the WP&YR railway's steam locomotive era. Highway maintenance camp to west. Average annual snowfall at Fraser is 721 cm/24 feet.

Distance marker southbound shows Skagway 36 km/22 miles.

S 22.7 (36.9 km) AH 75 (120.7 km) Fraser rest area to east is a large double-ended gravel turnout with viewing platform overlooking beautiful deep-green Bernard Lake; benches, litter bins. Interpretive signs about

Motorists from Skagway, AK, go through Canadian customs at Fraser, BC. The red building seen here is the depot for White Pass & Yukon Route Railway.
(©Kris Valencia, staff)

Fraser (excerpt follows):

"The present-day location of Canadian Customs is also the site of one of the WP&YR railway stations. The station was named Fraser, probably to honour a politician from eastern Canada who had helped the railway company in its early days. Fraser is located on the stretch of track between the Summit, site of the International border, and Bennett, at the south end of Bennett Lake. This section of track was built during the winter of 1898-99, a winter that saw exceptionally heavy snowfall and cold temperatures. It also involved cutting a railway roadbed through solid rock. Rock debris had to be hauled by hand or by horse-drawn wagons."

Distance marker northbound shows Carcross 70 km/44 miles, Whitehorse 144 km/90 miles.

S 24.9 (40 km) AH 73.2 (117.8 km) Shallow Lake to east.

S 25.9 (41.8 km) AH 71.8 (115.5 km) Gravel turnout to east has sign to remind drivers that a rest stop with garbage can and outhouse is 2 km/1.2 miles north of here.

S 27 (43.9 km) AH 70.7 (113.8 km) Highway crosses tracks of the White Pass & Yukon Route at **LOG CABIN** (Chilkoot Trail National Historic Site); large parking area, toilets, litter bins, interpretive signs. With completion of the railway in 1900, the North West Mounted Police moved their customs checkpoint from the summit to Log Cabin. Chilkoot Trail hikers end their hike here.

S 27.1 (44 km) AH 70.6 (113.6 km) Distance marker northbound shows Carcross 61 km/38 miles, Tagish 95 km/59 miles, Whitehorse 135 km/84 miles.

S 29.4 (47.2 km) AH 68.3 (109.9 km) Yukon Suspension Bridge. Man-made suspension bridge offers bird's eye view of Tutshi River; restaurant, gift shop and historical display. Admission charged. www.yukonsuspensionbridge.com

S 35.6 (57.8 km) AH 62.1 (99.9 km) Gravel turnout with lake view as highway parallels Tutshi Lake for several miles northbound. This large lake in the Tagish Highland supports lake trout and grayling. Be sure you have a British Columbia fishing license.

S 38.2 (62 km) AH 59.5 (95.8 km) Large

Camping at Conrad Yukon government campground, Milepost S 55.5/Kilometerpost 90 on the South Klondike Highway. *(Judy Nadon, staff)*

gravel turnouts overlooking Tutshi Lake next 0.6 mile/1 km northbound.

S 39.6 (64.5 km) **AH 58.1** (93.5 km) Gravel access road to scenic picnic area on Tutshi Lake; boat launch. *Large vehicles check turnaround space before driving in.*

S 42.4 (68.8 km) **AH 55.3** (89 km) Distance marker northbound shows Carcross 37 km/23 miles.

S 43 (70 km) **AH 54.7** (87.9 km) Gravel shoulder parking overlooking Tutshi Lake. Good photo op.

S 44 (71.3 km) **AH 53.7** (86.4 km) Begin 1.8-mile/2.9-km passing lane northbound.

S 46 (74.6 km) **AH 51.7** (83.2 km) To the east is the site of the Venus Mines concentrator (private property), which had a capacity of 150 tons per day. A drop in silver prices caused the Venus mill's closure in October 1981.

S 47.6 (77.1 km) **AH 50.1** (80.6 km) Begin 2-mile/3.2-km passing lane southbound

S 48.8 (79 km) **AH 48.9** (78.7 km) Gravel parking area with view.

S 49.2 (79.7 km) **AH 48.5** (78 km) Dall Creek. Watch for Dall sheep and mountain goats on Dall Peak to west. Large gravel turnout to east overlooking Windy Arm.

©Kris Valencia, staff

S 49.5 (80.3 km) **AH 48.2** (77.6 km) Gravel turnout to east with Yukon Larger than Life welcome sign at BC–YT border; interpretive signs on Dall sheep and mountain goats (look for both species in summer on Montana Mountain to the northwest, Racine Mountain to southwest).

Welcome to British Columbia sign southbound.

YUKON HIGHWAY 2

S 51 (82.5 km) **AH 46.7** (75.2 km) Small turnout to east and small turnout at gated tract to west, used by hikers.

S 51.5 (83.4 km) **AH 46.2** (74.4 km) Remnant of Venus silver mine mill to east (see **Milepost S 55**). The turnouts here have been blocked off to discourage travelers from climbing on this old structure.

S 52.2 (84.5 km) **AH 45.5** (73.2 km) Several turnouts adjacent highway in this area. Pooly Creek canyon, named for J.M. Pooly, who staked the first Venus claims in 1901. Watch for rocks on the road.

S 52.5 (85.2 km) **AH 45.2** (72.6 km) Gravel turnout to east offers unobstructed view of Windy Arm.

S 53.5 (86.7 km) **AH 44.2** (71.1 km) Concrete tramline support, another remnant from Venus silver mine days.

S 55 (88 km) **AH 42.7** (68.7 km) Remnant of framework from Venus Mill, built in 1908 to serve Venus mines. The first claim on Montana Mountain was staked by W. R. Young in 1899. New York financier Col. Joseph H. Conrad acquired most of the Montana Mountain claims and formed Conrad Consolidated Mines, which began gold exploration and mining in 1905. A town of about 300 people—Conrad City—sprang up along Windy Arm and an aerial tramway was built from the town up the side of Montana Mountain. Venus Mill proved uneconomical and Conrad was bankrupt in 1912. Yukon District Gold leased the mine briefly and operated it from 1918–1920 after which it closed for good.

Small mining operations continued over the years, lower down on the hillside with short-lived startups by various mining interests. United Keno Hill Mines acquired the mining claims and their Venus Mines division saw limited production of high-grade gold/silver veins from 1970–1971 and again in 1979–1980.

S 55.5 (90 km) **AH 42.2** (67.9 km) Turnoff to east for 0.5-mile/0.8-km gravel access road downhill to **Conrad Yukon government campground**. This campground is built on the Conrad City historic site (see **Milepost S 55**) above Windy Arm. The

campground offers 29 sites on a loop road with 2 pull-throughs; picnic shelter, firepits, firewood, toilets, bear-proof garbage containers; a playground and walking trails. Tent camping area planned. Camping fee $12.

S 58.7 (95 km) **AH 39** (62.8 km) Rest area and Bove Island Viewpoint; litter bin. In 1883, Lt. F. Schwatka, U.S. Army, named this body of water after Lt. Bove of the Italian navy, who had served with the Austro-Hungarian Expedition of 1872–1874. In 1887, Dr. G.M. Dawson, GSC, renamed the lake Tagish, its original First Nations name (but spelled Ta-Gish-Ai). Dawson left Bove's name on the island.

Magnificent views of Windy Arm and its islands (Bove is the larger island). Windy Arm is an extension of Tagish Lake. Lime Mountain (elev. 5,225 feet/1,593m) rises to the east beyond Bove Island.

S 60.7 (98.2 km) **AH 37** (59.5 km) Avalanche gates; large gravel turnout.

S 61.8 (99.8 km) **AH 35.9** (57.8 km) Highway descends northbound; trucks use low gear (sign).

S 62.2 (100.8 km) **AH 35.5** (57.1 km) Begin 0.8-mile/1.3-km passing lane southbound.

S 64.3 (104 km) **AH 33.4** (53.7 km) *Slow for posted speed zone northbound entering Carcross.*

S 64.4 (104.2 km) **AH 33.3** (53.5 km) Nares Lake (sign). Waterfront Drive turnoff to public dock and boat launch.

S 64.7 (104.7 km) **AH 33** (53.1 km) Natasheeni Village turnoff.

Caribou Mountain (elev. 5,645 feet/1,721m) is visible to the east.

S 65 (105.2 km) **AH 32.7** (52.6 km) Nares Bridge crosses the narrows between Lake Bennett and Nares Lake. Gravel parking with outhouses and litter bins at boat launch at north end of bridge. Larger lakes freeze to an ice depth of more than 3 feet/1m in winter, when air temperatures drop well below -40°F/-40°C. In spring and fall look for swans, teal, pintail, goldeneye and wigeon on Nares Lake. Fishing in **Lake Bennett** for lake trout, northern pike, Arctic grayling, whitefish and cisco.

S 65.2 (105.5 km) **AH 32.5** (52.3 km) Turnoff to west on Carcross Road for historic Carcross and for town center (description follows). Driving into town you will pass the police station and fire hall and the historic St. Saviours Anglican church and the Carcross Visitor Information Center.

Distance marker northbound shows Whitehorse 74 km/46 miles, Dawson City 612 km/380 miles.

No services southbound until Skagway. Log continues on page 662.

Carcross

On the shore of Lake Bennett, 44 miles/71 km southeast of Whitehorse. **Population:** 504. **Emergency Services:** on right entering town, **RCMP**, phone (867) 821-5555. **Fire Department**, Fire Hall on Carcross Road, phone (867) 821-2222. **Ambulance**, phone (867) 821-4444. **Health Center**, phone (867) 821-4444.

Visitor Information: Carcross Visitor Reception Center, part of a complex of small buildings called the Carcross Commons, is

White Pass & Yukon Route railway offers summer passenger service between Skagway, AK, and Carcross, YT. (©Kris Valencia, staff)

located in town center. The Commons house local tourist-oriented businesses. The colorful crests on the fronts of these buildings are representative of First Nations' clans. The Center is painted with the "Welcome Man" crest and is operated by Tourism Yukon. Open daily from 8 A.M. to 8 P.M., from May 1 to Sept. 30; phone (867) 821-4431. The visitor center has a wealth of travel information for both Yukon and Alaska.

Elevation: 2,175 feet/663m. **Climate:** Average temperature in January, -4.2°F/-20.1°C; in July, 55.4°F/13°C. Annual rainfall 11 inches, snowfall 2 to 3 feet. Driest month is April, wettest month August. **Radio:** 590-AM, CIKO-FM 97.5, CHON-FM 90.5, CKRW. **Television:** CBC, APTN.

Transportation: White Pass & Yukon Route offers train service to Carcross from Skagway, with a bus return to Skagway, Tuesday–Thursday and Sundays. Or you can take the bus to Carcross from Skagway and return by train to Skagway, Tuesday to Thursday and weekends. Available May 21 to Sept. 14, 2019. Reservations and passports required; more details at www.wpyr.com or see "Railroads" in TRAVEL PLANNING section.

Private Aircraft: Carcross airstrip, 0.3 mile/0.5 km north via highway; elev. 2,161 feet/659m; length 2,000 feet/610m.

Carcross has several gift shops and restaurants and a general store. The historic Carcross post office is open Mondays, Wednesdays and Fridays 8 A.M. to noon and 1–3:45 P.M.; Tuesday and Thursday from 10–11:45 A.M. Get a Carcross cancellation stamp.

The local Isabelle Pringle library is open Monday–Thursday with varied hours. Carcross' community pool is open late June through August, phone (867) 821-3211.

Several totems in downtown were carved by Native carver Keith Smarch, who also runs the carving studio in Carcross.

Lodging in Carcross located in Chilkoot Cabins. The Caribou Hotel, established in 1901 and a Yukon Heritage Site, has been under renovation; current status unknown.

Camping is available at Carcross government campground near the airstrip and south of town at Conrad Yukon government campground. Montana Services, on the highway, has a food store, RV Park, restaurant and gas.

Historic Carcross was formerly known as Caribou Crossing because of the large numbers of caribou that traversed the narrows here between Bennett and Nares lakes. In 1904 Bishop Bompas, who had established a school here for Native children in 1901, petitioned the government to change the name of the community to Carcross because of confusion in mail services due to duplicate names in Alaska, British Columbia and the Klondike.

©Judy Nadon, staff

Carcross became a stopping place for gold stampeders on their way to the Klondike goldfields. It was a major stop on the White Pass & Yukon Route railroad from 1900 until 1982, when the railroad ceased through train service. In the early days, passengers and freight transferred from rail to stern-wheelers at Carcross. The partially rebuilt hull of the old stern-wheeler *SS Tutshi* (too-shy), pictured above, makes up the **SS Tutshi Memorial**. The Tustshi burned

down in July 1990.

A cairn beside the railroad station marks the site where construction crews laying track for the White Pass & Yukon Route from Skagway met the crew from Whitehorse. The golden spike was set in place when the last rail was laid at Carcross on July 29, 1900. The construction project had begun May 27, 1898, during the height of the Klondike Gold Rush.

The White Pass & Yukon Route runs a popular trip down to Skagway from Carcross. See "Railroads" in the TRAVEL PLANNING section. Their ticket office is located in the train depot with a gift shop area and fascinating historical displays with archival photos and large-scale maps.

Walk down to the Bennett Lake Viewing Platform on the shore of Bennett Lake. The footpath begins adjacent the post office. This scenic overlook on the Carcross waterfront has picnic tables, an interpretive sign on the Klondike Gold Rush, 2 toilets and access to the beach.

©Kris Valencia, staff

Other visitor attractions include **St. Saviour's Anglican Church** (pictured above), built in 1902; the Royal Mail Carriage; and the little steam locomotive, *Duchess*. The *Duchess* traversed the 2.5-mile rail line—called the Taku Tram—between Taku Landing on Tagish Lake and Scotia Bay on Atlin Lake, from 1900 to 1920. It is on display

Carcross Desert—the world's smallest desert—is composed of sandy lake-bottom material left behind by a large glacial lake. *(©Kris Valencia, staff)*

near the depot and makes a terrific photo op.

Caribou Crossing Trading Post, with its collection of wildlife mounts and other attractions, is just 2 miles north of Carcross; see **Milepost S 67.2**.

For mountain bikers, Carcross has become quite a destination. The Carcross Tagish First Nations has constructed single-track bike trails on the 7,233-foot/2,205m Montana Mountain.

South Klondike Highway Log
(continued)

S 65.4 (105.9 km) **AH 32.3** (52 km) Montana Services to west with gas/diesel, convenience store, liquor sales and RV park. Picnic pavilion to east.

S 65.6 (106.1 km) **AH 32.1** (51.6 km) Carcross airstrip to east. Also access via side road to Carcross Tagish First Nation's Carcross Campground; 12 campsites, picnic tables, firewood, no water provided, outhouses, camping permit ($12).

S 65.7 (106.1 km) **AH 32** (51.5 km) Tagish Road leads east to Tagish Wilderness Lodge, Tagish and Atlin Road junction.

Junction with paved Tagish Road, which leads east to Tagish (20 miles/33 km), Atlin Road (33 miles/53 km) and the Alaska Highway at Jake's Corner (34 miles/55 km). See "Atlin–Tagish–Carcross Scenic Loop" on pages 193–194.

S 65.9 (106.4 km) **AH 31.8** (51.2 km) *Slow for posted speed zone southbound.*

Distance marker southbound shows Tagish 33 km/20 miles, Alaska Highway 54 km/33 miles, Atlin 150 km/93 miles.

S 66.1 (106.7 km) **AH 32.6** (52.5 km) *Slow for posted speed zone southbound.*

S 66.6 (107.5 km) **AH 31.1** (50 km) Turnout with litter bin, toilets, and point-of-interest sign about **Carcross Desert**. This unusual desert area of sand dunes, east of the highway, is the world's smallest desert and an International Biophysical Programme site for ecological studies. The desert is com-

posed of sandy lake-bottom material left behind by a large glacial lake. Strong winds off Lake Bennett make it difficult for vegetation to take hold here and yet it has an enormous variety of plants, including kinni-kinnick, a low trailing evergreen with small leathery leaves that are used for brewing tea.

S 67.2 (109 km) **AH 30.5** (49.1 km) Caribou Crossing Trading Post (www.caribou crossing.ca) has a tremendous collection of wildlife mounts, including a life-size woolly mammoth. Other attractions include the Historical Mountie Museum, dog sled rides, gift shop, freshly made old-fashioned donuts and locally roasted coffee in their cafe.

S 71.3 (115.4 km) **AH 26.4** (42.5 km) Spirit Lake Wilderness Resort.

S 72.7 (117.6 km) **AH 25** (40.2 km) Large turnout with litter bin and information signs overlooking beautiful **Emerald Lake** (pictured above), also called Rainbow Lake by Yukoners, to west. (Good view of lake by climbing the hill across from the turnout.)

The rainbow-like colors of the lake result from blue-green light waves reflecting off the white sediment of the lake bottom. This white sediment, called marl, consists of fragments of decomposed shell mixed with clay; it is usually found in shallow, freshwater lakes that have low oxygen levels during the summer months.

S 74.6 (120 km) **AH 23.1** (38.3 km) Paved turnout to west.

S 75.4 (122 km) **AH 22.3** (35.9 km) Highway follows base of **Caribou Mountain** (elev. 5,645 feet/1,721m). View of Montana Mountain to south, Caribou Mountain to east and Gray Ridge Range to the west between Kilometreposts 122 and 128. Flora

consists of jack and lodgepole pine.

S 78.9 (127.5 km) **AH 18.8** (30.2 km) Highway crosses Lewes Creek.

S 79.5 (128.6 km) **AH 18.2** (29.3 km) Access road west leads 1 mile/1.6 km to Lewes Lake.

S 84.6 (136.6 km) **AH 13.1** (21.1 km) Rat Lake to west.

S 86.4 (139.6 km) **AH 11.3** (18.2 km) Access road west to Robinson Roadhouse rest area with large gravel parking area with litter bin, toilets, information signs. In 1899, the White Pass & Yukon Route built a railroad siding at Robinson (named for Stikine Bill Robinson). Gold was discovered nearby in the early 1900s and a townsite was surveyed. A few buildings were constructed and a post office, manned by Charlie McConnell, operated from 1909 to 1915. Low mineral yields caused Robinson to be abandoned, but postmaster McConnell stayed and established one of the first ranches in the Yukon.

S 86.6 (139.9 km) **AH 11.1** (17.9 km) Annie Lake Road; access to Annie Lake golf course (0.8 mile/1.4 km). Hamlet of Lorne Community Center.

S 92 (148.4 km) **AH 5.7** (8.7 km) Trucks-only pullout to east for northbound traffic.

S 94.3 (152.3 km) **AH 3.4** (5.5 km) Turn-off to east for **Kookatsoon Lake Yukon Government Recreation Site** (day use only, no camping, gate locked at 10 P.M. daily); picnic tables, playground, fire pits, pit toilets, canoe launch. Kookatsoon Lake has a nice sandy beach and is shallow and usually warm enough for swimming in summer. Look for Bonaparte's gulls and Arctic terns nesting at the south end of the lake.

S 97 (156.5 km) **AH 0.7** (1.1 km) *Slow for posted speed zones northbound.*

S 97.7 (157.8 km) **AH 0 Junction** with the Alaska Highway; interpretive signs to west for traffic southbound on the Klondike Highway. Northbound traffic turn left/northwest for Whitehorse (about 12 miles/19 km from here); turn right/southeast for Watson Lake (422 km/262 miles).

Junction with the Alaska Highway. Turn to **Milepost DC 874.4** on page 196 in the ALASKA HIGHWAY section: Whitehorse-bound travelers continue with that log; travelers heading south down the Alaska Highway read that log back to front.

Distance marker southbound shows Carcross 52 km/32 miles, Tagish 84 km/52 miles, Skagway 158 km/98 miles.

Southbound: Distance from Skagway (S) is followed by distance from Alaska Highway (AH). Read log:

Milepost distance from Skagway reflects physical mileposts in Alaska. Kilometer distance from Skagway reflects physical kilometerposts in Canada and is not necessarily a metric conversion of the mileage figure.

Campbell Highway

CONNECTS: Watson Lake, YT, to Klondike Hwy.

Length: 362 miles   **Road Surface: 40% Paved, 60% Gravel**   **Season: Open all year**

(See map, page 664)

(See map, page 664)

Campbell Highway campgrounds tend to be uncrowded. This is Drury Creek Campground on Little Salmon Lake.
(©Judy Nadon, staff)

Named for Robert Campbell, the first white man to enter what is now known as Yukon, this all-weather road leads 362 miles/583 km northwest from the Alaska Highway at Watson Lake, to junction with the Klondike Highway just north of Carmacks. The Campbell Highway is both gravel and pavement, with ongoing road improvements. This road can be rough and slippery in winter.

The Campbell Highway is an alternative route to Dawson City. It is about 20 miles/32 km shorter than driving the Alaska Highway through to Whitehorse, then driving up the Klondike Highway to Dawson City, but it is a significantly rougher (and slower) road.

Between Watson Lake and the turnoff for Faro, a distance of 258 miles/414 km, the Campbell Highway is a mostly narrow gravel road with some paving and improved sections. Expect continued road construction in summer 2019, particularly around the Nahanni Range Road junction.

There is very little traffic on the highway between Watson Lake and Ross River. Services on this highway (food, gas, lodging) are available in Watson Lake, Ross River, Faro and Carmacks.

Faro is celebrating its 50th anniversary in 2019. Join the community for its Homecoming Festival, June 28 to July 7, 2019. Faro is home to the Campbell Region Interpretive Centre.

The 105-mile/169-km stretch of the Campbell Highway between Faro and the Klondike Highway is paved and generally wider, straighter, and more heavily traveled than the Ross River to Watson Lake portion.

The Campbell Highway junctions with the South Canol Road to the Alaska Highway and North Canol Road to Northwest Territories *(see CANOL ROAD section beginning on page 671 for logs)* and with the Nahanni Range Road to the Tungsten mine site.

The posted speed limit on the Campbell Highway is 70 to 90-kmph/43 to 55-mph. On winding sections with no centerline, keep to the right at corners

Watch your gas tank. Motorcyclists should carry auxiliary tanks. NOTE: Government campground fees are cash or check only (carry

Distance in miles	Carmacks	Dawson City	Faro	Ross River	Watson Lake
Carmacks		222	111	145	364
Dawson City	222		330	364	582
Faro	111	330		45	258
Ross River	145	364	45		225
Watson Lake	364	582	258	225	

Canadian funds).

You have a good chance of seeing black bears along this road as well as some lake scenery (although many views are obscured by trees and brush). This is a wilderness drive with long distances between services. *Drive with your headlights on at all times. Keep*

Campbell Highway
Watson Lake, YT, to Junction with Klondike Loop

© 2019 The MILEPOST®

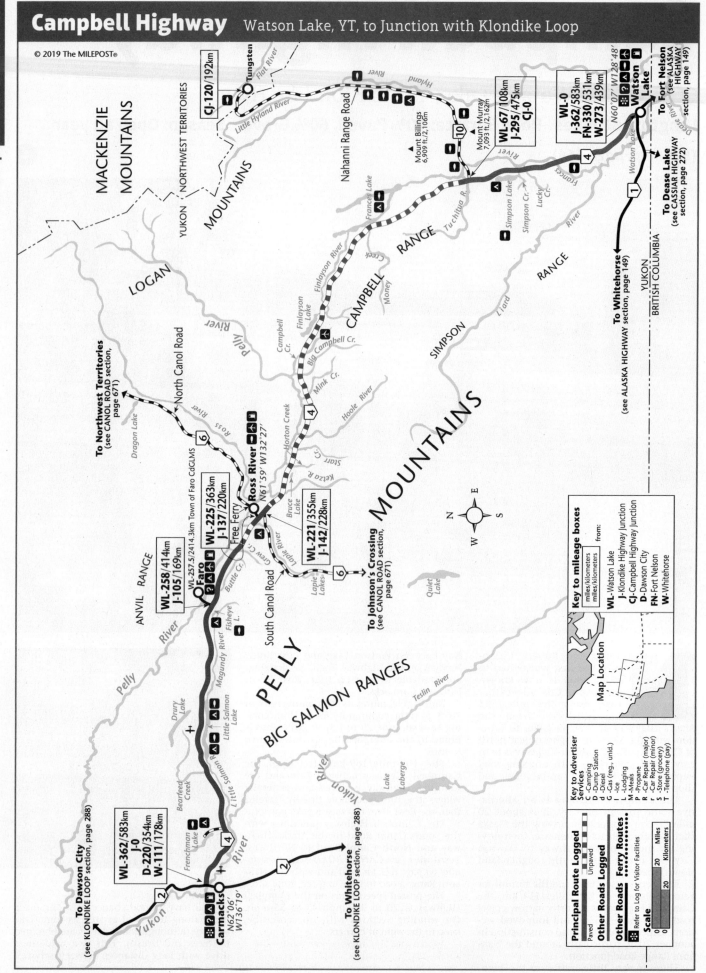

MACKENZIE MOUNTAINS

NORTHWEST TERRITORIES
YUKON

LOGAN MOUNTAINS

Tungsten
CJ-120/192km

Flat River

Little Hyland River

Hyland River

Nahanni Range Road

Mount Billings
6,909 ft./2,106m

Mount Murray
7,093 ft./2,162m

WL-67/108km
J-295/475km
CJ-0

WL-0/583km
J-362/583km
FN-330/531km
W-273/439km

N60°07' W128°48'

Watson Lake

To Fort Nelson
(see ALASKA HIGHWAY section, page 149)

To Dease Lake
(see CASSIAR HIGHWAY section, page 272)

To Whitehorse
(see ALASKA HIGHWAY section, page 149)

YUKON
BRITISH COLUMBIA

Dease River

Watson Lake

Frances River

Frances Lake

Simpson Lake

Simpson Cr.

Lucky Cr.

Liard River

Tuchitua R.

CAMPBELL RANGE

SIMPSON RANGE

Finlayson River

Finlayson Lake

Campbell Cr.

Big Campbell Cr.

Mink Cr.

Hoole River

Money Cr.

Horton Creek

Starr Cr.

Ketza R.

Bruce Lake

Ross River
N61°59' W132°27'

North Canol Road

To Northwest Territories
(see CANOL ROAD section, page 671)

Dragon Lake

Ross River

Pelly River

PELLY MOUNTAINS

WL-225/363km
J-137/220km

WL-257.5/214.3km Town of Faro CdGLMS

Free Ferry

Crew Cr.

WL-221/355km
J-142/228km

South Canol Road

Lapie River

Lapie Lakes

To Johnson's Crossing
(see CANOL ROAD section, page 671)

Quiet Lake

WL-258/414km
J-105/169km

Faro

ANVIL RANGE

Fisheye L.

Buttle Cr.

Magundy River

Little Salmon River

Drury Lake

Little Salmon Lake

Bearfeed Creek

Frenchman Lake

WL-362/583km
J-0
D-220/354km
W-111/178km

To Dawson City
(see KLONDIKE LOOP section, page 288)

Pelly River

Yukon River

BIG SALMON RANGES

PELLY

Teslin River

Lake Laberge

Carmacks
N62°06' W136°19'

To Whitehorse
(see KLONDIKE LOOP section, page 288)

N
W E
S

Key to mileage boxes
miles/kilometers
miles/kilometers
from:
WL–Watson Lake
J–Klondike Highway Junction
CJ–Campbell Highway Junction
D–Dawson City
FN–Fort Nelson
W–Whitehorse

Map Location

Key to Advertiser Services
C –Camping
D –Dump Station
d –Diesel
G –Gas (reg., unld.)
I –Ice
L –Lodging
M –Meals
P –Propane
R –Car Repair (major)
r –Car Repair (minor)
S –Store (grocery)
T –Telephone (pay)

Principal Route Logged
Paved
Unpaved
Other Roads Logged
Ferry Routes
Refer to Log for Visitor Facilities

Scale
0   20   Miles
0   20   Kilometers

www.themilepost.com

to right on corners and hills. Be prepared for rough road in construction and mining areas. Check current road conditions in Watson Lake at the visitor center or online at: 511yukon.ca.

The Robert Campbell Highway was completed in 1968 and closely follows sections of the fur trade route established by Robert Campbell. Campbell was a Hudson's Bay Co. trader who was sent into the region in the 1840s to find a route west into the unexplored central Yukon. He followed the Liard and Frances rivers, building a chain of posts along the way. His major discovery came in 1843, when he reached the Yukon River, which was to become the major transportation route within the Yukon.

Emergency Services: Dial 911 or phone the RCMP (5555) or Ambulance (4444) at: Watson Lake, phone (867) 536-5555/4444; Ross River, phone (867) 969-5555/4444; Faro, phone (867) 994-5555/4444; Carmacks, phone (867) 863-5555/4444.

Campbell Highway Log

Northbound: Distance from Watson Lake (WL) is followed by distance from junction with the Klondike Highway just north of Carmacks (J). Read log: ⬇

YUKON HIGHWAY 4 WEST

WL 0 J 362.2 (582.9 km) **WATSON LAKE;** all services including a hospital. Watson Lake Visitor Information Center and Watson Lake Sign Post Forest are located at this junction.

➕ 🅱 🔺

> **Junction** of the Campbell Highway with the Alaska Highway. Turn to description of Watson Lake beginning on page 184 in the ALASKA HIGHWAY section.

Watch for soft spots, rutted road, washboard and road construction northbound.

Check current road conditions at 511yukon. ca or with the Watson Lake Visitor Information Center.

WL 4.3 (6.9 km) **J 357.9** (576 km) Access road on right northbound to Mount Maichen ski hill; 2 lifts, 7 runs, a partial half pipe, and a full service ski chalet with viewing and eating areas; a concession and lounge; a rental shop for skiers and snowboarders. The mountain closes if the temperatures are below -13°F/-25°C.

The U.S. Air Force, based at the Watson Lake airport between 1943 and 1952, cleared the land for a ski run and built a small warm-up shed. In 1968, the area was turned over to the newly formed Watson Lake Ski Club whose members "dedicated their time, energy and personal resources to develop the ski area's facilities into what it is today."

WL 6.3 (10.1 km) **J 355.9** (572.7 km) Airport Road leads west 1.7 miles/2.7 km to Watson Lake Airport.

The terminal at the airport was built in 1942 and is a designated Heritage Building. Inside, historical photographs on the aviation history of this area are displayed.

WL 6.6 (10.6 km) **J 355.6** (572.3 km) Watson Creek. Tamarack is rare in Yukon, but this northern type of larch can be seen along here. Although a member of the pine family, it sheds its needles in the fall.

Northbound, the highway begins to

The south half of the Campbell Highway, between Watson Lake and Ross River, is mostly gravel road and lightly traveled. (©David L. Ranta, staff)

climb to a heavily timbered plateau and then heads north following the east bank of the Frances River.

WL 22.2 (35.7 km) **J 340** (547.2 km) **Tom Creek,** named after a First Nation's trapper whose cabin is at the mouth of the stream. Excellent fishing for grayling. 🐟

WL 24.9 (40.1 km) **J 337.3** (542.8 km) Turnout and access to lake.

WL 29.1 (46.9 km) **J 333.1** (536.1 km) Sa Dena Hes Mine access. This lead-zinc mine began production in August 1991, but due to low zinc prices ceased operations in November 1992. During the 14 months the project was in operation, the mine produced approximately 607,500 tons of concentrate containing 374,400 tons of payable zinc and 290,200 tons lead. The mine is currently in a state of permanent closure. Reclamation and closure activities began in 2013 and were completed in 2015.

WL 35.2 (56.6 km) **J 327** (526.2 km) Tuchitua Highway Maintenance section begins northbound.

WL 35.6 (57.3 km) **J 326.6** (525.6 km) **Frances River** bridge. Named by Robert Campbell for the wife of Sir George Simpson, governor of the Hudson's Bay Co. for 40 years, the Frances River is a tributary of the Liard River. The Frances River was part of Hudson's Bay Co.'s route into central Yukon for many years before being abandoned because of its dangerous rapids and canyons.

WL 46.1 (74.2 km) **J 316.1** (508.7 km) Lucky Creek.

WL 48.3 (77.8 km) **J 313.9** (505.2 km) Simpson Creek.

WL 50.5 (81.3 km) **J 311.7** (501.6 km) Access road leads west 1 mile/1.6 km to Yukon government **Simpson Lake Campground:** 10 campsites (1 pull-through), tables, firewood, outhouses, boat launch, dock, swimming beach, playground, kitchen shelter and water (boil water for drinking). Wheelchair accessible. Serviced mid-May to mid-September. Daily camping fee $12. Excellent fishing for lake trout, Arctic grayling and northern pike.

🔄 🔺

WL 54.7 (88 km) **J 301.5** (485.4 km) Improved pavement between Kilometerposts 88 and 97.

WL 57.6 (92.7 km) **J 304.6** (490.2 km) Large turnout with litter barrels.

WL 67 (107.8 km) **J 295.2** (475.1 km) **Junction** with Nahanni Range Road/Yukon Highway 10. The Nahanni Range (Tungsten) Road leads 120 miles/192 km to dead-end at a barricade, where a road continues on private property to **TUNGSTEN,** NWT, the company town for the Canadian Tungsten (CanTung) mine. *The Yukon government does not recommend this road for tourist travel.*

The CanTung deposit was first discovered in 1954. Production began in November 1962, and at its height Tungsten had 600 people, an RCMP post, 2 schools, a medical clinic and a jail. The mine has been shut down a number of times over the years, usually because of commodity prices. It reopened with production beginning again in October 2010, then closed down again in October 2015. When operating, CanTung produces more than 4 percent of the world's tungsten.

Construction of the Nahanni Range Road was begun in 1961 to provide access to the mining property. The road was completed in 1963 with the bridging of the Frances and Hyland rivers. Road improvements are expected to begin in 2019 and will include this junction with the Campbell Highway and at the border between Yukon and NWT to help access the area rich with mining potential. *There are no services along Nahanni Range Road.*

WL 68.7 (110.5 km) **J 293.5** (472.3 km) Yukon government Tuchitua River maintenance station to east, phone (867) 667-8511.

WL 90 (144.8 km) **J 272.2** (438 km) Jules Creek.

WL 97.8 (157 km) **J 264.4** (425.5 km) Distance marker northbound shows Ross River 221 km/137 miles, Faro 275 km/171 miles.

WL 98.2 (158 km) **J 264** (424.8 km) Distance marker southbound shows Watson Lake 160 km/99 miles.

Finlayson Lake viewpoint at Milepost WL 144.8 has a picnic area and information panels on caribou. (©David L. Ranta, staff)

WL 98.8 (159 km) **J 263.4** (423.9 km) 99 Mile Creek (not signed).

WL 104.6 (168.3 km) **J 257.6** (414.6 km) Caesar Creek (not signed).

WL 106.5 (171.4 km) **J 255.7** (411.5 km) Access road east leads to Yukon government **Frances Lake Campground** and boat launch. From highway, drive 0.6 mile/1 km east then turn left and drive 0.4 mile/0.6 km to campground. For boat launch, continue straight ahead instead of turning (it is 0.7 mile/1.1 km from highway).

The well-maintained campground has 24 sites (many on lakeshore), firewood, litter bins, picnic tables, firepits, kitchen shelter, water (boil water for drinking), outhouses and bear proof lockers. Serviced mid-May to mid-September. Daily camping permit ($12). The solitary peak between the two arms of **Frances Lake** is called Simpson Tower (elev. 5,500 feet/1,676m), named by Robert Campbell for Hudson's Bay Co. Governor Sir George Simpson.

Fishing for lake trout, Arctic grayling and northern pike.

WL 106.6 (171.5 km) **J 255.6** (411.3 km) Money Creek, named for Anton Money, a mining engineer and prospector who mined placer gold in this area between 1929 and 1946. Money later operated "The Village" service station at Mile 442 on the Alaska Highway.

Highway climbs 8 percent grade northbound.

WL 106.9 (172.1 km) **J 255.3** (410.8 km) View of Frances Lake.

WL 108.2 (174 km) **J 254** (408.8 km) Road narrows northbound, gravel continues.

WL 111.1 (178.8 km) **J 251.1** (404.1 km) Dick Creek (not signed).

WL 118 (190 km) **J 244.2** (393 km) Access road to Yukon Zinc's Wolverine Mine, a high grade zinc-silver-copper-lead-gold underground mine, with on-site milling capabilities. The majority of the concentrate from Wolverine was trucked south to the port at Stewart, BC. Operations began in 2011 and it was placed on care and mainte-nance, indefinitely in in 2015.

WL 120.9 (194.6 km) **J 241.3** (388.3 km) Highway descends Finlayson River valley northbound. Mountains to the west are part of the Campbell Range.

WL 123.6 (198.9 km) **J 238.6** (384 km) Light Creek (not signed).

WL 126.2 (203.1 km) **J 236** (379.8 km) Van Bibber Creek (not signed).

WL 129.7 (208.6 km) **J 232.5** (374.2 km) Entering Tatchun Fire Management Zone northbound.

WL 133.4 (214.5 km) **J 228.8** (368.2 km) Distance marker northbound shows Ross River 171 km/106 miles, Faro 225 km/140 miles.

WL 143 (230.1 km) **J 219.2** (352.7 km) Finlayson Creek (not signed).

The creek was named by Robert Campbell in 1840 for Chief Factor Duncan Finlayson, who later became director of the Hudson's Bay Co. Placer gold mined at the mouth of Finlayson River in 1875 is believed to be some of the first gold mined in the territory. Finlayson Lake (elev. 3,100 feet/945m), on the Continental Divide, separates watersheds of Mackenzie and Yukon rivers.

WL 143.4 (230.8 km) **J 218.8** (352.1 km) Access road east to Finlayson Lake Floatplane base.

Highway climbs 8 percent grade northbound.

WL 144.1 (231.9 km) **J 218.1** (351 km) Private side road to mineral exploration at Kudz Ze Kayah. Part of the R15 Project, located in the Yukon Tanana Terrane (YTT) of southeastern Yukon that hosts numerous other volcanic-hosted massive sulfide deposits including the high-grade, poly-metallic Wolverine deposit, the GP4F deposit, and the Kudz Ze Kayah deposit.

WL 144.8 (233.1 km) **J 217.4** (349.9 km) Turnout to east is **Finlayson Lake Viewpoint** with picnic area, observation platform and information panels on Finlayson caribou herd. The herd population was just over 3,000 animals in 2007, according to the most recent survey available. The herd's winter range is east of Ross River in lowland forest.

WL 146.6 (235.9 km) **J 215.6** (347 km) *CAUTION: Watch for moose* next 20 kms/12 miles northbound.

WL 153 (246.2 km) **J 209.2** (336.7 km) **Private Aircraft:** Finlayson Lake airstrip to south; elev. 3,300 feet/1,006m; length 2,100 feet/640m; gravel. No services.

WL 157 (252.6 km) **J 205.2** (330.2 km) Distance marker northbound shows Ross River 121 km/75 miles, Faro 175 km/109 miles.

WL 160.4 (258.2 km) **J 201.8** (324.7 km) Campbell Creek. Robert Campbell followed this creek to the Pelly River in 1840.

WL 166.3 (267.7 km) **J 195.9** (315.3 km) Bridge over Big Campbell Creek, which flows into Pelly River at Pelly Banks. Robert Campbell named the river and banks after Hudson's Bay Co. Governor Sir John Henry Pelly. Campbell built a trading post here in 1846; never successful, it burned down in 1849. Isaac Taylor and William S. Drury later operated a trading post at Pelly Banks, one of a string of successful posts established by their firm in remote spots throughout the Yukon from 1899 on.

The highway follows the Pelly River for the next 90 miles/145 km. Highway climbs steeply northbound.

WL 173.9 (279.9 km) **J 188.3** (303 km) Mink Creek culvert.

WL 187.3 (301.4 km) **J 174.9** (281.5 km) Distance marker northbound shows Ross River 71 km/44 miles, Faro 125 km/78 km.

WL 188.2 (302.8 km) **J 174** (280 km) Bridge over Hoole River; turnout to north at west end of bridge. Confluence of the Hoole and Pelly rivers. Dig out your gold pan—this river once yielded gold. A walking trail leads into Hoole Canyon, which has interesting volcanic rock formations. Go online for a brochure on recreational gold panning: www.emr.gov.yk.ca/mining/pdf/recreational_gold_panning_brochure_rvsd.pdf or check with the Watson Lake Visitor Information Center.

WL 194.1 (312.4 km) **J 168.1** (270.5 km) Star Creek culvert.

WL 200.8 (322.9 km) **J 161.4** (259.7 km) Horton Creek.

WL 201.1 (323.4 km) **J 161.1** (259.2 km) Private side road (not maintained) leads south 27 miles/44 km through the Ketza River Valley to the Ketza River Property. The first gold bar was poured at Ketza River mine in April 1984, and the mine operated from July 1988 until October 1990. The property was abandoned in 2015 and Yukon government took over its care. The Ketza River hard-rock gold deposit was first discovered in 1947. No visitor facilities.

The Ketza is a scenic river/mountain valley and a good area for canoeing, kayaking, hiking, climbing, mountain biking and gold panning. The valley has 3 formerly active gold mines and an old silver mine.

WL 211.7 (340.7 km) **J 150.5** (242.2 km) Ketza River. St. Cyr Range to southwest.

WL 212.9 (342.6 km) **J 149.3** (240.3 km) Little Ketza Creek.

WL 215 (345.7 km) **J 147.2** (236.8 km) Beautiful Creek culvert.

WL 218.4 (351.5 km) **J 143.8** (231.4 km) **Coffee Lake** to south; local swimming hole, stocked trout fishing.

WL 220.5 (354.5 km) **J 141.7** (228 km) **Junction** with South Canol Road; floatplane base on Jackfish Lake.

Junction of the Campbell Highway with the South Canol Road. Read log of South Canol Road backwards beginning on page 673 the CANOL ROAD section.

The 137-mile/220-km South Canol Road connects the Alaska Highway near Johnson's Crossing (food, gas, lodging) and to the Campbell Highway near Ross River (description begins below). *WARNING: There are no facilities or communities along the South Canol Road. Be sure to check your gas supply before you go.*

WL 225.4 (362.7 km) **J 136.8** (220.2 km) Turnoff Campbell Highway to main access road leads 7 miles/11.2 km to Ross River.

Ross River

WL 225.4 (362.7 km) **J 136.8** (220.2 km) Located on the Pelly River. **Population: 411. Emergency Services:** RCMP, phone (867) 969-5555. **Health Center,** 24-hour nurse on call and ambulance, phone (867) 969-4444. **Visitor Information:** In Faro at the Campbell Region Interpretive Center. **Radio:** CBC 990 (local AM station), CHON 90.5 FM (road reports and weather), CKRW-FM (Faro). **Transportation:** No scheduled air service. **Private Aircraft:** Ross River airstrip; elev. 2,408 feet/734m; length 5,500 feet/1,676m; gravel; fuel 40.

Ross River is a supply and communication base for prospectors testing and mining mineral bodies in this region. It was named by Robert Campbell in 1843 for Chief Trader Donald Ross of the Hudson's Bay Co. Ross River is one of 2 Kaska Dena communities in the Yukon.

With the building of the Canol pipeline service road in WWII and the completion of the Robert Campbell Highway in 1968, Ross River was linked by road to the rest of the territory. Originally situated on the north side of the Pelly River, the town has been in its present location on the southwest bank of the river since 1964.

The Dene General Store has a gas station with diesel, groceries and some merchandise (open Monday to Friday 9 A.M. to 6 P.M., noon to 5 P.M. weekends), phone (867) 969-2280. There is a Toronto–Dominion bank (no ATM), open Monday and Wednesday–Friday noon–3 P.M.; and a post office (open 11 A.M. to 2 P.M. Monday–Friday). Internet access is available at the Community Campus of Yukon College and at the public library.

The nearest campground is Lapie Canyon (see **Milepost WL 226.5**).

Ross River, located in the heart of the Tintina Trench, is a jumping-off point for big game hunters and canoeists. Canoeists traveling the Pelly River can launch just downriver from the ferry crossing. Experienced canoeists recommend camping on the Pelly's many gravel bars and islets to avoid bears, bugs and the danger of accidentally setting tundra fires. The Pelly has many sweepers, sleepers and gravel shallows, some gravel shoals, and extensive channeling. There are 2 sets of rapids between Ross River and the mouth of the Pelly: Fish Hook and Granite Canyon. Water is potable (boil first), firewood available and wildlife plentiful. Inquire locally about river conditions before setting out.

Pelly Barge crosses the Pelly River at Ross River, providing access to the North Canol Road.
(©Earl Brown)

Wildlife viewing is very popular around Ross River and along the Campbell Highway. Species include moose, black and grizzly bears, wolves, lynx, Fannin sheep, Finlayson woodland caribou and a variety of waterfowl and migratory birds.

Rock hounds check Pelly River gravels for jaspers and the occasional agate, and plant lovers keep your eye out for the numerous Yukon endemic plants in the area.

The footbridge across the Pelly River at Ross River is a 70-year-old suspension bridge that was repaired in 2018. It is a favorite photo stop for visitors and offers essential pedestrian access for community members. The government-operated Pelly Barge across the Pelly River runs almost underneath the bridge on an underwater cable. Normal daily schedule in season (May to mid–October) has been 8 A.M. to noon and 1–5 P.M. Inquire locally for current times or online at www.hpw.gov.yk.ca/trans/maintenance/yukon_ferries.html.

Across the river, the **North Canol Road** leads 144 miles/232 km to Macmillan Pass at the Northwest Territories border. The North Canol Road is a narrow, winding, rough road that some motorists have compared to a roller coaster. All bridges on the North Canol are 1-lane. Road surface can be very slippery when wet. *Not recommended during wet weather and not recommended for RVs or trailers.* Subject to closure due to washouts. *See log of the North Canol Road beginning on page 671, and read the introduction to the CANOL ROAD section.*

For current road conditions on the North Canol Road or Campbell Highway, inquire locally and visit www.511yukon.ca.

Campbell Highway Log
(continued)

WL 225.4 (362.7 km) **J 136.8** (220.2 km) Main access road leads 7 miles/11 km to Ross River (see preceding description).

WL 225.5 (362.9 km) **J 136.7** (220 km) Double-ended rest area with outhouses and litter bins.

WL 226.4 (364.4 km) **J 135.8** (218.5 km) Lapie River bridge and picturesque **Lapie River Canyon.** Turnout to north at west end of bridge. The Lapie River flows into the Pelly River from Lapie Lakes on the South Canol Road. There is a walking trail to the river and canyon from Lapie Canyon Yukon government campground *(see next entry).*

WL 226.5 (364.5 km) **J 135.7** (218.4 km) Turnoff to south for **Lapie Canyon Campground** (description follows); drive downhill 0.3 mile/0.5 km (keep left at fork).

This Yukon government campground has 18 campsites (5 pull–throughs), firewood, tables, firepits, a group picnic area, kitchen shelters, walk-in tent sites and water (boil water for drinking). Serviced mid-May to mid-September. Daily camping permit ($12). Short scenic trails to the **Lapie River.** Hiking trail with bird watching.

WL 229.1 (368.5 km) **J 133.1** (214.2 km) Danger Creek.

WL 233.3 (375.4 km) **J 128.9** (207.4 km) Double-ended turnout.

WL 235 (378.1 km) **J 127.2** (204.8 km) Small turnout beside pond to west.

WL 252.3 (406 km) **J 109.9** (176.9 km) Buttle Creek, named for Roy Buttle, a trapper, prospector and trader who lived here in the early 1900s and at one time owned a trading post at Ross River.

WL 257.5 (414.3 km) **J 104.7** (168.5 km) Turn on paved Mitchell Road for 5.6 miles/9 km northeast for the community of **FARO,** then turn right at intersection with point of interest sign about Faro. *(See description of Faro on pages 668-669.)* Road to Faro also accesses airport and **Johnson Lake Campground,** 3.5 km/2.2 miles on Faro Road, with 16 sites (7 pull-throughs), outhouses, litter bins, water (boil first), firewood and kitchen shelter. Serviced mid-May to mid-September. Daily camping permit $12. This lake is also a floatplane base for Faro.

(Continues on page 670)

Faro

Don't miss the Campbell Region Interpretive Cente (here and top inset). Camp at the adjacent John Connolly Municipal RV Park.
(©Judy Nadon, staff)

Located in east-central Yukon, 220 road miles/354 km from Whitehorse. **Population: 375. Emergency Services:** Dial 911. **RCMP,** phone (867) 994-5555. **Fire Department,** phone (867) 994-2222. **Nursing Station/ Ambulance,** phone (867) 994-4444.

Visitor Information: Campbell Region Interpretive Center, located across from John Connolly RV Park. Open first weekend in May to mid-September daily 9 A.M. to 5 P.M.; June–August 8 A.M. to 6 P.M.; off season tours may be arranged by contacting the Town Office. The center is a must-stop, with historical displays, local and regional information and free WiFi. Brochure of area hiking trails available. Contact Faro Town Office, P.O. Box 580, Faro, YT Y0B 1K0; phone (867) 994-2728; www.faroyukon.ca; email admin-faro@faroyukon.ca.

Climate: Temperatures range from -51°F/-46°C in winter to a summer maximum of 84°F/29°C. **Radio:** CBC-FM 105.1 (weather alerts), CKRW-FM 98.7, CHON-FM 90.5 (road reports and weather). **Television:** CBC and satellite channels.

Private Aircraft: Faro airport; 1.5 miles/2.4 km south; elev. 2,351 feet/717m; length 4,000 feet/1,219m; gravel.

A former mining town, named after a card game, Faro lies on the northern escarpment of the Tintina Trench. Many places in town offer a commanding view of the Pelly River.

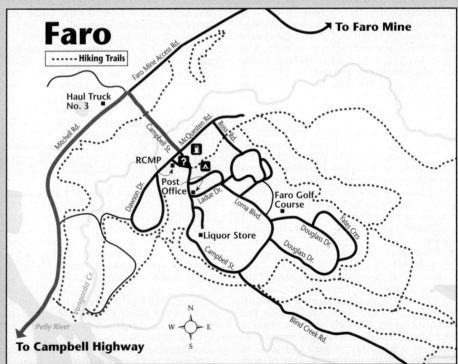

Faro

‑ ‑ ‑ ‑ **Hiking Trails**

To Faro Mine

Faro Mine Access Rd.

Haul Truck No. 3

Mitchell Rd.

Campbell St.

McQuesten Rd.

Ross Rd.

RCMP

Dawson Dr.

Post Office

Ladue Dr.

Lorna Blvd.

Faro Golf Course

Yates Cres.

Liquor Store

Campbell St.

Douglass Dr.

Douglass Dr.

Vangorda Cr.

Pelly River

To Campbell Highway

Blind Creek Rd.

N W E S

The community celebrates 50 years in 2019! Join in the year-long celebrations with a special reunion focus for events from June 28 to July 7, 2019. Get specifics and additional information at their Facebook site: TownofFaro or by email: farois turning50@gmail.com.

Lodging & Services

The Faro Studio Hotel has a lounge, restaurant (breakfast, lunch, dinner), ATM and rooms for rent. There are several bed and breakfasts in Faro and a vacation rental.

The Gas Station is open 7 days a week, has both gas and diesel and takes cash, debit and all major credit cards. For questions on hours please phone VanGorda Enterprises (867) 689-2251.

Other services in town include the Discovery Store grocery, Faro Hardware store, liquor store, post office and recreation center with seasonal indoor swimming pool and squash courts. Catholic and Protestant churches are located here.

Camping

Faro has the John Connolly municipal campground and RV park with 20- and 30-amp electrical hookups, water, showers, laundromat and sani-dump ($7.50/or free to registered campers). Camping fees begin at $15 for tenters/sites without hook-up, $27 for full hook-up (showers and firewood included in these fees). A short nature trail leads from the campground to Van Gorder Falls viewing platform.

Attractions

Dena Cho Trail. Take a hike on the 67.7 km/42 mile Dena Cho Trail and follow in the footsteps of the traditional Kaska people. The trail spans the distance between Ross River and Faro and there are 2 cabins en route for overnight stays. Be aware that if water levels are high when you travel, this can be a dangerous route.

A public boat ramp is available for exploring the Pelly River and at the stocked Fisheye Lake day-use recreation area.

Play Golf. Faro has a unique, "urban," 9-hole golf course that plays through the middle of town. Rent golf carts and equipment at the Campbell Region Interpretive Center. July 2019 will be the 22nd annual golf tournament.

A bit farther up Mitchell Road, look for the **Faro Arboretum** on the right. The most northerly arboretum in Canada, it has viewing decks, interpretive panels and walking trails showcasing native plants and animals. The trail to the Arboreteum is steep but there are interpretive signs and viewing decks along the way. The gravel access road continues 13.6 miles/22 km north to the Faro Mine Complex gate.

©Judy Nadon, staff

The Anvil Range lead-silver and zinc mine, one of the largest open-pit mines in the world at 25 square km, operated off and on from 1969 until 1998. Check out the **Ore Haul Truck No. 3** (pictured above), on Canada's list of Large Roadside Attractions. The truck is capable of carrying 65 tons of ore!

The **Van Gorder Falls Trail** departs from the Campbell Region Interpretive Center. This 1.5 km/0.9 mile trail leads to a viewing deck over the falls. You may extend your hike by turning off on the **Wolf Trail** on your return portion. This trail leads to the Faro mine site. Or, veer off on the **Fox Trail** and get in some steep hill climbs as it winds through cranberry rich forest.

Circle the community with an easy **Bear**

Trail hike. Photo worthy views include the Pelly River Valley. Or hike the "Mountain of Everything" otherwise known as Mount Mye which is more a fascinating rock than a mountain. It is just northeast of Faro and its name came from the productive hunting enjoyed by First Nations people in the area.

View Wildlife. An all-season observation cabin and isolated photographer's blind for wildlife viewing at the Mount Mye Sheep Viewing Center. Viewing areas are accessible via a gravel road skirting the Fannin sheep grazing area and are within 4 miles/6.4 km of town. On the way there, turn off at sign for **Blind Creek Salmon weir**; interpretive signs about chinook (king) salmon cycle.

Blind Creek is a salmon spawning stream that flows to the Pelly River. The weir enables sampling of the fish to learn more about the chinook. It also offers a fascinating and educational visitor experience when, in mid-July through mid-August, the chinook salmon return to spawn. Most salmon are 5–6 years old when they return. Staff on hand to count the spawning salmon will also provide information to visitors regarding this weir and the fish that they're counting. Access road is not recommended for RVs.

Special Events. Faro hosts a variety of events throughout the year, including the annual Crane & Sheep Viewing Festival in May, Faro Golf Tournament in July and regular fireside chats during Bocce Tournaments and occasional market days through summer.

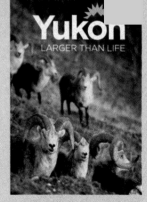

Dinner on the firepit and a lakeside seat at Little Salmon Lake Campground.
(©Judy Nadon, staff)

Campbell Highway Log
(continued from page 667)

WL 257.5 (414.3 km) **J 104.7** (168.5 km) Paved Mitchell Road leads 5.6 miles/9 km northeast to **Faro** *(see description on pages 668-669).*

WL 257.6 (414.5 km) **J 104.6** (168.3 km) Large rest area with outhouses, litter bins and information kiosk just west of this junction.

WL 259.3 (419.5 km) **J 102.9** (165.6 km) Short access road to parking for day-use area on **Fisheye Lake**; boating, rainbow trout fishing.

WL 269.6 (433.9 km) **J 92.6** (149 km) Large turnout to south.

WL 290 (466.7 km) **J 72.2** (116.2 km) Good view westbound of **Little Salmon Lake.** The Campbell Highway follows the north shore of this lake. Fishing for northern pike, Arctic grayling, lake trout.

WL 290.9 (468.1 km) **J 71.3** (114.7 km) Short access road south to **Drury Creek Campground.** This Yukon government campground is situated at the east end of **Little Salmon Lake** and is serviced mid-May to mid-September. It has 10 campsites (5 pull–throughs), boat launch, fish filleting table, kitchen shelter, outhouses, picnic tables, playground, group firepit, water, and a daily camping fee $12. Good fishing for northern pike, Arctic grayling, whitefish, lake trout 2 to 5 lbs., June 15–July.

WL 291.1 (468.5 km) **J 71.1** (114.4 km) Drury Creek bridge. Drury Creek Yukon government maintenance station to north, phone (867) 667-8596.

WL 291.3 (468.8 km) **J 70.9** (114.1 km) Distance marker northbound shows Carmacks 111 km/69 miles, Whitehorse 294 km/183 miles, Dawson City 469 km/291 miles.

WL 292.1 (470 km) **J 70.1** (112.8 km) Turnout with litter bin to south.

WL 311.8 (501.9 km) **J 50.4** (81.1 km) Steep, narrow, winding access road south to Yukon government **Little Salmon Lake Campground;** serviced mid-May to mid-September; 15 campsites (7 pull–through sites), boat launch, water, picnic tables, outhouses, firepits, playground and kitchen shelter. Daily camping fee $12. Look for fishing restrictions regarding lake trout.

WL 315.1 (506.9 km) **J 47.1** (75.8 km) Bearfeed Creek, a tributary of Little Salmon River. Access to creek to north at west end of bridge.

Highway follows Little Salmon River westbound.

WL 333.8 (537.2 km) **J 28.4** (45.7 km) Picnic spot on Little Salmon River, which flows into the Yukon River.

WL 337.5 (543.3 km) **J 24.7** (39.7 km) **Junction** with Frenchman Road (narrow, gravel) which leads north to Yukon government campgrounds (serviced mid-May to mid-September); descriptions follow.

Follow road 2.8 miles/4.5 km for **Frenchman Lake Campground;** 10 sites (2 pull-throughs), boat launch, daily camping fee $12. *Government of Yukon Campgrounds and Recreation Sites Guide* calls this a "small, cozy campgrounds offering good access to Frenchman Lake for boating and swimming from the dock." Fishing for trout, pike and Arctic grayling. Continue 5.2 miles/8.4 km on Frenchman Road from this junction for **Nunatak Campground;** 15 sites (4 pull-throughs) either on Frenchman Lake or in the forest; daily camping fee $12; boat

launch. Frenchman Road loops around to **Tatchun Lake Campground** (another 15.5 miles/25 km) with 20 sites and a dock; good place to paddle. Boat launch is 1.2 miles/2 km away on Frenchman Road.

Frenchman Road then continues 5.2 miles/8.4 km to junction with the Klondike Highway, 17 miles/27 km north of Carmacks *(see **Milepost J 118.5** on page 296 in the KLONDIKE LOOP section).* Total driving distance on Frenchman Road is 28.7 miles/46.2 km. The stretch between Nunatuk and Tatchun Lake can be quite rutted.

WL 345.6 (555.7 km) **J 16.6** (26.7 km) Turnout with litter bins and outhouses to north. **Eagles Nest Bluff** to south overlooks Yukon River; sign reads:

"The worst accident in the history of the territory's riverboat travel occurred here at Eagle Rock, on the Yukon River. In September 1906, the sternwheeler Columbian exploded and burned, killing 5 men and badly burning another. The steamer was carrying a crew of 25 men and a full cargo, including cattle and 3 tons of blasting powder destined for the Tantalus Butte coal mine, 30 miles downriver.

"The fire started when Phil Murray, the deckhand, showed his loaded gun to Edward Morgan. Morgan, ironically the fireman on watch, accidentally fired the weapon into a load of blasting powder stored on deck. The powder exploded and a sheet of flame swept the boat.

"Captain J.O. Williams was protected in the wheelhouse, but could not work the steering or communicate with the engine room. He raced down to the freight deck and told the engineer to stop the engines. As they headed into a bend in the river, he ordered the engines started again to ram the bank. After the bow hit, the stern swung round in the current and Williams ordered full astern to back the vessel up on the shore. His quick thinking allowed the crew to jump ashore and prevented the disaster from being even worse."

WL 359.3 (578.3 km) **J 2.9** (4.6 km) **Private Aircraft:** Carmacks airstrip to south; elev. 1,770 feet/539m; length 5,200 feet/1,585m; gravel.

WL 360 (579.4) **J 2.2** (3.5 km) View of Tantalus Butte coal mine on hill to the north, named by U.S. Army Lt. Frederick Schwatka in 1883, overlooks the junction of Campbell and Klondike highways.

WL 362.2 (582.9 km) **J 0 Junction.** Turn south on the Klondike Highway for Carmacks (2 miles/3.2 km), the nearest gas stop; turn north for Dawson City (222 miles/357 km). Coal Mine Campground is located at this junction.

Junction with the North Klondike Highway (Yukon Highway 2). Turn to **Milepost J 103.5** on page 295 in the KLONDIKE LOOP section for highway log.

Southbound: Distance from Watson Lake (WL) is followed by distance from junction with the Klondike Highway just north of Carmacks (J). Read log:

Canol Road

CONNECTS: Johnson's Crossing, Alaska Hwy., to NWT Border

Length: 286 miles   Road Surface: Gravel   Season: Closed in winter

(See map, page 672)

(See map, page 672)

View of the North Canol Road as it approaches the Yukon–Northwest Territories border. (©Earl Brown)

The Canol Road was built in 1942–1944, a 513-mile/825-km route to reach the important oil fields at Norman Wells, NWT, on the Mackenzie River. It was declared a National Historic Site in 1990. Today, the Canol Road (Yukon Highway 6) ends for vehicle traffic at the NWT border. A scenic route, it is accessible by foot, bike, car, or plane; the rivers along the road are popular with those who canoe and kayak; and the numerous fish-filled lakes in the area are accessible by road or floatplane. There are also many opportunities for camping. *NOTE: The Yukon Department of Tourism does not recommend the use of campers or trailers on this road. (Our field editor suffered $450 worth of damage to his camper on this route.)*

The Canol Road was part of the Canol (Canadian Oil) Project, which included a 4-inch-diameter pipeline, a telephone line, refinery, airfields, pumping stations, tank farms, wells and camps. Only about a million barrels of oil were pumped to Whitehorse before the war ended in 1945 and the $134 million project was abandoned. In 1985 the pipeline was opened to Zama, AB and oil began to flow. Today, Norman Wells oil production is operated by

Imperial Oil and includes about 100 employees/contractors.

The road was rebuilt in the 1950s, and today is open to summer traffic. It is maintained to minimum standards in summer and is closed to traffic and not maintained in winter. The Pelly Barge also closes for the winter. The Canol Road between Johnson's Crossing on the Alaska Highway and Ross River on the Campbell Highway is referred to as the South Canol Road, while the road between Ross River and the YT–NWT border is referred to as the North Canol Road.

The 137-mile/220-km South Canol Road is a narrow winding road which crests the Big Salmon Range (elev. about 4,000 feet/1,219m) and threads its way above Lapie Canyon via a difficult but scenic stretch of road. Reconstruction on the South Canol has replaced many old bridges with culverts, but there are still a few 1-lane wooden bridges and the road can be rough with trees that block the road after a storm. There are occasional road closures due to washouts. Driving time is about 4 hours 1-way; plan to be self-sufficient, there is little traffic along this route. Use caution on steep hills and sharp corners. *This road is not recommended for any vehicles in wet weather.*

The 144-mile/232-km North Canol Road

Distance in miles	Alaska Hwy. Jct.	Ross River	NWT Border
Alaska Hwy. Jct.		142	286
Ross River	142		144
NWT Border	286	144	

is also a narrow, winding, rough road that some motorists have compared to a roller coaster. All bridges on the North Canol are 1-lane, and the road surface can be very slippery when wet. *It is not recommended for travel during wet weather and not meant for RVs or trailers. Subject to closure due to washouts.*

Inquiries on current road conditions may be made at Johnson's Crossing, or check with the Yukon Dept. of Highways at (867) 456-7623, or in Yukon dial 511, or visit www.511yukon.ca before driving this road. *Drive with headlights on at all times! Make sure*

Canol Road Alaska Highway Junction, YT, to NWT Border

© 2019 The MILEPOST®

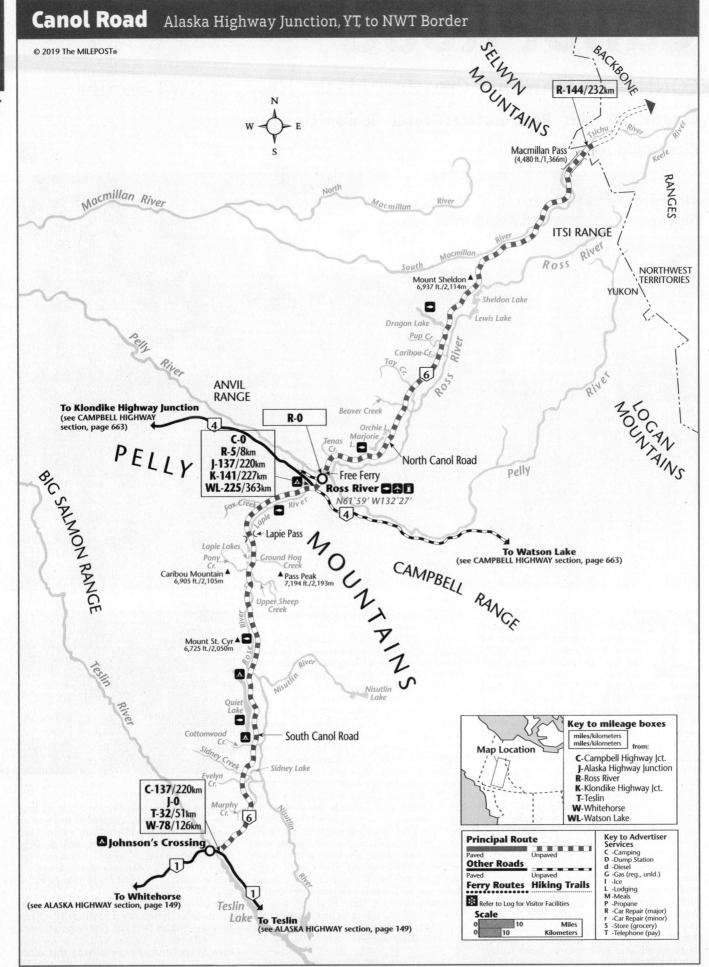

SELWYN MOUNTAINS

BACKBONE

R-144/232km

Tsichu River

Macmillan Pass
(4,480 ft./1,366m)

Keele River

ITSI RANGE

RANGES

South Macmillan River

Ross River

NORTHWEST
TERRITORIES

YUKON

LOGAN
MOUNTAINS

Mount Sheldon
6,937 ft./2,114m

Sheldon Lake
Lewis Lake

Dragon Lake
Pup Cr.
Caribou Cr.
Tay Cr.

6

North Macmillan River

Macmillan River

North

Pelly River

ANVIL
RANGE

To Klondike Highway Junction
(see CAMPBELL HIGHWAY
section, page 663)

4

R-0

Beaver Creek

Orchie L.
Marjorie
L.

Tenas Cr.

North Canol Road

P E L L Y

C-0
R-5/8km
J-137/220km
K-141/227km
WL-225/363km

Fox Creek

Lapie River

Free Ferry

Ross River
N61°59' W132°27'

4

Pelly

BIG SALMON RANGE

Lapie Pass

Lapie Lakes
Pony
Cr.

*Ground Hog
Creek*

M O U N T A I N S

CAMPBELL RANGE

To Watson Lake
(see CAMPBELL HIGHWAY section, page 663)

Caribou Mountain ▲
6,905 ft./2,105m

Pass Peak ▲
7,194 ft./2,193m

*Upper Sheep
Creek*

Ross River

Mount St. Cyr ▲
6,725 ft./2,050m

Nisutlin River

*Nisutlin
Lake*

Teslin River

Quiet
Lake

Cottonwood
Cr.

South Canol Road

Sidney Creek

Sidney Lake

*Evelyn
Cr.*

C-137/220km
J-0
T-32/51km
W-78/126km

Murphy
Cr.

6

Johnson's Crossing

Nisutlin River

1

To Whitehorse
(see ALASKA HIGHWAY section, page 149)

*Teslin
Lake*

1

To Teslin
(see ALASKA HIGHWAY section, page 149)

Map Location

Key to mileage boxes
miles/kilometers
miles/kilometers from:

C-Campbell Highway Jct.
J-Alaska Highway Junction
R-Ross River
K-Klondike Highway Jct.
T-Teslin
W-Whitehorse
WL-Watson Lake

Principal Route
Paved   Unpaved
Other Roads
Paved   Unpaved
Ferry Routes   Hiking Trails

Refer to Log for Visitor Facilities

Scale
0   10   Miles
0   10   Kilometers

Key to Advertiser Services
C -Camping
D -Dump Station
d -Diesel
G -Gas (reg., unld.)
I -Ice
L -Lodging
M -Meals
P -Propane
R -Car Repair (major)
r -Car Repair (minor)
S -Store (grocery)
T -Telephone (pay)

your tires are in good shape and carry at least 1 spare and all necessary changeover tools.

WARNING: The only facilities on the Canol Road are at Ross River on the Campbell Highway and at Johnson's Crossing on the Alaska Highway. Be sure to check your gas supply before you go.

Emergency Services: In Ross River, dial 411 or (867) 969-4444 for ambulance; or phone the RCMP at (867) 969-5555.

South Canol Road

Distance from the junction with the Alaska Highway (J) is followed by distance from the Campbell Highway junction (C). Kilometer figures in the log from the Alaska Highway junction reflect the location of physical kilometerposts when they occur.

YUKON HIGHWAY 6

J 0 C 136.8 (220.2 km) Rest area with parking, outhouses, litter bin and interpretive signs on the history and construction of Canol Road. Several WWII vehicles from the Canol Project are displayed at this rest stop.

©Earl Brown

Junction of the Canol Road (Yukon Highway 6) with the Alaska Highway (Yukon Highway 1). Turn to **Milepost DC 808.2** on page 192 in the ALASKA HIGHWAY section for log.

Just beyond the rest area are signs indicating current status of Canol Road. *Road is unmaintained and gated in winter.*

For services *before* you begin this route, Johnson's Crossing is 0.7 mile/1.1 km west on the Alaska Highway, and has food, gas/diesel, store and camping.

J 3.7 (6 km) **C 133.1** (214 km) Short, rough access road leads to **Haircut Lake**; trout fishing. Difficult access and limited parking.

J 3.9 (6.2 km) **C 132.9** (213.8 km) Fourmile Creek. Road begins ascent across the Big Salmon Range to the summit (elev. about 4,000 feet/1,219m). Snow possible at summit early October to late spring.

J 13.9 (22.4 km) **C 122.9** (197.8 km) Moose Creek. Small gravel turnout.

J 17.3 (27.8 km) **C 119.5** (192.3 km) 17 Mile Creek.

J 19.4 (31.2 km) **C 117.4** (188.9 km) Murphy Creek.

J 27 (43.4 km) **C 109.8** (176.7 km) Evelyn Creek 1-lane wooden bridge.

J 28.7 (46.2 km) **C 108.1** (174 km) Sidney Creek culvert.

J 30.6 (49.2 km) **C 106.2** (170.9 km) Access road east to Sidney Lake. Nice little lake and good place to camp.

Road follows the Nisutlin River, seen to

One-lane bridges are the rule rather than the exception on the Canol Road. (©Earl Brown)

the east for the next 30 miles/48 km until the Rose River beyond Quiet Lake.

J 30.9 (49.7 km) **C 105.9** (170.4 km) Turnout to east.

J 39.1 (62.9 km) **C 97.7** (157.2 km) Good view of Pelly Mountains ahead. Road crosses Cottonwood Creek.

J 42 (67.6 km) **C 94.8** (152.5 km) Access road east 0.4 mile/0.6 km to Nisutlin River Recreation Site, viewpoint, popular canoe put-in, boat launch, day-use area with interpretive signs, firepits, tables, litter bins and outhouse. Look for wildlife.

J 47.8 (76.9 km) **C 89** (143.2 km) **Quiet Lake South Yukon government campground**; 12 sites (1 pull–through), daily camping fee $12, boat launch, picnic tables, water (boil), kitchen shelter, firewood; serviced mid-May to early September. Steep hills northbound to Quiet Lake.

J 54.7 (88 km) **C 82.1** (132.1 km) Lake Creek. Road now follows **Quiet Lake** to west; good fishing for lake trout, northern pike and Arctic grayling.

J 56 (90.1 km) **C 80.8** (130 km) Turnout with litter barrels and point of interest sign overlooking Quiet Lake. This is the largest of 3 lakes that form the headwaters of the Big Salmon River system. The 17-mile-/28-km-long lake was named in 1887 by John McCormack, 1 of 4 miners who prospected the Big Salmon River from its mouth on the Yukon River to its source. Although they did find some gold, the river and lakes have become better known for their good fishing and fine scenery. Until the completion of the South Canol Road in the 1940s, this area was reached mainly by boating and portaging hundreds of miles up the Teslin and Nisutlin rivers.

J 61.2 (98.5 km) **C 75.6** (121.6 km) Turnoff west for **Quiet Lake North Yukon government campground**; 10 sites, daily camping fee $12, tables, firepits, kitchen shelter, day-use area with picnic sites, water; serviced mid-May to early September. Entry point for canoeists on the Big Salmon River. Boat launch and fishing, salmon spawn in river, August–September. *CAUTION: Watch for bears.*

J 61.5 (99 km) **C 75.3** (121.2 km) Yukon government Quiet Lake maintenance camp on left northbound. A vintage Canol Project dump truck and pull grader are on display in front of the camp. There are no traveler

©Susan Hay

services here, but the crew at the station has a satellite phone for emergency use only.

J 62.6 (100.7 km) **C 74.2** (119.4 km) Distance marker northbound shows Ross River 126 km.

J 63.7 (102 km) **C 73.1** (117.6 km) Steep hill and panoramic view of mountains and valley.

J 65.5 (105.4 km) **C 71.3** (114.7 km) 1-lane Bailey bridge across Rose River No. 1. The road now follows the valley of the Rose River into Lapie Pass northbound. According to R.C. Coutts in *Yukon: Places and Names*, Oliver Rose prospected extensively in this area in the early 1900s. He came to the Yukon from Quebec.

J 70.4 (113.3 km) **C 66.4** (106.8 km) Canol Creek culvert.

J 71.9 (115.7 km) **C 64.9** (104.4 km) Deer Creek.

J 75.7 (121.8 km) **C 61.1** (98.3 km) Gravel Creek culvert.

J 81.1 (130 km) **C 55.7** (89.6 km) Road crosses creek (name unknown) in culvert.

J 83.7 (134 km) **C 53.1** (85.4 km) Dodge Creek culvert.

J 87.1 (140 km) **C 49.7** (80 km) Rose River No. 2 culvert.

J 89.7 (144.3 km) **C 47.1** (75.8 km) Rose River No. 3 culvert.

J 91.5 (147.2 km) **C 45.3** (72.9 km) Rose River No. 4 culvert.

J 93.8 (151 km) **C 43** (69.2 km) Rose River No. 5 culvert.

J 95.1 (153 km) **C 41.7** (67.1 km) Upper

North Canol Road crosses the Macmillan River 6 times before ending—for most travelers—about 144 miles north of Ross River. (©Earl Brown)

North Canol Road

The North Canol Road leads 144 miles/232 km to the NWT border. Physical kilometerposts along road reflect distance from the Alaska Highway junction. **Distance from Ross River (R) is shown.**
WARNING: There are no services along the North Canol Road. Subject to closures. Inquire locally before attempting to drive. Vehicles with trailers and RVs not recommended.

R 0 ROSS RIVER. *See description of Ross River on page 667 in the CAMPBELL HIGHWAY section.* Yukon government **Pelly River Barge** (free) carries passengers and vehicles across the river between 8 A.M. and 5 P.M. daily from May to mid–October. See website for more on ferry: www.hpw.gov.yk.ca/trans/maintenance/yukon_ferries.html.

There is a 319m/1,047 foot footbridge crossing the river. Built in WWII to support the oil pipeline it offers needed pedestrian access to the hunting and ritual areas across the river and is a favorite photo op and photo taking vantage point for visitors.

R 0.6 (1 km) Road to east leads to original site of Ross River and the Kaska village.

R 0.9 (1.4 km) Second access road east to old Ross River and Indian village. Canol Road follows the Ross River.

R 2.1 (3.4 km) *CAUTION: Slide area, watch for falling rocks.*

R 6.8 (10.9 km) Tenas Creek 1-lane bridge.

R 20.9 (33.6 km) **Marjorie Creek.** Locals report good Arctic grayling fishing.

R 21 (33.8 km) Marjorie Lake to west.

R 28.1 (45.2 km) West to Orchie Lake with boat launch.

R 31.9 (51.3 km) Gravel Creek 1-lane bridge.

R 33.4 (53.7 km) Flat Creek 1-lane bridge.

R 37 (59.5 km) Beaver Creek 1-lane bridge.

R 41.8 (67.2 km) 180 Mile Creek 1-lane bridge.

R 43.9 (70.6 km) Tay River 1-lane bridge. *Yukon: Places & Names* states that Robert Campbell named this stream, a Pelly River tributary, after the "River Tay" in his ancestral home of Scotland.

R 46.3 (74.5 km) Blue Creek 1-lane bridge.

R 48.1 (77.4 km) Kilometerpost 306.

R 57.6 (92.7 km) Clifford's Slough to the east.

R 58.6 (94.3 km) Steep hill to 1-lane bridge over Caribou Creek.

R 61.8 (99.4 km) Pup Creek 1-lane bridge.

R 64.8 (104.3 km) Turnout to west. Steep hill.

R 65.1 (104.7 km) Turnout to **Dragon Lake;** unmaintained campground, pack it in, pack it out. Locals report excellent pike and trout fishing in early spring. Rock hounds check roadsides and borrow pits for chert.

R 65.4 (105.2 km) Kilometerpost 334. Large, level gravel turnout to west overlooking Dragon Lake; boat launch.

R 69.9 (112.5 km) Road to Twin Creek.

R 70.8 (113.9 km) Airstrip.

R 71 (114.2 km) 1-lane bridge over Twin Creek No. 1. Yukon government maintenance camp.

R 71.1 (114.4 km) 1-lane bridge over

Sheep Creek joins the Rose River. Pass Peak (elev. 7,194 feet/2,193m).

J 95.9 (154.3 km) **C 40.9** (65.8 km) Solar panels to the west are part of the Yukon College's correlated international study of seismic activity along a 1000 km line that covers from sea level to 1500m. This earthquake monitoring station is one of 27 installed along or near the Canol Road. Part of a multi-year study, they operated through the summer of 2018 to collect data regarding seismic activity.

J 96.4 (155.1 km) **C 40.4** (65 km) Rose River No. 6.

J 96.8 (155.8 km) **C 40** (64.4 km) Pony Creek.

J 97.1 (156.2 km) **C 39.7** (63.9 km) Rose Lake to east (3 unserviced campsites).

J 97.5 (156.9 km) **C 39.3** (63.2 km) Pony Creek. Caribou Mountain (elev. 6,905 feet/2,105m) to west.

J 101.1 (162.7 km) **C 35.7** (57.4 km) Lakes to west are part of **Lapie Lakes** chain, headwaters of the Lapie River. These features were named by Dr. George M. Dawson of the Geological Survey of Canada in 1887 for Lapie, a Fort Liard hunter who accompanied explorer Robert Campbell. A short dirt road provides access to the lakeshore. Watch for moose and nesting waterfowl. Unmaintained camping area, trout fishing and boat launch. Short walking trail to Ian H. Thomson Falls. Old gold exploration trails in the area are great for hiking and mountain biking.

J 102.5 (165 km) **C 34.3** (55.2 km) Access road west to **Lapie Lakes.** Good place to camp; excellent lake trout fishing. There is also a gravel road between the lakes that leads east to the Groundhog Creek area. The creek leads to **Seagull Lakes,** which have excellent Arctic grayling fishing.

J 107.4 (172.8 km) **C 29.4** (47.3 km) **Lapie River** No. 1 culvert. Ponds reported good for Arctic grayling fishing. *NOTE: Watch for horses on the road.*

J 107.5 (173 km) **C 29.3** (47.1 km) Ahead northbound is Barite Mountain (elevation approximately 6,500 feet/1,981m).

J 119.3 (192 km) **C 17.5** (28.1 km) Another earthquake monitoring station (see **Milepost J 95.9** for more details).

J 120.7 (194.2 km) **C 16.1** (25.9 km) Lapie River Canyon next 11 miles/18 km; road climbs to an elevation of about 500 feet/152m above the river. *CAUTION: Narrow road, watch for rocks.*

J 123.3 (198.4 km) **C 13.5** (21.7 km) Kilometerpost 200. Lapie River to east.

J 126.3 (203.2 km) **C 10.5** (16.9 km) Turnouts to east overlook Lapie River Canyon. Toilets, litter bins.

J 132.3 (212.9 km) **C 4.5** (7.2 km) Narrow 1-lane bridge over Lapie River No. 2. Point of interest sign on north end of bridge about the **Lapie River Canyon.** The old Lapie Canyon walking trail is a great place for a short hike and scenic photos. Look for stone sheep in mountains.

J 133 (214 km) **C 3.8** (6.1 km) Erosional features called hoodoos can be seen in the clay banks rising above the road.

J 133.3 (214.5 km) **C 3.5** (5.6 km) Ash layer can be seen in clay bank on right side of road.

©David L. Ranta, staff

J 135.6 (218.2 km) **C 1.2** (1.9 km) Jackfish Lake to west; floatplane dock.

J 136.8 (220 km) **C 0** Campbell Highway **junction.** Go west 5 miles/8 km for access road to Ross River for fuel and all services.

Junction of the South Canol Road with the Campbell Highway. Turn to **Milepost WL 220.5** on page 666 in the CAMPBELL HIGHWAY section for log.

North Canol Road offers WWII vehicles, great scenery and a bumpy ride. (©Earl Brown)

Twin Creek No. 2. Good views of Mount Sheldon.

R 75.1 (120.8 km) Kilometerpost 350. **Mount Sheldon** (elev. 6,937 feet/2,114m) ahead northbound; a very beautiful and distinguishable peak on the Canol Road.

R 76.4 (123 km) Kilometerpost 352. Lewis and Field lake, visible from here, part of a 3-lake chain, with Sheldon Lake the farthest north (see **Milepost R 79.8**).

R 77.6 (124.9 km) Kilometerpost 354. Riddell Creek 1-lane bridge. Tip of **Mount Riddell** (elev. 3,665 feet/1,114m) can be seen to the west; named for Robert Riddell, the first white trapper and explorer of the area.

R 78.8 (126.8 km) View of Sheldon Lake ahead, Field Lake to east.

R 79.8 (128.4 km) Kilometerpost 363. Access road east to Sheldon Lake. Named by Charles Sheldon, Sheldon Lake had a trading post and a sawmill here in 1943. The lake has a sandy beach and is great for camping; popular float plane lake.

R 82.7 (133.1 km) Sheldon Creek 1-lane bridge. Road climbs, leaving Ross River valley and entering Macmillan Valley northbound.

R 89.7 (144.3 km) *Steep hill.* Road may wash out during heavy rains. Deep ditches along roadside help channel water.

R 91.4 (147.1 km) Moose Creek 1-lane bridge.

R 91.6 (147.4 km) Milepost 230.

R 92.3 (148.5 km) Kilometerpost 378. Spectacular scenery.

R 93.8 (151 km) First of several WWII vehicle dumps to west. Wannigans, or skid shacks, were used as living quarters by Canol Road workers during construction of the road. These small buildings were strategically located along the route so the workers far from base camp had a place to overnight.

R 94 (151.3 km) First glimpse of the South Macmillan River northbound.

R 94.7 (152.4 km) Kilometerpost 382. Old Canol project equipment dump.

R 97.8 (157.4 km) Boulder Creek 1-lane bridge.

R 98.5 (158.5 km) Access road west to South Macmillan River where boats can be launched. Locals advise launching boats here rather than from the bridge at **Milepost R 113.6**, which washes out periodically and leaves dangerous debris in the river. Popular but challenging canoe trip.

R 100.8 (162.5 km) Kilometerpost 392. Itsi Range comes into view northbound.

R 104.5 (168.2 km) Kilometerpost 398. View of the South Macmillan River.

R 105.3 (169.4 km) View of Selwyn Mountains, named in 1901 by Joseph Keele of the Geological Survey of Canada for Dr. Alfred Richard Selwyn (1824–1902), a distinguished geologist in England.

R 111 (178.6 km) Kilometerpost 408.6. Itsi Creek 1-lane bridge.

R 112.2 (180.5 km) Wagon Creek 1-lane bridge.

R 113.6 (182.8 km) Turnout to east on South Macmillan River. 1-lane Bailey bridge over South Macmillan River No. 1.

Robert Campbell, a Hudson's Bay Co. explorer on a journey down the Pelly River in 1843, named this major tributary of the Pelly after Chief Factor James McMillan, who had sponsored Campbell's employment with the company.

R 115.1 (185.2 km) Access road on left northbound leads about 7 miles/11 km to Yukon Barite Mine.

R 118.1 (190.6 km) Solar panels/earthquake sensors (see **Milepost J 95.9** on the South Canol Road for more information.

R 118.9 (191.3 km) Jeff Creek 1-lane bridge.

R 121.2 (195 km) Hess Creek 1-lane bridge. Bears in area.

R 123.2 (198.3 km) Gravel turnout to west. 1-lane bridge over Dewhurst Creek.

R 127.5 (205.2 km) Entering **Macmillan Pass**, "Mac Pass" (elev. 4,480 feet/1,366m). This area is very scenic in late summer and fall (snow is possible); good place to camp.

R 129.4 (208.2 km) 1-lane bridge over Macmillan River No. 2.

R 129.5 (208.4 km) Abandoned Army

vehicles from the Canol Project. *NOTE: This large cache of trucks and equipment is protected under Yukon's Historic Resources Act, do NOT touch or remove.*

R 133.6 (215 km) To the west is the Jason deposit, a zinc, lead and silver property first staked in 1974 by Ogilvie Joint Venture.1-lane bridge over Sekie Creek No. 1. Do not drink this water.

R 136.4 (219.5 km) Access to Macmillan airstrip. Earthquake monitoring site. To the east is the Tom property, a lead, zinc and silver deposit first staked in 1951 by Hudson Bay Mining and Smelting.

CAUTION: Watch for road washouts.

R 137.7 (221.6 km) 1-lane bridge over Macmillan River No. 3.

R 141.8 (228.2 km) 1-lane bridge over Macmillan River No. 4.

R 142.9 (230 km) 1-lane bridge over Macmillan River No. 5.

R 144.1 (231.9 km) 1-lane bridge over Macmillan River No. 6. Mount Yara to west; repeater station. Ahead is the Tsichu River valley and the Selwyn Mountains. The Mac-Tung tungsten deposit is located on Mount Allan in the Selwyn Range.

©Susan Hay

R 144.2 (232 km) **YT–NWT border**; vehicle turnaround. From here to Norman Wells it is 221 miles/355 km of former mining road now utilized by backpackers. Check out "Hike the Canol Trail" at http://spectacularnwt.com/story/best-hardest-hike. Guided hikes may be possible, see the Norman Wells website: www.normanwells.com/lifestyle/tourism-norman-wells for more information.

Dempster Highway

CONNECTS: Klondike Highway to Inuvik, NWT

Length: 456 miles   Road Surface: Gravel   Season: Open all year

New all-season road from Inuvik to Tuktoyaktuk ends here at the Arctic Ocean. The Dempster Highway ends at Inuvik. (©Dianne & Joe Hofbeck)

Distance in miles	Dawson City	Ft. McPherson	Inuvik	Klondike Hwy.
Dawson City		367	481	25
Ft. McPherson	367		114	342
Inuvik	481	114		456
Klondike Hwy.	25	342	456	

The Dempster Highway (Yukon Highway 5, NWT Highway 8) begins about 25 miles/40 km east of Dawson City, YT, at its junction with the Klondike Highway *(see KLONDIKE LOOP on page 288)* and leads 456 miles/734 km northeast to Inuvik, NWT. From Inuvik, the newly opened Mackenzie Valley Highway/NWT 10 leads 83 miles/134 km to Tuktoyaktuk on the Arctic Ocean *(see "Road to Tuk" page 684).*

The Dempster Highway can be driven in 10 to 14 hours, but it is strongly recommended that motorists slow down and enjoy the trip, allowing extra time for hiking, camping, fishing, wildlife viewing (especially birds) and the spectacular photo opportunities this remote road affords.

Motorists looking for a shorter side trip from the Klondike Highway might just make the 44-mile/71-km drive up to the Tombstone Interpretive Center, a popular day trip alternative. Extend your stay with an overnight at the Tombstone Mountain Campground, then retrace your route the next day. Or drive 229 miles/369 km to the approximate half-way point at Eagle Plains Hotel, overnight, and return.

Construction of the Dempster Highway began in 1959 and was finally completed in 1978, although it did not officially open until Discovery Day weekend in 1979. It was built to provide access to the Canadian Arctic and to accommodate oil and gas exploration activity. It was named for Inspector William John Duncan Dempster of the RCMP.

The first 5 miles/8 km of the Dempster are seal-coated, and the last 6 miles/10 km are paved, but the rest of the road is gravel. Although in relatively good condition, this highway requires drivers pay attention at all times for sudden changes in road surface, including frost heaves, potholes, boggy or slick stretches, crushed shale (hard on tires),

Major Attractions:

©Kris Valencia, staff

Lost Patrol Gravesite, Tombstone Interpretive Center, Igloo Church, Arctic Circle Crossing, Tuktoyaktuk

Highest Summit:
North Fork Pass 4,593 ft.

Dempster Highway   Klondike Highway Junction to Inuvik, NWT

© 2019 The MILEPOST®

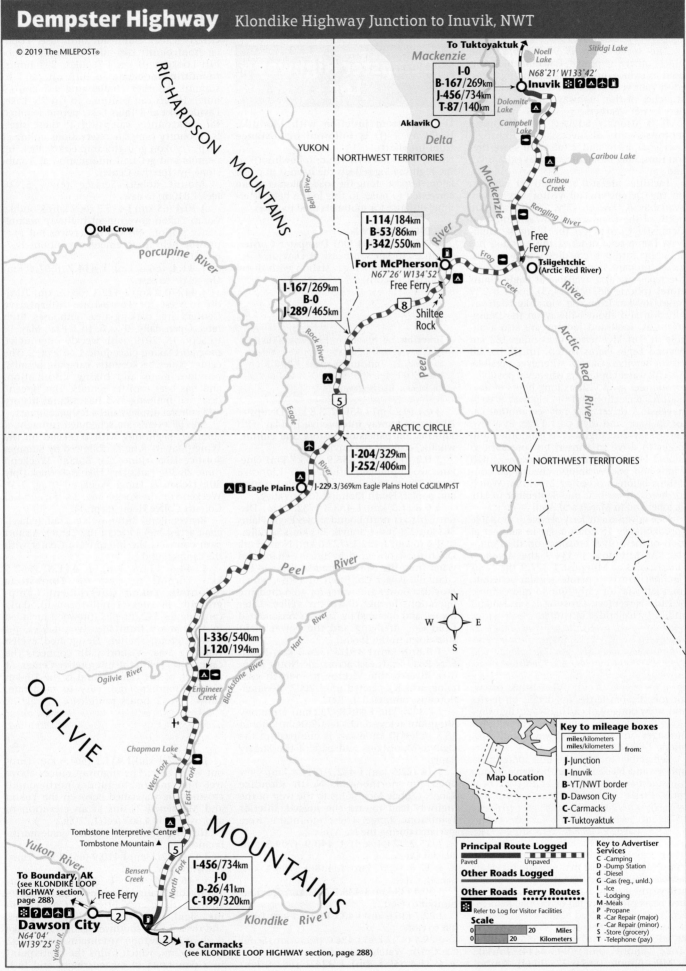

To Tuktoyaktuk

Mackenzie

Noell Lake

Sitidgi Lake

N68°21' W133°42'

I-0
B-167/269km
J-456/734km
T-87/140km

Inuvik ❄?▲⛽🛈

Dolomite Lake

Delta

Aklavik

YUKON

NORTHWEST TERRITORIES

Mackenzie River

Campbell Lake

Caribou Lake

Caribou Creek

Rengling River

Free Ferry

RICHARDSON MOUNTAINS

Bell River

I-114/184km
B-53/86km
J-342/550km

Fort McPherson
N67°26' W134°52'

Free Ferry

Tsiigehtchic
(Arctic Red River)

Frog Creek

Arctic Red River

Old Crow

Porcupine River

I-167/269km
B-0
J-289/465km

8

Rock River

Shiltee Rock

×

Peel River

5

ARCTIC CIRCLE

YUKON | NORTHWEST TERRITORIES

✈

I-204/329km
J-252/406km

River

▲⛽ **Eagle Plains**   J-229.3/369km Eagle Plains Hotel CdGILMPrST

Peel River

Hart River

N

W ✦ E

S

I-336/540km
J-120/194km

▲⛽

Ogilvie River

Blackstone River

Engineer Creek

✝

Chapman Lake

⛽

OGILVIE MOUNTAINS

West fork

East fork

▲

Tombstone Interpretive Centre
Tombstone Mountain ▲

5

Bensen Creek

North fork

To Boundary, AK
(see KLONDIKE LOOP
HIGHWAY section,
page 288)

Yukon River

Free Ferry

❄?▲⛽🛈

2

Dawson City
N64°04'
W139°25'

Yukon R.

I-456/734km
J-0
D-26/41km
C-199/320km

Klondike River

2 **To Carmacks**
(see KLONDIKE LOOP HIGHWAY section, page 288)

Key to mileage boxes

miles/kilometers
miles/kilometers   from:

J-Junction
I-Inuvik
B-YT/NWT border
D-Dawson City
C-Carmacks
T-Tuktoyaktuk

Map Location

Principal Route Logged

Paved ▬▬▬   Unpaved ▬▬▬

Other Roads Logged

Other Roads   Ferry Routes

❄ Refer to Log for Visitor Facilities

Scale

0 — 20 Miles
0 — 20 Kilometers

Key to Advertiser Services

C -Camping
D -Dump Station
d -Diesel
G -Gas (reg., unld.)
I -Ice
L -Lodging
M -Meals
P -Propane
R -Car Repair (major)
r -Car Repair (minor)
S -Store (grocery)
T -Telephone (pay)

and other drivers. Drivers should pull-over (if space allows) for oncoming trucks or to allow trucks to pass. *Drive with your headlights on at all times.*

The speed limit is 90-kmph/55-mph unless otherwise posted. Calcium chloride is used to reduce dust and as a bonding agent; wash your vehicle as soon as practical. Some stretches of this highway can be very slippery in wet weather!

It is strongly advised that Dempster motorists carry all necessary tire changeover equipment and 2 full-sized spare tires (on rims, fully inflated) as well as extra water and gas.

Facilities are still few and far between on the Dempster. Full visitor services are available in Dawson City, 25 miles/40 km north of the Dempster Highway turnoff (at Dempster Corner) on the Klondike Highway. Dempster Corner at the junction has a public cardlock gas/diesel station. Gas, diesel, propane, food, lodging, and car and tire repair are also available at **Eagle Plains Hotel** (phone 867/993-2453), located 229 miles/369 km from the Klondike Highway junction and about halfway on the Dempster. Gas, food and lodging are also available in Fort McPherson (113 miles/182 km beyond Eagle Plains Hotel). Inuvik has all visitor services. Gas up whenever possible. Also fill water containers whenever possible.

Summer gives visitors long hours of daylight for recreation and the highway is well-traveled: A driver may not see another car for an hour, and then pass 4 cars in a row. Locals say the highway is smoother and easier to drive in winter, but precautions should be taken against cold weather, high winds and poor visibility; check road conditions before proceeding in winter. Watch for herds of caribou mid-September to late October and in March and April.

Free government ferry service is available approximately 15 hours a day in summer at each of the 2 river crossings on the Dempster: At **Milepost J 334.9** the *Abraham Francis*; and at **Milepost J 377.9** the *Louis Cardinal*. Ferries operate regular schedule from late May or early June to mid-October or early November. Crossing is on demand and/or by ice bridge in winter. *"Ferries in the NWT can close with little or no notice due to low water levels, ice conditions, or other factors. Caution should be used on landings and approaches. Always check road bulletins before traveling to ensure ferries on your route are operating normal hours."* Visit https://www.inf.gov.nt.ca/en/ferries for details on ferries and www.dot.gov.nt.ca/Highways/Highway–Conditions for road conditions. For recorded messages on current highway conditions, phone 1-800-661-0750.

Remember to pack the bug spray: mosquitoes and black flies can be fierce during the summer. Also remember to pack bear spray. *Conservation officers have warned that anybody traveling on the Dempster Highway should take precautions to avoid a bear encounter, and cyclists should be sure to have bear spray handy at all times.* In 2017, an aggressive grizzly bear or bears approached a bicyclist and motorcyclist in 2 separate incidents between Kilometers 230 and 270. Officials believe these may have been food habituated bears previously fed by people. Remember: A fed bear is a dead bear.

Emergency Services: Dawson City: RCMP, phone (867) 993-5555; **Ambulance,** phone (867) 993-4444. Inuvik: **RCMP,** phone (867) 777-1111; **Ambu-**lance, phone (867) 777-4444. Tuktoyaktuk: **RCMP,** phone (867) 977-1111; **Hospital** phone (867) 977-2321.

Dempster Highway Log

Distance from junction with Klondike Highway 2 (J) is followed by distance from Inuvik (I).

NOTE: The kilometer figure following (J) in the highway log reflects the nearest physical kilometerpost along the road. Kilometers are converted to miles in this log to help determine distance for motorists used to miles.

YUKON HIGHWAY 5

J 0 I 456.1 (734 km) Dempster Corner, 25 miles/40 km southeast of Dawson City. AFD public cardlock gas station with diesel at northeast corner. *NOTE: Next gas northbound is at Eagle Plains, 229 miles/369 km from here.*

🅱

Junction of Klondike Highway (Yukon Highway 2) and Dempster Highway (Yukon Highway 5). Turn to **Milepost J 298.3** on page 300 in the KLONDIKE LOOP section for log of Klondike Highway.

J 0.1 (0.2 km) I 456 (733.8 km) Dempster Highway Gateway Interpretive Display with information panels on history and culture, wildlife, ecology and driving tips.

J 0.2 (0.3 km) I 455.9 (733.7 km) One-lane wood-planked bridge over Klondike River. The road follows the wooded (spruce and poplar) North Klondike River Valley.

J 0.8 (1.3 km) I 455.3 (732.7 km) Distance marker northbound shows Eagle Plains 363 km/226 miles, Inuvik 735 km/457 miles.

J 4 (6 km) I 452.1 (727.6 km) North Fork Ditch (now obscured by brush) channeled water from the North Klondike River to the Granville Power Co. (built in 1909), which provided power and water for gold-dredging operations farther down the valley. Later owned and operated by Yukon Consolidated Gold Co., dredging and the power plant shut down in the 1960s.

J 4.8 (8 km) I 451.3 (726.3 km) North Fork Road leads east across the North Klondike River to the Viceroy heap-leach gold mine, which operated until 2002. Reclamation was completed in 2005.

J 7.3 (12 km) I 448.8 (722 km) Antimony Mountain (elev. 6,693 feet/2,040m), about 18.5 miles/30 km away, is one peak of the Ogilvie Mountains and part of the Snowy Range.

J 14 (22.5 km) I 442.1 (711.4 km) View opens up northbound. North Klondike Range, Ogilvie Mountains to the west of the highway lead toward the rugged, interior Tombstone Range. These mountains were glaciated during the Ice Age.

J 15.2 (24.4 km) I 440.9 (709.5 km) Glacier Creek.

J 17.8 (28.6 km) I 438.3 (705.4 km) Bensen Creek.

J 20.4 (33 km) I 435.7 (701 km) Spacious turnout to west.

J 22.7 (36.6 km) I 433.4 (697.4 km) Turnout to east.

J 29.4 (47.3 km) I 426.7 (686.7 km) Scout Car Creek. Watch for grouse.

J 31.4 (50.5 km) I 424.7 (683.5 km) Tombstone Territorial Park (northbound sign).

J 36.5 (58.5 km) I 419.6 (675.5 km) Grizzly Creek trailhead; outhouse. Popular frontcountry day-hike to Mount Monolith Lookout (6 km/3.7 miles, 3–4 hours, roundtrip, moderate to difficult) and to summit (another challenging 1.5 km/0.9 mile). Hikers can continue to Grizzly Lake, Divide Lake and Talus Lake; permit required for backcountry campsites at these sites. Backcountry campsite reservations online at https://yukon.goingtocamp.com/. Pick up permits and get trail information at Tombstone Interpretive Center.

Mount Robert Service (elev. 5,938 feet/1,810m) to east.

J 40.4 (65 km) I 415.7 (669 km) Klondike Camp Yukon government highway maintenance station. No visitor services but may provide help in an emergency, phone 867-667-8691.

J 41.4 (66.6 km) I 414.7 (667.4 km) Gravel pit to east.

J 44 (70.8 km) I 412.1 (663.2 km) Turnoff to west for **Tombstone Interpretive Center**; large parking area, outhouses, litter bins. Open daily, 9 A.M. to 5 P.M., May 18 to Sept. 15, 2019, with weekly interpretive programs taking place June 1 to Sept. 2. The center issues backcountry camping permits, provides maps and hiking information, and has bear canister rentals. The "green" designed building also has natural history and cultural displays and a resource library.

Special events are scheduled throughout summer, beginning with Weekend on the Wing (May 31-June 2), followed by Summer Solstice Hike (June 21); Botany Weekend (June 28-30); Parks Day Hike & Potluck (July 20); Lichen & Fungi Weekend (Aug. 2-4); Weekend on the Rocks (Aug. 23-25); and Fall Colours Coffee House (Sept. 7).

Beaver Pond Interpretive Trail (wheelchair accessible) adjacent the Center. A short path connects the Interpretive Center with the campground.

J 44.5 (71.5 km) I 411.8 (662.5 km) Turnoff to west for **Tombstone Mountain Yukon Government Campground**; 48 sites (1 pull-through), daily camping fee $12, firepits (firewood included in fee), water from the river, tables, pit toilets, group shelter. Designated cyclist camping area. A short path connects the campground with the Interpretive Center. At the back of the campground is the 1.6-km North Klondike Trail: easy to moderate, allow 1 to 2 hours roundtrip. *CAUTION: Hikers should be bear aware. Inquire about recent bear activity in the area before setting out.*

▲

J 45 (72.4 km) I 411.1 (661.6 km) Turnout with view. The highway moves above tree line and on to tundra northbound, crossing the watershed between the Yukon and Mackenzie basins at an elevation of approximately 4,003 feet/1,220m.

Highway climbs 10 percent grade northbound.

J 45.2 (72.7 km) I 410.9 (661.3 km) Turnout with view.

J 46 (74 km) I 410.1 (660 km) Tombstone Range Viewpoint; large double-ended parking area, litter bin ("No Camping" sign). Good views of North Fork Pass and river. To the southwest is the needle-like peak of Tombstone Mountain (elev. 7,192 feet/2,192m), which forms the centerpoint in a panorama of ragged ridges and lush green tundra slopes. To the north is the East Fork Blackstone River valley; on each side are the Ogilvie Mountains, which rise to elevations of 6,890 feet/2,100m. Watch for Dall sheep, grizzlies, hoary marmots and ptarmigan. The Tombstone, Cloudy and Blackstone mountain ranges are identified as a Special Management Area by the Yukon Government. Look for Northern Wheatear nesting in nearby cliffs.

J 46.2 (74.6 km) **I 409.9** (659.6 km) Side road east to Northwestel microwave tower accesses Goldensides Mountain trailhead (1.5 km/0.9 mile, allow 30 minutes to 1 hour one-way). Popular day hike, rated moderate, with views of North Klondike Valley.

J 47.7 (76.6 km) **I 408.4** (657.4 km) Game management unit boundary (signed)

J 48.6 (78.2 km) **I 407.5** (655.8 km) Hart River Winter Road trailhead to east, parking area to west. Easy to moderate hiking on former mineral exploration road; also suitable for cycling, ATVs and motorbikes (must stay on road) but not for vehicles. Road can be very rough and is very muddy in wet weather. It is 5 km/3.1 miles to Hart Road summit, 9.5 km/5.9 miles to Park boundary.

J 49.3 (79.3 km) **I 406.8** (654.7 km) **North Fork Pass Summit**, elev. 4,593 feet/1,400m, is the highest point on the Dempster Highway and the continental divide between the Yukon River watershed, where rivers flow west to the Bering Sea, and the Mackenzie River system, where rivers flow north into the Beaufort Sea.

J 50 (80.4 km) **I 406.1** (653.5 km) Double-ended turnout to east. Wildflowers abundant in late June, early July. Good bird-watching area. A hike up the mountain slopes increases the chance of seeing pika, marmots, ptarmigan and golden eagles. Also watch for gyrfalcon, which hunt ptarmigan. *NOTE: Do not hike here during lambing season in May and June to avoid disturbing the sheep.*

J 52 (83.5 km) **I 404.1** (650.3 km) Anglecomb Peak (also called Sheep Mountain) is a lambing and nursery habitat for Dall sheep during May and June. This is also a frequent nesting area for a pair of golden eagles.

J 53.3 (85.8 km) **I 402.8** (648.2 km) First crossing of East Fork Blackstone River.

J 54.6 (87.9 km) **I 401.5** (646.1 km) White fireweed in summer.

J 56.4 (90.8 km) **I 399.7** (643.2 km) Guide and outfitters camp to east.

CAUTION: Watch for horses on road.

The Blackstone Uplands, stretching from North Fork Pass to Chapman Lake, are a rich area for birdlife (long-tailed jaegers, gyrfalcons, peregrine falcons, red-throated loons, whimbrels, upland sandpipers and long-tailed ducks) and big game hunting for Dall sheep and grizzly bear. The open tundra vegetation here is similar to high Arctic tundra.

J 62.6 (100.7 km) **I 393.5** (633.2 km) Distance marker northbound shows Eagle Plains 261 km/162 miles, Inuvik 633 km/393 miles.

Distance marker southbound shows Dawson 142 km/88 miles, Whitehorse 600 km/373 miles.

J 63.7 (102.5 km) **I 392.4** (631.5 km) Turnout with information panels, viewing platform for Two Moose Lake and litter bins. You may see moose, which are relatively scarce in the Blackstone Uplands. Bird watching includes Northern pintail, scaup, American wigeon, Northern shoveller and harlequin ducks.

J 66.9 (107.5 km) **I 389.2** (626.5 km) Double-ended pullout to east with outhouse, litter and recycling bins. Access to Black-

Tombstone Interpretive Center at Milepost J 44 offers special summer events and interpretive programs as well as camping permits, maps and hiking help. (©Kris Valencia, staff)

stone River.

J 70.3 (113 km) **I 385.8** (621 km) Parking area to east with memorial to local residents Joseph and Annie Henry.

J 71.3 (114.8 km) **I 384.8** (619.3 km) First crossing of **West Fork Blackstone River.** Watch for arctic terns. Good fishing for Dolly Varden and grayling a short distance downstream where the west and east forks of the Blackstone join to form the Blackstone River, which the road now follows. After the river crossing, 2 low, cone-shaped mounds called pingos are visible upriver about 5 miles/8 km.

J 72.1 (116 km) **I 384** (618 km) Turnout to west with litter bin, interpretive signs. Tombstone Territorial Park boundary (sign). Commemorative road sign about sled dog patrols of the Royal North West Mounted Police. View of **Chapman Lake**, one of the few lakes close to the highway that is large enough to permit floatplane operations. The lake is named for Ernest Chapman, a local trader, trapper and prospector. Common loons nest on island.

Porcupine caribou herd (estimated at 218,000 in 2017) sometimes crosses the highway in this area in mid-October.

J 77 (124 km) **I 379.1** (610 km) **Private Aircraft:** Government airstrip side of road; elev. 3,100 feet/945m; length 3,000 feet/914m.

J 85.7 (138 km) **I 370.4** (596 km) Note black or reddish hematite in the pale limestone to the west. When cut and polished, black hematite is known as Alaska black diamond.

J 95.2 (153 km) **I 360.9** (581.1 km) Turnouts at **Windy Pass Summit** (elev. 3,478 feet/1,060m). This is part of eastern Beringia, which escaped glaciation during the Ice Age and allowed refuge for some unique flora and fauna. This is the start of the Northern Ogilvie Mountains, which are more rounded and more sparsely vegetated than mountains to the south. Nicknamed the Limestone Hills, dolomite rock outcroppings eroded by wind and weather and rocky rubble slopes characterize this range.

J 100.1 (161 km) **I 356** (573 km) Engi-

neer Creek, a tributary of the Ogilvie River, was renamed from Big Creek in 1971 to commemorate Dept. of Public Works engineers who worked on the Dempster Highway.

Iron oxide, limestone, gypsum, salt- and sulfide-bearing sediments dissolve in rain water and color the creek and earth in reds and orange-brown hues. The distinctive smell is from the aptly-named Sulfur Springs nearby. *Do not drink creek water!*

J 108.6 (174.7 km) **I 347.5** (559.3 km) Turnout.

J 110.6 (178 km) **I 345.5** (556 km) Look for sheep on rocky hillsides.

J 120.4 (193.8 km) **I 335.7** (540.2 km) Turnoff to east for **Engineer Creek Yukon Government Campground**; 11 sites, daily camping fee $12, fireplaces, firewood, water, picnic tables, pit toilets, screened kitchen shelter with stove and tables. *Bring mosquito repellent; mosquito nets also recommended. Grayling fishing.*

Sapper Hill, across Engineer Creek from the campground, is a massive castellated hill of dolomite exhibiting huge and interesting rock formations. It was named in 1971 in honor of the Third Royal Canadian Engineers who built the Ogilvie River bridge. "Sapper" is a nickname for an army engineer. The Gwich'in name is Chu Akan.

J 121.2 (195 km) **I 334.9** (539 km) Engineer Creek bridge.

J 121.5 (195.5 km) **I 334.6** (538.5 km) The 360-foot/110-m Ogilvie River Bridge (metal decking), also called Jeckell Bridge. Built by the Canadian Armed Forces Engineers as a training exercise, it is named in honor of Allan Jeckell, controller of the Yukon from 1932 to 1946. Yukon Highway Maintenance compound to west at north end of bridge.

J 123 (197.8 km) **I 333.1** (536.2 km) Northbound, the highway traverses the Ogilvie River valley. *NOTE: The steep valley sides are prone to avalanches in winter; watch for signs indicating avalanche areas.* The Ogilvie River and Ogilvie Mountains were named in honor of William Ogilvie, a highly respected Dominion land surveyor and commissioner

Miles of gravel road—over hills, along ridges and across mountain passes—make up the Dempster en route to Inuvik. (©Kris Valencia, staff)

of the Yukon during the Klondike Gold Rush.

Good views of unglaciated, castle-like outcroppings of rock, known as tors, on mountain to north. Also watch for bird nests in the shale embankments along the highway.

J 123.7 (198.8 km) **I 332.4** (535.2 km) Distance marker southbound shows Dawson City 240 km/149 miles, Whitehorse 698 km/434 miles.

J 137.5 (221.2 km) **I 318.6** (512.7 km) Rest area to east on river with litter barrels. Elephant Rock is on mountain ridge to east—use binoculars. This is one example of the many tors in this area, and was named because of its resemblance to an elephant but also because they were common here 8,000 years ago. Archaeological discoveries have found both elephant and wooly mammoth bones in the area. Easy access to **Ogilvie River**; good grayling fishing.

J 137.6 (221.5 km) **I 318.5** (512.6 km) Davies Creek.

J 139.2 (224 km) **I 316.9** (510 km) Churchwood Hill. Fascinating mountain—last of the Ogilvie Mountains northbound—of broken rock and shale. The Gwich'in call this Beaver House Mountain because they say a giant beaver occupied this mountain during Beringia. (Beringia refers to a large, ice-free land area that occurred during the last ice age in northern Yukon and Alaska. Stop by the Yukon Beringia Interpretive Center in Whitehorse for more information.)

Dolomite cliff faces along road. Look for peregrine falcon nests.

J 147.3 (237 km) **I 308.8** (497 km) Ogil-

vie airstrip. The great gray owl, one of Canada's largest owls, is known to nest as far north as this area. These impressive birds may be seen hunting during the day.

J 151.4 (243.6 km) **I 304.7** (490.4 km) Northbound sign reads: "Welcome, you are now entering Vuntut Gwitchin Settlement Lands."

J 152 (244.6 km) **I 304.1** (489.4 km) Road narrows in places as highway climbs Seven Mile Hill, the escarpment of the Eagle Plains plateau.

J 160.9 (259 km) **I 295.2** (475 km) Panoramic **Ogilvie Ridge/Gwazhal Kak Viewpoint** is a large double-ended turnout with interpretive panels on the geology of the area; outhouse, litter bins. Lowbush cranberries in August.

Northbound, the road traverses a high ridge (elev. 1,969 feet/600m), with broad sweeps and easy grades, crossing the continental divide for a second time northbound. Waters on the southeast side of the road flow to the Beaufort Sea; waters on the northwest side of the road flow to the Bering Sea.

This is one of the few unglaciated areas in Canada, with a landscape shaped by wind and water erosion rather than by ice. Views of Mount Cronkhite and Mount McCullum to the southeast.

J 169.5 (272.5 km) **I 286.6** (461.3 km) Large dirt turnout to east, microwave tower to west.

J 185 (297.9 km) **I 271.1** (436.3 km) Large turnout to east. Evidence of forest fires northbound for many miles.

J 192.6 (310 km) **I 263.5** (424 km) Distance marker southbound shows Dawson City 346 km/215 miles, Whitehorse 804

km/500 miles.

J 201.6 (324.5 km) **I 254.5** (409.6 km) Double-ended turnout with litter bins and outhouses. Road widens to act as an airstrip when needed. No parking or stopping on this section of road, use turnouts.

J 219.4 (353 km) **I 236.7** (381 km) Large turnout to west.

J 224.8 (361.8 km) **I 231.3** (372.2 km) Distance marker northbound shows Eagle Plains Lodge 7 km/4 miles, Inuvik 379 km/236 miles.

J 229.3 (369 km) **I 226.8** (365 km) **Mile 231. EAGLE PLAINS** (pop. approx. 8); **Eagle Plains Hotel** (description follows), open year-round.

©Kris Valencia, staff

Eagle Plains Hotel. Located midway on the Dempster, this year-round facility is an oasis in the wilderness. 32 hotel rooms, satellite TV, plus restaurant and lounge. WiFi available in lobby. Full camping facilities with electrical hookups. Showers, store, minor repairs, tires, gas/diesel/propane. Road and area information. Check out our historical photos. Phone (867) 993-2453; eagleplains@northwestel.net. See display ad this page. [ADVERTISEMENT]

An interesting and crucial stop for Dempster Highway travelers, the hotel was built in 1978, just before completion of the Dempster Highway. Construction of the hotel was an engineering challenge with engineers having to consider the permafrost in the area and find a place where the bedrock was at the surface. The hotel was built on this natural pad, thus avoiding the costly process of building on pilings.

Eagle Plains Hotel offers rooms (reservations recommended); a restaurant (menu is posted outside the dining room, they stop serving dinner at 7 P.M.); and a comfortable bar/lounge. A wonderful collection of historical photographs—including one of Albert Johnson, the Mad Trapper of Rat River—are displayed in the hotel's common areas.

The adjacent service station has gas, diesel, propane, and tire and minor repairs. There is also a campground next to the hotel with electrical hookups.

J 234.6 (377.8 km) **I 221.5** (356.5 km) Eagle River bridge. Like the Ogilvie Bridge, it was built by the Dept. of National Defense as a training exercise. In contrast to the other rivers seen from the Dempster, the Eagle is a more sluggish, silt-laden stream with unstable banks. It is the main drainage channel for the western slopes of the Richardson Mountains. The **Eagle River** and its tributaries provide good grayling fishing. Canoeists leave here bound for Alaska via the Porcupine and Yukon rivers.

J 241.7 (389 km) **I 214.4** (345 km) Road widens and acts as an emergency airstrip; no stopping. **Private Aircraft:** Eagle Plains airstrip; elev. 2,365 feet/721m; length 2,500 feet/762m; gravel.

J 252 (405.5 km) **I 204.1** (328.5 km) Large double-ended turnout at **Arctic Circle Crossing**, N 66°33'; interpretive sign, picnic tables, litter bins, outhouses.

On June 21, the sun does not fall below the horizon for 6 weeks at this latitude.

Highway crosses Arctic tundra on an elevated berm beside the Richardson Mountains; sweeping views. The unglaciated Richardson Mountains, which extend almost to the Arctic Ocean, were named for Sir John Richardson, surgeon and naturalist on both of Sir John Franklin's overland expeditions to the Arctic Ocean.

J 252.4 (406 km) **I 203.7** (327.8 km) Turnout.

J 253.4 (407.6 km) **I 202.7** (326.2 km) Distance marker northbound shows NWT border 57 km/35 miles, Fort McPherson 142 km/88 miles.

J 257.9 (415 km) **I 198.2** (319 km) Glacier Creek.

J 276.6 (445.2 km) **I 179.5** (288.9 km) Large garage building to east, turnout with interpretive boards about Porcupine caribou herd. You may spot them from this area, from September through May.

J 277 (445.8 km) **I 179.1** (288.2 km) **Rock River Yukon Government Campground** to west; 17 sites (3 pull–throughs), daily camping fee $12, tables, kitchen shelter, water, firepits, outhouses. *NOTE: Black flies and mosquitoes can be fierce; bring repellent.*

J 277.4 (446.4 km) **I 178.7** (287.6 km) Rock River (culvert). Highway climbs northbound

J 288.6 (464.4 km) **I 167.5** (269.5 km) Large turnout to west; monument to Al Wright, a highway engineer with Public Works Canada, who was responsible for the routing of the Dempster Highway and for whom Wright Pass is named.

Distance marker northbound shows Fort McPherson 85 km/53 miles, Tsiigehtchic 142 km/88 miles, Inuvik 270 km/168 miles.

J 288.9 (465 km) **I 167.2** (269.1 km) Large turnout to east with litter bins and interpretive signs at **YT-NWT Border**. Highway crosses **Wright Pass** (elev. 3,000 feet/915m) and the Continental Divide in the Richardson Mountains. West of here, water flows to the Pacific Ocean. East of here, water flows to the Arctic Ocean. Good photo spot and hiking area. *CAUTION: watch for grizzly bears!*

TIME ZONE CHANGE: Yukon observes Pacific standard time; Northwest Territories is on Mountain standard time.

Highway descends, road narrows, northbound.

NOTE: Seat-belt use required by law in Yukon Territory (southbound sign).

NWT HIGHWAY 8

Distance from YT-NWT border (B) is followed by distance from junction with Klondike Highway 2 (J) and distance from Inuvik (I). Kilometerposts northbound (white numerals on a blue background) now indicate distance from YT–NWT border.
NOTE: The kilometer figure following the (B) in the highway log reflects the nearest physical kilometerpost along this section of the highway.

B 0 J 288.9 (465 km) **I 167.2** (269.1 km) **YT-NWT Border.**

B 8.7 (14.2 km) **J 297.6** (478.9 km) **I 158.5** (255.1 km) **James Creek**; good grayling fishing. Former maintenance camp, good spot to park overnight.

B 11.8 (19 km) **J 300.7** (483.9 km) **I 155.4** (250.1 km) Sign advises no passing next 7 km/4.3 miles as the highway winds through mountain valley.

B 14.6 (23.6 km) **J 303.5** (488.4 km) **I 152.6** (245.6 km) Northbound, the highway descends 2,300 feet/853m to the Peel River crossing, 31 miles/50 km ahead.

B 22.3 (36 km) **J 311.2** (500.8 km) **I 144.9** (233.2 km) Distance marker northbound shows Fort McPherson 50 km/31 miles, Tsiigehtchic 110 km/68 miles, and Inuvik 235 km/146 miles.

B 27.3 (44 km) **J 316.2** (508.9 km) **I 139.9** (225.1 km) Side road leads down to Midway Lake; no services. Midway Lake Music Festival a celebration of Gwich'in culture it has live music, dance, story telling and food, held the first long weekend in August; phone (867) 952-2712.

B 30.4 (49 km) **J 319.3** (513.8 km) **I 136.8** (220.2 km) **Private Aircraft:** Highway widens to form Midway airstrip; length 3,000 feet/914m.

B 40.5 (65.2 km) **J 329.4** (530.1 km) **I 126.7** (203.9 km) **Tetlit Gwinjik Territorial Park Viewpoint** to east; interpretive panels, litter bins. Short walk up to viewing platform; views of Richardson Mountains, Peel River Valley, Mackenzie River Delta and Fort McPherson.

B 46 (74 km) **J 334.9** (539 km) **I 121.2** (195 km) **Peel River Crossing**, locally called Eight Mile because it is situated 8 miles/12.8 km south of Fort McPherson. This free government ferry—the CF *Abraham Francis*—is a double-ended cable ferry: Drive on, drive off. Ferry operates approximately 15 hours a day (9 A.M. to 1 A.M.) from late May or early June to mid-October or first week in November. Phone toll free 1-800-661-0750 for information on ferry crossings, road conditions and weather. Crossing is on demand and/or by ice bridge in winter.

The level of the Peel River changes rapidly in spring and summer in response to meltwater from the mountains and ice jams on the Mackenzie River. The alluvial flood plain is covered by muskeg on the flats, and scrubby alder and stunted black spruce on the valley sides.

NOTE: Extreme high and low water level fluctuations may cause delays in ferry service.

B 47.1 (75.8 km) **J 336** (540.7 km) **I 120.1** (193.3 km) **Nitainlaii Territorial Park Interpretive Center** to west. The center is open 12 hours a day June 1 to September 1. Exhibits and displays show Gwich'in traditional ways of life. See the photo of the polar bear who wandered down to this area. And ask for your copy of the *Certificate of the Arctic Circle Chapter Order of Adventurers.*

The **Nitainlaii Territorial Park Campground** is adjacent the interpretive center with registration on-site upon arrival; $22.50 (CAD)/night; 23 campsites, camping permit required, potable water, firewood, pit toilets, shower building and kitchen shelter available.

B 51.7 (83.4 km) **J 340.6** (548.1 km) **I 115.5** (185.9 km) Access road east to Fort McPherson airport.

B 53 (85.5 km) **J 341.9** (550.2 km) **I 114.2** (183.8 km) **Junction** with access road which leads west to Fort McPherson (Tetl'it Zheh); description follows.

Fort McPherson

Located on the Peel River, 24 miles/38 km from its junction with the Mackenzie River; 100 miles/160 km southwest of Aklavik by boat along Peel Channel. **Population:** 700. **Emergency Services:** RCMP, phone (867) 952-1111. **Health Center,** phone (867) 952-2586.

Visitor Information: Contact Hamlet of Fort McPherson, phone (867) 952-2428; http://spectacularnwt.com. Radio: CBC 680.

Transportation: Air—Aklak Air provides scheduled air service from Inuvik during breakup and freezeup.

Private Aircraft: Fort McPherson airstrip; N 67°24', W 134°51'; elev. 142 feet/43m; length 3,500 feet/1,067m; gravel.

This is a pleasant Gwich'in community with 2 grocery/general stores and 2 service stations with gas/diesel. Lodging at the Peel River Inn, an Inns North location, phone 1-888-866-6784. Fort McPherson Tent and Canvas factory produces canvas items; outlet shop at factory for shoppers. Fort McPherson is an alcohol-restricted community and there are strict limits on transported quantities allowed. To be compliant, do not bring more than you could reasonably consume in one day.

Fort McPherson was named in 1848 for Murdoch McPherson, chief trader of the Hudson's Bay Co., which had established its first posts in the area 8 years before. Between 1849 and 1859 there were frequent feuds with neighboring Inuit, who later moved farther north to the Aklavik area, where they established a fur-trading post.

In addition to subsistence fishing and hunting, income is earned from trapping (mostly muskrat and mink), handicrafts, government employment, and commercial enterprises.

Photos and artifacts depicting the history and way of life of the community are displayed in the Chief Julius School. **The Lost Patrol Gravesite** is in the cemetery outside the Anglican church. Buried there are Inspector Francis J. Fitzgerald and 3 men from the ill-fated North West Mounted Police patrol of 1910–1911 between Fort McPherson and Dawson. A plaque inside the church commemorates the Lost Patrol. The original church, St. Matthew's, was built in 1860. It was replaced about 100 years later by the present-day church.

Inspector Fitzgerald and the men had left Fort McPherson on Dec. 21, 1910, carrying mail and dispatches to Dawson City. By Feb. 20, 1911, the men had not yet arrived in Dawson, nearly a month overdue. A search party led by Corporal W.J.D. Dempster was sent to look for the missing patrol. On March 22, 1911, Dempster discovered their frozen bodies only 26 miles from where they had started. Lack of knowledge of the trail, coupled with too few rations, had doomed the 4-man patrol. One of the last entries in Fitzgerald's diary, quoted in Dick North's *The Lost Patrol*, an account of their journey, reads: "We have now only 10 pounds of flour and 8 pounds of bacon and some dried fish. My last hope is gone. ... We have been a week looking for a river to take us over the divide, but there are dozens of rivers, and I am at a loss."

Free government ferries transport motorists across the Mackenzie and Peel rivers.
(©Kris Valencia, staff)

Dempster Highway Log
(continued)

B 53 (85.5 km) **J 341.9** (550.2 km) **I 114.2** (183.8 km) **Junction** with access road west to Fort McPherson. Distance marker northbound shows Tsiigehtchic 57 km/35 miles, Inuvik 185 km/115 miles.

B 65.3 (105 km) **J 354.2** (570 km) **I 101.9** (164 km) Microwave tower to east.

B 68.4 (110 km) **J 357.3** (575 km) **I 98.8** (159 km) Northbound, the highway passes through area of numerous lakes and densely forested terrain, a change due to the more productive conditions provided by the lower elevation, nutrient-rich soil and warmer climate of the Mackenzie River Delta.

B 76.1 (122.5 km) **J 365** (587.4 km) **I 91.1** (146.6 km) **Frog Creek**; grayling, pike. Road east to picnic area.

B 88.5 (142.5 km) **J 377.4** (607.3 km)

I 78.7 (126.7 km) South bank line-up for **Mackenzie River Crossing**. Free government ferry MV *Louis Cardinal* operates approximately 15 hours a day (8:15 A.M. to 11:15 P.M.) from early June to late October. Double-ended ferry: Drive on, drive off. Crossing is on demand and/or by ice bridge in winter. Phone 1-800-661-0750 for current status.

Motorcyclists should be especially careful in this area due to dust and gravel. Always drive with headlights on!

The ferry travels between landings on either side of the Mackenzie River and also provides access to **TSIIGEHTCHIC**, formerly **ARCTIC RED RIVER**, a small Gwichya Gwich'in community (pop. 172) located at the confluence of the Mackenzie and Arctic Red rivers (visible from ferry landing). Tsiigehtchic has a grocery store, post office and pay phone.

The Arctic Red River (Tsiigehnjik) was declared a Canadian Heritage River in 1993. Tsiigehnjik, the Gwich'in name for the river, winds its way out of the Mackenzie Mountains and flows into the Mackenzie River at Tsiigehtchic. The Gwichya Gwich'in have long used and traveled the river for fishing, hunting and trapping.

B 110.7 (178.1 km) **J 399.6** (643 km) **I 56.5** (90.9 km) Highway descends northbound to **Rengling River**; grayling. Large turnout to east on north side of river.

B 114 (183.5 km) **J 402.9** (648.4 km) **I 53.2** (85.6 km) Microwave tower to east.

B 115.3 (185.7 km) **J 404.2** (650.4 km) **I 51.9** (83.5 km) Begin 13-mile/21-km stretch of straight highway northbound.

B 118.3 (190.3 km) **J 407.2** (655.2 km) **I 48.9** (78.7 km) Neilo Creek.

B 119.5 (192.3 km) **J 408.4** (657.2 km) **I 47.7** (76.8 km) Lynx Creek.

B 120.7 (194.3 km) **J 409.6** (659.2 km) **I 46.5** (74.8 km) Distance marker northbound shows Inuvik 75 km/47 miles.

B 126.3 (203.3 km) **J 415.2** (668.2 km) **I 40.9** (65.8 km) Moose Lake to east; watch for waterfowl.

B 129.8 (208.9 km) **J 418.7** (673.8 km) **I 37.4** (60.2 km) Rabbit Creek.

B 137.1 (220.7 km) **J 426** (685.6 km) **I 30.1** (48.4 km) **Vadzaih Van Tshik Campground** to east; registration is on-site upon arrival. $22.50 (CAD)/night. 11 sites, tables, firewood, firepits, barbecue pits and toilets. Adjacent to Caribou Creek.

B 137.3 (220.9 km) **J 426.2** (685.8 km) **I 29.9** (48.1 km) Caribou Creek bridge. Day-use area to east at north end of bridge.

B 143.9 (231.5 km) **J 432.8** (696.4 km) **I 23.3** (37.5 km) Benoit Lake (sign).

B 144.3 (232.3 km) **J 433.2** (697.2 km) **I 22.9** (36.9 km) **Titheqehchii Vitail Lookout** to west; parking. Very scenic 10-minute walk to viewing platform with information signs overlooking Campbell Lake.

B 145 (233.4 km) **J 433.9** (698.3 km) **I 22.2** (35.7 km) View of Campbell Lake to west.

B 145.6 (234.3 km) **J 434.5** (699.2 km) **I 21.6** (34.8 km) **Gwich'in Territorial Park Campground**; registration is on-site upon arrival, $22.50 (CAD)/night; 29 non-powered campsites and 4 tent sites; firepits, potable water, kitchen shelter and toilets. Beach access, boat launch and fishing at **Campbell Lake**.

B 151.6 (244 km) **J 440.5** (708.9 km) **I 15.6** (25.1 km) **Ehjuu Njik (part of Gwich'in Territorial Park)** day-use area downhill to west; picnic tables, firepits, firewood, outhouses. Arctic grayling fishing in **Cabin Creek**.

B 153.5 (247 km) **J 442.4** (711.9 km) **I 13.7** (22 km) **Nihtak (in Gwich'in Territorial Park)** day-use area to north by Campbell Creek; 8 picnic sites with firewood, tables, firepits and toilets. Boat launch on south side of highway. Creek flows a short distance to Campbell Lake. Bring mosquito repellent. Good fishing for pike and whitefish, some sheefish (inconnu).

B 161 (259.2 km) **J 450** (724.1 km) **I 6.1** (9.8 km) "Y" **junction** at Airport Road; northbound travelers turn left for airport, keep to right for Inuvik. Southbound travelers continue straight for airport, keep to

right then turn left for Dempster Highway.

Pavement begins northbound, slow for frost heaves.

Distance markers southbound show Eagle Plains 356 km/221 miles, Dawson City, 767 km/477 miles, Whitehorse 1220 km/758 miles, Tsiigehtchic 114 km/71 miles, Fort McPherson 172 km/107 miles, Yukon Border 257 km/160 miles.

B 164.9 (265.4 km) **J 453.8** (730.3 km) **I 2.3** (3.7 km) Turnoff to west on 0.5-mile gravel access road for **Jak Territorial Park and Campground**; 36 campsites (11 powered sites, 25 non-powered sites), 13 pull-through, kitchen shelter, playground, firewood, water, showers; $28 (CAD)/night powered site or $22.50 (CAD)/night for non-powered. Reserve sites at www.NWTparks.ca. Amenities also include a canoe launch, walking trails, lookout tower with views of Mackenzie River Delta and the Richardson Mountains, and interpretive signage.

B 166.4 (267.8 km) **J 455.3** (732.7 km) **I 0.8** (1.3 km) Turnoff for **Arctic Chalet** and **Arctic Adventure Tours**, phone 1-800-685-9417.

B 167.2 (269.1 km) **J 456.1** (734 km) **I 0** Turnoff for Inuvik town center via Mackenzie Road (description follows); Nova Inn.

Continue on Marine Bypass Road to skirt Inuvik and **junction** with Navy Road to Tuktoyaktuk Highway, opened in November 2017. The 83-mile/134-km all-season highway provides year-round land connection to the Arctic Ocean community of Tuktoyatuk (*see description in "Road to Tuk" feature on page 684*).

Inuvik

Situated on the east channel of the Mackenzie River, some 60 air miles/96 km south of the Beaufort Sea, at the end of the Dempster Highway. **Population**: 3,243, Gwich'in, Inuvialuit. **Emergency Services**: RCMP, phone (867) 777-1111. **Hospital**, Inuvik Regional, phone (867) 777-8000. **Ambulance**, phone (867) 777-4444. **Fire Department**, phone (867) 777-2222.

Visitor Information: Western Arctic Regional Visitor Center on Mackenzie Road across from the hospital; phone (867) 777-4727 in summer or 777-7237 year-round; www.trulyarctic.ca, www.inuvik.ca. The center is open 9 A.M. to 7 P.M. daily, June 1 to September; interactive displays, excellent cultural and wildlife displays, clean restrooms and knowledgeable staff.

Elevation: 224 feet/68m. **Climate**: May 24 marks 57 days of midnight sun. The sun begins to set on July 19; on Dec. 6, the sun sets and does not rise until Jan. 6. Average annual precipitation 4 inches rainfall, 69 inches snowfall. July mean high 67°F/19°C, mean low 45°F/7°C. January mean high is -11°F/-24°C, mean low is -30°F/-35°C. **Radio**

Drive down to the public boat launch in Inuvik to watch boat traffic on the Mackenzie River. (©Kris Valencia, staff)

and **Television:** CBC and local. **Newspaper:** *The Drum* (weekly).

Private Aircraft: Mike Zubko Airport (daily jet service) 8 miles/14 km from city; elev. 220 feet/67m; length 6,000 feet/1,829m; asphalt; fuel 80, 100.

Inuvik, meaning "The Place of Man," is the largest Canadian community north of the Arctic Circle, and the major government, transportation and communication center for Canada's western Arctic. Construction of the town began in 1955 and was completed in 1961.

Inuvik is constructed on permafrost, so a unique utilidor system carries water, sewage and heating systems between buildings. Inquire at the Visitor Center about utilidor and permafrost exhibits.

Inuvik was the main supply base for the petrochemical exploration of the delta until Tuktoyaktuk took over that role as activity centered in the Beaufort Sea. In Inuvik, some hunting, fishing and trapping is done, but most people earn wages in government and private enterprises, particularly in transportation, tourism and construction. As the delta is one of the richest muskrat areas in the world, Inuvik is the western center for shipping furs south.

The town's official monument says, in part, that Inuvik was "the first community north of the Arctic Circle built to provide the normal facilities of a Canadian town." There is a post office, territorial liquor store,

a library, a bank (CIBC) and churches. Inuvik also has one of the most northerly mosques in the world, brought here by road and river from Manitoba. There are 2 gas stations with gas, diesel and car wash; propane, auto repair and towing are available. The town has a hardware, grocery, general stores, gift shops and a pharmacy.

Transportation

Air: Inuvik Airport is a transportation hub for the western Arctic. Scheduled services via Air North, phone 1-800-661-0407; Aklak Air, phone (867) 777-3777; Canadian North, phone 1-800-661-1505; and First Air, phone 1-800-267-1247.

Highways: Dempster Highway, open year-round except for when rivers are freezing or thawing (ferry crossing of 2 rivers/ice bridge in winter). Highway to Tuktoyaktuk and Arctic Ocean open year-round (87 miles/140 km). Winter road to Aklavik (73 miles/117 km). 24-hr. emergency roadside assistance, phone (867) 777-4747 or 678-5410 after hours.

Bus: MGM Services offers on-demand bus service to and from Inuvik; call (867) 777-4295 for information.

Taxi: United Taxi at (867) 777-5050; Delta Cabs at (867) 777-5100.

Lodging & Services

Accommodations downtown at the very nice **Capital Suites** (1-877-669-9444) and

Road to Tuk

The 134-km/83-mile Inuvik to Tuktoyaktuk highway (also known as the Mackenzie Valley Highway and Highway 10) is an all-weather 2-lane gravel road that replaces the former winter ice road that connected the 2 communities. This new year-round route crosses more than 300 culverts and 8 bridges, and travels through the grazing area of Canada's only domestic reindeer herd. Also along the way is the Pingo National Landmark, a collection of 8 ice hills, including the world's second tallest.

An all-season road was first proposed in the early 1960s, but construction did not begin until 2013. The bulk of the construction activities were planned for the winter months to preserve the permafrost. Additionally, a geotextile fabric was placed between the ground and construction materials along the entire highway. About half of the road is located on Inuvialuit private lands. The road opened to the public on November 15, 2017.

Dianne and Joe Hofbeck and friends drove the new highway in 2 vans during the latter half of September 2018, enjoying beautiful weather. They found the road "easy to travel along, although there were not many turnouts and none with facilities or garbage cans. We had a little difficulty finding our way out of Inuvik to the beginning of the Tuk road, but after that we just enjoyed our journey, watching the tamarack and black spruce disappear and the arctic lakes and tundra take their place. That time of the year some of the facilities in Tuk were already closed, but the Hotel and Gramma's Kitchen (serving hamburgers and smoked whitefish) were still open. It is a trip into a

©Dianne & Joe Hofbeck

land that still belongs to the wildlife and the First Nations people who have chosen to remain there."

Road grading is ongoing. Watch for steep drop-offs at the road edge. There is a large dirt parking area with picnic tables at the end of the road in Tuktoyaktuk, at the Arctic Ocean. *The MILEPOST®* met a number of people who traveled the new road last summer, including one visitor who was turned back because his rig was deemed too heavy for current road conditions. Posted maximum load is 63,500 kg, but it may be that the newness of the road combined with weather conditions created temporary restrictions. Current road conditions are posted at www.dot.gov.nt.ca/Highways/Highway-Conditions.

The hamlet of **TUKTOYAKTUK** (pop. 965) offers some visitor services. These include 2 gas stations; lodging at 4 B&B-style locations (Smitty's, Hunters, Tuktu and End of the Road Inn); convenience store and restaurant (open daily 11 A.M. to 2 P.M. and 7 P.M. to 9 P.M.); Gramma's Kitchen & Takeout; a post office, church, airport, store, ATM, camping and firewood.

Visitor Information: www.tuktoyaktuk.ca.

A largely Inuvialuit population, languages spoken here include Inuvialuktun and English. The community was founded in 1928 when the Hudson Bay Company created a post here and its first name was Port Brabant. For those interested in Inuvialuit history and culture, this is a cultural hub. It is also one of the few places in Canada that has a road to where you can take a dip in the Arctic Ocean if you are so inclined. Special events include the Beluga Jamboree in April and the Pingo Music Festival in August.

Mackenzie Hotel. Nova Inn at junction of access road and Dempster Highway. Turnoff for **Arctic Chalet** (description follows) just south of Inuvik access road.

Arctic Chalet and Arctic Adventure Tours. Experience something uniquely Northern at the best rates in town. Charming log home and full-service cabins and 1 honeymoon cabin in a beautiful lakeside setting on the edge of Inuvik. Wireless internet, telephone and satellite TV; kitchenettes with breakfast foods. Walking trails. Specializing in tours to Tuktoyaktuk and Herschel Island and much more. www.arcticchalet.com; Phone (867) 777-3535; 1-800-685-9417. [ADVERTISEMENT]

There are various restaurants and fast-food outlets; gas stations, a carwash, tire repair; groceries; clothing stores; and Northern arts and crafts stores.

Roads End golf course is one of the first sights you see on your way into Inuvik. It has a driving range and there are no green fees; 24 hour access in summer.

The Midnight Sun Complex includes a fitness center, hockey and curling rinks, a popular canteen, and a fantastic aquatic center with leisure pool, 4-lane pool, hot tub, steam room, sauna, and a waterslide (190 feet long). Phone (867) 777-8640.

Camping

In town, **Happy Valley Territorial Park Campground** has 36 sites (19 sites with power, 15 without power, and a group tent site); nightly fee $22.50–$28 (CAD); hot showers, laundromat, firewood, water; fee charged; open June 1–Sept. 1. Services include 24-hour reception and security; phone (867) 777-3652. Just 2 miles/4 km south of town (see log) is Jak Territorial Park, with 36 campsites.

Attractions

Igloo Church, The most photographed landmark in Inuvik, Our Lady of Victory Roman Catholic Church or "the Igloo Church" owes its distinctive architecture and construction to a community effort over the course of 2 years. Completed in 1958, the Igloo Church's interior is decorated with stations of the cross painted by one of the Delta's most famous Inuvialuit artists, Mona Thrasher. Visitors are welcomed with tours offered in the summer months. Located at 180 Mackenzie Rd.; phone (867) 777-2236.

Great Northern Arts Festival. This 10-day fine arts and performing arts event celebrates its 31st Anniversary in 2019. The festival features a 5,000 sq. ft. gallery, 60+ workshops and evenings of dance, song and stories. Dedicated to showcasing the talent of Northwest Territories, Yukon, Nunavut and the larger circumpolar region, it delivers unique Northern programming. Try your hand at print making, experience traditional drumming and dancing, meet stone carvers and shop for mukluks, paintings, jewelry and more. The festival is scheduled for July 12–21, 2019; www.gnaf.org.

The Mackenzie River Delta, second largest delta in North America and an important wildlife corridor to the Arctic, is 40 miles/64 km wide and 60 miles/97 km long. A maze of lakes, channels and islands, the delta supports a variety of bird life, fish and muskrats. Boat tours of the Mackenzie River are available. Watch activity on the Mackenzie River from Inuvik Waterfront Park.

Stop by Parks Canada at 81 Kingmingya Rd. and learn more about fly-in trips to Ivvavik, Tuktut Nogait and Aulavik national parks. The parks protect a variety of unique landscapes, flora and fauna. Phone (867) 777-8800.

Fly/drive to TUKTOYAKTUK, or "Tuk," an Inuvialuit village on the shores of the Arctic Ocean. Accessible by air or the new all-season gravel highway (see "The Road to Tuk" above), Arctic Adventure Tours offers tours to Tuktoyaktuk.

Fly/boat tour to AKLAVIK (pop. 590), 36 miles/58 km southwest of Inuvik by air, by ice road in winter. An important center for muskrat harvesting it is also the final resting place of Albert Johnson, "The Mad Trapper of Rat River." Johnson wounded one Mountie and killed another in 2 separate run-ins with the RCMP, who initially were responding to complaints that Johnson was tampering with Native trap lines. The ensuing manhunt became famous in the North, as Johnson eluded Mounties for 48 days during the winter of 1931–1932. Johnson was killed in a shoot-out on Feb. 17, 1932.

Deh Cho Route

CONNECTS: Grimshaw, AB, to the Alaska Highway via Northwest Territories

Length: 795 miles   **Road Surface: 70% Paved, 30% Gravel**   **Season: Open all year**

(See map, page 686)

`35` `49` `2` `1` `2` `3` `4` `5` `6` `7` `77`

Stopping for a photo op at the 60th Parallel Territorial Park and Visitor Center at the Alberta–NWT border. *(©Earl Brown)*

Major Attractions:

©Judy Nadon, staff

Prince of Wales Northern Heritage Center, Waterfalls, Nahanni & Wood Buffalo National Parks

Named after the Mackenzie River—Deh Cho is Slavey Dene for "big river"— the Deh Cho route is a 795-mile/1,279-km wilderness loop connecting Grimshaw in the Peace River region of northern Alberta with the Alaska Highway in British Columbia by way of the Mackenzie River region of Northwest Territories. The Deh Cho also provides access to an additional 700 miles/1,127 km of the Northwest Territories road system.

This route begins for northbound travelers in either Grande Prairie or Valleyview, Alberta. The Grande Prairie route (via Alberta Highway 2) leads 104 miles/167 km north via historic Dunvegan to Grimshaw and then via Alberta Highway 35 (the Mackenzie Highway) to Northwest Territories. The Valleyview route (via Alberta Highways 49 and 2) leads 99 miles/160 km north to connect with Alberta Highway 35/Mackenzie Highway. (The official Deh Cho route offers a loop route that includes the distance between Grande Prairie to Dawson Creek; if you choose to follow that portion, turn to the EAST ACCESS ROUTE for a log

Distance in miles	Alaska Hwy.	Ft. Resolution	Ft. Simpson	Ft. Smith	Grimshaw	Yellowknife
Alaska Hwy.		563	282	636	795	596
Ft. Resolution	563		357	185	459	389
Ft. Simpson	282	357		430	588	390
Ft. Smith	636	185	430		532	462
Grimshaw	795	459	588	532		620
Yellowknife	596	389	390	462	620	

of those miles.)

From the Alberta/NWT border, the Deh Cho Route continues north and west as NWT Highway 1 (the Waterfalls Route) to Checkpoint and the junction with the Liard Trail (NWT Highway 7/BC Highway 77). The Deh

Deh Cho Route Grimshaw, AB, to Alaska Hwy, BC via NWT Highways

© 2019 The MILEPOST®

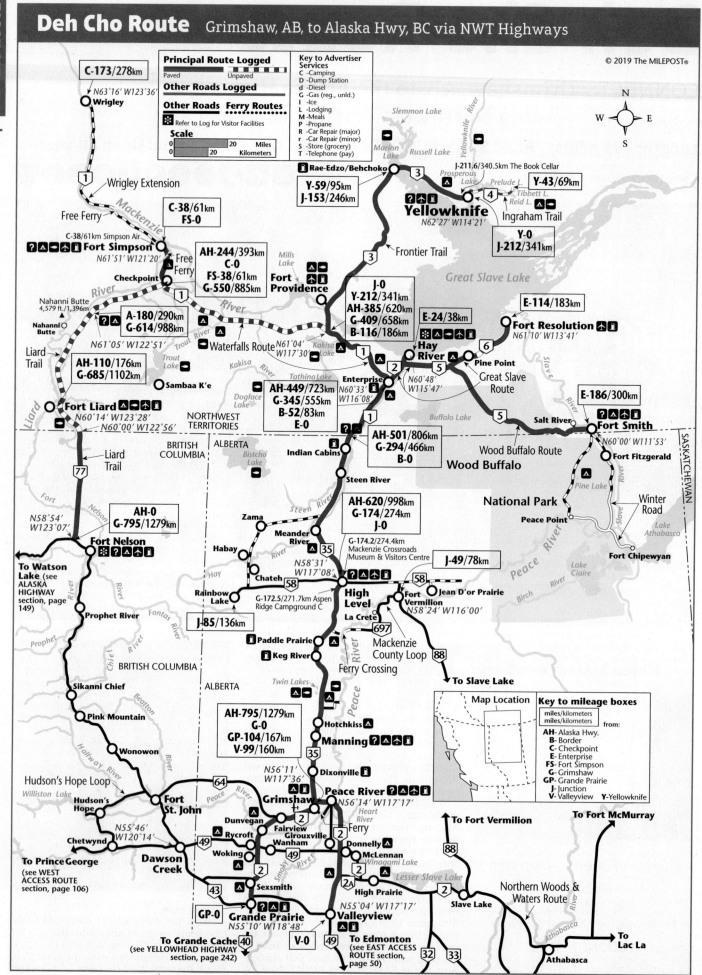

Principal Route Logged
Paved ▬▬▬ Unpaved ▬ ▬ ▬

Other Roads Logged ▬▬▬

Other Roads ······· **Ferry Routes** ·•·•·•·

❄ Refer to Log for Visitor Facilities

Scale
0 _____ 20 Miles
0 _____ 20 Kilometers

Key to Advertiser Services
C - Camping
D - Dump Station
d - Diesel
G - Gas (reg., unld.)
I - Ice
L - Lodging
M - Meals
P - Propane
R - Car Repair (major)
r - Car Repair (minor)
S - Store (grocery)
T - Telephone (pay)

C-173/278km
N63°16' W123°36'
Wrigley

Wrigley Extension

Free Ferry

Mackenzie River

C-38/61km Simpson Air
Fort Simpson
N61°51' W121°20'

C-38/61km
FS-0

Free Ferry

Checkpoint

Nahanni Butte
4,579 ft./1,396m
Nahanni Butte

A-180/290km
G-614/988km
N61°05' W122°51'

AH-244/393km
C-0
FS-38/61km
G-550/885km

Fort Providence

Mills Lake

Liard Trail

AH-110/176km
G-685/1102km

Trout River
Trout Lake

Sambaa K'e

Liard River

Fort Liard
N60°14' W123°28'
N60°00' W122°56'

NORTHWEST TERRITORIES

BRITISH COLUMBIA   ALBERTA

Kakisa River
Dogface Lake

Waterfalls Route
N61°04' W117°30'

AH-449/723km
G-345/555km
B-52/83km
E-0

Enterprise
N60°33' W116°08'

Kakisa Lake
Tathina Lake

J-0
Y-212/341km
AH-385/620km
G-409/658km
B-116/186km

Hay River
N60°48' W115°47'

Pine Point
Great Slave Route

Slemmon Lake
Marion Lake
Russell Lake
Yellowknife River

Rae-Edzo/Behchoko

Y-59/95km
J-153/246km

J-211.6/340.5km The Book Cellar
Prosperous Lake
Prelude L.   Tibbett L.
Reid L.

Y-43/69km

Yellowknife
N62°27' W114°21'

Ingraham Trail

Y-0
J-212/341km

Frontier Trail

Great Slave Lake

E-24/38km
E-114/183km

Fort Resolution
N61°10' W113°41'

Salt River

E-186/300km
Fort Smith
N60°00' W111°53'

SASKATCHEWAN

Fort Fitzgerald

Slave River

Winter Road

Pine Lake

Peace Point

Fort Chipewyan
Lake Athabasca
Lake Claire

Wood Buffalo Route

Wood Buffalo

AH-501/806km
G-294/466km
B-0

Indian Cabins

Steen River

Bistcho Lake

AH-620/998km
G-174/274km
J-0

Zama
Meander River

G-174.2/274.4km
Mackenzie Crossroads
Museum & Visitors Centre

Habay

Steen River

National Park

J-49/78km

58
High Level

Fort Vermilion
N58°24' W116°00'

Jean D'or Prairie

Chateh
58

Rainbow Lake
G-172.5/271.7km Aspen
Ridge Campground C

La Crete
697
Mackenzie County Loop
88

Ferry Crossing

J-85/136km

Paddle Prairie

Keg River

BRITISH COLUMBIA

ALBERTA

Twin Lakes

AH-0
G-795/1279km
N58°54' W123°07'

Fort Nelson

To Watson Lake (see ALASKA HIGHWAY section, page 149)

Prophet River

Sikanni Chief

Pink Mountain

Wonowon

Hudson's Hope Loop
Williston Lake
Hudson's Hope

Fort St. John

Chetwynd

To Prince George (see WEST ACCESS ROUTE section, page 106)

Dawson Creek

43

GP-0

Grande Prairie
N55°10' W118°48'

To Grande Cache (see YELLOWHEAD HIGHWAY section, page 242)

40

V-0
49

Dunvegan
Rycroft
Woking
Sexsmith

AH-795/1279km
G-0
GP-104/167km
V-99/160km

Hotchkiss

Manning

Dixonville
35
N56°11' W117°36'

Grimshaw
N56°14' W117°17'

Peace River

Fairview
Girouxville
Wanham

Donnelly
McLennan
Winagami Lake

High Prairie
N55°04' W117°17'

To Edmonton (see EAST ACCESS ROUTE section, page 50)

49

32   33

Slave Lake

Lesser Slave Lake

88

To Fort Vermilion

To Fort McMurray

Northern Woods & Waters Route

Athabasca River

To Lac La

Athabasca

To Slave Lake

Heart River
Ferry

Peace River

Map Location

Key to mileage boxes
miles/kilometers
miles/kilometers from:
AH - Alaska Hwy.
B - Border
C - Checkpoint
E - Enterprise
FS - Fort Simpson
G - Grimshaw
GP - Grande Prairie
J - Junction
V - Valleyview
Y - Yellowknife

N55°46' W120°14'
1

Halfway River
Beatton River
Fontas River
Chief River
Prophet River
Nelson River
Fort Nelson River

64
49
2
2A

www.themilepost.com

Cho "loop" is completed as the Liard Trail intersects with the Alaska Highway about 18 miles/29 km north of Fort Nelson, BC.

Connecting routes—or side trips—along the Deh Cho Route through Northwest Territories that are logged in this section are: Highway 1/Heritage Route, from Checkpoint to Fort Simpson and Wrigley; Great Slave Route, from Enterprise to Hay River and Fort Resolution; Wood Buffalo Route, from its junction with Highway 6 south to Fort Smith; and Frontier Trail, from its junction with Highway 1 to Yellowknife.

Expect 2-lane paved highway in Alberta and on NWT Highways 1, 2, 3, 5 and 6. Road surface remains mostly gravel with some paved sections on NWT Highway 1 to Fort Simpson and Wrigley. The Liard Trail, a relatively straight 2-lane road, is mostly gravel in Northwest Territories and chip-seal/pavement in British Columbia to the Alaska Highway. In addition to these highways, Northwest Territories maintains winter ice roads to Fort Good Hope, Sambaa k'e (formerly Trout Lake), Wekweètì, Whatì and Gamètì.

Gravel road can be muddy when wet and dusty when dry. "Dust-free zones" on gravel roads are treated with calcium chloride; wash your vehicle when possible. Watch for moose, black bear, wood bison and grouse along the road.

Free NWT ferries provide passenger and vehicle service in summer across the Liard River to Fort Simpson and across the Mackenzie River to Wrigley. In winter, traffic crosses on the ice. For current road conditions, phone 1-800-661-0750 or visit www.dot.gov.nt.ca/Highways/Highway–Conditions. Ferry information is at https://www.inf.gov.nt.ca/en/ferries. Tourist information at https://spectacularnwt.com. Campground information at nwtparks.ca.

Deh Cho Route: From Valleyview

Distance from Valleyview (V) is shown.

ALBERTA HIGHWAY 49

V 0 Junction of Highways 43 and 49. Continue north on Highway 49 or go west on 43 to Grande Prairie. Visitor Center is 2 miles east on Highway 43. **VALLEYVIEW** (pop. 1,863). See description of Valleyview beginning on page 75 in the EAST ACCESS ROUTE section.

V 1.2 (1.9 km) *Begin posted speed zone* at Welcome to Valleyview sign. Distance marker northbound shows Guy 57 km/35 miles, Donnelly Corners 76 km/47 miles, Peace River 176 km/109 miles.

V 1.9 (3.1 km) **Junction** with Highway 669. Turnoff to east for Sunset House (26 km/16 miles).

V 3.8 (6.1 km) Sturgeon Creek.

V 16.4 (26.4 km) New Fish Creek Road.

V 18.6 (29.9 km) **East Dollar Lake** to west; day-use area with picnic tables, litter bins, toilets, boat launch. Stocked with rainbow trout, popular local fishing spot.

V 24.6 (39.6 km) **Junction** with Highway 676 West to Whitemud Creek.

V 26.8 (43.1 km) Little Smoky River Ski Area to west. A common sight along the road are small rectangular ponds, called "dugouts," that are used to water livestock.

V 28.5 (45.9 km) Little Smoky River.

V 29.6 (47.6 km) Distance marker southbound shows Valleyview 47 km/29 miles, Grande Prairie 156 km/97 miles, Edmonton 385 km/239 miles.

V 29.7 (47.8 km) **Junction** with Highway 2A east to High Prairie (32 km/19 miles) and Edmonton.

V 30.9 (49.7 km) Turnout with litter/recycling bins to east. Information board on Francophone Settlement and Alberta history.

V 35.7 (57.4 km) Community of **GUY** (pop. 40), pronounced Gee, to east. Access road leads west 11 km/7 miles to Five Star Golf Course. The primary industry here is honey production.

V 39.7 (63.9 km) **Junction** with Highway 679 East which leads 20 km/12.4 miles to Highway 2.

V 47.9 (77.1 km) **Junction** of Highway 49 and 2 (**Donnelly Corners**). Continue north on Highway 2 for Peace River. Go east 5 km/3 miles for camping. The community of **DONNELLY** (pop. 342) has a restaurant, store, a library and a museum. 15 campsites west side of village (follow signs, 1.5 km via gravel road).

Turn west on Highway 2 for **FAHLER** (pop. 1,047), Alberta's largest honey producer (an estimated 5 million lbs. annually). Community is 5 km/3 miles from highway 49 and the Fahler Municipal Campground is on the east edge of town, right behind the visitor center. Open May 1–Sept. 30; 30 sites, water, playground restrooms/showerhouse, sani-dump. Fee was $25–$30 CAD in 2018. Free firewood. Phone (780) 837-6817.

ALBERTA HIGHWAY 2

V 59.3 (95.4 km) Side road leads 11 km/7 miles west to **JEAN COTE** (pop. approx. 65)

V 66.2 (106.5 km) ACC Road leads east 9 km/5.6 miles to Reno.

V 70 (112.6 km) **NAMPA** (pop. 364) Visitor Information Center and Nampa & District Museum to North (open Sunday-Saturday, during the summer months) from 10 A.M. to 5 P.M., $12 family, $5 Adult, $2 Student, under 6 Free); phone (780) 322-2777, www.nampamuseum.ca.

Nampa was founded in 1917 when the East Dunvegan and BC Railway Company built a line through the area. Today, grain is shipped from Richardson Pioneer Grain terminals, located at the north side of town. Visitor facilities include a motel, B&B, restaurant, grocery and retail stores; service station, a library, curling rink/arena, ball diamonds and tennis courts. Camping at Mill Brown Memorial Municipal Campground, 6 sites, power hookups and trails.

V 70.1 (112.8 km) **Junction** with Highway 683 West to Highway 744 (10 km/6 miles).

V 71 (114.3 km) North Heart River bridge.

V 81.9 (131.8 km) **Junction** with Highway 688 East to St. Isadore (7 km/4.3 miles) and to **junction** with Highway 986 (24 km/15 miles), the main east-west route connecting Peace River to Highway 88/Bicentennial Highway at Red Earth Creek.

V 82.7 (133.1 km) Cecil Thompson Park; picnic area adjacent pond. Peace River Equestrian Center and Fairgrounds.

V 85.9 (138.2 km) Turnout to east with information sign about Peace River. Rendez-Vous RV Park & Storage with 60 fully serviced sites used by crews but also open to the traveling public ($40–$45 CAD); phone (780) 618-1345.

Peace River

V 86.7 (139.5 km) Located on the banks of the Peace River, 15 miles/24 km northeast of Grimshaw (Mile 0 of the Mackenzie Highway), in Northern Sunrise County. **Population: 6,842. Emergency Services: Ambulance** and **Fire Department**, phone 911. **RCMP**, Peace River Detachment, phone (780) 624-6611. **Hospital**, Peace River Community Health Care Center (www.albertahealthservices.ca), phone (780) 624-7500.

Visitor Information: Take a hard left

Fahler honey bee honors the town's status as Alberta's largest honey producer.
(©Judy Nadon, staff)

Oilfield pumpjacks on Highway 35 north of Guy. The majority of Canada's oil sands are located in northern Alberta. (©Earl Brown)

after you have gone under the overpass to reach the NAR station at the east entrance to downtown, open mid-May to mid-September; (780) 624-4166. Online visit www.mightypeace.com.

Elevation: 1,066 feet/325m. **Private Aircraft:** Peace River airport, 6 miles/10 km west; elev. 1,873 feet/571m; length 5,000 feet/1,524m; asphalt; fuel; terminal.

An important transportation center on the Peace River, the town of Peace River was incorporated in 1919. Today, Peace River is a center for government services in the region. Area industry includes a pulp mill, gas and oil and farming.

Visitor facilities include 8 hotels/motels and many restaurants. Visitors will find WiFi available throughout downtown Peace River. Peace River has a Super Walmart. Camping at Lions Club Campground, phone (780) 624-2120, and at Citadel Ridge RV Park, phone (780) 618-5585, both on the west side of the river south of Highway 2.

The **Peace River Museum** on the south side of town along the river (10302–99th St.), houses archives and exhibits on Sir Alexander Mackenzie, the fur trade and local history. Open Monday to Saturday 10 A.M. to 5 P.M., year-round; phone (780) 624-4261. Admission fee $2 CAD. Website: www.peaceriver.ca; email museum@peaceriver.ca.

Visitors can take a historic walking tour to various points of interest around town. The tour includes the statue of **Twelve-Foot Davis**, a gold miner who struck it rich on a 12-foot strip of land between 2 larger claims in the Cariboo gold fields.

Deh Cho Route Log
(continued)

V 87.5 (140.8 km) Peace River bridge.

V 88.4 (142.3 km) Esso gas/diesel station/convenience store. **Junction** with Highway 684 south to Peace River Lions Campground, Citadel Ridge RV Park and Shaftesbury Ferry to Tangent Campground.

V 89.2 (143.6 km) **Junction** with Highway 743 North Weberville Road and Peace

River pulp mill to east, hospital to west. Hotel and stoplight. Super 8, grocery store, gas/diesel stations, fast food and restaurants, Walmart and Canadian Tire.

V 89.9 (144.7 km) Turnout to south with information sign about Peace River.

V 91.2 (146.8 km) Highway descends 7 percent grade northbound.

V 93 (150 km) Peace River airport to south.

V 94.3 (151.8 km) Roma Junction with Highway 2A to Grimshaw (12 km/7 miles southwest).

V 95.4 (153.5 km) Turnoff for Mighty Peace Golf Course (2 km/1.2 miles); 18 holes, licensed dining room, pro shop.

V 97.7 (157.2) Turnoff to south for Wilderness Park; picnic tables, outhouses, hiking trails, fishing (1 km on gravel).

V 99.4 (159.9 km) **Junction** with Highway 35 (Mackenzie Highway) to Northwest Territories.

*Turn to **Milepost G 2.8** in the "Deh Cho Route: Mackenzie Highway," log on page 690.*

Deh Cho Route: From Grande Prairie

Distance from Grande Prairie (GP) is shown.

ALBERTA HIGHWAY 2

GP 0 Junction of Highways 43 East and Highway 2 North. **GRANDE PRAIRIE** (pop. 68,556) city center 4.5 miles south; all services. *See description beginning on page 75 in the EAST ACCESS ROUTE section.*

GP 0.5 (0.8 km) Distance marker northbound shows Rycroft 61 km/38 miles, Fairview 106 km/66 miles, Peace River 189 km/117 miles.

GP 1 (1.6 km) Stoplight at 84th Street (County Crossing), hotels, fast-food, Shell gas/diesel station.

GP 1.9 (3.1 km) First access to Clairmont, FasGas gas/diesel station.

GP 2.5 (4 km) Turnoff to Clairmont for camping.

GP 2.9 (4.7 km) Railroad crossing.

GP 3.9 (6.3 km) Begin 4-lane divided freeway northbound, end divided highway southbound. Bear Lake Park camping (12 km/7.5 miles west).

GP 6.1 (9.8 km) **Junction** with Highway 672 West to Hythe on Highway 43, 52 km/32 miles. Morningview RV Park and Golf Course (6 km/3.7 miles to east).

GP 8.3 (13.4 km) Heritage Park Campground.

GP 8.7 (14 km) Turnoff to **SEXSMITH** (pop. 2,620), sometimes called the "Grain Capital of Alberta." Heritage Park Campground at the south entrance to city. Husky gas/diesel station with food store.

GP 10.3 (16.6 km) **Junction** with Highway 59 West to La Grace (39 miles/63 km) on Highway 43, and junction with Highway 674 East to Teepee Creek and Highway 733 (15 miles/24 km).

GP 11.5 (18.5 km) End 4-lane divided freeway northbound, begin 2-lane undivided highway.

GP 13.3 (21.4 km) Spruce Meadows Golf Course and Campground 3 km to east; 80 sites with full hook-ups; $35 CAD.

GP 20 (32.2 km) Saddle Hills County (northbound sign).

GP 27.3 (43.9 km) Turnoff to Woking (5 km), Chinook Valley Golf Resort; camping (10 km/6.2 miles east), full and partial hook-ups and sani-dump station; $20–$32 CAD.

GP 28.3 (45.5 km) **Junction** with Highway 677 East to Peoria and Highway 833 (26 km/16 miles). Kakut Lake camping (May–September; phone (780) 694-2643; 24 sites $25 non-powered, $30 power, free firewood) and fishing (11 km/6.8 miles).

GP 30.9 (49.7 km) Saddle River.

GP 38.1 (61.3 km) Vehicle inspection station to east with litter bins.

GP 38.9 (62.6 km) **Junction** with Highway 49. Town of **RYCROFT** to west (pop. 638, surrounding area pop. 5,500). Husky gas/diesel, propane, restaurant, lodging and groceries. Town website: www.rycroft.ca, (780) 765-3652. Nardam Campground is just outside Rycroft on Highway 49 (2 km west); $35 CAD with hookups, $15 CAD without. Fishing in stocked lake.

GP 41.8 (67.3 km) Spirit River.

GP 47.4 (76.3 km) Long paved turnout to east with litter/recycling bins is also a brake-check inspection stop prior to steep decent ahead.

GP 47.9 (77.1 km) Highway descends northbound to Dunvegan Bridge across the Peace River. *CAUTION: Deer crossing, some frost heaves and sharp curves.*

GP 51.1 (82.2 km) Turnoff west for Dunvegan Boat Launch on the Peace River.

GP 51.3 (82.6 km) Dunvegan Bridge crosses Peace River. This is Alberta's only motor vehicle suspension bridge.

GP 52 (83.7 km) Entrance to **Dunvegan Provincial Park & Historic Site.** Visitor

Center open daily 10 A.M. to 6 P.M., mid-May to Labor Day; summer phone (780) 835-7150, or visit www.albertaparks.ca. Interpretive program admission $5 CAD adults, $4 CAD seniors, $2 CAD youth/$14 CAD family. Historic Dunvegan is the site of one of Alberta's earliest Hudson's Bay posts and Oblate missions. Several of the 19th century log buildings have been restored and furnished in meticulous detail, including the Rectory, St. Charles Mission Church and the Hudson's Bay Factor's House. Visit the nearby market gardens, which are still farmed as they were a hundred years ago.

Adjacent campground has 65 sites (28 with electrical hookups, 3 handicap accessible), firewood, table, pit toilets, sani-dump ($5 CAD) and phone. Camping fee is $34 CAD (15-amp power). Phone (780) 538-5350. ⓐ

If you head west under Highway 2, you will see the Factor's House and a vantage point for looking at the river and bridge; outhouses. Beyond it, "The Maples" is a beautiful picnic area with horseshoe pits, picnic shelter and chemical toilets and steps that lead down to the rivers edge. Be respectful in this park, homeowners live just beyond the edge of it.

GP 55.2 (88.8 km) Highway climbs steep grade next 2.2 miles northbound.

GP 56.9 (91.6 km) Turnout to west with litter/recycling bins, information boards on Peace River.

GP 60.2 (96.9 km) **Junction** with Highway 64 North is to the west for Hines Creek (28 km/17 miles) and Fort St. John (192 km/119 miles).

GP 63.8 (102.7 km) Turnout with information board on Alberta's history.

GP 67 (107.8 km) *Slow for speed zone.* Fairview is an agriculture center for the northwest Peace River region.

Fairview

GP 67.5 (108.6 km) **Junction** with Highway 732 and Highway 64A. Highway forks: turn right northbound for continuation of Highway 2; go straight for access to downtown Fairview. **Population**: 2,998. **Emergency Services**: RCMP, phone (780) 835-2211; **Hospital**, phone (780) 835-6100.

Visitor Information: The Visitor Information Center, part of the Fairview Chamber of Commerce is located in the Lancaster Building at 10316 109 St., Ste's 111 and 116. Open Monday–Thursday 8 A.M. to 4 P.M., Friday 9 A.M. to 4 P.M. (780) 835-5999. The Fine Arts Center for Northern Art is located at the south end of town and open May to September. Phone (780) 835-2697 or visit www.fairview.ca.

Fairview has hotels/motels, fast-food outlets, restaurants, museums, golf course and aquatic center. The Fairview Pioneer Museum, located at Cummings Lake Park, 1 km/0.6 mile north of Fairview, is open May to September.

Cummings Park Recreation Area 2 km north of Fairview on Highway 732 has a day-use area, ball parks and a campground with showers and powered sites; camping fee $25 CAD/night with electric hookup. Good perch fishing. Trail circles lake for an 11 km/6 mile walk. Phone (780) 835-5461.

The George Lake Campground is 1.9 miles/3 km south of Hines Creek on Highway 64. Open May to October, with 30 sites, hiking trails, a lake, free firewood, paddle-wheeler rides, and washroom with showers. Phone (780) 494-2419.

Deh Cho Route Log

(continued)

GP 73.7 (118.6 km) Blue Sky, picnic and skiing to west. Distance marker northbound shows Whitelaw 12 km/7 miles, Brownvale 67 km/42 miles.

GP 76.7 (123.4 km) Leith River (Little Burnt).

GP 81.3 (130.8 km) **Junction** with Highway 735 North to Whitelaw (1 km).

GP 90 (144.8 km) **Junction** with 737 North for Brownvale. Picnicking, North Peace Museum.

GP 97 (156.1 km) Turnoff to west for Berwyn. Library, cafe, camping. ⓐ

GP 97.1 (156.3 km) Distance marker northbound shows Grimshaw 11 km/7 miles, Peace River 37 km/23 miles.

GP 100.1 (160.9) Turnoff for Shaftsbury Road to Shaftsbury Ferry and Highway 684 (16 km/10 miles).

GP 103.8 (167 km) **Junction** with 685 West to hospital. Welcome to Grimshaw (sign).

GP 103.5 (166.6 km) *Begin speed zone.* Fast food and lodging.

Grimshaw

GP 104 (167.4 km) **G 0 AH 794.5** (1278.5 km) Mile 0 of the Mackenzie Highway, monument at Grimshaw Visitor Center; turnoff for City Center. **Population**: 2,718. **Emergency Services**: Dial 911. RCMP, phone (780) 332-4666. **Hospital and Ambulance**, phone (780) 332-6500.

Visitor Information: Visitor Center open Monday–Fridays 10 A.M. to 5 P.M. NAR railway car adjacent the centennial monument marking Mile 0 of the Mackenzie Highway. Online visit www.grimshaw.ca.

Grimshaw has 2 motels including the Dee-Jay Motel, a hotel, restaurants, service stations, car washes, a laundromat, a recreation park and other shops and other services. Camping at Queen Elizabeth Provincial Park 1.9 miles north of town. The Lac Cardinal Pioneer Village Museum is adjacent the provincial park.

Named for pioneer doctor M.E. Grimshaw, the community developed as a shipping center for surrounding farms with the arrival of the railroad in 1921. Grimshaw gained town status in February 1953. Local resources are wheat and grains, livestock, gravel, lumber, gas and oil.

Deh Cho Route: Mackenzie Highway

Distance from Grimshaw (G) is followed by distance from Alaska Highway (AH) via Northwest Territories.

ALBERTA HIGHWAY 35

G 0 AH 794.5 (1278.5 km) **GRIMSHAW**, Mile 0 of the Mackenzie Highway; see preceding description. Travelers going to Peace River go east 2 miles on Highway 35 to junction with Highway 2, then turn south to follow Highway 2 to Peace River, then Valleyview.

G 1.9 (3 km) **AH 792.6** (1275.5 km) **Queen Elizabeth Provincial Park**, 5 km/3 miles west on Lac Cardinal via side road; day-use area with boat launch; 36 unserviced sites and 20 powered campsites; picnic shelter, firewood, firepits, toilets, playground, swimming, trails, sani-dump. Phone (780) 624-6486. Nightly fee $27 CAD/unserviced and $34 CAD power sites (cash). Group camping available. Lac Cardinal is only 6 feet deep. ⓐ

Adjacent the park is **Lac Cardinal Pioneer Village Museum** (donation), open mid-May to mid-September, 11 A.M. to 5 P.M. daily, and North Peace Stampede Grounds. Annual Pioneer Days the second weekend

Stop by the Grimshaw Visitor Center and photograph the Mile Zero Mackenzie Highway monument and NAR railway car adjacent. (©Earl Brown)

of August with horse and wagon rides, and demonstrations. Beyond the entrance to the museum there are dry campsites in a field, camping fee $10 CAD/night.

G 2.8 (4.6 km) **AH 791.7** (1274 km) **Junction** of Highways 35 and 2 East.

G 4.1 (6.6 km) **AH 790.4** (1272 km) Turnout to east with litter barrels. Pine Bluff information boards and McKenzie River.

G 6.9 (11.1 km) **AH 787.6** (1267.5 km) Vehicle inspection station; pay phone, recycle bin, litter bin.

G 7.7 (12.4 km) **AH 786.8** (1266.2 km) Bear Creek Drive and the Creek Golf Course & Campground, 1 mile to west.

G 8.6 (13.8 km) **AH 785.9** (1264.7 km) **Junction** with SR 737 which leads west 20 km/12.4 miles to **Figure 8 Lake Provincial Recreation Area**; open April 27–Oct. 12; 27 campsites (no hookups), firepits, firewood$, water, tables, outhouses, boat launch, hiking trails. Camping fee is $27 CAD, cash or check/Canadian funds only. Lake stocked with rainbow trout; no gas motors.

G 12.3 (19.7 km) **AH 782.2** (1258.7 km) Road widens to 4-lane divided highway northbound.

G 12.5 (20.1 km) **AH 782** (1258.5 km) **Junction** with Highway 986 East to Peace River (30 km/19 miles) and Highway 88/Red Earth Creek (162 km/101 miles).

G 13 (20.9 km) **AH 781.5** (1257.6 km) Road narrows to 2 lanes northbound. Pass with care.

G 23 (37 km) **AH 771.5** (1241.5 km) Whitemud River bridge.

G 24.8 (39.9 km) **AH 769.7** (1238.7 km) **Junction** with Highway 689 west at **DIXONVILLE** (pop. 100, surrounding area 300); gas station, general store. Dixonville Museum is housed in a 100-year-old building that was formerly a trading post. Shady Lane Campground has 22 treed campsites. Phone (780) 971-3865.

G 26.9 (43.3 km) **AH 767.6** (1235.2 km) **Sulphur Lake** Road (dirt and gravel) leads west to junction with Highway 689. Sulphur Lake Provincial Campground is 55 km/34 miles west via 689. Open May 6 7–Oct. 11 user maintained; 11 sites, $10 CAD cash or check only, boat launch, fishing, swimming. There is no firewood or potable water provided.

CAUTION: Watch for deer northbound.

G 28.4 (45.7 km) **AH 766.1** (1233 km) Roadside turnout to west with litter/recycling bins.

G 39.1 (62.9 km) **AH 755.4** (1215.7 km) **Junction** with SR 690 east to hamlet of Deadwood (11 km/7 miles).

G 45.1 (72.5 km) **AH 749.4** (1206 km) Buchanan Creek.

G 47.5 (76.4 km) **AH 747** (1202 km) North Star to east.

G 49.6 (79.8 km) **AH 744.9** (1198.8 km) RV park to west; 15 sites with power, tables, firepits, outhouses.

G 51.4 (82.7 km) **AH 743.1** (1195.9 km) **Junction** with Highway 691. Turnoff for Battle River Pioneer Museum (1 km). Buildings open 1–6 P.M. daily, May and September, 10 A.M. to 6 P.M. July and August. Donations appreciated. Phone (780) 836-2374.

CAUTION: Slow for speed zone and pedestrians northbound through Manning.

Manning

G 52 (83.7 km) **AH 742.5** (1194.9 km) Located 122 miles/196 km south of High Level; a 45-minute drive north of Grimshaw. **Population:** 1,183. **Emergency Services:** Dial 911. **Visitor Information:** Visitors Information Center is located on the main street; look for the mighty moose. A campground and sanidump are just west of the visitor center. For more information, go to www.manning.ca or phone (780) 836-3606.

Manning has motels/hotels, restaurants, a municipal campground (9 sites with power and water, $25 CAD), a pharmacy and drug mart, gas stations (diesel). There is a grocery store and other shops and services.

Named for an Alberta premier, Manning was established in 1947. The railway from Roma, AB, to Pine Point, NWT, reached Manning in September 1962. Today, Manning is a service center and jumping-off point for hunters and fishermen, emphasized by the large moose statue in the city.

Attractions include the Old Hospital Gallery & Museum in city center. Built by volunteers in 1937, it is located on Main Street. See what life was like for an early missionary nurse. For a tour of the Old Hospital, please see the Tourist Information Center.

Mackenzie Highway Log
(continued)

G 52.1 (83.8 km) **AH 742.4** (1194.7 km) Notikewin River.

G 53.8 (86.6 km) **AH 740.7** (1192 km) Manning airport to west.

G 54.2 (87.2 km) **AH 740.3** (1191.4 km) Truck stop, gas/diesel.

G 55.5 (89.3 km) **AH 739** (1189.3 km) Community of Notikewin to west. Historically known as "Big Prairie."

G 59.9 (96.4 km) **AH 736.6** (1185.4 km) Railroad crossing.

G 60.6 (97.5 km) **AH 735.9** (1184.3 km) Turnout to west with litter bin.

G 61.6 (99.1 km) **AH 732.9** (1179.5 km) Hotchkiss River bridge. Historically known as the "Second Battle."

G 61.7 (99.3 km) **AH 732.8** (1179.3 km) Hotchkiss Community Club Park to east in the **Hotchkiss River** valley; 10 sites, picnic shelter, tables, firepits, fishing, outhouses and water pump.

G 62.2 (100.1 km) **AH 732.3** (1178.5 km) Condy Meadows Golf Course and Campground to east.

G 66 (106.2 km) **AH 728.5** (1172.3 km) *CAUTION: Steep, sharp bends, rough pavement.*

G 66.5 (107 km) **AH 728** (1171.5 km) Chinchaga Forestry Road to west.

G 67.8 (109.1 km) **AH 726.7** (1169.5 km) Meikle River bridge. Historically known as the "Third Battle." *CAUTION: Steep, sharp bends northbound.*

G 68.8 (110.7 km) **AH 725.7** (1167.9 km) Hawk Hills Road to east. Railroad crossing. Communication tower to west.

G 72 (115.9 km) **AH 722.5** (1162.7 km) Roadside turnout with litter bins to west.

G 75 (120.7 km) **AH 719.5** (1157.9 km) **Junction** with Highway 692 and access to

Notikewin Provincial Park (18.6 miles/30 km), with camping open May–October (19 sites), $23 CAD per night; free firewood, outhouses and firepits, no potable water. Day-use area, hiking trails, good wildlife viewing, picnicking and fishing for walleye and pike on the Notikewin and Peace rivers. Narrow portions of the access road make this unsuitable for large 5th wheelers or long trailers. Phone (780) 624-6486.

G 89.4 (143.9 km) **AH 705.1** (1134.7 km) Twin Lakes Lodge to east; they are the caretakers for the Twin Lakes Campground—if they appear closed, knock for service.

©Earl Brown

G 89.8 (144.5 km) **AH 704.7** (1134.1 km) **Twin Lakes Campground**, 0.5 mile west; open May–Oct. 12, 49 campsites, no hookups, $25 CAD fee ($2 senior discount), firewood$, picnic shelter, firepits, tables, outhouses, no potable water, beach, boat launch (no gas motors), playground, hiking trails; small store and office at entrance. Fish for stocked rainbow trout from June–September. Phone (780) 624-6486.

G 96.4 (155.1 km) **AH 698.1** (1123.5 km) Roadside turnout to west with litter bins.

G 104 (167.4 km) **AH 690.5** (1111.2 km) Kemp Creek.

G 112.2 (180.6 km) **AH 682.3** (1098 km) **Junction** with Highway 695 East to Carcajou.

G 113.4 (176.6 km) **AH 681.1** (1096.1 km) Keg River bridge. The community of **KEG RIVER** (pop. approx. 400). Keg River Cabins; food, gas, diesel, convenience store, liquor store, post office, bus station, lodging. There are some bison ranches in the area.

G 116.5 (181.4 km) **AH 678** (1091.1 km) **Junction** with Secondary Road 695 West. This paved road leads 14.5 km/9 miles to Keg River Post. A spot once rich in fur trade history, the post has Peace River Constituency's first MLA, "Allie" Brick, buried in its cemetery.

G 130.3 (203.9 km) **AH 664.2** (1068.9 km) **PADDLE PRAIRIE** (pop. approx. 544) has a gas bar, school and store. Paddle Prairie is a Métis settlement. The Métis culture, a combination of French and Amer-Indian, played a key role in the fur trade and development of northwestern Canada.

G 135.1 (211.5 km) **AH 659.4** (1061.2 km) Roadside turnout to west with litter bins and recycle bins.

G 137 (218.6 km) **AH 657.5** (1058.1 km) **Junction** with Highway 697, a 2-lane paved highway that helps form the "Mackenzie County Loop" drive through La Crete, Tomkin's Landing and Fort Vermilion back to Highway 35 at High Level.

Junction with Highway 697 east to La Crete and Fort Vermilion. See "Mackenzie County Loop" on page 692.

G 141.8 (222.2 km) **AH 652.7** (1050.4 km) Entering Mackenzie County (northbound sign).

G 145.5 (234.2 km) **AH 649** (1035.3 km) Turnout to east with litter bins and recycling.

G 147.2 (231 km) **AH 647.3** (1041.7 km) Chuckegg Creek.

G 154.2 (242.4 km) **AH 640.3** (1030.4 km) Roadside turnout with litter bins and recycle bins to west. Watch for waterfowl in small lakes along highway.

G 161 (253.3 km) **AH 633.5** (1019.5 km) Road dips at Bede Creek.

G 161.7 (254.4 km) **AH 632.8** (1018.4 km) Road dips at Parma Creek.

G 166.1 (261.4 km) **AH 628.4** (1011.3 km) Melito Creek.

G 168.1 (264.6 km) **AH 626.4** (1008.1 km) Railroad crossing.

G 168.4 (265.1 km) **AH 626.1** (1007.6 km) Norbord OSB Plant to east.

G 171.2 (269.8 km) **AH 623.3** (1003.1 km) Truck weigh station. Interpretive sign about Fort Vermilion.

G 172.5 (271.7 km) **AH 622** (1001 km) **Aspen Ridge Campground.** See display ad this page.

G 174 (274 km) **AH 620.5** (998.6 km) **Junction** with Highway 58 West, which leads 136 km/85 miles to **RAINBOW LAKE** (pop. 870), a service community for oil and natural gas development in the region.

High Level

G 174.2 (274.4 km) **AH 620.3** (998.2 km) Museum and Tourist Information Center and service road. High Level is located at the junction of Highways 35 and 58. **Population:** 3,992. **Emergency Services:** Dial 911 for **RCMP, Ambulance** and **Fire Department. Northwest Health Center,** phone (780) 841-3200

Visitor Information: Southeast edge of town at **Mackenzie Crossroads Museum & Visitors Center.** The center has extensive local and regional information for Alberta and the Northwest Territories; museum displays; free internet access; road and weather reports; and gift shop with authentic, local handicrafts. Fishing licenses for the Northwest Territories are sold here. Rest area with picnic tables. Open 9 A.M. to 8 P.M. daily in summer. Address: 10803–96th St., phone (780) 926-4811; www.highlevel.ca.

Private Aircraft: Scheduled air service to High Level airport, 7.5 miles/12 km north; elev. 1,110 feet/338m; length 5,000 feet/1,524m; asphalt; fuel 80, 100, Jet B. Footner Lake floatplane base, 0.6 mile/1 km west.

In 1786 fur traders arrived in the area but it wasn't until 1947 that the first settlers arrived. High Level began as a small settlement on the Mackenzie Highway after WWII. It grew with the oil boom of the 1960s and completion of the railroad to Pine Point. High Level has a strong agricultural economy (and the most northerly grain elevators in North America); 2 major forestry companies; and serves as a service center for the Mackenzie County region.

Visitor services include: major motels (Quality Inn & Suites, Days Inn, EconoLodge, Best Western, Super 8, Flamingo Inn); fast-food outlets, restaurants; 24-hour gas station; grocery and hardware stores, laundromats and car washes. The community offers a hospital, banks, schools, churches and a library.

Camping 1.7 miles/2.7 km south of town at **Aspen Ridge Campground.** Treed sites, full hookups, 41 RV sites and laundry facilities.

Dump station and freshwater fill-up are located at the corner of 94th Street and 105th Avenue, just northeast of the Visitors Center.

Recreation includes an 18-hole golf course and RV campsites, indoor swimming pool, skateboard park, playgrounds, splash park, tennis courts, ball diamonds, walking trails, cycling, boating, canoeing, snowmobile trails, ice arena, outdoor skate park and curling rinks, hunting (moose, caribou, deer, bear) and fishing for northern pike, perch, walleye, whitefish, goldeye and Arctic grayling.

Mackenzie Crossroads Museum & Visitors Centre. See display ad this page.

NOTE: Limited gas stations along the way until Enterprise, approximately 170 miles/274 km north.

Mackenzie Highway Log
(continued)

G 174.9 (275.5 km) **AH 619.6** (997.1 km) **Junction** with Highway 58 East to Jean D'Or Prairie (125 km/77 miles, paved/gravel). Highway 58 leads 78 km/49 miles east (paved) to Fort Vermilion, the oldest settlement in Alberta, and junctions with Highway 697 to La Crete, forming the "Mackenzie County Loop" for travelers.

High Level's Mackenzie Crossroads Museum & Visitors Centre is a fun and informative stop.
(©Susan Hay)

The Mackenzie County Loop

Mackenzie County (mackenziecounty.com) is larger than the Province of New Brunswick. Explore just part of this huge area by taking this 125-mile/200-km loop off the Mackenzie Highway through La Crete and Fort Vermilion.

Highway 697 leads 18 km/11 miles east from **Milepost G 137** on the Mackenzie Highway (Alberta 35) to cross the Peace River at **Tompkin's Landing**, via a free ferry which operates 24 hours a day, except in heavy fog or low water, and carries 4–6 vehicles. Travel is via an ice bridge in the winter months. The **LaCrete Ferry Campground** has spacious campsites (some overlook river) and electrical hookups; open May to September; phone (780) 841-2705.

Highway 697 continues east through Buffalo Head Prairie, which has a small store and gas, to **LA CRETE** (pop. 3,000), 87 km/54 miles northeast of Highway 35.

La Crete serves an area of 7,000 but continues to have the charm of the Mennonite settlers that founded it. Established in the early 1900s, La Crete celebrates Farmer's Day in June and Pioneer Days in September. Many events take place throughout the year and La Crete has all visitor services including a hotel with full RV hookups.

La Crete Mennonite Heritage Village has unique buildings and farming artifacts. It is open May to September 8 A.M. to 5 P.M. weekdays and is 3 km/1 mile southwest of town; phone (780) 928-4447.

Most of the town speaks Plattdeutsch, or "low German," while "high German" is mainly reserved for church services. English is spoken at the town businesses, which include restaurants and a motel with 86 rooms that also offers electrical hookups for RVs. Jubilee Park is a new scenic park with gazebo, a bridge, pond with colored fountains, walking paths, benches and lighting. Reinland Park in town has a day-use area, sani-dump, playground and picnic shelter.

Visit the Chamber of Commerce for maps and brochures, stamps, and souvenirs; 10500–100 St., Unit 1, phone (780) 928-2278; www.LaCreteChamber.com.

From La Crete, drive northeast 25 miles/40 km via Highway 697 to junction with Highway 88 and access to the hamlet of **FORT VERMILION** (pop. 871), the oldest settlement in Alberta, established in 1788. Visitor facilities include hotels, restaurants, grocery and liquor stores. Fort Vermilion has a 36-bed hospital (phone 780/927-3761) and a Provincial Court. The community library at 5103 River Rd., is open Monday to Saturday, 12:30–5:30 P.M.; till 8 P.M. on Tuesdays and Thursdays.

Stop in at the Visitor Center and Museum, June–August; phone (780) 927-3216. It is housed in a 1923-built building and one of 25 historic sites in Fort Vermilion. Visit the Fort Vermilion Heritage Center Museum and log house for a look at First Nations and fur trade history. A walk through the site includes the Trappers Shack. Built in 1912–1916. Other historic buildings include a Hudson's Bay store, Kratzs' Clinic, a Catholic mission site and St. Luke's Anglican Cemetery. Open June–August; (780) 927-4603; fvhc@hotmail.ca.

Camping at Fort Vermilion's Heritage Bicentennial Park (D.A. Thomas Park), day-use facilities, boat launch and fishing; phone (780) 927-4222. **Fort Vermilion Provincial Recreation Area (Bridge Campground)**, located 10 km/6.2 miles west of town on Highway 88, has 8 non-serviced campsites; open May 12–Sept. 14.

Highway 88/Bicentennial Highway continues south 410 km/255 miles to Slave Lake. Stop at Red Earth Creek, 243 km/151 miles south of Fort Vermilion, for gas stations/convenience stores on Highway 88 en route to Slave Lake.

When you leave Fort Vermilion you are only 79 km/49 miles west of High Level via Highway 58. Along the way is the **Machesis Lake Forest Provincial Recreation Area** (drive 30 km/16 miles east on 58 then 17 km/9 miles south); 20 campsites, boat launch and fishing.

Return to Milepost G 137 or Milepost G 174.9

Zama, which is the southern terminal of the interprovincial pipeline, carrying Norman Wells crude to Edmonton refineries.

Zama has a full-service campground and Cardlocks grocery store (phone 780/683-2215 for more information). The Zama Library doubles as a visitor center and has internet access. It is open Sundays 1–4 P.M., Tuesdays and Thursdays 7–9 P.M. Zama Community Park has a fish pond. It is adjacent the hamlet's RV park offering full services, picnic area, sani-dump, firepits and playground.

Many fishing lakes are in this area; local air charters are available to take you to them.

G 232.3 (368 km) **AH 562.2** (904.7 km) Slavey Creek.

G 241 (382 km) **AH 553.5** (890.7 km) Railroad crossing.

G 242.8 (384.8 km) **AH 551.7** (887.8 km) Paved turnout with litter/recycling bins to west.

G 249.5 (395.4 km) **AH 545** (877.1 km) Lutose Creek.

G 262.2 (416 km) **AH 532.3** (856.6 km) Steen River bridge.

G 263.2 (417.6 km) **AH 531.3** (855 km) Access road west to Steen River Gas Plant (13 km/8 miles).

G 265.6 (421.5 km) **AH 528.9** (851.2 km) **STEEN RIVER** (pop. approx. 25) to east; no services.

G 265.8 (421.8 km) **AH 528.7** (850.8 km) Steen River Forestry Tanker Base to west. Grass airstrip.

G 270 (428.6 km) **AH 524.5** (844.1 km) Jackpot Creek.

G 276.2 (438.6 km) **AH 518.3** (834.1 km) Road crosses creek. Improved road, northbound to border.

G 284 (450.7 km) **AH 510.5** (821.5 km) **INDIAN CABINS** (pop. 10); gas/diesel, cafe, lodging, showers, liquor, pay phone and native crafts. The Indian cabins that gave this settlement its name are gone, but nearby is a First Nations cemetery with spirit houses. Historic log church.

G 285.3 (452.5 km) **AH 509.2** (819.5 km) Delphine Creek.

G 287.3 (455.7 km) **AH 507.2** (816.2 km) Microwave tower to east.

G 293.5 (465.8 km) **AH 501** (806.3 km) 60th parallel. Border between Alberta and Northwest Territories. The Mackenzie Highway now changes from Alberta Highway 35 to NWT Highway 1, the Waterfalls Route.

Deh Cho Route: Waterfalls Route

Distance from AB–NWT border (B) is followed by distance from Grimshaw (G) and distance from the Alaska Highway (AH).

Kilometerposts on Highway 1 reflect distance from AB–NWT border.

NWT HIGHWAY 1

B 0 G 293.5 AH 501 (806.3 km) **AB–NWT border, 60th Parallel Territorial Park and Visitor Center.** The visitor center is open mid-May to mid-September; brochures, maps, fishing licenses, camping permits, litter bins, pay phone, drinking water and free coffee. Dene (First Nations) arts and crafts are on display. Check here on road and ferry conditions before proceeding.

IMPORTANT: All NWT government

See "Mackenzie County Loop" log on this page.

G 177.1 (279 km) **AH 617.4** (993.6 km) Golf and country club to east; clubhouse, grass greens 18 holes, pro shop, power carts and camping facilities.

G 181.7 (286.5 km) **AH 612.8** (986.2 km) Turnoff to west for High Level Airport.
CAUTION: Watch for deer northbound and for logging truck activity heading south.

G 194.4 (306.9 km) **AH 600.1** (965.7 km) Turnoff to west for Hutch Lake recreation area, 11 sites, boat launch, fishing and swimming. Phone (780) 926-2201.

G 196.5 (310.3 km) **AH 598** (962.4 km) Roadside turnouts with litter bins both sides of highway.

G 206.8 (327 km) **AH 587.7** (945.8 km) Wooden railway bridge to east.

G 218.7 (346.2 km) **AH 575.8** (926.6 km)

MEANDER RIVER (pop. 289); no highway services. Fish the Meander River where it meets Hay River for pike and walleye.

G 224.9 (356.3 km) **AH 569.6** (916.6 km) Roadside turnout to west with litter and recycling bins.

G 227 (359.5 km) **AH 567.5** (913.3 km) The Mackenzie Highway crosses the Hay River here and follows it north into Northwest Territories. Great Slave Lake Railway bridge over Hay River to east. This railway line extends 607 km/377 miles from Roma Junction near Peace River, AB, to Hay River, NWT, on the shore of Great Slave Lake. (A 87-km/54-mile branch line extended the line to the now-defunct lead–zinc mine at Pine Point, NWT.) Opened in 1964, the line carries mining shipments south and fuel and supplies north to Hay River.

G 227.5 (360.3 km) **AH 567** (912.5 km) Gravel road leads west 63 km/39 miles to ZAMA (pop. 250), an oilfield community. Drilling and related operations take place at

campsite fees must be paid in Canadian cash. They do not accept credit cards, checks or U.S. cash at the parks. Plan ahead as there are few ATMs in this region. If you would like to pay with a credit card, book your campsite online at NWTparks.ca.

60th Parallel Territorial Park Campground and picnic area adjacent visitor center; 7 dry, level, non-powered campsites on treed loop. Sani-dump station, washrooms, picnic sites, kitchen shelter and toilet at end of campground road overlooks Hay River; unmaintained boat launch, fishing. A short walking trail around a pond leads to the 60th Parallel Monument.

Northbound, the highway to Enterprise is designated "Highway of Heroes" in honor of the sacrifices made by armed forces, police and emergency responders who have died while in the line of duty.

Distance marker northbound shows Hay River 120 km/75 miles; Fort Simpson 474 km/295 miles; Wrigley 695 km/432 miles; Fort Providence 222 km/138 miles; Yellowknife 532 km/331 miles; Fort Smith 380 km/236 miles.

NOTE: Fines are double for drivers speeding through school or construction zones and triple for those driving without a valid license. Driving without insurance is a $1,700 fine plus a victim surcharge that totals $1,955.

B 1.7 (2.9 km) **G 295.2 AH 499.3** (803.5 km) **Reindeer Creek**; pike, pickerel.

B 20.4 (32.9 km) **G 313.9 AH 480.6** (773.4 km) Distance marker northbound shows Enterprise 50 km/31 miles, Hay River 88 km/55 miles, Fort Simpson 442 km/275 miles.

B 25.5 (40.9 km) **G 319 AH 475.5** (765.2 km) Swede Creek.

B 26.1 (42 km) **G 319.6 AH 474.9** (764.3 km) Large dirt turnout, toilets and gravel stockpile to west.

B 40.4 (65.1 km) **G 333.9 AH 460.6** (741.2 km) Mink Creek.

Judy Nadon, staff

B 45 (72 km) **G 338.5 AH 456** (733.8 km) Turnoff to east for **Twin Falls Gorge Territorial Park, Alexandra Falls** day use area; toilets, litter bins, picnic shelters and interpretive signs. Paved parking area and gravel walkway to falls viewpoint, overlooking the Hay River, which plunges 33m/109 feet to form **Alexandra Falls** (pictured above). Excellent photo opportunities; walk down stairs to top of falls. *Use extreme caution when accessing areas past the staircase, as the rocks can be slippery.* A 3-km/1.9-mile trail through mixed boreal forest (with good canyon views) connects with Louise Falls.

B 46.4 (74.6 km) **G 339.9 AH 454.6** (731.6 km) Turnoff to east for **Twin Falls Gorge Territorial Park, Louise Falls Campground**; nice reception area just off of road. Large building nearby with interpretive center for registration before turning into the campground loops. Camping fee $28 CAD; 26 powered campsites, tables, toilets,

firepits, firewood, tent pads, sani-dump station, potable water at site (no RV fillup). Drive in 0.3 mile for picnic area with kitchen shelter, playground. Showers and laundry facility are in Loop B (8 A.M. to 8 P.M.). Campsite reservations may be made at NWTparks.ca.

Pleasant trail to viewpoint overlooking 3-tiered **Louise Falls**, which drops 50 feet/15m. Walk down stairs to top of falls. Look for fossils at edge of falls. A 1.9-mile/3-km trails connects with Alexandra Falls.

B 48.2 (77.5 km) **G 341.7 AH 452.8** (728.7 km) **Escarpment Creek** picnic and group camping area; 12 powered sites, tables, shelter, toilets, firepits, garbage container, water. Spectacular series of waterfalls on Escarpment Creek; access from north side of creek. A 4.4-km/2.6-mile trail connects to Louise Falls.

B 51.5 (83.2 km) **G 345 AH 449.5** (723.4 km) **ENTERPRISE** (pop. 90), a highway community with food, gas/diesel, motel/cafe and B&B, grocery store, pay phone. Enterprise Regional Tourist Info Center in old weigh station; open daily in summer; phone (867) 984-3017. Native crafts, restaurant and lodging at motel and B&B. Minor vehicle repair available. View of Hay River Gorge just east of the highway. Look for sandhill cranes in this area.

Slow for posted speed zone.

B 51.6 (83.3 km) **G 345.1 AH 449.4** (723.2 km) "Y" intersection of Highways 1 and 2. Northbound travelers keep left for Yellowknife, right for Hay River. (Kilometerposts are white, on the right side of road.)

Junction of Highway 1 with Highway 2 to Hay River; see "Great Slave Route" on page 694 for log.

B 51.9 (83.8 km) **G 345.4 AH 449.1** (722.7 km) Weigh station.

B 56.4 (90.7 km) **G 349.9 AH 444.6** (715.5 km) Microwave tower to north.

Judy Nadon, staff

B 74.8 (120.4 km) **G 368.3 AH 426.2** (685 km) **McNallie Creek Territorial Park** day use area with picnic tables, outhouses, firepits, litter bins, viewing platform and short trail to waterfall (pictured above). Plaque explains origin of name.

B 74.7 (120.2 km) **G 368.2 AH 426.3** (686 km) Paved double-ended turnout north.

B 84.4 (135.7 km) **G 377.9 AH 416.6** (670.3) Distance marker shows Fort Providence 90 km/60 miles, Fort Simpson 340 km/211 miles.

B 76.5 (122.9 km) **G 370 AH 424.5** (683.1 km) Double-ended paved turnout to north with picnic tables, litter bins and no toilets. *CAUTION: Failing edge. Supervise children and dogs.*

B 104 (167.1 km) **G 397.5 AH 397** (638.9 km) Access road leads south 6.8

km/4.2 miles to **Lady Evelyn Falls Territorial Campground** and continues another 4 miles/7.4 km to the Slavey village of **KAKISA** (pop. 40) and **Kakisa Lake**.

The Kakisa River drops 49 feet/15m over an escarpment to form **Lady Evelyn Falls**. Staircase down to viewing platform. Hiking trail to base of falls; swimming, fishing and wading. Ample parking, interpretive display, territorial campground with 23 sites with power, camping fee $28 CAD, 7 picnic sites (including a group picnic shelter), showers, toilets, tables, firepits, firewood$, garbage containers, water pump, kitchen shelters, laundry facility and visitor center. Reservations at NWTparks.ca.

B 104.9 (168.5 km) **G 398.4 AH 396.1** (637.4 km) Kakisa River bridge.

B 105.1 (168.8 km) **G 398.6 AH 395.9** (637.1 km) **Kakisa River Territorial Park**; day-use only picnic area with tables, toilets, fireplaces and firewood$. Hiking trail to Lady Evelyn Falls. Good fishing in **Kakisa River** for Arctic grayling.

B 115.5 (185.6 km) **G 409 AH 385.5** (620.4 km) Double-ended turnout to east with litter bins, toilet. Informational boards here about the Deh Cho route.

B 115.7 (186 km) **G 409.2 AH 385.3** (620 km) Turnoff to north for Highway 3 to Yellowknife.

Junction of Highway 1 with Highway 3, which leads 211 miles/340 km north to Yellowknife. See "Frontier Trail" log page 695.

B 115.9 (186.5 km) **G 409 AH 385.1** (619.7 km) Distance marker westbound shows Liard Highway Junction 225 km/140 miles, Fort Simpson 287 km/178 miles.

B 130 (208 km) **G 423.5 AH 371** Next Services 280 km/174 miles in Fort Simpson (westbound sign).

B 141.9 (227 km) **G 435.4 AH 359.1** (577.9 km) Pavement ends, gravel begins, westbound.

B 144.1 (233 km) **G 437.6 AH 356.9** (574.4 km) Turnout with litter bins and outhouse to south.

B 154.7 (248.8 km) **G 448.2 AH 346.3** (557.2 km) Distance marker eastbound shows Fort Providence 100 km/62 miles, Enterprise 168 km/104 miles, Fort Resolution 350 km/217 miles.

B 158.6 (255 km) **G 452.1 AH 342.4** (551 km) Double-ended turnout to north with litter bins.

B 160.8 (258.5 km) **G 454.3 AH 340.2** (547.5 km) Microwave tower to north.

B 162 (260.7 km) **G 455.5 AH 339** (545.5 km) **Axe Handle Creek**; fishing.

B 172.5 (277.4 km) **G 466 AH 328.5** (528.7 km) **Bouvier Creek**; good fishing in spring.

B 173.5 (279 km) **G 467 AH 327.5** (527 km) Turnout with litter bins to south.

B 180.1 (289.4 km) **G 473.6 AH 320.9** (516.4 km) Double-ended turnout with litter bins, toilet east side of Wallace Creek. Scenic canyon to north; trail access on west side of creek; 15-minute walk to waterfall.

B 183.8 (295.2 km) **G 476.6 AH 317.9** (511.6 km) Gravel access to north at east end of **Redknife River** bridge; local fishing spot for pickerel and Arctic grayling.

(Continues on page 697)

Great Slave Route: Highways 2 & 6

Porrit Landing in Hay River. The community is located on the south shore of Great Slave Lake at the mouth of the Hay River. (©Judy Nadon, staff)

The Great Slave Lake Route begins at the junction of Highways 1 and 2 at Enterprise. Highway 2 leads north 24 miles/38 km to the community of Hay River, the largest shipping center in the north. Highway 2 also junctions with Highway 5, which connects with Highway 6 to the historic town of Fort Resolution on the south shore of Great Slave Lake.

Distance from Enterprise (E) is shown.

Highway 2 is paved from Enterprise to Hay River. Kilometerposts along the highway reflect distance from Enterprise. *There are no services between Hay River and Fort Resolution.*

NWT HIGHWAY 2

E 0 **Junction** with Highway 1 at Enterprise, **Milepost B 51.6.**

E 8.5 (13.6 km) Paradise Gardens.

E 15.7 (25.3 km) Hay River Golf Course; large log clubhouse, driving range, 9 holes (par 36), artificial greens. 10 powered RV sites available, $22.50 CAD/night, sani-dump on site. Phone (867) 874-6290; Website: hayrivergolfclub.com.

E 17.2 (28.5 km) Double-ended turnout with litter bin.

E 19.8 (31.9 km) **Junction** with Highway 5, which connects with Highway 6 to Fort Resolution.

Hay River

E 23.6 (38 km) **H 0** Hay River is 3.8 miles from the junction of Highways 2 and 5 via the Hay River Highway (Highway 2). Located on the south shore of Great Slave Lake at the mouth of the Hay River. **Population:** 3,606. **Emergency Services: RCMP**, phone (867) 874-1111. **Fire Department**, phone (867) 874-2222. **Ambulance**, phone (867) 874-9333. **Hospital**, phone (867) 874-8000.

Visitor Information: Visitor Information Center, just east of the highway; phone (867) 874-3180. Open daily, 8 A.M. to 8 P.M., Monday to Thursday, 8:30 A.M.

to 9 P.M. Friday to Sunday from late May to early September. Open 9 A.M. to 5 P.M. Monday to Friday from Mid-September to early May. There is a sani-dump and potable water located here. Also visit www.hayriver.com under 'Tourism' menu for businesses/services listing, Attractions and Events/Festivals or www.hayriverchamber.com; email: tourism@hayriver.com. Sani-dump available at the Hay River Center. Local artisan shop, washroom facilities, coffee, water and free WiFi.

Transportation: Air—Scheduled service. **Bus**—Double 'A' Ventures Express Bus Services (867) 874-1117 . **Rental cars**—Budget Rental (867) 875-7677.

Private Aircraft: Hay River airport; elev. 543 feet/165m; length 6,000 feet/1,830m, paved; 4,000 feet/1,219m, gravel; fuel 100, Jet B.

Visitor services include food, gas and lodging; supermarkets and Home Hardware; recreation center with aquatic center; banks; and other services. Outdoor Saturday market mid-June to mid-September at Fisherman's Wharf. Check out the Dene Cultural Center.

Hay River was established in 1868 with the building of a Hudson's Bay Co. post. Today, the community is the transfer point from highway and rail to barges on Great Slave Lake bound for arctic and subarctic communities. Hay River harbor is also home port of the Mackenzie River barge fleet that plies the river in summer.

Hay River Territorial Park and Campground on Vale Island on Great Slave Lake (10 km/6 miles past the visitor center, follow signs); 33 sites all with power, some pull-throughs, hookups, showers, firewood$, toilets, potable water, sani-dump station and firepits, outdoor gym; camping fee, open mid-May to mid-September. The beach park offers picnic sites, firepits, toilets, swimming and playground. Reservations at NWTparks.ca. Also beachfront camping in Hay River at 2 Seasons Adventures, Castaways and powered sites at the Hay River Golf Course.

Visit **Yamozha Kue** (the Dene Cultural Institute) accessed by the Katlodeeche Reserve road, across from Hay River. Gift shop and

books available; http://spectacularnwt.com/attraction/dene-cultural-institute.

Great Slave Lake, northern pike up to 40 lbs.; Inconnu (sheefish); Arctic grayling; good pickerel fishing in Hay River from bank.

NWT HIGHWAY 5

E 19.8 (31.9 km) **Junction** with Highway 5, which connects with Highway 6 to Fort Resolution.

E 21.1 (34 km) Railroad and auto bridge crosses Hay River.

E 21.3 (34.3 km) Access Road leads north 3.7 miles/5.9 km to the Katlodeeche First Nation Reserve, located on the east channel of the Hay River, across from the own of Hay River. One of only 2 Indian reserves in the Northwest Territories, Hay River Reserve is the home of the K'atl'odeeche First Nation. Most of the residents are South Slavey Dene.

E 50.1 (80.6 km) Good gravel road leads 1.6 km/1 mile north to **Polar Lake**; no motorboats allowed. Day-use fee $5 CAD; camping $10 CAD/night. Playground and good bird watching.

E 54 (86.9 km) Buffalo River bridge.

E 54.4 (87.5 km) Turnout to north with outhouse, litter barrel and map.

E 57.6 (92.7 km) **Junction** with Highway 5 to Fort Smith. *See "Wood Buffalo Route" log on page 700. Continue on Highway 6.*

NWT HIGHWAY 6

E 70.8 (113.9 km) Main access road north to **PINE POINT** (abandoned); no services. Pine Point was built in the 1960s by Cominco Ltd. The open-pit lead-zinc mine shut down in 1987.

E 76 (121.7 km) Pavement ends, gravel begins, eastbound.

E 89.9 (144.7 km) Turnoff to north for Dawson Landing viewpoint on Great Slave Lake, accessible via a 40-km/25-mile bush road (not recommended in wet weather).

E 94 (151.3 km) Turnout to north with litter barrel.

E 99.4 (160 km) **Little Buffalo River Crossing Territorial Park** to south; 20 powered campsites, nightly camping fee $22.50 CAD, picnic tables, kitchen shelter, firewood$, toilets, litter barrels, boat launch and fantastic walleye fishing in the spring. Reservations at NWTparks.ca.

E 99.5 (160.1 km) Bridge over **Little Buffalo River**. Good fishing for northern pike and walleye.

E 113.5 (182.7 km) **FORT RESOLUTION** (pop. 524), located on the south shore of Great Slave Lake on Resolution Bay. **Emergency Services: RCMP**, phone (867) 394-1111.

Visitor Information: Stop in at the Dene Noo Community Council.

The oldest Chipewyan and Métis town in NWT, it was founded in 1791 by the Hudson's Bay Co. post as the earliest fur trading post on Great Slave Lake. Today's economy is based on trapping, fishing, and a logging and sawmill operation.

Visitor services include food, gas and groceries and a service station. Canada Post outlet located in Northern Store.

Frontier Trail: Highway 3 to Yellowknife

Highway 3 is a wide, paved, all-weather road in good condition leading 211 miles/341 km from its junction with Highway 1 to Yellowknife. The Deh Cho Bridge spans the Mackenzie River. Gas is available at Fort Providence, Behchoko and in Yellowknife.

Distance from junction of Highways 1 and 3 (J) is shown.

NWT HIGHWAY 3

J 0 Highway 3 leads north 211 miles/341 km to Yellowknife from **Milepost B 115.5** on Highway 1.

J 12.7 (20.4 km) Dory Point Territorial Park (day use only); picnic area to east with 5 sites and screened in kitchen shelter with large center fire pit for cooking, no drinking water; overlooking Mackenzie River with view of passing riverboats.

J 14.8 (23.8 km) South bank of the Mackenzie River and approach to Deh Cho Bridge. Construction of the $185-million cablestay bridge across the Mackenzie River took 4 years. It officially opened Nov. 30, 2012, marking the end of a long history of ferry and ice road transport only across the Mackenzie River. It is the longest joint-less bridge in North America with a total length of 1,045m/3,428 feet.

There are tolls for commercial vehicles greater than 4,500 kg/9,920 lb. See fees and options for payment at: www.dot.gov.nt.ca/Highways/Tolling.

J 15.6 (25.1 km) North bank of the Mackenzie River.

J 16.2 (26 km) Mackenzie Bison Sanctuary next 92.6 km/57 miles. "Watch for Bison" sign. *Use EXTREME CAUTION driving Highway 3: Slow down and watch for bison on highway north from the river crossing!*

J 16.3 (26.2 km) Turnout to west with picnic tables, litter bins and information boards.

J 19.5 (31.4 km) Big River Service Center has gas/diesel, propane; a boat launch; motel and lounge; full-service restaurant (overlooking the Mackenzie River) and groceries. *NOTE: Next gas available northbound is in Rae (Behchoko) 228 km/142 miles. For southbound travelers, no gas until Enterprise or Fort Simpson.*

J 20.9 (33.6 km) **Fort Providence Territorial Park** 2 km/1.2 miles west located in poplars are 32 powered sites, nightly camping fee $28 CAD, showers, information center, screened kitchen, sani-dump, walking trails and WiFi. Reservations at NWT parks.ca. Good fishing.

J 22.6 (36.4 km) **Junction** with access road which leads 5 km/3.1 miles west to **FORT PROVIDENCE** (approx. pop. 748); food and lodging at Snow Shoe Inn; medical clinic.

A Roman Catholic mission was established at Fort Providence in 1861. (Our Lady of Fort Providence church is a major landmark.) Although noted for its early agricultural endeavors, Fort Providence is traditionally a trapping community.

Moose hair embroidery is found in local gift shops and local craftswomen are also noted for their porcupine quill work, knitting, fur garments and accessories.

Yellowknife is a unique city, located on the shore of Great Slave Lake. Photo ops abound.
(©David L. Ranta, staff)

Historical monument, boat launch and picnic sites on the **Mackenzie River.** Spectacular photo opportunities here for sunsets on the river. Also good bird watching for eagles, sandhill cranes and other birds. Guides, cabins, boats and air charters available locally. Good to excellent fishing. Northern pike to 30 lbs., May 30 to September, use large Red Devils; Arctic grayling and pickerel from 1 to 6 lbs., June–September, use anything (small Red Devils will do).

NOTE: No services on highway from here to Yellowknife (193 miles/310 km). You can find gas/fuel at **Milepost J 152.9** by turning off at junction for Behchoko (130 miles north of Fort Providence).

J 32.5 (52.3 km) Occasional loose gravel northbound.

CAUTION: Watch for bison on highway! A Yellowknife resident offered the tip that if you see a bison on a rise pointing downhill with his head down, he's likely getting ready to charge. Use caution if you stop to take photographs; stay in your vehicle and maintain a safe distance.

J 42.5 (68.4 km) Double-ended turnout to east with litter bin.

J 44 (70.8 km) *CAUTION: Watch for herds of bison alongside or standing in the middle of the road.*

J 51.7 (83.2 km) Double-ended turnout to west with litter bins and outhouses. Information boards on wood bison are here and at several additional turnouts northbound.

J 64.5 (103.8 km) Gravel breaks northbound.

J 75.8 (122 km) Chan Lake Territorial Park day use area to east. Double-ended parking area with picnic shelter, litter bins and outhouse. Watch for waterfowl.

J 77.5 (124.7 km) Turnout to east with litter bin.

J 86.4 (139 km) Double-ended turnout to east with litter bins.

J 90.5 (145.6 km) Double-ended turnout to west.

J 100.7 (162.1 km) Double-ended turnout with litter bin to east.

J 130.4 (209.8 km) Double-ended turnout with litter bins to east. Northbound travelers may notice the trees are getting shorter as you move farther north.

J 141.9 (228.4 km) Highway descends northbound to **Mosquito Creek.** Fishing for pickerel and whitefish; closed May and June, open season July through April.

J 144.8 (233 km) North Arm Territorial Park day use area on the shores of Great Slave Lake to east; tables, toilets, firewood and firepits. Lowbush cranberries and other berries in area. Boat launch. *CAUTION: Beware of bears.*

J 148.1 (236 km) Rolling frost heaves begin here, northbound to Yellowknife.

J 148.9 (239.6 km) **Junction** with winter ice road north to communities of Wha Ti (formerly Lac La Marte) and Rae Lakes (Gameti).

J 149.5 (240.6 km) **Junction** with access road west to community of Edzo, no services (see description at **Milepost J 152.9**).

Watch for frost heaves and gravel breaks north to Yellowknife. Highway turns east for northbound travelers.

J 152.2 (245 km) Bridge over **Frank Channel,** which extends from the head of the North Arm of Great Slave Lake to the Aboriginal village of Rae. Boating and fishing for whitefish.

J 152.9 (246 km) **Junction** with road which leads west 6.2 miles/10 km to **BEHCHOKO**, which includes the 2 hamlets of **Rae–Edzo** (descriptions follow); website: www.tlicho.ca/community/behchoko. **Population:** 1,926. **Emergency Services:** RCMP, in Rae, phone (867) 392-1111. **Nursing station (Emergencies)**, in Rae, phone (867) 392-6075.

Rae, located on Marion Lake, is the largest Dogrib community in the territory. Rae has a large general store, a post office, 2 motels, a restaurant and gas stations (one with deli/inside seating). The mission church at Rae has a tipi-style entrance. Inquire locally about buying local crafts (beaded jackets, slippers, etc.).

Edzo is a residential community a few kilometers away from Rae. Edzo was developed in 1965 by the government to provide

Shop for unique Northern art in Yellowknife. (©David L. Ranta, staff)

schools and a sanitation system.

J 159.9 (257.3 km) Turnout to west with litter bins.

J 160.1 (257.6 km) Stagg River bridge. After crossing the North Arm of Great Slave Lake, the highway swings southeast toward Yellowknife. Winding road to Yellowknife, good opportunities to see waterfowl in the many small lakes.

J 175 (280.1 km) Double-ended turnout to south with litter bins.

J 189.7 (305.3 km) Double-ended turnout to north with litter bin.

J 207.5 (334 km) Yellowknife Golf Club to north; 18 holes, sand fairways, artificial greens, pro shop, licensed clubhouse. Non-profit club with 300 members, welcomes visitors. Built on the Canadian Pre-Cambrian Shield, the course is mostly sand and bedrock. Each player gets a small piece of carpet to take along on the round as their own portable turf. Site of the June 21 Midnight Tournament. Some modified rules have been adopted by this Far North golf course, among them: "No penalty assessed when ball carried off by raven." Website: https://yellowknifegolf.com/.

J 208.5 (335.5 km) Yellowknife airport to south.

J 208.7 (335.9 km) Turnoff to north for Fred Henne Territorial Park day use area Long Lake Beach at Long Lake; picnic sites,

boat launch, snack bar, sandy beach and swimming.

J 209.2 (336.7 km) Old Airport Road access to Yellowknife; 3.5 km/2.2 miles to Walmart, 4.5 km/2.8 miles to Franklin Avenue. Wardair Bristol freighter to the south. A plaque commemorates the Bristol freighter, which was the first wheel-equipped aircraft to land at the North Pole.

J 209.4 (337 km) Turnoff to north for **Fred Henne Territorial Park**. Well-maintained public campground with approximately 100 vehicle sites and 12 walk-in tent pads. Non-powered, 15-amp and 30-amp sites available; most are back-in, some pull-throughs. Wheelchair accessible. Canadian cash only for camping fees. Generators are permitted. There are kitchen shelters, dump station, playground, swimming, firewood, outhouses firepits, showers, laundromat, WiFi and pay phone. Daily and seasonal rates available. Reservations at NWTparks.ca. Open from mid-May to mid-September. Campground gates close at 10:30 P.M. [A]

J 210 (338 km) Small turnout overlooking Jack Fish Lake south, litter bin.

J 210.4 (338.6 km) **Junction** with Highway 4/Ingraham Trail; *see log on page 697.* Turn south for Yellowknife *(description follows).*

Yellowknife   [icons]

J 211.6 (340.5 km) Intersection of Highway 3 and Franklin Avenue in downtown Yellowknife. Yellowknife is located on the north shore of Great Slave Lake, approximately 940 miles/1,513 km from Edmonton, AB. **Population:** 19,234. **Emergency Services: RCMP**, phone (867) 669-1111. **Fire Department** and **Ambulance**, phone (867) 873-2222; **Hospital**, Stanton Yellowknife, phone (867) 669-4111.

Visitor Information: The Northern Frontier Visitor Center closed permanently in October 2017; a temporary visitor center was opened at City Hall. Inquire locally about visitor center status or contact Northwest Territories Tourism, P.O. Box 610, Yellowknife, NT X1A 2N5. Phone 1-800-661-0788 or (867) 873-5007; website spectacularnwt.com.

Private Aircraft: Yellowknife airport; elev. 674 feet/205m; length 7,500 feet/2,286m; asphalt; fuel 100/130, Jet B. Float-plane bases located at East Bay and West Bay of Latham Island.

Transportation: Air—Scheduled air service to Edmonton and Calgary aboard First Air Canadian North, Air Canada Jazz, West-Jet. Several carriers serve Yellowknife and Arctic communities. Charter service available. **Bus**—Available via Frontier Coachlines Tuesday--Sunday. **Taxi**—2 taxi companies. **Rentals**—Several major car rental agencies; boat, canoe and houseboat rentals.

Yellowknife is a modern city where you can experience rustic nature and traditional culture without missing out on urban amenities.

Yellowknife became capital of the Northwest Territories in 1967, developing as a mining, transportation and government administrative center for the territories. The Northwest Territories Legislative Assembly building is located on Frame Lake (tours are available).

European settlers arrived in the 1930s with the discovery of gold in the area and radium at Great Bear Lake. Cominco poured its first gold brick in 1938. WWII intervened and gold mining was halted until Giant Yellowknife Mines began mining again on May 12, 1948. The road connecting the city with the provinces was completed in 1960.

The discovery of diamonds north of Yellowknife at Lac de Gras in 1992, set off a rush of claim stakers, and Yellowknife is now the service center for several diamond mines. An estimated 150 companies have staked claims in an area stretching from north of Yellowknife to the Arctic coast, and east from the North Arm of Great Slave Lake to Hudson Bay. In winter, the Ingraham Trail (NWT Highway 4) is used as part of the 380-mile/612-km ice road to Lupin Gold Mine, which now extends to Lac de Gras, heart of the diamond rush, and Contwoyto Lake.

Lodging & Services

Accommodations at Super 8 and other hotels/motels, inns and B&Bs. There are many restaurants to choose from and a micro-brewery to enjoy. There are major-chain retail stores here such as Walmart. Gas stations and all other visitor services available. Northern books can be found downtown at **The Book Cellar**. Celebrating 40 years in 2019, the Book Cellar specializes in stories and topics of the great north.

The Book Cellar. See display ad on this page.

Attractions

The Prince of Wales Northern Heritage Center, built to collect, preserve, document, exhibit, study and interpret the North's natural and cultural history, is located on Frame Lake, accessible via 48th Street or by way of a pedestrian causeway behind City Hall. Do not miss the moose-skin boat or the video about the construction of this craft. The narrative and historic photos about missionaries making their way North are also excellent. Good overview of aviation history in NWT.

Walking tour. Explore Old Town—"The Rock"—the area surrounding Bush Pilot's Monument, including Ragged Ass Road. Eat at the historic (1937) Wildcat Cafe, which operates from mid-June to mid-September; phone (867) 873-4004 for hours. Walk around Latham Island to see historic structures and modern buildings with very innovative architectural solutions to the problem of building on solid rock.

There is an app available to guide visitors through Yellowknife's Old Town. Go to website: experienceyellowknife.com/content/yellowknife-old-town-soundwalk or visit the app store and search for "Yellowknife Old Town Soundwalk."

Downtown, stop in at the **Diamond Display** at the Diamond Center on the corner of 49th Street and 51st Avenue.

Walk along the popular **Frame Lake Trail** (8 km/5 mile loop) with its views of Yellowknife's skyline, including the Legislative Assembly buildings. "Will and Kate" visited and planted bushes near the "Hope Garden" on their visit in summer 2011.

Summer events. Various special events mark June 21, the longest day of the year and also Aboriginal Day, a territorial holiday. Canada Day (July 1) is a national holiday celebrated with a parade, music and games.

Take a tour by boat or van, enjoy fish fry

dinners on the lake, take a flightseeing tour by floatplane, or explore the waters along the Ingraham Trail by canoe or Great Slave Lake by cruiseboat.

Ingraham Trail is a 43-mile/69-km road leading northeast of Yellowknife to picnicking, camping, fishing, canoeing and bird watching opportunities (see log below).

Ingraham Trail

Distance from Yellowknife (Y) is shown.

NWT Highway 4 Ingraham Trail

Y 0 Junction of Highways 3 and 4.

Y 2.9 (4.7 km) Side road leads north 5 km/3 miles to Vee Lake.

Y 4.7 (7.5 km) Yellowknife River bridge.

Y 4.8 (7.7 km) **Yellowknife River** picnic area with boat launch, 6 picnic sites, firewood, firepits and toilets. Good fishing for northern pike and Arctic grayling.

Y 12.2 (19.7 km) **Prosperous Lake** boat launch to north with toilets; fishing.

Y 14.9 (24 km) **Madeline Lake** picnic area to north with boat launch, picnic sites, firewood, firepits, toilets and fishing.

Y 16.4 (26.4 km) **Pontoon Lake** picnic area to south with picnic sites, firewood, firepits, toilets and boat launch. Fishing for northern pike, whitefish, cisco and suckers.

Y 17.4 (28 km) Side road leads north 1.6 km/1 mile to **Prelude Lake Territorial Campground**; 67 non-powered campsites, 12 tent sites, $22.50/$15 CAD, 20 picnic sites, firewood, water, showers, sani-dump station, toilets, marina, boat launch, swimming. Prelude Wildlife hiking trail. Fishing for lake trout, Arctic grayling, whitefish, cisco, burbot, suckers and northern pike.

Y 27.3 (44 km) Powder Point Territorial Park on Prelude Lake, north; parking area and toilets. Boat launch for canoeists doing the route into Hidden Lake Territorial Park, Lower Cameron River, or 4-day trip to Yellowknife River bridge.

Y 28.4 (45.8 km) **Hidden Lake Picnic Area** and Cameron River Falls trailhead to north; parking and toilets. A 1-km/0.6-mile trail leads to cliffs overlooking Cameron River Falls. Pedestrian bridge over river.

Y 28.8 (46 km) Pavement ends, gravel begins, eastbound.

Y 33.5 (53.9 km) Bridge across Cameron River; parking area, toilets, picnicking, canoeing, hiking and swimming.

Y 34.4 (55.3 km) Informal campsites on sand esker overlooking Cameron River next 0.3 km eastbound.

Y 36.7 (59 km) **Reid Lake Territorial Campground** with 65 non-powered campsites, $22.50 CAD, 11 tent sites $15 CAD, 10 picnic sites, wheelchair accessible, firewood$, kitchen shelter, showers, swimming, hiking trail, playground, boat launch and fishing. Canoe launch point for Upper Cameron River and Jennejohn Lake routes. CAUTION: Watch for bears.

Y 42.8 (68.9 km) Tibbitt Lake. End of road. Pensive Lakes canoe route (advanced).

(Continued from page 693)

B 195 (313.5 km) G **488.5** AH **306** (492.4 km) Morrisey Creek.

B 200.1 (321.3 km) G **493.6** AH **300.9** (484.2 km) Winter ice road leads south 126 km/78 miles to **SAMBAA K'E** (pop. 92), a traditional Dene settlement formerly known as **Trout Lake**, after the body of water. Fishing for lake trout and pickerel/walleye. Fly-in, no road access, in summer.

B 202.1 (324.5 km) G **495.6** AH **298.9** (481 km) Trout River bridge. View of Sambaa Deh Falls to north from bridge. You can walk down to the falls for a better look, but you will have to park at the Territorial Park. Good fishing hole below the falls north of the bridge. Hike 0.6 mile/1 km north on west side of river to access to **Trout River Canyon**. Fossils are embedded in the rocks along the Trout River.

B 202 (324.3 km) G **494.7** AH **299.8** (482.5 km) Turnoff to **Sambaa Deh Falls Territorial Park** just east of Trout River bridge. Beautiful information center with brochures and visitor guides regarding area attractions. Well-maintained campground with 20 large, non-powered, wooded campsites, picnic tables, viewing platforms, playground, litter barrels, immaculate showers, kitchen shelter, firepits, firewood, water; $22.50 CAD. Emergency phone. **RCMP**, phone (867) 695-1111. Visitor center, parking and picnic area. Sambaa Deh Falls can be seen from the highway bridge. From the campground's Loop B, hike 0.6 mile/1 km south to **Coral Falls**. Good trout fishing.

B 202.7 (326.2 km) G **496.3** AH **298.2** (479.9 km) Trailhead parking for Trout River Canyon trails to see fossils embedded in rocks along the river.

B 206.5 (331.6 km) G **500** AH **294.5** (474 km) Emergency survival cabin and turnout with litter bins to north.

B 206.7 (332 km) G **500.2** AH **294.3** (473.6 km) Distance marker westbound shows Fort Simpson 140 km/87 miles, Fort Liard 300 km/186 miles, Wrigley 355 km/220 miles.

B 234 (375.4 km) G **527.5** AH **267** (429.7 km) Double-ended turnout to north with litter barrel and information sign on Jean Marie River.

B 234.1 (375.5 km) G **527.6** AH **266.9** (429.5 km) **Junction** with an all-weather, gravel road leading 27 km/17 miles to community of **JEAN MARIE RIVER** (pop. 64), located on the south shore of the Mackenzie River at the confluence with the Jean Marie River. A very traditional community known for its Native crafts. Visitors are welcome to visit traditional camps along the road. Please respect private property.

Visitor Information: Available from friendly staff at the Band Office in the large brown building in front of the central playground. If the office is closed, ask anyone you see in the community.

Services here include an undeveloped camping area (located near airport); picnic site on the river; Lucy's Bed & Breakfast and gas. Arts and crafts available; inquire at the Band Office. There is a co-op store, territorial government offices and nursing station here. Local crafts include beaded moose hide and moose hair tuftings. The historic tugboat Jean Marie River rests up shore, retired from shipping lumber down the Mackenzie to Arctic communities. Good photo oppor-

tunity. Ask about guided boat tours.

B 234.4 (376 km) G **527.9** AH **266.6** (429 km) Sign here says to phone (867) 695-1111 for RCMP Emergency in this area.

B 236.2 (379 km) G **529.7** AH **264.8** (426.1 km) Emergency survival cabin and turnout to north with outhouse and litter bins.

B 236.8 (380 km) G **530.3** AH **264.2** (425.2 km) Distance marker westbound shows Fort Simpson 60 km/37 miles, Fort Liard 250 km/155 miles, Wrigley 305 km/190 miles.

B 242 (388 km) G **535.5** AH **259** (416.8 km) Pipeline camp and pump station to north. Highway crosses pipeline. Microwave tower visible to south.

B 246 (395 km) G **540.4** AH **254.1** (406.6 km) Gravel ends, pavement begins, westbound. Pavement ends, gravel begins, eastbound.

B 256.5 (412 km) G **550** AH **244.5** (393.5 km) Jean Marie River bridge.

B 256.7 (412.3 km) G **550.2** AH **244.3** (393.1 km) "Checkpoint" at junction with the Liard Highway. No visitor services.

Junction of Highway 1 with the Liard Trail (Highway 7). Continue with this log for the Liard Trail to Fort Liard and junction with the Alaska Highway. See "Heritage Route" on page 698 for continuation of Highway 1 to Fort Simpson and Wrigley.

Deh Cho Route: Liard Trail

Distance from Grimshaw (G) is followed by distance from junction with Highway 1 (J) and distance from the Alaska Highway (AH).
Kilometerposts southbound on Highway 7 reflect distance from BC–NWT border. Kilometerposts eastbound on Highway 1 reflect distance from NWT–Alberta border. You need Canadian cash to pay for camping in territorial parks. Many places do not accept credit cards, checks or U.S. cash. Use credit cards to make online reservations at NWT parks.ca.

HIGHWAY 7

G **550.2** J **0** AH **244.3** (393.2 km) **Junction** of Highways 1 and 7 at Checkpoint; no services. The Liard Trail is named for the Liard River Valley through which it runs for most of its length. In French, Liard means "black poplar," and this wilderness highway (officially opened in June 1984) is a corridor through a forest of white and black spruce, trembling aspen and balsam poplar.

G **550.3** J **0.1** (0.2 km) AH **244.2** (393 km) Pavement ends, gravel begins, southbound on Liard Trail. **Emergency services:** RCMP, phone (867) 770-1111.

G **550.8** J **0.6** (1 km) AH **243.7** (392.1 km) Double-ended turnout with litter bins and interpretive signs about the Liard Highway.

G **552.7** J **2.5** (4 km) AH **241.8** (389.1 km) Distance marker southbound shows BC/NWT border 250 km/155 miles, Alaska Highway 400 km/249 miles.

G **566.4** J **15.9** (25.6 km) AH **228.1** (367.1 km) NorthwesTel Microwave tower
(Continues on page 699)

Heritage Route: Fort Simpson

The Hudson's Bay Co. began its post here in 1822. At that time the fort was renamed after Sir George Simpson, one of the first governors of the combined North West Co. and Hudson's Bay Co. Fort Simpson served as the Mackenzie District headquarters for the Hudson's Bay Co. fur-trading operation. Its key location on the Mackenzie River also made Fort Simpson an important transportation center. Anglican and Catholic missions were established here in 1858 and 1894.

Highway 1 continues northwest from Checkpoint to Fort Simpson as the Heritage Route. Driving distance from the junction of Highway 1 with the Liard Trail at Checkpoint is 38 miles/61 km. This route crosses the Liard River via ferry in summer, ice road in winter. Fort Simpson is the gateway to Nahanni National Park Reserve.

Distance from Checkpoint (C) is shown. Physical kilometerposts reflect distance from Alberta border.

NWT HIGHWAY 1

C 0 **Junction** of Highway 1 with the Liard Trail (Highway 7) at Checkpoint. *Turn to Deh Cho Route log on page 697 for description of the Liard Trail to Fort Liard and the Alaska Highway.* Continue with this log for Fort Simpson and Wrigley.

A popular stop at one time, Checkpoint no longer offers visitor services.

C 26.6 (42.8 km) Free government-operated **Liard River** (South Mackenzie) ferry, the *Lafferty*, operates daily late May through October from 8 A.M. to 11:30 P.M., 7 days a week; on demand until 11:45 P.M. Crossing time is 6 minutes. Capacity is 8 cars or 2 trucks, with a maximum total weight of 130,269 lbs./59,090 kg. An ice bridge opens for light vehicles (to 6,614 lbs./3,000 kg) usually by late November; heavier vehicles can cross as ice thickens. *NOTE: This crossing is subject to extreme high and low water level fluctuations which may cause delays. No crossing possible during breakup (about mid-April to mid-May) and freeze-up (mid-October to mid-November).* For crossing information, phone 1-800-661-0750 or visit: www.dot.gov.nt.ca/Highways/Highway-Conditions.

C 35.7 (57.5 km) **Junction** of NWT Highway 1 with Fort Simpson access road. NWT Highway 1 turns and continues to Wrigley. Fort Simpson access road leads 2.3 miles/3.8 km to Fort Simpson; description follows.

Fort Simpson

C 38 (61 km) Located on an island at the confluence of the Mackenzie and Liard rivers. **Population:** 1,238. **Emergency Services: RCMP,** phone (867) 695-3111. **Health Center** with 1 doctor, daytime phone (867) 695-7000 or (867) 695-3232 for after hours emergencies. **Fire Department** (volunteer), phone (867) 695-2222.

Visitor Information: Very nice Visitor Information Center with a wealth of historic photos and historical displays. A movie theater shows films. The visitor center is open 9 A.M. to 8 P.M. weekdays, noon–8 P.M. weekends, from May to September. Winter hours are 1–4 P.M. weekdays only. Ask for a Historical Walking Tours booklet and guide. Phone (867) 695-3182; fsvic@northwestel.net. Also visit www.fortsimpson.com.

Nahanni National Park Reserve office is at 10002 100 St., open daily June 15–Labor Day weekend, 8 A.M. to noon and 1–5 P.M.; weekdays the rest of the year, 8:30 A.M. to noon and 1–5 P.M. year-round. Phone (867) 695-7750; summer phone for 24-hour park emergency duty officer (867) 695-3732.

Transportation: Air—Scheduled service to Yellowknife and Whitehorse, YT. Charter services available. **Rental cars**—Available. **Taxi service**—Available.

Private Aircraft: Fort Simpson airport; elev. 554 feet/169m; length 6,000 feet/1,829m; asphalt; fuel 100, Jet B. Fort Simpson Island; elev. 405 feet/123m; length 3,000 feet/914m; gravel; fuel 100, Jet B.

Fort Simpson or Łíídljj K<u>ų</u>ę (Deh Cho First Nations meaning "the place where the rivers come together") is the administrative headquarters for the Deh Cho (Big River) region. It is the oldest continuously occupied site on the Mackenzie River, dating from 1804 when the North West Co. established its Fort of the Forks. There is a National Historic Site plaque on the bank of the Mackenzie overlooking the confluence and another National Historic Site plaque commemorating Ehdaa a traditional gathering place of the Dehcho First Nations. Ehdaa is adjacent the Territorial campground on the river flats. It is home to the world's largest wooden tipi.

Fort Simpson continues to be an important center for the Northwest Territories water transport system. Visitors may walk along the high banks of the Mackenzie River and watch the boat traffic and floatplanes.

NWT Highway 1 leads north from Fort Simpson to **WRIGLEY** (pop. 146), home of the Pehdzeh Ki First Nation; limited visitor services. Driving time to Wrigley, 137 miles/221 km from here, is approximately 3 hours. Allow at least 2 hours from Wrigley to the N'Dulee/Camsell Bend ferry/ice crossing of the Mackenzie River. The MV *Johnny Berens* operates daily, late May–October.

Lodging & Services

Fort Simpson is a full-service community. Accommodations at motels and bed-and-breakfasts.

There are 2 restaurants; 2 gas stations, one with repair service (unleaded and propane available); 2 grocery stores, department store, hardware store, a bank, laundromat, post office, and 1 craft shop. Small engine repair shop and mechanics available. Diesel available at Imperial Oil bulk plant Monday through Friday.

Recreational facilities include an arena, curling rink, gym, ball diamond, tennis and small indoor pool; a 9-hole golf course (longest hole is 475 yards) with clubhouse and gear rental ($15 day pass) and a boat launch at government wharf.

One of the easiest places to get down to the water is by Albert Faille's cabin on Mackenzie Drive. Faille was a well-known Fort Simpson pioneer and prospector.

Camping at **Fort Simpson Territorial Park** on village access road; 21 powered campsites $28 CAD, 11 non-powered campsites $22.50 CAD, 4 picnic sites, playground, interpretive area, sani-dump station, water,

The free government ferry Lafferty carries passengers and vehicles across the Liard River.
(©Earl Brown)

firewood$, kitchen shelter; showers. Reservations at NWTparks.ca

Attractions

Shopping. Fort Simpson features Dene crafts, such as birch-bark baskets, bead-work, moosehide crafts, northern carvings and other hand made crafts.

©Earl Brown

Fort Simpson Heritage Park, overlooking the National Historic Site Ehdaa, also known as the Papal Grounds where Pope John Paul II landed in 1987, features the McPherson House, built in 1936 and home to local pioneers George and Lucy McPherson and "Doc" Marion. Some old structures are from the Experimental Farm, or Research Station, which operated at Fort Simpson for more than 20 years.

Fort Simpson is also a jumping-off point for fly-in trips with **Simpson Air** to **Nahanni National Park Reserve**. The park is a UNESCO world heritage site, and is globally renowned for its diverse landforms, waterways, wildlife, forests and First Nations history. Visitors are welcomed to the land by the Dehcho First Nations, whose ancestors have called Nah?a Dehé home for untold centuries (the question mark is not a mistake, it represents pronunciation of a glottal stop). Nahanni is a Dehcho First Nations gift to Canada, and Canada's gift to the world.

Howard's Pass Access Road on the west boundary of the park is a 700-km/435-mile one-way, unserviced remote dirt/gravel mining operations road. To use this route, you must first obtain a permit signed by the Superintendents of both Nahanni National Park Reserve and Nááts'įhch'oh National Park Reserve. Please contact Nahanni NPR office prior to travel.

The park is accessed predominantly by aircraft for day flightseeing tours and overnight recreation. On average it takes 1 to 2 hours to fly into the park from Fort Simpson, depending on aircraft and destination.

Located southwest of Fort Simpson near the Yukon border, air charter companies operate day-trip flightseeing tours to Little Doctor and Glacier lakes, Ram Plateau, Cirque of the Unclimbables, the Ragged Range and Virginia Falls on the South Nahanni River. Virginia Falls in Nahanni National Park Reserve are 300 feet/90m high, twice as high as Niagara Falls. One of the most popular attractions, for experienced river paddlers is running the South Nahanni River or its tributaries, the Flat River, the Broken Skull River and the Little Nahanni River.

The park has a mandatory reservation, registration and de-registration system for overnight use. A Northern Backcountry Excursion Permit (annual or daily fee) is required. Contact Nahanni National Park Reserve; phone (867) 695-7750; email nahanni.info@pc.gc.ca; website www.pc.gc.ca/nahanni.

Simpson Air. See display ad on facing page.

(Continued from page 697)
to east. Vegetation changes northbound to muskeg with black spruce, tamarack and jack pine.

G 571.3 J 21 (33.8 km) **AH 223.3** (367.1 km) Southbound, begin 40 km/25 miles of rough frost heaves.

G 571.7 J 21.5 (34.6 km) **AH 223.4** (359.5 km) *Slow for one-lane metal-decked* bridge over **Poplar River.** Good Arctic grayling and pike fishing in Poplar River culverts.

G 582.7 J 32.5 (52.3 km) **AH 209** (387 km) Highway descends both directions to Birch River bridge (elev. 256m/840 feet).

G 585.1 J 34.9 (56.2 km) **AH 205** (379.7 km) Double-ended turnout with litter bins, outhouse. Informal campsite.

G 593.5 J 43.3 (69.7 km) **AH 201** (323.5 km) Microwave tower to east.

G 612.6 J 62.4 (100.4 km) **AH 181.9** (292.7 km) Entrance to Lindberg Landing; guest cabins, reservations required.

G 614.2 J 64 (103 km) **AH 180.3** (290.2 km) Entrance to **Blackstone Territorial Park and Campground.** The visitor information building, built with local logs, is located on the bank of the Liard River with superb views of Nahanni Butte (elev. 4,579 feet/1,396m). The center is staffed and open from mid-May to Oct. 1.

There are 19 non-powered campsites with tables and firepits. Room accommodation for rent with 2 beds, tables, wood stove, outdoor firepit and parking for $60CAD/night. Campground offers kitchen shelter with wood-burning stove, firewood$, hand-pump water and garbage containers, boat dock, playground and state-of-the-art restroom and shower facility. No phone, no WiFi. Camping fee $22.50 CAD. The boat launch is usable only in high water early in the season; use boat launch at Cadillac Landing or Lindberg's Landing during low water. The area offers wildlife and bird viewing, great scenery, river canoeing and other activities. [camping icon]

G 616.7 J 66.5 (107 km) Blackstone River bridge.

G 617 J 66.8 (107.5 km) **AH 177.5** (285.7 km) Blackstone River Park to west; picnic area with litter bins and outhouse.

G 617.1 J 66.9 (107.7 km) **AH 177.4** (285.5 km) Upper Blackstone River bridge.

G 618 J 67.8 (109.1 km) **AH 176.5** (284 km) Microwave tower to east.

G 627.3 J 77.1 (124 km) **AH 167.2** (269.1 km) Turnoff to west for winter ice road that leads 22.3 km/13.8 miles to the Dene settlement of **NAHANNI BUTTE** (pop. 116), at the confluence of the South Nahanni and Liard rivers. Summer access by boat, floatplane or by wheeled plane using the village's all-weather runway. Boats to Nahanni Butte can be arranged at Blackstone Territorial Park.

This is a busy outfitting area in season for deer, elk, grizzly and wood bison.

G 629.7 J 79.5 (127.9 km) **AH 164.8** (265.2 km) Road widens for an emergency airstrip; elev. 156m/512 feet.

G 635.7 J 85.5 (137.6 km) **AH 158.8** (255.6 km) Netla River bridge. The Netla River Delta is an important waterfowl breeding habitat, and Native fishing and hunting area.

G 644.6 J 94.4 (152 km) **AH 149.9** (241.2 km) Views of Mackenzie Mountains southbound. Road widens for an emergency airstrip; elev. 299m/981 feet.

G 646.3 J 96.1 (154.7 km) **AH 148.2** (238.5 km) *Limited visibility southbound* as road crests hill.

G 658.8 J 107.6 (173.2 km) **AH 135.7** (218.4 km) Distance marker southbound shows Fort Liard 50 km/31 miles, Fort Nelson 250 km/155 miles. *CAUTION Watch for buffalo in this area.*

G 660 J 109.8 (176.7 km) **AH 134.5** (216.5 km) Double-ended turnout to west with interpretive signs, litter bins and outhouse.

G 668.1 J 117.9 (189.7 km) **AH 126.4** (203.4 km) Big Island Creek bridge (elev. 252m/827 feet). Good views of Liard Range to the west and northwest for the next 21 km/13 miles northbound.

G 671 J 120.8 (194.4 km) **AH 123.5** (198.7 km) Rabbit Creek.

G 679.5 J 129.3 (208 km) **AH 115** (185.1 km) **Muskeg River** bridge (elev. 248m/814 feet). River access and interpretive sign to west at north end of bridge. Gravel bars on the river make a good rest area, small rigs only. Swimming; fishing for pike, pickerel and freshwater clams. [fishing icon]

G 685 J 134.8 (216.9 km) **AH 109.5** (176.2 km) **Junction** with Fort Liard Access Road. From this junction it is 2.7 km/1.7 miles to Hay Lakes Campground and 5.6 km/3.5 miles to a Native crafts store and a gas/diesel station. Double-ended turnout with interpretive signs west of junction on access road. [fishing icon] [camping icon]

Views from road into Fort Liard across the Liard River of Mount Coty (elev. 830m/2,715 feet) and Pointed Mountain (elev. 1,405m/4,610 feet) at the southern tip of the Liard Range.

NOTE: Begin posted speed zone through town.

Fort Liard

[gas/food/lodging/camping icons]

G 685 J 134.8 (216.9 km) **AH 109.5** (176.2 km) Located on the south bank of the Liard River near its confluence with the Petitot River (known locally as Black River because of its color), about 50 miles/80 km south of Nahanni Butte. **Population:** 584. **Emergency Services:** RCMP, phone (867) 770-1111. **Fire Department**, phone (867) 770-2222. **Health Center**, phone (867) 770-4301.

Visitor Information: Visitor Information Center/Acho Dene Native Crafts (closed Sundays), phone (867) 770-4161. Visitor information also available from Hamlet of Fort Liard; phone (867) 770-4104; www.fortliard.com.

Elevation: 686 feet/209m. **Climate:** Comparatively mild considering Fort Liard's geographical location. Fort Liard is known as the "tropics of the Territories." **Radio and Television:** CBC radio (microwave) and CKLB 101.9 from Yellowknife; CBC Television (Anik), APTN and private satellite receivers. Bell cellular service available.

Private Aircraft: Liard airstrip; elev. 700 feet/213m; length 2,950 feet/899m; gravel.

Transportation: Air—no charter service locally, arrange from Fort Simpson or Fort Nelson. **Barge**—Nonscheduled barge service in summer.

This small, well-laid-out hamlet of both traditional log homes and new modern housing is located among tall poplar, spruce

(Continues on page 701)

Wood Buffalo Route: Highway 5

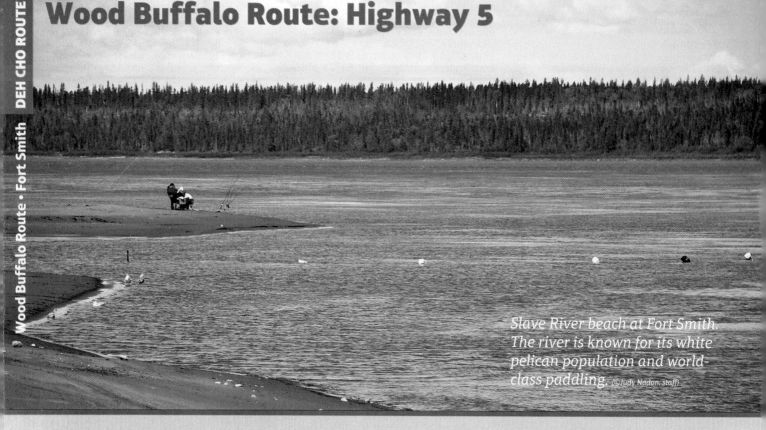

Slave River beach at Fort Smith. The river is known for its white pelican population and world-class paddling. (©Judy Nadon, staff)

Highway 5 (paved in 2017, in good condition for RVers and travelers with trailers) leads 166 miles/267 km from its junction with Highway 2 to the community of Fort Smith.

Distance from Enterprise (E) is shown.

There are no services between Hay River and Fort Smith.

NWT Highway 5 Wood Buffalo Route

E 19.8 (31.9 km) **Junction** with Highway 2 to Hay River and Enterprise.

E 21.1 (34 km) Railroad and auto bridge crosses Hay River.

E 21.3 (34.3 km) Access road leads north 5.9 km/3.7 miles to Hay River Reserve and Dene Cultural Center.

E 54 (86.9 km) Buffalo River bridge.

E 54.4 (87.5 km) Turnout to north with outhouse, litter barrel and map.

E 57.6 (92.7 km) **Junction** with Highway 6 to Fort Resolution; *(see "Great Slave Lake Route" log on page 694).* Continue on Highway 5 south for Fort Smith.

E 74.3 (119.6 km) Turnoff for **Sandy Lake**, 13 km/8 miles south; swimming, sandy beach, fishing for northern pike.

E 79.8 (128.4 km) Entrance to Wood Buffalo National Park. Established in 1922 to protect Canada's largest free roaming herd of wood bison. **Wood Buffalo National Park** (a UNESCO World Heritage Site) is a vast wilderness area larger than the size of Switzerland. Its total size is 44,741 square kilometers with the greater portion located in the northeast corner of Alberta and the Wood Buffalo National Park and Visitor Reception Center are located in Fort Smith, NT and Fort Chipewyan, AB. The park is open year-round and a variety of outdoor activities and cultural experiences draw visitors from around the world. For more information, contact Wood Buffalo National Park, Box 750, Fort Smith, NT X0E 0P0;

phone (867) 872-7960. Website: www.parkscanada.gc.ca/WoodBuffalo.

E 82 (132 km) Picnic area with tables, toilets, firewood and playground to north at Angus Fire Tower. Giant sinkhole here is typical of karst topography.

E 94 (151.2 km) Turnout to south with litter barrel, toilets and interpretive signs on bison and the Nyarling River. *CAUTION: Watch for wood bison.*

E 130 (209.2 km) Highway crosses Sass River. Shallow lakes from here south to Preble Creek provide nesting areas for whooping cranes.

E 135.3 (217.7 km) Highway crosses Preble Creek.

E 143.6 (231.1 km) Turnout with washrooms, litter barrel, walking trail and interpretive signs on whooping crane nesting grounds.

E 150.3 (241.9 km) Little Buffalo River bridge.

E 153.5 (247 km) Access road leads 1 km/0.6 mile to **Little Buffalo River Falls Territorial Park** with shelter, firepits, picnic tables, sani-dump, 6 non-powered sites, toilets, tent platforms, interpretive trail and boat/canoe launch, fishing. Park is open mid-May to mid-September. Camping fee is $22.50 CAD; self-register at kiosk.

E 163.5 (263.1 km) Turnoff for Parsons Lake Road (narrow gravel) which leads south 8 miles/13 km to **Salt Plains Overlook**; interpretive exhibit and viewing telescope. Gravel parking area with tables, firepits and toilets at overlook. A hiking trail down to Salt Plains (proper footwear is essential).

Springs at the edge of a high escarpment bring salt to the surface and spread it across the huge flat plain; only plants adapted to high salinity can grow here. Fine view of a unique environment. Some 227 species of birds are known to migrate through here. More information on the Salt Plains is avail-

able at the Park office, Visitor Reception Center in town.

CAUTION: Parsons Lake Road beyond the overlook is a narrow wilderness road that may be impassable in wet weather and/or blocked by fallen trees. Four-wheel drive strongly recommended.

E 166.6 (268.1 km) Salt River bridge.

E 170.8 (274.9 km) Good gravel side road leads 16 km/10 miles north to settlement of **Salt River**; campground, small-boat launch, and fishing for pike, walleye, inconnu and goldeye.

E 176.3 (283.7 km) Access road north to old Bell Rock, where goods portaged from Fort Fitzgerald were loaded on boats bound for Great Slave Lake and the Mackenzie River.

E 181.6 (292.3 km) Double-ended turnout with litter bin.

E 181.9 (292.8 km) Turnoff to north for Fort Smith airport and **Queen Elizabeth Territorial Park** 24 powered sites, camping fee $28 CAD, picnic sites, toilets, water, kitchen shelter, showers, sani-dump station, firewood, firepits and playground. Reserve at NWTparks.ca.

Short hike from campground to bluff overlooking Rapids of the Drowned on the Slave River; look for pelicans feeding here.

Fort Smith

E 186.4 (300 km) Located on the Slave River. **Population:** 2,396. **Emergency Services:** RCMP, phone (867) 872-1111. **Fire Department**, phone (867) 872-2222. **Ambulance**, phone (867) 872-3111. **Health Center**, phone (867) 872-6200.

Visitor Information: Town of Fort Smith

Visitor Center is open in the summer, phone (867) 872-3065; email townoffortsmith@fortsmith.ca.

The **Wood Buffalo National Park Visitor Center**, located at 149 McDougal Rd., is open year-round, 8:30 to noon and 1–5 P.M., weekdays, closed holidays (fall-spring) and every day from 8:30 A.M. to 6 P.M. in the summer. Phone (867) 872-7960; email wbnp.info@pc.gc.ca; website www.pc.gc.ca/en/pn-np/nt/woodbuffalo.

Transportation: Air—Scheduled and charter service available. Northwestern Air (867/872-2216, ext. 401) offers flightseeing tours of the area. **Bus**—Frontier Coachlines, phone (867) 874-2566. **Rental trucks**—Visa Truck Rental (867) 872-5121.

Private Aircraft: Fort Smith airport; elev. 666 feet/203m; length, 6,000 feet/1,829m; asphalt; fuel 80, 100.

Fort Smith began as a trading post at a favorite campsite of the portagers traveling the 1,600-mile/2575-km water passage from Fort McMurray to the Arctic Ocean. The 4 sets of rapids, named (south to north) Cassette, Pelican, Mountain and the Rapids of the Drowned, separate the Northwest Territories from Alberta. In 1872, Hudson's Bay Co. established a permanent post, and the Roman Catholic mission was built here in 1876. By 1911 the settlement had become a major trading post for the area.

There are 2 hotels/motels, multiple bed and breakfasts, 2 grocery stores, post office, 3 gift shops, several restaurants and a take-out place, a bar, convenience store, gas stations and several repair service locations.

Attractions include an interpretive display at **Wood Buffalo National Park** Visitor Reception Center. Daily guided tours and fun events are scheduled throughout the summer months. Wood Buffalo National Park was established in 1922 to protect the last remaining herd of bison in northern Canada. It also serves to protect the Canada Northern Boreal Plains and the Peace-Athabasca Delta.

The excellent **Northern Life Museum & Cultural Center** showcases Native basketry, the fur trade and birdlife, especially the miraculous comeback of the Whooping Crane. Open Monday–Saturday, 10 A.M. to 5 P.M., June through August; weekdays only, September through May.

Fort Smith Mission Park historic site which includes the fascinating grotto, is open May 15–Sept. 15. The park provides a self-guided tour of the site.

Tee-up with a view of Slave River Rapids at the 9-hole **Pelican Rapids Golf Course.**

A lookout with viewing telescope is located at the north edge of town, overlooking the Slave River. Enjoy the network of walking trails along the riverbank. The Slave River offers world-class paddling opportunities for intermediate and expert paddlers.

Walk down to **Rapids of the Drowned** to watch the most northerly colony of nesting white pelicans fishing for walleyes, eels and suckers; interpretive sign at overlook.

Drive out to Pine Lake in Wood Buffalo National Park. Watch for bison, black bears and other wildlife. There are 2 cabins for rent on Pine Lake. Non-powered campsites at **Pine Lake Campground** for RVs/tents, with 3 pull-through sites, dump station, firepits, firewood; $15.70 CAD. Day-use area with beautiful beach, picnic sites, flush toilets, kitchen shelter, and playground. Located 61 km/38 miles south of Fort Smith.

(continued from page 699)

and birch trees on the south bank of the Liard River. Forestry and tourism, along with government and community services support the local economy. Fort Liard residents are well known for the high quality of their birch-bark baskets and porcupine quill workmanship.

The North West Co. established a trading post near here at the confluence of the Liard and Petitot rivers called Riviere aux Liards in 1805. The post was abandoned after the massacre of more than a dozen residents by Indians. It was taken over by the Hudson's Bay Co. in 1821 and re-established in 1822 when the 2 companies merged. The well-known geologist Charles Camsell was born at Fort Liard in 1876.

Lodging, groceries, ATM, hardware and sundries available at Liard Valley General Store and Motel (at the far end of main street). Gas, diesel, propane and fishing and hunting licenses available here at the Fort Liard Fuel Center (which includes Sisters Cafe, crafts and groceries). Post office, groceries and ATM at the Northern. ATM at the Liard Valley General Store. There is the modern Echo Dene School. There is no bank in Fort Liard.

Stop in at the native crafts store to shop for quill-decorated birchbark berry baskets and bowls (a Fort Liard specialty), beaded moccasins and mukluks, moose-hair tufting, miniature birchbark canoes and many other traditional native handicrafts.

Community-run Hay Lake Campground has 12 campsites (no power or hook-ups), sani-dump, potable water, free firewood, picnic tables, cooking shelter, toilets and a hiking trail around the lake. Bring insect repellent. There is no charge for these sites.

Recreation and sightseeing in the area including fishing (for pike, pickerel, goldeye and spring Arctic grayling) at the confluence of the Liard and Petitot rivers.

Deh Cho Route Log

(continued)

G 685 J 134.8 (216.9 km) **AH 109.5** (176.2 km) **Junction** with Fort Liard Access Road: Hay Lakes Campground 1.7 miles/2.7 km west; gas station 3.5 miles/5.6 km west.

G 686 J 135.8 (218.5 km) **AH 108.5** (174.6 km) Vehicle inspection station to east (closed for many years). Parking.

G 696.1 J 145.9 (234.8 km) **AH 98.5** (158.5 km) Gravel ends, pavement begins, southbound. Northbound, gravel road may be slippery when wet.

G 708.2 J 158 (254.3 km) **AH 86.3** (138.9 km) Double-ended turnout to east with litter bins.

G 708.5 J 158.3 (254.7 km) **BC–NWT border.** *TIME ZONE CHANGE: British Columbia observes Pacific standard time, Northwest Territories observes Mountain.*

Distance marker southbound shows Alaska Highway 134 km/83 miles, Fort Nelson 161 km/100 miles. *CAUTION: Northbound travelers watch for buffalo on road.*

G 710.6 J 160.4 (258.1 km) **AH 83.9** (135 km) Highway descends in both directions to Petitot River bridge. The **Petitot River** was named for Father Petitot, an Oblate missionary who came to this area from France in the 1860s. It is said to have the warmest swimming water in British Columbia (70°F/21°C). Good bird-watching area. Also freshwater clams, pike and pickerel; Arctic grayling. ☞

The Petitot River bridge was the site of

the official opening of the Liard Highway on June 23, 1984. The Liard Highway replaced the old Fort Simpson winter road that joined Fort Nelson and Fort Simpson. The original Simpson Trail was first blazed in November 1942 by Alaska Highway engineers, including the 648th, Company A detachment.

G 712 J 161.8 (260.4 km) **AH 82.5** (132.8 km) Crest of Petitot River hill; 10 percent grades.

G 721 J 170.8 (274.9 km) **AH 73.5** (45.7 km) Gravel turnout to west.

G 724.4 J 174.2 (280.3 km) **AH 70.1** (112.8 km) Bridge over Deasum Creek (elev. 490m/1,608 feet). Good bird-watching area.

G 724.9 J 174.7 (281.1 km) **AH 69.6** (112 km) There are several roads in this area used by the forest, oil and gas industries.

G 730.6 J 180.4 (290.3 km) **AH 63.9** (102.8 km) Long paved turnout to west.

G 753.8 J 203.6 (327.7 km) **AH 40.7** (65.5 km) Tshinia Creek.

G 757.7 J 207.5 (333.9 km) **AH 36.8** (59.2 km) Paved turnout to east.

©Earl Brown

G 768 J 217.8 (350.5 km) **AH 26.5** (42.6 km) **Fort Nelson River Bridge** (elev. 298m/978 feet). After nearly 35 years, the "temporary" single-lane Acrow bridge here was replaced with a conventional 2-lane cement-surfaced bridge in 2017 (pictured above). The former bridge was the longest Acrow bridge in the world at 1,410 feet/430m. It was also very narrow at 14 feet/4m wide. The Acrow bridge, formerly called the Bailey bridge after its designer, Sir Donald Bailey, was designed for rapid construction using interchangeable steel panels coupled with pins.

G 767.9 J 217.7 (350.3 km) **AH 26.6** (42.8 km) Rest area to west at north end of bridge with outhouse, concrete picnic table and litter bins.

G 771.2 J 221 (355.7 km) **AH 23.3** (37.5 km) Long paved turnout to east with litter bins.

G 780 J 229.8 (369.8 km) **AH 14.5** (23.3 km) Stanolind Creek. Beaver dams to west.

G 786.7 J 236.5 (380.7 km) **AH 7.8** (12.5 km) **Beaver Lake Recreation Site** to east. Narrow, bumpy dirt road access to user maintained camping area (not appropriate for mid- to large-size rigs); 6 small sites, dumpster, outhouse. ▲

G 794.5 J 244.3 (393.2 km) **AH 0 Junction** of Liard Trail and the Alaska Highway. From this junction it is 29 km/18 miles to Fort Nelson, BC; 181 km/113 miles to Fort Liard, NWT; 454 km/282 miles to Fort Simpson; 651 km/405 miles to Fort Providence; and 959 km/596 miles to Yellowknife. *NOTE: Next gas stops northbound are Fort Liard, Fort Simpson and Fort Providence.*

Junction with the Alaska Highway. Turn to **Milepost DC 301** on page 176 in the ALASKA HIGHWAY section.

Index